BUS

DIRECTORY OF FOREIGN FIRMS OPERATING IN THE UNITED STATES

13th Edition

Edited & Published by Uniworld Business Publications, Inc.

Uniworld Business Publications, Inc.
3 Clark Road
Millis, MA 02054
Tel. and Fax.: 508.376.6006
info@uniworldbp.com
www.uniworldbp.com

First Edition	1969
Second Edition	1972
Third Edition	1975
Fourth Edition	1978
Fifth Edition	1986
Sixth Edition	1989
Seventh Edition	1992
Eighth Edition	1995
Ninth Edition	1998
Tenth Edition	2000
Eleventh Edition	2002
Twelfth Edition	2004
Thirteenth Edition	2006

Published by
Uniworld Business Publications, Inc.
3 Clark Road
Millis, MA 02054

ISBN: 0-8360-0054-4

Printed in the United States of America

Table Of Contents

PART ONE

FOREIGN FIRMS OPERATING IN THE UNITED STATES   1
(Grouped by Country)

PART TWO
ALPHABETICAL LISTING OF FOREIGN FIRMS — 1523

PART THREE
ALPHABETICAL LISTING OF AMERICAN AFFILIATES — 1579

PART FOUR
NAICS CODE INDEX — 1687

PART FIVE
PUBLISHER'S NOTES – Related Publications — 1709

Introduction

This is the 13th Edition of **DIRECTORY OF FOREIGN FIRMS OPERATING IN THE UNITED STATES.** First published in 1969, it has been an authoritative and valuable source of information for corporations, government agencies, organizations, institutions, and individuals involved in many forms of international commerce or investment. The current edition contains over 3,500 foreign firms headquartered in 86 countries and nearly 10,000 businesses in the US that they own, wholly, or in part. The U.S. headquarters and selected locations of each branch, subsidiary or affiliate are listed.

Source and Accuracy of Listings

Firms in the 13th Edition are actively researched by our staff on an on going basis. The primary sources of information for all entries are direct corporate information and/or annual reports provided by them. Direct telephone, fax, web, and e-mail contact were used extensively for verification and clarification, as well as print and electronic media. Overseas companies in the 12th Edition, which no longer have a US subsidiary, were deleted, as were US firms whose ownership by foreign firms had ceased. Nearly 650 new firms were identified as the beneficial owner of companies operating in the US, while over 400 were removed from the 13th Edition.

The aim of this Directory is to provide accurate, up-to-date listings, but the Editor and Publisher cannot guarantee that the information received from a company or other source is correct. Also, as extensive as this Directory may be, it does not claim to be all-inclusive. It contains only what has been disclosed to us. In addition, the designations and listings are not to be considered definitive as to legal status or the relationship between the foreign and American firms. Some US companies included here are technically owned by other US companies that, in turn, are owned by non-US firms. "Foreign-owned," therefore, refers to the ultimate owner. Also, no assumptions should be made if the percentage of ownership is not specified. Neither the direct nor indirect nature of ownership, nor the degree of participation, is of primary importance to the purpose of this directory.

In a compilation of this scope inaccuracies are inevitable. It would be appreciated if the reader would inform the Publisher of inaccuracies so corrections can be made in all future publications.

Acknowledgements

We thank, most sincerely, the many company representatives who cooperated generously in providing information for this directory, and those who assisted in its preparation; *Publisher* – M. Christopher Shimkin; *Associate Editor* - Lynn Sherwood; *Researchers* – Cissy Hull-Allen and Tracy Antonowicz.

Barbara D. Fiorito, *Editor*
Uniworld Business Publications, Inc.

Key to Abbreviations

The following abbreviations have been used in the Directory

A/C	Air Conditioning	Equip	Equipment
Access	Accessories	Exch	Exchange
Adv	Advertising	Exec	Executive
Affil	Affiliate(d)	Exp	Export(er)
Agcy	Agent/Agency	EVP	Executive Vice President
Agric	Agriculture	Fax	Facsimile
Arch	Architect(ural)	Fin	Financial/Finance
Assur	Assurance	Fl	Floor
Auto	Automotive	For	Foreign
Aux	Auxiliary	Furn	Furniture
Bldg	Building	Fwdg	Forwarding
Bus	Business	Gds	Goods
CEO	Chief Executive Officer	Gen	General
COO	Chief Operating Officer	Gov	Governor
Chem	Chemical	Hdwe	Hardware
Chmn	Chairman	Hos	Hospital
Cir	Circulation	Hydr	Hydraulic(s)
Corn	Components	Imp	Import(er)
Coml	Commercial	Ind	Industrial/Industry
Commun	Communications	Inf	Information
Conslt	Consultant/Consulting	Ins	Insurance
Constr	Construction	Inspec	Inspect(ion)
Cont	Controller	Instru	Instrument
Corp	Corporate	Intl	International
Cust	Customer	Invest	Investment
Dept	Department	JV	Joint Venture
Devel	Development	Lab	Laboratory
Diag	Diagnostic	Liq	Liquid
Dir	Director	Mach	Machine(ry)
Dist	District	Maint	Maintenance
Distr	Distributor/Distribution	Mat	Material
Divers	Diversified	Mdse	Merchandise
Dom	Domestic	Mdsng	Merchandising
Econ	Economist	Meas	Measurement
Educ	Education(al)	Med	Medical
Elec	Electrical	Mfg	Manufacturing
Electr	Electronic	Mfr.	Manufacture(r)
Emp	Employee(s)	Mgmt	Management
Engr	Engineer(ing)	Mng	Managing
Envi	Environmental	Mgr	Manager

(continued)

Mkt	Market	Rel	Relations
Mktg	Marketing	Rep	Representative
Mil	Million	Ret	Retail(er)
Oper	Operation	Rev	Revenue
Ops	Operations	Rfg	Refining
Orgn	Organization(al)	Rwy	Railway
Pass	Passenger	Sci	Scientific
Petrol	Petroleum	Spec	Special(ty)/Specialized
Pharm	Pharmaceutical	Sta	Station
Plt	Plant	Subs	Subsidiary
Prdt(s)	Product(s)	Super	Supervision
Pres	President	SVP	Senior Vice President
Prin	Principal	Sys	System
Print	Printing	TV	Television
Prod	Process(ing)	Tech	Technical/Technology
Prod	Production	Tel	Telephone
Prog	Programming	Telecom	Telecommunications
Ptnr	Partner	Temp	Temperature
Pub	Publishing	Trans	Transmission
Publ	Publisher	Transp	Transport(ation)
R&D	Research & Development	VP	Vice President
Recre	Recreation(al)	Whl	Wholesale(r)
Refrig	Refrigeration	Whse	Warehouse
Reins	Reinsurance		

Company Designations

Abbreviation	*Term*	*Country*
AB	Aktiebolag	Sweden
AG	Aktiengesellschaft	Austria, Germany, Switzerland
AS	Anonim Sirketi	Turkey
A/S	Aktieselskab	Denmark
	Aksjeselskap	Norway
BV	Beslotene Vennootschap	Netherlands
CA	Compania Anonima	Venezuela
CIE	Compagnie	Belgium, France
CO	Company	Canada, England, U.S.
CORP	Corporation	England, U.S.
GMBH	Gesellschaft mit beschrankter Haftung	Austria, Germany
INC	Incorporated	Canada, England, U.S.
KG	Kommanditgesellschaft	Germany
KK	Kabushiki Kaisha	Japan
LTD	Limited	Canada, England, U.S.
Mli	Maatschappij	Netherlands
NV	Naamioze Vennoostchap	Belgium, Netherlands
OYJ	Osakeyhtio	Finland
P/L	Proprietary Limited	Australia
PLC	Public Limited Company	England, Scotland
PT	Perusahaan Terbatas	Indonesia
SA	Sociedad Anonima	Argentina, Brazil, Colombia Spain, Venezuela
	Societe Anonyme	Belgium, France, Switzerland
SpA	Societa per Azioni	Italy
SPRL	Societe de Personnes a Responsabilite Limitee	Belgium
SRL, srl	Societa a Responsabilita Limitata	Italy

Notes on Alphabetizing

Alphabetizing in this directory is by computer sort, which places numerals before letters; and among names, places blanks, hyphens and ampersands before letters. Thus, 3D Co. precedes A Z Co., which precedes A-Z Co., which precedes A&Z Co., which precedes Abiz Co.

Names such as The Jones Corp., Charles Jones Inc., and L. M. Jones & Co. are alphabetized conventionally: all will be found under J.

Names, which consist of initials, only (e.g., LFM Co.) are in strict alphabetical order: Lewis Corp., LFM Co., and Lintz Inc.

While the custom in most countries is to place company designations (Co., Inc., etc.) at the end of the firm's name, that is not always the case. For example, Finland's "Oyj" and Sweden's "AB" sometimes appear at the end and sometimes at the beginning of the company's name. In this directory they have been disregarded in alphabetizing. The reader is advised to check more than one location when looking for a firm whose listing might be affected by the company designation.

Special Notes

North American Industry Classification System (NAICS)

We have included the North American Industry Classification System (NAICS revised 2002) as the numeric industrial classification search tool. The official U.S. Census Bureau listing of all NAICS is available at **www.census.gov/epcd/naics02/**

Revenue Figures

All revenue (Rev) figures have been converted to US $ and are quoted in millions.

FOREIGN FIRMS OPERATING IN THE UNITED STATES
(Grouped by Country)

Part One groups foreign firms by country. Within each country, the foreign firms are listed alphabetically noted by a bullet. The American firm(s) owned by or affiliated with the foreign firm is indented.

Argentina

- **AEROLINEAS ARGENTINAS SA**
  Aerolíneas Argentinas Terminal, Ezeiza International Airport, Ezeiza, 1014 Buenos Aires, Argentina
  CEO: Daniel Burlas, CEO   Tel: 54-11-5480-6111
  Bus: *Airline transport services.*   Fax: 54-11-5480-6111
                                             www.aerolineas.com.ar
  NAICS: 481111

    AEROLINEAS ARGENTINAS
    45 Rockefeller Plaza, New York, New York 10111-0100
    CEO: Edwardo Avadia   Tel: (212) 698-2050   %FO: 100
    Bus: *Airlines transport services.*   Fax: (212) 698-2050

    AEROLINEAS ARGENTINAS
    5805 Blue Lagoon Dr., Miami, Florida 33126-2053
    CEO: Juan Dimichele   Tel: (305) 261-0100   %FO: 100
    Bus: *Airlines transport services.*   Fax: (305) 261-0100

    AEROLINEAS ARGENTINAS
    JFK International Airport, Jamaica, New York 11432
    CEO: Silvia Faretera   Tel: (718) 632-1721   %FO: 100
    Bus: *Airlines transport services.*   Fax: (718) 632-1721

    AEROLINEAS ARGENTINAS
    5065 Westheimer Rd., Houston, Texas 77056-5605
    CEO: Edwardo Abadia   Tel: (713) 522-9877   %FO: 100
    Bus: *Airlines transport services.*   Fax: (713) 522-9877

    AEROLINEAS ARGENTINAS
    3101 Burgundy Rd., Alexandria, Virginia 22303-1211
    CEO: Maria Graciano   Tel: (703) 960-1679   %FO: 100
    Bus: *Airlines transport services.*   Fax: (703) 960-1679

- **ALLENDE & BREA**
  Maipu 1300, 10 Piso, 1006 Buenos Aires, Argentina
  CEO: Osvaldo J. Marzorati, PR   Tel: 54-11-4318-9900
  Bus: *International law firm.*   Fax: 54-11-4313-9999   Emp: 100
                                            www.allendebrea.com
  NAICS: 541110

    ALLENDE & BREA
    885 Woodstock Rd., Ste. 430, Atlanta, Georgia 30075
    CEO: Paula B. Holfeld   Tel: (770) 906-5696   %FO: 100
    Bus: *International law firm.*   Fax: (770) 906-5696

    ALLENDE & BREA
    201 South Biscayne Blvd., 34/F, Miami, Florida 33131
    CEO: Daniel Korn   Tel: (305) 351-0760   %FO: 100
    Bus: *International law firm.*   Fax: (305) 371-5732

- **BANCO DE GALICIA Y BUENOS AIRES**
  General Juan D. Peron 407, 2 Piso, C1038AAI Buenos Aires, Argentina
  CEO: Antonio R. Garces, CEO   Tel: 54-11-329-6000   Rev: $1,700
  Bus: *General banking services.*   Fax: 54-11-329-6100   Emp: 8,865
                                       www.bancogalicia.com.ar
  NAICS: 522110

    BANCO DE GALICIA Y BUENOS AIRES
    300 Park Ave., 20/F, New York, New York 10022
    CEO: Hector E. Arzeno, EVP   Tel: (212) 906-3700   %FO: 100
    Bus: *General banking services.* Fax: (212) 906-3777

- **BANCO DE LA NACION ARGENTINA**
  Bartolmoe Mitre, 326, 1036 Buenos Aires, Argentina
  CEO: Felisa Josefina Miceli, Pres. & CEO   Tel: 54-11-347-6000   Rev: $1,792
  Bus: *Commercial banking services.*   Fax: 54-11-347-8097   Emp: 8,865
                                               www.bna.com.ar
  NAICS: 522110

    BANCO DE LA NACION ARGENTINA
    299 Park Ave., 2/F, New York, New York 10171
    CEO: George Volpini, Sr. Prtn.   Tel: (212) 303-0600   %FO: 100
    Bus: *Commercial banking services.* Fax: (212)303-0805

    BANCO DE LA NACION ARGENTINA
    777 Brickell Ave., Miami, Florida 33131
    CEO: Arturo Almado, Mgr.   Tel: (305) 371-7500   %FO: 100
    Bus: *Commercial banking services.* Fax: (305) 374-7805

- **CENTER GROUP**
  Cerrito, 1070 - 2º Piso, 1010 Buenos Aires, Argentina
  CEO: Viviana Maggiori, CEO   Tel: 54-11-4375-6200
  Bus: *Management consulting and logistics services.* Fax: 54-11-4816-0909
                                                    www.centergroup.net
  NAICS: 541611

    CENTER GROUP
    600 Brickell Ave., Ste. 300 East, Miami, Florida 33131
    CEO: Claudio Cury   Tel: (305) 371-1300   %FO: 100
    Bus: *Management consulting and logistics* Fax: (305) 675-2467
      services.

- **CLAXSON INTERACTIVE GROUP INC.**
  Avenida Melian 2752, C1430EYH Buenos Aires, Argentina
  CEO: Roberto Vivo-Chaneton, CEO   Tel: 54-11-4546-8000   Rev: $82
  Bus: *Multimedia company providing branded* Fax: 54-11-4546-8000   Emp: 954
    entertainment content targeted to Spanish and www.claxson.com
    Portuguese speakers around the world.
  NAICS: 512110, 512191, 515111, 515120, 516110

CLAXSON INTERACTIVE GROUP INC.
404 Washington Ave., 8/F, Miami, Florida 33139
CEO: Samira Montoya   Tel: (305) 894-3500   %FO: 100
Bus: *Entertainment content for Spanish and*   Fax: (305) 894-3600
       Portuguese-speaking audiences.

● **IMPSAT FIBER NETWORKS, INC.**
Elvira Rawson de Dellepiane 150, Piso 8, C1107BCA Buenos Aires, Argentina
CEO: Ricardo A. Verdaguer, CEO   Tel: 54-11-5170-0000   Rev: $227
Bus: *Voice and data telecommunications services.*   Fax: 54-11-5170-6500   Emp: 1,270
                                                              www.impsat.com
NAICS: 517410, 517910

   IMPSAT FIBER NETWORKS USA
   2040 North Dixie Hwy., Wilton Manors, Florida 33305
   CEO: Mauricio Ceballos, Mgr.   Tel: (954) 779-7171   %FO: 100
   Bus: *Voice and data telecommunications services.* Fax: (954) 779-3766

● **SIDERAR S.A.I.C**
Avenida Leandro N. Alem 1067, 1001 Buenos Aires, Argentina
CEO: Paolo Rocca, CEO   Tel: 54-11-4318-2044   Rev: $1,232
Bus: *Mfr. flat rolled steel.*   Fax: 54-11-4313-2092   Emp: 4,729
                                                              www.siderar.com.ar
NAICS: 331221

   SIDERAR CORPORATION
   2200 West Loop South, Ste. 750, Houston, Texas 77041
   CEO: Mario Vespa   Tel: (713) 767-4400   %FO: 100
   Bus: *Flat rolled steel manufacture and sales..*   Fax: (713) 767-4444

Australia

- **ALTIUM LIMITED**
  12A Rodborough Rd., Frenchs Forest NSW 2086, Australia
  CEO: Nick Martin, CEO   Tel: 61-2-9975-7710   Rev: $30
  Bus: *Computer design software manufacture.*   Fax: 61-2-9975-7720   Emp: 300
        www.altium.com
  NAICS: 541511

    ALTIUM INC.
    17140 Bernardo Center Dr., Ste. 100, San Diego, California 92128
    CEO: Bruce Edwards   Tel: (858) 485-4600   %FO: 100
    Bus: *Computer design software manufacture.*   Fax: (858) 485-4610

- **AMCOR LTD.**
  679 Victoria St., Abbotsford VIC 3067, Australia
  CEO: Louis Lachal, CEO   Tel: 61-3-9226-9000   Rev: $7,231
  Bus: *Paper and wood products and packaging*   Fax: 61-3-9226-9050   Emp: 20
  manufacture and sales.   www.amcor.com.au
  NAICS: 321999, 322299

    AMCOR FLEXIBLES
    747 Bowman Ave., Hagerstown, Maryland 21740-6871
    CEO: David Bradley, Gen. Mgr.   Tel: (301) 745-5000   %FO: 100
    Bus: *Paper and wood products and packaging*   Fax: (301) 745-5005
    manufacture and sales.

    AMCOR FLEXIBLES
    150 Horner Ave., Ashland, Massachusetts 01721-0227
    CEO: Kerry Turner, Operations Mgr.   Tel: (508) 881-2440   %FO: 100
    Bus: *Paper and wood products and packaging*   Fax: (508) 881-7234
    manufacture and sales.

    AMCOR FLEXIBLES
    4101 Lien Rd., Madison, Wisconsin 53707-7730
    CEO: Todd Hurd, Operations Mgr.   Tel: (608) 249-0404   %FO: 100
    Bus: *Paper and wood products and packaging*   Fax: (608) 249-4175
    manufacture and sales.

    AMCOR FLEXIBLES
    220 Shreve St., Mount Holly, New Jersey 08060-0158
    CEO: Michael Orye, Dir.   Tel: (609) 267-5900   %FO: 100
    Bus: *Paper and wood products and packaging*   Fax: (609) 267-7437
    manufacture and sales.

    AMCOR FLEXIBLES
    1919 South Butterfield Rd., Mundelein, Illinois 60060-9735
    CEO: Thomas Haney, Gen. Mgr.   Tel: (847) 362-9000   %FO: 100
    Bus: *Paper and wood products and packaging*   Fax: (847) 918-4600
    manufacture and sales.

AMCOR PACKAGING USA INC.
43700 Gen Mar, Novi, Michigan 48375
CEO: Bob Humberger, Mgr.   Tel: (248) 347-7590   %FO: 100
Bus: *Glass containers manufacture.*   Fax: (248) 347-7590

AMCOR PACKAGING USA INC.
10521 South Highway M 52, Manchester, Michigan 48158
CEO: William Long, Mgr.   Tel: (734) 428-9741   %FO: 100
Bus: *Polyethylene terephthalate (PET) plastic*   Fax: (734) 428-9741
  bottles manufacture.

AMCOR PACKAGING USA INC.
6600 Valley View St., Buena Park, California 90620
CEO: Louis Lachal, VP   Tel: (714) 562-2001   %FO: 100
Bus: *Holding company for sales of paper and*   Fax: (714) 562-2030
  wood products.

AMCOR PET PACKAGING
750 Expressway Dr., Itasca, Illinois 60143
CEO: Randy Kluber, Plant Mgr.   Tel: (630) 773-3235   %FO: 100
Bus: *Polyethylene terephthalate (PET) plastic*   Fax: (630) 773-3260

AMCOR PET PACKAGING
6974 Schantz Rd., Allentown, Pennsylvania 18106
CEO: Bob Kaczynski, Plant Mgr.   Tel: (610) 871-9000   %FO: 100
Bus: *Polyethylene terephthalate (PET) plastic*   Fax: (610) 871-9050

AMCOR PET PACKAGING
180 Jackson Plaza, Ann Arbor, Michigan 48103
CEO: William Long, Pres.   Tel: (734) 428-9741   %FO: 100
Bus: *Polyethylene terephthalate (PET) plastic*   Fax: (734) 302-2298

AMCOR PET PACKAGING
3700 Lakeside Dr., Ste. 470, Miramar, Florida 33027
CEO: Jorge Sanz, Mktg.   Tel: (954) 704-4552   %FO: 100
Bus: *Polyethylene terephthalate (PET) plastic*   Fax: (954) 704-0443

AMCOR PET PACKAGING
753 Central Florida Pkwy., Orlando, Florida 32824
CEO: Sam Schmeber, Plant Mgr.   Tel: (407) 859-7560   %FO: 100
Bus: *Polyethylene terephthalate (PET) plastic*   Fax: (407) 857-6436

AMCOR PET PACKAGING
801 Memorial Dr., Nicholasville, Kentucky 40356
CEO: Larry Saula, Plant Mgr.   Tel: (859) 885-6087   %FO: 100
Bus: *Polyethylene terephthalate (PET) plastic*   Fax: (859) 885-7484

AMCOR PET PACKAGING
3201 Bearing Dr., Franklin, Indiana 46131
CEO: Tom Balk, Plant Mgr.   Tel: (317) 736-4313   %FO: 100
Bus: *Polyethylene terephthalate (PET) plastic*   Fax: (317) 736-4067

Australia

AMCOR PET PACKAGING
4234 Fleetwood Rd., Ft. Worth, Texas 76155
CEO: Mike Simpson, Plant Mgr.
Bus: *Polyethylene terephthalate (PET) plastic*

Tel: (817) 267-5917
Fax: (817) 267-9913

%FO: 100

AMCOR PET PACKAGING
4990 Ironton St., Denver, Colorado 80239
CEO: Jeff Cowan, Plant Mgr.
Bus: *Polyethylene terephthalate (PET) plastic*

Tel: (303) 371-1350
Fax: (303) 373-0450

%FO: 100

AMCOR PET PACKAGING
2110 Yates Ave., Commerce, California 90040
CEO: John Salo, Plant Mgr.
Bus: *Polyethylene terephthalate (PET) plastic*

Tel: (323) 838-6300
Fax: (323) 838-6309

%FO: 100

AMCOR PET PACKAGING
2425 S. Watney Way, Fairfield, California 94533
CEO: Jay Blessing, Dir.
Bus: *Polyethylene terephthalate (PET) plastic*

Tel: (707) 399-6500
Fax: (707) 421-1999

%FO: 100

AMCOR PET PACKAGING
401 Nestle Way, Lathrop, California 95330
CEO: Dan Silva, Mgr.
Bus: *Polyethylene terephthalate (PET) plastic*

Tel: (209) 858-9252
Fax: (209) 858-0248

%FO: 100

AMCOR PET PACKAGING
3045-32nd Ave. SW, Tumwater, Washington 98512
CEO: Bruce Lind
Bus: *Polyethylene terephthalate (PET) plastic*

Tel: (360) 943-2527
Fax: (360) 943-2587

%FO: 100

AMCOR PET PACKAGING
1080 Jenkins Brothers Rd., Blythewood, South Carolina 29016
CEO: Jeff McGrory, Plant Mgr.
Bus: *Polyethylene terephthalate (PET) plastic*

Tel: (803) 691-7000
Fax: (803) 691-7100

%FO: 100

AMCOR PET PACKAGING
9939 Widmer Rd., Lenexa, Kansas 66215
CEO: Roger Justice, Plant Mgr.
Bus: *Polyethylene terephthalate (PET) plastic*

Tel: (913) 894-2211
Fax: (913) 319-0995

%FO: 100

AMCOR PET PACKAGING R & D CENTER
10521 S. Hwy M-52, Manchester, Michigan 48158
CEO: Russell Hubbard, VP
Bus: *Polyethylene terephthalate (PET) plastic*

Tel: (734) 428-9741
Fax: (734) 428-4622

%FO: 100

AMCOR PLASTUBE
1167 Ridgewood Circle, Lake In The Hills, Illinois 60156
CEO: Jennifer Hackett, Mktg.
Bus: *Paper and wood products and packaging
manufacture and sales.*

Tel: (847) 854-7760
Fax: (847) 854-7763

%FO: 100

AMCOR SUNCLIPSE
6600 Valley View St., Buena Park, California 90620
CEO: Eric Bloom, Pres. & CEO
Bus: *Paper and wood products and packaging manufacture and sales.*

Tel: (714) 562-6000
Fax: (714) 562-6059

%FO: 100

BERICAP (JV)
401 North Michigan Ave., Ste. 2525, Chicago, Illinois 60611-4212
CEO: Ludger Roedder, Sales Mgr.
Bus: *Paper and wood products and packaging manufacture and sales.*

Tel: (312) 832-9013
Fax: (312) 832-9018

%FO: 100

BERICAP (JV)
1671-B Champagne Ave., Ontario, California 91761
CEO: Stephen Buckley, Plant Mgr.
Bus: *Paper and wood products and packaging manufacture and sales.*

Tel: (909) 390-5518
Fax: (909) 390-5597

%FO: 100

● **ANIMAL LOGIC GROUP __ THE**
Fox Studios Australia, Bldg. 54/FSA, #19, Driver Ave., Moore Park NSW 1363, Australia
CEO: Zareh Nalbandian, Mng. Dir.
Bus: *Commercial and television visual effects; software developer.*
NAICS: 511210, 512110, 512191, 512199

Tel: 61-2-9383-4800
Fax: 61-2-9383-4801
www.animallogic.com

THE ANIMAL LOGIC GROUP
1117 Abbot Kinney Blvd., Venice, California 90291
CEO: Maury Strong, Exec. Dir.
Bus: *Commercial and television visual effects.*

Tel: (310) 664-8765
Fax: (310) 664-9355

%FO: 100

● **ANSELL LIMITED**
Level 3, 678 Victoria St., Richmond VIC 3121, Australia
CEO: Douglas D. Tough, Chmn.
Bus: *Latex and rubber products and needles manufacture.*
NAICS: 334517, 339112, 339113, 339114, 423450, 811219

Tel: 61-3-9264-0888
Fax: 61-3-9264-0886
www.ansell.com

Rev: $880
Emp: 16,000

ANSELL HEALTHCARE INC.
200 Schulz Dr., Red Bank, New Jersey 07701
CEO: Roland Nonnenmacher, CEO
Bus: *Industrial and medical gloves manufacture and distribution.*

Tel: (732) 345-5400
Fax: (732) 345-9695

%FO: 100

● **ARISTOCRAT LEISURE LIMITED**
71 Longueville Rd. Lane, Cove NSW 2066, Australia
CEO: Paul Oneile, CEO
Bus: *Mfr. video gaming machines.*

NAICS: 334310

Tel: 61-2-9413-6300
Fax: 61-2-9420-1354
www.aristocrat.com.au

Rev: $886
Emp: 2,080

ARISTOCRAT TECHNOLOGIES INC.
7230 Amigo St., Las Vegas, Nevada 89119
CEO: M. Gavin Isaacs, HR
Bus: *Mfr. video gaming machines.*

Tel: (702) 270-1000
Fax: (702) 270-1469

%FO: 100
Emp: 120

- **ASI ENTERTAINMENT INC.**
  Factory 2/12, Candlebark Court, Research VIC 3095, Australia
  CEO: Ronald J. Chapman, Pres.
  Bus: *Supplies in-flight video entertainment systems to airlines and ground communications.*
  Tel: 61-3-9437-1233
  Fax: 61-3-9437-1299
  www.asig.com
  Emp: 3
  NAICS: 334119, 511210

  ASI ENTERTAINMENT
  101 North Brand Blvd., Ste. 1700, Glendale, California 91203-2628
  CEO: Bill Tayler, CEO
  Bus: *Specializes in research for television programming.*
  Tel: (818) 637-5600
  Fax:
  %FO: 100

  ASI ENTERTAINMENT
  15200 E. Girard Ave., Aurora, Colorado 80014-3988
  CEO: Ronald Chapman, Pres.
  Bus: *Software & Airline data*
  Tel: (970) 881-3573
  Fax:
  Emp: 4

  CASTLER
  1 University Plaza, Ste. 8, Hackensack, New Jersey 07601-6207
  CEO: Richard Feldman, Mgr.
  Bus: *Commercial research.*
  Tel: (201) 489-4889
  Fax:
  %FO: 100

- **AUSTAL LIMITED**
  100 Clarence Beach Rd., Henderson WA 6166, Australia
  CEO: John Rothwell, Exec. Chmn.
  Bus: *Design and construction of customized aluminum vessels.*
  Tel: 61-8-9410-1111
  Fax: 61-8-9410-2564
  www.austal.com
  Rev: $214
  Emp: 1,209
  NAICS: 336611

  AUSTAL USA
  100 Dunlap Dr., PO Box 1049, Mobile, Alabama 36633
  CEO: Chris Pemberton, VP Sales
  Bus: *Ship manufacturing and sales.*
  Tel: (251) 434-8000
  Fax: (251) 434-8080
  %FO: 100

- **AUSTRALIA & NEW ZEALAND BANKING GROUP LTD.**
  Level 6, 100 Queen St., Melbourne VIC 3000, Australia
  CEO: John McFarlane, CEO
  Bus: *International banking services.*
  Tel: 61-3-9273-6141
  Fax: 61-3-9273-6142
  www.anz.com.au
  Rev: $12,736
  Emp: 28,755
  NAICS: 522110, 522293

  AUSTRALIA & NEW ZEALAND BANKING GROUP LTD.
  1177 Ave. of the Americas, 6/F, New York, New York 10036
  CEO: R. Scott McInnis, EVP
  Bus: *International banking services.*
  Tel: (212) 801-9800
  Fax: (212) 801-9859
  %FO: 100

- **AUSTRALIAN BROADCASTING CORP.**
  700 Harris St., Ultimo, Sydney NSW 2007, Australia
  CEO: John Gallagher, CEO
  Bus: *Television and radio broadcasting.*
  Tel: 61-2-9339-1500
  Fax: 61-2-9333-5305
  www.abc.net.au
  Rev: $579
  Emp: 4,700
  NAICS: 515111, 515120

AUSTRALIAN BROADCASTING CORP.
45 Rockefeller Plaza, Ste. 2710, New York, New York 10011
CEO: Maggie M. Jones, Mgr.   Tel: (212) 332-2540   %FO: 100
Bus: *TV and radio broadcasting.*   Fax: (212) 813-2497

● **AVENUE GROUP INC.**
34-36 Punt Rd., Melbourne VIC 3181, Australia
CEO: Levi Mochkin, CEO   Tel: 61-3-9533-7800
Bus: *Petroleum exploration; oil and gas.*   Fax: 61-3-9533-7900
www.avenuegroupinc.com
NAICS: 211111, 213111, 213112

   AVENUE ENERGY INC.
   17547 Venture Blvd., Ste. 305, Encino, California 91316
   CEO: Norman Singer   Tel: (818) 465-1200   %FO: 100
   Bus: *Oil and gas exploration.*   Fax: (818) 301-2708

● **BARBEQUES GALORE LIMITED**
327 Chisholm Rd., Sydney NSW 2144, Australia
CEO: Sam Linz, Chmn. & CEO   Tel: 61-2-9704-4177   Rev: $225
Bus: *Mfr. grills, smokers, sauces, cookbooks and*   Fax: 61-2-9704-4201   Emp: 1,174
barbecue accessories.   www.bbqgalore.com
NAICS: 335221, 442299, 443111

   BARBEQUES GALORE U.S.
   15041 Blake Pkwy., Irvine, California 92602
   CEO: Sydney Selati, CEO   Tel: (949) 597-2400   %FO: 100
   Bus: *Mfr. grills, smokers, sauces.*   Fax: (949) 597-2435

   BARBEQUES GALORE U.S.
   13274 Jamboree, Irvine, California 92620
   CEO: George Gonzales, Mgr.   Tel: (714) 505-0893   %FO: 100
   Bus: *Mfr. grills, smokers, sauces.*   Fax: (714) 505-0894

● **BHP BILLITON LIMITED**
180 Lonsdale St., Melbourne VIC 3000, Australia
CEO: Charles W. Goodyear, CEO   Tel: 61-3-9609-3333   Rev: $23,513
Bus: *Exploration of petroleum, copper, steel and*   Fax: 61-3-9609-3015   Emp: 35,000
minerals. (JV of BHP BILLITON PLC. UK)   www.bhpbilliton.com
NAICS: 212113, 212234, 213112

   BHP BILLITON
   1360 Post Oak Blvd., Ste. 150, Houston, Texas 77056
   CEO: Tom Oddie   Tel: (713) 961-8500   %FO: 100
   Bus: *Mining silver, gold zinc and lead. (JV with*   Fax: (713) 961-8400
   Hecla Mining).

   BHP STEEL BUILDING PRODUCTS USA
   2110 Enterprise Blvd., West Sacramento, California 95691
   CEO: Jeff Freidman   Tel: (916) 372-6851   %FO: 100
   Bus: *Roofing products manufacture.*   Fax: (916) 372-7606

● **BILLABONG INTERNATIONAL LTD.**
1 Billabong Place, Burleigh Heads QLD 4220, Australia
CEO: Derek O'Neill, CEO
Bus: *Sporting products, including surfboards,*
snowboards, skateboards and sports apparel
manufacture.

Tel: 61-75-589-9899
Fax: 61-75-589-9800
www.billabongcorporate.com

Rev: $467
Emp: 1,321

NAICS: 315211, 315212, 315223, 315224, 315232, 315299, 315991, 315999, 424320, 424330, 424340, 448110,
448120, 448130, 448140, 448190, 448210,
448310, 448320, 453998, 532220

    BILLABONG USA, INC.
    117 Waterworks Way, Irvine, California 92618
    CEO: Paul Naude, Pres.
    Bus: *Mfr. sporting products, including*
       surfboards, snowboards, skateboards and

Tel: (949) 753-7222
Fax: (949) 753-7223

%FO: 100
Emp: 200

● **BLUESCOPE STEEL LTD.**
120 Collins St., Level 11, Melbourne VIC 3000, Australia
CEO: Graham Kraehe, Chmn.
Bus: *Coated steel mfr/dist.*

Tel: 61-3-9666-4000
Fax: 61-3-9666-4111
www.bluescopesteel.com

Rev: $3,980
Emp: 16,000

NAICS: 331111

    BUTLER MANUFACTURING CO.
    1540 Genessee St., Kansas City, Missouri 64102
    CEO: Patrick Finan, Pres.
    Bus: *Pre-engineered building mfr; aluminum*
       supplier and construction management
       services.

Tel: (816) 968-3000
Fax: (816) 968-3279

%FO: 100
Emp: 4,300

    CASTRIP LLC (JV)
    2100 Rexford Rd., Ste. 420, Charlotte, North Carolina 28211
    CEO: Peter Campbell, Mktg. Dir.
    Bus: *Steel mfg. technology.*

Tel: (704) 972-1820
Fax: (704) 972-1829

%FO: 48

    NORTH STAR STEEL INC. (JV)
    3601 W. 76th St., Ste 300, Edina, Minnesota 55435
    CEO: Jon Ruth, Pres.
    Bus: *Steel mfg. technology.*

Tel: (952) 367-3500
Fax: (952) 367-3082

%FO: 50

● **BORAL LIMITED**
Level 39, AMP Centre, 50 Bridge St., Sydney NSW 2000, Australia
CEO: Rodney T. Pearse, Dir.
Bus: *Building and construction materials (bricks,*
timber, tiles manufacture); and energy
marketing/exploration.

Tel: 61-2-9220-6300
Fax: 61-2-9233-6605
www.boral.com.au

Rev: $2,863
Emp: 13,194

NAICS: 212313, 212319, 212321, 212392, 213111, 321911, 327121, 327331, 327332, 327390, 327420, 327991,
327999, 332321, 423320

    BORAL INDUSTRIES, INC.
    200 Mansell Ct. East, Ste. 310, Roswell, Georgia 30076
    CEO: Emery Severin, Pres.
    Bus: *Building & construction materials*
       manufacturing/distribution.

Tel: (770) 645-4500
Fax: (770) 645-2888

%FO: 100
Emp: 1,900

BORAL MATERIAL TECHNOLOGIES INC.
45 NE Loop 410, Ste. 700, San Antonio, Texas 78216
CEO: Bob Kepford, Pres.   Tel: (210) 349-4069   %FO: 100
Bus: *Building & construction materials*   Fax: (210) 349-8512   Emp: 330
    manufacturing/distribution.

BORAL MATERIAL TECHNOLOGIES INC.
10851 N. Black Canyon Hwy., Phoenix, Arizona 85029-4755
CEO: David Allen, Mgr.   Tel: (602) 861-5100   %FO: 100
Bus: *Building & construction materials*   Fax: (602) 861-0885
    manufacturing/distribution.

BORAL MATERIAL TECHNOLOGIES INC.
10817 Notus Lane, Ste. E-102, El Paso, Texas 79935
CEO: Gary Skelton, Gen. Mgr.   Tel: (915) 591-2149   %FO: 100
Bus: *Building & construction materials*   Fax: (915) 494-1299
    manufacturing/distribution.

BORAL MATERIAL TECHNOLOGIES INC.
227 Pearl St., Auburndale, Florida 33823-3153
CEO: Paul B. Bieber, Mgr.   Tel: (863) 967-6626
Bus: *Building & construction materials*   Fax: (863) 967-6626
    manufacturing/distribution.

MONIER LIFETILE
6500 Brem Ln., Gilroy, California 95020
CEO: Lewis Garcia   Tel: (408) 847-2721   %FO: 100
Bus: *Mfr. concrete tiles.*   Fax: (408) 847-2721

US TILE
909 Railroad St, Corona, California 92882 1906
CEO: Greg Heydenreich   Tel: (909) 737-0200   %FO: 100
Bus: *Mfr. clay roof tiles.*   Fax: (909) 734-9591

● **BOWEN & GROVES PTY LTD.**
92 Victor Crescent, Ste. 2, Narre Warren VIC 3805, Australia
CEO: Geoff Groves, CEO   Tel: 61-3-9705-2244
Bus: *Enterprise Resource Planning (ERP) software*   Fax: 61-3-9705-2944
    manufacture.   www.bowen-groves.com
NAICS: 511210

    BOWEN & GROVES PTY LTD.
    1682 Langley Ave., Irvine, California 92614
    CEO: Aleta Kane, COO   Tel: (949) 260-0344   %FO: 100
    Bus: *ERP software manufacture and sales.*   Fax: (949) 260-0343

● **BRAMBLES INDUSTRIES LIMITED**
Level 40, Gateway, 1 Macquarie Place, Sydney NSW2000, Australia
CEO: David J. Turner, CEO   Tel: 61-2-9256-5222   Rev: $5,382
Bus: *Materials handling, industrial services and*   Fax: 61-2-9256-5299   Emp: 28,199
    equipment operations.   www.brambles.com
NAICS: 333922, 333924, 333993, 334513, 335314, 488510, 511210, 541614, 561410, 562111

Australia

BRAMBLES AUSTRALIA
105 Harborcrest Dr., Seabrook, Texas 77586
CEO: John Marcussen   Tel: (281) 326-7336
Bus: *Industrial plant services*   Fax:

BRAMBLES INDUSTRIES (CHEP)
8517 S. Park Cir., Orlando, Florida 32819
CEO: David Mezzanotte, Pres.   Tel: (407) 563-2000
Bus: *Support activities for transportation*   Fax: (407) 563-2001   Emp: 7,704

BRAMBLES INDUSTRIES (INTERLAKE
1230 E. Diehl Rd., Ste. 400, Naperville, Illinois 60563
CEO: Mike Gonzales, Pres. & CEO   Tel: (630) 245-8800
Bus: *Mfr. of automotive & aerospace parts &*   Fax: (630) 245-8906
    materials

BRAMBLES INDUSTRIES (RECALL)
1 Recall Center, 180 Technology Pkwy., Rm. 100, Norcross, Georgia 30092
CEO: Alfredo Trujilo, Pres.   Tel: (770) 776-1000   %FO: 100
Bus: *Information & records management services* Fax: (770) 776-1001   Emp: 3,856

● **CHEMGENEX PHARMACEUTICALS LTD.**
1 Pigdon's Rd., Geelong VIC 3217, Australia
CEO: Greg Collier, CEO   Tel: 61-3-5227-2752   Rev: $2
Bus: *Targeted medicine development.*   Fax: 61-3-5227-1322   Emp: 8
                                                        www.chemgenex.com/wt/home/index
   NAICS: 325411, 325412, 325414

    CHEMGENEX PHARMACEUTICALS LTD.
   3475 Edison Way, Ste. M, Menlo Park, California 94025
   CEO: Dennis Brown, Pres.   Tel: (650) 474-9800   %FO: 100
   Bus: *Develops targeted medicine.*   Fax: (650) 474-9808

● **COMMONWEALTH BANK OF AUSTRALIA**
Level 1, 48 Martin Place, Sydney NSW 1155, Australia
CEO: David V. Murray, CEO & Mng. Dir.   Tel: 61-2-9378-2000   Rev: $15,176
Bus: *General banking, investment and life insurance* Fax: 61-2-9378-3317   Emp: 36,296
    services.   www.commbank.com.au
   NAICS: 522110, 522210, 522292, 523920, 523930, 524210

    COMMONWEALTH BANK OF AUSTRALIA
   599 Lexington Ave., 17/F, New York, New York 10022
   CEO: Patrick Hidreth   Tel: (212) 848-9200   %FO: 100
   Bus: *International banking services.*   Fax: (212) 336-7725

● **COMPUTERSHARE LTD.**
Yarra Falls, 452 Johnson St., Abbotsford VIC 3067, Australia
CEO: Christopher John Morris, CEO   Tel: 61-3-9415-5050   Rev: $653
Bus: *Financial market service provider.*   Fax: 61-3-9473-2500   Emp: 8,000
                                                        www.computershare.com.au
   NAICS: 523999

COMPUTERSHARE INVESTOR SERVICES U.S.A.
2 N. LaSalle St., 3/F, Chicago, Illinois 60602
CEO: Steven Rothbloom, Mng. Dir.
Bus: *Financial market services provider.*

Tel: (312) 588-4990
Fax: (312) 601-4332

%FO: 100

● **CSL LTD.**
45 Poplar Rd., Parkville VIC 3052, Australia
CEO: Brian A. McNamee, CEO & Mng. Dir.
Bus: *Specialty biopharmaceutical mfg.*

Tel: 61-3-9389-1911
Fax: 61-3-9389-1434
www.csl.com.au

Rev: $1,138

NAICS: 325411, 325412, 325414

ZLB BEHRING LLC
1020 First Ave., King of Prussia, Pennsylvania 19406
CEO: Peter Turner, Pres.
Bus: *Plasma collection.*

Tel: (610) 878-4000
Fax: (610) 878-4009

%FO: 100

● **CSR LIMITED**
9 Help St., Level 1, Chatswood NSW 2067, Australia
CEO: Alexander Norman Brennan, Mng. Dir.
Bus: *Building and construction materials; real estate
and sugar industry investments.*

Tel: 61-2-9235-8000
Fax: 61-2-9235-8044
www.csr.com.au

Rev: $1,484
Emp: 1,535

NAICS: 311311, 311312, 327121, 327123, 327331, 327332, 327390, 327420, 331312

RINKER MATERIALS CORPORATION
1501 Belvedere Rd., West Palm Beach, Florida 33406
CEO: David Clarke, Pres. & CEO
Bus: *Building and construction materials.*

Tel: (800) 226-5521
Fax: (561) 820-8309

%FO: 100
Emp: 10,695

● **FINEWRAP AUSTRALIA PTY LTD.**
4 Edward St., Oakleigh VIC 3166, Australia
CEO: Greg Rosshandler, Mng. Dir.
Bus: *Flexible packaging production.*

Tel: 61-3-9568-3966
Fax: 61-3-9569-9373
www.finewrap.com.au

NAICS: 326199

FINEWRAP USA, INC.
1902 Kimberly Park Dr., Dalton, Georgia 30720
CEO: Greg Rosshandler, Pres.
Bus: *Flexible packaging sales and distribution.*

Tel: (706) 226-9551
Fax: (706) 259-6861

Emp: 40

● **FOSTER'S GROUP LIMITED**
77 Southbank Blvd., Southbank VIC 3006, Australia
CEO: Trevor O'Hoy, CEO
Bus: *Brewing and sales of beer.*

Tel: 61-3-9633-2000
Fax: 61-3-9633-2002
www.fostersgroup.com

Rev: $2,696
Emp: 9,300

NAICS: 312120, 312130

BERINGER BLASS WINE ESTATES LTD.
610 Airpark Rd., Napa, California 94558
CEO: Jamie Odell, Pres.
Bus: *Winemakers.*

Tel: (707) 259-4500
Fax: (707) 259-4542

Emp: 3,800

INTERNATIONAL WINE ACCESSORIES (IWA)
10246 Miller Rd., Dallas, Texas 75238
CEO: Bob Orenstein   Tel: (214) 349-6097
Bus: *Wine accessories.*   Fax: (214) 349-8712

MILLER BREWING COMPANY
3939 West Highland Blvd., Milwaukee, Wisconsin 53208-2866
CEO: Norman Adami, Dir.   Tel: (414) 931-2000
Bus: *Wholesale beer and ale brewer.*   Fax: (414) 931-3735

● **GOLDMAN SACHS JB WERE PTY LTD.**
Level 16, 101 Collins St., Melbourne VIC 3000, Australia
CEO: Terry Campbell, Chmn. & CEO   Tel: 61-3-9679-1534   Rev: $305
Bus: *Financial services: securities.*   Fax: Emp: 1,400
                                     www.gsjbwere.com
NAICS: 523110

    GOLDMAN SACHS TRUST
    1 New York Plaza, Level 42, New York, New York 10004
    CEO: Henry Paulson, CEO   Tel: (212) 357-6550   %FO: 100
    Bus: *Financial services; securities.*   Fax: (212) 357-1100   Emp: 400

● **HITWISE PTY LTD.**
580 St. Kilda Rd., Level 7, Melbourne VIC 3004, Australia
CEO: Andrew Walsh, CEO   Tel: 61-3-8530-2400
Bus: *Publisher of Internet traffic information for*   Fax: 61-3-9529-8907
marketers.   www.hitwise.com
NAICS: 541910

    HITWISE USA INC.
    41 East 11th St., 11/F, New York, New York 10003
    CEO: Chris Maher   Tel: (212) 331-1280   %FO: 100
    Bus: *Publisher of Internet traffic information for*   Fax: (212) 331-1285
    marketers.

● **HOYTS CINEMAS LIMITED**
Hoyts Center, 505-523 George St., Sydney NSW 2000, Australia
CEO: Stuart McInnes, CEO   Tel: 61-2-9273-7373   Rev: $312
Bus: *Owns and operates theater chains.*   Fax: 61-2-9273-7358   Emp: 6,500
                                         www.hoyts.com.au
NAICS: 512120, 512131

    HOYTS CINEMAS CORPORATION
    One Exeter Plaza, Boston, Massachusetts 02116
    CEO: Peter A. Ivany, Chmn.   Tel: (617) 646-5700   %FO: 100
    Bus: *Owns and operates theater chains.*   Fax: Emp: 2,000

● **ILUKA RESOURCES LTD.**
Level 5, 553 Hay St., Perth WA 6000, Australia
CEO: Dr. Richard Aldous, CEO   Tel: 61-8-9221-7611
Bus: *Titanium minerals, tin, coal and quicklime.*   Fax: 61-8-9221-7744
                                               www.iluka.com
NAICS: 331491

ILUKA RESOURCES INC.
1301 Riverplace Blvd., Ste. 700, Jacksonville, Florida 32207
CEO: Elizabeth Revell   Tel: (904) 421-4020   %FO: 100
Bus: *Non-metallic mineral services.*   Fax: (904) 421-4029

ILUKA RESOURCES INC.
12472 St. John Church Rd., Stony Creek, Virginia 23822
CEO: Elizabeth Revell   Tel: (434) 246-8016
Bus: *Mining mineral sands.*   Fax: (434) 246-3039

ILUKA RESOURCES, INC.
1223 Warner Rd., Green Cove Springs, Florida 32043
CEO: Ted Goodman, Gen. Mgr.   Tel: (904) 284-9832   %FO: 100
Bus: *Non-metallic mineral services.*   Fax: (904) 284-4006

● **INTEROIL CORPORATION**
Orchid Plaza, 79-88 Abbott St., Ste 2, Cairns QLD 4870, Australia
CEO: Phil E. Mulacek, Chmn. & Pres. & CEO   Tel: 61-7-4046-4600   Rev: $70
Bus: *Oil refinery, retail and exploration.* Fax: 61-7-4031-4565
                                              www.interoil.com
NAICS: 211111, 213111

   INTEROIL CORPORATION
   25025 I-45 North, Ste. 420, The Woodlands, Texas 77387
   CEO: Christian M. Vinson, CEO   Tel: (281) 292-1800   %FO: 100
   Bus: *Oil refinery.*   Fax: (281) 292-0888

● **LEND LEASE CORPORATION LIMITED**
Level 46, Tower Bldg., Australia Square, Sydney NSW 2000, Australia
CEO: Greg A. Clarke, CEO & Mng. Dir.   Tel: 61-2-9236-6111   Rev: $6,709
Bus: *Engaged in the management of property funds.*   Fax: 61-2-9252-2192   Emp: 9,060
                                             www.lendlease.com.au
NAICS: 236220, 237210, 522310, 531120, 531190

   BOVIS LEND LEASE
   200 Park Ave., New York, New York 10166
   CEO: Peter A. Marchetto, COO   Tel: (212) 592-6800   %FO: 100
   Bus: *Real estate investment.*   Fax: (212) 592-6988   Emp: 592

● **LONELY PLANET PUBLICATIONS**
Locked Bag 1, Footscray VIC 3011, Australia
CEO: Judy Slatyer, CEO   Tel: 61-3-8379-8000
Bus: *Travel guide publisher.*   Fax: 61-3-8379-8111
                                           www.lonelyplanet.com
NAICS: 511130

   LONELY PLANET PUBLICATIONS
   150 Linden St., Oakland, California 94067-2538
   CEO: Greg Mand   Tel: (510) 893-8555   %FO: 100
   Bus: *Travel guide publishers*   Fax: (510) 893-8563

- **MACQUARIE BANK LIMITED**
  No. 1 Martin Place, Sydney NSW 2000, Australia
  CEO: Allan E. Moss, CEO & Mng. Dir.   Tel: 61-2-8232-3333   Rev: $2,595
  Bus: *Engaged in investment banking.*   Fax: 61-2-8232-7780   Emp: 4,700
                                                 www.macquarie.com.au
  NAICS: 522110, 523110, 523120, 523130, 523140, 523920, 523930

  > **MACQUARIE BANK**
  > 1420 Fifth Ave., Ste. 2975, Seattle, Washington 98101
  > CEO: Arthur Porter, CEO   Tel: (206) 674-3380   %FO: 100
  > Bus: *Investment banking.*   Fax: (206) 674-3394   Emp: 6

  > **MACQUARIE BANK**
  > 1 North Wacker Dr., Ste. 900, Chicago, Illinois 60606
  > CEO: Donald Suter, member   Tel: (312) 499-8500   %FO: 100
  > Bus: *Investment banking.*   Fax: Emp: 40

  > **MACQUARIE BANK**
  > Rockefeller Center, 600 Fifth Ave., 21/F, New York, New York 10020
  > CEO: Kim Mills, EVP   Tel: (212) 548-6555   %FO: 100
  > Bus: *Investment banking.*   Fax: (212) 399-8930   Emp: 150

  > **MACQUARIE ELECTRONICS**
  > 11440 W. Bernardo Ct., San Diego, California 92127
  > CEO: David Coons, Pres.   Tel: (858) 207-1092
  > Bus: *Security broker dealer.*   Fax:

  > **MACQUARIE INFRASTRUCTURE CO. TRUST**
  > 600 5th Ave., 21/F, New York, New York 10020
  > CEO: Peter Stokes, CEO   Tel: (212) 548-6538
  > Bus: *Airport management services.*   Fax: Emp: 6,500

- **MAYNE GROUP LTD.**
  390 St. Kilda Rd., Level 21, Melbourne VIC 3004, Australia
  CEO: Stuart B. James, CEO   Tel: 61-3-9868-0700   Rev: $3,479
  Bus: *Healthcare & pharmaceutical provider.*   Fax: 61-3-9867-1179   Emp: 15,300
                                                 www.maynegroup.com
  NAICS: 325411, 325412, 424210

  > **MAYNE PHARMA (USA) INC.**
  > 650 From Rd., Mack-Cali Centre II, 2/F, Paramus, New Jersey 07652
  > CEO: Stuart Hinchen, Pres.   Tel: (201) 225-5500   %FO: 100
  > Bus: *Pharmaceutical manufacturer*   Fax: (201) 225-5515

- **MEAT & LIVESTOCK AUSTRALIA LTD.**
  165 Walker St., Level 1, North Sydney NSW 2060, Australia
  CEO: David Charles Crombie, Dir.   Tel: 61-2-9463-9333   Rev: $96
  Bus: *Promotion and marketing of Australian meat and*   Fax: 61-2-9463-9393   Emp: 213
       livestock.   www.mla.com.au
  NAICS: 541613

MEAT AND LIVESTOCK AUSTRALIA LTD.
1401 K St. NW, Ste. 602, Washington, District of Columbia 20005
CEO: David Palmer, CEO   Tel: (202) 521-2551   %FO: 100
Bus: *Promotion and marketing of Australian meat*   Fax: (202) 521-2699
     and livestock.

● **METAL STORM LTD.**
Level 34, Central Plaza 1, 345 Queen St., Brisbane QLD 4000, Australia
CEO: David A. Smith, CEO   Tel: 61-7-3221-9733   Rev: $4
Bus: *Defense technology development.*   Fax: 61-7-3221-9788
     www.metalstorm.com
NAICS: 332993

    METAL STORM INC.
    4350 N. Fairfax Dr., Ste. 810, Arlington, Virginia 22203
    CEO: Peter Pursey, Mgr.   Tel: (703) 248-8218   %FO: 100
    Bus: *Defense technology development.*   Fax: (703) 248-8262

● **MINCOM LIMITED**
193 Turbot St., Brisbane QLD4000, Australia
CEO: Alan J. McElrea, CEO & Mng. Dir.   Tel: 61-7-3303-3333   Rev: $103
Bus: *Mfr. computer software.*   Fax: 61-7-3303-3232   Emp: 1,000
     www.mincom.com
NAICS: 541511, 541512, 541519

    MINCOM, INC.
    9635 S Maroon Cir., Ste. 100, Englewood, Colorado 80112
    CEO: Ricky Rogers, Pres.   Tel: (303) 446-9000   %FO: 100
    Bus: *Mfr./sales computer software.*   Fax: (303) 446-8664   Emp: 200

● **MYOB LIMITED**
12 Wesley Ct., Burwood East VIC 3151, Australia
CEO: Craig Winkler, CEO   Tel: 61-3-9222-9700   Rev: $40
Bus: *Business management software manufacturer.*   Fax: 61-3-9222-9798   Emp: 450
     www.myob.com
NAICS: 511210

    MYOB US, INC.
    300 Roundhill Dr., Rockaway, New Jersey 07866
    CEO: Cynthia Mackewicz, Gen. Mgr.   Tel: (973) 586-2200   %FO: 100
    Bus: *Business management software*   Fax: (973) 586-2229   Emp: 70
     manufacturer.

● **NATIONAL AUSTRALIA BANK LIMITED**
500 Bourke St., 24/F, Melbourne VIC 3000, Australia
CEO: John M. Stewart, CEO & Mng. Dir.   Tel: 61-3-8641-3500   Rev: $22,055
Bus: *International banking, investment and insurance*   Fax: 61-3-9208-5695   Emp: 43,517
    services.   www.nagroup.com
NAICS: 522110, 522210, 522291, 522292, 522293, 523920, 523930

NATIONAL AUSTRALIA BANK LTD.
245 Park Ave., 28/F, New York, New York 10167
CEO: Thomas W. Hunersen, EVP   Tel: (212) 916-9500   %FO: 100
Bus: *International banking, investment and*   Fax: (212) 983-1969
      insurance services.

● **NOVOGEN LIMITED**
140 Wicks Rd., North Ryde NSW 2113, Australia
CEO: Christopher Naughton, CEO   Tel: 61-2-9878-088   Rev: $11
Bus: *Non-prescription pharmaceuticals manufacture.*   Fax: 61-2-9878-0055   Emp: 67
      www.novogen.com
NAICS: 325411, 325412
    NOVOGEN INC.
    1 Landmark Square, Ste. 240, Stamford, Connecticut 06901
    CEO: Warren Lancaster, VP   Tel: (203) 327-1188
    Bus: *Development of prescription drugs*   Fax: (203) 327-0011   Emp: 10

● **OPTISCAN IMAGING LTD.**
15-17 Normansby Rd., Notting Hill VIC 3168, Australia
CEO: Matthew Barnett, CEO   Tel: 61-3-9538-3333
Bus: *Development and application of microscopic*   Fax: 61-3-9562-7742   Emp: 29
      imaging technologies.   www.optiscan.com
NAICS: 334510, 339112
    OPTISCAN IMAGING LTD.
    555 Industrial Dr., Hartland, Wisconsin 53029
    CEO: Pam Werner   Tel: (262) 369-9510   %FO: 100
    Bus: *Development and application of microscopic*   Fax: (262) 369-9805
      imaging technologies.

● **ORBITAL CORPORATION LIMITED**
1 Whipple St., Balcatta WA 6021, Australia
CEO: Peter Chapman Cook, CEO   Tel: 61-8-9441-2311   Rev: $12
Bus: *Direct fuel injection technology to reduce fuel use*   Fax: 61-8 9441-2133   Emp: 93
      and emissions in engines.   www.orbeng.com.au
NAICS: 336312
    ORBITAL CORPORATION LTD.
    389 W. Hunters Creek Rd., Lapeer, Michigan 48446
    CEO: Robert A. Schmidt, Sales Dir.   Tel: (810) 245-0621
    Bus: *Engaged in direct fuel injection*   Fax: (810) 277-2183

    SYNERJECT LLC
    201 Enterprise Dr., Newport News, Virginia 23603
    CEO: Stephanie Tagliante   Tel: (757) 890-4900   %FO: 50
    Bus: *Engaged in direct fuel injection technology*   Fax: (757) 890-4933   Emp: 75
      to reduce fuel use and emissions in

- **ORICA LIMITED**
Level 9, 1 Nicholson St., Melbourne VIC 3002, Australia
CEO: Malcolm W. Broomhead, CEO
Bus: *Chemicals and explosives manufacturer.*

Tel: 61-3-9665-7111
Fax: 61-3-9665-7937
www.orica.com.

Rev: $3,393
Emp: 10,111

NAICS: 325181, 325211, 325212, 325510, 325611, 325920, 325998, 424690

> **ORICA USA INC.**
> 33101 E. Quincy Ave., Watkins, Colorado 80137
> CEO: Donald Brinker, Pres.
> Bus: *Chemical Manufacturer*
>
> Tel: (303) 268-5000
> Fax: (303) 268-5250

- **PETSEC ENERGY LTD.**
Level 13, 1 Alfred St., Sydney NSW 2000, Australia
CEO: Terrence N. Fern, Chmn. & CEO
Bus: *Exploration and production of oil and gas.*

Tel: 61-2-9247-4605
Fax: 61-2-9251-2410
www.petsec.com

Rev: $45
Emp: 17

NAICS: 211111

> **PETSEC ENERGY INC.**
> 143 Ridgeway Dr., Lafayette, Louisiana 70503
> CEO: Ross A. Keogh, VP
> Bus: *Engaged in exploration and production of oil and gas.*
>
> Tel: (337) 989-1942
> Fax: (337) 981-8784
>
> %FO: 100

- **PRANA BIOTECHNOLOGY LTD.**
Level 2, 369 Royal Parade, Parkville VIC 3052, Australia
CEO: Geoffrey P. Kempler, Chmn.
Bus: *Development of therapies for neurodegenerative conditions.*

Tel: 61-3-9349-4906
Fax: 61-3-9348-0377
www.pranabio.com

Rev: $1
Emp: 12

NAICS: 325411, 325414

> **PRANA BIOTECHNOLOGY LTD.**
> 700 Canal St., Stamford, Connecticut 06902
> CEO: Jon Alsenas, CEO
> Bus: *Development of therapies for neurodegenerative conditions.*
>
> Tel: (203) 328-3097
> Fax: (203) 328-3738
>
> %FO: 100

- **PROTEOME SYSTEMS LIMITED**
Locked Bag 2073, North Ryde NSW 1670, Australia
CEO: Stephen Porges, CEO
Bus: *Proteomics research: discovery and diagnostics and technology.*

Tel: 61-2-9889-1830
Fax: 61-2-9889-1805
www.proteomesystems.com

NAICS: 541710

> **PROTEOME SYSTEMS INC.**
> 6 Gill St., Woburn, Massachusetts 01801
> CEO: William Emhiser
> Bus: *Product manufacture.*
>
> Tel: (781) 932-9477
> Fax: (781) 932-9294
>
> %FO: 100

- **PUBLISHING & BROADCASTING LTD.**
2/F, 54 Park St., Sydney NSW 1028, Australia
CEO: John H. Alexander, CEO & Mng. Dir.   Tel: 61-2-9282-8000   Rev: $2,186
Bus: *Media and entertainment company.*   Fax: 61-2-9282-8828   Emp: 8,270
    www.pbl.com.au
NAICS: 511120, 721120

    ACP NY BUREAU
    Ste. 803, The Soho Building, 110 Greene St., New York, New York 10012
    CEO: Lesley Jackson, Bureau Chief   Tel: (212) 966-5300   %FO: 100
    Bus: *Magazine publishing.*   Fax: (212) 966-1118

    CHANNEL 9 AUSTRALIA INC.
    Ste. 1500, 6255 Sunset Blvd., Los Angeles, California 90028
    CEO: Robert Penfold,   Tel: (323) 461-3853   %FO: 100
    Bus: *Media and entertainment company.*   Fax: (323) 462-4849

- **QANTAS AIRWAYS LTD.**
Qantas Centre, Level 9, Bldg. A, 203 Coward St., Mascot NSW 2020, Australia
CEO: Geoff Dixon, CEO   Tel: 61-2-9691-3636   Rev: $7,832
Bus: *Commercial airline and hotel operators.*   Fax: 61-2-9691-3339   Emp: 33,862
    www.qantas.com.au
NAICS: 481111, 481112, 481212

    QANTAS AIRWAYS LTD.
    841 Apollo St., Ste. 400, El Segundo, California 90245
    CEO: Howard Goldberg, VP Sales   Tel: (310) 726-1400   %FO: 100
    Bus: *Air transport services.*   Fax: (310) 726-1484

- **QBE INSURANCE GROUP LIMITED**
82 Pitt St., Sydney NSW 2000, Australia
CEO: Frank O'Halloran, CEO   Tel: 61-2-9375-4444   Rev: $7,016
Bus: *General insurance.*   Fax: 61-2-9235-3166   Emp: 6,746
    www.qbe.com.
NAICS: 524114, 524126

    QBE INSURANCE CORPORATION
    Wall St. Plaza, 88 Pine St., 16/F, New York, New York 10005-1404
    CEO: Timothy Kenny, Pres.   Tel: (212) 422-1212   %FO: 100
    Bus: *Engaged in general insurance.*   Fax: (212) 422-1313   Emp: 50

- **RESERVE BANK OF AUSTRALIA**
65 Martin Place, Sydney NSW 2000, Australia
CEO: Ian J. Macfarlane, Gov.   Tel: 61-2-9551-8111   Rev: $2,122
Bus: *Central Bank of Australia.*   Fax: 61-2-9551-8000   Emp: 830
    www.rba.gov.au
NAICS: 521110

    RESERVE BANK OF AUSTRALIA, NY REPRESENTATIVE OFFICE
    1 Liberty Plaza, 46/F, New York, New York 10006-1404
    CEO: James Whitelaw, Chief Rep.   Tel: (212) 566-8466   %FO: 100
    Bus: *Australia's central bank.*   Fax: (212) 566-8501

- **RIDLEY CORPORATION LIMITED**
  12 Castlereagh St., 10/F, Sydney NSW 2000, Australia
  CEO: Matthew Bickford-Smith, CEO & Mng. Dir.
  Bus: *Animal feed production.*

  Tel: 61-2-8227-6100
  Fax: 61-2-8227-6002
  www.ridley.com.au

  Rev: $813
  Emp: 2,064

  NAICS: 212399, 311111, 311119

  HUBBARD FEEDS INC.
  104 Oak St., Botkins, Ohio 45306
  CEO: Jack Tracy, Mgr.
  Bus: *Feed products manufacture.*

  Tel: (937) 693-6393
  Fax: (937) 693-3657

  %FO: 100
  Emp: 60

  HUBBARD FEEDS INC.
  424 North Riverfront Dr., Mankato, Minnesota 56002
  CEO: Werner Brown, Mgr.
  Bus: *Feed products manufacture.*

  Tel: (507) 388-9400
  Fax: (507) 388-9415

- **RINKER GROUP LIMITED**
  Level 8, Tower B, 799 Pacific Hwy., Chatswood NSW 2067, Australia
  CEO: David Vincent Clarke, CEO & Mng. Dir.
  Bus: *Heavy building materials manufacture and acquisition.*

  Tel: 61-2-9412-6600
  Fax: 61-2-9412-6601
  www.rinker.com.au

  Rev: $4,312
  Emp: 13,279

  NAICS: 212312, 212319, 212321, 327310, 327331, 327420

  FLORIDA MATERIALS
  1501 Belvedere Rd., West Palm Beach, Florida 33406
  CEO: Will Glusac, Pres.
  Bus: *Construction and building materials manufacture.*

  Tel: (800) 226-5521
  Fax: (561) 820-8309

  %FO: 100

  HYDRO CONDUIT CORPORATION
  6560 Langfield Rd. Bldg 3, Houston, Texas 77092
  CEO: Duncan Gage, Pres.
  Bus: *Construction and building materials manufacture.*

  Tel: (832) 590-5300
  Fax: (852) 590-5399

  %FO: 100

  RINKER MATERIALS CORPORATION
  69 Neck Rd., Westfield, Massachusetts 01085
  CEO: James Lyons
  Bus: *Construction and building materials manufacture.*

  Tel: (413) 562-8547
  Fax: (413) 562-8547

  %FO: 100

  RINKER MATERIALS CORPORATION
  11840 Alico Rd., Ft. Myers, Florida 33913
  CEO: Rodney Keller
  Bus: *Quarry.*

  Tel: (239) 267-5555
  Fax: (239) 267-5555

  %FO: 100

  RINKER MATERIALS CORPORATION
  1501 Belvedere Rd., West Palm Beach, Florida 33406
  CEO: David Clarke, Pres. & CEO
  Bus: *Construction and building materials manufacture.*

  Tel: (800) 226-5521
  Fax: (561) 820-8309

  %FO: 100

Australia

- **RIO TINTO GROUP**
  55 Collins St. Level 33, Melbourne VIC 3001, Australia
  CEO: R. Leigh Clifford, CEO & Mng. Dir.   Tel: 61-3-9283-3333   Rev: $11,344
  Bus: *Mining, metals and industrial minerals.*   Fax: 61-3-9283-3707   Emp: 33,000
      www.riotinto.com
  NAICS: 212111, 212112, 212113, 212210, 212231, 212234, 212291, 212299, 212325, 212391, 212399, 213113, 213114, 324199, 331312

  KENNECOTT ENERGY GROUP
  505 South Gillette Ave., Gillette, Wyoming 82717
  CEO: Bret Clayton, Pres. & CEO   Tel: (307) 687-6000
  Bus: *Electricity and coal.*   Fax: (307) 687-6015   Emp: 1,770

  KENNECOTT EXPLORATION CO.
  224 North 2200 West, Salt Lake City, Utah 84116
  CEO: John V. Main, Pres. & CEO   Tel: (801) 238-2400   %FO: 100
  Bus: *Mining, metals and industrial minerals.*   Fax: (801) 238-2480   Emp: 70

  KENNECOTT GREENS CREEK MINING CO.
  3000 Vintage Blvd., Ste. 200, PO Box 32199, Juneau, Alaska 99801
  CEO: Adrian F. Jackman, Pres. & CEO   Tel: (907) 789-8100
  Bus: *Gold, silver, zinc & lead mining*   Fax: (901) 789-8108

  KENNECOTT MINERALS CO.
  224 N. 2200 West, Salt Lake City, Utah 84116
  CEO: Adrian F. Jackman, CEO   Tel: (801) 238-2492
  Bus: *Gold & silver mining & milling*   Fax: (801) 238-2488

  KENNECOTT UTAH COPPER CORPORATION
  8362 W. 10200 South, Bingham Canyon, Utah 84006
  CEO: William Champion, Pres. & CEO   Tel: (801) 569-6000   %FO: 100
  Bus: *Mining, metals and industrial minerals.*   Fax: (801) 569-6045   Emp: 1,113

  LUZENAC AMERICA, INC.
  345 Inverness Dr. South, Ste. 310, Centennial, Colorado 80112
  CEO: Jon Godla, VP Operations   Tel: (303) 643-0400   %FO: 100
  Bus: *Mining, metals and industrial minerals.*   Fax: (303) 643-0446   Emp: 562

  U.S. BORAX AND CHEMICAL CORPORATION
  26877 Tourney Rd., Valencia, California 91355
  CEO: Gary Goldberg, Pres. & CEO   Tel: (661) 287-5400   %FO: 100
  Bus: *Mining, metals and industrial minerals.*   Fax: (661) 287-5495   Emp: 1,200

- **SANTOS LTD.**
  Level 29, Santos House, 91 King William St., Adelaide WA 5000, Australia
  CEO: John Ellice-Flint, CEO & Mng. Dir.   Tel: 61-8-8218-5111   Rev: $1,102
  Bus: *Engaged in oil and gas production.*   Fax: 61-8-8218-5274   Emp: 1,700
      www.santos.com.au
  NAICS: 211111, 211112, 213111, 213112, 333132, 541360

  SANTOS USA CORPORATION
  10111 Richmond Ave., Ste. 500, Houston, Texas 77042
  CEO: Kathleen Hogenson, Pres.   Tel: (713) 986-1700   %FO: 100
  Bus: *Engaged in oil and gas production.*   Fax: (713) 986-4200   Emp: 41

- **SIMS GROUP LIMITED**
  Level 6, 41 McLaren St., North Sydney NSW 2060, Australia
  CEO: Jeremy Sutcliffe, CEO   Tel: 61-2-9956-9100   Rev: $1,609
  Bus: *Metal recycling services.*   Fax: 61-2-9954-9680   Emp: 2,200
      www.sims-group.com
  NAICS: 423930

      SIMS GROUP USA
      600 S. 4th St., Richmond, California 94804
      CEO: Rick Jansen   Tel: (510) 412-5300   %FO: 100
      Bus: *Metal recycling services.*   Fax: (510) 412-5421

- **TELSTRA CORPORATION LIMITED**
  242 Exhibition St., Melbourne VIC 3000, Australia
  CEO: Donald G. McGauchie, Chmn.   Tel: 61-3-9634-6400   Rev: $14,410
  Bus: *Telecommunications services.*   Fax: 61-3-9632-3215   Emp: 41,941
      www.telstra.com.au
  NAICS: 511140, 515210, 517110, 517212, 517410, 517510, 517910, 518111, 518210, 519190, 541219, 541511, 561421, 561499, 811213

      TELSTRA INC.
      611 Wilshire Blvd., Los Angeles, California 90017-2928
      CEO: Lawrence Reilly, Mgr.   Tel: (213) 347-2888
      Bus: *Communication services*   Fax: Emp: 3

- **TRANSURBAN GROUP**
  Level 43 Rialto South Tower, 525 Collins St., Melbourne VIC 3000, Australia
  CEO: Kim Edwards, Mng. Dir.   Tel: 61-3-9612-6999
  Bus: *Develops and operates electronic toll roads.*   Fax: 61-3-9649-7380
      www.transurban.com.au
  NAICS: 488490

      FLUOR VIRGINIA INC./TRANSURBAN USA INC.
      1101 Wilson Blvd., Ste. 1900, Arlington, Virginia 22209
      CEO: Michael Kulper, VP North America   Tel: (703) 351-1204   %FO: 100
      Bus: *Develops and operates electronic toll roads.*   Fax: (703) 469-1593

- **WATTYL LIMITED**
  4 Steel St., Blacktown NSW 2148, Australia
  CEO: H. Van Hummel, CEO   Tel: 61-2-9621-6255   Rev: $369
  Bus: *Paints and coatings manufacture.*   Fax: 61-2-9621-9351   Emp: 1,967
      www.wattyl.com.au
  NAICS: 325211, 325510

      WATTYL (US) LTD.
      308 Old County Rd., Edgewater, Florida 32132
      CEO: Robert Hechler, Pres.   Tel: (386) 428-6461   %FO: 100
      Bus: *Paint and coatings sales and distribution*   Fax: (386) 427-7130   Emp: 400

Australia

- **WESTFIELD GROUP**
  Level 24, 100 William St., Sydney NSW 2011, Australia
  CEO: Frank P. Lowy, Chmn.   Tel: 61-2-9358-7000   Rev: $2,092
  Bus: *Design, building and managing shopping centers.*   Fax: 61-2-9358-7077
                                                               www.westfield.com.au
  NAICS: 236220, 531120, 531190, 531312, 531390
  > **WESTFIELD AMERICA TRUST**
  > 11601 Wilshire Blvd., 12/F, Los Angeles, California 90025
  > CEO: Richard E. Green, Pres.   Tel: (310) 478-4456   %FO: 100
  > Bus: *Engaged in leasing, operating and*   Fax: (310) 478-1267   Emp: 990
  >   *developing shopping centers.*

- **WESTPAC BANKING CORP**
  60 Martin Place, Level 25, Sydney NSW 2000, Australia
  CEO: David R. Morgan, Pres. & CEO   Tel: 61-2-9226-3143   Rev: $11,780
  Bus: *International banking and insurance services.*   Fax: 61-2-9226-1539   Emp: 27,013
                                                               www.westpac.com.au
  NAICS: 522110, 523920, 525910
  > **WESTPAC BANKING CORP**
  > 575 Fifth Ave., 39/F, New York, New York 10017-2422
  > CEO: Jim Tate, Mng. Prtn.   Tel: (212) 551-1800   %FO: 100
  > Bus: *General international banking services.*   Fax: (212) 818-2800   Emp: 445

- **WMC RESOURCES LIMITED**
  IBM Centre, 60 City Rd., 16/F, Southbank VIC 3006, Australia
  CEO: Christopher Campbell, CEO & Mng. Dir.   Tel: 61-3-9685-6000   Rev: $2,989
  Bus: *Engaged in mining of alumina, copper, gold nickel*   Fax: 61-3-9686-3569   Emp: 4,863
        and phosphate.   www.wmc.com.au
  NAICS: 212221, 212231, 212234, 212299, 236220, 531120
  > **WMC CORPORATE SERVICES INC.**
  > 8008 East Arapahoe Ct., Ste. 110, Englewood, Colorado 80112
  > CEO: Bart Suchomel, Pres.   Tel: (720) 554-8300   %FO: 100
  > Bus: *Engaged in mining exploration.*   Fax: (720) 554-8370   Emp: 15

- **WOODSIDE PETROLEUM LTD.**
  240 St. George's Terrace, Perth WA 6000, Australia
  CEO: Don Voelte, Mng. Dir.   Tel: 61-8-9348-4000   Rev: $1,542
  Bus: *Oil and gas exploration and production.*   Fax: 61-8-9348-5539   Emp: 2,219
                                                               www.woodside.com.au
  NAICS: 211111, 211112
  > **WOODSIDE ENERGY (USA) INC.**
  > Sage Plaza, 5151 San Felipe, 12/F, Houston, Texas 77056
  > CEO: Agu Kanstler, Dir.   Tel: (713) 963-8490   %FO: 100
  > Bus: *Oil and gas exploration and production.*   Fax: (713) 969-8868

- **WORLEYPARSONS ENGINEERING PTY LTD.**
  Level 6 Qui Bldg., 250 St. Georges Terrace, Perth WA 6000, Australia
  CEO: David Shane Mofflin, Dir.   Tel: 61-8-9278-8111   Rev: $249
  Bus: *Provider of engineering services.*   Fax: Emp: 1,010
                                           www.worley.com.au
  NAICS: 541330

  PARSONS E&C
  125 West Huntington Dr., Arcadia, California 91007
  CEO: Jeff Osborne   Tel: (626) 294-3300   %FO: 100
  Bus: *Provider of engineering services.*   Fax: (626) 294-3322

  PARSONS E&C
  2675 Morgantown Rd., Reading, Pennsylvania 19607
  CEO: Kenneth Ericson,   Tel: (610) 855-2000   %FO: 100
  Bus: *Provider of engineering services.*   Fax: (610) 855-2001

  PARSONS E&C
  633 Chestnut St., Ste. 400, Chattanooga, Tennessee 37450
  CEO: William.D.Griffith   Tel: (423) 757-8020   %FO: 100
  Bus: *Provider of engineering services.*   Fax: (423) 266-0922

  WORLEYPARSONS
  5 Greenway Plaza, Ste. 1000, Houston, Texas 77046
  CEO: Robert Looper   Tel: (713) 407-5000
  Bus: *Provider of engineering services.*   Fax: (713) 350-1300

Austria

- **ANDRITZ AG**
  Stattegger Strasse 18, A-8045 Graz, Austria
  CEO: Wolfgang Leitner, Pres. & CEO   Tel: 43-316-6902-0   Rev: $1,538
  Bus: *Engaged in the supply of customized plants,*   Fax: 43-316-6902-415   Emp: 4,600
       systems, and services for specialized industries.   www.andritz.com
  NAICS: 115210, 332912, 333291, 333298

  ANDRITZ INC.
  Sprout-Matodor, 53018-158th St., Garden City, Minnesota 56034
  CEO: Joel Eberhart, Mgr.   Tel: (507) 549-3779   %FO: 100
  Bus: *Conventional feed application.*   Fax: (507) 549-3779

  ANDRITZ INC.
  35 Sherman St., Muncy, Pennsylvania 17756
  CEO: Gary A. Krick, Pres.   Tel: (570) 546-1575   %FO: 100
  Bus: *Rotary and diverter valves.*   Fax: (570) 546-1615

  ANDRITZ INC.
  7225 Sheffield Place, Cumming, Georgia 30040
  CEO: Michael A. Snyder, Customer Service   Tel: (570) 546-1265   %FO: 100
  Bus: *Engaged in the supply of customized plants,*   Fax: (570) 546-1615
       systems, and services for specialized
       industries.

  ANDRITZ INC.
  10745 Westside Pkwy., Alpharetta, Georgia 30004
  CEO: William R. Enterline, Mgr.   Tel: (678) 947-1588   %FO: 100
  Bus: *Ethanol and corn wet milling.*   Fax: (678) 947-1588

  ATLANTIC PROCESS SYSTEMS
  13579 State Route 87, Williamsport, Pennsylvania 17701
  CEO: H. William Alsted, Rep.   Tel: (570) 478-2244   %FO: 100
  Bus: *Wood/Fiber-Plastic composites.*   Fax: (570) 478-2333

  ROCKEY INDUSTRIAL SALES
  112 Lamplighter Lane, McMurray, Pennsylvania 15317
  CEO: Ron Rockey, Rep.   Tel: (724) 941-1416   %FO: 100
  Bus: *Biofuels.*   Fax: (724) 941-7623

- **AUSTRIAMICROSYSTEMS AG**
  Schloss, A-8141 Schloss Premstatten, Austria
  CEO: John A. Heugle, CEO   Tel: 43-3136-5000   Rev: $219
  Bus: *Electronics and semiconductor manufacture.*   Fax: 43-3136-52501   Emp: 819
                                   www.austriamicrosystems.com
  NAICS: 334413

  AUSTRIAMICROSYSTEMS USA INC.
  8601 Six Forks Rd., Ste. 400, Raleigh, North Carolina 27615
  CEO: Ronald Tingl   Tel: (919) 676-5292   %FO: 100
  Bus: *Semiconductor manufacture and sales.*   Fax: (509) 696-2713

• AUSTRIAN AIRLINES GROUP
Fontanastrassa 1, A-1107 Vienna, Austria
CEO: Vagn Sorensen, Chmn.
Bus: *Commercial air transport services.*

Tel: 43-1-683511
Fax: 43-1-685505
www.austrianair.com

Rev: $2,560
Emp: 7,167

NAICS: 481111

AUSTRIAN AIRLINES GROUP
150 N. Michigan Ave., Chicago, Illinois 11357
CEO: W. Wolk, Mgr.
Bus: *Air transport services.*

Tel: (312) 629-1199
Fax: (312) 629-0667

%FO: 100
Emp: 70

• BERNDORF BAND GMBH
Leobersdorfer Strasse 26, A-2560 Berndorf, Austria
CEO: Karin Sidan, Mktg. Dir.
Bus: *Engineering and manufacturing of solid steel belts and continuous steel belt conveyor systems.*

Tel: 43-2672-800-292
Fax: 43-2672-841-76
www.berndorf-band.at

Emp: 300

NAICS: 332618, 333922

BERNDORF HUECK NORTH AMERICA, INC.
2525 Bath Rd., Elgin, Illinois 60123
CEO: Maurice Farissier
Bus: *Mfr./distributor of conveyor systems and related equipment.*

Tel: (847) 931-5264
Fax: (847) 931-5299

%FO: 100
Emp: 32

• BOEHLER-UDDEHOLM AG
Modecenterstr. 14/A/3, A-1030 Vienna, Austria
CEO: Georg Reiser, Mng. Dir.
Bus: *Mfr. and production of high-performance steels for drills and mining tools.*

Tel: 43-17-9869-0190
Fax: 43-17-9869-0166
www.bohler-uddeholm.com

Rev: $1,274
Emp: 11,800

NAICS: 333132, 532412

BOEHLER-UDDEHOLM AMERICA INC.
4902 Tollview Dr., Rolling Meadows, Illinois 60008-3729
CEO: Mark Appleton, Pres.
Bus: *Sales/distribution of high-performance steels.*

Tel: (847) 577-2220
Fax: (847) 577-8028

%FO: 100

BOEHLER-UDDEHOLM SPECIALTY METALS INC.
2306 Eastover Dr., South Boston, Virginia 24592
CEO: George Kelley
Bus: *Cutting tool applications, including high speed steel and powdered metal.*

Tel: (434) 575-7994
Fax: (434) 575-7997

%FO: 100

• EMCO MAIER GMBH
Salvachtal Bundesstr., Nord 58, PO Box 131, A-5400 Hallein, Austria
CEO: Herbert Maier, Pres.
Bus: *Mfr. industrial machinery.*

Tel: 43-6245-891-0
Fax: 43-6245-869-65
www.emco.co.at

NAICS: 333319

Austria

EMCO MAIER CORPORATION
2841 Charter St., Columbus, Ohio 43228-4607
CEO: Michael Wicken, Pres.
Bus: *Mfr./distribution industrial machinery.*

Tel: (614) 771-5991
Fax: (614) 771-5990

%FO: 100

● **ERSTE BANK AG**
Graben 21, A-1010 Vienna, Austria
CEO: Andreas Treichl, Chmn.
Bus: *Commercial banking, real estate financing and
asset management.*
NAICS: 522110

Tel: 43-5-0100-10100
Fax: 43-5-0100-10100
www.erstebank.at

Rev: $8,333
Emp: 36,661

ERSTE BANK
280 Park Ave. Frnt. 1, W. Bldg., 32/F, New York, New York 10017
CEO: Hans Krikava, Mgr.
Bus: *Commercial banking, real estate financing
and asset management.*

Tel: (212) 984-5600
Fax: (212) 986-1423

%FO: 100

● **GLOCK GMBH**
PO Box 9, A-2232 Deutsch-Wagram, Austria
CEO: Gaston Glock, Pres.
Bus: *Supplies pistols to armies and civilians.*

NAICS: 332994, 339920

Tel: 43-2247-90300-0
Fax: 43-2247-90300-312
www.glock.com

GLOCK INC.
6000 Highlands Pkwy., Smyrna, Georgia 30082
CEO: Gaston H. Glock, Pres.
Bus: *Sales of pistols.*

Tel: (770) 432-1202
Fax: (770) 433-8719

%FO: 100
Emp: 90

● **GRASS HOLDING AG**
Grass Platz 1, A-6973 Hochst, Austria
CEO: Jurgen Ahlfeld, Chmn. & CEO
Bus: *Mfr. hinges, brackets and other steel fittings for
use in kitchen and household furniture.*
NAICS: 332510

Tel: 43-5578-701-0
Fax: 43-5578-701-59
www.grass.at

Rev: $104
Emp: 490

GRASS AMERICA INC.
PO Box 1019, 1202 Hwy. 66 South, Kernersville, North Carolina 27284
CEO: Alfred Grass Jr., Pres.
Bus: *Distribution/sales hinges, brackets and
other steel fittings for use in office and
household furniture.*

Tel: (336) 996-4041
Fax: (336) 996-5149

%FO: 100
Emp: 260

● **MIBA AKTIENGESELLSCAFT**
Dr. Mitterbauer, Strasse 3, A-4663 Laakirchen, Austria
CEO: Peter Mitterbauer, Chmn.
Bus: *Automotive component mfr.*

NAICS: 336211

Tel: 43-7613-2541-0
Fax: 43-7613-2541-2172
www.miba-at.com

Rev: $365
Emp: 2,498

MIBA BEARINGS US LLC
North State Rte. 60, McConnelsville, Ohio 43756
CEO: Ted McConnell   Tel: (740) 962-4242   %FO: 100
Bus: *Automotive component mfr.*   Fax:

MIBA HYDRAMECHANICA CORP.
6625 Cobb Dr., Sterling Heights, Michigan 48312
CEO: Perhard Reisner, VP   Tel: (586) 939-0620   %FO: 100
Bus: *Automotive component mfr.*   Fax:

- **RED BULL GMBH**
Am Brunnen 1, A-5330 Fuschi am See, Austria
CEO: Norbert Krailhamer, Pres.   Tel: 43-662-6582-0   Rev: $2,000
Bus: *Non-alcoholic, energy drink manufacture.*   Fax: 43-662-6582-7010   Emp: 1,850
                                         www.redbull.com
NAICS: 312111

  RED BULL NORTH AMERICA, INC.
  2525 Colorado Blvd., Ste. 320, Santa Monica, California 90404
  CEO: Dan Ginsberg, CEO   Tel: (310) 393-4647
  Bus: *Sales of non-alcoholic, energy drink.*   Fax: (310) 320-2361   Emp: 640

- **ROSENBAUER INTERNATIONAL AG**
Paschinger Str. 90, A-4060 Leonding Osterreich, Austria
CEO: Julian Wagner, Pres. & CEO   Tel: 43-732-6794-0
Bus: *Fire-fighting technology; vehicles, components*   Fax: 43-732-6794-83
  and equipment.   www.rosenbauer.co.at
NAICS: 336120

  ROSENBAUER AMERICA
  25900 Fallbrook Ave., Wyoming, Minnesota 55092
  CEO: Joe Williams, Pres.   Tel: (651) 462-1000   %FO: 100
  Bus: *Engaged in fire-fighting technology;*   Fax: (651) 462-1700
    vehicles, components and equipment.

- **D. SWAROVSKI AND COMPANY**
Swarovskistr. 30, A-6112 Wattens, Austria
CEO: Gernot Langes-Swarovski, CFO   Tel: 43-5224-5002317
Bus: *Mfr. crystal jewelry and cutting materials.*   Fax: 43-5224-54807   Emp: 9,200
                                         www.swarovski.com
NAICS: 327215, 339914

  SWAROVSKI NORTH AMERICA LTD.
  230 5th Ave., New York, New York 10001
  CEO: Nadja Swarovski   Tel: (212) 683-6991   %FO: 100
  Bus: *Crystal fiber optics, architectural crystal*   Fax: (212) 481-3960
    panels and decorative crystal down lights
    and spots.

  SWAROVSKI NORTH AMERICA LTD.
  1 Kenney Dr., Cranston, Rhode Island 02920-4468
  CEO: Daniel J. Cohen, Pres.   Tel: (401) 463-6400   %FO: 100
  Bus: *Mfr. fashion jewelry, gifts and collectors*   Fax: (401) 463-3261   Emp: 700
    objects.

- **TOPCALL INTERNATIONAL AG**
Talpagasse 1, A-1230 Vienna, Austria
CEO: Christoph Stockert, CEO   Tel: 43-1-86353-0   Rev: $37
Bus: *Engaged in management and communication*   Fax: 43-1-86353-21   Emp: 220
business solutions.   www.topcall.com
NAICS: 511210

> **TOPCALL CORPORATION**
> 203 N. La Salle St., Ste. 2100, Chicago, Illinois 60601
> CEO: Charles Randall   Tel: (773) 239-1655   %FO: 100
> Bus: *Engaged in management and communication* Fax: (773) 239-5850
> *business solutions.*

> **TOPCALL CORPORATION**
> 14800 Quorum Dr. Suite 540, Dallas, Texas 75254
> CEO: Richard Gilbert   Tel: (972) 404-0071   %FO: 100
> Bus: *Engaged in management and communication* Fax: (972) 404-0071
> *business solutions.*

> **TOPCALL CORPORATION**
> 533 Airport Boulevard, Suite 400, Burlingame, California 94010
> CEO: Christoph Stockert   Tel: (610) 560-4340   %FO: 100
> Bus: *Engaged in management and communication* Fax: (610) 560-4340
> *business solutions.*

> **TOPCALL CORPORATION**
> 200 Chester Field Pkwy., Malvern, Pennsylvania 19355
> CEO: Ryan O'Neil   Tel: (610) 240-4300   %FO: 100
> Bus: *Engaged in management and communication* Fax: (610) 240-4340
> *business solutions.*

> **TOPCALL CORPORATION**
> 16245 Laguna Canyon Rd., Irvine, California 92618
> CEO: Denis O'Neil, Pres.   Tel: (949) 453-8691   %FO: 100
> Bus: *Engaged in management and communication* Fax: (949) 453-8691
> *business solutions.*

> **TOPCALL CORPORATION**
> 1200 Abernathy Rd., Ste. 1700, Atlanta, Georgia 30338
> CEO: Christoph Stockert   Tel: (770) 998-2494   %FO: 100
> Bus: *Engaged in management and communication* Fax: (770) 998-2494
> *business solutions.*

- **TREIBACHER SCHLEIFMITTEL AG**
Seebach 2, PO Box 1, A-9523 Villach, Austria
CEO: Bernd Durstberger, CEO   Tel: 43-4242-41885-0
Bus: *Abrasives manufacture.*   Fax: 43-4242-42653
     www.treibacher.at
NAICS: 327910

> **TREIBACHER SCHLEIFMITTEL INC.**
> 2000 College Ave., Niagara Falls, New York 14302
> CEO: Richard A. Davis, CEO   Tel: (716) 286-1250   %FO: 100
> Bus: *Abrasives manufacture and sales.*   Fax: (716) 286-1224

TREIBACHER SCHLEIFMITTEL INC.
Box 158, Highway 49 South, Andersonville, Georgia 31711
CEO: Jackie Palmer, Mgr.   Tel: (229) 924-5866   %FO: 100
Bus: *Abrasives manufacture and sales.*   Fax: (229) 924-7792

• **VA TECHNOLOGIE AG**
Lunzerstr. 65, A-4031 Linz, Austria
CEO: Erich Becker, Chmn.   Tel: 43-732-6986-9222   Rev: $5,555
Bus: *Metallurgical, energy and environmental*   Fax: 43-732-6980-3416   Emp: 16,562
engineering services; steel milling technology,   www.vatech.at
hydroelectric turbines and industrial gas cleaning
systems.
NAICS: 213112, 236210, 237110, 237120, 237130, 237990, 333516, 333611, 541330

SHAPE TECHNOLOGY
Penn Centre West, Bldg. One, Ste. 211, Pittsburgh, Pennsylvania 15276
CEO: Randy Smerk, Pres.   Tel: (412) 490-9202
Bus: *Sale and service of metals.*   Fax: (412) 490-9037   Emp: 5

VA TECH
Lincoln Bldg., 60 E. 42nd. St., Ste. 4510, New York, New York 10165
CEO: J. Lee   Tel: (212) 922-2000
Bus: *Metallurgical, energy and environmental*   Fax: (212) 922-3810
engineering services; steel milling
technology, hydroelectric turbines and
industrial gas cleaning systems.

VA TECH ELIN USA CORPORATION
501 Technology Dr., Canonsburg, Pennsylvania 15317
CEO: Walter Paminger, CEO   Tel: (724) 514-8454   %FO: 100
Bus: *Transformers manufacture.*   Fax: Emp: 30

VA TECH ELIN USA CORPORATION
48 Miller Ave., Jackson, Tennessee 38305
CEO: Robert Kelly, Mgr.   Tel: (901) 664-7644   %FO: 100
Bus: *Transformers manufacture and service.*   Fax: (901) 664-5372

VA TECH MAERICA
501 Technology Dr., Canonsburg, Pennsylvania 15317
CEO: Alan Helgerman, Pres.   Tel: (724) 514-8500   %FO: 100
Bus: *Metallurgical, energy and environmental*   Fax: (724) 514-8354   Emp: 700
engineering services; steel milling
technology, hydroelectric turbines and
industrial gas cleaning systems.

VAI AUTOMATION, INC.
2390 Pipestone Rd., Benton Harbor, Michigan 49022
CEO: B. Ropp, Mgr.   Tel: (800) 860-1968   %FO: 100
Bus: *Metallurgical, energy and environmental*   Fax: (269) 926-6854
engineering services.

- **VAE GMBH**
  Rotenturmstr. 5-9, A-1010 Vienna, Austria
  CEO: Marc Kaddoura, CEO
  Bus: *Mfr. railway switches and related electronic*
     equipment.
  NAICS: 332312, 332510, 332999

  Tel: 43-1-531-180
  Fax: 43-1-531-18222
  www.voestalpine.com

  Rev: $674
  Emp: 3,540

  > **VAE NORTRAK NORTH AMERICA INC.**
  > 1740 Pacific Ave., Cheyenne, Wyoming 82007
  > CEO: Al Tuningley
  > Bus: *Mfr. railroad track work and supplies.*
  >
  > Tel: (307) 778-8700
  > Fax: (307) 778-8777
  >
  > %FO: 100

- **VOESTALPINE AG**
  Voest-Alpine Str. 1, A-4020 Linz, Austria
  CEO: Rudoplh Streicher, Chmn.
  Bus: *Mfr. mechanical cutting equipment for mining of*
     coal and rocks. (JV with Sandvik Tamrock,
  NAICS: 331111, 331210, 331221, 331222

  Tel: 43-732-6585-0
  Fax: 43-732-6980-8981
  www.voestalpine.com

  Rev: $5,655
  Emp: 23,216

  > **VAE NORTRAK NORTH AMERICA INC.**
  > 1740 Pacific Ave., Cheyenne, Wyoming 82007
  > CEO: Al Tuningley, Pres.
  > Bus: *Metal fabrication.*
  >
  > Tel: (307) 778-8700
  > Fax: (307) 778-8777
  >
  > %FO: 100
  > Emp: 400

  > **VOESTALPINE USA**
  > 500 Mamaroneck Ave., Ste. 310, Harrison, New York 10528
  > CEO: Josef Welser, Chmn.
  > Bus: *Sales/distribution of high-quality steel flat*
  >   *and long products.*
  >
  > Tel: (914) 899-3706
  > Fax: (914) 381-0509
  >
  > %FO: 100

- **WIENERBERGER AG**
  Wienerbergerstr. 7, Wienerberg City, Vienna Twin Tower, A-1100 Vienna, Austria
  CEO: Wolfgang Reithofer, CEO
  Bus: *Engaged in manufacture of building materials and*
     real estate development.
  NAICS: 236220, 327122, 327123, 525930, 531110, 531120, 531130, 531190, 531312

  Tel: 43-1-601-92-0
  Fax: 43-1-601-92-466
  www.wienerberger.com

  Rev: $2,293
  Emp: 12,237

  > **GENERAL SHALE BRICK, INC.**
  > 3211 North Roan St., Johnson City, Tennessee 37601
  > CEO: Richard L. Green, Pres. & CEO
  > Bus: *U.S. headquarters. Mfr. facing bricks,*
  >   *concrete block, lightweight aggregates and*
  >   *sand.*
  >
  > Tel: (423) 282-4661
  > Fax: (423) 282-0491
  >
  > %FO: 100
  > Emp: 1,886

- **WINTERSTEIGER**
  J.M. Dimmel Strasse 9, Oberosterreich, A-4910 Ried, Austria
  CEO: Gunther Kamml, CEO
  Bus: *Ski tuning machines, agricultural machines,*
     woodworking machines.
  NAICS: 333111, 333210

  Tel: 43-7752-919-0
  Fax: 43-7752-919-57
  www.wintersteiger.com

  Rev: $35
  Emp: 300

WINTERSTEIGER
217 Wright Brothers Dr., Salt Lake City, Utah 84116
CEO: Fritz Hoeckner, CEO
Bus: *Ski tuning machines, agricultural machines, woodworking machines.*
Tel: (801) 355-6550
Fax: (801) 355-6541
%FO: 100
Emp: 25

● **WITTMANN ROBOT GMBH**
Lichtblaustr. 10, A-1220 Vienna, Austria
CEO: Dr. Werner Wittmann, Pres.
Bus: *Mfr. of water flow regulators, temperature controllers and automation systems for plastic industry.*
Tel: 43-1-250-390
Fax: 43-1-259-7170
www.wittmann-robot.com
Emp: 260

NAICS: 334111, 334290, 334512, 334514

WITTMANN ROBOT AND AUTOMATION SYSTEMS INC.
1 Technology Park Dr., Torrington, Connecticut 06790
CEO: Werner Wittmann, CEO
Bus: *Automation systems for plastic industry manufacture.*
Tel: (860) 496-9603
Fax: (860) 482-2069
%FO: 100
Emp: 75

● **WOLFORD AG**
Wolfordstr. 1-2, A-6901 Bregenz, Austria
CEO: Holger Dahmen, CEO
Bus: *Mfr. hosiery, lingerie, bodysuits and swimwear.*
Tel: 43-5574-690-2448
Fax: 43-5574-690-1219
www.wolford.com
Rev: $119
Emp: 1,560

NAICS: 315111, 315221

WOLFORD AMERICA
540 Madison Ave., 34/F, New York, New York 10022
CEO: Karen Schnider, Pres.
Bus: *Sales/distribution of hosiery and lingerie.*
Tel: (212) 453-5556
Fax: (212) 453-5563
%FO: 100
Emp: 15

WOLFORD BOUTIQUES
540 Madison Ave., 34/F, New York, New York 10022
CEO: Wilson Lee, Mgr.
Bus: *Sales/distribution of hosiery and lingerie.*
Tel: (212) 453-5556
Fax: (212) 453-5563

● **ZUMTOBEL AG**
Hochster Str. 8, A-6850 Dornbirn, Austria
CEO: Jurg Zumtobel, Chmn.
Bus: *Mfr. lighting fixtures.*
Tel: 43-5572-5090
Fax: 43-5572-5096-01
www.zumtobel.com
Rev: $1,368
Emp: 7,643

NAICS: 335110, 335121, 335122, 335129, 335314

TRIDONIC INC.
4405 International Blvd., Ste. B-113, Norcross, Georgia 30093
CEO: Walter Ziegler, CEO
Bus: *Dist. of lighting equipment*
Tel: (770) 717-0556
Fax: (770) 717-7969
Emp: 5

ZUMTOBEL STAFF LIGHTING, INC.
3300 Rte. 9W, Highland, New York 12528
CEO: Wolfgang Egger, Pres.
Bus: *Mfr. lighting fixtures.*
Tel: (845) 691-6262
Fax: (914) 691-6289
%FO: 100
Emp: 193

Bahamas

- **KERZNER INTERNATIONAL LIMITED**
  Atlantis, Coral Towers, Executive Offices, Paradise Island C5, Bahamas
  CEO: Howard B. Kerzner, CEO   Tel: 242-363-6000   Rev: $621
  Bus: *Casino and resort operator.*   Fax: 242-363-5401   Emp: 11,870
  www.kerzner.com
  NAICS: 713290, 721120, 722110, 722410
  - **KERZNER INTERNATIONAL LIMITED**
    1000 S. Pine Island Rd., Plantation, Florida 33324
    CEO: Omar Palacios, VP   Tel: (954) 809-2263   %FO: 100
    Bus: *Casino and resort operator.*   Fax: (954) 809-2346

- **STEINER LEISURE LIMITED**
  Saffrey Square, Ste. 104A, Nassau, Bahamas
  CEO: Leonard I. Fluxman, CEO   Tel: 242-356-0006   Rev: $342
  Bus: *Operates spas on cruise ship lines.*   Fax: 242-356-6260   Emp: 3,464
  www.steinerleisure.com
  NAICS: 446120, 488999, 611310, 611519, 611699, 713940, 812111, 812112, 812113, 812199, 812990
  - **STEINER USA INC.**
    770 South Dixie Hwy., Ste. 200, Coral Gables, Florida 33146
    CEO: Marc D. Jacobson, Mgr.   Tel: (305) 358-9002   %FO: 100
    Bus: *Manages spas on cruise ship lines.*   Fax: (305) 358-9954

Bahrain

- **AHLI UNITED BANK B.S.C.**
  Al Seef, Bldg. 2495, Rd. 2832, Manama 428, Bahrain
  CEO: Adel A. El-Labban, CEO & Mng. Dir.
  Bus: *Private banking, asset management, commercial lending and finance.*
  Tel: 973-17-585-858
  Fax: 973-17-580-569
  www.ahliunited.com
  Rev: $372
  Emp: 561
  NAICS: 522110, 522291, 522292, 522293, 523110, 523920, 523930
  - **THE UNITED BANK OF KUWAIT PLC**
    126 East 56th St., 3/F, New York, New York 10022
    CEO: Paul Sleight, Gen. Mgr.
    Bus: *International banking services.*
    Tel: (212) 906-8500
    Fax: (212) 319-4762
    %FO: 100
    Emp: 18

- **ARAB BANKING CORPORATION**
  PO Box 5698, ABC Tower, Diplomatic Area, Manama, Bahrain
  CEO: Ghazi M. Abdul-Jawad, Chmn.
  Bus: *International banking services.*
  Tel: 973-17-532-235
  Fax: 973-17-533-062
  www.arabbanking.com
  Rev: $665
  Emp: 5,266
  NAICS: 522110
  - **ARAB BANKING CORPORATION**
    277 Park Ave., 32/F, New York, New York 10172
    CEO: Robert Ivosevich, VP
    Bus: *International banking services.*
    Tel: (212) 583-4774
    Fax: (212) 583-4873
    %FO: 100

- **GULF INTERNATIONAL BANK (GIB)**
  Al-Dowali Building, 3 Palace Avenue, 3 Palace Avenue, Manama, Bahrain
  CEO: Dr. Khaled M. Al-Fayez, CEO
  Bus: *Corporate and institutional banking, investment banking, asset management, treasury and financial markets.*
  Tel: 973-17-534-000
  Fax: 973-17-522-633
  www.gibonline.com
  NAICS: 522110, 523110, 523920
  - **GULF INVESTMENT CORPORATION**
    330 Madison Ave., New York, New York 10017
    CEO: Gregga Baxter, Sr. Prtn.
    Bus: *International banking services.*
    Tel: (212) 922-2300
    Fax: (212) 922-2309
    %FO: 100

- **INVESTCORP SA**
  Investcorp House, PO Box 5340, Manama, Bahrain
  CEO: Nemir A. Kirdar, CEO
  Bus: *Asset management and global investment.*
  Tel: 973-17-532-000
  Fax: 973-17-530-816
  www.investcorp.com
  Rev: $289
  Emp: 275
  NAICS: 523999
  - **INVESTCORP**
    280 Park Ave., New York, New York 10017
    CEO: John R. Fraser, Mng. Dir.
    Bus: *Asset management and global investment.*
    Tel: (212) 599-4700
    Fax: (212) 983-7073
    %FO: 100

Bangladesh

- **BANGLADESH BIMAN AIRLINES CORPORATION**
Balaka, Zia International Airport, Kurmitola Dhaka 1206, Bangladesh
CEO: M. Mahmudur Rahman, Mktg. Dir.
Bus: *Airline transport services.*
Tel: 880-2-897400-29
Fax: 880-2-9560151-10
www.bimanair.com

NAICS: 481111

BANGLADESH BIMAN AIRLINES CORPORATION
211 East 43rd St., Ste. 602, New York, New York 10017
CEO: Badrul Kamal
Bus: *Airlines services.*
Tel: (212) 808-4523
Fax: (212) 808-4589
%FO: 100

Belgium

- **AGFA-GEVAERT NV**
Septestraat 27, B-2640 Mortsel, Belgium
CEO: Ludo Verhoeven, Chmn. & CEO   Tel: 32-3-444-2111   Rev: $5,131
Bus: *Photographic and electronic imaging equipment*   Fax: 32-3-444-7094   Emp: 16,224
  manufacturer.   www.agfa.com
NAICS: 333315

  AGFA CORPORATION
  100 Challenger Rd., Ridgefield Park, New Jersey 07660-2199
  CEO: Dany Claeys, VP   Tel: (201) 440-2500   %FO: 100
  Bus: *Photographic, imaging technologies.*   Fax: (201) 440-5733

- **BARCO N.V.**
President Kennedy Park 35, B-8500 Kortrijk, Belgium
CEO: Martin De Prycker, CEO   Tel: 32-56-2332-11   Rev: $789
Bus: *Designs large-screen projection and visualization*   Fax: 32-56-2622-62   Emp: 4,022
  solutions, and optical systems for visual   www.barco.com
NAICS: 333293, 333315, 334119, 335314

  BARCO FOLSOM
  11101 A Trade Center Dr., Rancho Cordova, California 95670
  CEO: Stephan Paridaen   Tel: (916) 859-2500
  Bus: *Mfr. of radio & TV commercial equipment.*   Fax: (916) 859-2515

  BARCO MEDIA
  1651 North 1000 West, Logan, Utah 84321
  CEO: Michael Mulcahy, Pres.   Tel: (435) 753-2224
  Bus: *Mfr. of computer controlled electronic signs.*   Fax: (435) 752-8513   Emp: 65

  BARCO ORTHOGON LLC
  29 South New York Rd., Ste. 400, Smithville, New Jersey 08201
  CEO: Joe Galushka, member   Tel: (609) 404-1111   %FO: 100
  Bus: *Computer software, custom computer*   Fax: (609) 404-0007
  programming.

  BARCO SIMULATION
  600 Bellbrook Ave., Xenia, Ohio 45385
  CEO: Steve McCullugh, VP   Tel: (937) 372-7579
  Bus: *Mfr. of radio & TV commercial equipment.*   Fax: (937) 372-8645   Emp: 117

  BARCO VISUAL SOLUTIONS
  3240 Town Point Dr., Kennesaw, Georgia 30144
  CEO: Tom Burdette, member   Tel: (770) 218-3200   %FO: 100
  Bus: *Projection equipment & supplies.*   Fax: (770) 218-3250   Emp: 175

  BARCOVIEW
  Amberglen Business Center, 1600 N.W. Compton Dr., Beaverton, Oregon 97006
  CEO: Ray Phillips, member   Tel: (503) 690-1550
  Bus: *Innovative display technology.*   Fax: (503) 690-1525   Emp: 40

BARCOVIEW LLC
3059 Premiere Pkwy., Duluth, Georgia 30097
CEO: Hugh David Scott, member
Bus: *Innovative display technology.*
Tel: (678) 475-8000
Fax: (678) 475-8100
%FO: 100
Emp: 285

VOXAR INC.
945 Concord St., Framingham, Massachusetts 01701
CEO: Andrew Bissell, CEO
Bus: *Sale of medical /hospital equipment.*
Tel: (508) 620-9446
Fax: (508) 620-9447

● **BDO INTERNATIONAL BV**
Boulevard de la Woluwe 60, B-1200 Brussels, Belgium
CEO: Frans J. Samyn, CEO
Bus: *Accounting and auditing services.*
Tel: 32-2-778-0130
Fax: 32-2-771-4443
www.bdoglobal.com
Rev: $3,017
Emp: 25,118

NAICS: 541211, 541213, 541214, 541219, 541611

BDO SEIDMAN LLP
130 East Randolph, Ste. 2800, Chicago, Illinois 60601
CEO: Jack Weisbaum, CEO
Bus: *Accounting services.*
Tel: (312) 240-1236
Fax: (312) 240-3311
%FO: 100

BDO SEIDMAN LLP
99 Monroe, NW, Ste. 800, Grand Rapids, Michigan 49503-2698
CEO: Rich Rottman
Bus: *Accounting services.*
Tel: (616) 774-7000
Fax: (616) 776-3680
%FO: 100

BDO SEIDMAN LLP
330 Madison Ave., New York, New York 10017
CEO: Jack Wilson
Bus: *Accounting services.*
Tel: (212) 885-8000
Fax: (212) 697-1299
%FO: 100

● **NV BEKAERT SA**
President Kennedy Park 18, B-8500 Kortrijk, Belgium
CEO: Joseph De Neve, Pres.
Bus: *Mfr. producer of high-grade steel cord, steel wire and fences.*
Tel: 32-56-230-511
Fax: 32-56-230543
www.bekaert.com
Rev: $1,800
Emp: 15,000

NAICS: 326113, 331222, 332618

BEKAERT CORP.
2121 Latimer Dr., Muskegon, Michigan 49442
CEO: Nancy Laurie, Pres.
Bus: *Mfr. wire and wire products.*
Tel: (231) 777-2575
Fax: (231) 773-4863
%FO: 100

BEKAERT CORP.
1 Bekaert Dr., Rogers, Arkansas 72756-1948
CEO: Debra Wood
Bus: *Mfr. advanced materials.*
Tel: (479) 631-7661
Fax: (479) 631-7661
%FO: 100

BEKAERT CORP.
2000 Isaac Shelby Dr., Shelbyville, Kentucky 40065-9129
CEO: Sung Deok Kim
Bus: *Wire products manufacture.*
Tel: (502) 633-6722
Fax: (502) 633-6722
%FO: 100

BEKAERT CORP.
301 Darlington Dr., SE, PO Box 1205, Rome, Georgia 30161
CEO: Richard J. Hammond, Pres. Tel: (706) 235-4481 %FO: 100
Bus: *Mfr. steel cord.* Fax: (706) 235-2160

BEKAERT CORP.
PO Box 13159, Research Triangle Park, North Carolina 27709-3159
CEO: Albert Busch, Pres. Tel: (919) 485-8995 %FO: 100
Bus: *Mfr. advanced materials.* Fax: (919) 485-8993

BEKAERT CORP.
8401 N.W. 53rd Terrace, Ste. 109, Miami, Florida 33166
CEO: Marc Holvoet, Pres. Tel: (305) 463-8979 %FO: 100
Bus: *Mfr. steel cord and wire.* Fax: (305) 463-8959

BEKAERT CORPORATION
3200 West Market St., Ste. 300, Akron, Ohio 44333
CEO: Guido Haezebrouck, Pres. & CEO Tel: (330) 867-3325 %FO: 100
Bus: *U.S. headquarters for production of high-* Fax: (330) 873-3424
  grade steel cord, steel wire and fences.

BEKAERT CORPORATION
1395 South Marietta Pkwy., Marietta, Georgia 30067-5026
CEO: Tom Lloyd, Pres. Tel: (770) 514-2668 %FO: 100
Bus: *Mfr. steel wire & wire products.* Fax: (770) 514-2251

● **BROWNING INTERNATIONAL SA**
Parc Indust des Hauts-Sarts, 3, ème Ave. 25, B-4040 Herstal, Belgium
CEO: Philippe Tenneson, Pres. Tel: 32-42-405-211
Bus: *Hunting, shooting and fishing products.* Fax: 32-42-405-212
  www.browningint.com
NAICS: 332211, 332994, 339920

 BROWNING ARMS COMPANY
 One Browning Place, Morgan, Utah 84050-9326
 CEO: Charles Guevremont, Pres. Tel: (801) 876-2711 %FO: 100
 Bus: *Distributor hunting, fishing & shooting* Fax: (801) 876-3331
  products.

● **THE CAPITAL MARKETS COMPANY (CAPCO)**
Prins Boudewijnlaan 43, B-2650 Edegem, Belgium
CEO: Rob Heyvaert, Chmn. & CEO Tel: 32-3-740-1000
Bus: *Technology services and products to financial* Fax: 32-3-740-1001
  industry. www.capco.com
NAICS: 541511

 CAPCO REFERENCE DATA SERVICES INC.
 111 West Evelyn Ave., Ste. 206, Sunnyvale, California 94086
 CEO: Predrag Dizdarevic, Pres. Tel: (408) 522-9900 %FO: 100
 Bus: *Technology services.* Fax: (408) 522-9911

THE CAPITAL MARKETS COMPANY
120 Broadway, 15/F, New York, New York 10271
CEO: Rob Heyvaert, Pres.   Tel: (212) 284-8600   %FO: 100
Bus: *Technology services.*   Fax: (212) 284-8601

THE CAPITAL MARKETS COMPANY
One Montgomery St., 37/F, San Francisco, California 94101
CEO: Joe Anastasio   Tel: (415) 445-0968   %FO: 100
Bus: *Technology services.*   Fax: (415) 445-9173

● **CYTEC SURFACE SPECIALITIES**
Anderlecht Str. 33, B-1620 Drogenbos, Belgium
CEO: Ben Van Assche, CEO   Tel: 32-2-559-99-99   Rev: $3,723
Bus: *Plastic foam products manufacture.*   Fax: 32-2-559-99-00   Emp: 11,559
                                  www.surfacespecialties.com
NAICS: 325191, 325211, 325221

CYTEC CARBON FIBERS LLC
301 E. Carmel Dr., Ste. 100, Carmel, Indiana 46032
CEO: Dave Wanker   Tel: (317) 705-6565   %FO: 100
Bus: *Mfr. engineered materials.*   Fax: (317) 705-6588

CYTEC CARBON FIBERS LLC
800 Cel River Rd., Rock Hill, South Carolina 29730
CEO: David Snyder   Tel: (803) 328-3390   %FO: 100
Bus: *Mfr. carbon fibers.*   Fax: (803) 329-6560

CYTEC ENGINEERED MATERIALS INC.
1937 W. Main St., Stamford, Connecticut 06904
CEO: James P. Cronin   Tel: (203) 321-2200   %FO: 100
Bus: *Mfr. polymer additives and coating and*   Fax: (203) 321-3398
performance chemicals.

CYTEC ENGINEERED MATERIALS INC.
5916 Pkwy. Plaza Blvd., Charlotte, North Carolina 28217
CEO: Sharon Young   Tel: (704) 423-8900   %FO: 100
Bus: *Mfr. coatings and performance chemicals.*   Fax: (704) 423-8946

CYTEC ENGINEERED MATERIALS INC.
1 Heilman Ave., Willow Island, West Virginia 26134
CEO: David Wanker   Tel: (304) 665-2422   %FO: 100
Bus: *Mfr. coatings and performance chemicals.*   Fax: (304) 665-2455

CYTEC ENGINEERED MATERIALS INC.
10800 River Rd., Westwego, Louisiana 70094
CEO: Thomas Call   Tel: (504) 431-9511   %FO: 100
Bus: *Mfr. coatings and performance chemicals.*   Fax: (504) 431-6354

CYTEC ENGINEERED MATERIALS INC.
South Cherry St., Wallingford, Connecticut 06492
CEO: Robert A Leitzman   Tel: (203) 269-4481   %FO: 100
Bus: *Mfr. coatings and performance chemicals.*   Fax: (203) 269-5574

CYTEC ENGINEERED MATERIALS INC.
1440 N. Kraemer Blvd., Anaheim, California 92806
CEO: James P. Cronin   Tel: (714) 630-9400   %FO: 100
Bus: *Mfr. engineered materials.*   Fax: (714) 630-9410

CYTEC ENGINEERED MATERIALS INC.
5 Garret Mountain Plaza, West Paterson, New Jersey 07424
CEO: David Lilley   Tel: (973) 357-3100   %FO: 100
Bus: *Mfr. water treatment chemicals.*   Fax: (973) 357-3065

CYTEC ENGINEERED MATERIALS INC.
4300 Jackson ST., Greenville, Texas 75401
CEO: Robin Prokop   Tel: (903) 457-8500   %FO: 100
Bus: *Mfr. engineered materials.*   Fax: (903) 457-8598

CYTEC ENGINEERED MATERIALS INC.
501 W. 3rd St., Winona, Minnesota 55987
CEO: Scott Jackelf   Tel: (507) 454-3611   %FO: 100
Bus: *Mfr. engineered materials.*   Fax: (507) 452-8195

CYTEC ENGINEERED MATERIALS INC.
645 N. Cypress St., Orange, California 92867
CEO: Joe Morris   Tel: (714) 639-2050   %FO: 100
Bus: *Mfr. engineered materials.*   Fax: (714) 532-4096

CYTEC ENGINEERED MATERIALS INC.
1300 Revolution St., Harve de Grace, Maryland 21078
CEO: Jay Tavormina   Tel: (410) 939-1910   %FO: 100
Bus: *Mfr. engineered materials.*   Fax: (410) 939-8100

CYTEC ENGINEERED MATERIALS INC.
2085 E. Technology Cir., Ste. 300, Tempe, Arizona 85284
CEO: Steven C. Speak, Pres.   Tel: (480) 730-2000   %FO: 100
Bus: *Mfr. engineered materials.*   Fax: (480) 730-2088

CYTEC INDUSTRIES INC.
10800 River Rd., Westwego, Louisiana 70094
CEO: Thomas Call   Tel: (504) 431-9511   %FO: 100
Bus: *Mfr. chemicals.*   Fax: (504) 431-6354

CYTEC INDUSTRIES INC.
850 3rd Ave., Longview, Washington 98632
CEO: Ed Elsner   Tel: (360) 425-6532   %FO: 100
Bus: *Mfr. chemicals.*   Fax: (360) 425-8840

CYTEC INDUSTRIES INC.
1405 Buffalo St., Olean, New York 14760
CEO: Gerret M. Peters   Tel: (716) 372-9650   %FO: 100
Bus: *Mfr. water treatment chemicals.*   Fax: (716) 372-1594

● **DECEUNINCK NV**
Bruggesteenweg 164, 8830, Hooglede-Gits, B-8800 Roeselare, Belgium
CEO: Clement De Meersman, CEO   Tel: 32-51-239-211   Rev: $794
Bus: *Building products manufacture including PVC*   Fax: 32-51-22-79-93   Emp: 3,043
    doors and window frames, floor and wall   www.deceuninck.com
NAICS: 321911, 326140, 326192

    DECEUNINCK NORTH AMERICAN
    351 N. Garver Rd., Monroe, Ohio 45050
    CEO: Darwin G. Brown   Tel: (513) 539-4444   %FO: 100
    Bus: *Building products manufacture including*   Fax: (513) 539-5404
        PVC doors and window frames, floor and
        wall coverings.

● **DELHAIZE GROUP**
Rue Osseghemstraat 53, Molenbeek-St.-Jean, B-1080 Brussels, Belgium
CEO: Pierre-Olivier Beckers, Pres. & CEO   Tel: 32-2-412-2111   Rev: $24,344
Bus: *General merchandise and food retailers.*   Fax: 32-2-412-2194   Emp: 141,711
              www.delhaizegroup.com
NAICS: 445110, 445120, 453910

    DELHAIZE AMERICA
    2110 Executive Dr., Salisbury, North Carolina 28145-1330
    CEO: Bill McCanless, Chmn. & CEO   Tel: (704) 633-8250   %FO: 51
    Bus: *Supermarket chain.*   Fax: (704) 636-5024   Emp: 105,395

    FOOD LION
    2110 Executive Dr., Salisbury, North Carolina 28145
    CEO: Rick Anicetti, Pres. & CEO   Tel: (704) 633-8250
    Bus: *Grocery retail.*   Fax: (704) 636-5024

    HANNAFORD BROS. CO.
    145 Pleasant Hill Rd., Scarborough, Maine 04074
    CEO: Ronald C. Hodge, Pres. & CEO   Tel: (207) 883-2911
    Bus: *Grocery retail.*   Fax: (207) 885-3165

    J.H. HARVEY CO., LLC
    727 S. Davis St., Nashville, Georgia 31639
    CEO: J. H. Harvey Jr., Pres.   Tel: (229) 686-7654
    Bus: *Grocery retail.*   Fax: (229) 686-2927   Emp: 3,500

    KASH N' KARRY FOOD STORES, INC.
    3801 Sugar Palm Dr., Tampa, Florida 33619
    CEO: Shelley G. Broader, CEO   Tel: (813) 620-1139
    Bus: *Grocery retail.*   Fax: (813) 626-9550

● **DEXIA NV/SA**
Square de Meeus, 1, B-1000 Brussels, Belgium
CEO: Pierre Richard, CEO   Tel: 32-2-213-5700   Rev: $20,949
Bus: *Financial institution engaged in asset*   Fax: 32-2-213-5701   Emp: 23,865
    management, public works loans and insurance.   www.dexia.com
    (JV with Dexia France)
NAICS: 522110, 522293, 522294, 523130, 523140

ARTESIA MORTGAGE CAPITAL CORP.
1180 NW Maple St., Issaquah, Washington 98027
CEO: Guy Cools, Mng. Dir.   Tel: (425) 313-4600
Bus: *Commercial mortgages*   Fax: (425) 313-1005   Emp: 34

ASTRIS FINANCE
1730 K St., Ste. 900, Washington, District of Columbia 20006
CEO: Terry A. Powers, Mng. Dir.   Tel: (202) 223-9420
Bus: *Consulting company*   Fax: Emp: 3

DEXIA BANK
445 Park Ave., 7/F, New York, New York 10022
CEO: Marc Brugiere, Gen. Dir.   Tel: (212) 705-0700
Bus: *Commercial bank*   Fax: (212) 705-0701   Emp: 29

DEXIA CREDIT
445 Park Ave., New York, New York 10022
CEO: Marc Brugiere, Gen. Dir.   Tel: (212) 515-7000   %FO: 100
Bus: *General banking services.*   Fax: (212) 753-5522   Emp: 60

DEXIA SECURITIES USA INC.
747 Third Ave, 22/F, New York, New York 10017
CEO: Nils Geenen, Exec. Dir.   Tel: (212) 376-0130   %FO: 100
Bus: *Brokerage services.*   Fax: (212) 376-0139   Emp: 4

FINANCIAL SECURITY ASSURANCE HOLDINGS LTD.
350 Park Ave., New York, New York 10022
CEO: Robert P. Cochran, Chmn. & CEO   Tel: (212) 826-0100
Bus: *Surety insurance*   Fax: (212) 688-3101   Emp: 345

• **DHL WORLDWIDE NETWORK**
De Kleetlaan 1, B-1831 Diegem-Machelen, Belgium
CEO: Peter E. Kruse, CEO   Tel: 32-2-713-4000   Rev: $27,570
Bus: *Worldwide logistics and freight forwarding*   Fax: 32-2-713-5000   Emp: 160,754
                                       www.dhl.com
NAICS: 488510, 492110

ASTAR AIR CARGO, INC.
2 South Biscayne Blvd., Ste. 3663, Miami, Florida 33131
CEO: John H. Dasburg, Pres. & CEO   Tel: (305) 982-0501
Bus: *Aircraft freight forwarding services.*   Fax: (305) 416-9564

DHL DANZAS AIR & OCEAN NORTH AMERICA
33 Washington St., 14/F, Newark, New Jersey 07102
CEO: Hans Toggweiler   Tel: (973) 639-1989
Bus: *Freight forwarding and logistics services.*   Fax: (973) 639-1985

DHL HOLDINGS USA
1200 S. Pine Island Rd., Ste. 600, Plantation, Florida 33324
CEO: John P. Mullen   Tel: (954) 888-7000   %FO: 100
Bus: *Logistics and freight forwarding services.*   Fax: (954) 888-7310

- **ESKO-GRAPHICS**
Kortrijksesteenweg 1095, B-9051 Gent, Belgium
CEO: Magda Deruytter, Sales   Tel: 32-9-216-9211   Rev: $83
Bus: *Mfr. pre-press, scanning equipment.*   Fax: 32-9-216-9464   Emp: 800
    www.esko-graphics.com
NAICS: 333293

    ESKO-GRAPHICS
    1955 Vaughn Rd., Ste. 101, Kennesaw, Georgia 30144
    CEO: Kim Graven, Pres.   Tel: (770) 427-5700   %FO: 100
    Bus: *Pre-press working process and press ready*   Fax: (770) 427-7844   Emp: 178
      printing plates.

    ESKO-GRAPHICS
    40 Westover Rd., Ludlow, Massachusetts 01056
    CEO: Simon James, Principal   Tel: (413) 583-4100   %FO: 100
    Bus: *Pre-press working process and press ready*   Fax: (413) 589-0990   Emp: 12
      printing plates.

- **ETEX GROUP SA**
Avenue de Tervueren 361, B-1150 Brussels, Belgium
CEO: Canio L. Corbo, Chmn.   Tel: 32-2-778-1211
Bus: *Mfr. building materials and systems, including*   Fax: 32-2-778-1212   Emp: 24,000
   roofs, plastics, boards, floors and walls.   www.etexgroup.com
NAICS: 326199

    CANPLAS INC.
    11402 East 53rd Ave., Ste. 200, Denver, Colorado 80239
    CEO: Mike Gilroy, Pres.   Tel: (303) 373-1918   %FO: 100
    Bus: *Mfr. injection molded components for the*   Fax: (303) 373-1923
      construction industry.

    CÉRAMICA SAN LORENZO INC.
    10012 Norwalk Blvd., Ste. 110, Santa Fe Springs, California 90670
    CEO: David Santibanez   Tel: (562) 944-3957   %FO: 100
    Bus: *Mfr. building materials.*   Fax: (562) 944-3198

- **HAMON & CIE SA**
50-58 rue Capouillet, B-1060 Brussels, Belgium
CEO: Francis Lambilliotte, CEO   Tel: 32-2-535-1239
Bus: *Air pollution control and equipment.*   Fax: 32-2-537-0039
    www.hamon.com
NAICS: 335314, 335931, 541330, 561210

    HAMON
    58 East Main St., PO Box 1500, Somerville, New Jersey 08876
    CEO: Pier Havier, CEO   Tel: (908) 685-4000   %FO: 100
    Bus: *Air-pollution-control devices manufacture*   Fax: (908) 333-2152   Emp: 232

    HAMON THERMAL TRANSFER CORP.
    50 North Linden St., Duquesne, Pennsylvania 15110
    CEO: Timothy W. Ottie, Pres.   Tel: (412) 460-4004
    Bus: *Mfr. of electrostatic precipitator, & high*   Fax: (412) 466-2899   Emp: 135
      temp heat recovery products.

- **ICOS VISION SYSTEMS CORPORATION N.V.**
Research Park Haasrode, Esperantolaan 8, B-3001 Heverlee, Belgium
CEO: Antoon DeProft, Pres. & CEO   Tel: 32-16-39-8220   Rev: $121
Bus: *Machine vision and inspection systems*   Fax: 32-16-40-0067   Emp: 262
    manufacture for electronic and automotive   www.icos.be
NAICS: 333295, 333295, 333314

   ICOS VISION SYSTEMS INC.
   2000 Wyatt Dr., Ste. 13, Santa Clara, California 95054
   CEO: Dale Christman   Tel: (408) 567-9511   %FO: 100
   Bus: *Machine vision and inspection systems*   Fax: (408) 567-9512
    manufacture for electronic and automotive
    industries.

   ICOS VISION SYSTEMS INC.
   17 Hornbeam Hill Rd., Chelmsford, Massachusetts 01824
   CEO: Paul Boucher   Tel: (978) 256-3402   %FO: 100
   Bus: *Process control systems manufacture.*   Fax: (978) 256-3402

- **INBEV**
Brouweriiplein 1, B-3000 Leuven, Belgium
CEO: John F. Brock, CEO   Tel: 32-16-24-7111   Rev: $8,842
Bus: *Brews beers (Rolling Rock, Labatt, & Tecate);*   Fax: 32-16-24-7407   Emp: 50,000
   bottles soft drinks, juices and water; operates   www.inbev.com
   restaurants.
NAICS: 311421, 312111, 312120

   INBEV USA
   101 Merritt 7, PO Box 5075, Norwalk, Connecticut 06856
   CEO: Carlos Brito, Pres. & CEO   Tel: (203) 750-6600
   Bus: *Bottling & distribution.*   Fax: (203) 750-6699

- **KBCGROUP NV**
Havenlaan 2, B-1080 Brussels, Belgium
CEO: Willy Duron, Pres. & CEO   Tel: 32-2-429-4916   Rev: $25,626
Bus: *General banking services.*   Fax: 32-2-429-4416   Emp: 51,000
    www.kbc.be
NAICS: 522110, 524113, 524128

   KBC BANK NV
   245 Peachtree Center Ave., Marquis One Tower, Ste. 2550, Atlanta, Georgia 30303
   CEO: Michael Sawicki, Reg. Mgr.   Tel: (404) 584-5466   %FO: 100
   Bus: *International banking services.*   Fax: (404) 584-5465

   KBC BANK NV
   515 South Figueroa St., Ste. 1920, Los Angeles, California 90071
   CEO: Thomas Jackson, Reg. Mgr.   Tel: (213) 624-0401   %FO: 100
   Bus: *International banking services.*   Fax: (213) 629-5801

   KBC BANK NV
   125 West 55th St., 10/F, New York, New York 10019
   CEO: Hendrik Scheerlinck, Gen. Mgr.   Tel: (212) 541-0600   %FO: 100
   Bus: *International banking services.*   Fax: (212) 956-5580

● **MAGOTTEAUX INTERNATIONAL S.A.**
Rue A. Dumont, B-4051 Chevremont, Belgium
CEO: Walter Mersch, Gen. Mgr.   Tel: 32-43-617-550   Rev: $40
Bus: *White iron grinding media, iron and steel castings* Fax: Emp: 510
manufacture.   www.magotteaux.com
NAICS: 331511, 331513

    MAGGOTTEAUX INC.
    1 Maryland Farms, Ste. 200, Brentwood, Tennessee 37027
    CEO: Bill Early, Mgr.   Tel: (615) 385-3055
    Bus: *Industrial machinery and equipment*   Fax: (615) 297-6743

    MAGOTTEAUX - PULASKI INC.
    2360 Industrial Loop Rd., PO Box 518, Pulaski, Tennessee 38478
    CEO: Walter Mersch, Pres.   Tel: (931) 363-7471
    Bus: *Grinding media castings*   Fax: (931) 363-6918   Emp: 591

    WOLLASTON ALLOYS INC.
    205 Wood Rd., Braintree, Massachusetts 02184
    CEO: Walter Mersch, Chmn.   Tel: (781) 848-3333   %FO: 100
    Bus: *Copper, Steel, Nonferrous Metal Foundries* Fax: (781) 848-3993   Emp: 130

● **MEDECINS SANS FRONTIERES**
Rue de la Tourelle, 39, B-1090 Brussels, Belgium
CEO: Marine Buissonniere, Gen. Mgr.   Tel: 32-2-280-1881
Bus: *International association of volunteer medical* Fax: 32-2-280-0173
professionals known as Doctors Without Borders. www.msf.org
NAICS: 813212, 813311

    DOCTORS WITHOUT BORDERS
    6 East 39th St., 8/F, New York, New York 10016
    CEO: Martha Carey   Tel: (212) 679-6800   %FO: 100
    Bus: *International association of volunteer*   Fax: (212) 679-7016
    medical professionals.

● **PICANOL GROUP NV**
Ter Waarde 50, B-8900 Ieper, Belgium
CEO: Patrick Steverlynck, Pres.   Tel: 32-57-22-2111
Bus: *Weaving machine & parts manufacture and sale;* Fax: 32-57-22-2220   Emp: 985
technical service for installation & training.   www.picanolgroup.com
NAICS: 333292

    GTP STEEL HEDDLE INC.
    1801 Rutherford Rd., PO Box 5519, Greenville, South Carolina 29606
    CEO: James C. Thomas, Pres.   Tel: (864) 288-5475   %FO: 100
    Bus: *Sale weaving machine & parts, technical* Fax: (864) 297-5081   Emp: 50
    service for installation & training.

- **PUNCH INTERNATIONAL NV**
Duwijckstraat 17, B-2500 Lier, Belgium
CEO: Guido Dumarey, Pres. & CEO
Bus: *Electronic components manufacture.*

Tel: 32-3-443-1911
Fax: 32-3-443-1906
www.punchinternational.com

Rev: $293
Emp: 3,108

NAICS: 333293, 334119, 334220, 334419, 335999

 PUNCH COMPONENTS
 505 N. Cable Rd., Lima, Ohio 45805
 CEO: Kevin Perry, Plant Mgr.
 Bus: *Electronic components manufacture and distribution.*

 Tel: (419) 224-1242
 Fax: (419) 224-1243

 Emp: 30

- **S.W.I.F.T.**
Avenue Adele 1, B-1310 La Hulpe, Belgium
CEO: Leonard H. Schrank, CEO
Bus: *Global communications.*

Tel: 32-2-655-3111
Fax: 32-2-655-3226
www.swift.com

Rev: $692
Emp: 1,708

NAICS: 516110, 518111, 522320, 541519, 928120

 S.I.D.E AMERICA CORP.
 245 Park Ave., 39/F, New York, New York 10167
 CEO: Rao Sanapala
 Bus: *Engaged in international banking.*

 Tel: (212) 792-4211
 Fax: (212) 792-4001

 S.I.D.E AMERICA CORP.
 445 S. Figueroa St., Ste. 2700, Los Angeles, California 90071
 CEO: Roy Sudeepto
 Bus: *Engaged in international banking.*

 Tel: (213) 612-7799
 Fax: (213) 612-7797

 S.W.I.F.T. PAN AMERICAS
 9615 Center St., Manassas, Virginia 20110
 CEO: Joe Eng, CEO
 Bus: *Engaged in international banking.*

 Tel: (703) 365-6397
 Fax:

 %FO: 100

 S.W.I.F.T. PAN AMERICAS
 200 Park Ave., 38/F, New York, New York 10166
 CEO: Leonard Schrank, CEO
 Bus: *Engaged in international banking.*

 Tel: (212) 455-1800
 Fax: (212) 455-1817

 %FO: 100
 Emp: 50

- **SOCIETY FOR WORLDWIDE INTERBANK FINANCIAL TELECOMMUNICATIONS**
Avenue Adele 1, B-1310 La Hulpe, Belgium
CEO: Leonard H. Schrank, CEO
Bus: *Financial services; transaction processing and settlement.*

Tel: 32-2-655-3111
Fax: 32-2-655-3226
www.swift.com

Rev: $757
Emp: 1,737

NAICS: 522320

 SOCIETY FOR WORLDWIDE INTERBANK FINANCIAL TELECOMMUNICATIONS
 7 Times Sq., 45/F, New York, New York 10036
 CEO: Ranita Massuda
 Bus: *Financial services; transaction processing and settlement.*

 Tel: (212) 455-1800
 Fax: (212) 455-1817

 %FO: 100

● **SOCONORD GROUP**
Avenue Louise 287/15, B-1050 Brussels, Belgium
CEO: Daniel Gheysens, Dir.   Tel: 32-2-640-7430
Bus: *Engaged in pipes and tubular products for the*   Fax: 32-2-647-7297   Emp: 500
gas and oil industry.   www.soconord.com
NAICS: 332996

   SOCONORD CORPORATION
   340 North Houston Pkwy., Ste. 275, Houston, Texas 77060-2415
   CEO: Daniel Gheysens, Dir.   Tel: (281) 820-9400   %FO: 100
   Bus: *Sales/distribution of pipes and tubular*   Fax: (281) 820-5800
   products for the gas and oil industry.

● **SOLVAY SA**
Rue du Prince Albert 33, B-1050 Brussels, Belgium
CEO: Alois Michielsen, Chmn.   Tel: 32-2-509-6111   Rev: $9,485
Bus: *Plastics, chemicals and pharmaceuticals*   Fax: 32-2-509-6617   Emp: 30,000
manufacture   www.solvay.com
NAICS: 325181, 325188, 325199, 325211, 325221, 325222, 325411, 325412, 325414, 326113, 326199

   AMERICAN SODA
   2717 County Rd. 215, Parachute, Colorado 81636
   CEO: Charlie Yates, Gen. Mgr.   Tel: (970) 285-0408
   Bus: *Mfr. Industrial metals & minerals.*   Fax: (970) 285-0448   Emp: 117

   BP SOLVAY POLYETHYLENE NORTH AMERICA
   PO Box 1000, Deer Park, Texas 77536
   CEO: Gary Miertschin   Tel: (713) 307-3000   %FO: JV
   Bus: *HDPE production.*   Fax: (713) 307-3548

   HEDWIN CORPORATION
   1600 Roland Heights Ave., Baltimore, Maryland 21211
   CEO: David Rubley, Pres.   Tel: (410) 467-8209
   Bus: *Manufacture of liners to service both*   Fax: (410) 467-1761
   shipping and in-plant processing

   INERGY AUTOMOTIVE SYSTEMS
   2710 Bellingham Rd., Ste. 400, Troy, Michigan 48084
   CEO: James A. Squatrito, Pres.   Tel: (248) 743-5700
   Bus: *Auto parts manufacturing.*   Fax: (248) 743-1469   Emp: 882

   PEPTISYNTHA, INC.
   20910 Higgins Ct., Torrance, California 90501
   CEO: Satish Joshi   Tel: (310) 782-7534   %FO: 100
   Bus: *Pharmaceuticals manufacture and sales.*   Fax: (310) 782-7352

   PIPELIFE JET STREAM, INC.
   PO Box 190, Siloam Springs, Arkansas 72761
   CEO: Donald Baird   Tel: (501) 524-5151   %FO: 100
   Bus: *Plastic pipe manufacture.*   Fax: (501) 524-5156

SOLVAY ADVANCED POLYMERS
12210 Blazer Rd., Cheyenne, Wyoming 82001
CEO: Scott Gullette, VP
Bus: *Polymers.*

Tel: (307) 634-9229
Fax: (307) 634-9003

%FO: 100

SOLVAY ADVANCED POLYMERS, INC.
4500 McGinnis Ferry Rd., Alpharetta, Georgia 30005
CEO: Joseph D. Greulich
Bus: *Chemicals.*

Tel: (770) 772-8200
Fax: (770) 772-8747

%FO: 100

SOLVAY AUTOMOTIVE INC.
2710 Bellingham Dr., Troy, Michigan 48083
CEO: Norman Johnston, Pres.
Bus: *Mfr. gas tanks and plastic parts for auto
    industry; design, test, mfr. blow-molded
    plastic components.*

Tel: (248) 526-9563
Fax: (248) 435-3957

%FO: 100
Emp: 516

SOLVAY CHEMICALS, INC.
3333 Richmond Ave., Houston, Texas 77098
CEO: David G. Birney, Pres. & CEO
Bus: *Holding company. U.S. headquarters.*

Tel: (713) 525-6500
Fax: (713) 525-7806

%FO: 100
Emp: 9,601

SOLVAY CHEMICALS, INC.
3333 Richmond Ave., Houston, Texas 77227
CEO: Gary Hall, Pres.
Bus: *Mfr./distribution peroxygen chemicals.*

Tel: (713) 525-6500
Fax: (713) 524-9032

%FO: 100

SOLVAY DRAKA
6900 Elm St., City of Commerce, California 90040
CEO: Mark Stern, VP Mktg.
Bus: *Provides competencies in calendaring &
    extrusion of medical film & sheeting, PVC
    compounds, Press Polished PVC sheets &
    specialty laminate products.*

Tel: (323) 725-0050
Fax: (323) 725-1283

SOLVAY ENGINEERED POLYMERS
1200 Harmon Rd., Auburn Hills, Michigan 48326
CEO: Pierre Joris, Pres.
Bus: *Mfr. thermoplastic polyolefin for auto
    industry.*

Tel: (248) 391-9500
Fax: (248) 391-9501

%FO: 100

SOLVAY PHARMACEUTICALS, INC.
901 Sawyer Rd., Marietta, Georgia 30062
CEO: Harold H. Shlevin, Pres. & CEO
Bus: *Pharmaceutical manufacture.*

Tel: (770) 578-9000
Fax: (770) 578-5597

%FO: 100

SOLVAY SOLEXIS
10 Leonard Lane, Thorofare, New Jersey 08086
CEO: Diana Roman, Mktg.
Bus: *Fluoropolymers manufacture.*

Tel: (856) 853-8119
Fax: (856) 853-6405

%FO: 100

UNIMED PHARMACEUTICALS, INC.
901 Sawyer Rd., Marietta, Georgia 30062
CEO: Jean-Louis Anspach, Pres. & CEO
Bus: *Pharmaceuticals manufacture and sales.*

Tel: (770) 578-9000
Fax: (770) 578-5597

%FO: 100

- **SUEZ-TRACTEBEL S.A.**
1, Place du Trone, B-1000 Brussels, Belgium
CEO: Jean-Pierre Hansen, CEO
Bus: *Electricity and gas, energy and services.*
Tel: 32-2-510-7111
Fax: 32-2-510-7330
www.tractebel.be
Rev: $40,012
Emp: 87,300

NAICS: 221111, 221112, 221113, 221119, 221121, 221122, 221210, 221310, 237110, 237120, 237130, 238990, 424720, 454319, 486210, 523130, 523140,
541330, 541519, 541618, 541620, 541690, 561210, 811213

  SUEZ ENERGY RESOURCES NA
  1990 Post Oak Blvd., Ste. 1900, Houston, Texas 77056
  CEO: Zin Smati, Pres. & CEO
  Bus: *Retail energy marketing.*
  Tel: (713) 636-0000
  Fax: (713) 599-2601
  Emp: 100

  SUEZ LNG NA
  1 Liberty Square, Ste.11, Boston, Massachusetts 02109
  CEO: Richard Grant, CEO
  Bus: *LNG storage, transport & commercialization.*
  Tel: (617) 526-8300
  Fax:
  Emp: 40

- **UBIZEN NV**
Philipssite 5, B-3001 Leuven, Belgium
CEO: Stijn Bijnens, CEO
Bus: *Computer security services*
Tel: 32-16-28-70-00
Fax: 32-16-28-71-00
www.ubizen.com
Rev: $21
Emp: 300

NAICS: 541511, 541512

  UBIZEN INC.
  125 Maiden Lane, 15/F, New York, New York 10038
  CEO: Dirk Peeters
  Bus: *Computer security services.*
  Tel: (212) 240-9300
  Fax: (212) 240-9301
  %FO: 100

- **UCB CHEMICALS CORPORATION, DIV. SURFACE SPECIALTIES**
Allee de la Recherche 60, B-1070 Brussels, Belgium
CEO: Roch F. Doliveux, Chmn. & CEO
Bus: *Specialty chemicals and resins manufacture.*
Tel: 32-2-599-9999
Fax: 32-2-599-9900
www.ucb-group.com
Rev: $4,185
Emp: 11,403

NAICS: 325411, 325412

  UCB INC.
  2000 Lake Park Dr., Smyrna, Georgia 30080
  CEO: Larry Golen, Pres.
  Bus: *Mfr. specialty chemicals.*
  Tel: (770) 434-6188
  Fax: (770) 437-5749
  %FO: 100
  Emp: 430

  UCB PHARMA INC.
  1950 Lake Park Dr., Smyrna, Georgia 30080
  CEO: Anthony Tebbutt, Pres.
  Bus: *Mfr. prescription medicines.*
  Tel: (770) 970-7500
  Fax: (770) 970-8344
  %FO: 100

- **N.V. UMICORE S.A.**
Rue du Marias 31, B-1000 Brussels, Belgium
CEO: Thomas Leysen, CEO
Bus: *Zinc, copper, precious metals, and advanced materials manufacture.*
Tel: 32-2-227-7111
Fax: 32-2-227-7900
www.umicore.com
Rev: $5,871
Emp: 11,470

NAICS: 212221, 212231, 212234, 212299, 213114

UMICORE GROUP
3120 Highwoods Blvd., Magnolia Bldg. 3120, Ste. 104, Raleigh, North Carolina 27604
CEO: Marc Van Sande, Pres.   Tel: (919) 874-7156
Bus: *Nonferrous metals*   Fax: (919) 874-7195   Emp: 200

Belize

- **CARLISLE HOLDINGS LIMITED**
  60 Market Square, PO Box 1764, Belize City, Belize
  CEO: Michael A. Ashcroft, CEO
  Bus: *Supplies outsourced facilities services and
         staffing services to a broad range of commercial,
         industrial and municipal clients.*
  NAICS: 561310, 561320, 561720

  Tel: 501-2-72660
  Fax: 501-2-75854
  www.carlisleholdings.com

  Rev: $1,380
  Emp: 36,300

  CARLISLE GROUP
  625 N. Michigan Ave., Ste. 2100, Chicago, Illinois 60611
  CEO: Max DeZara, Pres.
  Bus: *Engaged in a full range of facilities
         services, including janitorial, landscaping,
         security services & general repair &*

  Tel: (312) 587-3030
  Fax: (312) 587-0491

  %FO: 100

  ONESOURCE, DIV. CARLISLE GROUP US
  1600 Parkwood Circle, Atlanta, Georgia 30339
  CEO: Cheryl Jones, Pres.
  Bus: *Engaged in a full range of facilities
         services, including janitorial, landscaping,
         security services & general repair &*

  Tel: (770) 436-9900
  Fax: (770) 226-8512

  %FO: 100
  Emp: 42,000

Bermuda

- **ACCENTURE LTD.**
22 Victoria St., Hamilton HM 12, Bermuda
CEO: Joe W. Forehand, Chmn. & CEO
Bus: *Engaged in management and technology*

Tel: 44-1-296-8262
Fax: 44-1-296-4245
www.accenture.com

Rev: $13,397
Emp: 83,000

NAICS: 541511, 541611

ACCENTURE LTD.
1501 S. McPac Expwy., Ste. 300, Austin, Texas 78746
CEO: Douglas Doerr
Bus: *Engaged in management and technology consulting.*

Tel: (512) 472-2323
Fax: (512) 476-7765

%FO: 100

ACCENTURE LTD.
2929 Allen Pkwy., Ste. 2000, Houston, Texas 77019-7107
CEO: Lillian Watkins
Bus: *Engaged in management and technology consulting.*

Tel: (713) 837-1500
Fax: (713) 837-1593

%FO: 100

ACCENTURE LTD.
One Financial Plaza, Hartford, Connecticut 06103
CEO: Glenn A. Sieber
Bus: *Engaged in management and technology consulting.*

Tel: (860) 756-2000
Fax: (860) 756-2888

%FO: 100

ACCENTURE LTD.
128 Third St. South, St. Petersburg, Florida 33701
CEO: David Straube
Bus: *Engaged in management and technology consulting.*

Tel: (727) 897-7000
Fax: (727) 897-7099

%FO: 100

ACCENTURE LTD.
1345 Ave. of the Americas, New York, New York 10105
CEO: William D. Green
Bus: *Engaged in management and technology consulting.*

Tel: (917) 452-4400
Fax: (917) 527-9915

%FO: 100

ACCENTURE LTD.
200 Public Square, Ste. 1900, Cleveland, Ohio 44114
CEO: Wendy O'Donnell
Bus: *Engaged in management and technology consulting.*

Tel: (216) 535-5000
Fax: (216) 535-5350

%FO: 100

ACCENTURE LTD.
133 Peachtree St. NE, Ste. 2600, Atlanta, Georgia 30303
CEO: Robert C. Clauser
Bus: *Engaged in management and technology consulting.*

Tel: (404) 880-9100
Fax: (404) 589-4200

%FO: 100

Bermuda

ACCENTURE LTD.
100 William St., Wellesley, Massachusetts 02181-9151
CEO: Thomas Davenport   Tel: (617) 454-4000   %FO: 100
Bus: *Engaged in management and technology*   Fax: (617) 454-4001
    consulting.

ACCENTURE LTD.
100 North Tryon St., Ste. 3900, Charlotte, North Carolina 28202-4000
CEO: Michelle Brown   Tel: (704) 332-6411   %FO: 100
Bus: *Engaged in management and technology*   Fax: (704) 370-5700
    consulting.

ACCENTURE LTD.
161 North Clark St., Chicago, Illinois 60601
CEO: Michael R. Naset   Tel: (312) 693-0161   %FO: 100
Bus: *Engaged in management and technology*   Fax: (312) 652-2329
    consulting.

ACCENTURE LTD.
201 East Fourth St., Ste.1600, Cincinnati, Ohio 45202
CEO: Michael E. Hughes   Tel: (513) 455-1001   %FO: 100
Bus: *Engaged in management and technology*   Fax: (513) 455-1600
    consulting.

ACCENTURE LTD.
7500 College Blvd., Ste. 1400, Overland Park, Kansas 66210
CEO: David Straube   Tel: (913) 319-1000   %FO: 100
Bus: *Engaged in management and technology*   Fax: (913) 319-1900
    consulting.

ACCENTURE LTD.
111 Washington Ave., Albany, New York 12210
CEO: Andrew Stengel   Tel: (518) 462-4762   %FO: 100
Bus: *Engaged in management and technology*   Fax: (518) 462-4762
    consulting.

ACCENTURE LTD.
Two Hannover Square, Ste. 1520, Raleigh, North Carolina 27601
CEO: Charlotte Trudel   Tel: (919) 836-1200   %FO: 100
Bus: *Engaged in management and technology*   Fax: (919) 821-0561
    consulting.

ACCENTURE LTD.
One Market St., 38/F, San Francisco, California 94105
CEO: LaMae Allen   Tel: (415) 537-5000   %FO: 100
Bus: *Engaged in management and technology*   Fax: (415) 537-5038
    consulting.

ACCENTURE LTD.
901 Main St., Ste. 5400, Dallas, Texas 75202
CEO: Mike Hickey   Tel: (214) 853-1000   %FO: 100
Bus: *Engaged in management and technology*   Fax: (214) 853-2000
    consulting.

ACCENTURE LTD.
605 Fifth Ave. South, Ste. 800, Seattle, Washington 98104
CEO: David Andrews
Bus: *Engaged in management and technology consulting.*
Tel: (206) 839-2000
Fax: (206) 839-2008
%FO: 100

ACCENTURE LTD.
1010 Market St., St. Louis, Missouri 63101
CEO: David Straube
Bus: *Engaged in management and technology consulting.*
Tel: (314) 345-3000
Fax: (314) 345-3505
%FO: 100

ACCENTURE LTD.
11951 Freedom Dr., Reston, Virginia 20190
CEO: Charlotte Trudel
Bus: *Engaged in management and technology consulting.*
Tel: (703) 947-2000
Fax: (703) 947-2200
%FO: 100

ACCENTURE LTD.
One Biscayne Tower, Ste. 2000, Miami, Florida 33131
CEO: David Straube
Bus: *Engaged in management and technology consulting.*
Tel: (786) 425-7000
Fax: (305) 358-3122
%FO: 100

ACCENTURE LTD.
2101 Rosecrans Ave., Ste. 3300, El Segundo, California 90245
CEO: Tim Brennan
Bus: *Engaged in management and technology consulting.*
Tel: (310) 726-2700
Fax: (310) 726-2950
%FO: 100

ACCENTURE LTD.
112 East Jefferson St., Tallahassee, Florida 32301
CEO: David Wilkins
Bus: *Engaged in management and technology consulting.*
Tel: (850) 513-0620
Fax: (850) 513-3500
%FO: 100

ACCENTURE LTD.
2527 Camino Ramon, Ste. 170, San Ramon, California 94583
CEO: Robert C. Clauser
Bus: *Engaged in management and technology consulting.*
Tel: (925) 358-7000
Fax: (925) 358-7200
%FO: 100

AVANADE INC.
2211 Elliott Ave., Seattle, Washington 98121-1692
CEO: Mitchell C. Hill, Pres.
Bus: *Information technology services.*
Tel: (206) 239-5600
Fax: (206) 239-5605
%FO: 100

INDELIQ, INC.
1 North Franklin, Ste. 220, Chicago, Illinois 60606
CEO: Jim Richey, Pres.
Bus: *Management training services.*
Tel: (312) 442-6600
Fax: (312) 442-6606
%FO: 100

- **ACE LIMITED**
  17 Woodbourne Avenue, Hamilton HM 08, Bermuda
  CEO: Evan G. Greenberg, Pres.   Tel: 44-1-295-5200   Rev: $12,329
  Bus: *Engaged in property and casual insurance.* Fax: 44-1-295-5221   Emp: 9,200
                                                     www.ace.bm
  NAICS: 524126

     ACE CASUALTY SOLUTIONS
     1601 Chestnut St., Philadelphia, Pennsylvania 19103
     CEO: Brian E. Dowd   Tel: (215) 640-1000   %FO: 100
     Bus: *Engaged in casualty insurance services.* Fax: (215) 640-1484

     ACE HOLDING USA
     1601 Chestnut St., PO Box 41484, Philadelphia, Pennsylvania 19101-1484
     CEO: Dominic J. Frederico, Pres. & CEO   Tel: (215) 640-1000   %FO: 100
     Bus: *Engaged in property and casual insurance.*   Fax: (215) 640-2489

     ACE TEMPEST RE USA
     281 Tresser Blvd., Ste. 500, Stamford, Connecticut 06901
     CEO: Jacques Q. Bonneau, Pres.   Tel: (203) 328-7000   %FO: 100
     Bus: *Engaged in property and casual insurance.*   Fax: (203) 328-7003

     ACE WESTCHESTER SPECIALTY
     500 Colonial Center Pkwy., Ste. 200, Roswell, Georgia 30076
     CEO: Dennis Crosby   Tel: (678) 795-4000   %FO: 100
     Bus: *Specialty property and casualty products*   Fax: (678) 795-4190
         insurance.

     ESIS INC., DIV. ACE LIMITED
     1133 Ave. of the Americas, New York, New York 10036
     CEO: Carl Cincotta   Tel: (212) 703-7160   %FO: 100
     Bus: *Risk management services.*   Fax: (212) 703-7160

- **AMERICAN SAFETY INSURANCE HOLDINGS LTD.**
  44 Church St., Hamilton HM HX, Bermuda
  CEO: Stephen R. Crim, CEO   Tel: 44-1-296-8560   Rev: $214
  Bus: *Insurance services.*   Fax: 44-1-296-8561   Emp: 113
                                                     www.americansafetygroup.com
  NAICS: 524126

     AMERICAN SAFETY INSURANCE HOLDINGS
     1845 The Exchange, Ste. 200, Atlanta, Georgia 30339
     CEO: Joseph D. Scollo Jr., Pres.   Tel: (770) 916-1908   %FO: 100
     Bus: *Insurance services.*   Fax: (770) 916-0618   Emp: 130

- **ARCH CAPITAL GROUP LTD.**
  Wessex House, 45 Reid St., Hamilton HM 12, Bermuda
  CEO: Constantine Iordanou, Pres. & CEO   Tel: 44-1-278-9250   Rev: $3,104
  Bus: *Property and casualty insurer.*   Fax: 44-1-278-9250   Emp: 900
                                                     www.archcapgroup.com
  NAICS: 524126

ARCH REINSURANCE COMPANY
20 Horseneck Lane, Greenwich, Connecticut 06830
CEO: Constantine Iordanou
Bus: *Property and casualty insurance.*

Tel: (203) 862-4300
Fax: (203) 862-4300

%FO: 100

● **B+H OCEAN CARRIERS LTD.**
Par LaVille Place, 14 Par-la-Ville Rd., 3/F, Hamilton HM JX, Bermuda
CEO: Michael S. Hudner, CEO
Bus: *Dry bulk and liquid cargo transport.*

Tel: 44-1-295-6875
Fax: 44-1-295-6796
www.bhocean.com

Rev: $55
Emp: 300

NAICS: 483111

    B+H OCEAN CARRIERS, DIV. NAVINVEST MARINE
    One Little Harbor Landing, Portsmouth, Rhode Island 02871
    CEO: John LeFrere
    Bus: *Engaged in dry bulk and liquid cargo transport.*

    Tel: (401) 682-1100
    Fax: (401) 682-1122

    %FO: 100

● **BACARDI LIMITED**
65 Pitts Bay Rd., Pembroke HM 08, Bermuda
CEO: Andreas Gembler, Pres. & CEO
Bus: *Mfr. wine and spirits, including Bacardi rum, Martini vermouth, Dewar's scotch and Bombay*

Tel: 44-1-295-4345
Fax: 44-1-292-0562
www.bacardi.com

Rev: $3,300
Emp: 6,000

NAICS: 312140

    BACARDI MARTINI USA
    2100 Biscayne Boulevard, Miami, Florida 33137
    CEO: Eduardo Sardina
    Bus: *Sales/distribution of wine and spirits, including Bacardi rum and Martini vermouth.*

    Tel: (305) 573-8511
    Fax: (305) 576-7507

    %FO: 100

● **THE BANK OF BERMUDA LTD.**
6 Front St., Hamilton HM 11, Bermuda
CEO: Phillip M. Butterfield, CEO
Bus: *International commercial banking and trust services.*

Tel: 44-1-295-4000
Fax: 44-1-295-7093
www.bankofbermuda.bm

Rev: $466

NAICS: 522110, 523110, 523910, 523920, 523930, 523991, 523999, 525910, 525920, 551111

    BANK OF BERMUDA (NEW YORK) LTD
    100 Wall St., New York, New York 10005
    CEO: Fred Busk, Pres.
    Bus: *International banking & trust services.*

    Tel: (212) 747-9300
    Fax: (212) 747-9393

    %FO: 100
    Emp: 40

● **BERMUDA DEPARTMENT OF TOURISM**
PO Box 465, Hamilton HM BX, Bermuda
CEO: Gary Phillips, Dir.
Bus: *Engaged in tourism and travel.*

Tel: 44-1-292-0023
Fax: 44-1-292-7537
www.bermudatourism.com

NAICS: 561591, 561599

BERMUDA DEPARTMENT OF TOURISM
310 Madison Ave., Ste. 201, New York, New York 10017
CEO: Richard Eve, Dir.   Tel: (212) 818-9800   %FO: 100
Bus: *Engaged in tourism and travel.*   Fax: (212) 983-5289

● **EVEREST RE GROUP LTD.**
Wessex House, 45 Reid St., 2/F, Hamilton HM DX, Bermuda
CEO: Joseph V. Taranto, Chmn. & CEO   Tel: 44-1-295-0006   Rev: $5,009
Bus: *Underwriter of property and casualty*   Fax: Emp: 606
                                                                            www.everestre.com
NAICS: 524126, 524130

    EVEREST RE GROUP
    461 Fifth Ave., 5/F, New York, New York 10017-6234
    CEO: Joseph Turanto, Principal   Tel: (646) 746-2700   %FO: 100
    Bus: *Engaged in insurance services.*   Fax: (646) 746-2751

    EVEREST RE GROUP
    1200 Brickell Ave., Ste. 600, Miami, Florida 33131
    CEO: Larry A. Frakes   Tel: (305) 371-8200   %FO: 100
    Bus: *Engaged in insurance services.*   Fax: (305) 789-3936

    EVEREST RE GROUP
    10 South Wacker Dr., Ste. 2135, Chicago, Illinois 60606
    CEO: Mark Seelen, Mgr.   Tel: (312) 660-0012   %FO: 100
    Bus: *Engaged in insurance services.*   Fax: (312) 660-0032

    EVEREST RE GROUP
    1111 Broadway, Ste. 2050, Oakland, California 94607
    CEO: Nancy B. Caravaca, Mgr.   Tel: (510) 273-4660   %FO: 100
    Bus: *Engaged in insurance services.*   Fax: (510) 267-0751

    EVEREST REINSURANCE COMPANY
    477 Martinsville Rd., Liberty Corner, New Jersey 07938-0830
    CEO: Larry A. Frakes, Pres. & CEO   Tel: (908) 604-3000   %FO: 100
    Bus: *Engaged in re-insurance.*   Fax: (908) 604-3322   Emp: 377

● **GLOBAL CROSSING LTD.**
Wessex House, 45 Reid St., Hamilton HM 12, Bermuda
CEO: John J. Legere, CEO   Tel: 44-1-296-8600   Rev: $2,932
Bus: *Data transport telecommunications.*   Fax: 44-1-296-8607   Emp: 4,000
                                                                            www.globalcrossing.com
NAICS: 517110, 517910, 518210, 519190, 561499

    GLOBAL CROSSING INC.
    200 Park Ave., Ste. 300, Florham Park, New Jersey 07932
    CEO: John J. Legere, CEO   Tel: (973) 937-0100   %FO: 100
    Bus: *Engaged in data transport*   Fax: (973) 360-0148   Emp: 3,600
       telecommunications.

GLOBAL CROSSING INC.
12010 Sunset Hills Rd., 4/F, Reston, Virginia 20190
CEO: Joseph Clayton, VP   Tel: (703) 464-3300   %FO: 100
Bus: *Engaged in data transport*   Fax:
   telecommunications.

GLOBAL CROSSING INC.
100 Ashford Center North, Ste. 560, Atlanta, Georgia 30338
CEO: Tel: (404) 250-6577
Bus: *Engaged in data transport*   Fax:
   telecommunications.

GLOBAL CROSSING INC.
Wall St. Plaza, 88 Pine St., New York, New York 10005
CEO: James M. Demitrieus, Pres.   Tel: (212) 825-9060
Bus: *Networking services*   Fax: Emp: 175

GLOBAL CROSSING INC.
1120 Pittsford-Victor Rd., Pittsford, New York 14534
CEO: David Carey   Tel: (973) 410-8300
Bus: *Long distance communications*   Fax: Emp: 3,200

GLOBAL CROSSING INC.
435 West Commercial St., East Rochester, New York 14445
CEO: Bob Calissendorss   Tel: (585) 777-1000
Bus: *Project Development*   Fax:

GLOBAL CROSSING INC.
1221 Brickell Ave., 16/F, Miami, Florida 33131
CEO: Jeramiah Carr, Pres.   Tel: (305) 808-5900
Bus: *Electrical repair*   Fax:

• LAZARD LLC
Clarendon House, 2 Church St., Hamilton HM 11, Bermuda
CEO: Bruce Wasserstein, Chmn. & CEO   Tel: 44-1-295-1422   Rev: $1,328
Bus: *Investment banking services.*   Fax: Emp: 2,343
   www.lazard.com
NAICS: 523110, 523120, 523130, 523140, 523920, 523991, 523999, 525110, 525120, 525190, 525910, 525920,
525990, 551111

LAZARD ASSET MANAGEMENT
225 South Sixth St., Ste. 3390, Minneapolis, Minnesota 55402
CEO: Gerald Mazzari, COO   Tel: (612) 341-8171   %FO: 100
Bus: *Venture capital services.*   Fax:

LAZARD FRERES & CO.
JP Morgan Chase Tower, 600 Travis St., Ste. 2300, Houston, Texas 77002
CEO: Theresa Cullinan Caulfield, HR   Tel: (713) 236-4600   %FO: 100
Bus: *Venture capital services.*   Fax: (713) 236-4620

LAZARD FRERES & CO.
1999 Ave. of the Stars, Ste. 1140, Los Angeles, California 90067
CEO: Theresa Cullinan Caulfield, HR   Tel: (310) 601-3400   %FO: 100
Bus: *Venture capital services.*   Fax: (310) 601-3401

LAZARD FRERES COMPANY
4 Embarcadero Center, Ste. 650, San Francisco, California 94111
CEO: David Locala, Mgr.
Bus: *Investment banking services.*
Tel: (415) 623-5000
Fax: (415) 421-5050
%FO: 100
Emp: 25

LAZARD FRERES COMPANY
3414 Peachtree Rd., Ste. 705, Atlanta, Georgia 30326
CEO: Kenneth Jacobs, Chmn.
Bus: *Investment banking services.*
Tel: (404) 442-2144
Fax: (404) 442-2155
%FO: 100

LAZARD FRERES COMPANY
200 West Madison St., Ste. 2200, Chicago, Illinois 60606
CEO: John Adams, Mgr.
Bus: *Investment banking services.*
Tel: (312) 407-6600
Fax: (312) 407-6620
%FO: 100
Emp: 40

LAZARD TECHNOLOGY PARTNERS (LTP)
30 Rockefeller Plaza, New York, New York 10020
CEO: Michel David-Weill, Owner
Bus: *Venture capital services.*
Tel: (212) 632-6000
Fax: (212) 632-6060
%FO: 100
Emp: 1,300

● **MUTUAL RISK MANAGEMENT LTD.**
44 Church St., Hamilton HM 12, Bermuda
CEO: Robert A. Mulderig, Chmn. & CEO
Bus: *Engaged in risk insurance.*
Tel: 44-1-295-5688
Fax: 44-1-292-1867
www.mutrisk.com
Rev: $498
Emp: 1,373

NAICS: 523999, 524126, 524128, 525190, 525910, 525920, 525990

   COMMONWEALTH RISK SERVICE
   One Logan Sq., Ste. 1500, Philadelphia, Pennsylvania 19103
   CEO: Richard Turner, CEO
   Bus: *Engaged in insurance services.*
Tel: (215) 963-1600
Fax: (215) 963-1205
%FO: 100

● **ORIENT-EXPRESS HOTELS LTD.**
22 Victoria St., Hamilton HM 12, Bermuda
CEO: Simon M. C. Sherwood, Pres.
Bus: *Manager of luxury hotels.*
Tel: 44-1-295-2244
Fax: 44-1-292-8666
www.orient-expresshotels.com
Rev: $357
Emp: 5,500

NAICS: 721110

   21 CLUB
   21 West 52nd St., New York, New York 10019
   CEO: James Sherwood, Pres.
   Bus: *Restaurant and private dining.*
Tel: (212) 582-1900
Fax:
%FO: 100
Emp: 160

   CHARLESTON PLACE
   205 Meeting St., Charleston, South Carolina 29401
   CEO: Paul Stracey, Gen. Mgr.
   Bus: *Hotel operations.*
Tel: (843) 722-4900
Fax:
%FO: 100
Emp: 575

   KESWICK HALL
   701 Club Dr., Keswick, Virginia 22947
   CEO: Michael Pownall
   Bus: *Resort hotel.*
Tel: (434) 979-3440
Fax: (434) 977-4171
%FO: 100

ORIENT-EXPRESS HOTELS LTD.
1155 Ave. of the Americas, New York, New York 10036
CEO: James B. Sherwood, Chmn.   Tel: (212) 302-5055   %FO: 100
Bus: *Hotel operator.*   Fax: (212) 302-5073   Emp: 5,100

THE INN AT PERRY CABIN
308 Watkins Lane, St Michaels, Maryland 21663
CEO: Roy Barker, Pres.   Tel: (410) 745-2200   %FO: 100
Bus: *Resort hotel.*   Fax: (410) 745-3348   Emp: 60

WINDSOR COURT HOTEL
300 Gravier St., New Orleans, Louisiana 70130
CEO: Chris Whipple, Controller   Tel: (504) 523-6000   %FO: 100
Bus: *Manager of luxury hotel.*   Fax: (504) 596-4513   Emp: 500

• **PARTNER RE LTD.**
Wellesley House, 96 Pitts Bay Rd., Pembroke HM 08, Bermuda
CEO: Patrick Thiele, Pres. & CEO   Tel: 44-1-292-0888   Rev: $4,173
Bus: *Engaged in reinsurance.*   Fax: 44-1-292-7010   Emp: 913
                                         www.partnerre.com
NAICS: 524130
PARTNER REINSURANCE CO OF THE US
One Greenwich Plaza, Greenwich, Connecticut 06830
CEO: Scott D. Moore, Pres. & CEO   Tel: (203) 485-4200   %FO: 100
Bus: *Reinsurance services.*   Fax: (203) 485-4300   Emp: 150

• **PXRE GROUP LTD.**
PXRE House, 110 Pitts Bay Rd., Pembroke HM 08, Bermuda
CEO: Jeffrey L. Radke, Pres. & CEO   Tel: 44-1-296-5858   Rev: $336
Bus: *Provides re-insurance.*   Fax: 44-1-296-6162   Emp: 62
                                         www.pxregroup.com
NAICS: 524130
PXRE REINSURANCE COMPANY
399 Thornall St., 14/F, Edison, New Jersey 08837
CEO: Eugene J. Servchek, SVP   Tel: (732) 906-8100   %FO: 100
Bus: *Engaged in re-insurance.*   Fax: (732) 906-9283

• **RENAISSANCE RE HOLDINGS LTD.**
Renaissance House, 8-20 East Broadway, Pembroke HM 19, Bermuda
CEO: James N. Stanard, Chmn. & CEO   Tel: 44-1-295-4513   Rev: $1,568
Bus: *Catastrophe reinsurance.*   Fax: 44-1-292-9453   Emp: 156
                                         www.renre.com
NAICS: 524126, 524130
DESOTO INSURANCE COMPANY
PO Box 901002, Ft. Worth, Texas 76113-2002
CEO: Robert L. Ricker, Pres.   Tel: (877) 843-4554   %FO: 100
Bus: *Engaged in catastrophe reinsurance.*   Fax: (877) 843-4554

GLENCOE US HOLDINGS LTD.
5080 Spectrum Dr., Ste. 900, Addison, Texas 75001
CEO: David Heatherly, Pres.   Tel: (972) 664-7000
Bus: *Provider of Insurance.*   Fax: (972) 994-9746   Emp: 60

• **SEA CONTAINERS LTD.**
Canon's Court, 21 Victoria St., Hamilton HM12, Bermuda
CEO: James B. Sherwood, Chmn. & Pres. & CEO   Tel: 44-1-295-2244   Rev: $1,743
Bus: *Passenger transport services.*   Fax: 44-1-292-8666   Emp: 14,500
                                                 www.seacontainers.com
NAICS: 483111

    SEA CONTAINERS AMERICA, INC.
    1114 Ave. of the Americas, New York, New York 10036
    CEO: Robin Lynch, Pres.   Tel: (212) 302-5070   %FO: 100
    Bus: *Marine container leasing companies. (JV of* Fax: Emp: 970
        GE Capital)

    SEASTREAK AMERICA INC.
    2 1st Ave., Atlantic Highlands, New Jersey 07716
    CEO: Robin Lynch, Pres.   Tel: (732) 872-2628   %FO: 100
    Bus: *Passenger ferry services.*   Fax: Emp: 20

• **SILVERSTAR HOLDINGS, LTD.**
Clarendon House, Church St., Hamilton HM CX, Bermuda
CEO: Michael Levy, Chmn.   Tel: 44-1-295-1422   Rev: $3
Bus: *Holding company for college football fantasy* Fax: 44-1-292-4720   Emp: 5
  sports games.   www.silverstarholdings.com
NAICS: 334413, 511210, 516110

    SILVERSTAR HOLDINGS LTD.
    6100 Glades Rd., Ste. 305, Boca Raton, Florida 33434
    CEO: Clive Kabatznik, Pres. & CEO   Tel: (561) 479-0040   %FO: 100
    Bus: *Holding company investing in profitable* Fax: (561) 479-0757   Emp: 5
      businesses.

• **W. P. STEWART & CO. LTD.**
Trinity Hall, 43 Cedar Ave., P.O. Box HM 2905, Hamilton HM LX, Bermuda
CEO: Henry B. Smith, Pres. & CEO   Tel: 44-1-295-8585   Rev: $152
Bus: *Asset management services.*   Fax: 44-1-296-6823   Emp: 106
                                                 www.wpstewart.com
NAICS: 522110, 522390, 523120, 523910, 523920, 523930, 523991, 523999, 525910, 525920, 525990

    W. P. STEWART & CO.
    527 Madison Ave., 20/F, New York, New York 10022
    CEO: Robert Rohn, Chmn.   Tel: (212) 750-8585   %FO: 100
    Bus: *Asset management.*   Fax: (212) 980-8039   Emp: 50

    W.P. STEWART ASSET MANAGEMENT (NA), INC.
    1 Jericho Plaza, 2/F, Jericho, New York 11753
    CEO: Rocco Macary, CFO   Tel: (516) 942-6688
    Bus: *Investment advice*   Fax: (516) 935-1274   Emp: 2

W.P. STEWART ASSET MANAGEMENT (NA), INC.
One Union St., Ste. 302, Portland, Maine 04101
CEO: P. Jefferson Kimball, Pres.   Tel: (207) 775-6700
Bus: *Management consulting services*   Fax: (207) 775-1665   Emp: 4

● **TELEGLOBE INTERNATIONAL HOLDINGS LTD.**
10 Queen St., PO Box HM1154, Hamilton HM EX, Bermuda
CEO: Gerald Porter Strong, Pres. & CEO   Tel: 44-1-296-4856   Rev: $1,002
Bus: *International telecommunications services and* Fax: Emp: 800
    products.   www.teleglobe.com
NAICS: 517110, 517910, 518210, 561499

    TELEGLOBE COMMUNICATIONS CORP.
    306 Alcazar Ave., Ste. 204, Coral Gables, Florida 33134
    CEO: Gerald Strong, Pres. & CEO   Tel: (305) 443-9444
    Bus: *Provides telecommunications services.*   Fax: (305) 445-6495

    TELEGLOBE COMMUNICATIONS CORP.
    750 College Rd. East, Princeton, New Jersey 08540
    CEO: Gerald Strong, Pres. & CEO   Tel: (609) 750-3333   %FO: 100
    Bus: *Provides telecommunications services.*   Fax: (609) 419-1511

    TELEGLOBE COMMUNICATIONS CORP.
    12010 Sunset Hills Rd., Reston, Virginia 20190
    CEO: Gerald Strong, Pres. & CEO   Tel: (703) 766-3100   %FO: 100
    Bus: *Provides telecommunications services.*   Fax: (703) 733-3102   Emp: 75

● **TYCO INTERNATIONAL, LTD.**
The Zurich Centre 2/F, 90 Pitts Bay Rd., Pembroke HM 08, Bermuda
CEO: Edward D. Breen, Chmn. & CEO   Tel: 44-1-292-8674   Rev: $40,153
Bus: *Engaged in security monitoring/fire protection* Fax: 44-1-295-9647   Emp: 260,000
    services, disposable medical products/surgical www.tyco.com
    instruments, undersea fiber optic cables,
    electrical connectors and industrial valves and
NAICS: 315999, 325212, 325412, 326220, 326291, 326299, 332618, 332911, 332912, 333298, 333996, 334119,
334210, 334290, 334412, 334413, 334418,
         334419, 334510, 334512, 334514, 334519, 335314, 335921, 335931, 335999, 339112, 339113, 339999,
423690, 517910, 561499, 561621, 922160

    ADT SECURITY SERVICES, INC.
    1 Town Center Rd., Boca Raton, Florida 33486
    CEO: Michael Snyder, Pres.   Tel: (561) 988-3600
    Bus: *Integrated security systems*   Fax: (561) 988-3601   Emp: 11,109

    AFC CABLE SYSTEMS, INC.
    275 Duchaine Blvd., New Bedford, Massachusetts 02745
    CEO: Robert Pereira, VP Operations   Tel: (508) 998-1131
    Bus: *Wire & cable manufacturing.*   Fax: (508) 998-1447

    ALLIED TUBE & CONDUIT
    16100 South Lathrop Ave., Harvey, Illinois 60426
    CEO: Ed Breen, CEO   Tel: (708) 339-1610   %FO: 100
    Bus: *Mfr. tubular and pipe products.*   Fax: (708) 339-2399

Bermuda

ANSUL INCORPORATED
1 Stanton St., Marinette, Wisconsin 54143
CEO: Mark VanDover, Pres.
Bus: *Chemicals*

Tel: (715) 735-7411
Fax: (715) 732-3469

Emp: 645

EARTH TECH
300 Oceangate, Long Beach, California 90802
CEO: Alan P. Krusi, Pres.
Bus: *Environmental services.*

Tel: (562) 951-2000
Fax: (562) 951-2100

%FO: 100
Emp: 8,500

GRAPHIC CONTROLS LLC
400 Exchange St., Buffalo, New York 14204
CEO: Sam Heleba, Gen. Mgr.
Bus: *Medical equipment & supplies*

Tel: (716) 853-7500
Fax: (800) 347-2420

Emp: 1,430

M/A-COM, INC.
1011 Pawtucket Blvd., Lowell, Massachusetts 01853
CEO: David Coughlan, Pres.
Bus: *Communications chips*

Tel: (978) 442-5000
Fax: (978) 453-9128

MALLINCKRODT INC.
675 McDonnell Blvd., Hazelwood, Missouri 63042
CEO: Michael J. Collins, Pres.
Bus: *Pharmaceuticals manufacturing*

Tel: (314) 654-2000
Fax: (314) 654-5381

RADIONICS
22 Terry Ave., Burlington, Massachusetts 01803
CEO: Russ Linderman, Pres.
Bus: *Health care products*

Tel: (781) 272-1233
Fax: (781) 272-2428

Emp: 250

SIMPLEX GRINNELL
50 Technology Dr., Westminster, Massachusetts 01441
CEO: Dean Seavers, Pres.
Bus: *Security & monitoring equipment*

Tel: (978) 731-2500
Fax: (978) 731-7856

TYCO ELECTRONICS
PO Box 3608, Harrisburg, Pennsylvania 17105-3608
CEO: Juergen Gromer, Pres.
Bus: *Mfr. electrical and electronic connectors
and connector assemblies.*

Tel: (717) 564-0100
Fax: (717) 986-7575

%FO: 100

TYCO ENGINEERED PRODUCTS AND SERVICES, INC.
3 Holland Way, Exeter, New Hampshire 03833
CEO: Thomas J. Lynch, Pres.
Bus: *Cabling products manufacture.*

Tel: (603) 773-9499
Fax: (603) 778-9249

%FO: 100
Emp: 28,000

TYCO FIRE & BUILDING PRODUCTS
451 North Cannon Ave., Lansdale, Pennsylvania 19446
CEO: Robert Brinkman, Pres.
Bus: *Fluid control equipment, pump, seal & valve
manufacturing*

Tel: (215) 362-0700
Fax: (215) 362-5385

Emp: 1,200

TYCO FIRE AND SECURITY SERVICES
One Town Center Rd., Boca Raton, Florida 33486
CEO: David E. Robinson, Pres. Tel: (561) 988-7200 %FO: 100
Bus: *Provides fire protection.* Fax: (561) 988-3673 Emp: 100,000

TYCO HEALTHCARE GROUP
15 Hampshire St., Mansfield, Massachusetts 02048
CEO: Richard J. Meelia, Pres. & CEO Tel: (508) 261-8000 %FO: 100
Bus: *Mfr. health care products.* Fax: (508) 261-8145

TYCO INTERNATIONAL LTD.
9 Roszel Rd., Princeton, New Jersey 08540
CEO: Christopher J. Coughlin Tel: (609) 720-4200
Bus: *Security monitoring/fire protection services,* Fax: (603) 720-4208
    disposable medical products/surgical
    instruments, undersea fiber optic cables,
    electrical connectors & industrial valves &
    plastic films.

TYCO PLASTICS AND ADHESIVES
7 Roszel Rd., Princeton, New Jersey 08540
CEO: Terry Sutter, Pres. Tel: (609) 720-4200 %FO: 100
Bus: *Produces industrial and consumer products.* Fax: (609) 720-4200 Emp: 4,400

TYCO TELECOMMUNICATIONS LTD.
60 Columbia Rd., Morristown, New Jersey 07960
CEO: Juergen W. Gromer, Pres. Tel: (973) 656-8000
Bus: *Telecommunications infrastructure* Fax: (973) 656-8131
    development

UNITED STATES SURGICAL CORP.
150 Glover Ave., Norwalk, Connecticut 06856
CEO: Allen Panzer, Pres. Tel: (203) 845-1000 %FO: 100
Bus: *Mfr. surgical staplers.* Fax: (203) 845-4257

● **WHITE MOUNTAINS RE GROUP LTD.**
12 Church St., Ste. 322, Hamilton HM 11, Bermuda
CEO: Steven E. Fass, Pres. & CEO Tel: 44-1-296-6011 Rev: $850
Bus: *Financial services holding company.* Fax: 44-1-296-9904 Emp: 255
    www.wtmre.com
NAICS: 524126, 524130, 551111

FOLKSAMERICA REINSURANCE COMPANY
120 North LaSalle, Ste. 2700, Chicago, Illinois 60602
CEO: Robert Larson Tel: (312) 357-7000 %FO: 100
Bus: *Engaged in insurance services.* Fax: (312) 357-7029

FOLKSAMERICA REINSURANCE COMPANY
599 West Putnam Ave., Greenwich, Connecticut 06831
CEO: Peter Haley, SVP Tel: (203) 618-3200 %FO: 100
Bus: *Engaged in insurance services.* Fax: (203) 618-3250

FOLKSAMERICA REINSURANCE COMPANY
800 Douglas Rd., 10/F, Coral Gables, Florida 33134
CEO: Rafael A. Saer, SVP   Tel: (305) 444-6660   %FO: 100
Bus: *Engaged in insurance services.*   Fax: (305) 444-7727

FOLKSAMERICA REINSURANCE COMPANY
One Liberty Plaza, 19/F, New York, New York 10006
CEO: Edward J. Stanco, Pres.   Tel: (212) 312-2500   %FO: 100
Bus: *Engaged in insurance services.*   Fax: (212) 385-2279

INTERNATIONAL MARINE UNDERWRITERS
77 Water St., New York, New York 10005-4488
CEO: James Zrebies, HR   Tel: (212) 440-6500   %FO: 100
Bus: *Property and casualty insurance.*   Fax: (212) 440-6689

ONEBEACON INSURANCE GROUP
One Beacon St., Boston, Massachusetts 02108
CEO: Mike Miller, Pres. & CEO   Tel: (617) 725-6283   %FO: 100
Bus: *Property and casualty insurance.*   Fax: (617) 725-6709

ONEBEACON INSURANCE GROUP
707 Sable Oaks Dr., South Portland, Maine 04106-3279
CEO: Susan Libby   Tel: (207) 791-1790   %FO: 100
Bus: *Property and casualty insurance.*   Fax: (207) 791-1790

ONEBEACON INSURANCE GROUP
5901-B Peachtree Dunwoody Rd., Atlanta, Georgia 30328
CEO: Michael Preston   Tel: (404) 682-4900   %FO: 100
Bus: *Engaged in insurance services.*   Fax: (404) 682-4902

ONEBEACON INSURANCE GROUP
50 California St., Ste. 850, San Francisco, California 94111
CEO: Toni Mitchell   Tel: (415) 343-3500   %FO: 100
Bus: *Engaged in insurance services.*   Fax: (415) 343-3502

ONEBEACON INSURANCE GROUP
1200 Sixth Ave., Suite 1810, Seattle, Washington 98101
CEO: Mark McGregor   Tel: (206) 587-6555   %FO: 100
Bus: *Engaged in insurance services.*   Fax: (206) 587-3281

ONEBEACON INSURANCE GROUP
2401 East Katella Ave., Ste. 500, Anaheim, California 92806
CEO: Bob Bell   Tel: (714) 923-2101   %FO: 100
Bus: *Engaged in insurance services.*   Fax: (714) 923-2128

ONEBEACON INSURANCE GROUP
131 Morristown Rd., Baskingridge, New Jersey 07920
CEO: Joe Armeni   Tel: (908) 766-8742   %FO: 100
Bus: *Engaged in insurance services.*   Fax: (908) 766-8639

ONEBEACON INSURANCE GROUP
29 North Wacker Dr., Ste. 900, Chicago, Illinois 60605
CEO: David Gutman   Tel: (312) 821-4700   %FO: 100
Bus: *Engaged in insurance services.*   Fax: (312) 634-2044

ONEBEACON INSURANCE GROUP
100 Corporate Pl., 3/F, Rocky Hill, Connecticut 06067
CEO: Phil Spencer   Tel: (860) 256-2820   %FO: 100
Bus: *Engaged in insurance services.*   Fax: (888) 545-4788

ONEBEACON INSURANCE GROUP
707 Sable Oaks Dr., South Portland, Maine 04106
CEO: Norma Fossett   Tel: (207) 791-1790   %FO: 100
Bus: *Engaged in insurance services.*   Fax: (207) 791-1790

WHITE MOUNTAINS INSURANCE GROUP
80 South Main St., Hanover, New Hampshire 03755-2053
CEO: David T. Foy, EVP   Tel: (603) 643-1567   %FO: 100
Bus: *Engaged in insurance services.*   Fax: (603) 643-4562

- **XL CAPITAL LTD.**
XL House, One Bermudiana Rd., Hamilton HM 11, Bermuda
CEO: Brian M. O'Hara, Pres. & CEO   Tel: 44-1-292-8515   Rev: $10,176
Bus: *Global insurance, reinsurance, and financial*   Fax: 44-1-292-5280   Emp: 3,527
    products and services.   www.xlcapital.com
NAICS: 523920, 524126, 524130

  INDIAN HARBOR INSURANCE COMPANY
  70 Seaview Ave., Stamford, Connecticut 06902
  CEO: Ken Meagher   Tel: (203) 964-5309   %FO: 100
  Bus: *Insurance services.*   Fax: (203) 964-5309

  XL AEROSPACE
  1111 Chapala St., Ste. 300, Santa Barbara, California 93101
  CEO: Charles A. Rudd   Tel: (805) 897-1111   %FO: 100
  Bus: *Insurance sales.*   Fax: (805) 897-1112

  XL CAPITAL
  2353 Alexandria Dr., Ste. 260, Lexington, Kentucky 40504
  CEO: Clive Tobin   Tel: (859) 219-1368   %FO: 100
  Bus: *Insurance services.*   Fax: (859) 219-1368

  XL CAPITAL INVESTMENT PARTNERS
  1221 6th Ave., 32/F, New York, New York 10020
  CEO: Sarah E. Street   Tel: (646) 658-5928   %FO: 100
  Bus: *Insurance services.*   Fax: (646) 658-5928

  XL ENVIRONMENTAL
  520 Eagleview Blvd., Exton, Pennsylvania 19341
  CEO: Richard Corbett   Tel: (610) 458-9109   %FO: 100
  Bus: *Insurance sales.*   Fax: (610) 458-9109

  XL INSURANCE
  190 South LaSalle St., Ste. 950, Chicago, Illinois 60603
  CEO: Brian D. Udolph   Tel: (312) 444-6500   %FO: 100
  Bus: *Insurance sales.*   Fax: (312) 444-6501

Bermuda

XL MARINE AND OFFSHORE ENERGY
99 Park Ave., 3/F, New York, New York 10016
CEO: Ricardo Garcia
Bus: *Marine insurance services.*
Tel: (212) 894-9250
Fax: (212) 894-9424
%FO: 100

XL REINSURANCE AMERICA INC.
70 Seaview Ave., Stamford, Connecticut 06902
CEO: Dennis Kane, Pres.
Bus: *Insurance sales.*
Tel: (203) 964-5566
Fax: (203) 964-1494
%FO: 100

XL REINSURANCE AMERICA, INC.
1990 North California Blvd., Ste. 740, Walnut Creek, California 94546
CEO: John Oster
Bus: *Insurance services.*
Tel: (925) 974-8200
Fax: (925) 974-8275
%FO: 100

XL REINSURANCE AMERICA, INC.
10 South Wacker Dr., Ste. 1915, Chicago, Illinois 60606
CEO: James Clausing
Bus: *Insurance services.*
Tel: (312) 876-7200
Fax: (312) 876-1399
%FO: 100

XL REINSURANCE AMERICA, INC.
115 Perimeter Center Pl., Ste. 545, Atlanta, Georgia 30346
CEO: Rob N. Wilson
Bus: *Insurance services.*
Tel: (770) 677-4200
Fax: (770) 604-9092
%FO: 100

XL REINSURANCE AMERICA, INC.
2 Logan Square, Ste. 2010, Philadelphia, Pennsylvania 19103
CEO: W. Scott Yeomans
Bus: *Insurance services.*
Tel: (215) 988-8001
Fax: (215) 988-0182
%FO: 100

XL REINSURANCE AMERICA, INC.
111 Broadway, Ste. 1802, New York, New York 10006
CEO: Bill Rosa
Bus: *Insurance services.*
Tel: (212) 820-6100
Fax: (212) 346-9826

Brazil

- **ALTUS SISTEMAS DE INFORMATICA SA**
Av. Theodomiro Porta da Fonseca, 3101 Lt. 01, Bairro Duque de Caxias, 93020-161 Sao Leopoldo RS, Brazil
CEO: Ricardo Felizzola, Pres.　　Tel: 55-51-589-9500　　Rev: $12
Bus: *Mfr. industrial automation systems.*　　Fax: 55-51-589-9501　　Emp: 150
　　www.altus.com.br
NAICS: 423690, 541512

  ALTUS AUTOMATION SYSTEMS CORP., INC.
  11870 West State Rd. 84, Ste. C10, Davies, Florida 33325
  CEO: Ricardo M. B. Felizzola, Pres.　　Tel: (954) 382-1455　　%FO: 100
  Bus: *Electronics, computers, relays & Industrial controls.*　　Fax: (954) 382-2526

- **AMIL ASSISTENCIA MEDICA INTERNACIONAL LTDA.**
Avenida Nove de Julho 5143, Jd. Paulista, 01407 Sao Paulo SP, Brazil
CEO: Edson de Godoy Bueno, Chmn. & Pres.　　Tel: 55-11-3067-1210　　Rev: $2,000
Bus: *Health care services.*　　Fax: 55-11-3079-3333　　Emp: 9,000
　　www.amil.com.br
NAICS: 524114

  AMIL INTERNATIONAL INSURANCE CO.
  9229 Waterford Centre Blvd., Ste. 500, Austin, Texas 78758-7504
  CEO: Marco Santos, CEO　　Tel: (512) 349-2645　　%FO: 100
  Bus: *Physician owned health insurance provider.*　　Fax: (512) 349-4329

- **ARACRUZ CELULOSE SA**
Rua Lauro Muller 116, 21o./222o. Andares, 22299-900 Rio de Janeiro RJ, Brazil
CEO: Carlos Augusto Lira Aguiar, Pres.　　Tel: 55-21-3820-8111　　Rev: $1,167
Bus: *Pulp mills, forestry services.*　　Fax: 55-21-3820-8202　　Emp: 1,680
　　www.aracruz.com.br
NAICS: 322110

  ARACRUZ CELULOSE USA INC.
  16300 NE 19th Ave., Ste. 210, North Miami Beach, Florida 33162
  CEO: Carlos Aguiar　　Tel: (305) 940-9762　　%FO: 100
  Bus: *Paper & pulp mills; forestry services.*　　Fax: (305) 940-9763　　Emp: 5

- **ARBI GROUP SA**
Av. Almirante Borroso 52, 11o. Andar, 20031-000 Rio de Janeiro RJ, Brazil
CEO: Daniel B. Birmann, Pres.　　Tel: 55-21-212-8282　　Rev: $996
Bus: *Investment advisor services.*　　Fax: 55-21-220-5232　　Emp: 1,200
　　www.arbisf.com
NAICS: 523930

  ARBI TRANSNATIONAL, INC.
  601 California St., Suite 615, San Francisco, California 94108
  CEO: Terry Vogt, Pres.　　Tel: (415) 989-2884　　%FO: 100
  Bus: *Investment advisory.*　　Fax: (415) 989-2904　　Emp: 6

- **BANCO BRADESCO SA**
Cidade de Deus, Predio Novo, Osasco, 06029-900 Sao Paulo SP, Brazil
CEO: Marcio Artur Laurelli Cypriano, Chmn. Tel: 55-11-3235-9566 Rev: $12,367
Bus: *Commercial banking services.* Fax: 55-11-3235-9161 Emp: 75,000
www.bradesco.com.br
NAICS: 522110

  BANCO BRADESCO SA
  450 Park Ave., Ste. 3200, New York, New York 10022
  CEO: Edison Antonelli, Mgr. Tel: (212) 688-9855 %FO: 100
  Bus: *International commercial banking services.* Fax: (212) 754-4032 Emp: 30

- **BANCO DO BRASIL**
SBS Qd. 01 Bloco C, Edifício Sede III, 24th Fl., 70073-901 Brasilia DF, Brazil
CEO: Rossano Maranhao, CEO Tel: 55-61-310-3409 Rev: $16,064
Bus: *Commercial banking services.* Fax: 55-61-310-2561 Emp: 82,671
www.bancobrasil.com.br
NAICS: 522110

  BANCO DO BRASIL S.A.
  2 South Biscayne Blvd., Ste. 3870, Miami, Florida 33131
  CEO: Max Zelmancowicz, Gen. Mgr. Tel: (305) 358-3586 %FO: 100
  Bus: *International commercial banking services.* Fax: (305) 577-0541

  BANCO DO BRASIL S.A.
  2020 K St NW, Ste. 450, Washington, District of Columbia 20006
  CEO: Paul T. Medeiros, Mgr. Tel: (202) 857-0320 %FO: 100
  Bus: *International commercial banking services.* Fax: (202) 872-8649 Emp: 100

  BANCO DO BRASIL S.A.
  600 Fifth Ave., 3/F, New York, New York 10036
  CEO: Manuel Do Espirito Santo Neto, Mgr. Tel: (212) 626-7000 %FO: 100
  Bus: *Savings institution.* Fax: (212) 626-7045 Emp: 210

  BANCO DO BRASIL S.A.
  2 North LaSalle St., Ste. 2005, Chicago, Illinois 60602
  CEO: Francisco Driguerio, Rep. Tel: (312) 236-9766 %FO: 100
  Bus: *International commercial banking services.* Fax: (312) 236-1591

- **BANCO DO ESTADO DO PARANA SA**
Rua Maximo Joao Kopp, 274, Santa Candida, 82630-900 Curitiba, Brazil
CEO: Antonio B. Hermosilllo, Chmn. Tel: 55-41-351-7688 Rev: $3,000
Bus: *General banking services.* Fax: 55-41-351-7245 Emp: 10,000
www.banestado.com.br
NAICS: 522110

  BANESTADO SA
  125 West 55th St., Ste. 900, New York, New York 10019
  CEO: Gilson Girardi Tel: (212) 956-0011 %FO: 100
  Bus: *International commercial banking services.* Fax: (212) 956-0011 Emp: 10

• BANCO DO ESTADO DO RIO GRANDE DO SUL SA
Rua Capitao Montanha 177, 90018-900 Porto Alegre RS, Brazil
CEO: Ario Zimmermann, Chmn.   Tel: 55-51-3215-1515
Bus: *General banking services.*   Fax: 55-51-3215-1716   Emp: 10,000
www.banrisul.com.br

NAICS: 522110

BANRISUL SA
500 Fifth Ave., Ste. 2310, New York, New York 10110
CEO: Carlos Becker, Mgr.   Tel: (212) 827-0390   %FO: 100
Bus: *Banking services.*   Fax: (212) 869-0844   Emp: 4

• BANCO ITAU HOLDING FINANCEIRA S.A.
Praca Alfredo Egydio de Souzo, Aranha, 100, 04344-902 Sao Paulo SP, Brazil
CEO: Roberto Egydio Setubal, Chmn. & Pres. & CEO   Tel: 55-11-5019-1549   Rev: $10,023
Bus: *Investment and commercial banking.*   Fax: 55-11-5019-1133   Emp: 42,450
www.itau.com.br

NAICS: 522110, 522220, 522292, 522293, 523110, 523120, 523920, 523930

BANCO ITAU HOLDING FINANCEIRA S.A.
540 Madison Ave., New York, New York 10022
CEO: Marcelo Sanchez, Mgr.   Tel: (212) 486-1309   %FO: 100
Bus: *International banking services.*   Fax: (212) 888-9342   Emp: 30

• BANCO MERCANTIL DE SAO PAULO
Ave. Paulista, 1450, CEP 01310-917 Sao Paulo SP, Brazil
CEO: Gastao Augusto de Bueno Vidigal, CEO   Tel: 55-11-3145-2121
Bus: *Banking services.*   Fax: 55-11-3145-3180
www.finasa.com.br

NAICS: 522110

BANCO MERCANTIL DE SAO PAULO
450 Park Ave., 14/F, New York, New York 10022
CEO: Charles Ryan   Tel: (212) 888-0030   %FO: 100
Bus: *Banking services.*   Fax: (212) 888-4631

• BM & F - BOLSA DE MERCADORIAS & FUTUROS
Praca Antonio Prado 48, 01010-901 Sao Paulo SP, Brazil
CEO: Edemir Pinto, CEO   Tel: 55-11-3119-2000   Rev: $82
Bus: *Commodities, futures, and options exchanges.*   Fax: 55-11-3242-7565   Emp: 450
www.bmf.com.br

NAICS: 523210

BM & F USA
61 Broadway, Ste. 2605, New York, New York 10006
CEO: Joao L. Amaral, Dir.   Tel: (212) 750-4197   %FO: 100
Bus: *International financial advisory firm.*   Fax: (212) 750-4198   Emp: 3

- **COMPANHIA CACIQUE DE CAFE SOLUVEL**
Av. das Nações Unidas 10989, 10o - 11o. Andares, 04578-000 Sao Paulo SP, Brazil
CEO: Sérgio Coimbra, Pres.   Tel: 55-11-3054-8200
Bus: *Mfr. roasted coffee.*   Fax: 55-11-3849-7278   Emp: 2,000
                                                             www.cafepele.com.br
NAICS: 311920
  BRASTRADE (BRAZILIAN TRADING COMPANY, INC.)
  120 Wall St., Suite 1801, New York, New York 10005
  CEO: Cergio Pereira, Pres.   Tel: (212) 363-2575   %FO: 100
  Bus: *Coffee brokers & dealers.*   Fax: (212) 514-6119   Emp: 11

- **COMPANHIA VALE DO RIO DOCE**
Avenida Graca Aranha 26, 20030-000 Rio de Janeiro, Brazil
CEO: Roger Agnelli, CEO   Tel: 55-21-3814-4477   Rev: $8,066
Bus: *Provides mining and exposition of iron ore.*   Fax: 55-21-3814-4040   Emp: 29,632
                                                             www.vale.com.br
NAICS: 212111, 212112, 212210, 212234, 212299, 212324, 212391, 213114, 331111, 331312
  RIO DOCE AMERICA INC.
  546 Fifth Ave., 12/F, New York, New York 10036
  CEO: Vincente Wright, Pres.   Tel: (212) 589-9800   %FO: 100
  Bus: *Iron ore & wood pulp*   Fax: (212) 391-4546   Emp: 8

- **DEMAREST E ALMEIDA**
Alameda Campinas 1070, 01404-002 Sao Paulo SP, Brazil
CEO: Altamiro Boscoli, Ptnr.   Tel: 55-11-888-1800
Bus: *International law firm.*   Fax: 55-11-888-1700
                                                             www.demarest.com.br
NAICS: 541110
  DEMAREST E. ALMEIDA
  509 Madison Ave., Ste. 506, New York, New York 10169
  CEO: Isabelle Franco, Prtn.   Tel: (212) 371-9191   %FO: 100
  Bus: *International law firm.*   Fax: (212) 371-5551

- **DURATEX SA**
Av. Paulista 1938, 01310-200 Sao Paulo SP, Brazil
CEO: Olavo Egydio Setubal, EVP   Tel: 55-11-3179-7733
Bus: *Mfr./sale hardboard and particle board.*   Fax: 55-11-3179-7707
                                                             www.duratex.com.br
NAICS: 321219
  DURATEX NORTH AMERICA, INC.
  1208 Eastchester Dr., Ste. 202, High Point, North Carolina 27265
  CEO: Phillip Kusiak   Tel: (336) 885-1500   %FO: 100
  Bus: *Mfr./sale hardboard & particleboard.*   Fax: (336) 885-1501

● **EMBRAER, EMPRESA BRASILEIRA DE AERONAUTICA S.A.**
Avenida Brigadeiro Faria Lima, 2170, 12227-901 Sao Jose dos Campos SC, Brazil
CEO: Mauricio N. Botelho, Pres.   Tel: 55-12-3927-1000   Rev: $3,440
Bus: *Mfr. aircraft, engines and parts.*   Fax: 55-12-3922-6070   Emp: 12,974
                  www.embraer.com.br
NAICS: 336413

  EMBRAER AIRCRAFT MAINTENANCE SERVICES, INC.
  10 Airways Blvd., Nashville, Tennessee 37217
  CEO: Robert Davis   Tel: (615) 367-2100   %FO: 100
  Bus: *Aircraft engines and parts.* Fax: (615) 367-4327

● **GERDAU SA**
Avenida Farrapos 1811, Porto Alegre, 90220-005 Rio Grande do Sul, Brazil
CEO: Jorge Gerdau Johannpeter, Chmn. & Pres. Tel: 55-51-3323-2000 Rev: $6,952
Bus: *Long-rolled steel manufacture.*   Fax: 55-51-3323-2080 Emp: 20,160
                  www.gerdau.com.br
NAICS: 331111, 331221, 331222, 332618

  AMERISTEEL STEEL MILL
  801 Gerdau Ameristeel Rd., Jackson, Tennessee 38305
  CEO: W G Manuel, Mgr.   Tel: (731) 424-5600   %FO: 100
  Bus: *Mfr. long-rolled steel.*   Fax: (731) 422-4247

  AMERISTEEL STEEL MILL
  6601 Lakeview Rd., Charlotte, North Carolina 28269
  CEO: Anthony Read, Operations Mgr. Tel: (704) 596-0361
  Bus: *Mfr. wire rod coils and steel rod, bar &* Fax: (704) 597-5031
   structural shapes.

  AMERISTEEL STEEL MILL
  1919 Tennessee Ave., Knoxville, Tennessee 37921
  CEO: Ed Woodward, Exec. Dir. Tel: (865) 546-5472   %FO: 100
  Bus: *Mfr. long-rolled steel.*   Fax: (865) 637-8293

  AMERISTEEL STEEL MILL
  16770 Rebar Rd., Baldwin, Florida 32234
  CEO: Don Shumake   Tel: (904) 266-4261
  Bus: *Mfr. wire rod coils and steel rod, bar &* Fax: (904) 266-4244
   structural shapes.

  AMERISTEEL STEEL MILL
  384 Old Grassdale Rd. NE, Cartersville, Georgia 30121
  CEO: Donny Shumake, Mgr.   Tel: (770) 387-3300
  Bus: *Mfr. wire rod coils and steel rod, bar &* Fax: (770) 387-3327
   structural shapes.

  AMERISTEEL STEEL MILL
  North Crossman Rd., Sayreville, New Jersey 08871-0249
  CEO: Bill Rider, VP   Tel: (732) 721-6600   %FO: 100
  Bus: *Mfr. wire rod coils and steel rod, bar &* Fax: (732) 721-8784   Emp: 300
   structural shapes.

GALLATIN STEEL COMPANY
4831 US Hwy. 42 West, Ghent, Kentucky 41045-9704
CEO: Don B. Daily, Pres.   Tel: (859) 567-3100
Bus: *Mfr. wire rod coils and steel rod, bar &*   Fax: (859) 567-3165   Emp: 380
structural shapes.

GERDAU
5100 W. Lemon St., Ste. 312, Tampa, Florida 33609
CEO: Philip E. Casey, CEO   Tel: (813) 286-8383
Bus: *Steel production.*   Fax: (813) 207-2328   Emp: 2,300

GERDAU AMERISTEEL
1500-2500 West 3rd St., Wilton, Iowa 52778
CEO: Tel: (563) 732-3231
Bus: *Steel production.*   Fax: (563) 732-4587

GERDAU AMERISTEEL
1678 Red Rock Rd., St. Paul, Minnesota 55119
CEO: Jerry Goodwald, Mgr.   Tel: (651) 731-5600
Bus: *Mfr. of cold rolled steel.*   Fax: (651) 731-5699

GERDAU AMERISTEEL
PO Box 3869, Beaumont, Texas 77704
CEO: Greg Bott   Tel: (409) 768-1211
Bus: *Steel production.*   Fax:

GERDAU AMERISTEEL
1035 Shar-Cal Rd., Calvert City, Kentucky 42029
CEO: Mark Quiring   Tel: (270) 395-3100
Bus: *Steel production.*   Fax: (270) 395-7861

GERDAU AMERISTEEL CORPORATION
4221 Boy Scout Blvd., Ste. 600, Tampa, Florida 33607
CEO: Phillip E. Casey, Pres. & CEO   Tel: (813) 286-8383   %FO: 100
Bus: *Mfr. long-rolled steel.*   Fax: (813) 207-2328   Emp: 2,200

GERDAU AMERISTEEL RARITAN INC.
225 Elm St., Perth Amboy, New Jersey 08862
CEO: Robert Bullard, VP   Tel: (732) 442-1600   %FO: 100
Bus: *Mfr. wire rod coils and steel rod, bar &*   Fax: (732) 442-3957   Emp: 300
structural shapes.

● **MANGELS INDUSTRIAL S.A.**
Rua Verbo Divino 1488, 3 andar, Bloco A, 04719-904 Sao Paulo SP, Brazil
CEO: Robert M. Mangels, Pres.   Tel: 55-11-5188-8800   Rev: $128
Bus: *Motor vehicle wheels, parts and accessories.*   Fax: 55-11-5181-0155   Emp: 1,800
www.mangels.com.br
NAICS: 332313, 336399

MANGELS USA INC.
652 Rembrandt Cir., Corona, California 92882
CEO: Mark R. Mangels, Pres.   Tel: (909) 737-2117   %FO: 100
Bus: *Mfr. wheels, parts and accessories.*   Fax: (909) 737-0292   Emp: 3

- **NET SERVICOS DE COMMUNICAO S.A.**
Rua Verbo Divino, 1356, 04719-002 Sao Paulo SP, Brazil
CEO: Francisco Tosta Valim Filho, CEO   Tel: 55-11-5186-2606   Rev: $574
Bus: *Cable television broadcasting.*   Fax: 55-11-5186-2606   Emp: 3,100
www.nettv.globo.com
NAICS: 515120, 515210, 517110, 517510, 517910, 518111, 518210, 519190
  - **GLOBO INTERNATIONAL**
  157 Chambers St., 15/F, New York, New York 10007
  CEO: Amaury Soares, Pres.   Tel: (917) 551-3500
  Bus: *Communication services*   Fax: Emp: 20

- **ODEBRECHT S.A.**
Av. Luis Viana, 2841, Paralela, Edificio Odebrecht, 41827-900 Salvador Bahia, Brazil
CEO: Pedro Novis, Pres. & CEO   Tel: 55-71-2105-1111   Rev: $8,184
Bus: *Holding company engaged in engineering,*   Fax: 55-71-230-0701
construction and offshore drilling.   www.odebrecht.com.br
NAICS: 213111, 237310, 237990, 325110, 325120, 325199, 325211, 325212, 488490
  - **ODEBRECH CONSTRUCTION, INC.**
  201 Alhambra Cir., Ste. 1400, Coral Cables, Florida 33134
  CEO: Luiz A. Rocha, Pres. & CEO   Tel: (305) 341-8800   %FO: 100
  Bus: *Engaged in heavy construction.*   Fax: (305) 569-1500

- **PETROBRAS SA**
Avenida Republica do Chile 65, sala 401E, 20031-912 Rio de Janeiro, Brazil
CEO: Jose Eduardo de Barros Dutra, Pres. & CEO   Tel: 55-21-2534-1510   Rev: $37,452
Bus: *Oil and gas exploration.*   Fax: 55-21-2534-6055   Emp: 53,666
www.petrobras.com.br
NAICS: 211111, 211112, 213111, 213112, 221210, 324110, 324191, 333132, 424710, 424720, 445120, 447110, 447190, 454311, 454312, 454319, 486110, 486210, 486910, 541360
  - **PETROBRAS AMERICA**
  570 Lexington Ave., 43/F, New York, New York 10022
  CEO: Theodore M. Helms, Gen. Mgr.   Tel: (212) 829-1517
  Bus: *Oil & gas exploration.*   Fax: (212) 832-5300
  - **PETROBRAS USA**
  10777 Westheimer Rd., Ste. 1200, Houston, Texas 77042
  CEO: Renato Tadeu Bertani, Gen. Mgr.   Tel: (713) 781-9798
  Bus: *Oil and gas exploration.*   Fax: Emp: 57

- **POLITEC LTDA.**
SIG Quadra 4 lote 173, 70610-440 Brasília DF, Brazil
CEO: Hélio Santos Oliveira, Dir. Sales   Tel: 55-61-3038-6800   Rev: $122
Bus: *Temporary help services*   Fax: 55-61-344-0276   Emp: 5,000
www.politec.com
NAICS: 561320
  - **POLITEC INC.**
  12007 Sunrise Valley Dr., Ste. 420, Reston, Virginia 20191
  CEO: Dalton Luz   Tel: (703) 476-0100   %FO: 100
  Bus: *Temporary help services*   Fax: (703) 476-0503

- **SÃO PAULO ALPARGATAS S.A.**
  Rua Urussuí 300, 04542-903 Sao Paulo SP, Brazil
  CEO: Marcio Luiz Simoes Utsch, Pres. & CEO
  Bus: *Textiles manufacturer.*

  Tel: 55-11-384-77295
  Fax: 55-11-
  www.alpargatas.com.br

  Rev: $293
  Emp: 11,000

  NAICS: 316213

  EXPASA FLORIDA, INC.
  10661 N. Kendall Dr., Miami, Florida 33176
  CEO: Francisco S. morales Cespede, Pres.
  Bus: *Industrial machinery & equipment*

  Tel: (305) 279-7810
  Fax: (305) 274-8207

  %FO: 100
  Emp: 2

- **SMAR EQUIPAMENTOS INDUSTRIAS LTDA.**
  Rua Dr. Antonio Furlan Jr., 1028, 14170-480 Sertaozinho SP, Brazil
  CEO: Antonio Jose Zamproni, CEO
  Bus: *Ind. measurement instruments, display & control, and machinery.*

  Tel: 55-16-3946-3510
  Fax: 55-16-3946-3554
  www.smar.com.br

  Rev: $19
  Emp: 1,100

  NAICS: 334513

  SMAR INTERNATIONAL CORPORATION
  6001 Stonington St., Ste. 100, Houston, Texas 77040
  CEO: Steve Hayden
  Bus: *Ind. measurement instruments, display and control machinery*

  Tel: (713) 849-2021
  Fax: (713) 849-2022

  %FO: 100

  SMAR RESEARCH CORPORATION
  4250 Veterans Memorial Hwy., Holbrook, New York 11741
  CEO: Edmundo Gorini, CEO
  Bus: *Mfr. of process control instruments.*

  Tel: (631) 737-3111
  Fax: (631) 737-3892

  %FO: 100
  Emp: 18

- **H. STERN JEWELERS**
  Rua Garcia Davila 113, Ipanema, 22421-010 Rio de Janeiro, Brazil
  CEO: Roberto Stern, CEO
  Bus: *High-end jewelry manufacture.*

  Tel: 55-21-2259-7442
  Fax: 55-21-2259-7442
  www.hstern.com.br

  NAICS: 339911

  H. STERN JEWELERS
  Waldorf Astoria Hotel, 301 Park Ave., New York, New York 10022
  CEO: Ronaldo Stern
  Bus: *Mfr./sales of high-end jewelry.*

  Tel: (212) 753-5595
  Fax: (212) 753-5595

  %FO: 100

  H. STERN JEWELERS
  Fontainebleau Hotel, 4441 Collins Ave., Miami, Florida 33140
  CEO: Andrea Hansen
  Bus: *Mfr./sales of high-end jewelry.*

  Tel: (305) 534-6426
  Fax: (395) 673-6783

  %FO: 100

  H. STERN JEWELERS
  645 Fifth Ave., New York, New York 10022
  CEO: Ronaldo Stern, Pres.
  Bus: *Mfr./sales of high-end jewelry.*

  Tel: (212) 688-0300
  Fax: (212) 888-5137

  %FO: 100

● **UNIBANCO HOLDINGS SA**
Av. Eusaebio Matoso 891, 4o. Andar, 05423-180 Sao Paulo SP, Brazil
CEO: Pedro Moreira Salles, CEO   Tel: 55-11-3097-1313   Rev: $4,627
Bus: *Commercial banking services.*   Fax: 55-11-3813-6182   Emp: 27,625
       www.unibanco.com.br
NAICS: 522110

    UNIBANCO NEW YORK
    65 East 55th St., 29/F, New York, New York 10022
    CEO: William Bethlem, Gen. Mgr.   Tel: (212) 832-1700   %FO: 100
    Bus: *Commercial banking.*   Fax: (212) 752-2076   Emp: 27

● **VARIG BRAZILIAN AIRLINES SA**
Rua 18 de Novembro No. 800, Sao Joao, Porto Alegre, 90240-040 Rio Grande do Sul, Brazil
CEO: Carlos L. M. Pereira e Souza, Pres. & CEO   Tel: 55-51-3358-7039   Rev: $3,328
Bus: *International commercial air transport services.*   Fax: 55-51-3358-7001   Emp: 15,000
       www.varig.com.br
NAICS: 481111

    VARIG BRAZILIAN AIRLINES
    985 Waimanu St., Honolulu, Hawaii 96814
    CEO: Antonio Lopez, Mgr.   Tel: (808) 593-2400   %FO: 100
    Bus: *Commercial air transport services.*   Fax: (808) 593-2400

    VARIG BRAZILIAN AIRLINES
    177 Post St., Ste. 890, San Francisco, California 94108
    CEO: Roger Pacheco, Gen. Mgr.   Tel: (415) 986-5737   %FO: 100
    Bus: *Commercial air transport services.*   Fax: (415) 986-5737

    VARIG BRAZILIAN AIRLINES
    71 South Central Ave., 2/F, Valley Stream, New York 11580
    CEO: Claudio F. Rocha, Principal   Tel: (516) 825-6200   %FO: 100
    Bus: *Commercial air transport services.*   Fax:

    VARIG BRAZILIAN AIRLINES
    149 Jewett St., PO Box 314, Georgetown, Massachusetts 01833
    CEO: Lawrence Thorsen Jr., Pres.   Tel: (978) 352-8238   %FO: 100
    Bus: *Airport services.*   Fax:

    VARIG BRAZILIAN AIRLINES
    5600 West Century Blvd., Los Angeles, California 90045
    CEO: Louis Nebto, Mgr.   Tel: (310) 646-7890   %FO: 100
    Bus: *Commercial air transport services.*   Fax: (310) 646-7890

    VARIG BRAZILIAN AIRLINES
    3334 Richmond Ave., Ste. 11, Houston, Texas 77098
    CEO: Louise Garcia, Mgr.   Tel: (713) 524-6092   %FO: 100
    Bus: *Commercial air transport services.*   Fax: (713) 524-6092

    VARIG BRAZILIAN AIRLINES
    380 World Way, Los Angeles, California 90045
    CEO: Vilma Vargas, Mgr.   Tel: (310) 646-2190   %FO: 100
    Bus: *Commercial air transport services.*   Fax: (310) 646-2190   Emp: 120

VARIG BRAZILIAN AIRLINES
3400 Peachtree Rd. NE, Atlanta, Georgia 30326
CEO: George Soesman, Mgr.   Tel: (404) 261-4846   %FO: 100
Bus: *Commercial air transport services.*   Fax: (404) 261-4846

VARIG BRAZILIAN AIRLINES
20 Park Plaza, Ste. 1206, Boston, Massachusetts 02116
CEO: Henrique Marques Jr., Mgr.   Tel: (617) 542-5202   %FO: 100
Bus: *Commercial air transport services.*   Fax: (617) 542-5202

VARIG BRAZILIAN AIRLINES
9463B Airport Blvd., Orlando, Florida 32827
CEO: Marcella Bottini, Mgr.   Tel: (407) 825-3935   %FO: 100
Bus: *Commercial air transport services.*   Fax: (407) 825-3935

VARIG BRAZILIAN AIRLINES
1411 Commerce Way, Hialeah, Florida 33016
CEO: Bruno Borghini, Mgr.   Tel: (305) 262-1440   %FO: 100
Bus: *Commercial air transport services.*   Fax: Emp: 20

VARIG BRAZILIAN AIRLINES
6000 N. Terminal, Atlanta, Georgia 30320
CEO: John Selgistine, Mgr.   Tel: (404) 761-7769   %FO: 100
Bus: *Commercial air transport services.*   Fax: (404) 761-7769

VARIG BRAZILIAN AIRLINES
380 Madison Ave., 17/F, New York, New York 10017
CEO: Alberto Fajerman   Tel: (212) 850-8259   %FO: 100
Bus: *Commercial air transport services.*   Fax: (212) 850-8201

VARIG BRAZILIAN AIRLINES
5815 NW 18th St., Miami, Florida 33126
CEO: Paulo Cordeiro, Mgr.   Tel: (305) 526-5965   %FO: 100
Bus: *Commercial air transport services.*   Fax: (305) 526-5965

● **VOTORANTIM PARTICIPACOES**
Rua Amauri, 255
r, 01448-000 Sao Paulo SP, Brazil
CEO: José Ermirio de Moraes Neto, Pres.   Tel: 55-11-3704-3300   Rev: $2,000
Bus: *Mfr. cement, paper, chemicals and allied products.* Fax: 55-11-3167-1550   Emp: 25,600
                                                www.vcp.com.br
NAICS: 322121, 322299, 325199, 327310, 327320

ST. MARYS CEMENT
1914 White Oak Lane, Dixon, Illinois 61021
CEO: Dan Carney   Tel: (815) 284-3357   %FO: 100
Bus: *Cement manufacturing.*   Fax: (815) 284-3314

ST. MARYS CEMENT
250 Jefferson Ave., Cleveland, Ohio 44113
CEO: Dan Kull   Tel: (216) 579-1911   %FO: 100
Bus: *Cement manufacturing.*   Fax: (216) 579-0625

ST. MARYS CEMENT
1801 Spring St., Manitowoc, Michigan 54220
CEO:
Bus: *Cement manufacturing.*
Tel: (920) 682-6552
Fax: (920) 682-6554
%FO: 100

ST. MARYS CEMENT
1975 S. Carferry Dr., Milwaukee, Wisconsin 53207
CEO: Joe Baker
Bus: *Cement manufacturing.*
Tel: (414) 486-7660
Fax: (414) 486-7659
%FO: 100

ST. MARYS CEMENT
924 McDonald St., Green Bay, Wisconsin 54303
CEO: Larry Hilbert
Bus: *Cement manufacturing.*
Tel: (920) 435-8590
Fax: (920) 435-8504
%FO: 100

ST. MARYS CEMENT
2006 S. Kinnickinnic Ave., Milwaukee, Wisconsin 54220
CEO:
Bus: *Cement manufacturing.*
Tel: (414) 481-6777
Fax: (414) 481-7783
%FO: 100

ST. MARYS CEMENT
2301 Front St., Toledo, Ohio 43605
CEO:
Bus: *Cement manufacturing.*
Tel: (419) 697-1141
Fax: (419) 697-1511
%FO: 100

ST. MARYS CEMENT
14531 Industrial Pkwy, Marysville, Ohio 43040
CEO:
Bus: *Cement manufacturing.*
Tel: (937) 642-4573
Fax: (937) 642-2438
%FO: 100

ST. MARYS CEMENT
389 Ganson St., Buffalo, New York 14203
CEO:
Bus: *Cement manufacturing.*
Tel: (716) 854-1222
Fax: (716) 854-1229
%FO: 100

ST. MARYS CEMENT
160000 Bells Bay Rd., Charlevoix, Michigan 49720
CEO: Ron Plocki
Bus: *Cement manufacturing.*
Tel: (231) 547-9971
Fax: (231) 547-6202
%FO: 100

ST. MARYS CEMENT
555 W. 2nd. St., Ferrysburg, Michigan 49409
CEO:
Bus: *Cement manufacturing.*
Tel: (616) 846-8553
Fax: (616) 846-9482
%FO: 100

ST. MARYS CEMENT
640 E. South St., Schoolcraft, Michigan 49087-9715
CEO:
Bus: *Cement manufacturing.*
Tel: (616) 679-5253
Fax: (616) 679-5254
%FO: 100

ST. MARYS CEMENT
12101 S. Doty Ave., Chicago, Illinois 60633
CEO:
Bus: *Cement manufacturing.*
Tel: (216) 579-1911
Fax: (216) 579-0625
%FO: 100

ST. MARYS CEMENT
400 Seahorse Dr., Waukegan, Illinois 60085
CEO: Tel: (847) 662-0006   %FO: 100
Bus: *Cement manufacturing.*   Fax: (847) 662-0007

ST. MARYS CEMENT
9333 Dearborn St., Detroit, Michigan 48209
CEO: Tel: (313) 842-4600   %FO: 100
Bus: *Cement manufacturing.*   Fax: (313) 842-4555

SUWANNEE AMERICAN CEMENT
5117 US Highway 27, Brandford, Florida 32008
CEO: Dana Moran, Gen. Mgr.   Tel: (386) 935-0966   %FO: 50
Bus: *Cement manufacturing.*   Fax: (386) 935-1155

VOTORANTIM INTERNATIONAL NORTH AMERICA, INC.
111 Continental Dr., Ste. 111, Newark, Delaware 19713
CEO: Andre Clark, Gen. Mgr.   Tel: (302) 454-8300   %FO: 100
Bus: *Import/export commodity sales office.* Fax: (302) 454-8309   Emp: 6

● **WEG INDUSTRIAS SA**
Av. Prefeito Waldemar Grubba 3300, 1 Andar, Santa Catarina, 89256-900 Jaragua do Sul SC, Brazil
CEO: Decio Da Silva, Pres.   Tel: 55-47-372-4000   Rev: $484
Bus: *Electric motors manufacture and sales.* Fax: 55-47-372-4010   Emp: 11,919
                                               www.weg.com.br
NAICS: 335311, 335312

WEG ELECTRIC MOTORS CORP
2631 Lindsey Privado Dr., Ontario, California 91761
CEO: Bill Frawley, Mgr.   Tel: (909) 390-5030   %FO: 100
Bus: *Electric motors manufacture and sales.* Fax: (909) 390-1190

WEG ELECTRIC MOTORS CORP.
295 S. Prospect Ave., Itasca, Illinois 60143
CEO: Tony Hood   Tel: (630) 773-8735
Bus: *Electric motors manufacture and sales.* Fax: (630) 773-8797

WEG ELECTRIC MOTORS CORPORATION
11705 W. 83rd Terr., Bldg. I, Ste. 100, Lenexa, Kansas 66215
CEO: Tony Hood   Tel: (913) 492-7000   %FO: 100
Bus: *Electric motors manufacture and sales.* Fax: (913) 492-6999

WEG ELECTRIC MOTORS CORPORATION
1327 Northbrook Pkwy., Suwannee, Georgia 30024
CEO: Walter Janssen, Pres.   Tel: (770) 338-5656   %FO: 100
Bus: *Electric motors manufacture and sales.* Fax: (770) 338-1632   Emp: 158

WEG ELECTRIC MOTORS CORPORATION
2100 Brighton Henrietta, Town Line Rd., Rochester, New York 14623
CEO: Ralph Scharle, Mgr.   Tel: (585) 240-1000   %FO: 100
Bus: *Electric motors manufacture and sales.* Fax: (585) 240-1067

Bulgaria

- **BALKAN BULGARIAN AIRLINES**
Sofia Airport, BG-1540 Sofia, Bulgaria
CEO: Ianko Guenadiev Stoimenov, VP
Bus: *Airline transport services.*

Tel: 359-2-984-489
Fax: 359-2-984-489
www.balkan.com

NAICS: 481111

   BALKAN BULGARIAN AIRLINES
   437 Madison Ave., 32/F, New York, New York 10022
   CEO: Radonja Radorvic
   Bus: *Airline services.*

   Tel: (212) 371-2047
   Fax: (212) 371-6618

   %FO: 100

Canada

● **180 CONNECT INC.**
609 14th St. NW, Ste. 400, Calgary AB T2N 2A1, Canada
CEO: Peter Giacalone, CEO   Tel: 403-269-1119   Rev: $89
Bus: *Provides cable, satellite, and telephone-system*   Fax: 403-269-1141   Emp: 3,300
     installation and maintenance services.   www.180connect.net
NAICS: 237130, 237990, 238990, 517910, 531390, 541690, 811213

     180 CONNECT INC.
     837 Lee Rd., Orlando, Florida 32810
     CEO: Claudia A. Di Maio   Tel: (407) 644-9333   %FO: 100
     Bus: *Cable TV line installation.*   Fax: (407) 644-9333

     180 CONNECT INC.
     6365 NW 6th Way, Ste. 200, Ft. Lauderdale, Florida 33309
     CEO: Robert Newell   Tel: (954) 678-3499   %FO: 100
     Bus: *Provides technical support.*   Fax: (954) 252-3885

● **20-20 TECHNOLOGIES INC.**
400 Armand-Frappier Blvd., Laval QC H7V 4B4, Canada
CEO: Jean Mignault   Tel: 514-332-4110   Rev: $33
Bus: *Computer aided interior design software.*   Fax: 514-334-6043   Emp: 280
     www.2020technologies.com
NAICS: 511210

     20-20 TECHNOLOGIES
     8933 Weston Way, Ste.17, Jacksonville, Florida 32256
     CEO: Mark Couture, VP   Tel: (904) 363-2226   %FO: 100
     Bus: *Computer aided interior design software*   Fax: (904) 363-2212

     20-20 TECHNOLOGIES
     99 Monroe NW, Ste.400, Grand Rapids, Michigan 49503-2651
     CEO: Tim Mroz, VP   Tel: (616) 454-0000   %FO: 100
     Bus: *Computer aided interior design software*   Fax: (616) 454-4140

● **5 BY 5 SOFTWARE VENTURES LTD.**
138 - 4th Ave. SE, Ste.355, Calgary AB T2G 4ZG, Canada
CEO: Bob Tretiak, CEO   Tel: 403 290-1406
Bus: *Enterprise application integration software*   Fax: 403-206-7197
     www.5by5software.com
NAICS: 511210

     5BY5 SOFTWARE VENTURES LTD
     4456 Longfellow Dr., Ste. 100, Plano, Texas 75093
     CEO: Clint Regehr, VP   Tel: (972) 612-2300   %FO: 100
     Bus: *Enterprise application integration software*   Fax: (972) 612-2284
     and service

- **724 SOLUTIONS INC.**
20 York Mills Rd., Ste. 201, Toronto ON M2P 2C2, Canada

CEO: John J. Sims, Chmn.	Tel: 416-226-2900	Rev: $15
Bus: *Provides online banking and financial services over wireless devices.*	Fax: 416-226-4456	Emp: 115
	www.724.com	

NAICS: 511210

    724 SOLUTIONS INC.
    1221 State St., Ste. 200, Santa Barbara, California 93101

CEO: Elda Rudd, PR	Tel: (805) 884-8308	%FO: 100
Bus: *Online banking and financial services over wireless devices.*	Fax: (805) 884-8311	

- **AASTRA TECHNOLOGIES LIMITED**
115 Snow Boulevard, Concord ON L4K 4N9, Canada

CEO: Anthony P. Shen, CEO	Tel: 905-760-4200	Rev: $148
Bus: *Telephones and broadcast communications networks manufacture.*	Fax: 905-760-4233	
	www.aastra.com	

NAICS: 334210, 334220

    AASTRA CVX NETWORK ACCESS
    8 Federal St., Billerica, Massachusetts 01821

CEO: Anthony Shen	Tel: (905) 436-4200	%FO: 100
Bus: *Telephones and broadcast communications networks sales.*	Fax: (905) 436-4200	

    AASTRA DIGITAL VIDEO
    1160 Route 22 East, Bridgewater, New Jersey 08807

CEO: John Mailhot	Tel: (908) 927-1319	%FO: 100
Bus: *Telephones digital video and broadcast communications networks sales.*	Fax: (908) 927-1233	

- **ABER DIAMOND CORP.**
PO Box 4569, Station A, Toronto ON M5W 4T9, Canada

CEO: Robert A. Gannicott, CEO	Tel: 416-362-2237	Rev: $385
Bus: *diamond production*	Fax: 416-362-2230	Emp: 55
	www.aber.ca	

NAICS: 212399, 213115

    HARRY WINSTON INC.
    718 5th Ave., New York, New York 10019

CEO: Thomas J. O'Neill, CEO	Tel: (212) 245-2000	%FO: 51
Bus: *Purchaser of diamonds and gems*	Fax: (212) 765-8809	

- **ABITIBI-CONSOLIDATED INC.**
1155 Metcalfe St., Ste. 800, Montreal QC H3B 5H2, Canada

CEO: John W. Weaver, Pres. & CEO	Tel: 514-875-2160	Rev: $5,800
Bus: *Newsprint, ground wood paper, pulp, and lumber manufacture.*	Fax: 514-394-2272	Emp: 14,000
	www.abicon.com	

NAICS: 321213, 322122

ABITIBI CONSOLIDATED
Four Gannett Dr., White Plains, New York 10604
CEO: David Schirmer, Pres. Tel: (914) 640-8600 %FO: 100
Bus: *U.S. headquarters.* Fax: (914) 640-8900

ABITIBI CONSOLIDATED SALES CORPORATION
5505 Natural Bridge Rd., St. Louis, Missouri 63120
CEO: Stefanie Fairless, VP Tel: (314) 381-3700 %FO: 100
Bus: *Paper recycling.* Fax: (314) 381-3733

ABITIBI CONSOLIDATED SALES CORPORATION
390 East Ray Rd., Chandler, Arizona 85225
CEO: Al Gomez, Mgr. Tel: (480) 821-0003 %FO: 100
Bus: *Uncoated ground wood papers, newsprint,* Fax: (480) 899-7670
market pulp manufacture.

ABITIBI CONSOLIDATED SALES CORPORATION
1923 Meridian St., Arlington, Texas 76011
CEO: Darrell Clemons Tel: (817) 275-6397 %FO: 100
Bus: *Paper sales.* Fax: (817) 275-6412

ABITIBI RECYCLING, INC.
510 Division St., Kansas City, Kansas 66103
CEO: Donna Utter, Mgr. Tel: (913) 722-9022 %FO: 100
Bus: *Paper recycling.* Fax: (913) 722-9060

ABITIBI RECYCLING, INC.
4939 Gasmer Dr., Houston, Texas 77035
CEO: Pattie Foster, Pres. Tel: (713) 723-6397 %FO: 100
Bus: *Paper recycling.* Fax: (713) 723-3562

ABITIBI-CONSOLIDATED INC.
360 South Main St., Sand Springs, Oklahoma 74063
CEO: Michael Hixon Tel: (918) 246-9100 %FO: 100
Bus: *Paper recycling.* Fax: (918) 246-9101

ABITIBI-CONSOLIDATED SALES
PO Box 3375, St. Charles, Illinois 60174
CEO: Kevin Rush, VP Tel: (630) 587-1300 %FO: 100
Bus: *Sales.* Fax: (630) 587-8740

● **ABLEAUCTIONS.COM, INC.**
1963 Lougheed Highway, Coquitlam BC V3K 3T8, Canada
CEO: Abdul Ladha, CEO Tel: 604-521-2253 Rev: $4
Bus: *High tech b2b and consumer* Fax: 604-521-5093 Emp: 36
auctioneer,conducting auctions live with internet www.ableauctions.com
NAICS: 454112

ABLEAUCTIONS.COM, INC.
1222 46th Ave. East, Fife, Washington 98424
CEO: Chad Ehli, VP Tel: (253) 926-1122 %FO: 100
Bus: *On-line auction house.* Fax: (253) 922-6849

- **ABMAST INC.**
6935 Picard, Saint-Hyacinthe QC J2S 1H3, Canada
CEO: A. Sterzi, CEO
Bus: *Abrasives equipment manufacture.*

  Tel: 450-774-4660
  Fax: 450-7740554
  www.abmast.com

  NAICS: 423840

  ABMAST ABRASIVES CORP.
  91 Carey Rd., Queensbury, New York 12804
  CEO: Andre Simard, Mgr.
  Bus: *Abrasives supplies.*

  Tel: (800) 361-2297
  Fax: (800) 300-2420

  %FO: 100

- **ABSOLUTE SOFTWARE CORP.**
111 Dunsmuir St., Ste. 800, Vancouver BC V6B 6A3, Canada
CEO: John Livingston
Bus: *Computer theft recovery and tracking software*

  Tel: 604-730-9851
  Fax: 604-730-2621
  www.absolute.com

  Rev: $6
  Emp: 80

  NAICS: 511210

  ABSOLUTE SOFTWARE CORP.
  10655 NE 4th St., Ste.400, Bellevue, Washington 98004
  CEO: Rob Chase
  Bus: *Computer theft and recovery software*

  Tel: (425) 943-6470
  Fax: (425) 943-6401

  %FO: 100

- **ACCORD FINANCIAL CORP.**
77 Bloor St. West, Ste.1803, Toronto ON M5S 1M2, Canada
CEO: Ken Hitzig
Bus: *Accounts receivable management and financial services*

  Tel: 416-961-0007
  Fax: 416-961-9443
  www.accordfinancial.com

  Rev: $20
  Emp: 120

  NAICS: 522298

  ACCORD FINANCIAL INC.
  PO Box 6704, Greenville, South Carolina 29606
  CEO: Tom Henderson, Pres.
  Bus: *Financial services*

  Tel: (864) 271-4384
  Fax: (864) 242-0863

  %FO: 100

- **ACCOVIA INC.**
2 Place Alexis-Nihon, 3500 de Maisonneuve Blvd. West, Montreal QC H3Z 3C1, Canada
CEO: Claude Guay
Bus: *E-commerce software and services*

  Tel: 514-931-4433
  Fax: 514-931-4818
  www.accovia.com

  NAICS: 511210, 561510

  ACCOVIA INC.
  1400 Logan St., Schaumburg, Illinois 60193
  CEO: Claude Guay
  Bus: *E-commerce software and services.*

  Tel: (847) 885-2695
  Fax: (801) 881-1135

  %FO: 100

- **ACD SYSTEMS LTD.**
  2261 Keating Cross Rd.,, Gateway Park, Block C, Saanichton BC V8M 2C3, Canada
  CEO: Douglas Vandekerkhove, Chmn. & CEO   Tel: 250-544-6700   Rev: $19
  Bus: *Digital software manufacture.*   Fax: 250-544-0291   Emp: 120
                                                                            www.acdsystems.com

  NAICS: 541511

    ACD SYSTEMS OF AMERICA INC.
    1150 NW 72 Ave., Ste. 180, Miami, Florida 33126
    CEO: C. Christensen, Sales   Tel: (305) 596-5644   %FO: 100
    Bus: *Digital software manufacture.*   Fax: (305) 406-9802

- **ACLARO SOFTWORKS**
  1900A 11th St. SE, Calgary AB T2G 3G2, Canada
  CEO: Christoph Faig, Pres. & CEO   Tel: 403-299-6612
  Bus: *Oil and gas software manufacturer.*   Fax: 403-247-8797
                                                                            www.aclaro.com

  NAICS: 541511

    ACLARO SOFTWORKS
    11000 Richmond, Ste. 610, Houston, Texas 77056
    CEO: Kevin Rooney, VP   Tel: (713) 781-2000   %FO: 100
    Bus: *Oil and gas software manufacturer.*   Fax: (713) 781-2049

- **ACTIONFRONT DATA RECOVERY LABS, INC.**
  340 Ferrier St., Ste. 100, Markham ON L3R 2Z5, Canada
  CEO: Nicolas Majors, Exec. Chmn.   Tel: 905-474-2220   Rev: $5
  Bus: *Computer data recovery and diagnostic products*   Fax: 905-474-2220   Emp: 45
       manufacture and services.   www.actionfront.com
  NAICS: 541511, 541513, 611420

    ACTIONFRONT DATA RECOVERY LABS, INC.
    14643 Dallas Pkwy., Ste. 560, Dallas, Texas 75254
    CEO: Ron Austin   Tel: (972) 560-0027   %FO: 100
    Bus: *Computer diagnostic and recovery services.*   Fax: (972) 560-0027

    ACTIONFRONT DATA RECOVERY LABS, INC.
    Technology Park, 2 Sun Ct., Ste. 375, Norcross, Georgia 30092
    CEO: Phil Graham, Mgr.   Tel: (770) 300-0744   %FO: 100
    Bus: *Computer diagnostic and recovery services.*   Fax: (770) 300-0744

    ACTIONFRONT DATA RECOVERY LABS, INC.
    3333 Bowers Ave., Ste. 235, Santa Clara, California 95054
    CEO: Craig Jones   Tel: (408) 987-0430   %FO: 100
    Bus: *Computer diagnostic and recovery services.*   Fax: (408) 987-0430

    ACTIONFRONT DATA RECOVERY LABS, INC.
    Schaumburg Corporate Center, 1501 E. Woodfield Road, Ste. 201N, Schaumburg, Illinois 60173
    CEO: Ron Austin   Tel: (847) 413-2376   %FO: 100
    Bus: *Computer diagnostic and recovery services.*   Fax: (847) 413-2376

- **ADB SYSTEMS INTERNATIONAL INC.**
  302 The East Mall, Ste. 300, Toronto ON M9B 6C7, Canada
  CEO: Jeffrey Lymburner, CEO   Tel: 416-640-0400   Rev: $4
  Bus: *Asset management applications and services.*   Fax: 905-672-5705   Emp: 50
  www.adbsys.com
  NAICS: 518210

  > **ADB SYSTEMS INTERNATIONAL INC.**
  > 3001 North Rocky Point Dr., Ste. 200, Tampa, Florida 33607
  > CEO: Aidan Rowsome   Tel: (813) 636-8205   %FO: 100
  > Bus: *Asset management applications and services.*   Fax: (813) 636-8205

- **ADF GROUP INC.**
  300 Henry-Bessemer, Terrebonne QC J6Y IT3, Canada
  CEO: Jean Paschini, CEO   Tel: 450-965-1911   Rev: $228
  Bus: *Design, engineer, fabrication and erection of architectural metal work and complex steel superstructures.*   Fax: 450-965-8558   Emp: 975
  www.adfgroup.com
  NAICS: 332323, 541420

  > **ADF INTERNATIONAL, INC.**
  > 3661 NW 126th Ave., Coral Springs, Florida 33065
  > CEO: Alexander Bergel   Tel: (954) 340-8854   %FO: 100
  > Bus: *Structural steel elements manufacture and sales.*   Fax: (954) 340-8856

- **AECON GROUP INC., JV HOCHTIEF AG**
  3660 Midland Avenue, Toronto ON M1V 4V3, Canada
  CEO: John M. Beck, Pres. & CEO   Tel: 416-754-8735   Rev: $412
  Bus: *Provides services in construction and engineering. (JV Hochtief AG)*   Fax: 416-754-8736   Emp: 13,000
  www.armbro.ca
  NAICS: 541330

  > **AECON BUILDING INC.**
  > 19217 36th Ave. West, Lynnwood, Washington 98036
  > CEO: George Kramer, VP   Tel: (425) 774-2945   %FO: 100
  > Bus: *Commercial construction services.*   Fax: (425) 771-8094

- **AESIGN EVERTRUST INC.**
  192 Fairhaven, Hudson QB J0P 1H0, Canada
  CEO: Thomas Gosnell   Tel: 450-458-0905
  Bus: *Developer of software to store and manage digital assets*   Fax: 450-458-7616
  www.evertrust.net
  NAICS: 511210

  > **EVERTRUST.NET USA LLC**
  > 3260 Rohrer Dr., Lafayete, California 94549
  > CEO: Thomas Gosnell   Tel: (925) 284-4303   %FO: 100
  > Bus: *Developer of software to store and manage digital assets.*   Fax: (925) 299-2933

• **AETERNA ZENTARIS INC.**
1405 Parc-Technologique Blvd., Quebec City QC G1P 4P5, Canada
CEO: Gilles R. Gagnon   Tel: 418-652-8525   Rev: $194
Bus: *Biopharmaceuticals*   Fax: 418*652-0881
                                         www.aeternazentaris.com
NAICS: 325411, 325412
   ECHELON BIOSCIENCES INC.
   111 Eighth Ave., 13/F, New York, New York 10011
   CEO: W. Tim Miller,   Tel: (212) 894-8638   %FO: 100
   Bus: *Biopharmaceuticals.*   Fax:

• **AFI INTERNATIONAL GROUP INC.**
8160 Parkhill Dr., Milton ON L9T 5V7, Canada
CEO: Darrell Parsons   Tel: 905-693-0746
Bus: *Security services for individuals* Fax: 905-693-1213
                                         www.accufax.on.ca
NAICS: 561612
   AFI USA
   5100 S. Cleveland Ave., Ste. 318-171, Ft. Myers, Florida 33907
   CEO: Jim Rovers, VP Int. Ops., VP Operations Tel: (866) 273-7072 %FO: 100
   Bus: *Security services*   Fax:

• **AFM HOSPITALITY CORP.**
135 Queens Plate, Ste.400, Toronto ON M9W 6V1, Canada
CEO: Lawrence P. Horwitz   Tel: 416-361-1010   Rev: $10
Bus: *Franchiser of hotel chains*   Fax: 416-361-9577
                                         www.afmcorp.com
NAICS: 721110
   NORTHWEST LODGING INTERNATIONAL INC.
   2101 Fourth Ave., Ste. 1020, Seattle, Washington 98121
   CEO: Tracey Kundey, COO   Tel: (206) 443-3550   %FO: 100
   Bus: *Lodging*   Fax: (206) 727-2207

• **AGRICORE UNITED**
TD Centre, 201 Portage Ave., 28th Fl., Winnipeg, Manitoba R3C 3A7, Canada
CEO: Brian Hayward, CEO   Tel: 204-944-5411   Rev: $2,072
Bus: *Grain handling and merchandising cooperative.* Fax: 204-944-5454   Emp: 2,743
                                         www.agricoreunited.com
NAICS: 311512, 311513, 424430
   AGRICORE UNITED, C/O ADM
   4666 Faries Pkwy., Decatur, Illinois 62525
   CEO: G. Allen Andreas   Tel: (217) 424-5200
   Bus: *Grain cooperative.*   Fax: (217) 424-6196

• AGRIUM INC.
13131 Lake Fraser Drive SE, Calgary AB T2J 7E8, Canada
CEO: Michael M. Wilson, Pres. & CEO
Bus: *Fertilizers and wholesale and retail plant growth nutrients manufacturer.*
NAICS: 212391, 325311, 325312, 325314

Tel: 403-225-7000
Fax: 403-225-7609
www.agrium.com

Rev: $2,838
Emp: 4,667

AGRIUM INC.
4582 South Ulster St., Ste. 1700, Denver, Colorado 80237
CEO: J. Muse, Dir. Sales
Bus: *Fertilizers and wholesale and retail plant growth nutrients manufacturer.*

Tel: (303) 804-4400
Fax: (303) 804-4482

%FO: 100

• AIR CANADA
Air Canada Centre, 7373 Cote-Vertu Blvd. West, Saint-Laurent QC H4Y 1H4, Canada
CEO: Robert A. Milton, CEO
Bus: *Commercial air transport services.*

Tel: 514-422-5000
Fax: 514-422-5739
www.aircanada.ca

Rev: $6,463
Emp: 39,730

NAICS: 481111

AIR CANADA
500 Terminal E, Boston, Massachusetts 02128-2015
CEO: Catherine McKenzie, CEO
Bus: *Commercial air transport services.*

Tel: (617) 569-1418
Fax: (617) 569-1418

%FO: 100

• AIRBOSS OF AMERICA CORP.
16441 Yonge St., Newmarket ON L3X 2G8, Canada
CEO: Robert L. Hagerman, CEO
Bus: *Develops, manufactures and sells high quality, proprietary rubber-based products offering enhanced performance and productivity.*
NAICS: 316211, 316213, 316214, 316219, 325212, 326113, 326199, 326211, 326220, 326291, 326299, 332618, 332722, 337125, 339993, 423130, 423710, 424610

Tel: 905-751-1188
Fax: 905-751-1101
www.airbossofamerica.com

Rev: $160
Emp: 761

AIRBOSS OF AMERICA INC
436 Melony LANE, Tallmadge, Ohio 44278
CEO: John Hagerman
Bus: *Develop/mfr. and sells high quality, proprietary rubber-based products offering enhanced performance and productivity.*

Tel: (330) 630-3181
Fax: (330) 630-3181

%FO: 100

AIRBOSS POLYMER PRODUCTS INC.
9229 Ward Pkwy., Ste. 206, Kansas City, Missouri 64114
CEO: Robert Magnuson, Pres.
Bus: *Develop/mfr. and sells high quality, proprietary rubber-based products offering enhanced performance and productivity.*

Tel: (816) 822-7599
Fax: (816) 822-0150

%FO: 100

AIRBOSS TIRES CO.
200 Veterans Blvd., South Haven, Michigan 49090
CEO: Wayne Unrath, Pres.
Bus: *Develop/mfr. and sells high quality, proprietary rubber-based products offering enhanced performance and productivity.*

Tel: (269) 637-6356
Fax: (269) 637-8955

%FO: 100

● **ALCAN INC.**
1188 Sherbrooke St. West, Montreal QC H3A 3G2, Canada
CEO: Travis Engen, Pres. & CEO   Tel: 514-848-8000   Rev: $24,885
Bus: *Mfr. aluminum & packaging industries, bauxite*   Fax: 514-848-8115   Emp: 82,500
mining, alumina refining, specialty chemicals,   www.alcan.com
power generation, aluminum smelting, recycling &
packaging.
NAICS: 213114, 331312, 331315, 331319, 331521, 332312, 332431

ALCAN CABLE
867 N. Bank Rd., Roseburg, Oregon 97470
CEO: Ian Hewett   Tel: (541) 672-4200   %FO: 100
Bus: *Engineered cable products.*   Fax: (541) 673-3501

ALCAN COMPOSITES
10 Fairway Ct., PO Box 195, Northvale, New Jersey 07647
CEO: George Dohn   Tel: (201) 767-1400   %FO: 100
Bus: *Balsa wood composites.*   Fax: (201) 387-6631

ALCAN FOIL PRODUCTS INC.
1513 Redding Dr., La Grange, Georgia 30240
CEO: Tom Woods   Tel: (706) 812-2000   %FO: 100
Bus: *Packaging.*   Fax: (706) 812-2000

ALCAN PACKAGING
1108 North State Rd. 3, Westport, Indiana 47283
CEO: Larry Capper   Tel: (812) 591-2332   %FO: 100
Bus: *Pharmaceutical packaging.*   Fax: (812) 591-2313

ALCAN PACKAGING
2301 Industrial Dr., Neenah, Wisconsin 54956
CEO: Jim Britt   Tel: (920) 727-6000   %FO: 100
Bus: *Food packaging.*   Fax: (920) 727-6742

ALCAN PACKAGING
175 Western Ave., Neenah, Wisconsin 54956
CEO: Jim Britt   Tel: (920) 727-6000   %FO: 100
Bus: *Food packaging.*   Fax: (920) 727-6742

ALCAN PACKAGING
595 Madison Ave., 10/F, New York, New York 10022
CEO: Jon Alexander   Tel: (212) 371-5100   %FO: 100
Bus: *Beauty packaging.*   Fax: (212) 829-9539

ALCAN PACKAGING
150 26th Ave. SE, Minneapolis, Minnesota 55414
CEO: Gerry Bartz   Tel: (612) 378-3300   %FO: 100
Bus: *Food packaging.*   Fax: (612) 378-3380

ALCAN PACKAGING
6590 Central Ave., Newark, California 94560
CEO: Tom Brehm   Tel: (510) 797-3710   %FO: 100
Bus: *Food packaging.*   Fax: (510) 797-6194

ALCAN PACKAGING
445 Dividend Dr., Peachtree City, Georgia 30269
CEO: Ron Syrkos   Tel: (770) 486-9095   %FO: 100
Bus: *Tobacco packaging.*   Fax: (770) 486-9015

ALCAN PACKAGING
Century Rd., PO Box 68, Ravenswood, West Virginia 26164
CEO: Steve Abelman   Tel: (304) 273-7000   %FO: 100
Bus: *Packaging.*   Fax: (304) 273-6544

ALCAN PACKAGING
701 Algroup Way, Chester, Virginia 23836
CEO: Sylvie Bergeron   Tel: (804) 748-3470   %FO: 100
Bus: *Tobacco packaging.*   Fax: (804) 748-3471

ALCAN PACKAGING
3033 East 16th St., Russellville, Arkansas 72802
CEO: Mike Frazier   Tel: (479) 880-8077   %FO: 100
Bus: *Food packaging.*   Fax: (479) 880-8337

ALCAN PACKAGING
2450 Alvarado St., PO Box 1954, San Leandro, California 94577-0293
CEO: Tom Brehm   Tel: (510) 352-2262   %FO: 100
Bus: *Food packaging.*   Fax: (510) 614-3145

ALCAN PACKAGING
9404 Hwy 2096, Robards, Kentucky 42452
CEO: Steve Salt   Tel: (270) 521-7811   %FO: 100
Bus: *Aluminum can recycling.*   Fax: (270) 521-7811

ALCAN PACKAGING
1209 New Tullahoma Hwy, PO Box 747, Shelbyville, Tennessee 37160
CEO: Roy Turner   Tel: (931) 684-4161   %FO: 100
Bus: *Beauty packaging.*   Fax: (931) 684-2878

ALCAN PACKAGING
3600 Alabama Ave., St. Louis Park, Minnesota 55416
CEO: Gerry Bartz   Tel: (612) 378-3300   %FO: 100
Bus: *Food packaging.*   Fax: (612) 378-3380

ALCAN PACKAGING
908 W. Verdigris Pkwy., Catoosa, Oklahoma 74015
CEO: Luis Bogran   Tel: (918) 739-4900   %FO: 100
Bus: *Food packaging.*   Fax: (918) 739-4002

ALCAN PACKAGING
111 Wheaton Ave., Youngsville, North Carolina 27596
CEO: Ronnie Vaught   Tel: (919) 556-9715   %FO: 100
Bus: *Pharmaceutical packaging.*   Fax: (919) 556-9508

ALCAN PACKAGING
625 Sharp St., Millville, New Jersey 08332
CEO: Bill Lamanteer   Tel: (856) 825-1400   %FO: 100
Bus: *Pharmaceutical packaging.*   Fax: (856) 327-1826

ALCAN PACKAGING
1200 North 10th St., Millville, New Jersey 08332
CEO: Larry Capper   Tel: (856) 825-0400   %FO: 100
Bus: *Pharmaceutical packaging.*   Fax: (856) 293-6307

ALCAN PACKAGING
3040 J Rd., Syracuse, Nebraska 68446
CEO: Larry Capper   Tel: (402) 269-2261   %FO: 100
Bus: *Pharmaceutical packaging.*   Fax: (402) 269-3481

ALCAN PACKAGING
2425 S. Wabash Ave., PO Box 686, Centralia, Illinois 62801
CEO: Terri Sieminski   Tel: (618) 532-7304   %FO: 100
Bus: *Pharmaceutical packaging.*   Fax: (618) 532-7747

ALCAN PACKAGING
3055 Sweeten Creek Rd, PO Box 5258, Asheville, North Carolina 28813
CEO: Jesse Blake   Tel: (828) 274-1611   %FO: 100
Bus: *Pharmaceutical packaging.*   Fax: (828) 274-4947

ALCAN PACKAGING
6161 N. 64th St., Milwaukee, Wisconsin 53218
CEO: Bret Melton   Tel: (414) 431-2200   %FO: 100
Bus: *Pharmaceutical packaging.*   Fax: (414) 431-2200

ALCAN PACKAGING
535 N. Exchange Ct., Aurora, Illinois 60504
CEO: Paul Scolan   Tel: (630) 851-7757   %FO: 100
Bus: *Aluminum extruded packaging.*   Fax: (630) 851-7757

ALCAN PACKAGING
475 North Kirk Rd., Batavia, Illinois 60510
CEO: Tom Nelson   Tel: (630) 879-5850   %FO: 100
Bus: *Food packaging.*   Fax: (630) 879-1695

ALCAN PACKAGING
975 West Main St., Bellevue, Ohio 44811
CEO: Bruce Zemba   Tel: (419) 483-4343   %FO: 100
Bus: *Food packaging.*   Fax: (419) 483-2834

ALCAN PACKAGING
5303 St.Charles Rd., Bellwood, Illinois 60104
CEO: Tom Nelson   Tel: (708) 544-1600   %FO: 100
Bus: *Food packaging.*   Fax: (708) 544-1600

ALCAN PACKAGING
6850 Midland Industrial Dr., Shelbyville, Kentucky 40065
CEO: Tim Saarinen   Tel: (502) 647-2300   %FO: 100
Bus: *Composites engineering.*   Fax: (502) 647-2211

ALCAN PACKAGING
1633 Wheaton Ave., Millville, New Jersey 08332
CEO: Bill Lamanteer   Tel: (856) 825-1400   %FO: 100
Bus: *Pharmaceutical packaging.*   Fax: (856) 327-1826

ALCAN PACKAGING
307 2nd St., Boscobel, Wisconsin 53805
CEO: Randy Frey   Tel: (608) 375-5610   %FO: 100
Bus: *Food packaging.*   Fax: (608) 375-5633

ALCAN PACKAGING
194 Duckworth Dr., Chase City, Virginia 23924
CEO: Larry Capper   Tel: (804) 372-5113   %FO: 100
Bus: *Pharmaceutical packaging.* Fax: (804) 372-2267

ALCAN PACKAGING
8770 West Bryn Mawr Ave., Chicago, Illinois 60631-3542
CEO: Pete Mathias   Tel: (773) 399-8000   %FO: 100
Bus: *Food packaging.*   Fax: (773) 399-8648

ALCAN PACKAGING
1101 Wheaton Ave., Millville, New Jersey 08332
CEO: Larry Capper   Tel: (856) 825-0400   %FO: 100
Bus: *Pharmaceutical packaging.* Fax: (856) 293-6307

ALCAN PACKAGING
5425 Broadway St., American Canyon, California 94503
CEO: Frederic Catteau   Tel: (707) 257-6481   %FO: 100
Bus: *Food packaging.*   Fax: (707) 257-8028

ALCAN PACKAGING
1000 North 10th St., Millville, New Jersey 08332
CEO: Paula Leach   Tel: (856) 825-1100   %FO: 100
Bus: *Pharmaceutical packaging.* Fax: (856) 825-1131

ALCAN PACKAGING
2400 Baglyos Circle, Bethlehem, Pennsylvania 18020
CEO: Rick Sury   Tel: (484) 898-5000   %FO: 100
Bus: *Pharmaceutical packaging.* Fax: (484) 898-5019

ALCAN PACKAGING
3 Ravinia Dr., Ste. 1600, Atlanta, Georgia 30346-2133
CEO: Rhonda Buckley   Tel: (770) 394-9886   %FO: 100
Bus: *Aluminum extruded packaging.* Fax: (770) 394-9070

ALCAN PACKAGING
1500 East Aurora Ave., Des Moines, Iowa 50313
CEO: John Carlberg   Tel: (515) 265-2501   %FO: 100
Bus: *Food packaging.*   Fax: (515) 266-3561

ALCAN PACKAGING
271 River St., Menasha, Wisconsin 54952
CEO: Jim Britt   Tel: (920) 727-6000   %FO: 100
Bus: *Food packaging.*   Fax: (920) 727-6742

ALCAN PACKAGING
100 Kenpak Lane, PO Box 49, Marshall, North Carolina 28753
CEO: Renee Anderson   Tel: (828) 649-3800   %FO: 100
Bus: *Pharmaceutical packaging.* Fax: (828) 649-3350

ALCAN PACKAGING
PO Box 686, Centralia, Illinois 62801
CEO: Jerry Miles Tel: (618) 532-7304 %FO: 100
Bus: *Beauty packaging.* Fax: (618) 532-7747

ALCAN PACKAGING
2 Frassetto Way, Lincoln Park, New Jersey 07035
CEO: Bill Lamenteer Tel: (973) 628-7602 %FO: 100
Bus: *Beauty packaging.* Fax: (973) 628-7574

ALCAN PACKAGING
3210 North Progress Ave., Joplin, Missouri 64801
CEO: Mark Allan Tel: (417) 781-1120 %FO: 100
Bus: *Packaging.* Fax: (417) 781-1120

ALCAN PACKAGING
1731 S. Mt. Prospect Rd., Des Plaines, Illinois 60018
CEO: Terri Sieminski Tel: (847) 298-5626 %FO: 100
Bus: *Global pharmaceutical packaging.* Fax: (847) 827-0773

REXAM BEVERAGE CANS AMERICA
8770 Bryn Mawr Ave., Chicago, Illinois 60631
CEO: Harry Barto Tel: (773) 399-3000 %FO: 100
Bus: *Packages beverages.* Fax: (773) 399-3354

TECHPACK/CMI, DIV. ALCAN
20 Melville Park Rd., Melville, New York 11747
CEO: Alain Chevassus Tel: (631) 531-5700 %FO: 100
Bus: *Packaging.* Fax: (631) 531-5700

● **ALGOMA CENTRAL CORP.**
289 Bay St., Sault St. Marie, ON P6A 5P6, Canada
CEO: Tim S. Dool Tel: 905-687-7888
Bus: *Barge and tanker service* Fax:
www.algonet.com
NAICS: 483113, 483211

ALGOMA TANKERS (USA) INC.
One Cleveland Centre, 1375 East 9th St., Ste. 1210, Cleveland, Ohio 44114
CEO: Tim S. Dool Tel: (216) 771-1999 %FO: 100
Bus: *Barge and tanker service* Fax:

MARBULK SHIPPING INC.
55 Tozer Rd., Beverly, Massachusetts 01915
CEO: Egon Oldendorff Tel: (978) 299-1090 %FO: 100
Bus: *Barge and tanker service* Fax:

● **ALGORITHMICS INCORPORATED**
185 Spadina Avenue, Toronto ON M5T 2C6, Canada
CEO: Stephen W. Joynt, CEO Tel: 416-217-1500 Rev: $77
Bus: *Risk management software manufacture.* Fax: 416-971-6100 Emp: 550
www.algorithmics.com
NAICS: 511210

ALGORITHMICS INCORPORATED
196 Mercer St., 8/F, New York, New York 10012
CEO: Jeffrey Bagg   Tel: (212) 625-5260   %FO: 100
Bus: *Risk management software manufacture.*   Fax: (212) 625-9604

• **ALIAS SYSTEMS INC.**
210 King St. East, Toronto ON M5A 1J7, Canada
CEO: Doug Walker   Tel: 416-362-9181
Bus: *Maker of 3D graphics software*   Fax: 416-369-6140
                                            www.alias.com
NAICS: 511210

    ALIAS SYSTEMS INC.
    11 Penn Plaza, 5/F, New York, New York 10001
    CEO: Dave Wharry   Tel: (212) 946-2832   %FO: 100
    Bus: *3D graphics software.*   Fax: (212) 946-2808

    ALIAS SYSTEMS INC.
    795 Folsom St., Ste.1069, San Francisco, California 94107
    CEO: Jim Lorenz   Tel: (415) 848-3030   %FO: 100
    Bus: *3D graphics software.*   Fax: (415) 848-2754

    ALIAS SYSTEMS INC.
    1600 Parkdale Rd., Ste. 100, Rochester, Michigan 48304
    CEO: Ashin Bose, Dir.   Tel: (248) 656-0226   %FO: 100
    Bus: *3D graphics software.*   Fax: (248) 656-0252   Emp: 15

    ALIAS SYSTEMS INC.
    2020 Howell Mill Rd., Ste. C-354, Atlanta, Georgia 30318
    CEO: Dave Wharry   Tel: (404) 367-9949   %FO: 100
    Bus: *3D graphics software.*   Fax: (404) 367-8066

    ALIAS SYSTEMS INC.
    1601 Cloverfield Blvd., 2/F South Tower, Santa Monica, California 90404
    CEO: Doug Walker, CEO   Tel: (310) 460-3697   %FO: 100
    Bus: *3D graphics software.*   Fax: (310) 460-3693

• **ALLIANCE ATLANTIS COMMUNICATIONS INC.**
121 Bloor St. East, Ste.1500, Toronto ON M4W 3M5, Canada
CEO: Michael I. M. MacMillan, Chmn.   Tel: 416-934-7144   Rev: $848
Bus: *Broadcaster and international distributor of filmed*   Fax: 416-967-5884   Emp: 900
    entertainment for TV and cinema.   www.allianceatlantis.com
NAICS: 512110

    ALLIANCE ATLANTIS COMMUNICATIONS
    301 N. Canon Dr., Ste. 321, Beverly Hills, California 90210
    CEO: Kathy Berk   Tel: (310) 275-5501   %FO: 100
    Bus: *Engaged in production and distribution of*   Fax: (310) 275-5502
    films and TV shows.

- **ALLIANCE PIPELINE**
  600, 605 5th Ave. SW, Calgary AB T2P 3H5, Canada
  CEO: Murray P. Birch, Pres.   Tel: 403-266-4464   Rev: $640
  Bus: *Operates natural gas pipelines* Fax: 403-266-4495
                www.alliance-pipeline.com
  NAICS: 486210

    ALLIANCE PIPELINE
    6385 Old Shady Oak Rd., Ste. 150, Eden Prairie, Minnesota 55344
    CEO: Keith Palmer   Tel: (952) 944-3183 %FO: 100
    Bus: *Operates natural gas pipeline* Fax: (952) 944-9166

    ALLIANCE PIPELINE
    1520 8th St. SE, Valley City, North Dakota 58072
    CEO: Leighton Smith   Tel: (701) 845-1929 %FO: 100
    Bus: *Operates natural gas pipeline* Fax: Emp: 5

    ALLIANCE PIPELINE
    1208 E. Summit St., Maquoketa, Iowa 52060
    CEO: Greg Devens   Tel: (563) 652-0532 %FO: 100
    Bus: *Operates natural gas pipeline* Fax: Emp: 7

    ALLIANCE PIPELINE
    1990 Lookout Dr., North Mankato, Minnesota 56003
    CEO: Rick Bartlett   Tel: (507) 625-2404 %FO: 100
    Bus: *Operates natural gas pipeline* Fax: Emp: 6

- **ALPHA PRO TECH, LTD.**
  60 Centurian Drive, Ste. 112, Markham ON L3R 9R 2, Canada
  CEO: Sheldon Hoffman, CEO   Tel: 905-479-0654   Rev: $25
  Bus: *Protective apparel manufacture for medical,* Fax: 905-479-9732 Emp: 121
    dental, industrial and food service industries. www.alphaprotech.com
  NAICS: 315225

    ALPHA PRO TECH, INC.
    2224 Cypress St., Valdosta, Georgia 31602
    CEO: Dan Montgomery, Plant Mgr. Tel: (229) 242-1931 %FO: 100
    Bus: *Automated shoe cover and laminating* Fax: (229) 242-1947
    manufacture.

    ALPHA PRO TECH, INC.
    615 North Parker Dr., Janesville, Wisconsin 53545
    CEO: Bill Steinke, Mgr.   Tel: (608) 755-1385 %FO: 100
    Bus: *Medical fleece and pet products* Fax: (608) 755-1408
    manufacturing.

    ALPHA PRO TECH, INC.
    1287 West Fairway Dr., Nogales, Arizona 85621
    CEO: Joe Santasiere, Plant Mgr. Tel: (520) 281-0127 %FO: 100
    Bus: *Apparel and shields manufacture.* Fax: (520) 281-2642

ALPHA PRO TECH, INC.
903 West Center, Salt Lake City, Utah 84054
CEO: John Jensen, Plant Mgr.
Bus: *Hygiene mask manufacture.*
Tel: (801) 298-3240
Fax: (801) 298-3648
%FO: 100

● **ALUMA ENTERPRISES INC.**
4810 Dufferin St., Toronto ON M3H 5S8, Canada
CEO: Jim Demitrieus, CEO
Bus: *Forming system products manufacture for high-rise concrete construction.*
Tel: 416-665-7222
Fax: 416-665-5934
www.aluma.com
NAICS: 327331, 327390, 332323

    ALUMA SYSTEMS USA
    5240 East Great SW Pkwy., Atlanta, Georgia 30336
    CEO: Tim Monk
    Bus: *Formwork, shoring and scaffold rental.*
    Tel: (404) 699-0979
    Fax: (404) 699-2570
    %FO: 100

    ALUMA SYSTEMS USA
    1111 North Loop West, Houston, Texas 77008
    CEO: Caroline Champness, VP
    Bus: *Formwork, shoring and scaffold rental.*
    Tel: (713) 802-9055
    Fax: (713) 802-9054
    %FO: 100

    ALUMA SYSTEMS USA
    6711 Industrial Dr., Beltsville, Maryland 20705
    CEO: John Knowles
    Bus: *Forming system products manufacture for high-rise concrete construction.*
    Tel: (301) 937-5090
    Fax: (301) 937-3829
    %FO: 100

● **AMF HOSPITALITY CORPORATION**
135 Queens Plate, Ste. 400, Toronto ON M9W 6V1, Canada
CEO: Lawrence P. Horwitz, Mng. Dir.
Bus: *Hotel chain franchise.*
Tel: 604-276-1360
Fax: 604-276-1122
www.afmcorp.com
NAICS: 721110

    AFM HOSPITALITY CORPORATION
    2101 Fourth Ave., Ste. 1020, Seattle, Washington 98121
    CEO: Lawrence P. Horwitz
    Bus: *Hotel management services.*
    Tel: (206) 443-2570
    Fax: (206) 727-2207
    %FO: 100

● **ANACHEMIA CANADA LTD.**
255 rue Norman, Ville St. Pierre QC H8R 1A3, Canada
CEO: Martin Robinson, Pres.
Bus: *Chemicals manufacture and lab equipment distribution.*
Tel: 514-489-5711
Fax: 514-363-5281
www.anachemia.com
NAICS: 325199, 423490

    ANACHEMIA CHEMICALS
    3 Lincoln Boulevard, Rouses Point, New York 12979
    CEO: Russell Lavigne, Mgr.
    Bus: *Chemicals distribution and marketing.*
    Tel: (518) 297-4444
    Fax: (518) 297-2960
    %FO: 100

ANACHEMIA CHEMICALS
23 Pleasant St., Newburyport, Massachusetts 01950
CEO: Douglas Crossman, Mgr.   Tel: (978) 462-1066   %FO: 100
Bus: *Industrial inorganic chemicals*   Fax: (978) 462-1066
     manufacturing.

ANACHEMIA SCIENCE
738 Spice Island Dr., Sparks, Nevada 89431
CEO: Wes Walker, Mgr.   Tel: (775) 331-2300   %FO: 100
Bus: *Chemicals distribution and marketing.*   Fax: (775) 331-2646

• **ANGIOTECH PHARMACEUTICALS INC.**
1618 Station St., Vancouver BC V6A 1B6, Canada
CEO: William L. Hunter, Pres. & CEO   Tel: 604-221-7676   Rev: $131
Bus: *Drug-coated medical devices and biomaterials*   Fax: 604-221-2330   Emp: 150
     manufacture.   www.angiotech.com
  NAICS: 325411, 325412

    ANGIOTECH BIOCOATINGS CORP.
    336 Summit Point Dr., Henrietta, New York 14467
    CEO: Margaret Lydon, Gen. Mgr.   Tel: (585) 321-1130   %FO: 100
    Bus: *Mfr./development of pharmaceutical and*   Fax: (585) 321-1575
         surgical products.

    ANGIOTECH PHARMACEUTICALS, INC.
    101 North Bend Way, Ste. 201, North Bend, Washington 98045
    CEO: David McMasters   Tel: (425) 831-3090   %FO: 100
    Bus: *Drug-coated medical devices and*   Fax: (425) 831-3039
         biomaterials manufacture.

    ANGIOTECH PHARMACEUTICALS, INC.
    2500 Faber Place, Palo Alto, California 94303
    CEO: Gary Ingenit   Tel: (650) 320-5500   %FO: 100
    Bus: *Drug-coated medical devices and*   Fax: (650) 320-5511
         biomaterials manufacture.

    NEUCOLL INC.
    105 Cooper Ct., Los Gatos, California 95032-7604
    CEO: Roy Fiebiger, Pres. & CEO   Tel: (408) 583-3000   %FO: 100
    Bus: *Mfr./development of pharmaceutical and*   Fax: (408) 583-3002
         surgical products.

• **ANTARCTICA SYSTEMS INC.**
700 W. Pender St., St. 1203, Vancouver BC V6C 1G8, Canada
CEO: Barry Yates, Pres. & CEO   Tel: 604-873-6100
Bus: *Software developer*   Fax: 604-873-6188
                                 www.antarctica.net
  NAICS: 511210

    ANTARCTICA SYSTEMS INC.
    390 Park Ave., 18/F, New York, New York 10022-4698
    CEO: Barry Yates   Tel: (212) 906-3501
    Bus: *Software developer*   Fax: (212) 906-4666

• API ELECTRONICS GROUP CORP.

505 University Ave., Ste. 1400, Toronto ON M5G 1X3, Canada
CEO: Phillip DeZwirek, Chmn. & CEO
Bus: *Mfr. of electronic components.*

Tel: 416-593-6543
Fax: 416-593-4658
www.apielectronics.com

Rev: $11
Emp: 182

NAICS: 334417, 334419

API ELECTRONICS CORP.
375 Rabro Dr., Hauppauge, New York 11788
CEO: Thomas W. Mills Jr.
Bus: *Manufacturer of electronic components.*

Tel: (631) 582-6767
Fax: (631) 582-6771

%FO: 100

• APOLLO GOLD CORP.

204 Black St., Ste. 300, Whitehorse YK Y1A 2M9, Canada
CEO: R. David Russell, Pres. & CEO
Bus: *Mining operations*

Tel: 867-668-5252
Fax:
www.apollogold.com

Rev: $65
Emp: 403

NAICS: 212221

APOLLO GOLD CORP.
5655 S. Yosemite St., Ste.200, Greenwood, Colorado 80111-3220
CEO: Wade W. Bristol, VP Operations
Bus: *Mining operations.*

Tel: (720) 886-9656
Fax: (720) 482-0957

%FO: 100

• ARMSTRONG, S.A. LTD.

23 Bertrand Avenue, Scarborough ON M1L 2P3, Canada
CEO: Charles A. Armstrong, Pres.
Bus: *Pumps and pumping equipment manufacture.*

Tel: 416-755-2291
Fax: 416-759-9101
www.armstrongpumps.com

Emp: 200

NAICS: 333911, 333913

ARMSTRONG PUMPS INC.
93 East Ave., North Tonawanda, New York 14120
CEO: Charles Armstrong, VP
Bus: *Pumps and pumping equipment manufacture.*

Tel: (716) 693-8813
Fax: (716) 693-8970

%FO: 100
Emp: 100

• ASSANTE CORPORATION

130 King St., Ste. 2950, Toronto ON M5X 1A9, Canada
CEO: Joseph C. Canavan, CEO
Bus: *Asset management services.*

Tel: 204-943-7201
Fax: 204-957-5865
www.assante.com

NAICS: 523991, 523999, 525910

ASSANTE CORPORATION
280 Park Ave., 5/F, New York, New York 10017
CEO: Martin Weinberg, Mgr.
Bus: *Asset management services.*

Tel: (212) 907-8000
Fax: (212) 907-8089

%FO: 100

ASSANTE CORPORATION
10100 Santa Monica Blvd., Ste. 1300, Los Angeles, California 90067
CEO: Denise Hart, Mgr.
Bus: *Asset management services.*

Tel: (310) 277-4657
Fax: (310) 277-9232

%FO: 100

ASSANTE CORPORATION
1190 Saratoga Ave., Ste. 200, San Jose, California 95129
CEO: Adam Dooley, Mgr.   Tel: (204) 954-5188   %FO: 100
Bus: *Asset management services.*   Fax: (204) 247-1108

ASSANTE CORPORATION
16030 Ventura Blvd., Ste. 380, Encino, California 91436
CEO: Robert Philpott, Mgr.   Tel: (818) 905-9500   %FO: 100
Bus: *Asset management services.*   Fax: (818) 905-6832

ASSANTE CORPORATION
PO Box 637, Roanoke, Indiana 46783
CEO: Roosevelt Barnes, Mgr.   Tel: (260) 672-9480   %FO: 100
Bus: *Asset management services.*   Fax: (260) 672-1310

ASSANTE CORPORATION
500 Newport Center Dr., Ste. 800, Newport Beach, California 92660
CEO: Jeff Moorad, Mgr.   Tel: (949) 720-8700   %FO: 100
Bus: *Asset management services.*   Fax: (949) 720-1331

● **AT PLASTICS INC.**
134 Kennedy Rd. South, Brampton ON L6W 3G5, Canada
CEO: Gary L. Connaughty, Pres. & CEO   Tel: 905-451-9985   Rev: $174
Bus: *Mfr. of resins and plastics*   Fax: 905-451-7650   Emp: 374
                                          www.atplastics.com
NAICS: 325211

   AT PLASTICS, FILMS
   200 Westpark Dr. #250, Peachtree City, Georgia 30269
   CEO: Thomas P. Gipson   Tel: (678) 364-8848   %FO: 100
   Bus: *Manufacturer of resins and plastics* Fax: (678) 364-8847

● **ATI TECHNOLOGIES INC.**
1 Commerce Valley Drive East, Thornhill ON L3T 7X6, Canada
CEO: David Orton, CEO   Tel: 905-852-2600   Rev: $1,020
Bus: *Mfr. graphics accelerator chips.*   Fax: 905-882-2620   Emp: 2,100
                                          www.atitech.ca
NAICS: 334413, 334418

   ATI RESEARCH, INC
   4555 Great America Pkwy., Santa Clara, California 95054
   CEO: L. Chen   Tel: (408) 572-6000   %FO: 100
   Bus: *Chip research.*   Fax: (408) 492-1015

   ATI RESEARCH, INC
   62 Forest St., Marlborough, Massachusetts 01752-1978
   CEO: Dan Worthmann   Tel: (508) 303-3920   %FO: 100
   Bus: *Chip research.*   Fax:

- **ATLANTIS SUBMARINES, INC.**
  210 West 6th Avenue, Ste. 200, Vancouver BC V5Y 1K8, Canada
  CEO: Dennis Hurd, Pres. & CEO
  Bus: *Passenger submarine travel adventures.*
  Tel: 604-875-1367
  Fax: 604-875-0833
  www.atlantisadventures.net
  Rev: $47
  Emp: 450

  NAICS: 487210

  ### ATLANTIS SUBMARINES HAWAII
  1600 Kapiolani Boulevard, Honolulu Oahu, Hawaii 96815
  CEO: Ronald Williams, Mgr.
  Bus: *Passenger submarine travel adventures.*
  Tel: (808) 973-9840
  Fax: (808) 973-9840
  %FO: 100

  ### ATLANTIS SUBMARINES INC.
  1001 W Cypress Creek Rd., Ft. Lauderdale, Florida 33309
  CEO: Laura Martin, Mgr.
  Bus: *Passenger submarine travel adventures.*
  Tel: (954) 779-1095
  Fax: (954) 779-1095
  %FO: 100

- **ATRIUM BIOTECHNOLOGIES INC.**
  1405 Parc-Technologique Blvd., Quebec City QC G1P 4P5, Canada
  CEO: Luc Dupont, Pres. & CEO
  Bus: *Cosmetic and nutrition pharmaceuticals*
  Tel: 418-652-1116
  Fax: 418-652-0151
  www.atrium-bio.com
  Rev: $147
  Emp: 234

  NAICS: 325998

  ### ATRIUM BIOTECHNOLOGIES
  490 Boston Post Rd., Sudbury, Massachusetts 01776`
  CEO: Serge Yelle
  Bus: *Cosmetic and nutrition pharmaceuticals*
  Tel: (866) 628-2355
  Fax: (866) 866-6661
  %FO: 100

  ### PURE ENCAPSULATIONS INC.
  490 Boston Post Rd., Sudbury, Massachusetts 01776
  CEO: Ray Hamel
  Bus: *Cosmetic and nutrition pharmaceuticals*
  Tel: (978) 443-1999
  Fax: (978) 443-4230
  %FO: 100

- **ATS AUTOMATION TOOLING SYSTEMS INC.**
  250 Royal Oak Rd., Cambridge ON N3H 4R6, Canada
  CEO: Ron J. Jutras, Pres. & CEO
  Bus: *Mfr. automated production and test systems.*
  Tel: 519-653-6500
  Fax: 519-653-6533
  www.atsautomation.com
  Rev: $345
  Emp: 3,185

  NAICS: 334513, 335314

  ### ATS CAROLINA
  1510 Cedar Line Dr., Rock Hill, South Carolina 29731
  CEO: Klaus D. Woerner, CEO
  Bus: *Mfr. automated production and test systems.*
  Tel: (803) 324-9300
  Fax: (803) 324-9360
  %FO: 100

  ### ATS MICHIGAN SALES & SERVICE INC.
  7060 Kensington Rd., Brighton, Michigan 48116
  CEO: Klaus D. Woerner, CEO
  Bus: *Mfr. automated production and test systems.*
  Tel: (248) 446-5006
  Fax: (248) 446-5007
  %FO: 100

ATS OHIO INC.
425 Enterprise Dr., Lewis Center, Ohio 43035
CEO: William Robinson, CEO   Tel: (614) 888-2344   %FO: 100
Bus: *Mfr. automated production and test systems.* Fax: (614) 888-9875

ATS SOUTHWEST
10900 North Stallard Place, Tucson, Arizona 85737
CEO: Doug Desalvo, Gen. Mgr.   Tel: (520) 575-9446   %FO: 100
Bus: *Mfr. automated production and test systems.* Fax: (520) 575-9622   Emp: 25

ATS SYSTEMS CALIFORNIA, INC.
4763 Bennett Dr., Livermore, California 94550
CEO: Mike Cybulski, VP   Tel: (925) 606-1302   %FO: 100
Bus: *Mfr. automated production and test systems.* Fax: (925) 606-1305

ATS SYSTEMS OREGON INC.
2121 NE Jack London St., Corvallis, Oregon 97330
CEO: Bill Robinson   Tel: (541) 758-3329   %FO: 100
Bus: *Mfr. automated production and test systems.* Fax: (541) 758-9022

● **AUDIOTECH HEALTHCARE CORPORATION**
175 Second Avenue, Ste. 760, Kamloops BC V2C SW1, Canada
CEO: Osvaldo Iadarola, CEO   Tel: 250-372-5847
Bus: *Operates hearing service clinics.*   Fax: 250-372-3859
                                              www.audiotech.org
NAICS: 423450

    THE HEARING CLINIC
    32 Madison Professional Park, 360 E. Main St., Rexburg, Idaho 83401
    CEO: Travis Ribgy, Pres.   Tel: (208) 356-0766   %FO: 100
    Bus: *Operates hearing service clinics.* Fax: (208) 356-0766

    THE HEARING CLINIC
    1662 John Adams Pkwy., Idaho Falls, Idaho 83401
    CEO: Dr. Gerald Mill, Mgr.   Tel: (208) 529-1514   %FO: 100
    Bus: *Operates hearing service clinics.* Fax: (208) 529-1514

● **AUTOMODULAR CORPORATION**
20 Toronto St., Ste. 420, Toronto ON M5C 2B8, Canada
CEO: Michael Blair, CEO   Tel: 416-861-0662   Rev: $83
Bus: *Sequencing services for auto manufacturing.* Fax: 416-861-0063   Emp: 1,100
                                              www.automodular.com
NAICS: 336111, 423120

    AUTOMODULAR ASSEMBLIES INC.
    1701 Henn Parkway, Lordstown, Ohio 48090
    CEO: Chris Nutt   Tel: (330) 824-3461   %FO: 100
    Bus: *Assembly services.*   Fax: (330) 324-3418

    TEC-MAR DISTRIBUTION SERVICES, INC.
    18406 Telegraph Rd., Brownstown, Michigan 48183
    CEO: Ernie Wassmann   Tel: (734) 955-2115   %FO: 100
    Bus: *Distribution services.*   Fax: (734) 955-2114

- **AVOTUS CORP.**
110 Matheson Blvd. W, Ste.300, Mississauga ON L5R 4G7, Canada
CEO: Frederick Lizza, Pres. & CEO   Tel: 905-890-9199   Rev: $25
Bus: *Software developer*   Fax: 905-890-9707
                                                 www.avotus.com
NAICS: 511210

  AVOTUS CORP.
  430 Mountain Ave., Murray Hill, New Jersey 07974
  CEO: Chuck Machlin, VP North America   Tel: (908) 464-7570   %FO: 100
  Bus: *Software developer, Expense management*   Fax: (908) 464-2052
       operations

  AVOTUS CORP.
  1001 Bay Hill Dr., 2/F, San Bruno, California 94066
  CEO: Lisa Welch, VP North America   Tel: (888) 294-3126   %FO: 100
  Bus: *Software developer*   Fax: (866) 323-8596

  AVOTUS CORP.
  Burlington Center, 4/F, 35 Corporate Dr., Burlington, Massachusetts 01803
  CEO: Jo Martell, VP North America   Tel: (877) 286-8871   %FO: 100
  Bus: *Software developer*   Fax: (781) 685-4763

  AVOTUS CORP.
  One Stamford Plaza, 263 Tressor Blvd., 9/F, Stamford, Connecticut 06901
  CEO: Fred Lizza, VP North America   Tel: (877) 286-8871   %FO: 100
  Bus: *Software developer*   Fax: (203) 564-1402

- **AXCAN PHARMA INC.**
597 Laurier Boulevard, Mont-Saint-Hilaie QC J3H 6C4, Canada
CEO: Leon Gosselin, CEO   Tel: 450-467-5138   Rev: $243
Bus: *Pharmaceutical manufacture.*   Fax: 450-464-9979   Emp: 394
                                                 www.axcan.com
NAICS: 325411, 325412

  AXCAN PHARMA INC.
  22 Inverness Center Pkwy., Birmingham, Alabama 35242
  CEO: Roddie Thurman   Tel: (205) 991-8085   %FO: 100
  Bus: *Pharmaceutical manufacture.*   Fax: (205) 991-8176

- **AZCAR TECHNOLOGIES INC.**
3235 14th Ave., Markham ON L3R 0H3, Canada
CEO: Stephen Pumple, Chmn. & Pres. & CEO   Tel: 905-470-2545
Bus: *Information Technology Services*   Fax: 905-470-2559
                                                  www.azcar.com
NAICS: 334310, 532490, 541512

  AZCAR USA INC.
  121 Hillpointe Dr., Ste. 700, Canonsburg, Pennsylvania 15317
  CEO: David George, Chmn.   Tel: (724) 873-0800   %FO: 100
  Bus: *Information technology services.*   Fax: (724) 873-4770

- **BADGER DAYLIGHTING INC.**
715 5th Ave, SW, Ste. 2820, Calgary AB T2P 2X6, Canada
CEO: Tor Wilson, Pres. & CEO   Tel: 403-264-8500   Rev: $49
Bus: *Industrial manufacturing*   Fax: 403-228-9773   Emp: 112
                                       www.badgerinc.com
NAICS: 332912, 332919, 333132, 333996
  BADGER DAYLIGHTING INC.
  1300 East U.S. Highway 136, Ste. E, Pittsboro, Indiana 46167
  CEO: Dan Hutchinson, VP North America   Tel: (888) 726-9146   %FO: 100
  Bus: *Industrial equipment manufacturer*   Fax:

- **BALLARD POWER SYSTEMS INC.**
4343 North Fraser Way, Burnaby BC V5J 5J9, Canada
CEO: John W. Sheridan, Pres. & CEO   Tel: 604-454-0900   Rev: $81
Bus: *Develops fuel cell power systems.*   Fax: 604-454-4700   Emp: 1,100
                                       www.ballard.com
NAICS: 335311, 335999, 336111
  BALLARD MATERIAL PRODUCTS
  Two Industrial Ave., Lowell, Massachusetts 01851-5199
  CEO: Ross Witschonke   Tel: (978) 452-8961   %FO: 100
  Bus: *Material products.*   Fax: (978) 454-5617

  BALLARD POWER SYSTEMS CORPORATION
  15001 North Commerce Dr., Dearborn, Michigan 48120-1216
  CEO: Firoz Rasul, VP   Tel: (313) 583-5980   %FO: 100
  Bus: *Provides fuel cell power systems.*   Fax: (313) 583-5980

- **BANK OF MONTREAL**
1 First Canadian Place, 100 King St. West, Toronto ON M5X 1A1, Canada
CEO: F. Anthony Comper, Pres. & CEO   Tel: 416-867-5000   Rev: $10,833
Bus: *Commercial banking services.*   Fax: 416-867-6793   Emp: 33,593
                                       www.bmo.com
NAICS: 522110, 522291, 522292, 523120, 523920, 523930, 524210
  BMO NESBITT BURNS CORP.
  111 West Monroe St., Chicago, Illinois 60603
  CEO: Sally Larson Sargent, Mng. Dir.   Tel: (312) 461-2121   %FO: 100
  Bus: *Investment banking services.*   Fax: (312) 461-3869

  HARRIS BANKCORP INC.
  111 West Monroe St., Chicago, Illinois 60603
  CEO: Sally Larson Sargent, Pres. & CEO   Tel: (312) 461-2121   %FO: 100
  Bus: *Commercial banking services.*   Fax: (312) 461-7869   Emp: 7,200

  HARRISDIRECT LLC
  Harborside Financial Center, 501 Plaza II, Jersey City, New Jersey 07311
  CEO: Charles N. Piermarini, Pres. & CEO   Tel: (201) 308-2525
  Bus: *Online retail brokerages*   Fax: (201) 413-5268

● **THE BANK OF NOVA SCOTIA**
44 King St. West, Toronto ON M5H 1H1, Canada
CEO: Richard E. Waugh, Pres. & CEO
Bus: *Provides commercial, corporate, investment and*
international banking services.
Tel: 416-866-6161
Fax: 416-866-3750
www.scotiabank.ca
Rev: $13,531
Emp: 48,000
NAICS: 522110, 523110, 523120, 523920, 523930

SCOTIABANK
One Liberty Plaza, 165 Broadway, 26/F, New York, New York 10006
CEO: Bill Ebbels, Mng. Dir.
Bus: *Banking services.*
Tel: (212) 225-5000
Fax: (212) 225-5090
%FO: 100

SCOTIABANK
580 California St., Ste. 2100, San Francisco, California 94104
CEO: James York, Mng. Dir.
Bus: *Corporate, investment banking and capital*
market services.
Tel: (415) 986-1100
Fax: (415) 397-0791
%FO: 100

SCOTIABANK
888 SW Fifth Ave., Ste. 750, Portland, Oregon 97204
CEO: James York, Mng. Dir.
Bus: *Corporate, investment banking and capital*
market services.
Tel: (503) 222-4396
Fax: (503) 222-5502
%FO: 100

SCOTIABANK
1100 Louisiana St., Ste. 3000, Houston, Texas 77002
CEO: Mark Ammerman, Mng. Dir.
Bus: *Corporate, investment banking and capital*
market services.
Tel: (713) 752-0900
Fax: (713) 752-2425
%FO: 100

SCOTIABANK
600 Peachtree St. NE, Ste. 2700, Atlanta, Georgia 30308
CEO: Chris Allen, Mng. Dir.
Bus: *Corporate, investment banking and capital*
market services.
Tel: (404) 877-1500
Fax: (404) 888-8998
%FO: 100

SCOTIABANK
181 West Madison St., Chicago, Illinois 60602
CEO: Dave Vishny, Mng. Dir.
Bus: *Corporate, investment banking and capital*
market services.
Tel: (312) 201-4100
Fax: (312) 201-4108
%FO: 100

● **BARRICK GOLD CORP.**
Canada Trust Tower, 161 Bay St., Ste. 3700, Toronto ON M5J 2S1, Canada
CEO: Gregory C. Wilkins, Pres. & CEO
Bus: *Gold mining.*
Tel: 416-861-9911
Fax: 416-861-2492
www.barrick.com
Rev: $1,935
Emp: 7,100
NAICS: 212221, 213114

BARRICK GOLD CORPORATION
136 East South Temple, Ste. 1050, Salt Lake City, Utah 84111-1180
CEO: Gregory Lang, VP
Bus: *Gold mining operations.*
Tel: (801) 990-3770
Fax: (801) 359-0875
%FO: 100

BARRICK GOLDSTRIKE MINES, INC.
PO Box 29, Elko, Nevada 89803
CEO: Mike Feehan, Gen. Mgr.   Tel: (775) 778-8183   %FO: 100
Bus: *Goldmine*   Fax: (775) 738-7643

ROUND MOUNTAIN GOLD
PO Box 480, Round Mountain, Nevada 89045
CEO: Mike Iannacchione, Gen. Mgr.   Tel: (775) 377-2366   %FO: 100
Bus: *Goldmine.*   Fax: (775) 377-3240

- **BATA SHOE ORGANIZATION**
59 Wynford Dr., North York ON M3C 1K3, Canada
CEO: Thomas G. Bata Jr., Pres.   Tel: 416-446-2011
Bus: *Children's shoes, athletic and seasonal footwear,*   Fax: 416-446-2175
      industrial boots and casual and dress shoes   www.bata.com
      manufacture and sales.
NAICS: 315999, 316211, 316212, 316213, 316214, 316219, 316992, 316993, 316999, 424340, 448210
  BATA SHOE COMPANY INC.
  4501 Pulaski Highway, Belcamp, Maryland 21017
  CEO: B. Baker, Pres.   Tel: (410) 272-2000   %FO: 100
  Bus: *Rubber, canvas and plastic footwear.*   Fax: (410) 272-3346

- **BCE INC. (BELL CANADA ENTERPRISES)**
1000 de la Gauchetiere Quest, Suite 3700, Montreal QC H3B 4Y7, Canada
CEO: Michael J. Sabia, Pres. & CEO   Tel: 514-870-8777   Rev: $15,995
Bus: *Provides communications and telecommunications* Fax: 514-786-3970   Emp: 61,739
      services.   www.bce.com
NAICS: 454112, 511110, 511140, 515120, 515210, 517110, 517212, 518111
  BCE EMERGIS
  2273 Research Blvd., 4/F., Rockville, Maryland 20850
  CEO: Spiro Karadimas   Tel: (301) 548-1000   %FO: 100
  Bus: *Information technology.*   Fax: (301) 548-1000

- **BELL GLOBEMEDIA INC.**
9 Channel Nine Court, Scarborough ON M1S 4B5, Canada
CEO: Ivan Fecan, Pres. & CEO   Tel: 416-332-5700   Rev: $1,178
Bus: *Engaged in broadcasting and newspaper.*   Fax: 416-332-5022
                                      www.bellglobemedia.com
NAICS: 511110, 512110, 512120, 512191, 515210
  CTV WASHINGTON NEWS BUREAU
  2000 M St. N.W., Ste. 330, Washington, District of Columbia 20036
  CEO: Tom Clark, Bureau Chief   Tel: (202) 466-3595   %FO: 100
  Bus: *News bureau.*   Fax: (202) 296-2025

  GLOBE & MAIL NEWS BUREAU
  c/o Dow Jones & Co., 200 Liberty St., 16/F, New York, New York 10281
  CEO: Susanne Craig   Tel: (212) 416-3246   %FO: 100
  Bus: *News bureau.*   Fax: (212) 416-3246

- **BELLVILLE RODAIR INTERNATIONAL**
3710 Nashua Dr., Mississauga ON L4V 1M5, Canada
CEO: Jeff Cullen, Pres.   Tel: 905-671-4655   Rev: $23
Bus: *Freight forwarding and logistics management*   Fax: 905-671-4414
                                              www.rodair.com
NAICS: 488510, 541614

    BELLVILLE RODAIR INT., INC.
    2120 E. Raymond St. #20, Phoenix, Arizona 85034
    CEO: Oliver Adam, Mgr.   Tel: (602) 244-1011   %FO: 100
    Bus: *Freight forwarder and logistics management.* Fax: (602) 225-5917

    BELLVILLE RODAIR INT., INC.
    Miami Industrial Trade Ctr., 8473 N.W. 74th St., Miami, Florida 33166
    CEO: Paul McAuley, Branch Mgr.   Tel: (305) 436-1813   %FO: 100
    Bus: *Freight forwarder and logistics management.* Fax: (305) 436-8514

    BELLVILLE RODAIR INT., INC.
    9133 S. La Cienega Blvd., Ste. 225, Inglewood, California 90301
    CEO: Chris Matthews, Branch Mgr.   Tel: (310) 215-8844   %FO: 100
    Bus: *Freight forwarder and logistics management.* Fax: (310) 215-8855

    BELLVILLE RODAIR INT., INC.
    8910 Lawndale, Suite A, Houston, Texas 77012
    CEO: Paul McAuley, Branch Mgr.   Tel: (713) 921-5544   %FO: 100
    Bus: *Freight forwarder and logistics management.* Fax: (713) 923-9005

    BELLVILLE RODAIR INT., INC.
    171 Cooper Ave., Unit 110, Tonawanda, New York 14150
    CEO: Jonathan Minkensky, Branch Mgr.   Tel: (716) 877-9432   %FO: 100
    Bus: *Freight forwarding and logistics management* Fax: (716) 877-9034

    RODAIR INTERNATIONAL INC.
    1094 Globe Ave., Mountainside, New Jersey 07082
    CEO: Jeff Cullen, CEO   Tel: (908) 789-4900   %FO: 100
    Bus: *Freight forwarding and logistics management* Fax: (908) 789-4906

- **BELZBERG TECHNOLOGIES INC.**
40 King St. West, 34th Fl., Toronto ON M5H 3Y2, Canada
CEO: Sidney H. Belzberg, Chmn. & Pres. & CEO   Tel: 416-360-1812   Rev: $18
Bus: *Management software.*   Fax: 416-360-0039   Emp: 116
                                             www.belzberg.com
NAICS: 511210

    BELZBERG TECHNOLOGIES INC.
    55 Broad St., 28/F, New York, New York 10004
    CEO: Alicia Belzberg   Tel: (212) 943-1400   %FO: 100
    Bus: *Management software.*   Fax: (212) 943-1515

● **BENNETT ENVIRONMENTAL INC.**
1540 Cornwall Rd., Ste. 208, Oakville ON L6J 7W5, Canada
CEO: Allan G. Bulckaert, Pres. & CEO
Bus: *Environmental consulting services*

Tel: 905-339-1540
Fax: 905-339-0016
www.bennettenv.com

Rev: $21
Emp: 85

NAICS: 541620, 562213, 562910

BENNETT ENVIRONMENTAL INC.
288 Littleton Rd, #32, Westford, Massachusetts 01886
CEO: Bill Eaton, Dir. Sales
Bus: *Environmental consulting services*

Tel: (978) 692-9990
Fax: (978) 692-7779

%FO: 100

● **BERG CHILLING SYSTEMS INC.**
51 Nantucket Blvd., Scarborough ON M1P 2N5, Canada
CEO: Donald Berggren, CEO
Bus: *Industrial refrigeration design and manufacture.*

Tel: 416-755-2221
Fax: 416-755-3874
www.berg-group.com

Emp: 100

NAICS: 333415, 334519

BERG MANUFACTURING CORPORATION
818 Harrison St., Ste. 206, Oak Park, Illinois 60101
CEO: John Kirow, Mgr.
Bus: *Industrial refrigeration manufacture.*

Tel: (708) 358-9800
Fax: (708) 358-9801

%FO: 100

● **BERNARD CALLEBAUT CHOCOLATERIE**
1313 First St. SE, Calgary AB T2G 5L1, Canada
CEO: Bernard Callebaut, Chmn. & Pres.
Bus: *High quality confectioner and artisan chocolatier.*

Tel: 403-265-5777
Fax: 403-265-7738
www.bernardcallebaut.com

NAICS: 311320, 311330, 311340, 424450

BERNARD C. CHOCOLATERIE
440 - 5th St., Lake Oswego, Oregon 97034
CEO: Ron Cameron
Bus: *High quality, decorative chocolates.*

Tel: (503) 675-7500
Fax: (503) 675-0500

%FO: 100

BERNARD C. CHOCOLATERIE
15211 North Kierland Blvd, Ste. 160, Scottsdale, Arizona 85254
CEO: Murray Kuzek
Bus: *High quality, decorative chocolates.*

Tel: (480) 315-1002
Fax: (480) 315-1003

%FO: 100

BERNARD C. CHOCOLATERIE
Sunset Corners, 825 South Waukegan Rd., Lake Forest, Illinois 60045
CEO: Helen Shum, Mgr.
Bus: *High quality, decorative chocolates.*

Tel: (847) 283-9927
Fax: (847) 283-9928

%FO: 100

● **BIOMIRA INC.**
2011 94th St., Edmonton AB T6N 1H1, Canada
CEO: T. Alexander McPherson, CEO
Bus: *Synthetic vaccines manufacture.*

Tel: 780-450-3761
Fax: 780-450-4772
www.biomira.com

Rev: $4
Emp: 115

NAICS: 325414

BIOMIRA USA INC.
1002 East Park Blvd., Cranbury, New Jersey 08512
CEO: Alex McPherson, MD   Tel: (609) 655-5300   %FO: 100
Bus: *Synthetic vaccines manufacture and sales.*   Fax: (609) 655-5145

● **BIONICHE LIFE SCIENCES INC.**
231 Dundas St. East, Belleville ON K8N 1E2, Canada
CEO: Graeme McRae, Pres. & CEO   Tel: 613-966-8058   Rev: $40
Bus: *Pharmaceutical manufacturer*   Fax: 613-966-4177   Emp: 300
     www.bioniche.com
NAICS: 325412, 325414

     AB TECHNOLOGY
     1335 NE Terre View Dr., Pullman, Washington 99163
     CEO: Alyssa Hood, Dir.   Tel: (509) 335-4047   %FO: 100
     Bus: *Pharmaceutical manufacturer*   Fax: (509) 335-1064

     BIONICHE ANIMAL HEALTH USA, INC.
     1551 Jennings Mill Rd., Ste. 3200A, Bogart, Georgia 30622
     CEO: Jim Phillips, Pres.   Tel: (706) 549-4503   %FO: 100
     Bus: *Pharmaceutical manufacturer*   Fax: (706) 548-0659

● **BIOVAIL CORPORATION**
7150 Mississauga Rd., Mississauga ON L5N 8M5, Canada
CEO: Douglas J.P. Squires, CEO   Tel: 905-286-3000   Rev: $890
Bus: *Formulation, clinical testing, registration,*   Fax: 905-286-3050   Emp: 1,958
     manufacturing, sale and promotion of   www.biovail.com
     pharmaceutical products.
NAICS: 325412

     BIOVAIL PHARMACEUTICALS, INC.
     700 Route 202/206 North, Bridgewater, New Jersey 08807
     CEO: Kathleen Milligan   Tel: (908) 927-1400   %FO: 100
     Bus: *Developer and manufacturer of innovative*   Fax: (908) 927-1401
     nutritional supplements and foods.

     BIOVAIL TECHNOLOGIES LTD.
     3701 Concorde Pkwy., Chantilly, Virginia 20151
     CEO: David Tierney   Tel: (703) 480-6000   %FO: 100
     Bus: *Pharmaceuticals.*   Fax: (703) 480-5735

     NUTRAVAIL TECHNOLOGIES INC.
     14790 Flint Lee Rd., Chantilly, Virginia 20151
     CEO: Marc Canton, Mgr.   Tel: (703) 222-6340   %FO: 100
     Bus: *Developer and manufacturer of innovative*   Fax: (703) 961-1836
     nutritional supplements and foods.

● **BLAKES LLP**
199 Bay St., Ste. 2800, Toronto ON M5L 1A9, Canada
CEO: James Christie, Chmn.   Tel: 416-863-2400
Bus: *Full service law firm.*   Fax: 416-863-2653   Emp: 1,500
     www.blakes.com
NAICS: 541110

BLAKE, CASSELS & GRAYDON LLP
65 East 55th St., Ste. 2304, New York, New York 10022
CEO: Michael Gans							Tel:	(212) 893-8200				%FO: 100
Bus: *Full service law firm.*						Fax:	(212) 829-9500

BLAKE, CASSELS & GRAYDON LLP
181 W. Madison St., Ste. 3610, Chicago, Illinois 60602
CEO: Geoffrey Belsher						Tel:	(312) 739-3610				%FO: 100
Bus: *Full service law firm.*						Fax:	(312) 739-3611

● **BOMBARDIER INC.**
800 Rene-Levesque Blvd., Montreal QC H3N 1Y8, Canada
CEO: Laurent Beaudoin, Chmn. & CEO				Tel:	514-861-9481				Rev: $16,025
Bus: *Mfr. civil aircraft, business jets and railway*			Fax:	514-861-7053				Emp: 64,600
    equipment.						www.bombardier.com
NAICS: 333618, 336411

    BOMBARDIER CAPITAL
    1600 Mountain View Dr., Colchester, Vermont 05446
    CEO: George Calver, VP					Tel:	(802) 654-8100				%FO: 100
    Bus: *Financing and leasing services.*			Fax:	(802) 654-8421

    BOMBARDIER CAPITAL
    12735 Gran Bay Pkwy. West, Jacksonville, Florida 32258
    CEO: Bryan Peters						Tel:	(904) 288-1000				%FO: 100
    Bus: *Financing and leasing services.*			Fax:	(904) 288-1920

    BOMBARDIER FLEXJET
    3400 Waterview Pkwy., Ste. 400, Richardson, Texas 75080
    CEO: Clifford Dickman, Pres.				Tel:	(972) 720-2800				%FO: 100
    Bus: *Fractional jet ownership services.*			Fax:	(972) 720-2475

    BOMBARDIER SKYJET
    3040 Williams Dr., Ste. 404, Fairfax, Virginia 22031
    CEO: Alexandre Monnier, VP				Tel:	(703) 584-3330				%FO: 100
    Bus: *Private jet charter.*					Fax:	(703) 584-3361

    LEARJET INC.
    One Learjet Way, Wichita, Kansas 67277
    CEO: James Ziegler, VP					Tel:	(316) 946-2000				%FO: 100
    Bus: *Mfr. executive aircraft.*				Fax:	(316) 946-5767

● **BONAR PLASTICS**
423 Highway 36 South, Lindsay ON K9V 4R8, Canada
CEO: Larry Hughes, Mktg. Dir.					Tel:	705-328-1805
Bus: *Molded plastics manufacture.*				Fax:	705-328-1805
									www.bonarplastics.com
NAICS: 326199

    BONAR PLASTICS INC.
    8257 Blakeland Dr., Littleton, Colorado 80125
    CEO: Kevin Matovcik						Tel:	(303) 791-8593				%FO: 100
    Bus: *Molded plastics manufacture.*			Fax:	(303) 791-8593

BONAR PLASTICS INC.
375 Walt Sanders Dr., Newman, Georgia 30265
CEO: Susan Burns   Tel: (770) 251-8264   %FO: 100
Bus: *Molded plastics manufacture.*   Fax: (770) 251-8275

BONAR PLASTICS INC.
6111 S. 6th Way, Ridgefield, Washington 98642
CEO: John Bielby   Tel: (360) 887-2230   %FO: 100
Bus: *Molded plastics manufacture.*   Fax: (360) 887-3553

BONAR PLASTICS INC.
1005 Atlantic Dr., West Chicago, Illinois 60185
CEO: Jeffrey J. Thompson   Tel: (630) 293-0303   %FO: 100
Bus: *Molded plastics manufacture.*   Fax: (630) 293-0930

● **BRAINHUNTER.COM**
99 Atlantic Ave., Ste. 200, Toronto ON M6K 3J8, Canada
CEO: John McKimm, Chmn. & CEO   Tel: 416-588-7111   Rev: $8
Bus: *Executive search.*   Fax: 416-588-9239   Emp: 25
                                           www.brainhunter.com
NAICS: 541511, 541512, 541513, 541618, 541690, 561310, 561320

    BRAINHUNTER.COM
    1364 Beverley Rd., Ste. 100, McLean, Virginia 22102
    CEO: Raj Singh   Tel: (703) 288-0525   %FO: 100
    Bus: *Executive search services.*   Fax: (703) 288-0665

    BRAINHUNTER.COM
    111 Pine St., Ste. 1650, San Francisco, California 94111
    CEO: Raj Singh   Tel: (415) 421-3309   %FO: 100
    Bus: *Executive search services.*   Fax: (415) 377-4221

● **BRASCAN CORPORATION**
Ste.300, BCE Place, 181 Bay St., Toronto ON M5J 2T3, Canada
CEO: Robert J. Harding, CEO   Tel: 416-363-9491   Rev: $4,027
Bus: *Commercial property investment*   Fax: 416-363-2856   Emp: 55,000
                                           www.brascancorp.com
NAICS: 212231, 212299, 523920, 523930, 531120, 531190

    BRASCAN ASSET MANAGEMENT
    One Liberty Plaza, New York, New York 10006
    CEO: George E. Myhal, Chmn.   Tel: (212) 417-7195   %FO: 100
    Bus: *Asset management services*   Fax: (212) 417-7000

● **BRIDGES TRANSITIONS INC.**
1404 Hunter Court, Ste. 7B, Kelowna BC V1X 6E6, Canada
CEO: John H. Simmons, CEO   Tel: 250-869-4200   Rev: $10
Bus: *Self-directed career and educational software*   Fax: 250-869-4201   Emp: 100
   manufacturer.   www.bridges.com
NAICS: 511210

Canada

BRIDGES TRANSITIONS INC.
336-37B Highway 97N, Oroville, Washington 98844
CEO: Norm Thompson, VP
Bus: *Self-directed career and educational
    software sales.*

Tel: (250) 869-4200
Fax: (250) 869-4201

%FO: 100

● **BROOKFIELD COMMERCIAL PROPERTIES, LTD.**
181 Bay St., Ste. 4300, PO Box 739, Toronto ON M5J 2T3, Canada
CEO: Ric Clark, Pres. & CEO
Bus: *Develops commercial and retail real estate.*

Tel: 416-369-8200
Fax: 416-369-0973
www.brookfield.ca

Rev: $1,825
Emp: 2,500

NAICS: 525930

BROOKFIELD HOMES
500 La Gonda Way, Danville, California 94526
CEO: John Ryan, Pres.
Bus: *Develop commercial and retail real estate.*

Tel: (925) 743-8000
Fax: (925) 743-8000

%FO: 100

BROOKFIELD HOMES
3090 Bristol St., Ste. 200, Costa Mesa, California 92626
CEO: K. Grant, Pres.
Bus: *Develop commercial and retail real estate.*

Tel: (714) 427-6868
Fax: (714) 427-6869

%FO: 100

● **BURNTSAND INC.**
201-300 The East Mall, Toronto ON M9B 6B7, Canada
CEO: James R. Yeates, Chmn.
Bus: *E-commerce and consulting.*

Tel: 416-234-3800
Fax: 416-234-3900
www.burntsand.com

Rev: $41
Emp: 250

NAICS: 454111

BURNTSAND INC.
311 Arsenal St., Watertown, Massachusetts 02472
CEO: Martin Glover
Bus: *Engaged in e-commerce and consulting.*

Tel: (617) 923-6500
Fax: (617) 923-6500

%FO: 100

BURNTSAND PACIFIC INC.
S17 Route One South, Ste. 5600, Iselin, New Jersey 08830
CEO: Rick Higger, VP
Bus: *Engaged in e-commerce and consulting.*

Tel: (732) 404-9400
Fax: (732) 404-1400

%FO: 100

● **THE CADILLAC FAIRVIEW CORPORATION LIMITED**
20 Queen St. West, 5th Fl., Toronto ON M5H 3R4, Canada
CEO: L. Peter Sharpe, CEO
Bus: *Retail property management of shopping centers.*

Tel: 416-598-8200
Fax: 416-598-8607
www.cadillacfairview.com

NAICS: 531312

CASCADE MALL, DIV. CADILLAC FAIRVIEW CORP.
2 Concourse Pkwy NE, Atlanta, Georgia 30328
CEO: L. Peter Sharpe
Bus: *Retail property management of shopping
    centers.*

Tel: (770) 399-8440
Fax: (770) 399-8440

%FO: 100

- **CAE INC.**
  8585 Cote de Liesse, Saint-Laurent, Montreal QC H4T 1G6, Canada
  CEO: Robert E. Brown, Pres. & CEO   Tel: 514-341-6780   Rev: $817
  Bus: *Flight simulators, forest product machinery and*   Fax: 514-341-7699   Emp: 5,500
     equipment manufacture and training services.   www.cae.ca
  NAICS: 423810, 532412

     CAE USA INC.
  4501 Airport Way, Gateway Park, Denver, Colorado 80239
  CEO: Michael Fedele   Tel: (303) 373-3210
  Bus: *Training center.*   Fax: (303) 373-0695

     CAE USA INC.
  2929 W. Airfield Dr., D/FW Airport Box 619119, Dallas, Texas 75261
  CEO: Jeff Roberts, Sales   Tel: (972) 456-8092
  Bus: *Aviation training and sales.*   Fax: (972) 456-8383

     CAE USA INC.
  12424 Research Pkwy., Ste. 101, Orlando, Florida 32826
  CEO: Joseph O'Connell   Tel: (407) 277-2112
  Bus: *Flight training services and sales.*   Fax: (407) 277-2014

     CAE USA INC.
  PO Box 311323, Enterprise, Alabama 36331-1323
  CEO: Angel de la Cruz, Mgr.   Tel: (334) 393-3892
  Bus: *Flight training services and sales.*   Fax: (334) 393-3940

     CAE USA, INC.
  4650 Diplomacy Rd., Fort Worth, Texas 76155
  CEO: Ian Darnley, Mgr.   Tel: (817) 868-8700   %FO: 100
  Bus: *Mfr. flight simulators.*   Fax: (817) 868-8711

     CAE USA, INC.
  4908 Tampa West Blvd., Tampa, Florida 33634
  CEO: John Lenyo, CEO   Tel: (813) 885-7481   %FO: 100
  Bus: *Mfr. flight simulators.*   Fax: (813) 887-1419

- **THE CANADA LIFE ASSURANCE COMPANY, SUB GREAT WESTERN LIFE**
  330 University Avenue, Toronto ON M5G 1R8, Canada
  CEO: Raymond L. McFeetors, CEO   Tel: 416-597-1440   Rev: $5,464
  Bus: *Group life and long-term disability insurance.*   Fax: 416-597-8849   Emp: 6,770
     www.canadalife.com
  NAICS: 524113, 524128

     CANADA LIFE INSURANCE COMPANY
  2000 S. Colorado Blvd., Denver, Colorado 80222
  CEO: Jeff Heggie   Tel: (303) 782-4800   %FO: 100
  Bus: *Group life and long-term disability*   Fax: (303) 782-4800
     insurance.

     CANADA LIFE INSURANCE COMPANY
  410 Saw Mill River Rd., Ardsley, New York 10502
  CEO: Ishbel M. Lucas   Tel: (914) 693-2300   %FO: 100
  Bus: *Group life and long-term disability*   Fax: (914) 674-2532
     insurance.

Canada

- **CANADIAN BROADCASTING CORPORATION**
  250 Lanark Avenue, Ottawa ON K1Y 14E, Canada
  CEO: Robert Rabinovitch, CEO
  Bus: *TV and radio network operations.*

  Tel: 613-724-1200
  Fax: 613-724-5707
  www.cbc.ca

  Rev: $389
  Emp: 7,500

  NAICS: 515112, 515120

    CANADIAN BROADCASTING CORPORATION
    747 Third Ave., Ste. 8C, New York, New York 10017
    CEO: Eva Efryscak, VP
    Bus: *TV and radio network operations.*

    Tel: (212) 546-0500
    Fax: (212) 546-0501

    %FO: 100

- **CANADIAN IMPERIAL BANK OF COMMERCE (CIBC)**
  Commerce Court, 25 King St., Toronto ON M5L 1A2, Canada
  CEO: Gerald T. McCaughey, Pres. & CEO
  Bus: *General banking services.*

  Tel: 416-980-2210
  Fax: 416-980-5026
  www.cibc.com

  Rev: $13,701
  Emp: 37,280

  NAICS: 522110, 522293

    CANADIAN IMPERIAL BANK OF COMMERCE
    425 Lexington Ave., New York, New York 10017
    CEO: Michael G. Capatides
    Bus: *Commercial and investment banking,*
         securities brokerage & asset management
         services.

    Tel: (212) 667-7000
    Fax: (212) 885-4936

    %FO: 100
    Emp: 300

    CANADIAN IMPERIAL BANK OF COMMERCE
    200 West Madison St., Ste. 2300, Chicago, Illinois 60606
    CEO: George Knight
    Bus: *Commercial and investment banking,*
         securities brokerage & asset management
         services.

    Tel: (312) 368-1160
    Fax: (312) 368-1160

    %FO: 100

- **CANADIAN NATIONAL RAILWAY COMPANY**
  935 de la Gauchetiere St. West, Montreal QC H3B 2M9, Canada
  CEO: E. Hunter Harrison, Pres. & CEO
  Bus: *Railway and intermodal transportation;*
       telecommunications.

  Tel: 514-399-5430
  Fax: 204-987-9310
  www.cn.ca

  Rev: $5,457
  Emp: 21,489

  NAICS: 482111, 482112, 517212

    CANADIAN NATIONAL RAILWAY COMPANY
    455 North Cityfront Plaza Dr., Chicago, Illinois 60611-5504
    CEO: Jack Burke, VP
    Bus: *Operates freight railroad services.*

    Tel: (312) 755-7500
    Fax: (312) 755-7839

    %FO: 100

    CANADIAN NATIONAL RAILWAY COMPANY
    2075 West 43rd St., Chicago, Illinois 60609
    CEO: Martha Topell
    Bus: *Transportation center.*

    Tel: (773) 869-9534
    Fax: (773) 869-9534

    %FO: 100

    CANADIAN NATIONAL RAILWAY COMPANY
    590 West Alcy Rd., Memphis, Tennessee 38109
    CEO: J. Roland
    Bus: *Operates freight railroad services.*

    Tel: (901) 789-6376
    Fax: (901) 789-6381

    %FO: 100

CANADIAN NATIONAL RAILWAY COMPANY
17641 Ashland Ave., Homewood, Illinois 60430
CEO: E. Hunter Harrison
Bus: *Operates freight railroad services.*
Tel: (708) 332-3500
Fax: (708) 332-3500
%FO: 100

CANADIAN NATIONAL RAILWAY COMPANY
2800 Livernois Ave., Ste. 300, Troy, Michigan 48083-1222
CEO: Mark Hallman
Bus: *Operates freight railroad services.*
Tel: (601) 592-1814
Fax: (601) 592-1818
%FO: 100

CN CARGOFLO - BATTLE CREEK
420 W. Jameson, Battle Creek, Michigan 49014
CEO: Sean Voelkle
Bus: *Operates freight railroad services.*
Tel: (269) 966-5353
Fax: (269) 966-5355
%FO: 100

CN CARGOFLO - CHICAGO
16750 Center Ave., Harvey, Michigan 60426
CEO: Martha Topei, Facilities Mgr.
Bus: *Operates freight railroad services.*
Tel: (708) 332-3686
Fax: (708) 332-3603
%FO: 100

CN CARGOFLO - CINCINNATI
670 Lunken Park Drive, Cincinnati, Ohio 45246
CEO: Martha Topei, Facilities Mgr.
Bus: *Operates freight railroad services.*
Tel: (708) 332-3686
Fax: (708) 332-3603
%FO: 100

● **CANADIAN PACIFIC RAILWAY LIMITED**
Gulf Canada Square, Ste.500, 401 9th Ave. SW, Calgary AB T2P 4Z4, Canada
CEO: J. Edward Newall, Chmn.
Bus: *Freight railroad*
Tel: 403-319-7000
Fax: 403-319-7567
www.cpr.ca
Rev: $3,253
Emp: 16,056

NAICS: 482111, 482112, 488510

SOO LINE RAILROAD COMPANY
501 Marquette Ave., Minneapolis, Minnesota 55402
CEO: J. Edward Newall
Bus: *Freight railroad.*
Tel: (612) 851-5658
Fax:
%FO: 100
Emp: 2,656

● **CANADIAN REAL ESTATE INVESTMENT TRUST**
130 Bloor St. West, Ste.1001, Toronto ON M5S 1N5, Canada
CEO: Stephen E. Johnson, Pres. & CEO
Bus: *Real Estate Investment Trusts*
Tel: 416-628-7771
Fax: 416-628-7777
www.creit.ca
Rev: $148

NAICS: 525930

CREIT MANAGEMENT L.P.
The Shops at Oak Brook Place, 2155 West 22nd St., Oak Brook, Illinois 60521
CEO: Rudy Banducci, Mgr.
Bus: *Real Estate Investment Trusts*
Tel: (312) 726-4260
Fax: (312) 977-0919
%FO: 100

Canada

● **CANADIAN STANDARDS ASSOCIATION**
5060 Spectrum Way, Ste. 100, Mississauga ON L4W 5N6, Canada
CEO: Rob M. Griffin, Pres. & CEO   Tel: 416-747-4000   Rev: $134
Bus: *Pipe line safety standards.*   Fax: 416-747-2473   Emp: 1,200
                                          www.csa.ca
NAICS: 541380, 541690

> **CSA AMERICA**
> 8501 East Pleasant Valley Rd., Cleveland, Ohio 44131-5575
> CEO: Spencer P. Grieco   Tel: (216) 524-4990   %FO: 100
> Bus: *Pipe line safety standards.*   Fax: (216) 520-8979

● **CANADIAN TECHNICAL TAPE LTD., DIV. CTT GROUP**
455 Cote Vertu Rd., Montreal QC H4N 1E8, Canada
CEO: Alice Cohen, CEO   Tel: 514-334-1510   Rev: $37
Bus: *Mfr. pressure sensitive tapes.*   Fax: 514-745-0764   Emp: 300
                                    www.cttgroup.com
NAICS: 322222

> **CANTECH INDUSTRIES INC.**
> 2222 Eddie Williams Rd., Johnson City, Tennessee 37601
> CEO: Leonard Cohen, Plant Mgr.   Tel: (423) 928-8331   %FO: 100
> Bus: *Mfr. pressure sensitive tapes.*   Fax: (423) 928-0311

● **CANAM GROUP INC.**
270, chemin Du Tremblay, Boucherville QC J4B 5X9, Canada
CEO: Marcel Dutil, Chmn. & CEO   Tel: 450-641-4000   Rev: $638
Bus: *Mfr. steel joists and structural steel components,*   Fax: 450-641-4001   Emp: 4,361
     concrete flooring systems.   www.canammanac.com
NAICS: 321999, 332111, 332312, 442210

> **CANAM USA**
> 14521 West 86th Terrace, Lenexa, Kansas 66215
> CEO: Sam Blatchford, Pres. & CEO   Tel: (913) 384-9809   %FO: 100
> Bus: *Metal fabricators manufacture and sales.*   Fax: (913) 384-9816

> **CANAM USA**
> 14481 Fairway Dr., Eden Prairie, Minnesota 55344
> CEO: Sam Blatchford, Pres. & CEO   Tel: (952) 475-9165   %FO: 100
> Bus: *Metal fabricators manufacture and sales.*   Fax: (952) 475-2710

> **CANAM USA**
> 30 Hill Rd. South, Pickerington, Ohio 43147
> CEO: Sam Blatchford, Pres. & CEO   Tel: (614) 920-0949   %FO: 100
> Bus: *Metal fabricators manufacture and sales.*   Fax: (614) 920-0937

> **CANAM USA**
> 5605 Hidden Valley Rd., Russiaville, Indiana 46979
> CEO: Sam Blatchford, Pres. & CEO   Tel: (765) 883-1135   %FO: 100
> Bus: *Metal fabricators manufacture and sales.*   Fax: (765) 883-1138

CANAM USA
540 Truman St., Bolingbrook, Illinois 60440
CEO: Sam Blatchford, Pres. & CEO   Tel: (630) 961-5944   %FO: 100
Bus: *Metal fabricators manufacture and sales.*   Fax: (630) 961-5945

CANAM USA
553 Waterside Dr., Hypoluxo, Florida 33462
CEO: Sam Blatchford, Pres. & CEO   Tel: (561) 547-7469   %FO: 100
Bus: *Metal fabricators manufacture and sales.*   Fax: (561) 540-2571

CANAM USA
11008 Blake Lane, Bealton, Virginia 22712
CEO: Sam Blatchford, Pres. & CEO   Tel: (540) 439-1475   %FO: 100
Bus: *Metal fabricators manufacture and sales.*   Fax: (540) 439-1479

CANAM USA
1012 Hampstead Rd., Wynnewood, Pennsylvania 19096
CEO: Sam Blatchford, Pres. & CEO   Tel: (610) 896-4790   %FO: 100
Bus: *Metal fabricators manufacture and sales.*   Fax: (610) 896-4815

CANAM USA
2081 Holcom Springs Rd., Gold Hill, Oregon 97525
CEO: Sam Blatchford, Pres. & CEO   Tel: (541) 855-9057   %FO: 100
Bus: *Metal fabricators manufacture and sales.*   Fax: (541) 855-2027

CANAM USA
50 Eastman St., Easton, Massachusetts 02334-1245
CEO: Sam Blatchford, Pres. & CEO   Tel: (508) 238-4500   %FO: 100
Bus: *Metal fabricators manufacture and sales.*   Fax: (508) 238-8253

CANAM USA
2219 Canyon Creek Dr., Lafayette, Indiana 47909
CEO: Mike Eckert   Tel: (765) 471-7300   %FO: 100
Bus: *Metal fabricators manufacture and sales.*   Fax: (765) 471-7303

CANAM USA
613 Sheffield Lane, Bolingbrook, Illinois 60440
CEO: Sam Blatchford, Pres. & CEO   Tel: (630) 427-1003   %FO: 100
Bus: *Metal fabricators manufacture and sales.*   Fax: (630) 427-9046

CANAM USA
388 La Purisma Way, Oceanside, California 92057
CEO: Sam Blatchford, Pres. & CEO   Tel: (760) 439-5339   %FO: 100
Bus: *Metal fabricators manufacture and sales.*   Fax: (760) 269-3403

CANAM USA
139 Hawthorne Way, Chittenango, New York 13037-1010
CEO: Sam Blatchford, Pres. & CEO   Tel: (315) 687-5870   %FO: 100
Bus: *Metal fabricators manufacture and sales.*   Fax: (315) 687-3701

CANAM USA
210 Silent Bluff Dr., San Antonio, Texas 78216
CEO: Sam Blatchford, Pres. & CEO   Tel: (210) 495-0105   %FO: 100
Bus: *Metal fabricators manufacture and sales.*   Fax: (210) 495-0141

Canada

CANAM USA
13243 Harpers Ferry Rd., Purcellville, Virginia 20132
CEO: Sam Blatchford, Pres. & CEO   Tel: (540) 668-7766   %FO: 100
Bus: *Metal fabricators manufacture and sales.*   Fax: (540) 668-7767

CANAM USA
4010 Clay St., PO Box 285, Point of Rocks, Maryland 21777-0285
CEO: Sam Blatchford, Pres. & CEO   Tel: (301) 874-5141   %FO: 100
Bus: *Metal fabricators manufacture and sales.*   Fax: (301) 874-5685

CANAM USA
240 N.W. Gilman Blvd., Ste. G, Issaquah, Washington 98027
CEO: Sam Blatchford, Pres. & CEO   Tel: (425) 392-2935   %FO: 100
Bus: *Metal fabricators manufacture and sales.*   Fax: (425) 392-3149

CANAM USA
2000 West Main St., Washington, Missouri 63090-1008
CEO: Sam Blatchford, Pres. & CEO   Tel: (636) 239-6716   %FO: 100
Bus: *Metal fabricators manufacture and sales.*   Fax: (636) 239-4135

CANAM USA
140 South Ellis Rd., Jacksonville, Florida 32254
CEO: Sam Blatchford, Pres. & CEO   Tel: (904) 781-0898   %FO: 100
Bus: *Metal fabricators manufacture and sales.*   Fax: (904) 781-2004

CANAM USA
2002 Morgan Rd., Sunnyside, Washington 98944
CEO: Sam Blatchford, Pres. & CEO   Tel: (509) 837-7008   %FO: 100
Bus: *Metal fabricators manufacture and sales.*   Fax: (509) 839-0383

CANAM USA
PO Box 296, Phoenix, Maryland 21131-0296
CEO: Sam Blatchford, Pres. & CEO   Tel: (410) 472-4327   %FO: 100
Bus: *Metal fabricators manufacture and sales.*   Fax: (410) 472-4827

CANAM USA
3280 St. Andrews Dr., Chambersburg, Pennsylvania 17201
CEO: Sam Blatchford, Pres. & CEO   Tel: (717) 263-7432   %FO: 100
Bus: *Metal fabricators manufacture and sales.*   Fax: (717) 263-7542

HAMBRO STRUCTURAL SYSTEMS
450 East Hillsboro Blvd., Deerfield Beach, Florida 33441
CEO: Mike Ramano   Tel: (954) 571-3030   %FO: 100
Bus: *Metal fabricators manufacture and sales.*   Fax: (954) 571-3051

MUROX, DIV. CANAM STEEL CORP.
21966 Emily Lane, Frankfort, Illinois 60423
CEO: Pierre Arcand   Tel: (815) 464-6735   %FO: 100
Bus: *Building products manufacture and sales.*   Fax: (815) 464-6738

STRUCTAL US
4010 Clay St., Point of Rocks, Maryland 21777
CEO: Michel Lafrance   Tel: (301) 874-5141   %FO: 100
Bus: *Heavy steel construction.*   Fax: (301) 874-5075

SUN BUILDING SYSTEMS
PO Box 686, Stanwood, Washington 98292
CEO: Bill Dreyer, Sales
Bus: *Pre-engineering building products manufacture.*

Tel: (360) 387-3987
Fax: (360) 387-8033

%FO: 100

● **CANFOR CORPORATION**
Bentall 5, 1500-550 Burrard St., Vancouver BC V6C 2C1, Canada
CEO: Peter J. G. Bentley, Pres. & CEO
Bus: *Producer of softwood lumber and market pulp.*

Tel: 604-661-5241
Fax: 604-661-5235
www.canfor.com

Rev: $1,618
Emp: 6,656

NAICS: 423310

CANFOR (USA) CORPORATION
4395 Curtis Rd., Bellingham, Washington 98225
CEO: George Layton, Mng. Dir.
Bus: *Mfr. pulp, paper, wood products.*

Tel: (360) 647-2434
Fax: (360) 647-2437

%FO: 100

● **CANGENE CORPORATION**
104 Chancellor Matheson Rd., Winnipeg MB R3T 5Y3, Canada
CEO: John Langstaff, Pres. & CEO
Bus: *Plasma products manufacture.*

Tel: 204-278-4200
Fax: 204-269-7003
www.cangene.com

Rev: $118
Emp: 600

NAICS: 424210

BIO-THERAPEUTIC LABORATORIES
14435 Sherman Way, Ste. 115, Van Nuys, California 91405
CEO: D. Gunn
Bus: *Plasma products.*

Tel: (818) 989-0611
Fax: (818) 989-4930

%FO: 100

FREDERICKS BIOLOGICALS
Unit #5,1713-G Rosemont Ave., Frederick, Maryland 21702-4199
CEO: Mark Langstaff
Bus: *Plasma products.*

Tel: (301) 696-8110
Fax: (301) 696-8113

%FO: 100

MID-FLORIDA BIOLOGICALS
380 South North Lake Blvd., Ste. 1024, Altamonte Springs, Florida 32701
CEO: K. Clifford
Bus: *Plasma products.*

Tel: (407) 628-4248
Fax: (407) 628-4249

%FO: 100

● **CANTOL LIMITED**
9729 Cote de Liesse, Dorval QC H9P 1A3, Canada
CEO: Elmer Snethen, CEO
Bus: *Commercial cleaning chemicals manufacture.*

Tel: 905-475-1584
Fax: 905-475-6141
www.cantol.com

Rev: $5
Emp: 55

NAICS: 424690

CANTOL LIMITED
2211 N. American St., Philadelphia, Pennsylvania 19133
CEO: Jennifer Kane
Bus: *Commercial cleaning chemicals manufacture.*

Tel: (215) 425-1966
Fax: (215) 425-1468

%FO: 100

CANTOL LIMITED
6870 Hawthorn Park Dr., Indianapolis, Indiana 46220
CEO: Richard Petsche   Tel: (317) 842-1865   %FO: 100
Bus: *Commercial cleaning chemicals manufacture.* Fax: (317) 568-1436

● **CARBIZ.COM INC.**
3044 Bloor St. West, Ste. 930, Toronto ON M8X 2Y8, Canada
CEO: Ross R. Lye, CEO   Tel: 416-391-2994
Bus: *Software manufacture for auto industry.*   Fax: 416-391-4824   Emp: 50
                                              www.carbiz.com
NAICS: 541511
    CARBIZ.COM INC.
    7560 Commerce Ct., Sarasota, Florida 34243
    CEO: Rick Reeves   Tel: (941) 953-3812   %FO: 100
    Bus: *Auto industry software manufacture and*   Fax: (941) 953-3812
        sales.

● **CARDIOME PHARMA CORP.**
6190 Agronomy Rd., 6/F, Vancouver BC V6T 1Z3, Canada
CEO: Mark C. Rogers, Chmn.   Tel: 604-677-6905   Rev: $22
Bus: *Mfr. of pharmaceuticals*   Fax: 604-677-6915   Emp: 63
                                              www.cardiome.com
NAICS: 325411
    CARDIOME PHARMA CORP.
    1111 Brickell Ave., Ste. 1113, Miami, Florida 33131
    CEO: Bob Rieder   Tel: (305) 913-7167
    Bus: *Manufacturer of pharmaceuticals*   Fax: (305) 913-4101

● **CARIS**
115 Waggoner's Ln., Florenceville NB E3B 2L4, Canada
CEO: Salem E. Masry, Pres. & CEO   Tel: 506-458-8533   Rev: $13
Bus: *Software publisher*   Fax: 506-459-3849   Emp: 148
                                              www.caris.com
NAICS: 511210
    CARIS USA
    3239A Corporate Ct., Ellicott City, Maryland 21042
    CEO: Frederick Ganjon, Pres.   Tel: (410) 418-8907   %FO: 100
    Bus: *Software publisher.*   Fax: (410) 418-8957

● **CASCADES INC.**
404 Marie-Victorin Blvd., PO Box 30, Kingsey Falls PQ J0A 1B0, Canada
CEO: Alain Lemaire, Pres. & CEO   Tel: 819-363-5100   Rev: $2,701
Bus: *Paper and packaging products and boxboard*   Fax: 819-363-5155   Emp: 15,800
    sheeting manufacture.   www.cascades.com
NAICS: 322121, 322130
    CASCADES INC.
    2255 Global Way, Hebron, Kentucky 41048
    CEO: Mark P. Roy, EVP   Tel: (606) 586-1100   %FO: 100
    Bus: *Mfr. paper and packaging products.*   Fax: (606) 334-6941

CASCADES TISSUE GROUP
148 Hudson River Rd., Waterford, New York 12198
CEO: Gary Hayden   Tel: (518) 238-1900   %FO: 100
Bus: *Private label tissue manufacture.*   Fax: (518) 238-1919

CASCADES TISSUE GROUP
PO Box 2028, Eau Claire, Wisconsin 54702
CEO: Stephan E. Doyon, Mgr.   Tel: (715) 834-3461   %FO: 100
Bus: *Tissue paper manufacturing.*   Fax: (715) 833-3172

CASCADES TISSUE GROUP
805 Midway Rd., Rockingham, North Carolina 28380
CEO: Gary Hayden   Tel: (910) 895-4033   %FO: 100
Bus: *Tissue paper manufacturing.*   Fax: (910) 895-9887

NORAMPAC INDUSTRIES INC.
4001 Packard Rd., Niagara Falls, New York 14303
CEO: Sal Sciarrino   Tel: (716) 285-3681   %FO: 100
Bus: *Corrugated packaging manufacture.*   Fax: (716) 285-3767

NORAMPAC INDUSTRIES INC.
1755 Elmwood Ave., Buffalo, New York 14207-2409
CEO: Chuck Grimm, Mgr.   Tel: (716) 876-1555   %FO: 100
Bus: *Corrugated packaging manufacture.*   Fax: (716) 876-1555

● **CASEWARE INTERNATIONAL INC.**
145 King St. East, 2nd Fl., Toronto ON M5C 2YB, Canada
CEO: Dwight Wainman, CEO   Tel: 416-867-9504
Bus: *Accounting and auditing software manufacture.*   Fax: 416-867-1906
                                                    www.caseware.com
NAICS: 511210, 541511

   CASEWARE INTERNATIONAL INC.
2425B Channing Way, Ste. 590, Berkeley, California 94704
CEO: Joyce Fisher, HR   Tel: (416) 867-1906
Bus: *Accounting and auditing software*   Fax: (416) 867-1906
    manufacture.

● **CCL INDUSTRIES INC.**
105 Gordon Baker Rd., Ste. 800, Willowdale ON M2H 3P8, Canada
CEO: Donald G. Lang, Pres. & CEO   Tel: 416-756-8500   Rev: $1,173
Bus: *Container, packaging and label manufacture for*   Fax: 416-391-5558   Emp: 6,100
    major corporations.   www.cclind.com
NAICS: 321920, 322211, 322212, 322222, 322223, 322224, 323110, 561910

   CCL DISPENSING INC.
901 Technology Way, Libertyville, Illinois 60048
CEO: Jim Dorsch   Tel: (847) 816-9400   %FO: 100
Bus: *Plastic packaging manufacture.*   Fax: (847) 816-4898

   CCL LABEL, INC.
1 West Hegeler Lane, Danville, Illinois 61832-8398
CEO: Brenda White   Tel: (217) 442-1400   %FO: 100
Bus: *Label manufacture.*   Fax: (217) 442-0902

CCL LABEL, INC.
15 Controls Dr., Shelton, Connecticut 06484
CEO: Serge De Paoli   Tel: (203) 926-1253   %FO: 100
Bus: *Label manufacture.*   Fax: (203) 926-9324

CCL LABEL, INC.
161 Worcester Rd., Framingham, Massachusetts 01701
CEO: Geoff Martin   Tel: (508) 872-4511   %FO: 100
Bus: *Label manufacture.*   Fax: (508) 872-7671

CCL PLASTIC PACKAGING INC.
2501 West Rosecrans Ave., Los Angeles, California 90059
CEO: Ray Cooney   Tel: (310) 635-4444   %FO: 100
Bus: *Plastic packaging manufacture.*   Fax: (310) 635-3877

CCL PLASTIC PACKAGING INC.
1 Lasley Ave., Wilkes Barre, Pennsylvania 18706
CEO: Marie Ditchfield   Tel: (570) 824-8485   %FO: 100
Bus: *Plastic packaging manufacture.*   Fax: (570) 824-8480

● **CELESTICA INC.**
1150 Eglinton Avenue East, Toronto ON M3C 1H7, Canada
CEO: Stephen W. Delaney, Pres. & CEO   Tel: 416-448-5800   Rev: $8,840
Bus: *Engaged in providing services to electronics*   Fax: 416-448-4810   Emp: 46,000
     computer manufacturers.   www.celestica.com
NAICS: 334119, 334412, 334413, 334417, 334418, 334419

     CELESTICA INC.
     7400 Scott Hamilton Drive, Little Rock, Arkansas 72209
     CEO: Joe S. Ackerman   Tel: (501) 562-4411   %FO: 100
     Bus: *Engaged in providing services to*   Fax: (501) 562-4779
     electronics computer manufacturers.

     CELESTICA INC.
     7345 IBM Drive, Charlotte, North Carolina 28262
     CEO: Eugene Polistuk   Tel: (704) 945-4000   %FO: 100
     Bus: *Engaged in providing services to*   Fax: (704) 945-4099
     electronics computer manufacturers.

     CELESTICA INC.
     4300 Round Lake Rd., Arden Hills, Minnesota 55112
     CEO: Gary Moore   Tel: (651) 604-2400   %FO: 100
     Bus: *Engaged in providing services to*   Fax: (651) 604-2420
     electronics computer manufacturers.

     CELESTICA INC.
     9 Northeastern Blvd., Salem, New Hampshire 03079
     CEO: Stephen Delaney   Tel: (603) 890-8000   %FO: 100
     Bus: *Engaged in providing services to*   Fax: (603) 890-8450
     electronics computer manufacturers.

     CELESTICA INC.
     1811 Sardis Rd. North, Charlotte, North Carolina 28270
     CEO: Scott James   Tel: (704) 847-6232   %FO: 100
     Bus: *Engaged in providing services to*   Fax: (704) 847-6232
     electronics computer manufacturers.

CELESTICA INC.
4616 West Howard lane, Bldg. 1, Ste. 100, Austin, Texas 78728
CEO: James Armstrong   Tel: (512) 310-7540   %FO: 100
Bus: *Engaged in providing services to*   Fax: (512) 310-0951
     electronics computer manufacturers.

CELESTICA INC.
1615 East Washington St., Mt. Pleasant, Iowa 52641
CEO: Chuck Finley, Pres.   Tel: (319) 385-9271   %FO: 100
Bus: *Engaged in providing services to*   Fax: (319) 385-5244
     electronics computer manufacturers.

CELESTICA INC.
4701 Technology Pkwy., Ft. Collins, Colorado 80525
CEO: Stephen Delaney   Tel: (970) 207-5000   %FO: 100
Bus: *Engaged in providing services to*   Fax: (970) 207-5290
     electronics computer manufacturers.

CELESTICA INC.
5325 Hellyer Ave., San Jose, California 95138
CEO: Joel Bustos   Tel: (408) 574-6000   %FO: 100
Bus: *Engaged in providing services to*   Fax: (408) 229-6075
     electronics computer manufacturers.

● **CERTICOM CORPORATION**
5520 Explorer Dr., 4th Fl, Mississauga ON L4W 5L1, Canada
CEO: Ian M. McKinnon, CEO   Tel: 905-507-4220   Rev: $12
Bus: *Digital software products manufacture.*   Fax: 905-507-4230   Emp: 125
                                        www.certicom.com
NAICS: 541511, 541519

CERTICOM CORPORATION
1800 Alexander Bell Dr., Ste. 400, Reston, Virginia 20191
CEO: David Sequino, VP Sales   Tel: (703) 234-2357   %FO: 100
Bus: *Digital software products manufacture and*   Fax: (703) 234-2356
     sales.

CERTICOM CORPORATION
1810 Gateway Dr., Ste. 200, San Mateo, California 94404
CEO: Ian McKinnon   Tel: (650) 655-3950   %FO: 100
Bus: *Digital software products manufacture and*   Fax: (650) 655-3961
     sales.

● **CFS GROUP INC**
103 The East Mall, Etobicoke ON M8Z 5X9, Canada
CEO: Michael Kawaja, Pres.   Tel: 416-237-1234   Rev: $85
Bus: *Mfr. of adhesives, coatings, and emulsion*   Fax: 416-237-1227   Emp: 226
                                        www.ifscos.com
NAICS: 325510, 325520, 325998

IFS COATINGS INC.
3601 North I-35, PO Box 1211, Gainesville, Texas 76241
CEO: Michael Nordin   Tel: (940) 668-1062   %FO: 100
Bus: *Manufacturer of coatings*   Fax: (940) 668-1061

IFS COATINGS INC.
3601 North I-35, PO Box 1211, Gainesville, Texas 76241
CEO: Glenn Mason   Tel: (940) 668-1062   %FO: 100
Bus: *Manufacturer of adhesives, coatings, and*   Fax: (940) 668-1061
    emulsion polymers

IFS INDUSTRIES INC.
2222 Lonnecker Dr., Garland, Texas 75041
CEO: Michael Kawaja   Tel: (972) 864-2202   %FO: 100
Bus: *Manufacturer of adhesives, coatings, and*   Fax: (972) 278-5595
    emulsion polymers

IFS INDUSTRIES INC.
450 Fenton Lane, Ste. 901, West Chicago, Illinois 60185
CEO: Christopher Tamkei   Tel: (630) 562-9677   %FO: 100
Bus: *Manufacturer of adhesives, coatings, and*   Fax: (630) 562-9678
    emulsion polymers

IFS INDUSTRIES INC.
400 Orrton Ave., Reading, Pennsylvania 19603
CEO: Michael Kawaja   Tel: (610) 378-1381   %FO: 100
Bus: *Manufacturer of adhesives, coatings, and*   Fax: (610) 378-5080
    emulsion polymers

● **CGI GROUP INC.**
1130 Sherbrooke St. West, 5th Fl., Montreal QC H3A 2M8, Canada
CEO: Serge Godin, CEO   Tel: 514-841-3200   Rev: $1,367
Bus: *Independent information technology and business*   Fax: 514-841-3299   Emp: 20,000
    process services.   www.cgi.ca
NAICS: 541512, 541513

CGI GROUP INC.
12 Corporate Woods Blvd., Albany, New York 12211
CEO: William Cunningham   Tel: (518) 434-0294   %FO: 100
Bus: *Engaged in information technology services.*   Fax: (518) 434-3697

CGI GROUP INC.
20 N. Clark St., Chicago, Illinois 60602
CEO: Julie Creed   Tel: (312) 269-0275   %FO: 100
Bus: *Engaged in information technology services.*   Fax: (312) 269-1218

CGI GROUP INC.
600 Federal St., Andover, Massachusetts 01810
CEO: Serge Godin   Tel: (978) 946-3000   %FO: 100
Bus: *Engaged in information technology services.*   Fax: (978) 686-0130

CGI GROUP INC.
1225 North Loop West, Ste. 825, Houston, Texas 77008
CEO: Barbara Graff, Sr. Prtn.   Tel: (713) 868-5537   %FO: 100
Bus: *Engaged in information technology services.*   Fax: (713) 868-4014

CGI GROUP INC.
One Chase Manhattan Plaza, 36/F., New York, New York 10005
CEO: Bob Sember, Sr. Prtn.   Tel: (212) 612-3600   %FO: 100
Bus: *Engaged in information technology services.*   Fax: (212) 612-3636

- **CHANCERY SOFTWARE LTD.**
  3001 Wayburne Dr., Ste. 275, Burnaby BC V5G 4W3, Canada
  CEO: Paul Kellenberger, CEO   Tel: 604-294-1233   Rev: $30
  Bus: *Software publisher*   Fax: 604-294-2225   Emp: 200
                                       www.chancery.com

  NAICS: 511210

  > **CHANCERY SOFTWARE**
  > 3500-188th St. SW, Ste. 430, Lynnwood, Washington 98037
  > CEO: Chris Sherman, EVP   Tel: (800) 999-9931   %FO: 100
  > Bus: *Software publisher*   Fax:

- **CIBC (CANADIAN IMPERIAL BANK OF COMMERCE) WORLD MARKETS**
  BCE Place, 161 Bay St., Toronto ON M5J 2S8, Canada
  CEO: Brian G. Shaw, Chmn. & CEO   Tel: 416-594-7000
  Bus: *Brokerage and investment banking services.*   Fax: 416-956-6958
                                           www.cibcwm.com

  NAICS: 523110

  > **CIBC WORLD MARKETS**
  > 2420 Sand Hill Rd., Ste. 300, Menlo Park, California 94025-6942
  > CEO: Eric Risley   Tel: (650) 234-2400   %FO: 100
  > Bus: *Brokerage and investment banking services.*   Fax: (650) 234-2405

  > **CIBC WORLD MARKETS**
  > 300 Madison, New York, New York 10017
  > CEO: Gerald McCouthey   Tel: (212) 856-4000   %FO: 100
  > Bus: *Brokerage and investment banking services.*   Fax: (212) 856-4000

  > **CIBC WORLD MARKETS**
  > 1 Post St., Ste. 3550, San Francisco, California 94104-5250
  > CEO: Earl Lum   Tel: (415) 399-5700   %FO: 100
  > Bus: *Brokerage and investment banking services.*   Fax: (415) 399-5700

- **CIMTEK AUTOMATION SYSTEMS INC.**
  5328 John Lucas Dr., Burlington ON L7L 6A6, Canada
  CEO: Stan Smith, Pres. & CEO   Tel: 905-331-6338   Rev: $18
  Bus: *Instrument manufacturer*   Fax: 905-331-6339   Emp: 110
                                        www.cimtek.com

  NAICS: 334513, 334515

  > **CIMTEK AUTOMATION SYSTEMS**
  > 3114 S. Lafountain St., Kokomo, Indiana 46902
  > CEO: Salvador Jaramillo   Tel: (765) 455-1900   %FO: 100
  > Bus: *Instrument manufacturer*   Fax: (765) 455-1919

  > **CIMTEK AUTOMATION SYSTEMS**
  > 33045 Hamilton Ct. East, Ste. 105, Farmington Hills, Michigan 48334
  > CEO: Mike Miller   Tel: (248) 324-0859   %FO: 100
  > Bus: *Instrument manufacturer*   Fax: (248) 324-3945

Canada

• **CINRAM INTERNATIONAL INC.**
2255 Markham Rd., Scarborough ON M1B 2W3, Canada
CEO: Isodore Philosophe, CEO
Bus: *Pre-recorded videotapes manufacture.*

Tel: 416-298-8190
Fax: 416-298-0612
www.cinram.com

Rev: $890
Emp: 9,500

NAICS: 334612

> **CINRAM INTERNATIONAL INC.**
> 1600 Rich Rd., Richmond, Indiana 47374
> CEO: Nelda Fratellio
> Bus: *Pre-recorded videotapes manufacture and sales.*
>
> Tel: (765) 962-9511
> Fax: (765) 962-1564
>
> %FO: 100

> **CINRAM INTERNATIONAL INC.**
> 4905 Moores Mill Rd., Huntsville, Alabama 35811
> CEO: Larry Tabb
> Bus: *Pre-recorded videotapes manufacture and sales.*
>
> Tel: (256) 859-9042
> Fax: (256) 859-9932
>
> %FO: 100

> **CINRAM MANUFACTURING**
> 6110 Peachtree St., Commerce, California 90040
> CEO: Tom Arboit
> Bus: *Pre-recorded videotapes manufacture and sales.*
>
> Tel: (323) 725-6900
> Fax: (323) 725-6900
>
> %FO: 100

> **CINRAM MANUFACTURING**
> 1400 East Lackawanna Ave., Olyphant, Pennsylvania 18448
> CEO: Kevin Cleary
> Bus: *Pre-recorded videotapes manufacture and sales.*
>
> Tel: (570) 383-3291
> Fax: (570) 383-3291
>
> %FO: 100

• **CIRQUE DU SOLEIL INC.**
8400 Second Avenue, Montreal QC H1Z 4M6, Canada
CEO: Guy Laliberté, CEO
Bus: *Cirque Du Soleil (Circus of the Sun) is a circus art performance troupe.*

Tel: 514-722-2324
Fax: 514-722-3692
www.cirquedusoleil.com

Rev: $327
Emp: 2,100

NAICS: 711190

> **CIRQUE DU SOLEIL INC.**
> 1478 East Buena Vista Dr., Lake Buena Vista, Florida 32830
> CEO: Guy Laliberte
> Bus: *Cirque Du Soleil (Circus of the Sun) is a circus art performance troupe.*
>
> Tel: (407) 934-9200
> Fax: (407) 934-9200
>
> %FO: 100

> **CIRQUE DU SOLEIL INC.**
> 875 Beach Blvd., Biloxi, Mississippi 39530
> CEO: Jerry Nadal
> Bus: *Cirque Du Soleil (Circus of the Sun) is a circus art performance troupe.*
>
> Tel: (228) 386-7790
> Fax: (228) 386-7790
>
> %FO: 100

> **CIRQUE DU SOLEIL INC.**
> 3600 Las Vegas Boulevard South, Las Vegas, Nevada 89109
> CEO: Jeff Herd, Pres.
> Bus: *Cirque Du Soleil (Circus of the Sun) is a circus art performance troupe.*
>
> Tel: (702) 693-7790
> Fax: (702) 693-7768
>
> %FO: 100

- **CITYEXPRESS CORPORATION**
1727 West Broadway, Ste. 200, Vancouver BC V6J 4W6, Canada
CEO: Phil Dubois, CEO   Tel: 604-638-3800   Rev: $
Bus: *On-line auction services.*   Fax: 604-638-3808   Emp: 25
     www.cityxpress.com
NAICS: 454112

     CITYEXPRESS CORPORATION
     6234 McCormick Woods Dr., Port Orchard, Washington 98367
     CEO: Jim MacKay   Tel: (360) 895-5374   %FO: 100
     Bus: *On-line auction services.*   Fax: (360) 895-0476

- **CLARKE INC.**
6009 Quinpool Rd., Halifax NS M9B 6J8, Canada
CEO: George Armoyan, CEO   Tel: 416-695-7711   Rev: $175
Bus: *Truck freight transport services.*   Fax: 416-695-9544   Emp: 1,300
     www.clarkelink.com
NAICS: 484110, 484121, 484122

     CLARKE LOGISTICS
     101 Lindenwood Dr., Malvern, Pennsylvania 19380
     CEO: Ann Marie J. Haskins   Tel: (610) 431-7878   %FO: 100
     Bus: *Truck freight transport services.*   Fax: (610) 431-4336

     CLARKE LOGISTICS
     8840 Wilshire Blvd., 2/F, Beverly Hills, California 90211
     CEO: Steven Goodman   Tel: (310) 358-3234   %FO: 100
     Bus: *Truck freight transport services.*   Fax: (310) 358-3284

     CLARKE LOGISTICS
     4210-198th St., SW, Ste. 212, Lynwood, Washington 98036
     CEO: Kevin Turner   Tel: (425) 672-3060   %FO: 100
     Bus: *Truck freight transport services.*   Fax: (425) 672-3061

     CLARKE LOGISTICS
     6990 Village Pkwy, 1/F, Dublin, California 94568
     CEO: George Norstrom   Tel: (925) 803-2905   %FO: 100
     Bus: *Truck freight transport services.*   Fax: (925) 803-0822

     CLARKE LOGISTICS
     11803 Grant Rd. Ste. 209, Cypress, Texas 77429
     CEO: Tanya Williams   Tel: (281) 320-9930   %FO: 100
     Bus: *Truck freight transport services.*   Fax: (281) 320-0656

     CLARKE LOGISTICS
     900 Ridge Rd., Homewood, Illinois 60430
     CEO: John Glennon   Tel: (708) 647-7900   %FO: 100
     Bus: *Truck freight transport services.*   Fax: (708) 647-7961

     CLARKE LOGISTICS
     2500 Mt. Mariah, Bldg. H, Ste. 250, Memphis, Tennessee 38115
     CEO: Wray Williams   Tel: (901) 362-1310   %FO: 100
     Bus: *Truck freight transport services.*   Fax: (901) 360-8240

- **CLEARLY CANADIAN BEVERAGE CORPORATION**
  2489 Bellevue Avenue, West Vancouver BC V7V 1E1, Canada
  CEO: Douglas L. Mason, CEO   Tel: 604-922-8100   Rev: $13
  Bus: *Mfr. beverages.*   Fax: 604-922-8195   Emp: 30
                                      www.clearly.ca
  NAICS: 312111

    CC BEVERAGE CORPORATION
    1650 Port Dr., Burlington, Washington 98233
    CEO: Tom Koltai, PR   Tel: (360) 757-4441   %FO: 100
    Bus: *Mfr. beverages.*   Fax: (360) 757-4441

- **CLEARWATER SEAFOODS INCOME FUND**
  757 Bedford Highway, Bedford NS B4A 3Z7, Canada
  CEO: Colin E. MacDonald, Chmn.   Tel: 902-443-0550   Rev: $9
  Bus: *Seafood processing.*   Fax: 902-443-7797   Emp: 800
                                      www.clrwater.ca
  NAICS: 311712

    CLEARWATER SEAFOODS INCOME FUND
    7608 Oswego Rd., Liverpool, New York 13090
    CEO: Mike Middleton   Tel: (315) 652-1454   %FO: 100
    Bus: *Seafood processing.*   Fax: (315) 652-1454

    CLEARWATER SEAFOODS INCOME FUND
    556 S. Highway 27, Unit B, Minneola, Florida 34755
    CEO: Andrew Fisher   Tel: (352) 394-4116   %FO: 100
    Bus: *Seafood processing.*   Fax: (352) 394-2659

- **CLINICARE CORPORATION**
  3553-31st St. NW, Ste. 300, Calgary AB T2L 2K7, Canada
  CEO: Dennis Niebergal, CEO   Tel: 403-259-2273   Rev: $4
  Bus: *Electronic medical records manufacturer.*   Fax: 403-259-2400   Emp: 42
                                      www.clinicare.com
  NAICS: 541511, 541513

    CHARTCARE CORPORATION
    7403 Lakewood Dr. West, Ste. 12, Lakewood, Washington 98499
    CEO: Dennis Niebergal   Tel: (253) 472-7013   %FO: 100
    Bus: *Electronic medical records manufacturer.*   Fax: (253) 475-9278

- **CLOVERDALE PAINT INC.**
  6950 King George Hwy., Surrey BC V3W 4Z1, Canada
  CEO: Charles A. Mordy, Pres.   Tel: 604-596-6261   Rev: $87
  Bus: *Paint manufacturer*   Fax: 604-597-2677   Emp: 650
                                      www.cloverdalepaint.com
  NAICS: 325510, 424950

    CLOVERDALE PAINT
    570 South Michigan St., Seattle, Washington 98108
    CEO: Al Mordy   Tel: (206) 762-9274   %FO: 100
    Bus: *Paint manufacturer*   Fax: (206) 762-9312

● **CMC ELECTRONICS INC.**
600 Dr. Frederik Philips Blvd., Saint-Laurent QC H4M 2S9, Canada
CEO: Jean-Pierre Mortreux, Pres. & CEO   Tel: 514-748-3148   Rev: $200
Bus: *Aviation Electronics manufacturer*   Fax: 5147483100
     www.cmcelectronics.ca
NAICS: 336413, 336415

     CMC ELECTRONICS INC.
     84 North Dugan Rd., PO Box 250, Sugar Grove, Illinois 60554-0250
     CEO: Jean-Pierre Mortreux   Tel: (630) 466-4343   %FO: 100
     Bus: *Aviation electronics*   Fax: (630) 466-4358

● **COGNOS INCORPORATED**
3755 Riverside Drive, PO Box 9707, Ottawa ON K1G 4K9, Canada
CEO: Renato Zambonini, CEO   Tel: 613-738-1440   Rev: $826
Bus: *Development and marketing of computer software.* Fax: 613-738-0002   Emp: 3,297
     www.cognos.com
NAICS: 511210

     COGNOS CORPORATION
     Two Discovery Square, 12012 Sunset Hills Rd., Reston, Virginia 20190
     CEO: Venetia Rush   Tel: (571) 262-2100   %FO: 100
     Bus: *Marketing/sales computer software.*   Fax: (571) 262-2100

     COGNOS CORPORATION
     67 South Bedford St., Ste. 1005, Burlington, Massachusetts 01803-5164
     CEO: Nancy DeFilippis, Pres.   Tel: (781) 229-6600   %FO: 100
     Bus: *Marketing/sales computer software.*   Fax: (781) 229-9844   Emp: 205

     COGNOS CORPORATION
     405 Sherrin Ave., Louisville, Kentucky 40207
     CEO: Kim Smith   Tel: (502) 896-2673   %FO: 100
     Bus: *Marketing/sales computer software.*   Fax: (502) 896-2673

     COGNOS CORPORATION
     425 North Martingale Rd., Suite 600, Schaumburg, Illinois 60173-2207
     CEO: Robbie Ellis   Tel: (847) 285-2900   %FO: 100
     Bus: *Marketing/sales computer software.*   Fax: (847) 240-0252

     COGNOS CORPORATION
     7702 E Doubletree Ranch Rd., Scottsdale, Arizona 85258
     CEO: Doug Barton, VP   Tel: (480) 607-4375   %FO: 100
     Bus: *Marketing/sales computer software.*   Fax: (480) 607-4375

     COGNOS CORPORATION
     10900 NE 4th St., Suite 1030, Seattle, Washington 98004
     CEO: Thomas Griggs   Tel: (425) 698-6405   %FO: 100
     Bus: *Marketing/sales computer software.*   Fax: (425) 698-6405

• **COM DEV INTERNATIONAL LTD.**
  155 Sheldon Dr., Cambridge ON N1R 7H6, Canada
  CEO: John Keating, CEO   Tel: 519-622-2300   Rev: $69
  Bus: *Wireless communications manufacturer*   Fax: 519-622-1691   Emp: 660
                                                   www.comdev.ca

  NAICS: 334210, 334220, 334290, 334413
      COM DEV INTERNATIONAL LTD.
      , Marina del Rey, California 90292
      CEO: Glenn Barney   Tel: (310) 823-5575   %FO: 100
      Bus: *Wireless communications manufacturer.* Fax: (310) 577-3702

• **COMPUTER MODELLING GROUP LTD.**
  3553 31st St. NW, Ste. 150, Calgary AB T2L 2K6, Canada
  CEO: Kenneth M. Dedeluk, Pres.   Tel: 403-531-1300   Rev: $9
  Bus: *Computer software engineering and consulting* Fax: 403-282-1823   Emp: 55
       services.   www.cmgl.ca
  NAICS: 541511, 541512, 541611
      CMG INC.
      450 Gears Rd., Ste. 860, Houston, Texas 77067
      CEO: Gerald Jacobs   Tel: (281) 872-8500   %FO: 100
      Bus: *Computer software engineering and*   Fax: (281) 872-8577
           consulting services.

• **CON-WAY CANADA EXPRESS, INC.**
  5425 Dixie Rd., Ste. 202, Mississauga ON L4W 1E6, Canada
  CEO: David L. Miller, CEO   Tel: 905-602-9477
  Bus: *Freight transportation services.*   Fax: 905-602-9477   Emp: 2,900
                                                   www.con-way.com
  NAICS: 488510
      CON-WAY WESTERN EXPRESS
      6301 Beach Blvd., Ste. 300, Buena Park, California 90621
      CEO: Kevin M. Hartman, Pres.   Tel: (714) 562-0110   %FO: 100
      Bus: *Freight transportation services.*   Fax: (714) 562-0110

• **COOKIE JAR GROUP**
  1055 Rene-Levesque East, Ste.900, Montreal QC H2L 4S5, Canada
  CEO: Michael Hirsh, CEO   Tel: 514-843-7070
  Bus: *Motion picture and video production*   Fax: 514-843-6773
                                                   www.cinar.com
  NAICS: 512110, 512191
      CARSON-DELLOSA PUBLISHING CO., INC.
      7027 Albert Pick Rd., Greensboro, North Carolina 27409
      CEO: Scott McCaw, CEO   Tel: (336) 632-0084   %FO: 100
      Bus: *Educational materials*   Fax: (336) 632-0087

      COOKIE JAR ENTERTAINMENT INC.
      4500 Wilshire Blvd., 1/F, Los Angeles, California 90010
      CEO: Toper Taylor, Pres. & COO   Tel: (323) 954-4552   %FO: 100
      Bus: *Motion picture and video production*   Fax:

HIGHREACH LEARNING
1337 Hundred Oaks Dr., Ste. FF, Charlotte, North Carolina 28217
CEO: Richard Lugo, VP
Bus: *Motion picture and video production*

Tel: (704) 357-0112
Fax: (704) 357-0608

%FO: 100

● **COOLBRANDS INTERNATIONAL INC.**
8300 Woodbine Avenue, 5th Fl., Markham ON L3R 9Y7, Canada
CEO: David J. Stein, CEO
Bus: *Frozen yogurt deserts manufacture.*

Tel: 905-479-8762
Fax: 905-479-5235
www.yogenfruz.com

Rev: $487
Emp: 1,305

NAICS: 311520

COOLBRANDS INTERNATIONAL INC.
4175 Veterans Hwy., 3/F, Ronkonkoma, New York 11775
CEO: Joe Arancio
Bus: *Mfr. frozen ice cream deserts.*

Tel: (631) 737-9700
Fax: (631) 737-9792

%FO: 100

● **COREL CORPORATION**
1600 Carling Avenue, Ottawa ON K1Z BR7, Canada
CEO: David Dobson, CEO
Bus: *Publishing and graphics software.*

Tel: 613-728-8200
Fax: 613-728-9790
www.corel.com

NAICS: 511210, 541511

COREL CORPORATION
8144 Walnut Hill Lane, Ste. 1050, Dallas, Texas 75231
CEO: Jenna Brouillette
Bus: *Publishing and graphics software sales.*

Tel: (469) 232-1000
Fax: (469) 232-1194

%FO: 100

● **CORE-MARK INTERNATIONAL INC.**
7800 Riverfront Gate, Burnaby BC V5J 5L3, Canada
CEO: J. Michael Walsh, Pres. & CEO
Bus: *Full-service distributors of packaged consumer products to the convenience retail industry in North America.*

Tel: 604-430-2181
Fax:
www.coremark.com

NAICS: 424410

CORE-MARK INTERNATIONAL INC.
2311 East 48th St., Los Angeles, California 90058
CEO: J. Michael Walsh
Bus: *Food wholesale distributor.*

Tel: (323) 583-6531
Fax: (323) 589-1828

%FO: 100

CORE-MARK INTERNATIONAL INC.
1035 Nathan Lane N., Plymouth, Minnesota 55441
CEO: Pete Willmott
Bus: *Food wholesale distributor.*

Tel: (763) 545-3700
Fax: (763) 545-3700

%FO: 100

CORE-MARK INTERNATIONAL INC.
6401 Will Rogers Blvd., Ste. 200, Fort Worth, Texas 76134
CEO: Chris L. Walsh
Bus: *Food wholesale distributor.*

Tel: (817) 293-5558
Fax: (817) 293-5558

%FO: 100

Canada

CORE-MARK INTERNATIONAL INC.
5600 Second St. N.W., Albuquerque, New Mexico 87107
CEO: Chris L. Walsh   Tel: (505) 343-9577   %FO: 100
Bus: *Food wholesale distributor.*   Fax: (505) 343-9577

CORE-MARK INTERNATIONAL INC.
3797 Windsor Dr., Aurora, Colorado 80011
CEO: Chris L. Walsh   Tel: (303) 373-2300   %FO: 100
Bus: *Food wholesale distributor.*   Fax: (303) 373-2300

CORE-MARK INTERNATIONAL INC.
395 Oyster Point Blvd., Ste. 415, South San Francisco, California 94080
CEO: Gary Christensen, VP   Tel: (650) 589-9445   %FO: 100
Bus: *Purchasing and tobacco.*   Fax: (650) 589-3182

CORE-MARK INTERNATIONAL INC.
353 Meyer Circle, Corona, California 91720
CEO: Michelle Shaw   Tel: (951) 736-1591   %FO: 100
Bus: *Food wholesale distributor.*   Fax: (951) 736-1591

CORE-MARK INTERNATIONAL INC.
200 Core-Mark Ct., Bakersfield, California 93307
CEO: J. Michael Walsh   Tel: (661) 366-2673   %FO: 100
Bus: *Food wholesale distributor.*   Fax: (661) 366-5178

CORE-MARK INTERNATIONAL INC.
31300 Medallion Dr., Hayward, California 94544
CEO: J. Michael Walsh   Tel: (510) 487-3000   %FO: 100
Bus: *Food wholesale distributor.*   Fax:

CORE-MARK INTERNATIONAL INC.
3970 Pell Circle, Sacramento, California 95838
CEO: J. Michael Walsh   Tel: (916) 927-0795   %FO: 100
Bus: *Food wholesale distributor.*   Fax:

CORE-MARK INTERNATIONAL INC.
303 N.E. F St., Grants Pass, Oregon 97526
CEO: Jack Cooper   Tel: (541) 476-6651   %FO: 100
Bus: *Food wholesale distributor.*   Fax: (541) 476-6651

CORE-MARK INTERNATIONAL INC.
13551 S.E. Johnson, Portland, Oregon 97222
CEO: B. Barry   Tel: (503) 652-0200   %FO: 100
Bus: *Food wholesale distributor.*   Fax: (503) 652-1079

CORE-MARK INTERNATIONAL INC.
1015 Dyer Rd., Spokane, Washington 99212
CEO: Ian Johnstone   Tel: (509) 535-9768   %FO: 100
Bus: *Food wholesale distributor.*   Fax: (509) 535-9768

CORE-MARK INTERNATIONAL INC.
3950 W. Harmon, Las Vegas, Nevada 89103
CEO: Chris L. Walsh   Tel: (702) 876-5220   %FO: 100
Bus: *Food wholesale distributor.*   Fax: (702) 876-5220

- **CORETEC INC.**
  8150 Sheppard Ave. East, Toronto ON M1B 5K2, Canada
  CEO: Paul Langston, Chmn. & Pres. & CEO   Tel: 416-208-2100   Rev: $66
  Bus: *Electronic assembly*   Fax: 416-208-2195   Emp: 500
     www.coretec-inc.com

  NAICS: 334412, 334418

     CORETEC CLEVELAND INC.
     7 Ascot Pkwy., Cuyahoga Falls, Ohio 44223
     CEO: Jeffrey Canavor   Tel: (330) 572-3400   %FO: 100
     Bus: *PCB manufacturing*   Fax: (330) 572-3434   Emp: 50

     CORETEC DENVER INC.
     10570 Bradford Rd., Littleton, Colorado 80127
     CEO: Jeffrey Canavor   Tel: (303) 972-4105   %FO: 100
     Bus: *PCB manufacturing*   Fax: (303) 904-6199   Emp: 80

- **COSSETTE COMMUNICATION GROUP INC.**
  801 Chemin St.-Louis, Ste. 200, Quebec City QC G1S 1C1, Canada
  CEO: Claude Lessard, CEO   Tel: 418-647-2727   Rev: $143
  Bus: *Advertising and marketing services.*   Fax: 418-647-2564   Emp: 1,300
     www.cossette.com

  NAICS: 541613, 541810

     COSSETTE POST
     415 Madison Ave., New York, New York 10017-1163
     CEO: Peter Post, CEO   Tel: (212) 753-4700   %FO: 100
     Bus: *Advertising and marketing services.*   Fax: (212) 755-0284   Emp: 77

     PAINEPR
     1900 MacArthur Blvd., 8/F, Irvine, California 92612
     CEO: David Paine   Tel: (949) 809-6700   %FO: 100
     Bus: *Public relations firm.*   Fax: (949) 260-1116

     PAINEPR
     660 South Figueroa St., 7/F, Los Angeles, California 90017
     CEO: Eric Borsum   Tel: (213) 430-0480   %FO: 100
     Bus: *Public relations firm.*   Fax: (213) 430-0494

     PAINEPR
     1370 Broadway, 9/F, New York, New York 10018
     CEO: Beth Balsam   Tel: (212) 868-7199   %FO: 100
     Bus: *Public relations firm.*   Fax: (212) 868-7206

- **COTT CORPORATION**
  207 Queen's Quay West, Ste. 340, Toronto ON M5J 1A7, Canada
  CEO: Frank E. Weise III, Chmn.   Tel: 416-203-3898   Rev: $1,646
  Bus: *Mfr. bottled and canned soft drinks/carbonated*   Fax: 416-203-8171   Emp: 3,236
     waters.   www.cott.com
  NAICS: 312111

COTT BEVERAGES
4211 West Boy Scout Blvd., Ste. 290, Tampa, Florida 33607
CEO: Frank Weise, CEO   Tel: (813) 313-1800   %FO: 100
Bus: *US headquarters for soft drinks.*   Fax: Emp: 1,500

● **CPI PLASTICS GROUP LTD.**
979 Gana Court, Mississauga ON L5S 1N9, Canada
CEO: Ronald W. Mitchell, CEO   Tel: 416-798-9333   Rev: $112
Bus: *Thermoplastics manufacture.*   Fax: 416-798-9229   Emp: 1,000
                                          www.cpiplastics.com
NAICS: 325199, 326122
  CPI PLASTICS GROUP LTD.
  1042A Mitchell Jellison Dr. North, Elkhart, Indiana 46516
  CEO: Ron Mitchell   Tel: (219) 294-1263   %FO: 100
  Bus: *Thermoplastics manufacture and sales.*   Fax: (219) 294-1261

● **CREATION TECHNOLOGIES INC.**
3939 North Fraser Way, Burnaby BC V5J 5J2, Canada
CEO: Geoff Reed, CEO   Tel: 604-430-4336   Rev: $55
Bus: *Circuit board manufacturing.*   Fax: 604-430-4337   Emp: 800
                                          www.creationtech.com
NAICS: 334412
  CREATION TECHNOLOGIES
  2250 W. Southbranch Blvd., Oak Creek, Wisconsin 53154
  CEO: Patrick Ciriacks   Tel: (414) 761-0400   %FO: 100
  Bus: *Circuit board manufacturing and sales.*   Fax: (414) 761-0582

● **CREDITRON INC.**
10 Kingsbridge Garden Circle, Ste. 801, Mississauga ON L5R 3K6, Canada
CEO: Wally Vogel, CEO   Tel: 905-890-7800
Bus: *Hardware and software manufacture.* Fax: 905-890-3242
                                          www.creditron.com
NAICS: 541511
  CREDITRON CORPORATION
  2700 N. Main St., Ste. 310, Santa Ana, California 92705
  CEO: Wally Vogel   Tel: (702) 566-3834   %FO: 100
  Bus: *Hardware and software manufacture and*   Fax: (702) 566-3834
   sales.

● **CSI WIRELESS INC.**
4110 9th St., SE, Calgary AB T2G 3C4, Canada
CEO: Stephen Verhoeff, CEO   Tel: 403-259-3311   Rev: $34
Bus: *Wireless communications network equipment*   Fax: 403-259-8866   Emp: 135
 manufacture.   www.csi-wireless.com
NAICS: 334210

CSI WIRELESS INC.
1001 Murphy Ranch Rd., Bldg. 3, Milpitas, California 95035
CEO: Scott Terry
Bus: *Wireless communications network equipment manufacture and sales.*
Tel: (408) 434-0685
Fax: (408) 433-9647
%FO: 100
Emp: 20

SATLOC LLC
7560 E. Redfield Rd., Ste. B, Scottsdale, Arizona 85260
CEO: Stephen Verhoeff
Bus: *Wireless communications network equipment manufacture and sales.*
Tel: (480) 348-9919
Fax: (480) 348-6370
%FO: 100

● **CYBERPLEX INC.**
267 Richmond St. West, Toronto ON M5V 3M6, Canada
CEO: W. Dean Hopkins, CEO
Bus: *Provides web site design and marketing and e-commerce solutions and services.*
Tel: 416-597-8889
Fax: 416-597-2345
www.cyberplex.com
Rev: $6
Emp: 70
NAICS: 454111, 541511

CYBERPLEX INC.
7000 North Mopac, Ste. 150, Austin, Texas 78731
CEO: Paul Saper, VP
Bus: *Provides web site design and marketing and e-commerce solutions and services.*
Tel: (512) 795-3095
Fax: (512) 343-6175
%FO: 100

CYBERPLEX INC.
1870 The Exchange, Ste. 100, Atlanta, Georgia 30339
CEO: Paul Saper
Bus: *Provides web site design and marketing and e-commerce solutions and services.*
Tel: (770) 850-8500
Fax: (770) 951-7008
%FO: 100

● **DALSA CORPORATION**
605 McMurray Rd., Waterloo ON N2V 2E9, Canada
CEO: Savvas Chamberlain, Chmn. & CEO
Bus: *Silicon chips and digital camera components manufacture.*
Tel: 519-886-6000
Fax: 519-886-8023
www.dalsa.com
Rev: $106
Emp: 775
NAICS: 334413

DALSA CORECO
900 Middlesex Tpke., Bldg. B, Billerica, Massachusetts 01821
CEO: Keith Reuben
Bus: *Software manufacturer.*
Tel: (978) 670-2000
Fax: (978) 670-2010
%FO: 100

DALSA CORPORATION
5055 Corporate Plaza Dr., Colorado Springs, Colorado 80919
CEO: David W. Gardner
Bus: *Silicon chips and digital camera components manufacture and sales.*
Tel: (719) 599-7700
Fax: (719) 599-7775
%FO: 100

● **DANFOSS TURBOCOR COMPRESSORS, INC.**
1850 Trans-Canada Hwy., Dorval QC H9P 2N4, Canada
CEO: Joe Orosz, Pres.
Bus: *Oil-free compressors manufacture.*
Tel: 514-421-0523
Fax: 514-421-4277
www.turbocor.com
NAICS: 333415, 333912

Canada

DANFOSS TURBOCOR COMPRESSORS INC.
3120 South Ave., La Crosse, Wisconsin 54601
CEO: Joe Orosz, Pres.
Bus: *Oil-free compressors sales and distribution.*
Tel: (608) 787-8145
Fax: (608) 787-0012
%FO: 100

● **DATAMARK SYSTEMS GROUP INC.**
909 Upton St., LaSalle QC H8R 2V1, Canada
CEO: Jeffrey Zunenshine, Pres.
Bus: *Customized business forms manufacture.*
Tel: 514-367-4468
Fax: 514-663-7720
www.datamark.com
Rev: $88
Emp: 750

NAICS: 323116

DATAMARK SYSTEMS GROUP INC.
2305 President's Dr., Salt Lake City, Utah 84160
CEO: Rod Hadean
Bus: *Customized business forms manufacture and sales.*
Tel: (801) 886-0102
Fax: (801) 886-0102
%FO: 100

DATAMARK SYSTEMS GROUP INC.
11011 King St., Overland Park, Kansas 66210
CEO:
Bus: *Customized business forms manufacture and sales.*
Tel: (913) 338-0070
Fax: (913) 338-0075
%FO: 100

● **DATAMIRROR CORPORATION**
3100 Steeles Avenue East, Ste. 700, Markham ON L3R 8T3, Canada
CEO: Nigel W. Stokes, CEO
Bus: *Mfr. database software.*
Tel: 905-425-0310
Fax: 905-415-0340
www.datamirror.com
Rev: $43
Emp: 232

NAICS: 511210

DATAMIRROR CORPORATION
5000 Birch St., Suite 3000, Newport Beach, California 92660
CEO: Alex Rodriduez
Bus: *Mfr. database software.*
Tel: (949) 476-3638
Fax: (949) 752-2160
%FO: 100

DATAMIRROR CORPORATION
1600 Golf Rd., Ste. 1200, Rolling Meadows, Illinois 60008
CEO: P. Kirk Dixon
Bus: *Mfr. database software.*
Tel: (847) 981-5066
Fax: (847) 981-5061
%FO: 100

DATAMIRROR CORPORATION
3350 Riverwood Pkwy., Ste. 1900, Atlanta, Georgia 30339
CEO: Stewart A. Ritchie
Bus: *Mfr. database software.*
Tel: (630) 573-2927
Fax: (630) 954-0650
%FO: 100

DATAMIRROR CORPORATION
90 Park Ave., 16/F, New York, New York 10021
CEO: Samuel Webster, Mgr.
Bus: *Mfr. database software.*
Tel: (212) 984-0608
Fax: (212) 351-5098
%FO: 100

- **DATAWAVE SYSTEMS, INC.**
  13575 Commerce Pkwy., Ste. 110, Richmond BC V6V 2L1, Canada
  CEO: Josh Emanuel, CEO   Tel: 604-295-1800   Rev: $18
  Bus: *Engaged in merchandising of prepaid phone cards.* Fax: 604-874-1503   Emp: 80
           www.datawave.ca
  NAICS: 517310

      DATAWAVE SYSTEMS, INC.
      625 West Ridge Pike, Ste. C106, Conshohocken, Pennsylvania 19428
      CEO: David C. Bryan, VP   Tel: (610) 825-6224   %FO: 100
      Bus: *Engaged in merchandising of prepaid phone* Fax: (610) 825-9266
          cards.

- **DAVIES WARD PHILLIPS & VINEBERG LLP**
  1 First Canadian Place, 44th Fl., Toronto ON M5X 1B1, Canada
  CEO: William O'Reilly, CEO   Tel: 416-863-0900
  Bus: *International law firm.*   Fax: 416-863-5573   Emp: 240
           www.dwpv.com
  NAICS: 541110

      DAVIES WARD PHILLIPS & VINEBERG LLP
      625 Madison Ave., 12/F, New York, New York 10022
      CEO: Steven H. Levin, Prtn.   Tel: (212) 308-8866   %FO: 100
      Bus: *International law firm.*   Fax: (212) 308-0132

- **DECTRON INTERNATIONALE INC.**
  4300 Poirier Boulevard, Montreal QC H4R 2C5, Canada
  CEO: Ness Lakdawala, Chmn. & Pres. & CEO   Tel: 514-334-9609   Rev: $37
  Bus: *Dehumidification, air-conditioning and refrigeration* Fax: 514-334-9184   Emp: 500
      product manufacture.   www.dectron.com
  NAICS: 333412, 333415, 423730

      DECTRON INTERNATIONALE INC.
      10935 Crabapple Rd., 202-B, Roswell, Georgia 30075
      CEO: Brian Monk   Tel: (770) 649-0102   %FO: 100
      Bus: *Refrigeration and air-conditioning product* Fax: (770) 649-0243
          manufacture and sales.

      INTERNATIONAL WATER MAKERS, INC.
      1639 W McNab Rd., Pompano Beach, Florida 33069
      CEO: Tel: (954) 783-3900   %FO: 100
      Bus: *Air conditioning services.*   Fax: (954) 783-3900

- **DENSIGRAPHIX INC.**
  1100 Parent, Saint-Bruno QC J3V 6L8, Canada
  CEO: Camille Cotran, Chmn. & CEO   Tel: 450-441-1300   Rev: $15
  Bus: *Mfr. parts and supplies for copiers and printers,* Fax: 450-441-1105
      including toner, drums, blades and fuser rollers. www.densi.com
  NAICS: 322233

DENSIGRAPHIX INC.
6030 N. Bailey Ave., Ste.100, Amherst, New York 14226
CEO: John Brohman
Bus: *Mfr. parts and supplies for copiers and printers.*
Tel: (905) 501-9655
Fax: (905) 501-9324
%FO: 100

• **THE DESCARTES SYSTEMS GROUP INC.**
120 Randall Dr., Waterloo ON N2V 1C6, Canada
CEO: Arthur Mesher, CEO
Bus: *Supply chain management software manufacture.*
Tel: 519-746-8110
Fax: 519-747-0082
www.descartes.com
Rev: $46
Emp: 404
NAICS: 511210, 518210, 541511, 541512, 541513, 541519, 611420, 811212, 811213, 811219

DESCARTES SYSTEMS GROUP
Powers Ferry Business Park, 203 Powers Ferry Rd. NW, Bldg. 500, Ste. 510, Atlanta, Georgia 30339
CEO: Bruce Gordon
Bus: *Mfr. supply chain management software.*
Tel: (678) 247-0400
Fax: (678) 247-0400
%FO: 100

DESCARTES SYSTEMS GROUP
200 Hightower Blvd., Pittsburgh, Pennsylvania 15205-1123
CEO: Manuel Pietra, Mgr.
Bus: *Mfr. supply chain management software.*
Tel: (412) 788-2466
Fax: (412) 788-4821
%FO: 100
Emp: 80

• **DIAMOND DISCOVERIES INTERNATIONAL CORPORATION**
750 W. Pender St., Ste. 804, Vancouver BC V6C 2T7, Canada
CEO: John Kowalchuk, CEO
Bus: *Mineral exploration.*
Tel: 514-842-3343
Fax: 514-499-9315
www.diamonddiscoveries.com
Emp: 5
NAICS: 212399, 213115

DIAMOND DISCOVERIES INTERNATIONAL CORPORATION
119 West 23rd St., New York, New York 10011
CEO: Tom Franzone
Bus: *Mineral exploration.*
Tel: (212) 741-8934
Fax: (212) 972-1677
%FO: 100

• **DOFASCO, INC.**
1330 Burlington St. East, Hamilton ON L8N 3J5, Canada
CEO: Donald A. Pether, Pres. & CEO
Bus: *Steel and steel products manufacture.*
Tel: 905-544-3761
Fax: 905-548-4935
www.dofasco.ca
Rev: $2,746
Emp: 8,000
NAICS: 331111, 331210, 331221

DOFASCO MARION
PO Box 588, 689 West Fairground St., Marion, Ohio 43301
CEO: Don A. Pether, Dir.
Bus: *Steel pipe & tubes*
Tel: (740) 382-3979
Fax: (740) 375-2236
Emp: 123

DOFASCO, U.S.A., INC.
26899 Northwest Hwy., Southfield, Michigan 48034
CEO: L. Allan Root, Pres.
Bus: *Mfr./sale steel and steel products.*
Tel: (248) 357-3090
Fax: (248) 357-9888
%FO: 100
Emp: 10

GALLATIN STEEL COMPANY
4831 US Hwy., 42 West, Ghent, Kentucky 41045
CEO: Don B. Daily, Pres.
Bus: *Steel production*

Tel: (859) 567-3100
Fax: (859) 567-3165

%FO: JV
Emp: 380

POWERLASERS
PO Box 939, 2 Kexon Dr., Pioneer, Ohio 43554
CEO: Joe Neri, Pres.
Bus: *Automotive stamping*

Tel: (419) 737-3180
Fax: (419) 737-3181

Emp: 92

• **DOMTAR INC.**
395 de Maisonneuve Blvd. West, Montreal QC H3A 1L6, Canada
CEO: Raymond Royer, CEO
Bus: *Specialty paper manufacture.*

Tel: 800-267-2040
Fax: 800-267-4050
www.domtar.com

Rev: $4,263
Emp: 10,600

NAICS: 322121

DOMTAR INC.
10 Peachtree Place NE, Atlanta, Georgia 30309-3931
CEO: Roger Brear
Bus: *Specialty paper manufacture and sales.*

Tel: (404) 532-1140
Fax: (404) 532-1140

%FO: 100

• **DOREL INDUSTRIES INC.**
1255 Greene Ave., Ste. 300, Montreal QC H3Z 2A4, Canada
CEO: Martin Schwartz, Chmn.
Bus: *Mfr. general household furniture, including juvenile furnishings.*

Tel: 514-523-5701
Fax: 514-523-5701
www.dorel.com

Rev: $1,685
Emp: 4,800

NAICS: 336991, 337122, 337124, 337125, 337129, 337215, 337910

AMERIWOOD INDUSTRIES
305 East South First St., Wright City, Missouri 63390
CEO: Bob Klassen
Bus: *Mfr. household furnishings, including juvenile furniture.*

Tel: (636) 745-3351
Fax: (636) 745-1007

%FO: 100

DOREL JUVENILE GROUP
2525 State St., Columbus, Indiana 47201
CEO: Bruce M. Cazenave, Pres.
Bus: *Mfr. juvenile furniture & vehicles, padded seats.*

Tel: (812) 372-0141
Fax: (812) 372-0911

%FO: 100
Emp: 1,100

DOREL JUVENILE GROUP USA
45 Dan Rd., Canton, Massachusetts 02021
CEO: Bruce M. Cazenave
Bus: *Juvenile furniture manufacture.*

Tel: (781) 364-3297
Fax: (781) 364-3215

%FO: 100

• **EAGLE PRECISION TECHNOLOGIES INC.**
565 West St., PO Box 786, Brantford ON N3T 5R7, Canada
CEO: Douglas W. Boughner, CEO
Bus: *Machinery and equipment manufacture.*

Tel: 519-756-5223
Fax: 519-756-9062
www.eaglept.com

Rev: $26
Emp: 200

NAICS: 333319

EAGLE TECHNOLOGIES SERVICES LTD.
1445 Brookville Way, Ste. D, Indianapolis, Indiana 46239
CEO: Doug Boughner
Bus: *Electronic parts and service manufacture.*
Tel: (317) 308-2600
Fax: (317) 308-2610
%FO: 100

● **EDGETECH SERVICES, INC.**
18 Wynford Drive, Ste. 615, Toronto ON M3C 3S2, Canada
CEO: Xavier Roy, Chmn.
Bus: *IT security services.*
Tel: 416-441-4046
Fax: 416-441-0697
www.mwsp.com
Rev: $2
Emp: 36

NAICS: 541511

EDGETECH CONSULTING, INC.
462 East 17th St., Ste. C#37, Costa Mesa, California 92627
CEO: Steve Norris
Bus: *IT security services.*
Tel: (949) 623-8444
Fax: (949) 623-8444
%FO: 100

● **EICON NETWORKS CORP.**
9800 Cavendish Blvd., Montreal QC H4M 2V9, Canada
CEO: Nick Jensen, CEO
Bus: *Mfr. specialty semiconductors.*
Tel: 514-745-5500
Fax: 514-745-5588
www.eicon.com

NAICS: 334290, 511210

EICON NETWORKS
Parkway Centre II, 2805 N. Dallas Pkwy., Ste. 200, Plano, Texas 75093
CEO: David Brennan, Principal
Bus: *Mfr. specialty semiconductors.*
Tel: (972) 473-4500
Fax: (972) 473-4510
%FO: 100
Emp: 40

● **EIGER TECHNOLOGY, INC.**
330 Bay St., Ste. 602, Toronto ON M5H 2S8, Canada
CEO: Gerry A. Racicot, Pres.
Bus: *Internet capable electronic device manufacture.*
Tel: 416-216-8659
Fax: 416-216-1164
www.eigertechnology.com
Rev: $12
Emp: 82

NAICS: 523999, 525990, 551112

K-TRONIK INDUSTRIES CORP.
290 Vincent Ave., 3/F, Hackensack, New Jersey 07601
CEO: Robert Kimm
Bus: *Internet capable electronic device manufacture and sales.*
Tel: (201) 488-4600
Fax: (201) 488-8480
%FO: 100

● **ELLISDON CONSTRUCTION LTD.**
2045 Oxford St., London ON N5V 1Z7, Canada
CEO: Geoffrey M. Smith, Pres. & CEO
Bus: *Construction management.*
Tel: 770-303-4240
Fax: 770-303-4242
www.ellisdon.com

NAICS: 236220

ELLISDON CONSTRUCTION LTD.
6520 Powers Ferry Rd., Ste. 370, Atlanta, Georgia 30339
CEO: Geoffrey M. Smith, Mgr.
Bus: *Construction management.*
Tel: (770) 303-4240
Fax: (770) 303-4242
%FO: 100

ELLISDON CONSTRUCTION LTD.
21500 Haggerty Rd., Ste. 200, Northville, Michigan 48167
CEO: Matthew Tunnard, VP   Tel: (248) 348-8800   %FO: 100
Bus: *Construction management.*   Fax: (248) 348-1010

● **EMCO LTD.**
1108 Dundas St., London ON N5W 3A7, Canada
CEO: William Ricketts, Pres. & CEO   Tel: 519-645-3900   Rev: $850
Bus: *Mfr. fluid handling systems and equipment.*   Fax: 519-645-2465   Emp: 2,850
    www.emcoltd.com

NAICS: 334513

    METCRAFT INC. (POWER SOAK SYSTEMS)
    13910 Kessler Dr., Grandview, Missouri 64030
    CEO: Pete Corpeny, Pres.   Tel: (816) 761-3250   %FO: 100
    Bus: *Stainless steel, wash tank systems*   Fax: (816) 761-0544   Emp: 60
    manufacture for institutional, and commercial
    markets.

● **EMERA INC.**
1894 Barrington St., PO Box 910, Halifax NS B3J 2W5, Canada
CEO: Christopher G. Huskilson, CEO   Tel: 902-428-6250   Rev: $951
Bus: *Energy services, oil, diesel fuel, gas and*   Fax: 902-428-6181   Emp: 2,359
    www.emera.com

NAICS: 324110

    BANGOR HYDRO ELECTRIC COMPANY
    33 State St., PO Box 932, Bangor, Maine 04401
    CEO: Raymond Robinson, Pres.   Tel: (207) 945-5621   %FO: 100
    Bus: *Provides electrical services.*   Fax: (207) 947-2414

● **EMERGIS INC.**
1000 de Serigny, Longueuil QC J4K 5B1, Canada
CEO: Francois Cote, Pres. & CEO   Tel: 450-928-6000   Rev: $244
Bus: *Software publisher*   Fax: 450-928-6344   Emp: 2,025
    www.emergis.com

NAICS: 511210

    EMERGIS INC.
    1600 International Dr., Ste. 200, McLean, Virginia 22102
    CEO: Tel: (888) 726-8802   %FO: 100
    Bus: *Developer of e-commerce software*   Fax:

● **ENBRIDGE INC.**
3000 Fifth Ave. Place, 425 First Street SW, Calgary AB T2P 3L8, Canada
CEO: Patrick D. Daniel, CEO   Tel: 403-231-3900   Rev: $5,450
Bus: *Crude petroleum pipelines and natural gas*   Fax: 403-231-3920   Emp: 4,185
    distribution and utility.   www.enbridge.com
NAICS: 211112, 486110

ENBRIDGE ENERGY COMPANY, INC.
1100 Louisiana St., Ste. 3300, Houston, Texas 77002-5217
CEO: Larry Springer   Tel: (713) 821-2000   %FO: 100
Bus: *Liquid petroleum and natural gas pipelines*   Fax: (713) 821-2232
     operations.

● **ENCANA CORPORATION**
855 - 2nd St. SW, Ste. 1800, Calgary AB T2P 2S5, Canada
CEO: Gwyn Morgan, Chmn.   Tel: 403-290-2000   Rev: $10,200
Bus: *Engaged in oil exploration and production.*   Fax: 403-290-2950   Emp: 3,850
                                      www.pcp.ca
  NAICS: 211111, 211112

    ENCANA OIL & GAS INC.
    3601 C St., Ste. 1334, Anchorage, Alaska 99503
    CEO: Paul Myers   Tel: (907) 770-3700   %FO: 100
    Bus: *Specialty chemicals and natural gas liquids,*   Fax: (907) 770-3636
        magnesium; operates gas pipelines;
        property development.

    ENCANA OIL & GAS INC.
    950 17th St., Ste. 1700, Denver, Colorado 80202
    CEO: Roger J. Biemans   Tel: (303) 623-2300   %FO: 100
    Bus: *Specialty chemicals and natural gas liquids,*   Fax: (303) 623-2400
        magnesium; operates gas pipelines;
        property development.

● **ENERFLEX SYSTEMS LTD.**
4700 47th St. SE, Calgary AB T2B 3R1, Canada
CEO: J. Blair Goertzen, Pres. & CEO   Tel: 403-236-6800   Rev: $462
Bus: *Oil & Gas Exploration*   Fax: 403-236-6816   Emp: 2,000
                                      www.enerflex.com
  NAICS: 333132

    EFX COMPRESSION USA
    1800 W. Loop S, Ste. 1565, Houston, Texas 77027
    CEO: Thomas D. Gamble, VP North America   Tel: (713) 355-6645   %FO: 100
    Bus: *Oil & Gas Exploration*   Fax: (713) 355-1067

● **ENGHOUSE SYSTEMS LIMITED**
80 Tiverton Court, Ste. 800, Markham ON L3R 0G4, Canada
CEO: Stephen J. Sadler, CEO   Tel: 905-946-3200   Rev: $49
Bus: *GIS software manufacture.*   Fax: 905-946-3201   Emp: 500
                                      www.enghouse.com
  NAICS: 511210

    SYNTELLECT LTD.
    30 Mansell Court, Ste. 10, Roswell, Georgia 30076
    CEO: Steve Dodenhoff   Tel: (678) 256-7737   %FO: 100
    Bus: *Software developer*   Fax: (678) 256-7755

SYNTELLECT LTD.
16610 N. Black Canyon Hwy, Ste.100, Phoenix, Arizona 85053
CEO: Steve Dodenhoff, Pres.　　　　Tel: (602) 789-2800　　　%FO: 100
Bus: *Software developer*　　　　　Fax: (602) 789-2899

• **ENSIGN ENERGY SERVICES INC.**
400 Fifth Avenue SW, Ste. 900, Calgary AB T2P OL6, Canada
CEO: Selby W. Porter, Pres.　　　Tel: 403-262-1361　　　Rev: $879
Bus: *Engaged in oil field services.*　Fax: 403-262-8215　　Emp: 7,300
　　　　　　　　　　　　　　　www.ensigngroup.com
NAICS: 213111, 213112

　CAZA DRILLING
　7001 Charity Ave., Bakersfield, California 93308
　CEO: Terry Ellis　　　　　　Tel: (661) 589-0111　　　%FO: 100
　Bus: *Drilling services.*　　　Fax: (661) 559-0283

　CAZA DRILLING
　1801 Broadway, Ste. 360, Denver, Colorado 80202
　CEO: Steve Grimes, Pres.　　Tel: (303) 292-1206　　　%FO: 100
　Bus: *Drilling services.*　　　Fax: (303) 292-5843

• **EPIC DATA INTERNATIONAL INC.**
6300 River Rd., Richmond BC V6X1X5, Canada
CEO: Peter Murphy, CEO　　　Tel: 604-273-9146　　　Rev: $19
Bus: *Information systems data.*　Fax: 604-273-1830　　Emp: 92
　　　　　　　　　　　　　　　www.epicdata.com
NAICS: 541511, 541519

　EPIC DATA INTERNATIONAL INC.
　1500 Perimeter Pkwy., Ste. 330, Huntsville, Alabama 35806
　CEO: Ralph Yeomans　　　　Tel: (256) 536-0812　　　%FO: 100
　Bus: *Sales support and information.*　Fax: (256) 536-0872

　EPIC DATA INTERNATIONAL INC.
　635 South Cherry Lane, White Settlement, Texas 76108
　CEO: Greg Watkin　　　　　Tel: (817) 367-0805　　　%FO: 100
　Bus: *Sales support and information.*　Fax: (817) 367-3946

• **EXCO TECHNOLOGIES LIMITED**
130 Spy Court, 2nd Fl., Markham ON L3R 5H6, Canada
CEO: Brian A. Robbins, Pres. & CEO　Tel: 905-477-3065　Rev: $135
Bus: *Casting and extrusion technology for automobile*　Fax: 905-477-2449　Emp: 2,125
　industry.　　　　　　　　　www.excocorp.com
NAICS: 333513

　POLYTECH NETTING INDUSTRIEST
　631 East Big Beaver Rd., Troy, Michigan 48083
　CEO: Don Moore　　　　　Tel: (248) 680-9020　　　%FO: 100
　Bus: *Casting and extrusion technology for*　Fax: (248) 680-9024
　　automobile industry.

Canada

- **EXFO ELECTRO-OPTICAL ENGINEERING INC.**
  465 Godin Avenue, Vanier QC G1M 3G7, Canada
  CEO: Germain Lamonde, CEO
  Bus: *Fiber optic testing.*

  Tel: 418-683-0211
  Fax: 418-683-2170
  www.exfo.com

  Rev: $75
  Emp: 600

  NAICS: 335921

  EXFO AMERICA
  4275 Kellway Circle, Ste. 122, Addison, Texas 75001
  CEO: Benoit Fleury
  Bus: *Fiber optic testing.*

  Tel: (972) 836-0100
  Fax: (972) 836-0164

  %FO: 100

- **EXTENDICARE INC.**
  3000 Steeles Avenue East, Markham ON L3R 9W2, Canada
  CEO: Mel A. Rhinelander, Pres. & CEO
  Bus: *Operators of long-term care, medical specialty
  services, including sub acute care and
  rehabilitative therapy services, medical supplies
  and services.*

  Tel: 905-470-4000
  Fax: 905-470-5588
  www.extendicare.com

  Rev: $1,456
  Emp: 35,800

  NAICS: 621498, 621610, 623110, 623311, 623312, 623990, 624110, 624120, 624190, 624310

  ALLEN HOUSE
  1406 E. 19th, Atlantic, Iowa 50022
  CEO: Linda Judkins
  Bus: *Long-term care and assisted living facilities.*

  Tel: (712) 243-3820
  Fax: (712) 243-6707

  %FO: 100

  ARBORS AT NEW CASTLE
  32 Buena Vista Dr., New Castle, Delaware 19720
  CEO: Donna Winegar
  Bus: *Long-term care and assisted living facilities.*

  Tel: (302) 328-2580
  Fax: (302) 328-2036

  %FO: 100

  AURORA HOUSE
  675 W. Broadway Rd., Apache Junction, Arizona 85220
  CEO: Joan Lumbard
  Bus: *Long-term care and assisted living facilities.*

  Tel: (480) 288-1791
  Fax: (480) 671-9660

  %FO: 100

  BELL OAKS TERRACE
  4200 Wyntree Dr., Newburgh, Indiana 47630
  CEO: Carol Felger
  Bus: *Long-term care and assisted living facilities.*

  Tel: (812) 858-0488
  Fax: (812) 858-3762

  %FO: 100

  CLARK HOUSE
  1401 N. Polk St., Moscow, Idaho 83843
  CEO: Carol Vandal-Carroll
  Bus: *Long-term care and assisted living facilities.*

  Tel: (208) 882-3438
  Fax: (208) 882-3369

  %FO: 100

  DRESHER HILL EXTENDICARE INC.
  1390 Camp Hill Rd., Fort Washington, Pennsylvania 19034
  CEO: Terry Tressler
  Bus: *Long-term care and assisted living facilities.*

  Tel: (215) 641-1710
  Fax: (215) 641-1710

  %FO: 100

EXTENDICARE FACILITIES INC.
950 S. Saint Andrews St., Dothan, Alabama 36301
CEO: David Dennis
Bus: *Long-term care and assisted living facilities.*
Tel: (334) 793-1177
Fax: (334) 793-1177
%FO: 100

EXTENDICARE FACILITIES INC.
111 W. Michigan St., Milwaukee, Wisconsin 53203
CEO: Bob Beyer, COO
Bus: *Long-term care and assisted living facilities.*
Tel: (414) 908-8000
Fax: (414) 908-8059
%FO: 100

THE HIGHLANDS
225 Norfleet Dr., Somerset, Kentucky 42501
CEO: Deborah Westfall
Bus: *Long-term care and assisted living facilities.*
Tel: (606) 678-5865
Fax: (606) 451-1216
%FO: 100

● **FAIRFAX FINANCIAL HOLDINGS LIMITED**
95 Wellington St. West, Ste. 800, Toronto ON M5J 2N7, Canada
CEO: V. Prem Watsa, Chmn. & CEO
Bus: *Engaged in life, property and casualty insurance and investment management.*
NAICS: 523930, 524113, 524126
Tel: 416-367-4941
Fax: 416-367-4946
www.fairfax.ca
Rev: $5,793
Emp: 9,000

CRUM & FORSTER HOLDINGS INC.
1600 Market St., 39/F, Philadelphia, Pennsylvania 19103
CEO: Jim Avato
Bus: *Engaged in property and casualty insurance.*
Tel: (215) 982-3500
Fax: (215) 982-3500
%FO: 100

CRUM & FORSTER HOLDINGS INC.
7000 Central Pkwy., Ste. 950, Atlanta, Georgia 30328
CEO: Lou Snage
Bus: *Engaged in property and casualty insurance.*
Tel: (770) 990-2071
Fax: (770) 990-2071
%FO: 100

CRUM & FORSTER HOLDINGS INC.
60 State St., Boston, Massachusetts 02109
CEO: Eileen Currie
Bus: *Engaged in property and casualty insurance.*
Tel: (617) 406-3000
Fax: (617) 406-3009
%FO: 100

CRUM & FORSTER HOLDINGS INC.
One Market, Ste. 310, San Francisco, California 94105
CEO: Joe Dillon
Bus: *Engaged in property and casualty insurance.*
Tel: (415) 541-3200
Fax: (415) 541-3201
%FO: 100

CRUM & FORSTER HOLDINGS INC.
10 South Wacker Dr., Ste. 2220, Chicago, Illinois 60606
CEO: Michael Poehlmann
Bus: *Engaged in property and casualty insurance.*
Tel: (312) 596-6610
Fax: (312) 596-6610
%FO: 100

CRUM & FORSTER HOLDINGS INC.
725 S. Figueroa ST., Ste. 2300, Los Angeles, California 90017
CEO: Mark Owens
Bus: *Engaged in property and casualty insurance.*
Tel: (213) 797-3101
Fax: (213) 797-3139
%FO: 100

Canada

CRUM & FORSTER HOLDINGS, INC.
305 Madison Ave., Morristown, New Jersey 07960
CEO: Nikolas Antonopoulos, CEO
Bus: *Engaged in insurance services.*
Tel: (973) 490-6600
Fax: (973) 490-6600
%FO: 100

FAIRMONT SPECIALTY INSURANCE COMPANY
PO Box 2807, Houston, Texas 77252
CEO: Linda Jordan, Pres.
Bus: *Engaged in property and casualty insurance.*
Tel: (713) 954-8100
Fax: (713) 954-8335
%FO: 100

FALCON INSURANCE AGENCY
PO Box 92409, Austin, Texas 78709-2409
CEO: John R. Allen
Bus: *Aviation insurance.*
Tel: (512) 891-8473
Fax: (512) 891-8473
%FO: 100

HUDSON INSURANCE COMPANY
140 Broadway, 39/F, New York, New York 10005
CEO: Chris Gallagher, Pres.
Bus: *Insurance.*
Tel: (212) 978-2800
Fax: (212) 344-2973
%FO: 100

KAYE OF CONNECTICUT, DIV. HUB
1221 Post Rd. East, Westport, Connecticut 06880
CEO: Jeff Rubin
Bus: *Insurance services.*
Tel: (203) 291-1800
Fax: (203) 291-1800

ODYSSEY AMERICA REINSURANCE CORPORATION
1200 Brickell Ave., Miami, Florida 33131
CEO: Arturo E. Falcon
Bus: *Engaged in reinsurance.*
Tel: (305) 577-4244
Fax: (305) 577-9895
%FO: 100

ODYSSEY AMERICA US CASUALTY TREATY
300 First Stamford Place, Stamford, Connecticut 06902
CEO: Brian D. Quinn
Bus: *US casualty treaty.*
Tel: (203) 977-8000
Fax: (203) 356-0196
%FO: 100

ODYSSEY RE FACULTATIVE RISK
22 Cortlandt St., 18/F, New York, New York 10007
CEO: Christopher T. Suarez, SVP
Bus: *Engaged in property and casualty insurance.*
Tel: (212) 978-2700
Fax: (212) 385-2795
%FO: 100

ODYSSEY RE HOLDINGS CORP.
140 Broadway, 39/F, New York, New York 10005
CEO: Andrew A. Barnard
Bus: *Insurance.*
Tel: (212) 978-4700
Fax: (212) 432-0145
%FO: 100

ODYSSEY RE HOLDINGS INC.
300 First Stamford Place, Stamford, Connecticut 06902
CEO: Andrew A. Barnard, CEO
Bus: *Engaged in treaty reinsurance.*
Tel: (203) 977-8000
Fax: (203) 940-8183
%FO: 100

- **FAIRMONT HOTELS & RESORTS INC.**
Canadian Pacific Tower, 100 Wellington St. West, Ste. 1600, Toronto ON M5K 1B7, Canada
CEO: William R. Fatt, CEO & Mng. Dir.   Tel: 416-874-2600   Rev: $769
Bus: *Management of luxury hotels and resorts.*   Fax: 416-874-2601   Emp: 30,000
                                                www.fairmont.com

NAICS: 525930, 721110

    FAIRMONT HOTELS & RESORTS INC.
    950 Mason St., San Francisco, California 94108
    CEO: Ed Mace, Partner   Tel: (415) 772-5000   %FO: 100
    Bus: *Engaged in hotel management.*   Fax: (415) 772-5013   Emp: 2,645

    FAIRMONT OLYMPIC HOTEL
    411 University St., Seattle, Washington 98101
    CEO: Dennis Clark, Gen. Mgr.   Tel: (206) 621-1700   %FO: 100
    Bus: *Luxury hotel.*   Fax: (206) 682-9633   Emp: 500

    THE FAIRMONT CHICAGO
    200 N. Columbus Dr., Chicago, Illinois 60601
    CEO: Kevin Frid, Gen. Mgr.   Tel: (312) 819-7464   %FO: 100
    Bus: *Engaged in hotel management.*   Fax: Emp: 730

    THE FAIRMONT COPLEY PLAZA
    138 St. James Ave., Boston, Massachusetts 02116
    CEO: Jon Crellin, Gen. Mgr.   Tel: (617) 267-5300   %FO: 100
    Bus: *Engaged in hotel management.*   Fax: (617) 247-6681   Emp: 350

    THE FAIRMONT DALLAS
    1717 North Akard St., Dallas, Texas 75201
    CEO: Frank Naboulsi, Gen. Mgr.   Tel: (214) 720-2020   %FO: 100
    Bus: *Engaged in hotel management.*   Fax: (214) 720-7403   Emp: 500

    THE FAIRMONT KANSAS CITY AT THE PLAZA
    401 NW Parkway, Kansas City, Missouri 64150
    CEO: Michael Pendergast, Gen. Mgr.   Tel: (816) 756-1500   %FO: 100
    Bus: *Engaged in hotel management.*   Fax: (816) 303-0734   Emp: 120

    THE FAIRMONT KEA LANI
    4100 Wailea Alanui Dr., Kihei, Hawaii 96753
    CEO: Bill Fatt, Pres.   Tel: (808) 875-4100   %FO: 100
    Bus: *Engaged in hotel management.*   Fax: (808) 875-1200   Emp: 520

    THE FAIRMONT MIRAMAR HOTEL
    101 Wilshire Blvd., Santa Monica, California 90401
    CEO: Matt Di Napoli, Pres.   Tel: (310) 576-7777   %FO: 100
    Bus: *Engaged in hotel management.*   Fax: (310) 458-7912   Emp: 260

    THE FAIRMONT NEW ORLEANS
    123 Baronne St., New Orleans, Louisiana 70112
    CEO: Ray Tackaberry, Mgr.   Tel: (504) 529-7111   %FO: 100
    Bus: *Engaged in hotel management.*   Fax: (504) 529-4764   Emp: 500

THE FAIRMONT SAN JOSE
170 South Market St., San Jose, California 95113
CEO: Edward Mace, CEO
Bus: *Engaged in hotel management.*
Tel: (408) 998-1900
Fax: (408) 287-1648
%FO: 100
Emp: 500

THE FAIRMONT SCOTTSDALE PRINCESS
7575 East Princess Dr., Scottsdale, Arizona 85255
CEO: Kiaran MacDonald, Gen. Mgr.
Bus: *Engaged in hotel management.*
Tel: (480) 585-4848
Fax: (480) 585-0086
%FO: 100
Emp: 1,150

THE PLAZA
Fifth Ave. at Central Park South, New York, New York 10019
CEO: Gary Schweikert, Mgr.
Bus: *Engaged in hotel management.*
Tel: (212) 759-3000
Fax: (212) 546-5324
%FO: 100

● **FALCONBRIDGE LIMITED**
BCE Place, 181 Bay St., Ste. 200, Toronto ON M5J 2T3, Canada
CEO: Derek G. Pannell, CEO
Bus: *Nickel mining company.*
Tel: 416-982-7111
Fax: 416-982-7423
www.falconbridge.com
Rev: $6,978
Emp: 14,500
NAICS: 212234

FALCONBRIDGE US, INC.
4955 Steubenville Pike, Ste. 245, Pittsburgh, Pennsylvania 15205
CEO: Thomas Aurila, Pres.
Bus: *Nickel mining.*
Tel: (412) 787-0220
Fax: (412) 787-0287
%FO: 100

● **FANEUIL GROUP_ THE**
363 Broadway, Ste.1600, Winnipeg MB R3C 3N9, Canada
CEO: Brian Cornick, CEO
Bus: *Market research*
Tel: 204-934-1900
Fax: 204-987-9310
www.faneuil.com
Rev: $45
Emp: 1,700
NAICS: 541910

FANEUIL GROUP_ THE
1 Bridge St., Ste.101, Newton, Massachusetts 02458
CEO: Brian Cornick
Bus: *Market research*
Tel: (617) 742-4888
Fax: (617) 742-3666
%FO: 100

● **FARMS.COM LTD.**
148 Fullerton St., Ste. 1400, London ON N6A 5P3, Canada
CEO: J. Douglas Maus, Pres. & CEO
Bus: *Software tool and Internet site.*
Tel: 519-438-5729
Fax: 519-438-3152
www.farms.com
NAICS: 511210, 516110

PIGCHAMP INC.
426 South 17th St., Ames, Iowa 50010
CEO: Joe Dales
Bus: *Software tool and Internet site.*
Tel: (800) 672-7187
Fax: (515) 233-7187
%FO: 100

- **FINANCIAL MODELS COMPANY INC.**
  5255 Orbitor Dr., Mississauga ON L4W 5M6, Canada
  CEO: Normand A. Boulanger, Pres. & CEO   Tel: 905-629-8000   Rev: $54
  Bus: *Investment management software and*   Fax: 905-629-0022   Emp: 385
  professional management services.   www.fmco.com
  NAICS: 511210

      FINANCIAL MODELS COMPANY INC.
      477 Madison Ave., 3/F, New York, New York 10022
      CEO: Stamos Katotakis, Pres.   Tel: (212) 319-9730   %FO: 100
      Bus: *Investment management software and*   Fax: (212) 319-9739   Emp: 50
      professional management services.

      FINANCIAL MODELS COMPANY INC.
      1201 Camino Del Mar, Del Mar, California 92014
      CEO: Stamos Katotakis, Pres.   Tel: (858) 259-4308   %FO: 100
      Bus: *Investment management software and*   Fax: (858) 259-4309
      professional management services.

- **FINCENTRIC CORPORATION**
  13571 Commerce Pkwy., Ste. 200, Richmond BC V6V 2R2, Canada
  CEO: Robert Nygren, Pres. & CEO   Tel: 604-278-6470   Rev: $40
  Bus: *Financial software manufacturer.*   Fax: 604-214-4900   Emp: 275
      www.fincentric.com
  NAICS: 511210

      FINCENTRIC CORPORATION
      1800 Pembroke Dr., Ste. 300, Orlando, Florida 32810
      CEO: Jack Allison, SVP   Tel: (407) 667-3429   %FO: 100
      Bus: *Mfr. of financial software.*   Fax: (407) 667-3430

      FINCENTRIC CORPORATION
      1200 Route 22 East, Bridgewater, New Jersey 08807
      CEO: Alice D. Laberge, CEO   Tel: (908) 253-3599   %FO: 100
      Bus: *Financial software manufacture.*   Fax: (908) 203-4706

- **FIRST CAPITAL REALTY INC.**
  Canada Trust Tower, 161 Bay Street, Ste. 2820, Toronto ON M5J 1S1, Canada
  CEO: Dori J. Segal, Pres. & CEO   Tel: 416-504-4114   Rev: $184
  Bus: *Operates shopping centers and retail properties.*   Fax: 416-941-1655   Emp: 70
      www.firstcapitalrealty.ca
  NAICS: 531312

      EQUITY ONE INC.
      1696 NE Miami Gardens Dr., Ste. 1, North Miami Beach, Florida 33179
      CEO: Howard Sipzner, EVP   Tel: (305) 944-7988   %FO: 100
      Bus: *Operates shopping centers and retail*   Fax: (305) 944-7986
      properties.

- **FIRSTSERVICE CORPORATION**
  1140 Bay St., Ste. 4000, Toronto ON M5S 2B4, Canada
  CEO: Jay S. Hennick, CEO   Tel: 416-960-9500   Rev: $812
  Bus: *Residential property management; commercial real* Fax: 416-960-5333   Emp: 11,000
       estate; swimming pool maintenance, landscaping, www.firstservice.com
       painting and property inspection.
  NAICS: 238320, 335999, 531110, 531190, 531312, 531390, 561612, 561730

  CALIFORNIA CLOSETS COMPANY, INC.
  1000 Fourth St., Ste. 800, San Rafael, California 94901
  CEO: Anthony Vidergauz, Pres.   Tel: (415) 256-8500   %FO: 100
  Bus: *Mfr. closet shelving systems and organizing* Fax: (415) 256-8501
       systems.

  COLLEGE PRO PAINTERS LTD.
  71 Second Ave., 2/F, Waltham, Massachusetts 02451
  CEO: Richard Oller, Pres.   Tel: (781) 250-0802   %FO: 100
  Bus: *Engaged in painting services.*   Fax: (781) 250-0817

  COLLIERS INTERNATIONAL PROPERTY CONSULTANTS
  601 Union St., Ste. 5300, Seattle, Washington 98101
  CEO: Morris Groberman, VP   Tel: (206) 223-0866   %FO: 100
  Bus: *Commercial real estate management.*   Fax: (206) 223-1427

  COLLIERS INTERNATIONAL PROPERTY CONSULTANTS
  50 Milk St., 20/F, Boston, Massachusetts 02109
  CEO: Margaret Wigglesworth, Pres.   Tel: (617) 722-0221   %FO: 100
  Bus: *Commercial real estate management.*   Fax: (617) 722-0224

  COLLIERS INTERNATIONAL PROPERTY CONSULTANTS
  444 South Flower St., Ste. 2200, Los Angeles, California 90071
  CEO: Bill DuBrowa, mgr   Tel: (213) 627-1214   %FO: 100
  Bus: *Commercial real estate management.*   Fax: (213) 627-2700

  FLOOR COVERINGS INTERNATIONAL
  200 Technology Ct., Ste. 1200, Smyrna, Georgia 30082
  CEO: Thomas W. Wood, Pres.   Tel: (770) 874-7600   %FO: 100
  Bus: *Floor coverings and installation.*   Fax: (770) 874-7605

  PAUL DAVIS RESTORATION
  One Independent Dr., Ste. 2300, Jacksonville, Florida 32202
  CEO: Scott Baker, Pres.   Tel: (904) 737-2779   %FO: 100
  Bus: *Residential and commercial loss mitigation,* Fax: (904) 737-4204
       reconstruction and restoration services.

  PILLAR TO POST INC.
  13902 North Dale Mabry, Ste. 300, Tampa, Florida 33618
  CEO: Dan Steward, Pres.   Tel: (813) 962-4461   %FO: 100
  Bus: *Home inspection franchise.*   Fax: (813) 963-5301

  STAINED GLASS OVERLAY, INC.
  1827 North Case St., Orange, California 92865
  CEO: Cathy Cooper, Pres.   Tel: (714) 974-6124   %FO: 100
  Bus: *Mfr. stained glass.*   Fax: (714) 974-6529

THE WENTWORTH GROUP
901 South Tropper Rd., Norristown, Pennsylvania 19403-2312
CEO: David Readinger, Pres.   Tel: (610) 650-0600   %FO: 100
Bus: *Engaged in real estate management,*   Fax: (610) 650-0700
      marketing, financial and consulting

- **FLINT ENERGY SERVICES LTD.**
300-5th Ave. SW, Ste. 700, Calgary AB T2P 3C4, Canada
CEO: William J. Lingard, Pres. & CEO   Tel: 403-218-7100   Rev: $503
Bus: *Oil & Gas operations support*   Fax: 403-215-5445
                                                www.flint-energy.com
NAICS: 213112, 333132

FLINT ENERGY SERVICES LTD.
Box 368, 1409 W. Stovall Rd., Wilburton, Oklahoma 74578
CEO: Ronnie Wynn   Tel: (918) 465-5684   %FO: 100
Bus: *Oil & gas operations support.*   Fax: (918) 465-3725

FLINT ENERGY SERVICES LTD.
One Memorial Place, Ste. 500, 7633 East 63rd Pl., Tulsa, Oklahoma 74133
CEO: Paul Boechler   Tel: (918) 294-3030   %FO: 100
Bus: *Oil & gas operations support.*   Fax: (918) 307-8960

FLINT ENERGY SERVICES LTD.
2180 Renauna, Casper, Wyoming 82601
CEO: Pat Keefe   Tel: (307) 237-8345   %FO: 100
Bus: *Oil & gas operations support.*   Fax: (307) 234-1530

FLINT ENERGY SERVICES LTD.
1 Memorial Place, 7633 E. 63rd Pl., Ste. 500, Tulsa, Oklahoma 74133
CEO: Paul Boechler, Pres.   Tel: (918) 294-3030   %FO: 100
Bus: *Oil & gas operations support.*   Fax: (918) 307-8960

FLINT ENERGY SERVICES LTD.
1391 Denver Ave., Fort Lupton, Colorado 80621
CEO: Tom Hogelin   Tel: (303) 857-2791   %FO: 100
Bus: *Oil & gas operations support.*   Fax: (303) 857-2791

FLINT ENERGY SERVICES LTD.
2 County Rd., 5569, Farmington, New Mexico 87401
CEO: Lloyd Stewart   Tel: (505) 325-5081   %FO: 100
Bus: *Oil & gas operations support.*   Fax: (505) 326-0371

FLINT ENERGY SERVICES LTD.
1700 W. Seven Mile Rd., Mission, Texas 78572
CEO: Dustin Roach   Tel: (956) 585-9779   %FO: 100
Bus: *Oil & gas operations support.*   Fax: (956) 585-9694

FLINT ENERGY SERVICES LTD.
PO Box 248, Boulder, Wyoming 82923
CEO: Paul Boechler   Tel: (307) 537-3225   %FO: 100
Bus: *Oil & gas operations support.*   Fax: (307) 537-3228

FLINT ENERGY SERVICES LTD.
Box 2049, Kilgore, Texas 75663
CEO: Wesley Mahone
Bus: *Oil & gas operations support.*
Tel: (903) 983-1486
Fax: (903) 984-2383
%FO: 100

FLINT ENERGY SERVICES LTD.
341 Interstate 45, Fairfield, Texas 75840
CEO: Brenda Ferguson
Bus: *Oil & gas operations support.*
Tel: (903) 389-8716
Fax: (903) 389-7495
%FO: 100

FLINT ENERGY SERVICES LTD.
1908A Chico Highway, Bridgeport, Texas 76426-2222
CEO: Paul Boechler
Bus: *Oil & gas operations support.*
Tel: (940) 683-4181
Fax: (940) 683-3710
%FO: 100

FLINT ENERGY SERVICES LTD.
Box 249, Rock Springs, Wyoming 82902
CEO: Paul Boechler
Bus: *Oil & gas operations support.*
Tel: (307) 362-0300
Fax: (307) 362-0400
%FO: 100

FLINT ENERGY SERVICES LTD.
Sub. District of Farmington, PO Box 739, Ignacio, Colorado 81137
CEO: Kenny Raines
Bus: *Oil & gas operations support.*
Tel: (970) 563-0489
Fax: (970) 247-2413
%FO: 100

FLINT ENERGY SERVICES LTD.
Box 145, 1391 Denver Ave., Ft. Lupton, Colorado 80621
CEO: Tom Hogelin
Bus: *Oil & gas operations support.*
Tel: (303) 857-2791
Fax: (303) 892-1820
%FO: 100

FLINT ENERGY SERVICES LTD.
PO Box 766, 1629 Airport Road, Rifle, Colorado 81650
CEO: Ken Hale
Bus: *Oil & gas operations support.*
Tel: (970) 625-4265
Fax: (970) 625-4268
%FO: 100

FLINT ENERGY SERVICES LTD.
Box 1147, Odessa, Texas 79760
CEO: Jeffe Sinney
Bus: *Oil & gas operations support.*
Tel: (432) 332-0687
Fax: (432) 332-3603
%FO: 100

● **FOUR SEASONS HOTELS**
1165 Leslie St., Toronto ON M3C 2K8, Canada
CEO: Isadore Sharp, Chmn. & CEO
Bus: *First class hotel and resort chain.*
Tel: 416-449-1750
Fax: 416-441-4374
www.fourseasons.com
Rev: $190
Emp: 27,720

NAICS: 721110

FOUR SEASONS & REGENT HOTELS
2777 Stemmons Freeway, Ste. 1632, Dallas, Texas 75207
CEO: Craig Reid
Bus: *Worldwide sales office.*
Tel: (214) 634-7200
Fax: (214) 634-7208

FOUR SEASONS & REGENT HOTELS
505 Park Ave., 6/F, New York, New York 10022
CEO: Rene Beauchamp
Bus: *Worldwide sales office.*
Tel: (212) 980-0101
Fax: (212) 980-8270

FOUR SEASONS & REGENT HOTELS
350 South Beverly Dr., Ste. 220, Beverly Hills, California 90212-4814
CEO: Michael Erickson
Bus: *Worldwide sales office.*
Tel: (310) 286-7545
Fax: (310) 274-2620

FOUR SEASONS HOTELS
1025 Thomas Jefferson St., NW, Ste. 306-E, Washington, District of Columbia 20007
CEO: Christopher Hunsberger
Bus: *Worldwide sales office.*
Tel: (202) 333-7141
Fax: (202) 337-8035

FOUR SEASONS REGENT HOTELS & RESORTS
75 Fourteenth St., Atlanta, Georgia 30309
CEO: Thomas Hubler
Bus: *Worldwide sales office.*
Tel: (404) 249-1580
Fax: (404) 249-7226

FOUR SEASONS RESORTS & HOTELS
900 North Michigan Ave., Ste. 804, Chicago, Illinois 60611
CEO: Thomas Hubler
Bus: *Worldwide sales office.*
Tel: (312) 944-4949
Fax: (312) 944-6798

FOUR SEASONS RESORTS & HOTELS
690 Newport Center Dr., Newport Beach, California 92660
CEO: Carrie Olson
Bus: *Worldwide sales office.*
Tel: (949) 759-0808
Fax: (949) 759-0568

• **FPI LTD. (FISHERY PRODUCTS INTERNATIONAL)**
PO Box 550, St. Johns NF A1C 5L1, Canada
CEO: Derrick H. Rowe, CEO
Bus: *Harvesting, processing and global sourcing of seafood.*
Tel: 709-570-0000
Fax: 709-570-0479
www.fpil.com
NAICS: 311712

OCEAN CUISINE INTERNATIONAL
18 Electronics Ave., Danvers, Massachusetts 01923
CEO: Kevin Cronan, Dir.
Bus: *Supplies frozen seafood products.*
Tel: (978) 777-2660
Fax: (978) 777-7458
%FO: 100

• **FRASER MILNER CASGRAIN LLP**
1 First Canadian Place, Toronto ON M5X 1B2, Canada
CEO: Chris Pinnington, Mng. Prtn.
Bus: *Full service law firm.*
Tel: 416-863-4511
Fax: 416-863-4592
www.fmc-law.com
Emp: 1,000
NAICS: 541110

FRASER MILNER CASGRAIN LLP
1 Rockefeller Plaza, Ste. 1528, New York, New York 10020
CEO: Richard A. Scott
Bus: *Full service law firm.*
Tel: (212) 218-2995
Fax: (212) 218-2972
%FO: 100

- **FREEBALANCE, INC.**
1101 Prince of Wales Drive, Ste. 210, Ottawa ON K2C 3W7, Canada
CEO: Bruce Lazenby, Pres. & CEO　　　　Tel: 613-236-5150　　　Rev: $7
Bus: *Financial management software.*　　　Fax: 613-236-7785　　　Emp: 60
　　　　　　　　　　　　　　　　　　　　　www.freebalance.com
NAICS: 511210

　　FREEBALANCE, INC.
　　1655 N. Fort Myer Dr., Ste. 700, Rosslyn, Virginia 22209
　　CEO: Bruce Lazenby　　　　　　　　Tel: (703) 351-5247　　　%FO: 100
　　Bus: *Financial management software.*　Fax: (703) 351-5293

- **GAZ METROPOLITAN AND COMPANY, LIMITED PARTNERSHIP**
1717 du Havre St., Montreal QC H2K 2X3, Canada
CEO: Robert Tessier, Pres. & CEO　　　Tel: 514-598-3444　　　Rev: $1,800
Bus: *Natural Gas Distribution*　　　　　Fax: 514-598-3144　　　Emp: 1,500
　　　　　　　　　　　　　　　　　　　　www.gazmet.com
NAICS: 221210, 486210

　　VERMONT GAS SYSTEMS
　　165 Lake St., Saint Albans, Vermont 05478
　　CEO: A. Donald Gilbert　　　　　　　Tel: (802) 524-6559　　　%FO: 100
　　Bus: *Natural gas distribution*　　　　Fax:

　　VERMONT GAS SYSTEMS
　　PO Box 467, Burlington, Vermont 05402-0467
　　CEO: Scott Scholten　　　　　　　　Tel: (802) 863-4511　　　%FO: 100
　　Bus: *Natural gas distribution*　　　　Fax:

- **GEAC COMPUTER CORPORATION LTD.**
11 Allstate Parkway, Ste. 300, Markham ON L3R 9T8, Canada
CEO: Charles S. Jones, Pres. & CEO　　Tel: 905-475-0525　　　Rev: $444
Bus: *Automation systems manufacture software for*　Fax: 905-475-3847　　Emp: 250
　　　diverse industries and services.　　www.geac.com
NAICS: 511210

　　GEAC
　　13831 NW Freeway, Ste. 550, Houston, Texas 77040
　　CEO: Mike Greenough, Mktg.　　　　Tel: (713) 690-2674　　　%FO: 100
　　Bus: *Software to property management.*　Fax: (713) 690-0330

　　GEAC
　　66 Perimeter Center East, Atlanta, Georgia 30346
　　CEO: Jeff Murphy, Principal　　　　　Tel: (404) 239-2000　　　%FO: 100
　　Bus: *Business applications software.*　Fax: (404) 239-2404　　　Emp: 969

　　GEAC
　　3707 West Cherry St., Tampa, Florida 33607
　　CEO: Blaine Camp, Mgr.　　　　　　Tel: (813) 874-3344　　　%FO: 100
　　Bus: *Custom computer programming.*　Fax: (813) 874-3773　　　Emp: 100

GEAC INTEREALTY
1951 Kidwell Dr., Vienna, Virginia 22182
CEO: Bryan Forman, Pres.
Bus: *Data processing services.*

Tel: (703) 760-9877
Fax:

%FO: 100
Emp: 400

GEAC MPC
555 Briarwood Circle, Ann Arbor, Michigan 48108
CEO: Charles Jones, Pres.
Bus: *Prepackaged software.*

Tel: (734) 994-4800
Fax: (734) 994-0341

%FO: 100
Emp: 1,000

GEAC NORTH AMERICA
120 Turnpike Rd., 2/F, Southborough, Massachusetts 01772
CEO: John Caldwell, Pres.
Bus: *Sale of computers, peripherals, computer maintenance & repair.*

Tel: (508) 871-5000
Fax: (508) 871-5887

%FO: 100
Emp: 1,200

GEAC PUBLIC SAFETY
5509 West Gray St., Ste. 100, Tampa, Florida 33609
CEO: Molly Crews, Gen. Mgr.
Bus: *Publishing custom computer programming.*

Tel: (813) 207-6911
Fax: (813) 207-6941

Emp: 48

GEAC RESTAURANT SYSTEMS INC.
175 Ledge St., Nashua, New Hampshire 03060
CEO: David Poole, Gen. Mgr.
Bus: *Provides restaurant enterprise solutions.*

Tel: (603) 889-5152
Fax: (603) 889-7538

%FO: 100
Emp: 100

● **GEMCOM SOFTWARE INTERNATIONAL INC.**
1285 W. Hastings St., Ste. 1100, Vancouver BC V6E 3X1, Canada
CEO: Rick Moignard, Pres. & CEO
Bus: *Software publisher*

Tel: 604-684-6550
Fax: 604-684-3541
www.gemcomsoftware.com

Rev: $11

NAICS: 511210

GEMCOM USA INC.
1755 East Plumb Lane, Ste. 118, Reno, Nevada 89502-3691
CEO: Cameron Reed, VP North America
Bus: *Software publisher*

Tel: (775) 323-2236
Fax: (775) 323-6980

%FO: 100

● **GENERAL MINERALS CORPORATION**
580 Hornby St., Ste. 880, Vancouver BC V6C 3B6, Canada
CEO: Ralph G. Fitch, Chmn. & Pres. & CEO
Bus: *Exploration of copper, silver, and gold reserves.*

Tel: 604-684-0693
Fax: 604-684-0642
www.generalminerals.com

NAICS: 212221, 212222, 212234

GENERAL MINERALS CORPORATION
4201 East Yale Ave., Ste. 230, Denver, Colorado 80222
CEO: L.A. Dick, Dir.
Bus: *Exploration of copper, silver, and gold reserves.*

Tel: (303) 584-0606
Fax: (303) 758-2063

%FO: 100
Emp: 40

● **GLOBAL THERMOELECTRIC INC.**
3700 78th Ave. SE, Ste. 9, Calgary AB T2C 2L8, Canada
CEO: Peter Garrett, Pres. & CEO
Bus: *Thermoelectric generators manufacture and sales.*

Tel: 403-236-5556
Fax: 403-236-5575
www.globalte.com

Rev: $1,300
Emp: 275

NAICS: 335311, 335312, 335999

    GLOBAL THERMOELECTRIC INC.
    16760 Hedgecroft Dr., Ste. 614, Houston, Texas 77060
    CEO: Paul Crilly, VP
    Bus: *Thermoelectric generators manufacture and sales.*

    Tel: (281) 445-1515
    Fax: (281) 445-6060

    %FO: 100

● **GOLDCORP INC.**
200 Burrard St., Ste. 1560, Vancouver BC V6C 3L6, Canada
CEO: Ian W. Telfer, CEO
Bus: *Operates gold mines.*

Tel: 604-696-3000
Fax: 604-696-3001
www.goldcorp.com

Rev: $191
Emp: 330

NAICS: 212221, 212231, 212299

    WHARF RESOURCES
    10928 Wharf Rd, Lead, South Dakota 57754
    CEO: Ron Evertt, Mgr.
    Bus: *Precious metals mining; gold bullion, silver bullion.*

    Tel: (605) 584-1441
    Fax: (605) 584-4188

    %FO: 100

● **GOLDEN SPIRIT GAMING LTD.**
1288 Alberni St., Ste. 806, Vancouver BC V6E 4N5, Canada
CEO: Robert Klein, Pres.
Bus: *Online poker gaming.*

Tel: 604-664-0499
Fax: 604-664-0498
www.goldenspirit.ws

Emp: 2

NAICS: 713290

    GOLDEN SPIRIT GAMING LTD.
    177 Telegraph Rd., Ste. 560, Bellingham, Washington 98226
    CEO: Abdul Rahmen Aref, Chmn.
    Bus: *Online poker.*

    Tel: (888) 488-6882
    Fax: (888) 488-6882

    %FO: 100

● **GOLDER ASSOCIATES LTD.**
2390 Argentia Rd., Mississauga ON L5N 5Z7, Canada
CEO: Brian Conlin, Pres.
Bus: *Group of consulting companies, specializing in ground engineering and environmental services.*

Tel: 905-567-4444
Fax:
www.golder.com

Rev: $180
Emp: 1,500

NAICS: 541310, 541330, 541490

    GOLDER ASSOCIATES
    Lee Park, Ste. 225, 1100 Hector St., Conshohocken, Pennsylvania 19428
    CEO: Joe Kostusiak
    Bus: *Engineering and environmental services.*

    Tel: (610) 941-8173
    Fax: (610) 941-8174

    %FO: 100

GOLDER ASSOCIATES
409 Main St., Ste. 252, Amherst, Massachusetts 01002
CEO: Todd Rees   Tel: (413) 253-9772   %FO: 100
Bus: *Engineering and environmental services.*   Fax: (413) 253-4267

GOLDER ASSOCIATES
4910 Alameda Blvd., Ste. A, Albuquerque, New Mexico 87113-1736
CEO: Bob Newcomer   Tel: (505) 821-3043   %FO: 100
Bus: *Engineering and environmental services.*   Fax: (505) 821-5273

GOLDER ASSOCIATES
6420 Congress Ave., Ste. 2000, Boca Raton, Florida 33487
CEO: Craig Ash   Tel: (561) 994-9910   %FO: 100
Bus: *Engineering and environmental services.*   Fax: (561) 994-9393

GOLDER ASSOCIATES
8933 Western Way, Ste. 12, Jacksonville, Florida 32256
CEO: Mark Swallow   Tel: (904) 363-3430   %FO: 100
Bus: *Engineering and environmental services.*   Fax: (904) 363-3445

GOLDER ASSOCIATES
5100 W. Lemon St., Ste.114, Tampa, Florida 33609
CEO: Anthony Grasso   Tel: (813) 287-1717   %FO: 100
Bus: *Engineering and environmental services.*   Fax: (813) 287-1716

GOLDER ASSOCIATES
18300 NE Union Hill Rd., Ste. 200, Redmond, Washington 98052
CEO: Doug Dunster   Tel: (425) 883-0777   %FO: 100
Bus: *Engineering and environmental services.*   Fax: (425) 882-5498

GOLDER ASSOCIATES
1200 W. Ironwood Dr., Ste. 102, Coeur d'Alene, Idaho 83814
CEO: Tim Martin   Tel: (208) 676-9933   %FO: 100
Bus: *Engineering and environmental services.*   Fax: (208) 676-8602

GOLDER ASSOCIATES
1551 Hillshire Dr., Ste. A, Las Vegas, Nevada 89134
CEO: W. Mark Nutt   Tel: (702) 794-1394   %FO: 100
Bus: *Engineering and environmental services.*   Fax: (702) 794-5040

GOLDER ASSOCIATES
The Wingate Bldg., 4900 Koger Blvd., Ste 140, Greensboro, North Carolina 27407
CEO: Christopher M. Gee   Tel: (336) 852-4903   %FO: 100
Bus: *Engineering and environmental services.*   Fax: (336) 852-4904

GOLDER ASSOCIATES
28 School St., PO Box 944, East Granby, Connecticut 06026-0944
CEO: John Carroll   Tel: (860) 653-7042   %FO: 100
Bus: *Engineering and environmental services.*   Fax: (860) 653-7056

GOLDER ASSOCIATES
500 Century Plaza Dr., Ste. 190, Houston, Texas 77073
CEO: Charlie Dominguez   Tel: (281) 821-6868   %FO: 100
Bus: *Engineering and environmental services.*   Fax: (281) 821-6870

Canada

GOLDER ASSOCIATES
15851 South US 27, Ste. 50, Lansing, Michigan 48906
CEO: David List
Bus: *Engineering and environmental services.*
Tel: (517) 482-2262
Fax: (517) 482-2460
%FO: 100

GOLDER ASSOCIATES
540 North Commercial St., Ste. 250, Manchester, New Hampshire 03101-1146
CEO: Alistair Macdonald
Bus: *Engineering and environmental services.*
Tel: (603) 668-0880
Fax: (603) 668-1199
%FO: 100

GOLDER ASSOCIATES
1751 West County Rd. B, Ste. 220, Roseville, Minnesota 55113
CEO: Mark Sandfort
Bus: *Engineering and environmental services.*
Tel: (651) 697-9737
Fax: (651) 697-9735
%FO: 100

GOLDER ASSOCIATES
1750 Abbott Rd., Ste. 200, Anchorage, Alaska 99507-3443
CEO: Bob Dugan
Bus: *Engineering and environmental services.*
Tel: (907) 344-6001
Fax: (907) 344-6011
%FO: 100

GOLDER ASSOCIATES
4445 SW Barbur Blvd., Ste. 101, Portland, Oregon 97239
CEO: Bob Long
Bus: *Engineering and environmental services.*
Tel: (503) 241-9404
Fax: (503) 241-9403
%FO: 100

GOLDER ASSOCIATES
The Federal Trust Bldg., 24 Commerce St., Ste. 430, Newark, New Jersey 07102
CEO: Mark McNeilly
Bus: *Engineering and environmental services.*
Tel: (973) 621-0777
Fax: (973) 621-7725
%FO: 100

GOLDER ASSOCIATES
136 S. Illinois Ave., Ste. 204, Oak Ridge, Tennessee 37830
CEO: W. Timothy Griffin
Bus: *Engineering and environmental services.*
Tel: (865) 483-9201
Fax: (865) 483-3952
%FO: 100

GOLDER ASSOCIATES
3730 Chamblee Tucker Rd., Atlanta, Georgia 30341
CEO: Steve Moeller
Bus: *Engineering and environmental services.*
Tel: (770) 496-1893
Fax: (770) 934-9476
%FO: 100

GOLDER ASSOCIATES
103 Harpswell Rd., Brunswick, Maine 04011-7821
CEO: Mark Peterson
Bus: *Engineering and environmental services.*
Tel: (207) 373-1520
Fax: (207) 373-1516
%FO: 100

GOLDER ASSOCIATES
12860 West Cedar Dr., Ste. 206, Lakewood, Colorado 80228
CEO: Matthew J. Barrett
Bus: *Engineering and environmental services.*
Tel: (303) 969-9270
Fax: (303) 969-0468
%FO: 100

GOLDER ASSOCIATES
400 14th St. SE, Ste. 1, Decatur, Alabama 35601
CEO: Tim Leeth
Bus: *Engineering and environmental services.*
Tel: (256) 350-2051
Fax: (256) 350-3491
%FO: 100

GOLDER ASSOCIATES
44 Union Blvd., Ste. 300, Lakewood, Colorado 80228
CEO: Randy March
Bus: *Engineering and environmental services.*
Tel: (303) 980-0540
Fax: (303) 985-2080
%FO: 100

GOLDER ASSOCIATES
1630 Heritage Landing, Ste. 103, St. Charles, Missouri 63303
CEO: Bob Glazier
Bus: *Engineering and environmental services.*
Tel: (636) 936-1554
Fax: (636) 936-1135
%FO: 100

GOLDER ASSOCIATES
2221 Niagara Falls Blvd., Ste. 9, Niagara Falls, New York 14304
CEO: Brian C. Senefelder
Bus: *Engineering and environmental services.*
Tel: (716) 215-0650
Fax: (716) 215-0655
%FO: 100

GOLDER ASSOCIATES
1009 Enterprise Way, Ste. 350, Roseville, California 95678
CEO: David Cochrane
Bus: *Engineering and environmental services.*
Tel: (916) 786-2424
Fax: (916) 786-2434
%FO: 100

GOLDER ASSOCIATES
230 Commerce, Ste. 200, Irvine, California 92602
CEO: Alan Hull
Bus: *Engineering and environmental services.*
Tel: (714) 508-4400
Fax: (714) 508-4401
%FO: 100

GOLDER ASSOCIATES
Blackstone Center, 302 SE 36th St., Omaha, Nebraska 68131
CEO: Jack Monzingo
Bus: *Engineering and environmental services.*
Tel: (402) 203-7466
Fax:
%FO: 100

GOLDER ASSOCIATES
3719 Saunders Ave., Richmond, Virginia 23227
CEO: Chris Gee
Bus: *Engineering and environmental services.*
Tel: (804) 358-7900
Fax: (804) 358-2900
%FO: 100

GOLDER ASSOCIATES
1730 North Oracle Rd., Ste. 210, Tucson, Arizona 85708
CEO: David Kidd
Bus: *Engineering and environmental services.*
Tel: (520) 888-8818
Fax: (520) 888-8817
%FO: 100

GOLDER ASSOCIATES
2580 Wyandotte St., Ste. G, Mountain View, California 94043
CEO: Bill Fowler
Bus: *Engineering and environmental services.*
Tel: (650) 386-3828
Fax: (650) 386-3815
%FO: 100

GOLDER ASSOCIATES
6241 NW23rd St., Ste. 500, Gainesville, Florida 32653
CEO: Benny Susi
Bus: *Engineering and environmental services.*
Tel: (352) 336-5600
Fax: (352) 336-6603

GOLDER ASSOCIATES
309 South 4th St., Ste. 201, Laramie, Wyoming 82070
CEO: Archie Reeve
Bus: *Engineering and environmental services.*
Tel: (307) 742-0842
Fax: (307) 742-0872
%FO: 100

GOLDER ASSOCIATES
1951 Old Cuthbert Rd., Ste. 301, Cherry Hill, New Jersey 08034
CEO: Pete Swinick   Tel: (856) 616-8166   %FO: 100
Bus: *Engineering and environmental services.*   Fax: (856) 616-1874

GOLDER ASSOCIATES
2525 Tiller Lane, Ste. 208, Columbus, Ohio 43231
CEO: Sheryl R. Smith   Tel: (614) 899-9288   %FO: 100
Bus: *Engineering and environmental services.*   Fax: (614) 899-9290

GOLDER ASSOCIATES
51229 Century Ct., Wixom, Michigan 48393
CEO: Paul Sgricca   Tel: (248) 295-0135   %FO: 100
Bus: *Engineering and environmental services.*   Fax: (248) 295-0133

GOLDER ASSOCIATES
6165 Ridgeview Ct., Ste. F, Reno, Nevada 89509
CEO: Graeme Major   Tel: (775) 828-9604   %FO: 100
Bus: *Engineering and environmental services.*   Fax: (775) 828-9645

● **GOODFELLOW INC.**
225 Goodfellow St., Delson QC J5B 1V5, Canada
CEO: Richard Goodfellow, Pres. & CEO   Tel: 450-635-6511   Rev: $406
Bus: *Lumber and wood products manufacture.*   Fax: 450-635-3729   Emp: 805
                              www.goodfellowinc.com
NAICS: 321211, 321212, 321213, 321219, 321911, 321918, 321999

    GOODFELLOW INC.
    171 Clinton St., Watertown, New York 13601
    CEO: Peter Thurston, Mgr.   Tel: (315) 782-2109   %FO: 100
    Bus: *Lumber and wood products sales and*   Fax: (315) 782-2722
          distribution.

    GOODFELLOW INC.
    1024 6th Ave. South, Seattle, Washington 98134
    CEO: Nace Hentschell, Gen. Mgr.   Tel: (206) 622-0917   %FO: 100
    Bus: *Hardwood flooring sales and distribution.*   Fax: (206) 622-7012   Emp: 20

    GOODFELLOW INC.
    368 Pepsi Rd., Manchester, New Hampshire 03109
    CEO: Steve Guertin, Mgr.   Tel: (603) 623-9811   %FO: 100
    Bus: *Lumber and wood products sales and*   Fax: (603) 623-9484   Emp: 700
          distribution.

● **GORAN CAPITAL INC.**
2 Eva Rd., Ste. 200, Etobicoke ON M9C 2A8, Canada
CEO: Douglas H. Symons, Pres. & CEO   Tel: 416-622-0660   Rev: $128
Bus: *Engaged in property and casualty insurance and*   Fax: 416-622-8809   Emp: 350
    auto and crop insurance.   www.sigins.com
NAICS: 524126, 524130

GORAN CAPITAL
4720 Kingsway Dr., Ste. 5, Indianapolis, Indiana 46205
CEO: Douglas Symons, Pres.
Bus: *Insurance agent.*
Tel: (317) 259-6400
Fax:
%FO: 100

SUPERIOR INSURANCE
4720 Kingsway Dr., Ste. 5, Indianapolis, Indiana 46205
CEO: Douglas Symons, Pres.
Bus: *Insurance agent.*
Tel: (317) 259-6429
Fax:
%FO: 100
Emp: 850

SYMONS INSURANCE GROUP
4720 Kingsway Dr., Indianapolis, Indiana 46205
CEO: Douglas H. Symons, Chmn. & Pres. & CEO
Bus: *Engaged in non-standard auto insurance.*
Tel: (317) 259-6300
Fax: (317) 259-6395
%FO: 100

SYMONS INTERNATIONAL GROUP
2300 Glades Rd., Ste. 135E, Boca Raton, Florida 33431
CEO: Douglas Symons, Pres.
Bus: *Insurance agent.*
Tel: (561) 392-1323
Fax:
Emp: 7

● **GREAT-WEST LIFECO INC.**
100 Osborne St. North, Winnipeg MB R3C 3A5, Canada
CEO: William T. McCallum, Pres. & CEO
Bus: *Provides group executive benefit planning and health and life insurance services.*
Tel: 204-946-1190
Fax: 204-946-4129
www.greatwestlifeco.com
Rev: $10,373
Emp: 13,800
NAICS: 523991, 523999, 524113, 524114, 524130, 525110, 525120, 525190, 525910, 525920, 525990

CANADA LIFE FINANCIAL CORP.
6201 Powers Ferry Rd., Ste. 100, Atlanta, Georgia 30339
CEO: Ron Beetam, Pres.
Bus: *Insurance agents*
Tel: (770) 953-1959
Fax:

GREAT-WEST LIFE & ANNUITY INSURANCE COMPANY
8505 E. Orchard Rd., Greenwood Village, Colorado 80111
CEO: William T. McCallum, Pres. & CEO
Bus: *Provides executive benefit planning and health and life insurance services.*
Tel: (303) 737-3000
Fax: (303) 737-3198
%FO: 100
Emp: 6,200

ONE HEALTH PLAN
8505 E. Orchard Rd., Greenwood Village, Colorado 80111
CEO: William T. McCallum, Pres. & CEO
Bus: *Health care services*
Tel: (303) 737-3000
Fax: (303) 737-3146

● **GROUPE LAPERRIERE & VERREAULT INC.**
25 des Forget St., Ste. 420, Trois-Rivieres QC G9A 6A7, Canada
CEO: Laurent Verreault, Chmn. & Pres. & CEO
Bus: *Mfr. machinery for paper and pulp manufacture.*
Tel: 819-371-8265
Fax: 819-373-4439
www.glv.com
Rev: $419
Emp: 1,400
NAICS: 333291

DORR-OLIVER EIMCO USA INC.
600 Vestavia Pkwy., Ste. 203, Birmingham, Alabama 35216
CEO: Allan Arthur, CEO
Bus: *Sales of machinery for paper and pulp.*
Tel: (205) 822-1730
Fax: (205) 979-5345
%FO: 100

DORR-OLIVER EIMCO USA INC.
8711 Pyott Rd., Lake In The Hills, Illinois 60156
CEO: Dan Igrisan, CEO
Bus: *Sales of machinery for paper and pulp.*
Tel: (815) 356-0050
Fax: (815) 356-0055
%FO: 100

DORR-OLIVER EIMCO USA INC.
1186 Thorn Run, Ste. 130, Pittsburgh, Pennsylvania 15108
CEO: Laurent Verreault, Exec. Dir.
Bus: *Sales & engineering - machinery for paper and pulp.*
Tel: (412) 604-6060
Fax: (412) 604-6061
%FO: 100

EIMCO WATER TECHNOLOGIES
2850 South Decker Lake Dr., Salt Lake City, Utah 84119
CEO: Nick Babyak, member
Bus: *Water treatment plant.*
Tel: (801) 526-2400
Fax: (801) 526-2910
%FO: 100
Emp: 48

GL&V USA
219 Roswell At., Ste. 130, Alpharetta, Georgia 30004
CEO: Laurent Verreault, CEO
Bus: *Recausticizing.*
Tel: (770) 394-6200
Fax: (770) 396-7504
%FO: 100

GL&V USA
141 Burke St., Nashua, New Hampshire 03060
CEO: Laurent Verreault, CEO
Bus: *Sales & engineering - machinery for paper and pulp.*
Tel: (603) 882-2711
Fax: (603) 598-7832
%FO: 100

GL&V USA
175 Crystal St., PO Box 846, Lenox, Massachusetts 01240
CEO: M. Winders, Chmn.
Bus: *Mfr. machinery for paper and pulp.*
Tel: (413) 637-2424
Fax: (413) 637-3740
%FO: 100
Emp: 150

GL&V USA
609 Hamilton St., Ste. 2, Allentown, Pennsylvania 18101
CEO: Laurent Verreault, CEO
Bus: *Sale of pumps.*
Tel: (610) 740-1015
Fax: (610) 744-0233
%FO: 100

GL&V USA
100 Laval Blvd., Lawrenceville, Georgia 30043
CEO: Laurent Verreault, CEO
Bus: *Mfr. machinery for paper and pulp.*
Tel: (770) 963-2100
Fax: (770) 339-6132
%FO: 100

GL&V USA
27 Allen St., Hudson Falls, New York 12839
CEO: Frances Dunsmore, CEO
Bus: *Mfr. of paper industries machinery.*
Tel: (518) 747-2444
Fax: (518) 747-1334
%FO: 100
Emp: 103

● **GSW INC.**
2020 Winston Park Dr., Ste. 100, Oakville ON L6H 6X7, Canada
CEO: John A. Barford, Chmn.
Bus: *Mfr. of water and building products*
Tel: 905-829-1197
Fax: 905-829-0092
www.gswinc.com
Rev: $392
Emp: 2,000

NAICS: 333415, 423730

American Water Heater Company
500 Princeton Rd, Johnson City, Tennessee 37601
CEO: Robert Trudeau, Pres.   Tel: (423) 283-8000   %FO: 100
Bus: *Manufacturer of residential and commercial*   Fax: (423) 283-8050   Emp: 1,200
    water heaters

● **HABANERO RESOURCES INC.**
789 West Pender St., Ste. 1205, Vancouver BC V6C 1H2, Canada
CEO: Jason Gigliotti, Pres.   Tel: 604-646-6900
Bus: *Gas exploration.*   Fax: 604-689-1733
                                      www.habaneroresources

NAICS: 211111, 213111

   HABANERO OIL & GAS
   802 Rio Grande St., Austin, Texas 78701
   CEO: John Ruwwe, Pres.   Tel: (512) 476-5500
   Bus: *Oil & gas exploration.*   Fax:

● **HAEMACURE CORPORATION**
2001 University St., Ste. 430, Montreal QC H3A 2A6, Canada
CEO: Marc Paquin, Pres. & CEO   Tel: 514-282-3350
Bus: *Medical sealants and adhesives manufacture and*   Fax: 514-282-3358   Emp: 16
    sales.   www.haemacure.com
NAICS: 339113, 423450

   HAEMACURE CORPORATION
   One Sarasota Tower, Ste. 206, Two North Tamiami Trail, Sarasota, Florida 34236
   CEO: Marc Paquin, Pres.   Tel: (941) 364-3700   %FO: 100
   Bus: *Medical sealants and adhesives sales and*   Fax: (941) 365-1051   Emp: 35
       distribution.

● **HAMMOND MANUFACTURING COMPANY LIMITED**
394 Edinburgh Rd. North, Guelph ON N1H 1E5, Canada
CEO: Robert F. Hammond, Chmn. & CEO   Tel: 519-822-2960   Rev: $50
Bus: *Electrical and electronic component enclosures*   Fax: 519-822-8987   Emp: 479
    manufacture.   www.hammfg.com
NAICS: 334416, 335311, 335999

   HAMMOND MANUFACTURING COMPANY LIMITED
   475 Cayuga Rd., Cheektowaga, New York 14225
   CEO: Robert F. Hammond, Pres.   Tel: (716) 630-7030   %FO: 100
   Bus: *Electrical and electronic component*   Fax: (716) 630-7042   Emp: 14
       enclosures manufacture and sales..

● **HAMMOND POWER SOLUTIONS INC.**
595 Southgate Dr., Guelph ON N1G 3W6, Canada
CEO: William G. Hammond, CEO   Tel: 519-822-2441   Rev: $57
Bus: *Designs and manufactures transformers and*   Fax: 519822-4366   Emp: 450
    related electrical products.   www.hammondpowersolutions.com
NAICS: 335311

HAMMOND POWER SOLUTIONS INC.
17715 Susana Rd., Compton, California 90224
CEO: Curtis Gullick, Plant Mgr.
Bus: *Mining operation electrical products manufacture.*

Tel: (310) 537-4690
Fax: (310) 537-7506

%FO: 100

● **HARLEQUIN ENTERPRISES LTD.**
225 Duncan Mill Rd., 4/F, Don Mills ON M3B 3K9, Canada
CEO: Donna Hayes, Pres. & CEO
Bus: *Publishing.*

Tel: 416-445-5860
Fax: 416-445-8655
www.eharlequin.com

Rev: $452
Emp: 1,200

NAICS: 511130

HARLEQUIN BOOKS
3010 Walden Ave., Depew, New York 14043
CEO: Donna Hayes, Pres.
Bus: *Book distribution.*

Tel: (716) 684-1800
Fax: (716) 684-5066

%FO: 100
Emp: 200

● **HATCH ACRES**
1235 North Service Rd. West, Oakville ON L6M 2W2, Canada
CEO: Tony Hilton, Pres.
Bus: *Engineering services.*

Tel: 905-469-3400
Fax: 905-469-3404
www.hatchacres.com

Emp: 1,100

NAICS: 541330

ACRES INTERNATIONAL CORPORATION
100 Sylvan Pkwy., Amherst, New York 14228
CEO: S. Gill, VP
Bus: *Engineering services.*

Tel: (716) 689-3737
Fax: (716) 689-3749

%FO: 100
Emp: 65

ACRES INTERNATIONAL CORPORATION
6 Nickerson St., Ste. 101, Seattle, Washington 98109
CEO: Robin Charlwood, Mgr.
Bus: *Engineering services.*

Tel: (206) 352-5730
Fax: (206) 352-5734

%FO: 100
Emp: 11

● **HEMOSOL CORP.**
2585 Meadowpine Blvd., Mississauga ON L5N 8H9, Canada
CEO: Lee Hartwell, CEO
Bus: *Mfr. blood substitute.*

Tel: 905-286-6200
Fax: 905-286-6300
www.hemosol.com

NAICS: 325412, 325414

HEMOSOL USA INC.
8 Wood Hollow Rd., Ste. 301, Parsippany, New Jersey 07054
CEO: Lee Hartwell, CEO
Bus: *Mfr. blood substitute.*

Tel: (973) 781-0200
Fax: (973) 781-9840

%FO: 100

● **HEROUX-DEVTEK INC.**
Ste.658, East Tower, Complexe Saint-Charles, 1111 Saint-Charles St. Quest, Longueuil QC J4K 5G4, Canada
CEO: Gilles Labbe, Pres.
Bus: *Mfr. of landing gear and aerospace products*

Tel: 450-679-3330
Fax: 450-679-3666
www.herouxdevtek.com

Rev: $163

NAICS: 336412, 336413

Heroux-Devteck, Inc.
382 Circle Freeway Dr., Cincinnati, Ohio 45246
CEO: Alvin Cook, Pres.
Bus: *Mfr. gas turbines*
Tel: (513) 619-1222
Fax: (513) 619-1225
%FO: 100

PROGRESSIVE INC.
1030 Commercial Blvd. North, Arlington, Texas 76001
CEO: Guinn D. Crousen, Pres.
Bus: *Aerospace.*
Tel: (817) 465-3221
Fax: (817) 465-1289
%FO: 100

● **HIGH LINER FOODS INCORPORATED**
100 Battery Point, Lunenburg NS B0J 2C0, Canada
CEO: Henry E. Demone, Pres. & CEO
Bus: *Frozen foods processing.*
Tel: 902-634-8811
Fax: 902-634-4785
www.highlinerfoods.com
Rev: $244
Emp: 1,061

NAICS: 311412, 311712

HIGH LINER FOODS INCORPORATED
1 Highliner Ave., Box 839, Portsmouth, New Hampshire 03801
CEO: Henry Demone, Pres. & COO
Bus: *Frozen foods processing and sales.*
Tel: (603) 431-6865
Fax: (603) 431-6865
%FO: 100
Emp: 260

● **HOLLINGER, INC.**
10 Toronto St., Toronto ON M5C 2B7, Canada
CEO: Randall C. Benson, CEO
Bus: *International newspaper publishing.*
Tel: 416-363-8721
Fax: 416-364-2088
www.hollingerinc.com

NAICS: 511110, 511120, 516110

CHICAGO SUN-TIMES
350 N. Orleans St., Chicago, Illinois 60654
CEO: David Radler
Bus: *Daily newspaper.*
Tel: (312) 321-3000
Fax: (312) 321-0629
%FO: 100
Emp: 1,500

HOLLINGER INTERNATIONAL INC.
712 Fifth Ave., 18/F, New York, New York 10022
CEO: Gordon A. Paris, Chmn. & Pres. & CEO
Bus: *Newspaper publishing.*
Tel: (212) 586-5666
Fax: (212) 974-0978
%FO: 17
Emp: 6,728

HOLLINGER INTERNATIONAL INC.
401 N. Wabash Ave., Ste. 740, Chicago, Illinois 60611
CEO: F. David Radler, Pres.
Bus: *Newspaper publishing.*
Tel: (312) 321-2299
Fax: (312) 321-0629
%FO: 100
Emp: 3,100

● **HOOD PACKAGING CORPORATION**
2380 McDowell Rd., Burlington ON L7R 4A1, Canada
CEO: John H. McCabe, Pres. & CEO
Bus: *Multiwall and small paper bags manufacture.*
Tel: 905-637-5611
Fax: 905-637-9954
www.hoodpkg.com
Rev: $190
Emp: 200

NAICS: 322221, 322223

HOOD PACKAGING INC.
2410 North Lyndon St., Tyler, Texas 75702
CEO: Gulam Harji, mgr
Bus: *Plant facility for plastic film and bag manufacture.*
Tel: (903) 593-1793
Fax: (903) 595-6019
%FO: 100

● **HUMMINGBIRD LTD.**
1 Sparks Ave., Toronto ON M2H 2W1, Canada
CEO: Alan B. Litwin, Pres. & CEO
Bus: *Software manufacture.*
Tel: 416-496-2200
Fax: 416-496-2207
www.hummingbird.com
Rev: $220
Emp: 1,430

NAICS: 511210

HUMMINGBIRD USA INC.
124 Marriot Dr., Tallahassee, Florida 32301
CEO: Andrew Pery
Bus: *Mfr. software.*
Tel: (850) 942-3627
Fax: (850) 656-5559
%FO: 100

HUMMINGBIRD USA INC.
25 Burlington Mall Rd., 4/F, Burlington, Massachusetts 01803
CEO: Michelle Felice, Mgr.
Bus: *Mfr. software.*
Tel: (781) 273-3800
Fax: (781) 272-3693
%FO: 100
Emp: 20

HUMMINGBIRD USA INC.
8601 Six Forks Rd., Ste. 400, Raleigh, North Carolina 27615
CEO: Donna Johnson, Principal
Bus: *Mfr. software.*
Tel: (919) 831-8989
Fax: (919) 831-8990
%FO: 100
Emp: 20

HUMMINGBIRD USA INC.
304 Park Ave. South, 9/F, New York, New York 10010
CEO: Inder Duggal, CEO
Bus: *Mfr. software.*
Tel: (212) 353-7500
Fax: (212) 353-7600
%FO: 100
Emp: 70

HUMMINGBIRD USA INC.
13601 Preston Rd., Ste. 900, East Dallas, Texas 75240
CEO: Frank Sorkin, Chmn.
Bus: *Software.*
Tel: (972) 892-0300
Fax: (972) 788-4199
%FO: 100

HUMMINGBIRD USA INC.
480 San Antonio Rd., Ste. 200, Mountain View, California 94040
CEO: Kim Kaku, Mgr.
Bus: *Software.*
Tel: (650) 917-7300
Fax: (650) 917-7310
%FO: 100
Emp: 25

HUMMINGBIRD USA INC.
1415 West 22nd St., Tower Floor, Oak Brook, Illinois 90523
CEO: Fred Sorkin, Pres.
Bus: *Software.*
Tel: (630) 684-2222
Fax: (630) 684-2326
%FO: 100
Emp: 100

HUMMINGBIRD USA INC.
5000 Birch St., Ste. 3000, West Tower, Newport Beach, California 92660
CEO: Joey Bitdashtoo, Mgr.
Bus: *Software.*
Tel: (949) 260-2047
Fax: (949) 475-6879
%FO: 100

HUMMINGBIRD USA INC.
1575 Eye St. NW, Ste. 240, Washington, District of Columbia 20005
CEO: Dick Kann, Mgr.   Tel: (202) 741-1000   %FO: 100
Bus: *Computer programming.* Fax: (202) 741-1020   Emp: 12

RED DOT SOLUTIONS CORP.
1 Battery Park Plaza, 25/F, New York, New York 10004
CEO: Detlef Kamps, Pres. & CEO   Tel: (212) 425-3988   %FO: 100
Bus: *Content & document management software.* Fax: (212) 425-3987

● **HUSKY INJECTION MOLDING SYSTEMS LTD.**
500 Queen St. South, Bolton ON L7E 5S5, Canada
CEO: Robert Schad, Pres. & CEO   Tel: 905-951-5000   Rev: $774
Bus: *Mfr. injection molding equipment for manufacture* Fax: 905-951-5324   Emp: 3,039
  of plastic products.   www.husky.ca
NAICS: 333220, 333993

    HUSKY INJECTION MOLDING SYSTEMS INC
    3 Travis Grove, Pittsford, New York 14534
    CEO: John Galt, Pres.   Tel: (585) 586-7320   %FO: 100
    Bus: *Mfr. Industry machinery.* Fax:

    HUSKY INJECTION MOLDING SYSTEMS INC
    3505 Cadillac Ave., Ste. N4, Costa Mesa, California 92626
    CEO: Michael Smith, Mgr.   Tel: (714) 545-8200   %FO: 100
    Bus: *Mfr. of plastic products.* Fax: Emp: 14

    HUSKY INJECTION MOLDING SYSTEMS INC
    344 Troy Rd., Rochester, New York 14618
    CEO: Michael Marshall, Mgr.   Tel: (585) 242-9040   %FO: 100
    Bus: *Mfr. of industry machinery.* Fax:

    HUSKY INJECTION MOLDING SYSTEMS INC
    5215 N O'Connor Blvd., Irving, Texas 75039
    CEO: Wayne Harper, Mgr.   Tel: (972) 831-7340   %FO: 100
    Bus: *Mfr. of plastic products.* Fax: Emp: 5

    HUSKY INJECTION MOLDING SYSTEMS INC
    100 Husky Dr., Peachtree City, Georgia 30269
    CEO: John Elward, Mgr.   Tel: (770) 487-6234   %FO: 100
    Bus: *Mfr. of injection molding products.* Fax:

    HUSKY INJECTION MOLDING SYSTEMS INC
    5301 Blue Lagoon Dr., Miami, Florida 33126
    CEO: Rod Selem, Pres.   Tel: (305) 261-3003   %FO: 100
    Bus: *Mfr. of plastic products.* Fax: Emp: 73

    HUSKY INJECTION MOLDING SYSTEMS INC
    2 Village Cir., Ste. 525, Roanoke, Texas 76262
    CEO: Robert Schad, Pres.   Tel: (817) 222-9440   %FO: 100
    Bus: *Sale of industrial equipment.* Fax:

HUSKY INJECTION MOLDING SYSTEMS LTD.
115 Catamount Dr., Milton, Vermont 05468
CEO: Tim Loucks, Gen. Mgr.   Tel: (802) 859-8000   %FO: 100
Bus: *Sale of plastic injection molding machinery.*   Fax: Emp: 75

HUSKY INJECTION MOLDING SYSTEMS LTD.
400 Milford Pkwy., Milford, Ohio 45150
CEO: Michael Diletti, Mgr.   Tel: (513) 965-8080   %FO: 100
Bus: *Mfr. injection molding equipment for*   Fax: (513) 965-8080   Emp: 12
      manufacture of plastic products.

HUSKY INJECTION MOLDING SYSTEMS LTD.
45145 West Twelve Mile Rd., Novi, Michigan 48377
CEO: Trevor Jones, Gen. Mgr.   Tel: (248) 735-6300   %FO: 100
Bus: *Mfr. injection molding equipment for*   Fax: (248) 735-6400   Emp: 40
      manufacture of plastic products.

HUSKY INJECTION MOLDING SYSTEMS LTD.
105 Terry Dr., Ste. 119, Newtown, Pennsylvania 18940
CEO: Robert Schad, Pres.   Tel: (215) 497-9700   %FO: 100
Bus: *Mfr. injection molding equipment for*   Fax: (215) 497-9700
      manufacture of plastic products.

HUSKY INJECTION MOLDING SYSTEMS LTD.
55 Amherst Villa Rd., Buffalo, New York 14225
CEO: Robert Schad, CEO   Tel: (716) 630-7300   %FO: 100
Bus: *Plastic injection molding machinery.*   Fax: Emp: 668

HUSKY INJECTION MOLDING SYSTEMS LTD.
5 Lan Dr., Ste. 100, Westford, Massachusetts 01886
CEO: Michael Urquhart, Pres.   Tel: (978) 392-1411   %FO: 100
Bus: *Mfr. injection molding equipment for*   Fax: Emp: 25
      manufacture of plastic products.

• **ID BIOMEDICAL CORPORATION**
1630 Waterfront Center, 200 Burrard St., Vancouver BC V6C 3L6, Canada
CEO: Anthony F. Holler, CEO   Tel: 604-431-9314   Rev: $43
Bus: *Gene therapy.*   Fax: 604-431-9378   Emp: 154
                                         www.idbiomed.com
NAICS: 325413

ID BIOMEDICAL CORP.
30 Bearfoot Rd., Northborough, Massachusetts 01532
CEO: Todd Patrick, Pres.   Tel: (508) 351-9944   %FO: 100
Bus: *Engaged in gene therapy.*   Fax: (508) 351-9675

ID BIOMEDICAL CORPORATION
6996 Columbia Gateway Dr., Ste. 103, Columbia, Maryland 21046
CEO: Louis Fries, VP   Tel: (410) 312-0121   %FO: 100
Bus: *Engaged in gene therapy.*   Fax: (410) 312-0125   Emp: 4

ID BIOMEDICAL CORPORATION
19204 North Creek Pkwy., Ste. 100, Bothell, Washington 98011
CEO: Todd Patrick, Pres.   Tel: (425) 482-2601   %FO: 100
Bus: *Engaged in gene therapy.*   Fax: (425) 482-2502   Emp: 58

● **IMAX CORPORATION**
2525 Speakman Dr., Mississauga ON L5K 1B1, Canada
CEO: Richard L. Gelfond, Co-Chair
Bus: *Mfr. and leasing of projection and sound systems
for IMAX giant screen theaters.*
NAICS: 512110, 512120, 512131, 512199

Tel: 905-403-6500
Fax: 905-403-6450
www.imax.com

Rev: $136
Emp: 363

> **DAVID KEIGHLEY PRODUCTIONS 70 MM INC.**
> 959 Seward St., Los Angeles, California 90038
> CEO: Gerald Mantonya, Principal
> Bus: *Cinematic presentations together with
> IMAX, IMAX 3D and the development of the
> highest quality digital production and*
>
> Tel: (323) 255-5500
> Fax:
>
> %FO: 100

> **DAVID KEIGHLEY PRODUCTIONS 70 MM INC.**
> 3003 Exposition Blvd., Santa Monica, California 90404
> CEO: David B. Keighley, Pres.
> Bus: *Engaged in laboratory post production and
> image quality assurance.*
>
> Tel: (310) 255-5500
> Fax:
>
> %FO: 100
> Emp: 35

● **IMPERIAL PARKING CORPORATION**
601 West Cordova St., Ste. 300, Vancouver BC V6B 1G1, Canada
CEO: Herbert Anderson Jr., CEO
Bus: *Parking facilities.*

Tel: 604-681-7311
Fax: 604-681-4098
www.impark.com

Rev: $154
Emp: 3,400

NAICS: 812930

> **IMPERIAL PARKING CORPORATION**
> 510 Walnut St., Ste. 250, Philadelphia, Pennsylvania 19106
> CEO: Collen Niese, VP
> Bus: *Parking facilities.*
>
> Tel: (215) 931-4300
> Fax: (215) 574-0837
>
> %FO: 100

● **INCO LIMITED**
145 King St. West, Ste. 1500, Toronto ON M5H 4B7, Canada
CEO: Scott M. Hand, Chmn. & CEO
Bus: *Mines/processes nickel, copper, precious metals,
cobalt.*
NAICS: 212221, 212222, 212231, 212299, 213114

Tel: 416-361-7511
Fax: 416-361-7781
www.inco.com

Rev: $4,278
Emp: 10,973

> **INMETCO**
> PO Box 720, 245 Potersville Rd., Ellwood City, Pennsylvania 16117
> CEO: Scott Hand, Pres.
> Bus: *Mfr. nickel, copper and precious metals.*
>
> Tel: (724) 758-2800
> Fax: (724) 758-2845
>
> %FO: 100
> Emp: 120

> **INTERNATIONAL NICKEL INC.**
> Park 80 West, Plaza 2, Saddle Brook, New Jersey 07663
> CEO: David J. Anderson, Pres.
> Bus: *Sale of primary nickel & other nonferrous
> metals.*
>
> Tel: (201) 368-4800
> Fax: (201) 368-4858
>
> %FO: 100
> Emp: 31

INTERNATIONAL NICKEL INC.
North Central Center, 1100 NW Loop 410, Ste. 700, San Antonio, Texas 78213
CEO: David J. Anderson, Pres.   Tel: (210) 336-8714   %FO: 100
Bus: *Sale of primary nickel & other nonferrous*   Fax:
metals.

NOVAMET SPECIALTY PRODUCTS CORP
681 Lawlins Rd., Wyckoff, New Jersey 07481
CEO: Louis F. Koehler, Pres.   Tel: (201) 891-7976   %FO: 100
Bus: *Mfr. of flakes & powder products for*   Fax: (201) 891-9467   Emp: 25
coatings industry.

• **INFOWAVE SOFTWARE INC.**
4664 Lougheed Hwy., Ste. 188, Burnaby BC V5C 5T5, Canada
CEO: James W. Suttie, CEO   Tel: 604-473-3600   Rev: $1
Bus: *Develops, markets and sells software solutions*   Fax: 604-473-3699   Emp: 40
for the wireless computing business.   www.infowave.com
NAICS: 511210, 541511

INFOWAVE SOFTWARE
4301 North Fairfax Dr., Ste. 200, Reston, Virginia 20191
CEO: Randy Brouckman   Tel: (703) 247-0500   %FO: 100
Bus: *Develops software for wireless*   Fax: (703) 284-1759
communications.

• **INNOVA SYBRON DENTAL SPECIALTIES**
522 University Ave., Ste. 1200, Toronto ON M5G 1W7, Canada
CEO: Michael A. Kehoe, Chmn. & Pres. & CEO   Tel: 416-340-8818   Rev: $13
Bus: *Dental device manufacturing.*   Fax: 416-340-0415   Emp: 150
    www.innovalife.com
NAICS: 339114

ATTACHMENTS INTERNATIONAL INC.
600 S. Amphlett Blvd., San Mateo, California 94402-1325
CEO: Peter Staubli, Pres.   Tel: (650) 340-0393   %FO: 100
Bus: *Dental restoration parts manufacture and*   Fax: (650) 340-8423   Emp: 12
sales.

• **INSYSTEMS CORPORATION**
19 Allstate Pkwy., Ste. 400, Markham ON L3R 5A4, Canada
CEO: Neil Betteridge, Dir.   Tel: 905-513-1400   Rev: $45
Bus: *Portal and document management software*   Fax: 905-513-1419   Emp: 100
manufacture and sales.   www.insystems.com
NAICS: 511210

INSYSTEMS CORPORATION
109 Norfolk Ave., Roanoke, Virginia 24011
CEO: Neil Betteridge, Dir.   Tel: (905) 513-1400   %FO: 100
Bus: *Portal and document management software*   Fax: (905) 513-1419
sales.

INSYSTEMS CORPORATION
PO Box 1167, 600 Albany Rd., Dayton, Ohio 45401
CEO: Michael Egan, Pres.
Bus: *Portal and document management software sales.*

Tel: (540) 344-7344
Fax:

%FO: 100
Emp: 75

● **INTERMAP TECHNOLOGIES CORPORATION**
1000, 736-8th Ave. SW, Calgary AB T2P 1H4, Canada
CEO: Brian L. Bullock, Pres. & CEO
Bus: *Provides mapping and surveying services.*

Tel: 403-266-0900
Fax: 403-265-0499
www.intermaptechnologies.com

Rev: $18
Emp: 276

NAICS: 541330, 541360

INTERMAP TECHNOLOGIES CORPORATION
400 Inverness Pkwy South, Ste. 330, Englewood, Colorado 80112
CEO: Brian Bullock, CEO
Bus: *Provides mapping and surveying services.*

Tel: (303) 708-0955
Fax: (303) 708-0952

%FO: 100
Emp: 25

● **INTERNATIONAL ABSORBENTS INC.**
1569 Dempsey Rd., North Vancouver BC V7K 1S8, Canada
CEO: Gordon L. Ellis, Chmn. & Pres. & CEO
Bus: *Mfr. biodegradable absorption products.*

Tel: 604-681-6181
Fax: 604-904-4105
www.absorbent.com

Rev: $22
Emp: 117

NAICS: 322299, 424130

ABSORBENTS CORP.
6960 Salashan Pkwy., Ferndale, Washington 92848
CEO: Duglas E. Ellis, Pres. & COO
Bus: *Mfr. and sales of biodegradable absorption products.*

Tel: (360) 734-7415
Fax: (360) 671-1588

%FO: 100
Emp: 100

● **INTERPIPE INC.**
R.R.#3, 3320 Miles Rd., Mount Hope ON L0R 1W0, Canada
CEO: Mbianni Bianco, Pres.
Bus: *Steel pipe manufacture.*

Tel: 905-679-6999
Fax: 905-679-6544
www.interpipe.com

NAICS: 331210, 332919, 423830

INTERPIPE INC.
12651 Briar Forest Dr., Houston, Texas 77077
CEO: Horst Stratmann, Chmn.
Bus: *Steel pipe sales.*

Tel: (281) 531-7700
Fax: (281) 531-7700

%FO: 100
Emp: 14

● **INTERTAPE POLYMER GROUP**
110 E. Montee de Liesse, Saint-Laurent QC H4T 1N4, Canada
CEO: Melbourne F. Yull, Chmn. & CEO
Bus: *Packaging and masking tape manufacture and sales.*

Tel: 514-731-7591
Fax: 514-731-5039
www.intertapepolymer.com

Rev: $692
Emp: 2,600

NAICS: 322222, 326112, 333993

INTERTAPE POLYMER GROUP
3647 Cortez Rd West, Bradenton, Florida 34210
CEO: Dale McSween, Pres.
Bus: *Sales/distribution of packing/masking tape.*
Tel: (941) 727-5788
Fax: (941) 727-1568
%FO: 100

• **INTIER AUTOMOTIVE INC.**
521 Newpark Blvd., Newmarket ON L3Y 4X7, Canada
CEO: Donald R. Walker, Chmn. & Pres. & CEO
Bus: *Automotive seating systems manufacture and*
NAICS: 336360
Tel: 905-898-5200
Fax: 905-898-6093
www.intier.com
Rev: $5,474
Emp: 24,100

INTIER AUTOMOTIVE INC.
39600 Lewis Dr., Novi, Michigan 48377
CEO: Tom Apostolis, Pres.
Bus: *Automotive seating systems sales.*
Tel: (248) 567-4000
Fax: (248) 567-5420
%FO: 100
Emp: 2,500

• **INTRAWEST CORPORATION**
200 Burrard St., Ste. 800, Vancouver BC V6C 3L6, Canada
CEO: Joe S. Houssian, Chmn. & Pres. & CEO
Bus: *Owns and operates ski resorts and affiliated hotels and restaurants.*
NAICS: 611620, 713920, 713990, 721110, 721199
Tel: 604-669-9777
Fax: 604-669-0605
www.intrawest.com
Rev: $1,544
Emp: 21,900

ABERCROMBIE & KENT
1520 Kensington Rd., Ste. 212, Oak Brook, Illinois 60523
CEO: Geoffrey J. W. Kent, Chmn. & CEO
Bus: *Travel agencies.*
Tel: (630) 954-2944
Fax: (630) 954-3324

COPPER MOUNTAIN
PO Box 3001, 209 Ten Mile Circle, Frisco, Colorado 80443
CEO: David Barry, COO
Bus: *Operates a ski resort.*
Tel: (970) 968-2882
Fax: (970) 968-3155
%FO: 100
Emp: 350

INTRAWEST GOLF
14646 North Kierland Blvd., Ste. 210, Scottsdale, Arizona 85254
CEO: Jim McLaughlin, Pres.
Bus: *Luxury golf resort accommodation.*
Tel: (480) 874-2200
Fax: (480) 874-2610
%FO: 100
Emp: 30

INTRAWEST/SQUAW CORP.
PO Box 3710, 1910 Squaw Valley Rd., Olympic Valley, California 96146
CEO: Alexander C. Cushing, Chmn.
Bus: *Ski Lodge.*
Tel: (530) 584-1000
Fax: (530) 584-0100
%FO: 100
Emp: 250

KEYSTONE REAL ESTATE
PO Box 8876, 574 County Rd. 5, Keystone, Colorado 80435
CEO: Renie Kelly Hunt,
Bus: *Colorado real estate.*
Tel: (970) 496-4522
Fax: (970) 496-4524
%FO: 100

MOUNTAIN CREEK
200 Rte. 94, Vernon Hills, New Jersey 07462
CEO: Charles Blier, VP
Bus: *Ski resort.*
Tel: (973) 827-3900
Fax: (973) 209-3363
%FO: 100
Emp: 200

SANDESTIN GOLF & BEACH RESORT
9300 Emerald Coast Pkwy. West, Sandestin, Florida 32550
CEO: Michael Stange, Gen. Mgr.   Tel: (850) 267-8000   %FO: 100
Bus: *Resort hotel.*   Fax: (850) 267-8222   Emp: 1,200

SNOWSHOE MOUNTAIN
PO Box 10, 1 Snowshoe Dr., Snowshoe, West Virginia 26209
CEO: Joe Houssian, Pres.   Tel: (304) 572-1000   %FO: 100
Bus: *Hotel operations.*   Fax: (304) 572-5616   Emp: 1,400

SOLITUDE RESORT DEVELOPMENT
12000 Big Cottonwood Canyon, Solitude, Utah 84121
CEO: Gary L De Seelhorst, Chmn.   Tel: (435) 649-4803   %FO: 100
Bus: *Hotel operations.*   Fax: (435) 649-6581   Emp: 450

STRATTON MOUNTAIN
R.R. #1 Box 145, South Londonderry, Vermont 05155
CEO: Jan Dlouhy, Pres.   Tel: (802) 297-2200   %FO: 100
Bus: *Hotel operations.*   Fax: (802) 297-4395

WINTER PARK RESORT
PO Box 36, Winter Park, Colorado 80436
CEO: Gary De Frange, Pres.   Tel: (970) 726-5514   %FO: 100
Bus: *Ski Lodge.*   Fax: (970) 726-5993   Emp: 300

• **INTRINSYC SOFTWARE INTERNATIONAL, INC.**
700 W. Pender St., 10/F, Vancouver BC V6C 1G8, Canada
CEO: Derek Spratt, CEO   Tel: 604-801-6461   Rev: $11
Bus: *Managing systems software.*   Fax: 604-801-6417   Emp: 125
        www.intrinsyc.com
NAICS: 511210

    INTRINSYC SOFTWARE INTERNATIONAL, INC.
    11130 NE 33rd Place, Bellevue, Washington 98004
    CEO: Derek Spratt, CEO   Tel: (425) 732-4950   %FO: 100
    Bus: *Systems software sales.*   Fax: (425) 732-4901

• **IPL INC.**
140 Commerciale St., Saint-Damine QC G0R 2Y0, Canada
CEO: Julien Metivier, CEO   Tel: 418-789-2880   Rev: $165
Bus: *Industrial plastic products manufacture and*   Fax: 418-789-3153   Emp: 1,000
        www.ipl-plastics.com
NAICS: 326199

    IPL PRODUCTS LTD.
    640 Lincoln St., Worcester, Massachusetts 01605
    CEO: John Hallock   Tel: (508) 351-6050   %FO: 100
    Bus: *Develop/mfr. reusable plastic containers*   Fax: (508) 351-6044
        and totes.

    JATCO, INC.
    725 Zwissig Way, Union City, California 94587
    CEO: Paul Appelblom   Tel: (510) 487-0888   %FO: 100
    Bus: *Plastics manufacture.*   Fax: (510) 487-1880

● **IPSCO, INC.**
PO Box 1670, Armour Rd., Regina SK S4P 3C7, Canada
CEO: David Suterland, Pres. & CEO   Tel: 306-924-7700   Rev: $2,453
Bus: *Steel and pipe manufacturing.*   Fax: 306-924-7500   Emp: 2,601
                                                     www.ipsco.com
NAICS: 331210, 331221, 331513, 332116

   IPSCO INC.
   PO Box 64303, St. Paul, Minnesota 55164
   CEO: Joseph Folio, Mgr.   Tel: (651) 631-9031   %FO: 100
   Bus: *Steel manufacture and sales.*   Fax: (651) 631-9670   Emp: 50

   IPSCO INC.
   650 Warrenville Rd., Ste. 500, Lisle, Illinois 60532
   CEO: David Sutherland, Pres.   Tel: (630) 810-4800   %FO: 100
   Bus: *Steel manufacture and sales.*   Fax: (630) 810-4600   Emp: 550

   IPSCO INC.
   13609 Industrial Rd., Ste. 114, Houston, Texas 77015
   CEO: Peter Vojvodich, Mgr.   Tel: (713) 341-7700   %FO: 100
   Bus: *Steel manufacture and sales.*   Fax: (713) 455-0668   Emp: 40

   IPSCO INC.
   12400 Highway 43 North, Axis, Alabama 36505
   CEO: Paul Wilson, Mgr.   Tel: (251) 662-4400   %FO: 100
   Bus: *Steel manufacture and sales.*   Fax: (251) 662-4360   Emp: 300

   IPSCO STEEL, INC.
   1770 Bill Sharp Blvd., Muscatine, Iowa 52761
   CEO: Richard Acquaviva, Mgr.   Tel: (563) 381-5300   %FO: 100
   Bus: *Steel mill operators.*   Fax: (563) 381-5322   Emp: 250

   IPSCO TUBULARS INC.
   2011 Seventh Ave., PO Box 18, Comanche, Iowa 52730
   CEO: David Green, Mgr.   Tel: (319) 242-0000   %FO: 100
   Bus: *Steel pipe mill operator.*   Fax: (319) 242-9408   Emp: 204

   IPSCO TUBULARS INC.
   5460 North State Hwy. 137, Blytheville, Arkansas 72315
   CEO: Ken McLean, Mgr.   Tel: (870) 763-7700   %FO: 100
   Bus: *Steel manufacture and sales.*   Fax: (870) 763-7991

   IPSCO TUBULARS INC.
   1201 R St., Geneva, Nebraska 68361
   CEO: Russ Reinke, Mgr.   Tel: (402) 759-4401   %FO: 100
   Bus: *Steel pipe mill.*   Fax: (402) 759-3088   Emp: 25

● **ISOTECHNIKA INC.**
2100 College Plaza, 8215 112th St., Edmonton AB T6G 2C8, Canada
CEO: Robert Foster, Chmn. & CEO   Tel: 780-487-1600   Rev: $1
Bus: *Drug and pharmaceutical manufacture and sales.*   Fax: 780-484-4105   Emp: 90
                                                     www.isotechnika.com
NAICS: 325412, 541710

ISOTECHNIKA INC.
17301 North Perimeter Dr., Scottsdale, Arizona 85255
CEO: Joseph Koziak, Mgr.   Tel: (480) 505-0540   %FO: 100
Bus: *Mfr. of Biopharmaceuticals &*   Fax: (480) 505-0545
   biotherapeutics.

● **IVACO INC.**
1 Place Alexis Nihon, 3400 de Maisonneuve W., Ste. 1501, Montreal QC H3Z 3B8, Canada
CEO: Gordon Silverman, Pres. & CEO   Tel: 514-288-4545
Bus: *Steel and wire rods manufacture.*   Fax: 514-284-9414
                                           www.ivaco.com
   NAICS: 331111

   IVACO STEEL MILLS USA INC.
   3001 West Big Beaver Rd., Troy, Michigan 48084
   CEO: Gordon Silverman, Pres. & CEO   Tel: (248) 649-8888   %FO: 100
   Bus: *Mfr. fastener products.*   Fax: (248) 649-6116

   IVACO, INC.
   920 Providence Rd., Ste. 305, Baltimore, Maryland 21286
   CEO: Donald Habersack, Mgr.   Tel: (410) 823-7696   %FO: 100
   Bus: *Mfr. wire products and wire rod processing.*   Fax:

   VERMONT FASTENERS MANUFACTURING
   50 Jonergin Dr., Swanton, Vermont 05488
   CEO: Peter Kasper, Mgr.   Tel: (802) 868-3663   %FO: 100
   Bus: *Produces high strength steel fasteners for*   Fax: (802) 868-2089   Emp: 9
      the construction industry.

● **IVANHOE ENERGY INC.**
654-999 Canada Place, Vancouver BC V6C 3E1, Canada
CEO: E. Leon Daniel, Pres. & CEO   Tel: 604-688-8323   Rev: $18
Bus: *Energy.*   Fax: 604-688-7168   Emp: 137
                                           www.ivanhoe-energy.com
   NAICS: 211111, 211112, 324110

   IVANHOE ENERGY USA INC.
   5060 California Ave., Ste. 400, PO Box 9279, Bakersfield, California 93389
   CEO: E. Leon Daniel, Pres.   Tel: (661) 869-2887   %FO: 100
   Bus: *Engaged in energy.*   Fax: (661) 869-2820   Emp: 20

● **JACQUES WHITFORD GROUP**
3 Spectacle Lake Dr., Dartmouth NS B3B 1W8, Canada
CEO: Bob Youden, CEO   Tel: 902-468-7777   Rev: $72
Bus: *Environmental, geotechnical and risk management* Fax: 902-468-9009   Emp: 900
   consultants.   www.jacqueswhitford.com
   NAICS: 541330, 541611, 541690, 551111, 812990

   JACQUES WHITFORD
   24 Albion Rd., Ste. 220, Lincoln, Rhode Island 02865
   CEO: Stan Genega, Pres.   Tel: (401) 312-8005   %FO: 100
   Bus: *Business Consulting*   Fax: (401) 312-8010   Emp: 11

JACQUES WHITFORD
75 Pearl St., Ste. 410, Portland, Maine 04101
CEO: Stan Genega, Pres.   Tel: (207) 761-7790
Bus: *Engineering services*   Fax: (207) 761-7631

JACQUES WHITFORD
5 W. Main St., Ste. 109, Elmsford, New York 10523
CEO: Stan Genega, Pres.   Tel: (914) 592-1804
Bus: *Geological & engineering consulting* Fax: (914) 592-1805   Emp: 10

JACQUES WHITFORD
1920 S. Highland Ave., Ste. 114, Lombard, Illinois 60148
CEO: Stan Genega, Pres.   Tel: (630) 495-3813
Bus: *Geological consultant*   Fax: (630) 495-3817

JACQUES WHITFORD COMPANY INC.
27 Congress St., Portsmouth, New Hampshire 03801
CEO: Stan Genega, Pres.   Tel: (603) 431-4899   %FO: 100
Bus: *Environmental, geotechnical and risk* Fax: (603) 431-5982   Emp: 120
    management consultants.

JACQUES WHITFORD COMPANY INC.
450 South Gravers Rd., Ste. 105, Plymouth Meeting, Pennsylvania 19462
CEO: Stan Genega, Pres.   Tel: (484) 322-0301   %FO: 100
Bus: *Environmental consulting*   Fax: (484) 322-0302

JACQUES WHITFORD COMPANY INC.
800 West Cummings Park, Ste. 5650, Woburn, Massachusetts 01801
CEO: Stan Genega, Pres.   Tel: (781) 935-9281   %FO: 100
Bus: *Environmental, geotechnical and risk* Fax: (781) 935-9307
    management consultants.

● **THE JEAN COUTU GROUP (PJC) INC.**
530 Beriault St., Longueuil QC J4G 1SI, Canada
CEO: Jean Coutu, Chmn.   Tel: 450-646-9611   Rev: $2,925
Bus: *Owns and operates chain drugstores, including* Fax: 450-646-5649   Emp: 9,780
    Jean Coutu, Maxi Drug and Brooks Pharmacy. www.jeancoutu.com
NAICS: 446110, 446120, 531120, 531312, 531390

   BROOKS PHARMACY
   50 Service Rd., Warwick, Rhode Island 02886
   CEO: Michel Coutu, SVP   Tel: (401) 825-3900   %FO: 100
   Bus: *Owns and operates chain drugstores.* Fax: (401) 825-3996

● **THE JIM PATTISON GROUP**
1067 West Cordova St., Ste. 1800, Vancouver BC V6C 1C7, Canada
CEO: Jimmy Pattison, CEO   Tel: 604-688-6764
Bus: *Plastic signs and industrial machinery* Fax: 604-687-2601   Emp: 27,000
                                          www.jimpattison.com
NAICS: 333512, 423990

ALASKA NEWS
325 West Potter Dr., Anchorage, Alaska 99518
CEO: Mike Beck, Pres.   Tel: (907) 563-3251
Bus: *Wholesale books & periodicals*   Fax: (907) 261-8523   Emp: 50

COROPLAST
4501 Spring Valley Rd., Dallas, Texas 75244
CEO: Ken Vandervelde, Pres.   Tel: (972) 392-2241
Bus: *Rubber & plastic product*   Fax: (972) 392-2242   Emp: 151

GENPAK
68 Warren St., Glens Falls, New York 12801
CEO: Jim Pattison, Chmn.   Tel: (518) 798-9511
Bus: *Plastic products*   Fax: (518) 798-3302   Emp: 1,115

GREAT ATLANTIC NEWS
4070 Shirley Dr. S.W., Atlanta, Georgia 30336
CEO: Charlie Gee, Mgr.   Tel: (404) 691-2800
Bus: *Books, periodicals, & newspapers*   Fax: (404) 691-3147

GREAT MIDATLANTIC NEWS
2571 Saradan Dr., Jackson, Michigan 49202
CEO: John Swett, Principal   Tel: (517) 784-7163
Bus: *Wholesale periodicals.*   Fax: (517) 784-0075   Emp: 800

GREAT PACIFIC NEWS COMPANY, INC.
3400 D Industry Dr. E., Fife, Washington 98424
CEO: Mike Cooke, Pres.   Tel: (253) 922-8011
Bus: *Books, periodicals, & newspapers*   Fax: (253) 896-5028   Emp: 1,500

PATTISON SIGN GROUP
5500 Peachtree Industrial Blvd., Norcross, Georgia 30071
CEO: Jim Pattison Jr., CEO   Tel: (770) 455-8831   %FO: 100
Bus: *Signs & advertising specialties*   Fax: (770) 454-7383   Emp: 100

RIPLEY'S ENTERTAINMENT, INC.
7576 Kingspointe Pkwy., Ste. 188, Orlando, Florida 32819
CEO: Bob Masterson, Pres.   Tel: (407) 345-8010
Bus: *Amusement parks, arcades, attractions*   Fax: (407) 345-0801   Emp: 225

SELECT MEDIA SERVICES
1685 Boggs Rd., Ste. 400, Duluth, Georgia 30096
CEO: John Seebach, member   Tel: (678) 380-9880
Bus: *Wholesale books & periodicals*   Fax: (678) 380-8870   Emp: 119

THE NEWS GROUP
4070 Shirley Dr. S.W., Atlanta, Georgia 30336
CEO: John Seebach, Pres.   Tel: (404) 691-2800
Bus: *Wholesale periodicals.*   Fax: (404) 691-3147   Emp: 201

- **KATZ GROUP CANADA LTD.**
  10104 103rd Ave., Ste.1702, Bell Tower, Edmonton AB T5J 0H8, Canada
  CEO: Larry Latowsky, Pres.   Tel: 780-990-0505   Rev: $4,510
  Bus: *Owner of pharmacies*   Fax: 780-425-6118   Emp: 15,000
                                      www.katzgroup.com
  NAICS: 446110

  > **SNYDER'S DRUG STORES, INC.**
  > 14525 Hwy. 7, Minnetonka, Minnesota 55345
  > CEO: Andrew A. Giancamilli, CEO   Tel: (952) 935-5441   %FO: 100
  > Bus: *Owner of drug stores*   Fax: (952) 936-2512   Emp: 1,580

- **KELMAN TECHNOLOGIES INC.**
  540 5th Ave. SW, Ste. 600, Calgary AB T2P 0M2, Canada
  CEO: Rene VandenBrand, Pres. & CEO   Tel: 403-262-5220   Rev: $17
  Bus: *Seismic data management services.*   Fax: 402-263-1518   Emp: 171
                                               www.kelman.com
  NAICS: 518210, 541690

  > **KELMAN TECHNOLOGIES INC.**
  > 1800 S. Dairy Ashford, Ste. 222, Houston, Texas 77077
  > CEO: Paul Huff, Mgr.   Tel: (281) 293-0537   %FO: 100
  > Bus: *Seismic processing services.* Fax: (281) 293-0641

  > **KELMAN TECHNOLOGIES INC.**
  > Union Plaza, 3030 Northwest Expressway, Ste. 1727, Oklahoma City, Oklahoma 73112
  > CEO: Rene VandenBrand, Pres. & CEO   Tel: (405) 606-4123   %FO: 100
  > Bus: *Seismic processing services.*   Fax: (405) 606-4128

  > **KELMAN TECHNOLOGIES INC.**
  > Mile High Center, 1700 Broadway, Ste. 414, Denver, Colorado 80290
  > CEO: Barry Newman, Mgr.   Tel: (303) 832-5086   %FO: 100
  > Bus: *Seismic processing services.* Fax: (303) 832-6014

- **KINAXIS**
  700 Silver Seven Rd., Ottawa ON K2V 1C3, Canada
  CEO: Douglas P. Colbeth, Chmn. & Pres. & CEO   Tel: 613-592-5780   Rev: $17
  Bus: *Web-based application and Manufacturing Insight* Fax: 613-592-0584   Emp: 121
      software sales.   www.kinaxis.com
  NAICS: 511210

  > **KINAXIS**
  > 40 E. Chicago Ave., Ste. 391, Chicago, Illinois 60611
  > CEO: Kelli-Ann Underhill   Tel: (866) 236-3249   %FO: 100
  > Bus: *Management & Logistics software.* Fax: (866) 236-3249

- **KINGSWAY FINANCIAL SERVICES INC.**
  5310 Explorer Dr., Ste. 200, Mississauga ON L4W 5H8, Canada
  CEO: William G. Star, Chmn. & Pres. & CEO   Tel: 905-629-7888   Rev: $2,031
  Bus: *Provides casualty and property insurance*   Fax: 905-629-5008   Emp: 2,027
                                                     www.kingsway-financial.com
  NAICS: 524126

AMERICAN COUNTRY INSURANCE COMPANY
150 Northwest Point Blvd., Elk Grove Village, Illinois 60007
CEO: Roger T. Beck, Pres. & CEO   Tel: (847) 700-8200   %FO: 100
Bus: *Provides casualty and property insurance*   Fax: (847) 700-8280
    services.

AMERICAN SERVICE INSURANCE
150 Northwest Point Blvd., Elk Grove Village, Illinois 60007
CEO: John T. Clark, Pres.   Tel: (847) 472-6700
Bus: *Fire/casualty insurance.*   Fax: (847) 228-3920   Emp: 130

AVALON RISK MANAGEMENT, INC.
84 Wharf St., Salem, Massachusetts 01970
CEO: Michael S. Brown   Tel: (978) 740-5677   %FO: 100
Bus: *Provides casualty and property insurance*   Fax: (978) 740-6627
    services.

HAMILTON RISK MANAGEMENT CO.
3155 N.W. 77th Ave., Miami, Florida 33122
CEO: Roberto Espin Jr., Chmn.   Tel: (305) 716-6000
Bus: *Fire casualty insurance.*   Fax: (305) 716-6404   Emp: 250

KINGSWAY AMERICA INC.
150 Northwest Point Blvd., Elk Grove Village, Illinois 60007
CEO: W. Shaun Jackson, VP   Tel: (847) 871-6400   %FO: 100
Bus: *Provides casualty and property insurance*   Fax: (847) 264-2700
    services.

LINCOLN GENERAL INSURANCE CO.
3350 Whiteford Rd., PO Box 3709, York, Pennsylvania 17402
CEO: William G. Star, Pres.   Tel: (717) 757-0000
Bus: *Commercial physical damage insurance.*   Fax: (717) 751-0165   Emp: 87

SOUTHERN UNITED FIRE INSURNACE CO.
One Southern Way, PO Box 190421, Mobile, Alabama 36619
CEO: Richard D. Murray, Pres.   Tel: (800) 677-7834
Bus: *Automobile insurance.*   Fax: Emp: 156

UNIVERSAL CASUALTY CO.
150 Northwest Point Blvd., Elk Grove Village, Illinois 60007
CEO: Marshall Romanz, Pres.   Tel: (847) 700-9100
Bus: *Insurance Company.*   Fax: (847) 700-9170   Emp: 125

● **KINROSS GOLD CORPORATION**
40 King St. West, 52/F, Scotia Plaza, Toronto ON M5H 3Y2, Canada
CEO: Tye W. Burt, Pres. & CEO   Tel: 416-365-5123   Rev: $572
Bus: *Gold mining.*   Fax: 416-363-6622   Emp: 6,400
    www.kinross.com

NAICS: 212221, 212222, 213114

    FAIRBANKS GOLD MINING, INC.
    1 Fort Knox Rd., Fairbanks, Alaska 99712
    CEO: John Wild, VP & Gen. Mgr.   Tel: (907) 488-4653
    Bus: *Exploration & developing./ Gold ore mining.*   Fax: (907) 490-2290   Emp: 360

KINROSS GOLD
681 Sierra Rose Dr., Ste. B, Reno, Nevada 89509
CEO: Richard Dye, VP   Tel: (775) 829-1000
Bus: *Gold ore mining.*   Fax: (775) 829-1666   Emp: 1,573

KINROSS GOLD
Hwy. 376, Round Mountain, Nevada 89045
CEO: Mike Doyle, Gen. Mgr.   Tel: (775) 377-2366
Bus: *Gold & silver ore mining.*   Fax: Emp: 509

KINROSS GOLD
363 Fish Hatchery Rd., Republic, Washington 99166
CEO: Robert Taylor, VP   Tel: (509) 775-3157
Bus: *Gold ore mining petroleum refiner.* Fax: Emp: 109

KINROSS GOLD
185 S. State St., Ste. 820, Salt Lake City, Utah 84111
CEO: Richard Dye, VP   Tel: (801) 363-9152
Bus: *Gold & silver mining.*   Fax: Emp: 15

● **LASIDO INC.**
19420 Clark-Graham Ave., Baie d'Urfe QC H9X 3R8, Canada
CEO: Robert Godin, Pres. & CEO   Tel: 514-457-7977
Bus: *Acoustic guitar manufacture.*   Fax: 514-457-5774
                                        www.lasido.com
NAICS: 339992

    GUITABEC USA INC.
    42 Industrial Park Rd., Berlin, New Hampshire 03570
    CEO: Robert Godin, Pres.   Tel: (603) 752-1432   %FO: 100
    Bus: *Acoustic guitar manufacture and sales.* Fax: (603) 752-1432 Emp: 32

● **LE CHATEAU INC.**
5695 Ferrier St., Montreal QC H4P 1N1, Canada
CEO: Herschel H. Segal, Chmn. & CEO   Tel: 514-738-7000
Bus: *Clothing manufacture and sales.* Fax: 514-783-3670   Emp: 2,000
                                        www.le-chateau.com
NAICS: 315211, 315212, 316213, 316214, 448110, 448120, 448130, 448140, 448150

    LE CHATEAU INC.
    704 Broadway, New York, New York 10011
    CEO: Terri Frank, Mgr.   Tel: (212) 674-5560   %FO: 100
    Bus: *Clothing sales.*   Fax: (212) 674-5560

    LE CHATEAU INC.
    73061 El Paseo, Palm Desert, California 92260
    CEO: Richard Vincent, Mgr.   Tel: (760) 568-9400   %FO: 100
    Bus: *Clothing sales.*   Fax: Emp: 5

    LE CHATEAU INC.
    34 West 34th St., New York, New York 10001
    CEO: Tracine Hampton, Mgr.   Tel: (212) 967-0025   %FO: 100
    Bus: *Clothing sales.*   Fax: (212) 967-6901

LE CHATEAU INC.
314 N. Beverly Dr., Beverly Hills, California 90210
CEO: Mike Stern, Pres.   Tel: (310) 271-9801   %FO: 100
Bus: *Clothing sales.*   Fax: Emp: 16

• **LEADING BRANDS, INC.**
1500 West Georgia St., Ste. 1800, Vancouver BC V6G 2Z6, Canada
CEO: Ralph D. McRae, Chmn. & Pres. & CEO   Tel: 604-685-5200   Rev: $34
Bus: *Soft drinks bottler and distributor.* Fax: 604-685-5249   Emp: 188
                                              www.lbix.com
NAICS: 312111
    LEADING BRANDS, INC.
    880 Canal St., Stamford, Connecticut 06902
    CEO: Howard E. Wishner, Pres.   Tel: (203) 323-9435   %FO: 100
    Bus: *Soft drinks bottler and distributor.* Fax: (203) 323-9461

• **LEDCOR GROUP OF COMPANIES**
1067 W. Cordova St., Ste. 1200, Vancouver BC V6C 1C7, Canada
CEO: David Lede, Chmn. & CEO   Tel: 604-681-7500
Bus: *Engaged in construction.*   Fax: 604-681-4385
                                            www.ledcor.com
NAICS: 236210, 237120, 237310, 237990
    LEDCOR GROUP OF COMPANIES
    9466 Black Mountain Rd., Ste. 250, San Diego, California 92126
    CEO: Mike Fisher Sr., VP   Tel: (858) 527-6400   %FO: 100
    Bus: *Construction services.*   Fax: (858) 527-6410

• **LEGACY HOTELS REAL ESTATE INVESTMENT TRUST**
100 Wellington St. West, Ste. 2000, Calgary AB M5K 1H1, Canada
CEO: Neil J. Labatte, Pres. & CEO   Tel: 416-860-6100   Rev: $626
Bus: *Hotel management services.*   Fax: 416-860-6101   Emp: 9,000
                                            www.legacyhotels.ca
NAICS: 525930, 721110
    FAIRMONT HOTELS & RESORTS
    100 Boyes Blvd., Sonoma, California 95476
    CEO: William Fatt, CEO   Tel: (707) 938-9000   %FO: 100
    Bus: *Hotel services.*   Fax:

    FAIRMONT HOTELS & RESORTS
    1 Kaikaina St., Kailua, Hawaii 96734
    CEO: William Fatt, CEO   Tel: (808) 885-2000   %FO: 100
    Bus: *Hotel services.*   Fax: Emp: 90

    FAIRMONT HOTELS & RESORTS
    1100 N Glebe Rd., Ste. 1070, Arlington, Virginia 22201
    CEO: William Fatt, CEO   Tel: (703) 524-2201   %FO: 100
    Bus: *Hotel services.*   Fax:

FAIRMONT WASHINGTON DC
2401 M St. NW, Washington, District of Columbia 20037
CEO: William Fatt, CEO   Tel: (202) 429-2400   %FO: 100
Bus: *Hotel services.*   Fax: (202) 457-5010

● **LEITCH TECHNOLOGY CORPORATION**
150 Ferrand Dr., Ste. 700, Toronto ON M3C 3E5, Canada
CEO: Timothy E. Thorsteinson, Pres. & CEO   Tel: 416-445-9640   Rev: $113
Bus: *Mfr. products for processing audio and video*   Fax: 416-443-3088   Emp: 791
  signals.   www.leitch.com
NAICS: 334220, 334310, 512110, 512191, 512199

  LEITCH INC.
  377 Rector Place, Ste. 24E, New York, New York 10280
  CEO: Chris Ziemer   Tel: (212) 786-1473   %FO: 100
  Bus: *Mfr./sales of products for processing audio*   Fax: (201) 242-0271
    and video signals.

  LEITCH INC.
  11 Spiral Dr., Ste. 10, Florence, Kentucky 41042
  CEO: Marlene Franklin   Tel: (859) 371-5533   %FO: 100
  Bus: *Mfr./sales of products for processing audio*   Fax: (859) 371-3729
    and video signals.

  LEITCH INC.
  207 Duke Dr., Kokomo, Indiana 46902
  CEO: Jon Powell   Tel: (765) 864-0982   %FO: 100
  Bus: *Mfr./sales of products for processing audio*   Fax: (765) 864-0968
    and video signals.

  LEITCH INC.
  15222 68th Place North, Maple Grove, Minnesota 55372
  CEO: Mark Sharp   Tel: (763) 551-9730   %FO: 100
  Bus: *Mfr./sales of products for processing audio*   Fax:
    and video signals.

  LEITCH INC.
  11807 Ridge View Circle, Clermont, Florida 34711
  CEO: Mark Rodgers   Tel: (352) 242-1875   %FO: 100
  Bus: *Mfr./sales of products for processing audio*   Fax: (352) 242-9168
    and video signals.

  LEITCH INC.
  42808 N. Livingstone Way, Anthem, Arizona 85086
  CEO: Juan Noboa   Tel: (480) 664-9541   %FO: 100
  Bus: *Mfr./sales of products for processing audio*   Fax:
    and video signals.

  LEITCH INC.
  One Bridge Plaza, Ste. 350, Fort Lee, New Jersey 07024
  CEO: John Newton   Tel: (201) 242-0271   %FO: 100
  Bus: *Mfr./sales of products for processing audio*   Fax: (201) 242-0272
    and video signals.

LEITCH INC.
4400 Vanowen St., Burbank, California 91505
CEO: Steve Roth, Controller
Bus: *Mfr./sales of products for processing audio and video signals.*

Tel: (818) 843-7004
Fax: (818) 842-8945

%FO: 100
Emp: 63

LEITCH INC.
6511 NE Alameda St., Portland, Oregon 97213
CEO: Dave Hagerty
Bus: *Mfr./sales of products for processing audio and video signals.*

Tel: (503) 228-2384
Fax:

%FO: 100

LEITCH INC.
3400 Preakness Dr., Flower Mound, Texas 75028
CEO: Jon Ulfsrud
Bus: *Mfr./sales of products for processing audio and video signals.*

Tel: (972) 899-2633
Fax:

%FO: 100

LEITCH INC.
4512 Lake Park Dr., Ackworth, Georgia 30101
CEO: Chris Soresi
Bus: *Mfr./sales of products for processing audio and video signals.*

Tel: (678) 575-3104
Fax:

%FO: 100

LEITCH INC.
7 James Hayward Rd., Glen Mills, Pennsylvania 19342
CEO: Richard Cooper
Bus: *Mfr./sales of products for processing audio and video signals.*

Tel: (484) 410-6743
Fax:

%FO: 100

LEITCH INC.
920 Corporate Lane, Chesapeake, Virginia 23320-3641
CEO: Mike Gardner
Bus: *Mfr./sales of products for processing audio and video signals.*

Tel: (757) 548-2300
Fax: (757) 548-4088

%FO: 100
Emp: 100

LEITCH INC.
7090 Cerney Circle, Castle Rock, Colorado 80104
CEO: Brad Torr, Mgr.
Bus: *Mfr./sales of products for processing audio and video signals.*

Tel: (303) 814-6801
Fax: (303) 814-6803

%FO: 100
Emp: 5

LEITCH LATIN AMERICA
14750 NW 77th Ct., Ste. 320, Miami Lakes, Florida 33016
CEO: Ariel Sardinas
Bus: *Mfr./sales of products for processing audio and video signals.*

Tel: (305) 512-0045
Fax: (305) 362-0034

%FO: 100

● **LINAMAR CORPORATION**
287 Speedvale Ave. West, Guelph ON N1H 1C5, Canada
CEO: Linda S. Hasenfratz, CEO & Mng. Dir.
Bus: *Mfr. precision machine components.*

Tel: 519-836-7550
Fax: 519-824-8479
www.linamar.com

Rev: $1,182
Emp: 9,400

NAICS: 336312, 336399

EAGLE MANUFACTURING LLC
7100 Industrial Rd., Florence, Kentucky 41042
CEO: Bruce Reed, Gen. Mgr.   Tel: (859) 282-5900   %FO: 100
Bus: *Mfr. precision machine components.*   Fax: (859) 282-5925   Emp: 146

LINAMAR SALES CORP.
Raleigh Office Center, 25300 Telegraph Rd., Ste. 450, Southfield, Michigan 48034
CEO: Linda S. Hasenfratz, Pres. & CEO   Tel: (248) 355-3533   %FO: 100
Bus: *Mfr. precision machine components.*   Fax: (248) 355-3558

LINAMAR USA INC.
9401 Harrison Rd., Romulus, Michigan 48174
CEO: Linda S. Hasenfratz, Pres. & CEO   Tel: (734) 946-0610   %FO: 100
Bus: *Mfr. precision machine components.*   Fax: (734) 946-9660

MACLAREN PERFORMANCE TECHNOLOGIES INC.
32233 W. Eight Mile Rd., Livonia, Michigan 48152
CEO: Wiley R. McCoy, CEO   Tel: (248) 477-6240
Bus: *Mfr. of auto parts*   Fax: (248) 477-3349

SKYJACK MANUFACTURING
3810 460th Ave., Emmetsburg, Iowa 50536
CEO: Lloyd Spaulding, Pres.   Tel: (712) 852-2724   %FO: 100
Bus: *Mfr. aerial lifts.*   Fax: (712) 852-2952   Emp: 400

● **LINDSEY MORDEN GROUP INC.**
70 University Ave., Ste. 1200, Toronto ON M5J 2M4, Canada
CEO: Jan Christiansen, Pres. & CEO   Tel: 416-596-8020   Rev: $352
Bus: *Insurance claims services.*   Fax: 416-596-6510   Emp: 3,384
      www.lindseymordengroupinc.com
NAICS: 524291

    CUNNINGHAM LINDSEY U.S., INC.
    405 State Hwy., 121 Bypass, Bldg. A, Ste. 200, Lewisville, Texas 75067
    CEO: Jan Christiansen, Pres. & CEO   Tel: (214) 488-5139
    Bus: *Risk management.*   Fax: (214) 488-6767

    VALE NATIONAL TRAINING CENTER
    5070 Ritter Rd., Ste. 130, Mechanicsburg, Pennsylvania 17055
    CEO: Ron Smith, Mgr.   Tel: (717) 790-9950   %FO: 100
    Bus: *Insurance claims services.*   Fax: (717) 790-9506

    VALE NATIONAL TRAINING CENTER
    2424 East Randol Mill Rd., Arlington, Texas 76011
    CEO: Steve Le Claire, Pres.   Tel: (817) 633-4800   %FO: 100
    Bus: *Insurance claims services.*   Fax: (817) 633-2922   Emp: 13

    VALE NATIONAL TRAINING CENTER
    2590 North Grove Industrial Dr., Ste. 105, Fresno, California 93727
    CEO: Gene Hensley, Sales Mgr.   Tel: (559) 252-8138   %FO: 100
    Bus: *Insurance claims services.*   Fax: (559) 252-2539

- **LIONS GATE ENTERTAINMENT CORPORATION**
  555 Brooksbank Ave., North Vancouver BC V7J 355, Canada
  CEO: Jon Feitheimer, Chmn. & CEO
  Bus: *Production and distribution of independent films.*

  Tel: 604-983-5555
  Fax: 604-983-5554
  www.lionsgatefilms.com

  Rev: $843
  Emp: 316

  NAICS: 512110, 512120, 512191, 512199

  LIONS GATE TELEVISION CORPORATION
  2700 Colorado Ave., Ste. 200, Santa Monica, California 90404
  CEO: Kevin Beggs, Pres.
  Bus: *Independent film production and distribution.*

  Tel: (310) 449-9200
  Fax: (310) 255-3870

  %FO: 100

- **LIQUIDATION WORLD INC.**
  3880 29th St. NE, Calgary AB T1Y 6B6, Canada
  CEO: Jonathan Hill, Pres. & CEO
  Bus: *Discount & variety retail.*

  Tel: 403-250-1222
  Fax: 403-291-1306
  www.liquidationworld.com

  Rev: $128
  Emp: 1,800

  NAICS: 445110, 452990

  LIQUIDATION WORLD INC.
  7714 North Division St., Spokane, Washington 99208
  CEO: Dana Marlow, Mgr.
  Bus: *Discount stores.*

  Tel: (509) 482-3111
  Fax:

  LIQUIDATION WORLD INC.
  3101 Penland Pkwy., Ste. 8, Anchorage, Alaska 99507
  CEO: Dale Gilespie, Pres.
  Bus: *Discount stores.*

  Tel: (907) 277-7511
  Fax:

  LIQUIDATION WORLD INC.
  6945 Overland Rd., Boise, Idaho 83704
  CEO: Mike Gable, Mgr.
  Bus: *Discount stores.*

  Tel: (208) 321-0185
  Fax:

  %FO: 100

  LIQUIDATION WORLD INC.
  4800 10th Ave. South, Great Falls, Montana 59405
  CEO: Scott Schaff, Mgr.
  Bus: *Discount stores.*

  Tel: (406) 761-3600
  Fax:

  %FO: 100
  Emp: 8

- **LMI (LASER MEASUREMENT INTERNATIONAL INC.)**
  1673 Cliveden Avenue, Delta BC V4G IH5, Canada
  CEO: Leonard Metcalfe, CEO
  Bus: *Mfr. optoelectronic monitoring and measuring equipment.*

  Tel: 604-636-1011
  Fax: 604-516-8368
  www.lmint.com

  NAICS: 334510

  LMI SELCOM INC.
  21455 Melrose Ave., Ste. 22, Southfield, Michigan 48075
  CEO: Anna Lofgren, VP & Gen. Mgr.
  Bus: *Optoelectronic monitoring/measuring equipment.*

  Tel: (248) 355-5900
  Fax: (248) 355-3283

  %FO: 100
  Emp: 10

● **LML PAYMENT SYSTEMS INC.**
1140 West Pender St., Ste. 1680, Vancouver BC V6E 4G1, Canada
CEO: Patrick H. Gaines, Chmn. & Pres. & CEO Tel: 604-689-4440 Rev: $7
Bus: *Provides check verification and electronic* Fax: 604-689-4413 Emp: 86
  payment system software. www.lmlpayment.com
NAICS: 522320, 561440

  LML PAYMENT SYSTEMS CORP.
  4141 N. Granite Reef Rd., Ste. 241, Scottsdale, Arizona 85251
  CEO: Bob Peyton, Pres. Tel: (480) 425-4700 %FO: 100
  Bus: *Mfr. of calculating equipment.* Fax: (480) 425-4750 Emp: 20

  LML PAYMENT SYSTEMS CORP.
  1024 N. West St., Wichita, Kansas 67203
  CEO: Bob Peyton, Pres. Tel: (316) 943-2000 %FO: 100
  Bus: *Mfr. of calculating equipment.* Fax: (316) 943-1280

  LML PAYMENT SYSTEMS CORP.
  1330 Riverbend Dr., Ste. 600, Dallas, Texas 75247
  CEO: Patrick Gaines, Pres. Tel: (214) 678-2000 %FO: 100
  Bus: *Provides check verification and electronic* Fax: (214) 678-2001 Emp: 85
    payment system software.

● **LOGISTEC CORPORATION**
360 St. Jacques St., Ste. 1500, Montreal QC H2Y 1P5, Canada
CEO: Madeleine Paquin, Pres. & CEO Tel: 514-844-9381 Rev: $154
Bus: *Ship loading and unloading services.* Fax: 514-843-5217 Emp: 540
  www.logistec.com
NAICS: 488320

  LOGISTEC CORPORATION
  100 Waterfront St., PO Box 9411, New Haven, Connecticut 06534
  CEO: Madeleine Paquin, VP Tel: (203) 469-1391 %FO: 100
  Bus: *Ship loading and unloading services.* Fax: (203) 469-0905 Emp: 240

● **LONGVIEW SOLUTIONS INC.**
65 Allstate Pkwy., Ste. 200, Markham ON L3R 9X1, Canada
CEO: Mark E. Burton, Pres. & CEO Tel: 905-940-1510
Bus: *Finance software manufacture and sales.* Fax: 905-940-8310 Emp: 150
  www.longview.com
NAICS: 511210

  LONGVIEW SOLUTIONS INC.
  1974 Sproul Rd., Ste. 402, Broomall, Pennsylvania 19008
  CEO: Matthew B. Townley, Pres. Tel: (610) 325-3295 %FO: 100
  Bus: *Software development.* Fax: (610) 325-8851 Emp: 19

  LONGVIEW SOLUTIONS INC.
  15 Salt Creek Lane, Ste. 314, Hinsdale, Illinois 60521
  CEO: Margaret Stuart, VP Tel: (630) 321-0202 %FO: 100
  Bus: *Computer software & services.* Fax: (630) 321-0220

LONGVIEW SOLUTIONS INC.
Eight Tower Bridge, 161 Washington St., Ste. 750, Conshohocken, Pennsylvania 19428
CEO: Margaret Stuart, VP   Tel: (610) 828-7915   %FO: 100
Bus: *Software development.*   Fax: (610) 828-7916

LONGVIEW SOLUTIONS INC.
Concourse Centre, 5 Concourse Pkwy., Ste. 3000, Atlanta, Georgia 30328
CEO: Margaret Stuart, VP   Tel: (770) 399-3138   %FO: 100
Bus: *Computer software & services.*   Fax: (770) 392-3303

LONGVIEW SOLUTIONS INC.
101 Park East Blvd., Ste. 600, Plano, Texas 75074
CEO: Margaret Stuart, VP   Tel: (972) 516-3810   %FO: 100
Bus: *Computer software & services.*   Fax: (972) 516-3869

● **LORING WARD INTERNATIONAL LTD.**
360 Main St., 15th Fl., Winnipeg MB R3C 3Z3, Canada
CEO: Donald J. Herrema, CEO   Tel: 204-954-5150   Rev: $72
Bus: *Mutual funds and asset management services.*   Fax: 204-954-5102   Emp: 350
www.loringward.com
NAICS: 523991, 523999, 525990

LORING WARD INC.
10100 Santa Monica Blvd., Ste. 1300, Los Angeles, California 90067
CEO: Nicole Katz, Mng. Dir.   Tel: (310) 277-4657   %FO: 100
Bus: *Financial and business management*   Fax: (310) 277-9232
services.

LORING WARD INC.
16030 Ventura Blvd.,, Ste. 380, Encino, California 91436
CEO: Bob Philpott, Mng. Dir.   Tel: (818) 905-9500   %FO: 100
Bus: *Financial and business management*   Fax: (818) 905-6823
services.

LORING WARD INC.
280 Park Ave., 5/F East, New York, New York 10017
CEO: Barry Klarberg, Mng. Dir.   Tel: (212) 907-8000   %FO: 100
Bus: *Financial and business management*   Fax: (212) 907-8089
services.

● **MAAX INC.**
1010 Sherbrooke St. West, Ste. 1610, Montreal QC H3A 2R7, Canada
CEO: Andre Heroux, Pres. & CEO   Tel: 418-387-4155   Rev: $520
Bus: *Designs and manufactures acrylic and fiberglass*   Fax: 418-386-4520   Emp: 3,800
showers and bathtubs.   www.maax.com
NAICS: 332322, 332911, 332912, 332913, 332919, 337110, 423390, 423720, 423740

COLEMAN SPAS BY MAAX
25605 South Arizona Ave., Chandler, Arizona 85248
CEO: Russell Suchon, CFO   Tel: (480) 895-0598
Bus: *Mfr. plastic pluming fixtures/sale of pluming*   Fax: (480) 895-7926   Emp: 150
equipment.

KEYSTONE BY MAAX
505 Keystone Rd., Southampton, Pennsylvania 18966
CEO: Placid Pulong, Pres.   Tel: (215) 355-0660   %FO: 100
Bus: *Mfr. shower doors., plastic pluming fixtures.*   Fax: Emp: 100

MAAX AKER
2121 Walter Glaub Dr., Plymouth, Indiana 46563
CEO: Andre Heroux, Pres. & CEO
Bus: *Fiberglass bath ware manufacture.*
Tel: (574) 936-3838
Fax: (574) 936-8294
%FO: 100

MAAX PEARL
9224 73rd Ave. North, Minneapolis, Minnesota 55428
CEO: Andre Heroux, Pres.
Bus: *Mfr. acrylic and fiberglass showers and
    bathtubs.*
Tel: (736) 424-3335
Fax: (763) 424-9808
%FO: 100

MAXX USA INC.
1625 James C. Rodgers Rd., Valdosta, Georgia 31603
CEO: Andre Heroux, Pres. & CEO
Bus: *Fiberglass showers and whirlpool
    manufacture.*
Tel: (229) 247-2364
Fax: (229) 247-4967
%FO: 100
Emp: 100

• **MACDONALD, DETTWILER AND ASSOCIATES LTD.**
13800 Commerce Pkwy., Richmond BC V6V 2J3, Canada
CEO: Daniel E. Friedmann, Pres. & CEO
Bus: *Information technology services for property
    evaluation.*
Tel: 604-278-3411
Fax: 604-231-2750
www.mda.ca
Rev: $624
Emp: 2,500

NAICS:　334220, 334290, 334511, 336414, 511210, 541511, 541512, 541519, 927110

DATAQUICK.COM
9620 Towne Centre Dr., San Diego, California 92121
CEO: Marshall Prentice, Pres.
Bus: *Real estate information solutions provider.*
Tel: (858) 597-3100
Fax: (858) 455-7406
%FO: 100
Emp: 150

DYNACS INC.
1300 Hercules, Ste. 210, Houston, Texas 77057
CEO: Mike Mantell, Pres.
Bus: *Information technology services.*
Tel: (281) 226-5200
Fax: (281) 226-5205
Emp: 250

EARTH SATELLITE CORP.
6011 Executive Blvd., Ste. 400, Rockville, Maryland 20852
CEO: Douglas Hall, Pres.
Bus: *Engineering & consulting services.*
Tel: (240) 833-8200
Fax: (240) 833-8201
Emp: 135

MARSHALL & SWIFT BOECKH
915 Wilshire Blvd., Ste. 800, Los Angeles, California 90017
CEO: Daniel Friedman, Pres. & CEO
Bus: *Aerospace & defense.*
Tel: (213) 683-9000
Fax: (213) 683-9010

MD ATLANTIC TECHNOLOGIES INC.
2227 Drake Ave. SW, Bldg. 14, Huntsville, Alabama 35805
CEO: Mark Brooks
Bus: *Aerospace & defense.*
Tel: (256) 882-7788
Fax: (256) 882-7774

- **MAD CATZ INTERACTIVE, INC.**
  2425 Matheson Blvd. E., 7/F, Mississauga ON L4W 5K4, Canada
  CEO: Darren Richardson, Pres. & CEO   Tel: 619-683-9830   Rev: $99
  Bus: *Video game accessories manufacturer.*   Fax: 619-683-9839   Emp: 85
                                                www.madcatz.com
  NAICS: 334310, 339932

    MAD CATZ INTERACTIVE, INC.
    7480 Mission Valley Rd., Ste. 101, San Diego, California 92108
    CEO: Darren Richardson, Pres. & CEO   Tel: (619) 683-9830   %FO: 100
    Bus: *Video game accessories manufacture and*   Fax: (619) 683-9839   Emp: 137
        sales.

- **MAGELLAN AEROSPACE CORPORATION**
  3160 Derry Rd. East, Mississauga ON L4T 1A9, Canada
  CEO: Richard A. Neill, Pres. & CEO   Tel: 905-677-1889   Rev: $476
  Bus: *Leading global supplier of technologically*   Fax: 905-677-5658   Emp: 3,500
      advanced aerospace systems and components.   www.magellanaerospace.com
  NAICS: 334511, 336411, 336412, 336413, 336414, 336415, 336419, 811310, 927110

    MAGELLAN AEROSPACE CORP.
    4 Fifth St., Peabody, Massachusetts 01960
    CEO: Richard Neill, CEO   Tel: (978) 977-6001   %FO: 100
    Bus: *Aircraft/aerospace parts and assemblies.*   Fax: (978) 532-1222

    MIDDLETON AEROSPACE CORPORATION
    206 South Main St., Middleton, Massachusetts 01949
    CEO: Steve Tosi, Pres.   Tel: (978) 977-6001   %FO: 100
    Bus: *Aircraft/aerospace parts and assemblies.*   Fax: Emp: 145

- **MAGNA ENTERTAINMENT CORPORATION**
  337 Magna Dr., Aurora ON L4G 7K1, Canada
  CEO: W. Thomas Hodgson, Pres. & CEO   Tel: 905-726-2462   Rev: $732
  Bus: *Engaged in racetrack management.*   Fax: 905-726-7164   Emp: 5,300
                                                www.magnaent.com
  NAICS: 512110, 512199, 525930, 531390, 711212, 713290

    AMTOTE INTERNATIONAL, INC.
    11200 Pepper Rd., Hunt Valley, Maryland 21031
    CEO: Jim Corckran, CEO   Tel: (410) 771-8700   %FO: 30
    Bus: *Business services to racing associations*   Fax: Emp: 300

    GOLDEN GATE FIELDS
    1100 Eastshore Hwy., Albany, California 94710
    CEO: Peter W. Tunney, Gen. Mgr.   Tel: (510) 559-7300   %FO: 100
    Bus: *Engaged in racetrack management.*   Fax: Emp: 140

    GREAT LAKES DOWNS
    4800 Harvey St., Muskegon, Michigan 49444
    CEO: Amy MacNeil, Gen. Mgr.   Tel: (231) 799-2400   %FO: 100
    Bus: *Engaged in racetrack management.*   Fax: Emp: 35

GULFSTREAM PARK
901 S. Federal Hwy., Hallandale, Florida 33009
CEO: R. Douglas Donn, Pres. Tel: (954) 454-7000 %FO: 100
Bus: *Engaged in racetrack management.* Fax: Emp: 75

LAUREL PARK
Racetrack Rd., RR198, Laurel, Maryland 20724
CEO: Joseph A. DeFrancis, Mng. Prtn. Tel: (301) 725-0400 %FO: 100
Bus: *Engaged in racetrack management.* Fax: Emp: 600

LONE STAR PARK AT GRAND PRAIRIE
1000 Lone Star Pkwy., Grand Prairie, Texas 75050
CEO: Bob Kaminski, Prtn. Tel: (972) 263-7223 %FO: 100
Bus: *Engaged in racetrack management.* Fax: Emp: 700

PIMLICO RACE COURSE
5200 Park Heights Ave., Baltimore, Maryland 21215
CEO: Joseph A. DeFrancis, Pres. Tel: (410) 542-9400 %FO: 100
Bus: *Engaged in racetrack management.* Fax: Emp: 500

PORTLAND MEADOWS
1001 N. Schmeer Rd., Portland, Oregon 97217
CEO: Greg Bloemke, Pres. Tel: (503) 289-3405 %FO: 100
Bus: *Engaged in racetrack management.* Fax: Emp: 8

REMINGTON PARK
1 Remington Place, Oklahoma City, Oklahoma 73111
CEO: James Nicol, Pres. Tel: (405) 424-1000 %FO: 100
Bus: *Engaged in racetrack management.* Fax: Emp: 250

SANTA ANITA PARK
285 W. Huntington Dr., Arcadia, California 91007
CEO: Scott Derudy, Mgr. Tel: (626) 574-6322 %FO: 100
Bus: *Engaged in racetrack management.* Fax:

THE MEADOWS
Racetrack Rd., Meadow Lands, Pennsylvania 15347
CEO: Michael Jeannot, Mgr. Tel: (724) 225-7900 %FO: 100
Bus: *Race track operation* Fax:

THISTLEDOWN RACE TRACK
21501 Emery Rd., Cleveland, Ohio 44128
CEO: Jim McAlpine, Pres. Tel: (216) 662-8600 %FO: 100
Bus: *Engaged in racetrack management.* Fax: (216) 662-8600 Emp: 200

● **MAGNA INTERNATIONAL INC.**
337 Magna Dr., Aurora ON L4G 7K1, Canada
CEO: Frank Stronach, Chmn. Tel: 905-726-2462 Rev: $20,653
Bus: *Auto parts manufacturing* Fax: 905-726-7164 Emp: 81,000
www.magnaint.com

NAICS: 336211, 336322, 336360, 336370, 336399

COSMA INTERNATIONAL
1807 E. Maple Rd., Troy, Michigan 48083-4212
CEO: Horst Prelog
Bus: *Automotive parts manufacturing.*

Tel: (248) 524-5300
Fax: (248) 524-4674

%FO: 100
Emp: 800

INTIER AUTOMOTIVE INTERIORS USA
39600 Lewis Dr., Ste. 3000, Novi, Michigan 48377
CEO: Scott Paradise, EVP
Bus: *Design and engineering of interior
        components
        and systems for the automotive industry.*

Tel: (248) 567-4000
Fax: (248) 567-5430

%FO: 100

MAGNA DONNELLY
49 West Third St., Holland, Michigan 49423
CEO: Beverly Snyder
Bus: *Design and engineering of interior
        components
        and systems for the automotive industry.*

Tel: (616) 786-7000
Fax: (616) 786-6034

%FO: 100

MAGNA INTERNATIONAL OF AMERICA
600 Wilshire Dr., Troy, Michigan 48084-1625
CEO: Molly Fitzpatrick
Bus: *Automotive parts manufacturing.*

Tel: (248) 729-2500
Fax: (248) 729-2520

%FO: 100

MAGNA STEYR
2950 Waterview Dr., Rochester Hills, Michigan 48309
CEO: August Hofbauer, Pres.
Bus: *Automotive engineering and design
        services.*

Tel: (248) 844-2400
Fax: (248) 844-2400

%FO: 100

TESMA INTERNATIONAL OF AMERICA INC.
23300 Haggerty Rd., Farmington Hills, Michigan 48335
CEO: Jane Sokoloski
Bus: *Automotive parts manufacturing.*

Tel: (248) 888-5513
Fax: (248) 427-1458

%FO: 100

● **MAINFRAME ENTERTAINMENT INC.**
2025 West Broadway, Ste. 200, Vancouver BC V6J 1Z6, Canada
CEO: Rick Mischel, CEO
Bus: *Produces computer animation for TV and video
        products.*
NAICS: 512110, 512191, 512199

Tel: 604-714-2600
Fax: 604-714-2641
www.mainframe.ca

Rev: $12
Emp: 258

MAINFRAME ENTERTAINMENT INC.
2049 Century Park East, Ste. 2130, Los Angeles, California 90067
CEO: Rick Mischel, CEO
Bus: *Produces computer animation for TV and
        video products.*

Tel: (310) 556-2221
Fax: (310) 556-0975

%FO: 100

MAINFRAME USA
12020 Chandler Blvd., North Hollywood, California 91607
CEO: Rick Mischel, CEO
Bus: *Produces computer animation for TV and
        video products.*

Tel: (818) 738-1338
Fax: (818) 506-5805

● **MANULIFE FINANCIAL CORPORATION**
200 Bloor St., East, NT 11, Toronto ON M4W 1E5, Canada
CEO: Dominic D'Alessandro, Pres. & CEO   Tel: 416-926-3000   Rev: $22,627
Bus: *Life insurance, group life and health and financial*   Fax: 416-926-5410   Emp: 13,000
     services.   www.manulife.com
   NAICS: 522190, 522292, 522310, 523930, 523999, 524113, 524114, 524128, 524130, 525190, 525910, 525920,
525990, 531120, 531190, 531312, 531390

     ESSEX CORP.
     825 3rd Ave., #37, New York, New York 10022
     CEO: Kevin E. Crowe, Chmn. & CEO   Tel: (212) 371-0303   %FO: 100
     Bus: *Outsources financial products & services*   Fax: (212) 486-0535   Emp: 140
     marketing.

     MANULIFE FINANCIAL
     John Hancock Place, Boston, Massachusetts 02117
     CEO: John D. DesPrez III, Pres. & CEO   Tel: (617) 572-6000   %FO: 100
     Bus: *Life insurance.*   Fax: (617) 572-9799   Emp: 3,914

     MANULIFE FINANCIAL
     4170 Ashford Dunwoody Rd, Atlanta, Georgia 30319
     CEO: Dominic Delasandro   Tel: (404) 252-6973   %FO: 100
     Bus: *Life insurance.*   Fax: (404) 252-6973

     MANULIFE FINANCIAL
     680 Washington Blvd., Stamford, Connecticut 06901
     CEO: Mike Nicola   Tel: (203) 602-7500   %FO: 100
     Bus: *Insurance agents.*   Fax: (203) 602-7557

     MANULIFE FINANCIAL CORPORATION
     100 Pringle Ave., Ste. 310, Walnut Creek, California 94596
     CEO: Cheryl Aboussie   Tel: (925) 935-7400   %FO: 100
     Bus: *Mutual funds, annuities.*   Fax: (925) 935-8425

     MANULIFE USA INC.
     6400 Sheridan Dr., Ste. 220, Williamsville, New York 14201
     CEO: Greg Mack   Tel: (716) 626-4034   %FO: 100
     Bus: *Financial services.*   Fax: (716) 626-4034

     MANULIFE WOOD LOGAN
     680 Washington Blvd., 9/F, Stamford, Connecticut 06901
     CEO: Robert T. Cassato   Tel: (203) 602-7500   %FO: 100
     Bus: *Financial services.*   Fax: (203) 602-7557

● **MAPLE LEAF FOODS INC.**
30 St. Clair Ave. West, Ste. 1500, Toronto ON M4V 3A2, Canada
CEO: G. Wallace F. McCain, Chmn.   Tel: 416-926-2000   Rev: $5,283
Bus: *Processed and canned foods and animal feeds.*   Fax: 416-926-2018   Emp: 22,784
     www.mapleleaf.com
   NAICS: 115210, 311111, 311119, 311422, 311611, 311612, 311613, 311812, 311823, 311941, 311991

MAPLE LEAF BAKERY, INC.
1011 East Touhy Ave., Ste. 500, Des Plaines, Illinois 60018
CEO: Douglas J. MacFarlane, Pres.   Tel: (847) 655-8100   %FO: 100
Bus: *Mfr./distributes fresh, processed and*   Fax: (847) 655-8110   Emp: 620
    canned foods and animal feeds.

MAPLE LEAF FOODS USA
220 South Orange Ave., Livingston, New Jersey 07039
CEO: Richard Lan, Pres.   Tel: (973) 597-1991   %FO: 100
Bus: *Mfr./distributes fresh, processed and*   Fax: (973) 597-1183
    canned foods and animal feeds.

MAPLE LEAF FOODS USA
1955 Blue Hills Dr., Roanoke, Virginia 24012
CEO: Al Saunter, VP   Tel: (540) 343-2404   %FO: 100
Bus: *Mfr. of bread bakery products.*   Fax: Emp: 160

- **MASONITE INTERNATIONAL CORPORATION**
1600 Britannia Rd. East, Mississauga ON L4W 1J2, Canada
CEO: Philip S. Orsino, Pres. & CEO   Tel: 905-670-6500   Rev: $2,200
Bus: *Mfr. interior and exterior doors.*   Fax: 905-670-6520   Emp: 14,000
                                                     www.masonite.com
NAICS: 321911, 332321

  MASONITE INTERNATIONAL
  1 North Dale Mabry, Ste. 950, Tampa, Florida 33609
  CEO: Philip S. Orsino, Pres.   Tel: (813) 877-2726   %FO: 100
  Bus: *Mfr./sales interior and exterior doors.*   Fax: (813) 876-1435   Emp: 100

- **MATRIKON INC.**
10405 Jasper Ave., Ste. 1800, Edmonton AB T5J 3N4, Canada
CEO: Nizar J. Somji, CEO   Tel: 780-448-1010   Rev: $41
Bus: *Automation software.*   Fax: 780-448-9191   Emp: 465
                                                     www.matrikon.com
NAICS: 511210

  MATRIKON INC.
  30275 Bainbridge Rd., Ste. A5, Solon, Ohio 44139
  CEO: Cory Engel, VP   Tel: (440) 519-1919   %FO: 100
  Bus: *Automation software sales.*   Fax: (440) 519-1260

  MATRIKON INC.
  1120 Ave. of the Americas, 4/F, New York, New York 10036
  CEO: Cory Engel, VP   Tel: (212) 626-6644
  Bus: *Manufacturing, warehousing & industrial*   Fax: (212) 626-6645
      software.

  MATRIKON INTERNATIONAL, INC.
  1551 Wall St., Ste. 280, St. Charles, Mississippi 63303
  CEO: Cory Engel, VP   Tel: (314) 218-7065   %FO: 100
  Bus: *Manufacturing, warehousing & industrial*   Fax: (636) 573-0030
      software.

MATRIKON INTERNATIONAL, INC.
1330 Post Oak Blvd., Ste. 1600, Houston, Texas 77056
CEO: Cory Engel, VP
Bus: *Manufacturing, warehousing & industrial software.*

Tel: (713) 963-4677
Fax: (713) 963-4676

%FO: 100

● **McCAIN FOODS, LTD.**
107 Main St., Florenceville NB E7L 1B2, Canada
CEO: Dale F. Morrison, Pres. & CEO
Bus: *Food processing, storage and transport.*

Tel: 506-392-5541
Fax: 506-392-6062
www.mccain.com

Rev: $4,311
Emp: 20,000

NAICS: 311411, 311412, 311520, 311813

MC CAIN FOODS USA, INC.
2905 Butterfield Rd., Oak Brook, Illinois 60523
CEO: Gilles Lessard, Pres.
Bus: *Mfr. potato & vegetable specialties, pizza products.*

Tel: (630) 472-0420
Fax: (630) 472-0450

%FO: 100
Emp: 4,100

MCCAIN FOODS USA
11Gregg St., Lodi, New Jersey 07644
CEO: Tim Driscoll, Pres.
Bus: *Mfr. of frozen specialties.*

Tel: (201) 368-0600
Fax:

Emp: 160

● **McCARTHY TETRAULT LLP**
Toronto Dominion Tower, Ste. 4700, Toronto ON M5K 1E6, Canada
CEO: Kirby Chown, Mng. Prtn.
Bus: *Full service law firm.*

Tel: 416-362-1812
Fax: 416-868-0673
www.mccarthy.ca

Emp: 1,000

NAICS: 541110

McCARTHY TETRAULT LLP
One New York Plaza, 25/F, New York, New York 10004
CEO: David M. Armstrong, Mng. Prtn.
Bus: *Full service law firm.*

Tel: (212) 785-6410
Fax: (212) 785-6438

%FO: 100

● **MDC PARTNERS**
45 Hazelton Ave., Toronto ON M5R 2E3, Canada
CEO: Miles S. Nadal, Chmn. & Pres. & CEO
Bus: *Full-service marketing and communications.*

Tel: 416-960-9000
Fax: 416-960-9555
www.mdccorp.com

Rev: $317
Emp: 4,030

NAICS: 323110, 323119, 323121, 323122, 541430, 541613, 541810, 541830, 541850, 541860, 541870, 541890, 541910

ACCENT
400 Missouri Ave., Ste. 107, Jeffersonville, Indiana 47130
CEO: Kevin Foley, Pres.
Bus: *Marketing communications.*

Tel: (812) 206-6200
Fax: (812) 206-6201

%FO: 100

BANJO STRATEGIC ENTERTAINMENT
39 Mesa, Ste. 206, San Francisco, California 94129
CEO: Pat Madden, Pres.
Bus: *Marketing communications.*

Tel: (415) 561-6600
Fax: (415) 561-6605

%FO: 100

BRATSKEIR AND CO.
400 Lafayette St., 5/F, New York, New York 10003
CEO: Lauren Kuschner, Pres.   Tel: (212) 679-2233   %FO: 100
Bus: *Marketing communications.*   Fax: (212) 460-0432

CLIFF FREEMAN AND PARTNERS
375 Hudson St., New York, New York 10014
CEO: Cliff Freeman, Chmn. & COO   Tel: (212) 463-3200   %FO: 25
Bus: *Advertising agency.*   Fax: (212) 463-3225

COLLE AND MCVOY, INC.
8500 Normandale Lake Blvd., Ste. 2400, Minneapolis, Minnesota 55437
CEO: John Jarvis, Pres. & CEO   Tel: (952) 852-7500   %FO: 100
Bus: *Sales promotion & specialized marketing*   Fax: (952) 852-8100   Emp: 230
  services.

CRISPIN PORTER AND BOGUSKY
3390 Mary St., Ste. 300, Coconut Grove, Florida 33133
CEO: Chuck Porter, Chmn.   Tel: (305) 859-2070   %FO: 100
Bus: *Advertising agency.*   Fax: (305) 854-3419

DOTGLU LLC
160 Varick St., 4/F, New York, New York 10013
CEO: Steve Thibodeau, Pres.   Tel: (212) 462-1300   %FO: 100
Bus: *Marketing communications.*   Fax: (212) 633-1719

FLETCHER MARTIN LLC
303 Peachtree Center Ave., Ste. 625, Atlanta, Georgia 30303
CEO: Andy Fletcher, Pres. & CEO   Tel: (404) 221-1188   %FO: 100
Bus: *Advertising agency.*   Fax: (404) 223-1136

HELLO DESIGN
8684 Washington Blvd., Culver City, California 90232
CEO: David Lai, CEO   Tel: (310) 839-4885   %FO: 100
Bus: *Marketing communications.*   Fax: (310) 829-4886

KIRSHENBAUM BOND & PARTNERS, LLC
160 Varick St., 4/F, New York, New York 10013
CEO: Stephen Fick, COO   Tel: (212) 633-0080   %FO: 100
Bus: *Advertising agency.*   Fax: (212) 463-8643   Emp: 240

LIME PUBLIC RELATIONS & PROMOTION
160 Varick St., 4/F, New York, New York 10013
CEO: Claudis Strauss, Pres.   Tel: (212) 337-6000   %FO: 100
Bus: *Marketing communications.*   Fax: (212) 633-1711

MACKENZIE MARKETING
505 North Hwy 169, Ste. 350, Minneapolis, Minnesota 55441
CEO: Andrew Mackenzie, Pres.   Tel: (763) 417-7305   %FO: 100
Bus: *Marketing communications.*   Fax: (763) 417-7301

MARGEOTES FERTITTA POWELL LLC
411 Lafayette St., 6/F, New York, New York 10003
CEO: George Fertitta, Chmn. & CEO   Tel: (212) 979-6600   %FO: 100
Bus: *Advertising agency.*   Fax: (212) 475-3827

MDC PARTNERS
375 Hudson St., 8/F, New York, New York 10014
CEO: Katie Kempner   Tel: (212) 463-2777   %FO: 100
Bus: *Marketing and advertising.*   Fax: (212) 463-2777

MOBIUM CREATIVE GROUP
444 North Michigan Ave., 27/F, Chicago, Illinois 60611
CEO: Guy Gangi, Mng. Prtn.   Tel: (312) 527-0500   %FO: 100
Bus: *Advertising agency.*   Fax: (312) 527-7230   Emp: 35

MONO
2902 Garfield Ave. South, Minneapolis, Minnesota 55408
CEO: James Scott, Mng. Prtn.   Tel: (612) 822-4135   %FO: 100
Bus: *Advertising agency.*   Fax: (612) 822-4136

NORTHSTAR RESEARCH PARTNERS
The Chrysler Bldg., 7700 Irvine Center Dr., Ste. 210, Irvine, California 92618
CEO: Stephen Tile, Pres.   Tel: (949) 453-7372   %FO: 100
Bus: *Marketing communications.*   Fax: (949) 453-7374

NORTHSTAR RESEARCH PARTNERS
6 Times Square Plaza, Ste. 803, New York, New York 10036
CEO: Stephen Tile, Pres.   Tel: (212) 354-9500   %FO: 100
Bus: *Marketing communications.*   Fax: (212) 354-9501

SOURCE MARKETING LLC
15 Ketchum St., Westport, Connecticut 06880
CEO: Howard Steinberg, Chmn. & CEO   Tel: (203) 291-4000   %FO: 100
Bus: *Marketing communications.*   Fax: (203) 291-4010

TARGETCOM LLC
444 North Michigan Ave., 27/F, Chicago, Illinois 60611
CEO: Nora Ligurotis, Pres.   Tel: (312) 822-1100   %FO: 100
Bus: *Marketing communications.*   Fax: (312) 822-9628

THE MEDIA KITCHEN
160 Varick St., 4/F, New York, New York 10013
CEO: Paul Woolmington, CEO   Tel: (646) 336-9400   %FO: 100
Bus: *Marketing communications.*   Fax: (646) 336-6627

VITROROBERTSON, LLC
625 Broadway, 4/F, San Diego, California 92101
CEO: John Vitro, CEO   Tel: (619) 234-0408   %FO: 100
Bus: *Advertising agency.*   Fax: (619) 234-4015   Emp: 49

● **MDS INC.**
100 International Blvd., Toronto ON M9W 6J6, Canada
CEO: Stephen P. DeFalco, CEO   Tel: 416-675-7661   Rev: $1,447
Bus: *Distributes medical supplies and home health care*   Fax: 416-675-0688   Emp: 10,000
    products and provides management of automated   www.mdsintl.com
    lab systems.
NAICS: 325413, 325414, 339111, 541380, 541710, 621511, 621512

MDS DIAGNOSTIC SERVICES
5361 N.W 33rd Ave., Ft. Lauderdale, Florida 33309
CEO: David S. Zaccardelli, VP   Tel: (954) 777-0018   %FO: 100
Bus: *Distributes medical supplies and home*   Fax: Emp: 56
     health care products and provides
     management of automated lab systems.

MDS PHARMA SERVICES
22011 30th Dr. SE, Bothell, Washington 98021
CEO: Douglas Squires, Pres.   Tel: (425) 487-8200   %FO: 100
Bus: *Distributes medical supplies and home*   Fax: (425) 487-3787
     health care products and provides
     management of automated lab systems.

MDS PHARMA SERVICES
245 First St., Ste. 1800, Cambridge, Massachusetts 02142
CEO: Stephen DeFalco, CEO   Tel: (617) 444-8550   %FO: 100
Bus: *Chemical & bacterial testing research.*   Fax: (253) 484-4262

MDS PHARMA SERVICES
15360 Barranca Pkwy., Irvine, California 92618
CEO: Stephen DeFalco, CEO   Tel: (949) 450-8345   %FO: 100
Bus: *Business consulting services.*   Fax: (949) 450-8350   Emp: 100

MDS PHARMA SERVICES
5415 West Laurel St., Tampa, Florida 33607
CEO: David Zaccardelli, VP   Tel: (813) 286-0404   %FO: 100
Bus: *Contract pharmaceutical research &*   Fax: (813) 286-1105   Emp: 56
     development.

MDS PHARMA SERVICES
2237 Poydras St., New Orleans, Louisiana 70119
CEO: Steve Hurley, Mgr.   Tel: (504) 826-5000   %FO: 100
Bus: *Medical research.*   Fax: (504) 826-5088   Emp: 42

MDS PHARMA SERVICES
The Triad, 2200 Renaissance Blvd., Ste. 400, King of Prussia, Pennsylvania 19406
CEO: Douglas Squires, Pres.   Tel: (610) 239-7900   %FO: 100
Bus: *Chemical & bacterial testing research.*   Fax: (610) 239-7111   Emp: 3,042

MDS PHARMA SERVICES
621 Rose St., PO Box 80837, Lincoln, Nebraska 68502
CEO: Stephen DeFalco, CEO   Tel: (402) 476-2811   %FO: 100
Bus: *Chemical & bacterial testing research.*   Fax: (402) 476-7598

MDS PHARMA SERVICES
4747 East Beautiful Lane, Phoenix, Arizona 85044
CEO: Stephen DeFalco, CEO   Tel: (602) 437-0097   %FO: 100
Bus: *Chemical & bacterial testing research.*   Fax: (602) 437-3386

MDS SCIEX
1170 Veterans Blvd., Ste. 200, South San Francisco, California 94080
CEO: Stephen DeFalco, CEO   Tel: (650) 635-4380   %FO: 100
Bus: *Chemical & bacterial testing research.*   Fax:

● **MDSI MOBILE DATA SOLUTIONS INC.**
10271 Shellbridge Way, Richmond BC V6X 2W8, Canada
CEO: Erik Dysthe, Chmn. & Pres. & CEO   Tel: 604-207-6000   Rev: $50
Bus: *Mfr. field service operations software.*   Fax: 604-207-6060   Emp: 333
                                                  www.mdsi-advantex.com
NAICS: 511210, 541511

    MDSI MOBILE DATA SOLUTIONS INC.
    500 Park Blvd., Ste. 776, Itasca, Illinois 60143
    CEO: Ken Miller, Pres.   Tel: (630) 875-2800   %FO: 100
    Bus: *Field service operations software sales and*   Fax: (630) 775-1552   Emp: 170
       distribution.

● **A. R. MEDICOM INC.**
1200 55th Ave., Lachine QC H8T 3J8, Canada
CEO: M. Ronald Reuben, Pres.   Tel: 514-636-6262
Bus: *Dental and medical professional-use supplies.*   Fax: 514-636-6266   Emp: 100
                                                  www.medicom.ca
NAICS: 339114

    MEDICOM USA
    295 Firetower Rd., Tonawanda, New York 14150
    CEO: Ian Levine, Pres.   Tel: (716) 695-0258   %FO: 100
    Bus: *Mfr. of disposable medical & hospital*   Fax:
       equipment.

● **MEDISOLUTION LTD.**
110 Cremazie Blvd. West, 12/F, Montreal QC H2P 1B9, Canada
CEO: Allan D. Lin, Pres. & CEO   Tel: 514-850-5000   Rev: $38
Bus: *Health care information management software.*   Fax: 514-850-5005   Emp: 335
                                                  www.medisolution.com
NAICS: 511210, 541511, 541512, 541519

    MEDISOLUTION LTD.
    2999 N. 44th St., Ste. 308, Phoenix, Arizona 85018
    CEO: Allan D. Lin, Pres. & CEO   Tel: (602) 269-8373   %FO: 100
    Bus: *Health care information management*   Fax: (602) 269-6462
       software sales.

● **METHANEX CORPORATION**
1800 Waterfront Centre, 200 Burrard St., Vancouver BC V6C 3M1, Canada
CEO: Bruce Aitken, Pres. & CEO   Tel: 604-661-2600   Rev: $1,719
Bus: *Mfr. methanol.*   Fax: 604-661-2676   Emp: 733
                                                  www.methanex.com
NAICS: 325199

    METHANEX CORPORATION
    15301 Dallas Pkwy., Ste. 1150, Addison, Texas 75001
    CEO: Ron Britton, VP   Tel: (972) 702-0909   %FO: 100
    Bus: *Mfr. methanol.*   Fax: (972) 233-1266   Emp: 44

METHANEX CORPORATION
3 Kingwood Place, Ste. 220, 800 Rockmead Dr., Kingwood, Texas 77339
CEO: Jorge Yanez, Mgr.   Tel: (281) 358-0455   %FO: 100
Bus: *Engineering.*   Fax: (281) 348-9626

METHANEX CORPORATION
100 Wilson Blvd., Ste. 2705, Arlington, Virginia 22209
CEO: Andrew Browning   Tel: (703) 248-6100   %FO: 100
Bus: *Government relations.*   Fax: (703) 248-6120

- **MINACOM**
  80 Queen St., Ste. 501, Montreal QC H3C 2N5, Canada
  CEO: Michael Nadeau, Pres. & CEO   Tel: 514-879-9111   Rev: $8
  Bus: *Develops and markets QoS and test management* Fax: 514-879-9333   Emp: 75
       systems.   www.minacom.com`
  NAICS: 511210

  MINACOM
  8034 7th Place South, West Palm Beach, Florida 33411
  CEO: Charles Coutu   Tel: (561) 790-2268   %FO: 100
  Bus: *Develops and markets QoS and test*   Fax: (561) 790-1162
       management systems.

  MINACOM
  11921 Freedom Dr., Ste. 550, Reston, Virginia 20190
  CEO: Charles Coutu   Tel: (703) 478-2382   %FO: 100
  Bus: *Develops and markets QoS and test*   Fax: (703) 904-4399
       management systems.

- **MINACS WORLDWIDE INC.**
  180 Duncan Mill Rd., Toronto ON M3B 1Z6, Canada
  CEO: Elaine Minacs, Chmn. & Pres. & CEO   Tel: 416-380-3800   Rev: $228
  Bus: *CRM services, including design and management* Fax: 416-380-3830   Emp: 4,500
       of customized, multimedia contact centers.   www.minacs.com
  NAICS: 511210, 541519, 541611, 541860, 541910

  MINACS WORLDWIDE INC.
  34115 W. Twelve Mile Rd., Farmington Hills, Michigan 48331
  CEO: Elaine Minacs, Pres.   Tel: (248) 553-8355   %FO: 100
  Bus: *Business services management consulting* Fax: (248) 488-3696   Emp: 1,160
       services.

- **MITEL NETWORKS CORPORATION**
  350 Legett Dr., PO Box 13089, Kanata ON K2K 2W7, Canada
  CEO: Don Smith, CEO & Mng. Dir.   Tel: 613-592-2122   Rev: $341
  Bus: *Semiconductor devices, components & integrated* Fax: 613-592-4784   Emp: 1,849
       circuits, telephone systems and call centers   www.mitel.com
       design and manufacture.
  NAICS: 334210, 334290, 334413

MITEL NETWORKS
3200 Bristol St., Ste. 200, Costa Mesa, California 92626
CEO: David Schiler, Mgr.   Tel:　(714) 435-4006
Bus:　*Mfr./sales semiconductor devices,*   Fax:　(714) 431-3073
　　　components & integrated circuits, telephone
　　　and call centers.

MITEL NETWORKS
120 Interstate N. Pkwy., Bldg. 400, Ste. 450, Atlanta, Georgia 30339
CEO: Matt Hickey, Mgr.   Tel:　(770) 952-6275
Bus:　*Mfr./sales semiconductor devices,*   Fax:　(770) 956-9625
　　　components & integrated circuits, telephone
　　　and call centers.

MITEL NETWORKS
Bishop Ranch 2, Bldg. 1, 2680 Bishop Dr., Ste. 280, San Ramon, California 94583
CEO: Lynn Griffin, Mgr.   Tel:　(925) 275-9050
Bus:　*Mfr./sales semiconductor devices,*   Fax:　(925) 275-9068
　　　components & integrated circuits, telephone
　　　and call centers.

MITEL NETWORKS
3 Park Ave., 31/F, New York, New York 10016
CEO: Jack Stoddard, Mgr.   Tel:　(212) 683-4455
Bus:　*Mfr./sales semiconductor devices,*   Fax:　(212) 779-2667
　　　components & integrated circuits, telephone
　　　and call centers.

MITEL NETWORKS
1833 Centre Point Cir., Naperville, Illinois 60563
CEO: Bruce Wood   Tel:　(630) 505-8200
Bus:　*Mfr./sales semiconductor devices,*   Fax:　(630) 505-8200
　　　components & integrated circuits, telephone
　　　and call centers.

MITEL NETWORKS
120 Interstate North Pkwy., Atlanta, Georgia 30339
CEO: Matt Hickey   Tel:　(770) 952-7248
Bus:　*Mfr./sales semiconductor devices,*   Fax:　(770) 952-7248
　　　components & integrated circuits, telephone
　　　and call centers.

MITEL NETWORKS
800 Corporate Dr., Ste. 221, Ft. Lauderdale, Florida 33334
CEO: Matt Hickey, VP Mktg.   Tel:　(954) 928-0604
Bus:　*Mfr./sales semiconductor devices,*   Fax:　(954) 928-0688
　　　components & integrated circuits, telephone
　　　and call centers.

MITEL NETWORKS
Karlyn Bldg., Irvine, California 92617
CEO: David Schuler   Tel:　(949) 737-7000
Bus:　*Mfr./sales semiconductor devices,*   Fax:　(949) 737-7000
　　　components & integrated circuits, telephone
　　　and call centers.

MITEL NETWORKS CORPORATION
205 Van Buren St., Ste. 400, Herndon, Virginia 20170
CEO: Don Smith, CEO
Bus: *Semiconductor devices, components & integrated circuits, telephone systems and call centers design and manufacture.*

Tel: (703) 318-7020
Fax:

%FO: 100
Emp: 2,000

● **MKS INC.**
410 Albert St., Waterloo ON N2L 3V3, Canada
CEO: Philip C. Deck, Chmn. & CEO
Bus: *Software manufacture.*

Tel: 519-884-2251
Fax: 519-884-8861
www.mks.com

Rev: $32
Emp: 250

NAICS: 511210, 518210, 541511, 541512, 541519, 611420

MKS INTEROPERABILITY INC.
12450 Fair Lakes Circle, Ste. 400, Fairfax, Virginia 22033
CEO: Patrick Higbie, CEO
Bus: *Software manufacture and sales.*

Tel: (703) 803-3343
Fax: (703) 803-3344

%FO: 100
Emp: 40

MKS SOFTWARE INC.
1815 South Meyers Rd., Ste. 220, Oakbrook Terrace, Illinois 60181
CEO: Philip Deck, Chmn.
Bus: *Software manufacture and sales.*

Tel: (630) 827-4900
Fax: (630) 629-9167

%FO: 100
Emp: 253

● **MOBILE CLIMATE CONTROL INDUSTRIES INC.**
80 Kincort St., Toronto ON M6M 5G1, Canada
CEO: Marianne B. Mannerheim, Chmn. & CEO
Bus: *Mfr. air conditioning and heating systems for public transit operations.*

Tel: 416-242-5858
Fax: 416-242-6406
www.mccii.com

Rev: $54
Emp: 400

NAICS: 333415

MOBILE CLIMATE CONTROL INDUSTRIES INC.
2200 Dwyer Ave., Utica, New York 13501
CEO: Marianne Mannierheim, Pres.
Bus: *Air conditioning and heating systems sales and distribution.*

Tel: (315) 738-1500
Fax: (315) 738-1919

%FO: 100
Emp: 470

MOBILE CLIMATE CONTROL INDUSTRIES INC.
426 Winnebago Ave., Fairmont, Minnesota 56031
CEO: Tim Hested, Mgr.
Bus: *Air conditioning and heating systems sales and distribution.*

Tel: (507) 238-2783
Fax: (507) 238-4151

%FO: 100

● **MONARCH INDUSTRIES LTD.**
51 Burmac Rd., Winnipeg MB R3C 3E4, Canada
CEO: Michael Friedman, Pres.
Bus: *Centrifugal pumps manufacture, concrete mixers, hydraulic cylinders, water systems, self priming pumps.*

Tel: 204-786-7921
Fax: 204-889-9120
www.monarchinc.com

Rev: $81
Emp: 540

NAICS: 333120, 333911, 333995

MONARCH INDUSTRIES, INC.
99 Main St., Warren, Rhode Island 02885
CEO: Michael Anania, Mgr.   Tel: (800) 669-9663
Bus: *Mfr. centrifugal pumps.*   Fax:

● **MOSAID TECHNOLOGIES INCORPORATED**
11 Hines Rd., Kanata ON K2K 2X1, Canada
CEO: George J. J. Cwynar, Pres. & CEO   Tel: 613-599-9539   Rev: $21
Bus: *Semiconductors.*   Fax: 613-591-8148   Emp: 67
                                           www.mosaid.com

NAICS: 333295, 334413

    MOSAID SYSTEMS INC.
    3375 Scott Blvd., Ste. 206, Santa Clara, California 95054
    CEO: Glenn Evans, Pres.   Tel: (408) 727-7199   %FO: 100
    Bus: *Semiconductors manufacture.* Fax: (408) 727-0479   Emp: 15

● **MOUNTAIN PROVINCE DIAMONDS INC.**
21 Nesbitt Dr., Toronto ON M4W 2G2, Canada
CEO: Elizabeth Kirkwood, Chmn.   Tel: 416-364-6928
Bus: *Diamond exploration. (JV of DeBeers).* Fax: 416-364-0618
                                             www.mountainprovince.com

NAICS: 212399

    MOUNTAIN PROVINCE DIAMONDS INC.
    3633 East Inland Empire Blvd., Ste. 465, Ontario, California 91764
    CEO: Jan Vandersande, Pres. & CEO   Tel: (909) 466-1411   %FO: 100
    Bus: *Diamond exploration.*   Fax: (906) 466-1409

● **MTI GLOBAL INC.**
7391 Pacific Circle, Mississauga ON L5T 2A4, Canada
CEO: William J. Neill, Pres. & CEO   Tel: 905-564-9700   Rev: $31
Bus: *Silicone based insulation products design and* Fax: 905-564-8886   Emp: 300
    manufacture.   www.magnifoam.com

NAICS: 325211, 325212, 336399, 336413

    MAGNIFOAM TECHNOLOGY INTERNATIONAL INC.
    8020 Whitepine Rd., Richmond, Virginia 23237
    CEO: William J. Neil, Pres.   Tel: (804) 714-0001   %FO: 100
    Bus: *Mfr. of flexible cellular foam.* Fax: (804) 714-1539   Emp: 11

● **MUNICIPAL SOLUTIONS GROUP, INC.**
4464 Markham St., Ste.1108, Victoria BC V8Z 7X8, Canada
CEO: Iain McLean, CEO   Tel: 250-475-6600   Rev: $4
Bus: *Automation software manufacture.*   Fax: 250-475-6080   Emp: 50
                                            www.municipalsolutions.com

NAICS: 511210

    MUNICIPAL SOLUTIONS GROUP, INC.
    2043 Grove St., Denver, Colorado 80211
    CEO: Robert Bennett, Pres.   Tel: (303) 458-5979   %FO: 100
    Bus: *Automation software manufacture and* Fax: (303) 433-4682
      sales.

- **NATIONAL BANK OF CANADA**
National Bank Tower, 600 de la Gauchetiere West, Montreal QC H3B 4L2, Canada
CEO: Real Raymond, Pres. & CEO   Tel: 514-394-5000   Rev: $3,914
Bus: *General banking services.*   Fax: 514-394-8434   Emp: 16,555
www.nbc.ca
NAICS: 522110, 523110, 523120, 523920, 523930, 525110, 525910

  NATBANK
  Pompano Marketplace, 1231 S. Federal Hwy., Pompano Beach, Florida 33062
  CEO: Tel: (954) 781-4005   %FO: 100
  Bus: *Commercial banking.*   Fax: (954) 781-8791

  NATBANK
  Oakwood Plaza, 4031 Oakwood Blvd., Hollywood, Florida 33020
  CEO: Tel: (954) 922-9992   %FO: 100
  Bus: *General banking services.*   Fax: (954) 922-9916

  NATIONAL BANK OF CANADA
  125 West 55th St., New York, New York 10019
  CEO: Kenneth S. Feldman   Tel: (212) 532-8585   %FO: 100
  Bus: *Commercial banking.*   Fax: (212) 632-8616

- **NBS TECHNOLOGIES**
703 Evans Ave., Ste. 400, Toronto ON M9C 5E9, Canada
CEO: David Nylan, Pres. & CEO   Tel: 416-621-1911
Bus: *Electronic business equipment.*   Fax: 416-621-8875
www.nbstech.com
NAICS: 334113, 334119, 511210, 518210, 561499

  NBS CARD TECHNOLOGY CORPORATION
  70 Eisenhower Dr., Paramus, New Jersey 07652
  CEO: Nayri Artun, Pres.   Tel: (201) 845-7373   %FO: 100
  Bus: *Engaged in card technology.*   Fax: (201) 845-3337   Emp: 140

  NBS TECHNOLOGIES
  10925 Bren Rd. East, Minneapolis, Minnesota 55343
  CEO: David Tushee, Mgr.   Tel: (952) 912-9400   %FO: 100
  Bus: *Custom computer programming services.*   Fax: (952) 912-9439   Emp: 20

- **NECHO SYSTEMS CORPORATION**
6275 Northam Drive., Bldg. 1, Toronto ON L4V 1YB, Canada
CEO: Jeremy Davis, Pres.   Tel: 905-671-5500   Rev: $10
Bus: *Expense management automation software*   Fax: 905-671-5530   Emp: 125
  manufacture.   www.necho.com
NAICS: 511210, 541511

  NECHO SYSTEMS CORPORATION
  233 Needham St., Paragon Towers, Ste. 300, Newton, Massachusetts 02164
  CEO: Malcolm Ward   Tel: (617) 965-7447   %FO: 100
  Bus: *Expense management automation software*   Fax: (617) 965-3399
     manufacture and sales.

- **THE NEWS GROUP (DIV. JIM PATTISON GROUP)**
  3320 South Service Rd., 2/F, Burlington ON L7N 3M6, Canada
  CEO: Glen Clark, Pres.
  Bus: *Plastics and industrial machinery manufacture.*

  Tel: 905-681-1113
  Fax: 905-681-3615
  www.thenewsgroup.com

  NAICS: 424920

  ALASKA NEWS INC.
  325 West Potter Dr., Anchorage, Alaska 99518
  CEO: John Seebach, Pres.
  Bus: *Periodical supplier*

  Tel: (907) 563-3251
  Fax: (907) 261-8523

  Emp: 50

  GREAT ATLANTIC NEWS LLC
  4070 Shirley Dr. S.W., Atlanta, Georgia 30336
  CEO: John Seebach, Pres.
  Bus: *Periodical supplier.*

  Tel: (404) 691-2800
  Fax: (404) 691-3417

  %FO: 100
  Emp: 201

  GREAT MIDWEST NEWS
  2571 Saradan Dr., Jackson, Michigan 49202
  CEO: John Swett, VP
  Bus: *Periodical supplier.*

  Tel: (517) 784-7163
  Fax: (517) 784-0075

  %FO: 100
  Emp: 800

  GREAT PACIFIC NEWS CO., INC.
  3400 D Industry Dr. E., Fife, Washington 98424
  CEO: Mike Cooke, Pres.
  Bus: *Periodical supplier*

  Tel: (253) 922-8011
  Fax: (253) 896-5027

  Emp: 1,500

- **NEXEN INC.**
  801 7th Ave. Southwest, Calgary AB T2P 3P7, Canada
  CEO: Charles W. Fischer, Pres. & CEO
  Bus: *Oil and gas chemicals*

  Tel: 403-699-4000
  Fax: 403-699-5800
  www.nexeninc.com

  Rev: $3,166
  Emp: 3,247

  NAICS: 211111, 213111, 213112

  NEXEN PETROLEUM USA INC.
  12790 Merit Dr., Ste. 800, Dallas, Texas 75251
  CEO: Doug Otten, SVP
  Bus: *Oil and gas chemicals*

  Tel: (972) 450-4600
  Fax: (972) 450-4729

  %FO: 100

- **NORAMPAC INC.**
  1061 Paren t St., St. Bruno QC J3V 6R7, Canada
  CEO: Marc-Andre Depin, Pres. & CEO
  Bus: *Packaging products manufacture, including boxes and bags. (JV of Cascades and Domtar)*

  Tel: 450-461-8600
  Fax: 450-461-8636
  www.norampac.com

  Rev: $1,050
  Emp: 4,900

  NAICS: 322211, 322212, 322213, 322214, 322215, 322221, 322224

  NORAMPAC INC.
  Bldg. 801 Corporation Park, Schenectady, New York 12302
  CEO: Marc-Andre Depin, Pres.
  Bus: *Mfr. of corrugated products.*

  Tel: (518) 346-6151
  Fax: (518) 346-8504

  %FO: 100
  Emp: 150

NORAMPAC INC.
4001 Packard Rd., Niagara Falls, New York 14303
CEO: Sal Sciarrino, Treasurer
Bus: *Mfr. corrugated paper.*
Tel: (716) 285-3681
Fax: (716) 285-3767
%FO: 100
Emp: 138

NORAMPAC INC.
1755 Elmwood Ave., Buffalo, New York 14207
CEO: Chuck Grimm, Mgr.
Bus: *Mfr. corrugated paper.*
Tel: (716) 876-1555
Fax: (716) 876-8596
%FO: 100
Emp: 100

NORAMPAC INC.
One AIM Place, 4444 Walden Ave., Lancaster, New York 14086
CEO: Marc-Andre Depin, Pres. & CEO
Bus: *Mfr. corrugated paper.*
Tel: (716) 651-2000
Fax: (716) 651-4444
%FO: 100
Emp: 128

NORAMPAC INC.
55-15 Grand Ave., Maspeth, New York 11378
CEO: Matthew Densen, Gen. Mgr.
Bus: *Mfr. of corrugated products.*
Tel: (718) 386-3200
Fax: (718) 386-7370
%FO: 100
Emp: 260

NORAMPAC INC.
720 Thompson Rd., PO Box 246, Thompson, Connecticut 06277
CEO: Randy Johnson, CEO
Bus: *Design & manufacture of corrugated
packaging containers.*
Tel: (860) 923-9563
Fax: (860) 923-3707
%FO: 100
Emp: 120

NORAMPAC INC.
175 Pioneer Dr., Pioneer Industrial Park, PO Box 746, Leominster, Massachusetts 01453
CEO: Bill Ferzoco, Gen. Mgr.
Bus: *Mfr. of corrugated products.*
Tel: (978) 537-1676
Fax: (978) 537-9119
%FO: 100
Emp: 152

● **NORBORD INC. (FORMERLY NEXFOR)**
Suite 500, 1 Toronto St., Toronto ON M5C 2W4, Canada
CEO: J. Barrie A. Shineton, CEO
Bus: *Mfr. wooden panels and wooden building*
Tel: 416-643-8820
Fax: 416-643-8827
www.nexfor.com
Rev: $1,193
Emp: 6,500
NAICS: 321113, 321211, 321219, 321912, 322110, 322222, 322299

NORBORD INC.
2301 SE Stallings Dr., Nacogdoches, Texas 75963
CEO: J. Barrie Shineton
Bus: *Mfr. wooden panels and wooden building
products.*
Tel: (936) 568-8000
Fax: (936) 568-8046
%FO: 100

NORBORD INC.
500 Nexfor Blvd., Jefferson, Texas 75657
CEO: Peter Wijnbergen
Bus: *Mfr. wooden panels and wooden building
products.*
Tel: (903) 665-5800
Fax: (903) 665-5897
%FO: 100

- **NORTEL NETWORKS CORPORATION**
  8200 Dixie Rd., Ste. 100, Brampton ON L6T 5P6, Canada
  CEO: William A. Owens, CEO
  Bus: *Global supplier of communications networks and services for data and telephony, engaged in remote information processing systems.*
  NAICS: 334210, 334220, 334290, 541512

  Tel: 905-863-0000
  Fax: 905-863-8408
  www.nortelnetworks.com

  Rev: $9,828
  Emp: 34,150

  AC TECHNOLOGIES
  2751 Prosperity Ave., Ste. 500, Fairfax, Virginia 22031
  CEO: Leo Choi, VP
  Bus: *Information technology services.*

  Tel: (703) 698-4300
  Fax: (703) 698-4381

  Emp: 350

  INTERGRATED INFORMATION TECHNOLOGY CORP.
  4725 S. Monaco St., Ste. 300, Denver, Colorado 80237
  CEO: Francisco Garcia, Pres. & CEO
  Bus: *Information technology services.*

  Tel: (303) 796-8799
  Fax: (303) 796-9506

  Emp: 250

  NORTEL NETWORKS
  4001 E. Chapel Hill-Nelson Hwy., Research Triangle Park, North Carolina 27709
  CEO: Steve Schilling, Pres.
  Bus: *Engaged in remote information processing systems.*

  Tel: (919) 992-5000
  Fax:

  %FO: 100

  NORTEL NETWORKS
  2221 Lakeside Blvd., Richardson, Texas 75082-4399
  CEO: Ron Young, Mgr.
  Bus: *Engaged in remote information processing systems.*

  Tel: (972) 684-1000
  Fax: (972) 684-1000

  %FO: 100

  NORTEL NETWORKS
  4655 Great America Pkwy., Santa Clara, California 95054
  CEO: Frank Dunn, CEO
  Bus: *Engaged in remote information processing systems.*

  Tel: (408) 495-2400
  Fax:

  %FO: 100

  NORTEL NETWORKS
  600 Technology Park Dr., Billerica, Massachusetts 01821
  CEO: John Ross, CEO
  Bus: *Computer integrated & systems design*

  Tel: (978) 670-8888
  Fax:

  NORTEL PEC
  12730 Fair Lakes Cir., Fairfax, Virginia 22033
  CEO: David C. Karlgaard, Chmn. & CEO
  Bus: *Information technology services.*

  Tel: (703) 679-4900
  Fax: (703) 679-4901

  Emp: 1,991

- **NORTHSTAR AEROSPACE**
  105 Bedford Rd., Toronto ON M5R 2K4, Canada
  CEO: Mark Emery, Pres. & CEO
  Bus: *Mfr. flight critical parts for military aircraft applications and non-flight critical parts for commercial aircraft.*
  NAICS: 336412, 336413, 541330, 811219, 811310

  Tel: 416-364-5852
  Fax: 416-362-5334
  www.northstar-aerospace.com

  Rev: $131
  Emp: 768

D-VELCO MANUFACTURING OF ARIZONA, INC.
401 South 36th St., Phoenix, Arizona 85034
CEO: John Marris, Pres.
Bus: *engineering, manufacturing and testing of high precision aerospace products.*

Tel: (602) 275-4406
Fax: (602) 275-1071

%FO: 100
Emp: 171

NORTHSTAR AEROSPACE
6006 W. 73rd St., Bedford Park, Illinois 60638
CEO: Mark Emery, CEO
Bus: *Mfr. flight critical parts for military aircraft applications and non-flight critical parts for commercial aircraft.*

Tel: (708) 728-2000
Fax: (708) 728-2009

%FO: 100
Emp: 230

NORTHSTAR AEROSPACE TURBINE ENGINE SERVICE GROUP
Northstar Stroud Municipal Airport, PO Box 460, Stroud, Oklahoma 74079
CEO:
Bus: *Overhaul and repair turboprop engines.*

Tel: (918) 968-9561
Fax: (918) 968-9564

%FO: 100

● NOVA CHEMICALS CORPORATION
1000 7th Ave. Southwest, Calgary AB T2P 5C6, Canada
CEO: Jeffrey M. Lipton, Pres. & CEO
Bus: *Mfr. chemicals, including polyethylene and polystyrene.*
NAICS: 325110, 325199, 325211

Tel: 403-750-3600
Fax: 403-269-7410
www.novachem.com

Rev: $5,270
Emp: 4,115

NOVA CHEMICALS CORP.
950 Nova Chemical Blvd., Decatur, Alabama 35601
CEO: Lynn Sinell, Principal
Bus: *Mfr. chemicals, including polyethylene and polystyrene.*

Tel: (256) 306-4800
Fax:

Emp: 45

NOVA CHEMICALS CORP.
800 Rockmead Dr., Ste. 212, Humble, Texas 77339
CEO: Rick Seguin, Mgr.
Bus: *Mfr. chemicals, including polyethylene and polystyrene.*

Tel: (281) 359-7889
Fax:

NOVA CHEMICALS CORP.
12222 Port Dr., Pasadena, Texas 77507
CEO: Bill Bispeck, Mgr.
Bus: *Mfr. chemicals, including polyethylene and polystyrene.*

Tel: (281) 474-1000
Fax:

NOVA CHEMICALS CORPORATION
950 Worcester St., Indian Orchard, Massachusetts 01151
CEO: James Joyce, Mgr.
Bus: *Mfr. chemicals, including polyethylene and polystyrene.*

Tel: (413) 781-1441
Fax:

%FO: 100

NOVA CHEMICALS CORPORATION
5100 Bainbridge Blvd., Chesapeake, Virginia 23320
CEO: Pete Graham, Mgr.
Bus: *Mfr. chemicals, including polyethylene and polystyrene.*

Tel: (757) 494-2500
Fax:

%FO: 100

NOVA CHEMICALS CORPORATION
400 Frankfort Rd., Monaca, Pennsylvania 15061
CEO: Ian MacDonald, Mgr.   Tel: (724) 770-5542   %FO: 100
Bus: *Mfr. chemicals, including polyethylene and*   Fax:
polystyrene.

NOVA CHEMICALS CORPORATION
1550 Coraopolis Heights Rd., Moon Township, Pennsylvania 15108
CEO: Jeff Lipton, CEO   Tel: (412) 490-4000   %FO: 100
Bus: *Mfr. chemicals, including polyethylene and*   Fax: (412) 490-4155   Emp: 1,500
polystyrene.

NOVA CHEMICALS CORPORATION
97 Township Rd., PO Box 600, Belpre, Ohio 45714
CEO: Cliff Hardaway, Operations Mgr.   Tel: (740) 568-3200   %FO: 100
Bus: *Mfr. chemicals, including polyethylene and*   Fax:
polystyrene.

● **NOVAMERICAN STEEL INC.**
6001 Irwin St., LaSalle QC H8N 1A1, Canada
CEO: D. Bryan Jones, Chmn. & Pres. & CEO   Tel: 514-335-6682   Rev: $769
Bus: *Mfr./distributes steel products.*   Fax: 514-683-5285   Emp: 1,104
                                                      www.novamerican.com
NAICS: 331221, 331222, 331312

   AMERICAN STEEL AND ALUMINUM CORPORATION
   4601 Crown Rd., Liverpool, New York 13088
   CEO: Jack Chaney, Mgr.   Tel: (315) 451-6990   %FO: 100
   Bus: *Mfr./distribute steel products.*   Fax: (315) 451-8946

   AMERICAN STEEL AND ALUMINUM CORPORATION
   2751 Spring Garden Dr., Middletown, Pennsylvania 17057
   CEO: James Post, Mgr.   Tel: (717) 939-7861   %FO: 100
   Bus: *Mfr./distribute steel products.*   Fax: (717) 939-3264

   AMERICAN STEEL AND ALUMINUM CORPORATION
   425 Homestead Ave., Hartford, Connecticut 06112
   CEO: Joseph Pfeffer, Mgr.   Tel: (860) 527-2681   %FO: 100
   Bus: *Mfr./distribute steel products.*   Fax: (860) 244-9563

   AMERICAN STEEL AND ALUMINUM CORPORATION
   197 Dexter St., Cumberland, Rhode Island 02864
   CEO: Mark Wilwerth, Mgr.   Tel: (401) 728-8000   %FO: 100
   Bus: *Mfr./distribute steel products.*   Fax: (401) 726-6980

   AMERICAN STEEL AND ALUMINUM CORPORATION
   27 Elm St., Auburn, Massachusetts 01501
   CEO: Mike Ryan, Mgr.   Tel: (508) 832-9681   %FO: 100
   Bus: *Mfr./distribute steel products.*   Fax: (508) 832-3719

   AMERICAN STEEL AND ALUMINUM CORPORATION
   1080 University Ave., Norwood, Massachusetts 02062
   CEO: Stephen Shaw, Pres. & COO   Tel: (781) 762-8014   %FO: 100
   Bus: *Mfr./distribute steel products.*   Fax: (781) 762-8804   Emp: 123

AMERICAN STEEL AND ALUMINUM CORPORATION
115 Wallace Ave., South Portland, Maine 04106
CEO: Peter Brissette, Mgr.
Bus: *Mfr./distribute steel products.*

Tel: (207) 772-4641
Fax: (207) 772-0359

%FO: 100

AMERICAN STEEL AND ALUMINUM CORPORATION
One West Albany Dr., Albany, New York 12205
CEO: Dan Day, Mgr.
Bus: *Mfr./distribute steel products.*

Tel: (518) 489-3281
Fax: (518) 489-0007

%FO: 100

AMERICAN STEEL AND ALUMINUM CORPORATION
600 Dean Sievers Place, Morrisville, Pennsylvania 19067
CEO: Bill Ward, Mgr.
Bus: *Mfr./distribute steel products.*

Tel: (215) 295-8813
Fax: (215) 295-8798

%FO: 100

AMERICAN STEEL AND ALUMINUM CORPORATION
11111 Leadbetter Rd., Ashland, Virginia 23005
CEO: Neil Snellings, Mgr.
Bus: *Mfr./distribute steel products.*

Tel: (804) 798-6031
Fax: (804) 798-4010

%FO: 100

NOVA TUBE, LLC
PO Box 1179, Jeffersonville, Indiana 47130
CEO: Chuck Yingst, Gen. Mgr.
Bus: *Mfr./distribute steel products.*

Tel: (812) 285-9796
Fax: (812) 285-8832

%FO: 100

• **NOVATEL INC.**
1120 68th Ave., Calgary AB T2E 8S5, Canada
CEO: Jonathan W. Ladd, Pres. & CEO
Bus: *Mfr. receiver units, antennas and components.*

Tel: 403-295-4500
Fax: 403-295-4901
www.novatel.com

Rev: $45
Emp: 205

NAICS: 334220, 334419, 334511

NOVATEL INC.
1303 Coryell St., League City, Texas 77573
CEO: Steve Duncombe, Mgr.
Bus: *Sale of electronic navigation equipment.*

Tel: (281) 554-9081
Fax: (403) 295-4901

%FO: 100

• **NQL DRILLING TOOLS INC.**
1507 4th St., Nisku AB T9E 7M9, Canada
CEO: Kevin Nugent, Pres. & CEO
Bus: *Tools and drills manufacture.*

Tel: 780-955-8828
Fax: 780-955-3309
www.nql.com

Rev: $61
Emp: 500

NAICS: 213111, 333132

NQL ENERGY SERVICES US, INC.
10404 Mula Rd., Stafford, Texas 77477
CEO:
Bus: *Tools and drills manufacture and sales.*

Tel: (281) 568-1336
Fax: (281) 568-1405

%FO: 100

Canada

● **NSB RETAIL SYSTEMS PLC**
2800 Trans-Canada Hwy., Pointe-Claire QC H9R 1B1, Canada
CEO: Nikaila S. Beckett, CEO   Tel: 514-426-0822   Rev: $87
Bus: *Mfr. retail software.*   Fax: 514-426-0824   Emp: 742
    www.nsbgroup.com

NAICS: 511210

    NSB RETAIL USA, INC.
    400 Venure Dr., Lewis Center, Ohio 43035
    CEO: Howard Stotland, Pres.   Tel: (614) 840-1400   %FO: 100
    Bus: *Computer software development*   Fax: (614) 840-1401   Emp: 90

● **THE NU-GRO CORPORATION**
10 Craig St., Brantford ON N3R 7J1, Canada
CEO: John D. Hill, Pres. & CEO   Tel: 519-757-0077   Rev: $138
Bus: *Horticultural products manufacture.*   Fax: 519-757-0080   Emp: 520
    www.nu-gro.com

NAICS: 325311, 325312, 325314, 325320, 453910

    NU-GRO TECHNOLOGIES, INC.
    2680 Horizon Dr. SE, Ste. F5, Grand Rapids, Michigan 49546
    CEO: John Hill, Pres.   Tel: (616) 949-9733   %FO: 100
    Bus: *Horticultural products sales and distribution.*   Fax: (616) 949-4882   Emp: 40

● **NURUN INC.**
711 de la Commune St. West, Montreal QC H3C 1X6, Canada
CEO: Jacques-Herve Roubert, Pres. & CEO   Tel: 514-392-1292   Rev: $51
Bus: *E-commerce services.*   Fax: 514-392-0911   Emp: 600
    www.nurun.com

NAICS: 541511, 541613, 541690, 541830

    NURUN INC.
    55 Broad St., 24/F, New York, New York 10004
    CEO: Jacques-Herve Roubert, Pres.   Tel: (212) 825-5290   %FO: 100
    Bus: *Engaged in e-commerce.*   Fax: (212) 826-5628   Emp: 25

    NURUN INC.
    Penobscot Bldg., 645 Griswold, Ste. 1300, Detroit, Michigan 48226
    CEO: Jacques-Herve Roubert, Pres.   Tel: (313) 237-6880   %FO: 100
    Bus: *Engaged in e-commerce.*   Fax: (313) 237-6888

    NURUN INC.
    75 Fifth St. NW, Ste. 600, Atlanta, Georgia 30308
    CEO: Jacques-Herve Roubert, Pres.   Tel: (404) 591-1600   %FO: 100
    Bus: *Engaged in e-commerce.*   Fax: (404) 876-7226

● **NYMOX PHARMACEUTICAL CORPORATION**
9900 Cavendish Blvd., Saint-Laurent QC H4M 2V2, Canada
CEO: Paul Averback, Chmn. & Pres. & CEO   Tel: 514-332-3222   Rev: $1
Bus: *Biotechnology.*   Fax: 514-332-2227   Emp: 16
    www.nymox.com

NAICS: 325413

NYMOX CORPORATION
Heights Plaza, 777 Terrace Ave., 3/F, Hasbrouck Heights, New Jersey 07604
CEO: Matthew McTonville, Principal   Tel: (800) 936-9669   %FO: 100
Bus: *Diagnostic test research.*   Fax: (514) 332-2227

NYMOX CORPORATION
230 West Passaic St., Maywood, New Jersey 07607
CEO: Paul Averback, Pres.   Tel: (201) 368-5700   %FO: 100
Bus: *Engaged in biotechnology.*   Fax: (514) 332-2227   Emp: 38

● **OASIS TECHNOLOGY LTD.**
20 York Mills Rd., 4/F, PO Box 700, Toronto ON M2P 2C2, Canada
CEO: David Pasieka, Pres. & CEO   Tel: 416-228-8000
Bus: *Payment processing software manufacture.*   Fax: 416-228-8881
www.oasis-technology.com
NAICS: 511210

   E FUNDS CORPORATION
   Gainey Center II, 8501 North Scottsdale Rd., Ste. 300, Scottsdale, Arizona 85253
   CEO: Paul F. Walsh, Chmn. & CEO   Tel: (480) 629-7700
   Bus: *Transaction Processing & settlement.*   Fax: (480) 629-7701   Emp: 5,500

   OASIS TECHNOLOGY LTD
   2400 N. Commerce Pkwy., Ste. 306, Weston, Florida 33326
   CEO: Gustabo Alesso, VP   Tel: (954) 384-7894   %FO: 100
   Bus: *Payment processing software manufacture*   Fax: (954) 384-8046   Emp: 6
   and sales.

● **ONEX CORPORATION**
161 Bay St., 49/F, Toronto ON M5J 2S1, Canada
CEO: Gerald W. Schwartz, Pres. & CEO   Tel: 416-362-7711   Rev: $13,214
Bus: *Holding company engaged in airline catering,*   Fax: 416-362-6803   Emp: 102,000
electronics manufacturing, auto and building   www.onexcorp.com
products and telecommunications.
NAICS: 523999

   AMERICAN MEDICAL RESPONSE
   6200 S. Syracuse Way # 200, Greenwood Village, Colorado 80011
   CEO: William A. Sanger, CEO   Tel: (303) 495-1200
   Bus: *Medical practice management & services*   Fax: (303) 495-1295   Emp: 17,800

   CLIENTLOGIC CORPORATION
   3102 West End Ave., Ste. 900, Nashville, Tennessee 37203
   CEO: David E. Garner, Pres. & CEO   Tel: (615) 301-7100   %FO: 100
   Bus: *Provides outsourced customer service.*   Fax: (615) 301-7150   Emp: 20,300

   COSMETIC ESSENCE INC.
   2182 Rte. 35 South, Holmdel, New Jersey 07733
   CEO: John Croddick Sr., Pres. & CEO   Tel: (732) 888-7788
   Bus: *Personal care products*   Fax: (732) 888-6086   Emp: 1,400

EMCARE HOLDINGS
1717 Main St., Ste. 5200, Dallas, Texas 75201
CEO: William A. Sanger, CEO
Bus: *Medical practice management & services*
Tel: (214) 712-2000
Fax: (214) 712-2444
Emp: 5,000

ONEX INVESTMENT CORP.
712 Fifth Ave., New York, New York 10019
CEO: Gerald W. Schwartz, Chmn.
Bus: *Engaged in finance.*
Tel: (212) 582-2211
Fax: (212) 582-2211
%FO: 100

• **ONTARIO DIE COMPANY INTERNATIONAL**
235 Gage Ave., Kitchener ON N2M 2C9, Canada
CEO: Gary Levene, Pres.
Bus: *Mfr. die cuts and machinery leasing.*
Tel: 519-745-1002
Fax: 519-745-0051
www.ontariodie.com

NAICS: 332212, 532490

ONTARIO DIE INTERNATIONAL INC.
2735 20th St., Port Huron, Michigan 48060
CEO: Gary Levene, Pres.
Bus: *Mfr. of dies, tools, jigs & fixtures*
Tel: (810) 987-5060
Fax: (810) 987-3688
%FO: 100
Emp: 200

ONTARIO DIE INTERNATIONAL INC.
110 Hickory Dr., Simpsonville, South Carolina 29681
CEO: John Bak, Mgr.
Bus: *Mfr. hand & edge tools*
Tel: (864) 297-1191
Fax:

ONTARIO DIE INTERNATIONAL INC.
9641 Plaza Circle, El Paso, Texas 79927
CEO: Derek Stewart, Mgr.
Bus: *Mfr. of dies, tools, jigs, & fixtures*
Tel: (915) 858-1900
Fax: (915) 858-6964
%FO: 100

• **OPEN TEXT CORPORATION**
185 Columbia St. West, Waterloo ON N2L 5Z5, Canada
CEO: John Shackleton, Pres. & CEO
Bus: *Mfr. software products.*
Tel: 519-888-7111
Fax: 519-888-0677
www.opentext.com
Rev: $291
Emp: 2,105

NAICS: 511210, 518210, 541511, 541512, 541519, 611420

ARTESIA TECHNOLOGIES, INC.
700 King Farm Blvd., Ste. 400, Rockville, Maryland 20850
CEO: Chris Veator, CEO
Bus: *Asset management software.*
Tel: (301) 548-7850
Fax: (301) 548-4015
Emp: 50

OPEN TEXT CORPORATION
8717 Research Dr., Irvine, California 92618
CEO: Ronald M. Vangell, Pres.
Bus: *Mfr. software products.*
Tel: (949) 784-8000
Fax: (949) 784-8200
Emp: 70

OPEN TEXT CORPORATION
200 State St., 12/F, Boston, Massachusetts 02109
CEO: Thomas Jenkins, CEO
Bus: *Mfr. software products.*
Tel: (617) 378-3364
Fax: (617) 737-9308

OPEN TEXT CORPORATION
100 Tri-State International Pkwy., Lincolnshire, Illinois 60069
CEO: Thomas Jenkins, CEO   Tel: (847) 267-9330
Bus: *Mfr. software products.*   Fax: (847) 267-9332   Emp: 90

OPEN TEXT CORPORATION
39209 Six Mile Rd., Ste. 250, Livonia, Michigan 48152
CEO: Renee Dobson, CEO   Tel: (734) 542-5955   %FO: 100
Bus: *Mfr. software products.*   Fax: (734) 542-1805

OPEN TEXT CORPORATION
6500 Emerald Pkwy., Ste. 200, Dublin, Ohio 43016-3297
CEO: Thomas Jenkins, Mgr.   Tel: (614) 761-7290   %FO: 100
Bus: *Mfr. software products.*   Fax: (614) 761-7290

OPEN TEXT CORPORATION
80 Wolf Rd., Ste. 302, Albany, New York 12205-1608
CEO: Joe Knudson, Mgr.   Tel: (518) 446-0490   %FO: 100
Bus: *Mfr. software products.*   Fax: (518) 446-0792

- **OPPENHEIMER HOLDINGS INC**
20 Eglinton Ave. W, Ste. 1110, PO Box 2015, Toronto ON M4R 1K8, Canada
CEO: Albert G. Lowenthal, Chmn. & CEO   Tel: 416-322-1515   Rev: $655
Bus: *Securities brokerage and investments.*   Fax: 416-322-7007   Emp: 2,854
    www.opco.com
NAICS: 523110, 523120, 523920, 523930, 523991, 523999, 525110, 525120, 525190, 525910, 525920, 525990

    OPPENHEIMER & CO. INC.
    125 Broad St., New York, New York 10004
    CEO: Albert Lowenthal, Chmn.   Tel: (212) 668-8000   %FO: 100
    Bus: *Securities brokerage and investments.*   Fax: (212) 943-8728   Emp: 3,255

- **OPTIMAL PAYMENTS INC.**
2 Place Alexis-Nihon, 3500 de Maisonneuve Blvd. West, Ste. 700, Montreal QC H3Z 3C1, Canada
CEO: Mitchell A. Garber, Pres. & CEO   Tel: 514-738-8885   Rev: $43
Bus: *Transaction software manufacture.*   Fax: 514-738-2284   Emp: 150
    www.optimalpayments.com
NAICS: 511210

    NATIONAL PROCESSING SERVICES
    4036 Telegraph Rd., STE. 205, Bloomfield Hills, Michigan 48302
    CEO: Jimmy Nafso   Tel: (248) 540-7900   %FO: 100
    Bus: *Mfr. transaction software.*   Fax: (248) 333-1175

- **OSLER LLP**
1 First Canadian Place, Ste. 6100, PO Box 50, Toronto ON M5X 1B8, Canada
CEO: Dale Ponder, Mng. Prtn.   Tel: 416-362-2111   Rev: $83
Bus: *Canadian law firm, barristers and solicitors;*   Fax: 416-862-6666   Emp: 1,100
    patent and trade-mark agents.   www.osler.com
NAICS: 541110

OSLER
1221 Ave. of the Americas, 26/F., New York, New York 10020
CEO: Rob Lando, Mng. Prtn.   Tel: (212) 867-5800   %FO: 100
Bus: *Law practice.*   Fax: (212) 867-5802

● **PACIFIC RIM MINING CORPORATION**
625 Howe St., Ste. 410, Vancouver BC V6C 2T6, Canada
CEO: Thomas C. Shrake, CEO   Tel: 604-689-1976   Rev: $12
Bus: *Gold mining.*   Fax: 604-689-1978   Emp: 134
                                     www.pacrim-mining.com
NAICS: 212221

    PACIFIC RIM MINING CORPORATION
    3545 Airway Dr., Ste. 105, Reno, Nevada 89511
    CEO: Catherine McLeod-Seltzer   Tel: (775) 852-5888   %FO: 100
    Bus: *Gold mining.*   Fax: (775) 852-0323

● **PASON SYSTEMS INC.**
6130 3rd St. SE, Calgary AB T2H 1K4, Canada
CEO: Jim Hill, Pres. & CEO   Tel: 403-301-3400   Rev: $101
Bus: *Design, manufacture and rental of specialized*   Fax: 403-301-3499   Emp: 318
drilling instrumentation systems software.   www.pason.com
NAICS: 333132, 511210

    PASON SYSTEMS INC.
    1424 North Sam Houston Pkwy. E., Houston, Texas 77032
    CEO: Ben Thomas, Mgr.   Tel: (281) 227-0600   %FO: 100
    Bus: *Design, manufacture and rental of*   Fax: (281) 227-0602   Emp: 6
    specialized drilling instrumentation systems
    software.

    PASON SYSTEMS INC.
    16100 Table Mountain Pkwy., Ste. 100, Golden, Colorado 80403
    CEO: James Hill, Pres.   Tel: (720) 880-2000   %FO: 100
    Bus: *Design, manufacture and rental of*   Fax: (720) 880-0016   Emp: 120
    specialized drilling instrumentation systems
    software.

● **PATHEON INC.**
7070 Mississauga Rd, Ste.350, Mississauga ON L5N 7J8, Canada
CEO: Peter A. W. Green, Chmn.   Tel: 905-821-4001   Rev: $386
Bus: *Mfr. pharmaceuticals*   Fax: 905-812-6709   Emp: 3,800
                                        www.patheon.com
NAICS: 325411, 325412

    PATHEON INC.
    2110 East Galbraith Rd., Cincinnati, Ohio 45237
    CEO: Cline V. Bennett, Pres.   Tel: (513) 948-9111   %FO: 100
    Bus: *Manufacturer pharmaceuticals*   Fax:

● **H. PAULIN & CO. LIMITED**
55 Milne Ave., Toronto ON M1L 4N3, Canada
CEO: Richard C. Paulin, Pres.
Bus: *Manufactures and distributes fasteners, fluid system products, automotive parts, and screw machine components.*
NAICS: 332722, 339993

Tel: 416-694-3351
Fax: 416-694-1869
www.hpaulin.com

Rev: $117
Emp: 375

   H. PAULIN & CO. LIMITED
   12400 Plaza Dr., Unit 1, Parma, Ohio 44130
   CEO: Bob Finch, Gen. Mgr.
   Bus: *Manufactures and distributes fasteners, fluid system products, automotive parts, and screw machine components.*

   Tel: (216) 433-7633
   Fax: (216) 433-7622

   %FO: 100

● **PCL EMPLOYEES HOLDINGS LTD.**
5410 - 99th St., Bldg. 2, Edmonton AB T6E 3P4, Canada
CEO: Ross S. Grieve, Pres. & CEO
Bus: *Industrial, civil and commercial construction.*
NAICS: 236210, 236220, 237310, 238990

Tel: 780-435-9711
Fax: 780-436-2247
www.pcl.ca

Rev: $3,000
Emp: 6,800

   PCL CIVIL CONSTRUCTORS, INC.
   3810 Northdale Blvd., Ste. 200, Tampa, Florida 33624
   CEO: Jerry Harder, Mgr.
   Bus: *Engaged in industrial, civil and commercial construction.*

   Tel: (813) 264-9500
   Fax: (813) 264-9500

   %FO: 100

   PCL CIVIL CONSTRUCTORS, INC.
   2000 South Colorado Blvd., Tower Two, Ste. 2500, Denver, Colorado 80222
   CEO: Peter Beaupre, Pres. & COO
   Bus: *U.S. headquarters location for industrial, civil and commercial construction.*

   Tel: (303) 365-6500
   Fax: (303) 365-6590

   %FO: 100
   Emp: 650

   PCL CONSTRUCTION SERVICES INC.
   12200 Nicollet Ave. S, Burnsville, Minnesota 55337
   CEO: Fred G. Auch, Mgr.
   Bus: *Engaged in industrial, civil and commercial construction.*

   Tel: (952) 882-9600
   Fax: (952) 882-9600

   %FO: 100
   Emp: 1,900

   PCL CONSTRUCTION SERVICES, INC.
   15405 Southeast 37th St., Ste. 200, Bellevue, Washington 98006
   CEO: Ed Olsgard, Mgr.
   Bus: *Engaged in industrial, civil and commercial construction.*

   Tel: (424) 454-8020
   Fax: (425) 454-5924

   %FO: 100
   Emp: 50

   PCL CONSTRUCTION SERVICES, INC.
   1729 West Greentree Dr., Ste. 105, Tempe, Arizona 85254
   CEO: Luis Ventoza, VP
   Bus: *Engaged in industrial, civil and commercial construction.*

   Tel: (480) 829-6333
   Fax: (480) 829-8252

   %FO: 100
   Emp: 24

PCL CONSTRUCTION SERVICES, INC.
6675 West Blvd., Ste. 200, Orlando, Florida 32821
CEO: Deron Brown, Mgr.   Tel: (407) 363-0059   %FO: 100
Bus: *Engaged in industrial, civil and commercial*   Fax: (407) 363-0171   Emp: 70
construction.

PCL CONSTRUCTION SERVICES, INC.
200 Burchett St., Glendale, California 91203
CEO: Will Painter, Mgr.   Tel: (818) 246-3481   %FO: 100
Bus: *Engaged in industrial, civil and commercial*   Fax: (818) 247-5775   Emp: 75
construction.

● **PCL PACKAGING CORPORATION**
2300 Speers Rd., Oakville ON L6L 2XB, Canada
CEO: Paul Senov, Pres. & CEO   Tel: 905-827-8071   Rev: $125
Bus: *Plastic grocery bag manufacture.*   Fax: 905-827-8924   Emp: 550
                                                 www.pclpackaging.com

NAICS: 326111

　　　PCL PACKAGING CORPORATION
　　　455 Somerset Ave., Bldg. #3, North Dighton, Massachusetts 02764
　　　CEO: Wayne Kochuk, Mgr.   Tel: (508) 880-7640   %FO: 100
　　　Bus: *Plastic grocery bag manufacture and sales.*   Fax: Emp: 100

　　　PCL PACKAGING CORPORATION
　　　33500 Lockheed Ave., Pueblo, Colorado 81001
　　　CEO: Bill Swinimer, CEO   Tel: (719) 948-2800   %FO: 100
　　　Bus: *Plastic grocery bag manufacture and sales.*   Fax: Emp: 70

● **PERLE SYSTEMS LIMITED**
60 Renfrew Dr., Ste. 100, Markham ON L3R OE1, Canada
CEO: Joseph E. Perle, Chmn. & Pres. & CEO   Tel: 905-475-6070   Rev: $31
Bus: *Communications hardware manufacture and sales.* Fax: 905-475-2377   Emp: 100
                                                 www.perle.com

NAICS: 334111, 334290

　　　PERLE SYSTEMS LIMITED
　　　830 Fesslers Pkwy., Ste. 106, Nashville, Tennessee 37210
　　　CEO: Jeff Pack, Pres.   Tel: (615) 872-0770   %FO: 100
　　　Bus: *Communications hardware manufacture and*   Fax: (615) 748-1678   Emp: 150
　　　sales.

● **PLACER DOME INC.**
1055 Dunsmuir St, Ste. 1600, Vancouver BC V7X 1P1, Canada
CEO: Peter W. Tomsett, Pres. & CEO   Tel: 604-682-7082   Rev: $1,946
Bus: *Mineral exploration, development and production.* Fax: 604-682-7092   Emp: 17,400
                                                 www.placerdome.com

NAICS: 212221, 212222, 213115

　　　BALD MOUNTAIN MINE
　　　Box 2706, Elko, Nevada 89803
　　　CEO: Al Frank, Mgr.   Tel: (775) 237-7100   %FO: 100
　　　Bus: *Mining.*   Fax: (775) 237-7101

CORTEZ GOLD MINES
HC66 Box 1250, Crescent Valley, Nevada 89821
CEO: William Martinich, Principal   Tel: (775) 468-4400   %FO: 100
Bus: *Mining.*   Fax: (775) 468-4496   Emp: 430

GOLDEN SUNLIGHT MINES, INC.
453 Montana Highway 2 East, Whitehall, Montana 59759
CEO: Bill Hayes, CEO   Tel: (406) 287-3257
Bus: *Mining.*   Fax: (406) 287-2035   Emp: 181

PLACER DOME INC.
1125 Seventeenth St., Ste. 2310, Denver, Colorado 80202
CEO: Bill Hayes, CEO   Tel: (303) 675-0055   %FO: 100
Bus: *Mineral exploration, development and* Fax: (303) 675-0707   Emp: 6
    production.

TURQUOISE RIDGE MINE
PO Box 220-HC66, Golconda, Nevada 89414-9702
CEO: William Hayes, Pres.   Tel: (775) 529-5001   %FO: 100
Bus: *Mining.*   Fax: (775) 529-0752   Emp: 300

● **PMC-SIERRA, INC.**
100-2700 Production Way, Burnaby BC V5A 4X1, Canada
CEO: Robert L. Bailey, Pres. & CEO   Tel: 604-415-6000   Rev: $300
Bus: *Mfr. broadband chips for network infrastructure* Fax: 604-415-6200   Emp: 900
    applications.   www.pmc-sierra.com
NAICS: 334413

PMC-SIERRA, INC.
Mission Towers One, 3975 Frredom Circle, Santa Clara, California 95054
CEO: Robert Bailey, Pres. & CEO   Tel: (408) 239-8000   %FO: 100
Bus: *Mfr. broadband chips for network*   Fax: (408) 492-1157   Emp: 951
    infrastructure applications.

PMC-SIERRA, INC.
One Copley Pkwy., Ste. 306, Morrisville, North Carolina 27560
CEO: Kevin Reno, Mgr.   Tel: (919) 460-5411   %FO: 100
Bus: *Mfr. broadband chips for network*   Fax: (919) 468-2470   Emp: 4
    infrastructure applications.

PMC-SIERRA, INC.
850 Central Pkwy. East, Ste. 140, Plano, Texas 75074
CEO: John Hayden, Mgr.   Tel: (972) 423-4135   %FO: 100
Bus: *Mfr. broadband chips for network*   Fax: (972) 424-1041
    infrastructure applications.

PMC-SIERRA, INC.
1500 West Park Dr., Ste. 240, Westborough, Massachusetts 01581
CFO: Constantinos Bekis, Mgr.   Tel: (508) 475-4650   %FO: 100
Bus: *Mfr. broadband chips for network*   Fax: (508) 366-0267   Emp: 11
    infrastructure applications.

- **POLYAIR INTER PACK INC.**
  330 Humberline Dr., Toronto ON M9W 1R5, Canada
  CEO: Henry Schnurbach, Pres. & CEO
  Bus: *Mfr. protective foam packaging materials.*

  Tel: 416-679-6600
  Fax: 416-679-6610
  www.polyair.com

  Rev: $192
  Emp: 1,200

  NAICS: 326112, 334512, 335999, 423720, 423730

  POLYAIR INTER PACK INC.
  1600 Kelly Blvd., Ste. 140, Carrollton, Texas 75006
  CEO: Raymond Vershum, VP
  Bus: *Mfr. protective foam packaging materials.*

  Tel: (972) 820-6484
  Fax: (972) 820-6899

  %FO: 100

  POLYAIR INTER PACK INC.
  6035-B LeGrange Blvd., Atlanta, Georgia 30336
  CEO: Dino Claussen, Mgr.
  Bus: *Mfr. protective foam packaging materials.*

  Tel: (404) 344-4413
  Fax: (404) 629-6148

  %FO: 100
  Emp: 8

  POLYAIR INTER PACK INC.
  1100 Performance Place, Youngstown, Ohio 44502
  CEO: Ray Vershum, Mgr.
  Bus: *Mfr. protective foam packaging materials.*

  Tel: (330) 744-8812
  Fax: (330) 744-1228

  %FO: 100
  Emp: 125

  POLYAIR INTER PACK INC.
  300 Spencer Mattingly Lane, Bardstown, Kentucky 40004
  CEO: Joe Osborne, Mgr.
  Bus: *Mfr. protective foam packaging materials.*

  Tel: (502) 348-7020
  Fax: (502) 348-5511

  %FO: 100
  Emp: 54

  POLYAIR INTER PACK INC.
  1692 Jenks Dr., Ste. 102, Corona, California 92880
  CEO: Jim Higgins, VP Mktg.
  Bus: *Mfr. protective foam packaging materials.*

  Tel: (909) 737-7125
  Fax: (909) 737-8021

  %FO: 100

  POLYAIR INTER PACK INC.
  808 East 113th St., Chicago, Illinois 60628
  CEO: Henry Schnurbach, Pres.
  Bus: *Mfr. protective foam packaging materials.*

  Tel: (773) 995-1818
  Fax: (773) 995-7725

  %FO: 100

  POLYAIR INTER PACK INC.
  495 Meadow Lane, Carlstadt, New Jersey 07072
  CEO: Chris Franch, Pres.
  Bus: *Mfr. protective foam packaging materials.*

  Tel: (201) 804-1700
  Fax: (201) 804-1710

  %FO: 100
  Emp: 72

- **POLYTAINERS INC.**
  197 Norseman St., Toronto ON M8Z 2R5, Canada
  CEO: Robert K. Barrett, Pres.
  Bus: *Plastic containers manufacture.*

  Tel: 416-239-7311
  Fax: 416-239-0596
  www.polytainersinc.com

  NAICS: 322215, 326160

  POLYTAINERS INC.
  1400 SE Douglas St., Lee's Summit, Missouri 64036
  CEO: Robert Barrett, Pres.
  Bus: *Plastic containers manufacture and sales.*

  Tel: (816) 246-6100
  Fax: (816) 246-4897

  %FO: 100
  Emp: 150

- **POTASH CORPORATION OF SASKATCHEWAN INC. (PCS)**
500-122 1st Ave. South, Saskatoon SK S7K 7G3, Canada
CEO: William J. Doyle, Pres. & CEO Tel: 306-933-8500 Rev: $3,244
Bus: *Engaged in producing fertilizers.* Fax: 306-933-8844 Emp: 4,906
www.potashcorp.com
NAICS: 325181, 325311, 325312, 325320

PCS NITROGEN
1900 Fort Amanda Rd., Lima, Ohio 45805
CEO: Don Johnson, Gen. Mgr. Tel: (419) 226-1200 %FO: 100
Bus: *Mfr. ammonia, nitric acid, urea solutions,* Fax: Emp: 5
prill & granular urea.

PCS NITROGEN
23 Columbia Nitrogen Rd., Augusta, Georgia 30901
CEO: Keith Thornton, Gen. Mgr. Tel: (706) 849-6100 %FO: 100
Bus: *Mfr. anhydrous ammonia, urea, nitric acid,* Fax: Emp: 112
liquid carbon dioxide, ammonium nitrate, &
liquid fertilizers.

PCS PHOSPHATE
Hwy.3115 Hwy. 30, Box 307, Geismar, Louisiana 70734
CEO: Fred Elliott, Gen. Mgr. Tel: (225) 621-1500 %FO: 100
Bus: *Mfr. of phosphate fertilizer.* Fax: Emp: 138

PCS PHOSPHATE
301 State Line Ave., Joplin, Missouri 64802
CEO: Paul Shoup, Operations Mgr. Tel: (417) 624-5225 %FO: 100
Bus: *Mfr. of dicalcium phosphate.* Fax: Emp: 35

PCS PHOSPHATE INC.
E. Garfield St., PO Box 171, Weeping Water, Nebraska 68463
CEO: William Donohue, Operations Mgr. Tel: (402) 267-2915 %FO: 100
Bus: *Engaged in minimizing emissions through the* Fax: Emp: 46
use of advanced control technology.

PCS PHOSPHATE INC.
2660 East U.S. Rte. 6, Marseilles, Illinois 61341
CEO: Bob Startzer, Operations Mgr. Tel: (815) 795-5111 %FO: 100
Bus: *Engaged in minimizing emissions through the* Fax: Emp: 36
use of advanced control technology.

PCS PHOSPHATE INC.
1530 NC Hwy. 306 S., Box 48, Aurora, North Carolina 27806
CEO: Richard C. Atwood, Gen. Mgr. Tel: (252) 322-4111 %FO: 100
Bus: *Engaged in minimizing emissions through the* Fax: Emp: 1,033
use of advanced control technology.

PCS PHOSPHATE INC.
PO Box 300, 15843 Southeast 78th St., White Springs, Florida 32096
CEO: Paul Barrett, Gen. Mgr. Tel: (386) 397-8101 %FO: 100
Bus: *Engaged in minimizing emissions through the* Fax: Emp: 912
use of advanced control technology.

POTASH CORP.
1101 Skokie Blvd., Ste. 400, Northbrook, Illinois 60062
CEO: Thomas Regan, Mgr.   Tel: (847) 849-4200   %FO: 100
Bus: *Rock mining.*   Fax: (847) 849-4673   Emp: 200

• **POWER FINANCIAL LTD.**
751 Victoria Sq., Montreal QC H2Y 2J3, Canada
CEO: R. Jeffrey Orr, Pres. & CEO   Tel: 514-286-7400   Rev: $16,020
Bus: *Holding company.*   Fax: 514-286-7424
    www.powerfinancial.com
NAICS: 523910, 523991, 523999, 524113, 524114, 525110, 525120, 525190, 525910, 525920, 525990, 551112

    CANADA LIFE FINANCIAL CORP.
    6201 Power Ferry Rd., Ste. 100, Atlanta, Georgia 30339
    CEO: Ron Beetam, Pres.   Tel: (770) 953-1959
    Bus: *Insurance company*   Fax:

    GREAT-WEST LIFE & ANNUITY INSURANCE COMPANY
    8515 East Orchard Rd., Greenwood Village, Colorado 80111
    CEO: William T. McCallum, Pres. & CEO   Tel: (303) 737-3000   %FO: 100
    Bus: *Life & health insurance and annuities.*   Fax: (303) 737-3198   Emp: 6,200

    ONE HEALTH PLAN
    8505 E. Orchard Rd., Greenwood Village, Colorado 80111
    CEO: William T. McCallum, Pres. & CEO   Tel: (303) 737-3000
    Bus: *Health care services*   Fax: (303) 737-3146

• **POWER MEASUREMENT, INC. (Sub. of Schneider Electric SA)**
2195 Keating Cross Rd., Saanichton BC V8M 2A5, Canada
CEO: J. Bradford Forth, Pres. & CEO   Tel: 250-652-7100   Rev: $50
Bus: *Energy management software manufacture.*   Fax: 250-652-0411   Emp: 250
    www.pwrm.com
NAICS: 334512, 334513, 334514, 334515

    POWER MEASUREMENT, INC.
    33533 West 12 Mile Rd., Farmington Hills, Michigan 48331
    CEO: Gary Moody, Mgr.   Tel: (248) 324-2400   %FO: 100
    Bus: *Energy management software manufacture*   Fax: Emp: 12
    and sales.

    POWER MEASUREMENT, INC.
    1075 Easton Ave., Ste. 2, Somerset, New Jersey 08873
    CEO: Brad Forth, Pres.   Tel: (732) 937-9881   %FO: 100
    Bus: *Energy management software manufacture*   Fax:
    and sales.

    POWER MEASUREMENT, INC.
    105 Westpark Dr., Ste. 410, Brentwood, Tennessee 37027
    CEO: Brad Forth, Pres.   Tel: (615) 372-1532   %FO: 100
    Bus: *Energy management software manufacture*   Fax: Emp: 54
    and sales.

- **PRECISION DRILLING CORPORATION**
  150 6th Avenue SW, Ste. 4200, Calgary AB T2P 3Y7, Canada
  CEO: Hank B. Swartout, Chmn. & Pres. & CEO Tel: 403-716-4500 Rev: $1,938
  Bus: *Oil well drilling contractor.* Fax: 403-716-4867 Emp: 12,000
               www.precisiondrilling.com
  NAICS: 213111

    PRECISION DRILLING CORPORATION
    363 North Sam Houston Pkwy. East, Ste. 1700, Houston, Texas 77060
    CEO: Dale E. Tremblay Tel: (281) 260-5600 %FO: 100
    Bus: *Oil well drilling contractor.* Fax: (281) 260-5670

- **PREMIER SALONS INTERNATIONAL, INC.**
  3780 14th Ave., Ste. 106, Markham ON L3R 9Y5, Canada
  CEO: Brian Luborsky, CEO Tel: 905-470-7850 Rev: $125
  Bus: *Hair care salons.* Fax: 905-470-8174 Emp: 3,200
              www.premiersalons.com
  NAICS: 812112

    PREMIER SALONS INTERNATIONAL
    5421 Feltl Rd., Ste. 110, Hopkins, Minnesota 55343-3943
    CEO: Brian Luborsky, Chmn. Tel: (905) 470-7850 %FO: 100
    Bus: *Hair care products sale and distribution.* Fax: (905) 470-8174

    PREMIER SALONS INTERNATIONAL
    8341 10th Ave. North, Golden Valley, Minnesota 55427
    CEO: Brian Luborsky, Chmn. Tel: (763) 513-7200 %FO: 100
    Bus: *Beauty salons & hair care products.* Fax: (905) 470-8174 Emp: 50

- **PREVOST CAR INC.**
  35 Gagnon Blvd., Sainte-Claire QC G0R 2V0, Canada
  CEO: Gaetan Bolduc, Pres. Tel: 418-883-3391
  Bus: *Mfr. intercity coaches and special purpose* Fax: 418-883-4157 Emp: 1,500
   vehicles. (JV Volvo Bus and Henly's Group Plc) www.prevostcar.com
  NAICS: 336213, 336510

    PREVOST CAR INC.
    3384 De Forest Circle, Mira Loma, California 91752
    CEO: Rocky Burke, Mgr. Tel: (877) 507-7386
    Bus: *Sales/service intercity coaches & special* Fax: (951) 360-2567
     purpose vehicles.

    PREVOST CAR INC.
    15200 Frye Rd., Fort Worth, Texas 76155
    CEO: Don Arlett, Mgr. Tel: (817) 685-0250
    Bus: *Sales/service intercity coaches & special* Fax: (817) 685-0460
     purpose vehicles.

    PREVOST CAR INC.
    2200 Point Blvd., Ste. 100, Elgin, Illinois 60123
    CEO: Jack Forbes, Mgr. Tel: (800) 799-9938
    Bus: *Sales/service intercity coaches & special* Fax: (847) 844-7682
     purpose vehicles.

PREVOST CAR INC.
201 South Ave., South Plainfield, New Jersey 07080
CEO: Gaetan Bolduc, Pres.   Tel: (908) 222-7211
Bus: *Sales/service intercity coaches & special*   Fax: (908) 222-7304   Emp: 150
      purpose vehicles.

PREVOST CAR INC.
6931 Business Park Blvd., North Jacksonville, Florida 32256
CEO: Eric Olsen, Mgr.   Tel: (904) 886-4555   %FO: 100
Bus: *Sales/service intercity coaches & special*   Fax: (904) 886-7369
      purpose vehicles.

PREVOST CAR INC.
529 Hickory Hill Blvd., Whites Creek, Tennessee 37189
CEO: Wayne Kackley, Mgr.   Tel: (615) 299-8881   %FO: 100
Bus: *Sales/service intercity coaches & special*   Fax: (615) 299-8865
      purpose vehicles.

● **PROVIDENT ENERGY TRUST**
112 4th Ave., SW, Ste.700, Calgary AB T2P 0H3, Canada
CEO: Thomas W. Buchanan, CEO   Tel: 403-296-2233   Rev: $1,001
Bus: *Manager of oil and gas production properties*   Fax: 403-294-0111   Emp: 319
                                         www.providentenergy.com
NAICS: 211111, 211112, 525920

   BREITBURN ENERGY COMPANY LLC
   Two Allen Center, 1200 Smith St., Ste. 2885, Houston, Texas 77002
   CEO: Thurmon Andress   Tel: (713) 739-8112   %FO: 100
   Bus: *Oil & Gas Production*   Fax: (713) 739-8115

   BREITBURN ENERGY COMPANY LLC
   515 S. Flower St., Ste. 4800, Los Angeles, California 90071
   CEO: Hal Washburn, CEO   Tel: (213) 225-5900   %FO: 100
   Bus: *Oil & Gas Production*   Fax: (213) 225-5916   Emp: 100

● **PUROLATOR COURIER LTD.**
5995 Avebury Rd., Ste. 100, Mississauga ON L5R 3T8, Canada
CEO: Robert C. Johnson, Pres. & CEO   Tel: 905-712-1084   Rev: $960
Bus: *Express delivery services*   Fax: 905-712-6739   Emp: 12,500
                                         www.purolator.com
NAICS: 492110

   PUROLATOR COURIER USA
   165 EAB Plaza, West Tower, 6/F, Uniondale, New York 11556
   CEO: John Costanzo, Pres.   Tel: (516) 522-2552   %FO: 100
   Bus: *Express delivery services*   Fax: (516) 522-2559

● **QLT INC.**
887 Great Northern Way, Vancouver BC V5T 4T5, Canada
CEO: Paul J. Hastings, Pres. & CEO   Tel: 604-707-7000   Rev: $186
Bus: *Developer of pharmaceuticals*   Fax: 604-707-7001   Emp: 474
                                         www.qltinc.com
NAICS: 325411, 325412

QLT USA INC.
2579 Midpoint Dr., Fort Collins, Colorado 80525
CEO: MIchael Duncan, Pres.
Bus: *Developer of pharmaceuticals*

Tel: (970) 482-5868
Fax: (970) 482-9735

%FO: 100

● **QMI, DIV. CSA GROUP**
20 Carlson Court, Suite 100, Toronto ON M9W 7K6, Canada
CEO: Rob M. Griffin, Pres. & CEO
Bus: *Engaged in national and international management system registration and certification.*
NAICS: 541710, 813910

Tel: 416-401-8700
Fax: 416-401-8650
www.qmi.com

CSA AMERICA INC.
8501 East Pleasant Valley Rd., Cleveland, Ohio 44131
CEO: Spencer Grieco
Bus: *Track standards and regulations.*

Tel: (216) 524-4990
Fax: (216) 520-8979

%FO: 100

QUALITY MANAGEMENT INSTITUTE (QMI)
13206 Glen Erica Dr., Houston, Texas 77069
CEO: Mike White
Bus: *Engaged in national and international management system registration and certification.*

Tel: (281) 895-9417
Fax: (281) 895-9360

%FO: 100

QUALITY MANAGEMENT INSTITUTE (QMI)
8501 East Pleasant Valley Rd., Cleveland, Ohio 44131
CEO: Demo Stavros, Mgr.
Bus: *Engaged in national and international management system registration and certification.*

Tel: (216) 901-1911
Fax: (216) 520-8967

%FO: 100

QUALITY MANAGEMENT INSTITUTE (QMI)
2805 Barranca Pkwy., Irvine, California 92606
CEO: Harold Hodder
Bus: *Engaged in national and international management system registration and certification.*

Tel: (949) 733-4333
Fax: (949) 733-4316

%FO: 100

● **QUEBECOR WORLD INC.**
612 Saint-Jacques St., Montreal QC H3C 4M8, Canada
CEO: Pierre Karl Peladeau, Pres. & CEO
Bus: *Commercial printing services and distributors of French language books and CD-ROMS.*
NAICS: 323110, 323111, 323115, 323117, 323119, 323121, 323122, 488510, 541430, 541860

Tel: 514-954-0101
Fax: 514-954-9624
www.quebecorworld.com

Rev: $6,622
Emp: 37,000

QUEBECOR WORLD (USA) CORP.
291 State St., North Haven, Connecticut 06473
CEO: Pierre Karl Peladeau, Pres.
Bus: *Lithographic print gravure printing.*

Tel: (203) 288-2468
Fax: (203) 248-6478

%FO: 100
Emp: 30,000

QUEBECOR WORLD NORTH AMERICA
340 Pemberwick Rd., Greenwich, Connecticut 06831
CEO: Pierre Karl Peladeau, Pres. & CEO
Bus: *Distributes print and digital information.*

Tel: (203) 532-4200
Fax: (203) 532-3480

%FO: 100

● **QUEENSTAKE RESOURCES LTD.**
204 Lambert St., Ste. 200, Whitehorse YK Y1A 3T2, Canada
CEO: Dorian L. Nicol, Pres. & CEO   Tel: 867-667-7885   Rev: $98
Bus: *Gold mining and exploration.*   Fax: Emp: 442
                                        www.queenstake.com

NAICS: 212221

    QUEENSTAKE RESOURCES LTD.
    Jerritt Canyon, HC31 Box 78, Elko, Nevada 89801
    CEO: Greg Struble, Mgr.   Tel: (775) 738-5006   %FO: 100
    Bus: *Gold ores.*   Fax: (775) 758-9231

    QUEENSTAKE RESOURCES LTD.
    999 18th St., Ste. 2940, Denver, Colorado 80202
    CEO: Dorian Nicol, Pres.   Tel: (303) 297-1557   %FO: 100
    Bus: *Gold mining and exploration.*   Fax: (303) 297-1587   Emp: 420

● **RAINBOW GROUP OF COMPANIES INC.**
107, 10108 1125th St., Edmonton AB T5N 4B6, Canada
CEO: Neil McLennan, Chmn. & Pres.   Tel: 780-452-0073   Rev: $1
Bus: *Infrared sensor technology design and* Fax: 780-452-1765
                                             www.rbpgroup.com

NAICS: 334519

    QWIP TECHNOLOGIES INC.
    2400 Lincoln Ave., Altadena, California 91001
    CEO: Margo Kaufmann, CFO   Tel: (626) 296-6432   %FO: 100
    Bus: *Infrared sensor technology design and* Fax: (626) 296-6442   Emp: 12
    manufacture and sales.

● **RAND A TECHNOLOGY CORPORATION**
5285 Solar Dr., Mississauga ON L4W 5B8, Canada
CEO: Frank Baldesarra, Pres. & CEO   Tel: 905-625-2000   Rev: $141
Bus: *Knowledge-based solutions for the engineering* Fax: 905-625-8535   Emp: 828
community.   www.rand.com
NAICS: 423420, 423430, 423440, 518210, 541511, 541512, 541519, 611420

    RAND WORLDWIDE
    4168 Crossgate Dr., Cincinnati, Ohio 45236
    CEO: Brian Semkiwl, Pres.   Tel: (513) 891-6776   %FO: 100
    Bus: *Resale of software and hardware.*   Fax: (513) 792-6892

    RAND WORLDWIDE
    190 North Main St., Natick, Massachusetts 01760
    CEO: Brian Semkiwl   Tel: (508) 655-0885   %FO: 100
    Bus: *Resale of software and hardware.*   Fax: (508) 655-4196

    RAND WORLDWIDE
    14651 Dallas Pkwy., The Princeton, Ste. 127, Dallas, Texas 75254
    CEO: Brian Semkiwl   Tel: (972) 991-1404   %FO: 100
    Bus: *Resale of software and hardware.*   Fax: (972) 991-1447

RAND WORLDWIDE
2030 E. Algonquin Rd., Ste. 402, Schaumburg, Illinois 60173
CEO: Brian Semkiwl   Tel: (847) 303-6460   %FO: 100
Bus: *Resale of software and hardware.*   Fax: (847) 303-6471

RAND WORLDWIDE
12660 West North Ave., Brookfield, Wisconsin 53005
CEO: Brian Semkiwl   Tel: (262) 797-0900   %FO: 100
Bus: *Resale of software and hardware.*   Fax: (262) 797-0930

RAND WORLDWIDE
1 Lahser Center, Ste. 225, 26400 Lahser Rd., Southfield, Michigan 48034
CEO: Brian Semkiwl   Tel: (248) 352-2779   %FO: 100
Bus: *Resale of software and hardware.*   Fax: (248) 352-5260

RAND WORLDWIDE
4600 A- Montgomery Blvd. N.E., Ste. 205, Albuquerque, New Mexico 87109
CEO: Brian Semkiwl   Tel: (505) 884-0284
Bus: *Resale of software and hardware.*   Fax: (505) 884-0286

RAND WORLDWIDE
8401 University Executive Park, Ste. 103, Charlotte, North Carolina 28262
CEO: Brian Semkiwl   Tel: (704) 510-2145   %FO: 100
Bus: *Resale of software and hardware.*   Fax: (704) 510-2239

RAND WORLDWIDE
8001 Sweet Valley Dr., Valley View, Ohio 45236
CEO: Brian Semkiwl   Tel: (216) 834-8300
Bus: *Resale of software and hardware.*   Fax: (216) 834-8301

RAND WORLDWIDE
250 West Main St., Ste. 100, Charlottesville, Virginia 22902
CEO: Brian Semkiwl   Tel: (434) 817-7908
Bus: *Resale of software and hardware.*   Fax: (434) 817-4393

● **RAYCO-WYLIE SYSTEMS**
2440, avenue Dalton, Sainte-Foy QC G1P 3X1, Canada
CEO: Norman Hinse, CEO   Tel: 418-266-6600
Bus: *Engaged in supply crane and heavy equipment* Fax: 418-266-6610   Emp: 100
    monitoring and safety systems.   www.raycotech.com
NAICS: 333923

    RAYCO-WYLIE SYSTEMS
    1020 9th Ave., SW, Ste. 124, Bessemer, Alabama 35022
    CEO: Ray Hays, Pres. & CEO   Tel: (205) 481-2080   %FO: 100
    Bus: *Distribution/service crane safety systems.* Fax: (205) 481-2081   Emp: 5

● **RBC DOMINION SECURITIES, DIV. ROYAL BANK OF CANADA**
Royal Bank Plaza, 200 Bay St., Toronto ON M5J 2W7, Canada
CEO: Charles M. Winograd, Pres. & CEO Tel: 416-842-2000
Bus: *Investment broker.*   Fax: 416-842-2100   Emp: 2,000
                               www.rbccm.com
NAICS: 523110, 523120, 523130, 523140, 523210, 523910, 523930, 523999

RBC DOMINION SECURITIES, INC.
1 Liberty Plaza, 165 Broadway, New York, New York 10006
CEO: Bruce MacDonald, Pres.   Tel: (212) 858-7000   %FO: 100
Bus: *Investment broker.*   Fax: (212) 428-6200   Emp: 300

● **RECOCHEM INC.**
850 Montee de Liesse, Montreal QC H4T 1P4, Canada
CEO: Richard E. Boudreaux, Pres. & CEO   Tel: 514-341-3550
Bus: *Chemicals manufacture and sales.*   Fax: 514-341-6553   Emp: 450
                                           www.recochem.com
NAICS: 424690, 424910

    RECOCHEM (USA)
    182 West Central St., Ste. 303d, Natick, Massachusetts 01760-3756
    CEO: Joseph Kuchar, VP   Tel: (508) 650-5800   %FO: 100
    Bus: *Chemicals manufacture and sales.*   Fax: (508) 651-0294

● **REKO INTERNATIONAL GROUP INC.**
5390 Brandan Lane, Oldcastle ON N0R 1L0, Canada
CEO: Steve Reko, Pres. & CEO   Tel: 519-737-6974   Rev: $72
Bus: *Designs and manufacture plastic injection moulds.* Fax: 519-737-6975   Emp: 500
                                                  www.rekointl.com
NAICS: 332116

    PROTO-TECHNIQUES INC.
    23333 Griswold Rd., South Lyon Township, Michigan 48178
    CEO: Steve Reko, Pres.   Tel: (248) 486-0066   %FO: 100
    Bus: *Mfr. metal prototype parts and stamping*   Fax: (248) 486-3470
        dies for the
        automotive and industrial parts markets.

● **RESEARCH IN MOTION LIMITED**
295 Phillip St., Waterloo ON N2L 3W8, Canada
CEO: Michael Lazaridis, CEO   Tel: 519-888-7465   Rev: $1,350
Bus: *Mfr. Handheld computer and accessories,*   Fax: 519-888-7884   Emp: 2,223
    computer software and networking equipment.   www.rim.net
NAICS: 334111, 334290, 511210

    RESEARCH IN MOTION LIMITED
    122 West John Carpenter Pkwy., Ste. 430, Irving, Texas 75039
    CEO: Mark Guibert   Tel: (972) 650-6126   %FO: 100
    Bus: *Handheld computers and wireless software*   Fax: (972) 650-2006
        manufacture.

● **REXEL CANADA ELECTRICAL INC.**
5600 Keaton Crescent, Mississauga ON L5R 3G3, Canada
CEO: John A. Hanna, CEO   Tel: 905-712-4004   Rev: $11,577
Bus: *Mfr. electrical supplies.*   Fax: 905-568-2987   Emp: 22,100
                                     www.rexal.ca
NAICS: 423610, 423690

REXEL, INC.
301 46th Ct., Meridian, Mississippi 39305
CEO: Tim Hogan, Pres.
Bus: *Mfr. and sales electrical supplies.*
Tel: (601) 693-4141
Fax: (601) 693-6225
%FO: 100
Emp: 9

REXEL, INC.
6600 LBJ Freeway, Ste. 180, Dallas, Texas 75240
CEO: Mike Cox, VP
Bus: *Mfr. and sales electrical supplies.*
Tel: (972) 450-8556
Fax: (972) 308-9733
%FO: 100

REXEL, INC.
1049 Prince Georges Blvd., Upper Marlboro, Maryland 20774
CEO: Dennis Marshall, Pres.
Bus: *Mfr. and sales electrical supplies.*
Tel: (301) 249-5005
Fax: (301) 390-4216
%FO: 100
Emp: 43

REXEL, INC.
1340 Corporate Dr., Ste. 500, Hudson, Ohio 44236
CEO: Mike Cox, VP
Bus: *Mfr. and sales electrical supplies.*
Tel: (330) 463-5550
Fax: (330) 463-5509
%FO: 100

REXEL, INC.
6606 LBJ Freeway, Ste. 200, Dallas, Texas 75240
CEO: Richard Waterman, CEO
Bus: *Mfr. and sales electrical supplies.*
Tel: (972) 387-3600
Fax:
%FO: 100
Emp: 4,322

REXEL, INC.
1051 Winderley Place, Ste. 303, Maitland, Florida 32751
CEO: Mike Cox, VP
Bus: *Mfr. and sales electrical supplies.*
Tel: (407) 660-1303
Fax: (407) 660-2184
%FO: 100

REXEL, INC.
1990 N. California Blvd., Ste. 1055, Walnut Creek, California 94596
CEO: Joe Lucas, Mgr.
Bus: *Mfr. and sales electrical supplies.*
Tel: (925) 952-4295
Fax: (925) 952-4296
%FO: 100
Emp: 5

REXEL, INC.
2627 W. 6th Ave., Denver, Colorado 80204
CEO: Mike Cox, VP
Bus: *Mfr. and sales electrical supplies.*
Tel: (303) 629-7721
Fax: (303) 629-0133
%FO: 100

• **RITCHIE BROS. AUCTIONEERS INC.**
6500 River Rd., Richmond BC V6X 4G5, Canada
CEO: David Edward Ritchie, Chmn. & CEO
Bus: *Auctioneer.*
Tel: 604-273-7564
Fax: 604-273-6873
www.rbauction.com
Rev: $182
Emp: 615

NAICS: 423830, 453998, 561990

RITCHIE BROS. AUCTIONEERS
3901 Faulkner Dr., Lincoln, Nebraska 68516
CEO: David Ritchie, Chmn.
Bus: *Auctioneer.*
Tel: (402) 421-3631
Fax: (402) 421-1738
%FO: 100
Emp: 1,500

- **ROYAL BANK OF CANADA**
  200 Bay St., Royal Bank Plaza, Toronto ON M5J 2J5, Canada
  CEO: Gordon Nixon, Pres. & CEO   Tel: 416-974-5151   Rev: $20,672
  Bus: *General banking and brokerage services.*   Fax: 416-955-7800   Emp: 57,795
                                            www.rbc.com
  NAICS: 522110, 522220, 522291, 522292, 522293, 523110, 523920, 523930, 524210

  RBC DAIN RAUSCHER
  Dain Rauscher Plaza, 60 S. 6th St., Minneapolis, Minnesota 55402-4422
  CEO: Brian F. Peters, Pres. & CEO   Tel: (612) 371-2711   %FO: 100
  Bus: *Engaged in corporate, institutional and*   Fax: (612) 371-7619
       individual investment services.

  RBC FINANCIAL GROUP
  One Liberty Plaza, New York, New York 10006-1404
  CEO: Gordon M. Nixon   Tel: (212) 428-6200   %FO: 100
  Bus: *Commercial banking services.*   Fax: (212) 428-2329

  RBC INSURANCE
  2000 Wade Hampton Blvd., Greenville, South Carolina 29615
  CEO: William James Westlake, Chmn. & CEO   Tel: (864) 609-8111
  Bus: *Insurance services.*   Fax: (864) 292-4211

  RBC MORTGAGE COMPANY
  13100 Northwest Fwy., Ste. 200, Houston, Texas 77040
  CEO: Jonathon Threadqill, Pres. & CEO   Tel: (713) 939-7094
  Bus: *Mortgage banking*   Fax: (713) 939-9203

- **ROYAL GROUP TECHNOLOGIES LTD.**
  1 Royal Gate Blvd., Woodbridge ON L4L 8Z7, Canada
  CEO: Lawrence J. Blanford, Pres. & CEO   Tel: 905-264-0701   Rev: $1,520
  Bus: *Mfr. construction materials; roofing, plumbing and* Fax: 905-264-0702 Emp: 9,000
       flooring.   www.royalgrouptech.com
  NAICS: 238340, 321918, 332913, 423390, 488999, 541614

  ROYAL MOULDINGS INC.
  135 Bear Creek Rd., PO Box 610, Marion, Virginia 24354
  CEO: Larry L. Davis, Pres.   Tel: (276) 783-8161   %FO: 100
  Bus: *Mfr./distribution construction materials;*   Fax: (276) 782-3292   Emp: 750
       moldings.

- **RUSSEL METALS INC.**
  1900 Minnesota Ct., Ste. 210, Mississauga ON L5N 3C9, Canada
  CEO: Edward M. Siegel Jr., Pres. & CEO   Tel: 905-819-7777   Rev: $2,007
  Bus: *Engaged in steel distribution.*   Fax: 905-819-7409   Emp: 2,680
                                            www.russelmetals.com
  NAICS: 423510

  ARROW STEEL PROCESSORS
  8710 Clinton Dr., Houston, Texas 77029
  CEO: Brian R. Hedges   Tel: (713) 673-0666   %FO: 100
  Bus: *Engaged in steel distribution.*   Fax: (713) 673-3308

BALDWIN INTERNATIONAL
30403 Bruce Industrial Pkwy., Solon, Ohio 44139
CEO: Edward Siegle, Pres.   Tel: (440) 248-9500   %FO: 100
Bus: *Engaged in steel distribution.*   Fax: (440) 248-7899   Emp: 20

CONTINENTAL WOOD TRADING
1990 Post Oak Blvd., Ste. 1550, Houston, Texas 77056
CEO: Brian R. Hedges   Tel: (713) 629-1701   %FO: 100
Bus: *Engaged in steel distribution.*   Fax: (713) 629-1701

PIONEER PIPE
2203 Timberloch Place, Ste. 125-1, The Woodlands, Houston, Texas 77380
CEO: Brian R. Hedges   Tel: (281) 292-2875
Bus: *Engaged in steel distribution.*   Fax: (281) 292-2875

PIONEER PIPE
1660 Lincoln St., Ste. 2300, Denver, Colorado 80264
CEO: Mike Harris, SVP   Tel: (303) 289-3201   %FO: 100
Bus: *Mfr. steel pipe & tubes.*   Fax: (303) 824-0083   Emp: 36

PIONEER PIPE
1610 West 200 South, Lindon, Utah 84042
CEO: Mike Houghton, Mgr.   Tel: (801) 224-8739   %FO: 100
Bus: *Mfr. of steel pipe/tubes.*   Fax: (801) 224-8752   Emp: 4

RUSSEL METALS WILLIAMS BAHCALL
895 Hinkle St., Green Bay, Wisconsin 54303
CEO: Donald Schuelke, VP   Tel: (800) 875-7624   %FO: 100
Bus: *Metals service center.*   Fax: (920) 496-3199   Emp: 45

RUSSELL METALS INC.
975 North Meade St., PO Box 1054, Appleton, Wisconsin 54912
CEO: Rod Smith, Gen. Mgr.   Tel: (800) 875-7624   %FO: 100
Bus: *Engaged in steel distribution.*   Fax: (920) 730-5857   Emp: 175

RUSSELL METALS INC.
999 West Armour Ave., Milwaukee, Wisconsin 53221
CEO: Rod Smith, Mgr.   Tel: (414) 481-7100   %FO: 100
Bus: *Wholesale steel.*   Fax: (414) 481-7120   Emp: 2

SPARTAN STEEL PRODUCTS
2942 Evergreen Pkwy., Ste. 207, Evergreen, Colorado 80439
CEO: Brian R. Hedges   Tel: (303) 670-9048
Bus: *Engaged in steel distribution.*   Fax: (303) 670-9569

SUNBELT GROUP INC.
7300 W. 110th St., Ste. 660, Overland Park, Kansas 66210
CEO: Greg Eidman   Tel: (913) 491-6660   %FO: 100
Bus: *Engaged in steel distribution.*   Fax: (913) 491-6742

SUNBELT GROUP INC.
1990 Post Oak Blvd., Ste. 950, Houston, Texas 77056
CEO: Greg Eidman, Pres.   Tel: (713) 840-0550   %FO: 100
Bus: *Engaged in steel distribution.*   Fax: (713) 840-8727   Emp: 41

● **SAMUEL MANU-TECH INC.**
185 The West Mall, Ste. 1500, Toronto ON M9C 5L5, Canada
CEO: Mark C. Samuel, Chmn. & Pres. & CEO   Tel: 416-626-2190   Rev: $697
Bus: *Steel tubing and rolled form products and plastic*   Fax: 416-626-5969   Emp: 2,132
       strapping manufacture.   www.samuelmanutech.com
   NAICS: 326113, 326199, 332919, 332996, 333518, 333993, 423830, 423840

   AMCA MACHINERY
   1876 Midland Rd., PO Box 3166, Rock Hill, South Carolina 29732
   CEO: John Dalla Rosa, Pres.   Tel: (803) 327-1216   %FO: 100
   Bus: *Mfr. of conveyors & conveying equipment.*   Fax: (803) 327-1216   Emp: 15

   ENERGY STEEL PRODUCTS
   10002 Windfern Rd., Houston, Texas 77064
   CEO: R. Levine   Tel: (281) 955-0903
   Bus: *Steel and plastic strapping manufacture,*   Fax: (281) 955-2965
         sales and distribution.

   ENERGY STEEL PRODUCTS
   8540 Cobb Center, Ste. 300, Kennesaw, Georgia 30144
   CEO: Chris Columbus, Mgr.   Tel: (770) 428-3201   %FO: 100
   Bus: *Steel and plastic strapping manufacture,*   Fax: (770) 421-9356
         sales and distribution.

   ENERGY STEEL PRODUCTS
   1191 W. Hawthorne Lane, West Chicago, Illinois 60185
   CEO: Christopher T. Franco, Mgr.   Tel: (630) 876-9388   %FO: 100
   Bus: *Steel and plastic strapping manufacture,*   Fax: (630) 876-9373   Emp: 10
         sales and distribution.

   ISP STITCHING & BINDERY PRODUCTS
   3911 South Memorial Dr., Racine, Wisconsin 53403
   CEO: Roy Wilkinson, Gen. Mgr.   Tel: (262) 632-5115   %FO: 100
   Bus: *Mfr. of industrial stitching machinery.*   Fax: (262) 632-5115   Emp: 80

   SAMUEL STEEL PICKLING COMPANY
   1400 Enterprise Pkwy., Twinsburg, Ohio 44087
   CEO: Rick L. Snyder, Gen. Mgr.   Tel: (330) 963-3777   %FO: 100
   Bus: *Steel and plastic strapping manufacture,*   Fax: (330) 963-0770   Emp: 70
         sales and distribution.

   SAMUEL STRAPPING SYSTEMS US
   1401 Davey Rd., Woodridge, Illinois 60517
   CEO: Robert W. Hickey, Pres.   Tel: (630) 783-8900   %FO: 100
   Bus: *Mfr. of fabricated metal products.*   Fax: (630) 783-8901   Emp: 419

   SAMUEL STRAPPING SYSTEMS US
   3900 Groves Rd., Columbus, Ohio 43232
   CEO: Robert W. Hickey, Mgr.   Tel: (614) 864-3400   %FO: 100
   Bus: *Mfr. of packaging machinery.*   Fax: (614) 864-3708   Emp: 70

   SAMUEL STRAPPING SYSTEMS US
   640 Cel River Rd., Rock Hill, South Carolina 29730
   CEO: Jess Shaver, Mgr.   Tel: (803) 325-1616   %FO: 100
   Bus: *Mfr. of steel strappings.*   Fax: (803) 325-1616   Emp: 35

SAMUEL STRAPPING SYSTEMS US
2000K Boyer Dr., Fort Mill, South Carolina 29708
CEO: Rick Dean, Mgr.   Tel: (803) 802-3203   %FO: 100
Bus: *Mfr. of steel strappings.*   Fax: (803) 802-3209   Emp: 50

SAMUEL STRAPPING SYSTEMS USA INC.
623 Fisher Rd., Longview, Texas 75604
CEO: Bobby Gosschalk, Gen. Mgr.   Tel: (903) 759-2761   %FO: 100
Bus: *Sale of packaging equipment & machinery*   Fax: (903) 759-2308   Emp: 54
    supplies.

SAMUEL/SEKISUI JUSHI STRAPPING LLC
110 Dent Dr., Cartersville, Georgia 30121
CEO: Toshi Yamada, Pres.   Tel: (770) 386-8837   %FO: 100
Bus: *Mfr. of plastic strapping.*   Fax: (770) 387-0315   Emp: 70

STEEL FAB
17074 & 17403 Lee Hwy., Abingdon, Virginia 24210
CEO: Michael V. Newlands, Gen. Mgr.   Tel: (276) 628-3843   %FO: 100
Bus: *Mfr. of fabricated plate work & air/gas*   Fax: (276) 628-7865   Emp: 95
    compressors.

- ## SAND TECHNOLOGY INC.
215 Redfern, Ste. 410, Westmount QC H3Z 3L5, Canada
CEO: Arthur G. Ritchie, Chmn. & Pres. & CEO   Tel: 514-939-3477   Rev: $4
Bus: *Mfr. analytical processing software.*   Fax: 514-939-2042   Emp: 70
    www.sanddtechnology.com

NAICS: 511210

SAND TECHNOLOGY CORP.
1616 Anderson Rd., Ste. 203, McLean, Virginia 22101
CEO: George Wicker, Pres.   Tel: (703) 286-0913   %FO: 100
Bus: *Mfr./sales analytical processing software.*   Fax:

SAND TECHNOLOGY CORPORATION
754A Lexington Ave., Kenilworth, New Jersey 07033
CEO: George Wicker, Pres.   Tel: (732) 750-4848   %FO: 100
Bus: *Mfr./sales analytical processing software.*   Fax: (732) 750-4848

- ## SANDWELL INTERNATIONAL, INC.
Park Place, 666 Burrard St., Vancouver BC V6C 2XB, Canada
CEO: Alan Pyatt, Chmn. & Pres. & CEO   Tel: 604-684-0055   Rev: $65
Bus: *Engineering design and construction*   Fax: 604-684-7533   Emp: 550
    www.sandwell.com

NAICS: 541330

SANDWELL INC.
7500 San Felipe, Ste. 600, Houston, Texas 77063
CEO: Bill Maddock, Mgr.   Tel: (713) 914-8110   %FO: 100
Bus: *Engineering, planning, design, project &*   Fax: (713) 914-8111
    construction management

SANDWELL INC.
2300 Lake Park Dr., Ste. 150, Smyrna, Georgia 30080
CEO: Joe Tomsula, VP & Gen. Mgr.   Tel: (770) 433-9336   %FO: 100
Bus: *Engineering, planning, design, project &*   Fax: (770) 433-9518   Emp: 51
construction management

● **SAPUTO INC.**
6869 Metropolitan Blvd. East, Saint-Leonard QC H1P 1X8, Canada
CEO: Lino A. Saputo Jr., Pres. & CEO   Tel: 514-328-6662   Rev: $2,729
Bus: *Mfr. mozzarella and specialty cheeses, butter and* Fax: 514-328-3364   Emp: 8,500
whey protein.   www.saputo.com
NAICS: 311513, 311812

   SAPUTO CHEESE USA INC.
   25 Tri State International Office Centre, Ste. 250, Lincolnshire, Illinois 60069
   CEO: Dino Dello Sbarba, Pres. & COO   Tel: (847) 267-1100   %FO: 100
   Bus: *Mfr. cheeses.*   Fax: (847) 267-1110   Emp: 2,100

● **SE GLOBAL EQUITIES CORPORATION**
777 W. Broadway, Ste. 1200, Vancouver BC V5Z 4J7, Canada
CEO: Toby Chu, Chmn. & CEO   Tel: 604-871-9909   Rev: $2
Bus: *Investment brokerage services.*   Fax: 604-871-9919   Emp: 12
                                                    www.seglobal.com
NAICS: 511210, 522320, 523120, 523910

   SE GLOBAL EQUITIES CORPORATION
   1142 S. Diamond Bar Blvd., Diamond Bar, California 91765
   CEO: Cedric M. Swirsky, Pres.   Tel: (909) 598-6855   %FO: 100
   Bus: *Investment brokerage services.*   Fax: (909) 594-4547

   SE GLOBAL EQUITIES CORPORATION
   1569 Fairway Dr., Ste. 222, Walnut, California 91789
   CEO: Darryl Sloan, Mgr.   Tel: (909) 598-6855   %FO: 100
   Bus: *Investment brokerage services.*   Fax: (909) 598-9077

● **SENVEST CAPITAL INC.**
1140 de Maisonneuve Blvd. West, Ste. 1180, Montreal QC H3A 1M8, Canada
CEO: Victor Mashaal, Chmn. & Pres.   Tel: 514-281-8082   Rev: $20
Bus: *Investment banking services.*   Fax: 514-281-0166   Emp: 11
                                                    www.senvest.com
NAICS: 523110, 523910, 551112

   SENVEST INTERNATIONAL LLC
   110 East 55th St., 16/F, New York, New York 10019
   CEO: Richard Mashaal, Pres.   Tel: (212) 977-2466   %FO: 100
   Bus: *Investment banking services.*   Fax: (212) 489-1248   Emp: 7

● **SHAWCOR LTD.**
25 Bethridge Rd., Toronto ON M9W 1M7, Canada
CEO: Geoffrey F. Hyland, Pres. & CEO   Tel: 416-743-7111   Rev: $717
Bus: *Pipeline coatings manufacture.*   Fax: 416-743-7199   Emp: 4,784
                                                    www.shawcor.com
NAICS: 237120, 326112, 333132

BREDERO SHAW LLC
2350 N. Sam Houston Pkwy. E., Ste. 500, Houston, Texas 77032
CEO: G. Hyland, Pres.   Tel: (281) 886-2350   %FO: 100
Bus: *Pipeline coatings for the oil and gas*   Fax: (281) 886-2351
     industry.

CANUSA-CPS
2408 Timerloch Place, Bldg. C-8, The Woodlands, Texas 77380
CEO: Nick Gritis   Tel: (281) 367-8866   %FO: 100
Bus: *Mfr. pipeline protection systems.*   Fax: (281) 367-4304

DSG-CANUSA
173 Commerce Blvd., Loveland, Ohio 45140
CEO: Jim Huntebrinker, Mgr.   Tel: (513) 683-7800   %FO: 100
Bus: *Mfr. pipeline protection systems.*   Fax: (513) 683-7809   Emp: 40

OMSCO
6300 Navigation, PO Box 230589, Houston, Texas 77223
CEO: L.W.J. Hutchison, Gen. Mgr.   Tel: (713) 844-3700   %FO: 100
Bus: *Mfr. valves and pipes.*   Fax: (713) 926-7103

SHAW PIPELINE SERVICES
15411 W. Vantage Pkwy., Ste. 200, Houston, Texas 77032
CEO: Les Hutchison, Mgr.   Tel: (832) 601-0850   %FO: 100
Bus: *Pipeline coatings for the oil and gas*   Fax: (281) 442-1593   Emp: 30
     industry.

SHAW PIPELINE SERVICES INC.
5435 S. 101st. East Ave., Tulsa, Oklahoma 74146
CEO: Johnny Peters, Gen. Mgr.   Tel: (918) 627-8288   %FO: 100
Bus: *Pipeline coatings for the oil and gas*   Fax: (918) 627-0020
     industry.

SHAWFLEX
, Cleveland, Ohio 60602
CEO: Tel: (330) 688-4001
Bus: *Pipeline coatings manufacture.*   Fax: (330) 688-4013

● **SIBERCORE TECHNOLOGIES**
1 Hines Rd., Unit 100, Ottawa ON K2K 3C7, Canada
CEO: Adam Chowaniec, Chmn.   Tel: 613-271-8100
Bus: *Design and manufacture integrated circuits.*   Fax: 613-271-8444
                                         www.sibercore.com

NAICS: 334413

   SIBERCORE TECHNOLOGIES
   999 Governor Dr., Ste. 103, El Dorado Hills, California 95762
   CEO: Adam Chowaniec, Chmn.   Tel: (916) 941-7960   %FO: 100
   Bus: *Design and manufacture integrated circuits.*   Fax: (916) 941-8572

● **SIERRA SYSTEMS GROUP INC.**
1177 W. Hastings St., Ste.2500, Vancouver BC V6E 2K3, Canada
CEO: Iraj Pourian, CEO   Tel: 604-688-1371   Rev: $112
Bus: *Information technology services*   Fax: 604-688-6482   Emp: 912
                                         www.sierrasystems.com

NAICS: 541511, 541512, 541513

SIERRA SYSTEMS GROUP INC.
901 South Mo-Pac Expressway, Barton Oaks Plaza Three, Ste. 130, Austin, Texas 78746
CEO: R.M. Meisner, EVP   Tel: (512) 583-2300   %FO: 100
Bus: *Information technology services.*   Fax: (512) 583-2334

SIERRA SYSTEMS GROUP INC.
10900 North East 8th St., Ste. 1110, Bellevue, Washington 98004
CEO: K.M. Meisner, EVP   Tel: (425) 688-7724   %FO: 100
Bus: *Information technology services.*   Fax: (425) 451-4430

SIERRA SYSTEMS GROUP INC.
400 North Continental Blvd., Ste. 300, El Segundo, California 90245
CEO: R.M. Meisner, EVP   Tel: (310) 536-6288   %FO: 100
Bus: *Information technology services.*   Fax: (310) 536-6282

SIERRA SYSTEMS GROUP INC.
100 Pearl St., 14/F, Hartford, Connecticut 06103-4506
CEO: R.M. Meisner, EVP   Tel: (860) 249-7008   %FO: 100
Bus: *Information technology services.*   Fax: (860) 249-7001

SIERRA SYSTEMS GROUP INC.
15455 Dallas Pkwy., Ste. 600, Addison, Texas 75001
CEO: R.M. Meisner, EVP   Tel: (972) 556-2121   %FO: 100
Bus: *Information technology services.*   Fax: (972) 869-3155

SIERRA SYSTEMS GROUP INC.
111 Market St. NE, Ste. 225, Olympia, Washington 98501
CEO: Kent Meisner, EVP   Tel: (360) 357-5668   %FO: 100
Bus: *Information technology services.*   Fax: (360) 754-0480

● **SIERRA WIRELESS, INC.**
13811 Wireless Way, Richmond BC V6V 3A4, Canada
CEO: David B. Stucliffe, Pres. & CEO   Tel: 604-231-1100   Rev: $211
Bus: *Mfr. modems and software for wireless* Fax: 604-231-1109   Emp: 227
   communication.   www.sierrawireless.com
NAICS: 334210, 334220, 334290, 334418, 541511

   SIERRA WIRELESS
   2290 Cosmos Ct., Carlsbad, California 92011
   CEO: Jim Kirkpatrick, VP   Tel: (760) 476-8604   %FO: 100
   Bus: *Engaged in radiotelephone communications* Fax: Emp: 82

● **SIMEXIWERKS INC.**
511 King St. West, Ste. 130, Toronto ON M5V 1K4, Canada
CEO: Michael Needham, Pres. & CEO   Tel: 416-597-1585   Rev: $32
Bus: *Designs motion simulation machines.*   Fax: 416-597-0530   Emp: 90
                                           www.simex-iwerks.com
NAICS: 713990

   SIMEX IWERKS
   2644 Slow Flight Dr., Daytona Beach, Florida 32124
   CEO: David Needham   Tel: (386) 767-2101   %FO: 100
   Bus: *Designs motion simulation machines.* Fax: (376) 767-2163

SIMEX IWERKS
4520 Valerio St., Burbank, California 91505
CEO: Mike Frueh
Bus: *Designs motion simulation machines.*

Tel: (818) 841-7766
Fax: (818) 840-6192

%FO: 100

• **A.G. SIMPSON AUTOMOTIVE SYSTEMS**
675 Progress Ave., Scarborough ON M1H 2W9, Canada
CEO: Joseph Leon, Co-Pres.
Bus: *Mfr. bumper systems, metal brackets, fuel tank straps and tailgates.*
NAICS: 336211, 336312, 336370

Tel: 416-438-6650
Fax: 416-431-8756
www.agsimpson.com

Rev: $409
Emp: 3,000

AG SIMPSON AUTOMOTIVE
1304 East Maple Rd., Troy, Michigan 48083
CEO: Robert DiNatale, Sales Mgr.
Bus: *Sale of automotive products.*

Tel: (248) 925-5600
Fax: (248) 925-5600

%FO: 100
Emp: 35

TROY BUMPER
1304 East Maple Rd., Troy, Michigan 48034
CEO: Dave Kesselring, Dir.
Bus: *Mfr. bumper systems, metal brackets, fuel tank straps and tailgates.*

Tel: (248) 925-5600
Fax: (248) 616-0865

%FO: 100
Emp: 70

• **SINCLAIR TECHNOLOGIES LTD.**
85 Mary St., Aurora ON L4G 6X5, Canada
CEO: Calven S. Iwata, Pres. & CEO
Bus: *Mfr. antennas & filters for radio communication systems.*
NAICS: 334220, 334413

Tel: 905-727-0165
Fax: 905-727-0861
www.sinctech.com

Emp: 170

SINCLAIR TECHNOLOGIES INC.
55 Oriskany Dr., Tonawanda, New York 14150
CEO: David Ralston, Pres.
Bus: *Mfr./distribution of high-quality fixed & mobile antennas, filters, receiver multi-couplers, transmitter combiners & related components.*

Tel: (905) 727-0165
Fax: (905) 727-0861

%FO: 100
Emp: 30

• **SKYJACK, INC.**
55 Campbell Rd., Guelph ON N1H 1B9, Canada
CEO: Lloyd Spalding, Pres. & CEO
Bus: *Aerial work platforms manufacture.*

NAICS: 333120

Tel: 519-837-0888
Fax: 519-837-8104
www.skyjackinc.com

Rev: $155
Emp: 1,100

SKYJACK, INC.
3810 460th Ave., Emmetsburg, Iowa 50536
CEO: Lloyd Spalding, Pres.
Bus: *Mfr. scissor lift work platforms.*

Tel: (712) 852-2724
Fax: (712) 852-2952

%FO: 100
Emp: 400

SKYJACK, INC.
3451 Swenson Ave., St. Charles, Illinois 60174
CEO: Chuck Burls, Gen. Mgr.
Bus: *Mfr. scissor lift work platforms.*

Tel: (630) 262-0005
Fax: (630) 262-0006

%FO: 100

- **SLATER STEEL INC.**
Markborough Place, 6711 Mississauga Rd., Ste. 202, Mississauga ON L5N 2W3, Canada
CEO: Anthony F. Griffiths, Chmn.   Tel: 905-567-1822   Rev: $480
Bus: *Steel products and special steel, hardware for*   Fax: 905-567-0946   Emp: 1,466
electric transmission.   www.slater.com
NAICS: 331111, 331221

> **SLATER STEEL INC.**
> 2400 Taylor St. West, Fort Wayne, Indiana 46802
> CEO: Bruce Kennedy, VP   Tel: (219) 434-2800   %FO: 100
> Bus: *Mfr. specialty alloys.*   Fax: (219) 434-2801   Emp: 400

- **SMTC CORPORATION**
635 Hood Rd., Markham ON L3R 4N6, Canada
CEO: John E. Caldwell, Pres. & CEO   Tel: 905-479-1810   Rev: $245
Bus: *Mfr. electronics.*   Fax: 905-479-1877   Emp: 921
www.smtc.com
NAICS: 334412, 334418

> **SMTC PENSAR DESIGN**
> 2302 Trade Zone Blvd., San Jose, California 95131
> CEO: Paul Walker, Pres.   Tel: (408) 934-7100   %FO: 100
> Bus: *Mfr. electronics.*   Fax: (408) 934-7101   Emp: 100

> **SMTC PENSAR DESIGN**
> 109 Constitution Blvd., Unit 160, Franklin, Massachusetts 02038
> CEO: Shelia Chartier, VP   Tel: (508) 520-5800   %FO: 100
> Bus: *Mfr. electronics.*   Fax: (508) 553-9351   Emp: 120

> **SMTC PENSAR DESIGN**
> 2222 E. Pensar Dr., Appleton, Wisconsin 54911
> CEO: Robe Deback   Tel: (920) 739-4355   %FO: 100
> Bus: *Mfr. electronics.*   Fax: (920) 739-9615

- **SNC LAVALIN GROUP INC.**
455 Rene-Levesque Blvd. West, Montreal QC H2Z 1Z3, Canada
CEO: Jacques Lamarre, Pres. & CEO   Tel: 514-393-1000   Rev: $2,861
Bus: *Engaged in pulp, paper, pharmaceuticals,*   Fax: 514-866-0795   Emp: 11,000
biotechnology, chemicals, petroleum, agriculture   www.snclavalin.com
and engineering.
NAICS: 236210, 237110, 237120, 237130, 237310, 237990, 541330

> **SNC LAVALIN AMERICA INC.**
> 6585 Penn Ave., Pittsburgh, Pennsylvania 15206
> CEO: Bob Grier, Mgr.   Tel: (412) 363-9000   %FO: 100
> Bus: *Heavy construction services.*   Fax: (412) 365-3303

> **SNC LAVALIN CONSTRUCTORS INC.**
> 15011 NE 36th St., Redmond, Washington 98052
> CEO: John H. Gillis, COO   Tel: (425) 896-4000   %FO: 100
> Bus: *Commercial & heavy construction.*   Fax: (425) 896-4040   Emp: 5,000

SNC LAVALIN INTERNATIONAL, INC.
5775 DTC Blvd., Ste. 200, Englewood, Colorado 80111
CEO: Jacquese Laramee, Pres.
Bus: *Engaged in pulp, paper, pharmaceuticals,*
biotechnology, chemicals, petroleum,
agriculture and engineering.

Tel: (303) 689-9144
Fax: (303) 689-9148

%FO: 100

SNC LAVALIN INTERNATIONAL, INC.
1666 K St. NW, 7/F, Washington, District of Columbia 20006
CEO: Frank Sutcliffe, VP
Bus: *Engaged in pulp, paper, pharmaceuticals,*
biotechnology, chemicals, petroleum,
agriculture and engineering.

Tel: (202) 293-7601
Fax: (202) 887-7018

%FO: 100

SNC LAVALIN INTERNATIONAL, INC.
9009 West Loop South, Ste. 800, Houston, Texas 77096
CEO: James M. Walters, Pres.
Bus: *Engaged in pulp, paper, pharmaceuticals,*
biotechnology, chemicals, petroleum,
agriculture and engineering.

Tel: (713) 667-9162
Fax: (713) 667-0010

%FO: 100
Emp: 500

● **SOBEYS CANADA INC.**
115 King St., Stellarton NS B0K 1S0, Canada
CEO: William G. McEwan, Pres. & CEO
Bus: *Retail groceries.*

Tel: 902-752-8371
Fax: 902-928-1101
www.sobeys.com

Rev: $8,057
Emp: 75,000

NAICS: 424410, 424480, 424490, 445110, 446110

SOBEYS PRODUCE, INC.
1903 S. Congress Ave., Boynton Beach, Florida 33426
CEO: Myron Wolfe, Pres.
Bus: *Wholesale food distribution, supermarkets*
and drug stores.

Tel: (561) 731-2722
Fax: (561) 731-1463

%FO: 26
Emp: 8

● **SOFTCHOICE CORPORATION**
173 Dufferin St., Ste. 200, Toronto ON M6K 3H7, Canada
CEO: David MacDonald, Pres.
Bus: *Software services.*

Tel: 416-588-9000
Fax: 416-588-9001
www.softchoice.com

Rev: $523
Emp: 536

NAICS: 423430

SOFTCHOICE CORPORATION
314 West Superior, Ste. 301, Chicago, Illinois 60610
CEO: David MacDonald, Pres.
Bus: *Software services.*

Tel: (312) 655-9000
Fax: (312) 655-9001

%FO: 100

● **SOLCORP**
177 Lakeshore Blvd. East, Toronto ON M5A 1B7, Canada
CEO: Michael Dufton, Pres. & CEO
Bus: *Software solutions and consulting services.*

Tel: 416-673-9900
Fax: 416-573-6200
www.solcorp.com

Rev: $95
Emp: 700

NAICS: 511210, 518210, 541511, 541512, 541519, 611420

SOLCORP
1333 Butterfield Rd., Ste. 500, Downers Grove, Illinois 60515-5631
CEO: Mark Cline, VP   Tel: (630) 960-4604   %FO: 100
Bus: *Software solutions and consulting services.*   Fax: (630) 960-4607   Emp: 50

● **SOMA NETWORKS, INC.**
312 Adelaide St. West, Ste. 600, Toronto ON M5V 1R2, Canada
CEO: Yatish Pathak, Pres. & CEO   Tel: 416-977-1414
Bus: *Wireless networking equipment manufacture.*   Fax: 416-977-1505
                                          www.somanetworks.com
NAICS: 334220

   SOMA NETWORKS, INC.
   400 Industrial Dr., Ste. 200, Richardson, Texas 75081
   CEO: Mark Rau, Mgr.   Tel: (972) 739-3100   %FO: 100
   Bus: *Wireless networking equipment*   Fax: (972) 739-3113   Emp: 3
      manufacture.
   SOMA NETWORKS, INC.
   185 Berry St., Ste. 4600, San Francisco, California 94107
   CEO: Yatish Pathak, Pres.   Tel: (415) 882-6500   %FO: 100
   Bus: *Wireless networking equipment*   Fax: (415) 882-6501   Emp: 35
      manufacture.

● **SPECTRAL DIAGNOSTICS INC.**
135-2 The West Mall, Toronto ON M9C 1C2, Canada
CEO: Paul M. Walker, Pres. & CEO   Tel: 416-626-3233   Rev: $9
Bus: *Mfr. blood test kits for health care professionals.*   Fax: 416-626-7383   Emp: 70
                                          www.spectraldx.com
NAICS: 325413

   SPECTRAL DIAGNOSTICS INC.
   85 First St., White Stone, Virginia 22578
   CEO: Donna Edmonds, VP   Tel: (804) 435-9850   %FO: 100
   Bus: *Blood test kits for health care*   Fax: (804) 435-9851   Emp: 30
      professionals.

● **SPECTRUM SIGNAL PROCESSING INC.**
2700 Production Way, Ste. 300, Burnaby BC V5A 4X1, Canada
CEO: Pascal Spotheifer, Pres. & CEO   Tel: 604-421-5422   Rev: $18
Bus: *Engaged in software and wireless systems.*   Fax: 604-421-1764   Emp: 88
                                          www.spectrumsignal.com
NAICS: 334210, 334220, 334290, 334413, 334511

   SPECTRUM SIGNAL PROCESSING INC.
   6630 Eli Whitney Dr., Columbia, Maryland 21046
   CEO: James Atkins, Pres.   Tel: (410) 872-0202   %FO: 100
   Bus: *Engaged in software and wireless systems.*   Fax: (410) 872-0201   Emp: 20

   SPECTRUM SIGNAL PROCESSING INC.
   116 South River Rd., Bldg. C, Bedford, New Hampshire 03110
   CEO: Steve Fetter   Tel: (603) 629-0088   %FO: 100
   Bus: *Engaged in software and wireless systems.*   Fax: (603) 629-9994

SPECTRUM SIGNAL PROCESSING INC.
4010 Moorpark Ave., Ste. 215, San Jose, California 95117
CEO: Mark Murray   Tel: (408) 241-0000   %FO: 100
Bus: *Engaged in software and wireless systems.*   Fax: (408) 241-0033

• **SPEEDWARE CORPORATION INC.**
9999 Cavendish Blvd., Ste. 100, Saint-Laurent QC H4M 2X5, Canada
CEO: Andrew Gutman, Pres. & CEO   Tel: 514-747-7007   Rev: $19
Bus: *Application development software manufacture.*   Fax: 514-747-3380   Emp: 234
                                     www.corporate.speedware.com
NAICS: 511210
    ACTIVANT SOLUTIONS
    804 Las Cimas Pkwy., Ste. 200, Austin, Texas 78746
    CEO: A. Laurence Jones, Pres. & CEO   Tel: (512) 328-2300   %FO: 100
    Bus: *Enterprise resource planning software.*   Fax: (512) 278-5223   Emp: 1,200

    ECS, DIV. SPEEDWARE CORPORATION
    5 Independence Pointe, Greenville, South Carolina 29602
    CEO: Andrew Gutman, Pres. & CEO   Tel: (864) 234-7676   %FO: 100
    Bus: *Application development software sales.*   Fax: (864) 987-6400

• **SR TELECOM INC.**
8150 Trans-Canada Hwy., Saint-Laurent QC H4S 1M5, Canada
CEO: William Aziz, CEO   Tel: 514-335-1210   Rev: $103
Bus: *Wireless network infrastructure equipment*   Fax: 514-334-7783   Emp: 987
    manufacture.   www.srtelecom.com
NAICS: 334220
    SR TELECOM INC.
    600 North Pine Island Rd., Ste. 150, Plantation, Florida 33324
    CEO: Don Sonntag, Mgr.   Tel: (954) 874-1639   %FO: 100
    Bus: *Wireless network infrastructure equipment*   Fax: (954) 423-4238
    manufacture and sales.

    SRT TELECOMMUNICATIONS LTD.
    3350 SW 148th Ave., Ste. 110, Miramar, Florida 33027
    CEO: William Aziz, CEO   Tel: (954) 874-1639   %FO: 100
    Bus: *Wireless network infrastructure equipment*   Fax:
    manufacture and sales.

• **ST. LAWRENCE CEMENT GROUP, INC.**
1945 Graham Blvd., Mount Royal QC H3R 1H1, Canada
CEO: Philippe Arto, Pres. & CEO   Tel: 514-340-1881   Rev: $1,061
Bus: *Cement, concrete, aggregates, construction*   Fax: 514-342-8154   Emp: 2,900
                                     www.stlawrencecement.com
NAICS: 212311, 212312, 212319, 212321, 327310, 327320
    HOLCIM U.S. INC.
    6211 North Ann Arbor Rd., PO Box 122, Dundee, Michigan 48131
    CEO: Patrick Dolberg, Pres. & CEO   Tel: (734) 529-2411   %FO: 100
    Bus: *Mfr./distribution cement.*   Fax: (734) 529-5512   Emp: 2,389

INDEPENDENT CEMENT CORPORATION
3 Columbia Circle, Albany, New York 12203
CEO: Dennis Skidmore, VP
Bus: *Mfr./distribution cement.*

Tel: (518) 452-3563
Fax: (518) 452-3045

%FO: 100
Emp: 2,000

● **STANTEC INC.**
10160-112 St., Edmonton AB T5K 2L6, Canada
CEO: Anthony P. Franceschini, Pres. & CEO
Bus: *Architectural and engineering services*

Tel: 780-917-7000
Fax: 780-917-7330
www.stantec.com

Rev: $302
Emp: 4,000

NAICS: 541310, 541330, 541420, 541611, 561210

    STANTEC INC.
    Ste. 100, 51 Century Blvd., Nashville, Tennessee 37214
    CEO: Michael Delvizis, Principal
    Bus: *Architectural and engineering services.*

Tel: (615) 885-1144
Fax: (615) 885-1102

%FO: 100

    STANTEC INC.
    Ste. 100, 6980 Sierra Center Parkway, Reno, Nevada 89511
    CEO: Curt Chapman, Principal
    Bus: *Architectural and engineering services.*

Tel: (775) 850-0777
Fax: (775) 850-0787

%FO: 100

    STANTEC INC.
    Unit D, 9 Princess Rd., Lawrenceville, New Jersey 08648
    CEO: Sameh Zaghloul, Principal
    Bus: *Architectural and engineering services.*

Tel: (609) 895-6662
Fax: (609) 895-8822

%FO: 100

    STANTEC INC.
    109 Great Oaks Blvd., Albany, New York 12203-7905
    CEO: Paul Bohl, Sr. Mgr.
    Bus: *Architectural and engineering services.*

Tel: (518) 464-1717
Fax: (518) 464-6767

%FO: 100

    STANTEC INC.
    Bldg. 40-4, 1701 North Street, Endicott, New York 13760
    CEO: Jerry Serbonich, Mgr.
    Bus: *Architectural and engineering services.*

Tel: (607) 755-9800
Fax: (607) 755-9850

%FO: 100

    STANTEC INC.
    Ste. 250, 300 Meridian Centre, Rochester, New York 14618
    CEO: Mark Lang, VP
    Bus: *Architectural and engineering services.*

Tel: (585) 475-1440
Fax: (585) 272-1814

%FO: 100

    STANTEC INC.
    Ste. 108, 150 Lawrence Bell Dr., Amherst, New York 14221
    CEO: Sameh Zaghloul, Principal
    Bus: *Architectural and engineering services.*

Tel: (716) 631-8030
Fax: (716) 632-4808

%FO: 100

    STANTEC INC.
    990 Morrison Dr., Charleston, South Carolina 29403
    CEO: Eddie Porcher, Assoc. VP
    Bus: *Architectural and engineering services.*

Tel: (843) 577-4926
Fax: (843) 723-0440

%FO: 100

STANTEC INC.
Ste. 300, 2127 Ayrsley Town Blvd., Charlotte, North Carolina 28273
CEO: Richard Keagy, Principal Tel: (704) 329-0900 %FO: 100
Bus: *Architectural and engineering services.* Fax: (704) 329-0905

STANTEC INC.
Ste. 310, 2135 South Cherry St., Denver, Colorado 80222
CEO: Michael Unger, Principal Tel: (303) 758-4058 %FO: 100
Bus: *Architectural and engineering services.* Fax: (303) 758-4828

STANTEC INC.
209 South Meldrum, Fort Collins, Colorado 80521-2603
CEO: Bret Cummock, Mgr. Tel: (970) 482-5922 %FO: 100
Bus: *Architectural and engineering services.* Fax: (970) 482-6368

STANTEC INC.
7251 West Charleston Blvd., Las Vegas, Nevada 89117
CEO: Victor Neufeld, VP Tel: (702) 258-0115 %FO: 100
Bus: *Architectural and engineering services.* Fax: (702) 258-4956

STANTEC INC.
Ste. 300, 801 Jones Franklin Rd., Raleigh, North Carolina 27606
CEO: Kenneth Smith, Principal Tel: (919) 851-6866 %FO: 100
Bus: *Architectural and engineering services.* Fax: (919) 851-7024

STANTEC INC.
8211 South 48th St., Phoenix, Arizona 85044
CEO: Tim Lines, VP Tel: (602) 438-2200 %FO: 100
Bus: *Architectural and engineering services.* Fax: (602) 431-9562

STANTEC INC.
Ste. 200, 150 Oak Plaza Blvd., Winston-Salem, North Carolina 27105
CEO: Randal Pool, Principal Tel: (336) 759-7400 %FO: 100
Bus: *Architectural and engineering services.* Fax: (336) 759-7900

STANTEC INC.
201 North Bonita Ave., Tucson, Arizona 85745-2999
CEO: John Take, Principal Tel: (520) 750-7474 %FO: 100
Bus: *Architectural and engineering services.* Fax: (520) 750-7470

STANTEC INC.
Ste. 300, 3995 South 700 East, Salt Lake City, Utah 84107
CEO: Ken Watson, Principal Tel: (801) 261-0090 %FO: 100
Bus: *Architectural and engineering services.* Fax: (801) 266-1671

STANTEC INC.
2590 Venture Oaks Way, Sacramento, California 95833-3288
CEO: Dan Tomie, VP Tel: (916) 569-2500 %FO: 100
Bus: *Architectural and engineering services.* Fax: (916) 921-9274

STANTEC INC.
Ste. 300, 1800 Bayberry Ct., Richmond, Virginia 23226
CEO: Randall Harris, Assoc. VP Tel: (804) 285-9021 %FO: 100
Bus: *Architectural and engineering services.* Fax: (804) 285-0991

THE KEITH COMPANIES INC.
19 Technology Dr., Irvine, California 92618-2334
CEO: Aram H. Keith, Chmn. & CEO   Tel: (949) 923-6000   %FO: 100
Bus: *Engineering services*   Fax: (949) 923-6121   Emp: 830

● **STELCO, INC.**
386 Wilcox St., Hamilton ON L8L 8K5, Canada
CEO: Courtney Pratt, Pres. & CEO   Tel: 905-528-2511   Rev: $2,116
Bus: *Blast furnaces and steel mills.*   Fax: 905-308-7007   Emp: 9,143
          www.stelco.ca
NAICS: 331221, 331222

  CAMROSE PIPE CO.
  1000 SW Broadway, Ste. 2200, Portland, Oregon 97205
  CEO: Ray Adams, CFO   Tel: (503) 223-9228   %FO: 40
  Bus: *Mfr. steel pipe.*   Fax: Emp: 84

  STELCO INC.
  2855 Coolridge Hwy., Ste. 203, Troy, Michigan 48084
  CEO: Linc Simpson, Principal   Tel: (248) 649-3460   %FO: 100
  Bus: *Mfr. hot and cold rolled steel sheets.*   Fax: (248) 649-1104   Emp: 3

● **STELLA-JONES INC.**
4269 Sainte-Catherine St. West, 7/F, Westmount QC H3Z 1P7, Canada
CEO: Brian McManus, Pres, & CEO   Tel: 514-934-8666   Rev: $61
Bus: *Production and manufacture of treated wood*   Fax: 514-934-5327   Emp: 200
    poles serving electrical utilities and   www.stella-jones.com
    telecommunication companies.
NAICS: 321113, 321114, 321999

  WEBSTER WOOD PRESERVING CO.
  County Trunk Hwy. U, PO Box 297, Bangor, Wisconsin 54614
  CEO: Paul D. Webster, Pres.   Tel: (608) 486-2341   %FO: 100
  Bus: *Wood preservation.*   Fax: Emp: 35

● **STOCKGROUP INFORMATION SYSTEMS INC.**
795 West Pender St., Ste. 500, Vancouver BC V6C 2T7, Canada
CEO: Marcus A. New, Pres. & CEO   Tel: 604-331-0995   Rev: $4
Bus: *Financial software manufacture.*   Fax: 604-331-1194   Emp: 47
          www.stockgroup.com
NAICS: 511210, 516110, 519110, 519190

  STOCKGROUP
  599 Lexington Ave., Ste. 4102, New York, New York 10020
  CEO: Marcus New, Principal   Tel: (212) 319-1740   %FO: 100
  Bus: *Mfr. of financial software.*   Fax: (212) 319-4438

● **STRESSGEN BIOTECHNOLGIES CORPORATION**
4243 Glanford Ave., Ste. 350, Victoria BC V8Z 4B9, Canada
CEO: Gregory M. McKee, Pres. & CEO   Tel: 250-744-2811   Rev: $1
Bus: *Pharmaceutical and biotechnology.*   Fax: 250-744-2877   Emp: 103
          www.stressgen.com
NAICS: 325412

STRESSGEN BIOTECHNOLGIES CORPORATION
6055 Lusk Blvd., San Diego, California 92121
CEO: Gregory McKee, Pres.   Tel: (858) 202-4900   %FO: 100
Bus: *Pharmaceutical and biotechnology.*   Fax: (858) 450-6849

• **SUN LIFE FINANCIAL INC.**
150 King St. West, 6/F, Toronto ON M5H 1J9, Canada
CEO: Donald A. Stewart, CEO & Mng. Dir.   Tel: 416-979-9966   Rev: $18,125
Bus: *Insurance, pensions and mutual funds.*   Fax: 416-585-7892   Emp: 13,570
www.sunlife.com
NAICS: 523991, 523999, 524113, 524114, 524292, 525110, 525120, 525190, 525910, 525920, 525990

MASSACHUSETTS FINANCIAL SERVICES COMPANY
500 Boylston St., Boston, Massachusetts 02116
CEO: Robert J. Manning, Pres. & CEO   Tel: (617) 954-5000   %FO: 100
Bus: *Investment management services.*   Fax: (617) 954-6620

SUN LIFE FINANCIAL SERVICES
One Sun Life Executive Park, Wellesley Hills, Massachusetts 02481
CEO: Robert C. Salipante, Pres.   Tel: (781) 237-6030   %FO: 100
Bus: *Insurance, pensions and mutual funds.*   Fax: Emp: 2,292

• **SUNCOR ENERGY INC.**
112 4th Ave. SW, PO Box 38, Calgary AB T2P 2V5, Canada
CEO: Richard L. George, Pres. & CEO   Tel: 403-269-8100   Rev: $6,856
Bus: *Oil and natural gas exploration.*   Fax: 403-269-6200   Emp: 4,605
www.suncor.com
NAICS: 211111, 211112, 324110, 324191, 324199, 424710, 424720, 447190, 454311, 454312, 454319

SUNCOR ENERGY INC.
District Region Pipeline Office, 2234 West Lincoln Way, Cheyenne, Wyoming 82001
CEO: Mike Ashar, Pres.   Tel: (307) 634-1853   %FO: 100
Bus: *Oil and natural gas exploration.*   Fax: (304) 637-6633

SUNCOR ENERGY INC.
5801 Brighton Blvd., Commerce City, Colorado 80022
CEO: Mike Ashar, Pres.   Tel: (303) 286-5701   %FO: 100
Bus: *Oil and natural gas exploration.*   Fax: (303) 286-5702   Emp: 625

SUNCOR ENERGY INC.
7800 E. Orchard Rd., Ste. 300, Greenwood Village, Colorado 80111
CEO: Mike Ashar, Pres.   Tel: (303) 793-8000   %FO: 100
Bus: *Oil and natural gas exploration.*   Fax: (303) 793-8003

• **SUNOPTA, INC.**
2838 Bovaird Dr. West, Norval ON L0P 1KO, Canada
CEO: Jeremy N. Kendall, Chmn. & CEO   Tel: 905-445-1990   Rev: $306
Bus: *Organic corn and soy products manufacture.*   Fax: 905-455-2529   Emp: 910
www.sunopta.com
NAICS: 311222, 311223, 311225, 424410, 424490, 562111, 562119, 562212, 562213, 562219, 562910, 562920

SUNOPTA FOOD GROUP LLC
5850 Opus Pkwy., Ste. 150, Minnetonka, Minnesota 55343
CEO: Allan Routh, Pres.   Tel: (952) 939-3949   %FO: 100
Bus: *Sale of groceries.*   Fax: Emp: 12

● **SYNDESIS LIMITED**
30 Fulton Way, Richmond Hill ON L4B 1E6, Canada
CEO: John Lochow, Pres. & CEO   Tel: 905-886-7818
Bus: *Telecommunications software manufacture.*   Fax: 905-886-9076
    www.syndesis.com
NAICS: 511210

    COMANAGE CORPORATION
    12330 Perry Highway, Ste. 107, Wexford, Pennsylvania 15090
    CEO: Adam Boone   Tel: (412) 318-6000   %FO: 100
    Bus: *Telecommunications software sales.*   Fax: (412) 318-2400

● **SYSTECH RETAIL SYSTEMS INC.**
5800 Ambler Dr., Ste. 215, Mississauga ON L4W 4J4, Canada
CEO: David w. Shonerd, Pres. & CEO   Tel: 905-507-4333   Rev: $16
Bus: *Developer, integrator and supporter of best-in-*   Fax: 905-507-2325   Emp: 274
    class solutions for supermarket, general   www.openfieldsolutions.com
    merchandise and hospitality chains.
NAICS: 541511, 541512

    SYSTECH RETAIL SYSTEMS INC.
    5510 Six Forks Rd., Ste. 200, Raleigh, North Carolina 27609
    CEO: Dave Shonerd, Pres.   Tel: (919) 844-7301   %FO: 100
    Bus: *Developer, integrator and supporter of best-*   Fax: (919) 866-1152   Emp: 400
    in-class solutions for supermarket, general
    merchandise and hospitality chains.

● **SYSTEMS XCELLENCE, INC.**
555 Industrial Dr., Milton ON L9T 5E1, Canada
CEO: Gordon S. Glenn, Pres. & CEO   Tel: 905-876-4741   Rev: $33
Bus: *Information management software for*   Fax: 905-878-8869   Emp: 260
    pharmaceutical companies.   www.sxc.com
NAICS: 511210, 518210, 541519

    HEALTH BUSINESS SYSTEMS, INC.
    738 Louis Dr., Warminster, Pennsylvania 18974
    CEO: Louis Greenberg, Pres.   Tel: (215) 442-9300
    Bus: *Sale of computer equipment & programs.*   Fax: (215) 442-7555   Emp: 85

    SXC HEALTH SOLUTIONS, INC.
    7047 E. Greenway Pkwy., Ste. 360, Scottsdale, Arizona 85254
    CEO: Gordon Glenn, CEO   Tel: (480) 609-8060
    Bus: *Information management software for*   Fax: (480) 609-8070
    pharmaceutical companies.

SYSTEMS XCELLENCE, INC.
2505 S. Finley Rd., Ste. 110, Lombard, Illinois 60148
CEO: Gordon Glenn, CEO
Bus: *Information management software for pharmaceutical companies.*

Tel: (630) 268-3600
Fax: (630) 268-0008

%FO: 100
Emp: 215

• **TAIGA FOREST PRODUCTS LTD.**
4710 Kingsway, Ste. 800, Burnaby BC V5H 4M2, Canada
CEO: Tong Kooi Ong, Chmn. & CEO
Bus: *Lumber wholesaler.*

Tel: 604-438-1471
Fax: 604-439-4242
www.taigaforest.com

Rev: $1,092
Emp: 524

NAICS: 321114, 321213, 321219, 321999, 324122

TAIGA FOREST PRODUCTS LTD.
PO Box 402, Custer, Washington 98240
CEO: John Steele, Mgr.
Bus: *Lumber wholesaler.*

Tel: (800) 663-1470
Fax:

%FO: 100

• **TARKETT INC.**
1001 Yamaska St. East, Farnham QC J2N 1J7, Canada
CEO: Marc Assa, CEO
Bus: *Flooring manufacture.*

Tel: 450-293-3173
Fax: 450-293-6644
www.domcotarkett.com

Rev: $425
Emp: 2,235

NAICS: 321918

TARKETT INC.
1705 Oliver St., Houston, Texas 77007
CEO: Diane Martel, VP Mktg.
Bus: *Flooring manufacture and sales.*

Tel: (713) 344-2858
Fax: (713) 869-0859

%FO: 100

• **THE TDL GROUP LTD., DIV. WENDY'S**
874 Sinclair Rd., Oakville ON L6K 2 Y1, Canada
CEO: Paul D. House, Pres. & CEO
Bus: *Coffee and baked goods chain, Tim Horton's.*

Tel: 905-845-6511
Fax: 905-845-0265
www.timhortons.com

Rev: $807
Emp: 760

NAICS: 722211

HORTONS TIM
19575 Victor Pkwy., Ste. 170, Livonia, Michigan 48152
CEO: Christos G. Laganos, VP
Bus: *Coffee and baked goods chain.*

Tel: (734) 779-0100
Fax: (734) 779-0147

%FO: 100

TIM HORTONS
4150 Tuller Rd., Ste.236, Dublin, Ohio 43017
CEO: Chris Laganos, Pres.
Bus: *Coffee and baked goods chain.*

Tel: (614) 791-4200
Fax: (614) 791-4235

%FO: 100
Emp: 34

• **TDS AUTOMOTIVE**
100 Milverton Dr., Ste. 600, Mississauga ON L5R 4H1, Canada
CEO: Joe Opdeweegh, Pres. & CEO
Bus: *Material logistical services for auto industry.*

Tel: 905-755-6100
Fax: 905-755-6160
www.tdsautomotive.com

NAICS: 336399

TDS AUTOMOTIVE
22701 Trolley Industrial Dr., Ste. C, Taylor, Michigan 48180
CEO: Paul McQuinter, Pres. & CEO   Tel: (248) 377-4700   %FO: 100
Bus: *Mfr. of industrial machinery.*   Fax: (248) 340-1180

TDS AUTOMOTIVE
11191 Lappin, Detroit, Michigan 48234
CEO: John Donaldson, Mgr.   Tel: (313) 371-3867   %FO: 100
Bus: *Mfr. of industrial machinery.*   Fax: (313) 371-8314

TDS AUTOMOTIVE
17800 Dix Toledo Rd., Riverview, Michigan 48192
CEO: Paul McQuinter, Pres. & CEO   Tel: (248) 377-4700   %FO: 100
Bus: *Mfr. of industry machinery.*   Fax: (248) 340-1180

TDS AUTOMOTIVE
20495 Pennsylvania Rd., Brownstown, Michigan 48192
CEO: Paul McQuinter, Pres. & CEO   Tel: (519) 645-6060   %FO: 100
Bus: *Material logistical services for auto industry.*   Fax: (519) 645-6080

TDS AUTOMOTIVE
1331 North Main St., Mount Pleasant, Tennessee 38474
CEO: Bobbi Allison, Mgr.   Tel: (931) 379-9700   %FO: 100
Bus: *Mfr. of industry machinery, motor vehicle*   Fax: (931) 379-9907   Emp: 45
       parts & accessories.

TDS AUTOMOTIVE
2851 High Meadow Circle, Ste. 250, Auburn Hills, Michigan 48326
CEO: Paul McQuinter, Pres. & CEO   Tel: (248) 377-4700   %FO: 100
Bus: *Mfr. of industrial machinery.*   Fax: (248) 340-1180

● **TECK COMINCO CORPORATION**
200 Burrard St., Ste. 600, Vancouver BC V6C 3L9, Canada
CEO: Donald R. Lindsay, Pres. & CEO   Tel: 604-687-1117   Rev: $2,845
Bus: *Integrated natural resource mining.*   Fax: 604-687-6100   Emp: 6,710
                                               www.teckcominco.com
NAICS: 212111, 212112, 212113, 212221, 212222, 212231, 212234, 212299, 213113, 213114, 324199

TECK COMINCO ADVANCED MATERIALS, INC.
13670 Danielson St., Ste. H & I, PO Box 1390, Poway, California 92074
CEO: Douglas Magoon, Pres.   Tel: (858) 391-2935   %FO: 100
Bus: *Mining of gold, coal and copper.*   Fax: (858) 391-2934   Emp: 5

TECK COMINCO AMERICA INC.
15918 East Euclid Ave., Spokane, Washington 99216
CEO: D. Thompson, Pres.   Tel: (509) 747-6111   %FO: 100
Bus: *Mining of gold, coal and copper.*   Fax: (509) 459-4400   Emp: 510

● **TECSYS INC.**
87 Prince St., 5/F, Montreal QC H3C 2M7, Canada
CEO: Peter Brereton, Pres. & CEO   Tel: 514-866-0001   Rev: $18
Bus: *Supply chain management software manufacture.*   Fax: 514-866-1805   Emp: 224
                                               www.tecsys.com
NAICS: 423430, 511210

TECSYS U.S., INC.
1515 Woodfield Rd., Ste. 330, Schaumburg, Illinois 60173
CEO: Peter Brereton, Pres.
Bus: *Supply chain management software sales.*

Tel: (847) 969-8800
Fax: (847) 969-0380

%FO: 100
Emp: 24

● **TEKNION CORPORATION**
1150 Flint Rd., Toronto ON M3J 2J5, Canada
CEO: David Feldberg, Pres. & CEO
Bus: *Portable sheetrock walls manufacture.*

Tel: 416-661-3370
Fax: 416-661-7970
www.teknion.com

Rev: $419
Emp: 3,150

NAICS: 337211, 337214, 337215

TEKNION CORP.
1048 Merchandise Mart, Chicago, Illinois 60654
CEO: Pattie Ferrell, Mgr.
Bus: *Mfr./sales portable sheetrock walls.*

Tel: (312) 321-1286
Fax: (312) 321-1388

%FO: 100
Emp: 8

TEKNION CORP.
2424 N. Federal Hwy., Ste. 351, Boca Raton, Florida 33431
CEO: Daniel Welbes, Mgr.
Bus: *Mfr./sales portable sheetrock walls.*

Tel: (561) 382-7732
Fax: (561) 392-7048

%FO: 100
Emp: 3

TEKNION CORPORATION
900 17th St., NW, Ste. 200, Washington, District of Columbia 20006
CEO: James Herring, Mgr.
Bus: *Mfr./sales portable sheetrock walls.*

Tel: (202) 378-6460
Fax: (202) 378-6490

%FO: 100
Emp: 7

TEKNION CORPORATION
2828 North Harwood St., Ste. 1700, Dallas, Texas 75201
CEO: Stephen Silver
Bus: *Mfr./sales portable sheetrock walls.*

Tel: (214) 764-6500
Fax: (214) 764-6550

%FO: 100

TEKNION CORPORATION
150 East 58th St., 12/F, New York, New York 10155
CEO: Christopher Stevenson, Mgr.
Bus: *Mfr./sales portable sheetrock walls.*

Tel: (212) 750-7850
Fax: (212) 750-7996

%FO: 100
Emp: 10

TEKNION CORPORATION
1200 Brickell Ave., Ste. 650, Miami, Florida 33133
CEO: Daniel Walbes, Mgr.
Bus: *Mfr./sales portable sheetrock walls.*

Tel: (305) 373-6310
Fax: (305) 373-6305

%FO: 100
Emp: 6

TEKNION CORPORATION
Pinnacle Bldg., 3455 Peachtree Rd. N.E., Ste. 100, Atlanta, Georgia 30326
CEO: Andrew Blake, Mgr.
Bus: *Mfr./sales portable sheetrock walls.*

Tel: (404) 266-1911
Fax: (404) 266-2811

%FO: 100
Emp: 12

TEKNION CORPORATION
631 Wilshire Blvd., 2/F Ste. B, Santa Monica, California 90401
CEO: Randy Kemp, Mgr.
Bus: *Mfr./sales portable sheetrock walls.*

Tel: (310) 300-3800
Fax: (310) 300-3224

%FO: 100
Emp: 8

TEKNION CORPORATION
5201 Great American Pkwy., Ste. 446, Santa Clara, California 95054
CEO: Andrew Cicisly, Mgr.
Bus: *Mfr./sales portable sheetrock walls.*
Tel: (408) 970-0891
Fax: (408) 970-0894
%FO: 100
Emp: 5

TEKNION CORPORATION
268 Summer St., Ste. 105, Boston, Massachusetts 02210
CEO: David Fallon, Mgr.
Bus: *Mfr./sales portable sheetrock walls.*
Tel: (617) 487-6960
Fax: (617) 487-6980
%FO: 100

TEKNION LLC
12000 Horizon Way, Mt. Laurel, New Jersey 08054
CEO: Stephen L. Silver, Pres.
Bus: *Mfr./sales portable sheetrock walls.*
Tel: (856) 596-7608
Fax: (856) 596-8088
%FO: 100
Emp: 242

● **TEMBEC INC.**
800 Rene-Levesque Blvd. West, Ste. 1050, Montreal QC H3B 1X9, Canada
CEO: Frank A. Dottori, Pres. & CEO
Bus: *Pulp, lumber, timber and flooring manufacture and sales.*
NAICS: 113310, 321113, 321219, 321918, 322110, 322130
Tel: 514-871-0137
Fax: 514-397-0896
www.tembec.ca
Rev: $2,886
Emp: 10,047

TEMBEC INC.
501 B St., Ste. 3, Marysville, California 95901
CEO: James Haas, Mgr.
Bus: *Pulp, lumber, timber and flooring manufacture and sales.*
Tel: (530) 743-4388
Fax: (530) 743-4392
%FO: 100

TEMBEC INC.
2112 Sylvan Ave., PO Box 2570, Toledo, Ohio 43606
CEO: Robert Zalkowitz, Chmn.
Bus: *Pulp, lumber, timber and flooring manufacture and sales.*
Tel: (419) 244-5856
Fax: (419) 244-9206
%FO: 100
Emp: 46

TEMBEC INC.
16045 Business Pkwy., Hagerstown, Maryland 21740
CEO: Frank A. Dottori
Bus: *Pulp, lumber, timber and flooring manufacture and sales.*
Tel: (301) 791-1582
Fax: (301) 791-3643
%FO: 100

● **TESCO CORPORATION**
6204 6A St. SE, Calgary AB T2H 2B7, Canada
CEO: Julio M. Quintana, CEO & Mng. Dir.
Bus: *Drilling equipment for oil and gas industry.*
NAICS: 333132
Tel: 403-233-0757
Fax: 403-252-3362
www.tescocorp.com
Rev: $149
Emp: 875

TESCO CORPORATION
11330 Brittmoore Park Dr., Houston, Texas 77041
CEO: Julio M. Quintana, Pres.
Bus: *Drilling equipment for oil and gas industry.*
Tel: (713) 849-5900
Fax: (713) 849-0075
%FO: 100
Emp: 201

- **TESMA INTERNATIONAL INC.**
  1000 Tesma Way, Concord ON L4K 5R8, Canada
  CEO: Manfred Gingl, Chmn. & CEO
  Bus: *Engine and fueling components manufacture.*

  Tel: 905-417-2100
  Fax: 905-417-2101
  www.magnapowertrain.com

  Rev: $1,377
  Emp: 5,000

  NAICS: 336312, 336350, 336399

  TESMA INTERNATIONAL INC.
  23300 Haggerty Rd., Ste. 200, Farmington Hills, Michigan 48335
  CEO: Manfred Gingl, Chmn.
  Bus: *Engine and fueling components sales.*

  Tel: (248) 888-5550
  Fax: (248) 427-1458

  %FO: 100
  Emp: 35

  TESMA INTERNATIONAL INC.
  6363 E. 14 Mile Rd., Sterling Heights, Michigan 48312
  CEO: Joe Gusumano, Gen. Mgr.
  Bus: *Mfr. of automotive stamping.*

  Tel: (586) 264-8180
  Fax:

  %FO: 100
  Emp: 150

- **THINKFILM COMPANY**
  2300 Yonge St., Ste. 906, Toronto ON M4P 1E4, Canada
  CEO: Jeff Sackman, CEO
  Bus: *Independent film distribution.*

  Tel: 416-488-0037
  Fax: 416-488-0031
  www.thinkfilmcompany.com

  NAICS: 512110

  THINKFILM COMPANY
  155 Ave. of the Americas, New York, New York 10013
  CEO: Jeff Sackman
  Bus: *Independent film distribution.*

  Tel: (646) 293-9400
  Fax: (646) 293-9407

  %FO: 100

- **THINKPATH INC.**
  201 Westcreek Blvd., Ste. 400, Brampton ON L6T 5S6, Canada
  CEO: Declan A. French, CEO
  Bus: *Provides information technology and engineering
  services.*

  Tel: 905-460-3040
  Fax: 905-460-3050
  www.thinkpath.com

  Rev: $11
  Emp: 37

  NAICS: 541330, 541420, 561310, 561320

  CAD CAM, DIV. THINKPATH
  9887 Fourth St., North Ste. 235, St. Petersburg, Florida 33702
  CEO: Ed Godwin
  Bus: *Engaged in engineering services and
  support.*

  Tel: (727) 578-0700
  Fax: (727) 578-0479

  THINKPATH.COM INC.
  25840 Sherwood, Warren, Michigan 48091
  CEO: Rick Simon, Mgr.
  Bus: *Engaged in engineering services and
  support.*

  Tel: (586) 754-2700
  Fax: (586) 754-2800

  %FO: 100

  THINKPATH.COM INC.
  2800 East River Rd., 4/F, Dayton, Ohio 45439
  CEO: Robert J. Trick, VP
  Bus: *Engaged in engineering services and
  support.*

  Tel: (937) 643-4100
  Fax: (937) 643-4110

  %FO: 100

THINKPATH.COM INC.
155 Tri-County Pkwy., Suite 110, Cincinnati, Ohio 45256
CEO: Dave Hoffman Tel: (513) 326-4760 %FO: 100
Bus: *Engaged in engineering services and* Fax: (513) 326-4765
  support.

THINKPATH.COM INC.
1941 Savage Rd., Ste. 400C, Charleston, South Carolina 29407
CEO: Jeff Sheidow, Mgr. Tel: (843) 556-2511 %FO: 100
Bus: *Engaged in engineering services and* Fax: (843) 556-1920
  support.

● **THE THOMSON CORPORATION**
Toronto-Dominion Bank Tower, 66 Wellington St. West, Toronto ON M5K 1A1, Canada
CEO: Richard J. Harrington, Pres. & CEO Tel: 416-360-8700 Rev: $8,098
Bus: *Provides integrated information solutions to* Fax: 416-360-8812 Emp: 39,550
  business and professional markets. www.thomson.com
NAICS: 323117, 511120, 511130, 511140, 512110, 516110, 518112, 519110, 519190

FINDLAW
610 Opperman Dr., Eagan, Minnesota 55123
CEO: Deborah Monroe, Pres. & CEO Tel: (651) 687-7000
Bus: *Internet content providers.* Fax: (800) 392-6206

LIQUENT, INC.
101 Gibraltar Rd., Ste. 200, Horsham, Pennsylvania 19044
CEO: Richard J. Riegel, Gen. Mgr. Tel: (215) 328-4444
Bus: *Content & document management software.* Fax: (215) 328-4445

NETG, INC.
14624 N. Scottsdale Rd., Ste. 300, Scottsdale, Arizona 85254
CEO: Joe Dougherty, Pres. Tel: (480) 315-4000
Bus: *Education & training software.* Fax: (480) 315-4001 Emp: 617

OMGEO LLC
22 Thomson Place, Boston, Massachusetts 02210
CEO: Adam Bryan, Pres. & CEO Tel: (866) 496-6436
Bus: *Computer software.* Fax: (617) 772-5330 Emp: 500

THE DIALOG CORP.
11000 Regency Pkwy., Ste. 10, Cary, North Carolina 27511
CEO: Ciaran Morton, Gen. Mgr. Tel: (919) 462-8600
Bus: *Information collection & delivery.* Fax: (919) 468-9890

THE THOMSON CORP. USA INC.
Metro Center, 1 Station Place, Stamford, Connecticut 06902
CEO: Richard Harrington, Pres. Tel: (203) 539-8000 %FO: 100
Bus: *Newspaper, books & periodicals printing &* Fax:
  publishing.

THOMPSON LEARNING
200 First Stamford Place, 4/F, Stamford, Connecticut 06902
CEO: Ronald H. Schlosser, Pres. & CEO Tel: (203) 539-8000 %FO: 100
Bus: *Provider of data, commentary, and analysis* Fax: (203) 328-8301 Emp: 9,100
  to investment bankers, M&A professionals,
  and venture capitalists.

THOMSOM PROMETRIC
1000 Lancaster St., Baltimore, Maryland 21202
CEO: Michael Brannick, Pres. & CEO
Bus: *Education & training software.*
Tel: (443) 923-8000
Fax: (443) 923-6735

THOMSON ELITE
5100 W. Goldleaf Circle, Ste. 100, Los Angeles, California 90056
CEO: Christopher K. Poole, Pres. & CEO
Bus: *Financial services, legal, government software.*
Tel: (323) 642-5200
Fax: (323) 642-5400

THOMSON FINANCIAL
195 Broadway, New York, New York 10007
CEO: Sharon Rowlands, Pres. & CEO
Bus: *Provides financial information to investment bankers and stockbrokers.*
Tel: (646) 822-2000
Fax: (646) 822-3220
%FO: 100
Emp: 8,200

THOMSON GALE
27500 Drake Rd., Farmington Hills, Michigan 48331
CEO: Gordon T. Macomber, Pres.
Bus: *Internet education services.*
Tel: (248) 699-4253
Fax: (800) 414-5043
Emp: 1,232

THOMSON LEGAL & REGULATORY NORTH AMERICA
610 Opperman Dr., Eagan, Minnesota 55123
CEO: Brian Hall, Pres.
Bus: *Provides legal information.*
Tel: (651) 687-7000
Fax:
%FO: 100
Emp: 7,004

THOMSON PROFESSIONAL & REGULATORY, INC.
395 Hudson St., New York, New York 10014
CEO: Roy M. Martin, CEO
Bus: *Accounting & finance software.*
Tel: (212) 367-6300
Fax: (212) 367-6305
Emp: 2,500

THOMSON SCIENTIFIC
3501 Market St., Philadelphia, Pennsylvania 19104
CEO: Vin Caraher, Pres. & CEO
Bus: *Information Collection & delivery.*
Tel: (215) 386-0100
Fax: (215) 386-2911

THOMSON SCIENTIFIC & HEALTHCARE
200 First Stamford Place, 4/F, Stamford, Connecticut 06902
CEO: Robert Cullen, Mgr.
Bus: *Information retrieval services.*
Tel: (203) 539-8000
Fax:
%FO: 100

THOMSON TRADEWEB, LLC
Harborside Financial Center, 2200 Plaza Five, Jersey City, New Jersey 07311
CEO: James Toffey, CEO
Bus: *Fixed income trading.*
Tel: (201) 536-6540
Fax: (203) 915-3160

THOMSON WEST
610 Opperman Dr., Eagan, Minnesota 55123
CEO: Peter Warwick, Pres. & CEO
Bus: *Directories & book publishers.*
Tel: (651) 687-7000
Fax: (651) 687-5827

● **THRILLTIME ENTERTAINMENT INTERNATIONAL, INC.**
322-4585 Canada Way, Ste. 322, Burnaby BC V5G 4L6, Canada
CEO: Ralph Procevlat, Chmn. & Pres.   Tel: 604-294-8084   Rev: $1
Bus: *Design and manufacture of amusement park rides.* Fax: 604-294-8709   Emp: 5
                                         www.thrilltime.com
NAICS: 713110, 713990

   SKYCOASTER, INC.
   2985 North 935 East, Layton, Utah 84040
   CEO: Tel: (801) 771-0303   %FO: 100
   Bus: *Design and manufacture of amusement park* Fax: (801) 771-0505
   rides.

● **TIMMINCO LIMITED**
Sunlife Financial Tower, 150 King St. West, Ste. 2401, Toronto ON M5H 1J9, Canada
CEO: Charles H. Entrekin Jr., Chmn. & CEO   Tel: 416-364-5171   Rev: $77
Bus: *Engaged in the production of non-ferrous metals.* Fax: 416-364-3451   Emp: 376
                                         www.timminco.com
NAICS: 212299

   TIMMINCO TECHNOLOGY CORP.
   3595 Moline St., Aurora, Colorado 80010
   CEO: Scott Shook, Dir.   Tel: (303) 367-0960   %FO: 100
   Bus: *Sales and distribution of non-ferrous metals.* Fax: (303) 363-1532   Emp: 150

● **TLC VISION CORPORATION**
5280 Solar Dr., Ste. 300, Mississauga ON L4W 5M8, Canada
CEO: James C. Wachtman, Pres. & CEO   Tel: 905-602-2020   Rev: $242
Bus: *Operates laser eye clinics.*   Fax: 905-602-2025   Emp: 1,138
                                         www.tlcv.com
NAICS: 621320, 621498

   TLC VISION CORPORATION
   540 Maryville Centre Dr., Ste. 200, St. Louis, Missouri 63141
   CEO: Elias Vamvakas, Chmn.   Tel: (314) 434-6900   %FO: 100
   Bus: *Laser eye clinic.*   Fax: (314) 434-2424   Emp: 911

● **TOROMONT INDUSTRIES LTD.**
3131 Highway 7 West, PO Box 5511, Concord ON L4K 1B7, Canada
CEO: Hugo T. Sorensen, Pres. & CEO   Tel: 416-667-5511   Rev: $1,234
Bus: *Mfr. refrigeration and heating equipment and* Fax: 416-667-5555   Emp: 4,000
distribution of construction equipment.   www.toromont.com
NAICS: 333412, 423740, 423810, 532412, 532490

   AERO TECH MANUFACTURING INC.
   395 West 1100 North, North Salt Lake, Utah 84054
   CEO: Tim Riley, Pres.   Tel: (801) 292-0493   %FO: 100
   Bus: *Refrigeration equipment.*   Fax: (801) 292-9908   Emp: 420

   TOROMONT INDUSTRIES LTD.
   10815 Telge Rd., Houston, Texas 77095
   CEO: Jerry Fraelic, CEO   Tel: (281) 345-9300   %FO: 100
   Bus: *Mfr. of refrig/heat equipment.* Fax: (281) 345-7434   Emp: 98

● **THE TORONTO-DOMINION BANK**
Toronto-Dominion Centre, King St. West and Bay St., Toronto ON M5K 1A2, Canada
CEO: W. Edmund Clark, Pres. & CEO   Tel: 416-982-8222   Rev: $13,136
Bus: *Banking and financial services.*   Fax: 416-982-5671   Emp: 42,843
                                                           www.td.com
NAICS: 522110, 522210, 522292, 523110, 523120, 523920, 523930

TD BANKNORTH INC.
2 Portland Sq., Portland, Maine 04112
CEO: William J. Ryan, Chmn. & Pres. & CEO   Tel: (207) 761-8500
Bus: *Super regional banks*   Fax: (207) 761-8534   Emp: 7,200

TD SECURITIES INC.
31 West 52nd St., New York, New York 10019-6101
CEO: Brendan O'Halloran, Pres.   Tel: (212) 827-7300   %FO: 100
Bus: *Investment banking services.*   Fax: (212) 827-7232   Emp: 41

TD WATERHOUSE GROUP, INC.
100 Wall St., 28/F, New York, New York 10005
CEO: Timothy P. Pinnington, Pres. & CEO   Tel: (212) 806-3500   %FO: 100
Bus: *Investment banking services.*   Fax: (212) 785-1636

● **TORSTAR CORPORATION**
One Yonge St., Toronto ON M5E 1P9, Canada
CEO: J. Robert Pritchard, Pres. & CEO   Tel: 416-869-4010   Rev: $1,280
Bus: *Publishes romance novels.*   Fax: 416-869-4183   Emp: 6,880
                                                           www.torstar.com
NAICS: 454111, 454113, 511110, 511130

HARLEQUIN
3010 Walden Ave., Depew, New York 14043
CEO: Donna Hayes, Pres.   Tel: (716) 684-1800   %FO: 100
Bus: *Publishes romance novels.*   Fax: Emp: 200

TRANSIT TELEVISION NETWORK
8544 Commodity Cir., Orlando, Florida 32819
CEO: Marc Plogstedt, Chmn.   Tel: (407) 226-0204
Bus: *Transit broadcasting.*   Fax: Emp: 54

● **TORYS LLP**
79 Wellington St. West, Ste. 3000, Box 270, TD Centre, Toronto ON M5K 1N2, Canada
CEO: Les Viner, Mng. Prtn.   Tel: 416-865-0040   Rev: $60
Bus: *International business law firm.*   Fax: 416-865-7380   Emp: 800
                                                           www.torys.com
NAICS: 541110

TORYS LLP
237 Park Ave., New York, New York 10017-3142
CEO: Charles E. Dorkey III, Chmn.   Tel: (212) 880-6000   %FO: 100
Bus: *Business law firm.*   Fax: (212) 682-0200   Emp: 145

● **TRACTEL SWINGSTAGE LTD.**
1615 Warden Ave., Scarborough ON M1R 2T3, Canada
CEO: Therry Bertrand, Pres.   Tel: 416-298-8822   Rev: $22
Bus: *Engineering lifting and materials handling,*   Fax: 416-298-1053   Emp: 122
   electronic load measuring and fall arrest   www.tractel.com
   equipment.
NAICS: 332999

    TRACTEL SWINGSTAGE
    315 Cloverleaf Dr., Ste. E, Baldwin Park, California 91706
    CEO: Allee Kamarek, Mgr.   Tel: (626) 937-6727   %FO: 100
    Bus: *Engineering lifting and materials handling,*   Fax: (626) 937-6730
       electronic load measuring and fall arrest
       equipment.

    TRACTEL SWINGSTAGE
    110 Shawmut Rd., Canton, Massachusetts 01021
    CEO: Thierry Bertrand, Pres.   Tel: (781) 401-3288   %FO: 100
    Bus: *Engineering lifting and materials handling,*   Fax: (781) 828-3642   Emp: 25
       electronic load measuring and fall arrest
       equipment.

● **TRANSALTA CORPORATION**
110 12th Ave. SW, Calgary AB T2R 0G7, Canada
CEO: Stephen G. Snyder, Pres. & CEO   Tel: 403-267-7110   Rev: $2,365
Bus: *Energy management; electric and gas.*   Fax: 403-267-2590   Emp: 2,505
                                          www.transalta.com
NAICS: 221111, 221112, 221119, 221121, 424720, 523130, 523140

    IPP ENERGY LLC
    22 Charles St., Binghamton, New York 13905
    CEO: Richard Langhammer, Pres.   Tel: (607) 773-3307
    Bus: *Power plant.*   Fax: Emp: 5

    POWER RESOURCES INC.
    500 Refinery Rd., Big Spring, Texas 79720
    CEO: Abel Gregory, Pres.   Tel: (432) 263-3940
    Bus: *Power plant.*   Fax: Emp: 19

    SARANAC POWER PARTNERS
    99 Weed St., PO Box 2985, Plattsburgh, New York 12901
    CEO: David Solkol, CEO   Tel: (518) 563-1072   %FO: 37
    Bus: *Electricity cogeneration.*   Fax: Emp: 25

    TRANS ALTA ENERGY MARKETING
    4004 Kruse Way Place, Ste. 150, Lake Oswego, Oregon 97035
    CEO: Denise Hill, Mgr.   Tel: (503) 675-3800   %FO: 100
    Bus: *Engaged in energy management; electric*   Fax: (503) 675-3808   Emp: 7
       and gas.

    TRANSALTA CENTRALIA GENERATION LLC
    913 Big Hanaford Rd., Centralia, Washington 98531
    CEO: Richard Langhammer, Mgr.   Tel: (360) 736-9901
    Bus: *Electric generation.*   Fax: Emp: 800

TRANSALTA CENTRALIA MINING LLC
913 Big Hanaford Rd., Centralia, Washington 98531
CEO: Steve Snyder, CEO   Tel: (360) 736-9901
Bus: *Bituminous coal mining.*   Fax: Emp: 630

TRANSALTA CORP.
1126 S. Gold St., Ste. 207, Centralia, Washington 98531
CEO: Brian Clewes, SVP   Tel: (360) 330-0275   %FO: 100
Bus: *Electric services.*   Fax:

TRANSALTA ENERGY CORP.
151 West St., Ste. 30, Annapolis, Maryland 21401
CEO: Julie Ryan, Principal   Tel: (410) 295-1746   %FO: 100
Bus: *Sale of energy products.*   Fax:

● **TRANSAT A.T. INC.**
Place du Parc, 300 Leo- Pariseau St., Ste. 600, Montreal QC H2X 4C2, Canada
CEO: Jean-Marc Eustache, Chmn. & Pres. & CEO   Tel: 514-987-1660   Rev: $1,593
Bus: *Travel services.*   Fax: 514-987-8035   Emp: 4,658
      www.transat.com
NAICS: 561510, 561520

      AIR TRANSAT HOLIDAYS USA
      140 S. Federal Hwy., 2/F, Dania, Florida 33004
      CEO: Lina Decesare, Pres.   Tel: (954) 920-3138   %FO: 100
      Bus: *Travel services.*   Fax: (954) 920-3969   Emp: 20

● **TRANSCANADA CORPORATION**
TransCanada Tower, 450-1 st St. SW, Calgary AB T2P 5H1, Canada
CEO: Harold N. Kvisle, Pres. & CEO   Tel: 403-920-2000   Rev: $4,256
Bus: *Natural gas marketing and transmission and*   Fax: 403-920-2200   Emp: 2,473
      electric power generation.   www.transcanada.com
NAICS: 221111, 221112, 221113, 221119, 221121, 221122, 486210

      GAS TRANSMISSION NORTHWEST CORP.
      1400 SW 5th Ave., Ste. 900, Portland, Oregon 97201
      CEO: Jeff Rush, VP & Gen. Mgr.   Tel: (503) 833-4000
      Bus: *Natural gas pipelines.*   Fax: (503) 833-4930   Emp: 189

      NORTH BAJA PIPELINE LLC
      1400 SW 5th Ave., Ste. 900, Portland, Oregon 97201
      CEO: Harold Kvisle, CEO   Tel: (503) 833-4000
      Bus: *Oil & gas transportation.*   Fax: (503) 833-4930

      TC PIPELINES, LP
      110 Turnpike Rd., Ste. 203, Westborough, Massachusetts 01581
      CEO: Ronald Turner, Pres. & CEO   Tel: (508) 871-7046   %FO: 100
      Bus: *Power plant supplier.*   Fax: (508) 871-7047

- **TRANSCONTINENTAL INC.**
  1, Place Ville Marie, Ste. 3315, Montreal QC H3B 3N2, Canada
  CEO: Luc Desjardins, Pres. & CEO   Tel: 514-954-4000   Rev: $1,449
  Bus: *Flyers, direct marketing products, books and* Fax: 514-954-4016   Emp: 11,266
      newspapers printing.   www.transcontinental-gtc.com
  NAICS: 323110, 323111, 323115, 323117, 323119, 323121, 334612, 511110, 511120

  JETSON DIREST MAIL SERVICES INC.
  100 Industrial Dr., Hamburg, Pennsylvania 19526
  CEO: Vincent Carosella, CEO   Tel: (610) 562-1000
  Bus: *Business services*   Fax: (610) 562-9702   Emp: 982

  ROSS-ELLIS U.S.A.
  67 Irving Place, 9/F, Valley Stream, New York 11580
  CEO: Nina Sheldon, Pres.   Tel: (212) 260-9200
  Bus: *Commercial printing*   Fax: (212) 260-2143   Emp: 2

  ROSS-ELLIS U.S.A. INC.
  8550 Balboa Blvd., Ste. 200, Northridge, California 91325
  CEO: Nina Thomas Sheldon, Owner   Tel: (818) 993-4767
  Bus: *Publishing.*   Fax: (818) 993-4760   Emp: 8

  TRANSCONTINENTAL DIRECT U.S.A. INC.
  75 Hawk Rd., Warminster, Pennsylvania 18974
  CEO: Don McKenzie, Pres. & CEO   Tel: (215) 672-6900
  Bus: *Business services*   Fax: (215) 957-4366

- **TRIMAC CORPORATION**
  800 5th Ave. SW, Ste. 2100, PO Box 3500, Calgary AB T2P 2P9, Canada
  CEO: Terry J. Owen, Pres. & CEO   Tel: 403-298-5100   Rev: $464
  Bus: *Liquid and dry bulk transportation services.* Fax: 403-298-5146   Emp: 3,214
                                                 www.trimac.com
  NAICS: 484230, 488510, 541614

  HARRIS TRANSPORTATION COMPANY, LLC
  3077 NW St., Helens Rd., Portland, Oregon 97210
  CEO: Brian Harris, Pres.   Tel: (503) 552-5800
  Bus: *Trucking for petroleum products.*   Fax: Emp: 105

  TRIMAC CORPORATION
  3663 N. Sam Houston Pkwy. E, Ste. 300, Gateway I, Houston, Texas 77032
  CEO: Jeff McCaig, Pres. & CEO   Tel: (281) 985-0000   %FO: 100
  Bus: *Long distance trucking.*   Fax: (281) 449-4888   Emp: 1,700

- **TRIVERSITY INC.**
  3550 Victoria Park Ave., Ste. 400, Toronto ON M2H 2N5, Canada
  CEO: David Thomas, Pres. & CEO   Tel: 416-791-7100   Rev: $31
  Bus: *Computer software & services.*   Fax: 416-791-7101   Emp: 245
                                                  www.triversity.com
  NAICS: 511210

TRIVERSITY CORPORATION
311 Sinclair St., Bristol, Pennsylvania 19007
CEO: David Thomas, Pres.
Bus: *Computer software & services.*

Tel: (215) 785-4321
Fax: (215) 785-5329

%FO: 100
Emp: 100

● **TROJAN TECHNOLOGIES INC.**
3020 Gore Rd., London ON N5V 4T7, Canada
CEO: Marvin R. DeVries, Pres. & CEO
Bus: *UV lighting systems and wastewater treatment systems manufacture.*
NAICS: 333319

Tel: 519-457-3400
Fax: 519-457-3030
www.trojanuv.com

Rev: $20
Emp: 350

PUREFLOW ULTRAVIOLET
1750 Spectrum Dr., Lawrenceville, Georgia 30043
CEO: Richard Combs, Pres.
Bus: *Distributor of industrial ultra-violet equipment.*

Tel: (770) 277-6330
Fax: (770) 277-6344

%FO: 100
Emp: 11

U.S. PEROXIDE
23 Morningwood Dr., Laguna Niguel, California 92677
CEO: Scott Duggan, Pres.
Bus: *Sale of chemicals.*

Tel: (404) 589-9381
Fax: (404) 589-9778

%FO: 100
Emp: 19

● **TUCOWS INC.**
96 Mowat Ave., Toronto ON M6K 3M1, Canada
CEO: Elliot Noss, Pres. & CEO
Bus: *Computer software & services.*

Tel: 416-535-0123
Fax: 416-531-5584
www.tucows.com

Rev: $45
Emp: 160

NAICS: 511210, 516110, 518210, 519190, 541519

TUCOWS INC.
4100 Pier North Dr., Ste. A, Flint, Michigan 48504
CEO: Scott Swedorski, Pres.
Bus: *Computer software & services.*

Tel: (810) 720-1155
Fax: (810) 720-0520

%FO: 100
Emp: 73

● **TUNDRA SEMICONDUCTOR CORPORATION**
603 March Rd., Ottawa ON K2K 2M5, Canada
CEO: Jim Roche, Pres. & CEO
Bus: *Mfg. electronics and semiconductor products.*

Tel: 613-592-0714
Fax: 613-592-1320
www.tundra.com

Rev: $51
Emp: 200

NAICS: 334413

TUNDRA SEMICONDUCTOR CORPORATION
39 Darling Ave., South Portland, Maine 04106
CEO: Jim Roche, Pres. & CEO
Bus: *Mfr. electronics & semiconductor products.*

Tel: (207) 773-2662
Fax: (207) 773-1550

%FO: 100

TUNDRA SEMICONDUCTOR CORPORATION
4100 Alpha Rd., Ste. 900, Dallas, Texas 75244
CEO: Jim Roche, Pres. & CEO
Bus: *Mfr. electronics & semiconductor products.*

Tel: (214) 420-9315
Fax: (214) 420-9316

%FO: 100

- **TURBOSONIC TECHNOLOGIES, INC.**
550 Parkside Dr., Ste. A-14, Waterloo ON N2L 5V4, Canada
CEO: Edward F. Spink, Chmn. & CEO   Tel: 519-885-5513   Rev: $5
Bus: *Air pollution control equipment manufacture.*   Fax: 519-885-6992   Emp: 31
                                            www.turbosonic.com
  NAICS: 562211, 562219, 562998

    TURBOSONIC TECHNOLOGIES, INC.
    239 New Rd., Bldg. B, Ste. 205, Parsippany, New Jersey 07054
    CEO: Jorgen Hedenhag, Gen. Mgr.   Tel: (973) 224-9544   %FO: 100
    Bus: *Air pollution control equipment manufacture* Fax: (973) 224-9545
        and sales.

- **TWIN MINING CORPORATION**
155 University Ave., Ste. 1250, Toronto ON M5H 3B7, Canada
CEO: Hermann Derbuch, Chmn. & Pres. & CEO   Tel: 416-777-0013
Bus: *Diamond exploration.*   Fax: 416-777-0014
                                            www.twinmining.com
  NAICS: 212221, 212299

    TWIN MINING CORPORATION
    1509 Tyrell Lane, Ste. B, Boise, Idaho 83706
    CEO: Douglas Glaspey, Mgr.   Tel: (208) 424-1028   %FO: 100
    Bus: *Diamond exploration.*   Fax: (208) 424-1030

- **UAP INC.**
7025 Ontario St. East, Montreal QC H1N 2B3, Canada
CEO: Larry Samuelson, CEO   Tel: 514-256-5031   Rev: $750
Bus: *Replacement parts for autos and trucks.*   Fax: 514-256-8469   Emp: 4,000
                                            www.uapinc.com
  NAICS: 336399, 423120, 423140, 441310

    GENUINE PARTS COMPANY
    2999 Circle 75 Pkwy., Atlanta, Georgia 30339
    CEO: Thomas C. Gallagher, Chmn. & Pres. &   Tel: (770) 953-1700   %FO: 100
    Bus: *Auto parts distribution and sales.*   Fax: (770) 956-2211   Emp: 31,200

- **UNIBOARD**
2540 Daniel-Johnson Blvd., Ste. 500, Laval QC H7T 2S3, Canada
CEO: Guy Lacroix, Pres. & CEO   Tel: 450-682-5240   Rev: $434
Bus: *Particleboard manufacture.*   Fax: 450-682-0550   Emp: 1,360
                                            www.uniboard.com
  NAICS: 321219, 321918, 423310

    UNIBOARD
    1600 N. Main St., Fostoria, Ohio 44830
    CEO: Cam Gentile, Chmn.   Tel: (419) 435-6674   %FO: 100
    Bus: *Particleboard manufacture and sales.*   Fax: Emp: 90

- **UNI-SELECT INC.**
170 Industrial Blvd., Boucherville QC J4B 2X3, Canada
CEO: Jacques Landreville, Pres. & CEO
Bus: *Automotive, heavy parts manufacture.*

Tel: 450-641-2440
Fax: 450-449-4908
www.uni-select.com

Rev: $654
Emp: 3,200

NAICS: 423120

MIDDLE ATLANTIC WAREHOUSE DISTRIBUTOR, INC.
601 Vickers St., Tonawanda, New York 14150
CEO: Clay E. Buzzard, CEO
Bus: *Auto parts retail.*

Tel: (716) 694-0200
Fax: (716) 694-0796

%FO: 100

UNI-SELECT INC.
601 Vickers St., PO Box 308, Tonawanda, New York 14150
CEO: Jim Buzzard, VP
Bus: *Automotive, heavy parts manufacture and sales.*

Tel: (716) 694-0200
Fax: (716) 694-1469

%FO: 100

- **VAN HOUTTE INC.**
8300 19th Ave., Montreal QC H1Z 4J8, Canada
CEO: Jean-Yves Monette, Pres. & CEO
Bus: *Gourmet and specialty coffees. (JV of Keurig Inc.)*

Tel: 514-593-7711
Fax: 514-593-8755
www.vanhoutte.com

Rev: $251
Emp: 1,800

NAICS: 311920, 722213

KEURIG INC.
101 Edgewater Dr., Wakefield, Massachusetts 01880
CEO: Nick Lazaris, Pres. & CEO
Bus: *Gourmet and specialty coffees.*

Tel: (781) 246-3466
Fax: (781) 246-3499

Emp: 95

VAN HOUTTE USA
208 Parkway View Dr., Pittsburgh, Pennsylvania 15205
CEO: Roger Cohen, Pres. & CEO
Bus: *Gourmet and specialty coffees.*

Tel: (800) 361-5628
Fax:

%FO: 100

- **VECTOR AEROSPACE CORPORATION**
34 Harvey Rd., St. Johns NF A1C 5K5, Canada
CEO: Donald K. Jackson, Chmn. & Pres. & CEO
Bus: *Turbine engine repairs.*

Tel: 709-724-4500
Fax: 709-724-4544
www.vectoraerospace.ca

Rev: $264
Emp: 1,100

NAICS: 541330, 811219, 811310

ATLANTIC TURBINES USA INC.
1603 Hart St., Southlake, Texas 76092
CEO: Russell Starr, VP
Bus: *Engineering repairs.*

Tel: (817) 416-7926
Fax: (817) 421-2706

%FO: 100
Emp: 15

HELIPRO CORPORATION INTERNATIONAL
2000 W Bakerview Rd., Hangar D, Bellingham, Washington 98226
CEO: Mike Druet, Pres.
Bus: *Aircraft repair.*

Tel: (360) 734-3532
Fax: (360) 734-3193

%FO: 100
Emp: 46

HELIPRO CORPORATION INTERNATIONAL
21839 Bill Benton Lane, Andalusia, Alabama 36421
CEO: Mark Topping, Mgr.   Tel: (334) 222-1277   %FO: 100
Bus: *Aircraft repair.*   Fax: (334) 222-1954   Emp: 22

HELIPRO CORPORATION INTERNATIONAL
318 Paseo Tersoro, Walnut, California 91789
CEO: Roy Foo, Pres.   Tel: (909) 594-8835   %FO: 100
Bus: *Aircraft repair.*   Fax: (909) 594-2584

● **VELAN INC.**
7007 Cote de Liesse, Montreal QC H4T 1G2, Canada
CEO: A. K. Velan, CEO   Tel: 514-748-7743
Bus: *Forged and cast pressure valves manufacture.*   Fax: 514-748-8635
                                               www.velan.com
NAICS: 332911, 332912, 332919, 333995, 333996

   VELAN-VALVE CORPORATION
   94 Ave. C, Williston, Vermont 05495
   CEO: Adolph K. Velan, CEO   Tel: (802) 863-2562   %FO: 100
   Bus: *Mfr. Industrial valves.*   Fax: (802) 862-4014   Emp: 214

● **VERTIGOXMEDIA, INC.**
147 Saint-Paul West, Ste. 100, Montreal QC H2Y 1Z5, Canada
CEO: David Wilkins, Pres. & CEO   Tel: 514-397-0955
Bus: *Software manufacture.*   Fax: 514-397-0954
                                               www.vertigoxmedia.com
NAICS: 511210

   VERTIGOXMEDIA, INC.
   7418 Hitching Post Dr., Park City, Utah 84098
   CEO: Darin Crosby   Tel: (435) 655-7138   %FO: 100
   Bus: *Software sales.*   Fax: (435) 655-7139

● **VINCOR INTERNATIONAL INC.**
441 Courtneypark Dr. East, Mississauga ON L5T 2V3, Canada
CEO: Donald L. Triggs, Pres. & CEO   Tel: 905-564-6900   Rev: $364
Bus: *Wine production.*   Fax: 905-564-6909   Emp: 2,210
                                               www.vincorinternational.com
NAICS: 312130

   HOGUE CELLARS LTD.
   2800 Lee Rd., Prosser, Washington 99350-5520
   CEO: David Copeland, Mgr.   Tel: (509) 786-4557   %FO: 100
   Bus: *Grape growing for wine production.*   Fax: (509) 786-4580   Emp: 60

   R. H. PHILLIPS WINERY
   26836 County Rd. 12A, Esparto, California 95627
   CEO: Mike Jaeger, Pres.   Tel: (530) 662-3215   %FO: 100
   Bus: *Wine production.*   Fax: (530) 662-2880   Emp: 250

- **VISIPHOR CORPORATION**
  1075 W. Georgia St., Ste. 1630, Vancouver BC V6E 3C9, Canada
  CEO: Roy D. Trivett, Pres. & CEO   Tel: 604-684-2449   Rev: $1
  Bus: *Image identification software manufacture.*   Fax: 604-684-9314   Emp: 25
                                                        www.visiphor.com
  NAICS: 511210
  > **VISIPHOR CORPORATION**
  > 725 15th St., NW, Ste. 805, Washington, District of Columbia 20005
  > CEO: Roy Trivett, Pres. & CEO   Tel: (202) 628-7817
  > Bus: *Image recognition software manufacture.*   Fax:

- **VITRAN CORPORATION INC.**
  185 The West Mall, Ste. 701, Toronto ON M9C 5L5, Canada
  CEO: Richard E. Gaetz, Pres. & CEO   Tel: 416-596-7664   Rev: $375
  Bus: *Freight shipping and logistics services.*   Fax: 416-596-8039   Emp: 2,498
                                                        www.vitran.com
  NAICS: 484121, 484122, 488510, 541614
  > **FRONTIER TRANSPORT CO.**
  > 1560 W. Raymond St., Indianapolis, Indiana 46221
  > CEO: Steve Cook, Pres.   Tel: (317) 636-2242   %FO: 100
  > Bus: *Long distance & local trucking*   Fax: (317) 636-4690   Emp: 80

  > **VITRAN EXPRESS INC.**
  > 6500 East 30th St., Indianapolis, Indiana 46219
  > CEO: David Kimack, Pres.   Tel: (317) 803-6400   %FO: 100
  > Bus: *Freight shipping and logistics services.*   Fax: (317) 543-1228   Emp: 1,500

  > **VITRAN LOGISTICS**
  > 9870 Highway 92, Ste. 110, Woodstock, Georgia 30188
  > CEO: Richard E. Gaetz, CEO   Tel: (770) 517-7744   %FO: 100
  > Bus: *Freight forwarding & consolidation.*   Fax: (770) 517-4774   Emp: 46

  > **VITRAN LOGISTICS**
  > 12465 Lewis St., Ste. 102, Garden Grove, California 92840
  > CEO: Adrian Valera, Mgr.   Tel: (714) 748-4042   %FO: 100
  > Bus: *Freight forwarding & consolidation.*   Fax: (714) 748-4047   Emp: 8

- **VIXS SYSTEMS, INC.**
  2235 Sheppard Ave. East, Ste. 1705, Toronto ON M2J 5B5, Canada
  CEO: Sally J. Daub, Pres. & CEO   Tel: 416-646-2000
  Bus: *Microprocessors manufacture.*   Fax: 416-646-1042
                                                        www.vixs.com
  NAICS: 334413
  > **VIXS SYSTEMS, INC.**
  > 108 Wild Basin Rd., Ste. 210, Austin, Texas 78746
  > CEO: James T. Reinhart, Pres.   Tel: (512) 732-2740   %FO: 100
  > Bus: *Microprocessors manufacture and sales..*   Fax: (512) 732-2741

- **VOORTMAN COOKIES LTD.**
4455 North Service Rd., Burlington ON L7L 4X7, Canada
CEO: Harry Voortman, Pres.
Bus: *Cookie manufacture.*

Tel: 905-335-9500
Fax: 905-332-5499
www.voortman.com

Rev: $60
Emp: 300

NAICS: 311821

  VOORTMAN COOKIES LTD.
  PO Box 4562, Buffalo, New York 14240
  CEO: Adrian Voortman, VP
  Bus: *Cookie sales and distribution.*

  Tel: (905) 335-9500
  Fax: (905) 332-5499

  %FO: 100

- **WAJAX LIMITED**
3280 Wharton Way, Mississauga ON L4X 2C5, Canada
CEO: Neil D. Manning, Pres. & CEO
Bus: *Mfr. industrial machinery*

Tel: 905-212-3300
Fax: 905-212-3350
www.wajax.com

Rev: $770
Emp: 2,357

NAICS: 423830

  SPENCER INDUSTRIES INC.
  19308 68th Ave. South, Kent, Washington 98032
  CEO: Jerry Randecker, Pres.
  Bus: *Manufacturer industrial equipment*

  Tel: (253) 796-1100
  Fax: (800) 367-5646

  %FO: 100

- **WATERSAVE LOGIC CORP.**
1166 Alberni St., Ste. 1100, Vancouver BC V6E 3Z3, Canada
CEO: David G. Nelson, Chmn.
Bus: *Ceramic sanitary ware and vitreous china
manufacture.*

Tel: 604-688-9484
Fax: 604-683-2235
www.watersavelogic.com

NAICS: 423720

  WP INDUSTRIES INC.
  14405 Best Ave., Norwalk, California 90650
  CEO: Walter O'Rourke, Pres. & CEO
  Bus: *Mfr. ceramic sanitary ware.*

  Tel: (562) 229-0910
  Fax: (562) 229-0930

  %FO: 100
  Emp: 20

- **WAWANESA MUTUAL INSURANCE COMPANY**
900-191 Broadway, Winnipeg MB R3C 3P1, Canada
CEO: Gregg J. Hanson, Pres. & CEO
Bus: *Engaged in property and casualty insurance.*

Tel: 204-985-3923
Fax: 204-942-7724
www.wawanesa.com

NAICS: 524113, 524126

  WAWANESA MUTUAL INSURANCE COMPANY
  9050 Friars Rd., San Diego, California 92108
  CEO: David J. Goss, Secretary
  Bus: *Engaged in property and casualty insurance.*

  Tel: (858) 874-5300
  Fax: (858) 715-5970

  %FO: 100
  Emp: 500

- **WENTWORTH TECHNOLOGIES CO.**
5330 Mainway Dr., Burlington ON L7L 5Z1, Canada
CEO: Walter T. Kuskowski, Pres. & CEO
Bus: *Industrial machinery manufacture.*

Tel: 905-332-1096
Fax: 905-332-7802
www.wentworthtechnologies.com

Rev: $100
Emp: 200

NAICS: 326199, 332997, 333513

> **ACCURATE MOLD USA INC.**
> 852 Scholz Dr., Vandalia, Ohio 45377
> CEO: William Chapelear, VP & Gen. Mgr.
> Bus: *Industrial machinery manufacture.*
>
> Tel: (937) 898-8460
> Fax: (937) 898-1992
>
> %FO: 100

> **ELECTRA FORM INDUSTRIES (EFI)**
> 852 Scholz Dr., Vandalia, Ohio 45377
> CEO: Brian Karns, Gen. Mgr.
> Bus: *Industrial machinery manufacture.*
>
> Tel: (937) 898-8460
> Fax: (937) 898-1750
>
> %FO: 100
> Emp: 60

- **WENZEL DOWNHOLE TOOLS LTD.**
736 6th Ave. SW, Ste. 500, Calgary AB T2P 3T7, Canada
CEO: Harvie Andre, Pres. & CEO
Bus: *Drilling tools manufacture.*

Tel: 403-262-3050
Fax: 403-265-8154
www.downhole.com

NAICS: 333132

> **WENZEL DOWNHOLE TOOLS LTD.**
> 1820 Pyrite Rd., Casper, Wyoming 82604
> CEO: Leonard Linde, Mgr.
> Bus: *Drilling tools sales and distribution.*
>
> Tel: (307) 266-1580
> Fax: (307) 266-1656
>
> %FO: 100

> **WENZEL DOWNHOLE TOOLS LTD.**
> 4205 FM 1485 Rd., Conroe, Texas 77306
> CEO: Murice Minvielle, Dir.
> Bus: *Drilling tools sales and distribution.*
>
> Tel: (936) 441-1480
> Fax: (936) 756-5335
>
> %FO: 100
> Emp: 13

- **WESCAST INDUSTRIES INC.**
150 Savannah Oaks Dr., Brantford ON N3T 5L8, Canada
CEO: Edward G. Frackowiak, Chmn. & CEO
Bus: *Exhaust manifolds manufacture.*

Tel: 519-750-0000
Fax: 519-750-1628
www.wescast.com

Rev: $341
Emp: 2,077

NAICS: 333995

> **WESCAST USA INC.**
> 6300 18½ Mile Rd., Sterling Heights, Michigan 48314
> CEO: Chris Gaige, Mgr.
> Bus: *Exhaust manifolds sales.*
>
> Tel: (586) 323-2278
> Fax: (586) 323-2329
>
> %FO: 100

- **WEST FRASER TIMBER CO. LTD.**
501-858 Beatty St., Vancouver BC V6B 1C1, Canada
CEO: Henry H. Ketcham III, Chmn. & Pres. & CEO
Bus: *Lumber, fiberboard, pulp and paper manufacture.*

Tel: 604-895-2700
Fax: 604-681-6061
www.westfrasertimber.ca

Rev: $1,165
Emp: 4,000

NAICS: 113110, 321113, 321211, 321219, 322110, 322122, 322299, 424130

WEST FRASER (SOUTH) INC.
6481 Hwy. 34 North, PO Box 1, Joyce, Louisiana 71440
CEO: Henry H. Ketcham
Bus: *Lumber, fiberboard, pulp and paper sales and distribution.*
Tel: (318) 648-3300
Fax: (318) 648-3447
%FO: 100

WEST FRASER (SOUTH) INC.
502 Olin Ave., PO Box 460, Huttig, Arkansas 71747
CEO: Herman Boykin
Bus: *Lumber, fiberboard, pulp and paper sales and distribution.*
Tel: (870) 943-2211
Fax: (870) 943-3121
%FO: 100

WEST FRASER (SOUTH) INC.
401 Thomas Rd., Ste. 2, West Monroe, Louisiana 71292
CEO: Henry H. Kethchum, Pres.
Bus: *Lumber, fiberboard, pulp and paper sales and distribution..*
Tel: (318) 340-6000
Fax: (318) 340-6064
%FO: 100
Emp: 22

● **THE WESTAIM CORPORATION**
144 4th Ave. Southwest, Calgary AB T2P 3N4, Canada
CEO: Barry M. Heck, Pres. & CEO
Bus: *Mfr. pharmaceuticals.*
Tel: 403-237-7272
Fax: 403-237-6565
www.westaim.com
Rev: $30
Emp: 344

NAICS: 212299, 325412, 325998, 334419, 339113

NUCRYST PHARMACEUTICALS
50 Audubon Rd., Ste. B, Wakefield, Massachusetts 01880
CEO: Scott Gillis, Pres.
Bus: *Pharmaceutical sales.*
Tel: (781) 224-1444
Fax: (781) 246-6002
Emp: 28

● **GEORGE WESTON LIMITED**
22 St. Clair Avenue East, Toronto ON M4T 2S7, Canada
CEO: W. Galen Weston, Chmn. & Pres.
Bus: *Bakery and confectionery products, groceries, fisheries.*
Tel: 416-922-2500
Fax: 416-922-4395
www.weston.ca
Rev: $22,553
Emp: 145,860

NAICS: 311320, 311340, 311812, 311999, 541710

GEORGE WESTON BAKERIES
PO Box 535, Totowa, New Jersey 07511
CEO: Gary J. Prince
Bus: *Mfr. bakery products*
Tel: (973) 785-7601
Fax: (973) 785-0009
%FO: 100

GEORGE WESTON BAKERIES
55 Paradise La., Bayshore, New York 11706
CEO: Gary J. Prince
Bus: *Mfr./distribution crackers & cookies.*
Tel: (631) 273-6000
Fax: (631) 273-2654
%FO: 100

INTERBAKE FOODS INC.
2821 Emerywood Pkwy., Ste. 210, Richmond, Virginia 23294
CEO: Raymond Baxter, Pres.
Bus: *Mfr./distribution crackers & cookies.*
Tel: (804) 755-7107
Fax: (804) 755-7173
%FO: 100

INTERBAKE FOODS INC.
1910 W. Temple St., Los Angeles, California 90026
CEO: Randy Obrien   Tel: (213) 484-8161   %FO: 100
Bus: *Mfr./distribution crackers & cookies.*   Fax: (213) 484-8161

INTERBAKE FOODS INC.
Rd.#5, Box 386, Drum Ave., Somerset, Pennsylvania 15501
CEO: Tim Miller   Tel: (814) 445-9685   %FO: 100
Bus: *Mfr./distribution crackers & cookies.*   Fax: (814) 445-9685

INTERBAKE FOODS INC.
PO Box 1869, Columbus, Ohio 43216
CEO: Scott Fullbright   Tel: (612) 294-4931   %FO: 100
Bus: *Mfr./distribution crackers & cookies.*   Fax: (612) 294-4931

INTERBAKE FOODS INC.
891 Newark Ave., Elizabeth, New Jersey 07208-3599
CEO: Scott Stone   Tel: (908) 527-7000   %FO: 100
Bus: *Mfr./distribution crackers & cookies.*   Fax: (908) 527-7000

INTERBAKE FOODS INC.
900 Terminal Place, Richmond, Virginia 23220-1918
CEO: Nick Kantner   Tel: (804) 257-7446   %FO: 100
Bus: *Mfr./distribution crackers & cookies.*   Fax: (804) 257-7446

INTERBAKE FOODS INC.
One Devilsfood Dr., North Sioux City, South Dakota 57049-5134
CEO: Dean G. Duzik   Tel: (605) 232-4900   %FO: 100
Bus: *Mfr./distribution crackers & cookies.*   Fax: (605) 232-4900

INTERBAKE FOODS INC.
1122 Lincoln St., Green Bay, Wisconsin 54303
CEO: Hank Zirbel   Tel: (920) 497-7669   %FO: 100
Bus: *Mfr./distribution crackers & cookies.*   Fax: (920) 497-7669

MAPLEHURST BAKERIES INC.
50 Maplehurst Dr., Brownsburg, Indiana 46112
CEO: Paul Durlacher   Tel: (317) 858-9000   %FO: 100
Bus: *Mfr./distribution crackers & cookies.*   Fax: (317) 858-9001

WESTON FOODS
255 Business Center Dr., Ste. 200, Horsham, Pennsylvania 19044
CEO: Gary J. Prince   Tel: (215) 672-8010   %FO: 100
Bus: *Mfr./distribution crackers & cookies.*   Fax: (215) 672-6988

● **WI-LAN INC.**
2891 Sunridge Way NE, Calgary AB T1Y 7K7, Canada
CEO: William Dunbar, Pres. & CEO   Tel: 403-273-9133
Bus: *Wireless network access equipment manufacture.* Fax: 403-273-5100
www.wi-lan.com
NAICS: 334119, 334220, 334290

Canada

WI-LAN INC.
2201 Wilson Blvd., Arlington, Virginia 22201
CEO: James Merrigan, Sales
Bus: *Mfr. of wireless networks access equipment.*
Tel: (703) 310-7976
Fax: (202) 318-4011
%FO: 100

● **WINPAK LTD.**
100 Saulteaux Crescent, Winnipeg MB R3J 3T3, Canada
CEO: Bruce J. Berry, Pres. & CEO
Bus: *Packaging machines manufacture.*
Tel: 204-889-1015
Fax: 204-888-7806
www.winpak.com
Rev: $328
Emp: 1,812

NAICS: 322215, 322223, 326111, 326112, 333993

WINPAK LTD.
PO Box 14748, Minneapolis, Minnesota 55414
CEO: Rod Degeus, Controller
Bus: *Portion packaging solutions.*
Tel: (204) 889-1015
Fax:
%FO: 100
Emp: 30

● **WIRELESS MATRIX CORPORATION**
1530 27th Ave. NE, Ste. 102, Calgary AB T2E 7S6, Canada
CEO: Rich Carlson, CEO
Bus: *Wireless network development.*
Tel: 403-250-3949
Fax: 403-150-8163
www.wirelessmatrixcorp.com
Rev: $28
Emp: 130

NAICS: 488999, 517212, 517410, 517910, 519190, 561499

WIRELESS MATRIX CORPORATION
Sunrise Technology Park, 12369-B Sunrise Valley Dr., Reston, Virginia 20191
CEO: John Herring, Pres.
Bus: *Satellite services.*
Tel: (703) 262-0500
Fax: (703) 262-0380
%FO: 100
Emp: 126

● **W. C. WOOD COMPANY LIMITED**
5 Arthur St. South, PO Box 750, Guelph ON N1H 6L9, Canada
CEO: John F. Wood, Pres. & CEO
Bus: *Mfr. refrigerators and freezers.*
Tel: 519-823-9663
Fax: 519-821-4451
www.4.wcwood.com

NAICS: 335221, 335222

W. C. WOOD COMPANY LIMITED
677 Woodland Dr., PO Box 310, Ottawa, Ohio 45875
CEO: John F. Wood, Pres.
Bus: *Refrigerator and freezer sales and distribution.*
Tel: (419) 523-9663
Fax: (419) 523-4826
%FO: 100

● **THE WOODBRIDGE GROUP**
4240 Sherwoodtowne Blvd., Mississauga ON L4Z 2G6, Canada
CEO: T. Robert Beamish, Chmn.
Bus: *Automotive urethane technologies.*
Tel: 905-896-3626
Fax: 905-896-9262
www.woodbridgegroup.com
Rev: $800
Emp: 4,500

NAICS: 326140, 326150, 326199, 336360

WOODBRIDGE SALES & ENGINEERING INC.
1515 Equity Dr., Ste. 100, Troy, Michigan 48084
CEO: Hugh W. Sloan Jr., Pres.   Tel: (248) 288-0100   %FO: 100
Bus: *Sales and engineering of plastic materials,*   Fax: (248) 288-1640   Emp: 121
    auto parts, resins.

● **WORKBRAIN, INC.**
250 Ferrand Dr., Ste. 1200, Toronto ON M3C 3G8, Canada
CEO: David Ossip, Pres. & CEO   Tel: 416-421-6700   Rev: $57
Bus: *Workforce management software manufacture.*   Fax: 416-421-8440   Emp: 472
    www.workbrain.com

NAICS: 511210

    WORKBRAIN, INC.
    3440 Preston Ridge Rd., Ste. 100, Alpharetta, Georgia 30005
    CEO: David Ossip, Pres.   Tel: (678) 713-6014   %FO: 100
    Bus: *Workforce management software sales.*   Fax: (678) 713-6020   Emp: 110

    WORKBRAIN, INC.
    100 Bayview Circle, Ste. 340, Newport Beach, California 92660
    CEO: David Ossip, Pres.   Tel: (949) 753-5454   %FO: 100
    Bus: *Workforce management software sales.*   Fax: (949) 856-2627

● **WORKSTREAM INC.**
495 March Rd., Ste. 300, Ottawa ON K2K 3G1, Canada
CEO: Michael Mullarkey, Chmn. & CEO   Tel: 613-270-0619   Rev: $27
Bus: *Job site software manufacture.*   Fax: 613-270-0776   Emp: 199
    www.workstreaminc.com

NAICS: 511210, 561310, 561320

    ALLEN AND ASSOCIATES
    2600 Lake Lucien Dr., Ste. 235, Maitland, Florida 32751
    CEO: Michael Mullarkey, CEO   Tel: (866) 953-8800
    Bus: *Staffing services.*   Fax: (407) 475-5502   Emp: 108

    PROACT TECHNOLOGIES CORP.
    120 Bloomingdale Rd., Ste. 404, White Plains, New York 10605
    CEO: Greg Rorke, Pres. & CEO   Tel: (914) 872-8000
    Bus: *Human resources & workforce management.* Fax: (914) 872-8100   Emp: 70

● **XANTREX TECHNOLOGY**
8999 Nelson Way, Burnaby BC V5A 4B5, Canada
CEO: John R. Wallace, CEO   Tel: 604-422-8595   Rev: $136
Bus: *Power electronic devices manufacture.*   Fax: 604-420-1591   Emp: 500
    www.xantrex.com

NAICS: 334416, 335999

    XANTREX TECHNOLOGY
    541 Roske Dr., Ste. D, Elkhart, Indiana 46516
    CEO: Ben Kerstig, Mgr.   Tel: (574) 294-5858   %FO: 100
    Bus: *Sells advanced power electronics.*   Fax: Emp: 5

XANTREX TECHNOLOGY
161 S. Vasco Rd., Ste. G, Livermore, California 94551
CEO: Ray Hudson, VP
Bus: *Mfr. of electrical industrial equipment & supplies.*

Tel: (925) 245-5400
Fax: (925) 245-1022

%FO: 100
Emp: 50

XANTREX TECHNOLOGY
5916 195th St. NE, Arlington, Washington 98223
CEO: Ron Pitt, Principal
Bus: *Power electronic devices sales and distribution.*

Tel: (360) 435-8826
Fax: (360) 925-5144

%FO: 100

- **XENOS GROUP INC.**
95 Mural St., Ste. 201, Richmond Hill ON L4B 3G2, Canada
CEO: Stuart Butts, Chmn. & CEO
Bus: *Content management software.*

Tel: 905-709-1020
Fax: 905-709-1023
www.xenos.com

Rev: $13
Emp: 87

NAICS: 511210

XENOS GROUP INC.
1909 Woodall Rodgers Fwy., Ste. 575, Dallas, Texas 75201
CEO: Jim Farmer, Pres.
Bus: *Content management software.*

Tel: (972) 857-0776
Fax: (972) 857-0979

%FO: 100

- **XENTEL DM INCORPORATED**
8000 Jane St., Tower A, Ste. 401, Concord ON L4K 5B8, Canada
CEO: Michael P. Platz, Chmn. & CEO
Bus: *Direct marketing services.*

Tel: 416-633-4646
Fax: 416-433-4643
www.xentel.com

Rev: $108
Emp: 3,000

NAICS: 541613, 541820, 541890

XENTEL DM INCORPORATED
101 SE 3rd Ave., Ste. 203, Ft. Lauderdale, Florida 33301
CEO: Michael Platz, Chmn.
Bus: *Direct marketing services.*

Tel: (954) 522-5200
Fax: (954) 524-5183

%FO: 100
Emp: 900

- **XPLORE TECHNOLOGIES CORP.**
6535-B Mississauga Rd., Mississauga ON L5N 1A6, Canada
CEO: Brian Groh, Chmn. & Pres. & CEO
Bus: *Wireless computing systems.*

Tel: 905-814-9122
Fax: 905-814-9124
www.xploretech.com

Rev: $25
Emp: 70

NAICS: 334111

XPLORE TECHNOLOGIES CORP. OF AMERICA
14000 Summit Dr., Ste. 900, Austin, Texas 78728
CEO: Brian Groh, Pres.
Bus: *Computer services.*

Tel: (512) 336-7797
Fax: (512) 336-7791

%FO: 100
Emp: 75

- **XWAVE SOLUTIONS INC.**
40 Higgins Line, PO Box 13543, St. Johns NF A1B 4B8, Canada
CEO: Paul Kent, COO
Bus: *Information technology solutions.*

Tel: 709-724-7500
Fax: 709-724-7555
www.xwave.com

Rev: $285
Emp: 1,900

NAICS: 423430, 541511, 541512, 541519

  XWAVE SOLUTIONS INC
  57 Atlantic Place, South Portland, Maine 04106
  CEO: BJ Carter, Mgr.
  Bus: *Information technology solutions.*

  Tel: (207) 774-2104
  Fax: (207) 772-2400

  %FO: 100

  XWAVE SOLUTIONS INC.
  151 Capitol St., PO Box 495, Augusta, Maine 04332
  CEO: BJ Carter, Mgr.
  Bus: *Information technology solutions.*

  Tel: (207) 622-9772
  Fax: (207) 623-5984

  %FO: 100
  Emp: 49

- **YAK COMMUNICATIONS INC.**
300 Consillium Pl., Ste. 500, Scarborough ON M1H 3G2, Canada
CEO: Charles Zwebner, CEO
Bus: *International, discount calling services.*

Tel: 647-722-2752
Fax: 647-722-2767
www.yak.ca

Rev: $81
Emp: 150

NAICS: 517110, 517310, 517910, 561499

  YAK COMMUNICATIONS INC.
  20803 Biscayne Blvd., Ste. 305, Aventura, Florida 33180
  CEO: Larry Turel, PR
  Bus: *International, discount calling services.*

  Tel: (305) 933-8322
  Fax: (305) 933-6833

  %FO: 100

- **YORKVILLE SOUND INC.**
550 Granite Court, Pickering ON L1W 3Y8, Canada
CEO: Jack Long, CEO
Bus: *Professional audio equipment manufacture.*

Tel: 905-837-8481
Fax: 905-839-5776
www.yorkville.com

Emp: 200

NAICS: 334310

  YORKVILLE SOUND INC.
  4625 Witmer Industrial Estate, Niagara Falls, New York 14305
  CEO: Terry Sherwood, Mgr.
  Bus: *Professional audio equipment sales.*

  Tel: (716) 297-2920
  Fax: (716) 297-3689

  %FO: 100
  Emp: 9

- **YOTTA YOTTA, INC.**
6020 104th St., Edmonton AB T6H 5S4, Canada
CEO: Barton Y. Shigemura, Pres. & CEO
Bus: *Software manufacture.*

Tel: 780-989-6800
Fax: 780-989-6868
www.yottayotta.com

Rev: $100
Emp: 120

NAICS: 511210

  YOTTA YOTTA, INC.
  211 North Union St., Ste. 100, Alexandria, Virginia 22314
  CEO: Barton Y. Shigemura, Pres. & CEO
  Bus: *Software sales.*

  Tel: (703) 684-4892
  Fax: (703) 838-5564

  %FO: 100

- **ZENON ENVIRONMENTAL INC.**
  3239 Dundas St. W., Oakville ON L6M 4B2, Canada
  CEO: Andrew Benedek, CEO
  Bus: *Mfr. and sales of membrane-filtration products and equipment for water filtration systems.*
  NAICS: 333319

  Tel: 905-465-3030
  Fax: 905-465-3050
  www.zenon.com

  Rev: $142
  Emp: 1,051

  ZENON ENVIRONMENTAL INC.
  3800 Oceanic Dr., Ste. 113, San Diego, California 92056
  CEO: Steve Watzeck
  Bus: *Sales of membrane-filtration products and equipment for water filtration systems.*

  Tel: (760) 547-2160
  Fax: (760) 547-2161

  %FO: 100

  ZENON ENVIRONMENTAL INC.
  5051 Commercial Circle, Ste. B, Concord, California 94250
  CEO: Paul Schuler
  Bus: *Sales of membrane-filtration products and equipment for water filtration systems.*

  Tel: (925) 246-8190
  Fax: (925) 246-8199

  %FO: 100

- **ZI CORPORATION**
  840 7th Avenue SW, Ste. 2100, Calgary AB T2P 3G2, Canada
  CEO: Michael E. Lobsinger, CEO
  Bus: *Software for wireless headsets.*

  Tel: 403-233-8875
  Fax: 403-233-8878
  www.zicorp.com

  Rev: $13
  Emp: 119

  NAICS: 511210

  ZI CORPORATION
  2121 N California Blvd., Ste. 290, Walnut Creek, California 94596
  CEO: Roland Williams
  Bus: *Software manufacture and sales.*

  Tel: (925) 974-3370
  Fax: (925) 974-3371

  %FO: 100

- **ZYNG INTERNATIONAL LLC**
  4710 St. Ambroise St., Ste. 320, Montreal QC H4C 2C7, Canada
  CEO: Dan Rowe, CEO
  Bus: *Restaurant operator.*

  Tel: 514-288-8800
  Fax: 514-939-8808
  www.zyng.com

  NAICS: 722110

  ZYNG INTERNATIONAL LLC
  132 King St., 2/F, Alexandria, Virginia 22314
  CEO: Dan Rowe, CEO
  Bus: *Restaurant franchises.*

  Tel: (703) 549-5332
  Fax: (703) 549-0740

  %FO: 100

Cayman Islands

- **APEX SILVER MINES LIMITED**
Walker House, Mary St., George Town, Grand Cayman, Cayman Islands
CEO: Jeffrey G. Clevenger, Pres. & CEO   Tel: 345-949-0050
Bus: *Silver, zinc and lead mining.*   Fax: 345-949-8062   Emp: 115
www.apexsilver.com

  NAICS: 212222, 212231, 212299
  APEX SILVER MINES LIMITED
  1700 Lincoln St., Ste. 3050, Denver, Colorado 80203
  CEO: Jeffrey G. Clevenger   Tel: (303) 839-5060
  Bus: *Mining.*   Fax: (303) 839-5907

- **CAYMAN AIRWAYS**
233 Owen Roberts Dr., George Town, Grand Cayman, Cayman Islands
CEO: Michael Adam, Pres. & CEO   Tel: 345-949-8200
Bus: *Airline carrier.*   Fax: 345-949-7607
www.caymanairways.com

  NAICS: 481111, 481112, 481212
  CAYMAN AIRWAYS
  8400 NW 52nd St., Ste. 210, Miami, Florida 33166
  CEO: Marjorie Henriques, Mgr.   Tel: (305) 266-4141   %FO: 100
  Bus: *Airline carrier.*   Fax: (305) 267-2925   Emp: 11

- **FRESH DEL MONTE PRODUCE, INC.**
Walker House, Mary St., George Town, Grand Cayman, Cayman Islands
CEO: Mohammad Abu-Ghazaleh, Chmn. & CEO   Tel: 345-949-0100   Rev: $2,906
Bus: *Producer of fresh fruit*   Fax: Emp: 35,000
www.freshdelmonte.com

  NAICS: 111339, 311421
  FRESH DEL MONTE PRODUCE INC.
  241 Sevilla Ave., Coral Gables, Florida 33134
  CEO: M. Bryce Edmonson, SVP   Tel: (305) 520-8400   %FO: 100
  Bus: *Supplier of fresh fruit*   Fax: (305) 567-0320

- **GARMIN LTD.**
Harbour Place, 5/F., 113 South Church Street, George Town, Grand Cayman, Cayman Islands
CEO: Min H. Kao, Co-Chair   Tel: 345-946-5203   Rev: $763
Bus: *Digital navigation products manufacture.*   Fax: 345-945-2197   Emp: 2,484
www.garmin.com

  NAICS: 334220, 334290, 334511
  GARMIN INTERNATIONAL INC.
  1200 East 151st St., Olathe, Kansas 66062
  CEO: Kevin S. Rauckman, Pres.   Tel: (913) 397-8200   %FO: 100
  Bus: *Digital navigation products manufacture and*   Fax: (913) 397-8282
  sales.

- **O2MICRO INTERNATIONAL LIMITED**
The Grand Pavillion, West Bay Road, George Town, Grand Cayman, Cayman Islands
CEO: Sterling Du, CEO   Tel: 345-945-1110   Rev: $92
Bus: *Mfr. integrated circuits.*   Fax: 345-945-1110   Emp: 426
                                         www.o2micro.com
  NAICS: 334413
      O2MICRO USA INC.
  2700 Pecan St. West, Ste. 400, Pflugerville, Texas 78660
  CEO: Marc Cram   Tel: (512) 990-3246   %FO: 100
  Bus: *Mfr./sales integrated circuits.* Fax: (512) 990-3246

      O2MICRO USA INC.
  3118 Patrick Henry Dr., Santa Clara, California 95054
  CEO: Sterling Du, VP   Tel: (408) 987-5920   %FO: 100
  Bus: *Mfr./sales integrated circuits.* Fax: (408) 987-5920

      O2MICRO USA INC.
  9950 Cypresswood Dr., Ste. 211, Houston, Texas 77070
  CEO: Tania Hall   Tel: (832) 237-8800   %FO: 100
  Bus: *Mfr./sales integrated circuits.* Fax: (832) 237-8800

- **UNITED AMERICA INDEMNITY, LTD.**
Walker House, 87 Mary St., George Town, Grand Cayman, Cayman Islands
CEO: Edward J. Noonan, Pres. & CEO   Tel: 345-949-0100   Rev: $254
Bus: *Property and casualty insurance services.* Fax: Emp: 680
                                         www.ungl.ky
  NAICS: 524126
      PENN-AMERICA GROUP, INC.
  420 S. York Rd., Hatboro, Pennsylvania 19040
  CEO: Joseph F. Morris, Pres. & CEO   Tel: (215) 443-3600   %FO: 100
  Bus: *Property and casualty insurance.* Fax: (215) 443-3603   Emp: 120

      UNITED AMERICA INDEMNITY, LTD.
  3 Bala Plaza East, Ste. 300, Bala Cynwyd, Pennsylvania 19004
  CEO: James Maguire Jr., Pres.   Tel: (610) 664-1500   %FO: 100
  Bus: *Property and casualty insurance services.* Fax: (610) 660-8882 Emp: 350

- **XCELERA INC.**
PO Box 309, Ugland House, South Church St., George Town, Grand Cayman, Cayman Islands
CEO: Alexander M. Vik, Chmn. & CEO   Tel: 203-622-1606
Bus: *Internet startups.*   Fax: 203-622-1610
                                         www.xcelera.com
  NAICS: 425110, 454111, 516110, 518112, 523999, 551112
      FIRM LTD.
  Watergate Tower 1, 1900 Powell St., Ste. 200, Emeryville, California 94608
  CEO: Henning Hansen, Pres.   Tel: (510) 653-8527   %FO: 14
  Bus: *Survey & reporting software.*   Fax: (510) 653-8584

FIRM LTD.
424 W33rd St., Ste. 410, New York, New York 10001
CEO: Henning Hansen, Pres.
Bus: *Survey & reporting software.*
Tel: (212) 660-1800
Fax: (212) 268-0354
%FO: 14

INEO USA INC.
1300 Crescent Green, Ste. 135, Cary, North Carolina 27511
CEO: Gustav Vik, CEO
Bus: *Business consulting services.*
Tel: (919) 319-1099
Fax: (919) 468-5987
%FO: 100

MIRROR IMAGE INTERNET, INC.
2 Highwood Dr., Tewksbury, Massachusetts 01876
CEO: Alexander M. Vik, Chmn. & CEO
Bus: *Internet imaging.*
Tel: (781) 376-1100
Fax: (781) 376-1110
%FO: 99
Emp: 77

PROTEGRITY USA CORP.
15 Bank St., Stamford, Connecticut 06901
CEO: Gordon Rapkin, CEO
Bus: *Database security.*
Tel: (203) 326-7200
Fax:
%FO: 100
Emp: 45

SCENE 7, INC., DIV. XCELERA INC.
6 Hamilton Landing, Ste. 150, Novato, California 94949
CEO: Douglas Mack, CEO
Bus: *Internet startups.*
Tel: (415) 506-6000
Fax: (415) 884-9920

276

Channel Islands, U.K.

● **AMDOCS LIMITED**
Tower Hill House, Le Bordage, Ste. 5, St. Peter Port, Guernsey GY1 3QT, Channel Islands, U.K.
CEO: Dov Baharav, Pres. & CEO   Tel: 972-9-776-2222   Rev: $1,773
Bus: *Billing and order management systems for*   Fax: 972-9-776-2120   Emp: 10,600
    communications providers and business support   www.amdocs.com
    systems for directory publishing companies.
NAICS: 541614

    AMDOCS MANAGEMENT LIMITED
    1390 Timberlake Manor Pkwy., St. Louis, Missouri 63017
    CEO: Gary Smith   Tel: (314) 212-7000
    Bus: *Operations support software manufacture.*   Fax: (314) 213-7500

Chile

- **BANCO DE CHILE**
Ahumada 251, Piso 3, Santiago, Chile
CEO: Pablo Granifo Lavin, Pres.
Bus: *Commercial banking services.*

Tel: 56-2-637-1111
Fax: 56-2-637-3434
www.bancochile.cl

Rev: $1,165
Emp: 8,650

NAICS: 522110

  BANCO DE CHILE
  200 South Biscayne Boulevard, 27/F, Miami, Florida 33131-5307
  CEO: Matias Herrera, Gen. Mgr.
  Bus: *International banking services.*

  Tel: (305) 373-0041
  Fax: (305) 373-6465

  %FO: 100
  Emp: 10

  BANCO DE CHILE
  535 Madison Ave., 9/F, New York, New York 10022
  CEO: Eduardo Omegna, Gen. Mgr.
  Bus: *General banking services.*

  Tel: (212) 758-0909
  Fax: (212) 593-9770

  %FO: 100
  Emp: 33

- **BANCO SANTANDER CHILE**
Bandera 140, F3, Santiago, Chile
CEO: Oscar Von Chrismar, CEO
Bus: *Commercial banking services.*

Tel: 56-2-320-2000
Fax: 56-2-320-8877
www.santandersantiago.cl

Rev: $1,910
Emp: 7,561

NAICS: 522110, 523920, 523930, 524210

  BANCO SANTANDER
  45 East 53rd St., Ste. 900, New York, New York 10022
  CEO: Daniel Keane, SVP
  Bus: *Commercial banking services.*

  Tel: (212) 350-3400
  Fax:

  %FO: 100
  Emp: 500

- **CELULOSA ARAUCO Y CONSTITUCION SA**
Ave. El Golf 150, 14th Fl., Las Condes, Santiago, Chile
CEO: Matias Domeyko, CEO
Bus: *Timber and forest plantations.*

Tel: 56-2461-7200
Fax: 56-2461-7542
www.arauco.cl

Rev: $2,075
Emp: 4,728

NAICS: 113210, 113310, 321113, 321912

  ARAUCO WOOD PRODUCTS, INC.
  5901 C Peachtree Dunwood Rd., NE, Ste. 370, Atlanta, Georgia 30328
  CEO: Charles Kimber
  Bus: *Timber sales.*

  Tel: (770) 379-9270
  Fax: (770) 379-9288

  %FO: 100

- **CHILE FAST**
Manquelhue Norte 44, Apoquindo 5856, Las Condes Santiago, Chile
CEO: Ana Maria Carey, Mgr.
Bus: *Engaged in tourism and cargo transport.*

Tel: 56-2-201-3611
Fax: 56-2-240-0450
www.fastair.cl

NAICS: 481111, 481212, 561520

CHILE FAST TOURS
82 Wall St., Ste. 1009, New York, New York 10005
CEO: Cecilia Carey, Pres.
Bus: *Engaged in tourism and cargo transport.*

Tel: (212) 344-4690
Fax: (212) 344-0004

%FO: JV
Emp: 2

● **CHILESAT CORP SA**
Rinconada El Salto 202, Huechuraba, Santiago, Chile
CEO: Alejandro Rojas Pinaud, CEO
Bus: *International and domestic telephone services.*

Tel: 56-2-380-0170
Fax: 56-2-382-5142
www.telex.cl

Rev: $75
Emp: 560

NAICS: 517110, 517910, 518210, 519190

TEXCOM WIRELESS LTD.
PO Box 266916, Houston, Texas 77207
CEO: J. J. Trogdon
Bus: *International and domestic long international phone services.*

Tel: (713) 649-0616
Fax: (713) 645-6411

%FO: 100

● **COMPANIA CERVECERIAS UNIDAS, SA**
Bandera 84, 6th Fl., Santiago, Chile
CEO: Patricio Jottar Nasrallah, CEO
Bus: *Beer brewery. 20% JV of Anheuser-Busch*

Tel: 56-2-427-3000
Fax: 56-2-427-3222
www.ccu-sa.com

Rev: $646
Emp: 4,000

NAICS: 424810

ANHEUSTER-BUSCH COMPANIES, INC.
1 Busch Place, St. Louis, Missouri 63118
CEO: Patrick T. Stokes, Pres.
Bus: *Brews beer.*

Tel: (314) 577-2000
Fax: (314) 577-2900

%FO: JV

● **COMPANIA SUD AMERICANA DE VAPORES SA**
Plaza Sotomayor 50, Valparaiso, Chile
CEO: Ricardo Claro Valdés, CEO
Bus: *Cargo container carrier, handling and logistics services.*

Tel: 56-32-203-000
Fax: 56-32-203-333
www.csav.cl

Rev: $1,675
Emp: 5,234

NAICS: 483111, 488310, 488320

AMERICAN TRANSPORT GROUP CSAV
99 Wood Ave. South, 9/F, Iselin, New Jersey 08830
CEO: Dan Klein
Bus: *Cargo container carrier, handling and logistics services.*

Tel: (732) 635-2600
Fax: (732) 635-2601

%FO: 100

● **CORPORACION NACIONAL DE COBRE DE CHILE (CODELCO)**
Huerfanos 1270, 150-D, Santiago, Chile
CEO: Juan Villarzu Rohde, Pres. & CEO
Bus: *Operates mines and generates and distributes electric power.*

Tel: 56-2-690-3000
Fax: 56-2-690-3059
www.codelco.com

Rev: $3,782
Emp: 16,595

NAICS: 212234, 212299, 213114

CODELCO USA INC.
177 Broad St., 14/F, Stamford, Connecticut 06901
CEO: Joan Dennen, VP
Bus: *Sales agent of copper & molybdenum ores*

Tel: (203) 425-4321
Fax: (203) 425-4322

%FO: 100

● **CSAV (COMPAÑIA SUD AMERICANA DE VAPORES)**
Plaza Sotomayor 50, PO Box 49-V, 236171, Valparaiso, Chile
CEO: Ricardo Claro Vaides, Chmn.
Bus: *Cargo and freight handling services.*

Tel: 56-32-203000
Fax: 56-32-203333
www.csav.cl

Rev: $1,674
Emp: 5,234

NAICS: 481112, 484121

CSAV/CHILEAN LINE INC.
99 Wood Ave., Ste. 9, Iselin, New Jersey 08830
CEO: Mario Dabove
Bus: *Cargo and freight handling services.*

Tel: (732) 635-2600
Fax: (732) 635-2601

%FO: 100

CSAV/CHILEAN LINE INC.
249 East Ocean Blvd., Ste. 1000, Los Angeles, California 90802
CEO: Eric K. Chang, Pres.
Bus: *Cargo and freight handling services.*

Tel: (562) 983-7699
Fax: (562) 983-7668

%FO: 100

● **EMPRESAS CMPC SA**
Agustinas 1343, Piso 9, Casilla 279, Correo Central, Santiago, Chile
CEO: Arturo Mackenna, CEO
Bus: *Wood and paper products manufacture.*

Tel: 56-2-441-2000
Fax: 56-2-671-1957
www.cmpc.cl

Rev: $1,672
Emp: 8,573

NAICS: 321912, 423310

CMPC USA
3330 Cumberland Blvd SE, Atlanta, Georgia 30339
CEO: Pablo Sufan
Bus: *Wood and paper products.*

Tel: (770) 933-6237
Fax: (770) 933-6237

%FO: 100

● **LAN AIRLINES S.A.**
Avenida Americo Vespucio, Sur 901, Renca, Santiago, Chile
CEO: Enrique Cueto Plaza, CEO
Bus: *International commercial air transport.*

Tel: 56-2-565-2525
Fax: 56-2-565-3973
www7.lan.com

Rev: $2,093
Emp: 13,414

NAICS: 481111, 481112, 481212

LAN CHILE AIRLINES
1960 East Grand Ave., Ste. 530, El Segundo, California 90245
CEO: Ivan Zika, Sales
Bus: *International commercial air transport
services.*

Tel: (310) 416-9061
Fax: (310) 416-9864

%FO: 100

LAN CHILE AIRLINES
JFK International Airport, Concourse A-Terminal 4, Jamaica, New York 11430
CEO: Rolando Burgis, Mgr.
Bus: *International commercial air transport
services.*

Tel: (718) 751-4580
Fax: (718) 751-4537

%FO: 100

LAN CHILE AIRLINES
630 Fifth Ave., Ste. 809, New York, New York 10111
CEO: Luis E. Riquelme, VP   Tel: (212) 582-3250   %FO: 100
Bus: *International commercial air transport*   Fax: (212) 582-6863
     services.

LAN CHILE AIRLINES
Miami International Airport, Concourse A- Level 2, Miami, Florida 33122
CEO: Robert Banchi, Mgr.   Tel: (305) 670-9999   %FO: 100
Bus: *International commercial air transport*   Fax: (305) 670-9599
     services.

● **SOCIEDAD QUIMICA Y MINERA DE CHILE S.A.**
SQM El Trovado, 4285 Las Condes, Santiago, Chile
CEO: Patricio Contesse Gonzalez, CEO   Tel: 56-2-425-2000   Rev: $788
Bus: *Production and distribution of specialty fertilizers*   Fax: 56-2-425-2493   Emp: 3,418
     and industrial chemicals.   www.sqm.com
NAICS: 325188, 325199, 325311, 325312

SQM NORTH AMERICA INC.
3101 Towercreek Pkwy., Ste. 450, Atlanta, Georgia 30339
CEO: Ignacio Ruiz, Pres.   Tel: (770) 916-9400   %FO: 100
Bus: *Mfr./sales of nitrate, nitrogenous fertilizers.*   Fax: (770) 916-9401   Emp: 47

China PRC

- **AGRICULTURAL BANK OF CHINA**
  Jia 23, Fuxing Rd., Beijing 100036, China PRC
  CEO: Mingsheng Yang, CEO
  Bus: *Banking services.*

  Tel: 86-10-6842-4548
  Fax: 86-10-6842-4548
  www.abocn.com

  NAICS: 522110

  > **AGRICULTURAL BANK OF CHINA**
  > 375 Park Ave., Ste. 2504, New York, New York 10152
  > CEO: Yang Kun
  > Bus: *Banking services.*
  >
  > Tel: (212) 888-8998
  > Fax: (212) 888-8998
  >
  > %FO: 100

- **AIR CHINA**
  Beijing Capital International Airport, Beijing 100621, China PRC
  CEO: Ma Xulun, Pres.
  Bus: *Commercial air transport services.*

  Tel: 86-10-6456-3201
  Fax: 86-10-6456-3831
  www.airchina.com

  Rev: $996
  Emp: 14,000

  NAICS: 481111, 481212

  > **AIR CHINA INTERNATIONAL INC.**
  > 24858 Rockaway Blvd., Ste. 2, Jamaica, New York 11422-3151
  > CEO: Jy Hong
  > Bus: *Commercial air transport services.*
  >
  > Tel: (718) 528-0300
  > Fax: (718) 528-0300
  >
  > %FO: 100

  > **AIR CHINA INTERNATIONAL INC.**
  > 400 Oyster Point Blvd., South San Francisco, California 94080-1904
  > CEO: Wing Kun Tam, Gen. Mgr.
  > Bus: *Freight transport services.*
  >
  > Tel: (650) 737-0888
  > Fax: (650) 737-0888
  >
  > %FO: 100

  > **AIR CHINA INTERNATIONAL INC.**
  > 200 World Way, Ste. 2, Los Angeles, California 90045-5844
  > CEO: Xushing Liu, Sales Mgr.
  > Bus: *Commercial air transport services.*
  >
  > Tel: (310) 215-1188
  > Fax: (310) 215-1188
  >
  > %FO: 100

- **ALIBABA.COM CORPORATION**
  6/F Chuangye Mansion, East Software Park, 99 Huaxing Rd., Hangzhou, Zhejiang, China PRC
  CEO: Jack Ma, Chmn. & CEO
  Bus: *Electronic online services*

  Tel: 86-571-8502-2088
  Fax: 86-571-8815-7866
  www.alibaba.com

  Rev: $68
  Emp: 2,000

  NAICS: 454111, 454112, 454390

  > **Alibaba.com Corporation**
  > 39899 Balentine Dr., Ste. 355, Newark, California 94560
  > CEO: Annie Jie Xu, CEO
  > Bus: *Electronic online services*
  >
  > Tel: (510) 438-7980
  > Fax: (510) 438-7981
  >
  > %FO: 100

- **ASIAINFO HOLDINGS, INC.**
  6 Zhongguancun South St., 4th Fl., Haidian District, Beijing 100086, China PRC
  CEO: Steve Zhang, Pres. & CEO
  Bus: *Software manufacturer.*
  Tel: 86-10-6250-1658
  Fax: 86-10-6250-1893
  www.asiainfo.com
  Rev: $106
  Emp: 2,000
  NAICS: 511210
  - **ASIAINFO HOLDINGS, INC.**
    5201 Great American Pkwy., Ste. 429, Santa Clara, California 95054
    CEO: Cindy Yang
    Bus: *Software manufacturer.*
    Tel: (408) 970-9788
    Fax: (408) 970-9366
    %FO: 100

- **AXL MUSICAL INSTRUMENTS CO.**
  1068 YongXin Rd., XuHang Town, JiaDing District, Shanghai 200434, China PRC
  CEO: Alan Liu, CEO
  Bus: *Musical instruments manufacture, including*
  pianos and woodwind instruments.
  Tel: 86-21-6561-0998
  Fax: 86-21-6561-7268
  www.axlusa.com
  NAICS: 339992
  - **AXL MUSICAL INSTRUMENTS CO.**
    380 Valley Dr., Brisbane, California 94005
    CEO: Karol Yao
    Bus: *Musical instruments sales and distribution,*
    including pianos and woodwind instruments.
    Tel: (415) 508-1398
    Fax: (415) 508-1396
    %FO: 100

- **BANK OF CHINA**
  1 Fuxingmen Nei Dajie, Beijing 100818, China PRC
  CEO: Xiao Gang, Chmn. & Pres.
  Bus: *Commercial banking services.*
  Tel: 86-10-6659-6688
  Fax: 86-10-6659-3777
  www.bank-of-china.com
  Rev: $15,000
  Emp: 188,000
  NAICS: 522110, 522210, 523920, 523930, 524210
  - **BANK OF CHINA**
    42 East Broadway, New York, New York 10002
    CEO: Ernest Li, Mktg. Dir.
    Bus: *International banking services.*
    Tel: (212) 925-2355
    Fax: (212) 431-6157
    %FO: 100
  - **BANK OF CHINA**
    444 South Flower St., Ste. 3900, Los Angeles, California 90071
    CEO: Happy Lieu, Mgr.
    Bus: *International banking services.*
    Tel: (213) 688-8700
    Fax: (213) 688-0198
    %FO: 100
  - **BANK OF CHINA**
    410 Madison Ave., New York, New York 10017
    CEO: Bailing Zheng, Mgr.
    Bus: *International banking services.*
    Tel: (212) 935-3101
    Fax: (212) 593-1831
    %FO: 100

- **CHINA EASTERN AIRLINES CORPORATION LIMITED**
  2550 Hongqiao Rd., Hongqiao International Airport, Shanghai 200335, China PRC
  CEO: Luo Chaogeng, Pres.
  Bus: *Passenger and cargo airline services.*
  Tel: 86-21-6268-6268
  Fax: 86-21-6268-8668
  www.cea.com.cn
  Rev: $1,725
  Emp: 16,435
  NAICS: 481111, 481212

CHINA EASTERN AIRLINES
Tom Bradley International Terminal, 380 World Way, Los Angeles, California 90045
CEO: Zhang Jianzhong   Tel: (310) 646-1849   %FO: 100
Bus: *Passenger airline services.*   Fax: (310) 645-1758

CHINA EASTERN AIRLINES
55 South Lake Ave., Ste. 120, Pasadena, California 91101
CEO: Zhang Jianzhong   Tel: (818) 583-1500   %FO: 100
Bus: *Passenger and cargo airline services.*   Fax: (818) 583-1515

CHINA EASTERN AIRLINES
O'Hare International Airport, PO Box 6608, Chicago, Illinois 60601
CEO: Zhang Jianzhong   Tel: (773) 686-0107   %FO: 100
Bus: *Cargo airline services.*   Fax: (773) 686-0125

● **CHINA NATIONAL PETROLEUM CORPORATION**
6 Liu Pu Kang Jie, Xicheng District, Beijing 100724, China PRC
CEO: Chen Geng, Pres.   Tel: 86-10-6209-4114   Rev: $47,046
Bus: *Oil and gas exploration.*   Fax: 86-10-6209-4806   Emp: 102,400
    www.cnpc.com.cn
NAICS: 211111, 211112, 213111, 213112, 324110, 324191, 324199, 333132, 424710, 424720, 447190, 454311, 454312, 454319, 541360

CHINA NATIONAL PETROLEUM CORPORATION
1080 West Sam Houston Pkwy., Houston, Texas 77043-5021
CEO: Zheng Chen   Tel: (713) 465-7382   %FO: 100
Bus: *Oil and gas exploration.*   Fax: (713) 465-5865

● **CHINA OCEAN SHIPPING COMPANY**
158 Fuxingmennei St., Beijing 100031, China PRC
CEO: Jiafu Wei, Pres. & CEO   Tel: 86-10-6649-3388
Bus: *Marine transport services.*   Fax: 86-10-6649-2266
    www.cosco.com.cn
NAICS: 336611, 483111, 488510, 561520

COSCO NORTH AMERICA INC.
8326 Cricket Lake Dr., Charlotte, North Carolina 28277-9844
CEO: Ronald B. McLauchlin   Tel: (704) 544-1249   %FO: 100
Bus: *Marine transport services.*   Fax: (704) 544-1249

COSCO NORTH AMERICA INC.
1201 Roberts Blvd. NW, Kennesaw, Georgia 30144-3693
CEO: Jeff Hall   Tel: (770) 419-1123   %FO: 100
Bus: *Marine transport services.*   Fax: (770) 419-1123

COSCO NORTH AMERICA INC.
100 Lighting Way, Ste. 101, Secaucus, New Jersey 07094
CEO: Zhang Liyong   Tel: (201) 422-0500   %FO: 100
Bus: *Marine transport services.*   Fax: (201) 422-8928

- **CHINA SOUTHERN AIRLINES COMPANY LTD.**
  278 Ji Chang Rd., Guangzhou, Guangdong, Guangdong 510405, China PRC
  CEO: Si Xian Min, CEO
  Bus: *International passenger and cargo carrier, engaged in operation of hotels, restaurants and duty-free shops.*
  Tel: 86-20-8613-0870
  Fax: 86-20-8613-0873
  www.cs-air.com
  Rev: $2,896
  Emp: 17,569
  NAICS: 481111, 481112, 481212, 721110
    CHINA SOUTHERN AIRLINES COMPANY LTD.
    6300 Wilshire Blvd., Los Angeles, California 90048
    CEO: Benny Wei, Mgr.
    Bus: *International passenger and cargo carrier, engaged in operation of hotels, restaurants and duty-free shops.*
    Tel: (323) 653-8088
    Fax: (323) 653-8066
    %FO: 100

- **CHINA STATE CONSTRUCTION ENGINEERING CORPORATION**
  37 Maizidian St., Chaoyang, Beijing 100026, China PRC
  CEO: Sun Wenjie, CEO
  Bus: *Construction and engineering.*
  Tel: 86-10-8527-6677
  Fax: 86-10-8527-5566
  www.cscec.com
  Rev: $6,400
  Emp: 60,000
  NAICS: 236210, 236220, 237110, 237120, 237130, 237990, 541330
    CHINA CONSTRUCTION AMERICA
    525 Washington Blvd., Ste. 2688, Jersey City, New Jersey 07310
    CEO: Mason Gao, Pres.
    Bus: *Construction and engineering services.*
    Tel: (201) 876-2788
    Fax: (201) 876-6737
    %FO: 100

- **CITIG GROUP**
  Capital Mansion 6, Xinuan Nanlu, Beijing 10004, China PRC
  CEO: Kong Dan, CEO
  Bus: *Engaged in overseeing the government's international investments.*
  Tel: 86-10-6466-8866
  Fax: 86-10-6466-1186
  www.citic.com
  Rev: $4,190
  Emp: 20,000
  NAICS: 921190
    CITIFOR INC.
    701 Fifth Ave.,, Ste. 7272, Seattle, Washington 98104-7090
    CEO: Sun Xinguo, Pres.
    Bus: *Engaged in international investments.*
    Tel: (206) 622-3770
    Fax: (206) 622-6714
    %FO: 100

- **COFCO INTERNATIONAL**
  COFCO Plaza, Tower A, Room 1002, 8 Jian Guo Men Nei Ave., Beijing 100005, China PRC
  CEO: Zhou Mingchen, Chmn.
  Bus: *Import and exports of grains and foodstuffs.*
  Tel: 86-10-6526-8888
  Fax: 86-10-6527-6028
  www.cofco.com.
  Rev: $12,100
  Emp: 28,000
  NAICS: 111110, 111120, 111130, 111140, 111150, 111160, 111930, 111991, 112120, 112310, 112320, 112512, 114112, 311211, 311212, 311213, 311222,
  311223, 311225, 311311, 311312, 311320, 311330, 312111, 312130, 332431, 332439, 531120, 531190, 531312, 531390, 721110
    BNU CORPORATION
    COFCO Chinese Cultural Center, 668 North 44th St., Ste. 228, Phoenix, Arizona 85008-6547
    CEO: Elizabeth Mann, Pres.
    Bus: *Engaged in commodity trading.*
    Tel: (602) 273-7268
    Fax: (602) 273-7129
    %FO: 100
    Emp: 125

CEROIL FOOD INC.
910 Sylvan Ave., 1/F, Englewood Cliffs, New Jersey 07632
CEO: Jin Jiakai, Pres.   Tel: (201) 568-6788   %FO: 100
Bus: *Engaged in commodity trading.*   Fax: (201) 569-2008

COFCO CAPITAL CORPORATION
Three First National Plaza, 70 West Madison St., Ste. 2430, Chicago, Illinois 60602
CEO: Chen Qinan,   Tel: (312) 855-9010
Bus: *Engaged in commodity trading.*   Fax: (312) 855-9011

• **COL CHINA ONLINE INTERNATIONAL**
922 Heng Shan Rd., 27th Fl., Shanghai 200030, China PRC
CEO: Chi Keung Wong, CEO   Tel: 86-21-6447-9982
Bus: *Information technology services.*   Fax: 86-21-6447-7930   Emp: 30
                                            www.col-chinaonline.com

NAICS: 541611

    COL CHINA ONLINE INTERNATIONAL
    3176 South Peoria Ct., Aurora, Colorado 80014
    CEO: Mark K. Shaner   Tel: (303) 695-8530   %FO: 100
    Bus: *Information technology services.*   Fax: (303) 696-7396

• **ETERNAL TECHNOLOGIES GROUP**
235 Nanjing Rd., Ste. 04-06, 28/F, Block A, Tianjin 300052, China PRC
CEO: Jiansheng Wei, CEO   Tel: 86-22-2721-7020   Rev: $15
Bus: *Agricultural genetics; animal-embryo production.* Fax: 86-22-2721-7030   Emp: 35
                                            www.eternalprc.com

NAICS: 541710

    ETERNAL TECHNOLOGIES GROUP
    1301 Travis St., Ste. 1200, Houston, Texas 77000
    CEO: Dan Gray   Tel: (954) 974-3475   %FO: 100
    Bus: *Genetics.*   Fax: (954) 974-3475

• **HAIER GROUP COMPANY**
1 Haier Rd., Hi-Tech Zone, Qingdao, Shandong 266101, China PRC
CEO: Zhang Ruimin, Chmn. & CEO   Tel: 86-532-893-9999   Rev: $8,725
Bus: *Mfr. refrigerators and home appliances.* Fax: 86-532-893-8666   Emp: 30,000
                                            www.haier.com

NAICS: 334111, 334310, 335211, 335212, 335221, 335224, 335228

    HAIER AMERICA
    1356 Broadway, New York, New York 10018
    CEO: Michael Jemal, Pres. & CEO   Tel: (212) 594-3330   %FO: 100
    Bus: *Refrigerators and home appliances Fax: (212) 594-9667   Emp: 105
        manufacture and sales.*

    HAIER AMERICA
    50 Haier Blvd., Camden, South Carolina 29020
    CEO: Michael Jemal, Pres. & CEO   Tel: (803) 424-5960   %FO: 100
    Bus: *Refrigerator manufacture.*   Fax: (803) 424-8424   Emp: 150

● **INDUSTRIAL AND COMMERCIAL BANK OF CHINA**
No. 55, Fuxingmennei Street, Beijing 100031, China PRC
CEO: Jiang Jianqing, CEO   Tel: 86-10-6588-8888
Bus: *State-owned commercial bank.*   Fax: 86-10-6588-9999
     www.icbc.com.cn
NAICS: 521110, 522110

     INDUSTRIAL AND COMMERCIAL BANK OF CHINA
     375 Park Ave., Ste. 3508, New York, New York 10152
     CEO: Lido Wang   Tel: (212) 838-7799   %FO: 100
     Bus: *Bank services.*   Fax: (212) 838-5770

● **JINPAN INTERNATIONAL**
100 Industry Ave., Jinpan Development Area, Haikou, Hainan 570216, China PRC
CEO: Li Zhiyuan, Chmn. & Pres. & CEO   Tel: 86-898-6681-1746
Bus: *Cast resin transformer manufacturer.*   Fax: 86-896-6681-8820
     www.jst.com.cn
NAICS: 334416

     JINPAN INTERNATIONAL
     560 Sylvan Ave., 3/F, Englewood Cliffs, New Jersey 07632
     CEO: Yuqing Jing, Pres.   Tel: (201) 227-0680   %FO: 100
     Bus: *Cast resin transformer sales and distribution.* Fax: (201) 227-0685

● **JUN HE LAW OFFICE**
China Resources Bldg., 20th Fl., 8 Jianguomenbei Avenue, Beijing 100005, China PRC
CEO: Xiaolin Zhou, Prtn.   Tel: 86-10-8519-1300
Bus: *International law firm.*   Fax: 86-10-8519-1350   Emp: 85
     www.junhe.com
NAICS: 541110

     JUN HE LAW OFFICE
     500 Fifth Ave., Ste. 1930, New York, New York 10110
     CEO: Xiaolin Zhou   Tel: (212) 775-8610   %FO: 100
     Bus: *International law firm.*   Fax: (212) 775-8533

● **SEMICONDUCTOR MANUFACTURING INTERNATIONAL CORPORATION**
18 Ahangjiang Rd., Pudong New Area, Shanghai 201203, China PRC
CEO: Richard Chang, Pres. & CEO   Tel: 86-21-5080-2000   Rev: $975
Bus: *Semiconductor manufacture.*   Fax: 86-21-5080-2868   Emp: 7,640
     www.smics.com
NAICS: 334413

     SEMICONDUCTOR MANUFACTURING INTERNATIONAL CORPORATION
     45757 Northport Loop West, Fremont, California 94538
     CEO: Samuel Wang, Pres.   Tel: (510) 492-2025   %FO: 100
     Bus: *Semiconductor manufacture.*   Fax: (510) 651-1242

● **SHANGHAI AUTOMOTIVE INDUSTRY CORPORATION**
489 Wei Hai Rd., Shanghai 200041, China PRC
CEO: Hu Mao Yuan, Pres.
Bus: *Cars, buses, trucks and auto parts manufacturer.*
Tel: 86-21-2201-1888
Fax: 86-21-2201-1777
www.saicgroup.com
Rev: $11,743
Emp: 64,343
NAICS: 333111, 336111, 336120, 336211, 336399, 336991

SAIC USA INC.
3391 Sage Dr., Rockford, Illinois 61114
CEO: Minge Zhang, Mgr.
Bus: *Mfr. of motors & generators.*
Tel: (815) 877-8832
Fax:
%FO: 100

SAIC USA INC.
1301 W. Long Lake Rd., Troy, Michigan 48098
CEO: Yong Zhou Chen, Pres.
Bus: *Cars, buses, trucks and auto parts manufacturer.*
Tel: (248) 267-9117
Fax:
%FO: 100
Emp: 20

● **SHANGHAI BAOSTEEL GROUP CORPORATION**
Baosteel Tower, Pudian Rd., 370 Pudong New District, Shanghai, China PRC
CEO: Xie Qihua, Chmn.
Bus: *Steel production.*
Tel: 86-21-5835-8888
Fax: 86-21-6840-4832
www.baosteel.com
Rev: $14,534
Emp: 127,000
NAICS: 331111, 331222, 331513

BAOSTEEL AMERICA INC.
401 Hackensack Ave., Hackensack, New Jersey 07601
CEO: Xu Lejiang, Pres.
Bus: *Steel production.*
Tel: (201) 457-1144
Fax: (201) 457-0909
%FO: 100

● **SINA CORP.**
1468 Nan Jing Rd. West, United Plaza, Ste. 1802, Shanghai 200040, China PRC
CEO: Yan Wang, CEO
Bus: *Operates Chinese Web portals.*
Tel: 86-21-6289-5678
Fax: 86-21-6279-3803
www.sina.com
Rev: $200
Emp: 1,760
NAICS: 516110, 518111, 518112

SINA CORP.
2988 Campus Dr., San Mateo, California 94403
CEO: Hurst Lin, Pres.
Bus: *Operates Chinese Web portals.*
Tel: (650) 638-9228
Fax: (650) 638-9268
%FO: 100
Emp: 30

● **SINOCHEM (CHINA NATIONAL CHEMICALS IMPORT & EXPORT)**
Sinochem Tower, A2 Fuxingmenwai Dajie, Beijing 100045, China PRC
CEO: Liu Deshu, Pres. & CEO
Bus: *Chemicals, petroleum, rubber and plastics manufacture.*
Tel: 86-10-831-6017
Fax: 86-10-841-5588
www.sinochem.com
Rev: $18,760
Emp: 7,660
NAICS: 325110, 326199, 326299, 424690

SINOCHEM AMERICAN INC.
1330 Post Oak Blvd., Ste. 2500, Houston, Texas 77056
CEO: Yu Chen, Pres.   Tel: (713) 263-8880   %FO: 100
Bus: *Chemicals, petroleum, rubber and plastics*   Fax: (713) 212-0258   Emp: 350
    manufacture and sales.

SINOCHEM USA
1330 Post Oak Blvd., Ste. 2500, Houston, Texas 77056
CEO: Lin Min Gu, Pres.   Tel: (713) 686-0700
Bus: *Chemicals & pharmaceuticals.*   Fax: (713) 686-6801   Emp: 10

U.S. CHEM RESOURCES, INC.
2701 N. Rocky Point Dr., Tampa, Florida 33607
CEO: Yang Hong, Pres.   Tel: (813) 282-0300   %FO: 100
Bus: *Chemicals manufacture.*   Fax: (813) 289-2954   Emp: 10

• **SINOPEC (CHINA PETROLEUM AND CHEMICAL COMPANY)**
6A Huixin East St., Chaoyang District, Beijing 100029, China PRC
CEO: Wang Tianpu, Pres.   Tel: 86-10-6499-0060   Rev: $74,870
Bus: *Mfr. ethylene and petroleum-based fuels and oils,* Fax: 86-10-6499-0022   Emp: 389,451
    including benzene. (JV with Union Carbide Corp.,   www.sinopec.com.cn
    US)
    NAICS: 211111, 211112, 213111, 213112, 221210, 324110, 324191, 324199, 333132, 424710, 424720, 447110,
447190, 454311, 454312, 454319, 486110,
        486210, 486910, 541360

    SINOPEC-USA COMPANY
    150 East 52nd St., 28/F, New York, New York 10022
    CEO: Kaige Xu, Pres.   Tel: (212) 759-5085   %FO: 100
    Bus: *Petrochemicals.*   Fax: (212) 759-6882   Emp: 10

• **SINOTRANS LIMITED**
Sinotrans Plaza, A43 Xizhimen, Beidajie, Beijing 100044, China PRC
CEO: Zhang Jianwei, CEO   Tel: 86-10-6229-6666   Rev: $2,103
Bus: *Air, ocean, road and rail freight forwarding*   Fax: 86-10-6229-6600   Emp: 13,200
    services.   www.sinotrans.com
NAICS: 481212, 483111

    CHINA INTEROCEAN TRANSPORT INC.
    2300 E. Higgins Rd., Ste. 213A, Chicago, Illinois 60007
    CEO: M. Xijin, Mgr.   Tel: (847) 437-5900   %FO: 100
    Bus: *Freight forwarding services.*   Fax: (847) 437-5902

    CHINA INTEROCEAN TRANSPORT INC. (CIT)
    JFK Airport Bldg. #75, North Hangar Road, Ste. 203, Jamaica, New York 11430
    CEO: Jinshan Lu   Tel: (718) 656-3098   %FO: 100
    Bus: *Freight forwarding services.*   Fax: (718) 656-3098

    SINO-AM MARINE (CIT)
    601 E. Linden Ave., Linden, New Jersey 07036
    CEO: Min Liu, Mgr.   Tel: (908) 862-0800   %FO: 100
    Bus: *Freight forwarding services.*   Fax: (908) 862-0876

SINOTRANS SHIPPING AGENCY INC.
301 W. Warner Rd., Ste. 131, Tempe, Arizona 85284
CEO: J. Owens
Bus: *Freight forwarding services.*

Tel: (480) 763-9060
Fax: (480) 961-1070

%FO: 100

● **VERISILICON HOLDINGS CO. LTD.**
200 Zhangheng Rd., 3/F, Bldg. 1, Zhangjiang Hi-Tech Park, Pudong, Shanghai 201204, China PRC
CEO: Wei Ming Dai, Chmn. & Pres. & CEO
Bus: *Integrated circuit design manufacture.*

Tel: 86-21-5131-1118
Fax: 86-21-5131-1119
www.verisilicon.com

NAICS: 334413, 511210, 541690, 541990

VERISILICON HOLDINGS CO. LTD.
4699 Old Ironsides Dr., Ste. 270, Santa Clara, California 95054
CEO: Bill Wang, Gen. Mgr.
Bus: *Integrated circuit design manufacture.*

Tel: (408) 844-8560
Fax: (408) 844-8563

%FO: 100

Colombia

- **AEROVIAS NACIONALES DE COLOMBIA SA**
  Avenida Eldorado, No. 93-30, Bogota, Colombia
  CEO: Fabio Villegas Ramlrez, Pres. & CEO   Tel: 57-1-413-9511
  Bus: *Airline transport services.*   Fax: 57-1-413-9702
                                                     www.avianca.com

  NAICS: 481111

  - **AVIANCA AIRLINES**
    720 Fifth Ave., New York, New York 10019
    CEO: Fabio Villegas Ramirez   Tel: (212) 399-0824   %FO: 100
    Bus: *Airline carrier.*   Fax: (212) 399-0828

  - **AVIANCA AIRLINES**
    800 West 6th St., Ste. 310, Los Angeles, California 90017-2706
    CEO: Fabio Villegas Ramirez   Tel: (213) 626-9147   %FO: 100
    Bus: *Airline carrier.*   Fax: (213) 626-9147

  - **AVIANCA AIRLINES**
    2025 18th St., Bldg. 2203, Miami, Florida 33159
    CEO: Fabio Villegas Ramirez   Tel: (305) 871-2042   %FO: 100
    Bus: *Cargo sales.*   Fax: (305) 871-2042

  - **AVIANCA AIRLINES**
    JFK Airport Bldg. 534248, Jamaica, New York 11432
    CEO: Ruben Jovine   Tel: (718) 632-1467   %FO: 100
    Bus: *Airline carrier.*   Fax: (718) 632-1467

- **BANCAFE (BANCO CAFETERO)**
  Calle 28 #13A-15, Apartado Aereo, 240332 Bogota, Colombia
  CEO: Gilberto Gomez-Arango, Pres.   Tel: 57-1-284-6800
  Bus: *International banking services.*   Fax: 57-1-286-8893   Emp: 6,900
                                            www.bancafe.com

  NAICS: 522110

  - **BANCAFE INTERNATIONAL MIAMI**
    801 Brickell Ave., PH-1, Miami, Florida 33131
    CEO: Alfredo Quintero, Pres.   Tel: (305) 372-9909   %FO: 100
    Bus: *International banking services.*   Fax: (305) 372-1797   Emp: 35

- **BANCO COLPATRIA SA**
  Carretera 13, 93B-11 Floor 1, Bogota, Colombia
  CEO: Santiago Perdomo Maldonado, Pres.   Tel: 57-1-661-1104
  Bus: *International banking services.*   Fax: 57-1-616-1184   Emp: 500
                                            www.colpatria.com.co

  NAICS: 522110

BANCO COLPATRIA S.A.
801 Brickell Ave., Ste. 2360, Miami, Florida 33131
CEO: Carlos R. Pancheco, Mgr.   Tel: (305) 374-4026   %FO: 100
Bus: *International banking services.*   Fax: (305) 372-0605   Emp: 5

● **BANCOLOMBIA S.A.**
Calle 50, No. 51-66, Medellin, Colombia
CEO: Jorge Londono Saldarriaga, Pres. & CEO   Tel: 57-4-511-5516   Rev: $1,065
Bus: *Provides banking services.*   Fax: 57-4-510-8779   Emp: 8,000
    www.bancolombia.com.co
NAICS: 522110, 522291, 522293

BANCOLOMBIA S.A.
1111 Brickell Ave., Ste. 1550, Miami, Florida 33131
CEO: Santiago Villa, Gen. Mgr.   Tel: (305) 373-3969   %FO: 100
Bus: *Banking and financial services.*   Fax: (305) 373-6853

Costa Rica

- **BANCO INTERNACIONAL DE COSTA RICA, S.A.**
  Barrio Tournon, 6116-1000 San Jose, Costa Rica
  CEO: Alfonso Guardia Mora, Pres.   Tel: 506-243-1000   Rev: $14
  Bus: *International banking services.*   Fax: 506-233-5479   Emp: 109
                 www.bicsa.com

  NAICS: 522110

    BANCO INTERNACIONAL DE COSTA RICA, S.A.
    4000 Ponce De Leon Blvd, Ste. 600, Miami, Florida 33146
    CEO: Percy A. Elbrecht, Mgr.   Tel: (305) 374-0855   %FO: 100
    Bus: *Banking services.*   Fax: (305) 381-6971

- **CAFÉ BRITT COFFEE CORPORATION**
  400 Meters West la Comandancia, Heredia, Costa Rica
  CEO: Steven J. Aronson, CEO   Tel: 506-261-0707   Rev: $21
  Bus: *Coffee manufacture and sales.*   Fax: 506-260-1456   Emp: 200
                 www.cafebritt.com

  NAICS: 311920

    CAFE BRITT GOURMET COFFEE
    81 Wayne Rd., Newton, Massachusetts 02459
    CEO: Jerry Backer   Tel: (617) 244-7585   %FO: 100
    Bus: *Coffee sales and distribution.* Fax: (617) 244-7585

Croatia

- **PLIVA D.D.**
Ulica Grada Vukovara 49, 10000 Zagreb, Croatia
CEO: Zeljko Covic, CEO
Bus: *Develop and production of pharmaceuticals.*

Tel: 385-161-20-999
Fax: 385-161-11-011
www.pliva.hr

Rev: $1,077
Emp: 6,780

NAICS: 325412

PLIVA INC.
72 Eagle Rock Ave., East Hanover, New Jersey 07936
CEO: David Berthold
Bus: *Pharmaceuticals.*

Tel: (973) 386-5566
Fax: (973) 386-5566

%FO: 100

PLIVA USA INC.
150 East 58th St., New York, New York 10155
CEO: D. Nevjestic, Pres.
Bus: *Pharmaceuticals.*

Tel: (212) 832-8970
Fax: (212) 593-0448

Cyprus

- **CYPRUS AIRWAYS LTD.**
  21 Alkeou St., Engomi, CY-2404 Nicosia, Cyprus
  CEO: Eleni Kaloyirou, CFO
  Bus: *Commercial air transport services.*

  Tel: 357-22-661-054
  Fax: 357-22-663-167
  www.cyprusair.com

  Rev: $302
  Emp: 2,000

  NAICS: 481111

  CYPRUS AIRWAYS LTD.
  71 W. 35th St., New York, New York 10001
  CEO: Ted Ermogenous
  Bus: *Commercial air transport services.*

  Tel: (212) 714-2190
  Fax:

  %FO: 100

Czech Republic

- **CESKE AEROLINIE AS**
  Prague Ruzynì Airport, 160 08 Prague, Czech Republic
  CEO: Jaroslav Tvrdik, Pres.
  Bus: *Commercial air transport services.*

  Tel: 420-220-104-310
  Fax: 420-224-81-04-26
  www.csa.cz

  Rev: $435
  Emp: 4,455

  NAICS: 481111

    CZECH AIRLINES LTD.
    1350 Ave. of the Americas, Ste. 601, New York, New York 10036
    CEO: Miroslav Belovsky, Gen. Mgr.
    Bus: *Commercial air transport services.*

    Tel: (212) 765-6022
    Fax: (212) 765-6588

    %FO: 100

    CZECH AIRLINES LTD.
    16743 Porter Rd., Jamaica, New York 11434
    CEO: Marek Drvota, Dir.
    Bus: *Commercial air transport services.*

    Tel: (718) 656-1237
    Fax: (718) 656-1237

    %FO: 100

- **MORAVIA WORLDWIDE**
  Hilleho 4, 602 00 Brno, Czech Republic
  CEO: Katerina Forstingerova, CEO & Mng. Dir.
  Bus: *Globalization solution provider, including product testing, multilingual publishing and technical translation.*

  Tel: 420-545-552-222
  Fax: 420-545-552-233
  www.moraviaworldwide.com

  NAICS: 516110, 519110, 519190, 541930, 611420, 611630, 611710, 624310

    MORAVIA IT, INC.
    199 East Thousand Oaks Blvd., Thousand Oaks, California 91360
    CEO: Joseph Didamo, Pres.
    Bus: *Globalization solution provider; localization & product testing services, internationalization, multilingual publishing & technical translation.*

    Tel: (805) 557-1700
    Fax: (805) 557-1702

    %FO: 100
    Emp: 7

- **PRECIOSA AS**
  Opletalova Cp. 3197, 466 00 Jablonec Nad Nisou, Czech Republic
  CEO: Karel Kamir, Dir.
  Bus: *Design and manufacture of glass cutting and polishing machines, machine-cut glass stones, light fittings and cut crystal figurines.*

  Tel: 420-488-115555
  Fax: 420-428-311761
  www.preciosa.com

  Emp: 4,000

  NAICS: 327212, 333999

    PRECIOSA INTERNATIONAL, INC.
    41 Madison Ave., 16/F, New York, New York 10010
    CEO: Michael Kamir, Pres.
    Bus: *Sales/distribution of machine-cut glass stones, including beads, fancy stones and chandelier trimmings.*

    Tel: (212) 889-3741
    Fax: (212) 684-1874

    %FO: 100

- **UNIPLET GROUP**
  Kloknerova 9, 148 00 Prague 4, Czech Republic
  CEO: Otakar Curda, VP
  Bus: *Small diameter hosiery knitting machines manufacture.*
  NAICS: 333292, 333298, 421830

  Tel: 420-255-701-333
  Fax: 420-255-701--312
  www.uniplet.cz

      TRUSTFIN USA - UNIPLET CO. LTD.
      6012-A Old Pineville Rd., Charlotte, North Carolina 28217
      CEO: Otto Curda, VP
      Bus: *Sales, service and support for hosiery knitting machines.*

  Tel: (704) 521-9303
  Fax: (704) 521-8379

  %FO: 100
  Emp: 4

Denmark

- **AARHUS UNITED A/S**
M.P. Bruuns Gade 27, Postboks 50, DK-8000 Aarhus, Denmark
CEO: Erik Hojsholt, CEO
Bus: *Specialty manufacturer of vegetable fats for the international food industry.*
NAICS: 311225
Tel: 45-87-30-6000
Fax: 45-87-30-6012
www.aarhus.com
Rev: $578
Emp: 2,100

  AARHUS INC.
131 Marsh St., Port Newark, New Jersey 07114
CEO: Edmund Wilson, Mgr.
Bus: *specialty fats and oils manufacturer.*
Tel: (973) 344-1300
Fax: (973) 344-9049
%FO: 100

- **ALK-ABELLÓ LABORATORIES AS, DIV. CHR. HANSEN GROUP**
Boge Alle 6-8, DK-2970 Horsholm, Denmark
CEO: Jens Bager, Pres. & CEO
Bus: *Develops allergy products for the diagnosis, prevention and cure of allergies.*
NAICS: 325412
Tel: 45-45-74-7445
Fax: 45-45-74-8690
www.alk-abello.com

  ALK-ABELLO LABORATORIES INC.
1700 Royston Lane, Round Rock, Texas 78664
CEO: Karsten Jorgensen, Pres.
Bus: *Develops allergy products for the diagnosis, prevention and cure of allergies and the relief of symptoms.*
Tel: (512) 251-0037
Fax: (512) 251-8450
%FO: 100
Emp: 165

  ALK-ABELLO NEW YORK
35 Channel Dr., Port Washington, New York 11050
CEO: Karsten Jorgensen
Bus: *Allergy medicine manufacture.*
Tel: (516) 767-1800
Fax: (516) 767-4229
%FO: 100

  BIOPOL LABORATORY, INC.
327 East Pacific Ave., Spokane, Washington 99202
CEO: Miles W. Guralnick, Pres.
Bus: *Allergy medication development and manufacture.*
Tel: (509) 456-7794
Fax: (509) 456-7965
%FO: 100

  VESPA LABORATORIES INC.
1095 Upper Georges Valley Rd., Spring Mills, Pennsylvania 16875
CEO: Miles W. Guralnick, Pres.
Bus: *Allergy manufacture.*
Tel: (814) 422-8165
Fax: (814) 422-8424
%FO: 100
Emp: 18

- **ARLA FOODS AMBA**
Skanderborgvej 277, PO Box 2400, DK-8260 Viby, Denmark
CEO: Knud Erik Jensen, Chmn.
Bus: *Engaged in production of fresh milk products, cheeses, yogurts and specialty products.*
NAICS: 311511, 311513, 311514
Tel: 45-89-38-1000
Fax: 45-86-28-1691
www.arlafoods.com
Rev: $7,884
Emp: 20,855

MEDIPHARM INC.
10215 Dennis Dr., Des Moines, Iowa 50322
CEO: Mark Richards, Dir.   Tel: (515) 254-1280   %FO: 100
Bus: *Engaged in concentrates and cultures for*   Fax: (515) 254-1356
the food industry.

● **BANG & OLUFSEN A/S**
Peter Bangs Vej 15, DK-7600 Struer, Denmark
CEO: Torben B. Sorensen, Pres. & CEO   Tel: 45-96-84-1122   Rev: $595
Bus: *Mfr. electronics.*   Fax: 45-97-85-1888   Emp: 2,717
                                              www.bang-olufsen.com
NAICS: 334310, 423620

   BANG & OLUFSEN
   780 West Dundee Rd., Arlington Heights, Illinois 60004
   CEO: Kim Gravesen   Tel: (847) 590-4900   %FO: 100
   Bus: *Sales of electronic equipment.*   Fax: (847) 590-4900

   BANG & OLUFSEN
   3500 Peachtree Rd., Atlanta, Georgia 30326
   CEO: Joey Pratt   Tel: (404) 233-5445   %FO: 100
   Bus: *Sales of electronic equipment.*   Fax: (404) 233-3980

   BANG & OLUFSEN
   86 Greenwich Ave., Greenwich, Connecticut 06830
   CEO: Kim Gravesen   Tel: (203) 625-3388   %FO: 100
   Bus: *Sales of electronic equipment.*   Fax: (203) 625-8666

   BANG & OLUFSEN
   330 Columbus Ave., New York, New York 10023
   CEO: George Doxiades   Tel: (212) 501-0926   %FO: 100
   Bus: *Sales of electronic equipment.*   Fax: (212) 501-9530

   BANG & OLUFSEN
   Roosevelt Field Mall, Ste. 2082, Garden City, New York 11530
   CEO: Michael Aagaard Andersen   Tel: (516) 248-4198   %FO: 100
   Bus: *Sales of electronic equipment.*   Fax: (516) 248-4430

   BANG & OLUFSEN
   35 The Shops at Mission Viejo, Mission Viejo, California 92691
   CEO: Michael Ostergaard   Tel: (949) 365-1899   %FO: 100
   Bus: *Sales of electronic equipment.*   Fax: (949) 365-1897

● **BOREALIS A/S**
Parallelvej 16, DK-2800 Kongens Lyngby, Denmark
CEO: John Taylor, CEO   Tel: 45-4596-6000   Rev: $3,285
Bus: *Plastic resins manufacture.*   Fax: 45-4596-6123   Emp: 5,300
                                              www.borealisgroup.com
NAICS: 325211
   BOREALIS COMPOUNDS
   176 Thomas Rd., Port Murray, New Jersey 07865
   CEO: Laurence Jones   Tel: (908) 850-6200   %FO: 100
   Bus: *Plastic resins manufacture and sales.* Fax: (908) 850-1236

- **CARLSBERG A/S**
  1, Valby Langgade, DK-2500 Valby, Denmark
  CEO: Nils S. Andersen, CEO
  Bus: *Beer brewing.*

  Tel: 45-3327-2727
  Fax: 45-3327-4850
  www.carlsberg.com

  Rev: $6,850
  Emp: 150

  NAICS: 312120

    LABATT USA
    101 Merritt 7, PO Box 5075, Norwalk, Connecticut 06856
    CEO: Simon C. Thorpe, Mgr.
    Bus: *Beer sales and distribution.*

    Tel: (203) 750-6600
    Fax: (203) 750-6699

    %FO: JV

- **COWI A/S**
  Parallelvej 2, Kongens Lyngby, DK-2800 Copenhagen, Denmark
  CEO: Klaus Henrik Ostenfeld, Mng. Dir.
  Bus: *International consulting group*

  Tel: 45-45-972-211
  Fax:
  www.cowi.com

  Rev: $453
  Emp: 1,942

  NAICS: 541330

    BEN C. GERWICK INC.
    20 California St., Ste. 400, San Francisco, California 94111
    CEO: Robert Bittner
    Bus: *Major marine structure construction.*

    Tel: (415) 398-8972
    Fax: (415) 398-0433

    %FO: 95

- **L DAEHNFELDT A/S**
  Faaborgvej 248 B, DK-5250 Odense C, Denmark
  CEO: Joe Messer, Dir.
  Bus: *Engaged in seed production and sales.*

  Tel: 45-66-17-5506
  Fax: 45-66-17-5505
  www.daehnfeldt.com

  NAICS: 111199

    DAEHNFELDT INC.
    PO Box 38, North Manchester, Indiana 46962-0038
    CEO: Joe Messer, Pres.
    Bus: *Seed production and sales.*

    Tel: (219) 982-7969
    Fax: (219) 982-7970

    %FO: 100
    Emp: 18

- **DAKOCYTOMATION A/S**
  Produktionsvej 42, DK-2600 Glostrup, Denmark
  CEO: Jes Ostergaard, CEO
  Bus: *Research equipment manufacturer.*

  Tel: 45-4485-9500
  Fax: 45-4485-9595
  www.dakocytomation.com

  Rev: $278
  Emp: 1,300

  NAICS: 334510, 334517, 339111, 339113

    DAKOCYTOMATION INC.
    4850 Innovation Dr., Fort Collins, Colorado 80525
    CEO: Sonja Wulff, PR
    Bus: *Research equipment manufacture and sales.*

    Tel: (970) 226-2200
    Fax: (970) 226-0107

    %FO: 100

    DAKOCYTOMATION INC.
    6392 Via Real, Carpentaria, California 93013
    CEO: Klaus Kjeldal
    Bus: *Research equipment manufacture and sales.*

    Tel: (805) 566-6655
    Fax: (805) 684-5935

    %FO: 100

- **DANFOSS A/S**
Danfoss Center, DK-6430 Nordborg, Denmark
CEO: Jorgen Mads Clausen, Pres.
Bus: *Refrigeration controls, heating and water controls and motion controls.*
NAICS: 334512

Tel: 45-7488-2222
Fax: 45-7488-0949
www.danfoss.com

Rev: $2,008
Emp: 18,000

DANFOSS AUTOMATIC CONTROLS
3435 Box Hill Corporate Center Dr., Ste. C, Abingdon, Maryland 21009
CEO: Karen Smith
Bus: *Mfr. controls.*

Tel: (443) 512-0266
Fax: (443) 512-0270

%FO: 100

DANFOSS BAUER
31 Schoolhouse Rd., Somerset, New Jersey 08873
CEO: Steven Blazak
Bus: *Mfr. of DC electronic frequency converters.*

Tel: (732) 469-8770
Fax: (732) 469-8773

%FO: 100

DANFOSS COMMERCIAL COMPRESSORS LTD.
1775-G MacLeod Dr., Lawrenceville, Georgia 30243
CEO: D. McDonald, VP
Bus: *Mfr. refrigerant compressors and condensing units.*

Tel: (678) 377-5100
Fax: (678) 377-5101

%FO: 100
Emp: 60

DANFOSS DRIVES
4401 N. Bell School Rd., Loves Park, Illinois 61111
CEO: Sven Ruder
Bus: *Motion controls manufacture.*

Tel: (815) 639-8600
Fax: (815) 639-8000

%FO: 100

DANFOSS FLOMATIC CORPORATION
145 Murray St., Glens Falls, New York 12801-4424
CEO: Bo Andersson, Pres.
Bus: *Mfr./sale check valves, foot valves, back flow preventers, control valves.*

Tel: (518) 761-9797
Fax: (518) 761-9798

%FO: JV
Emp: 50

DANFOSS FLUID POWER
1201 Pelzer Highway, Easley, South Carolina 29642
CEO: Hans J. Cornett, Dir.
Bus: *Mfr. hydraulic components.*

Tel: (864) 855-2884
Fax: (864) 855-5885

%FO: 100

DANFOSS GRAHAM
PO Box 245041, Milwaukee, Wisconsin 53224
CEO: Charles G. Manz, EVP
Bus: *Mfr. of DC electronic frequency converters.*

Tel: (414) 355-8800
Fax: (414) 355-6117

%FO: 100
Emp: 130

DANFOSS INC.
7941 Corporate Dr., Baltimore, Maryland 21236
CEO: Kjeld Stærk, Pres.
Bus: *Burner components, industrial controls, air conditioning and refrigeration manufacture.*

Tel: (410) 931-8250
Fax: (410) 931-8256

%FO: 100
Emp: 142

DANFOSS WATER & WASTEWATER
8800 W. Bradley Rd., Milwaukee, Wisconsin 53224
CEO: Curt Monhart
Bus: *Water processing.*

Tel: (414) 365-8602
Fax: (414) 355-6117

%FO: 100

INSTRUMARK INTERNATIONAL
1124 Wrigley Way, Milpitas, California 95035
CEO: Bernard Brown, Pres.
Bus: *Mfr. flow products.*

Tel: (408) 262-0717
Fax: (408) 262-3610

%FO: 100

SAUER-DANFOSS INC.
2800 East 13th St., Ames, Iowa 50010
CEO: David J. Anderson, Pres.
Bus: *Engineered hydraulic and electronic systems manufacture.*

Tel: (515) 239-6364
Fax: (515) 239-6443

● **DANIONICS LIMITED, JV GP BATTERIES INTERNATIONAL**
Sivlandvaenget 3, DK-5260 Odense, Denmark
CEO: Niels Kryger Andersen, CEO
Bus: *Rechargeable and alkaline batteries manufacture.*

Tel: 45- 6591-8130
Fax: 45-6591-5130
www.gpbatteries.com.sg

Rev: $372
Emp: 9,500

NAICS: 335912

GP BATTERIES INTERNATIONAL LIMITED
11235 West Bernardo Ct., San Diego, California 92127
CEO: Victor Lo Chung Wing, CEO
Bus: *Rechargeable and alkaline batteries manufacture and sales.*

Tel: (858) 674-6099
Fax: (858) 674-6496

%FO: 100

● **DANISCO A/S**
Langebrogade 1, PO Box 17, DK-1001 Copenhagen K, Denmark
CEO: Alf Duch-Pedersen, CEO
Bus: *Food and beverages, sweeteners, food ingredients and packaging.*

Tel: 45-32-66-2000
Fax: 45-32-66-2175
www.danisco.com

Rev: $2,640
Emp: 8,295

NAICS: 311221, 311311, 311312, 311313, 311942

DANISCO
4 New Century Pkwy., New Century, Kansas 66031
CEO: Germain Despres, Pres.
Bus: *Food ingredients and flavors.*

Tel: (913) 764-8100
Fax: (913) 764-5407

%FO: 100
Emp: 276

DANISCO AMERICA
440 Saw Mill River Rd., Ardsley, New York 10502
CEO: Irene Gil, Mgr.
Bus: *Mfr./sale food ingredients.*

Tel: (913) 764-8100
Fax:

%FO: 100
Emp: 35

DANISCO ANIMAL NUTRITION
411 East Gano Ave., St. Louis, Missouri 63147
CEO: Kaj-Erik Monten, Principal
Bus: *Nutritional advice & support for the feed industry.*

Tel: (314) 231-7766
Fax:

%FO: 100
Emp: 8

DANISCO INGREDIENTS USA, INC.
4509 S. 50th St., St. Joseph, Missouri 64507
CEO: Gary King, Mgr.
Bus: *Mfr./sale food ingredients.*

Tel: (314) 436-3133
Fax: (314) 436-1049

%FO: 100
Emp: 71

DANISCO USA INC.
10994 Three Mile Rd., Thomson, Illinois 61285
CEO: Craig Myers, Mgr.   Tel: (815) 259-3311   %FO: 100
Bus: *Mfr. of sweeteners.*   Fax: Emp: 80

DANISCO USA INC.
2802 Walton Commons West, Madison, Wisconsin 53718
CEO: Ronald Weiss, Mgr.   Tel: (608) 224-1850   %FO: 100
Bus: *Mfr./sale food ingredients.*   Fax: Emp: 93

DANISCO USA INC.
34796 Lencioni Ave., Rte. 1, Bakersfield, California 93308
CEO: Sylvia Thornton, Mgr.   Tel: (661) 392-4400   %FO: 100
Bus: *Mfr./sale food ingredients.*   Fax: Emp: 3

DANISCO USA INC.
33 W. Pfizer Dr., Terre Haute, Indiana 47802
CEO: Douglas W. Cartwright, Mgr.   Tel: (812) 299-6700   %FO: 100
Bus: *Mfr./sale food ingredients.*   Fax: Emp: 85

DANISCO USA INC.
10 New Maple Ave. 653, Pine Brook, New Jersey 07058
CEO: Robert Sauchinitz   Tel: (973) 227-8507   %FO: 100
Bus: *Mfr./sale food ingredients.*   Fax: Emp: 3

DANISCO USA, INC.
3919 Kidron Rd., Lakeland, Florida 33811
CEO: Gil Escobar, VP   Tel: (863) 646-0165   %FO: 100
Bus: *Food ingredients and flavors.*   Fax: (863) 646-0991   Emp: 53

GENENCOR INTERNATIONAL INC.
925 Page Mill Rd., Palo Alto, California 94304
CEO: Robert H. Mayer, Chmn. & Pres. & CEO   Tel: (650) 846-7500
Bus: *Mfr. enzymes.*   Fax: (650) 845-6500   Emp: 1,271

● **DANISH CROWN AMBA**
Marsvej 43, DK-8900 Randers, Denmark
CEO: Kjeld Johannesen, CEO   Tel: 45-8919-1919   Rev: $6,301
Bus: *Meat processing operations.*   Fax: 45-8644-8066   Emp: 23m053
                                         www.danishcrown.dk

NAICS: 112111, 112210, 311611, 311612

   DANISH CROWN USA INC.
   11 Commerce Dr., Cranford, New Jersey 07016
   CEO: Kjeld Johannesen   Tel: (908) 931-9733   %FO: 100
   Bus: *Mfr. sliced deli meats.*   Fax: (908) 931-9747

   PLUMROSE USA INC.
   101 East George E. Allen Dr., Booneville, Mississippi 38829
   CEO: Freddy Mortensen   Tel: (662) 728-6291   %FO: 100
   Bus: *Deli meat products.*   Fax: (662) 728-6291

PLUMROSE USA INC.
52650 23rd Ave., Council Bluffs, Iowa 51501
CEO: Curtis Thompson
Bus: *Deli meats and bacon products.*

Tel: (712) 388-8058
Fax: (712) 388-9317

%FO: 100

PLUMROSE USA INC.
125 N. Coley Rd., Tupelo, Mississippi 38801
CEO: James Ameling
Bus: *Deli meat products.*

Tel: (662) 840-6831
Fax: (662) 840-6076

%FO: 100

PLUMROSE USA INC.
PO Box 1066, Elkhart, Indiana 46516
CEO: Mike Wilfert
Bus: *Bacon products.*

Tel: (574) 295-8190
Fax: (574) 294-5335

%FO: 100

PLUMROSE USA INC.
7 Lexington Ave., East Brunswick, New Jersey 08816
CEO: John Arends
Bus: *Mfr. sliced deli meats.*

Tel: (732) 257-6600
Fax: (732) 257-6644

%FO: 100

SUNHILL FOOD OF VERMONT
14 Jonergin Dr., Swanton, Vermont 05488
CEO: Carsten Jacobson
Bus: *Ribs and barbeque products.*

Tel: (802) 868-7314
Fax: (802) 868-3264

%FO: 100

● **DANSKE BANK A/S**
Holmens Kanal 2-12, DK-1092 Copenhagen, Denmark
CEO: Peter Straarup, Chmn.
Bus: *General commercial banking services.*

Tel: 45-33-44-0000
Fax: 45-33-44-1708
www.danskebank.com

Rev: $14,228
Emp: 16,235

NAICS: 522110

DANSKE BANK
299 Park Ave., 4/F, New York, New York 10171
CEO: Brent V. Christensen, Gen. Mgr.
Bus: *International commercial banking services.*

Tel: (212) 984-8400
Fax: (212) 370-9239

%FO: 100

● **DFDS A/S**
Sundkrogsgade 11, DK-2100 Copenhagen K, Denmark
CEO: Ole Frie, CEO
Bus: *Shipping line, engaged in travel and transport
services.*

Tel: 45-33-42-3342
Fax: 45-33-42-3341
www.dfds.dk

Rev: $531
Emp: 4,185

NAICS: 483111, 483112

DFDS DAN TRANSPORT CORPORATION
5959 W. Century Blvd., Los Angeles, California 90045
CEO: Tina Larsen, Pres.
Bus: *Engaged in international freight forwarding.*

Tel: (310) 216-4242
Fax: (310) 216-4242

%FO: 100

DFDS SEAWAYS (USA) INC.
6801 Lake Worth Rd., Ste. 107, Lake Worth, Florida 33467
CEO: Mike Zacchilli, Dir.
Bus: *Marketing/reservations travel & transport.*

Tel: (561) 649-8124
Fax: (561) 649-8124

%FO: 100
Emp: 5

- **ENKOTEC A/S**
  Sverigesvej 26, DK-8660 Skanderborg, Denmark
  CEO: Svend-Helge Sorensen, Pres.
  Bus: *Mfr. rotary forming nail machines and cold*

  Tel: 45-86-52-4444
  Fax: 45-86-52-4813
  www.encotech.com

  Emp: 60

  NAICS: 332322

  ENKOTEC CO INC
  31200 Solon Rd., Ste. 16, Cleveland, Ohio 44139-3523
  CEO: Jan Sorige, Pres.
  Bus: *Sale/service rotary forming nail machines, and cold formers.*

  Tel: (440) 349-2800
  Fax: (440) 349-3575

  %FO: 100
  Emp: 7

- **FLS INDUSTRIES A/S**
  Vigerslev AllE 77, DK-2500 Valby, Denmark
  CEO: Jorgen Worning, Chmn.
  Bus: *Engineering, building materials, real estate, aerospace services.*

  Tel: 45-3618-1800
  Fax: 45-3630-4441
  www.flsmidth.com

  Rev: $2,698
  Emp: 5,667

  NAICS: 237130, 327310, 811310

  F. L. SMIDTH INC.
  2040 Ave. C, Bethlehem, Pennsylvania 18017
  CEO: Lea Demilio, Pres.
  Bus: *Supplier of custom equipment, systems, products & processes for cement, pulp, paper, mining, and chemical industry.*

  Tel: (610) 264-6011
  Fax: (610) 264-6170

  %FO: 100
  Emp: 1,250

  FFE MINERALS
  3235 Schonersville Rd., Bethlehem, Pennsylvania 18017
  CEO: George Robles
  Bus: *Engineering and building materials.*

  Tcl: (610) 264-6900
  Fax: (610) 264-6996

  FLSMIDTH INC.
  3225 Schoenersville Rd., Bethlehem, Pennsylvania 18017
  CEO: Rafael Martinez Alejandre, Mgr.
  Bus: *Supplier of custom equipment, systems, products.*

  Tel: (610) 264-6044
  Fax: (610) 264-6045

  %FO: 100

  FLSMIDTH MANUFACTURING
  600 South 10th St., Allentown, Pennsylvania 18103
  CEO: Robert Miller, Mgr.
  Bus: *Mfr. of custom equipment*

  Tel: (610) 770-7400
  Fax: (610) 770-7429

  FLSMIDTH MANUFACTURING
  236 South Cherry St., Manheim, Pennsylvania 17545
  CEO: Frank Olejack, Exec. Dir.
  Bus: *Mfr. of custom equipment*

  Tel: (717) 665-2224
  Fax: (717) 664-9217

- **FLSMIDTH A/S**
  Vigerslev Alle 77, Valby, DK-2500 Copenhagen, Denmark
  CEO: Jorgen Huno Rasmussen, CEO
  Bus: *Mfr. cement products.*

  Tel: 45-3618-1000
  Fax: 45-3630-1820
  www.flsmidth.com

  NAICS: 212312, 327320

FLSMIDTH INC.
2040 Ave. C, Bethlehem, Pennsylvania 18017
CEO: Rafael Martinez Alejandre
Bus: *Mfr. cement and cement products.*
Tel: (610) 264-6011
Fax: (610) 264-6170
%FO: 100

● **FOSS ELECTRIC A/S**
Slangerupgade 69, PO Box 260, DK-3400 Hillerod, Denmark
CEO: Peter Foss, Pres.
Bus: *Electronic equipment, measure control devices.*
Tel: 45-70-203-380
Fax: 45-70-203-381
www.foss.dk
Emp: 1,100

NAICS: 334513

FOSS NIRSYSTEMS
7703 Montpelier Rd., Ste. 1, Laurel, Maryland 20723
CEO: Philip Irving, Pres.
Bus: *Near-infrared spectroscopic instrumentation manufacture and distribution.*
Tel: (301) 680-9600
Fax: (301) 236-0134
%FO: 100
Emp: 100

FOSS NORTH AMERICA
7682 Executive Dr., Eden Prairie, Minnesota 55344
CEO: Robert Wang, Pres.
Bus: *Sale/service analytical instruments for dairy, food & feed industry.*
Tel: (952) 974-9892
Fax: (952) 974-9823
%FO: 100
Emp: 78

R & D ENTERPRISES
26 Lynne Dr., Hollis, New Hampshire 03049
CEO: David B. Geller
Bus: *Mfr. of fragrances & flavors.*
Tel: (603) 465-6577
Fax: (603) 465-6588

● **GN RESOUND AS, SUB. GN GREAT NORDIC**
Markaervej 2A, Postbox 224, DK-2630 Taastrup, Denmark
CEO: Jesper Mailind, CEO
Bus: *Mfr. and sales of audio logical diagnostic systems and measurement equipment.*
Tel: 45-72-11-1111
Fax: 45-72-11-1188
www.gnresound-group.com

NAICS: 334510, 339113

GN RESOUND CORPORATION
220 Saginaw Centre, Redwood City, California 94063
CEO: Peter Nolan, SVP
Bus: *Mfr. and sales of audio logical diagnostic systems and measurement equipment.*
Tel: (650) 780-7800
Fax: (650) 367-0675
%FO: 100

GN RESOUND NORTH AMERICA
8001 Bloomington Freeway, Bloomington, Minnesota 55420
CEO: Alan P. Dozier, VP
Bus: *Sales of audio logical diagnostic systems and measurement equipment.*
Tel: (952) 769-8000
Fax: (952) 769-8001
%FO: 100

● **GN STORE NORD A/S**
Markaervej 2 A, PO Box 249, DK-2630 Taastrup, Denmark
CEO: Jorn Kildegaard, Pres. & CEO
Bus: *Mfr. hearing healthcare products and services.*
Tel: 45-72-111-888
Fax: 45-72-111-889
www.gn.com
Rev: $1,017
Emp: 4,500

NAICS: 334290, 334510

BELTONE ELECTRONICS CORP.
4201 W. Victoria St., Chicago, Illinois 60646
CEO: Lawrence Posen, Pres.   Tel: (773) 583-3600   %FO: 100
Bus: *Hearing instruments and fitting systems mfr.*   Fax: (773) 583-3980

GN JABRA NORTH AMERICA
700 E. Butterfield Rd., Ste. 150, Lombard, Illinois 60148
CEO: David Hogan, VP Sales   Tel: (630) 442-6900   %FO: 100
Bus: *Mfr. hands-free communication products for*   Fax: (630) 371-2628
   the mobile consumer market.

HELLO DIRECT, INC.
75 Northeastern Blvd., Nashua, New Hampshire 03062
CEO: Terry Flynn, Gen. Mgr.   Tel: (603) 598-1100   %FO: 100
Bus: *Sales telephones and accessories,*   Fax: (603) 598-1122
   recording, distance-conferencing, and VOIP

● **HALDOR TOPSOE A/S**
Nymollevej 55, Kongens Lyngby, DK-2800 Copenhagen, Denmark
CEO: Giorgio Marcello Girola, Mng. Dir.   Tel: 45-45-27-2000   Rev: $355
Bus: *Engineering and licensing, chemical process*   Fax: 45-45-27-2999   Emp: 1,200
   research, development, manufacture and sale   www.haldortopsoe.com
   catalyst.
NAICS: 325320, 325998, 333415, 541330, 541720

   HALDOR TOPSOE INC.
   770 The City Dr., Ste. 8400, Orange, California 92668
   CEO: Niels K. Sorensen, VP   Tel: (714) 621-3800   %FO: 100
   Bus: *Marketing and sales catalysts.*   Fax: (714) 748-4188   Emp: 10

   HALDOR TOPSOE INC.
   17629 El Camino Real, Houston, Texas 77058-2901
   CEO: Niels K. Sorensen, VP   Tel: (281) 228-5000   %FO: 100
   Bus: *Marketing and sales catalysts.*   Fax: (281) 228-5019   Emp: 196

● **CHRISTIAN HANSEN HOLDING A/S**
Boge Alle 10-12, DK-2970 Horsholm, Denmark
CEO: Jens Bager, Pres. & CEO   Tel: 45-4574-7474   Rev: $725
Bus: *Supplies ingredients; food industry,*   Fax: 45-4574-8888   Emp: 3,681
   pharmaceuticals and diagnostics for specific   www.chr-hansen.com
   allergy disease treatment.
NAICS: 325199, 325412, 325998, 541380, 541710, 621511, 621512

   CHR HANSEN INC.
   2400 East 130th St., Chicago, Illinois 60633
   CEO: Jack Slater, Operations Mgr.   Tel: (773) 646-2203   %FO: 100
   Bus: *Mfr. of food preparations.*   Fax: Emp: 18

   CHR HANSEN INC.
   1595 MacArthur Blvd., Mahwah, New Jersey 07430
   CEO: Peter O'Connor, Mgr.   Tel: (201) 818-1200   %FO: 100
   Bus: *Compound blend flavors manufacture.*   Fax: (201) 818-2173   Emp: 120

CHR HANSEN INC.
110 Liberty Ct., Elyria, Ohio 44035
CEO: Tim Alt, Mgr.   Tel: (440) 324-6060   %FO: 100
Bus: *Ingredient technology.*   Fax: (440) 324-2747

CHR HANSEN INC.
199 1st St., Gretna, Louisiana 70053
CEO: David Sonnier, Mgr.   Tel: (504) 367-7727   %FO: 100
Bus: *Mfr. of molasses.*   Fax: Emp: 13

CHR HANSEN INC.
3558 NW 97th Blvd., Gainesville, Florida 32606
CEO: Mike Valentine, Mgr.   Tel: (352) 332-9455   %FO: 100
Bus: *Mfr. of food ingredients.*   Fax: (352) 332-9939   Emp: 8

CHRISTIAN HANSEN INC. BIOSYSTEMS
9015 West Maple St., Milwaukee, Wisconsin 53214
CEO: David R. Carpenter, Pres. & CEO   Tel: (414) 607-5700   %FO: 100
Bus: *Mfr. supplies for dairy and agricultural*   Fax: (414) 607-5959   Emp: 700
industry.

● **HARDI INTERNATIONAL A/S**
Helgeshoj Alle 38, DK-2630 Taastrup, Denmark
CEO: Niels Jorn Rahbek, Dir.   Tel: 45-43-58-8500
Bus: *Mfr. agricultural sprayers.*   Fax: 45-43-58-8520   Emp: 750
www.hardi.dk

NAICS: 333111, 333112

    HARDI, INC.
    1500 West 76th St., Davenport, Iowa 52806-1356
    CEO: Thomas Kingenbaw, Mgr.   Tel: (563) 386-1730   %FO: 100
    Bus: *Mfr./distribution agricultural sprayers.*   Fax: (563) 386-1710

● **LABOTEK A/S**
Strobjergvej 29, DK-3600 Frederikssund, Denmark
CEO: Peter Jurgensen, CEO   Tel: 45-48-21-8411
Bus: *Auxiliary plastic processing equipment.*   Fax: 45-48-21-8000   Emp: 100
www.labotek.com

NAICS: 333999

    V-TECH ENGINEERING, INC.
    118 East Wabash St., Bluffton, Indiana 46714
    CEO: Bo Alstoft, Rep.   Tel: (260) 824-4322   %FO: 100
    Bus: *Manufacture auxiliary equipment and*   Fax: (260) 824-4335
    centralized systems for the plastics industry.

● **J. LAURITZEN A/S (JL)**
28 Sankt Annae Plads, PO Box 2147, DK-1291 Copenhagen, Denmark
CEO: Torben Janholt, Pres. & CEO   Tel: 45-33-96-8000   Rev: $420
Bus: *Ship owner and operator.*   Fax: 45-33-96-8001   Emp: 1,041
www.j-lauritzen.com

NAICS: 483111, 488510

J. LAURITZEN (USA) INC.
4 Landmark Square, Ste. 150, Stamford, Connecticut 06901
CEO: Jens Ditlev Lauritzen, Pres.　　　　Tel: (203) 961-8661　　　%FO: 100
Bus: *Ship owner & operator.*　　　　　　Fax: (203) 964-0350　　　Emp: 8

LAURITZEN COOL
105 East Port Hueneme Rd., PO Box 639, Port Hueneme, California 93044
CEO: Mats Jansson, Pres.　　　　　　　　Tel: (805) 488-1222　　　%FO: 100
Bus: *Steamship agent for water transportation.*　Fax: (805) 986-8320

LAURITZEN KOSAN
2600 SW 30th Ave., Ft. Lauderdale, Florida 33312
CEO: Jan Kastrup-Nielsen, Pres.　　　　Tel: (954) 584-0524　　　%FO: 100
Bus: *Shipping and tanker services.*　　Fax: (954) 584-0037

● **LEGO GROUP A/S**
Aastvej 1, DK-7190 Billund, Denmark
CEO: Jorgen Vig Knudstorp, CEO　　　　Tel: 45-79-50-6070　　　Rev: $1,422
Bus: *Educational toys; plastic bricks.*　　Fax: 45-75-35-2725　　　Emp: 8,278
　　　　　　　　　　　　　　　　　　　　www.lego.com

NAICS: 339932, 451120, 713110

LEGO SYSTEMS, INC.
555 Taylor Rd., PO Box 1600, Enfield, Connecticut 06083
CEO: Peter Eio, Pres.　　　　　　　　　Tel: (860) 763-3211　　　%FO: 100
Bus: *Educational toys; plastic bricks.*　　Fax: (860) 763-6680　　　Emp: 1,450

● **A. P. MOLLER MAERSK A/S**
Esplanaden 50, DK-1098 Copenhagen K, Denmark
CEO: Michael Pram Ramussen, Chmn.　　Tel: 45-3363-3363　　　Rev: $30,421
Bus: *Engaged in shipping, exploration for and*　Fax: 45-3363-4108　　　Emp: 62,300
　　production of oil and gas, shipbuilding, aviation,　www.apmoller.com
　　industry, supermarkets and EDP services.

NAICS: 211111, 213111, 336611, 445110, 481111, 481112, 483111

APM TERMINALS NORTH AMERICA
6000 Carnegie Blvd., Charlotte, North Carolina 28209
CEO: Anthony Scioscia, Pres. & CEO　　Tel: (704) 571-2000
Bus: *Port, harbor & marine terminal management*　Fax: (704) 571-4967　　Emp: 500

HUDD DISTRIBUTION SERVICES, INC.
5011 Firestone Pl., South Gate, California 90280
CEO: Jeff Larson, Pres.　　　　　　　　Tel: (323) 568-2500
Bus: *Warehousing & distribution services*　Fax: (323) 568-2692

MAERSK INC.
Giralda Farms, Madison, New Jersey 07940
CEO: John Clancy, Chmn.　　　　　　　Tel: (973) 514-5000　　　%FO: 100
Bus: *Engaged in shipping.*　　　　　　Fax: (973) 514-5410　　　Emp: 3,000

MAERSK INC.
790 NW 107th Ave., Ste. 400, Miami, Florida 33172
CEO: Timothy Nolan, Mgr.　　　　　　　Tel: (305) 220-4440　　　%FO: 100
Bus: *Engaged in shipping.*　　　　　　Fax:

MAERSK SEALAND INC.
115 Perimeter Center Pl., NE, Atlanta, Georgia 30346-1274
CEO: Pamela Lake, Sales Dir.
Bus: *Engaged in shipping.*
Tel: (770) 395-9676
Fax:
%FO: 100

● **NILFISK-ADVANCE GROUP**
Sognevej 25, DK-2605 Broendby, Denmark
CEO: Johan Molin, Pres. & CEO
Bus: *Mfr. equipment for professional cleaning.*
Tel: 45-43-23-8100
Fax: 45-43-43-7700
www.nilfisk-advance.com
Rev: $456
Emp: 2,049

NAICS: 327910, 333319, 339994

NILFISK-ADVANCE AMERICA INC.
300 Technology Dr., Malvern, Pennsylvania 19355
CEO: Paul Miller, VP
Bus: *Mfr. specialty vacuum cleaners.*
Tel: (610) 647-6420
Fax: (610) 647-6427
%FO: 100
Emp: 48

NILFISK-ADVANCE INC.
14600 21st Ave. North, Plymouth, Minnesota 55447
CEO: Christian Cornelius-Knutson, CEO
Bus: *Mfr. equipment for professional cleaning; commercial and industrial floor care.*
Tel: (763) 745-3500
Fax: (763) 745-3718
%FO: 100
Emp: 582

● **NIRO A/S, DIV. GEA**
Gladsaxevej 305, P.O. Box 45, DK-2860 Soeborg, Denmark
CEO: Niels Graugaard, Pres.
Bus: *Industrial spray & fluid bed dryers, homogenizers, membrane filtration, extraction. heating & cooling plants for processing liquid & solid materials.*
Tel: 45-39-545-454
Fax: 45-39-545-800
www.niro.com
Rev: $192
Emp: 415

NAICS: 237110, 238290, 334512

NIRO INC.
9165 Rumsey Rd., Columbia, Maryland 21045
CEO: Steven M. Kaplan, Pres.
Bus: *Mfr./sale industrial drying agglomeration equipment, consulting, industrial testing facilities. Spare parts, repairs & marketing.*
Tel: (410) 997-8700
Fax: (410) 997-5021
%FO: 100
Emp: 325

NIRO INC., FOOD AND DAIRY DIV.
1600 O'Keefe Rd., PO Box 268, Hudson, Wisconsin 54016
CEO: Christian Svensgaard, VP
Bus: *Mfr./sale industrial drying agglomeration equipment, consulting, industrial testing facilities. Food and dairy division.*
Tel: (715) 386-9371
Fax: (715) 386-9376
%FO: 100
Emp: 220

● **NOVO NORDISK A/S**
Novo Alle, DK-2880 Bagsvaerd, Denmark
CEO: Lars Rebien Sorensen, Pres. & CEO
Bus: *Pharmaceuticals company: leader in diabetes care, mfr./markets pharmaceutical products.*
Tel: 45-44-44-8888
Fax: 45-44-49-0555
www.novonordisk.com
Rev: $5,327
Emp: 20,285

NAICS: 325411, 325412, 334510

NOVO NORDISK , INC.
100 College Rd. West, Princeton, New Jersey 08540
CEO: Martin Soeters, Pres.　　　　　　　　　Tel:　(609) 987-5800　　　%FO: 100
Bus: *Pharmaceutical sales.*　　　　　　　　　Fax:　(609) 921-8082　　　Emp: 390

NOVO NORDISK PHARMACEUTICAL IND., INC.
3612 Powhatan Rd., Clayton, North Carolina 27520
CEO: John R. Pratt, VP　　　　　　　　　　　Tel:　(919) 550-2200　　　%FO: 100
Bus: *Mfr./sales pharmaceuticals.*　　　　　　Fax:　(919) 553-4057　　　Emp: 329

ZYMOGENETICS INC.
1201 East Lake Ave. East, Seattle, Washington 98102
CEO: Bruce L.A. Carter, Chmn. & Pres. & CEO　Tel:　(206) 442-6600　　　%FO: 100
Bus: *Biotechnology research and development.*　Fax:　(206) 442-6608　　　Emp: 410

● **OLICOM A/S**
Kongevejen 239, DK-2830 Virum, Denmark
CEO: Boji Rinhart, Pres. & CEO　　　　　　　Tel:　45-45-27-0000　　　Rev: $207
Bus: *Complete networking services.*　　　　　Fax:　45-45-27-0101　　　Emp: 750
　　　　　　　　　　　　　　　　　　　　　www.olicom.dk

NAICS:　541512

　　OLICOM USA INC.
　　740 E. Campbell Rd., Ste. 900, Richardson, Texas 75081
　　CEO: Max Jensen, Pres.　　　　　　　　　Tel:　(972) 301-4688　　　%FO: 100
　　Bus: *Complete networking solutions.*　　　Fax:　(972) 302-4689　　　Emp: 80

● **ORTOFON DK**
Telegrafvej 5, DK-2750 Ballerup, Denmark
CEO: Benny Nielsen, Pres.　　　　　　　　　Tel:　45-44-68-1033
Bus: *Mfr. phonograph cartridges.*　　　　　　Fax:　45-44-68-0970　　　Emp: 100
　　　　　　　　　　　　　　　　　　　　　www.ortofon.dk

NAICS:　334510

　　ORTOFON INC.
　　1363-42 Veterans Highway, Hauppauge, New York 11788
　　CEO: Russell Brown, VP　　　　　　　　　Tel:　(631) 979-5828　　　%FO: 100
　　Bus: *Phonograph cartridges.*　　　　　　　Fax:　(631) 979-5920

● **PHASE ONE DENMARK A/S**
Roskildevej 39, DK-2000 Frederiksberg, Denmark
CEO: Pernille Reddik, CEO　　　　　　　　　Tel:　45-36-46-0111
Bus: *Mfr. direct digital imaging camera equipment.*　Fax:　45-36-46-0222
　　　　　　　　　　　　　　　　　　　　　www.phaseone.com

NAICS:　334119

　　PHASE ONE INC.
　　200 Broadhollow Rd., Ste. 12, Melville, New York 11747
　　CEO: Stephen Kiernan, Pres.　　　　　　　Tel:　(516) 547-8900　　　%FO: 100
　　Bus: *Sales and service direct digital imaging*　Fax:　(516) 547-9898　　　Emp: 18
　　　　　camera equipment.

- **RADIOMETER A/S**
  Akandevej 21, Bronshoj, DK-2700 Copenhagen, Denmark
  CEO: Peter Kurstein, Pres. & CEO
  Bus: *Electronic instruments for science, medicine and industry.*
  NAICS: 332212, 334512, 334513, 334515, 335313

  Tel: 45-38-273827
  Fax: 45-38-272727
  www.radiometer.com

  Rev: $225
  Emp: 1,680

  ### RADIOMETER AMERICA INC.
  810 Sharon Dr., Ste. 1, Westlake, Ohio 44145
  CEO: Russell Christian, Pres.
  Bus: *Mfr./sale electronic instruments for science, medicine & industry.*

  Tel: (440) 871-8900
  Fax: (440) 871-8117

  %FO: 100
  Emp: 193

- **SCAN SHIPPING SERVICES LIMITED**
  18-50 Snorresgade, DK-2300 Copenhagen, Denmark
  CEO: A. Simonsen, Chmn.
  Bus: *International shipping and transport.*
  NAICS: 488510

  Tel: 45-32-66-8100
  Fax: 45-32-57-4900
  www.scan-group.com

  Emp: 420

  ### SCAN HOUSE - SHIPCO TRANSPORT
  80 Washington St., Hoboken, New Jersey 07030
  CEO: Klaus Jepsen, Pres.
  Bus: *International shipping and transport.*

  Tel: (201) 216-1500
  Fax: (201) 216-9550

  %FO: 100
  Emp: 250

  ### SHIPCO TRANSPORT
  770 Atlanta S. Pkwy, Ste. C, Atlanta, Georgia 30349
  CEO: Thomas Olsen
  Bus: *International shipping and transport.*

  Tel: (404) 767-0246
  Fax: (404) 767-0534

  %FO: 100

  ### SHIPCO TRANSPORT
  20 Pulaski St., Bayonne, New Jersey 07002
  CEO: Christine Barahona
  Bus: *International shipping and transport.*

  Tel: (201) 356-3500
  Fax: (201) 356-3550

  %FO: 100

  ### SHIPCO TRANSPORT
  101 W. Walnut St., Gardena, California 90248
  CEO: Glen Thompson
  Bus: *International shipping and transport.*

  Tel: (310) 538-0888
  Fax: (310) 538-0787

  %FO: 100

  ### SHIPCO TRANSPORT
  925 W. Thorndale Ave,, Itasca, Illinois 60143
  CEO: Jacob Bluhme
  Bus: *International shipping and transport.*

  Tel: (630) 616-9100
  Fax: (630) 616-9105

  %FO: 100

  ### SHIPCO TRANSPORT
  501 S. Airport Blvd., Ste. 212, S. San Francisco, California 94080
  CEO: Klaus Jepsen
  Bus: *International shipping and transport.*

  Tel: (650) 588-0363
  Fax: (650) 588-0364

  %FO: 100

  ### SHIPCO TRANSPORT
  14900 Interurban Ave. S, Ste. 215, Tukwila, Washington 98168
  CEO: Klaus Jepsen
  Bus: *International shipping and transport.*

  Tel: (206) 444-7447
  Fax: (206) 444-5329

  %FO: 100

SHIPCO TRANSPORT
2430 Mall Dr., Ste. 200, N. Charleston, North Carolina 29406
CEO: Joyce A. Hansen   Tel: (843) 744-8336   %FO: 100
Bus: *International shipping and transport.*   Fax: (843) 744-5226

SHIPCO TRANSPORT
10255 NW 116th Way, Ste. 3, Medley, Florida 33178
CEO: Jesper Hvidberg   Tel: (305) 591-3900   %FO: 100
Bus: *International shipping and transport.*   Fax: (305) 863-1802

SHIPCO TRANSPORT
1235 North Loop West., Houston, Texas 77008
CEO: Klaus Jepsen   Tel: (713) 861-2100   %FO: 100
Bus: *International shipping and transport.*   Fax: (713) 861-0055

● **SOPHUS BERENDSEN A/S**
Islands Brygge 57, DK-2300 Copenhagen, Denmark
CEO: Chister Strom, CEO   Tel: 45-39-53-8500
Bus: *Provides healthcare, pest control, laundry &*   Fax: 45-39-53-8585
     textile services; distribution, industrial parts;   www.berendsen.com
     hydraulics/electronics.
NAICS: 313111, 333292, 424310, 523991, 523999, 561790, 812310

     BERENDSEN INC.
     401 S. Boston Ave., Tulsa, Oklahoma 74103
     CEO: Tom Froberg, Pres.   Tel: (918) 592-3781   %FO: 100
     Bus: *Distribution, industrial parts;*   Fax: Emp: 800
       hydraulics/electronics.

● **TACONIC**
Bomholtvej 10, Box 1079, DK-8680 Ry, Denmark
CEO: Samuel Phelan, CEO   Tel: 45-70-23-0405
Bus: *Biotechnology.*   Fax: 45-86-84-1699
       www.taconic.com
NAICS: 112990

     TACONIC ANMED
     7676 Standish Place, Rockville, Maryland 20855
     CEO: Steven Weisbroth, Pres.   Tel: (301) 762-0366   %FO: 100
     Bus: *Laboratory animal health and*   Fax: (301) 762-7438
       biopharmaceutical product safety.

     TACONIC BIOTECHNOLOGY
     1 University Place, Rensselaer, New York 12144
     CEO: Ron Bussian   Tel: (518) 257-2030   %FO: 100
     Bus: *Laboratory animal health and*   Fax: (518) 257-2031
       biopharmaceutical product safety.

     TACONIC FARMS INC.
     273 Hover Ave., Germantown, New York 12526
     CEO: Todd Little, Pres.   Tel: (518) 537-6208   %FO: 100
     Bus: *Breeding facility.*   Fax: (518) 537-3316

TACONIC FARMS INC.
3100 Camino Del Sol, Oxnard, California 93030
CEO: John Mussmacher   Tel: (805) 981-2884   %FO: 100
Bus: *Biotechnology.*   Fax: (805) 981-2893

TACONIC FARMS INC.
One Hudson City Centre, Hudson, New York 12534
CEO: Eric Arlund   Tel: (518) 426-3269   %FO: 100
Bus: *Biotechnology.*   Fax: (518) 537-7287

● **TDC A/S**
Norregade 21, DK-0900 Copenhagen C, Denmark
CEO: Henning Dyremose, Pres. & CEO   Tel: 45-33-43-7777   Rev: $8,220
Bus: *Provider of telecommunications services.*   Fax: 45-33-43-7678   Emp: 20,573
                                         www.tdc.dk
NAICS: 511140, 515210, 517110, 517211, 517212, 517510, 517910, 518111, 518210, 519190, 541219, 561499

TDC CARRIER SERVICES, INC.
111 Pavonia Ave., Ste. 901, Jersey City, New Jersey 07310
CEO: Datson Vogel, Pres.   Tel: (201) 795-7262   %FO: 100
Bus: *Telecommunications and data*   Fax: (201) 222-0150   Emp: 6
communications services.

● **THOLSTRUP CHEESE A/S**
Halskestr. 9, DK-40880 Ratingen, Denmark
CEO: Finn Schioett Hansen, CEO   Tel: 45-7556-2822
Bus: *Mfr. cheese and dairy products.*   Fax: 45-7556-2822
                                         www.sagacheese.com
NAICS: 311513

THOLSTRUP DAIRIES INC.
6366 Norton Center Dr., Muskegon, Michigan 49441
CEO: Fin Hansen, Mgr.   Tel: (231) 798-4371   %FO: 100
Bus: *Sales/distribution of cheese and dairy*   Fax: (231) 798-4371
products.

● **TYTEX A/S**
Industrivej 21, Ringkobing, DK-7430 Ikast, Denmark
CEO: Peter Aggersbjerg, Pres. & CEO   Tel: 45-96-60-4200   Rev: $44
Bus: *Mfr. medical textile products.*   Fax: 45-96-60-4201   Emp: 150
                                         www.tytex.dk
NAICS: 313312, 424490

TYTEX, INC.
601 Park East Dr., Highland Corporate Park, Woonsocket, Rhode Island 02895
CEO: David Gaspar, Mgr.   Tel: (401) 762-4100   %FO: 100
Bus: *Mfr./sale textiles.*   Fax: (401) 762-4262

• **UNIBANK A/S**
Torvegade 2, DK-1256 Copenhagen, Denmark
CEO: Knud Sorensen, Chmn.   Tel: 45-33-33-3333
Bus: *Commercial banking services.*   Fax: 45-33-33-6262
                                             www.unibank.dk
NAICS: 522110

    UNIBANK A/S - NEW YORK BRANCH
    701 Brickell Ave., Ste. 1700, Miami, Florida 33131
    CEO: Joseph M. Guerra   Tel: (305) 577-6000   %FO: 100
    Bus: *International banking services.*   Fax: (305) 577-6083

• **VESTAS WIND SYSTEMS A/S**
Alsvej 21, DK-8900 Randers, Denmark
CEO: Svend Sigaard, Pres. & CEO   Tel: 45-97-30000   Rev: $2,074
Bus: *Mfr. install, maintain wind turbines and wind*   Fax: 45-97-300001   Emp: 6,394
    turbine projects.   www.vestas.com
NAICS: 335311, 335312, 335999

    VESTAS-AMERICAN WIND
    2850 W. Golf Rd., Ste. 405, Rolling Meadows, Illinois 60008
    CEO: Tom Carbone   Tel: (847) 806-9500
    Bus: *Mfr. turbines & turbine generator sets*   Fax: (847) 806-9100

    VESTAS-AMERICAN WIND TECHNOLOGY, INC.
    111 SW Columbia St., Ste. 480, Portland, Oregon 97201
    CEO: Henrik Norremark, Pres.   Tel: (503) 327-2000   %FO: 100
    Bus: *Mfr./sales of wind turbines*   Fax: (503) 327-2001   Emp: 248

• **VIKING LIFE-SAVING EQUIPMENT A/S**
Saedding Ringvej 13, DK-6710 Esbjerg V, Denmark
CEO: Kjeld Amann, Mng. Dir.   Tel: 45-76-11-8100   Rev: $118
Bus: *Life rafts, escape systems, survival and*   Fax: 45-79-11-8101   Emp: 301
    protection suits, mob rescue boats.   www.viking-life.com
NAICS: 424320, 448190, 561990

    VIKING LIFE-SAVING EQUIPMENT
    (AMERICA) INC.
    1400 NW 159 St., Ste. 101, Miami, Florida 33169
    CEO: Jens O Bjerre-Madsen, Pres.   Tel: (305) 314-5800   %FO: 100
    Bus: *Life rafts, marine escape systems, survival*   Fax: (305) 614-5810   Emp: 23
    a protection suits, water-activated lights,
    thermal protective aides.

Dominican Republic

● **TRICOM, S.A.**
Avenida Lope de Vega 95, Ensanche Naco, Santo Domingo, Dominican Republic
CEO: Hector Castro Noboa, Pres.   Tel: 809-476-4997   Rev: $207
Bus: *Basic and long-distance telephone, cellular and*   Fax: 809-476-4412   Emp: 1,469
     paging services and telecommunications systems   www.tricom.net
     and equipment.
NAICS: 517110, 517212

   TRICOM USA
   One Exchange Place, Ste. 400, Jersey City, New Jersey 07302
   CEO: Hank Perea, Pres.   Tel: (201) 324-0078   %FO: 100
   Bus: *Sales of long-distance telephone, cellular*   Fax: (201) 324-0688
        and paging services and
        telecommunications systems and equipment.

Egypt

- **EGYPTAIR**
Cairo International Airport, Airport Rd., Cairo, Egypt
CEO: Sherif Galal, Chmn. & CEO   Tel: 20-2-267-4700
Bus: *International commercial air transport services.*   Fax: 20-2-267-4555   Emp: 3,000
      www.egyptair.com.eg
NAICS: 481111

    EGYPTAIR
    PO Box 660, Elmhurst, Illinois 60126
    CEO: Tel: (630) 832-4141   %FO: 100
    Bus: *Commercial air transport services.*   Fax: (630) 832-9292

    EGYPTAIR
    9841 Airport Blvd., Los Angeles, California 90045
    CEO: Hassan Solomon   Tel: (310) 215-3900   %FO: 100
    Bus: *Commercial air transport services.*   Fax: (310) 215-9574

    EGYPTAIR
    720 Fifth Ave., New York, New York 10019
    CEO: Hisham Nabih, VP   Tel: (212) 581-5600   %FO: 100
    Bus: *Commercial air transport services.*   Fax: (212) 586-6599

    EGYPTAIR CARGO
    159-11 Rockaway Blvd., Jamaica, New York 11434
    CEO: Samir El Shanawany, Mgr.   Tel: (718) 656-8627   %FO: 100
    Bus: *Commercial air transport services.*   Fax: (718) 949-6410

El Salvador

● **GRUPO TACA**
Paseo General Escalon y 71 Avenida, Norte, Centro Comercial Galerias, Local 21, San Salvador, El Salvador
CEO: Roberto Kriete, Chmn. & CEO   Tel: 503-298-1560   Rev: $700
Bus: *Provides airline passenger and cargo services.*   Fax: 503-298-3064   Emp: 6,500
                                          www.taca.com
NAICS: 481111, 481112, 481212

GRUPO TACA
6824 Veterans Blvd., Metairie, Louisiana 70003
CEO: Peter Massina, Mgr.   Tel: (504) 887-7671   %FO: 100
Bus: *Airline passenger and cargo services.*   Fax:

GRUPO TACA
7795 West Flagler St., Ste. 45, Mall of the Americas, Miami, Florida 33144
CEO: Jim Eberthart, Mgr.   Tel: (800) 400-8222   %FO: 100
Bus: *Airline passenger and cargo services.*   Fax:

GRUPO TACA
25 West 45th St., Ste. 503, New York, New York 10036
CEO: Harazio Rodriguez, Mgr.   Tel: (212) 997-3398   %FO: 100
Bus: *Airline passenger and cargo services.*   Fax:

GRUPO TACA
6710 Van Nuys Blvd., Van Nuys, California 91405
CEO: Tel: (818) 988-0022   %FO: 100
Bus: *Airline passenger and cargo services.*   Fax:

GRUPO TACA
1776 G St., Ste. 103, Washington, District of Columbia 20006
CEO: Gloria Granillo, Mgr.   Tel: (202) 833-2076   %FO: 100
Bus: *Airline passenger and cargo services.*   Fax:

GRUPO TACA
3600 Wilshire Blvd., Ste.100, Los Angeles, California 90010
CEO: Mauel Jaquet, Mgr.   Tel: (213) 385-9424   %FO: 100
Bus: *Airline passenger and cargo services.*   Fax:

GRUPO TACA
5601A Bellaire Blvd., Houston, Texas 77057
CEO: Feberico Bloch, Pres.   Tel: (800) 400-8222   %FO: 100
Bus: *Airline passenger and cargo services.*   Fax:

GRUPO TACA
139 Meridian St., East Boston, Massachusetts 02128
CEO: Tel: (800) 400-8222   %FO: 100
Bus: *Airline passenger and cargo services.*   Fax:

El Salvador

GRUPO TACA
3338 17th St., Ste.100A, San Francisco, California 94110
CEO: Phil Kline   Tel: (415) 252-0130   %FO: 100
Bus: *Airline passenger and cargo services.*   Fax:

England, U.K.

- **3i GROUP PLC**
  91 Waterloo Rd., London SE1 8XP, England, U.K.
  CEO: Philip Yea, CEO
  Bus: *International venture capital investments and buyouts.*
  NAICS: 523991

  Tel: 44-207-928-3131
  Fax: 44-207-928-0058
  www.3i.com

  Rev: $480
  Emp: 750

  3i CORPORATION
  275 Middlefield Rd., Menlo Park, California 94025
  CEO: Katja Gehrt
  Bus: *Business Internet and telecommunications.*

  Tel: (650) 843-3131
  Fax: (650) 470-3201

  %FO: 100

  3i CORPORATION
  880 Winter St., Ste. 330, Waltham, Massachusetts 02451
  CEO: Allan Ferguson
  Bus: *Business Internet and telecommunications.*

  Tel: (781) 890-8300
  Fax: (781) 890-8301

  %FO: 100

- **4IMPRINT GROUP PLC**
  Park 17, Moss Ln., Whitefield, Manchester M45 8FJ, England, U.K.
  CEO: Ken Minton, CEO
  Bus: *Sources and sells printed, promotional merchandise through direct marketing, partner services and corporate and premium promotions.*
  NAICS: 541613

  Tel: 44-161-272-4000
  Fax: 44-161-272-4001
  www.uk2.4imprint.com

  Rev: $180
  Emp: 663

  4IMPRINT INC.
  101 Commerce St., Oshkosh, Wisconsin 54901
  CEO: John Lord
  Bus: *Printed, promotional merchandise.*

  Tel: (920) 236-7272
  Fax: (920) 236-7282

  %FO: 100

- **THE 600 GROUP PLC**
  600 House, Landmark Court, Revie Rd., Leeds LS11 8JT, England, U.K.
  CEO: Andrew James Dick, Mng. Dir.
  Bus: *Machine tools, machine tool accessories, lasers and engineering products manufacturing.*
  NAICS: 333512, 333513

  Tel: 44-113-277-6100
  Fax: 44-113-276-5600
  www.the600group.com

  Rev: $121
  Emp: 644

  CLAUSING INDUSTRIAL INC.
  811 Eisenhower Dr. South, Goshen, Indiana 46526
  CEO: Tracy Dwight
  Bus: *Service center.*

  Tel: (574) 533-0371
  Fax: (574) 533-0403

  %FO: 100
  Emp: 100

  CLAUSING INDUSTRIAL INC.
  1819 North Pitcher St., Kalamazoo, Michigan 49007
  CEO: Dennis Pepper, Sales
  Bus: *Mfr. industrial machinery, drills and equipment.*

  Tel: (269) 345-7155
  Fax: (269) 345-5945

  %FO: 100
  Emp: 100

- **A&G GROUP**
8 Grafton St., London W1S 4EL, England, U.K.
CEO: Gianluca Brozzetti, CEO
Bus: *Accessories, clothing, jewelry, leather, and silver goods manufacture and sales.*
NAICS: 334518, 339911, 339913, 442299

Tel: 44-870-905-0767
Fax: 44-870-905-0768
www.a-ggroup.com

    A&G GROUP USA INC.
    725 Fifth Ave., New York, New York 10022
    CEO: Robert Donofrio, CEO
    Bus: *Mfr. jewelry.*

    Tel: (212) 688-1811
    Fax: (212) 826-3746

    %FO: 100

- **ABBEY NATIONAL PLC, SUB. SCH**
2 Triton Square, Regent's Place, London NW1 3AN, England, U.K.
CEO: Francisco Gomez-Roldan, CEO
Bus: *Retail banking services.*

Tel: 44-870-607-6000
Fax: 44-207-486-2764
www.abbeynational.com

Rev: $12,973
Emp: 27,725

NAICS: 523110

    ABBEY NATIONAL TREASURY SERVICES PLC
    400 Atlantic St., Ste. 200, Stamford, Connecticut 06901
    CEO: Robert Ferrari
    Bus: *Retail banking services.*

    Tel: (203) 355-7900
    Fax: (203) 355-8072

    %FO: 100

- **ABINGWORTH MANAGEMENT LTD.**
38 Jermyn St., London SW1Y 6DN, England, U.K.
CEO: Stephen Bunting, Mng. Dir.
Bus: *Venture capital services, specializing in the biotechnology and medical fields.*
NAICS: 523910

Tel: 44-207-534-1500
Fax: 44-207-287-0480
www.abingworth.com

Rev: $9
Emp: 15

    ABINGWORTH MANAGEMENT INC.
    2465 East Bayshore Rd., Ste. 348, Palo Alto, California 94303
    CEO: Jonathan MacQuitty
    Bus: *Venture capital services, specializing in the biotechnology and medical fields.*

    Tel: (650) 565-8299
    Fax: (650) 565-8295

    %FO: 100

- **ACAL PLC**
Acal House, 2 Chancellor Ct., Occam Rd., Guilford, Surrey GU2 7AH, England, U.K.
CEO: A. J. Laughton, CEO
Bus: *Electronic component distribution and support.*

Tel: 44-1483-544-500
Fax: 44-1483-544-550
www.acalplc.co.uk

Rev: $491
Emp: 1,037

NAICS: 423610, 423690

    ACAL FLORIDA
    5944 Coral Ridge Dr., Coral Springs, Florida 33076
    CEO: Mike Rivera, Sales Mgr.
    Bus: *Electronic component distribution and support.*

    Tel: (954) 345-8278
    Fax: (954) 255-6468

    %FO: 100

ACAL NEW YORK INC.
10 Cutter Mill Rd., Ste. 203, Great Neck, New York 11021
CEO: Helen Rosalia, Sales Mgr.   Tel: (516) 487-9870   %FO: 100
Bus: *Electronic component distribution and*   Fax: (516) 487-9342
support.

● **ACAMBIS PLC**
Peterhouse Technology Park, 100 Fulbourn Rd., Cambridge CB1 9PT, England, U.K.
CEO: Gordon Cameron, CEO   Tel: 44-122-327-5300   Rev: $163
Bus: *Biotechnology company discovering, developing*   Fax: 44-122-341-6300   Emp: 320
and manufacturing   www.acambis.com
novel vaccines.
NAICS: 541710

   ACAMBIS INC.
   38 Sidney St., Cambridge, Massachusetts 02139
   CEO: Gordon Cameron, Pres.   Tel: (617) 494-1339   %FO: 100
   Bus: *Development of oral and nasal vaccines.*   Fax: (617) 494-1741

● **ACTINIC SOFTWARE LTD.**
Locke King House, 2 Balfour Road, Weybridge Surrey KT13 8HD, England, U.K.
CEO: Christopher D. Barling, COO   Tel: 44-845-129-4888   Rev: $2
Bus: *E-commerce software manufacturer.*   Fax: 44-1932-871001   Emp: 21
                        www.actinic.co.uk
NAICS: 511210, 541511

   SURE SOLUTIONS INC.
   105 Curtis Place, Manasquan, New Jersey 08736
   CEO: Brian Johnson, Mgr.   Tel: (732) 528-7636   %FO: 100
   Bus: *Mfr. e-commerce software products.*   Fax: (732) 528-0951

● **ACTIX LTD.**
200, Hammersmith Rd., Hammersmith, London W6 7DL, England, U.K.
CEO: Robert W. A. Dobson, CEO   Tel: 44-20-8735-6300   Rev: $28
Bus: *Software manufacture.*   Fax: 44-20-8735-6301   Emp: 116
                        www.actix.com
NAICS: 511210

   ACTIX INC.
   1851 Alexander Bell Dr., Reston, Virginia 20191
   CEO: Desmond Owens   Tel: (703) 740-8900   %FO: 100
   Bus: *Software manufacture and sales.*   Fax: (703) 740-8908

● **ADEPTRA, LTD.**
Forbury Court, 12 Forbury Road, London SW1V 1JZ, England, U.K.
CEO: Phil Wilson, CEO   Tel: 44-118-938-7000
Bus: *Customer relationship management technology.*   Fax: 44-118-938-7022   Emp: 50
                        www.adeptra.co.uk
NAICS: 541511

ADEPTRA INC.
383 Main Ave.. 4/F, Norwalk, Connecticut 06851
CEO: Vytas Kisielius, Sales
Bus: *Engaged in customer relationship management technology.*

Tel: (203) 956-2600
Fax: (203) 355-2300

%FO: 100

● **ADVANCED COMPOSITES GROUP LTD.**
Composites House, Sinclair Close, Heanor Gate Industrial Estate, Derbyshire DE75 7SP, England, U.K.
CEO: Alan Brian Moore, CEO
Bus: *Composite materials manufacture.*

Tel: 44-1773-766-200
Fax: 44-1773-530-245
www.advanced-composites.com

NAICS: 326199, 327993, 336415

    ADVANCED COMPOSITES GROUP
    5350 S. 129th East Ave., Tulsa, Oklahoma 74134
    CEO: Steve Larby, Sales
    Bus: *Composite materials manufacture and sales.*

    Tel: (918) 252-3922
    Fax: (918) 252-7371

    %FO: 100

● **AEA TECHNOLOGY PLC**
329 Harwell, Didcot Oxfordshire OX11 ORA, England, U.K.
CEO: Andrew McCree, CEO
Bus: *Creates industrial plants and provides waste management.*

Tel: 44-1235-521840
Fax: 44-1235-432916
www.aeat.co.uk

Rev: $459
Emp: 3,035

NAICS: 924110

    AEA TECHNOLOGY ENGINEERING SERVICES, INC.
    1100 Jardin Ave., Ste. 350, Richland, Washington 99352
    CEO: Katie Klute
    Bus: *Creates industrial plants and provides waste management.*

    Tel: (509) 946-5854
    Fax: (509) 946-5856

    %FO: 100

    AEA TECHNOLOGY ENGINEERING SERVICES, INC.
    1301 Moran Rd., Ste. 202, Herndon, Virginia 20170
    CEO: Laurie Judd
    Bus: *Creates industrial plants and provides waste management.*

    Tel: (703) 433-0720
    Fax: (703) 433-9745

    %FO: 100

    AEA TECHNOLOGY ENGINEERING SERVICES, INC.
    241 Curry Hollow Rd., Pittsburgh, Pennsylvania 15236-4696
    CEO: Van B. Walker
    Bus: *Creates industrial plants and provides waste management.*

    Tel: (412) 655-1200
    Fax: (412) 655-2928

    %FO: 100

    AEA TECHNOLOGY ENGINEERING SERVICES, INC.
    184 B Rolling Hill Rd., Mooresville, North Carolina 28117
    CEO: Robert Mullens
    Bus: *Creates industrial plants and provides waste management.*

    Tel: (704) 799-2708
    Fax: (704) 799-6426

    %FO: 100

    AEA TECHNOLOGY ENGINEERING SOFTWARE, INC.
    4960 Robert Mathews Pkwy., Ste. B, El Dorado Hills, California 95762
    CEO: Dan White
    Bus: *Creates industrial plants and provides waste management.*

    Tel: (916) 939-0246
    Fax: (916) 939-0342

    %FO: 100

AEA TECHNOLOGY QSA, INC.
6765 Langley Dr., Baton Rouge, Louisiana 70809
CEO: Curt Auzenne
Bus: *Creates industrial plants and provides
waste management.*

Tel: (225) 751-5893
Fax: (225) 756-0365

%FO: 100

AEA TECHNOLOGY QSA, INC.
40 North Ave., Burlington, Massachusetts 01803
CEO: Hank Kaczowka
Bus: *Creates industrial plants and provides
waste management.*

Tel: (781) 505-8250
Fax: (781) 229-2279

%FO: 100

● AEGIS GROUP PLC
43-45 Portman Square, London W1H 6LY, England, U.K.
CEO: Robert E. Lerwill, CEO
Bus: *Media buying and planning services.*

Tel: 44-207-070-7700
Fax: 44-207-070-7800
www.aegisplc.com

Rev: $1,154
Emp: 8,538

NAICS: 541613, 541830, 541910

CARAT INTERACTIVE
360 Newbury St., Boston, Massachusetts 02115
CEO: Toby Gabriner, Pres.
Bus: *Engaged in media buying and planning
services.*

Tel: (617) 449-4100
Fax: (617) 449-4200

%FO: 100
Emp: 271

MMA/ CARAT INC.
15 River Rd., Ste. 101, Wilson, Connecticut 06897
CEO: Randy Stone, CEO
Bus: *Management consulting*

Tel: (203) 834-3300
Fax: (203) 834-3333

Emp: 10

SYNOVATE NORTH AMERICA
222 S. Riverside, Chicago, Illinois 60606
CEO: Robert Philpott, CEO
Bus: *Commercial nonphysical research*

Tel: (312) 526-4530
Fax: (312) 526-4099

%FO: 100
Emp: 1,500

VELOCITY SPORT & ENTERTAINMENT
10 Westport Rd., Wilson, Connecticut 06897
CEO: Michelle Berg, VP
Bus: *Marketing & Public Relations*

Tel: (203) 571-5500
Fax: (203) 571-5501

Emp: 90

● AEROSYSTEMS INTERNATIONAL LTD.
Enigma Park, Grovewood Rd., Malvern, Worcestershire WR142GD, England, U.K.
CEO: Scott Roy, CEO
Bus: *Design and manufacture of software-intensive
systems for the defense industry.*

Tel: 44-1684-858-700
Fax: 44-1684-858-700
www.aeroint.com

Rev: $93
Emp: 341

NAICS: 336414, 511210, 927110

AEROSYSTEMS INTERNATIONAL INC.
13501 Ingenuity Dr., Ste. 204, Orlando, Florida 32826
CEO: Emma Taylor
Bus: *Software systems manufacture.*

Tel: (407) 381-0329
Fax: (407) 381-0329

%FO: 100

- **AGA FOODSERVICE GROUP PLC**
  4 Arleston Way, Shirley Solihull, West Midlands B90 4LH, England, U.K.
  CEO: William B. McGrath, CEO   Tel: 44-121-711-6000   Rev: $698
  Bus: *Food service equipment and commercial kitchen*   Fax: 44-121-711-6001   Emp: 4,745
        equipment manufacture.   www.agafoodservice.co
  NAICS: 238290

        HARRINGTON INDUSTRIAL PLASTICS INC.
        14480 Yorba Ave., Chino, California 91710
        CEO: William McCollum   Tel: (909) 597-8641   %FO: 100
        Bus: *Food service equipment and commercial*   Fax: (909) 597-9826
             kitchen equipment manufacture.

- **AGGREGATE INDUSTRIES, PLC**
  Bardon Hall, Copt Oak Rd., Markfield, Leicestershire LE67 9PJ, England, U.K.
  CEO: Peter Tom, Pres. & CEO   Tel: 44-153-081-6600   Rev: $2,593
  Bus: *Aggregates, paving contracting and soil*   Fax: 44-153-081-6666   Emp: 8,545
        remediation services.   www.aggregate.com
  NAICS: 115112, 327992

        AGGREGATE INDUSTRIES MANAGEMENT, INC.
        13900 Piney Meetinghouse Rd., Rockville, Maryland 20850
        CEO: Michael Hayes   Tel: (301) 284-3600   %FO: 100
        Bus: *Building materials sales and distribution.*   Fax: (301) 284-3645

        AGGREGATE INDUSTRIES, INC.
        1700 Egbert Ave.
        CEO: 1707 Latta St., Goshen, Indiana 46528   Scott Stine, Mgr.   Tel: (574) 533-0415

        Bus: *Building materials sales and distribution.*   Fax: (574) 534-4528

        AGGREGATE INDUSTRIES, INC.
        1715 Broadway, Saugus, Massachusetts 01906
        CEO: David Tidmarsh, Mgr.   Tel: (781) 941-7200   %FO: 100
        Bus: *Building materials sales and distribution.*   Fax: (781) 341-2440   Emp: 500

        AGGREGATE INDUSTRIES, INC.
        8075 Creekside Dr., Ste. 200, Kalamazoo, Michigan 49024
        CEO: Brent Cook, Pres.   Tel: (616) 236-9640   %FO: 100
        Bus: *Building materials sales and distribution.*   Fax: (616) 321-3838   Emp: 100

- **AIM GROUP PLC**
  16 Carlton Crescent, Southampton, Hampshire SO15 2ES, England, U.K.
  CEO: Jeffrey C. Smith, Chmn. & CEO   Tel: 44-2380-335-111   Rev: $88
  Bus: *Aircraft interior components and equipment*   Fax: 44-2380-229-733   Emp: 725
        manufacture.   www.aimaviation.com
  NAICS: 336413

        AIM AVIATION INC.
        705 Southwest Seventh Ave., Renton, Washington 98055
        CEO: Mark Ptensky, Pres.   Tel: (425) 235-2750   %FO: 100
        Bus: *Sales/distribution of aircraft interiors,*   Fax: (425) 228-0761   Emp: 150
             assemblies & parts.

● **AIR PARTNER PLC**
Platinum House, Gatwick Rd., Crawley, West Sussex RH 10 2RP, England, U.K.
CEO: David C. W. Savile, Chmn.   Tel: 44-1293-549-555   Rev: $183
Bus: *Corporate aircraft charters.*   Fax: 44-1293-539-263   Emp: 112
                                         www.airpartner.com
  NAICS: 481211

  AIR PARTNER INC.
  1100 Lee Wagener Blvd., Ste. 326, Ft. Lauderdale, Florida 33315
  CEO: David Savile   Tel: (954) 359-4300   %FO: 100
  Bus: *Corporate aircraft charters.*   Fax: (954) 359-3930

  AIR PARTNER INC.
  1 Rockefeller Plaza, Ste. 1424, New York, New York 10020
  CEO: Jo Jeffs, Pres.   Tel: (212) 252-1002   %FO: 100
  Bus: *Corporate aircraft charters.*   Fax: (212) 792-4191

  AIR PARTNER USA INC.
  1101 30th St. NW, Ste. 500, Washington, District of Columbia 20007
  CEO: Sue Hazord   Tel: (202) 625-6600   %FO: 100
  Bus: *Corporate aircraft charters.*   Fax: (202) 625-6600

● **AIRCLAIMS LTD.**
Cardinal Point, Newell Road Heathrow Airport, London TW 6 2AS, England, U.K.
CEO: Derek Hammond Giles, Mng. Dir.   Tel: 44-208-897-1066
Bus: *Information and aviation loss adjusting services.*   Fax: 44-208-897-0300
                                         www.airclaims.co.uk
  NAICS.   524291, 541990

  AIRCLAIMS, INC.
  3000 C Airway Ave., Ste. 150, Costa Mesa, California 92626
  CEO: Rob Grundy, Mgr.   Tel: (714) 437-3103   %FO: 100
  Bus: *Aviation claims/loss adjustments.*   Fax: (714) 437-3132

  AIRCLAIMS, INC.
  7270 Northwest 12th St., Ste. 800, Miami, Florida 33126
  CEO: Kenneth Forsyth, Mgr.   Tel: (305) 597-5666   %FO: 100
  Bus: *Aviation claims/loss adjustments.*   Fax: (305) 639-2555

  AIRCLAIMS, INC.
  PO Box 45153, Seattle, Washington 98451
  CEO: Bill Garcia, Mgr.   Tel: (206) 528-7400   %FO: 100
  Bus: *Aviation claims/loss adjustments.*   Fax: (206) 528-7500

● **AIT GROUP PLC**
Smith Centre, Fairmile, Henley-on-Thames, Oxfordshire RG9 6AB, England, U.K.
CEO: Nicholas J. S. Randall, CEO   Tel: 44-1491-416600
Bus: *CRM (customer relationship management)*   Fax: 44-1491-416600
     software manufacture.   www.aitgroup.com
  NAICS: 511210

AIT USA INC.
639 Research Pkwy., Ste. 100, Meriden, Connecticut 06450
CEO: Rob Chase
Bus: *CRM software manufacture and sales.*
Tel: (203) 630-1942
Fax: (203) 630-1942
%FO: 100

● **ALAN DICK & COMPANY LTD.**
The Barlands, London Rd., Cheltenham, Gloucestershire GL52 6UT, England, U.K.
CEO: Callum A. Dick, CEO
Bus: *Wireless telecommunications networks.*
Tel: 44-1242-518-500
Fax: 44-1242-510-191
www.alandick.co.uk
Emp: 2,800

NAICS: 334210, 334290, 334310

ALAN DICK & COMPANY
26 Town Forest, Webster, Massachusetts 01570
CEO: Brian Lancaster
Bus: *Wireless telecommunications.*
Tel: (508) 640-0032
Fax: (508) 640-0035
%FO: 100

● **ALFRED DUNHILL OF LONDON**
48 Jermyn St., London SW1Y 6DL, England, U.K.
CEO: Richard Dunhill, Chmn.
Bus: *Tobacconists and men's luxury goods, including leather products and accessories.*
Tel: 44-20-7290-8606
Fax: 44-20-7491-1489
www.alfreddunhill.net
NAICS: 312221, 316999, 453991

ALFRED DUNHILL OF LONDON
201 North Rodeo Dr., # B, Beverly Hills, California 90210
CEO: Todd Thoman
Bus: *Sales/distribution of tobacco and tobacco products, clothing, leather goods, and*
Tel: (310) 274-5351
Fax: (310) 274-5351
%FO: 100

ALFRED DUNHILL OF LONDON INC.
450 Park Ave., New York, New York 10022
CEO: Vincent Robin, Pres.
Bus: *Sales/distribution of tobacco and tobacco products, clothing, leather goods, and*
Tel: (212) 888-4000
Fax: (212) 750-8841
%FO: 100

● **ALFRED MC ALPINE PLC**
Kinnaird House, 1 Pall Mall East, London SW1Y 5AZ, England, U.K.
CEO: Ian M. Grice, CEO
Bus: *Construction, building and civil engineering.*
Tel: 44-207-930-6255
Fax: 44-207-839-6902
www.alfredmcalpineplc.com
Rev: $1,544
Emp: 7,794

NAICS: 236220, 237110, 237120, 237130, 237310, 237990

HILLTOP SLATE
PO Box 201, Rte. 22A, Middle Granville, New York 12804
CEO: David Thomas, Pres.
Bus: *Producers of natural slate*
Tel: (518) 642-2270
Fax: (518) 642-1220
%FO: 100
Emp: 30

- **ALLEN & OVERY**
  One New Change, London EC4M 9QQ, England, U.K.
  CEO: Guy Berringer, Sr. Prtn.   Tel: 44-207-330-3000
  Bus: *International law firm.*   Fax: 44-207-330-9999   Emp: 4,000
                                        www.allenovery.com
  NAICS: 541110

  ALLEN & OVERY
  1221 Ave. of the Americas, New York, New York 10020
  CEO: Ken Rivlin   Tel: (212) 610-6300   %FO: 100
  Bus: *International law firm.*   Fax: (212) 610-6399   Emp: 100

- **ALLIED DOMECQ PLC., DIV PERNOD RICARD**
  The Pavilions, Bridgwater Rd., Bedminster Down, Bristol BS13 8AR, England, U.K.
  CEO: Philip Bowman, CEO   Tel: 44-117-978-5000   Rev: $5,823
  Bus: *International spirits manufacturing and retailing* Fax: 44-117-978-5300   Emp: 11,685
       group: wine, spirits, frozen foods, desserts, tea www.allieddomecq.co.uk
       and coffee.
  NAICS: 311412, 311920, 312130, 312140

  ALLIED DOMECQ NORTH AMERICA CORP.
  355 Riverside Ave., Westport, Connecticut 06880
  CEO: Jim Clerkin, Pres. & CEO   Tel: (203) 221-5400   %FO: 100
  Bus: *Sales and marketing company for distilled* Fax: (203) 221-5444   Emp: 100
       spirits.

  ALLIED DOMECQ WINES USA
  375 Healdsburg Ave., 2/F, Healdsburg, California 95448-4137
  CEO: William A. Newlands Jr., Pres. Tel: (707) 433-8268   %FO: 100
  Bus: *Sales and marketing for wine products.* Fax: (707) 433-3538   Emp: 150

  DUNKIN' BRANDS, INC.
  130 Royall St., Canton, Massachusetts 02021
  CEO: Jon L. Luther, CEO   Tel: (781) 737-3000   %FO: 100
  Bus: *Specialty eateries.*   Fax: (781) 737-4000   Emp: 1,200

  MAKER'S MARK DISTILLERY, INC.
  6200 Dutchman's Lane, Ste. 103, Louisville, Kentucky 40205
  CEO: T. William Samuels, Pres.   Tel: (502) 459-7884   %FO: 100
  Bus: *Distillery of bourbon whiskey.* Fax: (502) 459-2026

- **ALI SERVE SYSTEMS LTD.**
  St. George's House, Knoll Rd., Camberloy, Surrey GU15 3SY, England, U.K.
  CEO: A. K. Sen, CEO   Tel: 44-870-850-0081
  Bus: *Software services.*   Fax: 44-870-850-0082
                                        www.allservesystems.com
  NAICS: 541511, 541512, 541513

  ALLSERVE SYSTEMS INC.
  204 n. Center Dr., Commerce Ctr., North Brunswick, New Jersey 08902
  CEO: Krishna Chari   Tel: (732) 297-9977   %FO: 100
  Bus: *Software services.*   Fax: (732) 297-9382

- **ALPHAMERIC PLC**
Bishopsgate House, Broadford Park, Shalford, Guildford, Surrey GU4 8ED, England, U.K.
CEO: Alan Morcombe, CEO   Tel: 44-1483-293-971   Rev: $96
Bus: *Software and hardware manufacture.*   Fax: 44-1483-293-977   Emp: 700
                                                www.alphameric.com
NAICS: 334111, 511210
    ALPHAMERIC
    4766 Park Granada, Ste. 112, Calabasas, California 91302
    CEO: Jillian Girard   Tel: (818) 223-0343   %FO: 100
    Bus: *Software and hardware manufacture and*   Fax: (818) 223-0249
         sales.

- **ALTERIAN PLC**
Century Place, Newfoundland Street, Bristol BS2 9AG, England, U.K.
CEO: David Justin Eldridge, CEO   Tel: 44-117-970-3200   Rev: $10
Bus: *Provides analytical software solutions.*   Fax: 44-117-970-3201   Emp: 68
                                                www.alterian.com
NAICS: 511210, 541511
    ALTERIAN, INC.
    One North LaSalle, Ste. 4300, Chicago, Illinois 60602
    CEO: Brett Kilpatrick   Tel: (312) 704-1700   %FO: 100
    Bus: *Provides analytical software solutions.*   Fax: (312) 704-1701

- **AMALGAMATED METAL CORPORATION PLC**
55 Bishopsgate, London EC2N 3AH, England, U.K.
CEO: V. H. Sher, CEO   Tel: 44-207-626-4521   Rev: $768
Bus: *Mfr./distribution and trading of metals, chemicals*   Fax: 44-207-623-6015   Emp: 1,600
     and building products.   www.amcgroup.com
NAICS: 325412, 325510, 331513, 332112
    AMALGAMATE INC.
    50 Main St., 12/F, White Plains, New York 10606
    CEO: C. J. Moreton, Gen. Mgr.   Tel: (914) 286-2300   %FO: 100
    Bus: *Sales of non-ferrous metals, commodity*   Fax: (914) 286-2330
         chemicals and essential oils.

- **AMARIN CORPORATION PLC**
7 Curzon St., London W1J 5HG, England, U.K.
CEO: Richard A. B. Stewart, CEO   Tel: 44-207-499-9009   Rev: $65
Bus: *Innovative pharmaceutical product development*   Fax: 44-207-499-9004   Emp: 84
     of proprietary topical & transdermal drug delivery   www.amarincorp.com
     technologies, improving established drugs.
NAICS: 325412
    AMARIN PHARMACEUTICALS
    25 Independence Boulevard, Warren, New Jersey 07059
    CEO: Eric Liebler, VP   Tel: (908) 580-5535   %FO: 100
    Bus: *Research and development and sale and*   Fax: (908) 580-9390
         marketing of pain management
         pharmaceuticals.

• **AMEC, PLC**
65 Carter Lane, London EC4V SHF, England, U.K.
CEO: Peter J. Mason, CEO
Bus: *Engineering and construction.*

Tel: 44-207-634-0000
Fax: 44-201-634-0001
www.amec.co.uk

Rev: $8,971
Emp: 43,660

NAICS: 237990, 541330

AMEC
6600 North Andrews Ave., Ste. 590, Ft. Lauderdale, Florida 33309
CEO: Carl Walters
Bus: *Engaged in engineering and construction.*
Tel: (954) 771-6677
Fax: (954) 771-6694
%FO: 100

AMEC
239 Littleton Rd., Ste. 1B, Westford, Massachusetts 01886
CEO: Elaine Moore, CEO
Bus: *Engaged in engineering and construction.*
Tel: (978) 692-9090
Fax: (978) 692-6633
%FO: 100

AMEC
1633 Broadway, 24/F, New York, New York 10019
CEO: Roland Ferrera, CEO
Bus: *Engaged in engineering and construction.*
Tel: (212) 484-0300
Fax: (212) 484-0580
%FO: 100

AMEC
311 California St., Ste. 200, San Francisco, California 94104
CEO: George Speights
Bus: *Engaged in engineering and construction.*
Tel: (415) 399-0905
Fax: (415) 399-0945
%FO: 100

AMEC
7101 Wisconsin Ave., Ste. 1403, Bethesda, Maryland 20814
CEO: Mack McGaughan, CEO
Bus: *Engaged in engineering and construction.*
Tel: (301) 657-3370
Fax: (301) 657-3075
%FO: 100

AMEC
125 South Wacker Dr., 2/F, Chicago, Illinois 60606
CEO: Muhammad Azim, CEO
Bus: *Engaged in engineering and construction.*
Tel: (312) 541-1600
Fax: (312) 541-1754
%FO: 100

AMEC
9800 West Kincey Ave., Ste. 190, Huntersville, North Carolina 28078
CEO: Helen Corley
Bus: *Earth and environmental services.*
Tel: (704) 875-3570
Fax: (704) 875-8718
%FO: 100

AMEC
1979 Lakeside Pkwy., Ste. 500, Tucker, Georgia 30084
CEO: Shannon Keal
Bus: *Earth and environmental services.*
Tel: (770) 688-2500
Fax: (770) 688-2501
%FO: 100

AMEC
1290 North Hancock St., Ste. 102, Anaheim, California 92807
CEO: Jeff Davies
Bus: *Earth and environmental services.*
Tel: (714) 779-2591
Fax: (714) 779-8377
%FO: 100

AMEC
8519 Jefferson NE, Albuquerque, New Mexico 87113
CEO: Mike Schulz   Tel: (505) 821-1801   %FO: 100
Bus: *Earth and environmental services.*   Fax: (505) 821-7371

AMEC
4455 Brookfield Corporate Dr., Ste. 100, Chantilly, Virginia 20151
CEO: Jake Bliek   Tel: (703) 448-3700   %FO: 100
Bus: *Engaged in engineering and construction.*   Fax: (703) 448-3701

AMEC
1401 I (Eye) St. NW, Ste. 1000, Washington, District of Columbia 20005
CEO: Lauren Gallagher   Tel: (202) 350-5700   %FO: 100
Bus: *Engaged in engineering and construction.*   Fax: (202) 350-5701

AMEC
3232 West Virginia Ave., Phoenix, Arizona 85009
CEO: Steve Myers   Tel: (602) 272-6848   %FO: 100
Bus: *Construction management.*   Fax: (602) 272-7239

AMEC
200 Lincoln St., 4/F, Boston, Massachusetts 02111
CEO: Joseph Bearak   Tel: (617) 695-2225   %FO: 100
Bus: *Construction management.*   Fax: (617) 695-2211

● **AMVESCAP PLC**
30 Finsbury Square, London EC2A 1AG, England, U.K.
CEO: Charles W. Brady, CEO   Tel: 44-207-638-0731   Rev: $2,221
Bus: *Institutional and retail investment advisory*   Fax: 44-207-065-3962   Emp: 7,069
services and mutual funds distribution.   www.amvescap.com
NAICS: 523110, 525910

   AIM MANAGEMENT GROUP, INC.
   11 Greenway Plaza, Ste. 100, Houston, Texas 77046
   CEO: Robert H. Graham, CEO   Tel: (713) 626-1919   %FO: 100
   Bus: *Institutional and retail investment advisory*   Fax: (713) 214-7565   Emp: 2,100
   services, mutual funds distribution.

   AMVESCAP USA INC.
   1315 Peachtree St., NE, Atlanta, Georgia 30309
   CEO: Bill Hensel, Dir.   Tel: (404) 479-2886   %FO: 100
   Bus: *Investment management services.*   Fax: (404) 479-1095

   INVESCO FUNDS GROUP, INC.
   3003 East 3rd Ave., Denver, Colorado 80206
   CEO: Ilene Despain, CEO   Tel: (303) 930-2700   %FO: 100
   Bus: *Asset management.*   Fax: (303) 930-2700

● **ANGLE TECHNOLOGY GROUP**
Surrey Technology Centre, Surrey Research Park, Guilford GU2 7YG, England, U.K.
CEO: Andrew Newland, CEO   Tel: 44-1483-295-830
Bus: *Management consultant services.*   Fax: 44-1483-295-836
                                     www.angletechnology.com
NAICS: 213114, 541611

ANGLE TECHNOLOGY INC.
2214 Rock Hill Rd., Herndon, Virginia 20170
CEO: Gary P. Evans
Bus: *Management consulting services.*

Tel: (703) 326-9185
Fax: (703) 326-9185

%FO: 100

● **APATECH LTD.**
327 Mile End Rd., London E1 4NS, England, U.K.
CEO: Simon C. Cartmell, CEO
Bus: *Synthetic bone graft technologies and materials*
manufacture.
NAICS: 339113, 541710

Tel: 40-20-7882-7502
Fax: 40-20-7882-7503
www.apatech.com

Emp: 7

APATECH INC.
2 Hampshire St., Foxborough, Massachusetts 02035
CEO: Stephen J. Czick, Pres.
Bus: *Synthetic bone graft technologies.*

Tel: (508) 543-0700
Fax: (508) 543-5551

%FO: 100

● **APPLIED OPTICAL TECHNOLOGIES PLC**
40 Phoenix Rd., Crowther District 3, Tyne and Wear NE38 0AD, England, U.K.
CEO: David A. Mahony, Chmn.
Bus: *Mfr. anti-counterfeiting and tamper-resistant*
devices, security photo ID pouches and security
seals and labels.
NAICS: 322225, 322233, 323110

Tel: 44-191-417-5434
Fax: 44-191-417-6591
www.aotgroup.com

Rev: $48
Emp: 258

APPLIED OPTICAL TECHNOLOGIES INC.
535 16th St., Ste. 920, Denver, Colorado 80202
CEO: Mark Turnage, CEO
Bus: *Mfr. anti-counterfeiting and tamper-resistant*
devices, security photo ID pouches, and
security seals and labels.

Tel: (303) 534-4500
Fax: (303) 534-1010

%FO: 100

APPLIED OPTICAL TECHNOLOGIES INC.
21132 Old York Rd., Parkton, Maryland 21120
CEO: Rick Salomone, Pres.
Bus: *Mfr. anti-counterfeiting and tamper-resistant*
devices, security photo ID pouches, and
security seals and labels.

Tel: (410) 357-4491
Fax: (410) 357-4485

%FO: 100

APPLIED OPTICAL TECHNOLOGIES INC.
1857 Colonial Village Ln., Lancaster, Pennsylvania 17601
CEO: Jeff Davis
Bus: *Mfr. holographic labels, laminates and foils.*

Tel: (717) 293-4110
Fax:

%FO: 100

● **APPLIED PRODUCT SOLUTIONS LTD. (APS)**
Unit 36, Mere View Industrial Estate, Yaxley Peterborough PE7 3HF, England, U.K.
CEO: Nic Berg, CEO
Bus: *Mfr. refrigeration equipment..*

NAICS: 333415

Tel: 44-173-324-3777
Fax: 44-173-324-3888
www.productsolutions.co.uk

VIRGINIA KMP CORPORATION
4100 Platinum Way, Dallas, Texas 75237
CEO: Mark Vagle, Pres.
Bus: *Refrigeration equipment manufacturers.*
Tel: (214) 330-7731
Fax: (214) 337-8854
%FO: 100
Emp: 100

● **APV BAKER INC.**
Manor Drive, Paston Parkway, Peterborough PE4 7AP, England, U.K.
CEO: David Marshall, Pres.
Bus: *Markets specialized process plants and*
equipment for food and beverage industry.
Tel: 44-173-328-3000
Fax: 44-173-328-3001
www.apvbaker.com
Rev: $471
Emp: 2,753
NAICS: 311511, 423720

    APV BAKER INC.
    1200 West Ash St., PO Box 1718, Goldsboro, North Carolina 27530
    CEO: Robert H. Rander, Mgr.
    Bus: *Mfr. process packaging equipment for*
    bakery/cereal industry.
    Tel: (919) 731-5302
    Fax: (919) 731-5455
    %FO: 100

● **ARM HOLDINGS PLC**
Peterhouse Tech Park, 110 Fulbourn Rd., Cambridge CB1 9NJ, England, U.K.
CEO: Warren East, CEO
Bus: *Develops and licenses microprocessors for fax*
modems, cell phones and hand-held computers.
Tel: 44-122-340-0400
Fax: 44-122-340-0410
www.arm.com
Rev: $293
Emp: 740
NAICS: 334413

    ARM, INC.
    5 East St., Franklin, Massachusetts 02038
    CEO: Mark Lewin
    Bus: *Develops & licenses microprocessors for*
    fax modems, cell phones and hand-held
    computers.
    Tel: (508) 520-1905
    Fax: (508) 520-1907
    %FO: 100

    ARM, INC.
    27922 NE Quail Creek Dr., Redmond, Washington 98053
    CEO: Erik Ploof
    Bus: *Develops & licenses microprocessors for*
    fax modems, cell phones and hand-held
    computers.
    Tel: (425) 880-6033
    Fax: (425) 880-6034
    %FO: 100

    ARTISAN COMPONENTS INC.
    141 Caspian Ct., Sunnyvale, California 94089
    CEO: James Hogan
    Bus: *Develops & licenses microprocessors for*
    fax modems, cell phones and hand-held
    computers.
    Tel: (408) 734-5600
    Fax: (408) 734-5050
    %FO: 100

    KEIL SOFTWARE INC.
    1501 10th Street, Suite 110, Plano, Texas 75074
    CEO: Jon Ward
    Bus: *Develops & licenses microprocessors for*
    fax modems, cell phones and hand-held
    computers.
    Tel: (972) 312-1107
    Fax: (972) 312-1159
    %FO: 100

- **ARUP GROUP LTD.**
13 Fitzroy St., London W1T 4BQ, England, U.K.
CEO: Terry Hill, Chmn.
Bus: *Architectural and engineering services.*

Tel: 44-20-7636-1531
Fax: 44-20-7580-3924
www.arup.com

Rev: $726
Emp: 7,000

NAICS: 541310, 541330, 541340, 541490

ARUP GROUP
7670 Woodway, Ste. 162, Houston, Texas 77063
CEO: Brian Raine
Bus: *Architectural and engineering services.*

Tel: (713) 783-2787
Fax: (713) 783-1565

%FO: 100

ARUP GROUP
1500 West Park Dr., Ste. 180, Westborough, Massachusetts 01581
CEO: Jeff Tubbs
Bus: *Architectural and engineering services.*

Tel: (508) 616-9990
Fax: (508) 616-9991

%FO: 100

ARUP GROUP
403 Columbia St., Ste. 220, Seattle, Washington 98104
CEO: Gary Lawrence
Bus: *Architectural and engineering services.*

Tel: (206) 749-9674
Fax: (206) 749-0665

%FO: 100

ARUP GROUP
901 Market St., Ste. 260, San Francisco, California 94103
CEO: Mike Kaye
Bus: *Architectural and engineering services.*

Tel: (415) 957-9445
Fax: (415) 957-9096

%FO: 100

ARUP GROUP
2440 South Sepulveda Blvd,, Ste. 180, Los Angeles, California 90064
CEO: Steve Carter
Bus: *Architectural and engineering services.*

Tel: (310) 312-5040
Fax: (310) 312-5788

%FO: 100

ARUP GROUP
1625 W. Big Beaver, Ste. C, Troy, Michigan 48084
CEO: Jim Hadden, CEO
Bus: *Architectural and engineering services.*

Tel: (248) 822-5050
Fax: (248) 822-4072

%FO: 100

ARUP GROUP
35 East Wacker Dr., Ste.1800, Chicago, Illinois 60601
CEO: Nancy Hamilton
Bus: *Architectural and engineering services.*

Tel: (312) 849-5610
Fax: (312) 849-5611

%FO: 100

ARUP GROUP
955 Massachusetts Ave., Boston, Massachusetts 02139
CEO: Ray Crane
Bus: *Architectural and engineering services.*

Tel: (617) 864-2987
Fax: (617) 864-6178

%FO: 100

ARUP GROUP
155 Ave. of the Americas, New York, New York 10013
CEO: Gregory Hodkinson, Chmn.
Bus: *Architectural and engineering services.*

Tel: (212) 229-2669
Fax: (212) 229-1056

%FO: 100

- **ASHTEAD GROUP PLC**
King's Court, 41-51 Kingston Rd., Leatherhead Surrey KT22 7AP, England, U.K.
CEO: George B. Burnett, CEO   Tel: 44-1372-362-300   Rev: $866
Bus: *Engaged in rental of industrial equipment and*   Fax: 44-1372-376-610   Emp: 3,729
tools, electronic survey, inspection and testing   www.ashtead-group.com
equipment.
NAICS: 532412, 532490

   ASHTEAD TECHNOLOGY, INC.
   3311 Preston Ave., Pasadena, Texas 77505
   CEO: Andy Holroyd, Pres.   Tel: (281) 991-1448   %FO: 100
   Bus: *Engaged in rental of industrial equipment*   Fax: (281) 991-1449
   and tools, electronic survey, inspection and
   testing equipment.

   ASHTEAD TECHNOLOGY, INC.
   1057 East Henrietta Rd., Rochester, New York 14623
   CEO: Doug Allen, VP   Tel: (585) 424-2140   %FO: 100
   Bus: *Engaged in rental of industrial equipment*   Fax: (585) 424-2140
   and tools, electronic survey, inspection and
   testing equipment.

   RESPONSE RENTALS, DIV. ASHTEAD TECHNOLOGY
   19407 Park Row, Ste. 170, Houston, Texas 77084
   CEO: Andy Holroyd, SVP   Tel: (281) 398-9533   %FO: 100
   Bus: *Engaged in international survey and*   Fax: (281) 398-3052
   inspection equipment rentals.

   SUNBELT RENTALS, INC.
   611 Templeton Ave., Charlotte, North Carolina 28203
   CEO: Charles L. Miller III, Pres. & CEO   Tel: (704) 969-0250   %FO: 100
   Bus: *Provides rental solutions.*   Fax: (704) 348-5722

- **ASSOCIATED BRITISH FOODS PLC**
Weston Centre, 10 Grosvenor St., London W1K 4QY, England, U.K.
CEO: Martin Adamson, Chmn.   Tel: 44-207-399-6500   Rev: $9,290
Bus: *Mfr. food products.*   Fax: 44-207-399-6580   Emp: 35,584
www.abf.co.uk
NAICS: 311111, 311119, 311221, 311311, 311312, 311313, 311330, 311514, 311612, 311821, 311822, 311823,
311930, 311941, 311942, 315111, 315119,
315191, 315192, 315211, 315212, 315221, 315222, 315223, 315224, 315228, 315231, 315232, 315233,
315234, 315239, 315291, 315292,
315299, 315991, 315992, 315993, 315999, 316211, 316212, 316213, 316214, 316219, 316992, 316993,
316999

   ACH FOOD COMPANY, INC.
   7171 Goodlett Farms Pkwy., Memphis, Tennessee 38016
   CEO: Dan Antonelli   Tel: (901) 381-3000   %FO: 100
   Bus: *Food products marketing and distribution.*   Fax: (901) 381-2968

   ACH FOOD COMPANY, INC.
   7171 Goodlett Farms Pkwy., Cordova, Tennessee 38018
   CEO: Dan Antonelli, Pres. & CEO   Tel: (901) 381-3000   %FO: 100
   Bus: *Food products sales and distribution.*   Fax: (901) 381-2968   Emp: 1,500

   PGP INTERNATIONAL
   PO Box 2060, 351 Hanson Way, Woodland, California 95776
   CEO: Zachary Wochok   Tel: (530) 662-5056
   Bus: *Rice Milling*   Fax: (530) 662-6074

SPI PHARMA
321 Cherry Lane, New Castle, Delaware 19720
CEO: John Burrows, Pres.   Tel: (302) 576-8554
Bus: *Industrial organic chemicals*   Fax: (302) 576-8567   Emp: 368

SPI POLYOLS
321 Cherry Lane, New Castle, Delaware 19720
CEO: John Burrows, CEO   Tel: (302) 576-8600
Bus: *Industrial organic chemicals*   Fax: (302) 576-8569   Emp: 288

● **ASSOCIATED BRITISH PORTS HOLDINGS PLC**
150 Holborn St., London EC1N 2LR, England, U.K.
CEO: Bo Lerenius, CEO   Tel: 44-207-430-1177 Rev: $690
Bus: *Port operator providing container handling,* Fax: 44-207-430-1384 Emp: 3,500
  dredging and docking, storage and distribution. www.abports.co.uk
NAICS: 488310, 488320, 488510, 493110, 541614

  AMERICAN PORT SERVICES, INC.
  9240 Blount Island Blvd., Jacksonville, Florida 32226-4028
  CEO: James Davis   Tel: (904) 751-4391
  Bus: *Port operator for automobile processing.* Fax: (904) 751-4391

● **ASSOCIATED NEWSPAPERS, LTD.**
Northcliffe House, 2 Derry St., Kensington, London W85 TT, England, U.K.
CEO: Kevin J. Beatty, Mng. Dir.   Tel: 44-207-938-6000 Rev: $1,600
Bus: *UK newspaper group.*   Fax: 44-207-938-6000 Emp: 3,485
           www.associatednewspapers.co.uk
NAICS: 511110, 516110

  ASSOCIATED NEWSPAPERS N.A., INC.
  1921 Gallows Rd., Ste. 600, Vienna, Virginia 22182
  CEO: John K. Sturm, Bureau Chief Tel: (703) 902-1600 %FO: 100
  Bus: *Newspaper editorial bureau for UK news* Fax: (703) 917-0636 Emp: 4
    group.

● **ASTRAZENECA INTERNATIONAL**
15 Stanhope Gate, London W1K 1LN, England, U.K.
CEO: Tom McKillop, CEO   Tel: 44-207-304-5000 Rev: $21,426
Bus: *Pharmaceutical products manufacture.* Fax: 44-207-304-5183 Emp: 64,000
           www.astrazeneca.com
NAICS: 311412, 325411, 325412, 339112, 339113, 339114

  ASTRAZENECA PHARMACEUTICALS
  725 Chesterbrook Blvd., Wayne, Pennsylvania 19087-5677
  CEO: David R.Brennan, CEO   Tel: (610) 695-1000 %FO: 100
  Bus: *Research, product development and* Fax: (610) 695-1280
    marketing of pharmaceuticals.

  ASTRAZENECA PHARMACEUTICALS
  1800 Concord Pike, PO Box 15437, Wilmington, Delaware 19850
  CEO: David R. Brennan, CEO   Tel: (302) 886-3000 %FO: 100
  Bus: *Research, product development and* Fax: (302) 886-2972 Emp: 8,000
    marketing of pharmaceuticals.

ASTRAZENECA PHARMACEUTICALS
1250 Eye St. NW, Ste. 804, Washington, District of Columbia 20005
CEO: Rich Ckley, VP   Tel: (202) 289-2570
Bus: *Pharmaceutical preparations*   Fax: (202) 289-2580

ASTRAZENECA PHARMACEUTICALS
50 Otis St., PO Box 4500, Westborough, Massachusetts 01581
CEO: Ivan R. Rowley, Pres.   Tel: (508) 366-1100   %FO: 100
Bus: *Research, product development and*   Fax: (508) 366-7406   Emp: 801
marketing of pharmaceuticals.

ASTRAZENECA PHARMACEUTICALS
587 Old Baltimore Pike, Newark, Delaware 19702
CEO: W. R. Matthews   Tel: (302) 286-3500   %FO: 100
Bus: *Research, product development and*   Fax: (302) 286-4097
marketing of pharmaceuticals.

● **WS ATKINS PLC**
Woodcote Grove, Ashley Rd., Epsom, Surrey KT18 5BW, England, U.K.
CEO: Keith Clarke, CEO   Tel: 44-137-272-6140   Rev: $1,810
Bus: *Engaged in management consulting services.*   Fax: 44-137-274-0055   Emp: 13,691
                                             www.atkinsglobal.com
NAICS: 541310, 541320, 541330, 541370, 541410, 541512

ATKINS HANSCOMB FAITHFUL & GOULD
11200 Richmond Ave., Ste. 300, Houston, Texas 77082
CEO: Tim Horner   Tel: (281) 558-8701   %FO: 100
Bus: *Management consultants.*   Fax: (281) 558-8707

ATKINS HANSCOMB FAITHFUL & GOULD
11 East 26th St., 18/F, New York, New York 10010
CEO: Brian McDonough   Tel: (212) 252-7070   %FO: 100
Bus: *Management consultant services.*   Fax: (212) 213-1138

ATKINS HANSCOMB FAITHFUL & GOULD
One World Trade Center, Ste. 841, Long Beach, California 98031
CEO: Len Marshall   Tel: (562) 983-8080   %FO: 100
Bus: *Management consultant services.*   Fax: (562) 983-8082

HANSCOMB FAITHFUL & GOULD
100 Canal Pointe Blvd., Princeton, New Jersey 08540
CEO: Chris Taylor   Tel: (609) 514-0900   %FO: 100
Bus: *Management consultants.*   Fax: (609) 514-9888

● **AUTONOMY CORPORATION PLC**
Cambridge Park, Cowley Rd., Cambridge CB4 0WZ, England, U.K.
CEO: Michael R. Lynch, Mng. Dir.   Tel: 44-122-344-8000   Rev: $54
Bus: *Mfr. software for on-line media and publishing*   Fax: 44-122-344-8001   Emp: 242
companies.   www.autonomy.com
NAICS: 511210

AUTONOMY INC.
411 Borel Ave., Ste. 100 S., San Mateo, California 94402
CEO: Patrick Ryan, Mktg.　　　　　　　Tel: (650) 573-3210　　　%FO: 100
Bus: *Mfr. software for on-line media and*　Fax: (650) 573-3211
　　　publishing companies.

● **AUTOTYPE INTERNATIONAL LTD.**
Grove Rd., Wantage, Oxon OX127 B2, England, U.K.
CEO: Peter Levinsohn, Mng. Dir.　　　　Tel: 44-123-577-1111　　Rev: $394
Bus: *Mfr. of specialty films and chemicals for the*　Fax: 44-123-577-1196　　Emp: 250
　　　electronics industry, screen printing, digital　www.autotype.com
　　　display printing and industrial applications.
NAICS: 325411

　　　AUTOTYPE AMERICAS INC.
　　　2050 Hammond Dr., Schaumburg, Illinois 60173-3810
　　　CEO: Phil McGugan, Pres.　　　　Tel: (847) 303-5900　　　%FO: 100
　　　Bus: *Mfr. films/chemicals for the screen and print*　Fax: (847) 303-5225
　　　　　industry.

● **AVECIA GROUP PLC**
Hexagon House, Blackley, Manchester M9 8ZS, England, U.K.
CEO: Jeremy Scudamore, CEO　　　　　Tel: 44-161-740-1460　　Rev: $784
Bus: *Fine and specialty chemicals mfr.*　　Fax: 44-161-795-6005　　Emp: 2
　　　　　　　　　　　　　　　　　　　　www.avecia.com
NAICS: 325199, 325910, 325992

　　　AVECIA BIOTECHNOLOGY INC.
　　　155 Fortune Blvd., Milford, Massachusetts 01757
　　　CEO: Robert W. Porter　　　　　　Tel: (508) 482-7500　　　%FO: 100
　　　Bus: *Fine and specialty chemicals mfr. -DNA*　Fax: (508) 482-7510
　　　　　medicine division.

　　　AVECIA INC.
　　　1405 Foulk Rd., Wilmington, Delaware 19803
　　　CEO: Shelly Adams, Sales Dir.　　　Tel: (302) 477-8000　　　%FO: 100
　　　Bus: *Fine and specialty chemicals mfr.*　Fax: (302) 477-8150

　　　AVECIA INC.
　　　213 Cherry lane, PO Box 231, New Castle, Delaware 19720
　　　CEO: Robert W. Porter　　　　　　Tel: (302) 472-1245　　　%FO: 100
　　　Bus: *Fine and specialty chemicals mfr. -mfg.*　Fax: (302) 472-1029
　　　　　site.

● **AVENT HOLDINGS LTD.**
North London Business Park, Oakleigh Rd. S, New Southgate, London N11 1SS, England, U.K.
CEO: Beth Christie, CEO　　　　　　　Tel: 44-208-365-5700　　Rev: $210
Bus: *Baby care products manufacture.*　　Fax: 44-208-365-5701　　Emp: 900
　　　　　　　　　　　　　　　　　　　　www.avent.com
NAICS: 339999

　　　AVENT AMERICA INC.
　　　475 Supreme Dr., Bensenville, Illinois 60106
　　　CEO: Edward Atkin　　　　　　　Tel: (630) 350-2600　　　%FO: 100
　　　Bus: *Baby care products manufacture.*　Fax: (630) 766-5078

- **AVESCO PLC**
Unit E2, Sussex Manor Business Park, Gatwick Rd., Crawley, West Sussex RH10 9NH, England, U.K.
CEO: David John Nicholson, CEO   Tel: 44-1293-583-400   Rev: $99
Bus: *Provider of audio-visual services.*   Fax: 44-1293-583-410   Emp: 400
                                        www.avesco.co.uk
   NAICS: 334310, 512191, 532490
   ### CREATIVE TECHNOLOGY
   10501 Delta Pkwy., Schiller Park, Illinois 60176
   CEO: Jeff Meyer   Tel: (847) 671-9670   %FO: 100
   Bus: *Provider of video, audio & IT solutions.*   Fax: (847) 671-9676

   ### CREATIVE TECHNOLOGY
   2501 Monarch St., Hangar 22, Alameda, California 94501
   CEO: Stephen Gray   Tel: (510) 217-2700   %FO: 100
   Bus: *Provider of video, audio & IT solutions.*   Fax: (510) 217-2874

   ### CREATIVE TECHNOLOGY
   20675 Nordhoff St., Chatsworth, California 91311
   CEO: Sean Leo   Tel: (818) 464-7500   %FO: 100
   Bus: *Provider of video, audio & IT solutions.*   Fax: (818) 464-7502

   ### CREATIVE TECHNOLOGY
   Patrick Commerce Center, 6170 South McLeod Drive, Bldg. E, Las Vegas, Nevada 89120
   CEO: Herb Brandt   Tel: (866) 841-2858   %FO: 100
   Bus: *Provider of video, audio & IT solutions.*   Fax:

- **AVEVA GROUP PLC**
High Cross, Madingley Rd., Cambridge CB3 0HB, England, U.K.
CEO: Richard Longdon, CEO   Tel: 44-122-355-6655   Rev: $70
Bus: *Software and IT provider.*   Fax: Emp: 326
                                        www.aveva.com
   NAICS: 511210, 541512, 541690
   ### AVEVA INC.
   10370 Richmond Ave., Ste. 400, Houston, Texas 77042
   CEO: Matthew McKinley, EVP   Tel: (713) 977-1225   %FO: 100
   Bus: *Software and IT provider.*   Fax: (713) 977-1231

   ### AVEVA INC.
   800 Delaware Ave., Ste. 300, Wilmington, Delaware 19801
   CEO: Nick Dunlop   Tel: (302) 427-8600   %FO: 100
   Bus: *Software and IT provider.*   Fax: (302) 427-8118

- **AVIVA PLC**
PO Box 420, St. Helen's 1 Undershaft, London EC3P 3DQ, England, U.K.
CEO: Richard Harvey, CEO   Tel: 44-207-283-2000   Rev: $78,581
Bus: *General insurance underwriters and investment*   Fax: 44-207-283-2753   Emp: 60,740
   advisory services.   www.cgugroup.com
   NAICS: 523920, 524127

AVIVA LIFE INSURANCE COMPANY
108 Myrtle St., Quincy, Massachusetts 02171
CEO: Hans L. Carstensen III, SVP
Bus: *Insurance services.*

Tel: (617) 786-2110
Fax: (617) 786-2319

%FO: 100

● **AVON RUBBER PLC**
Manvers House, Kingston Rd., Bradford-on-Avon, Wiltshire BA15 1AA, England, U.K.
CEO: Terry Stead, CEO
Bus: *Polymers engineering for auto hoses and dairy
    cow tubes.*

Tel: 44-1225-861-100
Fax: 44-1225-861-199
www.avon-rubber.com

Rev: $430
Emp: 4,281

NAICS: 325211, 325212

AVON ENGINEERED FABRICATIONS
1200 Martin Luther King Blvd., Picayune, Michigan 39466
CEO: David Poole
Bus: *Polymers manufacture.*

Tel: (601) 799-1217
Fax: (601) 799-1360

%FO: 100

AVON MILK-RITE USA
110 Lincoln St., Johnson Creek, Wisconsin 53038
CEO: Allen Coates
Bus: *Dairy cow tubes manufacture.*

Tel: (920) 699-3431
Fax: (920) 699-2344

%FO: 100

AVON RUBBER & PLASTICS INC.
805 W. 13th St., Cadillac, Michigan 49601
CEO: Roger Hunt
Bus: *Polymers engineering for auto hoses and
    dairy cow tubes.*

Tel: (231) 775-6571
Fax: (231) 775-7304

%FO: 100

AVON ZATEC
475h Paramount Dr., Raynham, Massachusetts 02767
CEO: Charles Bruckman
Bus: *Copy machine polyurethane cleaning blades
    manufacture.*

Tel: (508) 880-3388
Fax: (508) 880-5772

%FO: 100

● **AXON GROUP PLC**
AxonCentre, Church Rd., Egham, Surrey TW20 9QB, England, U.K.
CEO: Mark Hunter, CEO
Bus: *Business transformation consultancy.*

Tel: 44-1784-480-800
Fax: 44-1784-480-900
www.axonglobal.com

Rev: $116
Emp: 547

NAICS: 541512, 541513, 541519, 611420

BYWATER INC.
2 Stamford Landing, 68 Southfield Ave., Stamford, Connecticut 06902
CEO: Kevin Fiala
Bus: *Business transformation consultancy.*

Tel: (203) 973-0344
Fax: (203) 973-0345

%FO: 100
Emp: 75

● **BAA PLC**
130 Wilton Rd., London SW1V 1LQ, England, U.K.
CEO: Mike Clasper, CEO
Bus: *Airport management and operations.*

Tel: 44-207-932-6642
Fax: 44-207-932-6757
www.baa.co.uk

Rev: $3,596
Emp: 12,533

NAICS: 488119, 488190

England, U.K.

BAA INDIANAPOLIS INC.
2500 South High School Rd., Indianapolis, Indiana 46241
CEO: Patrick Dooley, Pres.
Tel: (317) 487-5003
%FO: 100
Bus: *Airport management and operations.*
Fax: (317) 487-5034
Emp: 199

BAA PITTSBURGH INC.
Pittsburgh Intl Airport, PO Box 12318, Pittsburgh, Pennsylvania 15231-0318
CEO: Kelly Quaresima, VP
Tel: (412) 472-5180
%FO: 100
Bus: *Airport management and operations.*
Fax: (412) 472-5190
Emp: 8

BAA USA
PO Box 8719, Baltimore, Maryland 21240
CEO: Mark Knight, Dir.
Tel: (410) 859-9201
%FO: 100
Bus: *Airport management and operations.*
Fax: (410) 859-9204

● **BABCOCK INTERNATIONAL GROUP PLC**
2 Cavendish Sq., London W!G 0PX, England, U.K.
CEO: Peter I. Rogers, CEO
Tel: 44-20-7291-5000
Rev: $825
Bus: *Provides engineering services, facilities*
Fax: 44-20-7291-5055
Emp: 6,110
management and training.
www.babcock.co.uk
NAICS: 541330, 541710, 811219

BABCOCK EAGLETON INC.
3900 Essex Ln., Ste. 300, Houston, Texas 77027
CEO: Duain Cagle, Pres.
Tel: (713) 871-8787
%FO: 100
Bus: *Provides engineering and contracting*
Fax: (713) 871-1914
services to the pipeline industry.

● **BAE SYSTEMS, PLC**
6 Carlton Gardens, London SW1Y 5AD, England, U.K.
CEO: Michael John Turner, CEO
Tel: 44-1252-373-232
Rev: $14,911
Bus: *Mfr. aerospace products, commercial and military*
Fax: 44-1252-383-000
Emp: 68,400
aircraft, artillery, missiles, defense systems.
www.baesystems.com
NAICS: 332993, 332995, 334511, 336411, 336413, 336414, 336415, 336419, 336611, 336612, 336992, 811219, 811310, 927110, 928110

AIRBUS NORTH AMERICA
198 Van Buren St., Ste. 300, Herndon, Virginia 20170\
CEO: Henri Courpron, Pres. & CEO
Tel: (703) 834-3400
Bus: *Mfr. of commercial aircrafts.*
Fax: (703) 834-3340

BAE SYSTEMS ELECTRONICS & INTEGRATED SOLUTIONS
65 Spit Brook Rd., Nashua, New Hampshire 03061
CEO: Walter P. Havenstein, Pres.
Tel: (603) 885-3653
%FO: 100
Bus: *Computer services*
Fax:
Emp: 8,900

BAE SYSTEMS LAND & ARMAMENTS
1525 Wilson Blvd., Ste. 700, Arlington, Virginia 22209
CEO: Thomas W. Rabaut, Pres. & CEO
Tel: (703) 312-6100
%FO: 100
Bus: *Mfr. of weaponry & related products*
Fax: (703) 312-6111
Emp: 8,150

BAE SYSTEMS NA
1601 Research Blvd., Rockville, Maryland 20850
CEO: Mark H. Ronald, Pres. & CEO   Tel: (301) 838-6000   %FO: 100
Bus: *Sale & support aerospace products &*   Fax: (301) 838-6925   Emp: 24,628
operations.

BAE SYSTEMS SAN DIEGO SHIP REPAIR
2205 E. Belt, Foot of Sampson St., San Diego, California 92113
CEO: Robert Kilpatrick, Pres.   Tel: (619) 238-1000
Bus: *Aerospace & defense maintenance &*   Fax: (619) 239-1751
services.

BAE SYSTEMS SHIP REPAIR
750 W. Berkley Ave., Norfolk, Virginia 23523
CEO: Alexander J. Krekrich, Pres.   Tel: (757) 494-4000
Bus: *Mfr. of military ships & submarines.*   Fax: (757) 494-4184   Emp: 2,200

BAE SYSTEMS STEEL PRODUCTS DIVISION
2101 W. 10th St., Anniston, Alabama 36202
CEO: Robert Houston, Gen. Mgr.   Tel: (256) 237-2841
Bus: *Metal fabrication.*   Fax: (256) 235-9699

BAE SYSTEMS TECHNOLOGY SOLUTIONS & SERVICES
1601 Research Blvd., Rockville, Maryland 20850
CEO: Larry Wise, Pres.   Tel: (301) 738-4000
Bus: *Aerospace & defense.*   Fax: (301) 738-4643   Emp: 25,628

MBDA
5701 Lindero Canton Rd., Ste. 4-100, Westlake Village, California 91362
CEO: Dr. John Smith, Pres.   Tel: (818) 991-0300
Bus: *Aerospace & defense.*   Fax: (818) 991-4669   Emp: 90

SAAB BARRACUDA LLC
608 E. McNeil St., Lillington, North Carolina 27546
CEO: Robert Martin, Pres. & CEO   Tel: (910) 893-2094
Bus: *Mfr. aerospace & defense parts.*   Fax: (910) 893-8807   Emp: 100

● **BAKER TILLY INTERNATIONAL LTD.**
2 Bloomsbury St., London WC1B 3ST, England, U.K.
CEO: Geoff Barnes, Pres. & CEO   Tel: 44-20-7314-6875   Rev: $1,820
Bus: *Accounting and business services.*   Fax: 44-20-7314-6876   Emp: 186,000
                                                  www.bakertillyinternational.com

NAICS: 541211, 541213, 541611, 541618

BAKER TILLY INTERNATIONAL LTD.
c/o Blum Shapiro & Co., PC, 29 S. Main St., West Hartford, Connecticut 06107
CEO: David B. Rosenthal, Chmn.   Tel: (860) 561-4000   %FO: 100
Bus: *Accounting and business services.*   Fax: (860) 521-9241

● **BALFOUR BEATTY PLC**
130 Wilton Rd., London SW1V 1LQ, England, U.K.
CEO: Ian P. Tyler, CEO   Tel: 44-207-216-6800   Rev: $3,585
Bus: *Engineering for power, construction and*   Fax: 44-207-216-6950   Emp: 24,000
communications industries.   www.balfourbeatty.com

NAICS: 237990

BALFOUR BEATTY CONSTRUCTION INC.
999 Peachtree St. NE, Ste. 200, Atlanta, Georgia 30309
CEO: William Ogle, CEO   Tel: (404) 875-0356   %FO: 100
Bus: *Construction management.*   Fax: (404) 607-7319   Emp: 1,100

● **BALLI GROUP PLC**
5 Stanhope Gate, London W1Y 5LA, England, U.K.
CEO: Vahid Alaghband, Pres.   Tel: 44-20-7306-2000   Rev: $1,400
Bus: *Engaged in trading steel and steel raw materials.*   Fax: 44-20-7491-9000
                                       www.balli.co.uk
NAICS: 423510, 523130

   BALLI STEEL PIPE USA
   1800 St. James Place, Houston, Texas 77056
   CEO: Jeffrey McCarthy, Pres.   Tel: (713) 627-7321   %FO: 100
   Bus: *Steel manufacture.*   Fax: (713) 627-7321

   BALLI WEBCO INTERNATIONAL
   210 Three Springs Dr., Ste. 2, Weirton, West Virginia 26062
   CEO: F. William Weber   Tel: (304) 723-6101   %FO: 100
   Bus: *Steel manufacture.*   Fax: (304) 723-6102

● **BALTIMORE TECHNOLOGIES PLC**
Innovation House, Hemel Hempstead, Hertfordshire HP2 7DN, England, U.K.
CEO: Timothy Lovell, COO   Tel: 44-1442-342-600   Rev: $32
Bus: *E-commerce hardware manufacture.*   Fax: 44-1442-266-438   Emp: 223
                                       www.baltimoreplc.com
NAICS: 334119, 511210

   BALTIMORE TECHNOLOGIES INC
   77 A St., Needham Heights, Massachusetts 02494
   CEO: Dennis Kelly   Tel: (781) 455-3333   %FO: 100
   Bus: *E-commerce hardware sales.*   Fax: (781) 455-4005

● **BARCLAYS PLC**
1 Churchill Place, London E14 5HP, England, U.K.
CEO: John S. Varley, CEO   Tel: 44-207-116-1000   Rev: $40,016
Bus: *International investment banking and asset*   Fax: Emp: 77,000
   management services.   www.barclays.com
NAICS: 522110, 522210, 522220, 522292, 523130, 523920, 523930

   BARCLAYS CAPITAL
   200 Park Ave, 35/F, New York, New York 10166
   CEO: Juliet Jones, CEO   Tel: (212) 412-4000
   Bus: *Security brokers & dealers* Fax: (212) 412-7300   Emp: 224

   BARCLAYS GLOBAL INVESTORS
   101 California St., San Francisco, California 94111
   CEO: Craig Lewis, CEO   Tel: (415) 765-4700   %FO: 100
   Bus: *International investment banking and asset*   Fax: (415) 765-4760   Emp: 3,000
      management services.

JUNIPER FINANCIAL CORP.
100 S. West St., Wilmington, Delaware 19801
CEO: Richard Vague, Chmn. & CEO   Tel: (302) 888-1400
Bus: *Business services*   Fax: (302) 888-0405   Emp: 350

● **BARRATT DEVELOPMENTS PLC**
Wingrove House, Ponteland Rd., Newcastle NE5 3DP, England, U.K.
CEO: Sir Lawrence Barratt, Pres.   Tel: 44-191-286-6811   Rev: $4,546
Bus: *Property investment, building and development.*   Fax: 44-191-271-2242   Emp: 4,578
www.barratthomes.co.uk

NAICS: 236115, 237210

    BARRATT AMERICAN INC.
    5950 Priestly Dr., Carlsbad, California 92008
    CEO: Michael D. Pattinson, Pres. & CEO   Tel: (760) 431-0800   %FO: 100
    Bus: *Property investment, building and*   Fax: (760) 931-9270   Emp: 115
        development.

● **BARTLE BOGLE HEGARTY LTD.**
60 Kingly St., London W1B 5DS, England, U.K.
CEO: Nigel Bogle, CEO   Tel: 44-20-7734-1677   Rev: $100
Bus: *Advertising agency.*   Fax: 44-20-7437-3666   Emp: 550
www.bbh.co.uk

NAICS: 541810

    BBH LTD.
    7 W. 22nd St., New York, New York 10010
    CEO: Gwyn Jones, CEO   Tel: (212) 812-6600   %FO: 100
    Bus: *Advertising agency.*   Fax: (212) 243-4110

● **BBA GROUP, PLC.**
20 Balderton St., London W1K 6TL, England, U.K.
CEO: Roy V. McGlone, CEO   Tel: 44-20-7514-3999   Rev: $2,300
Bus: *Aviation and materials technology.*   Fax: 44-20-7408-2318   Emp: 12,850
www.bbagroup.com

NAICS: 322291, 811310

    BBA AVIATION SERVICES GROUP
    201 South Orange Ave., Ste.1425, Orlando, Florida 32801
    CEO: Gary Boekenkamp   Tel: (407) 648-7230
    Bus: *Flight support for business & commercial*   Fax: (407) 206-5357
        aircraft; turbine engine repair & overhaul;
        component repair, overhaul & distribution.

    BBA FIBERWEB INC.
    5110 Maryland Way, Ste. 280, Brentwood, Tennessee 37027
    CEO: John Matheny   Tel: (615) 847-7503   %FO: 100
    Bus: *Mfr. nonwoven spun bonded products.*   Fax: (615) 847-7063

    BBA NONWOVENS
    3120 Commodity Lane, Green Bay, Wisconsin 54303
    CEO: Dave Imeson, Pres. & CEO   Tel: (920) 336-0222   %FO: 100
    Bus: *Mfr. nonwovens.*   Fax: (920) 336-3418

BBA NONWOVENS
PO Box 579, Bethune, South Carolina 29009
CEO: Bill Bunn
Bus: *Mfr. nonwovens.*

Tel: (843) 334-6211
Fax: (843) 334-6462

%FO: 100

BBA NONWOVENS
3720 Grant St., Washougal, Washington 98671
CEO: Gary Drews, Mgr.
Bus: *Mfr. nonwovens.*

Tel: (360) 835-8787
Fax: (360) 835-2546

%FO: 100

BBA NONWOVENS
PO Box 3, Colrain, Massachusetts 01340
CEO: Albert Sheridan
Bus: *Mfr. nonwovens.*

Tel: (413) 624-3471
Fax: (413) 624-5590

%FO: 100

BBA US HOLDINGS, INC.
401 Edgewater Place, Ste. 670, Wakefield, Massachusetts 01880
CEO: Roberto Quarta, Pres.
Bus: *U.S. holding company.*

Tel: (781) 246-8900
Fax: (781) 245-3227

%FO: 100

● **BEAZLEY GROUP PLC**
1 Aldgate, Aldgate, London EC3N 1AA, England, U.K.
CEO: Andrew Beazley, CEO
Bus: *Insurance underwriter.*

Tel: 44-20-7667-0623
Fax: 44-20-7667-0624
www.beazley.com

Rev: $588
Emp: 160

NAICS: 524126

BEAZLEY USA
822 North Highway A1A, Ste. 202, Ponte Vedra Beach, Florida 32082
CEO: King Flynn
Bus: *Insurance underwriters.*

Tel: (904) 567-1220
Fax: (904) 567-1230

%FO: 100

BEAZLEY USA
20 Stanford Dr., Farmington, Connecticut 06032
CEO: Nicholas Bozzo
Bus: *Insurance underwriters.*

Tel: (860) 677-3700
Fax: (860) 679-0247

%FO: 100

● **BELRON**
The King's Observatory, Old Deer Park, Richmond Surrey TW9 2AE, England, U.K.
CEO: Gary Lubner, CEO
Bus: *Auto glass repair and replacement.*

Tel: 44-20-8332-0099
Fax: 44-20-8948-7323
www.belron.com

Rev: $800
Emp: 8,200

NAICS: 327215, 811122

SAFELITE AUTO GLASS
2400 Farmers Dr., Columbus, Ohio 43216
CEO: Dan Wilson, Pres. & CEO
Bus: *Engaged in auto glass repair and replacement.*

Tel: (614) 210-9000
Fax: (614) 210-9451

%FO: 50

• BENFIELD GROUP LIMITED
55 Bishopsgate, London EC2N 3BD, England, U.K.
CEO: Grahame Chilton, Chmn.   Tel: 44-207-578-7000   Rev: $209
Bus: *Engaged in risk insurance and investment.*   Fax: 44-207-578-7001   Emp: 350
www.benfieldgroup.com
NAICS: 524126, 524128, 524130, 524210

BENFIELD GROUP
5000 North Akara, Ste. 3700, Dallas, Texas 75201
CEO: Brant Chandler, Dir.   Tel: (214) 756-7000   %FO: 100
Bus: *Engaged in risk insurance and investment.*   Fax: (214) 756-7001

BENFIELD GROUP
140 Broadway, Ste. 32, New York, New York 10005
CEO: Kevin Markowski   Tel: (917) 320-4500   %FO: 100
Bus: *Engaged in risk insurance and investment.*   Fax: (917) 320-4659

BENFIELD GROUP
3600 West 80th St., Minneapolis, Minnesota 55431
CEO: Paul Karon, Dir.   Tel: (952) 886-8000   %FO: 100
Bus: *Engaged in risk insurance and investment.*   Fax: (952) 886-8001

BENFIELD GROUP
3655 North Point Pkwy., Ste. 300, Alpharetta, Georgia 30005
CEO: Bill Fleischhacker, Dir.   Tel: (678) 297-0784   %FO: 100
Bus: *Engaged in risk insurance and investment.*   Fax: (678) 297-0844

• BERMANS
Pioneer Buildings, 65/67 Dale Street, Liverpool L2 2NS, England, U.K.
CEO: Keith Berman, Pres.   Tel: 44-151-224-0500
Bus: *Law firm services.*   Fax: 44-151-236-2107
www.bermans.co.uk
NAICS: 541110

BERMANS ASSOCIATES
1775 Broadway, Ste. 608, New York, New York 10019
CEO: Keith Berman, Pres.   Tel: (212) 956-7767   %FO: 100
Bus: *English solicitors and international attorneys.*   Fax: (212) 956-1099

• BESPAK PLC
Blackhill Dr., Featherstone Rd., Wolverton Mill South, Milton Keynes MK12 5TS, England, U.K.
CEO: Mark Throdahl, CEO   Tel: 44-1553-691000   Rev: $141
Bus: *Pharmaceuticals valve delivery systems, specialty valves, pumps.*   Fax: 44-1553-693728   Emp: 560
www.bespak.com
NAICS: 333913, 334510, 339112, 339113

BESPAK HOLDINGS INC.
2450 Laura Duncan Rd., Apex, North Carolina 27502
CEO: Tom Addison, Mgr.   Tel: (919) 387-0112   %FO: 100
Bus: *Mfr./distribution pharmaceuticals valve delivery systems, specialty valves, pumps.*   Fax: (919) 387-0116   Emp: 100

● **BEVAN FUNNELL LIMITED**
Reprodux House, Norton Rd., New Haven, East Sussex BN9 0BZ, England, U.K.
CEO: T. Cooke, Chmn.   Tel: 44-127-351-3762
Bus: *Distributes antique reproductions and classic*   Fax: 44-127-351-6735
    English furniture.   www.bevan-funnell.co.uk
NAICS: 423210

    BEVAN FUNNELL, LTD.
    909 W Market Center Dr., PO Box 1109, High Point, North Carolina 27261
    CEO: Barry Bevan Funnell, VP   Tel: (336) 889-4800   %FO: 100
    Bus: *Sales/distribution/service of antique*   Fax: (336) 889-7037
        reproductions.

● **BG GROUP PLC**
100 Thames Valley Park Dr., Reading, Berkshire RG6 1PT, England, U.K.
CEO: Frank Chapman, CEO   Tel: 44-118-935-3222   Rev: $7,826
Bus: *Gas and oil exploration.*   Fax: 44-118-935-3233   Emp: 5,175
                                        www.bg-group.com
NAICS: 211111

    BRITISH GAS U.S. HOLDINGS, INC.
    5444 Westheimer, Ste. 1775, Houston, Texas 77056
    CEO: Elizabeth Spomer, VP   Tel: (713) 622-7100   %FO: 100
    Bus: *Distributes and sells gas, implements*   Fax: (713) 622-7244
        exploration and provides technological
        support.

● **BIOTRACE LIMITED**
The Science Park, Bridgend CF31 3NA, England, U.K.
CEO: Ian R. Johnson   Tel: 44-165-664-1400
Bus: *Mfr. rapid tests for hygiene monitoring and*   Fax: 44-165-676-8835
    microbial screening in the food, industrial and   www.biotrace.com
    environmental markets.
NAICS: 325414, 333298, 334511, 334516, 339111, 541710

    BIOTRACE LIFE SCIENCES
    7537 State Rd., Cincinnati, Ohio 45255
    CEO: Chad Way, Mgr.   Tel: (513) 842-0410
    Bus: *Mfr. test equipment*   Fax: (513) 842-0416

    BIOTRACE, INTERNATIONAL
    21312 30th Dr. SE #110, Bothell, Washington 98021
    CEO: Ron Aube, VP   Tel: (425) 398-7993   %FO: 100
    Bus: *Mfr. rapid tests for hygiene monitoring and*   Fax: (425) 398-7993
        microbial screening in the food, industrial
        and environmental markets.

● **BLACKWELL PUBLISHING LTD.**
9600 Garsington Rd., Oxford OX42DQ, England, U.K.
CEO: Rene Olivieri, CEO   Tel: 44-186-577-6868   Rev: $250
Bus: *Book publisher.*   Fax: 44-186-571-4591   Emp: 607
                                        www.blackwellpublishing.com
NAICS: 511130

BLACKWELL PUBLISHING INC.
350 Main St., Malden, Massachusetts 02148
CEO: Amy Yodanis, VP Mktg.
Bus: *Book publishing.*

Tel: (781) 388-8200
Fax: (781) 388-8210

%FO: 100

BLACKWELL PUBLISHING INC.
2121 State Ave., Ames, Iowa 50014
CEO: Sally Clayton, Dir. Sales
Bus: *Book publishing.*

Tel: (515) 292-0140
Fax: (515) 292-3348

%FO: 100

● **BLOOMSBURY PUBLISHING PLC**
36 Soho Sq., London W1D 3QY, England, U.K.
CEO: Nigel Newton, CEO
Bus: *Book publishing.*

Tel: 44-20-7494-2111
Fax: 44-20-7434-0151
www.bloomsburymagazine.com

Rev: $163
Emp: 250

NAICS: 511130

BLOOMSBURY USA
175 Fifth Ave., New York, New York 10010
CEO: Gillian Blake
Bus: *Book publisher.*

Tel: (212) 674-5151
Fax: (212) 780-0115

%FO: 100

WALKER PUBLISHING COMPANY INC.
104 Fifth Ave., New York, New York 10011
CEO: Karen Rinaldi
Bus: *Book publisher.*

Tel: (212) 727-8300
Fax: (212) 727-0984

%FO: 100

● **THE BOC GROUP PLC**
Chertsey Rd., Windlesham, Surrey GU20 6HJ, England, U.K.
CEO: Anthony E. Isaac, CEO
Bus: *Mfr. gases and related products and services.*

Tel: 44-1276-477222
Fax: 44-1276-471333
www.boc.com

Rev: $7,042
Emp: 43,383

NAICS: 325120, 333295, 488510

BOC EDWARDS
301 Ballardvale St., Wilmington, Massachusetts 01887
CEO: Mike Cole, Pres.
Bus: *Mfr. high vacuum equipment and service pumps.*

Tel: (978) 658-5410
Fax: (978) 658-7969

%FO: 100

BOC EDWARDS
575 Mountain Ave., Murray Hill, New Jersey 07974
CEO: Glenn Rush, Pres.
Bus: *Mfr. industrial gases.*

Tel: (908) 665-2400
Fax: (908) 464-9015

%FO: 100
Emp: 9,700

BOC EDWARDS
3901 Burton Dr., Santa Clara, California 95054
CEO: Dr. Kenneth Aitchison
Bus: *Mfr. industrial gases.*

Tel: (408) 496-1177
Fax: (408) 496-1188

BOC EDWARDS PHARMACEUTICAL SYSTEMS
2175 Military Rd., Tonawanda, New York 14150
CEO: Simon Hunton
Bus: *Mfr. pharmaceutical freeze dryers.*

Tel: (716) 695-6354
Fax: (716) 695-6354

BOC EDWARDS TEMESCAL
4569-d Las Positas Rd., Livermore, California 94551
CEO: Jim Golden   Tel: (925) 371-4170   %FO: 100
Bus: *Mfr. industrial gases.*   Fax: (925) 371-4172

• **THE BODY SHOP INTERNATIONAL PLC**
Watersmead, Littlehampton, West Sussex BN17 6LS, England, U.K.
CEO: Peter Saunders, CEO   Tel: 44-190-373-1500   Rev: $636
Bus: *Mfr. and sales of health and beauty products.*   Fax: 44-190-372-6250 Emp: 5,860
                                              www.the-body-shop.com
  NAICS: 325620
    THE BODY SHOP, INC.
    5036 One World Way, PO Box 1409, Wake Forest, North Carolina 27587
    CEO: Joanne Calabrese, CEO   Tel: (919) 554-4900   %FO: 100
    Bus: *Retailer health and beauty products.*   Fax: (919) 554-4361   Emp: 1,000

• **BODYCOTE INTERNATIONAL PLC**
Hulley Rd., Macclesfield, Cheshire SK10 2SG, England, U.K.
CEO: J. D. Hubbard, CEO   Tel: 44-1625-505-300   Rev: $881
Bus: *Heat treatments and manufacture of metallurgical*   Fax: 44-1625-505-313 Emp: 7,154
    coatings.   www.bodycote.com
  NAICS: 332116, 332811
    BODYCOTE METALLURGICAL COATINGS
    111 K-Tech Lane, Hot Springs, Arkansas 71913-9140
    CEO: David Hair, Pres.   Tel: (501) 760-1696   %FO: 100
    Bus: *Heat treatments and manufacture of*   Fax: (501) 760-1695   Emp: 12
      metallurgical coatings.

    BODYCOTE OMNITEST, INC.
    4302 Dayco St., Houston, Texas 77092-4406
    CEO: Ian Nicol, CEO   Tel: (713) 939-8690   %FO: 100
    Bus: *Heat treatments and manufacture of*   Fax: (713) 939-0249   Emp: 20
      metallurgical coatings.

    BODYCOTE THERMAL PROCESSING
    4208 South 74th East Ave., Tulsa, Oklahoma 74145-4709
    CEO: Edward Grott, Mgr.   Tel: (918) 627-7324   %FO: 100
    Bus: *Heat treatments and manufacture of*   Fax: (918) 627-0008
      metallurgical coatings.

    BODYCOTE THERMAL PROCESSING
    1520 North 170th East Ave., Tulsa, Oklahoma 74116
    CEO: Denton Cornelison, Mgr.   Tel: (918) 834-0855   %FO: 100
    Bus: *Heat treatments and manufacture of*   Fax: (918) 437-9460
      metallurgical coatings.

    BODYCOTE THERMAL PROCESSING
    5001 L.B.J. Fwy., Dallas, Texas 75244-6120
    CEO: Jeannie Clark, CFO   Tel: (214) 904-2420   %FO: 100
    Bus: *Heat treatments and manufacture of*   Fax: (214) 904-2424   Emp: 893
      metallurgical coatings.

BODYCOTE THERMAL PROCESSING
675 Christian Lane, Berlin, Connecticut 06037-1425
CEO: Al Hutwagner, Mgr.   Tel: (860) 225-7691   %FO: 100
Bus: *Heat treatments and manufacture of*   Fax: (860) 229-3891
    metallurgical coatings.

BODYCOTE THERMAL PROCESSING
1975 N. Ruby St., Melrose Park, Illinois 60160-1109
CEO: Kelly Phillips, Mgr.   Tel: (708) 344-4080   %FO: 100
Bus: *Heat treatments and manufacture of*   Fax: (708) 344-4010
    metallurgical coatings.

BODYCOTE THERMAL PROCESSING
8580 North Haggerty Rd., Canton, Michigan 48187-2095
CEO: Rick Smith, Mgr.   Tel: (734) 451-2264   %FO: 100
Bus: *Heat treatments and manufacture of*   Fax: (734) 451-2803
    metallurgical coatings.

BODYCOTE THERMAL PROCESSING
6924 South Eastern Ave., Oklahoma City, Oklahoma 73149-5221
CEO: Steven Cargill, Gen. Mgr.   Tel: (405) 670-5710   %FO: 100
Bus: *Heat treatments and manufacture of*   Fax: (405) 672-3306
    metallurgical coatings.

• **BOOTS GROUP PLC**
One Thane Rd. West, Nottingham NG2 3AA, England, U.K.
CEO: Richard Baker, CEO   Tel: 44-115-950-6111   Rev: $9,722
Bus: *Operates drug stores and manufactures over-the-* Fax: 44-115-959-2727   Emp: 68,910
    counter drug products.   www.boots-plc.co.uk
NAICS: 325412, 446110

BOOTS HEALTHCARE USA INC.
177 Broad St., Stamford, Connecticut 06901
CEO: Robert Urbain, CEO   Tel: (203) 355-8200   %FO: 100
Bus: *Skin care product sales.*   Fax: (203) 355-8201   Emp: 900

• **BOVIS LEND LEASE**
York House, 23 Kingsway, London WC2B 6UJ, England, U.K.
CEO: Greg Clarke, CEO   Tel: 44-20-7379-0222   Rev: $6,744
Bus: *Provides construction and project management* Fax: 44-20-7395-7678   Emp: 7,500
    services.   www.bovislendlease.com
NAICS: 237990

BOVIS LEND LEASE INC.
One North Wacker Dr., Ste. 850, Chicago, Illinois 60606
CEO: Jeff Riemer   Tel: (312) 245-1000   %FO: 100
Bus: *Construction and project management* Fax: (312) 245-1379
    services.

BOVIS LEND LEASE INC.
2550 West Tyvola Rd., Ste. 600, Charlotte, North Carolina 28217
CEO: Louis Mosley   Tel: (704) 357-1919   %FO: 100
Bus: *Construction and project management* Fax: (704) 357-2854
    services.

England, U.K.

BOVIS LEND LEASE INC.
111 West Rich St., Ste. 280, Columbus, Ohio 43215
CEO: George Keppler   Tel: (614) 621-4148   %FO: 100
Bus: *Construction and project management services.*   Fax: (614) 621-4149

BOVIS LEND LEASE INC.
800 West 6th St., Ste. 1250, Los Angeles, California 90017
CEO: Todd Pennington   Tel: (213) 430-4660   %FO: 100
Bus: *Construction and project management services.*   Fax: (213) 430-4699

BOVIS LEND LEASE INC.
80 SW 8th St., Ste. 1800, Miami, Florida 33130
CEO: Steven Hood   Tel: (305) 373-8006   %FO: 100
Bus: *Construction and project management services.*   Fax: (305) 373-8082

BOVIS LEND LEASE INC.
1801 West End Ave., Ste. 600, Nashville, Tennessee 37203
CEO: Terry Brantley   Tel: (615) 963-2600   %FO: 100
Bus: *Construction and project management services.*   Fax: (615) 963-2662

BOVIS LEND LEASE INC.
200 Park Ave., New York, New York 10166
CEO: James Abadie   Tel: (212) 592-6700   %FO: 100
Bus: *Construction and project management services.*   Fax: (212) 592-6988

BOVIS LEND LEASE INC.
300 South Orange Ave., Ste. 1500, Orlando, Florida 32801
CEO: Rod Creach   Tel: (407) 551-1000   %FO: 100
Bus: *Construction and project management services.*   Fax: (407) 551-1001

BOVIS LEND LEASE INC.
821 Alexander Rd., Princeton, New Jersey 08540
CEO: Robert Thomsen   Tel: (901) 951-0500   %FO: 100
Bus: *Construction and project management services.*   Fax: (901) 951-0038

BOVIS LEND LEASE INC.
8540 Colonnade Center Dr., Ste. 201, Raleigh, North Carolina 27615
CEO: Brad Eller   Tel: (919) 841-5100   %FO: 100
Bus: *Construction and project management services.*   Fax: (919) 841-5200

BOVIS LEND LEASE INC.
33 New Montgomery St., Ste. 220, San Francisco, California 94105
CEO: Bruce Berardi   Tel: (415) 512-0586   %FO: 100
Bus: *Construction and project management services.*   Fax: (415) 512-0589

BOVIS LEND LEASE INC.
7315 Wisconsin Ave., 14/F. West, Bethesda, Maryland 20814
CEO: Stephen S. Conley
Bus: *Construction and project management
    services.*
Tel: (301) 951-3800
Fax: (301) 951-3151
%FO: 100

BOVIS LEND LEASE INC.
5909 Peachtree, Dunwoody Rd., Atlanta, Georgia 30328
CEO: Michael Hampton
Bus: *Construction and project management
    services.*
Tel: (770) 481-9380
Fax: (770) 481-9893
%FO: 100

BOVIS LEND LEASE INC.
909 Lake Carolyn Pkwy., Ste. 900, Irving, Texas 75039
CEO: Jeff Jones
Bus: *Construction and project management
    services.*
Tel: (469) 977-4300
Fax: (469) 977-4301
%FO: 100

BOVIS LEND LEASE LMB INC.
767 Warren Rd., Ithaca, New York 14850
CEO: Mark Balling
Bus: *Construction and project management
    services.*
Tel: (607) 266-3000
Fax: (607) 266-3009
%FO: 100

BOVIS LEND LEASE LMB INC.
99 Chauncy St., 11/F, Boston, Massachusetts 02111
CEO: Joseph Farrell
Bus: *Construction and project management
    services.*
Tel: (617) 598-4300
Fax: (617) 598-4399
%FO: 100

● **BP PLC**
1 St. James Place, London SW1Y 4PD, England, U.K.
CEO: Peter D. Sutherland, CEO
Bus: *Oil and natural resources, exploration, production
    and distribution.*
Tel: 44-20-7496-4000
Fax: 44-20-7496-4630
www.bp.com
Rev: $285,059
Emp: 102,900
NAICS: 211111, 211112, 213111, 213112, 221210, 324110, 324191, 324199, 325110, 325120, 325131, 325132, 325181, 325188, 325191, 325192, 325193,
325199, 325211, 325212, 325221, 325222, 333132, 424710, 424720, 445120, 447110, 447190, 454311, 454319, 486110, 486210, 486910, 541360

ARCO ALUMINUM INC.
9960 Corporate Campus Dr., Ste. 3000, Louisville, Kentucky 40223
CEO: Patrick Franc, Pres.
Bus: *Aluminum production*
Tel: (502) 566-5700
Fax: (502) 566-5740
Emp: 32

BP
535 Madison Ave., 22/F, New York, New York 10022
CEO: Peggy Chandler, Mgr.
Bus: *Gasoline service station*
Tel: (212) 421-5010
Fax: (212) 421-5010

BP
333 South Hope St., Los Angeles, California 90071
CEO: Mike Buzzacott
Bus: *Petroleum exploration, refining and sales.*
Tel: (310) 549-6204
Fax: (310) 549-6204

England, U.K.

BP CHEMICALS
28100 Torch Park Way, Warrenville, Illinois 60555
CEO: Mike Buzzacott
Bus: *Petroleum exploration, refining and sales.*
Tel: (877) 701-2726
Fax: (877) 701-2726

BP ENERGY COMPANY
501 Westlake Park Blvd., Houston, Texas 77079
CEO: Tim Bullock, Pres.
Bus: *Petroleum Refiner*
Tel: (281) 366-2000
Fax: (281) 366-7569
Emp: 150

BP EXPLORATION ALASKA INC.
900 East Benson Blvd., Anchorage, Alaska 99508
CEO: Jean Wall
Bus: *Exploration, production oil and gas.*
Tel: (907) 564-5111
Fax: (907) 564-5441
%FO: 100

BP NGL
28100 Torch Pkwy., Warrenville, Illinois 60555
CEO: Jeanne Johns, Gen. Mgr.
Bus: *Oil & Gas*
Tel: (630) 836-5000
Fax: (630) 836-6535

BP SOLAR INC.
989 Corporate Blvd., Linthicum, Maryland 21090
CEO: Lee Edwards
Bus: *Mfr. photovoltaic products.*
Tel: (410) 981-0240
Fax: (410) 981-0278
%FO: 100

BP SOLAR INTERNATIONAL
630 Solares Crt., Frederick, Maryland 21703
CEO: Steve Westwell, Pres.
Bus: *Alternative energy sources*
Tel: (301) 698-4200
Fax: (301) 698-4201

CASTROL CONSUMER NORTH AMERICA INC.
1500 Valley Rd., Wayne, New Jersey 07470
CEO: Mike Dearden, CEO
Bus: *Sales of petroleum & petroleum products*
Tel: (973) 633-2200
Fax: (973) 633-9867

INNOVENE
200 E. Randolph St., 25/F & 26/F, Chicago, Illinois 60601
CEO: Ralph C. Alexander, CEO
Bus: *Chemical & petrochemical Mfr.*
Tel: (312) 873-8700
Fax: (312) 873-8906
Emp: 8,500

LOGAN ALUMINIUM
6920 Lewisburg Rd., Russelville, Kentucky 42276
CEO: Mike Harris, Pres.
Bus: *Aluminum production*
Tel: (270) 755-6000
Fax: (270) 755-6617
Emp: 980

OLYMPIC PIPE LINE CO.
2201 Lind Ave. SW, Ste. 270, Renton, Washington 98055
CEO: Bobby Tally, Pres.
Bus: *Oil & gas transportation & storage*
Tel: (425) 235-7736
Fax: (425) 271-5320

● **BPB LTD.**
Park House, 15 Bath Rd., Slough SL1 3UF, England, U.K.
CEO: Richard J. Cousins, CEO   Tel: 44-175-389-8800   Rev: $3,100
Bus: *Mfr. plasterboard, insulation and flooring.*   Fax: 44-175-389-8888   Emp: 12,775
www.bpb.com
NAICS: 321219, 321999, 322130, 326192, 327420, 423310

    BPB AMERICA, INC.
    5301 West Cypress St., Tampa, Florida 33607
    CEO: Pam Bush, Mktg.   Tel: (813) 286-3900   %FO: 100
    Bus: *Mfr. plasterboard.*   Fax: (813) 286-3991

    BPB MARCO
    8105 Industrial St., Junction City, Kansas 66441
    CEO: Jeff Dushak, mgr   Tel: (785) 762-2994   %FO: 100
    Bus: *Mfr. plasterboard.*   Fax: (785) 762-6442

● **BRADMAN LAKE GROUP LTD.**
Yelverton Rd., Brislington, Bristol SW1A 1NP, England, U.K.
CEO: Graham Hayes, CEO   Tel: 44-117-971-5228   Rev: $75
Bus: *Mfr. Of industrial automation & industrial control*   Fax: 44-117-977-5514   Emp: 400
    products.   www.bradmanlakegroup.com
NAICS: 333993, 334513

    BRADMAN LAKE INC.
    9201 D Forsyth Park Dr., Charlotte, North Carolina 28273
    CEO: David Mills   Tel: (704) 588-3301   %FO: 100
    Bus: *Mfr. of packaging machinery.*   Fax: (704) 588-3302   Emp: 60

● **BREK ENERGY CORPORATION**
346 Kensington High St., 3/F, London W14 8NS, England, U.K.
CEO: Richard N. Jeffs, CEO   Tel: 44-20-7471-9898
Bus: *Oil and gas exploration.*   Fax: 44-20-7371-6668
www.brekenergy.com
NAICS: 211111, 213111

    GASCO ENERGY
    14 Inverness Dr. East, Suite 236-H, Englewood, Colorado 80112
    CEO: Michael K. Decker, COO   Tel: (303) 483-0044   %FO: 100
    Bus: *Acquires and explores petroleum and*   Fax: (303) 483-0011
    natural gas properties in the US.

● **BRIDON INTERNATIONAL LIMITED**
Carr Hill, Doncaster, South Yorkshire DN4 8DG, England, U.K.
CEO: Stephen Brimble, Mng. Dir.   Tel: 44-1302-344010   Rev: $2,376
Bus: *Steel wire manufacture.*   Fax: 44-1302-382263
www.bridon.com
NAICS: 331222

    BRIDON AMERICAN
    C280 New Commerce Blvd., Wilkes Barre, Pennsylvania 18706
    CEO: David Sleightholm   Tel: (570) 822-3349   %FO: 100
    Bus: *Steel wire manufacture and sales.*   Fax: (570) 822-9180

- **BRINTONS LTD**
Exchange St., Kidderminster DY10 1AG, England, U.K.
CEO: Stewart Crofts, Chmn.   Tel: 44-156-282-0000   Rev: $151
Bus: *Mfr. carpets.*   Fax: 44-156-251-2321   Emp: 2,000
                                               www.brintons.co.uk
  NAICS: 314110
    BRINTONS AXMINSTER, INC.
    1000 Cobb Place Blvd., Kennesaw, Georgia 30144
    CEO: Deborah Adams   Tel: (678) 594-9300
    Bus: *Import/sale of carpets.*   Fax: (678) 594-9301

- **BRITAX INTERNATIONAL LTD.**
Seton House, Warwick Technology Park, Warwick CV34 6DE, England, U.K.
CEO: Bernard D. Brogan, CEO   Tel: 44-192-640-0040   Rev: $960
Bus: *Mfr. auto components, consumer and special*   Fax: 44-192-640-6350   Emp: 6,800
      products, including aircraft equipment, vehicle   www.britax.com
      leasing and childcare products.
  NAICS: 336360, 336413, 337125, 532111
    BRITAX CHILD SAFETY, INC.
    13501 South Ridge Dr., Charlotte, North Carolina 28273
    CEO: Thomas Baloga, Pres.   Tel: (704) 409-1700   %FO: 100
    Bus: *Mfr. childcare products.*   Fax: (704) 409-1710

    BRITAX INTERNATIONAL INC.
    10986 North Warson Rd., St. Louis, Missouri 63114
    CEO: John M. Kusek   Tel: (314) 426-2700   %FO: 100
    Bus: *Vehicle safety products manufacture.*   Fax: (314) 426-2700

- **BRITISH AIRWAYS PLC**
Waterside, Harmondsworth, London UB7 0GB, England, U.K.
CEO: Roderick Eddington, CEO   Tel: 44-208-759-5511   Rev: $13,933
Bus: *International air transport services.* Fax: 44-208-759-4314   Emp: 51,939
                                               www.british-airways.com
  NAICS: 481111
    BRITISH AIRWAYS (US), INC.
    1175 Peachtree Walk NE, Atlanta, Georgia 30309-3950
    CEO: Roy Linkner   Tel: (404) 685-3250   %FO: 100
    Bus: *Airlines transport services.*   Fax: (404) 685-3250

    BRITISH AIRWAYS (US), INC.
    516 Express Center Dr., Chicago, Illinois 60688
    CEO: Barbara Wilson   Tel: (773) 894-4130
    Bus: *Airlines transport services.*   Fax:

    BRITISH AIRWAYS (US), INC.
    91 Miami International Airport, Miami, Florida 33159
    CEO: Tony J. King   Tel: (305) 526-7825
    Bus: *Airlines transport services.*   Fax: (305) 526-7825

- **BAT INDUSTRIES (BRITISH AMERICAN TOBACCO PLC)**
Globe House, 4 Temple Place, London WC2R 2PG, England, U.K.
CEO: Paul Adams, CEO & Mng. Dir.
Bus: *Tobacco products manufacturing, including Kent, Benson & Hedges and Rothmans.*
NAICS: 312221

Tel: 44-207-845-1000
Fax: 44-207-240-0555
www.bat.com

Rev: $60,988
Emp: 86,941

> **REYNOLDS AMERICAN INC.**
> 401 N. Main St., Winston-Salem, North Carolina 27102
> CEO: Susan M. Ivey, Pres. & CEO
> Bus: *Cigarettes, cigars & smokeless tobacco products*
>
> Tel: (336) 741-2000
> Fax: (336) 741-4238
>
> Emp: 9,400

- **BRITISH BROADCASTING CORPORATION**
Broadcasting House, Portland Place, London W1A 1AA, England, U.K.
CEO: John Smith, Dir.
Bus: *Engaged in international radio and television broadcasting.*
NAICS: 515111, 515120

Tel: 44-207-580-4468
Fax: 44-207-765-1181
www.bbc.co.uk

Rev: $4,823
Emp: 25,560

> **BBC AMERICA, INC.**
> 7475 Wisconsin Ave., Ste. 110, Bethesda, Maryland 20814
> CEO: Scott Langerman, CEO
> Bus: *Engaged in international television broadcasting.*
>
> Tel: (301) 347-2233
> Fax: (301) 656-8591
>
> %FO: 100

- **BRITISH NUCLEAR FUELS PLC**
1100 Daresbury Park, Warrington WA4 4GB, England, U.K.
CEO: Michael D. Parker, CEO
Bus: *Mfr. Nuclear fuels and owns and manages nuclear power plants, as well as nuclear waste clean up services.*
NAICS: 212291, 213114

Tel: 44-1925-832-000
Fax: 44-1925-822-711
www.bnfl.com

Rev: $3,223
Emp: 1,000

> **BNFL INC.**
> 1970 East 17th St., Idaho Falls, Idaho 83404
> CEO: Paul Young
> Bus: *Nuclear power related services.*
>
> Tel: (208) 524-8484
> Fax: (208) 524-4442
>
> %FO: 100

> **BNFL INC.**
> 10306 Eaton Place, Ste. 450, Fairfax, Virginia 22030
> CEO: Pauline Calder
> Bus: *Nuclear power related services.*
>
> Tel: (703) 385-7100
> Fax: (703) 385-7128
>
> %FO: 100

> **BNFL INC.**
> 2345 Stevens Dr., Ste. 200, Richland, Washington 99352
> CEO: Paul S. Townson
> Bus: *Nuclear power related services.*
>
> Tel: (509) 371-8006
> Fax: (509) 371-1906
>
> %FO: 100

> **BNFL INC.**
> 5801 Bluff Rd., Columbia, South Carolina 29209
> CEO: Darlene Elliott
> Bus: *Nuclear power related services.*
>
> Tel: (803) 647-1016
> Fax: (803) 647-1016
>
> %FO: 100

BNFL INC.
9781 S Meridian Blvd., Ste. 100, Englewood, Colorado 80112
CEO: Colin Boardman
Bus: *Nuclear power related services.*
Tel: (303) 874-1660
Fax: (303) 874-1674
%FO: 100

FAUSKE & ASSOCIATES
16W070 83rd St., Burr Ridge, Illinois 60521
CEO: Hans K. Fauske
Bus: *Nuclear power related services.*
Tel: (630) 323-8750
Fax: (630) 986-5481
%FO: 100

WESTINGHOUSE NUCLEAR SERVICES
4350 Northern Pike, Monroeville, Pennsylvania 15146
CEO: Stephen R. Tritch
Bus: *Design work and start-up help for new nuclear power plants.*
Tel: (412) 374-4111
Fax: (412) 374-3851
%FO: 100

● **BRITISH STANDARDS INSTITUTION**
389 Chiswick High Rd., London W4 4AL, England, U.K.
CEO: Stevan Breeze, CEO
Bus: *Certification services and industry standards applications and publishing and distribution.*
NAICS: 541380, 541690, 541990
Tel: 44-20-8996-9000
Fax: 44-20-8996-7001
www.bsi-global.com
Rev: $422
Emp: 5,357

BSI MANAGEMENT SYSTEMS AMERICA
12110 Sunset Hills Rd., Ste. 200, Reston, Virginia 20190
CEO: Gary Pearsons, Mgr.
Bus: *Management systems registration and training services.*
Tel: (703) 437-9000
Fax: (703) 437-9001
%FO: 100

● **BRITISH VITA PLC**
Oldham Rd., Middleton, Manchester M24 2DB, England, U.K.
CEO: David A. Campbell, CEO
Bus: *Foam and foam products manufacture.*
NAICS: 325211, 325222
Tel: 44-161-643-1133
Fax: 44-161-653-5411
www.britishvita.com
Rev: $1,671
Emp: 8,260

CREST FOAM INDUSTRIES INC.
100 Carol Place, Moonachie, New Jersey 07074-1387
CEO: Michael Curti, Pres.
Bus: *Mfr. controlled pore reticulated polyurethane foams for industrial*
Tel: (201) 807-0809
Fax: (201) 807-1113
%FO: 100
Emp: 68

HYPERLAST NORTH AMERICA
2003 Amnicola Highway, Chattanooga, Tennessee 37406
CEO: Brian Howard
Bus: *Mfr. polyurethane resins*
Tel: (423) 697-0400
Fax: (423) 697-0424

VITA NONWOVENS
2215 Shore Dr., High Point, North Carolina 27263
CEO: Rob Stoller, VP
Bus: *Mfr. polyester fiberfill*
Tel: (336) 431-7187
Fax: (336) 431-0693

VITA NONWOVENS
6389 FM3009, Ste. 202, Tri-County Industrial Park, Schertz, Texas 78154
CEO: Alan Ball
Bus: *Business services*
Tel: (210) 651-3735
Fax: (210) 651-4630

VITA NONWOVENS
9403 Avionics Dr., Fort Wayne, Indiana 46809
CEO: Alan Ball
Bus: *Plastics foam products*
Tel: (260) 747-0990
Fax: (260) 747-2012

VITAFOAM INC.
PO Box 5069, 1900 Stuart St., Chattanooga, Tennessee 37406
CEO: Scott Riley, Gen. Mgr.
Bus: *Home furnishings*
Tel: (423) 698-3408
Fax: (423) 698-0706

VITAFOAM INC.
1116 South Veteran's Blvd., PO Box 1767, Tupelo, Mississippi 38802
CEO: Kerry Davis, Mgr.
Bus: *Mfr. plastics materials & resins*
Tel: (662) 842-0123
Fax: (662) 841-0631

VITAFOAM INC.
2222 Surrett Dr., High Point, North Carolina 27263
CEO: Bill Lucas, Pres. & CEO
Bus: *polyurethane foam packaging*
Tel: (336) 431-1171
Fax: (336) 431-7747
Emp: 719

VITAFOAM INC.
4100 Pleasant Garden Rd., Greensboro, North Carolina 27406
CEO: Britt Keaton, VP
Bus: *Mfr. plastics material*
Tel: (336) 378-9620
Fax: (336) 273-0238

VIS IMPERIAL
1230 Sunset Dr., Thomasville, Georgia 31792
CEO: Charles Hays, Gen. Mgr.
Bus: *Mfr. foam products.*
Tel: (229) 228-6914
Fax: (229) 228-7712
%FO: 100
Emp: 35

● **BT GROUP PLC**
BT Centre, 81 Newgate St., London EC1A 7AJ, England, U.K.
CEO: Ben J. M. Verwaayen, CEO
Bus: *Telecommunications and information
systems/services.*
Tel: 44-207-356-5000
Fax: 44-207-356-5520
www.btplc.com
Rev: $35,194
Emp: 102,100
NAICS: 517110, 517211, 517212, 517410, 517910, 518111, 518210, 519190, 541513, 561499

BT AMERICAS, INC.
350 Madison Ave., 6/F, New York, New York 10017
CEO: Chuck Pol, CEO
Bus: *Telecommunications services.*
Tel: (646) 487-3902
Fax: (646) 487-3902
%FO: 100

BT INFONET
2160 E. Grand Ave., El Segundo, California 90245-1022
CEO: Jose A. Collazo, CEO
Bus: *Provider of managed global network
communications services.*
Tel: (310) 335-2600
Fax: (310) 335-4507
%FO: 100
Emp: 1,085

SYNTEGRA USA INC.
4201 Lexington Ave., North Arden Hills, Minnesota 55126
CEO: Rob Morrison
Bus: *IT consulting services.*
Tel: (651) 415-4401
Fax: (651) 415-4891
%FO: 100

● **BUNZL PLC**
110 Park St., London W1Y 3RB, England, U.K.
CEO: Anthony J. Habgood, Chmn.
Bus: *Plastic products manufacture, marketing and distribution of building materials, paper and plastic disposables.*
NAICS: 326199, 423390
Tel: 44-207-495-4950
Fax: 44-207-495-4953
www.bunzl.com
Rev: $5,168
Emp: 14,635

BUNZL USA INC.
701 Emerson Rd., St. Louis, Missouri 63141
CEO: Patrick L. Larmon, Pres.
Bus: *Distribution of paper & plastic products, building materials.*
Tel: (314) 997-5959
Fax: (314) 997-1405
%FO: 100

● **BURBERRY LIMITED**
18-22 Haymarket, London SW1 4DQ, England, U.K.
CEO: Rose Marie Bravo, CEO
Bus: *Men's, women's and baby designer apparel and accessories.*
NAICS: 316992, 448110, 448120, 448150, 448320
Tel: 44-207-968-0000
Fax: 44-207-318-2666
www.burberry.com
Rev: $1,234
Emp: 3,869

BURBERRY LTD.
9 East 57th St., New York, New York 10022
CEO: Eugenia Ulasewicz
Bus: *Men's, women's and baby designer apparel and accessories.*
Tel: (212) 407-7100
Fax: (212) 407-7100

BURBERRY LTD.
South Park Mall, 4400 Sharon Rd., Charlotte, North Carolina 28211
CEO: Eugenia Ulasewicz
Bus: *Men's, women's and baby designer apparel and accessories.*
Tel: (704) 365-3310
Fax: (704) 365-3310
%FO: 100

BURBERRY LTD.
The Mall at Short Hills, 1200 Morris Turnpike, Short Hills, New Jersey 07078
CEO: Eugenia Ulasewicz
Bus: *Men's, women's and baby designer apparel and accessories.*
Tel: (973) 379-7100
Fax: (973) 379-7100

BURBERRY LTD.
The Grand Canal Shoppes at The Venetian, Las Vegas Blvd. South, Las Vegas, Nevada 89109
CEO: Eugenia Ulasewicz
Bus: *Men's, women's and baby designer apparel and accessories.*
Tel: (702) 735-2600
Fax: (702) 735-2600

BURBERRY LTD.
The Plaza at King of Prussia Mall, 160 Gulph Rd., King of Prussia, Pennsylvania 19406
CEO: Eugenia Ulasewicz
Bus: *Men's, women's and baby designer apparel and accessories.*
Tel: (610) 878-9300
Fax: (610) 878-9300
%FO: 100

BURBERRY LTD.
North Park Center, 316 North Park Center, Dallas, Texas 75225
CEO: Eugenia Ulasewicz   Tel: (214) 369-1100   %FO: 100
Bus: *Men's, women's and baby designer apparel*   Fax: (214) 369-1100
and accessories.

BURBERRY LTD.
Somerset Collection, 2801 West Big Beaver Rd., Troy, Michigan 48084
CEO: Eugenia Ulasewicz   Tel: (248) 643-8555
Bus: *Men's, women's and baby designer apparel*   Fax: (248) 643-8555
and accessories.

BURBERRY LTD.
Tysons Galleria, 1739 International Dr., McLean, Virginia 22102
CEO: Eugenia Ulasewicz   Tel: (703) 288-1700   %FO: 100
Bus: *Men's, women's and baby designer apparel*   Fax: (703) 288-1700
and accessories.

BURBERRY LTD.
9560 Wilshire Blvd., Beverly Hills, California 90212
CEO: Eugenia Ulasewicz   Tel: (310) 550-4500   %FO: 100
Bus: *Men's, women's and baby designer apparel*   Fax: (310) 550-4500
and accessories.

BURBERRY LTD.
Cherry Creek Shopping Ctr., 3000 East First Ave., Denver, Colorado 80206
CEO: Eugenia Ulasewicz   Tel: (303) 388-2700   %FO: 100
Bus: *Men's, women's and baby designer apparel*   Fax: (303) 388-2700
and accessories.

BURBERRY LTD.
Lenox Square, 3393 Peachtree Rd., Atlanta, Georgia 30326
CEO: Eugenia Ulasewicz   Tel: (404) 231-5550   %FO: 100
Bus: *Men's, women's and baby designer apparel*   Fax: (404) 231-5550
and accessories.

BURBERRY LTD.
7014 East Camelback Rd., Scottsdale, Arizona 85251
CEO: Eugenia Ulasewicz   Tel: (480) 947-4400   %FO: 100
Bus: *Men's, women's and baby designer apparel*   Fax: (480) 947-4400
and accessories.

BURBERRY LTD.
1300 Connecticut Ave., NW, Washington, District of Columbia 20036
CEO: Eugenia Ulasewicz   Tel: (202) 463-3000   %FO: 100
Bus: *Men's, women's and baby designer apparel*   Fax: (202) 463-3000
and accessories.

BURBERRY LTD.
Town Center at Boca Raton, 6000 Glades Rd., Boca Raton, Florida 33431
CEO: Eugenia Ulasewicz   Tel: (561) 392-8050
Bus: *Men's, women's and baby designer apparel*   Fax: (561) 392-8050
and accessories.

BURBERRY LTD.
Ala Moana Center, 1450 Ala Moana Blvd., Honolulu, Hawaii 96814
CEO: Eugenia Ulasewicz　　　　　　　　　Tel: (808) 951-6999
Bus: *Men's, women's and baby designer apparel*　Fax: (808) 951-6999
and accessories.

BURBERRY LTD.
633 N. Michigan Ave., Chicago, Illinois 60611
CEO: Sheryl Dyer　　　　　　　　　　　Tel: (312) 787-2500　　　　%FO: 100
Bus: *Men's, women's and baby designer apparel*　Fax: (312) 787-7252
and accessories.

BURBERRY LTD.
356 Boylston St., Boston, Massachusetts 02116
CEO: V. Digironimo　　　　　　　　　　Tel: (617) 236-1000　　　　%FO: 100
Bus: *Men's, women's and baby designer apparel*　Fax: (617) 236-1000
and accessories.

BURBERRY LTD.
1350 Ave. of the Americas, 30/F, New York, New York 10019
CEO: Michael Scimeca, Pres. & CEO　　　Tel: (212) 757-3700　　　　%FO: 100
Bus: *Men's, women's and baby designer apparel*　Fax: (212) 246-9440
and accessories.

● **BUSINESS TRAVEL INTERNATIONAL**
Abby House, 282 Farnborough Rd., Hampshire D-GU14 7NJ, England, U.K.
CEO: John Fentener van Vlissingen, Chmn.　Tel: 44-1252-370-777　　Rev: $169
Bus: *Travel agency.*　　　　　　　　　Fax:　　　　　　　　　　Emp: 300
　　　　　　　　　　　　　　　　　　www.bti-worldwide.com

NAICS: 561510

　　WORLD TRAVEL BTI
　　1055 Lenox Park Blvd., 4/F, Ste. 420, Atlanta, Georgia 30319
　　CEO: Michael A. Buckman, CEO　　　Tel: (404) 841-6600　　　%FO: 100
　　Bus: *Travel agency.*　　　　　　　Fax: (404) 814-2983

● **C&J CLARK INTERNATIONAL LTD.**
40 High St., Somerset BA16 0YA, England, U.K.
CEO: Peter Bolliger, CEO　　　　　　　Tel: 44-1458-443-131　　Rev: $1,325
Bus: *Mfr./sale of shoes and shoe components.*　Fax: 44-1458-447-547　Emp: 15,275
　　　　　　　　　　　　　　　　　　www.clarks.co.uk

NAICS: 316211, 316213, 316214, 316219

　　THE CLARK COMPANIES NORTH AMERICA (CCNA)
　　156 Oak St., Newton Upper Falls, Massachusetts 02164
　　CEO: Dick Scheerer, Pres.　　　　　Tel: (617) 964-1222　　　%FO: 100
　　Bus: *Shoes and shoe components manufacture,*　Fax: (617) 243-4199
　　including brands Clarks and Bostonian.

● **C2C SYSTEMS LIMITED**
6 Richfield Place, Reading RG1 8EQ, England, U.K.
CEO: Robert David Hunt, CEO　　　　　Tel: 44-118-951-1211
Bus: *Software development.*　　　　　Fax: 44-118-951-1111
　　　　　　　　　　　　　　　　　　www.c2c.com

NAICS: 511210

C2C SYSTEMS LIMITED
1 Federal St., Bldg. 101-R, Springfield, Massachusetts 01105-1222
CEO: Jonathan Brown
Bus: *Software development.*
Tel: (413) 739-8575
Fax: (413) 739-4980
%FO: 100

● **CADBURY SCHWEPPES PLC**
25 Berkeley Square, London W1X 6HT, England, U.K.
CEO: H. Todd Stitzer, CEO
Bus: *Mfr./franchiser confectionery products and soft drinks, including Snapple, Mystic and Stewart's root beer.*
Tel: 44-207-409-1313
Fax: 44-207-830 5200
www.cadburyschweppes.com
Rev: $12,918
Emp: 58,442
NAICS: 311320, 311421, 312111

> **CADBURY SCHWEPPES**
> 5301 Legacy Dr., Plano, Texas 75204
> CEO: Gil M. Cassagne, Pres. & CEO
> Bus: *Mfr. fruit drinks, franchise soft drinks.*
> Tel: (972) 673-7000
> Fax: (972) 673-7980
> %FO: 100
> Emp: 2,700

> **DR. PEPPER BOTTLING COMPANY**
> 2304 Century Center Blvd., Irving, Texas 75062
> CEO: Jim Trebilcock, CEO
> Bus: *Soft drink bottler and distribution.*
> Tel: (972) 579-1024
> Fax: (972) 721-8147
> %FO: 100

> **ORANGINA USA COMPANY INC.**
> 156 East 46th St., New York, New York 10017-2632
> CEO: Lou Warner, Pres.
> Bus: *Soft drinks.*
> Tel: (212) 455-9400
> Fax: (212) 455-9400

> **YOO HOO INDUSTRIES INC.**
> 600 Commercial Ave., Carlstadt, New Jersey 07072 2602
> CEO: Brian O'Byrne
> Bus: *Beverages.*
> Tel: (201) 933-0070
> Fax: (201) 933-5360

● **CAMBRIDGE CONSULTANTS LTD.**
Science Park, Milton Rd., Cambridge CB4 0DW, England, U.K.
CEO: Brian Moon, CEO
Bus: *Business consulting services.*
Tel: 44-122-342-0024
Fax: 44-122-342-3373
www.cambridgeconsultants.com
Rev: $57
Emp: 84
NAICS: 541611, 541614, 541618, 541620

> **CAMBRIDGE CONSULTANTS**
> 451 D St., Boston, Massachusetts 02210
> CEO: Andrew Diston, Mng. Dir.
> Bus: *Business consulting services.*
> Tel: (617) 532-4700
> Fax: (617) 737-9889
> %FO: 100

● **CAPITAL & COUNTIES PLC**
40 Broadway, London SW1H 0BU, England, U.K.
CEO: John Saggers, Mng. Dir.
Bus: *Develops, invests in and manages commercial real estate.*
Tel: 44-20-7887-7000
Fax: 44-20-7887-0000
www.capital-and-counties.com
Rev: $97
Emp: 108
NAICS: 237210, 531120, 531190, 531312, 531390

CAPITAL & COUNTIES
100 The Embarcadero, Ste. 200, San Francisco, California 94105
CEO: Turner Newton, CEO
Bus: *Develops, invests in and manages commercial real estate.*
Tel: (415) 421-5100
Fax: (415) 421-6021
%FO: 100

● **CAPITAL CHRISTIAN & TIMBERS**
22 Bedford Square, London WC1B 3HH, England, U.K.
CEO: Marisa Kacary, CEO
Bus: *Executive search firm.*
Tel: 44-207-462-6200
Fax: 44-207-462-6201
www.capitalconsulting.com
NAICS: 541612

CHRISTIAN & TIMBERS
24 New England Executive Park, Burlington, Massachusetts 01803
CEO: Jennifer M. Burgess
Bus: *Executive search firm.*
Tel: (781) 229-9515
Fax: (781) 229-8608
%FO: 100

CHRISTIAN & TIMBERS
2180 Sand Hill Rd., Ste. 300, Menlo Park, California 94025
CEO: Robert L. Forman
Bus: *Executive search firm.*
Tel: (650) 798-0980
Fax: (650) 854-8026
%FO: 100

CHRISTIAN & TIMBERS
875 15th St. NW, Ste. 901, Washington, District of Columbia 20005
CEO: Richard W. Herman
Bus: *Executive search firm.*
Tel: (202) 730-7910
Fax: (202) 730-7910
%FO: 100

CHRISTIAN & TIMBERS
1177 Ave. of the Americas, New York, New York 10036
CEO: Daniel C. Barr
Bus: *Executive search firm.*
Tel: (212) 588-3500
Fax: (212) 688-5754
%FO: 100

CHRISTIAN & TIMBERS
25825 Science Park Dr., Ste. 200, Cleveland, Ohio 44122
CEO: Helen Briggs
Bus: *Executive search firm.*
Tel: (216) 464-8710
Fax: (216) 464-6160
%FO: 100

CHRISTIAN & TIMBERS
10211 Wincopin Circle, Columbia, Maryland 21044
CEO: Ernest W. Brittingham
Bus: *Executive search firm.*
Tel: (410) 393-0001
Fax: (410) 872-0208
%FO: 100

● **CAPITAL SAFETY GROUP LTD.**
6 Canon Harnett Court, Warren Farm, Wolverton Mill, Milton Keynes MK1 25NF, England, U.K.
CEO: Paul T.Trinder, CEO
Bus: *Rescue and fall protection equipment manufacture.*
Tel: 44-190-831-7600
Fax: 44-190-831-7611
www.capitalsafety.com
NAICS: 333311

CAPITAL SAFETY INC.
3965 Pepin Ave., Red Wing, Minnesota 55066
CEO: Pat Velasco, Pres.
Bus: *Mfr. of safety equipment.*
Tel: (651) 388-8282
Fax: (651) 388-5065
%FO: 100
Emp: 500

DBI/SALA
3965 Pepin Ave., Red Wing, Minnesota 55066
CEO: Pat Velasco, Pres.   Tel: (651) 388-8282
Bus: *Mfr. metal products.*   Fax: (651) 388-5065   Emp: 500

SINCO
701 Middle St., Middletown, Connecticut 06457
CEO: Mark Gibb, Pres.   Tel: (860) 632-0500
Bus: *Mfr. metal products.*   Fax: (860) 632-1509   Emp: 500

● **CARCLO PLC**
Springstone House, 27 Dewsbury Rd., Ossett, West Yorkshire WF5 9WS, England, U.K.
CEO: Ian Williamson, CEO   Tel: 44-1924-268-040   Rev: $212
Bus: *Plastic and specialty wire mfr.* Fax: 44-1924-283-226   Emp: 2,040
                                         www.carclo-plc.com
NAICS: 326220

    CTP CARRERA CORP.
    600 Depot St., Latrobe, Pennsylvania 15650-1617
    CEO: Douglas Wood, Pres.   Tel: (724) 539-1833   %FO: 100
    Bus: *Plastics mfr.*   Fax: (724) 539-6620

● **CARNIVAL PLC**
5 Gainsford St., London SE1 2NE, England, U.K.
CEO: Micky Arison, CEO   Tel: 44-20-7940-5381   Rev: $2,043
Bus: *Cruise operator.*   Fax: 44-20-7940-5382   Emp: 66,000
                                          www.carnivalcorp.com
NAICS: 483112

    CARNIVAL CORPORATION
    3655 NW 87th Ave., Miami, Florida 33178-2418
    CEO: Howard S. Frank   Tel: (305) 599-2600   %FO: 100
    Bus: *Cruise line.*   Fax: (305) 599-2600

    COSTA CRUISE LINES NV
    200 South Park Rd., Ste. 200, Hollywood, Florida 33021-8541
    CEO: Dino Schibuola, Pres.   Tel: (305) 358-7325   %FO: 100
    Bus: *Cruise line.*   Fax: (305) 375-0676   Emp: 320

● **THE CATALYST GROUP**
Dolphin House, St. Peter St., Winchester, Hampshire SO23 8BW, England, U.K.
CEO: John Scholes, Mng. Dir.   Tel: 44-1962-840-816
Bus: *Investment banking services.*   Fax: 44-845-280-1888
                                         www.it-catalyst.com
NAICS: 523110, 523120, 523130, 523140, 523930

    THE CATALYST GROUP
    470 Atlantic Ave., 4/F, Boston, Massachusetts 02210
    CEO: Robert Dunn   Tel: (617) 273-8121   %FO: 100
    Bus: *Investment banking services.* Fax: (617) 273-8121

THE CATALYST GROUP
4611 Bee Cave Rd., Ste. 108, Austin, Texas 78746
CEO: Ken Bresnen
Bus: *Investment banking services.*
Tel: (512) 327-9988
Fax: (512) 327-9988
%FO: 100

● **CAZENOVE GROUP PLC**
20 Moorgate, London EC2R 6DA, England, U.K.
CEO: Robert Pickering, Chmn.
Bus: *Securities brokerage, money management and investment banking services.*
Tel: 44-207-588-2828
Fax: 44-207-606-9205
www.cazenove.co.uk
Emp: 900
NAICS: 523110, 523120

CAZENOVE & COMPANY
640 Fifth Ave., 16/F, New York, New York 10019
CEO: Charles Garnett
Bus: *Securities broker/dealer, money management, and investment banking.*
Tel: (212) 376-1225
Fax: (212) 376-6160
%FO: 100
Emp: 32

● **CEDAR OPEN ACCOUNTS**
78 Portsmouth Rd., Cobham Surrey KT11 1HY, England, U.K.
CEO: Fiona Timothy, CEO
Bus: *Provides business software solutions and global enterprise consulting.*
Tel: 44-193-258-4000
Fax: 44-193-258-4001
www.cedargroup.co.uk
Rev: $81
Emp: 300
NAICS: 511210, 541511, 541512, 541519, 541618

CEDAR CONSULTING, INC.
57 Wingate St., Haverhill, Massachusetts 01832
CEO: Kerri Connelly
Bus: *Provides business software solutions and global enterprise consulting.*
Tel: (978) 372-0770
Fax: (978) 374-4382
%FO: 100

CEDAR CONSULTING, INC.
7475 Wisconsin Ave., Ste. 1050, Bethesda, Maryland 20814
CEO: Tom Rump
Bus: *Provides business software solutions and global enterprise consulting.*
Tel: (301) 951-4299
Fax: (301) 951-8724
%FO: 100

CEDAR CONSULTING, INC.
100 East Pratt St., 16/F, Baltimore, Maryland 21202
CEO: Neil Boyer
Bus: *Provides business software solutions and global enterprise consulting.*
Tel: (410) 576-1515
Fax: (410) 752-2879
%FO: 100

● **CELERANT CONSULTING LIMITED**
Avalon House, 72 Lower Mortlake Rd., London TW9 2JY, England, U.K.
CEO: Ian P. Clarkson, CEO
Bus: *Management consulting services.*
Tel: 44-20-8338-5000
Fax: 44-20-8338-5001
www.celerantconsulting.com
Rev: $162
Emp: 500
NAICS: 541611, 541614, 541618

CELERANT CONSULTING
Technology Center of Excellence, 67 Middle St. 3/F, Lowell, Massachusetts 01852
CEO: Ian P. Clarkson, CEO
Bus: *Management consulting services.*
Tel: (781) 674-0400
Fax: (978) 454-5200
%FO: 100

CELERANT CONSULTING INC.
45 Hayden Ave., Lexington, Massachusetts 02421
CEO: Bill Jeffrey
Bus: *Management consulting services.*

Tel: (781) 674-0400
Fax: (781) 274-7204

%FO: 100

● **CELLTECH GROUP PLC, DIV. UCB**
208 Bath Road, Slough Berkshire SL1 4EN, England, U.K.
CEO: Goran A. Ando, CEO
Bus: *Mfr. pharmaceuticals.*

Tel: 44-175-353-4655
Fax: 44-175-353-6632
www.celltechgroup.com

Rev: $630
Emp: 8,300

NAICS: 325411, 325412

CELLTECH PHARMACUETICALS
755 Jefferson Rd., Rochester, New York 14603
CEO: Ian Garland, COO
Bus: *Mfr. pharmaceuticals.*

Tel: (585) 475-9000
Fax: (585) 272-3926

%FO: 100

● **CELOXICA LIMITED**
66 Milton Park, Abingdon, Oxfordshire OX14 4RX, England, U.K.
CEO: Philip E. Bishop, CEO
Bus: *Software design.*

Tel: 44-1235-863656
Fax: 44-1235-863648
www.celoxica.com

Rev: $4
Emp: 65

NAICS: 511210

CELOXICA INC.
4516 Seton Center, Austin, Texas 78759
CEO: Jeff Jussel, Sales
Bus: *Software design and sales.*

Tel: (512) 795-8170
Fax: (512) 795-8167

%FO: 100

● **CELSIS INTERNATIONAL PLC**
Lyndon House, Kings Court, Newmarket, Suffolk CB8 7SG, England, U.K.
CEO: Jay LeCoque, Pres. & CEO
Bus: *Rapid diagnostic and monitoring systems
manufacture.*

Tel: 44-1638-600-151
Fax: 44-1638-600-160
www.celsis.com

Rev: $50
Emp: 178

NAICS: 334516, 541710

CELSIS INTERNATIONAL
6200 S. Lindbergh Blvd., St. Louis, Missouri 63123
CEO: Anne Pickles
Bus: *Mfr. and sales rapid diagnostic and
monitoring systems.*

Tel: (314) 487-6776
Fax: (314) 487-8991

%FO: 100

CELSIS INTERNATIONAL
165 Fieldcrest Ave., Edison, New Jersey 08837
CEO: Jenny Parsons
Bus: *Mfr. and sales rapid diagnostic and
monitoring systems.*

Tel: (732) 346-5210
Fax: (732) 346-5210

%FO: 100

CELSIS INTERNATIONAL
400 W. Erie, Ste. 300, Chicago, Illinois 60610
CEO: Arthur Holden
Bus: *Mfr. and sales rapid diagnostic and
monitoring systems.*

Tel: (312) 476-1200
Fax: (312) 476-1201

%FO: 100

- **CHAPELTHORPE PLC**
Chapelthorpe Hall, Church Lane, Wakefield, West Yorkshire WF4 3JB, England, U.K.
CEO: Brian Leckie, CEO
Bus: *Fiber, coating and umbrella frame mfr.*
Tel: 44-1924-248-200
Fax: 44-1924-248-222
www.chapelthorpe.com
Rev: $221
Emp: 815
NAICS: 325211, 325212, 325221, 339920

  DRAKE EXTRUSION
  PO Box 4868, Martinsville, Virginia 24115-4868
  CEO: John Parkinson, CEO
  Bus: *Research and development of polypropylene fiber technology.*
  Tel: (276) 632-0159
  Fax: (276) 632-0981
  %FO: 100

- **CHARLES TAYLOR CONSULTING PLC**
Essex House, 12-13 Essex, London WC2R 3AA, England, U.K.
CEO: John S. M. Rowe, Chmn. & CEO
Bus: *Insurance services.*
Tel: 44-20-7759-4955
Fax: 44-20-7759-4949
www.charlestaylorconsulting.com
Rev: $121
Emp: 720
NAICS: 524291, 524292, 541613

  BATEMAN CHAPMAN
  1980 Post Oak Blvd., Ste. 1890, Houston, Texas 77056
  CEO: Bill Rothhammer
  Bus: *Insurance services.*
  Tel: (713) 840-1642
  Fax: (713) 840-8030
  %FO: 100

  CHARLES TAYLOR CONSULTING
  12700 Park Central Dr., Ste. 1705, Dallas, Texas 75251
  CEO: Joe Roach
  Bus: *Insurance services.*
  Tel: (972) 770-1480
  Fax: (972) 770-1485
  %FO: 100

  CHARLES TAYLOR P&I MANAGEMENT
  40 Exchange Place, New York, New York 10005-2701
  CEO: Paul Barnes
  Bus: *Insurance services.*
  Tel: (212) 809-8085
  Fax: (212) 968-1978
  %FO: 100

  CTC AVIATION
  16415 Addison Rd., Ste. 800, Addison, Texas 75001-3268
  CEO: Richard Boeschen
  Bus: *Insurance services.*
  Tel: (972) 447-2050
  Fax: (972) 447-9050
  %FO: 100

  CTC AVIATION
  990 South Second St., Ste. 6, Ronkonkoma, New York 11779
  CEO: John Young
  Bus: *Insurance services.*
  Tel: (631) 285-6934
  Fax: (631) 285-6938
  %FO: 100

  CTC AVIATION
  411 Aviation Way, Frederick, Maryland 21701
  CEO: Gregg Pike
  Bus: *Insurance services.*
  Tel: (301) 694-4215
  Fax: (301) 694-4389
  %FO: 100

  CTC AVIATION
  514 Earth City Expressway, Ste. 241, Earth City, Missouri 63045
  CEO: Russell Day
  Bus: *Insurance services.*
  Tel: (314) 739-4526
  Fax: (314) 739-4990
  %FO: 100

CTC AVIATION
810 Bear Tavern Rd., Ste. 103, West Trenton, New Jersey 08628
CEO: Larry Belmont
Bus: *Insurance services.*
Tel: (609) 538-8502
Fax: (609) 538-8526
%FO: 100

CTC AVIATION
901 Rainier Ave. North, Ste. B201, Renton, Washington 98055
CEO: Bob Cole
Bus: *Insurance services.*
Tel: (206) 772-9315
Fax: (206) 772-3790
%FO: 100

CTC AVIATION
3555 Maguire Blvd., Ste. 204, Orlando, Florida 32803-3726
CEO: Steve Homenda
Bus: *Insurance services.*
Tel: (407) 894-1634
Fax: (407) 894-7731
%FO: 100

CTC AVIATION
16501 Sherman Way, Ste. 100, Van Nuys, California 91406
CEO: Scott McGinnis
Bus: *Insurance services.*
Tel: (818) 785-3513
Fax: (818) 785-0087
%FO: 100

CTC SERVICES AVIATION
2764 Compass Dr., Ste. 245, Grand Junction, Colorado 81506
CEO: Greg Heiss
Bus: *Insurance services.*
Tel: (970) 255-0300
Fax: (970) 255-0304
%FO: 100

CTS SERVICES PROPERTY & CASUALTY
5201 Blue Lagoon Dr., Ste. 884, Miami, Florida 33126
CEO: David Perry
Bus: *Insurance services.*
Tel: (305) 629-3683
Fax: (305) 629-3520
%FO: 100

SIGNAL ADMINISTRATION INC.
64 Danbury Rd., Wilton, Connecticut 06897
CEO: Richard Wood
Bus: *Insurance services.*
Tel: (203) 761-6060
Fax: (203) 761-6174
%FO: 100

● **CHARTER PLC**
52 Grosvenor Gardens, London SW1W 0AU, England, U.K.
CEO: David Gawler, Chmn. & CEO
Bus: *Equipment and machinery mfr.*
Tel: 44-20-7881-7800
Fax: 44-20-7259-9338
www.charterplc.com
Rev: $1,677
Emp: 9,040

NAICS: 333298, 333513

HOWDEN BUFFALO INC.
2029 W. DeKalb St., Camden, South Carolina 29020
CEO: Dave McDowell, Mng. Dir.
Bus: *Mfr. air movement equipment.*
Tel: (803) 713-2200
Fax: (803) 713-2222
%FO: 100

● **CHEMRING GROUP PLC**
1650 Parkway, Whiteley, Fareham, Hampshire PO15 7AH, England, U.K.
CEO: David Price, CEO
Bus: *Aerospace and defense countermeasures and marine and military electronics manufacture.*
Tel: 44-1489-881-880
Fax: 44-1489-881-123
www.chemring.co.uk
Rev: $232
Emp: 1,633

NAICS: 332995, 334290, 334419, 334511, 336413, 336992, 928110

ALLOY SURFACES INC.
121 North Commerce Dr., Chester Township, Pennsylvania 19014
CEO: John LaFemina, Pres.   Tel: (610) 497-7979   %FO: 100
Bus: *Self-protection technology services.*   Fax: (610) 497-7979

KILGORE FLARES CO., LLC
155 Kilgore Dr., Toone, Tennessee 38381
CEO: Thomas W. Plummer, VP Sales   Tel: (731) 658-5231   %FO: 100
Bus: *Scrap magnesium supplier.*   Fax: (731) 658-4173

● **CHLORIDE GROUP PLC**
Abford House, 15 Wilton Rd., London SW1V 1LT, England, U.K.
CEO: Keith Hodgkinson, CEO   Tel: 44-207-834-5500   Rev: $280
Bus: *Mfr. batteries, lighting fixtures, non-electric*   Fax: 44-207-630-0563   Emp: 1,414
   transformers.   www.chloridegroup.com
NAICS: 335121, 335122, 335129, 335311, 335911, 335912

   ONEAC CORPORATION
   27944 North Bradley Rd., Libertyville, Illinois 60048
   CEO: Theodore Antonitis, Pres.   Tel: (847) 816-6000   %FO: 100
   Bus: *Design/mfr. products that provide the*   Fax: (847) 680-5124
      highest level of protection against power
      and data line disturbances.

● **CHRISTIE'S INTERNATIONAL PLC**
8 King St., St. James's, London SW1Y 6QT, England, U.K.
CEO: Marc Porter, Pres.   Tel: 44-207-839-9060   Rev: $500
Bus: *Auctioneering company dealing in fine art.*   Fax: 44-207-839-1611   Emp: 2,500
      www.christies.com
NAICS: 454390, 561990

   CHRISTIE'S FINE ART AUCTINEERS
   360 North Camden Dr., Beverly Hills, California 90210
   CEO: Andrea Fiuczynski, Pres.   Tel: (310) 385-2600   %FO: 100
   Bus: *Auctioning of fine art.*   Fax: (310) 385-0247

   CHRISTIE'S FINE ART AUCTINEERS
   550 Bienville St., New Orleans, Louisiana 70130
   CEO: Susan Brennan   Tel: (504) 522-0008   %FO: 100
   Bus: *Auctioning of fine art.*   Fax: (504) 522-0008

   CHRISTIE'S FINE ART AUCTINEERS
   20 Rockefeller Plaza, New York, New York 10020
   CEO: Edward Dolman, CEO   Tel: (212) 636-2000   %FO: 100
   Bus: *Auctioning of fine art.*   Fax: (212) 636-2399

● **CHUBB, DIV. UTC**
Staines Rd. West, Chubb House, Sunbury on Thames, Middlesex TW16 7AR, England, U.K.
CEO: Olivier Robert, CEO   Tel: 44-1932-785588
Bus: *Security and fire protection services.*   Fax: 44-1932 738600   Emp: 48,000
      www.chubb.co.uk
NAICS: 334290, 334519

CHUBB, INC.
903 N. Bowser Rd., Ste. 250, Richardson, Texas 75081
CEO: Brenda Harrison
Bus: *Security and fire protection services.*
Tel: (972) 690-4691
Fax: (972) 690-4691
%FO: 100

CHUBB, INC.
4410 Dillon Lane, Ste. 38, Corpus Christi, Texas 78415
CEO: Mike Hickey
Bus: *Security and fire protection services.*
Tel: (361) 985-2761
Fax: (361) 985-2761

CHUBB, INC.
1209 E. Jasmine, Ste. B, McAllen, Texas 78501
CEO: Rudy Perez
Bus: *Security and fire protection services.*
Tel: (956) 618-1096
Fax: (956) 618-1096
%FO: 100

● **CIVICA PLC**
2 Burston Rd., London SW15 6AR, England, U.K.
CEO: Simon Richard Downing, CEO
Bus: *Software and services provider.*
Tel: 44-20-7760-2800
Fax: 44-20-7760-2888
www.civica.co.uk
Rev: $187
Emp: 456

NAICS: 511210

CREATIVE MICROSYSTEMS INC.
52 Hillside Ct., Englewood, Ohio 45322
CEO: Rick Fortman
Bus: *Software and services provider.*
Tel: (800) 686-9313
Fax: (937) 836-1036
%FO: 100

● **CLARKSON PLC**
St. Magnus House, 3 Lower Thames St., London EC3R 6HE, England, U.K.
CEO: Richard Fulford-Smith, CEO
Bus: *Integrated shipping services.*
Tel: 44-20-7334-0000
Fax: 44-20-7626-2967
www.clarksons.co.uk
Rev: $168
Emp: 329

NAICS: 483111

CLARKSON SHIPPING SERVICES USA INC.
1333 w. Loop S., Ste 1525, Houston, Texas 77027
CEO: Mike Reardon
Bus: *Integrated shipping services.*
Tel: (713) 235-7400
Fax: (713) 235-7449
%FO: 100

OVERSEAS WIBORG CHARTERING CO.
7 Mt. Lassen Dr., Ste. A-121, San Rafael, California 94003
CEO: Niels Hoy
Bus: *Integrated shipping services.*
Tel: (415) 479-2706
Fax: (415) 479-2841
%FO: 100

● **CLEARSPEED TECHNOLOGY LTD.**
3110 Great Western Court, Hunts Ground Rd., Bristol BS34 BHP, England, U.K.
CEO: Tom Beese, CEO
Bus: *Mfr. microprocessors.*
Tel: 44-117-317-2000
Fax: 44-117-317-2002
www.clearspeed.com
Rev: $
Emp: 28

NAICS: 334413

CLEARSPEED TECHNOLOGY LTD.
3031 Tisch Way, Ste. 502, San Jose, California 95128
CEO: Mike Calise
Bus: *Developer of high-performance, low-power, programmable microprocessor solutions.*

Tel: (408) 557-2067
Fax: (408) 557-9054

%FO: 100

● **CLESTRA HAUSERMAN LTD.**
Hamilton House, 3 North St., Carshalton, London SM5 2HZ, England, U.K.
CEO: Michel Douay, Chmn.
Bus: *Designs, produces and installs relocatable steel partitions and ceilings.*
NAICS: 236220, 238350, 238910, 238990

Tel: 44-20-8773-2121
Fax: 44-20-8773-4793
www.clestra.com

Rev: $200
Emp: 1,200

CLESTRA HAUSERMAN
PO Box 906, 4259 Swamp Rd., Ste. 108, Doylestown, Pennsylvania 18901
CEO: David R. Harkins Jr., Sales
Bus: *Designs, produces and installs relocatable steel partitions and ceilings.*

Tel: (267) 880-3700
Fax: (267) 880-3705

%FO: 100

● **CLIFFORD CHANCE LLP**
10 Upper Bank St., London E14 5JJ, England, U.K.
CEO: Peter Cornell, Mng. Prtn.
Bus: *International law.*

NAICS: 541110, 541199

Tel: 44-207-600-1000
Fax: 44-207-600 5555
www.cliffordchance.com

Rev: $1,350
Emp: 7,200

CLIFFORD CHANCE US LLP
31 W. 52nd St., New York, New York 10019
CEO: Craig Medwick, Mng. Prtn.
Bus: *International law firm.*

Tel: (212) 878-8000
Fax: (212) 878-8375

%FO: 100
Emp: 7,500

CLIFFORD CHANCE US LLP
2001 K St. NW, Washington, District of Columbia 20006
CEO: Leiv Blad, Mgr.
Bus: *International law.*

Tel: (202) 912-5000
Fax: (202) 912-6000

%FO: 100

CLIFFORD CHANCE US LLP
990 Marsh Rd., Menlo Park, California 94025
CEO: Daniel Harris, Mng. Prtn.
Bus: *International law.*

Tel: (650) 566-4300
Fax: (650) 566-4399

%FO: 100

● **CLINICAL COMPUTING PLC**
2 Kew Bridge Rd., Brentford, London TWF 0JF, England, U.K.
CEO: Jack Richardson, CEO
Bus: *Design and marketing of health care management software.*
NAICS: 511210

Tel: 44-20-8747-8744
Fax: 44-20-8747-8745
www.ccl.com

Rev: $41
Emp: 3

CLINICAL COMPUTING
801-B West Eighth St., Ste. 510, Cincinnati, Ohio 45203
CEO: Doug Colyer, Sales
Bus: *Design and marketing of health care management software.*

Tel: (513) 651-3803
Fax: (513) 651-5813

%FO: 100

• CMS CAMERON MCKENNA LLP
Mitre House, 160 Aldersgate St., London EC1A 4DD, England, U.K.
CEO: Richard Price, Sr. Prtn.   Tel: 44-207-367-3000
Bus: *International law firm.*   Fax: 44-207-367-2000
                                         www.law-now.com
NAICS: 541110
    CMS BUREAU FRANCIS LEFEBVRE
    712 Fifth Ave., New York, New York 10019
    CEO: Carina Levintoff, Partner   Tel: (212) 246-8045   %FO: 100
    Bus: *International law office.*   Fax: (212) 246-2951

• COATS HOLDINGS, DIV. GUINESS PEAT
1 The Square, Stockley Park, Uxbridge, London UB11 1TD, England, U.K.
CEO: Mike Smithyman, Pres.   Tel: 44-20-8210-5000   Rev: $1,784
Bus: *Mfr. textiles, yarns, fabrics and precision*   Fax: 44-20-8210-5030   Emp: 31,135
   engineering products.   www.coats.com
NAICS: 313112, 313113
    COATS VIYELLA NORTH AMERICA, INC.
    4135 South Stream Dr., Charlotte, North Carolina 28217
    CEO: Max Perks, Mgr.   Tel: (704) 329-5800   %FO: 100
    Bus: *U.S. holding company.*   Fax: (704) 329-5820   Emp: 180

• COBHAM PLC
Brook Rd., Wimborne, Dorset BH21 2BJ, England, U.K.
CEO: Gordon F. Page, Chmn.   Tel: 44-120-288-2020   Rev: $1,480
Bus: *Mfr. fuel tanks and air-to-air flight refueling*   Fax: 44-120-284-0523   Emp: 8,990
   equipment.   www.cobham.com
NAICS: 336413
    CARLETON TECHNOLOGIES INC.
    10 Cobham Dr., Orchard Park, New York 14127
    CEO: Padraig H. Cawdery   Tel: (716) 662-0006   %FO: 100
    Bus: *Mfr. pneumatic systems and life support*   Fax: (716) 662-0747
    equipment.

    CONAX FLORIDA CORPORATION
    2801 75th St. North, St. Petersburg, Florida 33710
    CEO: Jeff Eckhart   Tel: (727) 345-8000   %FO: 100
    Bus: *Mfr. electro-explosive actuated valves, life*   Fax: (727) 345-4217
    preserver auto inflators and gas storage
    systems.

• COBRA BIOMANUFCTURING PLC
Stephenson Bldg., The Science Park, Keele, Staffordshire ST5 5SP, England, U.K.
CEO: David Thatcher, CEO   Tel: 44-1782-714-101   Rev: $4
Bus: *Biopharmaceuticals and gene medicines*   Fax: 44-1782-714-168   Emp: 75
   manufacture.   www.cobrabio.com
NAICS: 325411

COBRA BIOMANUFACTURING INC.
3020 El Cerrito Plaza, Ste. 300, El Cerrito, California 94530
CEO: Cathy Smith
Bus: *Biopharmaceuticals and gene medicines manufacture and sales.*
Tel: (510) 233-3107
Fax: (510) 233-3437
%FO: 100

COBRA BIOMANUFACTURING INC.
500 N. Michigan Ave., Ste. 300, Chicago, Illinois 60611
CEO: Jason Rahal
Bus: *Biopharmaceuticals and gene medicines manufacture and sales.*
Tel: (773) 865-2411
Fax: (773) 506-6513
%FO: 100

● **CODASCISYS PLC**
Methuen Park, Chippenham, Wiltshire SN14 0GB, England, U.K.
CEO: Graham Steinsberg, CEO
Bus: *Financial software and information technology services.*
NAICS: 511210, 541511, 541512, 541519
Tel: 44-1249-466466
Fax: 44-1249-466664
www.codascisys.co.uk
Rev: $131
Emp: 845

CODA FINANCIALS USA
350 Indiana St., Ste. 601, Golden, Colorado 80401
CEO: Kevin Roberts, VP
Bus: *Accounting software manufacture.*
Tel: (303) 216-9220
Fax: (303) 216-0321
%FO: 100

CODA FINANCIALS USA
1155 Elm St., 7/F, Manchester, New Hampshire 03101
CEO: Sherri Gray
Bus: *Accounting software manufacture.*
Tel: (603) 471-1700
Fax: (603) 471-1717
%FO: 100

● **THE CODEMASTERS SOFTWARE COMPANY**
Stoneythorpe, Southam Leamington Spa, Warwickshire CV47 2DL, England, U.K.
CEO: Nicholas C. Wheelwright, Mng. Dir.
Bus: *Software developer and publisher.*
NAICS: 511210
Tel: 44-1926-814-132
Fax: 44-1926-817-595
www.codemasters.co.uk

CODEMASTERS USA
350 5th Ave., 59/F, New York, New York 10118
CEO: Marc Bennett, Pres.
Bus: *Develops and publishes software.*
Tel: (212) 601-2670
Fax: (212) 601-2649
%FO: 100

● **CODIMA TECHNOLOGIES INC.**
191 Victoria St., Victoria Station House, London SW1E 5NE, England, U.K.
CEO: Christer Mattsson, CEO
Bus: *Network management software manufacture.*
NAICS: 511210
Tel: 44-171-448-508
Fax: 44-171-541-67
www.codimatech.com

CODIMA TECHNOLOGIES INC.
101 Bill Smith Blvd., King of Prussia Inn, King of Prussia, Pennsylvania 19406
CEO: David Williams, Sales
Bus: *Network software manufacture.*
Tel: (610) 579-9435
Fax: (610) 482-9166
%FO: 100

- **COLLINS STEWART TULLETT PLC**
88 Wood St., 9th Fl., London EC2V 7QR, England, U.K.
CEO: Terry Smith, CEO
Bus: *Inter-dealer broker (IDB) services.*
Tel: 44-20-7523-8000
Fax: 44-20-7523-8131
www.collins-stewart.com
Rev: $1,122
Emp: 2,092
NAICS: 523120

  COLLINS STEWART INC.
  101 Hudson St., 24/F, Jersey City, New Jersey 07302
  CEO: Edward Tereskiewicz
  Bus: *Inter-dealer broker (IDB) services.*
  Tel: (201) 557-5000
  Fax: (201) 557-5995
  %FO: 100

  COLLINS STEWART INC.
  50 Federal St., 7/F, Boston, Massachusetts 02110
  CEO: Richard McDonald
  Bus: *Inter-dealer broker (IDB) services.*
  Tel: (617) 556-2600
  Fax: (617) 357-5592
  %FO: 100

  COLLINS STEWART INC.
  444 Madison Ave., 41/F, New York, New York 10022
  CEO: Mark Perkins
  Bus: *Inter-dealer broker (IDB) services.*
  Tel: (212) 652-9000
  Fax: (212) 652-9050
  %FO: 100

  COLLINS STEWART INC.
  108 Corporate Park Dr., White Plains, New York 10604
  CEO: Shawn McLoughlin
  Bus: *Inter-dealer broker (IDB) services.*
  Tel: (914) 694-6412
  Fax: (914) 696-1329
  %FO: 100

  TULLETT LIBERTY INC.
  80 Pine St., 28/F, New York, New York 10005
  CEO: Mark Perkins
  Bus: *Inter-dealer broker (IDB) services.*
  Tel: (212) 208-2000
  Fax: (212) 208-2019
  %FO: 100

- **COMPASS GROUP PLC**
Cowley House, Guildford St., Chertsey, Surrey KT16 9BA, England, U.K.
CEO: Michael J. Bailey, CEO
Bus: *Food service contract and catering, restaurant and food outlets.*
Tel: 44-193-257-3000
Fax: 44-193-256-9956
www.compass-group.com
Rev: $21,175
Emp: 402,375
NAICS: 722110, 722211, 722310

  CANTEEN CORPORATION
  216 W Diversey Ave., Elmhurst, Illinois 60126
  CEO: Bob Smith
  Bus: *Provides food service.*
  Tel: (630) 833-3666
  Fax: (630) 832-3927
  %FO: 100

  COMPASS GROUP FOOD SERVICE CORP
  2400 Yorkmont Rd., Charlotte, North Carolina 28217
  CEO: Gary R. Green
  Bus: *Provides food service.*
  Tel: (704) 329-4000
  Fax: (704) 329-4160
  %FO: 100

- **CONTROL RISKS GROUP**
  Cottons Ctr., Cottons Lane, London SE1 2QG, England, U.K.
  CEO: Christopher Kemball, Dir.   Tel: 44-207-970-2100   Rev: $116
  Bus: *Advice on Fraud Prevention, Investigations, Due*   Fax: 44-207-970-2222   Emp: 411
      Diligence, Money Laundering and other services   www.crg.com
  NAICS: 541611, 561613

  CONTROL RISKS GROUP
  550 S. Hope St., Ste. 2330, Los Angeles, California 90071
  CEO: Eline Carey, Mgr.   Tel: (213) 996-7560
  Bus: *Security Consulting*   Fax: (213) 624-1634

  CONTROL RISKS GROUP
  1600 K St. NW, Ste. 450, Washington, District of Columbia 20006
  CEO: Andreas Carleton-Smith, Pres.   Tel: (202) 449-3330
  Bus: *Security consulting*   Fax: (202) 449-3325   Emp: 35

  CONTROL RISKS GROUP
  19 West 44th St., Ste. 412, New York, New York 10036
  CEO: Dana Kelly, Mgr.   Tel: (212) 967-3955
  Bus: *Security Consulting*   Fax: (212) 967-3956

- **COOKSON GROUP PLC**
  265 Strand, London WC2R 1DB, England, U.K.
  CEO: Nicholas Robin Salmon, CEO   Tel: 44-207-766-4500   Rev: $2,916
  Bus: *Industrial materials manufacture.*   Fax: 44-207-747-6600   Emp: 15,653
                                               www.cooksongroup.co.uk
  NAICS: 212221, 212222, 327124

  COOKSON ELECTRONICS ASSEMBLY MATERIALS
  600 Route 440, Jersey City, New Jersey 07304
  CEO: David Zerfoss   Tel: (201) 434-6778   %FO: 100
  Bus: *Assembly materials manufacture.*   Fax: (201) 434-7508

  COOKSON ELECTRONICS INC.
  50 Sims Ave., Providence, Rhode Island 02909
  CEO: Stephen Corbett, Mgr.   Tel: (401) 228-8800   %FO: 100
  Bus: *Precious metals manufacture.*   Fax: (401) 228-8879

- **CORIN GROUP PLC**
  The Corinium Centre, Cirencester, Gloucestershire GL7 1YJ, England, U.K.
  CEO: Ian Paling, CEO   Tel: 44-1285-659-866   Rev: $49
  Bus: *Designs and manufactures reconstructive* Fax: 44-1285-658-960   Emp: 227
      orthopedic devices.   www.corin.co.uk
  NAICS: 334510, 339112, 339113

  CORIN USA INC.
  10500 University Center Dr., Ste. 190, Tampa, Florida 33612
  CEO: Roger Salvati, VP Sales   Tel: (813) 977-4469   %FO: 100
  Bus: *Manufacture and sales reconstructive*   Fax: (813) 979-0042
      orthopedic devices.

- **CORPORATE SERVICES GROUP PLC**
  800 The Boulevard, Capability Green Luton, London LU1 3BA, England, U.K.
  CEO: John Rowley, CEO
  Bus: *Temporary staff services.*

  Tel: 44-1582-692-692
  Fax: 44-1582-698-698
  www.corporateservices.co.uk

  Rev: $932
  Emp: 1,967

  NAICS: 561320

  > **CORPORATE SERVICES GROUP**
  > 1775 St. James Place, Ste. 300, Houston, Texas 77056
  > CEO: Steven R. Drexel, PR
  > Bus: *Temporary staff services.*
  >
  > Tel: (713) 438-1400
  > Fax: (713) 438-1763
  >
  > %FO: 100

- **CORUS GROUP, PLC**
  30 Millbank, London SW1P 4WY, England, U.K.
  CEO: Philippe Varin, CEO
  Bus: *Steel production, rolling, processing and distribution.*

  Tel: 44-20-7717-4444
  Fax: 44-20-7717-4455
  www.corusgroup.com

  Rev: $17,891
  Emp: 48,300

  NAICS: 331111, 331210, 331221, 331222, 331312

  > **CORUS INTERNATIONAL AMERICAS**
  > 475 N. Martingale Rd., Ste. 400, Schaumburg, Illinois 60173
  > CEO: Jeffrey W. Hoye, Pres.
  > Bus: *US Steel sales*
  >
  > Tel: (847) 619-0400
  > Fax: (847) 619-0468
  >
  > Emp: 30

  > **THOMAS STEEL STRIP CORP.**
  > Delaware Ave., N.W., Warren, Ohio 44485
  > CEO: Denny Wist, Pres. & CEO
  > Bus: *Steel production*
  >
  > Tel: (330) 841-6222
  > Fax: (330) 841-6430
  >
  > %FO: 100

- **COSWORTH TECHNOLOGY LTD.**
  Costin House, St. James Mill Rd., Northampton NN5 5TZ, England, U.K.
  CEO: Norbert Südhaus, CEO
  Bus: *Mfr. aluminum alloy casting power trains and vehicle engine parts with sand casting*

  Tel: 44-870-157-3000
  Fax: 44-870-157-3100
  www.cosworth-technology.co.uk

  NAICS: 333511, 333516, 333613

  > **COSWORTH INTELLIGENT CONTROLS INC.**
  > 41000 Vincenti Ct., Novi, Michigan 48375
  > CEO: Dale Henriksen, Sales
  > Bus: *Mfr. aluminum alloy casting power trains and vehicle engine parts with sand casting technology.*
  >
  > Tel: (248) 471-5000
  > Fax: (248) 471-3680
  >
  > %FO: 100

- **CP SHIPS LIMITED**
  62-65 Trafalgar Sq., London WC2N 5DY, England, U.K.
  CEO: Raymond R. Miles, CEO
  Bus: *Container carrier.*

  Tel: 44-207-389-1100
  Fax: 44-207389-6841
  www.cpships.com

  Rev: $2,687
  Emp: 1,000

  NAICS: 483111

LYKES LINES LTD.
401 E. Jackson St., Ste. 401, Tampa, Florida 33602
CEO: Michael Cunningham   Tel: (813) 276-4600   %FO: 100
Bus: *Container carrier shipping line.*   Fax: (813) 276-4878

● **CRAMER SYSTEMS EUROPE LIMITED**
Cramer House, The Square, Lower Bristol Rd., Bath BA2 3BH, England, U.K.
CEO: Jerry Crook, CEO   Tel: 44-122-547-1300
Bus: *Management network software.*   Fax: 44-122-547-1301
                                        www.cramer.com
NAICS: 511210

    CRAMER SYSTEMS INC.
    1593 Spring Hill Rd., Ste. 530, Vienna, Virginia 22182
    CEO: Stephen Hurn   Tel: (571) 633-4440   %FO: 100
    Bus: *Software sales.*   Fax: (571) 633-4441

● **CRODA INTERNATIONAL PLC**
Cowick Hall, Snaith, Goole, East Yorkshire DN14 9AA, England, U.K.
CEO: Michael Humphrey, CEO   Tel: 44-140-586-0551   Rev: $539
Bus: *Specialty chemicals manufacture.*   Fax: 44-140-586-0202   Emp: 1,691
                                          www.croda.co.uk
NAICS: 325199

    CRODA INC.
    300 A Columbus Circle, Edison, New Jersey 08837
    CEO: Robert Comber, VP   Tel: (732) 417-0800   %FO: 100
    Bus: *Chemical specialties*   Fax: (732) 417-0804

    SEDERMA INC.
    300 A Columbus Circle, Edison, New Jersey 08837
    CEO: Kevin Gallagher   Tel: (732) 417-0800   %FO: 100
    Bus: *Active ingredients for skin care.*   Fax: (732) 417-0804

● **CSR (CAMBRIDGE SILICON RADIO)**
Cambridge Science Park, Cowley RD., Cambridge CB4 0WH, England, U.K.
CEO: John S. Hodgson, CEO   Tel: 44-122-369-2000   Rev: $488
Bus: *Design and manufacture of radio chips.*   Fax: 44-122--69-2001   Emp: 248
                                          www.csr.com
NAICS: 334413

    CSR INC.
    1651 N. Collins Blvd., Ste. 210, Richardson, Texas 75080
    CEO: Simon Finch   Tel: (972) 238-2300   %FO: 100
    Bus: *Design and manufacture of radio chips.*   Fax: (972) 231-1440

● **CSS STELLAR PLC**
Drury House, 34-43 Russell St., Covent Garden, London WC2B 5HA, England, U.K.
CEO: Sean Kelly, CEO   Tel: 44-20-7078-1400   Rev: $150
Bus: *Sports and entertainment marketing group.*   Fax: 44-20-707801401   Emp: 503
                                          www.css-stellar.com
NAICS: 541840, 711410

HAMBRIC SPORTS MANAGEMENT
2515 McKinney Ave., Ste. 940, Dallas, Texas 75201
CEO: Rocky Hambric   Tel: (214) 720-7179   %FO: 100
Bus: *Sports and entertainment marketing group.*   Fax:

PFD NY
373 Park Ave. South, 5/F, New York, New York 10016
CEO: Zoe Pagnamenta   Tel: (917) 256-0707   %FO: 100
Bus: *Sports and entertainment marketing group.*   Fax: (212) 685-9635

THE GEM GROUP
5 Concourse Pkwy., Ste. 1000, Atlanta, Georgia 30328
CEO: Keith McCracken, CEO   Tel: (678) 259-9400   %FO: 100
Bus: *Sports and entertainment marketing group.*   Fax: (678) 259-9600

THE GEM GROUP
373 Park Ave. South, 5/F, New York, New York 10016
CEO: Margo Vallone   Tel: (212) 448-9200   %FO: 100
Bus: *Sports and entertainment marketing group.*   Fax: (212) 685-9635

THE GEM GROUP
5900 Rowland Rd., Minnetonka, Minnesota 55343
CEO: Keith McCracken, CEO   Tel: (952) 831-6313   %FO: 100
Bus: *Sports and entertainment marketing group.*   Fax: (952) 653-5900

THE GEM GROUP
2801 Youngfield, Ste. 210, Golden, Colorado 80401
CEO: Tip Nunn   Tel: (303) 237-0616   %FO: 100
Bus: *Sports and entertainment marketing group.*   Fax: (303) 237-0609

THE GEM GROUP
1402 Toplea, Euless, Texas 76040
CEO: Rosie Crews   Tel: (817) 684-0366   %FO: 100
Bus: *Sports and entertainment marketing group.*   Fax: (817) 684-0365

● DAILY MAIL AND GENERAL TRUST (DMGT) PLC
Northcliffe House, 2 Derry Street, Kensington, London W8 5TT, England, U.K.
CEO: Charles J. F. Sinclair, CEO   Tel: 44-207-938-6000   Rev: $3,792
Bus: *Media holding company.*   Fax: 44-207-937-3745   Emp: 18,737
www.dmgt.co.uk

NAICS: 511110, 511120, 541840

DMG INFORMATION (DMGI)
68 Southfield Ave., Ste. 210, Stamford, Connecticut 06902
CEO: Martin Morgan   Tel: (203) 973-2940   %FO: 100
Bus: *Business to business information.*   Fax: (203) 973-2995

RISK MANAGEMENT SOLUTIONS (RMSI)
744 Broad St., 14/F, Newark, New Jersey 07102
CEO: Hemant Shah, Pres.   Tel: (973) 848-4900   %FO: 100
Bus: *Provides products and services for the*   Fax: (973) 848-4901
quantification and management of natural
hazard risks.

RISK MANAGEMENT SOLUTIONS (RMSI)
7015 Gateway Blvd., Newark, California 94560
CEO: Smita Khoot, Pres.
Bus: *Provides products and services for the quantification and management of natural hazard risks.*

Tel: (510) 505-2500
Fax: (510) 505-2501

%FO: 100

● **DANKA BUSINESS SYSTEMS PLC**
Masters House, 107 Hammersmith Rd., London W14 0QH, England, U.K.
CEO: Todd L. Mavis, Chmn.
Bus: *Mfr./distributes photocopiers, fax machines and paper supplies.*
NAICS: 333313, 333315

Tel: 44-207-605-0150
Fax: 44-207-603-8448
www.danka.com

Rev: $1,233
Emp: 7,700

DANKA BUSINESS SYSTEMS
11101 Roosevelt Blvd. North, St. Petersburg, Florida 33716
CEO: P. Lang Lowrey III, Pres.
Bus: *Sales/distribution of photocopiers and fax machines.*

Tel: (727) 576-6003
Fax: (727) 579-0832

%FO: 100

DANKA OFFICE IMAGING CO.
801 Cromwell Park Dr., Ste. 107, Glen Burnie, Maryland 21061
CEO: James Morrell
Bus: *Office machines and equipment sales.*

Tel: (410) 553-3875
Fax: (410) 553-3890

%FO: 100

DANKA OFFICE IMAGING CO.
90 Park Ave., 11/F, New York, New York 10016
CEO: Eurel Tobicas
Bus: *Office machines sales and service.*

Tel: (917) 542-2400
Fax: (917) 542-2400

%FO: 100

DANKA OFFICE IMAGING CO.
1601 Trapelo Rd., Ste. 264, Waltham, Massachusetts 02451
CEO: Ray Patten
Bus: *Office machines sales and service.*

Tel: (781) 464-7600
Fax: (781) 464-7620

%FO: 100

● **DATA CONNECTION LIMITED**
100 Church St., Enfield, London EN2 6BQ, England, U.K.
CEO: Phil McConnell, CEO
Bus: *Designs and sells messaging and networking software.*
NAICS: 511210

Tel: 44-208-366-1177
Fax: 44-208-363-1468
www.dataconnection.com

Rev: $52
Emp: 300

DATA CONNECTION CORPORATION
12007 Sunrise Valley Dr., Ste. 250, Reston, Virginia 20191
CEO: Ian Ferguson
Bus: *Network software sales.*

Tel: (703) 715-4914
Fax: (703) 480-0499

%FO: 100

DATA CONNECTION CORPORATION
1411 Harbor Bay Pkwy., Ste. 1003, Alameda, California 94502
CEO: Carol Daniels, Sales
Bus: *Network software sales.*

Tel: (510) 748-8230
Fax: (510) 748-8230

%FO: 100

● **DATAMONITOR PLC**
108-110 Finchley Rd., London NW3 5JJ, England, U.K.
CEO: Michael T. Danson, CEO
Bus: *Engaged in market analysis.*

Tel: 44-207-675-7000
Fax: 44-207-675-7500
www.datamonitor.com

Rev: $66
Emp: 543

NAICS: 541910

DATAMONITOR INC.
1 Park Ave., New York, New York 10016-5802
CEO: Brian Huff, PR
Bus: *Engaged in market analysis for the
technology industry.*

Tel: (212) 686-7400
Fax: (212) 686-2626

%FO: 100

● **DAVID HALSALL INTERNATIONAL LTD.**
Eastham House, Copse Rd., Fleetwood, Lancashire FY7 7NY, England, U.K.
CEO: Graham Wilson Halsall, CEO
Bus: *Mfr. toys, Christmas decorations, stationery and
gifts and seasonal furniture.*

Tel: 44-125-377-5533
Fax: 44-125-387-8711
www.dhalsall.com

NAICS: 339931, 339932

DAVID HALSALL LTD.
200 Fifth Ave., Rm. 335, New York, New York 10017
CEO: David Alan Halsall
Bus: *Mfr. toys, Christmas decorations, stationery
and gifts and seasonal furniture.*

Tel: (212) 675-3535
Fax: (212) 807-2600

%FO: 100

● **DAWSON INTERNATIONAL PLC**
Lochieven Mills, Kinross KY13 8GL, England, U.K.
CEO: Mike Hartley, Chmn.
Bus: *Mfr. and distributos cashmere products.*

Tel: 44-1577-867000
Fax: 44-1577-867010
www.dawson-International.co.uk

Rev: $98
Emp: 908

NAICS: 315993, 315999

DAWSON-FORTE CASHMERE
499 Seventh Ave., 17/F, South, New York, New York 10018
CEO: Debbie Davidson
Bus: *Cashmere products.*

Tel: (212) 997-2524
Fax: (212) 869-2853

%FO: 100

● **DDD GROUP PLC**
c/o Cargil Management Services, 90 Gloucester Pl., London W1U 6EH, England, U.K.
CEO: Paul Kristensen, Chmn.
Bus: *Computer software manufacture.*

Tel: 44-117-957-3666
Fax: 44-780-154-0358
www.ddd.com

NAICS: 511210

DDD GROUP
3000 Ocean Park Blvd., Ste. 1025, Santa Monica, California 90404
CEO: Chris Yewdall, Pres.
Bus: *Software manufacture.*

Tel: (310) 566-3340
Fax: (310) 566-3380

%FO: 100

- **DECHRA PHARMACEUTICALS PLC**
  Dechra House, Jamage Industrial Estate, Talke Pits, Stroke-on-Trent ST7 1XW, England, U.K.
  CEO: Michael Redmond, Chmn.   Tel: 44-178-277-1100   Rev: $338
  Bus: *Mfr. of veterinary pharmaceuticals*   Fax: 44-178-277-3366   Emp: 643
                         www.dechra.com
  NAICS: 325411, 325412

       DECHRA VETERINARY PRODUCTS
       7505 NW Tiffany Springs Pkwy., Ste. 210, Kansas City, Missouri 64153
       CEO: Mike Edwards, Pres.   Tel: (866) 933-2472   %FO: 100
       Bus: *Manufacturer of veterinary pharmaceuticals.*   Fax:

- **DELCAM PLC**
  Talbot Way, Small Heath Business Park, Birmingham B10 OHJ, England, U.K.
  CEO: Hugh R.O. Humphreys, Mng. Dir.   Tel: 44-121-766-5544   Rev: $36
  Bus: *Mfr. software for design and manufacturing.*   Fax: 44-121-766-5511   Emp: 309
                         www.delcam.com
  NAICS: 511210

       AXSYS INCORPORATED
       29627 West Tech Dr., Wixom, Michigan 48393
       CEO: Steve Braykovich, Pres. & CEO   Tel: (248) 926-8810   %FO: 100
       Bus: *Mfr. software for design and manufacturing.*   Fax: (248) 926-9085

       PROGRAMMING PLUS, INC.
       17685 West Lincoln Ave., New Berlin, Wisconsin 53146
       CEO: Thomas Bently, CEO   Tel: (262) 786-3500   %FO: 100
       Bus: *Mfr. software for design and manufacturing.*   Fax: (262) 786-3501

       ROMER CIMCORE INC.
       27240 Haggerty Rd., Suite, Farmington Hills, Michigan 48331
       CEO: Paul Evans   Tel: (248) 324-5100   %FO: 100
       Bus: *Mfr. electronic measuring machines.*   Fax: (248) 324-0525

       ROMER CIMCORE INC.
       5145 Avenida Encinas, Carlsbad, California 92008
       CEO: Thomas Moran   Tel: (760) 438-1725   %FO: 100
       Bus: *Mfr. electronic measuring machines.*   Fax: (760) 438-3512

       SURFWARE, INC., DIV. PROGRAMMING PLUS
       5703 Corsa Ave., Westlake Village, California 91362
       CEO: Linda Voge, CEO   Tel: (818) 991-1960   %FO: 100
       Bus: *Mfr. software for design and manufacturing.*   Fax: (818) 991-1980

- **DELTA PLC**
  One Kingsway, 7th Fl., London WC2B 6NP, England, U.K.
  CEO: Todd Atkinson, CEO   Tel: 44-207-836-3535   Rev: $930
  Bus: *Engineering, specializing in electrical, electrolytic*   Fax: 44-207-836-4511   Emp: 10,000
      manganese and galvanizing.   www.deltaplc.com
  NAICS: 541330

DELTA TECHNICAL SALES INC.
11911 NE First St., Bellevue, Washington 98005
CEO: Steve Mowe, Pres.
Bus: *Engineering, specializing in electrical, electrolytic manganese and galvanizing.*

Tel: (425) 688-0812
Fax: (425) 688-0813

%FO: 100

DELTA TECHNICAL SALES INC.
15050 SW Koll Pkwy., Beaverton, Oregon 97006
CEO: Bret Gutzka, Sales
Bus: *Engineering, specializing in electrical, electrolytic manganese and galvanizing.*

Tel: (503) 646-7747
Fax: (503) 646-7747

%FO: 100

● **DENISON INTERNATIONAL PLC**
Masters House, 107 Hammersmith Rd., London W14 0QH, England, U.K.
CEO: David L. Weir, CEO
Bus: *Mfr. hydraulic products for industrial machinery.*

Tel: 44-207-603-1515
Fax: 44-207-603-8448
www.denisonhydraulics.com

Rev: $158
Emp: 1,150

NAICS: 333995

DENISON HYDRAULICS INC.
14249 Industrial Pkwy., Marysville, Ohio 43040
CEO: Colin Keith, Mgr.
Bus: *Mfr. hydraulic products for industrial machinery.*

Tel: (937) 644-3915
Fax: (937) 644-3915

%FO: 100

● **DENNIS PUBLISHING LTD.**
30 Cleveland St., London W1P 5FF, England, U.K.
CEO: Felix Dennis, Chmn.
Bus: *Magazine publisher.*

Tel: 44-207-907-6000
Fax: 44-207-907-6020
www.theden.co.uk

Rev: $345
Emp: 640

NAICS: 511120, 512110, 516110

DENNIS PUBLISHING INC.
1040 Sixth Ave., New York, New York 10018
CEO: Stephen Colvin, Pub.
Bus: *Magazine publishing.*

Tel: (212) 302-2626
Fax: (212) 302-2635

%FO: 100

● **DENSITRON TECHNOLOGIES PLC**
Unit 4, Airport Trading Estate, Biggin Hill, Kent TN16 3BW, England, U.K.
CEO: Phil Lawler, Chmn.
Bus: *Design, manufacture and distribution of computer and public information displays.*

Tel: 44-1959-542-000
Fax: 44-1959-542-001
www.densitron.com

Rev: $50
Emp: 210

NAICS: 334111, 334113, 334119

DENSITRON CORPORATION
10400-4 Pioneer Blvd., Santa Fe Springs, California 90670
CEO: Grahame R. Falconer
Bus: *Industrial computers & peripherals sales and distribution.*

Tel: (562) 941-5000
Fax: (562) 941-5757

%FO: 100

● **DETICA GROUP PLC**
Surrey Research Park, Guildford, Surrey GU2 7YP, England, U.K.
CEO: Tom Black, CEO   Tel: 44-1483-442-000   Rev: $98
Bus: *IT consulting services.*   Fax: 44-1483-442-144   Emp: 492
                                             www.detica.com
NAICS: 511210, 541511, 541512
    DETICA INC.
    10440 Little Patuxent Pkwy., Stes. 300/900, Columbia, Maryland 21044
    CEO: Dean Bakeris, mgr   Tel: (410) 884-4010   %FO: 100
    Bus: *IT consulting services.*   Fax: (410) 740-5684

● **DIAGEO PLC**
8 Henrietta Place, London W1G 0MD, England, U.K.
CEO: Paul S. Walsh, CEO   Tel: 44-20-7927-5200   Rev: $16,161
Bus: *Distributor of food (Burger King), wines and*   Fax: 44-20-7927-4600   Emp: 23,720
   spirits. DIAGEO-Guinness USA Inc.   www.diageo.co.uk
NAICS: 312120, 312140
    CHALONE WINE GROUP
    621 Airpark Rd., Napa, California 94558
    CEO: Thomas B. Selfridge, Pres. & CEO   Tel: (707) 254-4200
    Bus: *Winemakers.*   Fax: (707) 254-4201   Emp: 170

    DIAGEO CHATEAU & ESTATE WINES CO.
    240 Gateway Rd. West, Napa, California 94558
    CEO: Ray Chadwick, Pres.   Tel: (707) 299-2700
    Bus: *Winemakers.*   Fax:

    DIAGEO NORTH AMERICA
    Six Landmark Square, Stamford, Connecticut 06901
    CEO: Ivan M. Menezes, Pres. & CEO   Tel: (203) 299-2100   %FO: 100
    Bus: *Import/distribution of wines and spirits.*   Fax: (203) 359-7402

    EDNA VALLEY VINEYARD
    2585 Biddle Ranch Rd., San Luis Obispo, California 93401
    CEO: Tom Selfridge, CEO   Tel: (805) 544-9594
    Bus: *Winemakers.*   Fax: (805) 544-7292   Emp: 45

● **DIAGONAL PLC**
Wey Court, Farnham, Surrey GU9 7PT, England, U.K.
CEO: David Beresford, Mng. Dir.   Tel: 44-1252-736-666   Rev: $97
Bus: *Provider of information technology consulting*   Fax: 44-1252-736-677   Emp: 418
   services.   www.diagonal.co.uk
NAICS: 541511, 541512
    DIAGONAL CONSULTING INC.
    690 Lee Rd., Ste. 320, Wayne, Pennsylvania 19087
    CEO: Paul Scherer, Pres.   Tel: (484) 329-2080   %FO: 100
    Bus: *Provider of information technology*   Fax: (484) 329-2081
      consulting services.

- **DICOM GROUP PLC**
Beechwood, Chineham Business Park, Basingstoke, Hampshire RG24 8 WA, England, U.K.
CEO: Arnold von Buren, CEO | Tel: 44-870-777-3767 | Rev: $283
Bus: *Document and data management software.* | Fax: 44-870-777-3768 | Emp: 846
| www.dicomgroup.com |
NAICS: 511210, 561410, 561439

  KOFAX IMAGE PRODUCTS INC.
  16245 Laguna Canyon Rd., Irvine, California 92618
  CEO: David Oldfield | Tel: (949) 727-1733 | %FO: 100
  Bus: *Electronic document capture.* | Fax: (949) 727-3144 |

  TOPCALL CORPORATION
  16245 Laguna Canyon Rd., Irvine, California 92618
  CEO: Christoph Stockart | Tel: (610) 240-4300 | %FO: 100
  Bus: *Electronic document capture.* | Fax: (610) 240-4340 |

  TOPCALL CORPORATION
  14800 Quorum Dr., Ste. 540, Dallas, Texas 75254
  CEO: Ryan Apos | Tel: (972) 404-0071 | %FO: 100
  Bus: *Electronic document capture.* | Fax: (972) 404-0071 |

  TOPCALL CORPORATION
  200 Chester Field Pkwy., Malvern, Pennsylvania 19355
  CEO: Denis O'Neil | Tel: (610) 560-0519 | %FO: 100
  Bus: *Electronic document capture.* | Fax: (610) 240-4372 |

  TOPCALL CORPORATION
  203 N. LaSalle St., Ste. 2100, Chicago, Illinois 60601
  CEO: Joel Embry | Tel: (773) 239-1655 | %FO: 100
  Bus: *Electronic document capture.* | Fax: (773) 239-1655 |

- **DIGICA LTD.**
Phoenix House, Colliers Way, Nottingham NG8 6AT, England, U.K.
CEO: Mark Howling, CEO | Tel: 44-115-977-1177 | Rev: $16
Bus: *Engaged in outsourcing, providing end-to-end* | Fax: 44-115-977-7000 | Emp: 125
business and technology management solutions. | www.digica.com |
NAICS: 541519, 541611

  DIGICA USA, INC.
  3434 US Highway 22, Ste. 150, Branchburg, New Jersey 08876-6011
  CEO: Gerry Goodwin, Mgr. | Tel: (908) 526-8488 | %FO: 100
  Bus: *Engaged in outsourcing, providing end-to-* | Fax: (908) 526-3036 |
  end business and technology management
  solutions.

- **DOMNICK HUNTER GROUP PLC**
Durham RD., Birtley, Durham DH3 2SF, England, U.K.
CEO: Colin T. Billiet, CEO | Tel: 44-191-410-5121 | Rev: $279
Bus: *Mfr. and design compressed air treatment* | Fax: 44-191-410-4497 | Emp: 1,783
| www.domnickh.co.uk |
NAICS: 333411, 333412

DOMNICK HUNTER INC.
756 Edgewood Ave., Wood Dale, Illinois 60191
CEO: Jim Tomczyk
Bus: *Mfr. and sales compressed air treatment
products.*

Tel: (630) 238-1375
Fax: (630) 238-3062

%FO: 100

DOMNICK HUNTER INC.
5900 Northwoods Pkwy., Ste. B, Charlotte, North Carolina 28269
CEO: Chris Churchill
Bus: *Mfr. and sales compressed air treatment
products.*

Tel: (704) 921-9303
Fax: (704) 921-1960

%FO: 100

• **DONCASTERS PLC, SUB. ROYAL BANK PRIVATE EQUITY**
28-30 Derby Rd., Melbourne, Derbyshire DE73 1FE, England, U.K.
CEO: Eric Lewis, CEO
Bus: *Airfoils and castings manufacture.*

Tel: 44-1332-864-900
Fax: 44-1332-864-888
www.doncasters.com

Rev: $380
Emp: 5,500

NAICS: 332116, 336370, 336399, 336412, 339914

DONCASTERS INC.
PO Box 2050, Springfield, Massachusetts 01102-2050
CEO: David Simm, Pres. & CEO
Bus: *Mfr. iron and steel forgings.*

Tel: (413) 785-1801
Fax: (413) 785-5680

%FO: 100

DONCASTERS INC.
36 Spring Lane, Farmington, Connecticut 06032
CEO: Jay Horrocks
Bus: *Mfr. airfoils and castings.*

Tel: (860) 677-1376
Fax: (860) 677-4720

%FO: 100

DONCASTERS PRECISION CASTINGS INC.
PO Box 1146, Groton, Connecticut 06840-1146
CEO: Bruce Ebright, Pres. & CEO
Bus: *Mfr. airfoils and castings.*

Tel: (860) 449-1603
Fax: (860) 449-1615

%FO: 100

PED MANUFACTURING
PO Box 1990, Oregon City, Oregon 97045
CEO: Chris Andersen, Mgr.
Bus: *Mfr. airfoils and castings.*

Tel: (503) 656-9653
Fax: (503) 656-1788

%FO: 100

TRUCAST INC.
81 Mawsons Way, Newberry, South Carolina 29108
CEO: Chris Pritchard
Bus: *Mfr. airfoils and castings.*

Tel: (803) 276-5353
Fax: (803) 276-6340

• **DOUGHTY HANSON & CO.**
45 Pall Mall, London SW1Y 5JG, England, U.K.
CEO: Nigel E. Doughty, Dir.
Bus: *Engaged in venture capital.*

Tel: 44-207-663-9300
Fax: 44-207-663-9350
www.doughtyhanson.com

NAICS: 523910, 523999

DOUGHTY HANSON & CO.
152 West 57th St., 47/F, New York, New York 10019
CEO: Peggy Doisselle
Bus: *Engaged in venture capital.*

Tel: (212) 641-3700
Fax: (212) 641-3750

%FO: 100

● **DOWDING & MILLS PLC**
Camp Hill,, Birmingham B12 0JJ, England, U.K.
CEO: Tudor Davies, CEO
Bus: *Provides electrical and electronic services.*

Tel: 44-121-766-6161
Fax: 44-121-766-1345
www.dowdingandmills.co.uk

Rev: $186
Emp: 1,766

NAICS: 541330, 811212, 811219, 811310

EQUIPMENT MAINTENANCE SERVICES INC.
2412 West Durango, Phoenix, Arizona 85009
CEO: Rick Hooper
Bus: *Engineering, electronics and calibration services.*

Tel: (602) 258-8545
Fax: (602) 258-9242

%FO: 100

EQUIPMENT MAINTENANCE SERVICES INC.
1025 Troy King Rd., Farmington, New Mexico 87401
CEO: Ed Sansing
Bus: *Engineering, electronics and calibration services.*

Tel: (505) 327-6055
Fax: (505) 326-3402

%FO: 100

EQUIPMENT MAINTENANCE SERVICES INC.
3382 Bird Dr., Gillette, Wyoming 82716
CEO: Dave Allen
Bus: *Engineering, electronics and calibration services.*

Tel: (307) 682-8733
Fax: (307) 682-6432

%FO: 100

EQUIPMENT MAINTENANCE SERVICES INC.
5190 Idaho St., Elko, Nevada 89801
CEO: Bill Douglas
Bus: *Engineering, electronics and calibration services.*

Tel: (775) 753-6311
Fax: (775) 753-8173

%FO: 100

● **DRESDNER KLEINWORT WASSERSTEIN PLC**
20 Fenchurch St., London EC3P 3DB, England, U.K.
CEO: Andrew Pisker, CEO
Bus: *Investment bank products and services.*

Tel: 44-207-623-8000
Fax: 44-207-623-4069
www.drkw.com

Emp: 8,000

NAICS: 523110

DRESDNER KLEINWORT WASSERSTEIN NA INC.
350 California St., 18/F, San Francisco, California 94104
CEO: John Faukner, Mgr.
Bus: *Investment bank products and services.*

Tel: (415) 288-3100
Fax: (415) 288-3130

%FO: 100

DRESDNER KLEINWORT WASSERSTEIN NA INC.
101 California St., Ste. 4200, San Francisco, California 94111
CEO: Susan Stein, Mgr.
Bus: *Investment bank products and services.*

Tel: (415) 677-4800
Fax: (415) 677-4804

%FO: 100

DRESDNER KLEINWORT WASSERSTEIN NA INC.
3 First National Plaza, Ste. 5700, Chicago, Illinois 60602
CEO: John Simpson, Mgr.   Tel: (312) 263-2020   %FO: 100
Bus: *Investment bank products and services.* Fax: (312) 558-9245

DRESDNER KLEINWORT WASSERSTEIN NA INC.
1301 Ave. of the Americas, New York, New York 10019
CEO: Bruce Wasserstein, Chmn.   Tel: (212) 969-2700   %FO: 100
Bus: *Investment bank products and services.* Fax: (212) 429-2127   Emp: 766

- **DTZ HOLDINGS PLC**
  1 Curzon St., London W1A 5PZ, England, U.K.
  CEO: Timothy David Melville-Ross, Chmn.   Tel: 44-207-408-1161   Rev: $295
  Bus: *Commercial real estate services.*   Fax: 44-207-643-6000   Emp: 8,000
       www.dtz.com
  NAICS: 531120, 531190, 531210, 531312, 531390

  AEW CAPITAL MANAGEMENT
  World Trade Center East, 2 Seaport Lane, Boston, Massachusetts 02210
  CEO: Joseph Azrack, Pres.   Tel: (617) 261-9000   %FO: 100
  Bus: *Engaged in real estate investment advisory.* Fax: (617) 261-9555   Emp: 224

  AEW CAPITAL MANAGEMENT, INC.
  601 South Figueroa St., Los Angeles, California 90017
  CEO: Tom Mullahey   Tel: (213) 689-3111   %FO: 100
  Bus: *Engaged in real estate investment advisory* Fax: (213) 629-9160
      services.

  THE STAUBACH COMPANY
  15601 Dallas Pkwy., Ste. 400, Addison, Texas 75001
  CEO: Roger T. Staubach, Chmn. & CEO   Tel: (972) 361-5000   %FO: 100
  Bus: *Engaged in commercial real estate advisory* Fax: (972) 361-5912   Emp: 1,100
      services.

- **DUNLOP SPORTS GROUP**
  Maxfly Court, Riverside Way
  Wakefield 41, Camberley GU15 3YL, England, U.K.
  CEO: Phil Parnell, CEO   Tel: 44-127-680-3399
  Bus: *Mfr. sporting and athletic goods.*   Fax: 44-127-667-9680
       www.slazenger.co.uk
  NAICS: 339920

  FOCUS GOLF SYSTEMS INC.
  25 Draper St., Greenville, South Carolina 29611
  CEO: Dan Murphy, VP   Tel: (864) 271-0201   %FO: 100
  Bus: *Sales and distribution of sporting and* Fax: (864) 527-7881
      athletic goods.

- **E2V TECHNOLOGIES PLC**
  106 Waterhouse Ln., Chelmsford, Essex CM1 3QU, England, U.K.
  CEO: Keith Attwood, CEO   Tel: 44-1245-493493   Rev: $178
  Bus: *Mfr. high-powered vacuum tubes.*   Fax: 44-1245-492492
       www.e2vtechnologies.com
  NAICS: 334411, 335999

E2V TECHNOLOGIES INC.
4 Westchester Plaza, Elmsford, New York 10523
CEO: Rudy Winter   Tel: (914) 592-6050   %FO: 100
Bus: *Mfr. high-powered vacuum tubes.*   Fax: (914) 592-5148

● **EASYSCREEN PLC**
78 Cannon St., London EC4N 6HH, England, U.K.
CEO: Philip H. Docker,Chmn.   Tel: 44-207-645-4600   Rev: $4
Bus: *Mfr. software to financial institutions for trading*   Fax: 44-207-645-4667   Emp: 40
    on electronic derivatives exchanges.   www.easyscreen.com
NAICS: 541511

    EASYSCREEN INC.
    330 Madison Ave., 6/F, New York, New York 10017
    CEO: Giles Castle, Mng. Dir.   Tel: (212) 404-7008   %FO: 100
    Bus: *Mfr. software to financial institutions for*   Fax: (212) 404-7022
      trading on electronic derivatives

    EASYSCREEN INC.
    101 North Wacker Dr., Ste. 602, Chicago, Illinois 60606
    CEO: Tonya Aarts, Mng. Dir.   Tel: (312) 939-9185   %FO: 100
    Bus: *Mfr. software to financial institutions for*   Fax: (312) 939-9188
      trading on electronic derivatives

● **ECL GROUP PLC (EXPLORATION CONSULTANTS GROUP)**
Highland Farm, Greys Rd., Henley-on-Thames, Oxfordshire RG9 4PR, England, U.K.
CEO: Ashti Abdullah, CEO   Tel: 44-1291-415-400
Bus: *Software and mapping database for oil and gas*   Fax: 44-1491-415-415
    industry.   www.ecqc.com
NAICS: 541511

    EXPLORATION CONSULTANTS GROUP
    9801 Westheimer Rd., Ste. 1060, Houston, Texas 77042
    CEO: Dietrich Landis   Tel: (713) 784-5800   %FO: 100
    Bus: *Oil and gas support services.*   Fax: (713) 974-3687

● **THE ECONOMIST GROUP LIMITED, SUB. PEARSON**
25 St. James's St., London SW1A 1HG, England, U.K.
CEO: Helen Alexander, CEO   Tel: 44-207-830-7000   Rev: $300
Bus: *International business and political news*   Fax: 44-207-839-2968   Emp: 960
    publication. (JV Pearson, UK)   www.economistgroup.com
NAICS: 511120

    CFO PUBLISHING T&RM
    253 Summer St., Boston, Massachusetts 02210
    CEO: Roy Harris   Tel: (617) 345-9700   %FO: 100
    Bus: *Publishing.*   Fax: (617) 951-4090

    ROLL CALL INC.
    50 F St. NW, Ste. 700, Washington, District of Columbia 20001
    CEO: Tim Curran   Tel: (202) 824-6800   %FO: 100
    Bus: *Editorial offices.*   Fax: (202) 824-0902

THE ECONOMIST
111 West 57th St., 8/F, New York, New York 10019
CEO: Helen Alexander   Tel: (212) 541-5730   %FO: 100
Bus: *Publishes/distributes newspaper.* Fax: (212) 541-9379

THE ECONOMIST EDITORIAL DIV.
35 East Wacker Dr., Ste. 1960, Chicago, Illinois 60601
CEO: James A. Mack   Tel: (312) 853-3835   %FO: 100
Bus: *Editorial offices.*   Fax: (312) 704-0448

THE ECONOMIST/SHENANDOAH VALLEY PRESS
Route 55 East, Strasburg, Virginia 22657
CEO: Helen Alexander   Tel: (540) 465-4833   %FO: 100
Bus: *Production facilities.*   Fax: (540) 465-4835

• **EIDOS PLC**
Wimbledon Bridge House, 1 Hartfield Road, Wimbledon, London SW19 3RU, England, U.K.
CEO: Jane Cavanagh, CEO   Tel: 44-208-636-3000   Rev: $243
Bus: *Develops and manufactures video games.* Fax: 44-208-636-3001   Emp: 696
                                         www.eidos.com
NAICS: 334613, 511210

    EIDOS INTERACTIVE USA, INC
    651 Brannan St., 4/F, San Francisco, California 94107
    CEO: Graeme Bayless, Pres.   Tel: (415) 547-1200   %FO: 100
    Bus: *Sales and marketing of video games.* Fax: (415) 547-1201

• **ELATERAL LIMITED**
Elateral House, Crosby Way, Farnham, Surrey GU16 7XX, England, U.K.
CEO: Paul Goater, CEO   Tel: 44-125-274-0740   Rev: $1
Bus: *Provides on-line printing services.* Fax: 44-125-274-0741   Emp: 20
                                         www.elateral.com
NAICS: 323119

    ELATERAL INC.
    5050 El Camino Real, Ste. 202, Los Altos, California 94024
    CEO: Kathy Mandle   Tel: (650) 969-4666   %FO: 100
    Bus: *Provides on-line printing services.* Fax: (650) 969-4667

• **ELECTROCOMPONENTS PLC**
International Management Centre, 5000 Oxford Business Park South, Oxford OX4 2BH, England, U.K.
CEO: Ian Mason, CEO   Tel: 44-186-520-4000   Rev: $1,386
Bus: *Distributes electronic, electrical and mechanical* Fax: 44-186-520-7400   Emp: 4,973
   components and tools.   www.electrocomponents.com
NAICS: 423610, 423690

    ALLIED ELECTRONICS INC.
    7410 Pebble Dr., Ft. Worth, Texas 76118
    CEO: Lee Davidson   Tel: (800) 433-5700   %FO: 100
    Bus: *Distributes electronic, electrical and* Fax: (817) 595-6444
       mechanical components and tools.

- **ELEMENTIS PLC**
Elementis House, 56 Kinston Rd., Staines, Surrey TW18 4ES, England, U.K.
CEO: Geoff Gaywood, CEO
Bus: *Chemicals manufacture.*
Tel: 44-1784-22-7000
Fax: 44-1784-46-0731
www.elementis.com
Rev: $655
Emp: 2,204
NAICS: 325131, 325132, 325188, 325211, 325212, 325998

ELEMENTIS CHROMIUM LP
5408 Holly Shelter Rd., Castle Hayne, North Carolina 28429
CEO: Gene Renzaglia, Principal
Bus: *Produces chemicals.*
Tel: (910) 675-7200
Fax: (910) 675-7210
%FO: 100

ELEMENTIS PIGMENTS INC.
2051 Lynch Ave., East St. Louis, Illinois 62204
CEO: David Dutro, Pres.
Bus: *Produces chemicals.*
Tel: (618) 646-2100
Fax: (618) 646-2178
%FO: 100
Emp: 400

ELEMENTIS SPECIALTIES, INC
329 Wyckoffs Mill Rd., Hightstown, New Jersey 08520
CEO: Neil Carr, Mng. Dir.
Bus: *Chemicals*
Tel: (609) 443-2500
Fax: (609) 443-2422
Emp: 700

- **EMAP PLC**
Wentworth House, Wentworth St., Peterborough PE1 1DS, England, U.K.
CEO: Tom Moloney, CEO
Bus: *Magazine publisher.*
Tel: 44-173-321-3700
Fax: 44-173-331-2115
www.emap.com
Rev: $1,917
Emp: 5,807
NAICS: 511120, 515111, 515112, 561920

EMAP BUSINESS COMMUNICATIONS
420 Lexington Ave., New York, New York 10170
CEO: Catherine Sodoci
Bus: *Magazine publishing.*
Tel: (212) 599-5209
Fax: (212) 599-5209
%FO: 100

FHM MAGAZINE
110 Fifth Ave., New York, New York 10011
CEO: Andrew Ormson
Bus: *Magazine publishing.*
Tel: (212) 201-6700
Fax: (212) 201-6980
%FO: 100

MAGAZINE SPECS
110 Fifth Ave., New York, New York 10010
CEO: Matthew Bolshaw
Bus: *Magazine publishing.*
Tel: (212) 886-2845
Fax: (212) 886-2845
%FO: 100

- **EMI GROUP PLC**
27 Wrights Lane, London W8 5SW, England, U.K.
CEO: Eric L. Nicoli, Chmn.
Bus: *Entertainment, consumer electronics, recorded music, music publishing and retail sale of recorded music and video.*
Tel: 44-207-795-7000
Fax: 44-207-795-7296
www.emigroup.com
Rev: $3,872
Emp: 8,000
NAICS: 334220, 423990, 511210, 512220

CAPITOL RECORDS
1750 North Vine St., Hollywood, California 90028
CEO: Andrew Slater, Pres.   Tel: (323) 462-6252   %FO: 100
Bus: *Full service music company.* Fax: (323) 467-6550

EMI MUSIC PUBLISHING
1290 Ave. of the Americas, New York, New York 10104
CEO: Roger Faxon, CEO   Tel: (212) 492-1200   %FO: 100
Bus: *Recorded music, music publishing.* Fax: (212) 245-4115

VIRGIN RECORDS AMERICA, INC.
150 5th Ave., New York, New York 10010
CEO: Matt Serletic, Chmn.   Tel: (212) 786-8200   %FO: 100
Bus: *Recorded music, music publishing.* Fax: (212) 786-8343

VIRGIN RECORDS AMERICA, INC.
5750 Wilshire Blvd., Los Angeles, California 90036
CEO: Ray Cooper   Tel: (323) 426-6252   %FO: 100
Bus: *Recorded music, music publishing.* Fax: (323) 426-6252

● **EMPIRE INTERACTIVE PLC**
The Spires, 677 High Rd., London N12 0DA, England, U.K.
CEO: Ian Higgins, CEO   Tel: 44-20-8343-7337   Rev: $57
Bus: *Publisher of software games.* Fax: 44-20-8343-7447   Emp: 121
                                   www.empireinteractive.com
NAICS: 511210

   EMPIRE INTERACTIVE
   580 California St., 16/F, San Francisco, California 94104
   CEO: James Lamorticelli, Gen. Mgr. Tel: (415) 439-4854   %FO: 100
   Bus: *Publisher of software games.* Fax: (415) 439-4928

● **ENGEL & VOLKERS**
Alameda House, 90-100 Sydney Street, London SW3 6NJ, England, U.K.
CEO: Marie Harrison   Tel: 44-207-351-6767
Bus: *Real estate.*   Fax: 44-207-351-6448   Emp: 1,000
                                   www.engelvoelkers.co.uk
NAICS: 531210

   ENGEL & VOLKERS
   4901 Tamiami Trail North, Naples, Florida 34103
   CEO: Cheryl D. Turner   Tel: (239) 213-4000   %FO: 100
   Bus: *Real estate sales.*   Fax: (239) 435-0138

   ENGEL & VOLKERS
   20 Main St., Southampton, New York 11968
   CEO: Patrick O'Shea   Tel: (631) 287-9260   %FO: 100
   Bus: *Real estate sales.*   Fax: (631) 287-9261

- **ENNSTONE PLC**
Breedon Quarry, Breedon-on-the-Hill, Derby DE73 1AN, England, U.K.
CEO: C. Vaughan McLeod, CEO   Tel: 44-133-269-4444   Rev: $156
Bus: *Producer of aggregates, ready mixed concrete,*   Fax: 44-133-269-4445   Emp: 689
asphalt, natural
stone and reconstituted building products
NAICS: 237310

  COLONIAL CONCRETE INC.
  PO Box 5237, Falmouth, Virginia 22403
  CEO: Mark A. Elliott, Pres.   Tel: (540) 371-1787   %FO: 100
  Bus: *Asphalt and concrete manufacture and*   Fax: (540) 899-9148
  sales.

- **ENODIS PLC**
Washington House, 40-41 Conduit St., London W1S 2YQ, England, U.K.
CEO: David S. McCulloch, CEO   Tel: 44-20-7304-6000   Rev: $1,189
Bus: *Engaged in manufacture of commercial food*   Fax: 44-20-7304-6001   Emp: 6,261
equipment and building materials.   www.enodis.com
NAICS: 333319, 333415

  CLEVELAND RANGE, INC.
  1333 E. 179th St., Cleveland, Ohio 44110
  CEO: Richard Cutler, Pres.   Tel: (216) 481-4900
  Bus: *Food services & food retail equipment*   Fax: (216) 481-3782   Emp: 220
  manufacturing.

  ENODIS CORPORATION
  2227 Welbilt Blvd., New Port Richey, Florida 34655
  CEO: Kevin Fink, Pres.   Tel: (727) 375-7010
  Bus: *Food service & food retail equipment*   Fax: (727) 375-0894   Emp: 6,000
  manufacturing.

  FRYMASTER
  8700 Line Ave., Shreveport, Louisiana 71106
  CEO: Gene Baugh, Pres.   Tel: (318) 865-1711
  Bus: *Food service & food retail equipment*   Fax: (318) 868-5987   Emp: 750
  manufacturing

  KYSOR//WARREN
  5201 Transport Blvd., Columbus, Georgia 31907
  CEO: Ralph Schmitt, Pres.   Tel: (706) 568-1514
  Bus: *Food service & food retail equipment*   Fax: (705) 568-8990
  manufacturing

  LINCOLN FOODSERVICE PRODUCTS, INC.
  1111 N. Hadley Rd., Fort Wayne, Indiana 46804
  CEO: Mike Hicks, Pres.   Tel: (260) 459-8200
  Bus: *Food service & food retail equipment*   Fax: (260) 436-0735   Emp: 500
  manufacturing

  SCOTSMAN GROUP, INC.
  775 Corporate Woods Pkwy., Vernon Hills, Illinois 60061
  CEO: Randall C. Rossi, Pres.   Tel: (847) 215-4550   %FO: 100
  Bus: *Mfr. coolers and freezers and beverage*   Fax: (847) 913-9844   Emp: 2,500
  systems.

THE DELFIELD CO.
980 S. Isabella Rd., Mt. Pleasant, Michigan 48858
CEO: Robert Nerbonne, Pres.   Tel: (989) 773-7981
Bus: *Food service & food retail equipment*   Fax: (800) 669-0619
manufacturing

- **ENVIRONMENTAL RESOURCES MANAGEMENT LIMITED (ERM GROUP)**
8 Cavendish Square, London W1G 0ER, England, U.K.
CEO: Peter T. Regan, CEO   Tel: 44-20-7465-7200   Rev: $218
Bus: *Environmental consulting services.*   Fax: 44-20-7465-7272   Emp: 2,400
www.erm.com

NAICS: 541620

ERM GROUP
350 Eagleview Blvd., Ste. 200, Exton, Pennsylvania 19341-1155
CEO: John Deal   Tel: (610) 524-3500   %FO: 100
Bus: *Environmental consulting services.*   Fax: (610) 524-7335

ERM GROUP
475 Park Ave. South, 29/F, New York, New York 10016
CEO: Carlo Alberto Marcoaldi   Tel: (212) 447-1900   %FO: 100
Bus: *Environmental consulting services.*   Fax: (212) 447-1904

ERM GROUP
11350 N. Meridian St., Ste. 220, Carmel, Indiana 46032
CEO: David Jordan   Tel: (317) 706-2000   %FO: 100
Bus: *Environmental consulting services.*   Fax: (317) 706-2010

ERM GROUP
3501 N. Causeway Blvd., Ste. 200, Metairie, Louisiana 70002
CEO: Jim Pastene   Tel: (504) 831-6700   %FO: 100
Bus: *Environmental consulting services.*   Fax: (504) 831-6742

ERM GROUP
250 Phillips Blvd., Ste. 280, Ewing, New Jersey 08618
CEO: Pete Sudano   Tel: (609) 895-0050   %FO: 100
Bus: *Environmental consulting services.*   Fax: (609) 895-0111

ERM GROUP
7700 Chevy Chase Dr., Ste. 110, Austin, Texas 78752
CEO: Mark Stuckey   Tel: (512) 459-4700   %FO: 100
Bus: *Environmental consulting services.*   Fax: (512) 459-4711

ERM GROUP
102 West 500 South, Ste. 650, Salt Lake City, Utah 84101-2334
CEO: Dave Wilson   Tel: (801) 595-8400   %FO: 100
Bus: *Environmental consulting services.*   Fax: (801) 595-8484

ERM GROUP
11676 Perry Highway, Suite 3300, Wexford, Pennsylvania 15090
CEO: Steve Lewandowski   Tel: (724) 933-5444   %FO: 100
Bus: *Environmental consulting services.*   Fax: (724) 933-5464

● **ESAB HOLDINGS LTD., SUB. CHARTER**
50 Curzon St., London W1J 7UW, England, U.K.
CEO: Jon Templeman, CEO
Bus: *Welding and cutting equipment manufacture.*

Tel: 44-20-7491-6800
Fax: 44-20-7629-8181
www.esab.com

Rev: $1,197
Emp: 6,357

NAICS: 333512, 333992

ESAB WELDING
411 South Ebenezer Rd., Florence, South Carolina 29501
CEO: Jill Heiden, Sales
Bus: *Welding and cutting equipment manufacture and sales.*

Tel: (843) 669-4411
Fax: (843) 664-4258

%FO: 100

● **ESSELTE AB**
Waterside House, Cowley Business Park, Middlesex, Uxbridge UB8 2HR, England, U.K.
CEO: Richard John Startin, Dir.
Bus: *Office equipment and stationery, packaging, printing and bookbinding, cartography, school equipment, publishing manufacture; book shops.*

Tel: 44-189-587-8700
Fax: 44-189-587-8810
www.esselte.com

Rev: $105
Emp: 10,000

NAICS: 323116, 551112

DYMO CORPORATION
44 Commerce Rd., Stamford, Connecticut 06902-4561
CEO: Chris Curran
Bus: *Mfr. labeling tags & printers*

Tel: (203) 355-9000
Fax:

ESSELTE CORPORATION
48 South Service Rd., Melville, New York 11747
CEO: Gary J. Brooks
Bus: *Bar coding systems, labeling systems labels & tags, printer supplies & consumables, imprinting services.*

Tel: (631) 675-5700
Fax: (631) 675-3320

%FO: 100

XYRON
7400 E. Tierra Buena Lane, Scottsdale, Arizona 85260
CEO:
Bus: *Mfr. labeling tags & printers*

Tel: (480) 443-9419
Fax: (480) 443-0118

● **EUROMONEY INSTITUTIONAL INVESTOR PLC**
Nestor House, Playhouse Yard, London EC4V 5EX, England, U.K.
CEO: Sir Patrick Sergeant, Pres.
Bus: *Publisher of financial magazines.*

Tel: 44-207-779-8888
Fax: 44-207-779-8658
www.euromoneyplc.com

Rev: $314
Emp: 1,552

NAICS: 511120, 511130, 511140, 516110, 561920, 611430, 611699

INSTITUTIONAL INVESTOR INC.
450 5th St. NW, Ste. 1- C53, Washington, District of Columbia 20001
CEO: Jenifer Burchman, Mgr.
Bus: *Publisher of financial, on-line and print, magazine.*

Tel: (202) 393-4233
Fax:

%FO: 100

INSTITUTIONAL INVESTOR INC.
225 Park Ave. South, New York, New York 10003
CEO: Lisa Myers, Pres.   Tel: (212) 224-3300   %FO: 100
Bus: *Publisher of financial, on-line and print,*   Fax: (212) 224-3300
     magazine.

● **EUROPEAN COLOUR PLC**
Hempshaw Lane, Greater Manchester, Stockport SK1 4LG, England, U.K.
CEO: Steve Smith, Chmn.   Tel: 44-161-476-7112   Rev: $51
Bus: *Mfr. of organic pigments.*   Fax: 44-161-480-9852   Emp: 196
                                              www.ecplc.com
NAICS: 325510, 424950

    EC PIGMENTS USA
    749 Quequechan St., PO Box 5360, Fall River, Massachusetts 02723
    CEO: John W. Combs, Jr., Sales Mgr.   Tel: (508) 676-3481   %FO: 100
    Bus: *Manufacturer of organic pigments.*   Fax: (508) 676-9011

● **EUROPEAN METAL RECYCLING LIMITED**
Sirius House, Delta Crescent, Westbrook, Warrington WA5 7NSS, England, U.K.
CEO: Colin Iles, Mng. Dir.   Tel: 44-1925-715-400   Rev: $1,561
Bus: *Metal recycler.*   Fax: 44-1925-713-470   Emp: 1,364
                                              www.emrltd.com
NAICS: 423930, 562111, 562212, 562219, 562920

    EUROPEAN METAL RECYCLING LIMITED
    508 Westport Ave., Norwalk, Connecticut 06851
    CEO: Richard Codero   Tel: (203) 750-8226   %FO: 100
    Bus: *Metal recycler.*   Fax: (203) 750-8227

● **EXEL PLC**
Ocean House, The Ring, Bracknell, Berkshire RG12 1AW, England, U.K.
CEO: John M. Allan, Dir.   Tel: 44-134-430-2000   Rev: $8,865
Bus: *Supplies logistic services and home moving*   Fax: 44-134-430-2000   Emp: 74,000
                                              www.exel.com
NAICS: 484210

    EXEL GLOBAL LOGISTICS INC.
    1143 SBC Center Pkwy., San Antonio, Texas 78219
    CEO: Tammy Anderson   Tel: (210) 224-0605   %FO: 100
    Bus: *Supplies logistic services.*   Fax: (210) 224-0605

    EXEL GLOBAL LOGISTICS INC.
    21500 Aerospace Pkwy, Columbus, Ohio 44142
    CEO: Jim Matcham, Pres.   Tel: (440) 243-5900   %FO: 100
    Bus: *Supplies logistic services.*   Fax: (440) 826-0515

    EXEL GLOBAL LOGISTICS INC.
    2225 Air Cargo Rd., Wichita, Kansas 67209
    CEO: Richard Devers   Tel: (316) 946-0120   %FO: 100
    Bus: *Supplies logistic services.*   Fax: (316) 946-0120

EXEL GLOBAL LOGISTICS INC.
230-39 International Airport Center Blvd., Ste. 1000, Jamaica, New York 11213
CEO: Debra Kampell
Bus: *Supplies logistic services.*
Tel: (718) 995-9519
Fax: (718) 276-6601
%FO: 100

EXEL GLOBAL LOGISTICS INC.
4120 Point Eden Way 200, Hayward, California 94545
CEO: Michael Fountain
Bus: *Supplies logistic services.*
Tel: (510) 731-3333
Fax: (510) 731-3434
%FO: 100

EXEL GLOBAL LOGISTICS INC.
2151 South Park Dr., Hebron, Kentucky 41048
CEO: Thomas Voss
Bus: *Supplies logistic services.*
Tel: (859) 586-2900
Fax: (859) 586-2900
%FO: 100

● **EXITECH LTD.**
Oxford Industrial Park, Yarnton, Oxford OX5 1QU, England, U.K.
CEO: Malcolm Gower, CEO
Bus: *Micromachining and micro fabrication equipment manufacture.*
NAICS: 334413
Tel: 44-186-529-0400
Fax: 44-186-529-0401
www.exitech.co.uk
Rev: $18
Emp: 68

EXITECH INC.
1125 East Hillsdale Blvd., Ste. 106, Foster City, California 94404
CEO: Herbert Pummer
Bus: *Micromachining and micro fabrication equipment manufacture and sales.*
Tel: (650) 212-1411
Fax: (650) 212-1511
%FO: 100

● **EXPRO INTERNATIONAL GROUP PLC**
Reading Bridge House, Reading, Berkshire RG1 8PL, England, U.K.
CEO: Graeme F. Coutts, CEO
Bus: *Engaged in oil field services.*
NAICS: 213112
Tel: 44 118-959-1341
Fax: 44-118-958-9000
www.expro.co.uk
Rev: $357
Emp: 1,765

EXPRO AMERICAS INC.
324A Hardware Rd., Broussard, Louisiana 70518-7806
CEO: Stan Wall
Bus: *Engaged in oil field services.*
Tel: (337) 839-9600
Fax: (337) 839-9600
%FO: 100

EXPRO AMERICAS INC.
580 Westlake Park Rd., Ste. 1500, Houston, Texas 77079
CEO: Stan Wall, SVP
Bus: *Engaged in oil field services.*
Tel: (281) 597-9010
Fax: (281) 497-8402
%FO: 100

SURFACE PRODUCTION SYSTEMS INC.
580 Westlake Park Blvd., Suite 1501, Houston, Texas 77079
CEO: Kevin Galvin
Bus: *Onshore Offshore production facilities.*
Tel: (281) 589-1808
Fax: (281) 589-2638
%FO: 100

• **FCX INTERNATIONAL PLC**
68 Baker St., Weybridge, Surrey KT13 8AL, England, U.K.
CEO: John A. Perkins, Chmn.
Bus: *Mfr. flow control products, industrial tools and packaging.*
NAICS: 334513

Tel: 44-193-283-7700
Fax: 44-193-282-0204
www.fc-x.com

Rev: $485
Emp: 1,100

FCX PERFORMANCE INC.
373 East Route 46 West, Fairfield, New Jersey 07004
CEO: Michael Magee, CEO
Bus: *Distributes valves, instrumentation & corrosion piping and hose systems for industrial & high-purity flow control applications.*

Tel: (973) 575-8350
Fax: (973) 575-5228

%FO: 100

FCX PERFORMANCE INC.
300 Oak St., Unite 400, Pembroke, Massachusetts 02359
CEO: Brian Scalata, Mgr.
Bus: *Distributes valves, instrumentation & corrosion piping and hose systems for industrial & high-purity flow control applications.*

Tel: (781) 826-7866
Fax: (781) 826-4698

%FO: 100

FCX SIMCO CONTROLS
9715 Kincaid Dr., Indianapolis, Indiana 46038
CEO: Dale Greenlee, CEO
Bus: *Distributes valves, instrumentation & corrosion piping and hose systems for industrial & high-purity flow control applications.*

Tel: (317) 577-0982
Fax: (317) 577-0985

%FO: 100

FCX SIMCO CONTROLS
3000 East 14th Ave., Columbus, Ohio 43219
CEO: Charles M. Simon, Pres.
Bus: *Distributes valves, instrumentation & corrosion piping and hose systems for industrial & high-purity flow control applications.*

Tel: (614) 253-1996
Fax: (614) 253-1996

%FO: 100

FCX SIMONE ENGINEERING
N106 W13131 Bradley Way, Germantown, Wisconsin 53022
CEO: Dennis Barney
Bus: *Distributes valves, instrumentation & corrosion piping and hose systems for industrial & high-purity flow control applications.*

Tel: (262) 512-4000
Fax: (262) 512-4111

%FO: 100

FCX SIMONE ENGINEERING
1355 Sherman Rd., Ste. 501, Hiawatha, Iowa 52233
CEO: Keith Ochs, CEO
Bus: *Distributes valves, instrumentation & corrosion piping and hose systems for industrial & high-purity flow control applications.*

Tel: (319) 294-8445
Fax: (319) 294-8446

%FO: 100

- **FENNER GROUP**
Marfleet Hull, East Yorkshire HU9 5RA, England, U.K.
CEO: John Pratt, Mng. Dir.
Bus: *Reinforced polymer technology manufacturing; heavyweight belting.*
NAICS: 316999

Tel: 44-1482-781234	Rev: $470
Fax: 44-1482-785438	Emp: 3,900
www.fenner.com	

  FENNER DRIVES, INC.
  311 West Stiegel St., Manheim, Pennsylvania 17545
  CEO: Robin Palmer, VP
  Bus: *Mfr./sale fluid power equipment and industrial belting.*

Tel: (717) 665-2421	%FO: 100
Fax: (717) 665-2649	Emp: 350

  GEORGIA DUCK CONVEYOR BELTING
  21 Laredo Dr., Scottdale, Georgia 30079
  CEO: Jim Prescott, Pres.
  Bus: *Mfr. premium conveyor belting.*

Tel: (404) 294-5272	%FO: 100
Fax: (404) 296-5165	

  SCANDURA CONVEYOR BELTING USA
  PO Box 30606, Charlotte, North Carolina 28273
  CEO: Robert Mullen, Pres.
  Bus: *Conveyor belting manufacture.*

Tel: (704) 943-5669	%FO: 100
Fax: (704) 334-7126	

- **FFASTFILL PLC**
1-3 Norton Folgate, London E1 6DB, England, U.K.
CEO: Keith Todd, CEO
Bus: *Designs and markets software to traders, brokers and clearers that enables trading on electronic exchanges.*
NAICS: 541511

Tel: 44-207-665-8900	Rev: $2
Fax: 44-207-665-8905	Emp: 50
www.ffastfill.com	

  FFASTFILL INC.
  30 South Wacker Dr., Ste. 1716, Chicago, Illinois 60606
  CEO: Jim Oliff, CEO
  Bus: *Designs and markets software to traders, brokers and clearers that enables trading on electronic exchanges.*

Tel: (312) 637-7090	%FO: 100
Fax: (312) 637-7097	

- **FILTRONA PLC**
201-249 Avebury Blvd., Milton Keynes MK9 1AU, England, U.K.
CEO: Mark Harper, CEO
Bus: *Mfr cigarette filters and specialty fiber and plastic products.*
NAICS: 325211, 325520

Tel: 44-1908-359-100	Rev: $90
Fax: 44-1908-359-102	Emp: 5,200
www.filtrona.com	

  ALLIANCE PLASTICS INC.
  3123 Station Rd., Erie, Pennsylvania 16510
  CEO: Mike Conley
  Bus: *Packaging distribution.*

Tel: (814) 899-7671	%FO: 100
Fax: (814) 898-1638	

FILTRONA EXTRUSION PHILADELPHIA INC.
16 Progress Dr., Morrisville, Pennsylvania 19067
CEO: Tony Herbert, Pres.
Bus: *Mfr. extruded profile shapes, sheet and specialty tubes for OEM's.*

Tel: (215) 736-2553
Fax: (215) 736-9346

%FO: 100

IFS NORTH AMERICA INC.
3716 E. Columbia St., Tucson, Arizona 85714
CEO: John Bridges, VP
Bus: *Mfr. software.*

Tel: (520) 512-2000
Fax: (520) 512-2000

%FO: 100

MSI PRODUCTS INC.
9110 Meadow Vista, Houston, Texas 77064
CEO: John Bravo
Bus: *Mfr. thread protectors and pipe protection products.*

Tel: (281) 890-4595
Fax: (281) 890-0543

%FO: 100

PAYNE INC.
1625 Ashton Park Dr., Colonial Heights, Virginia 23834
CEO: M. Richmond
Bus: *Mfr. tear tape.*

Tel: (804) 518-1803
Fax: (804) 518-1809

%FO: 100

● **FILTRONIC PLC**
The Waterfront at Salts Mill Rd., Saltaire Shipley, West Yorkshire BD18 3TT, England, U.K.
CEO: John Roulston, CEO
Bus: *Wireless electronics, including amplifiers and related products manufacture.*
NAICS: 334419

Tel: 44-127-453-0622
Fax: 44-127-453-1561
www.filtronic.com

Rev: $435
Emp: 3,369

FILTRONIC COMTEK, INC.
31901 Comtek Lane, Salisbury, Maryland 21804-1788
CEO: Biba Aidoo
Bus: *Mfr. wireless electronics.*

Tel: (410) 341-7766
Fax: (410) 548-4750

%FO: 100

FILTRONIC COMTEK, INC.
300 Park Blvd., Ste. 260, Itasca, Illinois 60143
CEO: Paul Balashewski
Bus: *Mfr. wireless electronics.*

Tel: (630) 775-1000
Fax: (630) 775-1050

%FO: 100

FILTRONIC COMTEK, INC.
21 Continental Boulevard, Merrimack, New Hampshire 03054
CEO: Joe Nicewicz
Bus: *Mfr. wireless electronics.*

Tel: (603) 424-8404
Fax: (603) 424-7947

%FO: 100

FILTRONIC SIGTEK, INC.
9075 Guilford Rd., Ste. C-1, Columbia, Maryland 21046
CEO: Katie Conway, Pres.
Bus: *Engaged in broadband access*

Tel: (410) 290-3918
Fax: (410) 290-8146

%FO: 100

- **FINANCIAL OBJECTS PLC**
  7 Dials Village, 45 Monmouth St., Convent Garden, London WC2H 9DG, England, U.K.
  CEO: Roger Foster, CEO | Tel: 44-20-7836-3010 | Rev: $21
  Bus: *Core banking systems and international banking* | Fax: 44-20-7240-3324 | Emp: 150
  software manufacture. | www.finobj.com
  NAICS: 541511
  - **FINANCIAL OBJECTS PLC**
    330 Madison Ave., 26/F, New York, New York 10017
    CEO: Karim Peermohamed | Tel: (212) 697-8990 | %FO: 100
    Bus: *Custom computer programming services.* | Fax: (212) 986-4331

- **FIRCROFT ENGINEERING SERVICES LTD.**
  Trinity House, 114 Northenden Rd., Greater Manchester M33 3FZ, England, U.K.
  CEO: John Urpi, Mng. Dir. | Tel: 44-161-905-2020 | Rev: $235
  Bus: *Clerical, technical and engineering staffing* | Fax: 44-161-969-1743 | Emp: 560
  services. | www.fircroft.co.uk
  NAICS: 541612, 561330
  - **FIRCROFT ENGINEERING SERVICES INC.**
    5100 Westheimer, Ste. 200, Houston, Texas 77056
    CEO: Dave Mahoney | Tel: (713) 968-9264 | %FO: 100
    Bus: *Clerical, technical and engineering staffing* | Fax: (713) 968-9265
    services.

- **FIREWORKS ENTERTAINMENT, INC.**
  Tennyson House, 159-165 Great Portland St., London W1W 5PA, England, U.K.
  CEO: Greg Phillips, CEO | Tel: 44-207-307-6309
  Bus: *Produces, finances and distributes television* | Fax: 44-207-307-6399
  programs and motion picture films worldwide. | www.fireworksentertainment.com
  NAICS: 512110
  - **FIREWORKS TELEVISION, INC.**
    421 South Beverly Dr., Beverly Hills, California 90212
    CEO: Saralo MacGregor | Tel: (310) 789-4750 | %FO: 100
    Bus: *Produces, finances and distributes* | Fax: (310) 789-4799
    television programs and motion picture films

- **FIRST TECHNOLOGY PLC**
  9 High St., Egham, Surrey TW20 9EA, England, U.K.
  CEO: Fred Westlake, Chmn. | Tel: 44-134-462-2322 | Rev: $211
  Bus: *Mfr. vehicle safety products.* | Fax: 44-134-462-2773 | Emp: 1,805
  | www.firsttech.oo.uk
  NAICS: 336399
  - **FIRST TECHNOLOGY AUTOMOTIVE, INC.**
    PO Box 480, Grand Blanc, Michigan 48439
    CEO: John Shepherd, Pres. | Tel: (810) 695-8333 | %FO: 100
    Bus: *Mfr. vehicle safety products.* | Fax: (810) 695-0589

FIRST TECHNOLOGY AUTOMOTIVE, INC.
228 Northeast Rd., Standish, Maine 04084
CEO: Jeffrey G. Wood, Pres.   Tel: (207) 642-4535   %FO: 100
Bus: *Mfr. optical sensors and crash dummies*   Fax: (207) 642-0198
      used by the automotive industry.

FIRST TECHNOLOGY INC.
47460 Galleon Dr., Plymouth, Michigan 48170
CEO: Gordie Morgan   Tel: (734) 451-7878   %FO: 100
Bus: *Mfr. vehicle safety products.*   Fax: (734) 451-9549

FIRST TECHNOLOGY INC.
28411 Northwestern Highway, Southfield, Michigan 48034
CEO: Jeffrey G. Wood   Tel: (248) 353-6200   %FO: 100
Bus: *Mfr. vehicle safety products.*   Fax: (248) 353-8333

HITEC, DIV. FIRST TECHNOLOGY INC.
537 Great Rd., Littleton, Massachusetts 01460
CEO: Jerrold Beeney   Tel: (978) 742-9032   %FO: 100
Bus: *Mfr. strain gauge-based transducers.*   Fax: (978) 742-9033

● **FKI PLC**
15-19 New Fetter Lane, London EC4A 1LY, England, U.K.
CEO: Paul Heiden, CEO   Tel: 44-207-832-0000   Rev: $2,456
Bus: *Automated sorting, material handling & lifting*   Fax: 44-207-832-0001   Emp: 14,133
      equipment, hardware products, electric motors,   www.fki.co.uk
      generators, measurement & control devices.
NAICS: 333923, 335312, 423830

   BELWITH INTERNATIONAL, LTD.
   PO Box 127, Grandville, Michigan 49468-0127
   CEO: Von Williamson, VP   Tel: (616) 531-4300   %FO: 100
   Bus: *Process control systems.*   Fax: (616) 531 5670

   BRIDON AMERICAN CORPORATION
   PO Box 6000, Wilkes Barre, Pennsylvania 18773
   CEO: Robert Madden, Dir. Sales   Tel: (570) 822-3349   %FO: 100
   Bus: *Manufacturer of steel wire and wire*   Fax: (570) 822-9180
         rope solutions.

   BRISTOL BABCOCK INC.
   1100 Buckingham St., Watertown, Connecticut 06795
   CEO: Jack Kelly, Pres.   Tel: (860) 945-2200   %FO: 100
   Bus: *Manufacture flow computers, pressure*   Fax: (860) 945-2213
         gauges, process control systems and
         transmitters.

   FAULTLESS CASTER
   1421 North Garvin St., Evansville, Indiana 47711-4487
   CEO: Don Laux, Pres.   Tel: (812) 425-1011   %FO: 100
   Bus: *Process control systems manufacture.*   Fax: (812) 421-7328

FKI ROTATING MACHINES INC.
2000 Governor's Circle West, Ste. F, Houston, Texas 77092
CEO: Charlie Mallon, Sales   Tel: (281) 580-1314   %FO: 100
Bus: *Rotating machines manufacture.*   Fax: (281) 580-5801

KEELER BRASS HARDWARE COMPANY
955 Godfrey Ave., SW, Grand Rapids, Michigan 49503-5087
CEO: Becky Jones, Sales   Tel: (616) 247-4000   %FO: 100
Bus: *Sales and distribution of brass hardware.*   Fax: (616) 247-4060

NORTH AMERICA
10045 International Blvd., Cincinnati, Ohio 45246
CEO: George King, Pres.   Tel: (513) 874-0788   %FO: 100
Bus: *Material handling solutions manufacture.*   Fax: (513) 881-5251   Emp: 700

WEBER-KNAPP
441 Chandler St., Jamestown, New York 14702-0518
CEO: Rex E. McCray, Pres.   Tel: (716) 484-9135   %FO: 100
Bus: *Process control systems.*   Fax: (716) 484-9142

● **FLOMERICS GROUP PLC**
81 Bridge Rd., Hampton Court, London KT8 9HH, England, U.K.
CEO: Gary Carter, CEO   Tel: 44-20-8487-3000   Rev: $20
Bus: *Software development.*   Fax: 44-20-8487-3001   Emp: 117
    www.flomerics.com
NAICS: 541511

FLOMERICS INC.
257 Turnpike Rd., Ste. 100, Southborough, Massachusetts 01772
CEO: David Johns   Tel: (508) 357-2012   %FO: 100
Bus: *Software development and sales.*   Fax: (508) 357-2013

FLOMERICS INC.
4699 Old Ironside Dr., Ste. 390, Santa Clara, California 95054
CEO: Sherman Ikemoto   Tel: (408) 562-9100   %FO: 100
Bus: *Software development and sales.*   Fax: (408) 562-9101

FLOMERICS INC.
410 South Melrose Dr., Ste. 102, Vista, California 92083
CEO: Fred German   Tel: (760) 643-4028   %FO: 100
Bus: *Software development and sales.*   Fax: (760) 643-4128

FLOMERICS INC.
1106 Clayton Lane, Ste. 525W, Austin, Texas 78723
CEO: Sarang Shidore   Tel: (512) 420-9273   %FO: 100
Bus: *Web product development.*   Fax: (512) 420-9485

● **FORMSCAN PLC**
Apex House, West End, Frome, Somerset BA11 3AS, England, U.K.
CEO: John F. Harvey, Mng. Dir.   Tel: 44-1373-452555   Rev: $7
Bus: *Software and consulting services.*   Fax: 44-1373-461269   Emp: 50
    www.formscan.com
NAICS: 541511

FORMSCAN INC.
20 Gilbert Ave., Ste. 101, Smithtown, New York 11787
CEO: William T. Riley
Bus: *Software and consulting services.*
Tel: (631) 361-5021
Fax: (631) 361-4955
%FO: 100

● **FOSECO INTERNATIONAL LTD.**
Coleshill Rd., Fazeley, Tamworth, Staffordshire B78 3TL, England, U.K.
CEO: Roland Johnson, Mktg. Dir.
Bus: *Foundry performance products manufacture and production of metallurgical chemicals.*
Tel: 44-182-726-2021
Fax: 44-182-728-3725
www.foseco.com
NAICS: 236210, 332997

　FOSECO METALLURGICAL INC.
　6550 Eastland Rd., Cleveland, Ohio 44142
　CEO: Roger Stanbridge
　Bus: *Sales/distribution of industrial chemicals.*
　Tel: (440) 826-4548
　Fax: (440) 816-7087

　FOSECO-MORVAL INC.
　3152 Dublin Lane, Bessemer, Alabama 35022
　CEO: Tom Shewfelt
　Bus: *Custom pattern molder providing manufacture and supply of patterns and services to the foam foundry industry.*
　Tel: (205) 425-6220
　Fax: (205) 425-6220
　%FO: 100

● **FRENCH CONNECTION GROUP PLC**
30 Old Burlington St., London W1S 3NL, England, U.K.
CEO: Stephen Marks, Chmn.
Bus: *Mfr. women's clothing; chain stores.*
Tel: 44-207-399-7000
Fax: 44-207-399-7001
www.frenchconnection.com
Rev: $487
Emp: 2,424
NAICS: 315211, 315212, 315223, 315224, 315232, 315234, 315239, 315299, 315999, 316992, 316993, 325620, 448110, 448120

　FRENCH CONNECTION
　512 Seventh Ave., 25/F, New York, New York 10018
　CEO: Andrea S. Hyde, Pres.
　Bus: *Showroom; women's clothing.*
　Tel: (212) 221-3157
　Fax:
　%FO: 100

　THE FRENCH CONNECTION GROUP
　18402 Jamaica Ave., Hollis, New York 11423
　CEO: Stephen Marks, Pres.
　Bus: *U.S. headquarters office; women's clothing chain.*
　Tel: (718) 465-0500
　Fax: (718) 465-0550
　%FO: 100

● **FRESHFIELDS BRUCKHAUS DERINGER LLP**
65 Fleet St., London EC4Y 1HS, England, U.K.
CEO: Hugh Crisp, Mng. Prtn.
Bus: *International business law.*
Tel: 44-207-936-4000
Fax: 44-207-832-7001
www.freshfields.co.uk
Emp: 690
NAICS: 541110

　FRESHFIELDS BRUCKHAUS DERINGER LLP
　520 Madison Ave., 34/F, New York, New York 10022
　CEO: Ted Burke
　Bus: *International law firm.*
　Tel: (212) 277-4000
　Fax: (212) 277-4001
　%FO: 100
　Emp: 8

FRESHFIELDS BRUCKHAUS DERINGER LLP
1300 I St. NW, 12/F East, Washington, District of Columbia 20005-3314
CEO: Gregory May
Bus: *International law firm.*
Tel: (202) 777-4500
Fax: (202) 777-4545
%FO: 100

● **FULCRUM PHARMA PLC**
Kodak House, Station Rd., Hemel Hempstead, Hertfordshire HP1 1JY, England, U.K.
CEO: Sir Charles F. George, Chmn.
Bus: *Drug development services.*
Tel: 44-1442-283-600
Fax: 44-1442-283-613
www.fulcrumpharma.com
Rev: $20
Emp: 44
NAICS: 325411, 325412, 541710, 621511

> **FULCRUM PHARMA**
> 2803 Slater Rd., Ste. 125, Morrisville, North Carolina 27560
> CEO: Bruce J. McCreedy, Pres.
> Bus: *Drug development services.*
> Tel: (919) 226-1440
> Fax: (919) 226-1441
> %FO: 100

● **FUTURE PLC**
Beauford Ct., 30 Monmouth St., Bath BA1 2BW, England, U.K.
CEO: Roger G. Parry, Chmn.
Bus: *Publisher of magazines.*
Tel: 44-122-544-2244
Fax: 44-122-544-6019
www.futureplc.com
Rev: $239
Emp: 1,058
NAICS: 511120

> **FUTURE NETWORK USA INC.**
> 149 Fifth Ave., 9/F, New York, New York 10010
> CEO: Jonathan Simpson-Bint, Pres.
> Bus: *Publisher of magazines.*
> Tel: (212) 768-2966
> Fax:
> %FO: 100

> **FUTURE NETWORK USA INC.**
> 245 Townpark Dr., Ste. 660, Kennesaw, Georgia 30144
> CEO: Jonathan Simpson-Bint, Pres.
> Bus: *Publisher of magazines.*
> Tel: (678) 594-4044
> Fax:
> %FO: 100

> **FUTURE NETWORK USA INC.**
> 150 North Hill Dr., Ste. 40, Brisbane, California 94005
> CEO: Jonathan Simpson-Bint, Pres.
> Bus: *Publisher of magazines.*
> Tel: (415) 468-4684
> Fax: (415) 468-4686
> %FO: 100

● **GAFFNEY, CLINE & ASSOCIATES LTD.**
Bentley Hall, Blacknest, Alton, Hampshire GY34 4PU, England, U.K.
CEO: Peter Gaffney, CEO
Bus: *Provides management and commercial advice to the global oil and gas industry.*
Tel: 44-1420-525366
Fax: 44-1420-525367
www.gaffney-cline.com
Rev: $15
Emp: 61
NAICS: 541614, 541690

> **GAFFNEY, CLINE & ASSOCIATES**
> 1360 Post Oak Blvd., Ste. 2500, Houston, Texas 77056
> CEO: W. B. Cline
> Bus: *Integrated technical and management advice.*
> Tel: (713) 850-9955
> Fax: (713) 850-9966
> %FO: 100

- **GAMES WORKSHOP GROUP PLC**
  Willow Rd., Lenton, Nottingham NG7 2WS, England, U.K.
  CEO: Thomas H. F. Kirby, CEO
  Bus: *Designs and manufactures model soldiers, game systems and accessories for tabletop war*
  NAICS: 339932

  Tel: 44-115-916-8100
  Fax: 44-115-916-8111
  www.games-workshop.com

  Rev: $278
  Emp: 3,177

  > **GAMES WORKSHOP USA INC.**
  > 6721 Baymeadow Dr., Glen Burnie, Maryland 21060
  > CEO: John Stallard
  > Bus: *Designs and manufactures model soldiers, game systems and accessories for tabletop war gaming.*
  >
  > Tel: (410) 590-1400
  > Fax: (410) 590-6700
  >
  > %FO: 100

- **GE SEACO**
  Sea Containers House, 20 Upper Ground, London SE1 9PF, England, U.K.
  CEO: Angus R. Frew, SVP
  Bus: *Freight leasing services. (JV of GE Capital and Sea Containers).*
  NAICS: 532411

  Tel: 44-20-7805-5600
  Fax: 44-20-7805-5900
  www.geseaco.com

  > **GE SEACO AMERICA, INC.**
  > 7200 NW 19th St., Ste. 702, Miami, Florida 33126
  > CEO: Lowell Thomas, Mgr.
  > Bus: *Marine container leasing companies. (JV of GE Capital)*
  >
  > Tel: (305) 594-4244
  > Fax: (305) 591-7214
  >
  > %FO: 100

  > **GE SEACO AMERICA, INC.**
  > 1114 Ave. of the Americas, 38/F, New York, New York 10036
  > CEO: Robin Lynch, Pres.
  > Bus: *Freight leasing services.*
  >
  > Tel: (212) 302-5070
  > Fax: (212) 921-4353
  >
  > %FO: 100
  > Emp: 200

  > **GE SEACO AMERICA, INC.**
  > 3478 Buskirk Ave., Pleasant Hill, Ste. 1000, San Francisco, California 94523
  > CEO: Chris Laskaris, Mgr.
  > Bus: *Marine container leasing companies. (JV of GE Capital)*
  >
  > Tel: (925) 746-4231
  > Fax: (925) 746-7109
  >
  > %FO: 100

  > **GE SEACO AMERICA, INC.**
  > 1601 Oceanic St., Charleston, South Carolina 29405
  > CEO: Paul Dacey, VP
  > Bus: *Accounting services for operations.*
  >
  > Tel: (843) 723-8833
  > Fax: (843) 723-5861
  >
  > %FO: 100

- **THE GENERICS GROUP AG**
  Harston Mill. Harston, Cambridge CB2 5GG, England, U.K.
  CEO: Gordon Edge, Chmn.
  Bus: *Engaged in integrated technology consulting, development and investment.*
  NAICS: 523910, 523999, 525990, 551112

  Tel: 44-122-387-5200
  Fax: 44-122-387-5201
  www.genericsgroup.com

  Rev: $30
  Emp: 208

SCIENTIFIC GENERICS INC.
Reservoir Place, 1601 Trapelo Rd., Ste. 154, Waltham, Massachusetts 02451
CEO: Peter Hyde, Pres.   Tel: (781) 290-0500   %FO: 100
Bus: *Engaged in integrated technology*   Fax: (781) 290-0501   Emp: 20
consulting, development and investment.

SCIENTIFIC GENERICS INC.
11403 Cronhill Dr., Ste. B, Owings Mills, Maryland 21117
CEO: Daniel Flicos, Pres.   Tel: (410) 654-0090   %FO: 100
Bus: *Engaged in integrated technology*   Fax: (410) 654-0138   Emp: 15
consulting, development and investment.

● **GENETIX GROUP PLC**
Queensway, New Milton, Hampshire BH25 5NN, England, U.K.
CEO: Mark A. Reid, CEO   Tel: 44-1425-624-600   Rev: $23
Bus: *Biotechnology.*   Fax: 44-1425-624-700   Emp: 100
                                           www.genetix.co.uk
NAICS: 541519

GENETIX USA INC.
56 Roland St., Ste.106, Charlestown, Massachusetts 02129-1223
CEO: James A. Bull, Pres.   Tel: (617) 776-6100   %FO: 100
Bus: *Engaged in biotechnology.*   Fax: (617) 776-6100

● **GET GROUP PLC**
Key Point, 3-17 High St., Hertfordshire, Potters Bar EN6 5AJ, England, U.K.
CEO: Lance Joseph, CEO   Tel: 44-1707-6-01707   Rev: $115
Bus: *Distributor of decorative lighting fixtures, switch* Fax: 44-1707-6-01701   Emp: 280
plates, wiring components, circuit breakers, and www.getplc.co.uk
other equip.
NAICS: 335931, 335999, 423610

GET ASIA LTD.
8770 Old Southwick Pass, Alpharetta, Georgia 30022
CEO: David Kaplan   Tel: (678) 641-9252   %FO: 100
Bus: *Distributor of decorative lighting fixtures,* Fax: (770) 569-1036
switch plates, and other equip.

● **GFI GROUP INC.**
25 Christopher St., London EC2A 2BS, England, U.K.
CEO: Colin Heffron, Pres.   Tel: 44-20-7422-1000   Rev: $385
Bus: *Inter-dealer brokerage services.*   Fax: 44-20-7877-8065   Emp: 868
                                           www.gfigroup.com
NAICS: 511210, 523120

GFI GROUP INC.
100 Wall St., New York, New York 10005
CEO: Donald Fewer, Mng. Dir.   Tel: (212) 968-4100   %FO: 100
Bus: *Inter-dealer brokerage services.*   Fax: (212) 968-4124

- **GKN PLC**
PO Box 55, Ipsley Church Lane, Redditch, Worcestershire B98 0TL, England, U.K.
CEO: Roy Brown, Chmn.   Tel: 44-152-751-7715   Rev: $8,152
Bus: *Mfr. automotive components.*   Fax: 44-152-751-7700   Emp: 47,900
                                       www.gknplc.com
    NAICS: 336312, 336350, 336411, 336992

    GKN AEROSPACE CHEM-TRONICS, INC.
    1150 West Bradley Ave., El Cajon, California 92020
    CEO: James Legler, Pres.   Tel: (619) 448-2320   %FO: 100
    Bus: *Engaged in aerospace components and*   Fax: Emp: 915
    aviation repair.

    GKN AEROSPACE TRANSPARENCY SYSTEMS
    12122 Western Ave., Garden Grove, California 92841
    CEO: James E. Dauw, Pres.   Tel: (714) 893-7531
    Bus: *Plastic products*   Fax: Emp: 321

    GKN AMERICA CORP.
    550 Warrenville Rd., Lisle, Illinois 60532
    CEO: Grey Denham, Pres.   Tel: (630) 719-7204
    Bus: *Motor vehicle parts & accessories*   Fax: Emp: 3,000

    GKN AUTOMOTIVE INC.
    6400 Durham Rd., Timberlake, North Carolina 27583
    CEO: Thomas R. Stone, CEO   Tel: (336) 364-6200
    Bus: *Automotive parts manufacturing*   Fax: (336) 364-6460

    SINTER METALS
    3300 University Dr., Auburn Hills, Michigan 48326-2362
    CEO: Kenneth Sparks, Pres.   Tel: (248) 371-0800   %FO: 100
    Bus: *Metal fabrication*   Fax: (248) 371-0809

- **GLAXOSMITHKLINE PLC**
980 Great West Rd., Brentford, London TW8 9GS, England, U.K.
CEO: Jean-Pierre Garnier, CEO   Tel: 44-20-8047-5000   Rev: $39,032
Bus: *Development/mfr./marketing human and animal*   Fax: 44-20-8047-7807   Emp: 100,019
health care products, over-counter medicines;   www.gsk.com
clinical lab testing services; healthcare services.
    NAICS: 325411, 325412, 325620

    GLAXOSMITHKLINE
    One Franklin Plaza, Philadelphia, Pennsylvania 19101
    CEO: Jean-Pierre Garnier, CEO   Tel: (215) 751-5000   %FO: 100
    Bus: *Develop /mfr./marketing human & animal*   Fax: (215) 751-3233   Emp: 24,036
    healthcare products, over-counter
    medicines; clinical lab testing services;
    healthcare services.

    GLAXOSMITHKLINE
    5 Moore Dr., PO Box 13398, Research Triangle Park, North Carolina 27709
    CEO: George Marrow, Pres.   Tel: (919) 483-2100   %FO: 100
    Bus: *Mfr. pharmaceuticals.*   Fax: (919) 483-2412   Emp: 8,500

● **GLENDINNING MANAGEMENT CONSULTANTS**
1 Station Rd., Addlestone, Surrey KT15 2AG, England, U.K.
CEO: Peter Swift, CEO
Bus: *Marketing consulting services.*

Tel: 44-1932-833600
Fax: 44-1932-833601
www.glendinning.co.uk

Rev: $15
Emp: 56

NAICS: 541611, 541613, 611430

   GLENDINNING MANAGEMENT CONSULTANTS
   10 Mountainview Rd., 1/F, Upper Saddle River, New Jersey 07458
   CEO: Alastair Cochrane, Pres.
   Bus: *Consulting services.*

   Tel: (201) 760-8650
   Fax: (201) 760-8655

   %FO: 100
   Emp: 6

● **GLOBAL INSURANCE SOLUTIONS**
34 Leadenhall St., London EC3A 1AX, England, U.K.
CEO: Roger Townsend, CEO
Bus: *Mfr. software for the insurance and reinsurance industries.*

Tel: 44-20-7780-6999
Fax: 44-20-7780-6998
www.rebusis.com

NAICS: 541511

   GLOBAL INSURANCE SOLUTIONS
   300 Lighting Way, 1/F, Secaucus, New Jersey 07094
   CEO: Martyn Sutton, Pres.
   Bus: *Software for the insurance and reinsurance industries.*

   Tel: (201) 223-2900
   Fax: (201) 223-2744

   %FO: 100

● **GLOTEL PLC**
The Communications Bldg., 48 Leicester Sq., 7/F, London WC2H 7LT, England, U.K.
CEO: Les Clark, Chmn.
Bus: *Recruiting services.*

Tel: 44-20-7484-3000
Fax: 44-20-7484-3001
www.glotel.co.uk

Rev: $165
Emp: 180

NAICS: 561310, 561320

   GLOTEL INC.
   The Alliance Center, 3500 Lenox Rd., Ste. 1850, Atlanta, Georgia 30326
   CEO: Greg Lynch
   Bus: *Recruiting services.*

   Tel: (404) 926-0025
   Fax: (404) 926-0013

   %FO: 100

   GLOTEL INC.
   10 Post Office Square, Ste. 700, Boston, Massachusetts 02109
   CEO: Andrew Baker, CEO
   Bus: *Recruiting services.*

   Tel: (610) 338-5134
   Fax: (610) 338-9340

   %FO: 100
   Emp: 65

   GLOTEL INC.
   350 S. Mill Ave., Ste. 202B, Tempe, Arizona 85281
   CEO: Kim Pope, Mgr.
   Bus: *Recruiting services.*

   Tel: (480) 829-8162
   Fax: (480) 829-1863

   %FO: 100

   GLOTEL INC.
   30 South Wacker Dr., Ste. 3900, Chicago, Illinois 60606
   CEO: Greg Lynch
   Bus: *Recruiting services.*

   Tel: (312) 715-0699
   Fax: (312) 715-0756

   %FO: 100

GLOTEL INC.
Parkview Tower, 1150 First Ave., Ste. 105, King of Prussia, Pennsylvania 19406
CEO: Andy Baker, Principal   Tel: (610) 757-6000   %FO: 100
Bus: *Recruiting services.*   Fax: (610) 757-6006

GLOTEL INC.
3811 Turtle Creek Blvd., Ste. 1820, Dallas, Texas 75219
CEO: Peter Trivedi, Mgr.   Tel: (214) 922-8930   %FO: 100
Bus: *Recruiting services.*   Fax: (214) 922-8285   Emp: 8

GLOTEL INC.
388 Market St., Ste. 1000, San Francisco, California 94111
CEO: Kara Reiter, Dir.   Tel: (415) 283-4999   %FO: 100
Bus: *Recruiting services.*   Fax: (415) 283-4998   Emp: 13

GLOTEL INC.
7101 York Ave. South, Ste. 374, Edina, Minnesota 55435
CEO: Tim Davis   Tel: (952) 921-3333   %FO: 100
Bus: *Recruiting services.*   Fax: (952) 921-3334

GLOTEL INC.
400 Madison Ave., Ste. 5D, New York, New York 10019
CEO: Heidi Madden, Mgr.   Tel: (212) 223-4090   %FO: 100
Bus: *Recruiting services.*   Fax: (212) 223-5124

GLOTEL INC.
8500 College Blvd., Overland Park, Kansas 66210
CEO: Greg Lynch   Tel: (913) 338-7103   %FO: 100
Bus: *Recruiting services.*   Fax: (913) 663-9905

GLOTEL INC.
1001 Brickell Bay Dr., Ste. 2016, Miami, Florida 33131
CEO: Greg Lynch   Tel: (305) 341-8990   %FO: 100
Bus: *Recruiting services.*   Fax: (305) 416-9529

GLOTEL INC.
150 Almaden Blvd., Ste. 1340, San Jose, California 95113
CEO: Andy Barton, Mgr.   Tel: (408) 795-1100   %FO: 100
Bus: *Recruiting services.*   Fax: (408) 795-1101

● **GOLIATH INTERNATIONAL TOOLS LTD.**
Goliath House, Newtown Row, Aston, Birmingham B6 4NQ, England, U.K.
CEO: Norman E. Moore, Pres.   Tel: 44-121-359-6621
Bus: *Mfr. threading tapes and ties.*   Fax: 44-121-359-6882   Emp: 200
                                      www.goliathinternational.com
NAICS: 315191
    GOLIATH THREADING TOOLS INC.
    9092 Telegraph Rd., Redford, Michigan 48239
    CEO: Norman E. Moore, Pres.   Tel: (313) 538-0999   %FO: 100
    Bus: *Distribution threading taps & dies.*   Fax: (313) 538-8099   Emp: 3

- **GRANADA INTERNATIONAL**
48 Leicester Square, London WC2H 7FB, England, U.K.
CEO: Patrice Andrews, VP
Bus: *Motion picture production and distribution*

Tel: 44-20-7493-7677
Fax: 44-20-7491-1441
www.int.granadamedia.com/international

NAICS: 512110, 512120, 512191, 512199

  GRANADA AMERICA
  15303 Ventura Blvd., Bldg. C, Ste. 800, Sherman Oaks, California 91403
  CEO: Scott Siegler, Pres.
  Bus: *Motion picture & video production*

  Tel: (818) 455-4600
  Fax:

  %FO: 100
  Emp: 13

- **WILLIAM GRANT & SONS LTD.**
Independence House, 84 Lower Mortlake Rd., Richmond, London TW9 2HS, England, U.K.
CEO: Roland van Bommel, CEO
Bus: *Distillery/exporter liquor.*

Tel: 44-20-8332-1188
Fax: 44-20-8332-1695
www.williamgrant.com

NAICS: 312140

  WILLIAM GRANT & SON INC
  130 Fieldcrest Ave., Edison, New Jersey 08837
  CEO: Derek Anderson, Pres.
  Bus: *Distillery/importer liquor.*

  Tel: (732) 225-9000
  Fax: (732) 225-0950

  %FO: 100
  Emp: 1

- **R. GRIGGS GROUP LIMITED**
Cobbs Lane, Wallaston, Northamptonshire NN29 7SW, England, U.K.
CEO: Stephen W. Griggs, Pres.
Bus: *Specialty footwear manufacture, including Doc Martens.*

Tel: 44-1933-653-281
Fax: 44-1933-662-848
www.drmartens.com

Rev: $280
Emp: 3,100

NAICS: 316213, 316214

  DR. MARTENS AIRWAIR USA
  10 NW 10th Ave., Portland, Oregon 97209
  CEO: Bill Cohen, Pres.
  Bus: *Specialty footwear manufacture and sales.*

  Tel: (503) 222-6300
  Fax: (503) 222-6880

  %FO: 100

- **GROSVENOR GROUP HOLDINGS LIMITED**
70 Grosvenor St., London W1K 3JP, England, U.K.
CEO: Jeremy Newsum, CEO
Bus: *Acquires, manages and develops real estate properties.*

Tel: 44-20-7408-0988
Fax: 44-20-7629-9115
www.grosvenor.com

Rev: $163
Emp: 373

NAICS: 531110, 531190, 531390

  GROSVENOR AMERICAS INC.
  One Embarcadero Center, Ste. 3900, San Francisco, California 94111
  CEO: Alan Chamorro
  Bus: *Acquires, manages and develops real estate properties.*

  Tel: (415) 434-0175
  Fax: (415) 434-2742

  %FO: 100

GROSVENOR USA LIMITED
1701 Pennsylvania Ave. NW., Ste. 1050, Washington, District of Columbia 20006
CEO: Ashleigh Simpson   Tel: (202) 293-1235   %FO: 100
Bus: *Acquires, manages and develops real*   Fax: (202) 785-2632
    estate properties.

● **GROUP 4 SECURICOR PLC**
The Manor, Manor Royal, Gatwick, Sussex RH10 9UN, England, U.K.
CEO: Lars Norby Johansen, CEO   Tel: 44-20-8770-7000   Rev: $7,493
Bus: *Engaged in security systems.*   Fax: 44-20-8722-2000   Emp: 332,000
                                         www.group4securicor.com
NAICS: 334290, 334511, 334519, 335999, 561611, 561612, 561621

AMAG TECHNOLOGY
20701 Manhattan Place, Torrance, California 90501
CEO: Robert A. Sawyer, Pres.   Tel: (310) 518-2380
Bus: *Mfr. computer access control security*   Fax: (310) 834-0685   Emp: 30
    systems

COGNISA SECURITY, INC.
2000 River Edge Pkwy., Ste. GL-100, Atlanta, Georgia 30328
CEO: Keith Badham, Pres. & CEO   Tel: (877) 246-4176   %FO: 100
Bus: *Provides security products & services*   Fax: (770) 541-5399   Emp: 6,500

SECURICOR EMS
30201 Aventura, Rancho Santa Margarita, California 92688
CEO: Fiona Walters, Pres.   Tel: (949) 635-1600
Bus: *Search & navigation equipment*   Fax: (949) 635-1626   Emp: 96

SECURICOR INTERNATIONAL VALUABLES TRANSPORT
JFK International Airport, Bldg. 79, North Boundary, Jamaica, New York 11430
CEO: Murray Rose, Dir.   Tel: (718) 244-6206
Bus: *Freight transportation arrangements.*   Fax: (718) 244-1345   Emp: 12

SECURICOR NEW CENTURY
9609 Gayton Rd., Ste. 100, Richmond, Virginia 23233
CEO: Gail Browne, Pres.   Tel: (804) 754-1100
Bus: *Youth correction center management &*   Fax: (804) 741-9515   Emp: 1,118
    consulting

WACKENHUT CORPORATION
4200 Wackenhut Dr., Ste. 100, Palm Beach Gardens, Florida 33410-4243
CEO: Gary A. Sanders, CEO   Tel: (561) 622-5656   %FO: 100
Bus: *Provides security products & services*   Fax: (561) 691-6423

WACKENHUT SERVICES, INC.
7121 Fairway Dr., Ste. 301, Palm Beach Gardens, Florida 33418
CEO: James L. Long, CEO   Tel: (561) 472-0600   %FO: 100
Bus: *Security products & services*   Fax: (561) 472-3679   Emp: 397

- **GUARDIAN MEDIA GROUP**
  75 Farringdon Rd., London EC1M 3JY, England, U.K.
  CEO: Paul Myners, CEO
  Bus: *Newspaper and magazine publishing and regional radio stations.*
  NAICS: 511110, 511120, 515111, 515210

  Tel: 44-207-713-4452
  Fax: 44-207-242-0679
  www.gmgplc.co.uk

  Rev: $560
  Emp: 3,170

  GUARDIAN WEEKLY
  PO Box 2515, Champlain, New York 12919
  CEO: Patrick Ensor, Sales Mgr.
  Bus: *Magazine publishing.*

  Tel: (514) 737-2525
  Fax: (514) 697-3490

  %FO: 100

- **GUS PLC, GREAT UNIVERSAL STORES**
  1 Stanhope Gate, London W1K 1AF, England, U.K.
  CEO: John W. Peace, CEO
  Bus: *Provider of global information solutions, consumer credit reporting, logistics and customer care and multi-channel retailing.*
  NAICS: 442299, 443111, 443112, 448140, 448150, 454113, 561450

  Tel: 44-207-495-0070
  Fax: 44-207-495-1567
  www.gusplc.co.uk

  Rev: $13,781
  Emp: 76,263

  EXPERIAN NORTH AMERICA
  475 Anton Blvd., Costa Mesa, California 92626
  CEO: Donald A. Robert, CEO
  Bus: *Credit reporting agency.*

  Tel: (714) 830-7000
  Fax: (714) 830-2449

  %FO: 100

- **HALCROW GROUP LTD.**
  Vineyard House, 44 Brook Green, London W6 7BY, England, U.K.
  CEO: Peter J. Gammie, CEO
  Bus: *Provides planning, design and management services.*
  NAICS: 541330, 541490, 541620

  Tel: 44-207-602-7282
  Fax: 44-207-603-0095
  www.halcrow.com

  Rev: $356
  Emp: 4,000

  HALCROW
  2111 Wilson Blvd., Ste. 600, Arlington, Virginia 22201
  CEO: Charles Oldham
  Bus: *Provides international management, planning and design services.*

  Tel: (703) 351-5025
  Fax: (703) 312-7068

  %FO: 100

  HALCROW
  22 Cortlandt St., New York, New York 10007
  CEO: Jonathan Goldstick
  Bus: *Provides international planning, management and design services.*

  Tel: (212) 608-4963
  Fax: (212) 608-5059

  %FO: 100

  HPA LLC
  1939 Harrison St., Ste. 730, Oakland, California 94612
  CEO: Gayle Johnson
  Bus: *Provides international management, planning and design services.*

  Tel: (510) 452-0040
  Fax: (510) 452-0041

  %FO: 100

  HPA LLC
  6700 East Pacific Coast Highway, Ste. 180, Long Beach, California 90803
  CEO: Ken Forssen
  Bus: *Provides international management, planning and design services.*

  Tel: (562) 493-8300
  Fax: (562) 493-8308

  %FO: 100

HPA LLC
4010 Boy Scout Blvd., Ste. 580, Tampa, Florida 33607
CEO: Todd Stockberger Tel: (813) 876-6800 %FO: 100
Bus: *Provides international management, planning* Fax: (813) 876-6700
and design services.

HPA LLC
8130 Baymeadows Circle W., Ste. 206, Jacksonville, Florida 32256
CEO: Paul Starr Tel: (904) 733-3180 %FO: 100
Bus: *Provides international management, planning* Fax: (904) 733-3343
and design services.

● **HALMA PLC**
Misbourne Court, Rectory Way, Amersham, Buckinghamshire HP7 0DE, England, U.K.
CEO: Andrew J. Williams, CEO Tel: 44-149-472-1111 Rev: $534
Bus: *Supplies environmental control, fire and gas* Fax: 44-149-472-8032 Emp: 2,925
detection, safety and security products and www.halma.com
NAICS: 334220, 334419, 334511, 334519, 335999, 423690

AIR PRODUCTS AND CONTROLS, INC.
1749 East Highwood,, Bldg. G, Pontiac, Michigan 48340
CEO: Jim Ludwig, Pres. Tel: (248) 332-3900 %FO: 100
Bus: *Duct detectors manufacture for smoke* Fax: (248) 332-8807
control systems.

AQUIONICS INC.
21 Kenton Lands Rd., Erlanger, Kentucky 41018
CEO: Jon McClean, Pres. Tel: (859) 341-0710 %FO: 100
Bus: *Ultraviolet equipment manufacture for water* Fax: (859) 341-0350
sterilization & disinfection.

B.E.A INC.
100 Enterprise Dr., RIDC Park West, Pittsburgh, Pennsylvania 15275
CEO: Patrick Maercier Tel: (412) 249-4100
Bus: *Elevator & Door Safety manufacturer..* Fax: (412) 249-4101

BIO-CHEM VALVE INC.
85 Fulton St., Boonton, New Jersey 07005
CEO: George Gaydos, Pres. Tel: (973) 263-3001 %FO: 100
Bus: *Miniature valves manufacture for scientific* Fax: (973) 263-2880
instruments.

DIBA INDUSTRIES
4 Precision Rd., Danbury, Connecticut 06810
CEO: Chuck Dubois, Pres. Tel: (203) 744-0773
Bus: *Medical, life science and scientific* Fax: (203) 744-0663
instruments

ELECTRONIC MICRO SYSTEMS, INC
125 Ricefield Lane, Hauppauge, New York 11788
CEO: Mike Bryne, Pres. Tel: (631) 864-4770 %FO: 100
Bus: *Elevator electronics manufacture.* Fax: (631) 864-4770

FLUID CONSERVATIN SYSTEMS INC.
2001 Ford Circle, Ste. F, Milford, Ohio 45150
CEO: Tom McGee, VP Operations Tel: (513) 831-9335 %FO: 100
Bus: *Underground water leaks diagnostic* Fax: (513) 831-9336
equipment manufacture.

HALMA HOLDINGS, INC.
3100 East Kemper Rd., Cincinnati, Ohio 45241
CEO: Steve Sowell, CFO Tel: (513) 772-5501 %FO: 100
Bus: *U.S. headquarters holding company; firms* Fax: (513) 772-5507
supply environmental control, fire & gas
detection, safety & security products &
services.

IPC POWER RESISTORS INTL INC.
167 Gap Way, Erlanger, Kentucky 41018-3130
CEO: Richard Field, Pres. Tel: (859) 282-2900 %FO: 100
Bus: *Heavy-duty electrical resistors manufacture.* Fax: (859) 282-2907

JANUS ELEVATOR PRODUCTS INC.
125 Ricefield Lane, Hauppauge, New York 11788
CEO: Mike Byrne, Pres. Tel: (631) 864-3699 %FO: 100
Bus: *Elevator controls manufacture.* Fax: (631) 864-2631

KEELER INSTRUMENTS INC.
456 Parkway, Lawrence Park Industrial Estate, Broomall, Pennsylvania 19008
CEO: David J. Keeler, Pres. Tel: (610) 353-4350 %FO: 100
Bus: *Distribution of optical equipment.* Fax: (610) 353-7814

MARATHON SENSORS INC.
3100 East Kemper Rd., Cincinnati, Ohio 45241
CEO: Eric S. Boltz, Pres. Tel: (513) 772-1000 %FO: 100
Bus: *Control equipment manufacture for heat* Fax: (513) 326-7090
treatment and boiler efficiency.

MONITOR CONTROLS INC
125 Ricefield Lane, Hauppauge, New York 11788
CEO: John Farella, Pres. Tel: (631) 543-4334 %FO: 100
Bus: *Elevator signal fixtures.* Fax: (631) 543-4372

MOSEBACH MANUFACTURING COMPANY
1417 McLaughlin Run Rd., Pittsburgh, Pennsylvania 15241
CEO: Gordon Denny, Pres. Tel: (412) 220-0200 %FO: 100
Bus: *High power electrical resistors manufacture.* Fax: (412) 220-0236

OCEAN OPTICS
830 Douglas Ave., Dunedin, Florida 34698
CEO: Mike Morris, Pres. Tel: (727) 733-2447
Bus: *Miniature fiber optics manufacturer.* Fax: (727) 733-3962

OKLAHOMA SAFETY EQUIPMENT CO. INC.
PO Box 1327, 1701 West Tacoma, Broken Arrow, Oklahoma 74013
CEO: Joe M. Ragosta, Pres. Tel: (918) 258-5626 %FO: 100
Bus: *Process bursting disks manufacture.* Fax: (918) 251-2809

PERMA PURE INC.
8 Executive Dr., Toms River, New Jersey 08754
CEO: David A. Leighty, Pres.
Bus: *Provides systems for removal of moisture from gas samples.*

Tel: (732) 244-0010
Fax: (732) 244-8140

%FO: 100

POST GLOVER LIFELINK INC.
PO Box 18666, 4750 Olympic Blvd., Erlanger, Kentucky 41018
CEO: Judith Kathman, Pres.
Bus: *Electrical patient safety equipment for hospitals.*

Tel: (859) 283-0778
Fax: (859) 372-6144

%FO: 100

POST GLOVER RESISTORS INC.
4750 Olympic Blvd., Erlanger, Kentucky 41018-3141
CEO: John Whincup, Pres.
Bus: *High Power electrical resistors*

Tel: (859) 283-0778
Fax: (859) 283-2978

VOLK OPTICAL INC.
7893 Enterprise Dr., Mentor, Ohio 44060
CEO: Pete L. Mastores, Pres.
Bus: *Ophthalmic lenses manufacture.*

Tel: (440) 942-6161
Fax: (440) 942-2257

%FO: 100

● **HAMPSON INDUSTRIES PLC**
7 Harbour Bldgs., Waterfront West, Dudley Rd., Brierley Hill, West Midlands DY5 1LN, England, U.K.
CEO: Kim S. Ward, CEO
Bus: *Mfr. aerospace, automotive and industrial engineering products.*

Tel: 44-1384-485-345
Fax: 44-1384-472-962
www.hampson-industries.plc.uk

Rev: $125
Emp: 1,180

NAICS: 336411, 336412, 336413, 541330

    BOLSAN COMPANY INC.
    163 Linwood Rd., Eighty Four, Pennsylvania 15330
    CEO: Chris Felcho
    Bus: *Mfr. engineering products.*

    Tel: (724) 225-0446
    Fax: (724) 225-8268

    %FO: 100

    BOLSAN WEST INC.
    226B N. Sherman Ave., Corona, California 92882
    CEO: Larry Glasman Jr.
    Bus: *Mfr. engineering products.*

    Tel: (909) 278-8197
    Fax: (909) 278-0956

    %FO: 100

    TEXSTARS INC.
    802 Ave. J. East, Grand Prairie, Texas 75050
    CEO: Grey Frye
    Bus: *Mfr. aviation and transportation products*

    Tel: (972) 647-1366
    Fax: (972) 641-2800

    %FO: 100

● **HANSON PLC**
1 Grosvenor Place, London SW1X 7JH, England, U.K.
CEO: Alan J. Murray, CEO
Bus: *Building materials supplies and equipment.*

Tel: 44-207-245-1245
Fax: 44-207-235-3455
www.hansonplc.com

Rev: $6,642
Emp: 27,400

NAICS: 212311, 212312, 212319, 212321, 327310, 327320, 327331, 327332, 327390

HANSON AGGREGATES EAST
2300 Gateway Centre Blvd., Morrisville, North Carolina 27560
CEO: C. Howard (Ward) Nye, Pres.
Bus: *Produces construction aggregates and hot mix asphalt.*
Tel: (919) 380-2500
Fax: (919) 380-2522
%FO: 100
Emp: 3,000

HANSON AGGREGATES NORTH AMERICA
8505 Freeport Pkwy., Ste. 138, Irving, Texas 75063
CEO: James Kitzmiller, Pres.
Bus: *Mfr. cement.*
Tel: (972) 621-0345
Fax: (972) 621-0505
%FO: 100
Emp: 5,400

HANSON BRICK & TILE
15720 John J. Delaney Dr., Ste. 555, Charlotte, North Carolina 28277
CEO: Richard Manning, Pres.
Bus: *Building materials; brick and tile.*
Tel: (704) 341-8750
Fax: (704) 341-8735
%FO: 100

HANSON BUILDING PRODUCTS NORTH AMERICA
3500 Maple Ave., Dallas, Texas 75219
CEO: Richard Manning, Pres.
Bus: *Mfr. concrete pipe and precast concrete products.*
Tel: (214) 525-5500
Fax: (214) 525-5817
%FO: 100
Emp: 5,800

HANSON NORTH AMERICA
1333 Campus Pkwy., Monmouth Shores Corporate Park, Neptune, New Jersey 07753
CEO: Alan J. Murray, Pres.
Bus: *Supplier of aggregates, cement and road materials; construction services.*
Tel: (732) 919-9777
Fax: (732) 919-1149
%FO: 100
Emp: 14,872

HANSON PIPE & PRODUCTS
3500 Maple Ave., Ste. 1500, Dallas, Texas 75219
CEO: Joseph W. Alridge, CFO
Bus: *Concrete & cement*
Tel: (214) 525-5500
Fax: (214) 525-5817
Emp: 3,800

● **HARVEY NASH GROUP PLC**
13 Bruton St.,, London W1J 6QA, England, U.K.
CEO: Ian Kirkpatrick, Chmn.
Bus: *Provider of executive search, IT permanent placement and temporary staffing.*
NAICS: 541612
Tel: 44-20-7333-0033
Fax: 44-20-7333-0032
www.harveynash.com
Rev: $238
Emp: 374

HARVEY NASH GROUP PLC
1700 Park St., Ste.212, Naperville, Illinois 60563
CEO: Mark McGee, VP
Bus: *Provider of executive search, IT permanent and temporary staffing.*
Tel: (630) 369-9300
Fax: (630) 369-7698
%FO: 100

HARVEY NASH GROUP PLC
3 Park Ave., 33/F, New York, New York 10016
CEO: Jayne Gill, VP
Bus: *Provider of executive search, IT permanent and temporary staffing.*
Tel: (212) 481-1317
Fax: (212) 481-1319
%FO: 100

HARVEY NASH GROUP PLC
Stratis Business Center, 101 Eisenhower Pkwy, Ste. 300, Roseland, New Jersey 07068
CEO: Robert J. Miano, Pres.   Tel: (973) 795-1234   %FO: 100
Bus: *Provider of executive search, IT permanent*   Fax: (973) 795-1238
    and temporary staffing.

HARVEY NASH GROUP PLC
455 Market St., Ste. 1190, San Francisco, California 94105
CEO: Chris Beisler, VP   Tel: (415) 901-0910   %FO: 100
Bus: *Provider of executive search, IT permanent*   Fax: (415) 901-0920
    and temporary staffing.

HARVEY NASH GROUP PLC
1123 Auraria Pkwy, Ste.100, Denver, Colorado 80204
CEO: Chris Beisler, VP   Tel: (303) 299-9090   %FO: 100
Bus: *Provider of executive search, IT permanent*   Fax: (303) 296-8855
    and temporary staffing.

HARVEY NASH GROUP PLC
1 Corporate Dr., 5/F, Ste.522, Shelton, Connecticut 06484
CEO: Anna Frazzetto, VP   Tel: (203) 225-0544   %FO: 100
Bus: *Provider of executive search, IT permanent*   Fax: (203) 225-0560
    and temporary staffing.

HARVEY NASH GROUP PLC
2505 2nd Ave., Ste. 705, Seattle, Washington 98121
CEO: Sean Horan, VP   Tel: (206) 956-9200   %FO: 100
Bus: *Provider of executive search, IT permanent*   Fax: (206) 956-0474
    and temporary staffing.

HARVEY NASH GROUP PLC
16214 Marshfield Dr., Tampa, Florida 33607
CEO: Mark McGee, VP   Tel: (813) 961-2281   %FO: 100
Bus: *Provider of executive search, IT permanent*   Fax: (813) 961-1893
    and temporary staffing.

HARVEY NASH GROUP PLC
3 Park Ave., 33/F, New York, New York 10016
CEO: Alistar Robinson, Mng. Dir.   Tel: (646) 752-2292   %FO: 100
Bus: *Provider of executive search.*   Fax: (212) 481-3264

● **THE HAYMARKET GROUP**
174 Hammersmith Rd., London W67 JP, England, U.K.
CEO: Michael Heseltine, Chmn.   Tel: 44-20-8267-5000
Bus: *Magazine publisher.*   Fax: 44-20-8267-4268
                       www.haymarketgroup.co.uk

NAICS: 511120, 516110, 561920

    THE HAYMARKET GROUP
    114 W. 26th St., 3/F, New York, New York 10001
    CEO: Maria Schummette   Tel: (646) 638-6000   %FO: 100
    Bus: *Magazine publishing.*   Fax: (646) 638-6113

● **HEATH LAMBERT GROUP LIMITED**
Friary Court, 65 Crutched Friars, London EC3N 2NP, England, U.K.
CEO: Adrian Colosso, CEO
Bus: *Insurance and reinsurance brokers.*

Tel: 44-207-560-3000
Fax: 44-207-560-3540
www.heathlambert.com

NAICS: 524210

EDWARD LLOYD LIMITED
100 Merrick Rd., Ste. 210W, Rockville Centre, New York 11570
CEO: John Mannix
Bus: *Insurance and reinsurance services.*

Tel: (516) 763-9320
Fax: (516) 763-6722

%FO: 100

HEALTH INSURANCE BROKING HOLDINGS
3100 Monticello Ave., Dallas, Texas 75205
CEO: Michelle De La Cruz
Bus: *Insurance and reinsurance services.*

Tel: (214) 561-7000
Fax: (214) 523-1576

%FO: 100

HEALTH INSURANCE BROKING HOLDINGS
300 S. Wacker Dr., Ste. 1080, Chicago, Illinois 60606
CEO: D. Barnett
Bus: *Insurance and reinsurance services.*

Tel: (312) 986-0404
Fax: (312) 986-0491

%FO: 100

● **HENDERSON GROUP PLC**
4 Broadgate, London EC2M 2DA, England, U.K.
CEO: Roger Yates, CEO
Bus: *Provider of investment, insurance, financial planning, and portfolio management services.*

Tel: 44-20-7638-5757
Fax: 44-20-7818-1820
www.hhg.com

Rev: $6,397
Emp: 3,100

NAICS: 523120, 523920, 523930, 523999, 525910

HENDERSON GROUP INVESTORS NA INC.
737 North Michigan Ave., Ste. 1950, Chicago, Illinois 60611
CEO: Charles H. Wartzebach, Mng. Dir.
Bus: *Provider of investment, insurance, financial planning, and portfolio management services.*

Tel: (312) 397-1122
Fax: (312) 397-1494

%FO: 100

HENDERSON GROUP INVESTORS NA INC.
1 Financial Plaza, 755 Main St., 19/F, Hartford, Connecticut 06103
CEO: Douglas G. Denyer, CFO
Bus: *Provider of investment, insurance, financial planning, and portfolio management services.*

Tel: (860) 723-8600
Fax: (860) 723-8601

%FO: 100

● **HENLYS GROUP PLC**
Unit 1, Imperial Place Maxwell Rd., Elstree Way, Borehamwood, Hertfordshire WD6 1JJ, England, U.K.
CEO: T. Allan Welsh, CEO
Bus: *Mfr. motor vehicles and automobile bodies.*

Tel: 44-20-8953-9953
Fax: 44-20-8207-2477
www.henlys.com

Rev: $504
Emp: 2,864

NAICS: 336111

AUTO SAFETY HOUSE
2630 W. Buckeye Rd., Phoenix, Arizona 85009
CEO: Ernesto Salazar, Sales
Bus: *Commercial bus distributor.*

Tel: (602) 269-9721
Fax: (602) 278-3916

%FO: 100

BLUE BIRD CORPORATION
402 Blue Bird Blvd., Fort Valley, Georgia 31030
CEO: Jeffrey Bust
Bus: *Mfr. commercial buses, high-end motor coaches and school buses.*

Tel: (478) 825-2021
Fax: (478) 822-2457

%FO: 100

● **HERBERT ARNOLD GMBH & CO. KG**
Weilstr. 6, Weilburg 35781, England, U.K.
CEO: Wolfram Arnold, Pres.
Bus: *Fiber optic, TV and quartz-working machinery.*

Tel: 44-190-822-2500
Fax: 44-190-822-2564
www.h-arnold.de

Emp: 70

NAICS: 334417

HEATHWAY INC.
4030 Skyron Dr., Ste. C, Doylestown, Pennsylvania 18901
CEO: Charles Glover, Pres.
Bus: *Electronic parts & equipment*

Tel: (215) 348-2881
Fax:

Emp: 6

● **HERBERT SMITH LLP**
Exchange House, Primrose St., London EC2A 2HS, England, U.K.
CEO: David Gold, Mng. Prtn.
Bus: *International law firm.*

Tel: 44-207-374-8000
Fax: 44-207-374-0888
www.herbertsmith.com

Rev: $444
Emp: 1,900

NAICS: 541110

STIBBE USA INC.
350 Park Ave., 28/F, New York, New York 10022
CEO: Hans Witteveen, Mng. Prtn.
Bus: *International law firm.*

Tel: (212) 972-4000
Fax: (212) 972-4929

%FO: 100

● **HEYWOOD WILLIAMS GROUP PLC**
Waverley, Edgerton Rd., Huddersfield, West Yorkshire HD3 3AR, England, U.K.
CEO: Robert Barr, CEO
Bus: *Holding company: manufactured housing, home fabrication and hardware markets.*

Tel: 44-1484-487200
Fax: 44-1484-547511
www.heywoodwilliams.com

Rev: $700
Emp: 2,200

NAICS: 332321, 551112

NORTH AMERICAN PROFILES GROUP
2287 Route 292, Holmes, New York 12531
CEO: Ralph J. Vasami
Bus: *Mfr. vinyl windows and doors.*

Tel: (845) 855-1738
Fax: (845) 855-1058

%FO: 100

WESTLAKE CHEMICAL CORPORATION
2801 Post Oak Blvd., Ste. 600, Houston, Texas 77056
CEO: Albert Chao, Pres.
Bus: *Mfr./supplier of petrochemicals, polymers and fabricated products.*

Tel: (713) 960-9111
Fax: (713) 963-1590

%FO: 100

- **HILTON GROUP PLC**
Maple Court, Central Park, Reeds Crescent, Watford Hertfordshire WD24 4QQ, England, U.K.
CEO: David M. C. Michels, CEO   Tel: 44-20-7856-8000   Rev: $15,877
Bus: *Leisure industry, gaming, real estate, hotels,*   Fax: 44-20-7856-8001   Emp: 84,500
                                        www.hiltongroup.com

NAICS: 531311, 713290, 713940, 721110, 722410

  HILTON HOTELS CORPORATION
  9336 Civic Center Dr., Beverly Hills, California 90210
  CEO: Stephen F. Bollenbach, Chmn. & CEO   Tel: (310) 278-4321
  Bus: *Hotel services.*   Fax: (310) 205-7678   Emp: 70,000

- **HIT ENTERTAINMENT LIMITED**
Maple House, 149-150 Tottenham Court Rd., London WIT 7NF, England, U.K.
CEO: Rob Lawes, CEO   Tel: 44-20-7554-2500   Rev: $269
Bus: *Children's TV programming distribution.*   Fax: 44-20-7388-9321   Emp: 412
                                        www.hitentertainment.com

NAICS: 511130, 512110, 512191, 512199, 533110, 711110, 711130, 711190, 711320

  HIT ENTERTAINMENT USA INC.
  830 S. Greenville Ave., Allen, Texas 75002
  CEO: Debbie Ries   Tel: (972) 390-6000   %FO: 100
  Bus: *Children's TV programming distribution.*   Fax: (972) 390-6000

  HIT ENTERTAINMENT USA INC.
  1133 Broadway, Ste. 1520, New York, New York 10010
  CEO: Charlie Caminada   Tel: (212) 463-9623   %FO: 100
  Bus: *Children's TV programming distribution.*   Fax: (212) 463-9626

- **HOGG ROBINSON PLC**
Abbey House, 282 Farnborough Rd., Hampshire, Farnborough GU14 7NJ, England, U.K.
CEO: David J.C. Radcliffe, CEO   Tel: 44-1252-372-000
Bus: *Business travel services*   Fax: 44-1252-371-200
                                        www.hoggrobinson.co.uk

NAICS: 561510, 561520, 561599

  SEA GATE TRAVEL GROUP LLC
  16 E. 34th St., 3/F, New York, New York 10016
  CEO: Dan Green, CEO   Tel: (212) 404-8800   %FO: 100
  Bus: *Business travel services*   Fax: (212) 481-2881   Emp: 320

- **HOMESERVE PLC**
Cable Dr., West Midlands, Walsall WS2 7BN, England, U.K.
CEO: Brian Howard Whilly, Chmn.   Tel: 44-1922-426-262   Rev: $580
Bus: *Provider of emergency plumbing, electrical, and*   Fax: 44-1922-427-904   Emp: 3,928
    gas services.   www.homeserve.co.uk
NAICS: 237110, 237130, 541620, 561210, 561790

  HOME SERVICE USA
  3401 NW 82nd Ave., Ste.220, Miami, Florida 33122
  CEO: Jerome McManus, Gen. Mgr.   Tel: (305) 477-2764   %FO: 100
  Bus: *Provider of emergency plumbing, electrical,*   Fax: (305) 477-2862
    and gas services.

- **HSBC HOLDINGS PLC**
8 Canada Sq., London E14 5HQ, England, U.K.
CEO: Stephen K. Green, CEO   Tel: 44-207-991-8888   Rev: $70,860
Bus: *Banking, trade, financial and insurance services.*   Fax: 44-207-992-4880   Emp: 253,000
www.hsbc.com
NAICS: 522110, 522220, 522291, 522292, 522293, 522294, 523110, 523120, 523920, 524210, 525910, 551111

   DECISION ONE MORTGAGE COMPANY, LLC
   6060 J.A. Jones Dr., Charlotte, North Carolina 28287
   CEO: J.C. Faulkner, Pres.   Tel: (704) 887-2700
   Bus: *Mortgage banking & related services*   Fax: (704) 887-2777   Emp: 1,500

   HSBC BANK USA
   1 HSBC Center, Buffalo, New York 14203
   CEO: William F. Aldinger, Pres.   Tel: (716) 841-2424
   Bus: *Commercial banking*   Fax: (716) 841-5391   Emp: 17,821

   HSBC CARD SERVICES
   1441 Schilling Place, Salinas, California 93902
   CEO: Siddarth N. Mehta, Vice Chmn.   Tel: (831) 754-1400
   Bus: *Credit cards*   Fax: (831) 755-2940

   HSBC FINANCE CORP.
   2700 Sanders Rd., Prospect Heights, Illinois 60070
   CEO: Siddarth N. Mehta, Chmn. & CEO   Tel: (847) 564-5000
   Bus: *Personal lending*   Fax: (847) 205-7401   Emp: 31,500

   HSBC NORTH AMERICA HOLDINGS INC.
   2700 Sanders Rd., Prospect Heights, Illinois 60070
   CEO: Siddath N. Mehta, Chmn. & CEO   Tel: (704) 564-5000
   Bus: *Financial services*   Fax:

   HSBC PRIVATE BANK
   2954 Adventura Blvd., Aventura, Florida 33180
   CEO: Stephen K. Green, Chmn.   Tel: (305) 935-3066
   Bus: *Banking*   Fax: (305) 937-6373

   HSBC USA INC.
   452 Fifth Ave., New York, New York 10018
   CEO: Martin J. G. Glynn, Pres. & CEO   Tel: (212) 525-3735   %FO: 100
   Bus: *International banking and trade financing*   Fax: Emp: 10,800
   services.

   THE BANK OF BERMUDA
   100 Wall St., 17/F, New York, New York 10005
   CEO: Fred Busk, Pres.   Tel: (212) 747-9300
   Bus: *Foreign trade & international banks*   Fax: (212) 747-9393   Emp: 40

- **HUNTING PLC**
3 Cockspur St., London SW1Y 5BQ, England, U.K.
CEO: Dennis L. Proctor, CEO   Tel: 44-20-7321-0123   Rev: $2,417
Bus: *Oil and natural gas.*   Fax: 44-20-7839-2072   Emp: 2,188
www.hunting.plc.uk

NAICS: 221210, 486110, 486210, 486910

HUNTING OILFIELD SERVICES
Two Northpoint Dr., Ste. 500, Houston, Texas 77060
CEO: Dennis L. Proctor
Bus: *Oilfield services.*
Tel: (281) 442-7382
Fax: (281) 442-2487
%FO: 100

● **HUNTLEIGH TECHNOLOGY PLC**
310 Dallow Rd., Luton LU1 1TD, England, U.K.
CEO: Julian D. Schild, Chmn.
Bus: *Mfr. of medical equipment.*
Tel: 44-1582-413-104
Fax: 44-1582-402-589
www.huntleigh-technology.com
Rev: $383
Emp: 2,530

NAICS: 334510, 339113

HUNTLEIGH HEALTHCARE LLC
40 Christopher Way, Eatontown, New Jersey 07724-3327
CEO: Chris Daughtery
Bus: *Manufacturer of medical equipment.*
Tel: (732) 578-9898
Fax: (732) 578-9889
%FO: 100

HUNTLEIGH HEALTHCARE LLC
2602 North West 97th Ave., Miami, Florida 33172
CEO: Joe Cristobal, Mgr.
Bus: *Manufacturer of medical equipment*
Tel: (305) 463-0526
Fax: (305) 463-0216
%FO: 100

● **IBSTOCK BRICK LIMITED**
Leicester Rd., Ibstock, Leicestershire LE67 6HS, England, U.K.
CEO: Wayne Sheppard, CEO
Bus: *Mfr. of high quality clay facing bricks and paving.*
Tel: 44-153-026-1999
Fax: 44-153-025-7457
www.ibstock.uk.com

NAICS: 327124, 327310, 327331

GLEN-GERY CORPORATION
1166 Spring St., Wyomissing, Pennsylvania 19610-6001
CEO: Ronald J. Hunsicker, Pres. & CEO
Bus: *Mfr. brick, brickwork design and services.*
Tel: (610) 374-4011
Fax: (610) 374-1622
%FO: 100
Emp: 1,200

● **ICAP PLC**
2 Broadgate, London EC2M 7UR, England, U.K.
CEO: Michael A. Spencer, CEO
Bus: *Wholesale broker of derivatives, money markets and securities.*
Tel: 44-20-7000-5000
Fax: 44-20-7000-5975
www.icap.com
Rev: $1,463
Emp: 2,860

NAICS: 523120, 523130, 523140, 523910, 523920, 523930

BROKERTEC
Harborside Financial Center, Plaza 5, 11/F, Jersey City, New Jersey 07311-3988
CEO: Stephen McDermott, COO
Bus: *Wholesale broker of derivatives, money markets, and securities.*
Tel: (201) 209-7832
Fax:
%FO: 100

ICAP ENERGY INC.
9931 Corporate Campus Dr., Louisville, Kentucky 40223
CEO: Richard Rosenberg
Bus: *Wholesale broker of energy derivatives.*
Tel: (502) 327-1400
Fax: (502) 327-1407
%FO: 100

ICAP ENERGY INC.
6320 Quadrangle Dr., Ste. 380, Chapel Hill, North Carolina 27517
CEO: Tom Hahn   Tel: (919) 969-9779   %FO: 100
Bus: *Wholesale broker of energy derivatives.*   Fax: (919) 969-9802

ICAP ENERGY INC.
1650 Post Oak Blvd, Ste. 740, Houston, Texas 77056
CEO: Spencer Vosko   Tel: (713) 355-4600   %FO: 100
Bus: *Wholesale broker of energy derivatives.*   Fax: (713) 355-1983

ICAP ENERGY INC.
Harborside Financial Center, 1100 Plaza Five, 12/F, Jersey City, New Jersey 07311
CEO: Carole Server   Tel: (212) 341-6500   %FO: 100
Bus: *Wholesale broker of energy derivatives.*   Fax: (212) 341-9599

● **IMAGINATION TECHNOLOGIES GROUP PLC**
Imagination House, Home Park Estate, Kings Langley, Hertfordshire WD4 8LZ, England, U.K.
CEO: Hossein Yassaie, CEO   Tel: 44-1923-260-511   Rev: $57
Bus: *Mfr. electronic entertainment, including audio and*   Fax: 44-1923-268-969   Emp: 273
 video systems for PC's.   www.imgtec.com
NAICS: 334119, 334413

   IMAGINATION TECHNOLOGIES INC.
   16870 W. Bernardo Dr., Ste. 407, San Diego, California 92127
   CEO: David McBrien   Tel: (858) 674-6644   %FO: 100
   Bus: *Mfr. and sales electronic entertainment,*   Fax: (858) 674-6645
    including audio and video systems for PC's.

● **IMI PLC**
Lakeside, Solihull Pkwy., Birmingham Business Park, Birmingham B37 7XY, England, U.K.
CEO: Martin J. Lamb, CEO & Mng. Dir. Tel: 44-121-717-3700   Rev: $3,103
Bus: *Holding company. Mfr. building products, liquid*   Fax: 44-121-356-3526   Emp: 17,063
 dispensers and designs engineering systems.   www.imiplc.com
NAICS: 332322, 332911, 332912, 332913, 332919, 333995, 333996, 423390, 423720

   CONTROL COMPONENTS INC.
   22591 Avenida Empresa, Rancho Santa Margarita, California 92688
   CEO: Stuart Carson, Pres.   Tel: (949) 858-1877   %FO: 100
   Bus: *Mfr./sale/service control valves for power,*   Fax: (949) 858-1878   Emp: 900
    oil, gas and petrochemicals industry.

   DCI MARKETING INC.
   2727 W. Good Hope Rd., Milwaukee, Wisconsin 53209
   CEO: Alan LaFreniere, Pres.   Tel: (414) 228-7000   %FO: 100
   Bus: *Direct marketing services.*   Fax: (414) 228-3421

   IMI CORNELIUS INC.
   101 Broadway West, Osseo, Minnesota 55369
   CEO: Martin Lamb, CEO   Tel: (763) 488-8200   %FO: 100
   Bus: *Mfr. beverage dispensing systems and*   Fax: (763) 488-4298   Emp: 2,000
    equipment.

IMI NORGREN COMPANY
5400 South Delaware St., Littleton, Colorado 80120
CEO: Mark Shellenberger, Pres.   Tel: (303) 794-2611   %FO: 100
Bus: *Mfr. pneumatic products.*   Fax: (303) 795-9487   Emp: 573

● **IMPERIAL CHEMICAL INDUSTRIES PLC**
20 Manchester Sq., London W1U 3AN, England, U.K.
CEO: John D. G. McAdam, CEO   Tel: 44-20-7009-5000   Rev: $10,738
Bus: *Mfr. industrial and special chemicals,*   Fax: 44-20-7009-5007   Emp: 33,300
agrochemical seeds, pharmaceuticals, films,   www.ici.com
paints, explosives, fibers, acrylics.
NAICS: 311930, 311942, 325131, 325132, 325181, 325188, 325199, 325212, 325221, 325222, 325510, 325520, 325620, 325920, 444120

ABLESTIK LABORATORIES
20021 Susana Rd., Rancho Dominguez, California 90221
CEO: Alan Syzdek, Pres.   Tel: (310) 764-4600
Bus: *Mfr. specialty chemicals.*   Fax: (310) 764-2545   Emp: 326

ACHESON COLLOIDS COMPANY
1600 Washington Ave., Port Huron, Michigan 48060
CEO: William H. Powell, CEO   Tel: (810) 984-5581   %FO: 100
Bus: *Mfr. electronic and engineering materials.*   Fax: (810) 984-1446

ICI AMERICAN
10 Finderne Ave., Bridgewater, New Jersey 08807
CEO: John R. Danzeisen, Chmn.   Tel: (908) 685-5000
Bus: *Mfr. specialty chemicals.*   Fax: (908) 685-5005   Emp: 15,240

ICI PAINTS NORTH AMERICA INC.
15885 W. Sprague Rd., Strongsville, Ohio 44136
CEO: Larry B. Pocellato, CEO   Tel: (440) 297-8000   %FO: 100
Bus: *Paints and coatings manufacture.*   Fax: (440) 297-8900   Emp: 7,000

NATIONAL STARCH & CHEMICAL COMPANY
10 Finderne Ave., Bridgewater, New Jersey 08807
CEO: William H. Powell, Chmn. & CEO   Tel: (908) 685-5000   %FO: 100
Bus: *Mfr./sales adhesives and specialty*   Fax: (908) 685-5005   Emp: 9,410
synthetic polymers.

UNIQEMA
1000 Uniqema Blvd., New Castle, Delaware 19720
CEO: Leonard J. Berlik, CEO   Tel: (302) 574-3252   %FO: 100
Bus: *Mfr. specialty chemicals.*   Fax: Emp: 2,950

● **INCAT INTERNATIONAL PLC**
INCAT House, Prospect Way, Luton Airport LU2 9QH, England, U.K.
CEO: Ulrich Herter, CEO   Tel: 44-1582-878-750   Rev: $117
Bus: *Design software and related engineering and*   Fax: 44-1582-878-751   Emp: 650
technical services.   www2.incat.com
NAICS: 511210

INCAT NORTH AMERICA INC.
3040 Charlevoix Dr. S.E., Grand Rapids, Michigan 49546
CEO: Patrick Malkowski   Tel: (616) 942-4744   %FO: 100
Bus: *Design software and related engineering*   Fax: (616) 942-5390
     and technical services.

INCAT NORTH AMERICA INC.
26351 Curtis Wright Pkwy., Ste. B, Richmond Heights, Ohio 44143
CEO: Karl Engler   Tel: (216) 797-0007   %FO: 100
Bus: *Design software and related engineering*   Fax: (216) 797-0077
     and technical services.

INCAT NORTH AMERICA INC.
1215-F Lyons Rd., Dayton, Ohio 45458
CEO: Jim Jordan   Tel: (937) 428-7521   %FO: 100
Bus: *Design software and related engineering*   Fax: (937) 428-7526
     and technical services.

INCAT NORTH AMERICA INC.
One Glenlake Pkwy., Ste. 700, Atlanta, Georgia 30328
CEO: George Ingols   Tel: (678) 638-6133   %FO: 100
Bus: *Design software and related engineering*   Fax: (678) 638-6134
     and technical services.

INCAT NORTH AMERICA INC.
41370 Bridge St., Novi, Michigan 48375
CEO: Joseph Ben-Gal, VP   Tel: (248) 426-1482   %FO: 100
Bus: *Design software and related engineering*   Fax: (248) 426-8398
     and technical services.

INCAT NORTH AMERICA INC.
5215 Old Orchard Rd., Suite 360, Skokie, Illinois 60077
CEO: Mark Human   Tel: (847) 663-1966   %FO: 100
Bus: *Design software and related engineering*   Fax: (847) 663-1968
     and technical services.

● **INCEPTA GROUP PLC**
3 London Wall Bldgs., London Wall, London EC2M 5SY, England, U.K.
CEO: Rt. Hon. Francis Anthony Aylmer Maude,   Tel: 44-207-282-2800   Rev: $457
Bus: *Advertising, marketing and public relations.* Fax: 44-207-282-8030   Emp: 2,058
                                                www.incepta.com
NAICS: 541613, 541810, 541820, 541830, 541850, 541870, 541890

    BROAD STREET
    44 Pleasant St., Watertown, Massachusetts 02472
    CEO: Lee Rubenstein, Pres.   Tel: (617) 924-3737
    Bus: *Motion picture & video production*   Fax: (617) 924-3373   Emp: 30

    BROAD STREET
    920 Broadway, New York, New York 10010
    CEO: Adam Selig, Pres. & CEO   Tel: (212) 780-5700
    Bus: *Business services.*   Fax: (212) 780-5710   Emp: 56

CAPITAL BRIDGE
111 River St., Ste. 1001, Hoboken, New Jersey 07030
CEO: Chris Taylor
Bus: *Advertising, marketing and public relations.*
Tel: (201) 499-3500
Fax: (201) 499-3600

CITIGATE ALBERT FRANK
850 Third Ave., 11/F, New York, New York 10022
CEO: Richard Nicholas, Chmn.
Bus: *Engaged in advertising.*
Tel: (212) 508-3400
Fax: (212) 508-3544
%FO: 100
Emp: 75

CITIGATE CUNNINGHAM
1530 Page Mill Rd., Palo Alto, California 94304
CEO: Paul Bergevin, Pres.
Bus: *Customized communications/technology programs.*
Tel: (650) 858-3700
Fax: (650) 858-3702
%FO: 100
Emp: 50

CITIGATE HUDSON
62 West 45th St., 5/F, New York, New York 10036
CEO: David Mittereder, Pres.
Bus: *Computer related services.*
Tel: (212) 840-0008
Fax: (212) 840-9490
Emp: 36

CITIGATE SARD VERBINNEN
630 Third Ave., New York, New York 10017
CEO: Paul Verbinnen, Pres.
Bus: *Public relations services*
Tel: (212) 687-8080
Fax: (212) 687-8344
Emp: 45

CITIGATE SARD VERBINNEN
343 West Erie St., Ste. 600, Chicago, Illinois 60610
CEO: Susan Silk, Mng. Dir.
Bus: *Advertising services.*
Tel: (312) 944-7398
Fax: (312) 944-7785
Emp: 13

INCEPTA ONLINE
111 River St., Hoboken, New Jersey 07030
CEO: Patricia Baronowski
Bus: *Advertising, marketing and public relations services.*
Tel: (201) 499-3500
Fax:

LLOYD NORTHOVER
850 Third Ave., New York, New York 10022
CEO: Simon Thackway
Bus: *Advertising, marketing and public relations.*
Tel: (212) 508-3400
Fax: (212) 508-3511

RED MANDARIN
850 Third Ave., New York, New York 10022
CEO: Fiona Young
Bus: *Advertising, marketing and public relations.*
Tel: (212) 508-3446
Fax: (212) 508-3592

● **INCISIVE MEDIA PLC**
Haymarket House, 28 Haymarket, London SW1Y 4RX, England, U.K.
CEO: Timothy Grainger Weller, CEO
Bus: *Provider of business information on risk management, retail investment, insurance, mortgage, and capital markets.*
Tel: 44-20-7484-9700
Fax: 44-20-7930-2238
www.incisivemedia.com
Rev: $90
Emp: 414

NAICS: 511120, 511199, 519110

INCISIVE RISK WATERS GROUP INC.
270 Lafayette St., Ste.700, New York, New York 10012
CEO: Richard Bravo   Tel: (212) 925-6990   %FO: 100
Bus: *Provider of business information*   Fax: (212) 925-7585
   publications.

● **INEOS FLUOR LIMITED**
PO Box 13, The Heath, Runcorn, Cheshire WA7 4QF, England, U.K.
CEO: Thomas P. Crotty, CEO   Tel: 44-1928-515-525   Rev: $198
Bus: *Mfr. fluorinated chemicals and intermediates.*   Fax: 44-1928-513-890   Emp: 256
   www.ineosfluor.com
   NAICS: 325199

   INEOS FLUOR AMERICAS LLC
   4990 B ICI Rd., Hwy. 75, PO Box 30, St. Gabriel, Louisiana 70776
   CEO: John Pacillo   Tel: (225) 642-0094   %FO: 100
   Bus: *Mfr. fluorinated chemicals and*   Fax: (225) 642-8629
      intermediates.

● **INEOS GROUP LIMITED**
Hawkslease, Chapel Lane, Lyndhurst, Hampshire SO43 7FF, England, U.K.
CEO: James A. Ratcliffe, CEO   Tel: 44-23-8028-7067   Rev: $4,623
Bus: *Mfr. and production of chlor-alkali products.*   Fax: 44-23-8028-7054   Emp: 7,000
   www.ineos.com
   NAICS: 325110, 325181, 325188, 325199, 325211, 325613

   INEOS CHLOR AMERICAS INC.
   300 Dickinson Dr., Ste 300, Chadds Ford, Pennsylvania 19317
   CEO: Lou Gatti   Tel: (484) 840-1870   %FO: 100
   Bus: *Mfr. chlor-alkali products.*   Fax: (484) 840-0639

   INEOS FILMS INC.
   1389 School House Rd., Delaware City, Delaware 19706
   CEO: John Rebrovic   Tel: (302) 838-4000   %FO: 100
   Bus: *Mfr. chlor-alkali products*   Fax: (302) 838-3222

   INEOS FLUOR AMERICAS INC.
   PO Box 30, St. Gabriel, Louisiana 70776
   CEO: Tony Kaye   Tel: (225) 642-0094   %FO: 100
   Bus: *Mfr. chlor-alkali products.*   Fax: (225) 642-8629

   INEOS FLUOR AMERICAS INC.
   2925 Briarpark, Ste. 879, Houston, Texas 77042
   CEO: T. P. Crotty   Tel: (713) 243-6200   %FO: 100
   Bus: *Mfr. chlor-alkali products.*   Fax: (713) 243-6220

   INEOS PHENOL
   7770 Rangeline Rd., Theodore, Alabama 36582
   CEO: Dr. Alberto Spera   Tel: (251) 443-3000   %FO: 100
   Bus: *Mfr. chlor-alkali products.*   Fax: (251) 443-3001

   INEOS SILICAS AMERICAS LLC
   111 Ingalls Ave., Joliet, Illinois 60435
   CEO: Patrick Murphy   Tel: (815) 727-3651   %FO: 100
   Bus: *Mfr. chlor-alkali products.*   Fax: (815) 727-5312

- **INEOS OXIDE LTD., SUB. INEOS GROUP**
Hawkslease House, Chapel Lane, Lyndhurst, Hampshire SO43 7FG, England, U.K.
CEO: James A. Ratcliffe, CEO
Bus: *Mfr. chemicals; ethylene oxide (EO) and ethylene glycol (EG).*
NAICS: 325199

Tel: 44-23-8028-7067
Fax: 44-23-8028-7054
www.ineosoxide.com

Rev: $806
Emp: 550

> **INEOS OXIDE INC.**
> Box 718, Plaquemine, Louisiana 70765
> CEO: Roland Lambotte
> Bus: *Mfr. chemicals.*
>
> Tel: (225) 242-3005
> Fax: (225) 242-3062
>
> %FO: 100

> **INEOS OXIDE INC.**
> 2925 Briarpark, Ste. 870, Houston, Texas 77042
> CEO: Bob Learman
> Bus: *Mfr. chemicals.*
>
> Tel: (713) 243-6200
> Fax: (713) 243-6220
>
> %FO: 100

- **INFAST GROUP PLC, SUB. ANIXER INTERNATIONAL**
Waterwells Dr., Quedgeley, Gloucester GL2 2FR, England, U.K.
CEO: Dennis J. Letham, CEO
Bus: *Supply chain management services to auto and industrial companies.*
NAICS: 488510, 541614

Tel: 44-1452-880-500
Fax: 44-1452-880-590
www.infast.com

Rev: $317
Emp: 1,274

> **INFAST USA**
> 2314 Norman Rd., Lancaster, Pennsylvania 17601
> CEO: Bill Vajda
> Bus: *Supply chain management services.*
>
> Tel: (800) 262-8449
> Fax: (770) 442-1027
>
> %FO: 100

> **INFAST USA**
> 1219 W. North Front St., Grand Island, Nebraska 68801
> CEO: Bill Vajda
> Bus: *Supply chain management services.*
>
> Tel: (800) 262-8449
> Fax: (770) 442-1027
>
> %FO: 100

> **INFAST USA**
> 600 Roundhouse Rd., Lewistown, Pennsylvania 17044
> CEO: Roberta Hughes
> Bus: *Supply chain management services.*
>
> Tel: (800) 262-8449
> Fax: (770) 442-1027
>
> %FO: 100

> **INFAST USA**
> 1360 Grandview Pkwy., Sturtevant, Wisconsin 53177
> CEO: Bill Vajda
> Bus: *Supply chain management services.*
>
> Tel: (800) 262-8449
> Fax: (770) 442-1027
>
> %FO: 100

> **INFAST USA**
> 709 Industrial Blvd., Dublin, Georgia 31021
> CEO: Bill Vajda
> Bus: *Supply chain management services.*
>
> Tel: (800) 262-8449
> Fax: (770) 442-1027
>
> %FO: 100

> **INFAST USA**
> 1810 Grassland Pkwy., Alpharetta, Georgia 30004
> CEO: Robert Sternick
> Bus: *Supply chain management services.*
>
> Tel: (800) 262-8449
> Fax: (770) 442-1027
>
> %FO: 100

● **INGENTA PLC**
3-4 Riverside Court, Lower Bristol Rd., Bath BA2 3DZ, England, U.K.
CEO: Simon Dessain, CEO   Tel: 44-122-536-1000   Rev: $14
Bus: *Provides marketing support to publishers and*   Fax: 44-122-536-1155   Emp: 150
    website development.   www.ingenta.com
NAICS: 541613

    INGENTA INC.
    44 Brattle St., 4/F, Cambridge, Massachusetts 02138
    CEO: Mike Tavares, VP   Tel: (617) 395-4000   %FO: 100
    Bus: *Provides marketing support to publishers.*   Fax: (617) 395-4099

    INGENTA INC.
    12 Bassett St., Providence, Rhode Island 02903
    CEO: David Durand, HR   Tel: (401) 331-2014   %FO: 100
    Bus: *Engaged in website development.*   Fax: (401) 331-2015

    PUBLISHERS COMMUNICATION GROUP (PCG)
    875 Massachusetts Ave., 7/F, Cambridge, Massachusetts 02139
    CEO: Claire M. Ginn   Tel: (617) 497-6514   %FO: 100
    Bus: *Engaged in website development.*   Fax: (617) 354-6875

● **INMARSAT GLOBAL**
99 City Rd., London EC1Y 1AX, England, U.K.
CEO: Andrew Sukawaty, CEO   Tel: 44-207-728-1256   Rev: $470
Bus: *Provides satellite communications services.*   Fax: 44-207-726-1179   Emp: 514
    www.inmarsat.com
NAICS: 517410

    INMARSAT NORTH AMERICA
    201 Biscayne Blvd., Miami, Florida 33131
    CEO: Michael Butler   Tel: (305) 913-7521   %FO: 100
    Bus: *Broadband communications solutions to*   Fax: (305) 913-6435
    enterprise, maritime and aeronautical users.

    INMARSAT NORTH AMERICA
    100 Wilson Blvd., Ste. 1425, Arlington, Virginia 22209
    CEO: Michael Butler   Tel: (703) 647-4760   %FO: 100
    Bus: *Broadband communications solutions to*   Fax: (703) 647-4761
    enterprise, maritime and aeronautical users.

● **THE INNOVATION GROUP PLC**
Yarmouth House, 1300 Parkway, Solent Business Park, Whiteley, Hampshire PO15 7AE, England, U.K.
CEO: Hassan Sadig, CEO   Tel: 44-148-956-5321   Rev: $104
Bus: *Mfr. financial software.*   Fax: 44-148-957-918   Emp: 1,028
    www.tigplc.com
NAICS: 511210, 541511

    THE INNOVATION GROUP
    6601 Ventnor Ave., Ste. 11, Ventnor City, New Jersey 08406
    CEO: Ernie D'Ambrosio   Tel: (609) 487-9585   %FO: 100
    Bus: *Mfr. financial software.*   Fax: (609) 487-9590

THE INNOVATION GROUP
7 Kenosia Ave., 1/F, Danbury, Connecticut 06810-7395
CEO: Ed Ossie, Mktg. Dir.
Bus: *Mfr. financial software.*

Tel: (203) 743-6000	%FO: 100
Fax: (203) 743-6003	

THE INNOVATION GROUP
120 Hayes St., Bel Air, Maryland 21-14
CEO: Paul Smolinski
Bus: *Mfr. financial software.*

Tel: (410) 638-8320	%FO: 100
Fax: (410) 638-7420	

THE INNOVATION GROUP
One Constitution Plaza, Ninth Floor, Hartford, Connecticut 06103
CEO: Paul Smolinski
Bus: *Mfr. financial software.*

Tel: (860) 218-9250	%FO: 100
Fax: (860) 727-0244	

THE INNOVATION GROUP
7800 College Blvd., 2/F, Overland Park, Kansas 66210
CEO: Paul Smolinski
Bus: *Mfr. financial software.*

Tel: (913) 888-4100	%FO: 100
Fax: (913) 562-3101	

● **INNOVIA FILMS LTD**
Wigton, Cumbria CA7 9BG, England, U.K.
CEO: Dennis Matthewman, Chmn.
Bus: *Mfr. of biaxially oriented polypropylene and cellulose films.*
NAICS: 325211, 325221, 325222, 325520

Tel: 44-169-734-2281	Rev: $454
Fax: 44-169-734-1417	Emp: 1,600
www.innoviafilms.com	

INNOVIA FILMS INC.
1950 Lake Park Dr., Smyrna, Georgia 30080
CEO: Margaret Boggess, Rep.
Bus: *Manufacturer of biaxially oriented polypropylene and cellulose films.*

Tel: (770) 970-8212	%FO: 100
Fax: (770) 970-8702	

● **INNOVISION RESEARCH & TECHNOLOGY PLC**
Ash Court, 23 Rose St., Wokingham RG40 1XS, England, U.K.
CEO: Marc A. Borrett, CEO
Bus: *Design and manufacture of customized radio frequency identification (RFID) chips.*
NAICS: 334413, 541618, 541690, 541710, 541990

Tel: 44-118-979-2000	Rev: $1
Fax: 44-118-979-1500	Emp: 56
www.innovision-group.com	

INNOVISION GROUP INC.
3308 Canyon Valley Trail, Plano, Texas 75023
CEO: Jim Ferguson
Bus: *Design and manufacture of customized radio frequency identification (RFID) chips.*

Tel: (214) 244-8216	%FO: 100
Fax: (214) 244-8216	

● **INSIGNIA SOLUTIONS PLC**
Insignia House, The Mercury Centre, Wycombe Lane, High Wycombe, Buckinghamshire HP10 0HH, England,
CEO: Mark E. McMillan, CEO
Bus: *Engaged in Internet technology.*
NAICS: 541519

Tel: 44-162-853-9500	Rev: $1
Fax: 44-162-853-9501	Emp: 32
www.insignia.com	

INSIGNIA SOLUTIONS INC.
41300 Christy St., Fremont, California 94538-3115
CEO: Mark Stevenson, VP   Tel: (510) 360-3700   %FO: 100
Bus: *Engaged in Internet technology.*   Fax: (510) 360-3701

● **INTEC TELECOM SYSTEMS PLC**
Wells Ct. 2, Albert Dr.
Woking, Surrey GU21 5UB, England, U.K.
CEO: Kevin D. Adams, CEO   Tel: 44-1483-745-800   Rev: $84
Bus: *Mfr. operational support services computer*   Fax: 44-1483-745-860   Emp: 529
    software.   www.intec-telecom-systems.com
NAICS: 517110, 517212, 517410, 517910, 518111, 541511

    INTEC TELECOM SYSTEMS PLC
    301 Perimeter Center North, Atlanta, Georgia 30346
    CEO: Fred Brott, Sales   Tel: (404) 705-2800   %FO: 100
    Bus: *Mfr. computer software.*   Fax: (770) 705-2805

● **INTELEK PLC**
Spitfire Way, South Marston Park, Swindon, Wiltshire SN3 4TR, England, U.K.
CEO: Ian D. Brodie, CEO   Tel: 44-179-827-000   Rev: $71
Bus: *Mfr. transceivers and amplifiers for satellites,*   Fax: 44-179-827-578   Emp: 499
    microwave boards and aerostructure components.   www.intelek.plc.uk
NAICS: 334417, 334419

    PARADISE DATACOM LLC
    1766 E. Evergreen St., Mesa, Arizona 85203
    CEO: Tony Radford   Tel: (602) 451-4805   %FO: 100
    Bus: *Mfr. satellite communication equipment.*   Fax: (602) 451-4805

    PARADISE DATACOM LLC
    2180 Satellite Blvd., Ste. 400, Duluth, Georgia 30097
    CEO: Tony Radford, VP Sales   Tel: (770) 239-1731   %FO: 100
    Bus: *Mfr. satellite communication equipment.*   Fax: (770) 368-1075

    PARADISE DATACOM LLC
    328 Innovation Blvd., State College, Pennsylvania 16803
    CEO: Kathy Baughman, VP   Tel: (814) 238-3450   %FO: 100
    Bus: *Mfr. satellite communication equipment.*   Fax: (814) 238-3829

● **INTERCYTEX LIMITED**
48 Grafton St., Manchester M13 9XX, England, U.K.
CEO: Nicolas Higgins, CEO   Tel: 44-161-606-7270
Bus: *Pharmaceutical cell-based treatments.*   Fax: 44-161-606-7320
    www.intercytex.net
NAICS: 325414

    INTERCYTEX RESEARCH
    175-E New Boston St., Woburn, Massachusetts 01801
    CEO: Jeff Teumer   Tel: (781) 569-0990   %FO: 100
    Bus: *Pharmaceutical cell-based treatments.*   Fax: (781) 569-6797

- **INTERNATIONAL GREETINGS PLC**
Belgrave House, Hatfield Business Park, Frobisher Way, Hatfield AL10 9TQ, England, U.K.
CEO: Anders Hedlund, Co-CEO
Bus: *Mfr. gift wrapping paper and related products.*

Tel: 44-1707-630-630
Fax: 44-1707-630-666
www.internationagreetings.co.uk

Rev: $231
Emp: 1,243

NAICS: 323110, 323111, 511191
  THE GIFT WRAP COMPANY
  338 Industrial Blvd., Midway, Georgia 31320
  CEO: Lawrence Louis, Pres.
  Bus: *Mfr. and sales of wrapping paper.*

  Tel: (912) 884-9727
  Fax:

  %FO: 100
  Emp: 185

- **INTERNATIONAL POWER PLC**
Senator House, 85 Queen Victoria St., London EC4V 4DP, England, U.K.
CEO: Philip G. Cox, CEO
Bus: *Generates and sells electricity.*

Tel: 44-207-320-8600
Fax: 44-207-320-8700
www.ipplc.com

Rev: $1,472
Emp: 2,750

NAICS: 221112, 221121, 523130, 523140
  AMERICAN NATIONAL POWER INC.
  62 Forest St., Ste. 102, Marlborough, Massachusetts 01752
  CEO: Ian Nutt, CEO
  Bus: *Independent power generators.*

  Tel: (508) 382-9300
  Fax:

  %FO: 100
  Emp: 81

- **INTEROUTE TELECOMMUNICATIONS PLC**
Barnard's Inn, 86 Fetter Ln., London EC4A 1EN, England, U.K.
CEO: Alan Lowe, CEO
Bus: *Fiber optic networks.*

Tel: 44-207-025-9000
Fax: 44-207-025-9888
www.interroute.com

NAICS: 517310, 517010, 518111, 519210, 519190, 561400
  INTEROUTE AMERICAS
  13010 Morris Rd., 6/F, Alpharetta, Georgia 30004
  CEO: Jay Belodoff, Dir.
  Bus: *Fiber optic networks.*

  Tel: (770) 576-1970
  Fax: (770) 576-3901

  %FO: 100

- **INTERTEK GROUP**
25 Saville Row, London W1S 2ES, England, U.K.
CEO: Wolfhart Hauser, CEO
Bus: *Engaged in product and commodity testing.*

Tel: 44-20-7396-3400
Fax: 44-20-7396-3480
www.intertek.com

Rev: $962
Emp: 12,717

NAICS: 541380, 541690, 541710
  CALEB BRETT USA
  Post Oak Tower, 5051 Westheimer, Ste. 1700, Houston, Texas 77056
  CEO: Jay Gutierrez, Pres.
  Bus: *Marine oil surveyors & cargo
    superintendents.*

  Tel: (713) 407-3500
  Fax: (713) 407-3594

  %FO: 100
  Emp: 900

  INTERTEK ETL SEMKO
  7250 Hudson Blvd., Oakdale, Minnesota 55128
  CEO: John Quigley
  Bus: *Product safety testing.*

  Tel: (651) 730-1188
  Fax: (651) 730-1282

  %FO: 100

INTERTEK ETL SEMKO
Omega Point Labs, 16015 Shady Falls Rd., Elmendorf, Texas 78112
CEO: John D. Nicholas   Tel: (210) 635-8100   %FO: 100
Bus: *Product safety testing.*   Fax: (210) 635-8133

INTERTEK ETL SEMKO
4850 Rhawn St., Philadelphia, Pennsylvania 19136
CEO: Michael Cucugliello   Tel: (215) 331-3530   %FO: 100
Bus: *Product safety testing.*   Fax: (215) 331-0508

INTERTEK TESTING SERVICES NA INC./ ETL SEMKO
70 Codman Hill Rd., Boxborough, Massachusetts 01719
CEO: Dennis Roth, Pres.   Tel: (607) 753-6711   %FO: 100
Bus: *Engineering testing lab.*   Fax: (607) 753-9891   Emp: 814

LABTEST INTERNATIONAL
70 Diamond Rd., Springfield, New Jersey 07081
CEO: Roque Corona, Pres.   Tel: (973) 346-5500   %FO: 100
Bus: *Commercial fabric testing.*   Fax: (973) 379-5232   Emp: 120

RAM CONSULTING
2107 Swift Dr., Ste. 200, Oak Brook, Illinois 60523
CEO: Eugene Rider, Pres.   Tel: (630) 623-6060   %FO: 100
Bus: *Consumer product testing.*   Fax: (630) 623-6074   Emp: 110

● **INVENSYS PLC**
Invensys House, Carlisle Place, London SW1P 1BX, England, U.K.
CEO: Rick Haythornthwaite, CEO   Tel: 44-20-7834-3848   Rev: $7,104
Bus: *Holding company for industrial manufacturing*   Fax: 44-20-7834-3879   Emp: 43,602
     companies.   www.invensys.com
NAICS: 333922, 334512, 334513, 335314

   INVENSYS BUILDING SYSTEMS
   1354 Clifford Ave., Loves Park, Illinois 61132
   CEO: John H. Duerden, Pres.   Tel: (815) 637-3000   %FO: 100
   Bus: *Environmental control solutions for the*   Fax: (815) 637-5300   Emp: 2,000
        commercial building industry.

   INVENSYS NORTH AMERICA
   33 Commercial St., Foxboro, Massachusetts 02035
   CEO: Michael Caliel, Pres.   Tel: (508) 543-8750   %FO: 100
   Bus: *Manufacturer of automatic temperature*   Fax: (508) 543-2735   Emp: 10,000
        controls

● **iORA LTD.**
1A, Intec 2, Intec Business Park, Wade St., Baskingstoke, Hampshire RG24 8NE, England, U.K.
CEO: Adrian Weekes, CEO   Tel: 44-1256-307800
Bus: *Web-based applications for mobile units.*   Fax: 44-1256-307801
                                          www.iora.com
NAICS: 541511, 541512, 541519

IORA USA
33 Wood Ave. South, Ste. 600, Iselin, New Jersey 08830
CEO: Paddy Falls   Tel: (732) 767-5300   %FO: 100
Bus: *Web-based applications for mobile units.*   Fax: (732) 791-4629

● **ITT MONEYCORP LTD.**
2 Sloane St., Knightsbridge, London SW1X 9LA, England, U.K.
CEO: Bassam Shlewet, Mng. Dir.   Tel: 44-20-7823-7400   Rev: $3,510
Bus: *Retail and wholesale currency services.*   Fax: 44-20-7823-7815   Emp: 150
    www.ittmoneycorp.com
NAICS: 523130, 523140

    MONEYCORP INC.
    5 Celebration Pl., Ste. 500, Celebration, Florida 34747
    CEO: Laura Dickinson   Tel: (321) 559-1050   %FO: 100
    Bus: *Retail and wholesale currency services.*   Fax: (321) 559-1002

● **JARDINE LLOYD THOMPSON GROUP PLC**
6 Crutched Friars, London EC3N 2PH, England, U.K.
CEO: Ken A. Carter, Chmn.   Tel: 44-207-528-4444   Rev: $902
Bus: *Insurance brokers.*   Fax: 40-207-528-4185   Emp: 5,003
    www.jltgroup.com
NAICS: 524114, 524126, 524210

    JARDINE LLOYD THOMPSON LLC
    5847 San Felipe, Ste. 2750, Houston, Texas 77057
    CEO: Rob Schanen, Mgr.   Tel: (832) 485-4000   %FO: 100
    Bus: *Insurance services.*   Fax: (832) 485-4001   Emp: 54

    JLT RE SOLUTIONS INC.
    Princeton Pike Corporate Center, 1009 Lenox Dr., Bldg. IV, Lawrenceville, New Jersey 08648
    CEO: Robert Cooney, CEO   Tel: (609) 896-0555   %FO: 100
    Bus: *Insurance services.*   Fax: (609) 896-2666   Emp: 42

    JLT SERVICES CORPORATION
    13 Cornell Rd., Latham, New York 12110
    CEO: Simon Curtis, Pres.   Tel: (518) 782-3000   %FO: 100
    Bus: *Insurance brokers.*   Fax: (518) 782-3032   Emp: 410

● **JC BAMFORD EXCAVATORS LTD**
Rochester, Straffordshire ST14 5JP, England, U.K.
CEO: John Patterson, CEO & Mng. Dir.   Tel: 44-188-959-0312   Rev: $1,295
Bus: *Construction and materials handling equipment*   Fax: 44-188-959-3455   Emp: 4,000
     manufacture.   www.jcb.com
NAICS: 333111, 333120, 522220, 524210

    JCB INC.
    2000 Bamford Blvd., Pooler, Georgia 31322
    CEO: Helmut Peters, Pres.   Tel: (912) 748-1118   %FO: 100
    Bus: *Mfr. construction and materials handling*   Fax: (912) 447-2299   Emp: 150
     equipment.

• **JIMMY CHOO LTD., DIV. LION CAPITAL**
Ixworth House, 37 Ixworth Pl., London SW3 3QH, England, U.K.
CEO: Robert Bensoussan, CEO
Bus: *Designs and manufactures shoes.*
Tel: 44-20-7591-7000
Fax: 44-20-7591-7077
www.jimmychoo.com
NAICS: 316214

    JIMMY CHOO INC.
    750 Lexington Ave., 16/F, New York, New York 10022
    CEO: Tony DiMasso, COO
    Bus: *Mfr. and sales of shoes.*
    Tel: (866) 584-6687
    Fax: (212) 319-9822
    %FO: 100

• **JOHNSON MATTHEY PLC**
2-4 Cockspur St., Trafalgar Square, London SW1Y 5BQ, England, U.K.
CEO: Neil A. P. Carson, CEO
Bus: *Refines & processes precious metals & rare minerals & produces pharmaceuticals & specialty chemicals.*
Tel: 44-207-269-8400
Fax: 44-207-269-8433
www.matthey.com
Rev: $8,203
Emp: 7,524
NAICS: 212221, 213114, 325131, 325188, 325192, 325199, 325510

    JOHNSON MATTHEY INC.
    435 Devon Park Dr., Ste. 600, Wayne, Pennsylvania 19087
    CEO: Neil A. P. Carson, CEO
    Bus: *Sale of platinum sheet, tube & wire to jewelers.*
    Tel: (610) 971-3000
    Fax: (610) 971-3022
    Emp: 1,650

• **KBC ADVANCED TECHNOLOGIES PLC**
KBC House, 42-50 Hersham Rd., Walton-on-Thames, Surrey KT12 1RZ, England, U.K.
CEO: Peter J. Close, CEO
Bus: *Technical consulting services to the hydrocarbon processing industry.*
Tel: 44-1932-242424
Fax: 44-1932-224214
www.kbcat.com
Rev: $56
Emp: 213
NAICS: 324110, 541690

    KBC ADVANCED TECHNOLOGIES
    14701 St. Mary's Ln., Ste. 300, Houston, Texas 77079
    CEO: J. Davis, Sales Dir.
    Bus: *Technical consulting services to the hydrocarbon processing industry.*
    Tel: (281) 293-8200
    Fax: (281) 293-8290
    %FO: 100

    KBC ADVANCED TECHNOLOGIES INC.
    14701 St. Mary's Ln., Ste. 300, Houston, Texas 77079
    CEO: C. Miller
    Bus: *Technical consulting services.*
    Tel: (281) 293-8200
    Fax: (281) 293-8290
    %FO: 100

    KBC ADVANCED TECHNOLOGIES INC.
    4 Campus Dr., 2/F, Parsippany, New Jersey 07054
    CEO: Geery Hickman
    Bus: *Technical consulting services.*
    Tel: (973) 889-8922
    Fax: (973) 889-8923
    %FO: 100

● **KELDA GROUP PLC**
Western House, Halifax Rd., Bradford, West Yorkshire BD6 2SZ, England, U.K.
CEO: Kevin Whiteman, CEO   Tel: 44-1274-600-111   Rev: $1,325
Bus: *Provides water and wastewater services.*   Fax: 44-1274-608-608   Emp: 3,461
                                         www.keldagroup.com
NAICS: 221310, 221320, 237210, 541519, 541618, 561210, 562111, 562212, 562213, 562219, 562920

   AQUARION COMPANY
   835 Main St., Bridgeport, Connecticut 06604
   CEO: Charles Firlotte, Pres. & CEO   Tel: (203) 335-2333   %FO: 100
   Bus: *Water management.*   Fax: (203) 336-5639

● **KELLER GROUP PLC**
Aztec House, 397-405 Archway Rd., London N6 4EY, England, U.K.
CEO: Justin R. Atkinson, CEO   Tel: 44-20-8341-6424   Rev: $1,148
Bus: *Concrete reinforcement and structural repair*   Fax: 44-20-8340-6981   Emp: 4,733
   engineering services.   www.keller.co.uk
NAICS: 236210, 236220, 238910, 541310, 541320, 541330, 541340

   CASE FOUNDATION COMPANY
   13065 40th St. North, Clearwater, Florida 33762-4219
   CEO: Nigel Osborn, Pres.   Tel: (727) 572-7740   %FO: 100
   Bus: *Contractor providing complete structural*   Fax: (727) 571-1393
        foundation systems.

   CASE FOUNDATION COMPANY
   PO Box 40, 1325 West Lake St., Roselle, Illinois 60172-3300
   CEO: John O'Malley, Pres.   Tel: (630) 529-2911   %FO: 100
   Bus: *Contractor providing complete structural*   Fax: (630) 529-4802
        foundation systems.

   CASE FOUNDATION COMPANY
   4022 E. Broadway Rd., Ste.103, Phoenix, Arizona 85040
   CEO: Todd Dustin, District Mgr.   Tel: (602) 454-0988   %FO: 100
   Bus: *Contractor providing complete structural*   Fax: (602) 454-2165
        foundation systems.

   CASE FOUNDATION COMPANY
   PO Box 338, 450 Parkway, Broomall, Pennsylvania 19008-0338
   CEO: Jim Cahill, VP   Tel: (610) 353-0600   %FO: 100
   Bus: *Contractor providing complete structural*   Fax: (610) 353-8409
        foundation systems.

   HAYWARD BAKER INC.
   1130 Annapolis Rd., Ste. 202, Odenton, Maryland 21113
   CEO: George R. Grisham   Tel: (410) 551-8200   %FO: 100
   Bus: *Ground modification services.*   Fax: (410) 551-1900

   MCKINNEY DRILLING COMPANY
   Rt.22, PO Box C, Delmont, Pennsylvania 15626
   CEO: Bill Maher, VP   Tel: (724) 468-4139   %FO: 100
   Bus: *Provider of drilling services.*   Fax: (724) 468-6877

MCKINNEY DRILLING COMPANY
8511 Backlick Rd., Lorton, Virginia 22079
CEO: Matthew Klanica, District Mgr.   Tel: (703) 550-9210   %FO: 100
Bus: *Provider of drilling services.*   Fax: (703) 550-9214

MCKINNEY DRILLING COMPANY
15800 IH-35, PO Box 957, Buda, Texas 79610
CEO: Neal Howard, VP   Tel: (512) 312-1525   %FO: 100
Bus: *Provider of drilling services.*   Fax: (512) 312-1618

MCKINNEY DRILLING COMPANY
7233 Division St., PO Box 46268, Bedford, Ohio 44146
CEO: Kevin Kingery, District Mgr.   Tel: (440) 439-4900   %FO: 100
Bus: *Provider of drilling services.*   Fax: (440) 439-5254

MCKINNEY DRILLING COMPANY
15850 Hwy 377 South, PO Box 126109, Ft. Worth, Texas 76126
CEO: Marshall Frye, District Mgr.   Tel: (817) 443-1465   %FO: 100
Bus: *Provider of drilling services.*   Fax: (817) 443-1463

MCKINNEY DRILLING COMPANY
119 Stewart Ln., Winfield, West Virginia 25213
CEO: James Gordon, District Mgr.   Tel: (304) 755-0143   %FO: 100
Bus: *Provider of drilling services.*   Fax: (304) 755-9644

MCKINNEY DRILLING COMPANY
2150 William St., Buffalo, New York 14206
CEO: Dale R. Howe, Jr., District Mgr.   Tel: (716) 897-4450   %FO: 100
Bus: *Provider of drilling services.*   Fax: (716) 897-5079

MCKINNEY DRILLING COMPANY
4631 E. Holmes Rd., Memphis, Tennessee 38118
CEO: Mike Kalder, District Mgr.   Tel: (901) 363-9421   %FO: 100
Bus: *Provider of drilling services.*   Fax: (901) 795-3880

MCKINNEY DRILLING COMPANY
1838 South Preston Hwy., Shepherdsville, Kentucky 40165
CEO: Lee Bradford, District Mgr.   Tel: (502) 955-8474   %FO: 100
Bus: *Provider of drilling services.*   Fax: (502) 955-8483

MCKINNEY DRILLING COMPANY
1265 Blairs Bridge Rd., Lithia Springs, Georgia 30122
CEO: Sammy Odum, District Mgr.   Tel: (770) 948-9521   %FO: 100
Bus: *Provider of drilling services.*   Fax: (770) 948-9553

MCKINNEY DRILLING COMPANY
1130 Annapolis Rd., Ste.103, Odenton, Maryland 21113
CEO: George Cloud, Pres.   Tel: (410) 874-1235   %FO: 100
Bus: *Provider of drilling services.*   Fax: (410) 551-1236

MCKINNEY DRILLING COMPANY
3150 Walnut St., PO Box 284, Colmar, Pennsylvania 18915
CEO: Martin McDermott, District Mgr.   Tel: (215) 643-0238   %FO: 100
Bus: *Provider of drilling services.*   Fax: (215) 822-3329

MCKINNEY DRILLING COMPANY
1024 East Mountain St., Kernersville, North Carolina 27284
CEO: Ronnie Sisk, District Mgr.   Tel: (336) 992-2300   %FO: 100
Bus: *Provider of drilling services.*   Fax: (336) 992-2429

SUNCOAST POST-TENSION LP
654 N. Sam Houston Pkwy. East, Ste. 110, Houston, Texas 77060
CEO: Larry E. Stadler   Tel: (281) 668-1840   %FO: 100
Bus: *Post-tension services.*   Fax: (281) 668-1864

● **KEWILL SYSTEMS PLC**
Ash House, Fairfield Ave., Staines, Surrey TW18 4AB, England, U.K.
CEO: Paul Nichols, CEO   Tel: 44-1784-495-722   Rev: $40
Bus: *Mfr. enterprise resource planning software.*   Fax: 44-1784-224-445   Emp: 272
www.kewill.com
NAICS: 511210

    KEWILL GROUP
    100 Nickerson Rd., Marlborough, Massachusetts 01752
    CEO: Paul Nichols, Pres.   Tel: (508) 229-4400   %FO: 100
    Bus: *Mfr. enterprise resource planning software.*   Fax: (508) 229-4404   Emp: 136

    KEWILL GROUP
    1230 East Diehl Rd., Naperville, Illinois 60563
    CEO: Paul Nichols   Tel: (630) 245-1111   %FO: 100
    Bus: *Mfr. enterprise resource planning software.*   Fax: (630) 245-1114

    TRADEPOINT SYSTEMS, LLC
    44 Franklin St., Nashua, New Hampshire 03064
    CEO: Christopher Crane, member   Tel: (603) 889-3200   %FO: 100
    Bus: *Sale of computer/peripheral freight*   Fax: (603) 889-9393   Emp: 85
    transportation arrangement.

● **KNOWLEDGE MANAGEMENT SOFTWARE PLC**
Unit 6B Whitworth Court, Manor Farm Rd., Runcorn, Cheshire WA7 1TE, England, U.K.
CEO: Ian Templeton, CEO   Tel: 44-870-160-1993
Bus: *Computer software and services.*   Fax: 44-870-143-6910
www.kmsoftware.com
NAICS: 511210, 541511, 541519

    STI KNOWLEDGE INC.
    Four Concourse Pkwy., Ste. 400, Atlanta, Georgia 30328
    CEO: Pete McGarahan, Chmn.   Tel: (770) 280-2630   %FO: 100
    Bus: *IT support services.*   Fax: (770) 280-2631

● **JAMES R. KNOWLES HOLDINGS PLC**
Vistorm House, 3200 Daresbury Park, Warrington WA4 4BU, England, U.K.
CEO: Brian S. Quinn, CEO   Tel: 44-8707-530-600   Rev: $57
Bus: *Business consulting, staffing, and support*   Fax: 44-8707-530-605   Emp: 366
services to the construction and engineering   www.jrknowles.com
NAICS: 541611

KNOWLES USA INC.
1620 Bella Vista Dr., Encinitas, California 92024
CEO: Gene Bennett   Tel: (760) 634-2683   %FO: 100
Bus: *Business consulting, staffing, and support*   Fax: (760) 436-5995
       services to the construction and
       engineering industries.

KNOWLES USA INC.
700 S. Flower St., Ste. 1100, Los Angeles, California 90017
CEO: Gene Bennett   Tel: (213) 892-6351   %FO: 100
Bus: *Business consulting, staffing, and support*   Fax: (213) 892-2284
       services to the construction and
       engineering industries.

KNOWLES USA INC.
1500 Market St., 12/F, Philadelphia, Pennsylvania 19103
CEO: Gene Bennett   Tel: (215) 246-3418   %FO: 100
Bus: *Business consulting, staffing, and support*   Fax: (215) 569-8228
       services to the construction and
       engineering industries.

● **KW INTERNATIONAL LIMITED**
The Triangle, 5 Hammersmith Grove, London SW6 0LG, England, U.K.
CEO: David Bucknall, CEO   Tel: 44-20-8834-8700
Bus: *Trading and risk management software.*   Fax: 44-20-8834-8747
                                                                          www.kwi.com
NAICS: 511210

       KW INTERNATIONAL LIMITED
       601 Jefferson, Ste. 3750, Houston, Texas 77002
       CEO: Carrie Gillette, Mktg.   Tel: (832) 366-1952   %FO: 100
       Bus: *Software manufacture.*   Fax: (832) 366-1958

● **LAING O'ROURKE PLC**
Bridge Place, Anchor Blvd., Admirals Park, Crossways, Dartford, Kent DA2 65N, England, U.K.
CEO: Ray O'Rourke, CEO   Tel: 44-1322-296-200
Bus: *Construction and engineering services.*   Fax: 44-1322-296-262
                                                                          www.laingorourke.com
NAICS: 236210, 236220, 237310, 237990, 541330
       JOHN LAING INTERNATIONAL LIMITED
       301 North Cascade Ave., Montrose, Colorado 81401
       CEO: Brian Emerton   Tel: (970) 249-9696   %FO: 100
       Bus: *Construction and engineering services.*   Fax: (970) 249-2651

● **THE LAIRD GROUP PLC**
3 St. James's Square, London SW1Y 4JU, England, U.K.
CEO: Peter Hill, CEO   Tel: 44-207-468-4040   Rev: $901
Bus: *Mfr. security systems and electronics.*   Fax: 44-207-839-2921   Emp: 8,375
                                                                          www.laird-plc.com
NAICS: 326199, 326299, 332510, 334419

CENTURION WIRELESS TECHNOLOGIES, INC.
3425 N. 44th St., Lincoln, Nebraska 68504
CEO: Gary L. Kuck, Chmn. & Pres. & CEO
Bus: *Wireless communications components.*
Tel: (402) 467-4491
Fax: (402) 467-4528
Emp: 1,365

LAIRD TECHNOLOGIES, INC.
Shielding Way, Delaware Water Gap, Pennsylvania 18327
CEO: Martin L. Rapp, CEO
Bus: *Electronic components.*
Tel: (570) 424-8510
Fax: (570) 424-6213
Emp: 1,100

● **LAND INSTRUMENTS INTERNATIONAL LTD.**
Stubley Lane, Dronfield, Derbyshire S18 1DJ, England, U.K.
CEO: Thomas Land, Chmn.
Bus: *Mfr. infrared temperature measuring instruments and devices.*
NAICS: 334513, 334516
Tel: 44-1246-41-7691
Fax: 44-1246-29-0274
www.landinst.com
Rev: $37
Emp: 300

    LAND INSTRUMENTS INTERNATIONAL
    10 Friends Lane, Newtown, Pennsylvania 18940
    CEO: Rich Shannon, Mgr.
    Bus: *Sale/distribution infrared temperature measuring instruments & devices.*
    Tel: (215) 504-8000
    Fax: (215) 504-0879
    %FO: 100

● **LAURA ASHLEY HOLDINGS PLC, SUB. UNITED INDUSTRIES**
27 Bagley's Lane, Fulham, London SW6 2AR, England, U.K.
CEO: Lillian Tan Lian Tee, CEO
Bus: *Retail clothing chain.*
NAICS: 442299, 448120, 448130, 448150
Tel: 44-207-880-5100
Fax: 44-207-880-5200
www.lauraashley.com
Rev: $515
Emp: 2,961

    LAURA ASHLEY INC.
    7000 Regent Pkwy., Fort Mill, South Carolina 29715
    CEO: Ivy Tan
    Bus: *Retail clothing chain.*
    Tel: (803) 396-7744
    Fax: (803) 396-7744
    %FO: 100

    LAURA ASHLEY INC.
    338 Goddard Blvd, King of Prussia, Pennsylvania 19406
    CEO: Suzanne Valter
    Bus: *Retail clothing chain.*
    Tel: (610) 354-9130
    Fax: (610) 354-9130
    %FO: 100

    LAURA ASHLEY INC.
    6 St. James Ave., Boston, Massachusetts 02116
    CEO: Andrea Collins, CEO
    Bus: *Retail clothing chain.*
    Tel: (617) 457-6000
    Fax: (617) 457-6060
    %FO: 100

    LAURA ASHLEY INC.
    200 Greenwich Ave., Greenwich, Connecticut 06830
    CEO: Suzie Smith
    Bus: *Retail clothing chain.*
    Tel: (203) 662-2382
    Fax: (203) 662-2382
    %FO: 100

    LAURA ASHLEY INC.
    Garden City Center, Cranston, Rhode Island 02907
    CEO: Stephen Cotter
    Bus: *Retail clothing chain.*
    Tel: (401) 946-1211
    Fax: (401) 946-1211
    %FO: 100

LAURA ASHLEY INC.
7875 Montgomery Rd., Cincinnati, Ohio 45236
CEO: Ivy Tan   Tel: (513) 793-5535   %FO: 100
Bus: *Retail clothing chain.*   Fax: (513) 793-5535

● **LE MERIDIEN HOTELS AND RESORTS**
166 High Holborn, London WC1V TT, England, U.K.
CEO: Robert E. Riley, Pres.   Tel: 44-20-7301-2000
Bus: *Luxury hotels owners and operators.*   Fax: 44-20-7301-2011
                                       www.lemeridien.com
NAICS: 721110, 721120

   FORTE & LE MERIDIEN HOTELS & RESORTS
   420 Lexington Ave., Suite 1718, New York, New York 10170
   CEO: Stephen Alexander, Mgr.   Tel: (212) 805-5000   %FO: 100
   Bus: *Luxury hotels owners and operators.*   Fax: (212) 805-5047

   LE PARKER MERIDIEN
   118 West 57th St., New York, New York 10019
   CEO: Steven Pipes, Mgr.   Tel: (212) 245-5000   %FO: 100
   Bus: *Luxury hotels owners and operators.*   Fax: (212) 307-1878

   THE VENETIAN
   3355 Las Vegas Blvd., Las Vegas, Nevada 89109
   CEO: Kirsten Dimond   Tel: (702) 414-3600   %FO: 100
   Bus: *Luxury hotels owners and operators.*   Fax: (702) 414-3600

● **LEGAL & GENERAL GROUP, PLC.**
Temple Court, 11 Queen Victoria St., London EC4N 4TP, England, U.K.
CEO: David Prosser, CEO   Tel: 44-207-528-6200   Rev: $68,099
Bus: *Provides life insurance.*   Fax: 44-207-528-6222   Emp: 8,807
                                       www.landg.com
NAICS: 522292, 522298, 522310, 523991, 523999, 524113, 524114, 525110, 525120, 525190, 525920, 525990, 531120, 531130, 531190

   BANNER LIFE INSURANCE COMPANY
   1701 Research Blvd., Rockville, Maryland 20850
   CEO: David S. Lenaburg, Pres.   Tel: (301) 279-4800   %FO: 100
   Bus: *Provides life insurance.*   Fax: (301) 294-6960   Emp: 250

● **LIBERTY INTERNATIONAL PLC**
40 Broadway, London SW1H 0BT, England, U.K.
CEO: David A. Fischel, CEO   Tel: 44-207-960-1200   Rev: $742
Bus: *Investor in retail and commercial property.*   Fax: 44-207-960-1333   Emp: 787
                                       www.liberty-international.co.uk
NAICS: 531120, 531190

   CAPITAL & COUNTIES
   100 The Embarcadero, Ste.200, San Francisco, California 94105
   CEO: Turner Newton, Pres.   Tel: (415) 421-5100   %FO: 100
   Bus: *Investor in retail and commercial property.*   Fax: (415) 421-6021

TAYLOR RAFFERTY
205 Lexington Ave., 8/F, New York, New York 10016
CEO: James Prout
Bus: *Investor in retail and commercial property.*
Tel: (212) 889-4350
Fax: (212) 683-2614
%FO: 100

● **LINKLATERS**
One Silk St., London EC2Y 8HQ, England, U.K.
CEO: Tony Angel, CEO
Bus: *International non-partnership association of European law firms.*
Tel: 44-207-456-2000
Fax: 44-207-456-2222
www.linklaters.com
NAICS: 541110

   LINKLATERS
   1345 Ave. of the Americas, 19/F, New York, New York 10105-0302
   CEO: Paul Wickes, Mng. Prtn.
   Bus: *International law firm.*
   Tel: (212) 424-9000
   Fax: (212) 424-9100
   %FO: 100
   Emp: 70

● **LISTER-PETTER, LTD.**
Long St., Dursley, Gloucestershire G11 4HS, England, U.K.
CEO: Bryan Draper, Dir.
Bus: *Mfr. diesel and marine engines and generators.*
Tel: 44-1453-544-141
Fax: 44-1453-546-732
www.lister-petter.co.uk
Rev: $23
Emp: 300
NAICS: 423120

   LISTER-PETTER INC.
   815 East 56 Highway, Olathe, Kansas 66061-4914
   CEO: Mike Meyer, CEO
   Bus: *Mfr./distribution diesel, marine & natural gas engines, generators.*
   Tel: (913) 764-3512
   Fax: (913) 764-5493
   %FO: 100
   Emp: 43

● **LLOYD'S**
One Lime St., London EC3M 7HA, England, U.K.
CEO: Nicholas E.T. Prettejohn, CEO
Bus: *Insurance market services.*
Tel: 44-207-327-1000
Fax: 44-207-327-5599
www.lloyds.com
Rev: $238
Emp: 582
NAICS: 524130, 524210

   LLOYD'S AMERICA LTD.
   590 Fifth Ave., 17/F, New York, New York 10036
   CEO: Winifred A Baker, Mgr.
   Bus: *Insurance agents, brokers & service*
   Tel: (212) 382-4060
   Fax: (212) 382-4070
   %FO: 100
   Emp: 10

● **LLOYD'S REGISTER GROUP**
71 Fenchurch St., London EC3M 4BS, England, U.K.
CEO: David G. Moorhouse, Chmn.
Bus: *Provider of ship classifications.*
Tel: 44-20-7709-9166
Fax: 44-20-7488-4796
www.lr.org
Rev: $663
Emp: 5,000
NAICS: 541690, 541990

   LLOYD'S REGISTER AMERICAS, INC.
   75 Executive Dr., Ste.112, Aurora, Illinois 60504
   CEO: Asrar Kazmi
   Bus: *Provider of ship classifications.*
   Tel: (630) 978-8400
   Fax: (630) 978-8850
   %FO: 100

LLOYD'S REGISTER AMERICAS INC.
1401 Enclave Pkwy., Ste.200, Houston, Texas 77077
CEO: Paul A. Huber, Pres.   Tel: (281) 675-3100   %FO: 100
Bus: *Provider of ship classifications.*   Fax: (281) 675-3139

LLOYD'S REGISTER NORTH AMERICA, INC.
32108 Alvarado Blvd. #369, Union City, California 94587-4000
CEO: Daniel Day, mgr   Tel: (510) 675-9880   %FO: 100
Bus: *Provider of ship classifications.*   Fax: (510) 675-9953

LLOYD'S REGISTER NORTH AMERICA, INC.
1000 S. Pine Island Rd., Ste.530, Plantation, Florida 33324
CEO: Graham Brown, VP Operations   Tel: (954) 236-3322   %FO: 100
Bus: *Provider of ship classifications.*   Fax: (954) 452-3128

LLOYD'S REGISTER NORTH AMERICA, INC.
c/o Delta Marine Industries, 1608 South 96th St., Seattle, Washington 98108-5198
CEO: Ches King, mgr   Tel: (206) 767-7157   %FO: 100
Bus: *Provider of ship classifications.*   Fax: (206) 767-7125

LLOYD'S REGISTER NORTH AMERICA, INC.
One World Trade Center, Ste.1880, Long Beach, California 90831
CEO: Steve Chen, Mgr.   Tel: (562) 495-4945   %FO: 100
Bus: *Provider of ship classifications.*   Fax: (562) 590-9524

LLOYD'S REGISTER NORTH AMERICA, INC.
725 Skippack Pike, Ste.3B5, Blue Bell, Pennsylvania 19422
CEO: Graeme Hyde   Tel: (215) 654-9909   %FO: 100
Bus: *Provider of ship classifications.*   Fax: (215) 654-9933

LLOYD'S REGISTER NORTH AMERICA, INC.
PO Box 51451, Jacksonville Beach, Florida 32240-1451
CEO: Darren Jenkins   Tel: (904) 220-6139   %FO: 100
Bus: *Provider of ship classifications.*   Fax: (904) 220-6135

LLOYD'S REGISTER NORTH AMERICA, INC.
Metrostar Plaza, 190 Middlesex Turnpike, Ste. 405, Iselin, New Jersey 08830
CEO: Tel: (732) 404-0222   %FO: 100
Bus: *Provider of ship classifications.*   Fax: (732) 404-0225

● **LLOYDS TSB GROUP PLC**
25 Gresham St., London EC2V 7HN, England, U.K.
CEO: J. Eric Daniels, CEO   Tel: 44-207-626-1500   Rev: $27,686
Bus: *Financial services group, commercial banking*   Fax: 44-207-489-3484   Emp: 71,609
     services.   www.lloydstsbgroup.co.uk
NAICS: 522110, 522292, 523920, 523930, 524113, 525110

LLOYDS BANK PLC
1251 Ave. of Americas, 3/F, New York, New York 10020
CEO: William Camposano, Principal   Tel: (212) 930-8916   %FO: 100
Bus: *International commercial banking services.*   Fax:

LLOYDS BANK PLC
2 South Biscayne Blvd., One Bicayne Tower, Ste. 3200, Miami, Florida 33131
CEO: John Alexander, VP   Tel: (305) 347-7140   %FO: 100
Bus: *International commercial banking services.*   Fax: (305) 371-8607

● **LOGICA CMG WORLDWIDE**
Stephenson House, 75 Hampstead Rd., London NW1 2PL, England, U.K.
CEO: Martin P. Read, CEO   Tel: 44-207-637-9111   Rev: $3,216
Bus: *Systems integration, consulting and software*   Fax: 44-207-468-7006   Emp: 19,695
  development.   www.logicacmg.com
NAICS: 541511, 541512, 541519, 611420

   LOGICA CMG INC.
   8525 120th Ave. NE, Ste. 300, Kirkland, Washington 98033
   CEO: DeWayne A. Nelon   Tel: (425) 827-5090   %FO: 100
   Bus: *Systems integration, consulting and*   Fax: (425) 827-5382
    software development.

   LOGICA CMG INC.
   32 Hartwell Ave., Lexington, Massachusetts 02421
   CEO: Jim Yates, CEO   Tel: (617) 476-8000   %FO: 100
   Bus: *Systems integration, consulting and*   Fax: (617) 476-8010   Emp: 700
    software development.

   LOGICA CMG INC.
   26999 Central Park Blvd., Ste. 380, Southfield, Michigan 48076
   CEO: John LeBlanc, Mgr.   Tel: (248) 352-6740   %FO: 100
   Bus: *Systems integration, consulting and*   Fax: (248) 352-6718   Emp: 170
    software development.

   LOGICA CMG INC.
   6404 International Pkwy., Ste. 2048, Plano, Texas 75093
   CEO: DeWayne A. Nelon, Mgr.   Tel: (972) 246-5400   %FO: 100
   Bus: *Systems integration, consulting and*   Fax: (972) 246-5401   Emp: 30
    software development.

   LOGICA CMG INC.
   10375 Richmond Ave., Ste. 1000, Houston, Texas 77042
   CEO: Jim Cypert, EVP   Tel: (713) 954-7000   %FO: 100
   Bus: *Systems integration, consulting and*   Fax: (713) 785-0880   Emp: 60
    software development.

   LOGICA CMG INC.
   Five PPG Place, Ste. 300, Pittsburgh, Pennsylvania 15222
   CEO: Scott Hill, CTO   Tel: (412) 642-6900   %FO: 100
   Bus: *Systems integration, consulting and*   Fax: (412) 642-6906   Emp: 5
    software development.

   LOGICA CMG INC.
   10900 Nuckols Rd., Ste. 400, Glen Allen, Virginia 23060
   CEO: Peter Oggel, Mgr.   Tel: (804) 762-5500   %FO: 100
   Bus: *Systems integration, consulting and*   Fax: (804) 762-5500
    software development.

LOGICA CMG INC.
655 Third Ave., Ste. 1800, New York, New York 10017
CEO: Don O'Brien, Mgr.
Bus: *Systems integration, consulting and software development.*

Tel: (212) 682-7411
Fax: (212) 682-0715

%FO: 100
Emp: 15

● **LOGICALIS GROUP**
110 Buckingham Ave., Slough SL1 4PF, England, U.K.
CEO: Jens Montanana, CEO
Bus: *IT network integration services and technology consulting.*
NAICS: 541511, 541512, 541513, 541519

Tel: 44-1753-797-100
Fax: 44-1753-819-284
www.logicalis.com

Rev: $363
Emp: 1

    LOGICALIS USA
    210 Interstate North Pkwy., Atlanta, Georgia 30339
    CEO: Terrence Flood
    Bus: *IT network integration services and technology consulting.*

Tel: (770) 980-6276
Fax: (770) 980-6276

%FO: 100

    LOGICALIS USA
    4555 Lake Forest Dr., Cincinnati, Ohio 45242
    CEO: Terrence Flood
    Bus: *IT network integration services and technology consulting.*

Tel: (513) 563-3018
Fax: (513) 563-3018

%FO: 100

    LOGICALIS USA
    1750 S. Telegraph Rd., Ste. 300, Bloomfield Hills, Michigan 48302
    CEO: Michael B. Cox, CEO
    Bus: *IT network integration services and technology consulting.*

Tel: (248) 745-5400
Fax: (248) 335-8715

%FO: 100

● **LONDON FORFAITING COMPANY PLC**
International House, 1 St. Katherine's Way, London E1W 1XA, England, U.K.
CEO: Andrew T.M. Freeman, CEO
Bus: *Short-term export finance services.*
NAICS: 522293, 522298

Tel: 44-207-481-3410
Fax: 44-207-480-7626
www.londonforfaiting.com

    LONDON FORFAITING COMPANY
    1180 Ave. of the Americas, Ste. 2020, New York, New York 10036
    CEO: Jeremy McGahan
    Bus: *Short-term export finance services.*

Tel: (212) 759-1919
Fax: (212) 377-2018

%FO: 100

● **LO-Q PLC**
New Close, Greenlands, Henley-on-Thames, Oxfordshire RG9 3AL, England, U.K.
CEO: Jeff McManus, CEO
Bus: *Mfr. theme park ride reservation systems.*
NAICS: 517211

Tel: 44-1491-577-210
Fax: 44-1491-577-270
www.lo-q.com

Rev: $1

    LO-Q VIRTUAL QUEUING INC.
    351 Thornton Rd., Ste. 119, Lithia Springs, Georgia 30122
    CEO: Leah Moss, Sales
    Bus: *Mfr. theme park ride reservation systems.*

Tel: (678) 838-6930
Fax: (678) 838-6932

%FO: 100

- **LOVELLS**
Atlantic House, Holborn Viaduct, London EC1A 2FG, England, U.K.
CEO: John Young, Chmn.
Bus: *International law firm.*

Tel: 44-207-296-2000
Fax: 44-207-296-2001
www.lovells.com

Emp: 3,200

NAICS: 541110, 541199

> **LOVELLS**
> 900 Third Ave., 16/F, New York, New York 10022
> CEO: Dave Alters, Mgr.
> Bus: *International law firm.*
>
> Tel: (212) 909-0600
> Fax: (212) 909-0666
>
> %FO: 100
> Emp: 50

> **LOVELLS**
> One IBM Plaza, 330 North Wabash Ave., Ste. 1900, Chicago, Illinois 60611
> CEO: Eric Haab, Mng. Prtn.
> Bus: *International law firm.*
>
> Tel: (312) 832-4400
> Fax: (312) 832-4444
>
> %FO: 100
> Emp: 98

- **LOW & BONAR PLC**
5A Praed St., 3rd Fl., London W2 1NJ, England, U.K.
CEO: Paul Forman, CEO
Bus: *Mfr. materials and plastics for flooring and fabrics.*

Tel: 44-20-7298-6820
Fax: 44-20-7298-6821
www.lowandbonar.com

Rev: $382
Emp: 2,253

NAICS: 326192, 326199

> **BONAR PLASTICS INC.**
> 8257 Blakeland Dr., Littleton, Colorado 80125
> CEO: Will Muzek, Sales
> Bus: *Mfr. materials and plastics for flooring and fabrics.*
>
> Tel: (303) 791-7866
> Fax: (303) 791-8593
>
> %FO: 100

- **LOWE & PARTNERS WORLDWIDE**
60 Sloane Ave., London SW3 3XB, England, U.K.
CEO: Tony Wright, Pres. & CEO
Bus: *Advertising and marketing services.*

Tel: 44-20-7894-5000
Fax: 44-20-7894-5050
www.loweworldwide.com

Rev: $413
Emp: 1,600

NAICS: 541613, 541810, 541850, 541890

> **LOWE & PARTNERS WORLDWIDE**
> 150 E. 42nd St., New York, New York 10017
> CEO: Kathleen Ruane
> Bus: *Advertising services.*
>
> Tel: (212) 605-8000
> Fax: (212) 605-5656
>
> %FO: 100

- **LOWE ALPINE GROUP LTD.**
Ann St., Kendal, Cumbria LA9 6AA, England, U.K.
CEO: John King, CEO
Bus: *Mfr. technical backpacks and outdoor apparel.*

Tel: 44-1539-740-840
Fax: 44-1539-726-314
www.lowealpine.com

NAICS: 339920

LOWE ALPINE SYSTEMS USA
190 Hanover St., Lebanon, New Hampshire 03766
CEO: Geoff O'Keeffe
Bus: *Mfr. technical backpacks and outdoor apparel.*

Tel: (603) 448-8827
Fax: (603) 448-8873

%FO: 100

● **LUCITE INTERNATIONAL**
Queens Gate, 15-17 Queens Terrace, Southampton SO14 3BP, England, U.K.
CEO: Ian R. Lambert, CEO
Bus: *Acrylics manufacture.*

NAICS: 325211

Tel: 44-870-240-4620
Fax: 44-870-240-4626
www.luciteinternational.com

Rev: $1,362
Emp: 2,091

LUCITE INTERNATIONAL
7275 Goodlett Farms Pkwy., Cordova, Tennessee 38016
CEO: Alan Ledger, VP
Bus: *Acrylics manufacture.*

Tel: (901) 381-2000
Fax: (901) 381-2266

%FO: 100

LUCITE INTERNATIONAL
6350 N. Twin City Hwy., Nederland, Texas 77627
CEO: Keith N. Rogers
Bus: *Acrylics manufacture.*

Tel: (409) 749-3400
Fax: (409) 749-3500

%FO: 100

LUCITE INTERNATIONAL
PO Box 13328, President's Island, Memphis, Tennessee 38113
CEO: J. Jefferson Davis
Bus: *Acrylics manufacture.*

Tel: (901) 942-0787
Fax: (901) 942-2377

%FO: 100

● **M&C SAATCHI PLC**
36 Golden Sq., London W1F 9EE, England, U.K.
CEO: Moray MacLennan, CEO
Bus: *Advertising services.*

NAICS: 541810, 541850, 541890

Tel: 44-20-7543-4500
Fax: 44-20-7543-4501
www.mcsaatchi.com

Rev: $415
Emp: 790

M&C SAATCHI
2032 Broadway, Santa Monica, California 90404
CEO: Huw Griffith
Bus: *Advertising services.*

Tel: (310) 401-6074
Fax: (310) 401-6070

%FO: 100

M&C SAATCHI
95 Fifth Ave., New York, New York 10003
CEO: Robert Fletcher
Bus: *Advertising services.*

Tel: (212) 655-8000
Fax: (212) 655-4301

%FO: 100

● **MACMILLAN PUBLISHERS LTD.**
4 Crinan St., London N1 9XW, England, U.K.
CEO: Richard Charkin, CEO
Bus: *Publishing conglomerate.*

NAICS: 511130

Tel: 44-207-843-4600
Fax: 44-207-843-4640
www.macmillan.co.uk

Emp: 1,900

BEDFORD FREEMAN WORTH
41 Madison Ave., New York, New York 10010
CEO: Joan Feinberg
Bus: *Science publishing.*

Tel: (212) 576-9400
Fax: (212) 481-1891

%FO: 100

DELTA SYSTEMS COMPANY INC.
1400 Miller Pkwy., McHenry, Illinois 60050
CEO: Steven Korte, Pres.
Bus: *Educational publishing.*

Tel: (815) 363-3582
Fax: (815) 363-2948

%FO: 100

GROVE'S DICTIONARIES INC., DIV. PALGRAVE
345 Park Ave. South, New York, New York 10010
CEO: Janice Kuta
Bus: *Dictionaries and on-line projects.*

Tel: (212) 689-9200
Fax: (212) 689-9711

%FO: 100

NATURE AMERICA INC
345 Park Ave. South, New York, New York 10010-1707
CEO: Howard Ratner, Pres.
Bus: *Publishing.*

Tel: (212) 726-9200
Fax: (212) 696-9006

%FO: 100

PALGRAVE MACMILLAN
175 Fifth Ave., New York, New York 10010
CEO: Garrett Kiely, COO
Bus: *Academic and scholarly book publishing.*

Tel: (212) 982-3900
Fax: (212) 777-6359

%FO: 100

PICADORE, DIV. MACMILLAN GROUP
175 Fifth Ave., New York, New York 10010
CEO: Ken Holland
Bus: *Book publishing.*

Tel: (212) 674-5151
Fax: (212) 253-9627

%FO: 100

SCIENTIFIC AMERICA
415 Madison Ave., New York, New York 10017
CEO: John Hanley
Bus: *Scientific publishing.*

Tel: (212) 754-0550
Fax: (212) 754-0550

%FO: 100

SINAUER ASSOCIATES
23 Plumtree Rd., Sunderland, Massachusetts 01375
CEO: Andrew Sinauer
Bus: *College textbook publishing.*

Tel: (413) 549-4300
Fax: (413) 549-1118

%FO: 100

ST. MARTIN'S PRESS, INC.
175 Fifth Ave., New York, New York 10010
CEO: Sally Richardson, Pres. & CEO
Bus: *Trade division; book publishing.*

Tel: (212) 726-0200
Fax: (212) 686-9491

%FO: 100
Emp: 500

● **MADGE LIMITED**
Madge House, Priors Way, Maidenhead SL6 2HP, England, U.K.
CEO: Martin Malina, CEO & Mng. Dir.
Bus: *Mfr. of token ring adapters for computer
    networking.*
NAICS: 334220, 334290, 541512

Tel: 44-162-840-8000
Fax: 44-162-840-8010
www.madge.com

Rev: $157
Emp: 600

MADGE LIMITED
39293 Plymouth Rd., Ste. 107H, Livonia, Michigan 48150
CEO: Kathleen Magill-Haas, Sales   Tel: (734) 432-7005   %FO: 100
Bus: *Mfr./sales of token ring adapters for*   Fax: (734) 432-7092
     computer networking.

● **THE MAN GROUP PLC**
Sugar Quay, Lower Thames St., London EC3R 6DU, England, U.K.
CEO: Stanley Fink, CEO   Tel: 44-207-144-1000   Rev: $1,595
Bus: *Financial services.*   Fax: 44-207-144-1923   Emp: 2,630
                                      www.mangroupplc.com
NAICS: 237990, 333293, 333611, 333618, 336112, 523120, 523140, 523910, 523920, 523930, 523999, 525910

    MAN FINANCIAL INC.
    717 Fifth Ave., 9/F, New York, New York 10022
    CEO: Ira Polk, Pres.   Tel: (212) 589-6200
    Bus: *Securities broker*   Fax: (212) 589-6215   Emp: 982

    MAN FINANCIAL INC.
    4800 Main St., Ste. 249, Kansas City, Missouri 64112
    CEO: Frank Stone, Gen. Mgr.   Tel: (816) 931-7620
    Bus: *Commodity contracts brokers, dealers*   Fax: (816) 931-6810

    MAN FINANCIAL INC.
    440 South LaSalle St., 20/F, Chicago, Illinois 60605
    CEO: John Goldsberry, Pres.   Tel: (312) 663-7500
    Bus: *Securities broker & dealer* Fax: (312) 663-7524   Emp: 500

    MAN INVESTMENTS
    123 North Wacker Dr., Ste. 2800, Chicago, Illinois 60606
    CEO: John M. Kelly, Pres.   Tel: (312) 881-6800
    Bus: *Securities broker & dealer* Fax: (312) 881-6700   Emp: 95

● **MANAGEMENT CONSULTING GROUP PLC**
Fleet Place House, 2 Fleet Place, Holborn Viaduct, London EC4M 7RF, England, U.K.
CEO: Kevin A. H. Parry, CEO   Tel: 44-20-7710-5000   Rev: $230
Bus: *Provider of human resource consulting services.*   Fax: 44-20-7710-5000   Emp: 757
                                      www.mcgplc.com
NAICS: 541612, 541618

    PARSONS CONSULTING
    333 W. Wacker Dr., Ste.1620, Chicago, Illinois 60606
    CEO: Tel: (312) 541-4692   %FO: 100
    Bus: *Provider of human resource consulting*   Fax:
         services.

    PROUDFOOT CONSULTING
    70 East 55th St., 5/F, New York, New York 10022
    CEO: Kevin Parry   Tel: (212) 755-2550   %FO: 100
    Bus: *Provider of human resource consulting*   Fax: (212) 679-5820
         services.

PROUDFOOT CONSULTING
11621 Kew Gardens Ave., Ste.200, Palm Beach Gardens, Florida 33410
CEO: Kevin Parry
Bus: *Provider of human resource consulting services.*

Tel: (561) 624-4377
Fax: (561) 656-2305

%FO: 100

• MANPOWER SOFTWARE PLC
48 Leicester Sq., London WC2H 7DB, England, U.K.
CEO: Richard James Morgan-Evans, CEO
Bus: *Workforce management software.*

Tel: 44-20-7389-9500
Fax: 44-20-7389-9588
www.manpowersoftware.com

Rev: $9
Emp: 61

NAICS: 511210

MANPOWER SOFTWARE INC.
2087 NW 87th Ave., Miami, Florida 33172
CEO: Lisa Harris, Sales
Bus: *Workforce management software.*

Tel: (305) 477-3779
Fax: (305) 477-3789

%FO: 100

• MARCONI CORPORATION PLC
New Century Park, Coventry, West Midlands CV3 1HJ, England, U.K.
CEO: Mike W. J. Parton, CEO
Bus: *Mfr. diagnostic and medical machines, medical equipment, imaging devices, and retail systems.*

Tel: 44-2476-562-000
Fax: 44-2476-567-000
www.marconi.com

Rev: $2,527
Emp: 32,000

NAICS: 334119, 334210, 334220, 334290

GREENSBORO ASSOCIATES INC.
3300 Battleground Ave., Ste. 301, Greensboro, North Carolina 27410
CEO: Douglas B. Kramer, VP
Bus: *Marconi Administrator*

Tel: (336) 545-7300
Fax: (336) 545-7340

Emp: 15

MARCONI
1000 Miller Ct. West, Norcross, Georgia 30071
CEO: Toni Counsil, Mgr.
Bus: *Business consulting services*

Tel: (800) 398-8867
Fax: (440) 353-2183

MARCONI
38683 Taylor Industrial Pkwy., North Ridgeville, Ohio 44039
CEO: Dennis Delcampo, Mgr.
Bus: *Computer peripherals equipment services.*

Tel: (800) 398-8867
Fax: (440) 353-2183

MARCONI BROADBAND ROUTING & SWITCHING DIV.
1000 Marconi Dr., Warrendale, Pennsylvania 15086-7502
CEO: Mwj Parton, Pres.
Bus: *Mfr. telecommunications systems, products and services.*

Tel: (886) 627-2664
Fax: (724) 742-6464

%FO: 100
Emp: 1,592

MARCONI NORTH AMERICA
1775 North Collins Blvd., Ste. 400, Richardson, Texas 75080
CEO: Chip Wagner, Pres.
Bus: *Wireless software and services manufacture.*

Tel: (972) 669-6300
Fax: (972) 669-6333

%FO: 100

MARCONI TEST SYSTEMS
2100 Reliance Pkwy., Bedford, Texas 76021
CEO: Joe Pajer
Bus: *Marketing, sales and engineering, access products.*

Tel: (817) 575-2609
Fax: (817) 575-2552

%FO: 100

● **MARCUS EVANS LTD.**
4 Cavendish Sq., London W1GO BX, England, U.K.
CEO: Marcus P.B. Evans, Chmn.
Bus: *Conference organizing services.*

Tel: 44-20-7499-0900
Fax: 44-20-7409-0990
www.marcusevans.com

Rev: $350
Emp: 2,000

NAICS: 561920

MARCUS EVANS INC.
5005 Rockside Rd., Ste. 921, Independence, Ohio 44131
CEO: Ryan Gano, Gen. Mgr.
Bus: *Conference organizing services.*

Tel: (216) 834-0169
Fax: (216) 834-0169

%FO: 100

MARCUS EVANS INC.
455 North Cityfront Plaza Dr., 9/F, Chicago, Illinois 60611
CEO: Paul Northover, Gen. Mgr.
Bus: *Conference organizing services.*

Tel: (312) 540-3000
Fax: (312) 540-3020

%FO: 100

MARCUS EVANS INC.
3250 W. Big Beaver Rd.,
CEO: Ste. 428, Troy, Michigan 48084
0400   %FO: 100

Tracy Ann Palmer, Gen. Mgr.   Tel: (248) 833-

Bus: *Conference organizing services.*

Fax: (248) 833-0403

MARCUS EVANS INC.
1600 Aspen Commons, Ste. 250, Middleton, Wisconsin 53562
CEO: Jason Driscoll, Gen. Mgr.
Bus: *Conference organizing services.*

Tel: (608) 824-8000
Fax: (608) 824-8010

%FO: 100

MARCUS EVANS INC.
1221 Lamar St., Ste.1328, Houston, Texas 77010
CEO: John Ksar, Gen. Mgr.
Bus: *Conference organizing services.*

Tel: (713) 650-6007
Fax: (713) 650-0796

%FO: 100

MARCUS EVANS INC.
20/F, 303 East Wacker Dr., Chicago, Illinois 60601
CEO: Paul Northover, Gen. Mgr.
Bus: *Conference organizing services.*

Tel: (312) 540-3000
Fax: (312) 540-3020

%FO: 100

MARCUS EVANS INC.
13520 Evening Creek Dr., Ste. 370, San Diego, California 92128
CEO: Marc Rosenberg, Gen. Mgr.
Bus: *Conference organizing services.*

Tel: (619) 685-8300
Fax: (619) 685-1177

%FO: 100

MARCUS EVANS INC.
380 Madison Ave., 16/F, New York, New York 10017
CEO: Andrew Johnson, Gen. Mgr.
Bus: *Conference organizing services.*

Tel: (212) 983-3500
Fax: (212) 983-8181

%FO: 100

MARCUS EVANS INC.
3340 Peachtree Rd, Ste. 2140, Atlanta, Georgia 30326
CEO: Paul Meakins, Gen. Mgr.   Tel: (404) 442-6994   %FO: 100
Bus: *Conference organizing services.*   Fax: (404) 442-6995

● **MARKS & SPENCER GROUP PLC**
Waterside House, 35 North Wharf Rd., London W2 1NW, England, U.K.
CEO: Stuart A. Rose, CEO   Tel: 44-207-935-4422   Rev: $15,157
Bus: *Retail stores, internationally markets clothing,*   Fax: 44-207-487-2679   Emp: 70,101
  food stuffs and household goods.   www.marksandspencer.com
NAICS: 442110, 442299, 445110, 445299, 452111, 522210, 524113, 525110, 722213

KING SUPER MARKETS, INC.
700 Lanidex Plaza, Parsippany, New Jersey 07054
CEO: Dan Portnoy, Chmn. & Pres. & CEO   Tel: (973) 463-6300   %FO: 100
Bus: *Chain store; retail foods.*   Fax: (973) 463-6512

● **MAYBORN GROUP PLC**
Worsley Bridge Rd., Lower Sydenham, London SE26 5HD, England, U.K.
CEO: Peter G. Sechiari, Chmn.   Tel: 44-20--8663-4801   Rev: $124
Bus: *Mfr. baby products.*   Fax: 44-20-8650-9876   Emp: 1,145
                                     www.mayborngrou.com
NAICS: 339999

MAYBORN USA INC.
321 S. Main St., Ste. 101, Providence, Rhode Island 02903
CEO: Marilyn Nevill   Tel: (401) 490-4700   %FO: 100
Bus: *Mfr. baby feeding products.*   Fax: (401) 490-4705

● **MC KECHNIE LTD.**
Precision House, Arden Rd., Alcester, Warwickshire B49 6HN, England, U.K.
CEO: Stuart Greville Moberley, CEO   Tel: 44-1789-761-020
Bus: *Mfr. of specialized engineering components and*   Fax: 44-1789-761-058
  engineering plastics.   www.mckechnie.co.uk
NAICS: 326199, 326291, 332722, 335314, 336399, 339993, 423710

AERO QUALITY SALES
47 Harbor View Ave., Stamford, Connecticut 06902
CEO: Mark Newton, Gen. Mgr.   Tel: (203) 351-8500   %FO: 100
Bus: *Aircraft battery distributor.* Fax: (203) 351-8555   Emp: 10

ARGER ENTERPRISES
350 South Rock Blvd., Reno, Nevada 89502
CEO: Malcolm McKay, Pres.   Tel: (775) 856-4141   %FO: 100
Bus: *Mfr. of aircraft parts.*   Fax: (775) 856-4334   Emp: 60

ELECTROMECH TECHNOLOGIES
2600 South Custer, Wichita, Kansas 67217
CEO: Chuck Gumbert, Pres.   Tel: (316) 941-0400   %FO: 100
Bus: *Mfr. of aircraft parts.*   Fax: (316) 942-4823   Emp: 200

HARTWELL CORPORATION
900 South Richfield Rd., Placentia, California 92870
CEO: Tariq Jesrai, Pres.   Tel: (714) 993-4200   %FO: 100
Bus: *Mfr. of aircraft hardware.*   Fax: (714) 579-4419   Emp: 270

JESSE INDUSTRIES
1215 Icehouse Rd., Sparks, Nevada 89431
CEO: Malcolm McKay, Pres.   Tel: (775) 359-2220   %FO: 100
Bus: *Machine shop.*   Fax: (775) 359-2348

MCKECHNIE TOOLING & ENGINEERING
501 Prairie Ave. Northwest, Staples, Minnesota 56479
CEO: Steve Palmer, Gen. Mgr.   Tel: (218) 894-1218   %FO: 100
Bus: *Sale of quality injection molds.*   Fax: (218) 894-3953   Emp: 35

MCKECHNIE VEHICLE COMPONENTS
12117 C.R. Koon (Hwy. 76), Newberry, South Carolina 29108
CEO: David A. Bisset, Operations Mgr.   Tel: (803) 364-3636   %FO: 100
Bus: *Mfr. of stainless steel trim rings, wheel*   Fax:
    covers, center caps & stainless steel
    claddings.

MCKECHNIE VEHICLE COMPONENTS
5440 Corporate Dr., Ste. 100, Troy, Michigan 48098
CEO: Mark Bennett, Pres.   Tel: (248) 641-4700   %FO: 100
Bus: *Mfr. of motor vehicle parts.*   Fax: Emp: 500

MCKECHNIE VEHICLE COMPONENTS
801 John C. Watts Dr., Nicholasville, Kentucky 40356
CEO: Alan Robson, Mgr.   Tel: (859) 887-2446   %FO: 100
Bus: *Mfr. of plastic products.*   Fax: Emp: 300

MCKECHNIE VEHICLE COMPONENTS
2201 Regency Rd., Ste. 701, Lexington, Kentucky 40503
CEO: Stuart Greville Moberley, CEO   Tel: (859) 276-5819   %FO: 100
Bus: *Mfr. of vehicle parts.*   Fax: (859) 276-5848

PSM FASTENER CORPORATION
12223 C.R. Koon Hwy., Newberry, South Carolina 29108
CEO: Bryan Lind, Mgr.   Tel: (803) 321-1300   %FO: 100
Bus: *Sale of industrial supplies.*   Fax: (803) 364-7377   Emp: 22

PTM INTERNATIONAL
8855 NW 35th Lane, Miami, Florida 33172
CEO: Stephen Henderson, Pres.   Tel: (305) 594-6500   %FO: 100
Bus: *Mfr. of aircraft engine components.*   Fax: (305) 594-9386   Emp: 25

TYEE AIRCRAFT
3008 100th St. Southwest, Everett, Washington 98204
CEO: Debbie Wick, Pres.   Tel: (425) 353-1256   %FO: 100
Bus: *Mfr. of aircraft parts & equipment.*   Fax: (425) 355-7097   Emp: 148

VALLEY-TODECO
12975 Bradley Ave., Sylmar, California 91342
CEO: William White, Pres.
Bus: *Mfr. of bolts, screws, rivets & power transmission equipment.*
Tel: (818) 367-2261
Fax: (818) 367-7431
%FO: 100
Emp: 120

WELCO TECHNOLOGIES
200 Technecenter Dr., Ste. 205, Cincinnati, Ohio 45150
CEO: Ralph Wallace, Mgr.
Bus: *Mfr. of electric motors.*
Tel: (513) 831-5335
Fax: (513) 831-4952
%FO: 100

● **MEDISYS PLC**
Dock Lane, Melton, Woodbridge, Suffolk IP12 1PE, England, U.K.
CEO: David Wong, Chmn.
Bus: *Medical products development and manufacture.*
Tel: 44-1394-387-333
Fax: 44-1394-380-152
www.medisys-group.com
Rev: $65
Emp: 313
NAICS: 334510, 336999, 339111, 339112, 339113

HYPOGUARD USA INC.
5182 W. 76th St., Minneapolis, Minnesota 55439
CEO: Dave Conn, Pres.
Bus: *Mfr. of surgical and medical instruments.*
Tel: (952) 646-3200
Fax:

HYPOGUARD USA INC.
One Corporate Center IV, 7301 Ohms Lane, Edina, Minnesota 55439
CEO: David Conn, Pres.
Bus: *Medical products development and manufacture.*
Tel: (952) 646-3200
Fax: (952) 646-3210
Emp: 147

● **MEGGITT PLC**
Farrs House Cowgrove, Wimborne, Dorset BH21 4EL, England, U.K.
CEO: Terence Twigger, CEO
Bus: *Electronics, aerospace, defense and industrial controls products manufacture..*
Tel: 44-1202-847-847
Fax: 44-1202-842-478
www.meggitt.com
Rev: $923
Emp: 4,424
NAICS: 334119, 334511, 336413

MEGGITT INC.
1915 Voyager Ave., Simi Valley, California 93063
CEO: Barney Rosenberg
Bus: *Produces aircraft fire detection and industrial fire and gas protection systems.*
Tel: (805) 526-5700
Fax: (805) 578-3400
%FO: 100

MEGGITT DEFENSE SYSTEMS
2672 Dow Ave., Tustin, California 92780
CEO: Roger Brum, Pres.
Bus: *Mfr. aerial towed vehicle systems.*
Tel: (714) 832-1333
Fax: (714) 832-6090
%FO: 100
Emp: 200

MEGGITT USA, INC.
1955 North Surveyor Ave., 2/F, Simi Valley, California 93063
CEO: Robert Soukup, VP
Bus: *Manufacturing of aerospace & defense products*
Tel: (805) 526-5700
Fax: (805) 526-4369
Emp: 1,435

● **MESSAGELABS GROUP LIMITED**
1240 Lansdowne Ct., Gloucester Business Park, Gloucester GL3 4AB, England, U.K.
CEO: Ben White, CEO
Bus: *Internet access and related services.*
Tel: 44-1452-627-627
Fax: 44-1452-627-787
www.messagelabsgroup.com

NAICS: 541511, 541512

MESSAGELABS INC.
512 Seventh Ave., 6/F, New York, New York 10018
CEO: Jos White
Bus: *Internet access and related services.*
Tel: (646) 519-8100
Fax: (646) 452-6570
%FO: 100

MESSAGELABS INC.
7760 France Ave. South, Ste. 1100, Bloomington, Minnesota 55435
CEO: Natasha Staley
Bus: *Internet access and related services.*
Tel: (952) 886-7541
Fax: (952) 886-7498
%FO: 100

● **METAL BULLETIN PLC**
Park House, Park Terrace, Worcester Park, London KT4 7HY, England, U.K.
CEO: Anthony R. Selvey, Chmn.
Bus: *Publishers of books, directories, and global news journals for the iron, steel and non-ferrous metals industries.*
Tel: 44-20-7827-9977
Fax: 44-20-8337-8943
www.metalbulletin.plc.uk
Rev: $78
Emp: 453

NAICS: 511110, 511120, 511130, 511140, 516110

METAL BULLETIN INC.
332 F Ave., Pittsburgh, Pennsylvania 15221
CEO: Thomas Balcerek, Branch Mgr.
Bus: *Book publishing*
Tel: (412) 824-5069
Fax:

METAL BULLETIN, INC.
1250 Broadway, 26/F, New York, New York 10001
CEO: Greg Newton, Pres.
Bus: *Publish magazine; conference organization service.*
Tel: (212) 213-6202
Fax:
%FO: 100
Emp: 130

● **METRO INTERNATIONAL SA**
Interpark House, 3rd Fl., 7 Down St., London W1J JAJ, England, U.K.
CEO: Pelle Toernberg, CEO
Bus: *Newspaper publishing.*
Tel: 44-20-7016-1300
Fax: 44-20-7016-1400
www.metro.lu
Rev: $302
Emp: 1,132

NAICS: 511110

BOSTON METRO PUBLISHING
320 Congress St., Boston, Massachusetts 02210
CEO: Bernard Petersen
Bus: *Newspaper publishing.*
Tel: (617) 210-9705
Fax: (617) 210-9705
%FO: 100

METRO NEW YORK INC.
44 Wall St., 8/F, New York, New York 10005
CEO: Michael Craig
Bus: *Newspaper publishing.*
Tel: (212) 952-1500
Fax: (212) 702-4559
%FO: 100

TPI METRO PHILADELPHIA
1 Penn Square West, 9/F, 30 S. 15th St., Philadelphia, Pennsylvania 19102
CEO: Ed Abrams   Tel: (215) 717-2600   %FO: 100
Bus: *Newspaper publishing.*   Fax: (215) 717-2664

● **MICE GROUP PLC**
10 Arley Park, Colliers Way, Arley, Coventry, West Midlands CV7 8HN, England, U.K.
CEO: Geoff Howard-Spink, Chmn.   Tel: 44-1676-542-000   Rev: $281
Bus: *Provider of marketing support services*   Fax: 44-1676-540-781   Emp: 1,575
    www.micegroup.com
NAICS: 541613, 541910, 561920

    MICE DALLAS
    700 Freeport Pkwy., Ste.200, Coppell, Texas 75019
    CEO: Mark Wilkinson   Tel: (469) 671-5031   %FO: 100
    Bus: *Designer of conference display exhibits.*   Fax: (469) 671-5053

    MICE DELTA
    15110 Pine Valley Blvd., Clermont, Florida 34711
    CEO: Frank Lasley   Tel: (407) 654-4332   %FO: 100
    Bus: *Provider of exhibit installation and*   Fax: (407) 654-1113
    dismantling services.

    MICE DELTA
    4147 W. 166th St., Oak Forest, Illinois 60452
    CEO: Frank Lasley   Tel: (708) 333-7310   %FO: 100
    Bus: *Provider of conference exhibit installation*   Fax: (312) 735-3630
    and dismantling services.

    MICE DISPLAYWORKS
    6481 Oak Canyon Rd., Irvine, California 92618-5202
    CEO: Herb Hite   Tel: (949) 654-0400   %FO: 100
    Bus: *Designer and producer of trade show*   Fax: (949) 654-0401
    exhibits and marketing strategies.

    MICE DISPLAYWORKS
    44380 Osgood Rd., Ste.101, Fremont, California 94539
    CEO: David Hardbarger   Tel: (510) 226-7001   %FO: 100
    Bus: *Designer and producer of trade show*   Fax: (510) 226-7008
    exhibits and marketing strategies.

    MICE DISPLAYWORKS
    9770 SW Nimbus, Beaverton, Oregon 97008-7172
    CEO: Daniel Hones   Tel: (503) 469-0900   %FO: 100
    Bus: *Provider of trade show exhibits and*   Fax: (503) 469-0800
    marketing strategies.

    MICE ICOM
    4504 St. James Dr., Plano, Texas 75024
    CEO: Nancy Norris   Tel: (469) 767-8338   %FO: 100
    Bus: *Provider of integrated communications and*   Fax: (972) 618-7146
    experimental marketing.

MICE ICOM
1201 W. Fifth St., Ste.T-320, Los Angeles, California 90017
CEO: Sue Cowie   Tel: (213) 572-0340   %FO: 100
Bus: *Provider of integrated communications and*   Fax: (323) 572-0357
      experimental marketing strategies.

MICE ICOM
57 East 11th St., New York, New York 10003
CEO: Bill Callejas   Tel: (212) 994-8840   %FO: 100
Bus: *Provider of strategic, creative, and*   Fax: (212) 994-8865
      production marketing services.

MICE INTERIORS
9160 S. McKemy, Ste.101, Tempe, Arizona 85284
CEO: Claudia Gerster   Tel: (480) 784-1700   %FO: 100
Bus: *Specialist in retail, real estate, and*   Fax: (480) 784-1708
      recreation facilities marketing.

MICE NORTH AMERICA
3326 Ponderosas Way, Ste. A, Las Vegas, Nevada 89118
CEO: Paul Mullen, CEO   Tel: (702) 644-9500   %FO: 100
Bus: *Event production and project management*   Fax: (702) 644-9400
      of conferences.

MICE NORTHAMERICA
1680 Executive Dr. South, Ste. 400, Duluth, Georgia 30096
CEO: Jay Subers   Tel: (678) 405-7900   %FO: 100
Bus: *Designer of conference exhibits.*   Fax: (678) 405-5380

MICE NORTHAMERICA
2755 Campus Dr., Ste.115, San Mateo, California 94403
CEO: Mark Hubbell   Tel: (650) 268-1780   %FO: 100
Bus: *Designer and producer of trade show*   Fax: (650) 268-1786
      exhibits and marketing strategies.

MICE NORTHAMERICA
3326 Ponderosa Way, Ste. A, Las Vegas, Nevada 89118
CEO: Stephen Bradley   Tel: (702) 644-9500   %FO: 100
Bus: *Provider of event production and*   Fax: (702) 644-9400
      conference management services.

MICE NORTHAMERICA
1520 Kensington, Ste.104, Oak Brook, Illinois 60523
CEO: Frank Vavpotic   Tel: (630) 891-0123   %FO: 100
Bus: *Designer of conference display exhibits.*   Fax: (630) 891-0124

MICE NORTHAMERICA
725 Gilfillan Ln., North Oaks, Minnesota 55127
CEO: Teri Mascotti   Tel: (612) 670-5550   %FO: 100
Bus: *Designer of conference exhibit displays.*   Fax: (651) 762-2793

- **MICHAEL PAGE INTERNATIONAL PLC**
  39-41 Parker St., London WC2B 5LN, England, U.K.
  CEO: Terence W. Benson, CEO
  Bus: *Engaged in recruitment.*

  Tel: 44-20-7831-2000
  Fax: 44-20-7269-2280
  www.michaelpage.co.uk

  Rev: $835
  Emp: 2,647

  NAICS: 541612, 561310, 561320

  > **MICHAEL PAGE INTERNATIONAL INC.**
  > 177 Broad St., Stamford, Connecticut 06901
  > CEO: Huw Rothwell, Mgr.
  > Bus: *Engaged in recruitment.*
  >
  > Tel: (203) 905-5250
  > Fax:
  >
  > %FO: 100

  > **MICHAEL PAGE INTERNATIONAL INC.**
  > 125 High St., 9/F, Boston, Massachusetts 02110
  > CEO: Terry Benson, CEO
  > Bus: *Engaged in recruitment.*
  >
  > Tel: (617) 428-3680
  > Fax:
  >
  > %FO: 100

  > **MICHAEL PAGE INTERNATIONAL INC.**
  > 99 Wood Ave. South, Iselin, New Jersey 08830
  > CEO: Ashley Hobkinson, Principal
  > Bus: *Engaged in recruitment.*
  >
  > Tel: (732) 623-4500
  > Fax: (732) 623-4500
  >
  > %FO: 100

  > **MICHAEL PAGE INTERNATIONAL INC.**
  > 405 Lexington Ave., 28/F, New York, New York 10174
  > CEO: Gary James, Mng. Dir.
  > Bus: *Engaged in recruitment.*
  >
  > Tel: (212) 661-4800
  > Fax: (212) 661-4800
  >
  > %FO: 100
  > Emp: 200

- **MICRO FOCUS INTERNATIONAL LTD.**
  22-30 Old Bath Rd., Newbury, Berkshire RG14 1QN, England, U.K.
  CEO: Anthony C. Hill, Chmn.
  Bus: *Develops and market software products.*

  Tel: 44 163 532 646
  Fax: 44-163-532-595
  www.microfocus.com

  Rev: $126
  Emp: 475

  NAICS: 511210

  > **MICRO FOCUS INC.**
  > 9420 Key West Ave., Rockville, Maryland 20850
  > CEO: Glenn R. Boyet, VP
  > Bus: *Development and marketing software
  > products.*
  >
  > Tel: (301) 838-5000
  > Fax: (301) 838-5432
  >
  > %FO: 100

  > **MICRO FOCUS INC.**
  > 15220 NW Greenbrier Pkwy., Ste. 340, Beaverton, Oregon 97006
  > CEO: Peter Young
  > Bus: *Development and marketing software
  > products.*
  >
  > Tel: (503) 716-1100
  > Fax: (503) 614-1862
  >
  > %FO: 100

  > **MICRO FOCUS INC.**
  > 1001 West Maude, Sunnyvale, California 94085
  > CEO: Michael Waters
  > Bus: *Development and marketing software
  > products.*
  >
  > Tel: (408) 222-0300
  > Fax: (408) 222-0303
  >
  > %FO: 100

MICRO FOCUS INC.
4825 Creekstone Dr., Durham, North Carolina 27560
CEO: Richard Levy
Bus: *Development and marketing software products.*
Tel: (919) 998-5260
Fax: (919) 998-5261
%FO: 100

MICRO FOCUS INC.
480 East Swedesford Rd., Wayne, Pennsylvania 19087
CEO: Richard Lloyd
Bus: *Development and marketing software products.*
Tel: (610) 263-3400
Fax: (610) 263-3700
%FO: 100

● **MICROGEN PLC**
11 Park St., Windsor SL4 1LU, England, U.K.
CEO: David J. Sherriff, Mng. Dir.
Bus: *Information management services.*
Tel: 44-1753-847-100
Fax: 44-1753-847-171
www.microgen.co.uk
Rev: $82
Emp: 500

NAICS: 511210, 541511, 541512

MICROGEN USA INC.
245 Park Ave., 39/F, New York, New York 10167
CEO: David J. Sherriff
Bus: *Information management services.*
Tel: (212) 792-4251
Fax: (212) 792-4001
%FO: 100

● **MILLENNIUM & COPTHORNE HOTELS PLC**
Scarsdale Place, Kensington, London W8 5SR, England, U.K.
CEO: Tony Potter, CEO
Bus: *Hotel management.*
Tel: 44-20-7872-2444
Fax: 44-20-7822-2460
www.millenniumhotels.com
Rev: $1,054
Emp: 12,448

NAICS: 721110

MILLENNIUM HOTEL
26 North St., Boston, Massachusetts 02109
CEO: Sudheer Raghaven, Pres.
Bus: *Hotel services.*
Tel: (617) 523-3600
Fax: (617) 523-2454
%FO: 100

MILLENNIUM HOTEL
200 S. 4th St., St. Louis, Missouri 63102
CEO: Keith Gundlefinger, Mgr.
Bus: *Hotel services.*
Tel: (314) 241-9500
Fax: (314) 241-6171
%FO: 100

MILLENNIUM HOTEL
163 E. Walton Pl., North Michigan Ave., Chicago, Illinois 60611
CEO: Sudheer Raghaven, Pres.
Bus: *Hotel services.*
Tel: (312) 751-8100
Fax: (312) 751-9205
%FO: 100

MILLENNIUM HOTEL
2025 Metro Center Blvd., Nashville, Tennessee 37228
CEO: Sudheer Raghaven, Pres.
Bus: *Hotel services.*
Tel: (615) 259-4343
Fax: (615) 313-1327
%FO: 100

MILLENNIUM HOTEL
2800 Campus Walk Ave., Durham, North Carolina 27705
CEO: Angelique Stallings, Mgr.   Tel: (919) 383-8575   %FO: 100
Bus: *Hotel services.*   Fax: (919) 383-8495

MILLENNIUM HOTEL
150 W. Fifth St., Cincinnati, Ohio 45202
CEO: Clyde Jeffries, Mgr.   Tel: (513) 352-2100   %FO: 100
Bus: *Hotel services.*   Fax: (513) 352-2148

MILLENNIUM HOTEL
1313 Nicollet Mall, Minneapolis, Minnesota 55403
CEO: Sudheer Raghaven, Pres.   Tel: (612) 332-6000   %FO: 100
Bus: *Hotel services.*   Fax: (612) 359-2160

MILLENNIUM HOTEL
145 W. 44 St., New York, New York 10036
CEO: Sudheer Raghaven, Pres.   Tel: (212) 768-4400   %FO: 100
Bus: *Hotel services.*   Fax: (212) 768-0847

MILLENNIUM HOTEL
506 S. Grand Ave., Los Angeles, California 90017
CEO: Ivan Lee, Mgr.   Tel: (213) 624-1011   %FO: 100
Bus: *Hotel services.*   Fax: (213) 612-1545

MILLENNIUM HOTEL
4800 Spenard Rd., Anchorage, Alaska 99517
CEO: Sudheer Raghaven, Pres.   Tel: (907) 243-2300   %FO: 100
Bus: *Hotel services.*   Fax: (907) 243-8815

MILLENNIUM HOTEL
2040 Walden Ave., Cheektowaga, New York 14225
CEO: Sudheer Raghaven, Pres.   Tel: (716) 681-2400   %FO: 100
Bus: *Hotel services.*   Fax: (716) 681-8067

MILLENNIUM HOTEL
1345 28th St., Boulder, Colorado 80302
CEO: Daniel Pirrallo, Mgr.   Tel: (303) 443-3850   %FO: 100
Bus: *Hotel services.*   Fax: (303) 443-1480

MILLENNIUM HOTEL PREMIER
133 W. 44th St., New York, New York 10036
CEO: Per Hellman, Mgr.   Tel: (212) 768-4400   %FO: 100
Bus: *Deluxe hotel services.*   Fax: (212) 768-0847

MILLENNIUM RESORT MCCORMICK RANCH
74501 N. Scottsdale Rd., Scottsdale, Arizona 85253
CEO: Tom Waite, Sales Dir.   Tel: (480) 948-5050   %FO: 100
Bus: *Deluxe resort accommodations*   Fax: (480) 991-5572

MILLENNIUM UN PLAZA HOTEL
1 United National Plaza, 44th Street, New York, New York 10017
CEO: Kate Simpson, Mgr.   Tel: (212) 758-1234   %FO: 100
Bus: *Hotel services.*   Fax: (212) 702-5051

● **MINORPLANET SYSTEMS PLC**
Greenwich House, 223 North St., Leeds LS7 2AA, England, U.K.

CEO: Terence Donovan, Chmn.	Tel: 44-113-383-6300	Rev: $60
Bus: *Mfr. satellite based tracking systems for trucking*	Fax: 44-113-383-6315	Emp: 620
fleets.	www.minorplanet.co.uk	

NAICS: 334519

> **REMOTE DYNAMICS INC.**
> 1155 Kas Dr., Richardson, Texas 75081
>
> | | | |
> |---|---|---|
> | CEO: Dennis R. Casey, Dir. | Tel: (972) 301-2000 | %FO: 100 |
> | Bus: *Fleet management solutions to service* | Fax: (972) 301-2403 | |
> | *vehicle fleets, long-haul truck fleets, and* | | |
> | *other mobile-asset fleets.* | | |

● **MISYS PLC**
Burleigh House, Chapel Oak, Salford Priors, Evesham, Worcestershire WR11 5SH, England, U.K.

CEO: J. Kevin Lomax, Mng. Dir.	Tel: 44-138-687-1373	Rev: $1,500
Bus: *Provider of healthcare information systems*	Fax: 44-138-687-1045	Emp: 6,500
software to physician organizations.	www.misys.co.uk	

NAICS: 511210, 541511

> **MISYS HEALTHCARE SYSTEMS, INC.**
> 8529 Six Forks Rd., Raleigh, North Carolina 27615
>
> | | | |
> |---|---|---|
> | CEO: Andrew Lawson, Pres. | Tel: (919) 847-8102 | %FO: 100 |
> | Bus: *Mfr. practice management software.* | Fax: (919) 846-1555 | |

● **MITCHELL GRIEVE LTD.**
Wolsey Rd., Coalville, Leicestershire LE67 3TS, England, U.K.

CEO: Chris Cashmore, Mgr.	Tel: 44-1530-510-565	
Bus: *Mfr. knitting needles and elements.*	Fax: 44-1530-510-458	Emp: 600
	www.mitchell-grieve.co.uk	

NAICS: 333292

> **MITCHELL GRIEVE (USA) INC.**
> 9600 Southern Pine Blvd., Charlotte, North Carolina 28273
>
> | | | |
> |---|---|---|
> | CEO: Paul Blount, Gen. Mgr. | Tel: (704) 525-0325 | %FO: 100 |
> | Bus: *Distribute needles and elements for knitting* | Fax: (704) 525-9471 | Emp: 5 |
> | *and hosiery industries, dental scalpels and* | | |
> | *blades.* | | |

● **MONADNOCK FOREST PRODUCTS INC.**
St. Martins House Business Centre, Ockham Road South, East Horsley, Surrey KT24 65N, England, U.K.

CEO: Jim DiPerri, CEO	Tel: 44-1483-285-551	Rev: $13
Bus: *Processing of hardwood and softwood products.*	Fax: 44-1483-285-175	Emp: 88
	www.mfphardwoods.com	

NAICS: 113110, 113210, 321912

> **MONADNOCK FOREST PRODUCTS INC.**
> 415 Squantum Rd., PO Box 600, Jaffrey, New Hampshire 03452
>
> | | | |
> |---|---|---|
> | CEO: Nick Taylor, Sales | Tel: (603) 532-4415 | %FO: 100 |
> | Bus: *Mfr. hardwoods and softwoods.* | Fax: (603) 532-7530 | |

● **MOORE STEPHENS INTERNATIONAL LIMITED**
St. Paul's House, Warwick Lane, London EC4P 4BN, England, U.K.
CEO: Richard Moore, Mng. Prtn.   Tel: 44-207-334-9191   Rev: $915
Bus: *Financial services.*   Fax: 44-207-334-7976   Emp: 13,059
    www.moorestephens.com
NAICS: 541110, 541211, 541219, 541611

    BURNSIDE & RICHEBARGER
    8700 Tesoro Dr., Ste. 340, San Antonio, Texas 78217
    CEO: Edward L. Rishebarger   Tel: (210) 820-3900   %FO: 100
    Bus: *Accounting and financial services.*   Fax: (210) 820-3226

    MOORE STEPEHENS WURTH FRAZER AND TORBET LLP
    2250 West Main St., Ste. B., Visalia, California 93291
    CEO: Robert A. Matlick   Tel: (559) 732-4135   %FO: 100
    Bus: *Accounting and financial services.*   Fax: (559) 732-7140

    MOORE STEPHENS APPLE INC.
    6690 Beta Dr., Mayfield Village, Ohio 44143
    CEO: Robert Turner   Tel: (440) 460-1980   %FO: 100
    Bus: *Accounting and financial services.*   Fax: (440) 460-1983

    MOORE STEPHENS APPLE, INC.
    29550 Detroit Rd., Westlake, Ohio 44145
    CEO: Stanley L. Apple   Tel: (440) 871-8288   %FO: 100
    Bus: *Accounting and financial services.*   Fax: (440) 871-6452

    MOORE STEPHENS APPLE, INC.
    340 North Ave., 3/F, Cranford, New Jersey 07016
    CEO: Joseph J. Corcoran   Tel: (908) 272-7000   %FO: 100
    Bus: *Accounting and financial services.*   Fax: (908) 272-7101

    MOORE STEPHENS APPLE, INC.
    1540 West Market St., Ste. 201, Akron, Ohio 44313
    CEO: David Gaino   Tel: (330) 867-7350   %FO: 100
    Bus: *Accounting and financial services.*   Fax: (330) 867-8866

    MOORE STEPHENS ATKINSON, LLC
    707 Broadway, NE, Ste. 400, Albuquerque, New Mexico 87102
    CEO: Henry C. South   Tel: (505) 843-6492   %FO: 100
    Bus: *Accounting and financial services.*   Fax: (505) 843-6817

    MOORE STEPHENS BANSLEY AND KIENER LLP
    8745 W. Higgins Rd., Ste. 200, Chicago, Illinois 60631
    CEO: Gerard J. Pater   Tel: (312) 236-4439   %FO: 100
    Bus: *Accounting and financial services.*   Fax: (312) 263-6935

    MOORE STEPHENS BEENE GARTER, PLC
    50 Monroe Ave., NW, Ste. 600, Grand Rapids, Michigan 49503
    CEO: Claude A. Titche   Tel: (616) 235-5200   %FO: 100
    Bus: *Accounting and financial services.*   Fax: (616) 235-5285

MOORE STEPHENS BENSON & MCLAUGHLIN
1400 Blanchard Plaza, 2201 - Sixth Ave., Seattle, Washington 98121
CEO: William R. Kauppila   Tel: (206) 441-3500   %FO: 100
Bus: *Accounting and financial services.*   Fax: (206) 441-1551

MOORE STEPHENS BONADIO LLP
171 Sully's Trail, Ste. 201, Pittsford, New York 14534
CEO: Gerald J. Archibald   Tel: (585) 381-1000   %FO: 100
Bus: *Accounting and financial services.*   Fax: (585) 381-3131

MOORE STEPHENS BROWN SMITH WALLACE LLC
104 N. Main St., St. Charles, Missouri 63301
CEO: Frank Megargel   Tel: (636) 255-3000   %FO: 100
Bus: *Accounting and financial services.*   Fax: (636) 947-6128

MOORE STEPHENS BROWN SMITH WALLACE LLC
1050 N. Lindberg Blvd., St. Louis, Missouri 63132
CEO: Sheldon L. Baron   Tel: (314) 983-1200   %FO: 100
Bus: *Accounting and financial services.*   Fax: (314) 983-1300

MOORE STEPHENS DOEREN MAYHEW, PC
755 W. Big Beaver Rd., Troy, Michigan 48084
CEO: Joseph A. Amine   Tel: (248) 244-3060   %FO: 100
Bus: *Accounting and financial services.*   Fax: (248) 244-3133

MOORE STEPHENS DUDLEY
2101 Magnolia Ave. South, Birmingham, Alabama 35205
CEO: C. R. Dudley Jr.   Tel: (205) 326-0402   %FO: 100
Bus: *Accounting and financial services.*   Fax: (205) 326-3384

MOORE STEPHENS ELLIOTT DAVIS LLC
PO Box 2278, Augusta, Georgia 30903
CEO: Michael W. Boliek   Tel: (706) 722-9090   %FO: 100
Bus: *Accounting and financial services.*   Fax: (706) 722-9092

MOORE STEPHENS FROST PLC
425 West Capitol, Ste. 3300, Little Rock, Arkansas 72201
CEO: Bob Childress   Tel: (501) 376-9241   %FO: 100
Bus: *Accounting and financial services.*   Fax: (501) 376-6256

MOORE STEPHENS HAYS, INC.
477 Madison Ave., New York, New York 10022
CEO: Martin R. Klein   Tel: (212) 572-5500   %FO: 100
Bus: *Accounting and financial services.*   Fax: (212) 572-5572

MOORE STEPHENS LOVELACE, P.A.
18167 US Highway 19 North, Ste. 650, Clearwater, Florida 33764
CEO: Alan P. Bandel   Tel: (727) 531-4477   %FO: 100
Bus: *Accounting and financial services.*   Fax: (727) 538-2154

MOORE STEPHENS LOVELACE, PA
307 West Park Ave., Ste. 202, Tallahassee, Florida 32301-1413
CEO: Steven R. Jones   Tel: (850) 224-4407   %FO: 100
Bus: *Accounting and financial services.*   Fax: (850) 222-3044

MOORE STEPHENS LOVELACE, PA
1201 South Orlando Ave., Ste. 400, Winter Park, Florida 32789-7192
CEO: Kevin D. Murphy   Tel: (407) 740-5400   %FO: 100
Bus: *Accounting and financial services.*   Fax: (407) 740-0012

MOORE STEPHENS MOHLER NIXON & WILLIAMS
2600 El Camino Real, Suite 405, Palo Alto, California 94306
CEO: Keith A. Byars   Tel: (650) 494-3901   %FO: 100
Bus: *Accounting and financial services.*   Fax: (650) 494-6756

MOORE STEPHENS MOHLER NIXON & WILLIAMS
635 Campbell Technology Pkwy., Ste. 100, Campbell, California 95008
CEO: John Murphy   Tel: (408) 369-2400   %FO: 100
Bus: *Accounting and financial services.*   Fax: (408) 879-9485

MOORE STEPHENS NORTH AMERICA INC.
7910 Woodmont Ave., Ste. 210, Bethesda, Maryland 20814
CEO: Alric H. Clay, Pres. & CEO   Tel: (301) 656-7100   %FO: 100
Bus: *Accounting and financial services.*   Fax: (301) 656-7797

MOORE STEPHENS REILLY, PC
424 Adams St., Milton, Massachusetts 02186
CEO: Frank T. Ardito   Tel: (617) 696-7789   %FO: 100
Bus: *Accounting and financial services.*   Fax: (617) 698-1803

MOORE STEPHENS TILLER, LLC
1612 Newcastle St., Ste. 200, Brunswick, Georgia 31520
CEO: James F. Barger   Tel: (912) 265-1750   %FO: 100
Bus: *Accounting and financial services.*   Fax: (912) 264-4976

MOORE STEPHENS TILLER, LLC
780 Johnson Ferry Rd., Ste. 325, Atlanta, Georgia 30342
CEO: Barry E. Fruchter   Tel: (404) 256-1606   %FO: 100
Bus: *Accounting and financial services.*   Fax: (404) 255-6114

MOORE STEPHENS TRAVIS WOLFF, LLP
5580 LBJ Freeway, Ste. 400, Dallas, Texas 75240
CEO: Kenneth W. McGill   Tel: (972) 991-7910   %FO: 100
Bus: *Accounting and financial services.*   Fax: (972) 490-4120

MOORE STEPHENS WATKINS MEEGAN LLC
7700 Wisconsin Ave., Ste. 500, Bethesda, Maryland 20814
CEO: Bruce B. Drury   Tel: (301) 654-7555   %FO: 100
Bus: *Accounting and financial services.*   Fax: (301) 656-9115

MOORE STEPHENS WATKINS MEEGAN LLC
8000 Towers Crescent Dr., Ste. 620, Vienna, Virginia 22182
CEO: Michael E. Meegan   Tel: (703) 761-4848   %FO: 100
Bus: *Accounting and financial services.*   Fax: (703) 761-4812

MOORE STEPHENS WATKINS MEEGAN, LLC
116 Defense Hwy., Ste. 501, Annapolis, Maryland 21401
CEO: J. Gloss   Tel: (410) 571-7766   %FO: 100
Bus: *Accounting and financial services.*   Fax: (410) 571-7764

MOORE STEPHENS WATKINS MEEGAN, LLC
1111 16th St. NW, Ste.400, Washington, District of Columbia 20036
CEO: Kirk S. Cranford, Mgr.   Tel: (202) 755-1616   %FO: 100
Bus: *Accounting and financial services.* Fax: (202) 296-0741

MOORE STEPHENS WATKINS MEEGAN, LLC
4800 Hampden Ln., 9/F, Bethesda, Maryland 20814-2932
CEO: Jim Wagenmann   Tel: (301) 654-7555   %FO: 100
Bus: *Accounting and financial services.* Fax: (301) 656-9115

MOORE STEPHENS WURTH FRAZER & TORBET LLP
14750 NW 77th Ct., Ste. 200, Miami Lakes, Florida 33016-1507
CEO: Julie A. Baird   Tel: (305) 819-9555   %FO: 100
Bus: *Accounting and financial services.* Fax: (305) 819-9955

● **THE MORGAN CRUCIBLE COMPANY**
Morgan House, Madeira Walk, Windsor SL4 1EP, England, U.K.
CEO: Warren Knowlton, CEO & Mng. Dir. Tel: 44-1753-837000 Rev: $1,533
Bus: *Mfr. specialized materials and components.* Fax: 44-1753-850872 Emp: 12,787
               www.morgancrucible.com
NAICS: 213114, 327124

MORGAN ADVANCED CERAMICS INC., GBC PRODUCTS
580 Monastery Dr., Latrobe, Pennsylvania 15650
CEO: Sharon Johnson, Mgr.   Tel: (724) 537-7791
Bus: *Mfr. of insulators for electronic components* Fax: (724) 537-4910   Emp: 2
  from pressed glass& porcelain.

MORGAN ADVANCED CERAMICS INC., WESGO CERAMICS
2425 Whipple Rd., Hayward, California 94544
CEO: Cristina N. Nguyen   Tel: (510) 491-1100
Bus: *Mfr. specialized materials and components.* Fax: (510) 491-1175

MORGAN ADVANCED CERAMICS, ALBEROX PRODUCTS
225 Theodore Rice Blvd., New Bedford, Massachusetts 02745
CEO: David Murray Jr., CFO   Tel: (508) 995-1725
Bus: *Mfr. of brazing alloys & high tech ceramics.* Fax: (508) 995-6954   Emp: 130

MORGAN ADVANCED CERAMICS, CVD PRODUCTS
4 Park Ave., Hudson, New Hampshire 03051
CEO: Victoria Gould   Tel: (603) 598-9122
Bus: *Mfr. abrasive products.*   Fax: (603) 598-9126   Emp: 40

MORGAN ADVANCED CERAMICS, DIAMONEX PRODUCTS
7331 William Ave., Allentown, Pennsylvania 18106
CEO: Fred Kimock, Pres.   Tel: (610) 366-7100
Bus: *Mfr. of jewelers material, porcelain electrical* Fax: (610) 366-7144   Emp: 25
  supplies, coating & engraving.

MORGAN ADVANCED CERAMICS, INC., WESGO/DURAMIC PRODUCTS
26 Madison Rd., Fairfield, New Jersey 07004
CEO: Israel L. Santos, Pres.   Tel: (973) 227-8877
Bus: *Mfr. of chemical preparation, brick* Fax: (973) 227-7135   Emp: 50
  structural tile, nonconductive wire, nonclay
  refractories, & porcelain electric supply.

MORGANITE CRUCIBLE INC.
22 North Plains Industrial Rd., Wallingford, Connecticut 06492
CEO: John Maxwell, Pres.
Bus: *Supply of crucibles, Mfr. Of furnaces for melting & holding metals & alloys.*
Tel: (203) 697-0808
Fax: (203) 265-6267
Emp: 100

MORGANITE, INC.
1 Morganite Dr., Dunn, North Carolina 28334
CEO: Fred Wollman, Pres.
Bus: *Mfr. carbon brushes*
Tel: (910) 892-8081
Fax: (910) 892-9600
%FO: 100

THERMAL CERAMICS, INC.
3102 Old Savannah Rd., Augusta, Georgia 30906
CEO: Matt Colbert, Pres.
Bus: *Mfr. of nonclay mineral, clay refractories, Sale of industrial supplies, mfr. Of mineral wool.*
Tel: (706) 796-4200
Fax: (706) 796-4398
Emp: 800

● **MOSAIC SOFTWARE HOLDINGS LIMITED**
Culverdon House, Abbots Way, Chertsey, Surrey KT16 9LE, England, U.K.
CEO: Johann Dreyer, CEO
Bus: *Electronic funds transfer and financial services transaction processing.*
Tel: 44-1932-574-700
Fax: 44-1932-574-701
www.mosaicsoftware.com
NAICS: 511210

MOSAIC SOFTWARE INC.
800 Fairway Dr., Ste. 198, Deerfield Beach, Florida 33441
CEO: Christopher D. Klein, EVP
Bus: *Software manufacture.*
Tel: (954) 426-1190
Fax: (954) 426-4430
%FO: 100

● **MOTT MACDONALD GROUP LTD.**
St. Anne House, 20-26 Wellesley Rd., Croydon, London CR9 2UL, England, U.K.
CEO: Keith J. Howells, Mng. Dir.
Bus: *Provides engineering, management and development consulting services.*
Tel: 44-20-8774-2000
Fax: 44-20-8681-5706
www.mottmac.com
Rev: $834
Emp: 6,858
NAICS: 236210, 237110, 237130, 237310, 541330

HATCH MOTT MACDONALD
1965 Greenspring Dr., Ste. B, Timonium, Maryland 21093
CEO: Bruce Burns
Bus: *Engineering, management and development consulting services.*
Tel: (410) 308-4810
Fax: (410) 308-4812
%FO: 100

HATCH MOTT MACDONALD/INE
8 Goffe St., Hadley, Massachusetts 01035-0778
CEO: Joe Barbalich
Bus: *Engineering, management and development consulting services.*
Tel: (413) 586-4074
Fax: (413) 586-6643
%FO: 100

HATCH MOTT MACDONALD/INE
1600 West Carson St., Gateway View Plaza, Pittsburgh, Pennsylvania 15219
CEO: Richard Steinhart
Bus: *Engineering, management and development consulting services.*
Tel: (412) 497-2900
Fax: (412) 497-2901
%FO: 100

HATCH MOTT MACDONALD/INE
c/o Baker Killam (JV), 5000 Overlook Ave. SW, Washington, District of Columbia 20032
CEO: Jim Poirier   Tel: (202) 787-2774   %FO: 100
Bus: *Engineering, management and development* Fax: (202) 787-2582
  consulting services.

HATCH MOTT MACDONALD/INE
511 North 12th Ave., Pensacola, Florida 32504
CEO: Charles Carlan   Tel: (850) 484-6011   %FO: 100
Bus: *Engineering, management and development* Fax: (850) 484-8199
  consulting services.

HATCH MOTT MACDONALD/INE
1110 Montimar Dr., Ste. 650, Mobile, Alabama 36609
CEO: Michael Christensen   Tel: (251) 343-4366   %FO: 100
Bus: *Engineering, management and development* Fax: (251) 343-6902
  consulting services.

HATCH MOTT MACDONALD/INE
27 Bleeker St., Millburn, New Jersey 07041
CEO: Nicholas M. DeNichilo, Pres.   Tel: (973) 379-3400   %FO: 100
Bus: *Engineering, management and development* Fax: (973) 376-1072
  consulting services.

HATCH MOTT MACDONALD/INE
15245 Shady Grove Rd., Ste. 340, Rockville, Maryland 20850
CEO: Jim Poirier   Tel: (240) 361-3000   %FO: 100
Bus: *Engineering, management and development* Fax: (240) 361-3020
  consulting services.

HATCH MOTT MACDONALD/INE
9330 Broadway St., Ste. 328, Pearland, Texas 77584
CEO: Eric Kleinhenz   Tel: (832) 736-9590   %FO: 100
Bus: *Engineering, management and development* Fax: (832) 736-9580
  consulting services.

HATCH MOTT MACDONALD/INE
1010 Oliver Rd., Ste. A, Monroe, Louisiana 71201
CEO: Tom Holtzclaw   Tel: (318) 329-0095   %FO: 100
Bus: *Engineering, management and development* Fax: (318) 329-0096
  consulting services.

HATCH MOTT MACDONALD/INE
c/o PSEG, 200 East 5th St., Paterson, New Jersey 07524
CEO: Tom Rudy   Tel: (973) 523-0019   %FO: 100
Bus: *Engineering, management and development* Fax: (973) 523-0053
  consulting services.

HATCH MOTT MACDONALD/INE
4100 S. Ferdon Blvd., Ste. C-6, Crestview, Florida 32536
CEO: Jim Weeks   Tel: (850) 423-7914   %FO: 100
Bus: *Engineering, management and development* Fax: (850) 423-7920
  consulting services.

HATCH MOTT MACDONALD/INE
173 River Dr., Passaic, New Jersey 07055-5708
CEO: David Knowles Tel: (973) 365-2692 %FO: 100
Bus: *Engineering, management and development* Fax: (973) 365-2698
consulting services.

HATCH MOTT MACDONALD/INE
833 Route 9 North, Cape May Court House, New Jersey 08210
CEO: Al Beninato Tel: (609) 465-9377 %FO: 100
Bus: *Engineering, management and development* Fax: (609) 465-5270
consulting services.

HATCH MOTT MACDONALD/INE
PO Box 334, Caldwell, New Jersey 07006
CEO: Bruce Kuhuthau Tel: (973) 575-0225 %FO: 100
Bus: *Engineering, management and development* Fax: (973) 575-8044
consulting services.

HATCH MOTT MACDONALD/INE
120 Beckrich Rd., Ste. 180, Panama City Beach, Florida 32407-2512
CEO: Bill Perry Tel: (850) 236-5831 %FO: 100
Bus: *Engineering, management and development* Fax: (850) 234-1952
consulting services.

HATCH MOTT MACDONALD/INE
3800 Esplanade Way, Ste. 150, Tallahassee, Florida 32311
CEO: James M. Bundy Tel: (850) 222-0334 %FO: 100
Bus: *Engineering, management and development* Fax: (850) 561-0205
consulting services.

HATCH MOTT MACDONALD/INE
10002 Princess Palm Ave., Tampa, Florida 33619
CEO: Bob Holt Tel: (813) 622-8848 %FO: 100
Bus: *Engineering, management and development* Fax: (813) 620 1631
consulting services.

HATCH MOTT MACDONALD/INE
c/o Union Pacific Railroad, 300 Pike Ave., Little Rock, Arkansas 72114
CEO: John Robison Tel: (501) 373-2099 %FO: 100
Bus: *Engineering, management and development* Fax: (501) 373-2947
consulting services.

HATCH MOTT MACDONALD/TNT
Gateway View Plaza, 1600 West Carson St., Pittsburgh, Pennsylvania 15219
CEO: William Palko Tel: (412) 497-2000 %FO: 100
Bus: *Engineering, management and development* Fax: (412) 497-2212
consulting services.

HATCH MOTT MACDONALD/TNT
3825 Hopyard Rd., Ste. 240, Pleasanton, California 94588
CEO: Joel Maniaci Tel: (925) 469-8010 %FO: 100
Bus: *Engineering, management and development* Fax: (925) 469-8011
consulting services.

HATCH MOTT MACDONALD/TNT
1801 North 1120 West, Provo, Utah 84604
CEO: Dan Isom   Tel: (801) 655-0468   %FO: 100
Bus: *Engineering, management and development* Fax: (801) 655-0656
      consulting services.

HATCH MOTT MACDONALD/TNT
817 Oakdale St., Folsom, California 95831
CEO: Guido Eyzaguirre   Tel: (916) 355-1083   %FO: 100
Bus: *Engineering, management and development* Fax: (916) 355-1082
      consulting services.

HATCH MOTT MACDONALD/TNT
c/o Arrowhead Tunnel Field Office, 6205 North Old Waterman Canyon Rd., San Bernardino, California
CEO: Gary Hemphill   Tel: (909) 475-1409   %FO: 100
Bus: *Engineering, management and development* Fax: (909) 475-1406
      consulting services.

HATCH MOTT MACDONALD/TNT
c/o Washington Infrastructure Services, Inc, 5814 Hardy Ave., #6, San Diego, California 92115
CEO: Keith J. Howells   Tel: (619) 265-5796   %FO: 100
Bus: *Engineering, management and development* Fax: (619) 265-3001
      consulting services.

HATCH MOTT MACDONALD/TNT
2727 Camino del Rio South, Ste. 244, San Diego, California 92108
CEO: Lee Warnock   Tel: (619) 858-1595   %FO: 100
Bus: *Engineering, management and development* Fax: (619) 858-1599
      consulting services.

HATCH MOTT MACDONALD/TNT
c/o MTA/LIRR Eastside Access Project Off., 469 7th Ave., 16/F, New York, New York 10018
CEO: John Moss   Tel: (212) 695-8637   %FO: 100
Bus: *Engineering, management and development* Fax: (212) 695-4590
      consulting services.

HATCH MOTT MACDONALD/TNT
c/o Route 880 Field Office, 425 Queens Lane, San Jose, California 95112
CEO: Keith J. Howells   Tel: (408) 452-1940   %FO: 100
Bus: *Engineering, management and development* Fax: (408) 452-7409
      consulting services.

HATCH MOTT MACDONALD/TNT
7311 Greenhaven Dr., Ste. 250, Sacramento, California 95831
CEO: Cara Strom   Tel. (916) 399-0580   %FO: 100
Bus: *Engineering, management and development* Fax: (916) 399-0582
      consulting services.

HATCH MOTT MACDONALD/TNT
21 Bleeker St., Millburn, New Jersey 07041-1008
CEO: Jerry Kroner   Tel: (973) 379-7110   %FO: 100
Bus: *Engineering, management and development* Fax: (973) 379-8970
      consulting services.

HATCH MOTT MACDONALD/TNT
879 Auzerais Ave., San Jose, California 95125
CEO: Keith J. Howells Tel: (408) 793-8730 %FO: 100
Bus: *Engineering, management and development* Fax:
consulting services.

HATCH MOTT MACDONALD/TNT
6 Nickerson St., Ste. 101, Seattle, Washington 98109
CEO: Steve Mauss Tel: (206) 838-2886 %FO: 100
Bus: *Engineering, management and development* Fax: (206) 284-7770
consulting services.

HATCH MOTT MACDONALD/TNT
401 S. Jackson St., Seattle, Washington 98104
CEO: Keith J. Howells Tel: (206) 398-5000 %FO: 100
Bus: *Engineering, management and development* Fax: (206) 689-3339
consulting services.

HATCH MOTT MACDONALD/TNT
c/o Route 85/101S Field Office, 6895 Via Del Oro, San Jose, California 95119
CEO: Keith J. Howells Tel: (408) 229-1989 %FO: 100
Bus: *Engineering, management and development* Fax: (408) 229-2343
consulting services.

HATCH MOTT MACDONALD/TNT
Rt. 7 Site, C/O NJDOT Field Office, 202 Belleville Ave., Belleville, New Jersey 07109
CEO: Keith J. Howells Tel: (973) 751-0889 %FO: 100
Bus: *Engineering, management and development* Fax:
consulting services.

HATCH MOTT MACDONALD/TNT
475 Park Ave. South, 10/F, New York, New York 10016-6901
CEO: Lee Abramson Tel: (212) 532-4111 %FO: 100
Bus: *Engineering, management and development* Fax: (212) 532-3907
consulting services.

HATCH MOTT MACDONALD/TNT
117 Milk St., Ste. 620, Boston, Massachusetts 02109
CEO: Steve Taylor Tel: (617) 422-0018 %FO: 100
Bus: *Engineering, management and development* Fax: (617) 422-0096
consulting services.

HATCH MOTT MACDONALD/TNT
c/o HNTB Corp., 2900 S. Quincy St., Ste. 200, Arlington, Virginia 22206
CEO: Colin R. Weeks Tel: (703) 824-5100 %FO: 100
Bus: *Engineering, management and development* Fax: (703) 671-6210
consulting services.

HATCH MOTT MACDONALD/TNT
16600 West Sprague Rd., Ste. 445, Cleveland, Ohio 44130
CEO: Mike Vitale Tel: (440) 243-8012 %FO: 100
Bus: *Engineering, management and development* Fax: (440) 243-8021
consulting services.

HATCH MOTT MACDONALD/TNT
6382 N. Arapahoe Ct., Parker, Colorado 80134
CEO: Michael Venter   Tel: (303) 828-0740   %FO: 100
Bus: *Engineering, management and development* Fax:
    consulting services.

HATCH MOTT MACDONALD/TNT
c/o CHS Designers, 228 South Wasatch Dr., Salt Lake City, Utah 84112
CEO: Jun Adela   Tel: (801) 466-8155   %FO: 100
Bus: *Engineering, management and development* Fax: (801) 466-8071
    consulting services.

HATCH MOTT MACDONALD/TNT
c/o STV, 225 Park Ave. South, New York, New York 10003
CEO: Gareth Mainwaring   Tel: (212) 777-4400   %FO: 100
Bus: *Engineering, management and development* Fax: (212) 529-5237
    consulting services.

● **MOWLEM PLC**
White Lion Court, Swan St., Isleworth, Middlesex TW7 6RN, England, U.K.
CEO: Simon N. Vivian, CEO & Mng. Dir.   Tel: 44-208-568-9111   Rev: $3,979
Bus: *Construction and engineering.*   Fax: 44-208-847-4802   Emp: 25,614
    www.mowlem.com
NAICS: 236220, 237310, 238130, 238140, 238910, 561210, 561720, 561790

    CHARTER BUILDERS INC.
    1501 LBJ Freeway, Ste. 700, Dallas, Texas 75234
    CEO: Charles E. DeVoe III, Pres.   Tel: (972) 484-4888   %FO: 100
    Bus: *Engaged in construction and engineering.*   Fax: (972) 484-4373   Emp: 120

● **THE MTL INSTRUMENTS GROUP**
Power Court, Luton LU1 3JJ, England, U.K.
CEO: Graeme Scott Philp, CEO   Tel: 44-1582-723-633   Rev: $122
Bus: *Mfr. industrial automation application technology*   Fax: 44-1582-422-283   Emp: 764
    products.   www.mtl-group.com
NAICS: 334513, 335314

    MTL INC.
    17350 Tomball Pkwy., Ste. 355, Houston, Texas 77064
    CEO: Jere Haney   Tel: (281) 571-8065   %FO: 100
    Bus: *Mfr. industrial automation application*   Fax: (281) 571-8069
    technology products.

    MTL INC.
    3421 Pebble Beach Dr., Wilmington, Delaware 19808
    CEO: Tim Koehler   Tel: (302) 368-4197   %FO: 100
    Bus: *Mfr. industrial automation application*   Fax: (302) 368-0996
    technology products.

    MTL INC.
    1483 Old Bridge Rd., Ste. 3, Woodbridge, Virginia 22192
    CEO: Don Long   Tel: (703) 494-6679   %FO: 100
    Bus: *Mfr. industrial automation application*   Fax: (703) 494-6068
    technology products.

MTL INC.
9 Merrill Industrial Dr., Hampton, New Hampshire 03842
CEO: Bob Hamm
Bus: *Mfr. industrial automation application technology products.*
Tel: (603) 926-0090
Fax: (603) 926-1899
%FO: 100

• **MUSIC SALES LIMITED**
8/9 Frith St., London W1D 3JB, England, U.K.
CEO: Robert Wise, Chmn. & Mng. Dir.
Bus: *Publishes printed music and music books.*
Tel: 44-20-7434-0066
Fax: 44-20-7287-6329
www.musicsales.com

NAICS: 451140, 454111, 511130, 511199

G. SCHIRMER SHAWNEE PRESS
257 Park Ave. South, 20/F, New York, New York 10010
CEO: Barrie Edwards, Pres.
Bus: *Publishes printed music and music books.*
Tel: (212) 254-2100
Fax: (212) 254-2013
%FO: 100
Emp: 97

MUSIC SALES LIMITED
1321 7th St., Ste. 300, Santa Monica, California 90401
CEO: Debbie Dumas, Mgr.
Bus: *Publishes printed music and music books.*
Tel: (310) 458-9861
Fax: (310) 458-9862
%FO: 100
Emp: 7

• **MYTRAVEL GROUP PLC (FORMERLY AIRTOURS)**
Parkway One, Parkway Business Centre, 300 Princess Rd., Manchester M14 7QU, England, U.K.
CEO: Peter McHugh, CEO
Bus: *Travel and tour operator.*
Tel: 44-161-23-232-066
Fax: 44-161-23-265-24
www.mytravelgroup.com
Rev: $6,382
Emp: 22,961

NAICS: 483112, 488999, 519190, 561510, 561520, 561599, 721110, 721191, 721199

LEXINGTON SERVICES CORPORATION, DIV. MYTRAVEL GROUP
2120 West Walnut Hill Lane, Irving, Texas 75038
CEO: Shawn Heaton, CFO
Bus: *Provider of reservations and centrally hosted technology services to hotels.*
Tel: (972) 714-0585
Fax:
Emp: 155

MY TRAVEL NORTH AMERICA INC.
1650 Sand Lake Rd., Ste. 300, Orlando, Florida 32809
CEO: Joan Grimbaldeston, Pres.
Bus: *Reservation management and distribution systems for the hospitality industry.*
Tel: (407) 850-2421
Fax:
%FO: 100
Emp: 50

• **NATIONAL EXPRESS GROUP PLC**
75 Davies St., London W1K 5HT, England, U.K.
CEO: Philip White, CEO
Bus: *Engaged in train, bus and coach transportation.*
Tel: 44-207-529-2000
Fax: 44-207-529-2100
www.nationalexpressgroup.com
Rev: $4,931
Emp: 41,222

NAICS: 485113, 485410, 485999

NATIONAL EXPRESS CORP.
9011 Mountain Ridge Dr., Ste. 200, Austin, Texas 78759
CEO: Brian Stock, CEO
Bus: *Bus services.*
Tel: (512) 343-6292
Fax: (512) 343-6596
%FO: 100

● **NATIONAL GRID PLC**
1-3 Strand, London WC2N 5EH, England, U.K.
CEO: Roger Urwin, CEO
Bus: *Electricity and gas services.*

Tel: 44-20-7004-3000
Fax: 44-20-7004-3004
www.ngtgroup.com

Rev: $16,103
Emp: 24,527

NAICS: 221121, 221122, 237120, 237130, 238210, 238990, 486210, 517910, 518210, 541330, 541519, 811213

   GRIDAMERICA LLC
   Key Tower, 127 Public Sq., 50/F, Cleveland, Ohio 44114
   CEO: Paul Halas, Pres.
   Bus: *Electric power transmission.*

   Tel: (216) 776-1900
   Fax: (216) 776-1599

   %FO: 100
   Emp: 54

   NARRAGANSETT ELECTRIC CO.
   280 Melrose St., Providence, Rhode Island 02901
   CEO: Cheryl LaFleur, Pres.
   Bus: *Electric utility.*

   Tel: (401) 784-7000
   Fax: (508) 389-2605

   %FO: 100
   Emp: 800

   NATIONAL GRID USA
   25 Research Dr., Westborough, Massachusetts 01582
   CEO: Michael E. Jesanis, CEO
   Bus: *Utility holding company.*

   Tel: (508) 389-2000
   Fax: (508) 389-2605

   %FO: 100
   Emp: 9,018

   NEW ENGLAND POWER COMPANY
   25 Research Dr., Westborough, Massachusetts 01582
   CEO: Stephen Lewis, Pres.
   Bus: *Electric power transmission.*

   Tel: (508) 389-2000
   Fax: (508) 389-2605

   %FO: 100
   Emp: 7

   NIAGARA MOHAWK POWER CORPORATION
   300 Erie Blvd. West, Syracuse, New York 13202
   CEO: William F. Edwards, Pres.
   Bus: *Electric utility.*

   Tel: (315) 474-1511
   Fax: (315) 460-7041

   %FO: 100
   Emp: 5,500

● **NCIPHER PLC**
Jupiter House, Station Rd., Cambridge CB1 2JD, England, U.K.
CEO: Alexander R. van Someren, CEO
Bus: *Mfr. computer hardware and software.*

Tel: 44-122-372-3600
Fax: 44-122-372-3601
www.ncipher.com

Rev: $27
Emp: 109

NAICS: 334290

   NCIPHER INC.
   2111 Wilson Blvd., Ste. 700, Arlington, Virginia 22201
   CEO: Colin Bastable, VP Sales
   Bus: *Mfr. computer hardware and software.*

   Tel: (703) 351-5019
   Fax: (703) 997-0849

   %FO: 100

   NCIPHER INC.
   500 Unicorn Park Dr., Woburn, Massachusetts 01801
   CEO: Ian K. Smith, Pres.
   Bus: *Mfr. computer hardware and software.*

   Tel: (781) 994-4000
   Fax: (781) 994-4001

   %FO: 100
   Emp: 150

   NCIPHER INC.
   92 Montvale Ave., Ste. 4500, Stoneham, Massachusetts 02180
   CEO: Alex van Someren, CEO
   Bus: *Mfr. computer hardware and software.*

   Tel: (781) 994-4000
   Fax: (781) 994-4001

   %FO: 100

● **NDS GROUP PLC**
1 London Rd., Staines, Middlesex TW18 4EX, England, U.K.
CEO: Abraham Peled, CEO
Bus: *Mfr. broadcast software.*

Tel: 44-208-476-8000
Fax: 44-208-476-8100
www.nds.com

Rev: $556
Emp: 2,012

NAICS: 511210

    NDS AMERICAS INC.
    3501 Jamboree Rd., Ste. 200, Newport Beach, California 92660
    CEO: Jim Britain, VP Sales
    Bus: *Mfr./sales broadcast software.*

    Tel: (949) 725-2500
    Fax: (949) 725-2505

    %FO: 100

● **NETCALL PLC**
10 Harding Way, St. Ives, Cambridgeshire PE27 3WR, England, U.K.
CEO: Henrik Bang, CEO
Bus: *Internet protocol (IP) telephone services.*

Tel: 44-1480-495-300
Fax: 44-1480-496-717
www.netcall.com

NAICS: 511210, 517910, 518210, 518210

    BRAHMACOM INC.
    32 Wexford St., Needham, Massachusetts 02494
    CEO: Barlow Keener
    Bus: *Internet protocol (IP) telephone services.*

    Tel: (781) 433-0333
    Fax: (781) 433-0333

    %FO: 100

    NETCALL USA, INC.
    PO Box 630553, Houston, Texas 77263-0553
    CEO: Jim Sutherland
    Bus: *Internet protocol (IP) telephone services.*

    Tel: (281) 531-9797
    Fax: (281) 752-0687

    %FO: 100

    NETCALL USA, INC.
    45R Blackburn Center, Gloucester, Massachusetts 01930
    CEO: Willliam J. Bouzan
    Bus: *Internet protocol (IP) telephone services.*

    Tel: (978) 281-5173
    Fax: (978) 281-5005

    %FO: 100

● **NTL INCORPORATED**
Bartley Wood Business Park, Bartley Way, Hook, Hampshire RG27 9UP, England, U.K.
CEO: Simon P. Duffy, CEO
Bus: *Cable TV operator.*

Tel: 44-1256-752-000
Fax: 44-1256-754-100
www.ntl.com

Rev: $3,800
Emp: 12,480

NAICS: 515210, 517110, 517510, 517910, 518111, 518210, 519190

    NTL INCORPORATED
    909 Third Ave., Ste. 2863, New York, New York 10022
    CEO: Simon Duffy, Pres.
    Bus: *Cable TV Services*

    Tel: (212) 906-8440
    Fax: (270) 569-2629

    Emp: 13,650

● **OCS GROUP LIMITED**
Trafford Bank House, 32 Brindley Rd., Manchester M16 9SA, England, U.K.
CEO: Chris Cracknell, CEO
Bus: *Property support services, airport transort and
      luggage delivery and sale of janitorial supplies.*

Tel: 44-8702-200-914
Fax: 44-208-651-4832
www.ocs.co.uk

Rev: $8,889
Emp: 54,300

NAICS: 561499

AVSEC SERVICES LLC
319 E. Watkins St., Phoenix, Arizona 85004
CEO: Richard Ollek   Tel: (602) 495-0074   %FO: 100
Bus: *Hygiene products and services.*   Fax: (602) 495-0074

CANNON HYGIENE / AWI OF VIRGINIA
508E Indian River Rd., Norfolk, Virginia 23523
CEO: Matt Gregory   Tel: (575) 543-7110   %FO: 100
Bus: *Hygiene products and services.*   Fax: (575) 543-2352

CANNON HYGIENE INC.
1600 Shore Rd., Naperville, Illinois 60563
CEO: Marc Clemends   Tel: (630) 753-9625   %FO: 100
Bus: *Hygiene products and services.*   Fax: (630) 753-9628

HYGIENIC SYSTEMS LTD.
PO Box 35272, Canton, Ohio 44735
CEO: Russell A. Parry   Tel: (330) 353-1815   %FO: 100
Bus: *Hygiene products and services.*   Fax: (330) 353-1815

● **OCTEL CORP.**
Global House, Bailey Lane, Manchester M90 4AA, England, U.K.
CEO: Paul W. Jennings, Pres. & CEO   Tel: 44-161-498-8889   Rev: $480
Bus: *Mfr. gas additives.*   Fax: 44-161-498-1899   Emp: 907
                                                                    www.octel-corp.com

NAICS: 325110, 325192, 325199, 325998

FINETEX INC.
410-418 Falmouth Ave., PO Box 216, Elmwood Park, New Jersey 07407
CEO: Roger Porter, Pres.   Tel: (201) 797-4686   %FO: 100
Bus: *Mfr. of industrial organic chemicals, surface*   Fax: (201) 797-6558   Emp: 75
      agent, toilet preparations.

OCTEL AMERICA INC.
220 Continental Dr., Newark, Delaware 19713
CEO: Dennis Kerrison, Pres.   Tel: (302) 454-8100   %FO: 100
Bus: *Mfr. gas additives.*   Fax: (302) 451-1380   Emp: 118

OCTEL PERFORMANCE CHEMICALS INC.
3901 F West McKinley Ave., Milwaukee, Wisconsin 53208
CEO: Warren Jones, Mgr.   Tel: (414) 342-5443   %FO: 100
Bus: *Mfr. of surface active agents. &*   Fax: (414) 342-7871   Emp: 25
      polish/sanitation goods.

OCTEL STARREON LLC
8375 South Willow St., Penthouse, Littleton, Colorado 80124
CEO: Mark McPherson, CEO   Tel: (303) 792-5554   %FO: 100
Bus: *Mfr. of petroleum refiner & chemical*   Fax: (303) 792-5668   Emp: 100
      preparations.

PROCHEM
510 W. Grimes Ave., High Point, North Carolina 27260
CEO: Seymour G. Hall, Pres.   Tel: (336) 882-3308   %FO: 100
Bus: *Mfr. of industrial organic chemicals/Mfr. Of*   Fax: (336) 889-6047   Emp: 42
      chemical preparations.

● **OLD MUTUAL PLC**
5/F., Old Mutual Place, 2 Lambeth Hill, London EC4V 4GG, England, U.K.
CEO: James H. Sutcliffe, CEO   Tel: 44-20-7002-7000   Rev: $21,038
Bus: *Engaged in life and general insurance, retail and*   Fax: 44-20-7002-7221   Emp: 41,336
commercial banking services.   www.oldmutual.com
NAICS: 522110, 522120, 522130, 522291, 522292, 523120, 523920, 523930, 523991, 523999, 524113, 524114, 525110, 525120, 525190, 525910, 525920, 525990

     FIDELITY AND GUARANTY LIFE INSURANCE COMPANY
     100 Fleet St., 6/F, Baltimore, Maryland 21202-1137
     CEO: Bruce Parker, Pres.   Tel: (410) 895-0100   %FO: 100
     Bus: *Life insurance.*   Fax: (410) 895-0132

     HEWES COMMUNICATION INC.
     509 Madison Ave., Ste. 904, New York, New York 10022-5501
     CEO: Tony Denninger   Tel: (212) 207-9452   %FO: 100
     Bus: *Real estate investment management.*   Fax: (212) 207-9475

     OLD MUTUAL US HOLDINGS INC.
     200 Clarendon Ave., 53/F, Boston, Massachusetts 02116
     CEO: Scott Powers, CEO   Tel: (617) 369-7300   %FO: 100
     Bus: *Life and general insurance, retail and*   Fax: (617) 369-7499
     commercial banking services.

     PROVIDENT INVESTMENT COUNSEL, INC.
     300 N. Lake Ave., Pasadena, California 91101-4106
     CEO: Thomas M. Mitchell, Chmn. & CEO   Tel: (626) 449-8500   %FO: 100
     Bus: *Investment management.*   Fax: (626) 356-0533

● **OPTO INTERNATIONAL LTD., DIV. STAMFORD GROUP**
Bayley St., Stalybridge, Cheshire SK 16 5LN, England, U.K.
CEO: David A. Openshaw, Mng. Dir.   Tel: 44-161-330-9136
Bus: *Mfr. clamps, tubing and display fixtures.*   Fax: 44-161-343-7332
     www.optoint.co.uk
NAICS: 331491, 333515, 337215

     OPTO INTERNATIONAL INC.
     220 Messner Dr., Ste. 215, Wheeling, Illinois 60090
     CEO: Graham R. Wood, Pres.   Tel: (847) 541-6786   %FO: 100
     Bus: *Sales/distribution of clamps, tubing and*   Fax: (847) 541-8160
     display fixtures.

● **ORTHOGON SYSTEMS LLC**
Linhay Business Park, Unit A1, Eastern Road, Ashburton, Devon TQ13 7UP, England, U.K.
CEO: Philip Andrew Bolt, CEO   Tel: 44-1364-655-500
Bus: *Wireless networking systems manufacture.*   Fax: 44-1364-654625
     www.orthogonsystems.com
NAICS: 334220

     ORTHOGON SYSTEMS LLC
     890 Winter St., Ste. 320, Waltham, Massachusetts 02451
     CEO: Matthew Burke   Tel: (603) 433-1353   %FO: 100
     Bus: *Wireless networking systems manufacture*   Fax: (603) 433-1353
     and sales

- **OSMETECH PLC**
Electra House Electra Way Crewe, Cheshire CW1 6WZ, England, U.K.
CEO: James White, CEO   Tel: 44-127-021-6444   Rev: $11
Bus: *Health products and services.*   Fax: 44-127-021-6030   Emp: 64
www.osmetech.plc.uk
NAICS: 334510, 339111, 339112, 339113

> **OSMETECH**
> 235 Hembree Park Dr., Roswell, Georgia 30076
> CEO: James White, CEO   Tel: (770) 510-4444
> Bus: *Mfr. of analytical instruments, medical &*   Fax: (771) 510-4445   Emp: 68
>   *hospital equipment*

> **OSMETECH INC.**
> 500 West Cummings Park, Ste. 4200, Woburn, Massachusetts 01801
> CEO: Donald Hetzel, Pres.   Tel: (781) 759-7112   %FO: 100
> Bus: *Mfr. of medical equipment & supplies*   Fax: (781) 759-1115

- **OXFORD BIOMEDICA PLC**
Medawar Centre, Robert Robinson Ave., Oxford OX4 4GA, England, U.K.
CEO: Peter Johnson, Chmn.   Tel: 44-186-578-3000   Rev: $1
Bus: *Gene based product treatment manufacture.*   Fax: 44-186-578-3001   Emp: 72
www.oxfordbiomedica.co.uk
NAICS: 325412

> **OXFORD BIOMEDICA INC.**
> 11622 El Camino Real, Ste. 100, San Diego, California 92130
> CEO: Jill Martin, Mgr.   Tel: (858) 677-6500   %FO: 100
> Bus: *Immunotherapy drug sales and distribution.*   Fax: (858) 677-6505

- **OXFORD INSTRUMENTS, PLC**
Old Station Way, Bynsham Witney, Oxfordshire OX8 1TL, England, U.K.
CEO: Jonathan Flint, CEO   Tel: 44-1865-88-1437   Rev: $365
Bus: *Patient monitoring systems manufacture.*   Fax: 44-1865-88-1944   Emp: 1,560
www.oxinst.com
NAICS: 339112

> **OXFORD INSTRUMENTS AMERICAN, INC.**
> 130A Baker Ave., Concord, Massachusetts 01742-2204
> CEO: Garry Ferguson, Pres.   Tel: (978) 369-9933   %FO: 100
> Bus: *Distribution of neurology products and*   Fax: (978) 369-6616
>   *accessories.*

- **P&O NEDLLOYD CONTAINER LINE LTD.**
Beagle House, Braham St., London E1 8EP, England, U.K.
CEO: Philip N. Green, CEO   Tel: 44-207-411-1000   Rev: $6,568
Bus: *Provides worldwide transport of containerized*   Fax: 44-207-441-1500   Emp: 9,000
  cargo.   www.ponl.com
NAICS: 483111, 488510

P&O NEDLLOYD
6 Hutton Centre Dr., Ste. 520, Santa Ana, California 92707
CEO: H. Warren, Principal
Bus: *Global container shipping services.*
Tel: (714) 754-6000
Fax: (714) 754-6001
%FO: 100
Emp: 60

P&O NEDLLOYD
330 S. Stiles St., Linden, New Jersey 07036
CEO: Gregg Prisco
Bus: *Global container shipping services.*
Tel: (908) 474-0303
Fax: (908) 474-0303
%FO: 100

P&O NEDLLOYD
4700 West Sam Houston Pkwy. N, Houston, Texas 77041
CEO: Armondo Martinez, Mgr.
Bus: *Global container shipping services.*
Tel: (832) 467-7000
Fax: (832) 467-7010
%FO: 100
Emp: 105

P&O NEDLLOYD
2500 Cumberland Pkwy., Ste. 400, Atlanta, Georgia 30339
CEO: Les Cutrona, VP
Bus: *Global container shipping services.*
Tel: (678) 309-7100
Fax: (678) 309-7113
%FO: 100

P&O NEDLLOYD
2001 York Rd., Ste. 500, Oak Brook, Illinois 60523
CEO: Mike Maselli, Mgr.
Bus: *Global container shipping services.*
Tel: (630) 891-7700
Fax: (630) 891-7710
%FO: 100
Emp: 70

P&O NEDLLOYD
3875 Faber Place Dr., Ste. 200, North Charleston, South Carolina 29405
CEO: Chuck Csernic, Gen. Mgr.
Bus: *Global container shipping services.*
Tel: (843) 566-7400
Fax: (843) 566-7411
%FO: 100

P&O NEDLLOYD LINES
One Meadowlands Plaza, 14/F, East Rutherford, New Jersey 07073
CEO: Michael White, EVP
Bus: *Global container shipping services.*
Tel: (201) 896-6200
Fax: (201) 896-6342
%FO: 100
Emp: 800

- **PA CONSULTING GROUP, LTD.**
123 Buckingham Palace Rd., London SW1W 9SR, England, U.K.
CEO: Bruce Tindale, CEO
Bus: *Engaged in technology consulting services.*
Tel: 44-207-730-9000
Fax: 44-207-333-5050
www.pa-consulting.com
Rev: $597
Emp: 3,053

NAICS: 541511, 541512, 541519

PA CONSULTING GROUP
One Memorial Dr., Cambridge, Massachusetts 02142
CEO: Alan Graham
Bus: *Engaged in technology consulting services.*
Tel: (617) 225-2700
Fax: (617) 225-2631
%FO: 100

PA CONSULTING GROUP
2711 Allen Blvd., Ste. 200, Middleton, Wisconsin 53562
CEO: Jeff Erickson
Bus: *Engaged in technology consulting services.*
Tel: (608) 827-7820
Fax: (608) 827-7815
%FO: 100

PA CONSULTING GROUP
405 Lexington Ave., New York, New York 10174
CEO: James Ward
Bus: *Engaged in technology consulting services.*
Tel: (212) 973-5900
Fax: (212) 973-5959
%FO: 100

PA CONSULTING GROUP
1776 I St. NW, Washington, District of Columbia 20006
CEO: Robert Hanfling
Bus: *Engaged in technology consulting services.*
Tel: (202) 223-6665
Fax: (202) 296-3858
%FO: 100

PA CONSULTING GROUP
315A Enterprise Dr., Plainsboro, New Jersey 08536
CEO: Julie Davern
Bus: *Engaged in technology consulting services.*
Tel: (609) 936-8300
Fax: (609) 936-8811
%FO: 100

PA CONSULTING GROUP
1750 Pennsylvania Ave. NW, Washington, District of Columbia 20006
CEO: David Casella
Bus: *Engaged in technology consulting services.*
Tel: (202) 442-2000
Fax: (202) 442-2001
%FO: 100

PA CONSULTING GROUP
520 South Grand Ave., Ste. 500, Los Angeles, California 90071
CEO: James Heidell
Bus: *Engaged in technology consulting services.*
Tel: (213) 689-1515
Fax: (213) 689-1129
%FO: 100

PA CONSULTING GROUP
311 South Wacker Dr., Ste. 6330, Chicago, Illinois 60606
CEO: John H. McCord
Bus: *Engaged in technology consulting services.*
Tel: (312) 566-9752
Fax: (312) 566-9753
%FO: 100

● **PACE MICRO TECHNOLOGY PLC**
Victoria Rd., Saltaire Shipley, West Yorkshire BD18 3LF, England, U.K.
CEO: John H. Dyson, CEO
Bus: *Mfr. digital satellite and cable TV set-top boxes.*
Tel: 44-1274-532-000
Fax: 44-1274-532-010
www.pace.co.uk
Rev: $440
Emp: 598

NAICS: 334220

PACE MICRO TECHNOLOGY AMERICAS
3701 FAU Boulevard, Ste. 200, Boca Raton, Florida 33431
CEO: Michael Pulli, Pres.
Bus: *Mfr. digital satellite and cable TV receivers.*
Tel: (561) 995-6000
Fax: (561) 995-6001
%FO: 100

● **PARADIGM GEOTECHNOLOGY BV**
Chobham House, Christchurch Way, Woking, Surrey GU21 1JG, England, U.K.
CEO: Eldad Weiss, COO
Bus: *Integrated software systems manufacture.*
Tel: 44-1483-758-000
Fax: 44-1483-758-001
www.paradigmgeo.com

NAICS: 541511

PARADIGM GEOTECHNOLOGY INC.
2 Memorial Plaza, 820 Gessner, Ste. 400, Houston, Texas 77024
CEO: John Turvill
Bus: *Integrated software systems manufacture and sales.*
Tel: (713) 393-4800
Fax: (713) 393-4801
%FO: 100

- **PARITY GROUP PLC**
  16 St. Martin's Le Grand, London EC1A 4NA, England, U.K.
  CEO: Philip E. Swinstead, CEO
  Bus: *Information technology services, including consulting, systems integration and technical staffing.*
  NAICS: 541310, 541612, 561320
  Tel: 44-20-7776-0800
  Fax: 44-20-7776-0801
  www.parity.net
  Rev: $327
  Emp: 818

  PARITY AMERICAS INC.
  200 Broadhollow Rd., Melville, New York 11747
  CEO: Don Wuerfl
  Bus: *IT consulting services.*
  Tel: (631) 393-5174
  Fax: (631) 393-5173
  %FO: 100

  PARITY AMERICAS INC.
  3295 River Exchange Dr., Ste. 300, Norcross, Georgia 30092
  CEO: David Yarbrough
  Bus: *IT consulting services.*
  Tel: (770) 840-8850
  Fax: (770) 840-8950
  %FO: 100

  PARITY AMERICAS INC.
  290 Linden Oaks Office Park, Rochester, New York 14625
  CEO: Christine Scheible
  Bus: *IT consulting services.*
  Tel: (585) 271-6740
  Fax: (585) 586-0605
  %FO: 100

  PARITY AMERICAS INC.
  5 Donovan Dr., Hopewell Junction, New York 12533
  CEO: Bruce Meyerson, VP
  Bus: *IT consulting services.*
  Tel: (845) 227-2800
  Fax: (845) 227-6820
  %FO: 100

  PARITY AMERICAS INC.
  39 Broadway, New York, New York 10006
  CEO: Lewis Mattson, Pres.
  Bus: *IT consulting services.*
  Tel: (212) 514-5600
  Fax: (212) 514-7246
  %FO: 100

- **PEARSON PLC**
  80 Strand Ave., London WC2R ORL, England, U.K.
  CEO: Marjorie M. Scardino, CEO
  Bus: *Newspapers and book publishing, visitor attractions, TV, investment banking.*
  NAICS: 511110, 511120, 511130, 511140, 511199, 516110, 519110, 519190, 611691, 611699, 611710
  Tel: 44-207-010-2000
  Fax: 44-207-010-6060
  www.pearson.com
  Rev: $7,514
  Emp: 33,389

  BENJAMIN CUMMINGS
  1301 Sansome St., San Francisco, California 94111
  CEO: Linda Davis, Pres.
  Bus: *Publishing & printing books.*
  Tel: (415) 402-2500
  Fax:
  %FO: 100

  COMSTOCK, INC.
  600 Mamaroneck Ave., Harrison, New York 10528
  CEO: Daniel Connell, Pres. & CEO
  Bus: *Information collection & delivery.*
  Tel: (914) 381-7000
  Fax: (914) 381-7022
  %FO: 100

  INTERACTIVE DATA CORPORATION
  22 Crosby Dr., Bedford, Massachusetts 01730
  CEO: Stuart J. Clark, Pres. & CEO
  Bus: *Subscription services.*
  Tel: (781) 687-8500
  Fax: (781) 687-8005
  %FO: 60
  Emp: 1,800

PEACHPIT PRESS
1249 8th St., Berkeley, California 94710
CEO: Nancy Aldrich-Ruenzel, VP   Tel: (510) 524-2178   %FO: 100
Bus: *Publisher.*   Fax: (510) 524-2221

PEARSON DIGITAL LEARNING
6710 E. Camelback Rd., Scottsdale, Arizona 85251
CEO: Bob Roliardi, Pres.   Tel: (480) 840-7700   %FO: 100
Bus: *Education & training services.*   Fax: (480) 840-7701

PEARSON EDUCATION
One Lake St., Upper Saddle River, New Jersey 07458
CEO: Marjorie M. Scardino, CEO   Tel: (201) 236-7000   %FO: 100
Bus: *Educational publisher.*   Fax: (201) 236-3290   Emp: 19,978

PEARSON GOVERNMENT SOLUTIONS, INC.
4250 North Fairfax Dr., Ste. 1200, Arlington, Virginia 22203
CEO: J. McNamara Curtis, Pres. & CEO   Tel: (703) 284-5600   %FO: 100
Bus: *Information technology services.* Fax: (703) 284-5628

THE PENGUIN GROUP
375 Hudson St., New York, New York 10014
CEO: David Shanks, CEO   Tel: (212) 366-2000   %FO: 100
Bus: *Publisher.*   Fax: Emp: 2,000

• **THE PENINSULAR & ORIENTAL STEAM NAVIGATION CO.**
79 Pall Mall, London SW1Y 5EJ, England, U.K.
CEO: Robert B. Woods, CEO   Tel: 44-20-7930-4343   Rev: $4,618
Bus: *Real estate investment and development, ocean* Fax: 44-20-7930-8572   Emp: 22,038
      passenger/cargo shipping, construction services. www.pogroup.com
NAICS: 483111, 483112, 525930
  P&O COLD LOGISTICS
  19840 Rancho Way, Dominguez Hills, California 90221
  CEO: Rick Loesel, Pres.   Tel: (310) 632-6265
  Bus: *Provides cold storage services.* Fax: (310) 632-8887

• **PENNA CONSULTING PLC**
15 Welbeck St., London W1G 9XT, England, U.K.
CEO: Michael G. Jolly, CEO   Tel: 44-20-7945-3505   Rev: $78
Bus: *Engaged in staffing and outsourcing.* Fax: 44-207-945-3506   Emp: 320
                                        www.e-penna.com
NAICS: 541611, 541612, 541618, 561310, 561320, 561990
  LEE HECHT INTERNATIONAL
  50 Tice Blvd., Woodcliff Lake, New Jersey 07677
  CEO: Paul R. O'Donnell, Pres. & COO   Tel: (201) 930-9333
  Bus: *Staffing services.*   Fax: (201) 307-0878   Emp: 850

● **PENNON GROUP PLC**
Peninsula House, Rydon Lane, Exeter, Devon EX2 7HR, England, U.K.
CEO: Robert J. Baty, CEO   Tel: 44-139-244-6677   Rev: $860
Bus: *Engaged in waste management and environmental* Fax: 44-139-243-4966   Emp: 2,600
    services.   www.pennon-group.co.uk
NAICS: 221119, 221310, 221320, 541519, 541618, 562111, 562212, 562213, 562920

     HART-LATIMER ASSOCIATES, INC.
     1150 East Chestnut Ave., Santa Ana, California 92701
     CEO: Harry Hart, Pres.   Tel: (714) 973-9200   %FO: 100
     Bus: *Engaged in waste management.*   Fax: (714) 973-4830   Emp: 10

● **PENTAGRAM DESIGN, INC.**
11 Needham Rd., London W11 2RP, England, U.K.
CEO: Michael Bierut, CEO   Tel: 44-20-7229-3477   Rev: $9
Bus: *Graphic arts design.*   Fax: 44-20-7227-9932   Emp: 48
             www.pentagram.com
NAICS: 541430

     PENTAGRAM DESIGN, INC.
     1508 West Fifth St., Austin, Texas 78703
     CEO: James Biber   Tel: (512) 476-3076   %FO: 100
     Bus: *Graphic arts design.*   Fax: (512) 476-5725

     PENTAGRAM DESIGN, INC.
     387 Tehama St., San Francisco, California 94103
     CEO: Brian Jacobs   Tel: (415) 896-0499   %FO: 100
     Bus: *Graphic arts design.*   Fax: (415) 896-0555

     PENTAGRAM DESIGN, INC.
     204 Fifth Ave., New York, New York 10010
     CEO: Robert Brunner   Tel: (212) 683-7000   %FO: 100
     Bus: *Graphic arts design.*   Fax: (212) 532-0181

● **PHOTO-ME INTERNATIONAL PLC**
Church Rd., Bookham, Surrey KT23 3EU, England, U.K.
CEO: Serge Crasnianski, CEO   Tel: 44-1372-453-399   Rev: $390
Bus: *Mfr. and operates coin-operated, photo booths.*   Fax: 44-1372-459-064   Emp: 1,819
             www.photo-me.co.uk
NAICS: 333315

     PHOTO-ME USA, INC.
     1123 N. Carrier Pkwy., Grand Prairie, Texas 75050
     CEO: Gary Gulley   Tel: (972) 606-1940   %FO: 100
     Bus: *Operates coin-operated, photo booths.*   Fax: (972) 606-0661

● **PILKINGTON PLC**
Prescot Rd., St. Helens, Merseyside WA10 3TT, England, U.K.
CEO: Stuart Chambers, CEO   Tel: 44-1744-288-82   Rev: $5,023
Bus: *Mfr. glass for the automobile industry.*   Fax: 44-1744-692-660   Emp: 24,700
             www.pilkington.com
NAICS: 327211, 336399

PILKINGTON NORTH AMERICA
811 Madison Ave., PO Box 799 811, Toledo, Ohio 43697
CEO: Alan Graham, Mgr.   Tel: (419) 247-3731   %FO: 100
Bus: *Manufactures products for the*   Fax: (419) 247-3821   Emp: 1,461
  architectural/commercial market, residential
  market, and fire-rated glass market.

● **PKF INTERNATIONAL**
Farringdon Place, 20 Farringdon Rd., London EC1M 3AP, England, U.K.
CEO: John Wosner, Chmn.   Tel: 44-20-7065-0000   Rev: $1,110
Bus: *Financial services; auditing, management &*   Fax: 44-20-7065-0650   Emp: 13,500
  technology consulting, forensic accounting,   www.pkf.com
  corporate finance, tax, and bankruptcy services.
NAICS: 541211, 541213, 541219, 541611, 541618, 541690, 561499

  PANNELL KERR FORSTER
  10304 Eaton Place, Ste. 440, Alexandria, Virginia 22030
  CEO: Kevin F. Reilly, Mng. Prtn.   Tel: (703) 385-8809
  Bus: *Financial services, accounting.*   Fax: (703) 385-8890

  PANNELL KERR FORSTER
  75 Federal St., 9/F, Boston, Massachusetts 02110
  CEO: Edward Nickles, Mng. Prtn.   Tel: (617) 753-9985
  Bus: *Financial services, accounting.*   Fax: (617) 753-9986

  PANNELL KERR FORSTER
  5847 San Felipe, Ste. 2400, Houston, Texas 77057
  CEO: Kenneth J. Guidry, Mng. Prtn.   Tel: (713) 860-1400
  Bus: *Financial services, accounting.*   Fax: (713) 355-3909

  PKF CAPITAL MARKETS GROUP
  4557 Turnberry Ct., Suite 100, Plano, Texas 75024
  CEO: Hank Wolpert   Tel: (972) 208-1820
  Bus: *Real estate services.*   Fax: (972) 208-1850

  PKF CONSULTING
  3340 Peachtree Rd., Ste. 580, Atlanta, Georgia 30326
  CEO: R. Mark Woodworth, Mng. Prtn.   Tel: (404) 842-1150
  Bus: *Financial services, accounting.*   Fax: (404) 842-1165

  PKF CONSULTING
  5 Post Oak Pkwy., Ste 1940, Houston, Texas 77027
  CEO: John Keeling, Mng. Prtn.   Tel: (713) 621-5252
  Bus: *Financial services, accounting.*   Fax: (713) 621-9494

  PKF CONSULTING
  29 Broadway, New York, New York 10006
  CEO: John W. Halloran, Mng. Prtn.   Tel: (212) 867-8000
  Bus: *Financial services, accounting.*   Fax: (212) 687-4346

  PKF CONSULTING
  400 South Hope St., Ste. 710, Los Angeles, California 90071
  CEO: Andrew A .Prentiss, Mng. Prtn.   Tel: (213) 891-9911
  Bus: *Financial services, accounting.*   Fax: (213) 891-9910

PKF CONSULTING
425 California St., Ste. 1650, San Francisco, California 94104
CEO: Thomas E. Callahan, Mng. Prtn.   Tel: (415) 421-5378
Bus: *Financial services, accounting.*   Fax: (415) 956-7708

PKF CONSULTING
865 S. Figueroa St., Ste. 104, Los Angeles, California 90017
CEO: Bruce Baltin, Mng. Prtn.   Tel: (213) 680-0900
Bus: *Financial services, accounting.*   Fax: (213) 623-8240

PKF CONSULTING
8 Penn Center Plaza, 19/F, Philadelphia, Pennsylvania 19103
CEO: John A. Fox, Mng. Prtn.   Tel: (215) 563-5300
Bus: *Financial services, accounting.*   Fax: (215) 563-1977

PKF CONSULTING
2034 Eisenhower Ave., Ste. 170, Alexandria, Virginia 22314
CEO: Thomas E. Callahan, Mng. Prtn.   Tel: (703) 684-5589
Bus: *Financial services, accounting.*   Fax: (703) 684-5598

PKF CONSULTING
2985 Tumbleweed Dr., Bozeman, Montana 59715
CEO: Chris Kraus, Mng. Prtn.   Tel: (406) 582-8189
Bus: *Financial services, accounting.*   Fax: (561) 658-8056

PKF CONSULTING
15301 Spectrum Dr., Ste 400, Addison, Texas 75001
CEO: Gregory C. Crown, Mng. Prtn.   Tel: (972) 364-0520
Bus: *Financial services, accounting.*   Fax: (972) 364-0521

PKF CONSULTING
2435 North Central Expwy, Suite 1200, Richardson, Texas 75080
CEO: Gregory C. Crown   Tel: (972) 364-0520
Bus: *Financial services, accounting.*   Fax: (972) 364-0521

PKF CONSULTING
8910 Purdue Rd., Suite 480, Indianapolis, Indiana 46268
CEO: Mark D. Eble   Tel: (317) 616-1815
Bus: *Financial services, accounting.*   Fax: (317) 616-1816

PKF CONSULTING
8 Penn Center Plaza, 19/F, Philadelphia, Pennsylvania 19103
CEO: David E. Arnold   Tel: (215) 563-5300
Bus: *Financial services, accounting.*   Fax: (215) 563-1977

● **PLANIT HOLDINGS PLC**
Inca House, Eureka Science & Business Park, Ashford, Kent TN25 4AB, England, U.K.
CEO: Trevor N. Semadeni, CEO   Tel: 44-1233-635-566   Rev: $48
Bus: *Design, manufacture and marketing of computer*   Fax: 44-1233-627-855   Emp: 375
     aided design (CAD) and sales software for the   www.planitholdings.com
     woodworking and furniture industries.
NAICS: 511210

PLANIT SOLUTIONS INC.
413 S Stream Blvd., Ste. 250, Charlotte, North Carolina 28208
CEO: Jessica Woodall   Tel: (704) 393-5551   %FO: 100
Bus: *Bath and kitchen design software.*   Fax: (704) 393-7320

PLANIT SOLUTIONS INC.
699 Perimeter Dr., Ste. 300, Lexington, Kentucky 40517
CEO: George Daum   Tel: (859) 269-8585   %FO: 100
Bus: *Design, manufacture and marketing of*   Fax: (859) 269-9821
computer aided design (CAD) software.

PLANIT SOLUTIONS INC.
3800 Palisades Dr., Tuscaloosa, Alabama 35405
CEO: George Daum, Pres.   Tel: (205) 556-9199   %FO: 100
Bus: *Design, manufacture and marketing of*   Fax: (205) 556-9199
computer aided design (CAD) software.

RADAN CIM INC.
10625 Railroad Ave., Ste. 201, Chisago City, Minnesota 55013
CEO: Doug Wood   Tel: (651) 257-2129   %FO: 100
Bus: *Design, manufacture and marketing of*   Fax: (651) 257-2129
computer aided design (CAD) software.

● **PLASMON PLC**
Whiting Way, Melbourn, Hertfordshire SG8 6EN, England, U.K.
CEO: Nigel Stret, CEO   Tel: 44-1763-262-963   Rev: $89
Bus: *Mfr. data storage systems.*   Fax: 44-1763-264-444   Emp: 412
          www.plasmon.co.uk
NAICS: 334112

    PLASMON USA INC.
    400 Inverness Pkwy., Ste. 310, Englewood, Colorado 80112
    CEO: Christopher Harris   Tel: (720) 873-2500   %FO: 100
    Bus: *Mfr. and sales data storage systems.*   Fax: (720) 873-2501

● **POLATIS LIMITED**
332/2 Cambridge Science Park, Cambridge CB4 0BZ, England, U.K.
CEO: Dave Lewis, CEO   Tel: 44-122-342-4200
Bus: *Develops and manufactures optical switches.*   Fax: 44-122-347-2015
          www.polatis.com
NAICS: 334210, 334419

    POLATIS USA
    5 Fortune Dr., Billerica, Massachusetts 01821
    CEO: Jeffrey Farmer, VP   Tel: (978) 670-4910   %FO: 100
    Bus: *Develop/mfr. optical switches.*   Fax: (978) 670-4915

● **PREMIER AUTOMOTIVE GROUP (PAG)**
17 Broadwick St., London W1F 0DJ, England, U.K.
CEO: Lewis W.K. Booth, CEO   Tel: 44-20-7025-6200   Rev: $2,760
Bus: *Oversees marketing, sales and distribution of*   Fax: 44-20-7025-6260   Emp: 1,000
Ford's U.S. brand autos.   www.premierautomotive.com
NAICS: 441110

PREMIER AUTOMOTIVE GROUP
One Premier Place, Irvine, California 92618
CEO: Wolfgang Reitzle
Bus: *Oversees marketing, sales and distribution of Ford's U.S. brand autos.*

Tel: (949) 341-5800
Fax: (949) 341-7776

%FO: 100

● **PREMIER FARNELL PLC**
150 Armley Rd., Leeds LS12 2QQ, England, U.K.
CEO: John R. Hirst, CEO & Exec.. Dir.
Bus: *Industrial and electronic components*

Tel: 44-870-129-8606
Fax: 44-870-129-8611
www.premierfarnell.co.uk

Rev: $1,395
Emp: 5,050

NAICS: 332919, 334417, 335931, 423610, 423690

AKRON BRASS COMPANY
343 Venture Blvd., PO Box 86, Wooster, Ohio 44691
CEO: Dan Peters, Superintendent
Bus: *Mfr. fire fighting equipment.*

Tel: (330) 264-5678
Fax:

%FO: 100

CADILLAC ELECTRIC
20700 Hubbell Ave., Ste. B, Oak Park, Michigan 48237
CEO: Jeff Green, Mktg. Dir.
Bus: *Sale of electronic equipment.*

Tel: (248) 967-1221
Fax:

MCM (AN INONE CO.)
650 Congress Park Dr., Centerville, Ohio 45459
CEO: Andrew Verey, CEO
Bus: *Distribution of electronics and related products.*

Tel: (800) 543-4330
Fax: (800) 765-6960

NEWARK INONE
4801 N. Ravenswood, Chicago, Illinois 60640
CEO: Paul Tallentire, Pres.
Bus: *Electronic component distribution & support.*

Tel: (773) 784-5100
Fax: (773) 907-5217

PREMIER FARNELL CORPORATION USA
7061 East Pleasant Valley Rd., Independence, Ohio 44131
CEO: Peter D Costello, Pres.
Bus: *Mfr. industrial and electronic components.*

Tel: (216) 525-4263
Fax: (216) 525-4509

%FO: 100
Emp: 4,000

TPC WIRE & CABLE
7061 E. Pleasant Valley Rd., Independence, Ohio 44131
CEO: Tom Dietz, Gen. Mgr.
Bus: *Mfr. electrical and electronic cord, cable and connectors for the industrial market.*

Tel: (216) 525-4400
Fax: (216) 525-4392

%FO: 100

● **PREMIER HEALTHCARE MANAGEMENT**
Provident House, 13 Russell Hill Rd., Purley, Surrey CR8 2LE, England, U.K.
CEO: Chris Eales, CEO
Bus: *Employment agencies and management services.*

Tel: 44-800-783-3311
Fax: 44-20-8763-9863
www.premierhealth.co.uk

NAICS: 524292, 541612, 621610

PREMIER HEALTHCARE PROFESSIONALS
1029 Windermere Crossing, Cumming, Georgia 30041
CEO: Chris Eales, CFO   Tel: (678) 460-1008   %FO: 100
Bus: *Health & allied services.*   Fax: Emp: 5

● **PRESSAC PLC**
Kedleston House, Aspen Rd., Derby DE21 7SS, England, U.K.
CEO: Chris J. S. Woodwark, CEO   Tel: 44-133-282-1340   Rev: $225
Bus: *Mfr. electrical and electronic components for the*   Fax: 44-133--82-1344   Emp: 3,800
auto telecommunications industry.   www.pressac.com
NAICS: 334419, 335314, 336399

   IN2CONNECT, INC.
   2304 Industrial Dr. SW, Cullman, Alabama 35055
   CEO: David Whittaker, Pres.   Tel: (256) 734-2110   %FO: 100
   Bus: *Mfr./sales electrical and electronic*   Fax: (256) 734-3123   Emp: 101
   components for the auto telecommunications
   industry.

   KAUMAGRAPH FLINT CORPORATION
   4705 Industrial Dr., Millington, Michigan 48746
   CEO: D. F. Taylor, Mng. Dir.   Tel: (518) 871-4550   %FO: 100
   Bus: *Mfr./sales electrical and electronic*   Fax: (517) 871-2291   Emp: 170
   components for the auto telecommunications
   industry.

● **PRODRIVE HOLDINGS LTD.**
Acorn Way, Wildmere Industrial Estate, Banbury, Oxfordshire OX16 3ER, England, U.K.
CEO: Andy Tempest, CEO   Tel: 44-1295-273-355   Rev: $222
Bus: *Motor sport and automotive technology.*   Fax: 44-1295-271-188   Emp: 900
      www.prodrive.com
NAICS: 711211, 711219, 711320

   PRODRIVE AT INC.
   41800 W. 11 Mile Rd., Novi, Michigan 48375
   CEO: A. Smith   Tel: (248) 380-5650   %FO: 100
   Bus: *Motorsport and automotive technology.*   Fax: (248) 380-5651

   PRODRIVE ENGELHARD LLC
   30844 Century Dr., Wixom, Michigan 48393
   CEO: Frank Briden   Tel: (248) 926-8200   %FO: 100
   Bus: *Motorsport and automotive technology.*   Fax: (248) 926-8300

   PRODRIVE USA
   1537-C East McFadden Ave., Santa Ana, California 92705
   CEO: Horacio Antonielli   Tel: (714) 541-4815   %FO: 100
   Bus: *Motorsport and automotive technology.*   Fax: (714) 541-4815

● **PROFESSIONAL STAFF LTD.**
Buckland House, Waterside Dr., Langley Business Park, Sough SL3 6EZ, England, U.K.
CEO: Andrew Wilson, Chmn.   Tel: 44-1753-580-540   Rev: $208
Bus: *Provides staffing services to clients in the*   Fax: 44-1753-540-962   Emp: 375
technology and science fields.   www.professional-staff.com
NAICS: 541512, 541612, 561310, 561320

THE WOOLF GROUP
5315 Highgate Dr., Ste. 102, Durham, North Carolina 27713
CEO: Faye Cochran-Woolf, Pres.
Bus: *Provides staffing services to clients in the technology and science fields.*

Tel: (919) 425-0155
Fax: (919) 425-0166

%FO: 100
Emp: 100

● **PROTHERICS PLC**
Heath Business & Technical Park, Runcom, Cheshire WA7 4 QF, England, U.K.
CEO: Andrew J. Heath, CEO
Bus: *Develops therapeutic vaccines.*

Tel: 44-192-851-8000
Fax: 44-192-851-8002
www.protherics.com

Rev: $38
Emp: 219

NAICS: 325414

PROTHERICS INC.
5214 Maryland Way, Ste. 405, Brentwood, Tennessee 37027
CEO: Saul Komisar
Bus: *Develops therapeutic vaccines.*

Tel: (615) 327-1027
Fax: (615) 320-1212

%FO: 100

● **PRUDENTIAL PLC**
Laurence Pountney Hill, London EC4R 0HH, England, U.K.
CEO: Mark Tucker, CEO
Bus: *Insurance and financial services.*

Tel: 44-207-220-7588
Fax: 44-207-548-3699
www.prudential.co.uk

Rev: $59,685
Emp: 21,500

NAICS: 522110, 522120, 522130, 522210, 522220, 522291, 522292, 522298, 523120, 523920, 523930, 523991, 523999, 524113, 525110, 525120, 525190, 525910, 525920, 525990

JACKSON NATIONAL LIFE DISTRIBUTORS, INC.
8055 E. Tufts Ave., 11/F, Denver, Colorado 80237
CEO: Clifford J. Jack, Pres. & CEO
Bus: *Life insurance*

Tel: (303) 846-3800
Fax: (303) 488-3599

JACKSON NATIONAL LIFE INSURANCE COMPANY
1 Corporate Way, Lansing, Michigan 48951
CEO: Clark P. Manning Jr., Pres. & CEO
Bus: *Life insurance and annuities.*

Tel: (517) 381-5500
Fax: (517) 706-5517

%FO: 100
Emp: 2,300

● **PSION PLC**
12 Park Crescent, London W1B 1PH, England, U.K.
CEO: Alistair Crawford, CEO
Bus: *Mfr. mini and hand-held computers.*

Tel: 44-20-7317-4100
Fax: 44-20-7258-7340
www.psion.com

Rev: $277
Emp: 1,002

NAICS: 334111

PSION TEKLOGIX INC.
150 Baker Ave. Ext., Concord, Massachusetts 01742
CEO: Robert Douglas, Pres.
Bus: *Sales of mini and hand-held computers.*

Tel: (978) 287-9669
Fax: (978) 287-0417

%FO: 100

PSION TEKLOGIX INC.
1810 Airhaven Exchange Blvd., Erlanger, Kentucky 41018
CEO: Robert Douglas, Dir.
Bus: *Sales of mini and hand-held computers.*

Tel: (859) 371-6006
Fax: (859) 371-6422

%FO: 100
Emp: 230

- **QAS LTD.**
Geroge West House, 2-3 Clapham, Common North Side, London SW4 0QL, England, U.K.
CEO: Simon B. Worth, Mng. Dir.   Tel: 44-20-7498-7777   Rev: $89
Bus: *Develops, markets and sells address verification*   Fax: 44-20-7498-0303   Emp: 356
        software.   www.qas.com
NAICS: 511210

  QAS CORP.
  19000 MacArthur Blvd., Ste. 500, Irvine, California 92612
  CEO: Anish Raivadera   Tel: (888) 727-2640   %FO: 100
  Bus: *Develops, markets and sells address*   Fax: (888) 727-2620
        verification software.

  QAS CORP.
  10 Exchange Place, 14/F, Jersey City, New Jersey 07302
  CEO: Fiona Stancombe, CFO   Tel: (201) 748-8010   %FO: 100
  Bus: *Develops, markets and sells address*   Fax: (201) 748-8110
        verification software.

  QAS CORP.
  515 North State St., Ste. 2340, Chicago, Illinois 60610
  CEO: Harry Meike, Mng. Dir.   Tel: (888) 278-6200   %FO: 100
  Bus: *Develops, markets and sells address*   Fax: (888) 260-9300
        verification software.

  QAS CORP.
  221 Main St., Ste. 1310, San Francisco, California 94105
  CEO: Harjinder Burrha   Tel: (888) 882-7203   %FO: 100
  Bus: *Develops, markets and sells address*   Fax: (888) 882-7204
        verification software.

  QAS CORP.
  529 Main St., Ste. 204, Charlestown, Massachusetts 02129
  CEO: Anthony Bickford, Chmn.   Tel: (888) 322-6201   %FO: 100
  Bus: *Develops, markets and sells address*   Fax: (888) 882-7082   Emp: 32
        verification software.

- **QINETIQ GROUP PLC**
Cody Technology Park, Ively Rd., Farnborough, Hampshire GU14 0LX, England, U.K.
CEO: Sir John Chisholm, Chmn.   Tel: 44-8700-100-942   Rev: $1,415
Bus: *Technical and scientific research services.*   Fax: 44-1252-393-399   Emp: 88,898
                                                 www.qinetiq.com
NAICS: 541710

  ELMCO WESTAR INC.
  6000 Technology Dr., Ste. N, Huntsville, Alabama 35805
  CEO: Garrett Martz   Tel: (256) 721-7700   %FO: 100
  Bus: *Global defense and systems engineering*   Fax: (256) 721-1816
        services.

  FOSTER-MILLER, INC.
  350 Second Ave., Waltham, Massachusetts 02451
  CEO: Charles Kojabashian, Chmn.   Tel: (781) 684-4000   %FO: 100
  Bus: *Mechanical engineers & commercial*   Fax: Emp: 675
        research.

QINETIQ INC.
9411 Lee Hwy., Ste. M, Fairfax, Virginia 22031
CEO: David Anderson, Pres.
Bus: *Technical and scientific research services.*

Tel: (703) 414-5454
Fax: (703) 413-4801

%FO: 100
Emp: 1,450

QINETIQ INC.
Four Crystal Park, 2345 Crystal Park, Ste. 909, Arlington, Virginia 22202
CEO: David Anderson, CEO
Bus: *R&D services/ high-tech div. &
implementation.*

Tel: (703) 414-5454
Fax: (703) 414-8161

%FO: 100
Emp: 50

QINETIQ TECHNOLOGY EXTENSION CORP.
2727 Hammer Ave., Annex A, Norco, California 92860
CEO: Malcom J. Baca, Pres.
Bus: *Information retrieval services.*

Tel: (951) 270-5357
Fax:

%FO: 100
Emp: 15

WESTAR AEROSPACE & DEFENSE GROUP
4 Research Park Dr., St. Louis, Missouri 63304
CEO: Jim Williford, EVP
Bus: *Technical and scientific research services.*

Tel: (636) 300-5000
Fax: (636) 300-5005

%FO: 100

WESTAR AEROSPACE & DEFENSE GROUP INC.
4950 Corporate Dr. NW, Ste. 125, Huntsville, Alabama 35805
CEO: Rod Bissell
Bus: *Global defense and systems engineering
services.*

Tel: (256) 430-1610
Fax: (256) 721-2436

%FO: 100

WESTAR DISPLAY TECHNOLOGIES, INC.
4 Research Park Dr., St. Charles, Missouri 63304
CEO: Dave Heiligenstein, Mng. Dir.
Bus: *Technical and scientific research services.*

Tel: (636) 300-5100
Fax: (636) 300-5105

%FO: 100

● RACAL INSTRUMENTS GROUP LTD.
29 Cobham Rd., Ferndown Industrial Estate, Dorset, Wimborne BH21 7PF, England, U.K.
CEO: W. McGinn, Mng. Dir.
Bus: *Test and measuring instruments manufacture.*

Tel: 44-1202-872-800
Fax: 44-1202-870-810
www.racalinstrumentsgroup.co.uk

NAICS: 332995

RACAL INSTRUMENTS INC.
4 Goodyear St., Irvine, California 92618
CEO: Gordon Taylor, Pres.
Bus: *Test and measuring instruments
manufacture.*

Tel: (949) 859-8999
Fax: (949) 859-7139

%FO: JV

● RADSTONE TECHNOLOGY PLC
Tove Valley Business Park, Towcester, Northamptonshire NN12 6PF, England, U.K.
CEO: Jeff L. Perrin, CEO
Bus: *Mfr. computer processors and software for the
military.*

Tel: 44-132-735-9444
Fax: 44-132-735-9662
www.radstone.co.uk

Rev: $80
Emp: 441

NAICS: 334119, 334418, 334419

RADSTONE TECHNOLOGY CORP.
296 Concord Rd., Billerica, Massachusetts 01821
CEO: Jeff Perrin, CEO
Bus: *Commercial physical research.*
Tel: (978) 671-9490
Fax: (978) 671-9488
%FO: 100

RADSTONE TECHNOLOGY CORP.
525 West Southern Ave., Mesa, Arizona 85210
CEO: Ed Saltou, Mgr.
Bus: *Computer related services.*
Tel: (480) 964-5407
Fax:
%FO: 100

RADSTONE TECHNOLOGY CORP.
3281 East Guasti Rd., Ste. 860, Ontario, California 91761
CEO: Charlie Paterson, Pres.
Bus: *Sale of computers/software.*
Tel: (909) 974-1141
Fax:
%FO: 100

RADSTONE TECHNOLOGY CORP.
50 Tice Rd., Woodcliff Lake, New Jersey 07677
CEO: Sandra Bartlett
Bus: *Mfr. computer processors and software for the military.*
Tel: (201) 391-2700
Fax: (201) 391-2899
%FO: 100
Emp: 27

RADSTONE TECHNOLOGY CORP.
119 North Maple St., Corona, California 92880
CEO: John Gurule
Bus: *Sale of computers/software.*
Tel: (951) 808-1711
Fax:
%FO: 100

● **THE RANK GROUP PLC**
6 Connaught Place, London W2 2EZ, England, U.K.
CEO: W. Alun Cathcart, Chmn.
Bus: *Hospitality, leisure and media businesses .*
Tel: 44-20-7706-1111
Fax: 44-20-7262-9886
www.rank.com
Rev: $3,725
Emp: 25,159

NAICS: 713990

DELUXE MEDIA SERVICES, INC.
568 Atrium Dr., Vernon Hills, Illinois 60061
CEO: Tom Vale
Bus: *Post production and distribution services.*
Tel: (847) 990-4100
Fax: (847) 549-8354
%FO: 100

HARD ROCK CAFE INTERNATIONAL, INC.
111 W. Crockett St., San Antonio, Texas 78205
CEO: Kim Creighton, HR
Bus: *Chain of theme restaurants.*
Tel: (210) 224-7625
Fax: (210) 224-7625
%FO: 100

HARD ROCK CAFE INTERNATIONAL, INC.
6100 Old Park Ln., Orlando, Florida 32819
CEO: Hamish Dodds, Pres.
Bus: *Chain of theme restaurants.*
Tel: (407) 445-7625
Fax: (407) 445-7937
%FO: 100
Emp: 3,000

HARD ROCK CAFE INTERNATIONAL, INC.
131 Clarendon St., Boston, Massachusetts 02116
CEO: Mike Kneidinger
Bus: *Chain of theme restaurants.*
Tel: (617) 424-7625
Fax: (617) 424-7625
%FO: 100

HARD ROCK CAFE INTERNATIONAL, INC.
2601 McKinney Ave., Dallas, Texas 75204
CEO: Mike Kneidinger
Bus: *Chain of theme restaurants.*
Tel: (214) 855-0007
Fax: (214) 855-0007
%FO: 100

HARD ROCK CAFE INTERNATIONAL, INC.
502 Texas Ave., Houston, Texas 77002
CEO: Mike Kneidinger
Bus: *Chain of theme restaurants.*
Tel: (713) 227-1392
Fax: (713) 227-1392
%FO: 100

HARD ROCK CAFE INTERNATIONAL, INC.
Bayside Marketplace, 401 Biscayne Blvd., Miami, Florida 33132
CEO: Oliver J. Munday
Bus: *Chain of theme restaurants.*
Tel: (305) 377-3110
Fax: (305) 377-3110
%FO: 100

HARD ROCK CAFE INTERNATIONAL, INC.
230 W. Station Square Dr., Pittsburgh, Pennsylvania 15219
CEO: Kim Creighton, HR
Bus: *Chain of theme restaurants.*
Tel: (412) 481-7625
Fax: (412) 481-7625
%FO: 100

HARD ROCK CAFE INTERNATIONAL, INC.
3 South 2nd St., Ste. 117, Phoenix, Arizona 85004
CEO: Kim Creighton, HR
Bus: *Chain of theme restaurants.*
Tel: (602) 261-7625
Fax: (602) 261-7625
%FO: 100

HARD ROCK CAFE INTERNATIONAL, INC.
Beach St. & The Embarcadero, Pier 39, San Francisco, California 94133
CEO: Kim Creighton, HR
Bus: *Chain of theme restaurants.*
Tel: (415) 956-2013
Fax: (415) 956-2013
%FO: 100

HARD ROCK CAFE INTERNATIONAL, INC.
999 E. St. NW, Washington, District of Columbia 20004
CEO: Kim Creighton, HR
Bus: *Chain of theme restaurants.*
Tel: (202) 737-7625
Fax: (202) 737-7625
%FO: 100

HARD ROCK CAFE INTERNATIONAL, INC.
8600 Beverly Blvd., Los Angeles, California 90048
CEO: Kim Creighton, HR
Bus: *Chain of theme restaurants.*
Tel: (310) 276-7605
Fax: (310) 276-7605
%FO: 100

HARD ROCK CAFE INTERNATIONAL, INC.
230 West Huron Rd., Cleveland, Ohio 44113
CEO: Rick Wittkopp
Bus: *Chain of theme restaurants.*
Tel: (216) 830-7625
Fax: (216) 830-7625
%FO: 100

HARD ROCK CAFE INTERNATIONAL, INC.
1501 Broadway, New York, New York 10036
CEO: Hamish Dodds
Bus: *Chain of theme restaurants.*
Tel: (212) 343-3355
Fax: (212) 938-1901
%FO: 100

HARD ROCK CAFE INTERNATIONAL, INC.
215 Peachtree St. NE, Atlanta, Georgia 30303
CEO: Sean Dee
Bus: *Chain of theme restaurants.*
Tel: (404) 688-7625
Fax: (404) 688-7625
%FO: 100

HARD ROCK CAFE INTERNATIONAL, INC.
1113-31 Market St., Philadelphia, Pennsylvania 19120
CEO: Kim Creighton, HR   Tel: (215) 238-1000   %FO: 100
Bus: *Chain of theme restaurants.*   Fax: (215) 238-1000

HARD ROCK CAFE INTERNATIONAL, INC.
63 West Ontario, Chicago, Illinois 60610
CEO: Oliver J. Munday   Tel: (312) 943-2252   %FO: 100
Bus: *Chain of theme restaurants.*   Fax: (312) 943-2252

HARD ROCK HOTEL & CASINO
4455 Paradise Rd., Las Vegas, Nevada 89109
CEO: Trevor Horwell   Tel: (702) 693-5021   %FO: 100
Bus: *Hotel and casino.*   Fax: (702) 693-5021

● **RAW COMMUNICATIONS LIMITED**
33 Aldgate House, London EC3N 1DL, England, U.K.
CEO: Ab Banerjee, CEO   Tel: 44-20-7369-7776
Bus: *Web cast and Online content providers.*   Fax: 44-20-7369-7021   Emp: 80
                                     www.rawcommunications.com
NAICS: 516110, 519190
      RAW COMMUNICATIONS INC.
      17 State St., 23/F, New York, New York 10004
      CEO: Simon Hague, Pres.   Tel: (212) 742-2222   %FO: 100
      Bus: *Web cast and Online content providers.*   Fax: (212) 742-8461

● **RAYMARINE PLC**
Quay Point, North Harbour Rd., Portsmouth PO6 3TD, England, U.K.
CEO: malcolm M. Miller, CEO   Tel: 44-23-9269-3611   Rev: $205
Bus: *Mfr. marine electronics.*   Fax: 44-23-9269-4642   Emp: 566
                                     www.raymarine.com
NAICS: 334511
      RAYMARINE USA INC.
      1800 NW 49th St., Ste. 130, Ft. Lauderdale, Florida 33309
      CEO: Terry Carlson   Tel: (954) 772-9228   %FO: 100
      Bus: *Design and engineering services for echo*   Fax: (954) 772-9228
           sounders and software.

      RAYMARINE USA INC.
      21 Manchester St., Merrimack, New Hampshire 03054
      CEO: Terry Carlson, Pres.   Tel: (603) 881-5200   %FO: 100
      Bus: *Mfr., marketing and distribution of marine*   Fax: (603) 864-4756
           electronics.

● **RECKITT BENCKISER PLC**
103-105 Bath Rd., Berkshire, Slough SL1 3UH, England, U.K.
CEO: Bart Becht, CEO & Mng. Dir.   Tel: 44-1753-217-800   Rev: $7,456
Bus: *Mfr. household cleaning products.*   Fax: 44-1753-217-899   Emp: 19,900
                                     www.reckittbenckiser.com
NAICS: 325412, 325611, 325612, 325613, 325620, 327910, 446120

RECKITT BENCKISER INC.
399 Interpace Pkwy., Morris Corporate Center IV, PO Box 225, Parsippany, New Jersey 07054
CEO: Javed Ahmed, EVP
Tel: (973) 404-2600
%FO: 100
Bus: *Mfr./marketing of household cleaning products.*
Fax: (973) 404-5700
Emp: 2,400

● **REED ELSEVIER GROUP**
1-3 Strand, London WC2N 5JR, England, U.K.
CEO: Crispin Davis, CEO
Tel: 44-207-930-7077
Rev: $9,270
Bus: *Publishing holding company; leading int'l publisher of scientific information. JV Reed Elsevier PLC, UK and Reed Elsevier NV, Netherlands*
Fax: 44-207-227-5799
www.reedelsevier.com
Emp: 35,100

NAICS: 511120, 511130, 511140, 511199, 516110, 519110, 519190, 561920

APPLIED DISCOVERY INC.
13427 NE 16th St., Ste. 200, Bellevue, Washington 98005
CEO: Michele Vivona, COO
Tel: (425) 467-3000
Bus: *Business services.*
Fax: (425) 467-3010
Emp: 130

CLASSROOM CONNECT INC.
8000 Marina Blvd., Ste. 400, Brisbane, California 94005
CEO: Jim Bowler, Pres. & CEO
Tel: (650) 351-5100
Bus: *Internet content providers.*
Fax: (650) 351-5300
Emp: 165

ELSEVIER INC.
1200 Chambers Rd., Ste. 210, Columbus, Ohio 43212
CEO: Russell Bausch, Mgr.
Tel: (614) 486-5502
%FO: 100
Bus: *Solutions for librarians.*
Fax: (614) 486-5509

ELSEVIER INC. CELL PRESS
600 Technology Square, 5/F, Cambridge, Massachusetts 02139
CEO: Lynne Herndon, CEO
Tel: (617) 661-7057
%FO: 100
Bus: *Science magazine.*
Fax: (617) 661-7061

ELSEVIER SCIENCE PUBLISHING INC.
655 Ave. of the Americas, New York, New York 10010
CEO: Karen Hunter, Pres.
Tel: (212) 989-5800
%FO: 100
Bus: *Publisher of science and medical journals.*
Fax: (212) 633-3990

GIFTS & DECORATIVE ACCESSORIES MAGAZINE
360 Park Ave. South, New York, New York 10010
CEO: Lawrence Oliver
Tel: (646) 746-6525
%FO: 100
Bus: *Gift trade magazine.*
Fax: (646) 746-7583

HARCOURT EDUCATION
6277 Sea Harbor Dr., Orlando, Florida 32887
CEO: Patrick J. Teirney, CEO
Tel: (407) 345-2000
%FO: 100
Bus: *Publisher of educational books.*
Fax: (407) 345-8388
Emp: 5,400

LEXIS NEXIS EXAMEN INC.
3831 N. Freeway Blvd., Ste. 200, Sacramento, California 95834
CEO: Kipp Johnson, CEO
Bus: *Outsourcing solution for the automated*
review and analysis of legal bills and
consulting services.

Tel: (916) 921-4300
Fax: (916) 921-4310

Emp: 75

LEXIS NEXIS INTERFACE SOFTWARE INC.
1420 Kensington Rd., Ste. 320, Oak Brook, Illinois 60523
CEO: Nathan Fineberg, COO
Bus: *Customer services management.*

Tel: (630) 572-1400
Fax: (630) 572-1818

LEXIS-NEXIS GROUP
9443 Springboro Pike, Miamisburg, Ohio 45342
CEO: Allan D. McLaughlin, CEO
Bus: *On-line information service; reference*
information & databases.

Tel: (937) 865-6800
Fax: (937) 847-3090

%FO: 100
Emp: 12,900

MDL INFORMATION SYSTEMS, INC.
14600 Catalina St., San Leandro, California 94577
CEO: Lars Barford, CEO
Bus: *Provides integrated solutions in the life*
science and chemical industries.

Tel: (510) 895-1313
Fax: (510) 483-4738

REED BUSINESS INFORMATION US
360 Park Ave. South, New York, New York 10010
CEO: James A. Casella, CEO
Bus: *U.S. headquarters for publishing holding*
company. JV of Reed Int'l plc, London
(50%) and Elsevier NV, Amsterdam (50%).

Tel: (646) 746-6400
Fax: (646) 746-7583

%FO: 100

REED ELSEVIER GROUP
125 Park Ave., 23/F, New York, New York 10017
CEO: Franchesca Schettni, Mgr.
Bus: *Periodicals.*

Tel: (212) 309-5498
Fax: (212) 309-5480

REED ELSEVIER INC.
11830 Westline Industrial, St. Louis, Missouri 63146-3313
CEO: Kathryn M. Downing
Bus: *Trade journals publishing.*

Tel: (314) 872-8370
Fax: (314) 432-1380

%FO: 100

REED ELSEVIER PUBLISHING, INC.
500 Plaza Dr., Secaucus, New Jersey 07096
CEO: Jim Casella, Sr. Prtn.
Bus: *Travel related publishing & services.*

Tel: (201) 902-2000
Fax: (201) 319-1726

%FO: 100

REED ELSEVIER US
1105 N. Market St., Wilmington, Delaware 19801
CEO: Mark Armour, Pres.
Bus: *Periodicals.*

Tel: (302) 427-2672
Fax: (302) 427-2672

Emp: 21,000

- **REFLEC PLC**
  Road One, Winsford Industrial Estate, Winsford, Cheshire CW7 3QQ, England, U.K.
  CEO: Peter Smith, CEO & Mng. Dir.
  Bus: *Mfr. & developer of retro-reflective inks, tapes,*
  ancillary products & plastic coatings for
  protective purposes for active wear and industrial
  NAICS: 322221, 322222, 325910, 325998

  Tel: 44-1606-593-911
  Fax: 44-1606-559-535
  www.reflec.com

  Rev: $3,706
  Emp: 75

  - **REFLEC USA CORP.**
    200 Homer Ave., Ste. 6B, Ashland, Massachusetts 01721
    CEO: Richard Smith, CEO
    Bus: *Develop/mfr. safety-enhancing retro-*
    reflective fabrics for active wear,
    outerwear, and industrial markets.

    Tel: (508) 231-0748
    Fax: (508) 231-1495

    %FO: 100
    Emp: 5

- **REFORMED SPIRITS COMPANY LTD**
  Plaza 535 King's Rd., London SW10 05Z, England, U.K.
  CEO: Andreas Versteegh, CEO
  Bus: *Mfr. gin and spirits.*

  Tel: 44-207-352-8697
  Fax: 44-207-351-9472
  www.millersgin.com

  NAICS: 312140

  - **REFORMED SPIRITS COMPANY**
    16375 NE 18th Ave., Ste. 204, North Miami Beach, Florida 33162
    CEO: Jean-Paul Benizri, Sales Dir.
    Bus: *Gin, spirits manufacture and sales.*

    Tel: (305) 919-9911
    Fax: (305) 999-9918

    %FO: 100

- **REGUS PLC**
  3000 Hillswood Dr., Chertsey, Surrey KT16 0RS, England, U.K.
  CEO: Mark Dixon, CEO
  Bus: *Engaged in temporary business support systems,*
  including office facilities, meeting rooms, multi-
  lingual staff and complete IT infrastructure.
  NAICS: 531190, 531312, 531390, 541513, 561439, 561990

  Tel: 44-1932-895-500
  Fax: 44-1932-895-501
  www.regus.com

  Rev: $456
  Emp: 2,000

  - **HQ GLOBAL WORKPLACES**
    15305 Dallas Pkwy., Ste. 1400, Addison, Texas 75001
    CEO: Stephen A. McNeely, CEO
    Bus: *Commercial property management.*

    Tel: (972) 361-8100
    Fax: (972) 361-8005

  - **REGUS BUSINESS CENTERS**
    263 Tresser Blvd., Stamford, Connecticut 06901
    CEO: Mark Dixon, Pres.
    Bus: *Operators of business suites*

    Tel: (203) 564-1930
    Fax:

    Emp: 400

- **RENISHAW PLC**
  New Mills, Wotton-under-Edge, Gloucestershire GL12 8JR, England, U.K.
  CEO: David R. McMurtry, Chmn. & CEO
  Bus: *Test probe and measurement systems*

  Tel: 44-145-524-524
  Fax: 44-145-524-901
  www.renishaw.com

  Rev: $231
  Emp: 1,679

  NAICS: 333314, 334513, 334515, 334519

England, U.K.

RENISHAW INC.
5277 Trillium Blvd., Hoffman Estates, Illinois 60192
CEO: John Deer, Chmn.   Tel: (847) 286-9953   %FO: 100
Bus: *Sales test probe and measurement*   Fax: (847) 286-9974   Emp: 84
  equipment.

● **RENOLD PLC**
Renold House, Styal Rd., Wythenshawe, Manchester M22 5WL, England, U.K.
CEO: Robert Davies, CEO   Tel: 44-161-498-4500   Rev: $351
Bus: *Transmission chain, gears, couplings, machine*   Fax: 44-161-437-7782   Emp: 2,653
  tools.   www.renold.com
  NAICS: 333298, 336312, 336350

  EDGETEK MACHINE CORPORATION
  17 Talcott Notch Rd., Farmington, Connecticut 06032
  CEO: Jim Carroll   Tel: (860) 409-7722   %FO: 100
  Bus: *Machine tools and rotors manufacture.* Fax: (860) 409-7730   Emp: 20

  RENOLD AJAX
  100 Bourne St., PO Box A, Westfield, New York 14787
  CEO: Thomas Murrer, Pres.   Tel: (716) 326-3121
  Bus: *Mfr./distribution of bush & gear couplings* Fax: (716) 326-6121   Emp: 300
    vibratory conveyors & power transmission
    equipment.

  RENOLD JEFFREY
  2305 Global Way, Hebron, Kentucky 41048
  CEO: Don Wood, Operations Mgr.   Tel: (800) 251-9012
  Bus: *Sale of industrial supplies & electrical*   Fax: (859) 334-8550   Emp: 30
    equipment.

  RENOLD JEFFREY
  2307 Maden Dr., Morristown, Tennessee 37813
  CEO: Jeffrey Reynold   Tel: (423) 586-1951   %FO: 100
  Bus: *Conveyor chain manufacture.*   Fax: (423) 581-2399

● **RENTOKIL INITIAL PLC**
Felcourt, East Grinsteadt, West Sussex RH19 2JY, England, U.K.
CEO: Brian D. McGowan, Chmn.   Tel: 44-134-283-3022   Rev: $4,207
Bus: *Transportation, electronic, leisure, industry,*   Fax: 44-134-232-6229   Emp: 94,064
  construction service, pest control.   www.rentokil-initial.com
  NAICS: 315225, 423610, 492110, 561210, 561612, 561621, 561710, 561720, 561730, 561740, 561790, 812331,
812332

  INITIAL HEALTHCARE SERVICES, INC.
  4067 Industrial Park Dr., Norcross, Georgia 30071
  CEO: Doug Fogwell   Tel: (770) 476-4871   %FO: 100
  Bus: *Healthcare services*   Fax: (770) 476-4871

  INITIAL SECURITY SERVICES
  3355 Cherry Ridge, Ste. 200, San Antonio, Texas 78230
  CEO: Randal R. Dorn   Tel: (210) 349-6321   %FO: 100
  Bus: *Security services.*   Fax: (210) 349-0213

RENTOKIL PEST CONTROL
4067 Industrial Park Dr., Norcross, Georgia 30071
CEO: Kevin Ward
Bus: *Pest Control*

Tel: (770) 623-1002
Fax: (770) 623-1477

%FO: 100

RENTOKIL, INC.
3750 West Deerfield Rd., Riverwoods, Illinois 60015
CEO: Jeff Mariola
Bus: *Plants and pest control specialists.*

Tel: (847) 634-4250
Fax: (847) 634-6820

%FO: 100

● **RESOURCE SOLUTIONS LTD.**
55 Strand, London WC2N 5WR, England, U.K.
CEO: Chance Wilson, CEO
Bus: *Human resources outsourcing.*

Tel: 44-20-7071-7000
Fax: 33-20-7915-8768
www.resourcesolutions.com

NAICS: 511210, 541612, 561310

RESOURCE SOLUTIONS INC.
7 Times Square, Ste. 1606, New York, New York 10036
CEO: Andrew Keys
Bus: *Human resources outsourcing.*

Tel: (212) 704-9900
Fax: (212) 704-4312

%FO: 100

● **RETAIL DECISIONS PLC**
Red House, Brookwood, Surrey GU24 0BL, England, U.K.
CEO: Caryle Clump, CEO
Bus: *Computer software manufacturer.*

Tel: 44-1483-728-700
Fax: 44-1483-488-895
www.redplc.com

Rev: $270
Emp: 48

NAICS: 511210, 522320, 541511, 541512

RETAIL DECISIONS
100 Village Ct., Ste. 102, Hazlet, New Jersey 07730
CEO: Carl C. Clump, CEO
Bus: *Computer software sales.*

Tel: (732) 888-0088
Fax: (732) 888-4396

%FO: 100
Emp: 66

RETAIL DECISIONS
525 University Ave., Ste. 230, Palo Alto, California 94301
CEO: Xavier Kris, Mng. Dir.
Bus: *Computer software sales.*

Tel: (650) 353-4990
Fax: (650) 328-1543

RETAIL DECISIONS
One State St., Providence, Rhode Island 02908
CEO: Xavier Kris, Mng. Dir.
Bus: *Computer software sales.*

Tel: (401) 228-2355
Fax: (401) 453-3622

%FO: 100

● **REUTERS GROUP PLC**
85 Fleet St., London EC4P 4AJ, England, U.K.
CEO: Thomas H. Glocer, CEO
Bus: *Produces and distributes news and financial information and photographs globally.*

Tel: 44-207-250-1122
Fax: 44-207-510-5896
www.reuters.com

Rev: $5,371
Emp: 16,500

NAICS: 519110

BT RADIANZ INC.
575 Lexington Ave., 12/F, New York, New York 10022
CEO: P. Howard Edelstein, CEO   Tel: (212) 415-4600   %FO: 100
Bus: *Business to Business financial service*   Fax: (212) 415-4600
      network providing access to information,
      service, and hosting services.

INSTINET CORPORATION
747 Third Ave., New York, New York 10017
CEO: Martin Langfield, CEO   Tel: (646) 223-4000   %FO: 100
Bus: *Produces brokerage services via an*   Fax: (646) 223-6137
      automated financial market access and
      information system.

LIPPER INC.
3 Times Sq., New York, New York 10036
CEO: Michael Peace   Tel: (877) 955-4773   %FO: 100
Bus: *Mutual funds research, news, data and*   Fax: (877) 955-4773
      analysis.

REUTERS AMERICA, INC.
445 South Figueroa St., Los Angeles, California 90071
CEO: Ben Silverman   Tel: (213) 680-4800   %FO: 100
Bus: *Produces and distributes news and*   Fax: (213) 680-4800
      financial information and photographs

REUTERS AMERICA, INC.
3 Times Square, New York, New York 10036
CEO: Michael O. Sanderson, CEO   Tel: (646) 223-4000   %FO: 100
Bus: *Produces and distributes news and*   Fax: (646) 436-1659
      financial information and photographs

REUTERS AMERICA, INC.
1333 H St. NW, Washington, District of Columbia 20005
CEO: Kathleen Silvassy, Dir.   Tel: (202) 898-8300   %FO: 100
Bus: *Produces and distributes news and*   Fax: (202) 898-8383
      financial information and photographs

REUTERS AMERICA, INC.
33 South King St., Ste. 514, Honolulu, Hawaii 96813
CEO: Sid Takare   Tel: (808) 538-6455   %FO: 100
Bus: *Produces and distributes news and*   Fax: (808) 538-6455
      financial information and photographs

REUTERS HEALTH INFORMATION
45 West 36th St., 12/F, New York, New York 10018
CEO: Dan McKillen, CEO   Tel: (212) 273-1700   %FO: 100
Bus: *Produces and distributes premiere health* Fax: (212) 273-1730
      and medical global daily news for
      professionals and consumers on the

TIBCO SOFTWARE INC.
15305 Dallas Pkwy., Ste. 300, Addison, Texas 75001
CEO: Todd Williams, CEO   Tel: (972) 387-7472   %FO: 100
Bus: *Mfr. software for enterprise solutions.*   Fax: (972) 387-7473

TIBCO SOFTWARE INC.
4 Cambridge Center, 4/F, Cambridge, Massachusetts 02142
CEO: Dawn Hanaphy, CEO
Bus: *Mfr. software for enterprise solutions.*
Tel: (617) 868-4700
Fax: (617) 499-4409
%FO: 100

TIBCO SOFTWARE INC.
3165 Porter Dr., Palo Alto, California 94304
CEO: Vivek Y. Ranadive, CEO
Bus: *Mfr. software for enterprise solutions.*
Tel: (650) 846-1000
Fax: (650) 846-1005
%FO: 100

TIBCO SOFTWARE INC.
5555 Glenridge Connector, Ste. 200, Atlanta, Georgia 30342
CEO: John Kwarsick, VP
Bus: *Mfr. software for enterprise solutions.*
Tel: (404) 257-4123
Fax: (404) 257-4124
%FO: 100

TIBCO SOFTWARE INC.
1600 Smith, Ste. 3890, Houston, Texas 77002
CEO: Brian Pierce, CEO
Bus: *Mfr. software for enterprise solutions.*
Tel: (713) 344-2050
Fax: (713) 344-2060
%FO: 100

TIBCO SOFTWARE INC.
100 West Big Beaver Rd., Troy, Michigan 48084
CEO: Jeff Blake, CEO
Bus: *Mfr. software for enterprise solutions.*
Tel: (248) 526-0530
Fax: (248) 526-0530
%FO: 100

TIBCO SOFTWARE INC.
200 West Franklin St., Ste. 250, Chapel Hill, North Carolina 27516
CEO: Mick Charles, CEO
Bus: *Mfr. software for enterprise solutions.*
Tel: (919) 969-6500
Fax: (919) 960-2572
%FO: 100

● **REXAM PLC**
4 Millbank, London SW1P 3XR, England, U.K.
CEO: Rolf Borjesson, Chmn.
Bus: *Mfr. of coated paper, film and specialty substrates for imaging and electronic*
NAICS: 326160, 327213
Tel: 44-20-7227-4100
Fax: 44-20-7227-4109
www.rexam.com
Rev: $5,907
Emp: 22,300

REXAM BEVERAGE CAN AMERICAS INC.
8770 W. Bryn Mawr Ave., Ste. 175, Chicago, Illinois 60631
CEO: Ron Lottman, CFO
Bus: *Beverage can packaging.*
Tel: (773) 399-3000
Fax: (773) 399-8088
Emp: 2,300

REXAM INC
4201 Congress St., Ste. 340, Charlotte, North Carolina 28209
CEO: Frank C. Brown, VP
Bus: *Corporate headquarters.*
Tel: (704) 551-1500
Fax: (704) 551-1572
%FO: 100
Emp: 750

● **RICARDO GROUP PLC**
Bridge Works, Shoreham-by-Sea, West Sussex BN43 5FG, England, U.K.
CEO: Rodney J. Westhead, CEO
Bus: *Engineering, design and consulting services to the automobile industry.*
NAICS: 541380
Tel: 44-127-345-5611
Fax: 44-127-346-4124
www.ricardo.com
Rev: $264
Emp: 1,738

RICARDO GROUP, INC.
7850 Grant St., Burr Ridge, Illinois 60527
CEO: Graham Weller, VP   Tel: (630) 789-0003   %FO: 100
Bus: *Engineering, design and consulting services*   Fax: (630) 789-0127   Emp: 60
      to the automobile industry.

RICARDO GROUP, INC.
40000 Ricardo Dr., Van Buren Township, Michigan 48111
CEO: Rodney Westhead, Chmn.   Tel: (734) 397-6666   %FO: 100
Bus: *Engineering, design and consulting services*   Fax: (734) 397-6677   Emp: 380
      to the automobile industry.

● **RICHMOND EVENTS LTD.**
St. Leonards House, St. Leonards Road, London SW14 7LY, England, U.K.
CEO: Mark Rayner, CEO   Tel: 44-20-8487-2200
Bus: *Cruise ship convention services.*   Fax: 44-20-8487-2300
                      www.richmondevents.com
NAICS: 561599, 561920

    RICHMOND EVENTS INC.
    48 West 38th St., 6/F, New York, New York 10018
    CEO: Cindy Edghill   Tel: (212) 651-8700   %FO: 100
    Bus: *Cruise ship convention services.*   Fax: (212) 651-8701

● **ROBOTIC TECHNOLOGY SYSTEMS PLC**
Northbank Industrial Park, Irlam, Great Manchester M44 5AY, England, U.K.
CEO: Craig Slater, CFO   Tel: 44-161-777-2000   Rev: $49
Bus: *Mfr. computer software.*   Fax: 44-161-777-2002   Emp: 308
                      www.rts-group.com
NAICS: 333298, 334513, 334519, 511210

    RTS LIFE SCIENCE INTERNATIONAL
    309 Fellowship Rd., Ste. 210, Mt. Laurel, New Jersey 08054
    CEO: Phil Johnson, Exec. Dir.   Tel: (856) 642-4095   %FO: 100
    Bus: *Mfr./sales computer software.*   Fax:

    RTS LIFE SCIENCE INTERNATIONAL
    609 Deep Valley Dr., Ste. 200, Rolling Hills Estates, California 90274
    CEO: Phil Johnson, Exec. Dir.   Tel: (310) 265-4420   %FO: 100
    Bus: *Mfr./sales computer software.*   Fax:

● **ROLLS ROYCE MARINE SYSTEMS AS**
P.O. Box 2000, Raynesway, Derbyshire, Derby DE21 7XX, England, U.K.
CEO: Saul Lanyado, Pres.   Tel: 44-133-266-1461   Rev: $39
Bus: *Mfr. diesel engines.*   Fax: 44-133-262-2935   Emp: 2,000
                      www.rolls-royce.com/marine
NAICS: 333618, 423830, 541330

    ROLLS ROYCE COMMERCIAL MARINE INC.
    10255 Richmond Ave., Houston, Texas 77042
    CEO: Richard Allianson   Tel: (713) 273-7700
    Bus: *Mfr. diesel engines.*   Fax:

ROLLS ROYCE MARINE INC.
110 Norfolk St., Walpole, Massachusetts 02081
CEO: Peter Gwyn, Pres.   Tel: (508) 668-9610   %FO: 100
Bus: *Mfr. diesel engines.*   Fax: (508) 668-2497   Emp: 250

ROLLS ROYCE MARINE INC.
200 James Dr. W, St. Rose, Louisiana 70087
CEO: Richard Allinson   Tel: (504) 464-4561
Bus: *Marine services.*   Fax: Emp: 95

ROLLS ROYCE NAVAL MARINE, INC.
3719 Industrial Rd., Pascagoula, Mississippi 39581
CEO: Patrick Marolda   Tel: (228) 762-0728
Bus: *M.fr. Industrial machinery.*   Fax:

ROLLS-ROYCE NAVAL MARINE, INC.
190 Admiral Cochrane Dr., Annapolis, Maryland 21401
CEO: Patrick Marolda   Tel: (410) 224-2130
Bus: *Mfr. industrial machinery.*   Fax:

● **ROLLS-ROYCE PLC**
65 Buckingham Gate, London SW1E 6AT, England, U.K.
CEO: John E. V. Rose, CEO   Tel: 44-207-222-9020   Rev: $10,036
Bus: *Turbine engines for aerospace, marine and* Fax: 44-207-227-9178   Emp: 35,200
     industrial power uses.   www.rolls-royce.com
NAICS: 333611, 336412

   ROLLS-ROYCE CORP.
   2001 South Tibbs Ave., Indianapolis, Indiana 46206
   CEO: James M. Guyette, Pres. & CEO   Tel: (317) 230-2000   %FO: 100
   Bus: *Sales/distribution engines for aerospace,* Fax: (317) 230-4020   Emp: 6,225
        marine and industry.

   ROLLS-ROYCE, INC.
   14850 Conference Center Dr., Chantilly, Virginia 20151
   CEO: James M. Guyette, Pres. & CEO   Tel: (703) 834-1700   %FO: 100
   Bus: *U.S. headquarters. Develops/mfr. turbine* Fax: (703) 709-6087
        engines for aerospace, marine and industrial
        power uses.

● **N. M. ROTHSCHILD & SONS LIMITED**
New Court, St. Swithin's Lane, London EC4P 4DU, England, U.K.
CEO: Baron David de Rothschild, Chmn.   Tel: 44-207-280-5000   Rev: $590
Bus: *Finance and investment banking.*   Fax: 44-207-929-1643   Emp: 2,000
                                            www.nmrothschild.com
NAICS: 523110, 523120, 523130, 523140, 523910, 523991, 523999, 525110, 525120, 525190, 525910, 525920,
525990, 551112

   N. M. ROTHSCHILD & SONS INC.
   370 Seventeenth St., Denver, Colorado 80202
   CEO: David de Rothschild, CEO   Tel: (303) 607-9890   %FO: 100
   Bus: *Engaged in finances and investment*   Fax: (303) 607-0998
        banking.

ROTHSCHILD NORTH AMERICA, INC.
1101 Connecticut Ave., NW, Ste. 700, Washington, District of Columbia 20036
CEO: Robert H. Andrew, Chmn.   Tel: (202) 862-1660   %FO: 100
Bus: *Engaged in finances and investment*   Fax: (202) 862-1699   Emp: 20
      banking.

ROTHSCHILD NORTH AMERICA, INC.
1251 Ave. of the Americas, 51/F, New York, New York 10020
CEO: Baron David de Rothschild, Chmn.   Tel: (212) 403-3500   %FO: 100
Bus: *Engaged in finances and investment*   Fax: (212) 403-3501   Emp: 72
      banking.

● **ROTORK PCL**
Rotork House, Brassmill Lane, Bath BA1 3JQ, England, U.K.
CEO: William H. Whiteley, CEO   Tel: 44-122-573-3200   Rev: $283
Bus: *Mfr. valve actuators.*   Fax: 44-122-573-3381   Emp: 1,140
                          www.rotork.com
NAICS: 332911, 332912, 332919, 333995, 333996, 334513

    ROTORK CONTROLS INC.
    PO Box 330, Plainfield, Illinois 60544-0330
    CEO: Michael English, Mgr.   Tel: (815) 436-1710   %FO: 100
    Bus: *Sales of valve and controls.*   Fax: (815) 436-1789

    ROTORK CONTROLS INC.
    504 Trade Center Blvd., Chesterfield, Missouri 63005
    CEO: Mark Franklin, Mgr.   Tel: (636) 681-1500
    Bus: *Mfr. of relays & industrial controls.* Fax: (636) 681-1500

    ROTORK CONTROLS INC.
    1945 Waverly, Napa, California 94558
    CEO: Tom DeGaetano, Mgr.   Tel: (707) 252-4679
    Bus: *Mfr. of relays & industrial controls.* Fax: (707) 252-4574

    ROTORK CONTROLS INC.
    885 Briarcliff Rd., Ste. 1, Atlanta, Georgia 30306
    CEO: Rob Lantz, Mgr.   Tel: (404) 377-8580   %FO: 100
    Bus: *Sales of valve and controls.*   Fax:

    ROTORK CONTROLS INC.
    2180 McDowell Blvd., Ste. B, Petaluma, California 94952
    CEO: David Littlejohns, Mgr.   Tel: (707) 769-4880   %FO: 100
    Bus: *Sales of valve and controls.*   Fax: (707) 769-4888

    ROTORK CONTROLS INC.
    675 Mile Crossing Blvd., Rochester, New York 14624
    CEO: Robert Arnold, Pres.   Tel: (585) 328-1550   %FO: 100
    Bus: *Mfr./sales valve actuators.*   Fax: (585) 328-5848   Emp: 131

    ROTORK CONTROLS INC.
    1325 Granger Rd., Lakewood, Ohio 44107
    CEO: Duane Hazen, Mgr.   Tel: (216) 221-2051
    Bus: *Mfr. of relays & industrial controls.* Fax: (216) 221-2077

- **ROYAL & SUN ALLIANCE INSURANCE GROUP PLC**
  30 Berkeley Square, London W1J 6EW, England, U.K.
  CEO: Andy Haste, CEO
  Bus: *Insurance services.*

  Tel: 44-20-7636-3450
  Fax: 44-207-636-3451
  www.royalsunalliance.com

  Rev: $26,074
  Emp: 32,000

  NAICS: 524113, 524126, 524128

  > **ROYAL & SUN ALLIANCE USA INC.**
  > 9300 Arrowpoint Blvd., Charlotte, North Carolina 28273-8135
  > CEO: John Tighe, Pres. & CEO
  > Bus: *Insurance services.*
  >
  > Tel: (704) 522-2000
  > Fax: (860) 674-6615
  >
  > %FO: 100

- **ROYAL DOULTON PLC**
  Sir Henry Doulton House, Forge Lane, Etruria, Stoke-on-Trent ST1 5NN, England, U.K.
  CEO: Wayne Nutbeen, CEO
  Bus: *Mfr. and distributor of fine china, crystal and ceramic tableware.*

  Tel: 44-1782-404-045
  Fax: 44-1782-404-254
  www.royaldoulton.company.com

  Rev: $241
  Emp: 5,545

  NAICS: 326199, 327112, 327212, 332211, 332214, 334518, 339912, 339999, 423220

  > **ROYAL DOULTON USA INC.**
  > 200 Cottontail Lane, Ste. B, Somerset, New Jersey 08873
  > CEO: R. Bruce McKerrall, VP
  > Bus: *Mfr./sales and distributor of ceramic tableware and giftware.*
  >
  > Tel: (732) 356-7880
  > Fax: (732) 764-4974
  >
  > %FO: 100
  > Emp: 400

- **ROYAL WORCESTER SPODE LTD.**
  Church St., Stoke-on-Trent ST4 1BX, England, U.K.
  CEO: Paul Wood, Mng. Dir.
  Bus: *Mfr. china and porcelain.*

  Tel: 44-1782-744-011
  Fax: 44-1782-744-220
  www.spode.co.uk

  NAICS: 327112, 327212, 332211, 332214, 334518, 339912, 339999, 423220

  > **ROYAL CHINA & PORCELAIN COMPANIES**
  > 1265 Glen Ave., Moorestown, New Jersey 08057-0912
  > CEO: Peter Cash, Pres.
  > Bus: *Mfr./sales china and porcelain.*
  >
  > Tel: (856) 866-2900
  > Fax: (856) 234-7984
  >
  > %FO: 100
  > Emp: 50

- **ROYALBLUE GROUP PLC**
  Dukes Court, Duke St., Woking, Surrey GU21 5BH, England, U.K.
  CEO: Chris J. F. Aspinwall, CEO
  Bus: *Mfr. global financial trading software.*

  Tel: 44-1483-206-300
  Fax: 44-1483-206-301
  www.royalblue.com

  Rev: $100
  Emp: 465

  NAICS: 511210, 518210, 541511, 541519

  > **ROYALBLUE GROUP, INC.**
  > 17 State St., 42/F, New York, New York 10004
  > CEO: Robert Thompson, Principal
  > Bus: *Mfr./sales global financial trading software.*
  >
  > Tel: (212) 269-9000
  > Fax: (212) 785-4327
  >
  > %FO: 100
  > Emp: 150

- **RPC GROUP PLC**
Lakeside House, Higham Ferrers, Northamptonshire NN10 8RP, England, U.K.
CEO: Ron J. E. Marsh, CEO & Mng. Dir.   Tel: 44-1933-410-064   Rev: $785
Bus: *Mfr. rigid plastic packaging, including printing and*   Fax: 44-1933-410-083   Emp: 5,535
labeling for related products.   www.rpc-group.com
NAICS: 322222, 326112, 326160, 326199
    RPC BRAMLAGE-WIKO USA, INC.
    415 Eagleview Blvd., Ste. 108, Exton, Pennsylvania 19341
    CEO: Ekhard Mugge, Pres.   Tel: (610) 321-0300   %FO: 75
    Bus: *Mfr. rigid plastic packaging.*   Fax: (610) 321-0394   Emp: 6

- **RWE THAMES WATER**
Clearwater Court, Vastern Rd., Reading RG1 8DB, England, U.K.
CEO: William J. Alexander, CEO   Tel: 44-118-373-8000   Rev: $5,545
Bus: *Supplies drinking water and environmental and*   Fax: 44-118-373-8916   Emp: 16,051
waste management products.   www.rwethameswater.com
NAICS: 221310, 221320, 237110, 237120, 237130, 541330, 541618, 541690, 561210
    AMERICAN WATER WORKS COMPANY, INC.
    1025 Laurel Oak Rd., Voorhees, New Jersey 08043
    CEO: Jeremy Pelczer, Pres. & CEO   Tel: (856) 346-8200   %FO: 100
    Bus: *Water utilities; related products and*   Fax: (856) 346-8360   Emp: 8,000
    services.
    PENNSYLVANIA-AMERICAN WATER CO.
    800 Hershey Park, Hershey, Pennsylvania 17033
    CEO: Daniel Warnock, Pres.   Tel: (717) 533-5000   %FO: 100
    Bus: *Water utilities.*   Fax: (717) 531-3251

- **M&C SAATCHI plc**
36 Golden Square, London W1F 9EE, England, U.K.
CEO: Moray MacLennan, Chmn.   Tel: 44-20-7543-4500   Rev: $415
Bus: *International advertising agency.*   Fax: 44-20-7543-4501   Emp: 790
www.mcsaatchi.com
NAICS: 541810
    SAATCHI LOS ANGELES __ M&C
    2032 Broadway, Santa Monica, California 90404
    CEO: Huw Griffith   Tel: (310) 401-6070   %FO: 100
    Bus: *International advertising agency.*   Fax: (310) 264-1910

    SAATCHI NEW YORK __ M&C
    95 Fifth Ave., 5/F, New York, New York 10003
    CEO: Robert Fletcher   Tel: (212) 655-8000   %FO: 100
    Bus: *International advertising agency.*   Fax: (212) 655-4301

- **SABMILLER PLC**
1 Stanhope Gate, London W1K 1AF, England, U.K.
CEO: Ernest A. Mackay, CEO   Tel: 44-20-7659-0100   Rev: $11,366
Bus: *Distributes and brews beer and bottled sodas for*   Fax: 44-20-7659-0111   Emp: 39,571
domestic use. (36% JV of Altria Group USA)   www.sabmiller.com
NAICS: 311411, 312111, 312112, 312120

JACOB LEINENKUGEL BREWING CO., INC.
1 Jefferson Ave., Chippewa Falls, Wisconsin 54729
CEO: Thomas J. Leinenkugel, Pres.   Tel: (715) 723-5558
Bus: *Breweries.*   Fax: (715) 723-7158

MILLER BREWING COMPANY
2020 Main St., Ste. 850, Irvine, California 92614
CEO: Alicia Berhow, Mgr.   Tel: (949) 608-6200   %FO: 100
Bus: *Mfr. of beer.*   Fax: Emp: 34

MILLER BREWING COMPANY
7001 South Fwy., Fort Worth, Texas 76134
CEO: James Jackson, Mgr.   Tel: (817) 551-3300   %FO: 100
Bus: *Brewery.*   Fax: Emp: 800

MILLER BREWING COMPANY
863 East Meadow Rd., Eden, North Carolina 27288
CEO: Patricia Henry, Mgr.   Tel: (336) 627-2100   %FO: 100
Bus: *Breweries.*   Fax: Emp: 750

MILLER BREWING COMPANY
3939 W. Highland Blvd., Milwaukee, Wisconsin 53201-2866
CEO: Norman J. Adami, Pres. & CEO   Tel: (414) 931-2000   %FO: 100
Bus: *Beer brewery.*   Fax: (414) 931-3735

MILLER BREWING COMPANY
2525 Wayne Madison Rd., Trenton, Ohio 45067
CEO: Dennis Puffer, Mgr.   Tel: (513) 896-9200   %FO: 100
Bus: *Breweries.*   Fax: Emp: 600

• **THE SAGE GROUP PLC**
North Park, Newcastle NE13 9AA, England, U.K.
CEO: Paul Walker, CEO   Tel: 44-191-294-3000   Rev: $1,237
Bus: *Mfr. PC accounting software.*   Fax: 44-191-294-0002
                                           www.sage.com
NAICS: 511210

ACCPAC INTERNATIONAL, INC.
6700 Koll Center Pkwy., Pleasanton, California 94566
CEO: Craig R. Downing, Gen. Mgr.   Tel: (925) 461-2625   %FO: 100
Bus: *Enterprise resource planning software.* Fax: (925) 461-5806

NONPROFIT SOLUTIONS, INC.
1821 University Ave. West, Ste. S256, St. Paul, Minnesota 55104
CEO: Jim Thalhuber, CEO   Tel: (651) 917-6240   %FO: 100
Bus: *Outsourcing solutions.*   Fax: (651) 917-1835

SAGE SOFTWARE SMALL BUSINESS, INC.
1505 Pavilion Place, Norcross, Georgia 30093
CEO: Douglas G. Meyer, Pres.   Tel: (770) 724-4000   %FO: 100
Bus: *Accounting & finance software.*   Fax: (770) 806-5166

SAGE SOFTWARE, INC.
56 Technology Dr., Irvine, California 92618
CEO: Ronald F. Verni, CEO
Bus: *Mfr./sales PC accounting software.*
Tel: (949) 753-1222
Fax: (949) 753-0374
%FO: 100

TIMBERLINE SOFTWARE CORP.
15195 NW Greenbrier Pkwy., Beaverton, Oregon 97006
CEO: Curtis L. Peltz, Pres. & Gen. Mgr.
Bus: *Accounting & finance software.*
Tel: (503) 690-6775
Fax: (503) 439-5700
%FO: 100

● **J. SAINSBURY PLC**
33 Holborn, London EC1N 2HT, England, U.K.
CEO: Justin King, CEO
Bus: *Engaged in retail food distribution, pig production, home improvement centers.*
NAICS: 445110, 445120
Tel: 44-207-695-6000
Fax: 44-207-695-7610
www.j-sainsbury.co.uk
Rev: $31,296
Emp: 180,200

SAINSBURY MARKET
12200 Wilshire Blvd., Los Angeles, California 90025
CEO: Bijan Moghaddam, Prtn.
Bus: *Supermarket*
Tel: (310) 826-4388
Fax:
%FO: 100
Emp: 3

● **SAPIENS INTERNATIONAL CORPORATION NV**
Harman House, Uxbridge, London UB8 1QQ, England, U.K.
CEO: Yitzhak Sharir, Pres. & CEO
Bus: *Mfr. software.*
NAICS: 511210, 541511, 541512, 541519, 611420
Tel: 44-1895-464-000
Fax: 44-1895-463-098
www.sapiens.com
Rev: $48
Emp: 464

SAPIENS AMERICAS
4000 Centre Green Way, Ste. 100, Cary, North Carolina 27513
CEO: Steven Bessellieu, Pres.
Bus: *Mfr./sales of software.*
Tel: (919) 405-1500
Fax: (919) 405-1700
%FO: 100
Emp: 60

● **SCAPA GROUP PLC**
Oakfield House, 93 Preston New Rd., Blackburn BB2 6AY, England, U.K.
CEO: Keith G. G. Hopkins, Chmn.
Bus: *Mfr. specialty products for the paper and printing industries.*
NAICS: 325211, 325520, 325992, 339113
Tel: 44-125-458-0123
Fax: 44-1254-517-64
www.scapa.com
Rev: $343
Emp: 1,708

SCAPA NORTH AMERICA
111 Vine St., Liverpool, New York 13088
CEO: Stuart Ganslaw, member
Bus: *Mfr. of plastic film.*
Tel: (315) 413-1111
Fax: (315) 413-1112
%FO: 100
Emp: 20

SCAPA NORTH AMERICA
746 Gotham Pkwy., Carlstadt, New Jersey 07072
CEO: Carmen Tirello, Mgr.
Bus: *Mfr. of pressure sensitive tapes.*
Tel: (201) 939-0565
Fax: (201) 939-0437
%FO: 100
Emp: 42

SCAPA NORTH AMERICA
540 North Oak St., Inglewood, California 90302
CEO: Stuart Ganslaw
Bus: *Mfr. of fabrics.*
Tel: (310) 419-0567
Fax: (310) 419-4150
%FO: 100

SCAPA NORTH AMERICA
111 Great Pond Dr., Windsor, Connecticut 06095
CEO: Ivan J. Fearnhead, Pres.
Bus: *Mfr. adhesive films and tapes.*
Tel: (860) 688-8000
Fax: (860) 688-7000
%FO: 100
Emp: 2,294

● **SCHRODERS PLC**
31 Gresham St., London EC2V 7QA, England, U.K.
CEO: Michael Dobson, CEO
Bus: *Asset management services.*
Tel: 44-20-7658-6000
Fax: 44-20-7658-6965
www.schroders.com
Rev: $994
Emp: 2,300

NAICS: 523991, 523999, 525990

SCHRODERS INVESTMENT MANAGEMENT INC.
601 Walnut St., Ste. L60-65, Philadelphia, Pennsylvania 19106
CEO: Patrick Vermeulen
Bus: *Asset management services.*
Tel: (215) 861-0997
Fax: (215) 861-0898
%FO: 100

SCHRODERS INVESTMENT MANAGEMENT INC.
875 Third Ave., 22/F, New York, New York 10022
CEO: Patrick Vermeulen
Bus: *Asset management services.*
Tel: (212) 641-3830
Fax: (212) 641-3985
%FO: 100

● **SCIENCE SYSTEMS PLC**
Methuen Park, Chippenham, Wiltshire SN14 0GB, England, U.K.
CEO: Mark Hampson, CEO
Bus: *Computer software and services.*
Tel: 44-1249-466466
Fax: 44-1249-466666
www.scisys.co.uk

NAICS: 541511, 541519

BANTEC INC.
2701 East Grauwyler Rd., Irvine, Texas 75061
CEO: Julie Brown
Bus: *Computer software and services.*
Tel: (972) 579-6000
Fax: (972) 579-6830

BEA SYSTEMS, INC.
2315 North First St., San Jose, California 95131
CEO: Alfred S. Chuang, Chmn. & Pres. & CEO
Bus: *Enterprise application integration software.*
Tel: (408) 570-8000
Fax: (408) 570-8901
Emp: 3,353

CODA FINANCIALS, INC.
15 Constitution Dr., Ste. 321, Bedford, New Hampshire 03110
CEO: Steve J. Pugh, CEO
Bus: *Financial accounting software.*
Tel: (603) 471-1700
Fax:
Emp: 25

CODA FINANCIALS, INC.
350 Indiana St., Ste. 601, Golden, Colorado 80401
CEO: Graham Steinsberg, CEO
Bus: *Accounting & finance software.*
Tel: (303) 216-9220
Fax: (303) 216-0321

HALEY SYSTEMS
2200 Georgetown Dr., Ste. 600, Sewickley, Pennsylvania 15143
CEO: Mark Juliano, CEO   Tel: (724) 934-7853
Bus: *Computer software development.*   Fax: (724) 934-7860   Emp: 14

ILOG INC.
1080 Linda Vista Ave., Mountain View, California 94043
CEO: Pierre Haren, Chmn.   Tel: (650) 567-8000
Bus: *Custom computer programming prepackaged* Fax: Emp: 586
    software services.

MAPINFO
1 Global View, Troy, New York 12180
CEO: Mark P. Cattini, Pres. & CEO   Tel: (518) 285-6000
Bus: *Engineering, Scientific & CAD/Cam Software.* Fax: (518) 285-6070   Emp: 800

ORACLE CORP.
500 Oracle Pkwy., Redwood Shores, California 94065
CEO: Lawrence J. Ellison, CEO   Tel: (650) 506-7000
Bus: *Database & file management software.*   Fax: (650) 506-7200   Emp: 2,886

● **SCOTT WILSON KIRKPATRICK & CO. LTD.**
Scott House, Basing View, Basingstoke RG21 4JG, England, U.K.
CEO: Geoff French, Chmn.   Tel: 44-125-646-1161   Rev: $154
Bus: *Provides a range of integrated planning,*   Fax: 44-125-646-0582   Emp: 3,500
    management and environmental services.   www.scottwilson.com
NAICS: 237310, 541330

    SCOTT WILSON
    49 South Main St., Yardley, Pennsylvania 19067
    CEO: Kaz Tabrizi   Tel: (215) 321-5855   %FO: 100
    Bus: *Provides a range of integrated planning,*   Fax:
        management and environmental services.

    SCOTT WILSON
    412 Wall St., Princeton, New Jersey 08540
    CEO: Kaz Tabrizi   Tel: (609) 430-9888   %FO: 100
    Bus: *Provides a range of integrated planning,*   Fax: (609) 430-9777
        management and environmental services.

● **SDL PLC**
Globe House, Clivemont Rd., Maidenhead SL6 7DY, England, U.K.
CEO: Mark J.Lancaster, Chmn. & CEO   Tel: 44-162-841-0100   Rev: $121
Bus: *Mfr. translation software and services.*   Fax: 44-162-841-0505   Emp: 1,270
     www.sdlintl.com
NAICS: 511210, 516110, 518112, 518210, 541511, 541512, 541519, 541690, 541930, 541990, 611420

    SDL USA INC.
    5994 w. Las Positas Blvd., Ste.115, Pleasanton, California 94588
    CEO: Mark Lancaster, Pres.   Tel: (877) 735-5106
    Bus: *Mfr./sales translation software.*   Fax: (650) 635-0360

SDL USA INC.
144 Railroad Ave., Ste. 222, Edmonds, Washington 98020
CEO: Mark Lancaster, CEO
Bus: *Mfr./sales translation software.*
Tel: (877) 735-5106
Fax: (425) 775-4235

SDL USA INC.
1704 Dorset Dr., Tarrytown, New York 10591
CEO: Mark Lancaster, Pres.
Bus: *Mfr./sales translation software.*
Tel: (877) 735-5106
Fax: (914) 366-4289

SDL USA INC.
600 North Bell Ave., Ste. 2701, Carnegie, Pennsylvania 15106
CEO: Mark Lancaster, Pres.
Bus: *Mfr./sales translation software.*
Tel: (877) 735-5106
Fax:
%FO: 100

SDL USA INC.
725 18th Ave., Salt Lake City, Utah 84103
CEO: Mark Lancaster, Pres.
Bus: *Mfr./sales translation software.*
Tel: (877) 735-5106
Fax: (801) 574-7733
%FO: 100

SDL USA INC.
5757 Central Ave., Ste. G, Boulder, Colorado 80301
CEO: Derek Patrick, Mgr.
Bus: *Mfr./sales translation software.*
Tel: (303) 440-0909
Fax: (303) 440-6369
%FO: 100
Emp: 24

SDL USA INC.
Granite Houe, 400 Amherst St., Ste. 402, Nashua, New Hampshire 03063
CEO: Mark Lancaster, Pres.
Bus: *Mfr./sales translation software.*
Tel: (603) 589-3900
Fax: (603) 589-3901
%FO: 100

SDL USA INC.
170 N. State St., Ste. A, Caro, Michigan 48732
CEO: Mark Lancaster, Pres.
Bus: *Mfr./sales translation software.*
Tel: (877) 735-5106
Fax: (989) 673-0667
%FO: 100

SDL USA INC.
1 N. La Salle, Ste. 1855, Chicago, Illinois 60602
CEO: Cristina Lancaster, Pres.
Bus: *Mfr./sales translation software.*
Tel: (877) 735-5106
Fax: (312) 658-0259
%FO: 100

SDL USA INC.
5700 Granite Pkwy., Ste. 410, Plano, Texas 75024
CEO: Mark Lancaster, Pres.
Bus: *Mfr./sales translation software.*
Tel: (214) 387-8500
Fax: (214) 387-9120
%FO: 100

SDL USA INC.
150 E. 9th At., Ste. 201, Durango, Colorado 81301
CEO: Mark Lancaster, Pres.
Bus: *Mfr./sales translation software.*
Tel: (877) 735-5106
Fax: (970) 247-2702
%FO: 100

TRADOS INC.
1292 Hammerwood Ave., Sunnyvale, California 94089
CEO: Joseph S. Campbell, Pres. & CEO
Bus: *Mfr. of language translation software.& consulting, support, training, & maintenance*
Tel: (408) 743-3500
Fax: (408) 743-3600

- **SENIOR PLC**
  Senior House, 59/61 High St., Rickmansworth, Hertfordshire WD3 1RH, England, U.K.
  CEO: Graham R. Menzies, CEO   Tel: 44-1923-775-547   Rev: $631
  Bus: *Aerospace and automotive components*   Fax: 44-1923-896-027   Emp: 5,149
       manufacture.   www.seniorplc.com
  NAICS: 332911, 332919, 332996, 336312, 336399, 336412, 336413, 336415

  SENIOR AUTOMOTIVE
  300 East Devon Ave., Bartlett, Illinois 60103
  CEO: Scott Swich, Mgr.   Tel: (630) 837-1811   %FO: 100
  Bus: *Mfr. exhaust products for automobiles.*   Fax: (630) 837-1847

  SENIOR AEROSPACE COMPOSITES
  2700 South Custer, Wichita, Kansas 67217
  CEO: Roy Best, CEO   Tel: (316) 942-3208   %FO: 100
  Bus: *Mfr. composites.*   Fax: (316) 942-5044

  SENIOR AEROSPACE JET PRODUCTS
  9106 Balboa Ave., San Diego, California 92123
  CEO: Ron Blair, Pres.   Tel: (858) 278-8400
  Bus: *Mfr. of complex machined rings & ring*   Fax: (858) 272-8768   Emp: 261
       components.

  SENIOR AEROSPACE KETEMA
  790 Greenfield Dr., El Cajon, California 92021
  CEO: Tom Brooks, Exec. Dir.   Tel: (619) 442-3451
  Bus: *Mfr. of unique fabrications using exotic*   Fax: (619) 441-5473
       materials for aircrafts.

  SENIOR AEROSPACE METAL BELLOWS
  1075 Providence Hwy., Sharon, Massachusetts 02067
  CEO: Peter Fontecchio, Pres.   Tel: (781) 784-1400   %FO: 100
  Bus: *Mfr./sales aerospace and automotive*   Fax: (781) 784-1405
       components.

  SENIOR AEROSPACE SSP
  2980 N. San Fernando Blvd., Burbank, California 91504
  CEO: Laurie Flemming, VP & Gen. Mgr.   Tel: (818) 260-2900   %FO: 100
  Bus: *Mfr./sales aerospace and automotive*   Fax: (818) 845-4205
       components.

  SENIOR FLEXONICS PATHWAY
  2400 Longhorn Industrial Dr., New Braunfels, Texas 78130
  CEO: Greg Perkins, Exec. Dir.   Tel: (830) 629-8080   %FO: 100
  Bus: *Mfr./sales aerospace and automotive*   Fax: (830) 629-6899
       components.

- **SERCO GROUP PLC**
  16 Bartley Wood Business Park, Bartley Way, Hook, Hampshire RG27 9UY, England, U.K.
  CEO: Christopher Rajendran Hyman, CEO   Tel: 44-1256-745900   Rev: $2,661
  Bus: *Provides facilities management and systems*   Fax: 44-1256-744111   Emp: 28,073
       engineering.   www.serco.com
  NAICS: 541511, 541512, 541519, 561210, 561790, 562112, 611710, 624310

SERCO GROUP
2650 Park Tower Dr., Ste. 800, Vienna, Virginia 22180
CEO: George Troendle, Pres. Tel: (571) 226-5000
Bus: *Computer design systems.* Fax: (703) 573-8215 Emp: 3,664

SERCO GROUP INC.
20 East Clementon Rd., Ste. 102, South Gibbsboro, New Jersey 08026
CEO: Brad King, CEO Tel: (856) 346-8800 %FO: 100
Bus: *Provides facilities management and systems* Fax: (856) 346-8463 Emp: 4,564
      engineering.

● SERVICE POWER TECHNOLOGIES PLC
Petersgate House, St. Petersgate Stockport, Manchester SK1 1HE, England, U.K.
CEO: Barry Welck, Chmn. Tel: 44-161-476-2277 Rev: $8
Bus: *Develops and sells artificial intelligence-based* Fax: 44-161-480-8088 Emp: 77
      software for the scheduling of field service www.servicepower.com
      personnel.
NAICS: 511210

SERVICE POWER TECHNOLOGIES
175 Admiral Cochrane Dr., Ste. 203, Annapolis, Maryland 21401
CEO: Paul Oliver, VP Operations Tel: (410) 571-6333 %FO: 100
Bus: *Mfr./sales computer software.* Fax: (410) 571-9330 Emp: 58

● SEVEN WORLDWIDE, INC.
St. Mark's House,, Shepherdess Walk, London N1 7LH, England, U.K.
CEO: Brian McGrath, Pres. Tel: 44-207-861-7777
Bus: *Visual communications projects, including graphic* Fax: 44-207-871-7702 Emp: 500
      imaging. www.sevenww.co.uk
NAICS: 323110, 323115, 323117, 323121, 323122, 541430, 541613, 541860, 541922

AMBROSI
200 W. Jackson Blvd., Ste. 800, Chicago, Illinois 60606
CEO: Dan Morrissey, Pres. Tel: (312) 666-9200 %FO: 100
Bus: *Advertising & marketing services.* Fax: (312) 360-0977 Emp: 450

SEVEN WORLDWIDE
450 W. 33rd St., New York, New York 10001
CEO: John R. Harris, CEO Tel: (212) 716-6600 %FO: 100
Bus: *Commercial printing.* Fax: (212) 716-6776

SEVEN WORLDWIDE, INC.
225 West Superior St., Chicago, Illinois 60610
CEO: Mark Rutter, Pres. Tel: (312) 943-0400 %FO: 100
Bus: *Engaged in promotional, packaging,* Fax: (312) 943-6186 Emp: 700
      advertising and imaging.

● SEVERN TRENT PLC
2297 Coventry Rd., Birmingham B26 3PU, England, U.K.
CEO: Colin Matthews, CEO Tel: 44-121-722-4000 Rev: $3,679
Bus: *Provides water and waste management services.* Fax: 44-121-722-4800 Emp: 15,793
      www.severn-trent.com
NAICS: 221310, 221320, 237110, 237120, 237130, 237210, 517110, 531120, 541330, 541519, 541618, 541620, 541690, 561210, 562111, 562212, 562213,
         562219, 562920, 562998

AEROTECH LABORATORIES
1501 West Knudsen Dr., Phoenix, Arizona 85027
CEO: Rachel Brydon Jannetta, CEO
Bus: *Environmental testing services.*
Tel: (623) 780-4800
Fax: (623) 780-7695
%FO: 100
Emp: 200

SEVERN TRENT LABORATORIES
10 Hazelwood Dr., Buffalo, New York 14228
CEO: Rachel Brydon Jannetta, Pres. & CEO
Bus: *Environmental services & equipment*
Tel: (716) 691-2600
Fax: (716) 691-2600

SEVERN TRENT SERVICES
580 Virginia Dr., Ste. 300, Fort Washington, Pennsylvania 19034
CEO: Leonard F. Graziano, Pres. & CEO
Bus: *Environmental services & equipment*
Tel: (215) 646-9201
Fax: (215) 283-6138
%FO: 100
Emp: 4,500

SEVERN TRENT SYSTEMS, INC.
16337 Park Row, Park 10, Houston, Texas 77084
CEO: Malcolm Shakespeare, Pres.
Bus: *Provides water and waste management services.*
Tel: (281) 578-4200
Fax: (281) 398-3550
%FO: 100
Emp: 80

● **SHIRE PHARMACEUTICALS GROUP PLC**
Hampshire International Business Park, Chineham, Basingstoke, Hampshire RG24 8EP, England, U.K.
CEO: Matthew W. Emmens, CEO
Bus: *Engaged in specialty pharmaceuticals.*
Tel: 44-1256-894-000
Fax: 44-1256-894-708
www.shire.com
Rev: $1,363
Emp: 1,833

NAICS: 325411, 325412

SHIRE GENETIC DISEASE UNIT
700 Main St., Cambridge, Massachusetts 02139
CEO: David Pendergast, VP
Bus: *Genetic disease.*
Tel: (617) 349-0200
Fax: (617) 613-4004

SHIRE LABORATORIES INC.
1550 East Guide Dr., Rockville, Maryland 20850
CEO: Jack Khattar, Pres. & CEO
Bus: *Engaged in drug delivery technologies.*
Tel: (301) 838-2500
Fax: (301) 838-2501
%FO: 100
Emp: 125

SHIRE PHARMACEUTICALS
725 Chesterbrook Blvd., Wayne, Pennsylvania 19087
CEO: Matthew Emmens, CEO
Bus: *Sale of drugs/sundries.*
Tel: (484) 595-8800
Fax: (484) 595-8200

SHIRE US MANUFACTURING
11200 Gundry Lane, Owings Mills, Maryland 21117
CEO: John Lee, VP
Bus: *Process bulk pharmaceutical powders.*
Tel: (410) 413-1000
Fax: (410) 413-2000
Emp: 100

● **SHL GROUP PLC**
The Pavillion, 1 Atwell Place, Thames Ditton, Surrey KT7 0NE, England, U.K.
CEO: John E. G. Bateson, CEO
Bus: *Human resources consulting services.*
Tel: 44-20-8355-8000
Fax: 44-20-8355-7000
www.shl.com
Rev: $127
Emp: 750

NAICS: 541612

SHL AMERICAS INC.
2555 55th St., Suite 201D, Boulder, Colorado 80301
CEO: Laurence Karsh
Bus: *Human resources services.*
Tel: (303) 442-5607
Fax: (303) 442-1184
%FO: 100

SHL AMERICAS INC.
200 South Wacker Dr., Ste. 1350, Chicago, Illinois 60606
CEO: Laurence Karsh
Bus: *Human resources services.*
Tel: (312) 655-8420
Fax: (312) 655-8421
%FO: 100

SHL AMERICAS INC.
100 Canal Pointe Boulevard Suite 110, Princeton, New Jersey 08540
CEO: Laurence Karsh
Bus: *Human resources services.*
Tel: (609) 520-1700
Fax: (609) 520-1774
%FO: 100

● **SIBELIUS SOFTWARE LTD.**
The Old Toy Factory, 20-22 City North, Fonthill Road, London N4 3HF, England, U.K.
CEO: Jeremy Silver, CEO
Bus: *Music software manufacture.*
Tel: 44-20-7561-7999
Fax: 44-20-7561-7888
www.sibelius.com

NAICS: 511210, 512230

SIBELIUS SOFTWARE USA INC.
1407 Oakland Blvd., Ste. 103, Walnut Creek, California 94546
CEO: Bill Reilly
Bus: *Music software manufacture and sales.*
Tel: (925) 280-0600
Fax: (925) 280-0008
%FO: 100

● **SIG PLC**
Hillsborough Works, Langsett Rd., Sheffield S6 2LW, England, U.K.
CEO: David Williams, CEO
Bus: *Mfr. and distribution of construction materials, dry lining, roofing, fire protection and commercial interior products.*
Tel: 44-114-285-6300
Fax: 44-114-285-6385
www.sigplc.co.uk
Rev: $2,637
Emp: 6,871

NAICS: 423390

BRANTON INDUSTRIES, INC
1101 Edwards Ave., Jefferson, Louisiana 70123
CEO: Jerry Malter, Mgr.
Bus: *Mfr./distribution of thermal and acoustical insulation*
Tel: (504) 733-7770
Fax: (504) 734-7818
%FO: 100

BRANTON INDUSTRIES, INC
12360 Leisure Rd., Baton Rouge, Louisiana 70807
CEO: Tresie Stiles, Mgr.
Bus: *Mfr./distribution of thermal and acoustical insulation*
Tel: (225) 775-1950
Fax: (725) 778-6700
%FO: 100
Emp: 11

BRANTON INDUSTRIES, INC
2405 Bell St., PO Box 3934, Shreveport, Louisiana 71103
CEO: John McCall, Mgr.
Bus: *Mfr./distribution of thermal and acoustical insulation*
Tel: (318) 424-2888
Fax: (318) 221-4239
%FO: 100

England, U.K.

BRANTON INDUSTRIES, INC
2735 Bailey Ave., Jacksonville, Mississippi 39213
CEO: Tom McKay, Mgr.   Tel: (601) 368-3000   %FO: 100
Bus: *Distribution of insulation.*   Fax: (301) 368-3002

BWI DISTRIBUTION, INC.
3805 Castlewood Rd., Richmond, Virginia 23234
CEO: Melody Driscoll, Mgr.   Tel: (804) 743-9091   %FO: 100
Bus: *Distribution of insulation.*   Fax: (804) 743-9097

BWI DISTRIBUTION, INC.
3020A Thurston Ave., Greensboro, North Carolina 27406
CEO: Frank Haynes, Mgr.   Tel: (336) 273-6245   %FO: 100
Bus: *Distribution of insulation.*   Fax: (336) 273-7604

BWI DISTRIBUTION, INC.
10942 Beaver Dam Rd., Hunt Valley, Maryland 21030
CEO: Barry Allen   Tel: (410) 785-4848   %FO: 100
Bus: *Distribution of insulation.*   Fax: (410) 785-4848

BWI DISTRIBUTION, INC.
6301-1 Gravel Ave., Alexandria, Virginia 22310
CEO: Judy Stephens   Tel: (703) 922-6530   %FO: 100
Bus: *Distribution of insulation.*   Fax: (703) 971-5917

BWI DISTRIBUTION, INC.
3805 Castlewood Rd., Richmond, Virginia 23234
CEO: Paget Sergeson   Tel: (804) 743-9091   %FO: 100
Bus: *Distribution of insulation.*   Fax: (804) 743-9091

BWI DISTRIBUTION, INC.
95 Sunbelt Blvd., Ste. C, Columbia, South Carolina 29203
CEO: Grady Sharpe   Tel: (803) 714-7151   %FO: 100
Bus: *Distribution of insulation.*   Fax: (803) 714-7152

BWI DISTRIBUTION, INC.
603 Howmet Dr., Hampton, Virginia 23661
CEO: Judy Stephens   Tel: (757) 826-3570   %FO: 100
Bus: *Distribution of insulation.*   Fax: (757) 826-4477

BWI DISTRIBUTION, INC.
1501 Piedmont Hwy., Piedmont, South Carolina 29673
CEO: T. D. Norman   Tel: (864) 299-1770   %FO: 100
Bus: *Distribution of insulation.*   Fax: (864) 299-5211

BWI DISTRIBUTION, INC.
10942 Beaver Dam Rd., Hunt Valley, Maryland 21030
CEO: Dana Vlk   Tel: (410) 785-4848   %FO: 100
Bus: *Distribution of insulation.*   Fax: (410) 785-4848

DISTRIBUTION INTERNATIONAL
202 Valley Forge, Port Arthur, Texas 77640
CEO: Kenny Commeaux, Mgr.   Tel: (409) 962-5684   %FO: 100
Bus: *Distribution of insulating construction* Fax: (409) 962-5684
     material.

DISTRIBUTION INTERNATIONAL
9000 Railroad Dr., Houston, Texas 77078
CEO: Frank Farese, Pres.
Bus: *Distribution of insulating construction material.*
Tel: (713) 428-3900
Fax: (713) 428-3900
%FO: 100

DISTRIBUTION INTERNATIONAL
138 Corporate Way, Pelham, Alabama 35124
CEO: David Hayes, Mgr.
Bus: *Distribution of insulating construction material.*
Tel: (205) 261-9810
Fax: (205) 621-9867
%FO: 100

DISTRIBUTION INTERNATIONAL
1217 North Tancahua, Corpus Christi, Texas 78469
CEO: Mike Golihar, Mgr.
Bus: *Distribution of insulating construction material.*
Tel: (361) 883-3651
Fax: (361) 883-3651
%FO: 100

DISTRIBUTION INTERNATIONAL
1250 Armour Ave., Mobile, Alabama 36617
CEO: Chad Wade, Mgr.
Bus: *Distribution of insulating construction material.*
Tel: (251) 471-4655
Fax: (251) 471-4655
%FO: 100

DISTRIBUTION INTERNATIONAL
1000 Riverbend, Ste. B, St. Rose, Louisiana 70087
CEO: Kevin Muller, Mgr.
Bus: *Distribution of insulating construction material.*
Tel: (504) 468-1800
Fax: (504) 468-1800
%FO: 100

KNIGHT SUPPLY
9000 Railwood Dr., Houston, Texas 77078
CEO: Fred Knight, Pres.
Bus: *Distribution of insulation.*
Tel: (713) 428-3800
Fax: (713) 428-3888
%FO: 100
Emp: 270

MIT INTERNATIONAL
9000 Railwood Dr., Houston, Texas 77078
CEO: Frank Farese, Pres.
Bus: *Distribute thermal & acoustical insulation*
Tel: (713) 675-0075
Fax: (713) 675-0075
%FO: 100

SIG ISF
4810 East Napoleon St., Sulphur, Louisiana 70663
CEO: Kenny Comeaux, Mgr.
Bus: *Distribution of insulating construction material*
Tel: (337) 625-4567
Fax: (337) 625-4567
%FO: 100

SIG SOUTHWEST, INC.
9000 Railwood Dr., Houston, Texas 77078
CEO: Frank Farese
Bus: *Mfr. of industrial products.*
Tel: (713) 428-3900
Fax: (713) 428-3999
%FO: 100
Emp: 270

WESTFLEX INDUSTRIAL
325 West 30th St., National City, California 91950
CEO: Dixon LeGros, Pres.
Bus: *Distribution of insulation.*
Tel: (619) 474-7400
Fax: (619) 474-7444
%FO: 100
Emp: 26

- **SIGNET GROUP PLC**
  Zenith House, The Hyde, London NW9 6EW, England, U.K.
  CEO: James McAdam, Chmn.   Tel: 44-870-909-0301   Rev: $3,040
  Bus: *Specialty jewelry retailer.*   Fax: 44-208-242-8590   Emp: 15,145
                                          www.signetgroupplc.com

  NAICS: 448310, 453220
  STERLING JEWELERS INC.
  375 Ghent Rd., Akron, Ohio 44333
  CEO: Terry Burman, Chmn. & CEO   Tel: (330) 668-5000   %FO: 100
  Bus: *Sale of jewelry & watches.*   Fax: (330) 668-5052   Emp: 9,900

- **SIMMONS & SIMMONS**
  City Point, 1 Ropemaker St., London EC2Y 9SS, England, U.K.
  CEO: Janet Gaymer, Sr. Mgr.   Tel: 44-207-628-2020   Rev: $374
  Bus: *Full service, international law firm.*   Fax: 44-207-628-2070   Emp: 800
                                          www.simmons-simmons.com

  NAICS: 541110
  SIMMONS & SIMMONS
  570 Lexington Ave., 28/F, New York, New York 10022
  CEO: Andrew Wingfield, Mng. Prtn.   Tel: (212) 688-6620   %FO: 100
  Bus: *Full service, international law firm.*   Fax: (212) 688-3237

- **SIRIUS FINANCIAL SOLUTIONS PLC**
  2500 The Crescent, Birmingham Business Park, Solihull, West Midlands B37 7YE, England, U.K.
  CEO: Stephen John Varrall, CEO   Tel: 44-121-779-8400   Rev: $42
  Bus: *Mfr. software for insurance companies.*   Fax: 44-121-779-8401   Emp: 268
                                          www.siriusgroup.co.uk

  NAICS: 511210
  SIRIUS FINANCIAL SYSTEMS INC.
  6300 S. Syracuse Way, Centennial, Colorado 80111
  CEO: Alaric Errington   Tel: (303) 209-5900   %FO: 100
  Bus: *Mfr. software.*   Fax: (303) 209-5901

- **SKYEPHARMA PLC**
  105 Piccadilly, London W1J 7NJ, England, U.K.
  CEO: Michael Ashton, CEO   Tel: 44-207-491-1777   Rev: $95
  Bus: *Pharmaceuticals manufacture.*   Fax: 44-207-491-3338   Emp: 466
                                          www.skyepharma.com

  NAICS: 325411, 325412
  SKYEPHARMA INC.
  10 East 63rd St., New York, New York 10021
  CEO: Sandra Houghton   Tel: (212) 753-5780   %FO: 100
  Bus: *Noncommercial research organizations*   Fax: (212) 759-3928

  SKYEPHARMA INC.
  10450 Science Center Dr., San Diego, California 92121
  CEO: Steven Thornton, CEO   Tel: (858) 625-2424   %FO: 100
  Bus: *Pharmaceuticals.*   Fax: (858) 625-2439

- **SLAUGHTER AND MAY**
One Bunhill Row, London EC1Y 8YY, England, U.K.
CEO: Tim Clark
Bus: *International law firm.*

Tel: 44-207-600-1200
Fax: 44-207-090-5000
www.slaughterandmay.com

NAICS: 541110

    SLAUGHTER AND MAY
    1270 Ave. of the Americas, New York, New York 10020
    CEO: Tim Pallister, Mgr.
    Bus: *International law firm.*

    Tel: (212) 632-4800
    Fax: (212) 632-4840

    %FO: 100
    Emp: 7

- **SLOUGH ESTATES PLC**
234 Bath Rd., Slough SL1 4EE, England, U.K.
CEO: Ian Coull, CEO
Bus: *Owns and manages commercial and retail properties.*

Tel: 44-1753-537-171
Fax: 44-1753-820-585
www.sloughestates.com

Rev: $609
Emp: 559

NAICS: 236210, 236220, 237210, 531120, 531190, 531312, 531390

    SLOUGH ESTATES USA INC.
    444 N. Michigan Ave., Ste. 323, Chicago, Illinois 60611
    CEO: Marshall D. Lees, Pres.
    Bus: *Management of commercial, industrial and properties.*

    Tel: (312) 755-0700
    Fax: (312) 755-0717

    %FO: 100
    Emp: 66

    TIPPERARY CORP.
    633 17th., Ste. 1550, Denver, Colorado 80202
    CEO: David L. Bradshaw, Chmn. & Pres. & CEO
    Bus: *Oil & gas exploration & production.*

    Tel: (303) 293-9379
    Fax: (303) 292-3428

    %FO: 54
    Emp: 8

- **SMITH & NEPHEW, INC.**
15 Adam St., London WC2N 6LA, England, U.K.
CEO: Chris J. O'Donnell, CEO
Bus: *Develop/mfr./marketing healthcare products; tissue repair and medical devices.*

Tel: 44-207-401-7646
Fax: 44-207-930-3353
www.smith-nephew.com

Rev: $2,394
Emp: 7,866

NAICS: 334510, 339111, 339112, 339113

    SMITH & NEPHEW INC.
    1450 Brooks Rd., Memphis, Tennessee 38116
    CEO: Larry Papasan, Chmn.
    Bus: *Mfr./sale surgical & medical products.*

    Tel: (901) 396-2121
    Fax: (901) 348-6207

    %FO: 100
    Emp: 1,396

    SMITH & NEPHEW INC..
    11775 Starkey Rd., PO Box 1970, Largo, Florida 33773
    CEO: Rodney Skaggs, Pres.
    Bus: *Mfr. surgical appliances & supplies.*

    Tel: (813) 392-1261
    Fax: (813) 299-3498

    %FO: 100
    Emp: 200

    SMITH & NEPHEW INC..
    150 Minuteman Rd., Andover, Massachusetts 01810
    CEO: Jim Taylor, Pres.
    Bus: *Mfr. of surgical & medical instruments.*

    Tel: (978) 749-1000
    Fax: (978) 749-1599

    %FO: 100
    Emp: 400

England, U.K.

● **D. S. SMITH PLC**
4-16 Artillery Row, London SW1P 1RZ, England, U.K.
CEO: Anthony D. Thorne, CEO
Bus: *Mfr. corrugated packaging and paper products.*

Tel: 44-207-932-5000
Fax: 44-207-932-5003
www.dssmith.uk.com

Rev: $2,640
Emp: 10,936

NAICS: 322211

DS SMITH PLASTICS
405 N. 75th Ave., Phoenix, Arizona 85043
CEO: Don Stidham
Bus: *Hi-tech packaging manufacturer.*

Tel: (623) 936-8440
Fax: (623) 936-5167

%FO: 100

DS SMITH WORLDWIDE DISPENSERS INC.
c/o Hedwin Corporation, 1600 Roland Heights Ave., Baltimore, Maryland 21211
CEO: Guy S. Shipley
Bus: *Mfr. injection-moulded plastic taps and
dispensing fitments.*

Tel: (410) 467-8209
Fax: (410) 467-1761

%FO: 100

DS SMITH WORLDWIDE DISPENSERS INC.
78 Second Ave. South, Lester Prairie, Minnesota 55354
CEO: Jerre Kachmar
Bus: *Mfr. injection-moulded plastic taps and
dispensing fitments.*

Tel: (320) 395-2553
Fax: (320) 395-2656

%FO: 100

RAPAK INC.
29959 Ahern Ave., Union City, California 94587
CEO: Chris Rutter
Bus: *Mfr. corrugated packaging and paper
products.*

Tel: (510) 324-0170
Fax: (510) 324-0180

%FO: 100

RAPAK INC.
737 Oakridge Dr., Romeoville, Illinois 60446
CEO: John Schwan
Bus: *Mfr. corrugated packaging and paper
products.*

Tel: (815) 372-3600
Fax: (815) 372-3636

%FO: 100

● **WH SMITH PLC**
Nations House, 103 Wigmore St., London W1U 1WH, England, U.K.
CEO: Kate Swann, CEO
Bus: *Engaged in publication of magazines and books
and distribution at airports.*

Tel: 44-20-7409-3222
Fax: 44-20-7514-9633
www.whsmithplc.com

Rev: $5,089
Emp: 28,804

NAICS: 451211, 451212, 451220, 511120, 511130

WH SMITH INC.
3200 Windy Hill Rd. SE, Atlanta, Georgia 30339
CEO: Sean Anderson, CEO
Bus: *Owns and operates news and gift stores
and bookstores in hotels and major airports.*

Tel: (770) 952-0705
Fax: (770) 951-1352

%FO: 100
Emp: 150

● **SMITHS GROUP PLC**
765 Finchley Rd., London NW11 8DS, England, U.K.
CEO: Keith O. Butler-Wheelhouse, CEO
Bus: *Aerospace, medical, sealing solutions and
engineering products.*

Tel: 44-208-458-3232
Fax: 44-208-458-4380
www.smiths-group.com

Rev: $4,975
Emp: 26,729

NAICS: 332322, 332999, 336413

JOHN CRANE NORTH AMERICA
6400 West Oakton St., Morton Grove, Illinois 60053
CEO: Robert Wasson, Pres.   Tel: (847) 967-2400   %FO: 100
Bus: *Mfr. mechanical seals.*   Fax: (847) 967-3915

LEA INTERNATIONAL
6520 Harney Rd., Tampa, Florida 33610
CEO: Shawn Thompson, Pres.   Tel: (813) 621-1324
Bus: *Mfr. surge suppression equipment*   Fax: (813) 621-8980   Emp: 45

MEDEX HOLDINGS CORPORATION
2231 Rutherford Rd., Carlsbad, California 92008
CEO: Dominick A. Arena, Pres. & CEO   Tel: (760) 602-4400
Bus: *Mfr. critical healthcare devices*   Fax: (760) 929-0147   Emp: 2,080

SMITHS AEROSPACE
3290 Patterson Ave. SE, Grand Rapids, Michigan 49512
CEO: John Ferrie, Mng. Dir.   Tel: (616) 241-7000   %FO: 100
Bus: *Design, develop and manufacturing plant.*   Fax: (616) 241-7533

SMITHS DETECTION
73 N. Vinedo Ave., Pasadena, California 91107
CEO: Steven Sunshine, Pres. & CEO   Tel: (626) 744-1700
Bus: *Biotechnology research Equipment*   Fax: (626) 744-1777

TRANSTECTOR SYSTEMS, INC.
10701 Airport Dr., Hayden Lake, Idaho 83835
CEO: Shawn Thompson, Mng. Dir.   Tel: (208) 772-8515   %FO: 100
Bus: *Mfr. electronic surge devices.*   Fax: (208) 762-6133   Emp: 150

● **SONY ERICSSON MOBILE COMMUNICATIONS AB**
Sony Ericsson House, 202 Hammersmith Rd., London W6 7 DN, England, U.K.
CEO: Gunilla Nordstrom, CEO   Tel: 44-208-762-5800   Rev: $8,900
Bus: *Mobile communications. JV of Sony and*   Fax: 44-208-762-5878   Emp: 5,000
                                    www.sonyericsson.com
NAICS: 334210, 334220
   SONY ERICSSON MOBILE COMMUNICATIONS NORTH AMERICA
   7001 Development Dr., Research Triangle Park, North Carolina 27709
   CEO: Urban Gillstrom, Pres.   Tel: (919) 472-7527   %FO: JV
   Bus: *Wireless telephone handsets.*   Fax: (919) 472-7451

● **SOPHEON PLC**
Unit 18, The Surrey Technology Centre, 40 Occam Rd., Surrey Research Park, Guildford, Surrey GU2 7YG,
CEO: Andy Michuda, CEO   Tel: 44-1483-685-735   Rev: $8
Bus: *Develops and provides knowledge management*   Fax: 44-1483-685-740   Emp: 58
   software, solutions and services.   www.sopheon.com
NAICS: 511210
   SOPHEON CORPORATION
   2850 Metro Dr., Minneapolis, Minnesota 55425
   CEO: Andrew L. Michuda, CEO   Tel: (952) 851-7500
   Bus: *Develops and provides knowledge*   Fax: (952) 852-7599
      management software,

SOPHEON CORPORATION
3050 Metro Dr., Ste. 200, Bloomington, Minnesota 55425
CEO: Andrew L. Michuda, CEO   Tel: (952) 851-7500   %FO: 100
Bus: *Develops and provides knowledge*   Fax: (952) 851-7599   Emp: 60
     management software, solutions and

SOPHEON CORPORATION
6870 West 52nd Ave., Ste. 215, Arvada, Colorado 80002
CEO: Andrew L. Michuda, CEO   Tel: (303) 736-4900   %FO: 100
Bus: *Develops and provides knowledge*   Fax: (303) 736-4949
     management software, solutions and

● **SOPHOS PLC**
The Pentagon, Abingdon Science Park, Abingdon, Oxfordshire OX14 3YP, England, U.K.
CEO: Jan Hruska, Co-CEO   Tel: 44-1235-559-933   Rev: $124
Bus: *Anti-virus software developers.*   Fax: 44-1235-559-935   Emp: 852
     www.sophos.com
NAICS: 511210

   SOPHOS, INC.
   6 Kimball Lane, 4/F, Lynnfield, Massachusetts 01940
   CEO: Stephen Munford, Pres.   Tel: (781) 973-0110   %FO: 100
   Bus: *Anti-virus software developers*   Fax: (781) 245-8620   Emp: 143

● **SPARK NETWORKS PLC**
73 Abbey Rd., London NW8 0AE, England, U.K.
CEO: David. E. Siminoff, CEO   Tel: 44-20-7644-8989   Rev: $65
Bus: *International dating services.*   Fax: 44-20-7644-8990   Emp: 170
     www.spark.net
NAICS: 516110

   SPARK NETWORKS PLC
   8383 Wilshire Blvd., Suite 800, Beverly Hills, California 90211
   CEO: David Siminoff   Tel: (323) 836-3000   %FO: 100
   Bus: *On-line dating services.*   Fax: (323) 836-3333

   SPARK NETWORKS PLC
   20111 Stevens Creek Blvd., Cupertino, California 95014
   CEO: David Siminoff   Tel: (408) 446-1826
   Bus: *On-line dating services.*   Fax: (408) 446-1826

   SPARK NETWORKS PLC
   455 Market St., Suite 1480, San Francisco, California 94105
   CEO: Gail Laguna   Tel: (323) 836-3000
   Bus: *On-line dating services.*   Fax: (323) 836-3333

   SPARK NETWORKS PLC
   3210 N. Canyon Rd., Suite 200, Provo, Utah 84604
   CEO: Ben Peterson   Tel: (801) 377-6411
   Bus: *On-line dating services.*   Fax: (801) 377-6411

● **SPECTRIS PLC**
Station Rd., Egham, Surrey TW20 9NP, England, U.K.
CEO: John W. Poulter, Chmn. & CEO
Bus: *Holding company: mfr. filtration, measuring and sensing equipment, and military control systems.*
NAICS: 334513, 335314

Tel: 44-1784-470-470
Fax: 44-1784-470-848
www.spectris.com

Rev: $1,010
Emp: 5,696

ARCOM CONTROL SYSTEMS, INC.
7500 West 161st St., Stilwell, Kansas 66085
CEO: Arlin Nipper, Pres.
Bus: *Mfr. bus-based computer boards, communication gateways, remote terminal units and industrial controls.*

Tel: (913) 549-1000
Fax: (913) 549-1001

%FO: 100
Emp: 25

BETA LASERMIKE, INC.
8001 Technology Blvd., Dayton, Ohio 45424
CEO: Dan Doster, Pres.
Bus: *Mfr. diameter gauging and process measurement products.*

Tel: (937) 233-9935
Fax: (937) 233-7284

%FO: 100
Emp: 111

BTG INC.
2815 Colonnades Ct., Norcross, Georgia 30071
CEO: Michael Watts, Pres.
Bus: *Pulp and paper processing.*

Tel: (770) 209-6912
Fax: (770) 447-8440

%FO: 100
Emp: 81

FUSION UV SYSTEMS, INC.
910 Clopper Rd., Gaithersburg, Maryland 20878
CEO: David Harbourne, Pres.
Bus: *Ultraviolet light processing technology for curing photosensitive inks, coating & adhesives in mfr. processes.*

Tel: (301) 527-2660
Fax: (301) 527-2661

%FO: 100
Emp: 180

IRCON, INC.
7300 N. Natchez Ave., Niles, Illinois 60714
CEO: M. A. Fay, Pres.
Bus: *Mfr. infrared non-contact temperature measuring instruments.*

Tel: (847) 967-5151
Fax: (847) 647-0948

%FO: 100
Emp: 880

LOMA SYSTEMS, INC.
283 East Lies Rd., Carol Stream, Illinois 60188
CEO: Gary Wilson, Pres.
Bus: *Food inspection systems manufacturer.*

Tel: (630) 588-0900
Fax: (630) 588-1394

%FO: 100
Emp: 80

MALVERN INSTRUMENTS INC.
10 Southville Rd., Southborough, Massachusetts 01772
CEO: Brian W. Dutko, Pres.
Bus: *Laboratory particle analysis instrumentation manufacture.*

Tel: (508) 480-0200
Fax: (508) 460-9692

%FO: 100
Emp: 46

MICROSCAN SYSTEMS, INC.
1201 Southwest 7th St., Renton, Washington 98055
CEO: Susan Snyder
Bus: *Mfr. high performance fixed mount bar code scanning & decoding instruments.*

Tel: (425) 226-5700
Fax: (425) 226-8250

%FO: 100

NDC INFRARED ENGINEERING LTD.
5314 Irwindale Ave., Irwindale, California 91706
CEO: Jim Psotka
Bus: *Design and manufacturing of on-line continuous process measuring instruments.*

Tel: (626) 960-3300
Fax: (626) 939-3870

%FO: 100

PANALYTICAL
12 Michigan Rd., Natick, Massachusetts 01760
CEO: Gjalt Kuiperes, Pres.
Bus: *X-ray equipment for industrial applications.*

Tel: (508) 647-1100
Fax: (508) 647-1115

Emp: 101

PARTICLE MEASURING SYSTEMS, INC.
5475 Airport Blvd., Boulder, Colorado 80301
CEO: Paul Kelly, Pres.
Bus: *Mfr. on-line laser based particle detection systems*

Tel: (303) 443-7100
Fax: (303) 449-6870

%FO: 100
Emp: 190

RED LION CONTROLS INC.
20 Willow Spring Circle, York, Pennsylvania 17402
CEO: Lindy Kuhn, Customer Service
Bus: *Mfr. digital control, sensing & measuring devices.*

Tel: (717) 767-6961
Fax: (717) 764-6587

%FO: 100

● **SPIRAX SARCO ENGINEERING PLC**
Charlton House, Cirencester Rd., Cheltenham, Gloucestershire GL53 8ER, England, U.K.
CEO: Marcus J. D. Steel, CEO
Bus: *Mfr. temperature controls, steam traps, pressure reduction, pipeline auxiliary.*
NAICS: 333911, 333996, 334513, 334514, 335314

Tel: 44-1242-521361
Fax: 44-1242-581470
www.spiraxsarcoengineering.com

Rev: $628
Emp: 4,104

SPIRAX SARCO INC.
1150 Northpoint Blvd., Blythewood, South Carolina 29016
CEO: Graham Marchand, Chmn.
Bus: *Mfr. temp control, steam traps, pressure reduction, pipeline auxiliary.*

Tel: (803) 714-2000
Fax: (803) 714-2222

%FO: 100
Emp: 295

WATSON-MARLOW BREDEL INC.
370 Upton Technology Park, Wilmington, Massachusetts 01887
CEO: James Whalen, CEO
Bus: *Dist. of industrial & laboratory metering & transfer pumps.*

Tel: (978) 658-6168
Fax: (978) 658-0041

Emp: 60

● **SPIRENT PLC**
Spirent House, Crawley Business Quarter, Fleming Way, Crawley West Sussex RH10 9QL, England, U.K.
CEO: John P. Weston, Chmn.
Bus: *Network technology.*
NAICS: 334210, 334220, 334290, 334515, 423610

Tel: 44-1293-767-676
Fax: 44-1293-767-677
www.spirent.com

Rev: $911
Emp: 4,482

HELLERMANN TYTON
PO Box 23055, Milwaukee, Wisconsin 53224
CEO: Jim Campion, Mng. Dir.
Bus: *Communication and power network products manufacturer.*

Tel: (414) 355-1130
Fax: (414) 355-7341

%FO: 100

SPIRENT COMMUNICATIONS INC.
541 Industrial Way West, PO Box 497, Eatontown, New Jersey 07724
CEO: Charles Simmons, Pres.   Tel: (732) 544-8700   %FO: 100
Bus: *Solutions for the electrical and*   Fax: (732) 544-8347   Emp: 110
    communications industries.

SPIRENT COMMUNICATIONS INC.
26750 Agoura Rd., Calabasas, California 91302
CEO: Kathy Arceo, Mgr.   Tel: (818) 676-2300
Bus: *Engineering services*   Fax: (818) 626-2700

SPIRENT COMMUNICATIONS INC.
1175 Borregas Ave., Sunnyvale, California 94089
CEO: Raymond Ng, Mgr.   Tel: (408) 541-1010
Bus: *Mfr. Instruments to measure electricity*   Fax: (408) 541-1090

SPIRENT COMMUNICATIONS OF ROCKVILLE, INC.
15200 Omega Dr., Rockville, Maryland 20850-3240
CEO: James Schleckser   Tel: (301) 590-3600   %FO: 100
Bus: *Automated test systems for*   Fax: (301) 590-3550
    telecommunications networks.

SPIRENT FEDERAL SYSTEMS INC.
22345 La Palma Ave., Yorba Linda, California 92887-3808
CEO: Ellen Hall, Pres.   Tel: (714) 692-6565   %FO: 100
Bus: *Communication and power network products*   Fax: (714) 692-6567   Emp: 15
    manufacturer.

SPIRENT FEDERAL SYSTEMS INC., CUSTOMER SUPPORT CENTRE
1331 Airport Freeway, Ste. 304, Euless, Texas 76040-4150
CEO: Ed Schwanke, Mgr.   Tel: (817) 508-6095   %FO: 100
Bus: *Advanced telecom test systems and*   Fax: (817) 508-6096
    implementing solutions.

● **SSL INTERNATIONAL PLC**
35 New Bridge St., London EC4V 6BW, England, U.K.
CEO: Gary Watts, CEO   Tel: 44-207-367-5760   Rev: $983
Bus: *Mfr. consumer health care products.*   Fax: 44-207-367-5790   Emp: 6,436
    www.ssl-international.com
NAICS: 325620

    SSL AMERICAS INC.
    3585 Engineering Dr., Ste. 200, Norcross, Georgia 30092
    CEO: Ron Plumridge, Pres.   Tel: (770) 582-2222   %FO: 100
    Bus: *Mfr. consumer health care products.*   Fax: (770) 582-2233   Emp: 40

● **ST. IVES PLC**
St. Ives House, Lavington St., London SE1 0NX, England, U.K.
CEO: Wayne Angstrom, Pres. & CEO   Tel: 44-207-928-8844   Rev: $747
Bus: *Commercial printing.*   Fax: 44-207-902-6572   Emp: 4,591
    www.st-ives.co.uk
NAICS: 323110, 323111, 323115, 323117, 323119, 323121

ST. IVES INC.
2025 McKinley St., Hollywood, Florida 33020
CEO: Wayne Angstrom, Pres.
Bus: *Periodical printing & publishing*

Tel: (954) 920-7300
Fax: (954) 925-4324

%FO: 100
Emp: 500

ST. IVES INC.
4437 East Forty-Ninth St., Cleveland, Ohio 44125
CEO: Mark Berkley, Gen. Mgr.
Bus: *Commercial printing*

Tel: (216) 271-5300
Fax: (216) 271-0623

%FO: 100
Emp: 331

ST. IVES. INC.
13349 NW 42nd. Ave., Miami, Florida 33054
CEO: Wayne Angstrom, Pres. & CEO
Bus: *Commercial printing*

Tel: (305) 685-7381
Fax: (305) 688-3260

• **STAGECOACH HOLDINGS PLC**
10 Dunkeld Rd., Perth, Tayside PHI 5TW, England, U.K.
CEO: Robert Speirs, Chmn.
Bus: *Engaged in transportation, including operation of
ferries, buses, railway units and airport services
businesses.*
NAICS: 485112, 485113, 485510, 485991

Tel: 44-173-844-2111
Fax: 44-173-864-3648
www.stagecoachgroup.com

Rev: $2,664
Emp: 29,163

    COACH USA, INC.
    160 S. Route 17 N., Paramus, New Jersey 07652
    CEO: Brian Souter, CEO
    Bus: *Provides charter and tour buses, taxi cab
    and airport shuttle services.*

Tel: (201) 225-7500
Fax: (201) 225-7590

%FO: 100

    GRAY LINE SAN FRANCISCO
    300 Toland St., San Francisco, California 94124
    CEO: Dan Eisentraeger, Pres.
    Bus: *Provides sightseeing tours.*

Tel: (415) 642-9400
Fax: (415) 642-1500

Emp: 130

• **STANDARD CHARTERED, PLC**
1 Aldermanbury Square, London EC2V 7SB, England, U.K.
CEO: Evan Mervyn Davies, CEO
Bus: *International banking.*

Tel: 44-207-280-7500
Fax: 44-207-280-7791
www.standardchartered.com

Rev: $7,714
Emp: 38,000

NAICS: 522110, 522310, 523920, 523930

    STANDARD CHARTERED, PLC.
    1 Madison Ave., New York, New York 10010
    CEO: James McCabe, Pres.
    Bus: *International banking services.*

Tel: (212) 667-0700
Fax: (212) 667-0380

%FO: 100
Emp: 11

• **STEMCOR HOLDINGS LTD.**
Level 27, City Point, 1 Ropemaker St., London EC2Y 9ST, England, U.K.
CEO: Julian Verden, Mng. Dir.
Bus: *International distribution of steel.*

Tel: 44-20-7775-3600
Fax: 44-20-7775-3679
www.stemcor.com

Rev: $5,350
Emp: 400

NAICS: 331210

STEMCOR USA INC.
350 Fifth Ave., Ste. 7815, New York, New York 10118
CEO: Peter Blohm, Pres.
Bus: *Steel distribution.*
Tel: (212) 563-0262
Fax: (212) 563-0403
%FO: 100

STEMCOR USA INC.
4400 N. Federal Hwy., Ste. 30, Boca Raton, Florida 33431
CEO: Peter Blohm, Pres.
Bus: *Steel distribution.*
Tel: (561) 417-9413
Fax: (561) 892-2479
%FO: 100

STEMCOR USA INC.
20 Corporate Park, Ste. 170, Irvine, California 92606
CEO: Peter Blohm
Bus: *Steel distribution.*
Tel: (949) 477-0686
Fax: (949) 477-0682
%FO: 100

STEMCOR USA INC.
1907 Jeanette Ave., St. Charles, Illinois 60174
CEO: Peter Blohm
Bus: *Steel distribution.*
Tel: (630) 513-7885
Fax: (630) 513-7889
%FO: 100

● **STERLING ENERGY PLC**
Mardall House, 7-9 Vaughan Rd., Harpenden, Hertfordshire AL5 4HU, England, U.K.
CEO: Harry G. Wilson, CEO
Bus: *Oil and natural gas exploration and production.*
Tel: 44-158-246-2121
Fax: 44-158-246-1221
www.sterlingenergyplc.com
Rev: $392

NAICS: 211111

STERLING ENERGY, INC.
15425 North Freeway, Ste. 160, Houston, Texas 77090
CEO: Robert P. Munn, VP
Bus: *Oil and natural gas exploration and production*
Tel: (281) 875-4835
Fax: (281) 875-0440
%FO: 100

● **STOCKCUBE PLC**
Plaza 535, Kings Rd., Ste. 1.23, London SW10 OSZ, England, U.K.
CEO: Julian Burney, CEO
Bus: *Provides financial services.*
Tel: 44-207-352-4001
Fax: 44-207-352-3185
www.stockcube.com
Rev: $5
Emp: 30

NAICS: 516110, 523920, 523930, 523999

CHARTCRAFT INC.
30 Church St., New Rochelle, New York 10801
CEO: John Gray, Pres.
Bus: *Financial services.*
Tel: (914) 632-0422
Fax: (914) 632-0335
%FO: 100
Emp: 22

● **STOLT OFFSHORE S.A.**
Dolphin House, Windmill Rd., Sunbury-on-Thames, Surrey TW16 7HT, England, U.K.
CEO: Tom Ehret, CEO
Bus: *Provides underwater engineering and construction services.*
Tel: 44-1932-773-700
Fax: 44-1932-773-701
www.sstoltoffshore.com
Rev: $1,242
Emp: 5,309

NAICS: 213112, 541330

STOLT OFFSHORE INC.
10787 Clay Rd., Houston, Texas 77041
CEO: Quinn J. Herbert, Pres.
Bus: *Provides underwater engineering and construction services.*

Tel: (713) 430-1100
Fax: (713) 461-0039

%FO: 100
Emp: 831

● STOLT-NIELSEN SA
Aldwych House, 71-91 Aldwych, London WC2B 4HN, England, U.K.
CEO: Niels G. Stolt-Nielsen, CEO
Bus: *International transport, storage and distribution specialty bulk liquids, sub sea contracting and aquaculture.*

Tel: 44-207-611-8960
Fax: 44-207-611-8965
www.stoltnielsen.com

Rev: $1,956
Emp: 7,259

NAICS: 114111, 213112, 311712, 424460, 483111

STOLTHAVEN NEW ORLEANS LLC
Stilthaven Terminals Division, 2444 English Turn Rd., Braithwaite, Louisiana 70040
CEO: Tom Sharon, Gen. Mgr.
Bus: *Bulk liquid storage.*

Tel: (504) 682-9989
Fax: (504) 682-9803

%FO: 100
Emp: 47

STOLT-NIELSEN TRANSPORT GROUP LTD.
15635 Jacintoport Blvd., Houston, Texas 77015
CEO: Owen Rogers, Controller
Bus: *Ship brokerage facilities.*

Tel: (281) 457-0303
Fax: (281) 860-5175

%FO: 100
Emp: 1,192

STOLT-NIELSEN TRANSPORT GROUP LTD.
800 Connecticut Ave., 4/F East, Norwalk, Connecticut 06854
CEO: Mickey Stayman
Bus: *International transport of specialty bulk liquids.*

Tel: (203) 838-7100
Fax: (203) 299-0067

%FO: 100

STOLT-NIELSEN TRANSPORT GROUP LTD.
Advanced Technology Center, 2021 Lakeshore Dr., Ste. 400, New Orleans, Louisiana 70122
CEO: Mickey Stayman
Bus: *Transportation services.*

Tel: (504) 304-2500
Fax: (504) 304-2511

%FO: 100

STOLT-NIELSEN TRANSPORTATION GROUP LTD.
8 Sound Shore Dr., Greenwich, Connecticut 06830
CEO: Reginald J.Lee, CEO
Bus: *International transport of specialty bulk liquids.*

Tel: (203) 625-9400
Fax: (203) 625-2525

%FO: 100
Emp: 4,500

● SUNGARD SHERWOOD SYSTEMS
Sherwood House, Eastworth Rd., Chertsey KT16 8DF, England, U.K.
CEO: Gavin Lavelle, CEO
Bus: *Software manufacture and outsourcing services for insurance markets.*

Tel: 44-1932-757575
Fax: 44-1932-757575
www.sherwoodinternational.com

Rev: $81
Emp: 475

NAICS: 511210

SHERWOOD INTERNATIONAL
200 Business Park Dr., Armonk, New York 10504
CEO: Gavin Lavelle
Bus: *Mfr./sales software for the insurance market.*

Tel: (914) 273-1717
Fax: (914) 273-7790

%FO: 100

SUNGARD DATA MANAGEMENT SOLUTIONS
888 7th Ave., 12/F, New York, New York 10106
CEO: Janet Crowley
Bus: *Market data distributor and data
management systems services.*
Tel: (212) 506-0300
Fax: (212) 977-7144
%FO: 100

SUNGARD DATA MANAGEMENT SOLUTIONS
112 West Park Dr., Mt. Laurel, New Jersey 08054
CEO: Ralph Koehrer
Bus: *Market data distributor and data
management systems services.*
Tel: (856) 235-7300
Fax: (856) 727-2147
%FO: 100

SUNGARD DATA MANAGEMENT SOLUTIONS
504 Totten Pond, 2/F, Waltham, Massachusetts 02451
CEO: Michiel Westerkamp
Bus: *Market data distributor and data
management systems services.*
Tel: (781) 890-7227
Fax: (781) 890-7449
%FO: 100

SUNGARD DATA MANAGEMENT SOLUTIONS
1331 Lamar St., Ste. 950, Houston, Texas 77010
CEO: Paul Bourke
Bus: *Market data distributor and data
management systems services.*
Tel: (713) 210-8000
Fax: (713) 210-8001
%FO: 100

SUNGARD DATA MANAGEMENT SOLUTIONS
1194 Oak Valley Dr. Ste 100, Ann Arbor, Michigan 48108
CEO: William Bingham
Bus: *Market data distributor and data
management systems services.*
Tel: (734) 332-4400
Fax: (734) 332-4440
%FO: 100

• **SUNSEEKER LIMITED LTD.**
27-31 W. Quay Rd., Poole BH15 1HX, England, U.K.
CEO: Robert Braithwaite, CEO
Bus: *Mfr. high-end powerboats, including yachts,
offshore cruisers and sports fishers.*
NAICS: 336612
Tel: 44-1202-381-111
Fax: 44-1202-382-222
www.sunseeker.com
Rev: $256
Emp: 1,258

SUNSEEKER FLORIDA LLC
825 NE 3rd St., Dania Beach, Florida 33004
CEO: J. Dagostino
Bus: *Mfr. powerboats and yachts.*
Tel: (954) 920-2433
Fax: (954) 920-0340
%FO: 100

SUNSEEKER MIDWEST
16011-154th St., St. Croix, Minnesota 55047
CEO: Mark Hatchard, Pres.
Bus: *Mfr. powerboats and yachts.*
Tel: (651) 433-5046
Fax: (651) 433-5457
%FO: 100

SUNSEEKER USA INC.
2001 SW 20th St., Ste. 106-B, Ft. Lauderdale, Florida 33315
CEO: Mark Hatchard, Pres.
Bus: *Mfr. powerboats and yachts.*
Tel: (954) 765-1234
Fax: (954) 920-0340
%FO: 100

THE SUNSEEKER CLUB AT CASTAWAYS
425 Davenport Ave., 2/F, New Rochelle, New York 10805
CEO: Mark Hatchard
Bus: *Mfr. powerboats and yachts.*
Tel: (914) 636-8444
Fax: (914) 235-9089
%FO: 100

- **SUPERCART PLC**
  3 The Mews, 16 Hollybush Lane, Sevenoaks, Kent TN13 3TH, England, U.K.
  CEO: Michael C. Wolfe, CEO
  Bus: *Designs and markets all-plastic shopping baskets and carts.*
  NAICS: 326199
  Tel: 44-1732 459898
  Fax: 44-1732 464301
  www.supercart.com
  Rev: $4
  Emp: 10

  SUPERCART NORTH AMERICA INC.
  177 Worcester St., Ste. 302, Wellesley Hills, Massachusetts 02481
  CEO: Martin Thoralf Deale
  Bus: *Designs and markets all-plastic shopping baskets and carts.*
  Tel: (781) 237-9464
  Fax: (781) 237-9465
  %FO: 100

- **SURFACE TECHNOLOGY SYSTEMS LTD.**
  Imperial Park, Newport NP10 8UJ, England, U.K.
  CEO: Mutsuo Mukuda, CEO
  Bus: *Design and manufacture of semiconductors and semiconductor related devices.*
  NAICS: 333295
  Tel: 44-1633-652400
  Fax: 44 1633 652405
  www.stsystems.com
  Emp: 250

  ST SYSTEMS USA INC.
  611 Veterans Blvd., Ste. 107, Redwood City, California 94063
  CEO: Todd Smith
  Bus: *Design and manufacture of semiconductors and semiconductor related devices.*
  Tel: (650) 569-3655
  Fax: (650) 569-3663
  %FO: 100

- **SURFCONTROL PLC**
  Riverside, Mountbatten Way, Congleton, Cheshire CW12 1DY, England, U.K.
  CEO: Patricia C. Sueltz, CEO
  Bus: *Mfr. Internet filtering software.*
  NAICS: 511210
  Tel: 44-1260-296-200
  Fax: 44-1260-296-201
  www.surfcontrol.com
  Rev: $87
  Emp: 464

  SURFCONTROL USA INC.
  1900 West Park Dr., Ste. 180, Westborough, Massachusetts 01581
  CEO: Susan Getgood, VP
  Bus: *Technical support.*
  Tel: (508) 870-7200
  Fax: (508) 870-7200
  %FO: 100

  SURFCONTROL USA INC.
  5550 Scotts Valley Dr., Scotts Valley, California 95066
  CEO: Kevin Blakeman, Pres.
  Bus: *Mfr./sales Internet filtering software.*
  Tel: (831) 440-2500
  Fax: (831) 440-2740
  %FO: 100

- **SUSTAINABILITY**
  20-22 Bedford Row, London WC1R 4EB, England, U.K.
  CEO: John Elkington, Chmn.
  Bus: *Int'l consultancy for business strategy and sustainable development, environmental improvement, social equity and economic development.*
  NAICS: 541611, 541620
  Tel: 44-20-7269-6900
  Fax: 44-20-7269-6901
  www.sustainability.com
  Emp: 20

SUSTAINABILITY
136 Dore St., San Francisco, California 94103
CEO: Mark Lee, Dir.
Bus: *International consultancy for business
strategy and sustainable development -
environmental improvement, social equity
and economic development.*

Tel: (415) 861-1545
Fax: (415) 861-1556

%FO: 100

SUSTAINABILITY
1150 Connecticut Ave., NW, Ste. 525, Washington, District of Columbia 20036
CEO: Jeff Erikson, Dir.
Bus: *International consultancy for business
strategy and sustainable development -
environmental improvement, social equity
and economic development.*

Tel: (202) 659-2898
Fax: (202) 659-1053

%FO: 100

- **JOHN SWIRE & SONS LTD.**
Swire House, 59 Buckingham Gate, London SW1E 6AJ, England, U.K.
CEO: James W. J. Hughes-Hallett, Chmn.
Bus: *Deep-sea shipping, cold storage, road transport,
and agricultural services.*

Tel: 44-20-7834-7717
Fax: 44-20-7630-0353
www.swire.com

NAICS: 483111, 493110, 493120, 493190

POLYNESIA LINE LTD.
810 Fifth Ave., Ste. 200, San Rafael, California 94901
CEO: Jens Jensen
Bus: *Maritime agency.*

Tel: (415) 256-1400
Fax: (415) 256-1401

%FO: 100

SWIRE PROPERTIES INC.
501 Brickell Key Dr., Ste. 600, Miami, Florida 33131
CEO: Stephen Owens
Bus: *Real estate development.*

Tel: (305) 371-3877
Fax: (305) 371-9324

UNITED STATES COLD STORAGE
PO Box 1106, 33400 Dowe Ave., Union City, California 94587
CEO: Dave Sweilem, Mgr.
Bus: *Refrigerated warehouse storage and freight
transport.*

Tel: (510) 489-8300
Fax: (510) 489-0698

%FO: 100

UNITED STATES COLD STORAGE
810 East Continental Ave., Tulare, California 93274
CEO: Brian Ford, Mgr.
Bus: *Refrigerated warehouse storage and freight
transport.*

Tel: (559) 686-1110
Fax: (559) 686-3827

%FO: 100

UNITED STATES COLD STORAGE
1400 N. MacArthur Dr., Tracy, California 95376
CEO: Stan Moya, VP & Gen. Mgr.
Bus: *Refrigerated warehouse storage and freight
transport.*

Tel: (209) 835-2653
Fax: (209) 835-4117

%FO: 100

UNITED STATES COLD STORAGE
3100 52nd Ave., Sacramento, California 95823
CEO: William Litton, VP & Gen. Mgr.
Bus: *Refrigerated warehouse storage and freight
transport.*

Tel: (916) 392-9160
Fax: (916) 392-5012

%FO: 100

UNITED STATES COLD STORAGE
2003 S. Cherry Ave., Fresno, California 93721
CEO: John Bodden, Jr., Mgr.   Tel: (559) 237-6145   %FO: 100
Bus: *Refrigerated warehouse storage and freight*   Fax: (559) 237-7214
     transport.

UNITED STATES COLD STORAGE
100 Dobbs Lane, Ste. 102, Cherry Hill, New Jersey 08034
CEO: David Harlan, Pres. & CEO   Tel: (856) 354-8181   %FO: 100
Bus: *Refrigerated warehouse storage and freight*   Fax: (856) 354-8199   Emp: 1,500
     transport.

UNITED STATES COLD STORAGE
W. Carlton Rd. & Santa Maria Ave., Laredo, Texas 78041
CEO: Luis Guardiola, VP & Gen. Mgr.   Tel: (956) 722-3951   %FO: 100
Bus: *Refrigerated warehouse storage and freight*   Fax: (956) 722-4325
     transport.

UNITED STATES COLD STORAGE
10711 Olive St., Omaha, Nebraska 68128
CEO: Tom Vaghy, VP & Gen. Mgr.   Tel: (402) 339-8855   %FO: 100
Bus: *Refrigerated warehouse storage and freight*   Fax: (402) 731-3955
     transport.

UNITED STATES COLD STORAGE
1021 E. Walnut Ave., Tulare, California 93274
CEO: Brian Ford, Mgr.   Tel: (559) 687-3320   %FO: 100
Bus: *Refrigerated warehouse storage and freight*   Fax: (559) 687-3330
     transport.

UNITED STATES COLD STORAGE
419 Milford-Harrington Hwy., PO Box 242, Milford, Delaware 19963
CEO: Ron Longhany, Mgr.   Tel: (302) 422-7536   %FO: 100
Bus: *Refrigerated warehouse storage and freight*   Fax: (302) 422-8420
     transport.

UNITED STATES COLD STORAGE
2901 Kenny Biggs Rd., Lumberton, North Carolina 28358
CEO: Darron Ezzell, Mgr.   Tel: (910) 739-1992   %FO: 100
Bus: *Refrigerated warehouse storage and freight*   Fax: (910) 739-1974
     transport.

UNITED STATES COLD STORAGE
1602 Island St., Laredo, Texas 78041
CEO: Luis Guardiola, VP & Gen. Mgr.   Tel: (956) 722-3951   %FO: 100
Bus: *Refrigerated warehouse storage and freight*   Fax: (956) 722-4325
     transport.

UNITED STATES COLD STORAGE
15 Emory St., Bethlehem, Pennsylvania 18015
CEO: Larry Alderfer, Dir.   Tel: (610) 433-7378   %FO: 100
Bus: *Refrigerated warehouse storage and freight*   Fax: (610) 433-7380
     transport.

UNITED STATES COLD STORAGE
2554 Downing Dr., Ft. Worth, Texas 76106
CEO: Frank Monroe, Mgr.
Bus: *Refrigerated warehouse storage and freight transport.*

Tel: (817) 624-1900
Fax: (817) 624-7190

%FO: 100

UNITED STATES COLD STORAGE
5150 Pulaski St., Dallas, Texas 75247
CEO: Brian Kroll, Mgr.
Bus: *Refrigerated warehouse storage and freight transport.*

Tel: (214) 631-4863
Fax: (214) 631-4615

%FO: 100

UNITED STATES COLD STORAGE
3300 E. Park Row. Dr., Arlington, Texas 76010
CEO: Michelle Grimes, Mgr.
Bus: *Refrigerated warehouse storage and freight transport.*

Tel: (817) 633-3070
Fax: (817) 649-3505

%FO: 100

UNITED STATES COLD STORAGE
125 Threet Industrial Blvd., Smyrna, Tennessee 37167
CEO: Marion Lucas, VP & Gen. Mgr.
Bus: *Refrigerated warehouse storage and freight transport.*

Tel: (615) 355-0047
Fax: (615) 355-0129

%FO: 100

UNITED STATES COLD STORAGE
1727 J.P. Hennessey Dr., LaVergne, Tennessee 37086
CEO: Marion Lucas, VP & Gen. Mgr.
Bus: *Refrigerated warehouse storage and freight transport.*

Tel: (615) 641-9800
Fax: (615) 641-3150

%FO: 100

UNITED STATES COLD STORAGE
1300 S. "O" St., Dinuba, California 93618
CEO: Gordon Petersen, Mgr.
Bus: *Refrigerated warehouse storage and freight transport.*

Tel: (559) 591-2680
Fax: (559) 591-7609

%FO: 100

UNITED STATES COLD STORAGE
240 Bruce Costin Rd., Warsaw, North Carolina 28398
CEO: Jesse Hooks, Mgr.
Bus: *Refrigerated warehouse storage and freight transport.*

Tel: (910) 293-7400
Fax: (910) 293-7090

%FO: 100

UNITED STATES COLD STORAGE
4302 South 30th St., Omaha, Nebraska 68107
CEO: Tom Vaghy, VP & Gen. Mgr.
Bus: *Refrigerated warehouse storage and freight transport.*

Tel: (402) 731-9900
Fax: (402) 731-3955

%FO: 100

UNITED STATES COLD STORAGE
601 Twin Rail Dr., PO Box 489, Minooka
CEO: Inooka, Illinois 60447
%FO: 100

Diane Stewart, Mgr.

Tel: (815) 467-0455

Bus: *Refrigerated warehouse storage and freight transport.*

Fax: (815) 467-0460

UNITED STATES COLD STORAGE
8424 West 47th St., PO Box 312, Lyons, Illinois 60534
CEO: John Otto, Operations Mgr.   Tel: (708) 442-6660   %FO: 100
Bus: *Refrigerated warehouse storage and freight*   Fax: (708) 443-0995
      transport.

UNITED STATES COLD STORAGE
11801 N.W. 102 Rd., Medley, Florida 33178
CEO: Joe Loffredo, VP & Gen. Mgr.   Tel: (305) 691-5391   %FO: 100
Bus: *Refrigerated warehouse storage and freight*   Fax: (305) 836-9159
      transport.

UNITED STATES COLD STORAGE
6501 District Blvd., Bakersfield, California 93313
CEO: Randy Dorrell, Mgr.   Tel: (661) 832-2653
Bus: *Refrigerated warehouse storage and freight*   Fax: (661) 832-5846
      transport.

UNITED STATES COLD STORAGE
1600 N. Crawford Av., Dinuba, California 93618
CEO: Gordon Petersen, Mgr.   Tel: (559) 591-6704   %FO: 100
Bus: *Refrigerated warehouse storage and freight*   Fax: (559) 591-4595
      transport.

UNITED STATES COLD STORAGE
2292 Sand Lake Rd., Orlando, Florida 32809
CEO: Althea Duncan, Mgr.   Tel: (407) 851-2410   %FO: 100
Bus: *Refrigerated warehouse storage and freight*   Fax: (407) 855-2981
      transport.

UNITED STATES COLD STORAGE
6983 N.W. 37th Ave., Miami, Florida 33147
CEO: Joe Loffredo, VP & Gen. Mgr.   Tel: (305) 691-5391   %FO: 100
Bus: *Refrigerated warehouse storage and freight*   Fax: (305) 836-9159
      transport.

● **SYGEN INTERNATIONAL PLC**
2 Kingston Business Park, Kingston Bagpuize, Oxfordshire OX13 5FE, England, U.K.
CEO: Phillip J. David, Pres. & CEO   Tel: 44-1865-822-275   Rev: $200
Bus: *Develops and markets breeding pigs.*   Fax: 44-1865-821-011   Emp: 1,261
                                                    www.sygeninternational.com
  NAICS: 112210

  PIC USA INC.
  PO Box 348, 3033 Nashville Rd., Franklin, Kentucky 42135
  CEO: Karol Pelletier, HR   Tel: (270) 586-9224   %FO: 90
  Bus: *Develops and markets breeding pigs.*   Fax: (270) 586-4190   Emp: 1,500

  SYGEN INTERNATIONAL PLC
  2929 Seventh St., Suite 130, Berkeley, California 94710
  CEO: Dennis Harms, SVP   Tel: (510) 848-8266
  Bus: *Develops and markets hogs and other farm*   Fax: (510) 848-0324
        animals

- **SYLTONE LTD.**
Springmill St., Bradford, Rawdon, West Yorkshire BD5 7HW, England, U.K.
CEO: Ross J. Centanni, Chmn.   Tel: 44-127-471-5240
Bus: *Mfr. compressors, valves, liquid pumps for tank*   Fax: 44-127-471-5241
trucks.   www.syltone.co.uk
NAICS: 333995, 333996, 532412, 532490

  SYLTONE INDUSTRIES LLC
  2501 Constant Comment Place, Louisville, Kentucky 40299
  CEO: Graham Killarney, Pres.   Tel: (502) 266-8767   %FO: 100
  Bus: *Mfr. Compressors, valves, liquid pumps for*   Fax: (502) 266-6689   Emp: 75
  tank trucks.

- **SYMBIAN LTD.**
2-6 Boundary Row, Southwark, London SE1 8HP, England, U.K.
CEO: Nigel Clifford, CEO   Tel: 44-20-7154-100   Rev: $81
Bus: *Develops and licenses software for the cell*   Fax: 44-20-7154-1860   Emp: 734
phone industry.   www.symbian.com
NAICS: 511210

  SYMBIAN LTD.
  390 Bridge Pkwy., Ste. 201, Redwood Shores, California 94065
  CEO: Cindy Perez, Mgr.   Tel: (650) 551-0240   %FO: 100
  Bus: *Develops & licenses software for the cell*   Fax: (650) 551-0241
  phone industry.

- **SYNERDEAL LTD.**
Business Innovation Centre, Binley Business Park, Coventry, West Midlands CV3 2TX, England, U.K.
CEO: Didier Picot, CEO   Tel: 44-24-76-43-01-00
Bus: *Reverse auction procurement systems*   Fax: 44-24-76-43-01-05
                                      www.synerdeal.com
NAICS: 511210, 541611, 541614, 541618, 561499

  SYNERDEAL
  1501 Third Ave., New York, New York 10028
  CEO: Didier Picot   Tel: (212) 517-1655   %FO: 100
  Bus: *Reverse auction procurement systems*   Fax: (212) 988-1632
  manufacture.

- **SYNOVATE**
26-28 Glasshouse Yard, 3/F, London EC1A 4JU, England, U.K.
CEO: Adrian Chedore, CEO   Tel: 44-20-7017-2500   Rev: $389
Bus: *Market research services.*   Fax: 44-20-7017-2510   Emp: 3,446
                                      www.synovate.com
NAICS: 541910

  SYNOVATE AMERICAS
  222 S. Riverside Plaza, Chicago, Illinois 60606
  CEO: Robert Philpott, EVP   Tel: (312) 526-4000   %FO: 100
  Bus: *Market research services.*   Fax: (312) 526-4099

SYNOVATE AMERICAS
3390 Peachtree Rd., NE, Atlanta, Georgia 30326
CEO: Casey Goodman   Tel: (678) 553-2076   %FO: 100
Bus: *Market research services.*   Fax: (678) 553-2081

SYNOVATE AMERICAS
One Apple Hill, Ste. 221, Natick, Massachusetts 01760
CEO: Mary De Bisschop, SVP   Tel: (508) 655-0777   %FO: 100
Bus: *Market research services.*   Fax: (508) 655-0033

SYNOVATE AMERICAS
1650 Tysons Blvd., Ste. 110, McLean, Virginia 22102
CEO: Leigh Seaver, SVP   Tel: (703) 790-9099   %FO: 100
Bus: *Market research services.*   Fax: (703) 790-9181

SYNOVATE AMERICAS
7900 S.E. 28th St., Ste. 200, Mercer Island, Washington 98040
CEO: Lindsay Holbrook, SVP   Tel: (206) 236-5970   %FO: 100
Bus: *Market research services.*   Fax: (206) 236-5971

SYNOVATE AMERICAS
25B Hanover Rd., Ste. 305, Florham Park, New Jersey 377-3900
CEO: Greg McMahon   Tel: (973) 377-3900   %FO: 100
Bus: *Market research services.*   Fax: (973) 377-3890

SYNOVATE AMERICAS
475 Branna St., Ste. 410, San Francisco, California 94107
CEO: Gary Williams, SVP   Tel: (415) 541-2880   %FO: 100
Bus: *Market research services.*   Fax: (415) 541-2881

SYNOVATE AMERICAS
5001 Spring Valley Rd., Ste. 130E, Dallas, Texas 75244
CEO: Kirk Blankenship, VP   Tel: (972) 387-5555   %FO: 100
Bus: *Market research services.*   Fax: (972) 387-4441

SYNOVATE AMERICAS
1200 MacArthur Blvd., 3/F, Mahwah, New Jersey 07430
CEO: Jackie Ilacqua, SVP   Tel: (201) 529-5540   %FO: 100
Bus: *Market research services.*   Fax: (201) 529-2659

SYNOVATE AMERICAS
16133 Ventura Blvd., Ste. 1000, Encino, California 91436
CEO: Larry Levin, EVP   Tel: (818) 380-1480   %FO: 100
Bus: *Market research services.*   Fax: (818) 380-1485

SYNOVATE AMERICAS
6730 N. West Ave., Ste. 103, Fresno, California 93711
CEO: Andrew Sorenson   Tel: (559) 451-2820   %FO: 100
Bus: *Market research services.*   Fax: (559) 451-2824

SYNOVATE AMERICAS
816 Congress Ave., Ste. 1680, Austin, Texas 78701
CEO: Susan Hart, VP   Tel: (512) 478-9500   %FO: 100
Bus: *Market research services.*   Fax: (512) 478-9501

SYNOVATE AMERICAS
360 Park Ave. S, 5/F, New York, New York 10010
CEO: Robert Skolnick, SVP
Bus: *Market research services.*

Tel: (212) 293-6100
Fax: (212) 293-6666

%FO: 100

SYNOVATE AMERICAS
201 E. Fifth St., Ste. 1340, Cincinnati, Ohio 45202
CEO: Pat Cowley, VP
Bus: *Market research services.*

Tel: (513) 322-3903
Fax: (513) 723-8734

%FO: 100

SYNOVATE DIVERSITY
8600 NW 17th St., Ste. 100, Miami, Florida 33126
CEO: Frank Szalay, VP
Bus: *Market research services.*

Tel: (305) 716-6800
Fax: (305) 716-6756

%FO: 100

SYNOVATE HEALTHCARE
9175 Guilford Rd., Columbia, Maryland 21046
CEO: Christy Larkin
Bus: *Market research services.*

Tel: (301) 317-1000
Fax: (310) 317-1201

%FO: 100

SYNOVATE MOTORESEARCH
306 S. Washington, Ste. 500, Royal Oak, Michigan 48067
CEO: Scott Miller, CEO
Bus: *Market research services.*

Tel: (248) 541-5311
Fax: (248) 541-5325

%FO: 100

● **SYSTEMS UNION GROUP PLC**
Systems Union House, 1 Lakeside Rd., Aerospace Centre, Farnborough, Hampshire GU14 6XP, England, U.K.
CEO: Paul Coleman, CEO
Bus: *Supply and service of accounting software.*

Tel: 44-125-255-6000
Fax: 44-125-255-6001
www.systemsunion.com

Rev: $201
Emp: 1,252

NAICS: 511210

SYSTEMS UNION INC.
3D/International Tower, 1900 W. Loop South, Ste. 970, Houston, Texas 77027
CEO: Mark A. Wolfendale, CEO
Bus: *Supply and service of accounting software.*

Tel: (713) 355-6100
Fax: (713) 355-4786

%FO: 100

SYSTEMS UNION INC.
7300Corporate Center Dr., Ste. 700, NW 19th St., Ste. 700, Miami, Florida 33126
CEO: Mark A. Wolfendale, CEO
Bus: *Computer software development*

Tel: (305) 594-8000
Fax: (305) 594-8001

Emp: 130

SYSTEMS UNION INC.
1800 Century Park East, 6/F, Los Angeles, California 90067
CEO: Antony Sweet
Bus: *Supply and service of accounting software.*

Tel: (310) 229-5775
Fax: (310) 229-5713

%FO: 100

SYSTEMS UNION INC.
1230 Ave. of the Americas, 7/F, New York, New York 10020
CEO: Chris O'Connor, Mgr.
Bus: *Supply and service of accounting software.*

Tel: (917) 639-4055
Fax: (917) 639-4065

%FO: 100

● **T & F INFORMA**
Mortier House, 37-41 Mortimer St., London W1T 3JH, England, U.K.
CEO: Peter S. Rigdy, CEO
Bus: *Publisher of academic books.*

Tel: 44-20-7017-5000
Fax: 44-20-7017-4286
www.tfinforma.com

Rev: $971
Emp: 4,000

NAICS: 511120, 511130, 519190, 561920

    INFORMA INVESTMENT SOLUTIONS, INC.
    4 Gannett Dr., White Plains, New York 10604
    CEO: Lac An Vuong, Mng. Dir.
    Bus: *Financial services, legal & government
        software.*

Tel: (914) 640-0200
Fax: (914) 694-6728

Emp: 100

    ROBBINS GIOIA
    11 Canal Center Plaza, Alexandria, Virginia 22314
    CEO: Jim Leto, CEO
    Bus: *Program management consulting services.*

Tel: (703) 548-7006
Fax:

Emp: 590

● **T.F. & J.H. BRAIME PLC**
Hunslett Rd., Leeds LS10 1JZ, England, U.K.
CEO: Oliver N.A. Braime, Chmn.
Bus: *Mfr. seamless pressings.*

Tel: 44-113-246-1800
Fax: 44-113-243-5021
www.braime.com

NAICS: 333921, 333922

    4B ELEVATOR COMPONENTS LTD.
    729 Sabrina Dr., East Peoria, Illinois 61611
    CEO: Johnny Wheat, SVP
    Bus: *Mfr. handling systems and bucket elevator
        or conveyor upgrades.*

Tel: (309) 698-5611
Fax: (309) 698-5615

%FO: 100

● **TADPOLE TECHNOLOGY PLC**
Cambridge Science Park, Trinity House, Cowley Rd., Cambridge CB4 OWZ, England, U.K.
CEO: David G. Lee, Chmn.
Bus: *Mfr. networking computers and software.*

Tel: 44-122-339-3522
Fax: 44-122-339-3879
www.tadpoletechnology.com

Rev: $9
Emp: 89

NAICS: 511210

    ENDEAVORS TECHNOLOGY/STREAM THEORY
    19700 Fairchild Rd., Ste. 350, Irvine, California 92612
    CEO: Steig Westerberg, Pres.
    Bus: *Mfr./sales software.*

Tel: (408) 790-2913
Fax: (408) 790-2918

%FO: 100

    TADPOLE TECHNOLOGY
    2231 Faraday Ave., Ste. 140, Carlsbad, California 92008
    CEO: Bernard Hulme, CEO
    Bus: *Mfr. of computer peripheral equipment.*

Tel: (760) 929-8345
Fax: (760) 692-0484

Emp: 75

    TADPOLE-CARTESIA
    2237 Faraday Ave., Ste. 120, Carlsbad, California 92008
    CEO: Jason Linley, Pres.
    Bus: *Mfr./sales software.*

Tel: (760) 929-8345
Fax: (760) 692-0484

%FO: 100
Emp: 75

- **TATE & LYLE PLC**
  Sugar Quay, Lower Thames St., London EC3R 6DQ, England, U.K.
  CEO: Iain Ferguson, CEO
  Bus: *Sugar refining, bulk liquid storage and agricultural consulting.*
  NAICS: 311221, 311311, 311312, 311313, 311930

  Tel: 44-207-626-6525
  Fax: 44-207-623-5213
  www.tate-lyle.co.uk

  Rev: $5,782
  Emp: 11,500

  TATE & LYLE
  2200 E. Eldorado St., Decatur, Illinois 62525
  CEO: D. Lynn Grider, Pres.
  Bus: *Corn refining.*

  Tel: (217) 421-4230
  Fax: (217) 421-2819

  %FO: 100
  Emp: 2,098

- **TAYLOR NELSON SOFRES PLC**
  Westgate, London W5 1UA, England, U.K.
  CEO: Mike Kirkham, CEO
  Bus: *Engaged in market research.*

  NAICS: 541910

  Tel: 44-208-967-0007
  Fax: 44-208-967-4060
  www.tns-global.com

  Rev: $1,404
  Emp: 11,150

  TNS INTERSEARCH
  401 Horsham Rd., Horsham, Pennsylvania 19044
  CEO: Bruce Shandler, Pres. & CEO
  Bus: *Market Research Services*

  Tel: (215) 442-9000
  Fax: (215) 442-9040

  %FO: 100
  Emp: 750

  TNS MEDIA INTELLIGENCE
  685 Third Ave., 4/F, New York, New York 10017
  CEO: Steven J. Fredricks, Pres. & CEO
  Bus: *Market Research Services*

  Tel: (212) 991-6000
  Fax: (212) 949-1963

  %FO: 100
  Emp: 607

  TNS TELECOMS
  101 Greenwood Ave., Ste. 502, Jenkintown, Pennsylvania 19046
  CEO: John Schiela, EVP
  Bus: *Market Research Services*

  Tel: (215) 886-9200
  Fax:

  Emp: 45

- **TAYLOR WOODROW PLC**
  2 Princes Way, Solihull, West Midlands B91 3ES, England, U.K.
  CEO: Norman Askew, Chmn.
  Bus: *Property development, housing, general construction and trading activities.*
  NAICS: 236115, 236116, 236117, 237210

  Tel: 44-121-600-8000
  Fax: 44-121-600-8001
  www.taylorwoodrow.com

  Rev: $3,542
  Emp: 6,000

  TAYLOR WOODROW, INC.
  8430 Enterprise Circle, Ste. 100, Bradenton, Florida 34202
  CEO: John R. Peshkin, CEO
  Bus: *Property development, housing and general construction.*

  Tel: (941) 554-2000
  Fax: (941) 554-3005

  %FO: 100

- **TBI PLC**
  159 New Bond St., 4/F, London W1S 2UD, England, U.K.
  CEO: G.Stanley Thomas, CEO
  Bus: *Airport management.*

  NAICS: 488119, 488190, 721110

  Tel: 44-207-408-7300
  Fax: 44-207-408-7321
  www.tbiplc.co.uk

  Rev: $340
  Emp: 2,129

ORLANDO SANFORD INTERNATIONAL, INC.
3200 Red Cleveland Blvd., Sanford, Florida 32773
CEO: Larry Gouldthorpe, Pres.   Tel: (407) 585-4500
Bus: *Airport services*   Fax: (407) 585-4545   Emp: 20

TBI (US), INC.
3222 Red Cleveland Blvd., Sanford, Florida 32773
CEO: Larry Gouldthorpe, Pres.   Tel: (407) 585-4555
Bus: *Airport management*   Fax: (407) 585-4545   Emp: 374

TBI CARGO, INC.
3216 Red Cleveland Blvd., Sanford, Florida 32773
CEO: Max Warriner, Pres.   Tel: (407) 585-4620
Bus: *Air transport services.*   Fax: (40) 585-4618   Emp: 15

● **TDS INC.**
Ducie House, 37 Ducie St., Manchester M1 2JW, England, U.K.
CEO: Roger A. Coomber, CEO   Tel: 44-161-236-7850   Rev: $1
Bus: *Telemedicine diagnostic services.*   Fax: 44-161-236-6654   Emp: 25
                                     www.tds-telemed.com

NAICS: 325412

    TDS INC., C/O SILLS CUMMIS
    One Riverfront Plaza, Newark, New Jersey 07102
    CEO: Ted Zangari   Tel: (973) 643-7000   %FO: 100
    Bus: *Telemedicine diagnostic services.*   Fax: (973) 643-6500

● **TEIKOKU PHARMA UK LTD.**
Central House, 1 Ballards Ln., London N3 1LQ, England, U.K.
CEO: Masahisa Kitagawa, CEO   Tel: 44-20-8349-8015   Rev: $620
Bus: *Pharmaceutical development.*   Fax: 44-20-8349-8619   Emp: 850
                                     www.teikoku.co.jp

NAICS: 325411, 325412

    TEIKOKU PHARMA USA INC.
    1718 Ringwood Ave., San Jose, California 95131
    CEO: Masahisa Kitagawa   Tel: (408) 501-1800   %FO: 100
    Bus: *Develops and manufactures a variety of*   Fax: (408) 501-1900
        medicated patches and ointments.

● **TELIRIS LTD.**
6 Braham St., 3rd Fl., London E18EE, England, U.K.
CEO: James Stewart Thomson, CEO   Tel: 44-207-702-6070
Bus: *Videoconferencing technology.* Fax: 44-207-702-2330
                                     www.teliris.com

NAICS: 334290, 334310

    TELIRIS LTD.
    12 E. 44th St., New York, New York 10017
    CEO: Steven Gage   Tel: (212) 490-1065   %FO: 100
    Bus: *Videoconferencing technology manufacture*   Fax: (212) 983-2707
        and sales.

● **TEQUILA**
82 Charing Cross Rd., London WC2H 0QB, England, U.K.
CEO: Jeremy Pagden, Pres. & CEO
Bus: *Advertising and marketing services.*

Tel: 44-207-557-6147
Fax: 44-207-7240-5463
www.tequila.com

NAICS: 541810, 541840, 541910

    TEQUILA
    5353 Grosvenor, Los Angeles, California 90066
    CEO: Kristi VandenBosch
    Bus: *Advertising and marketing services.*

Tel: (310) 305-5111
Fax: (310) 305-5111

%FO: 100

● **THE FUTURE NETWORK PLC**
30 Monmouth St., Bath BA1 2BW, England, U.K.
CEO: Greg Ingham, CEO
Bus: *Specialist consumer magazines publishing.*

Tel: 44-122-544-2244
Fax: 44-122-544-6019
www.futureplc.com

Rev: $265
Emp: 950

NAICS: 511120

    FUTURE NETWORK USA, INC.
    150 North Hill Dr., Brisbane, California 94005
    CEO: Jonathan Simpson-Bint, CEO
    Bus: *Engaged in magazine publishing.*

Tel: (415) 468-4684
Fax: (415) 468-4684

%FO: 100

    GUITAR ONE MAGAZINE
    149 Fifth Ave., New York, New York 10010
    CEO: Jeff Tyson, Sales
    Bus: *Engaged in magazine publishing.*

Tel: (212) 768-2966
Fax: (212) 944-9279

%FO: 100

● **THISTLE HOTELS LIMITED, DIV. BIL**
2 The Calls, Leeds, West Yorkshire LS2 7JU, England, U.K.
CEO: Arun Amarsi, CEO
Bus: *Luxury Hotels*

Tel: 44-113-243-9111
Fax: 44-113-244-5555
www.thistlehotels.com

Rev: $305
Emp: 2,912

NAICS: 721110

    THISTLE HOTELS PLC
    1800 East Lambert Rd., Ste. 220, Brea, California 92821
    CEO: James J. Enright, VP Sales
    Bus: *Luxury hotels*

Tel: (714) 256-8328
Fax: (714) 256-8329

● **TI AUTOMOTIVE LIMITED**
4650 Kingsgate, Oxford Business Park South, Cascade Way, Oxford OX4 2SU, England, U.K.
CEO: William J. Laule, Chmn. & CEO
Bus: *Mfr. of automotive parts.*

Tel: 44-1865-871-820
Fax: 44-1865-871-866
www.tiautomotive.com

Rev: $2,902
Emp: 21,350

NAICS: 336312, 336340, 336350, 336391, 336399

    TI AUTOMOTIVE
    12345 East Nine Mile Rd., Warren, Michigan 48090
    CEO: D. James Davis, Pres.
    Bus: *Mfr. of steel pipes & tubes, mfr. of rubber,*
        plastic hoses & belts.

Tel: (586) 758-4511
Fax: (586) 758-1131

%FO: 100
Emp: 2,588

TI AUTOMOTIVE
508 North Colony Rd., Meriden, Connecticut 06450
CEO: Jim Allen, Mgr.
Bus: *Manufacture of automotive parts.*

Tel: (203) 235-6180
Fax: (203) 235-2545

%FO: 100
Emp: 500

● **TISSUE SCIENCE LABORATORIES PLC**
Victoria House, Victoria Rd., Aldershot, Hampshire GU11 1EJ, England, U.K.
CEO: Martin Hunt, CEO
Bus: *Mfr. and distributes surgical supplies specializing in wound management and tissue implant products*www.tissuescience.com

Tel: 44-125-233-3002
Fax: 44-125-233-3010

Rev: $17
Emp: 79

NAICS: 325412, 325414, 339113, 541710

TSL NORTH AMERICA
1141 Clark St., Ste. D, Covington, Georgia 30014
CEO: Martin Hunt, Principal
Bus: *Mfr. and distributes surgical supplies specializing in wound management and tissue implant products*

Tel: (678) 342-7808
Fax: (678) 342-7844

%FO: 100

● **TOMKINS PLC**
East Putney House, 84 Upper Richmond Rd., London SW15 2ST, England, U.K.
CEO: David Newlands, Chmn.
Bus: *Industrial management services and manufacture of garden/leisure products, milling products and industrial products.*

Tel: 44-20-8871-4544
Fax: 44-20-8877-9700
www.tomkins.co.uk

Rev: $5,714
Emp: 36,720

NAICS: 332911, 332913, 332919, 333112, 336399

AIR SYSTEM COMPONENTS
1401 North Plano Rd., Richardson, Texas 75081
CEO: Terry O'Halloran, Pres.
Bus: *Mfr. HVAC components.*

Tel: (972) 680-9126
Fax: (972) 575-3372

%FO: 100
Emp: 2,079

DEARBORN MID-WEST CONVEYOR CO.
20334 Superior Rd., Taylor, Michigan 48180
CEO: Wes Paisley, Pres. & CEO
Bus: *Mfr. heavy duty conveyor equipment, postal and bulk system conveyors.*

Tel: (724) 288-4400
Fax: (734) 288-1914

%FO: 100

DEXTER AXLE COMPANY
2900 Industrial Pkwy E, PO Box 250, Elkhart, Indiana 46515
CEO: Mike Jones, Pres.
Bus: *Mfr. axles and wheels for trailers, motor homes and recreational vehicles.*

Tel: (574) 295-7888
Fax: (574) 295-1069

%FO: 100

GATES CORPORATION
1551 Wewatta St., Denver, Colorado 80202
CEO: Richard Bell, Pres.
Bus: *Mfr./distributor auto & industrial rubber products i.e.. belts, hose, and hydraulics.*

Tel: (303) 744-1911
Fax: (303) 744-4443

%FO: 100

HART & COOLEY, INC.
500 E. 8th St., Holland, Michigan 49423
CEO: Gary Henry, Pres.
Bus: *Mfr. residential heating and ventilating.*

Tel: (616) 392-7855
Fax: (616) 392-7971

%FO: 100
Emp: 1,950

LASCO BATHWARE, INC.
8101 East Kaiser Blvd., Anaheim, California 92808
CEO: Stacey Farley, Mgr. Tel: (800) 877-2005 %FO: 100
Bus: *Mfr. fiberglass showers and tubs.* Fax: (800) 775-2726

PHILIPS PRODUCTS, INC.
3221 Magnum Dr., Elkhart, Indiana 46516
CEO: Ronald Mason, Pres. Tel: (574) 296-0000 %FO: 100
Bus: *Mfr. aluminum/vinyl doors, windows, hoods,* Fax: (574) 296-0147 Emp: 6
and ventilating devices.

RUSKIN
3900 Dr. Greaves Rd., Kansas City, Missouri 64030
CEO: Tom Edwards, Pres. Tel: (816) 761-7476
Bus: *Mfr. of environmental controls* Fax: (816) 763-8102

STANT MANUFACTURING INC.
990 S. Broadway, Denver, Colorado 80209
CEO: David Carroll, Pres. Tel: (303) 744-1911 %FO: 100
Bus: *Mfr. of auto parts* Fax: (303) 744-4788

TOMKINS INDUSTRIES, INC.
1551 Wewatta St., Denver, Colorado 80202
CEO: Terry J. O'Halloran, Pres. Tel: (303) 744-1911
Bus: *Investment firm.* Fax: (303) 744-4443 Emp: 8,750

TRICO PRODUCTS
3255 West Hamlin Rd., Rochester Hills, Michigan 48309
CEO: David Cummings, Pres. Tel: (248) 371-1700 %FO: 100
Bus: *Mfr. wiper blades and refills.* Fax: (248) 371-8300 Emp: 4,500

● **TRANSITIVE TECHNOLOGIES LTD.**
The Triangle, hanging Ditch, Manchester M4 3TR, England, U.K.
CEO: Robert P. Wiederhold, CEO Tel: 44-161-836-2300 Rev: $2
Bus: *Software manufacture.* Fax: 44-161-836-2399 Emp: 8
www.transitive.com
NAICS: 541511

    TRANSITIVE TECHNOLOGIES INC.
    718 University Ave., Ste. 200, Los Gatos, California 95032
    CEO: Steven W. Mih Tel: (408) 399-6611 %FO: 100
    Bus: *Software manufacture and sales.* Fax: (408) 399-6610

● **TRAVELEX HOLDINGS LIMITED**
65 Kingsway, London WC2B 6TD, England, U.K.
CEO: Lloyd Dorfman, CEO Tel: 44-20-7400-4000 Rev: $970
Bus: *Foreign currency exchange services.* Fax: 44-20-7400-4001 Emp: 5,553
www.travelex.co.uk
NAICS: 522110, 522320, 525990

    TRAVELEX HOLDINGS AMERICA
    2121 North 117th Ave., Ste. 300, Omaha, Nebraska 68164
    CEO: Anthony R. Horne Tel: (402) 491-3200 %FO: 100
    Bus: *Foreign currency exchange services.* Fax: (402) 491-0016

TRAVELEX HOLDINGS AMERICA
29 Broadway, 1/F, New York, New York 10006
CEO: Anthony R. Horne   Tel: (212) 701-0499   %FO: 100
Bus: *Foreign currency exchange services.*   Fax: (212) 701-0497

TRAVELEX HOLDINGS AMERICA
1000 Franklin Ave., Ste. 100, Garden City, New York 11530
CEO: Anthony R. Horne, Mng. Dir.   Tel: (516) 663-5200   %FO: 100
Bus: *Foreign currency exchange services.*   Fax: (516) 663-5291

● **TREATT PLC**
Northern Way, Bury St. Edmunds, Suffolk IP32 6NL, England, U.K.
CEO: Hugo W. Bovill, Mng. Dir.   Tel: 44-128-470-2500   Rev: $53
Bus: *Flavors, fragrances and specialty chemicals*   Fax: 44-128-475-2888   Emp: 167
manufacture.   www.treatt.com
NAICS: 311930, 311942, 325188, 325199

    TREATT USA INC.
    4900 Lakeland Commerce Pkwy., Lakeland, Florida 33805
    CEO: Wayne Kegel, VP   Tel: (863) 668-9500   %FO: 100
    Bus: *Mfr. flavors, fragrances & specialty*   Fax: (863) 422-5930   Emp: 32
    chemicals.

● **TRIFAST PLC**
Bellbrook Park, Uckfield, East Sussex TN22 1QW, England, U.K.
CEO: Jim C. Barker, CEO   Tel: 44-1825-768-088   Rev: $187
Bus: *Mfr. and distributes industrial fasteners*   Fax: 44-1825-747-601   Emp: 947
   www.trfastenings.com
NAICS: 332722

    TR FASTENINGS
    23910 North 19th Ave., Ste. 54, Phoenix, Arizona 85027
    CEO: John Wilson   Tel: (623) 581-8082   %FO: 100
    Bus: *Mfr./distribute industrial fasteners*   Fax: (623) 581-0147

    TR FASTENINGS
    5770 Hannum Ave., Culver City, California 90232
    CEO: Mike Huntley, Pres.   Tel: (310) 215-0406   %FO: 100
    Bus: *Mfr./distribute industrial fasteners*   Fax: (310) 215-9769   Emp: 27

● **TRIKON TECHNOLOGIES, INC.**
Ringland Way, Newport NP18 2TA, England, U.K.
CEO: John MacNeil, Pres. & CEO   Tel: 44-1633-414-000   Rev: $37
Bus: *Electronics, semiconductor equipment and*   Fax: 44-1633-414-141   Emp: 214
materials manufacture.   www.trikon.com
NAICS: 333295, 334111, 334413

    TRIKON TECHNOLOGIES, INC.
    17835 New Hope St., Fountain Valley, California 92708
    CEO: John Macneil, CEO   Tel: (714) 968-4299
    Bus: *Electronics, semiconductor equipment and*   Fax: (714) 968-2594   Emp: 266
    materials manufacture.

● **TRIUMPH MOTORCYCLES LTD.**
Normandy Way, Hinkley, Leicestershire LE10 3BS, England, U.K.
CEO: John S. Bloor, Owner
Bus: *Mfr. of motorcycles and other small vehicles.*

Tel: 44-1455-251-700
Fax: 44-1455-453-005
www.triumph.co.uk

Rev: $2,111
Emp: 510

NAICS: 336991

TRIUMPH MOTORCYCLES AMERICA LTD.
385 W. Sanders Memorial Dr., Ste. 100, Newman, Georgia 30265
CEO: Mark Brady, CEO
Bus: *Manufacture & distribution of motorcycles
and other small vehicles.*

Tel: (678) 854-2010
Fax: (678) 854-2025

%FO: 100
Emp: 60

● **TT ELECTRONICS PLC**
Clive House, 12-18 Queens Rd., Weybridge, Surrey KT13 9XB, England, U.K.
CEO: Neil Rodgers, CEO
Bus: *Electronics, resistor film systems and industrial
engineering.*

Tel: 44-193-284-1310
Fax: 44-193-283-6450
www.ttelectronics.com

Rev: $949
Emp: 8,091

NAICS: 334412, 334414, 334415, 334416, 334417, 334418, 334419, 335311, 335312, 335313, 335314, 335921,
335931, 335999, 336312, 336321, 336322,
336399

AB AUTOMOTIVE INC.
PO Box 2240, 2500 Business Hwy. 70 East, Smithfield, North Carolina 27577
CEO: Robert A. Fletcher, Pres.
Bus: *Contact sensors and assemblies.*

Tel: (919) 934-5181
Fax: (919) 934-5186

%FO: 100
Emp: 110

BAS COMPONENTS INC.
1100 N. Meridian Rd., Youngstown, Ohio 45509
CEO: S.W.A. Comonte, Pres.
Bus: *High quality fasteners manufacture.*

Tel: (330) 793-9650
Fax: (330) 793-9620

%FO: 100
Emp: 10

BI TECHNOLOGIES
4200 Bonita Pl., Fullerton, California 92835
CEO: Ron Sullivan
Bus: *Automotive sensors manufacture.*

Tel: (714) 447-2300
Fax: (714) 447-2500

%FO: 100

IRC INC.
4222 South Staples St., Corpus Christi, Texas 78411
CEO: Steve Wade
Bus: *Advanced film division.*

Tel: (361) 992-7900
Fax: (361) 992-3377

%FO: 100

IRC INC.
736 Greenway Rd., PO Box 1860, Boone, North Carolina 28607
CEO: Allan Cole
Bus: *Film steel heater element manufacture.*

Tel: (828) 264-8861
Fax: (828) 264-8866

%FO: 100

IRC SHALCROSS
2500 Business Hwy. 70 East, PO Box 2240, Smithfield, North Carolina 27577
CEO: Allan Cole
Bus: *Resistor film systems manufacture.*

Tel: (919) 934-5181
Fax: (919) 934-5186

%FO: 100

OPTEK TECHNOLOGY INC.
1645 Wallace Dr., Carrollton, Texas 75006
CEO: Jerry Gallagher, Pres.   Tel: (972) 323-2200
Bus: *Mfr. of sensor chips.*   Fax: (972) 323-2396

- **TTP COMMUNICATIONS PLC**
Melbourn Science Park, Cambridge Rd., Melbourn Royston, Hertfordshire SG8 6HQ, England, U.K.
CEO: Anthony J. Milbourn, Mng. Dir.   Tel: 44-176-326-6266   Rev: $91
Bus: *Telecommunications equipment.*   Fax: 44-176-326-1216   Emp: 492
               www.ttpcom.com
    NAICS: 334210, 334413, 511210, 541710

    TTPCOM INC.
    3 Burlington Woods, Burlington, Massachusetts 01803
    CEO: Richard Walker   Tel: (781) 791-5200   %FO: 100
    Bus: *Telecommunications equipment.*   Fax: (781) 791-5201

    TTPCOM LTD.
    PO Box 461, Suwannee, Georgia 30024-0461
    CEO: Richard Walker   Tel: (770) 887-7694   %FO: 100
    Bus: *Telecommunications equipment.*   Fax: (770) 888-0354

- **THE TUSSAUDS GROUP LIMITED**
Silverglade, Leatherhead Rd., Chessington, Surrey KT9 QL, England, U.K.
CEO: Eric L. Nicoli, Chmn.   Tel: 44-870-429-2300   Rev: $199
Bus: *Entertainment attractions.*   Fax: 44-870-429-5500
               www.tussauds.com
    NAICS: 713110, 713990

    MADAME TUSSAUDS
    234 West 42nd St., New York, New York 10036
    CEO: Peter Phillipson, Pres.   Tel: (212) 512-9600   %FO: 100
    Bus: *Entertainment attractions.*   Fax: (212) 719-9440   Emp: 5

    MADAME TUSSAUDS
    3377 Las Vegas Blvd. South, Ste. 2001, Las Vegas, Nevada 89109
    CEO: Peter Phillipson, Pres.   Tel: (702) 862-7899
    Bus: *Entertainment attractions.*   Fax: (702) 862-7851

- **ULTRAFRAME PLC**
Enterprise Works, Salthill Rd., Clitheroe, Lancashire BB7 1PE, England, U.K.
CEO: David A. Moore, CEO   Tel: 44-1200-443311   Rev: $213
Bus: *Construction of manufactured buildings,*   Fax: 44-1200-425455   Emp: 1,108
     conservatories, sunrooms, roof systems.   www.ultraframe.co.uk
    NAICS: 321991, 321992, 332311, 453930

    FOUR SEASONS SUNROOMS LLC
    5005 Veterans Memorial Hwy., Holbrook, New York 11741
    CEO: Christopher Esposito, Pres.   Tel: (631) 563-4000   %FO: 100
    Bus: *Construction of manufactured buildings,*   Fax: (631) 563-4010
     conservatories, sunrooms, roof systems.

● **UMECO PLC**
Concorde House, 24 Warwick New Rd., Leamington Spa, Warwickshire CV32 5JG, England, U.K.
CEO: Clive J. Snowdon, CEO   Tel: 44-192-633-1800   Rev: $337
Bus: *Aerospace and defense products.*   Fax: 44-192-631-2680   Emp: 821
www.umeco.co.uk
NAICS: 423840, 541330, 541614, 811310

    ABSCOA INDUSTRIES, INC.
    1900 Robotics Place, PO Box 185369, Fort Worth, Texas 76118
    CEO: Robert Wilson, Pres.   Tel: (817) 284-4449   %FO: 100
    Bus: *Petroleum products industrial supplies &*   Fax: (817) 595-1554   Emp: 110
       trans equip.

    ADVANCED COMPOSITES GROUP INC.
    5350 South, 129th East Ave., Tulsa, Oklahoma 74134
    CEO: Adrian Potts, Pres.   Tel: (918) 252-3922
    Bus: *Rubber & Plastic Product Manufacturing*   Fax: (918) 252-7371

    RICHMOND AIRCRAFT PRODUCTS
    13503 Pumice St., Norwalk, California 90650
    CEO: Joerg Hubl, Pres.   Tel: (562) 404-2440   %FO: 100
    Bus: *Plastics materials & basic shapes*   Fax: (562) 404-9011   Emp: 30

    TLC
    702 Incentive Dr., Fort Wayne, Indiana 46825
    CEO: Marty Maringer, Pres.   Tel: (260) 490-6533
    Bus: *provides kits of components for the*   Fax: (260) 490-8454
       overhaul of military equipment & aircraft

● **UNILEVER PLC**
Unilever House, Blackfriars, PO Box 68, London EC4P 4BQ, England, U.K.
CEO: Patrick J. Cescau, CEO   Tel: 44-207-822-5252   Rev: $54,413
Bus: *Soaps and detergents, foods, chemicals,*   Fax: 44-207-822-5511   Emp: 223,000
personal products (J/V of UNILEVER NV,   www.unilever.com
NAICS: 311411, 311421, 311919, 311920, 311941, 311999, 322291, 325611, 325612, 325613, 325620, 327910, 424690, 446120

    SLIM FAST FOODS COMPANY
    777 S. Flagler Dr., West Palm Beach, Florida 33401
    CEO: John Rice, Pres.   Tel: (561) 833-9920   %FO: 100
    Bus: *Mfr. weight loss and weight maintenance*   Fax: (561) 822-2876
       food products.

    UNILEVER US, INC
    390 Park Ave., New York, New York 10022-4698
    CEO: Jim Duncan, Dir. Sales   Tel: (212) 888-1260   %FO: 100
    Bus: *Holding company.*   Fax: (212) 318-3800   Emp: 25,000

● **UNITED BUSINESS MEDIA PLC**
Ludgate House, 245 Blackfriars Rd., London SE1 9UY, England, U.K.
CEO: David Levin, CEO   Tel: 44-207-921-5000   Rev: $1,552
Bus: *Publishes trade and consumer*   Fax: 44-207-921-2728   Emp: 5,911
magazines/newspapers.   www.unitedbusinessmedia.com
NAICS: 511120, 516110, 519110, 519190, 541720, 541910

CMP MEDIA LLC
600 Community Dr., Manhasset, New York 11030
CEO: Steve Weitzner
Bus: *Publishes technology magazines.*

Tel: (516) 562-5000
Fax: (516) 562-7830

%FO: 100

PR NEWSWIRE ASSOCIATION LLC
810 7th Ave., 35/F, New York, New York 10019
CEO: David B. Armon, COO
Bus: *Distributor of corporate news and public relations materials.*

Tel: (212) 596-1500
Fax: (212) 541-6414

%FO: 100

● **V2 MUSIC GROUP, DIV. VIRGIN GROUP**
131 Holland Park Ave., London W11 4AT, England, U.K.
CEO: Tony Harlow, CEO
Bus: *Independent record label.*

Tel: 44-20-7471-3000
Fax: 44-20-7603-4796
www.v2music.com

NAICS: 512220

V2 MUSIC GROUP
14 East 4th St., 3/F, New York, New York 10012
CEO: Andy Gershon
Bus: *Independent record label.*

Tel: (212) 320-8500
Fax: (212) 320-8600

%FO: 100

● **VANCO PLC**
John Busch House, 277 London Rd., Iselworth, London TW7 5AX, England, U.K.
CEO: Allen Timpany, CEO
Bus: *Provides corporate communications networking services, security, management, etc.*
NAICS: 541511, 541512, 541513, 541519

Tel: 44-20-8636-1700
Fax: 44-20-8636-1701
www.canco.co.uk

Rev: $139
Emp: 344

VANCO USA
1420 Kensington Rd., Ste. 103, Oak Brook, Illinois 60523
CEO: Allen Timpany, CEO
Bus: *Provides corporate communications networking services, security, management, etc.*

Tel: (630) 218-5890
Fax: (630) 218-5891

● **VEOS PLC**
10 Greycoat Place, London SW1P 1SV, England, U.K.
CEO: Paul Lever, Chmn.
Bus: *Engaged in innovative, reproductive healthcare products for women.*
NAICS: 325412

Tel: 44-207-960-6066
Fax: 44-207-960-6696
www.veos.com

VEOS USA INC.
PO Box 331, Lake Forest, Illinois 60045
CEO: Paul Lewakowski, Mgr.
Bus: *Engaged in innovative, reproductive healthcare products for women.*

Tel: (847) 735-0003
Fax: (847) 735-0070

%FO: 100
Emp: 12

● **VICTREX PLC**
Victrex Technology Centre, Hillhouse Intl., Thornton Cleveleys, Lancashire FY5 4QD, England, U.K.
CEO: David Hummel, CEO
Bus: *Mfr. PEEK polymer thermoplastic.*
Tel: 44-1253-897-700
Fax: 44-1253-897-701
www.victrex.com
Rev: $127
Emp: 240
NAICS: 325211

   VICTREX USA INC.
   3A Caledon Ct., Greenville, South Carolina 29615
   CEO: Blair Souder, Pres.
   Bus: *Mfr. PEEK polymer thermoplastic.*
   Tel: (864) 672-7335
   Fax: (864) 672-7328
   %FO: 100

● **VINTEN BROADCAST LTD.**
Western Way, Bury St., Edmund, Suffolk IP33 3SP, England, U.K.
CEO: David Monkhouse, Sales
Bus: *Mfr./designs camera supports and dimensional animation.*
Tel: 44-128-475-2121
Fax: 44-128-475-0560
www.vinten.com
NAICS: 512191, 512199

   VINTEN INC.
   10295B NW 46th St., Sunrise, Florida 33351
   CEO: Joe Lantowski, Sales
   Bus: *Mfr. sales/distribution of camera supports.*
   Tel: (954) 572-4344
   Fax: (954) 572-4565

   VINTEN INC.
   2701 N. Ontario St., Burbank, California 91504
   CEO: Bob Low, Sales
   Bus: *Mfr. sales/distribution of camera supports.*
   Tel: (818) 847-1155
   Fax: (818) 847-1205

   VINTEN INC.
   709 Executive Blvd., Valley Cottage, New York 10989
   CEO: Len Donovan, Sales
   Bus: *Mfr. sales/distribution of camera supports.*
   Tel: (845) 268-0100
   Fax: (845) 268-0113
   %FO: 100

● **VIRGIN GROUP LTD.**
120 Campden Hill Rd., London W8 7AR, England, U.K.
CEO: Stephen Murphy, CEO
Bus: *Holding company: airline travel and hotels.*
Tel: 44-207-229-1282
Fax: 44-207-727-8200
www.virgin.com
Rev: $8,100
Emp: 35,000
NAICS: 334612, 423990, 451220, 481111, 485999, 511199, 512110, 512131, 512191, 512199, 512210, 512220, 512230, 512240, 515112, 517212, 517310, 517910, 518111, 518210, 519190, 532230, 561510, 561520, 561599

   V2 MUSIC GROUP
   14 E. 4th St., 3/F, New York, New York 10012
   CEO: Andy Gershon, Pres.
   Bus: *Music publishers and distributors*
   Tel: (212) 320-8500
   Fax: (212) 320-8600

   VIRGIN ATLANTIC AIRWAYS LTD.
   747 Belden Ave., Norwalk, Connecticut 06850
   CEO: Steve Ridgway, CEO
   Bus: *International commercial air transport services.*
   Tel: (203) 750-2570
   Fax: (203) 750-6480
   %FO: 100
   Emp: 500

England, U.K.

VIRGIN ENTERTAINMENT FROUP, INC.
5757 Wilshire Blvd., Ste. 300, Los Angeles, California 90036
CEO: Simon Wright, CEO
Bus: *Music, video, book & entertainment retail.*
Tel: (323) 935-1500
Fax: (323) 939-1993
Emp: 700

VIRGIN VACATIONS INC.
19021 120th Ave. NE, Ste. 102, Bothell, Washington 98011
CEO: Jeanne De Smedt, Pres.
Bus: *Vacation travel services.*
Tel: (888) 937-8474
Fax: (425) 424-9397
%FO: 100
Emp: 100

● **VITALOGRAPH LTD.**
Maids Moreton House, Buckingham MK18 1SW, England, U.K.
CEO: Barbara Martin, Pres.
Bus: *Mfr. spirometry and peak flow measuring
   equipment for the diagnosis and treatment of
   respiratory diseases.*
NAICS: 339112
Tel: 44-128-082-7120
Fax: 44-128-082-3302
www.vitalograph.co.uk
Emp: 160

VITALOGRAPH MEDICAL INSTRUMENTATION, INC.
13310 West 99th St., Lenexa, Kansas 66215
CEO: Phil Hemes, Pres.
Bus: *Pulmonary function testing equipment.*
Tel: (800) 255-6626
Fax: (913) 888-4259
%FO: 100

● **THE VITEC GROUP PLC**
1 Wheatfield Way, Kingston-upon-Thames, Surrey KT1 2TU, England, U.K.
CEO: Gareth Rhys Williams, CEO & Mng. Dir.
Bus: *Film and video equipment manufacture and*
NAICS: 334220, 334310, 512191, 512199, 532490
Tel: 44-20-8939-4650
Fax: 44-20-8939-4680
www.vitecgroup.com
Rev: $343
Emp: 1,624

ANTON/BAUER
14 Progress Dr., Shelton, Connecticut 06484
CEO: Alexander P. Desorbo, Pres.
Bus: *Mfr. of photographic equipment & primary
   batteries.*
Tel: (203) 929-1100
Fax: (203) 925-4988
Emp: 100

AUDIO SPECIALISTS GROUP
465 Herndon Pkwy., Herndon, Virginia 20170
CEO: Robert Nudo
Bus: *Professional audio equipment.*
Tel: (703) 471-7887
Fax: (703) 437-1107

BEXEL
2701 N. Ontario St., Burbank, California 91504
CEO: Tom Dickinson
Bus: *Audio & visual equipment & supply.*
Tel: (818) 841-5051
Fax: (818) 841-1572

BOGEN IMAGING
565 E. Crescent Ave., PO Box 506, Ramsey, New Jersey 07446
CEO: Paul Wilde, Pres.
Bus: *Sale of photographic equipment.*
Tel: (201) 818-9500
Fax: (201) 818-9177
Emp: 82

CLEAR-COM
4065 Hollis St., Emeryville, California 94608
CEO: Danny Burns, Pres.
Bus: *Mfr. of intercom systems.*
Tel: (510) 496-6666
Fax: (510) 496-6699
Emp: 75

OCONNOR
100 Kalmus Dr., Costa Mesa, California 92626
CEO: Joel Johnson, Gen. Mgr.
Bus: *Mfr. of photographic equipment.*
Tel: (714) 979-3993
Fax: (714) 957-8138
%FO: 100

● **VODAFONE GROUP**
Vodafone House, The Connection, Newbury, West Berkshire RG14 2FN, England, U.K.
CEO: Arun Sarin, CEO
Bus: *Provides digital mobile phones and equipment.*
(JV of Verizon Wireless).
Tel: 44-1635-33-251
Fax: 44-1635-45-713
www.vodafone.com
Rev: $64,505
Emp: 60,109
NAICS: 517110, 517212, 517910

VERIZON WIRELESS COMMUNICATIONS
1095 Ave. of the Americas, New York, New York 10036
CEO: Ivan G. Seidenberg, Chmn. & CEO
Bus: *Wireless telecommunications.*
Tel: (212) 395-2121
Fax: (212) 869-3265
%FO: JV
Emp: 210,000

● **VOLEX GROUP PLC**
Dornoch House, Kelvin Close, Birchwood Science Park, Warrington WA3 7JX, England, U.K.
CEO: John Corcoran, CEO
Bus: *Mfr. electronic and optical fiber cable assemblies.*
Tel: 44-192-583-0101
Fax: 44-192-583-0141
www.volex.com
Rev: $435
Emp: 9,297
NAICS: 331422, 332618, 423610

VOLEX INC.
1123 Industrial Dr. SW, Conover, North Carolina 28613
CEO: Mike Baer, Mgr.
Bus: *Mfr. of plastic products & electrical
equipment supplies.*
Tel: (828) 464-4546
Fax: (828) 464-8465
%FO: 100
Emp: 250

VOLEX INC.
5350 Lakeview Pkwy. S. Dr., Ste. D, Indianapolis, Indiana 46268
CEO: Jeff Deloughery, Mgr.
Bus: *Mfr. electronic and optical fiber cable
assemblies.*
Tel: (800) 246-2673
Fax: (800) 429-2498
%FO: 100
Emp: 25

VOLEX INC.
1900 Crown Colony Dr., Ste. 302, Quincy, Massachusetts 02169
CEO: Don Payzant, Pres.
Bus: *Mfr. of rubber & miscellaneous plastic
products.*
Tel: (617) 376-0555
Fax: (617) 376-0590
Emp: 2,300

VOLEX INC.
Quality Dr., Rte. 6, PO Box 201-H, Clinton, Arkansas 72031
CEO: Tom Baratka, Pres.
Bus: *Mfr. Electrical equipment & supplies.*
Tel: (501) 745-2444
Fax: (501) 745-4443
Emp: 75

VOLEX INC.
44250 Osgood Rd., Fremont, California 94539
CEO: Thomas Hagen, Pres.   Tel: (510) 360-5250   %FO: 100
Bus: *Mfr. fiber optic assemblies.*   Fax: (510) 354-0850   Emp: 200

● **WAGON PLC**
1 Kingmaker Court, Warwick Technology Park, Warwick CV34 6WG, England, U.K.
CEO: Pierre Vareille, CEO   Tel: 44-192-647-5000   Rev: $889
Bus: *Mfr. of automotive parts.*   Fax: 44-192-647-5050   Emp: 5,180
                                              www.wagon-plc.co.uk
NAICS: 332999, 336211, 336399
   WAGON AUTOMOTIVE USA
   25900 West Eleven Mile Rd., Southfield, Michigan 48393
   CEO: Tim Hatch, VP   Tel: (248) 262-2020   %FO: 100
   Bus: *Mfr. automotive parts.*   Fax: (248) 262-2020

● **WALKERS SHORTBREAD LTD.**
Aberlour on Spey, Moray AB38 9PD, England, U.K.
CEO: James N. Walker, CEO   Tel: 44-134-871-555   Rev: $133
Bus: *Mfr. packaged biscuits, cakes, fruitcakes and*   Fax: 44-134-871-355   Emp: 1,000
   shortbreads.   www.walkersshortbread.com
NAICS: 311821
   WALKERS USA INC.
   170Commerce Dr., Hauppauge, New York 11788
   CEO: Norman Barnes, Pres.   Tel: (631) 273-0011   %FO: 100
   Bus: *Mfr. shortbreads and biscuit products.*   Fax: (631) 273-0438

● **ROBERT WALTERS PLC**
55 Strand, London WC2N 5WR, England, U.K.
CEO: Robert C. Walters, CEO   Tel: 44-20-7379-3333   Rev: $279
Bus: *Engaged in outsourcing and recruitment.*   Fax: 44-20-7915-8714   Emp: 730
                                              www.robertwalters.com
NAICS: 541611, 541612, 561310, 561320
   ROBERT WALTERS USA INC.
   7 Times Square, Ste. 1606, New York, New York 10036
   CEO: Kurt Kraeger, CEO   Tel: (212) 704-9900   %FO: 100
   Bus: *Engaged in recruitment.*   Fax: (212) 704-4312   Emp: 11

● **WEETABIX LTD.**
Burton Latimer Kettering, Northamptonshire NN15 5JR, England, U.K.
CEO: Ken Wood, CEO   Tel: 44-1536-722-181
Bus: *Mfr. cereal and muesli.*   Fax: 44-1536-726-148
                                              www.weetabix.co.uk
NAICS: 311230, 311821
   WEETABIX CO. INC.
   20 Cameron St., Clinton, Massachusetts 01510
   CEO: Andy Harris, Mgr.   Tel: (978) 368-0991   %FO: 100
   Bus: *Mfr. cereal products.*   Fax: (978) 365-7268

- **WELLINGTON UNDERWRITING**
88 Leadenhall St., London EC3A 3BA, England, U.K.
CEO: John Barton, Chmn.
Bus: *Insurance brokers.*

NAICS: 524114, 524126

Tel: 40-207-337-2000
Fax: 40-207-337-2001
www.wellington.co.uk

Rev: $831
Emp: 385

WELLINGTON UNDERWRITING INC.
90 State House Square, Ste. 2, Hartford, Connecticut 06103
CEO: Stan Kott
Bus: *Insurance brokers.*

Tel: (860) 702-2900
Fax: (860) 801-1113

%FO: 100

WELLINGTON UNDERWRITING INC.
303 West Madison St., Suite 1250, Chicago, Illinois 60606
CEO: John Fliehler
Bus: *Insurance brokers.*

Tel: (312) 759-5522
Fax: (312) 759-5605

%FO: 100

- **WESTERNGECO**
Schlumberger House, Buckingham Gate, Gatewick Airport, West Sussex RH6 ONZ, England, U.K.
CEO: Dalton Jones, Pres.
Bus: *Reservoir imaging, oilfield services provider, monitoring and development services. (JV of Baker Hughes and Schlumberger)*

NAICS: 221310

Tel: 44-1293-556-655
Fax: 44-1293-556-940
www.westerngeco.com

Rev: $1,183
Emp: 9,000

BAKER HUGHES INCORPORATED
3900 Essex Ln., Ste. 1200, Houston, Texas 77027
CEO: Chad C. Deaton
Bus: *Oil and gas recovery services.*

Tel: (713) 439-8600
Fax: (713) 439-8699

%FO: JV

SCHLUMBERGER
2525 Gambell St., Ste 400, Anchorage, Alaska 99503
CEO: John Yearwood
Bus: *Oilfield services.*

Tel: (907) 273-1700
Fax: (907) 561-8394

%FO: 100

SCHLUMBERGER
200 Gillingham Ln., MD 200-11, Sugar Land, Texas 77478
CEO: Robert Drummond
Bus: *Oilfield services.*

Tel: (281) 285-8412
Fax: (281) 285-8523

%FO: 100

SCHLUMBERGER
300 Schlumberger Dr., Sugar Land, Texas 77478
CEO: Maurice Dijols
Bus: *Oilfield services.*

Tel: (281) 285-8500
Fax: (281) 285-8290

%FO: 100

SCHLUMBERGER LIMITED
153 East 53rd St., 57/F, New York, New York 10022
CEO: Andrew Gould, CEO
Bus: *Global technology.*

Tel: (212) 350-9400
Fax: (212) 350-9457

%FO: JV

SCHLUMBERGER-DOLL RESEARCH
36 Old Quarry Rd., Ridgefield, Connecticut 06877
CEO: Abigail Matteson
Bus: *Global technology.*

Tel: (203) 431-5000
Fax: (203) 431-5000

%FO: 100

England, U.K.

SCHLUMBERGERSEMA
5599 San Felipe, Houston, Texas 77056
CEO: Brad Kitterman
Bus: *Solutions center.*
Tel: (713) 513-2000
Fax: (713) 513-2000
%FO: 100

WESTERNGECO
10001 Richmond Ave., Houston, Texas 77042-4299
CEO: Maurice Nessim, Reg. Mgr.
Bus: *Reservoir imaging, monitoring and development services to the oil and gas industry.*
Tel: (713) 789-9600
Fax: (713) 789-0172
%FO: 100

● **WHATMAN PLC**
27 Great West Road, Brentford, Middlesex TW8 9BW, England, U.K.
CEO: William Emhiser, CEO
Bus: *Products and solutions in separations*
Tel: 44-208-326-1740
Fax: 44-208-326-1741
www.whatman.co.uk
Rev: $149
Emp: 749

NAICS: 334516

WHATMAN INC.
63 Community Dr., Sanford, Maine 04073
CEO: Helen Liu
Bus: *Lab filtration and chromatography products manufacture.*
Tel: (207) 459-7557
Fax: (207) 459-3099

WHATMAN INC.
200 Park Ave., Ste. 210, Florham Park, New Jersey 07932
CEO: David J. H. Smith, Pres.
Bus: *Sales/distribution of lab filtration and chromatography products.*
Tel: (973) 245-8300
Fax: (973) 245-8301
%FO: 100
Emp: 325

WHATMAN S&S BIOPATH INC.
2611 Mercer Ave., West Palm Beach, Florida 33401
CEO: Alan Edrick
Bus: *Engaged in life sciences.*
Tel: (561) 655-2302
Fax: (561) 655-2302
%FO: 100

WHATMAN SCHLEICHER & SCHUELL
10 Optical Ave., Keene, New Hampshire 03431
CEO: Dr. Robert Negm
Bus: *Mfr. filtration, paper products.*
Tel: (603) 352-3810
Fax: (603) 352-3627
%FO: 100

● **WHITEHEAD MANN GROUP PLC**
Ryder Ct., 14 Ryder St., London SW1Y 6QB, England, U.K.
CEO: C. J. Merry, CEO
Bus: *Executive search firm.*
Tel: 44-207-451-0499
Fax: 44-207-451-0498
www.wmann.com
Rev: $112
Emp: 297

NAICS: 541612

WHITEHEAD MANN GROUP PLC
90 South Cascade Ave., Ste. 1490, Colorado Springs, Colorado 80903
CEO: Jodi Taylor
Bus: *Executive search firm.*
Tel: (719) 227-5840
Fax: (719) 227-5840

WHITEHEAD MANN GROUP PLC
1 International Pl., 23/F, Boston, Massachusetts 02110
CEO: Durant A. Hunter
Bus: *Executive search firm.*
Tel: (617) 261-9696
Fax: (617) 261-9696

● **WILLIS GROUP HOLDINGS LIMITED**
Ten Trinity Square, London EC3P 3AX, England, U.K.
CEO: Joseph J. Plumeri, Chmn.
Bus: *Provides insurance and reinsurance brokerage and financial planning.*
NAICS: 524128, 524210
Tel: 44-23-7488-8111
Fax: 44-23-7488-8223
www.willis.com
Rev: $2,205
Emp: 15,800

STEWART SMITH GROUP INC.
88 Pine St., 17/F, New York, New York 10005
CEO: Mark M. Smith
Bus: *Insurance and reinsurance services.*
Tel: (212) 509-2700
Fax: (212) 509-3051
%FO: 100

WILLIS ADMINISTRATIVE SERVICES
1415 Murfreesboro Rd, Ste. 600, Nashville, Tennessee 37217
CEO: Fred Massa
Bus: *Insurance and reinsurance services.*
Tel: (615) 360-4560
Fax: (615) 360-2885
%FO: 100

WILLIS CARROON INC.
7650 Courtney Campbell Causeway, Ste. 920, Tampa, Florida 33607
CEO: Rob Allen
Bus: *Insurance and reinsurance services.*
Tel: (813) 281-2095
Fax: (813) 281-2234
%FO: 100

WILLIS CARROON INC.
Three Copley Pl., Ste. 300, Boston, Massachusetts 02116
CEO: David Jollin
Bus: *Insurance and reinsurance services.*
Tel: (617) 437-6900
Fax: (617) 247-1211
%FO: 100

WILLIS INSURANCE SERVICES
One Bush St., Ste. 900, San Francisco, California 94104
CEO: Claude Gallello
Bus: *Insurance and reinsurance services.*
Tel: (415) 981-1141
Fax: (415) 398-4986
%FO: 100

WILLIS INSURANCE SERVICES
2677 North Main St., Santa Ana, California 92705
CEO: Claude Gallello
Bus: *Insurance and reinsurance services.*
Tel: (714) 953-9521
Fax: (714) 953-6888
%FO: 100

WILLIS INSURANCE SERVICES
Two First Union Center, Ste. 2600, Charlotte, North Carolina 28282
CEO: Claude Gallello
Bus: *Insurance and reinsurance services.*
Tel: (704) 376-9161
Fax: (704) 342-3143
%FO: 100

WILLIS MANAGEMENT HAWAII LTD.
1001 Bishop St., Honolulu, Hawaii 96813
CEO: Jason Palmer
Bus: *Insurance and reinsurance services.*
Tel: (808) 521-0723
Fax: (808) 521-0724
%FO: 100

WILLIS NORTH AMERICA, INC.
26 Century Blvd., Nashville, Tennessee 37214-3695
CEO: Brian Johnson
Bus: *Insurance and reinsurance services.*
Tel: (615) 872-3000
Fax: (615) 872-3091
%FO: 100

WILLIS OF ALASKA INC.
4220 B St., Anchorage, Alaska 99503
CEO: Sherisa Crevier
Bus: *Insurance and reinsurance services.*
Tel: (907) 562-2266
Fax: (907) 562-2266
%FO: 100

WILLIS OF MARYLAND INC.
6700 Rockledge Dr., Bethesda, Maryland 20817
CEO: Brian Mack
Bus: *Insurance and reinsurance services.*
Tel: (301) 530-5050
Fax: (301) 897-8603
%FO: 100

WILLIS OF NEW HAMPSHIRE INC.
1 New Hampshire Ave., Ste. 200, Portsmouth, New Hampshire 03801
CEO: Bo Adams
Bus: *Insurance and reinsurance services.*
Tel: (603) 334-3000
Fax: (603) 334-3090
%FO: 100

WILLIS OF NEW YORK INC.
7 Hanover Sq., New York, New York 10004
CEO: Warren Isom
Bus: *Insurance and reinsurance services.*
Tel: (212) 344-8888
Fax: (212) 344-8511
%FO: 100

WILLIS OF NORTH AMERICA INC.
One Glenlake Pkwy., Atlanta, Georgia 30328
CEO: David S. Mohl
Bus: *Insurance and reinsurance services.*
Tel: (404) 224-5000
Fax: (404) 224-5001
%FO: 100

WILLIS OF PENNSYLVANIA INC.
444 Liberty Ave., Ste. 505, Pittsburgh, Pennsylvania 15222
CEO: Jeff Frank
Bus: *Insurance and reinsurance services.*
Tel: (412) 586-1400
Fax: (412) 586-3525
%FO: 100

WILLIS OF PORTLAND INC.
1800 SW 1st Ave., Ste. 400, Portland, Oregon 97201
CEO: Cynthia Hilton
Bus: *Insurance and reinsurance services.*
Tel: (503) 224-4155
Fax: (503) 274-2155
%FO: 100

WILLIS OF TEXAS INC.
13355 Noel Rd., Ste. 400, Dallas, Texas 75240
CEO: Ron Moore
Bus: *Insurance and reinsurance services.*
Tel: (972) 385-9800
Fax: (972) 385-9800
%FO: 100

WILLIS RISK SOLUTIONS
Seven Hanover Square, New York, New York 10004
CEO: Warren Isom
Bus: *Insurance and risk solutions.*
Tel: (212) 344-8888
Fax: (212) 344-8442
%FO: 100

WILLIS SPORTS & ENTERTAINMENT
1 Glenlake Pkwy., Atlanta, Georgia 30328
CEO: Michael Wright
Bus: *Insurance and reinsurance services.*
Tel: (404) 224-5090
Fax: (404) 224-5090
%FO: 100

● **GEORGE WIMPEY PLC**
Manning House, 22 Carlisle Pl., London SW1P 1JA, England, U.K.
CEO: Peter M. Johnson, CEO
Bus: *Homebuilding.*

Tel: 44-20-7802-9888
Fax: 44-20-7963-6366
www.wimpey.co.uk

Rev: $5,790
Emp: 5,967

NAICS: 236115, 236117, 237210

MORRISON HOMES, INC.
3655 Brookside Pkwy., Ste. 400, Alpharetta, Georgia 30022
CEO: Steven Parker, Pres. & CEO
Bus: *Home building.*

Tel: (770) 360-8700
Fax: (770) 360-8701

%FO: 100
Emp: 782

● **WINN & COALES DENSO LTD.**
Denso House, Chapel Rd., London SE27 OTR, England, U.K.
CEO: Joey Cox, Sales Mgr.
Bus: *Anti-corrosion and sealing products.*

Tel: 44-208-670-7511
Fax: 44-208-761-2456
www.denso.net

NAICS: 339991, 339999

DENSO NORTH AMERICA INC.
18211 Chisholm Trail, Houston, Texas 77060
CEO: Lucian Williams, Pres.
Bus: *Industrial supplies*

Tel: (281) 821-3355
Fax: (281) 821-0304

%FO: 100
Emp: 9

● **WOLSELEY PLC**
Arlington Business Park, Parkview 1220, Theale, West Berkshire RG7 46A, England, U.K.
CEO: Charles A. Banks, CEO
Bus: *Mfr. plumbing/heating supplies and equipment.*

Tel: 44-118-929-8700
Fax: 44-118-929-8701
www.wolseley.com

Rev: $18,120
Emp: 49,908

NAICS: 332913, 332919, 423310, 444190

FERGUSON ENTERPRISES, INC.
12500 Jefferson Ave., Newport News, Virginia 23602
CEO: Claude A. S. Hornsby III, Pres. & CEO
Bus: *Distribution and fabrication of plumbing products.*

Tel: (757) 874-7795
Fax: (757) 989-2501

%FO: 100

STOCK BUILDING SUPPLY INC.
4403 Bland Rd., Raleigh, North Carolina 27609
CEO: Fenton N. Hord, Pres. & CEO
Bus: *Building materials.*

Tel: (919) 431-1000
Fax: (919) 850-8280

%FO: 100
Emp: 9,043

THE PARNELL-MARTIN CO.
1315 n. Graham St., Charlotte, North Carolina 28206
CEO: Steady Cash, Chmn. & CEO
Bus: *Bldg. materials Retail & distribution*

Tel: (704) 375-8651
Fax: (704) 335-7156

Emp: 200

● **WPP GROUP PLC**
27 Farm St., London W1J 5RJ, England, U.K.
CEO: Martin S. Sorrell, CEO & Mng. Dir.
Bus: *Media and non-media marketing services group.*

Tel: 44-20-7408-2204
Fax: 44-20-7493-6819
www.wpp.com

Rev: $8,243
Emp: 59,932

NAICS: 541613, 541810, 541820, 541830, 541860, 541910

England, U.K.

A. EICOFF & COMPANY
401 North Michigan Ave., Chicago, Illinois 60611
CEO: Ronald Bilwas, Pres. & CEO
Bus: *Direct marketing services.*
Tel: (312) 527-7100
Fax: (312) 527-0458
%FO: 100
Emp: 91

BROUILLARD COMMUNICATIONS, INC.
466 Lexington Ave., New York, New York 10017
CEO: Bill Lyddan, Pres. & CEO
Bus: *Advertising.*
Tel: (212) 210-8563
Fax: (212) 210-8111
%FO: 100
Emp: 58

CENTER PARTNERS, INC.
4401 Innovation Dr., Fort Collins, Colorado 80525
CEO: David Geiger, CEO
Bus: *Direct marketing services.*
Tel: (970) 206-9000
Fax: (970) 282-9225
%FO: 100
Emp: 1,950

COMMONHEALTH
30 Lanidex Plaza West, Parsippany, New Jersey 07054
CEO: Matt Giegerich, Pres. & CEO
Bus: *Advertising.*
Tel: (973) 884-2200
Fax: (973) 560-7399
%FO: 100

EINSON FREEMAN, INC.
10 Mountainview Rd., Upper Saddle River, New Jersey 07458
CEO: Jean Mojo, Pres. & CEO
Bus: *Sales promotion & marketing services.*
Tel: (201) 760-8600
Fax: (201) 760-0479
%FO: 100

ENTERPRISE IG CORP.
1725 Montgomery St., San Francisco, California 94111
CEO: Dave Allen, CEO
Bus: *Advertising.*
Tel: (415) 391-9070
Fax: (415) 391-4080
%FO: 100
Emp: 60

FITCH: RPA
1266 Manning Pkwy., Powell, Ohio 43065
CEO: Todd Cameron, Pres. & CEO
Bus: *Advertising.*
Tel: (614) 885-3453
Fax: (614) 885-4289
%FO: 100

GREY GLOBAL GROUP INC.
777 3rd Ave., New York, New York 10017
CEO: Edward H. Meyer, Chmn. & Pres. & CEO
Bus: *Advertising & marketing.*
Tel: (212) 546-2000
Fax: (212) 546-1495
%FO: 100
Emp: 10,500

HILL AND KNOWLTON, INC.
466 Lexington Ave., 3/F, New York, New York 10017
CEO: Paul Taaffe, Chmn. & CEO
Bus: *Advertising services.*
Tel: (212) 885-0300
Fax: (212) 885-0570
%FO: 100

JWT
466 Lexington Ave., New York, New York 10017
CEO: Bob Jeffrey, Chmn. & CEO
Bus: *International advertising agency.*
Tel: (212) 210-7000
Fax: (212) 210-7299
%FO: 100
Emp: 8,500

OGILVY & MATHER WORLDWIDE
309 West 49th St., New York, New York 10019
CEO: Rochelle B. Lazarus, Chmn. & CEO
Bus: *International advertising agency.*
Tel: (212) 237-4000
Fax: (212) 237-5123
%FO: 100

OGILVY PUBLIC RELATIONS WORLDWIDE
825 8th Ave., World Wide Plaza, New York, New York 10019
CEO: Marcia Silverman, CEO
Bus: *Public relations.*
Tel: (212) 880-5200
Fax: (212) 370-4636
%FO: 100

THE GEPPETTO GROUP
95 Morton St., New York, New York 10014
CEO: Julie Halpin, CEO
Bus: *Advertising.*
Tel: (212) 462-8140
Fax: (212) 462-8197
%FO: 100

THE KANTAR GROUP
501 Kings Hwy. East, 4/F, Fairfield, Connecticut 06825
CEO: Eric Salama, Chmn. & CEO
Bus: *Market research.*
Tel: (203) 330-5200
Fax: (203) 330-5201
%FO: 100
Emp: 5,800

UNIWORLD GROUP, INC.
100 Ave. of the Americas, New York, New York 10013
CEO: Byron E. Lewis, Chmn. & CEO
Bus: *International advertising agency.*
Tel: (212) 219-1600
Fax: (212) 219-6395
%FO: 100

VML, INC.
250 Richards Rd., Ste. 255, Kansas City, Missouri 64116
CEO: Matt Anthony, CEO
Bus: *Advertising.*
Tel: (816) 283-0700
Fax: (816) 283-0954
%FO: 100

WPP GROUP USA, INC.
125 Park Ave., New York, New York 10017
CEO: Martin Sorrell, CEO
Bus: *Engaged in media and non-media
advertising, marketing services, public
relations, market research and
communications.*
Tel: (212) 632-2200
Fax: (212) 632-2222
%FO: 100
Emp: 26,120

YOUNG & RUBICAM, INC.
285 Madison Ave., New York, New York 10017
CEO: Ann M. Fudge, Chmn. & CEO
Bus: *International advertising agency.*
Tel: (212) 210-3000
Fax: (212) 210-4680
%FO: 100
Emp: 12,700

● **WSP GROUP PLC**
Buchanan House, 24-30 Holborn, London EC1N 2HS, England, U.K.
CEO: Christopher Cole, CEO
Bus: *Provides management and consultancy services.*
Tel: 44-207-314-5000
Fax: 44-207-314-5111
www.wspgroup.com
Rev: $594
Emp: 5,200

NAICS: 541310, 541330, 541490

FLACK & KURTZ
475 5th Ave., New York, New York 10017
CEO: Diane Dermer
Bus: *Provides engineering services.*
Tel: (212) 532-9600
Fax: (212) 689-7489
%FO: 100

FLACK & KURTZ
405 Howard St., Ste. 500, San Francisco, California 94105
CEO: Saied Nazeri
Bus: *Provides engineering services.*
Tel: (415) 398-3833
Fax: (415) 433-5311
%FO: 100

FLACK & KURTZ
1417 Fourth Ave., Ste. 400, Seattle, Washington 98101
CEO: Henry DiGregorio   Tel: (206) 342-9900   %FO: 100
Bus: *Provides engineering services.*   Fax: (206) 342-9901

FLACK & KURTZ
1201 Pennsylvania Ave. NW, Ste. 300, Washington, District of Columbia 20004
CEO: Henry DiGregorio   Tel: (202) 293-5951   %FO: 100
Bus: *Provides engineering services.*   Fax:

WSP CANTOR SEINUK
228 East 45th St., New York, New York 10017
CEO: Silvian Marcus, CEO   Tel: (212) 687-9888   %FO: 100
Bus: *Structural engineering firm*   Fax: (646) 487-5501

● **XYRATEX GROUP LIMITED**
Langstone Rd., Havant, Hampshire PO9 1SA, England, U.K.
CEO: Steve Barber, CEO   Tel: 44-23-9249-6000   Rev: $459
Bus: *Computer hardware manufacture.*   Fax: 44-23-9249-6001   Emp: 968
                                              www.xyratex.com
NAICS: 334111, 334112

    XYRATEX INTERNATIONAL
    840 Embarcadero Dr., Ste. 80, West Sacramento, California 95691
    CEO: Mark Sampson, Mgr.   Tel: (603) 642-7808   %FO: 100
    Bus: *Mfr. high performance network storage* Fax: (916) 375-8488
       systems.

    XYRATEX INTERNATIONAL
    2031 Concourse Dr., San Jose, California 95131
    CEO: Chris Sharman, Mgr.   Tel: (408) 894-0800   %FO: 100
    Bus: *Co-development, sales and support of*   Fax: (408) 894-0880
       storage systems and infrastructure

    XYRATEX INTERNATIONAL
    100 Technology Circle, Scotts Valley, California 95066
    CEO: Steve Barber, CEO   Tel: (831) 438-0701
    Bus: *Mfr. high performance network storage* Fax: (831) 438-0588
       systems.

    XYRATEX INTERNATIONAL
    1804 Centre Point Circle, Ste. 112, Naperville, Illinois 60563
    CEO: Steve Barber, CEO   Tel: (877) 997-2839
    Bus: *Mfr. high performance network storage* Fax: (630) 364-7601
       systems.

● **YELL GROUP PLC**
Queens Walk, Oxford Rd., Reading RG1 7PT, England, U.K.
CEO: John Condron, CEO   Tel: 44-118-959-2111   Rev: $2,167
Bus: *Telephone information service directory* Fax: 44-118-950-6988   Emp: 8,082
    publication.   www.yellgroup.com
NAICS: 511140, 519190

YELLOW BOOK INC.
1901 South Congress Ave., Boynton Beach, Florida 33426
CEO: Linda Terrizzi, Gen. Mgr.   Tel: (561) 734-8330   %FO: 100
Bus: *Publishes community and business*   Fax: Emp: 50
       directories.

YELLOW BOOK USA
6300 C St. SW, Cedar Rapids, Iowa 52404
CEO: Mark Hartung, Principal   Tel: (319) 366-1100   %FO: 100
Bus: *Publishes community and business*   Fax: Emp: 850
       directories.

YELLOW BOOK USA
193 EAB Plaza, Uniondale, New York 11556
CEO: Joseph Walsh, CEO   Tel: (516) 766-1900   %FO: 100
Bus: *Directories & yellow pages publishers.* Fax: (516) 766-1909

YELLOW BOOK USA
750 West Lake Cook Rd., Ste. 375, Buffalo Grove, Illinois 60089
CEO: Harry Dobbs, Mgr.   Tel: (847) 252-4800   %FO: 100
Bus: *Directories & yellow pages publishers.* Fax:

YELLOW BOOK USA
2560 Renaissance Blvd., King of Prussia, Pennsylvania 19406
CEO: Lorena Garagovzo, Mgr.   Tel: (610) 731-2500   %FO: 100
Bus: *Publishes leadership directories.*   Fax: Emp: 500

YELLOW BOOK USA
18881 Von Karman Ave., Ste. 600, Irvine, California 92616
CEO: John Bartlett, CFO   Tel: (949) 340-1200   %FO: 100
Bus: *Directories & yellow pages publishers.* Fax: Emp: 39

YELLOW BOOK USA
600 Vestavia Pkwy., Ste. 305, Birmingham, Alabama 35216
CEO: Michelle Haynes, Dir.   Tel: (205) 314-4700   %FO: 100
Bus: *Directories & yellow pages publishers.* Fax: Emp: 31

• **YULE CATTO & CO. PLC**
Central Rd., Temple Fields, Harlow, Essex CM20 2BH, England, U.K.
CEO: Alex Walker, CEO   Tel: 44-127-944-2791   Rev: $978
Bus: *Chemicals manufacturer.*   Fax: 44-127-964-1360   Emp: 3,630
                                               www.yulecatto.com
   NAICS: 325131, 325132, 325188, 325199, 325211, 325221, 325222, 325411, 325412, 325414, 325520, 325611,
325612, 325613, 325910, 325992

   ATLANCO
   2 Bomar St., Inman, South Carolina 29349
   CEO: Judy Hosa, Pres.   Tel: (864) 472-3832
   Bus: *Chemical products*   Fax: (864) 472-3584   Emp: 1

   PFW AROMA CHEMICALS
   235 Margaret King Ave., Ringwood, New Jersey 07456
   CEO: Max Vanvoorast, Dir.   Tel: (973) 962-1700
   Bus: *Chemical products*   Fax: (973) 962-4377   Emp: 2

UQUIFA, INC.
15 Blossom Lane, Golf, Illinois 60029
CEO: Michael East, VP Sales
Bus: *Chemical manufacturing*

Tel: (847) 729-8061
Fax: (847) 729-8062

● **ZENITH OPTIMEDIA**
23 Howland St., London W1T 4AY, England, U.K.
CEO: John PerrissSteve King, CEO
Bus: *Provides global media planning and buying*
    services. (JV Saatchi & Saatchi)
NAICS: 541830

Tel: 44-20-7961-1000
Fax: 44-20-7961-1113
www.zenithoptimedia.com

Rev: $8,200

    OPTIMEDIA
    375 Hudson St., 7/F, New York, New York 10014
    CEO: Michael Drexler, CEO
    Bus: *Advertising services.*

    Tel: (212) 820-3200
    Fax: (212) 820-3300

    Emp: 360

    ZENITH MEDIA SERVICES
    299 West Houston St., 10/F, New York, New York 10014
    CEO: Tim Jones, Pres.
    Bus: *Advertising services.*

    Tel: (212) 859-5100
    Fax: (212) 727-9494

    Emp: 360

    ZENITH MEDIA SERVICES INC.
    299 West Houston St., 10/F, New York, New York 10014
    CEO: Richard Hamilton, CEO
    Bus: *Provides media planning services.*

    Tel: (212) 859-5100
    Fax: (212) 727-9495

    %FO: JV
    Emp: 360

● **ZETEX PLC**
Zetex Technology Park, Chadderton, Oldham, Greater Manchester OL9 9LL, England, U.K.
CEO: Bob Conway, CEO
Bus: *Mfr. analog semiconductors.*

NAICS: 334413

Tel: 44-161-622-4444
Fax: 44-161-622-4446
www.zetex.com

Rev: $139
Emp: 755

    ZETEX INC.
    700 Veterans Memorial Hwy., Ste. 315, Hauppauge, New York 11788
    CEO: Neil Chadderton, Mgr.
    Bus: *Mfr. and sales analog semiconductors.*

    Tel: (631) 360-2222
    Fax: (631) 360-8222

    %FO: 100

● **ZEUS TECHNOLOGY LIMITED**
The Jeffreys Bldg., Cowley Rd., Cambridge CB4 0WS, England, U.K.
CEO: Paul Di Leo, CEO
Bus: *Mfr. computer software.*

NAICS: 511210

Tel: 44-122-352-5000
Fax: 44-122-352-5100
www.zeus.com

Rev: $5
Emp: 50

    ZEUS TECHNOLOGY
    5201 Great America Pkwy., Santa Clara, California 95054
    CEO: John Paterson, CEO
    Bus: *Mfr./sales computer software products.*

    Tel: (408) 350-9400
    Fax: (408) 350-9408

    %FO: 100

● **ZONE VISION ENTERPRISES LTD., SUB. UNITEDGLOBALCOM**
105-109 Salusbury Rd., London NW6 6RG, England, U.K.
CEO: Dermott Shortt, CEO
Bus: *Digital television, including film distribution.*

Tel: 44-20-7328-8808
Fax: 44-20-7624-3652
www.zonevision.co.uk

Rev: $46
Emp: 177

NAICS: 515120, 515210

HOT HOUSE MEDIA INC.
3399 Peachtree Rd., Ste. 700, Atlanta, Georgia 30326
CEO: Doug Orr
Bus: *Digital television, including film distribution.*

Tel: (404) 815-4606
Fax: (404) 685-0962

%FO: 100

ZONE VISION USA
637 Franklin St., Ste. 300, Denver, Colorado 80218
CEO: Monroe Rifkin
Bus: *Digital television, including film distribution.*

Tel: (303) 333-1215
Fax: (303) 322-3553

%FO: 100

● **ZOTEFOAMS PLC**
675 Mitcham Rd., Croydon, London CR9 3AL, England, U.K.
CEO: David Stirling, Mng. Dir.
Bus: *Mfr. protective foam padding for sports, health
care, autos, toys, life jackets and packaging.*

Tel: 44-20-8664-1600
Fax: 44-20-8664-1616
www.zotefoams.com

Rev: $49
Emp: 240

NAICS: 325212, 326299

ZOTEFOAMS INC.
55 Precision Dr., Walton, Kentucky 41094
CEO: Dan Catalano, Pres.
Bus: *Mfr. protective foam padding.*

Tel: (859) 371-4046
Fax: (859) 371-4734

%FO: 100

Ethiopia

- **ETHIOPIAN AIRLINES**
  Bole International Airlines, Addis Ababa, Ethiopia
  CEO: Ato Gima Wake, CEO
  Bus: *Airline transport services.*

  Tel: 251-615-110
  Fax: 251-611-474
  www.flyethiopian.com

  NAICS: 481111

  ETHIOPIAN AIRLINES
  336 East 45th St., 3/F, New York, New York 10017
  CEO: Girmaselassie Zewdu
  Bus: *Airlines services.*

  Tel: (212) 867-0095
  Fax: (212) 692-9589

  %FO: 100

Finland

- **AHLSTROM CORPORATION**
Etelaesplanadi 14, FIN-00130 Helsinki, Finland
CEO: Johan Gullichsen, Chmn.
Bus: *Fiber based materials and flexible packaging manufacturing.*
NAICS: 322214, 322222, 322299, 339113

Tel: 358-10-888-4712
Fax: 358-10-888-4799
www.ahlstrom.com

Rev: $820
Emp: 7,300

    AHLSTROM CAPITAL CORPORATION
    3820 Mansell Rd., Ste. 200, Alpharetta, Georgia 30022
    CEO: Brian Bezanson, Pres.
    Bus: *Pumps and specialty papers manufacturer.*

Tel: (770) 650-2100
Fax: (770) 650-2101

%FO: 100

    AHLSTROM CORPORATION
    122 West Butler St., Mt. Holly Springs, Pennsylvania 17065-0238
    CEO: Christopher Coates, VP
    Bus: *Engaged in life science and filtration process.*

Tel: (717) 486-3438
Fax: (717) 486-4863

%FO: 100

    AHLSTROM ENGINE FILTRATION, LLC
    PO Box 680, Taylorville, Illinois 62568
    CEO: Ken Andrews
    Bus: *Life science and filtration process.*

Tel: (217) 824-9611
Fax: (217) 824-9514

%FO: 100

    AHLSTROM ENGINE FILTRATION, LLC
    PO Box 1708, Madisonville, Kentucky 42431
    CEO: Jim Prescott
    Bus: *Fiber based materials and flexible packaging manufacture.*

Tel: (270) 821-0140
Fax: (270) 824-1526

%FO: 100

    AHLSTROM WINDSOR LOCKS
    2 Elm St., Windsor Locks, Connecticut 06096
    CEO: Randall Davis
    Bus: *Paper manufacture.*

Tel: (860) 654-8300
Fax: (860) 654-8338

%FO: 100

    ALHSTROM FIBERCOMPOSITES
    1 Canal Bank Rd., Windsor Locks, Connecticut 06096
    CEO: William Fitzpatrick, VP
    Bus: *Titanium equipment manufacture and sales.*

Tel: (860) 654-8300
Fax: (860) 654-8338

%FO: 100

- **AMER SPORTS CORPORATION**
Makelankatu 91, PO Box 130, FIN-00601 Helsinki, Finland
CEO: Roger Talermo, CEO
Bus: *Sporting goods equipment development and manufacture.*
NAICS: 339920

Tel: 358-9-757-7800
Fax: 358-9-757-8200
www.amersports.com

Rev: $1,276
Emp: 4,066

    ATOMIC SKI USA INC.
    9 Columbia Dr., Amherst, New Hampshire 03031
    CEO: Jack Baltz, Pres.
    Bus: *Marketing ski, snowboarding & skating equipment.*

Tel: (603) 880-6143
Fax: (603) 880-6099

%FO: 100
Emp: 30

PRECOR INCORPORATED
20031 142nd Ave. NE, PO Box 7202, Woodinville, Washington 98072-4002
CEO: Paul J. Byrne, Pres.   Tel: (425) 486-9292   %FO: 100
Bus: *Sports equipment manufacture.*   Fax: (425) 486-3856

SUUNTO USA INC.
2151 Las Palmas Dr., Ste. F, Carlsbad, California 92009
CEO: Dan Colliander   Tel: (760) 931-6788   %FO: 100
Bus: *Diving instruments and water sport suits,*   Fax: (760) 931-9875
     wrist top computers and field compasses
     manufacture.

WILSON SPORTING GOODS COMPANY
6435 NW Croeni Rd., Hillsboro, Oregon 97124
CEO: Mike Eggiman   Tel: (503) 531-5500   %FO: 100
Bus: *Sporting goods manufacture.*   Fax: (503) 531-5501

WILSON SPORTING GOODS COMPANY
8700 West Bryn Mawr Ave., Chicago, Illinois 60631
CEO: Steve Millea, Pres.   Tel: (773) 714-6400   %FO: 100
Bus: *Mfr./marketing sporting goods; racquet, golf*   Fax: (773) 714-4565   Emp: 3,049
     & team sports equipment & apparel.

● **DYNEA OY**
Siltasaarenkatu 18-20 A, FIN-00530 Helsinki, Finland
CEO: Roger Carlstedt, CEO   Tel: 358-10-585-2000   Rev: $1,471
Bus: *Adhesives manufacture.*   Fax: 358-10-585-2001   Emp: 3,137
                                   www.dynea.com
NAICS: 325520

DYNEA INC.
344 Tannehild Rd., Winnfield, Louisiana 71483
CEO: Tommy Provence   Tel: (318) 628-2139   %FO: 100
Bus: *Adhesive manufacture and sales.*   Fax: (318) 628-2238

DYNEA INC.
6175 American Rd., Toledo, Ohio 43612
CEO: Art Schermbeck   Tel: (419) 726-5013   %FO: 100
Bus: *Adhesive manufacture and sales.*   Fax: (419) 726-5988

DYNEA INC.
790 Corinth Rd., Manicure, North Carolina 17559
CEO: Bill Langley   Tel: (919) 542-2526   %FO: 100
Bus: *Adhesive manufacture and sales.*   Fax: (919) 542-2817

DYNEA INC.
PO Box 270, Springfield, Oregon 97477
CEO: Bill Langley   Tel: (541) 746-6501   %FO: 100
Bus: *Adhesive manufacture and sales.*   Fax: (541) 746-6273

DYNEA INC.
1600 Valley River Dr., Ste. 390, Eugene, Oregon 97401
CEO: Gary McClean   Tel: (541) 687-8840   %FO: 100
Bus: *Adhesive manufacture and sales.*   Fax: (541) 431-6813

DYNEA INC.
14139 US Highway 84 West, Andalusia, Alabama 36420
CEO: Steve Jimmerson
Bus: *Adhesive manufacture and sales.*
Tel: (334) 222-7581
Fax: (334) 222-3877
%FO: 100

DYNEA INC.
PO Box 2109, Welcome, North Carolina 27374
CEO: John Spanburg
Bus: *Adhesive manufacture and sales.*
Tel: (336) 731-1425
Fax: (336) 731-1433
%FO: 100

DYNEA OVERLAYS INC.
2301 N. Columbia Blvd., PO Box 17307, Portland, Oregon 97217
CEO: Rich Carroll
Bus: *Adhesive manufacture and sales.*
Tel: (503) 289-1111
Fax: (503) 978-2607
%FO: 100

DYNEA OVERLAYS INC.
10639 Hayward Ct., Hayward, Wisconsin 54843
CEO: Randy Schwartzhoff
Bus: *Adhesive manufacture and sales.*
Tel: (715) 634-5057
Fax: (715) 634-2361
%FO: 100

DYNEA OVERLAYS INC.
2144 Milwaukee Way, Tacoma, Washington 98421-2706
CEO: Bjorn Wahl
Bus: *Adhesive manufacture and sales.*
Tel: (253) 572-5600
Fax: (253) 627-2896
%FO: 100

• **ELCOTEQ NETWORK CORPORATION**
Sinimaentie 8, PO Box 8, FIN-02631 Espoo, Finland
CEO: Jouni Hartikainen, CEO
Bus: *Wireless communications products manufacture.*
Tel: 358-1041-311
Fax: 358-10413-1938
www.elcoteq.com
Rev: $4,028
Emp: 16,149

NAICS: 334210, 334419

ELCOTEQ, INC.
909 Lake Carolyn Pkwy., Ste. 500, Irving, Texas 75039
CEO: Doug Brenner
Bus: *Wireless communications products sales and distribution.*
Tel: (972) 401-9995
Fax: (972) 401-9606
%FO: 100

• **FATHAMMER LTD.**
Tammasaarenkatu 7-A, FIN-00180 Helsinki, Finland
CEO: Matti Airas, CEO
Bus: *3-D game tools manufacture for mobile devices.*
Tel: 358-9-694-4044
Fax: 358-9-693-3013
www.fathammer.com

NAICS: 541511, 541519

FATHAMMER USA INC.
1480 Seville Dr., Morgan Hill, California 95037
CEO: Brian Bruning
Bus: *3-D game tools manufacture for mobile devices.*
Tel: (408) 778-4631
Fax: (408) 778-3642
%FO: 100

Finland

- **FINNAIR OYJ**
Tietotie 11A, Helsinki-Vantaa Airport, FIN-01053 Helsinki, Finland
CEO: Keijo Suila, Pres. & CEO
Bus: *Passenger and cargo air transport services.*

  Tel: 358-9-818-8100
  Fax: 358-9-818-4092
  www.finnair.fi

  Rev: $2,317
  Emp: 9,522

  NAICS: 481111, 481212

  FINNAIR
  3600 W. Commercial Blvd., Ft. Lauderdale, Florida 33309
  CEO: Roland Adams
  Bus: *Passenger and cargo air transport services.*

  Tel: (954) 731-2110
  Fax: (954) 731-2110

  %FO: 100

  FINNAIR
  JFK Airport Bldg. 151, Jamaica, New York 11430
  CEO: Kari Tikkamen
  Bus: *Passenger and cargo air transport services.*

  Tel: (718) 656-8613
  Fax: (718) 656-8613

  %FO: 100

  FINNAIR
  228 East 45th St., New York, New York 10017
  CEO: Antero Lahtinen, Dir.
  Bus: *Passenger and cargo air transport services.*

  Tel: (212) 499-9000
  Fax: (212) 499-9036

  %FO: 100
  Emp: 100

- **FISKARS CORPORATION**
PO Box 235, Mannerheimintie 14A, FIN-00101 Helsinki, Finland
CEO: Heikki Allonen, Pres. & CEO
Bus: *Seasonal lawn, garden and recreation furniture and home, office and craft products manufacture.*

  Tel: 358-9-618-861
  Fax: 358-9-604-053
  www.fiskars.fi

  Rev: $814
  Emp: 3,448

  NAICS: 332211, 332212, 333991, 339944, 441210, 441229

  FISKARS BRANDS, INC.
  2537 Daniels St., Madison, Wisconsin 53718
  CEO: James S. Purdin, Pres. & CEO
  Bus: *Mfr. hand tools, power tools, lawn and garden equipment, school and office*

  Tel: (608) 259-1649
  Fax: (608) 294-4790

  %FO: 100
  Emp: 3,925

  FISKARS CONSUMER PRODUCTS INC.
  780 Carolina St., Sauk City, Wisconsin 53583-1369
  CEO: Joseph Petersen
  Bus: *Garden and outdoor living products.*

  Tel: (608) 643-4389
  Fax: (608) 643-4812

  %FO: 100
  Emp: 5,600

  FISKARS CONSUMER PRODUCTS INC.
  8300 Highland Dr., Wausau, Wisconsin 54401
  CEO: Lynn White, Controller
  Bus: *Power tools manufacture.*

  Tel: (715) 845-3802
  Fax: (715) 848-3342

  %FO: 100

  FISKARS CONSUMER PRODUCTS INC.
  7811 West Ave., Wausau, Wisconsin 54401
  CEO: Jeff Powell, Pres.
  Bus: *Crafts products manufacture.*

  Tel: (715) 842-2091
  Fax: (715) 848-3657

  %FO: 100

FISKARS HOME LEISURE DIV.
3000 West Orange Ave., Apopka, Florida 32703-3347
CEO: William Denton, Pres.
Bus: *Outdoor leisure products and American designer pottery manufacture.*
Tel: (407) 889-5533
Fax: (407) 889-7457
%FO: 100

FISKARS SCHOOL, OFFICE & CRAFT
2537 Daniels St., Madison, Wisconsin 53718
CEO: Chad Vincent, Pres.
Bus: *Hobby, craft, cutting, edging and trimming tools for school, home and office.*
Tel: (608) 259-1649
Fax: (608) 294-4790
%FO: 100

GERBER LEGENDARY BLADES
14200 SW 72nd Ave., Portland, Oregon 97224
CEO: Peter Favilla, VP
Bus: *Garden tools and blades manufacture.*
Tel: (503) 639-6161
Fax: (503) 620-3446
%FO: 100

POWER SENTRY
17300 Medina Rd., Ste. 800, Plymouth, Minnesota 55447
CEO: Mark Schaffner, Pres.
Bus: *Surge protectors manufacture.*
Tel: (763) 557-8889
Fax: (763) 557-8868
%FO: 100

● **F-SECURE CORPORATION**
Tammasaarenkatu 7, PL 24, FIN-00180 Helsinki, Finland
CEO: Risto Siilasmaa, Pres. & CEO
Bus: *Internet security and encryption software.*
Tel: 358-9-2520-0700
Fax: 358-9-2520-5001
www.f-secure.com
Rev: $37
Emp: 375

NAICS: 511210

F-SECURE, INC.
100 Century Ct., Ste. 700, San Jose, California 95112
CEO: Ilkka Starck, VP
Bus: *Mfr./sales Internet security and encryption software.*
Tel: (408) 938-6700
Fax: (408) 938-6701
%FO: 100
Emp: 50

● **HUHTAMAKI OYJ**
Lansituulentie 7, FIN-02100 Espoo, Finland
CEO: Heikki Takanen, CEO
Bus: *Consumer packaging; plastic, paper and disposable tableware.*
Tel: 358-9-686-881
Fax: 358-9-660-622
www.huhtamaki.com
Rev: $2,854
Emp: 15,531

NAICS: 322215, 322221, 322222, 339999

HUHTAMAKI AMERICAS
9201 Packaging Dr., De Soto, Kansas 66018
CEO: Clay Dunn, EVP
Bus: *Engaged in consumer packaging; plastic, paper and disposable tableware.*
Tel: (913) 583-3025
Fax: (913) 583-8781
%FO: 100
Emp: 3,000

HUHTAMAKI CONSUMER PRODUCTS INC.
4209 East Noakes St., Los Angeles, California 90023
CEO: Mark Pettigrew, Mgr.
Bus: *Mfr. of plastic foam products, plastic, folding paperboard box, sanitary food*
Tel: (323) 269-0151
Fax: (323) 269-3566
%FO: 100
Emp: 450

HUHTAMAKI CONSUMER PRODUCTS INC.
9201 Packaging Dr., De Soto, Kansas 66018
CEO: Mark Staton, Pres.
Bus: *Mfr. of laminated paper products.*
Tel: (913) 583-3025
Fax: (913) 583-8756
%FO: 100
Emp: 900

HUHTAMAKI CONSUMER PRODUCTS INC.
100 State St., Fulton, New York 13069
CEO: Tom Meucci, Dir.
Bus: *Mfr. of paper containers.*
Tel: (315) 593-5311
Fax: (315) 593-5345
%FO: 100
Emp: 585

HUHTAMAKI FLEXIBLES INC.
2400 Continental Blvd., Malvern, Pennsylvania 19355
CEO: Athos Ikonomou, Gen. Mgr.
Bus: *Mfr. of packaging paper & film.*
Tel: (484) 527-2000
Fax: (484) 527-2100
%FO: 100
Emp: 147

HUHTAMAKI FOODSERVICE, INC
402 N. 44th Ave., Ste. A, Phoenix, Arizona 85043
CEO: Don Towne, Mgr.
Bus: *Mfr. plastic food containers.*
Tel: (602) 477-3355
Fax: (602) 477-3370
%FO: 100
Emp: 75

HUHTAMAKI FOODSERVICE, INC.
5760 West Shaffer Rd., Coleman, Michigan 48618
CEO: Larry Terbush, Mgr.
Bus: *Mfr. of plastic products.*
Tel: (989) 633-8900
Fax: (989) 633-8991
%FO: 100
Emp: 250

HUHTAMAKI FOODSERVICE, INC.
5566 New Vienna Rd., New Vienna, Ohio 45159
CEO: Howard Liming, Mgr.
Bus: *Mfr. of plastic products.*
Tel: (937) 987-3020
Fax: (937) 987-3092
%FO: 100
Emp: 350

HUHTAMAKI FOODSERVICE, INC.
9201 Packaging Dr., De Soto, Kansas 66018
CEO: Kalle Tanhuanpaa, EVP
Bus: *Mfr. of packaging & containers.*
Tel: (913) 583-3025
Fax: (913) 583-8781
%FO: 100
Emp: 1,270

HUHTAMAKI FOODSERVICE, INC.
242 College Ave., Waterville, Maine 04903
CEO: Steve Bosse, Mgr.
Bus: *Mfr. of converted paper products, sanitary food containers & plastic products.*
Tel: (207) 873-3351
Fax: (207) 877-6254
%FO: 100
Emp: 550

HUHTAMAKI FOODSERVICE, INC.
6629 Indianapolis Blvd., Hammond, Indiana 46320
CEO: Rich Blastic, Mgr.
Bus: *Mfr. of cellulosic manmade fibers, packaging paper film.*
Tel: (219) 844-8950
Fax: (219) 845-0938
%FO: 100
Emp: 110

HUHTAMAKI FOODSERVICE, INC.
608 Mathis Mill Rd., Albertville, Alabama 35950
CEO: Kalle Tanhuanpaa
Bus: *Mfr. of molded paper products.*
Tel: (256) 894-1100
Fax: (256) 894-1138
%FO: 100
Emp: 142

HUHTAMAKI FOODSERVICE, INC.
8450 Gerber Rd., Sacramento, California 95828
CEO: Mike Wadsworth, Operations Mgr.   Tel: (916) 689-2020   %FO: 100
Bus: *Mfr. of fiber cans, drums & sanitary food*   Fax: (916) 689-1013   Emp: 250
  containers.

● **INSTRUMENTARIUM CORPORATION**
Kuortaneenkatu 2, PO Box 100, FIN-00031 Helsinki, Finland
CEO: Olli Riikkala, Pres. & CEO   Tel: 358-10-394-11
Bus: *Medical technology.*   Fax: 358-9-146-4172
   www.gehealthcare.com/fifi/

NAICS: 334510, 334517, 339111, 339112, 339113, 423450

DATEX-OHMEDA INC.
9155 South Dadeland Blvd., Miami, Florida 33156
CEO: Bill Beckman, Mgr.   Tel: (305) 670-8540   %FO: 100
Bus: *Medical technology.*   Fax: (305) 670-2316

DATEX-OHMEDA INC.
6892 Preston Rd., Keithville, Louisiana 71047
CEO: Don Lane, Mgr.   Tel: (318) 933-5723   %FO: 100
Bus: *Medical technology.*   Fax:

DATEX-OHMEDA INC.
3030 Ohmeda Dr., Madison, Wisconsin 53718
CEO: Richard Atkin, CEO   Tel: (608) 221-1551   %FO: 100
Bus: *Medical technology.*   Fax: (608) 222-9147   Emp: 1,400

DATEX-OHMEDA INC.
10 New England Business Center Dr., Andover, Massachusetts 01810
CEO: Joseph Davin, Mgr.   Tel: (978) 552-7000   %FO: 100
Bus: *Medical technology.*   Fax: (978) 552-7033   Emp: 30

INSTRUMENTARIUM IMAGING, INC.
4181 Latham St., Riverside, California 92501
CEO: Wolfram Klawitter, Pres.   Tel: (951) 781-2020   %FO: 100
Bus: *Mfr. of X-ray apparatus.*   Fax: Emp: 42

INSTRUMENTARIUM IMAGING, INC.
300 West Edgerton Ave., Milwaukee, Wisconsin 53207
CEO: Michael Palazzola, Pres.   Tel: (414) 747-1030   %FO: 100
Bus: *Medical technology.*   Fax: (414) 481-8665   Emp: 75

OHMEDA MEDICAL
60 Walnut Ave., Ste. 100, Clark, New Jersey 07066
CEO: Andrew Krakauer   Tel: (732) 815-7785   %FO: 100
Bus: *Medical technology.*   Fax: (732) 815-7786   Emp: 2

● **JAAKKO POYRY GROUP OYJ**
Jaakonkatu 3, PO Box 4, Vantaa, FIN-01621 Uusimaa, Finland
CEO: Erkki Pehu-Lehtonen, Pres. & CEO   Tel: 358-989-471   Rev: $474
Bus: *Consulting and engineering services.*   Fax: 358-9-878-5855   Emp: 4,635
   www.poyry.com

NAICS: 541310

JP MANAGEMENT CONSULTING
580 White Plains Rd., 3/F, Tarrytown, New York 10591-5183
CEO: Norman W. Lord, Pres.   Tel: (914) 332-4000   %FO: 100
Bus: *Architectural consulting.*   Fax: (914) 332-4411

MARATHON ENGINEERS/ARCHITECTS/PLANNERS LLC
PO Box 8028, 2323 East Capitol Dr., Appleton, Wisconsin 54912-8028
CEO: Chris Cox   Tel: (920) 954-2000   %FO: 100
Bus: *Engineering and architectural consulting.*   Fax: (920) 954-2020

• **KEMIRA OYJ**
Porkkalankatu 3, PO Box 330, FIN-00101 Helsinki, Finland
CEO: Esa Tirkkonen, CEO   Tel: 358-10-8611   Rev: $3,456
Bus: *Chemicals manufacture for paper products.* Fax: 358-10-862-1119   Emp: 9,714
                                         www.kemira.com

NAICS: 325131, 325181

   KEMIRA CHEMICALS, INC.
   315 North Madison St., Fortville, Indiana 46040
   CEO: Chris Conti, Mgr.   Tel: (317) 485-5117   %FO: 100
   Bus: *Mfr. of sodium silicate.*   Fax: (317) 485-6627   Emp: 29

   KEMIRA CHEMICALS, INC.
   148 State St., Macon, Georgia 31206
   CEO: John Pittman, Mgr.   Tel: (478) 743-7647   %FO: 100
   Bus: *Sale of chemicals/products.*   Fax: (478) 743-7649   Emp: 4

   KEMIRA CHEMICALS, INC.
   1525 Church St. Extension, Marietta, Georgia 30060
   CEO: Mark Gardner, Mgr.   Tel: (770) 422-1250   %FO: 100
   Bus: *Mfr./sale gum & wood chemicals.* Fax: (770) 423-1228   Emp: 175

   KEMIRA CHEMICALS, INC.
   430 Industrial Blvd., Midway, Georgia 31320
   CEO: Mark McMahan, Mgr.   Tel: (912) 884-7070   %FO: 100
   Bus: *Mfr./sale gum & wood chemicals.* Fax: (912) 884-2966   Emp: 10

   KEMIRA CHEMICALS, INC.
   2801 SE Columbia Way, Ste. 130, Vancouver, Washington 98661
   CEO: Brad Stephens, Mgr.   Tel: (360) 694-9815   %FO: 100
   Bus: *Sale of chemicals & products.*   Fax: (360) 694-9830   Emp: 4

   KEMIRA CHEMICALS, INC.
   1150 South 35th St., Washougal, Washington 98671
   CEO: Brad Stephens, Mgr.   Tel: (360) 835-8725   %FO: 100
   Bus: *Mfr. of chemical preparations & sale of* Fax: (360) 835-8729   Emp: 35
      chemical/products

   KEMIRA CHEMICALS, INC.
   1654 West Oak Dr., Marietta, Georgia 30062
   CEO: Mark Gardner, Mgr.   Tel: (770) 427-8431   %FO: 100
   Bus: *Mfr. of industrial organic & inorganic* Fax: Emp: 30
      chemicals

KEMIRA CHEMICALS, INC.
245 Townpark Dr., Ste. 200, Kennesaw, Georgia 30144
CEO: Seth Spurlock, Pres.   Tel: (770) 436-1542   %FO: 100
Bus: *Chemicals manufacture for paper products.*   Fax: (770) 436-3432

• **KONE CORPORATION**
Keilasatama 3, P.O. Box 7, FIN-02150 Espoo, Finland
CEO: Antti Herlin, Chmn. & CEO   Tel: 358-204-751   Rev: $7,182
Bus: *Mfr. elevators, rail-mounted cranes, cargo*   Fax: 358-204-75-4496   Emp: 33,021
     handling and access equipment.   www.kone.com
NAICS: 333921, 333922

   KONE, INC.
   One Kone Ct., Moline, Illinois 61265
   CEO: Heimo Makinen, Pres. & CEO   Tel: (309) 764-6771   %FO: 100
   Bus: *Mfr. hydraulic and traction elevators and*   Fax: (309) 743-5469
     escalators.

• **METSO CORPORATION**
Fabianinkatu 9 A, PO Box 1220, FIN-00101 Helsinki, Finland
CEO: Jorma Eloranta, Pres. & CEO   Tel: 358-20-484-100   Rev: $5,386
Bus: *Automation & information management application* Fax: 358-20-484-101   Emp: 22,802
     systems, machinery, automation & control   www.metso.com
     products for paper, packaging, construction &
NAICS: 322299, 333120, 333131, 333291, 334513, 336111

   METSO AUTOMATION INC.
   44 Bearfoot Rd., Northborough, Massachusetts 01532
   CEO: John Quinlivan, Pres.   Tel: (508) 852-0200   %FO: 100
   Bus: *Mfr. machines, valves & actuators.*   Fax: (508) 852-1175

   METSO AUTOMATION MAX CONTROLS INC.
   1180 Church Rd., Lansdale, Pennsylvania 19446
   CEO: Edward Coll, Pres.   Tel: (215) 393-3900   %FO: 100
   Bus: *Mfr. of process automation & control*   Fax: (215) 393-3921   Emp: 100
     systems.

   METSO MINERALS INDUSTRIES INC.
   20965 Crossroads Circle, Waukesha, Wisconsin 53186
   CEO: Hannu Melarti, Pres.   Tel: (262) 717-2500   %FO: 100
   Bus: *Mfr. of material handling equipment.*   Fax: (262) 717-2501   Emp: 1,173

   METSO PAPER USA, INC.
   2900 Courtyards Dr., Norcross, Georgia 30071
   CEO: Marco Marcheggiani, Pres.   Tel: (770) 263-7863   %FO: 100
   Bus: *Mfr./ Sale of pulp & paper mill machinery.*   Fax: (770) 441-9652   Emp: 1,500

   METSO USA
   133 Federal St., Ste. 302, Boston, Massachusetts 02110
   CEO: Hannu Melarti, Pres.   Tel: (617) 369-7850   %FO: 100
   Bus: *Financial holding company.*   Fax: (617) 369-7877   Emp: 3,873

METSO USA INC.
3100 Medlock Bridge Rd., Norcross, Georgia 30071
CEO: David Johnson, Pres.　　　　Tel: (770) 446-7818　　　%FO: 100
Bus: *Mfr. of control valves sales & distribution*　Fax: (770) 446-8794　　Emp: 600
　　　sensors scanners & DCS systems.

● **METSO MINERALS OY, DIV. METSO CORPORATION**
PO Box 307, Lokomonkatu 3, FIN-33101 Tampere, Finland
CEO: Bertel Langenskiold, Pres.　　Tel: 358-20-484-140　　Rev: $1,130
Bus: *Rock and mineral processing.*　　Fax: 358-20-484-141　　Emp: 11,495
　　　　　　　　　　　　　　　　www.metsominerals.com

NAICS: 333120, 333131, 333319, 333922

　　METSO MINERALS
　　20965 Crossroads Circle, Waukesha, Wisconsin 53186
　　CEO: Hannu Melarti, Pres.　　　Tel: (262) 717-2500　　%FO: 100
　　Bus: *Mfr. of material handling equipment.*　Fax: (262) 717-2501　Emp: 1,173

　　METSO MINERALS INDUSTRIES, INC.
　　1500 Corporate Dr., Ste. 300, Canonsburg, Pennsylvania 15317
　　CEO: Don Gaughennaugh, Pres.　　Tel: (412) 269-5298　　%FO: 100
　　Bus: *Mfr. of conveyors equipment construction*　Fax: (412) 269-5051　Emp: 100
　　　　machinery.

　　METSO MINERALS INDUSTRIES, INC.
　　416 Egypt Rd., Audubon, Pennsylvania 19403
　　CEO: Scott Hodge, Mgr.　　　　Tel: (610) 631-2900　　%FO: 100
　　Bus: *Minerals.*　　　　　　　Fax: (610) 631-9310

● **M-REAL CORPORATION**
Revontulentie 6, FIN-02100 Espoo, Finland
CEO: Hannu Anttila, Pres. & CEO　　Tel: 358-1046-11　　Rev: $7,448
Bus: *Paper manufacturer.*　　　　Fax: 358-1046-94355　Emp: 15,960
　　　　　　　　　　　　　　　　www.m-real.com

NAICS: 322130, 322222

　　KEMIART USA INC.
　　47 Cooper St., Woodbury, New Jersey 08096
　　CEO: Tom O'Brien　　　　　　Tel: (856) 686-5885　　%FO: 100
　　Bus: *Paperboard manufacturing and sales.*　Fax: (856) 686-5883

　　M-REAL USA CORPORATION
　　301 Merrit 7, Ste. 2, Norwalk, Connecticut 06851
　　CEO: Jorma Sahlstedt, Pres.　　Tel: (203) 229-7480　　%FO: 100
　　Bus: *Paper manufacturer.*　　　Fax: (203) 229-7499　　Emp: 8

● **MYLLYKOSKI PAPER OY**
46800 Anjalankoski, FIN-00180 Helsinki, Finland
CEO: Sverre Norrgard, Mng. Dir.　　Tel: 358-585-11　　　Rev: $423
Bus: *Paper manufacturer.*　　　　Fax: 358-5851-2501　　Emp: 861
　　　　　　　　　　　　　　　　www.myllykoskipaper.com

NAICS: 322121, 322222, 322233

MYLLYKOSKI NORTH AMERICA INC.
101 Merritt 7, 5/F, Norwalk, Connecticut 06851
CEO: Sverre Norrgard, Mng. Dir.
Bus: *Paper manufacture and sales.*

Tel: (203) 229-7400
Fax: (203) 229-7450

%FO: 100

● **NOKIA CORPORATION**
Keilalahdentie 4, FIN-00045 Espoo, Finland
CEO: Olli-Pekka Kallasvuo, Chmn. & CEO
Bus: *Telecommunications, mobile phones, base*

Tel: 358-7180-08000
Fax: 358-7180-38226
www.nokia.com

Rev: $39,645
Emp: 55,505

NAICS: 334119, 334220, 334515

NOKIA AMERICAS INC.
6000 Connection Dr., Irving, Texas 75039
CEO: Olli-Pekka Kallasvuo, Pres.
Bus: *Design, mfr. and sales electronics,*
telecommunications equipment.
Telecommunications U.S. headquarters.

Tel: (972) 894-5000
Fax: (972) 894-5050

%FO: 100
Emp: 7,300

NOKIA INC.
709 Westchester Ave., White Plains, New York 10604
CEO: Bill Seymour, Pres.
Bus: *Radio & TV communications equipment*
manufacture.

Tel: (914) 368-0555
Fax: (914) 368-0600

%FO: 100
Emp: 6,684

SYMBIAN
390 Bridge Pkwy., Ste. 201, Redwood Shores, California 94065
CEO: Nigel Clifford
Bus: *Mfr. of wireless communications software.*

Tel: (650) 551-0240
Fax: (650) 551-0241

%FO: 100

● **NOKIAN TYRES PLC**
Prikkalaistie 7, FIN-37101 Nokia, Finland
CEO: Kim Gran, CEO
Bus: *Mfr. tires and air pressure monitors.*

Tel: 358-3-340-7111
Fax: 358-3-342-0677
www.nokiantyres.com

Rev: $822
Emp: 2,323

NAICS: 326211

NOKIAN TYRES INC.
339 mason Rd., LaVergne, Tennessee 37086
CEO: Dennis Gaede
Bus: *Mfr. tires and air pressure monitors.*

Tel: (615) 287-0600
Fax: (615) 287-0610

%FO: 100

● **OUTOKUMPU OYJ**
Riihitontuntie 7, FIN-02201 Espoo, Finland
CEO: Juha Rantanen, Chmn. & CEO
Bus: *Stainless steel coil, wire, rod, and bar products*
manufacture.

Tel: 358-9421-1
Fax: 358-9421-3888
www.outokmpu.fi

Rev: $9,734
Emp: 19,465

NAICS: 332999

OUTOKUMPU ADVANCED SUPERCONDUCTORS INC.
1875 Thomaston Ave., Waterbury, Connecticut 06704
CEO: James Lajewski
Bus: *Air condition coils manufacture.*

Tel: (203) 753-5215
Fax: (203) 753-2096

%FO: 100

OUTOKUMPU AMERICAN BRASS
PO Box 981, Buffalo, New York 14240-0981
CEO: Todd Heusner, Pres.
Bus: *Mfr. brass products.*

Tel: (716) 879-6700
Fax: (716) 879-6735

%FO: 100

OUTOKUMPU COPPER FRANKLIN INC.
PO Box 539, Franklin, Kentucky 42135
CEO: Ron Beal, Pres.
Bus: *Mfr. copper products.*

Tel: (502) 586-8201
Fax: (502) 586-7404

%FO: 100

OUTOKUMPU COPPER NIPPERT INC.
801 Pittsburgh Dr., Delaware, Ohio 43015
CEO: Dirk Greywitt
Bus: *Air condition coils manufacture.*

Tel: (740) 363-1981
Fax: (740) 363-3847

%FO: 100

OUTOKUMPU COPPER USA, INC.
10771 East Easter Ave.,, Centennial, Colorado 80112
CEO: Travis Orser
Bus: *Mfr. base metals; stainless steel and
       copper products.*

Tel: (303) 792-3110
Fax: (303) 792-3110

%FO: 100

OUTOKUMPU COPPER USA, INC.
129 Fairfield Way, Bloomingdale, Illinois 60108
CEO: Ulf Anvin, Pres.
Bus: *Mfr./sale copper products.*

Tel: (630) 980-8400
Fax: (630) 980-8891

%FO: 100

OUTOKUMPU COPPER VALLEYCAST
553 Carter Ct., Kimberly, Wisconsin 54136
CEO: Stevens John
Bus: *Air condition coils manufacture.*

Tel: (920) 749-3820
Fax: (920) 749-3853

%FO: 100

OUTOKUMPU HEATCRAFT USA INC.
Box 948, Grenada, Mississippi 38902
CEO: Jim Laycock
Bus: *Air condition coils manufacture.*

Tel: (662) 229-2000
Fax: (662) 229-2000

%FO: 100

OUTOKUMPU STAINLESS PLATE INC.
PO Box 370, Newcastle, Indiana 47362
CEO: Mike Stateczny, EVP
Bus: *Plate products manufacture.*

Tel: (765) 529-0120
Fax: (765) 529-8177

%FO: 100

OUTOKUMPU TECHNOLOGY INC.
6100 Phillips Highway, Jacksonville, Florida 32216
CEO: Misty Dobbins
Bus: *Air condition coils manufacture.*

Tel: (904) 353-3681
Fax: (904) 353-8705

%FO: 100

● **RAUTARUUKKI OYJ**
Fredrikinkatu 51-53, FIN-90101 Helsinki, Finland
CEO: Mikko Hietanen, CFO
Bus: *Rolled steel sheets, pipes and tubes*

Tel: 358-9-417-711
Fax: 358-9-4177-6288
www.ruukki.com

Rev: $4,868
Emp: 12,126

NAICS: 331111, 331221, 423510

FINNSTEEL INC.
5 Revere Dr., Ste. 502, Northbrook, Illinois 60062
CEO: Tage L. Lindholm, Pres.
Bus: *Wholesale hot and cold rolled steel sheets, pipes and tubes.*

Tel: (847) 480-0420
Fax: (847) 480-9466

%FO: 100
Emp: 3

● **STORA ENSO OYJ**
Kanavaranta 1, P.O. Box 309, FIN-0010 Helsinki, Finland
CEO: Jukka Harmala, CEO
Bus: *Forest products and paper manufacturer.*

Tel: 358-20-46-131
Fax: 358-20-46-214-71
www.storaenso.com

Rev: $16,791
Emp: 43,779

NAICS: 113110, 321113, 322122, 322221, 322222, 322226, 322299, 424130

STORA ENSO NORTH AMERICA CORP.
231 1st Ave. North, Wisconsin Rapids, Wisconsin 54495-8050
CEO: Lars Bengtsson, Pres.
Bus: *Coated and super-calendered printing papers for brochures and magazines*

Tel: (715) 422-3111
Fax: (715) 422-3469

%FO: 100
Emp: 6,400

● **SUUNTO OY**
Valimotie 7, FIN-01510 Vantaa, Finland
CEO: Juha Pinomaa, Pres.
Bus: *Mfr. marine field compasses, professional instruments.*

Tel: 358-9-875-870
Fax: 358-9-8758-7300
www.suunto.com

Emp: 600

NAICS: 334518, 339920, 423940

SUUNTO USA
2151 Las Palmas Dr., Ste. F, Carlsbad, California 92009
CEO: Olivier Canler, Pres.
Bus: *Distribution/sale compasses, professional instruments, camping equipment.*

Tel: (760) 931-6788
Fax: (760) 931-9875

%FO: 100
Emp: 30

● **TAMFELT CORPORATION**
Yrittajankatu 21, FIN-33710 Tampere, Finland
CEO: Jyrki Nuutila, Pres. & CEO
Bus: *Mfr. industrial textiles.*

Tel: 358-3-363-9111
Fax: 358-3-356-0120
www.tamfelt.fi

Rev: $182
Emp: 1,380

NAICS: 313311

TAMFELT PMC, INC.
28 Draper Ln., Canton, Massachusetts 02021
CEO: Seppo Holkko, Pres.
Bus: *Mfr. industrial textiles.*

Tel: (781) 828-3350
Fax: (781) 828-0848

%FO: 100

● **UPM KYMMENE GROUP**
Etelaesplanadi 2, PO Box 380, FIN-00101 Helsinki, Finland
CEO: Jussi Pesonen, Pres. & CEO
Bus: *Mfr. forest industries and related products.*

Tel: 358-204-15-111
Fax: 358-204-15-110
www.upm-kymmene.com

Rev: $13,302
Emp: 33,433

NAICS: 113110, 321211, 322122, 322130, 322232, 322233, 322291, 424130

Finland

BLANDIN PAPER COMPANY
115 Southwest First St., Grand Rapids, Minnesota 57744
CEO: J. Kevin Lyden, Pres. & CEO   Tel: (218) 327-6200   %FO: 100
Bus: *Mfr. lightweight coated paper.*   Fax: (218) 327-6212   Emp: 860

ROSENLEW INC.
6387 Windfern Rd., Houston, Texas 77040
CEO: Chance Greene   Tel: (713) 461-0840   %FO: 100
Bus: *Paper packaging.*   Fax: (713) 461-0654   Emp: 80

UPM-KYMMENE, INC.
999 Oakmont Plaza Dr., Ste. 200, Westmont, Illinois 60559
CEO: Heikki Malinen, Pres.   Tel: (630) 850-3310   %FO: 100
Bus: *Distribution printing and writing papers.*   Fax: (630) 850-3322   Emp: 732

UPM-KYMMENE, INC.
1270 Avenue of the Americas, Ste. 203, New York, New York 10020
CEO: Heikki Malinen   Tel: (212) 218-8232
Bus: *Distribution printing and writing papers.*   Fax: (212) 218-8240

● **VAISALA OYJ**
Vanha Nurmijarventie 21, FIN-0167 Vantaa, Finland
CEO: Pekka Ketonen, Pres. & CEO   Tel: 358-9-894-91   Rev: $237
Bus: *Mfr. meteorological instruments.*   Fax: 358-9-8949-2227   Emp: 1,113
          www.vaisala.com

NAICS: 334511, 334516, 334519, 335999

VAISALA INC.
194 S. Taylor Ave., Louisville, Colorado 80027
CEO: Alan Reid, Pres.   Tel: (303) 499-1701
Bus: *Measuring & controlling devices*   Fax: (303) 499-1767   Emp: 210

VAISALA INC.
6980 Santa Teresa Blvd., San Jose, California 95119
CEO: Steven H. Chansky   Tel: (408) 578-3670
Bus: *Mfr. measuring & controlling devices*   Fax: (408) 578-3672

VAISALA, INC.
1120 NASA Rd., Ste. 220-E, Houston, Texas 77058
CEO: Cathy Barrett   Tel: (281) 335-9955   %FO: 100
Bus: *Mfr. meteorological instruments.*   Fax: (281) 335-9956

VAISALA, INC.
10-D Gill St., Woburn, Massachusetts 01801
CEO: Steven H. Chansky, Pres.   Tel: (781) 933-4500   %FO: 100
Bus: *Mfr. meteorological instruments.*   Fax: (781) 933-8029   Emp: 300

VAISALA, INC.
5600 Airport Blvd., PO Box 3659, Boulder, Colorado 80307
CEO: George Fredrick, Gen. Mgr.   Tel: (303) 499-1701   %FO: 100
Bus: *Mfr. measure & controlling devices*   Fax: (303) 499-1767   Emp: 17

VAISALA, INC.
2705 East Medina Rd., Tucson, Arizona 85706
CEO: Curtis Cowley, Mgr.
Bus: *Mfr. meteorological instruments.*

Tel: (520) 806-7300
Fax: (520) 741-2848

%FO: 100
Emp: 92

• **WARTSILA CORPORATION**
John Stenbergin Ranta 2, FIN-00531 Helsinki, Finland
CEO: Ole Johansson, Pres. & CEO
Bus: *Auto components manufacture.*

Tel: 358-10-709-0000
Fax: 358-10-709-5700
www.wartsila.com

NAICS: 336330, 336611

WARTSILA LIPS, INC.
3617 Koppens Ways, Chesapeake, Virginia 23323
CEO: Doug Fockler, Mgr.
Bus: *Auto components manufacture and sales.*

Tel: (757) 558-3625
Fax: (757) 558-3627

%FO: 100
Emp: 20

WARTSILA NORTH AMERICA, INC.
9625 Firdale Ave., Edmonds, Washington 98020
CEO: Mark Evans, Mgr.
Bus: *General auto repair*

Tel: (206) 903-9971
Fax: (206) 903-1048

%FO: 100
Emp: 10

WARTSILA NORTH AMERICA, INC.
2900 SW 42nd St., Ft. Lauderdale, Florida 33312
CEO: Rick Shilling, Mgr.
Bus: *Auto components manufacture and sales.*

Tel: (954) 327-4700
Fax: (954) 327-4877

%FO: 100
Emp: 50

WARTSILA NORTH AMERICA, INC.
16330 Air Center Blvd., Houston, Texas 77032
CEO: William Malacrida, Pres.
Bus: *Commercial & heavy construction.*

Tel: (281) 233-6200
Fax: (281) 233-6233

%FO: 100
Emp: 250

WARTSILA NORTH AMERICA, INC.
1313 MacArthur Ave., Harvey, Louisiana 70058
CEO: Paul Glandt, Mgr.
Bus: *Industrial equipment, auto repair.*

Tel: (504) 341-7201
Fax: (504) 341-1426

%FO: 100
Emp: 25

WARTSILA NORTH AMERICA, INC.
2140 Technology Place, Long Beach, California 90810
CEO: Paul Glandt, Mgr.
Bus: *Sale of industrial equipment.*

Tel: (562) 495-8484
Fax: (562) 495-8430

%FO: 100
Emp: 25

WARTSILA NORTH AMERICA, INC.
900 Bestgate Rd., Ste. 400, Annapolis, Maryland 21401
CEO: Jaako Eskola, Pres.
Bus: *Auto components manufacture and sales.*

Tel: (410) 573-2100
Fax: (410) 573-2200

%FO: 100
Emp: 10

WARTSILA NORTH AMERICA, INC.
1 Blue Hill Plaza, 3/F, Pearl River, New York 10965
CEO: William Malacrida, Mgr.
Bus: *Shipbuilding & repair.*

Tel: (914) 623-1212
Fax: (914) 623-3385

%FO: 100

Finland

WARTSILA NORTH AMERICA, INC.
26264 Twelve Trees Lane, Poulsbo, Washington 98370
CEO: Mark Greenwood, Mgr.   Tel: (360) 779-1444   %FO: 100
Bus: *Repair services.*   Fax: (360) 779-5927   Emp: 13

WARTSILA NORTH AMERICA, INC.
9422 Lafayette Ave., Bainbridge Island, Washington 98110
CEO: Thomas Carbone   Tel: (206) 780-2444   %FO: 100
Bus: *Auto components manufacture and sales.*   Fax: (206) 780-2999

France

- **ABB ENTRELEC, DIV. ABB LTD.**
  20, rue Childebert, F-69002 Lyon, France
  CEO: Pierre Bauer, Chmn. & CEO
  Bus: *Industrial connection and control products manufacture.*
  NAICS: 332722, 334419

  Tel: 33-4-7277-2737
  Fax: 33-4-7277-2757
  www.entrelec.com

  ABB ENTRELEC
  1950 Hurd Dr., Irving, Texas 75038
  CEO: Charles Oliver
  Bus: *Industrial connection and control products manufacture and sales.*

  Tel: (972) 550-9025
  Fax: (972) 550-9215

  %FO: 100

- **ACCESS COMMERCE**
  Rue Galilee, PB 555, F-31674 Labege Cedex, France
  CEO: Jacques Soumeillan, CEO
  Bus: *Software manufacturer.*

  NAICS: 541511

  Tel: 33-5-6139-7878
  Fax: 33-5-6139-7888
  www.access-commerce.com

  Rev: $12
  Emp: 100

  ACCESS COMMERCE
  1419 Lake Cook Rd., Deerfield, Illinois 60015
  CEO: Kurt Haller
  Bus: *Software manufacturer.*

  Tel: (847) 236-9061
  Fax: (847) 236-9124

  %FO: 100

- **ACCOR SA**
  2, rue de la Mare-Neuve, F-91021 Evry Cedex, France
  CEO: John Du Monceau, Vice Chmn.
  Bus: *Hotel owner/manager and catering; Sofitel, Motel 6 and Red Roof Inn.*
  NAICS: 713210, 721110

  Tel: 33-1-6936-8080
  Fax: 33-1-6936-7900
  www.accor.com

  Rev: $8,570
  Emp: 158,023

  ACCOR LODGING/MOTEL6 NORTH AMERICA
  14651 Dallas Pkwy., Ste. 500, Dallas, Texas 75240
  CEO: Michael Ferraro, VP Mktg.
  Bus: *Management of hotels (Sofitel, Motel 6) and restaurants.*

  Tel: (972) 386-6161
  Fax: (972) 991-2979

  %FO: 100

  ACCOR NORTH AMERICA CORPORATION
  245 Park Ave., 26/F., New York, New York 10167
  CEO: Georges LeMener, Pres.
  Bus: *Management of hotels (Sofitel, Motel 6) and restaurants.*

  Tel: (212) 949-5700
  Fax: (212) 490-0499

  %FO: 100
  Emp: 22,000

  CARLSON WAGONLIT TRAVEL INC.
  1405 Xenium Ln. North, Plymouth, Minnesota 55441
  CEO: Hubert Joly
  Bus: *Travel offices.*

  Tel: (763) 212-4000
  Fax: (763) 212-2219

- **AGENCE FRANCE-PRESSE**
  13, place de la Bourse, F-75002 Paris, France
  CEO: Bertrand Eveno, Chmn. & CEO
  Bus: *International news agency.*

  Tel: 33-1-4041-4646
  Fax: 33-1-4240-4632
  www.afp.com

  Rev: $300
  Emp: 3,000

  NAICS: 519110

  AGENCE FRANCE-PRESSE
  1500 K Street NW, Washington, District of Columbia 20005
  CEO: Georges Biannic, Mgr.
  Bus: *International news agency.*

  Tel: (202) 289-0700
  Fax: (202) 393-3752

  %FO: 100

  AGENCE FRANCE-PRESSE
  6430 Sunset Blvd., Ste. 702, Hollywood, California 90028
  CEO: Georges Biannic
  Bus: *International news agency.*

  Tel: (323) 463-0675
  Fax: (323) 463-4877

  %FO: 100

- **AGNES B.**
  194 rue de Rivoli, F-75001 Paris, France
  CEO: Agnes Trouble, CEO
  Bus: *Design and sales of clothes.*

  Tel: 33-1-4260-0341
  Fax: 33-1-4260-4561
  www.agnesb.net

  NAICS: 315233, 315299, 448120, 448150

  AGNES B.
  79 Greene St., New York, New York 10012
  CEO: Gregory Swift, CEO
  Bus: *Designer clothing sales.*

  Tel: (212) 548-9730
  Fax: (212) 548-9750

  %FO: 100
  Emp: 90

- **AIR FRANCE COMPAGNIE NATIONALE**
  45, rue de Paris, F-95747 Roissy CDG Cedex, France
  CEO: Jean-Cyril Spinetta, Chrm.
  Bus: *Commercial airline and catering services.*

  Tel: 33-1-4156-7800
  Fax: 33-1-4156-8419
  www.airfrance.com

  Rev: $10,900
  Emp: 70,150

  NAICS: 481111, 722310

  AIR FRANCE
  125 West 55th St., New York, New York 10019
  CEO: Jon Claude Protin, EVP
  Bus: *International air transport services.*

  Tel: (212) 830-4000
  Fax: (212) 830-4355

  %FO: 100
  Emp: 70

- **AIR LIQUIDE GROUP SA**
  75 Quai d'Orsay, F-75321 Paris Cedex 07, France
  CEO: Benoit Potier, CEO
  Bus: *Specializes in industrial and medical gases and
  related services.*
  NAICS: 325120

  Tel: 33-1-4062-5555
  Fax: 33-1-4555-5876
  www.airliquide.com

  Rev: $10,535
  Emp: 31,900

  AIR LIQUIDE AMERICA CORPORATION
  2700 Post Oak Blvd., Ste. 1800, Houston, Texas 77056
  CEO: Pierre DuFour
  Bus: *Engineering/construction services, welding,
  diving and medical equipment.*

  Tel: (713) 624-8000
  Fax: (713) 624-8030

  %FO: 100

AIR LIQUIDE ELECTRONICS SYSTEMS
2700 Post Oak Blvd., Ste. 1800, Houston, Texas 77056
CEO: Rich Jahr, Pres. & CEO
Bus: *Engineering/construction services, welding, diving and medical equipment.*
Tel: (713) 624-8000
Fax: (713) 624-8030
%FO: 100

AQUA-LUNG AMERICA
2340 Cousteau Ct., Vista, California 92083
CEO: Don Rockwell
Bus: *Mfr. diving equipment.*
Tel: (760) 597-5000
Fax: (760) 597-4900
%FO: 100

• **AIRBUS SAS**
1, Rond Point Maurice Bellonte, F-31707 Blagnac Cedex, France
CEO: NoEl Forgeard, Chmn.
Bus: *Aircraft manufacturer.*
Tel: 33-5-6193-3431
Fax: 33-5-6193-4955
www.airbus.com
Rev: $24,225
Emp: 50,000

NAICS: 336411

AIRBUS INDUSTRIE OF NORTH AMERICA, INC.
198 Van Buren St., Herndon, Virginia 20170
CEO: T. Allan McArtor, Pres.
Bus: *Provides after sales support for commercial aircraft.*
Tel: (703) 834-3400
Fax: (703) 834-3340
%FO: 100

• **ALCATEL SA**
54, rue La Boétie, F-75008 Paris Cedex 8, France
CEO: Mike Quigley, Pres. & COO
Bus: *Telecommunications.*
Tel: 33-1-4076-1010
Fax: 33-1-4076-1400
www.alcatel.com
Rev: $16,614
Emp: 55,718

NAICS: 517110

ALCATEL INTERNETWORKING INC.
720 S. Milpitas Blvd., Milpitas, California 95035
CEO: Tim Hember
Bus: *Supplies cable and telecommunications equipment.*
Tel: (408) 945-2200
Fax: (408) 945-2200
%FO: 100

ALCATEL INTERNETWORKING INC.
26801 West Agoura Rd., Calabasas, California 91301
CEO: Scott Berry
Bus: *Supplies cable and telecommunications equipment.*
Tel: (818) 880-3500
Fax: (818) 880-3505
%FO: 100

ALCATEL TELECOMMUNICATIONS CABLE
2512 Penny Rd., Claremont, North Carolina 28610
CEO: Christian Reinaudo, Dir.
Bus: *Supplies cable and telecommunications equipment.*
Tel: (828) 459-9787
Fax: (828) 459-9312
%FO: 100

ALCATEL USA, INC.
2301 Sugar Bush Rd., Raleigh, North Carolina 27612
CEO: Hubert de Pesquidoux, PR
Bus: *Supplies cable and telecommunications equipment.*
Tel: (919) 850-6000
Fax: (919) 850-6609
%FO: 100

ALCATEL USA, INC.
3400 W. Plano Pkwy., Plano, Texas 75075
CEO: Mike Quigley
Bus: *Supplies cable and telecommunications equipment.*

Tel: (972) 519-3000
Fax: (972) 519-2240

%FO: 100

● **ALDES AERAULIQUE**
20, Boulevard Joliot Curie, F-69694 Venissieux, France
CEO: Bruno Lacroix, CEO
Bus: *Mfr. ventilation, fire protection equipment & metal stamping.*
NAICS: 332322, 333411

Tel: 33-4-7877-1515
Fax: 33-4-7876-1597
www.aldes.com

Emp: 500

AMERICAN ALDES VENTILATION CORPORATION
4537 Northgate Ct., Sarasota, Florida 34234-2124
CEO: Dwight Shackelford, EVP
Bus: *Distribution ventilation products.*

Tel: (941) 351-3441
Fax: (941) 351-3442

%FO: 100
Emp: 6

● **ALSTOM SA**
25, Avenue Kleber, F-75795 Paris Cedex 16, France
CEO: Patrick Kron, Chmn. & CEO
Bus: *Power generation, power transmission, distribution and power conversion; and in transport through its activities in rail and marine.*
NAICS: 334416, 334513, 335311, 335312, 335314, 335999, 336510, 336611, 336999

Tel: 33-1-4755-2000
Fax: 33-1-4755-2599
www.alstom.com

Rev: $20,535
Emp: 76,811

ALSTOM
2000 Day Hill Rd., Windsor, Connecticut 06095
CEO: Tim Curran, Pres.
Bus: *Industrial manufacturing.*

Tel: (860) 285-3462
Fax: (860) 285-3840

Emp: 6,800

ALSTOM ENERGY
4 Skyline Dr., Hawthorne, New York 10532
CEO: Paul Jancek, Pres.
Bus: *Generators, motors, controls, valves, pumps, transportation and marine*

Tel: (914) 345-5137
Fax: (914) 345-5114

%FO: 20

ALSTOM POWER CONVERSION INC.
610 Epsilon Dr., Pittsburgh, Pennsylvania 15238
CEO: Shoun Kerbaugh, Pres.
Bus: *Mfr. of transformers*

Tel: (412) 967-0765
Fax: (412) 967-7660

%FO: 100
Emp: 250

ALSTOM USA
600 West Germantown Pike, Ste. 131, Plymouth Meeting, Pennsylvania 19462
CEO: John Valosky, Mgr.
Bus: *Generators, motors, controls, valves, pumps, transportation and marine*

Tel: (610) 832-8840
Fax: (610) 825-3269

%FO: 100

● **APEM SA**
Centre d'Affaires Paris-Nord, Tour Continental, P 200, F-93153 Le Blanc Mesnil Cedex, France
CEO: Pierre Ringue, CEO
Bus: *Mfr. switches, keyboards and assemblies.*
NAICS: 334119, 334119

Tel: 33-1-4814-9265
Fax: 33-1-4814-9284
www.apem.fr

Rev: $959
Emp: 378

APEM COMPONENTS INC.
PO Box 8288, Haverhill, Massachusetts 01835-0788
CEO: Georges Ranson
Bus: *Mfr. switches, keyboards and assemblies.*
Tel: (978) 372-1602
Fax: (978) 372-3534
%FO: 100

● **ARC INTERNATIONAL SA**
41, Avenue du General de Gaulle, F-62510 Arques, France
CEO: Patrick Gournay, Pres.
Bus: *Crystal, glassware and giftware manufacture.*
Tel: 33-3-21-95-46-47
Fax: 33-3-21-38-06-23
www.arc-international.com
Emp: 13,000

NAICS: 327211, 327212

ARC INTERNATIONAL NORTH AMERICA
Wade Boulevard, PO Box 5001, Millville, New Jersey 08332
CEO: Ron Biagi, CEO
Bus: *Lead crystal and glass dinner, stem, bar, cook/serve and giftware manufacture and sales.*
Tel: (609) 825-5620
Fax: (609) 696-3442
%FO: 100
Emp: 850

ARC INTERNATIONAL NORTH AMERICA
1665 Gladewood Dr., Alpharetta, Georgia 30005
CEO: Ron Kratz, CEO
Bus: *Mfr./sales lead crystal and glass dinner, stem, bar, cook/serve and giftware.*
Tel: (770) 751-6307
Fax: (770) 751-6081
%FO: 100

ARC INTERNATIONAL NORTH AMERICA
41 Madison Ave., 20/F, New York, New York 10010
CEO: Paul Wasserman, CEO
Bus: *Mfr./sales lead crystal and glass dinner, stem, bar, cook/serve and giftware.*
Tel: (212) 684-3680
Fax: (212) 532-8640
%FO: 100

ARC INTERNATIONAL NORTH AMERICA
96 Evergreen Rd., Cromwell, Connecticut 06416
CEO: Brian Rarey
Bus: *Lead crystal and glass dinner, stem, bar, cook/serve and giftware manufacture and sales.*
Tel: (860) 632-1370
Fax: (860) 632-1372

● **ARCHOS SA**
12 rue Ampere, F-91430 Igny, France
CEO: Henri Crohas, CEO
Bus: *Portable computer peripherals manufacture.*
Tel: 33-1-6933-1690
Fax: 33-1-6933-1699
www.archos.com
Rev: $81
Emp: 140

NAICS: 334119

ARCHOS USA INC.
3-A Goodyear, Irvine, California 92618
CEO: Marco delRosario, Sales
Bus: *Portable computer peripherals manufacture and sales.*
Tel: (949) 609-1483
Fax: (949) 609-1414
%FO: 100

- **AREVA GROUP**
  27-29 rue Le Peletier, F-75433 Paris Cedex 9, France
  CEO: Anne Lauvergeon, CEO
  Bus: *Fuel products and recycling services and mines uranium.*
  NAICS: 212291, 324199, 325998

  Tel: 33-1-4483-7100
  Fax: 33-1-4483-2500
  www.arevagroup.com

  Rev: $15,152
  Emp: 70,069

  - **AREVA ENTERPRISES INC.**
    4800 Hampden Lane, Ste. 100, Bethesda, Maryland 20814
    CEO: Andrew Cook, Pres. & COO
    Bus: *Nuclear fuel products & services.*

    Tel: (301) 652-9197
    Fax: (301) 652-5691

    %FO: 100

- **ARIANESPACE SA**
  Boulevard de l'Europe, B P 177, F-91006 Evry Cedex, France
  CEO: Jean-Yves Le Gall, Chmn. & CEO
  Bus: *Production/marketing/sales operations for launch services worldwide.*
  NAICS: 541614, 541890

  Tel: 33-1-6087-6000
  Fax: 33-1-6087-6247
  www.arianespace.com

  Rev: $700
  Emp: 380

  - **ARIANESPACE, INC.**
    601 13th St. NW, Ste. 710, Washington, District of Columbia 20005
    CEO: Suzanne Chambers
    Bus: *Satellite launching services.*

    Tel: (202) 628-3936
    Fax: (202) 628-3949

    %FO: 100
    Emp: 6

- **ATIC SERVICES**
  91 bis, rue du Cherche-Midi, F-75006 Paris, France
  CEO: Stéphane Lemoine, CEO
  Bus: *Coal import.*

  Tel: 33-235-711760
  Fax: 33-235-887519
  www.atics.fr

  Rev: $150
  Emp: 50

  NAICS: 213113

  - **ATIC SERVICES**
    122 East 42nd St., Rm. 3010, New York, New York 10168
    CEO: Denis Rousseau
    Bus: *Coal import and sales.*

    Tel: (212) 983-6210
    Fax: (212) 594-9506

    %FO: 100

- **ATOS ORIGIN**
  Tour Les Miroirs, Batiment C, 18, avenue d'Alsace, F-92926 Paris La Defense 3 Cedex, France
  CEO: Bernard Bourigeaud, CEO
  Bus: *Provides information technology and e-business solutions.*
  NAICS: 518210, 541511, 541512, 541513, 541519

  Tel: 33-1-5591-2000
  Fax: 331-5591-2005
  www.atosorigin.com

  Rev: $7,232
  Emp: 46,584

  - **ATOS ORIGIN INC.**
    5599 San Felipe St., Ste. 300, Houston, Texas 77056
    CEO: Paul Stewart, CEO
    Bus: *Computer integrated systems.*

    Tel: (713) 513-3000
    Fax: (713) 409-7204

    %FO: 100
    Emp: 350

● **AUCHAN GROUP**
200 rue de la Recherche, F-59650 Villeneuve d'Ascq Cedex, France
CEO: Christopher Dubrulle, Chmn.   Tel: 33-3-2837-6700   Rev: $36,032
Bus: *Retail supermarkets.*   Fax: 33-3-2067-5520   Emp: 15,600
                                         www.auchan.com
   NAICS: 443111, 443112, 444110, 444120, 444130, 445110, 448110, 448120, 448130, 448140, 448150, 448190,
452910, 453998

   AUCHAN USA, INC.
   7887 Katy Fwy, Ste. 250, Houston, Texas 77024
   CEO: Gerard Gallet, Pres.   Tel: (713) 263-1711   %FO: 100
   Bus: *Retail supermarkets.*   Fax: Emp: 550

● **AXA GROUP**
25, ave. Matignon, F-75008 Paris, France
CEO: Henri de Castries, Chmn. & CEO   Tel: 33-1-4075-5700   Rev: $124,369
Bus: *Global financial services; insurance, merchant*   Fax: 31-1-4075-4696   Emp: 74,584
    banking, securities broker/dealer, investment   www.axa.com
    advisory services.
   NAICS: 523991, 523999, 524113, 524126, 524130, 525110, 525120, 525190, 525910, 525920, 525990

   ALLIANCE CAPITAL MANAGEMENT CORPORATION
   1345 Ave. of the Americas, New York, New York 10105
   CEO: Gerald M. Lieberman, Pres.   Tel: (212) 969-1000   %FO: 36
   Bus: *Investment advisory services.*   Fax: (212) 969-2229   Emp: 4,100

   AXA ADVISORS
   1290 Ave. of the Americas, 8/F, New York, New York 10104
   CEO: John Lefferts, Pres.   Tel: (212) 314-4600   %FO: 100
   Bus: *Investment advisory services.*   Fax: (212) 314-2837   Emp: 3,999

   AXA EQUITABLE LIFE INSURANCE CO.
   1290 Ave. of the Americas, New York, New York 10104
   CEO: Christopher M. Condron, Pres. & CEO   Tel: (212) 554-1234
   Bus: *Life insurance*   Fax: Emp: 8,800

   AXA FINANCIAL INC.
   1290 Ave. of the Americas, New York, New York 10104
   CEO: Christopher M. Condron, Pres. & CEO   Tel: (212) 554-1234   %FO: 60
   Bus: *Insurance, investment & real estate* Fax: (212) 554-2320   Emp: 9,644
       management services.

   AXA ROSENBERG GROUP
   4 Orinda Way, Bldg. E, Orinda, California 94563
   CEO: Stephane Prunet, CEO   Tel: (925) 254-6464   %FO: 100
   Bus: *Engaged in investment management.*   Fax: (925) 253-0141

   SANFORD C. BERNSTEIN & CO.
   1345 Ave. of the Americas, New York, New York 10105
   CEO: Lisa A. Scalett, Chmn. & CEO   Tel: (212) 486-5800
   Bus: *Investment banking services.*   Fax: (212) 969-6189

THE ADVEST GROUP, INC.
90 State House Sq., Hartford, Connecticut 06103
CEO: Daniel J. Mullane, Pres. & CEO   Tel: (860) 509-1000
Bus: *Retail brokerage*   Fax: (860) 509-3849

● **AXALTO N.V.**
50, avenue Jean Jaures, F-92545 Montrouge, France
CEO: Olivier Piou, CEO   Tel: 33-1-46-00-6667   Rev: $960
Bus: *Microprocessor card provider.*   Fax: 33-1-46-00-6367   Emp: 4,500
                                             www.axalto.com

NAICS: 333313, 334119

AXALTO INC.
1601 Schlumberger Dr., Moorestown, New Jersey 08057
CEO: Eric Claudel   Tel: (888) 343-5773   %FO: 100
Bus: *Microprocessor card provider.*   Fax:

AXALTO INC.
8311 N. FM 620, Austin, Texas 78726
CEO: Paul Beverly, Pres.   Tel: (512) 257-3900   %FO: 100
Bus: *Microprocessor card provider.*   Fax: (512) 257-3881

AXALTO INC.
9800 Reisterstown Rd., Owings Mills, Maryland 21117
CEO: Eric Claudel   Tel: (410) 363-1600   %FO: 100
Bus: *Microprocessor card provider.*   Fax: (410) 363-3226

● **BACOU DALLOZ SA**
33 rue des Vanesses, F-95958 Roissy Cedex, France
CEO: Henri-Dominique Petit, CEO   Tel: 33-1-4990-7979   Rev: $998
Bus: *Mfr. personal protective equipment and safety*   Fax: 33-1-4990-7980   Emp: 6,254
     products; eye and ear protection, footwear and   www.bacou.com
     protective garments and gloves for the
NAICS: 314999, 339113, 339115, 423450

BACOU DALLOZ USA INC.
10 Thurber Blvd., Smithfield, Rhode Island 02917
CEO: Roger Gehring, SVP   Tel: (401) 233-0333   %FO: 100
Bus: *Sales/distribution of safety eyewear.* Fax: (401) 232-1830

● **BÉNÉTEAU S.A.**
Le Embruns 16, Boulevard de la Mer, F-85803 Saint-Gilles-Croix-Vie Cedex, France
CEO: Bruno Cathelinais, Pres.   Tel: 33-2-5126-8850   Rev: $862
Bus: *Building of sailboats and yachts.*   Fax: 33-2-5126-8864   Emp: 4,576
                                             www.beneteau.com

NAICS: 321991, 321992, 336611, 336612

BÉNÉTEAU USA INC.
410 Mill St., Ste. 101, Mount Pleasant, South Carolina 29464
CEO: Rachel Sweeney, Mktg. Dir.   Tel: (843) 805-5000   %FO: 100
Bus: *Sales of yachts.*   Fax: (843) 805-5010

- **SOCIETE BIC**
14, rue Jeanne d'Asnieres, F-92611 Clichy Cedex, France
CEO: Bruno Bich, CEO
Bus: *Electric razors, lighters, writing instruments and correction fluids manufacturing.*
NAICS: 335211, 339999

Tel: 33-1-4519-5200
Fax: 33-1-4519-5299
www.bicworld.com

Rev: $1,891
Emp: 8,706

> **BIC CORPORATION**
> 500 Bic Dr., Milford, Connecticut 06460
> CEO: Toshikazu Koike, Pres.
> Bus: *Mfr./distributor writing instruments, shavers, and lighters.*
>
> Tel: (203) 783-2000
> Fax: (203) 763-2108
>
> %FO: 100
> Emp: 1,500

- **BIOMERIEUX SA**
376 Chemin Orme, F-69280 Marcy l'Etoile, France
CEO: Alain Merieux, CEO
Bus: *Infectious disease pharmaceuticals.*

Tel: 33-4-7887-2000
Fax: 33-4-7887-2090
www.biomerieux.fr

Rev: $1,147
Emp: 5,300

NAICS: 325413, 325414, 424210

> **BIOMERIEUX USA**
> 100 Rodolphe St., Durham, North Carolina 27712
> CEO: Eric Bouvier, Pres. & CEO
> Bus: *Pharmaceutical research and development.*
>
> Tel: (919) 620-2000
> Fax: (919) 620-2009
>
> %FO: 100

- **BNP PARIBAS**
16, boulevard des Italiens, F-75009 Paris Cedex 09, France
CEO: Baudouin Prot, Chmn. & CEO
Bus: *Commercial and investment banking, and securities and asset management services.*
NAICS: 522110, 523110, 523920

Tel: 33-1-4014-4546
Fax: 33-1-4214-7546
www.bnpparibas.com

Rev: $52,095
Emp: 89,100

> **BANK OF THE WEST**
> 180 Montgomery St., San Francisco, California 94104
> CEO: Don J. McGrath
> Bus: *General commercial banking services.*
>
> Tel: (925) 942-8300
> Fax: (925) 943-1224
>
> %FO: 100

> **BNP PARIBAS CORPORATE FINANCE**
> 787 Seventh Ave., New York, New York 10019
> CEO: Everet Schenk, EVP
> Bus: *Merchant banking & investment advisory services.*
>
> Tel: (212) 841-2000
> Fax: (212) 841-2246
>
> %FO: 100

- **BOIRON LABORATOIRES**
20, rue de la Liberation, F-69110 Ste-Foy-les-Lyon, France
CEO: Patrick Caré, CEO
Bus: *Homeopathic pharmaceuticals manufacture.*

Tel: 33-4-7216-4000
Fax: 33-4-7859-6916
www.boiron.fr

Rev: $231
Emp: 2,400

NAICS: 325411

BOIRON BORNEMANN, INC.
98 C West Cochran St., Simi Valley, California 93065
CEO: Daniel Derseser, Mgr. Tel: (805) 582-9091 %FO: 100
Bus: *Mfr./distribution homeopathic medicines.* Fax: (805) 582-9091 Emp: 11

BOIRON BORNEMANN, INC.
6 Campus Blvd., Bldg. A, Newtown Square, Pennsylvania 19073
CEO: Thierry Boiron, Pres. Tel: (610) 325-7464 %FO: 100
Bus: *Mfr./distribution homeopathic medicines.* Fax: (610) 325-7480 Emp: 75

● **BONDUELLE SA**
Rue Nicolas Appert, F-59653 Lille-Villeneuve d'Ascq, France
CEO: Christophe Bonduelle, Mng. Dir. Tel: 33-3-2043-6060 Rev: $1,507
Bus: *Frozen and fresh vegetable distributor.* Fax: 33-3-2043-6000 Emp: 5,438
www.bonduelle.fr

NAICS: 424420, 424480

  BONDUELLE USA INC.
  50 Division St., Millington, New Jersey 07946
  CEO: Emmanuel Bommier, Sales Tel: (908) 604-2100 %FO: 100
  Bus: *Frozen and fresh vegetable distributor.* Fax: (908) 604-0757

● **BONGRAIN SA**
42, rue Rieussec, F-78220 Viroflay Cedex, France
CEO: Alex Bongrain, Pres. Tel: 33-1-3458-6300 Rev: $5,630
Bus: *Produces/distributes cheeses and other dairy* Fax: 33-1-3458-6685 Emp: 16,000
products. www.bongrain.com

NAICS: 311513, 311514

  ADVANCED FOOD PRODUCTS
  402 South Custer Ave., New Holland, Pennsylvania 17557
  CEO: Pierre Ragnet, Pres. Tel: (717) 355-8667
  Bus: *Mfr. of long-life products.* Fax: (717) 355-8848 Emp: 600

  BONGRAIN CHEESE
  400 South Custer Ave., New Holland, Pennsylvania 17557
  CEO: Jesse Hogan, Pres. Tel: (717) 355-8500
  Bus: *Mfr. Cream cheeses & soft pressed* Fax: (717) 355-8547 Emp: 335
  cheeses.

  SCHRATTER FOOD
  149 New Dutch Lane, Fairfield, New Jersey 07004
  CEO: Alain Voss, Pres. Tel: (973) 575-9120
  Bus: *Sales of cheese.* Fax: (973) 575-5010 Emp: 178

● **BOSTIK INC., SUB. TOTAL**
Tour Iris, 12 place de L'Iris, F-92062 La Defense Cedex, France
CEO: Andre Ladurelli, CEO Tel: 33-1-4796-9465 Rev: $975
Bus: *Adhesives manufacture.* Fax: 33-1-4796-9096 Emp: 4,500
www.bostikfindley.com

NAICS: 325520

BOSTIK INC.
1035 Louis Dr., Warminster, Pennsylvania 18974
CEO: John Duffy
Bus: *Adhesive manufacture and sales.*
Tel: (215) 957-0690
Fax: (215) 957-0716
%FO: 100

BOSTIK INC.
1500 Parker Rd., Conyers, Georgia 30094
CEO: Bob Homer
Bus: *Adhesive manufacture and sales.*
Tel: (770) 922-4545
Fax: (770) 929-0253
%FO: 100

BOSTIK INC.
7401 Intermodal Dr., Louisville, Kentucky 40258-
CEO: James Webb
Bus: *Adhesive manufacture and sales.*
Tel: (502) 933-4694
Fax: (502) 933-4694
%FO: 100

BOSTIK INC.
11320 Watertown Plank Rd., Wauwatosa, Wisconsin 53226
CEO: David H. Jackson
Bus: *Adhesive manufacture and sales.*
Tel: (414) 774-2250
Fax: (414) 479-0645
%FO: 100

● **BOUYGUES SA**
1, ave. Eugene Freyssinet, F-78061 Saint-Quentin-en-Yvelines, France
CEO: Martin Bouygues, CEO
Bus: *Construction, property development and telecommunications.*
NAICS: 236210, 236220, 517212
Tel: 33-1-3060-2111
Fax: 33-1-3060-4861
www.bouygues.fr
Rev: $23,300
Emp: 121,600

BARRETT PAVING MATERIALS INC.
3 Becker Farm Rd., Roseland, New Jersey 07068
CEO: George Ausseil
Bus: *Paving materials.*
Tel: (973) 533-1001
Fax: (973) 533-1020
%FO: 100

COLAS INC.
10 Madison Ave., 4/F, Morristown, New Jersey 07960
CEO: Michel Roullet
Bus: *Construction services.*
Tel: (973) 290-9082
Fax: (973) 290-9088
%FO: 100

DELTA COMPANIES INC.
114 South Silver Springs Rd., PO Box 880, Cape Girardeau, Michigan 63702
CEO: S. Lewis
Bus: *Construction services.*
Tel: (573) 334-5261
Fax: (573) 334-9576
%FO: 100

HRI INC.
1750 West College Ave., State College, Pennsylvania 16804
CEO: John R. Kulka
Bus: *Construction services.*
Tel: (814) 238-5071
Fax: (814) 238-0131
%FO: 100

IA CONSTRUCTION CORPORATION
PO Box 8, Concordville, Pennsylvania 19331
CEO: Robert Doucet
Bus: *Construction services.*
Tel: (610) 459-3136
Fax: (610) 459-2086
%FO: 100

REEVES CONSTRUCTION COMPANY
PO Box 547, Americus, Georgia 31709
CEO: Frank Whitaker, Pres.   Tel: (229) 924-7574   %FO: 100
Bus: *Construction services.*   Fax: (229) 924-8336

● **BULL**
Rue Jean Jaures, B.P. 68, F-78340 Les Clayes-sous-Bois, France
CEO: Didier Lamouche, Chmn. & CEO   Tel: 33-1-30-80-7000   Rev: $1,554
Bus: *Mfr. computer systems and networks; including*   Fax: 33-1-30-80-7373   Emp: 7,793
PC's, mainframes, smart cards, contract   www.bull.com
manufacturing services, systems integration and
software.
NAICS: 334111, 511210, 541511, 541512, 541519

BULL HN INFORMATION SYSTEMS, INC.
296 Concord Rd., Billerica, Massachusetts 01821
CEO: Jonathon Burbank, CEO   Tel: (978) 294-7999   %FO: 100
Bus: *Wholesale mainframe computers & computer* Fax: Emp: 500
related products

● **BUREAU VERITAS SA**
17 bis, Place des Relets, F-92400 Paris, France
CEO: Frank Piedelievre, CEO   Tel: 33-1-4054-6474   Rev: $897
Bus: *Technical services provider.*   Fax: 33-1-4054-6444   Emp: 12,850
                                               www.bureauveritas.com
NAICS: 541330, 541611, 541614, 541620, 924110

BUREAU VERITAS
515 West Fifth St., Jamestown, New York 14701
CEO: Randy Daugharthy   Tel: (716) 484-9002   %FO: 100
Bus: *Technical services provider.*   Fax: (716) 484-9003

BUREAU VERITAS
100 Northpointe Pkwy., Buffalo, New York 14228
CEO: Thomas Lynch   Tel: (716) 505-3300   %FO: 100
Bus: *Technical services provider.*   Fax: (716) 505-3301

BUREAU VERITAS
425 East Colorado St., Ste. 60, Glendale, California 91205
CEO: Mari Miller   Tel: (818) 549-2470   %FO: 100
Bus: *Technical services provider.*   Fax: (818) 548-2471

BUREAU VERITAS
50 Park Row West, Providence, Rhode Island 02903
CEO: David Osborne   Tel: (401) 273-7810   %FO: 100
Bus: *Technical services provider.*   Fax: (401) 273-7812

BUREAU VERITAS
224 Liberty St., Brockton, Massachusetts 02301
CEO: Kevin O'Brien   Tel: (508) 894-8000   %FO: 100
Bus: *Technical services provider.*   Fax: (508) 894-2669

BUREAU VERITAS
5001 West 80th St., Ste. 235, Bloomington, Minnesota 55437
CEO: David Osboune
Bus: *Technical services provider.*
Tel: (612) 844-0944
Fax: (612) 844-0911
%FO: 100

BUREAU VERITAS
2625 Butterfield Rd., Ste. 301N, Oak Brook, Illinois 60523
CEO: Joan Mattson
Bus: *Technical services provider.*
Tel: (630) 623-4690
Fax: (630) 623-4699
%FO: 100

BUREAU VERITAS
c/o Washington Labs, 7560 Lindberg Dr., Gaithersburg, Maryland 02879
CEO: Joann Dorsey
Bus: *Technical services provider.*
Tel: (301) 216-0506
Fax: (301) 216-0507
%FO: 100

• **BUSINESS INTERACTIF SA**
8, Rue Fournier, F-92110 Clichy, France
CEO: Francois de La Villardiere, Chmn. & Mng. Dir.
Bus: *Website consulting and design services.*
Tel: 33-1-4968-1212
Fax: 33-1-4968-1213
www.businessinteractif.com
Rev: $16
Emp: 200

NAICS: 541511

BUSINESS INTERACTIVE, INC.
151 West 19th St., 3/F, New York, New York 10011
CEO: D. Ellis
Bus: *Website consulting and design services.*
Tel: (212) 414-9243
Fax: (212) 414-9264
%FO: 100

• **BUSINESS OBJECTS, SA**
157-159 Rue Anatole, F-92300 Lavollois-Perret, France
CEO: Bernard Liautaud, CEO
Bus: *Business software development and marketing.*
Tel: 33-1-4125-2121
Fax: 33-1-4125-3100
www.businessobjects.com
Rev: $926
Emp: 3,834

NAICS: 541511

BUSINESS OBJECTS AMERICAS
3030 Orchard Pkwy., San Jose, California 95134
CEO: Tracy Eiler
Bus: *Mfr. software programs for corporate executives.*
Tel: (408) 953-6000
Fax: (408) 953-6001
%FO: 100

• **CAISSE DES DEPOTS ET CONSIGNATIONS**
56, rue de Lille, F-75356 Paris, France
CEO: Francis Mayer, Chmn. & CEO
Bus: *Financial services companies.*
Tel: 33-1-5850-0000
Fax: 33-1-5850-0246
www.caissedesdepots.fr
Rev: $10,900
Emp: 39,775

NAICS: 522110, 523110, 523991, 523999

CDC CAPITAL INC.
9 West 57th St., 36/F, New York, New York 10019
CEO: Luc De Clapiers, Pres. & CEO
Bus: *Financial trading and investment.*
Tel: (212) 891-6100
Fax: (212) 891-6295
%FO: 100
Emp: 52

IXIS ASSET MANAGEMENT NORTH AMERICA
399 Boylston St., Boston, Massachusetts 02116
CEO: Wendy D. Schoenfeld, VP   Tel: (617) 449-2100   %FO: 100
Bus: *Financial trading and investment.*   Fax: (617) 449-2197

● **CANAL PLUS SA**
85-89, Quai Andre Citroen, F-75015 Paris, France
CEO: Bertrand Meheut, Chmn.   Tel: 33-1-4425-1000   Rev: $2,780
Bus: *International telecommunications, TV*   Fax: 33-1-4425-1234   Emp: 3,800
  entertainment production and TV station   www.cplus.fr
  management. (34% ownership by Vivendi SA)
NAICS: 512110, 515120

  CANAL PLUS US
  301 N. Canon Dr., Ste. 228, Beverly Hills, California 90210-4722
  CEO: Robert Chamberlain, EVP   Tel: (310) 247-0994   %FO: 100
  Bus: *Film production and telecommunications.* Fax: (310) 247-0998

● **CAPGEMINI**
6-8, rue Duret, F-75017 Paris, France
CEO: Paul Hermelin, Exec. Chmn.   Tel: 33-1-5364-4444   Rev: $8,580
Bus: *Engaged in management consulting, computer* Fax: 33-1-5364-4445   Emp: 59,324
  services and information technology.   www.capgemini.com
NAICS: 541511, 541611, 541614

  CAPGEMINI
  5 Times Square, New York, New York 10036
  CEO: Salil Parekh, VP   Tel: (212) 934-8000   %FO: 100
  Bus: *Computer services and management*   Fax: (212) 934-8001   Emp: 3,200
    consulting.

  CAPGEMINI
  500 Woodward, Ste. 1620, Detroit, Michigan 48226
  CEO: Michael Wujciak   Tel: (313) 887-1400   %FO: 100
  Bus: *Computer services and management*   Fax: (313) 887-1401
    consulting.

  CAPGEMINI
  7701 Las Colinas Ridge, Ste. 600, Irving, Texas 75063
  CEO: Rick Tober   Tel: (972) 556-7000   %FO: 100
  Bus: *Computer services and management*   Fax: (972) 556-7001
    consulting.

  CAPGEMINI
  600 Memorial Drive, Suite 100, Cambridge, Massachusetts 02139
  CEO: Michael Callahan   Tel: (617) 768-5600   %FO: 100
  Bus: *Computer services and management*   Fax: (617) 768-5600
    consulting.

  CAPGEMINI
  1660 West Second St., Cleveland, Ohio 44113
  CEO: Kathy Valderrama, Pres.   Tel: (216) 373-4500   %FO: 100
  Bus: *Computer services and management*   Fax: (216) 373-4700
    consulting.

CAPGEMINI
111 North Canal St., Suite 1500, Chicago, Illinois 60606
CEO: Matt Manzella
Bus: *Computer services and management consulting.*
Tel: (312) 395-5000
Fax: (312) 395-5001
%FO: 100

CAPGEMINI
400 Broadacres Dr., 4/F, Bloomfield, New Jersey 07003
CEO: Lanny Cohen
Bus: *Computer services and management consulting.*
Tel: (973) 337-2700
Fax: (973) 337-2701
%FO: 100

CAPGEMINI
3315 North Oak Trafficway, Kansas City, Missouri 64116
CEO: Robert Cotton
Bus: *Computer services and management consulting.*
Tel: (816) 459-6000
Fax: (816) 459-6333
%FO: 100

CAPGEMINI
3 Paragon Way, Freehold, New Jersey 07728
CEO: Lanny Cohen
Bus: *Computer services and management consulting.*
Tel: (732) 358-8900
Fax: (732) 358-8803
%FO: 100

CAPGEMINI GOVERNMENT SOLUTIONS LLC
2250 Corporate Park Dr., Ste. 410, Herndon, Virginia 20171
CEO: Maria del Pilar Granados
Bus: *Computer services and management consulting.*
Tel: (571) 336-1600
Fax: (571) 336-1700
%FO: 100

● **CARTIER SA**
51 Rue Francois Premier, F-75008 Paris, France
CEO: Bernard Fornas, CEO
Bus: *Jewelry and watch manufacturer.*
Tel: 33-1-4074-6060
Fax: 33-1-4563-0565
www.cartier.com

NAICS: 334518, 339911, 423940, 448310

CARTIER INC.
231 Post St., San Francisco, California 94108
CEO: Wes Carroll
Bus: *Jewelry and watch sales.*
Tel: (415) 397-3180
Fax: (415) 397-7586
%FO: 100

CARTIER INTERNATIONAL INC.
653 Fifth Ave., New York, New York 10022
CEO: Simon Critchell
Bus: *Jewelry and watch sales.*
Tel: (212) 753-0111
Fax: (212) 753-0040
%FO: 100

● **CASINO GUICHARD-PERRACHON**
24, rue de la Montat, F-42008 Saint-Etienne Cedex 2, France
CEO: Jean-Charles Naouri, CEO
Bus: *Operates warehouse supermarkets.*
Tel: 33-4-7745-3131
Fax: 33-4-7721-8515
www.casine.fr
Rev: $28,848
Emp: 206,760

NAICS: 445110

SMART & FINAL FOODSERVICE DISTRIBUTORS INC.
, Stockton, California 95215
CEO: J. Edwin Furbee — Tel: (209) 948-1814 — %FO: 50
Bus: *Food distribution.* — Fax: (209) 467-3640

SMART & FINAL INC.
600 Citadel Dr., Commerce, California 90040
CEO: Etienne Snollaerts, Pres. & CEO — Tel: (323) 869-7608 — %FO: 50
Bus: *Operates warehouse-style grocery chain.* — Fax: (323) 869-7858 — Emp: 5,300

● **CEDRAT SA**
15, Chemin de Malacher, F-38246 Meylan, France
CEO: Bruno Ribard — Tel: 33-4-7690-5045
Bus: *CAD/CAM element analysis engineering,* — Fax: 33-4-7690-1609 — Emp: 40
agricultural planification. — www.cedrat.com
NAICS: 334290, 334413, 511210, 541512

  MAGSOFT CORPORATION
  20 Prospect St., Ballston Spa, New York 12020
  CEO: Sheppard Salon, Pres. — Tel: (518) 884-0505 — %FO: 100
  Bus: *Markets leading computer-aided-engineering* — Fax: (518) 884-8686 — Emp: 10
  (CAE) simulation tools.

● **CEGEDIM GROUP SA**
127-137, rue d'Aguesseau, F-92641 Boulogne, France
CEO: Jean-Claude Labrune, CEO — Tel: 33-1-4909-2200 — Rev: $580
Bus: *Information technology services.* — Fax: 33-1-4603-4595 — Emp: 3,851
— www.cegedim.fr
NAICS: 541511, 541512, 541519, 541910

  CAMM CORP INTERNATIONAL
  580 Sylvan Ave., Englewood Cliffs, New Jersey 07632
  CEO: Antoine Minkowski — Tel: (201) 871-5913 — %FO: 100
  Bus: *Measuring and monitoring of promotional* — Fax: (201) 871-0773
  investment.

  CEGEDIM GROUP
  610 W 150 Germantown Pike, Plymouth Meeting, Pennsylvania 19462
  CEO: Lawrence Reister — Tel: (610) 834-2470 — %FO: 100
  Bus: *Management services.* — Fax: (610) 834-2470

  DOCUBASE SYSTEMS
  2629 McCormick Dr., Ste.102, Clearwater, Florida 33759
  CEO: Yannick Tabanon — Tel: (727) 723-1484 — %FO: 100
  Bus: *Electronic document management solution* — Fax: (727) 723-0879
  services.

● **CEGID SA**
52 quai Paul Sédallian, F-69279 Lyon, France
CEO: Jean-Michel Aulas, CEO — Tel: 33-4-2629-5000 — Rev: $148
Bus: *Software and support services.* — Fax: 33-4-2629-5050 — Emp: 1,275
— www.cegid.fr
NAICS: 511210, 523991, 523999, 541511, 541519

CEGID USA INC.
76 Bedford St., Lexington, Massachusetts 02410
CEO: Sebastien Bourgeois
Bus: *Software and support services.*
Tel: (646) 241-4254
Fax: (617) 899-8831
%FO: 100

● **CEVA SANTE ANIMALE**
La Ballastiere, BP 126, F-33501 Libourne, France
CEO: Philippe Du Mesnil, CEO
Bus: *Animal health products manufacture.*
Tel: 33-5-5755-4040
Fax: 33-5-5755-4198
www.ceva.com
Rev: $140
Emp: 450

NAICS: 325412

BIOMUNE COMPANY
8906 Rosehill Rd., Lenexa, Kansas 66215
CEO: Ron Plylar
Bus: *Veterinary biological manufacturer.*
Tel: (913) 894-0230
Fax: (913) 894-0236
%FO: 100

● **CFF RECYCLING**
119 avenue du General Michel Bizot, F-75579 Paris Cedex, France
CEO: Daniel Derichebourg, CEO
Bus: *Used products recycling.*
Tel: 33-1-4475-4040
Fax: 33-1-4475-4322
www.cff.fr
Rev: $1,291
Emp: 2,488

NAICS: 423510, 423930, 562111

CFF RECYCLING USA
7501 Wallisville Rd., Houston, Texas 77020
CEO: Daniel Derichebourg
Bus: *Used products recycling.*
Tel: (713) 675-2281
Fax: (713) 675-2285
%FO: 100

CFF RECYCLING USA
5225 Fidelity St., Houston, Texas 77029
CEO: Rudy Couling
Bus: *Used products recycling.*
Tel: (713) 676-1256
Fax: (713) 676-1256
%FO: 100

● **CFM INTERNATIONAL, INC.**
Aerodrome de Villaroche, F-77019 Melun, France
CEO: Pierre Fabre, CEO
Bus: *Aircraft engine manufacture. JV of Snecma and General Electric.*
Tel: 33-1-6414-8866
Fax: 33-1-6479-8555
www.cfm56.com

NAICS: 336412

CFM INTERNATIONAL, INC.
PO Box 15514, One Neumann Way, Cincinnati, Ohio 45215-0514
CEO: Pierre Fabre
Bus: *Aircraft engine manufacture.*
Tel: (513) 563-4180
Fax: (513) 552-3329
%FO: 100

● **CHANEL SA**
135, Avenue Charles de Gaulle, F-92521 Neuilly-sur-Seine Cedex, France
CEO: Francoise Montenay, Pres. & CEO
Bus: *Mfr. ladies fashions, cosmetics, watches and jewelry.*
Tel: 33-1-4643-4000
Fax: 33-1-4747-6034
www.chanel.com

NAICS: 315212, 315299, 315999, 316214, 325620, 334518, 339911, 423940, 448120

CHANEL USA INC.
9 West 57th St., New York, New York 10022
CEO: Arie L. Kopelman, Pres.
Bus: *Mfr. ladies fashions, cosmetics, watches and jewelry.*

Tel: (212) 355-5050
Fax: (212) 752-1851

%FO: 100

● **CHARGEURS**
38, rue Marbeuf, F-75008 Paris, France
CEO: Eduardo Maline, CEO
Bus: *Wool processing and manufacture.*

Tel: 33-1-4953-1000
Fax: 33-1-4953-1001
www.chargeurs.fr

Rev: $1,157
Emp: 4,400

NAICS: 313210, 313221

IVEX NOVACEL, INC.
PO Box 95, 55 Tower Road, Newton, Massachusetts 02464
CEO: Robert Merriam, HR
Bus: *Protection films manufacture.*

Tel: (617) 527-4980
Fax: (617) 244-2051

%FO: 100

TROY LAMINATING & COATING IVEX
421 South Union St., Troy, Ohio 45373
CEO: Richard Corane
Bus: *Extrusion coating and laminating.*

Tel: (937) 335-5611
Fax: (937) 339-9223

%FO: 100

● **CIMENTS FRANCAIS**
22, Tour Ariane, F-92088 Paris La Defense, France
CEO: Yves-Rene Nanot, Chmn.
Bus: *Mfr./sale cement, ready mixed concrete and aggregates.*

Tel: 33-1-4291-7500
Fax: 33-1-4774-1135
www.cimfra.fr

Rev: $4,174
Emp: 12,011

NAICS: 327310, 327390, 327992

ESSROC CORP
PO Box 779, Bessemer, Pennsylvania 16112
CEO: Jim Grekon
Bus: *Cement plant.*

Tel: (724) 667-7702
Fax: (724) 667-1067

%FO: 100

ESSROC CORPORATION
3251 Bath Pike, Nazareth, Pennsylvania 18064
CEO: Rodolfo Danielli, Pres.
Bus: *Cement and construction materials.*

Tel: (610) 837-6725
Fax: (610) 837-9614

%FO: 100

● **CITEL-2CP**
12 Boulevard des Iles, F-92441 Issy-les-Moulineaux, France
CEO: Francois Guichard, Pres.
Bus: *Mfr. lightning and surge protectors for AC power, telephone, data and COXIAL lines.*

Tel: 33-1-4123-5023
Fax: 33-1-4123-5009
www.citel2cp.com

Rev: $22
Emp: 250

NAICS: 334417, 335931

CITEL, INC.
1515 NW 167th St., St. 5-223, Miami, Florida 33169
CEO: Fabrice A. Larmier, EVP
Bus: *Mfr./distribution of lightning and surge protectors for AC power, telephone, data and COXIAL lines.*

Tel: (305) 621-0022
Fax: (305) 621-0766

%FO: 100
Emp: 3

- **CLARINS S.A.**
4, rue Berteaux-Dumas, F-92200 Neuilly-sur-Seine Cedex, France
CEO: Christian Courtin-Clarins, Chmn.
Bus: *Produces/distributes skin care products and perfume.*
NAICS: 325620

Tel: 33-1-4738-1212
Fax: 33-1-4745-5576
www.clarins.fr

Rev: $1,280
Emp: 5,251

    CLARINS USA INC
    110 East 59th St., New York, New York 10022
    CEO: Joseph M. Horowitz, VP
    Bus: *Distribution/sales of skin care and perfume products.*

    Tel: (212) 980-1800
    Fax: (212) 308-1448

    %FO: 100

- **CLUB MEDITERRANEE SA**
11, rue de Cambrai, F-75957 Paris Cedex 19, France
CEO: Francois Salamon, Pres. & CEO
Bus: *Owns and operates vacation resorts, hotels, ships, planes.*
NAICS: 483112, 488999, 561520, 561599, 721199, 721310

Tel: 33-1-5335-3553
Fax: 33-1-5335-3273
www.clubmed.com

Rev: $1,914
Emp: 20,333

    CLUB MED INC.
    75 Valencia Dr., Ste. 900, Coral Gables, Florida 33134
    CEO: Philipe Bourguignon, Chmn.
    Bus: *Sales and management, vacation hotel, resorts, cruise ships.*

    Tel: (305) 925-9000
    Fax: (305) 443-9659

    %FO: 100
    Emp: 1,773

    CLUB MED SANDPIPER
    3500 Morningside Blvd. SE, Port Saint Lucie, Florida 34952
    CEO: Lionel Benzell, Mgr.
    Bus: *Resort hotel.*

    Tel: (772) 335-4400
    Fax:

    %FO: 100

    CRESTED BUTTE CLUB MED
    500 Gothic St., PO Box A, Crested Butte, Colorado 81225
    CEO: Edward Callaway, Pres.
    Bus: *Resort hotel.*

    Tel: (970) 349-4000
    Fax:

    %FO: 20
    Emp: 50

- **CMA-CGM GROUP**
4, quai d'Arenc, F-13235 Marseille Cedex 2, France
CEO: M. Jacques R. Saade, Chmn.
Bus: *Container shipping line.*

NAICS: 483111, 483211

Tel: 33-4-8891-9000
Fax: 33-4-8891-9095
www.cma-cgm.com

Rev: $4,854
Emp: 8,000

    CMA CGM AMERICA INC.
    5701 Lake Wright Dr., Norfolk, Virginia 23502
    CEO: H. Christensen, VP
    Bus: *Container shipping.*

    Tel: (757) 961-2100
    Fax: (757) 961-2151

    %FO: 100

    SDV USA INC.
    3950 Paramount Blvd., Lakewood, California 90712
    CEO: Rosetti Vong
    Bus: *Freight forwarding services.*

    Tel: (562) 377-0800
    Fax: (562) 377-0123

    %FO: 100

SDV USA INC.
195 Cottage St., Boston, Massachusetts 02128
CEO: Norman Pickering   Tel: (617) 887-2717   %FO: 100
Bus: *Freight forwarding services.*   Fax: (617) 887-2717

SDV USA INC.
150-10 132nd St., Jamaica, New York 11434
CEO: Philippe Naudin   Tel: (718) 525-8100   %FO: 100
Bus: *Freight forwarding services.*   Fax: (718) 525-8425

SDV USA INC.
3295 River Exchange Dr., Norcross, Georgia 30092
CEO: Yasser Dahmani   Tel: (770) 729-6728   %FO: 100
Bus: *Freight forwarding services.*   Fax: (770) 729-6734

SDV USA INC.
282 Roesler Ave., Glen Burnie, Maryland 21061
CEO: Charlie Gender   Tel: (410) 766-0212   %FO: 100
Bus: *Freight forwarding services.*   Fax: (410) 766-1619

SDV USA INC.
980 Atlantic Ave., Alameda, California 94501
CEO: Michele Kinchen   Tel: (510) 748-9450   %FO: 100
Bus: *Freight forwarding services.*   Fax: (510) 748-9800

SDV USA INC.
7172 NW 50th St., Miami, Florida 33166
CEO: Jean-Serge Martins   Tel: (305) 592-7222   %FO: 100
Bus: *Freight forwarding services.*   Fax: (305) 592-7222

● **COFACE HOLDING COMPANY**
12 cours Michelet, La Defense 10, F-92065 Paris, France
CEO: Francois David, CEO   Tel: 33-1-4902-2000   Rev: $1,361
Bus: *Provides credit information and short-term credit*   Fax: 33-1-4902-2741   Emp: 4,094
    insurance.   www.coface.com
NAICS: 524113, 524126

COFACE NORTH AMERICA
900 Church St., Ste. 2, New Haven, Connecticut 06510
CEO: Sebastien Bouvet, Mgr.   Tel: (203) 781-3800   %FO: 100
Bus: *Credit information and short-term credit*   Fax: (203) 781-3833
    insurance services.

COFACE NORTH AMERICA
50 Millstone Rd. Building 100, East Windsor, New Jersey 08520
CEO: Dora Gonczy, Mgr.   Tel: (609) 469-0441   %FO: 100
Bus: *Credit information and short-term credit*   Fax: (609) 490-1579
    insurance services.

COFACE NORTH AMERICA
1350 Broadway, 20/F, New York, New York 10018
CEO: Bob Frewen, Mgr.   Tel: (212) 389-6500   %FO: 100
Bus: *Credit information and short-term credit*   Fax: (877) 626-3223
    insurance services.

- **COLAS SA**
7, Place Rene Clair, F-92653 Boulogne-Billancourt, France
CEO: Alain Dupont, CEO
Bus: *Building and paving of roads.*
Tel: 33-1-4761-7500
Fax: 33-1-3761-7600
www.colas.fr
Rev: $9,321
Emp: 56,130

NAICS: 237310

COLAS INC.
10 Madison Ave., 4/F, Morristown, New Jersey 07960
CEO: Michel Roullet, Pres.
Bus: *Engaged in construction and building and paving of roads.*
Tel: (973) 290-9082
Fax: (973) 290-9088
%FO: 100

EASTERN BRIDGE COMPANY
2411 E Cherokee St., Blacksburg, South Carolina 29702
CEO: Kirsten Duffy
Bus: *Engaged in construction and building and paving of roads.*
Tel: (864) 936-3081
Fax: (864) 936-3084
%FO: 100

IA CONSTRUCTION CORPORATION
158 Lindsey Rd., Zelienople, Pennsylvania 16063
CEO: Robert Doucet, Pres.
Bus: *Engaged in construction and building and paving of roads.*
Tel: (724) 772-6630
Fax: (724) 772-6663
%FO: 100

SLOAN CONSTRUCTION COMPANY
1600 W Washington St., Greenville, South Carolina 29601
CEO: Randy Eller
Bus: *Engaged in construction and building and paving of roads.*
Tel: (864) 271-9090
Fax: (864) 235-5245
%FO: 100

SULLY-MILLER CONTRACTING COMPANY
1100 E Orangethorpe Ave., Anaheim, California 92801
CEO: Bruce Rieser
Bus: *Engaged in construction and building and paving of roads.*
Tel: (714) 578-9600
Fax: (714) 578-9600
%FO: 100

- **COMPAGNIE DE FIVES-LILLE**
38, rue de la Republique, F-93100 Montreuil-sous-Bois, France
CEO: Jacques Lefeuvre, CEO
Bus: *Thermal and mechanical equipment manufacture.*
Tel: 33-1-4988-3939
Fax: 33-1-4988-3900
www.fiveslille.com
Rev: $735
Emp: 7,000

NAICS: 332111, 333319, 333513, 333996

CINETIC AUTOMATION
23400 Halsted Rd., Farmington Hills, Michigan 48335-2878
CEO: Mike Dimichelle, HR
Bus: *Automotive manufacturing equipment.*
Tel: (248) 477-0800
Fax: (248) 615-2448
%FO: 100

CINETIC CLEANING & MACHINING
39001 Schoolcraft Rd., Livonia, Michigan 48150
CEO: Mark Pehrson
Bus: *Automotive manufacturing equipment.*
Tel: (734) 464-0100
Fax: (734) 953-7707
%FO: 100

DMS BLISS CORPORATION
400 Holiday Dr., Ste. 101, Pittsburgh, Pennsylvania 15220
CEO: Helmut Binder   Tel: (412) 922-5305   %FO: 100
Bus: *Steel equipment services.*   Fax: (412) 922-5306

FLETCHER SMITH INC.
2801 Ponce de Leon Blvd., Ste. 1055, Coral Gables, Florida 33134
CEO: Norma Perera   Tel: (305) 448-2845   %FO: 100
Bus: *Engineering architectural consulting*   Fax: (305) 448-0724
      services.

● **COMPAGNIE GENERALE DE GEOPHYSIQUE (CGG)**
1, rue Leon Migaux, F-91341 Massy Cedex, France
CEO: Robert Brunck, Chmn. & CEO   Tel: 33-1-6447-3000   Rev: $938
Bus: *Provides geophysical exploration and data*   Fax: 33-1-6447-3970   Emp: 3,669
      processing.   www.cgg.com
NAICS: 213112, 541330, 541360

    CGG AMERICAN SERVICES
    16430 Park Ten Place, Houston, Texas 77084
    CEO: Jonathon Miller   Tel: (281) 646-2400   %FO: 100
    Bus: *Provides geophysical exploration and data*   Fax: (281) 646-2640
        processing services.

    SERCEL INC.
    17200 Park Row, Houston, Texas 77084
    CEO: Thierry Le Roux, CEO   Tel: (281) 492-6688   %FO: 100
    Bus: *Geophysical equipment*   Fax: (281) 579-7505   Emp: 400

● **COMPAGNIE PLASTIC OMNIUM**
1, rue du Parc, F-92593 Levallois-Perret, France
CEO: Laurent Burelle, CEO   Tel: 33-1-4087-6400   Rev: $492
Bus: *Automobile parts manufacture.*   Fax: 33-1-4087-9662   Emp: 9,491
      www.plasticomnium.com
NAICS: 336399

    EPSCO INTERNATIONAL INC.
    2730 West Cardinal Dr., Beaumont, Texas 77705
    CEO: Charles Foux   Tel: (409) 842-1424   %FO: 100
    Bus: *Automobile parts manufacture and sales.*   Fax: (409) 842-1672

    EPSCO INTERNATIONAL INC.
    2851 Highway 90, Westlake, Louisiana 70669
    CEO: Charlie Foux   Tel: (318) 882-1340   %FO: 100
    Bus: *Automobile parts manufacture and sales.*   Fax: (318) 882-1632

    EPSCO INTERNATIONAL INC.
    717 Georgia St., Deer Park, Texas 77536-2513
    CEO: Don Hibbetts   Tel: (281) 930-1340   %FO: 100
    Bus: *Automobile parts manufacture and sales.*   Fax: (281) 930-1632

    PLASTIC OMNIUM INDUSTRIES INC.
    5100 Old Pearman Dairy Rd., Anderson, South Carolina 29625
    CEO: Philippe Claye   Tel: (864) 260-0000   %FO: 100
    Bus: *Automobile parts manufacture and sales.*   Fax: (864) 231-7537

PLASTIC OMNIUM ZARN INC.
5055 Cranswick Rd., Houston, Texas 77041
CEO: Shannon Horner
Bus: *Plastic automobile parts manufacture.*

Tel: (713) 460-3139
Fax: (713) 460-3139

%FO: 100

● **CREDIT AGRICOLE S.A.**
91-93, Blvd. Pasteur, F-75710 Paris 15, France
CEO: Jean Gaston Pierre Marie Victor Laurent, CEO
Bus: *General commercial banking, asset management, securities trading & insurance services.*

Tel: 33-1-4323-5202
Fax: 33-1-4323-3448
www.credit-agricole.fr

Rev: $45,754
Emp: 62,001

NAICS: 522110, 522292, 522298, 523110, 523920, 523930, 524210

    CALYON FINANCIAL
    550 W. Jackson Blvd., Ste. 500, Chicago, Illinois 60661
    CEO: Richard A. Ferina, Chmn. & CEO
    Bus: *Financial services*

    Tel: (312) 441-4200
    Fax: (312) 441-4201

    Emp: 390

    CALYON SECURITIES USA INC.
    1301 Ave. of the Americas, New York, New York 10019
    CEO: Francois Pages, Pres. & CEO
    Bus: *Financial services*

    Tel: (212) 261-7000
    Fax: (212) 459-3170

    CREDIT AGRICOLE INDOSUEZ
    55 East Monroe St., Ste. 4702, Chicago, Illinois 60603
    CEO: Walter Clark, Mgr.
    Bus: *Investment office*

    Tel: (312) 917-7550
    Fax:

    %FO: 100
    Emp: 15

    CRÉDIT AGRICOLE INDOSUEZ SECURITIES
    666 Third Ave., 8/F, New York, New York 10017
    CEO: Anthony West, CEO
    Bus: *Security brokers & dealers*

    Tel: (646) 658-2500
    Fax:

    %FO: 100
    Emp: 40

● **CREDIT INDUSTRIEL ET COMMERCIAL DE PARIS (CIC)**
6, avenue de Provence, F-75009 Paris, France
CEO: Michel Lucas, Pres. & CEO
Bus: *Provides retail, private and investment banking services.*

Tel: 33-1-4596-9696
Fax: 33-1-4596-9666
www.cic-banques.fr

Rev: $14,856
Emp: 24,001

NAICS: 522110

    CREDIT INDUSTRIEL ET COMMERCIAL DE PARIS
    520 Madison Ave., 37/F, New York, New York 10022
    CEO: Michel Lucas
    Bus: *Banking and financial services.*

    Tel: (212) 715-4444
    Fax: (212) 715-4441

    %FO: 100

● **CS COMMUNICATION & SYSTEMES**
1 ave. Newton, F-92142 Clamart Cedex, France
CEO: Francois Leraillez, CEO
Bus: *IT consulting services.*

Tel: 33-1-4128-4000
Fax: 33-1-41-28-4040
www.c-s.fr

Rev: $434
Emp: 3,391

NAICS: 541613

INTRANS GROUP INC.
55 Cherry Lane, Carle Place, New York 11514
CEO: Francois Ott
Bus: *IT consulting services.*

Tel: (516) 592-6100
Fax: (516) 484-5161

%FO: 100

● **GROUPE DANONE SA**
17 Blvd. Haussmann, F-75009 Paris, France
CEO: Franck Riboud, Chmn. & CEO
Bus: *Production and distribution of dairy and other branded food and beverage products worldwide.*
NAICS: 311511, 311513, 311520, 311821, 312112, 424430

Tel: 33-1-4435-2020
Fax: 33-1-4225-6716
www.danonegroup.com

Rev: $18,558
Emp: 89,449

DS WATERS OF AMERICA
5600 New Northside Dr., Atlanta, Georgia 30328
CEO: Willaim A. Holl, CEO
Bus: *Bottled water manufacturer*

Tel: (770) 933-1400
Fax: (770) 956-9495

Emp: 5,500

STONYFIELD FARM
10 Burton Dr., Londonderry, New Hampshire 03053
CEO: Gary Hirshberg, CEO
Bus: *Sale of dairy products*

Tel: (603) 437-4040
Fax: (603) 437-7594

Emp: 215

THE DANNON COMPANY
120 White Plains Rd., Tarrytown, New York 10591
CEO: Juan Carlos Dalto, Pres. & CEO
Bus: *Production and distribution of dairy products.*

Tel: (914) 366-9700
Fax: (914) 366-2805

%FO: 100

● **DASSAULT AVIATION SA**
9, Rond-Point des Champs-Elysées, Marcel Dassault, F-75008 Paris, France
CEO: Charles Edelstenne, Chmn. & CEO
Bus: *Luxury jets and military aircraft manufacture.*

Tel: 33-1-5376-9300
Fax: 33-1-5376-9320
www.dassault-aviation.com

Rev: $4,140
Emp: 11,950

NAICS: 332995, 334511, 336411, 336413

DASSAULT FALCON JET CORPORATION
Teterboro Airport, 200 Riser Rd., Little Ferry, New Jersey 07643
CEO: Jean Rosanvallon, Pres. & CEO
Bus: *Aircraft assembly, sales and service.*

Tel: (201) 440-6700
Fax: (201) 541-4619

%FO: 100
Emp: 180

DASSAULT SYSTEMES OF AMERICA
6320 Canoga Ave., 3/F, Woodland Hills, California 91367-2526
CEO: Philippe Forestier, CEO
Bus: *Develops CAD/CAM software for aerospace and automotive industries.*

Tel: (818) 999-2500
Fax: (818) 999-3535

%FO: 100

DELMIA CORPORATION
5500 New King St., Troy, Michigan 48098
CEO: Peter Schmitt, Pres.
Bus: *Produces software for digital manufacturing, robotics, NC verification & virtual prototyping.*

Tel: (248) 267-9696
Fax: (248) 267-8585

%FO: 100

ENOVIA CORPORATION
10926 David Taylor Dr., Charlotte, North Carolina 28262
CEO: Tony Hakola, CEO
Bus: *Provides software solutions to address the product development management market.*

Tel: (704) 944-8800
Fax: (704) 944-8888

%FO: 100

SOLIDWORKS CORPORATION
300 Baker Ave., Concord, Massachusetts 01742
CEO: John McEleney, CEO
Bus: *Provides modeling solutions for mechanical engineers.*

Tel: (978) 371-5111
Fax: (978) 371-5088

%FO: 100

● **DASSAULT SYSTEMS**
9 quai Marcel Dassault, F-92156 Suresnes, France
CEO: Bernard Charlès, CEO
Bus: *Enterprise software solutions.*

Tel: 33-1-4099-4099
Fax: 33-1-4204-4581
www.3ds.com

Rev: $1,079
Emp: 4,088

NAICS: 511210

DASSAULT SYSTEMES OF AMERICA CORP.
6320 Canoga Ave., Trillium East Tower, Woodland Hills, California 91367-2526
CEO: Philippe Forestier, VP
Bus: *Software development.*

Tel: (818) 999-2500
Fax: (818) 999-3535

%FO: 100

DELMIA CORPORATION
900 North Squirrel Rd., Ste. 100, Auburn Hills, Michigan 48326-2789
CEO: Philippe Charles, CEO
Bus: *Software and e-solutions for manufacturing firms.*

Tel: (248) 267-9696
Fax: (248) 267-8585

%FO: 100
Emp: 195

ENOVIA CORPORATION
10330 David Taylor Dr., Charlotte, North Carolina 28262
CEO: John Squire, VP
Bus: *Enterprise software solutions.*

Tel: (704) 264-8800
Fax: (704) 264-8888

%FO: 100

SOLIDWORKS CORPORATION
300 Baker Ave., Ext., Concord, Massachusetts 01742-2131
CEO: John McEleney, CEO
Bus: *3-D mechanical design software sales.*

Tel: (978) 371-5000
Fax: (978) 371-7303

%FO: 100
Emp: 460

● **DECLEOR PARIS**
31 rue Henri Rochefort, F-75017 Paris, France
CEO: Herve Lesieur, Chmn.
Bus: *Aromatherapy and phototherapy skin care*

Tel: 33-1-4212-7373
Fax: 33-1-4212-0241
www.decleor.com

NAICS: 325620

DECLEOR U.S.A., INC.
100 Tokeneke Rd., Darien, Connecticut 06820
CEO: Jacques Perusse, VP
Bus: *Distribution and sale of aromatherapy and phototherapy skin care products.*

Tel: (203) 656-7982
Fax: (203) 656-7814

%FO: 100

● **DELACHAUX SA**
119, ave. Louis Roche, BP 152, F-92231 Gennevilliers Cedex, France
CEO: Francois Delachaux, CEO   Tel: 33-1-4688-1500   Rev: $546
Bus: *Mfr. track laying equipment, elastic fastener*   Fax: 33-1-4688-1501   Emp: 2,158
     systems and electrification systems.   www.delachaux.fr
NAICS: 333220, 333513, 333516

     INSUL 8 CORPORATION
     10102 F. St., Omaha, Nebraska 68127
     CEO: Jerry Koetting   Tel: (402) 339-9300   %FO: 100
     Bus: *Mfr. electrical industrial apparatus.*   Fax: (402) 339-9627

     RAILTECH BOUTET USA INC.
     26 Interstate Dr., PO Box 69, Napoleon, Ohio 43545
     CEO: Hans Dolder   Tel: (419) 592-5050   %FO: 100
     Bus: *Mfr. rail aligning tools.*   Fax: (419) 599-3630

● **CHRISTIAN DIOR SA**
30, Avenue Montaigne, F-75008 Paris, France
CEO: Bernard Armault, Chmn. & CEO   Tel: 33-1-4413-2498   Rev: $16,270
Bus: *Designer fashion and accessories.*   Fax: 33-1-4413-2786   Emp: 58,246
     www.dior.com
NAICS: 315191, 315211, 315212, 315222, 315223, 315224, 315228, 315231, 315232, 315233, 315234, 315239, 315292, 315299, 315993, 315999, 316992, 316993, 316999

     BENEFIT COSMETICS LLC
     685 Market St., 7/F, San Francisco, California 94105
     CEO: Diane Miles, CEO   Tel: (415) 781-8153
     Bus: *Cosmetics & skin care.*   Fax: (415) 781-3930   Emp: 240

     CHRISTIAN DIOR
     712 Fifth Ave., 37/F, New York, New York 10019
     CEO: Donald Lewis   Tel: (212) 582-0500   %FO: 100
     Bus: *Designer fashion and accessories.*   Fax: (212) 582-1063

     CLICQUOT INC.
     8501 Hwy. 128, Philo, California 95466
     CEO: Mireille Guiliano, Pres. & CEO   Tel: (707) 895-2065   %FO: 100
     Bus: *Sparkling wines.*   Fax: (707) 895-2758

     CRUISE LINE HOLDINGS CO.
     8052 NW 14th St., Miami, Florida 33126
     CEO: Robin Norris, Pres.   Tel: (786) 845-7300
     Bus: *Floral & retail gifts.*   Fax: (305) 477-4522

     DFS GROUP LIMITED
     First Market Tower, 525 Market St., 33/F, San Francisco, California 94105
     CEO: Edward J. Brennan, Chmn. & Pres. & CEO   Tel: (415) 977-2700
     Bus: *Duty free shopping.*   Fax: (415) 977-4289

     DONNA KARAN INTERNATIONAL INC.
     550 7th Ave., New York, New York 10018
     CEO: Jeffry M. Aronsson, CEO   Tel: (212) 789-1500
     Bus: *Mfr. of apparel.*   Fax: (212) 768-6099

LVMH INC.
19 E. 57th St., New York, New York 10022
CEO: Bruce Ingram, CEO
Bus: *Mfr. of apparel.*
Tel: (212) 931-2700
Fax: (212) 931-2730

NEWTON VINEYARD LLC
2555 Madrona Ave., St. Helena, California 94574
CEO: Peter L. Newton, Pres.
Bus: *Winemakers.*
Tel: (707) 963-9000
Fax: (707) 963-5408
Emp: 200

SCHIEFFELIN & CO.
2 Park Ave., 17/F, New York, New York 10016
CEO: John Esposito, Pres. & CEO
Bus: *Wines and spirits.*
Tel: (212) 251-8200
Fax: (212) 251-8382
%FO: 100

SEPHORA USA LLC
First Market Tower, 525 Market St., 11/F, San Francisco, California 94105
CEO: David Suliteanu, Pres. & CEO
Bus: *Sale of cosmetics, beauty supply & perfume*
Tel: (415) 284-3300
Fax: (415) 284-3434

● **DOLLFUS MIEG & CIE (DMC)**
10, avenue Lefru-Rollin, F-75579 Paris, France
CEO: Jacques Boubal, Pres. & CEO
Bus: *Apparel fabrics and craft supplies manufacturer.*
Tel: 33-1-4928-1000
Fax: 33-1-4342-5654
www.dmc-cw.com
Rev: $340
Emp: 2,400

NAICS: 313311, 313312, 423920

VELCOREX OF FRANCE
1430 Broadway, 14/F, New York, New York 10018
CEO: David Sirkin, CEO
Bus: *Distributor embroidery threads.*
Tel: (212) 221-5959
Fax: (212) 221-5979
%FO: 100
Emp: 40

● **DOSATRON INTL SA**
Rue Pascal, BP 6, F-33370 Tresses, France
CEO: John D. Kelly, Pres.
Bus: *Non-electric proportional liquid dispensers manufacture.*
Tel: 33-5-5797-1111
Fax: 33-5-5797-1129
www.dosatron.com
Rev: $14
Emp: 100

NAICS: 332999, 333996

DOSATRON INTERNATIONAL INC.
2090 Sunnydale Blvd, Clearwater, Florida 33765
CEO: Edward D. Kelly
Bus: *Sale/distribution hydraulic injectors.*
Tel: (727) 443-5404
Fax: (727) 443-5404
%FO: 99
Emp: 12

● **EADS TELECOM**
Rue Jean-Pierre Timbaud, Montigny-le-Bretonneux, F-78063 Saint-Quentin-en-Yvelines, France
CEO: Patrick Jourdan, CEO
Bus: *Telecommunication services.*
Tel: 33-1-3460-8020
Fax: 33-1-3460-7022
www.eads-telecom.com

NAICS: 334210, 334220, 517212, 517410

EADS TELECOM NA
2811 Internet Blvd., Frisco, Texas 75034
CEO: George O'Brien
Bus: *Telecommunication services.*

Tel: (972) 855-8206
Fax: (972) 661-0331

%FO: 100

● **EDAP TMS SA**
Parc d'Activites la Poudrette, Lamartine, 4/6, rue du Dauphine, F-69120 Vaulx-en-Velin, France
CEO: Harel Beit-On, CEO
Bus: *Non-surgical medical device manufacture.*

Tel: 33-4-7215-3150
Fax: 33-4-7215-3151
www.edaptechnomed.com

Rev: $30
Emp: 122

NAICS: 334510, 334517, 339111, 339112, 339113

EDAP TECHNOMED INC.
100 Pinnacle Way, Ste. 100, Norcross, Georgia 30071
CEO: Antoine Tetard
Bus: *Non-surgical medical device manufacture and sales.*

Tel: (770) 446-9950
Fax: (770) 446-9951

%FO: 100

● **ELECTRICITE DE FRANCE (EDF)**
22-30 avenue de Wagram, F-75382 Paris Cedex 8, France
CEO: Pierre Gadonneix, Chmn. & CEO
Bus: *Generation/distribution electricity.*

Tel: 33-1-4042-2222
Fax: 33-1-4042-7940
www.edf.fr

Rev: $64,010
Emp: 156,152

NAICS: 221111, 221113, 221119, 221121, 221122, 221210, 237110, 237120, 237130, 424720, 486210, 523130, 541330, 541618, 541620, 541690, 561210

ATIC SERVICES
Empire State Bldg., 350 5th Ave., Ste. 1120, New York, New York 10118
CEO: Ghislaine Taylor, VP
Bus: *Coal mining*

Tel: (212) 947-7104
Fax: (212) 594-9506

ÉLECTRICITÉ DE FRANCE INTERNATIONAL NORTH AMERICA, INC.
1730 Rhode Island Ave., NW, Washington, District of Columbia 20036
CEO: Jean Cottave, mgr
Bus: *US headquarters of EDF; energy generator and distributor.*

Tel: (202) 429-2527
Fax: (202) 429-2532

%FO: 100

● **ELITE MODEL MANAGEMENT CORPORATION**
8 bis, rue Lecuirot, F-75014 Paris, France
CEO: Alan M. Jacobs, CEO
Bus: *Fashion model agency.*

Tel: 33-1-4044-3222
Fax: 33-1-4044-3280
www.elitemodel.com

NAICS: 711410

ELITE MODEL MANAGEMENT
111 East 22nd St., New York, New York 10010
CEO: Monique Pillard, Pres.
Bus: *Fashion model agency.*

Tel: (212) 529-9700
Fax: (212) 475-0572

%FO: 100

• **ERAMET**
Tour Maine-Montparnasse, 33, avenue du Maine, F-75755 Paris Cedex 15, France
CEO: Jacques Bacardats, CEO   Tel: 33-1-4538-4242   Rev: $3,438
Bus: *Mfr. specialty steels and super alloys.*   Fax: 33-1-4538-7425   Emp: 12,806
www.eramet.fr

NAICS: 212210, 212234, 212299, 325188, 331491

> **ERAMET NORTH AMERICA, INC.**
> 333 Rouser Rd., PO Box 1198, Coraopolis, Pennsylvania 15108
> CEO: Stephen Wilkinson   Tel: (412) 262-6200   %FO: 100
> Bus: *Mfr. specialty steels and super alloys.*   Fax: (412) 262-8761

• **ESI GROUP**
6, Rue Hamelin, F-75761 Paris Cedex 16, France
CEO: Alain de Rouvray, CEO   Tel: 33-1-5365-1414   Rev: $60
Bus: *Software products development and marketing.*   Fax: 33-1-5365-1412   Emp: 404
www.esi-group.com

NAICS: 334611, 511210

> **ESI NORTH AMERICA**
> 36800 Woodward Ave., Ste. 200, Bloomfield Hills, Michigan 48304
> CEO: Scott Hayward   Tel: (248) 203-0642   %FO: 100
> Bus: *Software products development and*   Fax: (248) 203-0696
> *marketing and sales.*

> **ESI NORTH AMERICA**
> 12555 High Bluff Dr., Ste. 310, San Diego, California 92130
> CEO: Andrew Cunningham   Tel: (858) 350-0057   %FO: 100
> Bus: *Software products development and*   Fax: (858) 350-8328
> *marketing and sales.*

• **ESKER SA**
10 rue des Emeraudes, F-69006 Lyon, France
CEO: Jean-Michel Berard, CEO   Tel: 33-4-7283-4646   Rev: $28
Bus: *Fax software manufacturer.*   Fax: 33-4-7283-4640   Emp: 269
www.esker.com

NAICS: 511210

> **ESKER USA INC.**
> 1212 Deming Way, Ste. 350, Madison, Wisconsin 53717
> CEO: Emmanuel Olivier, VP Sales   Tel: (608) 828-6000   %FO: 100
> Bus: *Fax software manufacture and sales.*   Fax: (608) 828-6001

• **ESSILOR INTERNATIONAL SA**
147, rue de Paris, F-94227 Charenton-le-Pont, France
CEO: Xavier Fontanet, CEO   Tel: 33-1-4977-4224   Rev: $3,083
Bus: *Optical products and supplies and corrective*   Fax: 33-1-4977-4420   Emp: 25,886
www.essilorgroupe.com

NAICS: 333314

ESSILOR OF AMERICA INC.
2400 118th Ave. North, St. Petersburg, Florida 33716
CEO: Mike Daly
Bus: *Optical lenses manufacturer.*
Tel: (727) 572-0844
Fax: (727) 572-8930
%FO: 100

ESSILOR OF AMERICA INC.
1100 Trappers Ct., Hugo, Minnesota 55038
CEO: Scott Pennock
Bus: *Optical lenses manufacturer.*
Tel: (651) 762-8612
Fax: (651) 762-8612
%FO: 100

ESSILOR OF AMERICA INC.
4925 West Cardinal Dr., Beaumont, Texas 77705
CEO: Doug Preston
Bus: *Optical lenses manufacturer.*
Tel: (409) 842-4113
Fax: (409) 842-4113
%FO: 100

ESSILOR OF AMERICA INC.
13515 North Stemmons Freeway, Dallas, Texas 75234
CEO: Hubert Sagnières
Bus: *Optical lenses manufacturer.*
Tel: (214) 496-4141
Fax: (972) 241-1162
%FO: 100

- **EULER HERMES**
1, rue Euler, F-75008 Paris, France
CEO: Nicolas Hein, CFO
Bus: *Provides credit insurance.*
Tel: 33-1-4070-5050
Fax: 33-1-4070-5017
www.eulerhermes.com
Rev: $2,448
Emp: 6,071

NAICS: 524128, 524291, 524298

EULER HERMES ACI
800 Red Brook Blvd., Owings Mills, Maryland 21117
CEO: Paul Overeem, Pres.
Bus: *Engaged in account receivable insurance, including credit insurance policies.*
Tel: (410) 753-0753
Fax: (410) 753-0952
%FO: 100
Emp: 300

- **EUROCOPTER SA**
Aeroport International de Marseille, F-13725 Marignane Cedex, France
CEO: Fabrice Bregier, Chmn.
Bus: *Mfr. helicopters.*
Tel: 33-4-4285-8585
Fax: 33-4-4285-8500
www.eurocopter.com
Rev: $2,630
Emp: 10,800

NAICS: 336411

AMERICAN EUROCOPTER CORPORATION
2701 Forum Dr., Grand Prairie, Texas 75052-7099
CEO: Linda Burket, CEO
Bus: *Assembly/sale helicopters.*
Tel: (972) 641-0000
Fax: (972) 641-3761
%FO: 100
Emp: 250

- **EUROFINS SCIENTIFIC**
Rue Pierre Adolphe Bobierre, F-44323 Nantes Cedex 3, France
CEO: Gilles G. Martin, Chmn. & CEO
Bus: *Product analysis services.*
Tel: 33-2-5183-2100
Fax: 33-2-5183-2111
www.eurofins.com
Rev: $212
Emp: 2,117

NAICS: 541380, 541710

EUROFINS SCIENTIFIC / PRODUCT SAFETY LABS
725 Cranbury Rd., East Brunswick, New Jersey 08816
CEO: Gary Wnorowski, Mgr.   Tel: (732) 254-4339   %FO: 100
Bus: *Commercial testing laboratories.*   Fax: (732) 355-3275   Emp: 20

EUROFINS SCIENTIFIC INC.
4500 Wadsworth, Ste. 110, Dayton, New Jersey 45414
CEO: Lars M.J. Reimann   Tel: (937) 276-7800   %FO: 100
Bus: *Testing laboratories.*   Fax: (937) 276-7805

EUROFINS SCIENTIFIC INC.
6555 Quince Rd., Ste. 202, Memphis, Tennessee 38119
CEO: Lars M.J. Reimann, Mgr.   Tel: (901) 272-7511   %FO: 100
Bus: *Analytical chemical testing labs.*   Fax: (901) 272-2926   Emp: 250

EUROFINS SCIENTIFIC INC.
345 Adams Ave., PO Box 2135, Memphis, Tennessee 38103
CEO: Doug Winters   Tel: (901) 521-4500   %FO: 100
Bus: *Testing laboratories.*   Fax: (901) 521-4510

EUROFINS SCIENTIFIC INC.
1365 Redwood Way, Petaluma, California 94954
CEO: Jules Skamarack   Tel: (707) 792-7300   %FO: 100
Bus: *Testing laboratories.*   Fax: (707) 792-7309

EUROFINS SCIENTIFIC INC.
3507 Delaware Ave., PO Box 1292, Des Moines, Iowa 50313
CEO: Ardin Backous, Mgr.   Tel: (515) 265-1461   %FO: 100
Bus: *Testing laboratories.*   Fax: (515) 266-5453   Emp: 35

EUROFINS SCIENTIFIC/PRODUCT SAFETY LABS
2394 Route 130, Dayton, New Jersey 08810
CEO: Ralph Shapiro, Mgr.   Tel: (732) 438-5100   %FO: 100
Bus: *Research laboratories.*   Fax: (732) 355-3275   Emp: 50

GENESCAN USA, INC.
2315 North Causeway Blvd., Ste. 200, Metairie, Louisiana 70001
CEO: Mike Russell   Tel: (504) 297-4330   %FO: 100
Bus: *Testing laboratories.*   Fax: (504) 297-4335

● **EUROP ASSISTANCE GROUP**
1, Promenade de la Bonnette, F-92633 Gennevilliers, France
CEO: Martin Vial, Chmn.   Tel: 33-1-4185-8585
Bus: *Travel assistance services and emergency*   Fax: 33-1-4185-8571
www.europassistance.fr
NAICS: 561510, 561599

WORLDWIDE ASSISTANCE SERVICES
1825 K St. NW, Ste. 1000, Washington, District of Columbia 20006
CEO: Jessica Ashley, CEO   Tel: (202) 331-1609   %FO: 100
Bus: *Travel assistance, travel emergency*   Fax: (202) 331-1588
network.

● **FACOM SA**
6/8, rue Gustave Eiffel, F-91420 Morangis, France
CEO: Thierry Paternot, CEO
Bus: *Hand tools manufacture.*

Tel: 33-1-6454-4545
Fax: 33-1-6909-6093
www.facom.fr

Rev: $555
Emp: 4,000

NAICS: 332212

FACOM TOOLS
5900 W. 55th St., Ste. B, McCook, Illinois 60525
CEO: Leonard O'Connell
Bus: *Mfr. hand tools.*

Tel: (708) 485-4574
Fax: (708) 485-4265

%FO: 100

● **FAIVELEY SA**
143, Blvd. Anatole France, Carrefour Pleyel, F-93285 Saint-Denis Cedex, France
CEO: Francois Faiveley, Chmn. & CEO
Bus: *Railroad equipment manufacture.*

Tel: 33-1-4813-6500
Fax: 33-1-4813-6554
www.faiveley.com

Rev: $379
Emp: 2,117

NAICS: 326199, 336510

FAIVELEY RAIL INC.
213 Welsh Pool Rd., Pickering Creek Industrial Park, Exton, Pennsylvania 19341
CEO: Francois Faiveley, Chmn.
Bus: *Mfr. railroad equipment.*

Tel: (610) 524-9110
Fax: (610) 524-9190

%FO: 100

● **FAURECIA SA**
2 rue Hennape, F-92735 Nanterre Cedex, France
CEO: Pierre Levi, CEO
Bus: *Auto parts manufacturer*

Tel: 33-1-7236-700
Fax: 33-1-7236-7007
www.faurecia.com

Rev: $12,706
Emp: 59,578

NAICS: 313312, 314129, 325620, 326199, 336330, 336360, 336399

FAURECIA AUTOMOTIVE SEATING INC.
907 Delta Council Dr., Cleveland, Mississippi 38732
CEO: Jacques Le Morvan
Bus: *Mfr. automotive seating.*

Tel: (662) 846-5252
Fax:

%FO: 100

FAURECIA EXHAUST SYSTEMS
543 Matzinger Rd., Toledo, Ohio 43612
CEO: Mark Stidham, Pres. & CEO
Bus: *Auto parts manufacturing.*

Tel: (419) 727-5000
Fax: (419) 727-5025

%FO: 100

FAURECIA INTERIOR SYSTEMS
101 International Blvd., Fountain Inn, South Carolina 29644
CEO: Jean-Michael Vallin, CEO
Bus: *Auto parts manufacturing.*

Tel: (864) 862-1900
Fax: (864) 862-7700

%FO: 100

FAURECIA INTERIOR SYSYTEMS
217 Lisa Dr., New Castle, Delaware 19720
CEO: Todd Goldie, mgr
Bus: *General warehousing & storage.*

Tel: (302) 395-9334
Fax:

SOMMER ALLIBERT US
101 International Blvd., Fountain Inn, South Carolina 29644
CEO: Jen Michelle Ballin, Pres.   Tel: (864) 862-8266   %FO: 100
Bus: *Auto & home supplies.*   Fax:

● **FIMALAC SA**
97, rue de Lille, F-75007 Paris, France
CEO: Marc Ladreit de Lacharrière, CEO   Tel: 33-1-4753-6150   Rev: $1,550
Bus: *Mfr. garage equipment, hand tools and produce*   Fax: 33-1-4553-6163   Emp: 47
furniture and operate credit agencies.   www.fimalac.fr
NAICS: 332212, 333991, 561450

    CASSINA USA INC.
    155 East 56th St., New York, New York 10022
    CEO: Denis Colacicco   Tel: (212) 245-2121   %FO: 100
    Bus: *Mfr. and sales of high quality, durable*   Fax: (212) 245-1340
    furniture products.

    FITCH RATINGS INC.
    1 State St. Plaza, New York, New York 10004
    CEO: Stephen W. Joynt   Tel: (212) 908-0500   %FO: 100
    Bus: *Credit rating agencies.*   Fax: (212) 908-0500

● **FLAMEL TECHNOLOGIES SA**
33, avenue du Docteur Georges Levy, F-69693 Venissieux Cedex, France
CEO: Stephen H. Willard, CEO   Tel: 33-4-7276-3434   Rev: $55
Bus: *Pharmaceutical manufacture of oral drug delivery*   Fax: 33-4-7276-3435   Emp: 200
systems.   www.flamel-technologies.fr
NAICS: 424210

    FLAMEL USA INC.
    2121 K St. NW, Ste. 650, Washington, District of Columbia 20037
    CEO: Charles Marlio, EVP   Tel: (202) 862-8400   %FO: 100
    Bus: *Mfr. oral drug delivery systems.*   Fax: (202) 862-3933

● **FRANCE TELECOM**
6, place d'Alleray, F-75505 Paris Cedex 15, France
CEO: Didier Lombard, Chmn. & CEO   Tel: 33-1-4444-2222   Rev: $63,879
Bus: *International telecommunications carrier.*   Fax: 33-1-4444-9595   Emp: 206,524
www.francetelecom.fr
NAICS: 511140, 515210, 517110, 517211, 517212, 517410, 517510, 517910, 518111, 518210, 519190, 541690, 561421, 561499

    EQUANT ATLANTA
    400 Galleria Pkwy. SE, Atlanta, Georgia 30339
    CEO: Charles Dehelly, Pres.   Tel: (678) 346-3000
    Bus: *Radio, telephone communications*   Fax: Emp: 400

    EQUANT WASHINGTON
    2355 Dulles Corner Blvd., Bldg. 3, Herndon, Virginia 20171
    CEO: Charles Dehelly, Pres.   Tel: (571) 643-7861
    Bus: *Telephone communications*   Fax: Emp: 2,000

FRANCE TELECOM LONG DISTANCE USA, LLC
2300 Corporate Park Dr., Ste. 600, Herndon, Virginia 20171
CEO: Janet Matulia, Pres.   Tel: (703) 375-4913
Bus: *Telephone communications*   Fax: (703) 375-4944   Emp: 172

FRANCE TELECOM NORTH AMERICA
1270 Ave. of the Americas, 28/F, New York, New York 10020
CEO: Sharyn Yensko, Pres.   Tel: (212) 332-2100   %FO: 100
Bus: *International telecommunications carrier.*   Fax: (212) 245-8605   Emp: 117

FRANCE TELECOM R&D BOSTON
175 Second St., Cambridge, Massachusetts 02142
CEO: Eric Dufresne, CEO   Tel: (617) 995-8000
Bus: *Business consulting*   Fax: (617) 995-8001   Emp: 12

FRANCE TELECOM R&D SAN FRANCISCO
801 Gateway Bldg., Ste. 500, South San Francisco, California 94080
CEO: Lionel Pelamourgues, member   Tel: (650) 875-1500
Bus: *Commercial nonphysical research*   Fax: Emp: 35

GLOBECAST US
7291 NW 74th St., Miami, Florida 33166
CEO: Robert Behar, Pres.   Tel: (305) 887-1600
Bus: *Cable & other pay television services* Fax: (305) 887-4424   Emp: 300

INNOVACOM US
1000 Marina Blvd., 3/F, Brisbane, California 94005
CEO: Frederic Veyssiere   Tel: (650) 876-1532
Bus: *Telecommunications.*   Fax: (650) 875-1505

ORANGE US
175 Second St., Cambridge, Massachusetts 02142
CEO: Richard Miner, VP   Tel: (617) 995-8000
Bus: *Commercial physical research.*   Fax: (617) 995-8001   Emp: 25

• **FROMAGERIES BEL**
4, rue d'Anjou, F-75008 Paris, France
CEO: Gerard Boivin, Chmn. & CEO   Tel: 33-1-4007-7250   Rev: $2,607
Bus: *Mfr. dairy products.*   Fax: 33-1-4007-7400   Emp: 9,700
                                             www.bel-group.com
NAICS: 311513

    BEL /KAUKAUNA USA, INC.
    1500 E. North St., Little Chute, Wisconsin 54140
    CEO: Robert Gilbert, Pres.   Tel: (920) 788-3524   %FO: 100
    Bus: *Sales/distribution of dairy products.*   Fax: (920) 788-9725   Emp: 350

    BEL /KAUKAUNA USA, INC.
    303 South Broadway, Ste. 430, New York, New York 10591
    CEO: Becky Ryan, Mgr.   Tel: (914) 366-8474   %FO: 100
    Bus: *Dairy products.*   Fax: Emp: 6

BEL /KAUKAUNA USA, INC.
602 West Main St., PO Box 468, Leitchfield, Kentucky 42755
CEO: John Plessis, Mgr.   Tel: (270) 259-4071   %FO: 100
Bus: *Mfr. of cheese & milk.*   Fax: Emp: 195

● **GAMELOFT SA**
35 Rue Greneta, F-75002 Paris, France
CEO: Michel Guillemot, CEO   Tel: 33-1-5816-2040   Rev: $32
Bus: *Video game publisher and manufacturer.*   Fax: 33-1-5816-2041   Emp: 400
www.gameloft.com
NAICS: 511210

    GAMELOFT USA INC.
    625 Third St., 3/F, San Francisco, California 94107
    CEO: Helene Juguet, Mgr.   Tel: (415) 547-4000   %FO: 100
    Bus: *Video game manufacture and sales.*   Fax: (415) 547-4001

    RED STORM ENTERTAINMENT
    3200 Gateway Ctr. Blvd., Morrisville, North Carolina 27560
    CEO: Steve Reid   Tel: (919) 460-1776   %FO: 100
    Bus: *Product development.*   Fax: (919) 468-3305

● **GAZ DE FRANCE**
23, rue Philibert Delorem, F-75840 Paris Cedex 17, France
CEO: Jean-Francois Cirelli, Chmn. & CEO   Tel: 33-1-4754-2020   Rev: $12,750
Bus: *Imports and distributes natural gas.*   Fax: 33-1-4227-2150   Emp: 25,357
www.gazdefrance.com
NAICS: 211111, 211112, 221210, 486210, 541330

    GDF ENERGY
    1515 Broadway, 43/F, New York, New York 10036
    CEO: Philippe Hochart, Pres.   Tel: (212) 302-0881
    Bus: *Oil & gas exploration services*   Fax: (212) 221-7816   Emp: 12

● **GENESYS SA**
Immeuble L'Acropole, 954-980, Ave. Jean Mermox, F-34999 Montpellier Cedex 2, France
CEO: Francois Legros, CEO   Tel: 33-4-9913-2767   Rev: $188
Bus: *Provides audio, data video and web-based*   Fax: 33-4-9913-2750   Emp: 982
   conferencing services worldwide.   www.genesys.com
NAICS: 517910, 519190, 561499

    GENESYS INC.
    9139 . Ridgeline Blvd., Highlands Ranch, Colorado 80129
    CEO: Jim Lysinger   Tel: (303) 267-1272   %FO: 100
    Bus: *Audio and video conferencing services.*   Fax: (303) 267-1282

● **GEODIS**
7-9 allees de l'Europe, F-92615 Clichy Cedex, France
CEO: Pierre Blayau, Chmn. & CEO   Tel: 33-1-5676-2600   Rev: $4,597
Bus: *Engaged in logistics services*   Fax: 33-1-5676-2626   Emp: 22,725
www.geodis.fr
NAICS: 483111, 484110, 484121, 484122, 484220, 484230, 488510, 493110, 541614

GEODIS VITESSE LOGISTICS INC.
333 North Michigan Ave., Ste. 1816, Chicago, Illinois 60601
CEO: Herbert Wennink, Dir. Tel: (312) 641-2805 %FO: 100
Bus: *European warehousing and distribution.* Fax: (312) 641-6733 Emp: 240

● **GL TRADE SA**
48 rue Notre-Dame des Victoires, F-75002 Paris, France
CEO: Pierre Gatignol, CEO Tel: 33-1-53-40-00-00 Rev: $205
Bus: *Provider of electronic trading platforms.* Fax: 33-1-53-40-01-40 Emp: 1,073
www.gltrade.fr
NAICS: 511210

GL CONSULTANTS INC.
440 S. LaSalle St., Ste.2202, Chicago, Illinois 60605
CEO: Gerard Varjacques, CEO Tel: (312) 386-2400 %FO: 100
Bus: *Provider of electronic trading platforms.* Fax: (312) 286-2448

● **GROSFILLEX SARL**
BP 2, Arbent, F-01107 Oyonnaux, France
CEO: Raymond Grosfillex, Pres. Tel: 33-4-7473-3030
Bus: *Mfr./sales furniture and home products.* Fax: 33-4-7473-3035 Emp: 1,200
www.grosfillex.com
NAICS: 337122, 337214

GROSFILLEX, INC.
230 Old West Penn Ave., Robesonia, Pennsylvania 19551
CEO: Carel Harmsen, CEO Tel: (610) 693-5835 %FO: 100
Bus: *Mfr/sales furniture & home products &* Fax: (610) 693-5414 Emp: 1,200
plastics

● **GROUPE LACTALIS**
10-20, rue Adolphe Beck, F-53089 Laval Cedex 9, France
CEO: Emmanuel Besnier, Chmn. Tel: 33-2-4359-4259 Rev: $7,205
Bus: *Production and distribution of dairy products.* Fax: 33-2-4349-4263 Emp: 16,500
www.lactalis.fr
NAICS: 115210, 311511, 311512, 311513, 311514, 311611

LACTALIS USA
950 Third Ave., 22/F, New York, New York 10022
CEO: Philippe Surget, Pres. Tel: (212) 758-6666 %FO: 100
Bus: *Mfr. cheese and dairy products.* Fax: (212) 758-7383

RONDELE ACQUISITION LLC
8100 Hwy. K, S., Merrill, Wisconsin 54452
CEO: Robert Constantino, Pres. & CEO Tel: (715) 675-3326 %FO: 100
Bus: *Mfr. of dairy products.* Fax: (715) 536-3028 Emp: 75

SORRENTO LACTALIS INC
2376 South Park Ave., Buffalo, New York 14220
CEO: Erick Boutry, Pres. & CEO Tel: (716) 823-6262 %FO: 100
Bus: *Mfr. cheese and dairy products.* Fax: (716) 823-6454

- **GROUPE LIMAGRAIN HOLDING**
  Rue Limagrain, BP 1, F-63720 Chappes, France
  CEO: Pierre Pagesse, Chmn. & Pres.   Tel: 33-4-7363-4000   Rev: $1,324
  Bus: *Production and sales of seeds.*   Fax: 33-4-7363-4044   Emp: 5,400
                                               www.limagrain.com

  NAICS: 311812, 325414

  ### AGRELIANT GENETICS LLC
  1122 East 169th St., Westfield, Illinois 46074
  CEO: Raphael Journel, Pres.   Tel: (317) 896-5551   %FO: 100
  Bus: *Seeds sales and distribution.*   Fax: (317) 896-9209   Emp: 400

  ### FERRY-MORSE SEED COMPANY
  600 Stephen Beale Dr., PO Box 1620, Fulton, Kentucky 42041
  CEO: Jack Simpson, Pres.   Tel: (270) 472-3400   %FO: 100
  Bus: *Seeds sales and distribution.*   Fax: (270) 472-3402   Emp: 125

  ### HARRIS MORAN SEED CO.
  555 Codoni Ave., Modesto, California 95352
  CEO: Bruno Carette, Pres.   Tel: (209) 579-7333   %FO: 100
  Bus: *Agricultural support & products.*   Fax: (209) 527-8684   Emp: 250

  ### VILMORIN INC.
  2551 North Dragoon St., Tucson, Arizona 85745
  CEO: Fransisco Tirado, CEO   Tel: (520) 884-0011   %FO: 100
  Bus: *Ornamental nursery.*   Fax: (520) 884-5102

- **GROUPE SEB**
  Les 4M, Chemin du Petit Bois, F-69134 Ecully Cedex, France
  CEO: Thierry de La Tour d'Artaise, Chmn. & CEO   Tel: 33-4-7218-1818   Rev: $3,191
  Bus: *Mfr./market electrical cooking and home care*   Fax: 33-4-7218-1655   Emp: 14,500
       appliances.   www.groupeseb.com
  NAICS: 327112, 332211, 332214, 335211, 335212, 335221, 335224

  ### ALL-CLAD
  424 Morganza Rd., Canonsburg, Pennsylvania 15317
  CEO: Marc Navarre, CEO   Tel: (724) 745-8300
  Bus: *Mfr. of cold rolled steel, metal stampings.*   Fax: (724) 746-5035   Emp: 70

  ### ROWENTA / MOULINEX / KRUPS
  196 Boston Ave., 4/F, Medford, Massachusetts 02155
  CEO: Tel: (781) 306-4660   %FO: 100
  Bus: *U.S. headquarters for sales/distribution*   Fax: (781) 396-1313
       electrical cooking & personal care
       appliances & household equipment

  ### T-FAL CORP.
  1 Boland Dr., Ste. 1, West Orange, New Jersey 07052
  CEO: Camille Hevert, Mgr.   Tel: (973) 736-0300
  Bus: *Sales/distribution of cooking equipment and*   Fax: (973) 575-7522
       household goods.

T-FAL CORPORATION
2121 Eden Rd., Millville, New Jersey 08332
CEO: Camille Hevert, Mgr.   Tel: (856) 825-6300   %FO: 100
Bus: *Sales/distribution of cooking equipment and* Fax: (856) 825-0222
      household goods.

● **GROUPE SILICOMP SA**
195 Rue Lavoisier, F-38330 Montbonnot-St-Martin, France
CEO: Jean-Michel Gliner, Chmn. & CEO   Tel: 33-4-7641-6666   Rev: $120
Bus: *IT services.*   Fax: 33-4-7641-6667   Emp: 931
                                                    www.silicomp.fr
  NAICS: 518210, 541511, 541512, 541519

  SILICOMP-AXEAN AMERICA
  7011 Koll Center Pkwy., Ste. 280, Pleasanton, California 94566
  CEO: Rajiv Agarwal, Pres.   Tel: (925) 931-4450   %FO: 100
  Bus: *Software development.*   Fax: (925) 931-4444   Emp: 45

● **GUERBET GROUP**
15, rue des Vanesses, F-93420 Villepinte, France
CEO: Philippe Decazes, Chmn. & CEO   Tel: 33-1-4591-5000   Rev: $338
Bus: *Medical imaging and specialty chemicals*   Fax: 33-1-4591-5199   Emp: 1,150
      manufacture.   www.guerbet-group.com
  NAICS: 325413

  ALTANA INC.
  60 Baylis Rd., Melville, New York 11747
  CEO: Paul McGarty, CEO   Tel: (631) 454-7677   %FO: 100
  Bus: *Mfr. of pharmaceuticals.*   Fax: (631) 454-6389

  GUERBET GROUP
  1185 West 2nd St., Bloomington, Indiana 47403
  CEO: Amy Lutes, Gen. Mgr.   Tel: (812) 333-0059   %FO: 100
  Bus: *Medical imaging and specialty chemicals*   Fax: (812) 333-0084   Emp: 21
      manufacture and sales.

  MALLINCKRODT INC.
  675 McDonnell Blvd., Hazelwood, Missouri 63042
  CEO: Michael J. Collins, Pres.   Tel: (314) 654-2000   %FO: 100
  Bus: *Mfr. of pharmaceuticals.*   Fax: (314) 654-5381

● **GUERLAIN SA**
68 Avenue Des Champs Elysees, F-78008 Paris, France
CEO: Renato Semerari, Chmn.   Tel: 33-1-4562-5257   Rev: $900
Bus: *Mfr. fragrances, cosmetics and skin products.* Fax: Emp: 259
                                                    www.guerlain.com
  NAICS: 325620
  GUERLAIN, INC.
  19 East 57th St., New York, New York 10022
  CEO: Patrick Waterfield, Pres.   Tel: (212) 931-2400   %FO: 100
  Bus: *Mfr./distribute fragrances and cosmetics.* Fax: (212) 931-2445   Emp: 152

- **HACHETTE FILIPACCHI MEDIAS**
  149-151, rue Anatol France, F-92300 Levallois-Perret, France
  CEO: Gerald de Roquemaurel, Chmn. & CEO   Tel: 33-1-4134-6000   Rev: $2,300
  Bus: *Publisher of culture and fashion magazines,*   Fax: 33-1-4134-7777   Emp: 8,590
       including Home, Metropolitan Home, Popular   www.hachette-filipacchi.com
       Photography, Woman's Day, Premier and Road
       and Track.
  NAICS: 511110, 511120, 516110

  > **CURTIS CIRCULATION CO.**
  > 730 River Rd., New Milford, New Jersey 07646
  > CEO: Joseph Walsh, Chmn. & CEO   Tel: (201) 634-7400   %FO: 100
  > Bus: *Press distributor.*   Fax: (201) 634-7499

  > **HFM US**
  > 1633 Broadway, 45/F, New York, New York 10019
  > CEO: Jack Klinger, Pres. & CEO   Tel: (212) 767-6000   %FO: 100
  > Bus: *Magazine publisher.*   Fax: (212) 767-5600   Emp: 2,050

- **HAVAS**
  2 allee de Longchamp, F-92281 Suresnes Cedex, France
  CEO: Alain de Pouzilhac, Chmn. & CEO   Tel: 33-1-5847-9000   Rev: $1,917
  Bus: *International advertising agency. (Sub of Havas*   Fax: 33-1-5847-9999   Emp: 16,343
       www.havas.com
  NAICS: 541613, 541720, 541810, 541820, 541830, 541840, 541850, 541860, 541870, 541890, 541910

  > **ARNOLD WORLDWIDE PARTNERS**
  > 101 Huntington Ave., Boston, Massachusetts 02199
  > CEO: Edward Eskandarian, Chmn. & CEO   Tel: (617) 587-8000
  > Bus: *Advertising services.*   Fax: (617) 587-8070   Emp: 1,800

  > **EURO RSCG 4D**
  > 920 Cassatt Rd., Ste. 300, Berwyn, Pennsylvania 19312
  > CEO: George Gallate, CEO   Tel: (610) 651-2600
  > Bus: *Advertising & marketing services.*   Fax: (610) 651-2643   Emp: 1,500

  > **EURO RSCG LIFE NRP**
  > 200 Madison Ave., 7/F, New York, New York 10016
  > CEO: Anthony J. Russo, CEO   Tel: (212) 845-4200   %FO: 100
  > Bus: *International advertising agency.*   Fax: (212) 845-4216   Emp: 70

  > **EURO RSCG MAGNET**
  > 110 Fifth Ave., 10/F, New York, New York 10011
  > CEO: Aaron Kwittken, CEO   Tel: (212) 367-6800   %FO: 100
  > Bus: *Public relations firm.*   Fax: (212) 367-7154   Emp: 140

  > **EURO RSCG NEW YORK, INC.**
  > 350 Hudson St., New York, New York 10014
  > CEO: Ron Berger, CEO   Tel: (212) 886-4100
  > Bus: *Advertising agencies*   Fax: (212) 886-4415

EURO RSCG WORLDWIDE
350 Hudson St., New York, New York 10014
CEO: James R. Heekin III, Chmn. & CEO   Tel: (212) 886-2000   %FO: 100
Bus: *International communications group of*   Fax: (212) 886-2016   Emp: 1,200
companies. Advertising; audiovisual;
publishing; travel & recreation.

MCKINNEY & SILVER
318 Blakewell St., Durham, North Carolina 27701
CEO: Brad Brinegar, CEO   Tel: (919) 313-0802
Bus: *Advertising agencies*   Fax: Emp: 140

MEDIA PLANNING GROUP
195 Broadway, 12/F, New York, New York 10007
CEO: Charlie Rutman, CEO   Tel: (212) 790-4800
Bus: *Advertising & marketing services.*   Fax: (212) 790-4823

WARSCHAWSKI PUBLIC RELATIONS
1501 Sulgrave Ave., Ste. 350, Baltimore, Maryland 21209
CEO: Davis Warschawski, Pres.   Tel: (410) 367-2700
Bus: *Advertising & marketing services.*   Fax: (410) 367-2400

• HERMES INTERNATIONAL SA
24, Faubourg Saint-Honore, F-75008 Paris, France
CEO: Jean-Louis Dumas, Chmn. & C0-CEO   Tel: 33-1-4017-4920   Rev: $1,544
Bus: *Men's and women's apparel, including leather*   Fax: 33-1-4017-4921   Emp: 5,594
handbags, silk scarves and ties.   www.hermes.com
NAICS: 315211, 315212, 315222, 315223, 315224, 315232, 315233, 315234, 315992, 315993, 315999, 316992,
325620, 333315, 334518, 339911, 339999,
     423410, 423940, 448150, 448320

HERMES OF PARIS
55 East 59th St., New York, New York 10022
CEO: Jean Louis Dumas, Chmn.   Tel: (212) 759-7585   %FO: 100
Bus: *Men's and women's apparel, including*   Fax: Emp: 350
leather handbags, silk scarves and ties.

• ILOG SA
9, rue de Verdun, F-94253 Gentilly Cedex, France
CEO: Pierre Haren, Chmn. & CEO   Tel: 33-1-4908-3500   Rev: $103
Bus: *Mfr. pre-built software component and related*   Fax: 33-1-4908-3510   Emp: 632
software.   www.ilog.com
NAICS: 511210, 541511, 541512, 541519, 611420

ILOG, INC.
1080 Linda Vista Ave., Mountain View, California 94043
CEO: Leo Hecke, VP Sales   Tel: (650) 567-8000   %FO: 100
Bus: *Mfr. software.*   Fax: (650) 567-8001   Emp: 586

ILOG, INC.
889 Alder Ave., Ste. 200, Incline Village, Nevada 89451
CEO: Bounthara Ing, CEO   Tel: (775) 831-2800   %FO: 100
Bus: *Mfr. software.*   Fax: (775) 831-7755

ILOG, INC.
4350 North Fairfax Dr., Ste. 800, Arlington, Virginia 22203
CEO: Bounthara Ing, CEO   Tel: (775) 881-2800   %FO: 100
Bus: *Mfr. software.*   Fax:

ILOG, INC.
144 Turnpike Rd., Ste. 130, Southborough, Massachusetts 01772
CEO: Bounthara Ing, CEO   Tel: (775) 881-2800   %FO: 100
Bus: *Mfr. software.*   Fax:

● **IMERYS**
Tour Maine-Montparnasse, 33, avenue du Maine, F-75755 Paris Cedex 15, France
CEO: Gerard Buffiere, CEO   Tel: 33-1-4538-4300   Rev: $4,030
Bus: *Produces building materials and industrial*   Fax: 33-1-4538-7478   Emp: 14,088
    minerals.   www.imerys.com
NAICS: 212393, 326199, 327121, 327124

   C-E MINERALS
   901 East 8th Ave., King of Prussia, Pennsylvania 19406
   CEO: Timothy J. McCarthy, Pres. & CEO   Tel: (610) 265-6880   %FO: 100
   Bus: *Mfr. industrial minerals.*   Fax: (610) 337-7163   Emp: 1,103

   IMERYS PIGMENTS FOR PAPER
   100 Mansell Ct. East, Ste. 300, Roswell, Georgia 30076
   CEO: Rich Ryan, EVP   Tel: (770) 594-0660   %FO: 100
   Bus: *Develops chemicals for paper manufacture.* Fax: (770) 645-3384   Emp: 1,000

   WORLD MINERALS, INC.
   130 Castillian Dr., Goleta, California 93117
   CEO: John Oskam, Chmn. & Pres. & CEO   Tel: (805) 562-0200
   Bus: *Industrial metals & minerals.*   Fax: (805) 562-0298   Emp: 1,591

● **INERGY AUTOMOTIVE SYSTEMS**
18 rue de Calais, F-75009 Paris, France
CEO: Pierre Lecocq, CEO & Mng. Dir.   Tel: 33-1-5602-2121   Rev: $1,637
Bus: *Automobile fuel delivery systems manufacture.*   Fax: 33-1-4526-1108   Emp: 4,500
                                    www.inergyautomotive.com
NAICS: 336399

   INERGY AUTOMOTIVE
   961 Berry Shoals Rd., Duncan, South Carolina 29334
   CEO: Mark Sullivan, Pres.   Tel: (864) 877-0584   %FO: 100
   Bus: *Distribution center.*   Fax:

   INERGY AUTOMOTIVE
   1775 Hillcrest Rd., Norcross, Georgia 30093
   CEO: Steve Paladino, Mgr.   Tel: (770) 381-8098   %FO: 100
   Bus: *Sequencing center.*   Fax: (770) 381-8561   Emp: 30

   INERGY AUTOMOTIVE
   2710 Bellingham Rd., Ste. 400, Troy, Michigan 48084
   CEO: James A. Squairito, Pres.   Tel: (248) 743-5700   %FO: 100
   Bus: *Mfr. of fuel systems for the automotive*   Fax: (248) 743-1469   Emp: 882
      industry.

INERGY AUTOMOTIVE
1549 West Beecher St., Adrian, Michigan 49221
CEO: Larry Town, Mgr.
Tel: (517) 265-1100
%FO: 100
Bus: *Mfr. of plastic products & motor vehicle*
Fax: (517) 265-1135
Emp: 242
parts & accessories.

INERGY AUTOMOTIVE
5100 Old Pearman Dairy Rd., Anderson, South Carolina 29265
CEO: Terry Medlin, Gen. Mgr.
Tel: (864) 260-0000
%FO: 100
Bus: *Mfr. of plastic products & motor vehicle*
Fax: (864) 231-7537
Emp: 277
parts & accessories.

INERGY AUTOMOTIVE
2585 West Maple Rd., Troy, Michigan 48083
CEO: Mark Sullivan, Pres. & CEO
Tel: (248) 655-4500
%FO: 100
Bus: *Automobile fuel delivery systems*
Fax: (248) 435-2504
manufacture and sales.

• **INFOGRAMES ENTERTAINMENT, SA**
1 Place Verazzano, F-69252 Lyon Cedex 09, France
CEO: Bruno Bonnell, CEO
Tel: 33-4-37643-000
Rev: $853
Bus: *Developer, publisher and distributor of interactive*
Fax: 33-4-37643-001
Emp: 1,511
entertainment software games.
www.infogrames.com
NAICS: 511210

   INFOGRAMES, INC.
   417 Fifth Ave., New York, New York 10016
   CEO: Nancy Bushkin, Pres.
   Tel: (212) 726-6500
   %FO: 98
   Bus: *Publisher and distributor of interactive*
   Fax: (212) 726-4222
   Emp: 800
   entertainment software games.

• **INFOVISTA SA**
6, rue de la Terre de Feu, Courtaboeuf, F-91952 Les Ulis Cedex, France
CEO: Gad Tobaly, CEO
Tel: 33-1-6486-7900
Rev: $35
Bus: *Mfr. software to monitor performance of computer*
Fax: 33-1-6486-7979
Emp: 190
networks.
www.infovista.com
NAICS: 511210

   INFOVISTA CORP.
   12950 Worldgate Dr., Ste. 250, Herndon, Virginia 20170
   CEO: Jack Allen, SVP
   Tel: (703) 435-2435
   %FO: 100
   Bus: *Mfr. software to monitor performance of*
   Fax: (703) 435-5122
   Emp: 58
   computer networks.

   INFOVISTA CORP.
   15455 Dallas Pkwy., Ste. 600, Dallas, Texas 75001
   CEO: Alain Tinguard, Chmn.
   Tel: (972) 764-3539
   %FO: 100
   Bus: *Mfr. software to monitor performance of*
   Fax: (972) 764-3224
   computer networks.

- **INGENICO S.A.**
  9, Quai de Dion Bouton, F-92816 Puteaux Cedex, France
  CEO: Amedeo d'Angelo, CEO & Mng. Dir.　　Tel: 33-1-4625-8200　　Rev: $583
  Bus: *Electronic payment and credit authorization*　Fax: 33-1-4772-5695　　Emp: 1,287
  　systems manufacture.　　　　　　　　　www.igenico.com
  NAICS: 333313, 334119
  - **INGENICO CORP.**
    1003 Mansell Rd., Atlanta, Georgia 30076
    CEO: L. Barry Thomson, Pres.　　　Tel: (770) 594-6000　　%FO: 100
    Bus: *Electronic payment and credit authorization*　Fax: (770) 594-6003
    　systems manufacture.

- **INTERNATIONAL METAL SERVICE**
  35, rue du pont, F-92522 Neuilly-sur-Seine Cedex, France
  CEO: Francois Faijean, Chmn.　　　Tel: 33-1-4192-0444　　Rev: $1,054
  Bus: *Processor of abrasion-resistant metal products.*　Fax: 33-1-4624-0596　　Emp: 1,594
  　　　　　　　　　　　　　　www.ims-group.com
  NAICS: 423510
  - **INTERNATIONAL METAL SERVICE**
    1550 Red Hollow Rd., Birmingham, Alabama 35217-0974
    CEO: Ed Moses, Mgr.　　　Tel: (205) 853-0300　　%FO: 100
    Bus: *Processor of abrasion-resistant metal*　Fax: (205) 583-7321
    　products.

- **INTERTECHNIQUE**
  61, rue Pierre Curie, BP 1, F-78373 Plaisir Cedex, France
  CEO: Wannick Assoud, CEO　　　Tel: 33-1-3054-8200　　Rev: $457
  Bus: *Flight oxygen masks manufacture.*　Fax: 33-1-3055-7161　　Emp: 3,200
  　　　　　　　　　　　　www.interetechnique.fr
  NAICS: 334514, 336413
  - **IN-EROS CORP.**
    1530 Glenn Curtis St., Carson, California 90746
    CEO: Denis Taieb, Pres.　　　Tel: (310) 884-7200　　%FO: 100
    Bus: *Mfr. / sale of aircraft parts & equipment.*　Fax:　　Emp: 27

  - **INTERTECHNIQUES SERVICES AMERICA**
    W175 N5737 Technology Dr., Menomonee Falls, Wisconsin 53051
    CEO: Ibrahim Youssef, Pres. & CEO　　Tel: (262) 293-1000　　%FO: 100
    Bus: *Mfr. of flight oxygen masks.*　Fax: (262) 293-1010

- **IPSOS SA**
  35 rue de Val de Marne, F-75013 Paris, France
  CEO: Jean-Marc Lech, Co-Chmn.　　　Tel: 33-1-41-98-90-00　　Rev: $826
  Bus: *Market research services.*　　Fax: 33-1-41-98-90-50　　Emp: 4,822
  　　　　　　　　　　　　www.ipsos.com
  NAICS: 541910

IPOS REID INC.
1101 Connecticut Ave., NW, Washington, District of Columbia 20036
CEO: Thomas Riehle
Bus: *Engaged in market research.*
Tel: (202) 463-7300
Fax: (202) 543-1635
%FO: 100

IPSOS INSIGHT INC.
416 Gallimore Dairy Rd., Greensboro, North Carolina 27409
CEO: Susan Simmons
Bus: *Engaged in market research.*
Tel: (336) 668-8320
Fax: (336) 668-7165
%FO: 100

IPSOS INSIGHT INC.
100 Charles Lindbergh Blvd., Uniondale, New York 11553
CEO: Lynne Armstrong
Bus: *Engaged in market research.*
Tel: (516) 507-3000
Fax: (516) 607-3300
%FO: 100

IPSOS INSIGHT INC.
111 North Canal St., Suite 405, Chicago, Illinois 60606
CEO: Matt Kleinschmit
Bus: *Engaged in market research.*
Tel: (312) 665-0600
Fax: (312) 665-0601
%FO: 100

IPSOS INSIGHT INC.
33 South Sixth St., Ste. 4540, Minneapolis, Minnesota 55402
CEO: Matt Kleinschmit
Bus: *Engaged in market research.*
Tel: (612) 904-6970
Fax: (612) 904-6980
%FO: 100

IPSOS INSIGHT INC.
1700 Broadway, 15/F, New York, New York 10019
CEO: Greg Mahon
Bus: *Engaged in market research.*
Tel: (212) 265-3200
Fax: (212) 265-3790
%FO: 100

IPSOS INSIGHT INC.
49 Stevenson St., 15/F, San Francisco, California 94105
CEO: Todd Board
Bus: *Engaged in market research.*
Tel: (415) 597-4000
Fax: (415) 597-4003
%FO: 100

IPSOS INSIGHT INC.
250 East Fifth St., Ste. 1110, Cincinnati, Ohio 45202
CEO: Diane Kosobud
Bus: *Engaged in market research.*
Tel: (513) 639-3700
Fax: (513) 381-1740
%FO: 100

IPSOS NOVACTION
3130 Crow Canyon Pl. Ste. 400, San Ramon, California 94583
CEO: Ed Wolkenmuth
Bus: *Engaged in market research.*
Tel: (925) 820-7350
Fax: (925) 820-1905
%FO: 100

IPSOS-ASI, INC.
301 Merritt 7, Norwalk, Connecticut 06851
CEO: John Lawlor, CEO
Bus: *Engaged in market research.*
Tel: (203) 840-3400
Fax: (203) 840-3450
%FO: 100

- **JCDECAUX SA**
  17 rue Soyer, F-92523 Neuilly-sur-Seine, France
  CEO: Jean-Francois Decaux, Chmn. & C0-CEO
  Bus: *Outdoor advertising services.*

  Tel: 33-1-3079-7979
  Fax: 33-1-3079-7791
  www.jcdecaux.com

  Rev: $2,225
  Emp: 6,900

  NAICS: 541850, 541870

  > **JCDECAUX NORTH AMERICA**
  > 3 Park Ave., 33/F, New York, New York 10016
  > CEO: Bernard Parisot, Mng. Dir.
  > Bus: *Outdoor advertising services.*
  >
  > Tel: (646) 834-1200
  > Fax: (646) 834-1201
  >
  > %FO: 100
  > Emp: 180

- **JEANTET & ASSOCIES**
  87, ave. Kleber, F-75784 Paris Cedex 16, France
  CEO: Renaud Glasson, Mgr.
  Bus: *International law firm.*

  Tel: 33-1-4505-8008
  Fax: 31-1-4704-2041
  www.jeantet.fr

  NAICS: 541110

  > **JEANTET & ASSOCIES**
  > 152 West 57th St., New York, New York 10019
  > CEO: Yvon Dreano, Partner
  > Bus: *International law firm.*
  >
  > Tel: (212) 314-9499
  > Fax: (212) 582-3806
  >
  > %FO: 100

- **LABINAL**
  9, avenue Franklin, F-78180 Montigny-le-Bretonneux, France
  CEO: Philippe Petitcolin, Chmn. & CEO
  Bus: *Designs, develops, builds and integrates electrical wiring solutions for the aerospace*

  Tel: 33-1-3085-4300
  Fax: 33-1-3085-4373
  www.labinal.com

  Rev: $580

  NAICS: 332618, 335929, 335931, 335932, 336413

  > **LABINAL -CORINTH, INC.**
  > 7801 South Stemmons, Ste. 100, Corinth, Texas 75831
  > CEO: Norman Jordan, Pres.
  > Bus: *Designs, develops, builds and integrates electrical wiring solutions for the aerospace industry.*
  >
  > Tel: (940) 497-7600
  > Fax: (940) 497-6976
  >
  > %FO: 100
  > Emp: 894

  > **LABINAL INC.**
  > 7505 Hardeson Rd., Ste. 100, Everett, Washington 98203
  > CEO: Franciose Tuerzeder, Principal
  > Bus: *Sale of electrical equipment.*
  >
  > Tel: (425) 438-1378
  > Fax: (425) 442-5932
  >
  > %FO: 100
  > Emp: 50

  > **LABINAL INC.**
  > 605 Highway 69A, 1 Labinal Way, Pryor Creek, Oklahoma 74361
  > CEO: Norman Jordan, Pres.
  > Bus: *Mfr. aircraft wiring harnesses.*
  >
  > Tel: (918) 824-0000
  > Fax: (918) 824-7092
  >
  > %FO: 100
  > Emp: 600

● **LABORATOIRES ARKOPHARMA SA**
LID de Carroa-le-Broc, 1, re avenue 2079M, F-06511 Carros, France
CEO: Philippe Rombi, CEO
Bus: *Nutritional supplements and herbal medicines*
manufacture.
NAICS: 325411, 325412

Tel: 33-4-9329-1128
Fax: 33-4-9329-1162
www.arkopharma.com

Rev: $288
Emp: 1,505

   ARKOPHARMA INC.
   19 Crosby Dr., Bedford, Massachusetts 01730
   CEO: Robert Beland, Pres.
   Bus: *Mfr. nutritional supplements and herbal*
   medicines.

   Tel: (781) 276-0505
   Fax: (781) 276-7335

   %FO: 100
   Emp: 60

● **LACIE GROUP SA**
17, rue Ampere, F-91349 Massy Cedex, France
CEO: Philippe Spruch, Chmn. & CEO
Bus: *Optical storage drives manufacture.*

Tel: 33-1-6932-8350
Fax: 33-1-6932-0760
www.lacie.com

Rev: $183
Emp: 440

NAICS: 334112
   LACIE LTD.
   22985 NW Evergreen Pkwy., Hillsboro, Oregon 97124
   CEO: Scott Philips, CEO
   Bus: *Mfr. of computer peripheral equipment.*

   Tel: (503) 844-4500
   Fax: (503) 844-4508

   %FO: 100
   Emp: 150

● **LAFARGE, S.A.**
61, rue de Belles Feuilles, F-75116 Paris Cedex 16, France
CEO: Bruno Lafont, COO
Bus: *Cement, concrete and aggregates, gypsum and*
specialty products manufacturer.
NAICS: 212311, 212319, 212321, 324121, 327112, 327310, 327320, 327390, 327420

Tel: 33-1-4434-1111
Fax: 33-1-4434-1200
www.lafarge.com

Rev: $19,555
Emp: 77,075

   LAFARGE NORTH AMERICA
   12950 Worldgate Dr., Ste. 500, Herndon, Virginia 20170
   CEO: Phillippe R. Rollier, Pres. & CEO
   Bus: *Cement and building materials manufacturer.*

   Tel: (703) 480-3600
   Fax: (703) 796-2218

   %FO: 50
   Emp: 15,300

● **LAGARDÈRE SCA**
4, rue de Presbourg, F-75016 Paris, France
CEO: Arnaud Lagardere, CEO
Bus: *Space, defense and transportation,*
communications and media.
NAICS: 323119, 336411, 336412, 336413, 336414, 336415, 336419, 451220, 511120, 511130, 515111, 515112, 515120, 515210, 516110, 517410, 517510, 517910, 518111, 519190, 927110

Tel: 33-1-4069-1600
Fax: 33-1-4069-2131
www.lagardere.fr

Rev: $11,770
Emp: 44,000

   CURTIS CIRCULATION COMPANY
   730 River Rd., New Milford, New Jersey 07646-3048
   CEO: Joe Walsh, CEO
   Bus: *press distributor*

   Tel: (201) 634-7400
   Fax: (201) 634-7499

HACHETTE FILIPACCHI HOLDINGS
1633 Broadway, New York, New York 10019
CEO: Gerald De Roquemaurel, CEO
Bus: *Magazine Publisher.*

Tel: (212) 767-6000
Fax: (212) 767-5810

%FO: 100
Emp: 2,050

HACHETTE FILIPACCHI MEDIA US
1633 Broadway, 45/F, New York, New York 10019
CEO: Jack Kliger, Pres. & CEO
Bus: *Magazine publishing.*

Tel: (212) 767-6000
Fax: (212) 767-5600

%FO: 100
Emp: 1,090

LAGARDERE ACTIVE NORTH AMERICA
1633 Broadway, 45/F, New York, New York 10019
CEO: Alain Lemarchand, CEO
Bus: *Public relations for publishing.*

Tel: (212) 767-6754
Fax: (212) 767-5635

%FO: 100
Emp: 1,864

RTM PRODUCTIONS
783 Old Hickory Blvd, Brentwood, Tennessee 37027
CEO: Joseph St. Lawrence, Pres.
Bus: *TV production.*

Tel: (615) 373-8838
Fax: (615) 373-0759

%FO: 100

● **L'AIR LIQUIDE SA**
75, Quai d'Orsay, F-75321 Paris Cedex 07, France
CEO: Benoit Potier, CEO
Bus: *Mfr. industrial gases.*

Tel: 33-1-4062-5555
Fax: 33-1-4062-5465
www.airliquide.com

Rev: $12,789
Emp: 35,900

NAICS: 325120

AIR LIQUIDE USA INC.
2700 Post Oak Blvd, Ste. 1800, Houston, Texas 77056
CEO: Pierre DuFour
Bus: *Mfr. industrial gases.*

Tel: (713) 624-8000
Fax: (713) 624-8085

%FO: 100

● **LE CARBONE LORRAINE COMPANY**
Immeuble La Fayette, 2-3, Place des Vosges, La Defense 5, F-92400 Courbevoie, France
CEO: Claude Cocozza, Chmn. & CEO
Bus: *Mfr. graphite brushes, permanent magnets and electrical protection devices for automobiles and machinery.*

Tel: 33-1-4691-5400
Fax: 33-1-4691-5401
www.carbonelorraine.com

Rev: $790
Emp: 6,800

NAICS: 335312, 335999, 336322

ASTROCOSMOS
3225 West Old Lincoln Way, PO Box 1229, Wooster, Ohio 44691
CEO: Gerhard Doerr, Pres.
Bus: *Mfr. of fabricated plate work.*

Tel: (330) 264-8639
Fax: (330) 264-4316

%FO: 100

CARBONE KIRKWOOD LLC
Hwy 15 & 460 West, 300 Industrial Park Rd., Farmville, Virginia 23901
CEO: Alan Grabiec, VP
Bus: *Mfr. of automotive carbon brushes.*

Tel: (434) 392-4111
Fax: (434) 395-8285

%FO: 100
Emp: 350

CARBONE LORRAINE NA
14 Eastmans Rd., Parsippany, New Jersey 07054
CEO: Kenny Green   Tel: (973) 503-0600   %FO: 100
Bus: *Mfr./sales/distribution of graphite brushes,*   Fax: (973) 503-0335
      permanent magnets and electrical protection
      devices.

CARBONE LORRAINE NORTH AMERICA
400 Myrtle Ave., Boonton, New Jersey 07004
CEO: Michael Coniglio, Pres.   Tel: (973) 541-4720   %FO: 100
Bus: *Mfr. of carbon brushes.*   Fax: (973) 541-1718   Emp: 1,061

CARBONE LORRAINE NORTH AMERICA CORP.
900 Harrison St., Bay City, Michigan 48708
CEO: Christopher Bommier, Gen. Mgr.   Tel: (989) 894-2911   %FO: 100
Bus: *Mfr. of nonferrous forgings.*   Fax: (989) 895-7740   Emp: 85

FERMAG INC.
47 Union Pacific Blvd., Ste. D, PO Box 1718, Laredo, Texas 78044
CEO: Gerard Brumel, CEO   Tel: (956) 717-3593   %FO: 100
Bus: *Mfr. of magnets for automotive electric*   Fax: Emp: 12
      parts.

FERRAZ SHAWMUT INC.
374 Merrimac St., Newburyport, Massachusetts 01950
CEO: William Trotman, Pres.   Tel: (978) 846-2662   %FO: 100
Bus: *Mfr. circuit protection equipment.* Fax: (978) 462-0181   Emp: 800

GMI METAULLICS, INC.
380 North Prairie Industrial Park, Mulberry, Florida 33860
CEO: Dennis Clements, Pres.   Tel: (863) 425-2866   %FO: 100
Bus: *Graphite heat exchangers manufacture and*   Fax: (863) 425-3296 Emp: 25
      repair.

GRAPHITE MATERIALS DIVISION
215 Stackpole St., St. Marys, Pennsylvania 15857
CEO: Edward Stumpoff, VP   Tel: (814) 781-1234   %FO: 100
Bus: *Mfr. of carbon/graphite products.* Fax: (814) 781-8570   Emp: 180

MIDLAND MATERIALS RESEARCH
2927 Venture Dr., Midland, Michigan 48640
CEO: James Gandy, Mgr.   Tel: (517) 835-7604   %FO: 100
Bus: *Coating graphite metals & machine shop.* Fax: (517) 835-2195   Emp: 18

● **LE DOMAINES BARONS DE ROTHSCHILD (LAFITE)**
33, rue de la Baume, F-75008 Paris, France
CEO: Eric de Rothschild, Chmn.   Tel: 33-1-5389-7800
Bus: *Distributes imported wines and domestic*   Fax: 33-1-5389-7801
      products. (JV with Chalone Wine Group, US) www.bpdr.com/
NAICS: 312130

CHALONE WINE GROUP LTD.
621 Airpark Rd., Napa, California 94559
CEO: Thomas B. Selfridge, Pres. & CEO
Bus: *Produces premium table wines and
     distributes imported wines. (Owns 20% of
     the Chateau Duhart-Milon estate in France.)*

Tel: (707) 254-4200
Fax: (707) 254-4201

%FO: JV

PASTERNAK WINE IMPORTS GROUP
500 Mamaroneck Ave., Harrison, New York 10528
CEO: James Galtieri
Bus: *Import and distribution of wine.*

Tel: (914) 630-8000
Fax: (914) 630-8120

%FO: JV

● **LECTRA SA**
16-18, rue Chalgrin, F-75016 Paris, France
CEO: Daniel Harari, CEO
Bus: *Mfr. software and equipment for apparel and
     textile manufacturers.*

Tel: 33-1-5364-4200
Fax: 33-1-5364-4300
www.lectra.com

Rev: $194
Emp: 1,350

NAICS: 334111, 334113, 334119, 511210, 518210, 541511, 541512, 541519, 611420

LECTRA INC.
1601 Galbraith Ave. SE, Grand Rapids, Michigan 49546
CEO: Christian Fernando, Dir.
Bus: *Sales software and equipment for apparel
     industry.*

Tel: (616) 464-4522
Fax: (616) 464-2485

%FO: 100

LECTRA INC.
889 Franklin Rd. SE, Marietta, Georgia 30067
CEO: Philippe Ribera, SVP
Bus: *Sales software and equipment for apparel
     industry.*

Tel: (770) 422-8050
Fax: (770) 422-1503

%FO: 100
Emp: 117

LECTRA INC.
5836 Corporate Ave., Ste. 110, Cypress, California 90630
CEO: Bill Beard, Mgr.
Bus: *Sales software and equipment for apparel
     industry.*

Tel: (714) 484-6600
Fax: (714) 484-6625

%FO: 100

LECTRA INC.
119 West 40th St., 3/F, New York, New York 10018
CEO: Phillippe Ribera
Bus: *Sales software and equipment for apparel
     industry.*

Tel: (212) 704-4004
Fax: (212) 704-0751

%FO: 100

LECTRA INC.
204 East Woodlawn Rd., Ste. 110, Bldg. 3, Charlotte, North Carolina 28217
CEO: Hugh Hayes, Mgr.
Bus: *Sales software and equipment for apparel
     industry.*

Tel: (704) 529-0094
Fax: (704) 529-0096

%FO: 100

● **LEGRAND SA**
128, ave du Marechal, de Lattre de Tassigny, F-8700 Limoges Cedex, France
CEO: Gilles Schnepp, Chmn. & CEO
Bus: *Electric wiring devices manufacture.*

Tel: 33-5-5506-8787
Fax: 33-5-5506-8888
www.legrandelectric.com

Rev: $3,991
Emp: 25,291

NAICS: 334210, 334416, 334419, 334512, 335121, 335122, 335129, 335311, 335314, 335931, 335999

ORTRONICS INC.
125 Eugene O'Neill Dr., New London, Connecticut 06320
CEO: Mark Panico, Pres.   Tel: (860) 445-3800   %FO: 100
Bus: *Electric wiring devices manufacture and*   Fax: (860) 445-2970   Emp: 100
sales.

PASS & SEYMOUR/LEGRAND
50 Boyd Ave., Syracuse, New York 13209
CEO: Michael Gambino, Pres.   Tel: (315) 468-6211   %FO: 100
Bus: *Mfr. electric wiring devices.*   Fax: (315) 463-6296   Emp: 2,739

THE WATT STOPPER, INC.
2800 De La Cruz Blvd., Santa Clara, California 95050
CEO: Jerry Mix, Pres.   Tel: (408) 988-5331   %FO: 100
Bus: *Manufacturer of lighting control products for*   Fax: (408) 988-5373
commercial buildings, schools, retail stores
and warehouses.

WIREMOLD CO.
60 Woodlawn St., PO Box 330639, West Hartford, Connecticut 06110
CEO: Arthur Byrne, Chmn.   Tel: (860) 233-6251   %FO: 100
Bus: *Mfr. of nonconductive wires.*   Fax: Emp: 1,300

● **LEGRIS INDUSTRIES**
74, rue de Paris, F-35704 Rennes Cedex 7, France
CEO: Hugues Robert, CEO   Tel: 33-2-9925-5500   Rev: $601
Bus: *Mfr. and sales of fluid controls.*   Fax: 33-2-9925-5650   Emp: 3,256
www.legris-industries.com
NAICS: 332911, 332912, 332919, 333922, 333924, 333999

    LEGRIS USA INC.
    7205 East Hampton Ave., Mesa, Arizona 85208
    CEO: Francois Brault, Chmn.   Tel: (480) 830-0216   %FO: 100
    Bus: *Sales of fluid controls.*   Fax: (480) 839-7556   Emp: 56

● **LINEDATA SERVICES SA**
19 rue d'Orleans, F-92523 Neuilly-sur-Seine Cedex, France
CEO: Anvaraly Jiva, Chmn. & CEO   Tel: 33-1-4777-6825   Rev: $126
Bus: *Software for asset management.*   Fax: 33-1-4708-1178   Emp: 602
www.linedata.com
NAICS: 511210, 541511, 541512, 541519

    LINEDATA SERVICES
    260 Franklin St., Boston, Massachusetts 02110
    CEO: Jack Wiener, COO   Tel: (617) 912-4700   %FO: 100
    Bus: *Software for asset management.*   Fax: (617) 912-4701   Emp: 51

● **L'OREAL SA**
41, rue Martre, F-92117 Clichy, France
CEO: Lindsay Owen-Jones, Chmn. & CEO   Tel: 33-1-4756-7000   Rev: $17,609
Bus: *Mfr. cosmetics, fragrances, hair care products,*   Fax: 33-1-4756-8002   Emp: 50,500
fashion publishing.   www.loreal.com
NAICS: 325620, 446120

KIEHL'S SINCE 1851 LLC
435 Hudson St., 5/F, New York, New York 10014
CEO: Philip Clough, Pres.
Bus: *Cosmetics & skin care products.*

Tel: (917) 606-2740
Fax: (917) 606-9536

Emp: 70

L'OREAL USA
575 Fifth Ave., New York, New York 10017
CEO: Jean-Paul Agon, Pres. & CEO
Bus: *Mfr./sale cosmetics, fragrances, hair care products.*

Tel: (212) 818-1500
Fax: (212) 984-4999

%FO: 100
Emp: 8,300

SOFT SHEEN / CARSON PRODUCTS, INC.
8552 S. Lafayette Ave., Chicago, Illinois 60620
CEO: Ronald DeNard, CFO
Bus: *Mfr. ethnic hair care products.*

Tel: (773) 962-5700
Fax: (773) 962-5741

%FO: 100

• LOUIS DREYFUS GROUP
87, ave. de la Grande Armee, F-75782 Paris Cedex 16, France
CEO: Gerard Louis-Dreyfus, Pres. & CEO
Bus: *Wholesalers of cereals, grains; ship-owners.*

Tel: 33-40-66-11-11
Fax: 33-45-01-70-28
www.louisdreyfus.com

NAICS: 112910, 113210, 115111, 115112, 115115, 115116, 115210, 237130, 238990, 311211, 311212, 311221, 311311, 311312, 311313, 311320, 324110, 325311, 325312, 325314, 325320, 424910, 517910, 541940

LOUIS DREYFUS CORPORATION
20 Westport Rd., Wilton, Connecticut 06897
CEO: Peter B. Griffin, Pres.
Bus: *Supplier of grains, cereals and seeds.*

Tel: (203) 791-2000
Fax: (203) 761-2088

%FO: 100

• LUZENAC GROUP
131 Avenue Charles de Gaulle, F-92200 Neuilly, France
CEO: Joachim Roeser, Pres. & CEO
Bus: *Producer of talk for personal care products, plastics, paints, ceramics, agriculture, and water purification.*

Tel: 33-1-4745-9040
Fax: 33-1-4747-5805
www.luzenac.com

Rev: $375
Emp: 1,500

NAICS: 212299

LUZENAC AMERICA, INC.
345 Inverness Dr. South, Ste.310, Centennial, Colorado 80112
CEO: Jon Godla, VP North America
Bus: *Miner and processor of talc.*

Tel: (303) 643-0400
Fax: (303) 643-0446

%FO: 100
Emp: 562

• LVMH MOET HENNESSY LOUIS VUITTON SA
22 avenue Montaigne, F-75008 Paris, France
CEO: Bernard J. Arnault, Chmn. & CEO
Bus: *Holding co. produces/ retails; wines/liquors; designer clothing; cosmetics/fragrances; shoes, luggage/leather goods.*

Tel: 33-1-4413-2222
Fax: 33-1-4413-2119
www.lvmh.com

Rev: $17,218
Emp: 59,840

NAICS: 312130, 312140, 315211, 315212, 315222, 315223, 315224, 315228, 315232, 315233, 315239, 315292, 315299, 315993, 315999, 316992, 316993, 316999, 325620, 334518, 339911, 423940, 424820, 425120, 446120, 448110, 448120, 448150, 448190, 448310, 448320, 453998

BENEFIT COSMETICS LLC
685 Market St., 7/F, San Francisco, California 94105
CEO: Diane Miles, CEO
Bus: *Cosmetics & skin care.*

Tel: (415) 781-8153
Fax: (415) 781-3930

Emp: 240

CLICQUOT INC.
8501 Hwy. 128, Philo, California 95466
CEO: Mireille Guiliano, Pres. & CEO   Tel: (707) 895-2065
Bus: *Winemakers.*   Fax: (707) 895-2758

CRUISE LINE HOLDIINGS CO.
8052 NW 14th St., Miami, Florida 33126
CEO: Robin Norris, Pres.   Tel: (786) 845-7300
Bus: *Floral & gifts retail.*   Fax: (305) 477-4522

DFS GROUP LTD.
First Market Tower, 525 Market St., 33/F, San Francisco, California 94105
CEO: Ed Brennan, Chmn. & Pres. & CEO   Tel: (415) 977-2700
Bus: *Operators of duty free shops in*   Fax: (415) 977-4289
       international air terminals.

DOMAINE CHANDON INC.
1 California Dr., Yountville, California 94599
CEO: Fredric Cumenal, CEO   Tel: (707) 944-8844
Bus: *Winemakers & restaurateurs.*   Fax: (707) 944-1123   Emp: 240

DONNA KARAN INTERNATIONAL
550 7th Ave., New York, New York 10018
CEO: Jeffry M. Aronsson, CEO   Tel: (212) 789-1500
Bus: *Mfr. of apparel.*   Fax: (212) 768-6099

LOUIS VUITTON USA INC.
19 East 57th St., New York, New York 10022
CEO: Bruce Ingram, CEO   Tel: (212) 931-2700   %FO: 100
Bus: *Handbags, leather goods, luggage.*   Fax: (212) 931-2730

NEWTON VINEYARD LLC
2555 Madrona Ave., St. Helena, California 94574
CEO: Peter L. Newton, Pres.   Tel: (707) 963-9000
Bus: *Winemakers.*   Fax: (707) 963-5408   Emp: 200

SCHIEFFELIN & CO.
2 Park Ave., 17/F, New York, New York 10016
CEO: John Esposito, Pres. & CEO   Tel: (212) 251-8200
Bus: *Mfr. alcoholic beverages.*   Fax: (212) 251-8382

SEPHORA USA
First Market Tower, 525 Market St., 11/F, San Francisco, California 94105
CEO: David Suliteanu, Pres. & CEO   Tel: (415) 284-3300
Bus: *Cosmetics, beauty supply & perfume retail.* Fax: (415) 284-3434

• **MANITOU BF SA**
430, rue de l'Aubiniere, F-44158 Ancenia Cedex, France
CEO: Marcel Braud, Chmn.   Tel: 33-2-4009-1011   Rev: $1,121
Bus: *Mfr. industrial vehicles.*   Fax: 33-2-4009-1703   Emp: 2,073
                                              www.manitou.com

  NAICS: 333120, 333924, 336999

KD MANITOU INC.
6401 Imperial Dr., Waco, Texas 76712
CEO: Serge Bosche, Dir.
Bus: *Mfr./dist. Masts, mastered trucks & rough
      terrain trucks*

Tel: (254) 799-0232
Fax: (254) 799-4433

%FO: 100
Emp: 125

● **MARTEK POWER**
Usine des Auberges, F-69770 Montrottier, France
CEO: Marcel Katz, Chmn.
Bus: *Design and manufacture of standard, modified
      standard and custom power supplies and DC/DC
      converters.*
NAICS: 335311

Tel: 33-1-6988-8397
Fax: 33-1-6988-8037
www.martekpower.fr

Emp: 1,400

MARTEK POWER ABBOTT, INC.
2727 South La Cienega Blvd., Los Angeles, California 90034
CEO: Steven Langer, Pres.
Bus: *Mfr. electronic power supplies.*

Tel: (310) 202-8820
Fax: (310) 836-1027

%FO: 100

MARTEK POWER, INC.
4115 Spencer St., Torrance, California 90503
CEO: Bill Standen, VP
Bus: *Mfr. electronic power supplies.*

Tel: (310) 542-8561
Fax: (310) 371-6331

%FO: 100
Emp: 740

● **MAYDREAM SA**
18-20, rue Jacques Dulud, F-92521 Neuilly-sur-Seine Cedex, France
CEO: Christopher J. Wynne, Pres. & CEO
Bus: *Engaged in marketing and public relations.*

NAICS: 516110, 518111, 518112, 541890

Tel: 33-1-4143-7193
Fax: 33-1-4637-3382
www.adforum.com/aboutus/aboutus.asp

ADFORUM MAYDREAM INC.
80 Park Ave., Hoboken, New Jersey 07030
CEO: Christopher Wynn, Pres.
Bus: *Internet host services & web design.*

Tel: (201) 792-3007
Fax: (201) 792-7234

%FO: 100
Emp: 10

● **MEDASYS SA**
Espace Technologique de St Aubin,, Immeuble Le Mercury, F-91193 Gif sur Yvette Cedex, France
CEO: Jean-Marie Lucani, Pres.
Bus: *Mfr. computer software.*

NAICS: 511210, 541511, 541512, 541519

Tel: 33-1-6933-7300
Fax: 33-1-6933-7301
www.medasys-digital-systems.fr

Rev: $68
Emp: 300

MEDASYS USA INC.
5301 Blue Lagoon Dr., Ste. 600, Miami, Florida 33126
CEO: Pierre Serafino
Bus: *Mfr. computer software.*

Tel: (305) 261-6025
Fax: (305) 261-9765

%FO: 100

• **MEGTEC SYSTEMS SA**
32-34, rue des Malines, F-91000 Lisses, France
CEO: Didier Durand, Dir.
Bus: *Mfr. press auxiliary equipment.*

Tel: 33-1-6989-4793
Fax: 33-1-6497-7414
www.megtec.com

Rev: $72
Emp: 800

NAICS: 333293

    MEGTEC SYSTEMS COMPANY INC.
    830 Prosper Rd., DePere, Wisconsin 54115
    CEO: Mohit Uberoi, Pres.
    Bus: *Mfr. equipment for printing, web coating,
    packaging, paper & tissue, and other
    industrial markets.*

Tel: (920) 336-5715
Fax: (920) 336-3404

%FO: 100

• **MEMSCAP**
Parc Tech des Fontaines, Bernin, F-38926 Crolles Cedex, France
CEO: Jean-Micel Karam, Chmn. & Pres. & CEO
Bus: *MEMS components manufacture.*

Tel: 33-4-7692-8500
Fax: 33-4-7692-8501
www.memscap.com

Rev: $12
Emp: 116

NAICS: 334419

    MEMSCAP INC.
    4021 Stirrup Creek Dr., Ste. 120, Durham, North Carolina 27703
    CEO: Ron Wages, Pres.
    Bus: *Mfr. of semiconductors.*

Tel: (919) 314-2200
Fax: (919) 314-2201

%FO: 100
Emp: 35

• **METROLOGIC GROUP**
6 Chemin du Vieux, F-38240 Meylan, France
CEO: Philippe Cimadomo, Chmn. & Pres. & CEO
Bus: *Design and manufacture of dimensional control
systems.*

Tel: 33-4-7604-3030
Fax: 33-4-7690-7571
www.metrologic.fr

Rev: $27
Emp: 86

NAICS: 334519

    GROUP SERVICES INC.
    24148 Research Dr., Farmington Hills, Michigan 48335
    CEO: Philippe Cinadomo, Pres.
    Bus: *Design and manufacture of dimensional
    control systems.*

Tel: (248) 426-9090
Fax: (248) 426-9095

%FO: 100
Emp: 9

• **MGE UPS SYSTEMS SA**
140 Avenue Jean Kuntzmann, Zirst Montbonnet, F-38334 Saint Ismier, France
CEO: Claude Graff, CEO
Bus: *Surge suppressors and power supplies*

Tel: 33-4-7618-3000
Fax: 33-4-7618-4000
www.mgeups.com

Rev: $576
Emp: 2,831

NAICS: 334416, 335311, 335999

    MGE UPS SYSTEMS INC.
    1660 Scenic Ave., Costa Mesa, California 92626
    CEO: Ray Prince, Pres.
    Bus: *Surge suppressors and power supplies
    manufacture and sales.*

Tel: (714) 557-1636
Fax: (714) 434-0865

%FO: 100
Emp: 540

- **COMPAGNIE GENERALE DES ETABLISSEMENTS MICHELIN**
  12, cours Sablon, F-63000 Clermont-Ferrand, France
  CEO: Edouard Michelin, Mng. Prtn. Tel: 33-4-7398-5900 Rev: $21,399
  Bus: *Mfr./distributes tires and rubber products.* Fax: 33-4-7398-5904 Emp: 126,474
   www.michelin.com
  NAICS: 326199, 326211, 334612, 336999, 423130, 511199

   MICHELIN NORTH AMERICA, INC.
   One Parkway South, PO Box 19001, Greenville, South Carolina 29615
   CEO: James Micali, Chmn. & Pres. Tel: (864) 458-5000 %FO: 100
   Bus: *Sales/distribution of passenger, light-truck,* Fax: (864) 458-6359 Emp: 23,453
    commercial-truck and earth-mover tires.

   TCI TIRE CENTERS, LLC
   310 Inglesby Pkwy., Duncan, South Carolina 29334
   CEO: Joe Finney, Pres. & CEO Tel: (864) 329-2700
   Bus: *Sale of auto parts.* Fax: (864) 329-2929 Emp: 2,400

- **MONTUPET SA**
  202, quai de Clichy, F-92112 Clichy Cedex, France
  CEO: Stephane Magnan, Pres. Tel: 33-1-4756-4756 Rev: $577
  Bus: *Design and manufacture of aluminum components* Fax: 33-1-4739-7793 Emp: 3,941
   for the car industry. www.ndu-montupet.demon.co.uk
  NAICS: 336312, 336340, 336399

   MONTUPET INC.
   17197 North Laurel Park Dr., Ste. 111, Livonia, Michigan 48152
   CEO: Stephane Magnan, Pres. Tel: (734) 462-0171 %FO: 100
   Bus: *Mfr. of automotive parts.* Fax: (734) 462-0174

- **NATEXIS BANQUES POPULAIRES S.A.**
  45, rue Saint-Dominique, F-75007 Paris, France
  CEO: Philippe Dupont, Chmn. & CEO Tel: 33-1-5832-3000 Rev: $8,339
  Bus: *Engaged in real estate, corporate lending and* Fax: 33-1-4039-6340 Emp: 12,532
   equity financing. www.nxbp.fr
  NAICS: 522110, 522220, 523110, 523120, 523920, 524210

   NEXTEXIS BANQUES POPULAIRES
   250 South Wacker Dr., Ste. 320, Chicago, Illinois 60606
   CEO: Francois Ladam, CEO Tel: (312) 382-7080
   Bus: *International banking services.* Fax: (312) 382-7088

   NEXTEXIS BANQUES POPULAIRES
   333 Clay St., Ste. 4340, Houston, Texas 77002
   CEO: Francois Ladam, CEO Tel: (713) 759-9401
   Bus: *International banking services.* Fax: (713) 759-9908

   NEXTEXIS BANQUES POPULAIRES
   1901 Ave. Of The Stars, Ste. 1901, Los Angeles, California 90067
   CEO: Mark Harrington, Mgr. Tel: (310) 203-8710 %FO: 100
   Bus: *International banking services.* Fax: (310) 203-8720

NEXTEXIS BANQUES POPULAIRES
1001 Brickell Bay Dr., Ste. 1714, Miami, Florida 33131
CEO: Francois Ladam, CEO   Tel: (305) 539-2844
Bus: *International banking services.*   Fax: (305) 539-2484

NEXTEXIS BANQUES POPULAIRES
125 Ave. of the Americas, 34/F, New York, New York 10020
CEO: Jean Richard, Mgr.   Tel: (212) 872-5000   %FO: 100
Bus: *International banking services.*   Fax: (212) 872-5045   Emp: 120

● **NEOPOST SA**
113, rue Jean-Marin Naudin, F-92220 Bagneax, France
CEO: Jean-Paul Villot, Chmn. & CEO   Tel: 33-1-4536-3000   Rev: $932
Bus: *Mfr. of office machinery.*   Fax: 33-1-4536-3170   Emp: 4,536
                                             www.neopost-group.com

NAICS: 333313, 333997

    HASLER INC.
    19 Forest Pkwy., Shelton, Connecticut 06484
    CEO: John Vavra, Pres. & CEO   Tel: (203) 926-1087   %FO: 100
    Bus: *Mfr./sale, & lease mailing and shipping*   Fax: (203) 929-6084   Emp: 350
       equipment.

    NEOPOST INC.
    6100 E. Shelby Dr., Ste. 4, Memphis, Tennessee 38141
    CEO: Robert Copeland, Mgr.   Tel: (901) 362-9442   %FO: 100
    Bus: *Sale of office equipment.*   Fax: Emp: 67

    NEOPOST USA INC.
    30955 Huntwood Ave., Hayward, California 94544-7084
    CEO: Hakan Orvell, CFO   Tel: (510) 489-6800   %FO: 100
    Bus: *Mailing and shipping equipment lease and*   Fax: (510) 475-5701   Emp: 1,000
       sales.

● **NESTLE WATERS**
20 rue Rouget de Lisle, F-92793 Issy Les Moulineaux, France
CEO: Carlo Maria Donati, Chmn. & CEO   Tel: 33-1-4123-3800   Rev: $7,068
Bus: *Bottled Water.*   Fax: 33-1-4123-6900   Emp: 27,600
                                             www.nestlewaters.com

NAICS: 312112

    NESTLE WATERS NORTH AMERICA
    777 W. Putnam Ave., Greenwich, Connecticut 06830
    CEO: Kim E. Jeffery, Pres. & CEO   Tel: (203) 531-4100   %FO: 100
    Bus: *Bottled water.*   Fax: (203) 863-0297

● **NETVALUE SA**
94 rue Lauriston, F-75116 Paris, France
CEO: Lennart Brag, CEO   Tel: 33-1-4291-1900   Rev: $6
Bus: *Services to Internet businesses, such as*   Fax: 33-1-4291-1901   Emp: 120
   researching and analyzing consumer use of the   www.netvalue.com
NAICS: 541910

NETVALUE USA INC.
427 Broadway, 4/F, New York, New York 10013
CEO: Jim Hatch
Bus: *PC and Internet-use tracking technology services.*

Tel: (917) 237-0530
Fax: (917) 237-0531

%FO: 100

● **NEXANS**
16 rue de Monceau, F-75008 Paris Cedex, France
CEO: Gerard Hauser, Chmn. & CEO
Bus: *Cables for infrastructure, industry and building.*

Tel: 33-1-5669-8400
Fax: 33-1-5669-8484
www.nexans.com

Rev: $5,673
Emp: 17,662

NAICS: 335314, 335921, 335999

NEXANS ENERGY USA INC.
25 Oakland Ave., Chester, New York 10918
CEO: Gordon Thursfield, Pres.
Bus: *Mfr. of non-ferrous insulated wire & cable.*

Tel: (845) 469-2141
Fax: (845) 469-9935

%FO: 100
Emp: 160

NEXANS INC. (BERK-TEK)
132 White Oak Rd., New Holland, Pennsylvania 17557
CEO: Kevin St. Cyr, Pres.
Bus: *Copper and fiber-optic cable products.*

Tel: (717) 354-6200
Fax: (717) 354-7944

%FO: 100
Emp: 450

NEXANS MAGNET WIRE USA INC.
2615 East Highway 146, PO Box 29, La Grange, Kentucky 40031
CEO: Gordon Thursfield, Pres.
Bus: *Mfr. of magnet wire.*

Tel: (502) 222-3222
Fax: (502) 222-7885

%FO: 100
Emp: 375

NEXANS USA INC.
132 White Oak Rd., New Holland, Pennsylvania 17557
CEO: Kevin St. Cyr, Pres.
Bus: *Non-ferrous wiredrawing & insulating.*

Tel: (717) 351-9398
Fax:

%FO: 100

● **NICOX SA**
Gala II, 2455 route des Dolines, F-06906 Sophia Antipolis, France
CEO: Michele Garufi, Chmn. & CEO
Bus: *Research pharmaceutical company.*

Tel: 33-4-9238-7020
Fax: 33-4-9238-7030
www.nicox.com

Rev: $5,600
Emp: 56

NAICS: 541710

AXICAN PHARMA INC.
22 Inverness Center Pkwy., Birmingham, Alabama 35242
CEO: Leon F. Gosselin, Chmn.
Bus: *Pharmaceutical manufacturer*

Tel: (205) 991-8085
Fax: (205) 991-8176

MERCK & CO., INC.
1 Merck Dr., PO Box 100, Whitehouse Station, New Jersey 08889
CEO: Richard T. Clark, Pres. & CEO
Bus: *Pharmaceutical & Medicine Manufacturing*

Tel: (908) 423-1000
Fax: (908) 735-1253

Emp: 63,000

PFIZER INC.
235 East 42nd St., New York, New York 10017
CEO: Hank McKinnell, Chmn. & CEO
Bus: *Pharmaceutical manufacturer*

Tel: (212) 573-2323
Fax: (212) 573-7857

Emp: 115,000

● **OBERTHUR CARD SYSTEMS**
71-73 rue des Hautes-Pature, 35 Ave. de l'Ile Saint Martin, F-92726 Nanterre, France
CEO: Pierre Barberis, CEO   Tel: 33-1-4785-5400   Rev: $540
Bus: *Engaged in supply of MasterCard, Visa, e-*   Fax: 33-1-5605-0582   Emp: 2,885
      commerce and pay-TV.   www.oberthurcs.com
NAICS: 333313

     OBERTHUR CARD SYSTEMS
     3150 E. Ana St., Rancho Dominguez, California 90221
     CEO: Philippe Tartavull, Pres.   Tel: (310) 884-7900   %FO: 100
     Bus: *Currency handling and security systems.*   Fax: (310) 884-7904   Emp: 353

     OBERTHUR CARD SYSTEMS
     4250 Pleasant Valley Rd., Chantilly, Virginia 20151
     CEO: Philippe Tartavul, Pres.   Tel: (703) 263-0100   %FO: 100
     Bus: *Currency handling and security systems.*   Fax: (703) 263-0503   Emp: 350

     OBERTHUR CARD SYSTEMS
     2764 Golfview Dr., Naperville, Illinois 60563
     CEO: Philippe Tartavul, Pres.   Tel: (630) 369-5400   %FO: 100
     Bus: *Currency handling and security systems.*   Fax: (630) 369-5999

     OBERTHUR CARD SYSTEMS, INC.
     Oaklands Corporate Center, 523 James Hance Ct., Exton, Pennsylvania 19341
     CEO: Philippe Tartavul, Pres.   Tel: (610) 524-2410   %FO: 100
     Bus: *Currency handling and security systems.*   Fax: (610) 524-2412   Emp: 200

● **OENEO**
7, Rue Louis Marat, F-75008 Paris Cedex, France
CEO: Gerard Epin, Chmn. & CEO   Tel: 33-1-5836-1090   Rev: $214
Bus: *Corks and barrels manufacture for wine industry.*   Fax: 33-1-4225-0341   Emp: 1,198
    www.sabate.com
NAICS: 321920, 332115

     OENEO CLOSURES USA
     902 Enterprise Way, Ste. M, Napa, California 94558
     CEO: Eric Mercier, Pres.   Tel: (707) 256-2830   %FO: 100
     Bus: *Mfr. of packaging & containers.*   Fax: (707) 256-2831

● **ONDEO DEGREMONT SA, SUB. SUEZ**
183, ave. de 18 Juin 1940, F-92500 Rueil-Malmaison, France
CEO: Thierry M. Mallet, CEO   Tel: 33-1-4625-6000   Rev: $1,000
Bus: *Water and wastewater treatment equipment.*   Fax: 33-1-4204-1699   Emp: 3,200
    www.degremont.fr
NAICS: 333319

     INFILCO DEGREMONT INC.
     PO Box 71390, Richmond, Virginia 23255
     CEO: Ilan Wilt   Tel: (804) 756-7600   %FO: 100
     Bus: *Water & wastewater treatment equipment.*   Fax: (804) 756-7643

INFILCO DEGREMONT INC.
1200 W Sierra Ln., Mequon, Wisconsin 53092
CEO: Joe Giannone   Tel: (262) 241-8017   %FO: 100
Bus: *Water & wastewater treatment equipment.*   Fax: (262) 241-8027

● **PERNOD RICARD SA**
12 place des Etats-Unis, F-75116 Paris, France
CEO: Patrick Ricard, Chmn. & CEO   Tel: 33-1-4100-4100   Rev: $12,254
Bus: *Mfr. spirits, liquors and wines.*   Fax: 33-1-4100-4141   Emp: 12,254
                                                    www.pernod-ricard.com/fr

NAICS: 311411, 312130, 312140

   ALLIED DOMECQ WINES USA
   375 Healdsburg Ave., 2/F, Healdsburg, California 95448
   CEO: William A. Newlands Jr., Pres. & CEO   Tel: (707) 433-8268   %FO: 100
   Bus: *Winemakers.*   Fax: (707) 433-3538   Emp: 550

   DUNKIN' BRANDS, INC.
   130 Royall St., Canton, Massachusetts 02021
   CEO: Jon L. Luther, CEO   Tel: (781) 737-3000   %FO: 100
   Bus: *Specialty eateries.*   Fax: (781) 737-4000   Emp: 1,200

   PERNOD RICARD USA
   777 Westchester Ave., White Plains, New York 10604
   CEO: Michael Bord, Pres. & CEO   Tel: (914) 539-4500   %FO: 100
   Bus: *Mfr. spirits, liquors and wines.*   Fax: (914) 539-4777

● **PINAULT-PRINTEMPS REDOUTE GROUP**
10, ave. Hoche, F-75381 Paris Cedex 08, France
CEO: Francois Henri Pinault, Chmn.   Tel: 33-1-4564-6100   Rev: $33,026
Bus: *Manages department stores, specialty stores and* Fax: 33-1-4490-6225   Emp: 95,397
     distributes, sells and rents construction   www.pprgroup.com

NAICS: 325620, 333120, 423610, 424320, 424330, 451211, 451220, 452111, 454111, 454113

   CHADWICK'S OF BOSTON, LTD.
   35 United Dr., West Bridgewater, Massachusetts 02379
   CEO: Eric Faintrey, Chmn. & CEO   Tel: (508) 583-8110   %FO: 100
   Bus: *Women's apparel catalog company.*   Fax: (508) 588-7994

   GUCCI AMERICA, INC.
   50 Hartz Way, Secaucus, New Jersey 07094
   CEO: Patrice Malone, Pres.   Tel: (201) 867-8800   %FO: 100
   Bus: *Sales/distribution of designer clothing and* Fax: (201) 392-2679
        leather goods. (JV w/LVMH, France)

   REDCATS USA
   463 7th Ave., New York, New York 10018
   CEO: Eric Faintreny, Chmn. & CEO   Tel: (212) 613-9500
   Bus: *Apparel & Accessories retail.*   Fax: (212) 613-9690

- **PINGUELY-HAULOTTE SA**
  La Peronniere, BP 9, F-42152 L'Horme, France
  CEO: Pierre Saubot, Chmn. & Mng. Dir.   Tel: 33-4-7729-2424   Rev: $389
  Bus: *Aerial platform manufacture.*   Fax: 33-4-7729-4395   Emp: 1,000
                                                 www.haulotte.com

  NAICS: 333120, 333923
     HAULOTTE USA INC.
     7135 Standard Dr., Hanover, Maryland 21076
     CEO: Daniel Damart, Pres.   Tel: (410) 712-4403   %FO: 100
     Bus: *Mfr./sales of aerial lifts.*   Fax: (410) 712-4419   Emp: 20

- **PORCHER INDUSTRIES**
  RN 85, F-38300 Badinieres, France
  CEO: Robert Porcher, CEO   Tel: 33-4-7443-1010   Rev: $400
  Bus: *Mfr. fabrics for technical applications.* Fax: 33-4-7492-1407   Emp: 4,200
                                                  www.porcher-ind.com

  NAICS: 313210, 327211
     BGF INDUSTRIES, INC.
     3815 Medford St., Los Angeles, California 90063
     CEO: Frank Cunningham   Tel: (323) 264-1353   %FO: 100
     Bus: *Glass fabrics for technical applications and* Fax: (323) 266-6430
     non-woven fabrics.

     BGF INDUSTRIES, INC.
     13 Kimberly Dr., Brookfield, Connecticut 06804
     CEO: Nick LaForgia   Tel: (203) 775-4994   %FO: 100
     Bus: *Glass fabrics for technical applications and* Fax: (203) 740-7458
     non-woven fabrics.

     BGF INDUSTRIES, INC.
     3802 Robert Porcher Way, Greensboro, North Carolina 27410
     CEO: Carla Frungillo   Tel: (336) 545-0011   %FO: 100
     Bus: *Glass fabrics for technical applications and* Fax: (336) 545-0233   Emp: 1,150
     non-woven fabrics.

- **PROSODIE**
  150, Rue Gallieni, F-92100 Boulogne-Billancourt, France
  CEO: Alain Bernard, CEO   Tel: 33-1-4684-1111   Rev: $189
  Bus: *On-line technical support and services.* Fax: 33-1-4684-0226   Emp: 600
                                                  www.prosodie.com

  NAICS: 541511, 541512
     PROSODIE NORTH AMERICA
     200 Barr Harbor Dr., Ste. 400, Conshohocken, Pennsylvania 19428
     CEO: Nicholas Dourassoff   Tel: (877) 453-5700   %FO: 100
     Bus: *On-line technical support and services.* Fax: (954) 343-5588

     PROSODIE NORTH AMERICA
     8411 W. Oakland Park Blvd., Ste. 300, Ft. Lauderdale, Florida 33351
     CEO: Nicholas Dourassoff   Tel: (877) 453-5700   %FO: 100
     Bus: *On-line technical support and services.* Fax: (954) 343-5588

PROSODIE NORTH AMERICA
6467 Main St., Ste. 202, Williamsville, New York 14421
CEO: Dana Love
Bus: *On-line technical support and services.*
Tel: (888) 633-3487
Fax: (954) 343-5588
%FO: 100

PROSODIE NORTH AMERICA
1 Front St., 6/F, San Francisco, California 94111
CEO: Nicholas Dourassoff
Bus: *On-line technical support and services.*
Tel: (866) 595-7757
Fax: (954) 343-5588
%FO: 100

- **PSA PEUGEOT CITROËN SA**
75, ave de la Grande-Armee, F-75116 Paris, France
CEO: Jean-Martin Folz, Chmn.
Bus: *Mfr. automobiles, parts and accessories.*
Tel: 33-1-4066-5511
Fax: 33-1-4066-5414
www.psa-peugeot-citroen.com
Rev: $68,292
Emp: 199,910

NAICS: 336111, 336112, 336399, 336991, 522291

FAURECIA EXHAUST SYSTEMS, INC.
543 Matzinger Rd., Toledo, Ohio 43612
CEO: Mark Stidham, Pres. & CEO
Bus: *Mfr. of auto parts*
Tel: (419) 727-5000
Fax: (419) 727-5025

FAURECIA INTERIOR SYSTEMS
101 International Blvd., Fountain Inn, South Carolina 29644
CEO: Jean-Michael Vallin, CEO
Bus: *Mfr. of auto parts*
Tel: (864) 862-1900
Fax: (864) 862-7700

PEUGEOT MOTORS OF AMERICA, INC.
150 Clove Rd., Ste. 5, Little Falls, New Jersey 07424
CEO: Pierre Peugeot, Chmn.
Bus: *Distribution/service automobiles.*
Tel: (973) 812-4444
Fax: (973) 812-2148
%FO: 100
Emp: 25

- **PSB INDUSTRIES SA**
BP 22, F-74001 Annecy Cedex, France
CEO: Jean-Baptiste Bosson, Pres.
Bus: *Mfr. and creation of packaging.*
Tel: 33-4-5009-0002
Fax: 33-4-5027-1178
www.psb-industries.com
Rev: $197
Emp: 1,239

NAICS: 322221, 322223, 326111, 326112, 326160

BAIKOWSKI MALAKOFF INC. (BMI)
PO Box 487, Malakoff, Texas 75148
CEO: Claude Djololian
Bus: *Mfr. and creation of packaging.*
Tel: (903) 489-1910
Fax: (903) 489-0849
%FO: 100

BIC (BAIKOWSKI INTERNATIONAL CORP.)
325 Westinghouse Blvd., Charlotte, North Carolina 28273
CEO: Justin Otto
Bus: *Mfr. and creation of packaging.*
Tel: (704) 587-7100
Fax: (704) 587-7106
%FO: 100

● **PUBLICIS GROUPE S.A.**
133, ave. des Champs Elysees, F-75008 Paris Cedex, France
CEO: Maurice Levy, Chmn. & CEO   Tel: 33-1-4443-7000   Rev: $4,850
Bus: *Advertising and public relations agencies, media*   Fax: 33-1-4443-7525   Emp: 35,166
      direct mail services and drugstores.   www.publicis.fr
NAICS: 541810, 541820, 541830

    ARC INTEGRATED MARKETING
    Greenwich Office Park 5, Greenwich, Connecticut 06831
    CEO: Caren Berlin   Tel: (203) 862-6000   %FO: 100
    Bus: *Sales promotion.*   Fax: (203) 862-6001

    ARC WORLDWIDE
    103 Carnegie Center, Ste. 106, Princeton, New Jersey 08540
    CEO: Dick Thomas, Pres. & CEO   Tel: (609) 720-1000   %FO: 100
    Bus: *Sales promotion.*   Fax: (609) 720-1380

    ARC WORLDWIDE
    35 West Wacker Dr., Chicago, Illinois 60601
    CEO: Nick Brien, Chmn. & CEO   Tel: (312) 220-3200   %FO: 100
    Bus: *Sales promotion.*   Fax: (312) 220-1995

    ARC WORLDWIDE
    1675 Broadway, 7/F, New York, New York 10019
    CEO: Nick Brien, Pres.   Tel: (646) 756-8950   %FO: 100
    Bus: *Sales promotion.*   Fax: (646) 756-8951

    BCOM3 GROUP
    35 West Wacker Dr., Chicago, Illinois 60601
    CEO: Arthur Selkowitz   Tel: (312) 220-5959   %FO: 20
    Bus: *Advertising & communications services.*   Fax: (312) 220-3299

    BIENESTAR LCG COMMUNICATIONS INC.
    41 Madison Ave., New York, New York 10010
    CEO: Shelly Lipton   Tel: (212) 894-6300   %FO: 100
    Bus: *Community marketing.*   Fax: (212) 894-6320   Emp: 70

    BROMLEY COMMUNICATIONS
    401 E. Houston, San Antonio, Texas 78205
    CEO: Enest Bromley, CEO   Tel: (210) 244-2000   %FO: 100
    Bus: *Advertising agency.*   Fax: (210) 244-2403

    BURRELL COMMUNICATIONS GROUP
    233 N. Michigan Ave., Chicago, Illinois 60601
    CEO: Thomas J. Burrell, CEO   Tel: (312) 297-9600   %FO: 49
    Bus: *Advertising agency.*   Fax: (312) 297-9601

    CAPPS DIGITAL
    35 W. Wacker Dr., Ste. 3000, Chicago, Illinois 60601
    CEO: Rick Capps, Pres. & CEO   Tel: (312) 220-0900   %FO: 100
    Bus: *Production and publishing company.*   Fax: (312) 220-1990

CHEMISTRI INC.
3310 W. Big Beaver Rd., Troy, Michigan 48084
CEO: Patrick Sherwood
Bus: *Advertising agency.*
Tel: (248) 458-8300
Fax: (248) 458-8736
%FO: 100

CONILL
375 Hudson St., New York, New York 10014
CEO: Celeb Windover, Dir.
Bus: *Community marketing.*
Tel: (212) 463-2500
Fax: (212) 463-2509
%FO: 100

DISCOVERY INST. OF MEDICAL EDUCATION
111 East Wacker Dr., Ste. 1800, Chicago, Illinois 60601-4505
CEO: Counce Hancock, MD, Dir.
Bus: *Healthcare communications.*
Tel: (312) 552-5100
Fax: (312) 552-5050
%FO: 100

DOUBLE PLATINUM
149 Fifth Ave., 14/F, New York, New York 10010
CEO: Stephanie K. Blackwood, CEO
Bus: *Advertising agency.*
Tel: (917) 534-5680
Fax: (917) 534-5625
%FO: 100

FALLON WORLDWIDE
50 South Sixth St., Minneapolis, Minnesota 55402
CEO: Pat Fallon, Chmn.
Bus: *Advertising agency.*
Tel: (612) 758-2345
Fax: (612) 758-2346
%FO: 100

HASS/MS&L
115 W. Liberty Rd., Ste. 200, Ann Arbor, Michigan 48104
CEO: Jud Branam, Mng. Dir.
Bus: *Public relations.*
Tel: (734) 214-1550
Fax: (734) 214-1551
%FO: 100

KAPLAN THALER GROUP
825 8th Ave., 34/F, New York, New York 10019
CEO: Linda Kaplan Thayer, CEO
Bus: *Advertising agency.*
Tel: (212) 474-5000
Fax: (212) 474-5702
%FO: 100

LEO BURNETT USA
520 Madison Ave., 9/F, New York, New York 10022
CEO: Tom Bernardin
Bus: *Advertising services.*
Tel: (212) 759-5959
Fax: (212) 752-4065

LEO BURNETT USA
35 West Wacker Dr., Chicago, Illinois 60601
CEO: Rich Stoddart, Chmn. & CEO
Bus: *Advertising services.*
Tel: (312) 220-5959
Fax: (312) 220-3299

LIFEBRANDS
1675 Broadway, New York, New York 10019
CEO: Lorraine Pastore, CEO
Bus: *Advertising and public relations agencies, media direct mail services and drugstores.*
Tel: (212) 468-3591
Fax: (212) 468-3590
%FO: 100

MANNING, SELVAGE & LEE
1675 Broadway, 9/F, New York, New York 10019
CEO: Mark Hass, CEO
Bus: *Public relations firm.*
Tel: (212) 468-4200
Fax: (212) 468-4175
%FO: 100

MARKETFORWARD
427 S. LaSalle, Chicago, Illinois 60605
CEO: Stephen Nesbit   Tel: (312) 220-1700   %FO: 100
Bus: *Marketing technology.*   Fax: (312) 220-1703

MASIUS
1675 Broadway, New York, New York 10019-5865
CEO: Andrew Porter, CEO   Tel: (212) 468-3300   %FO: 100
Bus: *Advertising agency.*   Fax: (212) 468-3304

MEDIAVEST
1675 Broadway, New York, New York 10019
CEO: Marston Allen   Tel: (212) 468-4000   %FO: 100
Bus: *Media consultants.*   Fax: (212) 468-4110

MOROCH LEO BURNETT USA
3625 North Hall, Ste. 1100, Dallas, Texas 75219
CEO: Pat Kempf   Tel: (214) 520-9700   %FO: 100
Bus: *Advertising agency.*   Fax: (214) 252-1719

NAZCA SAATCHI & SAATCHI
1101 Brickell Ave., Ste. 603-S, Miami, Florida 33131
CEO: Jose Antonio Cabrera   Tel: (305) 351-2900   %FO: 100
Bus: *Advertising agency.*   Fax: (305) 351-2899

NCI CONSULTING
2000 Lenox Dr., Ste. 100A, Lawrenceville, New Jersey 08648
CEO: Susan Lavine Coleman, Pres.   Tel: (609) 912-1444   %FO: 100
Bus: *Marketing and strategic consultants.*   Fax: (609) 912-0848

NELSON PROFESSIONAL SALES
2000 Lenox Dr., Ste. 100, Lawrenceville, New Jersey 08648
CEO: Deborah Kelleher, Pres.   Tel: (609) 896-4787   %FO: 100
Bus: *Marketing and management consulting.*   Fax: (609) 896-4789

PHARMACEUTICAL CORPORATION OF AMERICA
2000 Lenox Dr., Ste. 100A, Lawrenceville, New Jersey 08648
CEO: Steve Varon   Tel: (609) 896-4774   %FO: 100
Bus: *Marketing and strategic consulting.*   Fax: (609) 912-0844

PUBLICIS
168 North Ninth St., Ste. 250, Boise, Idaho 83702
CEO: Ramona Aschenbrener   Tel: (208) 395-8300   %FO: 100
Bus: *Advertising agency.*   Fax: (208) 395-8333

PUBLICIS
4 Herald Square, 950 6th Ave., New York, New York 10001
CEO: Susan M. Gianinno, Pres. & CEO   Tel: (212) 279-5550   %FO: 100
Bus: *Advertising agency.*   Fax: (212) 279-5560

PUBLICIS
424 2nd Ave. West, Seattle, Washington 98119
CEO: Randy Browning, Chmn. & CEO   Tel: (206) 285-2222   %FO: 100
Bus: *Advertising agency.*   Fax: (206) 286-8388

PUBLICIS
200 S. Meridian, Ste. 500, Indianapolis, Indiana 46225
CEO: Steve Price, Chmn. & CEO   Tel: (317) 639-5135   %FO: 100
Bus: *Advertising agency.*   Fax: (317) 639-5134

PUBLICIS DIALOG
424 Second Ave. West, Seattle, Washington 98119
CEO: Steve Bryant, Pres.   Tel: (206) 285-2222   %FO: 100
Bus: *Public relations.*   Fax: (206) 270-4656

PUBLICIS EHEALTH SOLUTIONS
1884 Lackland Hill Pkwy., Ste. 1, Saint Louis, Missouri 63146
CEO: Yaron Inbar   Tel: (314) 994-3030   %FO: 100
Bus: *Media technology.*   Fax: (314) 994-3133

PUBLICIS EVENTS
825 8th Ave., New York, New York 10019
CEO: Doreen Bonnami   Tel: (212) 474-6140   %FO: 100
Bus: *Event planning and execution.*   Fax: (212) 474-5700

PUBLICIS GROUPE MEDIA
35 West Wacker Drive, Chicago, Illinois 60601
CEO: Jack Klues, Chmn.   Tel: (312) 220-5586   %FO: 100
Bus: *Advertising and media services.* Fax: (312) 220-6549

PUBLICIS HAL RINEY & PARTNERS
1355 Peachtree St. NE, Atlanta, Georgia 30309-3212
CEO: Max Butler   Tel: (404) 575-4500   %FO: 100
Bus: *Advertising agency.*   Fax: (404) 575-4500

PUBLICIS HAL RINEY & PARTNERS
2001 The Embarcadero, San Francisco, California 94133
CEO: Karen C. Francis, Chmn.   Tel: (415) 293-2001   %FO: 100
Bus: *Advertising agency.*   Fax: (415) 293-2619   Emp: 360

PUBLICIS HEALTHCARE SPECIALTY GROUP
41 Madison Ave., New York, New York 10010
CEO: Ed Randy   Tel: (212) 448-5231   %FO: 100
Bus: *Healthcare services.*   Fax: (212) 684-3478

PUBLICIS SANCHEZ & LEVITAN
1790 Coral Way, 3/F, Miami, Florida 33145
CEO: Aida Levitan, Co-Chair   Tel: (305) 858-9495   %FO: 100
Bus: *Advertising agency.*   Fax: (305) 858-9461

PUBLICIS USA
4 Herald Square, 950 5th Ave., New York, New York 10001
CEO: Susan McManama Gianinno, Chmn. &   Tel: (212) 279-5550
Bus: *Advertising services.*   Fax: (212) 279-5560   Emp: 1,000

SAATCHI & SAATCHI BUSINESS
255 Woodcliff Dr., Ste. 200, Fairport, New York 14450
CEO: Christine Withers, Mng. Dir.   Tel: (585) 249-6100   %FO: 100
Bus: *Advertising agency.*   Fax: (585) 249-6161

SAATCHI & SAATCHI WORLDWIDE
375 Hudson St., New York, New York 10014-3620
CEO: Kevin J. Roberts, CEO   Tel: (212) 463-2000   %FO: 100
Bus: *Advertising agency.*   Fax: (212) 463-9855

SAATCHI & SAATCHI X
605 Lakeview Dr., Springdale, Arkansas 72764
CEO: Andy Murray   Tel: (479) 575-0200   %FO: 100
Bus: *Advertising agency.*   Fax: (479) 725-1136

SAATCHI & SAATCHI X
Chiquita Center, 150 E. 5th St., Ste. 610, Cincinnati, Ohio 45202
CEO: Andy Murray   Tel: (513) 369-7200   %FO: 100
Bus: *Advertising agency.*   Fax: (513) 369-0069

SMG IP
35 West Wacker Drive, Chicago, Illinois 60601
CEO: Renetta McCann, CEO   Tel: (312) 220-5586   %FO: 100
Bus: *Creation of media campaigns.*   Fax: (312) 220-6549

STARCOM NORTH AMERICA
35 West Wacker Dr., Chicago, Illinois 60601
CEO: Renetta McCann, CEO   Tel: (312) 220-3535   %FO: 100
Bus: *Media consulting.*   Fax: (312) 220-1515   Emp: 4,700

TAPESTRY
35 West Wacker Dr., Chicago, Illinois 60601
CEO: Nick Brien   Tel: (312) 220-5959   %FO: 100
Bus: *Community marketing.*   Fax: (312) 220-6561

TEAM ONE ADVERTISING
1960 East Grand Ave.., El Segundo, California 90245
CEO: Brian Sheehan, CEO   Tel: (310) 615-2000   %FO: 100
Bus: *Advertising agency.*   Fax: (310) 322-7565

WINNER & ASSOCIATES
16501 Ventura Blvd., Ste. 605, Encino, California 91436
CEO: Chuck Winner, Pres. & CEO   Tel: (818) 385-1900   %FO: 100
Bus: *Public relations agency.*   Fax: (818) 385-1867

● **RADIALL SA**
101, rue Philibert Hoffmann, F-93116 Rosny-sous-Bois, France
CEO: Pierre Gattaz, Chmn. & Pres. & CEO   Tel: 33-1-4935-3535   Rev: $222
Bus: *Mfr. coaxial connectors, microwave devices and*   Fax: 33-1-4854-6363   Emp: 1,585
     fiber optic connectors.   www.radiall.com
NAICS: 334417, 334419

     APPLIED ENGINEERING PRODUCTS
     104 J.W. Murphy Dr., New Haven, Connecticut 06513
     CEO: Benjamin Trivelli, Pres.   Tel: (203) 776-2813
     Bus: *Mfr. electronic connectors*   Fax: (203) 776-8294   Emp: 175

ELECTRONIC NOTE SPACE SYSTEMS
300 W. Esplanade Dr., Oxnard, California 93036
CEO: Peter Lust, Owner   Tel: (805) 981-9178
Bus: *Engineering services*   Fax: Emp: 5

RADIALL JERRIK
102 W. Julie Dr., Tempe, Arizona 85283
CEO: Andre Hernandez, Pres.   Tel: (480) 730-5700
Bus: *Mfr. conductive wiring devices.*   Fax: (480) 730-5800   Emp: 105

RADIALL LARSEN ANTENNA TECHNOLOGIES
3611 NE 112th Ave., Vancouver, Washington 98682
CEO: Dominique Pellizzari, Pres.   Tel: (360) 944-7551
Bus: *Mfr. electronic connectors.*   Fax: (360) 944-7556   Emp: 432

● **REMY COINTREAU GROUP**
21, boulevard Haussmann, F-75009 Paris, France
CEO: Jean-Marie Laborde, CEO   Tel: 33-1-4413-4413   Rev: $1,081
Bus: *Mfr. cognac and spirits.*   Fax: 33-1-4562-8252   Emp: 1,945
                                         www.remy-cointreau.com

NAICS: 312130, 312140
    REMY COINTREAU USA, INC.
    1350 Ave. of the Americas, New York, New York 10019
    CEO: James R. Chambers, Chmn.   Tel: (212) 399-4200   %FO: 100
    Bus: *Mfr. cognac and spirits.*   Fax: (212) 399-4265   Emp: 210

● **RENAULT, SA**
13-15, Quai Le Gallo, F-92513 Boulogne-Billancourt Cedex, France
CEO: Carlos Ghosn, Pres. & CEO   Tel: 33-1-7684-5050   Rev: $55,535
Bus: *Mfr. Renault & Mack vehicles; cars, trucks,*   Fax: 33-1-4104-5149   Emp: 130,573
    tractors.   www.renault.com
NAICS: 333924, 336111, 336112, 336120, 522291
    NISSAN NORTH AMERICA
    18501 S. Figueroa St., PO Box 191, Gardena, California 90248
    CEO: Carlos Ghosn, Pres. & CEO   Tel: (310) 771-3111
    Bus: *Automobile manufacturing*   Fax: (310) 516-7967

● **REXEL S.A.**
25, rue de Clichy, F-75009 Paris, France
CEO: Jean-Charles Pauze, Chmn. & CEO   Tel: 33-1-4285-8500   Rev: $8,358
Bus: *Distribution of electrical parts and installation*   Fax: 33-1-4526-2583   Emp: 25,366
    equipment.   www.rexel.com
NAICS: 423610, 423690
    BRAID ELECTRIC CO.
    299 Crown St., Nashville, Tennessee 37213
    CEO: Ben S. Gambill Jr., Pres.   Tel: (615) 242-6511   %FO: 100
    Bus: *Distributes electrical parts and supplies.*   Fax: (624) 242-9684   Emp: 95

REXEL INC.
1990 N. California Blvd., Ste. 1055, Walnut Creek, California 94596
CEO: Alan Rosenfeld
Bus: *Distributes electrical parts and supplies.*
Tel: (925) 952-4295
Fax: (925) 952-4296
%FO: 100

REXEL INC.
6700 LBJ Fwy., Ste. 3200, Dallas, Texas 75240
CEO: Dick Waterman, CEO
Bus: *Distributes electrical parts and supplies.*
Tel: (972) 387-3600
Fax: (972) 934-2056
%FO: 100

● **RHODIA SA**
26, Quai Alphonse Le Gallo, F-92512 Boulogne-Billancourt, France
CEO: Jean-Pierre Clamadieu, CEO
Bus: *Mfr. specialty chemicals and water treatment systems.*
Tel: 33-1-5538-4000
Fax: 33-1-5538-4471
www.rhodia.com
Rev: $7,154
Emp: 20,577

NAICS: 325199, 325211, 325222, 325412, 325510, 325613, 325998, 424950

RHODIA INC.
259 Prospect Plains Rd., PO Box 7500, Cranbury, New Jersey 08512-7500
CEO: Myron Galuskin, Pres.
Bus: *Mfr. specialty chemicals.*
Tel: (609) 860-4000
Fax: (609) 860-0464
%FO: 100
Emp: 2,410

● **RODRIGUEZ GROUP**
105 ave. des Freres Roustan, Palais Napoleon, F-06220 Golfe-Juan, France
CEO: Alexandre Rodriguez, Chmn. & CEO
Bus: *Yacht manufacture.*
Tel: 33-4-9721-8181
Fax: 33-4-9721-8717
www.rodriguezgroup.com
Rev: $453
Emp: 196

NAICS: 336612, 441222

BOB SAXON ASSOCIATES
1500 Cordova Rd., Ste. 314, Ft. Lauderdale, Florida 33316
CEO: Bob Saxon, Pres.
Bus: *Sale of recreational vehicles, motorcycles & boats.*
Tel: (954) 760-5801
Fax: (954) 467-8909
%FO: 100

CAMPER & NICHOLSONS INTERNATIONAL
Newport Shipyard, 1 Washington St., Newport, Rhode Island 02840
CEO: Sarah Montefiore, Mgr.
Bus: *Sale of recreational vehicles, motorcycles & boats.*
Tel: (401) 619-0075
Fax:
%FO: 100

CAMPER & NICHOLSONS INTERNATIONAL
450 Royal Palm Way, Palm Beach, Florida 33480
CEO: George Nicholson, Pres.
Bus: *Sale of recreational vehicles, motorcycles & boats.*
Tel: (561) 655-2121
Fax: (561) 655-2202
%FO: 100

CAMPER & NICHOLSONS INTERNATIONAL
801 Seabreeze Blvd., Ft. Lauderdale, Florida 33316
CEO: Sarah Montefiore, Mgr.
Bus: *Sale of recreational vehicles, motorcycles & boats.*
Tel: (954) 524-4250
Fax: (954) 524-4249
%FO: 100
Emp: 12

CAMPER & NICHOLSONS INTERNATIONAL
1651 Collins Ave., Miami Beach, Florida 33139
CEO: Sarah Montefiore, Mgr.   Tel: (305) 604-9191   %FO: 100
Bus: *Sale of recreational vehicles, motorcycles &* Fax: (305) 604-9196
boats.

CAMPER & NICHOLSONS INTERNATIONAL
1535 SE 17th St., Ft. Lauderdale, Florida 33316
CEO: Sarah Montefiore, Mgr.   Tel: (954) 760-5801   %FO: 100
Bus: *Yacht manufacture.*   Fax: (954) 467-4909

SNP BOAT SERVICE INC.
1515 S.E. 17th St., Ste. 115, Ft. Lauderdale, Florida 33316
CEO: Bassam Chahine, Mgr.   Tel: (954) 524-7310   %FO: 100
Bus: *Sale of recreational vehicles, motorcycles &* Fax: (954) 524-7578   Emp: 5
boats.

- **ROUTIN CORP.**
907 Rue Emile Romanet, BP 9428, F-73094 Chambery, France
CEO: Jean Clochet, Pres. & CEO   Tel: 33-4-792-56876
Bus: *Flavored syrups manufacture.*   Fax: 33-479-256-855
www.routin.com

NAICS: 311920, 311930

    ROUTIN AMERICA, INC., c/o PRAMEX
    1251 Ave. of the Americas, 34/F, New York, New York 10020
    CEO: Jerry Hureau, Pres.   Tel: (866) 438-1883   %FO: 100
    Bus: *Mfr./sales flavored syrups.* Fax: (866) 764-1883

- **ROYAL CANIN SA**
RN 113, F-30470 Aimargues, France
CEO: Henri Lagarde, Pres.   Tel: 33-4-6673-6400
Bus: *Pet food manufacture.*   Fax: 33-4-6783-4020   Emp: 2,200
www.royal-canin.com

NAICS: 311111, 311119, 541940, 812910

    ROYAL CANIN USA INC.
    5600 Mexico Rd., Ste. 2, St. Peters, Missouri 63376
    CEO: Stan Howton, Pres.   Tel: (636) 926-0003   %FO: 100
    Bus: *Pet food manufacture and sales.* Fax: (636) 926-3859   Emp: 196

- **SAFRAN**
2, blvd. du General Martial Valin, F-75015 Paris Cedex 15, France
CEO: Mario Colaiacovo, Chmn.   Tel: 33-1-4076-8080   Rev: $4,870
Bus: *Mfr. navigation, guidance and vehicle control* Fax: 33-1-4060-8102   Emp: 15,369
equipment, data processing and communications www.safran-group.com
systems, industrial equipment.

NAICS: 333313, 334119, 334220, 334511, 336411, 336412, 336413, 336415, 541330, 811219, 811310

    SAGEM MORPHO, INC.
    1145 Broadway Plaza, Ste. 200, Tacoma, Washington 98402
    CEO: Jean-Marc Suchier, Pres. & CEO Tel: (253) 383-3617   %FO: 100
    Bus: *Mfr./distributor industrial and auto* Fax: (253) 591-8856   Emp: 200
    equipment.

SNECMA USA, INC.
580 Waters Edge, Ste. 220, Lombard, Illinois 60148
CEO: Yves Imbert, Chmn. & CEO   Tel: (630) 705-5700   %FO: 100
Bus: *Mfr. of aerospace & defense parts.*   Fax: (630) 705-5704   Emp: 3,500

● **SAFT SA**
12, rue Sadi Carnot, F-93170 Bagnolet, France
CEO: John Searle, Chmn. & CEO   Tel: 33-1-4993-1918   Rev: $800
Bus: *Design and manufacture of industrial batteries.*   Fax: 33-1-4993-1950   Emp: 4,000
      www.saftbatteries.com
NAICS: 325613, 327910

    SAFT AMERICA INC.
    107 Beaver Ct., Cockeysville, Maryland 41077
    CEO: Guy Chagnon, Mgr.   Tel: (410) 771-3200   %FO: 100
    Bus: *Mfr. specialty batteries.*   Fax: (410) 771-1144

● **COMPAGNIE DE SAINT-GOBAIN**
Les Miroirs, 18, Avenue d'Alsace, F-92096 La Defense Cedex, France
CEO: Jean-Louis Beffa, Chmn. & CEO   Tel: 33-1-4762-3000   Rev: $37,141
Bus: *Processor of high performance polymer products,*   Fax: 33-1-4778-4503   Emp: 172,811
      including fluoropolymers, silicones, and high-   www.saint-gobain.com
      temperature thermoplastics.
NAICS: 325211, 327122, 327124, 327211, 327213, 332111

    CERTAINTEED CORPORATION
    750 East Swedesford Rd., Valley Forge, Pennsylvania 19482
    CEO: Peter R. Dachowski, Chmn. & Pres. & CEO   Tel: (610) 341-7000   %FO: 100
    Bus: *Mfr. plastic pumps and sprayers.*   Fax: (610) 341-7777   Emp: 7,000

    SAINT-GOBAIN ABRASIVES, INC.
    One New Bond St., Worcester, Massachusetts 01615
    CEO: Americo Denes, Pres.   Tel: (508) 795-5000   %FO: 100
    Bus: *Mfr. glass and building materials.*   Fax: (508) 795-5741   Emp: 3,494

    SAINT-GOBAIN BTI, INC.
    43 Bibber Pkwy., Brunswick, Maine 04011
    CEO: Phil Harmon, Operations Mgr.   Tel: (207) 729-7792
    Bus: *Mfr. of textiles*   Fax: (207) 729-7877

    SAINT-GOBAIN CALMAR INC.
    333 South Turnbull Canyon Rd., City of Industry, California 91745
    CEO: John McKernan, Pres. & CEO   Tel: (626) 330-3161   %FO: 100
    Bus: *Mfr. plastic pumps and sprayers.*   Fax: (626) 937-2764

    SAINT-GOBAIN CERAMICS & PLASTICS INC.
    1600 W. Lee St., Louisville, Kentucky 40210
    CEO: Roberto Caliari, Pres.   Tel: (502) 778-3311
    Bus: *Mfr. of plastic, fiber, glass, clay, & rubber*   Fax: (502) 775-7478   Emp: 6,050
      products

SAINT-GOBAIN CONTAINERS, INC.
1509 South Macedonia Ave., Muncie, Indiana 47302
CEO: Joseph R. Grewe, Pres. & CEO
Bus: *Mfr. glass containers.*

Tel: (765) 741-7000
Fax: (765) 741-7012

%FO: 100
Emp: 5,335

SAINT-GOBAIN CORPORATION
750 East Swedesford Rd., Valley Forge, Pennsylvania 19482
CEO: Jean-Francois Phelizon, Chmn. & Pres. &
Bus: *Mfr./sales fluid systems, extruded/molded*
Emp: 25,657
    silicone components and assemblies.

Tel: (610) 341-7000
CEO Fax:

%FO: 100
(610) 341-7777

● SALANS
9, rue Boissy d'Anglas, F-75008 Paris, France
CEO: Carl Salans, Pres.
Bus: *Multi-national law firm.*

Tel: 33-1-4268-4800
Fax: 33-1-4268-1545
www.salans.com

Emp: 350

NAICS: 541110

SALANS
620 Fifth Ave., Rockefeller Center, New York, New York 10020-2457
CEO: Richard Anderman, Partner
Bus: *Multinational law firm.*

Tel: (212) 632-5500
Fax: (212) 632-5555

%FO: 100
Emp: 162

● SANOFI-AVENTIS SA
174, avenue de France, F-75635 Paris Cedex 13, France
CEO: Jean-François Dehecq, Chmn.
Bus: *Healthcare and pharmaceutical drugs manufacture.*

Tel: 33-1-5377-4000
Fax: 33-1-5377-4133
www.sanofi-synthelabo.com

Rev: $30,000
Emp: 30,500

NAICS: 325411, 325412

SANOFI DIAGNOSTICS PASTEUR INC.
Discovery Dr., Swiftwater, Pennsylvania 18370
CEO: Damian Braga
Bus: *Develop/mfr./distributes preventative and*
    therapeutic vaccines.

Tel: (570) 839-7187
Fax: (570) 839-7235

SANOFI PHARMACEUTICALS INC.
90 Park Ave., New York, New York 10016-2499
CEO: Timothy Rothwell, Pres. & CEO
Bus: *Healthcare, skincare, fragrances, clothing*
    and household linens sales and distribution.

Tel: (212) 551-4000
Fax: (212) 551-4900

%FO: 100

SANOFI SYNTHELABO PHARMACEUTICALS
2633 Camino Ramon, San Ramon, California 94583
CEO: Tom Star
Bus: *Develop/mfr./distributes preventative and*
    therapeutic vaccines.

Tel: (925) 790-0720
Fax: (925) 790-0720

● SANSHA PARIS
52, rue de Clichy, F-75009 Paris, France
CEO: Franck Raoul-Duval, Pres.
Bus: *Mfr. ballet shoes.*

Tel: 33-1-4526-0138
Fax: 33-1-4526-0439
www.sansha.com

NAICS: 316219

SANSHA USA, INC.
Sansha Bldg., 2080 Mercantile Dr., Leland, North Carolina 28451
CEO: Philippe Saint-Paul, Mgr.   Tel: (910) 371-0101   %FO: 100
Bus: *Wholesale & retail ballet shoes.*   Fax: (910) 371-0187

SANSHA USA, INC.
888 8th Ave., Corner 53rd St., New York, New York 10019
CEO: Philippe Saint-Paul, Gen. Mgr.   Tel: (212) 246-6212   %FO: 100
Bus: *Sale of ballet shoes.*   Fax: (212) 246-2138

● **SCHNEIDER ELECTRIC SA**
43-45 boulevard Franklin-Roosevelt, F-92500 Rueil-Malmaison, France
CEO: Henri Lachmann, Chmn. & CEO   Tel: 33-1-41-29-7000   Rev: $14,138
Bus: *Mfr. voltage power distribution equipment and*   Fax: 33-1-41-29-7100   Emp: 85,000
electron mechanical industrial control components www.schneider-electric.com
and specializes in electrical contracting.
NAICS: 238210, 334419, 334512, 334513, 335211, 335311, 335312, 335314, 335931, 335999, 423610, 423690

ANDOVER CONTROLS CORP.
300 Brickstone Sq., Andover, Massachusetts 01810
CEO: William J. Lapointe, Pres. & CEO   Tel: (978) 470-0555
Bus: *Mfr. Industrial automation & industrial*   Fax: (978) 470-0946   Emp: 600
control products.

BEI TECHNOLOGIES INC.
1 Post St., Ste. 2500, San Francisco, California 94104
CEO: Charles Crocker   Tel: (415) 956-4477   %FO: 100
Bus: *Mfr. electronic sensors and engineered*   Fax: (415) 956-5564   Emp: 1,000
subsystems

JUNO LIGHTING INC.
1300 S. Wolf Rd., Des Plains, Illinois 60017
CEO: Thomas Bilbrough   Tel: (847) 827-9880   %FO: 100
Bus: *Mfr. light fixtures for commercial,*   Fax: (847) 296-4056   Emp: 1,000
institutional, and residential buildings.

KAVLICO CORP.
14501 Princeton Ave., Moorpark, California 93021
CEO: Terry O'Neal, Pres.   Tel: (805) 523-2000
Bus: *Industrial manufacturing.*   Fax: (805) 523-7125   Emp: 2,000

MGE UPS SYSTEMS INC.
1660 Scenic Ave., Costa Mesa, California 92626
CEO: Ray Prince, Pres.   Tel: (714) 557-1636
Bus: *Transformers & power conversion.*   Fax: (714) 434-0865   Emp: 540

SCHNEIDER NORTH AMERICA
1415 South Roselle Rd., Palatine, Illinois 60067
CEO: Dave Petratis, Pres.   Tel: (847) 397-2600   %FO: 100
Bus: *Mfr. electrical distribution equipment and*   Fax: (847) 397-8814   Emp: 17,045
systems.

- **SCOR SA**
  1 ave. du General de Gaulle, F-92074 La Defense Cedex, France
  CEO: Denis Kessler, Chmn. & CEO
  Bus: *Reinsurance services.*
  Tel: 33-1-4698-7000
  Fax: 33-1-4767-0409
  www.scor.com
  Rev: $4,730
  Emp: 1,176

  NAICS: 524130

  ### SCOR COMMERCIAL RISK RE-INSURANCE
  177 Broad St., PO Box 120019, Stamford, Connecticut 06912
  CEO: Pierre Charles
  Bus: *Property & casualty reinsurance services.*
  Tel: (203) 356-3440
  Fax: (203) 356-3480
  %FO: 100

  ### SCOR LIFE RE-INSURANCE COMPANY
  Colonnade Bldg. III, 15305 Dallas Pkwy., Addison, Texas 75001
  CEO: Yves Corcos, CEO
  Bus: *Property & casualty reinsurance services.*
  Tel: (972) 560-9500
  Fax: (972) 560-9535
  %FO: 100
  Emp: 32

  ### SCOR REINSURANCE
  101 California St., Ste. 2700, San Francisco, California 94111
  CEO: Steven Schreiber
  Bus: *Property & casualty reinsurance services.*
  Tel: (415) 765-1200
  Fax: (415) 397-8390
  %FO: 100

  ### SCOR REINSURANCE COMPANY
  1 Pierce Place, Ste. 600, PO Box 4049, Itasca, Illinois 60143-4049
  CEO: John Fitzpatrick, Mgr.
  Bus: *Property & casualty reinsurance services.*
  Tel: (630) 775-7300
  Fax: (630) 775-0846
  %FO: 100

  ### SCOR REINSURANCE COMPANY
  1401 Brickell Ave., Ste. 910, Miami, Florida 33131-3501
  CEO: Maria Vazquez, VP
  Bus: *Property & casualty reinsurance services.*
  Tel: (305) 679-9951
  Fax: (305) 679-9963
  %FO: 100

  ### SCOR U.S. CORPORATION
  1 Seaport Plaza, 199 Water St., Ste. 2100, New York, New York 10038-3526
  CEO: Henry Klekan Jr., Pres.
  Bus: *Property and casualty reinsurance
  services.*
  Tel: (212) 480-1900
  Fax: (212) 480-1328
  %FO: 100
  Emp: 230

- **SIDEL S.A.S.**
  Avenue de la Patrouille de France, Octeville sur Mer, BP 204, F-76053 La Havre Cedex, France
  CEO: Gerard Stricher, Pres. & CEO
  Bus: *Mfr. packaging machines for water and*
  Tel: 33-2-3285-8687
  Fax: 33-2-3285-8100
  www.sidel.com
  Rev: $1,125
  Emp: 4,060

  NAICS: 322211, 326160, 327213

  ### SIDEL INC.
  9480 Utica Ave., Ste. 605, Rancho Cucamonga, California 91730
  CEO: Martin Flores, Mgr.
  Bus: *Sales/Service of replacement parts for pet
  blow molding machines.*
  Tel: (909) 466-7799
  Fax: (909) 466-8778
  %FO: 100

SIDEL INC.
5600 Sun Ct., Norcross, Georgia 30092
CEO: Tehiery Parges, Pres.
Bus: *Sales/Service of replacements for pet blow molding machines.*

Tel: (770) 449-8058
Fax: (770) 447-0084

%FO: 100
Emp: 165

SIDEL INC.
6015 31st East St., Bradenton, Florida 34203
CEO: Mary Limpert, Sales
Bus: *Sales/Service of replacement parts for pet blow molding machines.*

Tel: (941) 727-1400
Fax: (941) 727-1200

%FO: 100

● **SIPA PRESS INC.**
101 Boulevard Murat, F-75016 Paris, France
CEO: Pierre-Yves Revol, Pres.
Bus: *Distribution of photo images.*

Tel: 33-1-4743-4743
Fax: 33-1-4743-4744
www.sipa.com

NAICS: 516110, 519110, 519190, 541922

SIPA PRESS INC.
307 7th Ave., Ste. 807, New York, New York 10001
CEO: Goksin Sipahioglu, Pres.
Bus: *Distribution of photo images.*

Tel: (212) 463-0150
Fax: (212) 463-0160

%FO: 100

● **SKIS ROSSIGNOL S.A.**
BP 329, F-38509 Voiron Cedex, France
CEO: Jacques-Henri Rodet, Chmn.
Bus: *Mfr. snow skis and poles.*

Tel: 33-4-7666-6565
Fax: 33-4-7665-6751
www.rossignol.com

Rev: $603
Emp: 2,902

NAICS: 315991, 315992, 315999, 339920

ROGER CLEVELAND GOLF COMPANY, INC.
5601 Skylab Rd., Cypress, California 92647
CEO: Greg Hopkins, Pres. & COO
Bus: *Golf equipment.*

Tel: (714) 889-1300
Fax: (714) 889-5890

Emp: 233

ROSSIGNOL
426 Industrial Ave., Williston, Vermont 05495
CEO: Franzois Goulet, Pres.
Bus: *Sale of skis and equipment.*

Tel: (802) 863-2511
Fax:

Emp: 233

ROSSIGNOL
Bldg. Y15 Freeport Center, PO Box 160218, Clearfield, Utah 84016
CEO: Ron Steel, Mgr.
Bus: *General warehousing.*

Tel: (801) 773-1321
Fax:

● **SNF FLOERGER SAS**
ZAC de Milleux, F-42163 Amdrezieux Cedex, France
CEO: Rene Pich, CEO
Bus: *Mfr. synthetic flocculants, including acrylamides and acrylates.*
NAICS: 325181, 325188, 325199

Tel: 33-4-7736-8600
Fax: 33-4-7736-8696
www.snf-floerger.com

Rev: $778
Emp: 1,700

France

653

PEARL RIVER POLYMERS INC.
PO Box 1650, I-59 North Exit 5A, Pearl River, Louisiana 70452
CEO: Scott Ramey
Bus: *Mfr. chemicals.*
Tel: (504) 863-5703
Fax: (504) 863-5703
%FO: 100

POLYCHEMIE INC.
3080 Port and Harbor Dr., St Louis, Mississippi 39502
CEO: Jerry Martin
Bus: *Mfr. chemicals.*
Tel: (228) 533-7127
Fax: (228) 533-7939
%FO: 100

SNF INC.
1 Chemical Plant Rd., Riceboro, Georgia 31323
CEO: Peter Nichols
Bus: *Mfr. chemicals.*
Tel: (912) 884-3366
Fax: (912) 884-5031
%FO: 100

● **SOCIETE DU LOUVRE**
10 ave. de Friedland, F-75008 Paris, France
CEO: Anne-Claire Taittinger, Mng. Dir.
Bus: *Luxury hotel group.*
Tel: 33-145-64-5000
Fax: 33-142-89-1310
www.societedulouvre.fr
Rev: $1,007
Emp: 7,370

NAICS: 325620, 327212, 721110

BACCARAT CRYSTAL
Ala Moana Center, 1450 Ala Moana Blvd., Honolulu, Hawaii 96814
CEO: Kimi Fukuda, Mgr.
Bus: *Sales of hand-cut crystal.*
Tel: (808) 943-6688
Fax: (808) 955-4699
%FO: 100

BACCARAT CRYSTAL
441 East Hopkins Ave., Aspen, Colorado 81611
CEO: Tanya Youngling, Mgr.
Bus: *Sales of hand-cut crystal.*
Tel: (970) 925-9299
Fax: (970) 925-8909
%FO: 100

BACCARAT CRYSTAL
238 Greenwich Ave., Greenwich, Connecticut 06830
CEO: Michele Quaranta, Mgr.
Bus: *Sales of hand-cut crystal.*
Tel: (203) 618-0900
Fax: (203) 618-9086
%FO: 100

BACCARAT CRYSTAL
South Coast Plaza, 3333 Bristol St., Costa Mesa, California 92626
CEO: Georgia Kaleb, Mgr.
Bus: *Sales of hand-cut crystal.*
Tel: (714) 435-9600
Fax: (714) 435-0703
%FO: 100

BACCARAT CRYSTAL
Union Square, 343 Powell St., San Francisco, California 94102
CEO: Kim Roberts, Mgr.
Bus: *Sales of hand-cut crystal.*
Tel: (415) 291-0600
Fax: (415) 291-9039
%FO: 100

BACCARAT CRYSTAL
73-111 El Paseo, Palm Desert, California 92260
CEO: Joyce Shampeny, Mgr.
Bus: *Sales of hand-cut crystal.*
Tel: (760) 346-6805
Fax: (760) 346-8498
%FO: 100

France

BACCARAT CRYSTAL
625 Madison Ave., New York, New York 10022
CEO: Richard Blachette, Mgr.
Bus: *Sales of hand-cut crystal.*

Tel: (212) 826-4100
Fax: (212) 826-5043

%FO: 100

BACCARAT CRYSTAL
13350 North Dallas Pkwy., Dallas, Texas 75240
CEO: Michelle Whiting, Mgr.
Bus: *Sales of hand-cut crystal.*

Tel: (972) 386-4100
Fax: (972) 386-7422

%FO: 100

BACCARAT CRYSTAL
Marshall Field's, 1/F, 111 North State St., Chicago, Illinois 60602
CEO: Carolyn Teeple, Mgr.
Bus: *Sales of hand-cut crystal.*

Tel: (312) 781-1000
Fax: (312) 781-3080

%FO: 100

BACCARAT CRYSTAL
The Galleria, 5085 Westheimer, Houston, Texas 77056
CEO: Bruce Padilla, Mgr.
Bus: *Sales of hand-cut crystal.*

Tel: (713) 572-4001
Fax: (713) 572-9573

%FO: 100

BACCARAT CRYSTAL
The Forum Shops at Caesars, 3500 Las Vegas Blvd. South, Ste. P-06, Las Vegas, Nevada 89109
CEO: Ruth Busser, Mgr.
Bus: *Sales of hand-cut crystal.*

Tel: (702) 693-6877
Fax: (702) 693-6738

%FO: 100

BACCARAT CRYSTAL
Somerset Collection, 2801 West Big Beaver Rd., Troy, Michigan 48084
CEO: Chris Coleman-Smith, Mgr.
Bus: *Sales of hand-cut crystal.*

Tel: (248) 822-2600
Fax: (248) 822-2082

%FO: 100

DOMAINE CARNEROS
1240 Duhig Rd., Napa, California 94559
CEO: Eileen Crane, Pres.
Bus: *Winery.*

Tel: (707) 257-0101
Fax: (707) 257-3020

%FO: 100
Emp: 25

HOTEL CHANDLER
12 E. 31st St., New York, New York 10016
CEO: Herb Chandler, Pres.
Bus: *Luxury hotel.*

Tel: (212) 889-6363
Fax: (212) 889-6699

%FO: 100

KOBRAND CORP.
134 East 40th St., New York, New York 10016
CEO: Charles Mueller, Chmn.
Bus: *Sale of wine & distilled beverages.*

Tel: (212) 490-9300
Fax: (212) 949-4645

%FO: 100
Emp: 150

THE COLONNADE HOTEL
120 Huntington Ave., Boston, Massachusetts 02116
CEO: Ronald Drucker, Pres.
Bus: *Luxury hotel.*

Tel: (617) 424-7000
Fax: (617) 424-1717

%FO: 100
Emp: 290

THE DYLAN HOTEL
52 East 41st St., New York, New York 10017
CEO: Christian Aldoy, Gen. Mgr.
Bus: *Luxury hotel.*

Tel: (212) 338-0500
Fax: (212) 338-0569

%FO: 100
Emp: 43

THE HELMSLEY PARK LANE HOTEL
36 Central Park South, New York, New York 10019
CEO: Leona Helmsley, Pres.   Tel: (212) 371-4000   %FO: 100
Bus: *Luxury hotel.*   Fax: (212) 319-9065

THE NEW YORK HELMSLEY
212 East 42nd St., New York, New York 10017
CEO: Leona Helmsley, Pres.   Tel: (212) 490-8900   %FO: 100
Bus: *Luxury hotel.*   Fax: (212) 986-4762   Emp: 400

● **SOCIÉTÉ GÉNÉRALE**
29, Boulevard Haussmann, F-75009 Paris, France
CEO: Daniel Bouton, Chmn. & CEO   Tel: 33-1-4214-2000   Rev: $20,000
Bus: *General commercial banking, private banking and* Fax: 33-1-4214-7555   Emp: 93,400
    asset management.   www.socgen.com
NAICS: 522110, 522293, 523110, 523920

    FIMAT USA INC.
    630 Fifth Ave., Ste. 500, New York, New York 10020-1001
    CEO: Cynthia Zeltwanger, COO   Tel: (646) 557-9000   %FO: 100
    Bus: *Securities broker/dealer.*   Fax: (646) 557-8480   Emp: 41

    SG COWEN & CO., LLC
    1221 Ave. of the Americas, New York, New York 10020
    CEO: Kim S. Fennebresque, CEO   Tel: (212) 278-4000   %FO: 100
    Bus: *International commercial banking services.* Fax: (212) 278-6789   Emp: 45

    SOCIETE GENERALE - Branch
    1221 Ave. of the Americas, New York, New York 10020
    CEO: Curt Welling   Tel: (212) 278-6000   %FO: 100
    Bus: *Investment management.*   Fax: (212) 278-6789

    SOCIETE GENERALE ENERGIE
    1221 Ave. of the Americas, 8/F, New York, New York 10020
    CEO: Christophe Leblanc, COO   Tel: (212) 278-5613   %FO: 100
    Bus: *Leasing and financing services.*   Fax: (212) 278-5689   Emp: 34

    THE TCW GROUP INC.
    865 S. Figueroa St., Ste. 1800, Los Angeles, California 90017
    CEO: Robert A. Day, Chmn. & CEO   Tel: (213) 244-0000   %FO: 60
    Bus: *Asset management services.*   Fax: (312) 244-0755

● **SODEXHO ALLIANCE**
3, ave. Newton, F-78180 Montigny-le-Bretonneux, France
CEO: Pierre Bellon, Chmn. & CEO   Tel: 33-1-3085-7500   Rev: $13,993
Bus: *Food and management services.*   Fax: 33-1-3043-0958   Emp: 312,975
    www.sodexho.com
NAICS: 561210, 561520, 722310, 722320, 722330

    RETAIL BRAND GROUP, LLC
    6081 Hamilton Blvd., Allentown, Pennsylvania 18106
    CEO: Damon Liever, Pres.   Tel: (610) 706-3900   %FO: 100
    Bus: *Casual dining restaurants.*   Fax: (610) 366-5466

SODEXHO, INC.
9801 Washingtonian Blvd., Gaithersburg, Maryland 20878
CEO: Richard Macedonia, Pres. & CEO
Bus: *Provides food and facilities management
    services.*
Tel: (301) 987-4500
Fax: (301) 987-4438
%FO: 100

UNIVERSAL SODEXHO
5749 Susitna Dr., Harahan, Louisiana 70123
CEO: Nicholas Japy, Pres. & CEO
Bus: *Foodservices.*
Tel: (504) 733-5761
Fax:
%FO: 100
Emp: 1,100

WOOD DINING SERVICES
6081 Hamilton Blvd., Allentown, Pennsylvania 18106
CEO: Robert C. Wood, Pres. & CEO
Bus: *Foodservices.*
Tel: (610) 395-3800
Fax: (610) 398-1599
%FO: 100
Emp: 14,000

● **SODIAAL SA**
170, bis blvd. du Montparnasse, F-75680 Paris Cedex 14, France
CEO: Gerard Budin, Chmn. & Mng. Dir.
Bus: *Mfr. milk ingredients for the food industry.*
Tel: 33-1-4410-9010
Fax: 33-1-4321-6299
www.sodiaal.fr
Rev: $3,300
Emp: 3,910

NAICS: 311511, 311513

  GENERAL MILLS INC./ YOPLAIT
  1 General Mills Blvd., Minneapolis, Minnesota 55426
  CEO: Ian Friendly, CEO
  Bus: *Sales/distribution of dairy products.*
  Tel: (763) 540-2311
  Fax:
  %FO: 100
  Emp: 90

● **SOGETI-TRANSICIEL SA**
6-8, rue Duret, F-75016 Paris, France
CEO: Luc-Francois Salvador, Chmn.
Bus: *Systems integration and IT services.*
Tel: 33-1-5844-5566
Fax: 33-1-5844-5570
www.sogeti-transiciel.com
Rev: $1,364
Emp: 14,000

NAICS: 541511, 541512

  SOGETI USA INC.
  7735 Paragon Rd., Ste. A, Dayton, Ohio 45459
  CEO: Navin Goel
  Bus: *Systems integration and IT services.*
  Tel: (937) 433-3334
  Fax: (937) 433-4048
  %FO: 100

● **SOITEC SA**
Parc Technologique des Fontaines, F-38190 Bernin, France
CEO: Andre Jacques Auberton-Herve, Chmn. & Pres.
    & CEO
Bus: *Semiconductor wafer manufacture.*
Tel: 33-4-7692-7500
Fax: 33-4-7692-7501
www.soitec.com
Rev: $107
Emp: 430

NAICS: 333295

  SOITEC USA INC.
  2 Centennial Dr., Peabody, Massachusetts 01960
  CEO: Andrew Wittkower, Pres.
  Bus: *Semiconductor wafer manufacture and sales.*
  Tel: (978) 531-2222
  Fax: (978) 531-2758
  %FO: 100
  Emp: 12

- **SOMFY SA**
  50 avenue Du Nouveau Monde, F-74307 Cluses, France
  CEO: Wilfrid Le Naour, CEO
  Bus: *Automatic controls and motors manufacture for awnings and interior blinds.*
  NAICS: 335312, 335314, 337920, 339999

  Tel: 33-4-5096-7000
  Fax: 33-4-6098-7089
  www.somfy.com

  Rev: $776
  Emp: 3,236

  SOMFY SYSTEMS INC.
  47 Commerce Dr., Cranbury, New Jersey 08512
  CEO: Bill Wilcox
  Bus: *Automatic controls and motors manufacture and sales for awnings and interior blinds.*

  Tel: (609) 395-1300
  Fax: (609) 395-1776

  %FO: 100

- **SONEPAR SA**
  43-47 avenue de la Grande Armee, F-75782 Paris Cedex 16, France
  CEO: Marie-Christine Coisne, Chmn. & CEO
  Bus: *Electrical equipment distribution; cables, trunkings, fittings, HVAC and lighting.*
  NAICS: 423610, 423690

  Tel: 33-1-5844-1313
  Fax: 33-1-5844-1300
  www.sonepar.com

  Rev: $8,284
  Emp: 19,700

  CAPITAL LIGHTING & SUPPLY, INC.
  3950 Wheeler Ave., Alexandria, Virginia 22304
  CEO: John Hardy, Pres.
  Bus: *Electrical products distribution.*

  Tel: (703) 823-6000
  Fax: (713) 823-1766

  %FO: 100

  COOPER ELECTRIC SUPPLY CO.
  70 Apple St., Tinton Falls, New Jersey 07724
  CEO: Greg Griswold, Pres.
  Bus: *Electrical products distribution.*

  Tel: (732) 747-2233
  Fax: (732) 576-8770

  %FO: 100
  Emp: 550

  EOFF ELECTRIC CO.
  1095 25th St. SE, Ste. A, Salem, Oregon 97301
  CEO: Jack Mumford, CEO
  Bus: *Electrical products distribution.*

  Tel: (503) 371-3633
  Fax: (503) 585-2286

  %FO: 100
  Emp: 140

  NORTHEAST ELECTRICAL DISTRIBUTORS
  135 Will Dr., Canton, Massachusetts 02021
  CEO: Carl D. Brand, Pres.
  Bus: *Electrical products distribution.*

  Tel: (781) 401-8500
  Fax: (781) 401-8596

  %FO: 100
  Emp: 288

  SONEPAR USA INC.
  1235 West Lakes Dr., Ste. 260, Berwyn, Pennsylvania 19312
  CEO: Tony Burr, Pres. & CEO
  Bus: *Electrical products manufacture and sales.*

  Tel: (610) 240-4950
  Fax: (610) 240-4951

  %FO: 100

  VIKING ELECTRIC SUPPLY
  451 Industrial Blvd. West, Minneapolis, Minnesota 55413
  CEO: Gregory Hames, Pres.
  Bus: *Electrical products distribution.*

  Tel: (612) 627-1300
  Fax: (612) 627-1310

  %FO: 100
  Emp: 450

- **SOPRA GROUP**
  9 bis, rue de Presbourg, F-75016 Paris, France
  CEO: Pierre Pasquier, Chmn. & Pres. & CEO
  Bus: *Information technology services.*

  Tel: 33-1-4067-2929
  Fax: 33-1-4067-2930
  www.sopra.com

  Rev: $858
  Emp: 7,500

  NAICS: 541511, 541512, 541519

  AXWAY, INC.
  3490 Piedmont Rd., Ste. 1220, Atlanta, Georgia 30305
  CEO: Paul Leiske, Gen. Mgr.
  Bus: *Information technology services.*

  Tel: (404) 842-7000
  Fax: (404) 842-7001

  %FO: 100

  VALORIS
  1101 Bloomfield St., Ste. C, Hoboken, New Jersey 07030
  CEO: Christine Goubet
  Bus: *Consulting & services.*

  Tel: (201) 216-0217
  Fax: (646) 405-1397

  %FO: 100

- **SOPREMA SA**
  14, rue de St Nazaire, BP 121, F-67025 Strasbourg, France
  CEO: Pierre E. Bindscheidler, CEO
  Bus: *Mfr./sale SBS modified roofing membranes.*

  Tel: 33-3-8879-8400
  Fax: 33-3-8879-8401
  www.soprema.fr

  Rev: $103
  Emp: 2,645

  NAICS: 238220, 324122

  SOPREMA INC
  310 Quadral Dr., Wadsworth, Ohio 44281-0471
  CEO: Pierre Bindschedler, Pres.
  Bus: *Mfr./sale SBS-modified roofing membranes.*

  Tel: (330) 334-0066
  Fax: (330) 334-4289

  %FO: 100
  Emp: 45

- **SOTHYS PARIS**
  128 rue du Faubourg Saint Honore, F-75008 Paris, France
  CEO: Bernard Mas, Chmn.
  Bus: *Skin care products.*

  Tel: 33-5-5517-4500
  Fax: 33-5-5523-3888
  www.sothys.com

  Emp: 200

  NAICS: 325620, 446120

  SOTHYS USA INC.
  1500 NW 94th Ave., Miami, Florida 33172
  CEO: Christian Garces, Pres.
  Bus: *Skin care products.*

  Tel: (305) 594-4222
  Fax: (305) 592-5785

  %FO: 100
  Emp: 43

- **SPOT IMAGE SA**
  5, rue des Satellites, BP 14 359, F-31030 Toulouse Cedex 4, France
  CEO: Herve Buchwalter, Chmn. & CEO
  Bus: *Satellite imagery provider.*

  Tel: 33-5-6219-4040
  Fax: 33-5-6219-4011
  www.spotimage.fr

  Rev: $46
  Emp: 213

  NAICS: 511199, 517410, 541330

  SPOT IMAGE CORPORATION
  14595 Avion Pkwy., Ste. 500, Chantilly, Virginia 20151
  CEO: Neal Carney, Pres.
  Bus: *Satellite imagery provider.*

  Tel: (703) 751-3100
  Fax: (703) 715-3120

  %FO: 100
  Emp: 14

- **STEDIM SA**
ZI des Paluds, Avenue de Jougues, BP 1051, F-13781 Aubagne, France
CEO: Thierry Favreau, CEO   Tel: 33-4-4284-5600   Rev: $87
Bus: *Sterile plastic container manufacture for*   Fax: 33-4-4284-5617   Emp: 442
     pharmaceutical industry.   www.stedim.com
   NAICS: 334510, 339111, 339112, 339113

     STEDIM, INC.
     1910 Mark Ct., Ste. 110, Concord, California 94520
     CEO: Chris Rombach, Pres.   Tel: (925) 689-6650   %FO: 100
     Bus: *Mfr. & design sterile single use bags for the*   Fax: (925) 689-6988   Emp: 65
       biopharmaceutical industry.

- **STRAT-X SA**
193-197, rue de Bercy, F-75582 Paris Cedex 12, France
CEO: Jean-Claude Larreche, Mng. Prtn.   Tel: 33-1-5346-6900
Bus: *Management development programs, strategic*   Fax: 33-1-5346-6901   Emp: 21
     planning and results- oriented consulting services.   www.stratx.fr
   NAICS: 541611, 541612

     STRAT-X INTERNATIONAL
     222 Third St., Ste. 3210, Cambridge, Massachusetts 02142
     CEO: Lucy Colombo, Mgr.   Tel: (617) 494-8282   %FO: 100
     Bus: *Management development programs,*   Fax: (617) 494-1421   Emp: 6
       strategic planning, results oriented
       consulting services.

- **SWORD GROUP**
9, avenue Charles de Gaulle, F-69370 Saint Didier au Mont d'Or, France
CEO: Jacques Mottard, Chmn. & Pres. & CEO   Tel: 33-4-7285-3740   Rev: $107
Bus: *IT consulting services.*   Fax: 33-4-7285-3780   Emp: 895
     www.sword-group.com
   NAICS: 541512

     SWORD GROUP
     1 New England Executive Park, Burlington, Massachusetts 01803
     CEO: ChristianTapia, Pres.   Tel: (781) 221-0365   %FO: 100
     Bus: *Computer related consulting & services.*   Fax:

     SWORD GROUP
     1250 Broadway, 18/F, New York, New York 10001
     CEO: ChristianTapia, Pres.   Tel: (212) 279-6734   %FO: 100
     Bus: *Computer related consulting & services.*   Fax: (212) 279-6733

     SWORD GROUP
     10921 Reed Hartman Corporate Center, Ste. 134,136 & 138, Cincinnati, Ohio 45242
     CEO: ChristianTapia, Pres.   Tel: (513) 792-7494
     Bus: *Computer related consulting & services.*   Fax:

- **SYSTAR, INC.**
171 Bureaux de la Colline, F-92213 Saint-Cloud Cedex, France
CEO: Guy T. Kuster, Chmn. & CEO
Bus: *Software manufacturer.*

Tel: 33-1-4911-4500
Fax: 33-1-4911-4545
www.systar.com

Rev: $13
Emp: 80

NAICS: 511210

SYSTAR, INC.
8000 Westpark Dr., Ste. 450, McLean, Virginia 22102
CEO: Laurent van Huffel, EVP
Bus: *Mfr./sales of software.*

Tel: (703) 556-8400
Fax: (703) 556-8430

%FO: 100
Emp: 20

- **SYSTRA**
5 Avenue Du Coq, F-75009 Paris, France
CEO: Philippe Citroen, Gen. Mgr.
Bus: *International consulting engineers for rail and urban transport.*

Tel: 33-1-4016-6100
Fax:
www.systra.com

Rev: $129
Emp: 1,100

NAICS: 541330

SYSTRA US
1515 Broad St., Bloomfield, New Jersey 07003-3069
CEO: James C. Greller, VP Mktg.
Bus: *International consulting engineers for rail and urban transport.*

Tel: (973) 893-6000
Fax: (973) 893-3131

%FO: 100

- **TAITTINGER SA**
9, Place Saint-Nicaise, F-51100 Rheims, France
CEO: Claude Taittinger, Chmn. & CEO
Bus: *Producer of champagne.*

Tel: 33-3-2685-4535
Fax: 33-3-2650-1430
www.taittinger.com

Rev: $119

NAICS: 312130, 721110

KOBRAND CORP.
134 East 40th St., New York, New York 10016
CEO: Charles Mueller, Chmn.
Bus: *Sale of wine/distilled beverages/eating places.*

Tel: (212) 490-9300
Fax: (212) 949-4645

Emp: 150

- **TAT GROUP**
47, rue Christiaan Huygens, F-37073 Tours Cedex, France
CEO: Rodolphe Marchais, Chmn. & CEO
Bus: *Mfr. aircraft equipment for major aviation and aerospace companies.*

Tel: 33-2-4742-3000
Fax: 33-2-4754-2950
www.tatgroup.com

NAICS: 532411, 811310

LIMCO AIREPAIR INC.
5304 South Lawton Ave., Tulsa, Oklahoma 74107
CEO: Shaul Menachem, Pres.
Bus: *Mfr. aircraft equipment for major aviation and aerospace companies.*

Tel: (918) 445-4300
Fax: (918) 446-2988

%FO: 100
Emp: 93

- **TECHNIP**
  Tour Technip, F-92973 Paris La Defense, France
  CEO: Daniel Valot, Chmn. & CEO
  Bus: *Oil and petrochemical engineering, construction and services.*
  NAICS: 213112, 236210, 237120, 237990, 333132

  Tel: 33-1-4778-2121
  Fax: 33-1-4778-3340
  www.technip-coflexip.com

  Rev: $6,964
  Emp: 19,000

  > **TECHNIP USA INC**
  > 1990 Post Oak Blvd., Houston, Texas 77056
  > CEO: Larry D. J. Pope, Pres. & CEO
  > Bus: *Engaged in engineering and construction.*
  >
  > Tel: (281) 249-2300
  > Fax: (281) 249-2325
  >
  > %FO: 100
  > Emp: 700

- **THALES COMPUTERS**
  150, rue Marcelin Berthelot, ZI de Toulon-Est . BP 244, F-83078 Toulon, France
  CEO: Alain Albarello, Chmn. & CEO
  Bus: *Computer technology services.*
  NAICS: 332995, 334111, 511210, 541511, 541512, 541519, 611420

  Tel: 33-4-9816-3400
  Fax: 33-4-9816-3401
  www.thales-computers.com

  Emp: 200

  > **THALES COMPUTERS**
  > 15455 Dallas Pkwy., Ste. 600, Addison, Texas 75001
  > CEO: Ed Holstien
  > Bus: *Computers.*
  >
  > Tel: (972) 764-5106
  > Fax: (972) 764-3430
  >
  > %FO: 100

  > **THALES COMPUTERS**
  > 3100 Spring Forest Rd., Raleigh, North Carolina 27616
  > CEO: Richard Goodell, Pres.
  > Bus: *Computers.*
  >
  > Tel: (919) 231-8000
  > Fax: (919) 231-8001

  > **THALES COMPUTERS**
  > 4456 Honeyglen Ct., Moorpark, California 93021
  > CEO: John De Leo
  > Bus: *Computers.*
  >
  > Tel: (805) 553-9454
  > Fax: (805) 531-9208
  >
  > %FO: 100

- **THALES GROUP**
  45 rue de Villiers, F-92526 Neuilly-sur-Seine, France
  CEO: Denis Ranque, Chmn. & CEO
  Bus: *Aerospace, defense, and information technology.*
  NAICS: 334511, 336412, 336413, 336414, 336419

  Tel: 33-1-5777-8000
  Fax: 33-1-5377-8659
  www.thalesgroup.com

  Rev: $13,267
  Emp: 57,439

  > **ARIANSPACE**
  > 601 13th St. NW, Ste. 710 N., Washington, District of Columbia 20005
  > CEO: Clayton Mowry, Pres.
  > Bus: *Satellite launch*
  >
  > Tel: (202) 628-3996
  > Fax: (202) 628-3949

  > **THALES**
  > 1 Corporate Commons, Ste. 302, 100 W. Common Blvd., New Castle, Delaware 19720
  > CEO: Dennis Ranque, Chmn.
  > Bus: *Electronic parts & equipment*
  >
  > Tel: (302) 326-4240
  > Fax: (302) 326-0837
  >
  > Emp: 434

THALES E-TRANSACTIONS
53 Perimeter Center East, Ste.175, Atlanta, Georgia 30346
CEO: William Peet, Pres.   Tel: (770) 393-2311
Bus: *Professional equipment*   Fax: (770) 393-2177   Emp: 32

THALES NORTH AMERICA
675 N. Washington St., Ste. 400, Alexandria, Virginia 22314
CEO: Lawrence Cavaiola, CEO   Tel: (703) 838-9685
Bus: *Management consulting services*   Fax: (703) 838-1688   Emp: 366

THALES RAYTHEON SYSTEMS CO. LTD.
1801 Hughes Dr., Fullerton, California 92834
CEO: Ron Levesque, CEO   Tel: (714) 446-3118
Bus: *Electronic parts& equipment*   Fax: (714) 446-3260   Emp: 750

● **THERMAL CERAMICS, INC.**
5 Boulevard Marcel Pourtout, F-92563 Rueil-Malmaison Cedex, France
CEO: John L. Simons, Chmn.   Tel: 33-1-4716-2223   Rev: $459
Bus: *Insulating fiber and firebricks manufacturer.*   Fax: 33-1-4716-2240   Emp: 2,600
www.thermalceramics.com

NAICS: 326150

    THERMAL CERAMICS, INC.
    2102 Old Savannah Rd., Augusta, Georgia 30906
    CEO: Miguel Pereyo   Tel: (706) 796-4200   %FO: 100
    Bus: *Insulating fiber and firebricks manufacture*   Fax: (706) 796-4398
        and sales.

● **THIEFFRY ET ASSOCIES**
23, ave. Hoche, F-75008 Paris, France
CEO: PatrickThieffry, Mng. Ptnr.   Tel: 33-1-4562-4554
Bus: *International law firm.*   Fax: 33-1-4225-8007
www.thieffry.com

NAICS: 541110

    THIEFFRY ET ASSOCIES
    630 Fifth Ave., Ste. 2518, New York, New York 10111
    CEO: Pierre Bailet, Mng. Assoc.   Tel: (212) 698-4550   %FO: 100
    Bus: *International law firm.*   Fax: (212) 698-4551

● **THOMSON SA**
46 Quai Alphonse Le Gallo, F-92100 Boulogne-Billancourt, France
CEO: Frank E. Dangeard, Chmn. & CEO   Tel: 33-1-4186-5000   Rev: $10,829
Bus: *Consumer electronics manufacturer.*   Fax: 33-1-4186-5859   Emp: 49,079
www.thomson.net

NAICS: 334210, 334310, 334411, 334419, 334611, 334612, 335211

    CONTENTGUARD, INC.
    6500 Rock Spring Dr., Ste. 110, Bethesda, Maryland 20817
    CEO: Bruce Giltin, CEO   Tel: (240) 694-1200
    Bus: *Content & document management software*   Fax: (240) 694-1297   Emp: 32

TECHNICOLOR INC.
3233 E. Mission Oaks Blvd., Camarillo, California 93012
CEO: Bana Banks, Dir.
Bus: *Film & video*
Tel: (805) 445-1122
Fax: (805) 445-4280

THOMSON INC.
10330 North Meridian St., Indianapolis, Indiana 46290
CEO: Dave Arland
Bus: *Consumer electronics manufacture and sales.*
Tel: (317) 587-4832
Fax: (317) 587-6708
%FO: 100

● **TONNELLERIE DEMPTOS SA**
BP 10, F-33 880 Saint Caprais de Bordeaux, France
CEO: Jerome Francois, CEO
Bus: *Barrel manufacture for wine.*
Tel: 33-5-5797-1250
Fax: 33-5-5678-7204
www.demptos.fr

NAICS: 321920

DEMPTOS NAPA COOPERAGE
1050 Soscol Ferry Rd., Napa, California 94558
CEO: Jerome Francois, Pres.
Bus: *Barrel manufacture for wine.*
Tel: (707) 257-2628
Fax: (707) 257-1622
%FO: 100
Emp: 50

● **TOTAL S.A..**
2, Place De La Coupole, La Defense 6, F-92400 Courbevoie, France
CEO: Thierry Desmarest, Chmn. & CEO
Bus: *Exploration, development and production of crude oil and gas and petrol-chemicals.*
Tel: 33-1-4744-5853
Fax: 33-1-4744-5824
www.total.com
Rev: $166,209
Emp: 111,401

NAICS: 211111, 211112, 213111, 221210, 324110, 324191, 324199, 333132, 424710, 424720, 447110, 447190, 454311, 454312, 454319, 486110, 486210, 486910, 541360

ARKEMA
2000 Market St.., Philadelphia, Pennsylvania 19103
CEO: Thierry Le Henaff, Chmn. & CEO
Bus: *Plastic & fiber manufacturing.*
Tel: (215) 419-7000
Fax: (215) 419-7591
%FO: 100
Emp: 19,300

BOSTIK
11320 Watertown Plank Rd., Wauwatosa, Wisconsin 53226
CEO: Michael A. Klonne, Pres.
Bus: *Industrial adhesives.*
Tel: (414) 774-2250
Fax: (414) 479-0645

COOK COMPOSITES and POLYMERS
820 E. 14th Ave., Kansas City, Missouri 64116
CEO: Charles E. Bennett, CEO
Bus: *Mfr. of gel coats, powder coating and composite resins, industrial cleaners and maintenance products.*
Tel: (816) 391-6000
Fax: (816) 391-6122
%FO: 100
Emp: 543

SARTOMER CHEMICAL, DIV. TOTAL FINA ELF
502 Thomas Jones Way, Exton, Pennsylvania 19341
CEO: Nicholas P. Trainer, Pres.
Bus: *Engaged in manufacture of resins and coatings and petro chemicals.*
Tel: (610) 363-4100
Fax: (610) 363-4140
%FO: 100
Emp: 373

TOTAL
444 Madison Ave., 42/F, New York, New York 10022
CEO: Robert Hammond, Pres.   Tel: (212) 922-3065
Bus: *Oil & gas explorations.*   Fax: (212) 922-3074   Emp: 2,371

TOTAL PETROCHEMICALS
15710 John F. Kennedy Blvd., Houston, Texas 77032
CEO: Jean-Pierre Seeuws, Pres.   Tel: (281) 227-5000
Bus: *Oil and gas exploration*   Fax: (281) 227-5025   Emp: 1,550

● **TRANSGENE S.A.**
11, rue de Molsheim, F-67082 Strasbourg Cedex, France
CEO: Philippe Archinard, CEO   Tel: 33-3-8827-9100   Rev: $3
Bus: *Biotechnology gene therapy R&D.*   Fax: 33-3-8822-5807   Emp: 170
        www.transgene.fr
NAICS: 325412

TRANSGENE INC.
5510 Nicholson Lane, Kensington, Maryland 20895-1078
CEO: Tel: (301) 816-5404
Bus: *Biotechnology gene therapy R&D.*   Fax: (301) 816-5439

● **UBI SOFT ENTERTAINMENT S.A.**
28, rue Armand Carrel, F-93108 Montreuil-sous-Bois, France
CEO: Yves Guillermot, Pres. & CEO   Tel: 33-1-4818-5000   Rev: $619
Bus: *Computer software & services, games &*   Fax: 33-1-4818-5282   Emp: 2,352
    entertainment software.   www.ubi.com
NAICS: 339932, 511210, 541519

RED STORM ENTERTAINMENT
3200 Gateway Centre Blvd., Ste. 100, Morrisville, North Carolina 27560
CEO: Yves Guillemont, Chmn. & CEO   Tel: (919) 460-1776
Bus: *Entertainment & games software.*   Fax: (919) 468-3305   Emp: 90

UBI SOFT ENTERTAINMENT, INC.
625 3rd. St., 3/F, San Francisco, California 94107
CEO: Laurent Detoc, Exec. Dir.   Tel: (415) 547-4000   %FO: 100
Bus: *Computer software & services, games &*   Fax: (415) 547-4001
    entertainment software.

WOLFPACK STUDIOS
3721 Executive Center Dr., Austin, Texas 78731
CEO: Yves Guillemot, Pres.   Tel: (512) 452-6200
Bus: *Sale of computers & peripherals.*   Fax: Emp: 25

● **VALEO SA**
43, rue Bayen, F-75017 Paris, France
CEO: Thierry Morin, Chmn. & CEO   Tel: 33-1-4055-2020   Rev: $12,875
Bus: *Mfr. automotive components.*   Fax: 33-1-4055-2171   Emp: 62,368
        www.valeo.com
NAICS: 336321, 336322, 336391, 336399

VALEO INC.
3000 University Dr., Auburn Hills, Michigan 48326
CEO: Hans-Peter Kunze, Dir.
Bus: *Mfr. automotive parts*

Tel: (248) 340-3000
Fax: (248) 340-8438

%FO: 100
Emp: 5,000

VALEO RAYTHEON SYSTEMS INC
3000 University Dr., Auburn Hills, Michigan 48326
CEO: Roland Lartigue, CEO
Bus: *Mfr. automotive parts*

Tel: (248) 340-3000
Fax: (248) 371-1122

%FO: 100

● **VALLOUREC SA**
130, rue de Silly, F-92100 Boulogne-Billancourt, France
CEO: Pierre Verluca, Chmn. & CEO
Bus: *Production of steel tubing.*

Tel: 33-1-4909-3800
Fax: 33-1-4909-3694
www.vallourec.fr

Rev: $4,144
Emp: 17,484

NAICS: 331210, 332996, 336312

V & M STAR
2669 Martin Luther King Jr. Blvd., Youngstown, Ohio 44510
CEO: Roger Lindgren, CEO
Bus: *Mfr. of seamless steel pipe.*

Tel: (330) 742-6300
Fax: (330) 742-6315

Emp: 570

V & M STAR, LP
8603 Sheldon Rd., Houston, Texas 77049
CEO: Jean-Yves LeCuziat, Chmn. & CEO
Bus: *Mfr. of hot-rolled seamless steel tubes.*

Tel: (281) 456-6000
Fax: (281) 456-0270

Emp: 561

VALLOUREC & MANNESMANN TUBES CORP.
1990 Post Oak Blvd., 14/F, Houston, Texas 77056-3813
CEO: David R Hamrick, Pres. & CEO
Bus: *Production of steel tubing.*

Tel: (713) 479-3200
Fax: (713) 479-3201

%FO: 100
Emp: 33

VALLOUREC INC.
414 Allegheny River Blvd., Ste. 202, Oakmont, Pennsylvania 15139
CEO: Robert Myers, Mgr.
Bus: *Production of steel tubing.*

Tel: (412) 828-7520
Fax: (412) 828-4386

%FO: 100

VALTIMET INC.
5501 Air Park Blvd., Morristown, Tennessee 37813
CEO: Alain Honnart, Pres.
Bus: *Mfr. of fabricated pipe fittings/ steel pipe tubes.*

Tel: (423) 587-1888
Fax: (423) 585-4215

Emp: 100

VAM PTS
19210 Hardy Rd., Houston, Texas 77073
CEO: Pierre Padovani, Chmn.
Bus: *Tubular pipe threading services.*

Tel: (281) 821-5510
Fax: (281) 821-7760

Emp: 158

● **VALTECH**
Immeuble Lavoisier, 4 place des Vosges, F-92052 La Defense, France
CEO: Jean-Yves Hardy, Chmn. & CEO
Bus: *E-commerce applications.*

Tel: 33-1-4188-2300
Fax: 33-1-4188-2301
www.valtech.com

Rev: $100
Emp: 639

NAICS: 511210, 541511, 541512, 541519

VALTECH INC.
8601 Six Forks Rd., Ste. 400, Raleigh, North Carolina 27615
CEO: Curis Hite, CEO   Tel: (919) 878-6690
Bus: *Management consulting for the software*   Fax: (413) 460-2724
     industry.

VALTECH INC.
5080 Spectrum Dr., Ste. 700 West, Addison, Texas 75001
CEO: Curtis Hite, Pres.   Tel: (972) 789-1200
Bus: *Management consulting for the software*   Fax: (972) 789-1340   Emp: 126
     industry.

VALTECH INC.
100 Wall St., New York, New York 10005
CEO: Curtis Hite, CEO   Tel: (212) 688-9900   %FO: 100
Bus: *Engaged in e-commerce applications.*   Fax: (212) 755-3368

VALTECH INC.
4610 South Ulster St., Denver, Colorado 80237
CEO: Cutis Hite, CEO   Tel: (720) 529-6100   %FO: 100
Bus: *Engaged in e-commerce applications.*   Fax: (720) 529-6161

VALTECH INC.
2 Allen Center, 1200 Smith St., 16/F, Houston, Texas 77002
CEO: Curtis Hite, CEO   Tel: (713) 659-3100   %FO: 100
Bus: *Engaged in e-commerce applications.*   Fax: (713) 353-4601

● **VEOLIA ENVIRONNEMENT, DIV. VIVENDI UNIVERSAL**
36-38 Avenue Kleber, F-75116 Paris, France
CEO: Henri Proglio, Chmn. & CEO   Tel: 33-1-7175-0000   Rev: $33,422
Bus: *Waste management, energy and water.*   Fax: 33-1-7171-1045   Emp: 309,563
                              www.veoliaenvironnement.com
NAICS: 221119, 221121, 221310, 221320, 485112, 485113, 485210, 541330, 541618, 541620, 541690, 561210, 562111, 562212

CONNEX NORTH AMERICA, INC.
8757 Georgia Ave., Ste. 1300, Silver Springs, Maryland 20910
CEO: Olivier Brousse, Pres. & CEO   Tel: (240) 485-2100
Bus: *Bus services*   Fax: (240) 485-2139

ONYX ENVIRONMENTAL SERVICES, L.L.C.
700 E. Butterfield Rd., Ste. 201, Lombard, Illinois 60148
CEO: Philippe Martin, Pres. & CEO   Tel: (630) 218-1500
Bus: *Remediation & environmental cleanup*   Fax: (630) 268-8973   Emp: 1,210
     services

ONYX NORTH AMERICA
700 E. Butterfield Rd., Ste. 201, Lombard, Illinois 60148
CEO: Michel Gourvennec, CEO   Tel: (630) 218-1500
Bus: *Solid waste services & recycling*   Fax: (630) 218-1828   Emp: 8,660

ONYX WASTE SERVICES, INC.
125 South 84th St., Ste. 200, Milwaukee, Wisconsin 53214
CEO: Paul R. Jenks, Pres. & CEO   Tel: (414) 479-7800   %FO: 100
Bus: *Solid waste services.*   Fax: (414) 479-7400   Emp: 3,700

VEOLIA WATER NORTH AMERICA OPERATING SERVICES, INC
14950 Heathrow Forest Pkwy., Ste. 200, Houston, Texas 77032
CEO: Michael M. Stark, Pres. & CEO — Tel: (281) 449-1500
Bus: *Water utilities.* — Fax: (281) 449-5970 — Emp: 3,100

● **VERRERIES BROSSE**
34 Rue Theodule Gerin, Vieux Rouen Sur Bresle, F-76390 Aumale, France
CEO: Giuseppe Breviari, Pres. — Tel: 33-2-3593-4502 — Rev: $28
Bus: *Distribution cosmetic and pharmaceuticals* — Fax: 33-2-3594-6944 — Emp: 295
  glassware. — www.zignago.com
NAICS: 327212, 423450

  BROSSE USA, INC.
  150 East 58th St., 21/F, New York, New York 10155
  CEO: Emanuel Mazzei, Pres. — Tel: (212) 832-1622 — %FO: 100
  Bus: *Mfr. /distribution glass containers for* — Fax: (212) 838-1995 — Emp: 4
    cosmetic/fragrance industry.

● **VICAT SA**
Tour Manhattan, 6 Place de l'Iris, F-92085 La Defense Cedex, France
CEO: Jacques Merceron-Vicat, Chmn. & CEO — Tel: 33-1-5886-8686 — Rev: $2,207
Bus: *Cement, chemicals and paper manufacture.* — Fax: 33-1-5886-8787 — Emp: 6,015
  www.vicat.com
NAICS: 212311, 212312, 212319, 212321, 327310, 327320

  NATIONAL CEMENT COMPANY OF ALABAMA
  2000 Southbridge Pkwy., Ste. 600, Birmingham, Alabama 35209
  CEO: Spencer Weitman, Pres. — Tel: (205) 423-2600 — %FO: 100
  Bus: *Cement, chemicals and paper manufacture.* — Fax: (205) 870-5777 — Emp: 150

  NATIONAL CEMENT COMPANY OF CALIFORNIA
  15821 Ventura Blvd., Ste. 475, Encino, California 91436
  CEO: D.J. Bidet, Pres. — Tel: (818) 728-5200 — %FO: 100
  Bus: *Cement, chemicals and paper manufacture.* — Fax: (818) 788-0615 — Emp: 1,254

● **VILMORIN CLAUSE & CIE**
4, quai de la Megisserie, F-75001 Paris, France
CEO: Daniel Cheron, CEO & Mng. Dir. — Tel: 33-4-7363-4195 — Rev: $595
Bus: *Producers of vegetable and flower seeds. (JV of* — Fax: 33-4-7363-4180 — Emp: 3,029
  Groupe Limagrain) — www.vilmorinclause.com
NAICS: 111219, 111422, 115114, 311119

  FERRY MORSE SEED COMPANY
  600 Stephen Beale Dr., PO Box 1620, Fulton, Kentucky 42041
  CEO: Jack Simpson, Pres. — Tel: (270) 472-3400 — %FO: 100
  Bus: *Sales/distribution of vegetable and flower* — Fax: (270) 472-3402 — Emp: 125
    seeds.

  HARRIS MORAN SEED COMPANY, INC.
  555 Codoni Ave., PO Box 4938, Modesto, California 95352
  CEO: Bruno Carette, Pres. — Tel: (209) 579-7333 — %FO: 100
  Bus: *Sales/distribution of vegetable and flower* — Fax: (209) 527-5312 — Emp: 250
    seeds.

HAZERA GENETICS
2250 E. Imperial Hwy., El Segundo, California 90245
CEO: Ely Saltz, CEO   Tel: (310) 563-2121
Bus: *Sales/distribution of vegetable and flower*   Fax: Emp: 5
seeds.

VILMORIN INC.
2551 North Dragon St., Tucson, Arizona 85745
CEO: Francisco Tirado, CEO   Tel: (520) 884-0011   %FO: 100
Bus: *Sales/distribution of vegetable and flower*   Fax: (520) 884-5102   Emp: 9
seeds.

● **VINCI**
1, Cours Ferdinand-de-Lesseps, F-92851 Rueil-Malmaison Cedex, France
CEO: Antoine Zacharias, Chmn. & CEO   Tel: 33-1-4716-3500   Rev: $22,733
Bus: *Construction.*   Fax: 33-1-4751-9102   Emp: 127,513
    www.groupe-vinci.com
NAICS: 236210, 236220, 237130, 237310, 237990, 488490, 541330, 812930

THE HUBBARD GROUP
1936 Lee Rd., Winter Park, Florida 32789
CEO: Luc Bodson, Pres.   Tel: (407) 645-5500   %FO: 100
Bus: *Engaged in construction.*   Fax: (407) 623-3865

WORLWIDE FLIGHT SERVICES, INC.
1925 W. John Carpenter Fwy., Ste. 450, Irving, Texas 75063
CEO: Oliver Bijaoui, Pres. & CEO   Tel: (800) 588-7484
Bus: *Airport management.*   Fax: (972) 629-5007   Emp: 9,300

● **VIRBAC SA**
13eme rue LID, F-06511 Carros Cedex, France
CEO: Jeanine Dick, Pres.   Tel: 33-4-9208-7100   Rev: $487
Bus: *Pharmaceutical manufacturer.*   Fax: 33-4-9208-7165   Emp: 2,200
    www.virbac.com

NAICS: 325411, 325412

VIRBAC CORPORATION
3200 Meacham Blvd., Fort Worth, Texas 76137
CEO: Erik Martinez, Pres. & CEO   Tel: (817) 831-5030   %FO: 100
Bus: *Animal health and pet care products sales.*   Fax: (817) 831-8327   Emp: 262

● **VIVENDI UNIVERSAL SA**
42, ave. de Friedland, F-75380 Paris Cedex 08, France
CEO: Jean-René Fourtou, Chmn. & CEO   Tel: 33-1-7171-1000   Rev: $29,026
Bus: *Telecommunications.*   Fax: 33-1-7171-1001   Emp: 55,451
    www.vivendiuniversal.com
NAICS: 334611, 334612, 511210, 512110, 512210, 512220, 512230, 515112, 515120, 515210, 517110, 517212, 517510, 517910

A&E TELEVISION NETWORKS
235 E. 45th St., New York, New York 10017
CEO: Abbe Raven, Pres. & CEO   Tel: (212) 210-1400
Bus: *Television cable, pay, & broadcast*   Fax: (212) 850-9370   Emp: 500
networks

BLIZZARD ENTERTAINMENT
PO Box 18979, Irvine, California 92623
CEO: Michael Morhaime, Pres.   Tel: (949) 955-1380
Bus: *Entertainment & games software.*   Fax: (949) 737-2000

BRAVO
30 Rockefeller Plaza, 14/F, New York, New York 10112
CEO: Lauren Zalaznick, Pres.   Tel: (212) 664-4444
Bus: *Cable, pay & broadcast television.*   Fax: (212) 664-5705

CANAL + GROUP
301 N. Canon Dr., Ste. 207, Beverly Hills, California 90210
CEO: Guy Lafarge   Tel: (310) 247-0994
Bus: *Pay TV operators.*   Fax: (310) 247-0998

CNBC, INC.
900 Sylvan Ave., Englewood Cliffs, New Jersey 07632
CEO: Pamela A. Thomas-Graham, Chmn.   Tel: (201) 735-2622
Bus: *Cable, pay & broadcast television.*   Fax: (201) 735-3200

FOCUS FEATURES
65 Bleecker St., 2/F, New York, New York 10012
CEO: James Schamus, Pres.   Tel: (212) 539-4000
Bus: *Motion picture production & distribution*   Fax: (212) 539-4099

INTERSCOPE GEFFEN A&M RECORDS
2220 Colorado Ave., Santa Monica, California 90404
CEO: Jimmy Iovine, Chmn.   Tel: (310) 865-1000
Bus: *Music publishing.*   Fax: (310) 965-7096

ISLAND DEF JAM
825 8th Ave., 28/F, New York, New York 10019
CEO: Antonio L.A. Reid, Chmn.   Tel: (212) 333-8000
Bus: *Music publishing.*   Fax: (212) 603-7931

MOTOWN RECORD COMPANY
1755 Broadway, 6/F, New York, New York 10019
CEO: Sylvia Rhone, Pres.   Tel: (212) 373-0750
Bus: *Music publishing.*   Fax: (212) 489-9096

MOVIE LINK
2120 Colorado Ave., 4/F, Santa Monica, California 90404
CEO: James Jim Ramo, CEO   Tel: (310) 264-4500
Bus: *Motion picture production & distribution*   Fax: (310) 264-4501

MSNBC CABLE
1 MSNBC Plaza, Secaucus, New Jersey 07094
CEO: Richard Kaplan, Pres.   Tel: (201) 583-5000
Bus: *Cable, pay & broadcast television.*   Fax: (201) 583-5453

MSNBC INTERACTIVE NEWS
1 Microsoft Way, Redmond, Washington 98052
CEO: Charles Tillinghast, Gen. Mgr.   Tel: (425) 882-8080
Bus: *Internet content providers.*   Fax: (425) 703-0415

NBC TELEVISION NETWORK
30 Rockefeller Plaza, New York, New York 10112
CEO: Randel A. Falco, Pres.   Tel: (212) 664-4444
Bus: *Television cable, pay, & broadcast*   Fax: (212) 664-4085
     networks

NBC UNIVERSAL
30 Rockefeller Plaza, New York, New York 10112
CEO: Robert C. Wright, Chmn. & CEO   Tel: (212) 664-4444
Bus: *Motion picture & video production*   Fax: (212) 664-4085

NBC UNIVERSAL CABLE
3000 W. Alameda Ave., Burbank, California 91523
CEO: David M. Zaslav, Pres.   Tel: (818) 840-4444
Bus: *Television cable, pay & broadcast*   Fax: (818) 840-4968
     networks.

NBC UNIVERSAL TELEVISION STUDIO
100 Universal City Plaza, Universal City, California 91608
CEO: Angela Bromstead, Pres.   Tel: (818) 777-1000
Bus: *television production & distribution* Fax: (818) 866-1430

PAXSON COMMUNICATION CORP.
601 Clearwater Park Rd., West Palm Beach, Florida 33401
CEO: Lowell W. Paxson, Chmn. & CEO   Tel: (561) 659-4122
Bus: *Television station groups.*   Fax: (561) 659-4252   Emp: 501

ROADRUNNER RECORDS
902 Broadway, 8/F, New York, New York 10010
CEO: Jonas Nachsin, Pres.   Tel: (212) 274-7500
Bus: *Music publishing.*   Fax: (212) 505-7469   Emp: 46

SCI FI CHANNEL
30 Rockefeller Center, New York, New York 10112
CEO: Bonnie Hammer, Pres.   Tel: (212) 413-5000
Bus: *Cable, pay & broadcast television.* Fax: (212) 413-6509

SEGA GAMEWORKS
600 N. Brand Blvd., 5/F, Glendale, California 91203
CEO: Ron Lam, CEO   Tel: (818) 254-4263
Bus: *Amusement parks, arcades*   Fax: (818) 254-4311

TELEMUNDO COMMUNICATIONS GROUP
2290 W. 8th Ave., Hialeah, Florida 33010
CEO: Donald Browne, Pres.   Tel: (305) 884-8200
Bus: *Television cable, pay & broadcast*   Fax: (305) 889-7980
     networks.

UNIVERSAL MUSIC ENTERPRISES
2220 Colorado Ave., Santa Monica, California 90404
CEO: Bruce Resnikoff, Pres.   Tel: (310) 865-5000
Bus: *Music publishing.*   Fax: (313) 865-5927

UNIVERSAL MUSIC GROUP
1755 Broadway, New York, New York 10019
CEO: Douglas Morris, Chmn. & CEO   Tel: (212) 841-8000
Bus: *Music publishing.*   Fax: (212) 331-2580   Emp: 10,700

UNIVERSAL MUSIC GROUP NASHVILLE
54 Music Sq. East, Ste. 300, Nashville, Tennessee 37203
CEO: Luke Lewis, Chmn.   Tel: (615) 524-7500
Bus: *Music publishing.*   Fax: (615) 524-7600

UNIVERSAL MUSIC PUBLISHING GROUP
2440 Sepulveda Blvd., Ste. 100, Los Angeles, California 90064
CEO: David Renzer, Chmn. & CEO   Tel: (310) 235-4700
Bus: *Music publishing.*   Fax: (310) 235-4900

UNIVERSAL PARKS & RESORTS
100 Universal City Plaza, Universal City, California 91608
CEO: Thomas L. Williams, Chmn. & CEO Tel: (818) 777-1000
Bus: *Amusement parks, arcades, & attractions* Fax: (818) 866-3600

UNIVERSAL PICTURES
100 Universal City Plaza, Universal City, California 91608
CEO: Rick Finkelstein, Pres. & COO   Tel: (818) 777-1000
Bus: *Motion picture production & distribution* Fax: (818) 777-6431

UNIVERSAL STUDIOS
100 Universal City Plaza, Universal City, California 91608
CEO: Ron Meyer, Pres. & COO   Tel: (818) 777-1000
Bus: *Motion picture production & distribution* Fax: (818) 866-3600

UNIVERSAL STUDIOS HOME ENTERTAINMENT
100 Universal City Plaza, Universal City, California 91608
CEO: Craig Kornblau, Pres.   Tel: (818) 777-1000
Bus: *Film & video*   Fax: (818) 866-3330

USA NETWORKS
30 Rockefeller Plaza, New York, New York 10112
CEO: Bonnie Hammer, Pres.   Tel: (212) 664-4444
Bus: *Television, cable, pay & broadcast* Fax: (212) 664-6365

VERVE MUSIC GROUP
1755 Broadway, 3/F, New York, New York 10019
CEO: Ron Goldstein, Pres. & CEO   Tel: (212) 331-2000
Bus: *Music publishing.*   Fax: (212) 331-2064

VIVENDI UNIVERSAL GAMES
6080 Center Dr., 10/F, Los Angeles, California 90045
CEO: Rene Penisson, Chmn.   Tel: (310) 431-4000
Bus: *Entertainment & games software.* Fax: (310) 342-0533

● **VIVENTURES PARTNERS SA**
21 Ave. Montaigne, F-75008 Paris, France
CEO: Philippe Charquet, Mng. Dir.   Tel: 33-1-5357-7700
Bus: *Engaged in venture capital.*   Fax: 33-1-5357-7718   Emp: 25
                          www.viventures.com
NAICS: 523999

VIVENTURES PARTNERS INC.
169 University Ave., 2/F, Palo Alto, California 94301
CEO: Thomas Heguy   Tel: (650) 566-8885   %FO: 100
Bus: *Venture capital.*   Fax: (650) 566-8882

● **VRANKEN POMMERY MONOPOLE**
5, Place Du General Gouraud, PO Box 1049, F-51689 Rheims Cedex 2, France
CEO: Paul-Francois Vranken, Pres.   Tel: 33-3-2661-6263   Rev: $316
Bus: *Production and distribution of champagne.*   Fax: 33-3-2661-6388   Emp: 557
www.vranken.net

NAICS: 312130

    VRANKEN AMERICA
    45 West 45th St., Ste. 905, New York, New York 10036
    CEO: Emanuel Des Mettre, Pres.   Tel: (212) 921-1215   %FO: 100
    Bus: *Sales and distribution of champagne.*   Fax: (212) 921-0204

● **WAVECOM SA**
3 Esplanade du Foncet, F-92442 Issy-les-Moulineaux, France
CEO: Aram Hekimian, CEO   Tel: 33-1-46-29-0800   Rev: $205
Bus: *Hardware and software manufacturer for wireless*   Fax: 33-1-46-29-0808   Emp: 516
    communications.   www.wavecom.com
NAICS: 334419

    WAVECOM INC.
    4810 Eastgate Mall, 2/F, San Diego, California 92121
    CEO: Pierre Piver, Pres.   Tel: (858) 362-0101   %FO: 100
    Bus: *Wholesale telecommunication equipment.*   Fax: (858) 558-5485   Emp: 32

● **WEBRASKA MOBILE TECHNOLOGIES SA**
22, rue Guynemer, F-78602 Maisons-Laffitte, France
CEO: Eric Node-Langlois, CEO   Tel: 33-1-3912-8800
Bus: *Provides wireless navigation, mapping and traffic-*   Fax: 33-1-3912-8888
    information services to carriers and car   www.webraska.com
    manufacturers.
NAICS: 488999, 517410, 517910, 519190, 561499

    WEBRASKA MOBILE TECHNOLOGIES
    12900 Saratoga Ave., Saratoga, California 95070
    CEO: Rama Aysola, Pres.   Tel: (408) 517-2200   %FO: 100
    Bus: *Provides wireless navigation, mapping and*   Fax: Emp: 120
    traffic-information services to carriers and
    car manufacturers.

● **XRT SA**
Tour Eve, Place Sud, La Defense 9, F-92806 Puteaux Cedex, France
CEO: Bruno Joseph, CEO   Tel: 33-1-46-92-6000   Rev: $55
Bus: *Software manufacturer.*   Fax: 33-1-46-92-6060   Emp: 350
www.xrt.com

NAICS: 511210, 541511, 541512, 541519, 611420

XRT USA INC.
1150 First Ave., Parkview Tower, Ste. 850, King of Prussia, Pennsylvania 19406
CEO: J.L. Alarcon, Gen. Mgr.   Tel: (610) 290-0300   %FO: 100
Bus: *Mfr./sales software.*   Fax: (610) 290-0308   Emp: 350

● **GROUPE ZODIAC SA**
2, rue Maurice Mallet, F-92137 Cedex Issy les Moulineaux, France
CEO: Jean-Louis Gerondeau, Chmn.   Tel: 33-1-4123-2323   Rev: $1,938
Bus: *Leisure marine inflatable products, aerospace*   Fax: 33-1-4648-7524   Emp: 11,237
safety products manufacture.   www.zodiac.fr
NAICS: 336412, 339920

C&D AEROSPACE INC.
5701 Bolsa Ave., Huntington Beach, California 92647
CEO: James E. Downey   Tel: (714) 934-0000   %FO: 100
Bus: *Airplane storage bins manufacture.*   Fax: (714) 934-0088

ZODIAC OF NORTH AMERICA INC.
540 Thompson Creek Rd., PO Box 400, Stevensville, Maryland 21666
CEO: Jean-Jacques Marie, Pres.   Tel: (410) 643-4141   %FO: 100
Bus: *Sales/distribution of leisure marine inflatable*   Fax: (410) 643-4491   Emp: 26
products and aerospace safety products.

French Guiana

- **EURO RESSOURCES S.A.**
  9, Lotissement Mont Joyeux, 97337 Cayenne, French Guiana
  CEO: Michel Juilland, Pres.
  Bus: *Exploration and development diamond and
  precious metal deposits.*
  NAICS: 212221, 212399

  Tel: 594-295-440
  Fax: 594-379-224
  www.gsr.com

  GOLDEN STAR RESOURCES LTD.
  10901 West Toller Dr., Ste. 300, Littleton, Colorado 80127
  CEO: Peter J. Bradford, Pres. & CEO
  Bus: *Mining & processing precious metals.*

  Tel: (303) 830-9000
  Fax: (303) 830-9094

  %FO: 100
  Emp: 1,150

Germany

- **ACLA-WERKE GMBH**
Frankfurter Strasse 142-190, D-51065 Cologne, Germany
CEO: Gerhard Kieffer, CEO
Bus: *Mfr. polyurethane molded parts.*
Tel: 49-221-697121
Fax: 49-221-699980
www.acla-werke.de
Emp: 600

NAICS: 326150

    ACLA USA INC.
    109 Thomson Park Dr., Cranberry Township, Pennsylvania 16066
    CEO: Andrew P. McIntyre, Pres.
    Bus: *Polyurethane molded parts manufacture and sales.*
    Tel: (412) 776-0099
    Fax: (412) 776-0477
    %FO: 100
    Emp: 5

- **ACO SEVERIN AHLMANN GMBH**
Am Ahlmannkai, Schleswig-Holstein, D-24782 Budelsdorf, Germany
CEO: Josef-Severin Ahlmann
Bus: *Polymer concrete, fiberglass and polypropylene trench drain systems and building products manufacture.*
Tel: 49-4331-3540
Fax: 49-4331-354130
www.aco-online.de
Rev: $157
Emp: 3,000

NAICS: 327390, 332919, 332996

    ACO POLYMER PRODUCTS, INC.
    12080 Ravenna Rd., PO Box 245, Chardon, Ohio 44024
    CEO: Derek Humphries, Pres.
    Bus: *Polymer concrete, fiberglass and polypropylene trench drain systems and building products manufacture.*
    Tel: (440) 285-7000
    Fax: (440) 285-7005
    %FO: 100
    Emp: 100

    AQUADUCT
    2819 Tophill Rd., Monroe, North Carolina 28110
    CEO: George Potter, Pres.
    Bus: *Construction materials*
    Tel: (704) 282-0400
    Fax: (704) 282-0403
    Emp: 20

- **ADIDAS-SALOMON AG**
Adi-Dassler-Strasse 1-2, Postfach 11 20, D-91074 Herzogenaurach, Germany
CEO: Herbert Hainer, Chmn. & CEO
Bus: *Footwear, sporting, athletic clothing and equipment manufacturer.*
Tel: 49-9132-84-0
Fax: 49-9132-84-2241
www.adidas.com
Rev: $7,866
Emp: 15,686

NAICS: 316211

    ADIDAS AMERICA, INC.
    9605 SW Nimbus Ave., Beaverton, Oregon 97008
    CEO: Jim Stutts, CEO
    Bus: *Athletic clothing, shoes.*
    Tel: (503) 972-2300
    Fax: (503) 797-4935
    %FO: 100
    Emp: 800

    ADIDAS ENTERTAINMENT PROMOTIONS
    3110 Main St., Ste. 225, Santa Monica, California 90405
    CEO: Russ Hopcus
    Bus: *Promotions.*
    Tel: (310) 396-5208
    Fax: (310) 396-5218

● **ADVA AG OPTICAL NETWORKING**
Fraunhoferstr. 9a, D-82152 Martinsried, Germany
CEO: Brian L. Protiva, CEO
Bus: *Optical communications products manufacture.*

Tel: 49-89-89-06-65-0
Fax: 49-89-89-06-65-199
www.advaoptical.com

Rev: $80
Emp: 400

NAICS: 333314

    ADVA OPTICAL NETWORKING INC.
    One International Blvd., Ste. 104, Mahwah, New Jersey 07495
    CEO: Alexa Schmidt, Mktg. Dir.
    Bus: *Marketing of optical communications products.*

Tel: (201) 258-8300
Fax: (201) 684-9200

%FO: 100

● **AEG ELEKTROFOTOGRAFIE GMBH**
Emil-Siepmann-Strasse 40, D-59581 Warstein-Belecke, Germany
CEO: Manfred Wagner, Chmn.
Bus: *Mfr. drums and photoconductors for a variety of imaging and printing markets.*
NAICS: 333293

Tel: 49-2902-861-359
Fax: 49-2902-861-350
www.aeg-photoconductor.com

Emp: 59,000

    AEG PHOTOCONDUCTOR CORPORATION
    27 Kiesland Ct., Hamilton, Ohio 45015
    CEO: Ron Roman, Mktg.
    Bus: *Mfr. photo-receptor drums.*

Tel: (513) 874-4939
Fax: (513) 874-5082

%FO: 100
Emp: 27

● **AERZENER MASCHINENFABRIK GMBH**
Reherweg 28, D-31855 Aerzen, Germany
CEO: Hans Jager, Pres.
Bus: *Blowers and compressors manufacture.*

Tel: 49-5154-810
Fax: 49-5154-81191
www.aerzener.de

NAICS: 532490

    AERZEN USA CORPORATION
    645 Sands Ct., Coatesville, Pennsylvania 19320
    CEO: K. Grant, Pres.
    Bus: *Sales/distribution of blowers and compressors.*

Tel: (610) 380-0244
Fax: (610) 380-0278

%FO: 100
Emp: 17

● **AIXTRON AG**
Kackertstrasse 15-17, D-52072 Aachen, Germany
CEO: Paul K. Hyland, CEO
Bus: *Semiconductor manufacture.*

Tel: 49-241-8909-0
Fax: 49-241-8909-445
www.aixtron.de

Rev: $115
Emp: 385

NAICS: 334413

    AIXTRON INC.
    1670 Barclay Blvd., Buffalo Grove, Illinois 60089
    CEO: Holger Juergensen
    Bus: *Semiconductor manufacture and sales.*

Tel: (847) 215-7335
Fax: (847) 215-7341

%FO: 100

- **ALDI GROUP**
Eckenbergstrasse 16, D-45307 Essen, Germany
CEO: Theo Albrecht, CEO
Bus: *Discount food retailer.*

  NAICS: 445110

  Tel: 49-201-8593-0
  Fax: 49-201-8593-319
  www.aldi.com

  Rev: $35,000

  ALDI
  1539 Alturas Dr., Burlingame, California 94010
  CEO: Vito Badalamenti, Sales
  Bus: *Discount food retailer.*

  Tel: (650) 342-9037
  Fax: (650) 342-9037

  %FO: 100

- **ALFRED KARCHER GMBH & CO.**
Alfred-KarcherStrasse 28-40, D-71349 Winnenden, Germany
CEO: Hartmut Jenner, Pres.
Bus: *Mfr. of cleaning equipment.*

  NAICS: 333319

  Tel: 49-7195-140
  Fax: 49-7195-142-212
  www.karcheruk.co.uk

  ALFRED KARCHER INC.
  2170 Satellite Blvd., Duluth, Georgia 30097-3799
  CEO: Joe James
  Bus: *Sales and support for high pressure washing products.*

  Tel: (732) 873-5002
  Fax: (732) 873-5002

  %FO: 100

- **ALLIANZ AG**
Koeniginstrasse 28, D-80802 Munich, Germany
CEO: Michael Diekmann, CEO
Bus: *Engaged in insurance; property and casualty insurance, life and health insurance,*

  NAICS: 524113, 524114, 524126

  Tel: 49-89-3800-0
  Fax: 49-89-3800-3425
  www.allianz.de

  Rev: $129,530
  Emp: 162,000

  ALLIANZ GLOBAL INVESTORS
  888 Newport Center Dr., Ste. 100, Newport Beach, California 92660
  CEO: Marna C. Whittington, CEO
  Bus: *Financial services.*

  Tel: (949) 219-2200
  Fax: (949) 219-2200

  %FO: 100

  ALLIANZ LIFE INSURANCE COMPANY OF NORTH AMERICA
  Box 1344, Minneapolis, Minnesota 55416
  CEO: Mark A. Zesbaugh, CEO
  Bus: *Fixed and variable annuities and life policies, group life and health, and long-term care products.*

  Tel: (763) 765-5200
  Fax: (763) 765-6500

  %FO: 100

  ALLIANZ OF AMERICA CORPORATION
  55 Greens Farms Rd., PO Box 5160, Westport, Connecticut 06881-5160
  CEO: Jan Carendi, CEO
  Bus: *Insurance services*

  Tel: (203) 221-8500
  Fax: (203) 221-8529

  %FO: 100

  CADENCE CAPITAL MANAGEMENT
  265 Franklin St, Boston, Massachusetts 02110
  CEO: Daniel P. Deter
  Bus: *Insurance.*

  Tel: (617) 624-3522
  Fax: (617) 722-0830

  %FO: 100

EULER HERMES ACI HOLDING INC.
800 Red Brook Blvd., Owings Mills, Maryland 21117
CEO: Paul Overeem
Bus: *Credit insurance services.*

Tel: (877) 883-3224
Fax: (877) 883-3224

%FO: 100

FIREMAN'S FUND AGRIBUSINESS
10895 Lowell Ave., Overland Park, Kansas 66210
CEO: Chuck Kavitsky
Bus: *Insurance services.*

Tel: (913) 338-7800
Fax: (913) 338-7888

%FO: 100

FIREMAN'S FUND MCGEE MARINE
One Market Plaza, Spear Street Tower, 11/F, San Francisco, California 94105
CEO: John M.Kozero, Pres.
Bus: *Marine insurance.*

Tel: (415) 899-2166
Fax: (415) 541-4441

%FO: 100

NFJ INVESTMENT GROUP
2121 San Jacinto St., Ste. 1840, Dallas, Texas 75201
CEO: Merrill L. Posey, Mng. Dir.
Bus: *Financial and investment services.*

Tel: (214) 754-1780
Fax: (214) 754-1780

%FO: 100

● **ALMATIS GMBH**
Olof-Palme-Str. 37, D-60439 Frankfurt, Germany
CEO: D. Oscar Groomes, CEO
Bus: *Mfr. alumina-based products.*

Tel: 49-69-957-3410
Fax: 49-69-957-341-13
www.almatis.com

Rev: $450
Emp: 900

NAICS: 325188

ALMATIS USA INC.
109 Highway 131, Vidalia, Louisiana 71373
CEO: Elise M. Mophett
Bus: *Mfr. alumina-based products.*

Tel: (318) 336-9601
Fax: (318) 336-9922

%FO: 100

ALMATIS USA INC.
501 West Park Rd., Leetsdale, Pennsylvania 15056
CEO: Alex De Bonth
Bus: *Mfr. alumina-based products.*

Tel: (412) 630-2800
Fax: (412) 630-2900

%FO: 100

ALMATIS USA INC.
4701 Alcoa Rd., Bauxite, Arkansas 72001
CEO: Edwin Black
Bus: *Mfr. alumina-based products.*

Tel: (501) 776-4654
Fax: (501) 776-4706

%FO: 100

● **ALTANA AG**
Herbert-Quandt-Haus, Am Pilgerrain 15, D-61352 Bad Homburg, Germany
CEO: Nikolaus Schweickart, CEO
Bus: *Pharmaceuticals, dietetics and infant foods
manufacturer.*

Tel: 49-6172-17-12-0
Fax: 49-6172-1712365
www.altana.com

Rev: $4,013
Emp: 10,783

NAICS: 311422, 325411

ALTANA PHARMA USA
60 Baylis Rd., Melville, New York 11747-3838
CEO: George Cole
Bus: *Pharmaceuticals, dietetics and infant foods
manufacturer.*

Tel: (631) 454-7677
Fax: (631) 454-7677

%FO: 100

ALTANA PHARMA USA
712 Fifth Ave., New York, New York 10019
CEO: Markus A Launer
Bus: *Pharmaceuticals, dietetics and infant foods manufacturer.*

Tel: (212) 974-9800
Fax: (212) 974-9800

%FO: 100

ALTANA PHARMA USA
210 Park Ave., Florham Park, New Jersey 07932
CEO: George Cole, Pres.
Bus: *Pharmaceuticals, dietetics and infant foods manufacturer.*

Tel: (973) 514-4240
Fax: (973) 514-4240

%FO: 100

● **ARTICON-INTEGRALIS AG**
Gutenbergstrasse 1, D-85737 Ismaning, Germany
CEO: Mark J. Silver, CEO
Bus: *Computer network and data security products manufacture.*
NAICS: 511210

Tel: 49-89-945733-0
Fax: 49-89-945733-49
www.articon-integralis.com

Rev: $220
Emp: 650

ARTICON-INTEGRALIS
111 Founders Plaza, 13/F, East Hartford, Connecticut 06108
CEO: Amy Blakley
Bus: *Computer network and data security products manufacture and sales.*

Tel: (860) 291-0851
Fax: (860) 291-0847

%FO: 100

● **ARVATO AG, SUB. BERTELSMANN**
Carl-Bertelsmann-Strasse 161, D-33311 Gutersloh, Germany
CEO: Harmut Ostrowski, CEO
Bus: *Media and business services.*
NAICS: 323110, 323117, 323119, 334611, 334612, 541840, 561422

Tel: 49-52-41-80-0
Fax: 49-52-41-80-3315
www.arvato.com

Rev: $3,756
Emp: 33,557

ARVATO SYSTEMS NORTH AMERICA INC.
6550 East 30th St., Indianapolis, Indiana 46219
CEO: Frank Zimmermann
Bus: *Digital content media services.*

Tel: (317) 542-6337
Fax: (317) 542-6337

ARVATO SYSTEMS NORTH AMERICA INC.
112 Hidden Lake Circle, Duncan, South Carolina 29334
CEO: George Mulling
Bus: *Digital content media services.*

Tel: (864) 433-5074
Fax: (864) 433-5074

ARVATO SYSTEMS NORTH AMERICA INC.
1540 Broadway, 11/F, New York, New York 10036
CEO: Anthony Yi
Bus: *Digital content media services.*

Tel: (212) 782-1225
Fax: (212) 782-7689

%FO: 100

SONOPRESS USA
109 Monticello Rd., Weaverville, North Carolina 28787-9442
CEO: Joe Mann-Stadt, Pres. & CEO
Bus: *Produces CD's for music, software and video.*

Tel: (828) 658-2000
Fax: (828) 658-2008

%FO: 100

- **ATB ANTRIEBSTECHNIK AG**
Silcherstrasse 74, D-73642 Welzheim, Germany
CEO: Dr. Mirko Kovats, Chmn.
Bus: *Mfr. electrical and mechanical motors and electrical equipment.*
NAICS: 423610

Tel: 49-7182-141
Fax: 49-7182-2887
www.atb.de

Rev: $144
Emp: 1,400

> **LOHER DRIVE SYSTEMS, INC.**
> 1240 Johnson Ferry Place, Marietta, Georgia 30086
> CEO: Dr. Joerg Recktenwald, Pres.
> Bus: *Mfr. standard motors for unregulated drive applications.*
>
> Tel: (770) 977-8650
> Fax: (770) 977-8650
>
> %FO: 100

- **AUDI, DIV. OF VOLKSWAGEN**
Finanzanalytik und Publizitat, I/FF 12, D-85045 Ingolstadt, Germany
CEO: Martin Winterkorn, CEO
Bus: *Automobile manufacturer.*
NAICS: 336111

Tel: 49-841-89-40300
Fax: 49-841-89-30900
www.audi.com

Rev: $33,426
Emp: 53,144

> **AUDI OF AMERICA, INC.**
> 3800 Hamlin Rd., Auburn Hills, Michigan 48326-2829
> CEO: Stephen Berkov, VP
> Bus: *Automobile manufacturer.*
>
> Tel: (248) 340-5000
> Fax: (248) 340-4960
>
> %FO: 100

- **AXA KONZERN AG, DIV. AXA**
Gereonsdriesch 9-11, D-50670 Cologne, Germany
CEO: Claas Kleyboldt, Chmn.
Bus: *Health, life, accident and pension insurance services.*
NAICS: 524113

Tel: 49-221-148-105
Fax: 49-221-148-22740
www.axa.de

Rev: $13,026
Emp: 8,196

> **AXA ART INSURANCE INC.**
> 4 West 58th St., 8/F, New York, New York 10019-2515
> CEO: Dietrich Von Frank, VP
> Bus: *Health, life, accident and pension insurance services.*
>
> Tel: (212) 415-8400
> Fax: (212) 415-8420
>
> %FO: 100

- **AXEL SPRINGER-VERLAG AG**
Axel-Springer-Platz 1, D-20350 Hamburg, Germany
CEO: Mathias Dopfner, CEO
Bus: *Publishing science, technical, medical books, journals & electronic media.*
NAICS: 511120, 511130, 516110

Tel: 49-40-347-22370
Fax: 49-40-347-29037
www.asv.de

Rev: $3,056
Emp: 11,694

> **SPRINGER-VERLAG NEW YORK INC.**
> 333 Meadowlands Pkwy., Secaucus, New Jersey 07094
> CEO: Dennis Looney
> Bus: *Science technical books, journals.*
>
> Tel: (201) 348-4033
> Fax: (201) 617-5975
>
> %FO: 100

SPRINGER-VERLAG NEW YORK INC.
175 Fifth Ave., New York, New York 10010
CEO: Peter Hendriks, Editor
Bus: *Science technical books, journals.*
Tel: (212) 460-1500
Fax: (212) 473-6272
%FO: 100
Emp: 250

● **AZO GMBH & COMPANY**
Rosenberger Straße 24, D-74706 Osterburken, Germany
CEO: Rudi Baumann, Mng. Dir.
Bus: *Ingredient automation systems manufacture.*
Tel: 49-6291-8920
Fax: 49-6291-8928
www.azo.de
Rev: $138
Emp: 767

NAICS: 423420

   AZO INC.
   4445 Malone Rd., Memphis, Tennessee 38118
   CEO: Robert F. Moore, Pres.
   Bus: *Ingredient automation systems manufacture.*
Tel: (901) 794-9480
Fax: (901) 794-9934
%FO: 100
Emp: 93

● **BAHLSEN GMBH & CO. KG**
Podbielskistrasse 11, D-30163 Hannover, Germany
CEO: Werner M. Bahlsen, Chmn.
Bus: *Mfr. biscuits and snacks.*
Tel: 49-511-960-0
Fax: 49-511-960-2749
www.bahlsen.de
Rev: $485
Emp: 3,900

NAICS: 311821

   BAHLSEN GMBH & CO.
   1335 North Fairfax Ave., Ste. 6, West Hollywood, California 90046
   CEO: Sonke Renk
   Bus: *Mfr. biscuits and snacks.*
Tel: (323) 850-7093
Fax: (323) 850-6693
%FO: 100

● **BASF AKTIENGESELLSCHAFT**
Carl-Bosch Str. 38, D-67056 Ludwigshafen, Germany
CEO: Jurgen Hambrecht, Chmn.
Bus: *Oil and gas, petrochemicals, agricultural, plastics and fibers, chemicals, dyestuffs, finishing, and consumer products.*
Tel: 49-621-60-0
Fax: 49-621-60-42525
www.basf.com
Rev: $51,573
Emp: 81,955

NAICS: 211111, 211112, 213111, 213112, 325110, 325120, 325131, 325132, 325181, 325188, 325192, 325199, 325211, 325212, 325221, 325222, 325311, 325312, 325320, 325510, 325520, 325998, 326199

   BASELL NORTH AMERICA
   912 Appleton Rd., Elkton, Maryland 21921
   CEO: Randy Woelfel, Pres.
   Bus: *Plastic & fiber manufacturing*
Tel: (410) 996-1600
Fax: (410) 996-2121
Emp: 1,500

   BASF CORPORATION
   100 Campus Dr., Florham Park, New Jersey 07932
   CEO: Klaus Peter Lobbe, Chmn. & CEO
   Bus: *Chemical manufacturing*
Tel: (973) 245-6000
Fax: (973) 245-6714
Emp: 11,002

● **CHRISTIAN BAUER GMBH & CO.**
Schorndorfer Str. 49, D-73642 Welzheim, Germany
CEO: Helmut Hutt, Gen Dir.   Tel: 49-7182-121
Bus: *Mfr. spring elements and precision components,*   Fax: 49-71821-2315   Emp: 536
       jewelry and precious metals.   www.bauersprings.com
NAICS: 332611

> **BAUER SPRINGS INC**
> 509 Parkway View Dr., Pittsburgh, Pennsylvania 15205
> CEO: Helmut Hutt, Pres.   Tel: (412) 787-7930   %FO: 100
> Bus: *Engineering/distribution disc springs.*   Fax: (412) 787-3882   Emp: 4

● **BAYER AG**
PF Centre Monheim, D-51368 Leverkusen, Germany
CEO: Werner Wenning, Chmn.   Tel: 49-2-1430-8992   Rev: $30,400
Bus: *Holding company for healthcare, imaging*   Fax: 49-2-1430-81146   Emp: 122,600
       technologies, agricultural, industrial products, www.bayer.com
       chemicals, polymer industries.
NAICS: 325314, 325411, 325412, 334517, 551112

> **BAYER CONSUMER CARE**
> 36 Columbia Rd., PO Box 1910, Morristown, New Jersey 07962-0910
> CEO: Timothy G. Hayes, Pres.   Tel: (973) 254-5000   %FO: 100
> Bus: *Consumer products division.*   Fax: (973) 408-8000

> **BAYER CORP.**
> 95 Chestnut Ridge Rd., Montvale, New Jersey 07645
> CEO: Gordon.Morrison   Tel: (201) 307-9700   %FO: 100
> Bus: *Crop science.*   Fax: (201) 307-9700

> **BAYER CORPORATION (US)**
> 100 Bayer Rd., Pittsburgh, Pennsylvania 15205-9741
> CEO: Attila Molnar, CEO   Tel: (412) 777-2000   %FO: 100
> Bus: *Headquarters US. Chemicals, healthcare,*   Fax: (412) 777-2447   Emp: 23,000
>   *imaging technologies, agricultural, industrial*
>   *products, chemicals, polymer industries.*

> **BAYER CORPORATION POLYMERS**
> 100 Bayer Rd., Pittsburgh, Pennsylvania 15205-9741
> CEO: Attila Molnar, Pres.   Tel: (412) 777-2000   %FO: 100
> Bus: *Mfr./sales industrial chemicals.*   Fax: (412) 777-4959

> **BAYER HEALTHCARE**
> 511 Benedict Ave., Tarrytown, New York 10591-5097
> CEO: Rolf Classon   Tel: (914) 631-8000   %FO: 100
> Bus: *Healthcare diagnostics division.*   Fax: (914) 524-2132

> **BAYER PHARMACEUTICAL DIV.**
> 400 Morgan Lane, West Haven, Connecticut 06516-4175
> CEO: Paolo Pucci, Pres.   Tel: (203) 812-2000   %FO: 100
> Bus: *R&D/mfr./sales ethical pharmaceuticals.*   Fax: (203) 812-5554

BIOLOGICAL PRODUCTS
79 T.W. Alexander Dr., Research Triangle Park, North Carolina 27709
CEO: Joseph A. Akers
Bus: *Hemostatis products.*
Tel: (919) 316-6396
Fax: (919) 316-6684
%FO: 100

● **BAYERISCHE HYPO-UND VEREINSBANK AG (HVB)**
Am Tucherpark 16, D-80538 Munich, Germany
CEO: Dieter Rampl, CEO
Bus: *General commercial banking services.*
Tel: 49-89-378-0
Fax: 49-89-378-27784
www.hvbgroup.com
Rev: $28,209
Emp: 57,806
NAICS: 522110, 522292, 522294, 522310, 523120, 523920, 523930

HVB CAPITAL MARKETS, INC.
150 East 42nd St., New York, New York 10017
CEO: George Medinger, Pres.
Bus: *International commercial banking services.*
Tel: (212) 672-6000
Fax: (212) 672-5500
%FO: 100
Emp: 300

HVB CORPORATES & MARKETS
150 East 42nd St., New York, New York 10017
CEO: Bernd Volk
Bus: *International commercial banking services.*
Tel: (212) 672-6000
Fax: (212) 672-5555

● **BAYERISCHE LANDESBANK**
Brienner Strasse 18, D-80333 Munich, Germany
CEO: Werner Schmidt, Chmn.
Bus: *General commercial banking services.*
Tel: 49-89-217-101
Fax: 49-89-217-13579
www.bayernlb.de
Rev: $17,113
Emp: 9,061
NAICS: 522110

BAYERISCHE LANDESBANK
560 Lexington Ave., New York, New York 10022
CEO: David John, VP
Bus: *International commercial banking services.*
Tel: (212) 310-9800
Fax: (212) 310-9841
%FO: 100
Emp: 170

● **BEATE UHSE AG**
Gutenbergstr. 12, D-24941 Flensburg, Germany
CEO: Ulrich Rotermund, Chmn.
Bus: *Adult entertainment and related lingerie, toys and videos, including latex manufacture and telephone sex networks.*
Tel: 49-461-9966-0
Fax: 49-461-9966-440
www.beate-uhse.ag
Rev: $379
Emp: 1,477
NAICS: 325212, 448110, 448120, 448150, 448190, 448190, 453998, 454111, 454113, 516110, 713990

DUTCH FINEST FANTASIES
20717 Marilla St., Chatsworth, California 91311
CEO: Gerard Cok
Bus: *Porn retailer.*
Tel: (818) 885-3300
Fax: (818) 885-5747
%FO: 100

● **BEHR GROUP**
Heilbronner Strasse 380, D-70469 Stuttgart, Germany
CEO: Dr. Markus Flik, Chmn.
Bus: *Mfr. automobile air conditioning and engine cooling systems.*
Tel: 49-711-896-3073
Fax: 49-711-896-3075
www.behrgroup.com
Rev: $17,100
Emp: 11,400
NAICS: 336391, 423730

BEHR AMERICA INC.
4500 Leeds Ave., Charleston, South Carolina 29405
CEO: Hans-Joachim Lange, Pres.   Tel: (843) 745-1233   %FO: 100
Bus: *Engine cooling and air conditioning for*   Fax: (843) 745-1285   Emp: 950
     automotive industry.

BEHR AMERICA, INC.
850 Ladd Rd., Bldg. A, Walled Lake, Michigan 48390-3026
CEO: Frank Mueller   Tel: (248) 624-7020   %FO: 100
Bus: *Engine cooling and air conditioning for*   Fax: (248) 624-9111
     automotive industry.

BEHR DAYTON THERMAL PRODUCTS INC.
1600 Webster St., Dayton, Ohio 45404
CEO: Wilhelm Baum   Tel: (937) 224-2383   %FO: 100
Bus: *Engine cooling and air conditioning for*   Fax: (937) 224-2383
     automotive industry.

BEHR HEAT TRANSFER SYSTEMS, INC.
47920 Fifth St., Canton, South Dakota 57013-5802
CEO: Mike Adams, Mgr.   Tel: (605) 764-2347   %FO: 100
Bus: *Engine cooling and air conditioning for*   Fax: (605) 764-1283
     automotive industry.

BEHR OF AMERICA INC., CLIMATE SYSTEMS
2301 Franklin Dr., Ft. Worth, Texas 76106
CEO: Harrel Alcorn   Tel: (817) 624-7267   %FO: 100
Bus: *Engine cooling and air conditioning for*   Fax: (817) 624-7267
     automotive industry.

● **BEIERSDORF AG**
Unnastrasse 48, D-20253 Hamburg, Germany
CEO: Thomas-Bernd Quaas, Chmn.   Tel: 49-40-4909-0   Rev: $4,970
Bus: *Mfr. toiletries, pharmaceuticals, medical products,* Fax: 49-40-4909-3434   Emp: 18,180
     tapes.   www.beiersdorf.com
NAICS: 325412, 325611, 325620

BEIERSDORF JOBST INC.
1348 Eagle Valley Dr., Greenwood, Indiana 46143
CEO: Jim Kenton, Mgr.   Tel: (317) 882-9785   %FO: 100
Bus: *Medical products manufacture.*   Fax: (317) 882-9785

BEIERSDORF JOBST, INC.
5825 Carnegie Boulevard, Charlotte, North Carolina 28209
CEO: Tammy Fischer, Pres.   Tel: (704) 554-9933   %FO: 100
Bus: *U.S. headquarters. Mfr. toiletries,*   Fax: (704) 553-5853
     pharmaceuticals, medical products, tapes.

BEIERSDORF, INC.
187 Danbury Rd., Wilton, Connecticut 06897
CEO: Rich Travers, Pres.   Tel: (203) 563-5800   %FO: 100
Bus: *Mfr. toiletries, medical products. Nivea &* Fax: (203) 563-5895   Emp: 400
     Eucerin brand products.

TESA TAPE INC.
5825 Carnegie Boulevard, Charlotte, North Carolina 28209
CEO: Daniel Germain, Pres.
Bus: *Mfr. pressure sensitive tape.*

Tel: (704) 554-0707
Fax: (704) 553-5853

%FO: 100
Emp: 100

● **BENEDIKT TASCHEN**
Hohenzollernring 53, D-50672 Cologne, Germany
CEO: Benedikt Taschen, CEO
Bus: *Publishing.*

Tel: 49-221-2018-00
Fax: 49-221-2549-19
www.taschen.com

NAICS: 511130

TASCHEN INC.
6671 Sunset Blvd., Ste. 1508, Los Angeles, California 90028
CEO: Paul Norton
Bus: *Publishing.*

Tel: (323) 463-4441
Fax: (323) 463-4442

%FO: 100

● **BENTELER AUTOMOTIVE GMBH & CO.**
An der Talle 27-31, D-33102 Paderborn, Germany
CEO: Hubertus Benteler, Pres.
Bus: *Mfr. automotive parts, steel tubing, machine
tooling and steel distribution.*

Tel: 49-5254-81-0
Fax: 49-5251-408-346
www.benteler.com

Rev: $2,500
Emp: 12,000

NAICS: 331210, 336399

BENTELER AUTOMOTIVE CORPORATION
9000 E Michigan, Galesburg, Michigan 49053
CEO: Bill Nieboer
Bus: *Mfr. of metal fabricated products: chassis,
front exhaust, impact management, and
stamping systems.*

Tel: (269) 665-4261
Fax: (269) 665-4261

%FO: 100

BENTELER AUTOMOTIVE CORPORATION
1780 Pond Run, Auburn Hills, Michigan 48326
CEO: Walter Frankiewicz, Pres.
Bus: *Mfr. of metal fabricated products: chassis,
front exhaust, impact management, and
stamping systems.*

Tel: (248) 377-9999
Fax: (248) 364-7142

%FO: 100
Emp: 1,800

BENTELER AUTOMOTIVE CORPORATION
3721 Hagen Dr. SE, Grand Rapids, Michigan 49548
CEO: Dave Passmore
Bus: *Mfr. of metal fabricated products: chassis,
front exhaust, impact management, and
stamping systems.*

Tel: (616) 245-4607
Fax: (616) 245-4607

%FO: 100

BENTELER AUTOMOTIVE CORPORATION
910 S. Eisenhower, Goshen, Indiana 46526
CEO: Ed Steinebach
Bus: *Mfr. of metal fabricated products: chassis,
front exhaust, impact management, and
stamping systems.*

Tel: (574) 534-1499
Fax: (574) 534-1499

%FO: 100

BENTELER AUTOMOTIVE CORPORATION
4401 N. Park Dr., Opelika, Alabama 36801
CEO: Rick Harman
Bus: *Mfr. of metal fabricated products: chassis, front exhaust, impact management, and stamping systems.*

Tel: (334) 364-1535
Fax: (334) 364-1535

%FO: 100

BENTELER STEEL & TUBE CORPORATION
1300 Post Oak Blvd., Ste. 2250, Houston, Texas 77056
CEO: Walter Frankiewicz
Bus: *Mfr. of metal fabricated products: chassis, front exhaust, impact management, and stamping systems.*

Tel: (713) 629-9111
Fax: (713) 629-9993

%FO: 100

● **BERTELSMANN AG**
Carl-Bertelsmann-Str. 270, D-33311 Gutersloh, Germany
CEO: Gunter Thielen, Chmn. & CEO
Bus: *International communications holding company. Publishing, printing, books, magazines, music, computer, TV and radio.*

Tel: 49-52-41-800
Fax: 49-52-41-80-9662
www.bertelsmann.de

Rev: $23,210
Emp: 76,266

NAICS: 323119, 454390, 511110, 511120, 511130, 512191, 512210, 512220, 512230, 512240, 512290, 515112, 515120, 515210, 516110, 518112, 519190, 541890, 541910, 551112, 711130

BMG MUSIC PUBLISHING
1540 Broadway, 39/F, New York, New York 10036-4098
CEO: Nicholas Firth, Chmn.
Bus: *Sales of music/recordings.*

Tel: (212) 930-4000
Fax: (212) 930-4263

%FO: 100
Emp: 575

BOOKS ON TAPE, INC.
2910 W. Garry Ave., Santa Ana, California 92704
CEO: Ron Prowell, Pres.
Bus: *Sale of music, video, book & entertainment*

Tel: (714) 825-0021
Fax: (714) 825-0756

BROWN PRINTING CO.
2300 Brown Ave., Waseca, Minnesota 56093
CEO: Tom Engdahl, Pres. & CEO
Bus: *Commercial printing*

Tel: (507) 835-2410
Fax: (507) 835-0420

CDNOW, INC.
1540 Broadway, New York, New York 10036
CEO: Stuart Goldfarb, Pres. & CEO
Bus: *Online retailer of music and music reviews.*

Tel: (212) 930-4932
Fax: (212) 930-4526

%FO: 100

COLUMBIA RECORDS GROUP
550 Madison Ave., New York, New York 10022
CEO: Steve Greenberg, Pres.
Bus: *Music publishing.*

Tel: (212) 833-8000
Fax: (212) 833-5401

EPIC RECORDS GROUP
550 Madison Ave., New York, New York 10022
CEO: Steve Barnett, Pres.
Bus: *Music publishing.*

Tel: (212) 833-8000
Fax: (212) 833-4818

FODORS LLC
1745 Broadway, New York, New York 10019
CEO: David Naggar, Pres.   Tel: (212) 572-2248
Bus: *Book publishing*   Fax:

GRUNER+JAHR USA
375 Lexington Ave., 10/F, New York, New York 10017
CEO: Lawrence Diamond, CFO   Tel: (212) 499-2000   %FO: 100
Bus: *Magazine publisher.*   Fax: (212) 499-2193

LOUD RECORDS, INC.
550 Madison Ave., New York, New York 10022
CEO: Steven Rifkin, CEO   Tel: (212) 833-8000
Bus: *Music publishing.*   Fax: (212) 833-4818

PROVIDENT MUSIC GROUP
741 Cool Springs Blvd., Franklin, Tennessee 37067
CEO: Terry Hemmings, Pres. & CEO   Tel: (615) 261-5909
Bus: *Music publishing.*   Fax: Emp: 99

RANDOM HOUSE, INC.
1745 Broadway, New York, New York 10019
CEO: Peter Olson, Chmn. & CEO   Tel: (212) 782-9000   %FO: 100
Bus: *Book publishing.*   Fax: (212) 302-7985   Emp: 5,338

RCA LABEL GROUP-NASHVILLE
1400 18th Ave. South, Nashville, Tennessee 37212
CEO: Joe Galante, Chmn.   Tel: (615) 301-4300   %FO: 100
Bus: *Music publishers and distributors*   Fax: (615) 301-4347

RCA MUSIC GROUP
745 5th Ave., New York, New York 10151
CEO: Clive Davis, Chmn.   Tel: (646) 840-5600   %FO: 100
Bus: *Sales of music/recordings.*   Fax: (646) 840-5791

RED DISTRIBUTION
79 Fifth Ave., New York, New York 10003
CEO: Bob Morelli, EVP & Gen. Mgr.   Tel: (212) 404-0600
Bus: *Music publishing.*   Fax: (212) 337-5252

SONY BMG MUSIC ENTERTAINMENT
550 Madison Ave., New York, New York 10022
CEO: Andrew R. Lack, CEO & Mng. Dir.   Tel: (212) 833-8000
Bus: *Music publishing.*   Fax: (212) 833-4818   Emp: 10,000

SONY MUSIC NASHVILLE
1400 18th Ave. South, Nashville, Tennessee 37212
CEO: John Grady, Pres.   Tel: (615) 858-1300
Bus: *Music publishing.*   Fax: (615) 858-1330

ZOMBA LABEL GROUP
137-139 W. 25th St., New York, New York 10001
CEO: Max Siegel, VP   Tel: (212) 727-0016
Bus: *Music publishing.*   Fax: (212) 924-0743

● **BERU GMBH**
Morikestrasse 155, D-71636 Ludwigsburg, Germany
CEO: Marco Freiherr von Maltzan, CEO
Bus: *Diesel glow plugs heating elements manufacture.*

Tel: 49-7141-132-0
Fax: 49-7141-132-350
www.beru.com

Rev: $431
Emp: 2,694

NAICS: 333415, 336321, 336322, 336399

   BERU CORPORATION
   1614 Mulford St., Evanston, Illinois 60202
   CEO: Suzanne Vail
   Bus: *Diesel glow plugs heating elements manufacture and sales.*

   Tel: (847) 570-9404
   Fax: (847) 570-9405

   %FO: 100

   BERU CORPORATION
   39555 Orchard Hill Place, Ste. 140, Novi, Michigan 48375
   CEO: Ulrich Ruetz
   Bus: *Diesel glow plugs heating elements manufacture and sales.*

   Tel: (248) 596-0081
   Fax: (248) 596-0083

   %FO: 100

● **BHF-BANK AKTIENGESELLSCHAFT**
Bockenheimer Landstr. 10, D-60323 Frankfurt am Main, Germany
CEO: Georg Baron von Ullmann, Chmn.
Bus: *Manages commercial and mortgage banks, financing companies and investment banking companies.*

Tel: 49-69-718-0
Fax: 49-69-718-2296
www.bhf-bank.de

Rev: $2,803
Emp: 2,900

NAICS: 522110, 522293, 523110

   BHF-BANK AKTIENGESELLSCHAFT
   590 Madison Ave., 30/F, New York, New York 10022
   CEO: Burkhart Frankenburger, Dir.
   Bus: *Investment banking services.*

   Tel: (212) 756-5500
   Fax: (212) 756-2729

   %FO: 100
   Emp: 100

● **BHK-HOLZ KUNSTSTOFF KG**
Heldfeld 5, D-33142 Buren, Germany
CEO: William Byrne, Chmn.
Bus: *Mfr. vinyl-wrapped drawer components, wall and ceiling paneling systems, flooring and decorative moldings.*

Tel: 49-295-16040
Fax: 49-295-17588
www.bhk.de

Emp: 750

NAICS: 238350, 321918, 423310

   BHK OF AMERICA INC.
   11 Bond St., PO Box 37, Central Valley, New York 10917
   CEO: Robert Kowalik, Pres.
   Bus: *Mfr./sale vinyl-wrapped and wood drawer components, furniture components.*

   Tel: (845) 928-6200
   Fax: (845) 928-2287

   %FO: 70
   Emp: 100

   BHK OF AMERICA INC.
   3045 Philpott Rd., South Boston, Virginia 24592
   CEO: Don Fus, Pres.
   Bus: *Mfr./sale vinyl-wrapped and wood drawer components, furniture components.*

   Tel: (434) 572-5500
   Fax: (434) 572-5503

   Emp: 100

- **BILFINGER BERGER AG**
  Carl-Reiss-Platz 1-5, Postfach 100562, D-68165 Mannheim, Germany
  CEO: Herbert Bodner, Chmn.
  Bus: *Construction and engineering services.*

  Tel: 49-621-4590
  Fax: 49-621-459-2366
  www.bilfingerberger.de

  Rev: $7,454
  Emp: 48,930

  NAICS: 541330

  ### FRU-CON CONSTRUCTION CORPORATION
  15933 Clayton Rd., PO Box 100, Ballwin, Missouri 63022-0100
  CEO: Mike Seidel, VP
  Bus: *Provides engineering, construction and project development.*

  Tel: (636) 391-6700
  Fax: (636) 391-4513

  ### FRU-CON HOLDING CORPORATION
  15933 Clayton Rd., PO Box 100, Ballwin, Missouri 63022-0100
  CEO: Harold Massey, Dir.
  Bus: *Full-service engineering construction.*

  Tel: (636) 391-6700
  Fax: (636) 391-4513

  %FO: 100
  Emp: 2,000

- **BAYERISCHE MOTOREN WERKE AG (BMW AG)**
  BMW Haus, Petuelring 130, D-80788 Munich, Germany
  CEO: Helmut Panke, Chmn.
  Bus: *Mfr. motor vehicles, motorbikes & engines.*

  Tel: 49-89-3822-4272
  Fax: 49-89-3822-4418
  www.bmw.com

  Rev: $44,300
  Emp: 101,400

  NAICS: 336111, 336112, 336312, 336991

  ### BMW MANUFACTURING CORPORATION
  1400 Hwy. 101 South, Greer, South Carolina 29651
  CEO: Clemens Schmitz-Justen, Pres.
  Bus: *Manufacturing facility.*

  Tel: (864) 968-6000
  Fax: (864) 968-6000

  %FO: 100

  ### BMW OF NORTH AMERICA, INC.
  300 Chestnut Ridge Rd., Woodcliff Lake, New Jersey 07675-1227
  CEO: Thomas Purves, VP
  Bus: *Sales of BMW automobiles and sports activity vehicles and financial services for*

  Tel: (201) 307-4000
  Fax: (201) 307-4000

  %FO: 100

  ### BMW OF NORTH AMERICA, INC.
  300 Chestnut Ridge Rd., Westwood, New Jersey 07677
  CEO: John Christman, VP
  Bus: *Import/distribution automobiles, motorcycles, parts & service.*

  Tel: (201) 391-8000
  Fax: (201) 307-4095

  %FO: 100
  Emp: 910

- **BOEHRINGER INGELHEIM GMBH**
  Bingerstrasse 173, D-55216 Ingelheim, Germany
  CEO: Alessandro Banchi, Chmn.
  Bus: *Mfr. prescription and veterinary drugs.*

  Tel: 49-6132-770
  Fax: 49-6132-77-3000
  www.boehringer-ingelheim.com

  Rev: $7,950
  Emp: 31,850

  NAICS: 325412, 541940

BEN VENUE LABORATORIES, INC.
300 North Field Rd., Bedford, Ohio 44146-4650
CEO: Thomas Russillo, Pres.   Tel: (440) 232-3320   %FO: 100
Bus: *Mfr. prescription and over-the-counter*   Fax: (440) 439-6398
      drugs.300 N. Field Rd.
      Bedford, OH 44146-4650

BOEHRINGER INGELHEIM CHEMICALS,
PO Box 1658, Petersburg, Virginia 23805-0658
CEO: Anthony Corso   Tel: (804) 504-8600   %FO: 100
Bus: *Mfr. prescription and veterinary drugs.* Fax: (804) 504-8637   Emp: 200

BOEHRINGER INGELHEIM CORP.
900 Ridgebury Rd., Ridgefield, Connecticut 06877-0368
CEO: Michael Kavanaugh, Vice Pres.   Tel: (203) 798-9988   %FO: 100
Bus: *Mfr. prescription and veterinary drugs.* Fax: (203) 791-6234

BOEHRINGER INGELHEIM VETMEDICA, INC.
2621 North Belt Hwy, St. Joseph, Missouri 64506-2002
CEO: George Heidgerken   Tel: (816) 233-2571   %FO: 100
Bus: *Research and development facility for*   Fax: (816) 233-4767   Emp: 600
      prescription and veterinary drugs.

ROXANE LABORATORIES, INC.
PO Box 16532, Columbus, Ohio 43216
CEO: Glenn Marina, VP Sales   Tel: (614) 276-4000   %FO: 100
Bus: *Engaged in palliative care and pain*   Fax: (614) 308-0236   Emp: 900
      management products.

● **ROBERT BOSCH GMBH**
Robert Bosch Platz 1, Postfach 10 60 50, D-70049 Stuttgart, Germany
CEO: Franz Fehrenbach, Chmn.   Tel: 49-711-8110   Rev: $28,100
Bus: *Automotive equipment, power tools, household* Fax: 49-711-8116630   Emp: 220,000
      appliances, automation systems and packaging   www.bosch.com
      machines manufacture.
NAICS: 333991, 336312, 423620

BOSCH POWER TOOL CORPORATION
4203 South Blvd., Charlotte, North Carolina 28209
CEO: Don Robertson   Tel: (704) 527-3745
Bus: *Power tools manufacture.*   Fax: (704) 527-3745

BOSCH POWER TOOLS
1401 Kirk St., Elk Grove Village, Illinois 60007
CEO: Kevin Coughlin, VP   Tel: (630) 860-0294   %FO: 100
Bus: *Tools manufacture.*   Fax: (630) 860-0294

BOSCH REXROTH CORP.
7505 Durand Ave., Sturtevant, Wisconsin 53177
CEO: Michael Erdmann, Pres. & CEO   Tel: (262) 554-8595   %FO: 100
Bus: *Provides custom solutions to maximize*   Fax: (262) 554-7117
      factory floor productivity, including
      industrial hydraulics, mobile hydraulics &
      pneumatics.

BOSCH REXROTH CORPORATION
5150 Prairie Stone Pkwy., Hoffman Estates, Illinois 60192
CEO: Wolfgang Dangel, Pres. & CEO   Tel: (847) 645-3705   %FO: 100
Bus: *Drives and motion control manufacture.(847)* Fax: (847) 645-0804
    645-3705

BOSCH REXROTH LINEAR MOTION
816 E. Third St., Buchanan, Michigan 49107
CEO: Ernst Iseli, VP   Tel: (269) 695-0151   %FO: 100
Bus: *Linear motion manufacture and assembly* Fax: (269) 695-5363
    technologies.

BOSCH REXROTH LINEAR MOTION
14001 S. Lakes Dr., Charlotte, North Carolina 28273
CEO: Wolfgang Dangel, VP   Tel: (704) 583-4338   %FO: 100
Bus: *Linear motion manufacture and assembly* Fax: (704) 583-0523
    technologies.

ROBERT BOSCH CORPORATION
38000 Hills Tech Dr., Farmington Hills, Michigan 48331-3417
CEO: Kurt Liedtke, Pres.   Tel: (248) 553-9000   %FO: 100
Bus: *Develop/mfr./distribution equipment for cars* Fax: (248) 553-1309
    and trucks.

ROBERT BOSCH CORPORATION
401 North Bendix Dr., South Bend, Indiana 46634-4001
CEO: Sigmar Micke, Pres.   Tel: (219) 237-2000   %FO: 100
Bus: *Develop/mfr./sale braking systems.* Fax: (219) 237-3242

ROBERT BOSCH TOOL CORPORATION
1800 West Central Rd., Mt. Prospect, Illinois 60056
CEO: Reiner Beutel   Tel: (224) 232-2000   %FO: 100
Bus: *Tool manufacture.*   Fax: (224) 232-2000

ROBERT BOSCH TOOL CORPORATION
2800 South 25th Ave., Broadview, Illinois 60153
CEO: Manfred Seitz, Pres.   Tel: (708) 865-5200   %FO: 100
Bus: *Tool manufacture.*   Fax: (708) 865-6430

● GEOBRA BRANDSTATTER GMBH & CO KG
Brandstatter Str. 2-10, D-90513 Zirndorf, Germany
CEO: Robert Benker, CEO   Tel: 49-911-966-60   Rev: $216
Bus: *Mfr. toys.*   Fax: 49-911-966-6120   Emp: 2,190
                                         www.playmobil.com

NAICS: 339931, 339932

PLAYMOBIL FUNPARK
PO Box 1226, Orlando, Florida 32802-1226
CEO: Jurgen Baudenbacher, Pres.   Tel: (407) 812-6336   %FO: 100
Bus: *Fun park.*   Fax: (407) 812-6336   Emp: 10

PLAYMOBIL USA INC.
26 Commerce Dr., Cranbury, New Jersey 08512
CEO: John Skrajewski, VP   Tel: (609) 395-5566   %FO: 100
Bus: *Sale/distribution toys.*   Fax: (609) 409-1288

● **BRENNTAG GROUP**
Stinnes-Platz 1, D-45472 Mulheim an der Ruhr, Germany
CEO: Dr. Klaus Engel, CEO   Tel: 49-208-7828-0   Rev: $6,274
Bus: *Distribution and logistics of industrial and*   Fax: 49-208-7828-698   Emp: 8,798
   specialty chemicals.   www.brenntag.com
NAICS: 325199

   BRENNTAG GREAT LAKES
   4420 N. Harley Davidson Ave., Wauwatosa, Wisconsin 53225
   CEO: Jim Holcomb, Pres.   Tel: (262) 252-3550   %FO: 100
   Bus: *Distribution of chemicals.*   Fax: (262) 252-5250

   BRENNTAG MID-SOUTH
   PO Box 20, Henderson, Kentucky 42419
   CEO: Joel Hopper   Tel: (270) 830-1200   %FO: 100
   Bus: *Distribution of chemicals.*   Fax: (270) 827-4767

   BRENNTAG, INC.
   Pottsville Pike & Huller Lane, PO Box 13788, Reading, Pennsylvania 19612-3786
   CEO: David Garner, Pres.   Tel: (610) 926-6100   %FO: 100
   Bus: *Distribution and manufacture of specialty*   Fax: (610) 926-0420
    chemicals.

   BRENNTAG, INC.
   10747 Patterson Place, Santa Fe Springs, California 90670
   CEO: Dick Scherrer, Pres.   Tel: (562) 903-9626   %FO: 100
   Bus: *Distribution of chemicals.*   Fax: (562) 903-9622

   BRENNTAG, INC.
   2000 East Pettigrew St., Durham, North Carolina 27703
   CEO: Dan Miller, Pres.   Tel: (919) 596-0681   %FO: 100
   Bus: *Distribution of chemicals.*   Fax: (919) 596-6438

   BRENNTAG, INC.
   610 Fisher Rd., Longview, Texas 75604
   CEO: Dawn McCubbins, HR   Tel: (903) 759-7151   %FO: 100
   Bus: *Distribution of chemicals.*   Fax: (903) 759-7548

   CHEMTECH SPECIALTIES
   5700 Tacony St., Philadelphia, Pennsylvania 19135
   CEO: Bruce Matta   Tel: (215) 537-1000   %FO: 100
   Bus: *Chemicals distribution.*   Fax: (215) 537-8575

   COASTAL CHEMICAL, INC.
   PO Box 820, Abbeyville, Louisiana 70511
   CEO: Randy King   Tel: (337) 898-0001   %FO: 100
   Bus: *Distribution of chemicals.*   Fax: (337) 893-8795

● **BRITA GMBH**
Heinrich-Hertz-Strasse 4, D-65232 Taunustein, Germany
CEO: Markus Hankammer, CEO   Tel: 49-6128-746-0   Rev: $222
Bus: *Household water filters manufacture.*   Fax: 49-6128-746-355   Emp: 610
     www.brita.com
NAICS: 221310

BRITA USA INC.
1221 Broadway, Oakland, California 94612
CEO: Charles Couric
Bus: *Household water filters manufacture and sales.*

Tel: (510) 271-1642
Fax: (510) 208-1575

%FO: 100

● **BSH Bosch und Siemens Hausgerate GmbH**
Carl-Wery-Str. 34, D-81739 Munich, Germany
CEO: Kurt-Ludwig Gutberlet, Pres. & CEO
Bus: *Mfr. of appliances*

Tel: 49-89-45-90-01
Fax: 49-89-45-90-21-28
www.bsh-group.com

Rev: $7,902
Emp: 34,407

NAICS: 335211, 335221, 335222, 335224, 335228

BSH Home Appliances Corporation
5551 McFadden Ave., Huntington Beach, California 92649
CEO: Franz Bosshard, Pres. & CEO
Bus: *Manufacturer of home appliances*

Tel: (714) 901-6600
Fax: (714) 901-5980

%FO: 100

● **BSN MEDICAL GMBH & CO.**
Quickbornstr. 24, D-20253 Hamburg, Germany
CEO: Graham Siddle, CEO
Bus: *Engaged in wound care, casting, bandaging and phlebotomy. (JV of Smith & Nephew UK and Beiersdorf AG Germany).*

Tel: 49-40-4909-0
Fax: 49-40-4909-3434
www.bsnmedical.com

Emp: 3,000

NAICS: 339112

BSN JOBST, INC.
5828 Carnegie Blvd., Charlotte, North Carolina 28209
CEO: Maurizio Ballicu, Pres.
Bus: *Electro medical equipment*

Tel: (704) 554-9933
Fax:

%FO: JV
Emp: 466

BSN MEDICAL INC.
5825 Carnegie Blvd., Charlotte, North Carolina 28209
CEO: Darrell Jenkins, Pres.
Bus: *Surgical appliances & supplies*

Tel: (704) 331-0600
Fax:

%FO: JV
Emp: 55

● **BUDERUS AG**
Sophienstrasse 30-32, D-35576 Wetzlar, Germany
CEO: Uwe Luders, CEO
Bus: *Heating and specialty steel products*

Tel: 49-6441-418-0
Fax: 49-6441-418-1901
www.buderus.de

Rev: $1,950
Emp: 9,575

NAICS: 331210, 331221, 333994

BUDERUS HYDRONIC SYSTEMS INC.
50 Wentworth Ave., Londonderry, New Hampshire 03053
CEO: Lou Vorsteveld
Bus: *Heating and specialty steel products manufacture and sales.*

Tel: (603) 522-1100
Fax: (603) 421-2719

%FO: 100

- **BUEHLER MOTOR GMBH**
  Anne-Frank-Strasse 33, D-90459 Nuremberg, Germany
  CEO: Christof Fuartwangler, CEO   Tel: 49-911-45040
  Bus: *Mfr. sub-fractional motors, gear motors and fans.*   Fax: 49-911-454626
                                          www.buehlermotor.de

  NAICS: 333612, 335312, 336322

  > **BUEHLER MOTOR GROUP**
  > PO Box 5069, Cary, North Carolina 27512
  > CEO: Bob Elder, HR   Tel: (919) 469-8522   %FO: 49
  > Bus: *Mfr. sub-fractional motors, gear motors &*   Fax: (919) 469-8522   Emp: 750
  >   *fans*

- **CARL ZEISS MEDITEC AG**
  Goeschwitzer Strasse 51-52, D-07745 Jena, Germany
  CEO: James L. Taylor, CEO   Tel: 49-3641-220-320   Rev: $290
  Bus: *Ophthalmic products manufacture.*   Fax: 49-3641-220-322   Emp: 801
                                          www.meditec.zeiss.com

  NAICS: 334510, 339111, 339112, 339113

  > **CARL ZEISS MEDITEC INC.**
  > 5160 Hacienda Dr., Dublin, California 94568
  > CEO: Ulrich Krauss   Tel: (925) 557-4100   %FO: 100
  > Bus: *Ophthalmic products manufacture and*   Fax: (925) 557-4101
  >   *sales.*

- **CE CONSUMER ELECTRONIC AG**
  Denninger Strasse 15, D-81679 Munich, Germany
  CEO: Friedrich Rettenberger, CEO   Tel: 49-89-9971-0   Rev: $337
  Bus: *Global broker of semiconductors, electronic*   Fax: 49-89-9971-1999   Emp: 400
         components and computer products.   www.consumer.de
  NAICS: 423430, 423690, 541511, 541519

  > **SND ELECTRONICS INC. (SND)**
  > 9 Cushing, Irvine, California 92618
  > CEO: Ereck Bettancourt   Tel: (949) 754-3064   %FO: 100
  > Bus: *Electronic components and computer*   Fax: (949) 754-4246
  >   *peripherals manufacture.*

  > **SND ELECTRONICS INC. (SND)**
  > 19621 Redwing St., Tarzana, California 91356
  > CEO: Rick Deckman   Tel: (818) 708-0824   %FO: 100
  > Bus: *Electronic components and computer*   Fax: (818) 708-9314
  >   *peripherals manufacture.*

  > **SND ELECTRONICS INC. (SND)**
  > 77 South Water St., Greenwich, Connecticut 06830
  > CEO: Christopher DeNisco, Pres.   Tel: (203) 532-1212   %FO: 100
  > Bus: *Electronic components and computer*   Fax: (203) 532-1382
  >   *peripherals manufacture.*

  > **VIRTUAL CHIP EXCHANGE INC.**
  > 140 Fell Ct., Hauppauge, New York 11788
  > CEO: Michael Wood   Tel: (631) 851-2800   %FO: 100
  > Bus: *Internet-based electronic components*   Fax: (631) 851-2810
  >   *exchange services.*

● **CELANESE AG**
Frankfurter Strasse 111, D-61476 Kronberg, Germany
CEO: Andreas Pohlmann, Chmn.
Bus: *Chemicals and pharmaceuticals manufacture.*

Tel: 49-69-305-16000
Fax: 49-69-305-16006
www.celanese.com

Rev: $3,789
Emp: 9,050

NAICS: 325188, 325211, 325222, 325411, 325998

CELANESE AMERICAS CORPORATION
550 U.S. Highway 202/206, Ste. 310, Bedminster, New Jersey 07921
CEO: C. J. Nelson, CFO
Bus: *Mfr. high performance technical polymers.*

Tel: (908) 901-4500
Fax: (908) 901-2190

%FO: 100

CELANESE CHEMICALS
1601 W. LBJ Fwy., Dallas, Texas 75234
CEO: David N. Weidman
Bus: *Commodity chemicals and acetate products manufacture.*

Tel: (972) 443-4000
Fax: (972) 443-4000

%FO: 100

● **CEYONIQ TECHNOLOGY GMBH**
Winter Str. 49, D-33649 Bielefeld, Germany
CEO: Juergen Schmoll, Chmn. & CEO
Bus: *Provides software and services for document management.*

Tel: 49-521-93-18-1000
Fax: 49-521-93-18-1111
www.ceyoniq.com/de/start.cfm

Rev: $91
Emp: 650

NAICS: 511210

TREEV LLC
13454 Sunrise Valley Dr., 4/F, Herndon, Virginia 20171
CEO: Jud Cairns, Pres. & CEO
Bus: *Provides innovative content lifecycle management solutions for businesses.*

Tel: (703) 478-2260
Fax: (703) 481-6920

%FO: 100

● **CHEMISCHE FABRIK BUDENHEIM (CFB)**
Rheinstrasse 27, D-55257 Budenheim, Germany
CEO: Dr. Christian Kohlpaintner, Chmn.
Bus: *Mfr. food products, wine, beer and soft drinks.*

Tel: 49-6139-890
Fax: 49-6139-73264
www.oetker.de

NAICS: 311999, 312111, 312120, 312130, 325188, 325221, 424690

GALLARD-SCHLESINGER INDUSTRIES INC.
245 Newtown Rd., Ste. 305, Plainview, New York 11803
CEO: Douglas Lim, Pres.
Bus: *Phosphates and ingredients R&D and high quality specialty chemicals.*

Tel: (516) 229-4000
Fax: (516) 229-4015

%FO: 100

● **CHIRON-WERKE GMBH & CO KG**
Talstr. 23, D-78532 Tuttlingen, Germany
CEO: Sean P. Lance, Pres.
Bus: *High speed manufacturing.*

Tel: 49-74-61-9400
Fax: 49-75-61-3159
www.chiron-werke.de

Emp: 650

NAICS: 333999

CHIRON AMERICA INC.
14201-G South Lakes Dr., 100950 Withers Cove Park Dr., Charlotte, North Carolina 28273
CEO: Hans Henning Winkler, Pres.   Tel: (704) 587-9526   %FO: 100
Bus: *CNC vertical machining centers.*   Fax: (704) 587-0485   Emp: 85

● **CHRISTIAN BAUER GMBH & COMPANY**
Schorndorfer Str. 49, D-73642 Welzheim, Germany
CEO: Helmut Hutt, Gen. Dir.   Tel: 49-7182-120
Bus: *Dual industry manufacture: precision disc springs* Fax: 49-7182-12315
  and wedding rings.   www.christianbauer.com
NAICS: 332611, 332612, 339911, 448310

    BAUER SPRINGS, INC.
    509 Pkwy View Dr., Dept. 110, Pittsburgh, Pennsylvania 15205
    CEO: Helmut Hutt, Mgr.   Tel: (412) 787-7930   %FO: 100
    Bus: *Precision disc springs manufacture and* Fax: (412) 787-3882
      sales.

    CHRISTIAN BAUER INC.
    1775 West Hibiscus Blvd., Melbourne, Florida 32901
    CEO: Tom Loback   Tel: (321) 951-4090   %FO: 100
    Bus: *Wholesale jewelry manufacture.*   Fax: (321) 951-4090

● **CLAAS KGAA**
Munsterstr. 33, D-33428 Harsewinkel, Germany
CEO: Helmut Claas, EVP   Tel: 49-5247-120
Bus: *Mfr./assembly harvesting equipment.* Fax: 49-5247-121927
                                           www.claas.de
NAICS: 333111

    CLAAS OF AMERICA INC.
    3030 Norcross Dr., PO Box 3008, Columbus, Indiana 47202-3008
    CEO: Theo Freye, Pres.   Tel: (812) 342-4441   %FO: 100
    Bus: *Mfr./assembly harvesting equipment.* Fax: (812) 342-3525   Emp: 19

● **COGNIS GMBH & CO.**
Rheinpromenade 1, D-40789 Monheim, Germany
CEO: Antonio Trius, CEO   Tel: 49-211-794-00   Rev: $4,192
Bus: *Mfr. specialty chemicals; additives for paints,* Fax: 49-211-798-4008   Emp: 8,059
  raw materials for printing inks, binders and   www.cognis.com
  hardeners for coatings and polymerization
NAICS: 325199, 325910

    COGNIS USA, INC.
    2430 North Huachuca Dr., Tucson, Arizona 85745
    CEO: Rachael Tocco, Sales   Tel: (520) 622-8891   %FO: 100
    Bus: *Specialty chemicals manufacture.* Fax: (520) 624-0912

    COGNIS USA, INC.
    1500 Old Stage Rd., Mauldin, South Carolina 29662
    CEO: Brenda Smith   Tel: (864) 963-4031   %FO: 100
    Bus: *Specialty chemicals manufacture and sales.* Fax: (864) 967-5156

COGNIS USA, INC.
2525 South Kensington Rd., Kankakee, Illinois 60901
CEO: Denny Ohomansiek
Bus: *Specialty chemicals manufacture and sales.*
Tel: (815) 932-6751
Fax: (815) 939-6472
%FO: 100

COGNIS USA, INC.
5051 Estecreek Dr., Cincinnati, Ohio 45232
CEO: Paul S. Allen, Mng. Dir.
Bus: *Specialty chemicals manufacture and sales.*
Tel: (717) 948-5364
Fax: (513) 482-5503
%FO: 100

COGNIS USA, INC.
300 Brookside Ave., Ambler, Pennsylvania 19002
CEO: Ed Van Yo
Bus: *Specialty chemicals manufacture and sales.*
Tel: (215) 628-1000
Fax: (215) 628-1200
%FO: 100

COGNIS USA, INC.
3304 Westinghouse Blvd., Charlotte, North Carolina 28273
CEO: Jeff Portfeild
Bus: *Textiles technology.*
Tel: (704) 587-3800
Fax: (704) 945-8804
%FO: 100

● **COMMERZBANK AG**
Kaiserplatz, D-60261 Frankfurt, Germany
CEO: Klaus-Peter Muller, Chmn.
Bus: *Commercial and investment banking services.*
Tel: 49-69-136-20
Fax: 49-69-285-389
www.commerzbank.com
Rev: $18,889
Emp: 32,377

NAICS: 522110, 522292, 522293, 523110, 523120, 523920, 523930

COMMERZBANK
2 World Financial Center, New York, New York 10281
CEO: Werner Bonsch, Mgr.
Bus: *International commercial and investment banking services.*
Tel: (212) 266-7200
Fax: (212) 266-7235

COMMERZBANK
1230 Peachtree St. NE, Promenade Two, Ste. 3500, Atlanta, Georgia 30309
CEO: Edward Forsberg, Mgr.
Bus: *International commercial and investment banking services.*
Tel: (404) 888-6500
Fax: (404) 888-6539

COMMERZBANK
20 South Clark St., Ste. 2700, Chicago, Illinois 60603
CEO: Tim Shortly, Mgr.
Bus: *International commercial and investment banking services.*
Tel: (312) 236-5300
Fax: (312) 236-2827

COMMERZBANK
633 W. 5th St., Ste. 6600, Los Angeles, California 90071
CEO: Christian Jagenberg, Mgr.
Bus: *International commercial and investment banking services.*
Tel: (213) 623-8223
Fax: (213) 623-0039

COMMERZBANK CAPITAL MARKETS CORP.
1251 Ave. of the Americas, New York, New York 10020
CEO: Bernd Loewen, Mgr.
Bus: *International commercial and investment banking services.*
Tel: (212) 703-4000
Fax: (212) 703-4001
%FO: 100
Emp: 200

COMMERZBANK FUTURES
209 W. Jackson Blvd., Ste. 600, Chicago, Illinois 60606
CEO: Edward Cartwright, Mgr.
Bus: *International commercial and investment banking services.*
Tel: (312) 360-1175
Fax: (312) 360-1176

● **CONERGY AG**
Anckelmannsplatz 1, D-20537 Hamburg, Germany
CEO: Hans-Martin Ruter, Chmn.
Bus: *Suppliers of regenerative energies.*
Tel: 49-40-2371-020
Fax: 49-40-2371-02-148
www.conergy.de
Rev: $388
Emp: 347

NAICS: 335311, 335999
CONERGY US
1730 Camino Carlos Rey, Ste. 103, Santa Fe, New Mexico 87507
CEO: Paul Benson, Pres.
Bus: *Supplier of regenerative energies.*
Tel: (505) 473-3800
Fax: (505) 473-3830
%FO: 100

● **CONTINENTAL AG**
Vahrenwalder Strasse 9, Postfach 169, D-30165 Hannover, Germany
CEO: Hubertus von Grunberg, CEO
Bus: *Mfr. tires and industrial rubber products, including brands Continental, Uniroyal and*
Tel: 49-511-93801
Fax: 49-511-9382766
www.conti.de
Rev: $17,182
Emp: 80,586

NAICS: 314992, 326199
CONTINENTAL TIRE NORTH AMERICA
1800 Continental Boulevard, Charlotte, North Carolina 28278
CEO: Alan Hippe, Pres.
Bus: *Mfr./sales and distribution of tires.*
Tel: (704) 583-3900
Fax: (704) 583-8698
%FO: 100
Emp: 8,000

● **COPERION HOLDING GMBH**
Theodor Str. 10, D-70469 Stuttgart, Germany
CEO: Norbert Bueter, CEO
Bus: *Compounding systems, bulk material systems and components manufacture.*
Tel: 49-711-897-2514
Fax: 49-711-897-3963
www.waeschle.de
Rev: $161
Emp: 808

NAICS: 332322, 333518, 333924, 333999, 423610, 541350
COPERION CORPORATION
285 Staffard Umberger Dr., PO Box 775, Wytheville, Virginia 24382
CEO: Jan van Bakergem
Bus: *Bulk solids handling conveyor systems.*
Tel: (276) 228-7717
Fax: (273) 228-7682

COPERION CORPORATION
30109 Ednil Dr., Bay Village, Ohio 44140
CEO: John H. Ogden
Bus: *Bulk solids handling conveyor systems.*
Tel: (440) 899-4960
Fax: (440) 899-4965
%FO: 100

COPERION CORPORATION
10424 Torrelle Dr., Charlotte, North Carolina 28277
CEO: Jan van Bakergem
Bus: *Bulk solids handling conveyor systems.*
Tel: (704) 759-9991
Fax: (704) 759-9983

COPERION CORPORATION
185 Hansen Ct., Ste. 100, Wood Dale, Illinois 60191
CEO: Robert Swanson, Mgr.　　　　　Tel: (630) 238-9300　　　%FO: 100
Bus: *Compounding systems, bulk material*　Fax:
systems and components manufacture.

COPERION CORPORATION
455 Kehoe Blvd., Ste. 109, Carol Stream, Illinois 60188
CEO: Jan Van Bakergem, CEO　　　　Tel: (630) 933-9100　　　%FO: 100
Bus: *Bulk solids handling conveyor systems.*　Fax: (630) 933-0400

COPERION CORPORATION
663 East Crescent Ave., Ramsey, New Jersey 07446
CEO: Jan Van Bakergem, Pres.　　　　Tel: (201) 327-6300　　　%FO: 100
Bus: *Bulk solids handling conveyor systems.*　Fax: (201) 825-6460　　Emp: 203

COPERION CORPORATION
230 Covington Dr., Bloomingdale, Illinois 60108
CEO: Paula Nurnberger, Pres.　　　　Tel: (630) 539-9100　　　%FO: 100
Bus: *Bulk solids handling conveyor systems.*　Fax: (630) 539-9196

- **COREOPTICS GMBH**
Nordostpark 12-14, D-90411 Nuremberg, Germany
CEO: Hamid Arabzadeh, CEO　　　　Tel: 49-911-941-516
Bus: *Transponder modules and integrated circuits*　Fax: 49-911-480-8682
manufacture.　　　　　　　　www.coreoptics.com
NAICS: 334413, 423690

　COREOPTICS INC.
　50 Bridge St., Ste. 308, Manchester, New Hampshire 03101
　CEO: Saeid Aramideh, VP　　　　　Tel: (603) 669-3309　　　%FO: 100
　Bus: *Transponder modules and integrated circuits*　Fax: (603) 669-6611
　manufacture and sales.

- **CYBIO AG**
Göschwitze Str. 40, D-07745 Jena, Germany
CEO: Heinz Daugart, CEO　　　　　Tel: 49-3641-351315　　Rev: $17
Bus: *Biotechnology and laboratory automation.*　Fax: 49-3641-351425　　Emp: 113
　　　　　　　　　　　　　　www.cybio-ag.com
NAICS: 334516

　CYBIO, INC.
　500 West Cummings Park, Ste. 1800, Woburn, Massachusetts 01801
　CEO: Robert Dall, Mktg.　　　　　Tel: (781) 376-9899　　%FO: 100
　Bus: *Engaged in biotechnology and laboratory*　Fax: (781) 376-9897
　automation.

- **D.LOGISTICS AG**
Johannes-Gutenberg-Str. 305, D-65719 Hofheim, Germany
CEO: Detlef W. Hubner, CEO　　　　Tel: 49-6122-5000　　　Rev: $429
Bus: *Provides logistics and logistics-related services,*　Fax: 49-6122-50-1306　Emp: 6,200
including consumer goods packaging solutions.　www.dlogistics.de
NAICS: 488510, 493110, 561910, 562111

J&J PACKAGING
8031 Golden Rd., Brookville, Indiana 47012
CEO: Rainer Monetha
Bus: *Packaging products manufacture.*
Tel: (765) 647-2571
Fax: (765) 647-3418

- ### DAIMLERCHRYSLER AG
Epplestr. 225, D-70546 Stuttgart, Germany
CEO: Juergen E. Schrempp, Chmn.
Bus: *Cars, trucks, commercial vehicles, aircraft
     engines and electronics manufacture.*
Tel: 49-711-17-0
Fax: 49-711-179-4022
www.daimlerchrysler.com
Rev: $192,433
Emp: 384,723

NAICS: 336111, 336112, 336120, 336211, 336399, 336510, 522291

AMERICAN LAFRANCE
8500 Palmetto Pkwy., North Charleston, South Carolina 29456
CEO: John Stevenson, Pres. & CEO
Bus: *Mfr. fire trucks and emergency vehicles.*
Tel: (843) 821-1800
Fax: (843) 821-1800
%FO: 100

DAIMLER-CHRYSLER NORTH AMERICA
1000 Chrysler Dr., Auburn Hills, Michigan 48326
CEO: Thomas W. LaSorda, COO
Bus: *Mfr. car, trucks, commercial vehicles.*
Tel: (248) 576-5741
Fax: (248) 576-4742
%FO: 100
Emp: 102,391

FREIGHTLINER LLC
4747 N. Channel Ave., Portland, Oregon 97217
CEO: Chris Patterson, Pres. & CEO
Bus: *Heavy truck manufacture.*
Tel: (503) 745-8000
Fax: (503) 745-8921
%FO: 100
Emp: 14,000

THOMAS BUILT BUSES INC.
1408 Courtesy Rd., High Point, North Carolina 27260
CEO: John O'Leary, Pres. & CEO
Bus: *Mfr. school buses.*
Tel: (336) 889-4871
Fax: (336) 881-6509
%FO: 100

- ### DBT (DEUTSCHE BERGBAU-TECHNIK) GMBH
Industriestrasse 1, D-44534 Luenen, Germany
CEO: William S. Tate, Pres. & CEO
Bus: *Design and manufacture of mining equipment and
     captive-guided transport systems for underground
     mining operations.*
Tel: 49-2306-709-0
Fax: 49-2306-709-1104
www.dbt.de

NAICS: 333131

DBT AMERICA INC.
2045 West Pike St., Houston, Pennsylvania 15342
CEO: William S. Tate, CEO
Bus: *Mfr./service of mining, hauling and
     transportation equipment.*
Tel: (724) 743-1200
Fax: (724) 743-1201
%FO: 100
Emp: 25

- ### DEGUSSA AG
Bennigsenplatz 1, D-40474 Dusseldorf, Germany
CEO: Utz-Hellmuth Felcht, CEO
Bus: *Specialty chemicals manufacture.*
Tel: 49-211-650-41-249
Fax: 49-211-650-41-377
www.degussa.com
Rev: $14,343
Emp: 46,997

NAICS: 311930, 311942, 325110, 325131, 325132, 325191, 325199, 325211, 325412, 325510, 325520

CREANOVA INC.
220 Davidson Ave., Somerset, New Jersey 08873
CEO: Dietmar Zorenboehmer, VP
Bus: *Provides high quality colorants and raw materials.*
Tel: (732) 560-6800
Fax: (732) 560-6950
%FO: 100

CREASORB DEGUSSA
2401 Doyle St., Greensboro, North Carolina 27406
CEO: James Hoeger
Bus: *Research and development of new and advanced absorbent polymer technologies*
Tel: (336) 333-3669
Fax: (336) 279-3586
%FO: 100

DEGUSSA BIOACTIVES US
PO Box 1609, Waukesha, Wisconsin 53187
CEO: Andy Dederich
Bus: *Food ingredients.*
Tel: (262) 547-5531
Fax: (262) 547-0587
%FO: 100

DEGUSSA CONSTRUCTION CHEMICALS AMERICAS
23700 Chagrin Boulevard, Cleveland, Ohio 44122
CEO: Konrad Wernthaler
Bus: *Chemicals manufacture.*
Tel: (952) 496-6369
Fax: (952) 233-8402
%FO: 100

DEGUSSA CORPORATION
379 Interpace Pkwy., Parsippany, New Jersey 07054-0677
CEO: John Salvatore
Bus: *Chemical production.*
Tel: (973) 541-8000
Fax: (973) 541-8072
%FO: 100

DEGUSSA FEED ADDITIVES
1701 Barrett Lakes Boulevard, Ste. 340, Kennesaw, Georgia 30144
CEO: John Dale
Bus: *Feed additives manufacture.*
Tel: (678) 797-4300
Fax: (678) 797-4313
%FO: 100

DEGUSSA INSPEC FOAMS INC.
101 East Park Boulevard, Ste. 201, Plano, Texas 75074
CEO: Stephanie Ayers
Bus: *Advanced polymer shapes.*
Tel: (972) 516-0702
Fax: (972) 516-0624
%FO: 100

DEGUSSA TEXTURANT SYSTEMS
3582 McCall Place, NE, Atlanta, Georgia 30340
CEO: Ed Baranski
Bus: *Food ingredients.*
Tel: (770) 455-3603
Fax: (770) 986-6216
%FO: 100

ROHMAX USA
723 Electronic Dr., Horsham, Pennsylvania 19044
CEO: Greg Bialy
Bus: *Chemicals and lubricating oils manufacture.*
Tel: (215) 706-5800
Fax: (215) 706-5801
%FO: 100

● **DEUTSCHE BANK AG**
Taunusanlage 12, D-60262 Frankfurt am Main, Germany
CEO: Josef Ackermann, CEO
Bus: *Commercial, private, investment and merchant banking services.*
Tel: 49-69-910-00
Fax: 49-69-910-38591
www.deutsche-bank.de
Rev: $60,631
Emp: 65,417
NAICS: 522110, 522220, 522292, 522293, 522294, 522310, 522390, 523110, 523120, 523130, 523140, 523920, 523930, 525110, 525910

DEUTSCHE BANK ALEX BROWN INC.
1 South St., 23/F, Baltimore, Maryland 21202
CEO: Fred Crozier, CEO
Bus: *Provides investment banking services.*
Tel: (410) 727-1700
Fax: (410) 895-3450
%FO: 100

DEUTSCHE BANK BERKSHIRE MORTGAGE
1 Beacon St., 14/F, Boston, Massachusetts 02108
CEO: Peter F. Donovan, CEO
Bus: *Mortgage banking & related services*
Tel: (617) 523-0066
Fax: (617) 556-8170

DEUTSCHE BANK SECURITIES INC.
60 Wall St., New York, New York 10019
CEO: Thomas Gahan, CEO
Bus: *Securities broker/dealer, investment banking & asset management services.*
Tel: (212) 469-5000
Fax: (212) 454-1706
%FO: 100

RREEF FUNDS LLC
101 California St., 26/F, San Francisco, California 94111
CEO: Stephen Steppe, Principal
Bus: *Commercial property management*
Tel: (415) 781-3300
Fax: (415) 391-9015

● **DEUTSCHE BOERSE**
Borsenplatz 4, D-60485 Frankfurt, Germany
CEO: Rolf E. Breuer, Chmn.
Bus: *Provider of financial securities exchange*
Tel: 49-69-2101-0
Fax: 49-69-2101-2005
www.deutsche-boerse.com
Rev: $2,082
Emp: 3,262

NAICS: 523210

DEUTSCHE BOERSE AG/EUREX
233 S. Wacker Dr., Ste. 2450, Chicago, Illinois 60606
CEO: Richard Heckinger, Rep.
Bus: *Provider of financial securities exchange platform.*
Tel: (312) 544-1100
Fax: (312) 544-1101
%FO: 100

● **DEUTSCHE BUNDESBANK**
Wilhelm-Epstein-Str. 14, D-60431 Frankfurt, Germany
CEO: Axel Weber, Pres.
Bus: *General banking services.*
Tel: 49-69-9566-1
Fax: 49-69-9566-3077
www.bundesbank.de

NAICS: 522110

DEUTSCHE BUNDESBANK
499 Park Ave., 25/F, New York, New York 10022
CEO: Horst Rinke, Pres.
Bus: *General banking services.*
Tel: (212) 688-3680
Fax: (212) 688-4274
%FO: 100
Emp: 5

● **DEUTSCHE LUFTHANSA AG**
Von-Gablenz-Str. 2-6, D-50679 Cologne 21, Germany
CEO: Wolfgang Mayrhuber, Chmn. & CEO
Bus: *International air transport services.*
Tel: 49-69-696-0
Fax: 49-69-696-6818
www.lufthansa.com
Rev: $20,029
Emp: 93,246

NAICS: 481111, 481112, 481212

AMADEUS GLOBAL TRAVEL DISTRIBUTION
9250 NW 36th St., AC04, Miami, Florida 33178
CEO: Tony McKinnon, member   Tel: (305) 499-6603
Bus: *Information services for airlines.*   Fax: (305) 499-6616   Emp: 550

E-TRAVEL BUSINESS UNIT
1000 Winter St., Ste. 4200, Waltham, Massachusetts 02451
CEO: Scott Gutz, CEO   Tel: (781) 622-5905
Bus: *Travel agency.*   Fax: (781) 522-9900   Emp: 130

HAWKER PACIFIC AEROSPACE
11240 Sherman Way, Sun Valley, California 91352
CEO: Richard A. Fortner, Pres. & CEO   Tel: (818) 765-6201
Bus: *Aerospace & defense maintenance &*   Fax: (818) 765-5759   Emp: 488
  service.

LSG LUFTHANSA SERVICE HOLDING AG
6191 N. State Hwy. 161, Irving, Texas 75038
CEO: Patrick Tolbert, CFO   Tel: (972) 793-9000
Bus: *Airline food catering.*   Fax: (972) 793-9738

LUFTHANSA
1640 Hempstead Tpke., East Meadow, New York 11554
CEO: Maier Funke, VP   Tel: (516) 296-9200   %FO: 100
Bus: *International air transport services.*   Fax: (516) 296-9660   Emp: 92

• **DEUTSCHE MESSE AG**
Messegelande, Niedersachsen, D-30521 Hannover, Germany
CEO: Sepp Dieter Heckmann, Chmn.   Tel: 49-511-890   Rev: $292
Bus: *Trade fairs operators.*   Fax: 49-511-8932626   Emp: 800
                                       www.messe.de
NAICS: 561920
  HANNOVER FAIRS USA INC.
  212 Carnegie Center, Ste. 203, Princeton, New Jersey 08540
  CEO: Joachim Schafer, Pres.   Tel: (609) 987-1202   %FO: 100
  Bus: *Trade fairs management & promotion.*   Fax: (609) 987-0092   Emp: 32

• **DEUTSCHE STEINZEUG CREMER & BREUER AG**
PO Box 2540, D-53015 Bonn, Germany
CEO: Manfred F. U. Rutten, CEO   Tel: 49-228-391-1006   Rev: $350
Bus: *Ceramics and clay pipes manufacture.*   Fax: 49-228-391-301006 Emp: 2,580
                                       www.deutsche-steinzeug.de
NAICS: 423320
  DEUTSCHE STEINZEUG AMERICA, INC. (DSA, INC.)
  367 Curie Dr., Alpharetta, Georgia 30005
  CEO: Joann Culbert   Tel: (770) 442-5500   %FO: 100
  Bus: *Ceramics and clay pipes manufacture and*   Fax: (770) 442-5502
    sales.

Germany

DEUTSCHE STEINZEUG AMERICA, INC. (DSA, INC.)
1239 Allec St., Anaheim, California 92805
CEO: Barbara G. Mohr
Bus: *Ceramics and clay pipes manufacture and sales.*

Tel: (714) 774-7750
Fax: (714) 774-7122

%FO: 100

• DEUTSCHE TELEKOM AG
Friedrich-Ebert-Allee 140, D-53113 Bonn, Germany
CEO: Kai-Uwe Ricke, CEO
Bus: *Provides telephone service, internet access and digital mobile communications services.*

Tel: 49-228-181-0
Fax: 49-228-181-8872
www.telekom.de

Rev: $78,404
Emp: 244,645

NAICS: 517110, 517211, 517212, 517910, 518111, 518210, 519190, 541511, 541512, 541519, 561421, 561499, 811213

DEUTSCHE TELEKOM, INC.
101 E. 52nd St., 17/f, New York, New York 10022
CEO: Jeffery A. Hedberg, CEO
Bus: *Engaged in telecommunications.*

Tel: (212) 424-2900
Fax: (212) 424-2989

%FO: 100
Emp: 23

T-MOBILE HOTSPOT
1601 N. Glenville Dr., Ste. 100, Richardson, Texas 75081
CEO: Robert P. Dotson, Pres. & CEO
Bus: *Wireless communication services.*

Tel: (972) 669-3262
Fax:

%FO: 100

T-MOBILE USA, INC.
12920 S.E. 38th St., Bellevue, Washington 98006
CEO: Robert P. Dotson, Pres. & CEO
Bus: *Wireless communications services.*

Tel: (425) 378-4000
Fax: (425) 378-4040

%FO: 100
Emp: 21,525

T-SYSTEMS NORTH AMERICA
701 Warrenville Rd., Lisle, Illinois 60532
CEO: Sean Parkinson, CEO
Bus: *Information technology services.*

Tel: (630) 493-6100
Fax: (630) 493-6111

%FO: 100
Emp: 350

• DEUTZ AG
Deutz-Muelheimer Strasse 147-149, D-51057 Cologne, Germany
CEO: Gordon Riske, CEO
Bus: *Mfr. diesel engines and industrial plant systems.*

Tel: 49-221-8220
Fax: 49-221-8222-004
www.deutz.de

Rev: $1,694
Emp: 5,472

NAICS: 333319, 333618

DEUTZ CORPORATION
3883 Steve Reynolds Boulevard, Norcross, Georgia 30093
CEO: Michael Letson, CEO
Bus: *Mfr. diesel engines and industrial plant systems.*

Tel: (770) 564-7100
Fax: (770) 564-7272

%FO: 100

HUMBOLDT WEDAG, INC.
400 Technology Pkwy., Norcross, Georgia 30092
CEO: Kenneth M. Hitcho, Pres.
Bus: *Provides design & product support in the area of industrial engineering.*

Tel: (770) 810-7300
Fax: (770) 810-7343

%FO: 100

- **DIALOG SEMICONDUCTOR PLC**
  Neus Strasse 95, D-73230 Kirchheim-Nabern, Germany
  CEO: Roland Pudelko, Pres. & CEO
  Bus: *Develops integrated circuits for wireless communications.*
  NAICS: 334413

  Tel: 49-7021-805-0
  Fax: 49-7021-805-100
  www.dialog-semiconductor.com

  Rev: $157
  Emp: 296

  > **DIALOG SEMICONDUCTOR**
  > 54 Old Highway 22, Clinton, New Jersey 08809
  > CEO: Erwin Hopf
  > Bus: *Develops integrated circuits for wireless communications.*
  >
  > Tel: (908) 238-0200
  > Fax: (908) 238-0201
  >
  > %FO: 100

- **FRIEDR. DICK GMBH**
  Kollwitzstrasse, 1, D-73728 Esslingen, Germany
  CEO: Wilhelm Leuze, CEO
  Bus: *Mfr. tools, machines and cutlery for food*

  NAICS: 332211, 333294

  Tel: 49-711-3994156
  Fax: 49-711-3994100
  www.dick.de

  Emp: 300

  > **FRIEDR. DICK CORPORATION**
  > 33 Allen Boulevard, Farmingdale, New York 11735
  > CEO: Karen Tech, Gen. Mgr.
  > Bus: *Distribution/sale cutlery.*
  >
  > Tel: (516) 454-6955
  > Fax: (516) 454-6184
  >
  > %FO: 100
  > Emp: 6

- **DIEHL STIFTUNG & CO.**
  Stephanstrasse 49, D-90478 Nuremberg, Germany
  CEO: Thomas Diehl, CEO
  Bus: *Defense products manufacture.*

  NAICS: 331222, 334414, 334419, 334511, 334512, 334515, 335999

  Tel: 49-911-947-20-24
  Fax: 49-911-947-30-24
  www.diehl.com

  Rev: $1,300
  Emp: 10,525

  > **DIEHL AVIONICS INC.**
  > 12001 Highway 280, Sterrett, Alabama 35147
  > CEO: Joe Sherman, EVP
  > Bus: *Electronic products manufacture.*
  >
  > Tel: (205) 678-7101
  > Fax: (205) 678-7119
  >
  > %FO: 100

  > **DIEHL CONTROLS INC.**
  > 1250 East Diehl Rd., Naperville, Illinois 60563
  > CEO: Wallace C. Leyshon
  > Bus: *Mfr. controls for the appliance industry.*
  >
  > Tel: (630) 955-9055
  > Fax: (630) 955-9065
  >
  > %FO: 100

  > **FRANCONIA INDUSTRIES INC.**
  > 411 Hackensack Ave., 10/F, Hackensack, New Jersey 07601
  > CEO: Peter Kretschmer
  > Bus: *Copper manufacture and sales.*
  >
  > Tel: (201) 487-1188
  > Fax: (201) 487-7827
  >
  > %FO: 100

- **DIENES-WERKE GMBH**
  Kolner Str. 7, D-51491 Overath, Germany
  CEO: Bernd Supe Dienes, Pres.
  Bus: *Solutions for industrial cutting applications.*

  NAICS: 332212, 333912

  Tel: 49-2206-605161
  Fax: 49-2206-605111
  www.dienes.de

  Emp: 250

DIENES CORPORATION
Spencer Corporate Park, Spencer, Massachusetts 01562-2498
CEO: William Shea, Mgr.   Tel: (508) 885-6301   %FO: 100
Bus: *Mfr. slitting tools and replacement parts for*   Fax: (508) 885-3452   Emp: 55
compressors.

● **DORMA GMBH**
Breckerfelder Straße 42-48, D-58256 Ennepetal, Germany
CEO: Michael Schadlich, CEO   Tel: 49-2333-793-0   Rev: $783
Bus: *Supplies door fixtures, including automatic and*   Fax: 49-2333-793-495   Emp: 5,510
revolving doors and door hardware.   www.dorma.com
NAICS: 332321, 332999, 335999

    DORMA GROUP NORTH AMERICA
    Dorma Dr., Drawer AC, Reamstown, Pennsylvania 17567-0411
    CEO: Larry O'Toole, Pres.   Tel: (717) 336-3881   %FO: 100
    Bus: *Supplies door fixtures, including automatic*   Fax: (717) 336-3881
    and revolving doors and door hardware.

● **ALOYS F. DORNBRACHT GMBH & CO.**
PO BOX 1454, D-58584 Iserlohn, Germany
CEO: Helmut Dornbracht, Chmn. & CEO   Tel: 49-2371-4330
Bus: *Mfr. design fittings and accessories for bath and*   Fax: 49-2371-433135
kitchens.   www.dornbracht.de
NAICS: 332913, 332999

    DORNBRACHT USA, INC.
    1700 Executive Dr. South, Ste. 600, Duluth, Georgia 30096
    CEO: Oliver Bleich, Mktg. Dir.   Tel: (770) 564-3599   %FO: 100
    Bus: *Mfr. design fittings and accessories for*   Fax: (770) 638-3316
    bath and kitchens.

● **DOUGLAS HOLDING AG**
Kabeler Str. 4, D-58099 Hagen, Germany
CEO: Henning Kreke, Chmn.   Tel: 49-2331-690-454   Rev: $1,673
Bus: *Perfume retailer.*   Fax: 49-2331-690-690   Emp: 18,039
                                                  www.douglas-holding.com
NAICS: 325620

    PARFUMERIE DOUGLAS
    156 Kings Highway North, Westport, Connecticut 06880
    CEO: Rita Donnerstag   Tel: (203) 226-2233   %FO: 100
    Bus: *Full-service, retail perfume store.*   Fax: (203) 226-2233

● **DRAEGER MEDICAL AG & CO.**
Moislinger Allee 53-55, D-23532 Luebeck, Germany
CEO: Dr. Wolfgang Reim, CEO   Tel: 49-451-882-808
Bus: *Medical equipment manufacture (35% JV Siemens*   Fax: 49-451-882-3197   Emp: 6,000
Medical).   www.draeger-medical.com
NAICS: 335999, 339112, 339113, 423450

DRAEGER SIEMENS MEDICAL, INC.
330 Jacksonville Rd., Hatboro, Pennsylvania 19040
CEO: Henning Lohse
Bus: *Mfr. infant medical devices.*

Tel: (215) 675-5200
Fax: (215) 675-5200

%FO: 100

DRAEGER SIEMENS MEDICAL, INC.
16 Electronics Ave., Danvers, Massachusetts 01923
CEO: Wilhelm Isenberg, Pres.
Bus: *Mfr. medical devices.*

Tel: (978) 907-7500
Fax: (978) 750-6879

%FO: 100

• **DRAGER SAFETY AG**
Revalstrasse 1, D-23560 Luebeck, Germany
CEO: Albert Jugel, Pres.
Bus: *Medical, safety and aerospace technology
   equipment.*

Tel: 49-451-882-2977
Fax: 49-451-882-3703
www.draeger-safety.com

Rev: $1,095
Emp: 10,800

NAICS: 334519, 335999, 339920, 561621

   DRAEGER SAFETY, INC.
   22010 Wilmington Ave., Carson, California 90745
   CEO: Patrica Wartoff
   Bus: *Mfr. safety equipment, respiratory
      protection products and gas detection*

   Tel: (310) 518-7188
   Fax: (310) 518-7699

   DRAEGER SAFETY, INC.
   505 Julie Rivers Dr., Sugar Land, Texas 77478
   CEO: Malcolm Watmough
   Bus: *Mfr. safety equipment, respiratory
      protection products and gas detection*

   Tel: (281) 498-1082
   Fax: (281) 498-5190

   %FO: 100

   DRAEGER SAFETY, INC.
   101 Technology Dr., PO Box 120, Pittsburgh, Pennsylvania 15230-0128
   CEO: Wesley J. Kenneweg, Pres.
   Bus: *Mfr. safety equipment, respiratory
      protection products and gas detection*

   Tel: (412) 787-8383
   Fax: (412) 787-2207

   %FO: 100
   Emp: 200

   DRAEGER SAFETY, INC.
   8356 Sterling St., Irving, Texas 75063
   CEO: Friedhelm Schellert
   Bus: *Mfr. safety equipment, respiratory
      protection products and gas detection*

   Tel: (972) 929-1100
   Fax: (972) 929-1105

• **DRESDNER BANK AG**
Jurgen-Ponto-Platz 1, D-60301 Frankfurt, Germany
CEO: Herbert Walter, Chmn.
Bus: *General banking services.*

Tel: 49-69-2630
Fax: 49-69-263-4831
www.dresdner-bank.de

Rev: $12,598
Emp: 42,060

NAICS: 522110, 522292, 523110, 523120, 523920, 523930

   DRESDNER BANK AG
   190 South LaSalle St., Chicago, Illinois 60603
   CEO: E. Ronald Holder, Mgr.
   Bus: *International commercial banking services.*

   Tel: (312) 444-1300
   Fax: (312) 444-1305

   %FO: 100

DRESDNER BANK LATIN AMERICA
801 Brickell Ave., 7/F, Miami, Florida 33132
CEO: Carmen C. Alvarez   Tel: (305) 373-0000
Bus: *Foreign bank & trade financing.*   Fax: (305) 530-0108

DRESDNER KLEINWORT WASSERSTEIN
1301 Ave. of the Americas, New York, New York 10019
CEO: Adam Parten   Tel: (212) 969-2700   %FO: 100
Bus: *Investment banking services.*   Fax: (212) 429-2127

● **DURKOPP ADLER AG**
Postdamer Strasse 190, D-33719 Bielefeld, Germany
CEO: Gerhard Vogel, Chmn.   Tel: 49-521-925-01   Rev: $182
Bus: *Mfr. industrial sewing equipment.*   Fax: 49-521-925-2645   Emp: 2,009
    www.duerkopp-adler.com
NAICS: 333298, 333922

    DURKOPP ADLER AMERICA INC.
    5875 Peachtree Industrial Blvd., Ste. 220, Norcross, Georgia 30092
    CEO: Norman Witthauser, Pres.   Tel: (770) 446-8162   %FO: 100
    Bus: *Sales/service industrial sewing equipment.*   Fax: (770) 448-1545   Emp: 100

    UNITED SEWING MACHINE SALES
    3230 Highland Ave. NE, Hickory, North Carolina 28601
    CEO: Buddy Jacomine   Tel: (828) 327-0115   %FO: 100
    Bus: *Sewing machine sales.*   Fax: (828) 327-3468

● **DURR AG**
Otto-Durr-Str. 8, D-70435 Stuttgart Zuffenhausen, Germany
CEO: Stephan Rojahn, CEO   Tel: 49-711-1361-095   Rev: $2,182
Bus: *Paint finishing systems, industrial cleaning*   Fax: 49-711-1361-455   Emp: 12,900
    systems and automation and conveyor systems.   www.durr.com
NAICS: 333922, 333999

    DURR INDUSTRIES INC.
    40600 Plymouth Rd., Plymouth, Michigan 48170-4297
    CEO: David S. Meynell, Mgr.   Tel: (734) 459-6800   %FO: 100
    Bus: *Paint finishing systems.*   Fax: (734) 459-5837

    PREMIER MANUFACTURING SUPPORT SERVICES L.P
    2828 Highland Ave., Norwood, Ohio 45212
    CEO: Michael A. Doyle   Tel: (513) 731-3590   %FO: 100
    Bus: *Manufacturing support services to the*   Fax: (513) 731-3658
    global automotive industry.

● **DZ BANK (DEUTSCHE GENOSSENSCHAFTSBANK)**
Am Platz der Republik, D-60265 Frankfurt am Main, Germany
CEO: Ulrich Brixner, Chmn. & CEO   Tel: 49-69-7447-2382   Rev: $2,860
Bus: *Commercial banking services.*   Fax: 49-69-7447-6784   Emp: 25,300
    www.dg.dzbank.de
NAICS: 522110, 522292, 522294, 522320, 522390

DZ BANK
DZ Bank Bldg., 609 5th Ave., New York, New York 10017
CEO: Oliver B'Oessnitz, Gen. Mgr.   Tel: (212) 745-1400   %FO: 100
Bus: *Commercial banking services.*   Fax: (212) 745-1550

DZ FINANCIAL MARKETS LLC
609 Fifth Ave., New York, New York 10017
CEO: Gerhard Summerer, Mgr.   Tel: (212) 745-1600   %FO: 100
Bus: *Financial services.*   Fax: (212) 745-1616   Emp: 100

● **E.ON AG**
E.ON-Platz 1, D-40479 Dusseldorf, Germany
CEO: Wulf H. Bernotat, Chmn. & CEO   Tel: 49-211-4579-0   Rev: $66,515
Bus: *Holding company engaged in utilities, energy and* Fax: 49-211-4579-501   Emp: 69,710
specialty chemicals.   www.eon.com
NAICS: 212111, 212112, 221111, 221112, 221113, 221119, 221121, 221122, 221210, 221310, 221320, 424720, 486210, 517212, 523130, 531110

CYRO INDUSTRIES
Rockaway 80 Corporate Center, 100 Enterprise Dr., Rockaway, New Jersey 07866
CEO: Robert Wurst, Pres.   Tel: (973) 442-6000
Bus: *Plastic & fiber manufacturing*   Fax: (973) 442-6117

DEGUSSA BUILDING SYSTEMS
889 Valley Park Dr., Shakopee, Minnesota 55379
CEO: Mike Galasso, Pres. & CEO   Tel: (952) 496-6000
Bus: *Specialty chemical manufacturing*   Fax: (952) 496-6062

DEGUSSA CORP.
379 Interpace Pkwy., Parsippany, New Jersey 07054
CEO: John Salvatore, Pres.   Tel: (973) 541-8000
Bus: *Specialty chemical manufacturing*   Fax: (973) 541-8013   Emp: 5,794

E.ON NORTH AMERICA, INC.
405 Lexington Ave., 57/F, New York, New York 10174
CEO: George Budenbender, Pres.   Tel: (646) 658-1962   %FO: 100
Bus: *Engaged in energy and specialty chemicals.* Fax: (212) 557-5189

KENTUCKY UTILTIES COMPANY
1 Quality St., Lexington, Kentucky 40507
CEO: Victor A. Staffieri, Chmn. & Pres. & CEO Tel: (859) 255-2100
Bus: *Electric utilities*   Fax: (502) 627-3609

LG&E ENERGY CORPORATION
220 West Main St., Louisville, Kentucky 40232
CEO: Victor A. Staffieri, Chmn. & Pres. & CEO Tel: (502) 627-2000   %FO: 100
Bus: *Engaged in energy and specialty chemicals.* Fax: (502) 627-3609   Emp: 3,521

STOCKHAUSEN, INC.
2401 Doyle St., Greensboro, North Carolina 27406
CEO: Peter Gursky, VP Operations   Tel: (336) 333-3500
Bus: *Specialty chemical manufacturing*   Fax: (336) 333-3545

- **EDEL MUSIC AG**
  Neumuhlen 17, D-22763 Hamburg, Germany
  CEO: Michael Haentjes, CEO
  Bus: *Distribution of music publishing, recordings and DVD manufacturing.*
  NAICS: 334612, 512220, 512230

  Tel: 49-40-890-85-0
  Fax: 49-40-890-85-310
  www.edel.com

  Rev: $160
  Emp: 740

    RED DISTRIBUTION COMPANY, DIV. EDEL MUSIC
    79 Fifth Ave., New York, New York 10003
    CEO: Bob Morelli
    Bus: *Heavy metal music distributor.*

    Tel: (212) 404-0600
    Fax: (212) 337-5252

    %FO: 100

- **EISENMANN KG**
  Tubinger Strasse 81, D-71032 Boblingen, Germany
  CEO: Gunther Dingler, CEO
  Bus: *Turnkey powder systems, energy saving ovens, efficient material flow systems and advanced controls.*
  NAICS: 325510, 333291, 333298, 334413

  Tel: 49-7031-780
  Fax: 49-7031-78-1000
  www.eisenmann.de

  Rev: $573
  Emp: 700

    EISENMANN, TEMTEK-ALLIED DIV.
    150 East Dartmoor Dr., Crystal Lake, Illinois 60014
    CEO: Klaus W. Lachmann
    Bus: *Ceramic and metallurgical systems.*

    Tel: (815) 455-4100
    Fax: (815) 455-1018

    %FO: 100

- **ELEKTRO-PHYSIK**
  Pasteurstr.15, D-50735 Cologne, Germany
  CEO: Klaus E. Steingroever, Dir.
  Bus: *Mfr. coating thickness testing gauges for quality control & corrosion prevention.*
  NAICS: 334513

  Tel: 49-221-752040
  Fax: 49-221-7520445
  www.elektrophysik.com

    ELECTRO-PHYSIK USA INC.
    770 West Algonquin Rd., Arlington Heights, Illinois 60005
    CEO: Aivars U. Freidenfelds, Vice Pres.
    Bus: *Coating thickness gauges distribution and sales.*

    Tel: (847) 437-6616
    Fax: (847) 437-0053

    %FO: 100

- **ELG HANIEL GmbH**
  Kremerskamp 16, D-47138 Duisburg, Germany
  CEO: Fredrich Terorde, Chmn.
  Bus: *Recycles and trades stainless steel scrap and processes metal alloys.*
  NAICS: 423510

  Tel: 49-203-4501-0
  Fax: 49-203-4501-251
  www.elg.de

  Rev: $1,589
  Emp: 785

    ELG METALS INC.
    8200 Port Rd., Louisville, Kentucky 40258
    CEO: Mark Schindler, Rep.
    Bus: *Recycles and trades stainless steel scrap and processes metal alloys.*

    Tel: (502) 933-2275
    Fax: (502) 933-2315

    %FO: 100

ELG METALS INC.
369 River Rd., McKeesport, Pennsylvania 15132
CEO: Alasdair J. Gledhill, Rep.
Bus: *Recycles and trades stainless steel scrap and processes metal alloys.*

Tel: (412) 672-9200
Fax: (412) 672-0824

%FO: 100

ELG METALS INC.
Southern Division, PO Box 955, Mobile, Alabama 36601-0955
CEO: Jeff Valentine, Rep.
Bus: *Recycles and trades stainless steel scrap and processes metal alloys.*

Tel: (251) 438-5600
Fax: (251) 438-5647

%FO: 100

ELG METALS INC.
Southern Division, 15134 Jacintoport Blvd., Houston, Texas 77213-6166
CEO: Andrew Wilk, Rep.
Bus: *Recycles and trades stainless steel scrap and processes metal alloys.*

Tel: (281) 457-2100
Fax: (281) 457-2500

%FO: 100

ELG METALS INC.
West Coast Division, 9400 Rayo Ave., South Gate, California 90280
CEO: Gary Brown, Rep.
Bus: *Recycles and trades stainless steel scrap and processes metal alloys.*

Tel: (323) 569-3545
Fax: (323) 569-4145

%FO: 100

ELG METALS INC.
103rd St. & Calumet River, Chicago, Illinois 60617-5721
CEO: Richard Jones, Rep.
Bus: *Recycles and trades stainless steel scrap and processes metal alloys.*

Tel: (773) 374-1500
Fax: (773) 374-1884

%FO: 100

ELG METALS INC.
145 Nassau St. #2E, New York, New York 10038
CEO: Chris Rohan, Rep.
Bus: *Recycles and trades stainless steel scrap and processes metal alloys.*

Tel: (212) 577-2312
Fax: (212) 577-2799

%FO: 100

● **ELMOS SEMICONDUCTOR AG**
Heinrich-Hertz Strasse, 1, D-44227 Dortmund, Germany
CEO: Knut S. Hinrichs, CEO
Bus: *Automobile integrated circuits manufacture.*

Tel: 49-231-75-490
Fax: 49-231-75-491-49
www.elmos.de

Rev: $115
Emp: 830

NAICS: 334413

ELMOS NORTH AMERICA, INC.
31700 W. 13 Mile, Ste. 110, Farmington Hills, Michigan 48334
CEO: Mike McCandlish
Bus: *Automobile integrated circuits manufacture and sales.*

Tel: (248) 865-3200
Fax: (248) 865-3203

%FO: 100

● **EPCOS AG**
St. Martin Str. 53, D-81669 Munich, Germany
CEO: Gerhard Pegam, CEO
Bus: *Passive electronic components manufacture.*

Tel: 49-89-636-09
Fax: 49-89-636-23549
www.epcos.com

Rev: $1,693
Emp: 15,587

NAICS: 334413

CRYSTAL TECHNOLOGY, INC., DIV. EPCOS
1040 East Meadow Circle, Palo Alto, California 94303
CEO: Georg Eberharter
Bus: *Mfr. of single crystals and components for OEM applications.*

Tel: (650) 856-7911
Fax: (650) 354-0173

%FO: 100

EPCOS, INC.
186 Wood Ave. South, Iselin, New Jersey 08830
CEO: Michael Pocsatko
Bus: *Passive electronic components manufacture and sales.*

Tel: (732) 906-4300
Fax: (732) 603-5935

%FO: 100

- **ERICH NETZSCH GHMB & CO.**
Gebrueder-Netzsch-Str. 19, D-95100 Selb, Germany
CEO: Thomas Netzsch, Chmn.
Bus: *Mfr. filter presses and dispersion pumps and equipment.*
NAICS: 333913

Tel: 49-92-87-75-0
Fax: 49-92-87-75-208
www.netzsch.com

NETZSCH INCORPORATED
119 Pickering Way, Exton, Pennsylvania 19341
CEO: Otto Max Schaefer, Pres.
Bus: *Mfr./sales/distribution of filter presses & dispersion equipment & pumps.*

Tel: (610) 363-8010
Fax: (610) 280-1229

%FO: 100
Emp: 75

NETZSCH INSTRUMENTS
37 North Ave., Burlington, Massachusetts 01803
CEO: Wolf-Dieter Emmerich, Pres.
Bus: *Mfr. thermal conductivity instruments & operates as a testing laboratory.*

Tel: (781) 272-5353
Fax: (781) 272-5225

Emp: 21

- **ESCADA AG**
Margaretha-Ley-Ring 1, D-85609 Aschheim/ Munich, Germany
CEO: Wolfgang Ley, CEO
Bus: *Design and manufacture of upscale women's apparel, accessories and fragrances.*
NAICS: 315212, 315231, 315232, 315233, 315234, 315999, 316214, 316992, 316993, 316999, 325620

Tel: 49-899-9440
Fax: 49-899-994-415-00
www.escada.com

Rev: $800
Emp: 4,167

ESCADA USA INC.
1412 Broadway, New York, New York 10018
CEO: Michelle Pesque, Mgr.
Bus: *Women's clothing.*

Tel: (800) 869-8424
Fax:

- **EUROHYPO AG**
Heffmann-Park 5, D-65760 Eschborn, Germany
CEO: Hendrik Gienow, CEO
Bus: *Mortgage lending.*

NAICS: 522310

Tel: 49-69-2548-28511
Fax: 49-69-2548-88511
www.eurohypo.com

Rev: $11,535
Emp: 2,400

EUROHYPO INC
6100 Center Dr., Ste. 925, Los Angeles, California 90045
CEO: Ed Balazs, VP
Bus: *Mortgage lending.*

Tel: (310) 215-1268
Fax: (310) 215-1277

EUROHYPO INC
123 North Wacker Dr., Ste. 2300, Chicago, Illinois 60606
CEO: Maureen Slentz, VP
Bus: *Mortgage lending.*

Tel: (312) 267-8860
Fax: (312) 267-8875

EUROHYPO INC.
1114 Ave. of the Americas, 29/F, New York, New York 10036
CEO: Johannes Boeckmann, VP
Bus: *Mortgage lending.*

Tel: (212) 479-5701
Fax: (212) 479-5800

%FO: 100

● **EVOTEC OAI AG**
Schnackenburgallee 114, D-22525 Hamburg, Germany
CEO: Joern Aldag, Pres. & CEO
Bus: *Drug research and discovery.*

Tel: 49-40-56081-0
Fax: 49-40-56081-222
www.evotecoai.com

Rev: $99
Emp: 639

NAICS: 325412, 541710

EVOTEC NORTH AMERICA
5 Turley Ct., North Potomac, Maryland 20878
CEO: Carsten Claussen, CEO
Bus: *Drug research and discovery.*

Tel: (240) 683-1199
Fax: (240) 683-8098

%FO: 100

● **FABER-CASTELL AG**
Numberger Strasse 2, D-90546 Stein, Germany
CEO: Wolfgang Graf von Faber-Castell, CEO
Bus: *Mfr. of pencils, fountain and roller pens and cosmetic products.*

Tel: 49-911-9965-0
Fax: 49-911-9965-760
www.faber-castell.de

Rev: $263
Emp: 5,500

NAICS: 325620, 339941

A. W. FABER-CASTELL CONSULTING USA, INC.
438 Main St., Bedminster, New Jersey 07921
CEO: Dante Del Vecchio
Bus: *Consulting services.*

Tel: (908) 470-4000
Fax: (908) 470-4000

%FO: 100

FABER-CASTELL COSMETICS, INC.
410 Jericho Turnpike, Jericho, New York 11753
CEO: Vincent Penna
Bus: *Mfr. cosmetic products.*

Tel: (516) 433-4064
Fax: (516) 433-4031

%FO: 100

FABER-CASTELL USA, INC.
9450 Allen Dr., Valley View, Cleveland, Ohio 44115
CEO: Jamie Gallagher
Bus: *Mfr. pencils, fountain and roller pens.*

Tel: (216) 589-4800
Fax: (216) 643-4660

%FO: 100

● **FAG KUGELFISCHER GEORG SCHAFER AG**
Georg-Schafer-Str. 30, D-97421 Schweinfurt, Germany
CEO: Robert Schullan, Chmn.
Bus: *Wholesale anti-friction bearings manufacture.*

Tel: 49-9721-910
Fax: 49-9721-91-3435
www.fag.de

Rev: $2,015
Emp: 16,200

NAICS: 332991, 333292, 333922, 333924, 333999

FAG AUTOMOTIVE, INC.
1750 East Big Beaver Rd., Troy, Michigan 48083
CEO: Mark Vachon, VP
Bus: *Automotive bearings products.*

Tel: (248) 528-4800
Fax: (248) 528-4827   Emp: 21

FAG BEARINGS CORPORATION
3900 Range Line Rd., Joplin, Missouri 64804
CEO: Gary Coonrad, Mgr.
Bus: *Ball & roller bearings*

Tel: (417) 781-3600
Fax: (417) 781-3605

FAG BEARINGS CORPORATION
200 Park Ave., Danbury, Connecticut 06810
CEO: Dieter Kuetemeier, Pres.
Bus: *Bearings manufacture and sales.*

Tel: (203) 790-5474   %FO: 100
Fax: (203) 830-8171   Emp: 300

THE BARDEN CORP.
200 Park Ave., Danbury, Connecticut 06810
CEO: John A. McCloskey, Pres.
Bus: *Mfr. of ball bearings components*

Tel: (203) 744-2211
Fax: (203) 744-3756   Emp: 600

● **FELIX SCHOELLER HOLDING GMBH**
Personalabteilung, Burg Gretesch, D-49086 Osnabruck, Germany
CEO: Kornelia Niekamp, Chmn.
Bus: *Mfr. specialty papers.*

Tel: 49-541-3800-307
Fax: 49-541-3800-782
www.felix-schoeller.com

NAICS: 322233

FELIX SCHOELLER TECHNICAL PAPERS INC.
PO Box 250, Pulaski, New York 13142
CEO: Richard E. Patterson Jones, CEO
Bus: *Paper products manufacture.*

Tel: (315) 298-5133   %FO: 100
Fax: (315) 298-4337

● **WILHELM FETTE GMBH, DIV. LEITZ GROUP**
Grabauer Strasse 24, D-2053 Schwarzenbek, Germany
CEO: Jorg Petersen, CEO
Bus: *Mfr. of precision metalwork cutters.*

Tel: 49-4151-120
Fax: 49-4151-12511   Emp: 1,200
www.fette.de

NAICS: 332212, 333515

FETTE AMERICA
400 Forge Way, Rockaway, New Jersey 07866
CEO: Rich Derickson, VP Sales
Bus: *Mfr. tablet presses.*

Tel: (973) 586-8722   %FO: 100
Fax: (973) 586-0450   Emp: 17

LMT-FETTE INC.
18013 Cleveland Pkwy., Suite 180, Cleveland, Ohio 44135
CEO: Brian Nowicki, Pres.
Bus: *Mfr. metal cutters.*

Tel: (216) 377-6130
Fax: (216) 377-0787

● **FJH AG**
Elsenheimerstr. 65, D-80687 Munich, Germany
CEO: Ulrich Korff, CEO
Bus: *Financial software manufacture.*

Tel: 49-89-769-01-0
Fax: 49-89-769-88-13
www.fjh.com

Rev: $92
Emp: 667

NAICS: 511210, 541512, 541519

   FJH US INC.
   512 Seventh Ave., 15/F, New York, New York 10018
   CEO: Marc Dutton, Dir.
   Bus: *Financial software manufacture and sales.*

   Tel: (212) 840-2618
   Fax: (212) 840-2693

   %FO: 100
   Emp: 12

● **FLUX GERAETE GMBH**
Talweg 12, D-75433 Maulbronn, Germany
CEO: Klaus Hann, Pres.
Bus: *Drum and container chemical transfer pumps
manufacture and distribution.*

Tel: 49-7043-1010
Fax: 49-7043-101555
www.flux-pumpen.de

NAICS: 333996

   FLUX PUMPS CORPORATION
   4330 Commerce Circle, Atlanta, Georgia 30336
   CEO: Michael T. O'Toole, Gen. Mgr.
   Bus: *Drum & container chemical transfer pumps
manufacture..*

   Tel: (404) 691-6010
   Fax: (404) 691-6314

   %FO: 100
   Emp: 5

● **FRANCOTYP-POSTALIA AG & CO.**
Triftweg 21-26, D-16542 Birkenwerder, Germany
CEO: Hans Christian Hiemenz, Mng. Dir.
Bus: *Postage meters, mail and shipping room systems
manufacture.*

Tel: 49-3303-525-0
Fax: 49-3303-525-799
www.francotyp.com

NAICS: 333293, 333313, 334119, 511210

   F-P MAILING SOLUTIONS
   140 North Mitchell Ct., Ste. 200, Addison, Illinois 60101
   CEO: Michael P. Doumas, Pres.
   Bus: *Distribution postage meters, mailing
machines, office equipment.*

   Tel: (630) 519-2600
   Fax: (630) 519-2499

   %FO: 100
   Emp: 50

● **FRANKL & KIRCHNER GMBH & CO. KG**
Scheffelstrasse 73, D-68723 Schwetzingen, Germany
CEO: Lotte Wiest, Pres.
Bus: *Electronic positioning motors for industrial sewing
equipment.*

Tel: 49-6202-2020
Fax: 49-6202-202115
www.efka.germany.net

NAICS: 335312, 335314

   EFKA OF AMERICA INC.
   3715 Northcrest Rd, Ste. 10, Atlanta, Georgia 30340
   CEO: J. D. Price, Sales
   Bus: *Electronic positioning motors sales and
service for industrial sewing equipment.*

   Tel: (770) 457-7006
   Fax: (770) 458-3899

   %FO: 100
   Emp: 12

- **FRANZ HANIEL & CIE GMBH**
  Franz-Haniel-Platz 1, D-47119 Duisburg, Germany
  CEO: Franz Markus Haniel, Chmn.
  Bus: *Pharmaceuticals, stainless-steel recycling and
     trading, washroom/work wear rental, aggregates
     and disaster recovery and property restoration.*
  NAICS: 327123, 327215, 424210, 541620, 562910, 812332

  Tel: 49-203-806-0
  Fax: 49-203-806-622
  www.haniel.de

  Rev: $33,168
  Emp: 53,200

  BELFOR USA GROUP, INC.
  185 Oakland Ave., Ste. 300, Birmingham, Michigan 48009
  CEO: Sheldon Yellen, CEO
  Bus: *Disaster restoration services.*

  Tel: (248) 594-1144
  Fax: (248) 594-3190

  %FO: 100
  Emp: 1,500

  ELG HANIEL METALS CORP.
  369 River Rd., McKeesport, Pennsylvania 15132
  CEO: Simon Merrills, CEO
  Bus: *Recycler of stainless steel & special alloys.*

  Tel: (413) 672-9200
  Fax: (413) 672-3236

  Emp: 265

- **FRANZ HERMLE & SOHN GMBH & CO.**
  Bahnhofstrasse 6, D-78559 Gosheim, Germany
  CEO: Gerd Hermle, Pres.
  Bus: *Mfr. of clocks and clock movements.*

  Tel: 49-7426-6010
  Fax: 49-7426-601333
  www.hermle-clocks.com

  Emp: 300

  NAICS: 334518

  HERMLE BLACK FOREST CLOCKS
  340 Industrial Park Dr, Amherst, Virginia 24521
  CEO: Alfred Hermle, Mgr.
  Bus: *Mfr. of clocks & clock movements, clock
     kits, Swiss screw machine parts.*

  Tel: (804) 946-7751
  Fax: (804) 946-7747

  %FO: 100
  Emp: 50

- **FRESENIUS MEDICAL CARE AG**
  Else-Kroner Strasse, 1, D-61346 Bad Homburg, Germany
  CEO: Dr. Ben Lipps, Chmn.
  Bus: *Healthcare operations in dialysis/renal services,
     dialysis products and homecare.*
  NAICS: 334510

  Tel: 49-6172-609-0
  Fax: 49-6172-609-2488
  www.fmc-ag.com

  Rev: $6,228
  Emp: 44,526

  FRESENIUS MEDICAL CARE NORTH AMERICA
  95 Hayden Ave., Lexington, Massachusetts 02421-7942
  CEO: Mats Wahlstrom, Pres. & CEO
  Bus: *Healthcare operations in dialysis/renal
     services, dialysis products and homecare.*

  Tel: (781) 402-9000
  Fax: (781) 402-9006

  %FO: 100

  OPTIMAL RENAL CARE LLC
  95 Hayden Ave., Lexington, Massachusetts 02421-7942
  CEO: David Tigue
  Bus: *Healthcare operations in dialysis/renal
     services, dialysis products and homecare.*

  Tel: (781) 402-9000
  Fax: (781) 402-9006

  %FO: 100

● **FREUDENBERG & CO. KOMMANDITGESELLSCHAFT**
Hohnerweg 2-4, D-69465 Weinheim, Germany
CEO: Dr. Peter Bettermann
Bus: *Seals, rubber, polymer, foam products and leather manufacturer.*
Tel: 49-6201-80-0
Fax: 49-6201-88-0
www.freudenberg.com
Rev: $4,000
Emp: 29,667
NAICS: 313210, 313221, 313311, 314110, 325212, 326113, 326291, 326299, 336312

> **FREUDENBERG NONWOVENS**
> 3400 Industrial Dr., Durham, North Carolina 27704-9429
> CEO: Walter Schwarz, Prtn.
> Bus: *Technical products division; mfr. nonwoven fabrics.*
> Tel: (919) 620-3900
> Fax: (919) 620-3909
> %FO: 100
> Emp: 750

> **FREUDENBERG NONWOVENS LTD. PARTNERSHIP**
> 2975 Pembroke Rd., Hopkinsville, Kentucky 42240-6802
> CEO: Hector Geist, VP
> Bus: *Filters sales and distribution.*
> Tel: (270) 886-0204
> Fax: (270) 886-7070
> %FO: 100

> **FREUDENBERG-NOK GENERAL PARTNERSHIP**
> 47690 East Anchor Ct., Plymouth, Michigan 48170
> CEO: Mohsen Sohi, Pres. & CEO
> Bus: *Seals, molded rubber & plastic components, vibration control systems, aftermarket rebuild kits manufacturer.*
> Tel: (734) 451-0020
> Fax: (734) 451-2547
> %FO: 100

● **FUCHS PETROLUB AG**
Friesenheimer Str. 17, D-68169 Mannheim, Germany
CEO: Dr. Manfred Fuchs, Chmn.
Bus: *Industrial lubricants manufacturer.*
Tel: 49-621-3802-0
Fax: 49-621-3802-190
www.fuchs-oil.de
Rev: $1,306
Emp: 4,220
NAICS: 324191, 325199

> **FUCHS LUBRICANTS CO.**
> 1001 Oakmead Dr., Arlington, Texas 76011
> CEO: Keith Brewer
> Bus: *Industrial lubricants manufacture.*
> Tel: (817) 640-0200
> Fax: (817) 649-8141
> %FO: 100

> **FUCHS LUBRICANTS CO.**
> PO Box 450, Waynesburg, Pennsylvania 15370
> CEO: John R. Elliot
> Bus: *Industrial lubricants manufacture.*
> Tel: (724) 627-3200
> Fax: (724) 852-2351
> %FO: 100

> **FUCHS LUBRICANTS CO.**
> 2601 New Cut Rd., Spartanburg, South Carolina 29303-6323
> CEO: J. Shepley
> Bus: *Industrial lubricants manufacture.*
> Tel: (864) 574-9300
> Fax: (864) 574-1591
> %FO: 100

> **FUCHS LUBRICANTS CO.**
> 17050 Lathrop Ave., Harvey, Illinois 60426
> CEO: L .Frank Kleinman, Chmn.
> Bus: *Industrial lubricants manufacture.*
> Tel: (708) 333-8900
> Fax: (708) 333-9180
> %FO: 100
> Emp: 515

FUCHS LUBRICANTS CO.
PO Box 9367, 120 Thirteenth St. West, Huntington, West Virginia 25704
CEO: Jack Yates   Tel: (304) 523-3716   %FO: 100
Bus: *Industrial lubricants manufacture.*   Fax: (304) 523-3751

FUCHS LUBRICANTS CO.
15556 Highway 216, Brookwood, Alabama 35444
CEO: Norman Hall   Tel: (205) 633-3526   %FO: 100
Bus: *Industrial lubricants manufacture.*   Fax: (205) 633-3527

FUCHS LUBRICANTS CO.
281 Silver Sands Rd., East Haven, Connecticut 06512
CEO: Chris Licursi   Tel: (203) 469-2336   %FO: 100
Bus: *Industrial lubricants manufacture.*   Fax: (203) 467-3223

FUCHS LUBRICANTS CO.
160 Weldon Pkwy., Maryland Heights, Missouri 63043
CEO: Tim Swearingen   Tel: (314) 997-4200   %FO: 100
Bus: *Industrial lubricants manufacture.*   Fax: (314) 997-6704

FUCHS LUBRICANTS CO.
17191 Walter P. Chrysler Freeway, Detroit, Michigan 48203
CEO: G. Przekop   Tel: (313) 891-3700   %FO: 100
Bus: *Industrial lubricants manufacture.*   Fax: (313) 891-1450

FUCHS LUBRICANTS CO.
1700 South Caton Ave., Baltimore, Maryland 21227-1100
CEO: Chris Licursi   Tel: (410) 368-5000   %FO: 100
Bus: *Industrial lubricants manufacture.*   Fax: (410) 368-5019

FUCHS LUBRICANTS CO.
3318 Pagosa Ct., Indianapolis, Indiana 46226
CEO: S. Deal   Tel: (317) 895-3907   %FO: 100
Bus: *Industrial lubricants manufacture.*   Fax: (317) 895-3908

FUCHS LUBRICANTS CO.
760 36th St. SE, Grand Rapids, Michigan 49548
CEO: Robert Cassidy   Tel: (616) 247-0363   %FO: 100
Bus: *Industrial lubricants manufacture.*   Fax: (616) 247-4856

FUCHS LUBRICANTS CO.
8036 Bavaria Rd., Twinsburg, Ohio 44087
CEO: Wolfgang Mueller, COO   Tel: (330) 963-0400   %FO: 100
Bus: *Industrial lubricants manufacture.*   Fax: (330) 963-3311   Emp: 200

FUCHS LUBRICANTS CO.
250 SW 14th Ave., Pompano Beach, Florida 33069
CEO: R. Nachenberg   Tel: (954) 782-9300   %FO: 100
Bus: *Industrial lubricants manufacture.*   Fax: (954) 781-5809

FUCHS LUBRICANTS CO.
105 Eighth St., PO Box M, Emlenton, Pennsylvania 16373
CEO: N. Marchak   Tel: (724) 867-5000   %FO: 100
Bus: *Industrial lubricants manufacture.*   Fax: (724) 867-1182

FUCHS LUBRICANTS CO.
250 SW 14th Ave., Pompano Beach, Florida 33069
CEO: Rick Nachenberg   Tel: (954) 782-9300   %FO: 100
Bus: *Industrial lubricants manufacture.* Fax: (954) 781-5809

FUCHS LUBRITECH DIVISION
2140 South 88th St., Kansas City, Kansas 66111-8701
CEO: Bill Kersey   Tel: (913) 422-4022   %FO: 100
Bus: *Industrial lubricants manufacture.* Fax: (913) 441-2333

● **JOSEF GARTNER GMBH**
Gartnerstrasse 20, D-89423 Gundelfingen, Germany
CEO: Dietrich Anders, CEO   Tel: 49-90-7384-0
Bus: *Door and gates and partitions manufacture.* Fax: 49-90-7384-2100
                                        www.josef-gartner.de

NAICS: 332321, 332323

JOSEF GARTNER USA INC.
1101 Perimeter Dr., Ste. 650, Schaumburg, Illinois 60173
CEO: Bernhard Rudolf   Tel: (847) 255-8133   %FO: 100
Bus: *Door and gates and partitions manufacture.* Fax: (847) 255-7881

● **GEA GROUP**
Dorstener Str. 484, D-44809 Bochum, Germany
CEO: Jorgen Heraeus, Chmn.   Tel: 49-234-9800   Rev: $7,424
Bus: *Develops and produces non-ferrous metals,* Fax: 49-234-9801-004   Emp: 29,189
chemicals, explosives and offers services for www.gea-group.com
transportation and engineering.
NAICS: 236210, 236220, 237990, 325998, 332410, 333294, 333319, 333415, 334513, 541330

GEA FILTRATION
1600 O'Keefe Rd., Hudson, Wisconsin 54016
CEO: Steve Kaplan   Tel: (715) 386-9371
Bus: *Mfr. industrial equipment.*   Fax: (715) 386-9376

GEA POWER COOLING SYSTEMS, INC.
610 West Ash St., 17/F, San Diego, California 92101
CEO: Thomas Tarnok, Pres.   Tel: (619) 232-7200   %FO: 100
Bus: *Engaged in heat rejection technology.* Fax: (619) 232-7177   Emp: 381

GEA/ FES SYSTEMS INC.
3475 Board Rd., York, Pennsylvania 17402
CEO: Ronald Eberhard, Pres.   Tel: (717) 767-6411   %FO: 100
Bus: *Mfr. of refrigeration equipment.* Fax: (717) 764-3627   Emp: 250

NIRO INC.
9165 Rumsey Rd., Columbia, Maryland 21045
CEO: Steven Kaplan, Pres.   Tel: (410) 997-8700   %FO: 100
Bus: *Mfr. liquid and powder processing* Fax: (410) 997-5021   Emp: 325
equipment.

TUCHENHAGEN
1000 Riverside St., Portland, Maine 04103
CEO: David W. Hamlin, member   Tel: (207) 797-9500   %FO: 100
Bus: *Sale of industrial equipment.*   Fax: Emp: 76

WESTFALIA SEPARATOR, INC.
100 Fairway Ct., Northvale, New Jersey 07647
CEO: Clement O'Donnell, Pres.
Bus: *Mfr. spare parts and centrifuges and systems.*
Tel: (201) 767-3900
Fax: (201) 767-3900
%FO: 100
Emp: 530

WESTFALIA-SURGE, INC.
1880 Country Farm Dr., Naperville, Illinois 60563-1000
CEO: Dirk Hejnal, Pres.
Bus: *Mfr. dairy equipment.*
Tel: (630) 369-8100
Fax: (630) 369-9875
%FO: 100
Emp: 324

● **GEDAS AG**
Carnotstr. 4, D-10587 Berlin, Germany
CEO: Axel Knobe, CEO
Bus: *Provides IT consulting and systems integration services to the auto industry.*
NAICS: 541511, 541512, 541519
Tel: 49-30-3997-2999
Fax: 49-30-3997-1970
www.gedas.com
Rev: $773
Emp: 4,930

GEDAS USA INC.
3499 Hamlin Rd., Rochester Hills, Michigan 48309
CEO: Francisco Celis
Bus: *Provides IT consulting and systems integration services to the auto industry.*
Tel: (248) 754-3100
Fax: (248) 754-3065
%FO: 100

● **GELITA GROUP**
Uferstr 7, D-69412 Eberbach, Germany
CEO: Jorg Siebert, Chmn.
Bus: *Mfr. gelatin.*
NAICS: 325199
Tel: 49-6271-8401
Fax: 49-6271-8427-00
www.gelita.com
Rev: $628
Emp: 2,500

GELITA USA INC.
2445 Port Neal Industrial Rd., Sergeant Bluff, Iowa 51054
CEO: Charles P. Markham, Pres.
Bus: *Mfr. gelatin.*
Tel: (712) 943-5516
Fax: (712) 943-3372
%FO: 100
Emp: 265

● **GENESCAN EUROPE AG**
Engesserstr. 4, D-79108 Freiburg, Germany
CEO: Wolfgang Senne, CEO
Bus: *Holding company provides microbiological and molecular biological testing of food and animal feed.*
NAICS: 541380, 551112
Tel: 49-761-5038-200
Fax: 49-761-5038-211
www.genescan.com

GENESCAN, INC.
2315 North Causeway Blvd., Ste. 200, Metairie, Louisiana 70001
CEO: Michael Russell, Pres.
Bus: *Testing laboratories.*
Tel: (504) 297-4330
Fax: (504) 297-4335
%FO: 100
Emp: 25

• GEORG VON HOLTZBRINCK GMBH

Gansheidestr. 26, D-70184 Stuttgart, Germany

CEO: Stefan von Holtzbrinck, Chmn.

Bus: *Engaged in magazine, book and newspaper publishing.*

NAICS: 511110, 511130

Tel: 49-711-2150-0
Fax: 49-711-2150-100
www.sholtzbrinck.com

Rev: $2,150
Emp: 11,500

BEDFORD, FREEMAN & WORTH

33 Irving Place, 10/F, New York, New York 10003-2332

CEO: Joan Feinberg, Pres.

Bus: *Trade book publishing.*

Tel: (212) 375-7000
Fax: (212) 561-8281

%FO: 100

FARRAR, STRAUS & GIROUX, INC.

19 Union Square West, New York, New York 10003

CEO: Jonathon Galassi, Pres.

Bus: *Book publishing.*

Tel: (212) 741-6900
Fax: (212) 206-5340

%FO: 100
Emp: 100

HOLTZBRINCK PUBLISHERS

175 Fifth Ave., New York, New York 10010-7703

CEO: John Sargent, CEO

Bus: *Trade and professional book publisher.*

Tel: (212) 674-5151
Fax: (310) 665-0900

%FO: 100

SCIENTIFIC AMERICAN

415 Madison Ave., 14/F, New York, New York 10017-7935

CEO: Gretchen G. Teichgraeber, Pres.

Bus: *Magazine and book publisher.*

Tel: (212) 754-0550
Fax: (212) 832-2998

%FO: 100
Emp: 228

ST. MARTIN'S PRESS, INC.

175 Fifth Ave., New York, New York 10010

CEO: Sally Richarson, Pres.

Bus: *Book publishing.*

Tel: (212) 674-5151
Fax: (212) 674-3179

%FO: 100
Emp: 455

W. H. FREEMAN & COMPANY

41 Madison Ave., 35/F, New York, New York 10010-2208

CEO: Lawrence Jankovic, CFO

Bus: *Trade and professional books publishing.*

Tel: (212) 576-9400
Fax: (212) 689-2383

%FO: 100
Emp: 300

• GERLING-KONZERN GLOBALE AG

Gereonshof 16, D-50670 Cologne, Germany

CEO: Bjorn Jansli, Chmn. & CEO

Bus: *Insurance holding company.*

NAICS: 524113, 524114, 524126, 524128, 524130

Tel: 49-221-144-1
Fax: 49-221-144-3319
www.gerling.com

Rev: $7,787
Emp: 7,406

GERLING AMERICA INSURANCE CO.

100 Park Ave., 28/F, New York, New York 10017

CEO: Peter Noack, Pres.

Bus: *Reinsurance products & services.*

Tel: (212) 756-2600
Fax: (212) 756-2605

%FO: 100
Emp: 106

- **GIESECKE & DEVRIENT GMBH**
  Prinzregentenstr. 159, D-81677 Munich, Germany
  CEO: Karsten Ottenberg, Chmn. & CEO   Tel: 49-8941-190   Rev: $992
  Bus: *Bank note and securities printing systems.*   Fax: 49-8941-19-1535   Emp: 7,000
                                              www.gdm.de
  NAICS: 323110, 323111, 323112, 323119, 333293, 333313, 541490

  GIESECKE & DEVRIENT AMERICA, INC.
  45925 Horseshoe Dr., Dulles, Virginia 20166
  CEO: William Berchtold, Pres.   Tel: (703) 480-2000   %FO: 100
  Bus: *Currency automation and services.*   Fax: (703) 480-2060   Emp: 650

  GIESECKE & DEVRIENT CARDTECH, INC.
  2020 Enterprise Pkwy., PO Box 1028, Twinsburg, Ohio 44087
  CEO: James Frye, Pres.   Tel: (330) 425-1515   %FO: 100
  Bus: *Smart cards and services.*   Fax: (330) 425-9105   Emp: 107

- **GILDEMEISTER AG**
  Gildemeisterstr. 60, I-33689 Bielefeld, Germany
  CEO: Hans Henning Offen, Chmn.   Tel: 49-5205-74-0   Rev: $1,434
  Bus: *Mfr. machine and cutting tools.*   Fax: 49-5205-74-3190   Emp: 5,174
                                              www.gildemeister.com
  NAICS: 333512, 333516

  DMG CHARLOTTE, INC.
  13509 S. Point Blvd., Ste. 190, Charlotte, North Carolina 28273
  CEO: Corey Johnson, Pres.   Tel: (704) 583-1193   %FO: 100
  Bus: *Mfr. machine and cutting tools.*   Fax: (704) 583-1149   Emp: 36

  DMG CHICAGO, INC.
  1665 Penny Lane, Schaumburg, Illinois 60173
  CEO: James Gondeck, Pres.   Tel: (847) 781-0277   %FO: 100
  Bus: *Sale of machine tools.*   Fax: (847) 781-0388   Emp: 40

  DMG LOS ANGELES, INC.
  5552 Cerritos Ave., Cypress, California 90630
  CEO: Mr. Pierce, Mng. Dir.   Tel: (714) 527-4981   %FO: 100
  Bus: *Mfr. machine and cutting tools.*   Fax: (714) 527-4986

- **GIRMES AG**
  Johannes-Girmes Str. 27, Nordrhein Westfalen, D-47929 Grefrath, Germany
  CEO: Dr. Dirk Busse, CEO   Tel: 49-2158-300   Rev: $193
  Bus: *Textiles and textile products manufacture.* Fax: 49-2158-30433   Emp: 900
                                              www.girmes.de
  NAICS: 313221, 314999, 424310

  J. L .DE BALL OF AMERICA LTD.
  111 West 40th St., Rm. 414, New York, New York 10018
  CEO: Paul Flay, Pres.   Tel: (212) 575-8613   %FO: 100
  Bus: *Marketing and trading textiles.*   Fax: (212) 575-8616   Emp: 5

• **GPC BIOTECH AG**
Fraunhoferstr. 20, D-82152 Munich, Germany
CEO: Bernd R. Seizinger, CEO
Bus: *Engaged in pharmaceutical research and technology.*
NAICS: 325412, 813212

Tel: 49-89-85-65-2600
Fax: 49-89-85-65-2610
www.gpc-biotech.com

Emp: 200

  GPC BIOTECH INC.
  101 College Rd. East, Princeton, New Jersey 08540
  CEO: Thomas McKearn, MD
  Bus: *Engaged in research and technology.*

  Tel: (609) 524-1000
  Fax: (609) 524-1050

  %FO: 100

  GPC BIOTECH INC.
  610 Lincoln St., Waltham, Massachusetts 02451
  CEO: Laurie Doyle
  Bus: *Engaged in research and technology.*

  Tel: (781) 890-9007
  Fax: (781) 890-9005

  %FO: 100

• **GREENLIGHT MEDIA AG**
Gormannstr. 22, D-10119 Berlin, Germany
CEO: Stefan Beiten, CEO
Bus: *Film production.*

NAICS: 512110, 512120, 512191, 512199

Tel: 49-30-72-6200-0
Fax: 49-30-42-6200-222
www.greenlightmedia.com

  GREENLIGHT MEDIA USA
  15000 Hayne St., Van Nuys, California 91411
  CEO: Heath McLaughlin, Pres.
  Bus: *Film production.*

  Tel: (818) 947-0099
  Fax: (818) 475-1488

  %FO: 100

• **GROB WERKE GMBH & CO KG**
Industriestr. 4, D-87712 Mindelheim, Germany
CEO: Burkhardt Grob, Owner
Bus: *Machine tools and assembly equipment manufacture.*
NAICS: 333512, 333999

Tel: 49-826-19960
Fax: 49-826-996268
www.grob.de

Rev: $245
Emp: 1,960

  GROB SYSTEMS,INC.
  1070 Navajo Dr., Bluffton, Ohio 45817
  CEO: Ralf Bronnenmeier, CEO
  Bus: *Mfr. machine tools & assembly equipment.*

  Tel: (419) 358-9015
  Fax: (419) 369-3331

  %FO: 100
  Emp: 194

• **GROHE WATER TECHNOLOGY AG & CO. KG**
PO Box 1361, D-58653 Hemer, Germany
CEO: David J. Haines, CEO
Bus: *Sanitary fittings and water technology products manufacture.*
NAICS: 332911, 332912, 332913, 423720

Tel: 49-2372-930
Fax: 49-2372-931-322
www.grohe.com

Rev: $1,243
Emp: 5,800

  GROHE AMERICA, INC.
  241 Covington Dr., Bloomingdale, Illinois 60108
  CEO: Bob Atkins, Pres.
  Bus: *Sanitary fittings and water technology products manufacture and sales.*

  Tel: (630) 582-7711
  Fax: (630) 872-5700

  %FO: 100

- **GROUP TECHNOLOGIES**
Ottostr. 4, D-76227 Karlsruhe, Germany
CEO: Jurgen W. Wege, Chmn. & CEO
Bus: *E-mail security software manufacture.*

Tel: 49-721-4901-0
Fax: 49-721-4901-199
www.group-technologies.com

NAICS: 511210

    GROUP TECHNOLOGIES
    120 Quarry Dr., Ste. B214, Milford, Massachusetts 01754
    CEO: Karl-Heinz Dahley, Pres.   Tel: (508) 473-3332   %FO: 100
    Bus: *Mfr. of security software.*   Fax: (508) 473-9940

    GROUP TECHNOLOGIES
    321 Fortune Blvd., Ste. 2, Milford, Massachusetts 01757
    CEO: Karl-Heinz Dahley, Pres.   Tel: (508) 473-3332   %FO: 100
    Bus: *Mfr. of e-mail security software.*   Fax: (508) 473-9940

- **GROZ-BECKERT K.G.**
Parkweg 2, D-72458 Albstadt, Germany
CEO: Dr. Thomas Linder, CEO
Bus: *Industrial knitting, sewing, felting tufting needles manufacture.*
NAICS: 333292, 339993

Tel: 49-74-31-100
Fax: 49-74-31-102777
www.groz-beckert.com
Emp: 6,000

    GROZ-BECKERT USA INC.
    3480 Lakemount Blvd., Mailing: P.O. Box 7131 Charlotte, NC 28241, Fort Mill, South Carolina 29708
    CEO: Henry Tio, VP   Tel: (803) 548-4769
    Bus: *Sewing needle products*   Fax: (803) 584-3544   Emp: 51

- **GUNOLD GMBH**
Obernburger Str. 125, D-63811 Stockstadt, Germany
CEO: Christoph Gunold, Mng. Dir.
Bus: *Distributor machine embroidery supplies, CAD computer systems, punching services for designs and consulting for embroidery industry.*
NAICS: 333292, 424310, 451130, 541512

Tel: 49-60-27-20080
Fax: 49-60-27-3772
www.gunold.de

    GUNOLD USA INC.
    980 Cobb Place Blvd. NW, Kennesaw, Georgia 30144
    CEO: James M. Geary, Pres.   Tel: (770) 421-0300   %FO: 100
    Bus: *Wholesale/distribution machine embroidery supplies, CAD computer system, punching services for designs, letter & appliqués cutting.*   Fax: (770) 421-0505   Emp: 50

- **HACOBA-TEXTILMASCHINEN GMBH**
Hatzfelder Str. 161, D-42281 Wuppertal, Germany
CEO: Ralf Lucht, Pres.
Bus: *Textile machinery and parts.*

Tel: 49-202 7091-0
Fax: 49-202-7091-214
www.hacoba.com

NAICS: 333292

HACOBA TEXTILE MACHINERY LP
11024 Nations Ford Rd., Pineville, North Carolina 28134
CEO: Eberhard Scheffer, Sales
Bus: *Sale/service textile machines.*
Tel: (704) 588-2781
Fax: (704) 588-4798
%FO: 100

● **HAFELE GMBH & CO.**
Adolf-Hafele Str. 1, Baden-Wuerttemberg, D-72202 Nagold, Germany
CEO: Hans Nock, Pres.
Bus: *Distribution of European furniture and cabinet hardware.*
Tel: 49-7452-950
Fax: 49-7452-95200
www.hafele.de
Rev: $259
Emp: 800
NAICS: 331111, 332212, 332510, 333515, 423710, 423830

HAFELE AMERICA COMPANY
3901 Cheyenne Dr., PO Box 4000, High Point, North Carolina 27263
CEO: John C. Hossli, Pres.
Bus: *Wholesaler of hardware for furniture & cabinets*
Tel: (336) 889-2322
Fax: (336) 431-3831
%FO: 100
Emp: 350

● **HAMBURG-SUD**
Ost-West-Str. 59-61, Postfach 111540, D-20457 Hamburg, Germany
CEO: Kochan Gunter, Chmn.
Bus: *Engaged in marine transport and logistics management.*
Tel: 49-40-3705-01
Fax: 49-40-3705-2313
www.hamburg-sued.com
Rev: $2,661
Emp: 3,462
NAICS: 483111

HAMBURG SUD NORTH AMERICA, INC.
1245 East Diehl Rd., Ste. 302, Naperville, Illinois 60563
CEO: Barbara Rogers
Bus: *Containerized shipping.*
Tel: (630) 955-1400
Fax: (630) 955-0974
%FO: 100

HAMBURG SUD NORTH AMERICA, INC.
11200 Metro Airport Center Dr., Ste. 105, Romulus, Michigan 48174
CEO: Sheryl Blessing, Mgr.
Bus: *Shipping agent.*
Tel: (734) 955-9000
Fax: (734) 955-9701
%FO: 100

HAMBURG SUD NORTH AMERICA, INC.
9485 Regency Square Blvd. North, Ste. 500, Jacksonville, Florida 33225
CEO: C. S. Jax
Bus: *Containerized shipping.*
Tel: (904) 722-2400
Fax: (904) 722-9069
%FO: 100

HAMBURG SUD NORTH AMERICA, INC.
8240 NW 52nd Terr., Ste. 505, Miami, Florida 33166
CEO: Milena Alicandu, Mgr.
Bus: *Sale of industrial service paper.*
Tel: (305) 471-7370
Fax: (305) 463-0518
%FO: 100
Emp: 47

HAMBURG SUD NORTH AMERICA, INC.
Curtis Center, Independence Square West, Ste. 1075W, Philadelphia, Pennsylvania 19106
CEO: Stephen George, Mgr.
Bus: *Containerized shipping.*
Tel: (215) 923-6900
Fax: (215) 625-9810
%FO: 100
Emp: 15

HAMBURG SUD NORTH AMERICA, INC.
333 Bush St., Ste. 2580, San Francisco, California 94104
CEO: Rhonda Short
Bus: *Containerized shipping.*
Tel: (415) 495-6300
Fax: (415) 295-2313
%FO: 100

HAMBURG SUD NORTH AMERICA, INC.
465 South St., Morristown, New Jersey 07960
CEO: Jay Hong, Pres.   Tel: (973) 775-5300   %FO: 100
Bus: *Shipping agent.*   Fax: (973) 775-5310   Emp: 400

HAMBURG SUD NORTH AMERICA, INC.
1225 North Loop West, Ste. 324, Houston, Texas 77008
CEO: Carol Whitefield, Mgr.   Tel: (713) 862-8077   %FO: 100
Bus: *Containerized shipping.*   Fax: (713) 862-8230

NORTON LILLY INTERNATIONAL, INC.
680 Iwilei Rd., Ste. 535, Honolulu, Hawaii 96817
CEO: Peter Wilson, Gen. Mgr.   Tel: (808) 544-0441   %FO: 100
Bus: *Containerized shipping.*   Fax: (808) 531-0858   Emp: 5

● **HANNOVER RUECKVERSICHERUNGS AG (HANNOVER RE)**
Karl-Wiechert-Allee 50, D-30625 Hannover, Germany
CEO: Wilhelm Zeller, Chmn.   Tel: 49-511-5604-0   Rev: $11,857
Bus: *Reinsurance.*   Fax: 49-511-5604-1188   Emp: 2,035
                                        www.hannover-re.com

NAICS: 334511, 524130

    CLARENDON NSURANCE GROUP
    7 Times Square, New York, New York 10036
    CEO: Detlef Steiner, Pres. & CEO   Tel: (212) 805-9700   %FO: 100
    Bus: *Provides property and casualty insurance.*   Fax: (212) 805-9800   Emp: 470

    HANNOVER LIFE REASSURANCE COMPANY OF AMERICA
    800 North Magnolia Ave., Ste. 1400, Orlando, Florida 32803
    CEO: Peter Schafer, Pres.   Tel: (407) 649-8411   %FO: 100
    Bus: *Reinsurance services.*   Fax: (407) 649-8322   Emp: 76

    INSURANCE CORP. OF HANNOVER
    500 Park Blvd., Ste. 1425, Itasca, Illinois 60143
    CEO: Stephen Fitzpatrick, Mgr.   Tel: (630) 250-5511
    Bus: *Accident/health insurance.*   Fax: Emp: 40

    INSURANCE CORP. OF HANNOVER
    150 N. Wacker Dr., 29/F, Chicago, Illinois 60606
    CEO: Lothar Becker, SVP   Tel: (312) 580-1900
    Bus: *Liability & property insurance.*   Fax: Emp: 120

● **HAPAG-LLOYD CONTAINER LINE GMBH, SUB. TUI**
Ballindamm 25, D-20095 Hamburg, Germany
CEO: Michael Behrendt, Chmn.   Tel: 49-40-3001-0   Rev: $3,670
Bus: *Freight container shipping, cruise line and travel.*   Fax: 49-40-3266-25   Emp: 3,937
                                        www.hapag-lloyd.com
NAICS: 483111, 483112, 483212, 488510, 493110, 561520

    HAPAG-LLOYD (AMERICA) INC
    7 East Congress St., Ste. 900, Savannah, Georgia 31401
    CEO: Edward Ramirez, Dir.   Tel: (912) 238-3510   %FO: 100
    Bus: *Ocean freight forwarding.*   Fax: (915) 238-3509

HAPAG-LLOYD (AMERICA) INC
2505 2nd Ave. Bldg., Ste. 605, Seattle, Washington 98121
CEO: Brad Crollard, Gen. Mgr.   Tel: (206) 448-6789   %FO: 100
Bus: *Ocean freight forwarding.*   Fax: (206) 448-6778

HAPAG-LLOYD (AMERICA) INC
8200 NW 33rd St., Ste. 301, Miami, Florida 33122
CEO: Ricardo Valdes   Tel: (305) 591-8410   %FO: 100
Bus: *Ocean freight forwarding.*   Fax: (305) 594-2374

HAPAG-LLOYD (AMERICA) INC
420 West 42nd St., Ste. 11, Kansas City, Missouri 64111
CEO: Douglas Ahrens, Mgr.   Tel: (816) 531-7185   %FO: 100
Bus: *Ocean freight forwarding.*   Fax: (816) 531-4753

HAPAG-LLOYD (AMERICA) INC
555 East Ocean Blvd., Ste. 300, Long Beach, California 90802
CEO: Frederick Coutinho, Gen. Mgr.   Tel: (888) 513-2180   %FO: 100
Bus: *Ocean freight forwarding.*   Fax: (562) 437-6656

HAPAG-LLOYD (AMERICA) INC
885 Kempsville Rd., Amelia Bldg., Ste. 320, Norfolk, Virginia 23502
CEO: Raymond A. Newlon, SVP   Tel: (877) 605-6533   %FO: 100
Bus: *Ocean freight forwarding.*   Fax: (757) 461-7628

HAPAG-LLOYD (AMERICA) INC.
222 Forbes Rd., Ste. 302, Braintree, Massachusetts 02184
CEO: Eric Brenner, Dir.   Tel: (781) 843-3300   %FO: 100
Bus: *Ocean freight forwarding.*   Fax: (781) 843-1805

HAPAG-LLOYD (AMERICA) INC.
PO Box 480114, Charlotte, North Carolina 28269
CEO: Debi Hanson, Mgr.   Tel: (704) 717-8330   %FO: 100
Bus: *Ocean freight forwarding.*   Fax: (704) 717-8339

HAPAG-LLOYD (AMERICA) INC.
3030 Warrenville Rd., Ste. 500, Lisle, Illinois 60532
CEO: Timothy Collins, SVP   Tel: (630) 527-9150   %FO: 100
Bus: *Ocean freight forwarding.*   Fax: (630) 527-4701

HAPAG-LLOYD (AMERICA) INC.
399 Hoes Lane, Piscataway, New Jersey 08854
CEO: Cameron Bowie, SVP   Tel: (877) 523-8300   %FO: 100
Bus: *Ocean freight forwarding.*   Fax: (732) 885-3745

HAPAG-LLOYD (AMERICA) INC.
24600 Center Ridge Rd., Ste. 120, Westlake, Ohio 44145
CEO: Peter Telari, Mgr.   Tel: (440) 835-4130   %FO: 100
Bus: *Ocean freight forwarding.*   Fax: (440) 835-5105

HAPAG-LLOYD (AMERICA) INC.
100 Meadowcreek Dr., Ste. 200, Corte Madera, California 94925
CEO: Wolfgang Freese, SVP   Tel: (415) 927-2900   %FO: 100
Bus: *Ocean freight forwarding.*   Fax: (415) 927-8833

HAPAG-LLOYD (AMERICA) INC.
1 Poston Rd., Ste. 195, Charleston, South Carolina 29407
CEO: David S. Buchanan, Mgr.   Tel: (843) 556-4052   %FO: 100
Bus: *Ocean freight forwarding.*   Fax: (843) 556-3169

HAPAG-LLOYD (AMERICA) INC.
245 Townpark Dr., Ste. 300, Kennesaw, Georgia 30144
CEO: Michelle Fowler, Dir.   Tel: (888) 851-4083   %FO: 100
Bus: *Ocean freight forwarding.*   Fax: (770) 419-2912

HAPAG-LLOYD (AMERICA) INC.
1015 Atlantic Blvd., Ste. 248, Atlantic Beach, Florida 32233
CEO: Raymond Jones, Mgr.   Tel: (904) 997-8989   %FO: 100
Bus: *Ocean freight forwarding.*   Fax: (904) 997-8283

HAPAG-LLOYD (AMERICA) INC.
30 Benmar Dr., Ste. 250, Houston, Texas 77060
CEO: David Meyer, Dir.   Tel: (866) 881-1374   %FO: 100
Bus: *Ocean freight forwarding.*   Fax: (281) 272-9523

HAPAG-LLOYD (AMERICA) INC.
PO Box 126347, Benbrook, Texas 76126
CEO: Carsten Seebers, Mgr.   Tel: (281) 405-4808   %FO: 100
Bus: *Ocean freight forwarding.*   Fax: (281) 272-9523

WALDRON NORTON LILLY INTERNATIONAL LLC
Pier 1, Control Tower, Honolulu, Hawaii 96813
CEO: Krystal Frank, Mgr.   Tel: (808) 545-2466   %FO: 100
Bus: *Ocean freight forwarding.*   Fax: (808) 537-2464

● **HARIBO GMBH & CO.**
Hans-Riegel-Str. 1, D-53129 Bonn, Germany
CEO: Hans Riegel, Mng. Dir.   Tel: 49-228-537-0   Rev: $570
Bus: *Gummi candies (Gummi Bear) manufacturer..*   Fax: 49-228-537-289   Emp: 2,000
                                       www.haribo.com
NAICS: 311340

HARIBO OF AMERICA, INC.
1825 Woodlawn Dr., Ste. 204, Baltimore, Maryland 21207
CEO: Christian Jegen, Pres. & CEO   Tel: (410) 265-8890   %FO: 100
Bus: *Candy (Gummi Bear) manufacturer and sales.*   Fax:(410) 265-8898

● **HAVER & BOECKER**
Carl Haver Platz 3, D-59282 Oelde, Germany
CEO: Reinhold Festge, Pres.   Tel: 49-25-22300   Rev: $128
Bus: *Mfr./engineering/sale/service individual*   Fax: 49-2522-30403   Emp: 1,375
     packaging systems.   www.haverboecker.com
NAICS: 331111, 332116

HAVER FILLING SYSTEMS INC.
400 Gees Mill Business Ct., PO Box 80937, Conyers, Georgia 30013
CEO: Reinhold Festage, Pres.   Tel: (770) 760-1130   %FO: 100
Bus: *Engineering/sale/service individual*   Fax: (770) 760-1181   Emp: 14
     packaging systems.

W.S. STYLER
Peach Orchard Rd., Salisbury, North Carolina 28144
CEO: Roy Tretchler, Mgr. Tel: (704) 633-5384
Bus: *Screening Media* Fax: (704) 633-5392

W.S. TYLER
8570 Tyler Blvd., Mentor, Ohio 44060
CEO: Larry Polk, Pres. Tel: (440) 974-1047
Bus: *Wire cloth products.* Fax: (440) 974-0921 Emp: 100

● **HEALY HUDSON AG**
Peter Sander Str. 32, D-55252 Mainz-Kastel, Germany
CEO: Christian Konhauser, CEO Tel: 49-6134-2980
Bus: *Software manufacture.* Fax: 49-6134-298105
 www.healy-hudson.com
 NAICS: 511210

 HEALY HUDSON
 1700 West Park Dr., Ste. 260, Westborough, Massachusetts 01581
 CEO: Susan Stevenson, Pres. Tel: (508) 870-5530 %FO: 100
 Bus: *Mfr./sales of software.* Fax: (508) 870-5533

● **HEIDELBERG CEMENT AG**
Berliner Str. 6, D-69120 Heidelberg, Germany
CEO: Fritz Jurgen Heckmann, Chmn. Tel: 49-6221-481-227 Rev: $9,452
Bus: *Mfr. construction materials, cement, concrete,* Fax: 49-6221-481-217 Emp: 42,062
 aggregates, brick and paperboard products. www.heidelbergcement.com
 NAICS: 212311, 212312, 212319, 212321, 212322, 213115, 327310, 327320, 327331, 327332, 327390, 327420,
327991

 LEHIGH CEMENT COMPANY
 7660 Imperial Way, Allentown, Pennsylvania 18195
 CEO: Helmut S. Erhard, Pres. & CEO Tel: (610) 366-4600 %FO: 100
 Bus: *Mfr. cement, aggregates, ready-mix cement.* Fax: (610) 366-4851 Emp: 6,000

● **HEIDELBERGER DRUCKMASCHINEN AG**
Kurfursten Anlage 52-60, D-69115 Heidelberg, Germany
CEO: Bernhard Schreier, Chmn. & CEO Tel: 49-6221-9200 Rev: $4,456
Bus: *solutions provider for the print media; printing* Fax: 49-6221-926999 Emp: 22,641
 presses and cutting, folding and binding www.heidelberg.com
 NAICS: 333293

 BAUMFOLDER CORP.
 1660 Campbell Rd., Sidney, Ohio 45365
 CEO: Ulrik Nygaard, Pres. Tel: (937) 492-1281 %FO: 100
 Bus: *Production of folding machines, drills,* Fax: (937) 492-7280 Emp: 80
 saddle stitchers, cutters, & collators.

 HEIDELBERG USA INC.
 1000 Gutenberg Dr., Kennesaw, Georgia 30144
 CEO: James P. Dunn, Pres. Tel: (770) 419-6600 %FO: 100
 Bus: *US Headquarters, Sales printing presses.* Fax: (770) 419-6550 Emp: 3,000

• **DR. JOHANNES HEIDENHAIN GMBH**
PO Box 1260, D-83292 Traunreut, Germany
CEO: Thomas Sesselmann, Mng. Dir.   Tel: 49-8669-31-3132   Rev: $476
Bus: *Mfr. optical rotary encoders.*   Fax: 49-8669-5061   Emp: 6,000
                                            www.heidenhain.de

   NAICS: 334413

    HEIDENHAIN CORPORATION
    333 State Pkwy., Schaumburg, Illinois 60173
    CEO: Rick J. Korte, Pres.   Tel: (847) 490-1191   %FO: 100
    Bus: *Mfr./sales optical rotary encoders.* Fax: (847) 490-3931   Emp: 75

• **HEINZ KETTLER**
Haupstr. 28, D-59463 Ense-Parsit, Germany
CEO: Heinz Kettler, Pres.   Tel: 49-2938-810   Rev: $504
Bus: *Children's bicycles and bicycle seats, patio*   Fax: 49-2938-2022   Emp: 2,000
    furniture, table tennis and exercise equipment   www.kettler.net
    and juvenile products.
   NAICS: 336991, 337122, 339920, 339932, 423910

    KETTLER INTERNATIONAL INC.
    PO Box 2747, Virginia Beach, Virginia 23450-2747
    CEO: Heinz Kettler, Pres.   Tel: (757) 427-2400   %FO: 100
    Bus: *Mfr. children's bicycles and bicycle seats,*   Fax: (757) 427-0183   Emp: 35
    patio furniture, table tennis and exercise
    equipment and juvenile products.

• **HELLA KGAA HUECK & CO.**
Rixbecker Str. 75, D-59552 Lippstadt, Germany
CEO: Rolf Breidenbach, CEO   Tel: 49-2941-380   Rev: $2,725
Bus: *Lamps and lighting equipment, pumps, control*   Fax: 49-2941-387133   Emp: 22,400
    modules manufacture.   www.hella.com
   NAICS: 336321

    HELLA INC.
    201 Kelly Dr., PO Box 2665, Peachtree City, Georgia 30269
    CEO: Linda Volckmann   Tel: (770) 631-7500   %FO: 100
    Bus: *Sale/distribution automotive lighting &*   Fax: (770) 631-7575
    accessories.

    HELLA LIGHTING CORP.
    7979 Park Place Rd., York, South Carolina 29745
    CEO: Dr. Raymund Heinen   Tel: (803) 684-1818   %FO: 100
    Bus: *Lighting Manufacturer*   Fax: (803) 628-1598   Emp: 100

    HELLA NORTH AMERICA, INC.
    43811 Plymouth Oaks Blvd., Plymouth, Michigan 48170
    CEO: Steve Hubble   Tel: (734) 414-0900   %FO: 100
    Bus: *Mfr. automotive relays & flashers for OEM*   Fax: (734) 414-5098
    marketing.

● **HELLMANN WORLDWIDE LOGISTICS GMBH**
Elbestr. 27, D-49090 Osnabruck, Germany
CEO: Jost Hellmann, Pres.
Bus: *Provides freight forwarding, logistics, customs
brokerage and warehousing services.*
NAICS: 481219, 483111, 483113, 488510, 493110

Tel: 49-541-605-0	Rev: $5,989
Fax: 49-541-605-1211	Emp: 2,034
www.hellmann.de	

   HELLMANN WORLDWIDE LOGISTICS, INC.
   10450 Doral Blvd., Miami, Florida 33178
   CEO: Karl Weyeneth, Pres. & CEO
   Bus: *Provides freight forwarding, logistics,
   customs brokerage and warehousing*

Tel: (305) 406-4500	%FO: 100
Fax: (305) 406-4519	Emp: 550

● **HELM AKTIENGESELLSCHAFT**
Nordkanalstr. 28, D-20097 Hamburg, Germany
CEO: Ulf Ganger, Chmn.
Bus: *Trading/distribution, warehousing, service
functions of medical, pharmaceuticals, chemicals,
plastics, steel, etc.*
NAICS: 325211, 325311, 325312, 325314, 325320, 325998

Tel: 49-40-23-750	Rev: $2,386
Fax: 49-40-23-75-1845	Emp: 1,101
www.helmag.com	

   HELM US CORPORATION
   1110 Centennial Ave., Piscataway, New Jersey 08854
   CEO: Andreas Weimann, Pres. & CEO
   Bus: *Chemical distribution*

Tel: (732) 981-1116	%FO: 100
Fax: (732) 981-0528	

● **HELMUT MAUELL GMBH**
Am Rosenhuegel 1-7, D-42553 Velbert, Germany
CEO: B. Mecking, CEO
Bus: *Control and display systems.*

NAICS: 334511, 335313, 511210

Tel: 49-2053-130	Rev: $35
Fax: 49-2053-13403	Emp: 420
www.mauell.com	

   MAUELL CORPORATION
   31 Old Cabin Hollow Rd., Dillsburg, Pennsylvania 17019
   CEO: Gary Suchy, Mgr.
   Bus: *Mosaic display panels.*

Tel: (717) 432-8686	%FO: 100
Fax: (717) 432-8688	

● **HENKEL KGAA**
Henklestr. 67, D-40191 Dusseldorf, Germany
CEO: Ulrich Lehner, Pres. & CEO
Bus: *Branded detergents, personal care products and
chemical products.*
NAICS: 325611, 325612, 325613, 325620, 325910, 327910, 446120

Tel: 49-211-7970	Rev: $11,844
Fax: 49-211-798-2484	Emp: 48,628
www.henkel.com	

   ECOLAB INC.
   370 Wabasha St., North St. Paul, Minnesota 55102
   CEO: Douglas M. Baker Jr., Pres. & CEO
   Bus: *Specialty Chemical Manufacturing*

Tel: (651) 293-2233	
Fax: (651) 293-2092	Emp: 21,300

HENKEL CONSUMER ADHESIVES INC.
32150 Just Imagine Dr., Avon, Ohio 44011
CEO: John Kahl, CEO
Bus: *Mfr. specialty chemicals for paper,*
coatings, textile, leather, and cosmetics
Tel: (440) 937-7000
Fax: (440) 937-7077
%FO: 100

HENKEL LOCTITE CORP.
1001 Trout Brook Crossing, Rocky Hill, Connecticut 06067
CEO: Julian Colquitt, Pres.
Bus: *Mfr. adhesives.*
Tel: (860) 571-5100
Fax: (860) 571-5465
%FO: 100

HENKEL OF AMERICA, INC.
2200 Renaissance Blvd., Ste. 200, Gulph Mills, Pennsylvania 19406
CEO: John Knudson, Pres.
Bus: *U.S. headquarters operation for*
manufacture of specialty chemicals.
Tel: (610) 270-8100
Fax: (610) 270-8104
%FO: 100
Emp: 4,181

SCHWARZKOPF & DEP INC.
2101 East Via Arado, Rancho Dominguez, California 90220
CEO: Tom Parr, Pres.
Bus: *Mfr. personal care products, including Dep*
styling hair gel, Lavoris mouthwash and
Porcelana skin products.
Tel: (310) 604-0777
Fax: (310) 537-2524

SOVEREIGN SPECIALTY CHEMICAL, INC.
123 W. Bartges St., Akron, Ohio 44311
CEO: John R. Knox, Pres. & COO
Bus: *Specialty chemical manufacturing*
Tel: (330) 374-2900
Fax: (330) 374-2860
Emp: 895

THE DIAL CORPORATION
15501 N. Dial Blvd., Scottsdale, Arizona 85260
CEO: Bradley A. Casper, Pres. & CEO
Bus: *Personal care products*
Tel: (480) 754-3425
Fax: (480) 754-1098
Emp: 2,500

• **HERAEUS HOLDING GMBH**
Heraeusstr. 12-14, D-63450 Hanau, Germany
CEO: Frank Heinricht, COO
Bus: *Holding company for mfr./distribution of metals,*
chemicals, sensors & glass.
NAICS: 331419, 334510, 339114, 423520
Tel: 49-6181-35-0
Fax: 49-6181-35-3550
www.heraeus.com
Rev: $9,304
Emp: 9,219

HERAEUS ELECTRO-NITE COMPANY
1 Summit Square 100, Philadelphia, Pennsylvania 19047
CEO: Michael Midash, Pres.
Bus: *Production of industrial temperature sensors.*
Tel: (215) 944-9000
Fax:
%FO: 100
Emp: 401

HERAEUS INCORPORATED
540 Madison Ave., 16/F, New York, New York 10022
CEO: John Burdsall, Pres.
Bus: *Trades precious metals.*
Tel: (212) 752-2705
Fax:
%FO: 100
Emp: 1,275

HERAEUS KULZER, INC.
99 Business Park Dr., Armonk, New York 10504
CEO: Christian Brutzer, Pres.
Bus: *Product solutions for the dental industry.*
Tel: (914) 273-8600
Fax:
%FO: 100
Emp: 210

HERAEUS METAL PROCESSING, INC.
13429 Alondra Blvd., Santa Fe Springs, California 90670
CEO: Gerhard Ritzert, Chmn.   Tel: (562) 921-7464   %FO: 100
Bus: *Chemical and powdered precious metals*   Fax: (562) 926-7899   Emp: 414
compounds manufacture.

HERAEUS PRECIOUS METALS MANAGEMENT, INC.
540 Madison Ave., New York, New York 10022
CEO: John Burdsall, Pres.   Tel: (212) 752-2180
Bus: *Metal brokers*   Fax: (212) 752-7141   Emp: 21

HERAEUS QUARTZTECH, INC.
15600 Bratton Lane, Austin, Texas 78728
CEO: Arno Pitzen, Pres.   Tel: (512) 251-5530   %FO: 100
Bus: *Fabricated quartz ware manufacture.*   Fax: (512) 990-3500   Emp: 100

HERAEUS SHIN-ETSU AMERICA INC.
4600 NW Pacific Rim Blvd., Camas, Washington 98607
CEO: Katsuhiko Kemmochi, Pres.   Tel: (360) 834-4004
Bus: *Pottery products*   Fax: Emp: 40

HERAEUS TENEVO
100 Heraeus Blvd., Buford, Georgia 30518
CEO: Guenter Bachmann, Chmn.   Tel: (770) 945-2275
Bus: *Industrial organic chemicals*   Fax: Emp: 168

VADNAIS TECHNOLOGIES CORP.
1375 Willow Lake Blvd., St. Paul, Minnesota 55110
CEO: Mark Kempf, Pres.   Tel: (651) 254-2621
Bus: *Steel springs*   Fax: Emp: 250

● **HETTICH GROUP GMBH**
Vahrenkampstr. 12-16, D-32278 Kirchlengern, Germany
CEO: Rainer Schwarz, Mgr.   Tel: 49-7433-3083-25   Rev: $400
Bus: *Furniture fittings and furniture accessories,*   Fax: 49-7433-3083-64   Emp: 4,800
designer handles, pulls and knobs manufacture.   www.hettich.com
NAICS: 337124

HETTICH AMERICA LLP
6225 Shiloh Rd., Alpharetta, Georgia 30005
CEO: Michael Gambill, Mktg.   Tel: (770) 887-3733   %FO: 100
Bus: *Mfr./distribution quality furniture hardware.*   Fax: (770) 887-0752   Emp: 70

● **HIRSCHMANN ELECTRONICS GMBH & CO. KG**
Stuttgarter Str.45-51, D-72654 Neckartenzlingen, Germany
CEO: Reinhard Sitzmann, Chmn.   Tel: 49-7127-140   Rev: $367
Bus: *Mfr. mobile antenna systems stationary receiving*   Fax: 49-7127-14-1214   Emp: 1,800
system, telecommunication equipment, connectors. www.hirschmann.com
NAICS: 334290, 334419, 423690, 541611

HIRSCHMANN ELECTRONICS
1665 Orchard Dr., Chambersburg, Pennsylvania 17201
CEO: David Joy   Tel: (240) 686-2300   %FO: 100
Bus: *Wholesale antennas.*   Fax: (240) 686-3589

HIRSCHMANN ELECTRONICS
1116 Centre Rd., Auburn Hills, Michigan 48326
CEO: Bjorn Heimerger, Mgr. Tel: (248) 373-7150
Bus: *Wholesale antennas.* Fax: (248) 276-2350

• HOCHTIEF, AG
Opernplatz 2, D-45128 Essen, Germany
CEO: Hans-Peter Keitel, CEO Tel: 49-201-824-0 Rev: $13,223
Bus: *Design and construction.* Fax: 49-201-824-2777 Emp: 34,039
www.hochtief.de
NAICS: 236210, 236220, 237130, 237310, 237990, 541310

THE TURNER CORPORATION
901 Main St., Ste. 4900, Dallas, Texas 75202
CEO: Thomas C. Leppert, Chmn. & CEO Tel: (214) 915-9600
Bus: *Engaged in design and construction.* Fax: (214) 915-9700 Emp: 5,000

TURNER CONSTRUCTION COMPANY
375 Hudson St., New York, New York 10014
CEO: Peter J. Davoren, Pres. & CEO Tel: (212) 229-6000 %FO: 100
Bus: *Construction and engineer services.* Fax: (212) 229-6390 Emp: 5,000

• HOERBIGER ORIGA GMBH
Industriestr. 8, D-70794 Fiderstadt, Germany
CEO: Johann Asperger, Mgr. Tel: 49-7158-170-30
Bus: *Electrical linear actuators, band cylinders,* Fax: 49-7158-648-70 Emp: 500
pneumatic valves & cylinders manufacture. www.hoerbiger-origa.com
NAICS: 332912, 333995, 339999

HOERBIGER-ORIGA CORPORATION
100 West Lake Dr., Glendale Heights, Illinois 60139
CEO: Joseph Hughes, Pres. Tel: (630) 871-8300 %FO: 100
Bus: *Electrical linear actuators, band cylinders,* Fax: (630) 871-1515 Emp: 55
pneumatic valves & cylinders manufacture.

• MATTH. HOHNER AG
Andreas-Koch-Str. 9, D-78647 Trossingen, Germany
CEO: Lyndle Volz, Pres. Tel: 49-7425-200 Rev: $76
Bus: *Mfr. musical instruments, amplifiers and* Fax: 49-7425-20-249 Emp: 370
accessories. www.hohner.de
NAICS: 339992

HOHNER INC.
100 Technology Park Dr., Glen Allen, Virginia 23059
CEO: Lyndle Volz, Pres. Tel: (804) 515-1900 %FO: 100
Bus: *Sale/service musical instruments, amplifiers* Fax: (804) 515-0840 Emp: 60
and accessories.

● **H. HOLTKAMP GMBH & CO., KG**
Betonstr. 19, Niedersachsen, D-49324 Melle, Germany
CEO: Thomas Holtkamp, Pres.
Bus: *Produce African violets.*

Tel: 49-54-227-070
Fax:
www.holtkamp.com

Rev: $32
Emp: 230

NAICS: 111421, 111422, 113210

HOLTKAMP GREENHOUSES INC.
1501 Lischey Ave., Nashville, Tennessee 37207
CEO: Reinhold Holtkamp Sr., Pres.
Bus: *African violets.*

Tel: (615) 228-2683
Fax: (615) 228-5831

%FO: 100
Emp: 90

● **HOLZHER REICH SPEZIALMASCHINEN GMBH**
Plochinger Str. 65, D-72622 Nurtingen, Germany
CEO: Wulf W. Reich, Mng. Dir.
Bus: *Mfr. industrial woodworking machines.*

Tel: 49-7022-702-0
Fax: 49-7022-702-101
www.holzher.de

Rev: $79
Emp: 447

NAICS: 333210, 333298

HOLZ-HER US, INC.
5120 Westinghouse Blvd., Charlotte, North Carolina 28273
CEO: Wulf W. Reich, Chmn.
Bus: *Industrial woodworking machines.*

Tel: (704) 587-3400
Fax: (704) 587-3412

%FO: 100
Emp: 79

● **HORMANN GMBH**
Hauptstr. 45-47, D-85614 Kirchseeon, Germany
CEO: Matthias Mullner, Mng. Dir.
Bus: *High power warning systems, electric
    engineering, swim pools, building facades.*
NAICS: 541330

Tel: 49-8091-52261
Fax: 49-8091-1275
www.hoermann-gmbh.de

Rev: $561
Emp: 3,599

HORMANN AMERICA
837 Arnold Dr., Ste. 600, Martinez, California 94533
CEO: Efraim Petel, Pres.
Bus: *Design, install & maintain public warning
    systems.*

Tel: (925) 228-2152
Fax: (925) 228-2114

Emp: 7

● **HUGO BOSS AG**
Dieselstr. 12, D-72555 Metzingen, Germany
CEO: Bruno E. Salzer, Chmn. & CEO
Bus: *Mfr./distribution of designer men's fashions.*

Tel: 49-7123-940
Fax: 49-7123-942-014
www.hugo-boss.com

Rev: $1,594
Emp: 6,942

NAICS: 315211, 315212, 315222, 315223, 315224, 315232, 315233, 315234, 315999, 325620, 448110, 448120

HUGO BOSS USA, INC.
601 W. 26th St., 8/F, New York, New York 10001
CEO: Tony Lucia, Pres.
Bus: *Mfr./distribution of designer men's fashions.*

Tel: (212) 940-0600
Fax: (212) 840-0619

%FO: 100
Emp: 511

- **HYPO REAL ESTATE HOLDING AG**
  Unsoldstrasse 2, D-80538 Munich, Germany
  CEO: Kurt F. Viermetz, Chmn.
  Bus: *Provider of products and services for finance of commercial real estate.*
  NAICS: 525930, 531190

  Tel: 49-89-20-30-07-0
  Fax: 49-89-20-30-07-783
  www.hyporealestate.com

  Rev: $11,534
  Emp: 1,416

  HYPO REAL ESTATE CAPITAL CORP.
  622 Third Ave., New York, New York 10017-6707
  CEO: Evan F. Denner, Dep. CEO
  Bus: *Provider of products and services for the finance of commercial real estate.*

  Tel: (212) 671-6300
  Fax: (212) 671-6402

  %FO: 100

- **IDS SCHEER AG**
  Altenkesseler Str. 17, D-66115 Saarbrucken, Germany
  CEO: Helmut Kruppke, Co-CEO
  Bus: *Software and business consulting services.*
  NAICS: 511210, 541511, 541512, 541519, 611420

  Tel: 49-681-210-0
  Fax: 49-681-210-1000
  www.ids-scheer.com

  Rev: $382
  Emp: 2,132

  IDS SCHEER, INC.
  1055 Westlakes Dr., Ste. 100, Berwyn, Pennsylvania 19312
  CEO: Mathias Kirchmer, Pres. & CEO
  Bus: *Software and business consulting services.*

  Tel: (610) 854-6800
  Fax: (610) 854-7382

  %FO: 100
  Emp: 38

  IDS SCHEER, INC.
  5555 Glenridge Connector, Ste. 650, Atlanta, Georgia 30342
  CEO: Jeffrey Michaels, Pres.
  Bus: *Software and business consulting services.*

  Tel: (404) 531-5100
  Fax: (404) 531-5102

  %FO: 100

- **IKA GROUP**
  Janke & Kunkel-Str. 10, D-79219 Staufen, Germany
  CEO: Andreas Reichert, Sales Dir.
  Bus: *Laboratory equipment manufacture.*
  NAICS: 334516, 334519

  Tel: 49-7633-8310
  Fax: 49-7633-83198
  www.ika.net

  Rev: $41
  Emp: 300

  IKA WORKS USA
  2635 North Chase Pkwy. SE, Wilmington, North Carolina 28405
  CEO: Rene Stiegelmann, Pres.
  Bus: *Mfr./sale lab/process equipment.*

  Tel: (910) 452-7059
  Fax: (910) 452-7693

  %FO: 100
  Emp: 63

- **IKB DEUTSCHE INDUSTRIEBANK AG**
  Wilhelm-Botzkes-Str. 1, D-40474 Dusseldorf, Germany
  CEO: Stefan Ortseife, Chmn. & Mng. Dir.
  Bus: *Provides long-term financing and consulting services.*
  NAICS: 522110, 522220, 522293, 522298, 522310, 523999

  Tel: 49-211-8221-0
  Fax: 49-211-8221-3959
  www.ikb.de

  Rev: $4,134
  Emp: 1,469

IKB CAPITAL CORPORATION
555 Madison Ave., 24/F, New York, New York 10022
CEO: Wolfgang Boeker, SVP   Tel: (212) 485-3600   %FO: 100
Bus: *Supplies long-term financing and consulting*   Fax: (212) 583-8800
    services.

● **IM INTERNATIONALMEDIA AG**
Cuvilliesstr. 25, D-81679 Munich, Germany
CEO: Moritz Bormann, Chmn. & CEO   Tel: 49-89-98-107-100   Rev: $255
Bus: *Engaged in motion picture development and*   Fax: 49-89-98-107-199   Emp: 51
    financing.   www.internationalmedia.de
   NAICS: 334612, 512120, 512199, 512210, 512220, 512240, 711130

   INTERMEDIA FILMS EQUITIES USA, INC
   9350 Civic Center Dr., Beverly Hills, California 90210
   CEO: Bahman Naraghi, COO   Tel: (310) 777-0007   %FO: 100
   Bus: *Motion picture production & distribution.*   Fax: (310) 777-0008   Emp: 24

● **IMI NORGREN HERION FLUIDTRONIC GMBH & CO.**
Stuttgarter Str. 120, D-70736 Fellbach, Germany
CEO: Eberhard Kleyersburg, Mgr.   Tel: 49-711-520-90
Bus: *Mfr. pneumatics, hydraulics, automatics,*   Fax: 49-711-520-9614   Emp: 2,500
    pressure and temperature devices, electric fluid   www.norgren.com
    power products, process valves.
   NAICS: 333999, 336340

   NORGREN AUTOMOTIVE DIVISION
   44831 Groesbeck Hwy., Box 787, Mt. Clemens, Michigan 48046
   CEO: Guy Potok, Pres.   Tel: (586) 463-3000   %FO: 100
   Bus: *Automotive manufacturing.*   Fax: (586) 465-2840   Emp: 250

   NORGREN INC.
   72 Spring Lane, Farmington, Connecticut 06032
   CEO: Nicholas Testanero   Tel: (860) 677-0272   %FO: 100
   Bus: *Pneumatic valve manufacture and sales.*   Fax: (860) 677-4999   Emp: 200

   NORGREN INC.
   5400 South Delaware St., Littleton, Colorado 80120
   CEO: Terry Weeber, Pres.   Tel: (303) 794-2611   %FO: 100
   Bus: *Fluid power products, process valves;*   Fax: (303) 795-9487   Emp: 673
    pneumatics, hydraulics, automatics,
    pressure and temperature devices.

● **INA-HOLDING SCHAEFFLER KG**
Industriestr. 1-3, D-91074 Herzogenaurach, Germany
CEO: Jurgen M. Geissinger, Pres. & CEO   Tel: 49-9132-820
Bus: *Roller bearings manufacture.*   Fax: 49-9132-824933
    www.ina.com
   NAICS: 332991

   INA LINEAR TECHNIK
   308 Springhill Farm Rd., Fort Mill, South Carolina 29715
   CEO: Dean May, Mgr.   Tel: (803) 548-8500   %FO: 100
   Bus: *Mfr. of roller bearings.*   Fax: (803) 548-8599   Emp: 70

INA USA CORP.
1298 New Cut Rd., PO Box 570, Spartanburg, South Carolina 29304
CEO: Bob Morella, Mgr.   Tel: (864) 583-4541   %FO: 100
Bus: *Mfr. of roller bearings & other automotive*   Fax: (864) 591-8890   Emp: 375
products.

INA USA CORP.
308 Springhill Farm Rd., Fort Mill, South Carolina 29715
CEO: Bruce G. Warmbold, Pres.   Tel: (803) 548-8500   %FO: 100
Bus: *Mfr./design, develop., sales of roller*   Fax: (803) 548-8599   Emp: 2,000
bearings.

INA USA CORP.
Hwy. 9 West, PO Box 390, Cheraw, South Carolina 29520
CEO: Jim Laenter, Mgr.   Tel: (843) 537-9341   %FO: 100
Bus: *Mfr. of roller bearings, engine components,* Fax: (843) 537-8752
rocker arms, tripod rollers & roller
assemblies for autos.

INA USA CORP.
1 Ina Dr., PO Box 390, Cheraw, South Carolina 29520
CEO: Cindy Yates, Mgr.   Tel: (843) 537-9341   %FO: 100
Bus: *Mfr. of roller bearings.*   Fax: (843) 537-8751

• **INDEX-WERKE GMBH & CO**
Plochinger Str. 92, D-73730 Esslingen, Germany
CEO: Waldachtal Klaus Frick, Dir.   Tel: 49-711-3191-0   Rev: $212
Bus: *Metalworking machine tools, turning automatics* Fax: 49-711-3191-587   Emp: 2,270
manufacture.   www.index-werke.de
NAICS: 333319

    INDEX CORPORATION
    14700 North Point Blvd., Noblesville, Indiana 46060
    CEO: Gary Sihler, Chmn.   Tel: (317) 770-6300   %FO: 100
    Bus: *Sales/service metalworking machine tools,* Fax: (317) 770-3166   Emp: 50
    turning automatics.

• **INEOS PHENOL GMBH**
Dechenstr. 3, D-45966 Gladbeck, Germany
CEO: Peter Bickert, CEO   Tel: 49-2043-958-302   Rev: $2,742
Bus: *Phenol and acetone chemical production.*   Fax: 49-2043-958-947   Emp: 650
                                       www.phenolchemie.com
NAICS: 325188

    INEOS PHENOL
    7770 Rangeline Rd., Theodore, Alabama 36582
    CEO: Alberto Spera, Mgr.   Tel: (251) 443-3000   %FO: 100
    Bus: *Mfr. of phenol & acetone products.*   Fax: (251) 443-3001   Emp: 320

    INEOS PHENOL
    7 Rosslare Ct., Cary, Illinois 60013
    CEO: Harold Swart, Mgr.   Tel: (847) 639-6902   %FO: 100
    Bus: *Phenol and acetone chemical production* Fax: (847) 639-7748
    and sales.

INEOS PHENOL
15 Shelton Rd., Quincy, Massachusetts 02169
CEO: Tim Mullally, Mgr.
Bus: *Phenol and acetone chemical production and sales.*

Tel: (617) 479-2838
Fax: (617) 479-2831

%FO: 100

● **INFINEON TECHNOLOGIES AG**
St.- Martin- Str. 53, D-81669 Munich, Germany
CEO: Wolfgang Ziebart, CEO
Bus: *Semiconductor manufacture.*

Tel: 49-89-234-0
Fax: 49-89-234-284-82
www.infineon.com

Rev: $8,946
Emp: 35,570

NAICS: 334412, 334413, 334414, 334415

INFINEON TECHNOLOGIES INC.
600 Technology Blvd., Sandston, Virginia 23150
CEO: Henry Becker, Mng. Dir.
Bus: *Mfr. of memory chips.*

Tel: (804) 952-6000
Fax: (804) 952-6000

%FO: 100
Emp: 1,800

INFINEON TECHNOLOGIES INC.
1730 North First St., San Jose, California 95112
CEO: Robert Lefort, Pres.
Bus: *Mfr. semiconductors.*

Tel: (408) 501-6000
Fax: (408) 501-2430

%FO: 100
Emp: 1,200

INFINEON TECHNOLOGIES INC.
459 Hurricane Lane, Williston, Vermont 05495
CEO: Frank Gelsdorf, Mgr.
Bus: *Mfr. semiconductors.*

Tel: (802) 764-1900
Fax: (802) 764-1902

%FO: 100
Emp: 65

INFINEON TECHNOLOGIES INC.
2070 Route 52, Zip 33A, Hopewell Junction, New York 12533
CEO: Wolfgang Mueller, Mgr.
Bus: *Mfr. semiconductors.*

Tel: (845) 892-9534
Fax: (845) 892-6648

%FO: 100

INFINEON TECHNOLOGIES INC.
755 College Rd. East, Princeton, New Jersey 08540
CEO: Jan Du Preez, Pres.
Bus: *Mfr. semiconductors.*

Tel: (609) 734-6513
Fax: (609) 734-3325

%FO: 100
Emp: 14

INFINEON TECHNOLOGIES INC.
3000 Centre Green Way, Cary, North Carolina 27513
CEO: Robert Lefort, Pres.
Bus: *Mfr. semiconductors.*

Tel: (919) 677-2700
Fax: (919) 678-1929

%FO: 100
Emp: 150

STARCORE LLC
8303 Mopac Expwy., Ste. A400, Austin, Texas 78759
CEO: Alex Bedarida, VP & Gen. Mgr.
Bus: *Mfr. of microprocessors, microcontrollers& DSPs.*

Tel: (512) 682-8500
Fax:

%FO: 100
Emp: 100

- **INSTITUT DR. FORSTER**
In Laisen 70, D-72766 Reutlingen, Germany
CEO: Martin Förster, Chrm.
Bus: *Mfr. non-destructive testing equipment.*

Tel: 49-7121-140-0
Fax: 49-7121-140-488
www.foerstergroup.de

Emp: 500

NAICS: 334510

FOERSTER INSTRUMENTS INC.
140 Industry Dr., RIDC Park West, Pittsburgh, Pennsylvania 15275-1028
CEO: Philip R. Warga, Pres.
Bus: *Mfr./distribution/service non-destructive testing equipment.*

Tel: (412) 788-8976
Fax: (412) 788-8984

%FO: 100
Emp: 50

FOERSTER SYSTEMS DIVISION
1484 Quaker Ct., Salem, Ohio 44460
CEO: Philip R. Warga
Bus: *Mfr./distribution/service non-destructive testing equipment.*

Tel: (330) 332-9100
Fax: (330) 332-9115

%FO: 100

- **INTERSHOP COMMUNICATIONS**
Intershop Tower, D-07740 Jena, Germany
CEO: Jurgen Schottler, CEO
Bus: *Management software manufacture.*

Tel: 49-3641-500
Fax: 49-3641-50-1002
www.intershop.com

Rev: $29
Emp: 278

NAICS: 511210, 541511

INTERSHOP COMMUNICATIONS
410 Townsend St., Ste. 125, San Francisco, California 94107
CEO: Gary DiOrio, Pres.
Bus: *Management software manufacture and sales.*

Tel: (415) 844-1500
Fax: (415) 844-3800

%FO: 100

- **IWKA AG**
Am Hardtwald 3, D-76275 Ettlingen, Germany
CEO: Hans lampert, CEO
Bus: *Mfr. industrial products including robots and factory machinery.*
NAICS: 333298, 333512, 333516, 334513, 336211

Tel: 49-721-143-325
Fax: 49-721-143-331
www.iwka.de

Rev: $2,870
Emp: 13,231

IWKA AUTOPROD INC.
5355 115th Ave. North, Clearwater, Florida 33760
CEO: Tom Riggins, SVP
Bus: *Mfr. bottling and liquid filling equipment.*

Tel: (727) 572-7753
Fax: (727) 573-0367

%FO: 100

KUKA ROBOTICS CORP.
22500 Key Dr., Clinton Township, Michigan 48036
CEO: Kevin Kozuszek
Bus: *Mfr. robots.*

Tel: (866) 873-5852
Fax: (866) 329-5852

%FO: 100

KUKA WELDING SYSTEMS + ROBOT CORP.
6600 Center Dr., Sterling Heights, Michigan 48312
CEO: Steve Schiff
Bus: *Mfr. assembly and welding systems.*

Tel: (586) 795-2000
Fax: (586) 978-0429

%FO: 100

PACKAGING TECHNOLOGIES
807 West Kimberly Rd., Davenport, Iowa 52806
CEO: Barry Shoulders
Bus: *Mfr. packaging equipment.*

Tel: (563) 391-1100
Fax: (563) 391-0017

%FO: 100

● **IXOS SOFTWARE AG**
Technopark 2, Werner-von-Siemens Ring 20, D-85630 Grasbrunn, Germany
CEO: John Shackleton, CEO
Bus: *Mfr. business document management software.*

Tel: 49-89-4629-0
Fax: 49-89-4629-1199
www.ixos.com

Rev: $162
Emp: 970

NAICS: 511210, 518210, 541511, 541512, 541519, 611420

IXOS SOFTWARE, INC.
19 Campus Blvd., Ste. 100, Newtown Square, Pennsylvania 19073
CEO: Rob Foore, Mgr.
Bus: *Mfr. business document management software.*

Tel: (610) 355-7467
Fax: (610) 355-7479

%FO: 100
Emp: 28

IXOS SOFTWARE, INC.
901 Mariner's Island Blvd., Ste. 625, San Mateo, California 94404
CEO: Matthew Suffoletto, Pres.
Bus: *Mfr. business document management software.*

Tel: (650) 294-5800
Fax: (650) 294-5836

%FO: 100
Emp: 800

OPEN TEXT CORPORATION
100 Tri-State International Pkwy., 3/F, Lincolnshire, Illinois 60069
CEO: Thomas Jenkins, CEO
Bus: *Mfr. software products.*

Tel: (847) 267-9330
Fax: (847) 267-9332

%FO: 100
Emp: 90

● **JAGENBERG AG**
Kempener Allee 30, D-47803 Krefeld, Germany
CEO: Stefan K. Kranzbuhler, Chmn.
Bus: *Mfr. machinery for paper mills and paper converting industry.*

Tel: 49-2151-9340-990
Fax: 49-2151-9340-9985
www.jagenberg.com

Emp: 2,000

NAICS: 333291

KAMPF MACHINERY CORP.
Kennedy Industrial Park, 900 River St., Unit H, Windsor, Connecticut 06095
CEO: Michael Schuvert, VP
Bus: *Sale of industrial equipment.*

Tel: (860) 640-0040
Fax: (860) 640-0046

Emp: 9

● **JUMO GMBH & CO. KG**
Moltkest. 13-31, D-36039 Fulda, Germany
CEO: Bernard Juchheim, Pres.
Bus: *Mfr. temperature, pressure and humidity sensors, transmitters, controls and recorders.*

Tel: 49-661-6003-0
Fax: 49-661-6003-500
www.jumo.de

Rev: $140
Emp: 1,591

NAICS: 334513, 334519, 423830

JUMO PROCESS CONTROL INC.
735 Fox Chase, Ste. 103, Coatesville, Pennsylvania 19320
CEO: Bernard Juchheim, Chmn.
Bus: *Sale/service temperature, pressure & humidity sensors, transmitters, controls & recorders.*

Tel: (610) 380-8002
Fax: (610) 380-8009

%FO: 100
Emp: 12

- **JUNGHEINRICH AG**
Friedrich-Eberrt-Damm 129, D-22047 Hamburg, Germany
CEO: Cletus von Pichler, Chmn.   Tel: 49-40-6948-0   Rev: $2,088
Bus: *Mfr. material handling equipment.*   Fax: 49-40-6948-1777   Emp: 9,008
                                          www.jungheinrich.de

NAICS: 333294, 532412
    JUNGHEINRICH LIFT TRUCK CORP. USA
    5701 Eastport Blvd., Richmond, Virginia 23231
    CEO: Dirk Von Holt, Pres.   Tel: (804) 737-6084   %FO: 100
    Bus: *Mfr./sales material handling equipment.*   Fax: (804) 737-6136   Emp: 110

- **KALENBORN KALPROTECT**
Asbacher Str. 50, D-53560 Vettelschoss, Germany
CEO: Michael W. Rokitta, Dir.   Tel: 49-2645-180
Bus: *Mfr. abrasion and corrosion-resistant linings and*   Fax: 49-2645-18112   Emp: 220
    pipelines.   www.kalenborn.de
NAICS: 332999
    ABRESIST CORPORATION
    5541 N. State Rd. 13, PO Box 38, Urbana, Indiana 46990
    CEO: Joe Accetta, Pres.   Tel: (260) 774-3327   %FO: 100
    Bus: *Mfr./sale/service abrasion and corrosion-*   Fax: (260) 774-8188   Emp: 40
    resistant linings and pipelines.

- **KAMPF GMBH & CO MASCHINENFABRIK**
Meuhlenerstrasse 36-42, D-51674 Wiehl, Germany
CEO: Walther Duerholt, CEO   Tel: 49-2262 810   Rev: $132
Bus: *Mfr./sale machines for paper, film and foil*   Fax: 49-2262 81208   Emp: 480
    converting industry.   www.kampf.de
NAICS: 333291, 333298
    KAMPF MACHINERY CORPORATION
    900 River St., Unit H, Windsor, Connecticut 06095
    CEO: James Gatcomb, Div. Mgr.   Tel: (860) 640-0040   %FO: 100
    Bus: *Sale/service machines for paper, film & foil*   Fax: (860) 640-0044   Emp: 50
    converting industry.

- **KHS MASCHINENBAU UND ANLAGENBAU AG**
Juchostr. 20, D-44143 Dortmund, Germany
CEO: Valentin Reisgen, Pres. & CAO   Tel: 49-231-569-0
Bus: *Packaging equipment manufacturer.*   Fax: 49-231-569-1541   Emp: 550
                                          www.khs-ag.de
NAICS: 333993
    KLOCKER KHS, INC
    800 Bahcall Ct., Waukesha, Wisconsin 53186
    CEO: Mark Arrant, Pres.   Tel: (262) 797-7200   %FO: 100
    Bus: *Sales, service and spare parts for*   Fax: (262) 797-0025   Emp: 400
    packaging equipment.

- **KILBENSCHMIDT PIERBURG AG**
  Rheinmetall Allee 1, D-40476 Dusseldorf, Germany
  CEO: Gerd Kleinert, CEO
  Bus: *Mfr. pistons, engine blocks, bearings, water
       pumps and injection moldings.*
  NAICS: 336211

  Tel: 49-211-473-4718
  Fax: 49-211-473-4157
  www.kolbenschmidt-pierburg.de

  Rev: $2,647
  Emp: 11,364

     KARL SCHMIDT UNISIA, ZOLLNER DIV.
     2425 Coliseum Blvd. South, Fort Wayne, Indiana 46803
     CEO: Mark Lennart
     Bus: *Mfr. pistons for car and truck engines.*

     Tel: (260) 426-8081
     Fax: (260) 423-2141

     %FO: 100

     KS BEARINGS INC.
     5 Southchase Ct., Fountain Inn, South Carolina 29644
     CEO: David H. Mosier
     Bus: *Mfr. metallic and steel bushings.*

     Tel: (864) 688-1400
     Fax: (864) 688-1401

     %FO: 100

- **C. KLINGSPOR GMBH**
  Huttenstr. 36, Hessen, D-35708 Haiger, Germany
  CEO: Klaus Toeller, Mng. Dir.
  Bus: *Mfr. coated and bonded abrasives.*

  Tel: 49-2773-9220
  Fax: 49-2773-922396
  www.klingspor.de

  Rev: $98
  Emp: 584

  NAICS: 212399, 327910, 423840

     KLINGSPOR ABRASIVES INC.
     2555 Tate Blvd. SE, PO Box 2367, Hickory, North Carolina 28603
     CEO: Christoph Klingspor, Pres.
     Bus: *Mfr. coated & bonded abrasives.*

     Tel: (828) 322-3030
     Fax: (828) 322-6060

     %FO: 100
     Emp: 321

- **KLOCKNER & CO. AG**
  Neudorfer Str. 3-5, D-47057 Duisburg, Germany
  CEO: Thomas Ludwig, Chmn. & CEO
  Bus: *Distributes steel and metal products.*

  Tel: 49-203-307-0
  Fax: 49-203-307-5000
  www.kloeckner.de

  Rev: $5
  Emp: 10,023

  NAICS: 423510

     NAMASCO CORPORATION
     500 Colonial Center Pkwy., Ste. 500, Roswell, Georgia 30076
     CEO: Bill Partalis, Pres. & CEO
     Bus: *Distributes steel and metal products.*

     Tel: (678) 259-8800
     Fax: (678) 259-8873

     %FO: 100
     Emp: 700

- **KLÖCKNER-WERKE AG**
  Opernplatz 2, D-60313 Frankfurt am Main, Germany
  CEO: Roland Flach, Chmn.
  Bus: *Mfr. automotive supplier, rigid films, filming and
       packaging technology.*
  NAICS: 326112, 333220, 333512, 333515, 333993

  Tel: 49-69-900-26507
  Fax: 49-69-900-26110
  www.kloecknerwerke.de

  Rev: $1,073
  Emp: 4,164

     KHS BARTELT, INC.
     5501 North Washington Blvd., Sarasota, Florida 34243
     CEO: Reno Cruz, Pres.
     Bus: *Mfr. of packaging machinery.*

     Tel: (941) 359-4000
     Fax:

     %FO: 100
     Emp: 81

KHS, INC.
880 Bahcall Ct., Waukesha, Wisconsin 53186
CEO: Mark Arrant, Pres.   Tel: (262) 797-7200   %FO: 100
Bus: *Mfr. of beverage & food processing*   Fax: Emp: 400
equipment.

REMAK OF NORTH AMERICA
2195 Arbor Tech Dr., Hebron, Kentucky 41048
CEO: Thomas Bar, Sales   Tel: (859) 372-3382   %FO: 100
Bus: *Mfr. of robots & robot system solutions.* Fax: (859) 525-8968

● **KLUBER LUBRICATION MUNCHEN KG**
Geisenhausenstr. 7, D-81379 Munich, Germany
CEO: Jorgen Becker, Pres. & CEO   Tel: 49-89-7876-0   Rev: $290
Bus: *Synthetic lubricants, lime-scale dissolvers, and* Fax: 49-89-7876-333   Emp: 1,500
oil/water separators manufacturer.   www.kluber.com
NAICS: 324191, 325199

   KLUBER LUBRICATION NORTH AMERICA
   9010 County Rd. 2120, Tyler, Texas 75707
   CEO: Glenn Boyle, Pres.   Tel: (903) 534-8021   %FO: 100
   Bus: *Mfr. of synthetic lubricants, lime-scale* Fax: (903) 581-4376
   dissolvers, and oil/water separators.

   KLUBER LUBRICATION NORTH AMERICA, INC.
   32 Industrial Dr., Londonderry, New Hampshire 03053
   CEO: Glenn Boyle, Pres.   Tel: (603) 647-4104   %FO: 100
   Bus: *Mfr. of synthetic lubricants, lime-scale* Fax: (603) 647-4105   Emp: 60
   dissolvers, and oil/water separators.

● **KNAUF GIPS KG**
Postfach 10, D-97343 Iphofen, Germany
CEO: Baldwin Knauf, Mng. Prtn.   Tel: 49-9323-310   Rev: $3,766
Bus: *Insulation and cushioning materials manufacture,* Fax: 49-9323-31277   Emp: 18,000
including closed cell foam plastic.   www.knauf.com
NAICS: 327420, 327993, 551112

   KNAUF INSULATION
   3502 43 St. SW, Lanett, Alabama 36863
   CEO: Bill Donnett, Mgr.   Tel: (334) 576-8141   %FO: 100
   Bus: *Mfr. of fiberglass insulation.*   Fax: (334) 576-2494   Emp: 300

   KNAUF INSULATION
   One Knauf Dr., Shelbyville, Indiana 46176
   CEO: Robert Britton, Pres.   Tel: (317) 398-4434   %FO: 100
   Bus: *Insulation and cushioning materials*   Fax: (317) 398-3675   Emp: 1,300
   manufacture and sales, including closed cell
   foam plastic.

   KNAUF POLYSTYRENE INC.
   2725 Henkle Dr., Lebanon, Ohio 45036
   CEO: Aser Woerlen, Mgr.   Tel: (513) 932-6923   %FO: 100
   Bus: *Insulation and cushioning materials*   Fax: (513) 932-3506   Emp: 12
   manufacture and sales, including closed cell
   foam plastic.

● **KOENIG & BAUER AG**
Friedrich-Koenig-Strasse 4, D-97080 Wurzburg, Germany
CEO: Albrecht Bolza-Schunemann, Pres. & CEO   Tel: 49-931-909-0   Rev: $1,941
Bus: *Mfr. of industrial equipment for printing services.*   Fax: 49-931-909-4101   Emp: 7,398
                                                              www.kba-print.de

NAICS: 333291

  KBA NORTH AMERICA INC.
  4651 Roswell Rd., F-505, Atlanta, Georgia 30342
  CEO: Heinz A. Schmid   Tel: (404) 256-2048   %FO: 100
  Bus: *Manufacturer of industrial machinery for*   Fax: (404) 256-0270
     printing services.

  KBA NORTH AMERICA INC.
  291 Hurricane Lane, Williston, Vermont 05495-0900
  CEO: Bob McKinney   Tel: (802) 878-9400   %FO: 100
  Bus: *Manufacturer of industrial machinery for*   Fax: (802) 878-3313
     printing services.

  KBA NORTH AMERICA INC.
  3900 East Market St., PO Box 12015, York, Pennsylvania 17402
  CEO: Gary L. Owen   Tel: (717) 505-1150   %FO: 100
  Bus: *Manufacturer of industrial machinery for*   Fax: (717) 505-1161
     printing services.

● **KOLBUS GMBH + CO. KG**
Osnabrucker Str. 77, D-32369 Rahden, Germany
CEO: Kai Buntemeyer, Mng. Dir.   Tel: 49-5771-71-0   Rev: $106
Bus: *Mfr. bookbinding machinery.*   Fax: 49-5771-71-333   Emp: 1,041
                                                www.kolbus.com

NAICS: 333293, 423830

  KOLBUS AMERICA, INC.
  812 Huron Rd., Ste. 750, Cleveland, Ohio 44115
  CEO: Robert Shafer, Pres.   Tel: (216) 931-5100   %FO: 100
  Bus: *Sales/distribution of bookbinding machinery.* Fax: (216) 931-5101 Emp: 45

● **KONTRON AG**
Oskar-von-Miller-Str. 1, D-85386 Eching, Germany
CEO: Hannes Niederhauser, Pres. & CEO   Tel: 49-81-65-77-0   Rev: $358
Bus: *Provides embedded computing solutions.*   Fax: 49-81-65-77-219   Emp: 1,832
                                                www.kontron.com

NAICS: 334413

  KONTRON AMERICA, INC.
  14118 Stowe Dr., Poway, California 92064
  CEO: Thomas Sparrvik   Tel: (858) 677-0877   %FO: 100
  Bus: *Provides embedded computing solutions.* Fax: (858) 677-0898   Emp: 200

  KONTRON AMERICA, INC.
  7610 Executive Dr., Eden Prairie, Minnesota 55344
  CEO: Dale Szymborski   Tel: (952) 974-7000   %FO: 100
  Bus: *Provides embedded computing solutions.* Fax: (952) 949-2791

KONTRON AMERICA, INC.
3178 Laurelview Ct., Fremont, California 94538
CEO: Matthias   Tel: (510) 661-2220   %FO: 100
Bus: *Provides embedded computing solutions.*   Huber   Fax: (510) 490-2360

KONTRON AMERICA, INC.
750 Holiday Dr., Building 9, Pittsburgh, Pennsylvania 15220
CEO: Sherry Schroeffel   Tel: (412) 921-3322   %FO: 100
Bus: *Provides embedded computing solutions.*   Fax: (412) 921-3356

● **KRAUSS-MAFFEI WEGMANN GMBH & CO KG**
Krauss-Maffei-Str. 11, D-80997 Munich, Germany
CEO: Manfred Bode, Chmn. & CEO   Tel: 49-89-8140-50   Rev: $418
Bus: *Mfr. plastics machinery, process equipment,* Fax: 49-89-8140-4900   Emp: 2,036
    armored tanks, locomotives, high-speed trains. www.kmweg.de
NAICS: 332993, 332995, 336413, 336992

    KRAUSS-MAFFEI CORPORATION
    7095 Industrial RD., Florence, Kentucky 41042
    CEO: Sandra K. Winter, Treasurer   Tel: (859) 283-0200   %FO: 100
    Bus: *Mfr./assembly/sale/service plastics*   Fax: (859) 283-9631   Emp: 147
       machinery, process equipment.

    WEGMANN USA, INC.
    30 Mill Race Dr., Lynchburg, Virginia 24502
    CEO: Charles T. Warren, Pres. & CEO   Tel: (434) 385-1580
    Bus: *Mfr. of iron/steel forgings, sheet metal* Fax: (434) 316-9450   Emp: 35
       work.

● **H. KRIEGHOFF GMBH**
Postfach 2610, Boschstrasse 22, D-89016 Ulm, Germany
CEO: Dieter Krieghoff, Pres.   Tel: 49-731-401820
Bus: *Mfr. hunting and sporting firearms.*   Fax: 49-731-4018270
                                                 www.krieghoff.de
NAICS: 332994

    KRIEGHOFF INTL, INC.
    7528 Easton Rd., PO Box 549, Ottsville, Pennsylvania 18942
    CEO: Norbert Haussmann, VP Operations   Tel: (610) 847-5173   %FO: 100
    Bus: *Importer/distributor hunting and sporting* Fax: (610) 847-8691   Emp: 15
       firearms.

● **KROHNE MESSTECHNIK GMBH & CO**
Ludwig-Krohne-Str. 5, D-47058 Duisburg, Germany
CEO: Stephan Neuburger, Mng. Dir.   Tel: 49-203-3010   Rev: $104
Bus: *Mfr. electromechanical & electronic flow and* Fax: 49-203-301389   Emp: 520
    liquid level measurement equipment.   www.krohne.com
NAICS: 334519, 423830

    KROHNE AMERICA INC.
    7 Dearborn Rd., Peabody, Massachusetts 01960
    CEO: Brian Elliott, Pres. & CEO   Tel: (978) 535-6060   %FO: 100
    Bus: *Mfr. electromechanical and electronic flow* Fax: (978) 535-1720
       and liquid level measurement equipment.

● **KRONES AG**
Bohmerwaldstr. 5, D-93068 Neutraubling, Germany
CEO: Volker Kronseder, CEO
Bus: *Mfr. labeling, bottle-filling and packaging
   equipment.*
NAICS: 333993

Tel: 49-9401-70-0
Fax: 49-9401-702488
www.krones.de

Rev: $2,079
Emp: 8,529

   KRONES INC.
   9600 S. 58th St., Franklin, Wisconsin 53132
   CEO: Heinz Sommer, CEO
   Bus: *Labeling, bottle-filling and packaging
      equipment.*

   Tel: (414) 409-4000
   Fax: (414) 409-4100

   %FO: 100
   Emp: 481

● **KRUPP BILSTEIN GMBH & CO.,**
August-Bilstein Str. 4, D-58256 Ennepetal, Germany
CEO: Hans Bohlman, Pres.
Bus: *Mfr. shock absorbers, car jacks and window
   hardware.*
NAICS: 336399, 423120

Tel: 49-23-33-7910
Fax: 49-23-33-79149-00
www.bilstein.de

Rev: $50
Emp: 248

   THYSSENKRUPP BILSTEIN OF AMERICA INC.
   14102 Stowe Dr., Poway, California 92064
   CEO: Doug Robertson, Pres.
   Bus: *Mfr. & sale of shock absorbers.*

   Tel: (858) 386-5900
   Fax: (858) 386-5901

   %FO: 100

● **KSB AG**
Johann-Klein-Str. 9, D-67227 Frankenthal, Germany
CEO: Josef Gerstner, Chmn.
Bus: *Pump and valve manufacture.*

NAICS: 332911, 332912, 332919, 333913, 333996

Tel: 49-623-386-0
Fax: 49-623-386-3401
www.ksb.de

Rev: $1,479
Emp: 12,281

   AMRI INC.
   2045 Silber Rd., Houston, Texas 77055
   CEO: William A. Leech, Pres.
   Bus: *Mfr. valves, pipe fittings*

   Tel: (713) 682-0000
   Fax: (713) 682-0080

   Emp: 45

   GIW INDUSTRIES
   5000 Wrightsboro Rd., Grovetown, Georgia 30813
   CEO: Dennis Zigler, Pres.
   Bus: *Mfr. pumps & pumping equipment*

   Tel: (706) 863-1011
   Fax: (706) 860-5897

   Emp: 300

   GIW INDUSTRIES-THOMSON
   968 Ferrous Rd. NE, Thomson, Georgia 30824
   CEO:
   Bus: *Mfr. pumps & pumping equipment*

   Tel: (706) 595-5950
   Fax: (706) 595-6963

   KSB INC.
   4415 Sarellen Rd., Richmond, Virginia 23231
   CEO: Karen Wood, Treasurer
   Bus: *Pump and valve manufacture and sales.*

   Tel: (804) 222-1818
   Fax: (804) 226-6961

   %FO: 100
   Emp: 508

- **KTR KUPPLUNGSTECHNIK GMBH**
Rodder Damm 170, D-48432 Rheine, Germany
CEO: Dr. Rainer Reichert, Mng. Dir.
Bus: *Mfr. mechanical power transmission equipment.*

Tel: 49-5971-798-0
Fax: 49-5971-798-698
www.ktr.com

Rev: $53
Emp: 250

NAICS: 333613

KTR CORPORATION
122 Anchor Rd., PO Box 9065, Michigan City, Indiana 46361
CEO: James Scott, Pres.
Bus: *Sale of mechanical power transmission equipment.*

Tel: (219) 872-9100
Fax: (219) 872-9150

%FO: 100
Emp: 35

- **LAMBDA PHYSIK AG**
Hans Blocker Str. 12, D-37079 Gottingen, Germany
CEO: John R. Ambroseo, Pres. & CEO
Bus: *Mfr. lasers for industrial, scientific, and medical applications.*

Tel: 49-551-6938-0
Fax: 49-551-6869-1
www.lambdaphysik.com

Rev: $86
Emp: 365

NAICS: 333314

LAMBDA PHYSIK USA INC.
3201 West Commercial Blvd., Ft. Lauderdale, Florida 33309
CEO: Dirk Basting, Pres.
Bus: *Sales of lasers for industrial, scientific, and medical applications.*

Tel: (954) 486-1500
Fax: (954) 486-1501

%FO: 100
Emp: 37

- **LANDESBANK BADEN-WURTTEMBERG**
Am Hauptbahnhof 2, D-70173 Stuttgart, Germany
CEO: Hans Dietmar Sauer, Chmn.
Bus: *International commercial bank.*

Tel: 49-711-127-0
Fax: 49-711-127-3278
www.lbbw.de

Rev: $19,980
Emp: 10,350

NAICS: 522110, 522292, 522320, 523920

LBBW NIEDERLASSUNG NEW YORK
280 Park Ave. West, 31/F, New York, New York 10017
CEO: Andreas Oberem, Gen. Mgr.
Bus: *International commercial banking services.*

Tel: (212) 584-1700
Fax: (212) 584-1799

- **LANDESBANK HESSEN-THÜRINGEN GIROZENTRALE**
Neue Mainzer Str. 52-58, D-60311 Frankfurt am Main, Germany
CEO: Gunther Merl, Chmn.
Bus: *International commercial banking services*

Tel: 49-69-91-3201
Fax: 49-69-29-1517
www.helaba.de

NAICS: 522110

LANDESBANK HESSEN-THURINGEN
420 Fifth Ave., 24/F, New York, New York 10018
CEO: Lee Duxbury, Gen. Mgr.
Bus: *International commercial banking services.*

Tel: (212) 703-5200
Fax: (212) 703-5256

%FO: 100
Emp: 60

● LANGENSCHEIDT KG
Mies-van-der-Rohe-Str. 1, D-80807 Munich, Germany
CEO: Stuart Dolgins, Pres.
Bus: *Publisher of maps.*

Tel: 49-89-36-096-0
Fax: 49-89-36-096-222
www.langenscheidt.de
Emp: 900

NAICS: 511130, 541930

AMERICAN MAP CORP.
4635 54th Rd., Maspeth, New York 11378
CEO: Stuart Dolgins, CEO
Bus: *Mfr./sale/distribution maps.*

Tel: (718) 784-0055
Fax:
Emp: 267

HAGSTROM MAP COMPANY, INC.
125 Maiden Lane, New York, New York 10038
CEO: Stuart Dolgins, Pres.
Bus: *Mfr./sale/distribution maps.*

Tel: (212) 785-5343
Fax:
%FO: 100

LANGENSCHEIDT PUBLISHERS, INC.
46-35 54th Rd., Maspeth, New York 11378
CEO: Stuart Dolgins, Pres.
Bus: *Mfr./sale/distribution maps.*

Tel: (718) 784-0055
Fax: (718) 784-0640
%FO: 100
Emp: 360

TRAKKER MAP INC
8350 Parkline Blvd., Orlando, Florida 32809
CEO: Stuart Dolgins, Pres.
Bus: *Maps manufacture, distribution and sales.*

Tel: (407) 447-6485
Fax: (407) 447-6485
%FO: 100
Emp: 15

● LANXESS AG
Bldg. K10, D-51368 Leverkusen, Germany
CEO: Rolf W. H. Stomberg, Chmn.
Bus: *Mfr. of chemicals, plastic colorants and inorganic pigments for paper and textile industries.*

Tel: 49-214-30-1
Fax: 49-214-30-31769
www.lanxess.com
Rev: $9,238
Emp: 19,659

NAICS: 325131, 325188, 325199

LANXESS CORPORATION
111 RIDC Park West Dr., Pittsburgh, Pennsylvania 15275-1112
CEO: Randall S. Dearth, Pres.
Bus: *Manufacturer of synthetic rubber products.*

Tel: (412) 809-1000
Fax:
%FO: 100

SYBRON CHEMICALS INC.
200 Birmingham Rd., Birmingham, New Jersey 08011
CEO: Ralf Matt, Pres.
Bus: *Manufacturer of ion exchange resins.*

Tel: (609) 893-1100
Fax: (609) 893-8641
%FO: 100

● LECHLER GMBH & CO KG
Ulmer Str. 128, D-72555 Metzingen, Germany
CEO: Juergen W. Frick, Dir.
Bus: *Mfr. of precision spray nozzles and nozzle accessories and agricultural products.*

Tel: 49-7123-962-0
Fax: 49-7123-962-444
www.lechler.de
Rev: $39
Emp: 245

NAICS: 333298, 333912, 339113, 423830

LECHLER INC.
445 Kautz Rd., St. Charles, Illinois 60174-5301
CEO: Ralph Fish, Mgr.
Bus: *Mfr. of precision spray nozzles and nozzle accessories and agricultural products.*

Tel: (630) 377-6611
Fax: (630) 377-6657

%FO: 100
Emp: 57

● **LEICA CAMERA, INC.**
Oskar Barnack-St. 11, D-35606 Solms, Germany
CEO: Hans Friderichs, Chmn.
Bus: *Mfr. of high quality camera equipment and*

Tel: 49-64-42-208-0
Fax: 49-64-42-208-333
www.leica-camera.com

Rev: $145
Emp: 1,296

NAICS: 333315

   LEICA CAMERA INC.
   156 Ludlow Ave., Northvale, New Jersey 07647
   CEO: Roger W. Horn, Pres.
   Bus: *Sales, distribution and parts for Leica camera equipment.*

Tel: (201) 767-7500
Fax: (201) 767-8666

%FO: 100

   LEICA CAMERA INC.
   1 Pearl Ct., Unit A, Allendale, New Jersey 07401
   CEO: Roger Horn, Pres.
   Bus: *Repair services, Sale of photo equipment & supplies.*

Tel: (201) 995-0051
Fax:

%FO: 100
Emp: 38

● **GEBR LEITZ GMBH & CO**
Leitzstr. 2, D-73447 Oberkochen, Germany
CEO: Dieter Brucklacher, CEO
Bus: *Mfr. woodworking tooling.*

Tel: 49-7364-9500
Fax: 49-7364-9506-62
www.leitz.org

Rev: $253
Emp: 3,267

NAICS: 332212

   LEITZ TOOLING SYSTEMS INC.
   4301 East Paris Ave., SE, Grand Rapids, Michigan 49512
   CEO: Terry Jacks, Mgr.
   Bus: *Mfr./sale/service woodworking tooling.*

Tel: (616) 698-7010
Fax: (616) 698-9270

%FO: 100

● **LEONI AG**
Marienstr. 7, D-90402 Nuremberg, Germany
CEO: Klaus probst, CEO
Bus: *Mfr. cables, wires and wiring systems for the automation, automotive, medical equipment and telecommunication industries.*

Tel: 49-911-2023-201
Fax: 49-911-2023-231
www.leoni.com

Rev: $1,701
Emp: 29,957

NAICS: 331222, 332618, 423610

   LEONI WIRING SYSTEMS
   43811 Plymouth Oaks Blvd., Plymouth Twp., Michigan 48170
   CEO: Matthias Schmitt
   Bus: *Mfr. wiring harnesses for the auto and commercial vehicle industries.*

Tel: (734) 414-5012
Fax: (734) 414-5001

%FO: 100

   LEONI WIRING SYSTEMS
   301 Griffith Rd., Chicopee, Massachusetts 01022
   CEO: Neville Crabbe
   Bus: *Mfr. cables, wires and wiring systems.*

Tel: (413) 593-6618
Fax: (413) 593-6639

%FO: 100

LEONI WIRING SYSTEMS
4618 Progress Dr., Columbus, Indiana 47201
CEO: Bob Bush
Bus: *Mfr. wiring harnesses for the commercial vehicle industry.*
Tel: (412) 376-7700
Fax: (412) 376-7700
%FO: 100

LEONI WIRING SYSTEMS
2861 N. Flowing Wells Rd., Ste. 121, Tucson, Arizona 85705
CEO: Alex Boekholt
Bus: *Mfr. wiring harnesses for the auto and commercial vehicle industries.*
Tel: (520) 741-0895
Fax: (520) 741-0864
%FO: 100

LEONI WIRING SYSTEMS
255 Industrial Row Dr., Troy, Michigan 48084
CEO: Mark Eisenmenger
Bus: *Mfr. cables, wires and wiring systems.*
Tel: (248) 655-1900
Fax: (248) 655-1905
%FO: 100

LEONI WIRING SYSTEMS
336 Main St., Ste. A, Rochester, Michigan 48307
CEO: Scott Wordsworth
Bus: *Mfr. cables, wires and wiring systems.*
Tel: (248) 650-3328
Fax: (248) 650-3365
%FO: 100

● **LINDE AG**
Abraham-Lincoln-Str. 21, D-65189 Wiesbaden, Germany
CEO: Wolfgang H. Reitzle, Chmn. & CEO
Bus: *Holding company. gas and engineering; material handling and refrigeration.*
NAICS: 236210, 325120, 333924
Tel: 49-611-770-0
Fax: 49-611-770-269
www.linde.de
Rev: $11,287
Emp: 46,662

HYDRO-CHEM
PO Box 869, Holly Hill, Georgia 30142
CEO: Richard R. Haggard
Bus: *Design/manufacture industrial gas systems.*
Tel: (770) 345-2222
Fax: (770) 345-2778
%FO: 100

LINDE BOC PROCESS PLANTS
8522 East 61st St., Tulsa, Oklahoma 74133
CEO: Steven M. Bertone, Pres.
Bus: *Design/manufacture industrial gas systems.*
Tel: (918) 250-8522
Fax: (918) 250-6915
%FO: 100
Emp: 400

LINDE GAS INC.
6055 Rockside Woods Blvd., Cleveland, Ohio 44131
CEO: Paul Herrgesell, Pres.
Bus: *Industrial gases.*
Tel: (216) 642-6600
Fax: (216) 642-7513
%FO: 100
Emp: 2,200

LINDE GAS INC.
c/o The Corporation Trust Company, 1209 Orange St., Wilmington, Delaware 19801
CEO: Steven M. Bertone
Bus: *Industrial gases.*
Tel: (302) 658-7581
Fax: (302) 658-2919

LINDE GROUP
2450 West Fifth North St., Summerville, South Carolina 29483
CEO: Mitchell Milovich, Pres.
Bus: *Pyrolysis, steam reforming and refinery, furnaces for the chemical, petrochemical and refining industries.*
Tel: (843) 875-8000
Fax: (843) 875-8329
%FO: 100
Emp: 1,012

SCIENTIFIC DESIGN COMPANY, INC.
49 Industrial Ave., Little Ferry, New Jersey 07643
CEO: Craig McLaughlin, Pres.   Tel: (201) 641-0500   %FO: 100
Bus: *Design/manufacture industrial gas systems.* Fax: (201) 641-6986   Emp: 76

SELAS FLUID PROCESSING CORP.
5 Sentry Pkwy. East, Ste. 204, Blue Bell, Pennsylvania 19422
CEO: Steven M. Bertone, Pres.   Tel: (610) 834-0300
Bus: *Engineering services.*   Fax: Emp: 80

THERMATRIX INC.
5 Sentry Pkwy. E, Ste. 204, Blue Bell, Pennsylvania 19422
CEO: Steven M. Bertone, Pres. & CEO   Tel: (610) 834-0300
Bus: *Environmental services & equipment.*   Fax: (610) 834-0473

● **LION BIOSCIENCE AG**
Waldhofer Str. 98, D-69123 Heidelberg, Germany
CEO: Thure Etzold, CEO   Tel: 49-6221-4038-0   Rev: $24
Bus: *Integrated IT solutions for the life science* Fax: 49-6221-4038-101   Emp: 177
                                                www.lionbioscience.com
    NAICS: 511210, 541511, 541512, 541710

    LION BIOSCIENCE INC.
    101 Main St., 17/F, Cambridge, Massachusetts 02142
    CEO: Joseph F. Donahue, Pres.   Tel: (617) 245-5400   %FO: 100
    Bus: *Engaged in biotechnology for drug*   Fax: (617) 245-5401   Emp: 29
         development.

    LION BIOSCIENCE INC.
    245 First St., 18/F, Cambridge, Massachusetts 02142
    CEO: Joseph F. Donahue, CEO   Tel: (617) 444-8485   %FO: 100
    Bus: *Engaged in biotechnology for drug*   Fax: (617) 444-8496
         development.

● **LOEHLE INTERNATIONAL MOVERS**
Heimsheimer Str. 29, D-70499 Stuttgart, Germany
CEO: Thomas Pfisterer, CEO   Tel: 49-711-282041
Bus: *Provides international packing, moving &* Fax: 49-711-2868329
                                                www.loehle.de
    NAICS: 488510

    KNOPF & LOEHLE INC.
    7259 Cross Park Dr., North Charleston, South Carolina 29418
    CEO: Siegfried J. Zarwel, Pres.   Tel: (843) 760-2501   %FO: 100
    Bus: *Provides international packing, moving &* Fax: (843) 760-2503   Emp: 6
         shipping.

    KNOPF INTERNATIONAL INC.
    1574 West 7th St., Monroe, Michigan 48161
    CEO: Siegfried J. Zarwel   Tel: (734) 457-0132   %FO: 100
    Bus: *Provides international packing, moving &* Fax: (734) 457-0132
         shipping.

KNOPF INTERNATIONAL INC.
201 Old Boiling Springs Rd., Ste. C, Greer, South Carolina 29650
CEO: Siegfried J. Zarwel
Bus: *Provides international packing, moving & shipping.*

Tel: (864) 281-9930
Fax:

%FO: 100

KNOPF INTERNATIONAL INC.
2397 South Dove St., Alexandria, Virginia 22314
CEO: Siegfried J. Zarwel, Pres.
Bus: *Provides international packing, moving & shipping.*

Tel: (703) 549-8585
Fax:

%FO: 100
Emp: 16

● **LTS LOHMANN THERAPEIE SYSTEME AG**
Lohmannstr. 2, D-56626 Andernach, Germany
CEO: Peter Schwarz, CEO
Bus: *Development and production of transdermal therapeutic systems.*
NAICS: 334510

Tel: 49-2632-99-0
Fax: 49-2632-99-2200
www.ltslohmann.com

Rev: $156
Emp: 862

LTS LOHMANN THERAPY-SYSTEMS CORP.
21 Henderson Dr., West Caldwell, New Jersey 07006
CEO: Patrick Walters, Pres.
Bus: *Engaged in development and production of transdermal therapeutic systems.*

Tel: (973) 244-2052
Fax: (973) 575-5174

%FO: 100
Emp: 225

● **MARKLIN & CIE GMBH**
Holzheimer Str. 8, D-73037 Goppingen, Germany
CEO: Fred Gates, CEO
Bus: *Toy train manufacturer.*

NAICS: 339932

Tel: 49-7161-608-286
Fax: 49-7161-608-222
www.marklin.de

MARKLIN, INC.
PO Box 319, 16988 W. Victor Rd., New Berlin, Wisconsin 53151-0559
CEO: Fred Gates
Bus: *Model train manufacturer.*

Tel: (262) 784-8854
Fax: (262) 784-8854

%FO: 100

● **MASCHINENFABRIK NIEHOFF GMBH & CO KG**
Further Str. 30, D-91126 Schwabach, Germany
CEO: Heinz Rockenhauser, CEO
Bus: *Mfr. machinery and equipment for non-ferrous wire and cable industry.*
NAICS: 335929

Tel: 49-9122-9770
Fax: 49-9122-977155
www.niehoff.de

Rev: $65
Emp: 395

NIEHOFF ENDEX, INC.
One Mallard Ct., Swedesboro, New Jersey 08085
CEO: Helmut Berghold, Pres.
Bus: *Sale/service machinery & equipment for non-ferrous wire & cable industry, distribution machinery & equipment for steel wire & cable industry.*

Tel: (856) 467-4884
Fax: (856) 467-0584

%FO: 100
Emp: 48

- **KARL MAYER TEXTILMASCHINENFABRIK GMBH**
Bruhlstr. 25, D-63179 Obertshausen, Germany
CEO: Fritz P. Mayer, Chmn.
Bus: *Mfr. warp knitting machinery and parts, warping equipment.*
NAICS: 333292

Tel: 49-6104-4020	Rev: $260
Fax: 49-6104-43574	Emp: 1,728
www.karlmayer.de	

> **MAYER TEXTILE MACHINE CORPORATION**
> 310 North Chimney Rock Rd., Greensboro, North Carolina 27409
> CEO: Michael Burke, VP
> Bus: *Mfr./distribution warp knitting machinery, parts and warping equipment.*
>
> Tel: (336) 294-1572   %FO: 100
> Fax: (336) 854-0251   Emp: 25

> **MAYER TEXTILE MACHINE CORPORATION**
> 310 Brighton Rd., Clifton, New Jersey 07012
> CEO: Gerd Rohmert, Pres.
> Bus: *Mfr./distribution warp knitting machinery, parts and warping equipment.*
>
> Tel: (973) 773-3350   %FO: 100
> Fax: (973) 473-3463   Emp: 140

- **MEDION AG**
Gansemarkt 16-18, D-45127 Essen, Germany
CEO: Gerd Brachmann, Chmn.
Bus: *Mfr. computers, peripherals, consumer electronics and telephony products.*
NAICS: 334111

Tel: 49-201-810-810	Rev: $3,579
Fax: 49-201-810-81227	Emp: 1,504
www.medion.com	

> **MEDION USA INC.**
> 1130 Lake Cook Rd., Ste. 340, Buffalo Grove, Illinois 60089
> CEO: Brian Firestone, Pres.
> Bus: *Mfr. computer products.*
>
> Tel: (866) 633-4660   %FO: 100
> Fax: (866) 633-4660

- **MELITTA**
Marienstr. 88, D-32 425 Minden, Germany
CEO: Jorg Bentz
Bus: *Mfr./marketing coffee & coffee related products; food preparation/preservation products; convenient products.*
NAICS: 311920, 335211

Tel: 49-571-4046-0	Rev: $1,000
Fax: 49-571-4046-8231	Emp: 4,500
www.melitta.de	

> **MELITTA NORTH AMERICA INC.**
> 13925 58th St. North, Clearwater, Florida 33760
> CEO: Martin Miller, CEO
> Bus: *Mfr. of coffee, coffee filters, & electronic coffee makers.*
>
> Tel: (727) 535-2111   %FO: 100
> Fax: (727) 535-7376   Emp: 150

- **MERCK KGAA**
Frankfurter Str. 250, D-64293 Darmstadt, Germany
CEO: Bernhard Scheuble, Chmn. & CEO
Bus: *Mfr. pharmaceuticals, chemicals and laboratory preparations.*
NAICS: 325411, 325412, 325520, 334419

Tel: 49-6151-72-0	Rev: $7,992
Fax: 49-6151-72-2000	Emp: 28,877
www.merck.de	

DEY, INC.
2751 Napa Valley Corporate Dr., Napa, California 94558
CEO: Mel Engle, CEO & Mng. Dir.   Tel: (707) 224-3200   %FO: 100
Bus: *Mfr./sales pharmaceuticals.*   Fax: (707) 224-0495

EMD BIOSCIENCES, INC.
10394 Pacific Center Ct., San Diego, California 92121
CEO: Octavio Diaz, CEO & Mng. Dir.   Tel: (858) 450-9600   %FO: 100
Bus: *Mfr./sales pharmaceuticals.*   Fax: (858) 453-3552

EMD CHEMICALS, INC.
480 S. Democrat Rd., Gibbstown, New Jersey 08027
CEO: Douglas S. Brown, CEO & Mng. Dir.   Tel: (856) 423-6300   %FO: 100
Bus: *Mfr./sales pharmaceuticals, chemicals and*   Fax: (856) 423-4389
    laboratory preparations.

EMD CHEMICALS, INC.
7 Skyline Dr., Hawthorne, New York 10532
CEO: Dougals S. Brown, CEO & Mng. Dir.   Tel: (914) 592-4660   %FO: 100
Bus: *Mfr. pharmaceuticals and organic and*   Fax: (914) 592-9469
    inorganic chemicals.

EMD LEXIGEN RESEARCH CENTER CORP.
45A Middlesex Turnpike, Bedford Campus, Billerica, Massachusetts 01821
CEO: Dr. Stephen Gillies, Pres. & CEO   Tel: (978) 294-1100
Bus: *Pharmaceuticals manufacture and sales.*   Fax: (978) 294-1101

EMD PHARMACEUTICALS, INC.
3211 Shannon Rd., Ste. 500, Durham, North Carolina 27707
CEO: Nancy J. Wysenski, Pres. & CEO   Tel: (919) 401-7100   %FO: 100
Bus: *Mfr./sales pharmaceuticals.*   Fax: (919) 401-7180

NITRAGIN INC.
13100 West Lisbon Rd., Ste. 600, Brookfield, Wisconsin 53005
CEO: Tom Winkofske, CEO & Mng. Dir.   Tel: (262) 957-2000   %FO: 100
Bus: *Pharmaceuticals.*   Fax: (262) 957-2121

• MERO SYSTEME GMBH & CO
Max-Mengeringhausen Str. 5, D-97084 Wurzburg, Germany
CEO: Gunther Troster, Mng. Dir.   Tel: 49-931-66-70-0
Bus: *Mfr. space frames, special structures/raised*   Fax: 49-931-66-70-404   Emp: 1,000
    floors, exhibits and displays.   www.mero.de
NAICS: 332312, 337215

MERO STRUCTURES INC.
W126 N8585 Westbrook Crossing, Menomonee Falls, Wisconsin 53021
CEO: Ian Collins, Pres.   Tel: (262) 255-5561   %FO: 100
Bus: *Space frames, special structures, exhibits*   Fax: (262) 255-6932   Emp: 70
    and displays.

MEROFORM SYSTEMS USA
429 West Levers Place, Orange, California 92867
CEO: Todd Koren, Pres.   Tel: (714) 974-8544   %FO: 100
Bus: *Tradeshow exhibit equipment distributor.*   Fax: (714) 283-2494   Emp: 35

- **MESSE DUSSELDORF GMBH**
  PO Box 10 10 06, D-40001 Dusseldorf, Germany
  CEO: Werner Matthias Dornscheidt, Chmn.   Tel: 49-211-4560-01
  Bus: *Organizes trade shows for medical, fashion and*   Fax: 49-211-4560-668   Emp: 600
  service industries.   www.messe-duesseldorf.de
  NAICS: 561920

  MESSE DUSSELDORF NORTH AMERICA
  150 N. Michigan Ave., Ste. 2920, Chicago, Illinois 60601
  CEO: Thomas Mitchell, VP   Tel: (312) 781-5180   %FO: 100
  Bus: *Promotes trade show program of Messe*   Fax: (312) 781-5188   Emp: 15
  Düsseldorf in the USA.

- **METRO HOLDING AG**
  Schulterstr. 1, D-40235 Dusseldorf, Germany
  CEO: Hans-Joachim Korber, Chmn. & CEO   Tel: 49-211-6886-0   Rev: $76,942
  Bus: *Holding company for department and electronic*   Fax: 49-211-6886-2178   Emp: 261,438
  stores and home improvement centers and   www.metro.de
  wholesale hypermarkets.
  NAICS: 443111, 443112, 444110, 444120, 444130, 445110, 452111, 551112

  JETRO CASH & CARRY ENTERPRISES, INC.
  15-24 132nd St., College Point, New York 11356
  CEO: Stanley Fleishman, Pres. & CEO   Tel: (718) 762-8700   %FO: JV
  Bus: *Distribution center for manufacturers.*   Fax: (718) 661-9627

- **LUCAS MEYER GMBH & COMPANY**
  Ausschlager Elbdeich 62, D-20539 Hamburg, Germany
  CEO: Peter Rohde, Pres.   Tel: 49-40-7895-50
  Bus: *Mfr. Lecithin soybeans..*   Fax: 49-40-7898-329
                                                   www.lucasmeyer.de
  NAICS: 111110, 325411

  LUCAS MEYER INC.
  765 East Pythian Ave., Decatur, Illinois 62526
  CEO: Peter Rhode, Pres.   Tel: (217) 875-3660   %FO: 100
  Bus: *Mfr. lecithin soybeans.*   Fax: (217) 877-5046   Emp: 11

- **MIELE & CIE GMBH**
  Carl-Miele-Str. 29, D-33332 Gutersloh, Germany
  CEO: Markus Miele, Mng. Dir.   Tel: 49-52-41-890
  Bus: *Mfr. commercial equipment & fitted kitchens, built-*   Fax: 49-52-41-89-2090   Emp: 15,000
  in appliances; washing & drying machines,   www.miele.de
  dishwashers, microwave ovens & vacuum
  NAICS: 238290, 335212, 335221, 335222, 335224

  MIELE, INC.
  555 Washington St., Wellesley, Massachusetts 02482
  CEO: Donna Lexo, Mgr.   Tel: (781) 431-2225   %FO: 100
  Bus: *Mfr. commercial equipment, fitted kitchens*   Fax: (781) 431-0003
  and built-in appliances.

MIELE, INC.
7680 North Federal Hwy., Boca Raton, Florida 33487
CEO: Danon Gorccynski, Mgr.
Bus: *Mfr. commercial equipment, fitted kitchens and built-in appliances.*
Tel: (561) 995-6809
Fax: (561) 995-8083
%FO: 100

MIELE, INC.
9 Independence Way, Princeton, New Jersey 08540
CEO: Nick Lord, Pres.
Bus: *Mfr. commercial equipment, fitted kitchens and built-in appliances.*
Tel: (609) 419-9898
Fax: (609) 419-4298
%FO: 100
Emp: 275

MIELE, INC.
189 North Robertson Blvd., Beverly Hills, California 90211
CEO: Adrian DiFuentes, Pres.
Bus: *Showroom for Miele products.*
Tel: (310) 855-9470
Fax: (310) 358-0238
%FO: 100

● **MOELLER-WEDEL GMBH**
Rosengarten 10, D-22880 Wedel, Germany
CEO: Dr. Martin Schmidt, Mng. Dir.
Bus: *Mfr. operating microscopes and eye examination equipment.*
NAICS: 339112
Tel: 49-4103-709-01
Fax: 49-4103-709-355
www.moeller-wedel.com
Rev: $22
Emp: 208

HAAG-STREIT USA INC.
5500 Courseview Dr., Mason, Ohio 45040
CEO: Christopher Blizzard, Pres.
Bus: *Mfr. and sales instruments and medical-practice equipment for ophthalmologists, optometrists and opticians.*
Tel: (513) 336-7255
Fax:
%FO: 100
Emp: 140

RELIANCE MEDICAL INC.
3535 King Hill Rd., Mason, Ohio 45040
CEO: Dennis Imwalle, Pres.
Bus: *Mfr. and sales instruments and medical-practice equipment for ophthalmologists, optometrists and opticians.*
Tel: (513) 398-3937
Fax:
%FO: 100
Emp: 105

● **MOTORCAR RADIATOR GMBH & CO**
Postfach 1346, D-34363 Hofgeismar, Germany
CEO: Dirk Pietzcker, Chmn. & Pres.
Bus: *Mfr. heat exchangers.*
NAICS: 332410
Tel: 49-5671-8830
Fax: 49-5671-3582
www.akg-gruppe.de
Rev: $140
Emp: 1,400

AKG OF AMERICA, INC.
7315 Oakwood St. Extension, PO Box 365, Mebane, North Carolina 27302
CEO: Heinrich J. Kuehne, VP
Bus: *Mfr./distribution heat exchangers and custom cooling systems.*
Tel: (919) 563-4286
Fax: (919) 563-6060
%FO: 100
Emp: 90

• **MUNCHENER RUCKVERSICHERUNGS-GESELLSCHAFT AKTIENGESELLSCHAFT**
Koniginstr. 107, D-80802 Munich, Germany
CEO: Nikolaus von Bomhard, Chmn.   Tel: 49-89-3891-0   Rev: $61,220
Bus: *Engaged in reinsurance services.*   Fax: 49-89-3990-56   Emp: 41,431
www.munichre.com
NAICS: 524113, 524114, 524126, 524130

   AMERICAN RE-INSURANCE COMPANY, DIV. MUNICH RE
   555 College Rd. East, Princeton, New Jersey 08543
   CEO: John P. Phelan, Chmn. & CEO   Tel: (609) 243-5558   %FO: 100
   Bus: *Reinsurance services*   Fax: (609) 243-4257   Emp: 1,327

   MUNICH AMERICAN REASSURANCE COMPANY
   56 Perimeter Center East, NE, Ste. 500, Atlanta, Georgia 30346-2290
   CEO: David M. Holland, Pres. & CEO   Tel: (770) 350-3200   %FO: 100
   Bus: *Reinsurance*   Fax: (770) 350-3300   Emp: 120

• **MWG-BIOTECH AG**
Anzinger Strasse 7a, D-85560 Ebersberg, Germany
CEO: Wolfgang Pieken, CEO   Tel: 49-8092-82890   Rev: $45
Bus: *Biotechnology.*   Fax: 49-8092-11084   Emp: 325
www.mwgbiotech.com
NAICS: 541710

   MWG-BIOTECH, INC.
   4170 Mendenhall Oaks Pkwy., High Point, North Carolina 27265
   CEO: Randi Charbonnet, Pres.   Tel: (336) 812-9995   %FO: 100
   Bus: *Engaged in biotechnology.*   Fax: (336) 812-9983

• **NBB CONTROLS & COMPONENTS AG**
Otto-Hahn-Str. 1-3, D-75248 Olbronn-Durrn, Germany
CEO: Thomas Burchard, CEO   Tel: 49-7237-999-0
Bus: *Radio remote control sales.*   Fax: 49-7237-999-199
www.nbb.de
NAICS: 334290, 421690

   NBB CONTROLS, INC.
   1572 East Parham Rd., Richmond, Virginia 23228-2360
   CEO: Wolfgang Bredow, Pres.   Tel: (804) 262-4846   %FO: 100
   Bus: *Industrial radio remote control sales.*   Fax: (804) 262-0596   Emp: 4

• **NEMETSCHEK AKTIENGESELLSCHAFT**
Konrad-Zuse-Platz 1, D-81829 Munich, Germany
CEO: Gerhard Weiss, CEO   Tel: 49-89-927-930   Rev: $132
Bus: *Mfr. CAD software for architects, contractors,*   Fax: 49-89-927-935-200   Emp: 750
   engineers and real estate managers.   www.nemetscheck.com
NAICS: 511210

   NEMETSCHEK NORTH AMERICA INC.
   7150 Riverwood Dr., Columbia, Maryland 21046
   CEO: Richard B. Diehl   Tel: (410) 290-5114   %FO: 100
   Bus: *Design and manufacture of CAD software.*   Fax: (410) 290-8050

- **NEUE HERBOLD MASCHINEN UND ANLAGENBAU GMBH**
  Wiesenstr. 44, D-74889 Sinshiem Reihen, Germany
  CEO: Peter Abraham, Mng. Dir.
  Bus: *Mfr. recycling equipment.*

  Tel: 49-7261-92480
  Fax: 49-7261-924899
  www.neue-herbold.com

  Emp: 50

  NAICS: 333319
  NEW HERBOLD INC.
  21 Eskow Rd., Worcester, Massachusetts 01604
  CEO: Edward Ronca, Pres.
  Bus: *Mfr./distribution of recycling equipment.*

  Tel: (508) 865-7355
  Fax: (508) 865-9975

  %FO: 100

- **NEUMAN & ESSER GROUP**
  Werkserasse o. Nr., D-52531 Ubach-Palenberg, Germany
  CEO: Klaus Peters, Chmn.
  Bus: *Compressors manufacture.*

  Tel: 49-2451-481-105
  Fax: 49-2451-481-139
  www.neuman-esser.de

  NAICS: 333912
  NEUMAN & ESSER USA
  1035 Dairy Ashford, Ste. 300, Houston, Texas 77079
  CEO: Milton DeLair
  Bus: *Mfr. compressors.*

  Tel: (281) 497-5113
  Fax: (281) 497-5047

- **OSRAM GMBH, SUB. SIEMENS AG**
  Hellabrunnerstr. 1, D-81543 Munich, Germany
  CEO: martin Goetzeler, CEO
  Bus: *Mfr. lighting products and film photography.*

  Tel: 49-89-62-130
  Fax: 49-89-62-132020
  www.osram.com

  Rev: $5,226
  Emp: 36,644

  NAICS: 335110, 335121, 335122, 335129, 335931
  OSRAM SYLVANIA INC.
  100 Endicott St., Danvers, Massachusetts 01923
  CEO: Charles F. Jerabek
  Bus: *Mfr. lighting products.*

  Tel: (978) 777-1900
  Fax: (978) 750-2152

  %FO: 100

- **OSSBERGER GMBH & CO.**
  Otto-Rieder-Str. 7, D-91781 Weissenburg/Bayern, Germany
  CEO: Karl Friedrich Ossberger, Pres. & CEO
  Bus: *Agricultural machinery manufacture.*

  Tel: 49-9141-9770
  Fax: 49-9141-97720
  www.ossberger.de

  NAICS: 326199, 333111, 336399
  OSSBERGER TURBINES, INC.
  3398 Stonewall Rd., PO Box 736, Hayes, Virginia 23072
  CEO: Karl F. Ossberger, Pres.
  Bus: *Agricultural machinery manufacture.*

  Tel: (804) 360-7992
  Fax:

- **OTTO GMBH & CO. KG**
  Wandsbeker Str. 3-7, D-2217 Hamburg, Germany
  CEO: Michael Otto, Chmn. & CEO
  Bus: *Engaged in mail order businesses.*

  Tel: 49-40-6461-401
  Fax: 49-40-6461-449
  www.ottogroup.com

  Rev: $17,879
  Emp: 55,406

  NAICS: 339920, 424340, 442110, 442299, 443111, 443112, 443120, 448110, 448120, 448130, 448140, 448210, 454111, 454113, 561510

  EDDIE BAUER HOLDINGS, INC.
  3500 Lacey Rd., Downers Grove, Illinois 60515
  CEO: Fabian Mansson, Pres. & CEO
  Bus: *Sportswear and home furnishings.*

  Tel: (630) 986-8800
  Fax: (630) 769-2012

  %FO: 100

  EUROMARKET DESIGNS INC.
  1250 Techny Rd., Northbrook, Illinois 60062
  CEO: Gordon Segal, CEO
  Bus: *Crate & Barrel catalog.*

  Tel: (847) 272-2888
  Fax: (847) 272-5366

  %FO: 100

  NEWPORT NEWS, INC.
  5100 City Line Rd., Hampton, Virginia 23630
  CEO: Geralynn Madonna, Pres. & COO
  Bus: *Women's clothing catalog sales.*

  Tel: (212) 986-2585
  Fax: (212) 916-8281

  %FO: 100

- **PANDATEL AG**
  Fasanenweg 25, D-22145 Hamburg, Germany
  CEO: Norbert Wienck, CEO
  Bus: *Mfr. optical telecommunication transmission equipment.*

  Tel: 49-40-664-140
  Fax: 49-40-664-5792
  www.pandatel.de

  Rev: $20
  Emp: 184

  NAICS: 333314

  PAN DACOM TELECOMMUNICATIONS INC.
  1095 Cranbury South River Rd., Ste. 24, Jamesburg, New Jersey 08831
  CEO: Ziaul Hasan
  Bus: *Mfr./sales optical telecommunication transmission equipment.*

  Tel: (732) 271-8680
  Fax: (732) 271-8689

  %FO: 100

- **PARI GMBH**
  Moosstr. 9, D-82319 Starnberg, Germany
  CEO: Paul Ritzau, CEO
  Bus: *Respiratory equipment manufacture.*

  Tel: 49-8151-279-0
  Fax: 49-8151-279-101
  www.pari.com

  Emp: 150

  NAICS: 334510, 339112

  PARI INNOVATIVE MANUFACTURERS
  2943 Oak Lake Blvd., Midlothian, Virginia 23112
  CEO: Lawrence Weinstein, Pres.
  Bus: *Respiratory products manufacture and sales.*

  Tel: (804) 639-7235
  Fax: (804) 253-0260

  %FO: 100
  Emp: 5

  PARI RESPIRATORY EQUIPMENT, INC.
  2943 Oak Lake Blvd., Midlothian, Virginia 23112
  CEO: Werner Gutmann, Pres.
  Bus: *Respiratory products manufacture and sales.*

  Tel: (804) 253-7274
  Fax: (804) 253-0260

  Emp: 28

- **PASSAVANT-ROEDIGER ANLAGENBAU GMBH**
Kinzigheimer Weg 104-106, D-63450 Hanau, Germany
CEO: Robert Huth, Mng. Dir.
Bus: *Engineering/design/construct waste water
treatment plants, mfr. related equipment.*
NAICS: 237110, 333319, 423610, 423830

Tel: 49-6181-3090
Fax: 49-6181-309111
www.passavant-roediger-anlagenbau.de

Rev: $235
Emp: 1,400

> **ROEDIGER PITTSBURGH INC.**
> 3812 Route 8 Allison Park, Pittsburgh, Pennsylvania 15101
> CEO: Charles Yetsconish, Pres.
> Bus: *Engineering/design/mfr. waste water
> treatment equipment.*
>
> Tel: (412) 487-6010
> Fax: (412) 487-6005
>
> %FO: 100
> Emp: 47

- **PEPPERL+FUCHS GMBH**
Koenigsberger Allee 87, D-68307 Mannheim, Germany
CEO: Leiter Beschaffung, Pres. & CEO
Bus: *Mfr. proximity sensors and electronic controls.*

Tel: 49-621-7760
Fax: 49-621-7761000
www.pepperl-fuchs.com

Emp: 2,500

NAICS: 334413

> **PEPPERL+FUCHS INC.**
> 1600 Enterprise Pkwy., Twinsburg, Ohio 44087
> CEO: Wolfgang A. Mueller
> Bus: *Enclosure protection systems division.*
>
> Tel: (330) 425-3555
> Fax: (330) 425-4607
>
> %FO: 100

> **PEPPERL+FUCHS INC.**
> 1600 Enterprise Pkwy., Twinsburg, Ohio 44087
> CEO: Dan Sweet, SVP
> Bus: *Mfr. proximity sensors and electronic
> controls.*
>
> Tel: (330) 425-3555
> Fax: (330) 425-4607
>
> %FO: 100
> Emp: 125

- **PERI GMBH**
PO Box 1264, Rudolf-Diesel Str. 19, D-89259 Weissenhorn, Germany
CEO: Artur Schworer, CEO
Bus: *Concrete formwork and scaffolding.*

Tel: 49-7309-9500
Fax: 49-7309-9510
www.peri.de

Rev: $311
Emp: 1,250

NAICS: 321219, 327390, 423310, 532490

> **PERI USA FORMWORK SYSTEMS, INC.(HEADQUARTERS)**
> 7272 Park Circle Dr., Ste. 200, Hanover, Maryland 21076
> CEO: Harvey Evans, VP
> Bus: *Distribution/sale/service concrete formwork
> and scaffolding.*
>
> Tel: (410) 712-7225
> Fax: (410) 712-7080

- **PETER WOLTERS SURFACE TECHNOLOGIES GMBH & CO. KG**
Busumer Str. 96, D-24768 Rendsburg, Germany
CEO: Peter Wolters, CEO
Bus: *Mfr. of tools for lapping, polishing and fine-
grinding.*
NAICS: 333295

Tel: 49-4331-458-0
Fax: 49-4331-458-290
www.peter-wolters.com

PETER WOLTERS OF AMERICA, INC.
14 High St., PO Box 1585, Plainville, Massachusetts 02762
CEO: Andrew Corsini, Pres.   Tel: (508) 695-7151   %FO: 100
Bus: *Chemical & allied products*   Fax: (508) 695-7154   Emp: 12

● **PFEIFFER VACUUM TECHNOLOGY AG**
Berliner Str. 43, D-35614 Asslar, Germany
CEO: Wolfgang Dondorf, Chmn. & CEO   Tel: 49-6441-802-0   Rev: $212
Bus: *Mfr. turbo molecular pumps and markets*   Fax: 49-6441-802-202   Emp: 745
components for vacuum technology.   www.pfeiffer-vacuum.com
NAICS: 333996

  PFEIFFER VACUUM TECHNOLOGY INC.
  24 Trafalgar Square, Nashua, New Hampshire 03063-1988
  CEO: Wolfgang Dondorf, CEO   Tel: (603) 578-6500   %FO: 100
  Bus: *Sales/distribution of turbo molecular pumps*   Fax: (603) 578-6550   Emp: 71
  and marketing of components for vacuum technology.

● **PFLEIDERER AG**
Ingolstadter Str. 51, D-92318 Newmarkt, Germany
CEO: Rolf H. Bufe, CEO   Tel: 49-9181-28-8044   Rev: $1,229
Bus: *Mfr. building supplies, including wood-based*   Fax: 49-9181-28-606   Emp: 4,429
furniture panels and turnkey solutions.   www.pfleiderer.de
NAICS: 221119, 221310, 221320, 326113

  NEWMARK INFRASTRUCTURE SOLUTIONS
  Box 815, Estill, South Carolina 29918
  CEO: Eric Larsen   Tel: (803) 625-3131   %FO: 100
  Bus: *Mfr. spun concrete and tubular steel poles.*   Fax: (803) 625-4722

  NEWMARK INFRASTRUCTURE SOLUTIONS
  11308 Highway 36, Bellville, Texas 77418
  CEO: G. Byrd   Tel: (979) 865-9137   %FO: 100
  Bus: *Mfr. spun concrete and tubular steel poles.*   Fax: (979) 865-5007

  NEWMARK INFRASTRUCTURE SOLUTIONS
  3129 35th St., Tuscaloosa, Alabama 35401
  CEO: David Brown   Tel: (205) 752-7653   %FO: 100
  Bus: *Mfr. spun concrete and tubular steel poles.*   Fax: (205) 752-8602

  NEWMARK INFRASTRUCTURE SOLUTIONS
  102 Sentry Dr., Mansfield, Texas 76063
  CEO: Jeff Steele   Tel: (817) 473-0226   %FO: 100
  Bus: *Mfr. spun concrete and tubular steel poles.*   Fax: (817) 473-1464

  NEWMARK INFRASTRUCTURE SOLUTIONS
  3970 Lenwood Rd., Barstow, California 92311
  CEO: C. Navarre   Tel: (760) 253-3070   %FO: 100
  Bus: *Mfr. spun concrete and tubular steel poles.*   Fax: (760) 253-3059

NEWMARK INFRASTRUCTURE SOLUTIONS
Box 1489, Bay Minette, Alabama 36507
CEO: K. Bateman
Bus: *Mfr. spun concrete and tubular steel poles.*
Tel: (251) 937-2800
Fax: (251) 937-0174
%FO: 100

NEWMARK INFRASTRUCTURE SOLUTIONS
4131 Hwy. 17 South, Bartow, Florida 33830
CEO: Jenny Brown
Bus: *Mfr. spun concrete and tubular steel poles.*
Tel: (863) 533-6465
Fax: (863) 533-2841
%FO: 100

NEWMARK INFRASTRUCTURE SOLUTIONS
Box 127, Claxton, Georgia 30417
CEO: Russell Belding
Bus: *Mfr. spun concrete and tubular steel poles.*
Tel: (912) 739-4970
Fax: (912) 739-2103
%FO: 100

NEWMARK INTERNATIONAL INC.
2 Perimeter Park South, Ste. 475, Birmingham, Alabama 35243
CEO: Doug Sherman
Bus: *Mfr. spun concrete and tubular steel poles.*
Tel: (205) 968-7200
Fax: (205) 968-7201
%FO: 100

VALMONT INDUSTRIES INC.
One Valmont Plaza, Omaha, Nebraska 68154
CEO: Mogens C. Bay
Bus: *Mfr. mechanized poles, towers and
structures for lighting,
traffic, utility and communications.*
Tel: (402) 963-1000
Fax: (402) 963-1198
%FO: 100

● **PHOENIX AG**
Hannoversche Str. 88, D-21079 Hamburg, Germany
CEO: Meinhard Liebing, CEO
Bus: *Mfr. acoustic systems and rubber products for
auto and industrial markets.*
NAICS: 336211
Tel: 49-40-7667-1521
Fax: 49-40-7667-2577
www.phoenix-ag.com
Rev: $1,395
Emp: 8,820

CONTITECH NORTH AMERICA, c/o INA BEARING
1750 E. Big Beaver Rd., Ste. 101, Troy, Michigan 48083
CEO: Andre Bogacz
Bus: *Automotive applications.*
Tel: (248) 528-4270
Fax: (248) 528-4318
%FO: 100

CONTITECH NORTH AMERICA, c/o INA BEARING
136 Summit Ave., Montvale, New Jersey 07645
CEO: Andre Bogacz
Bus: *Automotive applications.*
Tel: (201) 930-0600
Fax: (201) 930-0050
%FO: 100

PHOENIX NORTH AMERICA INC.
720 King Georges Post Rd., Ste. 3J, Fords, New Jersey 08863
CEO: Scott Poyner
Bus: *Mfr. acoustic systems and rubber products
for auto and industrial markets.*
Tel: (732) 346-5353
Fax: (732) 346-5355
%FO: 100

SANDUSKY ATHOL INTERNATIONAL
PO Box 105, Butner, North Carolina 27509
CEO: Jeffrey Post
Bus: *Mfr. polymer coated products.*
Tel: (919) 575-6523
Fax: (919) 575-9344
%FO: 100

Germany

SANDUSKY ATHOL INTERNATIONAL
27950 Orchard Lake, Ste. 101, Farmington Hills, Michigan 48334
CEO: Thomas J. Carstens Jr.   Tel: (248) 855-6100   %FO: 100
Bus: *Mfr. polymer coated products.*   Fax: (248) 855-6113

SANDUSKY ATHOL INTERNATIONAL
528 Townsend Ave., High Point, North Carolina 27264
CEO: Jeffrey Post   Tel: (919) 575-6523   %FO: 100
Bus: *Mfr. polymer coated products.*   Fax: (919) 575-9344

• **CARL AUG PICARD GMBH**
Hauptsitz, Haster Aue 9, D-42857 Remscheid, Germany
CEO: Klaus Picard, CEO   Tel: 49-2191-8930
Bus: *Precision grinding, wear parts & heat treating.*   Fax: 49-2191-893111   Emp: 400
                                     www.capicard.com
NAICS: 333512

  C. A . PICARD INC.
  305 Hill Brady Rd., Battle Creek, Michigan 49015
  CEO: Gunter Schramm, Pres.   Tel: (269) 962-2231   %FO: 100
  Bus: *Tooling for printed circuit board industry.*   Fax: (269) 962-4916   Emp: 129

  C.A. PICARD INC.
  Hwy. 36 East, PO Box 98, Belleville, Kansas 66935
  CEO: Ted Williams, Mgr.   Tel: (785) 527-5641   %FO: 100
  Bus: *Tooling for printed circuit board industry.*   Fax: (785) 527-5414   Emp: 25

  C.A. PICARD INC.
  689 Sugar Lane Ind. Pkwy., Elyria, Ohio 44035
  CEO: George Zambo, Pres.   Tel: (440) 366-5400   %FO: 100
  Bus: *Tooling for printed circuit board industry.*   Fax: (440) 366-5404   Emp: 12

• **POLYSIUS AG, DIV. THYSSEN KRUPP**
Graf-Galen-Str. 17, D-59269 Beckum, Germany
CEO: Jurgen Bauer, Chmn.   Tel: 49-2525-99-0
Bus: *Mfr. cement machinery and equipment.*   Fax: 49-2525-99-2100
                                     www.polysius.com
NAICS: 236210, 333120, 333999

  POLYSIUS CORPORATION
  180 Interstate North Pkwy., Ste. 300, Atlanta, Georgia 30339-2194
  CEO: Mark Terry, Pres.   Tel: (770) 955-3660   %FO: 100
  Bus: *Mfr. cement machinery and equipment.*   Fax: (770) 955-8789   Emp: 50

• **DR. ING. H.C.F. PORSCHE AG**
Porscheplatz 1, D-70435 Stuttgart, Germany
CEO: Helmut Sihler, Chmn.   Tel: 49-711-911-0   Rev: $7,645
Bus: *Mfr. and sales automobiles, engines and*   Fax: 49-711-911-5777   Emp: 11,668
     components.   www.porsche.com
NAICS: 336111

PORSCHE CARS OF NORTH AMERICA INC.
980 Hammond Dr., Ste. 1000, Atlanta, Georgia 30328
CEO: Peter Schwarzenbauer, Pres. & CEO
Bus: *Sales/distribution of automobiles.*

Tel: (770) 290-3500
Fax: (770) 290-3700

%FO: 100

● **PTR PRAEZISIONSTECHNIK GMBH**
Am Spitzen Sand 1, D-63477 Maintal, Germany
CEO: Ingo Kloss, Pres.
Bus: *Electron beam welders and electron beam job
shop services.*
NAICS: 335999

Tel: 49-6181-40940
Fax: 49-6181-409420
www.ptreb.com

> **PTR - PRECISION TECHNOLOGIES, INC.**
> 120 Post Rd., Enfield, Connecticut 06082-5625
> CEO: D. E. Powers
> Bus: *Electron beam welders, laser beam
> systems, electron beam job shop services.*
>
> Tel: (860) 741-2281
> Fax: (860) 745-7932
>
> %FO: 100
> Emp: 50

● **PUMA AG**
Wurzburgerstr. 13, D-91074 Herzogenaurach, Germany
CEO: Jochen Zeitz, Chmn. & CEO
Bus: *Mfr. athletic apparel and sports shoes.*

Tel: 49-9132-810
Fax: 49-9132-8122-46
www.puma.com

Rev: $2,087
Emp: 3,910

NAICS: 315222, 315223, 315224, 315228, 315232, 315234, 315239, 315299, 315991, 315992, 315999, 316211

> **PUMA NORTH AMERICA, INC.**
> 5 Lyberty Way, Westford, Massachusetts 01886
> CEO: Jay Piccola, Pres.
> Bus: *Mfr./sales athletic apparel and sports
> shoes.*
>
> Tel: (978) 698-1000
> Fax: (978) 698-1174
>
> %FO: 100
> Emp: 500

● **RACO ELEKTRO MASCHINEN GMBH**
Jesinghauserstr. 56-64, D-58332 Schwelm, Germany
CEO: Reinhard Wilke, Pres.
Bus: *Mfr. electric actuators and cylinders.*

Tel: 49-23-3640-090
Fax: 49-23-3640-0910
www.raco.de

NAICS: 333995

> **RACO INTERNATIONAL INC.**
> 3350 Industrial Blvd., PO Box 151, Bethel Park, Pennsylvania 15102
> CEO: Michael Bock
> Bus: *Mfr. environmentally safe, clean electric
> linear actuators and cylinders.*
>
> Tel: (412) 835-5744
> Fax: (412) 835-0338
>
> %FO: 100

● **RADEBERGER GRUPPE AG**
Darmstadter Landstr. 185, D-60589 Frankfurt, Germany
CEO: Ulrich Kallmeyer, Chmn.
Bus: *Brewery.*

Tel: 49-69-606-50
Fax: 49-69-606-5209
www.radeberger-gruppe.de

Rev: $905
Emp: 2,593

NAICS: 312111, 312112, 312120, 333294, 424810

BINDING BRAUEREI USA INC.
194 Main St., Norwalk, Connecticut 06851
CEO: Hans Schliebs, CEO
Bus: *Liquor and beer manufacturer.*

Tel: (203) 229-0111
Fax: (203) 229-0105

%FO: 100
Emp: 20

• **RAG AKTIENGESELLSCHAFT**
Rellinghauser Str. 3, D-45128 Essen, Germany
CEO: Werner Muller, Chmn.
Bus: *Engaged in mining, energy and technology.*

Tel: 49-201-177-02
Fax: 49-201-177-2050
www.rag.de

Rev: $16,147
Emp: 77,680

NAICS: 212111, 212112, 212113, 213113, 221111, 221112, 221113, 221119, 221121, 237990, 324199, 325199, 326199

CYRO INDUSTRIES
Rockaway 80 Corporate Center, 100 Enterprise Dr., Rockaway, New Jersey 07866
CEO: Robert Wurst, CFO
Bus: *Mfr. of plastic & fiber*

Tel: (973) 442-6000
Fax: (973) 442-6117

DEGUSSA BUILDING SYSTEMS
889 Valley Park Dr., Shakopee, Minnesota 55379
CEO: Mike Galasso, Pres. & CEO
Bus: *Mfr. of specialty chemical*

Tel: (952) 496-6000
Fax: (952) 496-6062

DEGUSSA CORP.
379 Interpace Pkwy., Parsippany, New Jersey 07054
CEO: John Salvatore, Pres. & CEO
Bus: *Mfr. of specialty chemicals*

Tel: (973) 541-8000
Fax: (973) 541-8013

Emp: 5,794

STOCKHAUSEN, INC.
2401 Doyle St., Greensboro, North Carolina 27406
CEO: Peter Gursky, VP Operations
Bus: *Mfr. of specialty chemicals*

Tel: (336) 333-3500
Fax: (336) 333-3545

• **REEMTSMA CIGARETTENFABRIKEN GMBH**
Max-Born-Str. 4, D-22761 Hamburg, Germany
CEO: Richard Gretler, Chmn.
Bus: *Mfr. cigarettes and fine tobacco products.*

Tel: 49-40-8220-0
Fax: 49-40-8220-1645
www.reemtsma.de

Rev: $2,080
Emp: 10,175

NAICS: 312221

WEST PARK TOBACCO USA, INC.
13293 Rivers Bend Blvd., Chester, Virginia 23836
CEO: Cheryl Ligon, Treasurer
Bus: *Mfr./distributor cigarettes and fine tobacco products.*

Tel: (804) 530-0031
Fax: (804) 530-9921

%FO: 100
Emp: 4

• **REIFENHAUSER GMBH & CO.**
Spicher Str. 46-48, D-53839 Troisdorf, Germany
CEO: Ulrich & Klaus Reifenhauser, Mng. Dir.
Bus: *Mfr. plastic extrusion equipment.*

Tel: 49-2241-481-0
Fax: 49-2241-408-778
www.reifenhauser.com

Rev: $214
Emp: 757

NAICS: 333220

REIFENHAUSER, INC.
2 Washington St., Ipswich, Massachusetts 01938
CEO: Richard Dexter II, Mgr.
Bus: *Sale/service & spare parts distribution plastic extrusion equipment.*

Tel: (978) 412-9700
Fax: (978) 412-9715

%FO: 100
Emp: 7

● **RENFERT GMBH & CO**
Untere Giewiesen 2, D-78247 Hilzingen, Germany
CEO: Klaus-Ulfert Rieger, Mng. Dir.
Bus: *Dental laboratory equipment manufacture.*

Tel: 49-7731-82080
Fax: 49-7731-820870
www.renfert.com

Emp: 140

NAICS: 339114

RENFERT USA INC.
3718 Illinois Ave., St. Charles, Illinois 60174
CEO: Richard Jakus, VP
Bus: *Distribution/service dental laboratory equipment.*

Tel: (630) 762-1803
Fax: (630) 762-9787

%FO: 100
Emp: 2

● **RENK AG**
Gogginger Str. 73, D-86159 Augsburg, Germany
CEO: Manfred Hirt, CEO
Bus: *Mfr./distributes industrial gears and vehicle transmissions.*

Tel: 49-821-5700-0
Fax: 49-821-5700-460
www.renk.de

Rev: $354
Emp: 1,514

NAICS: 333613, 334515, 336212, 336350

RENK CORPORATION
304 Tucapau Rd., Duncan, South Carolina 29344
CEO: Klaus Bock, VP
Bus: *Mfr./distributes industrial gears and vehicle transmissions.*

Tel: (864) 433-0069
Fax: (864) 433-0636

%FO: 100
Emp: 20

RENK LABECO CORPORATION
156 East Harrison St., Mooresville, Indiana 46158
CEO: Hans-Guenter Wagner, Dir.
Bus: *Turnkey test systems manufacture.*

Tel: (317) 831-2990
Fax: (317) 831-2990

%FO: 100
Emp: 8

● **RHEIN CHEMIE RHEINAU GMBH**
Duesseldorfer Strasse 23-27, D-68219 Mannheim, Germany
CEO: Anno Borkowsky, CEO
Bus: *Mfr. additives for rubber, lubricants, plastics, and polyurethane.*

Tel: 49-621-8907-0
Fax: 49-621-8907-675
www.rheinchemie.com

Rev: $349
Emp: 1,100

NAICS: 325211, 325212

RHEIN CHEMIE USA INC.
1014 Whitehead Rd., Trenton, New Jersey 08638
CEO: Bruce Ernst
Bus: *Polyurethanes and plastics manufacture.*

Tel: (609) 771-9100
Fax: (609) 771-0409

%FO: 100

RHEIN CHEMIE USA INC.
20482 Lake Rd., Cleveland, Ohio 44116
CEO: Anthony Cristiano
Bus: *Lubricant oil manufacture.*

Tel: (440) 333-7707
Fax: (440) 333-8353

%FO: 100

- **RITTALGMBH & CO. KG**
Auf dem Stutzelberg, D-35745 Herborn, Germany
CEO: Norbert Muller, CEO
Bus: *Mfr. electric/electronic enclosures.*

Tel: 49-2772-505-0
Fax: 49-2772-505-2319
www.rittal.com

Emp: 3,500

NAICS: 335999

  RITTAL CORPORATION
  One Rittal Place, Springfield, Ohio 45504
  CEO: Carie Ray, Pres.
  Bus: *Mfr. electric/electronic enclosures.*

  Tel: (937) 399-0500
  Fax: (937) 390-5599

  %FO: 100
  Emp: 700

- **ROHDE & SCHWARZ GMBH & CO.**
Muhldorfstr. 15, D-81671 Munich, Germany
CEO: Friedrich Schwarz, Pres. & CEO
Bus: *Mfr. test and measurement equipment.*

Tel: 49-89-41-290
Fax: 49-89-41-2912-164
www.rohde-schwarz.com

Rev: $1,000
Emp: 5,600

NAICS: 334210, 334220, 334290, 334515

  ROHDE & SCHWARZ
  8080 Tristar Dr., Ste. 120, Irving, Texas 75063
  CEO: Hans Guenter Titze, Mgr.
  Bus: *Mfr. test and measurement equipment.*

  Tel: (469) 713-5300
  Fax: (469) 713-5301

  %FO: 100
  Emp: 20

  ROHDE & SCHWARZ
  8661A Robert Fulton Dr., Columbia, Maryland 21046
  CEO: John Pannucci, Pres.
  Bus: *Sale of test measuring & communications electronic equipment.*

  Tel: (410) 910-7800
  Fax: (410) 910-7801

  %FO: 100
  Emp: 152

  ROHDE & SCHWARZ
  770 Irvine Center Dr., Ste. 100, Irvine, California 92618
  CEO: Friedrich Schawarz, CEO
  Bus: *Communication services.*

  Tel: (949) 885-7000
  Fax: (949) 885-7001

  %FO: 100

  ROHDE & SCHWARZ
  8905 SW Nimbus Ave., Ste. 240, Beaverton, Oregon 97008
  CEO: Friedrich Schawarz, Pres.
  Bus: *Communication services.*

  Tel: (503) 403-4700
  Fax: (503) 403-4701

  %FO: 100

- **ROHM GMBH & CO. KG, SUB. DEGUSSA**
Kirschenallee, D-64293 Darmstadt, Germany
CEO: Hans-Peter Schaufler, CEO
Bus: *Plastic polymers manufacture.*

Tel: 49-6151-1801
Fax: 49-6151-1802
www.roehm.de

NAICS: 325211

  CYRO INDUSTRIES, INC.
  100 Enterprise Dr., Rockaway, New Jersey 07866
  CEO: Robert Wurst
  Bus: *Acrylic plastic polymer and sheets manufacture.*

  Tel: (973) 442-6000
  Fax: (973) 442-6117

  %FO: 100

CYRO INDUSTRIES, INC.
25 Executive Blvd., Orange, Connecticut 06477
CEO: Alan Hollowchuck
Bus: *Acrylic plastic polymer and sheets manufacture.*

Tel: (203) 795-6081
Fax: (203) 795-5800

%FO: 100

CYRO INDUSTRIES, INC.
PO Box 591, Sanford, Maine 04073
CEO: Richard Healy
Bus: *Acrylic plastic polymer and sheets manufacture.*

Tel: (207) 324-6000
Fax: (207) 324-6000

%FO: 100

ROHM AMERICA INC.
2 Turner Pl., Piscataway, New Jersey 08854
CEO: Roger Cram
Bus: *Acrylic plastic polymer and sheets manufacture.*

Tel: (732) 981-5000
Fax: (732) 981-5275

%FO: 100

● **ROLAND BERGER STRATEGY CONSULTANTS GMBH**
Arabellastr. 33, D-81925 Munich, Germany
CEO: Burkhard Schwenker, CEO
Bus: *Management and strategy consulting services.*

Tel: 49-89-9230-0
Fax: 49-89-9230-8202
www.rolandberger.com

Rev: $723
Emp: 1,630

NAICS: 541611, 541618, 561499

ROLAND BERGER STRATEGY CONSULTANTS LLC
2401 w. Big Beaver Rd., Ste. 500, Troy, Michigan 48084
CEO: Wim Van Acker, Mng. Prtn.
Bus: *Management and strategy consulting services.*

Tel: (248) 729-5000
Fax: (248) 649-1794

%FO: 100

● **ROSENTHAL AG**
Philip-Rosenthal-Platz 1, D-95100 Selb, Germany
CEO: Ottmar C. Kusel, Chmn. & CEO
Bus: *Mfr. of china, crystal and flatware.*

Tel: 49-92-87-72-0
Fax: 49-92-87-72-225
www.int.rosenthal.de

Rev: $239
Emp: 2,100

NAICS: 327112, 327213, 332211, 423940

ROSENTHAL USA LTD.
355 Michele Place, Carlstadt, New Jersey 07072
CEO: George Simon, Pres.
Bus: *Wholesale distributor of imported china, crystal and flatware.*

Tel: (201) 804-8000
Fax: (201) 804-9300

%FO: 100
Emp: 35

● **ROVEMA VERPACKUNGSMASCHINEN GMBH**
Industriestr. 1, Hessen, D-35463 Fernwald, Germany
CEO: Walter Baur, Chmn. & Pres.
Bus: *Mfr. packaging machinery.*

Tel: 49-641-4090
Fax: 49-641-409-212
www.rovema.de

Rev: $106
Emp: 500

NAICS: 333993, 423830

ROVEMA PACKAGING MACHINES, INC.
650 Hurricane Shoals Rd. NW, Lawrenceville, Georgia 30045
CEO: Klaus Kraemer, Pres.
Bus: *Sale/service packaging machinery.*

Tel: (770) 513-9604
Fax: (770) 513-0814

%FO: 100

- **RUTGERS CHEMICALS AG**
  Heideacker 3, D-63457 Hanau, Germany
  CEO: Heribert Protzek, Chmn.   Tel: 49-6181-3990-0   Rev: $2,465
  Bus: *Specialty chemicals, coal tar-based intermediates*   Fax: 49-6181-3990-45   Emp: 12,750
       and plastics manufacture for road construction.   www.ruetgers-chemicals.de
  NAICS: 325110, 325188, 325192, 325199, 326199

  RUTGERS ORGANICS CORP.
  30 Old Augusta Rd., Piedmont, South Carolina 29673
  CEO: David Iden, Pres.   Tel: (864) 277-7000
  Bus: *Mfr. industrial organic chemicals.*   Fax: (864) 277-7807

  RUTGERS ORGANICS CORP.
  10740 Paddys Run Rd., Harrison, Ohio 45030
  CEO: Frank Caneta, Mgr.   Tel: (513) 738-1255
  Bus: *Mfr. industrial organic chemicals.*   Fax:

  RUTGERS ORGANICS CORPORATION
  201 Struble Rd., State College, Pennsylvania 16801
  CEO: David S. Johnson, Pres.   Tel: (814) 231-9270
  Bus: *Mfr. Industrial organic chemicals.*   Fax: Emp: 160

- **RUTGERS ORGANICS GMBH**
  Oppauerstr. 43, D-68305 Mannheim, Germany
  CEO: Eberhardt von Persall, Pres.   Tel: 49-621-7654-332
  Bus: *Mfr. fine chemicals and organic intermediates,*   Fax: 49-621-7654-454   Emp: 15,000
       including pyroplast fire protection systems.   www.ruetgers-organics.de
  NAICS: 424690

  RUETGERS ORGANICS CORPORATION
  201 Struble Rd., State College, Pennsylvania 16801
  CEO: David S. Johnson   Tel: (814) 238-2424   %FO: 100
  Bus: *Mfr. detergent intermediates, custom*   Fax: (814) 238-1567   Emp: 200
       organic synthesis

  RUETGERS ORGANICS CORPORATION
  4480 Lake Forest Dr., Cincinnati, Ohio 05242
  CEO: Frank Caneba   Tel: (513) 587-2800   %FO: 100
  Bus: *Mfr. detergent intermediates, custom*   Fax: (513) 587-2800
       organic synthesis

- **RWE AKTIENGESELLSCHAFT**
  Opernplatz 1, D-45128 Essen, Germany
  CEO: Harry J. M. Roels, Pres. & CEO   Tel: 49-201-1200   Rev: $55,918
  Bus: *Holding company: production/distribution of*   Fax: 49-201-12-15199   Emp: 97,777
       power, petroleum, mining, water, waste   www.rwe.com
       management, engineering and construction
  NAICS: 211111, 212111, 212112, 212210, 213113, 221121, 221122, 221210, 221310, 221320, 237990, 324199,
  423930, 424720, 486210, 523130, 523140,
           551112, 562111, 562119, 562212, 562213
  AMERICAN WATER WORKS COMPANY, INC.
  1025 Laurel Oak Rd., Voorhees, New Jersey 08043
  CEO: Jeremy Pelczer, Pres. & CEO   Tel: (856) 346-8200   %FO: 100
  Bus: *Provides water services.*   Fax: (856) 346-8360   Emp: 8,000

PENNSYLVANIA-AMERICAN WATER COMPANY
800 Hershey Park Dr., Hershey, Pennsylvania 17033
CEO: Daniel Warnock, Pres. Tel: (717) 533-5000
Bus: *Water supply & irrigation systems* Fax: (717) 531-3251

● **SAINT-GOBAIN DIAMANTWERKZEUGE GMBH & CO. KG**
Schutzenwall 13-17, D-22844 Nordestedt, Germany
CEO: Hans Robert Meyer, CEO Tel: 49-40-5258-0 Rev: $57
Bus: *Diamond hollow drills and small diamond tools and* Fax: 49-40-5258-215 Emp: 500
saw blades manufacture. www.winter-dtcbn.de
NAICS: 333131, 333514, 423840

SAINT-GOBAIN WINTER INC.
100 Wilhelm Winter St., PO Box 1006, Travelers Rest, South Carolina 29690
CEO: Pascal Riviere, Mgr. Tel: (864) 834-4145 %FO: 100
Bus: *Mfr./sale diamond cutting tools.* Fax: (864) 834-3730 Emp: 75

● **SAP AG**
Neurottstr. 16, D-69190 Walldorf, Germany
CEO: Henning Kagermann, Chmn. & CEO Tel: 49-6227-74-7474 Rev: $10,179
Bus: *Develop, manufacture, sales and service of* Fax: 49-6227-75-7575 Emp: 32,802
applications software. www.sap.com
NAICS: 511210

LIGHTHAMMER SOFTWARE DEVELOPMENT CORP.
350 Eagleview Blvd., Ste. 110, Exton, Pennsylvania 19341
CEO: Russell Fadel, CEO Tel: (610) 903-8000 %FO: 100
Bus: *Mfr. of Industrial software.* Fax: (610) 903-8006

SAP AMERICA INC.
3999 West Chester Pike, Newtown Square, Pennsylvania 19073
CEO: William R. McDermott, Pres. & CEO Tel: (610) 661-1000 %FO: 100
Bus: *Developer/mfr./distributor/service* Fax: (610) 355-3106
applications software.

TOMORROWNOW, INC.
1716 Briarcrest, Ste. 600, Bryan, Texas 77802
CEO: Andrew Nelson, Pres. & CEO Tel: (979) 595-1300 %FO: 100
Bus: *Support services for businesses.* Fax: (979) 595-1301 Emp: 70

● **SAP SYSTEMS INTEGRATION AG**
St. Petersburger Str. 9, D-01069 Dresden, Germany
CEO: Bernd-Michael Rumpf, CEO Tel: 49-351-4811-0 Rev: $414
Bus: *IT services; consulting, systems integration,* Fax: 49-351-4811-603 Emp: 1,800
application development and outsourcing. www.sap-si.com
NAICS: 541511, 541512

SAP SYSTEMS INTEGRATION AMERICA LLC
980 Hammond Dr., Ste. 1250, Atlanta, Georgia 30328
CEO: Mike Clurman, VP Tel: (770) 350-1860 %FO: 100
Bus: *IT services.* Fax: (770) 350-1864

• CARL SCHENCK AG, DIV. DURR AG

Landwehrstr. 55, D-64293 Darmstadt, Germany
CEO: Ralf Dieter, Chmn. Tel: 49-6151-320
Bus: *Engineering/mfr./instruments for weighing* Fax: 49-6151-32-1100
  balancing machines and testing systems. www.csd.de
NAICS: 333993

SCHENCK ACCURATE
746 E. Milwaukee St., Whitewater, Wisconsin 53190
CEO: Gregory Fream, Pres. Tel: (262) 473-2441 %FO: 100
Bus: *Mfr. metering and weighing devices.* Fax: (262) 473-2489 Emp: 125

SCHENCK MINING
80 Leetsdale Industrial Dr., Ste. 103, Leetsdale, Pennsylvania 15056
CEO: Scott Snyder, Mgr. Tel: (724) 266-2667 %FO: 100
Bus: *Mfr. of process control instruments.* Fax: (724) 266-2627 Emp: 10

SCHENCK ROTEC CORPORATION
100 Kay Industrial Dr., Orion, Michigan 48059
CEO: Mark Hass, Pres. Tel: (248) 377-2100 %FO: 100
Bus: *Mfr. materials testing, dynamometer system.* Fax: (248) 377-2102

SCHENCK TREBEL
535 Acorn St., Deer Park, New York 11729
CEO: Bertram Dittmar, Pres. Tel: (631) 242-4010 %FO: 100
Bus: *Mfr. industry balancing machine and related* Fax: (631) 242-5077 Emp: 70
  equipment.

SCHENCK WEIGHING SYSTEMS
81 Two Bridges Rd., Bldg. 2, Fairfield, New Jersey 07004
CEO: Ed Labarre, Mgr. Tel: (973) 882-4650 %FO: 100
Bus: *Mfr. weighing components.* Fax: (973) 882-3796

• SCHENKER AG

Alfredstr. 81, D-45130 Essen, Germany
CEO: Dr. Thomas Held, CEO Tel: 49-201-8781-0 Rev: $10,912
Bus: *Provides logistics solutions; land transport, sea* Fax: 49-201-8781-8495 Emp: 39,000
  and air. www.schenker.com
NAICS: 488510, 493110

SCHENKER USA INC.
150 Albany Ave., Freeport, New York 11520
CEO: Heiner Murmann, Pres. & CEO Tel: (516) 377-3000 %FO: 100
Bus: *Provides customs brokerage and logistics* Fax: (516) 377-3133
  solutions.

• SCHERING AG

Mullerstr. 178, D-13353 Berlin, Germany
CEO: Hubertus Erlen, Chmn. Tel: 49-30-468-1111 Rev: $6,647
Bus: *Mfr. pharmaceuticals.* Fax: 49-30-468-15305 Emp: 25,593
  www.schering.de/eng
NAICS: 325411, 325412

BERLEX BIOSCIENCES
2600 Hilltop Dr., PO Box 4099, Richmond, California 94804
CEO: Dale Stringfellow, Pres.
Bus: *Mfr. of pharmaceutical preparations.*
Tel: (510) 262-5000
Fax: (510) 262-7095

BERLEX LABORATORIES
21511 23rd. Dr. S.E., Bothell, Washington 98021
CEO: Reinhart Franzen
Bus: *Mfr. of pharmaceutical preparations.*
Tel: (425) 908-3300
Fax: (425) 908-3300

BERLEX LABORATORIES
1191 Second Ave., Ste. 1200, Seattle, Washington 98101
CEO: Reinhart Franzen
Bus: *Pharmaceutical preparations.*
Tel: (206) 254-7700
Fax: (206) 343-6379

BERLEX LABORATORIES, INC.
340 Changebridge Rd., Montville, New Jersey 07045-1000
CEO: Reinhart Franzen, Pres. & CEO
Bus: *U.S. holding company: ethical pharmaceuticals, agrochemicals.*
Tel: (973) 487-2000
Fax: (973) 487-2003
%FO: 100
Emp: 2,400

BERLEX LABORATORIES, INC.
6 Westbelt Rd., Wayne, New Jersey 07470-6808
CEO: Pat Johnson, Mgr.
Bus: *Sales/distribution of pharmaceuticals.*
Tel: (973) 694-4100
Fax: (973) 305-5490
%FO: 100

● **SCHLEICHER & SCHUELL MICROSCIENCE GMBH**
Hahnestr. 3, D-37586 Dassel, Germany
CEO: Dr. Werner Specht, Pres.
Bus: *Engaged in life sciences and manufacture of paper products.*
Tel: 49-5564-7910
Fax: 49-5564-72743
www.schleicher-schuell.com
Rev: $35
Emp: 200

NAICS: 322121, 541710

S&S BIOPATH INC.
2611 Mercer Ave., West Palm Beach, Florida 33401
CEO: Efrem Pesyna
Bus: *Engaged in life sciences.*
Tel: (561) 655-2302
Fax: (561) 655-2302
%FO: 100

SCHLEICHER & SCHUELL INC.
10 Optical Ave., Keene, New Hampshire 03431
CEO: Gary Henricksen
Bus: *Mfr. filtration, paper products.*
Tel: (603) 352-3810
Fax: (603) 352-3627
%FO: 100
Emp: 150

● **ADOLF SCHNORR GMBH & CO KG**
Stuttgarter Str. 37, D-71069 Sindelfingen, Germany
CEO: Andy Haunholter, Mng. Dir.
Bus: *Mfr. disc springs & safety washers.*
Tel: 49-7031-302-0
Fax: 49-7031-382-600
www.schnorr.de

NAICS: 332611

SCHNORR CORPORATION
4355 Varsity Dr., Ste. A, Ann Arbor, Michigan 48108
CEO: Axel Schremmer, Pres.
Bus: *Sales/distribution disc springs & safety washers.*

Tel: (734) 677-2683
Fax: (734) 975-0408

%FO: 100
Emp: 10

● **SCHOKINAG-SCHOKOLADE, DIV. HERRMANN GMBH**
Neckarvorlandstr. 21-25, D-68159 Mannheim, Germany
CEO: Hans-Joachim Herrmann, Gen. Mgr.
Bus: *Chocolate, cocoa and specialty chocolate products manufacture.*
NAICS: 311320

Tel: 49-621-107-82-0
Fax: 49-621-107-82-149
www.schokinag.de

Rev: $227
Emp: 190

SCHOKINAG CHOCOLATE NORTH AMERICA, INC.
5301 Office Park Dr., Ste. 200, Bakersfield, California 93309
CEO: Brian Workington, Pres.
Bus: *Chocolate, cocoa and specialty chocolate products manufacture.*

Tel: (800) 807-2465
Fax: (661) 322-1156

%FO: 100
Emp: 6

● **SCHOTT GLAS**
Hattenbergstr. 10, D-55122 Mainz, Germany
CEO: Udo Ungeheuer, Chmn.
Bus: *Mfr. specialty glass and fiber optic lighting components.*
NAICS: 327112, 327211, 332211, 332214, 334290, 334413, 334418, 334419, 335129, 335921, 339115, 339115, 339912, 339999, 423460

Tel: 49-6131-66-0
Fax: 49-6131-66-2000
www.schott.de

Rev: $2,494
Emp: 18,616

GEMTRON CORPORATION
615 Highway 68, Sweetwater, Tennessee 37874
CEO: Doug Roberts, Pres.
Bus: *Mfr. specialty glass for technical applications.*

Tel: (423) 337-3522
Fax: (423) 337-7979

%FO: 100

RWE SCHOTT SOLAR
4051 Alvis Ct., Rocklin, California 95677
CEO: Marc Roper
Bus: *Component manufacturer.*

Tel: (916) 625-9033
Fax: (916) 625-9032

%FO: 100

SCHOTT GLASS TECHNOLOGIES INC.
400 York Ave., Duryea, Pennsylvania 18642
CEO: Bruce Jennings, Pres.
Bus: *Mfr. optics for devices.*

Tel: (570) 457-7485
Fax: (570) 457-6960

%FO: 100

SCHOTT LITHOTEC USA CORP.
2323 S. Rd., Poughkeepsie, New York 12601
CEO: Dr. Martin Heming
Bus: *Micolithography.*

Tel: (845) 463-5300
Fax: (845) 463-5303

%FO: 100

SCHOTT NORTH AMERICA INC.
203 North Gables Blvd., Wheaton, Illinois 60187
CEO: Doug Roberts
Bus: *Mfr. electronics.*

Tel: (630) 344-0280
Fax: (630) 344-0282

%FO: 100

SCHOTT NORTH AMERICA INC.
555 Taxter Rd., Elmsford, New York 10523
CEO: Brian Lynch
Bus: *Mfr. and supplies standard and custom fiber optic lighting components for the lighting market.*
Tel: (914) 831-2200
Fax: (914) 831-2201
%FO: 100

SCHOTT NORTH AMERICA INC.
150 Calle Iglesia, San Clemente, California 92672
CEO: Tom Starrs
Bus: *Mfr. gas burner systems.*
Tel: (949) 492-0580
Fax: (949) 492-0506
%FO: 100

SCHOTT NORTH AMERICA INC.
122 Charleston St., Southbridge, Massachusetts 01550
CEO: Donald Miller, Pres.
Bus: *Electronic packaging.*
Tel: (508) 765-9744
Fax: (508) 764-6273
%FO: 100

SCHOTT NORTH AMERICA INC.
30 Lebanon Valley Pkwy., Lebanon, Pennsylvania 17042
CEO: Doug Roberts, Pres.
Bus: *Pharmaceutical packaging.*
Tel: (717) 228-4200
Fax: (717) 273-4730
%FO: 100

SCHOTT NORTH AMERICA INC.
62 Columbus St., Auburn, New York 13021
CEO: Doug Roberts, Pres.
Bus: *Mfr. fiber optics.*
Tel: (315) 255-2791
Fax: (315) 255-2695
%FO: 100

SCHOTT NORTH AMERICA INC.
1401 Tunnel Hill Varnell Rd., Dalton, Georgia 30720
CEO: Juergen Ausborn, Pres.
Bus: *Develops wet seal application and adhesive assembly process technology.*
Tel: (706) 694-2950
Fax: (706) 694-2951
%FO: 100

SCHOTT NORTH AMERICA INC.
5530 Shepherdsville Rd., Louisville, Kentucky 40228
CEO: Doug Roberts
Bus: *Develops wet seal application and adhesive assembly process technology.*
Tel: (502) 966-5126
Fax: (502) 966-4976
%FO: 100

● **SCHUMAG AG**
Nerscheider Weg 170, D-52076 Aachen, Germany
CEO: Dr. Joachim Graefe, Chmn.
Bus: *Mfr. of cold drawing, grinding, bar turning, bar straightening, progressive cold forming machines and precision parts.*
Tel: 49-2408-120
Fax: 49-2408-12256
www.schumag.de
Rev: $147
Emp: 1,000
NAICS: 333999

SCHUMAG-KIESERLING MACHINERY, INC.
155 Hudson Ave., Norwood, New Jersey 07648-0419
CEO: Harald Breme, Pres.
Bus: *Sales/service of cold drawing, grinding, bar turning, bar straightening machines and manufacturer of spare parts.*
Tel: (201) 767-6850
Fax: (201) 767-3341
%FO: 100
Emp: 16

- **SCHUNK GROUP GMBH**
  Parkstr. 1, D-06502 Thale, Germany
  CEO: Dagobert Kotzur, Mng. Dir.
  Bus: *Holding company: carbon and sintered metal technology; engineering ceramics, bearing and seal technology.*
  NAICS: 333513, 333612, 551112

  Tel: 49-3947-7200-0
  Fax: 49-3947-22-79
  www.schunk-group.com

  Emp: 7,120

  SCHUNK GRAPHITE TECHNOLOGY, INC.
  West 146 N9300 Held Dr., Menomonee Falls, Wisconsin 53051
  CEO: Heinz Volk, Pres.
  Bus: *Mfr. carbon/graphite products for purification and coating.*

  Tel: (262) 253-8720
  Fax: (262) 255-1391

  %FO: 100
  Emp: 175

  SCHUNK INEX CORP.
  9229 Olean Rd., Holland, New York 14080
  CEO: Michael Kasprzyk, Pres.
  Bus: *Mfr. of ceramic high temperature radiant tubes.*

  Tel: (716) 537-2270
  Fax: (716) 537-3218

  Emp: 16

  SCHUNK OF NORTH AMERICA
  W146 N9300 Held Dr., Menomonee Falls, Wisconsin 53051
  CEO: Heinz Volk, Pres.
  Bus: *Mfr. of mechanical graphite specialties & quartz crystal.*

  Tel: (262) 253-8720
  Fax: (262) 250-4856

  Emp: 300

  SCHUNK QUARTZ
  101 Inner Loop Rd., Georgetown, Texas 78626
  CEO: Wim Van Velzen, Pres.
  Bus: *Mfr. of quartz.*

  Tel: (512) 863-0033
  Fax: (512) 863-7376

  STAPLA ULTRASONICS CORP.
  375 Ballardvale St., Wilmington, Massachusetts 01887
  CEO: Saeed Mogadam, Pres.
  Bus: *Mfr. of electrical equipment, supplies mfr. Welding apparatus.*

  Tel: (978) 658-9400
  Fax: (978) 658-6550

  Emp: 28

  WEISS ENVIRONMENTAL TECHNOLOGY INC.
  W146 N9300 Held Dr., Menomonee Falls, Wisconsin 53051
  CEO: Heinz Volk, Pres.
  Bus: *Sale of environmental equipment.*

  Tel: (262) 253-8730
  Fax: (262) 255-1391

  XYCARB CERAMICS, INC.
  101 Inner Loop Rd., Georgetown, Texas 78626
  CEO: Wim Van Velzen, Pres.
  Bus: *Mfr. of electronic components, & semiconductors & related devices.*

  Tel: (512) 863-0033
  Fax: (512) 863-7376

  %FO: 100
  Emp: 50

- **SCHWARZ PHARMA AG**
  Alfred Nobelstrasse 10, D-40789 Monheim, Germany
  CEO: Patrick Schwarz-Schutte, Chmn.
  Bus: *Mfr./distribution ethical pharmaceutical products.*

  Tel: 49-2173-480
  Fax: 49-2173-481608
  www.schwarzpharma.com

  Rev: $1,291
  Emp: 3,813

  NAICS: 325411

SCHWARZ PHARMA INC.
6140 West Executive Dr., Mequon, Wisconsin 53092
CEO: Klaus Veitinger   Tel: (262) 238-9994   %FO: 100
Bus: *Gastrointestinal, cardiovascular and*   Fax: (262) 242-1641
pharmaceutical products.

SCHWARZ PHARMA INC.
103 Foulk Rd., Ste. 202, Wilmington, Delaware 19803
CEO: Detlef Thielgen, Pres.   Tel: (302) 656-1950   %FO: 100
Bus: *Gastrointestinal, cardiovascular and*   Fax: (302) 656-1950   Emp: 160
pharmaceutical products.

SCHWARZ PHARMA INC.
1101 C Ave., West Seymour, Indiana 47274
CEO: Klaus Veitinger, Mgr.   Tel: (812) 523-5468   %FO: 100
Bus: *Gastrointestinal, cardiovascular and*   Fax: (812) 523-1887
pharmaceutical products.

● **SEMIKRON INTL GMBH & CO**
Sigmundstrasse 200, D-90431 Nuremberg, Germany
CEO: Dirk Heidenreich, CEO   Tel: 49-911-6559-0
Bus: *Mfr. power semiconductors.*   Fax: 49-911-6559-262   Emp: 2,500
www.semikron.com
NAICS: 334413

SEMIKRON INTL INC.
3016 Fairhaven Ridge, Kennesaw, Georgia 30144
CEO: Gary Genet, Mgr.   Tel: (404) 713-0364   %FO: 100
Bus: *Mfr. power semiconductors.*   Fax: (678) 797-9514

SEMIKRON INTL INC.
4685 Pebble Dr., Elkhorn, Wisconsin 53121
CEO: David Ahler, Mgr.   Tel: (262) 743-1367   %FO: 100
Bus: *Mfr. power semiconductors.*   Fax: (262) 743-1368

SEMIKRON INTL INC.
23001 Stoneridge Mission, Viejo, California 92692
CEO: Dennis Isaac, Mgr.   Tel: (949) 586-9522   %FO: 100
Bus: *Mfr. power semiconductors.*   Fax: (949) 586-9822

SEMIKRON INTL INC.
11 Executive Dr., PO Box 66, Hudson, New Hampshire 03051
CEO: Thomas O'Reilley, Pres.   Tel: (603) 883-8102   %FO: 100
Bus: *Mfr. power semiconductors.*   Fax: (603) 883-8021   Emp: 55

SEMIKRON INTL INC.
561 Yarmouth Rd., Elk Grove Village, Illinois 60007
CEO: Don Vogt, Mgr.   Tel: (847) 437-8886   %FO: 100
Bus: *Mfr. power semiconductors.*   Fax: (847) 437-9899

SEMIKRON INTL INC.
17385 Parkside Dr., North Royalton, Ohio 44133
CEO: Andy Camardo, Mgr.   Tel: (440) 237-7095   %FO: 100
Bus: *Mfr. power semiconductors.*   Fax: (440) 237-1557

- **SENNHEISER ELECTRONIC GMBH & CO.**
  Am Labor 1, D-30900 Wedemark, Germany
  CEO: Volker Bartels, CEO
  Bus: *Consumer and professional audio equipment*
      manufacture.
  NAICS: 423620

  Tel: 49-5130-600-0
  Fax: 49-5130-600-300
  www.sennheiser.com

  SENNHEISER ELECTRONIC CORPORATION
  One Enterprise Dr., Old Lyme, Connecticut 06371
  CEO: John Falcone, Pres.
  Bus: *Consumer and professional audio equipment*
      manufacture.

  Tel: (860) 434-9190
  Fax: (860) 434-1759

  %FO: 100

- **SER SOLUTIONS GMBH**
  Innovationspark Rahms, D-53577 Neustadt/Wied, Germany
  CEO: Kurt-Werner Sikora, Mng. Dir.
  Bus: *Mfr. software.*

  NAICS: 511210

  Tel: 49-2683-984-0
  Fax: 49-2683-984-222
  www.ser.com

  Rev: $132
  Emp: 965

  SER SOLUTIONS, INC.
  Loudon Tech Center, 21680 Ridgetop Cir., Dulles, Virginia 20166
  CEO: Carl E. Mergele, Pres. & COO
  Bus: *Mfr. of content & document management*
      software.

  Tel: (703) 948-5500
  Fax: (703) 430-7738

  %FO: 100
  Emp: 360

- **SGL CARBON AG**
  Rheingaustr. 182, D-65203 Wiesbaden, Germany
  CEO: Robert J. Koehler, Chmn. & CEO
  Bus: *Mfr. graphite and carbon products.*

  NAICS: 331111, 335991

  Tel: 49-611-6029-100
  Fax: 49-611-6029-101
  www.sglcarbon.com

  Rev: $1,255
  Emp: 6,627

  CMS GRAPHITE
  342 Industrial Ave., Cheshire, Connecticut 06410
  CEO: Peter Hoffman, Pres.
  Bus: *Industrial applications.*

  Tel: (203) 272-1999
  Fax: (203) 272-1318

  %FO: 100

  HITCO CARBON COMPOSITES, INC.
  1600 West 135th St., Gardena, California 90249
  CEO: B.J. Schramm, CEO
  Bus: *Metal fabrication.*

  Tel: (310) 527-0700
  Fax: (310) 516-5714

  %FO: 100
  Emp: 240

  MGP LLC
  796 Fritztown Rd., Sinking Spring, Pennsylvania 19608
  CEO: Peter Hoffman, Pres.
  Bus: *Industrial applications.*

  Tel: (888) 745-6290
  Fax: (610) 670-4044

  %FO: 100

  SGL CARBON
  2607 Providence Hills Dr., Matthews, North Carolina 28105
  CEO: Peter Hoffman, Pres.
  Bus: *Automotive & mechanical applications.*

  Tel: (704) 814-7996
  Fax:

  %FO: 100

SGL CARBON CORPORATION
900 Theresa St., St. Marys, Pennsylvania 15857
CEO: Scott Edwards, member   Tel: (814) 781-2611   %FO: 100
Bus: *Mfr. graphite and carbon products.*   Fax: (814) 781-2697   Emp: 245

SGL CARBON CORPORATION
8600 William Ficklen Dr., Charlotte, North Carolina 28269
CEO: Peter Hoffman, Pres.   Tel: (704) 593-5100   %FO: 100
Bus: *U.S. headquarters location; mfr. graphite*   Fax: (704) 593-5117
and carbon products.

SGL TECHNIC INC.
28176 No. Ave. Stanford, Valencia, California 91355
CEO: B.J. Schramm, Pres.   Tel: (661) 257-0500   %FO: 100
Bus: *Expanded graphite.*   Fax: (661) 257-7742   Emp: 250

SGL TECHNIC INC.
21945 Drake Rd., Strongsville, Ohio 44149
CEO: Peter Hoffman, Pres.   Tel: (440) 572-3600   %FO: 100
Bus: *Mfr. graphite and carbon products.*   Fax: (440) 572-9570

SGL TECHNIC LTD.
1600 W. 135th St., Gardena, California 90249
CEO: Dan Layden   Tel: (310) 970-5806   %FO: 100
Bus: *Sale of plastic for automotive industry.*   Fax: (310) 516-5776   Emp: 250

● **SICK AG**
Sebastian-Kneipp-Str. 1, D-79183 Waldkirch, Germany
CEO: Anne-Kathrin Keutrich, CEO   Tel: 49-7681-202-0   Rev: $734
Bus: *Mfr. color sensors, contrast and luminescence*   Fax: 49-7681-202-3863   Emp: 3,953
scanners and encoders.   www.sick.com
NAICS: 334119, 334419, 334513, 335313, 335314, 335931, 339999

SICK INC.
800 Technology Center Dr., Ste. 6, Stoughton, Massachusetts 01072
CEO: Alberto Bertomeu   Tel: (781) 302-2500   %FO: 100
Bus: *Mfr. color sensors, contrast and*   Fax: (781) 828-3150
luminescence scanners and encoders.

SICK INC.
6900 W. 100th St., Minneapolis, Minnesota 55438
CEO: Alberto Bertomeu, Pres.   Tel: (952) 941-6780   %FO: 100
Bus: *Mfr. color sensors, contrast and*   Fax: (952) 941-9287
luminescence scanners and encoders.

SICK MAIHAK INC.
6300 Old Shakopee Rd., Ste. 124, Minneapolis, Minnesota 55438
CEO: Mark Penning, Pres.   Tel: (763) 201-9200   %FO: 100
Bus: *Mfr. color sensors, contrast and*   Fax: (763) 201-9210
luminescence scanners and encoders.

SICK STEGMANN INC.
7496 Webster St., Dayton, Ohio 75414
CEO: Gunther Stegmann, Pres.   Tel: (937) 454-1956   %FO: 100
Bus: *Mfr. color sensors, contrast and*   Fax: (937) 454-1955
luminescence scanners and encoders.

● **SIEGLING GMBH, DIV. FORBO GROUP**
Lilienthalstr.6-8, Niedersachsen, D-30179 Hannover, Germany
CEO:　Dr. Jan Lipton, Gen. Mgr.　　　　　　Tel:　49-511-6704-0　　　Rev: $70
Bus:　*Conveyor and processing belts manufacture.*　Fax:　49-511-6704-305　　Emp: 55
www.siegling.com

　NAICS:　326220, 333922, 423840

　　SIEGLING AMERICA, INC.
　　12201 Vanstory Rd., Huntersville, North Carolina　28078
　　CEO:　Wayne Hoffman, Pres.　　　　Tel:　(704) 948-0800
　　Bus:　*Conveyor belt manufacture and sales.*　Fax:　(704) 948-0995　　Emp: 240

● **SIEMENS AG**
Wittelsbacherplatz 2, D-80333 Munich, Germany
CEO:　Heinz-Joachim Neuburger, CEO　　Tel:　49-89-636-00　　　Rev: $93,455
Bus:　*Design/development/mfr. electrical and electronic*　Fax:　49-89-636-52000　　Emp: 430,000
　　system for industry.　　　　　　　www.siemens.com
　NAICS:　221330, 238210, 238220, 334111, 334210, 334220, 334290, 334310, 334413, 334513, 335129, 335311,
336399, 482111, 482112, 485112

　　ACUSON CORP.
　　1230 Shorebird Way, Mountain View, California　94043
　　CEO:　Erich R. Reinhardt, Pres. & CEO　Tel:　(650) 969-9112
　　Bus:　*Medical supplies & equipment*　　Fax:　(650) 943-7006

　　BSH HOME APPLIANCES CORP.
　　5551 McFadden Ave., Huntington Beach, California　92649
　　CEO:　Franz Bosshard, Pres. & CEO　　Tel:　(714) 901-6600
　　Bus:　*Mfr. of consumer appliances*　　Fax:　(714) 901-5980

　　CHANTRY NETWORKS INC.
　　200 West St., Ste. 401, Waltham, Massachusetts　02451
　　CEO:　Patrick Apfel, Pres. & CEO　　Tel:　(781) 547-0060
　　Bus:　*Wireless networking equipment.*　Fax:　(781) 547-0059

　　CTI MOLECULAR IMAGING INC.
　　810 Innovation Dr., Knoxville, Tennessee　37932
　　CEO:　Ronald Nutt, Pres. & CEO　　Tel:　(865) 218-2000
　　Bus:　*Medical supplies & equipment*　　Fax:　(865) 218-3000　　Emp: 963

　　FRAMATOME
　　3315 Old Forest Rd., Lynchburg, Virginia　24501
　　CEO:　Thomas Christopher, CEO　　Tel:　(434) 832-3000
　　Bus:　*fuel & engineering for the nuclear power*　Fax:　(434) 832-2997　　Emp: 3,400
　　　　industry

　　FUJITSU SIEMENS COMPUTERS
　　598 Gibraltar Dr., Milpitas, California　95035
　　CEO:　Guenter Frommel　　　　　Tel:　(408) 571-6000
　　Bus:　*Computer programming.*　　Fax:　(408) 571-6196

MYRIO CORP.
19015 N. Creek Pkwy., Ste. 105, Bothell, Washington 98011
CEO: Christopher B. Coles, Pres. & CEO   Tel: (425) 368-4400
Bus: *Messaging, conferencing & communications*   Fax: (425) 368-4500   Emp: 45
     software

NEW ENERGY ASSOCIATES, LLC
400 Interstate N. Pkwy., Ste. 1400, Atlanta, Georgia 30339
CEO: Ralph L. Genesi, CEO   Tel: (770) 779-2800
Bus: *Computer services*   Fax: (770) 779-1025   Emp: 125

OSRAM SYLVANIA
100 Endicott St., Danvers, Massachusetts 01923
CEO: Charles F. Jerabek, Pres.   Tel: (978) 777-1900
Bus: *Mfr. of lighting & other fixtures*   Fax: (978) 750-2152   Emp: 11,200

SIEMENS AIRFIELD SOLUTIONS, INC.
977 Gahanna Pkwy., Columbus, Ohio 43230-6610
CEO: Steve Rauch, Pres. & CEO   Tel: (614) 861-1304   %FO: 100
Bus: *Airport lighting products for runways, and*   Fax: (614) 864-2069
     taxiways.

SIEMENS AUTOMOTIVE CORPORATION
2400 Executive Hills Blvd., Auburn Hills, Michigan 48326-2980
CEO: John G. Sanderson, Pres.   Tel: (248) 209-4000
Bus: *Design/mfr. electronic components and*   Fax: (248) 209-4040   Emp: 6,425
     system or automotive industry.

SIEMENS BUILDING TECHNOLOGY
1000 Deerfield Pkwy., Buffalo Grove, Illinois 60089
CEO: Daryl Dulaney, Pres. & CEO   Tel: (847) 215-1000   %FO: 100
Bus: *Utility services.*   Fax: (847) 215-1093   Emp: 8,635

SIEMENS BUSINESS SERVICES, INC.
101 Merritt 7, Norwalk, Connecticut 06851
CEO: John A. McKenna Jr., CEO   Tel: (203) 642-2300   %FO: 100
Bus: *Information technology services.*   Fax: (203) 642-2399

SIEMENS COMMUNICATIOINS GROUP
900 Broken Sound Pkwy., Boca Raton, Florida 33487
CEO: George Nolen, Pres.   Tel: (561) 923-5000
Bus: *Developer & manufacturer of*   Fax: Emp: 105
     telecommunication systems

SIEMENS COMMUNICATIONS CPE
4849 Alpha Rd., Dallas, Texas 75244-4608
CEO: Paul Reitmeier, Pres.   Tel: (972) 852-1000
Bus: *Mfr. digital subscriber line (DSL) customer*   Fax: (972) 852-1001
     premises equipment (CPE).

SIEMENS CORPORATION
153 East 53rd St., New York, New York 10022
CEO: George C. Nolen, Pres. & CEO   Tel: (212) 258-4000   %FO: 100
Bus: *Holding company: electrical and electronic*   Fax: (212) 767-0580   Emp: 65,000
     systems.

SIEMENS ENERGY & AUTOMATION INC.
333 Old Milton Pkwy., Alpharetta, Georgia 30005
CEO: Aubert Martin, Pres. & CEO
Tel: (770) 751-2000 %FO: 100
Bus: *Mfr./markets a wide variety of electrical &* Fax: (770) 751-4333 Emp: 12,000
electronic equipment and systems in the
industrial & construction market segments.

SIEMENS LOGISTICS & ASSAMBLY SYSTEMS
507 Plymouth Ave., NE, Grand Rapids, Michigan 49505
CEO: Prashant Ranade, Pres.
Tel: (616) 913-6200
Bus: *Industrial manufacturing.* Fax: (616) 913-7701 Emp: 2,145

SIEMENS LOGISTICS & ASSAMBLY SYSTEMS
4400 Alafaya Trail, Orlando, Florida 32826
CEO: Randy Zwirn, Pres.
Tel: (407) 736-2000
Bus: *Supplies power generation equipment,* Fax: (407) 736-5008 Emp: 6,000
plants and services.

SIEMENS MEDICAL SOLUTIONS
51 Valley Stream Pkwy., Malvern, Pennsylvania 19355
CEO: Thomas N McCausland, Pres.
Tel: (888) 826-9702
Bus: *Medical, electro medical & speech &* Fax: Emp: 4,563
hearing equipment

SIEMENS TRANSPORTATION SYSTEMS
7464 French Rd., Sacramento, California 95828
CEO: Oliver O Hauck, Pres.
Tel: (916) 681-3000 %FO: 100
Bus: *Engaged in transportation.* Fax: (916) 681-3006 Emp: 1,000

SUPPLYON
7 W. Square Lake Rd., Bloomfield, Michigan 48302
CEO: John Kay, Pres.
Tel: (248) 758-2300
Bus: *Computer & software* Fax: (248) 758-2301

S-Y SYSTEMS TECHNOLOGIES AMERICA LLC
17000 Executive Plaza Dr., Dearborn, Michigan 48126
CEO: Robert Crumley, Pres.
Tel: (313) 768-3099
Bus: *Auto parts manufacturer* Fax: (313) 768-3232

SYMBIAN
390 Bridge Pkwy., Ste. 201, Redwood Shores, California 94065
CEO: Cindy Perez
Tel: (650) 551-0240
Bus: *Wireless communications.* Fax: (650) 551-0241

US FILTER
181 Thorn Hill Rd., Warrendale, Pennsylvania 15086
CEO: Andrew D. Seidel, Pres. & CEO
Tel: (724) 772-0044
Bus: *Environmental equipment & services* Fax: (724) 772-1360 Emp: 6,000

● **SINGULUS TECHNOLOGIES AG**
Hanauer Landstr. 103, D-63796 Kahl, Germany
CEO: Roland Lacher, CEO
Tel: 49-6188-440-0 Rev: $438
Bus: *CD and DVD replication machine manufacture.* Fax: 49-6188-440-110 Emp: 599
www.singulus.de

NAICS: 334112

SINGULUS TECHNOLOGIES
2815 Townsgate Rd., Ste. 115, Westlake Village, California 91361
CEO: Rick Nuffer   Tel: (805) 373-6216   %FO: 100
Bus: *CD and DVD replication machine*   Fax: (805) 371-7433
    manufacture.

SINGULUS TECHNOLOGIES
429D Hayden Station Rd., Windsor, Connecticut 06095
CEO: Dale Butrymowicz, VP   Tel: (860) 683-8000   %FO: 100
Bus: *CD and DVD replication machine*   Fax: (860) 683-8010
    manufacture.

● **SMITHS DETECTION**
Im Herzen 4, D-65205 Wiesbaden, Germany
CEO: Stephen Phipson, Mng. Dir.   Tel: 49-611-9412-0   Rev: $194
Bus: *Mfr. trace detection equipment, including x-ray*   Fax: 49-611-9412-229   Emp: 70
    inspection units for scanning mail and freight.   www.smithsdetection.com
NAICS: 334513, 334516

SMITHS DETECTION NORTH AMERICA INC.
30 Hook Mountain Rd., Pine Brook, New Jersey 07058
CEO: Bill Mawer   Tel: (973) 830-2100   %FO: 100
Bus: *Mfr. trace detection equipment.*   Fax: (973) 830-2200

SMITHS DETECTION NORTH AMERICA INC.
73 N. Vinedo Ave., Pasadena, California 91107
CEO: Steven Sunshine   Tel: (626) 744-1700   %FO: 100
Bus: *Mfr. electronic noses that use chemical*   Fax: (626) 744-1777
    sensors to sniff out explosives

● **SMS PLASTICS TECHNOLOGY**
Scherl 10, D-58540 Meinerzhagen, Germany
CEO: Dr. Heinrich Weiss, Chmn.   Tel: 49-2354-720   Rev: $446
Bus: *Plastic processing machinery manufacture.*   Fax: 49-2354-72575   Emp: 2,300
    www.sms-ag.de
NAICS: 326121, 331421, 333516, 423830, 541330

AMERICAN MAPLAN CORPORATION
823 South Bypass, PO Box 832, McPherson, Kansas 67460
CEO: Kurt Waldenhauer, Pres.   Tel: (620) 241-6843   %FO: 100
Bus: *Plastic processing machinery manufacture.*   Fax: (620) 241-0207   Emp: 65

BATTENFELD GLOUCESTER ENGINEERING CO. INC.
Blackburn Industrial Park, PO Box 900, Gloucester, Massachusetts 01931
CEO: Brian Marvelley, Pres.   Tel: (978) 281-1800
Bus: *Mfr. plastics working machinery*   Fax: (978) 282-9111   Emp: 410

BATTENFELD OF AMERICA
1620 Shanahan Dr., South Elgin, Illinois 60177
CEO: Ron Ricapito, VP   Tel: (847) 531-0015
Bus: *Industrial machinery & equipment*   Fax: (847) 531-0029

SOLVAY ENGINEERED POLYMERS
1200 Harmon Rd., Auburn Hills, Michigan 48326
CEO: Fredrick Young, Pres.
Bus: *Custom compound purchased resins*

Tel: (248) 391-9574
Fax: (248) 391-5887

Emp: 348

● SOFTWARE AG
Uhlandstr. 12, D-64297 Darmstadt, Germany
CEO: Karl-Heinz Streibich, CEO
Bus: *Mfr. software.*

Tel: 49-6151-92-0
Fax: 49-6151-92-1191
www.softwareag.com

Rev: $561
Emp: 2,505

NAICS: 511210

SOFTWARE AG INC.
11190 Sunrise Dr., Reston, Virginia 20191
CEO: Haskell Mayo, Pres.
Bus: *Sales/distribution of software.*

Tel: (703) 860-5050
Fax: (703) 391-6975

%FO: 100

● SOLO KLEINMOTOREN GMBH
Stuttgarter Str. 41, PO Box 60 01 52, D-71050 Sindelfingen, Germany
CEO: Andreas Emmerich, Mng. Dir.
Bus: *Mfr. chain saws, water pumps, lawnmowers, sprayers and trimmers.*

Tel: 49-7031-301-0
Fax: 49-7031-301-149
www.solo-germany.com

Rev: $53
Emp: 180

NAICS: 333111, 333112, 333611, 333991, 336991

SOLO, INC.
5100 Chestnut Ave., Newport News, Virginia 23605
CEO: Hans Emmerich, Chmn.
Bus: *Mfr. chain saws, sprayers & trimmers.*

Tel: (757) 245-4228
Fax: (757) 245-0800

%FO: 100
Emp: 100

● SPHERETEX GMBH
Eller Str. 101, D-40721 Hilden, Germany
CEO: Klaus Kolzer, Pres.
Bus: *High-tech core materials for fiberglass sandwich laminates.*

Tel: 49-2103-58993
Fax: 49-2103-589958
www.spheretex.com

Emp: 20

NAICS: 325221

SPHERETEX AMERICA INC.
PO Box 1936, Ponte Vedra Beach, Florida 32004
CEO: Juergen Boettcher, Pres.
Bus: *Sale/service high-tech core materials.*

Tel: (904) 273-0708
Fax: (904) 273-0709

%FO: 100

● STADA ARZNEIMITTEL AG
Stadastr. 2-18, D-61118 Bad Vilbel, Germany
CEO: Hartmut Retzlaff, CEO
Bus: *Pharmaceutical manufacture.*

Tel: 49-6101-603-0
Fax: 49-6101-603-259
www.stada.de

Rev: $1,110
Emp: 2,586

NAICS: 424210

STADA PHARMACEUTICALS INC.
5 Cedar Brook Dr., Cranbury, New Jersey 08512
CEO: Paul Evans
Bus: *Pharmaceutical manufacture.*

Tel: (609) 409-5555
Fax: (609) 977-3807

%FO: 100

• R. STAHL GMBH

Am Bahnhof 30, D-74638 Waldenburg, Germany
CEO: Martin Schomaker, CEO
Bus: *Mfr. electronic switchgear, intrinsic safety
    interface systems.*
NAICS: 335313

Tel: 49-7940-1280
Fax: 49-7940-17333
www.stahl.de

Rev: $100
Emp: 642

R. STAHL INC.
6420 Dorchester Rd., Charleston, South Carolina 29418
CEO: Scott Vogel
Bus: *Material handling products.*

Tel: (843) 767-1951
Fax: (843) 767-4366

R. STAHL INC.
45 Northwestern Dr., Salem, New Hampshire 03079
CEO: Bob Spang
Bus: *Suppliers of apparatus and systems for
    instrumentation, energy distribution and
    lighting in hazardous areas.*

Tel: (603) 870-9500
Fax: (603) 870-9290

%FO: 100
Emp: 25

• STAPLA ULTRASCHALL-TECHNIK GMBH

Am Sudpark 7c, PO Box 1527, D-65444 Kelsterbach, Frankfurt, Germany
CEO: Lother Nuss, Dir.
Bus: *Mfr. of ultrasonic metal welding products .*

Tel: 49-6107-71080
Fax: 49-6107-71085
www.staplaultrasonics.com

NAICS: 332313

STAPLA ULTRASONICS CORPORATION
375 Ballardvale St., Wilmington, Massachusetts 01887
CEO: Saeed Mogadam, Pres.
Bus: *Ultrasonic welding equipment manufacture.*

Tel: (978) 658-9400
Fax: (978) 658-6550

%FO: 100
Emp: 28

STAPLA ULTRASONICS CORPORATION
6008 Rinconcito Way, El Paso, Texas 79912
CEO: Saeed Mogadam
Bus: *Ultrasonic welding equipment manufacture.*

Tel: (915) 833-9913
Fax: (915) 833-9925

%FO: 100

• STEAG HAMA TECH AG

Ferdinand-von-Steinbeis-Ring 10, D75447 Sternenfels/Wurttemberg, Germany
CEO: Stefan Reineck, Pres. & CEO
Bus: *Optical disk machinery and equipment*

Tel: 49-7045-41-0
Fax: 49-7045-41-101
www.steag-hamatech.com

Rev: $170
Emp: 391

NAICS: 334310, 334519

STEAG HAMA TECH USA, INC.
2328 Walsh Ave., Santa Clara, California 95051
CEO: Uwe Dietze, Mgr.
Bus: *Optical disk machinery and equipment
    manufacture and sales.*

Tel: (408) 988-5211
Fax: (408) 988-5212

%FO: 100

STEAG HAMA TECH USA, INC.
2621 Ridgepoint Dr., Ste. 100, Austin, Texas 78754
CEO: Uwe Dietze, Pres.
Bus: *Optical disk machinery and equipment
    manufacture and sales.*

Tel: (512) 929-1880
Fax: (512) 929-1886

%FO: 100
Emp: 27

Germany

- **STIHL INTERNATIONAL GMBH**
Badstr.115, Baden-Wuerttemberg, D-71336 Waiblingen, Germany
CEO: Hans Peter Stihl, Chmn.   Tel: 49-7151-261-222   Rev: $1,426
Bus: *Mfr. outdoor power equipment.*   Fax: Emp: 1,574
www.stihl.com
NAICS: 333112, 333991, 423810, 551112

  STIHL INC.
  536 Viking Dr., Virginia Beach, Virginia 23450
  CEO: Fred J. Whyte, Pres.   Tel: (757) 486-9100   %FO: 100
  Bus: *Sales/distribution of outdoor power   Fax: (757) 486-9125
  equipment.*

- **STINNES AG**
Leipziger Platz 9, D-10117 Berlin, Germany
CEO: Hartmut Mehdorn, Chmn.   Tel: 49-30-297-54855   Rev: $16,914
Bus: *Transportation and logistics.*   Fax: 49-30-297-54029   Emp: 65,000
www.stinnes.de
NAICS: 212325, 325199, 332999, 482111, 488510, 493110, 541614

  SCHENKER INC.
  150 Albany Ave., Freeport, New York 11520
  CEO: Heiner Murmann, Pres. & CEO   Tel: (516) 377-3000
  Bus: *Transportation services*   Fax: (516) 377-3133

  STINNES CORPORATION
  120 White Plains Rd., Tarrytown, New York 10591
  CEO: Hans-Henni Maier, Pres.   Tel: (914) 366-7200   %FO: 100
  Bus: *Transportation and logistics.*   Fax: (914) 366-8226   Emp: 1,500

- **SUD-CHEMIE AG**
Lenbachplatz 6, D-80333 Munich, Germany
CEO: Hans Jurgen Wernicke, COO   Tel: 49-89-5110-0   Rev: $1,176
Bus: *Mfr. chemicals, bleaching products and   Fax: 49-89-5110-375   Emp: 51,080
thickening agents.*   www.sud-chemie.com
NAICS: 325110, 325188, 325192, 325199, 325211, 325510, 325612, 325613, 325910

  HYRADIX INC.
  175 West Oakton St., Des Plaines, Illinois 60018
  CEO: Robert L. Gray Jr., Pres.   Tel: (847) 391-1200   %FO: 100
  Bus: *Gas producers generators & other gas   Fax: Emp: 30
  related equipment.*

  SCIENTIFIC DESIGN COMPANY, INC.
  49 Industrial Dr., Little Ferry, New Jersey 07643
  CEO: Craig McLaughlin, Pres.   Tel: (201) 641-0500   %FO: 100
  Bus: *Mfr. of chemical catalysts & chemical   Fax: Emp: 76
  engineering services.*

  SUD-CHEMIE AIR PURIFICATION
  32 Fremont St., Needham, Massachusetts 02494
  CEO: Amiram Bar Ilan, Pres.   Tel: (781) 444-5188   %FO: 100
  Bus: *Mfr. of environmental controls, industrial   Fax: (781) 444-0130   Emp: 30
  inorganic chemicals.*

SUD-CHEMIE INC.
PO Box 32370, Louisville, Kentucky 40210
CEO: Thomas A. Marx, Pres. & CEO
Bus: *Mfr. of ammonia, fertilizers, & methanol.*
Tel: (502) 634-7200
Fax: (502) 634-7739
%FO: 100
Emp: 800

SUD-CHEMIE PERFORMANCE PACKAGING, INC.
926 South 8th St., PO Box 610, Colton, California 92324
CEO: Michelle Martin, Mgr.
Bus: *Mfr. of coated, laminated paper & nondurable goods.*
Tel: (909) 825-1793
Fax: (909) 825-6271
%FO: 100
Emp: 32

SUD-CHEMIE PERFORMANCE PACKAGING, INC.
Rio Grande Industrial Park, 101 Christine Dr., Belen, New Mexico 87002
CEO: Klause Linger, VP
Bus: *Mfr. of industrial inorganic chemicals, polish & sanitation goods.*
Tel: (505) 864-6691
Fax: (505) 864-9296
%FO: 100
Emp: 200

● **SUPFINA GRIESHABER GMBH & CO.**
Schmelzegrun 7, Wolfach, D-77709 Baden-Wuerttemberg, Germany
CEO: Karl-Heinz Koch, CEO
Bus: *Mfr. super finishing machines and attachments for polishing.*
NAICS: 333999
Tel: 49-7834-8660
Fax: 49-7834-866-111
www.supfina.com
Rev: $20
Emp: 200

SUPFINA MACHINE COMPANY
181 Circuit Dr., North Kingstown, Rhode Island 01852
CEO: Norbert Klotz, Pres.
Bus: *Mfr. super finishing machines & attachments.*
Tel: (401) 294-6600
Fax: (401) 294-6262
%FO: 100
Emp: 35

● **SUSS MICROTEC AG**
Schleissheimer Str. 90, D-85748 Garching, Germany
CEO: Franz Richter, CEO
Bus: *Development and manufacture of micro-optics equipment.*
NAICS: 333295
Tel: 49-89-320-070
Fax: 49-89-320-07450
www.suss.de
Rev: $139
Emp: 880

SUSS MICROTEC INC.
2065 Martin Ave., Ste.104, Santa Clara, California 95050
CEO: Joe Brown
Bus: *Development, manufacture and sales of micro-optics equipment.*
Tel: (408) 855-1055
Fax: (408) 844-9958
%FO: 100

SUSS MICROTEC INC.
228 Suss Dr., Waterbury Center, Vermont 05677
CEO: Jeff Dumas
Bus: *Development, manufacture and sales of micro-optics equipment.*
Tel: (802) 244-5181
Fax: (802) 244-5103
%FO: 100

SUSS MICROTEC INC.
8240 S. Kyrene Rd., Ste. 101, Tempe, Arizona 85284
CEO: Klaus Ruhmer
Bus: *Sales and service center for micro-optics equipment.*
Tel: (480) 557-9370
Fax: (480) 557-9371
%FO: 100

● **SYMRISE GMBH & CO. KG**
Muhlenfeldstr. 1, D-37603 Holzminden, Germany
CEO: Dr. Gerold Linzbach, CEO
Bus: *Flavors and fragrances.*

NAICS: 311942, 325188

Tel: 49-5531-900
Fax: 49-5531-90-1649
www.symrise.de

Rev: $1,425
Emp: 6,150

    SYMRISE INC.
    300 North St., Teterboro, New Jersey 07608
    CEO: Kara Rhodes
    Bus: *Flavors and fragrances.*

    Tel: (201) 288-3200
    Fax: (201) 462-2200

    %FO: 100

    SYMRISE INC.
    172 Industrial Pkwy., Branchburg, New Jersey 08876
    CEO: Emmanuel Laroche
    Bus: *Engineering, purchasing and product production.*

    Tel: (201) 288-3200
    Fax: (201) 462-2200

    %FO: 100

● **TAKKT AG**
Pressel Str. 12, D-70191 Stuttgart, Germany
CEO: Georg Gayer, Chmn. & CEO
Bus: *Mail order company for office, business and warehouse equipment.*
NAICS: 454113

Tel: 49-711-34658-0
Fax: 49-711-34658-100
www.takkt.de

Rev: $823
Emp: 1,860

    C&H DISTRIBUTORS, INC.
    770 South 70th St., PO Box 14770, Milwaukee, Wisconsin 53214
    CEO: Phillip J. Areddia, Pres. & CEO
    Bus: *Industrial machinery & equipment distribution*

    Tel: (414) 443-1700
    Fax: (800) 336-1331

    %FO: 100

    CONNEY SAFETY PRODUCTS
    3202 Latham Dr., PO Box 44190, Madison, Wisconsin 53744-4190
    CEO: Michael A. Stamn, Pres.
    Bus: *Clothing safety equipment & first aid kits & medical supplies*

    Tel: (888) 356-9100
    Fax: (800) 845-9095

    Emp: 175

● **TARKETT AKTIENGESELLSCHAFT**
Nachtweideweg 1-7, D-67227 Frankenthal, Germany
CEO: Marc Assa, Chmn. & CEO
Bus: *Mfr. hardwood flooring.*

NAICS: 326192, 327122, 339999

Tel: 49-623-3810
Fax: 49-623-3811-648
www.tarkett.com

Rev: $1,889
Emp: 6,883

    TARKETT NORTH AMERICA
    1139 Lehigh Ave., Whitehall, Pennsylvania 18052
    CEO: Robert W. Van Buren, Pres.
    Bus: *Mfr./sales hardwood flooring.*

    Tel: (610) 266-5500
    Fax:

    %FO: 100
    Emp: 1,460

- **TENGELMANN WARENHANDELSGESELLSCHAFT KG**
Wissollstr. 5-43, D-45478 Mulheim an der Ruhr, Germany
CEO: Erivan Haub, Chmn.   Tel: 49-208-5806-7601   Rev: $32,104
Bus: *Retail food chain.*   Fax: 49-208-5806-7605   Emp: 184,046
                                            www.tengelmann.de
NAICS: 311320, 311330, 311340, 424450, 444110, 444120, 444130, 445110, 446110

  ### FARMER JACK SUPERMARKETS
  18718 Borman Ave., Detroit, Michigan 48228
  CEO: Michael Cater, Pres.   Tel: (313) 270-1000
  Bus: *Retail food chain*   Fax: (313) 270-1333

  ### GREAT ATLANTIC & PACIFIC TEA COMPANY INC. (A&P)
  2 Paragon Dr., Montvale, New Jersey 07645
  CEO: Christian W. E. Haub, Chmn. & CEO   Tel: (201) 573-9700   %FO: 100
  Bus: *Retail food chain.*   Fax: (201) 571-8719   Emp: 73,000

  ### SUPER FRESH FOOD MARKETS
  1506 Woodlawn Dr., Gwynn Oak, Maryland 21207
  CEO: Harry Austin, VP Operations   Tel: (410) 594-7500
  Bus: *Retail food chain*   Fax: (410) 594-7619

  ### THE FOOD EMPORIUM, INC.
  20 Livingstone Ave., Dobbs Ferry, New York 10522
  CEO: Cheryl Palmer, Pres.   Tel: (914) 826-2300
  Bus: *Retail food chain*   Fax: (914) 826-2378   Emp: 6,500

  ### WALDBAUM, INC.
  133-11 20th Ave., College Point, New York 11356
  CEO: Robert Panasuk, Pres.   Tel: (718) 559-0903
  Bus: *Retail food chain.*   Fax: (718) 559-0901

- **TERROT STRICKMASCHINEN GMBH**
Durrheimer Str. 12, D-70372 Stuttgart, Germany
CEO: Thomas Archner, CEO   Tel: 49-711-5531-0
Bus: *Mfr. large diameter circular knitting machines.*   Fax: 49-711-5531-111   Emp: 700
                                            www.terrot.de
NAICS: 333292

  ### SEGGERT INTERNATIONAL, INC.
  777 Atwater Rd., Lake Oswego, Oregon 97034
  CEO: Silvia Papke, HR   Tel: (503) 635-7700   %FO: 100
  Bus: *Sale/service large diameter knitting*   Fax: (503) 636-8550
       machines.

  ### SEGGERT INTERNATIONAL, INC.
  9315 Lincoln Blvd., Ste. 2206, Los Angeles, California 90045
  CEO: Silvia Papke, HR   Tel: (310) 649-5681   %FO: 100
  Bus: *Sale/service large diameter knitting*   Fax: (310) 649-5681
       machines.

  ### TERROT KNITTING MACHINES INC.
  4808 Persimmon Ct., Monroe, North Carolina 28110
  CEO: Werner Boehringer, Pres.   Tel: (704) 283-9434   %FO: 100
  Bus: *Sale/service large diameter knitting*   Fax: (704) 289-9812
       machines.

- **THIES GMBH & CO.**
  Borkener Str. 155, D-48653 Coesfeld, Germany
  CEO: Erich Thies, Pres.
  Bus: *Mfr. textile dyeing equipment.*

  Tel: 49-2541-733-0
  Fax: 49-2541-733-299
  www.thiestextilmaschinen.de

  Emp: 500

  NAICS: 333292

  ### THIES CORPORATION
  PO Box 36010, 485 Bryant Blvd., Rock Hill, South Carolina 29732-0500
  CEO: Ronald Schrell, Pres.
  Bus: *Sale/service textile dyeing equipment.*

  Tel: (803) 366-4174
  Fax: (803) 366-8103

  %FO: 100
  Emp: 10

- **THYSSEN KRUPP AG**
  August-Thyssen-Str. 1, D-40211 Dusseldorf, Germany
  CEO: Ekkehard D. Schulz, Chmn.
  Bus: *Mfr. industrial materials, systems and
  components, including production of steel and
  manufacture of elevators and escalators.*

  Tel: 49-211-824-0
  Fax: 49-211-824-36000
  www.thyssenkrupp.com

  Rev: $48,489
  Emp: 187,678

  NAICS: 331111, 331210, 331221, 331222, 332312

  ### COPPER AND BRASS SALES
  22355 W. 11 Mile Rd., Southfield, Michigan 48034
  CEO: William G. Sabol, Pres.
  Bus: *Metals distribution*

  Tel: (248) 233-5700
  Fax: (248) 233-5777

  ### GIDDINGS & LEWIS, INC.
  142 Doty St., Fond du Lac, Wisconsin 54936
  CEO: Stephen Peterson, Pres. & CEO
  Bus: *Industrial machinery & equipment
  manufacturing*

  Tel: (920) 921-9400
  Fax: (920) 906-2522

  ### KEN-MAC METALS, INC.
  17901 Englewood Dr., Cleveland, Ohio 44130
  CEO: Larry E. Parsons, Pres.
  Bus: *Metals distribution*

  Tel: (440) 234-7500
  Fax: (440) 234-4459

  Emp: 202

  ### POLYSIUS
  180 Interstate North Pkwy., Ste. 300, Atlanta, Georgia 30339
  CEO:
  Bus: *Industrial manufacturing.*

  Tel: (770) 955-3660
  Fax: (770) 955-8789

  ### SAFWAY SERVICES INC.
  N19 W24200 Riverwood Dr., Waukesha, Wisconsin 53188
  CEO: Marc J. Wilson, Pres. & CEO
  Bus: *Industrial manufacturing.*

  Tel: (262) 523-6500
  Fax: (262) 523-9808

  Emp: 3,000

  ### THYSSEN KRUPP ELEVATOR
  15141 East Whittier Blvd., Ste. 420, Whittier, California 90603
  CEO: John Brant, Pres. & CEO
  Bus: *Mfr./sales/service elevators.*

  Tel: (562) 693-9491
  Fax: (562) 693-0028

  %FO: 100

THYSSENKRUPP BUDD
3155 W. Big Beaver Rd., Troy, Michigan 48007-2601
CEO: Wolfram Moersdorf, Chmn. & Pres. &
Bus: Elevator manufacture and sales.
Tel: (248) 643-3500
Fax: (248) 643-3687
%FO: 100
Emp: 11,000

THYSSENKRUPP MATERIALS NA
22355 W. 11 Mile Rd., Southfield, Michigan 48034
CEO: Joachim Limberg, Chmn. & Pres. & CEO
Bus: Industrial manufacturing.
Tel: (248) 233-5600
Fax: (248) 233-5699
Emp: 1,900

THYSSENKRUPP USA, INC.
3155 W. Big Beaver Rd., Troy, Michigan 48007
CEO: Siegfried Buschmann
Bus: Industrial manufacturing.
Tel: (248) 643-3929
Fax: (248) 643-3518

● **TQ3 TRAVEL SOLUTIONS GMBH**
Gustav-Deetjen-Allee 2-6, D-28215 Bremen, Germany
CEO: Marc Hildebrand, Pres. & CEO
Bus: Provides travel management services.
Tel: 49-421-3500-0
Fax: 49-421-3500-288
www.tq3.com
Rev: $11,000
Emp: 12,500

NAICS: 561510, 561599

TQ3 TRAVEL SOLUTIONS INC.
84 Inverness Circle East, Englewood, Colorado 80112
CEO: Edward S. Adams, Mng. Dir.
Bus: Provides travel management services.
Tel: (303) 706-0800
Fax: (303) 706-0770
%FO: 100

● **ALFRED TRONSER GMBH**
PO Box 63, D-75329 Engelsbrand, Germany
CEO: Michael Tronser, Pres.
Bus: Mfr. air dielectric & sapphire dielectric variable
capacitors design, microwave tuning elements,
precision machined, milled and tuned parts.
Tel: 49-7082-798-0
Fax: 49-7082-798155
www.tronser.com
Emp: 110

NAICS: 334414

TRONSER, INC.
3066 John Trush Blvd., Cazenovia, New York 13035
CEO: Michael Tronser, Pres.
Bus: Mfr. capacitors, microwave tuning elements.
Tel: (315) 655-9528
Fax: (315) 655-2149
%FO: 100
Emp: 6

● **TRUMPF GMBH & CO**
Johann-Maus-Str. 2, D-71254 Ditzingen, Germany
CEO: Berthold Leibinger, Pres.
Bus: Mfr. sheet metal fabricating equipment, punch
presses, laser processing centers, portable
power tools.
Tel: 49-7156-303-0
Fax: 49-7156-303-309
www.trumpf.com
Rev: $1,469
Emp: 5,561

NAICS: 332322, 333298

HUETTINGER ELECTRONIC INC.
111 Hyde Rd., Farmington, Connecticut 06032
CEO: Juergen Mertens, Pres.
Bus: Lasers and machine tools manufacture and
sales.
Tel: (860) 677-7930
Fax: (860) 678-8345
%FO: 100
Emp: 9

TRUMPF AMERICA INC.
Farmington Industrial Park, 111Hyde Rd., Farmington, Connecticut 06032
CEO: Rolf Biekert, Pres. & CEO   Tel: (860) 255-6000   %FO: 100
Bus: *Lasers and machine tools manufacture and*   Fax: (860) 255-6680   Emp: 550
sales.

● **T-SYSTEMS INTERNATIONAL GMBH**
Hahnstrasse 43d, D-60528 Frankfurt, Germany
CEO: Lothar Pauly, CEO   Tel: 49-69-665-31-0   Rev: $14,372
Bus: *Information and communication technology.*   Fax: 49-69-665-31-499   Emp: 39,500
www.t-systems.de

NAICS: 541511, 541512

    T-SYSTEMS NORTH AMERICA INC.
    701 Warrenville Rd., Ste. 100, Lisle, Illinois 60532
    CEO: Sean Parkinson   Tel: (630) 493-6100   %FO: 100
    Bus: *Information and communication technology.* Fax: (630) 493-6111

● **TUI AG (FORMERLY PREUSSAG)**
Karl-Wiechert-Allee 4, D-30625 Hannover, Germany
CEO: Dr. Michael H. Frenzel, Chmn.   Tel: 49-511-566-00   Rev: $24,615
Bus: *Steel and nonferrous metals production, trading,* Fax: 49-511-566-1098   Emp: 57,716
transport, information technology, energy and   www.tui.com
commodities.
NAICS: 481111, 561410, 561439, 561510, 561520, 561599, 721110

    TUI AMERICA
    1145 Broadway, Ste. 100, Tacoma, Washington 98402
    CEO: Ballu Khan, Pres.   Tel: (253) 830-3030   %FO: 100
    Bus: *Prepackaged software*   Fax: Emp: 75

● **TUV RHEINLAND BERLIN-BRANDENBURG EV**
Am Grauen Stein, D-51105 Cologne, Germany
CEO: Bruno Otto Braun, Pres. & CEO   Tel: 49-221-8060   Rev: $700
Bus: *International product safety testing and*   Fax: 49-221-8061760   Emp: 8,200
certification services.   www.de.tuv.com
NAICS: 541330, 541990

    TUV RHEINLAND OF NORTH AMERICA, INC.
    1815 Aston Ave., Ste. 104, Carlsbad, California 92008
    CEO: Korina Ortiz, Mgr.   Tel: (760) 929-1780   %FO: 100
    Bus: *International product safety testing and*   Fax: (760) 929-1781
    certification services.

    TUV RHEINLAND OF NORTH AMERICA, INC.
    2324 Ridgepoint Dr., Ste. E, Austin, Texas 78754-5214
    CEO: Michael Fliciinski, Mgr.   Tel: (512) 927-0070   %FO: 100
    Bus: *International product safety testing and*   Fax: (512) 927-0080
    certification services.

    TUV RHEINLAND OF NORTH AMERICA, INC.
    1300 Mass Ave., Ste. 103, Boxborough, Massachusetts 01719
    CEO: Gregor Dzialas   Tel: (978) 266-9500   %FO: 100
    Bus: *International product safety testing and*   Fax: (978) 266-9992
    certification services.

TUV RHEINLAND OF NORTH AMERICA, INC.
1945 Techny Rd., Unit 4, Northbrook, Illinois 60062-5357
CEO: Richard Hoekstra
Bus: *International product safety testing and certification services.*

Tel: (847) 562-9888
Fax: (847) 562-0688

%FO: 100

TUV RHEINLAND OF NORTH AMERICA, INC.
46979 Five Mile Rd., Plymouth, Michigan 48170
CEO: G. Bock
Bus: *International product safety testing and certification services.*

Tel: (734) 207-9852
Fax: (734) 207-9877

%FO: 100

TUV RHEINLAND OF NORTH AMERICA, INC.
1279 Quarry Lane, Ste. A, Pleasanton, California 94566
CEO: Ralf Bienert, Mgr.
Bus: *International product safety testing and certification services.*

Tel: (925) 249-9123
Fax: (925) 249-9124

%FO: 100

TUV RHEINLAND OF NORTH AMERICA, INC.
12 Commerce Rd., Newtown, Connecticut 06470
CEO: Stephan Schmitt, Pres.
Bus: *International product safety testing and certification services.*

Tel: (203) 426-0888
Fax: (203) 270-8883

%FO: 100
Emp: 200

TUV RHEINLAND OF NORTH AMERICA, INC.
7853 SW Cirrus Dr., Beaverton, Oregon 97008
CEO: James Mohr, Mgr.
Bus: *International product safety testing and certification services.*

Tel: (503) 469-8880
Fax: (503) 469-8881

%FO: 100

TUV RHEINLAND OF NORTH AMERICA, INC.
762 Park Ave., Youngsville, North Carolina 27596-9470
CEO: Bill Ronzio
Bus: *International product safety testing and certification services.*

Tel: (919) 554-3668
Fax: (919) 554-3542

%FO: 100

• **UNITECH MASCHINEN GMBH**
Clemens-Winkler-Str. 6, D-09116 Chemnitz, Germany
CEO: August Herzog, Mng. Dir.
Bus: *Fixed center crossheads and color change systems for wire extrusion.*
NAICS: 331421

Tel: 49-371-400-290
Fax: 49-371-400-2929
www.unitech-maschinen.de

Emp: 35

UNITEK NORTH AMERICA, INC.
One Evergreen Ave., Hamden, Connecticut 06518
CEO: Thomas J. Siedlarz, Pres.
Bus: *Fixed center crossheads and color change systems for wire extrusion.*

Tel: (203) 230-5947
Fax: (203) 230-9864

%FO: 80
Emp: 5

• **UNIVERSAL STRICKSYSTEME VERTRIEBS GMBH**
Deutschordenstr. 38, D-73461 Westhausen, Germany
CEO: Richard Geitner, Pres.
Bus: *Innovative flat bed knitting machines and pattern design workstations manufacture.*
NAICS: 333292, 423830

Tel: 49-7363-880
Fax: 49-7363-88202
www.universal.de

Emp: 1,000

UNIVERSAL KNITTING MACHINES CORP. OF AMERICA
820 Grand Blvd., Deer Park, New York 11729
CEO: Alfred Stojda, Pres.
Bus: *Knitting machines sales and distribution.*

Tel: (631) 242-2323
Fax:

%FO: 84
Emp: 6

● **VAI FUCHS, DIV. VOEST-ALPINE**
Reithallenstr. 1, D-77731 Willstatt-Legelshurst, Germany
CEO: Gerhard Fuchs, Pres.
Bus: *Electric steel making equipment manufacturer.*

Tel: 49-785-24100
Fax: 49-785-241141
www.fuchs-co.de

NAICS: 333319

VAI POMINI INC.
501 Technology Dr., Southpointe Industrial Park, Canonsburg, Pennsylvania 15317
CEO: Roland Fabris
Bus: *Electric steel making equipment manufacturer.*

Tel: (724) 514-8282
Fax: (724) 514-8281

VOEST ALPINE INDUSTRIES, INC.
501 Technology Dr., Southpointe Industrial Park, Canonsburg, Pennsylvania 15317
CEO: Jeff Noel
Bus: *Electric steel making equipment manufacturer.*

Tel: (724) 514-8500
Fax: (724) 514-8510

VOEST ALPINE INDUSTRIES, INC.
4201 Pottsville Pike, Reading, Pennsylvania 19605
CEO: Curt Stoyer
Bus: *Electric steel making equipment manufacturer.*

Tel: (610) 921-9101
Fax: (610) 921-1480

● **VARTA AG**
Am Leineufer 51, D-30419 Hannover, Germany
CEO: Uwe F. H. Ganzer, CEO
Bus: *Mfr. of batteries and plastics.*

Tel: 49-511-79-03-679
Fax: 49-511-79-03-609
www.varta.com

Rev: $216
Emp: 1,443

NAICS: 335911, 335912

JOHNSON CONTROLS INC.
5757 North Green Bay Ave., PO Box 591, Milwaukee, Wisconsin 53201
CEO: John M. Barth, Chmn. & Pres. & CEO
Bus: *Sale of electrical equipment, auto parts & supplies.*

Tel: (414) 524-1200
Fax: (414) 524-2077

%FO: 100
Emp: 123,000

SPECTRUM BRANDS
6 Concourse Pkwy., Ste. 3300, Atlanta, Georgia 30328
CEO: David A. Jones, Chmn. & CEO
Bus: *Power generation & storage.*

Tel: (770) 829-6200
Fax:

%FO: 100
Emp: 6,500

VARTA MICRO BATTERIES
1311 Mamaroneck Ave., Ste. 120, White Plains, New York 10605
CEO: Markus Warlitz, Dir.
Bus: *Sale of electrical equipment, auto parts & supplies.*

Tel: (800) 468-2782
Fax: (914) 345-0488

%FO: 100
Emp: 52

- **VERLAGSGRUPPE GEORG VON HOLTZBRINCK GMBH**
  Gansheiderstr. 26, D-70184 Stuttgart, Germany
  CEO: Stefan von Holtzbrinck, Chmn.
  Bus: *Engaged in publishing.*

  Tel: 49-711-2150-0
  Fax: 49-711-2150-100
  www.holtzbrinck.com

  Rev: $2,365
  Emp: 12,600

  NAICS: 511110, 511130

  FARRAR, STRAUS AND GIROUX
  19 Union Sq. West, New York, New York 10003
  CEO: Jonathon Galassi, Pres.
  Bus: *Book publishing*

  Tel: (212) 741-6900
  Fax: (212) 206-5340

  Emp: 100

  HENRY HOLT AND COMPANY, INC.
  175 Fifth Ave., New York, New York 10010
  CEO: John Sterling, Pres.
  Bus: *Book publishing.*

  Tel: (646) 307-5095
  Fax: (212) 633-0748

  %FO: 100

  HOLTZBRINCK PUBLISHERS, LLC
  175 Fifth Ave., New York, New York 10010
  CEO: John Sargent, CEO
  Bus: *Book Publishing.*

  Tel: (212) 674-5151
  Fax: (310) 665-0900

  ST. MARTIN'S PRESS, LLC
  175 Fifth Ave., New York, New York 10010
  CEO: Sally Richarson, Pres.
  Bus: *Book Publishing.*

  Tel: (212) 674-5151
  Fax: (212) 674-3179

  Emp: 455

- **VILLEROY & BOCH AG**
  Saaruferstr., D-66688 Mettlach, Germany
  CEO: Wendelin von Boch-Galhau, Chmn.
  Bus: *Tableware, ceramic tiles, plumbing fixtures manufacture.*

  Tel: 49-6864-81-0
  Fax:
  www.villeroyboch.com

  Rev: $1,657
  Emp: 11,000

  NAICS: 314129, 314999, 327112, 327212, 332211, 332214, 332912, 332913, 332919, 337121, 337122, 337124, 337125, 337129, 339912, 339999, 423210, 423220, 423720, 454113

  VILLEROY & BOCH TABLEWARE LTD.
  5 Vaughn Dr., #303, Princeton, New Jersey 08540
  CEO: Bernard Reuter, Pres.
  Bus: *Wholesale china dinnerware, crystal stemware and gifts.*

  Tel: (609) 734-7800
  Fax: (609) 520-8875

  %FO: 100

- **WILLY VOGEL AG**
  Motzener Str. 35/37, D-12227 Berlin, Germany
  CEO: Manfred E. Neubert, CEO
  Bus: *Mfr. lubrication equipment and devices for industry, fluid transfer pumps.*

  Tel: 49-30-720-020
  Fax: 49-30-720-111
  www.vogel-ag.com

  Rev: $118
  Emp: 945

  NAICS: 333911, 333999, 336312

  VOGEL LUBRICATION INC.
  1008 Jefferson Ave., Newport News, Virginia 23607
  CEO: Nice Pohlmann, Pres.
  Bus: *Centralized lubrication for industry, centralized lubrication for vehicles.*

  Tel: (757) 380-8585
  Fax: (757) 380-0709

  %FO: 100
  Emp: 50

● **VOITH FINCKH AG**
Sankt Poltener Straße 43, PO Box 2000, D-89522 Heidenheim, Germany
CEO: Hermut Kormann, CEO
Bus: *Hydroelectric turbines, paper machinery, power transmission engines, propellers and special drives and machine tools.*
NAICS: 313210, 333993

Tel: 49-7321-37-0
Fax: 49-7321-37-7000
www.voith.de

Rev: $4,021
Emp: 24,664

VOITH ANDRITZ TISSUE LLC
101 South Main St., Ste. 400, Janesville, Wisconsin 53545
CEO: Brad Dolbey
Bus: *Machine and paper technology.*

Tel: (608) 758-5920
Fax: (608) 758-5935

%FO: JV

VOITH FINCKH CORPORATION
8 Technology Dr., Belmont, New Hampshire 03110
CEO:
Bus: *Machine and paper technology.*

Tel: (603) 621-4148
Fax: (603) 621-4133

%FO: 100

VOITH PAPER INC.
2200 N. Roemer Rd., Appleton, Wisconsin 54911
CEO: Otto Heissenberger, Pres.
Bus: *Machine and paper technology.*

Tel: (920) 731-7724
Fax: (920) 731-0240

%FO: 100

VOITH PAPER INC.
2105 Water Ridge Pkwy, Charlotte, North Carolina 28217
CEO: Ray Hall
Bus: *Process control instruments.*

Tel: (704) 329-0050
Fax: (704) 329-0050

VOITH PAPER SERVICE SOUTHEAST, INC.
1831 Veterans Memorial Highway, Austell, Georgia 30168-0217
CEO: Tom Panter
Bus: *Plant location.*

Tel: (770) 948-8086
Fax: (770) 948-4613

%FO: JV

VOITH PAPER SERVICE WEST INC.
6654 NE 47th Ave., Portland, Oregon 97208
CEO: Donn Carrell
Bus: *Plant location.*

Tel: (503) 284-1440
Fax: (503) 288-3248

%FO: 100

VOITH SIEMENS HYDRO POWER
East Berlin Rd., PO Box 712, York, Pennsylvania 17405
CEO: Wolfgang Heine, EVP
Bus: *Mfr. hydroelectric turbines, digital & electro-hydraulic governors.*

Tel: (717) 792-7000
Fax: (717) 792-7263

%FO: JV
Emp: 550

VOITH SULZER PAPER TECHNOLOGY INC.
10 Commerce Pkwy., Farmington, New Hampshire 03835
CEO: Chris Turner
Bus: *Machine and paper technology.*

Tel: (603) 330-1088
Fax: (603) 330-1089

%FO: 100

VOITH TRANSMISSIONS, INC.
25 Winship Rd., York, Pennsylvania 17402
CEO: David M. Calveley, Pres.
Bus: *Designs, fabricates, distributes, & services Voith products, including bus transmissions & light rail transmissions, axle drives & torque converters.*

Tel: (717) 767-3200
Fax: (717) 767-3210

%FO: 100

VOITH TURBO
210 Harris Ave., Unit 1, Sacramento, California 95838
CEO: Fred Smith, Mgr.
Bus: *Sales, marketing, and service of drive line retarders.*

Tel: (916) 925-8241
Fax: (916) 925-4287

%FO: 100

• VOLKSWAGEN AG
Brieffach 1848-2, D-38436 Wolfsburg, Germany
CEO: Bernd Pischetsrieder, Chmn.
Bus: *Mfr. automobiles and parts.*

Tel: 49-53-61-90
Fax: 49-53-61-928282
www.volkswagen.de

Rev: $121,346
Emp: 342,502

NAICS: 336111, 522291, 532111

ROLLS-ROYCE MOTOR CARS, INC.
5136 Commerce Ave., Moorpark, California 93020
CEO: A. Stewart, Mng. Dir.
Bus: *Import/distribution/service motor vehicles.*

Tel: (310) 750-8381
Fax: (310) 750-8421

%FO: 100

ROLLS-ROYCE MOTOR CARS, INC. - SOUTHERN REGION
900 N. Federal Highway, Ste. 360, Boca Raton, Florida 33432
CEO: Gustavo Velazute, Reg. Dir.
Bus: *Import/distribution/service motor vehicles.*

Tel: (561) 750-8381
Fax: (561) 750-8421

%FO: 100

VOLKSWAGEN OF AMERICA
3800 Hamlin Rd., Auburn Hills, Michigan 48326
CEO: Frank Witter, CEO
Bus: *Import/marketing automobiles.*

Tel: (248) 340-5000
Fax: (248) 340-4930

%FO: 100

VORELCO INC.
3800 Hamlin Rd., Auburn Hills, Michigan 48326
CEO: William H. Devine, Gen. Mgr.
Bus: *Commercial and industrial building operator.*

Tel: (248) 340-5000
Fax: (248) 340-5525

%FO: 100
Emp: 40

• VOLLMER WERKE MASCHINENFABRIK GMBH
Ehinger Str. 34, P.O. Box 1760, D-88400 Biberach/Riss, Germany
CEO: Siegfried Knupfer, Chmn.
Bus: *Mfr. saw sharpening machines and systems.*

Tel: 49-7351-571-0
Fax: 49-7351-571-130
www.vollmer.de

Rev: $60
Emp: 458

NAICS: 333518, 423830, 541330

VOLLMER OF AMERICA
105 Broadway Ave., Carnegie, Pennsylvania 15106
CEO: Ralf Kraemer, Pres.
Bus: *distribution/service saw sharpening machines and systems.*

Tel: (412) 278-0655
Fax: (412) 278-0520

%FO: 100
Emp: 18

- **VON ARDENNE GMBH**
  Dresden Weifer Hirsch, Plattleite 19/29, D-01328 Dresden, Germany
  CEO: Dr. Peter Lenk, Pres. & CEO
  Bus: *Mfr. equipment, machinery and technology for*
        vacuum coatings and materials treatment.
  NAICS: 333298

  Tel: 49 351 2637-300
  Fax: 49 351 2637-308
  www.vaat.biz

  Emp: 200

  > **PELLMAN TECHNOLOGY INC.**
  > 815 Napa Valley Dr., Fort Collins, Colorado 80525
  > CEO: Mark Pellman, Pres.
  > Bus: *Coating technology.*
  >
  > Tel: (970) 691-0524
  > Fax: (970) 266-9551
  >
  > %FO: 100

- **VOSSLOH AG**
  Vosslohstr. 4, D-58791 Werdohl, Germany
  CEO: Burkhard Schuchmann, CEO
  Bus: *Mfr. and sales of railway products.*

  Tel: 49-2392-52-0
  Fax: 49-2392-52-219
  www.vossloh.de

  Rev: $1,258
  Emp: 4,481

  NAICS: 334416, 336510

  > **VOSSLOH-SCHWABE, INC.**
  > 55 Mayview Rd., Lawrence, Pennsylvania 15055
  > CEO: Stephen Minnici, Gen. Mgr.
  > Bus: *Mfr. and sales of railway products.*
  >
  > Tel: (724) 743-4770
  > Fax: (724) 743-4771
  >
  > %FO: 100

- **VOST ELECTRONIC AG**
  Platz 1, D-94130 Obernzell, Germany
  CEO: Bernd Kohler, CEO
  Bus: *Mfr. electronic components for the electronics*
        industry.
  NAICS: 334417, 334419

  Tel: 49-8591-9370
  Fax: 49-8591-937103
  www.vogt-electronic.com

  > **VOST ELECTRONIC NORTH AMERICA INC.**
  > 150 Purchase St., Ste. 8, Rye, New York 10580
  > CEO: Fred Amori, VP
  > Bus: *Mfr. electronic components for the*
  >   *electronics industry.*
  >
  > Tel: (914) 921-6900
  > Fax: (914) 921-6381
  >
  > %FO: 100

- **WACKER WERKE**
  Preusenstr. 41, Bayern, D-80809 Munich, Germany
  CEO: Ulrich Wacker, Chmn.
  Bus: *Mfr. light machinery.*

  Tel: 49-89-354-02-0
  Fax: 49-89-354-02-390
  www.wackergroup.com

  Rev: $125
  Emp: 900

  NAICS: 423810, 532412

  > **WACKER CORPORATION**
  > N. 92 W. 15000 Anthony Ave., Menomonee Falls, Wisconsin 53051-1504
  > CEO: Christopher Bernard, Pres. & CEO
  > Bus: *Mfr. light machinery.*
  >
  > Tel: (262) 255-0500
  > Fax: (262) 255-7177
  >
  > %FO: 100
  > Emp: 587

• WACKER-CHEMIE GMBH

Hans-Seidel-Platz 4, D-81737 Munich, Germany
CEO: Peter-Alexander Wacker, CEO
Bus: *Mfr. silicon and silanes to the personal computer, telecom and electronics industries.*
NAICS: 325110, 325199

Tel: 49-89-6279-01
Fax: 49-89-6279-1770
www.wacker.com

Rev: $3,468
Emp: 14,688

WACKER CHEMICAL CORPORATION

1 Wacker Dr., Eddyville, Iowa 52553
CEO: Steve Buller
Bus: *Mfr. silicon and silanes to the personal computer, telecom and electronics*

Tel: (641) 969-4817
Fax: (641) 969-4929

%FO: 100

• WALTER AG

Postfach 20 49, D-72010 Tubingen, Germany
CEO: Peter Witteczek, Pres. & CEO
Bus: *Mfr. tool machines.*

NAICS: 333512, 333515, 333518

Tel: 49-70-7170-1444
Fax: 49-70-7170-1530
www.walter-ag.de

Rev: $322
Emp: 1,968

WALTER GRINDERS, INC.

5160 Lad Land Dr., Fredericksburg, Virginia 22407
CEO: Dietmar Weselin, Pres.
Bus: *Sale of grinding and measuring machines.*

Tel: (540) 898-3700
Fax: (540) 898-2811

%FO: 90
Emp: 115

WALTER WAUKESHA INC.

1111 Sentry Dr., Waukesha, Wisconsin 53186
CEO: Muff Tanriverdi, Pres.
Bus: *Mfr. of cutting tools*

Tel: (262) 542-4426
Fax:

%FO: 100
Emp: 100

• WALTER DE GRUYTER PUBLISHERS

Genthiner Str. 13, D-10785 Berlin, Germany
CEO: Dr. Hans-Robert Cram, CEO
Bus: *Scholarly and scientific books and journals publishing.*
NAICS: 511120, 511130

Tel: 49-30-260050
Fax: 49-30-26005251
www.degruyter.com

Emp: 270

WALTER DE GRUYTER PUBLISHERS

500 Executive Blvd., Ossining, New York 10562
CEO: Patrick Alexander, Dir.
Bus: *Publisher; scholarly and scientific books and journals.*

Tel: (914) 762-5866
Fax: (914) 762-0371

%FO: 100

• WEIDMULLER INTERFACE INTERNATIONAL GMBH

Klingenbergstr. 16, Nordrhein, Westfalen, D-32758 Detmold, Germany
CEO: W. Schubl, Pres.
Bus: *Terminal blocks and connectors manufacture.*

NAICS: 334417, 335931

Tel: 49-5231-140
Fax: 49-5231-141175
www.weidmuller.de

Rev: $249
Emp: 1,360

WEIDMULLER INC.
821 Southlake Blvd., Richmond, Virginia 23236
CEO: Thomas Hagen, Chmn.   Tel: (804) 794-2877   %FO: 100
Bus: *Mfr./sale terminal blocks & connectors.* Fax: (804) 794-0252   Emp: 125

● **WELLA AG**
Berliner Allee 65, D-64274 Darmstadt, Germany
CEO: Heiner Gurtler, Pres.   Tel: 49-6151-340   Rev: $1,873
Bus: *Hair care products manufacture and sales.* Fax: 49-6151-34-3048   Emp: 17,040
                                          www.wella.com
NAICS: 325620, 446120

  BELVEDERE USA CORP.
  1 Belvedere Blvd., Belvedere, Illinois 61008
  CEO: Mark Waldron, Pres.   Tel: (815) 541-3131
  Bus: *Beauty supply manufacturing*   Fax: (815) 544-6747   Emp: 300

  GRAHAM WEBB
  5823 Newton Dr., Carlsbad, California 92008
  CEO: Rick Kornbluth, Pres.   Tel: (760) 918-3600
  Bus: *Mktg. & dist. Of hair care products* Fax: (760) 918-8106   Emp: 137

  SEBASTIAN INTERNATIONAL INC
  6109 DeSoto Ave., Woodland Hills, California 91367
  CEO: Steve Goddard, Pres.   Tel: (818) 999-5112
  Bus: *Sale of beauty supplies & hair care* Fax: (818) 712-7770   Emp: 80
       products

  WELLA CORPORATION
  6109 DeSoto Ave., Woodland Hills, California 91367
  CEO: Carsten Fischer, EVP   Tel: (818) 999-5112   %FO: 100
  Bus: *Mfr./sale hair care products.*   Fax: (818) 712-7770   Emp: 100

● **WERZALIT AG & CO**
Gronauer Str. 70, Baden-Wurttemberg, D-71720 Oberstenfeld, Germany
CEO: Gunter Heddemann, Chmn.   Tel: 49-7062-500   Rev: $71
Bus: *Molded wood products and veneers manufacture.* Fax: Emp: 800
                                          www.werzalit.de
NAICS: 321211, 321212, 321999, 423310

  WERZALIT OF AMERICA INC.
  40 Holley Ave., PO Box 373, Bradford, Pennsylvania 16701
  CEO: Robert H. Sefton, Pres.   Tel: (814) 362-3881   %FO: 100
  Bus: *Hardwood flooring mill*   Fax: (814) 362-4237   Emp: 51

● **WESTLB AG**
Herzogstr. 15, D-40217 Dusseldorf, Germany
CEO: Klaus-Michael Geiger, CEO   Tel: 49-211-826-01   Rev: $9,253
Bus: *Commercial banking services.*   Fax: 49-211-826-6119   Emp: 9,200
                                          www.westlb.com
NAICS: 521110, 522110, 522120, 522291, 522310, 523930, 551111

WESTLB ASSET MANAGEMENT USA INC.
5555 San Felipe Boulevard, 20/F, Houston, Texas 77056
CEO: Gregory Caudell   Tel: (713) 963-5200   %FO: 100
Bus: *Commercial banking and financial services.*   Fax: (713) 963-5200

WESTLB ASSET MANAGEMENT USA LLC
10 South Wacker Dr., Ste. 2960, Chicago, Illinois 60606
CEO: Tom Thompson   Tel: (312) 279-9300   %FO: 100
Bus: *Commercial banking and financial services.*   Fax: (312) 575-0222

WESTLB SECURITIES, INC.
1211 Ave. of the Americas, New York, New York 10036
CEO: Susan Mitchell   Tel: (212) 852-6000   %FO: 100
Bus: *Commercial banking and financial services.*   Fax: (212) 852-6300

● **WINCOR NIXDORF INTERNATIONAL GMBH**
Heinz-Nixdorf-Ring 1, D-33106 Paderborn, Germany
CEO: KarlpHeinz Stiller, CEO   Tel: 49-5251-693-30   Rev: $1,942
Bus: *Mfr. POS (point of sale) terminals.*   Fax: 49-5251-693-6767   Emp: 6,114
                                           www.wincor-nixdorf.com

NAICS: 334119
   WINCOR NIXDORF INC.
   2400 Grand Ave. Pkwy., Ste. 103, Austin, Texas 78728
   CEO: Saul Caprio, VP   Tel: (512) 252-5622   %FO: 100
   Bus: *Mfr. and sales POS terminals.*   Fax: (512) 252-5699

● **RICHARD WOLF GMBH**
Postfach 1164, D-75434 Knittlingen, Germany
CEO: Siegfried Karst, Mng. Dir.   Tel: 49-7043-350
Bus: *Produces endoscopes and modular system*   Fax: 49-7043-35300   Emp: 1,000
     solutions for all medical fields. www.richard-wolf.com
NAICS: 334510, 339112
   RICHARD WOLF MEDICAL INSTRUMENT CORPORATION
   353 Corporate Woods Pkwy., Vernon Hills, Illinois 60061
   CEO: Alfons Notheis, CEO   Tel: (847) 913-1113   %FO: 100
   Bus: *Mfr./distribution of surgical instruments.*   Fax: (847) 913-1488   Emp: 150

● **WORLD HOTELS AG**
Herriotstr. 1, D-60528 Frankfurt, Germany
CEO: Michael J. Ball, CEO   Tel: 49-69-6605-6423
Bus: *Hotel representation & reservation services.*   Fax: 49-69-6605-6196
                                           www.worldhotels.com

NAICS: 561510, 561599
   WORLDHOTELS
   6033 West Century Blvd., Ste. 690, Los Angeles, California 90045
   CEO: Thomas Griffiths, VP   Tel: (310) 568-8550   %FO: 100
   Bus: *Hotel representation & reservation.*   Fax: (310) 645-9440

WORLDHOTELS
2520 Coral Way, Miami, Florida 33145
CEO: Thomas Griffiths, VP
Bus: *Hotel representation & reservation.*
Tel: (305) 285-2400
Fax: (305) 285-2444
%FO: 100

WORLDHOTELS
2521 Oaklawn Ave., Ste. 113, Dallas, Texas 75219
CEO: Thomas Griffiths, VP
Bus: *Hotel representation & reservation.*
Tel: (214) 520-0238
Fax: (214) 520-0365
%FO: 100

WORLDHOTELS
106 West Calendar Ct., PMB 316, La Grange, Illinois 60525
CEO: Thomas Griffiths, VP
Bus: *Hotel representation & reservation.*
Tel: (708) 352-8960
Fax: (708) 352-8974
%FO: 100

WORLDHOTELS
152 West 57th St., 14/F, New York, New York 10019
CEO: Edward Brill, SVP
Bus: *Hotel representation & reservation.*
Tel: (212) 835-2534
Fax: (212) 956-2555
%FO: 100
Emp: 45

WORLDHOTELS
1935 South Plum Grove Rd., PMB 353, Palatine, Illinois 60067
CEO: Thomas Griffiths, VP
Bus: *Hotel representation & reservation.*
Tel: (847) 506-0944
Fax: (847) 506-0946
%FO: 100

● **WURTH GROUP**
Reinhold-Wurth-Str. 12-17, D-74653 Kunzelsau-Gaisbach, Germany
CEO: Walter Jaeger, Chmn.
Bus: *Fasteners manufacture and assembly technology.*
Tel: 49-79-40-15-0
Fax: 49-79-40-15-10-00
www.wuerth.com
Rev: $4,674
NAICS: 325510, 325520, 332722, 333991, 339993, 423710, 424950

ACTION BOLT & TOOL CO.
2051 Blue Heron Blvd. W., Riviera Beach, Florida 33404
CEO: Conrad Merklein, Pres.
Bus: *Wholesale nuts, rivets, screws & hand tools.*
Tel: (561) 845-8800
Fax: (561) 845-0255
Emp: 85

ADAMS NUT & BOLT CO.
PO Box 207, 10100 85th Ave. North, Maple Grove, Minnesota 55369
CEO: Gary Huck, Pres.
Bus: *Wholesale industrial fasteners.*
Tel: (763) 424-3374
Fax: (763) 493-0800
Emp: 120

BAER SUPPLY CO.
909 Forest Edge Dr., Vernon Hills, Illinois 60061
CEO: Jim Mulvaney, CEO
Bus: *Wholesale decorative & functional hardware.*
Tel: (847) 913-2237
Fax: (847) 913-9606
Emp: 400

BRIKKSEN INC.
11470 Hilguard Rd., Dallas, Texas 75243
CEO: Richard Pennington, CEO
Bus: *Stainless steel fasteners*
Tel: (214) 343-5703
Fax: (214) 348-6990
Emp: 15

ERGO ADHESIVES INC.
130 Lexington Pkwy., Lexington, North Carolina 27293
CEO: Robert Zihlmann, Pres.   Tel: (336) 956-4800
Bus: *Mfr. adhesives & sealants*   Fax: (336) 956-4890   Emp: 7

GRASS AMERICA
1202 Highway 66S, Kernersville, North Carolina 27284
CEO: Alfred Grass Jr., Pres.   Tel: (336) 996-4041
Bus: *Mfr.. & wholesale hinges & drawer glides* Fax: (336) 996-5149   Emp: 260

LOUIS AND COMPANY
Box 2253, Brea, California 92822
CEO: Jeffrey Louis, Pres.   Tel: (714) 529-1771   %FO: 100
Bus: *Industrial distributor of cabinet hardware,* Fax: (714) 990-6184   Emp: 364
woodworking supplies, surfacing products,
and machinery

MEPLA-ALFIT, INC.
PO Box 1666, Lexington, North Carolina 27293
CEO: Werner Boesch, Pres.   Tel: (336) 956-4600   %FO: 100
Bus: *Mfr. of functional hardware for cabinetry* Fax: (336) 956-4750   Emp: 66
and furniture.

REVCAR FASTENERS INC.
3845 Thirlane Rd., Roanoke, Virginia 24019
CEO: Aron Morthis, Mgr.   Tel: (540) 561-6565   %FO: 100
Bus: *Wholesale automotive supplies*   Fax: (540) 561-6577

SNIDER BOLT & SCREW
11503 Champions Way, Louisville, Kentucky 40299
CEO: Mark J.Cunningham, Pres.   Tel: (502) 968-2250   %FO: 100
Bus: *Industrial fasteners*   Fax: (502) 968-2278   Emp: 77

THE HARDWOOD GROUP INC.
PO Box 668 005, 4250 Golf Acres Dr., Charlotte, North Carolina 28266-8005
CEO: Robert Stolz, Pres.   Tel: (704) 394-2338   %FO: 100
Bus: *Mfr. hardwood flooring, molding, lumber,* Fax: (704) 391-9610   Emp: 203
plywood and decorative hardware.

TREND DISTRIBUTORS, INC.
2800 S.W. 42nd St., Ft. Lauderdale, Florida 33312
CEO: Craig Reyenga, Pres.   Tel: (954) 321-7220   %FO: 100
Bus: *Wholesale distributor of furniture & cabinet* Fax: (954) 321-7250   Emp: 65
hardware.

WURTH EASTERN MAINTENANCE AND INDUSTRIAL SUPPLIES, INC.
PO Box 8128, 199 White Oak Dr,, Berlin, Connecticut 06037
CEO: Robert Burbank   Tel: (860) 829-0556   %FO: 100
Bus: *Fasteners manufacture and assembly* Fax: (860) 829-0552
technology.

WURTH ELECTRONICS INC./ EMC & INDUCTIVE SOLUTIONS
91 Grant St., Ramsey, New Jersey 07446
CEO: Oliver Konz, Pres.   Tel: (201) 785-8800   %FO: 100
Bus: *Computers, peripherals & software* Fax: (201) 785-8810

WURTH INDUSTRY NETWORK OF NORTH AMERICA
Office Maple Grove/USA c/o Adams Nut & Bolt, 10100 85th Ave. North, PO Box 207, Maple Grove,
CEO: Minnesota 55369-4586   Gary Huck   Tel: (763) 424-
3374   %FO: 100

Bus: *Fasteners manufacture and assembly*   Fax: (763) 493-0800
      technology.

WURTH MCALLEN BOLT & SCREW
4403 West Military Hwy., McAllen, Texas 78503
CEO: L. Brice Chandler, Pres.   Tel: (956) 687-8596   %FO: 100
Bus: *Wholesale industrial supplies nuts, bolts,*   Fax: (956) 687-7940   Emp: 175
      screws, hardware.

WURTH USA INC.
Distribution Center Northeast, 93 Grant St., Ramsey, New Jersey 07446
CEO: Michael Kern, Pres.   Tel: (201) 825-2710
Bus: *Motor vehicle supplies & new parts*   Fax: (201) 825-3706   Emp: 353

WURTH/SERVICE SUPPLY INC.
4935 W. 86th St., Indianapolis, Indiana 46268
CEO: Alan Fein, Principal   Tel: (317) 704-1000   %FO: 100
Bus: *Motor vehicle supplies & new parts*   Fax: (317) 704-8701

• **X-FAB SEMICONDUCTOR FOUNDRIES AG**
Haarbergstr. 67, D-99097 Erfurt, Germany
CEO: Hans-Jurgen Straub, CEO   Tel: 49-361-427-6000   Rev: $194
Bus: *Provides contract manufacturing services for*   Fax: 49-361-427-60111   Emp: 1,000
      mixed-signal microchip companies.   www.xfab.com
NAICS: 334413, 511210

X-FAB SEMICONDUCTOR FOUNDRIES
1201 S. Alma School Rd., Mesa, Arizona 85210
CEO: Michael Gadberry   Tel: (480) 505-7036   %FO: 100
Bus: *Provides contract manufacturing services*   Fax: (480) 505-7036
      for mixed-signal microchip companies.

X-FAB SEMICONDUCTOR FOUNDRIES
1900 So. Norfolk St., Suite 350, San Mateo, California 94403
CEO: Carlos Stahr   Tel: (650) 577-2327   %FO: 100
Bus: *Provides contract manufacturing services*   Fax: (650) 577-2365
      for mixed-signal microchip companies.

X-FAB TEXAS INC.
2301 N. University Ave., Lubbock, Texas 79415
CEO: Andy Wilson, CEO   Tel: (806) 747-4400   %FO: 100
Bus: *Provides contract manufacturing services*   Fax: (806) 747-3111
      for mixed-signal microchip companies.

• **ZAPF CREATION AG**
Monchrodener Str. 13, D-96472 Rodental, Germany
CEO: Thomas Eichhorn, CEO   Tel: 49-95-63-7250   Rev: $253
Bus: *Mfr. functional dolls, collector dolls and*   Fax: 49-95-63-725116   Emp: 538
      accessories.   www.zapf-creation.com
NAICS: 339931, 339932

ZAPF CREATION US INC.
4901 Vineland Rd., Ste. 370, Orlando, Florida 32811
CEO: Sandra L. Crawford, Pres.   Tel: (407) 351-7702   %FO: 100
Bus: *Mfr. dolls and accessories.*   Fax: (407) 351-5274

● **ZF FRIEDRICHSHAFEN AG**
Allmannsweiler Str. 25, D-88038 Friedrichshafen, Germany
CEO: Siegfried Goll, CEO   Tel: 49-7541-770   Rev: $11,206
Bus: *Automotive supplier: axles, transmission and*   Fax: 49-7541-7790-8000   Emp: 53,197
     steering products for on/off highway and marine   www.zf-group.de
     markets.
NAICS: 336350

     SACHS AUTOMOTIVE OF AMERICA
     2107 Crooks Rd., Troy, Michigan 48084-5529
     CEO: Julio Caspari, Pres.   Tel: (248) 458-3600
     Bus: *Mfr. auto parts*   Fax: (248) 457-3601   Emp: 560

     SUPPLYON NORTH AMERICA
     7 W. Square Lake Rd., Bloomfield, Michigan 48302
     CEO: John Kay   Tel: (248) 758-2300
     Bus: *Internet auctions.*   Fax: (248) 758-2301

     ZF GROUP NORTH AMERICA
     15811 Centennial Dr., Northville, Michigan 48167
     CEO: Julio Caspari, Pres.   Tel: (734) 416-6200   %FO: 100
     Bus: *Mfr. auto parts*   Fax: (734) 416-8331

● **ZIMMERMANN & JANSEN GMBH**
Bahnstr. 52, D-52325 Duren, Germany
CEO: Holger Scubert, Dir.   Tel: 49-2421-6910
Bus: *Mfr. petrochemicals and glass manufacturing*   Fax: 49-2421-691200
     equipment.   www.zjgmbh.de
NAICS: 333298, 333319, 333999, 339999

     BACHMANN INDUSTRIES
     416 Lewiston Junction Rd., Auburn, Maine 04210
     CEO: William Fred Koch   Tel: (207) 784-1903
     Bus: *Mfr. petrochemicals and glass*   Fax: (207) 784-1904
       manufacturing equipment.

     ZIMMERMANN & JANSEN, INC.
     620 North Houston Ave., PO Box 3365, Humble, Texas 77338-3873
     CEO: Bredo Christensen, Pres.   Tel: (281) 446-8000   %FO: 100
     Bus: *Mfr. petrochemicals and glass*   Fax: (281) 446-8126
       manufacturing equipment.

Greece

- **NATIONAL BANK OF GREECE SA**
  86 Eolou St., GR-102 32 Athens, Greece
  CEO: Takis E. G. Arapoglou, Chmn. & CEO
  Bus: *State-controlled, commercial banking services.*
  Tel: 30-210-33-41000
  Fax: 30-210-48-06510
  www.nbg.gr
  Rev: $4,317
  Emp: 14,143

  NAICS: 522110, 522293, 522310, 523120, 523920, 523930, 523991, 523999, 525110, 525910

  > **ATLANTIC BANK OF NEW YORK**
  > 960 Ave. of Americas, New York, New York 10001
  > CEO: Thomas M. O'Brien, Pres. & CEO
  > Bus: *Banking.*
  > Tel: (212) 967-7425
  > Fax: (212) 714-7443
  > %FO: 100
  > Emp: 420

- **OLYMPIC AIRLINES SA**
  96-100 Syngrou Ave., GR-11741 Athens, Greece
  CEO: Stelios Paterakis, Mgr.
  Bus: *Commercial air transport services.*
  Tel: 30-210-926-9111
  Fax:
  www.olympicairlines.com

  NAICS: 481111

  > **OLYMPIC AIRWAYS**
  > Satellite Airlines Terminal, 125 Park Ave., New York, New York 10017
  > CEO: Fokas Drucelvidge
  > Bus: *Commercial air transport services.*
  > Tel: (212) 867-0970
  > Fax: (212) 867-0973
  > %FO: 100

  > **OLYMPIC AIRWAYS**
  > 333 North Michigan Ave., Ste. 1230, Chicago, Illinois 60601
  > CEO:
  > Bus: *Commercial air transport services.*
  > Tel: (312) 782-8878
  > Fax: (312) 782-8879
  > %FO: 100

  > **OLYMPIC AIRWAYS**
  > 1701 K St., NW, Ste. 801, Washington, District of Columbia 20006
  > CEO: V. Giannakopoulos
  > Bus: *Commercial air transport services.*
  > Tel: (202) 659-2511
  > Fax: (202) 659-2516
  > %FO: 100

  > **OLYMPIC AIRWAYS**
  > Terminal 1, JFK International Airport, Jamaica, New York 11430
  > CEO: Fokas Drucelvidge
  > Bus: *Commercial air transport services.*
  > Tel: (718) 751-2650
  > Fax: (718) 751-2671
  > %FO: 100

  > **OLYMPIC AIRWAYS**
  > 526 Statler Office Bldg., 20 Park Plaza, Boston, Massachusetts 02116
  > CEO: Demetri Costas
  > Bus: *Commercial air transport services.*
  > Tel: (617) 451-0500
  > Fax: (617) 451-2081
  > %FO: 100

  > **OLYMPIC AIRWAYS**
  > 7000 Austin St., Forest Hills, New York 11375
  > CEO: Christos Tsoutsanis
  > Bus: *Commercial air transport services.*
  > Tel: (718) 269-2200
  > Fax: (718) 269-2215
  > %FO: 100

OLYMPIC AIRWAYS
100 Biscayne Blvd., Ste. 1109, Miami, Florida 33132
CEO: Fokas Drucelvidge   Tel: (305) 372-9500   %FO: 100
Bus: *Commercial air transport services.*   Fax: (305) 372-9502

Hong Kong PRC

- **ALCO HOLDINGS LIMITED**
  11/F, Zung Fu Industrial Bldg., 1067 Kings Rd., Quarry Bay, Hong Kong PRC
  CEO: Kai Ching Leung, CEO   Tel: 852-2880-0698   Rev: $490
  Bus: *Contract electronics manufacture.*   Fax: 852-2880-0858   Emp: 14,000
      www.alco.com.hk
  NAICS: 335999

      ALCO ELECTRONICS LTD.
      6024 W. Maple Rd, Ste. 103, West Bloomfield, Michigan 48322
      CEO: S. Jorge   Tel: (248) 539-3883   %FO: 100
      Bus: *Contract electronics manufacture and sales.*   Fax: (248) 539-7989

- **ALPHA SPACECOM INCORPORATED**
  Progress Commercial Bldg., 7-17 Irving Street, Rm. 1305, Causeway Bay, Hong Kong PRC
  CEO: Terence F. Sien, CEO   Tel: 852-2972-2772
  Bus: *Broadband communications.*   Fax: 852-2972-2772
      www.alphaspacecom.com
  NAICS: 518111

      ALPHA SPACECOM INCORPORATED
      345 North Maple Dr., Ste. 295, Beverly Hills, California 90210
      CEO: Brian T. Brick, COO   Tel: (310) 276-6743   %FO: 100
      Bus: *Broadband communications.*   Fax: (310) 276-6783

- **ASAT HOLDINGS LIMITED**
  138 Texaco Rd., Tsuen Wan, New Territories, Hong Kong PRC
  CEO: Robert J. Gange, Pres. & CEO   Tel: 852-2408-7811   Rev: $214
  Bus: *Semiconductor manufacture.*   Fax: 852-2407-4056   Emp: 1,870
      www.asat.com
  NAICS: 334413

      ASAT INC.
      6701 Koll Center Pkwy., Ste. 200, Pleasanton, California 94566
      CEO: Darrell Baker   Tel: (925) 398-0400   %FO: 100
      Bus: *Semiconductor manufacture and sales.*   Fax: (925) 398-0388

      ASAT INC.
      PO Box 2369, Monument, Colorado 80132
      CEO: Corey Miller   Tel: (719) 487-0631   %FO: 100
      Bus: *Semiconductor manufacture and sales.*   Fax: (719) 623-0621

      ASAT INC.
      23436 Madero, High Park Center, Ste. 245, Mission Viejo, California 92691
      CEO: Rossana Chimileski   Tel: (949) 830-0965   %FO: 100
      Bus: *Semiconductor manufacture and sales.*   Fax: (949) 830-3505

ASAT INC.
48 Sword St., Ste. 203, Auburn, Massachusetts 01501
CEO: Mike Graves
Tel: (508) 755-2841
%FO: 100
Bus: *Semiconductor manufacture and sales.*
Fax: (508) 755-2843

ASAT INC.
3755 Capitol of Texas Hwy., Ste. 100, Austin, Texas 78701
CEO: Leo Higgins
Tel: (512) 383-8297
%FO: 100
Bus: *Semiconductor manufacture and sales.*
Fax: (512) 383-1590

• **THE BANK OF EAST ASIA, LIMITED**
Bank of East Asia Bldg., 10 Des Voeux Rd., 19/F, Central, Hong Kong PRC
CEO: David K. P. Li, Chmn. & CEO
Tel: 852-2842-3200
Rev: $1,049
Bus: *Provides commercial and retail banking services.*
Fax: 852-2845-9333
Emp: 5,700
www.hkbea.com
NAICS: 522110, 522210, 522291, 522292, 524210

THE BANK OF EAST ASIA, LIMITED
5773 Rosemead Blvd., Temple City, California 91780
CEO: Sammy Kwok, VP & Gen. Mgr.
Tel: (626) 656-8888
%FO: 100
Bus: *International commercial banking services.*
Fax: (626) 656-8899

THE BANK OF EAST ASIA, LIMITED
388 East Valley Blvd., Ste. 218, Alhambra, California 91801
CEO: Victor Li Man-fong, Gen. Mgr.
Tel: (626) 656-8818
%FO: 100
Bus: *International commercial banking services.*
Fax: (626) 656-8833
Emp: 56

THE BANK OF EAST ASIA, LIMITED
1675 Hanover Rd., City of Industry, California 91748
CEO: Gertrude Hu, VP & Gen. Mgr.
Tel: (626) 965-3938
%FO: 100
Bus: *International commercial banking services.*
Fax: (626) 965-5947

THE BANK OF EAST ASIA, LIMITED
135-20 39th Ave., Unit HL212, Flushing, New York 11354
CEO: Stanley Kung, SVP
Tel: (718) 886-9765
%FO: 100
Bus: *International commercial banking services.*
Fax: (718) 886-9775

THE BANK OF EAST ASIA, LIMITED
23133 Hawthorne Blvd., Ste. 100, Torrance, California 90505
CEO: Michael Tan, VP & Gen. Mgr.
Tel: (310) 802-7388
%FO: 100
Bus: *International commercial banking services.*
Fax: (310) 802-7399

THE BANK OF EAST ASIA, LIMITED
202 Canal St., 2/F, New York, New York 10013
CEO: Tang Peng-wah, CEO
Tel: (212) 238-8200
%FO: 100
Bus: *International commercial banking services.*
Fax: (212) 219-3211

• **CAFE DE CORAL HOLDINGS LIMITED**
5 Wo Sul St., 10/F, Cafe De Coral Centre, Fo Tan, Shatin, Hong Kong PRC
CEO: Sunny H. K. Lo, CEO
Tel: 852-2693-6218
Rev: $349
Bus: *Restaurant operator.*
Fax: 852-2695-0245
Emp: 9,000
www.cafedecoral.com
NAICS: 722110, 722211, 722213

DAI BAI DANG RESTAURANT
7736 N Blackstone Ave., Fresno, California 93711
CEO: Rosa L. F. Lau   Tel: (559) 448-8894   %FO: 100
Bus: *Asian restaurant chain.*   Fax: (559) 448-8896

FAN TING CHINA CAFÉ
1025-B Broadbeck Dr., Newbury Park, California 91320
CEO: Rosa L. F. Lau   Tel: (805) 375-4886   %FO: 100
Bus: *Asian restaurant chain.*   Fax: (805) 375-4886

MANCHU WOK USA
12912 Meadow Breeze Dr., Ste. 2, Wellington, Florida 33414
CEO: Mike Craig, mgr   Tel: (561) 798-7800   %FO: 100
Bus: *Asian restaurant chain.*   Fax: (561) 333-6663

● **CATHAY PACIFIC AIRWAYS LIMITED**
5th Fl., South Tower, 8 Scenic Road, Central, Hong Kong PRC
CEO: Philip N. L. Chen, CEO   Tel: 852-2747-1577   Rev: $3,809
Bus: *Commercial air transport services.*   Fax: 852-2560-1411   Emp: 14,600
                                www.cathaypacific-air.com
NAICS: 481111

    CATHAY PACIFIC AIRWAYS
    360 Post St., San Francisco, California 94108-4912
    CEO: Terry Kanat   Tel: (415) 982-3242   %FO: 100
    Bus: *Commercial air transport services.*   Fax: (415) 982-3242

    CATHAY PACIFIC AIRWAYS
    300 Continental Blvd., Ste. 500, El Segundo, California 90245
    CEO: Jake Olver, Pres.   Tel: (310) 615-1113   %FO: 100
    Bus: *U.S. headquarters.*   Fax: (310) 615-0042

● **CBR BREWING COMPANY, INC.**
23/F Hang Sang Causeway Bay Bldg., 28 Yee Wo Street, Causeway Bay, Hong Kong PRC
CEO: Daqing Zheng, CEO   Tel: 852-2866-2301   Rev: $79
Bus: *Brews, distributes and markets Pabst Blue*   Fax: 852-2866-7409   Emp: 1,522
   Ribbon beer.   www.cbrbrew.com
NAICS: 312120

    CBR BREWING COMPANY, INC.
    433 North Camden Dr., Ste. 600, Beverly Hills, California 90210
    CEO: Gary CK Lui   Tel: (310) 274-5172   %FO: 100
    Bus: *Brews, distributes and markets Pabst Blue*   Fax: (310) 550-8213
       Ribbon beer.

● **CDC CORPORATION**
18 Whitfield Rd., Causeway Bay, Hong Kong PRC
CEO: Peter Yip, Pres.   Tel: 852-2893-8200   Rev: $183
Bus: *Petroleum exploration, refining and sales.*   Fax: 852-2893-5245   Emp: 1,179
                                www.cdccorporation.net
NAICS: 211111, 324110, 511210, 516110, 519190, 541511, 541512

ASCENT SGI
373-E Route 46 West, Fairfield, New Jersey 07004
CEO: Rajan Vaz
Bus: *Software and business solutions.*
Tel: (973) 882-9797
Fax: (973) 882-9783
%FO: 100

ASCENT SGI
2700 Westchester Ave., Purchase, New York 10577
CEO: Sanjay Lall
Bus: *Software and business solutions.*
Tel: (914) 251-1300
Fax: (914) 251-1306
%FO: 100

CDC CORPORATION
405 Lexington Ave., 26/F, New York, New York 10174
CEO: Craig Celek
Bus: *Enterprise software.*
Tel: (212) 661-2160
Fax: (212) 591-9976
%FO: 100

IMI CORP.
521 Fellowship Rd., Ste. 140, Mt. Laurel, New Jersey 08054
CEO: Dan Bachrodt
Bus: *Software manufacture.*
Tel: (856) 793-4400
Fax: (856) 793-4401
%FO: 100

ROSS SYSTEMS INC.
Two Concourse Pkwy., Ste. 800, Atlanta, Georgia 30328
CEO: J. Patrick Tinley, Pres.
Bus: *Enterprise software.*
Tel: (770) 351-9600
Fax: (770) 351-0036
%FO: 100

● **CHINA PATENT AGENT (HK) LTD.**
22/F, Great Eagle Centre, 23 Harbour Rd, Wanchai, Hong Kong PRC
CEO: Ding Zhongze, Chmn.
Bus: *Intellectual property service; consultants, representatives & other legal services.*
NAICS: 541110, 541199, 922130
Tel: 852-2828-4688
Fax: 852-2827-1018
www.cpahkltd.com
Emp: 310

> **CHINA PATENT & TRADEMARK AGENT (USA) LTD.**
> 55 Broad St., 15/F, New York, New York 10004
> CEO: Sun Hongyou
> Bus: *Intellectual property service; consultants, representatives & other legal services.*
> Tel: (212) 809-8100
> Fax: (212) 809-8118
> %FO: 100
> Emp: 3

● **CHINADOTCOM CORPORATION**
34/F Citicorp Centre, 18 Whitfield Rd., Causeway Bay, Hong Kong PRC
CEO: Steven Chan, CEO
Bus: *Internet and software products manufacture.*
NAICS: 511210, 516110, 519190, 541511, 541512, 541519
Tel: 852-2893-8200
Fax: 852-2893-5245
www.cdccorporation.net
Rev: $183
Emp: 1,802

> **CHINADOTCOM CORPORATION**
> The Chrysler Bldg., 405 Lexington Ave., 26/F, New York, New York 10174
> CEO: Craig Celik, Mgr.
> Bus: *Internet and software products manufacture.*
> Tel: (212) 661-2160
> Fax: (212) 591-9976
> %FO: 100

> **ROSS SYSTEMS, INC.**
> 2 Concourse Pkwy., Ste. 800, Atlanta, Georgia 30328
> CEO: J. Patrick Tinley, CEO
> Bus: *Enterprise resource planning software.*
> Tel: (770) 351-9600
> Fax: (770) 351-0036
> %FO: 100

- **CITIC KA WAH BANK LTD.**
232 Des Voeux Rd., Central, Hong Kong PRC
CEO: Doreen Chan, Pres. & CEO
Bus: *General banking services.*

  Tel: 852-2545-7131
  Fax: 852-2541-7029
  www.citickawahbank.com

  Rev: $541
  Emp: 1,035

  NAICS: 522110

  CITIC KA WAH BANK LTD.
  323 West Blvd., Alhambra, California 91803
  CEO: Li Dong, VP
  Bus: *General banking services.*

  Tel: (626) 282-9820
  Fax: (626) 282-9399

  %FO: 100

  CITIC KA WAH BANK LTD.
  11 East Broadway, Glory China Tower, New York, New York 10038
  CEO: Peter Zhao, VP
  Bus: *General banking services.*

  Tel: (212) 732-8868
  Fax: (212) 791-3776

  %FO: 100
  Emp: 55

- **DSG INTERNATIONAL LIMITED**
17/F, Watson Centre, 16-22 Kung Yip Street, Kwai Chung, Hong Kong PRC
CEO: Brandon S.L. Wang, Pres. & CEO
Bus: *Mfr. personal care products.*

  Tel: 852-2484-4820
  Fax: 852-2480-4491
  www.dsgil.com

  Rev: $227
  Emp: 1,600

  NAICS: 325620

  ASSOCIATED HYGIENIC PRODUCTS LLC
  801 SE Assembly Ave., Vancouver, Washington 98661
  CEO: Steve Pankow
  Bus: *Manufacturing facility.*

  Tel: (360) 693-6688
  Fax: (360) 693-6688

  %FO: 100

  ASSOCIATED HYGIENIC PRODUCTS LLC
  4455 River Green Pkwy., Duluth, Georgia 30096
  CEO: Steve Pankow, CEO
  Bus: *Sales/distribution of personal care
       products.*

  Tel: (770) 497-9800
  Fax: (770) 623-8887

  %FO: 100

  ASSOCIATED HYGIENIC PRODUCTS LLC
  205 East Highland Dr., Oconto Falls, Wisconsin 54154
  CEO: Gary Arbusto
  Bus: *Sales/distribution of personal care
       products.*

  Tel: (920) 846-8444
  Fax: (920) 846-3026

  %FO: 100

- **ELEC & ELTEK INTERNATIONAL**
Unite B10, 3/F Merit Industrial Centre, 94 Tokwawan Road, Tokwawan, Central, Hong Kong PRC
CEO: Thomas K. Y. Tang, Chmn. & Mng. Dir.
Bus: *Designs and manufactures LCD and related
     magnetic products.*

  Tel: 852-2954-3333
  Fax: 852-2954-3304
  www.eleceltek.com

  Rev: $412
  Emp: 14,600

  NAICS: 334119, 334412, 334417, 334418, 334419

  E & E MAGNETIC PRODUCTS LTD.
  1183 Bordeaux Dr., Ste. 38, Sunnyvale, California 94089
  CEO: Michael Chan, Mgr.
  Bus: *Magnetic products manufacture and sales.*

  Tel: (408) 734-4223
  Fax: (408) 734-8352

  %FO: 100

- **ELEPHANT TALK COMMUNICATIONS, INC.**
  8/F, 145-149 Yeung Uk Rd., Tuesn Wan, Hong Kong PRC
  CEO: Russelle Choi, CEO
  Bus: *Long distance phone carrier.*
  Tel: 852-2707-0703
  Fax: 852-2707-0707
  www.elephanttalk.com
  Rev: $24
  Emp: 5

  NAICS: 517212

  ELEPHANT TALK COMMUNICATIONS, INC.
  438 E. Katella Ave., Ste. 217, Orange, California 92867
  CEO: Manu Ohri
  Bus: *Long distance phone carrier.*
  Tel: (714) 288-1570
  Fax: (714) 288-2045
  %FO: 100

- **GREAT EAGLE HOLDINGS LIMITED**
  Great Eagle Centre, 23 Harbour Rd., 33/F, Wanchai, Hong Kong PRC
  CEO: Lo Ying Shek, Chmn. & Mng. Dir.
  Bus: *Real estate operator of hotels and offices.*
  Tel: 852-2827-3668
  Fax: 852-2827-5799
  www.greateagle.com.hk
  Rev: $352
  Emp: 3,426

  NAICS: 236220, 237210, 531120, 531190, 531312, 531390

  THE LANGHAM BOSTON
  250 Franklin St., Boston, Massachusetts 02110
  CEO: Nigel Roberts, SVP
  Bus: *Luxury hotel.*
  Tel: (617) 451-1900
  Fax: (617) 423-2267
  %FO: 100

- **HECNY TRANSPORTATION INC.**
  111 Wai Yip St., Hecny Cargo Bldg., Kwun Tong, Kowloon, Hong Kong PRC
  CEO: Charlie Lee, Chmn.
  Bus: *Freight forwarding.*
  Tel: 852-2751-4328
  Fax: 852-2795-2910
  www.hecny.com

  NAICS: 488510, 511130

  HECNY BROKERAGE SERVICES
  1941 Williams Rd., Ste. 3C, Columbus, Ohio 43207
  CEO: Andy Tang, Mgr.
  Bus: *Air transport services.*
  Tel: (614) 491-1628
  Fax: (614) 491-1755

  HECNY GROUP
  1460 San Francisco St., Torrance, California 90501
  CEO: Charles Lee, Chmn.
  Bus: *Freight transportation arrangements.*
  Tel: (310) 347-3400
  Fax: (310) 347-3419
  Emp: 120

  HECNY TRANSPORATION INC.
  147-39 175th St., Ste. 100, Jamaica, New York 11434
  CEO: Tony Lee, Pres.
  Bus: *Engaged in freight forwarding.*
  Tel: (718) 656-5537
  Fax: (718) 632-8491
  %FO: 100
  Emp: 3

  HECNY TRANSPORTATION
  234 S W 43rd St., Ste. 2M/D, Renton, Washington 98055
  CEO: Desmond Leung
  Bus: *Business services*
  Tel: (425) 656-0431
  Fax: (425) 656-0435

HECNY TRANSPORTATION
Burrs Rd. Corporate Center, 116-B Burrs Rd., Westhampton, New Jersey 08060
CEO: Gary Yetter, Mgr.   Tel: (609) 267-3130
Bus: *Freight transportation arrangements.*   Fax: (310) 267-2868

HECNY TRANSPORTATION
150 North Hill Dr., Brisbane, California 94005
CEO: Charles Lee, Chmn.   Tel: (415) 468-0600
Bus: *Freight transportation arrangements.*   Fax: (415) 467-1775   Emp: 76

HECNY TRANSPORTATION INC.
2250 East Devon St., Ste. 115, Des Plaines, Illinois 60018
CEO: Jon Edwards   Tel: (915) 775-1258
Bus: *Freight transportation services.*   Fax: (915) 778-0581

HECNY TRANSPORTATION INC.
1280 South Main St., Ste. 105, Grapevine, Texas 76051
CEO: Young Oh, Mgr.   Tel: (817) 410-2332
Bus: *Freight transportation arrangements.*   Fax: (817) 329-5183

HECNY TRANSPORTATION INC.
7-A Founders Blvd., Ste. A, El Paso, Texas 79906
CEO: Jon Edwards, Mgr.   Tel: (915) 775-1258
Bus: *Freight transportation arrangements.*   Fax: (915) 778-0581

HECNY TRANSPORTATION INC.
2158 S. Lynhurst Dr., Indianapolis, Indiana 46241
CEO: Jon Edwards, Dir.   Tel: (317) 403-0874
Bus: *Freight transportation arrangements.*   Fax: (317) 244-6856

HECNY TRANSPORTATION INC.
1904 N. W. 82 Ave., Miami, Florida 33126
CEO: Tina Kao, Mgr.   Tel: (305) 594-5882
Bus: *Freight transport services.*   Fax: (305) 597-7084

● **TOMMY HILFIGER CORPORATION**
850-870 Lai Chi Kok Rd., 8/f, Cheung Sha Wan, Kowloon, Hong Kong PRC
CEO: Joel J. Horowitz, Co-Chair   Tel: 852-2216-0668   Rev: $1,876
Bus: *Design and manufacture of clothing, textiles and*   Fax: 852-2312-1368   Emp: 5,400
   accessories. JV Tommy Hilfiger USA   www.tommy.com
   NAICS: 314129, 314999, 315119, 315191, 315192, 315211, 315221, 315223, 315224, 315232, 315234, 315239,
315991, 315999, 316211, 316212, 316213,
                 316214, 325620, 339999, 423220
   TOMMY HILFIGER USA INC.
   25 West 39th St., New York, New York 10018
   CEO: Bob Rosenblatt, CEO   Tel: (212) 840-8888   %FO: 100
   Bus: *Sales/distribution of clothing and*   Fax: (212) 302-8718
      accessories.

● **THE HONG KONG & SHANGHAI HOTELS, LIMITED**
St. George's Bldg., 2 Ice House St., 8/F, Central, Hong Kong PRC
CEO: Kate Kelly, Mng. Dir.   Tel: 852-2840-7741   Rev: $324
Bus: *Owns and manages hotel properties.*   Fax: 852-2868-4770   Emp: 6,104
                                                 www.hshgroup.com
   NAICS: 541611

THE PENINSULA HOTEL
9882 Santa Monica Blvd., Beverly Hills, California 90212
CEO: Ali Kasikci, Mgr.   Tel: (310) 551-2888   %FO: 100
Bus: *Hotel property.*   Fax: (310) 788-2319

THE PENINSULA NEW YORK
700 Fifth Ave., New York, New York 10019
CEO: Niklaus Leuenberger, Mgr.   Tel: (212) 956-2888   %FO: 100
Bus: *Hotel chain.*   Fax:

● **HONG KONG TRADE DEVELOPMENT COUNCIL**
38/F, Convention Plaza, Office Tower, 1 Harbour Rd., Wanchai, Hong Kong PRC
CEO: Peter Woo, Chmn.   Tel: 852-2584-4333   Rev: $190
Bus: *Trade development for the Chinese mainland and* Fax: 852-2824-0249   Emp: 600
    the wider region.   www.tdctrade.com
NAICS: 561499, 926110

HONG KONG ECONOMIC & TRADE OFFICE
219 East 46th St., New York, New York 10017
CEO: Robin Chiu, Mgr.   Tel: (212) 838-8688   %FO: 100
Bus: *Trade development for the Chinese mainland* Fax: (212) 838-8941
    and the wider region.

HONG KONG TRADE DEVELOPMENT COUNCIL
333 North Michigan Ave., Ste. 2028, Chicago, Illinois 60601
CEO: James Yuen, Dir.   Tel: (312) 726-4515   %FO: 100
Bus: *Trade development for the Chinese mainland* Fax: (312) 726-2441
    and the wider region.

HONG KONG TRADE DEVELOPMENT COUNCIL
Los Angeles World Trade Centre, 350 S. Figueroa St., Ste. 139, Los Angeles, California 90071
CEO: Tony Wong, Mgr.   Tel: (213) 622-3194   %FO: 100
Bus: *Trade development for the Chinese mainland* Fax: (213) 613-1490
    and the wider region.

● **HUTCHISON WHAMPOA LIMITED**
Hutchison House, 22/F, 10 Harcourt Rd., Central, Hong Kong PRC
CEO: Li Ka-shing, Chmn.   Tel: 852-2128-1188   Rev: $17,309
Bus: *Food processing and distribution and hotel* Fax: 852-2128-1705   Emp: 182,000
    management.   www.hutchison-whampoa.com
NAICS: 211111, 211112, 213111, 213112, 221111, 221112, 221119, 221121, 221122, 221210, 311411, 311920, 312111, 312112, 424820, 445110, 446120, 488310, 488320, 517212, 531110, 531120, 531210, 531311, 531312, 531390, 541191, 721110

HUTCHISON WHAMPOA AMERICAS LIMITED
10900 NE 8th St., Ste. 1488, Bellevue, Washington 98004
CEO: Connie Wong, Pres.   Tel: (425) 709-8888   %FO: 100
Bus: *Engaged in food processing and distribution* Fax: (425) 709-8899   Emp: 10
    and hotel management.

● **IDT INTERNATIONAL LIMITED**
Block C, 9/Fl. Kaiser Estate, 41 Man Yue St., Hunghom, Kowloon, Hong Kong PRC
CEO: Raymond Chan, Chmn. & CEO   Tel: 852-2764-7873   Rev: $353
Bus: *LCD consumer electronics manufacture.* Fax: 852-2765-6620   Emp: 7,600
                       www.idthk.com

NAICS: 334111, 334210, 334310, 339932

OREGON SCIENTIFIC, INC., DIV. IDT
200 Friberg Pkwy., Ste. 1010, Westborough, Massachusetts 01581
CEO: Bill Uzell, EVP   Tel: (508) 475-0030   %FO: 100
Bus: *Mfr. of LCD products.*   Fax: (508) 519-0078

OREGON SCIENTIFIC, INC., DIV. IDT
19861 SW 95th Place, Tualatin, Oregon 97062
CEO: Paul S. Zimmerman, Pres.   Tel: (503) 783-5100   %FO: 100
Bus: *Mfr. of LCD technology.*   Fax: (503) 691-6208

OREGON SCIENTIFIC, INC., DIV. IDT
200 Fifth Ave., Ste. 757, New York, New York 10010
CEO: Ellen Careaga, VP   Tel: (212) 647-1608   %FO: 100
Bus: *Showroom services.*   Fax: (212) 647-0241

● **INTAC INTERNATIONAL INC.**
32/F Laws Commercial Plaza, 778 Cheung Sha Wan Rd., Kowloon, Hong Kong PRC
CEO: Wei Zhou, CEO   Tel: 852-2385-8789   Rev: $115
Bus: *On-line career development services.*   Fax: 852-2385-1621   Emp: 276
                                               www.intac.cn
NAICS: 611420, 611710, 624310
    INTAC INTERNATIONAL INC.
    12221 Merit Dr., Ste. 1350, Dallas, Texas 75251
    CEO: J. David Darnell, SVP   Tel: (469) 916-9891   %FO: JV
    Bus: *On-line career development services.* Fax: (469) 916-9892

● **JARDINE MATHESON HOLDINGS LTD.**
Jardine House 48/F, Central, Hong Kong PRC
CEO: Henry Keswick, Chmn.   Tel: 852-2843-8288   Rev: $8,970
Bus: *Engineering, construction, financial services,*   Fax: 852-2845-9005   Emp: 100,000
    marketing, distribution, real estate, luxury hotels,   www.jardines.com
    transportation services and food service.
NAICS: 236210, 236220, 237990, 441110, 441120, 445110, 446110, 524210, 531120, 531190, 531390, 541330,
721110
    MANDARIN ORIENTAL KAHALA
    5000 Kahala Ave., Honolulu, Hawaii 96816
    CEO: Dianna Shitanishi   Tel: (808) 739-8888   %FO: 100
    Bus: *Luxury hotel property.*   Fax:

    MANDARIN ORIENTAL MIAMI
    500 Brickell Key Dr., Miami, Florida 33131
    CEO: Jill DeMone   Tel: (305) 913-8288   %FO: 100
    Bus: *Luxury hotel property.*   Fax:

    MANDARIN ORIENTAL NEW YORK
    80 Columbus Circle, New York, New York 10023
    CEO: Eric Cruz   Tel: (212) 805-8800   %FO: 100
    Bus: *Luxury hotel property.*   Fax:

    MANDARIN ORIENTAL SAN FRANCISCO
    222 Sansome St., San Francisco, California 94104
    CEO: Wolfgang Hultner   Tel: (415) 276-9888   %FO: 100
    Bus: *Luxury hotel property.*   Fax:

MANDARIN ORIENTAL WASHINGTON DC
1330 Maryland Ave., Washington, District of Columbia 20024
CEO: Mark Politzer
Bus: *Luxury hotel property.*
Tel: (202) 554-8588
Fax:
%FO: 100

THE MARK - NEW YORK
25 East 77th St., New York, New York 10021
CEO: Wolfgang Hultner
Bus: *Luxury hotel property.*
Tel: (212) 744-4300
Fax:
%FO: 100

● **JOHNSON ELECTRIC GROUP**
6-22 Dai Shun St., Tai Po Industrial Estate, Tai Po, NT, Hong Kong PRC
CEO: Patrick S. C. Wang, Chmn. & CEO
Bus: *Electric micro motors design and manufacture.*
Tel: 852-755-299-00197
Fax: 852-755-299-00203
www.johnsonmotor.com
Rev: $1,051
Emp: 32,000

NAICS: 335312, 336399

JOHNSON ELECTRIC NORTH AMERICA
47660 Halyard Dr., Plymouth, Michigan 48170
CEO: Patrick Wang, Pres.
Bus: *Automotive products.*
Tel: (734) 392-5300
Fax: (734) 392-5388
%FO: 100
Emp: 550

JOHNSON ELECTRIC NORTH AMERICA
10 Progress Dr., Shelton, Connecticut 06484
CEO: Richard Wong, Pres.
Bus: *Electric motor mfr. for power tools, business equipment& personal products, home appliances & audio visuals.*
Tel: (203) 447-5362
Fax: (203) 447-5383
%FO: 100
Emp: 124

● **KYCE ENTERPRISE (HK) LTD.**
Merit Industrial Centre, 94 Tokwawan Road To Kwa Wan, Kowloon, Hong Kong PRC
CEO: Yuk Yun-Kit, Dir.
Bus: *Mfr. watches and consumer electronics.*
Tel: 852-3764-7255
Fax: 852-3764-1401
www.sinutex.com

NAICS: 423940, 443112

KYCE, INC.
4801 Metropolitan Ave., Ridgewood, New York 11385
CEO: Kevin Yuk, Pres.
Bus: *Import watches and consumer electronics.*
Tel: (718) 628-6282
Fax: (718) 628-1038
%FO: 100

● **LIU CHONG HING BANK, LTD.**
24 Des Voeux Rd., Central, Hong Kong PRC
CEO: Lit Man Liu, Pres.
Bus: *Commercial banking services.*
Tel: 852-2841-7417
Fax: 852-2845-9134
www.lchbank.com
Rev: $365

NAICS: 522110

LIU CHONG HING BANK LTD.
601 California St., Ste. 150, San Francisco, California 94108-2815
CEO: King Leung Chan, Mgr.
Bus: *International banking services.*
Tel: (415) 433-6404
Fax: (415) 433-0686
%FO: 100

- **LJ INTERNATIONAL INC.**
  21 Man Lok St., HungHom, Focal Industrial Centre, Block A, 12/F, Kowloon, Hong Kong PRC
  CEO: Lorenzo Y.C. Yih, Chmn. & Pres. & CEO   Tel: 852-2764-3622   Rev: $77
  Bus: *Precious and semi-precious jewelry manufacture.*   Fax: 852-2764-3783   Emp: 2,500
     www.ljintl.com

  NAICS: 334518, 339911, 339913, 423940, 448310

  > **LJ INTERNATIONAL**
  > 713 Brea Canyon Rd., Walnut, California 91789
  > CEO: Rowena Lin, CEO   Tel: (909) 979-8428
  > Bus: *Mfr. of jewelry & watches.*   Fax: (909) 979-8408   Emp: 10

- **LUNG CHEONG INTERNATIONAL HOLDINGS**
  1 Lok Yip Rd., Lung Cheong Bldg., On Lok Tsuen, Fanling, New Territories, Hong Kong PRC
  CEO: Lun Leung, Chmn.   Tel: 852-2677-6699   Rev: $99
  Bus: *Distributor of licensed toys and manufacturer of*   Fax: 852-2682-2161   Emp: 6,400
  radio control and electronic toys.   www.e-lci.com
  NAICS: 333315, 334111, 339932, 339999

  > **KID GALAXY, INC.**
  > 1 Sundial Ave., Ste. 310, Manchester, New Hampshire 03103
  > CEO: James Barkley, Pres. & CEO   Tel: (603) 645-6252   %FO: 100
  > Bus: *Bendable toy figures and mini remote control*   Fax: (603) 647-9416   Emp: 15
  > *vehicles manufacture.*

- **MANDARIN ORIENTAL INTERNATIONAL LIMITED**
  281 Gloucester Rd., Causeway Bay, Hong Kong PRC
  CEO: Percy Weatherall, Mng. Dir.   Tel: 852-2895-9288   Rev: $234
  Bus: *Manages high-end hotels.*   Fax: 852-2837-3500   Emp: 3,225
     www.mandarinoriental.com

  NAICS: 721110

  > **KAHALA MANDARIN ORIENTAL**
  > 5000 Kahala Ave., Honolulu, Hawaii 96816
  > CEO: Donald Bowman   Tel: (808) 739-8888
  > Bus: *Manages high-end hotels.*   Fax: (808) 739-8800

  > **MANDARIN ORIENTAL**
  > 80 Columbus Circle at 60th St., New York, New York 10023
  > CEO: Dan Devito, Mgr.   Tel: (212) 805-8800
  > Bus: *Manages high-end hotels.*   Fax: (212) 805-8888

  > **MANDARIN ORIENTAL**
  > 222 Sansome St., San Francisco, California 94104
  > CEO: Wolfgang K. Hultner, CEO   Tel: (415) 276-9888
  > Bus: *Manages high-end hotels.*   Fax: (415) 433-0289   Emp: 220

  > **MANDARIN ORIENTAL**
  > 509 Madison Ave., Ste. 1902, New York, New York 10022
  > CEO: Stasik Baabra, Mgr.   Tel: (212) 752-9710   %FO: 100
  > Bus: *Manages high-end hotels.*   Fax: (212) 207-8886

MANDARIN ORIENTAL
500 Brickell Key Dr., Miami, Florida 33131
CEO: Jorge Gonzales, VP
Bus: *Manages high-end hotels.*
Tel: (305) 913-8288
Fax: (305) 913-8300
%FO: 100

MANDARIN ORIENTAL
1330 Maryland Ave. SW, Washington, District of Columbia 20024
CEO: Derrell Sheaffer, Mgr.
Bus: *Manages high-end hotels.*
Tel: (202) 554-8588
Fax: (202) 554-8999

- **MEGAPOWER ELECTRONICS LTD.**
Harbour Centre Tower 1, 7th Fl., 1 Hok Cheung Street, Hunghom, Kowloon, Hong Kong PRC
CEO: Edmond Chow, Mng. Dir.
Bus: *LCD presentation projectors and display panels manufacture.*
NAICS: 334510
Tel: 852-2773-0292
Fax: 852-2362-4225
www.mega-power.com
Rev: $6
Emp: 100

    MEGAPOWER GRACE DISTRIBUTION INC.
    3353 West Cahuenga Blvd, Los Angeles, California 90068
    CEO: John Harnois, Mgr.
    Bus: *Sales and distribution of projectors.*
    Tel: (323) 876-7888
    Fax: (323) 876-8368

- **MEYER MANUFACTURING COMPANY LTD.**
382 Kwun Tong Rd., Kwun Tong, Kowloon, Hong Kong PRC
CEO: James K. P. Cheng, Chmn.
Bus: *Range-top cookware manufacture.*
NAICS: 332211, 332214
Tel: 852-2797-1288
Fax: 852-2763-5598
www.meyer.com

    MEYER CORPORATION COMPANY
    1 Meyer Plaza, Vallejo, California 94590
    CEO: Stanley K. S. Cheng, CEO
    Bus: *Range-top cookware manufacture and sales.*
    Tel: (707) 551-2800
    Fax: (707) 551-2951
    %FO: 100
    Emp: 210

- **ORIENT OVERSEAS INTERNATIONAL LTD.**
25 Harbour Rd., Harbour Centre 33/F, Wanchai, Hong Kong PRC
CEO: C. C. Tung, Chmn. & Pres. & CEO
Bus: *International steamship transport, freight forwarding.*
NAICS: 237210, 483111, 488310, 488320, 488510, 531110, 531120, 531190, 531390
Tel: 852-2833-3888
Fax: 852-2531-8234
www.ooilgroup.com
Rev: $4,140
Emp: 5,546

    OOCL (USA), INC.
    13831 North West Fwy., Ste. 360, Houston, Texas 77040
    CEO: Peter Sanders
    Bus: *International steamship transport, freight forwarding.*
    Tel: (713) 329-9200
    Fax: (713) 690-6292
    %FO: 100

    OOCL (USA), INC.
    8700 West Bryn Mawr Ave., Chicago, Illinois 60631
    CEO: Eric Witsaman
    Bus: *International steamship transport, freight forwarding.*
    Tel: (773) 399-1030
    Fax: (773) 380-6055
    %FO: 100

OOCL (USA), INC.
6155 Rockside Rd., Cleveland, Ohio 44131
CEO: Kevin Rowe
Bus: *International steamship transport, freight
      forwarding.*

Tel: (216) 901-5460   %FO: 100
Fax: (216) 901-5470

OOCL (USA), INC.
PO Box 5100, San Ramon, California 94583
CEO: Andy Lumley, Pres.
Bus: *International steamship transport, freight
      forwarding.*

Tel: (925) 358-6625   %FO: 100
Fax: (925) 358-6625

OOCL (USA), INC.
111 West Ocean Blvd., Ste. 1800, Long Beach, California 90802
CEO: Andy Lumley, Pres.
Bus: *International steamship transport, freight
      forwarding.*

Tel: (562) 499-2600   %FO: 100
Fax: (562) 435-2750

OOCL (USA), INC.
88 Pine St., 8/F, New York, New York 10005
CEO: Anthony D'Elia, Pres.
Bus: *International steamship transport, freight
      forwarding.*

Tel: (212) 428-2200   %FO: 100
Fax: (212) 428-2297   Emp: 60

● **OUTBLAZE LIMITED**
100 Cyberport Rd., Unit 1106-08, Cyberport 2, Hong Kong PRC
CEO: Yat Siu, CEO
Bus: *Software manufacture and IT services.*

Tel: 852-2534-1222
Fax: 852-2832-7807
www.outblaze.com

NAICS: 511210, 518210, 541512

OUTBLAZE LTD.
10 Marshall St., Old Greenwich, Connecticut 06870
CEO: Stefano Bensi, Mng. Dir.
Bus: *Mfr. of software and IT services and
      provides messaging services.*

Tel: (203) 286-1424   %FO: 100
Fax:

● **PACIFICNET INC.**
11 Sheung Yuet Rd., 601 New Bright Bldg. Room 601, Kowloon Bay, Kowloon, Hong Kong PRC
CEO: Tony C. W. Tong, Chmn. & CEO
Bus: *IT services.*

Tel: 852-2876-2900   Rev: $30
Fax: 852-2793-0689   Emp: 1,000
www.pacificnet.com

NAICS: 423430, 511210, 541511, 541512, 541519, 541618, 561499

PACIFICNET INC.
860 Blue Gentian Rd., Ste. 360, Eagan, Minnesota 55121
CEO: Tony Tong, CEO
Bus: *IT services.*

Tel: (651) 209-3102   %FO: 100
Fax: (651) 209-3103

PACIFICNET INC.
130 West 29th St., 6/F, New York, New York 10001
CEO: Desmond Ng, CEO
Bus: *IT services.*

Tel: (800) 693-8582   %FO: 100
Fax: (646) 349-1096

PACIFICNET INC.
416 Production St., North Aberdeen, South Dakota 57401
CEO: Desmond Ng, CEO   Tel: (605) 229-6678   %FO: 100
Bus: *IT services.*   Fax: (605) 229-0394

● **PCCW LIMITED**
PCCW Tower, Taikoo Place, 979 King's Rd., Quarry Bay 070, Hong Kong PRC
CEO: Richard T.K. Li, Chmn.   Tel: 852-2888-2888   Rev: $2,947
Bus: *Fiber-optic network and Internet services.*   Fax: 852-2877-8877   Emp: 12,450
www.pccw.com
NAICS: 511140, 517110, 517211, 517212, 517910, 518111, 518210, 519190, 541511, 541512, 541513, 541519, 561499

    PCCW LIMITED
    39 Broadway, Ste. 650, New York, New York 10006
    CEO: Alex Arena, CEO   Tel: (212) 389-6268   %FO: 100
    Bus: *Fiber-optic network and Internet services.*   Fax: (212) 389-6263

    PCCW LIMITED
    101 University Ave., Ste.240, Palo Alto, California 94301
    CEO: Alex Arena, CEO   Tel: (650) 687-2002   %FO: 100
    Bus: *Fiber-optic network and Internet services.*   Fax: (650) 687-2018

● **PENINSULA KNITTERS, LIMITED**
538 Castle Peak Rd., 31/F, Peninsula Tower, Cheung Sha Wan, Kowloon, Hong Kong PRC
CEO: Tai Fai Lam, Mng. Prtn.   Tel: 852-2375-0033
Bus: *Engaged in production of textiles and apparel.*   Fax: 852-2317-0017   Emp: 10,000
www.pkl.com.hk
NAICS: 315191, 315192, 424320

    BELFORD, INC.
    575 Fashion Ave., 24/F, New York, New York 10018
    CEO: Jack Fok, Pres.   Tel: (212) 944-2020   %FO: 100
    Bus: *Mfr. knitwear for men and women.*   Fax: (212) 944-0202   Emp: 25

● **PLAYMATES HOLDINGS LIMITED**
100 Canton Rd., Tsimshatsui, Kowloon, Hong Kong PRC
CEO: Shu Sing To, CEO   Tel: 852-2377-7388   Rev: $63
Bus: *Dolls and action figures manufacture.*   Fax: 852-2735-2058   Emp: 100
www.playmatestoys.com
NAICS: 339932

    PLAYMATES TOYS INC.
    600 Anton Blvd., Ste. 611, Costa Mesa, California 92626
    CEO: Lou Novak, Pres.   Tel: (714) 428-2000   %FO: 100
    Bus: *Dolls and action figures manufacture and sales.*   Fax: (714) 428-2220

● **RADICA GAMES LTD.**
2-12 Au Pui Wan St., Ste. V, 6/F, Fo Tan, Hong Kong PRC
CEO: Patrick S. Feely, CEO & Mng. Dir.   Tel: 852-2693-2238   Rev: $123
Bus: *Hand held electronic and mechanical games manufacture.*   Fax: 852-2695-9657   Emp: 4,480
www.radicagames.com
NAICS: 334119, 339932

RADICA USA, INC.
13628-A Beta Rd., Dallas, Texas 75244
CEO: Jeanne M. Olson, Pres.   Tel: (972) 490-4247
Bus: *Sales/distribution of hand held electronic* Fax: (972) 490-0765
    and mechanical games.

● **SHANGHAI COMMERCIAL BANK LTD.**
12 Queen's Rd., Central, Hong Kong PRC
CEO: John Kam-pak Yan, Chmn.   Tel: 852-2841-5415
Bus: *Commercial banking services.*   Fax: 852-2810-4623
                          www.shacombank.com.hk

  NAICS: 522110

    SHANGHAI COMMERCIAL BANK LTD.
    231 Sansome St., San Francisco, California 94104
    CEO: David Kwok, Mgr.   Tel: (415) 433-6700   %FO: 100
    Bus: *International commercial banking services.* Fax: (415) 433-0210   Emp: 25

    SHANGHAI COMMERCIAL BANK LTD.
    125 East 56th St., New York, New York 10022
    CEO: Timothy Chen, Mgr.   Tel: (212) 699-2800   %FO: 100
    Bus: *International commercial banking services.* Fax: (212) 699-2818   Emp: 25

    SHANGHAI COMMERCIAL BANK LTD.
    383 E. Valley Blvd., Alhambra, California 91801
    CEO: C. H. Kao, VP   Tel: (626) 300-8822   %FO: 100
    Bus: *International commercial banking services.* Fax: (626) 293-8833   Emp: 18

● **STAR CRUISES PLC**
Ocean Centre, 5 Canton Rd., Ste. 1501, Tsimshatsui, Kowloon SAR, Hong Kong PRC
CEO: Tan Sri Lim Kok Thay, Chmn. & Pres. & CEO Tel: 852-2378-2000   Rev: $1,636
Bus: *Cruise line.*   Fax: 852-2314-3809   Emp: 14,900
                          www.starcruises.com

  NAICS: 483112, 483114, 488999, 561510, 561520, 561599

    NORWEGIAN CRUISE LINE LIMITED
    7665 Corporate Center Dr., Miami, Florida 33126
    CEO: Colin Veitch, Pres.   Tel: (305) 436-4000   %FO: 100
    Bus: *Cruise line.*   Fax: (305) 436-4126   Emp: 12,000

● **SUNHAM & COMPANY, LTD.**
14 On Lan St., Central, Hong Kong PRC
CEO: A. Yung, Pres.   Tel: 852-2522-8388
Bus: *Mfr. linens.*   Fax:
                          www.sunham.com

  NAICS: 313210, 313230, 314129

    SUNHAM & COMPANY
    308 5th Ave., 2/F, New York, New York 10001
    CEO: Howard Yung, member   Tel: (212) 695-1218   %FO: 100
    Bus: *Home furnishings*   Fax: (212) 947-4793   Emp: 75

- **SWIRE PACIFIC LIMITED**
  88 Queens Way, 35/F, 2 Pacific Place, Central, Hong Kong PRC
  CEO: David M. Turnbull, Chmn.   Tel: 852-2840-8098   Rev: $842
  Bus: *Holding co.; commercial air and sea transport,*   Fax: 852-2526-9365   Emp: 60,400
       food/beverages, real estate & financial services,   www.swirepacific.com
       petroleum exploration, entertainment media.
  NAICS: 312111, 481111, 481112, 488310, 488320, 493190, 531120, 531190

  SWIRE COCA-COLA, USA
  12634 South 265 West, Draper, Utah 84020
  CEO: Jack Pelo, Pres. & CEO   Tel: (801) 816-5300   %FO: 100
  Bus: *Bottler/distributor of beverages.*   Fax: (801) 816-5342   Emp: 1,800

  SWIRE PACIFIC HOLDINGS INC.
  875 South West Temple St., Salt Lake City, Utah 84101
  CEO: David Turnbull, Chmn.   Tel: (801) 530-5300   %FO: 100
  Bus: *Commercial property investment./ Bottling &*   Fax: (801) 530-5342
       distribution.

  SWIRE PROPERTIES, INC.
  501 Brickell Key Dr., Ste. 600, Miami, Florida 33131
  CEO: Stephen Owens, Pres.   Tel: (305) 371-3877   %FO: 100
  Bus: *Property development.*   Fax: (305) 371-9324   Emp: 9

- **TAI PING CARPETS INTERNATIONAL LTD.**
  Tower A, 26/F, Regent Centre, 63 Wo Yi Hop Road, Kwai Chung, Hong Kong PRC
  CEO: James H. Kaplan, CEO   Tel: 852-2818-7668
  Bus: *Mfr. custom carpet and area rugs.*   Fax: 852-2845-9363
                                        www.taipingcarpets.com
  NAICS: 314110

  OPTIONS TAI PING CARPETS INC.
  715 Curtis Pkwy. SE, Calhoun, Georgia 30701
  CEO: Steven Brandon, VP   Tel: (706) 625-8905   %FO: 100
  Bus: *Sales and distribution of carpets.*   Fax: (706) 625-8719

  OPTIONS TAI PING CARPETS INC.
  860 Broadway, New York, New York 10003
  CEO: James Kaplan   Tel: (212) 979-2233   %FO: 100
  Bus: *Sales and distribution of carpets.*   Fax: (212) 979-1921

- **TECHTRONIC INDUSTRIES CO. LTD.**
  388 Castle Peak Rd., CDW Bldg., 24/F, New Territories, Hong Kong PRC
  CEO: Horst J. Pudwill, Chmn. & CEO   Tel: 852-2402-6888   Rev: $2,097
  Bus: *Power tools manufacture.*   Fax: 852-2413-5971   Emp: 21,549
                                        www.ttigroup.com
  NAICS: 333991
  HOMELITE CONSUMER PRODUCTS
  1428 Pearman Dairy Rd., Anderson, South Carolina 29625
  CEO: Horst J. Pudwill, CEO   Tel: (864) 226-6511   %FO: 100
  Bus: *Sale of lawn & garden equipment.*   Fax: (864) 261-9435   Emp: 75

MILWAUKEE ELECTRIC TOOL CORP.
13135 West Lisbon Rd., Brookfield, Wisconsin 53005
CEO: Daniel R. Perry, Pres. & CEO   Tel: (262) 781-3600   %FO: 100
Bus: *Mfr. of industrial machinery, equipment,*   Fax: (262) 781-3611
power tools, hand tools & lawn & garden
equipment.

OWT INDUSTRIES, INC.
256 Pumpkintown Hwy., PO Box 35, Pickens, South Carolina 29671
CEO: Horst Pudwill, Pres.   Tel: (864) 878-6331   %FO: 100
Bus: *Power tools manufacture and sales.*   Fax: (864) 878-7504   Emp: 800

ROYAL APPLIANCE MFG.
7005 Cochran Rd., Glenwillow, Ohio 44139
CEO: Paul R. D'Aloia, Pres.   Tel: (440) 996-2000   %FO: 100
Bus: *Appliance manufacture and sales.*   Fax: (440) 996-2027

TECHTRONIC INDUSTRIES NORTH AMERICA
1428 Pearman Dairy Rd., Anderson, South Carolina 29625
CEO: Horst Pudwell, Chmn.   Tel: (864) 226-6511   %FO: 100
Bus: *Mfr. of power driven hand tools, Sale of*   Fax: (864) 261-9435   Emp: 300
hardware, garden supplies.

● **TELEVISION BROADCASTS LIMITED**
TVB City, 77 Chun Choi St., Tseung Kwan O Industrial Estate, Kowloon, Hong Kong PRC
CEO: Louis Page, Mng. Dir.   Tel: 852-2335-9123   Rev: $426
Bus: *Chinese language television programming.*   Fax: 852-2358-1300   Emp: 5,242
                                        www.tvb.com.hk
  NAICS: 511120, 512110, 512191, 512199, 515120, 515210, 516110

  TVB USA INC.
  12 West 37th St., 5/F, New York, New York 10018
  CEO: Louis Page, Mng. Dir.   Tel: (212) 268-3888   %FO: 100
  Bus: *Chinese language television programming.*   Fax: (212) 268-8831

  TVB USA INC.
  39 Dorman Ave., San Francisco, California 94124
  CEO: Karman Liu, Mgr.   Tel: (415) 282-8228   %FO: 100
  Bus: *Chinese language television programming.*   Fax: (415) 282-8226   Emp: 10

  TVB USA INC.
  15411 Blackburn Ave., Norwalk, California 90650
  CEO: Philip Tan, Pres.   Tel: (562) 802-0220   %FO: 100
  Bus: *Chinese language television programming.*   Fax: (562) 802-5096   Emp: 55

● **TOMMY HILFIGER CORPORATION**
9/F Novel Industrial Bldg., 850 - 870 Lai Chi Kok Rd., Cheung Sha Wan, Kowloon, Hong Kong PRC
CEO: Joel J. Horowitz, Chmn.   Tel: 852-2216-0668   Rev: $1,876
Bus: *Apparel manufacturer*   Fax: 852-2312-1368   Emp: 5,400
                                        www.tommy.com
  NAICS: 315212, 315225

TOMMY HILFIGER USA INC.
25 W. 39th St., New York, New York 10018
CEO: Bob Rosenblah, Pres.
Bus: *Apparel manufacturer*
Tel: (212) 840-8888
Fax: (212) 548-1818
%FO: 100

• **VARITRONIX INTERNATIONAL LIMITED**
22 Chun Cheong St., Tseung Kwan O Industrial Estate, Tseung Kwan O, Hong Kong PRC
CEO: Tony T.H. Tsoi, CEO & Mng. Dir.
Bus: *Mfr. Liquid Crystal Displays (LCD)*
Tel: 852-2197-6000
Fax: 852-2343-9555
www.varitronix.com
Rev: $258
Emp: 4,760

NAICS: 334419

VL ELECTRONICS, INC.
3250 Wilshire Blvd., Ste. 1901, Los Angeles, California 90010
CEO: Chu Cheng Chang, Pres.
Bus: *Sales and distribution of electronics.*
Tel: (213) 738-8700
Fax: (213) 738-5340
%FO: 100
Emp: 12

• **VITASOY INTERNATIONAL HOLDINGS LIMITED**
1 Kin Wong St., Tuen Mun, New Territories, Hong Kong PRC
CEO: Winston Y. Lo, Chmn.
Bus: *Soy food products manufacture.*
Tel: 852-2466-0333
Fax: 852-3465-3441
www.vitasoy.com
Rev: $291
Emp: 2,321

NAICS: 311411, 311823, 311941

VITASOY INTERNATIONAL
1 New England Way, Ayer, Massachusetts 01432
CEO: Robert C. Jones, Pres. & CEO
Bus: *Soy food products manufacture and sales.*
Tel: (978) 772-6880
Fax: (978) 772-6881
%FO: 100
Emp: 217

• **VTECH HOLDINGS LIMITED**
23/F, Tai Ping Industrial Centre, Block 1, 57 Ting Kok Rd.,, New Territories, Hong Kong PRC
CEO: Andy Leung Hon Kwong, Chmn. & CEO
Bus: *Mfr. electronic learning games, toys, pre-
computer educational games and cordless phones.* www.vtech.com.hk
Tel: 852-2680-1000
Fax: 852-2665-5099
Rev: $915
Emp: 19,700

NAICS: 334210, 339932

VTECH COMMUNICATIONS INC.
9590 SW Gemini Dr., Ste. 120, Beaverton, Oregon 97008
CEO: Bruce Garfield
Bus: *Sales/distribution of telephones and
telecommunications equipment.*
Tel: (503) 596-1200
Fax: (503) 644-9887
%FO: 100

VTECH ELECTRONICS NORTH AMERICA
1155 W. Dundee Rd., Arlington Heights, Illinois 60004
CEO: Dennis W. Perry
Bus: *Sales/distribution of electronic learning
games, toys, pre-computer educational
games and cordless phones.*
Tel: (847) 400-3600
Fax: (847) 400-3601
%FO: 100

VTECH OEM INC.
12280 Saratoga-Sunnyvale Rd., Saratoga, California 95070
CEO: Gary Ashford
Bus: *Sales/distribution of telephones and
telecommunications equipment.*
Tel: (408) 252-8550
Fax: (408) 252-8555
%FO: 100

VTECH TELECOM LLC
545 Concord Ave., Ste. 12, Cambridge, Massachusetts 02138
CEO: Rolf Seichter
Bus: *Sales/distribution of telephones.*
Tel: (617) 576-3300
Fax: (617) 576-7753
%FO: 100

• **WING LUNG BANK LTD.**
45 Des Voeux Rd., Central, Hong Kong PRC
CEO: Michael Po-Ko Wu, Dir.
Bus: *Commercial banking services.*
Tel: 852-2826-8333
Fax: 852-2810-0592
www.winglungbank.com
Rev: $600
Emp: 1,250

NAICS: 522110

WING LUNG BANK LTD.
201 East Valley Boulevard, Alhambra, California 91801
CEO: W. K. Cheung
Bus: *International banking services.*
Tel: (213) 489-4193
Fax: (213) 489-3545
%FO: 100

WING LUNG BANK LTD.
445 South Figueroa St., Ste. 2270, Los Angeles, California 90070
CEO: W. K. Cheung
Bus: *International banking services.*
Tel: (213) 489-4193
Fax: (213) 489-3545
%FO: 100

• **WONGS KONG KING INTERNATIONAL**
414 Kwun Tong Rd., WKK Bldg., 2/F, Kowloon, Hong Kong PRC
CEO: Senta Wong, Chmn. & CEO
Bus: *Printed circuit boards manufacture.*
Tel: 852-2357-8888
Fax: 852-2357-8999
www.wkkintl.com

NAICS: 339932, 423620, 423830, 561510, 722211

WKK AMERICA INC.
1307 South Mary Ave., Ste. 201, Sunnyvale, California 94087
CEO: Bruce Bacon, Pres.
Bus: *Mfr./sales of circuit boards.*
Tel: (408) 738-3131
Fax: (408) 738-3166
%FO: 100

• **ZINDART LIMITED**
Flat D, 25/F, Blk. 1, Tai Ping Industrial Centre, 57 Ting Kok Rd., Tai Po NT, Hong Kong PRC
CEO: Peter A. J. Gardiner, Chmn. & CEO
Bus: *Mfr. die-cast and injection-molded toys and collectibles, pop-up books, puzzles and board games.*
Tel: 852-2665-6000
Fax: 852-2664-7066
www.zindart.com
Rev: $95
Emp: 11,175

NAICS: 339932, 339999, 511130

CORGI CLASSIC LTD.
430 West Erie St., Ste. 205, Chicago, Illinois 60610
CEO: David Davenport, Gen. Mgr.
Bus: *sales/distribution of die-cast and injection-molded toys and collectibles, pop-up books, puzzles and board games.*
Tel: (312) 302-9940
Fax:
%FO: 100
Emp: 7

ZINDART LTD., C/O CHINA VEST
160 Sansome St., 18/F, San Francisco, California 94104
CEO: C. Richard Tong, Pres. & CEO   Tel: (415) 276-8888   %FO: 100
Bus: *U.S. office for sales/distribution of die-cast*   Fax: (415) 276-8885
& injection-molded toys & collectibles, pop-
up books, puzzles & board games.

ZINDART, C/O WILLIAM DUNK PARTNERS INC.
251 S. Elliott Rd, Chapel Hill, North Carolina 27514
CEO: William Dunk, Pres.   Tel: (919) 929-4100   %FO: 100
Bus: *U.S. office for sales/distribution of die-cast*   Fax: Emp: 12
& injection-molded toys & collectibles, pop-
up books, puzzles & board games.

Hungary

- **GRAPHISOFT NV**
  Graphisoft Park 1, H-1031 Budapest, Hungary
  CEO: Dominic Gallello, CEO
  Bus: *Develops engineering software.*

  Tel: 36-1-437-3000
  Fax: 36-1-437-3099
  www.graphisoft.com

  Rev: $36
  Emp: 264

  NAICS: 511210

  GRAPHISOFT US INC.
  One Gateway Center, Ste. 302, Newton, Massachusetts 02458
  CEO: Don Henridge, Gen. Mgr.
  Bus: *Mfr. software.*

  Tel: (617) 485-4203
  Fax: (617) 485-4201

  %FO: 100
  Emp: 35

- **HEREND**
  8440 Herend, Kossuth Lajor Str. 140, Budapest, Hungary
  CEO: Robert Somogyi, Gen. Dir.
  Bus: *Hand-painted, porcelain figurines and china manufacture.*

  Tel: 36-88-523-185
  Fax: 36-88-261-518
  www.herend.com

  Emp: 1,550

  NAICS: 327112

  HEREND GUILD INC.
  21440 Pacific Blvd., PO Box 1358, Sterling, Virginia 20167
  CEO: Dianne G. Murphy, Pres.
  Bus: *Mfr. hand-painted, porcelain figurines and china.*

  Tel: (703) 450-1601
  Fax: (703) 450-1605

  Emp: 11

- **HUNGARIAN TELEPHONE AND CABLE CORP.**
  Terez Krt.46, H-1066 Budapest, Hungary
  CEO: Torben Holm, Pres. & CEO
  Bus: *Fixed line telephone services.*

  Tel: 36-47-47-700
  Fax: 36-47-40-350
  www.htcc.hu

  Rev: $69
  Emp: 600

  NAICS: 517110, 517910, 518210, 519190

  HUNGARIAN TELEPHONE AND CABLE CORP.
  1201 Third Ave., Ste. 3400, Seattle, Washington 98101
  CEO: Torben V. Holm, Chmn. & Pres. & CEO
  Bus: *Fixed line telephone services.*

  Tel: (206) 654-0204
  Fax: (206) 652-2911

  %FO: 100
  Emp: 900

- **MALEV HUNGARIAN AIRLINES**
  1097 Konyves Kalman Krt. 12-14, H-1051 Budapest, Hungary
  CEO: Laszlo Sandor, CEO
  Bus: *International airline carrier.*

  Tel: 36-1-235-3535
  Fax:
  www.malev.hu

  Emp: 2,830

  NAICS: 481111

  MALEV HUNGARIAN AIRLINES
  JFK International Airport, Terminal 3, 4/F, Ste. 4088, Jamaica, New York 11430
  CEO: Lalzlo Sandor, CEO
  Bus: *International airline carrier.*

  Tel: (708) 566-9944
  Fax:

  %FO: 100

MALEV HUNGARIAN AIRLINES
90 John St., Ste. 312, New York, New York 10038
CEO: Lalzlo Sandor   Tel: (212) 566-9944   %FO: 100
Bus: *International airline carrier.*   Fax: (212) 566-9950

● **NAGY ES TROCSANYI**
Ugocsa utca 4/B, H-1126 Budapest, Hungary
CEO: Tibor Bogdan, Mng. Prtn.   Tel: 36-1-487-8775
Bus: *International law firm.*   Fax: 36-1-487-8712
                                     www.nagyestrocsanyi.hu
NAICS: 541110
NAGY & TROCSANYI LLP
1114 Ave. of the Americas, New York, New York 10036
CEO: Andre H. Friedman, Mng. Prtn. Tel: (212) 626-4202   %FO: 100
Bus: *International law firm.*   Fax: (212) 626-4208

● **RICHTER GEDEON RT**
Gyomroi ut 19-21, H-1103 Budapest, Hungary
CEO: Andras Rado, Mng. Dir.   Tel: 36-1-431-4000   Rev: $670
Bus: *Mfr. pharmaceuticals.*   Fax: 36-1-260-6650   Emp: 5,619
                                     www.richter.hu
NAICS: 325411, 325412
GEDEON RICHTER USA INC.
1200 E. Ridgewood Ave., East Wing 3/F, Ridgewood, New Jersey 07450
CEO: Tibor Simon   Tel: (201) 445-8300   %FO: 100
Bus: *Mfr. and sales pharmaceuticals.* Fax: (201) 445-4848

Iceland

- **DECODE GENETICS, INC.**
  Sturlugata 8, IS-110 Reykjavik, Iceland
  CEO: Kari Stefansson, CEO
  Bus: *Drug development.*
  Tel: 354-570-1900
  Fax: 354-570-1903
  www.decode.com
  Rev: $42
  Emp: 429

  NAICS: 541710

    BIOSTRUCTURES GROUP
    7869 NE Day Rd., Bainbridge Island, Washington 98110
    CEO: Lance Stewart, VP
    Bus: *Drug development.*
    Tel: (206) 780-8535
    Fax: (206) 780-8549
    %FO: 100

    DECODE GENETICS, INC.
    1000 Winter St., Ste. 3100, Waltham, Massachusetts 02451
    CEO: Axel Nielsen
    Bus: *Drug development.*
    Tel: (781) 466-8833
    Fax: (781) 466-8686
    %FO: 100

    THERMOGEN, INC., DIV. DECODE GENETICS, INC.
    2501 Davey Rd., Woodridge, Illinois 60517
    CEO: Stuart Feinberg, Pres.
    Bus: *Drug development.*
    Tel: (630) 783-4600
    Fax: (630) 783-4646
    %FO: 100

- **THE ICELAND STEAMSHIP COMPANY LTD.**
  2 Korngordum, IS-104 Reykjavik, Iceland
  CEO: Benedikt Sveinsson, Chmn.
  Bus: *Engaged in transportation and investment.*
  Tel: 354-525-7000
  Fax: 354-525-7009
  www.eimskip.is
  Rev: $169
  Emp: 1,200

  NAICS: 483111, 483113, 483212, 484110, 525910

    EIMSKIP USA INC.
    1 Columbus Center, Ste. 500, Virginia Beach, Virginia 23462
    CEO: Annette Simons, Mgr.
    Bus: *Fully integrated transportation, ground operation, warehousing, coastal service, trucking and intermodal transportation.*
    Tel: (757) 627-4444
    Fax: (757) 627-9367
    %FO: 100

- **ICELANDAIR**
  101 Reykjavik Airport, IS-101 Reykjavik, Iceland
  CEO: Jon Karl Olafsson, Pres. & CEO
  Bus: *International passenger air carrier.*
  Tel: 354-505-0300
  Fax: 354-505-0330
  www.icelandair.is
  Rev: $183
  Emp: 1,280

  NAICS: 481111

    ICELANDAIR
    5950 Symphony Woods Rd., Ste. 410, Columbia, Maryland 21044
    CEO: Hlynur Elísson
    Bus: *International passenger air carrier.*
    Tel: (410) 715-1600
    Fax: (410) 715-3547
    %FO: 100

ICELANDAIR
90513 Airport Blvd., Orlando, Florida 32827
CEO: Siturdur Helgason
Bus: *International passenger air carrier.*

Tel: (407) 825-2343
Fax: (407) 825-2343

%FO: 100

• **ICELANDIC GROUP**
Borgartun 27, IS-105 Reykjavik, Iceland
CEO: Thorolfur Arnason, Pres. & CEO
Bus: *Importers and processors of frozen and fresh*

Tel: 354-560-7800
Fax: 354-562-1252
www.icelandic.is

Rev: $1,095
Emp: 2,769

NAICS: 114111, 311712, 424460

    ICELANDIC USA
    904 Woods Rd., Cambridge, Maryland 21613
    CEO: Jay Brooks, VP
    Bus: *Mfr. fresh/frozen fish*

    Tel: (410) 228-7500
    Fax: (410) 228-9222

    ICELANDIC USA
    60 Commercial St., Everett, Massachusetts 02149
    CEO: Rick Gordon
    Bus: *Storage of seafood*

    Tel: (617) 387-2050
    Fax: (617) 387-2249

    ICELANDIC USA
    501 Merritt 7, Norwalk, Connecticut 06851
    CEO: Magnus Gustafsson, Pres.
    Bus: *Frozen packaged seafood*

    Tel: (203) 852-1600
    Fax: (203) 866-4871

    Emp: 600

    ICELANDIC USA CORP.
    190 Enterprise Dr., Newport News, Virginia 23603
    CEO: Aevar Agnarsson, Pres. & CEO
    Bus: *Seafood product preparation & packaging*

    Tel: (757) 820-4000
    Fax: (757) 888-6250

    %FO: 100
    Emp: 800

• **KAUPTHING BUNADARBANKI**
Borgartun 19, IS-105 Reykjavik, Iceland
CEO: Hreidar Mar Sigurdsson, CEO
Bus: *Banking services.*

Tel: 354-525-6000
Fax: 354-525-6009
www.kaupthing.com

Rev: $1
Emp: 1,606

NAICS: 522110, 523110

    KAUPTHING NEW YORK
    230 Park Ave., Ste.1528, New York, New York 10169
    CEO: Robert Gibbons, Pres.
    Bus: *Banking services.*

    Tel: (212) 457-8700
    Fax: (212) 457-8725

    %FO: 100

• **MAREL HF**
9 Austurhraun 9, IS-210 Gardabaer, Iceland
CEO: Benedikt Sveinsson, Dir.
Bus: *Mfr. automation systems for the food industry;*
weighing and vision equipment and automatic
portioning machines for fish and meat industry.

Tel: 354-563-8000
Fax: 354-563-8001
www.marel.is

Rev: $79
Emp: 460

NAICS: 333111, 333294, 333997

MAREL USA
9745 Widmer Rd., Lenexa, Kansas 66215
CEO: Elinar Einarsson, Pres.   Tel: (913) 888-9110   %FO: 100
Bus: *Sales/distribution of weighing and portioning* Fax: (913) 888-9124   Emp: 36
     machines for fish and meat industry.

● **OSSUR**
Grjothals 5, IS-110 Reykjavik, Iceland
CEO: Jon Sigurdsson, Pres. & CEO   Tel: 354-515-1300
Bus: *Develop and manufacture prosthetic aids.*   Fax: 354-515-1366   Emp: 900
                               www.ossur.is
NAICS: 339112, 339113
    OSSUR NORTH AMERICA
    27412 Aliso Viejo Pkwy., Aliso Viejo, California 92656
    CEO: Eythor Bender, Pres.   Tel: (949) 362-3883   %FO: 100
    Bus: *Sales/distribution of prosthetic aids.* Fax: (949) 362-3888   Emp: 110

India

- **24/7 CUSTOMER INC.**
  1st Fl., Creator, International Tech Park, Whitefield, Bangalore 560 066, India
  CEO: P. V. Kannan, CEO
  Bus: *Voice mail and email based customer support services.*
  NAICS: 517910

  Tel: 91-80-841-0775
  Fax: 91-80-841-1787
  www.247customer.com

  > **24/7 CUSTOMER INC.**
  > 720 University Ave., Los Gatos, California 95032
  > CEO: Kathy Juve, Sales
  > Bus: *Voice mail and email based, customer service support services.*
  >
  > Tel: (408) 399-6205
  > Fax: (408) 399-5635
  >
  > %FO: 100

- **AIR INDIA LIMITED**
  Air India Building, Nariman Point, Mumbai 400 021, India
  CEO: V. Thulasidas, CEO
  Bus: *Air transport services.*
  NAICS: 481111

  Tel: 91-22-2279-6666
  Fax: 91-22-2202-1096
  www.airindia.com

  > **AIR INDIA**
  > 33 North Dearborn St., Chicago, Illinois 60602-3186
  > CEO: Rumy Khariwala
  > Bus: *Air transport services.*
  >
  > Tel: (312) 782-6263
  > Fax: (312) 782-6263
  >
  > %FO: 100

  > **AIR INDIA**
  > 14760 175th St., Jamaica, New York 11434
  > CEO: G. Kharat
  > Bus: *Air transport services.*
  >
  > Tel: (718) 632-0159
  > Fax: (718) 632-0159
  >
  > %FO: 100

  > **AIR INDIA**
  > 570 Lexington Ave., New York, New York 10022
  > CEO: M. Metz
  > Bus: *Air transport services.*
  >
  > Tel: (212) 407-1400
  > Fax: (212) 407-1400
  >
  > %FO: 100

  > **AIR INDIA**
  > 1612 K St. NW, Ste. 200, Washington, District of Columbia 20006-2805
  > CEO: G. T. Shivdasani
  > Bus: *Air transport services.*
  >
  > Tel: (202) 785-8770
  > Fax: (202) 785-8770
  >
  > %FO: 100

  > **AIR INDIA**
  > 5959 W. Century Blvd., Ste. 914, Los Angeles, California 90045
  > CEO: Lalit Kapur
  > Bus: *Air transport services.*
  >
  > Tel: (310) 348-5122
  > Fax: (310) 338-8481
  >
  > %FO: 100

- **ALLSEC TECHNOLOGIES LTD.**
  46B, Velachery Main Rd., Velachery, Chennai 600 042, India
  CEO: Ramamoorthy Jagadish, CEO
  Bus: *Outsourced business IT support services.*

  Tel: 91-44-2244-7070
  Fax: 91-44-2244-7077
  www.allsectech.com

  NAICS: 541513

  > **ALLSECTECH INC.**
  > 5 Independence Way, Princeton, New Jersey 08540
  > CEO: Rafael A. Martinez
  > Bus: *Outsourced business IT support services.*
  >
  > Tel: (609) 514-5189
  > Fax: (609) 452-8464
  >
  > %FO: 100

  > **ALLSECTECH INC.**
  > 3308 Chastain Landings Ct., Marietta, Georgia 30066
  > CEO: Rafael A. Martinez
  > Bus: *Outsourced business IT support services.*
  >
  > Tel: (770) 429-2744
  > Fax: (770) 429-7795
  >
  > %FO: 100

- **BANK OF BARODA**
  Suraj Plaza-1, Sayaji Ganj, Baroda 390005, India
  CEO: Dr. Anil K. Khandelwal, Chmn.
  Bus: *Commercial banking services.*

  Tel: 91-265-236-1852
  Fax: 91-265-236-2395
  www.bankofbaroda.com

  Rev: $1,269
  Emp: 45,900

  NAICS: 522110

  > **BANK OF BARODA**
  > One Park Ave., New York, New York 10016
  > CEO: A .D. Parulkar, CEO
  > Bus: *Banking services.*
  >
  > Tel: (212) 578-4550
  > Fax: (212) 578-4565
  >
  > %FO: 100

- **BANK OF INDIA**
  Star House, C - 5, "G" Block, Kurla Complex, Bandra East, Mumbai 400 051, India
  CEO: M. Venugopalan, CEO
  Bus: *Commercial banking services.*

  Tel: 91-22-5668-4444
  Fax: 91-22-5668-4444
  www.bankofindia.com

  NAICS: 522110, 522293

  > **BANK OF INDIA**
  > 555 California St., Ste. 4646, San Francisco, California 94104
  > CEO: Dr. Manoj Das
  > Bus: *Commercial banking services.*
  >
  > Tel: (415) 956-6326
  > Fax: (415) 956-6328
  >
  > %FO: 100

  > **BANK OF INDIA**
  > 277 Park Ave., New York, New York 10172
  > CEO: Anil Shah
  > Bus: *Commercial banking services.*
  >
  > Tel: (212) 753-6100
  > Fax: (212) 753-6100
  >
  > %FO: 100

- **BHARAT ELECTRONICS LTD.**
  25 MG Rd., 2nd Fl., Bangalore 560 001, India
  CEO: Y. Gopala Rao, Chmn.
  Bus: *Mfr. semiconductor devices, communication and
  radar systems.*

  Tel: 91-80-559-5001
  Fax: 91-80-558-4911
  www.bel-india.com

  Emp: 16,000

  NAICS: 334413, 334515

BHARAT ELECTRONICS LTD.
53 Hilton Ave., Garden City, New York 11530
CEO: K. Prakash
Bus: *Procurement of electronic components and export to India for in-house use.*

Tel: (516) 248-4020
Fax: (516) 741-5894

%FO: 100
Emp: 7

• **CROMPTON GREAVES LIMITED**
6th Fl., CG House, Dr. Annie Besant Road, Prabhadevi, Mumbai 400 025, India
CEO: S. M. Trehan, CEO
Bus: *Electronic products systems manufacture. (JV of Paxonet Communications USA)*
NAICS: 335999

Tel: 91-22-2423-7777
Fax: 91-22-2423-7788
www.cglonline.com

Rev: $401
Emp: 150

PAXONET COMMUNICATIONS INC.
4046 Clipper Ct., Fremont, California 94538
CEO: Chetan V. Sanghvi
Bus: *Developer of communication ICs and IP Cores.*

Tel: (510) 770-2277
Fax: (510) 770-2288

%FO: JV

• **DATAMATICS TECHNOLOGIES LTD.**
Unit 117-120, SDF4, Seepz, Andheri East, Mumbai, India
CEO: Manish Modi, CEO
Bus: *IT outsourcing services.*

Tel: 91-22-2829-0829
Fax: 91-22-2829-1673
www.datamaticstech.com

NAICS: 541512, 541513, 541519

DATAMATICS AMERICA INC.
31557 Schoolcraft Rd., Livonia, Michigan 48150-
CEO: Barry Lemay
Bus: *IT outsourcing services.*

Tel: (734) 525-4400
Fax: (734) 525-4400

%FO: 100

• **DR. REDDY'S LABORATORIES LIMITED**
7-1-27 Ameerpet, Andhra Pradesh, Hyderabad 500 016, India
CEO: K. Anji Reddy, Chmn.
Bus: *Mfr. pharmaceuticals*

Tel: 91-40-373-1946
Fax: 91-40-373-1955
www.drreddys.com

Rev: $464
Emp: 6,155

NAICS: 325411

DR. REDDY'S LABORATORIES LIMITED
200 Somerset Corp. Blvd., Bridgewater, New Jersey 08807
CEO: Jeffrey Wasserstein, EVP
Bus: *Manufacturer pharmaceuticals*

Tel: (908) 203-4900
Fax: (908) 203-4940

%FO: 100

DR. REDDY'S LABORATORIES LIMITED
355 Crestmont Dr., Fort Mill, South Carolina 29708
CEO: Mark Hartman, EVP
Bus: *Manufacturer pharmaceuticals*

Tel: (803) 802-1131
Fax: (866) 733-3939

%FO: 100

REDDY US THERAPEUTICS INC.
3065 Northwoods Circle, Norcross, Georgia 30071-1542
CEO:
Bus: *Manufacturer pharmaceuticals*

Tel: (770) 446-9500
Fax: (770) 446-1950

%FO: 100

- **EIH LTD.**
  7 Sham Nath Marg, Delhi 110 054, India
  CEO: P.R.S. Oberoi, Chmn.
  Bus: *Develops and manages hotel properties.*

  Tel: 91-112-389-0505
  Fax: 91-112-389-0582
  www.oberoihotels.com

  Rev: $700
  Emp: 12,000

  NAICS: 487210, 721110

  ### OBEROI GROUP OF HOTELS
  509 Madison Ave., Ste. 1906, New York, New York 10017
  CEO: Ketaki Narain, PR
  Bus: *Sales and bookings of hotel properties outside of the US.*

  Tel: (212) 223-8800
  Fax: (212) 223-8500

  %FO: 100
  Emp: 4

- **EPICENTER TECHNOLOGIES**
  Sigma, 10th Fl., Hirandanani Gardens, Powai, Mumbai 400-076, India
  CEO: Raj Thankappan, CEO
  Bus: *Call center technology services.*

  Tel: 91-22-570-5666
  Fax: 91-22-570-5039
  www.epicentertechnology.com

  NAICS: 561422

  ### EPICENTER TECHNOLOGIES
  11840 Nicholas St., Ste. 205, Omaha, Nebraska 68165
  CEO: Sylvia Hynes
  Bus: *Call center technology services.*

  Tel: (402) 493-1775
  Fax: (402) 493-0855

  %FO: 100

- **ESSEL PROPACK LIMITED**
  135, Continental Bldg., Dr. Annie Besant Rd, Worli, Mumbai 400 018, India
  CEO: Ashok Kumar Goel, Mng. Dir.
  Bus: *Specialty packaging*

  Tel: 91-22-2493-3280
  Fax: 91-22-2496-3137
  www.ep.esselgroup.com

  NAICS: 322214, 322215

  ### ESSEL PROPACK AMERICA LLC
  187 Cane Creek Blvd., Danville, Virginia 24540
  CEO: Anna Soden, Dir. Sales
  Bus: *Specialty packaging*

  Tel: (434) 822-8007
  Fax: (434) 822-8043

  %FO: 100

- **EXIMSOFT TECHNOLOGIES PVT. LTD.**
  63-B, 13th Cross, Bangalore 560 078, India
  CEO: PN Karanth, CEO
  Bus: *Knowledge management software manufacture.*

  Tel: 91-80-658-0466
  Fax: 91-80-658-3522
  www.eximsoft.com

  NAICS: 511210, 541511

  ### EXIMSOFT TECHNOLOGIES
  8995 Briarglen Rd., Eden Prairie, Minnesota 55347
  CEO: Rao Nagabhushan
  Bus: *Knowledge management software manufacture and sales.*

  Tel: (952) 906-0288
  Fax: (952) 906-0288

  %FO: 100

- **FOUR SOFT LTD.**
  5Q1A3, Cyber Towers, Hitec City, Madhapur, Hyderabad 500033, India
  CEO: Palem Srikanth Reddy, Chmn.
  Bus: *Information technology services and enterprise application integration services.*
  Tel: 91-40-2310-0600
  Fax: 91-40-2310-0602
  www.four-soft.com
  Rev: $150
  Emp: 1,270
  NAICS: 541511, 541512, 541519

  FOUR SOFT USA INC.
  538 Broadhollow Rd., Ste. 420E, Melville, New York 11747
  CEO: Alice Sciara
  Bus: *Engaged in information technology services.*
  Tel: (631) 752-7700
  Fax: (631) 752-7829
  %FO: 100

  FOUR SOFT USA INC.
  180 S. Western Ave., Carpentersville, Illinois 60110
  CEO: Jim Flanagan
  Bus: *Engaged in information technology services.*
  Tel: (847) 551-9563
  Fax: (847) 551-9563
  %FO: 100

  FOUR SOFT USA INC.
  1 Lincoln Blvd., Ste. 301, Rouses Point, New York 12979
  CEO: Linda Watson
  Bus: *Engaged in information technology services.*
  Tel: (518) 297-2047
  Fax: (518) 297-2680
  %FO: 100

- **HCL TECHNOLOGIES LTD.**
  A-10/11, Sector 3, Noida, Uttar Pradesh 201 301, India
  CEO: Shiv Nadar, Chmn. & CEO
  Bus: *IT consulting services.*
  Tel: 91-120-252-0917
  Fax: 91-120-253-0591
  www.hcltechnologies.com
  Rev: $568
  Emp: 16,358
  NAICS: 541511, 541512, 541519

  HCL TECHNOLOGIES
  1950 Old Gallows Rd., Ste. 555, Vienna, Virginia 22182
  CEO: James Devy, CEO
  Bus: *Business services.*
  Tel: (703) 891-0400
  Fax: (703) 891-0401
  %FO: 100
  Emp: 10

  HCL TECHNOLOGIES
  330 Potrero Ave., Sunnyvale, California 94086
  CEO: Raj Sirohi, Pres.
  Bus: *IT consulting services.*
  Tel: (408) 733-0480
  Fax: (408) 733-0482
  %FO: 100
  Emp: 871

  HCL TECHNOLOGIES
  25 Vreeland Rd., Bldg. B, Ste. 101, Florham Park, New Jersey 07932
  CEO: Padep Nair, Mgr.
  Bus: *Software consultant.*
  Tel: (973) 443-9690
  Fax: (973) 443-9692
  %FO: 100
  Emp: 10

  HCL TECHNOLOGIES
  1920 Main St., Ste. 225, Irvine, California 92614
  CEO: Subrat Mishra, Mgr.
  Bus: *Business consulting services.*
  Tel: (949) 863-3151
  Fax: (919) 863-3156
  %FO: 100
  Emp: 25

  HCL TECHNOLOGIES
  1400 Opus Place, Ste.650, Downers Grove, Illinois 60515
  CEO: Ramesh Pilai
  Bus: *Business services.*
  Tel: (630) 541-2451
  Fax: (630) 541-2450
  %FO: 100

HCL TECHNOLOGIES
100 West Big Beaver Rd., Ste. 200, Troy, Michigan 48084
CEO: Shiv Nadar   Tel: (248) 526-0568   %FO: 100
Bus: *Business services.*   Fax: (248) 526-0570

HCL TECHNOLOGIES
1055 Washington Blvd., 4/F, Stamford, Connecticut 06901
CEO: Ramesh Pilai, Mgr.   Tel: (203) 326-3000   %FO: 100
Bus: *Business services.*   Fax: (203) 462-3368

HCL TECHNOLOGIES
2601 Network Blvd., Ste. 400, Frisco, Texas 75034
CEO: Shiv Nadar   Tel: (972) 334-9733   %FO: 100
Bus: *Business services.*   Fax: (972) 334-9734

HCL TECHNOLOGIES
800 Bellevue Way NE, 4/F, Bellevue, Washington 98004
CEO: Shiv Nadar   Tel: (425) 646-2390   %FO: 100
Bus: *Business services.*   Fax: (425) 646-2391

HCL TECHNOLOGIES
11001 West 120th Ave., Ste. 400, Broomfield, Colorado 80021
CEO: Shiv Nadar   Tel: (303) 410-4297   %FO: 100
Bus: *Business services.*   Fax: (303) 410-4597

HCL TECHNOLOGIES
1400 Opus Place, Ste. 650, Downers Grove, Illinois 60515
CEO: Shiv Nadar   Tel: (630) 541-2451   %FO: 100
Bus: *Business services.*   Fax: (630) 541-2450

HCL TECHNOLOGIES
406 Farmington Ave., Ste. 1009, Farmington, Connecticut 06032
CEO: Ramesh Pilai, Gen. Mgr.   Tel: (860) 676-7759   %FO: 100
Bus: *Business services.*   Fax: (860) 676-7704

• **HEXAWARE TECHNOLOGIES, INC.**
  Millennium Business Park, Bldg. 152, TTC Industrial Area, Sector "A" Block, Mahape, Navi, Mumbai 400 701,
India
  CEO: Rusi Brij, Chmn. & CEO   Tel: 91-22-559-19-595   Rev: $77
  Bus: *Software services.*   Fax: 91-22-559-19-500   Emp: 2,343
                                           www.hexaware.com
    NAICS: 518210, 541511, 541512, 541513, 541519, 611420

HEXAWARE TECHNOLOGIES, INC.
792 South Main St., Ste. 206, Mansfield, Massachusetts 02048
CEO: Hari Murthy, Pres.   Tel: (508) 339-8162   %FO: 100
Bus: *Software services.*   Fax: (508) 339-9527

HEXAWARE TECHNOLOGIES, INC.
4343 Commerce Ct., Ste. 500, Lisle, Illinois 60532
CEO: Raj Padmaraj, Mgr.   Tel: (630) 955-0912   %FO: 100
Bus: *Software services.*   Fax: (630) 955-0997

HEXAWARE TECHNOLOGIES, INC.
1095 Cranbury South River Rd., Ste. 10, Jamesburg, New Jersey 08831
CEO: Rusi Brij, Mgr.   Tel: (609) 409-6950   %FO: 100
Bus: *Software services.*   Fax: (609) 409-6910   Emp: 350

HEXAWARE TECHNOLOGIES, INC.
1200 Abernathy Rd., Ste. 1700, Atlanta, Georgia 30328
CEO: Hari Murthy, Pres.   Tel: (770) 350-2676   %FO: 100
Bus: *Software services.*   Fax: (770) 551-8105

HEXAWARE TECHNOLOGIES, INC.
2591 Dallas Pkwy., Ste. 300, Frisco, Texas 75034
CEO: Hari Murthy, Pres.   Tel: (972) 731-4339   %FO: 100
Bus: *Software services.*   Fax:

HEXAWARE TECHNOLOGIES, INC.
2290 North First St., Ste. 204, San Jose, California 95131
CEO: Anurag Gupta, Mgr.   Tel: (408) 473-0400   %FO: 100
Bus: *Software services.*   Fax: (408) 473-0400

- **ICICI BANK LIMITED**
ICICI Bank Towers, Bandra-Kurla Complex, Mumbai 400051, India
CEO: Kundapur v. Kamath, CEO   Tel: 91-22-2653-1414   Rev: $2,896
Bus: *Commercial bank services.*   Fax: 91-22-2653-1167   Emp: 18,942
                                        www.icicibank.com
NAICS: 522110, 522293
  ICICI BANK NEW YORK
  500 Fifth Ave., Ste. 2830, New York, New York 10110
  CEO: Shri Madhav Kalyan, Mgr.   Tel: (646) 827-8484   %FO: 100
  Bus: *Commercial banking services.*   Fax: (646) 827-8435

- **IGATE GLOBAL SOLUTIONS LIMITED**
No. 1 Main Rd., Jakkasandra, Karnataka, Bangalore 560 034, India
CEO: Ashok Trivedi, Chmn.   Tel: 91-80-552-1701   Rev: $88
Bus: *Customs application software manufacture.* Fax: 91-80-552-1704 Emp: 1,700
                                        www.igate.com
NAICS: 541511, 541512, 541519
  IGATE CORPORATION
  1000 Commerce Dr., Ste. 500, Pittsburgh, Pennsylvania 15275
  CEO: Sunil Wadhwani, Chmn. & CEO   Tel: (412) 787-2100   %FO: 100
  Bus: *Customs application software manufacture* Fax: (412) 494-9272 Emp: 4,980
     and sales.

  IGATE CORPORATION
  2595 North Dallas Pkwy., Ste. 102, Frisco, Texas 75034
  CEO: Scott Solomon, Mgr.   Tel: (972) 377-7400   %FO: 100
  Bus: *Customs application software manufacture* Fax: (972) 377-7411
     and sales.

IGATE CORPORATION
6528 Kaiser Dr., Fremont, California 94555
CEO: Ashok Trivedi, Pres.
Bus: *Customs application software manufacture and sales.*
Tel: (510) 896-3000
Fax: (510) 896-3010
%FO: 100

IGATE MASTECH
1000 Commerce Dr., Ste. 500, Pittsburgh, Pennsylvania 15275
CEO: Steven J. Shangold, Pres.
Bus: *Provides information technology consulting & staffing augmentation services.*
Tel: (412) 787-2100
Fax: (412) 494-9272
%FO: 100
Emp: 1,225

● **INFINITE COMPUTER SOLUTIONS PVT.**
UG 7-9, Mohta Bldg., 4 Bhikaji Cama Place, New Delhi 110 066, India
CEO: Sanjay Govil, Chmn. & Pres.
Bus: *Computer solution services.*
Tel: 91-11-2616-8863
Fax: 91-11-2616-8875
www.consult-ics.com
Rev: $70
Emp: 1,050

NAICS: 541511, 541512, 541519

INFINITE COMPUTER SOLUTIONS INC.
3371 Brunswick Pike, Lawrence Commons, Ste. 116, Lawrenceville, New Jersey 08648
CEO: Upinder Zutshi
Bus: *Computer solution services.*
Tel: (609) 716-8600
Fax: (609) 716-8160
%FO: 100

INFINITE COMPUTER SOLUTIONS INC.
20250 Century Blvd., Germantown, Maryland 20874
CEO: Sanjay Govil, Pres.
Bus: *Computer solution services.*
Tel: (301) 944-1100
Fax: (301) 528-9040
%FO: 100
Emp: 300

INFINITE COMPUTER SOLUTIONS INC.
329 Bailey Ridge Dr., Morrisville, North Carolina 27560
CEO: John Laskey, Principal
Bus: *Computer solution services.*
Tel: (919) 678-1228
Fax: (919) 678-8027
%FO: 100

INFINITE COMPUTER SOLUTIONS INC.
3140 Dela Cruz Blvd., Ste. 108, Santa Clara, California 95054
CEO: Upinder Zutshi
Bus: *Computer solution services.*
Tel: (408) 855-9616
Fax: (408) 855-9490
%FO: 100

INFINITE COMPUTER SOLUTIONS INC.
1303 West Walnut Hill Lane, Ste. 225 & 301, Irving, Texas 75038
CEO: Upinder Zutshi
Bus: *Computer solution services.*
Tel: (214) 687-9200
Fax: (214) 687-9201
%FO: 100

INFINITE COMPUTER SOLUTIONS INC.
906 Highland St., Holliston, Massachusetts 01746
CEO: Upinder Zutshi
Bus: *Computer solution services.*
Tel: (508) 429-3233
Fax: (508) 429-6296
%FO: 100

INFINITE COMPUTER SOLUTIONS INC.
17 Mystic Way, Stoneybrook, New York 11790
CEO: Upinder Zutshi
Bus: *Computer solution services.*
Tel: (516) 883-3402
Fax:
%FO: 100

INFINITE COMPUTER SOLUTIONS INC.
3923 30th St. SE, Ruskin, Florida 33570
CEO: Upinder Zutshi   Tel: (813) 299-9939   %FO: 100
Bus: *Computer solution services.*   Fax:

INFINITE COMPUTER SOLUTIONS INC.
108 Powers Ct., Ste. 225, Sterling, Virginia 20166
CEO: Upinder Zutshi   Tel: (703) 575-7399   %FO: 100
Bus: *Computer solution services.*   Fax:

INFINITE COMPUTER SOLUTIONS INC.
8600 Hidden River Pkwy., Ste. 500, Tampa, Florida 33637
CEO: Upinder Zutshi   Tel: (813) 977-8883   %FO: 100
Bus: *Computer solution services.*   Fax:

INFINITE COMPUTER SOLUTIONS INC.
50 South St., Trumansburg, New York 14886
CEO: Upinder Zutshi   Tel: (607) 387-5156   %FO: 100
Bus: *Computer solution services.*   Fax:

● **INFOSYS TECHNOLOGY LIMITED**
Electronics City, Hosur Rd., Karnataka, Bangalore 560 100, India
CEO: N. R. Narayana Murthy, Chmn.   Tel: 91-80-2852-0261   Rev: $1,592
Bus: *Develops software products and provides*   Fax: 91-80-2852-0362   Emp: 36,800
   software services.   www.infosys.com
NAICS: 541511, 541512, 541513, 541519, 541611, 541614

INFOSYS TECHNOLOGY LTD.
205 108th Ave., NE, Ste. 550, Bellevue, Washington 98004
CEO: Pradep Prbhu, Mgr.   Tel: (425) 452-5300   %FO: 100
Bus: *Develops software products and provides*   Fax: (425) 452-8440
   software services.

INFOSYS TECHNOLOGY LTD.
Two Adams Place, Quincy, Massachusetts 02169
CEO: Paul Cole, Mgr.   Tel: (781) 356-3100   %FO: 100
Bus: *Develops software products and provides*   Fax: (781) 356-3150
   software services.

INFOSYS TECHNOLOGY LTD.
6100 Tennyson Pkwy., Ste. 200, Plano, Texas 75024
CEO: Romil Bahl   Tel: (469) 229-9400   %FO: 100
Bus: *Develops software products and provides*   Fax: (469) 229-9598   Emp: 2
   software services.

INFOSYS TECHNOLOGY LTD.
2300 Cabot Dr., Ste. 250, Lisle, Illinois 60532
CEO: Stephen Pratt   Tel: (630) 482-5000   %FO: 100
Bus: *Develops software products and provides*   Fax: (630) 505-9144
   software services.

INFOSYS TECHNOLOGY LTD.
2 Connell Dr., Ste. 4100, Berkeley Heights, New Jersey 07922
CEO: Shobha Meera, Mgr.   Tel: (908) 286-3100   %FO: 100
Bus: *Develops software products and provides*   Fax: (908) 286-3125
   software services.

INFOSYS TECHNOLOGY LTD.
10851 N. Black Canyon Fwy., Ste. 830, Phoenix, Arizona 85029
CEO: Stephen Pratt   Tel: (602) 944-4855   %FO: 100
Bus: *Develops software products and provides*   Fax: (602) 944-4879
     software services.

INFOSYS TECHNOLOGY LTD.
6607 Kaiser Dr., Fremont, California 94555
CEO: Stephen Pratt   Tel: (510) 742-3000   %FO: 100
Bus: *Develops software products and provides*   Fax: (510) 742-3090
     software services.

INFOSYS TECHNOLOGY LTD.
900 West Trade St., Ste. 750, Charlotte, North Carolina 28202
CEO: Stephen Pratt   Tel: (704) 264-1535
Bus: *Prepackaged software services*   Fax: (704) 264-1600   Emp: 2

INFOSYS TECHNOLOGY LTD.
1 Spectrum Pointe, Ste. 350, Lake Forest, California 92630
CEO: Raj Joshi, Mgr.   Tel: (949) 206-8400   %FO: 100
Bus: *Custom computer programming*   Fax: (949) 206-8499

INFOSYS TECHNOLOGY LTD.
12021 Sunset Hill Rd., Ste. 340, Reston, Virginia 20190
CEO: Stephen Pratt   Tel: (703) 481-3880
Bus: *Develops software products and provides*   Fax: (703) 481-3889
     software services.

INFOSYS TECHNOLOGY LTD.
400 Galleria Pkwy., Ste. 1490, Atlanta, Georgia 30339
CEO: Stephen Pratt   Tel: (770) 980-7955   %FO: 100
Bus: *Develops software products and provides*   Fax: (770) 980-7956
     software services.

● **INTERTEC COMMUNICAITONS LTD**
28 Shankar Mutt Rd., Karnataka, Bangalore 560 004, India
CEO: T. S. Ravi Chandar, Chmn. & CEO   Tel: 91-80-661-4706
Bus: *Application management software.*   Fax: 91-80-661-2075
                                        www.intertec1.com
NAICS: 511210, 541511, 541512, 541513, 541519, 611420

    INTERTEC AMERICA INC.
    425 Market St., Ste. 400, San Francisco, California 94105
    CEO: Lisa Thompson, Pres.   Tel: (415) 836-0656   %FO: 100
    Bus: *Application management software.*   Fax: (415) 284-1125

● **ITC INFOTECH INDIA LTD.**
Virginia House, 37, JL Nehru Rd., Kolkata 700 071, India
CEO: Anup Singh, Chmn.   Tel: 91-33-2288-1778
Bus: *IT services.*   Fax: 91-33-2288-2254
                                        www.itcinfotech.com
NAICS: 423430, 518210, 541511, 541512, 541513, 541519, 611420, 811212, 811213

ITC INFOTECH USA INC.
600 Alexander Park, Ste. 203, Princeton, New Jersey 08540
CEO: Ashwani Rishi, CEO   Tel: (609) 419-1110   %FO: 100
Bus: *IT services.*   Fax: (609) 419-1183   Emp: 28

ITC INFOTECH USA INC.
15255 North Frank Lloyd Wright Blvd., Apt. 1122, Scottsdale, Arizona 85260
CEO: Ashwani Rishi, CEO   Tel: (602) 743-9976   %FO: 100
Bus: *IT services.*   Fax:

ITC INFOTECH USA INC.
10440 Little Patuxent Pkwy., Ste. 935, Columbia, Maryland 21044
CEO: Ashwani Rishi, CEO   Tel: (410) 884-4093   %FO: 100
Bus: *IT services.*   Fax: (410) 884-4001

ITC INFOTECH USA INC.
2880 Zanker Rd., San Jose, California 95134
CEO: Avinash Bhokare, Mgr.   Tel: (408) 432-7284   %FO: 100
Bus: *IT services.*   Fax: (408) 432-7235

• **KPIT CUMMINS INFOSYSTEMS LIMITED**
KPIT House, Tejas Society, Kothrud Pune, Maharashtra 411 038, India
CEO: S. B. Ravi Pandit, Chmn. & CEO   Tel: 91-20-538-2358   Rev: $28
Bus: *Software development and maintenance systems.* Fax: 91-20-538-1141   Emp: 950
                                           www.kpitcummins.com
NAICS: 518210, 541511, 541512, 541513, 541519, 611420, 811212, 811213, 811219

   KPIT INFOSYSTEMS INC.
   33 Wood Ave., Iselin, New Jersey 08830
   CEO: Sachin Tikekar, COO   Tel: (732) 321-0921   %FO: 100
   Bus: *Customized software development.* Fax: (732) 321-0922

   KPIT INFOSYSTEMS INC.
   Techmart Center, 5201 Great America Pkwy., Ste. 457, Santa Clara, California 95054
   CEO: Myles O'Connor, Dir.   Tel: (408) 330-0910   %FO: 100
   Bus: *Customized software development.* Fax: (408) 330-0914

• **MASCON GLOBAL LIMITED**
4 Padma Complex, 320 Anna Salai, Chennai 600 035, India
CEO: Nandu Thondavadi, CEO   Tel: 91-44-2431-3101   Rev: $50
Bus: *IT consulting services.*   Fax: 91-44-2434-9330   Emp: 1,000
                                           www.masconit.com
NAICS: 541511, 541512, 541519, 611420

   MASCON GLOBAL LIMITED
   1699 E. Woodfield Rd., Ste. 200, Schaumburg, Illinois 60173
   CEO: Srini Sundaram, Mng. Prtn.   Tel: (847) 619-5005   %FO: 100
   Bus: *IT consulting services.*   Fax: (847) 969-9097

   MASCON GLOBAL LIMITED
   1405 Route 18S, Ste. 106, Old Bridge, New Jersey 08857
   CEO: Jayaraman Raghuraman, Mng. Prtn.   Tel: (732) 679-0770   %FO: 100
   Bus: *IT consulting services.*   Fax: (732) 679-0979

- **MASTEK, LTD.**
  #106 SDF IV, SEEPZ, Andheri East, Mumbai 400 096, India
  CEO: Sudhakar Ram, CEO   Tel: 91-22-5695-2222   Rev: $89
  Bus: *IT consulting and technology applications.*   Fax: 91-22-5695-1331   Emp: 2,200
  www.mastek.com
  NAICS: 518210, 541511, 541512, 541519, 611420

       MAJESCO SOFTWARE INC.
  2035 Lincoln Hwy., Ste. 3002, Edison, New Jersey 08817
  CEO: Sudhakar Ram, Pres.   Tel: (732) 590-6400   %FO: 100
  Bus: *Computer related services & programming.*   Fax: (732) 590-6422   Emp: 100

- **MISTRAL SOFTWARE PVT. LTD.**
  No. 60, Adarsh Regent, 100 Ft. Ring Rd., Domlur Extension, Karnataka, Bangalore 560 071, India
  CEO: Anees Ahmed, CEO   Tel: 91-80-2535-6400   Rev: $220
  Bus: *Software engineering services.*   Fax: 91-80-2535-6440   Emp: 165
  www.mistralsoftware.com
  NAICS: 541511, 541512, 541513, 541519

       MISTRAL SOFTWARE INC.
  2010 Crow Canyon Pl., Ste. 100, San Ramon, California 94583
  CEO: B. H. Narayanan   Tel: (925) 277-3453   %FO: 100
  Bus: *Software engineering services.*   Fax: (925) 277-3454

       MISTRAL SOFTWARE INC.
  26 Kessler Farm Dr., Ste. 418, Nashua, New Hampshire 03063
  CEO: Pankaj Shah   Tel: (603) 598-9637   %FO: 100
  Bus: *Software engineering services.*   Fax: (603) 339-2727

- **MPHASIS BFL LIMITED**
  139/1 Aditya Complex, Hosur Rd., Koramangala, Karnataka, Bangalore 560 095, India
  CEO: Jaithirth Rao, Chmn. & CEO   Tel: 91-80-552-2713   Rev: $132
  Bus: *IT consulting services and software development.*   Fax: 91-80-552-2719   Emp: 6,278
  www.mphasis.com
  NAICS: 511210, 541511, 541512, 541519, 541614, 541690, 561499

       MPHASIS
  5353 North 16th St., Ste. 400, Phoenix, Arizona 85016
  CEO: Fred Thierbach, Mgr.   Tel: (602) 604-3100   %FO: 100
  Bus: *Software developer & internet consultant.*   Fax: (602) 604-3115

       MPHASIS
  11600 Jones Rd., Cypress Center, Ste. 108/14, Houston, Texas 77070
  CEO: Dirak Bkrua, Mgr.   Tel: (281) 517-5108   %FO: 100
  Bus: *Software developer & internet consultant.*   Fax: (281) 517-5107

       MPHASIS
  3238 Players Club Circle, Ste. 55, Memphis, Tennessee 38125
  CEO: Kevin S. DeMilt, Mgr.   Tel: (901) 869-5705   %FO: 100
  Bus: *It services.*   Fax: (901) 748-3678

MPHASIS
11445 Johns Creek Pkwy., Ste. 300, Duluth, Georgia 30097
CEO: Sarathi Srinivasan, Mgr.
Bus: *IT consulting services and software development.*
Tel: (770) 448-8662
Fax: (770) 473-9294
%FO: 100

MPHASIS
1970 South Amphlett Blvd., Ste. 214, San Mateo, California 94402
CEO: Deb Barua, Mgr.
Bus: *IT consulting services and software development.*
Tel: (650) 378-8588
Fax: (650) 378-8531
%FO: 100

MPHASIS CORPORATION
460 Park Ave. South, Ste. 1101, New York, New York 10016
CEO: Arthur Flew, Pres.
Bus: *Software developer & internet consultant.*
Tel: (212) 686-6655
Fax: (212) 686-2422
%FO: 100
Emp: 100

● **NETGALACTIC INC.**
117-120, 80 Feet Rd., 4th Block, Koramangala, Karnataka 560 034, India
CEO: Paritosh Shah, CEO
Bus: *IT outsourcing services.*
Tel: 91-80-552-2996
Fax: 91-80-552-0371
www.netgalactic.com

NAICS: 541511, 541512, 541519

NETGALACTIC INC.
7906 Sleepy Brooke Ct., Springfield, Virginia 22039
CEO: Omer Faiyaz, Mgr.
Bus: *IT outsourcing services.*
Tel: (703) 652-0928
Fax: (703) 652-0928
%FO: 100

● **NIHILENT TECHNOLOGIES PRIVATE LIMITED**
Amar Avinash Corporate City, 11 Bund Garden Rd., 1/F, Maharashtra, Pune 411 001, India
CEO: L. C. Singh, Pres. & CEO
Bus: *IT service provider.*
Tel: 91-20-605-2253
Fax: 91-20-605-2093
www.nihilent.com

NAICS: 511210, 518210, 541511, 541512, 541513, 541519, 611420, 811212, 811213

NIHILENT TECHNOLOGIES, INC.
67 South Bedford St., Ste. 400 West, Burlington, Massachusetts 01803
CEO: Ashwini Khanna
Bus: *IT services.*
Tel: (781) 229-5812
Fax: (781) 674-9191
%FO: 100

● **NIIT LTD.**
8, Balaji Estate, Sudarshan Munjal Marg, Kalkaji, New Delhi 110 019, India
CEO: Rajendra S. Pawar, Chmn. & Mng. Dir.
Bus: *Educational and information technology (IT) services.*
Tel: 91-11-2648-2054
Fax: 91-11-2620-3333
www.niit.com
Rev: $160
Emp: 3,500

NAICS: 611420, 611430, 611699, 611710

NIIT USA INC.
1050 Crown Pointe Pkwy., 5/F, Atlanta, Georgia 30338
CEO: Ashish Basu, Pres.
Bus: *Educational and information technology (IT) services.*
Tel: (770) 551-9494
Fax: (770) 551-9229
%FO: 100
Emp: 100

- **PATNI COMPUTER SYSTEMS LTD.**
  Akruti, Rd. No: 21, MIDC Cross Road, Andheri (E), Mumbai 400 093, India
  CEO: Narendra K. Patni, CEO   Tel: 91-22-5693-0500   Rev: $188
  Bus: *Custom software development.*   Fax: 91-22-2832-1750   Emp: 5,600
                                                   www.patni.com
  NAICS: 541511

  > **PATNI COMPUTER SYSTEMS LTD.**
  > 17 W. 755 Butterfield Rd., Oak Brook, Illinois 60523
  > CEO: Prasenjit Paul   Tel: (630) 990-4585   %FO: 100
  > Bus: *Custom software development.*   Fax: (630) 990-4595

  > **PATNI COMPUTER SYSTEMS LTD.**
  > 2001 Killebrew Dr., Ste. 160, Minneapolis, Michigan 48076
  > CEO: Piyush Jain   Tel: (952) 854-6630   %FO: 100
  > Bus: *Custom software development.*   Fax: (952) 854-6630

  > **PATNI COMPUTER SYSTEMS LTD.**
  > 4390 US Route One, Ste. 230, Princeton, New Jersey 08540
  > CEO: Prasanna Satpathy   Tel: (609) 580-0011   %FO: 100
  > Bus: *Custom software development.*   Fax: (609) 580-0017

  > **PATNI COMPUTER SYSTEMS LTD.**
  > 101 Merritt 7, 5/F, Norwalk, Connecticut 06851
  > CEO: Ravindra Bhagwat   Tel: (203) 849-0309   %FO: 100
  > Bus: *Custom software development.*   Fax: (203) 849-0374

  > **PATNI COMPUTER SYSTEMS LTD.**
  > 5901 Peachtree Dunwoody Rd., Ste. A-410, Atlanta, Georgia 30328
  > CEO: Ganesh Iyer   Tel: (770) 395-0300   %FO: 100
  > Bus: *Custom software development.*   Fax: (770) 395-9911

  > **PATNI COMPUTER SYSTEMS LTD.**
  > 11260 Chester Rd Ste 600, Cincinnati, Ohio 45426
  > CEO: Ashish Hingorani   Tel: (513) 772-2072   %FO: 100
  > Bus: *Custom software development.*   Fax: (513) 772-5082

  > **PATNI COMPUTER SYSTEMS LTD.**
  > 940 South Coast Dr., Ste. 175, Costa Mesa, California 92626
  > CEO: Rajkumar Sansi   Tel: (714) 241-9555   %FO: 100
  > Bus: *Custom software development.*   Fax: (714) 241-9556

  > **PATNI COMPUTER SYSTEMS LTD.**
  > 238 Main St., Ste. 403, Cambridge, Massachusetts 02142
  > CEO: Shirish Nimgaonkar   Tel: (617) 354-7424   %FO: 100
  > Bus: *Custom software development.*   Fax: (617) 876-4711

- **PSI DATA SYSTEMS LIMITED**
  Shrutaa Complex,19 Primrose Rd., Bangalore 560 025, India
  CEO: Kumar Mangalam Birla, CEO   Tel: 91-80-5661-1300   Rev: $11
  Bus: *Customized software applications.*   Fax: 91-80-5661-1499   Emp: 72,000
                                                   www.psidata.com
  NAICS: 541511

PSI DATA SYSTEMS LIMITED
1 Bank St., Ste. 406, Stamford, Connecticut 06901
CEO: Nirmal P. Uppalapati   Tel: (203) 359-3992   %FO: 100
Bus: *Customized software applications.*   Fax: (203) 359-4662

● **QUALITY ENGINEERING AND SOFTWARE TECHNOLOGIES**
55 Whitefiled Main Rd., Quest Towers, Mahadevpura, Karnataka
, Karnataka, Bangalore 560 048, India
CEO: Ajit A. Prabhu, CEO   Tel: 91-80-511-90900
Bus: *Engineering consulting services.*   Fax: 91-80-511-90901
    www.quest-global.com
NAICS: 336312, 336412, 336611, 423430, 511210, 541330, 541420, 541511, 561310, 561320, 561330, 811310

    QUALITY ENGINEERING AND SOFTWARE TECHNOLOGIES
    1462 Erie Blvd., Schenectady, New York 12305
    CEO: James Gallo, Mgr.   Tel: (518) 370-3657   %FO: 100
    Bus: *Engineering consulting services.*   Fax: (518) 370-3593   Emp: 15

    QUALITY ENGINEERING AND SOFTWARE TECHNOLOGIES
    290 Roberts St., Ste. 202, East Hartford, Connecticut 06108
    CEO: Aravind Melligeri, Pres.   Tel: (860) 290-1145   %FO: 100
    Bus: *Engineering consulting services.*   Fax: (860) 371-2266   Emp: 75

    QUALITY ENGINEERING AND SOFTWARE TECHNOLOGIES
    24655 Southfield Rd., Ste. 110, Southfield, Michigan 48075
    CEO: Ajit A. Prabhu, CEO   Tel: (248) 443-8080   %FO: 100
    Bus: *Engineering consulting services.*   Fax: (248) 443-9790

● **RAMCO SYSTEMS LIMITED**
64, Sardar Patel Rd., Taramani, Chennai 600 113, India
CEO: P. R. Ramasubrahmaneya Rajha, Chmn.   Tel: 91-44-2235-4510   Rev: $19
Bus: *Enterprise management software.*   Fax: 91-44-2235-2884   Emp: 170
    www.ramco.com
NAICS: 511210

    RAMCO SYSTEMS LIMITED
    Crossroads Corporate Center, 3150 Brunswick Pike, Ste. 100, Lawrenceville, New Jersey 08648
    CEO: Michael C. Taylor, Pres. & CEO   Tel: (609) 620-4800   %FO: 100
    Bus: *Personalized enterprise solutions.*   Fax: (609) 620-4860   Emp: 105

● **RANBAXY LABORATORIES LIMITED**
Plot 90, Sector 32, Gurgaon, Haryana 122001, India
CEO: Tejendra Khanna, Chmn.   Tel: 91-124-513-5000   Rev: $1,265
Bus: *Mfr. pharmaceuticals*   Fax: Emp: 7,195
    www.ranbaxy.com
NAICS: 325411, 325412

    RANBAXY Pharmaceuticals Inc.
    600 College Rd. East, Ste. 2100, Princeton, New Jersey 08540
    CEO: Dipak Chattaraj, pres,   Tel: (609) 720-9200   %FO: 100
    Bus: *Manufacturer pharmaceuticals*   Fax: (609) 720-1155

- **DR. REDDY'S LABORATORIES LIMITED**
  7-1-27 Ameerpet, Hyderabad, Andhra Pradesh 500 016, India
  CEO: G. V. Prasad, Chmn. & CEO
  Bus: *Generic and branded pharmaceuticals development and manufacture.*
  NAICS: 325411, 325412, 325414
  Tel: 91-40-373-1946
  Fax: 91-40-373-1955
  www.drreddys.com
  Rev: $438
  Emp: 6,155

  - **DR. REDDY'S LABORATORIES INC.**
    200 Somerset Corp. Blvd., Bridgewater, New Jersey 08807
    CEO: Dennis Langer, Pres.
    Bus: *Sale of pharmaceutical products.*
    Tel: (908) 203-4900
    Fax: (908) 203-4940
    %FO: 100
    Emp: 50

  - **REDDY US THERAPEUTICS, INC.**
    3065 Northwoods Circle, Norcross, Georgia 30071
    CEO: Uday Saxena, Pres.
    Bus: *Research pharmaceutical solutions in therapeutic areas.*
    Tel: (770) 446-9500
    Fax: (770) 446-1950
    %FO: 100
    Emp: 21

- **REDIFF.COM INDIA LIMITED**
  Mahalaxmi Engineering Estate, /LJ First Cross Rd., 1/F, Mahim West, Mumbai 400 016, India
  CEO: Ajit Balakrishnan, Chmn. & Mng. Dir.
  Bus: *Internet portal services.*
  NAICS: 511110, 516110, 517310, 517910, 518111, 518112
  Tel: 91-22-2444-9144
  Fax: 91-22-2445-5346
  www.rediff.com
  Rev: $13
  Emp: 252

  - **INDIA ABROAD PUBLICATIONS, INC.**
    43 West 24th St., 7/F, New York, New York 10010
    CEO: Ajit Balakrishnan, Pres.
    Bus: *Weekly newspaper.*
    Tel: (212) 929-1727
    Fax: (212) 627-9503
    %FO: 100
    Emp: 60

- **SAHARA AIRLINES LIMITED**
  Dr. Gopaldas, Bhawan 28, 3/F, Barakamba Road, New Delhi 110001, India
  CEO: Uttam K. Bose, CEO
  Bus: *Air transport services.*
  NAICS: 481111
  Tel: 91-2332-6851-53
  Fax: 91-2375-5510
  www.airsahara.net

  - **SAHARA AIRLINES**
    3050 Post Oak Blvd., Houston, Texas 77056-6527
    CEO: Ravin Mehra
    Bus: *Air transport services.*
    Tel: (713) 622-3475
    Fax: (713) 622-3475
    %FO: 100

- **SATYAM COMPUTER SERVICES LTD.**
  Satyam Technology Center, Bahadurpallay Village, Qutubullapur, Mandal R.R. District Hyderabad, Andhra Pradesh 500 855, India
  CEO: B. Rama Raju, CEO & Mng. Dir.
  Bus: *Provides information technology services.*
  NAICS: 541511, 541512, 541519
  Tel: 91-40-5523-3505
  Fax: 91-40-2309-7515
  www.satyam.com
  Rev: $794
  Emp: 20,690

SATYAM COMPUTER SERVICES
1 Gatehall Dr., Ste. 301, Parsippany, New Jersey 07054
CEO: Rakesh Bhatia, VP
Bus: *Information technology services.*

Tel: (973) 656-0650
Fax: (973) 656-0653

%FO: 100
Emp: 80

SATYAM COMPUTER SERVICES
3945 Freedom Circle, Ste. 730, Santa Clara, California 95054
CEO: Pareen Dupta, VP
Bus: *Information technology services.*

Tel: (408) 988-3100
Fax: (408) 988-3876

%FO: 100
Emp: 20

SATYAM COMPUTER SERVICES
One Tower Lane, Ste. 2150, Oakbrook Terrace, Illinois 60181
CEO: Les Sowa, Mgr.
Bus: *Information technology services.*

Tel: (630) 928-0700
Fax: (630) 928-0701

%FO: 100
Emp: 35

SATYAM COMPUTER SERVICES
1000 Windward Concourse, Ste. 540, Alpharetta, Georgia 30005
CEO: Madhu Venkat, VP
Bus: *Information technology services.*

Tel: (770) 442-3111
Fax: (770) 442-3913

%FO: 100

SATYAM COMPUTER SERVICES
8500 Leesburg Pike, Ste. 202, Vienna, Virginia 22182
CEO: Shanmugam Bala, CFO
Bus: *Information technology services.*

Tel: (703) 734-2100
Fax: (703) 734-2110

%FO: 100
Emp: 17

● **SILVERLINE TECHNOLOGIES LTD.**
1405-1406 Maker Chamber V, Nariman Point, Mumbai 400-096, India
CEO: Ravi Subramanian, CEO & Mng. Dir.
Bus: *Software development and integration.*

Tel: 91-22-204-9161
Fax: 91-22-202-1131
www.silverline.com

Rev: $28
Emp: 2,600

NAICS: 541511, 541512, 541519

SILVERLINE TECHNOLOGIES, INC.
53 Knightsbridge Rd., Piscataway, New Jersey 08854
CEO: Ravi Siubramanian, CEO & Mng. Dir.
Bus: *Engaged in software development and integration.*

Tel: (732) 584-5300
Fax: (732) 584-5500

%FO: 100

● **SINGHANIA & COMPANY**
G107 Himalaya House, 23 Kasdurda Gandhi Marg, New Delhi 110 001, India
CEO: DC Singhania, Prtn.
Bus: *International law firm.*

Tel: 91-11-373-1400
Fax: 91-11-335-4050
www.singhania.com

NAICS: 541110

SINGHANIA & COMPANY
375 Park Ave., Ste. 1606, New York, New York 10152
CEO: DC Singhania
Bus: *International law firm.*

Tel: (212) 563-1222
Fax: (212) 563-1444

%FO: 100

- **SK GROUP INDIA**
  9, Chatrabhuj Jivandas House, 285, Princess Street, Mumbai 400 002, India
  CEO: Nitin Motani, CEO   Tel: 91-22-2000823
  Bus: *Narrow fabric manufacture, including hook and*   Fax: 91-22-2064687
       loop fastener tapes, knitted elastics, woven   www.skgroup.com
       elastics, webbings, laces and braided elastics.
  NAICS: 339993

  S KAY USA INC.
  110 East 9th St., Ste. C-782, Los Angeles, California 90079-2827
  CEO: Nitin Motani   Tel: (213) 683-0085   %FO: 100
  Bus: *Mfr. narrow fabric, including hook & loop*   Fax: (213) 683-0040
       fastener tapes, knitted elastics, woven
       elastics, webbings, laces & braided elastics.

- **SONATA SOFTWARE LIMITED**
  APS Trust Bldg., 1/4 Bull Temple Rd., N.R. Colony, Karnataka, Bangalore 560 019, India
  CEO: B. Ramaswamy, Pres.   Tel: 91-802-661-0330   Rev: $18
  Bus: *Software manufacture.*   Fax: 91-802-661-0972   Emp: 650
                                                 www.sonata-software.com
  NAICS: 541511, 541512, 541519

  SONATA SOFTWARE LIMITED
  212 Carnegie Centre, Ste. 206, Princeton, New Jersey 08540
  CEO: Venkat Ramani Ganapathy, Mgr.   Tel: (609) 919-6325   %FO: 100
  Bus: *Software sales.*   Fax: (609) 452-8467

  SONATA SOFTWARE LIMITED
  6507 Dumbarton Circle, Fremont, California 94555
  CEO: Thomas K Joseph, CEO   Tel: (510) 742-7213   %FO: 100
  Bus: *Software sales.*   Fax: (510) 791-7270   Emp: 110

  SONATA SOFTWARE LIMITED
  275 Grove St., Ste. 2-400, Newton, Massachusetts 02466
  CEO: Dev Prasad Igure, Mgr.   Tel: (617) 663-4866   %FO: 100
  Bus: *Software sales.*   Fax:

  SONATA SOFTWARE LIMITED
  10900 NE 8th St., Ste. 900, Bellevue, Washington 98004
  CEO: Srihari Kishen Prasad, Mgr.   Tel: (425) 450-4819   %FO: 100
  Bus: *Software sales.*   Fax: (425) 450-4821

  SONATA SOFTWARE LIMITED
  11330 Lakefield Dr., Bldg. 2, Ste. 200, Duluth, Georgia 30097
  CEO: Partho Mukherjee, Mgr.   Tel: (770) 814-4212   %FO: 100
  Bus: *Software sales.*   Fax: (678) 623-0236

- **STATE BANK OF INDIA**
  Madam Cama Rd., Mumbai 400 021, India
  CEO: Tara Shankar Bhattacharya, Mng. Dir.   Tel: 91-22-202-2426   Rev: $11,161
  Bus: *Commercial banking services.*   Fax: 91-22-285-2708   Emp: 207,039
                                                 www.statebankofindia.com
  NAICS: 522110, 522293, 524210

STATE BANK OF INDIA
460 Park Ave., 2/F, New York, New York 10022
CEO: Pratima Ram, Operations Mgr.   Tel: (212) 521-3200   %FO: 100
Bus: *International banking services.*   Fax: (212) 521-3360   Emp: 110

STATE BANK OF INDIA
19 South LaSalle St., Ste. 200, Chicago, Illinois 60603
CEO: Roger Goragagobalam   Tel: (312) 621-1200   %FO: 100
Bus: *International banking services.*   Fax: (312) 621-0740

STATE BANK OF INDIA
2001 Pennsylvania Ave. NW, Ste. 625, Washington, District of Columbia 20006
CEO: Ajid Lal   Tel: (202) 223-5579   %FO: 100
Bus: *International banking services.*   Fax: (202) 785-3739

STATE BANK OF INDIA
707 Wilshire Blvd., Ste. 1995, Los Angeles, California 90017
CEO: Kumar, CEO   Tel: (213) 623-7250   %FO: 100
Bus: *International banking services.*   Fax: (213) 622-2069

● **STATE TRADING CORP. OF INDIA LTD.**
Jawawar Vyapar Shawan, 1 Tolstoy Marg, New Delhi 110 001, India
CEO: Dr. Arvind Pandalai, Mng. Dir.   Tel: 91-11-233-13177   Rev: $900
Bus: *General commodities including chemicals, rice,*   Fax: 91-11-237-01191
wheat, tea, coffee, oils, textile/leather/sporting   www.stc.gov.in
goods & medical disposables.
NAICS: 311223, 311920, 424490, 424690

STATE TRADING CORP OF INDIA
350 Fifth Ave., Ste. 1124, New York, New York 10018
CEO: N.A N. Jeyakumar, Mgr.   Tel: (212) 244-3317   %FO: 100
Bus: *Trading company; organizes all products*   Fax: (212) 224-3319
from India.

● **TARANG SOFTWARE TECHNOLOGIES PVT. LTD.**
Tarang Towers #400/2, Whitefield Rd., Hoody, Karnataka, Bangalore 560048, India
CEO: V. Rama Kumar, Chmn. & CEO   Tel: 91-80-5115-7861
Bus: *Payment transaction software manufacture.*   Fax: 91-80-5115-7870
www.tarangtech.com
NAICS: 511210, 541511, 541512, 541519, 561320

TARANG SOFTWARE TECHNOLOGIES PVT. LTD.
450 N. Mathilda Ave., Bldg. M, Ste. 210, Sunnyvale, California 94086
CEO: V. Rama Kumar, CEO   Tel: (408) 733-9290   %FO: 100
Bus: *Payment transaction software manufacture*   Fax: (408) 733-9290
and sales.

● **TATA CONSULTANCY SERVICES LIMITED**
Air India Bldg., 11/F, Nariman Point, Mumbai 400 021, India
CEO: S. Ramadorai, CEO   Tel: 91-22-5550-9999   Rev: $1,614
Bus: *Consulting and outsourcing services, including*   Fax: 91-22-5550-9661   Emp: 600
offshore software development and systems   www.tcs.com
integration.
NAICS: 541511, 541512, 541519, 611420

TATA AMERICA INTERNATIONAL CORPORATION
425 Market St., Ste. 2250, San Francisco, California 94105
CEO: Vikram Talwar   Tel: (415) 955-2605   %FO: 100
Bus: *Technology consulting services.*   Fax: (415) 955-2794

TATA AMERICA INTERNATIONAL CORPORATION
111 Wood Ave. South, Iselin, New Jersey 08830
CEO: Viswanathan Swaminathan   Tel: (732) 321-9269   %FO: 100
Bus: *Technology consulting services.*   Fax: (732) 321-9269

TATA AMERICA INTERNATIONAL CORPORATION
14 Wall St., 20/F, New York, New York 10005
CEO: Rajib Bose   Tel: (212) 618-1980   %FO: 100
Bus: *Technology consulting services.*   Fax: (212) 618-1987

TATA AMERICA INTERNATIONAL CORPORATION
9401 Indian Creek Pkwy., Ste. 260, Overland Park, Kansas 66210
CEO: Debashish Chakraborti   Tel: (913) 906-0763   %FO: 100
Bus: *Technology consulting services.*   Fax: (913) 906-0764

TATA AMERICA INTERNATIONAL CORPORATION
1500 Market St., 12/F, Philadelphia, Pennsylvania 19102
CEO: K. Venugopal   Tel: (215) 246-3471   %FO: 100
Bus: *Technology consulting services.*   Fax: (215) 665-5771

TATA AMERICA INTERNATIONAL CORPORATION
20410 N. 19th Ave., Ste. 100, Phoenix, Arizona 85027
CEO: Haresh Tripathi   Tel: (602) 682-3502   %FO: 100
Bus: *Technology consulting services.*   Fax: (602) 682-3502

TATA AMERICA INTERNATIONAL CORPORATION
1910 Cochran Rd., Ste. 605, Pittsburgh, Pennsylvania 15220
CEO: Kanwar Singh   Tel: (412) 531-9276   %FO: 100
Bus: *Technology consulting services.*   Fax: (412) 531-3678

TATA AMERICA INTERNATIONAL CORPORATION
10260 SW Greenburg Rd., Ste. 400, Portland, Oregon 97223
CEO: Michael Barrett   Tel: (503) 293-8347   %FO: 100
Bus: *Technology consulting services.*   Fax: (503) 293-8499

TATA AMERICA INTERNATIONAL CORPORATION
12300 Twinbrook Pkwy., Ste. 420, Rockville, Maryland 20852
CEO: Narayan Iyer   Tel: (301) 231-4891   %FO: 100
Bus: *Technology consulting services.*   Fax: (301) 231-4892

TATA AMERICA INTERNATIONAL CORPORATION
3 Park Plaza, Irvine, California 92614
CEO: Atul Kapur   Tel: (949) 222-6570   %FO: 100
Bus: *Technology consulting services.*   Fax: (949) 752-6036

TATA AMERICA INTERNATIONAL CORPORATION
12730, High Bluff Dr., Ste. 120, San Diego, California 92130
CEO: Kamal Bhadada   Tel: (858) 259-4101   %FO: 100
Bus: *Technology consulting services.*   Fax: (858) 259-4104

TATA AMERICA INTERNATIONAL CORPORATION
4104 148th Ave., Bldg G., Redmond, Washington 98052
CEO: Sanjeev Khanna   Tel: (425) 497-7200   %FO: 100
Bus: *Technology consulting services.*   Fax: (425) 895-0158

TATA AMERICA INTERNATIONAL CORPORATION
3032 Bunker Hill Ln., Ste. 207, Santa Clara, California 95054
CEO: Abhay Srivastava   Tel: (408) 200-2942   %FO: 100
Bus: *Technology consulting services.*   Fax: (408) 200-2777

TATA AMERICA INTERNATIONAL CORPORATION
51 JFK Pkwy., Ste. 125, Short Hills, New Jersey 07078
CEO: Shashi Bhushan   Tel: (973) 218-2420   %FO: 100
Bus: *Technology consulting services.*   Fax: (973) 218-2401

TATA AMERICA INTERNATIONAL CORPORATION
101 Federal St., Ste. 1900, Boston, Massachusetts 02110
CEO: Ujjwal Mathur   Tel: (617) 342-3629   %FO: 100
Bus: *Technology consulting services.*   Fax: (617) 342-7233

TATA AMERICA INTERNATIONAL CORPORATION
424 Main St., Rm. 1812, Buffalo, New York 14202
CEO: Mukul Natu   Tel: (716) 853-1695   %FO: 100
Bus: *Technology consulting services.*   Fax: (716) 853-1695

TATA AMERICA INTERNATIONAL CORPORATION
115 Perimeter Center Pl., Ste. 1099, Atlanta, Georgia 30346
CEO: R . Siddharthan   Tel: (770) 396-1223   %FO: 100
Bus: *Technology consulting services.*   Fax: (770) 396-1239

TATA AMERICA INTERNATIONAL CORPORATION
8400 Normandale Lake Blvd., Ste. 920, Bloomington, Minnesota 55437
CEO: Ashu Tandon   Tel: (952) 921-3973   %FO: 100
Bus: *Technology consulting services.*   Fax: (952) 831-4109

TATA AMERICA INTERNATIONAL CORPORATION
80 S. 8th St., Ste. 900, Minneapolis, Minnesota 55402
CEO: J. Deva Prasad   Tel: (612) 349-5249   %FO: 100
Bus: *Technology consulting services.*   Fax: (612) 677-1936

TATA AMERICA INTERNATIONAL CORPORATION
101 Park Ave. 26/F, New York, New York 10178
CEO: Arup Gupta, Pres.   Tel: (212) 557-8038   %FO: 100
Bus: *Technology consulting services.*   Fax: (212) 867-8652

TATA AMERICA INTERNATIONAL CORPORATION
4000 Centre Green Way, Ste. 290, Cary, North Carolina 27513
CEO: Rajeev Wahi   Tel: (919) 678-9860   %FO: 100
Bus: *Technology consulting services.*   Fax: (919) 678-9863

TATA AMERICA INTERNATIONAL CORPORATION
3050 Post Oak Blvd., Ste. 699, Houston, Texas 77056
CEO: Alaguraj Balakrishnan   Tel: (713) 871-9898   %FO: 100
Bus: *Technology consulting services.*   Fax: (713) 871-9899

TATA AMERICA INTERNATIONAL CORPORATION
2825 Palmer St., Missoula, Montana 59808
CEO: Ashu Tandon
Bus: *Technology consulting services.*
Tel: (952) 921-3974
Fax: (952) 831-4109
%FO: 100

TATA AMERICA INTERNATIONAL CORPORATION
8800 Grand Oak Cir., Ste. 690, Tampa, Florida 33607
CEO: Deepak Kota
Bus: *Technology consulting services.*
Tel: (813) 615-2874
Fax: (813) 637-9677
%FO: 100

TATA AMERICA INTERNATIONAL CORPORATION
101 West Ohio St., 20/F, Indianapolis, Indiana 46204
CEO: Jayanta Banerjee
Bus: *Technology consulting services.*
Tel: (317) 977-2934
Fax: (317) 977-2926
%FO: 100

TATA AMERICA INTERNATIONAL CORPORATION
100 Pearl St., Hartford, Connecticut 06103
CEO: Mahesh Eswar
Bus: *Technology consulting services.*
Tel: (860) 249-7272
Fax: (860) 249-7270
%FO: 100

TATA AMERICA INTERNATIONAL CORPORATION
50 Utley Dr., Ste. 100, Camp Hill, Pennsylvania 17011
CEO: Raman Kumar
Bus: *Technology consulting services.*
Tel: (717) 737-4737
Fax: (717) 737-7587
%FO: 100

TATA AMERICA INTERNATIONAL CORPORATION
755 W. Big Beaver Rd., Troy, Michigan 48084
CEO: Satchi Sarangi
Bus: *Technology consulting services.*
Tel: (248) 362-8282
Fax: (248) 362-8292
%FO: 100

TATA AMERICA INTERNATIONAL CORPORATION
250 East Plaza, 18/F., Milwaukee, Wisconsin 53202
CEO: Raman Soni
Bus: *Technology consulting services.*
Tel: (414) 347-7842
Fax: (414) 203-1564
%FO: 100

TATA AMERICA INTERNATIONAL CORPORATION
3010 LBJ Fwy., Ste. 715, Dallas, Texas 75234
CEO: Ram Koduvayur
Bus: *Technology consulting services.*
Tel: (972) 484-6465
Fax: (972) 484-0450
%FO: 100

TATA AMERICA INTERNATIONAL CORPORATION
250 East 5th St., 15/F, Cincinnati, Ohio 45202
CEO: Arun Dhaka
Bus: *Technology consulting services.*
Tel: (513) 772-6603
Fax: (513) 772-9176
%FO: 100

TATA AMERICA INTERNATIONAL CORPORATION
200 S. Wacker Dr., Ste. 3100, Chicago, Illinois 60606
CEO: Sudhi Ranjan Sinha
Bus: *Technology consulting services.*
Tel: (312) 674-4593
Fax: (312) 674-4599
%FO: 100

TATA AMERICA INTERNATIONAL CORPORATION
1903 S. Congress Ave., Ste. 380, Boynton Beach, Florida 33426
CEO: Vikas Jain
Bus: *Technology consulting services.*
Tel: (561) 735-7811
Fax: (561) 735-7411
%FO: 100

TATA AMERICA INTERNATIONAL CORPORATION
999 18th St., Ste. 2700, Denver, Colorado 80202
CEO: Sapthagiri Chapalapalli   Tel: (303) 297-9282   %FO: 100
Bus: *Technology consulting services.*   Fax: (303) 297-9282

● **TATA GROUP**
Bombay House, 24 Homi Mody Street, Mumbai 400 001, India
CEO: Ratan N. Tata, Chmn.   Tel: 91-22-5665-8282   Rev: $13,921
Bus: *Mfr. steel and iron, automotive, and beverage*   Fax: 91-22-5665-8160   Emp: 220,219
  products.   www.tata.com
NAICS: 312111, 331111, 331210, 336211

  TATA INC.
  101 Park Ave., New York, New York 10178
  CEO: Bharat Wakhlu, Pres.   Tel: (212) 557-7979   %FO: 100
  Bus: *U.S. headquarters, diversified*   Fax: (212) 557-7987   Emp: 10
    conglomerate, engineering & locomotive,
    mfr. commercial vehicles, computer
    software, tea production, hotels, (US:
    Lexington Hotel, NY; Executive Plaza,

  TATA INC.
  1250 E. Diehl Rd., Ste. 102, Naperville, Illinois 60563
  CEO: Sarada Nair, Admin.   Tel: (630) 955-0227   %FO: 100
  Bus: *General Management, Illinois administration.*   Fax: (630) 955-0238   Emp: 5

● **TATA TEA LIMITED**
1 Bishop Lefroy Rd., Kolkata 700 020, India
CEO: R. N. Tata, Chmn.   Tel: 91-33-2281-3891
Bus: *Tea grower and marketing of coffee, tea and*   Fax: 91-33-2281-1199
          www.tata.com
NAICS: 311920

  TATA TEA INC.
  1001 West Dr. MLK Blvd., Plant City, Florida 33566
  CEO: V. Venkiteswaran, Pres.   Tel: (813) 754-2602   %FO: 100
  Bus: *Tea grower and marketing of coffee, tea*   Fax: (813) 754-2272
    and spices.

● **TCGIVEGA**
Global Village, Mysore Rd., Karnataka, Bangalore 560 059, India
CEO: Giri Devanur, CEO & Mng. Dir.   Tel: 91-80-2860-4444
Bus: *IT application management services.*   Fax: 91-80-2860-4175
          www.tcgivega.com
NAICS: 541511, 541512, 541513, 541519

  IVEGA CORPORATION
  115 Sansome St., Ste. 801, San Francisco, California 94104
  CEO: Giri Devanur, CEO   Tel: (415) 274-2699   %FO: 100
  Bus: *IT application management services.*   Fax: (415) 834-9508   Emp: 250

IVEGA CORPORATION
333 Thornall St., Edison, New Jersey 08837
CEO: Vivek Vaid, Sales
Bus: *IT application management services.*

Tel: (848) 333-9667
Fax:

%FO: 100
Emp: 300

- **TRANSWORKS INFORMATION SERVICES LTD.**
Teritex Bldg., Saki Vihar Rd., Mumbai 400 072, India
CEO: Prakash Gurbaxani, CEO
Bus: *Outsourcing services.*

Tel: 91-22-2857-2514
Fax: 91-22-2857-2517
www.transworks.com

Rev: $15
Emp: 2,500

NAICS: 561210, 561439

TRANSWORKS INFORMATION SERVICES LTD.
1999 South Bascom Ave., Ste. 700, Campbell, California 95008
CEO: Tanvir Ali Khan, Mgr.
Bus: *Outsourcing services.*

Tel: (408) 879-2399
Fax: (408) 879-2635

%FO: 100

- **VJIL CONSULTING LIMITED**
Usha Kiran, 1-8-165, S. D. Rd., Secunderabad, Andhra Pradesh 500 003, India
CEO: Shri Jalagam Venkat Rao, Chmn. & Mng. Dir.
Bus: *IT consulting services.*

Tel: 91-40-2781-0633
Fax: 91-40-2789-7814
www.vjil.com

NAICS: 541511, 541512, 541519

VJIL CONSULTING LIMITED
115 South Wilke Rd., Ste. 302, Arlington Heights, Illinois 60005
CEO: Satish Manchala, Exec. Dir.
Bus: *IT consulting services.*

Tel: (847) 483-8545
Fax: (847) 483-8552

%FO: 100

- **WIPRO LIMITED**
Wipro Campus, Doddakannelli, Sarjapur Rd., Bangalore 560 035, India
CEO: Azim H. Premji, Chmn. & CEO
Bus: *Information technology and software engineering.*

Tel: 91-80-2844-0011
Fax: 91-80-2844-0056
www.wiprocorporate.com

Rev: $1,863
Emp: 46,500

NAICS: 325611, 325620, 335110, 335121, 335122, 335931, 518210, 541511, 541512, 541513, 541519, 541611, 541612, 541614

WIPRO TECHNOLOGIES
1300 Crittenden Lane, 2/F, Mountain View, California 94043
CEO: Azim H. Premji, Chmn.
Bus: *Computer consulting.*

Tel: (650) 316-3555
Fax: (650) 316-3468

%FO: 100
Emp: 25,000

WIPRO TECHNOLOGIES
777 108th Ave. NE, Ste. 2040, Bellevue, Washington 98004
CEO: Kanwar Singh, Mgr.
Bus: *Custom computer programming.*

Tel: (425) 453-0129
Fax:

%FO: 100
Emp: 20

WIPRO TECHNOLOGIES
11921 Freedom Dr., Ste. 970, Herndon, Virginia 20190
CEO: Timothy Metlack, Mgr.
Bus: *Computer consulting services.*

Tel: (703) 668-8600
Fax:

%FO: 100

WIPRO TECHNOLOGIES
15455 NW Greenbrier Pkwy., Beaverton, Oregon 97006
CEO: Gopinathan Padyagh, Mgr. Tel: (503) 439-0825 %FO: 100
Bus: *Engaged in in information technology and* Fax: (503) 439-8426 Emp: 300
software engineering.

WIPRO TECHNOLOGIES
9801 Dupont Ave. S., Minneapolis, Minnesota 55431
CEO: Vivek Paul, Pres. Tel: (952) 948-9683 %FO: 100
Bus: *management consulting services.* Fax: Emp: 2

WIPRO TECHNOLOGIES
100 West 22nd St., Ste. 106, Lombard, Illinois 60148
CEO: Gautam Shah, Mgr. Tel: (630) 889-9184 %FO: 100
Bus: *Engaged in in information technology and* Fax: Emp: 10
software engineering.

WIPRO TECHNOLOGIES
220 Old New Brunswick Rd., Piscataway, New Jersey 08854
CEO: Sanjay Gupda, Mgr. Tel: (732) 465-0401 %FO: 100
Bus: *Custom computer programming.* Fax: Emp: 20

WIPRO TECHNOLOGIES
3430 East Jefferson Ave., Detroit, Michigan 48207
CEO: Koushik Ganguly, Mgr. Tel: (517) 381-5029 %FO: 100
Bus: *Automotive repair.* Fax:

Indonesia

- **BANK BNI (BANK NEGARA INDONESIA)**
  Jalan Jendral Sudirman Kav. 1, BNI Bldg., 1/F, Jakarta 10220, Indonesia
  CEO: Sigit Pramono, Pres.
  Bus: *International banking services.*

  Tel: 62-21-251-1946
  Fax: 62-21-570-0980
  www.bni.co.id

  Rev: $1,702
  Emp: 14,000

  NAICS: 522110

  BANK BNI
  55 Broadway, 26/F., New York, New York 10006
  CEO: Sigit Pramono, Gen. Mgr.
  Bus: *International banking services.*

  Tel: (212) 943-4750
  Fax: (212) 344-5723

  %FO: 100

- **PT GARUDA INDONESIA**
  Garuda Indonesia Bldg., Jalan Merdeka Selatan No. 13, Jakarta 10110, Indonesia
  CEO: Emirsyah Satar, CEO
  Bus: *Airlines services.*

  Tel: 62-21-231-0082
  Fax: 62-21-231-1679
  www.garuda-indonesia.com

  NAICS: 481111

  PT GARUDA INDONESIA
  9841 Airport Blvd., Ste. 1418, Los Angeles, California 90045
  CEO: M. Chanin
  Bus: *Airlines services.*

  Tel: (310) 348-9577
  Fax: (310) 216-7619

  %FO: 100

Iran

- **DR. ALEXANDER AGHAYAN & ASSOCIATES, INC.**
  83, Sarhang Sakhaee Avenue, Tehran 11354, Iran
  CEO: Dr. Alexander Aghayan, CEO
  Bus: *Engaged in patent and trademark law.*

  Tel: 98-21-670-5056
  Fax: 98-21-670-4858
  www.aghayan.com

  NAICS: 541110

  DR. ALEXANDER AGHAYAN & ASSOCIATES, INC.
  445 Park Ave., New York, New York 10022
  CEO: Alexander Aghayan, CEO
  Bus: *Engaged in patent and trademark law.*

  Tel: (212) 759-0303
  Fax: (212) 504-7951

  %FO: 100

- **BANK MELLI IRAN**
  Ferdoesi Avenue, Tehran 11354, Iran
  CEO: Ahmad Azizi, Chmn.
  Bus: *Banking services.*

  Tel: 98-21-3231
  Fax: 98-21-302813
  www.bank-melli-iran.com

  Emp: 32,000

  NAICS: 522110

  BANK MELLI IRAN
  628 Madison Ave., New York, New York 10022
  CEO: Reza Rahi, Chief Rep.
  Bus: *International banking services.*

  Tel: (212) 759-4700
  Fax: (212) 759-4704

  %FO: 100

Ireland

- **A&L GOODBODY SOLICITORS**
  International Financial Services Centre, North Wall Quay, Dublin 1, Ireland
  CEO: Paul Carroll, Mng. Prtn.   Tel: 353-1-649-2000
  Bus: *International law firm.*   Fax: 353-1-649-2649   Emp: 450
                                       www.algoodbody.ie

  NAICS: 541110

    A & L GOODBODY
    One Post Office Sq., 22/F, Boston, Massachusetts 02111
    CEO: Aidan Browne, Prtn.   Tel: (617) 338-3640   %FO: 100
    Bus: *International law firm.*   Fax: (617) 338-2880

    A & L GOODBODY
    10 Rockefeller Plaza, Ste. 816, New York, New York 10020
    CEO: Barry McGrath, Prtn.   Tel: (212) 582-4499   %FO: 100
    Bus: *International law firm.*   Fax: (212) 333-5126

- **AER LINGUS GROUP PLC**
  PO Box 180, Dublin Airport, Dublin, Ireland
  CEO: Dermot Mannion, CEO   Tel: 353-1-886-2103   Rev: $1,236
  Bus: *Commercial air transport services.* Fax: 353-1-886-3851   Emp: 3,900
                                       www.aerlingus.ie

  NAICS: 481111

    AER LINGUS
    538 Broadhollow Rd., Melville, New York 11747
    CEO: Jack Foley, SVP   Tel: (516) 577-5700   %FO: 100
    Bus: *International air transport services.* Fax: (516) 752-3600   Emp: 350

- **ALLIED IRISH BANKS PLC**
  Bankcentre, Ballsbridge, Dublin 4, Ireland
  CEO: Eugene J. Sheehy, CEO   Tel: 353-1-660-0311   Rev: $7,090
  Bus: *Commercial banking services.* Fax: 353-1-660-9137   Emp: 22,800
                                       www.aib.ie

  NAICS: 522110

    ALLIED IRISH BANKS
    333 Westchester Ave., White Plains, New York 10604
    CEO: C. Kieffer   Tel: (914) 684-2336
    Bus: *Commercial banking and trust services.* Fax: (914) 684-2336

    ALLIED IRISH BANKS
    405 Park Ave., New York, New York 10022
    CEO: Brian M. Leeney, EVP   Tel: (212) 339-8000   %FO: 100
    Bus: *International commercial banking services.* Fax: (212) 339-8008   Emp: 100

- **ANGLO IRISH BANK CORPORATION**
Stephen Court, 18/21 St. Stephen's Green, Dublin 2, Ireland
CEO: Sean P. FitzPatrick, Chmn.   Tel: 353-1-616-2000   Rev: $1,427
Bus: *Banking services.*   Fax: 353-1-616-2481   Emp: 1,031
                                       www.angloirishbank.ie
NAICS: 522110

  ANGLO IRISH BANK CORPORATION
  500 Park Ave., 6/F, New York, New York 10022
  CEO: Derek Keogh   Tel: (212) 588-1661   %FO: 100
  Bus: *Banking services.*   Fax: (646) 840-0896

  ANGLO IRISH BANK CORPORATION
  265 Franklin St., 19/F, Boston, Massachusetts 02110
  CEO: Paul Doyle, Pres. & CEO   Tel: (617) 720-2577   %FO: 100
  Bus: *Banking services.*   Fax: (617) 261-2783

- **BANK OF IRELAND**
Lower Baggot St., Dublin 2, Ireland
CEO: Brian J. Goggin, CEO   Tel: 353-1-661-5933   Rev: $7,127
Bus: *Banking services.*   Fax: 353-1-661-5671   Emp: 17,584
                                      www.bankofireland.ie
NAICS: 522110, 523920, 523930, 523999, 524113, 524210, 525110, 525910

  BANK OF IRELAND ASSET MANAGEMENT (U.S.)
  233 Wilshire Blvd., Ste. 830, Santa Monica, California 90401
  CEO: Leli Long, Mgr.   Tel: (310) 656-4440   %FO: 100
  Bus: *Foreign bank.*   Fax: (310) 395-0845

  BANK OF IRELAND ASSET MANAGEMENT (U.S.)
  Presidents Plaza I, 8600 West Bryn Mawr Ave., Ste. 530 North, Chicago, Illinois 60631
  CEO: Mary Fedorak   Tel: (773) 693-7194   %FO: 100
  Bus: *Foreign bank.*   Fax: (773) 693-7203

  BANK OF IRELAND ASSET MANAGEMENT (U.S.)
  75 Holly Hill Lane, Greenwich, Connecticut 06830
  CEO: Denis Curran, Exec. Dir.   Tel: (203) 869-0111   %FO: 100
  Bus: *Investment advisory services.* Fax: (203) 869-0268   Emp: 30

- **ARTHUR COX SOLICITORS**
Earlsfort Centre, Earlsfort Terrace, Dublin 2, Ireland
CEO: Padraig O'Riordain, Mng. Prtn. Tel: 353-1-618-0000
Bus: *International law firm.*   Fax: 353-1-618-0618   Emp: 450
                                     www.arthurcox.ie
NAICS: 541110

  ARTHUR COX
  570 Lexington Ave., 28/F, New York, New York 10022
  CEO: John Matson, Mng. Prtn.   Tel: (212) 759-0808   %FO: 100
  Bus: *International law firm.*   Fax: (212) 688-3237

- **CRH PLC**
  Belgard Castle, Clondalkin, Dublin 22, Ireland
  CEO: W. Liam O'Mahoney, CEO
  Bus: *Building materials manufacture and distribution.*

  Tel: 353-1-404-1000
  Fax: 353-1-404-1415
  www.crh.cie

  Rev: $16,635
  Emp: 54,239

  NAICS: 326199

  OLDCASTLE PRECAST, INC.
  4727 North Royal Atlanta Dr., Ste. A, Tucker, Georgia 30084
  CEO: Jan Olsen
  Bus: *Mfr. integrated aggregates.*

  Tel: (770) 270-5000
  Fax: (770) 270-5000

  %FO: 100

  OLDCASTLE PRECAST, INC.
  2820 A St. SE, Auburn, Washington 98071
  CEO: Jim Schack
  Bus: *Mfr./distribution of building materials.*

  Tel: (253) 833-2777
  Fax: (253) 939-9126

  %FO: 100

  OLDCASTLE PRECAST, INC.
  8392 Riverview Pkwy., Littleton, Colorado 80125
  CEO: Ray Rhees
  Bus: *Mfr. integrated aggregates.*

  Tel: (303) 791-1100
  Fax: (303) 791-9181

  %FO: 100

  THOMPSON-MCCULLY CO.
  230 South Michigan Ave., Coldwater, Michigan 49036
  CEO: Bob Thompson, CEO
  Bus: *Mfr. integrated aggregates.*

  Tel: (517) 279-6222
  Fax: (517) 279-6222

  %FO: 100

- **DATALEX PLC**
  Block U, East Point Business Park, Dublin 3, Ireland
  CEO: Michael Quinn, Pres. & CEO
  Bus: *Travel agency software.*

  Tel: 353-1-839-1787
  Fax: 353-1-839-1781
  www.datalex.com

  Rev: $29

  NAICS: 541511

  DATALEX COMMUNICATIONS USA, INC.
  1105 Sanctuary Park, Ste. 190, Alpharetta, Georgia 30004
  CEO: Bob Borgwat, PR
  Bus: *Travel agency software.*

  Tel: (770) 255-2400
  Fax: (770) 255-2500

  %FO: 100

- **DEPFA BANK PLC**
  International House, 3 Harbourmaster Place, Dublin 1, Ireland
  CEO: Gerhard E. Bruckermann, CEO
  Bus: *Engaged in property financing and investment
  banking solutions for public-sector authorities.*

  Tel: 353-1-607-1600
  Fax: 353-1-829-0213
  www.depfa.com

  Rev: $736
  Emp: 337

  NAICS: 523999

  DEPFA USA INC.
  30 North LaSalle St., Ste. 1510, Chicago, Illinois 60602
  CEO: Marnin Lebovits
  Bus: *Engaged in property financing.*

  Tel: (312) 332-9100
  Fax: (312) 332-9192

  %FO: 100

DEPFA USA INC.
623 Fifth Ave., 22/F, New York, New York 10022
CEO: Fulvio Dobrich, Pres. & CEO   Tel: (917) 286-2000   %FO: 100
Bus: *Engaged in property financing.*   Fax: (917) 286-2088

● **EIRCOM GROUP PLC**
114 St. Stephen's Green West, Dublin 2, Ireland
CEO: Philip M. G. Nolan, CEO   Tel: 353-1-671-4444   Rev: $2,069
Bus: *Engaged in telecommunications.*   Fax: 353-1-671-6916   Emp: 7,595
   www.eircom.com
NAICS: 334413, 517310

   EIRCOM USA LTD.
   2055 Gateway Place, Ste. 400, San Jose, California 95110
   CEO: Brad Montano, Mgr.   Tel: (408) 467-3863   %FO: 100
   Bus: *Engaged in telecommunications.*   Fax: (408) 441-9076

   TELECOM IRELAND
   1010 Washington Blvd., Stamford, Connecticut 06901
   CEO: Frank McQuillan, Mgr.   Tel: (203) 363-7171   %FO: 100
   Bus: *Engaged in telecommunications.*   Fax: (203) 363-7176

● **ELAN CORPORATION PLC**
Treasury Grand Bldg., Lower Canal St., Dublin 2, Ireland
CEO: G. Kelly Martin, Pres. & CEO   Tel: 353-1-709-4000   Rev: $482
Bus: *Pharmaceuticals and drug-delivery technology.*   Fax: 353-1-662-4949   Emp: 1,899
   www.elancom
NAICS: 325411

   ELAN CORPORATION
   3000 Horizon Dr., King of Prussia, Pennsylvania 19044
   CEO: David Czekai, VP   Tel: (610) 313-5100
   Bus: *Pharmaceuticals manufacturer.*   Fax: (610) 313-8845   Emp: 52

   ELAN CORPORATION
   7475 Lusk Blvd., San Diego, California 92121
   CEO: John Groom, Pres.   Tel: (858) 457-2553
   Bus: *Pharmaceuticals manufacturer*   Fax: (858) 457-2555

   ELAN CORPORATION
   225 Franklin St., 26/F, Boston, Massachusetts 02110-2804
   CEO: Peter Knights   Tel: (617) 217-2240
   Bus: *Pharmaceuticals manufacturer.*   Fax: (617) 217-2577

   ELAN CORPORATION
   800 Gateway Blvd., South San Francisco, California 94080
   CEO: John Groom, Pres.   Tel: (650) 877-0900   %FO: 100
   Bus: *Pharmaceuticals manufacture.*   Fax: (650) 877-7669   Emp: 727

   ELAN HOLDINGS
   1300 Gould Dr., SW, Gainesville, Georgia 30504
   CEO: Jim Bokin, Pres.   Tel: (770) 534-8239   %FO: 100
   Bus: *Pharmaceuticals manufacture.*   Fax: (770) 534-8247   Emp: 500

ELAN PHARMA INC.
875 Third Ave., 3/F, New York, New York 10022
CEO: Jack Howarth
Bus: *Pharmaceuticals manufacturer.*

Tel: (212) 407-5740
Fax: (212) 755-1043

%FO: 100

● **FINEOS CORPORATION**
Pembroke House, 8-10 Lower Pembroke Street, Dublin 2, Ireland
CEO: Michael Kelly, CEO
Bus: *Banking and insurance software.*

Tel: 353-1-639-9700
Fax: 353-1-639-9701
www.fineos.com

Rev: $21
Emp: 200

NAICS: 541511

FINEOS CORPORATION
24 Christopher Toppi Dr., South Portland, Maine 04106
CEO: Leo Corcoran, VP
Bus: *Banking and insurance software.*

Tel: (207) 879-0400
Fax: (207) 879-0900

%FO: 100

● **THE FITZPATRICK HOTEL GROUP**
14 Windsor Terrace, Dun Laoghaire, Dublin 2, Ireland
CEO: John Fitzpatrick, Chmn.
Bus: *Family owned and operated hotel group.*

Tel: 353-1-284-5656
Fax: 353-1-284-5655
www.fitzpatrickhotels.com

NAICS: 721110

FITZPATRICK CHICAGO HOTEL
166 E. Superior St., Chicago, Illinois 60611
CEO: Brian Sahy
Bus: *Hotels.*

Tel: (312) 787-6000
Fax: (312) 787-6133

%FO: 100

FITZPATRICK GRAND CENTRAL HOTEL
141 East 44th St., New York, New York 10017
CEO: Hilda Garvey, Gen. Mgr.
Bus: *Hotels.*

Tel: (212) 351-6800
Fax: (212) 818-1747

%FO: 100

FITZPATRICK MANHATTAN HOTEL
687 Lexington Ave., New York, New York 10021
CEO: Hilda Garvey, Gen. Mgr.
Bus: *Hotels.*

Tel: (212) 355-0100
Fax: (212) 308-5166

%FO: 100

● **FREIGHTWATCH GROUP LIMITED**
Landscape House, Baldonnell Business Park, Naas Road, Dublin 22, Ireland
CEO: Mick Moloney, CEO
Bus: *Transportation security services.*

Tel: 353-1-466-1799
Fax: 353-1-466-1756
www.freightwatchgroup.com

Rev: $6
Emp: 100

NAICS: 561612

FREIGHTWATCH GROUP LIMITED
1711 South Congress Ave., Ste. 205, Austin, Texas 78704
CEO: Kieran O'Connor
Bus: *Transportation security services.*

Tel: (512) 225-6490
Fax: (512) 225-6491

%FO: 100

- **FYFFES PLC**
  29 N. Anne St., Dublin 7, Ireland
  CEO: David. V. McCann, CEO
  Bus: *Import and distribution of fresh fruits, vegetables and flowers.*
  NAICS: 424480

  Tel: 353-1-887-2700
  Fax: 353-1-887-2751
  www.fyffes.com

  Rev: $2,500
  Emp: 2,979

  FYFFES INTERNATIONAL
  10100 w. Sample Rd., Ste. 405, Coral Springs, Florida 33065
  CEO: Dieter Otten
  Bus: *Import and distribution of fresh fruits, vegetables and flowers.*

  Tel: (954) 796-4230
  Fax: (954) 796-3095

  %FO: 100

- **GLANBIA PLC**
  Glanbia House, Kilkenny, Ireland
  CEO: John Moloney, Mng. Dir.
  Bus: *Dairy products.*

  Tel: 353-56-777-2200
  Fax: 353-56-777-2222
  www.glanbia.com

  Rev: $2,518
  Emp: 3,831

  NAICS: 311511, 311512, 311513, 311514, 311611

  GLANBIA NUTRITIONALS, INC.
  236 Washington St. South, Twin Falls, Idaho 83301
  CEO: John Lanigan, Mgr.
  Bus: *Global nutritional ingredients market.*

  Tel: (208) 733-3226
  Fax: (208) 733-3226

  %FO: 100
  Emp: 65

  GLANBIA NUTRITIONALS, INC.
  523 6th St., Monroe, Wisconsin 53566
  CEO: Jerry O'Dea, Pres.
  Bus: *Global nutritional ingredients market.*

  Tel: (608) 329-2800
  Fax: (608) 329-2800

  %FO: 100
  Emp: 25

  GLANBIA NUTRITIONALS, INC.
  1728 South 2300 East, Gooding, Idaho 83330
  CEO: John Lanigan, Gen. Mgr.
  Bus: *Global nutritional ingredients market.*

  Tel: (208) 934-8195
  Fax: (208) 934-8195

  %FO: 100
  Emp: 100

  GLANBIA NUTRITIONALS, INC.
  1373 Fillmore St., Twin Falls, Idaho 83301
  CEO: John Moloney
  Bus: *Global nutritional ingredients market.*

  Tel: (208) 733-7555
  Fax: (208) 733-7555

  %FO: 100
  Emp: 420

  GLANBIA NUTRITIONALS, INC.
  1572 East Hwy. 26, Richfield, Idaho 83349
  CEO: Owen Rice, Mgr.
  Bus: *Global nutritional ingredients market.*

  Tel: (208) 487-2545
  Fax:

  %FO: 100
  Emp: 60

- **GORANN LTD.**
  68 Harcourt St., Dublin 2, Ireland
  CEO: David Beatty, Pres. & CEO
  Bus: *Company start-up, product introduction and management consulting for the Irish consumer market.*
  NAICS: 541611

  Tel: 353-1-418-8112
  Fax: 353-1-633-5781
  www.gorann.com

GORANN INC.
350 Fifth Ave., Empire State Bldg., Ste. 5809, New York, New York 10118
CEO: David Beatty, Pres.   Tel: (212) 404-7340   %FO: 100
Bus: *Engaged in management consulting; start-up* Fax: Emp: 12
    to successful global organizations.

● **HEADWAY SOFTWARE LTD.**
Waterford Business Park, Confederation House, Waterford, Ireland
CEO: Pat Stuart, CEO   Tel: 353-86-174-0953
Bus: *Software manufacture.*   Fax: 419-793-1007
    www.headwaysoft.com

NAICS: 511210

    HEADWAY SOFTWARE LTD.
    Two Newton Place, 255 Washington St., Ste. 340, Newton, Massachusetts 02458
    CEO: Paul Hickey, Mgr.   Tel: (877) 432-3929   %FO: 100
    Bus: *Mfr. software.*   Fax: (419) 793-1007

● **IAWS GROUP PLC**
151 Thomas St., Dublin 8, Ireland
CEO: Owen Killian, CEO   Tel: 353-1-612-1200   Rev: $1,534
Bus: *Baking, foodservice, and wholesale food*   Fax: 353-1-612-1321   Emp: 3,093
    www.iaws.com

NAICS: 311811, 311812, 311813

    LA BREA BAKERY HOLDINGS INC
    15963 Strathern St., Van Nuys, California 91406-1313
    CEO: John Yamin, CEO   Tel: (818) 742-4242   %FO: 100
    Bus: *Producer of partially baked artisan breads.*   Fax: (818) 742-4276   Emp: 700

● **ICON PLC**
South County Business Park, Leopardstown, Dublin 18, Ireland
CEO: Peter Gray, CEO   Tel: 353-1-291-1100   Rev: $297
Bus: *Clinical drug trial services.*   Fax: 353-1-216-2700   Emp: 2,450
    www.iconclinical.com

NAICS: 541710

    BEACON BIOSCIENCE, INC.
    4259 West Swamp Rd., Ste. 410, Doylestown, Pennsylvania 18901
    CEO: Edward Gastineau, CEO   Tel: (215) 489-2626   %FO: 100
    Bus: *Clinical drug trial services.*   Fax: (215) 340-2674   Emp: 40

    GLOBOMAX LLC
    6031 University Blvd., Ste. 300, Ellicott City, Maryland 21043
    CEO: David Young, Mgr.   Tel: (410) 696-3000   %FO: 100
    Bus: *Clinical drug trial services.*   Fax: (410) 480-0776

    ICON CLINICAL RESEARCH
    100 Commerce Dr., Ste. 200, Newark, Delaware 19713
    CEO: Tim Saxton, Dir.   Tel: (215) 616-3570   %FO: 100
    Bus: *Clinical drug trial services.*   Fax: (302) 283-0146   Emp: 20

ICON CLINICAL RESEARCH
320 Seven Springs Way, Ste. 500, Brentwood, Tennessee 37027
CEO: John Climax, CEO   Tel: (615) 309-4200   %FO: 100
Bus: *Clinical drug trial services.*   Fax: (615) 661-7793   Emp: 65

ICON CLINICAL RESEARCH
10 Parkway North, Ste. 350, Deerfield, Illinois 60015
CEO: John Hubbard, Mgr.   Tel: (847) 580-4500   %FO: 100
Bus: *Clinical drug trial services.*   Fax: (847) 580-4360

ICON CLINICAL RESEARCH
13135 Dairy Ashford, Ste. 150, Sugar Land, Texas 77478
CEO: John Hubbard, Mgr.   Tel: (281) 295-4800   %FO: 100
Bus: *Clinical drug trial services.*   Fax: (281) 242-4890

ICON CLINICAL RESEARCH
555 Twin Dolphin Dr., Ste. 400, Redwood City, California 94065
CEO: Charles Dumond, CEO   Tel: (650) 620-2100   %FO: 100
Bus: *Clinical drug trial services.*   Fax: (650) 591-0611

ICON CLINICAL RESEARCH
4601 Creekstone Dr., Ste. 160, Durham, North Carolina 27703
CEO: John Hubbard, Mgr.   Tel: (919) 294-2200   %FO: 100
Bus: *Clinical drug trial services.*   Fax: (919) 294-2360

ICON CLINICAL RESEARCH
8105 Irvine Center Dr., Ste. 900, Irvine, California 92618
CEO: Bill Taaffe, CEO   Tel: (949) 585-8500   %FO: 100
Bus: *Clinical drug trial services.*   Fax: (949) 788-0930   Emp: 20

ICON CLINICAL RESEARCH
Lakepoint II, 3111 West Dr. Martin Luther King Blvd., Ste. 375, Tampa, Florida 33607
CEO: John Hubbard, Mgr.   Tel: (813) 350-8400   %FO: 100
Bus: *Clinical drug trial services.*   Fax: (813) 870-0699

ICON LABORATORIES INC.
123 Smith St., Farmingdale, New York 11735
CEO: Edward Caffrey, Pres.   Tel: (631) 777-8833   %FO: 100
Bus: *Clinical drug trial services.*   Fax: (631) 777-3904   Emp: 240

ICON LABORATORIES, INC.
345 Park Ave., New York, New York 10154
CEO: John Hubbard, Mgr.   Tel: (212) 688-4343   %FO: 100
Bus: *Clinical drug trial services.*   Fax: (212) 688-4074

ICON LABORATORIES, INC.
212 Church Rd., North Wales, Pennsylvania 19454
CEO: Bill Taaffe, CEO   Tel: (215) 616-3000   %FO: 100
Bus: *Clinical drug trial services.*   Fax: (215) 699-6288   Emp: 650

- **IONA TECHNOLOGIES PLC**
  The IONA Bldg., Shelbourne Road, Ballsbridge, Dublin 4, Ireland
  CEO: Peter M. Zotto, CEO   Tel: 353-1-637-2000   Rev: $68
  Bus: *Mfr. Web development software.*   Fax: 353-1-637-2888   Emp: 346
                                               www.iona.com
  NAICS: 541511
  - **IONA TECHNOLOGIES INC.**
    5400 Carillon Pt., Kirkland, Washington 98033
    CEO: Sarah Reed, Reg. Dir.   Tel: (576) 576-4083   %FO: 100
    Bus: *Sales Web development software.*   Fax: (576) 576-4084

  - **IONA TECHNOLOGIES INC.**
    816 Congress Ave., Ste. 1100, Austin, Texas 78701
    CEO: Jody Hunt, Reg. Dir.   Tel: (512) 485-4582   %FO: 100
    Bus: *Sales Web development software.*   Fax: (512) 473-3680

  - **IONA TECHNOLOGIES INC.**
    4600 South Ulster St., Ste. 300, Denver, Colorado 80237
    CEO: Sarah Reed, Reg. Dir.   Tel: (303) 486-0888   %FO: 100
    Bus: *Sales Web development software.*   Fax: (303) 486-0887

  - **IONA TECHNOLOGIES INC.**
    50 California St., San Francisco, California 94104
    CEO: Sarah Reed, Reg. Dir.   Tel: (415) 277-5432   %FO: 100
    Bus: *Sales Web development software.*   Fax: (415) 277-5430

  - **IONA TECHNOLOGIES INC.**
    200 West St., 4/F, Waltham, Massachusetts 02451
    CEO: Peter M. Zoto, Reg. Dir.   Tel: (781) 902-8000   %FO: 100
    Bus: *Sales Web development software.*   Fax: (781) 902-8001

- **IRISH DAIRY BOARD COOPERATIVE LTD.**
  Grattan House, Mount Street Lower, Dublin 2, Ireland
  CEO: Michael Cronin, Chmn.   Tel: 353-1-661-9599   Rev: $2,587
  Bus: *Dairy products manufacture, including butter and*   Fax: 353-1-661-2778   Emp: 3,133
       cheeses.   www.idb.ie
  NAICS: 311512, 311513, 311514, 424490
  - **DISTRIBUTION PLUS INC.**
    825 Green Bay Rd., Ste. 200, Wilmette, Illinois 60091
    CEO: Dan O'Connell, CEO   Tel: (847) 256-8289   %FO: 100
    Bus: *Dairy products manufacture, including butter*   Fax: (847) 256-8299
         and cheeses.

  - **DPI ARIZONA**
    246 South Robson St., Mesa, Arizona 85210
    CEO: Steven Forster, Pres.   Tel: (480) 969-9333   %FO: 100
    Bus: *Dairy products manufacture, including butter*   Fax: (480) 461-3645   Emp: 60
         and cheeses.

DPI MID ATLANTIC
1000 Prince Georges Blvd., Upper Marlboro, Maryland 20774
CEO: John Loveys, Pres.
Bus: *Wholesale distributor of dairy products.*
Tel: (301) 430-2200
Fax: (301) 430-2201
%FO: 100
Emp: 247

DPI MIDWEST
615 East Brook Dr., Arlington Heights, Illinois 60005
CEO: Frank Ryser, Pres.
Bus: *Wholesale distributor of dairy products.*
Tel: (847) 354-9704
Fax: (847) 364-9702
%FO: 100

DPI NORTHWEST
12360 SW Leveton Dr., Tualatin, Oregon 97062
CEO: Mark Dahm, Pres.
Bus: *Wholesale distributor of dairy products.*
Tel: (503) 692-0662
Fax: (503) 692-4776
%FO: 100
Emp: 140

DPI ROCKY MOUNTAIN
8125 East 88th Ave., Henderson, Colorado 80640
CEO: Jerre Snyder, Pres.
Bus: *Wholesale distributor of dairy products.*
Tel: (303) 301-1226
Fax: (303) 301-6931
%FO: 100

DPI SOUTHWEST
5840 Office Blvd., NE, Albuquerque, New Mexico 87109
CEO: Shelia Snyder, Pres.
Bus: *Wholesale distributor of dairy products.*
Tel: (505) 345-4488
Fax: (505) 345-4494
%FO: 100

DPI WEST
601 Rockefeller Ave., Ontario, California 91761
CEO: Jim DeKeyser, Pres.
Bus: *Wholesale distributor of dairy products.*
Tel: (909) 975-1019
Fax: (909) 975-7238
%FO: 100
Emp: 576

IRISH DAIRY BOARD, INC.
825 Green Bay Rd., Ste. 200, Wilmette, Illinois 60091
CEO: Daniel O'Connell, Pres.
Bus: *Purchase & resale of dairy products.*
Tel: (847) 256-8289
Fax: (847) 256-8299
%FO: 100
Emp: 498

● **JEFFERSON SMURFIT GROUP PLC**
Beech Hill, Clonskeagh, Dublin 4, Ireland
CEO: Gary W. McGann, CEO
Bus: *Corrugated paper and board, print, packaging and newsprint.*
Tel: 353-1-202-7000
Fax: 353-1-269-4481
www.smurfit-group.com
Rev: $6,554
Emp: 30,371
NAICS: 322211, 322214, 322223, 322224, 322299, 424130

JEFFERSON SMURFIT CORP. US
8182 Maryland Ave., Saint Louis, Missouri 63105
CEO: Michael W.J. Smurfit, Chmn.
Bus: *Mfr. paper and paperboard packaging.*
Tel: (314) 746-1100
Fax: (314) 746-1259
%FO: 50
Emp: 200

SMURFIT PACKAGING LLC
100 Sawgrass Corporate Place, Ft. Lauderdale, Florida 33323
CEO: Peter A. Cosgrove, Pres.
Bus: *Recycler & commercial offset printer.*
Tel: (954) 514-2600
Fax: (954) 514-2598
%FO: 100
Emp: 50

SMURFIT STONE CORP.
320 Parker St., Springfield, Massachusetts 01129
CEO: Robert Hirschhorn, Pres.   Tel: (413) 543-2311   %FO: 100
Bus: *Mfr. paper and paperboard packaging.*   Fax: Emp: 540

SMURFIT STONE CONTAINER CORPORATION
150 North Michigan Ave., Chicago, Illinois 60601
CEO: Patrick J. Moore, Chmn. & Pres. & CEO   Tel: (312) 346-6600   %FO: 100
Bus: *U.S. headquarters.*   Fax: (312) 580-2272   Emp: 35,300

● **JURYS DOYLE HOTEL GROUP PLC**
146 Pembroke Rd., Ballsbridge, Dublin 4, Ireland
CEO: Patrick A. McCann, CEO   Tel: 353-1-607-0070   Rev: $388
Bus: *Hotel group.*   Fax: 353-1-667-2370   Emp: 4,041
          www.jurys.com
NAICS: 721110

JURYS BOSTON HOTEL
350 Stuart St., Back Bay, Boston, Massachusetts 02116
CEO: Patrick McCann, CEO   Tel: (617) 266-7200   %FO: 100
Bus: *Hotel group.*   Fax: (617) 266-7203   Emp: 180

JURYS WASHINGTON HOTEL
1500 New Hampshire Ave. NW, Washington, District of Columbia 20036
CEO: Peter Hillary, Mgr.   Tel: (202) 483-6000   %FO: 100
Bus: *Hotel group.*   Fax: (202) 328-3265   Emp: 180

● **KERRY GROUP PLC**
Prince's St., Tralee, Kerry, Ireland
CEO: Hugh Friel, CEO & Mng. Dir.   Tel: 353-66-718-2000   Rev: $5,257
Bus: *Ingredients and food manufacture.*   Fax: 353-66-718-2961   Emp: 21,671
          www.kerrygroup.com
NAICS: 311411, 311511, 311512, 311612, 311822, 311930, 311942, 311999, 312112

KERRY BIO-SCIENCE AMERICAS
515 Sedge Blvd., Hoffman Estates, Illinois 60192
CEO: Stan McCarthy, Pres.   Tel: (847) 645-7340   %FO: 100
Bus: *Mfr. of specialty food ingredients.*   Fax: (847) 645-7341

KERRY INGREDIENTS NORTH AMERICA
100 East Grand Ave., Beloit, Wisconsin 53511
CEO: Stan McCarthy, Pres.   Tel: (608) 363-1200   %FO: 100
Bus: *Ingredients manufacture and sales.*   Fax: (608) 363-1429   Emp: 1,963

MASTERTASTE
6133 North River Rd., Ste. 670, Rosemont, Illinois 60018
CEO: Kevin Lane, Pres. & CEO   Tel: (847) 823-9300   %FO: 100
Bus: *Mfr. of flavorings, spices & other*   Fax:
    ingredients.

● **KINGSPAN GROUP PLC**
Dublin Rd., Kingscourt, Co. Cavan, Ireland
CEO: Gene M. Murtagh Jr., CEO
Bus: *Mfr. raised flooring.*

Tel: 353-42-969-8000
Fax: 353-42-966-7501
www.kingspan.com

Rev: $1,307
Emp: 3,351

NAICS: 332312

> **KINGSPAN CORPORATION**
> 25025 1-45 North, Ste. 525, The Woodlands, Texas 77387
> CEO: Michael Whelan, Pres.
> Bus: *Mfr./sales raised flooring.*
>
> Tel: (281) 364-6935
> Fax: (281) 364-6939
>
> %FO: 100

> **KINGSPAN CORPORATION**
> 7510 Montevideo Rd., Jessup, Maryland 20794
> CEO: Russel Shiels, Pres.
> Bus: *Mfr. access floor systems of steel & concrete combinations.*
>
> Tel: (410) 799-4200
> Fax:
>
> Emp: 960

● **MASON HAYES & CURRAN**
6 Fitzwilliam Sq., Dublin 2, Ireland
CEO: Declan Moylan, Mng. Prtn.
Bus: *Full service law firm.*

Tel: 353-1-614-5000
Fax: 353-1-614-5001
www.mhc.ie

Emp: 1,000

NAICS: 541110

> **MASON HAYES & CURRAN**
> 261 Madison Ave., Ste. 400, New York, New York 10016
> CEO: Daniel Walsh
> Bus: *Law practice.*
>
> Tel: (212) 973-9443
> Fax: (212) 681-0517
>
> %FO: 100

● **MATHESON ORMSBY PRENTICE**
30 Herbert St., Dublin 2, Ireland
CEO: Liam Quirke, Mng. Dir.
Bus: *Full service law firm.*

Tel: 353-1-619-9000
Fax: 353-1-619-9010
www.mop.ie

Emp: 400

NAICS: 541110

> **MATHESON ORMSBY PRENTICE**
> 245 Park Ave., New York, New York 10167
> CEO: Elizabeth O'Connor, Mng. Dir.
> Bus: *Full service law firm.*
>
> Tel: (212) 792-4141
> Fax: (212) 792-4131
>
> %FO: 100

● **OAKHILL GROUP PLC**
2a Sandymount Green, Sandymount, Dublin 4, Ireland
CEO: Dan O'Donohoe, Chmn.
Bus: *Engaged in printing and packaging.*

Tel: 353-1-240-1400
Fax: 353-1-240-1450
www.oakhillplc.com

Rev: $53
Emp: 350

NAICS: 323110, 323111, 323115, 323117, 323119, 323121, 541430

> **OAK HILL GROUP**
> 1320 Old Chain Bridge Rd., McLean, Virginia 22101
> CEO: Greg Hearne, Pres.
> Bus: *Management services.*
>
> Tel: (703) 761-1221
> Fax:
>
> Emp: 20

- **PRIMELEARNING GROUP LTD.**
Park House, Plassey Park Rd.,, National Technology Park, Limerick, Ireland
CEO: Terry O'Brien, CEO   Tel: 353-61-720000   Rev: $9
Bus: *Internet based e-learning software.*   Fax: 353-61-720001   Emp: 35
    www.primelearning.com

NAICS: 511210

    PRIMELEARNING GROUP
    410 Park Ave., 15/F, New York, New York 10022
    CEO: Fiona Howard   Tel: (917) 210-8173   %FO: 100
    Bus: *Internet based e-learning software.*   Fax: (917) 210-8182

- **RIVERDEEP INTERACTIVE LEARNING LTD.**
Styne House, 3/F, Upper Hatch St., Dublin 2, Ireland
CEO: Barry O'Callaghan, Chmn. & CEO   Tel: 353-1-670-7570   Rev: $52
Bus: *Mfr. web-based, educational software products.*   Fax: 353-1-670-7626   Emp: 159
    www.riverdeep.net

NAICS: 511210, 516110

    RIVERDEEP INC.
    100 Pine St., Ste. 1900, San Francisco, California 94111
    CEO: Barry O'Callaghan, CEO   Tel: (415) 659-2000
    Bus: *Mfr./sales of educational software.*   Fax: (415) 659-2020   Emp: 667

    RIVERDEEP INC.
    222 3rd Ave. SE, 4/F, Cedar Rapids, Iowa 52401
    CEO: Barry O'Callaghan, CEO   Tel: (319) 395-9686
    Bus: *Mfr./sales of educational software.*   Fax: (319) 395-0217

- **TRANSWARE PLC**
Transware House, South County, Business Park, Leopardstown, Dublin 18, Ireland
CEO: Devin Lynch, Pres. & CEO   Tel: 353-260-1997
Bus: *Business training software manufacture.*   Fax: 353-260-1947
    www.transwareplc.com

NAICS: 519190, 541930

    TRANSWARE
    7901 Stoneridge Dr., Ste. 500, Pleasanton, California 94588
    CEO: Thomas Kelly, Pres. & CEO   Tel: (925) 734-3000   %FO: 100
    Bus: *Business training software manufacture and*   Fax: (925) 224-8642
        sales.

- **TRINITY BIOTECH PLC**
IDA Business Park, Bray, Wicklow, Ireland
CEO: Brendan K. Farrell, Pres.   Tel: 353-1276-9800   Rev: $80
Bus: *Biotech company engaged in manufacture of*   Fax: 353-1276-9888   Emp: 675
    saliva and blood-based medical tests.   www.trinitybiotech.com
NAICS: 325413, 541512, 541710

    TRINITY BIOTECH USA
    1930 Innerbelt Business Center Dr., St. Louis, Missouri 63114
    CEO: George Fiedler, Gen. Mgr.   Tel: (314) 423-5565
    Bus: *Diagnostic substances.*   Fax:

TRINITY BIOTECH USA, INC.
4 Connell Dr., Berkeley Heights, New Jersey 07922
CEO: John Ferrera, CFO
Bus: *Mfr./sales of medical tests.*
Tel: (201) 803-3936
Fax:

TRINITY BIOTECH USA, INC.
2823 Girts Rd., Jamestown, New York 14701
CEO: Ian Woodwards, CEO
Bus: *Mfr./sales of medical tests.*
Tel: (716) 483-3851
Fax: (716) 488-1990
%FO: 100
Emp: 100

● **TRINTECH GROUP PLC**
Trintech House, South County Business Park, Leopardstown, Dublin 18, Ireland
CEO: Cyril P. McGuire, Chmn. & CEO
Bus: *Computer hardware and business equipment.*
Tel: 353-1-207-4000
Fax: 353-1-207-4005
www.trintech.com
Rev: $56
Emp: 315

NAICS: 334111, 334119

TRINTECH INC.
5 Independence Dr., Princeton, New Jersey 08540
CEO: Richard Wood, Mgr.
Bus: *Computer hardware and business equipment.*
Tel: (609) 919-6000
Fax: (609) 720-1020
%FO: 100

TRINTECH INC.
15851 Dallas Pkwy., Ste. 855, Addison, Texas 75001
CEO: Cyril McGuire, Mgr.
Bus: *Computer hardware and business equipment.*
Tel: (972) 701-9802
Fax: (972) 701-9337
%FO: 100
Emp: 80

TRINTECH INC.
1720 Walton Rd., Blue Bell, Pennsylvania 19462
CEO: Pat Moran, Mgr.
Bus: *Computer hardware and business equipment.*
Tel: (610) 825-9865
Fax:
%FO: 100

● **UNIDARE PLC**
Unidare House, Richview Office Park, Ste. 6, Clonskeagh, Dublin 14, Ireland
CEO: John J. Hayes, Chmn.
Bus: *Industrial products manufacture.*
Tel: 353-1-283-7111
Fax: 353-1-260-3177
www.unidare.ie
Rev: $257
Emp: 519

NAICS: 423830, 423840

ORS NASCO
2348 East Shawnee, Muskogee, Oklahoma 74403
CEO: William Scheller, Pres.
Bus: *Industrial products distribution.*
Tel: (918) 687-5441
Fax: (918) 682-5936
%FO: 100
Emp: 656

● **VISION CONSULTING**
Eastpoint Business Park, Fairview, Dublin 3, Ireland
CEO: Billy Glennon, CEO
Bus: *Business and information technology consulting services.*
Tel: 353-1-240-0200
Fax: 353-1-240-0201
www.vision.com
Rev: $41
Emp: 120

NAICS: 541511, 541512

VISION CONSULTING
110 E. 42ND St., Ste. 615, New York, New York 10017
CEO: Charles Follett
Bus: *Business and information technology consulting services.*
Tel: (212) 983-7250
Fax: (212) 983-7454
%FO: 100

• **WATERFORD WEDGWOOD PLC**
1-2 Upper Hatch St., Dublin 2, Ireland
CEO: Moira Gavin, Chmn.
Bus: *Manufacturing and marketing of lead crystal, china and cookware.*
NAICS: 327112, 327215
Tel: 353-1478-1855
Fax: 353-1478-4863
www.waterfordwedgwood.com
Rev: $1,024
Emp: 8,059

ALL-CLAD INC.
424 Morganza Rd., Canonsburg, Pennsylvania 15317
CEO: Peter Cameron
Bus: *Cookware and food preparation products manufacture.*
Tel: (724) 745-8300
Fax: (724) 746-5053
%FO: 100

WATERFORD WEDGWOOD USA INC
1330 Campus Pkwy., Wall, New Jersey 07719
CEO: John Foley, CEO
Bus: *Marketing of crystal and china.*
Tel: (732) 938-5800
Fax: (732) 938-7108
%FO: 100

• **WBT SYSTEMS LTD.**
Block 2, Harcourt Ctr., Harcourt St., Dublin 2, Ireland
CEO: Declan Kelly, CEO
Bus: *Enterprise e-learning software manufacture.*
NAICS: 511210
Tel: 353-1-417-0100
Fax: 353-1-478-5544
www.wbtsystems.com

WBT SYSTEMS
1601 Trapelo Rd., Waltham, Massachusetts 02451
CEO: Jim Whelan, VP & Gen. Mgr.
Bus: *Enterprise e-learning software manufacture.*
Tel: (781) 684-8270
Fax: (781) 684-8033
%FO: 100

• **XSIL LTD.**
Pearse St., Trinity Enterprise Centre, Ste. 3, Dublin 2, Ireland
CEO: Peter Conlon, CEO
Bus: *Semiconductor wafer manufacture.*
NAICS: 333295
Tel: 353-1-245-7500
Fax: 353-1-245-7501
www.xsil.com
Rev: $33
Emp: 120

XSIL USA INC.
4710 Bonnell Dr., Loveland, Colorado 80537
CEO: Dick Toftness, Mgr.
Bus: *Semiconductor wafer manufacture and sales.*
Tel: (970) 310-4994
Fax: (970) 613-9250
%FO: 100

Israel

- **ACS-TECH80 LTD.**
  Ramat Gabriel Industrial Park, PO Box 5668, Migdal Haemek 10500, Israel
  CEO: Ze'ev Kirshenboim, CEO
  Bus: *Programmable motion control products for automated systems.*
  NAICS: 561621

  Tel: 972-4-654-6440
  Fax: 972-6-654-6443
  www.acs-motion-control.com

  Rev: $8
  Emp: 75

  ACS-TECH80 INC.
  14700 28th Ave. North, Plymouth, Minnesota 55447
  CEO: Evan Reed
  Bus: *Mfr. programmable motion control products for automated systems.*

  Tel: (763) 559-7669
  Fax: (763) 559-0110

  %FO: 100

- **ALADDIN KNOWLEDGE SYSTEMS LTD.**
  15 Bein Oved St., Tel Aviv 61110, Israel
  CEO: Jacob Yanki Margalit, Chmn. & CEO
  Bus: *Sales, installation and service of software for security systems.*
  NAICS: 541511

  Tel: 972-3-636-2222
  Fax: 972-3-537-5796
  www.aks.com

  Rev: $69
  Emp: 351

  ALADDIN KNOWLEDGE SYSTEMS, INC.
  2920 N. Arlington Heights Rd., Arlington Heights, Illinois 60004
  CEO: Yanki Margalite, Pres.
  Bus: *Develop/sales/installation/service software for security systems.*

  Tel: (847) 808-0300
  Fax: (847) 808-0313

  %FO: 100

  ALADDIN KNOWLEDGE SYSTEMS, INC.
  360 West 31st St., Ste. 5110, New York, New York 10001
  CEO: Erez Rosen, Pres.
  Bus: *Develop/sales/installation/service software for security systems.*

  Tel: (212) 564-5678
  Fax: (212) 564-3377

  %FO: 100
  Emp: 18

- **ALBA-WALDENSIAN, INC.**
  28 Chida St., Bnei-Brak 51371, Israel
  CEO: Doug Dickson, CEO
  Bus: *Health products manufacture, including undergarments.*
  NAICS: 315119, 315192, 339113

  Tel: 972-3-579-8701
  Fax: 972-3-579-8715
  www.alba1.com

  ALBA-WALDENSIAN, INC.
  201 St. Germain Ave. SW, Valdese, North Carolina 28690
  CEO: Dan Miseka
  Bus: *Health products manufacture, including undergarments.*

  Tel: (828) 879-6500
  Fax: (828) 879-6559

- **ALLIANCE TIRE COMPANY**
  1 Fridlander St. Industrial Zone, Box 48, Hadera 38100, Israel
  CEO: Israel Chechik, Pres.   Tel: 972-6-624-0520   Rev: $96
  Bus: *Mfr. tires.*   Fax: 972-6-624-0520   Emp: 978
                                                          www.alliance.co.il

  NAICS: 326211
  - **ALLIANCE USA LTD.**
    204 Eaglerock Ave., Roseland, New Jersey 07068
    CEO: Leslie Gurland, Gen. Mgr.   Tel: (973) 364-5100   %FO: 100
    Bus: *Tire distribution.*   Fax: (973) 364-8177   Emp: 10

- **ALLOT COMMUNICATIONS**
  5 Hanagar St., Industrial Zone B, Hod-Hasharon 45800, Israel
  CEO: Eran Ziv, CEO   Tel: 972-9-761-9200   Rev: $100
  Bus: *Solutions for enterprises and IP service providers.* Fax: 972-9-744-3626 Emp: 115
                                                          www.allot.com

  NAICS: 334119, 541512
  - **ALLOT COMMUNICATIONS**
    250 Prairie Center Dr., Ste. 335, Eden Prairie, Minnesota 55344
    CEO: P. G. Narayanan, CEO   Tel: (952) 944-3100   %FO: 100
    Bus: *Solutions for enterprises and IP service*   Fax: (952) 944-3555
         providers.

  - **ALLOT COMMUNICATIONS**
    240E Twin Dolphin Dr., Redwood City, California 94065
    CEO: P. G. Narayanan, CEO   Tel: (650) 802-8550   %FO: 100
    Bus: *Solutions for enterprises and IP service*   Fax: (650) 802-8545
         providers.

- **ALVARION LTD.**
  21a HaBarzel St., Box 13139, Tel Aviv 61131, Israel
  CEO: Zvi Slonimski, CEO   Tel: 972-3-645-6262   Rev: $201
  Bus: *Broadband wireless network access equipment*   Fax: 972-3-645-6290   Emp: 743
       manufacture.   www.alvarion.com
  NAICS: 334119
  - **ALVARION, INC.**
    5858 Edison Place, Carlsbad, California 92008
    CEO: Joel Green   Tel: (760) 517-3100   %FO: 100
    Bus: *Broadband wireless network access*   Fax: (760) 517-3200
         equipment manufacture and sales.

- **AMERICAN ISRAELI PAPER MILLS LTD.**
  PO Box 142, Industrial Zone, Hadera 38101, Israel
  CEO: Avi Brener, CEO   Tel: 972-6-634-9349   Rev: $111
  Bus: *Mfr. paper and paper products.*   Fax: 972-6-633-9740   Emp: 3,133
                                                          www.aipm.co.il

  NAICS: 322121, 322299

GREEN LIND & McNULTY, INC.
1435 Morris Ave., Union, New Jersey 07083
CEO: Philip Y. Sardoff, Sr. Prtn.
Bus: *Investor relations consultant to American Israeli Paper mills, a mfr. of paper and paper products.*

Tel: (908) 686-7500
Fax: (908) 686-4757

%FO: 100

● **AREL COMMUNICATIONS AND SOFTWARE LTD.**
22 Einstein St., Science Park, Bldg. 2, Kiryat Weizman, Nes Ziona 74140, Israel
CEO: Philipe Szwarc, CEO
Bus: *Video conferencing software manufacture.*

Tel: 972-8-972-0880
Fax: 972-8-943-8106
www.arel.net

Rev: $4
Emp: 52

NAICS: 511210

AREL COMMUNICATIONS AND SOFTWARE INC.
1200 Ashwood Pkwy., Ste. 550, Atlanta, Georgia 30338
CEO: Moshe Ben-Yishai
Bus: *Video conferencing software manufacture and sales.*

Tel: (770) 396-8105
Fax: (770) 396-1755

%FO: 100

● **ATTUNITY LTD.**
Einstein Building, Carmel Business Park, Tirat Carmel 39101, Israel
CEO: Itzhak Ratner, CEO
Bus: *Business applications software manufacture.*

Tel: 972-4-855-9666
Fax: 972-4-857-6745
www.attunity.com

Rev: $17
Emp: 160

NAICS: 511210

ATTUNITY INC.
40 Audubon Rd., Wakefield, Massachusetts 01880
CEO: Terry Layo, VP
Bus: *Software sales and distribution.*

Tel: (781) 213-5200
Fax: (781) 213-5240

%FO: 100

● **AUDIOCODES LTD.**
1 Hayarden St., Airport City, Lod 70151, Israel
CEO: Shabtai Adlersberg, CEO
Bus: *Mfr. voice compression products for network*

Tel: 972-3-976-4000
Fax: 972-3-976-4040
www.audiocodes.com

Rev: $83
Emp: 328

NAICS: 334413

AUDIOCODES, INC.
27 World's Fair Dr., Somerset, New Jersey 08873
CEO: Stephanie Fennell
Bus: *Mfr. voice compression products for network use.*

Tel: (732) 469-0880
Fax: (732) 469-2298

%FO: 100

AUDIOCODES, INC.
101 West Renner Rd., Ste. 220, Richardson, Texas 75081
CEO: John D'Annunzio
Bus: *Mfr. voice compression products for network use.*

Tel: (972) 238-7976
Fax: (972) 238-8038

%FO: 100

AUDIOCODES, INC.
2099 Gateway Place, Ste. 500, San Jose, California 95110
CEO: Bruce Gellman, Pres.   Tel: (408) 441-1175   %FO: 100
Bus: *Mfr. voice compression products for*   Fax: (408) 451-9520
       network use.

AUDIOCODES, INC.
Deerfoot Office Park 257, Turnpike Rd., Ste. 320, Southborough, Massachusetts 01772
CEO: Ran Silberman, VP Sales   Tel: (508) 787-3800   %FO: 100
Bus: *Mfr. voice compression products for*   Fax: (508) 357-2043
       network use.

AUDIOCODES, INC.
8700 West Bryn Mawr, Ste. 720-S, Chicago, Illinois 60631
CEO: Rich Poole   Tel: (773) 695-9870   %FO: 100
Bus: *Mfr. voice compression products for*   Fax: (773) 695-9893
       network use.

● **BANK HAPOALIM BM**
50 Rothschild Blvd., Tel Aviv 66883, Israel
CEO: Zvi Ziv, CEO   Tel: 972-3-567-3333   Rev: $2,598
Bus: *Commercial banking services.*   Fax: 972-3-560-7028   Emp: 12,566
                                               www.bankhapoalim.co.il
  NAICS: 522110, 522292, 523110, 523920, 523930, 523991, 524210, 525910, 525920

   BANK HAPOALIM
   1177 Ave. of the Americas, 14/F, New York, New York 10036
   CEO: Shlomo Braun, Mgr.   Tel: (212) 782-2000   %FO: 100
   Bus: *Commercial banking branch office.*   Fax: (212) 782-2222   Emp: 240

   BANK HAPOALIM
   18851 NE 29th Ave., Ste. 800, Aventura, Florida 33180
   CEO: Haya Hover, Mgr.   Tel: (305) 466-7400   %FO: 100
   Bus: *Commercial bank.*   Fax: (305) 466-7699   Emp: 25

   BANK HAPOALIM
   225 North Michigan Ave., Chicago, Illinois 60601
   CEO: Azarya Ressler, SVP   Tel: (312) 228-6400   %FO: 100
   Bus: *Commercial banking branch office.*   Fax: (312) 228-6490   Emp: 12

● **BANK LEUMI LE ISRAEL B.M.**
24-32 Yehuda Halevi St., Tel Aviv 65546, Israel
CEO: Galia Maor, Pres. & CEO   Tel: 972-3-514-8111   Rev: $2,123
Bus: *Commercial banking services.*   Fax: 972-3-566-1872   Emp: 11,500
                                               www.bankleumi.co.il
  NAICS: 522110, 522210, 522292, 522310, 523120, 523920, 523930, 551111

   BANK LEUMI USA
   579 Fifth Ave., 3/F, New York, New York 10017
   CEO: Uzi Rosen, CEO   Tel: (917) 542-2343   %FO: 100
   Bus: *Commercial banking services.*   Fax: (917) 542-2254   Emp: 492

- **BARAN GROUP**
Baran House, Industrial Park, 8 Omarim Street, Omer 84965, Israel
CEO: Meir Dor, Chmn. & CEO   Tel: 972-8-620-0200   Rev: $183
Bus: *Engineering and consulting services and*   Fax: 972-8-620-0201   Emp: 1,300
telecommunications.   www.baran.co.il
NAICS: 236210, 237130, 237310, 237990, 517910, 541330, 541618

  BARAN GROUP
  805 Third Ave., 12/F, New York, New York 10022
  CEO: Alex Berd, CEO   Tel: (212) 207-4755   %FO: 100
  Bus: *Engineering and consulting services and*   Fax: (212) 207-4998
  telecommunications.

  BARAN GROUP
  104030 Rodgers Rd., Houston, Texas 77070
  CEO: Dee Farquhar, VP   Tel: (713) 973-6904   %FO: 100
  Bus: *Engineering and consulting services and*   Fax: (713) 973-0205
  telecommunications.

  BARAN TELECOM, INC.
  2355 Industrial Park Blvd., Cumming, Georgia 30041
  CEO: Ran Bukshpan, Chmn. & CEO   Tel: (678) 513-1501   %FO: 100
  Bus: *Engineering and consulting services and*   Fax: (678) 455-1153
  telecommunications.

  BARANTEC INC.
  Plaza 777 Passaic Ave., Ste. 4, Clifton, New Jersey 07012
  CEO: Diane Bersen, VP   Tel: (973) 779-8774   %FO: 100
  Bus: *Engineering and consulting services and*   Fax: (973) 779-8768   Emp: 10
  telecommunications.

- **BATM ADVANCED COMMUNICATIONS LTD.**
22 Hamelacha St., Bldg. 4, Rosh Ha'Ayin 48091, Israel
CEO: Zvi Marom, CEO   Tel: 972-3-938-6888   Rev: $49
Bus: *Mfr. networking and connectivity hardware.*   Fax: 972-3-938-6896   Emp: 250
www.batm.com
NAICS: 325221, 331491, 334210, 334290, 334310, 518111

  TELCO SYSTEMS, INC.
  2 Hampshire St., Ste. 3A, Foxboro, Massachusetts 02035-2897
  CEO: Ofer Bar-Ner, CEO   Tel: (781) 551-0300   %FO: 100
  Bus: *Mfr. networking and connectivity hardware.*   Fax: (781) 551-0538

- **BLUEPHOENIX SOLUTIONS LTD.**
8 Maskit St., PO Box 2062, Herzliyya 46120, Israel
CEO: Arik Kilman   Tel: 972-9-952-6100   Rev: $49

  Arik Kilman
  Arik Kilman, CEO
Bus: *Mfr. software.*   Fax: 972-9-952-6111   Emp: 500
www.bphx.com.
NAICS: 511210

BLUE PHOENIX SOLUTIONS LTD.
8000 Regency Pkwy., Cary, North Carolina 27511
CEO: Arik Kilman
Bus: *Mfr. software.*
Tel: (919) 380-5100
Fax: (919) 380-5111
%FO: 100

BLUE PHOENIX SOLUTIONS LTD.
45 West 25th St., New York, New York 10010
CEO: Ted Venema
Bus: *Mfr. software.*
Tel: (212) 947-5802
Fax: (212) 739-7449
%FO: 100

● **BVR SYSTEMS LTD.**
16 Hamelacha St., Afek Industrial Park, Rosh Ha'Ayin 48091, Israel
CEO: Aviv Tzidon, Chmn.
Bus: *Air, naval and ground, state-of-the-art simulation and training systems manufacture.*
Tel: 972-3-900-8000
Fax: 972-3-900-8030
www.bvrsystems.com
Rev: $13
Emp: 63
NAICS: 332995, 333319, 334511, 336413

ELISRA, INC.
10 East 53rd St., 25/F, New York, New York 10022
CEO: Arie Dolev
Bus: *Mfr./sales of air, naval and ground, state-of-the-art simulation and training systems.*
Tel: (212) 751-5018
Fax: (212) 751-5183
%FO: 100

● **CAMTEK LTD.**
Ramat Gavriel Ind. Zone, PO Box 544, Migdal Haemek 23150, Israel
CEO: Rafi Amit, CEO
Bus: *Mfr. intelligent optical inspection systems for the Printed Circuit Board (PCB), Semiconductor Packaging, and Microelectronics industries.*
Tel: 972-4-604-8100
Fax: 972-4-644-0523
www.camtek.co.il
Rev: $67
Emp: 265
NAICS: 334412

CAMTEK USA INC.
2000 Hyatt Dr., Santa Clara, California 95054
CEO: Tommy Weiss
Bus: *Sales of intelligent optical inspection systems for the Printed Circuit Board (PCB), Semiconductor Packaging, and Microelectronics industries.*
Tel: (408) 986-9540
Fax: (408) 986-9871
%FO: 100

CAMTEK USA INC.
3301 Route 66, Bldg. B, 2/F, Neptune, New Jersey 07753
CEO: Moshe Amit
Bus: *Sales of intelligent optical inspection systems for the Printed Circuit Board (PCB), Semiconductor Packaging, and Microelectronics industries.*
Tel: (732) 695-1333
Fax: (732) 542-7866
%FO: 100

● **CERAGON NETWORKS LTD.**
24 Raoul Wallenberg St., Tel Aviv 69719, Israel
CEO: Shraga Katz, CEO
Bus: *Network management software manufacture.*
Tel: 972-3-645-5733
Fax: 972-3-645-5499
www.ceragon.com
Rev: $55
Emp: 260
NAICS: 334119, 334220, 511210

CERAGON NETWORKS INC.
1 Chestnut St., Ste. 337, Nashua, New Hampshire 03060
CEO: Scott Sweetland
Bus: *Network management software manufacture and sales.*
Tel: (603) 886-8503
Fax: (603) 886-8523
%FO: 100

CERAGON NETWORKS INC.
10 Forest Ave., Paramus, New Jersey 07652
CEO: David Ackerman, Pres.
Bus: *Network management software manufacture and sales.*
Tel: (201) 845-6955
Fax: (201) 845-5665
%FO: 100

● **CHECK POINT SOFTWARE TECHNOLOGIES LTD.**
3A Jabotinsky St., Diamond Tower, Ramat Gan 52520, Israel
CEO: Gil Shwed, CEO
Bus: *Mfr. virus protection software.*
Tel: 972-3-753-4555
Fax: 972-3-575-9256
www.checkpoint.com
Rev: $515
Emp: 1,344

NAICS: 511210

CHECK POINT SOFTWARE TECHNOLOGIES LTD.
800 Bridge Pkwy., Redwood City, California 94065
CEO: Gil Shwed, VP
Bus: *Mfr. virus protection software.*
Tel: (650) 628-2000
Fax: (650) 654-4233
%FO: 100

CHECK POINT SOFTWARE TECHNOLOGIES LTD.
1704 Cabriole Mews, Virginia Beach, Virginia 23455
CEO: Dan Cavallaro
Bus: *Mfr. virus protection software.*
Tel: (757) 363-9894
Fax: (757) 363-9894
%FO: 100

CHECK POINT SOFTWARE TECHNOLOGIES LTD.
2505 North Highway 360, Ste. 800, Grand Prairie, Texas 75050
CEO: Bill Gerton
Bus: *Mfr. virus protection software.*
Tel: (817) 606-6600
Fax: (817) 652-9373
%FO: 100

● **CHIPX**
Advanced Technology Center, PO Box 2401, Haifa 31000, Israel
CEO: Amnon Fisher, Pres. & CEO
Bus: *Mfr. laser based turnkey systems for in-house prototype advanced application-specific integrated circuit (ASIC) products.*
Tel: 972-4-8550011
Fax: 972-4-8551122
www.chipx.co.il

NAICS: 333295

CHIP EXPRESS CORPORATION
2323 Owen St., Santa Clara, California 95054
CEO: Amnon Fisher, Pres. & CEO
Bus: *Develops internet applications and telecommunications software.*
Tel: (408) 988-2445
Fax: (408) 988-2449
%FO: 100
Emp: 95

● **CIMATRON LIMITED**
11 Gush Etzion St., Givat Shmuel 54030, Israel
CEO: Zvika Naggan, CEO
Bus: *CAD/CAM computer software manufacture.*
Tel: 972-3-531-2221
Fax: 972-3-531-2192
www.cimatron.com
Rev: $23
Emp: 215

NAICS: 511210

CIMATRON TECHNOLOGIES INC.
26800 Meadowbrook Rd., Ste. 113, Novi, Michigan 48377
CEO: Lisa Sterling   Tel: (248) 596-9700   %FO: 100
Bus: *CAD/CAM computer software manufacture* Fax: (248) 596-9741
     and sales.

● **CLICKSOFTWARE TECHNOLOGIES LTD.**
34 Habarzel St., Tel Aviv 69710, Israel
CEO: Moshe BenBassat, CEO   Tel: 972-3-765-9400   Rev: $22
Bus: *Mfr. Click Schedule software for corporations.* Fax: 972-3-765-9401   Emp: 154
     www.clicksoftware.com

  NAICS: 511210

    CLICKSOFTWARE, INC.
    70 Blanchard Rd., Burlington, Massachusetts 01830
    CEO: Tracy Shatford, Mgr.   Tel: (781) 272-5903   %FO: 100
    Bus: *Mfr. Click Schedule software for* Fax: (781) 272-6409
      corporations.

    CLICKSOFTWARE, INC.
    1999 South Bascom Ave., Campbell, California 95008-2216
    CEO: Mary Magnani   Tel: (408) 377-6088   %FO: 100
    Bus: *Mfr. Click Schedule software for* Fax: (408) 377-9088
      corporations.

● **COMMTOUCH SOFTWARE INC.**
1A Hatzoran St., PO Box 8511, Netanya 42504, Israel
CEO: Gideon Mantel, CEO   Tel: 972-9-863-6888   Rev: $2
Bus: *Management application software manufacture.* Fax: 972-9-863-6863   Emp: 45
     www.commtouch.com

  NAICS: 511210, 541511

    COMMTOUCH SOFTWARE INC.
    1300 Crittenden lane, Ste. 102, Mountain View, California 94043
    CEO: Gideon Mantel   Tel: (650) 864-2000   %FO: 100
    Bus: *Management application software* Fax: (650) 864-2002
      manufacture and sales.

● **COMPUGEN LTD.**
72 Pinchas Rosen St., Tel Aviv 69512, Israel
CEO: Mor Amitai, Pres. & CEO   Tel: 972-3-765-8585   Rev: $11
Bus: *Develops gene technology.* Fax: 972-3-765-8555   Emp: 175
     www.cgen.com

  NAICS: 541710

    COMPUGEN, INC.
    560 South Winchester Blvd., Ste.500, San Jose, California 95128
    CEO: Michelle Anderson, Office Mgr.   Tel: (408) 236-7336   %FO: 100
    Bus: *Develops gene technology.* Fax: (408) 236-7334

- **CONNECT ONE, LTD.**
  2 Hanagar St., Kfar Saba 44425, Israel
  CEO: Amir Friedman, CEO
  Bus: *Mfr. chips, software, and hardware, enabling efficient industrial, commercial and consumer devices, reducing time, cost and complexity of internet connection.*
  NAICS: 334119, 334413, 511210

  Tel: 972-9-760-0456
  Fax: 972-9-766-0461
  www.connectone.com

  CONNECT ONE SEMICONDUCTORS, INC.
  15818 N 9th Ave., Phoenix, Arizona 85023
  CEO: Richard Miller, VP
  Bus: *Mfr. chips, software, & hardware, enabling efficient industrial, commercial & consumer devices, reducing time, cost & complexity of internet connection.*

  Tel: (602) 493-5382
  Fax: (602) 493-5382

  %FO: 100

- **DELTA-GALIL INDUSTRIES LTD.**
  2 Kaufman St., Tel Aviv 68012, Israel
  CEO: Arnon Tiberg, CEO
  Bus: *Mfr. private label and licensed underwear.*

  Tel: 972-3-519-3636
  Fax: 972-5-519-3705
  www.deltagalil.com

  Rev: $654
  Emp: 14,200

  NAICS: 315192

  DELTA MILLS MARKETING INC.
  150 Meadowlands Pkwy., Secaucus, New Jersey 07094
  CEO: David Kastman
  Bus: *Mfr. private label and licensed underwear.*

  Tel: (201) 902-0055
  Fax: (201) 902-0070

  %FO: 100

  DELTA TEXTILES LTD.
  347 Fifth Ave., Ste. 503, New York, New York 10016
  CEO: Yossi Hajaj
  Bus: *Mfr. private label and licensed underwear.*

  Tel: (212) 481-3550
  Fax: (212) 481-3881

  %FO: 100

- **DRYKOR, LTD.**
  PO Box 17, Atlit 30300, Israel
  CEO: Joseph W. Lewis, CEO
  Bus: *Dehumidifiers and thermal air conditioners development and manufacture.*
  NAICS: 333415

  Tel: 972-4-954-1040
  Fax: 972-4-954-1041
  www.drykor.com

  DRYKOR, INC.
  205 Carnes Dr., Fayetteville, Georgia 30214
  CEO: Bruce Buchholz
  Bus: *Dehumidifiers and thermal air conditioners development, manufacture and sales.*

  Tel: (678) 817-0299
  Fax: (678) 817-1355

  %FO: 100

- **ECI TELECOM LTD.**
  30 Hasivim St., Petah Tikva 49133, Israel
  CEO: Doron Inbar, Pres. & CEO
  Bus: *Telecom equipment manufacturer.*

  Tel: 972-3-926-6555
  Fax: 972-3-926-6711
  www.ecitele.com

  Rev: $497
  Emp: 2,638

  NAICS: 334210, 334290

ECI TELECOM, INC.
1201 W. Cypress Creek Rd., Ft. Lauderdale, Florida 33309
CEO: Paul Ellett, Gen. Mgr.   Tel: (954) 772-3070   %FO: 100
Bus: *Digital cross-connect systems provider.*   Fax: (954) 351-4404   Emp: 70

ECTEL INC. USA
8211 West Broward Blvd., Ste. 460, Ft. Lauderdale, Florida 33324
CEO: Aaron Shech, Principal   Tel: (954) 465-2400   %FO: 100
Bus: *Marketing services & fraud software.*   Fax: (954) 335-1430

LAUREL NETWORKS, INC.
Omega Corporate Center, 1300 Omega Dr., Pittsburgh, Pennsylvania 15205
CEO: Don Pyle, CEO   Tel: (412) 809-4200   %FO: 100
Bus: *Optical switching & transmission equipment.*   Fax: (412) 809-4201   Emp: 138

VERAZ NETWORKS, INC.
926 Rock Ave., Ste. 20, San Jose, California 95131
CEO: Douglas Sabella, Pres. & CEO   Tel: (408) 750-9400   %FO: 100
Bus: *Networking & connectivity software.*   Fax: (408) 546-0081

● **ECTEL LTD.**
43 Hasivim St., Petah Tikva 49517, Israel
CEO: Harel Beit-On, CEO   Tel: 972-3-926-8200   Rev: $12
Bus: *Communications hardware and software*   Fax: 972-3-926-8282   Emp: 189
   manufacture.   www.ectel.com
NAICS: 541511, 541512

   ECTEL INC.
   8211 W. Broward Blvd., Suite 460, Ft. Lauderdale, Florida 33324
   CEO: Eitan Naor   Tel: (954) 465-2400   %FO: 100
   Bus: *Communications hardware and software*   Fax: (301) 351-4306
      manufacture and sales.

● **EDUSOFT LTD.**
16 Hamelacha St., Afek Industrial Park, Rosh Ha'Ayin 48091, Israel
CEO: Soly Kanes, Pres.   Tel: 972-3-900-2440   Rev: $7
Bus: *Multimedia educational software manufacture.*   Fax: 972-3-900-2401   Emp: 40
                                  www.edusoft.co.il
NAICS: 511210

   INNOVATIVE TECHNOLOGIES IN EDUCATION
   1181 S. Rogers Circle, Ste. 13, Boca Raton, Florida 33487
   CEO: Kim Jones, Pres.   Tel: (561) 953-0190   %FO: 100
   Bus: *Multimedia educational software.*   Fax: (561) 953-0188

● **EL AL ISRAEL AIRLINES LTD.**
PO Box 41, Ben Gurion Airport, Tel Aviv 70110, Israel
CEO: Israel Borovich, Chmn.   Tel: 972-3-971-6111   Rev: $1,386
Bus: *International air transport services.*   Fax: 972-3-972-1442   Emp: 5,417
                                 www.elal.co.il
NAICS: 561599

EL AL ISRAEL AIRLINES
Newark Airport, Newark, New Jersey 07114
CEO: Susanna Dikker
Bus: *International air transport services.*
Tel: (973) 643-3042
Fax: (973) 643-3042
%FO: 100

EL AL ISRAEL AIRLINES
407 Lincoln Rd., Ste. 4B, Miami, Florida 33139-3008
CEO: Shimshon Roth
Bus: *International air transport services.*
Tel: (305) 532-5441
Fax: (305) 532-5441
%FO: 100

EL AL ISRAEL AIRLINES
Cargo Bldg. 83-84, Jamaica, New York 11430
CEO: David Kilsten
Bus: *International air transport services.*
Tel: (718) 244-3176
Fax: (718) 244-3176
%FO: 100

EL AL ISRAEL AIRLINES
PO Box 488, Southfield, Michigan 48037-0488
CEO: Lynn Koppinger
Bus: *International air transport services.*
Tel: (248) 354-3777
Fax: (248) 354-3777
%FO: 100

EL AL ISRAEL AIRLINES
55 E Monroe St., Ste. 2950, Chicago, Illinois 60603
CEO: Dave Taylor
Bus: *International air transport services.*
Tel: (312) 516-3525
Fax: (312) 516-3525
%FO: 100

EL AL ISRAEL AIRLINES
120 West 45th St., 18/F, New York, New York 10036-9998
CEO: Michael Mayer, Pres.
Bus: *International air transport services.*
Tel: (212) 852-0600
Fax: (212) 768-9440
%FO: 100

EL AL ISRAEL AIRLINES
20 Park Plaza, Boston, Massachusetts 02166-4303
CEO: David Smith
Bus: *International air transport services.*
Tel: (617) 426-2651
Fax: (617) 426-2651
%FO: 100

EL AL ISRAEL AIRLINES
173 Rhode Island Ave. NW, Washington, District of Columbia 20001-1672
CEO: Katherine Jochon
Bus: *International air transport services.*
Tel: (202) 296-5440
Fax: (202) 296-5440
%FO: 100

EL AL ISRAEL AIRLINES
1515 Market St., Ste. 625, Philadelphia, Pennsylvania 19102
CEO: Yair Cohen
Bus: *International air transport services.*
Tel: (215) 563-8011
Fax: (215) 563-8011
%FO: 100

EL AL ISRAEL AIRLINES
380 World Way, Los Angeles, California 90045
CEO: Peter Kramer
Bus: *International air transport services.*
Tel: (310) 646-2906
Fax: (310) 646-1223
%FO: 100

EL AL ISRAEL AIRLINES
6040 Avion Dr., Ste. 333, Los Angeles, California 90045
CEO: Craig Wyman
Bus: *International air transport services.*
Tel: (310) 646-1223
Fax: (310) 646-1223
%FO: 100

● **ELBIT VISION SYSTEMS LTD.**
New Industrial Park, Bldg. 7, Yokneam 20692, Israel
CEO: Menashe Shohat, CEO   Tel: 972-4-9936-400   Rev: $11
Bus: *Automatic inspection systems manufacture.*   Fax: 972-4-989-4733   Emp: 132
     www.evs.co.il

NAICS: 334513, 334515, 335313

    ELBIT VISION SYSTEMS
    319 Garlington Rd., Ste. B4, Greenville, South Carolina 29615
    CEO: Sam Cohen   Tel: (864) 288-9777   %FO: 100
    Bus: *Automatic inspection systems manufacture*   Fax: (864) 288-9799
    and sales.

● **ELECTRONICS LINE 3000 LTD.**
2 Granit St., Kiryat Arieh 49130, Israel
CEO: Amir Hayek, CEO   Tel: 972-3-918-1333   Rev: $38
Bus: *Wireless and wired burglar alarm systems*   Fax: 972-3-922-0831   Emp: 270
manufacture.   www.elecline.com
NAICS: 238210

    ELECTRONICS LINE USA INC.
    5637 Arapahoe Ave., Boulder, Colorado 80303
    CEO: Mike Davis   Tel: (303) 938-1133   %FO: 100
    Bus: *Wireless and wired burglar alarm systems*   Fax: (303) 938-8062
    manufacture and sales.

    SECTEC GLOBAL
    200 Concord Plaza, Ste. 700, San Antonio, Texas 78216
    CEO: Robert G. Marbut   Tel: (210) 828-1700   %FO: 100
    Bus: *Wireless security systems.*   Fax: (210) 828-7300

    SECTEC GLOBAL
    156 West 56 St., Suite 1605, New York, New York 10019
    CEO: Karen Sussman   Tel: (212) 265-2400   %FO: 100
    Bus: *Wireless security systems.*   Fax: (212) 265-2419

● **ELRON ELECTRONIC INDUSTRIES LTD.**
3 Azrieli Center, 42nd Fl., Tel Aviv 67023, Israel
CEO: Doron Birger, Pres. & CEO   Tel: 972-3-607-5555   Rev: $16
Bus: *Develops internet applications and*   Fax: 972-3-607-5556   Emp: 22
telecommunications software.   www.elron.com
NAICS: 541511

    ELRON TELESOFT INC.
    7 New England Executive Park, Burlington, Massachusetts 01803
    CEO: Ray Boelig, CEO   Tel: (781) 744-6000   %FO: 100
    Bus: *Develops internet applications and*   Fax: (781) 744-6222
    telecommunications software.

    OREN SEMICONDUCTOR INC.
    2620 Augustine Dr., Suite 238, Santa Clara, California 95054
    CEO: Avraham Menachem,   Tel: (408) 330-0300   %FO: JV
    Bus: *Semiconductor manufacture.*   Fax: (408) 330-0305

- **ELTEK LTD.**
  4 Drezner St., Sgoola Industrial Zone, PO Box 159, Petah Tikva 49101, Israel
  CEO: Arieh Reichart, CEO
  Bus: *Printed circuit board manufacture.*

  Tel: 972-3-939-5050
  Fax: 972-3-930-9581
  www.eltekglobal.com

  Rev: $29
  Emp: 244

  NAICS: 334412

  > **ELTEK LTD.**
  > 55 Crystal Ave., PMB 289, Derry, New Hampshire 03038
  > CEO: Jim Barry
  > Bus: *Printed circuit board manufacture and sales.*
  >
  > Tel: (603) 329-5452
  > Fax: (603) 329-7047
  >
  > %FO: 100

- **E-SIM LTD.**
  Bynet Building, 19 Hartum St., 5 Kiryat Mada, Jerusalem 91450, Israel
  CEO: Marc Belzberg, CEO
  Bus: *Mfr. software to prototype and test products.*

  Tel: 972-2-587-0770
  Fax: 972-2-587-0773
  www.e-sim.com

  Rev: $4
  Emp: 57

  NAICS: 511210

  > **E-SIM INC**
  > 225 South Lake Ave., Ste. 300, Pasadena, California 91101
  > CEO: Ken Dixon
  > Bus: *Mfr. software to prototype and test products.*
  >
  > Tel: (626) 584-7810
  > Fax: (626) 584-7175
  >
  > %FO: 100

- **EXENT TECHNOLOGIES LTD.**
  10 Granit St., Petah Tikva 49125, Israel
  CEO: Zvi Levgoren, CEO
  Bus: *Develops Applications-on-Demand (AoD) technology to deliver computer software programs over IP networks in real time.*

  Tel: 972-3-924-3828
  Fax: 972-3-924-3930
  www.exent.com

  NAICS: 541511, 541519

  > **EXENT TECHNOLOGIES INC.**
  > 7910 Woodmont Ave., Ste. 430, Bethesda, Maryland 20814
  > CEO: Yoav Tzruya, VP Sales
  > Bus: *Sales of Applications-on-Demand (AoD) technology to deliver computer software programs over IP networks in real time.*
  >
  > Tel: (301) 652-7351
  > Fax: (301) 581-5925
  >
  > %FO: 100

- **EZCHIP TECHNOLOGIES INC.**
  1 Hatamar St., Yokneam 20692, Israel
  CEO: Eli Fruchter, CEO
  Bus: *Semiconductor manufacture.*

  Tel: 972-4-959-6666
  Fax: 972-4-959-4166
  www.ezchip.com

  NAICS: 334413

  > **EZCHIP TECHNOLOGIES INC.**
  > 900 East Hamilton Ave., Ste. 100, Campbell, California 95008
  > CEO: Rob O'Hara
  > Bus: *Semiconductor manufacture and sales.*
  >
  > Tel: (408) 879-7355
  > Fax: (408) 879-7357
  >
  > %FO: 100

- **FORMULA SYSTEMS LTD.**
  3 Abba Eban Blvd., Herzliyya 46725, Israel
  CEO: Gad Goldstein, CEO
  Bus: *Provides advanced data-driven solutions,
      services and products for e-commerce and
      business solutions.*
  NAICS: 541511, 541512, 541519

  Tel: 972-9-959-8954
  Fax: 972-9-959-8980
  www.formulasystems.com

  Rev: $457
  Emp: 3,500

    XTIVIA, INC.
    2035 Lincoln Highway, Ste. 2150, Edison, New Jersey 08817
    CEO: Tony Salerno, Pres.
    Bus: *Provides advanced data-driven solutions,
        services and products for e-commerce and
        business solutions.*

    Tel: (732) 248-9399
    Fax: (732) 248-5522

    %FO: 100

    XTIVIA, INC.
    45 West 25th St., 11/F, New York, New York 10010
    CEO: Nir Gryn
    Bus: *Provides advanced data-driven solutions,
        services and products for e-commerce and
        business solutions.*

    Tel: (212) 739-7464
    Fax: (212) 739-7448

    %FO: 100

    XTIVIA, INC.
    304 South 8th St., Ste. 201, Colorado Springs, Colorado 80905
    CEO: Dennis Robinson
    Bus: *Provides advanced data-driven solutions,
        services and products for e-commerce and
        business solutions.*

    Tel: (719) 685-3100
    Fax: (719) 685-3400

    %FO: 100

    XTIVIA, INC.
    911 West Anderson Lane, Suite 200, Austin, Texas 78757
    CEO: Barbara Glover
    Bus: *Provides advanced data-driven solutions,
        services and products for e-commerce and
        business solutions.*

    Tel: (512) 651-5050
    Fax: (512) 651-5069

    %FO: 100

- **THE GANDEN GROUP**
  Alrov Tower, 46 Rothschild Blvd., Tel Aviv 66883, Israel
  CEO: Nochi Dankner, CEO
  Bus: *Aviation security, transportation, technology and
      real estate.*
  NAICS: 336999, 523999, 531210, 561612, 561621

  Tel: 972-3-714-8888
  Fax: 972-3-714-8881
  www.Gs-3.com

    GS-3 (GANDEN SECURITY SERVICES SOLUTIONS)
    1555 Wilson Blvd., Ste. 504, Arlington, Virginia 22209
    CEO: Joel Feldschuh
    Bus: *Security services for airport facilities.*

    Tel: (703) 522-0946
    Fax: (703) 522-0958

    %FO: 100

- **GILAT SATELLITE NETWORKS LTD.**
  21 Yegia Kapayim St., Kiryat Arie, Petah Tikva 49130, Israel
  CEO: Amiram Levinberg, Chmn. & CEO
  Bus: *Mfr. satellite systems for data transmittal.*

  Tel: 972-3-925-2000
  Fax: 972-3-925-2222
  www.gilat.com

  Rev: $241
  Emp: 980

  NAICS: 334220

GILAT SATELLITE NETWORKING SYSTEMS
1750 Old Meadow Rd., McLean, Virginia 22102
CEO: Joshua Levinberg, EVP
Bus: *Communication services.*
Tel: (703) 848-1250
Fax: (703) 848-1122
%FO: 100

RSTAR CORPORATION
1560 Sawgrass Corporate Pkwy., Ste. 200, Sunrise, Florida 33323
CEO: Doron Gefen, CFO
Bus: *Internet & online service providers.*
Tel: (954) 858-1600
Fax: (954) 858-1777
%FO: 100
Emp: 125

SPACENET, INC.
1750 Old Meadow Rd., McLean, Virginia 22102
CEO: Bill Gerety, Pres. & CEO
Bus: *Mfr. satellite systems for data transmittal.*
Tel: (703) 848-1000
Fax: (703) 848-1012
%FO: 100
Emp: 200

● **GIVEN IMAGING LTD.**
13 Ha'Yetzira St., Yokneam 20692, Israel
CEO: Gavriel D. Meron, Pres. & CEO
Bus: *Mfr. minimally-invasive, disposable imaging capsule for diagnosing small intestine disorders and diseases.*
Tel: 972-4-909-7777
Fax: 972-4-959-2466
www.givenimaging.com
Rev: $65
Emp: 282

NAICS: 334510, 339112, 339113

GIVEN IMAGING, INC.
5555 Oakbrook Pkwy., Ste. 355, Norcross, Georgia 30093
CEO: Gavriel Meron, CEO
Bus: *Mfr. minimally-invasive, disposable imaging capsule for diagnosing small intestine disorders and diseases.*
Tel: (770) 662-0870
Fax: (770) 662-0510
%FO: 100
Emp: 45

● **GOTTEX MODELS LTD.**
1 Yoni Netanyahu St., New Industrial Zone, Yehuda 60376, Israel
CEO: Meir Guar, Pres.
Bus: *Mfr. swimwear.*
Tel: 972-3-538-7777
Fax: 972-3-533-3423
www.gottex.co.il

NAICS: 315212

GOTTEX INDUSTRIES, INC.
1411 Broadway, 29/F, New York, New York 10018
CEO: Uzi Evron, CEO
Bus: *Mfr. swimwear.*
Tel: (212) 354-1240
Fax: (212) 302-3851
%FO: 100

● **IAI ISRAEL AIRCRAFT INDUSTRIES LTD.**
Ben Gurion International Airport, Lod 70100, Israel
CEO: Moshe Keret, Pres. & CEO
Bus: *Aerospace industry: business jet aircraft, electronic systems, unmanned space vehicles; upgrade civilian & military aircraft.*
Tel: 972-3-935-3111
Fax: 972-3-935-8278
www.iai.co.il
Rev: $2,060
Emp: 14,500

NAICS: 336411, 336413, 336414, 541614, 811310, 927110

EMPIRE AERO CENTER
394 Hangar Rd., Bldg. 101, Griffis Airpark, Rome, New York 13441
CEO: Joseph Reinhurst, Pres.
Bus: *Mfr. aircraft.*
Tel: (315) 838-1530
Fax: (315) 838-1515
%FO: 100
Emp: 250

ISRAEL AIRCRAFT INDUSTRIES INTERNATIONAL INC.
1700 North Moore St., Ste. 1210, Arlington, Virginia 22209
CEO: Vigdor Berlin, VP   Tel: (703) 875-3729   %FO: 100
Bus: *Mfr. aircraft.*   Fax: (703) 875-3740   Emp: 20

ISRAEL AIRCRAFT INDUSTRIES INTERNATIONAL INC.
50 West 23rd St., New York, New York 10010
CEO: Mordechai Boness, Pres.   Tel: (212) 620-4404   %FO: 100
Bus: *Mfr. aircraft.*   Fax: (212) 620-1799   Emp: 675

- **IDE TECHNOLOGIES, LTD.**
  13 Zarchin Rd., P.O. Box 591, Ra'anana 43104, Israel
  CEO: Gustavo Kroneberg, VP   Tel: 972-9-747-9777
  Bus: *Water desalinization plants and water solutions.*   Fax: 972-9-747-9715
       www.ide-tech.com
  NAICS: 221310

  AMBIENT TECHNOLOGIES, INC.
  1877 SW 25 th St., Miami, Florida 33133
  CEO: Armando Chamorro, Pres.   Tel: (305) 937-0610   %FO: 100
  Bus: *Install/service water desalinization plants.*   Fax: (305) 937-2137

- **INGENEO TECHNOLOGIES LTD.**
  8 Maskit St., Herzliyya 46733, Israel
  CEO: Beni Basel, Gen. Mgr.   Tel: 972-9-952-6720
  Bus: *Customer relationship management software*   Fax:
         manufacture.   www.ingeneo.com
  NAICS: 511210

  INGENEO TECHNOLOGIES LTD.
  3455 Peachtree Rd., Atlanta, Georgia 30326
  CEO: Zehava Kashai, Mgr.   Tel: (404) 995-7050   %FO: 100
  Bus: *Customer relationship management software* Fax: (404) 995-7049
         sales.

- **ISRAEL AIRCRAFT INDUSTRIES LTD.**
  Ben Gurion International Airport, Lod 70100, Israel
  CEO: Moshe Keret, Pres. & CEO   Tel: 972-3-935-3111   Rev: $1,690
  Bus: *Mfr. business jet aircraft, electronic systems,*   Fax: 972-3-935-8278   Emp: 13,700
         unmanned space vehicles; upgrade civilian &   www.ibc.co.il
         military aircraft.
  NAICS: 336411, 336413, 336414, 541614, 811310, 927110

  EMPIRE AERO CENTER
  394 Hangar Rd., Bldg. 101, Griffis Airpark, Rome, New York 13441
  CEO: Joseph Reinhurst, Pres.   Tel: (315) 838-1530
  Bus: *Aircraft maintenance.*   Fax: (315) 838-1515   Emp: 250

  IAI INTERNATIONAL, INC.
  1700 North Moore St., Arlington, Virginia 22209
  CEO: Vigdor Berlin, VP   Tel: (703) 875-3729   %FO: 100
  Bus: *Mfr. of search & navigation equipment, sale*   Fax: (703) 875-3740   Emp: 20
         of transportation equipment.

ISRAEL AIRCRAFT INDUSTRIES INTERNATIONAL INC.
50 West 23rd St., New York, New York 10010
CEO: Mordechai Boness, Pres.
Bus: *Purchasing agent & sale of aircraft parts,*
marketing, repair, maintenance of aircraft.

Tel: (212) 620-4404
Fax: (212) 620-1799

Emp: 675

• **ISRAEL DISCOUNT BANK LTD.**
27 Yehuda Halevi St., Tel Aviv 65136, Israel
CEO: Giora Offer, Pres. & CEO
Bus: *Commercial banking services.*

Tel: 972-3-514-5549
Fax: 972-3-514-5246
www.discountbank.co.il

Rev: $1,165
Emp: 5,180

NAICS: 522110, 522210, 522220, 522293, 522310, 551111

    ISRAEL DISCOUNT BANK OF NY
    18851 NE 29th Ave., Ste. 600, Aventura, Florida 33180
    CEO: Arie Sheer, Pres.
    Bus: *Commercial banking services.*

Tel: (305) 682-3700
Fax: (305) 682-3777

%FO: 100
Emp: 38

    ISRAEL DISCOUNT BANK OF NY
    9401 Wilshire Blvd., Ste. 600, Beverly Hills, California 90212
    CEO: Yoav Peled, Mgr.
    Bus: *Commercial banking services.*

Tel: (310) 275-1411
Fax: (310) 859-1021

%FO: 100
Emp: 25

    ISRAEL DISCOUNT BANK OF NY
    1350 Broadway, New York, New York 10018
    CEO: Anthony Esposito, Mgr.
    Bus: *Commercial banking services.*

Tel: (212) 714-5660
Fax: (212) 714-1758

%FO: 100
Emp: 8

    ISRAEL DISCOUNT BANK OF NY
    511 Fifth Ave., New York, New York 10017
    CEO: Arie Sheer, Pres. & CEO
    Bus: *Commercial banking services.*

Tel: (212) 551-8145
Fax: (212) 370-9623

%FO: 100
Emp: 769

• **JACADA LTD.**
Droyanov House, 11 Galgalei Haplada St., Herzliyya 46722, Israel
CEO: Gideon Hollander, CEO
Bus: *Enterprise application integration software*
manufacture.

Tel: 972-9-952-5900
Fax: 972-9-952-5959
www.jacada.com

Rev: $20
Emp: 172

NAICS: 511210

    JACADA LTD.
    400 Perimeter Center Terr., Ste. 100, Atlanta, Georgia 30346
    CEO: Gideon Hollander, CEO
    Bus: *Enterprise application integration software*
    manufacture and sales.

Tel: (770) 352-1300
Fax: (770) 352-1313

%FO: 100
Emp: 85

• **LANOPTICS LTD.**
1 Hatamar St., Yokneam 20692, Israel
CEO: Meir Burstin, Chmn.
Bus: *Computer hardware and networking*
communication.

Tel: 972-4-959-6644
Fax: 972-4-959-4177
www.lanoptics.com

Rev: $5
Emp: 80

NAICS: 334413

EZCHIP TECHNOLOGIES LTD.
900 E. Hamilton Ave., Ste. 100, Campbell, California 95008
CEO: Eli Fruchter, Pres. & CEO
Bus: *Mfr. networking semiconductors chips.*
Tel: (408) 879-7355
Fax: (408) 879-7357
%FO: 100

● **LUMENIS LTD.**
Yokneam Industrial Park, Yokneam 20692, Israel
CEO: Jacob A. Frenkel, Chmn.
Bus: *Medical lasers manufacture.*
Tel: 972-4-959-9000
Fax: 972-4-959-9050
www.lumenis.com
Rev: $273
Emp: 900

NAICS: 334510, 339113

LUMENIS INC.
20 West 55th St., 9/F, New York, New York 10019
CEO: Kevin Morano, Mgr.
Bus: *Sale of medical and hospital equipment.*
Tel: (212) 515-4180
Fax: (212) 331-8200
%FO: 100

LUMENIS LTD.
2400 Condensa St., Santa Clara, California 95051
CEO: Abner Ray, Pres.
Bus: *Sales/distribution of medical lasers.*
Tel: (408) 764-3000
Fax: (408) 764-3999
%FO: 100
Emp: 600

● **MAGAL GROUP**
Industrial Zone, PO Box 70, Yehud 56000, Israel
CEO: Jacob Evan-Ezra, Chmn. & CEO
Bus: *Outdoor perimeter intrusion detection sensors and systems manufacture.*
Tel: 972-3-539-1444
Fax: 972-3-536-6245
www.magal-ssl.com
Rev: $61
Emp: 288

NAICS: 334419, 335999, 423690

PERIMETER PRODUCTS, INC.
43180 Osgood Rd., Fremont, California 94539
CEO: Martha A. Lee, Pres.
Bus: *Sales security systems.*
Tel: (510) 249-1450
Fax: (510) 249-1540
%FO: 100
Emp: 23

SENSTAR-STELLAR CORP.
43184 Osgood Rd., Freemont, California 94539
CEO: William J. Evenson, Pres.
Bus: *Marketing of security systems*
Tel: (510) 440-1000
Fax: (510) 440-8686
%FO: 100
Emp: 8

SMART INTERACTIVE SYSTEMS INC.
15-01 132nd St., College Point, New York 11356
CEO: Izar Dekel
Bus: *Real time security video monitoring*
Tel: (718) 661-6760
Fax: (718) 939-3644
%FO: 100

● **MAGIC SOFTWARE ENTERPRISES LTD.**
5 Haplada St., Or Yehuda 60218, Israel
CEO: Menachem Hasfari, CEO
Bus: *Provides of state-of-the-art application development technology and business solutions and training.*
Tel: 972-3-538-9292
Fax: 972-3-583-9393
www.magicsoftware.com
Rev: $65
Emp: 543

NAICS: 511210, 518210, 541511, 541512, 541519, 611420

MAGIC SOFTWARE ENTERPRISES, INC.
17310 Redhill Ave., Ste. 270, Irvine, California 92614
CEO: Doug Nohe, CEO
Bus: *Provides of state-of-the-art application development technology and business solutions and training.*

Tel: (949) 250-1718
Fax: (949) 250-7404

%FO: 100
Emp: 90

● **MAKHTESHIM-AGAN INDUSTRIES LTD.**
1 Azrieli Centre, Tel-Aviv 67012, Israel
CEO: Danny Biran, Chmn.
Bus: *Herbicides and insecticides manufacture.*

Tel: 972-3-694-7977
Fax: 972-3-609-5012
www.main.co.il

NAICS: 325188, 325199, 325320

MAKHTESHIM-AGAN NORTH AMERICA
2875 NE 191 St., Ste. PH3A, Aventura, Florida 33180
CEO: Lisa Khouri, Mgr.
Bus: *Herbicides and insecticides manufacture and sales.*

Tel: (305) 935-4974
Fax: (305) 935-5025

%FO: 100

MAKHTESHIM-AGAN NORTH AMERICA
4515 Falls of Neuse Rd., Ste. 300, Raleigh, North Carolina 27609
CEO: Daniel Porat, COO
Bus: *Herbicides and insecticides manufacture and sales.*

Tel: (919) 256-9300
Fax: (919) 256-9308

%FO: 100

MAKHTESHIM-AGAN NORTH AMERICA
551 Fifth Ave., Ste. 1100, New York, New York 10176
CEO: Moshe Givon, Pres.
Bus: *Herbicides and insecticides manufacture and sales.*

Tel: (212) 661-9800
Fax: (212) 661-9038

%FO: 100
Emp: 36

● **MENTERGY, LTD.**
16 Tiomkin, Jaffa, Tel Aviv 65783, Israel
CEO: Eitan Muchnik, Mgr.
Bus: *Provides e-learning products and services.*

Tel: 972-3-753-5624
Fax:
www.mentergy.com

Rev: $66
Emp: 750

NAICS: 511210, 611420

MENTERGY
2000 River Edge Pkwy., Ste. 850, Atlanta, Georgia 30328
CEO: Ron Zamir, Sr. Prtn.
Bus: *Provides e-learning products and services.*

Tel: (770) 612-9129
Fax: (770) 859-9110

%FO: 100

● **MER TELEMANAGEMENT SOLUTIONS LTD.**
22 Zarhin St., Ra'anana 43662, Israel
CEO: Eytan Bar, Pres. & CEO
Bus: *Mfr. software.*

Tel: 972-9-762-1777
Fax: 972-9-746-6597
www.mtsint.com

NAICS: 511210

MTS INTERNATIONAL
501 Hoes Lane, Ste. 202, Piscataway, New Jersey 08854
CEO: Roy Hess, Mgr.　　　　　　　　　　Tel: (732) 235-0900　　　%FO: 100
Bus: *Mfr. of software.*　　　　　　　　　　Fax: (732) 235-0906

MTS INTERNATIONAL
12600 SE 38th St., Ste. 250, Bellevue, Washington 98006
CEO: Eric Fay, VP　　　　　　　　　　　Tel: (425) 401-1000　　　%FO: 100
Bus: *Mfr. software.*　　　　　　　　　　　Fax: (425) 401-1700　　　Emp: 153

● **METALINK LTD.**
Yakum Business Park, Yakum 60972, Israel
CEO: Tzvika Shukhman, Chmn. & CEO　　　Tel: 972-9-960-5555　　　Rev: $22
Bus: *DSL chipsets manufacture for software*　Fax: 972-9-960-5544　　　Emp: 179
　　　programming interfaces.　　　　　　　www.metalink.co.il
NAICS: 334413

　　METALINK LTD.
　　Peachtree Pointe Office Park, 3260 Pointe Pkwy., Ste. 400, Norcross, Georgia 30092
　　CEO: Ron Cates, VP　　　　　　　　　Tel: (678) 325-5430　　　%FO: 100
　　Bus: *Mfr. of DSL chipsets for software*　　Fax: (770) 242-5998
　　　　programming interfaces.

● **MIND CTI LTD.**
Industrial Park, Bldg. 7, 2/F, Yokneam 20692, Israel
CEO: Monica Eisinger, Pres. & CEO　　　Tel: 972-4-993-6666　　　Rev: $18
Bus: *Mfr. software.*　　　　　　　　　　Fax: 972-4-993-7776　　　Emp: 183
　　　　　　　　　　　　　　　　　　www.mindcti.com
NAICS: 511210

　　MIND CTI INC.
　　777 Terrace Ave., Hasbrouck Heights, New Jersey 07604
　　CEO: Monica Eisinger, Pres. & CEO　　Tel: (201) 288-3900　　　%FO: 100
　　Bus: *Mfr./sales software.*　　　　　　Fax: (201) 288-4590

● **MOBILE ACCESS NETWORKS**
Ofek One Center Building B, Northern Industrial Zone, Lod 71293, Israel
CEO: Cathy Zatloukal, Pres. & CEO　　　Tel: 972-8-918-3888
Bus: *Fiber optic technology for the wireless industry.*　Fax: 972-8-918-3844
　　　　　　　　　　　　　　　　　　www.mobileaccess.com
NAICS: 334417, 335921

　　MOBILE ACCESS
　　8391 Old Courthouse Rd., Ste. 300, Vienna, Virginia 22182
　　CEO: Cathy Zatloukal, Pres.　　　　　Tel: (866) 436-9266　　　%FO: 100
　　Bus: *Telecommunications.*　　　　　Fax: (703) 848-0280　　　Emp: 70

● **M-SYSTEMS FLASH DISK PIONEERS LTD.**
7 Atir Yeda St., Kfar Saba 44425, Israel
CEO: Dov Moran, Chmn. & Pres. & CEO　Tel: 972-9-764-5000　　　Rev: $348
Bus: *Mfr. flash memory products and software.*　Fax: 972-3-548-8666　　Emp: 513
　　　　　　　　　　　　　　　　　　www.m-sys.com
NAICS: 334112, 334119, 334413

M-SYSTEMS INC.
555 North Mathilda Ave., Ste. 220, Sunnyvale, California 94085
CEO: Jerry Kolansky, Gen. Mgr.
Bus: *Mfr. of memory chips & modules.*

Tel: (408) 470-4440
Fax: (408) 470-4470

%FO: 100

• MYSTICOM LTD.
1 Hazoran St., PO Box 8364, Netanya 42504, Israel
CEO: Neil Vasant, CEO
Bus: *Data communications and computer chips.*

Tel: 972-9-863-6465
Fax: 972-9-863-6466
www.mysticom.com

NAICS: 334413

MYSTICOM INC.
1300 Crittenden Lane, Ste. 101, Mountain View, California 94043
CEO: Neil Vasant, CEO
Bus: *Engaged in data communications and computer chips.*

Tel: (650) 210-8080
Fax: (650) 210-9030

%FO: 100

MYSTICOM INC.
2323 Owen St., Santa Clara, California 95054
CEO: George Taylor, Mgr.
Bus: *Engaged in data communications and computer chips.*

Tel: (650) 210-8080
Fax: (650) 210-9030

%FO: 100

• NANO-OR TECHNOLOGIES LTD.
1 Yodfat St., Lod 71291, Israel
CEO: David Banitt, CEO
Bus: *Manufactures inspection and measurement devices based on its 3Dscope, a camera able to measure objects at the accuracy and resolution of nano-meters.*

Tel: 972-8-928-2801
Fax: 972-8-928-2805
www.nano-or.com

NAICS: 334513, 334519

NANO-OR TECHNOLOGIES LTD.
3350 Scott Blvd., Bldg. 55, Unit 2, Santa Clara, California 95054
CEO: Joseph Linde, Chmn.
Bus: *Mfr/sales of inspection and measurement devices based on its 3Dscope, a camera able to measure objects at the accuracy & resolution of nano-meters.*

Tel: (408) 588-9500
Fax: (408) 588-9501

%FO: 100

• NEGEVTECH LTD.
12 Hemada St., Rehovot 76122, Israel
CEO: Arnon Gat, Pres. & CEO
Bus: *Diagnostics equipment manufacture.*

Tel: 972-8-936-6050
Fax: 972-8-936-6051
www.negevtech.com

NAICS: 333295

NEGEVTECH INC.
2880 Lakeside Dr., Santa Clara, California 95054
CEO: Glyn Davies, Pres.
Bus: *Diagnostics equipment manufacture and sales.*

Tel: (408) 486-9831
Fax: (408) 486-9832

%FO: 100

- **NESS TECHNOLOGIES INC.**
Ness Tower, Atidim Industrial Park, Bldg. 4, Tel Aviv 61580, Israel
CEO: Raviv Zoller, Pres. & CEO
Bus: *Provides information technology.*
Tel: 972-3-766-6800
Fax: 972-3-766-6809
www.ness.com
Rev: $304
Emp: 5,025

  NAICS: 541511, 541512, 541513, 541519

    NESS GLOBAL SERVICES, INC.
    160 Technology Dr., Canonsburg, Pennsylvania 15317
    CEO: Rajeev Srivastava, Pres.
    Bus: *Information technology services.*
    Tel: (724) 745-7100
    Fax: (724) 745-6494
    %FO: 100

    NESS TECHNOLOGIES INC.
    2001 Gateway Place, Ste. 610 West, San Jose, California 95110
    CEO: Prasanna Oke, Pres.
    Bus: *Information technology services.*
    Tel: (408) 467-9340
    Fax: (408) 452-0299
    %FO: 100

    NESS TECHNOLOGIES, INC.
    3 University Plaza, Ste. 600, Hackensack, New Jersey 07601
    CEO: Raviv Zoller, CEO
    Bus: *Computer system design/related services.*
    Tel: (201) 488-7222
    Fax: (201) 488-5040
    %FO: 100
    Emp: 5,000

- **NETAFIM**
161 Arlozorov St., Tel Aviv 64922, Israel
CEO: Koby Milo, Mng. Dir.
Bus: *Mfr. distribution micro-irrigation components.*
Tel: 972-3-6919777
Fax: 972-3-6911962
www.netafim.com
Rev: $267
Emp: 1,767

  NAICS: 221310, 326220, 541618

    NETAFIM IRRIGATION USA INC.
    5470 East Home Ave., Fresno, California 93727
    CEO: Igal Aisenberg, Pres.
    Bus: *Mfr./distribution micro-irrigation components,*
    filters, micro-sprinklers.
    Tel: (559) 453-6800
    Fax: (559) 453-6803
    %FO: 100
    Emp: 150

- **NICE SYSTEMS LTD.**
8 Hapnina St., PO Box 690, Ra'anana 43107, Israel
CEO: Haim Shani, CEO
Bus: *Mfr. computer telephony integration systems.*
Tel: 972-9-775-3777
Fax: 972-9-743-4282
www.nice.com
Rev: $253
Emp: 1,072

  NAICS: 334112, 511210

    NICE SYSTEMS, INC.
    301 Route 17 North, 10/F, Rutherford, New Jersey 07070
    CEO: Jacob Fox, VP & Gen. Mgr.
    Bus: *Mfr. computer telephony integration*
    systems.
    Tel: (201) 964-2600
    Fax: (201) 964-2610
    %FO: 100

- **NOVA MEASURING INSTRUMENTS LTD.**
Weizmann Science Park, Bldg. 22, PO Box 266, Rehovot 76100, Israel
CEO: Giora Dishon, Pres. & CEO
Bus: *Optical monitoring systems manufacture.*
Tel: 972-8-938-7505
Fax: 972-8-940-7776
www.nova.co.il
Rev: $41
Emp: 239

  NAICS: 333295

NOVA MEASURING INSTRUMENTS LTD.
4050 East Cotton Center Blvd., Ste. 38, Phoenix, Arizona 85040
CEO: Ben Vinogradov, VP Tel: (602) 553-8899 %FO: 100
Bus: *Optical monitoring systems manufacture and* Fax: (602) 553-8898
sales.

NOVA MEASURING INSTRUMENTS LTD.
1270 Oakmead Pkwy., Ste. 215, Sunnyvale, California 94085
CEO: Ben Vinogradov, VP Tel: (408) 746-9921 %FO: 100
Bus: *Optical monitoring systems manufacture and* Fax: (408) 746-9728
sales.

● **NUR MACROPRINTERS LTD.**
12 Abba Hilel Silver St., PO Box 1281, Lod 71110, Israel
CEO: David Amir, Pres. & CEO Tel: 972-8-914-5555 Rev: $77
Bus: *Mfr. digital/color printers.* Fax: 972-8-921-1220 Emp: 328
www.nur.com

NAICS: 333293

  NUR AMERICA, INC.
  85 Oxford Dr., Moonachie, New Jersey 07074
  CEO: Nachum Korman, Pres. Tel: (201) 708-2100 %FO: 100
  Bus: *Digital color printers manufacture and sales.* Fax: (201) 708-2111 Emp: 60

● **ON TRACK INNOVATIONS (OTI) LTD.**
Z. H. R. Industrial Zone, P.O. Box 32, Rosh-Pina 12000, Israel
CEO: Oded Bashan, Chmn. & Pres. & CEO Tel: 972-4-686-8000 Rev: $23
Bus: *Smart cards software manufacture.* Fax: 972-4-693-8887 Emp: 218
www.oti.co.il

NAICS: 334119

  OTI AMERICA, INC.
  2 Executive Dr., Ste. 740, Fort Lee, New Jersey 07024
  CEO: Ohad Bashan, Pres. & CEO Tel: (201) 944-5200 %FO: 100
  Bus: *Mfr. of microprocessor-based smart cards.* Fax: (201) 944-3233

● **OPHIR OPTRONICS LTD.**
Science Based Industrial Park, Har Hotzvim, PO Box 45021, Jerusalem 91450, Israel
CEO: Dror Zerem, Mgr. Tel: 972-2-548-4444 Rev: $28
Bus: *Mfr. laser power energy instrumentation, FLIR &* Fax: 972-2-582-2338 Emp: 180
IR optical components. www.ophiropt.com
NAICS: 333314, 334419, 334511, 334519

  OPHIR OPTICS INC., OPTICS GROUP
  260-A Fordham Rd., Wilmington, Massachusetts 01887
  CEO: Dennis Cope, Pres. Tel: (978) 657-6410 %FO: 100
  Bus: *Mfr. of infrared lenses mirrors & optical* Fax: (978) 657-6056 Emp: 30
  assemblies.

  OPHIR OPTRONICS INC., LASER MEASUREMENT GROUP
  260-A Fordham Rd., Wilmington, Massachusetts 01887
  CEO: Yaacov Zerem, Pres. Tel: (978) 657-5553 %FO: 100
  Bus: *Distributor of laser test equipment.* Fax: (978) 657-6054 Emp: 13

- **OPTIBASE LTD.**
  7 Shenkar St., Herzliyya 46120, Israel
  CEO: Tom Wyler, Chmn. & Pres.   Tel: 972-9-970-9288   Rev: $21
  Bus: *Mfr. hardware and software products.*   Fax: 972-9-958-6099
                                                    www.optibase.com

  NAICS: 334310, 511210

  MEDIA 100 INC.
  450 Donald Lynch Blvd., Marlborough, Massachusetts 01752
  CEO: Amir Goren, Gen. Mgr.   Tel: (508) 460-1600
  Bus: *Multimedia graphics & publishing software.* Fax: (508) 481-8627

  OPTIBASE INC.
  1250 Space Park Way, Mountain View, California 94043
  CEO: Adam Schadle, Pres.   Tel: (650) 230-2400   %FO: 100
  Bus: *Mfr. hardware and software products.*   Fax: (650) 691-9998   Emp: 166

  OPTIBASE INC.
  156 Andover St., Ste. 210, Danvers, Massachusetts 01923
  CEO: Susan Dwyer, Mgr.   Tel: (978) 777-3800   %FO: 100
  Bus: *Mfr. hardware and software products.*   Fax: (978) 774-5766

- **ORBOTECH LTD.**
  Sanhedrin Blvd., North Industrial Zone, Yavne 81102, Israel
  CEO: Yochai Richter, Pres.   Tel: 972-8-942-3533   Rev: $315
  Bus: *Automated optical inspection equipment,*   Fax: 972-8-942-3897   Emp: 1,520
       CAD/CAM systems.   www.orbotech.com
  NAICS: 333314, 541512

  ORBOTECH INC.
  44 Manning Rd., Billerica, Massachusetts 01821
  CEO: Michelle Harnish, CEO   Tel: (978) 667-6037
  Bus: *Mfr./sale automated optical inspection*   Fax: (978) 667-9969
       equipment, CAD/CAM systems, pre-press
       image setters.

  ORBOTECH INC.
  2741 E. Walnut Ave., 1/F, Tustin, California 92780
  CEO: Michelle Harnish   Tel: (714) 545-6909
  Bus: *Mfr./sale automated optical inspection*   Fax: (714) 545-0866
       equipment, CAD/CAM systems, pre-press
       image setters.

  ORBOTECH INC.
  2841 Junction Ave., Ste. 101, San Jose, California 95134
  CEO: Michelle Harnish   Tel: (408) 432-3200
  Bus: *Mfr./sale automated optical inspection*   Fax: (408) 432-3286
       equipment, CAD/CAM systems, pre-press
       image setters.

- **ORCKIT COMMUNICATIONS LTD.**
  126 Yig'al Allon St., Tel Aviv 67443, Israel
  CEO: Eric Paneth, Chmn. & CEO
  Bus: *Mfr. high-speed digital modems.*

  Tel: 972-3-696-2121
  Fax: 972-3-696-5678
  www.orckit.com

  Rev: $11
  Emp: 181

  NAICS: 334210, 334290

  ORCKIT COMMUNICATIONS
  125 Half Mile Rd., Ste. 200, Red Bank, New Jersey 07701
  CEO: James Szeliga, Pres.
  Bus: *Sales/distribution high-speed digital modems.*

  Tel: (732) 933-2643
  Fax:

  %FO: 100
  Emp: 8

  ORCKIT COMMUNICATIONS
  110 Blue Ravine Rd., Ste. 160, Folsom, California 95630
  CEO: Nigel Cole, VP
  Bus: *Sales/distribution high-speed digital modems.*

  Tel: (916) 351-5600
  Fax:

  %FO: 100

- **ORMAT INDUSTRIES LTD.**
  Shydlowski Rd., New Industrial Area, Yavne 81100, Israel
  CEO: Yehuda Bronicki, Chmn.
  Bus: *Mfr. geothermal equipment.*

  Tel: 972-8-943-3777
  Fax: 972-8-943-9901
  www.ormat.com

  Rev: $116
  Emp: 600

  NAICS: 237990, 332313, 333611, 334119

  ORMAT TECHNOLOGIES, INC.
  980 Greg St., Sparks, Nevada 89431
  CEO: Yehudit Bronicki, CEO
  Bus: *Electric power distribution*

  Tel: (775) 356-9029
  Fax: (775) 356-9039

  %FO: 100
  Emp: 677

- **RADCOM LTD.**
  24 Raoul Wallenberg St., Tel Aviv 69719, Israel
  CEO: Arnon Toussia-Cohen, Pres. & CEO
  Bus: *Test equipment and software manufacture.*

  Tel: 972-3-645-5055
  Fax: 972-3-647-4681
  www.radcom.com

  Rev: $16
  Emp: 130

  NAICS: 334290, 334515, 511210, 541519

  RADCOM EQUIPMENT, INC.
  6 Forest Ave., Paramus, New Jersey 07652
  CEO: Avi Zamir, Pres.
  Bus: *Mfr./sales test equipment and software.*

  Tel: (201) 518-0033
  Fax: (201) 556-9030

  %FO: 100
  Emp: 25

- **RADVISION LTD.**
  24 Raoul Wallenberg St., Tel Aviv 69719, Israel
  CEO: Gadi Tamari, CEO
  Bus: *IT technology services.*

  Tel: 972-3-767-9300
  Fax: 972-3-767-9313
  www.radivision.com

  Rev: $64
  Emp: 335

  NAICS: 334210, 334290

  RADVISION LTD.
  2010 Corporate Ridge, Ste. 700, McLean, Virginia 22102
  CEO: Irit Machtey, HR
  Bus: *IT technology services.*

  Tel: (703) 827-8090
  Fax: (703) 827-8091

  %FO: 100

RADVISION LTD.
1290 Oakmead Pkwy., Ste. 111, Sunnyvale, California 94085
CEO: Boaz Raviv, Gen. Mgr.   Tel: (201) 689-6300   %FO: 100
Bus: *IT technology services.*   Fax: (408) 470-1501

RADVISION LTD.
8 Commerce Dr., Bedford, New Hampshire 03110
CEO: Boaz Raviv, Gen. Mgr.   Tel: (201) 689-6330   %FO: 100
Bus: *IT technology services.*   Fax: (201) 689-6251

RADVISION LTD.
17-17 State Hwy. 208, Ste. 300, Fair Lawn, New Jersey 07410
CEO: Meir Alon, VP   Tel: (201) 689-6300   %FO: 100
Bus: *IT technology services.*   Fax: (201) 689-6301   Emp: 135

● **RADWARE LTD.**
22 Raoul Wallenberg St., Tel Aviv 69710, Israel
CEO: Roy Zisapel, Pres. & CEO   Tel: 972-3-766-8666   Rev: $68
Bus: *Mfr. internet traffic hardware and software.*   Fax: 972-3-766-8655   Emp: 361
     www.radware.com

NAICS: 334119, 511210, 541511

    RADWARE INC.
    3505 Cadillac Ave., Ste. K1, Costa Mesa, California 92626
    CEO: Vik Desai, Pres.   Tel: (714) 436-9700
    Bus: *Mfr./sales internet traffic hardware and*   Fax: (714) 436-1941   Emp: 11
    software.

    RADWARE INC.
    909 Lake Carolyn Pkwy., Ste. 760, Irving, Texas 75039
    CEO: Roy Zisapel   Tel: (972) 910-8155
    Bus: *Mfr./sales internet traffic hardware and*   Fax: (972) 409-5964
    software.

    RADWARE, INC.
    575 Corporate Dr., Ste. 205, Mahwah, New Jersey 07430
    CEO: Roy Zisapel, CEO   Tel: (201) 512-9771   %FO: 100
    Bus: *Mfr./sales internet traffic hardware and*   Fax: (201) 512-9774   Emp: 96
    software.

● **RETALIX LTD.**
10 Zarhin St., Corex House, Ra'anana 43000, Israel
CEO: Barry Shaked, Chmn. & Pres. & CEO   Tel: 972-9-776-6677   Rev: $124
Bus: *Mfr. software for grocery industry.*   Fax: 972-9-740-0471   Emp: 650,920
     www.retalix.com

NAICS: 511210

    RETALIX USA INC.
    5213 Linbar Dr., Ste. 409, Nashville, Tennessee 37211
    CEO: Demetrius Doyle, Mgr.   Tel: (615) 832-0050
    Bus: *Sale of office equipment.*   Fax: (615) 832-0050

RETALIX USA INC.
2490 Technical Dr., Miamisburg, Ohio 45342
CEO: Barry Shaked, Pres.
Bus: *Sale of hand held electronic equipment.*
Tel: (937) 384-2277
Fax: (937) 384-2280
Emp: 155

RETALIX USA INC.
6100 Tennyson Pkwy., Ste. 150, Plano, Texas 75024
CEO: Jeffrey E. Yelton, Pres.
Bus: *Software sales and distribution.*
Tel: (469) 241-8400
Fax: (469) 241-0771
%FO: 100
Emp: 237

RETALIX USA INC.
7220 Aveinda Encinas, Ste. 206, Carlsbad, California 92009
CEO: Bob Smith, Sales
Bus: *Software sales and distribution.*
Tel: (760) 931-6940
Fax: (760) 931-6978
%FO: 100

RETALIX USA INC.
797 Commonwealth Dr., Warrendale, Pennsylvania 15086
CEO: Lynn Salmon, Controller
Bus: *Software sales and distribution.*
Tel: (724) 227-5544
Fax: (724) 776-0061
%FO: 100

STORE NEXT RETAIL TECHNOLOGIES USA
6100 Tennyson Pkwy., Ste. 130, Plano, Texas 75024
CEO: Ray Carlin, Pres. & CEO
Bus: *Software.*
Tel: (972) 265-4800
Fax: (972) 265-4801

TCI SOLUTIONS
5210 E. Willimas Circle, Ste. 300, Tucson, Arizona 85711
CEO: David R. Butler, Pres. & CEO
Bus: *Software management.*
Tel: (520) 298-7757
Fax: (520) 747-1660
Emp: 133

● **RIT TECHNOLOGIES LTD.**
24 Raoul Wallenberg St., Tel Aviv 69719, Israel
CEO: Doron Zinger, Pres. & CEO
Bus: *Mfr. hardware and software to track network computer cable connections.*
NAICS: 334119, 334417, 334418, 541511
Tel: 972-3-645-5151
Fax: 972-3-647-4115
www.rittech.com
Rev: $18
Emp: 132

RIT TECHNOLOGIES, INC.
900 Corporate Dr., Mahwah, New Jersey 07430
CEO: Motti Kleinmann, Pres.
Bus: *Sales/distribution of hardware and software products.*
Tel: (201) 512-1970
Fax: (201) 512-1286
%FO: 100
Emp: 7

● **ROBOGROUP T.E.K. LTD**
13 Hamelacha St., Afek Industrial Park, Rosh Ha'Ayin 48091, Israel
CEO: Rafael Aravot, Chmn. & CEO
Bus: *Robotics, motion control and smart memory technology.*
NAICS: 611420
Tel: 972-3-900-4170
Fax: 972-3-903-0994
www.robo-group.com
Rev: $14
Emp: 97

INTELITEK INC.
444 East Industrial Park Dr., Manchester, New Hampshire 03109
CEO: Brenda Quinn, Pres. Tel: (603) 625-8600 %FO: 100
Bus: *Robotics, motion control and smart memory* Fax: (603) 625-2137 Emp: 40
technology.

YET US INC.
409 North Lily Lake Rd., McHenry, Illinois 60051
CEO: Jim Piotrowski, Mgr. Tel: (815) 344-4868 %FO: 100
Bus: *Sale of motion control solutions* Fax: (877) 589-9727

YET US INC.
444 East Industrial Park Dr., Manchester, New Hampshire 03109
CEO: Mark Bourgeois, Pres. Tel: (603) 641-1822 %FO: 100
Bus: *Sale of motion control solutions.* Fax: (603) 641-1239

● **SCITEX CORPORATION LTD.**
3 Azrieli Center, Triangle Tower, 43/F, Tel Aviv 67023, Israel
CEO: Ami Erel, Chmn. Tel: 972-3-607-5855 Rev: $128
Bus: *Mfr. digital information systems.* Fax: 972-3-607-5756 Emp: 3,200
www.scitex.com

NAICS: 333293

XMPIE LTD.
41 Madison Ave., 25/F, New York, New York 10010
CEO: Jacob Aizkowitz, CEO Tel: (212) 479-5137 %FO: 100
Bus: *Software solution for direct marketers.* Fax: (212) 479-5187 Emp: 35

● **SCOPUS NETWORK TECHNOLOGIES LTD.**
10 Ha'amal St., Park Afek, Rosh Ha'Ayin 48092, Israel
CEO: David Mahlab, Pres. & CEO Tel: 972-3-900-7777
Bus: *Digital broadcasting equipment manufacture.* Fax: 972-3-900-7888
www.scopus.co.il

NAICS: 334210, 334220

SCOPUS NETWORK TECHNOLOGIES
100 Overlook Center Dr., Princeton, New Jersey 08540
CEO: Carlo Basile, Pres. Tel: (609) 987-8090 %FO: 100
Bus: *Supplier of digital compression technology* Fax: (609) 987-8095 Emp: 15
to the broadcasting industry.

● **SHELLCASE LTD.**
Manhat Technology Park, Bldg. 4, 4/F, PO Box 48328, Jerusalem 96251, Israel
CEO: Shlomo Oren, Pres. & CEO Tel: 972-2-679-8890 Rev: $6
Bus: *Advanced packaging technology.* Fax: 972-2-679-8850 Emp: 75
www.shellcase.com

NAICS: 334413

SHELLCASE INC.
642 Silver Ave., Half Moon Bay, California 94019
CEO: Shlomo Oran, Pres. Tel: (650) 712-4428 %FO: 100
Bus: *Advanced packaging technology.* Fax: (650) 712-8346

- **SILICOM LIMITED**
  8 Hanagar St., Kfar-Saba 44000, Israel
  CEO: Shaike Orbach, Pres. & CEO
  Bus: *Mfr. PC cards for portable and laptop computers.*

  Tel: 972-9-764-4555
  Fax: 972-9-765-1977
  www.silicom.co.il

  Rev: $5
  Emp: 38

  NAICS: 334119, 334290
  - **SILICOM CONNECTIVITY SOLUTIONS INC.**
    6 Forest Ave., Paramus, New Jersey 07652
    CEO: Mario Gamilo, Mgr.
    Bus: *Mfr. PC cards for portable and laptop computers.*

    Tel: (201) 843-1175
    Fax: (201) 843-1457

    %FO: 100

- **SMART LINK LTD.**
  7 Giborei St., New Industrial Zone, PO Box 8215, Netanya 42504, Israel
  CEO: Moty Mebel, CEO
  Bus: *Software-based modem manufacture.*

  Tel: 972-9-863-8000
  Fax: 972-9-865-6552
  www.smlink.com

  NAICS: 511210
  - **SMART LINK TECHNOLOGIES, INC.**
    57 Bedford St., Ste. 101, Lexington, Massachusetts 02420
    CEO: Benny Maytal, Pres.
    Bus: *Software-based modem manufacture and sales.*

    Tel: (781) 653-2000
    Fax: (781) 863-1899

    %FO: 100
    Emp: 7

- **SMARTEAM CORPORATION, DIV. DASSAULT SYSTEMES SA**
  5 Hagavish St., Ovadia House, Kfar Saba 44641, Israel
  CEO: Avinoam Nowogrodski, CEO
  Bus: *Computer software services.*

  Tel: 972-9-764-4000
  Fax: 972-9-764-4001
  www.smarteam.com

  NAICS: 511210, 518210, 541511, 541512, 541519, 611420
  - **SMARTEAM CORPORATION**
    PO Box 1645, Concord, Massachusetts 01742
    CEO: Shai Etzion, Mgr.
    Bus: *Engaged in computer software services.*

    Tel: (978) 318-5705
    Fax: (978) 318-5706

    %FO: 100

- **TARO PHARMACEUTICAL INDUSTRIES**
  14 Hakitor St., Haifa Bay 26110, Israel
  CEO: Aaron Levitt, Pres.
  Bus: *Pharmaceuticals manufacture.*

  Tel: 972-9-971-1800
  Fax: 972-9-955-7443
  www.taro.com

  Rev: $284
  Emp: 1,400

  NAICS: 325411, 325412
  - **TARO PHARMACEUTICALS USA INC.**
    5 Skyline Dr., Hawthorne, New York 10532
    CEO: Aaron Levitt, Pres.
    Bus: *Mfr. of pharmaceutical preparations/ Sale of drugs & sundries.*

    Tel: (914) 345-9001
    Fax: (914) 345-8728

    %FO: 100
    Emp: 325

- **TEFRON LTD.**
  Park Azurim, Derech Eim Hamoshovot 94, Petah Tikva 49527, Israel
  CEO: Yosef Shiran, Pres. & CEO   Tel: 972-3-60.-0215   Rev: $183
  Bus: *Lingerie manufacture and producer of seamless*   Fax: 972-3-922-9035   Emp: 2,082
        intimate apparel.   www.tefron.com
     NAICS: 315111, 315192, 315221, 315231

      ALBA WALDENSIAN, INC.
      350 5th Ave., Ste. 2210, New York, New York 10118
      CEO: Daniella Hami   Tel: (212) 239-8777   %FO: 100
      Bus: *Knitted textiles production.*   Fax:

      ALBA-WALDENSIAN
      201 St. Germain Ave. SW, Valdese, North Carolina 28690
      CEO: Dan Miseka, CEO   Tel: (828) 879-6500
      Bus: *manufacturers of Intimate Apparel*   Fax: (828) 879-6595   Emp: 25

- **TELRAD NETWORKS**
  Telrad Park Afek, 14 Hamelacha St., PO Box 488, Rosh Ha'Ayin 48091, Israel
  CEO: Zeev Eydlin, Controller   Tel: 972-3-915-7000   Rev: $112
  Bus: *Mfr. central office switching equipment, key*   Fax: 972-3-915-7555   Emp: 550
        systems, PBXs, ACDs, voice mail systems.   www.telrad.co.il
     NAICS: 517110

      TELRAD COMMATCH
      7770 Regents Rd., Ste. 113-252, San Diego, California 92122
      CEO: Aviv Ron, CEO   Tel: (888) 886-5651   %FO: 100
      Bus: *Cable TV Operators/Telecom carriers/ ISP &*   Fax:
        ITSP.

      TELRAD CONNEGY, INC.
      10 Executive Blvd., Farmingdale, New York 11735
      CEO: Rami Goraly, Pres. & CEO   Tel: (631) 420-8800   %FO: 100
      Bus: *Mfr./distribution/service business*   Fax: (631) 420-3938
        telecommunications products, voice mail
        systems, ISDN terminals & devices.

- **TEVA PHARMACEUTICALS IND LTD.**
  5 Basel St., PO Box 3190, Petah Tikva 49131, Israel
  CEO: Israel Makov, Pres. & CEO   Tel: 972-3-926-7267   Rev: $4,799
  Bus: *Mfr. pharmaceuticals, medical and veterinary*   Fax: 972-3-923-4050   Emp: 13,800
        supplies.   www.tevapharma.com
     NAICS: 325411, 325412

      BIOCRAFT
      API Production, 5000 Synder Dr., Mexico, Missouri 65265
      CEO: Max McGregor, Operations Mgr.   Tel: (573) 581-8080
      Bus: *Pharmaceutical productions.*   Fax: (573) 581-8085   Emp: 100

      IVAX CORP.
      4400 Biscayne Blvd., Miami, Florida 33137
      CEO: Philip Frost, Chmn. & CEO   Tel: (305) 575-6000
      Bus: *Generic drugs.*   Fax: (305) 575-6055   Emp: 10,100

PLANTEX INC.
2 University Plaza, Ste. 305, Hackensack, New Jersey 07601
CEO: George Svokos, Pres.   Tel: (201) 343-4141   %FO: 100
Bus: *Mfr. pharmaceutical ingredients for the*   Fax: (201) 343-3833   Emp: 12
worldwide generic pharmaceutical industry.

SICOR INC.
19 Hughes, Irvine, California 92618
CEO: Marvin Samson, Pres.   Tel: (949) 855-8210   %FO: 100
Bus: *Develop, manufacture and market*   Fax: (949) 855-8210   Emp: 1,851
pharmaceutical products.

TEVA NEUROSCIENCE
901 E. 104th St., Ste. 900, Kansas City, Missouri 64131
CEO: Larry Downey, CEO   Tel: (816) 508-5000   %FO: 100
Bus: *Research, treatment and pharmaceuticals*   Fax: (816) 508-5016
for treatment of neurological disorders.

TEVA PHARMACEUTICALS NORTH AMERICA
1090 Horsham Rd., North Wales, Pennsylvania 19454
CEO: William Marth, Pres. & CEO   Tel: (215) 591-3000   %FO: 100
Bus: *Research and development of generic*   Fax: (215) 591-8600   Emp: 1,025
pharmaceuticals.

● **TIGBUR LTD.**
14 Aba Hilel St., Ramat Gan 52506, Israel
CEO: Albert Benvenisti, Pres. & CEO   Tel: 972-3-576-2100
Bus: *Personnel placement.*   Fax: 972-3-576-2111
www.tigbur.com
NAICS: 561310

TIGBUR LTD.
31 East 32nd St., 3/F, New York, New York 10016
CEO: Doron Benvenisti, VP   Tel: (212) 867-0005   %FO: 100
Bus: *Temporary and permanent placement.*   Fax: (212) 867-0003

● **TOP IMAGE SYSTEMS, LTD.**
2 Habarzel St., Ramat Hahayel, Tel Aviv 69710, Israel
CEO: Ido Schechter, CEO   Tel: 972-3-767-9100   Rev: $11
Bus: *Wireless connectivity software manufacture.*   Fax: 972-3-648-6664   Emp: 75
www.topimagesystems.com
NAICS: 511210, 611420

TIS AMERICA, INC.
21356 Pagosa Ct., Boca Raton, Florida 33486
CEO: Gideon Shmuel, VP   Tel: (561) 417-3736   %FO: 100
Bus: *Wireless connectivity software*   Fax: (561) 347-1218
manufacture.

TIS AMERICA, INC.
591 North Ave., 3 Lakeside Office Park, Wakefield, Massachusetts 01880
CEO: Thomas Lavey, Chmn.   Tel: (781) 245-1154   %FO: 100
Bus: *Wireless connectivity software*   Fax: (781) 245-2999
manufacture.

● **TOWER SEMICONDUCTOR LTD.**
Ramat Gavriel Industrial Zone, PO Box 619, Migdal Haemek 23105, Israel
CEO: Russell C. Ellwanger, CEO   Tel: 972-4-650-6611   Rev: $126
Bus: *Mfr. computer chips.*   Fax: 972-4-654-7788   Emp: 1,369
      www.towersemi.com

NAICS: 334413

      TOWER SEMICONDUCTOR USA
      2350 Mission College Blvd., Santa Clara, California 95054
      CEO: Fra Drumm, VP   Tel: (408) 327-8900   %FO: 100
      Bus: *Mfr. of computer chips.*   Fax: (408) 969-9831   Emp: 17

● **TTI TEAM TELECOM INTERNATIONAL LTD.**
7 Martin Gahl St., Kiryat Arie, Petah Tikva 49512, Israel
CEO: Meir Lipshes, Chmn. & CEO   Tel: 972-3-926-9700   Rev: $38
Bus: *Computer software and services.*   Fax: 972-3-922-1249   Emp: 700
      www.tti-telecom.com

NAICS: 511210, 541511, 541519

      TTI TEAM TELECOM INTERNATIONAL LTD.
      2 Hudson Place, 6/F, Hoboken, New Jersey 07030
      CEO: Meir Lipshes, CEO   Tel: (201) 795-3883   %FO: 100
      Bus: *Computer software and services.*   Fax: (201) 795-3920   Emp: 566

● **UNITED MIZRAHI BANK LTD.**
13 Rothschild Blvd., Tel Aviv 65121, Israel
CEO: Eliezer Yones, Pres. & CEO   Tel: 972-3-567-9211
Bus: *Commercial banking services.*   Fax: 972-3-560-4780   Emp: 3,400
      www.mizrahi.co.il

NAICS: 522110

      UNITED MIZRAHI BANK LTD. - LA Branch
      611 Wilshire Blvd., Ste. 700, Los Angeles, California 90017
      CEO: Jacob Wintner, SVP   Tel: (213) 362-2999   %FO: 100
      Bus: *International commercial banking services.*   Fax: (213) 488-9783   Emp: 33

● **VALOR COMPUTERIZED SYSTEMS**
4 Faran St., Yavne 70600, Israel
CEO: Ofer Shofman, Pres. & CEO   Tel: 972-8-943-2430   Rev: $31
Bus: *Computer software and services.*   Fax: 972-8-943-2429   Emp: 218
      www.valor.com

NAICS: 511210

      VALOR COMPUTERIZED SYSTEMS
      27422 Portola Pkwy., Ste. 250, Foothill Ranch El Toro, California 92610
      CEO: Chuck Feingold, Pres.   Tel: (949) 586-5969
      Bus: *Mfr. of CAD software.*   Fax: (949) 586-1343   Emp: 25

- **VCON TELECOMMUNICATIONS LTD.**
  22 Maskit St., PO Box 12747, Herzliyya 46733, Israel
  CEO: David Ofek, CEO
  Bus: *Videoconferencing hardware and software
  manufacture.*
  NAICS: 334290, 334310

  Tel: 972-9-959-0059
  Fax: 972-9-9956-7244
  www.vcon.com

  Rev: $16

  EMBLAZE-VCON INC.
  2 University Plaza, Ste. 201, Hackensack, New Jersey 07601
  CEO: C. Gordon Daugherty IV, Mgr.
  Bus: *Videoconferencing hardware and software
  manufacture and sales.*

  Tel: (201) 883-1220
  Fax: (201) 883-1229

  %FO: 100
  Emp: 30

  VCON TELECOMMUNICATIONS
  10535 Boyer Blvd., Ste. 300, Austin, Texas 78758
  CEO: Andreas Wienhold, SVP
  Bus: *Videoconferencing hardware and software
  manufacture and sales.*

  Tel: (512) 583-7700
  Fax: (512) 583-7701

  %FO: 100

- **VIRYANET LTD.**
  8 HaMarpe St., Science Based, Industries Campus, Har Hotzvim, Jerusalem 91450, Israel
  CEO: Paul V. Brooks, Pres. & CEO
  Bus: *Mfr. application software.*

  NAICS: 511210

  Tel: 972-2-584-1000
  Fax: 972-2-581-5507
  www.viryanet.com

  Rev: $12
  Emp: 86

  VIRYANET USA LTD.
  2 Willow St., Southborough, Massachusetts 01745
  CEO: Paul Brooks, Pres.
  Bus: *Application software manufacture and
  sales.*

  Tel: (508) 490-8600
  Fax: (508) 490-8666

  %FO: 100
  Emp: 142

- **VOCALTEC COMMUNICATIONS LTD.**
  2 Maskit St., Herzliyya 46733, Israel
  CEO: Elon A. Ganor, Chmn. & CEO
  Bus: *Develops and manufactures voice and fax*

  NAICS: 334210, 334220, 334290

  Tel: 972-9-970-7777
  Fax: 972-9-956-1867
  www.vocaltec.com

  Rev: $5
  Emp: 101

  VOCALTEC COMMUNICATIONS, INC.
  2 Executive Dr., Ste. 592, Fort Lee, New Jersey 07024
  CEO: Elon Ganor, Chmn.
  Bus: *Mfr./sales voice and fax hardware.*

  Tel: (201) 228-7000
  Fax: (201) 363-8986

  %FO: 100
  Emp: 15

- **WAVES LTD.**
  Azrieli Center, The TriangleTower, 32st Fl., 132 Derech Petach-Tikva, Tel Aviv 67027, Israel
  CEO: Gilad Keren, CEO
  Bus: *Digital signal processing systems and software
  manufacture.*
  NAICS: 334310, 511210

  Tel: 972-3-608-4000
  Fax: 972-3-608-4056
  www.waves.com

WAVES, INC.
306 West Depot Ave., Ste. 100, Knoxville, Tennessee 37917
CEO: Garrett Soden
Bus: *Digital signal processing systems and software manufacture and sales.*
Tel: (865) 546-6115
Fax: (865) 546-8445
%FO: 100

● **ZAG INDUSTRIES LTD.**
19 Ha'Melacha St., New Industrial Zone, Rosh Ha'Ayin 48091, Israel
CEO: Seffi Janowski, Pres. & CEO
Bus: *Office products, lawn products and tool products manufacturer.*
Tel: 972-3-902-0200
Fax: 972-3-902-0222
www.zag.co.il
NAICS: 333112, 333313, 337127, 337211, 337214, 423420

   ZAG USA, INC.
   2 Executive Dr., Ste. 780, Fort Lee, New Jersey 07024
   CEO: Joseph Janowski, Pres.
   Bus: *Sales office products, lawn products and tool products.*
   Tel: (201) 242-1470
   Fax: (201) 242-1460
   %FO: 100
   Emp: 6

● **ZIM INTERGRATED SHIPPING SERVICES LTD.**
9 Andrei Sakharov St., Matam Scientific Industries Center, P.O. Box 1723, Haifa 31016, Israel
CEO: Dr. Yoram Sebba, Pres.
Bus: *Ship owner and operator.*
Tel: 972-4-865-2111
Fax: 972-4-865-2956
www.zim.co.il
Rev: $1,600
NAICS: 483111

   B&R AGENCY, DIV. ZIM
   4080 Woodcock Dr., Ste. 135, Jacksonville, Florida 32207
   CEO: Tom Haeussner, Mgr.
   Bus: *Ship owners and operators.*
   Tel: (904) 399-5693
   Fax: (904) 399-5577
   %FO: 100

   ZIM-AMERICAN ISRAEL SHIPPING CO INC.
   9950 Lawrence Ave., Ste. 215, Schiller Park, Illinois 60176
   CEO: Ken Hundret, Mgr.
   Bus: *Ship owners and operators.*
   Tel: (847) 671-7999
   Fax: (847) 671-7444
   %FO: 100

   ZIM-AMERICAN ISRAEL SHIPPING CO INC.
   321 St. Charles Ave., Ste. 700, New Orleans, Louisiana 70130
   CEO: T. O'Hara, Mgr.
   Bus: *Ship owners and operators.*
   Tel: (504) 524-1184
   Fax: (504) 525-8451
   %FO: 100

   ZIM-AMERICAN ISRAEL SHIPPING CO INC.
   555 E. Ocean Blvd., Ste. 700, Long Beach, California 90802
   CEO: Phillip T. Wright, VP
   Bus: *Ship owners and operators.*
   Tel: (562) 506-2820
   Fax: (562) 506-2860
   %FO: 100

   ZIM-AMERICAN ISRAEL SHIPPING CO INC.
   624 S. Grand, Ste. 800, Los Angeles, California 94612
   CEO: Karsten Lemke, Mgr.
   Bus: *Ship owners and operators.*
   Tel: (213) 688-4600
   Fax:
   %FO: 100

ZIM-AMERICAN ISRAEL SHIPPING CO INC.
5801 Lake Wright Dr., Norfolk, Virginia 23502
CEO: Shaul Cohen Mintz, Pres.   Tel: (757) 228-1300
Bus: *Ship owners and operators.*   Fax: (757) 228-1400   Emp: 320

ZIM-AMERICAN ISRAEL SHIPPING CO INC.
Maher Terminal, 4010 Tripoli St., Elizabeth, New Jersey 07201
CEO: Richard Piper, Mgr.   Tel: (908) 527-9405   %FO: 100
Bus: *Ship owners and operators.*   Fax:

ZIM-AMERICAN ISRAEL SHIPPING CO INC.
1900 North Loop West, Ste. 600, Houston, Texas 77018
CEO: Judy Ruddle, Mgr.   Tel: (713) 688-7447   %FO: 100
Bus: *Ship owners and operators.*   Fax: (713) 688-2180

ZIM-AMERICAN ISRAEL SHIPPING CO INC.
801 Broad St., Portsmouth, Virginia 23707
CEO: Doug Flowers, Mgr.   Tel: (757) 228-1314   %FO: 100
Bus: *Ship owners and operators.*   Fax:

Italy

- **3V SIGMA SpA.**
Piazza Liberta, 10, Via Tasso 58, I-24100 Bergamo, Italy
CEO: Giovanni Palandri, Chmn.
Bus: *Specialty chemicals and process equipment manufacture.*
NAICS: 325188, 325199
Tel: 39-035-4165-111
Fax: 39-035-235-031
www.3v.com
Rev: $112
Emp: 400

  3V INC.
1500 Harbor Boulevard, Weehawken, New Jersey 07087
CEO: Roger Dyer, EVP
Bus: *Mfr./sale specialty chemicals and process equipment.*
Tel: (201) 865-3600
Fax: (201) 865-1892
%FO: 100

- **AETHRA, SPA**
Via Matteo Ricci, 10, I-60020 Ancona, Italy
CEO: Giulio Viezzoli, CEO
Bus: *Communication equipment manufacture.*
NAICS: 334220
Tel: 39-071-2189-81
Fax: 39-071-8870-77
www.aethra.com

  AETHRA, INC.
701 Brickell Ave., Ste. 1390, Miami, Florida 33131
CEO: Giorgio Viezzoli
Bus: *Communication equipment manufacture and sales.*
Tel: (305) 375-0010
Fax: (305) 375-0655
%FO: 100

- **ALI GROUP**
Via Gobetti, 2a, Villa Fiorita, I-20063 Cernusco sul Naviglio, Italy
CEO: Luciano Berti, Chmn.
Bus: *Food service equipment manufacture.*
NAICS: 333319
Tel: 39-02-9210-4241
Fax: 39-02-9210-3841
www.aligroup.it

  ALADDIN TEMP-RITE
250 E. Main St., Henderson, Tennessee 37075
CEO: Hank Holt
Bus: *Institutional meal delivery systems.*
Tel: (615) 537-3600
Fax: (615) 537-3600
%FO: 100

- **ALITALIA SPA**
Via Alessandro Marchetti 111, I-00148 Rome, Italy
CEO: Giancarlo Cimoli, Chmn. & CEO
Bus: *Commercial air transport services.*
NAICS: 481111
Tel: 39-06-6562-2151
Fax: 39-06-6562-4733
www.alitalia.com
Rev: $5,553
Emp: 20,575

  ALITALIA AIRLINES
666 Fifth Ave., New York, New York 10103
CEO: Niels Wolfe
Bus: *International commercial air transport services.*
Tel: (212) 903-3300
Fax: (212) 903-3331
%FO: 100
Emp: 334

• **AMPLIFON SPA**
Via G. Ripamonti, 133, I-20141 Milan, Italy
CEO: Franco Moscetti, Mng. Dir.
Bus: *Hearing aid manufacture.*

NAICS: 334510

Tel: 39-02-5747-2331
Fax: 39-02-5730-0033
www.amplifon.it

Rev: $429
Emp: 2,290

AMPLIFON USA INC.
5000 Cheshire Lane North, Plymouth, Minnesota 55446
CEO: Paul D'Amico
Bus: *Hearing aid manufacture and sales.*

Tel: (763) 268-4000
Fax: (763) 268-4254

%FO: 100

NATIONAL HEARING CENTERS
5000 Cheshire Lane North, Plymouth, Minnesota 55446
CEO: Robert Wabler
Bus: *Hearing aid manufacture and sales.*

Tel: (763) 268-4000
Fax: (763) 268-4254

%FO: 100

SONUS USA INC.
5000 Cheshire Lane North, Plymouth, Minnesota 55446
CEO: Scott Klein
Bus: *Hearing aid manufacture and sales.*

Tel: (763) 268-4000
Fax: (763) 268-4254

%FO: 100

• **GIORGIO ARMANI SPA**
Via Borgonuovo 11, I-20121 Milan, Italy
CEO: Paolo Fontanelli, CEO
Bus: *Men's/women's clothing, eyewear and*

Tel: 39-02-723-181
Fax: 39-02-723-18-549
www.giorgioarmani.com

Rev: $1,360
Emp: 4,700

NAICS: 315211, 315212, 315222, 315223, 315224, 315228, 315232, 315233, 315234, 315239, 315292, 315299, 315993, 315999, 316993, 448110, 448120, 721110

GIORGIO ARMANI CORPORATION
114 Fifth Ave, 17/F, New York, New York 10011
CEO: Gaetano Sallorenzo, Pres.
Bus: *Men's and women's clothing, eyewear and accessories.*

Tel: (212) 366-9720
Fax: (212) 366-1685

%FO: 100
Emp: 850

• **ARQUATI SPA**
Via S. Vitale 3, Sala Baganza, I-43038 Parma, Italy
CEO: Vincenzo Orlando, Gen. Dir.
Bus: *Curtains, sun awnings, patio covers, picture frame moldings and furnishings manufacture.*

Tel: 39-0521-8321
Fax: 39-0521-832-388
www.arquati.it

Rev: $140
Emp: 2,000

NAICS: 314121, 314129, 337121, 337122, 337124, 337125, 337129, 337920, 339999, 423220

ARQUATI USA INC.
1433 W. Frankford Rd., Ste. 100, Carrollton, Texas 75007
CEO: Alberto Tanzi, Pres.
Bus: *Mfr. curtains, sun awnings, screens, patio covers, picture frame moldings and furnishings.*

Tel: (972) 466-0824
Fax: (972) 466-0561

%FO: 100
Emp: 50

- **ARTSANA SPA**
  Via S. Catelli, 1, I-20070 Grandate, Como, Italy
  CEO: Pietro Catelli, CEO
  Bus: *Baby products and health products manufacture.*

  Tel: 39-031-382-000
  Fax: 39-031-382-400
  www.artsana.com

  Rev: $1,525
  Emp: 6,700

  NAICS: 325620, 339113, 339999, 423450
    CHICCO USA INC.
    4E Easy St., Bound Brook, New Jersey 08805
    CEO: Alex Fazio
    Bus: *Chicco baby products sales.*

    Tel: (732) 805-9200
    Fax: (732) 805-3376

    %FO: 100

- **ASSICURAZIONI GENERALI, S.p.A.**
  Piazza Duca degli Abruzzi 2, Casella Poste 538, I-34132 Trieste, Italy
  CEO: Giovanni Perissinotto, Pres. & CEO
  Bus: *General insurance services.*

  Tel: 39-040-671-400
  Fax: 39-040-671-600
  www.generali.com

  Rev: $79,881
  Emp: 60,638

  NAICS: 524113, 524210
    GENERALI GLOBAL
    One Liberty Plaza, New York, New York 10006
    CEO: Christopher Carnicelli
    Bus: *General insurance services.*

    Tel: (212) 602-7600
    Fax: (305) 616-6399

    %FO: 100

- **AUTOGRILL SPA**
  Building Z, Rd. 5, Rozzano, I-20089 Milan, Italy
  CEO: Gianmario Tondato da Ruos, Chmn.
  Bus: *Provides restaurant concessions at airports, train stations and malls.*

  Tel: 39-02-4826-3444
  Fax: 39-02-4826-3444
  www.autogrill.it

  Rev: $4,103
  Emp: 36,460

  NAICS: 722211, 722213, 722310
    HMS HOST CORPORATION
    6600 Rockledge Dr., Bethesda, Maryland 20817
    CEO: John J. McCarthy, CEO
    Bus: *Provides restaurant and retail services.*

    Tel: (240) 694-4100
    Fax: (240) 694-4100

    %FO: 100

- **BANCA INTESA SPA**
  Via Monte di Pieta, 8, I-20121 Milan, Italy
  CEO: Corrado Passera, CEO & Mng. Dir.
  Bus: *International banking.*

  Tel: 39-02-879-11
  Fax: 39-02-879-42587
  www.bancaintesa.it

  Rev: $20,423
  Emp: 56,958

  NAICS: 522110, 522292, 522293, 523999
    BANK INTESA
    1 Williams St., New York, New York 10004
    CEO: Eduardo Bruno Bombieri, Mgr.
    Bus: *International banking services.*

    Tel: (212) 607-3500
    Fax: (212) 809-2124

    %FO: 100

- **BANCA CARIGE SPA**
  Via Cassa di Risparmio, 15, I-16100 Genoa, Italy
  CEO: Giovanni Berneschi, Chmn.
  Bus: *Retail banking services.*

  Tel: 39-010-5791
  Fax: 39-010-579-4000
  www.carige.it

  Rev: $1,437
  Emp: 3,719

  NAICS: 522110, 522293

  BANCA CARIGE USA
  375 Park Ave., Ste. 3605, New York, New York 10152
  CEO: Carlo Romairone
  Bus: *Retail banking services.*

  Tel: (212) 421-6010
  Fax: (212) 759-6785

  %FO: 100

- **BANCA CR FIRENZE (CASSA DI RISPARMIO DI FIRENZE)**
  Via Bufalini 6, I-50122 Florence, Italy
  CEO: M. Ulivagnoli, CEO
  Bus: *Commercial banking services.*

  Tel: 39-055-261-2900
  Fax: 39-055-261-2298
  www.bancacrfirenze.it

  Emp: 3,500

  NAICS: 522110

  CASSA DI RISPARMIO DI FIRENZE
  650 Fifth Ave., 16/F, New York, New York 10019
  CEO: Giovanni Bertacca, U.S. Rep.
  Bus: *International banking services.*

  Tel: (212) 421-6010
  Fax: (212) 759-6785

  %FO: 100
  Emp: 3

- **BANCA MONTE DEI PASCHI DI SIENA S.p.A. (BMPS)**
  Piazza Salimbene, 3, I-53100 Siena, Italy
  CEO: Emilio Gnutti, CEO
  Bus: *Commercial banking services.*

  Tel: 39-0577-294-111
  Fax: 39-0577-294-017
  www.mps.it

  Rev: $9,635
  Emp: 26,881

  NAICS: 522110, 522220, 523920, 523930

  BANCA MONTE DEI PASCHI DI SIENA SPA.
  55 East 59th St., 9/F, New York, New York 10022-1112
  CEO: Romeo Carlo Cella, Mgr.
  Bus: *Foreign bank, branches & agencies*

  Tel: (212) 891-3600
  Fax: (212) 891-3661

  %FO: 100

- **BANCA NAZIONALE DEL LAVORO**
  Via Vittorio Veneto 119, I-00187 Rome, Italy
  CEO: Angelo Novati, CFO
  Bus: *Commercial banking services.*

  Tel: 39-06-47021
  Fax: 39-06-47027336
  www.bnl.it

  Rev: $3,854
  Emp: 17,347

  NAICS: 522110, 522120, 522310, 523920, 523930, 523991

  BANCA NAZIONALE DEL LAVORO
  25 West 51st St., 36/F, New York, New York 10019
  CEO: Alessandro Di Giovanni
  Bus: *International banking services.*

  Tel: (212) 581-0710
  Fax: (212) 489-9088

  %FO: 100

  BANCA NAZIONALE DEL LAVORO
  55 West Monroe St., Ste. 3490, Chicago, Illinois 60603
  CEO: Alessandro Di Giovanni
  Bus: *International banking services.*

  Tel: (312) 444-9250
  Fax: (312) 444-9410

  %FO: 100

- **BANCA POPOLARE DI MILANO**
  Piazza Meda 4, I-20121 Milan, Italy
  CEO: Roberto Mazzotta, Chmn.
  Bus: *Commercial banking services.*

  Tel: 39-02-7700-1
  Fax: 39-02-7700-2280
  www.bpm.it

  Rev: $1,435
  Emp: 6,684

  NAICS: 522110

      BANCA POPOLARE DI MILANO
      375 Park Ave., 9/F, New York, New York 10152
      CEO: Gergio Cucalo, EVP
      Bus: *Commercial banking services.*

      Tel: (212) 758-5040
      Fax: (212) 838-1077

      %FO: 100
      Emp: 27

- **BANCO TOSCANA SPA**
  Firenze, Via Leone Pancaldo, 4, I-50157 Florence, Italy
  CEO: Paolo Mottura, CEO
  Bus: *Commerical banking services.*

  Tel: 39-055-43911
  Fax: 39-055-4379036
  www.bancatoscana.it

  Rev: $1,224
  Emp: 4,482

  NAICS: 522110, 522293

      BANCO TOSCANA USA
      55 East 59th St., New York, New York 10022
      CEO: Piero Faraoni
      Bus: *Commercial banking services.*

      Tel: (212) 891-3611
      Fax: (212) 891-3668

      %FO: 100

- **BARALAN INTERNATIONAL SPA**
  Baralan Building, Via Copernico, I-20090 Trezzano, Italy
  CEO: Luisa Kamelhar, Pres.
  Bus: *Mfr. cosmetic packaging.*

  Tel: 39-02-484-4961
  Fax: 39-02-484-2719
  www.baralan.com

  Emp: 100

  NAICS: 327213, 561910

      ARROWPAK INC.
      120-19 89th Ave., Richmond Hill, New York 11418
      CEO: Roland Baranes, Pres.
      Bus: *Sales/distribution cosmetic packaging.*

      Tel: (718) 849-1600
      Fax: (718) 849-1383

      %FO: JV
      Emp: 50

- **BARILLA HOLDING SPA**
  Via Mantova 166, I-43100 Parma, Italy
  CEO: Gianluca Bolla, CEO
  Bus: *Mfr. pasta, bread sticks, crackers and cookies.*

  Tel: 39-0521-2621
  Fax: 39-0521-270-621
  www.barilla.it

  Rev: $5,522
  Emp: 25,000

  NAICS: 311421, 311422, 311812, 311821, 311823

      BARILLA AMERICA INC.
      1200 Lakeside Dr., Bannockburn, Illinois 60015
      CEO: Carmen Buccini, Pres.
      Bus: *Mfr. pasta, break sticks, crackers and
          cookies.*

      Tel: (847) 405-7500
      Fax: (847) 405-7505

      %FO: 100
      Emp: 6,975

- **BEGHELLI SPA**
  Via Mozzeghine, 13/15, I-40050 Monteveglio Bologna, Italy
  CEO: Gian Pietro Beghelli, CEO
  Bus: *Emergency lighting systems manufacture and*

  Tel: 39-051-838-411
  Fax: 39-051-838-444
  www.beghelli.it

  Rev: $127
  Emp: 1,067

  NAICS: 334419, 335122, 335129, 335211

  BEGHELLI USA INC.
  3123 Commerce Pkwy., Pembroke Pines, Florida 33025-3944
  CEO: Dania La Spada
  Bus: *Emergency lighting systems manufacture and sales.*

  Tel: (954) 442-6600
  Fax: (954) 442-6677

  %FO: 100

- **BELL AGUSTA AIRCRAFT (BAAC)**
  Via Giovanni Agusta 520, I-21017 Cascina Costa di Samarato, Italy
  CEO: Amedeo Caporaletti, CEO
  Bus: *Helicopters and fixed-wing aircraft manufacturer.*

  Tel: 39-0331-229111
  Fax: 39-0331-229605
  www.augusta.it

  Emp: 6,000

  NAICS: 336411

  BELL/AGUSTA AEROSPACE CORP.
  PO Box 901073, Fort Worth, Texas 76101
  CEO: Louis Bartolotta, CEO
  Bus: *Helicopter marketing, sales & after-sale support.*

  Tel: (817) 278-9600
  Fax: (817) 278-9726

  %FO: 100
  Emp: 100

- **BENETTON GROUP, SPA**
  Via Villa Minelli 1, I-31050 Ponzano Veneto Treviso, Italy
  CEO: Silvano Cassano, CEO
  Bus: *Mfr. fashion apparel and accessories.*

  Tel: 39-0422-519111
  Fax: 39-0422-969501
  www.benetton.com

  Rev: $1,995
  Emp: 6,585

  NAICS: 448140, 448190

  BENETTON USA CORPORATION
  601 5th Ave., 4/F, New York, New York 10017
  CEO: Carlo Tunioli, VP
  Bus: *Mfr./sale of fashion apparel and accessories.*

  Tel: (212) 593-0290
  Fax: (212) 371-1438

  %FO: 100

- **FABBRICA D'ARMI PIETRO BERETTA**
  Via Pietro Beretta, 18, Gardone Val Trompia, I-25063 Brescia, Italy
  CEO: Ugo Gussalli Beretta, CEO
  Bus: *Gun and arms manufacture.*

  Tel: 39-030-8341-1
  Fax: 39-030-8341-421
  www.beretta.it

  Rev: $375
  Emp: 1,500

  NAICS: 332993, 332994, 339920

  BERETTA GALLERY
  718 Madison Ave., New York, New York 10021
  CEO: Patrick McDonald
  Bus: *Gun and arms sales.*

  Tel: (212) 319-3235
  Fax: (212) 207-8219

  %FO: 100

BERETTA GALLERY
41 Highland Park Village, Dallas, Texas 75205
CEO: Christopher Merritt
Bus: *Gun and arms sales.*

Tel: (214) 559-9800
Fax: (214) 559-9805

%FO: 100

BERETTA USA CORPORATION
17601 Beretta Dr., Accokeek, Maryland 20607
CEO: Christopher Merritt
Bus: *Gun and arms sales.*

Tel: (301) 283-2191
Fax: (301) 283-0435

%FO: 100

• **BIESSE SPA**
Via della Meccanica 16, I-61100 Pesaro, Italy
CEO: Roberto Selci, Pres.
Bus: *Mfr. woodworking equipment for furniture industry.*

Tel: 39-0721-439100
Fax: 39-0721-439499
www.biesse.it

Emp: 1,550

NAICS: 333210

   BIESSE GROUP AMERICA INC.
   4110 Meadow Oak Lane, Charlotte, North Carolina 28219-9849
   CEO: Federico Broccoli, CEO
   Bus: *Distribution/service woodworking
   equipment.*

   Tel: (704) 357-3131
   Fax: (704) 357-3130

   %FO: 80
   Emp: 45

• **BISCONTI & MERENDINO**
Piazza V. E. Orlando N. 33, I-90138 Palermo, Italy
CEO: Giuseppe Bisconti, Mng. Prtn.
Bus: *International law firm.*

Tel: 39-091-612-4005
Fax: 39-091-612-4230
www.studiobisconi.it

NAICS: 541110

   STUDIO LEGALE BISCONTI
   730 Fifth Ave., Ste. 1802, New York, New York 10019
   CEO: Andrea Bisconti, Mng. Prtn.
   Bus: *International law firm.*

   Tel: (212) 956-9400
   Fax: (212) 956-9405

   %FO: 100

• **BONDIOLI & PAVESI SPA**
Via Xxiii Aprile 35 A, I-46029 Suzzara, Italy
CEO: Edi Bondioli, Pres.
Bus: *Drive shafts, gear boxes, hydraulics*

Tel: 39-037-65141
Fax: 39-037-6531382
www.bypy.it

Rev: $85
Emp: 700

NAICS: 333999

   BONDIOLI & PAVESI INC.
   10252 Sycamore Dr., Ashland, Virginia 23005
   CEO: Franco Laghi, Pres.
   Bus: *Distributor drive shafts, gear boxes, and
   hydraulics*

   Tel: (804) 550-2224
   Fax: (804) 550-2837

   %FO: 100
   Emp: 27

• **BREMBO SPA**
Via Brembo 25, I-24035 Bergamo, Italy
CEO: Alberto Bombassei, Chmn.
Bus: *Mfr. brake components and components for autos.*

Tel: 39-035-605-111
Fax: 39-035-605-290
www.brembo.it

Rev: $795
Emp: 3,936

NAICS: 336340

BREMBO NORTH AMERICA, INC.
1585 Sunflower Ave., Costa Mesa, California 92626
CEO: Kenneth H. Miller, Pres.
Bus: *Mfr. braking components and components for autos.*

Tel: (714) 641-0104
Fax: (714) 641-5827

%FO: 100

● **BULGARI SPA**
Lungotevere Marzio 11, I-00186 Rome, Italy
CEO: Francesco Trapani, CEO
Bus: *Mfr. and sales of contemporary Italian jewelry and leather goods.*
NAICS: 339911, 448320

Tel: 39-06-688-10477
Fax: 39-06-688-10401
www.bulgari.it

Rev: $953
Emp: 1,824

BULGARI
605 East Cooper St., Aspen, Colorado 81611
CEO: Marla Marino, Pres.
Bus: *Retail store; sales of contemporary Italian jewelry and leather goods.*

Tel: (970) 925-6225
Fax: (970) 925-4418

%FO: 100

BULGARI
201 North Rodeo Dr., Beverly Hills, California 90210
CEO: Tobi Sargent, Pres.
Bus: *Retail store; sales of contemporary Italian jewelry and leather goods.*

Tel: (310) 858-9216
Fax: (310) 858-9226

%FO: 100

BULGARI
909 North Michigan Ave., Chicago, Illinois 60611
CEO: Christina Gilberti, Pres.
Bus: *Retail store; sales of contemporary Italian jewelry and leather goods.*

Tel: (312) 255-1313
Fax: (312) 255-1326

%FO: 100

BULGARI
9700 Collins Ave., Bal Harbour, Florida 33154
CEO: Mary Cunsoll, Pres.
Bus: *Retail store; sales of contemporary Italian jewelry and leather goods.*

Tel: (305) 861-8898
Fax: (305) 861-5718

%FO: 100

BULGARI CORPORATION OF AMERICA
730 Fifth Ave., New York, New York 10019-4105
CEO: Francesco Trapani
Bus: *Retail store; sales of contemporary Italian jewelry and leather goods.*

Tel: (212) 315-9000
Fax: (212) 315-9000

%FO: 100

BULGARI PERFUMES USA
9 West 57th St., New York, New York 10019
CEO: Francesco Trapini, Pres.
Bus: *Retail store; sales perfumes and cosmetics.*

Tel: (212) 315-9000
Fax: (212) 462-4001

%FO: 100

BULGARI PERFUMES USA
876 Centennial Ave., Piscataway, New Jersey 08854-3917
CEO: Marianne Decicco
Bus: *Retail store; sales of perfumes and cosmetics.*

Tel: (732) 885-5500
Fax: (732) 885-5500

%FO: 100

• **BUZZI UNICEM SPA**
Via Luigi Buzzi, 6, Casale Monferrato, I-15033 Alessandria, Italy
CEO: Alessandro Buzzi, CEO   Tel: 39-01-42416-111   Rev: $1,835
Bus: *Cement and concrete manufacture.*   Fax: 39-01-42416-464   Emp: 3,828
                                                                      www.buzziunicem.it
NAICS: 212321, 212324, 212325, 327310, 327320, 327331, 327332, 327390

    ALAMO CEMENT COMPANY
    6055 W. Green Mountain Rd., San Antonio, Texas 78266
    CEO: Ed Broach   Tel: (210) 208-1880   %FO: 100
    Bus: *Cement product manufacture.*   Fax: (210) 208-1881

    BUZZI UNICEM USA
    100 Broadhead Rd., Ste. 230, Bethlehem, Pennsylvania 18017
    CEO: Dave Nepereny   Tel: (610) 866-4400   %FO: 100
    Bus: *Cement product manufacture.*   Fax: (610) 866-9430

    BUZZI UNICEM USA
    1701 Chesterfield Airport Rd., Ste. 130, Chesterfield, Missouri 63005
    CEO: Rick Sutter   Tel: (636) 532-1060   %FO: 100
    Bus: *Cement product manufacture.*   Fax: (636) 532-3332

    BUZZI UNICEM USA INC.
    1104 East 167th St. South, Glenpool, Oklahoma 74033
    CEO: Robert Bivens   Tel: (918) 492-2121   %FO: 100
    Bus: *Cement product manufacture.*   Fax: (918) 481-5786

    BUZZI UNICEM USA INC.
    10401 North Meridian St., Indianapolis, Indiana 46290
    CEO: Michael Clarke   Tel: (317) 706-3314   %FO: 100
    Bus: *Cement product manufacture.*   Fax: (317) 706-3314

    HEARTLAND CEMENT COMPANY
    PO Box 428, Independence, Kansas 67301
    CEO: Larry Hooper   Tel: (316) 331-0200   %FO: 100
    Bus: *Cement product manufacture.*   Fax: (316) 331-3890

    HERCULES CEMENT COMPANY
    PO Box 69, Stockertown, Pennsylvania 18083
    CEO: Frank Stampf   Tel: (610) 759-6300   %FO: 100
    Bus: *Cement product manufacture.*   Fax: (610) 759-2661

    SIGNAL MOUNTAIN CEMENT
    348 Armour Dr., Atlanta, Georgia 30324
    CEO: Don Wellington   Tel: (404) 875-7091   %FO: 100
    Bus: *Cement product manufacture.*   Fax: (404) 875-7091

• **CAMOZZI GROUP**
Via Eritrea 20/I, I-25126 Brescia, Italy
CEO: Ettore Camozzi, CEO   Tel: 39-030-37921   Rev: $330
Bus: *Pneumatic component mfr.*   Fax: 39-030-240-0464   Emp: 1,900
                                                                      www.camozzi.it

NAICS: 423610, 423830

CAMOZZI PNEUMATICS INC.
2160 Redbud Blvd., Ste. 101, McKinney, Texas 75069
CEO: Vico Camozzi, Pres.
Bus: *Pneumatic component mfr.*

Tel: (972) 548-8885
Fax: (972) 548-2110

%FO: 100

MARZOLI INTERNATIONAL
100 Corporate Dr., Spartanburg, South Carolina 29303
CEO: Gary Romanstine
Bus: *Pneumatic component mfr.*

Tel: (864) 599-7100
Fax: (864) 599-7111

%FO: 100

● **CAPITALIA SPA (BANCA DI ROMA)**
via Marco Minghetti 17, I-00187 Rome, Italy
CEO: Cesare Geronzi, Chmn.
Bus: *Commercial banking services.*

Tel: 39-06-6707-1
Fax: 39-06-6707-0652
www.capitalia.it

Rev: $9,899
Emp: 28,264

NAICS: 522110

> **BANCA DI ROMA**
> 34 East 51st St., New York, New York 10022
> CEO: Alexander Voller, Mgr.
> Bus: *Commercial banking services.*
>
> Tel: (212) 407-1600
> Fax: (212) 407-1677
>
> %FO: 100
> Emp: 104

> **BANCA DI ROMA**
> 1 Market Plaza, Ste. 1000, San Francisco, California 94105
> CEO: Luca Balestra
> Bus: *Commercial banking services.*
>
> Tel: (415) 357-0800
> Fax: (415) 357-9869
>
> %FO: 100

● **CARRARO SPA**
Via Olmo 37, I-35011 Campodarsego Padua, Italy
CEO: Mario Carraro, Chmn. & CEO
Bus: *Mfr. components for cars and machinery,*
including axles, transmissions, tractors and

Tel: 39-049-921-9111
Fax: 39-049-928-9111
www.carraro.com

Rev: $489
Emp: 2,132

NAICS: 336350, 336399

> **CARRARO NORTH AMERICA, INC.**
> 2118 US Hwy. 41 S.E., Calhoun, Georgia 30701
> CEO: Tomaso Carraro, Pres.
> Bus: *Mfr. agricultural and construction equipment*
> *axles and transmissions.*
>
> Tel: (706) 625-2460
> Fax: (706) 625-3321
>
> %FO: 100
> Emp: 17

● **CEMBRE SPA**
Via Serenissima 9, I-25135 Brescia, Italy
CEO: Carlo Rosani, Chmn.
Bus: *Mfr. electrical connectors.*

Tel: 39-030-369-21
Fax: 39-030-336-5766
www.cembre.com

Rev: $89
Emp: 462

NAICS: 333991, 334417, 335313, 335314

> **CEMBRE**
> 70 Campus Plaza II, Edison, New Jersey 08837
> CEO: Carl Rosana, CEO
> Bus: *Mfr. electrical connectors.*
>
> Tel: (732) 225-7415
> Fax: (732) 225-7414
>
> %FO: 100

- **DAVIDE CENCI & MGT SRL**
Via Campo Marzio 1/7, I-00186 Rome, Italy
CEO: David Cenci, Pres.
Bus: *Design and manufacture of wearing apparel.*

Tel: 39-06-699-0681
Fax: 39-06-379-5900
www.davidecenci.com

Emp: 65

NAICS: 315228, 315239, 448110, 448120
  DAVIDE CENCI INC.
  801 Madison Ave., New York, New York 10021
  CEO: Paolo Cenci, VP
  Bus: *Retail men's wear.*

  Tel: (212) 628-5910
  Fax: (212) 439-1650

  %FO: 100
  Emp: 13

- **CIR S.P.A.**
Via Ciovassino, 1, I-20121 Milan, Italy
CEO: Rodolfo de Benedetti, CEO & Mng. Dir.
Bus: *Industrial holding company.*

Tel: 39-02-722-701
Fax: 39-02-722-70-309
www.cirgroup.it

Rev: $4,175
Emp: 10,324

NAICS: 523999, 525990, 551112
  CIR VENTURES
  505 Hamilton Ave., Ste. 210, Palo Alto, California 94301
  CEO: Giacomo Marini, Mng. Prtn.
  Bus: *Technology venture capital firm.*

  Tel: (650) 325-6699
  Fax: (650) 325-7799

  %FO: 100

- **COMAU SPA, SUB. OF FIAT GROUP**
Via Rivalta, 30, I-10095 Grugliasco, Torino, Italy
CEO: Carlo Mangiarino, CEO
Bus: *Sheet metal dies and welding equipment
manufacture.*

Tel: 39-022-684-9111
Fax: 39-011-789-356
www.comau.com

Rev: $2,340
Emp: 13,328

NAICS: 333514, 333992
  AUTODIE INTERNATIONAL INC.
  44 Coldbrook Northwest, Grand Rapids, Michigan 49503
  CEO: David Moore, Mgr.
  Bus: *Plastic and steel molds and dies
manufacture and sales to auto industry.*

  Tel: (616) 454-9361
  Fax: (616) 356-1539

  %FO: 100

  PROGRESIVE TOOL & INDUSTRIES CO./COMAU PICO
  21000 Telegraph Rd., Southfield, Michigan 48034
  CEO: Andrea Pappagallo, Pres.
  Bus: *Sheet metal dies and welding equipment
manufacture and sales.*

  Tel: (248) 353-8888
  Fax: (248) 368-2511

  %FO: 100

- **DANIELI & C. OFFICINE MECCANICHE**
Via Nazionale, 41, I-33042 Buttrio Udine, Italy
CEO: Gianpietro Benedetti, CEO
Bus: *Manufactures machinery for metal industry.*

Tel: 39-04-3259-81
Fax: 39-04-3259-8289
www.danieli.it

Rev: $1,389
Emp: 3,492

NAICS: 333131

DANIELI CORPORATION
800 Cranberry Woods Dr., Cranberry Township, Pennsylvania 16066
CEO: Mark M. Brandon, Pres.   Tel: (724) 778-5400   %FO: 100
Bus: *Manufactures machinery for metal industry.*   Fax: (724) 778-5401

● **DAVIDE CAMPARI-MILANO SPA**
Via Fillippo Turati 27, I-20121 Milan, Italy
CEO: Enzo Visone, CEO   Tel: 39-02-6225-343   Rev: $1,063
Bus: *Aperitif and cordial manufacturer.*   Fax: 39-02-6225-479   Emp: 1,545
                                             www.campari.com
NAICS: 312140, 424820

    SKYY SPIRITS
    1 Beach St., Ste. 300, San Francisco, California 94133
    CEO: Gerard Ruvo, Pres.   Tel: (415) 315-8000   %FO: JV
    Bus: *Vodka and Campari aperitif manufacture and*   Fax: (415) 315-8001
    sales.

● **DE LONGHI SPA**
Via Lodovico Seitz 47, I-31100 Treviso, Italy
CEO: Giuseppe De'Longhi, Chmn.   Tel: 39-0422-4131
Bus: *Mfr. small, household appliances.*   Fax: 39-0422-412420
                                             www.delonghi.com
NAICS: 333415, 335211, 335228

    DE LONGHI AMERICA, INC.
    Park 80 West Plaza One, 4/F, Saddle Brook, New Jersey 07663
    CEO: Maria Rita Perrone, Pres.   Tel: (201) 909-4000   %FO: 100
    Bus: *Mfr. household, air-conditioning, air-*   Fax: (201) 909-8550
    treatment and heating appliances.

● **DELLE VEDOVE LEVIGATRICI S.p.A.**
Viale Treviso 13A, I-33170 Pordenone, Italy
CEO: Gaetano Delle Vedove, Pres. & CEO   Tel: 39-0434-513711
Bus: *Woodworking machinery manufacture.*   Fax: 39-0434-572775   Emp: 50
                                             www.delllevedove.com
NAICS: 333210

    DELLE VEDOVE USA INC.
    6031 Harris Technology Blvd., Ste. G, Charlotte, North Carolina 28269
    CEO: Steve Bosley, VP & Gen. Mgr.   Tel: (704) 598-0020   %FO: 70
    Bus: *Sale/service woodworking equipment &*   Fax: (704) 598-3950   Emp: 19
    abrasives.

● **DELONGHI**
Via Lodovico Seitz, 47, I-31100 Treviso, Italy
CEO: Stefano Beraldo, CEO   Tel: 39-0422-4131   Rev: $1,727
Bus: *Home appliances manufacture.*   Fax: 39-0422-413-736   Emp: 7,184
                                             www.delonghi.com
NAICS: 335211, 335212, 335221

DELONGHI AMERICA INC.
Park 80 West Plaza One, 4/F, Saddle Brook, New Jersey 07663
CEO: Marco Beghin, Mktg. Dir.   Tel: (201) 909-4000   %FO: 100
Bus: *Mfr. home appliances.*   Fax: (201) 909-8550

● **DEROMA HOLDING SPA**
Via Pasubio 17, I-36034 Malo Vicenza, Italy
CEO: Valentino Ciscato, Chmn.   Tel: 39-0445-595-311
Bus: *Mfr. terra cotta pots.*   Fax: 39-0445-595-322
                                                  www.deroma.it
NAICS: 327112, 334518, 339999, 423220

    DEROMA
    4316 New River Hills Pkwy., Valrico, Florida 33594
    CEO: Stefano Cavinato, Pres.   Tel: (813) 643-7850
    Bus: *Home furnishings*   Fax:

    MARSHALL POTTERY INC.
    4901 Elysian Fields Rd., Marshall, Texas 75670
    CEO: Stefano Cavinato, Pres.   Tel: (903) 927-5400
    Bus: *Mfr. pottery products*   Fax: (903) 938-0222   Emp: 160

● **DIESEL S.p.A.**
Via Dell Industria 7, I-36060 Marostica, Vicenza, Italy
CEO: Renzo Rosso, CEO   Tel: 39-0424-477-555   Rev: $760
Bus: *Mfr. high-fashion clothing and accessories.*   Fax: 39-0424-708-061   Emp: 1,000
                                                  www.diesel.com
NAICS: 315299, 315991, 315999, 448120

    DIESEL INC.
    770 Lexington Ave., New York, New York 10021
    CEO: Panicko Philippou   Tel: (212) 308-0055   %FO: 100
    Bus: *Clothing and accessories sales.*   Fax: (212) 308-0055

    DIESEL INC.
    416 West Broadway, New York, New York 10012
    CEO: Panicko Philippou   Tel: (212) 343-3863   %FO: 100
    Bus: *Sales/distribution of high-fashion clothing*   Fax: (212) 434-2152
        and accessories.

    DIESEL INC.
    1340 Third St., Santa Monica, California 90401
    CEO: Sally Kaufman   Tel: (310) 899-3055   %FO: 100
    Bus: *Sales/distribution of high-fashion clothing*   Fax: (310) 899-3855
        and accessories.

    DIESEL INC.
    1450 Ala Moana Blvd., Honolulu, Hawaii 96814
    CEO: Panicko Philippou   Tel: (808) 955-3555   %FO: 100
    Bus: *Sales/distribution of high-fashion clothing*   Fax: (808) 955-7996
        and accessories.

DIESEL INC.
1507 Walnut St., Philadelphia, Pennsylvania 19107
CEO: Panicko Philippou
Bus: *Sales/distribution of high-fashion clothing
and accessories.*

Tel: (215) 561-2557
Fax: (215) 561-2557

%FO: 100

DIESEL INC.
400 Castro St., San Francisco, California 94114
CEO: Panicko Philippou
Bus: *Sales/distribution of high-fashion clothing
and accessories.*

Tel: (415) 621-5557
Fax: (415) 621-0321

%FO: 100

DIESEL INC.
923 Rush St., Chicago, Illinois 60611
CEO: Craig Leavitt
Bus: *Sales/distribution of high-fashion clothing
and accessories.*

Tel: (312) 255-0157
Fax: (312) 255-0158

%FO: 100

DIESEL INC.
30 Northwest 12th St., Portland, Oregon 97201
CEO: Craig Leavitt
Bus: *Sales/distribution of high-fashion clothing
and accessories.*

Tel: (503) 241-1355
Fax: (503) 241-7069

%FO: 100

DIESEL INC.
2500 Marcus Ave, New Hyde Park, New York 11042
CEO: Panicko Philippou
Bus: *Flagship store: sales/distribution of high-
fashion clothing and accessories.*

Tel: (516) 437-0970
Fax: (516) 437-0970

%FO: 100

DIESEL INC.
3000 East 1st Ave., Denver, Colorado 80206
CEO: Susan Jantzer
Bus: *Clothing and accessories sales.*

Tel: (303) 355-9555
Fax: (303) 355-9555

%FO: 100

DIESEL INC.
1249 Wisconsin Ave. NW, Washington, District of Columbia 20007
CEO: Panicko Philippou
Bus: *Sales/distribution of high-fashion clothing
and accessories.*

Tel: (202) 625-2780
Fax: (202) 625-2782

%FO: 100

● **DOLCE & GABBANA**
Via Santa Cecilia 7, I-20122 Milan, Italy
CEO: Domenico Dolce, Chmn. & CEO
Bus: *Mfr. men's and women's upscale, designer
clothing, fragrances and eyewear.*
NAICS: 316992, 325199, 423460, 448120

Tel: 39-02-7742-71
Fax: 39-02-7601-0600
www.dolcegabbana.it

Rev: $275
Emp: 900

DOLCE & GABBANA
660 Madison Ave., Ste. 10, New York, New York 10021
CEO: Eric Silverman
Bus: *Sales of men's and women's upscale,
designer clothing, fragrances and eyewear.*

Tel: (212) 750-0055
Fax: (212) 750-0055

%FO: 100

- **DUCATI MOTOR HOLDING SPA**
Via Cavalieri Ducati 3, I-40132 Bologna, Italy
CEO: Frederico Minoli, Chmn. & CEO
Bus: *Mfr. luxury, high-speed motorcycles and sport touring bikes.*
NAICS: 336991, 448110

Tel: 39-051-641-3111
Fax: 39-051-641-3223
www.ducati.com

Rev: $488
Emp: 1,162

    DUCATI NORTH AMERICA INC.
    10443 Bandley Dr., Cupertino, California 95014
    CEO: Michael Lock, CEO
    Bus: *Automobiles & other motor vehicles*

    Tel: (408) 253-0499
    Fax: (408) 253-4099

    Emp: 35

    DUCATI NORTH AMERICA, INC.
    237 West Pkwy., Pompton Plains, New Jersey 07444-1028
    CEO: Nicola Greco, CEO
    Bus: *Sales/distribution of luxury, high-speed motorcycles and sport touring bikes.*

    Tel: (973) 839-2600
    Fax: (973) 839-2331

    %FO: 100

- **ENI SPA**
Piazzale Enrico Mattei 1, I-00144 Rome, Italy
CEO: Paolo Scaroni, CEO
Bus: *Energy related product and services.*
NAICS: 211111, 211112, 213111, 213112, 221210, 324110, 324191, 324199, 325110, 325120, 325131, 325132, 325181, 325188, 325191, 325192, 325193, 325199, 333132, 424710, 424720, 447190, 454311, 454312, 454319, 486110, 486210, 486910, 541360

Tel: 39-06-59821
Fax: 39-06-5982-2141
www.eni.it

Rev: $79,084
Emp: 71,497

    AMERICAN AGIP CO. INC.
    666 Fifth Ave., New York, New York 10103
    CEO: Umberto Battalia, Pres. & CEO
    Bus: *Petrochemical business*

    Tel: (212) 887-0250
    Fax: (212) 887-0258

    Emp: 116

    ENI AMERICAS
    666 Fifth Ave., New York, New York 10103
    CEO: Enzo Viscusi, Mgr.
    Bus: *Group activity coordination.*

    Tel: (212) 887-0330
    Fax: (212) 246-0009

    %FO: 100

    ENI PETROLEUM CO. INC. & AGIP EXPLORATION CO.
    1201 Louisiana St., Ste. 3500, Houston, Texas 77002
    CEO: Frederico Arisi, Pres.
    Bus: *Crude petroleum & natural gas exploration*

    Tel: (713) 393-6100
    Fax:

    Emp: 80

    POLIMERI EUROPA AMERICAS INC.
    2000 West Loop South, Ste. 2010, Houston, Texas 77027
    CEO: Claudio Cignetti, Mgr.
    Bus: *Oil exploration/products, crude oil trading.*

    Tel: (713) 640-0700
    Fax:

    %FO: 100

    SAIPEM USA INC.
    15950 Park Row, Houston, Texas 77084
    CEO: Brian T. Fine, Pres.
    Bus: *Onshore/offshore drilling and pipelines.*

    Tel: (281) 552-5700
    Fax: (281) 552-5915

    %FO: 100
    Emp: 114

SNAMPROGETTI USA
1200 Smith St., Houston, Texas 77002
CEO: Alessandro Serpetti, Pres.
Bus: *Technology sales/service.*

Tel: (713) 655-7071
Fax: (713) 655-7764

%FO: 100
Emp: 5

SONSUB INTERNATIONAL
15950 Park Row, Houston, Texas 77084
CEO: Brian Fine, Pres. & CEO
Bus: *Sub-sea engineering services.*

Tel: (281) 552-5600
Fax: (281) 552-5910

%FO: 100
Emp: 220

● **GRUPPO ERMENEGILDO ZEGNA**
5 Via Forcella, I-20144 Milan, Italy
CEO: Paolo Zegna, Chmn.
Bus: *Mfr. upscale men's clothing.*

Tel: 39-02-58-103-787
Fax: 39-02-58-103-901
www.zegna.co.il

Rev: $727
Emp: 5,000

NAICS: 315228

  ERMENEGILDO ZEGNA CORPORATION
  301 N. Rodeo Dr., Beverly Hills, California 90210
  CEO: Tom Junk, Gen. Mgr.
  Bus: *Sales/distribution of menswear and
      sportswear.*

  Tel: (310) 247-8827
  Fax: (310) 247-8827

  %FO: 100

  ERMENEGILDO ZEGNA CORPORATION
  743 Fifth Ave., New York, New York 10022
  CEO: Andrea Pesaresi, CEO
  Bus: *Sales/distribution of menswear and
      sportswear.*

  Tel: (212) 421-4488
  Fax: (212) 421-4488

  %FO: 100

● **ESAOTE SPA**
Via Siffredi 58, I-16153 Genoa, Italy
CEO: Carlo Castellano, Chmn.
Bus: *Develops and manufactures ultrasound imaging
    (MRI).*

Tel: 39-010-6547-1
Fax: 39-010-6547-275
www.esaote.com

Rev: $3
Emp: 1,050

NAICS: 334510

  BIOSOUND ESAOTE INC.
  8000 Castleway Dr., PO Box 50858, Indianapolis, Indiana 46250
  CEO: Claudio Bertolini, Pres.
  Bus: *Develop/mfr. ultrasound imaging (MRI).*

  Tel: (317) 849-1793
  Fax: (317) 841-8616

  %FO: 100

● **SALVATORE FERRAGAMO ITALIA SPA**
Palazzo Feroni, Via dei Tornabuoni 2, I-50123 Florence, Italy
CEO: Ferruccio Ferragamo, CEO
Bus: *Clothing, belts, ties, handbags and scarves
    manufacture.*

Tel: 39-055-33-601
Fax: 39-055-33-60444
www.salvatoreferragamo.it

Rev: $568

NAICS: 315211, 315212, 315222, 315223, 315224, 315228, 315232, 315233, 315234, 315239, 315299, 315993,
315999, 316211, 316213, 316214, 316219,
       316991, 316992, 316993, 448150, 448210, 448320

  SALVATORE FERRAGAMO
  663 Fifth Ave., New York, New York 10022
  CEO: Ira Melnitsky, Pres.
  Bus: *Sales of clothing, belts, ties, handbags and
      scarves.*

  Tel: (212) 759-3822
  Fax:

  %FO: 100
  Emp: 76

● **FERRARI SPA**
Via Abetone Inferiore, 4, Maranello, I-41053 Modena, Italy
CEO: Luca Cordero de Montezemolo, Chmn. & Pres.   Tel: 39-05-3694-9111   Rev: $2,062
    & CEO
Bus: *Sports car manufacture.*   Fax: 39-05-3694-9714   Emp: 3,322
                                         www.ferrari.it
NAICS: 336111
    FERRARI USA INC.
    250 Sylvan Ave., Englewood Cliffs, New Jersey 07632
    CEO: Maurizio Parlato, Pres.   Tel: (201) 816-2600   %FO: 100
    Bus: *Sports car manufacture and sales.*   Fax: (201) 816-2626

● **FERRERO SPA**
Piazzale Pietro Ferrero, I-12051 Alba Cuneo, Italy
CEO: Pietro Ferreroi, Chmn. & CEO   Tel: 39-01-73-29-511   Rev: $5,664
Bus: *Mfr. confectionery products, including Nutella*   Fax: 39-01-73-363-034   Emp: 16,607
    Hazelnut Spread, Rocher chocolates and Tic Tac www.ferrero.it
    Breath Mints.
NAICS: 311320, 311340
    FERRERO USA INC.
    600 Cottontail Lane, Somerset, New Jersey 08873
    CEO: Martino Caretto, CEO   Tel: (732) 764-9300   %FO: 100
    Bus: *Mfr./repackaging sale confectionery goods.*   Fax: (732) 764-2700   Emp: 154

● **FILA HOLDINGS S.p.A.**
Strada 6 Palazzo L, I-20189 Rozzano Milanofiori, Italy
CEO: Dr. Michele Scannavini, Chmn.   Tel: 39-02-52823200   Rev: $842
Bus: *Sports footwear and clothing manufacture and*   Fax: 39-02-52823400   Emp: 2,300
    sales.   www.fila.com
  NAICS: 315211, 315212, 315223, 315224, 315228, 315291, 315299, 315991, 315999, 316211, 316212, 316213,
316214, 316219, 339920
    FILA U.S.A., INC.
    1 Fila Way, Sparks, Maryland 21152-3000
    CEO: Steve Wynne, Pres. & CEO   Tel: (410) 773-3000   %FO: 100
    Bus: *Sports footwear and clothing manufacture*   Fax: (410) 773-4989   Emp: 200
    and sales.

● **FINMECCANICA SpA**
Piazza Monte Grappa, 4, I-00195 Rome, Italy
CEO: Pier Francesco Guarguaglini, Chmn. & CEO   Tel: 39-06-324-731   Rev: $10,270
Bus: *Mfr. of helicopters, military aircraft, and defense* Fax: 39-06-320-8621   Emp: 51,026
    systems   www.finmeccanica.it
NAICS: 332993, 336411, 336413, 336414
    AUGUSTA AEROSPACE CORP.
    3050 Red Lion Rd., Philadelphia, Pennsylvania 19114
    CEO: Robert Budica, Pres. & CEO   Tel: (215) 281-1400
    Bus: *Aerospace & defense.*   Fax: (215) 281-1462   Emp: 100

UNION SWITCH & SIGNAL, INC.
1000 Technology Dr., Pittsburgh, Pennsylvania 15219
CEO: Kenneth Burk, Chmn. & CEO
Bus: *Mfr. of rail & truck equipment*

Tel: (412) 688-2400
Fax: (412) 688-2399

● **GEFRAN SPA**
Via Sebina, 74, Provaglio d'Iseo, I-25050 Brescia, Italy
CEO: Ennio Franceschetti, Chmn. & CEO
Bus: *Control systems manufacture.*

Tel: 39-030-9888-1
Fax: 39-030-9839-063
www.gefran.it

Rev: $92
Emp: 714

NAICS: 333298, 334512, 334513, 335313

    GEFRAN ISI, INC.
    8 Lowell Ave., Winchester, Massachusetts 01890
    CEO: Ennio Franceschetti, Pres.
    Bus: *Control systems manufacture and sales..*

    Tel: (781) 729-5249
    Fax: (781) 729-1468

    %FO: 100
    Emp: 29

● **GIANFRANCO FERRE SPA**
Via Pontaccio, 8, I-20121 Milan, Italy
CEO: Tonino Perna, Chmn.
Bus: *Mfr. clothing, yarns and fabrics.*

Tel: 39-02-721-341
Fax: 39-02-781-485
www.gianfrancoferre.com

NAICS: 313111, 313312, 315211, 315212, 315222, 315223, 315224, 315232, 315233, 315234, 315239, 315299, 315999, 325620, 448110, 448120

    GIANFRANCO FERRE USA
    712 Fifth Ave., 27/F, New York, New York 10019
    CEO: Enrico Di Muccio, CEO
    Bus: *Mfr. clothing, yarns and fabrics.*

    Tel: (212) 265-4166
    Fax: (212) 265-4144

    %FO: 100

● **GIULIANI**
Via del Lavoro 7, Quarto Inferiore, I-40050 Bologna, Italy
CEO: Tomaso Tarozzi, CEO
Bus: *Mfr. standard and customized machine tools for the global security industry.*

Tel: 39-051-603-7811
Fax: 39-051-603-7933
www.giulianico.com

NAICS: 333298, 333319

    BUCCI INDUSTRIES INC.
    9332 Forsyth Park Dr., Charlotte, North Carolina 28273
    CEO: Manfred Sprenger, Pres.
    Bus: *Transfer machines for the lock Industry manufacture.*

    Tel: (704) 583-8341
    Fax: (704) 583-8486

    %FO: 100
    Emp: 21

● **GRUPPO CERAMICHE RICCHETTI SPA**
Via Statale, 118/M, S.Antonino di Casalgrande, I-42013 Sassuolo Modena, Italy
CEO: Oscar Zannoni, Chmn.
Bus: *Glazed ceramic and stoneware tile manufacturer.*

Tel: 39-0536-99-2511
Fax: 39-0536-99-2515
www.ricchetti-group.com

Rev: $403
Emp: 2,386

NAICS: 212325, 327111, 327122, 327125

    RICCHETTI CERAMIC, INC.
    404 South Babcock St., Ste. 403, Melbourne, Florida 32901
    CEO: William Johnson, Pres.
    Bus: *Mfr. glazed ceramic and stoneware tile.*

    Tel: (321) 984-0505
    Fax: (321) 984-0503

    %FO: 100

- **GRUPPO ERMENEGILDO ZEGNA**
  5 Via Forcella, I-20144 Milan, Italy
  CEO: Gildo Zegna, Mng. Dir.   Tel: 39-0258-103787   Rev: $865
  Bus: *Menswear and sportswear manufacture.* Fax: 39-0258-103921   Emp: 5,000
          www.zegnaermenegildo.com
  NAICS: 313221, 315211, 315222, 315223, 315224, 315993, 424320, 448110

  - **ERMENEGILDO ZEGNA**
    743 Fifth Ave., New York, New York 10022
    CEO: Lauren Hansen, Mgr.   Tel: (212) 751-3468   %FO: 100
    Bus: *Menswear and sportswear manufacture.* Fax: (212) 750-6679

  - **ERMENEGILDO ZEGNA CORP.**
    100 West Forest Ave., Ste. A, Englewood, New Jersey 07631
    CEO: Robert Ackerman, Pres.   Tel: (201) 816-0921   %FO: 100
    Bus: *Sale of retail men's clothing.*   Fax: Emp: 220

- **GRUPPO GFT**
  Corso Emilia 6, I-10152 Torino, Italy
  CEO: Fabio Covarrubias Piffer, Pres.   Tel: 39-011-23971
  Bus: *Wearing apparel manufacture and distribution.* Fax: 39-011-2397319 Emp: 10,000
          www.sahza.it
  NAICS: 315999

  - **GFT USA CORPORATION**
    11 West 42nd St., New York, New York 10036
    CEO: Michael H. McLaughlin, EVP   Tel: (212) 302-8877   %FO: 100
    Bus: *Mfr. accessories, dress shirts, formalwear,* Fax: (212) 302-8889
         neckwear, outerwear, pants, sportswear
         and tailored clothing.

  - **RIVERSIDE MFG. CO., SUB. GFT USA CORP.**
    301 Riverside Dr., PO Box 460, Moultrie, Georgia 31776
    CEO: Larry Peoples,   Tel: (229) 985-5210   %FO: 100
    Bus: *Wardrobe, uniform and apparel manufacture.* Fax: (229) 890-2932

- **GRUPPO ITALIANO VINI SOC. COOP**
  Villa Belvedere, Calmasino, I-37010 Verona, Italy
  CEO: Rolando Chiossi, Chmn.   Tel: 39-045-626-9600
  Bus: *Wine vintner.*   Fax: 39-045-723-5772
          www.gruppoitalianovini.com
  NAICS: 312130

  - **FREDERICK WILDMAN & SONS LTD.**
    307 East 53rd St., New York, New York 10022
    CEO: Richard Cacciato, Pres.   Tel: (212) 355-0700   %FO: 100
    Bus: *Wine sales.*   Fax: (212) 355-4719   Emp: 85

● **I PELLETTIERI D'ITALIA S.p.A.**
Via Andrea Maffei 2, I-20135 Milan, Italy
CEO: Patrizio Bertelli, CEO
Bus: *Mfr. clothing line and leather goods.*

Tel: 39-0254-6701
Fax: 39-0255-1800-83
www.prada.com

Rev: $1,554
Emp: 2,000

NAICS: 315211, 315212, 315222, 315223, 315224, 315228, 315232, 315233, 315234, 315239, 315292, 315299, 315993, 315999, 316211, 316213, 316214, 316219, 316992, 316993, 448110, 448120

IPI USA (PRADA)
609 West 51st St., New York, New York 10019
CEO: Connie Darrow, Pres.
Bus: *Sales/distribution of Prada clothes and leather goods.*

Tel: (212) 307-9300
Fax: (212) 974-2919

%FO: 100
Emp: 475

PRADA USA CORP.
50 West 57th St., New York, New York 10019
CEO: Connie Darrow, Pres.
Bus: *Sale of apparel & accessories.*

Tel: (212) 307-9300
Fax: (212) 974-2919

%FO: 100

● **IDRA PRESSE SPA**
Via Triumplina, 41/43, I-25123 Brescia, Italy
CEO: Ernesto Domenico Musumeci, Pres.
Bus: *Metalworking products manufacture.*

Tel: 39-030-2011-1
Fax: 39-030-2000-625
www.prince-machine.com

Rev: $49
Emp: 150

NAICS: 332999, 333298

IDRA PRINCE, INC.
670 Windcrest Dr., Holland, Michigan 49423
CEO: Robert Hegel, Chmn.
Bus: *Metalworking products manufacture and sales..*

Tel: (616) 394-8248
Fax: (616) 394-1250

%FO: 100

● **IFI ISTITUTO FINANZIARIO INDUSTRIALE SPA**
Corso Matteotti 26, I-10121 Turin, Italy
CEO: Gianluigi Gabetti, Chmn.
Bus: *Holding company engaged in car manufacture, food production, packaging and insurance.*

Tel: 39-011-509-0266
Fax: 39-011-535-600
www.gruppoifi.com

Rev: $70,762
Emp: 179,790

NAICS: 311991, 336111, 523999, 524128, 551112, 711212

IFIL USA
375 Park Ave., 27/F, New York, New York 10152
CEO: Flexis Herlihy, Dir.
Bus: *Investment services.*

Tel: (212) 421-9700
Fax:

Emp: 4

RIVERWOOD INTERNATIONAL PACKAGING, INC.
3350 Riverwood Pkwy., Ste. 1400, Atlanta, Georgia 30339
CEO: Steven Saucier, COO
Bus: *Paperboard and packaging machinery manufacturing for the beverage and consumer products market.*

Tel: (770) 644-3000
Fax: (770) 644-2927

%FO: JV
Emp: 4,000

- **IMA (INDUSTRIA MACCHINE AUTOMATICHE SPA)**
Via Tosarelli 184, I-40055 Castenaso Bologna, Italy
CEO: Alberto Vacchi, Dir.
Bus: *Mfr. packaging machines for pharmaceuticals, cosmetics, and tea bags.*
NAICS: 333993

Tel: 39-05-1783-111	Rev: $496
Fax: 39-05-1784-422	Emp: 2,600
www.ima.it	

  IMA NORTH AMERICA, INC.
  211 Sinclair St., Bristol, Pennsylvania 19007
  CEO: William Crozier, Pres.
  Bus: *Mfr. packaging machines for pharmaceuticals.*

  Tel: (215) 826-8500   %FO: 100
  Fax: (215) 826-0400

- **IMPREGILO SPA**
Viale Italia 1, Sesto S. Giovanni, I-20099 Milan, Italy
CEO: Pier Giorgio Romiti, Chmn.
Bus: *Construction of dams, water systems and transportation infrastructures.*
NAICS: 236210, 236220, 237110, 237120, 237130, 237310, 237990, 488490, 541310, 541330

Tel: 39-02-244-22111   Rev: $3,681
Fax: 39-02-244-22293   Emp: 12,998
www.impregilo.it

  IMPREGILO HEALY
  2400 NW Front Ave., Portland, Oregon 97209
  CEO: Jim McDonald, Gen. Mgr.
  Bus: *Water, sewer & utility lines*

  Tel: (503) 595-4400
  Fax: Emp: 50

  IMPREGILO INTERNATIONAL USA INC.
  1910 South Highland Ave., Lombard, Illinois 60148
  CEO: Fulvio Castaldi, Pres.
  Bus: *Sales of heavy equipment.*

  Tel: (630) 678-3110   %FO: 100
  Fax: Emp: 200

- **IMT INTERMATO SPA**
Via Carego 14, I-21020 Crosio della Valle, Italy
CEO: Claudio Caprioli, Pres.
Bus: *Mfr. equipment for machining alloy aluminum wheels.*
NAICS: 333298

Tel: 39-0332-966-110   Rev: $45
Fax: 39-0332-966-033   Emp: 100
www.imtintermato.it

  IMT AMERICA INC
  18411 Sherman Way, Reseda, California 91335
  CEO: Francesco Chinaglia
  Bus: *Distributes equipment for machining light alloy aluminum parts.*

  Tel: (818) 705-1741   %FO: 100
  Fax: (818) 705-0462

- **INTERPUMP GROUP SPA**
Via E. Fermi 25, Calerno di S. Illario d'Enza, I-42040 Reggio, Italy
CEO: Giovanni Cavallini, Chmn.
Bus: *Mfr. high-pressure water plunger pumps.*
NAICS: 332911, 332912, 332919, 333995, 333996, 336312

Tel: 39-052-290-4311   Rev: $737
Fax: 39-052-290-4444   Emp: 2,292
www.interpumpgroup.it

GENERAL PUMP COMPANIES INC.
1174 Northland Dr., Mendota Heights, Minnesota 55120
CEO: Joe Campbell
Bus: *Centrifugal pumps manufacture and sales.*
Tel: (651) 454-6500
Fax: (651) 454-8015
%FO: 100

MUNCIE POWER PRODUCTS, INC.
PO Box 548, Muncie, Indiana 47305-2838
CEO: Joseph E. Wilson
Bus: *Sales high-pressure water plunger pumps.*
Tel: (765) 284-7721
Fax: (765) 284-6991
%FO: 100

● **IT HOLDING SPA**
Corso Monforte, 30, I-20122 Milan, Italy
CEO: Tonino Perna, CEO
Bus: *Mfr. high-end clothing apparel and accessories.*
Tel: 39-02-7630-391
Fax: 39-02-7800-16
www.itholding.it
Rev: $968
Emp: 1,720

NAICS: 315211, 315212

IT HOLDING USA INC.
85 Fifth Ave., 6/F, New York, New York 10003
CEO: Enrico Dimuccio
Bus: *Mfr. luxury clothing and accessories.*
Tel: (212) 413-4407
Fax: (212) 413-4438
%FO: 100

● **ITALCEMENTI SPA**
Via G. Camozzi 124, I-24121 Bergamo, Italy
CEO: Carlo Pesenti, CEO
Bus: *Cement, concrete and related construction materials manufacture.*
Tel: 39-035-396-111
Fax: 39-035-244-905
www.italcementigroup.com
Rev: $6,176
Emp: 17,570

NAICS: 212311, 212312, 212313, 212319, 212321, 327310, 327320

AXIM
8282 Middlebranch Rd., Middlebranch, Ohio 44652
CEO: David Nethercutt, VP
Bus: *Mfr. chemical preparations.*
Tel: (330) 966-0444
Fax: (330) 499-9275
%FO: 100
Emp: 62

ESSROC CEMENT CORP.
3251 Bath Pike, Nazareth, Pennsylvania 18064
CEO: Rodolfo Danielli, Chmn. & CEO
Bus: *Mfr./Sales concrete.*
Tel: (610) 837-6725
Fax: (610) 837-9614
%FO: 100

● **ITALDESIGN S.p.A.**
Via A Grandi 11, I-10024 Moncalieri Turin, Italy
CEO: Giorgetto Giugiaro, Chmn.
Bus: *Automotive research and construction.*
Tel: 39-01-689-1611
Fax: 39-01-647-0858
www.italdesign.it
Rev: $85
Emp: 750

NAICS: 541420

I.D.C. ITALDESIGN CALIFORNIA, INC.
6481 Oak Canyon Rd., Irvine, California 92620
CEO: Giorgetto Giugiaro, Pres. & CEO
Bus: *Automotive engineering, models and prototype building.*
Tel: (949) 654-0070
Fax: (949) 654-0077
%FO: 100
Emp: 50

- **IVECO SPA, DIV. FIAT GROUP**
  Via Puglia 35, I-10156 Turin, Italy
  CEO: Paolo Monferino, CEO
  Bus: *Manufacturer of industrial vehicles.*

  NAICS: 336120, 336211

    Tel: 39-011-007-2111   Rev: $10,215
    Fax: 39-011-007-4958   Emp: 31,000
    www.iveco.com

  ### IVECO NORTH AMERICA
  245 East North Ave., Carol Stream, Illinois 60188
  CEO: Luigi Carnino, Pres.
  Bus: *Sale of diesel engines.*

    Tel: (630) 260-4226   %FO: 100
    Fax:

- **COMPAGNIA ITALIANA DEI JOLLY HOTELS SpA**
  Via Bellini 6, Valdagno, I-36078 Vicenza, Italy
  CEO: Ugo Zanuso, Mng. Dir.
  Bus: *Hotel chain.*

  NAICS: 721110

    Tel: 39-04-4541-0000   Rev: $276
    Fax: 39-04-4541-1472   Emp: 2,428
    www.jollyhotels.it

  ### JOLLY HOTEL MADISON TOWERS
  22 East 38th St., New York, New York 10016
  CEO: Rosanna Coscia, Sales Mgr.
  Bus: *Hotels.*

    Tel: (212) 802-0600   %FO: 100
    Fax: (212) 447-0747

- **KINOMAT SPA**
  635 Via Enrico Fermi, I-21042 Caronno Pertusella, Italy
  CEO: Mario Falcone, Pres.
  Bus: *Mfr. coil winding equipment and automation systems.*
  NAICS: 333518, 334416

    Tel: 39-02-964531
    Fax: 39-02-96453300   Emp: 80
    www.kinomat.com

  ### MARSILLI NORTH AMERICA
  5410 Newport Dr., Ste. 40, Rolling Meadows, Illinois 60008
  CEO: Jay Lawes, Mgr.
  Bus: *Coil winding equipment and automation systems.*

    Tel: (847) 392-2599   %FO: 100
    Fax: (847) 392-2858

  ### MARSILLI NORTH AMERICA
  11445 Cronridge Dr., Owings Mills, Maryland 21117
  CEO: Marco Camardella, Pres.
  Bus: *Coil winding equipment and automation systems.*

    Tel: (410) 654-2425   %FO: 100
    Fax: Emp: 21

- **KRIZIA SPA**
  Via Manin 19, I-20121 Milan, Italy
  CEO: Mariuccia Mandelli, Chmn. & Mng. Dir.
  Bus: *Clothing and accessories manufacture.*

    Tel: 39-02-620-261   Rev: $20
    Fax: 39-02-654-013
    www.krizia.net

  NAICS: 315191, 315212, 315232, 315233, 315234, 315239, 315292, 315299, 315992, 315999, 316110, 316992, 316993, 316999, 448120, 721110

KRIZIA SPA BOUTIQUE
769 Madison Ave., New York, New York 10021
CEO: Aldo Pinto, Mng. Dir.
Bus: *Boutique clothing line.*

Tel: (212) 879-1211
Fax: (212) 472-7612

%FO: 100
Emp: 6

● **LEITNER SPA**
Brennerstr. 34, I-39049 Sterzing, Italy
CEO: Michael Seeber, Pres.
Bus: *Mfr. cable transportation systems, including ski-lifts, fixed & detachable chairlifts, gondolas, aerial tramways, sky rides & urban*
NAICS: 487110

Tel: 39-04-7272-2111
Fax: 39-04-7276-4884
www.leitner-lifts.com

Rev: $150
Emp: 542

   LEITNER-POMA OF AMERICA INC.
   PO Box 35, Route 100, Stockbridge, Vermont 05772
   CEO: Patricia Dykeman, Mgr.
   Bus: *Mfr. cable transportation systems, including ski-lifts, fixed and detachable chairlifts, gondolas, aerial tramways, sky rides and urban transportation.*

Tel: (802) 746-7955
Fax: (802) 746-7958

%FO: 100

   LEITNER-POMA OF AMERICA INC.
   2510 Foresight Circle, Grand Junction, Colorado 81505
   CEO: Jean Pierre Cathiard, Chmn.
   Bus: *Mfr. cable transportation systems, including ski-lifts, fixed and detachable chairlifts, gondolas, aerial tramways, sky rides and urban transportation.*

Tel: (970) 241-4442
Fax: (970) 241-3023

%FO: 100
Emp: 70

● **LOMBARDINI MOTORI S.p.A.**
Via Cav. del Lavoro A., Lombardini, 2, I-42100 Reggio Emilia, Italy
CEO: Giuliano Zucco, Pres.
Bus: *Industrial diesel engines manufacture.*

NAICS: 333618

Tel: 39-0522-3891
Fax: 39-0522-389503
www.lombardini.it

Rev: $235
Emp: 1,143

   LOMBARDINI USA INC.
   2150 Boggs Rd., Ste. 300, Duluth, Georgia 30096
   CEO: William P. Motague, CEO
   Bus: *Distribute industrial diesel engines.*

Tel: (770) 623-3554
Fax:

%FO: 100
Emp: 16

● **LUIGI LAVAZZA SPA**
Corso Novara 59, I-10154 Turin, Italy
CEO: Emilio Lavazza, Chmn.
Bus: *Producer of coffee beans.*

NAICS: 311920

Tel: 39-01-123-981
Fax: 39-01-123-98324
www.lavazza.it

Rev: $800
Emp: 500

   LAVAZZA PREMIUM COFFEES CORP.
   3 Park Ave., 28/F, New York, New York 10016
   CEO: Ennio Ranaboldo, Gen. Mgr.
   Bus: *Producer of coffee beans.*

Tel: (212) 725-8800
Fax: (212) 725-9475

%FO: 100
Emp: 25

- **LUXOTTICA GROUP, S.p.A.**
  Via Cantu, 2, I-20123 Milan, Italy
  CEO: Andrea Guerra, CEO   Tel: 39-02-863341   Rev: $4,410
  Bus: *Mfr. eyeglass frames, retail eye care and clothing* Fax: 39-0437-63223   Emp: 36,900
       stores.   www.luxottica.it
  NAICS: 339115, 446130, 448310, 621320

    EYEMED VISION CARE LLC
    4000 Luxottica Place, Mason, Ohio 45040
    CEO: Kerry Bradley, COO   Tel: (513) 765-6000   %FO: 100
    Bus: *Healthcare*   Fax: (513) 765-6388

    LENSCRAFTERS INC.
    4000 Luxottica Place, Mason, Ohio 45040
    CEO: Kerry Bradley, COO   Tel: (513) 765-6000   %FO: 100
    Bus: *Eyeglass frames and eye care retail stores.*   Fax: (513) 765-6249

    LUXOTTICA RETAIL
    4000 Luxottica Place, Mason, Ohio 45040
    CEO: Kerry Bradley, COO   Tel: (513) 765-6000   %FO: 100
    Bus: *Optical services.*   Fax: (513) 765-6249

    LUXOTTICA USA INC.
    44 Harbor Park Dr., Ste. 5, Port Washington, New York 11050
    CEO: Leonardo DelVecchio, Pres.   Tel: (516) 484-3800   %FO: 100
    Bus: *Real Estate.*   Fax: (800) 451-4839   Emp: 25

    PEARLE VISION, INC.
    4000 Luxottica Place, Mason, Ohio 45040
    CEO: Kerry Bradley, COO   Tel: (513) 765-6000   %FO: 100
    Bus: *Optical services.*   Fax: (513) 765-6249

    SUNGLASS HUT INTERNATIONAL, INC.
    4000 Luxottica Place, Mason, Ohio 45040
    CEO: Kerry Bradley, COO   Tel: (513) 765-6000   %FO: 100
    Bus: *Sunglasses.*   Fax: Emp: 10,000

    THINGS REMEMBERED, INC.
    5500 Avion Park Dr., Highland Heights, Ohio 44143
    CEO: Suzanne Sutter, Pres.   Tel: (440) 473-2000   %FO: 100
    Bus: *Floral & gifts.*   Fax: (440) 473-2018   Emp: 4,000

- **MANULI RUBBER INDUSTRIES SPA**
  Piazza della Repubblica 14/16, I-20124 Milan, Italy
  CEO: Dardanio Manuli, Chmn. & CEO   Tel: 39-02-627131   Rev: $310
  Bus: *Rubber components manufacturer and systems*   Fax: 39-02-62713-382   Emp: 3,300
       for transmitting fluids.   www.manulirubber.com
  NAICS: 326220, 336399

    MANULI HYDRAULICS INC.
    410 Keystone Dr., Ste. 410, Warrendale, Pennsylvania 15086
    CEO: Dardanio Manuli, Pres.   Tel: (724) 778-3380
    Bus: *Hydraulics sales & distribution*   Fax: (724) 778-3381   Emp: 11

MANULI OIL & MARINE USA INC.
2755 East Oakland Park Blvd., Ft. Lauderdale, Florida 33306
CEO: Robert Furness, Pres.
Bus: *Mfr. of rubber components and systems for transmitting fluids.*

Tel: (954) 561-3777
Fax: (954) 563-0644

%FO: 100
Emp: 5

MANULI RUBBER INDUSTRIES
5892 W. 71st. St., Indianapolis, Indiana 46278
CEO: Dardanio Manuli, CEO
Bus: *Mfr. of rubber & plastic product manufacturing*

Tel: (317) 280-0850
Fax: (317) 290-0247

● **MAPEI S.p.A.**
Via Cafiero, 22, I-20158 Milan, Italy
CEO: Giorgio Squinzi, Pres.
Bus: *Mfr. of adhesives and sealants.*

Tel: 39-0-237-6731
Fax: 39-0-237-673-214
www.mapei.it

Rev: $1,255
Emp: 3,000

NAICS: 325520

MAPEI CORP USA
1144 E. Newport Center Dr., Deerfield Beach, Florida 33442
CEO: Nicholas di Tempora, Pres.
Bus: *Manufacturer of adhesives and sealants*

Tel: (800) 426-2734
Fax: (954) 246-8801

%FO: 100

● **MARANGONI SPA**
Via E. Fermi, 11/B, I-37135 Verona, Italy
CEO: Mario Marangoni, Chmn. & Mng. Dir.
Bus: *Rethreading machinery manufacture.*

Tel: 39-045-921-5100
Fax: 39-045-820-2879
www.marangoni.com

Rev: $362

NAICS: 326211, 423130, 532490

MARANGONI TREAD INC.
712 Myatt Dr., Madison, Tennessee 37115
CEO: Bill Sweatman, Pres. & CEO
Bus: *Retreading machinery manufacture and sales.*

Tel: (615) 868-4050
Fax: (615) 868-0402

%FO: 100
Emp: 8

● **MARAZZI GRUPPO CERAMICHE SPA**
Viale Regina Pacis 39, Modena, I-41049 Sassuoto, Italy
CEO: Filippo Marazzi, Chmn. & Pres.
Bus: *Mfr. ceramic tile.*

Tel: 39-0536-860-111
Fax: 39-0536-860-644
www.marazi.it

Rev: $700
Emp: 4,000

NAICS: 327122

AMERICAN MARAZZI INC.
359 Clay Rd., Sunnyvale, Texas 75182
CEO: Filiippo Marazzi, Chmn.
Bus: *Mfr. ceramic tile.*

Tel: (972) 226-0110
Fax: (972) 226-2263

%FO: 100
Emp: 417

MONARCH CERAMIC TILE INC., DIV. AMERICAN MARAZZI
834 Rickwood Rd., Florence, Alabama 35630
CEO: Daniel J. Lasky, Pres.
Bus: *Mfr. ceramic tile.*

Tel: (256) 764-6181
Fax: (256) 760-8686

%FO: 100

- **MARCOLIN SPA**
  Localita Villanova 4, I-32013 Longarone Belluno, Italy
  CEO: Giovanni Marcolin Coffen, Chmn.
  Bus: *Designer eyewear manufacture.*

  Tel: 39-04-3777-7111
  Fax: 39-04-3777-2320
  www.marcolin.com

  Rev: $236
  Emp: 1,062

  NAICS: 339115, 423460

  MARCOLIN USA INC.
  7543 East Tierra Buena Lane, Scottsdale, Arizona 85260
  CEO: Antonio Bortuzzo, CEO
  Bus: *Sale of optical goods.*

  Tel: (888) 627-2654
  Fax: (888) 627-2671

  Emp: 300

- **NATUZZI S.p.A.**
  47, Via Iazzitiello, Santeramo in Colle, I-70029 Bari, Italy
  CEO: Pasquale Natuzzi, Chmn. & CEO
  Bus: *Mfr. of leather furniture.*

  Tel: 39-080-882-0111
  Fax: 39-080-882-0555
  www.natuzzi.com

  Rev: $1,021
  Emp: 6,230

  NAICS: 337121, 337122, 337124, 337125, 337129, 339999, 423210, 423220

  NATUZZI AMERICAS
  130 West Commerce Ave., High Point, North Carolina 27261
  CEO: Steve Bailey, Mgr.
  Bus: *Sales/distribution of leather furniture.*

  Tel: (336) 887-8300
  Fax:

  %FO: 100

- **OLIVETTI SPA**
  Via Jervis 77, Ivrea, I-10015 Torino, Italy
  CEO: Giovanni Ferrario, Chmn. & CEO
  Bus: *Mfr. office automation systems date processing
  products.*

  Tel: 39-0125-5200
  Fax: 39-0125-522524
  www.olivetti.it

  Rev: $822
  Emp: 2,395

  NAICS: 333293, 333313, 333315, 334119, 423420, 423430, 423440, 561499

  OLIVETTI CAPITAL MANAGEMENT
  15 Thomas Rd, Wellesley, Massachusetts 02482
  CEO: Jennifer Olivetti, Principal
  Bus: *Office equipment manufacturer.*

  Tel: (781) 237-9895
  Fax:

  ROYAL CONSUMER INFORMATION PRODUCTS
  379 Campus Dr, Somerset, New Jersey 08873
  CEO: Salomon Suwalsky, Pres.
  Bus: *Sales/marketing computers, office
  machinery, products and supplies.*

  Tel: (732) 627-9977
  Fax: (908) 526-8405

  %FO: 100
  Emp: 401

- **OTIM S.p.A.**
  Via Porro Lambertenghi 9, I-20159 Milan, Italy
  CEO: Mario Carniglia, Pres.
  Bus: *International freight forwarder.*

  Tel: 39-02-699121
  Fax: 39-02-69912245
  www.otim.it

  Rev: $5,976
  Emp: 39,350

  NAICS: 488510

  OTIM USA INC.
  320 Windsor Rd., Wood Ridge, New Jersey 07075
  CEO: Mario Carniglia, Pres.
  Bus: *Freight transportation.*

  Tel: (201) 933-6131
  Fax: (201) 624-7286

  %FO: 100

- **PARMALAT FINANZIARIA S.p.A.**
Piazza Ercules 9, I-20122 Milan, Italy
CEO: Enrico Bondi, Chmn. & CEO
Bus: *Produces milk and dairy products.*

Tel: 39-02-806-8801
Fax: 39-02-869-3863
www.parmalat.net

Rev: $5,355
Emp: 32,292

NAICS: 311421, 311511, 311514, 311821, 311999, 424430

  PARMALAT USA CORPORATION
  520 Main St., Wallington, New Jersey 07057
  CEO: Michael T. Rosicki, Pres.
  Bus: *Mfr. milk and dairy products.*

  Tel: (973) 777-2500
  Fax: (973) 777-7648

  %FO: 100
  Emp: 1,275

- **PARTECIPAZIONI ITALIANE SPA**
Viale della Repubblica, 34, I-27100 Pavi, Italy
CEO: Paolo Colombo, Chmn.
Bus: *Industrial sewing machines manufacture.*

Tel: 39-0382-5141
Fax: 39-0382-514211
www.necchi.it

Rev: $27
Emp: 53

NAICS: 333292

  ALLYN INTERNATIONAL CORP.
  1075 Santa Fe Dr., Denver, Colorado 80204
  CEO: Carolyn Rose-Borus, Pres.
  Bus: *Industrial sewing machines manufacture and sales.*

  Tel: (303) 825-5200
  Fax: (303) 825-5078

  %FO: 100
  Emp: 10

- **PERFETTI VAN MELLE SPA**
Via XXV, Aprile 7/9, Lainate, I-20020 Milan, Italy
CEO: A. Perfetti, Chmn.
Bus: *Candy and gum manufacture.*

Tel: 39-02-935-351
Fax: 39-02-937-3279
www.perfetti.it

Rev: $475
Emp: 3,039

NAICS: 311340

  PERFETTI VAN MELLE USA INC.
  3645 Turfway Rd., PO Box 18190, Erlanger, Kentucky 41018
  CEO: Ronald Korenhof, Pres. & CEO
  Bus: *Mfr./import candy.*

  Tel: (859) 283-1234
  Fax: (859) 283-1316

  %FO: 100
  Emp: 200

  PERFETTI VAN MELLE USA INC.
  151 North Hastings Lane, Buffalo Grove, Illinois 60089
  CEO: W. Dorhout Mees, COO
  Bus: *Mfr./import candy.*

  Tel: (841) 777-5650
  Fax: (841) 777-5654

  %FO: 100

- **FABIO PERINI S.p.A.**
Via per Mugnano 889, I-55100 Lucca, Italy
CEO: Martin Weickenmeier, Pres.
Bus: *Mfr. and sales tissue converting equipment.*

Tel: 39-0583-4601
Fax: 39-0583-435-543
www.fabioperini.com

Rev: $198
Emp: 630

NAICS: 333291

FABIO PERINI AMERICA, INC.
3060 South Ridge Rd., PO Box 28380, Green Bay, Wisconsin 54324
CEO: Michael Drage, Pres. & CEO   Tel: (920) 336-5000   %FO: 100
Bus: *Sales and distribution of tissue converting*   Fax: (920) 337-0363   Emp: 72
      equipment.

● **PERLIER SPA**
Corso Monforte 36, I-20122 Milan, Italy
CEO: Maria Elena Giraudi, Mng. Dir.   Tel: 39-02-76-008-125   Rev: $29
Bus: *Develops bath and body treatments and cosmetic* Fax: 39-02-76-009-207   Emp: 49
      products.   www.perlier.com
   NAICS: 325620

   PERLIER INC.
   555 Madison Ave., 11/F, New York, New York 10022
   CEO: Luigi Rivetty   Tel: (212) 750-1111   %FO: 100
   Bus: *Develops bath and body treatments and*   Fax: (212) 750-8930
         cosmetic products.

   PERLIER INC.
   300 Kennedy Dr., Sayreville, New Jersey 08872
   CEO: Gianluca Giraudi   Tel: (732) 727-1000   %FO: 100
   Bus: *Develops bath and body treatments and*   Fax: (732) 727-1000
         cosmetic products.

● **THE PERMASTEELISA GROUP**
Via Matte 21/23, Vittorio Veneto, I-31029 Treviso, Italy
CEO: Enzo Pavan, Chmn. & CEO   Tel: 39-0438-505-000   Rev: $1,138
Bus: *Curtain wall and commercial structure*   Fax: 39-0438-505-125   Emp: 4,780
      manufacture.   www.permasteelisa.com
   NAICS: 236210, 238170, 238390, 332311, 332322, 337211, 541310, 541330, 541410, 541420

   ALLIED BRONZE, LLC
   25-11 Hunters Point Ave, Long Island City, New York 11101
   CEO: Herbert Koenig, Pres.   Tel: (718) 361-8822   %FO: 100
   Bus: *Metal manufacture and sales.*   Fax: (718) 784-5523   Emp: 40

   GLASSALUM INTERNATIONAL CORP.
   7933 NW 71 St., Miami, Florida 33166
   CEO: Claudio Daniele, CEO   Tel: (305) 592-1212   %FO: 100
   Bus: *Mfr. aluminum products.*   Fax: (305) 599-1342   Emp: 200

   JOSEF GARTNER & CO.
   1101 Perimeter Dr., Ste. 650, Schaumburg, Illinois 60173
   CEO: Richard Hart, Gen. Mgr.   Tel: (847) 255-8133   %FO: 100
   Bus: *Glass/glazing contractor.*   Fax: (847) 255-7881   Emp: 17

   PERMASTEELISA CLADDING TECHNOLOGIES
   99 Addison Rd., PO Box 767, Windsor, Connecticut 06095
   CEO: Tom Casey, Mgr.   Tel: (860) 298-2000   %FO: 100
   Bus: *Industrial building, nonresidential*   Fax: (860) 298-2007   Emp: 5
         construction.

PERMASTEELISA CLADDING TECHNOLOGIES
2060 Centre Pointe Blvd., Ste. 10, Mendota Heights, Minnesota 55120
CEO: Mike Budd, Mgr.
Bus: *Commercial remodeling contractor.*
Tel: (651) 905-1515
Fax: (651) 905-1653
%FO: 100
Emp: 25

PERMASTEELISA CLADDING TECHNOLOGIES
100 Phoenix Ave., Enfield, Connecticut 06082
CEO: Alberto De Gobbi, Mgr.
Bus: *Commercial structure manufacture and sales.*
Tel: (860) 253-4485
Fax: (860) 745-8534
%FO: 100
Emp: 20

PERMASTEELISA CLADDING TECHNOLOGIES
229 North Sherman Ave., Corona, California 92882
CEO: Mark Pasveer, Mgr.
Bus: *Commercial structure manufacture and sales.*
Tel: (909) 736-5900
Fax: (909) 736-5901
%FO: 100
Emp: 20

PERMASTEELISA CLADDING TECHNOLOGIES
123 Day Hill Rd., Windsor, Connecticut 06095
CEO: Alberto De Gobbi, Pres.
Bus: *Commercial structure manufacture and sales.*
Tel: (860) 298-2000
Fax: (860) 298-2009
%FO: 100
Emp: 500

● **PIAGGIO SPA**
Viale Rinaldo Piaggio, 23, I-56025 Pontedera, Italy
CEO: Stefano Rosselli Del Turco, CEO
Bus: *Mfr. Vespa scoters.*
Tel: 39-0587-27-2111
Fax: 39-0587-27-2274
www.piaggio.com
Rev: $1,479
Emp: 6,000
NAICS: 336991

PIAGGIO AMERICA INC.
20003 South Rancho Way, Compton, California 90220
CEO: Paolo Timoni, Pres.
Bus: *Mfr. Vespa scooters.*
Tel: (310) 604-3980
Fax: (310) 604-3989
%FO: 100

PIAGGIO AMERICA INC.
160 E. 84th St., New York, New York 10028
CEO: Paolo Timoni
Bus: *Mfr. Vespa scooters.*
Tel: (212) 744-2100
Fax: (212) 744-2100
%FO: 100

● **PIRELLI & C S.p.A.**
Viale Sarca 222, I-20126 Milan, Italy
CEO: Marco Tronchetti Provera, Chmn. & CEO
Bus: *Mfr. tires, rubber products and plastics. (49% JV with Societe International Pirelli SA, Basel, Switzerland).*
Tel: 39-02-64421
Fax: 39-02-6442-4686
www.pirelli.com
Rev: $9,704
Emp: 37,154
NAICS: 326211, 335921, 335929, 424320, 424330, 424340, 525930

PIRELLI COMMUNICATIONS
246 Stoneridge Dr., 4/F, Columbia, South Carolina 29210
CEO: Mark Andrews, CEO
Bus: *Cable manufacture and sales.*
Tel: (803) 951-4800
Fax: (803) 808-4117
%FO: 100
Emp: 600

PIRELLI TIRE NA
100 Pirelli Dr., Rome, Georgia 30161
CEO: Sherwood Willard, member
Bus: *Mfr. tires, tubes, rubber products.*
Tel: (706) 235-3786
Fax: (706) 368-5832
%FO: 100
Emp: 775

● **POLIFORM, S.p.A.**
Via Montessanto No. 28, I-70022 Inverigo, Italy
CEO: Alberto Spinelli, Chmn.   Tel: 39-031-69951
Bus: *Mfr./sales of premium closet systems, wall units,*   Fax: 39-031-699444
       beds and dining room furniture.   www.poliform.it
NAICS: 326199, 337122

    POLIFORM CHICAGO
    1379 The Merchandise Mart, Chicago, Illinois 60654
    CEO: Gregory Herman, Mgr.   Tel: (312) 321-9600   %FO: 100
    Bus: *Sales/distribution of premium closet*   Fax: (312) 321-9797
        systems, wall units, beds and dining room

    POLIFORM MANHASSET
    1492 Northern Boulevard, Manhasset, New York 11030
    CEO: David A. Yarom   Tel: (516) 869-6600   %FO: 100
    Bus: *Sales/distribution of premium closet*   Fax: (516) 869-6565
        systems, wall units, beds and dining room

    POLIFORM USA, INC.
    150 East 58th St., New York, New York 10155
    CEO: David A. Yarom, Pres.   Tel: (212) 421-1220   %FO: 100
    Bus: *Sales/distribution of premium closet*   Fax: (212) 421-1600
        systems, wall units, beds and dining room

● **PREMUDA SPA**
Via CR Ceccardi 4/28, I-16121 Genoa, Italy
CEO: Stefano Rosina, Chmn. & Pres. & CEO   Tel: 39-010-544-41   Rev: $155
Bus: *Maritime transportation services.*   Fax: 39-010-553-1201   Emp: 100
                                                www.premuda.net

NAICS: 483111

    PREMUDA ATLANTIC INC.
    2700 Post Oak Blvd., Ste. 1160, Houston, Texas 77056
    CEO: Federico Beltrami   Tel: (713) 627-9955   %FO: 100
    Bus: *Maritime transportation services.*   Fax: (713) 627-9949

● **RATTI SPA**
Via Madonna 30, I-20070 Guanzate, Como, Italy
CEO: Donatella Ratti, Chmn.   Tel: 39-031-35-351   Rev: $150
Bus: *Mfr. printed silk fabrics.*   Fax: 39-031-3535-351   Emp: 917
                                                www.ratti.it

NAICS: 313210

    RATTI USA INC.
    8 West 40th St., New York, New York 10018
    CEO: Donatella Ratti, Pres.   Tel: (212) 391-2191   %FO: 100
    Bus: *Mfr. printed silk fabrics.*   Fax: (212) 391-0115   Emp: 4

- **RCS MEDIA GROUP SPA**
  Via Turati 16/18, I-20121 Milan, Italy
  CEO: Paolo Mieli, Chmn.
  Bus: *Bookstores engaged in publishing.*

  Tel: 39-02-622-91
  Fax: 39-02-622-9619
  www.rcsmediagroup.it

  Rev: $2,820
  Emp: 5,580

  NAICS: 451211, 511110, 511120, 511130

  RCS RIZZOLI CORPORATION
  300 Park Ave. South, New York, New York 10010
  CEO: Antonio Polito, Pres.
  Bus: *Engaged in bookstores and publishing.*

  Tel: (212) 387-3400
  Fax: (212) 387-3535

  %FO: 100
  Emp: 55

- **RECORDATI SPA**
  Via Matteo Civitali, 1, I-20148 Milan, Italy
  CEO: Giovanni Recordati, Chmn. & CEO
  Bus: *Pharmaceuticals and generic drugs manufacture.*

  Tel: 39-02-48787-1
  Fax: 39-02-4007-3747
  www.recordati.it

  Rev: $666
  Emp: 1,796

  NAICS: 325411, 325412

  RECORDATI CORPORATION
  35 Walnut Ave., Ste. 14, Clark, New Jersey 07066
  CEO: Giovanni Recordati, CEO
  Bus: *Sales and distribution of generic drugs.*

  Tel: (732) 882-0880
  Fax: (732) 882-0316

  %FO: 100
  Emp: 2

- **RITRAMA, S.p.A**
  Via della Guerrina 108, I-20052 Monza Milan, Italy
  CEO: Tomas Rink, CEO
  Bus: *Mfr. graphic art supplies and pressure sensitive film.*

  Tel: 39-039-83-9215
  Fax: 39-039-83-4718
  www.ritrama.com

  NAICS: 322222, 326113

  RITRAMA, INC.
  341 Eddy Rd., Cleveland, Ohio 44108
  CEO: Daniel Pierce, Mgr.
  Bus: *Mfr. of unsupported plastic film/ sheet.*

  Tel: (216) 851-2300
  Fax: (216) 851-1938

  %FO: 100
  Emp: 68

  RITRAMA, INC.
  800 Kasota Ave., Minneapolis, Minnesota 55414
  CEO: Thomas Rink, Chmn.
  Bus: *Mfr. of pressure sensitive adhesive coated films.*

  Tel: (612) 378-2277
  Fax: (612) 378-9327

  %FO: 100
  Emp: 190

- **SAECO INTERNATIONAL GROUP SpA**
  Via Panigali, 39, Gaggio Montano, I-40041 Bologna, Italy
  CEO: Nicolas De Gregorio, Mng. Dir.
  Bus: *Espresso and coffee machines manufacture.*

  Tel: 39-0534-771-111
  Fax: 39-0534-771-233
  www.saeco.com

  Rev: $527
  Emp: 2,172

  NAICS: 333319

SAECO USA INC.
7905 Cochran Rd., Ste. 100, Glenwillow, Ohio 44139
CEO: John McCann
Bus: *Espresso and coffee machines manufacture and sales.*
Tel: (440) 528-2000
Fax: (440) 542-9173
%FO: 100

● **SAES GETTERS SPA**
Viale Italia 77, I-20020 Lainate Milan, Italy
CEO: Paolo della Porta, Chmn. & Pres.
Bus: *Mfr. industrial equipment and components.*
Tel: 39-02-931781
Fax: 39-02-93178370
www.saesgetters.com
Rev: $193
Emp: 885

NAICS: 333295, 334419

SAES GETTERS USA INC.
1122 E. Cheyenne Mountain Blvd., Colorado Springs, Colorado 80906
CEO: Giulio Canale, CEO
Bus: *Mfr. industrial equipment and components.*
Tel: (719) 576-3200
Fax: (719) 576-5025

SAES GETTERS USA, INC.
5604 Valley Belt Rd., Independence Cleveland, Ohio 44131
CEO: Maurizio Alberini, Mgr.
Bus: *Mfr. industrial equipment and components.*
Tel: (216) 661-8488
Fax: (216) 661-8796

SAES PURE GAS, INC
4175 Santa Fe Rd., San Luis Obispo, California 93401
CEO: Howard McClary, CEO
Bus: *Mfr. industrial equipment and components.*
Tel: (805) 541-9299
Fax: (805) 541-9399
%FO: 100
Emp: 120

● **SAFILO SPA**
Zona Industriale, VII Strada 15, I-35129 Padua, Italy
CEO: Giannino Lorenzon, Co-CEO
Bus: *Mfr. eyeglass frames, sunglasses and goggles.*
Tel: 39-049-698-5111
Fax: 39-049-698-5354
www.safilo.com
Rev: $1,282
Emp: 6,513

NAICS: 339115, 423460

SAFILO USA INC.
801 Jefferson Rd., Parsippany, New Jersey 07054
CEO: Vittorio Tabacchi, Pres.
Bus: *Mfr./sales eyeglass frames, sunglasses and goggles.*
Tel: (973) 952-2800
Fax: (973) 560-1598
%FO: 100
Emp: 698

● **SAIPEM SPA**
Via Martiridi Cefalonia 67, San Donato Milanese, I-20097 Milan, Italy
CEO: Pietro Franco Tali, Chmn. & CEO
Bus: *Provides drilling and construction services to the oil and gas industries.*
Tel: 39-02-5201
Fax: 39-02-5204-4415
www.saipem.it
Rev: $5,153
Emp: 21,314

NAICS: 213111, 213112

DORIS INC.
820 Gessner Rd., Ste. 1200, Houston, Texas 77084
CEO: Brian T. Fine, Pres.
Bus: *Supply Services*
Tel: (832) 204-0700
Fax: (713) 973-2578
%FO: 100
Emp: 40

MOSS MARITIME INC.
15950 Park Row, Houston, Texas 77084
CEO: Svein Johnsen
Bus: *Provides drilling and construction services*
       to the oil and gas industries.
Tel: (281) 552-5900
Fax: (281) 552-5915
%FO: 100

PETROMARINE/ BCI ENGINEERING, INC.
15950 Park Row, Houston, Texas 77084
CEO: Pierro Paguati, Pres.
Bus: *Marine Engineering & Surveyors*
Tel: (281) 552-5800
Fax: (281) 552-5850
%FO: 100
Emp: 12

SAIPEM USA INC.
15950 Park Row, Houston, Texas 77084
CEO: Brian T. Fine, Pres.
Bus: *Provides drilling and construction services*
       to the oil and gas industries.
Tel: (281) 552-5700
Fax: (281) 552-5915
%FO: 100
Emp: 114

SONSUB INC.
15950 Park Row, Houston, Texas 77084
CEO: Brian T. Fine, Pres. & CEO
Bus: *Contractor to the international offshore oil*
       and gas industry and telecommunication.
Tel: (281) 552-5600
Fax: (281) 552-5910
%FO: 100
Emp: 220

● **SANPAOLO IMI SPA**
Piazza San Carlo 156, I-10121 Turin, Italy
CEO: Alfonso Iozzo, Mng. Dir.
Bus: *Banking.*
Tel: 39-01-5551
Fax: 39-01-513826
www.sanpaolo.it
Rev: $16,165

NAICS: 522110

SANPAOLO IMI BANK
245 Park Ave., New York, New York 10167
CEO: Roberto Civalleri, EVP
Bus: *Banking services.*
Tel: (212) 692-3000
Fax: (212) 599-5303
%FO: 100

● **SAVINO DEL BENE SPA**
Via dei Botteghino, 24/26, Scandicci, I-50018 Florence, Italy
CEO: Luciano Ciofi, CEO
Bus: *Freight forwarding services.*
Tel: 39-055-5-2191
Fax: 39-055-72-1288
www.sdb.it
Rev: $732
Emp: 1,553

NAICS: 488510

SAVINO DEL BENE USA INC.
3809-D Beam Rd., Charlotte, North Carolina 28217
CEO: Andrea Dal Pra, VP
Bus: *Freight forwarding services.*
Tel: (704) 423-0011
Fax: (704) 423-0015
%FO: 100

SAVINO DEL BENE USA INC.
11200 NW 25th St., Ste. 123, Miami, Florida 33172
CEO: Umberto Cella, VP
Bus: *Freight forwarding services.*
Tel: (305) 463-8844
Fax: (305) 463-7044
%FO: 100

Italy

SAVINO DEL BENE USA INC.
5324 Georgia Hwy. 85, Ste. 200, Atlanta, Georgia 30297
CEO: Silvia Roye, VP
Bus: *Freight forwarding services.*
Tel: (404) 762-9565
Fax: (404) 762-9599
%FO: 100

SAVINO DEL BENE USA INC.
100 Everett Ave., Ste. 15, Boston, Massachusetts 02150
CEO: Daniele Naldini, VP
Bus: *Freight forwarding services.*
Tel: (617) 884-0838
Fax: (617) 889-4224
%FO: 100

SAVINO DEL BENE USA INC.
463 North Oak St., Inglewood, California 90302
CEO: Andrea Fanti, VP
Bus: *Freight forwarding services.*
Tel: (310) 671-9969
Fax: (310) 671-9939
%FO: 100

SAVINO DEL BENE USA INC.
31 Airport Blvd., Ste. 31D, San Francisco, California 94080
CEO: Peter George, VP
Bus: *Freight forwarding services.*
Tel: (650) 837-9690
Fax: (650) 837-9670
%FO: 100

SAVINO DEL BENE USA INC.
149-10 183rd St., Jamaica, New York 11413
CEO: Giorgio Laccona, Pres.
Bus: *Freight forwarding services.*
Tel: (718) 906-2756
Fax: (718) 995-5018
%FO: 100

SAVINO DEL BENE USA INC.
1905 S. Mt. Prospect Rd., Unit D, Des Plaines, Illinois 60018
CEO: Mark Irwin, Pres.
Bus: *Freight forwarding services.*
Tel: (847) 321-5757
Fax: (847) 635-6257
%FO: 100

SAVINO DEL BENE USA INC.
1065 E. Northwest Hwy., Ste. 250, Grapevine, Texas 76051
CEO: Noe Rodriguez, VP
Bus: *Freight forwarding services.*
Tel: (817) 481-0602
Fax: (817) 481-0621
%FO: 100

SAVINO DEL BENE USA INC.
29288 Greens Rd., Ste. 750, Houston, Texas 77032
CEO: Anthony Piazza, Branch Mgr.
Bus: *Freight forwarding services.*
Tel: (281) 987-2030
Fax: (281) 987-3337
%FO: 100

SAVINO DEL BENE USA INC.
2580 S. 156th St., Rm. 207, Seattle, Washington 98158
CEO: Clay Egenes, Operations Mgr.
Bus: *Freight forwarding services.*
Tel: (206) 431-2800
Fax: (206) 431-5800
%FO: 100

● **SIRTI SPA**
Via Stamira d'Ancona 9, I-20127 Milan, Italy
CEO: Gianni Maria Chiarva, Chmn.
Bus: *Telecommunications and ICT design, construction and maintenance.*
Tel: 39-02-95-881
Fax: 39-02-95-883-333
www.sirti.it
Rev: $709
Emp: 4,725
NAICS: 237130, 237990, 238990, 517910, 531390, 541490, 541690, 811213

SODALIA NORTH AMERICA
12801 Worldgate Dr., Ste. 500, Herndon, Virginia 20170
CEO: Mike Bender, CEO & COO   Tel: (571) 203-7200   %FO: 100
Bus: *Telecommunications and ICT design,*   Fax: (571) 203-7201
    construction and maintenance.

● **SNIA S.P.A.**
Via Borgonuova, 14, I-20121 Milan, Italy
CEO: Carlo Vanoli, CEO   Tel: 39-02-633-21   Rev: $5,540
Bus: *Medical technology.*   Fax: 39-02-633-2311   Emp: 900
    www.snia.it
NAICS: 325181, 325188, 325199, 325311, 325312, 325320

    CARBOMEDICS, DIV. SNIA
    1300 East Anderson Lane, Austin, Texas 78752
    CEO: Charles D. Griffin, Pres.   Tel: (512) 435-3200   %FO: 100
    Bus: *Prosthetic heart valves manufacture.*   Fax: (512) 435-3350   Emp: 325

● **SOGEFI SPA**
Via Flavio Gioia 8, I-20149 Milan, Italy
CEO: Emanuele Bosio, CEO & Mng. Dir.   Tel: 39-02-467-501   Rev: $1,318
Bus: *Mfr. auto parts, including air and oil filters and*   Fax: 39-02-467-502-30   Emp: 6,303
    mufflers and horns.   www.sogefi.it
NAICS: 336330, 336399

    ALLEVARD SPRINGS
    600 Prichard Industrial Park, Prichard, West Virginia 25555
    CEO: Emanuele Bosio, CEO   Tel: (304) 781-7700
    Bus: *Mfr. of stabilizer bars & suspension*   Fax: (304) 486-9116   Emp: 10
    springs.

    SOGEFI FILTER
    3 Parklane Blvd., Ste. 730 W, Dearborn, Michigan 48126
    CEO: Emanuele Bosio, CEO   Tel: (313) 982-6320
    Bus: *Mfr. of auto parts*   Fax: (313) 982-6317

● **STARHOTELS SPA**
Viale Belfiore 27, I-50144 Florence, Italy
CEO: Ferruccio Fabri, Pres. & CEO   Tel: 39-055-36921   Rev: $129
Bus: *Four-star hotel chain.*   Fax: 39-055-36924   Emp: 800
    www.starhotels.it

NAICS: 721110

    THE MICHELANGELO HOTEL (STARHOTELS)
    152 West 51 St., New York, New York 10019
    CEO: Elisabetta Fabri, Pres.   Tel: (212) 765-1900   %FO: 100
    Bus: *178 room, 4-star hotel.*   Fax: (212) 541-6604   Emp: 120

● **STEFANEL SPA**
Via Postumia 85, Ponte di Piave, I-31047 Treviso, Italy
CEO: Elisa Lorenzon, Chmn.   Tel: 39-0422-8191   Rev: $1,101
Bus: *Knitwear and casual clothes manufacture.*   Fax: 39-0422-819342
    www.stefanel.it
  NAICS: 315191, 315211, 315212, 315222, 315223, 315224, 315228, 315232, 315233, 315234, 315239, 315299,
315999

STEFANEL
928 South Western Ave., Ste. 231, Los Angeles, California 90006
CEO: Carlo Stefanel, Pres.   Tel: (213) 385-9988   %FO: 100
Bus: *Sale of women's clothing.*   Fax:

● **TARGETTI SANKEY, SPA**
Via Pratese 164, I-50145 Florence, Italy
CEO: Giampaolo Targetti, Chmn. & Mng. Dir.   Tel: 39-055-37911   Rev: $209
Bus: *Contemporary-design interior and outdoor*   Fax: 39-055-3791266   Emp: 1,090
   commercial and upscale residential lighting   www.targetti.com
   products manufacture.
   NAICS: 335110, 335121, 335122, 335129, 335931
   TARGETTI NORTH AMERICA INC.
   1513 E. Saint Gertrude Place, Santa Ana, California 92705
   CEO: Lorenzo Targetti, Pres.   Tel: (714) 957-4900   %FO: 100
   Bus: *Mfr. specialty lighting and related products.*   Fax: (714) 957-1501   Emp: 91

● **TELECOM ITALIA S.p.A.**
Corso d'Italia 41, I-00198 Rome, Italy
CEO: Carlo Orazio Buora, CEO & Mng. Dir.   Tel: 39-06-36-881   Rev: $42,314
Bus: *Telecommunication services.*   Fax: 39-06-36-882-965   Emp: 91,365
                                              www.telecomitalia.it
   NAICS: 511140, 517110, 517211, 517212, 517310, 517410, 517910, 518111, 518210, 519190, 541519, 561421,
561499
   SODALIA NORTH AMERICA
   12801 Worldgate Dr., Ste. 500, Herndon, Virginia 20170
   CEO: Mike Bender, CEO & COO   Tel: (571) 203-7200   %FO: 100
   Bus: *Information technology services.*   Fax: (571) 203-7201

   TELECOM ITALIA OF NORTH AMERICA
   745 5th Ave., 27/F, New York, New York 10151
   CEO: Sal J. De Rosa, Pres.   Tel: (212) 755-5280   %FO: 100
   Bus: *Telecommunications services.*   Fax: Emp: 19

● **TREVI-FINANZIARIA INDUSTRIALE SpA**
201 Via Dismano, Forli-Cesena, I-47023 Cesena, Italy
CEO: Davide Trevisani, Chmn. & Pres.   Tel: 39-0547-319111   Rev: $454
Bus: *International engineering and architectural*   Fax: 39-0547-319313   Emp: 2,911
   services.   www.trevifin.com
   NAICS: 238910, 541310, 541330
   SOILMEC BRANHAM
   100 Woolridge, 105 E@3083, PO Box 2534, Conroe, Texas 77305
   CEO: Brando Ballerini, Pres.   Tel: (936) 441-1011
   Bus: *Mfr. oil & gas rigs.*   Fax: Emp: 6

   TREVI - ICOS CORPORATION
   250 Summer St., 4/F, Boston, Massachusetts 02210
   CEO: Ricardo Petrocelli, CEO   Tel: (617) 365-9955   %FO: 100
   Bus: *International engineering and architectural*   Fax: (617) 345-0041   Emp: 192
   services.

WAGNER CONSTRUCTION
12512 Highway 67, Lakeside, California 92040
CEO: Lee James Wagner, Pres.   Tel: (619) 873-2160
Bus: *Concrete contractor.*   Fax: Emp: 125

● **UNICREDIT S.p.A.**
Via Dante 1, I-16121 Genoa, Italy
CEO: Alessandro Profumo, CEO & Mng. Dir.   Tel: 39-02-8862-1   Rev: $22,298
Bus: *Commercial banking services.*   Fax: 39-02-8862-8503   Emp: 68,571
                                             www.unicredit.it

    NAICS: 522110, 523999, 524113, 524126, 525910

    HARBOR GLOBAL COMPANY LTD.
    1 Faneuil Hall Marketplace, 4/F, Boston, Massachusetts 02129
    CEO: Stephen G. Kasnet, Pres. & CEO   Tel: (617) 878-1600
    Bus: *Investment Firm.*   Fax: (617) 878-1699   Emp: 113

    PIONEER INVESTMENT MANAGEMENT USA INC.
    60 State St., Boston, Massachusetts 02109
    CEO: Osbert Hood, Pres. & CEO   Tel: (617) 742-7825
    Bus: *Asset Management.*   Fax: (617) 422-4274   Emp: 587

    UNICREDITO ITALIANO
    430 Park Ave., 9/F, New York, New York 10022
    CEO: Carmelo Mazza, SVP & Gen. Mgr.   Tel: (212) 546-9600   %FO: 100
    Bus: *International commercial banking services.*   Fax: (212) 546-9675

    UNICREDITO ITALIANO
    2 Prudential Plaza, 180 N. Stetson St., Ste. 1310, Chicago, Illinois 60601-6713
    CEO: Maurizio Brentegani   Tel: (312) 946-1111   %FO: 100
    Bus: *International commercial banking services.*   Fax: (312) 946-1112

● **UNIFOR SPA**
Via Isonzo 1, Turate, I-22078 Como, Italy
CEO: Benjamin Pardo, CEO   Tel: 39-02-967-191
Bus: *Contract furniture manufacturer.*   Fax: 39-02-967-50859
                                            www.unifor.it

    NAICS: 337122, 337124, 337125, 337211, 423210

    UNIFOR INC.
    149 Fifth Ave., 3/F, New York, New York 10010
    CEO: Benjamin Pardo, CEO   Tel: (212) 673-3434   %FO: 100
    Bus: *Contract furniture sales.*   Fax: (212) 673-7317   Emp: 8

● **GIANNI VERSACE**
Via Manzoni 38, I-20121 Milan, Italy
CEO: Santo Versace, Chmn. & Pres.   Tel: 39-02-760-931   Rev: $437
Bus: *Design/mfr./sale clothing, perfume, ceramics and*   Fax: 39-02-760-04122   Emp: 1,500
    tiles for home furnishings.   www.versace.it
    NAICS: 315211, 315212, 315222, 315223, 315224, 315228, 315232, 315233, 315234, 315239, 315292, 315299,
315993, 315999, 316992, 316993, 316999,
        325620, 448120

VERSACE COMPANY
3500 Peachtree Rd., Atlanta, Georgia 30326
CEO: Donatella Versace, Pres.   Tel: (404) 814-0664   %FO: 100
Bus: *Sale of men's & boys clothing.*   Fax: (404) 814-0664

VERSACE COMPANY
5015 Westheimer Rd., Ste. 2340, Houston, Texas 77056
CEO: Teresa Archer, Gen. Mgr.   Tel: (713) 623-8220   %FO: 100
Bus: *Sale of men & women's clothing.*   Fax: (713) 623-8220   Emp: 10

VERSACE COMPANY
9700 Collins Ave., 1/F, Bar Harbor, Florida 33154
CEO: Donatella Versace   Tel: (305) 864-0044
Bus: *Design/mfr./sale clothing, perfume, ceramics* Fax: (305) 864-0044
and tiles for home furnishings.

VERSACE COMPANY
160 North Gulph Rd., Ste. 5217, King of Prussia, Pennsylvania 19406
CEO: John Nadav, Pres.   Tel: (215) 500-8527   %FO: 100
Bus: *Design/mfr./sale clothing, perfume, ceramics* Fax: (215) 500-8527
and tiles for home furnishings.

VERSACE COMPANY
647 Fifth Ave., New York, New York 10022
CEO: Santo Versace, Pres.   Tel: (212) 317-0224   %FO: 100
Bus: *Sale of designer clothing.*   Fax: (212) 317-0224

VERSACE COMPANY
60 Post St., Crocker Galleria, San Francisco, California 94104
CEO: Matthew Mansell, Mgr.   Tel: (415) 616-0604   %FO: 100
Bus: *Design/mfr./sale clothing, perfume, ceramics* Fax: (415) 616-0604
and tiles for home furnishings.

VERSACE COMPANY
3500 Las Vegas Blvd., Las Vegas, Nevada 89109
CEO: Haresh Melwani, Pres.   Tel: (714) 751-7473   %FO: 100
Bus: *Design/mfr./sale clothing, perfume, ceramics* Fax: (714) 751-7473   Emp: 20
and tiles for home furnishings.

VERSACE COMPANY
13350 Dallas Pkwy., Ste. 1495, Dallas, Texas 75240
CEO: Alex Laynor, Mgr.   Tel: (972) 385-9155   %FO: 100
Bus: *Sale of customized clothing.*   Fax: (972) 385-9155

VERSACE COMPANY
248 North Rodeo Dr., Beverly Hills, California 90210
CEO: Suzanne Revisky, Mgr.   Tel: (310) 205-3921   %FO: 100
Bus: *Sale of designer clothing.*   Fax: (310) 205-3921

VERSACE COMPANY
3333 Bristol St., South Coast Plaza, Ste. 2207, Costa Mesa, California 92626
CEO: Mario Ruiz, Mgr.   Tel: (714) 751-7473   %FO: 100
Bus: *Design/mfr./sale clothing, perfume, ceramics* Fax: (714) 751-7473
and tiles for home furnishings.

VERSACE PROFUMI USA LTD.
645 Fifth Ave., Olympic Tower, 9/F, Ste. 905, New York, New York 10022
CEO: Marjorie Wollan, Pres. & CEO   Tel: (212) 935-4800   %FO: 100
Bus: *Design/mfr./dist. of fragrance & cosmetics.*   Fax: (212) 935-5476

● **WAM S.p.A.**
Via Cavour 338-338A, Modena, I-41030 Cavezzo, Italy
CEO: Valner Marchesini, Pres.   Tel: 39-0535-618111   Rev: $59
Bus: *Mfr. industrial and bulk handling equipment.*   Fax: 39-0535-618226   Emp: 326
www.wam.it
NAICS: 332919, 333999

    WAM CORPORATION OF AMERICA
    1300 Triad Blvd., Fort Worth, Texas 76131
    CEO: Max Magnani, Mgr.   Tel: (817) 232-2678
    Bus: *Mfr. of screw, drag, & shaftless screws*   Fax: (817) 232-2676
        conveyors, bucket elevators & standard
        conveyors.

    WAM INC.
    75 Boulderbrook Circle, Lawrenceville, Georgia 30045
    CEO: John Hasbrouck   Tel: (770) 339-6767
    Bus: *Tubular screw conveyors & dust collectors*   Fax: (770) 339-4727

● **ZAMBON GROUP, S.p.A.**
Via Lillo del Duca, 10, Bresso, I-20091 Milan, Italy
CEO: Paolo Pagliani, Pres.   Tel: 39-02-66-5241   Rev: $192
Bus: *Prescription/pharmaceutical products, fine*   Fax: 39-02-66-524979   Emp: 569
   chemicals and home health products.   www.zambongroup.com
NAICS: 325199, 325411, 325412, 325620, 424210, 424690

    ZAMBON CORPORATION
    301 Route 17, 2/F Ste. 205, Rutherford, New Jersey 07070
    CEO: Max Fehlmann, Pres.   Tel: (201) 939-4800   %FO: 100
    Bus: *Research & development of pharmaceutical*   Fax: (201) 939-4828
        preparations

Jamaica

- **AIR JAMAICA**
  4 St. Lucia Avenue, Kingston 5, Jamaica
  CEO: Vin Lawrence, Chmn.
  Bus: *Air passenger and cargo carrier.*

  Tel: 876-922-3460
  Fax: 876-929-5643
  www.airjamaica.com

  NAICS: 481111, 481212

  - **AIR JAMAICA**
    33 N. Dearborn, Chicago, Illinois 60602
    CEO: Rumy Khariwala
    Bus: *Air passenger and cargo carrier.*

    Tel: (312) 782-6263
    Fax: (312) 782-6263

    %FO: 100

  - **AIR JAMAICA**
    6000 N. Terminal Dr., Atlanta, Georgia 30320
    CEO: Lon Scanlan
    Bus: *Air passenger and cargo carrier.*

    Tel: (440) 761-2030
    Fax: (440) 761-2030

    %FO: 100

  - **AIR JAMAICA**
    1890 NW 82nd Ave., Miami, Florida 33126
    CEO: Frank Arboine
    Bus: *Air passenger and cargo carrier.*

    Tel: (305) 447-7704
    Fax: (305) 447-7704

    %FO: 100

Japan

- **ACHILLES CORPORATION**
  22, Daikyo-Cho, Shinjuku-ku, Tokyo 160-8885, Japan
  CEO: Takeshi Yagi, Pres.
  Bus: *Rubberized cloth, rubber footwear and supported and unsupported vinyl sheeting manufacturer.*
  NAICS: 316110, 325222

  Tel: 81-3-3341-5111
  Fax: 81-3-3225-4013
  www.achillesusa.com

  Rev: $990
  Emp: 2,444

  ACHILLES USA INC.
  1407 80th St. SW, Everett, Washington 98203
  CEO: Ted Becker, Pres.
  Bus: *Plastic film and sheeting manufacture.*

  Tel: (425) 353-7000
  Fax: (425) 347-5785

  %FO: 100
  Emp: 185

- **ADVANCED SOC PLATFORM CORPORATION**
  1120 Shimokuzawa, Sagamihara-City, Kanagawa 229-1134, Japan
  CEO: Keiichi Kawate, Pres. & CEO
  Bus: *Mfr. electronic fuses and fuse holders.*

  Tel: 81-42-775-6750
  Fax: 81-42-775-6799
  www.aspla.com

  Emp: 120

  NAICS: 335313

  SAN-O INDUSTRIAL CORPORATION
  1180 Lincoln Ave., Unit 8, Holbrook, New York 11741
  CEO: Neil Sato, Pres.
  Bus: *Mfr./sale electronic fuses and fuse holders.*

  Tel: (516) 472-6666
  Fax: (516) 472-6777

  Emp: 15

- **ADVANTEST CORPORATION**
  2-4-1, Nishi-Shinjuku, Shinjuku-ku, Tokyo 163-0880, Japan
  CEO: Hiroshi Oura, CEO
  Bus: *Research and development of electronic measurement and testing devices.*
  NAICS: 541710

  Tel: 81-3-3342-7500
  Fax: 81-3-3342-7510
  www.advantest.co.jp

  Rev: $1,648
  Emp: 3,544

  ADVANTEST AMERICA CORP.
  1510 Valley Center Pkwy., Ste. 110, Bethlehem, Pennsylvania 18017
  CEO: Jill Sciorra Sibert
  Bus: *Research and development of electronic measurement and testing devices.*

  Tel: (610) 758-8190
  Fax: (610) 758-8154

  %FO: 100

  ADVANTEST AMERICA CORP.
  509 Madison Ave., Ste. 1602, New York, New York 10024
  CEO: Amy Gold, Mktg.
  Bus: *Research and development of electronic measurement and testing devices.*

  Tel: (212) 753-0007
  Fax: (212) 753-1307

  %FO: 100

  ADVANTEST AMERICA INC.
  3201 Scott Blvd., Santa Clara, California 95054
  CEO: R. Keith Lee, Pres.
  Bus: *Electronic measurement and testing devices manufacture and distribution.*

  Tel: (408) 988-7700
  Fax: (408) 987-0691

  %FO: 100

ADVANTEST AMERICA INC.
258 Fernwood Ave., Edison, New Jersey 08837
CEO: Makoto Nakahara, Pres. & CEO　　Tel: (732) 346-2600　　%FO: 100
Bus: *Electronic measurement and testing devices*　Fax: (732) 346-2610
research and development.

● **AEON CO., LTD.**
1-5-1 Nakase, Mihama-ku, Chiba 261-8515, Japan
CEO: Toshiji Tokiwa, Chmn.　　　　Tel: 81-43-212-6042　　Rev: $36,237
Bus: *Operates specialty store chains and general*　Fax: 81-43-212-6849　　Emp: 194,978
merchandising stores. (Sub of AEON Group)　www.aeon.info
　NAICS: 445110, 445120, 445299, 446110, 448120, 448130, 452910, 522210, 531120, 531190

　　MYCAL CORP.
　　Mycal Dr., Soyflaking plant 21, Jefferson, Iowa 50129
　　CEO: Terry Tanaka, Gen. Mgr.　　　Tel: (515) 386-2100
　　Bus: *Department stores.*　　　　　Fax: (515) 386-3287

　　TALBOTS, INC.
　　1 Talbots Dr., Hingham, Massachusetts 02043
　　CEO: Arnold B. Zetcher, Chmn. & Pres. & CEO　Tel: (781) 749-7600　%FO: 100
　　Bus: *Operates retail clothing chain stores.*　　Fax: (781) 741-4369　Emp: 11,500

● **AIOI INSURANCE CO., INC.**
1-28-1 Ebisu, Shibuya-ku, Tokyo 150-8488, Japan
CEO: Akira Seshimo, Chmn.　　　　Tel: 81-3-5371-6000　　Rev: $10,158
Bus: *Insurance specializing in fire and marine*　Fax: 81-3-5371-6000　　Emp: 9,199
　　　　　　　　　　　　　　　　www.ioi-sonpo.co.jp
　NAICS: 524126

　　AIOI INSURANCE CO. OF AMERICA
　　757 Third Ave., New York, New York 10017
　　CEO: Akihiro Sasaso　　　　　　Tel: (212) 826-8110　　%FO: 100
　　Bus: *Property and casualty insurance*　Fax: (212) 826-8110

　　DTRIC INSURANCE CO., INC.
　　1600 Kapiolani Blvd., Ste. 1520, Honolulu, Hawaii 96814
　　CEO: Ronald Toyofuku　　　　　Tel: (808) 943-8742　　%FO: 75
　　Bus: *Property and casualty Insurance*　Fax: (808) 949-1927

● **AISAN INDUSTRY CO., LTD.**
1-1-1, Kyowa-cho, Obu, Aichi 474-8588, Japan
CEO: Tetsuya Oniki, Pres. & CEO　　Tel: 81-562-47-1131　　Rev: $1,166
Bus: *Mfr. electronic fuel injection products.*　Fax: 81-562-48-6357　　Emp: 4,824
　　　　　　　　　　　　　　　　www.aisan-ind.co.jp
　NAICS: 336211

　　FRANKLIN PRECISION INDUSTRY INC.
　　PO Box 369, 3220 Bowling Green Rd., Franklin, Kentucky 42135
　　CEO: Takeo Ogino　　　　　　Tel: (270) 586-4450　　%FO: 100
　　Bus: *Mfr. electronic fuel injection products.*　Fax: (270) 586-0180　　Emp: 500

- **AISIN SEIKI CO. LTD.**
2-1, Asahi-machi, Kariya, Aichi 448-8650, Japan
CEO: Kanshiro Toyoda, Pres.
Bus: *Mfr. auto parts; transmissions, brakes, cooling & lubrication, door frames & latches & car navigation systems, refrigeration & cutting equipment.*
NAICS: 333512, 336340, 336350

Tel: 81-566-24-8411
Fax: 81-566-24-8003
www.aisin.co.jp

Rev: $15,195
Emp: 56,386

AISIN AUTOMOTIVE CASTING TENNESSEE, INC.
221 Frank L. Diggs Dr., Clinton, Tennessee 37716
CEO: Yasuhito Yamauchi
Bus: *Mfr. Aluminum castings and machining.*

Tel: (865) 457-4581
Fax: (865) 457-4583

%FO: 100

AISIN AUTOMOTIVE CASTING, LLC
4870 E. Hwy 552, London, Kentucky 40744
CEO: Masaharu Goto
Bus: *Sales/distribution of auto components and home industrial equipment.*

Tel: (606) 878-6523
Fax: (606) 862-0430

%FO: 100

AISIN BRAKE & CHASSIS, INC.
10550 James Adams St., Terre Haute, Indiana 47802
CEO: Archie Kappel
Bus: *Mfr. brake system components.*

Tel: (812) 298-1617
Fax: (812) 298-1756

%FO: 100

AISIN DRIVETRAIN, INC.
1001 Industrial Way, Crothersville, Indiana 47229
CEO: Hitoshi Sumiya
Bus: *Mfr. industrial transmissions, torque converters.*

Tel: (812) 793-2427
Fax: (812) 793-3684

%FO: 100

AISIN ELECTRONICS INC.
199 Frank West Circle, Stockton, California 95206
CEO: Tomoo Ishikawa
Bus: *Mfr. electronic control units and sensors.*

Tel: (209) 983-4988
Fax: (209) 983-4989

%FO: 100

AISIN MFG. ILLINOIS LLC
11000 Redco Dr., Marion, Illinois 62959
CEO: Seiichi Takahashi, Pres.
Bus: *Auto body parts manufacture.*

Tel: (618) 998-8333
Fax: (618) 998-8383

%FO: 100
Emp: 1,600

AISIN USA MFG. INC.
1700 East Fourth St., Seymour, Indiana 47274
CEO: Tsutomo Yasui, Pres.
Bus: *Mfr. Automotive body components, door frames, seat adjusters.*

Tel: (812) 523-1969
Fax: (812) 523-1984

%FO: 100

ATTC MANUFACTURING, INC.
10455 State Rd. 37, Tell City, Indiana 47586
CEO: Kiyoshi Ohashi
Bus: *State-of-the-art automotive machining operations.*

Tel: (812) 547-5060
Fax: (812) 547-8390

%FO: 100

AW NORTH CAROLINA, INC.
4112 Old Oxford Hwy., Durham, North Carolina 27712
CEO: Colin P. Kerrigan, Mgr.   Tel: (919) 479-6550 %FO: 100
Bus: *Mfr. automotive transmissions.* Fax: (919) 479-6580

INTAT PRECISION, INC.
Box 488, Rushville, Indiana 46173
CEO: Donald Carson   Tel: (765) 932-5323 %FO: 100
Bus: *Gray and ductile iron castings.* Fax: (765) 932-3032

● **AJINOMOTO COMPANY INC.**
15-1, Kyobashi 1-chome, Chuo-ku, Tokyo 104, Japan
CEO: Kunio Egashira, Pres.   Tel: 81-3-5250-8111 Rev: $7,100
Bus: *Seasonings, amino acids, oil products and other* Fax: 81-3-5250-8293 Emp: 24,325
  foodstuffs and specialty chemicals. www.ajinomoto.com
NAICS: 311222, 311942

  AJINMOTO USA INC.
  Country Club Plaza, West 115 Century Rd., Paramus, New Jersey 07652
  CEO: Shinichi Suzuki, Pres. Tel: (201) 261-1789 %FO: 100
  Bus: *Mfr. food products, amino acids and* Fax: (201) 261-7857
   specialty chemicals.

● **ALL NIPPON AIRWAYS CO., LTD.**
1-5-2 Higashi-Shimbashi, Minato-ku, Tokyo 105-7133, Japan
CEO: Yoji Ohashi, Chmn.   Tel: 81-3-6735-1000 Rev: $9,080
Bus: *Commercial air transport and hotel services.* Fax: 81-3-5756-5659 Emp: 29,100
         www.ana.co.jp
NAICS: 481111

  ALL NIPPON AIRWAYS COMPANY, LTD.
  1251 Ave. of the Americas, 8/F., New York, New York 10111
  CEO: Yoshinobu Nishikawa, SVP Tel: (212) 840-3700 %FO: 100
  Bus: *International air transport services.* Fax: (212) 840-3704 Emp: 50

  ALL NIPPON AIRWAYS COMPANY, LTD.
  1350 Bayshore Hwy., Ste. 650, Burlingame, California 94010
  CEO: Hiroyuki Fujii   Tel: (650) 762-3300 %FO: 100
  Bus: *International air transport services.* Fax: (650) 762-3310

● **ALPINE ELECTRONICS INC.**
1-1-8, Nishi-Gotanda, Shinagawa-ku, Tokyo 141-8501, Japan
CEO: Kentaro Kutsuzawa, Pres. Tel: 81-3-3494-1101
Bus: *Audio, visual, navigation and security products* Fax: 81-3-3494-1109
  manufacture for the mobile environment. www.alpine.co.jp
NAICS: 334310, 334511

  ALPINE ELECTRONICS OF AMERICA INC.
  PO Box 430, 421 North Emerson Ave., Greenwood, Indiana 46142
  CEO: Bernard Pierce, Pres. Tel: (317) 881-7700 %FO: 100
  Bus: *Mfr. high-performance mobile electronics.* Fax: (317) 887-2415

ALPINE ELECTRONICS OF AMERICA INC.
19145 Gramercy Place, Torrance, California 90501
CEO: Toru Usami, VP
Bus: *Mfr. high-performance mobile electronics.*
Tel: (310) 326-8000
Fax: (310) 533-0369
%FO: 100

● **ALPS ELECTRIC CO., LTD.**
1-7, Yukigaya-otsuka-cho, Ota-Ku, Tokyo 145, Japan
CEO: Masataka Kataoka, Pres.
Bus: *Electric component and switches and communications devices manufacturer.*
NAICS: 334119, 334310, 334419
Tel: 81-3-3726-1211
Fax: 81-3-3728-1741
www.alps.co.jp
Rev: $5,866
Emp: 32,586

ALPS ELECTRIC NORTH AMERICA, INC.
30 Las Colinas Lane, San Jose, California 95119
CEO: Takahide Sato, Pres.
Bus: *Computers and peripheral components sales and distribution.*
Tel: (408) 361-6400
Fax: (408) 226-7301
%FO: 100
Emp: 321

ALPS ELECTRIC USA, INC.
30 Las Colinas Lane, San Jose, California 95119
CEO: Richard Kai, Pres.
Bus: *Custom switches, remote keyless entry systems, clock springs and sensors design and manufacture.*
Tel: (408) 361-6400
Fax: (408) 361-7301
%FO: 100
Emp: 62

● **AMADA LTD.**
200 Ishida, Isehara, Kanagawa 259-1196, Japan
CEO: E. Emori, Chmn.
Bus: *Engineering and machinery production.*
NAICS: 333319, 333512, 541511
Tel: 81-463-96-1111
Fax: 81-463-93-1323
www.amada.co.jp
Rev: $1,020
Emp: 2,360

AMADA AMERICA, INC.
7025 Firestone Blvd., Buena Park, California 90621
CEO: Katsumi Kamimura, Pres.
Bus: *Mfr./sales machine tools.*
Tel: (714) 739-2111
Fax: (714) 739-4099
%FO: 100

AMADA CUTTING TECHNOLOGIES INC.
14849 East Northam St., La Mirada, California 90638
CEO: Toshi Ichimura, Pres.
Bus: *Mfr. metal cutting machines.*
Tel: (714) 670-1704
Fax: (714) 670-2017
%FO: 100

● **AMANO ENZYME INC.**
1-2-7, Nishiki, Naka-ku, Nagoya 460-8630, Japan
CEO: Motoyuki Amano, Pres. & CEO
Bus: *Specialty enzyme pharmaceutical manufacture.*
NAICS: 325412
Tel: 81-52-211-3032
Fax: 81-52-211-3054
www.amano-enzyme.co.jp

AMANO ENZYME USA CO. LTD.
2150 Point Blvd., Elgin, Illinois 60123
CEO: John Diehl, Pres.
Bus: *Specialty enzyme pharmaceutical manufacture.*
Tel: (847) 649-0101
Fax: (847) 649-0205
%FO: 100
Emp: 12

● **ANRITSU CORPORATION**
1800 Onna, Atsugi, Kanagawa 243-8555, Japan
CEO: Akira Shiomi, Pres.   Tel: 81-462-23-1111   Rev: $742
Bus: *Mfr./sales optical and electronic measuring*   Fax: 81-46-225-8358   Emp: 3,568
       instruments, communications systems and   www.anritsu.co.jp
       computer peripherals.
NAICS: 333314, 334513, 335999

   ANRITSU COMPANY
   1155 East Collins Blvd., Ste. 100, Richardson, Texas 75081
   CEO: Sandy Bayles, Pres.   Tel: (972) 644-1777   %FO: 100
   Bus: *Mfr./sales electronic test instruments,*   Fax: (972) 644-3416
          systems and components.

   ANRITSU COMPANY
   490 Jarvis Dr., Morgan Hill, California 95037
   CEO: Frank Tiernan, Pres.   Tel: (408) 778-2000   %FO: 100
   Bus: *Mfr./sales electronic test instruments,*   Fax: (408) 277-8408
          systems and components.

   ANRITSU COMPANY
   10 New Maple Ave., Ste. 305, Pine Brook, New Jersey 07058-0836
   CEO: Keith Trevor   Tel: (973) 227-8999   %FO: 100
   Bus: *Engaged in sales and service of electronic*   Fax: (973) 575-0092
          test instruments, systems and components.

● **AOZORA BANK**
3-1, Kudan-minami 1-chome,, Chiyoda-ku, Tokyo 102-8660, Japan
CEO: Hirokazu Mizukami, CEO   Tel: 81-3-3263-1111   Rev: $1,301
Bus: *Credit banking, financing and investment banking.* Fax: 81-3-3239-8065   Emp: 1,345
                                                    www.aozorabank.co.jp
NAICS: 522110, 523110

   AOZORA BANK
   101 E. 52nd St., New York, New York 10022
   CEO: Akihiro Yamasak, Rep.   Tel: (212) 751-7330   %FO: 100
   Bus: *Financial banking services.*   Fax: (212) 751-0987

● **ARAKAWA CHEMICAL INDUSTRIES LTD.**
3-7, Hiranomachi, 1-chome Chuo-ku, Osaka 541-046, Japan
CEO: Nagahiro Suemura, Pres.   Tel: 81-6 6209 8580   Rev: $2,365
Bus: *Mfr./supplier rosin ester, absorbents,*   Fax: Emp: 635
       hydrocarbon and special resins.   www.arakawahem.co.jp
NAICS: 325991

   WUZHOU ARAKAWA CHEMICAL INDUSTRIES LTD.
   625 North Michigan Ave., Chicago, Illinois 60611
   CEO: Junichi Tatsumi, Pres.   Tel: (312) 642-1750   %FO: 100
   Bus: *Distributor/supplier rosin ester, absorbents,* Fax: (312) 642-0089   Emp: 6
          hydrocarbon and special resins.

- **ASACA CORPORATION**
3-2-28, Asahigaoka Hino-shi, Tokyo 191-0086, Japan
CEO: Takashi Shigezaki, Pres.
Bus: *Tape and disc storage disc systems and audio and video equipment manufacture. (JV of ShibaSoku Co.)*
NAICS: 334613
Tel: 81-4-2583-1211
Fax: 81-4-2586-9000
www.asaca.co.jp

  ASACA/SHIBA SOKU CORP.
  400 Corporate Circle, Ste. G, Golden, Colorado 80401
  CEO: Takashi Shigezaki, VP
  Bus: *Sales and services of professional color monitors.*
  Tel: (303) 278-1111
  Fax: (303) 278-0303
  %FO: JV

- **ASAHI BREWERIES, LTD.**
23-1, Azumabashi, 1 chome, Sumida-ku, Tokyo 130-8602, Japan
CEO: Kouichi Ikeda, Chmn.
Bus: *Engaged in production and marketing of alcoholic beverages and soft drinks.*
NAICS: 312111, 312120, 312140
Tel: 81-3-5608-5126
Fax: 81-3-5608-7121
www.asahibeer.co.jp
Rev: $14,007
Emp: 20,560

  ASAHI BEER USA INC.
  20000 Mariner Ave., Ste. 300, Torrance, California 90503
  CEO: Shigeo Fukuchi, Pres.
  Bus: *Market and sales of Asahi beer.*
  Tel: (310) 921-4000
  Fax: (310) 921-4001
  %FO: 100

- **ASAHI DENKA KOGYO K.K.**
Furukawa Bldg., 3-14, Nihonbashi-Muromachi 2-chome, Chuo-ku, Tokyo 103-8311, Japan
CEO: Masahiro Iwashita, Pres.
Bus: *Chemical products manufacture.*
NAICS: 325199
Tel: 81-3-5255-9015
Fax: 81-3-3246-2090
www.denka.co.jp
Rev: $1,338
Emp: 1,475

  DENKA CORPORATION
  780 Third Ave., 32/F, New York, New York 10017
  CEO: Toichi Takagi, VP
  Bus: *Service chemical products.*
  Tel: (212) 688-8700
  Fax: (212) 688-8727
  %FO: 100
  Emp: 3

- **ASAHI DIAMOND INDUSTRIAL CO.**
The New Otani Garden Ct., 11/F, 4-1 Kioicho, Chiyoda-Ku, Tokyo l02-0094, Japan
CEO: Mitsuo Takase, Pres.
Bus: *Diamond tools manufacturer.*
NAICS: 333515
Tel: 81-3-3222-6311
Fax: 81-3-3222-6305
www.asahidia.co.jp
Rev: $210
Emp: 1,658

  ASAHI DIAMOND AMERICA INC.
  9872 Windisch Rd., West Chester, Ohio 45069
  CEO: Takashi Kasagi, Pres.
  Bus: *Diamond tool manufacture and sales.*
  Tel: (513) 759-5222
  Fax: (513) 759-2885
  %FO: 100
  Emp: 3

- **ASAHI GLASS COMPANY, LTD.**
1-12-1, Yuraku-cho, Chiyoda-ku, Tokyo 100-8405, Japan
CEO: Masahiro Kadomatsu, Pres. & CEO
Bus: *Mfr. flat and fabricated glass, chemicals and ceramics and produces optical lenses.*
NAICS: 327212
Tel: 81-3-3218-5408
Fax: 81-3-3218-7805
www.agc.co.jp
Rev: $9,500
Emp: 48,360

  AGC AMERICAN INC.
  1401 S. Huron St., Ypsilanti, Michigan 48197
  CEO: Thomas Throop
  Bus: *Automotive glass and glazing systems.*
  Tel: (734) 547-2370
  Fax: (734) 547-2368

  ASAHI GLASS COMPANY INC.
  1465 W. Sandusky Ave., PO Box 819, Bellefontaine, Ohio 43311
  CEO: Robert Cobie
  Bus: *Sales/distribution of auto safety glass.*
  Tel: (513) 599-3131
  Fax: (513) 599-3322
  %FO: 100

  ASAHI GLASS FLUOROPOLYMERS USA INC.
  229 East 22nd St., Bayonne, New Jersey 07002-5002
  CEO: David Van Goor, Mgr.
  Bus: *Glass fluoropolymers manufacture.*
  Tel: (201) 858-8900
  Fax: (201) 858-8900
  %FO: 100

- **ASAHI KASEI CORPORATION**
Hibiya-Mitsui Bldg., 1-1-2 Yurakucho, Chiyoda-ku, Tokyo 100, Japan
CEO: Shiro Hiruta, Pres.
Bus: *Mfr. chemicals, medical products, plastics, fibers, textiles and construction materials.*
NAICS: 236115, 313210, 325314, 325510, 333292, 339113, 424910
Tel: 81-3-3507-2060
Fax: 81-3-3507-2495
www.asahi-kasei.co.jp
Rev: $11,866
Emp: 26,011

  ASAHI KASEI AMERICA, INC.
  535 Madison Ave., 33/F, New York, New York 10022-4212
  CEO: Eiichi Fujiwara, Pres.
  Bus: *Sales/distribution of chemicals, medical products and housing and construction materials.*
  Tel: (212) 371-9900
  Fax: (212) 371-9050
  %FO: 100

- **ASAHI MUTUAL LIFE INSURANCE COMPANY**
Tokai Bldg., 2-6-1, Ohte-machi, Chiyoda-ku, Tokyo 100-8103, Japan
CEO: Yuzuru Fujita, Pres.
Bus: *Life insurance services.*
NAICS: 524113
Tel: 81-3-6225-3111
Fax: 81-3-6225-3110
www.asahi-life.co.jp
Rev: $17,270
Emp: 12,150

  ASAHI AMERICA INC.
  PO Box 653, 35 Green Street, Malden, Massachusetts 02148
  CEO: Leslie B. Lewis, Pres.
  Bus: *Investment research.*
  Tel: (781) 321-5409
  Fax: (781) 321-4421
  %FO: 100
  Emp: 13

- **ASAHI ORGANIC CHEMICALS INDUSTRY CO., LTD.**
5955 Nakanose-machi, 2-chome, Nobeoka, Miyazaki 882-8688, Japan
CEO: Toru Okano, Chmn.
Bus: *Corrosion resistant thermoplastics manufacture.*

  Tel: 81-982-35-0880
  Fax: 81-982-35-9350
  www.asahi-yukizai.co.jp

  Rev: $307
  Emp: 1,056

  NAICS: 326199

  ASAHI AMERICA
  35 Green St., Malden, Massachusetts 02148
  CEO: Stephen Harrington, Pres. & CEO
  Bus: *Corrosion-resistant fluid flow products manufacture and distribution.*

  Tel: (781) 321-5409
  Fax: (781) 321-5409

  %FO: 100

- **ASATSU-DK, INC.**
13-1 Tsukiji 1-chome, Chuo-ku, Chuo-ku, Tokyo 104-8172, Japan
CEO: Masao Inagaki, Pres. & COO
Bus: *Advertising and marketing services.*

  Tel: 81-3-3547-2111
  Fax: 81-3-3547-2345
  www.asatsu-dk.co.jp

  Rev: $4,014
  Emp: 2,784

  NAICS: 541613, 541810

  ADK AMERICA, INC.
  420 Lexington Ave., 7/F, New York, New York 10011
  CEO: Dwain Taylor, Pres.
  Bus: *International advertising agency.*

  Tel: (646) 284-9800
  Fax: (646) 284-9825

  %FO: 100

- **ASICS CORPORATION**
1-1, Minatojima-Nakamachi, 7-chome, Chuo-ku, Kobe 650-8555, Japan
CEO: Kihachiro Onitsuka, Pres. & CEO
Bus: *Mfr. sporting goods and health related products.*

  Tel: 81-78-303-6888
  Fax: 81-78-303-2244
  www.asics.com

  Rev: $1,330
  Emp: 4,161

  NAICS: 316211, 339920

  ASICS AMERICA CORPORATION
  16275 Laguna Canyon Rd., Irvine, California 92618
  CEO: Richard Bourne, EVP
  Bus: *Athletic footwear, apparel, accessories & skiwear manufacture and sales.*

  Tel: (949) 453-8888
  Fax: (949) 453-0292

  %FO: 100
  Emp: 186

- **ASO PHARMACEUTICAL COMPANY, LTD.**
91-1, Tsukure, Kikuyo-machi, Kikuchi-gun,, Kumamoto 869-11, Japan
CEO: Tomohiro Ozaki, Pres.
Bus: *Health care and first aid products manufacture.*

  Tel: 81-96-232-2131
  Fax: 81-96-232-2137
  www.aso-pharm.co.jp

  Emp: 300

  NAICS: 325411, 325412

  ASO CORPORATION
  300 Sarasota Center Blvd., Sarasota, Florida 34240
  CEO: John D. Macaskill, Pres. & CEO
  Bus: *Mfr. first aid products and adhesive bandages.*

  Tel: (941) 379-0300
  Fax: (941) 378-9040

  %FO: 100
  Emp: 40

- **ASTELLAS PHARMA INC.**
3-11 Nihonbashi-Honcho, 2-chome, Chou-ku, Tokyo 103-8411, Japan
CEO: Toichi Takenaka, Pres. & CEO   Tel: 81-3-3244-3000   Rev: $4,839
Bus: *Mfr./distribution of pharmaceuticals.*   Fax: 81-3-3244-3272   Emp: 9,062
www.astellas.com
NAICS: 325411, 325412

  ASTELLAS PHARMA US, INC
  3125 Staley Rd., Grand Island, New York 14072
  CEO: Scott K. Aladeen   Tel: (716) 775-2200   %FO: 100
  Bus: *Pharmaceutical manufacture.*   Fax: (716) 775-2205

  ASTELLAS PHARMA US, INC.
  3 Parkway North, Deerfield, Illinois 60015
  CEO: Makoto Nishimura, Pres.   Tel: (847) 317-8800   %FO: 100
  Bus: *Pharmaceutical manufacture.*   Fax: (847) 317-7288

  ASTELLAS VENTURE CAPITAL LLC
  PO Box H, Los Altos, California 94023
  CEO: Masaki Doi, Pres. & CEO   Tel: (650) 926-0731   %FO: 100
  Bus: *Venture capital.*   Fax: (650) 926-0740

- **AUDIO-TECHNICA CORPORATION**
2206 Naruse Machida-Shi, Tokyo 194-8666, Japan
CEO: Hideo Matsushita, CEO   Tel: 81-4-2739-9111
Bus: *Professional sound equipment manufacture.*   Fax: 81-4-2739-9110
www.audio-technica.co.jp
NAICS: 334310

  AUDIO-TECHNICA USA INC.
  1221 Commerce Dr., Stow, Ohio 44224
  CEO: Philip Cajka, Pres. & CEO   Tel: (330) 686-2600   %FO: 100
  Bus: *Professional sound equipment distribution.*   Fax: (330) 686-0798

- **AUTOBACS SEVEN CO., LTD**
6-52, Toyosu 5-chome, Kotoku, Tokyo 135-8717, Japan
CEO: Koichi Sumino, Pres.   Tel: 81-3-6219-8700   Rev: $2,149
Bus: *Automotive products manufacture.*   Fax: 81-3-6219-8701   Emp: 4,008
www.autobacs-seven.com
NAICS: 441110

  AUTOBACS USA
  12645 Beach Boulevard, Stanton, California 90680
  CEO: Yasukiyo Tajima   Tel: (714) 903-9900   %FO: 100
  Bus: *Automotive products manufacture and*   Fax: (714) 903-9901
  sales.

- **THE BANK OF YOKOHAMA, LTD.**
3-1-1, Minatomirai, 3-chome, Nishi-ku, Yokohama 220-8611, Japan
CEO: Sadaaki Hirasawa, Pres. & CEO   Tel: 81-45-225-1111   Rev: $2,458
Bus: *General commercial banking services.*   Fax: 81-45-225-1160   Emp: 3,431
www.boy.co.jp
NAICS: 522110

BANK OF YOKOHAMA, LTD
405 Park Ave., Ste. 1101, New York, New York 10022
CEO: Shoichi Ohama, Rep.   Tel: (212) 750-0022   %FO: 100
Bus: *International commercial banking services.*   Fax: (212) 750-8008   Emp: 43

● **BRIDGESTONE CORPORATION**
10-1, Kyobashi, 1-chome, Chuo-ku, Tokyo 104-8340, Japan
CEO: Shigeo Watanabe, Pres. & CEO   Tel: 81-3-3567-0111   Rev: $23,439
Bus: *Mfr. rubber tires, chemical and industrial*   Fax: 81-3-3535-2553   Emp: 113,699
products, sporting goods and marine equipment.   www.bridgestone.co.jp
    NAICS: 316211, 325212, 326140, 326211, 332439, 333922, 333924, 333993, 333999, 336991, 339920, 423910

BRIDGESTONE AMERICA
535 Marriott Dr., Nashville, Tennessee 37214
CEO: Mark A. Emkes, Pres. & CEO   Tel: (615) 937-1000   %FO: 100
Bus: *Mfr./sales tires*   Fax: (615) 937-3621

● **BROTHER INDUSTRIES LTD.**
15-1, Nae Shiro-cho, Mizuho-ku, Nagoya 467, Japan
CEO: Seiichi Hirata, Pres.   Tel: 81-52-824-2511   Rev: $4,022
Bus: *Mfr. typewriters, microwave ovens, facsimile*   Fax: 81-52-824-3398   Emp: 17,450
machines, home & industrial sewing machinery.   www.brother.com
    NAICS: 333313, 335211, 443111

BROTHER INDUSTRIES, INC.
7777 North Brother Blvd., Memphis, Tennessee 38133-2738
CEO: Charles Stadler   Tel: (901) 377-7777   %FO: 100
Bus: *Typewriters and word processors*   Fax: (901) 372-1325
manufacture and sales.

BROTHER INTERNATIONAL CORPORATION
100 Somerset Corporate Blvd., Bridgewater, New Jersey 08807-0911
CEO: Toshikazu Koike, VP   Tel: (908) 704-1700   %FO: 100
Bus: *U.S. headquarters. Sales/marketing parent*   Fax: (908) 704-8235   Emp: 600
company products.

● **CALSONIC KANSEI CORPORATION**
5-24-15 Minamidal, Nakano-ku, Tokyo 164-8602, Japan
CEO: Takashi Kitajima, Pres. & CEO   Tel: 81-3-5285-0111   Rev: $5,861
Bus: *Mfr./distribution of automotive parts and modular*   Fax: 81-3-5285-0111   Emp: 15,613
systems.   www.calsonickansei.co.jp
    NAICS: 336399

CALSONIC NORTH AMERICA
One Calsonic Way, Shelbyville, Tennessee 37160
CEO: Elton Coleman   Tel: (931) 684-4490   %FO: 100
Bus: *Mfr. and distribution automotive parts.*   Fax:

- **CANON, INC.**
  30-2, Shimomaruko, 3-chome, Ohta-ku, Tokyo 146-8501, Japan
  CEO: Fujio Mitarai, Pres. & CEO   Tel: 81-3-3758-2111   Rev: $33,345
  Bus: *Office equipment, cameras, video, audio, medical* Fax: 81-3-5482-5135   Emp: 102,567
        & broadcast equipment manufacture.   www.canon.com
  NAICS: 333293, 333314, 333315

  > **CANON BUSINESS SOLUTIONS, INC.**
  > 300 Commerce Square Blvd., Burlington, New Jersey 08016
  > CEO: William Reed, Chmn.   Tel: (609) 387-8700   %FO: 100
  > Bus: *Mfr. business machines.*   Fax: Emp: 2,120
  >
  > **CANON BUSINESS SOLUTIONS CENTRAL, INC.**
  > 425 North Martingale Rd., Ste. 1400, Schaumburg, Illinois 60173
  > CEO: Emily Reynolds, Pres.   Tel: (847) 706-3400   %FO: 100
  > Bus: *Sales of business machines.*   Fax: (847) 706-3400   Emp: 400
  >
  > **CANON BUSINESS SOLUTIONS, INC.**
  > 110 West Walnut St., Gardena, California 90248
  > CEO: William Reed, Chmn.   Tel: (310) 217-3000   %FO: 100
  > Bus: *Sales of business machines.*   Fax: (310) 715-7050   Emp: 825
  >
  > **CANON DEVELOPENT AMERICAS, INC.**
  > 15975 Alton Pkwy., Irvine, California 92618
  > CEO: Michihiko Senoh, Pres.   Tel: (949) 932-3100
  > Bus: *Computer programming services.*   Fax: Emp: 200
  >
  > **CANON FINANCIAL SERVICES, INC.**
  > 158 Gaither Dr., Ste. 200, Mount Laurel, New Jersey 08054
  > CEO: Albert E. Smith, Pres.   Tel: (856) 813-1000   %FO: 100
  > Bus: *Equipment leasing*   Fax: Emp: 150
  >
  > **CANON INFORMATION TECHNOLOGY SERVICES, INC.**
  > 850 Greenbrier Circle, Ste. K, Chesapeake, Virginia 23320
  > CEO: Raymond A. Moritz, Pres.   Tel: (757) 579-7100   %FO: 100
  > Bus: *computer maintenance & repair.*   Fax: Emp: 500
  >
  > **CANON LATIN AMERICA, INC.**
  > 703 Waterford Way, Ste. 400, Miami, Florida 33126
  > CEO: Nobou Ijichi, Pres.   Tel: (305) 260-7400   %FO: 100
  > Bus: *Sales of cameras and office equipment.* Fax: (305) 260-7409   Emp: 54
  >
  > **CANON TECHNOLOGY SOLUTIONS**
  > 101 W. Elm St., Ste. 600, Conshohocken, Pennsylvania 19428
  > CEO: Kevin Swint, Pres.   Tel: (610) 277-1750
  > Bus: *Computer related services.*   Fax: Emp: 111
  >
  > **CANON U.S. LIFE SCIENCES**
  > 2110 Washington Blvd., Ste. 300, Arlington, Virginia 22204
  > CEO: Tel: (703) 807-3400
  > Bus: *Office equipment*   Fax: Emp: 2

CANON USA, INC.
One Canon Plaza, Lake Success, New York 11042
CEO: Yoroku Adachi, Pres. & CEO
Bus: *Mfr./distributor office equipment, cameras,*
video, audio, medical & broadcast
Tel: (516) 328-5000
Fax: (516) 328-5069
%FO: 100
Emp: 10,000

CANON, INC.
12000 Canon Blvd., Newport News, Virginia 23606
CEO: Takahoshi Hanagata, Pres. & CEO
Bus: *Mfr. copy machines, printers and toner.*
Tel: (757) 881-6000
Fax: (757) 881-6024
%FO: 100
Emp: 1,800

CUSTOM INTEGRATED TECHNOLOGY, INC.
120 Enterprise Dr., Newport News, Virginia 23606
CEO: Kenji Mori, Pres.
Bus: *Computer peripheral equipment.*
Tel: (757) 887-0211
Fax:
%FO: 100
Emp: 90

INDUSTRIAL RESOURCE TECHNOLOGIES, INC.
6000 Industrial Dr., Gloucester, Virginia 23601
CEO: Roger Simpson, Mgr.
Bus: *Photographic equipment & supplies*
Tel: (804) 695-7000
Fax:
%FO: 100
Emp: 120

● **CANON SOFTWARE INC.**
3-9-7 Mita, Minato-ku, Tokyo 108-8317, Japan
CEO: Akira Okada, Pres.
Bus: *Information technology services*
Tel: 81-3-3455-9911
Fax:
www.canon-soft.co.jp
Rev: $156
Emp: 901

NAICS: 511210, 541511

CANON SOFTWARE AMERICA, INC.
1 Canon Plaza, Lake Success, New York 11042-1198
CEO: Kinya Uchida, Pres.
Bus: *Information technology services.*
Tel: (516) 327-2176
Fax: (516) 327-2279
%FO: 100

● **CAPCOM CO. LTD**
3-1-3 Uchihirano-manchi, Chuo-ku, Osaka 540-0037, Japan
CEO: Kenzo Tsujimoto, Pres. & CEO
Bus: *Developer of entertainment and game software*
Tel: 81-6-6920-3600
Fax: 81-6-6920-5100
www.capcom.co.jp
Rev: $499
Emp: 1,206

NAICS: 511210

CAPCOM USA INC.
475 Oakmead Pkwy., Sunnyvale, California 94085
CEO: Kenzo Tsujimoto, CEO
Bus: *Developer of entertainment and game*
software
Tel: (408) 774-0500
Fax: (408) 774-3994
%FO: 100

● **CASIO COMPUTER CO., LTD.**
6-2, Hon-machi 1-chome, Shibuya-ku, Tokyo 151-8543, Japan
CEO: Kazuo Kashio, Pres.
Bus: *Mfr. electronic consumer products; calculators,*
watches, telecommunications equipment, cameras
and computers.
Tel: 81-3-5334-4111
Fax: 81-3-5334-4887
www.casio.co.jp
Rev: $4,956
Emp: 12,929

NAICS: 333313, 334111, 334119, 334220, 334518

CASIO INC.
570 Mount Pleasant Ave., Dover, New Jersey 07801
CEO: John B. Clough, Pres.
Bus: *Mfr./distribution electronic consumer products; calculators, watches, telecommunications equipment, cameras and computers.*
Tel: (973) 361-5400
Fax: (973) 361-3819
%FO: 100

● **THE CHIBA BANK, LTD.**
1-2, Chiba-Minato, Chuo-ku, Chiba 260-8720, Japan
CEO: Tadashi Takeyama, Pres.
Bus: *General commercial banking services.*
Tel: 81-43-245-1111
Fax: 81-43-244-6654
www.chibabank.co.jp
Rev: $1,977
Emp: 3,907

NAICS: 522110, 522210, 522291, 523110, 524210

THE CHIBA BANK, LTD.
1133 Ave. of the Americas, 15/F, New York, New York 10036
CEO: Masamichi Abe, Mgr.
Bus: *International commercial banking services.*
Tel: (212) 354-7777
Fax: (212) 354-8575
%FO: 100

● **CHIYODA CORPORATION**
2-12-1, Tsurumichuo, Tsurumi-ku, Yokohama 230-8601, Japan
CEO: Nobuo Seki, Pres. & CEO
Bus: *Provides facilities management services for construction and engineering.*
Tel: 81-45-521-1231
Fax: 81-45-503-0200
www.chiyoda-corp.com
Rev: $1,958
Emp: 3,588

NAICS: 236210, 237110, 237130, 237990, 541330

CHIYODA CORPORATION
1177 West Loop South, Ste. 1302, Houston, Texas 77027
CEO: Tamio Ohashi
Bus: *Provides facilities management services for construction and engineering.*
Tel: (713) 965-9005
Fax: (713) 965-0075
%FO: 100

● **CHORI COMPANY, LTD.**
4-7, Kawaramachi, 2-chome, Chuo-ku, Osaka 540-8603, Japan
CEO: Kenichi Tanaka, Pres.
Bus: *Textiles, chemical products and machinery.*
Tel: 81-6-6228-5000
Fax: 81-6-6228-5610
www.chori.co.jp
Rev: $2,531
Emp: 1,958

NAICS: 313311, 313312, 325199

CHORI AMERICA INC
1180 Ave. of the Americas, 21/F., New York, New York 10119-5498
CEO: Yoshikazu Masuda
Bus: *Textiles, chemical products and machinery*
Tel: (212) 563-3264
Fax: (212) 736-6392
%FO: 100

● **CHUBU ELECTRIC POWER CO. INC.**
1, Higashi-shincho, Higashi-ku, Nagoya 461-8680, Japan
CEO: Fumio Kawaguchi, Pres. & CEO
Bus: *Supplies electricity.*
Tel: 81-52-951-8211
Fax: 81-52-962-4624
www.chuden.co.jp
Rev: $19,835
Emp: 24,073

NAICS: 221111, 221112, 221113, 221121, 221122, 424720

CHUBU ELECTRIC POWER COMPANY INC.
900 17th St. NW, Ste. 1220, Washington, District of Columbia 20006
CEO: Tatsuo Yagi   Tel: (202) 775-1960   %FO: 100
Bus: *Supplies electric power.*   Fax: (202) 331-9256

● **CHUGAI PHARMACEUTICAL CO., LTD.**
1-9, Kyobashi, 2-chome, Chuo-ku, Tokyo 104-8301, Japan
CEO: Osamu Nagayama, Pres. & CEO   Tel: 81-3-3281-6611   Rev: $2,858
Bus: *Pharmaceuticals manufacture for bone and blood*   Fax: 81-3-3281-2828   Emp: 5,327
disorders and infectious diseases.   www.chugai-pharm.co.jp
NAICS: 325412, 424210

    CHUGAI PHARMA USA INC.
    444 Madison Ave., Ste. 1201, New York, New York 10022
    CEO: Abraham E. Cohen   Tel: (212) 486-7780   %FO: 100
    Bus: *Mfr. pharmaceuticals for bone and blood*   Fax: (212) 486-7780
    disorders and infectious diseases.

    CHUGAI PHARMA USA INC.
    One Crossroads Dr., Bedminster, New Jersey 07921
    CEO: David J. Mazzo, Pres. & CEO   Tel: (908) 947-2700   %FO: 100
    Bus: *Mfr. pharmaceuticals for bone and blood*   Fax: (908) 947-2662
    disorders and infectious diseases.

● **CHUGOKU BANK LTD.**
1-15-20, Marunouchi, Okayama 700-0823, Japan
CEO: Akira Nagashima, Pres.   Tel: 81-86-223-3111   Rev: $929
Bus: *International banking services.*   Fax: 81-86-234-6582   Emp: 4,394
          www.chugin.co.jp
NAICS: 522110

    CHUGOKU BANK LTD.
    1 World Trade Center, New York, New York 10048
    CEO: Makoto Inoue, Principal   Tel: (212) 321-3111   %FO: 100
    Bus: *General banking services.*   Fax:

● **CITIZEN WATCH COMPANY, LTD.**
6-1-12, Tanashi-cho, Nishi Tokyo-shi, Tokyo 188-8511, Japan
CEO: Makoto Umehara, Pres.   Tel: 81-3-42466-1231   Rev: $3,556
Bus: *Mfr. wrist-watches, information and electronic*   Fax: 81-3-42466-1280   Emp: 17,987
equipment and industrial equipment and   www.citizen.co.jp
instruments.
NAICS: 333298, 333999, 334119, 334510, 334518, 335999, 339112, 339911, 339913, 339999, 423220

    CBM AMERICA CORPORATION
    363 Van Ness Way, Ste. 404, Torrance, California 90501
    CEO: Peter J. Hawker, EVP   Tel: (310) 781-1460
    Bus: *Electronic products marketing and sales.*   Fax: (310) 781-9152

CITIZEN AMERICA CORP.
2102 Alton Pkwy, Unit A, Irvine, California 92606
CEO: Tetsuo Kashara, Pres.　　　　Tel: (949) 428-3700
Bus: *Sale of computers/peripheral, Mfr. Electric*　Fax:　　　　　　Emp: 31
measuring instruments, mfr. Of computer
peripherals

CITIZEN WATCH COMPANY OF AMERICA
1200 Wall St. West, Lyndhurst, New Jersey 07071
CEO: Laurence R. Grunstein, Pres.　　Tel: (201) 438-8150　　%FO: 100
Bus: *U.S. headquarters office.*　　　Fax: (201) 438-4161

MARUBENI CITIZEN-CINCOM, INC.
40 Boroline Rd., Allendale, New Jersey 07401
CEO: Atsuya Abe, Pres.　　　　Tel: (201) 818-0100　　%FO: 100
Bus: *Mfr. Industrial equipment & medical-hospital*　Fax: (201) 818-1877　Emp: 36
equipment

● **CLARION COMPANY, LTD.**
509 Kami-Toda, Toda, Saitama 335 8511, Japan
CEO: Tatsuhiko Izumi, Pres.　　　Tel: 81-48-443-1111　　Rev: $1,599
Bus: *Mfr. mobile electronics.*　　Fax: 81-48-445-3810　Emp: 9,211
　　　　　　　　　　www.clarion.co.jp
NAICS: 517212

　CLARION CORPORATION OF AMERICA
　661 West Redondo Beach Blvd., Gardena, California 90247
　CEO: Frank Pierce, Pres.　　　Tel: (310) 327-9100　　%FO: 100
　Bus: *Mfr./sale/service mobile electronics.*　Fax: (310) 327-1999　Emp: 500

● **COLUMBIA MUSIC ENTERTAINMENT LTD**
1-4-33 Roppongi 21 Mori Bldg, Roppongi, Minato-ku, Tokyo 106-8565, Japan
CEO: Strauss Zelnick, Pres.　　　Tel: 81-3-3588-2200　　Rev: $820
Bus: *Production, manufacturing, advertising and sales*　Fax: 81-3-3584-9647　Emp: 1,200
of audio and video software.　　www.elec.donon.co.jp
NAICS: 334210

　DENON DIGITAL LLC
　13 North Pasture Rd., Westport, Connecticut 06880
　CEO: Ed Simek　　　　Tel: (203) 454-4966　　%FO: 100
　Bus: *Distributes audio and video products.*　Fax: (203) 221-7932

　DENON DIGITAL LLC
　650 Fifth Ave., 31/F, New York, New York 10019
　CEO: Charles Cadmus　　　Tel: (646) 282-3356　　%FO: 100
　Bus: *Distributes audio and video products.*　Fax: (646) 282-3001

　DENON DIGITAL LLC
　1380 Monticello Rd., Madison, Georgia 30650
　CEO: Thomas Maddox　　　Tel: (706) 342-5105　　%FO: 100
　Bus: *Distributes audio and video products.*　Fax: (706) 484-4832

DENON DIGITAL LLC
13332 Dorfsmith Dr., Westminster, California 92683
CEO: Tony Nguyen   Tel: (714) 892-8500   %FO: 100
Bus: *Distributes audio and video products.*   Fax: (714) 892-3333

● **CORONA CORPORATION**
7-7, Higashi Shinbo, Sanjo, Niigata 955-8510, Japan
CEO: Tsutomu Uchida, Pres.   Tel: 81-256-32-2111   Rev: $550
Bus: *Kerosene heaters and air conditioners*   Fax: 81-256-35-6892   Emp: 2,279
                                                 www.corona.co.jp
NAICS: 333414, 333415, 335224
    CORONA USA CORPORATION
    2050 Center Ave., Ste. 4501, Fort Lee, New Jersey 07024
    CEO: T. Uchida   Tel: (201) 592-0123   %FO: 100
    Bus: *Sales/distribution of kerosene heaters and*   Fax: (201) 592-8848
      air conditioners.

● **COSMO OIL CO. LTD.**
1-1-1 Shibaura, Minato-ku, Tokyo 105-8528, Japan
CEO: Keiichiro Okabe, Chmn. & CEO   Tel: 81-3-3798-3211   Rev: $18,139
Bus: *Oil exploration, refining and sales.*   Fax: 81-3-3798-3237   Emp: 2,000
                                                 www.cosmo-oil.co.jp
NAICS: 324110, 324191, 424710, 424720, 447110, 447190, 454311, 454312, 454319
    COSMO OIL OF U.S.A.
    21250 Hawthorne Blvd., Ste. 765, Torrance, California 90503
    CEO: Yaichi Kimura   Tel: (310) 792-3863
    Bus: *Support for sales of petroleum products.*   Fax:

    COSMO OIL OF USA INC.
    150 East 52nd St., 22/F, New York, New York 10022
    CEO: Yaichi Kimura, CEO   Tel: (212) 486-3700   %FO: 100
    Bus: *Engineering and biotechnology.*   Fax: (212) 486-4715

● **CSK CORPORATION**
2-6-1, Nishi-Shinjuku, Shinjuku-ku, Tokyo 160-0227, Japan
CEO: Yoshito Fukuyama, CEO   Tel: 81-3-3344-1811   Rev: $3,581
Bus: *Information services; computer equipment,*   Fax: 81-3-5321-3939   Emp: 4,768
    publishing and telemarketing.   www.csk.co.jp
NAICS: 541519, 541611
    KIBO GROUP INC.
    14 Wall St., New York, New York 10005
    CEO: James Ryan   Tel: (212) 504-0200   %FO: 100
    Bus: *Provider of technology solutions to the*   Fax: (212) 504-0300
      financial services industry.

- **CYBOZU, INC.**
  Koraku Mori Bldg., 12th Fl., 1-4-14 Koraku, Bunkyo-Ku, Tokyo 112-0004, Japan
  CEO: Toru Sakamoto, Pres. & CEO   Tel: 81-3-5805-9035   Rev: $28
  Bus: *Internet ready-to-use software manufacture.*   Fax: 81-3-5805-9036   Emp: 135
      www.cybozu.co.jp

  NAICS: 511210

      CYBOZU CORPORATION
      235 Montgomery St., Ste. 1004, San Francisco, California 94104
      CEO: Yoshihisa Aono, CFO   Tel: (415) 421-1969   %FO: 100
      Bus: *Internet ready-to-use software manufacture*   Fax: (415) 421-3190
          and sales.

- **DAI NIPPON PRINTING CO LTD.**
  1-1, Ichigaya-Kagacho, 1-chome, Shijuku-ku, Tokyo 162-8001, Japan
  CEO: Yoshitoshi Kitajima, Pres.   Tel: 81-3-3266-2111   Rev: $15,658
  Bus: *Engaged in printing services.*   Fax: 81-3-5225-8239   Emp: 34,100
      www.dnp.co.jp

  NAICS: 323110

      DAI NIPPON IMS AMERICA CORP.
      3858 Carson St., Ste. 300, Torrance, California 90503
      CEO: Stephen Bishop   Tel: (310) 540-5123   %FO: 100
      Bus: *Decorative material products sales.*   Fax: (310) 543-3260

      DAI NIPPON IMS AMERICA CORP.
      4524 Enterprise Dr. NW, Concord, North Carolina 28027
      CEO: Masato Koike, Pres.   Tel: (704) 784-8100   %FO: 100
      Bus: *Thermal transfer ribbon manufacture.*   Fax: (704) 784-2777

      DNP AMERICA, INC.
      577 Airport Boulevard, Ste. 620, Burlingame, California 94010
      CEO: Kosuke Tago   Tel: (650) 558-4050   %FO: 100
      Bus: *Printing services.*   Fax: (650) 340-6095

      DNP AMERICA, INC.
      3235 Kifer Rd., Ste. 100, Santa Clara, California 95051
      CEO: Phino Funatsu   Tel: (408) 735-8880   %FO: 100
      Bus: *Electronic devices, semi-conductor*   Fax: (408) 735-0453
          materials.

      DNP AMERICA, INC.
      335 Madison Ave., 3/F, New York, New York 10017
      CEO: Yoji Yamakawa, Pres.   Tel: (212) 503-1060   %FO: 100
      Bus: *Printing sales.*   Fax: (212) 286-1501

      DNP ELECTRONICS AMERICA, LLC
      2391 Fenton St., Chula Vista, California 91914
      CEO: Masanori Sakoda   Tel: (619) 397-6700   %FO: 100
      Bus: *Precision electronic components*   Fax: (619) 397-6729
          manufacture.

- **DAICEL CHEMICAL INDUSTRIES, LTD.**
  1 Teppo-sho, Sakai, Osaka 590-8501, Japan
  CEO: Daisuke Ogawa, Pres. & CEO
  Bus: *Mfr. cellulose and organic chemical products.*

  Tel: 81-722-27-3111
  Fax: 81-722-27-3000
  www.daicel.co.jp

  Rev: $2,666
  Emp: 5,604

  NAICS: 325199, 325411

  ### CHIRAL TECHNOLOGIES INC.
  800 North Five Points Rd., West Chester, Pennsylvania 19380
  CEO: Thomas B. Lewis
  Bus: *Separation products and services for the pharmaceutical and related industries.*

  Tel: (610) 594-2100
  Fax: (610) 594-2325

  %FO: 100

  ### DAICEL (USA) INC.
  One Parker Plaza, 6/F, 400 Kolby Street, Fort Lee, New Jersey 07024
  CEO: Masato Sakai
  Bus: *Mfr. cellulose and organic chemical products.*

  Tel: (201) 461-4466
  Fax: (201) 461-2776

  %FO: 100

  ### DAICEL SAFETY SYSTEMS AMERICA, LLS
  720 Old Liberty Church Rd., Beaver Dam, Kentucky 42320
  CEO: Yashnori Iwai
  Bus: *Mfr. and sales of automotive airbag inflators.*

  Tel: (270) 274-2600
  Fax: (270) 274-0750

  %FO: 100

  ### THESIS CHEMISTRY
  7533 Tyler Blvd., Suite C, Mentor, Ohio 44060
  CEO: John Peterson
  Bus: *Chemistry services.*

  Tel: (440) 942-4295
  Fax: (440) 942-4375

  %FO: 100

- **DAIDO KOGYO CO LTD.**
  1-197 Kumasaka-Cho, Kaga City, Chuo-ku, Ishikawa 922-8686, Japan
  CEO: Shoichi Araya, Pres.
  Bus: *Chain and conveyors manufacture for industrial machinery.*

  Tel: 81-761-721234
  Fax: 81-761-726458
  www.daidocorp.com

  Emp: 100

  NAICS: 331513

  ### DAIDO CORPORATION
  1031 Fred White Blvd., Portland, Tennessee 37148
  CEO: Yoshiyuki Horie
  Bus: *Roller chain manufacturer.*

  Tel: (615) 323-4020
  Fax: (615) 323-4015

  %FO: 100

  ### DAIDO CORPORATION
  615 Pierce St., PO Box 6739, Somerset, New Jersey 08875-6739
  CEO: Mick Kusaka, Pres.
  Bus: *Roller chain manufacturer.*

  Tel: (732) 805-1900
  Fax: (732) 805-0122

  %FO: 100
  Emp: 140

- **DAIDO STEEL CO INC**
  1-11-18, Nishiki I-chome, Naka-ku, Nagoya 460, Japan
  CEO: Tsuyoshi Takayama, Pres.
  Bus: *Specialty steel products.*

  Tel: 81-52-201-5111
  Fax: 81-52-221-9268
  www.daido.co.jp

  Rev: $3,040
  Emp: 5,911

  NAICS: 331512

DAIDO STEEL (AMERICA) INC
1607 Ocean St., Ste. 3, Santa Cruz, California 95060
CEO: Yutaka Yoshida
Bus: *Importing and exporting, purchasing and*
selling steel,
industrial machinery, electrical machinery,
raw materials.

Tel: (831) 423-4217
Fax: (831) 423-4218

%FO: 100

DAIDO STEEL (AMERICA), INC.
1111 North Plaza Dr., Ste. 740, Schaumburg, Illinois 60173
CEO: Kimihiko Seki, Pres.
Bus: *Importing and exporting, purchasing and*
selling steel,
industrial machinery, electrical machinery,
raw materials.

Tel: (847) 517-7950
Fax: (847) 517-7950

%FO: 100
Emp: 10

INTERNATIONAL MOLD STEEL
6796 Powerline Dr., Florence, Kentucky 41042
CEO: Thomas Schade
Bus: *Importing and exporting, purchasing and*
selling steel,
industrial machinery, electrical machinery,
raw materials.

Tel: (859) 342-6000
Fax: (859) 342-6006

%FO: 100

OHIO STAR FORGE COMPANY
4000 Mahoning Ave., Warren, Ohio 44483
CEO: Jeffrey P. Downing, Pres.
Bus: *Mfr./sales small precision forgings.*

Tel: (330) 847-6360
Fax: (330) 847-6368

%FO: 100

OOZX USA INC.
10101 Caneel Dr., Knoxville, Tennessee 37931
CEO: Mack Ochiai
Bus: *Mfr. automobile parts.*

Tel: (423) 691-4000
Fax: (423) 539-9950

%FO: 100

● **DAIDOH LTD.**
3-1-16, Sotokanda, Chiyoda-ku, Tokyo 101-8619, Japan
CEO: Yoshiya Hatori, Chmn. & CEO
Bus: *Mfr. worsted fabrics and yarns; men's and*
women's apparel.
NAICS: 313111, 313210, 315232

Tel: 81-3-3257-5050
Fax: 81-3-3257-5051
www.daidon-limited.com

Rev: $126
Emp: 1,821

DAIDOH INTERNATIONAL INC.
119 West 57th St., Ste. 714, New York, New York 10019
CEO: Y. Hatori
Bus: *Import/export textile, apparel and*
furnishings.

Tel: (212) 581-8255
Fax:

%FO: 100

● **THE DAIEI, INC.**
4-1-1, Minatojima Nakamachi,, Chuo-ku Kobe, Hyogo 650-0046, Japan
CEO: Fumiko Hayashi, Chmn. & CEO
Bus: *Retail food and chain store operator.*
NAICS: 445110, 448110, 448120, 448130, 448140, 452112, 452910

Tel: 81-78-302-5001
Fax: 81-3-3433-9226
www.daiei.co.jp

Rev: $18,255
Emp: 23,560

DAIEI USA, INC.
801 Kahake St., Honolulu, Hawaii 96814
CEO: Isao Nakauchi, Chmn.
Bus: *Retail food and chain store operator.*

Tel: (808) 973-6600
Fax: (808) 941-6457

%FO: 100
Emp: 800

● **DAIHATSU MOTOR CO., LTD.**
1-1, Daihatsu-cho, Ikeda, Osaka 563-8651, Japan
CEO: Takaya Yamada, Pres.
Bus: *Mfr./sales passenger cars and commercial*

Tel: 81-72-754-3047
Fax: 81-72-753-6880
www.daihatsu.co.jp

Rev: $9,405
Emp: 27,543

NAICS: 336111

DAIHATSU AMERICA INC.
28 Centerpoint Dr., Ste. 120, La Palma, California 90623
CEO: Katsuhiko Okumura, Mng. Dir.
Bus: *Sales/distribution of cars and commercial vehicles.*

Tel: (714) 690-4700
Fax: (714) 690-4720

%FO: 100

● **DAIICHI CHUO KISEN KAISHA**
3-7-13 Toyo, Koto-ku, Tokyo 135-8364, Japan
CEO: Yasuhide Sakinaga, Pres.
Bus: *Engaged in the transportation of bulk cargo via marine transport.*

Tel: 81-3-5634-2243
Fax: 81-3-5634-2262
www.firstship.co.jp

Rev: $500
Emp: 200

NAICS: 483111

DAIICHI CHUO SHIPPING AMERICA, INC.
61 Broadway, New York, New York 10006
CEO: Hideko Ochiai
Bus: *Shipping agents and brokers.*

Tel: (212) 269-2677
Fax: (212) 269-2677

%FO: 100
Emp: 11

● **DAI-ICHI MUTUAL LIFE INSURANCE COMPANY**
13-1 Yurakucho-1-chome, Chiyoda-ku, Tokyo 100-8411, Japan
CEO: Tomijiro Morita, Chmn.
Bus: *Life insurance*

Tel: 81-3-3216-1211
Fax: 81-3-5221-4360
www.dai-ichi-life.co.jp

Rev: $44,437
Emp: 55,134

NAICS: 524113

DAI-ICHI LIFE INSURANCE USA INC.
1133 Ave. of the Americas, 28/F, New York, New York 10036
CEO: Masahiko Sakaguchi
Bus: *Life insurance*

Tel: (212) 350-7600
Fax: (212) 354-1866

%FO: 100

● **DAIICHI PHARMACEUTIAL CO. LTD.**
14-10, Nihonbashi, 3-chome, Chuo-ku, Tokyo 103-8234, Japan
CEO: Kiyoshi Morita, Pres. & CEO
Bus: *Research and distributes ethical pharmaceuticals and veterinary products.*
NAICS: 325411, 325412, 325413

Tel: 81-3-3272-0611
Fax: 81-3-3272-7348
www.daiichipharm.co.jp

Rev: $3,055
Emp: 7,379

DAIICHI PHARMACEUTICAL CORPORATION
11 Philips Pkwy., Montvale, New Jersey 07645
CEO: N. Marcellos, VP
Bus: *Pharmaceutical preparations*

Tel: (201) 573-7000
Fax: (201) 573-7650

%FO: 100
Emp: 350

● **DAIKIN INDUSTRIES, LTD.**
Umeda Center Bldg., 2-4-12, Nakazaki-Nishi,Kita-ku, Osaka 530-8323, Japan
CEO: Noriyuki Inoue, Chmn. & CEO   Tel: 81-6-6373-4312   Rev: $5,923
Bus: *Mfr. industrial pumps and refrigeration equipment,* Fax: 81-6-6373-4380   Emp: 16,816
  air-conditioning systems, medical equipment and www.daikin.com
  fluorochemicals.
NAICS: 332618, 335312, 335929, 336413, 423610, 423730, 511210, 811310

  DAIKIN AMERICA INC.
  20 Olympic Dr., Orangeburg, New York 10962
  CEO: Kiyohiko Ihara, Chmn.   Tel: (845) 365-9501
  Bus: *Mfr. commercial/industrial air conditioning* Fax: (845) 365-9545
    systems.

  DAIKIN U.S. CORPORATION, INC.
  375 Park Ave., Ste. 3308, New York, New York 10152
  CEO: Yoshinobu Noainoue, Pres.   Tel: (212) 935-4890   %FO: 100
  Bus: *Mfr. commercial/industrial air conditioning* Fax: (212) 935-4895   Emp: 23
    systems.

  MDA MANUFACTURING
  PO Box 2252, State Docks Rd., Decatur, Alabama 35609
  CEO: Cindy Hemback, Mgr.   Tel: (256) 306-0374
  Bus: *Industrial buildings & warehouses* Fax:

● **DAIMARU, INC.**
1-7-1 Shinsaibashi-Suji, Chuo-ku, Osaka 542-8501, Japan
CEO: Tsutomu Okuda, Pres.   Tel: 81-6-6271-1231   Rev: $6,000
Bus: *Department stores.*   Fax: 81-6-6245-1343   Emp: 600
                                         www.daimaru.co.jp
NAICS: 452111

  DAIMARU U.S.A., INC.
  52 Vanderbilt Ave., Rm. 1503, New York, New York 10017
  CEO: Masaki Kaseteni   Tel: (212) 681-8725   %FO: 100
  Bus: *Department stores.*   Fax: (212) 681-8725

● **DAINICHISEIKA COLOUR & CHEMICALS MFG. CO., LTD.**
1-7-6,Nihombashibakurocho, Chuo-ku, Tokyo 103-0002, Japan
CEO: Osamu Takahashi, Pres.   Tel: 81-3-3662-7111   Rev: $979
Bus: *Mfr. pigments and coloring agents for plastics* Fax: 81-3-3669-3936   Emp: 3,304
  and printing ink.   www.daicolor.co.jp
NAICS: 325131, 325199, 325910

  DAICOLOR-USA
  33 Sixth Ave., Paterson, New Jersey 07024
  CEO: Akira Ishizaka, Pres.   Tel: (973) 278-5170   %FO: 100
  Bus: *Mfr./sales/distribution of pigments and* Fax: (973) 279-1256
    dispersions.

  HI-TECH COLOR, INC.
  Midway Industrial Park, 1721 Midway Rd., Odenton, Maryland 21113
  CEO: Takashige Asai, Pres.   Tel: (410) 551-9871
  Bus: *Chemicals manufacture.*   Fax: (410) 672-3002   Emp: 17

● **DAINIPPON INK & CHEMICALS INC.**
DIC Building, 7-20, Nihonbashi, 3-chome, Chuo-Ku, Tokyo 103-8233, Japan
CEO: Koji Oe, Pres.   Tel: 81-3-3272-4511   Rev: $9,227
Bus: *Printing inks, supplies, machinery, chemicals,*   Fax: 81-3-3278-8558   Emp: 26,522
       imaging reprographic products, resins, plastics, www.dic.co.jp
       petrochemicals, building materials.
NAICS: 325131, 325132, 325211, 325510, 325910

DIC AMERICAS INC.
2400 Ellis Rd., Durham, North Carolina 27703-5543
CEO: Yoshiyuki Kawashima, CEO   Tel: (919) 990-7500   %FO: 100
Bus: *Mfr. synthetic resins and adhesives.*   Fax: (919) 990-7711   Emp: 3,500

DIC AMERICAS, INC.
222 Bridge Plaza South, Fort Lee, New Jersey 07024
CEO: Henri Dyner, Pres. & CEO   Tel: (201) 592-5100
Bus: *Mfr./sale printing inks and organic*   Fax: (201) 592-8232
       chemicals.

DIC IMAGING PRODUCTS INC.
7300 South 10th St., Oak Creek, Wisconsin 53154
CEO: Kazuyoshi Tsunumi, Pres.   Tel: (414) 764-5100   %FO: 100
Bus: *Toner and UV-curable coatings sales.*   Fax: (414) 764-5032

DYNARIC INC.
500 Frank W. Burr Blvd., Teaneck, New Jersey 07666
CEO: Joseph Martinez, Pres.   Tel: (201) 692-7700   %FO: 100
Bus: *Mfr. plastic strapping material.*   Fax: (201) 692-7757

EARTHRISE NUTRITIONALS
424 Payran St., Petaluma, California 94952
CEO: Yoshimichi Ota, Pres.   Tel: (707) 778-9078   %FO: 100
Bus: *Mfr./sale printing inks and organic*   Fax: (707) 778-9028
       chemicals.

PREMIER POLYMERS, INC.
4400 East Highway 6, Box 353, Alvin, Texas 77511
CEO: Neil Miller, Sales   Tel: (281) 331-8800   %FO: 99
Bus: *Mfr./sale printing inks and organic*   Fax: (281) 331-7444
       chemicals.

REICHHOLD, INC.
2400 Elis Rd., Durham, North Carolina 27703
CEO: John S. Gaither, Pres.   Tel: (919) 990-7500   %FO: 100
Bus: *Adhesives, coatings and polymer resins*   Fax: (919) 990-7711
       manufacture.

SUN CHEMICAL CORPORATION
35 Waterview Blvd., Parsippany, New Jersey 07054
CEO: Wes Lucas   Tel: (973) 404-6000   %FO: 100
Bus: *Inks and coatings manufacture.*   Fax: (973) 404-6001

- **DAINIPPON SCREEN MANUFACTURING CO LTD.**
  Tenjinkita-cho 1-1, Teranouchi-agaru, 4-chome, Horikawa-dori, Kamigyo-ku, Kyoto 602-8585, Japan
  CEO: Akira Ishida, Chmn. & Pres. & CEO   Tel: 81-75-414-7111   Rev: $1,817
  Bus: *Semiconductor equipment manufacturer*   Fax: 81-75-431-6500   Emp: 2,339
                                                   www.screen.co.jp

  NAICS: 333295

  > **DAINIPPON SCREEN ELECTRONICS INC.**
  > 820 Kifer Rd., Ste. B, Sunnyvale, California 94086-5214
  > CEO: James Beard   Tel: (408) 523-9140   %FO: 100
  > Bus: *Semiconductor manufacturer*   Fax: (408) 523-9150

- **DAIO PAPER CORPORATION**
  2-7-2 Yaesu, Chuo-ku, Tokyo 104-8468, Japan
  CEO: Toshitaka Ikawa, CEO   Tel: 81-3-3271-1442   Rev: $3,706
  Bus: *Pulp and paper manufacturer.*   Fax: 81-896-24-3860   Emp: 8,000
                                                   www.daio-paper.co.jp

  NAICS: 322121

  > **CALIFORNIA WOODFIBER CORPORATION**
  > 1890 Pkwy. Blvd., PO Box 753, West Sacramento, California 95691
  > CEO: Michihiko Tamaki,   Tel: (916) 371-3682   %FO: 80
  > Bus: *Mfr. woodchips for pulp.*   Fax: (916) 371-5060   Emp: 18

- **DAIWA SB INVESTMENTS LTD.**
  2-7-9 Nihonbashi, Chuo-ku, Tokyo 103-0027, Japan
  CEO: Shuichi Komori, Pres. & CEO   Tel: 81-3-3243-2915
  Bus: *Engaged in investment management.*   Fax: 81-3-3274-3717   Emp: 292
                                                   www.daiwasbi.co.jp

  NAICS: 523930

  > **DAIWA SB INVESTMENTS LTD.**
  > 1 Financial Square, 32 Old Slip, 11/F, New York, New York 10005
  > CEO: Kiyotaka Hoshino, Pres.   Tel: (212) 612-8500   %FO: 100
  > Bus: *Investment management.*   Fax: (212) 612-8518   Emp: 10

- **DAIWA SECURITIES GROUP INC.**
  6-4, Otemachi, 2-chome, Chiyoda-ku, Tokyo 100-8101, Japan
  CEO: Shigeharu Suzuki, Pres. & CEO   Tel: 81-3-3243-2100   Rev: $4,296
  Bus: *Engaged in wholesale securities.*   Fax: 81-3-3242-0955   Emp: 11,565
                                                   www.daiwa.co.jp

  NAICS: 523110

  > **DAIWA SECURITIES AMERICA INC.**
  > 32 Old Slip, Financial Square, New York, New York 10005
  > CEO: Yoshinari Hara, Pres.   Tel: (212) 612-7000   %FO: 100
  > Bus: *Investment banking and securities broker.* Fax: (212) 612-7100   Emp: 400

  > **DAIWA SECURITIES TRUST CO.**
  > One Evertrust Plaza, Jersey City, New Jersey 07302
  > CEO: E. Bauer, Pres.   Tel: (201) 333-7300   %FO: 100
  > Bus: *Investment banking and securities broker.* Fax: (201) 333-7726

- **DAIWA SEIKO INC.**
3-14-16 Maesawa, Higashi-kurume, Tokyo 203-8511, Japan
CEO: Tadao Kojima, Pres.
Bus: *Mfr. of athletic/outdoor gear and apparel*
Tel: 81-4-2475-2111
Fax: 81-4-2475-3334
www.daiwaseiko.co.jp
Rev: $466
Emp: 2,239

NAICS: 315228, 315239, 315991, 316211, 423910

    DAIWA CORPORATION
    12851 Midway Place, Cerritos, California 90703
    CEO: Tad Suzuki, Pres.
    Bus: *Manufacturer sporting goods and equipment*
    Tel: (562) 802-9589
    Fax: (562) 404-6212
    %FO: 100
    Emp: 103

- **DENKI KAGAKU KOGYO KABUSHIKI KAISHA**
Nihonbashi Mitsui Tower, 1-1, Nihonbashi-Muromachi 2-chome, Chuo-ku, Tokyo 103-8338, Japan
CEO: Tsuneo Yano, Chmn.
Bus: *Mfr. petrochemicals, chemical products, and construction materials*
Tel: 81-3-5290-5055
Fax: 81-3-5290-5059
www.denka.co.jp
Rev: $2,377
Emp: 5,618

NAICS: 325110, 325132, 325199, 325211

    THE DENKA GROUP
    780 Third Ave., 32/F, New York, New York 10017
    CEO: Toshio Hiruma, Pres.
    Bus: *Manufacturer petrochemicals, chemical products, and construction materials*
    Tel: (212) 688-8700
    Fax: (212) 688-8727
    %FO: 100

- **DENSO CORPORATION**
1-1, Showa-cho, Kariya, Aichi 448, Japan
CEO: Koichi Fukaya, Pres. & CEO
Bus: *Mfr. automotive components and systems technology.*
Tel: 81-566-25-5594
Fax: 81-566-25-4509
www.denso.co.jp
Rev: $24,255
Emp: 95,461

NAICS: 333415, 335999, 336340, 336350, 336399

    DENSO ENGINEERING SERVICES
    1840 Airport Exchange Blvd., Erlanger, Kentucky 41018-3195
    CEO: Mitsunobu Takeuchi
    Bus: *Auto starters and alternators manufacture.*
    Tel: (859) 525-7630
    Fax: (859) 525-7630
    %FO: 100

    DENSO INTERNATIONAL AMERICA
    24777 Denso Dr., PO Box 5133, Southfield, Michigan 48086-5133
    CEO: Mitsuo Matsushita, Chmn. & CEO
    Bus: *Automobile systems manufacture.*
    Tel: (248) 350-7500
    Fax: (248) 350-7772
    %FO: 100

    DENSO MANUFACTURING MICHIGAN, INC.
    400 Hill Brady Rd., Battle Creek, Michigan 49015-5606
    CEO: Akio Shikamura, Pres.
    Bus: *Mfr./sales of heaters, air conditioners and automotive components.*
    Tel: (269) 963-5393
    Fax: (269) 963-5393
    %FO: 100
    Emp: 6,000

    DENSO NORTH AMERICA INC.
    18211 Chisholm Trail, Houston, Texas 77060-1110
    CEO: Lucian Williams
    Bus: *Auto compounds manufacture.*
    Tel: (281) 821-3355
    Fax: (281) 821-3355
    %FO: 100

DENSO SALES CALIFORNIA, INC.
5770 Armada Dr., Carlsbad, California 92008-4608
CEO: Christina B. Jordan, EVP   Tel: (760) 804-3200   %FO: 100
Bus: *Automotive component manufacture.*   Fax: (760) 804-3280   Emp: 400

DENSO WIRELESS SYSTEMS INC.
3250 Business Park Dr., Vista, California 92083
CEO: Hidehiko Akatsuka, Pres.   Tel: (760) 734-4600   %FO: 100
Bus: *Mfr. cellular handsets.*   Fax: (760) 734-4685

● **DENTSU INC.**
1-8-1, Higashi-shimbashi, Minato-ku, Tokyo 105-7001, Japan
CEO: Tateo Mataki, Pres. & CEO   Tel: 81-3-6216-5111   Rev: $2,750
Bus: *Advertising and communications services.*   Fax: 81-3-5551-2013   Emp: 14,245
                                        www.dentsu.com
NAICS: 541613, 541810, 541820, 541830, 541840, 541850, 541860, 541870, 541890, 541910, 561422

DENTSU HOLDINGS USA INC.
488 Madison Ave., 23/F, New York, New York 10022
CEO: Naoki Kobuse, Chmn.   Tel: (212) 829-5120   %FO: 100
Bus: *Advertising and public relations.*   Fax: (212) 829-0009   Emp: 350

DENTSU, INC.
6080 Center Dr., 6/F, Los Angeles, California 90045
CEO: Tel: (310) 242-6845
Bus: *Advertising and public relations.*   Fax:

● **DESCENTE LTD.**
1-11-3, Dogashiba, Tennoji-ku, Osaka 543-0033, Japan
CEO: Yoshikazu Ishimoto, Chmn.   Tel: 81-6-6774-0365   Rev: $489
Bus: *Active sportswear manufacture and distribution.*   Fax: 81-6-6774-0367   Emp: 1,279
                                        www.descente.co.jp
NAICS: 423910, 424320, 424330

DESCENTE AMERICA INC.
7367 South Revere Pkwy., Ste. 2A, Englewood, Colorado 80112
CEO: Hideo Kiyoshige, Pres.   Tel: (303) 790-1155   %FO: 100
Bus: *Ski and golf apparel manufacture.*   Fax: (303) 790-2149

● **DISCO CORPORATION**
14-3 Higashi Kojiya 2-chome, Ota-ku, Tokyo 144-8650, Japan
CEO: Kenichi Sekiya, Chmn. & CEO   Tel: 81-3-3743-5813   Rev: $457
Bus: *Mfr. specialized cutting and polishing equipment*   Fax: 81-3-3743-5810   Emp: 1,670
                                        www.disco.co.jp
NAICS: 333295

CHRISTIAN DIOR
7931 SW Cirrus Dr., Beaverton, Oregon 97008-5971
CEO: Tel: (503) 644-0323   %FO: 100
Bus: *Manufacturer saws, grinders, and related*   Fax: (503) 643-8108
    machinery

DISCO HI-TEC AMERICA INC.
4411 South 40th St., Ste. D-5, Phoenix, Arizona 85040-2950
CEO: Tel: (602) 431-1412   %FO: 100
Bus: *Manufacturer saws, grinders, and related*   Fax: (602) 431-1437
machinery

DISCO HI-TEC AMERICA INC.
360 Harvey Rd., Bldg. B, Unit 202, Manchester, New Hampshire 03103
CEO: Tel: (603) 656-9019   %FO: 100
Bus: *Manufacturer saws, grinders, and related*   Fax: (603) 656-9018
machinery

DISCO HI-TEC AMERICA INC.
3000 Aerial Center Executive Park, Ste. 140, Morrisville, North Carolina 27560
CEO: Tel: (919) 468-6003   %FO: 100
Bus: *Manufacturer saws, grinders, and related*   Fax: (919) 468-6004
machinery

DISCO HI-TEC AMERICA INC.
3270 Scott Blvd., Santa Clara, California 95054-3011
CEO: Scott Sullivan   Tel: (408) 987-3776   %FO: 100
Bus: *Manufacturer saws, grinders, and related*   Fax: (408) 987-3785
machinery

DISCO HI-TEC AMERICA INC.
4392 Sunbelt Dr., Addison, Texas 75001
CEO: Tel: (972) 267-9500   %FO: 100
Bus: *Manufacturer saws, grinders, and related*   Fax: (972) 267-5612
machinery

DISCO-SEA AMERICA INC.
6850 Shiroh Rd. East, Ste. B1, Alpharetta, Georgia 30005
CEO: Tel: (770) 888-1442   %FO: 100
Bus: *Manufacturer saws, grinders, and related*   Fax: (770) 888-1472
machinery

● **DOWA MINING COMPANY LTD.**
8-2, Marunouchi 1-chome, Chiyoda-ku, Tokyo 100-8282, Japan
CEO: Hirokazu Yoshikawa, CEO   Tel: 81-3-3201-1061   Rev: $2,221
Bus: *Processing and sale of copper, zinc and gold.*   Fax: 81-3-3201-1259   Emp: 4,203
                                                        www.dowa.co.jp
NAICS: 212210, 212221, 212222, 212231, 212234, 212299, 213114

DOWA INTERNATIONAL CORP.
250 Park Ave., Ste. 911, New York, New York 10177
CEO: Kyoshi Harada   Tel: (212) 697-3217   %FO: 100
Bus: *Processing and sale of copper, zinc and*   Fax: (212) 697-3902
gold.

DOWA THT AMERICA, INC.
2130 South Woodland Circle, Bowling Green, Ohio 43402
CEO: Masanari Konomi   Tel: (419) 354-4144   %FO: 100
Bus: *Processing and sale of copper, zinc and*   Fax: (419) 354-6479
gold.

Japan

• EAST JAPAN RAILWAY COMPANY
2-2, Yoyogi 2-chome, Shibuya-ku, Tokyo 151-8578, Japan
CEO: Mutsutake Otsuka, Pres. & CEO   Tel: 81-3-5334-1310   Rev: $24,065
Bus: *National railway system.*   Fax: 81-3-5334-1297   Emp: 77,009
    www.jreast.co.jp
NAICS: 237210, 485112, 485999, 531120, 531190, 531312, 721110

EAST JAPAN RAILWAY COMPANY
One Rockefeller Plaza, New York, New York 10020
CEO: Mitsuo Higashi, Dir.   Tel: (212) 332-8686   %FO: 100
Bus: *Information and liaison office for East Japan*   Fax: (212) 332-8690
    Railway Company (non-commercial).

• EBARA CORPORATION
11-1, Haneda Asahi-cho, Ohta-ku, Tokyo 144-8510, Japan
CEO: Fumio Shimakawa, Pres.   Tel: 81-3-3743-6111   Rev: $4,806
Bus: *Mfr. water and air transportation systems,*   Fax: 81-3-3745-3356   Emp: 15,207
    precision machinery and communications   www.ebara.co.jp
NAICS: 221320, 237130, 332322, 332410, 332911, 332912, 332913, 332919, 333995, 333996, 423720, 423730, 541614

EBARA AMERICA CORPORATION
45 East Plumeria Dr., San Jose, California 95134
CEO: Matt Woodberry, VP   Tel: (408) 571-2250   %FO: 100
Bus: *Water and air transport systems and*   Fax: (408) 571-2259
    precision machinery manufacture and sales.

EBARA INTERNATIONAL
350 Salomon Circle, Sparks, Nevada 89434
CEO: Everett Hylton, CEO   Tel: (775) 356-2796
Bus: *Mfr. pumps equipment.*   Fax: (775) 356-2884   Emp: 155

EBARA INTERNATIONAL
1651 Cedar Line Dr., Rock Hill, South Carolina 29730
CEO: Martin Perlmutter, Mgr.   Tel: (803) 327-5005
Bus: *Mfr. conductive wire, pumps, pumping*   Fax: (803) 327-5097
    equip.

EBARA TECHNOLOGIES INC.
51 Main Ave., Sacramento, California 95838
CEO: Norio Kimura, Pres. & CEO   Tel: (916) 920-5451   %FO: 100
Bus: *Mfr. of equipment used in the production of*   Fax: (916) 830-1900   Emp: 225
    semiconductors

ELLIOTT ENERGY SYSTEMS
2901 SE Monroe St., Stuart, Florida 34997
CEO: Akiro Ushitora, Pres.   Tel: (772) 219-9449
Bus: *Wholesale micro turbine.*   Fax: (772) 219-9448   Emp: 100

ELLIOTT TURBOMACHINERY CO., INC.
901 N. Fourth St., Jeanette, Pennsylvania 15644
CEO: Donal P. Maloney, Pres. & CEO   Tel: (724) 527-2811
Bus: *Mfr. of power generating equipment.*   Fax: (725) 600-8442   Emp: 1,356

● **EIKI INDUSTRIAL COMPANY, LTD.**
4-12 Manzai-cho, Naniwa Bldg., Kita-ku, Osaka 530-91, Japan
CEO: Yukio Eiki, Pres.
Bus: *Mfr. film projectors and VCRs.*

Tel: 81-6-6311-9479
Fax: 81-6-6311-8486
www.eiki.com

NAICS: 334310

    EIKI INTERNATIONAL INC.
    30251 Esperanza, Rancho Santa Margarita, California 92688-2132
    CEO: Ken Kikuchi, Mgr.
    Bus: *Film projectors and VCRs.*

    Tel: (949) 457-7877
    Fax: (949) 457-7878

    %FO: 100

● **EISAI CO., LTD.**
4-6-10, Koishikawa, Bunkyo-ku, Tokyo 112-8088, Japan
CEO: Haruo Naito, Pres. & CEO
Bus: *Prescription and OTC pharmaceuticals and drug manufacturing equipment.*

Tel: 81-3-3817-5120
Fax: 81-3-3811-3077
www.eisai.co.jp

Rev: $4,735
Emp: 7,700

NAICS: 325412, 325413

    EISAI CORPORATION OF NORTH AMERICA
    Glenpointe Centre West, 5/F, 500 Frank W. Burr Blvd., Teaneck, New Jersey 07666
    CEO: Hajime Shimizu, Chmn. & CEO
    Bus: *Clinical & pharmaceutical research*

    Tel: (201) 692-1100
    Fax: (201) 692-1804

    %FO: 100
    Emp: 480

    EISAI MEDICAL RESEARCH INC.
    55 Challenger Rd., 5/F, Ridge Park, New Jersey 07660
    CEO: Mindell Seidlin, Pres.
    Bus: *Medical research*

    Tel: (201) 403-2500
    Fax: (201) 462-9351

    %FO: 100
    Emp: 9

    EISAI RESEARCH INSTITUTE OF BOSTON
    1 Corporate Dr., Andover, Massachusetts 01810
    CEO: Yoshito Kishi, Chmn.
    Bus: *Medical research in pharmaceutical research*

    Tel: (978) 794-1117
    Fax: (978) 688-9556

    %FO: 100
    Emp: 175

    EISAI USA
    3 University Plaza, Ste. 16, Hackensack, New Jersey 07601
    CEO: Michael De LA Montaigne, Pres.
    Bus: *wholesale pharmaceutical machinery & related parts*

    Tel: (201) 287-2111
    Fax: (201) 692-1972

    %FO: 100
    Emp: 10

● **ELMO COMPANY, LTD.**
6-14, Meizen-cho, Mizuho-ku, Nagoya 467-8567, Japan
CEO: Kazuhiko Ogura, Mgr.
Bus: *Mfr. electronic imaging equipment.*

Tel: 81-52-811-5143
Fax: 81-52-811-5243
www.elmo.co.jp

Emp: 500

NAICS: 334510

    ELMO MANUFACTURING CORPORATION
    1478 Old Country Rd., Plainview, New York 11803
    CEO: Stephen Yusko, EVP
    Bus: *Sale/service audio-visual, electronic imaging and CCTV products.*

    Tel: (516) 501-1400
    Fax: (516) 501-0429

    %FO: 100
    Emp: 30

- **ELPIDA MEMORY INC.**
  2-1 Yaesu 2-chome, Chuo-ku, Sumitomo Seimei Yaesu Bldg., 3/F, Tokyo, Japan
  CEO: Yukio Sakamoto, Pres. & CEO   Tel: 81-3-3281-1500   Rev: $951
  Bus: *Mfr. DRAM chips*   Fax: 81-3-3281-1571   Emp: 2,235
  www.elpida.com

  NAICS: 334112, 334413

  > **ELPIDA MEMORY USA INC.**
  > 9430 Research Blvd., Bldg. II, Ste. 340, Austin, Texas 78759
  > CEO: Ray Agrella, mgr   Tel: (512) 342-0500   %FO: 100
  > Bus: *Manufacturer DRAM chips*   Fax: (512) 342-0506

  > **ELPIDA MEMORY USA INC.**
  > 11 Daniel Lucy Way, Newburyport, Massachusetts 01950
  > CEO: Joe Marella, Mgr.   Tel: (978) 463-6224   %FO: 100
  > Bus: *Manufacturer DRAM chips*   Fax: (978) 463-6223

  > **ELPIDA MEMORY USA INC.**
  > 8521 Six Forks Rd., Ste. 270, Raleigh, North Carolina 27615
  > CEO: Dan Donabedian, Pres. & CEO   Tel: (919) 645-0330   %FO: 100
  > Bus: *Manufacturer DRAM chips*   Fax: (919) 645-0325

  > **ELPIDA MEMORY USA INC.**
  > 363 N. Sam Houston Pkwy E., Ste. 770, Houston, Texas 77060
  > CEO: David Lin, Sales Dir.   Tel: (281) 272-7171   %FO: 100
  > Bus: *Manufacturer DRAM chips*   Fax: (281) 272-7160

  > **ELPIDA MEMORY USA INC.**
  > 2001 Walsh Ave., Santa Clara, California 95050
  > CEO: Bijan Yazdani, Sales Dir.   Tel: (408) 970-6600   %FO: 100
  > Bus: *Manufacturer DRAM chips*   Fax: (408) 970-6999

- **EZAKI GLICO CO., LTD.**
  4-6-5, Utajima, Nishi-Yodogawaku, Osaka 555-8502, Japan
  CEO: Katsuhisa Ezaki, CEO   Tel: 81-6-6477-8352   Rev: $2,508
  Bus: *Mfr. confections, including cookies, candy and*   Fax: 81-6-6477-8250   Emp: 4,350
  ice cream and food supplements and stews.   www.glico.co.jp
  NAICS: 311320, 311330, 424450

  > **EZAKI GLICO USA CORP.**
  > 1420 Solana Dr., Belmont, California 94002
  > CEO: Eiichi Takano   Tel: (650) 631-7403   %FO: 100
  > Bus: *Biscuits and cookie manufacture.*   Fax: (650) 631-7402

- **FAMILYMART CO., LTD.**
  26-10, Higashi-Ikebukuro 4-chome, Toshima-ku, Tokyo 170-8404, Japan
  CEO: Michio Tanabe, CEO   Tel: 81-3-3989-6600   Rev: $2,403
  Bus: *Convenience store chain.*   Fax: 81-3-3989-6600   Emp: 5,458
  www.family.co.jp

  NAICS: 445120, 447110

FAMIMA CORPORATION
20000 Mariner Ave., Ste. 100, Torrance, California 90503
CEO: Shiro Inoue, Pres.
Bus: *Franchise specialty stores.*
Tel: (310) 214-1001
Fax: (310) 214-7200
%FO: 100

● **FANUC LIMITED**
3580, Shibokusa Aza-Komanba, Oshino, Yamanashi 401-0567, Japan
CEO: Shigeaki Oyama, Chmn.
Bus: *Industrial equipment research and production.*
Tel: 81-555-84-5555
Fax: 81-555-84-5512
www.fanuc.co.jp
Rev: $2,507
Emp: 6,000

NAICS: 333220, 334513, 335314

FANUC AMERICA
1800 Lakewood Blvd., Hoffman Estates, Illinois 60195
CEO:
Bus: *Industrial equipment sales and distribution.*
Tel: (847) 898-5000
Fax: (847) 898-5001
%FO: 100

FANUC ROBOTICS OF AMERICA, INC.
3900 West Hamlin Rd., Rochester Hills, Michigan 48309-3253
CEO: Rick Schneider, Pres. & CEO
Bus: *Industrial equipment sales and distribution.*
Tel: (248) 377-7000
Fax: (248) 276-4133
%FO: 100
Emp: 1,100

GE FANUC AUTOMATION NORTH AMERICA
2500 Austin Dr., Charlottesville, Virginia 22911
CEO: Jeff R. Garwood, Pres. & CEO
Bus: *Manufactures automation and control products*
Tel: (434) 978-5000
Fax: (434) 978-5205

● **FERROTEC CORPORATION**
1-4-14 Kyobashi, Chuo-ku, Tokyo 104-0031, Japan
CEO: Akira Yamamura, Pres. & CEO
Bus: *Production and sales of computer seals, vacuum seals, thermoelectric modules, and quartz products* www.ferrotec.co.jp
Tel: 81-3-3281-8808
Fax: 81-3-3281-8848
Rev: $150
Emp: 1,800

NAICS: 334417, 334419, 335999, 423610

FERROTEC USA CORPORATION
40 Simon St., Nashua, New Hampshire 03060-3075
CEO: Lucian Borduz, CEO
Bus: *Manufacturer fluids for sealing, sensing, lubrication, and heat transfer*
Tel: (603) 883-9800
Fax: (603) 883-2308
%FO: 100
Emp: 150

FERROTEC USA CORPORATION
3945 Freedom Circle, Ste. 670, Santa Clara, California 95054
CEO: Lucian Borduz, CEO
Bus: *Manufacturer fluids for sealing, sensing, lubrication, and heat transfer*
Tel: (408) 235-7618
Fax: (408) 235-7619
%FO: 100

● **FUJI ELECTRIC COMPANY, LTD.**
Gate City Ohsaki, East Tower, 11-2, Osaki, 1-chome, Shinagawa-ku, Tokyo 141-0032, Japan
CEO: Kunihiko Sawa, Pres. & CEO
Bus: *Electric and electronic devices, industrial/consumer electronics and specialty appliances manufacturer.*
Tel: 81-3-5435-7206
Fax: 81-3-5435-7486
www.fujielectric.co.jp
Rev: $8,105
Emp: 25,468

NAICS: 221320, 333294, 333311, 333313, 333415, 333996, 334416, 334419, 335311, 335312, 335313, 335314, 335931, 335999, 522220, 522291, 522292, 522293, 522294, 522298, 522310, 522390, 524210, 531120, 531130, 531190

FUJI ELECTRIC CORP. OF AMERICA
1 Park Plaza, Ste. 580, Irvine, California 92614
CEO: Yoichi Tsuyuguchi
Bus: *Electric & electronic products information
processing*

Tel: (949) 251-9600
Fax: (949) 251-9611

%FO: 100

FUJI ELECTRIC CORP. OF AMERICA
2532 Highlander Way, Carrollton, Texas 75006
CEO: Mike Meyer
Bus: *Electric & electronic products information
processing*

Tel: (972) 733-1700
Fax: (972) 381-9991

%FO: 100

FUJI ELECTRIC CORPORATION OF AMERICA, INC.
Park 80 West, Plaza 2, Saddle Brook, New Jersey 07663
CEO: Kazuo Sugiura, CEO
Bus: *Electric and electronic products &
information processing systems.*

Tel: (201) 712-0555
Fax: (201) 368-8258

%FO: 100
Emp: 32

● **FUJI HEAVY INDUSTRIES LTD.**
Subaru Bldg, 7-2 Nishi-Shinjuku, 1-chome, Shinjuku-ku, Tokyo 160-8316, Japan
CEO: Kyoji Takenaka, Pres. & CEO
Bus: *SUV automobiles, buses, railcars, aircraft
components, engines, and garbage trucks
manufacture.*

Tel: 81-3-3347-2111
Fax: 81-3-3347-2338
www.fhi.co.jp

Rev: $13,626
Emp: 27,296

NAICS: 333120, 333131, 336111, 336120, 336399, 336413

SUBARU OF AMERICA
2235 Rte. 70 West, Cherry Hill, New Jersey 08002
CEO: Kunio Ishigami, Pres.
Bus: *Cars and parts marketing and service and
accessories sales.*

Tel: (856) 488-8500
Fax: (856) 665-3346

%FO: 100
Emp: 30

SUBARU OF INDIANA AUTOMOTIVE, INC.
5500 State Rd. 38, East Lafayette, Indiana 47905
CEO: Hiroyuki Oikawa, Rep.
Bus: *Manufacturing facility.*

Tel: (765) 449-1111
Fax: (765) 449-6952

%FO: 100

SUBARU RESEARCH & DESIGN
6431 Global Dr., Cypress, California 90630
CEO: Yasuhiko Habara, Rep.
Bus: *Research & design of motor vehicles*

Tel: (714) 828-1875
Fax: (714) 828-2470

SUBARU RESEARCH & DESIGN
3995 Research Park Dr., Ann Arbor, Michigan 48108
CEO: Yasuhiko Habara, Rep.
Bus: *Research & design of motor vehicles.*

Tel: (734) 623-0075
Fax: (734) 623-0076

%FO: JV

● **FUJI PHOTO FILM CO., LTD.**
26-30, Nishiazabu, 2-chome, Minato-ku, Tokyo 106-8620, Japan
CEO: Shigetaka Komori, Pres. & CEO
Bus: *Photographic, reprographic, micrographic, audio
and visual, x-ray and graphic art supplies
manufacturing.*

Tel: 81-3-3406-2111
Fax: 81-3-3406-2173
www.fujifilm.co.jp

Rev: $23,580
Emp: 73,164

NAICS: 325992, 325998, 333293, 333298, 333314, 333315, 334112, 334119, 334613, 339112

FUJI PHOTO FILM USA, INC.
200 Summit Lake Dr., Valhalla, New York 10595
CEO: Atsushi Yoneda, Pres. & CEO
Bus: *Photographic & Optical equipment
Manufacturing*

Tel: (914) 789-8100
Fax: (914) 789-8295

● **FUJI TELEVISION NETWORK, INC.**
2-4-8 Daiba, Minato-ku, Tokyo 137-8088, Japan
CEO: Hisashi Hieda, Chmn. & CEO
Bus: *Television broadcast network, motion picture and
television production.*
NAICS: 512110, 515120

Tel: 81-3-5500-8888
Fax: 81-3-5500-8027
www.fujitv.co.jp

Rev: $4,316
Emp: 1,383

FUJI COMMUNICATIONS INTERNATIONAL,
10100 Santa Monica Blvd., Ste. 460, Los Angeles, California 90067
CEO: James Topham, Office Mgr.
Bus: *Broadcast and print news, broadcast
Japanese programming.*

Tel: (310) 553-5828
Fax:

%FO: 100

FUJI COMMUNICATIONS INTERNATIONAL,
330 National Press Building, 529 14th Street, NW, Washington, District of Columbia 20045
CEO: Nick Szechenyi, Bureau Chief
Bus: *Broadcast news agency.*

Tel: (202) 347-6070
Fax: (202) 347-0724

FUJI COMMUNICATIONS INTERNATIONAL, INC.
1357 Kapiolani Blvd., Ste. 1150, Honolulu, Hawaii 96814
CEO: Junji Kishikawa, Gen. Mgr.
Bus: *Entertainment and news broadcasting*

Tel: (808) 942-8184
Fax: (808) 946-3734

%FO: 100
Emp: 2

FUJI COMMUNICATIONS INTERNATIONAL, INC.
150 East 52nd St., 34/F, New York, New York 10022
CEO: Michael Schelp, Pres.
Bus: *Television production and distribution, news
agency, invest in film, music and
publishing, broadcast Japanese*

Tel: (212) 753-8100
Fax: (212) 688-0392

%FO: 100

● **FUJI XEROX CO., LTD.**
Akasaka Twin Tower East, 2-17-22, Akasaka 2-chome, Minato-ku, Tokyo 107-0052, Japan
CEO: Toshio Arima, CEO
Bus: *Office equipment manufacture, including digital
printers and copiers, fax machines and related
software.*
NAICS: 333293, 333315, 334119

Tel: 81-3-3585-3211
Fax: 81-3-3505-1609
www.fujixerox.co.jp

Rev: $9,487
Emp: 34,017

FX PALO ALTO LABORATORY INC.
3400 Hillview Ave., Bldg, 4, Palo Alto, California 94304
CEO: James Baker, Pres.
Bus: *Multimedia and communications technology
research.*

Tel: (650) 813-7765
Fax: (650) 813-7762

%FO: 100

XEROX INTERNATIONAL PARTNERS
3400 Hillview Ave., Bldg, 4, Palo Alto, California 94304
CEO: Sunil Gupta, Pres.
Bus: *OEM sales and support of laser printers.*

Tel: (650) 813-7700
Fax: (650) 813-7762

%FO: 100

- **FUJIKURA LTD.**
  5-1, Kiba, 1-chome, Koto-ku, Tokyo 135-8512, Japan
  CEO: Akira Tsujikawa, CEO
  Bus: *Mfr. wire and cable.*

  Tel: 81-3-5606-1030
  Fax: 81-3-5606-1502
  www.fujikura.co.jp

  Rev: $3,136
  Emp: 23,825

  NAICS: 331222, 331422, 332618, 333995, 334417, 335921, 335929, 336321, 423610

  AFL TELECOMMUNICATIONS
  830 Crescent Centre Dr., Ste. 600, Franklin, Tennessee 37067
  CEO: Craig Leyers
  Bus: *Mfr. fiber optic cable and components.*

  Tel: (615) 778-5729
  Fax: (615) 778-5734

  %FO: 100

  FUJIKURA AMERICA INC.
  11200 Westheimer Rd., Ste. 555, Houston, Texas 77042
  CEO: Junichi Kojima
  Bus: *Mfr. fiber optic cable and components.*

  Tel: (713) 784-8830
  Fax: (713) 784-8658

  %FO: 100

  FUJIKURA AMERICA INC.
  3001 Oakmead Village Dr., Santa Clara, California 95051-0811
  CEO: Hirokazu Hashimoto
  Bus: *Mfr. wire and cable.*

  Tel: (408) 748-6991
  Fax: (408) 727-3415

  %FO: 100

  FUJIKURA AMERICA INC.
  280 Interstate North Circle, Atlanta, Georgia 30339
  CEO: Mitsuji Hashimoto
  Bus: *Mfr. wire and cable.*

  Tel: (770) 956-7200
  Fax: (770) 956-9854

  %FO: 100

- **FUJITA CORPORATION**
  4-25-2 Sendagaya, Shibuya-ku, Tokyo 151-8570, Japan
  CEO: Keizo Harada, Pres. & CEO
  Bus: *Engineering and construction.*

  Tel: 81-3-3402-1911
  Fax: 81-3-3478-0729
  www.fujita.co.jp

  Rev: $2,870
  Emp: 3,309

  NAICS: 236210, 236220, 541330

  FUJITA CORPORATION USA, INC.
  101 Wilshire Blvd. #21, Santa Monica, California 90401
  CEO: Keizo Harada, Pres. & CEO
  Bus: *Engineering and construction services.*

  Tel: (310) 393-0787
  Fax: (310) 395-8130

  %FO: 100

- **FUJITEC COMPANY LTD.**
  28-10, Shoh, 1-chome, Ibaraki, Osaka 567-8510, Japan
  CEO: Kenji Otani, Chmn.
  Bus: *Elevators and escalators manufacture and sales.*

  Tel: 81-726-22-8151
  Fax: 81-726-22-1654
  www.fujitec.co.jp

  Rev: $862
  Emp: 7,278

  NAICS: 333921

  FUJITEC AMERICA INC.
  9701 Philadelphia Ct., Lanham, Maryland 20706
  CEO: Tom Petersen
  Bus: *Elevators and escalators sales and service.*

  Tel: (301) 918-4911
  Fax: (301) 918-8222

  %FO: 100

FUJITEC AMERICA INC.
900 Calcon Hook Rd., Ste. 22, Sharon Hill, Pennsylvania 19079
CEO: Bob Koleszarik, Mgr.   Tel: (610) 534-8985   %FO: 100
Bus: *Elevators and escalators sales and service.*   Fax: (610) 534-8951

FUJITEC AMERICA INC.
One Donna Dr., Wood Ridge, New Jersey 07075
CEO: Paul L. Pedretti, Pres.   Tel: (973) 890-4789   %FO: 100
Bus: *Elevators and escalators sales and service.*   Fax: (973) 890-4793

FUJITEC AMERICA INC.
13615 Welch Rd., Ste. 105, Dallas, Texas 75244
CEO: Jerry Cain   Tel: (972) 404-9984   %FO: 100
Bus: *Elevators and escalators sales and service.*   Fax: (972) 404-8491

FUJITEC AMERICA INC.
2624 Barrington Ct., Hayward, California 94545
CEO: Greg Rowe, Mgr.   Tel: (510) 780-9000   %FO: 100
Bus: *Elevators and escalators sales and service.*   Fax: (510) 780-9006

FUJITEC AMERICA INC.
6703 East Marginal Way South, Seattle, Washington 98108
CEO: Harvey Buntin, Mgr.   Tel: (206) 622-5565   %FO: 100
Bus: *Elevators and escalators sales and service.*   Fax: (206) 634-5688

FUJITEC AMERICA INC.
1225 Greenbriar Dr., Unit G, Chicago, Illinois 60101
CEO: Warren Diffenderfer, Mgr.   Tel: (630) 629-8808   %FO: 100
Bus: *Elevators and escalators sales and service.*   Fax: (630) 629-8851

FUJITEC AMERICA INC.
9009 Pinehill Lane, Ste. 212, Houston, Texas 77041
CEO: Jerry Cain, Mgr.   Tel: (713) 690-1990   %FO: 100
Bus: *Elevators and escalators sales and service.*   Fax: (713) 690-1506

FUJITEC AMERICA INC.
45A Teed Rive, Randolph, Massachusetts 02368
CEO: Tom Horan, Mgr.   Tel: (781) 961-7190   %FO: 100
Bus: *Elevators and escalators sales and service.*   Fax: (781) 961-7197

FUJITEC AMERICA, INC.
9881 Crescent Park Dr., West Chester, Ohio 45069
CEO: Curt Koslovsky   Tel: (513) 755-6100   %FO: 100
Bus: *Elevators and escalators sales and service.*   Fax: (513) 755-6215

FUJITEC AMERICA, INC.
401 Fujitec Dr., Lebanon, Ohio 45036
CEO: Vic Harada, Pres.   Tel: (513) 932-8000   %FO: 100
Bus: *Elevators and escalators sales and service.*   Fax: (513) 933-5517

FUJITEC AMERICA, INC.
2358 Perimeter Park Dr., Chamblee, Georgia 30341
CEO: Gary Krupp   Tel: (770) 457-2110   %FO: 100
Bus: *Elevators and escalators sales and service.*   Fax: (770) 457-2601

● **FUJITSU LTD.**
Shiodome City Center, 1-5-2, Higashi-Shimbashi, Minato-ku, Tokyo 105-7123, Japan
CEO: Naoyuki Akikusa, Chmn.   Tel: 81-3-6252-2220   Rev: $45,123
Bus: *Mfr. computer systems, telecommunications*   Fax: 81-3-6252-2783   Emp: 156,169
equipment, electrical components and   www.fujitsu.com
semiconductors.
NAICS: 333293, 333313, 333315, 334111, 334112, 334113, 334119, 334210, 334220, 334290, 334413, 334414,
334415, 335921, 423730, 511210, 541512,
541513, 541519, 611420

EUDYNA DEVICES INC.
2355 Zanker Rd., San Jose, California 95131
CEO: Warren Gould   Tel: (408) 232-9500
Bus: *Semiconductors.*   Fax: (408) 428-9111

FUJITSU COMPUTER PRODUCTS OF AMERICA, INC.
2904 Orchard Pkwy., San Jose, California 95134
CEO: Yoshihiko Masuda, Pres. & CEO   Tel: (408) 432-6333   %FO: 100
Bus: *R&D/mfr./sale electronic equipment.*   Fax: (408) 894-3606   Emp: 600

FUJITSU CONSULTING
333 Thornall St., Edison, New Jersey 08837
CEO: Michael J. Poehner, Pres. & CEO   Tel: (732) 549-4100
Bus: *Information technology.*   Fax: (732) 632-1826   Emp: 2,400

FUJITSU MICROELECTRONICS AMERICA INC.
1250 E. Arques Ave., Sunnyvale, California 94088
CEO: Kazuyuki Kawauchi, Pres. & CEO   Tel: (408) 737-5600
Bus: *Mfr. semiconductors.*   Fax: (408) 737-5999

FUJITSU NETWORK COMMUNICATIONS, INC.
2801 Telecom Pkwy., Richardson, Texas 75082
CEO: Takanobu Yoden, Pres. & CEO   Tel: (972) 690-6000   %FO: 100
Bus: *Mfr./sale telecommunications equipment.* Fax: (972) 479-6900

FUJITSU SIEMENS COMPUTERS
598 Gibraltar Dr., Milpitas, California 95035
CEO: Guenter Frommel   Tel: (408) 571-6000   %FO: 100
Bus: *Mfr. computer systems, telecommunications* Fax: (408) 571-6196
equipment, electrical components and
semiconductors.

FUJITSU SOFTWARE CORP.
1250 E. Arques Ave., Sunnyvale, California 94085
CEO: Shizuo Inagaki, Pres. & CEO   Tel: (408) 746-6300   %FO: 100
Bus: *Enterprise application integration software* Fax: (408) 746-6360

FUJITSU TRANSACTION SOLUTIONS
2801 Network Blvd., Frisco, Texas 75034
CEO: Austen Mulinder, Pres. & CEO   Tel: (972) 963-2300
Bus: *Computer hardware.*   Fax: (972) 963-8646   Emp: 1,400

SPANSION INC.
915 DeGuigne Dr., Sunnyvale, California 94088
CEO: Bertrand Cambou, Pres. & CEO   Tel: (408) 962-2500
Bus: *Semiconductors.*   Fax: (408) 962-2500   Emp: 7,500

- **FUJITSU TEN LTD.**
1-2-28, Gosho Dori, Hyogo-ku, Kobe 652, Japan
CEO: Takamitsu Tsuchimoto, Pres.
Bus: *Mfr. automotive audio, video, navigation and control systems.*
NAICS: 334310

Tel: 81-78-671-5081
Fax: 81-78-671-5325
www.fujitsu-ten.co.jp

Emp: 2,000

> **FUJITSU TEN CORP OF AMERICA**
> 47800 Halyard Dr., Plymouth, Michigan 48170
> CEO: Norihisa Sugata, Pres.
> Bus: *Mfr. automotive audio, video, navigation and control systems.*
>
> Tel: (734) 414-6620
> Fax: (734) 414-6660
>
> %FO: 100
> Emp: 50

- **FUKOKU MUTUAL LIFE INSURANCE COMPANY**
2-2-2 Uchisaiwai-cho, Chiyoda-ku, Tokyo 100-0011, Japan
CEO: Tomofumi Akiyama, Pres.
Bus: *Insurance services group allied with Mizuho Financial Group.*
NAICS: 523991, 523999, 524113, 524114, 524126, 525110, 525120, 525190, 525910, 525920, 525990

Tel: 81-3-3508-1101
Fax: 81-3-3581-7115
www.fukoku-life.co.jp

Rev: $8,395
Emp: 14,336

> **FUKOKU LIFE INTERNATIONAL (AMERICA) INC.**
> Times Square Tower, 7 Times Sq., 35/F, New York, New York 10036
> CEO: Ken Fukoki, Controller
> Bus: *Investment services.*
>
> Tel: (212) 221-7760
> Fax: (212) 221-7794
>
> %FO: 100
> Emp: 4

- **FUKUDA DENSHI CO., LTD.**
3-39-4, Hongo, Bunkyo-ku, Tokyo 113, Japan
CEO: Kotaro Fukuda, Pres.
Bus: *Mfr. medical equipment.*

NAICS: 334510, 334517

Tel: 81-3 3815-2121
Fax: 81-3 5684-1577
www.fukuda.co.jp

Emp: 500

> **FUKUDA DENSHI AMERICA CORP**
> 17725 NE 65th St., Redmond, Washington 98052
> CEO: Larry Walker, PR
> Bus: *Sales/service medical equipment.*
>
> Tel: (425) 881-7737
> Fax: (425) 869-2018
>
> %FO: 100
> Emp: 35

- **FUNAI ELECTRIC COMPANY LTD.**
7-7-1 Nakagaito, Daito, Osaka 574-0013, Japan
CEO: Tetsuro Funai, Pres.
Bus: *Mfr. household electrical appliances, including televisions, VCRs, DVDs, PCs, printers, telephones and fax machines.*
NAICS: 334112, 334119, 334210, 334310

Tel: 81-72-870-4303
Fax: 81-72-871-1112
www.funai.jp

Rev: $3,239
Emp: 21,049

> **FUNAI CORPORATION, INC.**
> 100 North St., Teterboro, New Jersey 07608
> CEO: Takeshi Ito
> Bus: *Sale of TV, VCRs, DVDs PCs, printers, telephones and fax machines.*
>
> Tel: (201) 288-2063
> Fax: (201) 288-8019
>
> %FO: 100

● **FURUKAWA ELECTRIC COMPANY LTD.**
6-1, Marunouchi, 2 chome, Chiyoda-ku, Tokyo 100-8322, Japan
CEO: Junnosuke Furukawa, Pres. Tel: 81-3-3286-3001 Rev: $7,003
Bus: *Mfr. electric wire and optical fiber cables.* Fax: 81-3-3286-3747 Emp: 25,880
www.furukawa.co.jp
NAICS: 212234, 331222, 331312, 331315, 331316, 331319, 331422, 331521, 332618, 335921, 335929, 335999

　　FURUKAWA AMERICA INC. (FAI)
　　Perryville Corporate Park, Bldg. 3, Clinton, New Jersey 08809
　　CEO: Katsu Mizushima, Pres. Tel: (908) 713-3525 %FO: 100
　　Bus: *Pump lasers, active components, passive* Fax: (908) 713-3515
　　　components and amplifiers sales.

　　FURUKAWA AMERICA INC. (FAI)
　　900 Lafayette St., Ste. 506, Santa Clara, California 95050
　　CEO: Arinobu Sato Tel: (408) 248-4884 %FO: 100
　　Bus: *Administrative sales office.* Fax: (408) 249-3094

　　FURUKAWA AMERICA INC. (FAI)
　　16151 Cairnway Dr., Ste., Houston, Texas 77084
　　CEO: Brad Fuqua Tel: (832) 391-3428 %FO: 100
　　Bus: *Fusion splicers, optical connectors, jumper* Fax: (832) 391-3429
　　　cords manufacture and sales.

　　FURUKAWA AMERICA INC. (FAI)
　　200 West Park Dr., Ste. 190, PO Box 502, Peachtree City, Georgia 30269
　　CEO: Amy L. Miller, Pres. Tel: (770) 487-1234 %FO: 100
　　Bus: *Fusion splicers, optical connectors, jumper* Fax: (770) 487-9910
　　　cords manufacture and sales.

● **FUTABA CORPORATION**
629 Oshiba, Mobara, Chiba 297- 8588, Japan
CEO: Reiji Hosoya, Chmn. Tel: 81-475-24-1111 Rev: $839
Bus: *Vacuum fluorescent displays and radio control* Fax: 81-475-23-1346 Emp: 6,996
　equipment manufacture. www.futaba.com
NAICS: 334419

　　FUTABA CORPORATION OF AMERICA
　　711 State Pkwy., Schaumburg, Illinois 60173-4530
　　CEO: Joe M. Dorris, Pres. Tel: (847) 884-1444 %FO: 100
　　Bus: *Vacuum fluorescent displays and radio* Fax: (847) 884-1444
　　　control equipment manufacture and sales.

● **GC CORPORATION**
76-1, Hasunumacho, Itabashi-ku, Tokyo 174-0052, Japan
CEO: Makoto Nakao, Pres. & CEO Tel: 81-3-3965-1221 Rev: $325
Bus: *Professional dental products manufacture.* Fax: 81-3-3965-3331 Emp: 701
www.gcdental.co.jp
NAICS: 339114

　　GC AMERICA INC.
　　3737 West 127th St., Alsip, Illinois 60803
　　CEO: Kent Fletcher, Pres. Tel: (708) 597-0900 %FO: 100
　　Bus: *Sales and distribution of dental products.* Fax: (708) 371-5148 Emp: 154

- **THE GIBRALTAR LIFE INSURANCE CO., LTD.**
Chiyoda Ku Nagatcho 2-13-10, Tokyo 100-8953, Japan
CEO: Timothy E. Feige, Pres.
Bus: *Insurance services.*

Tel: 81-3-5501-6001
Fax: 81-3-5501-5041
www.gib-life.co.jp

Rev: $12,500
Emp: 16,800

NAICS: 524113, 524126

  GIBRALTAR LIFE
  PO Box 340280, Austin, Texas 78734
  CEO: Tom Hanson, Owner
  Bus: *Representative office: insurance services.*

  Tel: (512) 263-3536
  Fax:

  %FO: 100

  GIBRALTAR NATIONAL INSURANCE CO. INC.
  1406 Cantrell Rd., Little Rock, Arkansas 72201
  CEO: Kelly Woolridge, Pres.
  Bus: *Insurance agents, brokers, & service*

  Tel: (501) 374-7755
  Fax:

- **GRAPHTEC CORPORATION**
503-10, Shinano-cho, Totsuka-ku, Yokohama 244-8503, Japan
CEO: Fumio Oku, Pres.
Bus: *Mfr. analog recorders and digital pen plotters, scanners and printers.*

Tel: 81-45-8256250
Fax: 81-45-8256396
www.graphteccorp.com

Rev: $111
Emp: 378

NAICS: 334119, 334310, 334517

  GRAPHIC TECHNOLOGY INC.
  9005 Junction Dr., Annapolis, Maryland 20710
  CEO: William Harrison
  Bus: *Prepress services.*

  Tel: (301) 317-0100
  Fax: (301) 317-0100

  WESTERN GRAPHTEC INC.
  11 Vanderbilt, Irvine, California 92618
  CEO: Kunio Minejima
  Bus: *Control instruments manufacture and sales.*

  Tel: (949) 855-9407
  Fax: (949) 855-9407

  %FO: 100

- **GS YUASA CORPORATION**
Nippon Seimei Shijo Bldg, 60 Tachiurinishimachi, Higashiiru, Higashino Toin, Shijodori, Shimogyo-ku, Kyoto 600-8007, Japan
CEO: Naruo Otsubo, Pres.
Bus: *Mfr. storage batteries, rectifiers and lighting equipment.*

Tel: 81-75-253-3800
Fax: 81-75-253-3801
www.gs-yuasa.com

Rev: $1,243
Emp: 9,162

NAICS: 335311, 335911, 335912, 335999, 336322

  GS BATTERY (USA) INC.
  1000 Mansell Exchange West, Ste. 350, Alpharetta, Georgia 30022
  CEO: Tadashi Shimizu, Pres.
  Bus: *Mfr. of storage batteries & primary batteries.*

  Tel: (678) 762-4818
  Fax: (678) 739-2133

  %FO: 100

  YUASA BATTERY, INC.
  2366 Bernville Rd., Reading, Pennsylvania 19605
  CEO: P Michael Ehlerman, CEO
  Bus: *Mfr. of storage batteries & primary batteries.*

  Tel: (866) 431-4784
  Fax:

  %FO: 100
  Emp: 300

YUASA BATTERY, INC.
2366 Bernville Rd., Reading, Pennsylvania 19605
CEO: P.Michael Ehlerman, CEO　　　　Tel: (610) 236-4100　　　　%FO: 87
Bus: *Mfr./distribute batteries.*　　　　Fax:　　　　Emp: 300

● **THE GUNMA BANK, LTD.**
194 Motosojamachi, Maebashi, Gunma 371-8611, Japan
CEO: Hiroshi Yomo, Pres.　　　　Tel: 81-272-52-1111　　　　Rev: $48,652
Bus: *Financial banking services.*　　　　Fax: 81-272-52-9721　　　　Emp: 3,115
　　　　www.gunmabank.co.jp

NAICS: 522110

　　THE GUNMA BANK, LTD.
　　245 Park Ave., 29/F, New York, New York 10167
　　CEO: Takashi Ooka, Mgr.　　　　Tel: (212) 949-8690　　　　%FO: 100
　　Bus: *Banking services.*　　　　Fax: (212) 867-1081　　　　Emp: 20

● **THE HACHIJUNI BANK LTD.**
178-8, Okada, Nagano 380-0935, Japan
CEO: Minoru Chino, Pres.　　　　Tel: 81-26-227-1182　　　　Rev: $1,155
Bus: *Commercial banking services.*　　　　Fax:　　　　Emp: 3,540
　　　　www.82bank.co.jp

NAICS: 522110

　　THE HACHIJUNI BANK LTD.
　　444 Madison Ave., 35/F, New York, New York 10022
　　CEO: Kazu Yoshi Araki, Mgr.　　　　Tel: (212) 557-1182　　　　%FO: 100
　　Bus: *International commercial banking services.*　　　　Fax: (212) 557-8026　　　　Emp: 13

● **HAKUHODO, INC.**
Gran Park Tower 4-1, 3 Chome, Minato-ku, Tokyo 108-8088, Japan
CEO: Takashi Shoji, Chmn.　　　　Tel: 81-3-5446-8111　　　　Rev: $685
Bus: *Advertising and communications services.*　　　　Fax: 81-3-5446-6227　　　　Emp: 3,500
　　　　www.hakuhodo.co.jp
　　NAICS: 512110, 512191, 512199, 541613, 541720, 541810, 541820, 541850, 541860, 541870, 541890, 541910,
561920

　　HAKUHODO ADVERTISING AMERICA, INC.
　　370 Lexington Ave., New York, New York 10017
　　CEO: Kolchiro Yabuki, Pres. & CEO　　　　Tel: (212) 661-8940　　　　%FO: 100
　　Bus: *Advertising agency.*　　　　Fax: (212) 490-1923

　　HAKUHODO ADVERTISING AMERICA, INC.
　　11111 Santa Monica Blvd., Los Angeles, California 90025
　　CEO: Kolchiro Yabuki　　　　Tel: (310) 444-1990　　　　%FO: 100
　　Bus: *Advertising agency.*　　　　Fax: (310) 444-9698

● **HAMADA PRINTING PRESS MFG CO.**
2-15-28, Mitejima, 2-chome, Nishi Yodogawa-ku, Osaka 555-0012, Japan
CEO: Takeshi Kajitani, Pres.　　　　Tel: 81-6-6472-1151　　　　Rev: $138
Bus: *Printing machinery and equipment manufacture.*　　　　Fax: 81-6-472-2704　　　　Emp: 555
　　　　www.hamada.co.jp
NAICS: 333293

HAMADA OF AMERICA,INC.
110 Arovista Ave., Brea, California 92821-3829
CEO: Kenichi Yokoe, Pres.   Tel: (714) 990-1999   %FO: 100
Bus: *Sheet-fed offset printing presses.*   Fax: (714) 990-1930   Emp: 20

● **HAMAMATSU PHOTONICS KK**
325-6 Sunayama-cho, Shizuoka Pref., Hamamatsu City 430-8587, Japan
CEO: Teruo Hiruma, Pres.   Tel: 81-53-452-2141   Rev: $453
Bus: *Photosensitive devices and systems.*   Fax: 81-53-456-7889   Emp: 3,021
                                                    www.hamamatsu.com

NAICS: 333314, 334411, 334413, 334513, 334515

    HAMAMATSU CORPORATION
    360 Foothill Rd., Bridgewater, New Jersey 08807
    CEO: Ralph Eno, Pres.   Tel: (908) 231-0960   %FO: 100
    Bus: *Distributor & support of electric components* Fax: (908) 231-1218   Emp: 150

    HAMAMATSU PHOTONICS SYSTEMS
    360 Foothill Rd., Bridgewater, New Jersey 08807
    CEO: Robert Wisner   Tel: (908) 231-0960   %FO: 100
    Bus: *Distributor & support of electric components* Fax: (908) 231-9374

    INSPEX INC.
    47 Manning Rd., Billerica, Massachusetts 01821
    CEO: Roberta Benson   Tel: (978) 667-5500
    Bus: *Management consulting*   Fax: (978) 663-0011

    UNIVERSAL SPECTRUM CORP.
    250 Wood Ave., Middlesex, New Jersey 08846
    CEO: Teruo Hiruma, Mgr.   Tel: (732) 805-1965
    Bus: *Electronic parts & equipment*   Fax: (732) 805-1966   Emp: 6

● **HANKYU EXPRESS INTERNATIONAL**
Hankyu Kotsusha Osaka Bldg., 6-4-18 Nishitemma , Kita-ku, Osaka 530-0047, Japan
CEO: Hiroshi Ojima, Pres.   Tel: 81-6-6366-1260   Rev: $336
Bus: *Provides railroad and line-haul operations.*   Fax: Emp: 2,296
                                                    www.hankyu.co.jp

NAICS: 488510, 522110, 561510

    HANKYU EXPRESS
    2222 Kalakaua Ave., Honolulu, Hawaii 96815
    CEO: Kapsuya Mihashi, Pres.   Tel: (808) 922-5061   %FO: 100
    Bus: *Operates travel agencies.*   Fax: Emp: 70

● **HANWA CO., LTD.**
4-3-9 Fushimi-machi, Chuo-ku, Osaka 541-8585, Japan
CEO: Shuji Kita, Pres. & CEO   Tel: 81-6-6206-3000   Rev: $7,118
Bus: *Trades in steel and stainless products, petroleum* Fax: 81-6-6206-3365   Emp: 1,294
    products and foodstuffs.   www.hanwa.co.jp
NAICS: 321999, 325110, 332999, 424420, 424720

HANWA AMERICAN CORP.
1920 Main St., Ste. 1020, Irvine, California 92614
CEO: Seiji Usui, Mgr.   Tel: (949) 955-2780
Bus: *Sale of steel products.*   Fax: (949) 955-2785

HANWA AMERICAN CORPORATION
9800 Richmond Ave., Ste. 515, Houston, Texas 77042
CEO: Yukio Iwata, Pres.   Tel: (713) 978-7904   %FO: 100
Bus: *Import of seafood.*   Fax: (713) 978-7790

HANWA AMERICAN CORPORATION
900 4th Ave., Ste. 1640, Seattle, Washington 98164
CEO: Hiroyuki Kajiwara, Mgr.   Tel: (206) 622-2102   %FO: 100
Bus: *Seafood & lumber manufacture and sales.* Fax: (206) 622-6464

HANWA AMERICAN CORPORATION
Parker Plaza, 400 Kelby St., 6/F, Fort Lee, New Jersey 07024
CEO: Yukio Iwata, Pres.   Tel: (201) 363-4500   %FO: 100
Bus: *U.S. headquarters.*   Fax: (201) 346-9890   Emp: 32

● **HARADA INDUSTRY CO LTD.**
4-17-13, Minami Ohi, 4-chome, Shinagawa-Ku, Tokyo 140-0013, Japan
CEO: Suichi Harada, Pres.   Tel: 81-3-3765-4321   Rev: $138
Bus: *Mfr. auto and communication antennas, electric* Fax: 81-33-763-0130   Emp: 2,285
  equipment, automotive access, household health www.harada.co.jp
  appliances.
NAICS: 334220, 334419, 334511, 335314, 335999
  HARADA INDUSTRY OF AMERICA ,INC.
  22925 Venture Dr., Novi, Michigan 48375
  CEO: Shoji Harada, Chmn.   Tel: (248) 374-9000   %FO: 100
  Bus: *Sales/distribution of auto antennas.* Fax: (248) 374-9100   Emp: 81

● **HASEKO CORPORATION**
2-32-1, Shiba, 2-chome, Minato-ku, Tokyo 105-0014, Japan
CEO: Toshihisa Dake, Pres.   Tel: 81-3-3456-5451   Rev: $3
Bus: *Construction, land development and engineering.* Fax: Emp: 3,293
                                           www.haseko.co.jp
NAICS: 236115, 236220, 531210, 541330
  HASEKO AMERICA, INC.
  91-1001 Kaimalie St., Ewa Beach, Hawaii 96706
  CEO: Koji Kato, Chmn.   Tel: (808) 536-3771   %FO: 100
  Bus: *Real estate development.*   Fax: Emp: 75

  HASEKO HAWAII INC.
  820 Mililani St., Ste. 820, Honolulu, Hawaii 96813
  CEO: Koji Kato, Chmn.   Tel: (808) 689-7772   %FO: 100
  Bus: *Develops high-rise condominiums, office* Fax: Emp: 60
    buildings, hotels & shopping centers.

• **HAZAMA CORPORATION**
2-5-8 Kita-Aoyama 2-Chome, Minato-ku, Tokyo 107-8658, Japan
CEO: Junichi Shimmyo, Pres. & CEO — Tel: 81-3-3405-1125 — Rev: $3,140
Bus: *General construction contractors.* — Fax: 81-3-3405-1568 — Emp: 3,100
www.hazama.co.jp
NAICS: 236210, 236220, 237990, 541330

   HAZAMA CORPORATION
   500 West Wilson Bridge Rd., Ste. 8, Worthington, Ohio 43085
   CEO: Matthew Grashil — Tel: (614) 985-4906 — %FO: 100
   Bus: *Construction/engineering services.* — Fax: (614) 985-4907 — Emp: 25

   HAZAMA CORPORATION
   1045 W. Redondo Beach Blvd., Ste. 200, Gardena, California 90247
   CEO: Tetsuo Tomoda, Pres. — Tel: (310) 352-3070 — %FO: 100
   Bus: *Construction/engineering services.* — Fax: (310) 352-3077 — Emp: 2

• **HINO MOTORS, LTD.**
3-1-1, Hinodai, 3-chome, Hino-shi, Tokyo 191-8860, Japan
CEO: Shoji Kondo, Pres. & CEO — Tel: 81-4-2586-5111 — Rev: $9,954
Bus: *diesel trucks and buses manufacture.* — Fax: 81-4-2586-5670 — Emp: 27,099
www.hino.co.jp
NAICS: 336120, 336211

   HINO MOTOR MANUFACTURING U.S.A., INC.
   451B North. Costa St., Corona, California 92880-2008
   CEO: Kimio Watanabe, Pres. — Tel: (909) 278-4466
   Bus: *Motor vehicle supplies & new parts* — Fax: (909) 278-9075 — Emp: 87

   HINO MOTOR SALES U.S.A., INC.
   2555 Telegraph Rd., Bloomfield, Michigan 48302-0954
   CEO: Nick Vermet — Tel: (248) 648-6400
   Bus: *Motor vehicle supplies & new parts* — Fax: (248) 648-6409

   HINO MOTOR SALES USA, INC.
   25 Corporate Dr., Orangeburg, New York 10962
   CEO: Mitsuo Kikuchi, Pres. — Tel: (845) 365-1400 — %FO: 100
   Bus: *Sales/distribution of diesel trucks and* — Fax: (845) 365-1409
   buses.

• **THE HIROSHIMA BANK LTD.**
3-8, Kamiya-cho, 1-chome, Naka-ku, Hiroshima 730-0031, Japan
CEO: Sho Takahashi, Pres. — Tel: 81-82-247-5151 — Rev: $1,374
Bus: *Commercial banking services.* — Fax: 81-82-240-5759 — Emp: 3,137
www.hirogin.co.jp
NAICS: 522110

   THE HIROSHIMA BANK LTD.
   444 Madison Ave., New York, New York 10022
   CEO: Nobu Shintani, Mgr. — Tel: (212) 644-8555 — %FO: 100
   Bus: *Commercial banking services.* — Fax: (212) 644-0905

- **HITACHI CABLE LTD.**
Otemachi Bldg., 6-1 Otemachi 1-chome, Chiyoda-ku, Tokyo 100-8166, Japan
CEO: Norio Sato, Pres. & CEO   Tel: 81-3-3216-1611   Rev: $3,223
Bus: *Mfr. coaxial and power cables, aluminum and*   Fax: 81-3-3214-5779   Emp: 13,590
magnet wire, fiber optic cable electronic   www.hitachi-cable.co.jp
components and rubber products.
NAICS: 326199, 331421, 331422, 332618, 334210, 334412, 334413, 334417, 334418, 334419, 335314, 335921, 335931

CNMP NETWORKS, INC.
1245 South Winchester Blvd., Ste. 208, San Jose, California 95128
CEO: Chao Z. Shi, Pres.   Tel: (408) 557-6602   %FO: 100
Bus: *Develop, mfr. and sale or information*   Fax: (408) 557-6601   Emp: 6
network devices.

HITACHI CABLE AMERICA, INC.
3031 Tisch Way, Ste. 807, San Jose, California 95128
CEO: Hiroyuki Myabe, Mgr.   Tel: (408) 260-2630   %FO: 100
Bus: *Sale of wires, cables, and materials for*   Fax: (408) 260-2756   Emp: 5
electronic components.

HITACHI CABLE AMERICA, INC.
3625 Del Amo Blvd., Ste. 385, Torrance, California 90503
CEO: Shigeo Yoshida, Mgr.   Tel: (310) 542-9680   %FO: 100
Bus: *Sale of wires, cables and materials for*   Fax: (310) 542-9610
electronic components

HITACHI CABLE AMERICA, INC.
10 Bank St., Ste. 680, White Plains, New York 10606
CEO: Tomoyuki Hatano, Pres.   Tel: (914) 993-0900   %FO: 100
Bus: *sale of wires, cables and material for*   Fax: (914) 993-0997   Emp: 26
electronic components

HITACHI CABLE INDIANA, INC.
5300 Grant Line Rd., New Albany, Indiana 47150
CEO: Akiro Kaneko, Pres.   Tel: (812) 945-9011   %FO: 100
Bus: *Mfr. / sale of rubber products.*   Fax: (812) 945-9006   Emp: 500

HITACHI CABLE MANCHESTER INC.
900 Holt Ave. East, Industrial Park, Manchester, New Hampshire 03109
CEO: Ronald J. Ruggiero, Pres.   Tel: (603) 669-4347   %FO: 100
Bus: *Mfr./Sale of wires and wire-processed*   Fax: (603) 669-6629   Emp: 130
products.

OXFORD WIRE & CABLE SERVICES, INC.
10 Industrial Dr., Oxford, Mississippi 38655
CEO: Yoshi Murakawa, Pres.   Tel: (601) 234-1410   %FO: 100
Bus: *Mfr. / sale of wires and cables*   Fax: (601) 234-1429   Emp: 38

- **HITACHI CHEMICAL CO., LTD.**
Shinjuku-Mitsui Bldg., 1-1 Nishi-Shinjuku 2-chrome, Shinjuku-ku, Tokyo 163-0449, Japan
CEO: Yasuji Nagase, Pres. & CEO   Tel: 81-3-3346-3111   Rev: $4,935
Bus: *Mfg. specialty chemicals & petrochemicals,*   Fax: 81-3-3346-2977   Emp: 16,764
paints, coatings, other finishing product, plastics   www.hitachi-chem.co.jp
& fibers, bathroom & kitchen fixtures.
NAICS: 325188, 325199, 325211, 325510, 325520, 325998, 332913, 333295, 424950

HITACHI CHEMICAL DIAGNOSTICS, INC
630 Clyde Ct., Mountain View, California 94043
CEO: Tetsuo Odashiro, CEO
Bus: *Mfr. specialty chemicals & petrochemicals, paints, coatings, other finishing product, plastics & fibers, bathroom & kitchen*

Tel: (650) 961-5501
Fax: (650) 969-2745

%FO: 100
Emp: 190

HITACHI CHEMICAL DUPONT MICROSYSTEMS LLC
250 Cheesequake Rd., Building 424, Parlin, New Jersey 08859
CEO: Phil Grifffin, Mgr.
Bus: *Mfr. specialty chemicals & petrochemicals, paints, coatings, other finishing product, plastics & fibers, bathroom & kitchen*

Tel: (732) 613-2175
Fax: (732) 613-2502

%FO: 100
Emp: 100

HITACHI CHEMICAL RESEARCH CENTER, INC.
1003 Health Sciences Rd., Irvine, California 92617
CEO: Munsok Kim, Pres. & CEO
Bus: *Mfr. specialty chemicals & petrochemicals, paints, coatings, other finishing product, plastics & fibers, bathroom & kitchen*

Tel: (949) 725-2721
Fax: (949) 725-2727

%FO: 100
Emp: 25

HITACHI OF AMERICA, LTD.
10080 North Wolfe Rd., Ste. SW3-200, Cupertino, California 95014
CEO: Tadao Kurosawa, Chmn.
Bus: *Mfr. specialty chemicals & petrochemicals, paints, coatings, other finishing product, plastics & fibers, bathroom & kitchen*

Tel: (408) 973-2200
Fax: (408) 873-2284

%FO: 100
Emp: 25

● HITACHI CONSTRUCTION MACHINERY CO., LTD.
2-5-1 Koraku, Bunkyo-ku, Tokyo 112-8563, Japan
CEO: Shungo Dazai, Pres. & CEO
Bus: *Construction equipment manufacture.*

Tel: 81-3-3830-8065
Fax: 81-3-3830-8224
www.hitachi-c-h.com

Rev: $3,807
Emp: 9,983

NAICS: 333120, 333131, 333923

DEERE-HITACHI CONSTRUCTION MACHINERY CORPORATION
1000 Deere Hitachi Rd., Kernersville, North Carolina 27285
CEO: Bill Horaney, Pres.
Bus: *Construction machinery manufacture.*

Tel: (336) 996-8100
Fax: (336) 996-8200

%FO: 100

● HITACHI HIGH-TECHNOLOGIES CORPORATION
24-14, Nishi-Shimbashi, 1-chome, Minato-ku, Tokyo 105-8717, Japan
CEO: Masaaki Hayashi, Pres. & CEO
Bus: *Marketing of scientific instruments.*

Tel: 81-3-3504-7111
Fax: 81-3-3504-7123
www.hitachi-hitec.com

Rev: $7,867
Emp: 10,043

NAICS: 333295, 334516

TECHNOLOGIES AMERICA, INC.
10 North Martingale Rd., Ste. 500, Schaumburg, Illinois 60173
CEO: Minoru Kurebayashi, VP & Gen. Mgr.
Bus: *Sale of electronics and scientific instruments.*

Tel: (847) 273-4141
Fax: (847) 273-4407

%FO: 100
Emp: 115

- **HITACHI KOKI CO., LTD.**
Shinagawa Inter City A, 2-15-1 Konan, Minato-ku, Tokyo 108-0075, Japan
CEO: Yasutsugu Takeda, Chmn.   Tel: 81-3-5783-0601   Rev: $614
Bus: *Power tools, printers, and scientific instruments*   Fax: 81-3-5783-0709   Emp: 3,976
  manufacture and sales..   www.hitachi-koki.com
NAICS: 333991, 334119

  HITACHI KOKI USA LTD.
  3950 Steve Reynolds Blvd., Norcross, Georgia 30093
  CEO: Shoichi Sakuma, Pres.   Tel: (770) 925-1774   %FO: 100
  Bus: *Power tools sales and distribution.*   Fax: (770) 564-7003   Emp: 150

- **HITACHI LTD.**
4-6 Kanda-Surugadai, Chiyoda-ku, Tokyo 101-8010, Japan
CEO: Etsuhiko Shoyama, Pres. & CEO   Tel: 81-3-3258-1111   Rev: $84,222
Bus: *Information systems and electronics, power and*   Fax: 81-3-3258-2375   Emp: 306,876
  industrial systems, consumer products and   www.hitachi.com
  materials.
NAICS: 325520, 332618, 333293, 333313, 333314, 333315, 334111, 334112, 334113, 334119, 334210, 334220,
334290, 334310, 335211, 335221, 335222,
        335224, 335228, 423620, 488510, 522291, 532490, 541614

  ELPIDA MEMORY
  2001 Walsh Ave., Santa Clara, California 95050
  CEO: Dan Donabedian, Pres.   Tel: (408) 970-6600
  Bus: *Electronics*   Fax: (408) 970-6999   Emp: 84

  GLOBAL NUCLEAR FUEL AMERICAS LLC
  3901 Castle Hayne Rd., Wilmington, North Carolina 28402
  CEO: John D. Fuller, Chmn. & CEO   Tel: (910) 675-5000
  Bus: *Specialty & exotic materials*   Fax: (910) 675-6666

  HITACHI AMERICA, LTD.
  50 Prospect Ave., Tarrytown, New York 10591
  CEO: Shigeharu Mano   Tel: (914) 332-5800   %FO: 100
  Bus: *Information systems and electronics, power*   Fax: (914) 332-5555
  and industrial systems, consumer products
  and materials.

  HITACHI AMERICA, LTD.
  2000 Sierra Point Pkwy., Brisbane, California 94005
  CEO: Masao Hisada, Pres. & CEO   Tel: (650) 589-8300   %FO: 100
  Bus: *Manufactures electronics and electrical* Fax: (650) 244-7920   Emp: 4,500
  products.

  HITACHI AUTOMOTIVE PRODUCTS
  955 Warwick Rd., Harrodsburg, Kentucky 40330
  CEO: Mark Fujisawa, Pres. & CEO   Tel: (859) 734-9451
  Bus: *Auto parts manufacturing*   Fax: (859) 734-5309   Emp: 1,150

  HITACHI CONSULTING CORPORATION
  2001 Bryan St., Ste. 3600, Dallas, Texas 75201
  CEO: Michael Travis, Pres. & COO   Tel: (214) 665-7000
  Bus: *Consulting*   Fax: (214) 665-7010

HITACHI DATA SYSTEMS CORPORATION
750 Central Expressway, Santa Clara, California 95050
CEO: Dave Roberson, Pres. & COO
Bus: *Manufactures electronics and electrical products.*

Tel: (408) 970-1000
Fax: (408) 727-8036

%FO: 100
Emp: 2,800

HITACHI GLOBAL STORAGE TECHNOLOGIES
5600 Cottle Rd., San Jose, California 95193
CEO: Hiroaki Nakanishi, CEO
Bus: *Magnetic disk storage*

Tel: (408) 717-5000
Fax: (408) 256-6770

Emp: 21,000

HITACHI HIGH TECHNOLOGIES CORPORATION
10 N. Martingale Rd., Ste. 500, Schaumburg, Illinois 60173
CEO: Masaaki Hatashi, Pres. & CEO
Bus: *Semiconductor equipment & materials*

Tel: (847) 273-4141
Fax: (847) 273-4407

Emp: 10,043

HITACHI MEDICAL SYSTEMS AMERICA
1959 Summit Commerce Park, Twinsburg, Ohio 44087
CEO: Richard L. Ernst, Pres. & CEO
Bus: *Medical Supplies & equipment*

Tel: (330) 425-1313
Fax: (330) 425-1410

HITACHI METALS LTD
2 Manhattanville Rd., Ste. 301, Purchase, New York 10577
CEO: Michiro Honda, Pres. & CEO
Bus: *Industrial manufacturing.*

Tel: (914) 694-9200
Fax: (914) 694-9279

Emp: 17,225

HITACHI TELECOM
3617 Pkwy. Ln., Norcross, Georgia 30092
CEO: Toshikazu Shimizu, Pres., Pres.
Bus: *Wireless telecommunications equipment.*

Tel: (770) 446-8820
Fax: (770) 242-1414

Emp: 55

RENESAS TECHNOLOGY CORP.
450 Holger Way, San Jose, California 95134
CEO: Satoru Ito, Pres. & CEO
Bus: *Semiconductors.*

Tel: (408) 382-7500
Fax: (408) 382-7501

SALIRA OPTICAL NETWORK SYSTEMS
3920 Freedom Circle, Ste. 101, Santa Clara, California 95054
CEO: Ross Bernard Lau, Pres. & CEO
Bus: *Optical switching & transmission equipment*

Tel: (408) 845-5200
Fax: (408) 845-5205

Emp: 70

SUPER H
3080 Olcott St., Ste. 130D, Santa Clara, California 95054
CEO: Don Higgins, CEO
Bus: *Semiconductors.*

Tel: (408) 980-9114
Fax: (408) 980-9114

WARD MANUFACTURING
117 Gulick St., Blossburg, Pennsylvania 16912
CEO: Arthur Guidi, Pres. & CEO
Bus: *Metal fabrication*

Tel: (570) 638-2131
Fax: (570) 638-3410

Emp: 989

● **HITACHI MAXELL, LTD**
2-18-2, Iidabashi, Chiyoda-ku, Tokyo 102-8567, Japan
CEO: Norio Akai, CEO
Bus: *CD and batteries manufacture.*

Tel: 81-726-238-101
Fax: 81-726-260-325
www.maxell.co.jp

Rev: $2,013
Emp: 5,034

NAICS: 334310, 335911

MAXELL CORPORATION OF AMERICA
22438 Route 208, Fairlawn, New Jersey 07410-2609
CEO: Daniel Lee, VP Mktg.
Bus: *CD and batteries manufacture.*

Tel: (201) 794-5900
Fax: (201) 794-5900

● **HITACHI METALS LTD.**
2-1 Shibaura 1-Chome, Minato-ku, Tokyo 105-8614, Japan
CEO: Michiro Honda, Pres. & CEO
Bus: *Custom metal products and specialty steel
manufacture.*

Tel: 81-3-5765-4000
Fax: 81-3-5765-8311
www.hitachi-metals.com

Rev: $3,976
Emp: 17,225

NAICS: 332112, 332912, 332996, 332999

AAP ST. MARY'S CORPORATION
1100 McKinley Ave., St. Mary's, Ohio 44885
CEO: Bruce Sakamoto, Pres.
Bus: *Mfr. aluminum wheels for automobiles.*

Tel: (419) 394-7840
Fax: (419) 394-4776

%FO: 100
Emp: 385

EASTERN COMPONENTS
11 Union Hill Rd., West Conshohoken, Pennsylvania 19428
CEO: Anthony J. Spadafora, Pres.
Bus: *Mfr. Distributors*

Tel: (610) 825-8610
Fax: (610) 825-6929

%FO: 100
Emp: 24

ELNA MAGNETICS
PO Box 395, 234 Tinker St., Woodstock, New York 12498
CEO: Joseph Ferraro, Pres.
Bus: *Mfr. distributors for electronic cores*

Tel: (845) 679-2497
Fax: (845) 679-7010

%FO: 100
Emp: 36

HI SPECIALTY AMERICA, INC.
Arona Rd., PO Box 442, Irwin, Pennsylvania 15642
CEO: Ernie Stricsck, Pres.
Bus: *Mfr. steel for cutting tool industry and
bearings.*

Tel: (412) 864-2370
Fax: (412) 864-0366

%FO: 100
Emp: 24

HITACHI MAXCO LTD.
3529 N.W. Yeon Ave., Portland, Oregon 97210
CEO: Scott Anderson, Mgr.
Bus: *Mfr. of power transmission equipment.*

Tel: (503) 228-6828
Fax: (503) 228-6703

%FO: 100
Emp: 6

HITACHI MAXCO, LTD.
1630 Cobb International Blvd., Kennesaw, Georgia 30152
CEO: Martin Bando, Pres.
Bus: *Mfr. metal products for the automobile
industry and sound portrait analyzers.*

Tel: (770) 424-9350
Fax: (770) 424-9145

%FO: 100
Emp: 218

HITACHI METALS AMERICA
21-1 South Arlington Heights Rd., Ste. 116, Arlington Heights, Illinois 60005
CEO: Harry Tanakca, Mgr.　　　　Tel: (847) 364-7200　　%FO: 100
Bus: *sale of metal products.*　　　Fax: (847) 364-7279　　Emp: 10

HITACHI METALS AMERICA, LTD.
2 Manhattanville Rd., Ste. 301, Purchase, New York 10577
CEO: Harry Tanaka, Pres.　　　　Tel: (914) 694-9200　　%FO: 100
Bus: *Custom metal products, magnetic products,*　Fax: (914) 694-9279　Emp: 2,400
　　specialty steel manufacture.

HITACHI METALS AMERICA, LTD.
2101 South Arlington Heights Rd., Arlington Heights, Illinois 60005
CEO: Harry Tanakca, Mgr.　　　　Tel: (847) 364-7200　　%FO: 100
Bus: *Mfr./sale custom metal products, magnetic*　Fax:　　　　Emp: 10
　　products, specialty steel.

HITACHI METALS AMERICA, LTD.
2107 North First St., Ste. 500, San Jose, California 95131
CEO: Juchi Kato, Pres.　　　　Tel: (408) 467-8900　　%FO: 100
Bus: *Custom metal products, magnetic products,*　Fax: (408) 467-8901
　　specialty steel.

HITACHI METALS AMERICA, LTD.
10700 Sikes Place, Ste. 240, Charlotte, North Carolina 28277
CEO: Robert Kaminski, Mgr.　　　Tel: (704) 321-1350　　%FO: 100
Bus: *Specialty metals.*　　　　Fax: (704) 321-1355

HITACHI METALS AMERICA, LTD.
41800 West Eleven Mile Rd., Ste. 100, Novi, Michigan 48375
CEO: Cassie Dundon, Mgr.　　　　Tel: (248) 465-6400　　%FO: 100
Bus: *Mfr./sale custom metal products, magnetic*　Fax: (248) 465-6020　Emp: 30
　　products, specialty steel.

HITACHI METALS AMERICA, LTD.
745 South Church St., Ste. 501, Murfreesboro, Tennessee 37130
CEO: Matt Takahashi　　　　　Tel: (615) 849-6900　　%FO: 100
Bus: *Custom metal products, magnetic products,*　Fax: (615) 849-8492
　　specialty steel manufacture.

HITACHI METALS NORTH CAROLINA
One Hitachi Metals Dr., China Grove, North Carolina 28023
CEO: Terry Mochida, Pres.　　　　Tel: (704) 855-2800　　%FO: 100
Bus: *Mfr./sale arc segment magnets for*　　Fax: (704) 855-2750　Emp: 150
　　automobile industry.

HN AUTOMOTIVE, INC.
Wellsboro Industrial Park, 9728 Route 287 10, Wellsboro, Pennsylvania 16901
CEO: Garry Heatley, Pres.　　　　Tel: (570) 724-5191　　%FO: 100
Bus: *Mfr. metal automotive parts.*　　Fax: (570) 724-4431　Emp: 80

HN AUTOMOTIVE, INC.
1500 Heartland Ave., Effingham, Illinois 62401
CEO: Kinzo Watanabe, Pres.　　　　Tel: (217) 342-5977　　%FO: 100
Bus: *Mfr. metal products for the automotive*　Fax: (217) 342-6933
　　industry.

MAXCESS TECHNOLOGIES, INC.
230 Deming Way, Summerville, South Carolina 29483
CEO: Andy Miarka, Pres.   Tel: (843) 821-1200   %FO: 100
Bus: *Mfr. of sheet metal , computer peripherals,*   Fax: Emp: 125
      fabricates plate work & hardware.

METGLAS, INC.
440 Allied Dr., Conway, South Carolina 29526
CEO: Taiji Yamada, Pres.   Tel: (843) 349-7319   %FO: 100
Bus: *Custom metal products and specialty steel*   Fax: (843) 349-6815   Emp: 135
      manufacture.

NEOMAX AMERICA, INC.
500 East Remington Rd., Ste. 106, Schaumburg, Illinois 60173
CEO: Tetsuo Toizume, Pres.   Tel: (847) 519-1100   %FO: 100
Bus: *Sale of ceramic & metal magnets.*   Fax: (847) 519-1180   Emp: 9

NEWPORT PRECISION, INC.
400 Cherry St., Newport, Tennessee 37821
CEO: Ted Komura, Pres.   Tel: (423) 623-3445   %FO: 100
Bus: *Mfr./sale vanes for power steering pumps.*   Fax: (423) 623-3449   Emp: 30

SINTERMET, LLC
North Park Dr., West Hills Industrial Park, Kittanning, Pennsylvania 16201
CEO: Paul C. Fleiner, Pres.   Tel: (724) 548-7631   %FO: 100
Bus: *Mfr. tungsten steel carbide rod mill rolls*   Fax: (724) 545-1824   Emp: 50
      and rotary knives

WARD MANUFACTURING, INC.
117 Gulick St., Blossburg, Pennsylvania 16912
CEO: Richard Stauffer, VP   Tel: (570) 638-2131   %FO: 100
Bus: *Mfr. pipe fittings & cast iron parts for*   Fax: (570) 638-3410   Emp: 989
      automobiles.

● **HITACHI ZOSEN CORPORATION**
7-89, Nanko-kita, 1-chome, Suminoe-ku, Osaka 559-8859, Japan
CEO: Takenao Shigefuji, Pres.   Tel: 81-6-6569-0001   Rev: $3,194
Bus: *Environmental systems & industrial plants,*   Fax: 81-6-6569-0002   Emp: 8,089
      shipbuilding & offshore & steel structures,   www.hitachizosen.co.jp
      construction machinery, logistics systems and
      machinery.
  NAICS: 236210, 236220, 237110, 237990, 333120, 334513, 335314, 541330, 541490, 541512, 562910

HITACHI ZOSEN USA LTD
301 South Perimeter Park Dr., Ste. 100, Nashville, Tennessee 37211
CEO: Takenao Shigefuji   Tel: (615) 781-4344   %FO: 100
Bus: *Sales/liaison shipbuilding repair offshore*   Fax: (615) 781-4361
      equipment.

HITACHI ZOSEN USA LTD.
767 Third Ave., 17/F, New York, New York 10017
CEO: Koichi Kaibuchi, Pres.   Tel: (212) 355-5650   %FO: 100
Bus: *Sales/liaison shipbuilding repair offshore*   Fax: (212) 308-4937   Emp: 22
      equipment.

HITACHI ZOSEN USA LTD.
1699 Wall St., Ste. 402, Mt. Prospect, Illinois 60056
CEO: Ken Inoue, Mgr.
Bus: *Sales/liaison shipbuilding repair offshore equipment.*
Tel: (847) 427-8353
Fax: (847) 427-1856
%FO: 100

HITACHI ZOSEN USA LTD.
10777 Westheimer Rd., Ste. 1075, Houston, Texas 77042
CEO: Andrew Newhouse, Mgr.
Bus: *Sales/liaison shipbuilding repair offshore equipment.*
Tel: (713) 532-9611
Fax: (713) 532-9533
%FO: 100

HITZ AMERICA
10777 Westheimer Rd., Ste. 1020, Houston, Texas 77042
CEO: Takashi Hayato, Pres.
Bus: *Engineering services*
Tel: (832) 204-5700
Fax: (832) 204-5710
Emp: 15

● **HITACHI-UNISIA AUTOMOTIVE, LTD.**
1370 Onna, Atsugi, Kanagawa 243-0032, Japan
CEO: Katsukuni Hisano, Pres.
Bus: *Automotive component supplier.*
Tel: 81-462-258025
Fax:
www.hitachi-unisia.co.jp
Rev: $1,495
Emp: 3,686

NAICS: 336399

KARL SCHMIDT UNISIA, INC.
1731 Industrial Pkwy. N, Marinette, Wisconsin 54143
CEO: Frank Pohlmann, CEO
Bus: *Pistons*
Tel: (715) 732-0181
Fax:
Emp: 1,500

UNISIA NORTH AMERICA
34500Grand River Ave., Farmington Hills, Michigan 48335
CEO: Motoki Kato, Pres.
Bus: *Development and sales of auto parts*
Tel: (248) 697-0000
Fax:
Emp: 30

UNISIA NORTH AMERICA
475 Alaska Ave., Torrance, California 90503
CEO: Hoshino Yujio, Mgr.
Bus: *Wholesale auto parts*
Tel: (310) 329-8855
Fax:

UNISIA NORTH AMERICA
1000 Unisia Dr., Monroe, Georgia 30655
CEO: Mineo Goto, Pres.
Bus: *Mfr. Evaporative purge controls, crank angle sensors, valve timing control systems & propeller shafts*
Tel: (770) 207-0050
Fax:
Emp: 94

ZUA AUTOPARTS, INC.
5750 McEver Rd., Ste. Z, Oakwood, Georgia 30566
CEO: Bernhard Freiermuth, Pres.
Bus: *Power steering pumps & gears*
Tel: (678) 455-8327
Fax:
Emp: 420

- **HOCHIKI CORPORATION**
  2-10-43, Kamiosaki, 2-chome, Shinagawa-ku, Tokyo 141-0021, Japan
  CEO: Eiichi Okada, Pres.   Tel: 81-3 3444-4111   Rev: $446
  Bus: *Fire alarms and TV equipment manufacture.*   Fax: 81-3 3444-4555   Emp: 1,425
                                               www.hochiki.co.jp

  NAICS: 333999, 334220, 334290

  HOCHIKI AMERICA CORPORATION
  7051 Village Dr., Ste. 100, Buena Park, California 90621
  CEO: Shunichi Shoji, Pres.   Tel: (714) 522-2246   %FO: 100
  Bus: *Fire alarms manufacture and distribution.*   Fax: (714) 522-2268   Emp: 72

- **THE HOKURIKU BANK, LTD.**
  1-2-26, Tsutsumicho-dori, Toyama 930-0046, Japan
  CEO: Shigeo Takagi, Pres.   Tel: 81-76-423-7111   Rev: $1,168
  Bus: *Provides banking and financial services.*   Fax: 81-76-491-6198   Emp: 3,134
                                               www.hokugin.co.jp

  NAICS: 522110

  THE HOKURIKU BANK LTD.
  780 South Ave., 28/F, New York, New York 10017
  CEO: Fumitoshi Fukasawa, Mgr.   Tel: (212) 355-3883   %FO: 100
  Bus: *Banking and financial services.*   Fax: (212) 355-3887

- **HOKURIKU ELECTRIC INDUSTRY CO.LTD.**
  3158 Shimo-okubo, Toyama 930-8686, Japan
  CEO: Masanari Nomura, Pres.   Tel: 81-76-441-2511   Rev: $3,000
  Bus: *Electronic and sensor components manufacture.*   Fax: 81-76-433-9985   Emp: 2,013
                                               www.rikuden.co.jp
  NAICS: 221111, 221112, 221113, 221121, 221122

  HOKURIKU USA CO., LTD.
  400 W. 24th St., Ste. B, National City, California 91950
  CEO: Masanari Nomura   Tel: (619) 477-7440   %FO: 100
  Bus: *Sales/distribution of film resistors and*   Fax: (619) 477-7440
     variable and high-voltage resistors.

  HOKURIKU USA COMPANY, LTD.
  2995 B Wall Triana Highway, Huntsville, Alabama 35824
  CEO: Masanari Nomura   Tel: (256) 772-9620   %FO: 100
  Bus: *Sales/distribution of film resistors and*   Fax: (256) 772-3475
     variable and high-voltage resistors.

  HOKURIKU USA COMPANY, LTD.
  200 N. Northwest Hwy., Barrington, Illinois 60010
  CEO: Masanari Nomura   Tel: (847) 382-9411   %FO: 100
  Bus: *Sales/distribution of film resistors and*   Fax: (847) 382-9412
     variable and high-voltage resistors.

- **HONDA MOTOR CO LTD.**
  2-1-1, Minami-Aoyama, 2-chome, Minato-ku, Tokyo 107-8556, Japan
  CEO: Takeo Fukui, Pres. & CEO   Tel: 81-3-3423-1111   Rev: $80,705
  Bus: *Mfr. automobiles, motorcycles & power products.*   Fax: 81-3-5412-1515   Emp: 131,600
                                         www.world.honda.com
  NAICS: 336111, 336112, 336991, 522291

  ### AMERICAN HONDA MOTOR COMPANY, INC.
  1919 Torrance Blvd., Torrance, California 90501-2722
  CEO: Koicji Kondo, Pres. & CEO   Tel: (310) 783-2000
  Bus: *Auto manufacturing*   Fax: (310) 783-2110   Emp: 15,000

  ### HONDA MOTOR CO., LTD.
  540 Madison Ave., 32/F, New York, New York 10022
  CEO: Koichi Kondo   Tel: (212) 355-9191
  Bus: *Auto manufacturing*   Fax: (212) 813-0260

  ### HONDA OF SOUTH CAROLINA MANUFACTURING, INC.
  1111 Honda Way, Timmonsville, South Carolina 29161
  CEO: Hideki Ikegawa, Pres.   Tel: (843) 346-8000
  Bus: *Motorcycle & other small engine vehicle   Fax:
  manufacturing*

- **HORIBA LTD.**
  2, Miyanohigashi-cho, Kisshoin, Minami-ku, Kyoto-shi 601-8305, Japan
  CEO: Masao Horiba, Chrm.   Tel: 81-75-312-9938   Rev: $655
  Bus: *Mfr. analyzer systems.*   Fax: 81-75-312-9936   Emp: 3,690
                                         www.horiba.co.jp
  NAICS: 334413, 334510

  ### HORIBA ABX DIAGNOSTICS
  34 Bunsen, Irvine, California 92618
  CEO: Michael A. Hawthorne   Tel: (949) 453-0500   %FO: 100
  Bus: *Mfr. scientific instruments and components.*   Fax: (949) 453-0600

  ### HORIBA INSTRUMENTS INC.
  5900 Hines Dr., Ann Arbor, Michigan 48108
  CEO: Rex Tapp, VP, VP   Tel: (734) 213-6555   %FO: 100
  Bus: *Mfr. analyzer systems.*   Fax: (734) 213-6525

  ### HORIBA INSTRUMENTS INC.
  17671 Armstrong Ave., Irvine, California 92714
  CEO: Neal Harvey, CEO   Tel: (949) 250-4811   %FO: 100
  Bus: *Mfr. analyzer systems.*   Fax: (949) 250-0924   Emp: 120

  ### HORIBA INSTRUMENTS INC.
  10240 SW Nimbus Ave., Portland, Oregon 97223
  CEO: Juichi Saito   Tel: (503) 624-9767   %FO: 100
  Bus: *Mfr. process control instruments.*   Fax: (503) 968-3236

  ### HORIBA JOBIN YVON
  3880 Park Ave., Edison, New Jersey 08820
  CEO: Andrew Whitley   Tel: (732) 494-8660   %FO: 100
  Bus: *Mfr. scientific instruments and components.*   Fax: (732) 549-5125

Japan

HORIBA STEC INCORPORATED
54 Heritage Circle, Hudson, New Hampshire 03051
CEO: Jim Woolsey
Bus: *Semiconductor instruments and systems manufacture.*

Tel: (603) 886-4167	%FO: 100
Fax: (603) 866-4267	

HORIBA STEC INCORPORATED
1080 E. Duane Ave., Ste. A, Sunnyvale, California 94085
CEO: Kensuke Nakagawa
Bus: *Semiconductor instruments and systems manufacture.*

Tel: (408) 730-8795	%FO: 100
Fax: (408) 730-8975	

HORIBA STEC INCORPORATED
2520 South Industrial Park Dr., Tempe, Arizona 85282
CEO: L. Dolley
Bus: *Crystal products manufacture.*

Tel: (602) 967-2283	%FO: 100
Fax: (602) 967-2283	

HORIBA STEC INCORPORATED
9701 Dessau Rd., Ste. 605, Austin, Texas 78754
CEO: Yvette Fisher
Bus: *Semiconductor instruments and systems manufacture.*

Tel: (513) 836-9560	%FO: 100
Fax: (512) 836-9560	

● **HOSHINO GAKKI CO. LTD.**
3-22 Shumoki-cho, Higashi-ku, Nagoya 461-8717, Japan
CEO: Tanaka Toshitsugu, CEO
Bus: *Musical instrument sales.*

Tel: 81-52-931-0381	Rev: $78
Fax: 81-52-932-2684	Emp: 280
www.hoshinogakki.co.jp	

NAICS: 339992

HOSHINO USA INC.
1726 Winchester Rd., Bensalem, Pennsylvania 19020
CEO: Bill Reim
Bus: *Musical instrument sales.*

Tel: (215) 638-8670	%FO: 100
Fax: (215) 245-8583	

● **HOSIDEN CORPORATION**
4-33 Kitakyuhoji 1-chome, Yao, Osaka 581-0071, Japan
CEO: Kenji Furuhashi, Pres. & CEO
Bus: *Electronic components manufacture.*

Tel: 81-729-93-1010	Rev: $2,133
Fax: 81-729-94-5101	Emp: 1,060
www.hosiden.co.jp	

NAICS: 334412, 334417, 334418

HOSIDEN AMERICA CORP
6815 Flanders Dr., Ste. 140, San Diego, California 92121
CEO: Yoshi Omori, Mgr.
Bus: *Sale of electronic components.*

Tel: (858) 558-8599	%FO: 100
Fax: (858) 558-9475	

HOSIDEN AMERICA CORP
3031 Tisch Way, Ste. 806, San Jose, California 95128
CEO: Tom Haraki, Pres.
Bus: *Sale of computers/ software.*

Tel: (408) 985-8780	%FO: 100
Fax: (408) 985-8785	

HOSIDEN AMERICA CORPORATION
120 E. State Pkwy., Schaumburg, Illinois 60173
CEO: Kenji Furuhashi, Pres.
Bus: *Electronic components manufacture.*

Tel: (847) 885-8870
Fax: (847) 885-0063

%FO: 100
Emp: 31

● **HOSOKAWA MICRON GROUP**
5-14, 2-chome, Kawaramachi Chuo-ku, Osaka 541-0048, Japan
CEO: Masuo Hosokawa, Chmn.
Bus: *Powder processing equipment and systems, environmental protection, filter media, plastics processing equipment.*
NAICS: 334419

Tel: 81-6-6233-3968
Fax: 81-6-6229-9261
www.hosokawa.com

Rev: $577
Emp: 421

HOSOKAWA ALPINE AMERICAN
5 Michigan Dr., Natick, Massachusetts 01760
CEO: David Nunes, Pres.
Bus: *Mfr. mono and co extrusion blown film systems.*

Tel: (508) 655-1123
Fax: (508) 655-9337

%FO: 100

HOSOKAWA AMERICAS INC.
780 Third Ave., New York, New York 10017
CEO: Simon Baker
Bus: *Marketing research services.*

Tel: (212) 826-3830
Fax: (212) 826-3830

%FO: 100

HOSOKAWA MICRON INTERNATIONAL INC.
333 NE Taft St., Minneapolis, Minnesota 55413
CEO: Paul Skogheim
Bus: *Mfr. powder processing equipment and systems.*

Tel: (612) 331-4370
Fax: (612) 627-1458

%FO: 100

HOSOKAWA MICRON INTERNATIONAL INC.
10 Chatham Rd., Summit, New Jersey 07901
CEO: Isao Sato
Bus: *Mfr. powder processing equipment and systems.*

Tel: (908) 273-6360
Fax: (908) 273-7432

Emp: 150

HOSOKAWA POLYMER SYSTEMS
63 Fuller Way, Berlin, Connecticut 06037
CEO: Doug Ort, Chmn.
Bus: *Mfr. pulverizers and auxiliary equipment for the plastics industry.*

Tel: (860) 828-0541
Fax: (860) 829-1313

%FO: 100

HOSOKAWA TECHNOLOGY SYSTEMS
8707 W. State St., Ste. C, Boise, Idaho 83703
CEO: Johann Walter
Bus: *Confectionery and bakery technology and systems.*

Tel: (208) 854-0755
Fax: (208) 854-0757

%FO: 100

● **HOYA CORPORATION**
7-5, Nakaochiai, 2-chome, Shinjuku-ku, Tokyo 161-0032, Japan
CEO: Hiroshi Suzuki, Pres.
Bus: *Mfr. ophthalmic goods.*

Tel: 81-3-3952-1151
Fax: 81-3-9352-1314
www.hoya.co.jp

Rev: $2,156
Emp: 21,234

NAICS: 333313, 333314, 339115

EAGLE OPTICS, INC.
591- F Thornton Rd., Lithia Springs, Georgia 30122
CEO: Mark Evett, Pres.   Tel: (770) 944-1800   %FO: 100
Bus: *Mfr. ophthalmic goods.*   Fax: Emp: 30

HOYA CORPORATION USA
101 Metro Dr., Ste. 500, San Jose, California 95110
CEO: Gerry Bottero, Pres.   Tel: (408) 441-0400   %FO: 100
Bus: *Mfr. ophthalmic goods.*   Fax: Emp: 600

HOYA CRYSTAL, INC.
41 Madison Ave., 9/F, New York, New York 10010
CEO: Jerald Bottero, Pres.   Tel: (212) 679-3100   %FO: 100
Bus: *Sales of crystals.*   Fax: Emp: 15

HOYA LENS OF AMERICA, INC.
13 Francis J. Clarke Circle, Bethel, Connecticut 06801
CEO: William Norwood, Pres.   Tel: (203) 790-0171   %FO: 100
Bus: *Mfr. ophthalmic goods.*   Fax: Emp: 120

HOYA LENS OF AMERICA, INC.
19750 South Vermont Ave., Torrance, California 90502
CEO: Bottero, Pres.   Tel: (310) 538-9310   %FO: 100
Bus: *Mfr. ophthalmic goods.*   Fax:

HOYA OPTICAL LABORATORIES
3531 North Martens St., Franklin Park, Illinois 60131
CEO: Paul Ingraffia Jr., Pres.   Tel: (847) 678-4700   %FO: 100
Bus: *Mfr. ophthalmic goods.*   Fax: Emp: 30

HOYA PHOTONICS, INC.
3150 Central Expressway, Santa Clara, California 95051
CEO: Fred Fink, CEO   Tel: (408) 727-3240   %FO: 100
Bus: *Mfr. ophthalmic goods.*   Fax:

● **IBIDEN CO., LTD.**
2-1 Kanda-cho, Ogaki, Gifu 503-8604, Japan
CEO: Yoshifumi Iwata, Pres.   Tel: 81-584-81-3111   Rev: $2,088
Bus: *Mfr. chemicals.*   Fax: 81-584-81-4676   Emp: 6,914
                                                        www.ibiden.co.jp
    NAICS: 325199, 325998

    IBIDEN USA CORP.
    4100 McEwen Rd., Suite 217, Dallas, Texas 75244
    CEO: Masahiro Mori   Tel: (972) 404-8730   %FO: 100
    Bus: *Mfr. chemicals.*   Fax: (972) 404-8735

    IBIDEN USA CORP.
    970 Knox St., Ste. A, Torrance, California 90502
    CEO: Masataka Ito   Tel: (310) 768-0519
    Bus: *Mfr. chemicals.*   Fax: (310) 768-0522

IBIDEN USA CORP.
2350 Mission College Blvd., Ste. 975, Santa Clara, California 95054
CEO: M. Kawasaki
Bus: *Mfr. chemicals.*
Tel: (408) 986-4343
Fax: (408) 986-4343
%FO: 100

IBIDEN USA CORP.
875 Toll Gate Rd., Elgin, Illinois 60123
CEO: Takashi Sakai
Bus: *Mfr. chemicals.*
Tel: (847) 608-4800
Fax: (847) 608-4800
%FO: 100

IBIDEN USA CORP.
33 Turnpike Rd., Ipswich, Massachusetts 01938
CEO: Takehiko Hayashi
Bus: *Mfr. chemicals.*
Tel: (978) 356-2966
Fax: (978) 356-4019
%FO: 100

IBIDEN USA CORP.
1300 N. McClintock Dr., Bldg. A, Chandler, Arizona 85226
CEO: Keiji Adachi
Bus: *Mfr. chemicals.*
Tel: (480) 726-8700
Fax: (480) 726-8700

● **IDEMITSU KOSAN CO., LTD.**
1-1, Marunouchi, 3-chome, Chiyoda-ku, Tokyo, Japan
CEO: Akira Idemitsu, Chmn.
Bus: *Refines crude oil and markets and distributes petroleum products.*
Tel: 81-3-3213-3115
Fax: 81-3-3213-9354
www.idemitsu.co.jp
Rev: $23,198
Emp: 6,306
NAICS: 324110, 324191, 324199, 424710, 424720, 447190, 454311, 454312, 454319

IDEMITSU APOLLO CORPORATION
1270 Ave. of the Americas, Ste. 420, New York, New York 10020
CEO: T. Kono, Pres.
Bus: *Sales/distribution of petroleum products.*
Tel: (212) 332-4820
Fax: (212) 322-4819
%FO: 100
Emp: 142

● **INTERNET INITIATIVE JAPAN INC.**
Jinbocho Mitsui Bldg., 1-105 Kanda Jinbo-cho, Chiyoda-ku, Tokyo 101-0051, Japan
CEO: Koichi Suzuki, Pres. & CEO
Bus: *Internet and online service provider*
Tel: 81-3-5205-6500
Fax: 81-3-5259-6311
www.iij.ad.jp
Rev: $389
Emp: 919
NAICS: 518111, 518210

INTERNET INITIATIVE JAPAN INC.
1211 Ave. of the Americas, Ste. 2900, New York, New York 10036
CEO: Isao Momota, Pres.
Bus: *Internet and online service provider.*
Tel: (212) 440-8080
Fax: (212) 869-9829
%FO: 100

INTERNET INITIATIVE JAPAN INC.
55 South Market St., Ste. 1600, San Jose, California 95113
CEO: Isao Momota, Pres.
Bus: *Internet and online service provider.*
Tel: (408) 224-2345
Fax: (408) 287-1025
%FO: 100

INTERNET INITIATIVE JAPAN INC.
990 West 190th St., Ste. 240, Torrance, California 90502
CEO: Isao Momota, Pres.
Bus: *Internet and online service provider.*
Tel: (310) 324-6007
Fax: (310) 324-2871
%FO: 100

- **ISETAN COMPANY, LTD.**
  3-14-1, Shinjuku, 3-chome, Shinjuku-ku, Tokyo 160-8001, Japan
  CEO: Nobukazu Muto, Pres. & CEO   Tel: 81-3-3352-1111   Rev: $5,820
  Bus: *Manages and operates department stores.*   Fax: 81-3-5273-5321   Emp: 9,009
                                                         www.isetan.co.jp
  NAICS: 452111, 561510

  > **ISETAN COMPANY, LTD.**
  > 1411 Broadway, Rm. 2550, New York, New York 10018
  > CEO: Tai Ogata, Mgr.   Tel: (212) 767-0300   %FO: 100
  > Bus: *Manages/operates department stores.*   Fax: (212) 767-0307

- **ISHIKAWAJIMA-HARIMA HEAVY INDUSTRIES COMPANY, LTD.**
  Shin Ohtemachi Bldg., 2-1 Ohtemachi, 2-chome, Chiyoda-ku, Tokyo 100-8182, Japan
  CEO: Mototsugu Ito, Pres. & CEO   Tel: 81-3-3244-5111   Rev: $9,915
  Bus: *Shipbuilding and repair, mfr. machinery, diesels,*   Fax: 81-3-3244-5131   Emp: 22,768
      boilers, bridges, etc.   www.ihi.co.jp
  NAICS: 333111, 333131, 333291, 333922, 334513, 335312, 335314, 336415, 336611

  > **CASTRIP LLC**
  > 2100 Rexford Rd., Ste. 420, Charlotte, North Carolina 28211
  > CEO: Brendan Killian, Mgr.   Tel: (704) 972-1820
  > Bus: *Steel production.*   Fax: (704) 972-1829

  > **COMPACT EXCAVATOR**
  > 202 Production Dr., PO Box 667, Elizabethtown, Kentucky 42701
  > CEO: Michael Smith, Pres.   Tel: (270) 737-1447
  > Bus: *Sale of compact excavators.*   Fax: (240) 737-1857   Emp: 16

  > **ICOMAC, INC.**
  > 2935 Dolphin Dr., Ste. 102, Elizabethtown, Kentucky 42701
  > CEO: Jenny Aldridge   Tel: (270) 737-9088
  > Bus: *Durable goods.*   Fax: (270) 737-9285

  > **IHI POWER-SYSTEMS AMERICA INC.**
  > 280 Park Ave., West Bldg., 30/F, New York, New York 10017
  > CEO: Mototsugu Ito   Tel: (212) 599-8100
  > Bus: *Durable goods.*   Fax: (212) 599-8111

  > **IHI PRESS TECHNOLOGY AMERICA, INC.**
  > 755 W. Big Beaver Rd., Troy, Michigan 48084
  > CEO: Hiroshi Horiguchi, Gen. Mgr.   Tel: (248) 244-9370   %FO: 100
  > Bus: *Shipbuilding and repair technical*   Fax: (248) 244-9062   Emp: 15
  >   *consultants; sale of ship-building material.*

  > **IHI SOUTHWEST TECHNOLOGIES INC.**
  > 6220 Culebra Rd., Ste. 177, San Antonio, Texas 78238
  > CEO: Bruce Jacobs, Pres.   Tel: (210) 256-4100
  > Bus: *Nondestructive examination/engineering* Fax: (210) 521-2311   Emp: 30
  >   *services.*

IHI TURBO AMERICA CO.
Rte. 16 West, RR3 BOX 36, Shelbyville, Illinois 62565
CEO: F. Nakamura, Pres.   Tel: (217) 774-9571
Bus: *Mfr. of turbo chargers, & valves.*   Fax: (217) 774-3834   Emp: 86

IHI VERSON PRESS TECHNOLOGY LLC
1355 East 93rd St., Door # 12, Chicago, Illinois 60619
CEO: Mototsugu Ito   Tel: (773) 356-6089
Bus: *Durable goods.*   Fax: (773) 356-8640

IHI, INC.
280 Park Ave., West Bldg., 30/F, New York, New York 10017
CEO: Noritaka Kosaka   Tel: (212) 599-8100   %FO: 100
Bus: *Shipbuilding and repair technical*   Fax: (212) 599-8111
    consultants; sale of ship-building material.

ISM AMERICA INC.
280 Park Ave., West Bldg., 30/F, New York, New York 10017
CEO: Katsiutoshi Nomura, CEO   Tel: (212) 599-8100
Bus: *Durable goods.*   Fax: (212) 599-8111

PERKINS SHIBAURA ENGINES LLC
325 Green Valley Rd., Griffin, Georgia 30224
CEO: Hae Sali, member   Tel: (770) 233-5896
Bus: *Mfr. of diesel engines.*   Fax: (770) 233-6352   Emp: 23

● **ISUZU MOTORS LTD.**
26-1, Minami-oi, 6-chome, Shinagawa-ku, Tokyo 140-8722, Japan
CEO: Yoshinori Ida, Pres.   Tel: 81-3 5471-1141   Rev: $13,540
Bus: *Mfr. motor vehicles, parts and accessories.*   Fax: 81-3-5471-1043   Emp: 18,130
                www.isuzu.co.jp
    NAICS: 336111, 336112

    AMERICAN ISUZU MOTORS, INC.
    13340 183rd St., Cerritos, California 90702
    CEO: J. Terry Maloney, Pres.   Tel: (562) 229-5000   %FO: 100
    Bus: *Sale/service trucks, sport utility vehicles.*   Fax: (562) 926-3082   Emp: 600

    GENERAL MOTORS ISUZU COMMERCIAL TRUCK
    13340 183rd. St., Cerritos, California 90702
    CEO: Gaku Nitta, Pres.   Tel: (562) 229-5000   %FO: 100
    Bus: *Mfr. commercial motor vehicles.*   Fax: (562) 229-3082   Emp: 200

● **ITO EN, LTD**
47-10, Honmachi, 3-chome, Shibuya-ku, Tokyo 151-8550, Japan
CEO: Hachiro Honjo, Pres.   Tel: 81-3-5371-7111   Rev: $2,178
Bus: *Coffee and tea production.*   Fax: 81-3-5371-7184   Emp: 4,229
                www.itoen.co.jp
    NAICS: 311920

ITO EN NORTH AMERICA, INC.
45 Main St., Ste. 3A, Brooklyn, New York 11201
CEO: Yosuke Honjo, Pres.   Tel: (718) 250-4000   %FO: 100
Bus: *Mfr. & sales of green tea & beverage* Fax: (718) 246-1325   Emp: 65
    products.

KAI NORTH AMERICA LLC
822 Madison Ave., New York, New York 10021
CEO: Rona Tison, Mgr.   Tel: (212) 988-7277   %FO: 100
Bus: *Restaurant management.*   Fax:

● **ITOCHU CORPORATION**
5-1, Kita Aoyama, 2 chome, Minato-ku, Tokyo 107-8077, Japan
CEO: Eizo Kobayashi, Pres. & CEO   Tel: 81-3-3497-2121   Rev: $5,865
Bus: *General international trading activities;* Fax: 81-3-3497-4141   Emp: 40,737
    construction, research, science and air lease www.itochu.co.jp
    divisions.
NAICS: 313111, 321113, 333295, 334113, 334119, 334220, 334419, 336411, 336413, 423430, 423450, 424410, 424690, 444190

CGB ENTERPRISES, INC.
1001 Hwy. 190 Service Rd. East, Ste. 200, Covington, Louisiana 70433
CEO: Kevin Adams, Pres. & CEO   Tel: (985) 867-3500   %FO: 100
Bus: *Agricultural support activities & products.* Fax: (985) 867-3506   Emp: 700

CHEMOIL CORPORATION
4 Embarcadero Center, Ste. 1100, San Francisco, California 94111
CEO: Robert V. Chandran, Pres. & CEO   Tel: (415) 268-2700   %FO: JV
Bus: *Marine bunker fuels.*   Fax: (415) 268-2701

ITOCHU INTERNATIONAL INC.
20 North Martingale Rd., Ste. 290, Schaumburg, Illinois 60173
CEO: John Romans, Mgr.   Tel: (847) 273-7000   %FO: 100
Bus: *Sale of chemicals & products.*   Fax: (847) 706-9349   Emp: 13

ITOCHU INTERNATIONAL INC.
4045 E. Thousand Oaks Blvd., Ste. 105, Westlake, California 91362
CEO: Ken Sellinger   Tel: (805) 379-4875   %FO: 100
Bus: *Foreign sea freight transportation.*   Fax: (805) 379-5966

ITOCHU INTERNATIONAL INC.
One S.W. Columbia St., Ste. 730, Portland, Oregon 97258
CEO: Toru Nishizaka, Sales Mgr.   Tel: (503) 227-6694   %FO: 100
Bus: *Mfr. of food preparations.*   Fax: (503) 226-3054   Emp: 4

ITOCHU INTERNATIONAL INC.
725 South Figueroa St., Ste. 3050, Los Angeles, California 90017
CEO: Katuyuki Pakapa, Mgr.   Tel: (213) 488-8300   %FO: 100
Bus: *General international trading activities in* Fax: (213) 614-0001
    cotton.

ITOCHU INTERNATIONAL INC.
180 Montgomery St., Ste. 2360, San Francisco, California 94104
CEO: Yoichi Okuda   Tel: (415) 399-3700   %FO: 100
Bus: *General international trading activities.* Fax: (415) 398-4648

ITOCHU INTERNATIONAL INC.
1300 Post Oak Blvd., Ste. 900, Houston, Texas 77056
CEO: Taijiro Sakagami, Mgr.
Bus: *General international trading activities.*

Tel: (713) 843-6500
Fax: (713) 843-6620

%FO: 100
Emp: 10

ITOCHU INTERNATIONAL INC.
Bank of America Plaza, 335 Madison Ave., 22/F, 23/F & 24/F, New York, New York 10017
CEO: Yoshio Akamatsu, Pres. & CEO
Bus: *General international trading activities.*

Tel: (212) 818-8000
Fax: (212) 818-8543

%FO: 100
Emp: 4,500

ITOCHU INTERNATIONAL INC.
2 Lafayette Centre, 1133 21st St.NW, Ste. 200, Washington, District of Columbia 20036
CEO: Taku Motloka, Gen. Mgr.
Bus: *General international trading activities.*

Tel: (202) 822-9082
Fax: (202) 822-9233

%FO: 100
Emp: 10

MARUBENI-ITOCHU STEEL AMERICA INC.
450 Lexington Ave., 34/F, New York, New York 10017
CEO: Hiroatsu Fujisawa, Pres. & CEO
Bus: *Steel service centers.*

Tel: (212) 450-0387
Fax: (212) 450-0790

%FO: 100
Emp: 1,202

MASTER-HALCO INC.
4000 W. Metropolitan Dr., Ste. 400, Orange, California 92868
CEO: Gregory Jendreas, Pres. & CEO
Bus: *Construction materials.*

Tel: (714) 385-0091
Fax: (714) 385-0107

%FO: 100
Emp: 1,615

PRIMESOURCE BUILDING PRODUCTS, INC.
2115 East Beltline Rd., Carrollton, Texas 75006
CEO: Charlie Choi, Chmn. & CEO
Bus: *Building materials retail & distribution.*

Tel: (972) 417-3701
Fax: (972) 416-3910

%FO: 100

SOS METALS, INC.
9050 Centre Pointe Dr., Ste. 200, West Chester, Ohio 45069
CEO: Toshio Adachi, Pres. & CEO
Bus: *Steel service centers.*

Tel: (513) 896-2700
Fax: (513) 896-2790

%FO: 100
Emp: 300

XYTEL CORPORATION
4220 S. Church St. Expansion, Roebuck, South Carolina 29376
CEO: Jay Khadye, Pres.
Bus: *Commercial & heavy construction.*

Tel: (864) 576-9777
Fax: (864) 576-9799

%FO: 100

• ITOHAM FOODS INC.
4-27 Takahata-cho, Hyogo, Nishinomiya City 6638586, Japan
CEO: Masami Ito, CEO
Bus: *Fresh and processed meat products manufacture and pharmaceutical drug research.*

Tel: 81-798-66-1231
Fax: 81-798-64-1140
www.itoham.co.jp

Rev: $4,664
Emp: 5,777

NAICS: 311611, 311612, 311613, 325412, 424440, 424820

AMERICAN PEPTIDE INC.
777 East Evelyn Ave., Sunnyvale, California 94088
CEO: Chris Bai
Bus: *Provides tools for peptide and protein research.*

Tel: (408) 733-7604
Fax: (408) 733-7603

%FO: 100

ITOHAM AMERICA INC.
3190 Corporate
CEO: Place, Hayward, California 94545　　　Ron Vincenzi　　　Tel: (510) 780-
4115　%FO: 100

　Bus: *Mfr. Italian specialty meat, and processed*　Fax: (510) 887-0882
　　　meat products.

WYOMING PREMIUM FARMS INC.
394 State Highway 26, Wheatland, Wyoming 82201
CEO: Doug Varushi　　　　　　　Tel: (307) 322-9285　　　%FO: 100
Bus: *Hog farm.*　　　　　　　　Fax: (307) 322-9285

● **ITO-YOKADA COMPANY, LTD.**
8-8, Nibancho, Chiyoda-ku, Tokyo 102-8450, Japan
CEO: Sakae Isaka, Pres. & COO　　　　Tel: 81-3-6238-2111　　Rev: $28,948
Bus: *Operates convenience stores (7-Eleven) and*　Fax: 81-3-6238-3492　Emp: 47,947
　　　specialty stores, department stores and　www.itoyokada.iyg.co.jp
　　　supermarkets.
　NAICS: 445110, 445120, 447110, 452111, 452910, 522210, 722110

7-ELEVEN, INC.
2711 North Haskell Ave., Dallas, Texas 75204
CEO: James W. Keyes, Pres. & CEO　　Tel: (214) 828-7011　　%FO: 73
Bus: *Operates convenience stores.*　　Fax: (214) 828-7848　　Emp: 31,500

ITO YOKADO CO.LTD.
1 Union Square, 600 University St., Ste. 1916, Seattle, Washington 98101
CEO: Hitoshi Yamanaka, Gen. Mgr.　　Tel: (206) 667-8973
Bus: *Commercial nonphysical research.*　Fax: (206) 667-8971

● **IWATANI INTERNATIONAL CORPORATION**
21-8 Nishi-Shimbashi 3- chome, Minato-ku, Tokyo 105-8458, Japan
CEO: Akiji Makino, Pres.　　　　　Tel: 81-3-5405-5741　　Rev: $5,223
Bus: *Consumer products, agricultural and medical*　Fax: 81-3-5405-5737　Emp: 6,598
　　　products, industrial gases/materials and　www.iwatani.co.jp
　　　construction.
　NAICS: 112210, 236115, 236116, 236117, 236118, 334413, 424690, 454312, 454319

IWATANI INTERNATIONAL CORPORATION OF AMERICA
385 Van Ness Ave., Ste.110, Torrance, California 90501
CEO: Akito Ovasa, Pres.　　　　　Tel: (310) 212-3331　　%FO: 100
Bus: *Sales of consumer products,*　　Fax: (310) 320-6477　　Emp: 15
　　　agricultural/medical products, industrial
　　　gases/materials and construction.

U.S. PORTABLE ENERGY CORP.
385 Van Ness Ave., Ste. 110, Torrance, California 90501
CEO: Chang SOO Hyun, Pres.　　　Tel: (310) 212-3632
Bus: *sale of gas canisters & burners*　Fax: (310) 320-6477　　Emp: 3

- **THE IYO BANK LTD.**
  1, Minami-Horibata-cho, Matsuyama 790-8514, Japan
  CEO: Shunsuke Aso, Pres.
  Bus: *Commercial banking services.*

  Tel: 81-89-941-1141
  Fax:
  www.iyobank.co.jp

  Rev: $770
  Emp: 2,892

  NAICS: 522110, 522120

  THE IYO BANK LTD.
  780 Third Ave., 18/F, New York, New York 10017
  CEO: Hiromichi Yoshikawa, Mgr.
  Bus: *Commercial banking services.*

  Tel: (212) 688-6031
  Fax: (212) 688-6420

  %FO: 100
  Emp: 10

- **JAFCO CO., LTD.**
  1-8-2, Marunochi, Chiyoda-ku, Tokyo 100-005, Japan
  CEO: Toshiaki Ito, Pres.
  Bus: *Capital ventures.*

  Tel: 81-3-5223-7536
  Fax: 81-3-5223-7561
  www.jafco.co.jp

  Rev: $169
  Emp: 358

  NAICS: 525990

  JAFCO AMERICA VENTURES, INC.
  505 Hamilton Ave., Ste. 310, Palo Alto, California 94301
  CEO: Joe Horowitz, Pres.
  Bus: *Engaged in capital ventures.*

  Tel: (650) 463-8800
  Fax: (650) 463-8801

  %FO: 100

  JAFCO AMERICA VENTURES, INC.
  One Boston Place, Ste. 2810, Boston, Massachusetts 02108
  CEO: Andy Goldfarb, Dir.
  Bus: *Engaged in capital ventures.*

  Tel: (617) 367-3510
  Fax: (617) 367-3532

  %FO: 100

- **JAPAN AIRLINES CORPORATION**
  4-11, Higashi-shinagawa, 2 chome, Shinagawa-ku, Tokyo 140-8605, Japan
  CEO: Toshiyuki Shinmachi, Pres. & CEO
  Bus: *International airline, hotels/catering.*

  Tel: 81-3-5769-6097
  Fax: 81-3-5460-5929
  www.jal.co.jp

  Rev: $18,286
  Emp: 54,053

  NAICS: 481111, 481112, 481212, 721110

  JAPAN AIRLINES
  461 Fifth Ave., New York, New York 10017
  CEO: Toshiyuki Shinmachi, CEO
  Bus: *International air transport services.*

  Tel: (212) 310-1454
  Fax: (212) 310-1230

  %FO: 100

- **JAPAN AVIATION ELECTRONICS INDUSTRY LTD.**
  21-2, Dogenzaka, 1-chome, Shibuya-ku, Tokyo 150-0043, Japan
  CEO: Masami Shinozaki, Pres.
  Bus: *Mfr. connectors and switches.*

  Tel: 81-3-3780-2711
  Fax: 81-3-3780-2733
  www.jae.co.jp

  Rev: $860
  Emp: 4,282

  NAICS: 334417, 334511, 335314

  JAE ELECTRONICS INC.
  142 Technology Dr., Ste. 100, Irvine, California 92618
  CEO: Yasuo Takagi, Pres.
  Bus: *Distribution/sale switches and connectors.*

  Tel: (949) 753-2600
  Fax: (949) 753-2699

  %FO: 100
  Emp: 261

JAE ELECTRONICS INC.
11555 SW Leveton Dr., Tualatin, Oregon 97062
CEO: Katsumi Watanabe, Pres.   Tel: (503) 692-1333
Bus: *Mfr. of electronic connectors.*   Fax: Emp: 252

• **JAPAN RADIO COMPANY, LTD.**
Nittochi Nishi-Shinjuku Bldg., 10-1 Nishi-Shinjuku 6-chome, Tokyo 160-8328, Japan
CEO: Yorihisa Suwa, Pres.   Tel: 81-3-3348-0151   Rev: $1,056
Bus: *Mfr. marine/land radio and navigation equipment.*   Fax: Emp: 8,739
                                                   www.jrc.co.jp
  NAICS: 334220, 334413, 334510, 334511

  JAPAN RADIO CO LTD.
  2125 Center Ave., Ste. 208, Fort Lee, New Jersey 07024
  CEO: Peter Kiko   Tel: (201) 242-1882   %FO: 100
  Bus: *Sale of marine/land radio and navigation* Fax: (201) 242-1885
        equipment.

  JAPAN RADIO COMPANY, LTD.
  1021 SW Klickitat Way, Bldg. D, Ste. 101, Seattle, Washington 98134
  CEO: Buddy Morgan   Tel: (206) 654-5644   %FO: 100
  Bus: *Sale of marine/land radio and navigation* Fax: (206) 654-7030
        equipment.

• **THE JAPAN STEEL WORKS, LTD.**
Hibiya Mitsui Bldg., 1-2, Yuraku-cho, 1-chome, Chiyoda-ku, Tokyo 100-8456, Japan
CEO: Masahisa Nagata, Pres.   Tel: 81-3-3501-6111   Rev: $1,290
Bus: *Produces defense equipment, steel products and* Fax: 81-3-3504-0727 Emp: 2,070
      industrial machinery.   www.jsw.co.jp
  NAICS: 331111, 331210, 331221, 333220

  JAPAN STEEL WORKS AMERICA INC.
  9801 Westheimer, Ste. 1050, Houston, Texas 77042
  CEO: Masahiko Taguchi, Mgr.   Tel: (713) 953-9151   %FO: 100
  Bus: *Mfr. steel products and industrial*   Fax: (713) 953-1439
        machinery.

  JAPAN STEEL WORKS AMERICA, INC.
  1211 Ave. of the Americas (6th Ave.), 43/F, New York, New York 10036
  CEO: Koichi Tokai, Pres.   Tel: (212) 490-2630   %FO: 100
  Bus: *Mfr. steel products and industrial*   Fax: (212) 490-2575   Emp: 8
        machinery.

  JSW PLASTICS MACHINERY, INC.
  1700 Cumberland Point Dr., Ste. 17, Marietta, Georgia 30067
  CEO: M. Greenwell   Tel: (770) 952-0269
  Bus: *Plastics & industrial machinery*   Fax: (770) 956-9058

  JSW PLASTICS MACHINERY, INC.
  24404 Catherine Industrial Dr., Ste. 310, Novi, Michigan 48375
  CEO: Tel: (248) 449-5422
  Bus: *Plastics & industrial machinery.*   Fax: (248) 449-6018

JSW PLASTICS MACHINERY, INC.
1300 Landmeier Rd., Elk Grove Village, Illinois 60007
CEO:
Bus: *Plastics & industrial machinery*
Tel: (847) 427-1100
Fax: (847) 427-1121

JSW PLASTICS MACHINERY, INC.
555 South Promenade Ave., Unit 104, Corona, California 92879
CEO:
Bus: *Plastics & industrial machinery*
Tel: (951) 898-0934
Fax: (951) 898-0944

• **JAPAN TOBACCO INC.**
2-1, Toranomon, 2-chome, Minato-ku, Tokyo 105-8422, Japan
CEO: Katsuhiko Honda, Pres. & CEO
Bus: *Mfr. tobacco, salt, food and pharmaceutical products.*
Tel: 81-3-3582-3111
Fax: 81-3-5572-1441
www.jti.co.jp
Rev: $43,782
Emp: 39,243
NAICS: 311411, 311421, 312111, 312221, 325411

   JAPAN TOBACCO INC.
   4700 Homewood Ct., Ste. 240, Raleigh, North Carolina 27609
   CEO: Yasuhiko Bunazowa, Mgr.
   Bus: *Mfr. tobacco, salt, food and pharmaceutical products.*
   Tel: (919) 782-1076
   Fax:
   %FO: 100
   Emp: 9

   JAPAN TOBACCO INTERNATIONAL USA INC.
   910 Sylvan Ave., Englewood Cliffs, New Jersey 07632
   CEO: Thomas Hirshfield, Pres.
   Bus: *Tobacco products manufacture and sales.*
   Tel: (201) 871-1210
   Fax: (201) 871-1210
   %FO: 100
   Emp: 58

• **JATCO LTD.**
700-1, Imaizumi, Fuji City, Shizuoka 417-0001, Japan
CEO: Shigeo Ishida, Pres. & CEO
Bus: *Import, sales and development of automatic transmissions and components.*
Tel: 81-54-553-9627
Fax: 81-54-553-9628
www.jatco.co.jp
Emp: 7,576
NAICS: 336399

   JATCO USA INC.
   30893 Century Dr., Wixom, Michigan 48393
   CEO: Tsuneaki Machida, Pres.
   Bus: *Import, sales and development of automatic transmissions and components.*
   Tel: (248) 668-7120
   Fax: (248) 668-9802
   %FO: 100

• **JEOL LTD.**
1-2, Musashino, 3-chome, Akishima Tokyo 196-8558, Japan
CEO: Terukazu Eto, Chmn. & CEO
Bus: *Scientific instruments manufacture, including electron optics and semiconductor and medical equipment.*
Tel: 81-42-543-1111
Fax: 81-42-546-3353
www.jeol.co.jp
Rev: $824
Emp: 3,086
NAICS: 333295, 333314, 334413, 334510, 334516

   JEOL USA, INC.
   5663 Stoneridge Dr., Ste. 122, Pleasanton, California 94588
   CEO: K. Yasutake, Pres.
   Bus: *Distribute/service scientific instruments.*
   Tel: (925) 737-1752
   Fax:
   %FO: 100

JEOL USA, INC.
11 Dearborn Rd., Peabody, Massachusetts 01960
CEO: Robert T. Santorelli, Pres. & CEO   Tel: (978) 535-5900   %FO: 100
Bus: *Distribute/service scientific instruments.*   Fax: (978) 536-2205   Emp: 320

• **JFE SHOJI HOLDINGS, INC.**
2-7-1, Otemachi Chiyoda-ku, Tokyo 100-8070, Japan
CEO: Hiroo Naruki, Pres. & CEO   Tel: 81-3-5203-5510   Rev: $11,165
Bus: *General trading company; heavy machinery and*   Fax: 81-3-5203-5289   Emp: 1,600
construction building materials. (50% JV Mitsui   www.jfe-shoji-hd.co.jp
Engineering & Shipbuilding Co. Ltd.)
NAICS: 424410, 424490, 424690, 444190

  AMERICAN SOY PRODUCTS, INC.
  1474 North Woodland Dr., Saline, Michigan 48176
  CEO: Hiroyasu Iwatsuki, CEO   Tel: (734) 429-2310   %FO: 100
  Bus: *Food manufacturing and sales.*   Fax: (734) 429-2112   Emp: 42

  JFE SHOJI TRADE AMERICA INC.
  45 Broadway, 18/F, New York, New York 10006
  CEO: Tatsuji Togawa, Pres.   Tel: (212) 841-7400   %FO: 100
  Bus: *Import and export of steel products. U.S.*   Fax: (212) 841-7465   Emp: 55
  headquarters.

  JFE SHOJI TRADE AMERICA INC.
  One World Trade Center, Ste. 450, Long Beach, California 90831
  CEO: Akira Suzuki, Mgr.   Tel: (562) 637-3500   %FO: 100
  Bus: *Mfr./sales of food.*   Fax: (562) 637-3501   Emp: 7

  JFE SHOJI TRADE AMERICA INC.
  10333 Richmond, Ste. 810, Houston, Texas 77042
  CEO: Yuji Sugiura   Tel: (713) 952-2591   %FO: 100
  Bus: *Welded steel pipe manufacturing.*   Fax: (713) 952-2595

  VEST INC.
  6023 Alcoa Ave., Los Angeles, California 90058
  CEO: Iwaki Sugimoto, Pres.   Tel: (323) 581-8823
  Bus: *Mfr. of welded steel pipe.*   Fax: (323) 581-3465   Emp: 125

• **JFE HOLDINGS, INC.**
1-2, Marunouchi, 1-chome, Chiyoda-ku, Tokyo 100-0005, Japan
CEO: Yoichi Shimogaichi, Pres. & CEO   Tel: 81-3-3217-4049   Rev: $23,416
Bus: *Steel products, shipbuilding, engineering, heavy*   Fax: 81-3-3214-6110   Emp: 52,577
industrial equipment, new material.   www.jfe-holdings.co.jp
NAICS: 331111, 331221, 331222, 332420, 333319, 334119, 334413, 336611, 541330, 541620, 551112, 562112,
562213, 562219

  CALIFORNIA STEEL INDUSTRIES, INC.
  14000 San Bernardino Ave., PO Box 5080, Fontana, California 92335
  CEO: Kyle Schulty   Tel: (909) 350-6300
  Bus: *Steel products, shipbuilding, engineering,*   Fax: (909) 350-6398
  heavy industrial equipment, new material.

JFE STEEL CORPORATION
10777 Westheimer Rd., Houston, Texas 77042
CEO: Hidenoki Tazawa
Bus: *Steel products, shipbuilding, engineering,
heavy industrial equipment, new material.*
Tel: (713) 532-0052
Fax: (713) 532-0062

JFE STEEL CORPORATION
2000 Town Ctr., Ste. 1900, Southfield, Michigan 48075
CEO: Shuji Kiyama, Mgr.
Bus: *Steel products, shipbuilding, engineering,
heavy industrial equipment, new material.*
Tel: (248) 351-6290
Fax:

KAWASAKI MICROELECTRONICS AMERICA, INC
2570 North First St., Ste. 301, San Jose, California 95131
CEO: Yukio Yamauchi
Bus: *Technical services for steel customers.*
Tel: (408) 570-0555
Fax:
%FO: 100

KAWASAKI MICROELECTRONICS AMERICA, INC
201 Edgewater Dr., Ste. 251, Wakefield, Massachusetts 01880
CEO: Jack Bittner
Bus: *Liaison office; information and technical
services for steel customers.*
Tel: (781) 224-4201
Fax:
%FO: 100

● **JGC CORPORATION**
2-3-1 Minato Mirai, Nishi-ku, Yokohama 220-6601, Japan
CEO: Yoshihiro Shigehisa, Chmn. & CEO
Bus: *Engineering, design, and commercial*
Tel: 81-45-682-1111
Fax: 81-45-682-1112
www.jpc.co.jp
Rev: $3,881
Emp: 4,063
NAICS: 236210, 237990, 325998, 541330

JGC (USA) INC.
10370 Richmond Ave., Ste. 800, Houston, Texas 77042
CEO:
Bus: *Engineering, design, and commercial
construction.*
Tel: (713) 789-1441
Fax: (713) 975-7874
%FO: 100

● **JIJI PRESS LTD.**
Jiji Press Bldg., 9/F, 5-15-8 Ginza, Chuo-ku, Tokyo 104-8178, Japan
CEO: Seizo Wakabayashi, Pres.
Bus: *News syndicate providing news services for
newspapers, TV and radio stations, and news
agencies in Japan and abroad.*
Tel: 81-3-3591-1111
Fax: 81-3-3508-1298
www.jinjapan.org
Rev: $495
Emp: 1,101
NAICS: 519110

JIJI PRESS AMERICA, LTD.
120 West 45th St., Ste. 1401, New York, New York 10036
CEO: Yoshikastsu Suguki, Pres.
Bus: *News agency.*
Tel: (212) 575-5830
Fax: (212) 764-3951
%FO: 100
Emp: 15

JIJI PRESS AMERICA, LTD.
175 West Jackson Blvd., Chicago, Illinois 60604
CEO: Yutaka Nakajima, Mgr.
Bus: *News agency.*
Tel: (312) 427-5865
Fax: (312) 427-5865
%FO: 100

JIJI PRESS AMERICA, LTD.
550 National Press Bldg., Washington, District of Columbia 20045
CEO: Sakakieab Juballa, Pres.   Tel: (202) 783-4330   %FO: 100
Bus: *News agency.*   Fax: (202) 783-4330

JIJI PRESS AMERICA, LTD.
455 S. Figueroa St., Ste. 2320, Los Angeles, California 90017
CEO: Naoki Odaira, Mgr.   Tel: (213) 488-0958   %FO: 100
Bus: *News agency.*   Fax: (213) 488-0958

JIJI PRESS AMERICA, LTD.
317 South Ashton Ave., Millbrae, California 94030
CEO: Malky Odaira, Controller   Tel: (650) 692-0108   %FO: 100
Bus: *News agency.*   Fax: (650) 692-0108

● **JSP CORPORATION**
3-4-2, Marunouchi, Chiyoda-ku, Tokyo 100-0005, Japan
CEO: Masaaki Harada, Chmn.   Tel: 81-3-6212-6300   Rev: $736
Bus: *Mfr. of foamed plastic products*   Fax: 81-3-6212-6302   Emp: 757
                                                www.co-jsp.co.jp
NAICS: 325211, 325212, 325221, 325222

    JSP INTERNATIONAL
    273 Great Valley Pkwy., Malvern, Pennsylvania 19355-1308
    CEO: Carl Moyer, Pres. & CEO   Tel: (610) 651-8600   %FO: 100
    Bus: *Manufacturer of expanded polypropylene*   Fax: (610) 651-8601
        beads.

● **JSR CORPORATION**
6-10 Tsukiji 5-chome, Chuo-ku, Tokyo 104-8410, Japan
CEO: Yoshinori Yoshida, CEO   Tel: 81-3-3206-2800   Rev: $2,674
Bus: *Mfr. synthetic and specialty rubbers and rubber-*   Fax: 81-3-3206-2809   Emp: 4,362
    based products.   www.jsr.co.jp
NAICS: 325211, 325212, 325221, 325222

    JSR AMERICA INC.
    312 Elm St., Ste. 1585, Cincinnati, Ohio 45202
    CEO: Yoshiaki Zama   Tel: (513) 421-6166   %FO: 100
    Bus: *Designs and provides materials for leading*   Fax: (513) 421-6148
        semiconductor manufacturers.

    JSR MICRO INC.
    1280 N. Mathilda Ave., Sunnyvale, California 94089
    CEO: Eric R. Johnson   Tel: (408) 543-8800   %FO: 100
    Bus: *Designs and provides materials for leading*   Fax: (408) 543-8999
        semiconductor manufacturers.

    TECHNO POLYMER AMERICA, INC.
    38777 W. Six Mile Rd., Ste. 204, Livonia, Michigan 48152
    CEO: Ikuo Watanabe   Tel: (734) 953-8843   %FO: 100
    Bus: *Resins and plastics manufacture.*   Fax: (734) 953-8973

● **JTB CORPORATION**
JTB Bldg., 2-3-11 Higashi-Shinagawa, Shinagawa-ku, Tokyo 100-0005, Japan
CEO: Takashi Sasaki, Pres. & CEO   Tel: 81-3-3284-7502   Rev: $10,323
Bus: *Travel services.*   Fax: 81-3-3284-7050
www.jtb.co.jp

NAICS: 519190, 561510, 561599

JTB HAWAII, INC.
2155 Kalakaua Ave., 9/F, Honolulu, Hawaii 96815-2335
CEO: Noriharu Takazawa, Pres. & CEO   Tel: (808) 922-0200   %FO: 100
Bus: *Travel services.*   Fax: (808) 926-9200   Emp: 400

JTB INC.
810 Seventh Ave., 34/F, New York, New York 10019
CEO: Toshio Matsugu   Tel: (212) 698-4900   %FO: 100
Bus: *Travel services.*   Fax: (212) 586-9686

● **KAGOME CO. LTD**
3-14-15 Nishiki, Naka-ku, Nagoya 460-0003, Japan
CEO: Koji Kioka, Pres. & CEO   Tel: 81-52-951-3571   Rev: $1,466
Bus: *Mfr. of sauces and condiments*   Fax: 81-52-968-2510   Emp: 1,942
www.kagome.co.jp

NAICS: 311421, 311941, 311942

KAGOME INC.
353 Vintage Park Dr., Ste. G, Foster City, California 94404
CEO: Don Polk, VP Sales   Tel: (650) 349-2271   %FO: 100
Bus: *Manufacturer of sauces and condiments*   Fax: (650) 349-6570

KAGOME INC.
333 Johnson Rd., Los Banos, California 93635-9768
CEO: Don Polk, VP Sales   Tel: (209) 826-8850   %FO: 100
Bus: *Manufacturer of sauces and condiments*   Fax: (209) 826-8858

● **KAJIMA CORPORATION**
2-7, Motoakasaka, 1-chome, Minato-ku, Tokyo 107-8388, Japan
CEO: Sadao Umeda, Pres.   Tel: 81-3-3404-3311   Rev: $15,352
Bus: *General contracting, architectural and*   Fax: 81-3-3470-1444   Emp: 9,910
engineering services.   www.kajima.co.jp
NAICS: 236220, 237310, 237990, 531210, 541310, 541330, 541620, 562910

INDUSTRIAL DEVELOPMENTS INTERNATIONAL INC.
3424 Peachtree Rd. NE, Ste. 1500, Atlanta, Georgia 30326
CEO: Henry D. Gregory, Pres. & CEO   Tel: (404) 479-4000
Bus: *Commercial property investment.*   Fax: (404) 479-4162

KAJIMA U.S.A. INC.
1251 Ave. of the Americas, 9/F, New York, New York 10020
CEO: Hiroaki Hoshino, Pres. & CEO   Tel: (212) 355-4571   %FO: 100
Bus: *Real estate investment & development and*   Fax: (212) 355-4576   Emp: 488
general contracting, architectural &
engineering services.

- **KANEBO, LTD.**
  20-20, Kaigan, 3-chome, Minato-ku, Tokyo 108-8080, Japan
  CEO: Takehiko Ogi, Pres.   Tel: 81-3-5446-3002   Rev: $4,143
  Bus: *Produces cosmetics and textiles.*   Fax: 81-3-5446-3027   Emp: 13,580
                                                     www.kanebo.co.jp
  NAICS: 325412, 325620, 446120
  - **KANEBO, LTD.**
    693 Fifth Ave., 17/F, New York, New York 10022
    CEO: Hiroshi Yuki, Pres.   Tel: (212) 339-9700   %FO: 100
    Bus: *Sales/distribution of cosmetics and textiles.*   Fax: (212) 750-3600

- **KANEKA CORPORATION**
  Asahi-Shimbun Bldg., 3-2-4, Nakanoshima Kita-ku, Osaka 530-8288, Japan
  CEO: Takeshi Furuta, Chmn.   Tel: 81-6-6226-5050   Rev: $3,789
  Bus: *Mfr. performance polymers, plastic products, food*   Fax: 81-6-6226-5037   Emp: 6,597
       products, electronic equipment, pharmaceuticals   www.kaneka.co.jp
       and medical devices.
  NAICS: 311223, 311999, 325181, 325211, 325411, 326199, 331222, 331422, 332618, 335999, 339112
  - **KANEKA AMERICA CORPORATION**
    546 Fifth Ave., 21/F, New York, New York 10036
    CEO: Kazuo Kuruma, Pres.   Tel: (212) 705-4340   %FO: 100
    Bus: *Public relations, Sales promotion marketing*   Fax: (212) 705-4350   Emp: 68
         research & advertising agency

  - **KANEKA CORP.**
    2 Northpoint Dr., Ste. 200, Houston, Texas 77060
    CEO: Dayl Hilpert, Mgr.   Tel: (281) 291-3136
    Bus: *Management consulting services*   Fax:

  - **KANEKA TEXAS HIGHTECH MATERIALS, CORPORATION**
    6161 Underwood Rd., Pasadena, Texas 77507
    CEO: Kazuhiko Makino, Pres.   Tel: (281) 291-4464   %FO: 100
    Bus: *Dry, condensed, evaporated products*   Fax: (281) 291-2110   Emp: 63

- **KANEMATSU CORPORATION**
  2-1, Shibaura 1-chome, Minato-ku, Tokyo 105-8005, Japan
  CEO: Tadashi Kurachi, Chmn.   Tel: 81-3-5440-8111   Rev: $7,748
  Bus: *International trading company engaged in*   Fax: 81-3-5440-6500   Emp: 4,194
       petroleum, machinery, textiles, metals and food   www.kanematsu.co.jp
       products.
  NAICS: 334413, 423430, 424410, 424480, 424490, 424690, 424720
  - **KANEMATSU (USA) INC**
    1785 Fox Dr., San Jose, California 95131
    CEO: Shunsuke Ambo, VP   Tel: (408) 501-1400   %FO: 100
    Bus: *Engaged in the trade of petroleum,*   Fax: (408) 501-1499   Emp: 20
         machinery, textiles, metals & food products.

KANEMATSU (USA) INC
114 West 47th St., 23/F, New York, New York 10036
CEO: Kazuo Fujisaki, Pres. Tel: (212) 704-9400 %FO: 100
Bus: *Engaged in the trade of petroleum,* Fax: (212) 704-9483
machinery, textiles, metals & food products.

KANEMATSU USA INC.
One SW Columbia St., Ste. 1450, Portland, Oregon 97258
CEO: Katsumi Morita, Gen. Mgr. Tel: (503) 224-7755 %FO: 100
Bus: *Sale of grain & filed beans/durable goods.* Fax: (503) 228-5067 Emp: 9

KANEMATSU USA INC.
2300 Boswell Rd., Ste. 206, Chula Vista, California 91914
CEO: Kazuo Shigemoto, Mng. Dir. Tel: (619) 656-2385 %FO: 100
Bus: *Mfr. of plastic resin, aluminum die cast* Fax: (619) 656-2386
parts & manufacturing -oriented

KANEMATSU USA INC.
333 South Hope St., Ste. 1125, Los Angeles, California 90071
CEO: Takashi Nagoya, Mng. Dir. Tel: (213) 620-6600 %FO: 100
Bus: *Mfr. of fabrics & textiles.* Fax: (213) 620-1050

KANEMATSU USA INC.
1800 Augusta Dr., Ste. 309, Houston, Texas 77057
CEO: Steve Kurihara, Gen. Mgr. Tel: (713) 975-7200 %FO: 100
Bus: *Sale of industrial equipment.* Fax: (713) 975-7966 Emp: 12

KANEMATSU USA INC.
543 West Algonquin Rd., Arlington Heights, Illinois 60005
CEO: I. Sakata Tel: (847) 981-5600 %FO: 100
Bus: *Sale of brick & stone/ Sale of sporting* Fax: (847) 981-6760 Emp: 50
recreational goods.

KANEMATSU USA INC.
100 Randolph Rd., Somerset, New Jersey 08873
CEO: Kevin Tanigawa, Mgr. Tel: (732) 271-7300 %FO: 100
Bus: *Sale of industrial supplies.* Fax: (732) 271-7370 Emp: 28

KANEMATSU USA INC.
75 Rockefeller Plaza, 52nd St., 22/F, New York, New York 10019
CEO: Masayuki Shimojima, Pres. Tel: (212) 704-9400 %FO: 100
Bus: *Electronic components distribution &* Fax: (212) 704-9483 Emp: 150
support.

● **THE KANSAI ELECTRIC POWER COMPANY, INC.**
3-22, Nakanoshima, 3-chome, Kita-ku, Osaka 530-8270, Japan
CEO: Yohsaku Fuji, Pres. Tel: 81-6-6441-8821 Rev: $24,045
Bus: *Electric utility.* Fax: 81-6-6447-7174 Emp: 33,935
www.kepco.co.jp
NAICS: 221111, 221112, 221113, 221119, 221121, 221122, 221210, 236220, 237130, 238210, 424720, 517910,
518111, 518210, 519190, 523130, 531312,
541330, 541511, 541512, 541513, 541519, 541618, 541690, 561210, 562111, 562212, 611420

THE KANSAI ELECTRIC POWER COMPANY, INC.
375 Park Ave., Ste. 2607, New York, New York 10152
CEO: Yozo Miyavaki, Mgr. Tel: (212) 758-3505 %FO: 100
Bus: *Electric utility.* Fax: (212) 832-3253

THE KANSAI ELECTRIC POWER COMPANY, INC.
2001 L St., NW, Ste. 801, Washington, District of Columbia 20036
CEO: Kenji Okada, Mgr.   Tel: (202) 659-1138   %FO: 100
Bus: *Electric utility.*   Fax: (202) 457-0272

● **KAO CORPORATION**
14-10, Nihonbashi Kayabacho, 1-chome, Chuo-ku, Tokyo 103-8210, Japan
CEO: Takuya Goto, Chmn.   Tel: 81-3-3660-7111   Rev: $8,544
Bus: *Mfr./sales personal care products,*   Fax: 81-3-3660-8978   Emp: 19,330
detergents/chemical products and information   www.kao.co.jp
technology products.
NAICS: 311222, 311223, 311225, 322291, 325199, 325211, 325611, 325612, 325613, 325620, 325910, 446120

> **ADM KOA**
> 4666 E. Faries Pkwy., Decatur, Illinois 62526
> CEO: Tetsuya Imamura, member   Tel: (217) 424-5200   %FO: 100
> Bus: *Mfr. Cooking oils*   Fax: Emp: 15
>
> **KAO BRANDS CO.**
> 2535 Spring Grove Ave., Cincinnati, Ohio 45214
> CEO: William Gentner, Pres. & CEO   Tel: (513) 421-1400
> Bus: *Mfr. personal care products*   Fax: (513) 263-7328   Emp: 560
>
> **KAO SPECIALTIES AMERICAS**
> PO Box 2316, 243 Woodbine St., High Point, North Carolina 27260
> CEO: Harvey Lowd, Principal   Tel: (336) 884-2214   %FO: 100
> Bus: *Mfr./sales chemicals.*   Fax: (336) 884-8975   Emp: 141

● **C.I. KASEI CO., LTD.**
18-1, Kyobashi, 1-Chome, Chuo-ku, Tokyo 104, Japan
CEO: Montonori Toyota, Pres.   Tel: 81-3-3535-4547   Rev: $420
Bus: *Mfr. plastics.*   Fax: 81-3-3535-4542   Emp: 831
                                 www.cik.co.jp
NAICS: 326199

> **BONSET AMERICA CORPORATION**
> 6107 Corporate Park Dr., Browns Summit, North Carolina 27214
> CEO: Hiroshi Suzuki, Pres.   Tel: (336) 375-0234   %FO: 100
> Bus: *Mfr. plastic shrink film.*   Fax: Emp: 98

● **KAWAI MUSICAL INSTRUMENTS MFG. CO., LTD.**
200, Terajima-cho, Hamamatsu, Shizuoka 430-8665, Japan
CEO: Hirotaka Kawai, Pres.   Tel: 81-53-457-1213   Rev: $656
Bus: *Pianos, electronic pianos and organs*   Fax: 81-53-457-1300   Emp: 3,295
manufacture and sales.   www.kawai.co.jp
NAICS: 332618, 339992, 443120

> **KAWAI AMERICA CORPORATION**
> 2055 E. University Dr., Compton, California 90220
> CEO: Jun Ando, Pres.   Tel: (310) 631-1771   %FO: 100
> Bus: *Pianos, electronic pianos and organs sales.*   Fax: (310) 604-6913   Emp: 2

• KAWASAKI HEAVY INDUSTRIES, LTD.
Kobe Crystal Tower, 1-3, Higashikawasaki-cho, 1-chome, Chou-ku, Kobe 650-8680, Japan
CEO: Masamoto Tazaki, Pres. & CEO   Tel: 81-78-371-9530   Rev: $10,983
Bus: *Mfr. heavy machinery and large-scale equipment*   Fax: 81-78-371-9568   Emp: 29,306
     for transportation, aerospace and industry.   www.khi.co.jp
NAICS: 333120, 333131, 334290, 336411, 336412, 336413, 336510, 336611, 336612, 336991, 336999

KAWASAKI HEAVY INDUSTRIES USA, INC.
599 Lexington Ave., Ste. 3901, New York, New York 10022
CEO: Yuichi Yamamoto, Pres.   Tel: (212) 759-4950   %FO: 100
Bus: *Industrial equipment manufacture and sales.*   Fax: (212) 759-6421   Emp: 10

KAWASAKI HEAVY INDUSTRIES, LTD.
333 Clay St., Ste. 4310, Houston, Texas 77002
CEO: Takea Takiyaki, Mgr.   Tel: (713) 654-8981   %FO: 100
Bus: *Mfr. machinery.*   Fax: (713) 654-8187

KAWASAKI RAIL CAR, INC.
29 Wells Ave., Bldg. 4, Yonkers, New York 10701
CEO: Yoshinori Kanehana, Pres.   Tel: (914) 376-4700   %FO: 100
Bus: *Transportation equipment manufacture and*   Fax: (914) 376-4779   Emp: 230
     sales.

• KAWASAKI KISEN KAISHA LTD.
Hibiya Central Bldg, 2-9, Nishi Shinbashi, 1-chome, Minato-ku, Tokyo 105-8421, Japan
CEO: Yasuhide Sakinaga, Chmn.   Tel: 81-3 3595-5063   Rev: $6,860
Bus: *Steamship company; cargo and cruise sea*   Fax: 81-3 3595-5001   Emp: 6,088
     www.kline.co.jp
NAICS: 483111, 488210, 488310, 488320, 488510, 493110

K LINE AMERICA
8730 Stony Point Pkwy., Ste. 400, Richmond, Virginia 23235
CEO: Shio Suzuki, CEO   Tel: (804) 560-3600   %FO: 100
Bus: *Liner services, car carrier tramp & tanker*   Fax: (804) 560-3463   Emp: 469
     operations.

• KAYABA INDUSTRY COMPANY, LTD.
World Trade Center Bldg., 2-4-1 Hammamtsucho, Minato-ku, Tokyo 105-0013, Japan
CEO: Tadahiko Ozawa, Pres.   Tel: 81-3-3435-3511   Rev: $1,487
Bus: *Mfr. marine, aircraft, auto, hydraulic and*   Fax: 81-3-3435-3580   Emp: 8,186
     construction parts and components.   www.kyb.co.jp
NAICS: 333996, 336350, 336399

KYB AMERICA
Bank of America Tower, 701 5th Ave., Ste. 1160, Seattle, Washington 98104
CEO: Satoshi Takase, Mgr.   Tel: (206) 386-5625   %FO: 100
Bus: *Mfr. of fluid power pumps.*   Fax: (206) 621-9448

KYB AMERICA
5790 Kateila Ave., Cypress, California 90630
CEO: Takahirn Kakamu, Mgr.   Tel: (562) 799-3862   %FO: 100
Bus: *Mfr. of motorcycles/bicycles.*   Fax: (562) 799-3863

KYB AMERICA
140 North Mitchell Ct., Addison, Illinois 60101
CEO: Shinichiro Maekawa, Pres. Tel: (630) 620-5555 %FO: 100
Bus: *Import/distribute auto shock absorbers,* Fax: (630) 620-8133 Emp: 65
industrial hydraulic motors and components.

KYB MANUFACTURING NORTH AMERICA
2625 N. Morton, Franklin, Indiana 46131
CEO: David Billingsley, Pres. Tel: (317) 736-7774 %FO: 100
Bus: *Mfr./sales automobile shock absorbers.* Fax: (317) 736-4618 Emp: 500

● **KDDI CORPORATION**
Garden Air Tower, 10-10 Iidabashi, 3-chome, Chiyoda-ku, Tokyo 102-8460, Japan
CEO: Tadashi Onodera, Pres. Tel: 81-3-6678-0692 Rev: $26,941
Bus: *Engaged in telecommunications.* Fax: 81-3-6678-0305 Emp: 13,128
www.kddi.com
NAICS: 334220, 517110, 517212, 517910, 518111, 561499

KDDI AMERICA, INC.
375 Park Ave., 7/F, New York, New York 10152
CEO: Naoki Kinoto, Pres. Tel: (212) 702-3720 %FO: 100
Bus: *Telecommunications.* Fax: (212) 702-3765 Emp: 205

KDDI AMERICA, INC.
1350 Bayshore Hwy., Ste. 580, Burlingame, California 94010
CEO: Shigeau Minatani, Pres. Tel: (650) 558-0005 %FO: 100
Bus: *Telecommunications.* Fax: (650) 401-3290

KDDI LABS USA INC.
100 Hamilton Ave., Ste. 225, Palo Alto, California 94301
CEO: Kazuo Hashimoto, Pres. Tel: (650) 566-8165
Bus: *Research and development.* Fax: (650) 566-8169 Emp: 4

● **KENWOOD CORPORATION**
2967-3, Ishikawa-machi, Hachioji, Tokyo 192-8525, Japan
CEO: Haruo Kawahara, Chmn. & CEO Tel: 81-4-2646-5111 Rev: $1,692
Bus: *Audio and communications equipment and test* Fax: 81-4-2646-7960 Emp: 8,820
and measurement instruments manufacture. www.kenwood.com
NAICS: 334310

KENWOOD USA CORP.
2201 E. Dominguez St., Long Beach, California 90810
CEO: Makoto Inukai, Pres. Tel: (310) 639-9000 %FO: 100
Bus: *Sales/service land mobile radio and marine* Fax: (310) 604-4488 Emp: 200
radio test equipment.

● **KEWPIE KABUSHIKI-KAISHA**
1-4-13 Shibuya, Shibuya-ku, Tokyo 150-0002, Japan
CEO: Gosuke Ohyama, Chmn. Tel: 81-3-3486-3331 Rev: $4,119
Bus: *Mfr. of sauces and condiments* Fax: 81-3-3498-1806 Emp: 8,192
www.kewpie.co.jp
NAICS: 311941, 311999, 424490

HENNINGSEN FOODS INC.
2700 Westchester Ave., Ste. 311, Purchase, New York 10577-2554
CEO: Kit Henningsen, VP Sales   Tel: (914) 701-4020   %FO: 100
Bus: *Manufacturer of sauces and condiments*   Fax: (914) 701-4050

Q&B FOODS, INC.
15547 First St., Irwindale, California 91706
CEO: Koh Matsumoto   Tel: (626) 334-5812   %FO: 100
Bus: *Manufacturer of sauces and condiments*   Fax: (626) 969-1587

● **KEYENCE CORPORATION**
1-3-14, Higashinakajima, Higashiyodogawa-Ku, Osaka 533-0033, Japan
CEO: Michio Sasaki, Pres.   Tel: 81-6-6379-2211   Rev: $901
Bus: *Mfr. sensors and instruments to measure*   Fax: 81-6-6379-2131   Emp: 2,250
    electricity and industrial instruments to measure   www.keyence.co.jp
    display/control process variables.
NAICS: 334511

    KEYENCE CORP. OF AMERICA
    50 Tice Blvd., Woodcliff Lake, New Jersey 07677
    CEO: Takemitsu Takizaki, Pres.   Tel: (201) 930-0100   %FO: 100
    Bus: *Mfr. sensors and measuring equipment.*   Fax: (201) 930-0099   Emp: 200

● **KIKKOMAN CORPORATION**
250 Noda, Chiba 278-8601, Japan
CEO: Yuzaburo Mogi, Chmn. & CEO   Tel: 81-471-23-5111   Rev: $3,168
Bus: *Mfr. soy related sauces, wine and*   Fax: 81-471-23-5200   Emp: 6,240
    www.kikkoman.co.jp
NAICS: 311941, 312111, 312130

    JAPAN HAWAII, INC.
    887 North Nimitz Hwy., Honolulu, Hawaii 96817
    CEO: Nobuyuki Enokido, Pres.   Tel: (808) 537-9528   %FO: 100
    Bus: *Sale of groceries.*   Fax: (808) 526-0389   Emp: 25

    JFC INTERNATIONAL, INC.
    540 Forbes Blvd., San Francisco, California 94080
    CEO: Hiroyuki Enomoto, Pres.   Tel: (650) 871-1660   %FO: 100
    Bus: *Sales/distribution of soy and related sauces*   Fax: (650) 952-3272   Emp: 573
    and food products.

    KIKKOMAN FOODS, INC.
    N 1365 Six Corners Rd., Walworth, Wisconsin 53184
    CEO: Yubaburo Mogi, Chmn.   Tel: (262) 275-6181   %FO: 100
    Bus: *Mfr. soy and related sauces.*   Fax: (262) 275-9452   Emp: 160

    KIKKOMAN FOODS, INC.
    1000 Glenn Dr., Folsom, California 95630
    CEO: Jim Howard, Mgr.   Tel: (916) 355-8078   %FO: 100
    Bus: *Mfr. of pickles/sauces & dressings.*   Fax: (916) 355-8083

KIKKOMAN INTERNATIONAL, INC.
50 California St., Ste. 3600, San Francisco, California 94111
CEO: Yuzaburo Mogi, Chmn.   Tel: (415) 956-7750   %FO: 100
Bus: *Mfr. soy and related sauces.*   Fax: (415) 956-7760   Emp: 45

KIKKOMAN MARKETING & PLANNING, INC.
675 Tollgate Rd., Ste. G, Elgin, Illinois 60123
CEO: Tsutomu Ueta, Pres.   Tel: (847) 622-9540   %FO: 100
Bus: *Research and development of flavors.*   Fax: (847) 622-9545

KMS SERVICE INC.
651 Gateway Blvd., Ste. 420, South San Francisco, California 94080
CEO: Naohiro Hara, Pres.   Tel: (650) 246-8600   %FO: 100
Bus: *Computer systems design.*   Fax: (650) 952-0455   Emp: 15

● **KINOKUNIYA COMPANY, LTD.**
3-13-11 Higashi, Shibuya-ku, Tokyo 150-8513, Japan
CEO: Osamu Matsubara, Chmn. & CEO   Tel: 81-3 3354-0131   Rev: $1,076
Bus: *Sales/distribution of books, magazines, printed*   Fax: 81-3-3354-2719   Emp: 3,000
and electronic publications.   www.kinokuniya.co.jp
NAICS: 511120, 511130, 516110

   KINOKUNIYA BOOK STORES OF AMERICA CO., LTD
   525 South Weller St., Seattle, Washington 98104
   CEO: Mikio Funaki, Mgr.   Tel: (206) 587-2477   %FO: 100
   Bus: *Distribution books and periodicals, related*   Fax: Emp: 14
   services.

   KINOKUNIYA BOOK STORES OF AMERICA CO., LTD
   1581 Webster St., San Francisco, California 94115
   CEO: Osamu Matsubara, Pres.   Tel: (415) 567-7625   %FO: 100
   Bus: *Books, magazines, printed and electronic*   Fax: Emp: 85
   publication.

   KINOKUNIYA BOOK STORES OF AMERICA CO., LTD
   123 Astronaut Ellison, South Onizuka St., Ste. 205, Los Angeles, California 90012
   CEO: Ko Ashkura, Mgr.   Tel: (213) 687-4480   %FO: 100
   Bus: *Distribution books and periodicals, related*   Fax: Emp: 23
   services.

   KINOKUNIYA BOOK STORES OF AMERICA CO., LTD
   3030 Harbor Blvd., Ste. G3, Costa Mesa, California 92626
   CEO: Osamu Matsubara, Pres.   Tel: (714) 662-2319   %FO: 100
   Bus: *Distribution books and periodicals, related*   Fax:
   services.

   KINOKUNIYA BOOK STORES OF AMERICA CO., LTD
   10500 SW Beaverton-Hillsdale Hwy., Beaverton, Oregon 97005
   CEO: Yoshi Kawcoe, Mgr.   Tel: (503) 641-6240   %FO: 100
   Bus: *Distribution books and periodicals, related*   Fax:
   services.

KINOKUNIYA BOOK STORES OF AMERICA CO., LTD
10 West 49th St., New York, New York 10020
CEO: Osamu Matsubara, Pres.
Bus: *Distribution books and periodicals, related services.*
Tel: (212) 765-7766
Fax:
%FO: 100
Emp: 45

KINOKUNIYA BOOK STORES OF AMERICA CO., LTD
3360 Palisades Center Dr., West Nyack, New York 10994
CEO: Osamu Matsubara, Pres.
Bus: *Distribution books and periodicals, related services.*
Tel: (845) 353-6600
Fax:
%FO: 100

KINOKUNIYA BOOK STORES OF AMERICA CO., LTD
685 Saratoga Ave., San Jose, California 95129
CEO: Aterumasa Fujieda, Mgr.
Bus: *Distribution books and periodicals, related services.*
Tel: (408) 252-1300
Fax:
%FO: 100
Emp: 12

● **KINTETSU WORLD EXPRESS, INC.**
Ohtemachi Bldg., 1-6-1, Ohtemachi, Chiyoda-ku, Tokyo 100-0004, Japan
CEO: Toshio Kumokawa, Chmn. & CEO
Bus: *Holding company engaged in international freight forwarding and customs brokerage, e-business solutions, rail, ocean, travel, hotel, restaurants and real estate.*
Tel: 81-3-3201-2580
Fax: 81-3-3201-2666
www.kwe.co.jp
Rev: $1,921
Emp: 5,535

NAICS: 488510, 493110, 551112, 561599

KINTETSU BLUE GRASS, INC.
100 Jericho Quadrangle, Ste. 326, Jericho, New York 11753
CEO: Robert Rice, mgr
Bus: *Freight transportation arrangements.*
Tel: (516) 933-7100
Fax: (516) 933-7701

KINTETSU WORLD EXPRESS, INC.
100 Jericho Quadrangle, Ste. 326, Jericho, New York 11753
CEO: Masa Hattori, Pres. & COO
Bus: *Provides e-business solutions.*
Tel: (516) 933-7100
Fax: (516) 933-7731
%FO: 100
Emp: 703

● **KIRIN BREWERY COMPANY, LTD.**
10-1, Shinkawa, 2-chome, Chuo-ku, Tokyo 104-8288, Japan
CEO: Koichiro Aramaki, Pres.
Bus: *Brewery.*
Tel: 81-3-5540-3411
Fax: 81-3-5540-3547
www.kirin.co.jp
Rev: $11,745
Emp: 22,160

NAICS: 312111, 312120, 312140, 325411, 325412, 541710, 621511

COCA-COLA BOTTLING CO. OF NORTHERN NEW ENGLAND, INC.
1 Executive Park Dr., Bedford, New Hampshire 03110
CEO: Wesley Elmer, Pres. & CEO
Bus: *Bottling & distribution.*
Tel: (603) 627-7871
Fax: (603) 627-6108

FOUR ROSES DISTILLERY
1224 Bonds Mill Rd., Lawrenceburg, Kentucky 40342
CEO: Mofoyasu Ishihara, CFO
Bus: *Distilled & blended liquors.*
Tel: (502) 839-3436
Fax: (502) 839-8338
Emp: 56

KIRIN BREWERY OF AMERICA
970 West 190th St., Ste. 890, Torrance, California 90502
CEO: Kazuhiro Tsukahara, Pres.   Tel: (310) 354-2400
Bus: *Distributor of beer & ale.*   Fax: (310) 354-5955   Emp: 23

KIRIN BREWERY OF AMERICA
2400 Broadway St., Ste. 240, Santa Monica, California 90404
CEO: Kazuhiro Tsuaahara, Pres.   Tel: (310) 829-2400   %FO: 100
Bus: *Import and distribution of beer.* Fax: (310) 829-0424   Emp: 23

RAYMOND VINEYARD AND CELLAR, INC.
849 Zinfandel Lane, St. Helena, California 94574
CEO: Roy Raymond Jr., Pres.   Tel: (707) 963-3141
Bus: *Alcoholic beverages.*   Fax: (707) 963-8498   Emp: 40

● **KITZ CORPORATION**
1-10-1, Nakase, Mihama-ku, Chiba 261-8577, Japan
CEO: Yuhsuke Shimizu, Pres. & CEO   Tel: 81-43-299-0111
Bus: *Fluid control equipment manufacture.*   Fax: 81-43-299-1740
                                        www.kitz.co.jp
NAICS: 332911

KITZ CORPORATION OF AMERICA
10750 Corporate Dr., Stafford, Texas 77477
CEO: Steve Twellman, Pres.   Tel: (281) 491-7333   %FO: 100
Bus: *Mfr./sales fluid control equipment.*   Fax: (281) 491-9402   Emp: 100

● **KOBE STEEL LTD.**
Shino Bldg., 10 -26 Wakinohamacho, 2-chome, Kobe 651-8585, Japan
CEO: Yasuo Inubushi, Pres. & CEO   Tel: 81-78-261-5111   Rev: $11,541
Bus: *Mfr. aluminum and copper products, steel,*   Fax: 81-78-261-4123   Emp: 26,179
industrial and construction machinery and   www.kobelco.co.jp
welding/cutting tools.
NAICS: 331111, 331221, 331222, 331312, 331316, 331491, 331492, 331513, 332312

KOBE STEEL USA INC.
535 Madison Ave., 34/F, New York, New York 10022
CEO: Tsukasa Kose, Pres.   Tel: (212) 751-9400   %FO: 100
Bus: *Steel production*   Fax: (212) 308-3116

KOBE STEEL USA, INC.
1000 Town Center, Ste. 340, Southfield, Michigan 48075
CEO: Masao Agui, Mgr.   Tel: (248) 827-7757   %FO: 100
Bus: *Mfr. steel and related materials.* Fax: (248) 827-7759

KOBELCO CONSTUCTION MACHINERY AMERICA
501 Richardson Rd., Calhoun, Georgia 30701
CEO: Jim McCullough, CEO   Tel: (706) 629-5572
Bus: *Construction mining & other heavy equipment* Fax: (706) 629-3952   Emp: 250

PRO-TEC COATING CO.
5000 County Rd., Ste. 5, Leipsic, Ohio 45856
CEO: Paul Worstell, Pres.   Tel: (419) 943-1100
Bus: *Metal fabrication*   Fax: (419) 943-1101   Emp: 230

● **KODANSHA INTL, LTD.**
2-12-21 Otowa, Bunkyo-ku, Tokyo 112-8001, Japan
CEO: Sawako Noma, Pres. & CEO   Tel: 81-3-5395-3410   Rev: $1,855
Bus: *Publisher of books and magazines.*   Fax: 81-3-3944-9908   Emp: 1,142
    www.kodansha.co.jp

NAICS: 511120, 511130

    KODANSHA AMERICA, INC.
    575 Lexington Ave., New York, New York 10022
    CEO: Sawako Noma, Chmn.   Tel: (917) 322-6223   %FO: 100
    Bus: *Publishing.*   Fax: (212) 935-6529

● **KOITO MANUFACTURING CO., LTD.**
4-8-3 Takanawa, Minato-ku, Tokyo 108-8711, Japan
CEO: Junsuke Kato, Chmn.   Tel: 81-3-3443-7111   Rev: $3,164
Bus: *Mfr. of automobile lighting equipment*   Fax: 81-3-3447-1520   Emp: 4,407
    www.koito.co.jp

NAICS: 336211

    NORTH AMERICAN LIGHTING INC.
    20 Industrial Park, Flora, Illinois 62839
    CEO: Daniel R. Robusto, pres,   Tel: (618) 662-4483   %FO: 100
    Bus: *Manufacturer of vehicle lighting products*   Fax: (618) 662-8143   Emp: 2,200

● **KOKUYO CO., LTD.**
1-1, Oimazato-minami 6-chome, Higashinari-ku, Osaka 537-8686, Japan
CEO: Akihiro Kuroda, Pres.   Tel: 81-6-6976-1221   Rev: $2,589
Bus: *Sales of office furniture and stationery supplies.*   Fax: 81-6-6975-0815   Emp: 4,191
    www.kokyo.co.jp
NAICS: 322121, 322130, 322231, 322232, 322233, 333313, 337214, 337215

    KOKUYO USA, INC.
    1931 North Meacham Rd., Ste. 350, Schaumburg, Illinois 60173
    CEO: Tetsuya Terada, Pres.   Tel: (847) 925-1900   %FO: 100
    Bus: *Sale of office furniture and stationery*   Fax: (847) 493-3210   Emp: 5
    supplies.

● **KOMATSU, LTD.**
2-3-6, Akasaka, Minato-ku, Tokyo 107-8414, Japan
CEO: Masahiro Sakane, Pres. & CEO   Tel: 81-3 5561-2687   Rev: $11,438
Bus: *Mfr. construction equipment, industrial machines*   Fax: 81-3 3561-4763   Emp: 31,635
    & presses.   www.komatsu.com
NAICS: 321992, 333111, 333120, 333131, 333513, 334411, 334413, 334419, 336120, 511210, 541330

    ADVANCED SILICON MATERIALS
    119140 Rick Jones Way, Silver Bow, Montana 59750
    CEO: Hideo Ueda, Chmn. & CEO   Tel: (406) 496-9898
    Bus: *Semiconductor equipment & materials*   Fax: (406) 496-9801   Emp: 350

    KOMATSU AMERICAN INTL CORPORATION
    440 North Fairway Dr., Vernon Hills, Illinois 60061-8112
    CEO: David W. Grzelak, Chmn. & CEO   Tel: (847) 970-4100   %FO: 100
    Bus: *Distribution heavy equipment.*   Fax: (847) 970-4187   Emp: 50

- **KONAMI CORPORATION**
  4-1, Marunouchi 2-chome, Chiyoda-ku, Tokyo 100-6330, Japan
  CEO: Kagemasa Kozuki, Chmn. & Pres. & CEO   Tel: 81-3-5220-0573   Rev: $2,427
  Bus: *Mfr. arcade and video games, casino machines,*   Fax: 81-3-5220-9900   Emp: 11,047
       electronic toys, and exercise equipment and   www.konami.co.jp
       software.
  NAICS: 339932, 511210, 713290, 713940

  KONAMI CORPORATION OF AMERICA
  1400 Bridge Pkwy., Ste. 101, Redwood City, California 94065
  CEO: Tomofumi Gopfubo, Pres.   Tel: (650) 654-5600   %FO: 100
  Bus: *Holding company.*   Fax: Emp: 200

  KONAMI DIGITAL ENTERTAINMENT, INC.
  2121 Ave. of the Stars, Ste. 900, Los Angeles, California 90067
  CEO: Naoki Okada, Pres.   Tel: (310) 228-1573   %FO: 100
  Bus: *Mfr. of toys.*   Fax: (310) 228-4677

  KONAMI DIGITAL ENTERTAINMENT, INC.
  1400 Bridge Pkwy., Ste. 101, Redwood City, California 94065
  CEO: Takuya Kozuki, Pres.   Tel: (650) 801-0266   %FO: 100
  Bus: *Mfr./marketing and distribution of video*   Fax: (650) 654-5690   Emp: 200
       camera software.

  KONAMI GAMING, INC.
  585 Trade Center Dr., Las Vegas, Nevada 89119
  CEO: Satoshi Sakamoto, CEO   Tel: (702) 367-0573   %FO: 100
  Bus: *Mfrs., designs, sells & services gaming*   Fax: (702) 367-0007   Emp: 150
       machines & casino management..

- **KONICA MINOLTA HOLDINGS HOLDINGS, INC.**
  1-6-1 Marunouchi, Chiyoda-ku, Tokyo 100-0005, Japan
  CEO: Fumio Iwai, Pres. & CEO   Tel: 81-3-6250-2100   Rev: $8,145
  Bus: *Photographic films, papers, chemicals, photo*   Fax: 81-3-3218-1368   Emp: 20,523
       equipment, business machines, cameras &   www.konicaminolta.com
       accessories, magnetic products.
  NAICS: 325992, 333293, 333313, 333314, 333315, 334119, 334510, 334517, 339112, 339113, 423410

  ALTERNATIVE BUSINESS SYSTEMS LLC
  5005 Russell Cir., Lincoln, Nebraska 68507
  CEO: H. Carl Little, Pres. & CEO   Tel: (402) 464-0555   %FO: 100
  Bus: *Computer products distribution & support.*   Fax: (402) 464-2030   Emp: 50

  KONICA MINOLTA BUSINESS SOLUTIONS USA INC.
  101 Williams Dr., Ramsey, New Jersey 07446
  CEO: Jun Haraguchi, Pres. & CEO   Tel: (201) 825-4000   %FO: 100
  Bus: *Office machines manufacture and sales.*   Fax: (201) 934-4669

  KONICA MINOLTA MEDICAL CORPORATION
  411 Newark Pompton Turnpike, Wayne, New Jersey 07470
  CEO: Jerry Leibowitz, CEO   Tel: (973) 633-1500   %FO: 100
  Bus: *Medical film processor, medical imaging*   Fax: (973) 523-7408   Emp: 150
       systems, film and accessories, clinical
       analysis equipment.

KONICA MINOLTA PHOTO IMAGING USA INC.
725 Darlington Ave., Mahwah, New Jersey 07430
CEO: Hideaki Iwama, Pres. & CEO   Tel: (201) 574-4000   %FO: 100
Bus: *Digital cameras and photographic equipment* Fax: (201) 574-4010
sales.

KONICA MINOLTA PRINTING SOLUTIONS USA INC.
1 Magnum Pass, Mobile, Alabama 36618
CEO: Shoei Yamana, Chmn. & CEO   Tel: (251) 633-4300   %FO: 100
Bus: *Color and monochrome laser printers*   Fax: (251) 633-0013
manufacture and sales.

● **KORG INC.**
4015-2, Yanokuchi, Inagi, Tokyo 206-0812, Japan
CEO: Tsutomu Katoh, Chmn.   Tel: 81-4-2379-5771
Bus: *Mfr. of musical instruments*   Fax: 81-4-2379-5773
                                         www.korg.co.jp
NAICS: 339992

   KORG USA, Inc.
   316 S. Service Rd., Melville, New York 11747-3201
   CEO: Michael Kovins, Pres. & CEO   Tel: (631) 390-6500   %FO: 100
   Bus: *Manufacturer of musical instruments* Fax: (631) 390-6501

● **KOYO SEIKO COMPANY, LTD.**
5-8, Minamisemba, 3-chome, Chuo-Ku, Osaka 542-8502, Japan
CEO: Kohshi Yoshida, Pres.   Tel: 81-6-6245-6087   Rev: $4,782
Bus: *Mfr. ball and roller bearings, auto steering gear,* Fax: 81-6-6244-0814   Emp: 6,003
machine tools, industry furnaces and seals. www.koyo-seiko.co.jp
NAICS: 336399

   KENTUCKY ADVANCED FORGE, LLC
   596 Triport Rd., Georgetown, Kentucky 40324
   CEO: Tadashi Futamura, member   Tel: (502) 863-7575   %FO: 100
   Bus: *Mfr./Sales of forged products.*   Fax: (502) 863-4923

   KOYO CORP OF USA
   1006 Northpoint Blvd., Blythewood, South Carolina 29016
   CEO: Robert Sullivan, Mgr.   Tel: (803) 691-4624   %FO: 100
   Bus: *Mfr. of bearings.*   Fax: (803) 691-4655   Emp: 150

   KOYO CORP OF USA
   2850 Magnolia St., Orangeburg, South Carolina 29115
   CEO: Jim Wakiya, Mgr.   Tel: (803) 536-6200   %FO: 100
   Bus: *Mfr. of bearings.*   Fax: (803) 534-0599

   KOYO CORPORATION OF USA, SALES DIV.
   29570 Clemens Rd., PO Box 45028, Westlake, Ohio 44145
   CEO: Tsutomu Nemoto, Pres.   Tel: (440) 835-1000   %FO: 100
   Bus: *Mfr./distribution anti-friction bearings and* Fax: (440) 835-9347   Emp: 1,000
   bearing units.

KOYO SEIKO CO., LTD. NORTH AMERICA
47771 Halyard Dr., Plymouth, Michigan 48170
CEO: Charles Brandt, Secretary
Bus: *Technical center.*
Tel: (734) 454-1500
Fax: (734) 454-4076
%FO: 100
Emp: 1,000

KOYO STEERING SYSTEMS OF NORTH AMERICA, INC.
47771 Halyard Dr., Plymouth, Michigan 48170
CEO: Charles Brandt, VP
Bus: *Regional integration (steerings)*
Tel: (734) 454-7039
Fax: (734) 454-7059
%FO: 100
Emp: 20

KOYO STEERING SYSTEMS OF TEXAS
4400 Sterlite Dr., Ennis, Texas 75119
CEO: Homer Rodden, Pres.
Bus: *Mfr. of steerings.*
Tel: (972) 245-0011
Fax:
%FO: 100

KOYO STEERING SYSTEMS OF USA INC.
555 International Pkwy., Daleville, Virginia 24083
CEO: Yoichi Kimoto, Pres.
Bus: *Mfr. / Sales of steerings.*
Tel: (540) 966-3505
Fax: (540) 966-3506
%FO: 100
Emp: 40

TENNESSEE KOYO STEERING SYSTEMS CO.
55 Excellence Way, Vonore, Tennessee 37885
CEO: Michael Bowers, Partner
Bus: *Mfr./Sales of steerings.*
Tel: (423) 884-9200
Fax: (423) 884-9295
%FO: 100
Emp: 40

• KUBOTA CORPORATION
2-47, Shikitsuhigashi, 1-chome, Naniwa-ku, Osaka 556-8601, Japan
CEO: Daisuke Hatakake, Pres.
Bus: *Tractors and farm machinery, ductile iron pipe, roofing and building materials manufacture.*
NAICS: 321992, 333111, 423320, 519110
Tel: 81-6-6648-2111
Fax: 81-6-6648-3862
www.kubota.co.jp
Rev: $9,173
Emp: 22,198

KUBOTA CREDIT CORPORATION
3401 Del Amo Blvd., Torrance, California 90503
CEO: Masato Yoshikawa, Pres.
Bus: *Corporate financial and administrative services.*
Tel: (310) 370-3370
Fax: (310) 370-2370
%FO: 100
Emp: 400

KUBOTA ENGINE AMERICA CORPORATION
505 Schelter Rd., Lincolnshire, Illinois 60069
CEO: Tad Umakoshi, Pres.
Bus: *Engine manufacture.*
Tel: (847) 955-2500
Fax: (847) 955-2699
Emp: 59

KUBOTA MFG, OF AMERICA CORPORATION
2715 Ramsey Rd., Gainesville, Georgia 30501
CEO: John Shiraishi, Pres.
Bus: *Mfr./distribution tractors and farm machinery, ductile iron pipe, roofing and building materials.*
Tel: (770) 532-0038
Fax: (770) 532-9057
%FO: 100
Emp: 1,300

KUBOTA TRACTOR CORP.
3401 Del Amo Blvd., Torrance, California 90503
CEO: Tetsuji Tomita, Pres.
Bus: *Farm & garden machinery*
Tel: (310) 370-3370
Fax: (310) 370-2370
Emp: 360

- **KUMON INSTITUTE OF EDUCATION CO., LTD.**
Osakaekimaedaini Bldg., 9/F, 1-2-2- Umeda Kita-ku, Osaka 530-0001, Japan
CEO: Yasuo Annaka, CEO   Tel: 81-6-4797-8787
Bus: *Tutoring and supplemental education services.*   Fax: 81-6-4797-8785
www.kumon.ne.jp
NAICS: 611691, 611699

   KUMON NORTH AMERICA INC.
   10 Elm St., Danvers, Massachusetts 01923
   CEO: Mathew Miskiman   Tel: (978) 739-4227   %FO: 100
   Bus: *Tutoring services.*   Fax: (978) 739-4727

   KUMON NORTH AMERICA INC.
   300 Frank W. Burr Blvd., 5/F, Teaneck, New Jersey 07666
   CEO: Matthew Lupsha   Tel: (201) 928-0777   %FO: 100
   Bus: *Tutoring services.*   Fax: (201) 928-1777

   KUMON NORTH AMERICA INC.
   4710 E. Elwood St., Ste. 15, Phoenix, Arizona 85040
   CEO: Shell Xu   Tel: (480) 784-2992   %FO: 100
   Bus: *Tutoring services.*   Fax: (480) 784-1677

   KUMON NORTH AMERICA INC.
   3950 Shackleford Rd., Ste. 325, Duluth, Georgia 30096
   CEO: Demitra Wilson   Tel: (678) 244-6284   %FO: 100
   Bus: *Tutoring services.*   Fax: (678) 244-6285

   KUMON NORTH AMERICA INC.
   2155 Butterfield Rd., Ste. 310, Troy, Michigan 48084
   CEO: Rasheda Williams   Tel: (248) 290-0450   %FO: 100
   Bus: *Tutoring services.*   Fax: (248) 649-2567

- **KURARAY CO., LTD.**
Shin-Hankyu Bldg., 1-12-39, Umeda Kita-ku, Osaka 530-8611, Japan
CEO: Hiroto Matsuo, Chmn.   Tel: 81-6-6348-2111   Rev: $3,144
Bus: *Mfr. synthetic fibers.*   Fax: 81-6-6348-2165   Emp: 6,760
www.kuraray.co.jp
NAICS: 313230, 314999, 325188, 325199, 325211, 325212, 339113, 339114, 541330, 541420, 541490

   EVAL COMPANY OF AMERICA
   2625 Bay Area Blvd., Ste. 300, Houston, Texas 77058
   CEO: Nobuya Tomita, Pres.   Tel: (281) 204-4610
   Bus: *Mfr./sale of plastic material/resins.*   Fax: (281) 204-4622   Emp: 90

   KURARAY AMERICA, INC.
   101 E. 52nd St., 26/F, New York, New York 10022
   CEO: Hiroaki Yoshino, Pres.   Tel: (212) 986-2230   %FO: 100
   Bus: *Mfr. of manmade leathers fine chemicals*   Fax: (212) 867-3543   Emp: 185
   resin.

SEPTON COMPANY OF AMERICA
11414 Choate Rd., Pasadena, Texas 77507
CEO: Masao Mizuno, Pres.
Bus: *Mfr. of plastic materials. resins & chemical preparations.*
Tel: (281) 909-5800
Fax: (281) 909-5801
Emp: 45

● **KUROI ELECTRIC COMPANY, LTD.**
27, Yawatacho Nishishichijo, Shimogyo-ku, Kyoto 600, Japan
CEO: Toshiro Matsura, Pres.
Bus: *Mfr. lighting products and electronics.*
Tel: 81-75-313-5191
Fax:
www.kuroi.co.jp
Rev: $106
Emp: 300

NAICS: 335121, 335121, 541511

KUROI INTL CORPORATION
497 Pini Rd., Watsonville, California 95076
CEO: Sumio Yonemoto, Pres.
Bus: *Mfr. lighting products and agricultural products.*
Tel: (831) 761-8977
Fax: (831) 761-3043
%FO: 100
Emp: 7

● **KYOCERA CORPORATION**
6, Takeda Tobadono-cho, Fushimi-ku, Kyoto 612-8501, Japan
CEO: Yasuo Nishiguchi, Chmn. & CEO
Bus: *Mfr. integrated ceramic packages for computers.*
Tel: 81-75-604-3500
Fax: 81-75-604-3501
www.kyocera.co.jp
Rev: $11,016
Emp: 7,870

NAICS: 327112, 332211, 332214, 333293, 333314, 333319, 333512, 333515, 334119, 334210, 334220, 334413, 334414, 334415, 334417, 334419, 336322, 336350, 339113, 339114, 339941, 532420, 541511, 541512, 541513, 541519

AVX CORPORATION
801 17th Ave. South, Myrtle Beach, South Carolina 29577
CEO: John S. Gilbertson, Pres. & CEO
Bus: *Mfr. passive electronic components.*
Tel: (843) 448-9411
Fax: (843) 448-7139
%FO: 100
Emp: 12,000

KYOCERA INTERNATIONAL INC.
8611 Balboa Ave., San Diego, California 92123-1580
CEO: Rodney Lanthorne, Pres.
Bus: *U.S. headquarters.*
Tel: (619) 576-2600
Fax: (619) 492-1456
%FO: 100

KYOCERA MITA AMERICA, INC.
225 Sand Rd., Fairfield, New Jersey 07004
CEO: Tony Pater, Pres.
Bus: *Printing & imaging equipment*
Tel: (973) 808-8444
Fax: (973) 882-6000

KYOCERA SOLAR, INC.
7812 East Acoma Dr., Scottsdale, Arizona 85260
CEO: Steven C. Hill, Pres.
Bus: *Mfr. solar electric generating systems.*
Tel: (480) 948-8003
Fax: (480) 483-6431
%FO: 100

KYOCERA TYCOM CORP.
17862 Fitch, Irvine, California 92614
CEO: Scott Yardley, Pres. & CEO
Bus: *Industrial machinery & equipment manufacturing*
Tel: (949) 955-0800
Fax: (949) 955-0880

KYOCERA WIRELESS CORP.
10300 Campus Point Dr., San Diego, California 92121
CEO: Tsuyoshi Mano, Pres.
Bus: *Wireless telecommunications equipment.*
Tel: (858) 882-2000
Fax: (858) 882-2010
Emp: 1,010

• KYOCERA MITA CORPORATION, DIV. KYOCERA GROUP
1-2-28 Tamatsukuri, Chuo-ku, Osaka 540-8585, Japan
CEO: Koji Seki, Chmn.
Bus: *Mfr. copiers, network-ready, multifunctional
document imaging systems and computer
peripherals.*
NAICS: 333293, 333313, 333315
Tel: 81-6-6764-3555
Fax: 81-6-6764-3980
www.kyoceramita.com

KYOCERA MITA AMERICA
201 Hansen Ct., Ste. 119, Wood Dale, Illinois 60191
CEO: Maria Flores, Principal
Bus: *Mfr. of copiers, fax machines, printers &
multi-function devices*
Tel: (630) 238-9982
Fax: (630) 238-9487
%FO: 100
Emp: 30

KYOCERA MITA AMERICA
14101 Alton Pkwy., PO Box 57006, Irvine, California 92618
CEO: Takuma Kimura, Mgr.
Bus: *Mfr. of copiers, fax machines, printers &
multi-function devices*
Tel: (949) 457-9000
Fax: (949) 457-9119
%FO: 100
Emp: 25

KYOCERA MITA AMERICA
2825 West Story Rd., Irving, Texas 75038
CEO: Hiro Kobayashi, Mgr.
Bus: *Mfr. of copiers, fax machines, printers &
multi-function devices*
Tel: (972) 550-8987
Fax: (972) 570-4704
%FO: 100
Emp: 75

KYOCERA MITA AMERICA
1500 Oakbrook Dr., Norcross, Georgia 30093
CEO: Nancy Hambly, Mgr.
Bus: *Mfr. of copiers, fax machines, printers &
multi-function devices*
Tel: (770) 729-9786
Fax: (770) 729-9873
%FO: 100
Emp: 30

KYOCERA MITA AMERICA, INC.
225 Sand Rd., PO Box 40008, Fairfield, New Jersey 07004
CEO: Tony Pater, Pres.
Bus: *Mfr. of copiers, fax machines, printers &
multi-function devices.*
Tel: (973) 808-8444
Fax: (973) 882-6000
%FO: 100

• KYODO NEWS
Shiodome Media Tower 15/F, 1-7-1 Higashi-Shimbashi, Minato-ku, Tokyo 105-7201, Japan
CEO: Ichiro Saita, Pres.
Bus: *Political, economic, business and cultural news
of Asia and the Pacific Rim to non-Japanese*
NAICS: 519110
Tel: 81-3625-28000
Fax: 81-3-5573-8018
www.kyodo.co.jp
Rev: $484
Emp: 1,848

KYODO NEWS INTERNATIONAL
747 3rd Ave., Ste. 1803, New York, New York 10017
CEO: Toshi Mitsudome
Bus: *News syndicates*
Tel: (212) 508-5440
Fax: (212) 508-5441
%FO: 100

- **KYOKUYO COMPANY LTD**
  Kousai Sanno Bldg., 3-5, 3-chome Akasaka, Minato-ku, Tokyo 107-0052, Japan
  CEO: Kiyokazu Fukui, Pres.   Tel: 81-3-5545-0701   Rev: $1,434
  Bus: *Seafood purveyor.*   Fax: 81-3-5545-0751   Emp: 1,353
                                                        www.kyokuyo.co.jp
     NAICS: 114111, 114112, 114119, 311711, 311712, 483111

       KYOKUYO AMERICA CORPORATION
       1200 Fifth Ave., Ste. 1301, Seattle, Washington 98101
       CEO: Hiroyuki Aoki, Pres.   Tel: (206) 405-2670   %FO: 100
       Bus: *Seafood purveyor.*   Fax: (206) 405-2671

- **KYOWA HAKKO KOGYO CO., LTD.**
  1-6-1, Ohtemachi, Chiyoda-ku, Tokyo 100-8185, Japan
  CEO: Dr. Tadashi Hirata, Chmn. & CEO   Tel: 81-3-3282-0007   Rev: $3,302
  Bus: *Develops, markets and manufactures*   Fax: 81-3-3284-1968   Emp: 6,294
       pharmaceuticals, chemicals, food products and   www.kyowa.co.jp
       alcoholic beverages.
     NAICS: 311111, 311412, 311942, 312130, 312140, 325110, 325120, 325181, 325188, 325199, 325320, 325411,
  325412

       BIOKYOWA INC,
       5469 Nash Rd., PO Box 1550, Cape Giradeau, Missouri 63702
       CEO: Satoru Akiyama, Pres.   Tel: (573) 335-4849
       Bus: *Mfr. animal food.*   Fax: Emp: 100

       BIOWA INC.
       212 Carnegie Center, Ste. 101, Princeton, New Jersey 08540
       CEO: Martina Molsbergen, Dir.   Tel: (609) 580-7500
       Bus: *Develops, markets and manufactures*   Fax: (609) 919-1108
       pharmaceuticals, chemicals, food products
       and alcoholic beverages.

       KYOWA AMERICA, INC.
       767 Third Ave., 19/F, New York, New York 10017
       CEO: Neil Sullivan, Dir. Sales   Tel: (212) 319-5353   %FO: 100
       Bus: *U.S. headquarters.*   Fax: (212) 421-1283

       KYOWA HAKKO U.S.A., INC.
       85 Enterprise, Ste. 430, Aliso Viejo, California 92656
       CEO: Koji Tashita, Mgr.   Tel: (949) 425-0707   %FO: 100
       Bus: *Sales/distribution of food products.*   Fax: (949) 425-0708   Emp: 2

       KYOWA PHARMACEUTICAL
       212 Carnegie Center, Ste. 101, Princeton, New Jersey 08540
       CEO: Shigeru Kobayashi, Pres.   Tel: (609) 919-1100   %FO: 100
       Bus: *Sales of pharmaceutical products.*   Fax: (609) 919-1111   Emp: 50

       SELECT SUPPLEMENTS, INC.
       5800 Newton Dr., Carlsbad, California 92008
       CEO: Toshifumi Asada, Pres.   Tel: (760) 431-7509
       Bus: *Support services.*   Fax: Emp: 14

● **MABUCHI MOTOR CO LTD.**
430 Matsuhidia, Matsudo, Chiba 270-2280, Japan
CEO: Shinji Kamei, Pres. & CEO
Bus: *DC motors manufacture for home electric appliances, precision machinery, auto machinery and supplies printers and power tools.*
NAICS: 333991, 334310, 335312, 811310

Tel: 81-47-384-1111
Fax: 81-47-385-5299
www.mabuchi-motor.co.jp

Rev: $964
Emp: 49,853

    MABUCHI MOTOR AMERICAN CORPORATION
    3001 West Big Beaver Rd., Ste. 520, Troy, Michigan 48084
    CEO: Yasuo Uehara, Pres.
    Bus: *Mfr./distributes DC motors for home electric appliances, precision machinery, auto machinery & supplies printers & power*

    Tel: (248) 816-3100
    Fax: (248) 816-3242

    %FO: 100
    Emp: 23

● **MAKINO MILLING MACHINE COMPANY**
3-19, Nakane, 2-chome, Meguro-ku, Tokyo 152-8578, Japan
CEO: Jiro Makino, Pres.
Bus: *Machine centers, systems, electric machinery, copy mills, engine lathes manufacture..*
NAICS: 333298, 333512, 333513, 333516

Tel: 81-3-3717-1151
Fax: 81-3-3725-2105
www.makino.co.jp

Rev: $794
Emp: 2,583

    MAKINO
    7680 Innovation Way, Mason, Ohio 45040
    CEO: Donald Lane, Pres.
    Bus: *Mfr./distribution machine tools and systems.*

    Tel: (513) 573-7200
    Fax: (513) 573-7360

    %FO: 100
    Emp: 300

● **MAKINO SEIKI CO.,LTD.**
4029, Nakatsu, Aikawa-machi, Aiko-gun, Kanagawa 243-0303, Japan
CEO: Tetsu Shimizu, Pres.
Bus: *Machine tool manufacture.*
NAICS: 333512, 333513

Tel: 88-462-85-5552
Fax: 88-462-85-5530
www.makinoseiki.co.jp

    MAKINO SEIKI
    901 Deerfield Pkwy., Buffalo Grove, Illinois 60089
    CEO:
    Bus: *Machine tool manufacture and sales.*

    Tel: (708) 215-2412
    Fax: (708) 215-0914

    %FO: 100

● **MAKITA CORPORATION**
3-11-8, Sumiyoshi-cho, Anjo Aichi 446-8502, Japan
CEO: Masahiko Goto, Pres.
Bus: *Portable electric power tools and accessories.*
NAICS: 332212, 332213, 333991

Tel: 81-566-98-1711
Fax: 81-566-98-6021
www.makita.co.jp

Rev: $1,820
Emp: 8,560

    MAKITA USA INC.
    14930 Northam St., La Mirada, California 90638-5753
    CEO: Hiroshi Okamoto, Pres. & CEO
    Bus: *Portable electric power tools & accessories.*

    Tel: (714) 522-8088
    Fax: (714) 522-8133

    %FO: 100
    Emp: 1,561

- **MARUBENI CORPORATION**
  4-2, Ohtemachi, 1-chome, Chiyoda-ku, Tokyo 100-8088, Japan
  CEO: Nobuo Katsumata, Pres. & CEO   Tel: 81-3-3282-2111   Rev: $3,876
  Bus: *Import/export metals, machinery, chemicals,*   Fax: 81-3-3282-4241   Emp: 24,417
  textiles, general merchandise, petroleum,   www.marubeni.co.jp
  agricultural and marine products.
  NAICS: 112111, 112112, 112210, 112511, 112512, 112519, 113210, 114111, 114112, 115210, 211111, 211112, 236116, 311212, 311222, 311223, 311225,
  311311, 311312, 311313, 311340, 311412, 311611, 311612, 311615, 311712, 311920, 312120, 312130, 312140, 313210, 313221, 313241,
  313249, 313311, 313312, 314121, 314129, 314912, 314991, 314992, 314999, 331312, 423430, 424410, 424460, 424520, 424690, 424720, 424810,
  424820, 424910, 425120, 531390

  MARUBENI AMERICA
  3945 Freedom Circle, McCandless Tower 1, Ste. 1000, Santa Clara, California 95054
  CEO: Kazuhiko Sakamoto   Tel: (408) 330-0808
  Bus: *Raw materials for semiconductors.*   Fax: (408) 330-0807   Emp: 18

  MARUBENI AMERICA CORPORATION
  450 Lexington Ave., 35/F, New York, New York 10017
  CEO: Kazuhiko Sakamoto, Pres. & CEO   Tel: (212) 450-0100   %FO: 100
  Bus: *Import/export metals, machinery, chemicals,*   Fax: (212) 450-0708   Emp: 4,545
  textiles, general merchandise, petroleum,
  agricultural & marine products.

  MARUBENI AMERICA CORPORATION
  1776 I St. NW, Ste. 725, Washington, District of Columbia 20006
  CEO: Kazuhiko Sakamoto   Tel: (202) 331-1167   %FO: 100
  Bus: *Farm supplies.*   Fax: (202) 331-1319   Emp: 4

  MARUBENI AMERICA CORPORATION
  333 S. Grand Ave., Ste. 2100, Los Angeles, California 90071
  CEO: Kazuhiko Sakamoto   Tel: (213) 972-2700   %FO: 100
  Bus: *Industrial machinery.*   Fax: (213) 626-1294

  MARUBENI AMERICAN CORPORATION
  8655 Ronda Dr., Canton, Michigan 48187
  CEO: Mark Ostraff, Mgr.   Tel: (734) 354-7940   %FO: 100
  Bus: *Industrial machinery*   Fax:

  MARUBENI AMERICAN CORPORATION
  101 California St., San Francisco, California 94111
  CEO: Keiji Shimizu   Tel: (415) 954-0100   %FO: 100
  Bus: *Import/export metals, machinery, chemicals,*   Fax: (415) 954-0100   Emp: 22
  textiles, general merchandise, petroleum,
  agricultural & marine products.

- **MARUBENI-ITOCHU STEEL INC.**
  Nihonbashi 1, Bldg. 4-1, Chuo-ku, Tokyo 1038247, Japan
  CEO: Akio Shigetomi, CEO   Tel: 81-3-5204-3300   Rev: $14,190
  Bus: *Mfr. of oil and gas industry tubular equipment*   Fax: 81-3-5204-3810   Emp: 634
  www.benichu.com
  NAICS: 331111, 331210, 331221, 331222

MARUBENI-ITOCHU STEEL AMERICA INC.
450 Lexington Ave., 34/F, New York, New York 10017
CEO: Mokoto Ishitani, Gen. Mgr.   Tel: (212) 450-0386   %FO: 100
Bus: *Manufacturer of steel tubular materials*   Fax: (212) 450-0790

● **MARUHA GROUP**
1-2, 1-chome Ohtemachi, Chiyoda-ku, Tokyo 100-8608, Japan
CEO: Yuji Igarashi, Pres. & CEO   Tel: 81-3-3216-0821   Rev: $7,174
Bus: *Provides refrigerated and cold storage services,*   Fax: 81-3-3216-0342   Emp: 15,749
food processing and plant management and   www.maruha.co.jp
engineering services.
NAICS: 114111, 114112, 114119, 311412, 311422, 311711, 311712, 311999, 424460, 493120, 541330

ALYESKA SEAFOODS
303 N.E. Northlake Way, Seattle, Washington 98105
CEO: William Weisfield, Pres.   Tel: (206) 547-2100
Bus: *Fish & seafood products.*   Fax: (206) 547-1808   Emp: 250

MARUHA CAPITAL INVESTMENT
1111 Third Ave., Ste. 2200, Seattle, Washington 98101
CEO: Yuji Igarashi, Pres. & CEO   Tel: (206) 382-0640   %FO: 100
Bus: *Investment services.*   Fax: (206) 625-0089   Emp: 400

SUPREME ALASKA SEAFOODS
4200 23rd. Ave., 3/F, Seattle, Washington 98199
CEO: F. Joseph Bersch, Pres.   Tel: (206) 281-8311
Bus: *Fresh. Frozen prepared fish*   Fax: (206) 281-8481   Emp: 110

TAIYO
405 Lexington Ave., 55/F, New York, New York 10174
CEO: Toshiko Yamaguchi, Dir.   Tel: (212) 297-9170
Bus: *Foreign trade & financing*   Fax: (212) 499-0577   Emp: 2

TRANS OCEAN PRODUCTS
350 W. Orchard Dr., Bellingham, Washington 98225
CEO: Rick Dutton   Tel: (360) 671-6886   %FO: 100
Bus: *Fish & seafood products.*   Fax: (360) 671-0354

WESTWARD SEAFOODS
1111 Third Ave., Ste. 2250, Seattle, Washington 98101
CEO: Fumito Kawa, Pres.   Tel: (206) 682-5949
Bus: *Fish & seafood products.*   Fax: (206) 682-1825   Emp: 235

● **MARUICHI STEEL TUBE LTD.**
9-10, 3-chome, Kitahorie, Nishi-ku, Osaka 550-0014, Japan
CEO: Seiji Yoshimura, Pres.   Tel: 81-6--6531-0101   Rev: $599
Bus: *Steel tubes manufacture.*   Fax: 81-66543-0190   Emp: 917
                                         www.maruichikokan.co.jp
NAICS: 331210

MARUICHI AMERICAN CORPORATION
11529 Greenstone Ave., PO Box 3187, Santa Fe Springs, California 90670
CEO: Riichi Soda, Pres.   Tel: (562) 903-8600
Bus: *Mfr. steel pipe and tubing.*   Fax: Emp: 85

- **MARUKAI CORPORATION KK**
  18-5, Kyomachibori, I-chome, Nishi-ku, Osaka 550, Japan
  CEO: Kenji Matsu, Pres.   Tel: 81-6-443-0071
  Bus: *Import/export general merchandise.*   Fax: 81-6-443-2182   Emp: 50
                                                           www.marukai.co.jp

  NAICS: 423990

    MARUKAI CORPORATION
    123 S. Onizuka St., #101, Los Angeles, California 90012
    CEO: Yu Komatsu, Mgr.   Tel: (213) 893-7200   %FO: 100
    Bus: *Sale/distribution of retail oriental goods.*   Fax: (213) 893-7211   Emp: 29

    MARUKAI CORPORATION
    1420 S Azusa Ave, West Covina, California 91791-4121
    CEO: Kotaro Ise, Mgr.   Tel: (626) 430-0900   %FO: 100
    Bus: *Department store engaged in sale of oriental* Fax: (626) 918-3825
       goods.

    MARUKAI CORPORATION
    1740 West Artesia Blvd., Gardena, California 90248
    CEO: Michiko Sango, Mgr.   Tel: (310) 660-6300   %FO: 100
    Bus: *Sale/distribution of retail oriental goods.*   Fax: (310) 660-6321

    MARUKAI CORPORATION
    2975 Harbor Blvd., Costa Mesa, California 92626
    CEO: Kanke Yoshitaka, Mgr.   Tel: (714) 751-8433   %FO: 100
    Bus: *Sale/distribution of retail oriental goods.*   Fax: (714) 751-8584   Emp: 10

    MARUKAI CORPORATION
    2310 Kamehameha Hwy., Honolulu, Hawaii 96819
    CEO: Hidejiro Matsu, Pres.   Tel: (808) 845-5051
    Bus: *Sale/distribution of retail oriental goods.*   Fax: Emp: 590

- **MARUZEN CHEMICAL TRADING CO., LTD.**
  25-10, Hatchobori 2-chome, Chuo-ku, Tokyo 104-0032, Japan
  CEO: Youichi Nonaka, CEO   Tel: 81-3-3551-1450
  Bus: *Chemicals manufacture.*   Fax: 81-3-3551-1426
                                                           www.chemiway.co.jp

  NAICS: 324199, 325110, 325193, 532230

    MARUZEN AMERICA INC.
    Three Riverway, Ste. 800, Houston, Texas 77056
    CEO: Youichi Nonaka, Pres.   Tel: (713) 966-5790   %FO: 100
    Bus: *Chemical manufacture.*   Fax: (713) 572-2285

- **MARUZEN COMPANY LIMITED**
  3-10, Nihombashi, 2 chome, Chuo-ku, Tokyo 103-8245, Japan
  CEO: Seishiro Murata, Pres. & CEO   Tel: 81-3-3272-7211   Rev: $1,105
  Bus: *Books and publications.*   Fax: 81-3-3272-7268   Emp: 3,258
                                                           www.maruzen.co.jp

  NAICS: 424920, 451211, 451220, 532230

MARUZEN INTERNATIONAL CO., LTD.
40 Seaview Dr., 2/F, Secaucus, New Jersey 07094
CEO: Youichi Nonaka
Bus: *Imported books and publications.*
Tel: (201) 865-4400
Fax: (201) 865-4845
%FO: 100

● **MATSUSHITA ELECTRIC INDUSTRIAL COMPANY, LTD.**
1006 Oaza Kadoma, Kadoma, Osaka 571-8501, Japan
CEO: Kunio Nakamura, Pres.
Bus: *Mfr. electronic and electric products for consumer, business and industry.*
Tel: 81-6-6908-1121
Fax: 81-6-6908-2351
www.matsushita.co.jp
Rev: $81,436
Emp: 288,324

NAICS: 333293, 333313, 334111, 334112, 334119, 334210, 334310, 334413, 334419, 335211, 335212, 335221, 335222, 335224, 335228

AROMAT CORP.
629 Central Ave., New Providence, New Jersey 07974
CEO: Takeshi Ishikawa, Pres.
Bus: *Electronic components*
Tel: (908) 464-3550
Fax: (905) 464-8513
Emp: 500

MATSUSHITA AVIONICS SYSTEMS CORPORATION
22333 29th Dr. SE, Bothell, Washington 98021
CEO: Takashi Mizuma, Pres.
Bus: *Supplies in-flight entertainment systems.*
Tel: (425) 415-9000
Fax: (425) 485-6175
%FO: 100
Emp: 1,100

MATSUSHITA ELECTRONIC COMPONENTS CO., LTD.
5105 South National Dr., Knoxville, Tennessee 37914
CEO: Yasutaka Kanamori, Pres.
Bus: *Electronic components*
Tel: (865) 673-0700
Fax: (865) 673-0309
Emp: 2,800

MATSUSHITA KOTOBUKI ELECTRONICS INDUSTRIES OF AMERICA INC.
2001 Kotobuki Way, Vancouver, Washington 98660
CEO: Satoshi Yamagami, Pres.
Bus: *Consumer electronics*
Tel: (360) 695-1338
Fax: (360) 695-3155
Emp: 530

PANASONIC COMPANY
One Panasonic Way, Secaucus, New Jersey 07094
CEO: Fujio Tsuji, CFO
Bus: *Mfr./wholesale consumer and industrial electronic products.*
Tel: (201) 348-7000
Fax: (201) 392-6007
%FO: 100

PANASONIC COMPUTER SOLUTIONS CO.
50 Meadowlands Pkwy., Secaucus, New Jersey 07094
CEO: Rance Poehler, Pres.
Bus: *Computer hardware.*
Tel: (201) 348-7000
Fax: (201) 392-4616

● **MAZDA MOTOR CORPORATION**
3-1, Shinchi, Fucho-cho, Aki-Gun, Hiroshima 730-8670, Japan
CEO: Hisakazu Imaki, Pres. & CEO
Bus: *Mfr. automobiles, machine tools and rock drills.*
Tel: 81-82-282-1111
Fax: 81-82-287-5190
www.mazda.co.jp
Rev: $27,604
Emp: 35,627

NAICS: 333120, 333319, 336111, 336112

AUTO ALLIANCE INTERNATIONAL
1 International Dr., Flat Rock, Michigan 48134
CEO: Phillip G. Spender, Pres. & COO
Bus: *Mfr. Automobiles*
Tel: (734) 782-7800
Fax: (734) 783-8216

MAZDA NORTH AMERICAN OPERATIONS
7755 Irvine Center Dr., Irvine, California 92623
CEO: James J. O'Sullivan, Pres. & CEO
Bus: *Mfr. automobiles, machine tools and rock drills.*
Tel: (949) 727-1990
Fax: (949) 727-6101
%FO: 100

• MEIDENSHA CORPORATION
Riverside Bldg., 36-2 Nihonbashi-Hakozakicho, Chuo-ku, Tokyo 103-8515, Japan
CEO: Keiji Kataoka, Pres.
Bus: *Energy, environment, industrial systems, information and communication and construction.*
NAICS: 333298, 333512
Tel: 81-3-5641-7000
Fax: 81-3-5641-7099
www.meidensha.co.jp
Rev: $1,719
Emp: 7,278

MEIDEN AMERICA INC.
27000 Meadowbrook Rd., Ste. 209, Novi, Michigan 48377
CEO: Yasumasa Nihei, Sales
Bus: *Products for utility, construction, metal and transportation industries.*
Tel: (248) 305-9903
Fax: (240) 305-9904
%FO: 100

• MEIJI SEIKA KAISHA LTD.
4-16-1 Hatchobori, Chuo-ku, Tokyo 104-8002, Japan
CEO: Naotada Sato, Pres. & CEO
Bus: *Mfr. foods, confectionery, pharmaceuticals and machinery.*
NAICS: 311320, 311330, 311340, 541940
Tel: 81-3-3272-6511
Fax: 81-3-3271-3528
www.meiji.co.jp
Rev: $3,492
Emp: 10,581

D. F. STAUFFER BISCUIT COMPANY, INC.
Belmont and Sixth Ave., York, Pennsylvania 17403
CEO: Haru Komatsu, Pres.
Bus: *Sale/distribution of confections and pharmaceuticals.*
Tel: (717) 843-9016
Fax: (717) 854-2387
%FO: 100

LAGUNA COOKIE COMPANY
4041 West Garry Ave., Santa Ana, California 92704
CEO: Mark McPeak, Gen. Mgr.
Bus: *Sale/distribution of confections and pharmaceuticals.*
Tel: (714) 546-6855
Fax: (714) 556-2491
%FO: 100
Emp: 100

MECOR, INC.
600 Corporate Circle, Ste. H, Golden, Colorado 80401
CEO: T. O'Brien
Bus: *Science based nutritional ingredients.*
Tel: (303) 216-2489
Fax: (303) 216-2477
%FO: 100

• MEIJI YASUDA LIFE INSURANCE COMPANY
1-9-1 Nishi-Shinjuku, Shinjuku-ku, Tokyo 169-8701, Japan
CEO: Ryotaro Kaneko, Pres.
Bus: *Life insurance services.*
NAICS: 523999, 524113, 525190, 525910, 525920, 525990
Tel: 81-3-3342-7111
Fax: 81-3-3215-8123
www.meijiyasuda.co.jp
Rev: $47,651
Emp: 49,412

MEIJI YASUDA AMERICA
865 S. Figueroa St., Ste. 2311, Los Angeles, California 90017
CEO: Nobuyuki Kamohara, VP & Gen. Mgr.
Bus: *Life insurance services.*
Tel: (213) 624-9200
Fax: (213) 624-0080
%FO: 100

MEIJI YASUDA AMERICA
630 5th Ave., Ste. 2650, New York, New York 10111
CEO: Toshihiko Yamashita, Pres.   Tel: (212) 332-4900
Bus: *Life insurance.*   Fax: (212) 332-4960

MEIJI YASUDA REALTY USA, INC.
630 Fifth Ave., Ste. 2650, New York, New York 10111
CEO: Hikari Takasugi, Pres.   Tel: (212) 332-4900
Bus: *Real estate.*   Fax: (212) 332-4961

PACIFIC GUARDIAN LIFE INS. CO. LTD.
865 S. Figueroa St., Ste. 2310, Los Angeles, California 90017
CEO: Norifumi Ichikawa, VP   Tel: (213) 236-0660
Bus: *Insurance agents, brokers, & services.*   Fax: (213) 236-0990

PACIFIC GUARDIAN LIFE INS. COMPANY LTD.
1440 Kapiolani Blvd., Ste. 1700, Honolulu, Hawaii 96814
CEO: Yoji Nakamura, Pres. & CEO   Tel: (808) 955-2236   %FO: 100
Bus: *Life insurance services.*   Fax: (808) 942-1290   Emp: 155

YASUDA ENTERPRISE DEVELOPMENT AMERICA, INC.
435 Tasso St., Ste. 205, Palo Alto, California 94301
CEO: Taisuke Yasuda, CEO   Tel: (650) 289-9733
Bus: *Business services.*   Fax: (650) 289-9415

● **MEIKO TRANS COMPANY, LTD.**
2-4-6 Irifune, Minato-ku, Nagoya, Japan
CEO: Noaharu Miwa, Pres.   Tel: 81-52-661-8111   Rev: $378
Bus: *Wholesale, trucking, stevedoring, freight*   Fax: 81-52-652-1680   Emp: 1,778
forwarding, customs house broker and air cargo   www.meiko.ca
agent.
NAICS: 484110, 488320, 493110

MEIKO AMERICA, INC.
1420 N. Sam Houston Pkwy. East, Ste. 100, Houston, Texas 77032
CEO: Mr. Fukuta, Mgr.   Tel: (281) 590-5252
Bus: *Ocean/Air Import & export.*   Fax: (281) 590-5567

MEIKO AMERICA, INC.
Mira Loma Warehouse 2, 12471 Riverside Dr., Mira Loma, California 91752
CEO: Mike Sole, Mgr.   Tel: (951) 360-0281
Bus: *Documents preparations for ocean & air*   Fax: Emp: 20
freight forwarding.

MEIKO AMERICA, INC.
1441 South Beltline Rd., Ste. 150, Coppell, Texas 75019
CEO: June Koremura, Mgr.   Tel: (972) 471-3736
Bus: *General warehouse & storage.*   Fax: (972) 462-1901

MEIKO AMERICA, INC.
Mira Loma Warehouse 1, 12300 Riverside Dr., Mira Loma, California 91753
CEO: Mike Sole, Mgr.   Tel: (951) 360-0281
Bus: *General warehousing & storage.*   Fax: Emp: 63

MEIKO AMERICA, INC.
888 A.E.C. Dr., Wood Dale, Illinois 60191
CEO: Roy Kageyama, Mgr.   Tel: (630) 766-1492
Bus: *Warehouse & customs freight forwarding*   Fax: (630) 766-1785
    broker.

MEIKO AMERICA, INC.
19600 Magellan Dr., Torrance, California 90502
CEO: Yoshiyuki Tsukamoto, Pres.   Tel: (310) 483-7401   %FO: 100
Bus: *Warehousing, trucking, freight forwarding,* Fax: (310) 483-7404   Emp: 181
    customs house broker and air cargo agent.

MEIKO AMERICA, INC.
1111 Honda Way, Timmonsville, South Carolina 29161
CEO: John R. Hedges, Mgr.   Tel: (843) 346-8086
Bus: *Freight transportation arrangements.* Fax: (843) 346-8073

MEIKO AMERICA, INC.
11590 Township Rd. 298, East Liberty, Ohio 43319
CEO: Hirofumi Suzuki, Mgr.   Tel: (937) 642-8207
Bus: *Freight transportation arrangements..* Fax: (937) 642-8416

MEIKO AMERICA, INC.
JFK Airport, Bldg. 14, Ste. 3, Jamaica, New York 11430
CEO: Joe Wang, Mgr.   Tel: (718) 917-6706
Bus: *Freight transportation arrangements, air* Fax: (718) 656-7795
    courier services.

MEIKO AMERICA, INC.
5 Marine View Plaza, Ste. 304, Hoboken, New Jersey 07030
CEO: Naoki Ishii, Mgr.   Tel: (201) 714-4700
Bus: *Freight transportation arrangements.* Fax: (201) 714-7670

MEIKO AMERICA, INC.
6412 South 216th St., Kent, Washington 98032
CEO: Kazuyoshi Ito, Mgr.   Tel: (253) 872-5939
Bus: *General warehousing & storage.*   Fax: (253) 872-5887

● **MIKIMOTO**
4-5-5, Ginza Chuo-ku, Tokyo 104-8145, Japan
CEO: Toyohiko Mikimoto, Pres.   Tel: 81-3-3535-4611
Bus: *Mfr. and sales of pearls and pearl jewelry.* Fax: 81-3-3535-4620
                                          www.mikimoto.com
    NAICS: 339911

    MIKIMOTO AMERICA CO.
    Regent Beverly Wilshire Hotel, 9500 Wilshire Blvd., Beverly Hills, California 90212
    CEO: Michiko Hidaka   Tel: (310) 205-8787   %FO: 100
    Bus: *Retail store for sales of pearls and pearl* Fax:
        jewelry.

    MIKIMOTO AMERICA CO.
    The Venetian, 3377 Las Vegas Blvd., Las Vegas, Nevada 89109
    CEO: Kikuichiro Ishii, Pres.   Tel: (702) 414-3900   %FO: 100
    Bus: *Retail store for sales of pearls and pearl* Fax: Emp: 10
        jewelry.

MIKIMOTO AMERICA CO.
South Coast Plaza, 3333 Bristol St., Costa Mesa, California 92626
CEO: Benard Barbilla, Mgr.   Tel: (714) 424-5440   %FO: 100
Bus: *Retail store for sales of pearls and pearl* Fax: Emp: 8
    jewelry.

MIKIMOTO AMERICA CO.
680 Fifth Ave., New York, New York 10019
CEO: Mitsuhiro Mitsui, CEO   Tel: (212) 457-4500   %FO: 100
Bus: *Sale of pearls, jewelry & watches.* Fax: (212) 457-4635   Emp: 110

MIKIMOTO AMERICA CO.
730 Fifth Ave., New York, New York 10019
CEO: Noel Garcia, Mgr.   Tel: (212) 457-4600   %FO: 100
Bus: *Retail store for sales of pearls and pearl* Fax:
    jewelry.

● **MIKUNI CORPORATION**
Mikuni Bldg., 6-13-11, Sotokanda, Chiyoda-ku, Tokyo 101-0021, Japan
CEO: Masaki Ikuta, Pres.   Tel: 81-3-3833-0392   Rev: $628
Bus: *Mfr. motor vehicle parts.*   Fax: 81-3-3836-4210   Emp: 4,168
     www.mikuni.co.jp

  NAICS: 336399

    MIKUNI AMERICAN CORPORATION
    8910 Mikuni Ave., Northridge, California 91324
    CEO: Masaki Ikuta, Chmn. & CEO   Tel: (818) 885-1242   %FO: 100
    Bus: *Distribution of motor vehicle parts.* Fax: (818) 993-6877   Emp: 67

    MIKUNI AMERICAN CORPORATION
    1599 Wilkening Rd., Schaumburg, Illinois 60173
    CEO: S. Ikuta, EVP   Tel: (847) 781-2000   %FO: 100
    Bus: *Distribution of motor vehicle parts.* Fax: (847) 490-9089

● **MILLEA HOLDINGS, INC.**
Otemachi First Sq., West Tower, 10/F, 1-5-1 Otemachi, Chiyoda-ku, Tokyo 100-0004, Japan
CEO: Kunio Ishihara, Pres.   Tel: 81-3-6212-3333   Rev: $25,536
Bus: *Insurance underwriter.*   Fax: 81-3-6212-3343   Emp: 19,779
     www.millea.co.jp

  NAICS: 523120, 523920, 523930, 524114, 524126, 524298

    TOKIO MARINE MANAGEMENT INC.
    230 Park Ave., New York, New York 10270
    CEO: Hiroshi Narimatsu, Pres.   Tel: (212) 297-6600   %FO: 100
    Bus: *Insurance underwriter for marine, fire,* Fax: (212) 297-6062   Emp: 350
     personal accident and auto.

● **MINEBEA CO., LTD.**
ARCO Tower, 1-8-1, Shimo-Meguro, 19/F, Meguro-ku, Tokyo 153-8662, Japan
CEO: Tsugio Yamamoto, Pres. & CEO   Tel: 81-3-5434-8611   Rev: $2,542
Bus: *Mfr. miniature and instrument ball bearings and* Fax: 81-3-5434-8601   Emp: 43,839
    components for aerospace, telecommunications www.minebea.co.jp
    and personal computers.
  NAICS: 332991

1046 Japan

HANSEN CORPORATION
901 South First St., Princeton, Indiana 47670
CEO: William K. Poyner, Pres.
Bus: *Mfr. of auto parts.*
Tel: (812) 385-3000
Fax: (812) 386-6387
%FO: 100

NEW HAMPSHIRE BALL BEARINGS INC.
155 Lexington Dr., Laconia, New Hampshire 03246
CEO: Richard Fleczok, VP
Bus: *Mfr. of ball bearings.*
Tel: (603) 524-0004
Fax: (603) 524-7422
%FO: 100
Emp: 500

NEW HAMPSHIRE BALL BEARINGS INC.
175 Jaffery Rd., Peterborough, New Hampshire 03458
CEO: Richard Reynells, Mgr.
Bus: *Mfr. of ball bearings.*
Tel: (603) 924-3311
Fax: (603) 924-6632
%FO: 100
Emp: 500

NEW HAMPSHIRE BALL BEARINGS INC.
9700 Independence Ave., Chatsworth, California 91311
CEO: Gary Yomantas, Pres.
Bus: *Mfr. of ball bearings.*
Tel: (818) 407-9300
Fax: (818) 407-5020
%FO: 100
Emp: 1,250

NMB TECHNOLOGIES CORPORATION
28700 Beck Rd., Wixom, Michigan 48393
CEO: Jim Myers, Mgr.
Bus: *Sale of industrial supplies.*
Tel: (248) 926-0026
Fax: (248) 926-0025
%FO: 100
Emp: 15

NMB TECHNOLOGIES CORPORATION
9730 Independence Ave., Chatsworth, California 91311
CEO: Myron Jones, Pres.
Bus: *Mfr. of miniature, steel, chrome & shielded bearing.*
Tel: (818) 341-3355
Fax: (818) 341-8207
%FO: 100

● **MISUMI CORPORATION**
4-43, Toyo 2-chome, Koto-ku, Tokyo 135-8458, Japan
CEO: Tadashi Saegusa, Chmn. & CEO
Bus: *Mfr. press die, plastic mold and automatic machine components.*
Tel: 81-3-647-7116
Fax: 81-3-647-7125
www.misumi.co.jp
Rev: $351
Emp: 390
NAICS: 333511

MISUMI USA
1105 Remington Rd., Ste. B, Schaumburg, Illinois 60173
CEO: Kaz Ishida, Pres.
Bus: *Sale press die, plastic mold and automatic machine components.*
Tel: (847) 843-9105
Fax: (847) 843-9107
%FO: 100
Emp: 12

● **MITSUBISHI CABLE INDUSTRIES LTD.**
4-1, Marunouchi 3-chome, Chiyoda-ku, Tokyo 100-8303, Japan
CEO: Hiroshi Okamoto, Pres.
Bus: *Mfr. cables and fiber optics.*
Tel: 81-3-3216-1551
Fax: 81-3-3201-3948
www.mitsubishi-cable.co.jp
Rev: $1,180
Emp: 2,981
NAICS: 335921

MITSUBISHI CABLE AMERICA, INC.
1050 Highland Dr., Suite A, Ann Arbor, Michigan 48108
CEO: Masahiko Hori, CEO
Bus: *Sales/service silica & plastic optical fibers, opti-electronic products, medical angiograms, automatic connectors, special gaskets.*

Tel: (734) 929-9375
Fax: (734) 929-9376

%FO: 100
Emp: 10

● MITSUBISHI CHEMICAL CORPORATION
33-8 Shiba 5 chome, Minato-ku, Tokyo 108-0014, Japan
CEO: Ryuichi Tomizawa, Pres. & CEO
Bus: *Mfr. and marketing carbon products, inorganic chemicals and pharmaceuticals.*

Tel: 81-3-6414-3730
Fax: 81-3-6414-3745
www.m-kagaku.co.jp

Rev: $18,225
Emp: 33,496

NAICS: 325110, 325131, 325132, 325182, 325188, 325192, 325193, 325199, 325211, 325212, 325221, 325222, 325412, 325910, 325992, 326199, 332999, 334112, 334413, 339999

MITSUBISHI CHEMICAL AMERICA, INC.
401 Volvo Pkwy., Chesapeake, Virginia 23320
CEO: John Canfield, VP
Bus: *Aluminum rolling & drawing*

Tel: (757) 382-5750
Fax: (757) 547-0119

MITSUBISHI CHEMICAL AMERICA, INC.
25 Independence Blvd., Ste. 201, Warren, New Jersey 07059
CEO: Tsuyoshi Itou
Bus: *Sales/distribution of carbon products, inorganic chemicals and pharmaceuticals.*

Tel: (908) 607-1950
Fax: (908) 607-1950

%FO: 100

MITSUBISHI CHEMICAL AMERICA, INC.
One North Lexington Ave., White Plains, New York 10601
CEO: Ken Ogasawara, Pres.
Bus: *Sales/distribution of carbon products, inorganic chemicals and pharmaceuticals.*

Tel: (914) 286-3600
Fax: (914) 681-0760

%FO: 100
Emp: 1,456

NOLTEX LLC
12220 Strang Rd., La Porte, Texas 77571
CEO: Joe Kelley
Bus: *Mfr. Soarnol resin.*

Tel: (281) 842-5000
Fax: (281) 842-5095

%FO: JV

SOARUS LLC
3930 N. Ventura Dr., Ste. 440, Arlington Heights, Illinois 60004
CEO: Mitsuzo Shida
Bus: *Mfr. Ethylene vinyl alcohol copolymer.*

Tel: (847) 255-1211
Fax: (847) 255-4343

%FO: JV

● MITSUBISHI CORPORATION
6-3 Marunouchi, 2-chome, Chiyoda-ku, Tokyo 100-8086, Japan
CEO: Mikio Sasaki, Chmn.
Bus: *Trading company: raw materials, chemicals, general merchandise.*

Tel: 81-3 3210-8580
Fax: 81-3 3210-8583
www.mitsubishi.co.jp

Rev: $15,094
Emp: 49,219

NAICS: 111191, 115210, 311211, 311222, 311223, 311225, 311920, 312111, 312112, 314999, 325181, 325199, 325211, 325212, 332410, 333298, 423510, 423520, 423990, 424410, 424430, 424690, 424710, 424940

INDIANA PACKERS CORPORATION
Highway 421 South, County Rd. 100 N., Delphi, Indiana 46923
CEO: Masao Watanabe, CEO
Bus: *Meat products*

Tel: (765) 564-3680
Fax: (765) 564-3684

MITSUBISHI INTERNATIONAL CORPORATION
655 3rd Ave., New York, New York 10017
CEO: Motoatsu Sakurai, Pres. & CEO
Bus: *Import/export; raw materials, chemicals, general merchandise.*
Tel: (212) 605-2000
Fax: (212) 605-2597
%FO: 100

● **MITSUBISHI ELECTRIC CORPORATION**
Mitsubishi Denki Bldg., 2-3, Marunouchi, 2-chome, Tokyo 100-8310, Japan
CEO: Tamotsu Nomakuchi, Pres. & CEO
Bus: *Mfr. electronics and electrical appliances.*
Tel: 81-3-3218-2111
Fax: 81-3-3218-2185
www.global.mitsubishielectric.com
Rev: $31,918
Emp: 98,988
NAICS: 221119, 221330, 332618, 333298, 333921, 334111, 334113, 334119, 334210, 334290, 334310, 334413, 334414, 334415, 334419, 334512, 334513,
335211, 335222, 335228, 335311, 335312, 335313, 335314, 335921, 335929, 335931, 335999, 336111, 336414, 336510, 423610, 423690,
423730, 811310

MITSUBISHI ELECTRIC AMERICA INC.
5665 Plaza Dr., PO Box 6007, Cypress, California 90630
CEO: K Kawakami, Chmn.
Bus: *Sales/distribution of electronics and electrical appliances.*
Tel: (714) 220-2500
Fax: (714) 229-3898
%FO: 100
Emp: 780

MITSUBISHI ELECTRIC MANUFACTURING CINCINNATI, INC.
4773 Bethany Rd., Mason, Ohio 45040
CEO: John Henry, Pres.
Bus: *Mfr./sales of alternators and starters.*
Tel: (513) 398-2220
Fax: (513) 398-1121
%FO: 100

MITSUBISHI ELECTRIC POWER PRODUCTS, INC.
512 Keystone Dr., Warrendale, Pennsylvania 15086
CEO: Roger Barna, Chmn.
Bus: *Mfr./sales of electric power products.*
Tel: (724) 772-2555
Fax: (724) 772-2146
%FO: 100

MITSUBISHI ELECTRIC RESEARCH LABORATORIES
201 Broadway, 8/F, Cambridge, Massachusetts 02139
CEO: Richard Waters, CEO
Bus: *Research center for computer electronics.*
Tel: (617) 621-7500
Fax: (617) 621-7548
%FO: 100

● **MITSUBISHI ESTATE COMPANY, LTD.**
Otemachi Bldg., 6-1, Otemachi 1-chome, Chiyoda-ku, Tokyo 100-8133, Japan
CEO: Keiji Kimura, Pres. & CEO
Bus: *Engaged in real estate development and hotel and resort management.*
Tel: 81-3-3287-5100
Fax: 81-3-3212-3757
www.mec.co.jp
Rev: $6,436
Emp: 17,732
NAICS: 236117, 236220, 237210, 531110, 531120, 531190, 531311, 531312, 531390, 541310, 541330, 721110

CUSHMAN & WAKEFIELD, INC.
51 W. 52nd St., New York, New York 10019
CEO: Bruce E. Mosler, Pres. & CEO
Bus: *Engaged in real estate development.*
Tel: (212) 841-7500
Fax: (212) 841-7767
%FO: 72
Emp: 11,000

ROCKEFELLER GROUP INC.
1221 Ave. of the Americas, New York, New York 10020-1001
CEO: Jonathan D. Green, Pres. & CEO
Bus: *Engaged in real estate development and hotel and resort management.*
Tel: (212) 282-2000
Fax: (212) 282-2179
%FO: 77

- **MITSUBISHI HEAVY INDUSTRIES LTD.**
  16-5, Konan 2-chome,, Minato-ku, Tokyo 108-8215, Japan
  CEO: Takashi Nishioka, Pres. & CEO   Tel: 81-3-6716-3111   Rev: $22,467
  Bus: *Machinery and plants, aerospace system,*   Fax: 81-3-6716-5800   Emp: 59,949
  shipbuilding and steel structures, R&D.   www.mhi.co.jp
  NAICS: 236210, 332312, 333120, 333319, 333924, 334511, 336411, 336412, 336414, 336415, 336611

  > **MITSUBISHI CATERPILLAR FORKLIFT AMERICA, INC.**
  > 2121 W. Sam Houston Pkwy. North, Houston, Texas 77043
  > CEO: Hideaki Niomiya, Pres.   Tel: (713) 365-1000
  > Bus: *Material handling equipment manufacturing.* Fax: (713) 365-1888   Emp: 1,000

  > **MITSUBISHI HEAVY INDUSTRIES AMERICAS, INC.**
  > 630 Fifth Ave., Ste. 3155, New York, New York 10111
  > CEO: Takumi Saito   Tel: (212) 969-9000   %FO: 100
  > Bus: *Industrial machinery and systems.*   Fax: (212) 262-3301

  > **MITSUBISHI POWER SYSTEMS, INC.**
  > 100 Colonial Center Pkwy., Lake Mary, Florida 32746
  > CEO: Noriaki Fuseya, Pres.   Tel: (407) 688-6100
  > Bus: *Construction & design services.*   Fax: (407) 688-6990   Emp: 250

- **MITSUBISHI LOGISTICS CORPORATION**
  1-19-1, Nihonbashi, Chuo-ku, Tokyo 103-8630, Japan
  CEO: Yasuaki Suzuki, Chmn.   Tel: 81-3-3278-6611   Rev: $1,454
  Bus: *Engaged in sea and air freight forwarding and* Fax: 81-3-3278-6694   Emp: 2,857
  warehousing.   www.mitsubishi-logistics.co.jp
  NAICS: 237210, 488310, 488320, 488510, 493110, 493120, 493130, 493190

  > **MITSUBISHI LOGISTICS AMERICA CORP.**
  > 1101 Andover Park West, Ste. 103, Seattle, Washington 98188
  > CEO: Kathleen Eisenman, Mgr.   Tel: (206) 575-7575   %FO: 100
  > Bus: *Freight transportation arrangement.*   Fax: (206) 575-3651

  > **MITSUBISHI LOGISTICS AMERICA CORP.**
  > 153-63 Rockaway Blvd., Jamaica, New York 11434
  > CEO: Thomas Suzuki, Mgr.   Tel: (718) 978-4400   %FO: 100
  > Bus: *Freight transportation arrangement.*   Fax: (718) 978-4433

  > **MITSUBISHI LOGISTICS AMERICA CORP.**
  > 650 Supreme Dr., Bensenville, Illinois 60106
  > CEO: Mark Tokita, Mgr.   Tel: (630) 350-1880   %FO: 100
  > Bus: *Freight transportation arrangement.*   Fax: (630) 350-2878   Emp: 14

  > **MITSUBISHI LOGISTICS AMERICA CORP.**
  > 61 Broadway, Ste. 1115, New York, New York 10006
  > CEO: Yuji Marushima, Pres.   Tel: (212) 968-0610   %FO: 100
  > Bus: *Freight forwarders, warehousing &*   Fax: (212) 968-0552   Emp: 80
  > *customhouse brokers.*

  > **MITSUBISHI LOGISTICS AMERICA CORP.**
  > 10500 Richmond Ave., Ste. 150, Houston, Texas 77042
  > CEO: Steve Sasaki, Mgr.   Tel: (713) 978-7433   %FO: 100
  > Bus: *Freight transportation arrangement.*   Fax: (713) 978-6872   Emp: 25

MITSUBISHI LOGISTICS AMERICA CORP.
11934 South LA Cienega Blvd., Hawthorne, California 90250
CEO: Hiroshi Nishikawa, Mgr.   Tel: (310) 643-7622   %FO: 100
Bus: *Freight transportation arrangement.*   Fax: (310) 643-7362   Emp: 15

MITSUBISHI LOGISTICS AMERICA CORP.
301 S. Perimeter Park Dr., Ste. 100, Nashville, Tennessee 37211
CEO: Yuji Marushima, Pres.   Tel: (615) 781-4256   %FO: 100
Bus: *Freight transportation arrangement.*   Fax: (615) 781-4243

MITSUBISHI LOGISTICS AMERICA CORP.
1799 Bayshore Hwy., Ste. 129, Burlingame, California 94010
CEO: Yuji Marushima, Pres.   Tel: (650) 552-9200   %FO: 100
Bus: *Freight transportation arrangement.*   Fax: (650) 552-9910

MITSUBISHI LOGISTICS AMERICA CORP.
1895 Phoenix Blvd., Ste. 150, Atlanta, Georgia 30349
CEO: Shigeru Wakita, Mgr.   Tel: (770) 994-7022   %FO: 100
Bus: *Freight transportation arrangement.*   Fax: (770) 994-7033   Emp: 7

MITSUBISHI WAREHOUSE CORP.
400 West Artesia Blvd., Compton, California 90220
CEO: Masataka Fukamachi, Mgr.   Tel: (310) 661-3560   %FO: 100
Bus: *Engaged in sea and air freight forwarding.*   Fax: (310) 631-7834

MITSUBISHI WAREHOUSE CORP.
3040 East Victoria St., Rancho Dominguez, California 90221
CEO: Soichiro Orihara, Pres.   Tel: (310) 886-5500   %FO: 100
Bus: *Engaged in sea and air freight forwarding.*   Fax: (310) 537-6126   Emp: 100

● **MITSUBISHI MATERIALS CORPORATION**
1-5-1, Otemachi, Chiyoda-ku, Tokyo 100-8117, Japan
CEO: Akihiko Ide, Pres.   Tel: 81-3-5252-5206   Rev: $8,976
Bus: *Non-ferrous metals, fabricated metals, electronic*   Fax: 81-3-5252-5272   Emp: 20,930
     material, aluminum cans, golden jewelry and semi- www.mmc.co.jp
     conductors.
NAICS: 331525, 333512

MITSUBISHI MATERIALS USA CORP.
61 Broadway, Ste. 1115, New York, New York 10006
CEO: Taizo Kondo, Pres.   Tel: (212) 968-0610   %FO: 100
Bus: *Metal fabrication.*   Fax: (212) 968-0552

MITSUBISHI MATERIALS USA CORP.
17401 Eastman, Irvine, California 92614
CEO: Taizo Kondo, Pres.   Tel: (949) 862-5100   %FO: 100
Bus: *Sale of cutting tools & machine tools.*   Fax: Emp: 129

MMC ELECTRONICS AMERICA INC.
1365 Wiley Rd., Ste. 149, Schaumburg, Illinois 60173
CEO: Toyoharu Tamura, Pres.   Tel: (847) 490-0222   %FO: 100
Bus: *Provides technical and sales support.*   Fax: (847) 490-0218   Emp: 9

MMC ELECTRONICS AMERICA INC.
1700 Wyatt Dr., Ste. 1, Santa Clara, California 95054
CEO: Eiko Omori, Mgr.   Tel: (408) 562-0000   %FO: 100
Bus: *Provides technical and sales support.*   Fax: (408) 562-0002

● **MITSUBISHI MOTORS CORPORATION**
2-16-4 Konan, Minato-ku, Tokyo 108-8410, Japan
CEO: Takashi Nishioka, Chmn. & CEO   Tel: 81-3-6719-2111   Rev: $23,849
Bus: *Mfr./sales of cars, diesel trucks and buses.*   Fax: 81-3-6719-0014   Emp: 43,624
                                          www.mitsubishi-motors.co.jp
NAICS: 336111, 336112, 336120

   MITSUBISHI FUSO TRUCK OF AMERICA, INC.
   2015 Center Square Rd., Bridgeport, New Jersey 08085
   CEO: Isao Toda, Pres.   Tel: (856) 467-4500   %FO: 100
   Bus: *Sales/distribution of trucks.*   Fax: (856) 467-4695

   MITSUBISHI MOTORS CREDIT OF AMERICA, INC.
   6363 Katella Ave., Cypress, California 90630
   CEO: Jeff Young, Pres. & CEO   Tel: (714) 372-6000
   Bus: *Financial services*   Fax: (714) 373-1020

   MITSUBISHI MOTORS NORTH AMERICA, INC.
   6400 Katella Ave., Cypress, California 90630-0064
   CEO: Hideyasu Tagaya, Chmn.   Tel: (714) 372-6000   %FO: 100
   Bus: *Sales/distribution of motors.*   Fax: (714) 373-1020

● **MITSUBISHI PAPER MILLS LIMITED**
Shin-Nisseki Bldg., 4-2, Marunouchi 3-chome, Chiyoda-ku, Tokyo 100-0005, Japan
CEO: Takeshi Sato, Pres.   Tel: 81-3-3213-3751   Rev: $2,243
Bus: *Mfr. specialty papers, photosensitive materials*   Fax: 81-3-3214-2338   Emp: 5,219
   and pulp.   web.infoweb.ne.jp/mpm/index.html
NAICS: 322121, 322130, 322211, 322222, 322226

   MITSUBISHI IMAGING, INC.MITSUBISHI IMAGING, INC.
   555 Theodore Fremd Ave., Rye, New York 10580
   CEO: Hiroshi Tomimasu, Pres.   Tel: (914) 925-3200   %FO: 100
   Bus: *Mfr. specialty papers, photosensitive*   Fax: (914) 921-2495   Emp: 80
   materials and pulp.

● **MITSUBISHI PHARMA , DIV. MITSUBISHI CHEMICAL HOLDINGS**
2-6-9, Hiranomachi, Chuo-ku, Osaka 541-0046, Japan
CEO: Takeshi Komine, Pres. & CEO   Tel: 81-6-6201-1600   Rev: $2,229
Bus: *Mfr. pharmaceuticals.*   Fax: 81-6-6233-2516   Emp: 6,122
                                          www.m-pharma.co.jp
NAICS: 325411, 325412

   MITSUBISHI PHARMA AMERICA INC.
   25 Independence Blvd., Ste. 201, Warren, New Jersey 07059
   CEO: Akiharo Narimatsu   Tel: (908) 607-1950   %FO: 100
   Bus: *Mfr. pharmaceuticals.*   Fax:

● **MITSUBISHI RAYON COMPANY, LTD.**
6-41, Konan 1-chome, Minato-ku, Tokyo 108-8506, Japan
CEO: Yoshiyuki Sumeragi, Pres.   Tel: 81-3-5495-3100   Rev: $2,931
Bus: *Mfr. synthetic fibers, films, resins, medical*   Fax: 81-3-5495-3184   Emp: 8,551
                                          www.mrc.co.jp
NAICS: 325211, 325212, 325221, 325222, 326199, 334418

> **MITSUBISHI RAYON AMERICA, INC.**
> 747 Third Ave., 19/F, New York, New York 10017
> CEO: Hiroyuki Sugao, Pres.   Tel: (212) 223-3043   %FO: 100
> Bus: *Synthetic, optical & carbon fibers, resins,*   Fax: (212) 223-3017   Emp: 77
>   *medical devices.*

● **MITSUBISHI STEEL MFG. CO., LTD.**
3-2-22, Harumi, Chuo-ku, Tokyo 104-8550, Japan
CEO: Akio Katoh, Pres. & CEO   Tel: 81-3-3536-3111   Rev: $871
Bus: *Steel castings and forgings manufacture.*   Fax: 81-3-3533-3123   Emp: 3,741
                                          www.mitsubishisteel.co.jp
NAICS: 332111, 332322

> **MSM US INC.**
> 3331 W. Big Beaver Rd., Ste. 310, Troy, Michigan 48084
> CEO: William Edwards, Mgr.   Tel: (248) 435-1775   %FO: 100
> Bus: *Mfr. coil springs, torsion bar springs,*   Fax: (248) 435-6704
>   *stabilizer bars and assemblies for*
>   *automobiles.*

> **MSM US INC.**
> 102 Bill Bryan Blvd., Hopkinsville, Kentucky 42240
> CEO: Robert Holt, Mgr.   Tel: (270) 887-3000   %FO: 100
> Bus: *Automobile suspensions manufacturing plant.* Fax: (270) 887-3004

● **MITSUBISHI UFJ FINANCIAL GROUP INC.**
7-1 Marunouchi 2-chome, Chiyoda-ku, Tokyo 100-8330, Japan
CEO: Nobuo Kuroyanagi, CEO   Tel: 81-3-3240-1111   Rev: $22,744
Bus: *Private investment banking services, deposit,*   Fax: 81-3-3240-8203   Emp: 43,600
     lending, leasing and trust services.   www.mufg.jp
NAICS: 522110, 523120, 523991, 525110, 525920

> **BANK OF TOKYO-MITSUBISHI TRUST COMPANY**
> 445 S. Figueroa St., Ste. 200, Los Angeles, California 90071
> CEO: Masaharu Takenaka   Tel: (213) 236-6100   %FO: 100
> Bus: *Banking services.*   Fax: (213) 236-6100

> **BANK OF TOKYO-MITSUBISHI TRUST COMPANY**
> 1909 K St., Washington, District of Columbia 20006
> CEO: Masaharu Takenaka   Tel: (202) 463-0477   %FO: 100
> Bus: *Banking services.*   Fax: (202) 463-0477

> **BANK OF TOKYO-MITSUBISHI TRUST COMPANY**
> 2001 Ross Ave., Ste. 3150, Dallas, Texas 75201
> CEO: John Merns   Tel: (214) 954-1200   %FO: 100
> Bus: *Banking services.*   Fax: (214) 954-1200

BANK OF TOKYO-MITSUBISHI TRUST COMPANY
133 Peachtree St. NE, Atlanta, Georgia 30303
CEO: Sean Shimono
Bus: *Banking services.*
Tel: (404) 577-2960
Fax: (404) 577-1155
%FO: 100

BANK OF TOKYO-MITSUBISHI TRUST COMPANY
1100 Louisiana St., Houston, Texas 77002-
CEO: Nasakai Yanava
Bus: *Banking services.*
Tel: (713) 658-1160
Fax: (713) 658-1160
%FO: 100

BANK OF TOKYO-MITSUBISHI TRUST COMPANY
227 W Monroe St., Ste. 2300, Chicago, Illinois 60606
CEO: Minoru Akimoto
Bus: *Banking services.*
Tel: (312) 696-4500
Fax: (312) 696-4500
%FO: 100

MITSUBISHI TRUST & BANKING CORP.
520 Madison Ave., New York, New York 10022
CEO: Kuniyashu Yamada, CEO
Bus: *Banking services.*
Tel: (212) 838-7700
Fax: (212) 838-7700
%FO: 100

MITSUBISHI UFJ FINANCIAL INC.
1251 Ave. of the Americas, New York, New York 10020
CEO: Mitsuhiro Yamawaki, VP
Bus: *Financial services.*
Tel: (212) 782-4000
Fax: (212) 782-4000
%FO: 100

TOKYO-MITSUBISHI FUTURES USA INC.
30 South Wacker Dr., Ste. 3910, Chicago, Illinois 60606
CEO: James Torkelson, Mgr.
Bus: *Banking services.*
Tel: (312) 930-2300
Fax:
%FO: 100

UNIONBANCAL CORPORATION
400 California St., San Francisco, California 94104
CEO: Takashi Morimura
Bus: *Banking services.*
Tel: (415) 705-7000
Fax: (415) 765-2220
%FO: 100

● **MITSUI & COMPANY, LTD.**
2-1, Ohtemachi 1-chome, Chiyoda-ku, Tokyo 100-0004, Japan
CEO: Shoei Utsuda, Pres. & CEO
Bus: *General trading company and administrative services for Mitsui Group.*
Tel: 81-3-3285-1111
Fax: 81-3-3285-9819
www.mitsui.co.jp
Rev: $32,895
Emp: 39,735

NAICS: 212299, 312111, 314999, 325414, 331491, 332111, 332112, 333120, 333131, 333292, 333298, 334119, 424410, 424490, 424690, 424710, 424720, 454312, 454319, 541710

MBK REAL ESTATE LTD.
175 Technology Dr., Irvine, California 92618
CEO: Stefan Markowitz, Pres.
Bus: *Residential real estate development.*
Tel: (949) 789-8300
Fax: (949) 789-9300
%FO: 100

MI-TECH STEEL, INC.
15415 Shelbyville Rd., Louisville, Kentucky 40253
CEO: Stuart N. Ray, Pres. & CEO
Bus: *Steel service center.*
Tel: (502) 245-2110
Fax: (502) 244-0182
%FO: 100

MITSUI & CO (USA) INC
1000 Town Centre, Ste. 1900, Southfield, Michigan 48075
CEO: Koichiro Ejiri
Bus: *Mfr. steel, machinery and general merchandise.*
Tel: (248) 357-3300
Fax: (248) 355-3572
%FO: 100
Emp: 31

MITSUI & CO (USA) INC.
601 South Figueroa St., Ste. 1900, Los Angeles, California 90017
CEO: Shozaburo Marayama, Mgr.
Bus: *Mfr. steel, machinery and general merchandise.*
Tel: (213) 896-1100
Fax: (213) 688-1138
%FO: 100
Emp: 52

MITSUI & CO (USA) INC.
200 SW Market St., Ste. 1830, Portland, Oregon 97201
CEO: N. Shimizu, Admin.
Bus: *Mfr. steel, machinery and general merchandise.*
Tel: (503) 226-3546
Fax: (503) 226-3520
%FO: 100
Emp: 8

MITSUI & CO (USA) INC.
1201 Third Ave., Ste. 5100, Seattle, Washington 98101
CEO: Yoshiharu Kurosawa, Sales
Bus: *Mfr. steel, machinery and general merchandise.*
Tel: (206) 223-5604
Fax: (206) 223-5618
%FO: 100
Emp: 30

MITSUI & CO (USA) INC.
1300 Post Oak Blvd., Ste. 1700, Houston, Texas 77056
CEO: Hobiyoshi Kawanopo, Sales Mgr.
Bus: *Mfr. steel, machinery and general merchandise.*
Tel: (713) 236-6100
Fax: (713) 236-6134
%FO: 100
Emp: 90

MITSUI & CO (USA) INC.
750 17th St., Ste. 400, Washington, District of Columbia 20006
CEO: Yeuji Takagi, Mgr.
Bus: *Mfr. steel, machinery and general merchandise.*
Tel: (202) 861-0660
Fax: (202) 861-0437
%FO: 100
Emp: 9

MITSUI & CO (USA) INC.
1 California St., Ste. 1500, San Francisco, California 94111
CEO: Yoshiyuki Enomoto, Gen. Mgr.
Bus: *Mfr. steel, machinery and general merchandise.*
Tel: (415) 765-1195
Fax: (415) 765-1190
%FO: 100

MITSUI & COMPANY, (USA) INC.
25 Century Blvd., Ste. 310, Nashville, Tennessee 37214
CEO: Akira Ishikawa, Mgr.
Bus: *Mfr. steel, machinery and general merchandise.*
Tel: (615) 885-5318
Fax: (615) 885-5321
%FO: 100
Emp: 100

MITSUI & COMPANY, (USA) INC.
Met Life Bldg., 200 Park Ave., 36/F, New York, New York 10166
CEO: Hiroshi Tada, Pres.
Bus: *General trading company: export/import, finance, investment, transportation and technology transfer.*
Tel: (212) 878-4000
Fax: (212) 878-4800
%FO: 100
Emp: 1,800

MITSUI & COMPANY, (USA) INC.
200 Public Square, BP Bldg., Ste. 29-5500, Cleveland, Ohio 44114
CEO: Al Kanetsky, VP
Bus: *Mfr. steel, machinery and general merchandise.*

Tel: (216) 696-8710
Fax: (216) 696-8574

%FO: 100
Emp: 15

MITSUI & COMPANY, (USA) INC.
200 East Randolph Dr., Ste. 5200, Chicago, Illinois 60601
CEO: John Fairchild, Mgr.
Bus: *Mfr. steel, machinery and general merchandise.*

Tel: (312) 540-4000
Fax: (312) 540-4001

%FO: 100
Emp: 40

ROAD MACHINERY LLC
716 South 7th St., Phoenix, Arizona 85034
CEO: Masao Tsukuda, Chmn. & CEO
Bus: *Industrial machinery & equipment.*

Tel: (602) 252-7121
Fax: (602) 253-9690

%FO: 100

TAMCO STEEL
12459B Arrow Hwy., Rancho Cucamonga, California 91739
CEO: Jack Stutz, Pres. & CEO
Bus: *Steel mill.*

Tel: (909) 899-0660
Fax: (909) 899-1910

%FO: 100

VENTURA FOODS, LLC
40 Pointe Dr., Brea, California 92821
CEO: Richard L. Mazer, CEO
Bus: *Mfr. of edible oils.*

Tel: (714) 257-3700
Fax: (714) 257-3702

%FO: 100
Emp: 1,800

• MITSUI CHEMICALS, INC.
Shiodome City Centre, 1-5-2 Higashi-Shimbashi, Minato-ku, Tokyo 105-7117, Japan
CEO: Hiroyuki Nakanishi, Chmn. & Pres.
Bus: *Mfr./sales chemical, pharmaceutical and electronic materials and products.*

Tel: 81-3-6253-2100
Fax: 81-3-6253-4245
www.mitsui-chem.co.jp

Rev: $10,313
Emp: 12,348

NAICS: 325110, 325188, 325192, 325193, 325199, 325211, 325212, 325221, 325222, 325311, 325312, 325320, 488510, 541330, 541614

ADVANCED COMPOSITES INC.
1062 Fourth Ave., Sidney, Ohio 45365
CEO: Yoichi Kawai, Pres.
Bus: *Mfr./sale of polypropylene compound.*

Tel: (937) 492-9187
Fax: (937) 498-4837

%FO: 100
Emp: 220

ANDERSON DEVELOPMENT CO.
1415 East Michigan St., Adrian, Michigan 49221
CEO: Larry Hardy, Pres.
Bus: *Mfr./develops specialty chemicals, including polyurethane & nitrogen trifluoride.*

Tel: (517) 263-2121
Fax: (517) 263-1000

%FO: 100
Emp: 140

ESCO COMPANY LTD. PARTNERSHIP
2340 Roberts St., PO Box 448, Muskegon, Michigan 49221
CEO: Bruce Rice, Principal
Bus: *Mfr./sale of color formers.*

Tel: (231) 726-3106
Fax: (231) 727-6452

%FO: 100
Emp: 82

IMAGE POLYMERS CO.
730 Main St., Wilmington, Massachusetts 01887
CEO: Steve Bagshaw, Pres.
Bus: *Develops & produces toner resin.*

Tel: (800) 241-3821
Fax: (978) 658-7882

%FO: 100
Emp: 23

MITSUI CHEMICALS AMERICA INC.
2099 Gateway Place, Ste. 260, San Jose, California 95110
CEO: Kenji Miyachi, Mgr.   Tel: (408) 453-0682   %FO: 100
Bus: *Sales/distribution of chemical,*   Fax: (408) 453-0684   Emp: 4
   pharmaceutical and electronic materials and
   products.

MITSUI CHEMICALS AMERICA, INC.
2500 Westchester Ave., Ste. 110, Purchase, New York 10577
CEO: Kensaku Maruyama, Pres.   Tel: (914) 253-0777   %FO: 100
Bus: *Sales/distribution of chemical,*   Fax: (914) 253-0790   Emp: 700
   pharmaceutical and electronic materials and
   products.

● **MITSUI ENGINEERING & SHIPBUILDING CO., LTD.**
6-4, Tsukiji 5-chome, Chuo-ku, Tokyo 104-8439, Japan
CEO: Takao Motoyama, Pres.   Tel: 81-3-3544-3147   Rev: $4,508
Bus: *Engaged in system engineering, shipbuilding,* Fax: 81-3-3544-3050   Emp: 10,676
   medical equipment, industrial machinery and   www.mes.co.jp
   pollution control plants.
NAICS: 236210, 237310, 321992, 336611, 541330

   ENGINEERS AND CONSTRUCTORS INTERNATIONAL, INC.
   14701 14925 Memorial Dr.., Bldg. A#100, Houston, Texas 77079
   CEO: Joseph C. Tate Jr., Pres.   Tel: (281) 584-9393   %FO: 100
   Bus: *Engineering, construction of & procurement* Fax: (281) 497-3614   Emp: 120
      of materials for chemical plant.

   MODEC INTERNATIONAL LLC
   1201 Dairy Ashford, Ste. 100, Houston, Texas 77079
   CEO: Shashank Karve, Pres.   Tel: (281) 496-1971   %FO: 100
   Bus: *Supplies offshore equipment, engineering &* Fax: (281) 496-9250   Emp: 100
      consultation on ocean development.

   PACECO CORPORATION
   3854 Bay Center Place, Hayward, California 94545
   CEO: Toru Takehara, Pres.   Tel: (510) 264-9288   %FO: 100
   Bus: *Development, engineering and sales of*   Fax: (510) 264-9280   Emp: 17
      PACECO cranes.

● **MITSUI FUDOSAN CO., LTD.**
Mitsui Main Bldg., 1-1 Nihonbashi, Muromachi, 2-chome, Chou-ku, Tokyo 103-0022, Japan
CEO: Hiromichi Iwasa, Pres. & CEO   Tel: 81-3-3246-3131   Rev: $10,550
Bus: *Engaged in real estate development, construction* Fax: 81-3-3246-3543 Emp: 12,808
   and financing.   www.mitsuifudosan.co.jp
NAICS: 236117, 236220, 237210, 525930, 531110, 531120, 531190, 531311, 531312, 531390

   MITSUI FUDOSAN AMERICA, INC.
   1251 Ave. of the Americas, Ste. 800, New York, New York 10020
   CEO: Kosei Murakami, Pres.   Tel: (212) 403-5600   %FO: 100
   Bus: *Engaged in real estate development,*   Fax: (212) 403-5657   Emp: 17
      construction and financing.

- **MITSUI MINING & SMELTING COMPANY, LTD.**
1-11-1, Osaki, Shinagawa-ku, Tokyo 141-8584, Japan
CEO: Shimpei Miyamura, Chmn. & CEO
Bus: *Mfr. non-ferrous metals.*
Tel: 81-3-5437-8028
Fax: 81-3-5437-8029
www.mitsui-kinzoku.co.jp
Rev: $3,729
Emp: 8,339
NAICS: 212231, 212234, 212299, 213114, 236210, 236220, 237110, 237120, 237130, 237310, 237990, 238910, 238990

GECOM CORPORATION
1025 Barachel Lane, Greensburg, Indiana 47240
CEO: Koji Nagashima, Pres.
Bus: *Mfr./Sales of functional parts for automobiles.*
Tel: (812) 663-2270
Fax: (812) 663-2230
%FO: 100
Emp: 3

MITSUI COMPONENTS (USA), INC.
602 South Swanson St., Casa Grande, Arizona 85222
CEO: Tomoyuki Doi, Pres.
Bus: *Mfr. of sales of die-cast products.*
Tel: (520) 836-5660
Fax:
%FO: 100
Emp: 55

MITSUI MINING & SMELTING COMPANY, (USA) INC.
461 Fifth Ave., New York, New York 10017
CEO: Nobuo Abe, Pres.
Bus: *Information services.*
Tel: (212) 679-9300
Fax: (212) 679-9303
%FO: 100

MITSUI ZINC POWDER LLC
302 Frankfort Rd., Monaca, Pennsylvania 15061
CEO: Nobutoshi Sakai, member
Bus: *Mfr. of zinc powder for batteries.*
Tel: (724) 728-8392
Fax:
%FO: 100
Emp: 16

OAK-MITSUI
80 First St., Hoosick Falls, New York 12090
CEO: Anthony Sirco, CFO
Bus: *Mfr. of copper foil for printed circuit boards.*
Tel: (518) 686-4961
Fax:
%FO: 100
Emp: 200

OAK-MITSUI PARTNERSHIP
29 Battleship Rd. Ext., PO Box 1709, Camden, South Carolina 29020
CEO: Jeff Gray, Pres.
Bus: *Mfr. of copper foil for printed circuit boards.*
Tel: (803) 425-7900
Fax:
%FO: 100
Emp: 60

- **MITSUI OSK LINES LTD.**
1-1, Toranomon, 2-chome, Minato-ku, Tokyo 105-8688, Japan
CEO: Akimitsu Ashida, Pres.
Bus: *International transport, sea, land and rail carriers, terminals, cruise ships and resorts, and real estate development.*
Tel: 81-3-3587-6224
Fax: 81-3-3587-7734
www.mol.co.jp
Rev: $9,440
Emp: 7,033
NAICS: 483111, 488310, 488320, 488510, 493110

GEARBULK HOLDING LTD.
3000 Bayport Dr., Tampa, Florida 33607
CEO: Kristian Jebsen, Pres.
Bus: *Freight forwarding.*
Tel: (813) 830-6000
Fax: (813) 830-6001
%FO: 100
Emp: 16

MITSUI OSK LINES (America) LTD.
2300 Clayton Rd., Ste. 1500, Concord, California 94520
CEO: George Hayashi, Pres.
Bus: *Marine transportation services.*
Tel: (925) 688-2600
Fax: (925) 688-2670
%FO: 100
Emp: 434

STAR-NET AMERICA, INC.
160 Fieldcrest Ave., Edison, New Jersey 08837
CEO: M. Hidaka, Pres.　　　　　　　　Tel: (732) 512-5200　　　%FO: 100
Bus: *Computer integrated systems design.*　Fax:　　　　　　　Emp: 40

TRANS PACIFIC CONTAINER SERVICE CORP.
920 W. Harry Bridges Blvd., Wilmington, California 90744
CEO: H. Sadamatsu, Pres.　　　　　　Tel: (310) 830-2000　　　%FO: 100
Bus: *Marine cargo handler freight transportation*　Fax:　　　Emp: 60
arrangements.

● **MITSUI SUMITOMO INSURANCE CO.**
27-2, Shinkawa 2-Chome, Chuo-ku, Tokyo 104-8252, Japan
CEO: Hiroyuki Uemura, Pres. & CEO　　Tel: 81-3-3297-1111　　Rev: $15,839
Bus: *Property and casualty insurance.*　Fax: 81-3-3297-6888　Emp: 13,675
　　　　　　　　　　　　　　　　　　www.ms-ins.com
NAICS: 523999, 524114, 524126, 524130, 525190, 525910, 525920, 525990

　　MITSUI SUMITOMO INSURANCE COMPANY OF AMERICA
　　10 Universal City Plaza, Universal City, California 91608
　　CEO: Kazuo Imazu, Mgr.　　　　　　Tel: (818) 509-7150　　%FO: 100
　　Bus: *Engaged in property and casualty insurance*　Fax:
　　services.

　　MITSUI SUMITOMO INSURANCE CO., LTD.
　　15 Independence Blvd., Warren, New Jersey 07059
　　CEO: Koji Yoshida, Pres.　　　　　　Tel: (908) 604-2900　　%FO: 100
　　Bus: *Engaged in property and casualty insurance*　Fax: (908) 604-2991　Emp: 197
　　services.

　　MITSUI SUMITOMO INSURANCE COMPANY
　　23200 Chagrin Blvd., Cleveland, Ohio 44122
　　CEO: Windy Sidel, VP　　　　　　　Tel: (216) 360-0202
　　Bus: *Fire, marine & casualty insurance*　Fax:

　　MITSUI SUMITOMO MARINE MANAGEMENT (USA), INC.
　　50 California St., Ste. 680, San Francisco, California 94111
　　CEO: Takashi Sorida, Mgr.　　　　　Tel: (415) 433-4270　　%FO: 100
　　Bus: *Engaged in property and casualty insurance*　Fax:
　　services.

　　SUMITOMO MITSUI ASSET MANAGEMENT INC.
　　101 E. 52nd St., 2/F, New York, New York 10022
　　CEO: Motoyuki Oka　　　　　　　　Tel: (212) 521-8300
　　Bus: *Insurance claim processing*　　Fax:　　　　　　　Emp: 8

● **MITSUI-SOKO CO., LTD.**
MSC Center Bldg.,, 22-23 Kaigan 3-chome, Minato-ku, Tokyo 108-0022, Japan
CEO: Kazuo Tamura, CEO　　　　　　Tel: 81-3-6400-8000　　Rev: $852
Bus: *Provides warehouse storage.*　　Fax: 81-3-6400-8079　Emp: 2,859
　　　　　　　　　　　　　　　　　　www.mitsui-soko.co.jp
NAICS: 484210, 488510, 493110, 493120, 493130, 493190, 519190

MITSUI-SOKO CO., LTD.
2125 Center Ave., Ste. 202, Fort Lee, New Jersey 07024
CEO: Tatsusuke Imaizumi, Mgr.   Tel: (201) 585-9399   %FO: 100
Bus: *Provides warehouse storage.*   Fax: (201) 585-2198

MITSUI-SOKO CO., LTD.
1651 Glenn Curtiss St., Carson, California 90746
CEO: H. Chijiiwa, Pres.   Tel: (310) 639-3060   %FO: 100
Bus: *Provides warehouse storage.*   Fax: (310) 639-4060   Emp: 70

MITSUI-SOKO CO., LTD.
101 Mark St., Chancellory Business Park, Bldg. 1, Ste. A, Wood Dale, Illinois 60191
CEO: Hioyuki Hamano, Mgr.   Tel: (630) 616-0990   %FO: 100
Bus: *Provides warehouse storage.*   Fax: (630) 616-0996

MITSUI-SOKO CO., LTD.
3 Butterfield Trail, Ste. 122, El Paso, Texas 79906
CEO: H. Hamano, Mgr.   Tel: (915) 772-3540   %FO: 100
Bus: *Provides warehouse storage.*   Fax: (915) 772-3728

MITSUI-SOKO CO., LTD.
1280 Lakes Pkwy., Lawrenceville, Georgia 30043
CEO: Jan Segars, Mgr.   Tel: (770) 931-4400   %FO: 100
Bus: *Provides warehouse storage.*   Fax: (770) 931-3700

MITSUI-SOKO CO., LTD.
6502 S. 216th St., Kent, Washington 98032
CEO: Kazumoto Baba, COO   Tel: (253) 239-4147   %FO: 100
Bus: *Provides warehouse storage.*   Fax: (253) 239-4148

● **MITSUKOSHI, LTD.**
1-4-1 Nihonbashi Muromachi, Chuo-ku, Tokyo 103-8001, Japan
CEO: Taneo Nakamura, Pres.   Tel: 81-3-3241-3311   Rev: $8,395
Bus: *Operates retail department stores.* Fax: 81-3-3242-4559   Emp: 11,829
                                         www.mitsukoshi.co.jp

NAICS: 452111, 452112

MITSUKOSHI USA, INC.
12 E. 49th St., 17/F, New York, New York 10017
CEO: Koji Nose, Pres.   Tel: (212) 753-5580   %FO: 100
Bus: *Sale/service restaurants, retail, exporting* Fax: (212) 355-7161   Emp: 315
     and interior decoration.

● **MITSUMI ELECTRIC CO., LTD.**
2-11-2, Tsurumaki, Tama, Tokyo 206-8567, Japan
CEO: Shigeru Moribe, Pres. & CEO   Tel: 81-4-2310-5333   Rev: $2,028
Bus: *Mfr. electronic components integrated circuits,* Fax: 81-4-2310-5158   Emp: 49,037
     keyboards, radio-frequency modulators, www.mitsumi.co.jp
     transformers, switches, adapters and
NAICS: 334112, 334119, 334220, 334290, 334413, 334419

MITSUMI ELECTRONICS CORP.
5808 West Campus Circle Dr., Irving, Texas 75063
CEO: Tom Iida, VP
Bus: *Sale of electronic components integrated
circuits, keyboards, mice, radio-frequency
modulators, transformers, switches,
adapters & connectors.*

Tel: (942) 550-7300
Fax: (942) 550-7424

%FO: 100
Emp: 40

MITSUMI ELECTRONICS CORPORATION
40000 Grand River Ave., Ste. 400, Novi, Michigan 48375
CEO: Jim McCaffrey
Bus: *Sale of electronic components integrated
circuits, keyboards, mice, radio-frequency
modulators, transformers, switches,
adapters & connectors.*

Tel: (238) 426-8448
Fax: (238) 426-8448

MITSUMI USA, INC.
4655 Old Ironside Dr., Ste. 320, Santa Clara, California 95054
CEO: Takashi Kumagai, Mgr.
Bus: *Sale of electronic components integrated
circuits, keyboards, mice, radio-frequency
modulators, transformers, switches,
adapters & connectors.*

Tel: (408) 970-0700
Fax: (408) 727-5337

%FO: 100
Emp: 20

MITSUMI USA, INC.
5 Centerpointe Dr., Ste. 400, Lake Oswego, Oregon 97035
CEO: David Clark, Mgr.
Bus: *Sale of electronic components integrated
circuits, keyboards, mice, radio-frequency
modulators, transformers, switches,
adapters & connectors.*

Tel: (503) 624-9128
Fax: (503) 620-3957

%FO: 100

MITSUMI USA, INC.
8880 Rio San Diego Dr., Ste. 800, 8/F, San Diego, California 92108
CEO: Keith Otani, Mgr.
Bus: *Sale of electronic components integrated
circuits, keyboards, mice, radio-frequency
modulators, transformers, switches,
adapters & connectors.*

Tel: (619) 209-6133
Fax: (619) 209-6134

%FO: 100

MITSUMI USA, INC.
7500 West Grand Ave., Ste. 23, Gurnee, Illinois 60031
CEO: Tom Hevrdejs, Mgr.
Bus: *Sale of electronic components integrated
circuits, keyboards, mice, radio-frequency
modulators, transformers, switches,
adapters & connectors.*

Tel: (847) 265-5030
Fax: (847) 265-5919

%FO: 100

● **MIURA CO.,LTD**
7 Horie-cho, Matsuyama, Ehime 799-2696, Japan
CEO: Yuji Takahashi, Pres.
Bus: *Mfr. steam and hot water boilers and food
machines.*
NAICS: 333294, 333414

Tel: 81-89-979-7123
Fax: 81-89-979-7117
www.miuraz.co.jp

Rev: $440
Emp: 1,476

MIURA BOILER USA, INC.
1945 South Myrtle Ave., Monrovia, California 91016-4854
CEO: Damon Erickson, Pres. Tel: (626) 305-6622 %FO: 100
Bus: *Sales and service of boilers.* Fax: (626) 305-6624

MIURA BOILER USA, INC.
600 Northgate Pkwy, Ste. M, Wheeling, Illinois 60090-3201
CEO: Mark Utzinger, VP Tel: (847) 465-0001 %FO: 100
Bus: *Sales and service of boilers.* Fax: (847) 465-0011 Emp: 10

● **MIYACHI TECHNOS CORPORATION**
Koyosha Bldg, 3/F, 5-48-5, Higashinippori, Arakawa-ku, Tokyo 116, Japan
CEO: Takasuke Miyauchi, Pres. Tel: 81-6-891-2211
Bus: *Mfr. welding controls, power supplies and* Fax: 81-6-891-7887 Emp: 250
industrial laser systems. www.miyachitechnos.co.jp
NAICS: 333512, 333992, 335999

   UNITEC MIYACHI INTERNATIONAL
   1900 Walker St., Monrovia, California 91017
   CEO: Jack D. Lantz, CEO Tel: (626) 303-5676 %FO: 100
   Bus: *Sales/service of welding controls, power* Fax: (626) 358-8048
   supplies and monitors.

● **MIZUHO FINANCIAL GROUP**
1-5-5, Otemachi, Chiyoda-ku, Tokyo 100-0004, Japan
CEO: Terunobu Maeda, Pres. & CEO Tel: 81-3-5224-1111 Rev: $31,644
Bus: *Commercial banking services.* Fax: 81-3-3215-4616 Emp: 26,575
   www.mizuho-fg.co.jp
NAICS: 522110

   DLIBJ ASSET MANAGEMENT USA INC.
   1133 Ave. of the Americas, 28/F, New York, New York 10036
   CEO: William R. Yost Tel: (212) 350-7650 %FO: 100
   Bus: *Financial services.* Fax: (212) 354-1883

   MIZUHO CAPITAL MARKETS CORP.
   1440 Broadway, 25/F, New York, New York 10018
   CEO: Takashi Kinoshita, Pres. Tel: (212) 547-1500 %FO: 100
   Bus: *Financial services.* Fax: (212) 299-0625 Emp: 140

   MIZUHO CORPORATE BANK
   311 South Wacker Dr., Ste. 2020, Chicago, Illinois 60661
   CEO: Esther Wilson Tel: (312) 855-1111 %FO: 100
   Bus: *Banking services* Fax: (312) 855-8200

   MIZUHO CORPORATE BANK (USA)
   1251 Ave. of the Americas, New York, New York 10020
   CEO: Masathugu Nagato, Gen. Mgr. Tel: (212) 282-3030 %FO: 100
   Bus: *Banking services.* Fax: (212) 282-4250 Emp: 500

   MIZUHO CORPORATE BANK OF CALIFORNIA
   350 South Grand Ave., Ste. 1500, Los Angeles, California 90071
   CEO: Takuo Yoshida, Chmn. Tel: (213) 243-4500 %FO: 100
   Bus: *Banking services.* Fax: (213) 243-4505 Emp: 95

MIZUHO SECURITIES USA, INC.
Waterfront Corporate Center, Bldg. 1, 111 River St., 11/F, Hoboken, New Jersey 07030
CEO: Bernard Jensen, Pres.   Tel: (201) 626-1000   %FO: 100
Bus: *Financial services.*   Fax: (201) 626-1577   Emp: 290

THE BRIDGEFORD GROUP, INC.
445 Park Ave., 20/F, New York, New York 10022
CEO: Haruhiko Masuda, CEO   Tel: (212) 705-0880   %FO: 100
Bus: *Financial services.*   Fax: (212) 755-8900   Emp: 9

● **MIZUHO TRUST & BANKING CO., LTD.**
2-1 Yaesu 1-chome, Chuo-ku, Tokyo 103-8670, Japan
CEO: Teruhiko Ikeda, Pres.   Tel: 81-3-3278-8111
Bus: *Financial and investment services.*   Fax: 81-3-3274-4670
                                     www.mizuho-tb.co.jp
NAICS: 522110, 523991, 523999

  MIZUHO TRUST & BANKING CO. (USA)
  666 Fifth Ave., Ste. 802, New York, New York 10103
  CEO: Akiyoshi Oba   Tel: (212) 373-5900   %FO: 100
  Bus: *Financial and investment services.*   Fax: (212) 354-1883

● **MIZUNO CORPORATION**
1-12-35, Nanko-kita, Suminoe-ku, Osaka 559-8510, Japan
CEO: Masato Mizuno, Pres.   Tel: 81-6-6614-8467   Rev: $1,332
Bus: *Mfr. sporting goods.*   Fax: 81-6-6614-8493   Emp: 4,034
                                     www.mizuno.com
NAICS: 339920

  MIZUNO USA INC.
  5601 Interstate View Dr., Morristown, Tennessee 37813
  CEO: Katsuhito Mizuno, Pres.   Tel: (423) 317-9876   %FO: 100
  Bus: *Mfr./sales sporting goods.*   Fax: (423) 317-9876   Emp: 23

  MIZUNO USA INC.
  4925 Avalon Ridge Pkwy., Norcross, Georgia 30071
  CEO: Robert Puccini, Pres. & CEO   Tel: (770) 441-5533   %FO: 100
  Bus: *Mfr./sales sporting goods.*   Fax: (770) 448-3234   Emp: 285

  MIZUNO USA INC.
  7415 SE 21st Ave., Portland, Oregon 97202
  CEO: Dave Lambert, Mgr.   Tel: (503) 233-3378   %FO: 100
  Bus: *Mfr./sales sporting goods.*   Fax: (503) 233-3378

● **MORI SEIKI CO., LTD.**
2-35-16 Meiki, Nakamura-ku, Aichi, Nagoya 450-0002, Japan
CEO: Masahiko Mori, Pres.   Tel: 81-52-587-1811   Rev: $655
Bus: *Mfr. of machine tools.*   Fax: Emp: 2,671
                                     www.moriseiki.co.jp
NAICS: 333512

MORI SEIKI USA
5740 Warland Dr., Cypress, California 90630
CEO: Shuji Yamashita, Mgr.
Bus: *Mfr. machine tools cutting equipment*
Tel: (562) 430-3800
Fax: (562) 430-5570

MORI SEIKI USA, INC.
9001 Currency St., Irving, Texas 75063
CEO: Yukio Mori, Chmn.
Bus: *Sales/distribution of machine tools.*
Tel: (972) 929-8321
Fax: (972) 929-8226
%FO: 100
Emp: 100

● **J. MORITA CORPORATION**
3-33-18, Tarumi-cho, Siuta City, Osaka 564-8650, Japan
CEO: Haruo Morita, Pres.
Bus: *Mfr./distributor of dental equipment and supplies.*
Tel: 81-6-6380-2525
Fax:
www.jmorita.com

NAICS: 339114

J. MORITA USA, INC.
9 Mason, Irvine, California 92618
CEO: Junichi Miyata, Pres.
Bus: *Mfr./distribution of furniture and dental instruments/equipment.*
Tel: (949) 581-9600
Fax: (949) 465-1095
%FO: 100
Emp: 49

● **MURATA MANUFACTURING COMPANY, LTD.**
26-10, Tenjin, 2-chome, Nagaokakyo, Kyoto 617-8555, Japan
CEO: Yasutaka Murata, Pres.
Bus: *Electronic components manufacture.*
Tel: 81-75-951-9111
Fax: 81-75-954-7720
www.murata.com
Rev: $3,921
Emp: 26,469

NAICS: 334210, 334220, 334290, 334413, 334414, 334415, 334416, 334419, 335311, 335999

MURATA ELECTRONICS NORTH AMERICA, INC.
2200 Lake Park Dr., Smyrna, Georgia 30080
CEO: Hiroshi Jozuka, EVP
Bus: *Electronic components manufacture and sales.*
Tel: (770) 436-1300
Fax: (770) 436-3030
%FO: 100
Emp: 1,200

● **MURATEC MURATA MACHINERY, LTD.**
136Mukaidaicho, Takeda, Fushimi-ku, Kyoto 612-8418, Japan
CEO: Junichi Murata, Chmn.
Bus: *Mfr./distribution of textile machinery, material handling equipment and machine tools.*
Tel: 81-75-672-8111
Fax:
www.muratec.co.jp
Rev: $1,046
Emp: 1,698

NAICS: 423610, 561499, 811412

MURATA MACHINERY USA, INC.
2120 I-85 South, Charlotte, North Carolina 28208
CEO: Masaharu Nishio, Pres.
Bus: *Industrial machinery & equipment*
Tel: (704) 394-8331
Fax:
%FO: 100
Emp: 122

MURATEC AMERICA, INC.
3301 East Plano Pkwy, Ste. 100, Plano, Texas 75074
CEO: Hideki Mori, Pres. & CEO
Bus: *Sales of multifunctional office equipment*
Tel: (469) 429-3300
Fax: (469) 429-3311
%FO: 100
Emp: 85

- **NABTESCO CORP.**
  9-18 Kaigan 1- chome, Minato-ku, Tokyo 105-0022, Japan
  CEO: Kazuyuki Matsumoto, Pres. & CEO   Tel: 81-3-3578-7070   Rev: $19
  Bus: *Mfr. textile machinery, industrial machinery and*   Fax: 81-3-3578-7237   Emp: 2,025
       aircraft parts.   www.nabtesco.com
  NAICS: 333292, 333298, 336413

  > **NABTESCO**
  > 17770 Northeast 78th Place, Redmond, Washington 98052-4960
  > CEO: Hiroshi Katada, Pres.   Tel: (425) 602-8400   %FO: 100
  > Bus: *Mfr./services aircraft parts.*   Fax: Emp: 38

- **NACHI-FUJIKOSHI CORP.**
  1-9-2 Higashi-Shinbashi, Minato-ku, Tokyo 105-0021, Japan
  CEO: Kensuke Imura, Pres.   Tel: 81-3-5568-5111   Rev: $1,449
  Bus: *Mfr. of industrial machinery*   Fax: 81-3-5568-5206   Emp: 5,320
                                     www.nachi-fujikoshi.co.jp
  NAICS: 333298, 333512, 333991

  > **NACHI AMERICA INC.**
  > 715 Pushville Rd., Greenwood, Indiana 46143
  > CEO: Shohei Ito, Chmn.   Tel: (317) 535-5527   %FO: 100
  > Bus: *Manufacturer industrial machinery.* Fax: (317) 535-3659

  > **NACHI AMERICA INC.**
  > 2315 N.W. 107th Ave., Miami, Florida 33172
  > CEO: Shohei Ito, Chmn.   Tel: (305) 591-0054   %FO: 100
  > Bus: *Manufacturer industrial machinery*   Fax: (305) 591-3110

  > **NACHI AMERICA INC.**
  > 12652 E. Alondra Blvd., Cerritos, California 90703
  > CEO: Shohei Ito, Chmn.   Tel: (562) 802-0055   %FO: 100
  > Bus: *Manufacturer industrial machinery*   Fax: (562) 802-2455

  > **NACHI AMERICA INC.**
  > 17500 Twenty-Three Mile Rd., Macomb, Michigan 48044
  > CEO: Shohei Ito, Chmn.   Tel: (586) 226-5151   %FO: 100
  > Bus: *Manufacturer industrial machinery*   Fax: (888) 383-8665

  > **NACHI ROBOTIC SYSTEMS INC.**
  > 22285 Roethel Dr., Novi, Michigan 48375
  > CEO: Shohei Ito, Chmn.   Tel: (248) 305-6545   %FO: 100
  > Bus: *Manufacturer robotic systems*   Fax: (248) 305-6542

- **NAGASE & CO. LTD.**
  1-1-17 Shinmachi,, Nishi-ku, Osaka 550-8668, Japan
  CEO: Hiroshi Nagase, Pres. & CEO   Tel: 81-6-6535-2114   Rev: $5,048
  Bus: *Development, production, sale and import and*   Fax: Emp: 2,884
       export of dyestuffs, chemicals, plastics, and   www.nagase.co.jp
       biochemical products.
  NAICS: 325132, 325192, 325199, 325211, 325320, 326199, 339112

NAGASE AMERICA CORPORATION
546 Fifth Ave., 16/F, New York, New York 10036
CEO: Fujio Okada, Pres.
Tel: (212) 703-1340
%FO: 100
Bus: *Engaged in development and manufacture of* Fax: (212) 398-0687
Emp: 24
chemicals.

NAGASE CALIFORNIA CORPORATION
710 Lakeway Dr., Ste. 135, Sunnyvale, California 94085
CEO: Hiroki Toda, Pres.
Tel: (408) 328-1520
%FO: 100
Bus: *Engaged in development and manufacture of* Fax: (408) 773-9567
Emp: 10
chemicals.

NAGASE PLASTICS AMERICA CORP.
39555 Orchard Hill Place, Crystal Glen Office Center, Ste. 356, Novi, Michigan 48375
CEO: Takao Nakano, COO
Tel: (248) 374-0490
%FO: 100
Bus: *Plastics manufacture.*
Fax: (248) 374-0497
Emp: 15

SOFIX CORPORATION
2800 Riverport Rd., Chattanooga, Tennessee 37406
CEO: Kazuhide Ohmaye, Pres.
Tel: (423) 624-3500
%FO: 100
Bus: *Specialty chemicals manufacture.*
Fax: (423) 624-3587
Emp: 35

● NAMBA PRESS WORKS COMPANY
8-3-8, Kojima-Ogawa, Kurashiki, Okayama 711, Japan
CEO: Shigezo Nanba, Chmn. & Pres.
Tel: 81-86-473-3111
Rev: $830
Bus: *Original equipment auto seating and related*
Fax: 81-86-473-4774
Emp: 243
products.
www.namba-press.co.jp
NAICS: 333111, 337127

BLOOMINGTON-NORMAL SEATING COMPANY
2031 Warehouse Rd., Normal, Illinois 61761
CEO: Hisato Inoue, Pres.
Tel: (309) 452-7878
%FO: JV
Bus: *Mfr. automotive seating systems.*
Fax: (309) 452-2312
Emp: 140

● NAMCO BANDAI HOLDINGS, INC.
Taiyo Life Shinagawa Bldg., 9/F, 16-2 Konan, Minato-ku, Tokyo 108-0075, Japan
CEO: Takeo Takasu, Pres. & CEO
Tel: 81-3-3847-5005
Rev: $2,491
Bus: *Character licensing, software for toys, mobile*
Fax: 81-3-3847-5067
Emp: 2,600
phones and amusement games.
www.bandainamco.co.jp
NAICS: 339931, 339932, 511210, 512110, 516110, 713990

BANDAI AMERICA INC.
5551 Katella Ave., Cypress, California 90630
CEO: Mark Tsuji, Pres.
Tel: (714) 816-9500
%FO: 100
Bus: *Character licensing, software for toys,*
Fax: (714) 816-6711
Emp: 60
mobile phones amusement games.

NAMCO AMERICA HOLDING CORP.
2055 Junction Ave., San Jose, California 95131
CEO: Akiyoshi Sarukawa
Tel: (408) 383-3900
%FO: 100
Bus: *Amusement facilities, coin-operated game*
Fax: (408) 383-0128
machines and home videogame software.

NAMCO HOMETEK INC.
4555 Great America Pkwy., Ste. 201, Santa Clara, California 95054
CEO: Nobuhiro Kasahara   Tel: (408) 235-2000   %FO: 100
Bus: *Arcade game manufacture.*   Fax: (408) 235-2005

● **NEC CORPORATION**
NEC Building, 7-1, Shiba 5-chome, Minato-ku, Tokyo 108-8001, Japan
CEO: Akinobu Kanasugi, Pres.   Tel: 81-3-3454-1111   Rev: $45,298
Bus: *Communication systems and equipment,*   Fax: 81-3-3798-1510   Emp: 143,393
   computers, industrial electronic systems,   www.nec.com
   NAICS: 333293, 333313, 333315, 334111, 334112, 334113, 334119, 334210, 334220, 334290, 334413, 541511,
   541512, 541513, 541519, 611420

   ACTIVE VOICE LLC
   2033 6th Ave., Ste. 500, Seattle, Washington 98121
   CEO: Victor T. Foria, Pres. & CEO   Tel: (206) 441-4700
   Bus: *Messaging, conferencing & communications*   Fax: (206) 441-4784   Emp: 85
      software

   ELPIDA MEMORY
   2001 Walsh Ave., Santa Clara, California 95050
   CEO: Dan Donabedian, Pres.   Tel: (408) 970-6600
   Bus: *Memory chips & modules*   Fax: (408) 970-6999   Emp: 84

   NEC AMERICA, INC.
   6555 N. State Highway 161, Irving, Texas 75039
   CEO: Kunitomo Matsuoka, Pres. & CEO   Tel: (214) 262-2000   %FO: 100
   Bus: *Mfr. advanced wireless communications*   Fax: (214) 262-2586
      products.

   NEC DISPLAY SOLUTIONS OF AMERICA
   500 Park Blvd., Ste. 1100, Itasca, Illinois 60143
   CEO: T.J. Trojan, Pres. & COO   Tel: (630) 467-3000
   Bus: *Computer hardware.*   Fax: (630) 467-3100   Emp: 160

   NEC ELECTRONICS CORP.
   2880 Scott Blvd., Santa Clara, California 95050
   CEO: Toshio Nakajima   Tel: (408) 588-6000
   Bus: *Electronics*   Fax: (408) 588-6130

   NEC FIBEROPTECH
   20400 Stevens Creek Blvd., Ste. 800, Cupertino, California 95014
   CEO: Yoshitaka Morimoto, Pres.   Tel: (408) 863-2000
   Bus: *Technical support for fiber optic devices*   Fax: (408) 863-2019

   NEC FINANCIAL SERVICES, INC.
   300 Frank W. Burr Blvd., Teaneck, New Jersey 07666
   CEO: Herschel Salan, Gen. Mgr.   Tel: (201) 287-8300
   Bus: *Commercial lending*   Fax: (800) 451-5360   Emp: 25

   NEC LABORATORIES AMERICA
   4 Independence Way, Princeton, New Jersey 08540
   CEO: Tel: (609) 520-1555
   Bus: *Basic research*   Fax: (609) 951-2481

NEC SOLUTIONS, INC.
10850 Gold Center Dr., Ste. 200, Rancho Cordova, California 95670
CEO: Tadao Kondo, Pres. & CEO   Tel: (916) 463-7000   %FO: 100
Bus: *Computer hardware.*   Fax: (916) 636-5656

NEC USA, INC.
8 Corporate Center Dr., Melville, New York 11747
CEO: Hirofumi Okuyama, Pres. & CEO   Tel: (516) 753-7021   %FO: 100
Bus: *Holding company. Communication systems*   Fax: (516) 753-7096
and equipment, computers, industrial
electronic systems, electronic devices.

NITEO PARTNERS
432 Park Ave. South, 13/F, New York, New York 10016
CEO: John Kelly, Pres.   Tel: (917) 256-5100
Bus: *E-business strategy & system integration*   Fax: (917) 256-5170   Emp: 160

NITEO PARTNERS
379 Thornall St., 5/F, Edison, New Jersey 08837
CEO: Suresh Nichani, COO   Tel: (732) 767-0400
Bus: *Information technology services.*   Fax: (732) 767-0401

NMI CORP.
6555 N. State Highway 161, Irving, Texas 75039
CEO: Tel: (214) 262-4068
Bus: *Sale of cellular phones & pagers*   Fax: (214) 262-4075

VIBREN TECHNOLOGIES INC.
80 Central St., Boxborough, Massachusetts 01719
CEO: Ken Takahashi, Chmn. & CEO   Tel: (978) 929-5500   %FO: 100
Bus: *Information technology services.*   Fax: (978) 635-6378   Emp: 70

• THE NEW OTANI COMPANY, LTD.
4-1, Kioi-cho, Chiyoda-ku, Tokyo 102-8578, Japan
CEO: Kazuhiko Otani, Pres. & CEO   Tel: 81-3-3265-1111
Bus: *Hotels management services.*   Fax: 81-3-3221-2619   Emp: 1,457
www.newotani.co.jp
NAICS: 721110

THE NEW OTANI HOTEL & GARDEN
120 South Los Angeles St., Los Angeles, California 90012
CEO: Chester Ikei, Pres.   Tel: (213) 629-1114   %FO: 100
Bus: *Hotels management services.*   Fax: (213) 620-9808   Emp: 250

THE NEW OTANI KAIMANA BEACH HOTEL
2863 Kalakaua Ave., Honolulu, Hawaii 96815
CEO: Kazhiko Otani, Pres.   Tel: (808) 923-1555   %FO: 100
Bus: *Hotels management services.*   Fax: (808) 922-9404   Emp: 180

- **NEWLONG MACHINE WORKS, LTD.**
14-14, Matsugaya, 1-chome, Taito-ku, Tokyo 111-0036, Japan
CEO: Yasuhiro Kondou, Pres.
Bus: *Mfr. automated/semi-automated, heavy-duty bag packaging/closing/filling/making equipment, and printing machines.*
NAICS: 333293, 333298, 333319, 333993

	Tel: 81-3-3843-0258	Rev: $300
	Fax: 81-3-3843-9963	Emp: 1,500
	www.newlong.com	

   AMERICAN - NEWLONG, INC.
   5310 South Harding St., Indianapolis, Indiana 46217
   CEO: Y. Kondo, Chmn.
   Bus: *Mfr. bag-making & packaging machines*

Tel: (317) 787-9421	%FO: 100
Fax: (317) 786-5225	Emp: 17

   NEWLONG LATIN AMERICA
   2700 N.W. 112th Ave., Miami, Florida 33172
   CEO: Masaaki Yokomori, Mgr.
   Bus: *Import/export packaging machinery*

Tel: (305) 406-1038	
Fax: (305) 406-1039	Emp: 4

- **NGK INSULATORS, LTD.**
2-56, Suda-Cho, Mizuho-ku, Nagoya 467-8530, Japan
CEO: Masaharu Shibata, Chmn. & CEO
Bus: *Mfr. surge arresters, air/water filters, noise absorption panels, sewage treatment systems and beryllium-copper products.*
NAICS: 237110, 237990, 327113, 327215, 327993, 332722, 334419, 334512, 335313, 335314, 335931

	Tel: 81-52-872-7171	Rev: $2,379
	Fax: 81-52-872-7690	Emp: 8,693
	www.ngk.co.jp	

   NGK INSULATORS, LTD
   2520 Mission College Blvd., Ste. 104, Santa Clara, California 95054
   CEO: Shun Matsushita, Pres.
   Bus: *Mfr. surge arresters, air/water filters, noise absorption panels, sewage treatment systems and beryllium-copper products.*

Tel: (408) 330-6900	%FO: 100
Fax: (408) 330-6905	

   NGK METALS CORP.
   917 US Hwy. 11 South, Sweetwater, Tennessee 37874
   CEO: Glade Nelson, Pres.
   Bus: *Copper Mining & Processing*

Tel: (423) 337-5500	%FO: 100
Fax: (423) 337-5540	

- **NGK SPARK PLUG CO., LTD.**
14-18 Takatsuji-cho, Mizuho-ku, Nagoya 467-8525, Japan
CEO: Sigenobu Kanagawa, Chmn.
Bus: *Mfr./distributor of spark plugs*

NAICS: 336211

	Tel: 81-52-872-5935	Rev: $2,166
	Fax: 81-52-872-5997	Emp: 5,324
	www.ngkntk.co.jp	

   NGK SPARK PLUGS USA, INC.
   6 Whatney, Irvine, California 92618
   CEO: Chikanori Abe, pres,
   Bus: *Manufacturer spark plugs*

Tel: (949) 855-8278	%FO: 100
Fax: (949) 855-8395	Emp: 600

   NGK SPARK PLUGS USA, INC.
   46929 Magellan, Wixom, Michigan 48393
   CEO: Chikanori Abe, pres,
   Bus: *Manufacturer spark plugs*

Tel: (248) 926-6900	%FO: 100
Fax: (248) 926-6910	Emp: 600

● **NHK SPRING, LTD.**
3-10 Fukuura, Kanazawa-ku, Yokohama 236-0004, Japan
CEO: Kenji Sasaki, Pres. & CEO
Bus: *Mfr. metal coils, wire, stabilizer bars, and accumulators.*
Tel: 81-45-786-7511
Fax:
www.nhkspg.co.jp
Rev: $2,659
Emp: 9,048
NAICS: 326150, 332116, 332611, 332612, 332618, 332996, 333512, 333513, 333922, 336330, 336340, 336399, 339991, 339999

GENERAL SEATING OF AMERICA INC.
2298 West State Rd. 28, Frankfort, Indiana 46041
CEO: Susumu Takahashi, Pres.
Bus: *Mfr. automotive seats*
Tel: (765) 659-4781
Fax: (765) 659-5591
%FO: 100
Emp: 325

NEW MATHER METALS, INC.
5270 North Detroit Ave., Toledo, Ohio 43612
CEO: Greg Andersen, Pres.
Bus: *Mfr. stabilizers*
Tel: (419) 476-9311
Fax: (419) 476-3466
%FO: 100
Emp: 325

NHK INTERNATIONAL CORPORATION
50706 Varsity Ct., Wixom, Michigan 48393
CEO: Katsuichi Ikeda, Pres.
Bus: *R&D engineering services for the automotive suspensions systems & marketing in computer & telecommunications*
Tel: (248) 926-0111
Fax: (248) 926-2002
%FO: 100
Emp: 30

NHK-ASSOCIATED SPRING SUSPENSION COMPONENTS INC.
3251 Nashville Rd., Bowling Green, Kentucky 42101
CEO: Takanori Sato, Pres.
Bus: *Mfr. metal coils, wire, stabilizers bars, and accumulators.*
Tel: (270) 842-4006
Fax: (270) 842-4618
%FO: 100
Emp: 214

● **NICHIA CORPORATION**
491 Oka, Kaminaki-cho, Tokushima 774-8601, Japan
CEO: Eiji Ogawa, Pres.
Bus: *Mfr. LEDs and laser diodes and fine chemicals.*
Tel: 81-884-22-2311
Fax: 81-884-21-0148
www.nichia.co.jp
Rev: $2,058
Emp: 3,482
NAICS: 333295

NICHIA AMERICA CORPORATION
3775 Hempland Rd., Mountville, Pennsylvania 17554
CEO: Aristides Wade, Sales
Bus: *LED's and laser diodes manufacture.*
Tel: (717) 285-2323
Fax: (717) 285-9378
%FO: 100

NICHIA AMERICA CORPORATION
3000 Town Center Dr., Ste. 2700, Southfield, Michigan 48075
CEO: Taiyo Yuden, Sales
Bus: *LED's and laser diodes manufacture.*
Tel: (248) 352-6575
Fax: (248) 352-6579
%FO: 100

NICHIA AMERICA CORPORATION
3878 Carson St., Ste. 205, Torrance, California 90503
CEO: Hiroki Oguro, Sales
Bus: *LED's and laser diodes manufacture.*
Tel: (310) 540-5667
Fax: (310) 540-5662
%FO: 100

- **NICHIREI CORPORATION**
  Nichirei Higashi-Ginza Bldg., 6-19-20, Tsukiji, Chuo-ku, Tokyo 104-8402, Japan
  CEO: Mitsudo Urano, Pres.   Tel: 81-3-3248-2235   Rev: $47,001
  Bus: *Produces and distributes frozen food and* Fax: 81-3-3248-2119   Emp: 5,770
       operates warehouses.   www.nichirei.co.jp
    NAICS: 111998, 311412, 311612, 311615, 311711, 311712, 311999, 424490, 531190, 531390

  NICHIREI USA INC.
  United Airlines Bldg., 2201 6th Ave., Ste. 1350, Seattle, Washington 98121
  CEO: Tetsuhisa Nakajima, Pres.   Tel: (206) 448-7800   %FO: 100
  Bus: *Mfr./distributes frozen food & operates*   Fax: (206) 443-5800   Emp: 11
       warehouses; engages in real estate,
       biotechnology & information services.

  NICHIREI USA INC.
  9500 South Dadeland Blvd., Ste. 703, Miami, Florida 33156-2824
  CEO: Sazalena Rodiigues, Mgr.   Tel: (305) 670-1365   %FO: 100
  Bus: *Mfr./distributes frozen food & operates*   Fax: (305) 670-2192   Emp: 3
       warehouses; engages in real estate,
       biotechnology & information services.

  TENGU CO.
  14420 Bloomfield Ave., Santa Fe Springs, California 90670
  CEO: Masuhisa Taniguchi, Pres.   Tel: (562) 483-7388
  Bus: *Mfr. of meat products.*   Fax: (562) 483-7389   Emp: 103

- **NICHIRO CORPORATION**
  Shin Yurakucho Bldg., 8/F, 12-1, Yuraku-cho 1-chome, Chiyoda-ku, Tokyo 100-0006, Japan
  CEO: Tatsuhiko Tanaka, Pres.   Tel: 81-3-3240-6211   Rev: $2,370
  Bus: *Seafood products.*   Fax: 81-3-5252-7966   Emp: 8,682
                                                   www.nichiro.co.jp
    NAICS: 311412, 311711, 311712, 311999

  GOLDEN ALASKA SEAFOODS, INC.
  2200 Sixth Ave., Ste. 707, Seattle, Washington 98121
  CEO: Larry Lavine, VP   Tel: (206) 441-1990   %FO: 100
  Bus: *Process frozen seafood.*   Fax: Emp: 115

  PETER PAN SEAFOODS, INC.
  2200 Sixth Ave., Seattle, Washington 98121
  CEO: Barry D. Collier, Pres. & CEO   Tel: (206) 728-6000   %FO: 100
  Bus: *Seafood distributor.*   Fax: (206) 441-9090   Emp: 376

- **NIDEC CORPORATION**
  338 Tonoshiro-cho, Kuze, Minami-ku, Kyoto 601-8205, Japan
  CEO: Shigenobu Nagamori, Chmn. & Pres. & CEO   Tel: 81-75-935-6140   Rev: $4,524
  Bus: *Mfr. spindle motors to service computer hard* Fax: 81-75-935-6141   Emp: 68,245
       drives.   www.nidec.co.jp
    NAICS: 334119, 334210, 334220, 334413, 334415, 334419, 335311, 335312, 335999, 336322, 811310

  NIDEC AMERICA CORP.
  100 River Ridge Dr., Norwood, Massachusetts 02062
  CEO: Mike Kulik, Mgr.   Tel: (781) 551-6818   %FO: 100
  Bus: *Mfr. of brushless dc motors & tube axial* Fax: Emp: 25
       fans.

NIDEC AMERICA CORP.
41700 Gardenbrook, Ste. 145, Novi, Michigan 48376
CEO: Shigenobu Nagamori, Pres.　　Tel: (248) 735-3851　　%FO: 100
Bus: *R&D for small high-precision motors, mid-*　Fax: (248) 735-3849
size motors and production engineering.

NIDEC AMERICA CORP.
7949 Woodley Ave., Van Nuys, California 91406
CEO: Tetsuo Inoue, Mgr.　　Tel: (818) 375-5094　　%FO: 100
Bus: *Mfr. of brushless dc motors & tube axial*　Fax: (818) 375-5095
fans.

NIDEC AMERICA CORP.
921 North Lake St., Aurora, Illinois 60506
CEO: Tetsuo Inoue, Mgr.　　Tel: (630) 892-5066　　%FO: 100
Bus: *Mfr. of brushless dc motors & tube axial*　Fax: (630) 892-5161
fans.

NIDEC AMERICA CORPORATION
3708 Mira Vista Dr., Austin, Texas 78732
CEO: Tetsuo Inoue, Mgr.　　Tel: (512) 266-6667　　%FO: 100
Bus: *R&D for small high-precision motors, mid-*　Fax: (512) 266-0601
size motors and production engineering.

NIDEC AMERICA CORPORATION
32026 Carte El Dorado, Temecula, California 92592
CEO: Shigenobu Nagamori, Pres.　　Tel: (909) 302-3498　　%FO: 100
Bus: *R&D for small high-precision motors, mid-*　Fax: (909) 302-3499
size motors and production engineering.

NIDEC AMERICA CORPORATION
318 Industrial Lane, PO Box 778, Torrington, Connecticut 06790
CEO: Shigenobu Nagamori, Chmn.　　Tel: (860) 482-4422　　%FO: 100
Bus: *R&D for small high-precision motors, mid-*　Fax: (860) 489-7201　　Emp: 220
size motors and production engineering.

NIDEC AMERICA CORPORATION
2160 Lundy Ave., Ste. 230, San Jose, California 95131
CEO: Sat Kaji, Mgr.　　Tel: (408) 432-9140　　%FO: 100
Bus: *R&D for small high-precision motors, mid-*　Fax: (408) 432-9621
size motors and production engineering.

NIDEC AMERICA CORPORATION
2011 Ken Pratt Blvd., Ste. 220, Longmont, Colorado 80501
CEO: Nick Combs, Mgr.　　Tel: (303) 651-1025　　%FO: 100
Bus: *R&D for small high-precision motors, mid-*　Fax: (303) 651-6816
size motors and production engineering.

NIDEC AMERICA CORPORATION
1710 West Main St., Ste. 221, Battle Ground, Washington 98604
CEO: Karl Mattson, Mgr.　　Tel: (360) 666-2445　　%FO: 100
Bus: *Mfr. of brushless dc motors & tube axial*　Fax: (360) 666-2447
fans.

NIDEC AMERICA CORPORATION
6860 Shingle Creek Pkwy., Ste. 111, Minneapolis, Minnesota 55430
CEO: Nick Combs, Mgr.　　Tel: (763) 561-6000　　%FO: 100
Bus: *R&D for small high-precision motors, mid-*　Fax: (763) 561-4500
size motors and production engineering.

- **NIHON KEIZAI SHIMBUN, INC.**
  1-9-5, Otemachi, Chiyoda-ku, Tokyo 100-66, Japan
  CEO: Ryoki Sugita, Pres.
  Bus: *Financial newspaper publisher, data bank
  services, broadcasting and exhibitions.*
  NAICS: 511110, 511120, 511130, 541513

  Tel: 81-3-3292-1813
  Fax: 81-3-3292-1813
  www.nni.nikkei.co.jp

  Emp: 4,400

  NIHON KEIZAI SHIMBUN AMERICA, INC.
  1325 Ave. of the Americas, Ste. 2500, New York, New York 10019
  CEO: Masami Wada, Pres.
  Bus: *Newspaper publisher, data bank services
  and research.*

  Tel: (212) 261-6200
  Fax: (212) 261-6209

  %FO: 100

  NIHON KEIZAI SHIMBUN AMERICA, INC.
  1 South Wacker Dr., Ste. 1150, Chicago, Illinois 60606-4616
  CEO: Ken Chiba
  Bus: *Newspaper publisher, data bank services
  and research.*

  Tel: (312) 726-9478
  Fax: (312) 726-9478

  %FO: 100

  NIHON KEIZAI SHIMBUN AMERICA, INC.
  815 Connecticut Ave. NW, Washington, District of Columbia 20006
  CEO: William Salbreiter
  Bus: *Newspaper publisher.*

  Tel: (202) 393-1388
  Fax: (202) 393-1388

  %FO: 100

- **NIHON PLAST CO., LTD.**
  218 Aoshima-cho, Fuji, Shizuoka 417-0047, Japan
  CEO: Makoto Hirose, Pres.
  Bus: *Mfr. airbags, engine components, instrument
  panels, steering wheels and interior trim parts.*
  NAICS: 336211

  Tel: 81-54-552-0481
  Fax: 81-54-553-5687
  www.wbs.ne.jp

  Rev: $728
  Emp: 2,800

  NEATON AUTO PRODUCTS MFG.
  975 S. Franklin St., Eaton, Ohio 45320
  CEO: Cindy Lopeman, HR
  Bus: *Automobile parts manufacture.*

  Tel: (937) 456-7103
  Fax: (937) 456-1437

  %FO: 100

- **NIKKO CORDIAL CORPORATION**
  6-5, Nihonbashi Kabuto-cho, Chuo-ku, Tokyo 103-8225, Japan
  CEO: Masashi Kaneko, Chmn.
  Bus: *Investment banking and brokerage.*

  Tel: 81-3-5644-3110
  Fax: 81-3-5644-4555
  www.nikko.co.jp

  Rev: $3,225
  Emp: 10,214

  NAICS: 523120, 523130, 523140, 523920, 523930, 523991, 523999, 525110, 525120, 525190, 525910, 525920, 525990

  NIKKO SECURITIES COMPANY
  535 Madison Ave., Ste. 2500, New York, New York 10022
  CEO: Masao Matsuda, Pres.
  Bus: *Investment banking/brokerage.*

  Tel: (212) 610-6100
  Fax: (212) 610-6140

  %FO: 100
  Emp: 22

- **NIKON CORPORATION**
  Fuji Bldg, 2-3 Marunouchi, 3-chome, Chiyoda-ku, Tokyo 100-8331, Japan
  CEO: Shoichiro Yoshida, Chmn. & CEO   Tel: 81-3-3214-5311   Rev: $4,793
  Bus: *Industrial equipment, imaging and information,*   Fax: 81-3-3216-1454   Emp: 13,636
       health and medical equipment and services.   www.nikon.com
  NAICS: 333295, 333298, 333314, 333315, 334510, 334516, 339112

  NIKON AMERICAS
  1300 Walt Whitman Rd., 2/F, Melville, New York 11747
  CEO: Yoshio Ichikawa, Pres.   Tel: (516) 547-4200   %FO: 100
  Bus: *Holding company.*   Fax: (516) 547-0299   Emp: 750

  NIKON INSTRUMENTS, INC.
  1300 Walt Whitman Rd., 2/F, Melville, New York 11747
  CEO: Hiro Kusaka, Pres.   Tel: (631) 547-4200   %FO: 100
  Bus: *Sale of biomedical & industrial instruments.*   Fax: Emp: 85

  NIKON PRECISION, INC.
  1399 Shoreway Rd., Belmont, California 94002
  CEO: Geoff Wild, Pres.   Tel: (650) 508-4674   %FO: 100
  Bus: *Sale of industrial equipment & electronic*   Fax: Emp: 700
       parts & equipment.

- **NINTENDO COMPANY, LTD.**
  11-1, Kamitobe Hokotate-cho, Minami-ku, Kyoto 601-8501, Japan
  CEO: Satoru Iwata, Pres.   Tel: 81-75-662-9600   Rev: $4,869
  Bus: *Develop/mfr. video games and video equipment.*   Fax: 81-75-662-9620   Emp: 2,975
                                              www.nintendo.co.jp
  NAICS: 334310, 339932, 511210

  NINTENDO OF AMERICA, INC.
  4820 150th Ave., NE, PO Box 957, Redmond, Washington 98052
  CEO: Tatsumi Kimishima, Pres.   Tel: (425) 882-2040   %FO: 100
  Bus: *Develop/mfr./distribution video games and*   Fax: (425) 882-3585
       video equipment.

  THE BASEBALL CLUB OF SEATTLE, L.P.
  1250 1st. South, Seattle, Washington 98134
  CEO: Howard Lincoln, Chmn. & CEO   Tel: (206) 346-4000   %FO: 50
  Bus: *Sports teams & organizations*   Fax: (206) 346-4100

- **NIPPON CARBIDE INDUSTRIES CO., INC.**
  2-11-19 Conan, Minato-ku, Tokyo 108-8466, Japan
  CEO: Tokushiro Hosada, Pres.   Tel: 81-3-5462-8200   Rev: $449
  Bus: *Chemicals, films, synthetic resins and electronic*   Fax: 81-3-5462-8244   Emp: 2,791
       materials manufacture.   www.carbide.co.jp
  NAICS: 325110, 325131, 325132, 325188, 325199

  NIPPON CARBIDE INDUSTRIES USA INC.
  3136 e. Victoria St., Rancho Dominguez, California 90221
  CEO: Dennis Johnson, Mgr.   Tel: (310) 632-7500   %FO: 100
  Bus: *Chemicals manufacture.*   Fax: (310) 632-1959

NIPPON CARBIDE INDUSTRIES USA INC.
1250 Perimeter Rd., Greenville, South Carolina 29605
CEO: John L. Wysocki, Mgr.   Tel: (864) 277-7717   %FO: 100
Bus: *Chemicals manufacture.*   Fax: (864) 277-8151

● **NIPPON CHEMICAL INDUSTRIAL CO., LTD.**
9-11-1, Komodo, Koto-ku, Tokyo 136-8515, Japan
CEO: Jun-ichi Tanahashi, Pres. & CEO   Tel: 81-3-3636-8111   Rev: $442
Bus: *Mfr. industrial chemicals.*   Fax: 81-3-3636-6817   Emp: 550
                                          www.nippon-chem.co.jp
NAICS: 325181, 325199, 325998

   JCI USA INC.
   1311 Mamaroneck Ave., Ste. 145, White Plains, New York 10605
   CEO: Nobuyuki Muramatsu   Tel: (914) 761-6555   %FO: 100
   Bus: *Sales of industrial chemicals.* Fax: (914) 761-6940   Emp: 2

● **NIPPON ELECTRIC GLASS CO., LTD.**
7-1 Saran, 2-chome Outs, Shiga 520-8639, Japan
CEO: Yuzo Izutsu, Pres.   Tel: 81-77-537-1700   Rev: $2,814
Bus: *Mfr. Industrial glass products, solar connectors,* Fax: 81-77-534-4967   Emp: 8,386
     electronic display components.   www.neg.co.jp
NAICS: 327211, 334419

   NIPPON ELECTRIC GLASS AMERICA, INC.
   650 East Devon, Ste. 110, Itasca, Illinois 60143
   CEO: Kiyoshi Asai, Pres.   Tel: (630) 285-8500   %FO: 100
   Bus: *Mfr. industrial glass products, solar* Fax: (630) 285-8510
        collectors, electronic display components.

   TECHNEGLAS, INC.
   707 East Jenkins Ave., Columbus, Ohio 43207
   CEO: Lawrence T. Hickey, Pres.   Tel: (614) 445-4700   %FO: 100
   Bus: *Mfr. industrial glass products, solar* Fax: (614) 445-4702   Emp: 1,200
        collectors, electronic display components.

● **NIPPON EXPRESS COMPANY, LTD.**
1-9-3, Higashi-Shimbashi, Minato-ku, Tokyo 105-8322, Japan
CEO: Masanori Kawai, Pres.   Tel: 81-3-6251-1111   Rev: $15,779
Bus: *Leasing, finance, import/export, real estate,* Fax: 81-3-6251-1111   Emp: 38,749
     equipment sales.   www.nittsu.co.jp
NAICS: 424710, 481212, 483111, 484110, 484121, 484122, 484210, 484220, 484230, 488510, 493110, 532120,
532411, 561510, 561520

   NIPPON EXPRESS TRAVEL USA, INC.
   720 Market St., 6/F, San Francisco, California 94102
   CEO: Masao Yamasaki, Pres.   Tel: (415) 421-1822   %FO: 100
   Bus: *Travel services.*   Fax: (415) 421-1809   Emp: 95

   NIPPON EXPRESS USA, INC.
   590 Madison Ave., Ste. 2401, New York, New York 10022
   CEO: Tadaaki Hashimoto, CEO   Tel: (212) 758-6100   %FO: 80
   Bus: *Freight forwarding, air/ocean cargo,* Fax: (212) 758-2595   Emp: 1,416
        household goods moving.

- **NIPPON FLOUR MILLS CO., LTD.**
  5-27-5, Sendagaya, Shibuya-ku, Tokyo 151-8537, Japan
  CEO: Masataka Horikawa, Pres.
  Bus: *Sales of flour and flour products for industrial and food service and pharmaceutical manufacture.*
  Tel: 81-3-3350-2311
  Fax: 81-3-5266-9320
  www.nippn.co.jp
  Rev: $2,043
  Emp: 2,335
  NAICS: 311111, 311119, 311211, 311212, 311230, 311423, 311811, 311812, 311813, 311821, 311822, 311823, 311830, 311941, 311991, 325412, 325413, 453910, 812910

  PASTA MONTANA INC.
  One Pasta Place, Great Falls, Montana 59401
  CEO: Katsutaro Nishihara, Pres. & CEO
  Bus: *Sales of flour and flour products for industrial and food service.*
  Tel: (406) 761-1516
  Fax: (406) 761-1516
  %FO: 100

- **NIPPON KAYAKU CO., LTD.**
  Tokyo Fuji Bldg., 11-2, Fujimi, 1-chome, Chiyoda-ku, Tokyo 102-8172, Japan
  CEO: Hajime Yoshitake, Mng. Dir.
  Bus: *Mfr. pharmaceuticals, agro chemicals and pesticides.*
  Tel: 81-3-3237-5044
  Fax: 81-3-3237-5085
  www.nipponkayaku.co.jp
  Rev: $1,160
  Emp: 1,920
  NAICS: 325320, 325411, 325412, 325413, 325520

  NIPPON KAYAKU AMERICA, INC.
  711 Westchester Ave., 2/F, White Plains, New York 10604
  CEO: Shinichi Ikenaga, Mng. Dir.
  Bus: *Mfr. pharmaceuticals, agri chemicals and pesticides.*
  Tel: (914) 686-6800
  Fax: (914) 686-6804
  %FO: 100

- **NIPPON KODO CO., LTD.**
  Ginza 4-9-1, Chuo-ku, Tokyo 104-8135, Japan
  CEO: Masayoshi Konaka, CEO
  Bus: *Home fragrance manufacture and sales.*
  Tel: 81-3-3541-3401
  Fax: 81-3-3541-3402
  www.nipponkodo.com
  Rev: $132
  Emp: 342
  NAICS: 325620, 423220

  NIPPON KODO INC.
  2771 Plaza del Amo, Ste. 806, Torrance, California 90503
  CEO: Yoshiyuki Tsuchiya, Pres.
  Bus: *Perfume manufacture.*
  Tel: (310) 320-8881
  Fax: (310) 320-8666
  %FO: 100

- **NIPPON LIFE INSURANCE COMPANY**
  3-5-12, Mabuchi, Chuo-ku, Osaka 541-8501, Japan
  CEO: Ikuo Uno, Chmn.
  Bus: *Life insurance.*
  Tel: 81-6-6209-5525
  Fax: 81-3-5510-7340
  www.nissay.co.jp
  Rev: $46,365
  Emp: 70,073
  NAICS: 236115, 236116, 236117, 237210, 522292, 522298, 522310, 523999, 524113, 525110, 525120, 525190, 525910, 525920, 525990, 531120, 531190, 531210, 531312, 531320, 531390, 541110

  NLI AMERICA
  757 3rd Ave., 26/F, New York, New York 10017
  CEO: Ken Curitore
  Bus: *Engaged in life insurance.*
  Tel: (212) 909-9894
  Fax: (212) 486-9054
  %FO: 100

NLI AMERICA
190 South LaSalle St., Ste. 1680, Chicago, Illinois 60603
CEO: Sharon Bakker   Tel: (312) 807-1123   %FO: 100
Bus: *Engaged in life insurance.*   Fax: (312) 807-1110

NLI AMERICA
5210 Maryland Way, Suite 302, Brentwood, Tennessee 37027
CEO: D. Varn   Tel: (615) 377-0416   %FO: 100
Bus: *Engaged in life insurance.*   Fax: (615) 376-4391

NLI AMERICA
7000 Central Parkway, Suite 1670, Atlanta, Georgia 30328
CEO: C. McKnight   Tel: (770) 551-1850   %FO: 100
Bus: *Engaged in life insurance.*   Fax: (770) 551-1858

NLI AMERICA
420 McKinley St., #111-609, Corona, California 92879
CEO: Arnold Andersen   Tel: (951) 734-4852   %FO: 100
Bus: *Engaged in life insurance.*   Fax: (951) 734-4852

NLI AMERICA
521 Fifth Ave., New York, New York 10175
CEO: A. Casatelli, Pres.   Tel: (212) 682-3000   %FO: 100
Bus: *Engaged in life insurance.*   Fax: (212) 682-3002   Emp: 100

NLI AMERICA
2203 Placer Dr., Bay Point, California 94565
CEO: Jeff Simon   Tel: (925) 458-5411   %FO: 100
Bus: *Engaged in life insurance.*   Fax: (925) 458-5407

NLI AMERICA
445 South Figueroa St., Ste. 2870, Los Angeles, California 90071
CEO: Sharon Bakker   Tel: (213) 430-9000   %FO: 100
Bus: *Engaged in life insurance.*   Fax: (213) 430-2010

• **NIPPON LIGHT METAL COMPANY LTD.**
NYK tennis Bldg., 2-20, Higashi-, Shinagawa, 2-chome,, Shingawa-ku, Tokyo 140-6828, Japan
CEO: Shigesato Sato, Pres. & CEO   Tel: 81-3-5461-9333   Rev: $5,038
Bus: *Aluminum production and distribution.*   Fax: 81-3-5461-9344   Emp: 12,598
                                       www.nikkeikin.co.jp
NAICS: 331315, 331316

  NIPPON LIGHT METAL COMPANY LTD.
  2131 Weston Dr., Hudson, Ohio 44236
  CEO: Shigesato Sato   Tel: (330) 463-5565   %FO: 100
  Bus: *Aluminum production and distribution.*   Fax: (330) 463-5672

• **NIPPON MEAT PACKERS INC.**
6-14, Minami-Honmachi, 3-chome, Chuo-ku, Osaka 541-0054, Japan
CEO: Yoshikiyo Fujii, Pres.   Tel: 81-6-6282-3031   Rev: $8,790
Bus: *Engaged in meat processing and services.*   Fax: 81-6-6282-1056   Emp: 2,926
                                       www.nipponham.co.jp
NAICS: 311513, 311611, 311612, 311615, 311712, 311999

NIPPON MEAT PACKERS
300 Pacific Coast Hwy., Huntington Beach, California 92648
CEO: Ken Hinohara, Pres.   Tel: (714) 374-5999   %FO: 100
Bus: *Sales/distribution of wholesale frozen*   Fax:
     foods.

NIPPON MEAT PACKERS
10350 Heritage Park Ctr.., Ste. 111, Santa Fe Springs, California 90670
CEO: Yoshikiyo Fujii, Pres.   Tel: (562) 903-3020
Bus: *Sales/distribution of wholesale frozen*   Fax: (562) 906-5080
     foods.

• **NIPPON METAL INDUSTRY COMPANY**
Shinjuku Mitsui Bldg., 2-1-1, Nishi-Shinjuku, Tokyo 163-0470, Japan
CEO: Hiroshi Miyata, Pres. & CEO   Tel: 81-3-3345-5555   Rev: $893
Bus: *Stainless steel manufacturer.*   Fax: 81-3-3345-5592   Emp: 929
      www.nikkinko.co.jp

NAICS: 331221

    NIPPON METAL INDUSTRY USA, INC.
    PO Box 250, Woodbury, Georgia 30293
    CEO: Fumiaki Watari   Tel: (706) 553-2146   %FO: 100
    Bus: *Sale stainless steel.*   Fax: (706) 553-2148

• **NIPPON MINING HOLDINGS, INC.**
2-10-1, Toranomon, Minato-ku, Tokyo 105-0001, Japan
CEO: Yasuyuki Shimizu, Pres. & CEO   Tel: 81-3-5573-5170   Rev: $20,963
Bus: *Holding company: oil and refinery, semi-conductor*   Fax: 81-3-5573-6784   Emp: 13,390
    materials   www.shinnikko-hd.co.jp
NAICS: 212210, 212231, 212299, 213114, 324110, 324191, 324199, 325411, 325412, 325413, 325414, 334413,
334516, 339111, 424710, 447190, 454311,
      454312, 454319, 541710, 551112, 621511, 621512

    GOULD ELECTRONICS INC.
    2929 W. Chandler Blvd., Chandler, Arizona 85224
    CEO: L. Joseph Huss, Pres. & CEO   Tel: (480) 899-0343   %FO: 100
    Bus: *Semiconductor equipment & materials*   Fax: (480) 963-2119   Emp: 2,730

    IRVINE SCIENTIFIC SALES COMPANY INC.
    2511 Daimler St., Santa Ana, California 92705
    CEO: Michael J. Kelly, Pres. & CEO   Tel: (949) 261-7800   %FO: 100
    Bus: *Medical devices*   Fax: (949) 261-6522   Emp: 103

    NIKKO MATERIALS USA
    125 North Price Rd., Chandler, Arizona 85224
    CEO: Keiji Katagiri, Pres.   Tel: (480) 732-9857   %FO: 100
    Bus: *Mfr. primary metal products, sheet metal*   Fax: (480) 899-0779   Emp: 64
    work

• **NIPPON OIL CORPORATION**
3-12 Nishi Shimbashi, 1-chome, Minato-ku, Tokyo 105-8412, Japan
CEO: Fumiaki Watari, Pres. & CEO   Tel: 81-3-3502-1131   Rev: $40,512
Bus: *Engaged in oil import and distribution.*   Fax: 81-3-3502-9352   Emp: 14,347
      www.eneos.co.jp
NAICS: 324110, 324191, 324199, 424710, 424720, 447110, 447190, 454311, 454312, 454319

NIPPON OIL EXPLORATION USA LTD.
5847 San Felipe St., Houston, Texas 77057
CEO: Austin Lyons, Pres.
Bus: *Engaged in oil import and distribution.*

Tel: (713) 260-7400
Fax: (713) 978-7800

%FO: 100
Emp: 25

NIPPON OIL USA LTD.
2680 Bishop Dr., Ste. 275, San Ramon, California 94583
CEO: Shigetaka Toyono, Pres.
Bus: *Oil & gas refining, marketing & distribution*

Tel: (925) 355-1101
Fax: (925) 355-1109

Emp: 16

● **NIPPON PAINT COMPANY, LTD.**
2-1-2, Oyo do-Kita, Kita-ku, Osaka 531-8511, Japan
CEO: Teruyoshi Fujishima, Pres.
Bus: *Mfr. and sales of powder coatings, automotive
coatings, pre-treatment chemicals and paint
protection film.*
NAICS: 325510, 325520

Tel: 81-6-6458-1111
Fax: 81-6-6455-9261
www.nipponpaint.co.jp

Rev: $1,881
Emp: 2,152

   MORTON NIPPON COATINGS
   2701 East 170th St., Lansing, Illinois 60438
   CEO: Teruyoshi Fujishima, Pres.
   Bus: *Mfr. paints and coatings.*

Tel: (708) 868-7403
Fax: (708) 868-7488

%FO: 100

   NIPPON PAINT RESEARCH INSTITUTE, INC.
   44382 Macomb Industrial Dr., Clinton Township, Michigan 48036
   CEO: Y Sakagughi, Pres.
   Bus: *Paints and coatings.*

Tel: (810) 954-2500
Fax: (810) 954-2504

%FO: 100

   NIPPON PAINT, INC.
   Glenpointe Centre West, 500 Frank W. Burr Blvd., Teaneck, New Jersey 07666
   CEO: Tatsuo Takeda, Pres.
   Bus: *Mfr. and sales of powder coatings,
   automotive coatings, pre-treatment
   chemicals and paint protection film.*

Tel: (201) 692-1111
Fax: (201) 692-0555

%FO: 100
Emp: 335

   NPA COATINGS
   11110 Berea Rd., Cleveland, Ohio 44102
   CEO: Samuel Rhue, Pres.
   Bus: *Mfr. and sales of powder coatings,
   automotive coatings, pre-treatment
   chemicals and paint protection film.*

Tel: (216) 651-5900
Fax: (216) 651-5902

%FO: 100
Emp: 215

● **NIPPON PAPER GROUP**
Shin Yurakucho Bldg., 1-12-1 Yurakucho, Chiyoda-ku, Tokyo 100-0006, Japan
CEO: Masatomo Nakamura, Pres.
Bus: *Mfr. newsprint & printing paper, household paper
goods, converted paper, soft drink & liquid
packaging, wood pulp, paperboard, lumber &
chemicals.*
NAICS: 113310, 312111, 321113, 322110, 322121, 322122, 322130, 322211, 322222, 322226, 322231, 322232, 322233, 322291, 322299, 424130

Tel: 81-3-3218-9300
Fax: 81-3-3216-5330
www.np-g.com

Rev: $11,290

NIPPON PAPER INDUSTRIES USA
1815 Marine Dr., PO Box 271, Port Angeles, Washington 98362
CEO: David Tamaki   Tel: (360) 457-4474   %FO: 100
Bus: *Production and sales of telephone directory*   Fax: (360) 452-6576
     paper.

NIPPON PAPER INDUSTRIES USA
2330 Scenic Hwy., Snellville, Georgia 30078
CEO: Naruaki Obuchi   Tel: (678) 252-2139   %FO: 100
Bus: *Research in procurement sources of North*   Fax: (678) 252-2140
     America

NIPPON PAPER INDUSTRIES USA
3001 Industrial Way, c/o Norpac, Longview, Washington 98632
CEO: Hideki Ushiro, Pres.   Tel: (360) 636-7110   %FO: 100
Bus: *Research of North America paper market.*   Fax: (360) 423-1514

NORTH PACIFIC PAPER CORP. (JV NIPPON & WEYERHAEUSER)
PO Box 2069, Longview, Washington 98632
CEO: Bill Baird, Pres.   Tel: (360) 636-6400   %FO: JV
Bus: *Production and sales of newsprint. (JV of*   Fax: (360) 423-1514   Emp: 524
     Nippon Paper and Weyerhaeuser)

● **NIPPON PISTON RING CO., LTD.**
5-12-10 Honmachi-Higashi, Saitama 338-8503, Japan
CEO: Fumiaki Moriya, CEO   Tel: 81-48-856-5011   Rev: $421
Bus: *Mfr. piston rings, cylinder liners, valve train parts*   Fax: 81-48-856-5036   Emp: 2,481
     and internal combustion engine parts.   www.npr.co.jp
   NAICS: 336211

     FEDERAL-MOGUL PISTON RINGS
     26555 Northwestern Hwy., Southfield, Michigan 48034
     CEO: Michael Sobieski   Tel: (248) 354-7700   %FO: 100
     Bus: *Mfr. auto parts.*   Fax: (248) 354-8950

     NPR OF AMERICA INC.
     16000 Canary Ave., La Mirada, California 90638
     CEO: Shigeo Hinohara   Tel: (562) 926-4407   %FO: 100
     Bus: *Mfr. auto parts.*   Fax: (562) 926-4407

● **NIPPON SHARYO, LTD.**
1-1 Sanbonmatsu-cho, Atsuta-ku, Nagoya 456-8691, Japan
CEO: Kazuhisa Matsuda, Pres. & CEO   Tel: 81-52-882-3328   Rev: $864
Bus: *Mfr. heavy equipment*   Fax: 81-52-882-3814   Emp: 2,050
     www.n-sharyo.co.jp
   NAICS: 336510, 423860

     NIPPON SHARYO USA INC.
     600 Third Ave., 28/F, New York, New York 10016
     CEO: Juntaro Miyako, VP   Tel: (212) 949-2228   %FO: 100
     Bus: *Manufacturer heavy equipment*   Fax: (212) 949-2229

- **NIPPON SHEET GLASS COMPANY, LTD.**
2-1-7 Kaigan, Minato-ku, Tokyo 105-8522, Japan
CEO: Yozo Izuhara, Chmn. & CEO
Bus: *Mfr. flat and safety glass, glass fiber and fiber optic products.*
NAICS: 327211, 334419, 336399
Tel: 81-3-5443-9500
Fax: 81-3-5443-9566
www.nsg.co.jp
Rev: $2,548
Emp: 11,392

  NSG AMERICA, INC.
  28 World's Fair Dr., Somerset, New Jersey 08873
  CEO: Simin Cai
  Bus: *Mfr. & sale of optoelectronic devices.*
  Tel: (732) 469-9650
  Fax: (732) 469-9654
  %FO: 100

- **NIPPON SHUPPAN HANBAI, INC.**
4-3, Kandasurugadai, Chiyoda-ku, Tokyo 101-0062, Japan
CEO: Naomasa Tsuruta, Pres. & CEO
Bus: *Book wholesaler.*
NAICS: 424920, 454111
Tel: 81-3-3233-1111
Fax: 81-3-3292-8521
www.nippan.co.jp
Rev: $6,961
Emp: 5,707

  NIPPON SHUPPAN HANBAI, INC.
  400 Forbes Blvd., Ste. 3, South San Francisco, California 94080
  CEO: Satomi Nakabayashi, Pres.
  Bus: *Book wholesaler.*
  Tel: (650) 871-3940
  Fax:
  %FO: 100
  Emp: 16

- **NIPPON SODA COMPANY, LTD.**
2-1, 2-Chome, Ohtemachi, Chiyoda-ku, Tokyo 100-8165, Japan
CEO: Katsunobu Inoue, Pres.
Bus: *Mfr. chemicals.*
NAICS: 325199
Tel: 81-3-3245-6054
Fax: 81-3-3245-6238
www.nippon-soda.co.jp
Rev: $1,280
Emp: 1,564

  NISSO AMERICA INC.
  45 Broadway, Ste. 2120, New York, New York 10006
  CEO: Takenibou Shimizu
  Bus: *Mfr. chemicals.*
  Tel: (212) 490-0350
  Fax: (212) 972-9361
  %FO: 100

  NISSO AMERICA, INC.
  13709 Progress Blvd., Alachua, Florida 32615-9544
  CEO: Isao Iwataki
  Bus: *Distribution of chemicals.*
  Tel: (386) 462-7031
  Fax: (386) 462-7031
  %FO: 100

  NISSO AMERICA, INC.
  220 East 42nd St., Ste. 3002, New York, New York 10017
  CEO: Takenobu Shimizu, CEO
  Bus: *Distribution of chemicals.*
  Tel: (212) 490-0350
  Fax: (212) 972-9361
  %FO: 100
  Emp: 4

  NOVUS INTERNATIONAL RESEARCH CENTER
  Missouri Research Park, 20 Research Park Dr., St. Charles, Missouri 63304
  CEO: W. Joseph Privott
  Bus: *Research of feed additives.*
  Tel: (636) 926-7400
  Fax: (636) 926-7405
  %FO: 100

NOVUS INTERNATIONAL, INC.
520 Maryville Center Dr., St. Louis, Missouri 63141
CEO: Thad W. Simons Jr., Pres. & COO   Tel: (314) 576-8406   %FO: 100
Bus: *Mfr. and sale of feed additives*   Fax: (314) 576-2148

● **NIPPON STEEL CORPORATION**
6-3 Otemachi 2- chome,, Chiyoda-ku, Tokyo 100-8071, Japan
CEO: Akira Chihara, Chmn.   Tel: 81-3-3242-4111   Rev: $27,696
Bus: *Mfr. steel products; engineering and construction*   Fax: 81-3-3275-5607   Emp: 46,233
    activities.   www.nsc.co.jp
NAICS: 237990, 331111, 331210, 331221, 331222, 332312

    NIPPON STEEL USA INC
    10 E. 50th St., 29/F, New York, New York 10022
    CEO: Masato Mori   Tel: (212) 486-7150
    Bus: *Ferrous and non-ferrous metals*   Fax: (212) 593-3049
    manufacture.

    NIPPON STEEL USA INC
    900 North Michigan Ave., Ste. 1820, Chicago, Illinois 60611
    CEO: Yutaka Hokura, Gen. Mgr.   Tel: (312) 751-0800
    Bus: *Commercial nonphysical research*   Fax: (312) 751-0345

    NIPPON STEEL USA, INC.
    780 Third Ave., 34/F, New York, New York 10017
    CEO: Masato Mori, Pres. & CEO   Tel: (212) 486-7150   %FO: 100
    Bus: *Ferrous and non-ferrous metals*   Fax: (212) 593-3049   Emp: 125
    manufacture.

● **NIPPON STEEL TRADING COMPANY**
Nittetsu ND Tower, 5-7 Kameido 1-chome, Koto-ku, Tokyo 136-8733, Japan
CEO: Tomio Yoshizawa, Pres. & CEO   Tel: 81-3-5627-2905   Rev: $8,098
Bus: *Supplies Steel products, smelting machinery and*   Fax: 81-3-5627-2650
    iron ore to the steel industry.   www.ns-net.co.jp
NAICS: 423510

    NIPPON STEEL TRADING COMPANY
    The Citicorp Center, 725 S. Figueroa St., Ste. 1860, Los Angeles, California 90017-6430
    CEO: Susuma Tedenuma, Pres.   Tel: (213) 485-9072   %FO: 100
    Bus: *Provides supplies to the steel industry.*   Fax: (213) 688-7579   Emp: 20

● **NIPPON SUISAN KAISHA, LTD.**
Nippon Bldg., 6-2 Otemachi, 2 chome, Chiyoda-ku, Chiyoda-ku, Tokyo 100-8686, Japan
CEO: Naoya Kakizoe, Pres. & CEO   Tel: 81-3-3244-7000   Rev: $4,682
Bus: *Mfr. various food products.*   Fax: 81-3-3244-7426   Emp: 11,787
    www.nissui.co.jp
NAICS: 114111, 114112, 114119, 311711, 311712, 325412, 424460

    FISHKING
    1320 Newton St., Los Angeles, California 90021
    CEO: Dennis Delaye, Pres. & CEO   Tel: (213) 746-1307
    Bus: *Fish & seafood distributors*   Fax: (213) 746-4008

GORTONS INC.
128 Rogers St., Gloucester, Massachusetts 01930
CEO: Steve Warhover, Pres. & CEO
Bus: *Canned & frozen fish*
Tel: (978) 283-3000
Fax: (978) 281-8295
Emp: 500

NIPPON SUISAN USA, INC.
15400 NE 90th St., Ste. 100, Redmond, Washington 98073
CEO: Kunihiko Koike, Pres. & CEO
Bus: *U.S. headquarters.*
Tel: (425) 869-1703
Fax: (425) 869-1615
%FO: 100

UNISEA INC.
15400 NE 90th St., Redmond, Washington 98073
CEO: Terry Shaff, Pres.
Bus: *Fish & seafood*
Tel: (425) 881-8181
Fax: (425) 861-5249
Emp: 250

● **THE NIPPON SYNTHETIC CHEMICAL INDUSTRY CO. LTD.**
Umeda Sky Bldg Tower East, 1-88 Oyodonaka 1-chome, Kita-ku, Osaka 531-0076, Japan
CEO: Yoshiaki Hirai, Pres.
Bus: *Mfr. specialty polymer chemicals*
Tel: 81-6-6440-5300
Fax: 81-6-6440-5330
www.nichigo.co.jp
Rev: $680
Emp: 1,496

NAICS: 325110, 325188, 325193, 325199

NIPPON GOHSEI (USA) CO. LTD.
12220 Strang Rd., La Porte, Texas 77571-9740
CEO: Masanori Fujikawa, Pres.
Bus: *Manufacturer specialty polymer chemicals*
Tel: (281) 842-5025
Fax: (281) 842-5023
%FO: 100

NOLTEX LLC
12220 Strang Rd., La Porte, Texas 77571-9740
CEO: Masanori Fujikawa, Pres.
Bus: *Manufacturer specialty polymer chemicals*
Tel: (281) 842-5000
Fax: (281) 842-5095
%FO: 100

SOARUS L.L.C.
3930 Ventura Dr., Ste. 355, Arlington Heights, Illinois 60004
CEO:
Bus: *Manufacturer specialty polymer chemicals*
Tel: (847) 255-1211
Fax: (847) 255-4343
%FO: 100

● **NIPPON TELEGRAPH & TELEPHONE CORP. (NTT)**
3-1, Otemachi, 2-chome, Chiyoda-ku, Tokyo 100-8116, Japan
CEO: Norio Wada, Pres.
Bus: *Engaged in telecommunication services.*
Tel: 81-3-5205-5581
Fax: 81-3-5205-5589
www.ntt.co.jp
Rev: $100,819
Emp: 205,288

NAICS: 517110, 517211, 517212, 517910, 518111, 518210, 519190, 561499

NTT AMERICA INC.
101 Park Ave., 41/F, New York, New York 10178
CEO: Tatsuo Kawasaki, Pres. & CEO
Bus: *Network services*
Tel: (212) 661-0810
Fax: (212) 661-1078
Emp: 180

NTT DATA CORP.
830 Third Ave., 3/F, New York, New York 10022
CEO: Takaashi Enomoto, Pres.
Bus: *Information technology services.*
Tel: (212) 355-3388
Fax:
Emp: 162

VERIO
8005 S. Chester St., Ste. 200, Englewood, Colorado 80112
CEO: Gregory A. Conley, Pres. & CEO
Bus: *Managed network services*
Tel: (303) 645-1900
Fax: (303) 792-5644

Emp: 3,000

● **NIPPON TELEVISION NETWORK CORP.**
1-6-1 Higashi Shimbashi, Minato-ku, Tokyo 105-7444, Japan
CEO: Kohei Manabe, Pres.
Bus: *Provides television broadcast services.*
Tel: 81-3-6215-1111
Fax: 81-3-5500-8249
www.ntv.co.jp

Rev: $3,108
Emp: 1,304

NAICS: 512110, 512120, 512191, 512199, 515120, 515210, 541860, 711211

NIPPON TELEVISION NETWORK
458 W. 25th St., San Mateo, California 94403
CEO: June Nakagawa, Mgr.
Bus: *Provides video production and web casting.*
Tel: (650) 349-4203
Fax:

NIPPON TELEVISION NETWORK
3000 West Alameda Ave., Burbank, California 91523-0001
CEO: Masaka Harukawa, Pres.
Bus: *Provides video production and web casting.*
Tel: (818) 954-0288
Fax: (818) 954-0288

%FO: 100

NTV INTERNATIONAL CORP.
50 Rockefeller Plaza, Ste. 940, New York, New York 10020
CEO: Jasaburo Hayahii, Pres.
Bus: *Provides video production and web casting.*
Tel: (212) 489-8390
Fax: (212) 489-8395

%FO: 100

● **NIPPON YUSEN KABUSHIKI KAISHA (NYK LINE)**
3-2, Marunouchi, 2-chome, Chiyoda-ku, Tokyo 100-0005, Japan
CEO: Koji Miyahara, Pres.
Bus: *Steamship operator and international
transportation.*
Tel: 81-3-3284-5151
Fax: 81-3-3284-6361
www.nyklline.com

Rev: $13,236
Emp: 1,739

NAICS: 483111, 483112, 483113, 488320, 488510, 561520

CERES TERMINALS INC.
1200 Harbor Blvd., Weehawken, New Jersey 07086
CEO: Thomas J. Simmers, Pres. & CEO
Bus: *Port, harbor & marine terminal management*
Tel: (201) 974-3800
Fax: (201) 974-3850

Emp: 276

CRYSTAL CRUISES, INC.
2049 Century Park East, Ste. 1400, Los Angeles, California 90067
CEO: Gregg Michel, Pres.
Bus: *Cruise ship tour operator.*
Tel: (310) 785-9300
Fax: (310) 785-0011

%FO: 100
Emp: 240

GST CORPORATION
8295 Tournament Dr., Ste. 150, Memphis, Tennessee 38125
CEO: Lanny Vaughn, Pres. & CEO
Bus: *Logistics services*
Tel: (901) 794-2225
Fax: (901) 362-8078

Emp: 520

NEW WAVE LOGISTICS
2417 E. Carson St., Ste. 200, Long Beach, California 90810
CEO: Yoshi Ogohchi, Pres.
Bus: *Freight transport services.*
Tel: (310) 518-0098
Fax:

Emp: 40

NIPPON YUSEN KAISHA
101 S. Capital Blvd., Boise, Idaho 83702
CEO: Kinichi Hirayama, CEO
Bus: *Mfr. relays & industrial controls*
Tel: (208) 363-8156
Fax:

NYK BULKSHIP USA INC.
5263-1 Intermodal Dr., Jacksonville, Florida 32226
CEO: Finn Roden, Pres.
Bus: *Trucking operator*
Tel: (904) 757-6610
Fax:

NYK BULKSHIP USA, INC.
925 Fell St. 3, Baltimore, Maryland 21231
CEO: Gary Hurley, Pres.
Bus: *International marine transport.*
Tel: (410) 534-4365
Fax:
%FO: 100

NYK LINE NORTH AMERICA
360 Interstate North Pkwy., Atlanta, Georgia 30339
CEO: Christopher Capodanno, Mgr.
Bus: *Water transportation*
Tel: (770) 955-8400
Fax:

NYK LINE NORTH AMERICA, INC.
300 Lighting Way, 5/F, Secaucus, New Jersey 07094
CEO: Hiroyuki Shimizu, Pres.
Bus: *International marine transport.*
Tel: (201) 330-3000
Fax: (201) 867-9059
%FO: 100
Emp: 1,235

NYK LOGISTICS, INC
2417 E. Carson St., Carson, California 90810
CEO: Akio Futami
Bus: *General warehousing*
Tel: (310) 522-2200
Fax:
Emp: 500

VEXURE
3131 St. Johns Bluff Rd. South, Jacksonville, Florida 32446
CEO: Al Steele, Chmn. & CEO
Bus: *Transportation services*
Tel: (904) 249-2010
Fax: (904) 394-0399
Emp: 140

YUSEN AIR & SEA SERVICE
377 Oak St., 3/F, Garden City, New York 11530
CEO: Sasatoshi Moriya, Pres.
Bus: *Travel agencies*
Tel: (516) 222-1777
Fax:
Emp: 388

● **NIPPONKOA INSURANCE COMPANY LIMITED**
3-7-3 Kasumigaseki, Chiyoda-ku, Tokyo 100-8965, Japan
CEO: Mutsuharu Okamoto, Chmn. & CEO
Bus: *Engaged in property and casualty insurance.*
Tel: 81-3-3593-3111
Fax: 81-3-3593-5388
www.nipponkoa.co.jp
Rev: $9,975
Emp: 8,321

NAICS: 524113, 524114, 524126

NIPPONKOA INSURANE COMPANY OF AMERICA
14 Wall St., Ste. 812, New York, New York 10005
CEO: Kozo Saito, Pres.
Bus: *Insurance agent.*
Tel: (212) 405-1650
Fax: (212) 405-1660
%FO: 100
Emp: 26

NIPPONKOA INSURANE COMPANY OF AMERICA
180 North LaSalle St., Ste. 2503, Chicago, Illinois 60601
CEO: Tomoyuki Yunoue, Mgr.   Tel: (312) 553-9344   %FO: 100
Bus: *Engaged in property and casualty insurance.* Fax: (312) 553-9347

NIPPONKOA INSURANE COMPANY OF AMERICA
601 South Figueroa St., Ste. 2100, Los Angeles, California 90071
CEO: Harumichi Ishu   Tel: (213) 833-2100   %FO: 100
Bus: *Engaged in property and casualty insurance.* Fax: (213) 833-2120

● **NISHI NIPPON RAILROAD CO., LTD.**
1-11-17, Tenjin 1-chome, Chuo-ku, Fukuoka 810-8570, Japan
CEO: Tsuguo Nagao, Pres.   Tel: 81-92-734-1553   Rev: $14,213
Bus: *Engaged in railway and coach services.* Fax: 81-92-781-2583   Emp: 2
    www.nishitetsu.co.jp
NAICS: 445110, 481111, 482111, 485119, 531210

    NNR AIRCARGO SERVICES (USA) INC.
    450 East Devon Ave., Ste. 260, Itasca, Illinois 60143
    CEO: Yoshio Nogami, Chmn.   Tel: (630) 773-1490   %FO: 100
    Bus: *Freight forwarding and customs house* Fax: (630) 773-1442   Emp: 280
      broker.

● **NISHIMOTO TRADING COMPANY LTD.**
1-38, Isobe-dori 4-chome, Chuo-ku, Kobe 651-0084, Japan
CEO: Tatsuzo Susaki, Pres.   Tel: 81-78-230-0111
Bus: *Supplies fresh fruits, vegetables and food* Fax: 81-78-230-0123   Emp: 50
    www.nishimototrading.com
NAICS: 424480

    DBA SEASIA
    19931 72nd Ave., South, Ste. 101, Kent, Washington 98032
    CEO: Michael Moriguchi   Tel: (893) 253-1000   %FO: 100
    Bus: *Sale/distribution of food products, fresh* Fax: (893) 253-1001
      fruits and vegetables.

    NISHIMOTO TRADING CO. OF AMERICA LTD.
    6630 Amberton Dr., Elkridge, Maryland 21075
    CEO: Andy Takahashi   Tel: (410) 540-4990   %FO: 100
    Bus: *Sale/distribution of food products, fresh* Fax: (410) 796-8101
      fruits and vegetables.

    NISHIMOTO TRADING COMPANY OF AMERICA, LTD.
    331 Libby St., Honolulu, Hawaii 96817
    CEO: Kazutaka Sato   Tel: (808) 832-7555   %FO: 100
    Bus: *Sale/distribution of food products, fresh* Fax: (808) 841-3853
      fruits and vegetables.

    NISHIMOTO TRADING COMPANY OF AMERICA, LTD.
    602 Washington Ave., Carlstadt, New Jersey 07072
    CEO: Toshiyuki Nishikawa   Tel: (201) 804-1600   %FO: 100
    Bus: *Sale/distribution of food products, fresh* Fax: (201) 635-9200
      fruits and vegetables.

NISHIMOTO TRADING COMPANY OF AMERICA, LTD.
1660 Helm Dr., Ste. 300, Las Vegas, Nevada 89119
CEO: Minoru Ichihara   Tel: (702) 262-6111   %FO: 100
Bus: *Sale/distribution of food products, fresh*   Fax: (702) 262-6222
fruits and vegetables.

NISHIMOTO TRADING COMPANY OF AMERICA, LTD.
340 Valley Dr., Brisbane, California 94005
CEO: Yoshiro Meiji   Tel: (415) 467-5300   %FO: 100
Bus: *Sale/distribution of food products, fresh*   Fax: (415) 467-9625
fruits and vegetables.

NISHIMOTO TRADING COMPANY OF AMERICA, LTD.
13409 Orden Dr., Bldg. J, Santa Fe Springs, California 90670
CEO: Ichiro Ken Sasaki, Pres.   Tel: (562) 802-1900   %FO: 100
Bus: *Sale/distribution of food products, fresh*   Fax: (562) 229-1720   Emp: 55
fruits and vegetables.

NISHIMOTO TRADING COMPANY OF AMERICA, LTD.
545 Fullerton Ave., Carol Steam, Illinois 60188
CEO: Toyoji Sugisawa   Tel: (630) 784-1500   %FO: 100
Bus: *Sale/distribution of food products, fresh*   Fax: (630) 784-9300
fruits and vegetables.

NISHIMOTO TRADING COMPANY OF AMERICA, LTD.
5065 Buford Hwy., Ste. 100, Norcross, Georgia 30071-2737
CEO: Mototsugu Ichikawa   Tel: (678) 966-0950   %FO: 100
Bus: *Sale/distribution of food products, fresh*   Fax: (678) 966-0950
fruits and vegetables.

NISHIMOTO TRADING COMPANY OF AMERICA, LTD.
8441 Arjons Dr., Ste. B, San Diego, California 92126
CEO: Kazuko Wu   Tel: (858) 547-4220   %FO: 100
Bus: *Sale/distribution of food products, fresh*   Fax: (858) 547-4999
fruits and vegetables.

NISHIMOTO TRADING COMPANY OF AMERICA, LTD.
3870 Paris St., Ste. 5, Denver, Colorado 80239
CEO: Kazuyuki Tokuhara   Tel: (303) 576-9111   %FO: 100
Bus: *Sale/distribution of food products, fresh*   Fax: (303) 576-9375
fruits and vegetables.

NISHIMOTO TRADING COMPANY OF AMERICA, LTD.
1401 B Lakeway Dr., Dallas, Texas 75057
CEO: Tadashi Higashiomori   Tel: (972) 221-4477   %FO: 100
Bus: *Sale/distribution of food products, fresh*   Fax: (972) 221-9494
fruits and vegetables.

NISHIMOTO TRADING COMPANY OF AMERICA, LTD.
3941 Commerce Pkwy., Miramar, Florida 33025
CEO: Hiroshi Kikumori   Tel: (954) 450-9111   %FO: 100
Bus: *Sale/distribution of food products, fresh*   Fax: (954) 450-9693
fruits and vegetables.

NISHIMOTO TRADING COMPANY OF AMERICA, LTD.
5522 W. Roosevelt, Ste. 6, Phoenix, Arizona 85034
CEO: Teijiro Sho, Pres. Tel: (602) 415-0011 %FO: 100
Bus: *Sale/distribution of food products, fresh* Fax: (602) 415-0011
fruits and vegetables.

• **NISSAN CHEMICAL INDUSTRIES, LTD.**
7-1, Kanda Nishiki-cho, 3-chome, Chiyoda-ku, Tokyo 101-0054, Japan
CEO: Nobuichiro Fujimoto, Pres. Tel: 81-3-3296-8320 Rev: $1,476
Bus: *Mfr. chemical fertilizers.* Fax: 81-3-3296-8210 Emp: 1,505
www.nissanchem.co.jp
NAICS: 325120, 325181, 325188, 325199, 325311, 325320, 325412, 325998, 424690

NISSAN CHEMICAL AMERICA CORP.
10777 Westheimer Rd., Ste. 150, Houston, Texas 77042
CEO: Kolchiro Yanagida, Pres. Tel: (713) 532-4745 %FO: 100
Bus: *Sale of chemicals.* Fax: Emp: 11

NISSAN CHEMICAL AMERICA CORPORATION
12330 Bay Area Blvd., Pasadena, Texas 77507
CEO: Susumu Kondo, Pres. Tel: (281) 291-0200 %FO: 100
Bus: *Mfr. of silica solution.* Fax:

• **NISSAN DIESEL MOTOR CO., LTD.**
1-1 Oaza, Ageo, Saitama 362-8523, Japan
CEO: Itaru Koeda, Chmn. Tel: 81-48-781-2301 Rev: $4,288
Bus: *Mfr. trucks, buses, tractors and other industrial* Fax: 81-48-781-6349 Emp: 9,959
vehicles. www.nissandiesel.co.jp
NAICS: 333924, 336120, 336211, 336340, 336350

NISSAN DIESEL AMERICA, INC.
5930 Campus Circle Dr., Irving, Texas 75063
CEO: Tetsuma Nieda, Pres. Tel: (972) 756-5500 %FO: 100
Bus: *Mfr. of truck trailers/ Sale of auto parts &* Fax: (972) 550-1255 Emp: 62
supplies.

• **NISSAN MOTOR COMPANY, LTD.**
17-1, Ginza, 6-chome, Chuo-ku, Tokyo 104-8023, Japan
CEO: Carlos Ghosn, Pres. & CEO Tel: 81-3-3543-5523 Rev: $70,087
Bus: *Mfr. cars, trucks, diesel and marine engines,* Fax: 81-3-5565-2228 Emp: 123,748
industrial machinery and vehicles, boats. (35% www.nissanmotors.com
interest Renault SA, France)
NAICS: 333618, 336111, 336112, 339999, 522291

NISSAN DIESEL MOTOR CO., LTD.
5930 Campus Circle Dr., Irving, Texas 75063
CEO: Satoshi Tanaka Tel: (972) 756-5500 %FO: 100
Bus: *Mfr./sales/distribution of automobiles.* Fax: (972) 550-1255

NISSAN FORKLIFT CORPORATION, NA
240 North Prospect St., Marengo, Illinois 60152
CEO: Takanobu Tokugawa, Pres. Tel: (815) 568-0061 %FO: 100
Bus: *Production/import/sale forklifts.* Fax: (815) 568-0179 Emp: 420

NISSAN NORTH AMERICA, INC
300 Nissan Dr., Canton, Mississippi 39046
CEO: Dave Boyer
Bus: *Sales/distribution of automobiles.*
Tel: (601) 855-8050
Fax: (601) 855-8055
%FO: 100
Emp: 5,300

NISSAN NORTH AMERICA, INC.
18051 South Figueroa St., Gardena, California 90248
CEO: Brian Witt, Pres. & CEO
Bus: *Sales/distribution of automobiles.*
Tel: (310) 532-3111
Fax: (310) 771-3343
%FO: 100

NISSAN TECHNICAL CENTER NORTH AMERICA
39001 Technical Center Dr., Farmington Hills, Michigan 48333
CEO: Mitsuhiko Yamashita, Pres.
Bus: *Engaged in research and development.*
Tel: (248) 488-4123
Fax: (248) 488-3901
%FO: 100

● **NISSHIN SEIFUN GROUP INC.**
1-25, Kanda-Nishiki-cho, Chiyoda-ku, Tokyo 101-8441, Japan
CEO: Osamu Shoda, Chmn.
Bus: *Mfr. fresh and processed foods, animal feed, pet food, pharmaceuticals and livestock farming.*
Tel: 81-3-5282-6650
Fax: 81-3-5282-6185
www.nisshin.com
Rev: $4,109
Emp: 5,185
NAICS: 112111, 112112, 112120, 112130, 112210, 112310, 112320, 112330, 112340, 112390, 112410, 112420, 112511, 112512, 112519, 112910, 112920,
112930, 112990, 114111, 114112, 114119, 115210, 311211, 311212, 311230, 311411, 311412, 311421, 311422, 311423, 311822, 311823,
311991, 325411, 325412, 325413, 325414, 424520, 424910, 722110, 722211, 722212, 722213, 722310, 722320

DYNAMESH, INC.
1555 West Hawthorne Lane, Ste. 4-E, West Chicago, Illinois 60185
CEO: Akio Ishizuka, Chmn.
Bus: *Mfr. and sale of screen printing*
Tel: (630) 293-5454
Fax: (630) 293-5647
%FO: 100
Emp: 20

FOOD MASTERS (PNW) CORP.
18420 50th Ave. East, Tacoma, Washington 98446
CEO: Akihiro Watanabe
Bus: *Mfr. fresh and processed foods, animal feed, pet food, pharmaceuticals and livestock farming.*
Tel: (253) 846-5230
Fax:
%FO: 100
Emp: 50

MEDALLION FOODS, INC.
18420 50th Ave. East, Tacoma, Washington 98446
CEO: Kiyohide Furukawa, Pres.
Bus: *Food preparations.*
Tel: (253) 846-2600
Fax: (253) 846-7161
%FO: 100
Emp: 50

OYC INTERNATIONAL, INC.
2 Elm Square, Andover, Massachusetts 01810
CEO: Mark Berman, Dir.
Bus: *Mfr. of pharmaceutical preparations.*
Tel: (978) 470-1980
Fax: (978) 470-2030
%FO: 100
Emp: 8

● **NISSHIN STEEL CO., LTD.**
Shinkokusai Bldg., 4-1 Marunouchi 3-chome, Chiyoda-ku, Tokyo 100-8366, Japan
CEO: Toshihiko Ono, Pres. & CEO
Bus: *Mfr. galvanized and aluminized and copper-plated steel sheets and strips.*
Tel: 81-3-3216-5511
Fax: 81-3-3214-1895
www.nisshn-steel.co.jp
Rev: $4,273
NAICS: 331111, 331221

NISSHIN STEEL USA, LLC
375 Park Ave., Ste. 1005, New York, New York 10152
CEO: Shoichi Ueda, Pres.
Bus: *Mfr. galvanized and aluminized steel products.*
Tel: (212) 317-3500
Fax: (212) 421-0496
%FO: 100

NORTH AMERICAN STAINLESS
6870 US Hwy., 42 East, Ghent, Kentucky 41045
CEO: Jose M. Cornejo, Pres. & CEO
Bus: *Mfr. of rolled steel shape & steel wire drawing.*
Tel: (502) 347-6000
Fax: (502) 347-6001
Emp: 575

WHEELING-NISSHIN, INC.
400 Penn and Main St., Follansbee, West Virginia 26037
CEO: Kazuo Yamamoto, Chmn. & CEO
Bus: *Mfr. of rolled steel shape.*
Tel: (304) 527-2800
Fax: (304) 527-0985
Emp: 180

• **NISSHINBO INDUSTRIES, INC.**
2-31-11, Ningyo-cho, Nihonbashi, Chuo-ku, Tokyo 103-8650, Japan
CEO: Yoshikazu Sashida, Pres.
Bus: *Engaged in manufacture of textile products, plastics, automobile brakes, paper and*
NAICS: 313210, 322291, 325211, 333512, 333513, 336340
Tel: 81-3-5965-8833
Fax: 81-3-5695-8970
www.nisshinbo.co.jp
Rev: $2,148
Emp: 9,875

NISSHINBO AUTOMOTIVE MANUFACTURING, INC.
14381 Industrial Park Blvd., Covington, Georgia 30014
CEO: Yukihiko Konno, Pres.
Bus: *Mfr./sales of brake linings.*
Tel: (770) 787-2002
Fax: (770) 788-6190
%FO: 100
Emp: 125

• **NISSIN CORPORATION**
6-84 Onoe-cho, Naka-ku, Yokohama 231-8477, Japan
CEO: Hiroshi Tsutsui, Pres.
Bus: *Air & ocean freight forwarding, customs brokerage and warehousing.*
NAICS: 488510
Tel: 81-45-671-6112
Fax: 81-45-671-6118
www.nissin-tw.co.jp
Rev: $1,028
Emp: 1,181

NISSIN INTERNATIONAL TRANSORT USA
Sharp Plaza, Mahwah, New Jersey 07430
CEO: M. Nakamura
Bus: *Air & ocean freight forwarding, customs brokerage and warehousing.*
Tel: (201) 529-8610
Fax: (201) 529-8589
%FO: 100

NISSIN INTERNATIONAL TRANSORT USA
490 Carlton Ct., South San Francisco, California 94080
CEO: N. Ban
Bus: *Air & ocean freight forwarding, customs brokerage and warehousing.*
Tel: (650) 360-2600
Fax: (650) 360-2626
%FO: 100

NISSIN INTERNATIONAL TRANSORT USA
68 Adcon Lane, Pell City, Alabama 35125
CEO: N. Goto
Bus: *Air & ocean freight forwarding, customs brokerage and warehousing.*
Tel: (205) 338-9092
Fax: (205) 338-9081
%FO: 100

NISSIN INTERNATIONAL TRANSORT USA
3131 No. Franklin Rd., Ste. H-1, Indianapolis, Indiana 46226
CEO: H. Hikita   Tel: (317) 895-4000   %FO: 100
Bus: *Air & ocean freight forwarding, customs*   Fax: (317) 895-4001
brokerage and warehousing.

NISSIN INTERNATIONAL TRANSORT USA
6094 Executive Blvd., Huber Heights, Ohio 45424
CEO: T. Kobayashi   Tel: (937) 237-1700   %FO: 100
Bus: *Air & ocean freight forwarding, customs*   Fax: (937) 237-1930
brokerage and warehousing.

NISSIN INTERNATIONAL TRANSORT USA
14353 Suntra Way, Marysville, Ohio 43040
CEO: F. Yajima   Tel: (937) 644-2503   %FO: 100
Bus: *Air & ocean freight forwarding, customs*   Fax: (937) 644-3146
brokerage and warehousing.

NISSIN INTERNATIONAL TRANSORT USA
5901 Bolsa Ave., Huntington Beach, California 92647
CEO: Y. Fujumoto   Tel: (714) 903-4649   %FO: 100
Bus: *Air & ocean freight forwarding, customs*   Fax: (714) 903-5943
brokerage and warehousing.

NISSIN INTERNATIONAL TRANSORT USA
10301 NW 108th St., Ste. 6, Miami, Florida 33178
CEO: K. Sonoda   Tel: (305) 884-5656   %FO: 100
Bus: *Air & ocean freight forwarding, customs*   Fax: (305) 884-6285
brokerage and warehousing.

NISSIN INTERNATIONAL TRANSORT USA
172-47 Baisley Blvd., Jamaica, New York 11434
CEO: H. Okutsu   Tel: (718) 525-2437   %FO: 100
Bus: *Air & ocean freight forwarding, customs*   Fax: (718) 525-2234
brokerage and warehousing.

NISSIN INTERNATIONAL TRANSORT USA
101 Mark St., Ste. 3, Wood Dale, Illinois 60191
CEO: S. Kikugawa   Tel: (630) 616-4000   %FO: 100
Bus: *Air & ocean freight forwarding, customs*   Fax: (630) 616-1098
brokerage and warehousing.

NISSIN INTERNATIONAL TRANSORT USA
3600 Lind Ave, SW, Ste. 120, Renton, Washington 98055
CEO: K. Yamano   Tel: (425) 656-5973   %FO: 100
Bus: *Air & ocean freight forwarding, customs*   Fax: (425) 656-5974
brokerage and warehousing.

NISSIN INTERNATIONAL TRANSORT USA
490 Carlton Ct., S. San Francisco, California 94080
CEO: N. Ban   Tel: (650) 360-2600   %FO: 100
Bus: *Air & ocean freight forwarding, customs*   Fax: (650) 360-2626
brokerage and warehousing.

NISSIN INTERNATIONAL TRANSORT USA
73 Southwoods Pkwy., Ste. 100, Atlanta, Georgia 30354
CEO: Y. Ninomiya   Tel: (404) 366-8565   %FO: 100
Bus: *Air & ocean freight forwarding, customs*
    brokerage and warehousing.   Fax: (404) 366-8932

NISSIN INTERNATIONAL TRANSORT USA
603 SE Assembly Ave., Ste. 100, Vancouver, Washington 98661
CEO: K. Yamano   Tel: (360) 693-5700   %FO: 100
Bus: *Air & ocean freight forwarding, customs*
    brokerage and warehousing.   Fax: (360) 693-5800

NISSIN INTERNATIONAL TRANSORT USA
US Headquarters, 1540 West 190th St., Torrance, California 90501
CEO: T. Shiomoto   Tel: (310) 222-5800   %FO: 100
Bus: *Air & ocean freight forwarding, customs*   Fax: (310) 787-7150   Emp: 300
    brokerage and warehousing.

NISSIN INTERNATIONAL TRANSORT USA
2275 Faraday Dr., Ste. 3, San Diego, California 92154-7927
CEO: Jose Maestro   Tel: (619) 710-0805   %FO: 100
Bus: *Air & ocean freight forwarding, customs*   Fax: (619) 710-0804
    brokerage and warehousing.

● **NISSIN FOOD PRODUCTS CO., LTD.**
1-1, 4-chome, Nishinakajima, Yodogawa-ku, Osaka 532-8524, Japan
CEO: Koki Ando, Pres.   Tel: 81-6-6305-7711   Rev: $3,029
Bus: *Mfr. food products and pharmaceuticals.*   Fax: 81-3-6304-1288   Emp: 6,176
     www.nissinfoods.co.jp
    NAICS: 311211, 311230, 311340, 311412, 311423, 311823

    NISSIN FOODS COMPANY, INC.
    2001 West Rosecrans Ave., Gardena, California 90249
    CEO: Tak Naruto, Pres.   Tel: (323) 321-6453   %FO: 100
    Bus: *Sales/distribution of soups, cereals and*   Fax: (323) 515-3751   Emp: 600
        desserts.

● **NITTA CORPORATION**
4-4-26, Sakuragawa, Naniwa-ku, Osaka 556-0022, Japan
CEO: Takehiko Nitta, Pres.   Tel: 81-6-6563-1211   Rev: $278
Bus: *Industrial belting, construction materials,*   Fax: 81-6-6563-1212   Emp: 1,448
    conveyor systems, air filtration products, hoses   www.nitta.co.jp
    and tubes, farming and forestry.
    NAICS: 333922

    NITTA CORPORATION OF AMERICA
    3790 Boyd Rd., PO Box 669, Suwannee, Georgia 30024
    CEO: Allison Ballard, Pres.   Tel: (770) 497-0212   %FO: 100
    Bus: *Production & sales of transmission &*   Fax: (770) 623-1398   Emp: 71
        conveyor belts.

● **NITTO BOSEKI COMPANY, LTD.**
4-1-28, Kudankita, Chiyoda ku, Tokyo 102-0073, Japan
CEO:　Atsuhiko Sagara, Pres.　　　　　　　　　　Tel:　81-3-3514-8675　　　　Rev: $1,205
Bus:　*Mfr. textiles, fibers, building materials and*　　Fax:　81-3-3514-8681　　　Emp: 4,018
　　　specialty chemicals.　　　　　　　　　　　　www.nittobo.co.jp
　NAICS:　236220, 237210, 321918, 325411, 325998, 326192, 326199, 327993

　　INTERNATIONAL IMMUNOLOGY CORPORATION
　　25549 Adams Ave., Murrieta, California 92562
　　CEO:　Yoshio Nakamura, Pres.　　　　　　　　Tel:　(951) 677-5629　　　%FO: 100
　　Bus:　*Mfr./sale biological bulk material for*　　　Fax:　　　　　　　　　　Emp: 42
　　　　　diagnostics industry.

　　NITTOBO AMERICA, INC.
　　22549 Adams Ave., Murrieta, California 92562
　　CEO:　Katsuhiro Katayama, Pres.　　　　　　　Tel:　(951) 677-9184
　　Bus:　*Investment company*　　　　　　　　　　Fax:　　　　　　　　　　　Emp: 97

● **NITTO DENKO CORPORATION**
1-1-2 Shimohozumi, Ibaraki, Osaka 567-8680, Japan
CEO:　Masamichi Takemoto, Pres.　　　　　　　　Tel:　81-726-22-2981　　　　Rev: $316
Bus:　*Industrial and electronic materials manufacture.*　Fax:　81-726-26-1505　　　Emp: 13,161
　　　　　　　　　　　　　　　　　　　　　　　　　www.nitto.com
　NAICS:　325211, 325520

　　AVEVA DRUG DELIVERY SYSTEMS
　　3250 Commerce Pkwy., Pembroke Pines, Florida 33025
　　CEO:　Wallace Reams, COO　　　　　　　　　　Tel:　(954) 430-3340
　　Bus:　*Mfr. of pharmaceutical preparations,*　　　Fax:　　　　　　　　　　Emp: 115
　　　　　commercial physical research, mfr. Of
　　　　　surgical & medical instruments.

　　GRAPHIC TECHNOLOGY, INC.
　　301 Gardner Dr., New Century, Kansas 66031
　　CEO:　R. Bardwell, Pres. & CEO　　　　　　　　Tel:　(913) 764-5550
　　Bus:　*Mfr. of bar code labels.*　　　　　　　　　Fax:　(913) 764-0320

　　HYDRANAUTICS
　　401 Jones Rd., Oceanside, California 92054
　　CEO:　Kenneth Klinko, Pres. & COO　　　　　　Tel:　(760) 901-2500
　　Bus:　*Mfr. of environmental services & equipment.*　Fax:　(760) 901-2578　　　Emp: 235

　　NITTO DENKO AMERICA INC.
　　48500 Freemont Blvd., Fremont, California 94538
　　CEO:　Kazuya Akiyama, Pres.　　　　　　　　　Tel:　(510) 445-5400　　　%FO: 100
　　Bus:　*Mfr. of ferromanganese.*　　　　　　　　Fax:　(510) 445-5480　　　Emp: 33

　　PERMACEL
　　US Hwy. 1, PO Box 671, New Brunswick, New Jersey 08903
　　CEO:　William J. Hayes, Pres.　　　　　　　　　Tel:　(732) 418-2400
　　Bus:　*Mfr. of pressure sensitive tapes, coated*　　Fax:　(732) 418-2474　　　Emp: 400
　　　　　films & automotive sealing materials.

● **NOF CORPORATION**
Yebisu Garden Place Tower, 20-3 Ebisu, 4-chiome, Shibuya-ku, Tokyo 150-6019, Japan
CEO: Youhei Nakajima, Pres. & CEO   Tel: 81-3-5424-6600   Rev: $1,301
Bus: *Mfr. petroleum-based chemicals and paints for*   Fax: 81-3-5424-6800   Emp: 3,599
ships and automobiles.   www.nof.co.jp
NAICS: 311222, 311223, 311225, 325110, 325199, 325211, 325510, 325613, 325920, 325998

   GEORGIA METAL COATINGS CO.
   3033 Adriatic Ct., Norcross, Georgia 30071
   CEO: George Palek, Pres.   Tel: (770) 446-3930
   Bus: *Metal corrosion prevention coating.*   Fax: (770) 446-3932   Emp: 10

   METAL COATINGS INTERNATIONAL INC.
   275 Industrial Pkwy., Chardon, Ohio 44024
   CEO: George Palek, Pres.   Tel: (440) 285-2231   %FO: 100
   Bus: *Production and sales of special corrosion* Fax: (440) 285-5009   Emp: 115
   prevention agents.

   MICHIGAN METAL COATINGS CO.
   2871 Research Dr., Rochester Hills, Michigan 48309
   CEO: George C. Palek, Pres.   Tel: (248) 853-3210   %FO: 100
   Bus: *Metal corrosion prevention coating.*   Fax: (248) 853-3260   Emp: 40

   NOF AMERICA CORP.
   11 Martine Ave., Ste. 1170, White Plains, New York 10606
   CEO: Kazuhiro Akama, Pres.   Tel: (914) 681-9790   %FO: 100
   Bus: *Import & export of chemicals.*   Fax: (914) 681-9791   Emp: 2

● **NOMURA HOLDINGS, INC.**
1-9-1, Nihonbashi, Chuo-ku, Tokyo 103-8645, Japan
CEO: Junichi Ujiie, Pres. & CEO   Tel: 81-3-5255-1000   Rev: $10,554
Bus: *International securities broker/dealer, investment* Fax: 81-3-3278-0420   Emp: 13,987
banking and asset management services.   www.nomura.com
NAICS: 523110, 523120, 523920, 523930, 523999, 524210, 525110, 525120, 525190, 525910, 525920, 525990

   NOMURA SECURITIES INTERNATIONAL, INC.
   2 World Financial Center, Bldg. B, New York, New York 10281
   CEO: Hideyuki Takahashi, Pres. & CEO   Tel: (212) 667-9300
   Bus: *U.S. Headquarters Securities brokers &*   Fax: (212) 667-1058   Emp: 900
   traders

● **NOMURA TRADING COMPANY, LTD.**
4-5, Bingo-machi, I-chome, Chuo-ku, Osaka 541, Japan
CEO: Yoshihisa Idesawa, CEO   Tel: 81-6-6268-8111
Bus: *Import/export general merchandise.*   Fax: 81-6-6268-8268   Emp: 600
                                                     www.nomuratrading.co.jp
NAICS: 111199, 113110, 311411, 314999, 325199

   NOMURA (AMERICA) CORPORATION
   970 West 190th St., Ste. 970, Torrance, California 90502
   CEO: A. Minamiyama, Mgr.   Tel: (310) 354-0059   %FO: 100
   Bus: *Import/export general merchandise.*   Fax: (310) 354-0079

NOMURA (AMERICA) CORPORATION
900 Fourth Ave., Seattle, Washington 98164
CEO: Hideyuki Takahashi, Mgr.
Bus: *Import/export general merchandise.*
Tel: (212) 667-9300
Fax: (212) 667-9300
%FO: 100

NOMURA (AMERICA) CORPORATION
747 Third Ave., 19/F, New York, New York 10017
CEO: Hideyuki Takahashi, CEO
Bus: *Import/export general merchandise.*
Tel: (212) 935-7151
Fax: (212) 935-6717
%FO: 100
Emp: 20

● **THE NORINCHUKIN BANK**
13-2, Yurakucho, 1-chome, Chiyoda-ku, CPO Box 364, Tokyo 100-8420, Japan
CEO: Hirofumi Ueno, Pres. & CEO
Bus: *Agricultural banking services.*
Tel: 81-3-3279-0111
Fax: 81-3-3218-5177
www.nochubank.or.jp
Rev: $10,804
Emp: 2,747

NAICS: 522110, 522298, 525110

THENORINCHUKIN BANK
245 Park Ave., 29/F, New York, New York 10167
CEO: Yoshiro Niiro, Gen. Mgr.
Bus: *Agricultural banking services.*
Tel: (212) 697-1717
Fax: (212) 697-5754
%FO: 100

● **NORITAKE CO., LIMITED**
3-1-36, Noritake-Shinmachi, Nishi-ku, Nagoya 451-8501, Japan
CEO: Takashi Iwasaki, Chmn.
Bus: *Mfr. china, stone and porcelain dinnerware.*
Tel: 81-52-561-7112
Fax: 81-52-561-9721
www.noritake.co.jp
Rev: $1,069
Emp: 5,923

NAICS: 327112, 333512, 333515, 334419, 339114

NORITAKE CO., LTD.
2635 Clearbrook Dr., Arlington Heights, Illinois 60005
CEO: Mike Surata, Mgr.
Bus: *Wholesale electronic parts/equipment & home furnishing.*
Tel: (847) 439-9020
Fax: (847) 593-2285
%FO: 100
Emp: 13

● **NORITSU KOKI COMPANY, LTD.**
Umehara 579-1, Wakayama 640-8550, Japan
CEO: Kanichi Nishimoto, Pres. & CEO
Bus: *Mfr. photo finishing equipment.*
Tel: 81-73-454-0307
Fax: 81-73-454-0420
www.noritsu.co.jp
Rev: $859
Emp: 1,836

NAICS: 333315, 443130

NORITSU AMERICA CORPORATION
6900 Noritsu Ave., Buena Park, California 90620
CEO: Kanichi Nishimoto, Chmn.
Bus: *Sales/service of photo finishing equipment*
Tel: (714) 521-9040
Fax: (714) 670-2049
%FO: 100
Emp: 472

● **NSK, LTD.**
Nissei Bldg., 1-6-3 Ohsaki, Shinagawa-ku, Tokyo 141-8560, Japan
CEO: Seiichi Asaka, Pres. & CEO
Bus: *Mfr. automotive products, steering system, seat belts, bearings, transmissions and clutches.*
Tel: 81-3-3779-7111
Fax: 81-3-3779-7431
www.nsk.com
Rev: $4,943
Emp: 19,772
NAICS: 332991, 532412, 532490, 541614

NSK CORPORATION
4200 Goss Rd., Ann Arbor, Michigan 48105
CEO: Ollie Martins, Pres.
Bus: *Mfr. of automotive bearings.*

Tel: (734) 913-7500
Fax: (734) 913-7740

%FO: 100
Emp: 142

● **NTN CORPORATION**
3-17, 1-chome, Kyomachi-bori, Nishi-ku, Osaka 550-0003, Japan
CEO: Yasunobu Suzuki, Pres.
Bus: *Mfr. bearings, joints and precision processing equipment.*

Tel: 81-6-6449-3528
Fax: 81-6-6443-3226
www.ntn.co.jp

Rev: $3,383
Emp: 11,885

NAICS: 332991

AMERICAN NTN BEARING MFG CORPORATION
9515 Winona Ave., Schiller Park, Illinois 60176
CEO: John Welch, Gen. Mgr.
Bus: *Mfr. bearings, wheel units.*

Tel: (847) 671-5450
Fax:

%FO: 100
Emp: 75

NTN BEARING CORP OF AMERICA
1600 East Bishop Ct., PO Box 7604, Mt. Prospect, Illinois 60056
CEO: Rick Thomas, Pres. & COO
Bus: *Engineering/sale anti-friction bearings & constant velocity joints.*

Tel: (847) 298-7500
Fax: (847) 699-9744

%FO: 100
Emp: 302

NTN BEARING CORP. OF AMERICA
1500 Holmes Rd., Elgin, Illinois 60123
CEO: Andy Kitajima, Pres.
Bus: *Mfr. of ball bearings.*

Tel: (847) 741-4545
Fax:

%FO: 100
Emp: 450

NTN BOWER CORPORATION
707 North Bower Rd., Macomb, Illinois 61455
CEO: Yasunori Terada, Pres.
Bus: *Sales of roller bearings.*

Tel: (309) 837-0440
Fax: (309) 837-0438

%FO: 100
Emp: 812

NTN DRIVESHAFT INC.
8251 South International Dr., Columbus, Indiana 47201
CEO: Nobuo Satoh, Pres.
Bus: *Mfr. constant velocity joints.*

Tel: (812) 342-7000
Fax: (812) 342-1155

%FO: 100
Emp: 780

NTN-BCA CORP.
401 West Lincoln Ave., Lititz, Pennsylvania 17543
CEO: Tom Kamachi, Pres.
Bus: *Mfr. of ball bearings.*

Tel: (717) 626-0164
Fax:

%FO: 100
Emp: 770

● **NTT DATA CORPORATION**
Toyosu Center Bldg., 3-3 Toyosu, 3-chome, Koto-ku, Tokyo 135-6033, Japan
CEO: Tomokazu Hamaguchi, Pres. & CEO
Bus: *Provides e-commerce solutions.*

Tel: 81-3-5546-8202
Fax: 81-3-5546-2405
www.nttdata.co.jp

Rev: $8,015
Emp: 17,389

NAICS: 541511, 541512, 541519

NTT AMERICA, INC.
101 Park Ave., 41/F, New York, New York 10178
CEO: Tatsuo Kwasaki, Pres. & CEO
Bus: *Managed network services.*

Tel: (212) 661-0810
Fax: (212) 661-1078

%FO: 54

NTT DATA INTERNATIONAL
830 Third Ave., 3/F, New York, New York 10022
CEO: Takashi Enomoto, Pres.
Bus: *Provides e-commerce solutions.*
Tel: (212) 355-3388
Fax:
%FO: 100
Emp: 162

NTT DATA USA, INC.
4005 Miranda Ave., Ste. 150, Palo Alto, California 94304
CEO: Kanbayashi, Principal
Bus: *Research & tie-up management.*
Tel: (650) 687-0640
Fax:
%FO: 100
Emp: 6

● **NTT DOCOMO, INC .**
1 Sanno Park Tower, 11-1 Nagatacho-2-chome, Chiyoda-ku, Tokyo 100-6150, Japan
CEO: Masao Nakamura, Pres. & CEO
Bus: *Provides wireless phone services.*
Tel: 81-3-5156-1111
Fax: 81-3-5156-0271
www.nttdocomo.com
Rev: $45,200
Emp: 21,527

NAICS: 443112, 517212, 517910, 561421

NIPPON TELEGRAPH AND TELEPHONE CORP.
101 Park Ave., 41/F, New York, New York 10178
CEO: Tatsuo Kawasaki
Bus: *telephone communications*
Tel: (212) 661-0810
Fax: (212) 661-1078
%FO: 63

NTT DOCOMO USA INC.
461 Fifth Ave., 24/F, New York, New York 10017
CEO: Nobuharu Ono, Pres.
Bus: *Provides wireless phone services.*
Tel: (212) 994-7222
Fax: (212) 994-7250
%FO: 100
Emp: 31

● **OBAYASHI CORPORATION**
Shinagawa Intercity, Tower B, 2-15-2, Konan, Minato-ku, Tokyo 108-8502, Japan
CEO: Shinji Mukasa, Pres. & CEO
Bus: *General building contractor.*
Tel: 81-3-5769-1111
Fax: 81-3-5769-1910
www.obayashi.co.jp
Rev: $13,060
Emp: 13,533

NAICS: 236116, 236220, 237130, 237990, 238120, 324121, 327320, 327331, 327390, 423310, 423320, 541310, 541330, 561210

E.W. HOWELL CO., INC.
113 Crossways Park Dr., Woodbury, New York 11797
CEO: Howard L. Powland, Pres.
Bus: *Construction.*
Tel: (516) 921-7100
Fax: (516) 921-0119
Emp: 200

OBAYASHI CORPORATION AMERICA INC.
592 Fifth Ave., 7/F, New York, New York 10036
CEO: Seiji Yabe, Pres.
Bus: *General building contractor.*
Tel: (212) 930-1020
Fax: (212) 704-9880
%FO: 100
Emp: 160

● **OGIHARA CORPORATION**
891-1 Minamiyajima-cho, Ota, Gunma 373-8630, Japan
CEO: Teruhisa Ogihara, Chmn.
Bus: *Automobile tool and die manufacturer.*
Tel: 81-276-38-1221
Fax: 81-276-38-5805
www.ogihara.co.jp
Emp: 650

NAICS: 333298, 336370

OGIHARA AMERICA CORPORATION
1480 West McPherson Park Dr., Howell, Michigan 48843
CEO: Tokio Ogihara, Pres.
Bus: *Stamped automotive panels and modules manufacturing.*
Tel: (517) 548-4900
Fax: (517) 548-6036
%FO: 100
Emp: 854

● **OJI PAPER COMPANY, LTD.**
Ginza 4-7-5, Chuo-Ku, Tokyo 104-0061, Japan
CEO: Shoichiro Suzuki, Pres. & CEO
Bus: *Mfr. paper, paperboard, pulp and converted products.*
Tel: 81-3-3563-1111
Fax: 81-3-3563-1135
www.ojipaper.co.jp
Rev: $11,174
Emp: 21,639

NAICS: 113310, 321113, 322110, 322121, 322122, 322130, 322211, 322222, 322226, 322232, 322233, 322291, 322299, 424130

OJI PAPER COMPANY, LTD.
One Union Square, Ste. 3015, Seattle, Washington 98101
CEO: Haruyoshi Harada, Mgr.
Bus: *Mfr. Printing & writing paper*
Tel: (206) 622-2820
Fax:
%FO: 100

OJI PAPER USA
20 Cummings St., Ware, Massachusetts 020821
CEO: Mitsuru Itsugi, Pres.
Bus: *Manufacturer of coated papers*
Tel: (413) 967-6204
Fax:
Emp: 357

OJI PAPER USA
1500 Main St., Springfield, Massachusetts 01103
CEO: Stephen Hefner, VP
Bus: *Manufacturer of coated & laminated paper*
Tel: (413) 736-3216
Fax:
%FO: 100

OJI YUKA SYNTHETIC PAPER CO. LTD.
1080 Holcomb Bridge Rd., Roswell, Georgia 30076
CEO: Oji Yuka, Mgr.
Bus: *Manufacturer of converted paper products*
Tel: (770) 587-6766
Fax:

● **OKAMOTO INDUSTRIES INC**
2-4-15 Shin-Yokohama, Kohoku-ku, Yokohama 222-0033, Japan
CEO: Taizo Hosoda, CEO
Bus: *Mfr. rubber and plastic products.*
Tel: 81-45-477-5231
Fax: 81-45-477-5235
www.okamoto.co.jp
Rev: $194
Emp: 218

NAICS: 326299

OKAMOTO CORP. (SEMICONDUCTOR EQUIPMENT DIV.)
3060 Scott Blvd., Santa Clara, California 95054
CEO: Bob Pinto, Mgr.
Bus: *Mfr. of semiconductors & related devices.*
Tel: (408) 654-8400
Fax: (408) 654-8405
%FO: 100
Emp: 16

OKAMOTO USA, CORP.
1342 Barclay Blvd., Buffalo Grove, Illinois 60089
CEO: Taizo Hosoda, Pres.
Bus: *Mfr. and sales of latex rubber products.*
Tel: (847) 520-7700
Fax: (847) 520-7980
%FO: 100
Emp: 20

- **OKAYA & COMPANY, LTD.**
4-18 Sakae, 2-chome, Naka-ku, Nagoya 460-8666, Japan
CEO: Tokuichi Okaya, Pres. & CEO   Tel: 81-52-204-8121   Rev: $4,910
Bus: *Wholesale iron and steel products, machinery and*   Fax: 81-52-204-8385   Emp: 2,979
      electrical products.   www.okaya.co.jp
    NAICS: 325510, 331492, 331513, 331528

    OKAYA USA INC.
    Mack-Cali Center III, 140 E. Ridgewood Ave., Paramus, New Jersey 07652
    CEO: Masahide Yamazaki, Pres.   Tel: (201) 734-7000   %FO: 100
    Bus: *Designs, manufactures and markets LCD*   Fax: (201) 734-7500   Emp: 50
      modules and panels, plasma panels, and
      other display products.

- **OKI ELECTRIC INDUSTRY COMPANY, LTD.**
7-12, Toranomon, 1-chome, Minato-ku, Tokyo 105-8460, Japan
CEO: Katsumasa Shinozuka, Pres. & CEO   Tel: 81-3-3501-3111   Rev: $6,193
Bus: *electronic equipment, including microelectronics,*   Fax: 81-3-3581-5522   Emp: 20,960
      office electronics equipment and   www.oki.com
      telecommunications products manufacture.
    NAICS: 333293, 333313, 333315, 334111, 334112, 334113, 334119, 334210, 334220, 334290, 334413, 334414,
334415, 335921, 335999

    OKI DATA CORP.
    2000 Bishops Gate Blvd., Mount Laurel, New Jersey 08054
    CEO: Stewart Krentzman, Pres. & CEO   Tel: (856) 235-2600   %FO: 100
    Bus: *Supplier of computer peripherals for*   Fax: (856) 222-5320   Emp: 500
      personal and general business computers.

    OKI NETWORK TECHNOLOGIES
    785 North Mary Ave., Sunnyvale, California 94085
    CEO: Michael Hata, Pres. & CEO   Tel: (408) 737-6477   %FO: 100
    Bus: *R&D, mfr./sales integrated circuits,*   Fax: (408) 737-6441   Emp: 150
      semiconductor products, and advanced
      electronics.

    OKI TELECOM, INC.
    1200 North Brook Park Way, Ste. 160, Suwannee, Georgia 30024
    CEO: Hirotaka Mizuno, CEO   Tel: (678) 252-5800   %FO: 100
    Bus: *Mfr. communications equipment*   Fax: Emp: 700

- **OKUMA CORPORATION**
5-25-1, Shimo-Oguchi, Ohguchi-cho, Niwa-gun, Aichi 480-0193, Japan
CEO: Junro Kashiwa, Pres. & CEO   Tel: 81-587-95-7820   Rev: $822
Bus: *Machine tools manufacture.*   Fax: 81-587-95-4807   Emp: 1,897
      www.okuma.co.jp
    NAICS: 333512

    OKUMA CORPORATION
    980 Knox St., Torrance, California 90502
    CEO: Peter Hazelhurst, Mgr.   Tel: (310) 715-7200   %FO: 100
    Bus: *Mfr. machine tools.*   Fax: (310) 630-5908   Emp: 20

OKUMA CORPORATION
15810 Centennial Dr., Northville, Michigan 48167
CEO: Tel: (734) 582-2100   %FO: 100
Bus: *Mfr. machine tools.*   Fax: (734) 582-2101

OKUMA CORPORATION
11900 Westhall Dr., Charlotte, North Carolina 28278
CEO: Yoshimaro Hanaki, Pres. & CEO   Tel: (704) 588-7000   %FO: 100
Bus: *Mfr. machine tools.*   Fax: (704) 588-6503

● **OLYMPUS CORPORATION**
Monolith, 3-1 Nishi-Shinjuku, 2-chome, Shinjuku-ku, Tokyo 163-0914, Japan
CEO: Tsuyoshi Kikukawa, Pres.   Tel: 81-3-3340-2111   Rev: $5,998
Bus: *Mfr./sales of healthcare equipment & devices,*   Fax: 81-3-3340-2062   Emp: 28,857
  imaging, information & industrial applications   www.olympus.co.jp
  35mm, APS & digital cameras, micro cassette &
  IC recorders, binoculars.
NAICS: 333293, 333314, 333315, 334112, 334119, 334510, 334516, 334519, 334613, 339111, 339112, 339113

OLYMPUS AMERICA, INC.
Two Corporate Center Dr., Melville, New York 11747-3157
CEO: F. Mark Gumz, Pres. & COO   Tel: (631) 844-5000   %FO: 100
Bus: *Distribution consumer and scientific*   Fax: (631) 844-5930   Emp: 2,000
  products.

OLYMPUS COMMUNICATION TECHNOLOGY OF AMERICA, INC.
9605 Scranton Rd., Ste. 830, San Diego, California 92121
CEO: Mark Gumz, Pres.   Tel: (858) 642-9700   %FO: 100
Bus: *Mfr. of communication equipment.*   Fax:

OLYMPUS IMAGING AMERICA
2 Corporate Center Dr., Melville, New York 11747
CEO: F. Mark Gumz, Pres.   Tel: (631) 844-5000   %FO: 100
Bus: *Mfr. of cameras, voice recorders magneto-*   Fax:
  optical disk drivers & mp3 type player.

OLYMPUS INTERGRATED TECHNOLOGIES AMERICA
180 Baytech Dr., San Jose, California 95134-2302
CEO: Larry Wang, VP   Tel: (408) 514-3900   %FO: 100
Bus: *Provides product and direct sales/service*   Fax:
  support for Olympus optical inspection and
  defect review products.

OLYMPUS LATIN AMERICA
6100 Blue Lagoon Dr., Ste. 390, Miami, Florida 33126
CEO: Brian Hladek, Pres.   Tel: (305) 266-2332   %FO: 100
Bus: *Sale of medical & hospital equipment.*   Fax:

OLYMPUS MEDICAL EQUIPMENT SERVICES AMERICA INC.
2 Corporate Center Dr., Melville, New York 11747
CEO: Mark Gumz, Pres.   Tel: (631) 844-5000   %FO: 100
Bus: *Sale of medical & hospital equipment.*   Fax: Emp: 50

OLYMPUS SURGICAL & INDUSTRIAL AMERICA INC.
One Corporate Dr., Orangeburg, New York 10962
CEO: Luke Calcrast, COO | Tel: (845) 398-9400 | %FO: 100
Bus: *Sale of optical goods/Medical & surgical supplies.* | Fax: | Emp: 106

● **OMRON CORPORATION**
Shiokoji Horikawa, Shimogyo-ku, Kyoto 600-8530, Japan
CEO: Hisao Sakuta, Pres. & CEO | Tel: 81-75-344-7000 | Rev: $5,537
Bus: *Mfr. automation components and systems.* | Fax: 81-75-344-7001 | Emp: 24,324
| www.omron.com |

NAICS: 334419, 334513, 334514, 335314

OMRON AUTOMOTIVE ELECTRONICS
29185 Cabot Dr., Novi, Michigan 48377
CEO: Khefuhiko Yabui, Pres. | Tel: (248) 893-0200 | %FO: 100
Bus: *Sales of automotive electronics.* | Fax: (248) 488-5430 | Emp: 20

OMRON AUTOMOTIVE ELECTRONICS
3709 Ohio Ave., St. Charles, Illinois 60174
CEO: Hisao Sakuta, CEO | Tel: (630) 443-6800 | %FO: 100
Bus: *Mfr. of automotive electronic components.* | Fax: (630) 443-6898 | Emp: 320

OMRON ELECTRONICS, INC.
1 Commerce Dr., Schaumburg, Illinois 60173
CEO: Tatsunosuke Goto, Chmn. & CEO | Tel: (847) 843-7900 | %FO: 100
Bus: *Engaged in sales and marketing of automation components and systems.* | Fax: (847) 843-7787 | Emp: 326

OMRON HEALTHCARE INC.
1200 Lakeside Dr., Bannockburn, Illinois 60015
CEO: Kazuo Saito, Chmn. | Tel: (847) 680-6200 | %FO: 100
Bus: *Sales of healthcare products.* | Fax: (847) 680-6269 | Emp: 120

● **ONO PHARMACEUTICAL COMPANY, LTD.**
1-8-2 Kyutaromachi, Chou-ku, Osaka 541-8564, Japan
CEO: Toshio Ueno, Chmn. & CEO | Tel: 81-6-6263-5670 | Rev: $1,150
Bus: *Pharmaceuticals manufacturing.* | Fax: | Emp: 2,696
| www.ono.co.jp |

NAICS: 325412

ONO PHARMA, INC.
2000 Lenox Dr., Ste. 101, Lawrenceville, New Jersey 08648
CEO: Katsura Kasahara, Pres. | Tel: (609) 219-1010
Bus: *Mfr./sales pharmaceuticals.* | Fax: (609) 219-9229 | Emp: 3

● **ONWARD KASHIYAMA CO., LTD.**
3-10-5 Nihonbashi, Chuo-ku, Tokyo 103-8239, Japan
CEO: Shigeru Uemura, Pres. & CEO | Tel: 81-3-3272-2371 | Rev: $2,578
Bus: *Mfr. and distribution of men's and women's* | Fax: 81-3-3272-2314 | Emp: 14,798
| www.onward.co.jp |

NAICS: 315211, 315225, 315233, 315999

ONWARD KASHIYAMA USA INC.
530 Seventh Ave., Ste. 29, New York, New York 10018
CEO: Hiroaki Sumi, Pres.
Bus: *Mfr. clothing.*
Tel: (212) 997-3600
Fax: (212) 997-5516
%FO: 100

● **ORIENTAL MOTOR CO., LTD.**
6-16-17, Ueno, Taito-ku, Tokyo 110, Japan
CEO: Yoshio Kuraishi, Pres.
Bus: *Mfr./sales small electric motors, drivers and fans.*
Tel: 81-3-3835-0684
Fax: 81-3-3835-1890
www.orientalmotor.co.jp
Rev: $355
Emp: 2,120
NAICS: 335312

ORIENTAL MOTOR USA CORPORATION
2580 West 237th St., Torrance, California 90505
CEO: Masatoshi Yamauchi, Pres.
Bus: *Technical support center: assembly/sale/distribute small motors, fans and drives.*
Tel: (310) 325-0040
Fax: (310) 515-2879
%FO: 100
Emp: 120

● **ORIX CORPORATION**
3-22-8, Shiba, Minato-ku, Tokyo 105-8683, Japan
CEO: Yoshihiko Miyauchi, Chmn. & CEO
Bus: *Equipment leasing, asset based lending and corporate financing.*
Tel: 81-3-5419-5102
Fax: 81-3-5419-5901
www.orix.co.jp
Rev: $7,073
Emp: 12,481
NAICS: 236115, 236116, 236117, 237210, 522110, 522190, 522220, 522293, 522298, 522310, 523120, 523920, 523930, 524113, 524126, 531120, 531130, 531190, 531210, 531311, 531312, 531320, 531390, 541110, 711211, 711219, 711310, 711320, 711410

ORIX EQUIPMENT FINANCE
600 Town Park Lane, 4/F, Kennesaw, Georgia 30144
CEO: Gary S Modesto, Mgr.
Bus: *Engaged in financing and leasing of capital equipment.*
Tel: (800) 999-3422
Fax:

ORIX REAL ESTATE
100 North Riverside Plaza, Ste. 1400, Chicago, Illinois 60606
CEO: David R. Brown, Pres. & CEO
Bus: *Engaged in development of industrial and office projects.*
Tel: (312) 669-6400
Fax: (312) 669-6464
Emp: 132

ORIX USA CORP.
1717 Main St., Ste. 900, Dallas, Texas 75201
CEO: James R. Thompson, Chmn. & CEO
Bus: *Engaged in servicing loans over commercial properties.*
Tel: (214) 237-2000
Fax: (214) 237-2018
%FO: 100

ORIX USA CORPORATION
1177 Ave. of the Americas, 10/F, New York, New York 10036
CEO: James R. Thompson, Pres. & CEO
Bus: *Engaged in equipment leasing, corporate financing and asset based lending.*
Tel: (212) 739-1600
Fax: (212) 739-1701
%FO: 100
Emp: 900

- **OSAKA GAS COMPANY, LTD.**
  4-1-2, Hiranomachi, Chuo-ku, Osaka 541-0046, Japan
  CEO: Hirofumi Shibano, Pres.   Tel: 81-6-6205-4715   Rev: $9,005
  Bus: *Produces and distributes gas.*   Fax: 81-6-6202-4637   Emp: 15,276
                                            www.osakagas.co.jp
    NAICS: 211111, 221112, 221122, 221210, 237120, 238990, 335221, 335228, 424710, 424720, 454311, 486210,
  561210, 561790

  OSAKA GAS COMPANY, LTD.
  375 Park Ave., Ste. 2109, New York, New York 10152
  CEO: Chiaki Gomi, Mgr.   Tel: (212) 980-1666   %FO: 100
  Bus: *Crude petroleum & natural gas*   Fax: (212) 832-0946

- **OTSUKA PHARMACEUTICAL COMPANY, LTD.**
  2-9, Kanda Tsukasa-cho, Chiyoda-ku, Tokyo 101-8535, Japan
  CEO: Tatsuo Higuchi, Pres.   Tel: 81-3-3292-0021   Rev: $3,293
  Bus: *Mfr. pharmaceuticals, chemicals, fertilizers,*   Fax: 81-3-3292-0021   Emp: 5,171
       foods, drinks and furniture.   www.otsuka.co.jp
    NAICS: 311999, 325311, 325312, 325411

  CAMBRIDGE ISOTAPE LABORATORIES INC.
  50 Frontage Rd., Andover, Massachusetts 01810
  CEO: Peter E. Dodwell   Tel: (978) 749-8000   %FO: 100
  Bus: *Mfr. pharmaceuticals.*   Fax: (978) 749-2768

  CG ROXANE LLC
  1210 State Highway, 395, Olancha, California 93549
  CEO: Ronan Papillaud   Tel: (760) 764-2885   %FO: 100
  Bus: *Mfr. spring water.*   Fax: (760) 764-2861

  CRYSTAL GEYSER WATER COMPANY
  501 Washington St., Calistoga, California 94515
  CEO: Peter Gordon   Tel: (707) 942-0500   %FO: 100
  Bus: *Mfr. natural beverages*   Fax: (707) 942-0647

  OTSUKA AMERICA, INC.
  2440 Research Boulevard, Rockville, Maryland 20850
  CEO: Hiromi Yoshikawa, VP   Tel: (301) 990-0030   %FO: 100
  Bus: *Clinical research and development.* Fax: (301) 990-0030

  OTSUKA AMERICA, INC.
  One Embarcadero Ctr., Ste. 2020, San Francisco, California 94111
  CEO: Hiromi Yoshikawa   Tel: (415) 986-5300   %FO: 100
  Bus: *Pharmaceuticals and chemicals.*   Fax: (415) 986-5300

  OTSUKA PHARMACEUTICAL FACTORY, INC.
  2655 Crescent Dr.,, Lafayette, Colorado 80026720
  CEO: Ryuichi Kisihgami, Mgr.   Tel: (720) 479-6400   %FO: 100
  Bus: *Mfr. pharmaceuticals.*   Fax: (720) 479-6499

  PHARMAVITE LLC
  8510 Balboa Blvd., Northridge, California 91325
  CEO: Brent Bailey   Tel: (818) 221-6200   %FO: 100
  Bus: *Mfr. nutraceutilcals.*   Fax: (818) 221-6611

RIDGE VINEYARDS INC.
17100 Monte Bello Rd., Cupertino, California 95014
CEO: Donn Reisen   Tel: (408) 867-3233   %FO: 100
Bus: *Mfr. wine.*   Fax: (408) 868-1350

TAIHO PHARMA USA INC.
210 Carnegie Center, Princeton, New Jersey 08540
CEO: Masayuki Kobayashi   Tel: (609) 750-5300   %FO: 100
Bus: *Development of pharmaceuticals.*   Fax: (609) 750-7450

● **OYO CORPORATION**
2-6, Kudan-kita, 4-chome, Chiyoda-ku, Tokyo 102-0073, Japan
CEO: Moriyuki Taya, Pres. & CEO   Tel: 81-3-3234-0811   Rev: $423
Bus: *Geophysical and geotechnical instruments*   Fax: 81-3-3234-0383   Emp: 2,729
     manufacture.   www.oyo.co.jp
NAICS: 334515, 541330, 541620

   BLACKHAWK GEOSERVICES INC., DIV. OYO
   301 Commercial Rd., Ste. B, Golden, Colorado 80401
   CEO: Richard J. Wold, Pres.   Tel: (303) 278-8700   %FO: 100
   Bus: *Geophysical contracting & consulting*   Fax: (303) 278-0789   Emp: 70
      services.

   GEOMETRICS, INC.
   2190 Fortune Dr., San Jose, California 95131
   CEO: Mike Prouty, Pres.   Tel: (408) 954-0522
   Bus: *Geophysical equipment.*   Fax: (408) 954-0902   Emp: 55

   GSSI
   13 Klein Dr., PO Box 97, North Salem, New Hampshire 03073
   CEO: Dennis Johnson, Pres.   Tel: (603) 893-1109
   Bus: *Mfr. of GPR, Ground Penetrating Radar.*   Fax: (603) 889-3984   Emp: 53

   KINEMETRICS, INC.
   222 Vista Ave., Pasadena, California 91107
   CEO: Ali Akal   Tel: (626) 795-2220
   Bus: *Earthquake monitoring equipment.*   Fax: (636) 795-0868   Emp: 69

   OYO CORPORATION
   9777 West Gulf Bank Rd., Ste. 5, Houston, Texas 77040
   CEO: Ernest M. Hall, Jr., Pres.   Tel: (713) 849-0804   %FO: 100
   Bus: *Mfr. measurement instruments.*   Fax: (713) 849-4915

   OYO GEOSPACE CORP.
   7007 Pinemont Dr., Houston, Texas 77040
   CEO: Gary D. Owens, Chmn.   Tel: (713) 986-4444
   Bus: *Seismic exploration business.*   Fax: (713) 986-4445   Emp: 748

● **PACIFIC CONSULTANTS INTERNATIONAL**
1-7-5 Sekedo, Tami-shi, Tokyo 206-8550, Japan
CEO: Itaru Mae, Pres.   Tel: 81-4-2372-6031   Rev: $167
Bus: *Engineering and management consulting services.*   Fax: 81-4-2372-6360   Emp: 364
       www.pci-world.com
NAICS: 541330, 541611

PCI AMERICAS
1100 Connecticut Ave. NW, Ste. 330, Washington, District of Columbia 20036
CEO: James Lange   Tel: (202) 331-2915   %FO: 100
Bus: *Engineering and management consulting*   Fax: (202) 331-2916
     services.

● **PALOMA INDUSTRIES LTD.**
6-23 Momozono-chu, Mizuho-ku, Nagoya 467-8585, Japan
CEO: Toshihiro Kobayashi, Pres.   Tel: 81-52-824-5031
Bus: *Mfr. gas powered home appliances, including air* Fax: 81-52-824-4366
     conditioners, heat pumps and furnaces.   www.paloma.co.jp
NAICS: 332410, 333414, 333415, 333996, 423720

   PALOMA INDUSTRIES INC.
   2151 Eastman Ave., Oxnard, California 93030
   CEO: Shinichi Kobayaski   Tel: (805) 278-5499   %FO: 100
   Bus: *Natural gas-powered equipment.*   Fax: (805) 278-5494

   RHEEM MANUFACTURING
   Box 17010, Fort Smith, Arkansas 72908
   CEO: William Lux   Tel: (479) 648-4900   %FO: 100
   Bus: *Mfr. of central heating and cooling*   Fax: (479) 648-4900
        products.
   RHEEM MANUFACTURING
   101 Bell Rd., Montgomery, Alabama 36117
   CEO: J. Mahoney   Tel: (334) 260-1500   %FO: 100
   Bus: *Central heating and cooling products.*   Fax: (334) 206-1562

● **PANASONIC MOBILE COMMUNICATIONS CO., LTD.**
4-3-1, Tsunashima-Higash, Kohoku-ku, Yokohama 223-8639, Japan
CEO: Yasuo Katsura, Pres.   Tel: 81-45-531-1231   Rev: $8,390
Bus: *Panasonic brand pagers, cell phones, network*   Fax: 81-45-542-5105   Emp: 16,570
     systems and surveillance equipment manufacture. www.panasonic.co.jp/pmc
NAICS: 334119, 334210, 334220, 334310, 334511, 334515, 335999

   PANASONIC MOBILE COMMUNICATIONS
   1225 North Brook Pkwy., Ste. 2-352, Suwannee, Georgia 30024
   CEO: Sumio Endo, CEO   Tel: (770) 338-6193
   Bus: *In-vehicle, multimedia systems and*   Fax: (770) 338-6210   Emp: 5
        components manufacture.

   SYMBIAN
   390 Bridge Pkwy., Ste. 201, Redwood Shores, California 94065
   CEO: Cindy Perez, Mgr.   Tel: (650) 551-0240
   Bus: *Wireless software.*   Fax: (650) 551-0241

● **PENTA-OCEAN CONSTRUCTION CO., LTD.**
2-8, Koraku, 2-chome, Bunkyo-ku, Tokyo 112-8576, Japan
CEO: Kazujiro Tetsumura, CEO   Tel: 81-3-3817-7181   Rev: $3,135
Bus: *Construction and marine engineering.*   Fax: 81-3-3817-7642   Emp: 3,767
                                          www.penta-ocean.co.jp
NAICS: 236220, 237310, 237990, 541310, 541330, 541620, 562910

PENTA-OCEAN CONSTRUCTION COMPANY
450 Park Ave., New York, New York 10022
CEO: Jun Ueno, EVP   Tel: (212) 421-5400   %FO: 100
Bus: *Engaged in construction and marine*   Fax: (212) 421-5452
       engineering.

● **PENTAX CORPORATION (FORMERLY ASAHI OPTICAL)**
2-36-9, Maenocho, Itabashi-ku, Chiyoda-ku, Tokyo 174-8369, Japan
CEO: Fumio Urano, Pres. & CEO   Tel: 81-3-3960-5151   Rev: $1,273
Bus: *Pentax cameras, binoculars, lenses, photo, video*   Fax: 81-3-3960-5226   Emp: 5,364
       components and accessories manufacture.   www.pentax.co.jp
   NAICS: 327215, 333315, 423410

   PENTAX OF AMERICA
   102 Chestnut Ridge Rd., Montvale, New Jersey 07645
   CEO: Ikuzo Okamoto   Tel: (201) 391-2680   %FO: 100
   Bus: *Mfr. video and fiber endoscopy equipment.*   Fax: (201) 391-2680

   PENTAX OF AMERICA
   501 W Lake St., Ste. 206, Elmhurst, Illinois 60126
   CEO: Jenn Behnkey   Tel: (630) 941-0909   %FO: 100
   Bus: *Mfr. medical equipment.*   Fax: (630) 941-0909

   PENTAX OF AMERICA
   600 12th St., Ste. 300, Golden, Colorado 80401
   CEO: Robert Bender, VP   Tel: (303) 799-8000   %FO: 100
   Bus: *Sales/distribution of cameras, binoculars,*   Fax: (303) 790-1131
       lenses, etc.

   PENTAX OF AMERICA
   8920 Kirby Dr., Houston, Texas 77054
   CEO: Warren Hickman   Tel: (713) 664-4095   %FO: 100
   Bus: *Mfr. medical equipment.*   Fax: (713) 664-4095

   PENTAX VISION, INC.
   Box 2300, 11545 Encore Circle, Hopkins, Minnesota 55343
   CEO: Mike Jacobson   Tel: (925) 945-2700   %FO: 100
   Bus: *Lenses manufacture.*   Fax: (612) 935-3987

● **PENTEL COMPANY, LTD.**
7-2, Nihombashikoamicho, Chuo-Ku,, Tokyo 103-0016, Japan
CEO: Keima Horie, CEO   Tel: 81-3-3667-3333
Bus: *Mfr. pens, mechanical pencils, industrial*   Fax: 81-3-3667-3331   Emp: 1,400
       machines and computers.   www.pentel.co.jp
   NAICS: 333999, 334411, 339941

   PENTEL OF AMERICA, LTD.
   2805 Columbia St., Torrance, California 90509
   CEO: Yukio Horie, VP   Tel: (310) 320-3831   %FO: 100
   Bus: *Pens, pencils and art materials.*   Fax: (310) 533-0697   Emp: 200

- **PILOT PEN CORPORATION**
  8-1, Nishi-Gotanda, 2-chome, Shinagawa-ku, Tokyo 141-8553, Japan
  CEO: Kiyoshi Takahashi, Pres.   Tel: 81-3-548-78111   Rev: $680
  Bus: *Mfr. writing instruments.*   Fax: 81-3-548-78181   Emp: 1,500
                                                  www.pilot.co.jp
  NAICS: 339941

    PILOT PEN CORPORATION OF AMERICA
    60 Commerce Dr., Trumbull, Connecticut 06611
    CEO: Ronald G. Shaw, Pres.   Tel: (203) 377-8800   %FO: 100
    Bus: *Sales/distribution of writing instruments*   Fax: (203) 377-4024   Emp: 240

- **PIONEER CORPORATION**
  4-1, Meguro, 1-chome, Meguro-ku, Tokyo 153-8654, Japan
  CEO: Kaneo Ito, Pres. & CEO   Tel: 81-3-3495-6774   Rev: $6,856
  Bus: *Mfr. electronics, video, music,*   Fax: 81-3-3495-4301   Emp: 39,362
      telecommunications products, consumer   www.pioneer.co.jp
  NAICS: 334210, 334310

    PIONEER ELECTRONICS (USA), INC.
    2265 E. 220th St., Long Beach, California 90810
    CEO: Rocky Matsubara, Pres.   Tel: (310) 952-2000   %FO: 100
    Bus: *Mfr. car stereos and home electronics.*   Fax: (310) 952-2199

    PIONEER SPEAKERS, INC.
    8701 Sempre Viva Rd., Ste. 100, San Diego, California 91910
    CEO: Mamoru Hashiba, Pres.   Tel: (619) 710-0850   %FO: 100
    Bus: *Mfr. of car stereo speakers.*   Fax: (619) 710-0851

- **RENESAS TECHNOLOGY CORPORATION**
  Marunouchi Bldg., 4-1, Marunouchi 2-chome, Chiyoda-ku, Tokyo 100-6334, Japan
  CEO: Satoru Ito, Pres. & CEO   Tel: 81-3-6250-5500   Rev: $7,510
  Bus: *Mfg. semiconductors, microprocessors, and*   Fax: 81-3-6250-5469   Emp: 27,200
      analog and memory chips. JV of Hitachi and   www.renesas.com
  NAICS: 334112, 334119, 334413, 334415

    RENESAS TECHNOLOGY AMERICA, INC.
    450 Holger Way, San Jose, California 95134-1368
    CEO: Daniel M. Mahoney Jr., Pres. & CEO   Tel: (408) 382-7500   %FO: 100
    Bus: *Mfr. semiconductors, microprocessors, and*   Fax: (408) 382-7501   Emp: 385
      analog and memory chips. JV of Hitachi and
      Mitsubishi.

    SUPERH, INC.
    3080 Olcott St., Ste. 130D, Santa Clara, California 95054
    CEO: Don Higgins, CEO   Tel: (408) 980-9114   %FO: 100
    Bus: *Mfr. of microprocessors & microcontrollers.*   Fax:

• RICOH COMPANY, LTD.

15-5, Minami-Aoyama, 1-chome, Minato-ku, Tokyo 107-8544, Japan

CEO: Masamitsu Sakurai, Pres. & CEO

Bus: *Mfr. and market multi-function digital office automation equipment, thermal media and imaging materials.*

Tel: 81-3-3479-3111
Fax: 81-3-3403-1578
www.ricoh.com

Rev: $16,852
Emp: 73,137

NAICS: 333293, 333313, 333314, 333315, 334112, 334119, 334413, 334414, 334415

LANIER WORLDWIDE INC.

2300 Parklake Dr. NE, Atlanta, Georgia 30345

CEO: Nori Goto, Pres. & CEO

Bus: *Computer products distribution & support.*

Tel: (770) 496-9500
Fax: (800) 252-9703

RICOH BUSINESS SYSTEMS, INC.

11-A Madison Rd., Fairfield, New Jersey 07004

CEO: Carl Davis, Pres.

Bus: *Printing & Imaging Equipment*

Tel: (973) 276-2500
Fax: (973) 808-1660

RICOH CORPORATION

5 Dedrick Place, West Caldwell, New Jersey 07006

CEO: Susumu Ichioka, Chmn. & CEO

Bus: *Mfr./sale/service copiers, facsimiles, cameras, scanners, printers, optical storage devices.*

Tel: (973) 882-2000
Fax: (973) 882-2048

%FO: 100
Emp: 11,000

SAVIN CORPORATION

333 Ludlow St., Stamford, Connecticut 06902

CEO: Thomas Salierno Jr., Pres.

Bus: *Printing & imaging equipment*

Tel: (203) 967-5000
Fax: (203) 967-5005

• RIKEN CORPORATION

13-5, Kudankita, 1-chome, Chiyoda-ku, Tokyo 102-8202, Japan

CEO: Toshio Koizumi, Pres.

Bus: *Mfr. electronics.*

Tel: 81-3-3230-3911
Fax: 81-3-3230-3913
www.riken.co.jp

Rev: $729
Emp: 3,600

NAICS: 336311

ALLIED RING CORP.

916 West State St., St. Johns, Michigan 48879

CEO: Mike Laisure

Bus: *Mfr. auto parts/piston rings.*

Tel: (989) 224-2384
Fax: (989) 224-3280

INTERMET CORP.

545 Corporate Dr., Ste. 200, Troy, Michigan 48098

CEO: Gary Ruff, Chmn. & CEO

Bus: *Mfr. of auto parts*

Tel: (248) 952-2500
Fax: (248) 952-2501

Emp: 5,652

RIKEN OF AMERICA INC.

4709 Golf Rd., Ste. 807, Skokie, Illinois 60076

CEO: Takuma Suzuki, Pres.

Bus: *Sales/distribution of electronic products.*

Tel: (847) 673-1400
Fax: (847) 673-1457

%FO: 100
Emp: 103

- **ROHM COMPANY, LTD.**
  21, Saiin Mizosaki-cho, Ukyo-ku, Kyoto 615-8585, Japan
  CEO: Kenichiro Sato, Pres. & CEO   Tel: 81-75-311-2121   Rev: $3,366
  Bus: *Mfr. diverse electronic components, including*   Fax: 81-75-315-0172   Emp: 18,591
      semiconductors.   www.rohm.com
  NAICS: 334413, 334414, 334415, 334416, 334419, 335311, 335999

    ROHM ELECTRONICS USA
    10145 Pacific Heights Blvd., Ste. 1000, San Diego, California 92121-4243
    CEO: Yoshi Kurahiashi, Pres.   Tel: (858) 625-3660   %FO: 100
    Bus: *Mktg./sale electronic components.*   Fax: (858) 625-3690   Emp: 20

- **ROHTO PHARMACEUTICAL COMPANY**
  1-8-1, Tatsumi-nishi, Ikuno-ku, Osaka 544-8666, Japan
  CEO: Kunio Yamada, Pres. & CEO   Tel: 81-6-6758-1231   Rev: $638
  Bus: *Mfr. eye lotions, gastrointestinal medicines and*   Fax: 81-6-6758-9820   Emp: 2,028
      skin care products.   www.rohto.co.jp
  NAICS: 325411, 325412, 325620

    THE MENTHOLATUM COMPANY
    707 Sterling Dr., Orchard Park, New York 14127
    CEO: Akiyoshi Yoshida, Pres. & CEO   Tel: (716) 677-2500   %FO: 100
    Bus: *Mfr. eye lotions, gastrointestinal medicines*   Fax: (716) 677-9528
        and skin care products.

- **ROLAND CORPORATION**
  20 Sonezakishinchi, 1-chome, Kita-ku, Osaka 530-0002, Japan
  CEO: Katsuyoshi Dan, Pres.   Tel: 81-6-6345-9800   Rev: $619
  Bus: *Mfr. musical equipment*   Fax: 81-6-6345-9792   Emp: 2,350
                                           www.roland.com
  NAICS: 339992

    ROLAND CORPORATION USA
    5100 S. Eastern Ave., Los Angeles, California 90040-2938
    CEO: Dennis Houlihan, pres,   Tel: (323) 890-3700   %FO: 100
    Bus: *Manufacturer musical instruments*   Fax: (323) 890-3701

- **RYOBI LTD.**
  762, Mesaki-cho, Fuchu, Hiroshima 726-8628, Japan
  CEO: Hiroshi Urakami, Chmn. & CEO   Tel: 81-847-41-1111   Rev: $1,470
  Bus: *Mfr. die castings, printing machinery, power tools*   Fax: 81-847-63-6111   Emp: 5,575
      and fishing tackle.   www.ryobi-group.co.jp
  NAICS: 333293, 333298, 333991

    RYOBI DIE CASTING INC.
    800 West Mausoleum Rd., Shelbyville, Indiana 46176
    CEO: Takashi Yokoyama, CEO   Tel: (317) 398-3398   %FO: 100
    Bus: *Mfr. die castings.*   Fax: (317) 398-2873   Emp: 827

    RYOBI FINANCE CORPORATION
    120 North LaSalle St., Ste. 1410, Chicago, Illinois 60602
    CEO: Takao Tanaka, Pres.   Tel: (312) 578-1990   %FO: 100
    Bus: *Finance company.*   Fax: Emp: 4

- **RYOSAN COMPANY, LTD.**
2-3-5 Higashi-Kanda, Chiyoda-ku, Tokyo 101-0031, Japan
CEO: Tatsuo Ui, Pres.
Bus: *Sale of semiconductors, LCD modules, workstations and manufacture electronic heat sinks and microchips.*
NAICS: 334413, 335991, 335999, 423690

Tel: 81-3-3862-2591
Fax: 81-3-3862-1395
www.ryosan.co.jp

Rev: $2,728
Emp: 1,123

    RYOSAN TECHNOLOGIES USA, INC.
    660 Baker St., Ste. 369, Costa Mesa, California 92626
    CEO: Toru Iwatani, Pres.
    Bus: *Sale of semiconductors, LCD modules, workstations and mfr. electronic heat sinks and microchips.*

    Tel: (714) 668-0170
    Fax:

    %FO: 100

    RYOSAN TECHNOLOGIES USA, INC.
    100 Century Center Ct., Ste. 504, San Jose, California 95112
    CEO: Makoto Cnaiachi, Pres.
    Bus: *Sale of semiconductors, LCD modules, workstations and mfr. electronic heat sinks and microchips.*

    Tel: (408) 441-9511
    Fax: (408) 441-9529

    %FO: 100

    RYOSAN TECHNOLOGIES USA, INC.
    5 Triangle Park Dr., Ste. 503, Cincinnati, Ohio 45246
    CEO: Toru Iwatani, Pres.
    Bus: *Sale of semiconductors, LCD modules, workstations and mfr. electronic heat sinks and microchips.*

    Tel: (513) 771-1610
    Fax: (513) 771-1628

    %FO: 100

- **S&B FOODS INC.**
18-6, Nihonbashi Kabuto-Cho, Chuo-ku, Tokyo 103-0026, Japan
CEO: Masaru Yamazaki, Pres.
Bus: *Mfr./import/export food products.*
NAICS: 311422, 311999

Tel: 81-3-3668-0551
Fax: 81-3-5970-6828
www.sbfoods.co.jp

Rev: $975
Emp: 1,459

    S&B INTERNATIONAL CORPORATION
    19300 South Hamilton Ave., Ste. 195, Gardena, California 90248
    CEO: Yukio Sato, VP
    Bus: *Import sales of S&B Food stuffs./Export of dried potato & onion.*

    Tel: (310) 327-7000
    Fax: (310) 327-0779

    %FO: 100

- **SAKATA INX CORPORATION**
1-4-25 Kohraku, Bunkyo-ku, Tokyo, Japan
CEO: Kazumi Suzuki, Pres.
Bus: *Mfr. copy machine toner*
NAICS: 325910

Tel: 81-3-5689-6600
Fax: 81-3-5689-6622
www.inx.co.jp

Rev: $906
Emp: 2,748

    INX INTERNATIONAL INK COMPANY
    150 North Martingale Rd., Ste. 700, Schaumburg, Illinois 60173
    CEO: Rick Clendenning, CEO
    Bus: *Manufacturer printing ink*

    Tel: (630) 382-1800
    Fax: (847) 969-9758

    %FO: 100

- **SANDEN CORPORATION**
  20 Kotobuki-cho, Isesaki, Gunma 372-8502, Japan
  CEO: Masayoshi Ushikubo, Chmn. & CEO   Tel: 81-270-24-1211   Rev: $2,000
  Bus: *Mfr. auto A/C systems, kerosene heaters,*   Fax: 81-270-24-5338   Emp: 3,000
       compressors and components, vending machines   www.sanden.co.jp
       and refrigerated showcases.
     NAICS: 333311, 333415, 336391
  > **SANDEN INTL (USA), INC.**
  > 601 S. Sanden Blvd., Wylie, Texas 75098
  > CEO: Seishi Kimura, Pres.   Tel: (972) 442-8400   %FO: 100
  > Bus: *Mfr./distribute mobile A/C compressors and*   Fax: (972) 442-8777   Emp: 897
  >   *components.*

- **THE SANKO STEAMSHIP CO., LTD.**
  2-3, Uchisaiwaicho, 2-chome, Chiyoda-ku, Tokyo 100-0011, Japan
  CEO: T. Matsui, CEO   Tel: 81-3-3507-8321   Rev: $925
  Bus: *Ship owner and operator.*   Fax: 81-3-3507-8324   Emp: 228
                                      www.sankoline.co.jp
     NAICS: 483111
  > **SANKO KISEN (USA) CORP**
  > 400 Poydras St., Ste. 1765, New Orleans, Louisiana 70130
  > CEO: Myles Lewis, Mgr.   Tel: (504) 561-8993   %FO: 100
  > Bus: *Ship owner representation.*   Fax: (504) 586-8831
  >
  > **SANKO KISEN (USA) CORPORATION**
  > 5 River Rd., Cos Cob, Connecticut 06807
  > CEO: Clifford C. Jagoe, VP   Tel: (203) 625-5584   %FO: 100
  > Bus: *Ship owner representation.*   Fax: (203) 625-7633   Emp: 12

- **SANKYO CO., LTD.**
  3-5-1 Nihonbashi-Hon-cho, Chuo-ku, Tokyo 103-8426, Japan
  CEO: Takashi Shoda, Pres.   Tel: 81-3-5255-7111   Rev: $5,645
  Bus: *Mfr. and markets pharmaceuticals and medical*   Fax: 81-3-5255-7035   Emp: 5,401
       devices.   www.sankyo.co.jp
     NAICS: 325320, 325411, 325412, 325520, 325998, 334510
  > **LUITPOLD PHARMACEUTICALS, INC.**
  > 1 Luitpold Dr., Shirley, New York 11967
  > CEO: Mary Helenek, Pres. & CEO   Tel: (631) 924-4000
  > Bus: *Mfr. of pharmaceuticals.*   Fax: (631) 924-1731
  >
  > **SANKYO PHARMA INC.**
  > 2 Hilton Ct., Parsippany, New Jersey 07054
  > CEO: J.P. Pieroni, Pres.   Tel: (973) 359-2600   %FO: 100
  > Bus: *Research, development & marketing of*   Fax: Emp: 1,500
  >   *pharmaceuticals.*

- **SANKYU INC.**
5-23, Kachidok,i 6-chome, Chuo-ku, Tokyo 104-0054, Japan
CEO: Kimikazu Nakamura, Pres. & CEO
Bus: *Engaged in marine and air cargo, trucking and shipping.*
NAICS: 236210, 488320, 488510

Tel: 81-3-3536-3939
Fax: 81-3-3536-3862
www.sankyu.co.jp

Rev: $3,048
Emp: 22,494

> **SANKYU INC.**
> 1555 Mittel Blvd., Ste. H, Wood Dale, Illinois 60191
> CEO: Yoshikazu Matsuzawa, Pres.
> Bus: *Engaged in marine and air cargo, trucking and shipping.*
>
> Tel: (630) 595-3009
> Fax: (630) 595-3314
>
> %FO: 100
> Emp: 45

> **SANKYU INC.**
> 24700 South Main St., Carson, California 90745
> CEO: David Westburn, Mgr.
> Bus: *Engaged in marine and air cargo, trucking and shipping and custom brokerage.*
>
> Tel: (310) 834-2245
> Fax: (310) 522-1952
>
> %FO: 100
> Emp: 37

- **SANRIO COMPANY, LTD.**
6-1, Osaki, 1-chome, Shinagawa-ku, Tokyo 141-8603, Japan
CEO: Shintaro Tsuji, Pres. & CEO
Bus: *Mfr./distributes character merchandise for*
NAICS: 339931, 339999, 511120, 511130, 511140, 511191, 511199, 512110, 713110, 722110

Tel: 81-3-3779-8111
Fax: 81-3-3779-8054
www.sanrio.co.jp

Rev: $984
Emp: 4,965

> **SANRIO, INC.**
> 570 Eccles Ave., South San Francisco, California 94080
> CEO: Kunihiko Tsuji, Pres.
> Bus: *Sales/distribution of children's gifts and accessories.*
>
> Tel: (650) 952-2880
> Fax: (650) 872-2730
>
> %FO: 100
> Emp: 400

- **SANWA SHUTTER CORPORATION**
Shinjuku Mitsui Bldg. 52/F, 2-1-1, Nishi-Shinjuku, Tokyo 163-0478, Japan
CEO: Toshitaka Takayama, Pres. & CEO
Bus: *Shutters, doors and window products*
NAICS: 332312, 332321

Tel: 81-3-3346-3019
Fax: 81-3-3346-3177
www.sanwa-ss.co.jp

Rev: $2,371
Emp: 8,625

> **HORTON AUTOMATICS**
> 4242 Baldwin Blvd., Corpus Christi, Texas 78405
> CEO: Bob Beckett, Mgr.
> Bus: *Mfr. of automated door systems.*
>
> Tel: (512) 829-3636
> Fax:

> **OVERHEAD DOOR CORPORATION**
> 1900 Crown Dr., Farmers Branch, Texas 75234
> CEO: Dennis Stone, Pres. & CEO
> Bus: *Mfr. garage doors and shutters.*
>
> Tel: (972) 233-6611
> Fax: (972) 233-0367
>
> %FO: 100
> Emp: 3,000

> **THE GENIE COMPANY**
> 22790 Lake Park Blvd., Alliance, Ohio 44601-3498
> CEO: Carl Adrien, Pres.
> Bus: *Mfr. of garage door operators.*
>
> Tel: (330) 821-5361
> Fax:
>
> Emp: 1,000

TODCO
1332 Fairground Rd., East Marion, Ohio 43302
CEO: Dan Ringert, Pres.
Bus: *Mfr. of doors and panels of trailers, truck, railway & marine.*
Tel: (740) 383-6376
Fax:

● **SANYEI CORPORATION**
1-2, Kotobuki, 4-chome, Taito-ku, Tokyo 111, Japan
CEO: Hiroyuki Mizutani, Pres.
Bus: *Import/export general merchandise.*
Tel: 81-3-3847-3500
Fax: 81-3-3842-0901
www.sanyeicorp.com
Rev: $129
Emp: 635

NAICS: 423210, 423620, 424340

SANYEI AMERICA CORPORATION
One Executive Dr., Fort Lee, New Jersey 07024
CEO: K. Obyashy, Pres.
Bus: *Import/export electronic merchandise.*
Tel: (201) 346-3939
Fax: (201) 346-3938
%FO: 100
Emp: 7

SANYEI AMERICA CORPORATION
201 Hennepin Ave. East, Ste. 202, Minneapolis, Minnesota 55414
CEO: Yoshi Kywi, Mgr.
Bus: *Import/export electronic merchandise.*
Tel: (612) 378-6068
Fax: (612) 378-6069
%FO: 100

● **SANYO ELECTRIC COMPANY, LTD.**
5-5, Keihan-Hondori , 2-chome, Moriguchi, Osaka 570-8677, Japan
CEO: Tomoyo Nonaka, Chmn. & CEO
Bus: *Mfr. audio and video equipment, commercial and consumer electric appliances, semiconductors, batteries, and components.*
Tel: 81-6-6991-1181
Fax: 81-6-6991-2086
www.sanyo.co.jp
Rev: $24,528
Emp: 82,337

NAICS: 325992, 333293, 333313, 333314, 333315, 333415, 334111, 334112, 334113, 334119, 334210, 334220, 334290, 334310, 334411, 334413, 334419, 335211, 335212, 335221, 335222, 335224, 335228, 335999, 337214

SANYO DENKI
468 Amapola Ave., Torrance, California 90501
CEO: Yoshi Terajima, Pres.
Bus: *Wholesale cooling fans for computers & value added assembler.*
Tel: (310) 783-5400
Fax:
Emp: 36

SANYO ELECTRONIC DEVICE CORPORATION
2055 Sanyo Ave., San Diego, California 92154
CEO: Masanori Nagai, Pres.
Bus: *Mfr./distribution/service audio & video equipment, commercial & consumer electric appliances, semi-conductors, batteries, & components.*
Tel: (619) 661-4134
Fax:
%FO: 100
Emp: 34

SANYO FISHER USA COMPANY
21605 Plummer St., Chatsworth, California 91311
CEO: S. Oka, Pres.
Bus: *Mfr./distribution/service audio equipment and components.*
Tel: (818) 717-2755
Fax:
%FO: 100
Emp: 29

SANYO MANUFACTURING CORPORATION
3333 Sanyo Rd., Forrest City, Arkansas 72335
CEO: Naoki Nakamura, Pres.
Bus: *Manufacturing operation; subsidiary of
Sanyo Electric Co., Ltd.*

Tel: (870) 633-5030
Fax: (870) 633-0650

%FO: 100
Emp: 600

SANYO NORTH AMERICA CORPORATION
2055 Sanyo Ave., San Diego, California 92154
CEO: Masafumi Matsunaga, Pres. & CEO
Bus: *Mfr./distribution/service audio & video
equipment, commercial & consumer electric
appliances, semi-conductors, batteries, &
components.*

Tel: (619) 661-1134
Fax: (619) 661-6795

%FO: 100

• **SANYO SPECIAL STEEL COMPANY, LTD. (SSSC)**
3007 Nakashima, Shikama-ku, Himeji 672-8677, Japan
CEO: Hiroki Sasaki, Pres.
Bus: *Mfr. specialty steel.*

Tel: 81-792-35-6003
Fax: 81-792-34-8571
www.sanyo-steel.co.jp

Emp: 1,340

NAICS: 331221

ADVANCED GREEN COMPONENTS, LLC
4005 Corporate Dr., Winchester, Kentucky 40391
CEO: Thomas F. Lucas, Pres.
Bus: *Mfr. of forged and machined rings for
bearings.*

Tel: (859) 737-6000
Fax: (859) 737-4666

%FO: 100
Emp: 65

SANYO SPECIAL STEEL COMPANY, LTD.
445 Park Ave., Ste. 2104, New York, New York 10022
CEO: Hajime Sakuma, Pres.
Bus: *Mfr. specialty steel.*

Tel: (212) 935-9033
Fax: (212) 980-8838

%FO: 100
Emp: 4

• **SANYO TRADING COMPANY, LTD.**
2-11, Kanda Nishiki-Cho, Chiyoda-ku, Tokyo 101-0054, Japan
CEO: Yoshimitsu Machida, Pres.
Bus: *Import/export rubber, agricultural and chemicals,
automotive parts, machinery materials, marine and
lumber products.*

Tel: 81-3-3233-5700
Fax: 81-3-3233-5777
www.sanyo-trading.co.jp

Rev: $350
Emp: 214

NAICS: 423120, 423440, 424690, 522293

SANYO CORPORATION OF AMERICA
529 Fifth Ave., 12/F, New York, New York 10036
CEO: Katsuji Yamada, Pres.
Bus: *Sale of industrial chemicals, plastics and
machinery.*

Tel: (212) 221-7890
Fax: (212) 221-7828

%FO: 100
Emp: 12

SANYO CORPORATION OF AMERICA
400 Olympic Corporate Center, 3940 Olympic Blvd., Erlanger, Kentucky 41018
CEO: Mark See, Pres.
Bus: *Sale of industrial chemicals, plastics and
machinery.*

Tel: (859) 372-6630
Fax: (859) 372-6631

%FO: 100

SANYO CORPORATION OF AMERICA
39111 West Six Mile Rd., Ste. 157, Livonia, Michigan 48152
CEO: Akifumi Suzuki, Mgr.   Tel: (734) 591-7257   %FO: 100
Bus: *Sale of industrial chemicals, plastics and* Fax: (734) 591-7406
     machinery.

● **SAPPORO HOLDINGS, LIMITED**
Yebisu Garden Place, 20-1 Ebisu 4-chome, Shibuya-ku, Tokyo 150-8522, Japan
CEO: Takao Murakami, Pres. & CEO   Tel: 81-3-5423-2111   Rev: $4,800
Bus: *Mfr. and imports beer soft drinks, wine and* Fax: 81-3-5423-2057   Emp: 7,341
    www.sapporoholdings.jp
NAICS: 236210, 236220, 237210, 312111, 312120, 424810, 722110

   SAPPORO USA, INC.
   391 North Emroy Ave., Elmhurst, Illinois 60126
   CEO: Garry Sutton, Pres.   Tel: (630) 993-0375   %FO: 100
   Bus: *Import/distribution of beer and production of* Fax:
      wine.

   SAPPORO USA, INC.
   18881 Von Karman Ave., Ste. 420, Irvine, California 92612
   CEO: Norifumi Sumiyoshi, Pres.   Tel: (949) 553-9733   %FO: 100
   Bus: *Import/distribution of beer and production of* Fax: (949) 553-9737 Emp: 15
      wine.

   SAPPORO USA, INC.
   666 Third Ave., New York, New York 10017
   CEO: Sumiyoshi Nori, Pres.   Tel: (212) 922-9165   %FO: 100
   Bus: *Import/distribution of beer and production of* Fax: (212) 922-9576 Emp: 7
      wine.

● **SECOM CO., LTD.**
5-1, Jingumae, 1-chome, Shibuya-ku, Tokyo 150-0001, Japan
CEO: Shohei Kimura, Pres. & CEO   Tel: 81-3-5775-8100   Rev: $4,992
Bus: *Provides security services and products.* Fax: 81-3-5775-8927 Emp: 26,232
    www.secom.co.jp
NAICS: 511210, 531120, 531190, 561612, 623312, 811219

   THE WESTEC SECURITY GROUP, INC.
   100 Bayview Circle, Ste. 5000, Newport Beach, California 92660
   CEO: Michael S. Kaye, Pres.   Tel: (949) 725-6200   %FO: 100
   Bus: *Provides security services and products.* Fax: (949) 725-6690 Emp: 300

   THE WESTEC SECURITY GROUP, INC.
   533 S Campbell Ave., Ste. K, Springfield, Missouri 65806-2011
   CEO: Joe Morris, Mgr.   Tel: (417) 887-7477   %FO: 100
   Bus: *Security systems manufacture and sales.* Fax: (417) 887-7477 Emp: 25

● **SEGA CORPORATION**
1-2-12, Haneda, 1-chome, Ohta-ku, Tokyo 144-8531, Japan
CEO: Hisao Oguchi, Pres. & COO   Tel: 81-3-5736-7111   Rev: $1,810
Bus: *Develop/mfr. video games and equipment.* Fax: 81-3-5736-7066 Emp: 10,760
   Entertainment facilities.   www.sega.co.jp
NAICS: 339932, 511210, 713120

SEGA GAMEWORKS
600 North Brand Blvd., 5/F, Glendale, California 91203
CEO: Ron Lam, CEO
Bus: *Amusement parks arcades*
Tel: (818) 254-4263
Fax:
%FO: 100
Emp: 1,300

SEGA OF AMERICA DREAMCAST, INC.
Townsend Center, 650 Townsend St., Ste. 575, San Francisco, California 94103
CEO: Hayao Nakayama, Pres. & COO
Bus: *Sale/service video games and equipment systems.*
Tel: (415) 701-6000
Fax: (415) 701-6001
%FO: 100
Emp: 180

SEGA OF AMERICA, INC.
Townsend Center, 650 Townsend St., Ste. 650, San Francisco, California 94103
CEO: Naoya Tsurumi, CEO
Bus: *Sale/service video games and equipment systems.*
Tel: (415) 701-6000
Fax: (415) 701-6001
%FO: 100
Emp: 350

● **SEIKA CORPORATION**
New-Tokyo Bldg., 3-1 Marunouchi 3-chome, Chiyoda-ku, Tokyo 100-0005, Japan
CEO: Terufumi Soejima, Pres.
Bus: *Importer and exporter of industrial machinery*
Tel: 81-3-5221-7109
Fax: 81-3-5221-7133
www.seika.com
Rev: $1,321
Emp: 342
NAICS: 423610, 423830, 423840

SEIKA MACHINERY INC.
3528 Torrance Blvd., Ste. 100, Torrance, California 90503
CEO: Michelle Ogihara
Bus: *Manufacturer electronics*
Tel: (310) 540-7310
Fax: (310) 540-7930
%FO: 100

● **SEIKO CORPORATION**
1-2-1 Shibura, Minato-ku, Tokyo 105-8459, Japan
CEO: Reijiro Hattori, Chmn.
Bus: *Mfr./sales of clocks/watches, eyeglass lenses/frames and golf clubs.*
Tel: 81-3-6401-2111
Fax: 81-3-6401-2216
www.seiko.co.jp
Rev: $1,924
Emp: 9,245
NAICS: 325620, 333314, 333315, 334111, 334518, 339115, 339911, 339920, 446120

SEIKO CORPORATION OF AMERICA, INC.
1111 MacArthur Blvd., Mahwah, New Jersey 07430
CEO: Toyoji Todaka, Pres.
Bus: *Sales of clocks/watches and golf clubs.*
Tel: (201) 529-5730
Fax: (201) 529-0132
%FO: 100
Emp: 400

SEIKO OPTICAL PRODUCTS, INC.
575 Corporate Dr., Mahwah, New Jersey 07430
CEO: Atsushi Iwasaki, Pres.
Bus: *Sales of eyeglass lenses and frames.*
Tel: (201) 529-9099
Fax: (201) 529-9019
%FO: 100
Emp: 50

● **SEIKO EPSON CORPORATION**
3-3-5 Owa, Suwa, Nagano 392-8502, Japan
CEO: Saburo Kusama, Pres.
Bus: *Mfr. printer mechanisms, liquid crystal displays, printers, computers and disk drives.*
Tel: 81-26-652-3131
Fax: 81-26-653-4844
www.epson.com
Rev: $13,378
Emp: 84,899
NAICS: 333293, 333315, 334111, 334112, 334113, 334119, 334310, 334411, 334413, 334414, 334415, 334518

EPSON AMERICA, INC.
3840 Kilroy Airport Way, Long Beach, California 90806
CEO: John Lang, Pres. & CEO   Tel: (562) 981-3840 %FO: 100
Bus: *Sales desktop and portable computers,* Fax: (562) 290-5220
printers, scanners and related equipment.

EPSON PORTLAND INC.
3950 Northwest Aloclek Place, Hillsboro, Oregon 97124
CEO: Randal McEvers, Mgr.   Tel: (503) 645-1118 %FO: 100
Bus: *Sales desktop and portable computers,* Fax: (503) 690-5450 Emp: 400
printers, scanners and related equipment.

● **SEINO TRANSPORTATION COMPANY, LTD.**
1,Taguchi-cho,Ogaki, Gifu 503-8501, Japan
CEO: Yoshikazu Taguchi, Chmn. & CEO Tel: 81-584-81-1111 Rev: $2,549
Bus: *Trucking, moving, air and sea transportation,* Fax: 81-584-82-5040 Emp: 20,895
warehousing and distribution. www.seino.co.jp
NAICS: 481212, 483111, 484121

 SEINO AMERICA, INC.
 8728 Aviation Blvd., Inglewood, California 90301
 CEO: Norizumi Fuma, Pres. Tel: (310) 215-0500 %FO: 100
 Bus: *International freight forwarding, moving,* Fax: (310) 215-3090 Emp: 78
 trade consulting and customs broker.

● **SEKI TECHNOTRON CORPORATION**
5-6-30 Kiba, Koto-ku, Tokyo 135-0042, Japan
CEO: Makoto Seki, Chmn. & Pres. & CEO Tel: 81-3-3820-1711 Rev: $78
Bus: *Distributor of specialized electronic equipment* Fax: 81-3-3820-1735 Emp: 109
   www.sekitech.biz
NAICS: 423610

 SEOCAL INC.
 2220 Martin Ave., Santa Clara, California 95050-2704
 CEO: Bob Johnson, EVP Tel: (408) 986-9190 %FO: 100
 Bus: *Distributor of specialized electronic* Fax: (408) 986-9191
 equipment

● **SEKISUI CHEMICAL COMPANY, LTD.**
4-4, Nishitenma, 2-chome, Kita-ku, Osaka 530-8565, Japan
CEO: Naotake Okubo, Pres. Tel: 81-6-365-4122 Rev: $7,713
Bus: *Molded plastic products and residential housing.* Fax: 81-6-365-4370 Emp: 15,782
   www.sekisui.co.jp
NAICS: 321991, 321992, 326112, 326113, 326199, 332311, 453930

 KLEERDEX CO.
 100 Gaither Dr., Ste. B, Mount Laurel, New Jersey 08054
 CEO: James Medalie, Pres. Tel: (856) 866-1700 %FO: 100
 Bus: *Mfr. of plastic materials.* Fax: (856) 866-9728 Emp: 130

 SEKISUI AMERICA CORP
 100 Gaither Dr., Ste. A, Mount Laurel, New Jersey 08054
 CEO: Tel: (856) 235-5115 %FO: 100
 Bus: *Mfr. of plastic foam products.* Fax: (856) 235-0097

SEKISUI AMERICA CORPORATION
666 Fifth Ave., 12/F, New York, New York 10103
CEO: Hirmou Mitsui, Treasurer
Bus: *Mfr./mktg. plastic products.*
Tel: (212) 489-3500
Fax: (212) 489-5100
%FO: 100
Emp: 850

SEKISUI PRODUCTS, LLC
550 Stephenson Hwy., Ste. 301, Troy, Michigan 48083
CEO: Richard Howe, Mgr.
Bus: *Mfr. of plastic foam products.*
Tel: (248) 307-0000
Fax: (248) 307-1680
%FO: 100

SEKISUI S-LEC AMERICA LLC
1786 Dividend Dr., Columbus, Ohio 43228
CEO: Matt Muramatsu, Mgr.
Bus: *Mfr. of automotive stampings.*
Tel: (614) 527-5250
Fax: (604) 527-5257
%FO: 100

SEKISUI TA INDUSTRIES LLC
100 S. Puente St., Brea, California 92821
CEO: Ernest Wong, Pres.
Bus: *Mfr. of industrial pressure sensitive tapes.*
Tel: (714) 255-7888
Fax: (714) 990-0440
%FO: 100
Emp: 190

VOLTEK LLC
100 Shepard St., Lawrence, Massachusetts 01843
CEO: Brian Norris, Pres.
Bus: *Mfr. of plastic foam products.*
Tel: (978) 685-2557
Fax: (978) 685-9861
%FO: 100
Emp: 110

● SEVEN-ELEVEN JAPAN CO. LTD., DIV. SEVEN & I HOLDINGS
8-8, Nibancho, Chiyoda-ku, Tokyo 102-8455, Japan
CEO: Toshifumi Suzuki, Chmn. & CEO
Bus: *Owns and operates convenience stores, food delivery services and e-commerce.*
NAICS: 454111, 492110, 722211
Tel: 81-3-6238-3711
Fax: 81-3-3261-2435
www.sej.co.jp
Rev: $4,343
Emp: 5,433

SEVEN ELEVEN (HAWAII) INC.
1755 Nuuanu Ave., Honolulu, Hawaii 98617
CEO: James Keyes, Pres.
Bus: *Convenience stores*
Tel: (808) 525-1711
Fax: (808) 523-5890
%FO: 100

● SHARP CORPORATION
22-22 Nagaike-cho, Abeno-ku, Osaka 545-8522, Japan
CEO: Katsuhiko Machida, Pres.
Bus: *Mfr. video and audio systems, appliances, office and information equipment and electronic components.*
NAICS: 333315, 334111, 334112, 334113, 334310, 334411, 334413, 334414, 334415, 334419, 335211, 335212, 335221, 335222, 335224
Tel: 81-6-6621-1221
Fax: 81-6-6627-1759
www.sharp.co.jp
Rev: $21,367
Emp: 46,164

SHARP ELECTRONICS CORPORATION
1 Sharp Plaza, Mahwah, New Jersey 07430-2135
CEO: Toshihiko Fujimoto, Chmn. & Pres.
Bus: *Mfr./sale/service video and audio systems, appliances, office and information equipment and electronic components.*
Tel: (201) 529-8200
Fax: (201) 529-8425
%FO: 100
Emp: 2,900

● **SHIBASOKU COMPANY, LTD.**
6-8, Shinbashi, 4-chome, Minato-ku, Tokyo 105-0004, Japan
CEO: Takashi Shigezaki, Pres. & CEO   Tel: 81-3-5401-3811   Rev: $120
Bus: *Mfr. audio and video test equipment. (JV of*   Fax: 81-3-5401-3815   Emp: 364
    ASACA Corp.)   www.shibasoku.co.jp
NAICS: 334310

    ASACA-SHIBASOKU CORPORATION OF AMERICA
    400 Corporate Circle, Ste. G, Golden, Colorado 80401
    CEO: Takashi Shigezaki, Pres.   Tel: (303) 278-1111
    Bus: *Sales/service of audio and video test*   Fax: (303) 278-0303   Emp: 11
        equipment.

    SHIBASOKU R&D CENTER INC.
    10 Bearfoot Rd., Ste. 2000, Northborough, Massachusetts 01532
    CEO: Takashi Shigezaki, Pres.   Tel: (508) 393-8555
    Bus: *Engineering services.*   Fax: (508) 393-8541   Emp: 7

● **SHIMADZU CORPORATION**
1, Nishinokyo-Kuwabaracho, Nakagyo-ku, Kyoto 604-8511, Japan
CEO: Hidetoshi Yajima, Chmn.   Tel: 81-75-823-1111   Rev: $2,063
Bus: *Laboratory instruments, aircraft equipment, and*   Fax: Emp: 7,930
    optical devices manufacture.   www.shimadzu.com
NAICS: 333298, 333314, 333997, 334516, 334517

    SHIMADZU MEDICAL SYSTEMS
    20101 S Vermont Ave., Torrance, California 90502
    CEO: Yoshinori Kakisaka, Pres.   Tel: (310) 217-8855   %FO: 100
    Bus: *Medical imaging equipment manufacture and*   Fax: (310) 217-0661   Emp: 100
        sales.

    SHIMADZU SCIENTIFIC INSTRUMENTS
    7102 Riverwood Dr., Columbia, Maryland 21046
    CEO: Osamo Ondo, Pres.   Tel: (410) 381-1227   %FO: 100
    Bus: *Laboratory instruments manufacture and*   Fax: (410) 371-1222
        sales.

● **SHIMIZU CORPORATION**
Seavans South, 1-2-3, Shibaura, 1-chome, Minato-ku, Tokyo 105-8007, Japan
CEO: Tetsuya Nomura, Pres. & CEO   Tel: 81-3-5441-1111   Rev: $14,678
Bus: *Engineering and construction.*   Fax: 81-3-5441-0526   Emp: 9,185
     www.shimz.co.jp
NAICS: 236116, 236210, 237310, 238190, 531120, 531190, 531312, 531390, 541310, 541330, 541620, 562910

    SHIMIZU AMERICA CORPORATION
    800 Wilshire Blvd., Ste. 800, Los Angeles, California 90177
    CEO: Kenji Nakagawa, Gen. Mgr.   Tel: (213) 362-7500   %FO: 100
    Bus: *General contractor, engineer and design.*   Fax: (213) 362-7511

    SHIMIZU AMERICA CORPORATION
    1820 Water Place, Ste. 255, Atlanta, Georgia 30339
    CEO: Shigeru Usui, Pres. & CEO   Tel: (770) 956-1123   %FO: 100
    Bus: *General contractor, engineer and design.*   Fax: (770) 956-7575   Emp: 84

SHIMIZU CORPORATION
461 Fifth Ave., 3/F, New York, New York 10017
CEO:
Bus: *Engineering and construction services.*
Tel: (212) 251-0050
Fax: (212) 251-1052

SHIMIZU CORPORATION
28 West 44th St., Ste. 1400, New York, New York 10036
CEO: Takahi Morita, Gen. Mgr.
Bus: *Engineering and construction services.*
Tel: (212) 223-7757
Fax: (212) 223-1930

● **SHIN-ETSU CHEMICAL COMPANY, LTD.**
6-1, Otemachi, 2-chome, Chiyoda-ku, Tokyo 100-0004, Japan
CEO: Chihiro Kanagawa, Pres. & CEO
Bus: *Mfr. specialty chemicals and high-tech materials.*
Tel: 81-3-3246-5091
Fax: 81-3-3246-5096
www.shinetsu.co.jp
Rev: $7,883
Emp: 17,384
NAICS: 236210, 237990, 238990, 325181, 325188, 325191, 325199, 325211, 325221, 325222, 334413

SEH AMERICA
4111 Northeast 112th Ave., Vancouver, Washington 98682
CEO: Steven Shimada, CEO
Bus: *Sales/marketing semiconductor silicon wafers.*
Tel: (360) 883-7000
Fax: (360) 254-6973
%FO: 100
Emp: 850

SEH AMERICA
715 East Route 10, Ste. 8, Randolph, New Jersey 07869
CEO: Mark Lima, CEO
Bus: *Electronic parts & equipment.*
Tel: (973) 361-7251
Fax: (973) 361-7252

SEH AMERICA
11882 Greenville Ave., Ste. 128, Dallas, Texas 75243
CEO: Steve Moore, VP
Bus: *Electronic parts & equipment.*
Tel: (972) 644-9784
Fax: (972) 690-3037

SHIN-ETSU CHEMICAL
46691 Mission Blvd., Ste. 300, Freemont, California 94539
CEO: Paul Uritani, Dir.
Bus: *Wholesale computers & computer equipment.*
Tel: (510) 659-9411
Fax:

SHIN-ETSU MAGNETICS INC.
2372 Qume Dr., Ste. B, San Jose, California 95131
CEO: Takashi Tanaka, Pres.
Bus: *Industrial supplies.*
Tel: (408) 383-9240
Fax: (408) 383-9245
Emp: 8

SHIN-ETSU MAGNETICS INC.
799 Roosevelt Rd., Bldg. 6, Ste. 215, Glen Ellyn, Illinois 60137
CEO: Shinji Fukui
Bus: *Mfr. specialty chemicals and high-tech materials.*
Tel: (630) 858-9340
Fax: (630) 858-9341

SHIN-ETSU MAGNETICS INC.
6600 City West Pkwy., #240, Eden Prairie, Minnesota 55334
CEO: Fhinji Fukui, Pres.
Bus: *Chemicals & products*
Tel: (952) 941-3370
Fax: (952) 941-3855
Emp: 10

SHINTECH INC.
3 Greenway Plaza, Ste. 1150, Houston, Texas 77046
CEO: Chigiro Kanagawa, Pres. & CEO   Tel: (713) 965-0713   %FO: 100
Bus: *Chemical & petrochemical manufacturing*   Fax: (713) 965-0629   Emp: 260

● **SHINKAWA LTD.**
2-51-1, Inadaira, Musashimurayama-shi, Tokyo 208-8585, Japan
CEO: Kenji Fujiyama, Chmn. & CEO   Tel: 81-4-2560-1231   Rev: $208
Bus: *Mfr. electronics.*   Fax: 81-4-2560-8485   Emp: 491
    www.shinkawa.com
NAICS: 333295
    SHINKAWA USA INC.
    1930 S. Alma School Rd., Ste. D-107, Mesa, Arizona 85210
    CEO: Sadashi Iida, Pres.   Tel: (480) 831-7988
    Bus: *Industrial machinery servicing.*   Fax: (480) 831-9480

● **SHINSEI BANK LIMITED**
1-8, Uchisaiwaicho, 2-chome, Chiyoda-ku, Tokyo 100-8501, Japan
CEO: Masamoto Yashiro, Pres. & CEO   Tel: 81-3-5511-5111   Rev: $1,541
Bus: *Commercial banking services.*   Fax: 81-3-5511-5505   Emp: 2,122
    www.shinseibank.com
NAICS: 522110
    SHINSEI BANK
    7 Times Square, 25/F, New York, New York 10036
    CEO: Kosaku Sakai   Tel: (646) 840-9700   %FO: 100
    Bus: *Financial services.*   Fax: (646) 840-9700

● **SHINSHO CORPORATION**
2-6-17 Kitahama, Chuo-ku, Osaka 541-8557, Japan
CEO: Tsuguto Moriwaki, Pres. & CEO   Tel: 81-6-6206-7001   Rev: $4,355
Bus: *Mfr. steel and metal products.*   Fax: 81-6-6206-7399   Emp: 838
    www.shinsho.co.jp
NAICS: 331111, 331210, 331221, 331222, 332322
    SHINSHO AMERICAN CORP.
    75 Windham Blvd., Verenes Industrial Park, Aiken, South Carolina 29801
    CEO: Ted Fukuda, Mgr.   Tel: (803) 641-6091   %FO: 100
    Bus: *Mfr. steel and metal products.*   Fax: (803) 541-6092   Emp: 10

    SHINSHO AMERICAN CORP.
    26200 Town Center Dr., Ste. 160, Novi, Michigan 48375
    CEO: Shutoku Ota, Mgr.   Tel: (248) 675-5569   %FO: 100
    Bus: *Mfr. steel and metal products.*   Fax: (248) 675-5575   Emp: 50

    SHINSHO AMERICAN CORP.
    1640 King St., Ste. C, Alexandria, Virginia 22314
    CEO: Satosha Muta, Principal   Tel: (703) 518-8878   %FO: 100
    Bus: *Mfr. steel and metal products.*   Fax: (703) 518-8838   Emp: 25

SHINSHO AMERICAN CORP.
2377 Crenshaw Blvd., Ste.108, Torrance, California 90501
CEO: Koichi Santo, Gen. Mgr.   Tel: (310) 782-8981   %FO: 100
Bus: *Mfr. steel and metal products.*   Fax: (310) 782-9056   Emp: 4

SHINSHO AMERICAN CORP.
45 Northwest Dr., PO Box 864, Plainville, Connecticut 06062
CEO: Hank Matsuo, Pres.   Tel: (860) 793-1232   %FO: 100
Bus: *Mfr. steel and metal products.*   Fax: (860) 793-1442

- **SHINTOA CORPORATION**
New Tokyo Bldg., 3-1, Marunouchi 3-chome, Chiyoda-ku, Tokyo 100-8383, Japan
CEO: Mr. Mitsuaki Iki   Tel: 81-3-3286-0546   Rev: $1,991
Bus: *Trading company.*   Fax: 81-3-3213-2451   Emp: 276
    www.shintoa.co.jp
NAICS: 522293

    SHINTOA INTL INC
    135 North Penn St., Ste. 1360, Indianapolis, Indiana 46204
    CEO: George Hidaka, Mgr.   Tel: (317) 917-1111   %FO: 100
    Bus: *Imports/exports of various merchandise.*   Fax:

    SHINTOA INTL, INC.
    970 West 190th St., Ste. 520, Torrance, California 90502
    CEO: Mark Sakakibara, Pres.   Tel: (310) 538-4898   %FO: 100
    Bus: *Imports/exports of various merchandise.*   Fax: Emp: 9

- **SHINWA KAIUN KAISHA, LTD.**
KDDI Otemachi Bldg., 14&15/F, 8-1 Otemachi, 1-chome, Chiyoda-ku, Tokyo 100-8108, Japan
CEO: Takahiko Kakei, Pres.   Tel: 81-3-5290-6400
Bus: *Shipping operator and tramp chartering and*   Fax: 81-3-5290-6230   Emp: 156
shipping agent.   www.shinwaship.com
NAICS: 483111, 488510

    SHINWA USA, INC.
    300 Harmon Meadow Blvd., 4/F, Secaucus, New Jersey 07094
    CEO: Hironobo Sato, Pres.   Tel: (201) 348-2101   %FO: 100
    Bus: *Marine transport operations, tramp*   Fax: (201) 319-0305   Emp: 8
chartering and shipping agency.

- **SHINYEI KAISHA**
77-1, Kyomachi, Chuo-ku, Kobe 651-0178, Japan
CEO: Shoichi Atarashi, Pres.   Tel: 81-78-392-6800   Rev: $359
Bus: *Trading: textiles, silk, electronics, agricultural &*   Fax: 81-78-392-0707   Emp: 675
marine products; mfr. electronics.   www.shinyei.co.jp
NAICS: 423830, 424310

    SHINYEI CORP OF AMERICA
    7252 Clairemont Mesa Blvd, San Diego, California 92111
    CEO: Kenji Nuki, Dir.   Tel: (858) 279-9940   %FO: 100
    Bus: *Sale of electronic parts & equipment.*   Fax: (858) 279-9945

SHINYEI CORP OF AMERICA
11 East 44th St., Ste. 700, New York, New York 10017
CEO: Hideo Akagawa, Pres.   Tel: (212) 682-4610   %FO: 100
Bus: *Sale of hardware textiles & electrical home*   Fax: (212) 286-8426   Emp: 9
appliances, exported processed foods,
recreational vehicles & lumber.

● **SHIONOGI & CO., LTD.**
1-8, Doshomachi, 3-chome, Chuo-ku, Osaka 541-0045, Japan
CEO: Motozo Shiono, Pres.   Tel: 81-6-6202-2161   Rev: $1,898
Bus: *Research, manufacture and marketing of*   Fax: 81-6-6229-9596   Emp: 5,589
pharmaceuticals and animal health products.   www.shionogi.co.jp
   NAICS: 325411, 325412

SHIONOGI QUALICAPS
6505 Franz Warner Pkwy., Whitsett, North Carolina 27377
CEO: Greg Bowers, Pres.   Tel: (336) 449-3900   %FO: 100
Bus: *Chemical preparations*   Fax: Emp: 176

SHIONOGI USA
100 Campus Dr., Florham Park, New Jersey 07932
CEO: Sapan A. Shah, Pres.   Tel: (973) 966-6900   %FO: 100
Bus: *Markets pharmaceutical, animal health*   Fax: (973) 966-2820   Emp: 20
products, agrochemicals and industrial
chemicals.

● **SHISEIDO COMPANY LTD.**
5-5, Ginza, 7-chome Chuo-ku, Tokyo 104-0061, Japan
CEO: Shinzo Maeda, Pres. & CEO   Tel: 81-3-3572-5111   Rev: $5,909
Bus: *Mfr./market cosmetics and healthcare products.*   Fax: 81-3-3289-1235   Emp: 24,839
                                         www.shiseido.co.jp
   NAICS: 325620, 446120

SHISEIDO COSMETICS AMERICA LTD.
178 Bauer Dr., Oakland, New Jersey 07436
CEO: Tosio Negami, Chmn. & CEO   Tel: (201) 337-3750   %FO: 100
Bus: *Mfr./marketing cosmetics and healthcare*   Fax: (201) 337-5083   Emp: 1,128
products.

SHISEIDO INTERNATIONAL CORP.
900 Third Ave., 15/F, New York, New York 10022
CEO: Yutaka Yamanouchi, Gen. Mgr.   Tel: (212) 805-2300   %FO: 100
Bus: *Mfr./sales beauty and healthcare products.*   Fax: (212) 688-0109   Emp: 300

ZOTOS INTERNATIONAL
100 Tokeneke Rd., Darien, Connecticut 06820
CEO: Robert Seidl, Pres. & CEO   Tel: (203) 655-8911   %FO: 100
Bus: *Mfr./marketing cosmetics and healthcare*   Fax: (203) 656-7890
products.

- **SHIZUOKA BANK, LTD.**
  2-1, Shimizukusanagi-kita, Shiizuoka 424-8677, Japan
  CEO: Soichiro Kamiya, Chmn.
  Bus: *Commercial banking services.*

  NAICS: 522110, 522310, 523110, 531320

  Tel: 81-543-45-5411
  Fax: 84-543-44-0090
  www.shizuokabank.co.jp

  Rev: $1,717
  Emp: 3,716

  SHIZUOKA BANK LTD.
  101 E. 52nd St., 4/F, New York, New York 10022
  CEO: Toshihiko Yamamoto, Mgr.
  Bus: *Commercial banking services.*

  Tel: (212) 319-6262
  Fax:

  %FO: 100

  SHIZUOKA BANK LTD.
  801 South Figueroa St., Ste. 800, Los Angeles, California 90017
  CEO: Shouji Fujita
  Bus: *Commercial banking services*

  Tel: (213) 622-3233
  Fax:

- **THE SHOKO CHUKIN BANK**
  10-17, Yaesu, 2-chome, Chuo-ku, Tokyo 104-0028, Japan
  CEO: Tadashi Ezaki, Pres.
  Bus: *Commercial banking services.*

  NAICS: 522110

  Tel: 81-3-3172-6111
  Fax: 81-3-3272-6169
  www.shokochukin.go.jp

  Emp: 6,000

  THE SHOKO CHUKIN BANK
  666 Fifth Ave., 9/F, New York, New York 10019
  CEO: Hiroshi Yamauchi, Mgr.
  Bus: *Commercial banking.*

  Tel: (212) 581-2800
  Fax: (212) 581-4850

  %FO: 100
  Emp: 20

- **SHOWA DENKO KK**
  13-9, Shiba Daimon, 1-chome, Minato-ku, Tokyo 105-8518, Japan
  CEO: Mitsuo Ohashi, Pres. & CEO
  Bus: *Chemicals and petrochemicals and ceramic materials.*

  NAICS: 325199, 331315, 332312

  Tel: 81-3-5470-3235
  Fax: 81-3-3436-2625
  www.sdk.co.jp

  Rev: $7,184
  Emp: 11,166

  SHOWA ALUMINUM CORP. OF AMERICA
  10500 Oday Harrison Rd., Mount Sterling, Ohio 43143
  CEO: Ted Shibata, Pres.
  Bus: *Mfr. of automotive parts & accessories, heat exchangers.*

  Tel: (740) 869-3333
  Fax:

  %FO: 100
  Emp: 476

  SHOWA DENKO AMERICA, INC.
  2800 Lakeside Dr., Santa Clara, California 95054
  CEO: Ted Shihcher Lin, CEO
  Bus: *Sale/distribution of chemicals.*

  Tel: (408) 327-8879
  Fax:

  %FO: 100
  Emp: 4

  SHOWA DENKO AMERICA, INC.
  489 Fifth Ave., 18/F, New York, New York 10017
  CEO: Atsushi Mizutani, Pres.
  Bus: *Sale/distribution of chemicals.*

  Tel: (212) 370-0033
  Fax: (212) 370-4566

  %FO: 100
  Emp: 10

SHOWA DENKO CARBON, INC.
478 Ridge Rd., Ridgeville, South Carolina 29472
CEO: Stephen L. Ulmer, Pres.   Tel: (843) 875-3200   %FO: 100
Bus: *Electrical products.*   Fax: (843) 875-2640   Emp: 200

● **SHOWA ELECTRIC WIRE & CABLE**
Tokyo Toranomon Bldg., 1-18 Toranomon 1-chome, Minato-ku, Tokyo 105-8444, Japan
CEO: Toshio Tomii, Pres. & CEO   Tel: 81-3-5532-1911   Rev: $1,032
Bus: *Electric power and telecommunications cables*   Fax: 81-3-3503-4506   Emp: 1,700
manufacture.   www.swcc.co.jp
NAICS: 326199, 326291, 331319, 333120, 335929

  SHOWA ELECTRIC AMERICA, INC.
  235 Montgomery St., Ste. 1142, San Francisco, California 94104
  CEO: Akihisa Takizawa, Mng. Dir.   Tel: (415) 781-5885   %FO: 100
  Bus: *Electric power and telecommunications*   Fax: (415) 781-1561
  cables manufacture and sales.

● **SMK CORPORATION**
5-5, Togoshi 6-chome, Shinagawa-ku, Tokyo 142-8511, Japan
CEO: Tetsuya Nakamura, CEO   Tel: 81-3-3785-1111   Rev: $485
Bus: *Electronic components manufacture.*   Fax: 81-3-3785-1878   Emp: 6,400
                                             www.smk.co.jp
NAICS: 334113, 334119, 334412, 334417, 334419, 335314, 335931

  SMK ELECTRONICS CORPORATION
  1055 Tierra Del Rey, Chula Vista, California 91910
  CEO: Tetsuya Nakamura, Pres.   Tel: (619) 216-6400   %FO: 100
  Bus: *Electronic components manufacture.*   Fax: (619) 216-6499

● **SOFTBANK CORPORATION**
1-9-1 Higashi Shinbashi, Minato-ku, Tokyo 105-7303, Japan
CEO: Masayoshi Son, Pres. & CEO   Tel: 81-3-5642-8000   Rev: $4,898
Bus: *Retailer; computer software and network*   Fax: 81-3-5543-0431   Emp: 6,662
products. Publisher of hi-tech magazines and   www.softbank.co.jp
invests in technology globally.
NAICS: 334119, 443120, 511120, 517910, 518111, 518210, 519190, 523999

  SOFTBANK CORP.
  300 Delaware Ave., Wilmington, Delaware 19801
  CEO: Ronald Fischer, Vice Chmn.   Tel: (302) 576-2713
  Bus: *Investment firm.*   Fax:

  SOFTBANK HOLDINGS, INC.
  1188 Centre St., Newton, Massachusetts 02159
  CEO: Masayoshi Sain, Pres.   Tel: (617) 928-9300   %FO: 100
  Bus: *U.S. headquarters. Retailer; computer*   Fax: (617) 928-9304   Emp: 3,025
  software & network products. Publisher of
  hi-tech magazines & invests in technology
  globally.

● **SOJITZ CORPORATION**
1-20, Akasaka 6-chome, Minato-ku, Tokyo 107-8655, Japan
CEO: Akio Dobashi, Pres. & CEO
Bus: *Import/export/trading; industrial development.*
Tel: 81-3-5520-5000
Fax: 81-3-5520-2390
www.sojitz-holdings.com
Rev: $55,487
Emp: 14,600
NAICS: 111910, 312210, 312229, 333518, 333922, 333923, 333924, 333993, 333999, 424710, 424940, 444190

BIAXIS PACKAGING SALES, INC.
2340 S. Arlington Heights Rd., Ste. 610, Arlington Heights, Illinois 60005
CEO: Yoshinori Suzuki, Pres.
Bus: *Sale of nylon film & plastic resins*
Tel: (847) 956-7320
Fax: (847) 956-7315
%FO: 100
Emp: 7

MAZAK LASER CORP.
140 East State Pkwy., Schaumburg, Illinois 60173
CEO: Glenn Berkhahn
Bus: *Import sale & aftercare of laser cutting machinery*
Tel: (847) 252-4511
Fax: (847) 252-4599
%FO: 100

METAL PROCESSING SYSTEMS, INC.
1096 National Pkwy., Schaumburg, Illinois 60173
CEO: Takehide Asada, Pres.
Bus: *Import, sale and aftercare of metal processing machines*
Tel: (847) 310-6363
Fax: (847) 310-6080
%FO: 100

METTON AMERICA, INC.
2727 Miller Cut Off Rd., La Porte, Texas 77571
CEO: Michifumi Watanabe
Bus: *Mfr. & sale of metton - DCPD resin.*
Tel: (281) 479-8078
Fax: (281) 479-4906
%FO: 100

NM PRODUCTS CORP.
6525 Daniel Burnham, Portage, Indiana 46368
CEO: Hiroki Kitajima, Pres.
Bus: *Wholesale of gasoline engines & related manufactured products*
Tel: (219) 764-5407
Fax: (219) 764-5455
%FO: 100

OAC INC.
17536 Von Karman Ave., Irvine, California 92614
CEO: Jun Matsumoto
Bus: *Sale of OAC-manufactured automatic exposure equipment, lamps & supplies.*
Tel: (949) 852-1551
Fax: (949) 852-1665
%FO: 100

SOJITZ CORPORATION OF AMERICA
701 Fifth Ave., Ste. 1160, Seattle, Washington 98104
CEO: Teruo Matsumura
Bus: *Sales/distribution of general commodities and food.*
Tel: (206) 622-4810
Fax: (206) 621-9448
%FO: 100

SOJITZ CORPORATION OF AMERICA
Pacwest Center, 1211 S.W.M.V, Fifth Ave., Ste. 2200, Portland, Oregon 97204
CEO: Matthew Kurtz, Mgr.
Bus: *Sales/distribution of general commodities and food.*
Tel: (503) 220-2200
Fax: (503) 241-0302
%FO: 100

SOJITZ CORPORATION OF AMERICA
1055 West 7th St., Ste. 3200, Los Angeles, California 90017
CEO: Masakazu Narumiya, Mgr.　　Tel:　(213) 688-0600　　%FO: 100
Bus: *Sales/distribution of general commodities*　Fax:　(213) 688-0660
　　and food.

SOJITZ CORPORATION OF AMERICA
Three Riverway, Ste. 800, Houston, Texas 77056
CEO: Louigi Pakueghi, Mgr.　　Tel:　(713) 961-5435　　%FO: 100
Bus: *Sales/distribution of general commodities*　Fax:　(713) 961-0723
　　and food.

SOJITZ CORPORATION OF AMERICA
c/o The Boeing Company, 5000 E. McDowell Rd., M530-B135, Mesa, Arizona 85215
CEO: Jun Matsumoto　　Tel:　(480) 891-7680　　%FO: 100
Bus: *Sales/distribution of general commodities*　Fax:　(480) 891-5479
　　and food.

SOJITZ CORPORATION OF AMERICA
300 Galleria Officentre, Ste. 112, Southfield, Michigan 48034
CEO: Takehid Asada, Mgr.　　Tel:　(248) 358-5400　　%FO: 100
Bus: *Sales/distribution of general commodities*　Fax:　(248) 358-0560
　　and food.

SOJITZ CORPORATION OF AMERICA
1211 Ave. of the Americas, 44/F, New York, New York 10036
CEO: Kazuo Sekikawa, Pres.　　Tel:　(212) 704-6500　　%FO: 100
Bus: *Sales/distribution of general commodities*　Fax:　(212) 704-6543　　Emp: 224
　　and food.

SOJITZ CORPORATION OF AMERICA
12310 N.E. 8th St., Ste. 200, Bellevue, Washington 98005
CEO: Kyoji Hagino, Mgr.　　Tel:　(425) 453-1100　　%FO: 100
Bus: *Sales/distribution of general commodities*　Fax:　(425) 455-2521
　　and food.

SOJITZ ENERGY VENTURE, INC.
New Castle County, Wilmington, Delaware 19801
CEO: M. Yoshizaki　　Tel:　(713) 966-5740　　%FO: 100
Bus: *Oil & gas development*　Fax:　(713) 961-0723

SOJITZ NOBLE ALLOYS CORP.
1211 Ave. of the Americas, New York, New York 10036
CEO: Kazuo Sekikawa　　Tel:　(212) 704-6622　　%FO: 100
Bus: *Investment in Strategic Minerals Corp.*　Fax:　(212) 704-6630
　　(Stratcor) a U.S. vanadium producer

STRATEGIC MINERALS CORP.
30 Main St., Ste. 300, Danbury, Connecticut 06810
CEO: William G. Beattie, Chmn.　　Tel:　(203) 790-1555　　%FO: 100
Bus: *Production & sale of vanadium*　Fax:　(203) 790-5750　　Emp: 450

SUNCROWN DEVELOPMENT INC.
8777 N. Gainey Center Dr., Ste. 162, Scottsdale, Arizona 85258
CEO: Masahiko Inoue, Treasurer　　Tel:　(480) 607-3900　　%FO: 100
Bus: *Real estate investment*　Fax:　(480) 607-3900　　Emp: 88

- **SOMPO JAPAN INSURANCE, INC.**
  26-1, Nishi-Shinjuku, 1-chome, Shinjuku-ku, Tokyo 160-8338, Japan
  CEO: Hiroshi Hirano, Pres. & CEO   Tel: 81-3-3349-3111   Rev: $14,500
  Bus: *Fire, property, casualty and auto insurance.*   Fax: 81-3-3349-4697   Emp: 15,800
  www.sompo-japan.co.jp
  NAICS: 523991, 523999, 524113, 524114, 524126, 524130, 525110, 525120, 525190, 525910, 525920, 525990

  SJA INSURANCE AGENCY,LLC
  11111 Camel Commons Blvd., 3/F, Charlotte, North Carolina 28226
  CEO: H. Clark Jackson   Tel: (704) 759-2200
  Bus: *Insurance services*   Fax:

  SOMPO JAPAN INSURANCE COMPANY
  1001 Bayhill Dr., Ste. 145, San Bruno, California 94066
  CEO: Gadahi Mipsui, Mgr.   Tel: (650) 737-0400
  Bus: *Insurance services*   Fax:

  SOMPO JAPAN INSURANCE COMPANY OF AMERICA
  Two World Financial Center, 43/F, 225 Liberty St., New York, New York 10281
  CEO: Hideo Haraguchi, Pres.   Tel: (212) 416-1200   %FO: 100
  Bus: *Insurance services.*   Fax: (212) 416-1280   Emp: 194

  SOMPO JAPAN INSURANCE COMPANY OF AMERICA
  120 North LaSalle St., Ste. 1220, Chicago, Illinois 60602
  CEO: Ryukichi Takao, Mgr.   Tel: (312) 782-0800   %FO: 100
  Bus: *Insurance services.*   Fax:

  SOMPO JAPAN INSURANCE COMPANY OF AMERICA
  777 S. Figueroa St., Ste. 4800, Los Angeles, California 90017
  CEO: Ichiro Kamimura, Mgr.   Tel: (213) 243-1850   %FO: 100
  Bus: *Insurance services.*   Fax: Emp: 2

  SOMPO JAPAN INSURANCE COMPANY OF AMERICA
  6 Concourse Pkwy., Ste. 2130, Atlanta, Georgia 30328
  CEO: Tracey Webb, VP   Tel: (770) 394-5644   %FO: 100
  Bus: *Insurance services.*   Fax:

  SOMPO JAPAN INSURANCE COMPANY OF AMERICA
  404 BNA Dr., Ste. 409, Nashville, Tennessee 37217
  CEO: Hideki Kawaguchi, Mgr.   Tel: (615) 366-8610   %FO: 100
  Bus: *Insurance services.*   Fax:

  YASUDA ENTERPRISE DEVELOPMENT AMERICA, INC.
  435 Tasso St., Ste. 205, Palo Alto, California 94301
  CEO: Taisuke Yasuda, CEO   Tel: (650) 289-9733
  Bus: *Business services*   Fax:

- **SONY CORPORATION**
  7-35, Kitashinagawa, 6-chome, Shinagawa-ku, Tokyo 141-0001, Japan
  CEO: Sir Howard Stringer, CEO   Tel: 81-3-5448-2111   Rev: $66,912
  Bus: *Mfr. audio, video, TV equipment, computer*   Fax: 81-3-5448-2244   Emp: 162,000
  peripherals, electronic communications;   www.sony.net
  entertainment product.
  NAICS: 334111, 334119, 334220, 334310, 334413, 334611, 334612, 339932, 512110, 512120, 512210, 512220,
  512230, 522110, 524113, 524126

AIWA BUSINESS CENTER
16530 Via Esprillo, Bldg. 3, San Diego, California 92127
CEO: Masaru Hirauchi, CEO   Tel: (858) 942-8166
Bus: *Audio equipment*   Fax:

COLUMBIA PICTURES
10202 W. Washington Blvd., Culver City, California 90232
CEO: Geoffrey Ammer, Pres.   Tel: (310) 244-4000
Bus: *Motion picture production & distribution*   Fax: (310) 244-2626

COLUMBIA RECORDS GROUP
550 Madison Ave., New York, New York 10022
CEO: Will Botwin, Chmn.   Tel: (212) 833-8000
Bus: *Music production.*   Fax: (212) 833-5401

COLUMBIA TRISTAR MOTION PICTURE GROUP
10202 W. Washington Blvd., Culver City, California 90232
CEO: Jeff Blake, Pres.   Tel: (310) 244-4000
Bus: *Motion picture production & distribution*   Fax: (310) 244-2626

EPIC RECORDS GROUP
550 Madison Ave., New York, New York 10022
CEO: Steve Barnett, Pres.   Tel: (212) 833-8000
Bus: *Music production.*   Fax: (212) 833-4818

GAME SHOW NETWORK
2150 Colorado Ave., Ste. 100, Santa Monica, California 90404
CEO: Richard Cronin, Pres. & CEO   Tel: (310) 244-2222
Bus: *Television cable, pay & broadcast networks*   Fax: (310) 255-6810

LOUD RECORDS
550 Madison Ave., New York, New York 10022
CEO: Steven Rifkin, CEO   Tel: (212) 833-8000
Bus: *Music production.*   Fax: (212) 833-4818

METRO-GOLDWYN-MAYER
10250 Constellation Blvd., Los Angeles, California 90067
CEO: Daniel J. Taylor, Pres.   Tel: (310) 449-3000
Bus: *Motion picture production & distribution*   Fax: (310) 449-8857   Emp: 1,440

MGM PICTURES
10250 Constellation Blvd., Los Angeles, California 90067
CEO: Alex Yemenidjian, Chmn. & CEO   Tel: (310) 449-3000
Bus: *Motion picture production & distribution*   Fax: (310) 449-8750

PROVIDENT MUSIC GROUP
741 Cool Springs Blvd., Franklin, Tennessee 37067
CEO: Terry Hemmings, Pres. & CEO   Tel: (615) 261-5909
Bus: *Music production.*   Fax: Emp: 99

RCA LABEL GROUP-NASHVILLE
1400 18th Ave. South, Nashville, Tennessee 37212
CEO: Joe Galante, Chmn.   Tel: (615) 301-4300
Bus: *Music production.*   Fax: (615) 301-4347

RCA MUSIC GROUP
745 5th Ave., New York, New York 10151
CEO: Charles Goldstuck, Pres. & COO
Bus: *Music production.*
Tel: (646) 840-5600
Fax: (646) 840-5791

RED DISTRIBUTION
79 Fifth Ave., New York, New York 10003
CEO: Bob Morelli, EVP & Gen. Mgr.
Bus: *Music production.*
Tel: (212) 404-0600
Fax: (212) 337-5252

SCREEN GEMS INC.
10202 W. Washington Blvd., Culver City, California 90232
CEO: Clinton Culpepper, Pres.
Bus: *Motion picture production & distribution*
Tel: (310) 244-4000
Fax: (310) 244-2626

SONY BMG MUSIC ENTERTAINMENT
550 Madison Ave., New York, New York 10022
CEO: Andrew R. Lack, CEO & Mng. Dir.
Bus: *Music production.*
Tel: (212) 833-8000
Fax: (212) 833-4818
%FO: JV
Emp: 10,000

SONY CORP OF AMERICA
550 Madison Ave., New York, New York 10022
CEO: Sir Robert Stringer, Chmn. & CEO
Bus: *U.S. headquarters for electronics and hardware-related products for global entertainment units.*
Tel: (212) 833-6800
Fax: (212) 833-6956
%FO: 100

SONY ELECTRONICS, INC.
16450 W. Bernardo Dr., San Diego, California 92127
CEO: Ryoji Chubachi, Pres. & CEO
Bus: *Electronics and entertainment businesses.*
Tel: (858) 942-2400
Fax: (858) 942-8201
%FO: 100
Emp: 26,000

SONY MUSIC NASHVILLE
34 Music Sq. East, Nashville, Tennessee 37203
CEO: John Grady, Pres.
Bus: *Music production.*
Tel: (615) 742-4321
Fax: (615) 254-3879

SONY ONLINE ENTERTAINMENT
8928 Terman Ct., San Diego, California 92121
CEO: John Smedley, Pres.
Bus: *Entertainment & games software*
Tel: (858) 577-3100
Fax: (858) 577-3313

SONY PICTURES CLASSICS
550 Madison Ave., 8/F, New York, New York 10022
CEO: Michael Barker, Pres.
Bus: *Motion picture production & distribution*
Tel: (212) 833-8833
Fax:
%FO: 100

SONY PICTURES DIGITAL ENTERTAINMENT
3960 Ince Blvd., Culver City, California 90232
CEO: Yair Landau, Pres.
Bus: *Digital production.*
Tel: (310) 840-8676
Fax: (310) 840-8390
%FO: 100

SONY PICTURES ENTERTAINMENT
10202 West Washington Blvd., Culver City, California 90232
CEO: Michael Lynton, Chmn. & CEO   Tel: (310) 244-4000   %FO: 100
Bus: *Mfr./distribution motion pictures &*   Fax: (310) 244-2626   Emp: 7
       television, including Loews Cineplex
       Entertainment theater chain, home video,
       studio operations, new entertainment
       technologies & licensed merchandise.

SONY PICTURES HOME ENTERTAINMENT
10202 W. Washington Blvd., Culver City, California 90232
CEO: Ben Feingold, Pres.   Tel: (310) 244-4000
Bus: *Film & video*   Fax: (310) 244-2626   Emp: 450

SONY PICTURES IMAGEWORKS INC.
9050 W. Washington Blvd., Culver City, California 90232
CEO: Tim Sarnoff, Pres.   Tel: (310) 840-8000   %FO: 100
Bus: *Provides visual effects.*   Fax: (310) 840-8100   Emp: 99

SONY PICTURES TELEVISION
10202 W. Washington Blvd., Culver City, California 90232
CEO: Steve Mosko, Pres.   Tel: (310) 244-4000
Bus: *Television production & distribution*   Fax: (310) 244-2626   Emp: 35

SONY/ATV MUSIC PUBLISHING LLC
2120 Colorado Ave., Santa Monica, California 90404
CEO: David Hockman, Chmn.   Tel: (310) 449-2120
Bus: *Music publishers and distributors*   Fax: (310) 449-2541

SYMBIAN LTD.
390 Bridge Pkwy., Ste. 201, Redwood Shores, California 94065
CEO: Nigel Clifford, CEO   Tel: (650) 551-0240
Bus: *Wireless software.*   Fax: (650) 551-0241

UNITED ARTISTS CORP.
10250 Constellation Blvd., Los Angeles, California 90067
CEO: Danny Rosett, Pres.   Tel: (310) 449-3000
Bus: *Motion picture production & distribution*   Fax:

ZOMBA LABEL GROUP
137-139 W. 25th St., New York, New York 10001
CEO: Barry Weiss, Pres. & CEO   Tel: (212) 727-0016
Bus: *Music production.*   Fax: (212) 924-0743

● **SPC ELECTRONICS CORPORATION**
2-1-3, Shibasaki Chofu-shi, Tokyo 182-8602, Japan
CEO: Hiroshi Miyazaki, Mgr.   Tel: 81-3-4248-18518   Rev: $191
Bus: *Satellite/terrestrial communication systems,*   Fax: 81-3-4248-18593   Emp: 1,000
       service. & maintenance industrial equipment, R&D www.spc.co.jp
       microwave & millimeter wave energy systems.
NAICS: 517410

SPC ELECTRONICS AMERICA, INC.
105 Technology Pkwy., Norcross, Georgia 30092
CEO: Hiroshi Miyazaki, Pres.
Bus: *R&D, service communication units and systems*

Tel: (770) 446-8626
Fax: (770) 441-2380

%FO: 100
Emp: 16

• SQUARE ENIX CO. LTD.
Shinjuku Bunka Quint Bldg., 3-22-7 Yoyogi, Shibuya-ku, Tokyo 151-8544, Japan
CEO: Yoichi Wada, CEO
Bus: *Software manufacture.*

Tel: 81-3-5333-1555
Fax: 81-3-5333-1554
www.square-enix.co.jp

Rev: $598
Emp: 1,412

NAICS: 511210

SQUARE ENIX USA, INC.
6060 Center Dr., Ste. 100, Los Angeles, California 90045
CEO: Kumiko Hakushi
Bus: *Software manufacture.*

Tel: (310) 846-0400
Fax: (310) 846-0403

%FO: 100

• STAR MICRONICS COMPANY, LTD.
20-10, Nakayoshida, Shizuoka 422-8654, Japan
CEO: Toshihiro Suzuki, Pres. & CEO
Bus: *Mfr. of precision electronic equipment and machine tools.*

Tel: 81-54-263-1111
Fax: 81-54-263-1057
www.star-micronics.co.jp

Rev: $397
Emp: 5,100

NAICS: 333293, 333313, 334119, 532490

STAR CNC MACHINE TOOL CORP.
123 Powerhouse Rd., PO Box 9, Roslyn Heights, New York 11577
CEO: Noriaki Okamoto, Pres.
Bus: *Industrial machinery & equipment*

Tel: (516) 484-0500
Fax: (516) 484-5820

Emp: 42

STAR MICRONICS AMERICA INC
1150 King Georges Post Rd., Edison, New Jersey 08837
CEO: Masashi Funasho, Pres.
Bus: *Mfr./sales of precision electronic equipment and machine tools.*

Tel: (732) 623-5500
Fax: (732) 623-5590

%FO: 100

• SUGINO MACHINE, LTD.
2410 Hongo, Uozu, Uozu 937-8511, Japan
CEO: Takara Sugino, Chmn.
Bus: *Mfr. machine tools and jet pumps.*

Tel: 81-765-24-5111
Fax: 81-765-24-5051
www.sugino.com

Emp: 750

NAICS: 333319, 336312

SUGINO CORP USA
6220 Blue Ridge Cutoff, Ste. 311, Kansas City, Missouri 64133-3700
CEO: Tom Wilson
Bus: *Machine tools, pumps and cutting systems.*

Tel: (816) 737-3797
Fax: (816) 737-3793

%FO: 100

SUGINO CORP USA
29700 Harper Ave. Ste. B, St. Clair Shores, Michigan 48082
CEO: Matt Savage
Bus: *Machine tools, pumps and cutting systems.*

Tel: (586) 415-8100
Fax: (586) 415-8103

%FO: 100

SUGINO CORP USA
8 Main St., Ste. 3, Westfield, Massachusetts 01085
CEO: Rich DeForge   Tel: (413) 568-9640   %FO: 100
Bus: *Machine tools, pumps and cutting systems.*   Fax: (413) 568-6092

SUGINO CORP USA
18525 Statesville Rd., Ste. D02, Cornelius, North Carolina 28031
CEO: Tom Wilson   Tel: (704) 655-0995   %FO: 100
Bus: *Machine tools, pumps and cutting systems.*   Fax: (704) 655-0995

SUGINO CORP USA
1380 Hamilton Pkwy., Itasca, Illinois 60143
CEO: John Fischer, Pres.   Tel: (630) 250-8585   %FO: 100
Bus: *Machine tools, pumps and cutting systems.*   Fax: (630) 250-8665   Emp: 30

● **SUMIKIN BUSSAN CORPORATION (DIV. SUMITOMO GROUP)**
6-2, Hommachi, 3-chome, Chuo-ku, Osaka 541-8544, Japan
CEO: Eiichi Euda, Pres. & CEO   Tel: 81-6-6244-8001   Rev: $8,450
Bus: *Mfr. textiles, iron, steel and industrial supplies.*   Fax: 81-6-6244-8009   Emp: 3,550
                                           www.sumibinbussan.co.jp.
  NAICS: 331221, 331222, 423510, 424410, 424480, 424490

  SUMIKIN BUSSAN INTERNATIONAL CORPORATION
  162 Fifth Ave., Ste. 902, New York, New York 10010
  CEO: Tetsuji Nishikawa   Tel: (212) 645-0009   %FO: 100
  Bus: *Sales/distribution of iron and steel*   Fax: (212) 645-0880
       products.

  SUMIKIN BUSSAN INTL CORP.
  1305 Wiley Rd., Ste. 130, Schaumburg, Illinois 60173
  CEO: Hiroyuki Takeda, Pres.   Tel: (847) 882-6300   %FO: 100
  Bus: *Sale of machinery, frozen packaged meats*   Fax: (847) 882-3725   Emp: 25
       & seafood. Mfr. of steel & non-ferrous metal
       products.

  SUMIKIN BUSSAN INTL CORP.
  18 Technology Dr., Ste. 144, Irvine, California 92618
  CEO: Tsuneaki Eguchi, Pres.   Tel: (949) 387-8100   %FO: 100
  Bus: *Sale of fabrics.*   Fax: (949) 387-8181

  SUMIKIN BUSSAN INTL CORP.
  1300 Remington Rd., Unit K, Schaumberg, Illinois 60173
  CEO: Jimmy Sugiguchi, Mgr.   Tel: (847) 882-9600   %FO: 100
  Bus: *Mfr. of steel & cold aluminum.*   Fax: (847) 882-9800

● **SUMITOMO BAKELITE COMPANY, LTD.**
Tennozu Parkside Bldg., 2-5-8, Higashishinagawa, Shinagawa-Ku,, Tokyo 104-0002, Japan
CEO: Tomitaro Ogawa, Pres.   Tel: 81-3-5462-4111   Rev: $992
Bus: *Mfr. chemical and plastic products.*   Fax: 81-3-5462-4873   Emp: 7,849
                                           www.sumibe.co.jp
  NAICS: 325199, 326199

DUREZ CORP.
14131 Midway Rd., Ste. 500, Addison, Texas 75001
CEO: John W. Fisher, CEO
Bus: *Mfr. of phenol resins & molding compounds.*
Tel: (972) 763-2800
Fax:
%FO: 100
Emp: 380

PROMERUS LLC
9921 Brecksville Rd., Brecksville, Ohio 44141
CEO: Malcolm Miles, COO
Bus: *Research & development.*
Tel: (440) 992-0300
Fax: (440) 922-0594
%FO: 100
Emp: 52

SUMITOMO PLASTICS AMERICA INC.
900 Lafayette St., Ste. 510, Santa Clara, California 95050
CEO: Hideaki Ezaki, Pres.
Bus: *Mfr./sale chemical and plastic products.*
Tel: (408) 243-8402
Fax: (408) 243-8405
%FO: 100
Emp: 398

VYNCOLIT NORTH AMERICA, INC.
24 Mill St., Manchester, Connecticut 06040
CEO: Henry Van Dijk, Pres.
Bus: *Mfr. of plastic composites.*
Tel: (860) 646-5500
Fax:
%FO: 100
Emp: 133

● **SUMITOMO CHEMICAL COMPANY, LTD.**
27-1, Shinkawa, 2-chome, Chuo-ku, Tokyo 104-8260, Japan
CEO: Hiromasa Yonekura, Pres.
Bus: *Mfr. industrial chemicals, fertilizers, fine chemicals, agrochemicals, and pharmaceuticals.*
Tel: 81-3-5543-5102
Fax: 81-3-5543-5901
www.sumitomo-chem.co.jp
Rev: $10,965
Emp: 19,036
NAICS: 221119, 325110, 325120, 325131, 325132, 325181, 325182, 325188, 325191, 325192, 325193, 325199, 325211, 325212, 325221, 325222, 325311, 325312, 325320, 325411, 325412, 325414, 325520, 325612, 325613, 325910

SUMITOMO CHEMICAL AMERICA INC
10077 Grogan's Mill Rd., Ste. 125, The Woodlands, Texas 77380
CEO: Simon Sellers
Bus: *Distribution/sales/service of specialty chemicals.*
Tel: (281) 298-7779
Fax: (281) 362-4103
%FO: 100

SUMITOMO CHEMICAL AMERICA INC
335 Madison Ave., Ste. 830, New York, New York 10017
CEO: Tetsu Wakabayashi, Pres.
Bus: *Distribution/sales/service of specialty chemicals.*
Tel: (212) 572-8200
Fax: (212) 572-8234
%FO: 100
Emp: 22

● **SUMITOMO CORPORATION**
1-8-11, Harumi, Chuo-ku, Tokyo 104-8610, Japan
CEO: Kenji Miyahara, Chmn.
Bus: *Worldwide trading group; administrative services.*
Tel: 81-3-5166-5000
Fax: 81-3-5166-6292
www.sumitomocorp.co.jp
Rev: $16,174
Emp: 33,799
NAICS: 221121, 311111, 311119, 321113, 327310, 327320, 332322, 333120, 333131, 423510, 424410, 424690, 424710, 441110, 515210, 522210, 532411

SUMITOMO CORPORATION OF AMERICA
600 Third Ave., New York, New York 10016
CEO: Atsushi Nishijo, Gen. Mgr.
Bus: *Trading and investment services.*
Tel: (212) 207-0700
Fax: (212) 207-0456
%FO: 100
Emp: 500

- **SUMITOMO ELECTRIC INDUSTRIES, INC.**
  5-33, Kitahama, 4-chome, Chuo-ku, Osaka 541-0041, Japan
  CEO: Norio Okayama, Chmn. & CEO   Tel: 81-6-6220-4141   Rev: $14,600
  Bus: *Mfr. electrical wire and cable, telecommunications*   Fax: 81-6-6222-3380   Emp: 87,415
       cable, specialty steel wire and automotive parts.   www.sei.co.jp
  NAICS: 331222, 331422, 331491, 332618, 335921, 335929, 336322, 423610

  EUDYNA DEVICES INC.
  2355 Zanker Rd., San Jose, California 95131
  CEO: Warren Gould   Tel: (408) 232-9500
  Bus: *Semiconductors.*   Fax: (408) 428-9111

  JUDD WIRE
  124 Turnpike Rd., Turner Falls, Massachusetts 01376
  CEO: Hidetoshi Kinuta, Pres.   Tel: (413) 863-4357   %FO: 100
  Bus: *Mfr. and sales of electronic wires*   Fax: Emp: 300

  SUMITOMO ELECTRIC LIGHTWAVE
  78 Alexander Dr., Research Triangle Park, North Carolina 27709
  CEO: Hiroaki Horima, CEO   Tel: (919) 514-8100   %FO: 100
  Bus: *Mfr. of optical fiber cable, ribbon-configured*   Fax: (919) 514-8100   Emp: 175
       network solutions, interconnect
       assemblies, fusion splicers.

  SUMITOMO ELECTRIC USA INC
  21221 S. Western Ave., Ste. 200, Torrance, California 90501
  CEO: Kawaguchi Teruaki, Gen. Mgr.   Tel: (310) 782-0227   %FO: 100
  Bus: *Sale semi conducting material, new material,*   Fax: (310) 782-0211
       optical fiber cable.

  SUMITOMO ELECTRIC USA, INC.
  One North Lexington Ave., White Plains, New York 10601
  CEO: Koji Shibata, Pres.   Tel: (914) 467-6001   %FO: 100
  Bus: *Sale semi conducting material, new material,*   Fax: (914) 467-6081   Emp: 370
       optical fiber cable.

  SUMITOMO ELECTRIC WINTEC AMERICA, INC.
  909 Industrial Dr., Edmonton, Kentucky 42129
  CEO: Masahara Kurata, Pres. & CEO   Tel: (502) 432-2233   %FO: JV
  Bus: *Mfr. Wire & electric cable*   Fax: (502) 432-2838

  SUMITOMO ELECTRIC WIRING SYSTEMS, INC.
  1018 Ashley St., PO Box 90031, Bowling Green, Kentucky 42103
  CEO: Moasayoshi Matsumoto, Chmn.   Tel: (270) 782-7397   %FO: 100
  Bus: *Mfr. wiring harnesses for automobiles.*   Fax: (270) 796-3063   Emp: 1,500

- **SUMITOMO FORESTRY CO., LTD.**
  Marunouchi Trust Tower Bldg. N.,, 1-8-1 Marunouchi, Chiyoda-ku, Tokyo 100-8270, Japan
  CEO: Ryu Yano, Pres. & CEO   Tel: 81-3-6730-3500   Rev: $6,724
  Bus: *Engaged in the import/sales of timber and*   Fax: 81-3-5322-6800   Emp: 12,858
       construction and marketing of custom built   www.sfc.co.jp
  NAICS: 236115, 236116, 236117, 236118, 321211, 321212, 541320

PACIFIC WOOD PRODUCTS LLC
16130 NE 85th St., Redmond, Washington 98052
CEO: Michael Goderich, member
Bus: *Wood products.*
Tel: (425) 885-1777
Fax:
%FO: 100
Emp: 4

SUMITOMO FORESTRY INC.
1000 Second Ave., Ste. 1220, Seattle, Washington 98104
CEO: Rita Muto, Pres.
Bus: *Engaged in exporting lumber.*
Tel: (206) 623-8840
Fax: (206) 345-0391
%FO: 100
Emp: 7

● **SUMITOMO HEAVY INDUSTRIES, LTD.**
9-11, Kita-Shinagawa, 5-chome, Shinagawa-ku, Tokyo 141-8686, Japan
CEO: Yoshio Hinoh, Pres. & CEO
Bus: *Mfr. industrial machineries, ships, bridges, defense systems, environmental systems and power transmissions.*
Tel: 81-3-5488-8336
Fax: 81-3-5488-8056
www.shi.co.jp/english/index.html
Rev: $4,570
Emp: 11,149
NAICS: 236210, 237310, 333120, 333921, 336611

    SUMITOMO HEAVY INDUSTRIES (USA) INC.
    666 Fifth Ave., 10/F, New York, New York 10103
    CEO: Seiichi Hasegawa, Pres.
    Bus: *Mfr. & sales of transmissions equipment & speed reducers.*
    Tel: (212) 459-2477
    Fax: (212) 459-2490
    %FO: 100

● **SUMITOMO METAL INDUSTRIES, LTD.**
5-33, Kitahama, 4-chome, Chou-ku, Osaka 541-0041, Japan
CEO: Hiroshi Shimozuma, Pres. & CEO
Bus: *Mfr. steel product; steel mill technology.*
Tel: 81-6-6220-5111
Fax: 81-6-6223-0305
www.sumitomometals.co.jp
Rev: $10,610
Emp: 24,744
NAICS: 331111, 331210, 331221

    SEYMOUR TUBING, INC.
    1515 E. 4th St. Rd., Seymour, Indiana 47274
    CEO: Y. Shirakawa, Pres.
    Bus: *Steel production*
    Tel: (812) 523-3638
    Fax: (812) 523-3648

    SUMIKIN BUSSAN INTERNATIONAL
    1305 Wiley Rd., Ste. 130, Schaumburg, Illinois 60173
    CEO: Hiroyuki Takeda, Pres.
    Bus: *Non-ferrous metal production*
    Tel: (847) 882-3643
    Fax:
    Emp: 25

    SUMITOMO METAL USA CORP
    900 4th Ave., Ste. 3950, Seattle, Washington 98164
    CEO: Ryoichi Suvuki, Pres.
    Bus: *Metal mining*
    Tel: (206) 405-2800
    Fax:

    SUMITOMO METAL USA CORPORATION
    8750 West Bryn Mawr Ave., Chicago, Illinois 60631-3508
    CEO: Seiichi Kawase, VP
    Bus: *Mfr. steel product; steel mill technology.*
    Tel: (773) 714-8130
    Fax: (773) 714-8183
    %FO: 100
    Emp: 12

- **SUMITOMO METAL MINING COMPANY, LTD.**
  5-11-3, Shinbashi, Minato-ku, Tokyo 105-8716, Japan
  CEO: Koichi Fukushima, Pres.   Tel: 81-3-3436-7701   Rev: $3,807
  Bus: *Engaged in mining and smelting, electronics and*   Fax: 81-3-3434-2215   Emp: 8,187
       metal fabrication.   www.smm.co.jp
  NAICS: 212221, 212222, 212231, 212234, 212299, 331421

  SMM USA, INC.
  4055 Calle Platino, Oceanside, California 92056
  CEO: Yoshi Yuki Tanaka, Pres.   Tel: (760) 941-4500   %FO: 100
  Bus: *Produces television frames.*   Fax: (760) 941-0900   Emp: 165

  SUMITOMO METAL MINING ARIZONA INC.
  900 4th Ave., Ste. 3950, Seattle, Washington 98164
  CEO: Ryoisihi Sufuki, Pres.   Tel: (206) 405-2800   %FO: 100
  Bus: *Engineering services.*   Fax: (206) 405-2814

  SUMITOMO METAL MINING USA INC.
  900 4th Ave., Ste. 3950, Seattle, Washington 98164
  CEO: Ryoichi Sufuki, Pres.   Tel: (206) 405-2800   %FO: 100
  Bus: *Produces television frames.*   Fax: (206) 405-2814   Emp: 8

- **SUMITOMO MITSUBISHI SILICON CORPORATION (SUMCO)**
  1-2-1 Shibaura, Minato-ku, Tokyo 105-8634, Japan
  CEO: Reijiro Mori, Pres.   Tel: 81-3-5444-0808
  Bus: *Mfr. silicon wafers used in the production of*   Fax: 81-3-5444-0809
       semiconductors.   www.sumcosi.com
  NAICS:

  SUMCO USA CORPORATION
  49090 Milmont Dr., Fremont, California 94538
  CEO: Janet Clark   Tel: (510) 440-7485   %FO: 100
  Bus: *Semiconductor manufacture.*   Fax: (510) 656-4200

  SUMCO USA CORPORATION
  19801 North Tatum Blvd., Phoenix, Arizona 85050
  CEO: Yasuo Tsujigo   Tel: (480) 473-6000   %FO: 100
  Bus: *Semiconductor manufacture.*   Fax: (480) 473-6100

  SUMCO USA CORPORATION
  1351 Tandem Ave. NE, Salem, Oregon 97303
  CEO: Janet Clark   Tel: (503) 371-0041   %FO: 100
  Bus: *Semiconductor manufacture.*   Fax: (503) 371-0406

- **SUMITOMO MITSUI FINANCIAL GROUP INC.**
  1-2, Yurakucho 1-chome, Chiyoda-ku, Tokyo 100-0006, Japan
  CEO: Masyuki Oku, Chmn. & Pres.   Tel: 81-3-5512-3411   Rev: $34,736
  Bus: *Commercial banking services.*   Fax: 81-3-5512-4429   Emp: 22,348
                                                   www.smfg.co.jp
  NAICS: 522110, 523110, 523130, 523140, 523920, 523930, 523991, 525920

SUMITOMO MITSUI BANKING CORPORATION
277 Park Ave., New York, New York 10172
CEO: Takao Umino   Tel: (212) 224-4000   %FO: 100
Bus: *International commercial banking services.*   Fax: (212) 593-9522

SUMITOMO MITSUI BANKING CORPORATION
777 S. Figueroa St., Ste. 2600, Los Angeles, California 90017
CEO: Toshishikiko Ogata   Tel: (213) 616-3000
Bus: *Commercial bank.*   Fax: (213) 623-6832

SUMITOMO MITSUI BANKING CORPORATION
515 South Figueroa St., Los Angeles, California 90071
CEO: Kazuo Gejo, Mgr.   Tel: (213) 489-6200   %FO: 100
Bus: *International commercial banking services.*   Fax: (213) 489-6254

SUMITOMO MITSUI BANKING CORPORATION
555 California St., Ste. 3350, San Francisco, California 94104
CEO: Takashi Sorida, Mgr.   Tel: (415) 616-3000
Bus: *Commercial bank.*   Fax: (415) 397-1475

● **SUMITOMO REALTY & DEVELOPMENT**
Shinjuku NS Bldg., 4-1, Nishi-Shinjuku, 2-chome, Shinjuku-ku, Tokyo 163-0820, Japan
CEO: Junji Takashima, Pres. & CEO   Tel: 81-3-3346-2342   Rev: $5,432
Bus: *Construction and development and leasing and*   Fax: 81-3-3346-1652   Emp: 6,937
managing office buildings.   www.sumitomo-rd.co.jp
NAICS: 236115, 236116, 236117, 236118, 236220, 237210, 531110, 531120, 531190, 531210, 531390

    SUMITOMO REALTY & DEVELOPMENT NY INC.
    805 Third Ave., 18/F, New York, New York 10022
    CEO: Tetsuya Fujita, Pres.   Tel: (212) 838-0401   %FO: 100
    Bus: *Engaged in development and leasing of*   Fax: (212) 838-0315
    office buildings.

● **SUMITOMO RUBBER INDUSTRIES LTD.**
3-6-9, Wakinohama-cho,, Chuo-ku, Kobe 651-0072, Japan
CEO: Mitsuaki Asai, Pres.   Tel: 81-78-265-3004   Rev: $4,564
Bus: *Mfr. rubber tires. (JV of Goodyear Tire & Rubber*   Fax: 81-78-265-3113   Emp: 15,034
Company).   www.srigroup.co.jp
NAICS: 325211, 326211, 326291, 339920

    FALKEN TIRE CORPORATION
    10404 6th St., Rancho Cucamonga, California 91730
    CEO: Hideo Honda, Pres. & COO   Tel: (909) 466-1116   %FO: 100
    Bus: *Mfr. of tires.*   Fax: (909) 466-1169

    GOODYEAR DUNLOP TIRES LTD.
    200 John James Audubon Pkwy., West Amherst, New York 14228
    CEO: James Galoppo, Chmn. & Pres.   Tel: (716) 639-5200   %FO: 100
    Bus: *Mfr. of tires.*   Fax: (716) 639-5017   Emp: 1,800

    SRIXON SPORTS USA
    1850 Beaver Ridge Circle, Norcross, Georgia 30071
    CEO: Shuhei Mimura, CEO   Tel: (770) 248-1991   %FO: 100
    Bus: *Sale of golf equipment.*   Fax: Emp: 50

THE GOODYEAR TIRE & RUBBER COMPANY
1144 East Market St., Akron, Ohio 44316
CEO: Robert Keegan, Chmn. & Pres. & CEO   Tel: (330) 796-2121   %FO: 100
Bus: *Mfr. of tires.*   Fax: (330) 796-2222   Emp: 84,000

TREADWAYS CORP.
2000 Campus Lane, East Norristown, Pennsylvania 19403
CEO: Dan G. Wire, CEO   Tel: (610) 615-8000   %FO: 100
Bus: *Mfr. of private-brand tires.*   Fax: (610) 615-8001   Emp: 182

● **THE SUMITOMO TRUST & BANKING CO., LTD.**
5-33, Kitahama, 4-chome, Chuo-ku, Osaka 540-8639, Japan
CEO: Yutaka Morita, Pres. & CEO   Tel: 81-6-6220-2121   Rev: $4,792
Bus: *Commercial banking services.*   Fax: 81-6-6220-2043   Emp: 4,843
                                                 www.sumitomotrust.co.jp
  NAICS: 522110, 523920, 523991, 525910, 525920
     SUMITOMO TRUST & BANKING CO USA
     111 River St., Hoboken, New Jersey 07030
     CEO: Takahiro Nomoto, Chmn.   Tel: (201) 420-9470   %FO: 100
     Bus: *Securities lending operations.*   Fax: Emp: 112

     SUMITOMO TRUST & BANKING COMPANY, USA
     527 Madison Ave., 4/F, New York, New York 10022
     CEO: Yutaka Morita   Tel: (212) 326-0600   %FO: 100
     Bus: *Commercial banking.*   Fax: (212) 644-3025

     SUMITOMO TRUST & BANKING COMPANY, USA
     10 South Wacker Dr., Ste. 2975, Chicago, Illinois 60606-7496
     CEO: Naoya Takeuchi, Mgr.   Tel: (312) 993-3400   %FO: 100
     Bus: *Commercial banking.*   Fax:

     SUMITOMO TRUST & BANKING COMPANY, USA
     777 S. Figueroa St., Los Angeles, California 90017-5800
     CEO: Toshishikiko Ogata   Tel: (213) 955-0800   %FO: 100
     Bus: *Commercial banking.*   Fax: (213) 955-0800

● **SUNTORY GROUP**
Dojimahama 2-1-40, Kita-ku, Osaka 530-8203, Japan
CEO: Nobutada Saji, Pres.   Tel: 81-6-6346-1131   Rev: $10,870
Bus: *Produces wine, liquors, malt beverages and* Fax: 81-6-6345-1169   Emp: 4,870
      specialty foods.   www.suntory.com
  NAICS: 115210, 311421, 311920, 311930, 311941, 311999, 312111, 312112, 312120, 312130, 312140, 325411,
  325412, 325414, 334111, 339920, 511120,
            511210, 531120, 531190, 531312, 541710, 713910, 721110, 722211, 722310
     DS WATER OF AMERICA
     5660 New Northside Dr., Atlanta, Georgia 30328
     CEO: William A. Holl, CEO   Tel: (770) 933-1400
     Bus: *Water & ice*   Fax: (770) 956-9495   Emp: 5,500

     PEPSI BOTTLING VENTURES, LLC
     4700 Homewood Ct., Ste. 200, Raleigh, North Carolina 27609
     CEO: Keith Reimer, Pres. & CEO   Tel: (919) 865-2300
     Bus: *Bottling & distribution of Pepsi-Cola* Fax: (919) 783-6925

RESTAURANT SUNTORY
2233 Kalakaua Ave., Ste. 307, Honolulu, Hawaii 96815
CEO: Masaru Uchida
Bus: *Japanese restaurant*
Tel: (808) 922-5511
Fax:
Emp: 55

SUNTORY INTERNATIONAL
1211 Ave of Americas, New York, New York 10036
CEO: Dave Hiroto, Pres.
Bus: *Sale of liquors, soft drink & bottled water*
Tel: (212) 836-3900
Fax:
Emp: 4,800

SUNTORY INTERNATIONAL
7 Times Square, 21/F, New York, New York 10036
CEO: Dave Y. Fukuyama
Bus: *Imports & markets Suntory products*
Tel: (212) 891-6600
Fax:

SUNTORY INTL CORPORATION
12 E. 49th St., 29/F, New York, New York 10017
CEO: Dave Y. Fukuyama, Pres. & CEO
Bus: *Wines, liquors, malt beverages and bottled water.*
Tel: (212) 836-3900
Fax: (212) 891-6601
%FO: 100

• **SUZUKI MOTOR CORPORATION**
300, Takatsuka, Hamamatsu, Shizuoka 432-8611, Japan
CEO: Osamu Suzuki, Chmn. & CEO
Bus: *Mfr./sale automobiles and motorcycles.*
Tel: 81-53-440-2061
Fax: 81-53-440-2776
www.globalsuzuki.com
Rev: $20,816
Emp: 13,700

NAICS: 336111, 336112, 336991, 441110, 441221

AMERICAN SUZUKI MOTOR CORPORATION
3251 East Imperial Hwy., Brea, California 92821
CEO: Rick Suzuki, Pres.
Bus: *Mfr./sale automobiles and motorcycles.*
Tel: (714) 996-7040
Fax: (714) 524-8499
%FO: 100

• **SYSMEX CORPORATION**
1-5-1, Wakinohara-Kaigandori, Chuo-ku, Kobe, Hyogo 651-0073, Japan
CEO: Hisashi Ietsugu, Pres. & CEO
Bus: *Mfr./developer of diagnostic instruments and reagents.*
Tel: 81-78-265-0500
Fax: 81-78-303-5640
www.sysmex.co.jp
Rev: $344
Emp: 959

NAICS: 334510

SYSMEX CORPORATION OF AMERICA
1 Nelson C White Pkwy., Mundelein, Illinois 60060
CEO: Kazuya Obe, Chmn.
Bus: *Medical equipment manufacture and sales.*
Tel: (847) 996-4500
Fax: (847) 996-4559
%FO: 100
Emp: 175

SYSMEX REAGENTS AMERICA INC.
10716 Reagan St., Los Alamitos, California 90720
CEO: Mike Kanagawa, Pres.
Bus: *Chemical preparations manufacture.*
Tel: (562) 799-4001
Fax:
%FO: 100
Emp: 17

- **TABUCHI ELECTRIC COMPANY, LTD.**
  12-20,Mitejima 1-chome, Nishiyodogawa-ku, Osaka 555-0012, Japan
  CEO: Teruhisa Tabuchi, Chmn.
  Bus: *Mfr. electronic components.*

  Tel: 81-6-6475-5111
  Fax: 81-6-6475-5136
  www.zbr.co.jp

  Rev: $127
  Emp: 4,402

  NAICS: 334419, 335311

  TABUCHI ELECTRIC COMPANY OF AMERICA
  65 Germantown Ct., Ste. 107, Cordova, Tennessee 38018
  CEO: Kaihoshi Toshihiro, Pres.
  Bus: *Mfr./sale electronic components.*

  Tel: (901) 757-2300
  Fax: (901) 757-1001

  %FO: 100

- **TAIHEIYO CEMENT CORPORATION**
  8-1, Akashi-cho, Chuo-ku, Tokyo 104-8518, Japan
  CEO: Fumio Sameshima, Pres.
  Bus: *Mfr. cement and cement products.*

  Tel: 81-3-5214-1520
  Fax: 81-3-5214-1707
  www.taiheiyo-cement.co.jp

  Rev: $8,325
  Emp: 22,206

  NAICS: 327310

  ARIZONA PORTLAND CEMENT
  2400 N. Central Ave., Ste. 308,, Phoenix, Arizona 85004
  CEO: Craig Starkey, Mgr.
  Bus: *Mfr. cement and cement products.*

  Tel: (602) 271-0069
  Fax: (602) 254-9027

  %FO: 100

  ARIZONA PORTLAND CEMENT
  11115 Casa Grande Hwy., Box 338, Rillito, Arizona 85654
  CEO: Dave Bittel, mgr
  Bus: *Mfr. cement and cement products.*

  Tel: (520) 682-2221
  Fax: (520) 682-4345

  %FO: 100

  CALIFORNIA PORTLAND CEMENT
  2025 East Financial Way, Glendora, California 91741
  CEO: James A. Repman, Pres.
  Bus: *Mfr. cement and cement products.*

  Tel: (626) 852-6200
  Fax: (626) 852-6217

  %FO: 100

  CALIFORNIA PORTLAND CEMENT
  695 S. Rancho Ave, Colton, California 92324
  CEO: Mike Robertson, mgr
  Bus: *Mfr. cement and cement products.*

  Tel: (909) 825-4260
  Fax: (909) 370-3306

  %FO: 100

  CALIFORNIA PORTLAND CEMENT
  9350 Oak Creek Rd., Mojave, California 93502
  CEO: Bruce Shafer, mgr
  Bus: *Mfr. cement and cement products.*

  Tel: (661) 824-2401
  Fax: (661) 824-4908

  %FO: 100

  CPC TRANSFER TERMINAL
  4928 Donovan Way, North Las Vegas, California 89081
  CEO: Jamie Padilla
  Bus: *Transfer terminal cement services.*

  Tel: (702) 632-0126
  Fax: (702) 632-0126

  %FO: 100

  CPC TRANSFER TERMINAL
  2201 W. Washington St., Stockton, California 95203
  CEO: Warren Burchett
  Bus: *Transfer terminal cement services.*

  Tel: (209) 469-0109
  Fax: (209) 469-0145

  %FO: 100

CPC TRANSFER TERMINAL
Berth 191, 401 Canal St., Wilmington, California 90748
CEO: Pete Bulthuis   Tel: (310) 835-5370   %FO: 100
Bus: *Transfer terminal cement services.*   Fax: (310) 830-3658

● **TAISEI CORPORATION**
25-1 Nishi-Shinjuku, Shinjuku-ku, Tokyo 163-0606, Japan
CEO: Osamu Hirashima, Chmn.   Tel: 81-3-3348-1111   Rev: $15,132
Bus: *Construction and civil engineering*   Fax: 81-3-3345-1386   Emp: 9,748
                                             www.taisei.co.jp
NAICS: 236210, 236220, 237310, 237990

    TAISEI CONSTRUCTION CORP.
    6261 Katella Ave., Ste. 200, Cypress, California 90630
    CEO: Kunihiko Nambu, Gen. Mgr.   Tel: (714) 886-1530   %FO: 100
    Bus: *Construction and civil engineering*   Fax: (714) 886-1546

    TAISEI CONSTRUCTION CORP.
    680 Iwilei Rd., Ste. 670, Honolulu, Hawaii 96817
    CEO: Kunihiko Nambu, Gen. Mgr.   Tel: (808) 536-6701   %FO: 100
    Bus: *Construction and civil engineering*   Fax: (808) 536-6771

● **TAISHO PHARMACEUTICAL CO., LTD.**
24-1, Takada 3-chome, Toshima-ku, Tokyo 170-8633, Japan
CEO: Akira Uehara, Chmn.   Tel: 81-3-3985-1111   Rev: $2,711
Bus: *Mfr./market pharmaceutical products and*   Fax: 81-3-3985-6485   Emp: 5,477
prescription drugs.   www.taisho.co.jp
NAICS: 325411, 325412

    TAISHO PHARMACEUTICAL R&D INC.
    350 Mount Kemble Ave., Morristown, New Jersey 07960-6646
    CEO: Junichi Fukudome   Tel: (973) 285-0870   %FO: 100
    Bus: *Pharmaceutical research and development.* Fax: (973) 285-1665

    TIASHO PHARMACEUTICALS CALIFORNIA INC.
    3878 Carson St., Ste. 216, Torrance, California 90503
    CEO: Jun Kuroda   Tel: (310) 543-2035   %FO: 100
    Bus: *Sales/distribution of pharmaceutical*   Fax: (310) 543-9636
    products.

● **TAIYO NIPPON SANSO CORPORATION**
16-7, Nishi-Shinbashi, 1-chome, Minato-ku, Tokyo 105-8442, Japan
CEO: Hiroshi Taguchi, Pres.   Tel: 81-3-3581-8200   Rev: $2,180
Bus: *Mfr. industrial gases and industrial gas equipment.* Fax: 81-3-3581-8755   Emp: 1,745
                                                         www.sanso.co.jp
NAICS: 325120, 333132

    MATHESON TRI-GAS, INC.
    621 NE 5th Terrace, Crystal River, Florida 34428
    CEO: Richard Good   Tel: (352) 563-1200   %FO: 100
    Bus: *Industrial gas manufacture.*   Fax: (352) 563-0371

MATHESON TRI-GAS, INC.
959 Route 46 East, Parsippany, New Jersey 07054-0624
CEO: James Samples, Pres.   Tel: (973) 257-1100   %FO: 100
Bus: *Industrial gas manufacture.*   Fax: (973) 257-9268

MATHESON TRI-GAS, INC.
625 Wool Creek Dr., San Jose, California 95112
CEO: Stefano Mangano   Tel: (408) 971-6500   %FO: 100
Bus: *Industrial gas manufacture.*   Fax: (408) 275-8643

MATHESON TRI-GAS, INC.
166 Keystone Dr., Montgomeryville, Pennsylvania 18936
CEO: Beth Sullivan   Tel: (215) 648-4026   %FO: 100
Bus: *Industrial gas manufacture.*   Fax: (215) 641-2714

MATHESON TRI-GAS, INC.
6775 Central Ave., Newark, California 94560
CEO: Rob Peetz   Tel: (510) 793-2559   %FO: 100
Bus: *Industrial gas manufacture.*   Fax: (510) 790-6241

MATHESON TRI-GAS, INC.
959 Rte. 46 East, Parsippany, New Jersey 07054-0624
CEO: James Samples, Pres. & COO   Tel: (973) 257-1100   %FO: 100
Bus: *Manufacturer of industrial gases and*   Fax: (973) 257-9393   Emp: 1,000
     related equipment

MATHESON TRI-GAS, INC.
161 Corporate Center, 6225 N. State Hwy 161, Ste. 200, Irving, Texas 75038
CEO: James Samples   Tel: (972) 870-7000   %FO: 100
Bus: *Manufacturer of industrial gases and*   Fax: (972) 870-0992
     related equipment

MATHESON TRI-GAS, INC.
625 Wool Creek Dr., San Jose, California 95112
CEO: Stefano Mangano   Tel: (408) 971-6500   %FO: 100
Bus: *Manufacturer of semiconductor gas related* Fax: (408) 275-8643
     equipment

MATHESON TRI-GAS, INC.
6775 Central Ave., Newark, California 94560
CEO: Rob Peetz   Tel: (510) 793-2559   %FO: 100
Bus: *Manufacturer of specialty gases*   Fax: (510) 790-6241

MATHESON TRI-GAS, INC.
2200 Houston Ave., Houston, Texas 77007
CEO: Scott Kallman   Tel: (713) 869-7351   %FO: 100
Bus: *Manufacturer of specialty gases*   Fax: (713) 869-0994

MATHESON TRI-GAS, INC.
166 Keystone Dr., Montgomeryville, Pennsylvania 18936
CEO: James Samples   Tel: (215) 641-2700   %FO: 100
Bus: *Manufacturer of specialty gases.*   Fax: (215) 619-0458

MATHESON TRI-GAS, INC.
2550 Dryhole Dr., Kyle, Texas 78640
CEO: Beverly Spencer   Tel: (512) 262-2129   %FO: 100
Bus: *Manufacturer of electronic gases*   Fax: (512) 262-4011

● **TAIYO YUDEN CO., LTD.**
6-16-20 Ueno, Taito-ku, Tokyo 110-0005, Japan
CEO: Tomiji Kobayashi, Pres. & CEO   Tel: 81-3-3833-5441   Rev: $1,546
Bus: *Mfr. electronics.*   Fax: 81-3-3835-4754   Emp: 17,194
                                               www.yuden.co.jp
NAICS: 334413, 334414, 334415

TAIYO YUDEN USA INC.
1320 Greenway Dr., Ste. 755, Irving, Texas 75038
CEO: Roy Bronder, Mgr.   Tel: (972) 870-0515   %FO: 100
Bus: *Mfr./sales electronics.*   Fax: (972) 870-1055

TAIYO YUDEN USA INC.
4020 West Chase Blvd., Ste. 390, Raleigh, North Carolina 27607
CEO: Akio Iida, VP   Tel: (919) 838-1875   %FO: 100
Bus: *Mfr./sales electronics.*   Fax: (919) 834-2616

TAIYO YUDEN USA INC.
2107 N. First St., Ste. 370, San Jose, California 95131
CEO: Akio Iida, VP   Tel: (408) 573-4150   %FO: 100
Bus: *Mfr./sales electronics.*   Fax: (408) 573-4159

TAIYO YUDEN USA INC.
1770 La Costa Meadows Dr., San Marcos, California 92078
CEO: Akio Iida, Treasurer   Tel: (760) 510-3200   %FO: 100
Bus: *Mfr./sales electronics.*   Fax: (760) 471-4021   Emp: 290

TAIYO YUDEN USA INC.
1930 North Thoreau Dr., Ste. 190, Schaumburg, Illinois 60173
CEO: Akio Iida, VP   Tel: (847) 925-0888   %FO: 100
Bus: *Mfr./sales electronics.*   Fax: (847) 925-0899   Emp: 125

TRDA INC.
10180 Telesis Ct., Ste. 120, San Diego, California 92121
CEO: Shoichi Sekiguchi, Pres.   Tel: (858) 554-0755   %FO: 100
Bus: *Mfr./sales electronics.*   Fax: (858) 455-7578   Emp: 21

● **TAKARA HOLDINGS INC.**
20 Naginatahoko-cho, Shijo-dori Karasuma, Higashi-iru,Shimogyo-ku, Kyoto 600-8688, Japan
CEO: Hisashi Ohmiya, Pres.   Tel: 81-75-241-5130   Rev: $1,864
Bus: *Mfr./import wines and liquors.*   Fax: 81-75-241-5185   Emp: 2,044
                                               www.takara.co.jp
NAICS: 312140, 325411, 325412, 325414, 541710, 541810, 541830, 541840, 621511

AGE INTERNATIONAL, INC.
229 W. Main St., Ste. 202, Frankfort, Kentucky 40602
CEO: Kazuhiro Kanauchi, Pres.   Tel: (502) 223-9874
Bus: *Sale of alcoholic beverages.*   Fax: (502) 223-9877   Emp: 5

TAKARA MIRUS BIO INC.
505 S. Rosa Rd., Ste. 101, Madison, Wisconsin 53719
CEO: Terry Sivesind, Gen. Mgr.   Tel: (608) 441-2844
Bus: *Sale of research reagents.*   Fax: (604) 441-2845   Emp: 10

TAKARA SAKE USA, INC.
708 Addison St., Berkeley, California 94710
CEO: Kazuyoshi Ito, Pres. & CEO   Tel: (510) 540-8250   %FO: 100
Bus: *Mfr. sake and wines.*   Fax: (510) 486-8758

● **TAKASHIMAYA COMPANY, LIMITED**
5-5, Namba, 5-chome, Chuo-ku, Osaka 542-8510, Japan
CEO: Koji Suzuki, Pres. & CEO   Tel: 81-6-6631-1101   Rev: $10,205
Bus: *Department store and restaurant owner/operator,* Fax: 81-6-6631-9850   Emp: 12,417
    direct marketing and design consulting services. www.takashimaya.co.jp
  NAICS: 236210, 236220, 237310, 237990, 422110, 441310, 441320, 452111, 522210, 531120, 531190, 531312,
531390, 541613

    TAKASHIMAYA ENTERPRISES, INC.
    401 Old Country Rd., Carle Place, New York 11514
    CEO: Jiro Shinohara, Pres.   Tel: (516) 997-4770   %FO: 100
    Bus: *U.S. headquarters. Department store and* Fax: (516) 997-4772   Emp: 40
      restaurant owner/operator, direct marketing
      and design consulting services.

    TAKASHIMAYA NEW YORK, INC.
    693 Fifth Ave., New York, New York 10022
    CEO: Tadahiko Hatano, Pres.   Tel: (212) 350-0100   %FO: 100
    Bus: *Department store and restaurant* Fax: (212) 350-0542   Emp: 60
      owner/operator, direct marketing and design
      consulting services.

● **TAKATA CORPORATION**
25 Mori Bldg., 4-30, Roppongi, 1-chome, Minato-ku, Tokyo 106, Japan
CEO: J. Takada, Pres.   Tel: 81-3-582-3222
Bus: *Mfr. industrial hose, lubricants, seat belts and air* Fax: 81-3-505-3022   Emp: 6,000
    bags.   www.takata.co.jp
  NAICS: 326220, 336360, 336399

    TAKATA FABRICATION CORPORATION
    2500 Takata Dr., Auburn Hills, Michigan 48326
    CEO: Tom Storrs, Pres.   Tel: (248) 873-8040   %FO: JV
    Bus: *Mfr./distribution seat belts.* Fax: (248) 373-2897

    TAKATA PETRI INC.
    2223 Dove St., Port Huron, Michigan 48060
    CEO: Alex Konig   Tel: (810) 985-9010   %FO: JV
    Bus: *Mfr. auto steering wheels.* Fax: (810) 985-4308

    TAKATA RESTRAINT SYSTEMS
    422 Gallimore Dairy Rd., Greensboro, North Carolina 27409
    CEO: Bruce Thames   Tel: (336) 665-6276   %FO: JV
    Bus: *Mfr. airbag modules and controls.* Fax: (336) 665-6276

TAKATA RESTRAINT SYSTEMS
629 Green Valley Rd., Greensboro, North Carolina 27408
CEO: J. Franklin Roe
Bus: *Mfr./distribution seat belts.*
Tel: (336) 547-1600
Fax: (336) 547-1681
%FO: JV

TAKATA SEAT BELTS INC.
4611 Wiseman Blvd., San Antonio, Texas 78251
CEO: Toshi Shimizu
Bus: *Seat belt and fabricated textile manufacture.*
Tel: (210) 250-5000
Fax: (210) 250-5059
%FO: JV

● **TAKEDA PHARMACEUTICAL COMPANY LTD.**
1-1, Doshomachi, 4-chome, Chuo-ku, Osaka 540-8645, Japan
CEO: Kunio Takeda, Chmn. & CEO
Bus: *Pharmaceuticals, bulk vitamins, agricultural and environmental products, agricultural chemicals manufacturer.*
NAICS: 325320, 325411, 325520
Tel: 81-6-6204-2111
Fax: 81-6-6204-2880
www.takeda.com
Rev: $10,284
Emp: 14,592

TAKEDA AMERICA HOLDINGS, INC..
555 Madison Ave., New York, New York 10022
CEO: I. Noguchi
Bus: *Holding company.*
Tel: (212) 421-6954
Fax: (212) 355-5243
%FO: 100

TAKEDA PHARMACEUTICAL NORTH AMERICA, INC.
475 Half Day Rd., Ste. 500, Lincolnshire, Illinois 60069
CEO: Mark Booth, Pres. & CEO
Bus: *Pharmaceutical preparations*
Tel: (847) 383-3000
Fax: (847) 383-3050
%FO: 100
Emp: 1,100

TAKEDA RESEARCH INVESTMENT
435 Tasso St., Ste. 300, Palo Alto, California 94301
CEO: Dr. Koichi Kato, Pres.
Bus: *Research and pharmaceutical preparations.*
Tel: (650) 328-2900
Fax: (650) 328-2922
Emp: 4

TAP PHARMACEUTICAL PRODUCTS INC.
675 North Field Dr., Lake Forest, Illinois 60045
CEO: Alan MacKenzie, Pres.
Bus: *Pharmaceutical manufacturer*
Tel: (847) 582-2000
Fax: (800) 830-6936
Emp: 3,300

● **TAKENAKA CORPORATION**
1-13, Hommachi, 4-chome, Chuo-ku, Chuo-ku, Osaka 541-0053, Japan
CEO: Toichi Takenaka, Pres. & CEO
Bus: *Planners, architects, engineers and builders.*
NAICS: 236210, 236220, 541330
Tel: 81-6-6252-1201
Fax: 81-3-3545-9083
www.takenaka.co.jp
Rev: $9,547
Emp: 11,805

TAK DEVELOPMENT
145 West 57th St., New York, New York 10019
CEO: Kirti Desai
Bus: *Real Estate development.*
Tel: (212) 489-6001
Fax: (212) 489-6002
%FO: 100

TAK HAWAII
Tupa Financial Center, Fort St. Tower, 745 Fort St., Ste. 1608, Honolulu, Hawaii 96813
CEO: Yo Su Ke Maezawa, Pres.
Bus: *Real Estate development.*
Tel: (808) 523-5899
Fax: (808) 523-9082
%FO: 100
Emp: 3

TAKENAKA (USA) CORPORATION
555 Pierce Rd., Ste. 190, Itasca, Illinois 60143
CEO: Shiro Toyomasu, Pres.
Bus: *Architectural services.*

Tel: (630) 250-3400
Fax: (630) 250-3433

%FO: 100
Emp: 45

● **TAKEUCHI PRECISION WORKS CO.**
246-16, Egoshi, Kurosuno, Izumimachi, Iwaki City, Fukushima Prefecture 971-8184, Japan
CEO: Mitsuo Takeuchi, Pres.
Bus: *Production and Sales of Linear Guides.*

Tel: 81-246-56-5281
Fax: 81-246-56-5282
www.tsklmb.com

Rev: $100
Emp: 130

NAICS: 335999

TKS AMERICA INC..
9668 Inter Ocean Dr., Cincinnati, Ohio 45246
CEO: Takeshi Takeuchi, Pres.
Bus: *Production and Sales of Linear Guides.*

Tel: (513) 942-4002
Fax: (513) 942-4003

%FO: 100
Emp: 20

● **TAKISAWA MACHINE TOOL COMPANY, LTD.**
983 Natsukawa, Okayama 701-0164, Japan
CEO: Yasumasa Kondo, Pres.
Bus: *Mfr. machine tools.*

Tel: 81-86-293-6111
Fax: 81-86-293-5571
www.takisawa.co.jp

Rev: $72
Emp: 212

NAICS: 333512

TAKISAWA USA, INC.
1571 Barclay Blvd., Buffalo Grove, Illinois 60089
CEO: Takao Todoroki, Pres.
Bus: *Sale of machine tools.*

Tel: (847) 419-0046
Fax: (847) 419-0043

%FO: 100
Emp: 11

● **TAMRON COMPANY, LTD.**
1385 Hasunuma, Minuma-ku, Saitama 337-8556, Japan
CEO: Morio Ono, Pres. & CEO
Bus: *Mfr. photo/video lenses, optical components,*
Broncia medium format cameras.

Tel: 81-3-3916-0131
Fax: 81-3-3916-1860
www.tamron.co.jp

Emp: 1,200

NAICS: 333314

TAMRON USA, INC.
10 Austin Blvd., Commack, New York 11725
CEO: Bruce Landau, Pres.
Bus: *Distribution photo & CCTV lenses, optical*
components.

Tel: (631) 858-8400
Fax: (631) 543-3963

%FO: 100
Emp: 44

● **TDK CORPORATION**
1-13-1, Nihonbashi, Chuo-ku, Tokyo 103-8272, Japan
CEO: Hajime Sawabe, Pres. & CEO
Bus: *Mfr. electronic materials, components and*
recording media.

Tel: 81-3-5201-7102
Fax: 81-3-5201-7114
www.tdk.co.jp

Rev: $6,148
Emp: 36,804

NAICS: 334112, 334119, 334414, 334415, 334419, 334613, 511210

HEADWAY TECHNOLOGIES, INC.
678 S. Hillview Dr., Milpitas, California 95035
CEO: M.Y. Chang, Pres. & CEO
Bus: *Electronic components.*

Tel: (408) 934-5300
Fax: (408) 934-5353

%FO: 100

HUSKO, INC.
100 S. Milpitas Dr., Milpitas, California 95035
CEO: Paul Ting, VP
Bus: *Research & development, sales & marketing of MR heads.*
Tel: (408) 956-7100
Fax: (408) 956-7171
%FO: 100
Emp: 80

TDK COMPONENTS USA, INC.
1 TDK Blvd., Peachtree City, Georgia 30269
CEO: Kunio Sato, Pres.
Bus: *Mfr. / Sale of electronic components.*
Tel: (770) 631-0410
Fax: (770) 631-0425
%FO: 100

TDK CORPORATION OF AMERICA
1221 E Business Center Dr., Mt. Prospect, Illinois 60056
CEO: Frank Avant, Pres.
Bus: *Sale of electronic materials and components.*
Tel: (847) 803-6100
Fax: (847) 803-6296
%FO: 100
Emp: 250

TDK ELECTRONICS CORP.
3190 East Miraloma Ave., Anaheim, California 92806
CEO: Robert Dietz, Principal
Bus: *Mfr. of multimedia storage, audio & video products.*
Tel: (714) 238-7900
Fax: (714) 632-1868
%FO: 100

TDK FERRITES CORP.
5900 North Harrison St., Shawnee, Oklahoma 74804
CEO: Yoshiharu Nanami, Pres.
Bus: *Mfr. of ceramic magnets.*
Tel: (405) 275-2100
Fax: (405) 878-0574
%FO: 100
Emp: 200

TDK INNOVETA INC.
840 Central Pkwy. East, Ste. 150, Plano, Texas 75074
CEO: Victor Lee, CEO
Bus: *Research, development design, Mfr. & sale of DC-DC converters.*
Tel: (972) 398-6884
Fax: (972) 398-9945
%FO: 100

TDK ONLINE SERVICES CORPORATION
901 Franklin Ave., Garden City, New York 11530
CEO: Kenichi Aoshima, CEO
Bus: *Semiconductor manufacture and sales.*
Tel: (516) 535-2600
Fax: (516) 294-7860
%FO: 100
Emp: 1,698

TDK R & D CORPORATION
4645 East Cotton Center Blvd., Ste. 199, Phoenix, Arizona 85040
CEO: Shunjiro Saito, Pres.
Bus: *Research & development & design of electronic components.*
Tel: (602) 458-9000
Fax: (602) 458-9055
%FO: 100
Emp: 31

TDK RF SOLUTIONS INC.
1101 Cypress Creek Rd., Cedar Park, Texas 78613
CEO: Norio Sasaki, Pres.
Bus: *Design & Mfr. of test systems used for noise measurements.*
Tel: (512) 258-9478
Fax: (512) 258-0740
%FO: 100
Emp: 35

● **TEAC CORPORATION**
3-7-3, Naka-cho, Musashino-shi, Tokyo 180-8550, Japan
CEO: Yoshiaki Sakai, Pres.
Bus: *Mfr. computer disk drives, data instrumentation recorders and audio recorders.*
Tel: 81-4-2252-5000
Fax: 81-4-2252-8959
www.teac.co.jp
Rev: $1,115
Emp: 6,727
NAICS: 334112, 334119, 334310, 334613, 339992

MERLIN ENGINEERING
1888 Embarcadero Rd., Palo Alto, California 94303
CEO: David Husted, Pres.
Bus: *Medical imaging.*

Tel: (650) 856-0900
Fax: (650) 858-2302

%FO: 100
Emp: 16

TASCAM INC.
7733 Telegraph Rd., Montebello, California 90640
CEO: Jim Mack, Mgr.
Bus: *Audio recorders manufacturer.*

Tel: (323) 726-0303
Fax: (323) 727-7656

%FO: 100

TEAC AMERICA, INC.
7733 Telegraph Rd., Montebello, California 90640
CEO: Hajime Yamaguchi, Pres.
Bus: *Mfr. computer disk drives, data
       instrumentation recorders and audio
       recorders.*

Tel: (323) 726-0303
Fax: (323) 727-7656

%FO: 100

• **TEIJIN LTD.**
6-7, Minami-Honmachi, 1-chome, Chuo-ku, Osaka 541-8587, Japan
CEO: Toru Nagashima, Pres. & CEO
Bus: *Mfr. synthetic fibers, raw materials for chemicals,
       pharmaceuticals and medical products.*

Tel: 81-6-6268-2132
Fax: 81-6-6268-3205
www.teijin.co.jp

Rev: $8,279
Emp: 18,960

NAICS: 325211, 325221, 325222, 325412, 333292, 333993, 334510, 336413, 339112

    DUPONT
    1007 Market St., Wilmington, Delaware 19898
    CEO: Charles O. Holliday Jr., Chmn. & CEO
    Bus: *Mfr. of plastic & fiber.*

    Tel: (302) 774-1000
    Fax: (302) 999-4399

    Emp: 1,780

    TEIJIN AMERICA, INC.
    101 East St., 27/F, New York, New York 10022
    CEO: Toru Nagashima, Pres. & CEO
    Bus: *Mfr. of plastic & fiber.*

    Tel: (212) 308-8744
    Fax: (212) 308-8902

    %FO: 100
    Emp: 85

    TEIJIN AMERICA, INC.
    600 Alexander Park, Princeton, New Jersey 08540
    CEO: Dr. Koyama, Pres.
    Bus: *Commercial physical & biological research.*

    Tel: (609) 716-7636
    Fax: (609) 716-7636

    %FO: 100
    Emp: 17

• **N. I. TEIJIN SHOJI**
Teijin Bldg., 6-7 Minami-hommachi, 1-chome, Chou-ku, Osaka 541-8540, Japan
CEO: Junji Morita, Pres.
Bus: *Export textiles and raw materials.*

Tel: 81-6-6266-8011
Fax: 81-6-6244-1217
www2.ni-teijinshoji.co.jp

NAICS: 314999

    N. I. TEIJIN SHOJI USA, INC.
    110 East 9th St., Ste. B-641, Los Angeles, California 90079
    CEO: Taiki Sugimoto, Mgr.
    Bus: *Import/export textiles, yarns, fibers, sleep
          and sportswear.*

    Tel: (213) 244-9900
    Fax:

    %FO: 100

N. I. TEIJIN SHOJI USA, INC.
42 West 39th St., 6/F, New York, New York 10018
CEO: Hiroshi Okuda, Pres. Tel: (212) 840-6900 %FO: 100
Bus: *Import/export textiles, yarns, fibers, sleep* Fax: Emp: 35
  and sportswear.

● TERUMO CORPORATION
44-1 2, Chome Hatagaya, Shibuya-ku, Tokyo 151-0072, Japan
CEO: Takashi Wachi, Chmn. & CEO Tel: 81-3-3374-8111 Rev: $2,037
Bus: *Pharmaceuticals and hospital supplies* Fax: 81-3-3374-8399 Emp: 9,094
  www.terumo.co.jp
NAICS: 325412, 334510, 335999, 339111, 339112, 339113

TERUMO CARDIOVASCULAR SYSTEMS (TCVS)
California Factory, 1311 Valencia Ave., Tustin, California 92780
CEO: Joel Kruger, Principal Tel: (714) 258-8001 %FO: 100
Bus: *Mfr. pharmaceuticals and hospital supplies.* Fax: (714) 258-3106

TERUMO CARDIOVASCULAR SYSTEMS (TCVS)
Massachusetts Factory, 28 Howe St., Ashland, Massachusetts 01721
CEO: Fred Howery, Mgr. Tel: (508) 881-2250 %FO: 100
Bus: *Mfr. pharmaceuticals and hospital supplies.* Fax: (508) 881-4858

TERUMO CARDIOVASCULAR SYSTEMS (TCVS)
Maryland Factory, West Plant, 125 Blue Ball Rd., Elkton, Maryland 21921
CEO: Mark A. Sutter Tel: (410) 392-8500 %FO: 100
Bus: *Mfr. pharmaceuticals and hospital supplies.* Fax: (410) 392-7218

TERUMO CARDIOVASCULAR SYSTEMS, CORP.
6180 Jackson Rd., Ann Arbor, Michigan 48103
CEO: Mark A. Sutter Tel: (734) 663-4145
Bus: *Mfr. of surgical and medical instruments.* Fax: (734) 741-6250

TERUMO CARDIOVASCULAR SYSTEMS, CORP.
Corporate Office, 6200 Jackson Rd., Ann Arbor, Michigan 48103-9300
CEO: Mark A. Sutter, Pres. Tel: (734) 663-4145 %FO: 100
Bus: *Mfr. pharmaceuticals and hospital supplies.* Fax: (734) 741-6057 Emp: 650

TERUMO MEDICAL CORPORATION
Maryland Factory, East Plant, 950 Elkton Blvd., Elkton, Maryland 21921
CEO: Kurt Horney, Mgr. Tel: (410) 392-8500 %FO: 100
Bus: *Mfr. pharmaceuticals and hospital supplies.* Fax: (410) 392-7171

TERUMO MEDICAL CORPORATION
2101 Cottontail Lane, Somerset, New Jersey 08873
CEO: Shogo Ninomiya, Pres. & CEO Tel: (732) 302-4900 %FO: 100
Bus: *Mfr. pharmaceuticals and hospital supplies.* Fax: (732) 302-3083 Emp: 1,137

● TOA CORPORATION
5, Yonbancho, Chiyoda-ku, Tokyo 102-8451, Japan
CEO: Masao Watanabe, CEO Tel: 81-3-3262-5102 Rev: $1,980
Bus: *Marine and civil engineering projects.* Fax: 81-3-3262-9536 Emp: 2,558
  www.toa-const.co.jp
NAICS: 236210, 236220, 237310, 237990, 541310, 541330

TOA ELECTRONICS, INC.
601 Gateway Blvd., Ste. 300, South San Francisco, California 94080
CEO: Steve Mate, Mktg. Tel: (650) 588-2538 %FO: 100
Bus: *Development, manufacturing and distribution* Fax: (650) 588-3349 Emp: 1,500
of professional and commercial sound
products.

● **TOAGOSEI CO. LTD.**
1-14-1, Nishi-Shinbashi, Minato-ku, Tokyo 105-8419, Japan
CEO: Bunshiro Fukuzawa, Chmn. Tel: 81-3-3597-7215 Rev: $1,399
Bus: *Mfr. chemicals, industrial coatings and* Fax: 81-3-3597-7217 Emp: 2,597
www.toagosei.co.jp
NAICS: 325120, 325188, 325199, 325211, 325311, 325312, 325320, 325412, 325998

BORDEN-TOAGOSEI AMERICA
180 East Broad St., 13/F, Columbus, Ohio 43215
CEO: Ronald Kesselman, Mgr. Tel: (614) 225-4000 %FO: 100
Bus: *Mfr. chemicals, industrial coatings and* Fax: (614) 225-7680
adhesives.

TOAGOSEI AMERICA
1450 West Main St., West Jefferson, Ohio 43162
CEO: Akira Komine, Pres. Tel: (614) 718-3855 %FO: 100
Bus: *Mfr. chemicals, industrial coatings and* Fax: (614) 718-3866 Emp: 60
adhesives.

TOAGOSEI AMERICA
180 E. Broad St., 13/F, Columbus, Ohio 43215
CEO: Ronald Kesselman Tel: (614) 225-4000 %FO: 100
Bus: *Mfr. chemicals, industrial coatings,* Fax: (614) 225-4000
adhesives and Krazy Glue.

● **TODA CORPORATION**
1-7-1 Kyobashi, Chuo-ku, Tokyo 104-8388, Japan
CEO: Hisao Kato, Pres. & CEO Tel: 81-3-3535-1591 Rev: $4,716
Bus: *Construction and real estate development.* Fax: 81-3-3561-5745 Emp: 4,925
www.toda.co.jp
NAICS: 236220, 237990, 541330

TODA AMERICA, INC.
5816 Corporate Ave., Ste. 160, Cypress, California 90630
CEO: Akinori Nakagawa, Pres. Tel: (714) 220-3141 %FO: 100
Bus: *Engaged in construction and real estate* Fax: (714) 220-1360
development.

● **TOHO TENAX CO., LTD.**
2-38-16, Hongo, Bunkyo-ku, Tokyo 113-8404, Japan
CEO: Yoshikuni Utsunomiya, CEO Tel: 81-3-5842-3700 Rev: $324
Bus: *Carbon fiber products manufacture.* Fax: 81-3-5842-3709 Emp: 1,289
www.tohotenax.com
NAICS: 313111, 313210, 325211, 325221, 325222, 326150

TOHO TENAX AMERICA INC.
121 Cardiff Valley Rd., Rockwood, Tennessee 37854
CEO: Peter W. Oswald, VP
Bus: *Carbon fiber products manufacture.*
Tel: (865) 354-8408
Fax: (865) 354-8409
%FO: 100

TOHO TENAX AMERICA INC.
18552 MacArthur Blvd., Ste. 325, Irvine, California 92612
CEO: Tom Lemire, VP
Bus: *Carbon fiber products manufacture.*
Tel: (949) 474-3278
Fax: (949) 474-3274
%FO: 100

TOHO TENAX AMERICA INC.
613-407 Brawley School Rd., Ste. 230, Mooresville, North Carolina 28117
CEO: Steve Hoye, Sales Mgr.
Bus: *Carbon fiber products manufacture.*
Tel: (704) 662-3012
Fax: (704) 662-3022
%FO: 100

● **TOHOKU ELECTRIC POWER CO., INC.**
7-1, Honcho 1-chome, Aoba-ku, Sendai, Miyagi 980-8550, Japan
CEO: Keiichi Makuta, Pres.
Bus: *Engaged in telecommunication, natural gas and electricity.*
Tel: 81-22-225-2111
Fax: 81-22-225-2550
www.tohoku-epco.co.jp
Rev: $14,793
Emp: 18,638

NAICS: 221111, 221112, 221113, 221121, 221122, 221210, 236220, 237990, 424720, 454312, 454319, 517910, 541330

TOHOKU ELECTRIC POWER COMPANY, INC.
55th State Plaza 65, New York, New York 10004
CEO: Minoru Sato, Mgr.
Bus: *Electric power company*
Tel: (212) 319-6200
Fax:
%FO: 100

● **TOKAI RIKA CO., LTD.**
3-260 Toyota, Oguchi-cho, Niwa-gun, Aichi 480-0195, Japan
CEO: Kiyoshi Kinoshita, Pres. & CEO
Bus: *Automobile switches and parts manufacture.*
Tel: 81-587-95-5211
Fax: 81-587-95-1917
www.tokai-rika.co.jp
Rev: $2,035
Emp: 8,450

NAICS: 333298, 334419, 334519, 335999, 336399

TAC MANUFACTURING, INC.
4111 County Farm Rd., Jackson, Michigan 49201
CEO: Nozomu Yamada
Bus: *Mfr. automobile steering wheels, air bags & shift levers.*
Tel: (517) 789-7000
Fax: (517) 789-5666

TRAM, INC.
47200 Port St., Plymouth, Michigan 48170
CEO: Yoshihei Iida
Bus: *Holding Co., automobile switches and parts manufacture.*
Tel: (734) 254-8500
Fax: (734) 254-8600
Emp: 90

TRIN, INC.
803 H.L.Thompson Jr. Dr., Ashley, Indiana 46705
CEO: Makato Goto
Bus: *Mfr. automobile switches and parts manufacture.*
Tel: (260) 587-9282
Fax: (260) 587-9285
Emp: 140

TRMI, INC.
100 Hill Brady Rd., Battle Creek, Michigan 49015
CEO: Masayuki Morita   Tel: (269) 966-0100
Bus: *Mfr. automobile switches and parts*   Fax: (269) 966-0143   Emp: 500
manufacture.

● **TOKYO BROADCASTING SYSTEM, INC.**
5-3-6 Akasaka, Minato-ku, Tokyo 107-8006, Japan
CEO: Hiroshi Inoue, CEO   Tel: 81-3-3746-1111   Rev: $2,793
Bus: *Commercial broadcasting services.*   Fax: 81-3-588-6378
    www.tbs.co.jp
NAICS: 512110, 512191, 515120, 515210, 517410

    TOKYO BROADCASTING SYSTEM INTERNATIONAL, INC.
    1370 Ave of the Americas, Ste. 1503, New York, New York 10019
    CEO: Togo Tajika   Tel: (212) 652-0006   %FO: 100
    Bus: *Japanese television.*   Fax: (212) 652-0006

    TOKYO BROADCASTING SYSTEM INTERNATIONAL, INC.
    1901 Ave. of The Stars, Los Angeles, California 90067
    CEO: Tsuneo Ofawa   Tel: (310) 556-2200   %FO: 100
    Bus: *News feature syndicate television.*   Fax: (310) 556-2200

● **THE TOKYO ELECTRIC POWER COMPANY, INC.**
1-3, Uchisaiwai-cho, 1-chome, Chiyoda-ku, Tokyo 100-8560, Japan
CEO: Tsunehisa Katsumata, Pres.   Tel: 81-3 4216-1111   Rev: $45,946
Bus: *Electric power generation and distribution.*   Fax: 81-3 4216-2539   Emp: 51,694
    www.tepco.co.jp
NAICS: 221111, 221112, 221113, 221119, 221121, 221122, 221210, 237130, 238210, 424710, 424720, 517110,
517910, 518111, 518210, 519190, 531120,
    531312, 541330

    TOKYO ELECTRIC POWER COMPANY, INC.
    1901 L St. NW, Ste. 720, Washington, District of Columbia 20036
    CEO: Tsunehisa Katsumata, Pres.   Tel: (202) 457-0790   %FO: 100
    Bus: *Electric power generation and distribution.*   Fax: (202) 457-0810

● **TOKYO ELECTRON LIMITED**
TBS Broadcast Center, 3-6, Akasaka, 5-chome, Minato-ku, Tokyo 107-8481, Japan
CEO: Tetsuro Higashi, Chmn. & CEO   Tel: 81-3-5561-7000   Rev: $5,014
Bus: *Mfr. medical and hospital equipment and industrial*   Fax: 81-3-5561-7400   Emp: 8,870
machinery.   www.tel.com
NAICS: 333295, 423430, 423440, 423620, 423690, 811212, 811213, 811219

    SUPERCRITICAL SYSTEMS, INC.
    2120 West Guadalupe Rd., Gilbert, Arizona 85233
    CEO: Max Biberger, Pres.   Tel: (480) 507-8100   %FO: 100
    Bus: *R&D & Mfr. of high pressure, supercritical*   Fax: (480) 507-3103
    CO_2 equipment.

    TIMBRE TECHNOLOGIES, INC.
    2953 Bunker Hill Lane, Ste. 301, Santa Clara, California 95054
    CEO: Allen Nolet, Pres.   Tel: (408) 200-1400   %FO: 100
    Bus: *Advanced software & hardware solutions*   Fax: (408) 200-1401   Emp: 51
    for stand-alone & in-line metrology

TOKYO ELECTRON INC. (MA)
123 Brimbal Ave., Beverly, Massachusetts 01915
CEO: Michael Jamison, Pres.
Bus: *Process & technical support for the UNITY etch system.*

Tel: (978) 921-0031
Fax: (978) 524-7099

%FO: 100
Emp: 62

TOKYO ELECTRON INC. (TX)
2400 Grove Blvd., Austin, Texas 78741
CEO: Kyoshi Sato, CEO
Bus: *Mfr. semiconductor manufacturing equipment.*

Tel: (512) 424-1000
Fax: (512) 424-1001

%FO: 100

● TOKYO GAS CO., LTD.
5-20, Kaigan 1-chome, Minato-ku, Tokyo 105-8527, Japan
CEO: Norio Ichino, Pres.
Bus: *Natural gas production and distribution.*

Tel: 81-3-5400-7561
Fax: 81-3-5472-5385
www.tokyo-gas.co.jp

Rev: $10,903
Emp: 8,753

NAICS: 211111, 211112, 221119, 221121, 237110, 237120, 237990, 238990, 324110, 335221, 335228, 424710, 424720, 486210, 531312, 541330, 541618, 541690, 561210

TOKYO GAS COMPANY
The Chrysler Bldg., 405 Lexington Ave., 33/F, New York, New York 10174
CEO: Norio Ichino, Pres.
Bus: *Natural gas production and distribution.*

Tel: (646) 865-0577
Fax: (646) 865-0592

%FO: 100

● TOKYO SEIMITSU COMPANY, LTD.
7-1, Shimorenjaku, 9-chome, Mitaka-shi, Tokyo 181-8515, Japan
CEO: Hideo Otsubo, Chmn.
Bus: *Precision measuring and semi-conductor machinery manufacture.*

Tel: 81-4-22481-1011
Fax: 81-4-2245-3636
www.accretech.jp

Rev: $353
Emp: 1,144

NAICS: 333295, 333298, 333515, 334511, 334515

ACCRETECH USA
800 E. Citation Ct., Ste. A, Boise, Idaho 83716
CEO: Chris Ellesmere-Jones, Mgr.
Bus: *Semiconductor equipment sector.*

Tel: (208) 429-6500
Fax: (208) 429-6555

ACCRETECH USA
2600 Telegraph Rd., Ste. 180, Bloomfield Hills, Michigan 48302
CEO: Michiaki Koda, CEO
Bus: *Sales and service of measuring instruments.*

Tel: (248) 332-0100
Fax: (248) 332-0700

%FO: 100
Emp: 105

ACCRETECH USA
1810 North Glenville, Ste. 124, Richardson, Texas 75081
CEO: Kevin Carlile, Mgr.
Bus: *Semiconductor equipment sector.*

Tel: (972) 735-0880
Fax: (972) 735-0890

ACCRETECH USA
39205 Country Club Dr., Ste. C-26, Farmington, Michigan 48331
CEO: April Scott, Mgr.
Bus: *Metrology equipment sector.*

Tel: (248) 489-5500
Fax: (248) 489-5503

ACCRETECH USA
1765 S. Main St., Ste. 121, Milpitas, California 95035
CEO: Patty Rhodes, Mgr.   Tel: (408) 719-2400
Bus: *Semiconductor equipment sector.*   Fax: (408) 719-2401

ACCRETECH USA
100 Michael Angelo Way, Ste. D 400, Austin, Texas 78728
CEO: Jill Dougherty   Tel: (512) 246-4500   %FO: 100
Bus: *Precision measuring and semi-conductor*   Fax: (512) 246-4501
     machinery manufacture.

ACCRETECH USA
48 Spruce St., Oakland, New Jersey 07436
CEO: Wes Charles   Tel: (201) 651-6700   %FO: 100
Bus: *Development & mfr. of Edge Grinders, wafer* Fax: (201) 651-6701
     polishers, edge polishing systems, wafer
     sorters and wafer scribers.

● **TOKYU CORPORATION**
5-6, Nanpeidai-cho, Shibuya-ku, Tokyo 150-8511, Japan
CEO: Toshiaki Koshimura, Pres.   Tel: 81-3-3477-6111   Rev: $11,581
Bus: *Transportation, development, hotels and*   Fax: 81-3-3462-1690   Emp: 30,967
     recreation, retail distribution.   www.tokyu.co.jp
NAICS: 236220, 237310, 485112, 485999, 713990, 721110

   TOKYU TRAVEL AMERICA
   21221 S. Western Ave., Ste. 210, Torrance, California 90501
   CEO: Ieharu Kaneko, Pres.   Tel: (310) 320-4722   %FO: 100
   Bus: *Travel agency.*   Fax: Emp: 64

● **TOMEN CORPORATION**
Tomen Marunouchi Bldg., 8-1 Marunouchi 3-chome, Chiyoda-ku, Tokyo 100-8623, Japan
CEO: Mahito Kageyama, Pres.   Tel: 81-3-5288-2111   Rev: $909
Bus: *General trading including chemicals, textiles,* Fax: 81-3-5288-9100 Emp: 5,871
     machinery and food.   www.tomen.co.jp
NAICS: 221119, 424410, 424480, 424490, 541512, 541513, 541519

   ARVESTA CORP.
   100 1st. St., Ste. 1700, San Francisco, California 94105
   CEO: Kimikazu Ushizaki, Pres.   Tel: (415) 536-3480
   Bus: *Mfr./sales of agricultural chemicals.* Fax: Emp: 100

   CASIO INC
   570 Mount Pleasant Ave., Dover, New Jersey 07801
   CEO: John B. Clough, Pres.   Tel: (973) 361-5400
   Bus: *Sales of Casio products*   Fax: (973) 537-8910

   DEWEY CHEMICAL
   5801 Broadway Ext., Ste. 305, Oklahoma City, Oklahoma 73118
   CEO: Kenichi Onishi, Pres.   Tel: (405) 848-8611
   Bus: *Production & sales of iodine.*   Fax:

Japan

EURUS ENERGY AMERICA CORP.
4660 La Jolla Village Dr., San Diego, California 92122
CEO: Mitsuru Sakaki, Pres.   Tel: (858) 638-7115
Bus: *Operation & management for wind power*   Fax: Emp: 6
    generation projects.

TOMEN AMERICA INC.
1285 Ave. of the Americas, New York, New York 10019
CEO: Tatsushi Yano, Pres.   Tel: (212) 397-4600   %FO: 100
Bus: *General trading company.*   Fax: (212) 582-2007   Emp: 200

TOYO COTTON
11611 Forest Central Dr., Dallas, Texas 75243
CEO: K. Yamaoka, Pres.   Tel: (214) 349-1376
Bus: *Sales of import & export of raw cotton.* Fax: Emp: 20

● **TOMOEGAWA PAPER CO., LTD.**
15-5 Kyobaashi 1-chome, Chuo-ku, Tokyo 104-8335, Japan
CEO: Yoshio Inoue, CEO   Tel: 81-3-3272-4111   Rev: $407
Bus: *Paper manufacture.*   Fax: 81-3-3272-4304   Emp: 1,488
    www.tomoegawa.co.jp
NAICS: 113110, 113210, 113310, 313230, 322110, 325211, 334290, 334412, 334413, 334417, 334418, 334419

   TOMOEGAWA (USA), INC.
   742 Glenn Ave., Wheeling, Illinois 60090
   CEO: Shigeru Yokoyama   Tel: (847) 541-3001   %FO: 100
   Bus: *Paper manufacture.*   Fax: (847) 459-7150

● **TOMY COMPANY, LTD.**
9-10 Tateishi 7-chome, Katsushika-ku, Tokyo 124-8511, Japan
CEO: Kantaro Tomiyama, CEO   Tel: 81-3-3693-9033
Bus: *Children's toys and games manufacture.* Fax: 81-3-3694-7403
    www.tomy.com
NAICS: 339931, 339932

   TOMY CORPORATION
   4695 Macarthur Ct., Ste. 10, Newport Beach, California 92660
   CEO: Koji Otsuka   Tel: (949) 955-1030   %FO: 100
   Bus: *Children's toys and games manufacture.* Fax: (949) 955-1030

● **TOPCON CORPORATION**
75-1 Hasunuma-cho, Itabashi-ku, Tokyo 174-8580, Japan
CEO: Soji Suzuki, CEO   Tel: 81-3-3558-2527   Rev: $677
Bus: *Electronic instrument manufacture.*   Fax: 81-3-3960-4214   Emp: 3,701
    www.topcon.com
NAICS: 334419, 334513, 334515

   TOPCON CORPORATION
   37 West Century Rd., Paramus, New Jersey 07652
   CEO: George Yoshino   Tel: (201) 261-9450   %FO: 100
   Bus: *Electronic instrument manufacture.* Fax: (201) 387-2710

TOPCON POSITIONING SYSTEMS, INC
7400 National Dr., Livermore, California 94550
CEO: Raymond O'Connor, Pres.   Tel: (925) 245-8300   %FO: 100
Bus: *Control device manufacture.*   Fax: (925) 245-8300

● **TOPPAN PRINTING COMPANY, LTD.**
1, Kanda Izumi-cho, Chiyoda-ku, Tokyo 101-0024, Japan
CEO: Naoki Adachi, Pres. & CEO   Tel: 81-3-3835-5111   Rev: $12,281
Bus: *Printing, publishing, packaging, semi-conductors,* Fax: 81-3-3835-0674   Emp: 32,517
interior decorating materials, securities.   www.toppan.co.jp
   NAICS: 322221, 322222, 323110, 323111, 323115, 323117, 323119, 323121, 323122, 326112, 334413, 334419,
339999, 541430

TOPPAN ELECTRONICS USA, INC.
3032 Bunker Hill Lane, Santa Clara, California 95054
CEO: Masahiko Tatewaki, Pres.   Tel: (408) 982-0944   %FO: 100
Bus: *Sales/distribution precision electronic* Fax: Emp: 19
components and packaging.

TOPPAN PHOTOMASKS
131 Old Settlers Blvd., Round Rock, Texas 78664
CEO: Marshall C. Turner, Pres. & CEO Tel: (512) 310-6500
Bus: *Semiconductor equipment & materials* Fax: (512) 255-9627   Emp: 1,600

TOPPAN PRINTING COMPANY, INC.
4551 Glencoe Ave., Ste. 230, Marina Del Rey, California 90292
CEO: Mary McGee, Mgr.   Tel: (310) 823-0050   %FO: 100
Bus: *Full service commercial printing.* Fax:

TOPPAN PRINTING COMPANY, INC.
650 Fifth Ave., 12/F, New York, New York 10019
CEO: Seshi Tanoue, Pres.   Tel: (212) 489-7740   %FO: 100
Bus: *Full service commercial printing.* Fax: (212) 969-9349   Emp: 200

TOPPAN PRINTING COMPANY, INC.
1100 Randolph Rd., Somerset, New Jersey 08873
CEO: Shingo Ohkado, Pres.   Tel: (732) 469-8400
Bus: *Commercial printing*   Fax:

● **TOPY INDUSTRIES LIMITED**
5-9, Yonban-cho, Chiyoda-ku, Tokyo 102-8448, Japan
CEO: Yoshiro Shimizu, Pres. & CEO   Tel: 81-3-3265-0111   Rev: $2,212
Bus: *Mfr. automobile wheels.*   Fax: 81-3-3262-0400   Emp: 4,849
                                     www.topy.co.jp
   NAICS: 331111, 331210, 331221, 331222, 331521

OTAY MESA METAL CORP.
22672 Lambert St., Ste. 616, Lake Forest, California 92630
CEO: Ryoji Kato, Pres.   Tel: (949) 458-1555   %FO: 100
Bus: *Sale of auto parts.*   Fax:

SUPERIOR INDUSTRIES INTERNATIONAL, INC.
7800 Woodley Ave., Van Nuys, California 91406
CEO: Steven J. Borick, Pres. & CEO   Tel: (818) 781-4973   %FO: 100
Bus: *Mfr. of auto parts.*   Fax: (818) 780-3500   Emp: 6,900

TOPY CORP.
980 Chenault Rd., Frankfort, Kentucky 40601
CEO: Horomu Okamoto, Pres.
Bus: *Mfr. of motor vehicle wheels.*
Tel: (502) 695-6163
Fax:
%FO: 100
Emp: 500

TOPY INTERNATIONAL
605C Enon Spring Rd. East, Smyrna, Tennessee 37167
CEO: Hiroshi Murakami, Pres.
Bus: *Mfr. of steel tracks for excavators.*
Tel: (615) 220-1780
Fax: (615) 220-1783
%FO: 100
Emp: 7

TOPY INTERNATIONAL
1375 Lunt Ave., Elk Grove Village, Illinois 60007
CEO: Katz Nagaoka, Pres.
Bus: *Mfr. automobile spring steel fasteners and components.*
Tel: (847) 439-6560
Fax: (847) 228-5299
%FO: 100
Emp: 59

TOPY PRECISION MFG., INC.
1651 Lively Blvd., Elk Grove, Illinois 60007
CEO: Katz Nagaoka, Pres.
Bus: *Sale of auto parts/supplies & industrial equipment.*
Tel: (847) 439-6560
Fax:
%FO: 100
Emp: 600

● **TORAY INDUSTRIES INC.**
Toray Bldg., 2-2-1 Nihonbashi-Muromachi, Chuo-ku, Tokyo 103-8666, Japan
CEO: Sadayuki Sakakibara, Pres. & CEO
Bus: *Mfr. fibers, plastics and chemicals.*
Tel: 81-3-3245-5111
Fax: 81-3-3245-5054
www.toray.co.jp
Rev: $10,304
Emp: 32,901

NAICS: 313111, 313210, 325211, 325222

TORAY CARBON FIBERS AMERICA
2030 Highway 20, Decatur, Alabama 35601
CEO: Minoru Yoshinaga, Pres.
Bus: *Mfr. polyacrylonitrile-based carbon fiber.*
Tel: (256) 260-2626
Fax: (256) 260-2627
%FO: 100
Emp: 86

TORAY COMPOSITE (AMERICA), INC.
19002 50th Ave. East, Tacoma, Washington 98446
CEO: Moriyuki Onishi, Pres.
Bus: *Mfr. carbon fiber prepreg products.*
Tel: (253) 846-1777
Fax: (253) 846-3897
%FO: 100
Emp: 190

TORAY FLUOROFIBERS (AMERICA) INC
2032 Hwy 20, Decatur, Alabama 35601
CEO: Kishio Miwa, Pres.
Bus: *Mfr. & mktg. of fluorofiber.*
Tel: (256) 260-5900
Fax: (256) 260-5910
%FO: 100
Emp: 55

TORAY INDUSTRIES AMERICA, INC.
461 Fifth Ave., 9/F, New York, New York 10017
CEO: Yasuke Orito, Pres.
Bus: *Mfr. man-made suede products.*
Tel: (212) 697-8150
Fax: (212) 972-4279
%FO: 100
Emp: 1,000

TORAY MEMBRANE AMERICA, INC.
65 Grove St., Watertown, Massachusetts 02472
CEO: Tfamotsu Yano, CEO
Bus: *Mfr./mktg. of romembra reverse osmosis membrane, sale of ultra filtration membranes & RO systems.*
Tel: (617) 972-8522
Fax: (617) 923-7077
%FO: 100
Emp: 33

TORAY PLASTICS (AMERICA) INC.
50 Belver Ave., North Kingstown, Rhode Island 02852
CEO: Hiroshi Ogihara, Pres. & CEO   Tel: (401) 294-4511   %FO: 100
Bus: *Mfr. of rubber & plastic products.*   Fax: (401) 294-2154   Emp: 800

TORAY RESIN COMPANY
888 West Big Beaver Rd., Ste. 290, Troy, Michigan 48084
CEO: Shinichi Tachibana, Pres.   Tel: (248) 269-8800   %FO: 100
Bus: *Mfr. nylon resin compounds.*   Fax: (248) 269-8900   Emp: 15

TORAY ULTRASUEDE
1450 Broadway, 15/F, New York, New York 10018
CEO: Yoshifumi Hamada, Pres.   Tel: (212) 382-1590   %FO: 100
Bus: *Sales of man-made suede & related*   Fax: (212) 382-1551   Emp: 31
products.

● **TOSHIBA CORPORATION**
1-1, Shibaura 1-chome, Minato-ku, Tokyo 105-8001, Japan
CEO: Tadashi Okamura, CEO   Tel: 81-3-3457-4511   Rev: $52,816
Bus: *Mfr. information & communications systems,*   Fax: 81-3-3455-1631   Emp: 166,651
information media & consumer products, power   www.toshiba.com
systems, industrial & electronic components.
NAICS: 333313, 333315, 334111, 334112, 334113, 334119, 334210, 334220, 334290, 334310, 334413, 334414,
334415, 335211, 335221, 335222, 335228,
335911, 335912, 336414, 339112, 423730, 423830, 519190

GLOBAL NUCLEAR FUEL AMERICAS, LLC
3901 Castle Hayne Rd., Wilmington, North Carolina 28402
CEO: John D. Fuller, Chmn. & CEO   Tel: (910) 675-5000
Bus: *Industrial manufacturing.*   Fax: (910) 675-6666

OFFICE COMMUNICATIONS SYSTEMS, INC.
10231 Kotzebue St., San Antonio, Texas 78217
CEO: James Magness, Pres.   Tel: (210) 357-2600
Bus: *Office products retail & distribution*   Fax: (210) 357-2665   Emp: 123

TMGE AUTOMATION SYSTEMS LLC
1501 Roanoke Blvd., Salem, Virginia 24153
CEO: Tomiharu Ishii, Pres. & CEO   Tel: (540) 387-5741
Bus: *Industrial manufacturing.*   Fax: (540) 387-7060

TOSHIBA AMERICA BUSINESS SOLUTIONS, INC.
2 Musick, Irvine, California 92618
CEO: Dennis Eversole, Pres.   Tel: (949) 462-6000
Bus: *Office products retail & distribution*   Fax: (949) 462-2900   Emp: 3,105

TOSHIBA AMERICA ELECTRONIC COMPONENTS, INC.
19900 MacArthur Blvd., Ste. 400, Irvine, California 92612
CEO: Takeaki Fukuyama, Pres. & CEO   Tel: (949) 623-2900
Bus: *Electronic components*   Fax: (949) 747-1805   Emp: 2,300

TOSHIBA AMERICA INC.
1251 Ave. of the Americas, 41/F, New York, New York 10020
CEO: Hideo Ito, CEO   Tel: (212) 596-0600   %FO: 100
Bus: *Consumer electronic and office equipment,*   Fax: (212) 593-3875
medical imaging systems and

TOSHIBA AMERICA INFORMATION SYSTEMS, INC.
9740 Irvine Blvd., Irvine, California 92618
CEO: Larry Meyer, VP Sales
Bus: *Mfr./sale of information and communication equipment.*

Tel: (949) 583-3700
Fax: (949) 587-6424

%FO: 100
Emp: 1,300

TOSHIBA AMERICA MEDICAL SYSTEMS, INC.
2441 Michelle Dr., Tustin, California 92780
CEO: Satoshi Tsunakawa, Pres.
Bus: *Mfr./sale medical equipment.*

Tel: (714) 730-5000
Fax: (714) 730-4022

%FO: 100

TOSHIBA SEMICONDUCTOR COMPANY
19900 MacArthur Blvd., Ste. 400, Irvine, California 92612
CEO: Masahi Muromachi
Bus: *Semiconductors.*

Tel: (949) 623-2900
Fax: (949) 474-1330

● **TOSHIBA MACHINE COMPANY, LTD.**
2068-3, Ooka, Numazu-shi, Shizuoka-ken, Numazu 410-8510, Japan
CEO: Reiji Nakajima, Pres.
Bus: *Mfr. machine tools, plastic machinery, die casting, printing press, etc.*
NAICS: 333511, 333513

Tel: 81-55-926-5141
Fax: 81-55-925-6501
www.toshiba-machine.co.jp

Rev: $116
Emp: 3,310

TOSHIBA MACHINE CO., AMERICA
755 Greenleaf Ave., Elk Grove Village, Illinois 60007
CEO: Masahisa Koyama, Pres.
Bus: *Import/distribution machine tools, injection molding, print & die-cast machinery and system robots.*

Tel: (847) 593-1616
Fax: (847) 593-0897

%FO: 100
Emp: 115

TOSHIBA MACHINE CO., AMERICA
1481 South Balboa Ave., Ontario, California 91761
CEO: Terry Estrada, Mgr.
Bus: *Sale of industrial equipment./Mfr. of misc. industry machinery.*

Tel: (909) 923-4009
Fax: (909) 923-7258

%FO: 100
Emp: 12

TOSHIBA MACHINE CO., AMERICA
1578 Sussex Turnpike, Randolph, New Jersey 07869
CEO: Hiroshi Iba
Bus: *Mfr. of plastic products.*

Tel: (973) 252-9956
Fax: (972) 252-9959

%FO: 100

TOSHIBA MACHINE CO., AMERICA
6478 Putnam Ford Dr., Ste. 106, Woodstock, Georgia 30189
CEO: Michael P. Welsh
Bus: *Mfr. of plastic products.*

Tel: (678) 494-8005
Fax: (678) 494-8006

%FO: 100

TOSHIBA MACHINE CO., AMERICA
10 Corporate Park Dr., Ste. C, Hopewell Junction, New York 12533
CEO: Hiroshi Iba
Bus: *Mfr. of plastic products.*

Tel: (845) 896-0692
Fax: (845) 896-1724

%FO: 100

- **TOSOH CORPORATION**
  3-8-2, Shiba, Minato-ku, Tokyo 105-8623, Japan
  CEO: Madoka Tashiro, Chmn. & CEO
  Bus: *Mfr./process chemicals, metals and raw*

  Tel: 81-3-5427-5118
  Fax: 81-3-5427-5198
  www.tosoh.com

  Rev: $4,585
  Emp: 1,196

  NAICS: 325110, 325181, 325188, 325192, 325193, 325199, 325211, 325212, 325221, 325222, 325311, 325312, 325520, 327310, 334516, 488510

  - **TOSOH USA INC**
    3600 Gantz Rd., Grove City, Ohio 43123
    CEO: Katsumi Ishikawa, Pres.
    Bus: *Mfr. of chemicals.*

    Tel: (614) 277-4348
    Fax: (614) 875-8066

    %FO: 100
    Emp: 600

- **TOTO LTD.**
  1-1, Nakashima 2-chome, Kokurakita-ku, Kitakyushu, Fukuoka 802-8601, Japan
  CEO: Masatoshi Shigefuchi, Chmn. & CEO
  Bus: *Mfr. and markets water related products for commercial, residential and public facilities.*

  Tel: 81-93-951-2707
  Fax: 81-93-922-6789
  www.toto.co.jp

  Rev: $4,429
  Emp: 17,192

  NAICS: 327124, 332911, 332913, 332998, 335224, 335228, 423720

  - **TOTO USA INC.**
    1155 Southern Rd., Morrow, Georgia 30260
    CEO: Kazuo Sako, Pres.
    Bus: *Mfr. and markets water related products for commercial, residential and public facilities.*

    Tel: (770) 282-8686
    Fax: (770) 282-8697

    %FO: 100

- **TOYO COTTON COMPANY**
  8-2, Utsubo-Honmachi, 1-Chome, Nishi-Ku, Osaka 550-0004, Japan
  CEO: Ken Yamaoko, CEO
  Bus: *Raw cotton trading.*

  Tel: 81-6-6479-1422
  Fax: 81-6-6479-1425
  www.toyocotton.com

  NAICS: 115113, 561499

  - **TOYO COTTON COMPANY**
    11611 Forest Central Dr., Dallas, Texas 75243
    CEO: Bill Adams
    Bus: *Raw cotton trading.*

    Tel: (214) 349-1376
    Fax: (214) 349-6490

    %FO: 100

- **TOYO SUISAN KAISHA, LTD.**
  2-13-40 Konan, Minato-ku, Tokyo 108-8501, Japan
  CEO: Hirofumi Miki, Pres.
  Bus: *Mfr. and sale glass and plastic containers and paper packaging products.*

  Tel: 81-3-3458-5111
  Fax: 81-3-3450-1381
  www.toyo-seikan.co.jp

  Rev: $6,307
  Emp: 5,372

  NAICS: 327213, 424130

  - **TOYO SEIKAN KAISHA USA**
    707 Skokie Blvd., Ste. 670, Northbrook, Illinois 60062
    CEO: Miyatani Yoshiki, Pres.
    Bus: *Mfr. and sale glass and plastic containers and paper packaging products.*

    Tel: (847) 509-3080
    Fax: (847) 509-3088

    %FO: 100

- **TOYO TIRE & RUBBER CO., LTD.**
  17-18, Edobori 1-chome, Nishi-ku, Osaka 550-8661, Japan
  CEO: Yoshio Kataoka, Pres. & CEO
  Bus: *Mfr. automobile tires.*
  Tel: 81-6-6441-8801
  Fax: 81-6-6446-2225
  www.toyo-rubber.co.jp
  Rev: $2,425
  Emp: 6,263
  NAICS: 325211, 326199, 326211, 326220, 326291, 336360, 336399

  GTY TIRE COMPANY
  PO Box 1029, Hwy. 142, South Mt. Vernon, Illinois 62864
  CEO: John C. Curry
  Bus: *Mfr. automobile tires.*
  Tel: (618) 246-2263
  Fax: (618) 246-2493
  %FO: 100

  NITTO TIRE NORTH AMERICA
  6261 Katella Ave., Ste. 2B, Cypress, California 90630
  CEO: Brian Chung, Mgr.
  Bus: *Sale of tires.*
  Tel: (714) 236-1863
  Fax: (714) 252-0008
  %FO: 100

  TOYO AUTOMOTIVE PARTS (USA) INC.
  521 Page Dr., Franklin, Kentucky 42134
  CEO: Yasou Ito, Pres.
  Bus: *Mfr. automobile tires.*
  Tel: (270) 598-4100
  Fax: (270) 586-4846
  %FO: 100
  Emp: 60

  TOYO TIRE (USA) CORP.
  6261 Katella Ave., Ste. 2B, Cypress, California 90630
  CEO: Yoshio Kataoka, Pres.
  Bus: *Mfr. of tires.*
  Tel: (714) 236-2080
  Fax: (714) 229-6199
  %FO: 100

  TOYO TIRE NORTH AMERICA, INC.
  7950 Troon Cir., Austell, Georgia 30168
  CEO: Gerald Brantley, PR
  Bus: *Sale of tires.*
  Tel: (770) 944-8696
  Fax:
  %FO: 100

- **TOYOBO CO., LTD.**
  2-2-8 Dojima Hama, Kita-ku, Osaka 530-8230, Japan
  CEO: Ryuzo Sakamoto, Pres. & CEO
  Bus: *Mfr. fiber and textiles.*
  Tel: 81-6-6348-3191
  Fax: 81-6-6348-3206
  www.toyobo.co.jp
  Rev: $3,531
  Emp: 10,831
  NAICS: 313111, 313210, 313230, 313311, 313312, 314992, 322221, 325211, 325412

  TOYOBO AMERICA, INC.
  950 Third Ave., 17/F, New York, New York 10022
  CEO: Masaki Yamanaka, Pres.
  Bus: *Fiber and textile products manufacture.*
  Tel: (212) 317-9245
  Fax: (212) 317-9280
  %FO: 100

- **TOYODA GOSEI CO., LTD.**
  1, Nagahata, Ochiai, Haruhi-cho, Nishikasugai-gun, Aichi 452-8564, Japan
  CEO: Takashi Matsuura, Pres.
  Bus: *Mfr. and sales of interior and exterior parts for automobiles.*
  Tel: 81-52-400-1055
  Fax: 81-52-409-7491
  www.toyoda-gosei.com
  Rev: $3,757
  Emp: 15,483
  NAICS: 334419, 336399

TOYODA GOSEI NORTH AMERICA
1400 Stevenson Hwy., Troy, Michigan 48083
CEO: Tsugio Kadowaki, Pres.
Bus: *Mfr. auto components.*
Tel: (248) 280-2100
Fax: (248) 280-2110
%FO: 100

TOYODA GOSEI TEXAS LLC
485 Quentin-Roosevelt, San Antonio, Texas 78226
CEO: Kanji Kumazawa, Sales
Bus: *Mfr. and sales of interior and exterior parts for automobiles.*
Tel: (248) 280-7461
Fax: (248) 927-2317
%FO: 100

● **TOYODA MACHINE WORKS**
1-1 Asahimachi, Kariya, Aichi 448-8652, Japan
CEO: Motohiko Yokoyama, Pres.
Bus: *Mfr. and sales of machine tools and auto parts.*
Tel: 81-566-255-412
Fax: 81-566-255-470
www.toyoda-kouki.co.jp
Rev: $2,047
Emp: 4,065
NAICS: 333512, 333513, 333514, 333515, 333516, 333518, 333911, 333912, 333992, 334513, 336330, 336350

TOYODA MACHINERY USA, INC.
316 West University Dr., Arlington Heights, Illinois 60004
CEO: Howard Michael, Pres. & CEO
Bus: *Mfr./distribute horizontal/vertical machining centers, grinders, machining cells &*
Tel: (847) 253-0340
Fax: (847) 253-0540
%FO: 100
Emp: 140

TOYODA-KOKI AUTOMOTIVE NORTH AMERICA, INC.
5932 Commerce Blvd., Morristown, Tennessee 37814
CEO: Max Biery, Pres.
Bus: *Mfr. of auto parts.*
Tel: (423) 585-0999
Fax: (423) 585-2941
%FO: 100
Emp: 545

● **TOYOSHIMA SPECIAL STEEL COMPANY, LTD.**
1-6, Sumiyoshi, 1-chome, Ikeda 563-0033, Japan
CEO: Susumu Tanabe, Chmn. & Pres.
Bus: *Springs, fork arms, earthmover equipment and auto spare parts.*
Tel: 81-722-61-2021
Fax:
www.kk-toyoshima.co.jp
Rev: $57
Emp: 220
NAICS: 332611, 336999

TOYOSHIMA SPECIAL STEEL USA
735 St. Paul St., Indianapolis, Indiana 46203
CEO: Nick Nishikawa, Pres.
Bus: *Mfr./distribute springs for trucks and automobiles.*
Tel: (317) 638-3511
Fax:
%FO: 100
Emp: 31

● **TOYOTA INDUSTRIES CORPORATION**
2-1, Toyoda-cho, Kariya, Aichi 448-8671, Japan
CEO: Tadashi Ishikawa, Pres.
Bus: *Mfr. textile machinery, industrial vehicles and engines.*
Tel: 81-566-22-2511
Fax: 81-566-27-5650
www.toyota-industries.com
Rev: $11,022
Emp: 27,431
NAICS: 333924, 334419, 336399

ACTIS MANUFACTURING LTD.
4051 Freeport Pkwy., Bldg. H, Ste.400, Grapevine, Texas 76051-231
CEO: Atsuhiro Hayakawa, Pres.
Bus: *Remanufacture of compressors for the compressor aftermarket*
Tel: (972) 724-3600
Fax: (972) 724-4741
Emp: 46

MICHIGAN AUTOMOTIVE COMPRESSOR, INC.
2400 North Dearing Rd., Parma, Michigan 49269
CEO: Kimio Kato, Pres.
Bus: *Mfr. textile machinery and industrial vehicles.*
Tel: (517) 622-7000
Fax: (517) 531-5680
%FO: 100
Emp: 879

TOYODA TEXTILE MACHINERY INC.
8300 Arrowbridge Blvd., Charlotte, North Carolina 28273
CEO: Osamu Miura, Pres.
Bus: *Sales of textile machinery and parts*
Tel: (704) 527-5400
Fax: (704) 527-3743
Emp: 17

TOYOTA INDUSTRIAL EQUIPMENT MFG INC.
5555 Inwood Dr., Columbus, Indiana 47201
CEO: Yoshimitsu Ogihara, Pres.
Bus: *Produces industrial vehicles and parts. (JV with Toyota Motor Corp.)*
Tel: (812) 342-0060
Fax: (812) 342-0064
%FO: 100
Emp: 624

TOYOTA INDUSTRIES NORTH AMERICA
10 North Martingale Rd., Ste. 400, Schaumburg, Illinois 60173
CEO: Yoshimitsu Ogihara, Pres.
Bus: *Holding company in USA*
Tel: (847) 466-1563
Fax: (847) 466-1564
Emp: 578

TOYOTA MATERIAL HANDLING USA
1 Park Plaza, Ste. 1000, Irvine, California 92614
CEO: Shankar Basu, Pres.
Bus: *Marketing and sales of industrial equipment*
Tel: (949) 474-1135
Fax: (949) 223-8000
Emp: 128

TOYOTA-LIFT OF LOS ANGELES
12907 Imperial Highway, Santa Fe Springs, California 90670-4715
CEO: Joseph Quinto, Pres.
Bus: *Marketing and sales of industrial equipment*
Tel: (562) 941-4155
Fax: (562) 941-4414

- **TOYOTA MOTOR CORPORATION**
1 Toyota-cho, Toyota City, Aichi 471-8571, Japan
CEO: Hiroshi Okuda, Chmn.
Bus: *Mfr. motor vehicles, prefab housing, telecommunications products.*
NAICS: 333120, 336111, 336112, 522291
Tel: 81-565-28-2121
Fax: 81-565-23-5800
www.toyota.com
Rev: $163,637
Emp: 264,410

TOYOTA MOTOR MANUFACTURING
25 Atlantic Ave., Erlanger, Kentucky 41018
CEO: Atsushi Niimi, Pres. & CEO
Bus: *Auto manufacturing*
Tel: (859) 746-4000
Fax: (859) 746-4190
Emp: 22,387

TOYOTA MOTOR NA INC.
9 West 57th St., Ste. 4900, New York, New York 10019
CEO: Hideaki Otaka, Pres. & CEO
Bus: *Auto manufacturing*
Tel: (212) 223-0303
Fax: (212) 759-7670
%FO: 100

TOYOTA MOTOR SALES USA, INC.
19001 South Western Ave., Torrance, California 90509
CEO: Yukitoshi Funo, Pres. & CEO
Bus: *Mktg./distribution motor vehicles.*
Tel: (310) 618-4000
Fax: (310) 618-7800
%FO: 100

- **TOYOTA TSUSHO CORPORATION**
4-9-8, Meieki, Nakamura-ku, Nagoya 450-0002, Japan
CEO: Masaaki Furikawa, Pres. & CEO — Tel: 81-52-584-5000 — Rev: $26,389
Bus: *Iron and steel, non-ferrous metals, machinery,* — Fax: 81-52-584-5663 — Emp: 11,792
vehicles, energy, textiles, general merchandise, — www.toyotsu.co.jp
chemicals, insurance services and products.
NAICS: 313311, 331111, 331210, 331221, 331222, 331491, 333512, 333513, 336112, 336999, 423120

  FEROLETO STEEL COMPANY, INC.
  300 Scofield Ave., Bridgeport, Connecticut 06605
  CEO: Yoshimi Takai, CEO — Tel: (203) 366-3263
  Bus: *Steel service centers* — Fax: (203) 366-8058 — Emp: 100

  TOYOTA TSUSHO AMERICA INC.
  437 Madison Ave., 29/F, New York, New York 10022
  CEO: Yoshimi Takai, CEO — Tel: (212) 418-0138
  Bus: *Steel service centers* — Fax: (212) 421-4066

  TOYOTA TSUSHO AMERICA, INC
  7300 Turfway Rd., Ste. 500, Florence, Kentucky 41042
  CEO: Takashi Hasegawa, Pres. — Tel: (859) 746-7800 — %FO: 100
  Bus: *Import/export and domestic trading.* — Fax: (859) 746-7817 — Emp: 1,200

  TRIM MASTERS, INC.
  1090 Industry Rd., Harrodsburg, Kentucky 40330
  CEO: Tadashi Naito, Pres. — Tel: (859) 734-6969
  Bus: *Mfr. of auto parts* — Fax: (859) 734-9666 — Emp: 3,400

- **TREND MICRO INC.**
Shinjuku MAYNDS Tower, 1-1, Yoyogi 2-chome, Shibuya-ku, Tokyo 151-0053, Japan
CEO: Steve Ming-Jang Chang, Chmn. — Tel: 81-3-5334-3650 — Rev: $604
Bus: *Computer software services.* — Fax: 81-3-5334-3651 — Emp: 2,466
www.trendmicro.com
NAICS: 511210, 541511, 541519

  TREND MICRO INC.
  10101 N. De Anza Blvd., Ste. 400, Cupertino, California 95014
  CEO: Steve Chang, Chmn. — Tel: (408) 257-1500 — %FO: 100
  Bus: *Computer software services.* — Fax: (408) 257-2003 — Emp: 300

- **TSUBAKI NAKASHIMA CO., LTD.**
19 Shakudo, Taimo-cho, Kita-Katsuragi-gun, Nara 639-2162, Japan
CEO: Takanori Kondoh, Pres. & CEO — Tel: 81-745-48-2891 — Rev: $275
Bus: *Mfr. of industrial machinery and equipment* — Fax: 81-745-48-6583 — Emp: 1,768
www008.upp.so-net.ne.jp/tsubaki/
NAICS: 333298

  HOOVER PRECISION PRODUCTS INC.
  2200 Pendley Rd., Cumming, Georgia 30041
  CEO: Joe Schmenk, Pres. & CEO — Tel: (770) 889-9223 — %FO: 100
  Bus: *Manufacturer of industrial machinery and* — Fax: (770) 889-0828 — Emp: 1,300
  equipment

- **TSUBAKIMOTO CHAIN COMPANY**
  Osaka Fukokuseimei Bldg., 2-4, Komatsubaracho, Kita-Ku, Osaka 530-0018, Japan
  CEO: Takashi Fukunaga, CEO   Tel: 81-3-3221-5612 Rev: $707
  Bus: *Mfr. chain and power transmission products and* Fax: 81-3-3221-5639 Emp: 4,709
    material handling systems.   www.tsubakimoto.co.jp
  NAICS: 332999, 333298, 333613

  BALLANTINE INC.
  840 McKinley St., Anoka, Minnesota 55303
  CEO: Al Chancellor   Tel: (763) 427-3959 %FO: 100
  Bus: *Sales of trencher parts.* Fax: (763) 427-2277

  BC&H COMPANY
  11010 Monroe Road, Matthews, North Carolina 28105
  CEO: Butch Cairnes   Tel: (704) 847-9131 %FO: 100
  Bus: *Distributor of ball bearings.* Fax: (704) 847-3651

  ROBCO INC.
  1523 Crescent Drive, Carrolton, Texas 75006
  CEO: Ron Haynes   Tel: (972) 242-3300 %FO: 100
  Bus: *Mfr. of drive chains, attachment chains,* Fax: (972) 245-2328
    engineering class chains, sprockets, and
    power transmission components.

  TSUBAKI CONVEYOR OF AMERICA INC.
  Box 710, 138 Davis St., Portland, Tennessee 37148
  CEO: Sadatsugu Sugimoto Tel: (615) 325-9221 %FO: 100
  Bus: *Mfr. and sales of materials handling* Fax: (615) 325-2442
    systems.

  US TSUBAKI INC.
  821 Main Street, Holyoke, Massachusetts 01040
  CEO: Sadatsugu Sugimoto Tel: (413) 536-1576 %FO: 100
  Bus: *Mfr. of drive chains, attachment chains,* Fax: (413) 534-8239
    engineering class chains, sprockets, and
    power transmission components.

  US TSUBAKI INC.
  1010 Edgewater Ave., Sandusky, Ohio 44870
  CEO: Frank Bobel   Tel: (419) 626-4560 %FO: 100
  Bus: *Mfr. of drive chains, attachment chains,* Fax: (419) 626-4560
    engineering class chains, sprockets, and
    power transmission components.

  US TSUBAKI INC.
  106 Lonczak Dr., Chicopee, Massachusetts 01022
  CEO: Mark Miller   Tel: (413) 593-1100 %FO: 100
  Bus: *Mfr. of drive chains, attachment chains,* Fax: (413) 593-9999
    engineering class chains, sprockets, and
    power transmission components.

  US TSUBAKI INC.
  301 E. Marquardt Dr., Wheeling, Illinois 60090
  CEO: Kenji Ohara   Tel: (847) 459-9500 %FO: 100
  Bus: *Mfr. of drive chains, attachment chains,* Fax: (847) 459-9515
    engineering class chains, sprockets, and
    power transmission components.

- **UBE INDUSTRIES LTD.**
  1978-96, Kogushi, Ube, Yamaguchi 755-8633, Japan
  CEO: Hiroaki Tamura, Pres. & CEO   Tel: 81-836-31-1111   Rev: $4,657
  Bus: *Petrochemicals, chemicals, cement, construction*   Fax: 81-836-21-2252   Emp: 11,397
        materials and machinery, coal, and plant   www.ube-ind.co.jp
        engineering services.
     NAICS: 237310, 325188, 325199, 325211, 325212, 325221, 325222, 327310, 327320, 532490

       UBE AMERICA
       55 East 59th St., 18/F, New York, New York 10022
       CEO: Kazuhiko Takahashi, Pres.   Tel: (212) 813-8300   %FO: 100
       Bus: *Export of UBE Group products and import*   Fax: (212) 826-0454   Emp: 13
          of raw materials to Japan.

       UBE MACHINERY INC.
       5700 South State Rd., Ann Arbor, Michigan 48108
       CEO: Mitsuhiro Kawamura, Pres.   Tel: (734) 741-7000   %FO: 100
       Bus: *Mfr./sales machinery.*   Fax: (734) 741-7017   Emp: 60

- **UCHIDA YOKO COMPANY, LTD.**
  2-4-7 Shinkawa, Chuo-ku, Chuo-ku, Tokyo 104-8282, Japan
  CEO: Hitoshi Hisata, Pres.   Tel: 81-3-5634-6056   Rev: $947
  Bus: *Metal office furniture manufacture.*   Fax: 81-3-5634-6802   Emp: 3,565
          www.uchida.co.jp
     NAICS: 337214, 423210, 423420, 423430, 423490

       CALLISON ARCHITECTURE INC.
       1420 5th Ave., Ste. 2400, Seattle, Washington 98101
       CEO: William Karst, CEO   Tel: (206) 623-4646
       Bus: *Architectural services*   Fax: Emp: 460

       OHAUS CORP.
       19 Chapin Rd. A, Pine Brook, New Jersey 07058
       CEO: Ted Xia, Pres.   Tel: (973) 377-9000
       Bus: *Laboratory apparatus & furniture*   Fax: Emp: 140

       PASCO SCIENTIFIC
       1799 Mclain Rd. NW, Acworth, Georgia 30101
       CEO: Alan Brown, Mgr.   Tel: (770) 422-3826
       Bus: *Professional equipment*   Fax:

       SPECTRUM SOFTWARE
       2140 Merritt Dr., Garland, Texas 74041
       CEO: Keith R. Coogan, CEO   Tel: (972) 840-6600
       Bus: *Computer products distribution & support.*   Fax: (972) 864-7878

       STEELCASE
       901 44th St. SE, Grand Rapids, Michigan 49508
       CEO: James P. Hackett, Pres. & CEO   Tel: (616) 247-2710
       Bus: *Office & business furniture, fixtures &*   Fax: (616) 475-2270   Emp: 14,500
          equipment

UCHIDA OF AMERICA CORPORATION
3535 Del Amo Blvd., Torrance, California 90503
CEO: Akihiro Fujisawa, Pres.   Tel: (310) 793-2200   %FO: 100
Bus: *Metal office furniture sales and distribution.*   Fax: (310) 793-2210   Emp: 45

● **ULVAC INC.**
2500 Hagisono, Chigasaki, Kanagawa 253-8543, Japan
CEO: Kyuzo Nakamura, Pres. & CEO   Tel: 81-467-89-2033   Rev: $1,457
Bus: *Mfr & sells vacuum equip. for semiconductors,*   Fax: 81-467-82-9114   Emp: 3,712
flat panel displays, disks and other electronic   www.ulvac.co.jp
devices and industrial applications
NAICS: 333295

   ULVAC TECHNOLOGIES INC.
   401 Griffin Brook Dr., Methuen, Massachusetts 01844-1883
   CEO: Hisaharu Obinata, Pres.   Tel: (978) 686-7550   %FO: 100
   Bus: *Mfr. sell, and conducts maintenance*   Fax: (978) 689-6300
   service for vacuum systems and

● **UNIDEN CORPORATION**
2-12-7, Hatchobori, Chuo-ku, Tokyo 104-8512, Japan
CEO: Satoru Omori, Pres.   Tel: 81-3-5543-2800   Rev: $774
Bus: *Mfr. telephone and radio communications*   Fax: 81-3-5543-2921   Emp: 21,401
equipment.   www.uniden.co.jp
NAICS: 334210, 334220, 334515

   UNIDEN AMERICA CORPORATION
   4700 Amon Carter Blvd., Ft. Worth, Texas 76155
   CEO: Rich Tosi   Tel: (817) 858-3300   %FO: 100
   Bus: *Mfr. telephone and radio communications*   Fax: (817) 858-3300
   equipment.

● **UNITIKA LTD.**
Osaka Center Bldg., 4-1-3 Kyutaro-machi, Chuo-ku, Osaka 541-8566, Japan
CEO: Otofumi Ohnishi, Pres.   Tel: 81-6-6281-5695   Rev: $2,053
Bus: *Fibers, textiles and plastics manufacture.*   Fax: 81-6-6281-5697   Emp: 6,214
www.unitika.co.jp
NAICS: 313210, 314999, 325211, 325222, 326199, 333319, 333994, 541330

   UNITIKA AMERICA CORPORATION
   257 W 39th St, New York, New York 10018
   CEO: Hisayasa Kaneshiro   Tel: (212) 398-5500   %FO: 100
   Bus: *Export/import textiles, fibers, plastics.*   Fax:

● **USHIO INC.**
Asahi-Tokai Bldg., 2-6-1 Otemachi, Tokyo 100-0004, Japan
CEO: Jiro Ushio, Chmn.   Tel: 81-3-3242-1811   Rev: $3,879
Bus: *Light sources, units and systems manufacture.*   Fax: 81-3-3242-1815   Emp: 394
www.ushio.co.jp
NAICS: 333314, 333315, 335110, 335121, 335122

CHRISTIE DIGITAL SYSTEMS USA, INC.
10550 Camden Dr., Cypress, California 90630
CEO: Jack Kline, Pres.   Tel: (714) 236-8610
Bus: *Light sources, units and systems*   Fax: (714) 503-3375
     manufacture.

USHIO AMERICA, INC.
5440 Cerritos Ave., Cypress, California 90630
CEO: Kenji Hamashima, Pres.   Tel: (714) 236-8600
Bus: *Light sources, units and systems*   Fax: (714) 229-3180   Emp: 650
     manufacture.

• **VICTOR COMPANY OF JAPAN, LTD.**
12, Moriya-cho, 3-Chome, Kanagawa-ku, Yokohama 221-8528, Japan
CEO: Masahikio Terada, Pres.   Tel: 81-45-450-1445   Rev: $8,727
Bus: *Mfr. electronic audio equipment.*   Fax: 81-45-450-1425   Emp: 35,580
                                               www.jvc-victor.co.jp
NAICS: 334310

  JVC CORPORATION
  1700 Valley Rd., Ste. 1, Wayne, New Jersey 07470
  CEO: Katsuhiko Hattori, Pres.   Tel: (973) 317-5000   %FO: 100
  Bus: *Mfr. electronic audio equipment.*   Fax: (973) 315-5010   Emp: 960

• **VIDEO RESEARCH LTD.**
2-1-1 Irifune, 2-Chome, Chuo-ku, Tokyo 104-0042, Japan
CEO: Tsuyoshi Takeuchi, Pres. & CEO   Tel: 81-3-5541-6506   Rev: $167
Bus: *Media market research*   Fax: 81-3-5541-6442   Emp: 379
                                               www.videor.co.jp
NAICS: 541910

  VIDEO RESEARCH USA INC.
  535 Fifth Ave., 2/F, New York, New York 10017
  CEO: Eiichiro Tsuchida, Pres. & CEO   Tel: (212) 557-8577   %FO: 100
  Bus: *Media research*   Fax: (212) 557-5157

• **WACOAL CORPORATION**
29, Nakajima-cho, Kisshoin, Minamiku, Kyoto 601-8530, Japan
CEO: Yoshikata Tsukamoto, Pres.   Tel: 81-75-682-5111   Rev: $1,564
Bus: *Mfr. lingerie, hosiery, underwear and outerwear.* Fax: 81-75-661-5603 Emp: 11,267
                                               www.wacoal.co.jp
NAICS: 315192, 315212, 315231, 315291

  WACOAL AMERICA INC.
  136 Madison Ave., New York, New York 10016
  CEO: Richard C. Murray, Pres. & COO   Tel: (212) 532-6100
  Bus: *Mfr. lingerie, hosiery, underwear and* Fax: (212) 696-5608
       outerwear.

  WACOAL SPORTS SCIENCE CORPORATION
  136 Madison Ave., New York, New York 10016
  CEO: John L.A. Wilson, VP   Tel: (212) 743-9662   %FO: 100
  Bus: *Patented anatomically correct performance* Fax: (212) 696-5608   Emp: 6
       sports apparel manufacture.

- **WACOM COMPANY, LIMITED**
  2-510-1 Toyonodai, Otone-Machi, Kitasaitaima-Gun, Saitama 349-1148, Japan
  CEO: Masahiko Yamada, Pres.   Tel: 81-48-0781-211   Rev: $111
  Bus: *Cordless and battery-free, pressure sensitive*   Fax: Emp: 464
       pens manufacture.   www.wacom.co.jp
  NAICS: 334119, 541512

  ### WACOM TECHNOLOGY CORPORATION
  1311 SE Cardinal Ct., Vancouver, Washington 98683
  CEO: Masahiko Yamada, Pres.   Tel: (360) 896-9833   %FO: 100
  Bus: *Computer peripheral equipment.*   Fax: Emp: 50

- **M. WATANABE & COMPANY, LTD.**
  2-16, Nihonbashi-Muromachi, 4 chome, Chuo-ku, Nanwa Nihonbashi Bldg., Tokyo 103-0022, Japan
  CEO: Masaki Kusuhara, Pres. & CEO   Tel: 81-3-3241-5231
  Bus: *Mfr. steel and brass tubing.* Fax: 81-3-3241-5208
                                        www.m-watanabe.co.jp
  NAICS: 331210, 331491

  ### QUARTZ SCIENTIFIC
  819 East St., Fairport Harbor, Ohio 44077
  CEO: Masaki Kusuhara, Chmn.   Tel: (440) 354-2186
  Bus: *Electronic components*   Fax: (440) 354-6381   Emp: 90

  ### WACOM CORP.
  146 Red Schoolhouse Rd., Spring Valley, New York 10977
  CEO: Masaki Kusuhara, Pres.   Tel: (914) 735-1303
  Bus: *Coal & other minerals*   Fax: (914) 735-3940   Emp: 28

  ### WACOM ENGINEERING CORP.
  300 Scott Blvd., Ste. 110, Santa Clara, California 95054
  CEO: Joe Deal   Tel: (408) 988-1673
  Bus: *Engineering & consulting services.*   Fax: (408) 988-2679

- **YAMAHA CORP**
  10-1, Nakazawa-cho, Hamamatsu, Shizuoka 430-8650, Japan
  CEO: Shuji Ito, Pres.   Tel: 81-53-460-2800   Rev: $5,107
  Bus: *Mfr. musical instruments, audio products,*   Fax: 81-53-460-2802   Emp: 23,903
       household and sporting goods, metal products,   www.global.yamaha.com
       furniture and recreational equipment.
  NAICS: 332999, 334310, 334413, 334417, 335129, 337121, 337122, 337124, 337125, 337129, 339920, 339992,
  339999, 423210, 423220, 423620, 423910,
          611610, 611630, 721110

  ### YAMAHA CORPORATION OF AMERICA
  6600 Orangethorpe Ave., Buena Park, California 90620
  CEO: Toshihiro Doi, Pres.   Tel: (714) 522-9011   %FO: 100
  Bus: *Distribution musical instruments and*   Fax: (714) 522-9961
       products; pianos, organs and computer

● **YAMAHA MOTOR CO., LTD.**
2500 Shingai Iwata, Shizuoka 438-8501, Japan
CEO: Toru Hasegawa, Pres.
Bus: *Mfr. motorized vehicles and parts, including golf carts and snowmobiles.*
NAICS: 336312, 336399, 336612, 336991, 336999

Tel: 81-53-832-1103
Fax: 81-53-837-4252
www.yamaha-motor.co.jp

Rev: $9,658
Emp: 33,694

   C&C MANUFACTURING
   650 Hickman Cir., Sanford, Florida 32771
   CEO: Steve Heaton, Gen. Mgr.
   Bus: *Boat manufacture.*

   Tel: (407) 321-7110
   Fax:

   SKEETER PRODUCTS INC.
   One Skeeter Rd., PO Box 230, Kilgore, Texas 75662
   CEO: Jeff Stone, VP
   Bus: *Mfr. and sales of boats.*

   Tel: (903) 984-0541
   Fax: (903) 984-7740

   %FO: 100
   Emp: 211

   TENNESSEE WATER CRAFTS, INC.
   2000 Cobia Dr, Vonore, Tennessee 37885
   CEO: Michel Mochida, Pres.
   Bus: *Boat manufacture.*

   Tel: (423) 884-6881
   Fax: (423) 884-6393

   YAMAHA GOLF CAR CO.
   261 Tiger Way, Peachtree City, Georgia 30269
   CEO: Chris Plummer
   Bus: *Marketing of golf carts*

   Tel: (770) 487-0554
   Fax:

   Emp: 2

   YAMAHA MOTOR CORPORATION USA
   6555 Katella Ave., Cypress, California 90630
   CEO: Shohei Kato, Pres.
   Bus: *Distribute/sales Yamaha products.*

   Tel: (714) 761-7300
   Fax: (714) 761-7302

   %FO: 100
   Emp: 3,700

   YAMAHA MOTOR MANUFACTURING CORP. OF AMERICA
   1270 Cahstain Rd. NW, Kennesaw, Georgia 30144
   CEO: Don George, Mgr.
   Bus: *Mfr. & mktg. of golf carts, mfr. Of personal watercraft & all-terrain vehicles*

   Tel: (770) 420-5700
   Fax:

● **YAMAMOTOYAMA CO LTD.**
2-5-2, Nihonbashi, Chuo-ku, Tokyo 103-0027, Japan
CEO: Kahei Yamamoto, Pres.
Bus: *Fish and sea foods, teas*

NAICS: 311711, 311920, 424460, 424490, 445299

Tel: 81-3-3271-3261
Fax:
www.yamamotoyama-usa.com

Rev: $90
Emp: 600

   YAMAMOTOYAMA OF AMERICA, INC.
   122 Voyager St., Pomona, California 91768
   CEO: Kahei Yamamoto, Chmn.
   Bus: *Tea, dried seaweed, real estate investments.*

   Tel: (909) 594-7356
   Fax: (909) 595-5849

   %FO: 100
   Emp: 190

● **YAMATO KOGYO CO., LTD.**
380 Kibi, Otsu-ku, Himeji, Hyogo 671-1192, Japan
CEO: Hiroyuki Inoue, Pres.   Tel: 81-792-73-1061   Rev: $674
Bus: *Mfr. of steel products, railway track materials,*   Fax: 81-792-73-9337
and heavy-duty fabricated products   www.yamatokogyo.co.jp
NAICS: 331111, 331210, 331221

    Nucor-Yamato Steel Company
    5929 E. State Hwy. 18, Armorel, Arkansas 72310
    CEO: Joe Stratman, Gen. Mgr.   Tel: (870) 762-5500   %FO: 100
    Bus: *Manufacturer of structural steel shapes*   Fax: (870) 762-1130

● **YAMATO TRANSPORT COMPANY, LTD.**
16-10, Ginza, 2-chome, Chuo-ku, Tokyo 104-8125, Japan
CEO: Keiji Aritomi, Chmn.   Tel: 81-3-3541-3411   Rev: $9,573
Bus: *Door-to-door parcel delivery services, moving &*   Fax: 81-3-5565-3428   Emp: 131,974
freight forwarding services.   www.kuronekoyamato.co.jp
NAICS: 484210, 484230, 488510, 492110, 541511, 541512, 541513, 541519

    YAMATO TRANSPORT USA INC
    755 Port America Place, Ste. 345, Grapevine, Texas 76051
    CEO: Takashi Kikuchi, Mgr.   Tel: (817) 481-9980
    Bus: *Freight transportation arrangements.*   Fax: (817) 421-3456

    YAMATO TRANSPORT USA INC
    4100 A Westfax Dr., Chantilly, Virginia 20151
    CEO: Hideyuki Kataoka, Mgr.   Tel: (703) 968-6896
    Bus: *Freight transportation arrangements.*   Fax: (703) 968-6899

    YAMATO TRANSPORT USA INC
    18202 80 th Ave., S. Kent, Washington 98032
    CEO: Shinji Kokage, Mgr.   Tel: (206) 292-9696
    Bus: *Freight transportation arrangements.*   Fax: (425) 251-9697

    YAMATO TRANSPORT USA INC
    23447 Cabot Blvd., Hayward, California 94545
    CEO: Teruo Egawa, Mgr.   Tel: (510) 259-0400
    Bus: *Freight transportation arrangements.*   Fax: (510) 259-0076

    YAMATO TRANSPORT USA INC
    3679 West 1987 South, Salt Lake City, Utah 84104
    CEO: Kunihiro Tanaka, Mgr.   Tel: (801) 886-9699
    Bus: *Freight transportation arrangements.*   Fax: (801) 886-9604

    YAMATO TRANSPORT USA INC
    5908 N.E. 112th Ave., Portland, Oregon 97220
    CEO: Seigo Kukushima, Mgr.   Tel: (503) 255-1885
    Bus: *Freight transportation arrangements.*   Fax: (503) 255-1938

    YAMATO TRANSPORT USA INC
    470 Metroplex Dr., Ste. 203, Nashville, Tennessee 37211
    CEO: Toru Hiyoshi   Tel: (615) 837-3870
    Bus: *Freight transportation arrangements.*   Fax: (615) 837-9323

YAMATO TRANSPORT USA INC
9005 Travis Dr., Las Milpas Industrial Park, Pharr, Texas 78577
CEO: Kenji Nakai, Mgr. Tel: (956) 782-9270
Bus: *Freight transportation arrangements.* Fax: (956) 782-9287

YAMATO TRANSPORT USA INC
18271 Bishop Ave., Carson, California 90746
CEO: Takeo Kosugi, Mgr. Tel: (310) 885-5400
Bus: *Freight transportation arrangements.* Fax: (310) 884-6994

YAMATO TRANSPORT USA INC
4646 Louisville Ave., Louisville, Kentucky 40209
CEO: Katsuyuki Tokuda, Mgr. Tel: (502) 375-1122
Bus: *Freight transport services.* Fax: (502) 375-1103

YAMATO TRANSPORT USA INC
9446 Old Katy Rd.#106, Houston, Texas 77055
CEO: Toru Hiyoshi Tel: (713) 984-8930
Bus: *Freight transportation arrangements.* Fax: (713) 467-9452

YAMATO TRANSPORT USA INC
99-1450A Koaha Place, Aiea, Hawaii 96701
CEO: Hisanori Kato, Mgr. Tel: (808) 422-6000
Bus: *Freight transportation arrangements.* Fax: (808) 422-3000

YAMATO TRANSPORT USA INC
11701 Metro Airport Center Dr., Ste. 103, Romulus, Michigan 48174
CEO: Masayuki Iizuka, Mgr. Tel: (734) 941-3240
Bus: *Freight transportation arrangements.* Fax: (734) 941-8848

YAMATO TRANSPORT USA INC
3033 International St., Columbus, Ohio 43228
CEO: Toyofumi Fujii, Mgr. Tel: (614) 850-7370
Bus: *Freight transportation arrangements.* Fax: (614) 850-7372

YAMATO TRANSPORT USA INC
920 North Dillon Dr., Wood Dale, Illinois 60191
CEO: Susan Friend, Mgr. Tel: (630) 595-8114
Bus: *Freight transportation arrangements.* Fax: (630) 595-2439

YAMATO TRANSPORT USA INC
3100 E. Piper Lane, Ste. E, Charlotte, North Carolina 28208
CEO: Osamu Shimozono, Mgr. Tel: (704) 329-7300
Bus: *Freight transportation arrangements.* Fax: (704) 329-7304

YAMATO TRANSPORT USA INC
4341 International Pkwy., Ste. 101, Atlanta, Georgia 30354
CEO: Makato Ishii, Mgr. Tel: (404) 363-6062
Bus: *Freight transportation arrangements.* Fax: (404) 362-1017

YAMATO TRANSPORT USA INC
8 State St., Woburn, Massachusetts 01801
CEO: Hideaki Yoshihara, Mgr. Tel: (781) 938-6400 %FO: 100
Bus: *Freight transportation arrangements.* Fax: (781) 938-6455

YAMATO TRANSPORT USA INC
1000 Old County Circle, Unit 108, Windsor Locks, Connecticut 06096
CEO: David Champigny, Mgr.   Tel: (860) 654-0690
Bus: *Freight transportation arrangements.*   Fax: (860) 654-1540

YAMATO TRANSPORT USA, INC.
80 Seaview Dr., Secaucus, New Jersey 07094
CEO: Toru Hiyoshi, Pres.   Tel: (201) 583-9696   %FO: 100
Bus: *Door-to-door parcel delivery services,*   Fax: (201) 583-9699   Emp: 285
    moving and freight forwarding services.

● **YAMAZAKI BAKING CO., LTD.**
10-1, Iwamoto-cho, 3-chome, Chiyoda-ku, Tokyo 101-8585, Japan
CEO: Nobuhiro Iijima   Tel: 81-3-3864-3111   Rev: $6,810
Bus: *Wholesale and retail bakery products.*   Fax: 81-3-3864-3109   Emp: 16,589
                            www.yamazakipan.co.jp
    NAICS: 311330, 311340, 311812, 445120, 445291, 722211

   YAMAZAKI BAKING CO., LTD.
   342 Madison Ave., Ste. 2016, New York, New York 10173
   CEO: Shigetomi Shimada, Principal   Tel: (212) 490-0055
   Bus: *Bakery*   Fax: (212) 490-0062

   YAMAZAKI BAKING CO., LTD.
   123 Japanese Village Plaza, Los Angeles, California 90012
   CEO: Kazumasa Tsugita, Pres.   Tel: (213) 624-2773
   Bus: *Retail bakeries*   Fax: Emp: 45

● **YAMAZAKI MAZAK CORPORATION**
1, Norifune, Oguchi, Oguchi-Cho, Niwa-Gun, Aichi 480-0100, Japan
CEO: Tomohisa Yamazaki, Pres.   Tel: 81-587-95-1131   Rev: $346
Bus: *Machine tool manufacture.*   Fax: Emp: 5,000
                            www.mazak.jp
    NAICS: 333513

   MAZAK CORPORATION
   8025 Production Dr., PO Box 970, Florence, Kentucky 41042
   CEO: Brian Papke, Pres. & CEO   Tel: (859) 342-1700   %FO: 100
   Bus: *Machine tool manufacture.*   Fax: (859) 342-1710   Emp: 830

● **YKK CORPORATION**
1 Kandaizumi-cho, Chiyoda-ku, Tokyo 101-8642, Japan
CEO: Tadahiro Yoshida, Pres. & CEO   Tel: 81-3-3864-2045   Rev: $5,281
Bus: *Mfr. zippers, buttons and clothing fasteners.*   Fax: 81-3-3866-5500   Emp: 35,551
                            www.ykk.com
    NAICS: 332321, 332999, 339993

   YKK CORPORATION OF AMERICA, INC.
   1 Parkway Ctr., 1850 Parkway Pl., SE, Ste. 300, Marietta, Georgia 30067
   CEO: Edward A. Gregory, Pres. & CEO   Tel: (770) 261-6120   %FO: 100
   Bus: *Zippers manufacture.*   Fax: (770) 261-6148

- **YOKOGAWA ELECTRIC CORPORATION**
2-9-32, Nakaco, Musashino-shi, Tokyo 180-8750, Japan
CEO: Isao Uchida, Pres. & CEO
Bus: *Mfr. measurement instruments.*

  Tel: 81-4-2252-5530
  Fax: 81-4-2255-6492
  www.yokogawa.co.jp

  Rev: $3,521
  Emp: 18,364

  NAICS: 334513, 334514, 334515, 335314, 518210
  ### YOKOGAWA CORP. OF AMERICA
  2 Dart Rd., Newman, Georgia 30265
  CEO: Shuzo Kaihori, Pres.
  Bus: *Mfr./sales measurement equipment.*

  Tel: (770) 254-0400
  Fax: (770) 254-0928

  %FO: 100
  Emp: 700

- **YOKOHAMA RUBBER COMPANY, LTD.**
36-11, Shimbashi, 5-chome, Minato-ku, Tokyo 105-8685, Japan
CEO: Tadanobu Nagumo, Pres.
Bus: *Mfr. automotive/aerospace/industrial rubber products.*

  Tel: 81-3-5400-4531
  Fax: 81-3-5400-4572
  www.yrc.co.jp

  Rev: $3,803
  Emp: 13,264

  NAICS: 237310, 326211, 326220, 326291, 326299, 336399, 336413, 339920
  ### YOKOHAMA TIRE CORP.
  601 S. Acacia Ave., Fullerton, California 92831
  CEO:
  Bus: *Tire development and manufacture.*

  Tel: (800) 423-4544
  Fax:

  %FO: 100

- **YUASA TRADING COMPANY, LTD.**
13-10, Nihonbashi Odenmacho, Chuo-ku, Tokyo 103-8570, Japan
CEO: Shigeyoshi Tani, Pres. & CEO
Bus: *Import and export of general merchandise.*

  Tel: 81-3-3665-6511
  Fax: 81-3-3665-6837
  www.yuasa.co.jp

  Rev: $3,705
  Emp: 1,512

  NAICS: 423310, 423610, 423810, 423830, 423840, 423990, 424410, 424490, 424510, 425120, 444190
  ### YUASA TRADING COMPANY (AMERICA) INC.
  60 East 42nd St., Rm. 2800, New York, New York 10165
  CEO: Yoshisumi Hagino, Pres.
  Bus: *Wholesale lumber industrial machinery.*

  Tel: (212) 867-8627
  Fax:

  %FO: 100
  Emp: 13

- **ZEON CORPORATION**
2-6-1, Marunouchi, Chiyoda-ku, Tokyo 100-8323, Japan
CEO: Naozumi Furukawa, Pres.
Bus: *Hydrocarbon resins manufacture.*

  Tel: 81-3-3216-1772
  Fax: 81-3-3216-0501
  www.zeon.co.jp

  Rev: $2,019
  Emp: 2,840

  NAICS: 325199, 325211, 325212
  ### ZEON CORPORATION
  4100 Bells Ln., Louisville, Kentucky 40211
  CEO: Gary W. Grindrod, Pres.
  Bus: *Mfr. and sale of synthetic rubbers.*

  Tel: (502) 775-7700
  Fax: (502) 775-7714

  %FO: 100
  Emp: 75

  ### ZEON CORPORATION
  4111 Bells Ln., Louisville, Kentucky 40211
  CEO: Dave Dargan
  Bus: *Research and development.*

  Tel: (502) 775-7765
  Fax: (502) 775-7783

  %FO: 100

ZEON CORPORATION
1301 W. 7th St., Hattiesburg, Michigan 39401
CEO: Dawson Wilkerson, Plant Mgr.
Bus: *Mfr./sale of synthetic rubbers.*

Tel: (601) 583-6020
Fax: (601) 583-6032

%FO: 100

● **ZERIA PHARMACEUTICAL CO., LTD.**
10-11 Nihombashikobunacho, Chuo-Ku, Tokyo 103-0024, Japan
CEO: Sachiaki Ibe, Pres.
Bus: *Pharmaceuticals and health foods manufacture
and distribution.*
NAICS: 325411, 325412

Tel: 81-3-3663-2351
Fax: 81-3-3663-4503
www.zeria.co.jp

Rev: $464
Emp: 1,362

    ZERIA USA, INC.
    51 E. 42nd St., Rm. 1507, New York, New York 10017
    CEO: Elio R. Loo, Pres.
    Bus: *Pharmaceuticals and healthcare sales and
    distribution.*

Tel: (212) 557-2535
Fax:

%FO: 100
Emp: 3

● **ZUKEN INC.**
2-25-1, Edahigashi, Tsuzuki-ku, Yokohama 224-8585, Japan
CEO: Makoto Kaneko, Pres.
Bus: *Mfr. computer software.*
NAICS: 511210, 541511, 541512, 541519, 541690, 541990, 611420

Tel: 81-45-942-1511
Fax: 81-45-942-1599
www.zuken.co.jp

Rev: $153
Emp: 604

    ZUKEN USA INC.
    238 Littleton Rd., Ste. 100, Westford, Massachusetts 01886
    CEO: J. Katsube, CEO
    Bus: *Mfr./sales computer software.*

Tel: (978) 692-4900
Fax: (978) 692-4725

%FO: 100
Emp: 20

Jordan

- **ARAMEX INTERNATIONAL LIMITED**
  2 Badr Shaker Alsayyab St., Amman 11196, Jordan
  CEO: Fadi Ghandour, Pres. & CEO
  Bus: *Provides freight forwarding, express package
  delivery and transportation services.*
  NAICS: 488510, 492110

  Tel: 962-6-552-2192
  Fax: 962-6-552-7461
  www.aramex.com

  Rev: $188
  Emp: 3,000

  - **ARAMEX INTERNATIONAL**
    6201 Leesburg Pike, Falls Church, Virginia 22044
    CEO: Marwan Mashal, Mgr.
    Bus: *Provides freight forwarding, express
    package delivery and transportation*

    Tel: (703) 534-0828
    Fax: (703) 534-1408

    %FO: 100

  - **ARAMEX INTERNATIONAL COURIER**
    147-29 182nd St., Jamaica, New York 11413
    CEO: Bibi Ali, Mgr.
    Bus: *Provides freight forwarding, express
    package delivery and transportation*

    Tel: (718) 553-8740
    Fax: (718) 553-8953

    %FO: 100
    Emp: 3,000

- **ROYAL JORDANIAN AIRLINES**
  Housing Bank Complex, Amman 11118, Jordan
  CEO: Samer A. Majali, Pres.
  Bus: *Commercial air transport services.*

  NAICS: 481111, 485999, 721110

  Tel: 962-65-607-300
  Fax:
  www.rja.com.jo

  Rev: $382
  Emp: -601,493

  - **ROYAL JORDANIAN AIRLINES**
    7200 NW 19th St., Miami, Florida 33126
    CEO: Jesus Cruz, Mgr.
    Bus: *Air transport services.*

    Tel: (305) 599-0800
    Fax:

  - **ROYAL JORDANIAN AIRLINES**
    1350 n. Michael Dr., Ste. D, Wood Dale, Illinois 60191
    CEO: Ray Meyhoefer, Mgr.
    Bus: *International commercial transportation.*

    Tel: (630) 595-3000
    Fax:

  - **ROYAL JORDANIAN AIRLINES**
    O'Hare International Airport, Chicago, Illinois 60602
    CEO: Michele Boulof, Mgr.
    Bus: *Air transport services.*

    Tel: (773) 686-6020
    Fax:

  - **ROYAL JORDANIAN AIRLINES(CARGO)**
    JFK Int'l Airport, Cargo Bldg., Room 3111, Jamaica, New York 11430
    CEO: Khalil Fanek, Mgr.
    Bus: *International commercial air transport
    services.*

    Tel: (718) 656-6030
    Fax: (718) 244-1821

    %FO: 100

ROYAL JORDANIAN AIRLINES(OFFICE)
6 Park Lane Blvd., Dearborn, Michigan 48126
CEO: Mukhlis Zaidat
Bus: *International commercial air transport
services.*
Tel: (313) 271-6663
Fax: (313) 271-6667
%FO: 100

ROYAL JORDANIAN AIRLINES(RESERVATIONS)
6 East 43rd St., 27/F, New York, New York 10017
CEO: Hussein Dabbas
Bus: *International commercial air transport
services.*
Tel: (212) 949-0060
Fax: (212) 949-0488
%FO: 100

ROYAL JORDANIAN AIRLINES(SALES)
6 Parklane Blvd., Ste. 122, Dearborn, Michigan 48126
CEO: Mukhlis Zaidat
Bus: *International commercial air transport
services.*
Tel: (313) 271-6663
Fax: (313) 271-6667
%FO: 100

Kenya

- **KENYA AIRWAYS**
  Barclays Plaza, 5/F, Loita St., PO Box 41010, Nairobi, Kenya
  CEO: Titus Naikuni, CEO & Mng. Dir.   Tel: 254-20-3274100
  Bus: *Airline transport services.*   Fax: 254-20-336252
                                                www.kenya-airways.com

  NAICS: 481111

  KENYA AIRWAYS
  401 North Michigan Ave., Ste. 865, Chicago, Illinois 60611
  CEO: Sampath Jayasekar, Mgr.   Tel: (312) 923-1012   %FO: 100
  Bus: *Airline transport services.*   Fax: (312) 822-0048

  KENYA AIRWAYS
  16250 Ventura Blvd., Ste. 115, Encino, California 91436
  CEO: Sam Kordi, Mgr.   Tel: (818) 990-5923   %FO: 100
  Bus: *Airline transport services.*   Fax: (818) 501-2098

  KENYA AIRWAYS
  350 Fifth Ave., Ste. 1421, New York, New York 10118
  CEO: Kirti Surendran, Mgr.   Tel: (212) 279-5394   %FO: 100
  Bus: *Airline transport services.*   Fax: (212) 279-6602

  KENYA AIRWAYS
  3050 Post Oak Blvd., Ste. 1320, Houston, Texas 77056
  CEO: Ravin Mehra, Mgr.   Tel: (713) 439-1012   %FO: 100
  Bus: *Airline transport services.*   Fax: (713) 626-1905

Kuwait

- **COMMERCIAL BANK OF KUWAIT (CBK)**
  Mubarak Al-Kabeer St., PO Box 2861, Safat 13029, Kuwait
  CEO: Jamel Abdelhameed Al Mutawa, CEO & Mng.   Tel: 965-241-1001
  Bus: *Commercial banking services.*   Fax: 965-245-0150
  www.banktijari.com
  NAICS: 522110

  - **COMMERCIAL BANK OF KUWAIT**
    1180 Ave. of the Americas, New York, New York 10036
    CEO: Norbert Tiedemann, Mgr.   Tel: (212) 398-9600   %FO: 100
    Bus: *International banking services.*   Fax: (212) 768-7606   Emp: 30

- **KUWAIT AIRWAYS CORP.**
  International Airport Building, Safat 13004, Kuwait
  CEO: Ahmed Faisal AL Zabin, Chmn.   Tel: 965-434-7777   Rev: $732
  Bus: *Commercial air transport services.*   Fax: 965-431-4726   Emp: 3,000
  www.kuwait-airways.com
  NAICS: 481111

  - **KUWAIT AIRWAYS CORP.**
    2015 S. Arlington Heights, Arlington Heights, Illinois 60005
    CEO: Arminak Youkhana, Sales Mgr.   Tel: (847) 437-5455
    Bus: *Air transport services.*   Fax:

  - **KUWAIT AIRWAYS CORPORATION**
    350 Park Ave., New York, New York 10022
    CEO: Waleed Bin Naji, Reg. Mgr.   Tel: (212) 319-1222   %FO: 100
    Bus: *International air transport.*   Fax:

- **KUWAIT PETROLEUM CORP**
  PO Box 26565, Safat 13126, Kuwait
  CEO: Hani Hussein, Chmn. & CEO   Tel: 965-240-0960
  Bus: *Integrated petroleum company.*   Fax: 965-240-7872
  www.kpc.com.kw
  NAICS: 211111, 211112, 213111, 213112, 324110, 324191, 324199, 333132, 424710, 424720

  - **KPC**
    Transco Tower, 2800 Post Oak Blvd., Ste. 5900, Houston, Texas 77056
    CEO: Mohammad Al Hadlaq   Tel: (713) 621-4646   %FO: 100
    Bus: *Oil drilling services.*   Fax: (713) 621-4797

- **THE NATIONAL BANK OF KUWAIT S.A.K.**
  Abdullah Al Ahmad, PO Box 95, Safat Kuwait 13001, Kuwait
  CEO: Ibrahim Dabdoub, CEO   Tel: 965-242-2011
  Bus: *Commercial banking services.*   Fax: 965-246-5190
  www.nbk.com
  NAICS: 522110, 522210, 522291, 522293, 523120, 523920, 523930, 525910, 921130

THE NATIONAL BANK OF KUWAIT S.A.K.
299 Park Ave., 20/F, New York, New York 10171
CEO: Muhammad Kamal, CEO
Bus: *International banking services.*

Tel: (212) 303-9800
Fax: (212) 319-8269

%FO: 100
Emp: 57

Lebanon

- **BANK AUDI**
Bank Audi Plaza, PO Box 11-2560 Riad El-Solh, Beirut, Lebanon
CEO: Samir N. Hanna, CEO   Tel: 961-1-994-000   Rev: $87
Bus: *Commercial banking services.*   Fax: 961-1-990-555   Emp: 100
    www.audi.com.lb
NAICS: 522110

     INTERAUDI BANK
     19 East 54th St., New York, New York 10022
     CEO: Joseph G. Audi, Pres.   Tel: (212) 833-1000   %FO: 100
     Bus: *International commercial banking services.*   Fax: (212) 833-1033   Emp: 66

     INTERAUDI BANK
     200 South Biscayne Boulevard Blvd., Ste. 2650, Miami, Florida 33131
     CEO: Nabil Achkar, Mgr.   Tel: (305) 373-0200   %FO: 100
     Bus: *International commercial banking services.*   Fax: (305) 373-0670

- **MIDDLE EAST AIRLINES (MEA)**
PO Box 206, Beirut International Airport, Beirut, Lebanon
CEO: Mohamad EL Hout, Gen. Dir.   Tel: 961-1-622222
Bus: *Commercial air transport services.*   Fax: 961-1-629279
    www.mea.com.lb
NAICS: 481111

     MIDDLE EAST AIRLINES
     9841 Airport Blvd., Ste. 810, Los Angeles, California 90045
     CEO: Habib Badaro, Mgr.   Tel: (310) 338-9124   %FO: 100
     Bus: *International air transport.*   Fax: (310) 338-9148

     MIDDLE EAST AIRLINES
     362 Fifth Ave., Ste. 701, New York, New York 10001
     CEO: Adib Kassis, Mgr.   Tel: (212) 244-6850   %FO: 100
     Bus: *International air transport.*   Fax: (212) 244-6860

Liechtenstein

- **BALZERS AG, DIV. UNAXIS HOLDING**
  18 Iramali, FL-9496 Balzers, Liechtenstein
  CEO: Dr. Hans Schulz, Pres. & CEO   Tel: 49-423-388-4785
  Bus: *Mfr. coated tools and film.*   Fax: 49-423-388-5419   Emp: 1,835
                                             www.balzers.com

  NAICS: 325510, 333319

  ### BALZERS, INC.
  2511 Technology Dr., Ste. 114, Elgin, Illinois 60123
  CEO: Christian Kunz   Tel: (847) 844-1753   %FO: 100
  Bus: *Mfr. coated tools and film.*   Fax: (847) 844-3306

  ### BALZERS, INC.
  1130 Industrial Pkwy. North, Brunswick, Ohio 44212
  CEO: Paul Faiken   Tel: (330) 220-7716   %FO: 100
  Bus: *Mfr. coated tools and film.*   Fax: (330) 220-6611

- **HILTI CORPORATION**
  Feldkircherstrasse 100, PB 333, FL-9494 Schaan, Liechtenstein
  CEO: Prof. Dr Pius Baschera, CEO   Tel: 41-4232-342111   Rev: $2,915
  Bus: *Drilling and fastening systems manufacture.*   Fax: 41-4232-342965   Emp: 15,120
                                             www.hilti.com
  NAICS: 332510, 333120, 333515, 333991, 339993, 423710, 423810, 423830, 423840

  ### HILTI CORPORATION
  5400 S. 122nd East Ave., Tulsa, Oklahoma 74146
  CEO: Gilbert L. Morris   Tel: (918) 252-6000   %FO: 100
  Bus: *Drilling and fastening systems manufacture*   Fax: (918) 254-0522
       and sales.

Luxembourg

● **ARCELOR SECTIONS COMMERCIAL SA**
66, rue de Luxembourg, L-4221 Esch-sur-Alzette, Luxembourg
CEO: Sylvie Petetin, Pres. & CEO   Tel: 352-5313-3007   Rev: $25,700
Bus: *Rolled steel manufacture.*   Fax: 352-5313-3095   Emp: 104,240
                                             www.arcelor.com

NAICS: 331111, 331221

  ARCELOR INTERNATIONAL AMERICA
  350 Hudson St., 4/F, New York, New York 10014
  CEO: Jacques Chabanier, Mgr.   Tel: (212) 520-7500   %FO: 100
  Bus: *Rolled steel manufacture.*   Fax: (212) 371-4493   Emp: 444

● **CLEARSTREAM BANKING INTERNATIONAL**
42 JF Kennedy Ave., L-1855 Luxembourg, Luxembourg
CEO: Stefan Lepp, Dir.   Tel: 352-2-43-0
Bus: *International banking and securities transactions.*   Fax: 352-2-43-3-8000
                                          www.clearstream.com

NAICS: 522110, 523110

  CLEARSTREAM BANKING
  350 Madison Ave., 23/F, New York, New York 10017
  CEO: Anthony Masiello, Chmn.   Tel: (212) 309-8888   %FO: 100
  Bus: *International banking and securities*   Fax: (212) 309-8889
        transactions.

● **THE CRONOS GROUP**
5, rue Guillaume Kroll, L-1882, Luxembourg
CEO: Dennis J. Tietz   Tel: 352-453-145   Rev: $137
Bus: *Engaged in leasing of intermodal containers to*   Fax: 352-453-147   Emp: 80
       marine carriers and transport operators.   www.cronos.com
NAICS: 332439

  CRONOS CONTAINERS INC.
  517 Route One South, Ste. 1000, Iselin, New Jersey 08830
  CEO: Thomas Lougren, Mgr.   Tel: (732) 602-0808   %FO: 100
  Bus: *Engaged in leasing of intermodal containers*   Fax: (732) 602-7722
        to marine carriers and transport operators.

● **ESPIRITO SANTO FINANCIAL GROUP (ESFG)**
231 Val des Bons Malades, L-2121 Luxembourg-Kirchberg, Luxembourg
CEO: Ricardo Espirito Silva, Chmn. & Pres.   Tel: 352-434945   Rev: $4,974
Bus: *General commercial banking services.*   Fax: 352-434-9454   Emp: 3,739
                                          www.esfg.com

NAICS: 522110

  BANCO ESPIRITO SANTO
  320 Park Ave., 29/F, New York, New York 10022
  CEO: Joaquim Garnecho, Gen. Mgr.   Tel: (212) 702-3410   %FO: 100
  Bus: *Commercial banking services.*   Fax: (212) 750-3888

ESPIRITO SANTO BANK
1395 Brickell Ave., Miami, Florida 33131
CEO: Victor C. Balestra, Pres.　　　　　　Tel: (305) 358-7700　　　%FO: 100
Bus: *Commercial banking services.*　　　　Fax: (305) 371-4410　　　Emp: 68

TAYLOR RAFFERTY ASSOCIATES
205 Lexington Ave., 7/F, New York, New York 10016
CEO: Brian Rafferty, Mng. Dir.　　　　　　Tel: (212) 889-4350　　　%FO: 100
Bus: *Commercial banking services.*　　　　Fax: (212) 696-4357　　　Emp: 80

● **GEMPLUS INTERNATIONAL SA**
46A, avenue J.F. Kennedy, L-1855 Luxembourg, Luxembourg
CEO: Alex J. Mandl, Pres. & CEO　　　　　Tel: 352-26-005-226　　　Rev: $1,172
Bus: *Mfr. of magnetic stripe cards (Smart Cards) and*　Fax: 352-26-005-832　　　Emp: 5,476
　　　software for access.　　　　　　　　www.gemplus.com
　NAICS: 333313

　　GEMPLUS CORPORATION
　　1350 Old Bayshore Hwy., Ste. 445, Burlingame, California 94010
　　CEO: Ron Macintosh, Pres.　　　　　　Tel: (650) 373-0200　　　%FO: 100
　　Bus: *Mfr. of magnetic stripe cards and software*　Fax: (650) 373-0201　　　Emp: 400
　　　　for access.

　　GEMPLUS CORPORATION
　　1655 Fort Myer Dr., Ste. 260, Arlington, Virginia 22209
　　CEO: Ernie Berger, EVP　　　　　　　Tel: (877) 291-1312　　　%FO: 100
　　Bus: *Mfr. of magnetic stripe cards and software*　Fax: (703) 373-5080
　　　　for access.

　　GEMPLUS CORPORATION
　　101 Park Dr., Montgomeryville, Pennsylvania 18936
　　CEO: Ronny DeTonnac, Pres.　　　　　Tel: (215) 390-2000　　　%FO: 100
　　Bus: *Mfr. of magnetic stripe cards and software*　Fax: (215) 390-2353　　　Emp: 400
　　　　for access.

　　GEMPLUS CORPORATION
　　16633 N Dallas Pkwy., Ste. 450, Addison, Texas 75001
　　CEO: Ernie Berger, EVP　　　　　　　Tel: (972) 726-1870　　　%FO: 100
　　Bus: *Mfr. of magnetic stripe cards and software*　Fax: (972) 726-1868
　　　　for access.

　　GEMPLUS CORPORATION
　　Keith Valley Business Center, One Progress Dr., 2/F, Horsham, Pennsylvania 19044
　　CEO: Carolyn Bach, Mgr.　　　　　　　Tel: (215) 390-2000　　　%FO: 100
　　Bus: *Mfr. of magnetic stripe cards and software*　Fax: (215) 390-2353　　　Emp: 50
　　　　for access.

● **MILLICOM INTERNATIONAL CELLULAR SA**
75 Route de Longwy, L-8080 Bertrange, Luxembourg
CEO: Marc Beuls, Pres. & CEO　　　　　Tel: 352-27-759-101　　　Rev: $921
Bus: *Cellular phone operations.*　　　　　Fax: 352-27-759-359　　　Emp: 2,269
　　　　　　　　　　　　　　　　　　www.millicom.com
　NAICS: 517212, 517910

MIT MILLICOM INTERNATIONAL
561 Acorn St., Ste. D, Deer Park, New York 11729
CEO: Thomas Cheng, Pres.   Tel: (631) 595-1515   %FO: 100
Bus: *Cellular phone operations.*   Fax:

● **SES GLOBAL SA**
Chateau de Betzdorf, L-6815 Betzdorf, Luxembourg
CEO: Romain Bausch, Pres. & CEO   Tel: 352-710-725-1   Rev: $1,564
Bus: *Saws, drills, and fastening systems manufacture*   Fax: 352-710-725-227   Emp: 985
     for the construction and building maintenance   www.ses-global.com
     industries.
  NAICS: 517212, 517410, 517910, 518210, 561499
    SES AMERICOM, INC.
    Four Research Way, Princeton, New Jersey 08540
    CEO: Edward D. Horowitz, Pres. & CEO   Tel: (609) 987-4000   %FO: 100
    Bus: *Saws, drills, and fastening systems*   Fax: (609) 987-4517
         manufacture and sales.

● **TENARIS SA**
46A, Avenue John F. Kennedy, L-1855 Luxembourg, Luxembourg
CEO: Paolo Rocca, CEO   Tel: 352-26-47-89-78   Rev: $3,800
Bus: *Mfr. seamless steel pipe.*   Fax: 352-26-47-89-79   Emp: 16,500
                              www.tenaris.com
  NAICS: 331210
    TENARIS PIPELINE SERVICE, INC.
    2200 West Loop South, Ste. 800, Houston, Texas 77027
    CEO: Hermann Buschor   Tel: (713) 767-4400   %FO: 100
    Bus: *Seamless steel pipe manufacture.*   Fax: (713) 767-4444

Malaysia

- **1ST SILICON MALAYSIA SDN BHD**
  1 Silicon Drive, Sama Jaya Free Industrial Zone, 93350 Kuching Sarawak, Malaysia
  CEO: William J. Nelson, CEO   Tel: 60-82-354-888   Rev: $83
  Bus: *Semiconductor foundry services.*   Fax: 60-82-363-330
  www.1stsilicom.com

  NAICS: 334413

  > **1ST SILICON AMERICA, INC.**
  > 2635 N. 1st St., Ste. 203, San Jose, California 95134
  > CEO: Claudio G. Loddo, CEO   Tel: (408) 943-8131   %FO: 100
  > Bus: *Semiconductor foundry services.*   Fax: (408) 943-8135

- **ACCTRAK 21 INTERNATIONAL LTD.**
  22, 2nd Fl., Jalan USJ 10/1E, 47620 UEP Subang Jaya, Malaysia
  CEO: Tim Loving, CEO   Tel: 60-3-5636-7484
  Bus: *Business management and accounting software*   Fax: 60-3-5635-6164
  for small and mid-size businesses.   www.acctrak21.com
  NAICS: 541511

  > **ACCTRAK 21 INTERNATIONAL LTD.**
  > 4600 S. Ulster St., Ste. 540, Denver, Colorado 80237
  > CEO: Steve Yulga   Tel: (888) 619-9399   %FO: 100
  > Bus: *Business management and accounting*   Fax: (888) 619-9399
  > *software for small and mid-size businesses.*

- **BANK NEGARA MALAYSIA**
  Jalan Dato' Onn, P.O. Box 10922, 50929 Kuala Lumpur, Malaysia
  CEO: Tan Sri Dato' Sri Dr. Zeti Alhatar Aziz, Chmn.   Tel: 60-3-2698-8044
  Bus: *Government bank.*   Fax: 60-3-2691-2990
  www.bnm.gov.my

  NAICS: 522110

  > **BANK NEGARA MALAYSIA**
  > 900 Third Ave., 18/F, New York, New York 10022
  > CEO: Sook Peng Tan, Mgr.   Tel: (212) 888-9220   %FO: 100
  > Bus: *Government & banking services.*   Fax: (212) 755-4561

- **MALAYAN BANKING BERHAD (MAYBANK)**
  Menara Maybank, 14/F, 100 Jalan Tun Perak, 50050 Kuala Lumpur, Malaysia
  CEO: Amirsham A. Aziz, Pres. & CEO   Tel: 60-3-2070-8833   Rev: $2,405
  Bus: *Commercial banking services.*   Fax: 60-3-2070-2611   Emp: 20,821
  www.maybank.com.my
  NAICS: 522110

  > **MALAYAN BANKING BERHAD (MAYBANK)**
  > 400 Park Ave., 9/F, New York, New York 10022
  > CEO: Wan Mohd. Fadzmi Wan Othman, Gen.   Tel: (212) 303-1300   %FO: 100
  > Bus: *International banking services.*   Fax: (212) 308-0109   Emp: 30

- **MALAYSIA AIRLINE SYSTEM BERHAD**
  MAS Bldg, 33/F, Jalan Sultan Ismail, 50250 Kuala Lumpur, Malaysia
  CEO: Dato' Abdul Rashid Khan, Gen. Mgr.   Tel: 60-3-261-0555   Rev: $1,982
  Bus: *International commercial air transport.*   Fax: 60-3-261-3472   Emp: 23,075
  www.malaysiaairlines.com
  NAICS: 481111, 561599

  ### MALAYSIA AIRLINES
  100 NE 3rd. Ave., Ste. 790, Ft. Lauderdale, Florida 33301
  CEO: Carlos Banks, Mgr.   Tel: (954) 767-0907   %FO: 100
  Bus: *International commercial air transport   Fax: (954) 767-0903
  services.*

  ### MALAYSIA AIRLINES
  100 North Sepulveda Blvd., Ste. 400, El Segundo, California 90245
  CEO: Ismail Talib, VP   Tel: (310) 535-9288   %FO: 100
  Bus: *International commercial air transport   Fax: (310) 535-9088
  services.*

  ### MALAYSIA AIRLINES
  1667 K. St. NW, Ste. 610, Washington, District of Columbia 20006
  CEO: Zeenet Koreshi, Mgr.   Tel: (202) 833-9180   %FO: 100
  Bus: *International commercial air transport   Fax: (202) 833-9178
  services.*

  ### MALAYSIA AIRLINES
  122 East 42nd St., Ste. 515, New York, New York 10168
  CEO: Tel: (212) 697-8994   %FO: 100
  Bus: *International commercial air transport   Fax: (212) 867-0325
  services.*

  ### MALAYSIA AIRLINES
  456 Montgomery St., Ste. 488, San Francisco, California 94104
  CEO: Henrik Von Rosen, Mgr.   Tel: (415) 788-0555   %FO: 100
  Bus: *International commercial air transport   Fax: (415) 788-6102
  services.*

- **OYL MANUFACTURING COMPANY SDN. BHD.**
  Jalan Pengapit 15/19, PO Box 7072, Shah Alam, Darul Ehsan, 40702 Selangor, Malaysia
  CEO: Foo Say Jan, Chmn.   Tel: 60-3-2164-3000   Rev: $1,167
  Bus: *Investment holding company: subsidiaries   Fax: 60-3-550-3730
  engaged in manufacture and distribution of   www.oyl.com.my
  heating, ventilation and air conditioning systems.*
  NAICS: 551112

  ### MC QUAY INTERNATIONAL INC.
  13600 Industrial Park Blvd., Minneapolis, Minnesota 55441
  CEO: Hugh Crowther   Tel: (763) 553-5177   %FO: 100
  Bus: *Heating, ventilation and air conditioning   Fax: (763) 553-5177
  systems manufacture.*

  ### MC QUAY LATIN AMERICA, INC.
  7205 NW 19th St., Ste. 408, Miami, Florida 33126
  CEO: Jose Ramos   Tel: (305) 716-8631   %FO: 100
  Bus: *Heating, ventilation and air conditioning   Fax: (305) 716-8643
  systems manufacture.*

● **SILTERRA MALAYSIA SDN. BHD.**
Kulim Hi-Tech Park, Lot 8, Phase 2, Kulim, 09000 Kedah, Malaysia
CEO: Bruce Gray, CEO   Tel: 60-4-403-3888   Rev: $150
Bus: *Semiconductor manufacture.*   Fax: 60-4-403-1675
                                         www.silterra.com
NAICS: 334413
    SILTERRA INC.
    1740 Technology Dr., Ste. 530, San Jose, California 95110
    CEO: Steve Della Rocchetta, EVP   Tel: (408) 530-0888   %FO: 100
    Bus: *Sale of electronic parts & equipment.*   Fax: (408) 530-0877   Emp: 18

Malta

- **GFI SOFTWARE LTD.**
  GFI House, San Andrea St., San Swann SGN 05, Malta
  CEO: Nicholas Paul Andrew Galea, Chmn.   Tel: 356-21-382-418   Rev: $4
  Bus: *Mfr. network security, content security and*   Fax: 356-21-382-419
      messaging software.   www.gfi.com
  NAICS: 511210

      GFI SOFTWARE, INC.
      15300 Weston Pkwy., Ste. 104, Cary, North Carolina 27513
      CEO: Thomas C. Kucmierz   Tel: (919) 379-3397   %FO: 100
      Bus: *Messaging and communications products*   Fax: (919) 379-3402
          manufacture.

Mexico

- **AEROVIAS DE MEXICO**
  Paseo de la Reforma 445, Cuauhtemoc, 06500 Mexico DF, Mexico
  CEO: Fernando Flores Perez, Dir.
  Bus: *Commercial air transport carrier.*
  Tel: 52-55-133-4000
  Fax: 52-55-133-4623
  www.aeromexico.com
  Rev: $1,306
  Emp: 6,650

  NAICS: 481219, 551112

  ### AEROMEXICO
  Geo. Bush Intercontinental Airport, Terminal "D", PO Box 60216, AMF Houston, Texas 77032
  CEO: Dennis Mancini, Mgr.
  Bus: *Air transport services.*
  Tel: (281) 372-3400
  Fax: (281) 372-3436
  %FO: 100

  ### AEROMEXICO
  Chicago O'Hare Int'l Airport Terminal 5, Room UL 132A, PO Box 66453, Chicago, Illinois 60666-0453
  CEO: Christopher Lopez, Pres.
  Bus: *Air transport services.*
  Tel: (773) 462-9472
  Fax: (773) 462-9471
  %FO: 100

  ### AEROMEXICO AIRLINES
  Logan Int'l Airport, 500 Terminal E., East Boston, Massachusetts 02128-1125
  CEO:
  Bus: *Air transport services.*
  Tel: (617) 569-9501
  Fax: (617) 634-6222
  %FO: 100

  ### AEROMEXICO AIRLINES
  JFK Int'l Airport, Terminal 1, Mezzanine, Jamaica, New York 11430
  CEO:
  Bus: *Air transport services.*
  Tel: (718) 751-2560
  Fax: (718) 553-6918
  %FO: 100

  ### AEROMEXICO AIRLINES
  Miami Int'l Airport, Concourse 5, 2/F, PO Box 996250, Miami, Florida 33299-6250
  CEO:
  Bus: *Air transport services.*
  Tel: (305) 868-4430
  Fax: (305) 869-4434
  %FO: 100

  ### AEROMEXICO AIRLINES
  Los Angeles Int'l Airport, Terminal 5, 500 World Way, Los Angeles, California 90045
  CEO:
  Bus: *Air transport services.*
  Tel: (310) 646-0338
  Fax: (310) 215-5058
  %FO: 100

  ### AEROMEXICO AIRLINES
  Dallas/Ft. Worth Int'l Airport Terminal E, Section "C" PO Box 610738, Dallas, Texas 75261
  CEO:
  Bus: *Air transport services.*
  Tel: (972) 574-6886
  Fax: (972) 574-8070
  %FO: 100

  ### AEROMEXICO AIRLINES
  ATL Hartsfield Int'l Airport Terminal So., 6000 S. Terminal Pkwy, Atlanta, Georgia 30320
  CEO:
  Bus: *Air transport services.*
  Tel: (404) 714-7059
  Fax: (404) 559-9975
  %FO: 100

AEROMEXICO AIRLINES
McCarran Int'l Airport Terminal 2, 5757 Wayne Newton Blvd., POB 11630, Las Vegas, Nevada 89111
CEO: Lizzete Trujillo, Mgr.　　　　　　　　　Tel: (702) 261-6114　　　　%FO: 100
Bus: *Air transport services.*　　　　　　　　Fax: (702) 261-6115　　　　Emp: 3

AEROMEXICO AIRLINES
3800 E. Sky Harbor Blvd., Phoenix, Arizona 85034
CEO: Casrlos Betancourt, Mgr.　　　　　　　Tel: (602) 231-8880　　　　%FO: 100
Bus: *Air transport services.*　　　　　　　　Fax: (602) 231-8880　　　　Emp: 15

AEROMEXICO AIRLINES
El Paso Int'l Airport, 6701 - Convair Rd., El Paso, Texas 79925
CEO:　　　　　　　　　　　　　　　　　　Tel: (915) 771-7478　　　　%FO: 100
Bus: *Air transport services.*　　　　　　　　Fax:

- **ALFA, S.A. de C.V.**
Avenida Gomez Morin 1111 Sur, Colonia Carrizalejo, San Pedro Garza Garcia, 66254 Nuevo Leon, Mexico
CEO: Dionisio Garza Medina, Chmn. & CEO　Tel: 52-81-8748-1111　　　Rev: $5,254
Bus: *Supplier of petrochemical synthetic fibers*　Fax: 52-81-8748-2552　　　Emp: 42,069
　　　　　　　　　　　　　　　　　　　　www.alfa.com.mx
NAICS: 325110

　　DAK AMERICAS
　　6324 Fairview Rd., Charlotte, North Carolina 28210
　　CEO: Hector Camberos, Pres.　　　　　　Tel: (704) 940-7562　　　%FO: 100
　　Bus: *Supplier of petrochemical synthetic fibers*　Fax: (704) 940-7501　　　Emp: 1,500

- **AMERICA MOVIL, SA DE CV**
Lago Alberto 366, Colonia Anahuac, 11320 Mexico DF, Mexico
CEO: Daniel Hajj Aboumrad, CEO　　　　　Tel: 52-55-2581-4411　　　Rev: $12,094
Bus: *Provides wireless phone service and telephone*　Fax: 52-55-5545-5550　　　Emp: 23,215
　　cards.　　　　　　　　　　　　　　　www.americamovil.com
NAICS: 517212

　　TRACFONE WIRELESS, INC.
　　8390 NW 25th St., Miami, Florida 33122
　　CEO: F. J. Pollak, CEO　　　　　　　　Tel: (305) 640-2000　　　%FO: 100
　　Bus: *Provides wireless phone services.*　　Fax: (305) 715-6921

- **BRYAN, GONZALEZ VARGAS Y GONZALEZ BAZ, S.C.**
Seneca 425, Polanco, 11560 Mexico DF, Mexico
CEO: Aureliano Gonzalez-Baz, Prtn.　　　　Tel: 52-55-5279-3600
Bus: *International law firm; Mexican and Latin*　Fax: 52-55-5279-3610　　　Emp: 250
　　American law.　　　　　　　　　　　www.bryanlex.com
NAICS: 541110

　　BRYAN, GONZALEZ VARGAS Y GONZALEZ BAZ, S.C.
　　16 East 52nd St., New York, New York 10022
　　CEO: Aureliano Gonzalez-Bez, Mng. Prtn.　Tel: (212) 355-5400　　　%FO: 100
　　Bus: *International law firm; Mexican and Latin*　Fax: (212) 355-6111
　　American law.

- **CEMEX S.A. DE C.V.**
  Avenida Ricardo Margain Zozaya, 325, Colonia del Valle Campestre, San Pedro Garza García, 66265 Nuevo Leon,

  CEO: Lorenzo H. Zambrano, CEO　　　　　Tel:　52-81-8888-8888　　　Rev: $8,148
  Bus: *Mfr. cement and concrete.*　　　　　　Fax:　52-81-8888-4417　　　Emp: 26,000
  　　　　　　　　　　　　　　　　　　　　　　　www.cemex.com
  NAICS:　212312, 212321, 327310, 327320, 327390, 327420

  CEMEX
  840 Gessner, Ste. 140, Houston, Texas　77024
  CEO: Gilberto Perez, Pres. & CEO　　　　Tel:　(713) 650-6200　　　%FO: 100
  Bus: *Mfr./distribution cement & concrete.*　Fax:　(713) 653-6815

  CEMEX
  1200 Smith St., Ste. 2400, Houston, Texas　77002
  CEO: Stephen R. Miley　　　　　　　　　Tel:　(713) 650-6200　　　%FO: 100
  Bus: *Mfr./distribution cement & concrete.*　Fax:　(713) 650-6200

  CEMEX
  590 Madison Ave., 41/F, New York, New York　10022
  CEO: Beate Melten, Chmn.　　　　　　　　Tel:　(212) 317-6000　　　%FO: 100
  Bus: *Mfr./distribution cement & concrete.*　Fax:　(212) 317-6047

- **CONTROLADORA COMERCIAL MEXICANA, S.A. DE C.V. (CCM)**
  Ave. Revolucion 780, Modulo 2, 03730 Mexico DF, Mexico
  CEO: Carlos Gonzalez Zabalegui, CEO　　Tel:　52-55-5270-9000　　　Rev: $3,085
  Bus: *Owns and manages supermarket and general*　Fax:　52-55-5371-7302　　　Emp: 33,000
  　　merchandise stores and restaurants.　　www.comerci.com.mx
  NAICS:　445110

  COSTCO COMPANIES
  999 Lake Dr., Issaquah, Washington　98027
  CEO: James D. Sinegal, Pres. & CEO　　Tel:　(425) 313-8100　　　%FO: JV
  Bus: *Operates Price/Costco warehouse clubs*　Fax:　(425) 313-8221
  　　(JV).

- **COPAMEX, S.A. de C.V.**
  Montes Apalaches 101, Residencial San Agustin, San Pedro Garza Garcia, 66260 Nuevo Leon, Mexico
  CEO: Juan B. Maldonado Quiroga, Chmn.　Tel:　52-81-8152-6000
  Bus: *Mfr. of consumer paper products*　　Fax:　52-81-8152-6129
  　　　　　　　　　　　　　　　　　　　　www.copamex.com
  NAICS:　322291, 322299

  COPAMEX NORTH AMERICA INC.
  1201 N. Watson Rd., Ste. 268, Arlington, Texas　76006
  CEO: Raymond A. Radcliff, Sales　　　　Tel:　(817) 652-8932　　　%FO: 100
  Bus: *Manufacturer of consumer paper products*　Fax:　(817) 652-8976

- **CORPORACION DURANGO, S.A. de C.V.**
  Potasio 150, Ciudad Industrial, 34220 Durango, Mexico
  CEO: Miguel Rincon, Chmn. & CEO　　　Tel:　52-618-514-1658　　　Rev: $608
  Bus: *Mfr. of packaging, paper, and wood products*　Fax:　52-618-814-1275　　　Emp: 7,587
  　　　　　　　　　　　　　　　　　　　　www.corpdgo.com
  NAICS:　321920, 322121, 322211, 322212, 322299

Durango-McKinley Paper Company
700 Sam Houston Rd., Dallas, Texas 75149
CEO: Prudencio Calderon
Bus: *Manufacturer of packaging, paper, and wood products.*

Tel: (972) 786-7000
Fax: (972) 786-7058

%FO: 100

● **CORPORACION INTERAMERICANA de ENTRETENIMIENTO, S.A. de C.V.**
Paseo de las Palmas 1005, Colonia Lomas de Chapultepec, 11000 Mexico DF, Mexico
CEO: Alejandro Soberon Kuri, Chmn. & CEO
Bus: *Producer and manager of live events*

Tel: 52-55-5201-9000
Fax: 52-55-5201-9401
www.cie-mexico.com.mx

Rev: $595
Emp: 10,891

NAICS: 711310, 713110, 713990

CIE USA Entertainment
200 W. 57th St., Ste.404, New York, New York 10019
CEO: Bruce E. Morgan, Pres.
Bus: *Producer and manager of live events*

Tel: (212) 586-0222
Fax: (212) 586-4695

%FO: 100

● **DESC, S.A. de C.V.**
Paseo de los Tamarindoes 400-B, Bosques de las Lomas, 05120 Mexico DF, Mexico
CEO: Fernando Senderos Mestre, Chmn. & CEO
Bus: *Mfr. auto parts and specialty chemicals. Real estate development. Food preparation.*

Tel: 52-55-5261-8000
Fax: 52-55-5261-8096
www.desc.com.mx

Rev: $2,130
Emp: 13,652

NAICS: 311711, 311712, 325182, 325520, 336211

AUTHENTIC SPECIALTY FOODS INC.
4340 Eucalyptus Ave., Chino, California 91710-9705
CEO: Ted Gardner, Pres.
Bus: *Manufacturer Mexican spices and sauces.*

Tel: (909) 631-2000
Fax: (909) 631-2100

%FO: 100

● **EDITORIAL TELEVISA SA de CV (Div. Grupo Televisa SA)**
Avenida Vasco de Quiroga #2000, Ed. E, Col. Santa Fe, Del. Alvaro Obregon, 01210 Mexico DF, Mexico
CEO: Eduardo Michelsen Delgado, CEO
Bus: *Spanish-language magazine publishers.*

Tel: 52-55-5261-2761
Fax: 52-55-5261-2704
www.esmas.com/get

NAICS: 511120

EDITORIAL TELEVISA CALIFORNIA
8383 Wilshire Blvd., Ste. 363, Beverly Hills, California 90211
CEO: Sergio Martinez
Bus: *Spanish-language magazine publishers.*

Tel: (323) 655-0535
Fax:

%FO: 100

EDITORIAL TELEVISA INTERNACIONAL
6355 NW 36th St., Miami, Florida 33166
CEO: David Taggart, Grp. Publisher
Bus: *Spanish-language magazine publisher.*

Tel: (305) 871-6400
Fax:

%FO: 100

EDITORIAL TELEVISA NEW YORK
964 Third Ave, 6/F, New York, New York 10155
CEO: David Taggart, Grp. Publisher
Bus: *Spanish-language magazine publisher.*

Tel: (212) 838-7220
Fax: (212) 838-8532

%FO: 100

- **ELAMEX, S.A. DE C.V.**
  Ave. Insurgentes No. 4145-B Oriente, 32340 Ciudad Juarez Chihuahua, Mexico
  CEO: Richard R. Harshman, Pres. & CEO   Tel: 52-16-649-1000   Rev: $98
  Bus: *Candy manufacturing and nut packaging*   Fax: 52-16-649-1000   Emp: 937
       operations, and manufacture of metal and plastic   www.elamex.com
       parts for the appliance and automotive industries.
     NAICS: 325212, 326113, 326211, 326220, 332111, 424450

  - **ELAMEX USA INC.**
    220 N. Kansas, Ste. 566, El Paso, Texas 79901
    CEO: Eloy S. Vallina, Chmn.   Tel: (915) 774-8333   %FO: 100
    Bus: *Mfr. printed circuit boards, fiber-optic*   Fax: (915) 298-3065
         cables, connectors, outlet strips, smoke
         detectors, medical products packaging &
         electronic switches.

  - **FRANKLIN CONNECTIONS**
    1800 Northwestern Dr., El Paso, Texas 79912
    CEO: Richard R. Harshman, Pres.   Tel: (915) 877-1173   %FO: 100
    Bus: *Nut processing and candy manufacture.*   Fax: (915) 877-1173

- **GRUMA, S.A. DE C.V.**
  Calzada del Valle 407, Oriente San Pedro, 66220 Garza Garcia NL, Mexico
  CEO: Roberto Gonzalez Barrera, Chmn. & CEO   Tel: 52-81-8399-3300   Rev: $2,243
  Bus: *Milled corn tortillas manufacturer. (JV with*   Fax: 52-81-8399-3294   Emp: 15,104
       Archer-Daniels-Midland U.S.)   www.gruma.com
     NAICS: 311211, 311830, 311919

  - **GRUMA CORPORATION**
    1159 Cottonwood Lane, Ste. 200, Irving, Texas 75038
    CEO: Jairo Senise, Pres. & CEO   Tel: (972) 232-5000   %FO: 50
    Bus: *Milled corn manufacture.*   Fax: (972) 232-5176

- **GRUPO BIMBO, SA**
  Prolongacion Paseo de la Reforma, 1000, Colonia Pena Blanca Santa Fe, Del. Alvaro Obregon, 01210 Mexico
  DF,
     CEO: Daniel Servitje, CEO   Tel: 52-55-5268-6600   Rev: $4,605
     Bus: *Commercial bakers of bread, tortillas, cookies and*   Fax: 52-55-5268-6847   Emp: 74,000
       cakes.   www.grupobimbo.com
     NAICS: 311340, 311812, 311821, 311830, 311919, 311941

  - **BIMBO BAKERIES USA, INC.**
    515 Jones St., Ft. Worth, Texas 76102
    CEO: Renaldo Reyna, Pres.   Tel: (817) 212-2000   %FO: 100
    Bus: *Commercial bakers of bread, tortillas,*   Fax: (817) 615-3186   Emp: 5,300
         cookies and cakes.

- **GRUPO CEMENTOS DE CHIHUAHUA, SA DE CV**
  Vicente Suarez y Sextra, Colonia Nombre de Dios, 31110 Chihuahua, Mexico
  CEO: Manuel A. Milan, Chmn.   Tel: 52-614-442-3100   Rev: $358
  Bus: *Mfr. cement, cement block and limestone*   Fax: 52-614-424-3377   Emp: 1,478
       aggregates.   www.gcc.com
     NAICS: 327310, 327331, 327992

GCC DACOTAH INC.
PO Box 360, Rapid City, South Dakota 57709-0360
CEO: Steve Zellmer
Bus: *Sales of cement and cement products.*
Tel: (605) 721-7100
Fax: (605) 721-7012
%FO: 100

GCC DACOTAH INC.
PO Box 100, Tijeras, New Mexico 87059
CEO: Joel Adams
Bus: *Sales of cement and cement products.*
Tel: (505) 281-3311
Fax: (505) 281-9126
%FO: 100

GCC RIO GRANDE INC.
4253 Montgomery NE, Albuquerque, New Mexico 87109
CEO: Richard D. Percival
Bus: *Sales of cement and cement products.*
Tel: (505) 281-3351
Fax: (505) 281-3353
%FO: 100

● **GRUPO FINANCIERO SANTANDER SERFIN S.A.**
Avenida Prolongacion Paseo de la, Reforma 500, Colonia Lomas de, Santa Fe, Delagacion Alvaro Obregon, 01219 Mexico DF, Mexico
CEO: Carol Gomez y Gomez, Chmn.
Bus: *Financial services; commercial and investment banking.*
NAICS: 522110, 523991, 524126
Tel: 52-55-5257-8000
Fax: 52-55-5269-2121
www.serfin.com.mx
Rev: $2,564
Emp: 11,853

    SANTANDER INVESTMENT
    45 E. 53rd St., Ste. 900, New York, New York 10022
    CEO: Chandra Boyle, CFO
    Bus: *Commercial banking.*
    Tel: (212) 350-3400
    Fax:
    %FO: 100
    Emp: 500

● **GRUPO GIGANTE, SA DE CV**
Ejercito Nacional 769-A, Delegacion, Miguel Hidalgo, 11520 Mexico DF, Mexico
CEO: Ángel Losada Moreno, Chmn. & Pres.
Bus: *General merchandise retail outlets. (JV Grupo Gigante, Radio Shack and Home Depot).*
NAICS: 445110
Tel: 52-55-5269-8186
Fax: 52-55-5269-8308
www.grupogigante.com.mx
Rev: $2,834
Emp: 35,831

    GIGANTE USA INC.
    270 N. Main St., Ste. 370, Santa Ana, California 92705
    CEO: Justo Frias, Pres.
    Bus: *General merchandise retail outlets.*
    Tel: (714) 664-0600
    Fax: (714) 664-0700
    %FO: 100

● **GRUPO IMSA, S.A. DE C.V.**
Avenida Batallon de San Patricio 111, Piso 26, Fraccionamiento Valle, Oriente, San Pedro Garza Garcia, 66269 Nuevo Leon, Mexico
CEO: Eugenio Clariond Reyes, Chmn. & CEO
Bus: *Mfr. steel, automotive and aluminum and construction products.*
NAICS: 331312, 332311
Tel: 52-81-8153-8300
Fax: 52-81-8153-8400
www.grupoimsa.com
Rev: $2,782
Emp: 15,722

    ASC PROFILES
    2110 Enterprise Blvd., West Sacramento, California 95691
    CEO: Joseph M. Coubal, Pres.
    Bus: *Mfr. of prefabricated metal bldgs and sheet metalwork.*
    Tel: (916) 372-0933
    Fax:
    Emp: 385

DAVIDSON LADDERS INC., DIV. LOUISVILLE LADDERS
700 Swan Dr., Smyrna, Tennessee 37167
CEO: Dave Patterson, Mgr.   Tel: (615) 459-6094   %FO: 100
Bus: *Mfr./sales aluminum ladders.*   Fax: (615) 223-6837   Emp: 130

IMSA INC.
222 Las Colinas Blvd. West, Irving, Texas 75039
CEO: Cesar Jarero, Pres.   Tel: (972) 831-7430
Bus: *Sale of steel, metal.*   Fax: Emp: 18

LOUISVILLE LADDERS INC.
7719 National Turnpike, Bldg. A, Louisville, Kentucky 40214
CEO: Carlos Morino, member   Tel: (502) 636-2811   %FO: 100
Bus: *Mfr./sales aluminum ladders.*   Fax: (502) 636-1014   Emp: 1,500

METL-SPAN
1497 North Kealy St., Lewisville, Texas 75057
CEO: Carl Hielscher, Pres.   Tel: (877) 585-9969   %FO: 100
Bus: *Mfr. of insulated metal panels for buildings.*   Fax: (972) 436-0648   Emp: 200

STABLIT AMERICA, GLASTEEL
425 Industrial Dr., Moscow, Tennessee 38057
CEO: Stephen Adkins, Pres.   Tel: (901) 877-3010
Bus: *Mfr. of fiberglass reinforced plastic panels.*   Fax: (901) 877-1388   Emp: 100

STEELSCAPE INC.
11200 Arrow Rte., Rancho Cucamonga, California 91730
CEO: Paul Zuckerman, Mgr.   Tel: (909) 987-4711
Bus: *Coil coating services.*   Fax: (909) 989-4470   Emp: 300

STEELSCAPE INC.
2995 Atlas Rd., Richmond, California 94806
CEO: David Catterlyn, Pres.   Tel: (510) 262-4888
Bus: *Coating & engraving services.*   Fax: (510) 223-0169   Emp: 175

STEELSCAPE, INC.
222 W. Kalama River Rd., Kalama, Washington 98625
CEO: Miguel Alvarez, Pres.   Tel: (360) 673-8200
Bus: *Mfr. of cold rolled, metallic coated, &*   Fax: (360) 673-8250   Emp: 420
custom painted steel coils.

UNITED PANEL
8 Wildon Dr., PO Box 188, Mt. Bethel, Pennsylvania 18343
CEO: Steve Atkins, Pres.   Tel: (610) 588-6871
Bus: *Mfr. of metal stampings, structural wood*   Fax: (610) 588-0536   Emp: 30
members, hardwood veneer plywood.

VARCO PRUDEN BUILDINGS
3200 Players Club Circle, Memphis, Tennessee 38125
CEO: David Zenger, Pres. & CEO   Tel: (901) 748-8000
Bus: *Mfr. of buildings.*   Fax: (901) 748-9200

- **GRUPO INDUSTRIAL MASECA**
  Avenida Enrique Herrerra 2307, Torre Martel, Col. Valle Oriente, San Pedro Garza Garcia, 64710 Nuevo Leon,
  CEO: Roberto Gonzalez Barrera, Chmn. & Pres. & CEO Tel: 52-81-8333-3800   Rev: $519
  Bus: *Mfr. ready-mixed corn flour to produce corn*   Fax: 52-81-8333-3287   Emp: 2,799
     tortillas, including Mission brand.   www.gimsa.com
  NAICS: 311822, 311830

  MISSION FOODS
  2110 Santa Fe Dr., Pueblo, Colorado 81006
  CEO: Ran Balalaman, Mgr.   Tel: (719) 543-4350   %FO: 100
  Bus: *Sales/distribution of Mission brand corn*   Fax: (719) 545-3681   Emp: 300
     flour products.

  MISSION FOODS
  1159 Cottonwood Lane, Ste. 200, Irving, Texas 75038
  CEO: Jairo Senise, Pres. & CEO   Tel: (972) 232-5200   %FO: 100
  Bus: *Sales/distribution of Mission brand corn*   Fax: (972) 232-5176   Emp: 4,900
     flour products.

- **GRUPO MEXICO SA DE CV**
  Avenida Baja California 200, Colonia Roma Sur, 06760 Mexico DF, Mexico
  CEO: German Larrea Mota-Velasco, CEO   Tel: 52-55-5080-0050   Rev: $4,206
  Bus: *Production of copper, silver and zinc.*   Fax: 52-55-5564-7677   Emp: 21,068
      www.gmexico.com
  NAICS: 212210, 212221, 212222, 212231, 212234, 212291, 212299, 213114, 482111, 482112

  ASARCO, INC.
  1150 North 7th Ave., Tucson, Arizona 85705
  CEO: Daniel Tellechea, Pres.   Tel: (520) 798-7500   %FO: 100
  Bus: *Mines smelts & refines copper, silver, lead,*   Fax: (520) 798-7780   Emp: 2,000
     gold & zinc.

  ASARCO, INC.
  2575 East Camelback Rd., Ste. 500, Phoenix, Arizona 85016
  CEO: German Larrea, Mgr.   Tel: (602) 977-6500   %FO: 100
  Bus: *Production of copper.*   Fax: (602) 977-6700   Emp: 60

  SOUTHERN COPPER
  2575 East Camelback Rd., Ste. 500, Phoenix, Arizona 85016
  CEO: Oscar Gonzalez Rocha, Pres.   Tel: (602) 977-6500   %FO: 100
  Bus: *Mfr. of integrated copper.*   Fax: (602) 977-6700   Emp: 3,544

- **GRUPO MINSA, SA DE CV**
  Prolongacion Toltecas 4, Los Reyes Ixtacala, Tlalnepantla, 54090 Mexico, Mexico
  CEO: Jose Cacho Ribeiro, Gen. Mgr.   Tel: 52-55-5722-1900
  Bus: *Mfr. corn flour.*   Fax: 52-55-5722-1905
      www.minsa.com
  NAICS: 311211

  MINSA USA INC.
  2049 Fernwood Ave., Red Oak, Iowa 51566
  CEO: Jose Luis Rebolleda, Pres.   Tel: (800) 701-5892   %FO: 100
  Bus: *Manufacturing plant for corn flour.*   Fax: Emp: 36

MINSA USA INC.
PO Box 484, Muleshoe, Texas 79347
CEO: Jose Luis Rebolleda, Pres.   Tel: (800) 852-8291
Bus: *Manufacturing plant for corn flour.*   Fax: Emp: 83

● **GRUPO PORCELANITE**
Bosque de Ciruelos, 130-9 piso, Col. Bosques de las Lomas, 11700 Mexico DF, Mexico
CEO: Alejandro Aboumrad Gabriel, Pres.   Tel: 52-55-52-469-912   Rev: $271
Bus: *Ceramic tile production.*   Fax: Emp: 2,500
                                                www.porcelanite.com

NAICS: 327122, 551112

　　PORCELANITE INC.
　　1184 Corporate Dr., Ste. E, Arlington, Texas 76006
　　CEO: Alejandro Aboumrad Gabriel, Chmn.   Tel: (817) 607-1500   %FO: 100
　　Bus: *Ceramic tile manufacturer.*   Fax: Emp: 21

● **GRUPO POSADAS, S.A. de C.V.**
Paseo de la Reforma 155, Col. Lomas de Chapultepec, 11000 Mexico DF, Mexico
CEO: Gaston Azcarraga Andrade, Chmn. & CEO   Tel: 52-55-5326-6919   Rev: $242
Bus: *Operator of resorts and hotels.*   Fax: 52-55-5326-6960
                                                www.posadas.com

NAICS: 721110

　　HOLIDAY INN
　　100 Padre Blvd., South Padre Island, Texas 78597
　　CEO: Mark Langdale   Tel: (956) 761-5401   %FO: 100
　　Bus: *Hotel operator*   Fax:

　　HOLIDAY INN
　　2000 S. 10th St., McAllen, Texas 78503
　　CEO: Mark Langdale   Tel: (956) 686-1741   %FO: 100
　　Bus: *Hotel operator*   Fax:

　　HOLIDAY INN
　　200 West Expressway 83, McAllen, Texas 78501
　　CEO: Mark Langdale   Tel: (956) 686-2471   %FO: 100
　　Bus: *Hotel operator*   Fax:

　　RESIDENCE INN
　　220 West Expressway 83, McAllen, Texas 78501
　　CEO: Mark Langdale   Tel: (956) 994-8626   %FO: 100
　　Bus: *Hotel operator*   Fax:

　　SHERATON FIESTA
　　310 Padre Blvd., South Padre Island, Texas 78597
　　CEO: Mark Langdale, Pres.   Tel: (956) 761-6551   %FO: 100
　　Bus: *Hotel operator*   Fax:

- **INTERNACIONAL DE CERAMICA, SA DE CV**
  Ave. Carlos Pacheco 7200, 31240 Chihuahua, Mexico
  CEO: Victor D. Almeida, Pres.
  Bus: *Mfr. glazed ceramic floor and wall tile.*

  Tel: 52-614-429-1127
  Fax: 52-614-429-1166
  www.interceramic.com

  NAICS: 327121

  - **INTERCERAMIC USA**
    2333 S. Jupiter Rd., Garland, Texas 75041
    CEO: Tom Shambo
    Bus: *Mfr. ceramic tiles.*

    Tel: (214) 503-5500
    Fax: (214) 503-5515

    %FO: 100

- **JUGOS DEL VALLE, S.A. de C.V.**
  Ejercito Nacional, No.904, 15/F, Colonia Polanco, 11560 Mexico DF, Mexico
  CEO: Roberto Albarran Campillo, Pres.
  Bus: *Mfr./distributor of juices.*

  Tel: 52-55-2581-6500
  Fax:
  www.jvalle.com.mx

  NAICS: 311411, 312111

  - **JUGOS DEL VALLE USA**
    6633 Portwest Dr., Ste.100, Houston, Texas 77024
    CEO: Miguel Longoria Villarreal, Mng. Dir.
    Bus: *Manufacturer and distributor of juices*

    Tel: (713) 622-2203
    Fax: (713) 622-2620

    %FO: 100

- **MEXICANA DE AVIACION SA DE CV**
  Aeropuerto Internacional Sala C, 15520 Mexico DF, Mexico
  CEO: Emilio Romano Mussali, CEO
  Bus: *International commercial air transport services.*

  Tel: 52-55-5448-0990
  Fax: 52-55-5571-2857
  www.mexicana.com.

  Emp: 6,000

  NAICS: 481111

  - **MEXICANA AIRLINES**
    7205 NW 19th St., Ste. 502, Miami, Florida 33126
    CEO: George Edelmann, Mgr.
    Bus: *Air transport services.*

    Tel: (800) 531-7921
    Fax:

    %FO: 100

  - **MEXICANA AIRLINES**
    One World Trade Center, 121 SW Salmon St., 11/F, Portland, Oregon 97205
    CEO: Jose Jimenez, Mgr.
    Bus: *Air transport services.*

    Tel: (800) 531-7921
    Fax:

    %FO: 100

  - **MEXICANA AIRLINES**
    9859 IH-10 West, Ste. 107, San Antonio, Texas 78230
    CEO: Samuel Cantu, Mgr.
    Bus: *Air transport services.*

    Tel: (800) 531-7921
    Fax:

    %FO: 100

  - **MEXICANA AIRLINES**
    14001 East Iliff Ave., Ste. 112, Aurora, Colorado 80014
    CEO: Martha Guillen, Mgr.
    Bus: *Air transport services.*

    Tel: (303) 337-8825
    Fax:

    %FO: 100

MEXICANA AIRLINES
420 Lexington Ave., Ste. 203, New York, New York 10170
CEO: Carolina Atai, Mgr.   Tel: (800) 531-7921   %FO: 100
Bus: *Air transport services.*   Fax:

MEXICANA AIRLINES
2466 East Desert Inn Rd., Ste. E, Las Vegas, Nevada 89121
CEO: Luz Elisa Pelaez Guzman, Mgr.   Tel: (702) 732-4082   %FO: 100
Bus: *Air transport services.*   Fax:

MEXICANA AIRLINES
195 East 4th Ave., 2/F, San Mateo, California 94401
CEO: Carlos Caso, Mgr.   Tel: (800) 531-7921   %FO: 100
Bus: *Air transport services.*   Fax:

MEXICANA AIRLINES
316 North Michigan Ave., Ste. 250, Chicago, Illinois 60601
CEO: Manuel Pliego, Mgr.   Tel: (800) 531-7921   %FO: 100
Bus: *Air transport services.*   Fax:

MEXICANA AIRLINES
6151 West Century Blvd., Ste. 1124, Los Angeles, California 90045
CEO: Marilys Villanueva-Ward, Mgr.   Tel: (800) 531-7921   %FO: 100
Bus: *Air transport services.*   Fax:

● **NACIONAL FINANCIERA SNC**
Ave. Insurgentes Sur 1971, Torre 4, Piso 11, Guadalupe Inn, Alvaro Obbregon, 01020 Mexico DF, Mexico
CEO: Mario Laborin Gomez, CEO & Mng. Dir.   Tel: 52-55-325-6000   Rev: $34
Bus: *Develops industry through Nafin (Nacional* Fax: Emp: 5,100
Financiera), long-term financing, foreign exchange www.nafinsa.com
operation and direct investment.
NAICS: 522293, 522298, 523110

NACIONAL FINANACIERA SNC
1615 L St. NW, Ste. 310, Washington, District of Columbia 20036
CEO: Jose Garcia Torres, Mgr.   Tel: (202) 338-9010
Bus: *Management consulting services.*   Fax:

NAFINSA SECURITIES, INC.
330 Madison Ave., Ste. 665, New York, New York 10017
CEO: Hector Villaescusa, Pres.   Tel: (646) 495-5175   %FO: 100
Bus: *Develops industry through Nafin (Nacional* Fax:
Financiera), long-term financing, foreign
exchange operation & direct investment.

● **PRODUCTOS LAMINADOS de MONTERREY, S.A. de C.V.**
Lazaro Cardenas, No. 1525 Pte., Colonia Nino Artillero, 64280 Monterrey, Mexico
CEO: Jose G. Garza Montemayor, Pres.   Tel: 52-81-8351-1625
Bus: *Fabricator of cold-rolled, hot-rolled and galvanized* Fax: 52-81-8351-0322
steel coils.   www.prolamsa.com
NAICS: 332111, 332312, 332721, 332999

PROLAMSA INC.
770 South Post Oak, Ste. 200, Houston, Texas 77056
CEO: Jean-Marie Diederichs, Gen. Mgr.   Tel: (281) 494-0900   %FO: 100
Bus: *Metal fabrication*   Fax: (281) 494-0990

● **SANLUIS CORPORACION, SA DE CV**
Monte Pelvoux 220, Piso 8, Colonia Lomas de Chapultepec, 11000 Mexico DF, Mexico
CEO: Antonio Madero Bracho, Chmn. & CEO   Tel: 52-55-5229-5800   Rev: $532
Bus: *Mfr. auto supplies.*   Fax: 52-55-5202-6604   Emp: 601
        www.sanluiscorp.com
NAICS: 336330, 336340

   SANLUIS RASSINI INTERNATIONAL INC.
   Magda Dr., Montpelier, Ohio 43543
   CEO: Jose Luis Resendiz, Pres.   Tel: (419) 485-1524   %FO: 100
   Bus: *Mfr./sales auto supplies.*   Fax:

   SANLUIS RASSINI INTERNATIONAL INC.
   14500 Beck Rd., Plymouth, Michigan 48170
   CEO: Robert J. Anderson, Pres.   Tel: (734) 454-4904   %FO: 100
   Bus: *Mfr./sales auto supplies.*   Fax: (734) 454-4914   Emp: 56

● **SAVIA, SA DE CV, DIV. GRUPO PULSAR**
Rio Sena 500 Poniente, Colonia del Valle, San Pedro, 66220 Garza Garcia NL, Mexico
CEO: Alfonso Romo Garza, Chmn. & CEO   Tel: 52-81-8173-5500   Rev: $130
Bus: *Diversified holdings including, property/casualty,*   Fax: 52-81-8173-5508   Emp: 1,500
   life, and health insurance and fruit and vegetable   www.savia.com.mx
   seed supplier and packager.
NAICS: 111211, 111419, 115116

   BIONOVA HOLDING CORPORATION
   9255 Customhouse Plaza, Ste. 1, San Diego, California 92154
   CEO: Jose Manuel Garcia, CEO   Tel: (609) 661-2560   %FO: 100
   Bus: *Engaged in biotechnology, genetic*   Fax: (609) 661-6499
   engineering and plant science technologies.

● **TELEFONOS DE MEXICO, S.A. DE C.V.**
Parque Via 198, oficina 701, Colonia Cuauhtemoc, 06599 Mexico DF, Mexico
CEO: Jaime Chico Pardo, CEO   Tel: 52-55-5703-3990   Rev: $12,457
Bus: *Provides local and long-distance telephone*   Fax: 52-55-5545-5550   Emp: 62,103
        www.telmex.com.mx
NAICS: 443112, 511140, 517110, 517211, 517212, 517910, 518111, 518210, 519190, 561499

   TELMEX USA
   4111 Buchanan Ave., Riverside, California 92503
   CEO: Hugo Alcaraz, Pres.   Tel: (951) 284-1464   %FO: 100
   Bus: *Engaged in telecommunications.*   Fax: Emp: 15

   TELVISTA
   19111 Dallas North Pkwy., Ste. 250, Dallas, Texas 75287
   CEO: Higinio Sanchez, Pres. & CEO   Tel: (972) 312-6000
   Bus: *Direct marketing services*   Fax: (972) 312-6107

- **TV AZTECA SA DE CV**
  Periferico Sur 4121, Colonia Fuentes del Pedregal, 14141 Mexico, DF, Mexico
  CEO: Mario San Roman Flores, CEO   Tel: 52-55-3099-1313   Rev: $739
  Bus: *Operates TV stations for Spanish-speaking*   Fax: 52-55-3099-1464   Emp: 4,228
         market and Internet portal.   www.tvazteca.com.mx
  NAICS: 334220

  AZTECA AMERICA
  1000 Universal Studios Plaza, Building 22A, Ste. 267, Orlando, Florida 32819
  CEO: Luis J. Echarte   Tel: (407) 224-5521   %FO: 100
  Bus: *Operates TV stations.*   Fax: (407) 224-5428

- **VECTOR SERVICIOS FINANCIEROS**
  Avenida Roble 565, Coloina Valle del Compestre, 66265 Garza Garcia NL, Mexico
  CEO: Raul Gerardo Faraas Arizpe, CEO   Tel: 52-81-318-3500
  Bus: *Securities broker/dealer.*   Fax: 52-81-318-3535   Emp: 350
                                                www.vector.com.mx
  NAICS: 523110

  VECTORMEX INCORPORATED
  475 Fifth Ave., Ste. 1500, New York, New York 10017
  CEO: Carlos Mena   Tel: (212) 407-5500   %FO: 100
  Bus: *Securities broker/dealer.*   Fax: (212) 407-5531   Emp: 25

- **VITRO, SA DE CV**
  Avenida Ricardo Margain Zozaya, 400, Colonia Valle del Campestre, San Pedro Garza Garcia, 66265 Nuevo
  Leon,
  CEO: Federico Sada Gonzalez, Pres. & CEO   Tel: 52-81-8863-1200   Rev: $2,348
  Bus: *Producer of glass.*   Fax: 52-81-8863-7839   Emp: 26
                                                www.vitro.com
  NAICS: 327112, 327211, 327213

  VITRO AMERICA INC.
  965 Ridge Lake Blvd., PO Box 171173, Memphis, Tennessee 38187
  CEO: Luis Gonzalez Sada, Pres. & CEO   Tel: (901) 767-7111   %FO: 100
  Bus: *Sale & distribution of building materials.*   Fax: (901) 682-3062

Monaco

- **JETCAM INTERNATIONAL HOLDING LIMITED**
Terrasses du Port, 2 Avenue des Ligures, MC-98000 Monaco, Monaco

CEO: Ivan Stern, CEO	Tel: 377-9797-1640	Rev: $5
Bus: *Software manufacture.*	Fax: 377-9350-7626	Emp: 40
	www.jetcam.com	

NAICS: 511210

    APS JETCAM
    744 North Brookdale Dr., Schaumburg, Illinois 60194

CEO: Ivan Stern	Tel: (847) 310-8512	%FO: 100
Bus: *Mfr./Sales of software.*	Fax: (847) 310-8548	

- **SEA HORSE INTERNATIONAL**
Chateau d'Azur, Block B, 44, blvd. d'Italie, 98000 Monte Carlo, Monaco

CEO: Capt. Assem Elbendary, Pres.	Tel: 377-9315-9657	
Bus: *Business of managing, mitigating and verifying*	Fax: 377-9315-9658	
losses arising from ocean marine claims.	www.shorse.com	

NAICS: 524291

    SEA HORSE INTERNATIONAL
    2052 Rockingham St., McLean, Virginia 22101

CEO: Captain Elbendary, Pres.	Tel: (703) 237-9046	%FO: 100
Bus: *Business of managing, mitigating and verifying losses arising from ocean marine claims.*	Fax: (703) 241-7562	

Morocco

- **ROYAL AIR MAROC**
  S4 Aeropuerto D'Anfa, 20200 Casablanca, Morocco
  CEO: Mohammed Berrada, Chmn.
  Bus: *Commercial air transport services.*

  Tel: 212-229-12-000
  Fax:
  www.royalairmaroc.com

  Rev: $584
  Emp: 5,534

  NAICS: 481111, 492110

  ROYAL AIR MAROC
  600 Brickell Ave., Ste. 301C, Miami, Florida 33131
  CEO: Hanine Arous, Mgr.
  Bus: *Air transport services.*

  Tel: (305) 372-2727
  Fax:

  ROYAL AIR MAROC
  55 East 59th St., Ste. 17B, New York, New York 10022
  CEO: Amm Agui, Gen. Mgr.
  Bus: *Commercial air transport services.*

  Tel: (212) 750-5115
  Fax: (212) 754-4215

  %FO: 100

Namibia

- **AIR NAMIBIA**
  Box 731, Jeans Street, Eros Airport, Windhoek, Namibia
  CEO: Sam Nujoma, Pres.
  Bus: *Airline transport services.*

  Tel: 264-61-2985111
  Fax: 264-61-2982160
  www.namibian.com.na

  NAICS: 481111

  AIR NAMIBIA
  12 West 37th St., 8/F, New York, New York 10018
  CEO: Henry Karpengar
  Bus: *Airlines services.*

  Tel: (212) 465-0619
  Fax: (212) 685-1561

Netherlands

- **AALBERTS INDUSTRIES N.V.**
Sandenburgerlaan 4, NL-3947 CS Langbroek, Netherlands
CEO: Jan Aalberts, Pres. & CEO   Tel: 31-343-565-080   Rev: $1,225
Bus: *Flow control system and industrial component mfr.*   Fax: 31-343-565-081   Emp: 6,785
   and distributor.   www.aalberts.nl
   NAICS: 332911, 332912, 332919

    ELKHART PRODUCTS CORPORATION
    700 Rainbow Rd., Geneva, Indiana 48740
    CEO: Dale Dieckbernd, Pres.   Tel: (260) 368-7246   %FO: 100
    Bus: *Copper plumbing fittings mfr.*   Fax: (260) 368-7889   Emp: 575

- **ABN AMRO HOLDING NV**
Gustav Mahlerlaan 10, NL-1182 PP Amsterdam, Netherlands
CEO: R. W. J. Groenink, CEO   Tel: 31-20-628-9393   Rev: $45,139
Bus: *Banking and financial services.*   Fax: 31-20-629-9111   Emp: 97,276
    www.abnamro.com
   NAICS: 523110

    ABN AMRO BANK N.V.
    200 S. Biscayne Blvd., 22/F, Miami, Florida 33131-1596
    CEO: Roberto Diaz De Villegas, Sr. Prtn.   Tel: (305) 372-1596   %FO: 100
    Bus: *Banking and financial services.*   Fax: (305) 372-2397

    ABN AMRO BANK N.V.
    101 California St., Ste. 4300, San Francisco, California 94111
    CEO: Phyliss Kai-Kee, Sr. Prtn.   Tel: (415) 984-3700   %FO: 100
    Bus: *International/domestic banking services.*   Fax: (415) 362-3524

    ABN AMRO BANK N.V.
    Three Riverway, Ste. 1700, Houston, Texas 77056
    CEO: Richard Schaeffer, Sr. Prtn.   Tel: (713) 629-6666   %FO: 100
    Bus: *Banking and financial services.*   Fax: (713) 629-7533

    ABN AMRO BANK N.V.
    135 South La Salle St., Ste. 6215, Chicago, Illinois 60603
    CEO: Norman R. Bobins, Sr. Prtn.   Tel: (312) 904-2957   %FO: 100
    Bus: *Banking and financial services.*   Fax: (312) 904-6521

    ABN AMRO BANK N.V.
    50 South Sixth St., Minneapolis, Minnesota 55402
    CEO: Ward Nixon, Mng. Dir.   Tel: (612) 337-9868   %FO: 100
    Bus: *Banking and financial services.*   Fax: (612) 338-8687

    ABN AMRO INC.
    55 East 52nd St., New York, New York 10055
    CEO: Richard Schaeffer, Sr. Prtn.   Tel: (212) 409-6010   %FO: 100
    Bus: *Global energy futures.*   Fax: (212) 409-6070

LASALLE BANK NORTH AMERICA
135 S. LaSalle St., Chicago, Illinois 60603
CEO: Norman R. Bobins, Pres.
Bus: *Retail banking services.*

Tel: (312) 904-2000
Fax: (312) 904-2579

LASALLE BANK NORTH AMERICA
2600 W. Big Beaver Rd., Troy, Michigan 48084
CEO: Mark A. Hoppe, Pres. & CEO
Bus: *Home mortgage services.*

Tel: (248) 643-9600
Fax: (248) 637-2701

● **ACORDIS BV**
Westervoortsedijk 73, 6827 AV, NL-6800 TC Arnhem, Netherlands
CEO: Folkert Blaisse, CEO
Bus: *Mfr. synthetic and specialty fibers, including acrylic, polyester and nylon.*
NAICS: 325221, 325222

Tel: 31-26-366-4444
Fax: 31-26-366-4692
www.acordis.com

Rev: $1,600
Emp: 11,000

CLAIFOIL, DIV. ACORDIS
9 South Virginia Ct., Englewood Cliffs, New Jersey 07632
CEO: Don Taylor
Bus: *Mfr./sales acetate fibers and textiles.*

Tel: (201) 541-2476
Fax: (201) 541-2478

%FO: 100

FORTAFIL FIBERS INC.
121 Cardiff Valley Rd., PO Box 357, Rockwood, Tennessee 37854
CEO: Peter Oswald
Bus: *Fibers.*

Tel: (865) 354-4120
Fax: (865) 354-4327

%FO: 100

POLYAMIDE HIGH PERFORMANCE INC.
7526 Akzo Boulevard, Scottsboro, Alabama 35769-8106
CEO: Adria Williams, Mgr.
Bus: *Plant for manufacture of industrial fibers.*

Tel: (256) 574-7200
Fax: (256) 574-7274

%FO: 100

● **AEGON N.V.**
AEGONplein 50, NL-2501 CE The Hague, Netherlands
CEO: Donald J. Shepard, Chmn.
Bus: *Insurance and financial services.*

Tel: 31-70-344-3210
Fax: 31-70-347-5238
www.aegon.be

Rev: $38,624
Emp: 27,446

NAICS: 522110, 524113, 524114, 525110, 525120, 525910, 525920

AEGON DIRECT MARKETING SERVICES
510 Park Ave., Baltimore, Maryland 21202
CEO: Karen Klein, Pres.
Bus: *Direct marketing campaigns for marketing life insurance products.*

Tel: (410) 685-5500
Fax: (410) 685-5500

%FO: 100

AEGON USA INC.
4333 Edgewater Rd., NE, Cedar Rapids, Iowa 52499
CEO: Patrick S. Baird
Bus: *Provides life insurance, accident and health insurance, annuity and investment products and mutual funds.*

Tel: (319) 398-8511
Fax: (319) 369-2147

%FO: 100
Emp: 14,308

AEGON USA INVESTMENT MANAGEMENT
4333 Edgewood Rd., NE, Cedar Rapids, Iowa 52499
CEO: Eric Goodman, Pres.   Tel: (319) 398-8511   %FO: 100
Bus: *Provides insurance services.*   Fax: (319) 369-2218   Emp: 324

AEGON USA REALTY ADVISORS
4333 Edgewater Rd., NE, Cedar Rapids, Iowa 52499
CEO: Frank W. Coe, Pres. & CEO   Tel: (319) 369-2783   %FO: 100
Bus: *Provides insurance services.*   Fax: (319) 369-2147

TRANSAMERICA FINANCE CORP.
9399 W. Higgins Rd., Ste. 600, Rosemont, Illinois 60018
CEO: Robert A. Watson   Tel: (847) 685-1100   %FO: 100
Bus: *life insurance, pensions, and related*   Fax: (847) 685-1100
      financial products.

● **AKZO NOBEL NV**
Velperweg 76, NL-6800 SB Arnhem, Netherlands
CEO: G.J. Wijers, Chmn.   Tel: 31-26-366-4433   Rev: $17,187
Bus: *Paints and coatings, chemicals, man-made fibers,*   Fax: 31-26-366-3250   Emp: 60,350
      salt and pharmaceuticals manufacture.   www.akzonobel.com
NAICS: 325132, 325199, 325411, 325510

    AKZO NOBEL CHEMICALS
    2625 Bay Area Blvd., Houston, Texas 77058
    CEO: Berthowld Raadsen   Tel: (281) 480-4747   %FO: 100
    Bus: *Mfr./sales resins.*   Fax: (281) 283-1519

    AKZO NOBEL CHEMICALS, INC.
    5 Livingstone Ave., Dobbs Ferry, New York 10522-3401
    CEO: Kelly Warenn   Tel: (914) 674-5000   %FO: 100
    Bus: *Chemicals manufacture.*   Fax: (914) 693-3417

    AKZO NOBEL COATINGS, INC.
    PO Box 7062, Troy, Michigan 48007
    CEO: Sandra Bersine, Mgr.   Tel: (248) 637-0400   %FO: 100
    Bus: *Mfr./sales plastic closures and over caps.*   Fax: (248) 649-3584

    AKZO NOBEL COATINGS, INC.
    340 Meadow Rd., Edison, New Jersey 08837
    CEO: Steve O'Brien   Tel: (732) 985-6262   %FO: 100
    Bus: *Mfr. distribution of industrial coatings.*   Fax: (732) 985-2203   Emp: 60

    AKZO NOBEL RESINS
    29782 White Otter Ln., Laguna Niguel, California 92677
    CEO: James Carmine   Tel: (912) 367-3616   %FO: 100
    Bus: *Chemical products manufacture.*   Fax: (912) 367-5754

    AKZO NOBEL RESINS
    8201 W 47th St., La Grange, Illinois 60525
    CEO: Jim Hatzfeld   Tel: (708) 447-7990   %FO: 100
    Bus: *Mfr./sales resins.*   Fax: (708) 447-7990

AKZO NOBEL, INC.
906 Fredricksburg Rd., Mount Juliet, Tennessee 37122
CEO: James Reddick, Mgr.   Tel: (615) 773-7120   %FO: 100
Bus: *Mfr. salt/basic chemicals, pharmaceuticals*   Fax: (615) 773-7120
  & coatings, plastics.

AKZO NOBEL, INC.
525 W. Van Buren St., Chicago, Illinois 60607
CEO: Conrad S. Kent, Pres.   Tel: (312) 906-7500   %FO: 100
Bus: *Mfr. salt/basic chemicals, pharmaceuticals*   Fax: (312) 906-7680
  & coatings, plastics.

ORGANON INTERNATIONAL INC.
56 Livingston Ave., Roseland, New Jersey 07068
CEO: A. T. M. Wilderbeek, Pres.   Tel: (973) 422-7698   %FO: 100
Bus: *Mfr. women's healthcare pharmaceuticals.*   Fax: (973) 325-4589   Emp: 15,000

● **AMMERAAL BELTECH BV**
PO Box 38, NL-1700 AA Heerhugowaard, Netherlands
CEO: I. A. Roberti, CEO   Tel: 31-72-575-1212
Bus: *Industrial conveyor belt manufacturer.*   Fax: 31-72-571-6455   Emp: 1,600
                                      www.ammeraalbeltech.com

NAICS: 326220

AMMERAAL BELTECH, INC.
1014 Santerre Dr., Grand Prairie, Texas 75050
CEO: John B. Gateley   Tel: (972) 647-8996   %FO: 100
Bus: *Conveyor belting sales and manufacture.*   Fax: (972) 660-2596

AMMERAAL BELTECH, INC.
3720 Three Mile Rd. NW, Grand Rapids, Michigan 49504
CEO: Tim Sneller, Mgr.   Tel: (616) 791-0162   %FO: 100
Bus: *Conveyor belting sales and manufacture.*   Fax: (616) 791-1067

AMMERAAL BELTECH, INC.
7501 Saint Louis Ave., Skokie, Illinois 60076
CEO: James Ekedahl, Pres.   Tel: (847) 673-6720   %FO: 100
Bus: *Conveyor belting sales and manufacture.*   Fax: (847) 673-6373

AMMERAAL BELTECH, INC.
2359 Verna Ct., San Leandro, California 94577
CEO: Terry Chatelle   Tel: (510) 352-3770   %FO: 100
Bus: *Conveyor belting sales and manufacture.*   Fax: (510) 352-4337

● **ANKER COAL COMPANY BV**
Vasteland 4, NL-3011 BK Rotterdam, Netherlands
CEO: Vitol Anker, Mng. Dir.   Tel: 31-10-452-9566   Rev: $250
Bus: *Sales and export of coal.*   Fax: 31-10-452-9073
                                      www.ankercoal.nv

NAICS: 324199

ANKER ENERGY CORPORATION, VANTRANS DIV.
2708 Cranberry Square, Morgantown, West Virginia 26505
CEO: George R. Desko
Bus: *Sales and export of coal.*
Tel: (304) 594-1616
Fax: (304) 594-3695
%FO: 100

PHILIPPI DEVELOPMENT, INC., SENTINEL MINES
Route 3, Box 146, Philippi, West Virginia 26416
CEO: Gary McCauley, Pres.
Bus: *Coal mining and preparation.*
Tel: (304) 457-1895
Fax: (304) 457-1005
%FO: 100

● **ARCADIS NV**
Utrechtseweg 68, NL-6812 AH Arnhem, Netherlands
CEO: Harrie L. J. Noy, Chmn.
Bus: *Engaged in international consulting, engineering and contracting.*
NAICS: 237990, 541330, 541611
Tel: 31-26-377-8911
Fax: 31-26-351-5235
www.arcadis.nl
Rev: $786
Emp: 9,277

ARCADIS G&M
35 East Wacker Dr., Ste. 1000, Chicago, Illinois 60601
CEO: Phillip Hutton, Pres.
Bus: *Engaged in environmental and engineering consulting services.*
Tel: (312) 263-6703
Fax: (312) 263-7897
%FO: 100

ARCADIS G&M
126 N. Jefferson St., Ste. 400, Milwaukee, Wisconsin 53202
CEO: Kathleen A. Niesen, Mgr.
Bus: *Engaged in environmental and engineering consulting services.*
Tel: (414) 276-7742
Fax: (414) 276-7603
%FO: 100

ARCADIS G&M
3000 Cabot Blvd. West, Ste. 3004, Langhorne, Pennsylvania 19047
CEO: Al Hanum, CEO
Bus: *Engaged in environmental and engineering consulting services.*
Tel: (215) 752-6840
Fax: (215) 752-6879
%FO: 100

ARCADIS G&M
1 Centerview Dr., Greensboro, North Carolina 27407
CEO: David Kane, Pres.
Bus: *Engaged in environmental and engineering consulting services.*
Tel: (336) 292-2271
Fax: (336) 855-5648
%FO: 100

ARCADIS G&M
25200 Telegraph Rd., Southfield, Michigan 48086
CEO: Loren Klevering
Bus: *Engaged in international consulting, engineering and contracting.*
Tel: (248) 936-8000
Fax: (248) 936-8111
%FO: 100

ARCADIS G&M
5608 Parkcrest Dr., Ste. 300, Austin, Texas 78731
CEO: Chuck Gurney, VP
Bus: *Engaged in environmental and engineering consulting services.*
Tel: (512) 451-1188
Fax: (512) 451-2930
%FO: 100

- **ASM INTERNATIONAL N.V.**
Jan van Eycklaan 10, NL-3723 BC Bilthoven, Netherlands
CEO: Arthur H. del Prado, Chmn. & CEO
Bus: *Mfr. semiconductor lithography equipment.*

Tel: 31-30-229-84-11
Fax: 31-30-228-74-69
www.asm.com

Rev: $1,021
Emp: 8,260

NAICS: 333295

  ASM AMERICA INC.
  97 East Brokaw Rd., Ste. 100, San Jose, California 95112-4209
  CEO: Doug Traina, Pres.
  Bus: *Mfr./sales semiconductor equipment.*

  Tel: (408) 451-0830
  Fax: (408) 451-0825

  %FO: 100

  ASM AMERICA INC.
  3440 East University Dr., Phoenix, Arizona 85034
  CEO: Terri Udelman, Pres.
  Bus: *Mfr./sales semiconductor equipment.*

  Tel: (602) 470-5700
  Fax: (602) 437-8497

  %FO: 100

  ASM AMERICA INC.
  107 Crooked Trail Extension, Woodstock, Connecticut 06281
  CEO: Ed Meyer
  Bus: *Mfr./sales semiconductor equipment.*

  Tel: (860) 974-1444
  Fax: (860) 974-1444

  %FO: 100

- **ASML HOLDING NV**
De Run 6501, NL-5504 Veldhoven, Netherlands
CEO: Eric Meurice, CEO
Bus: *Semiconductor manufacturing equipment.*

Tel: 31-40-268-4941
Fax: 31-40-268-3655
www.asml.com

Rev: $2,054
Emp: 5,970

NAICS: 333295

  ASML US, INC.
  8555 South River Pkwy., Tempe, Arizona 85284
  CEO: Martin A. van den Brink, EVP
  Bus: *Semiconductor manufacturing equipment.*

  Tel: (480) 383-4422
  Fax: (480) 383-3995

  %FO: 100

- **AVEBE B.A.**
Prins Hendrikplein 20, Veendam, NL-9641 GK Groningen, Netherlands
CEO: Eltjo Haselhoff, Dir.
Bus: *Engaged in potato milling, starches and*

Tel: 31-59-866-9111
Fax: 31-598-664368
www.avebe.com

Emp: 2,799

NAICS: 111211

  AVEBE AMERICA INC.
  4 Independence Way, Princeton, New Jersey 08540
  CEO: Fred Oostland, Pres.
  Bus: *Produces starches/chemicals.*

  Tel: (609) 520-1400
  Fax: (609) 520-1473

  %FO: 100

- **BALLAST NEDAM N.V.**
PO Box 1339, NL-3430 BH Nieuwegein, Netherlands
CEO: Rene H.P.W. Kottman, Chmn.
Bus: *Engineering, construction, dredging, excavation, ship-building, project management.*
NAICS: 237310, 237990, 336611

Tel: 31-30-2-85-3333
Fax: 31-30-2-85-4875
www.ballast-nedam.nl

Rev: $2,000
Emp: 8,500

BALLAST NEDAM CONSTRUCTION, INC.
2800 Biscayne Boulevard, Ste. 730, Miami, Florida 33137
CEO: Maurice J. Otto, Gen. Mgr.   Tel: (305) 576-6617   %FO: 100
Bus: *Construction and dredging equipment*   Fax: (305) 576-6890
services.

● **BASELL NV**
Hoeksteen 66, NL-2132 MS Hoofddorp, Netherlands
CEO: Volker Trautz, Pres. & CEO   Tel: 31-20 4468 644   Rev: $5,850
Bus: *Producer of polymers, including polypropylene*   Fax: 31-20 4468 666
and polyethylene. (JV Royal Dutch/Shell Group   www.basell.com
and BASF)
NAICS: 325188, 325211

    BASELL NORTH AMERICA INC.
    912 Appleton Rd., Elkton, Maryland 21921
    CEO: Randy Woelfel, Pres.   Tel: (410) 996-1600   %FO: 100
    Bus: *Polymers, including polypropylene and*   Fax: (410) 996-2121
    polyethylene sales and distribution.

● **BE SEMICONDUCTOR INDUSTRIES N.V.**
Marconilaan 4, NL-5151 DR Drunen, Netherlands
CEO: Richard W. Blickman, CEO   Tel: 31-41-638-4345   Rev: $87
Bus: *Produces integrated systems for semiconductor*   Fax: 31-416-384-344   Emp: 650
equipment industry.   www.besi.nl
NAICS: 333295, 334413

    BESI USA INC.
    224 E. Chilton Dr., Ste. 9, Chandler, Arizona 85225
    CEO: Robert Cole   Tel: (480) 497-8190   %FO: 100
    Bus: *Produces integrated systems for*   Fax: (480) 497-9104
    semiconductor equipment industry.

● **BORSTLAP BV**
Zevenheuvelenweg 44, NL-5048 AN Tilburg, Netherlands
CEO: Johannes M. A. Borstlap, Dir.   Tel: 31-13-594-1234   Rev: $66
Bus: *Metric fasteners.*   Fax: 31-13-594-1212   Emp: 900
    www.borstlap.com
NAICS: 339993

    FABORY USA LTD.
    PO Box 336, Fairplay, South Carolina 29643
    CEO: John Jordan, Pres.   Tel: (864) 972-2170   %FO: 100
    Bus: *Import/sales/distribution of metric fasteners*   Fax: (864) 972-2471
    and hardware.

    FABORY USA LTD.
    1360 Donaldson Rd., Ste. D, Erlanger, Kentucky 41018
    CEO: Patricia Hall, Pres.   Tel: (859) 282-8100   %FO: 100
    Bus: *Import/sales/distribution of metric fasteners*   Fax: (859) 282-8250
    and hardware.

FABORY USA LTD.
6095 Rickenbacker Rd., Los Angeles, California 90040
CEO: Doug Paulson, Mgr.   Tel: (323) 726-9944   %FO: 100
Bus: *Import/sales/distribution of metric fasteners* Fax: (323) 726-6718
and hardware.

FABORY USA LTD.
2240 29th St., Grand Rapids, Michigan 49508
CEO: Marty Goeree, Pres.   Tel: (616) 247-4777   %FO: 100
Bus: *Import/sales/distribution of metric fasteners* Fax: (616) 247-0408
and hardware.

FABORY USA LTD.
7110 Golden Ring Rd., Ste. 105, Baltimore, Maryland 21221
CEO: Dennis Mc Collum, Mgr.   Tel: (410) 780-0311   %FO: 100
Bus: *Import/sales/distribution of metric fasteners* Fax: (410) 780-0384
and hardware.

● **BUHRMANN N.V.**
Hoogoorddreef 62, NL-1100 BE Amsterdam, Netherlands
CEO: Frans H. J. Koffrie, Pres. & CEO   Tel: 31-20-651-1111   Rev: $7,503
Bus: *Graphic paper and packaging manufacture,* Fax: 31-20-651-1000   Emp: 18,000
distribute business machines and graphic system, www.buhrmann.com
paper/office products.
NAICS: 423490, 423830, 423840, 424120

ASAP SOFTWARE
850 Ashbury Dr., Buffalo Grove, Illinois 60089
CEO: Paul Jarvie, Pres.   Tel: (847) 465-3700
Bus: *Computer software, hardware services.* Fax: (847) 465-3277   Emp: 499

BUHRMANN US INC.
1 Environmental Way, Broomfield, Colorado 80021
CEO: Mark Hoffman, Pres.   Tel: (303) 664-2000   %FO: 100
Bus: *Mfr./sales/distribution of office and* Fax: (303) 664-3622   Emp: 13,300
computer supplies.

CORPORATE EXPRESS, INC.
1 Environmental Way, Broomfield, Colorado 80021
CEO: Mark Hoffman, Pres. & CEO   Tel: (303) 664-2000   %FO: 100
Bus: *Imaging and graphic supplies.* Fax: (303) 664-3474

● **CEBECO SEEDS GROUP**
Vijfhoevenlaan 4, Noord-Brabant, NL-5251 HH Vlijmen, Netherlands
CEO: Gerrit Van Straalen, Pres. & CEO   Tel: 31-73-518-8555   Rev: $81
Bus: *Wholesale, agricultural products; mfr., agricultural* Fax: 31-73-518-8666   Emp: 410
machinery and food products. www.cebeco-seeds-group.com
NAICS: 333111, 424910

CEBECO INTERNATIONAL SEEDS, INC.
820 West First St., PO Box 168, Halsey, Oregon 97348
CEO: Steve Johnson, Pres.   Tel: (541) 369-2251   %FO: 100
Bus: *Wholesale, agricultural products; mfr.,* Fax: (541) 369-2640
agricultural machinery and food products.

- **CFS B.V.**
Beekakker 11, DK-5761 EN Bakel, Netherlands
CEO: John-Ole Hansen, Dir.
Bus: *Mfr. industrial meat processing equipment.*

Tel: 31-492-34-9349
Fax: 31-492-34-3969
www.cfs.com

Rev: $168
Emp: 300

NAICS: 236220, 551112

  CFS NORTH AMERICA
  8000 North Dallas Pkwy., Frisco, Texas 75034
  CEO: Jan E. Kuhlmann, Pres.
  Bus: *Mfr. industrial meat processing equipment.*

  Tel: (214) 618-1100
  Fax: (214) 618-1301

  %FO: 100
  Emp: 154

  CFS NORTH AMERICA
  750 Cross Pointe Rd., Ste. W, Columbus, Ohio 43230
  CEO: Jan E. Kuhlmann, Pres.
  Bus: *Mfr. food products machinery*

  Tel: (614) 245-5000
  Fax: (614) 863-3296

- **CHICAGO BRIDGE & IRON COMPANY N.V.**
Polarisavenue 31, NL-2132 JH Hoofddorp, Netherlands
CEO: Gerald M. Glenn, Chmn. & CEO
Bus: *Engineering and construction specializing in bulk liquid terminals.*

Tel: 31-20-568-5660
Fax: 31-20-568-5661
www.chicago-bridge.com

Rev: $1,897
Emp: 11,000

NAICS: 237120, 237990, 332999

  CALLIDUS TECHNOLOGIES
  7130 South Lewis Ave., Ste. 635, Tulsa, Oklahoma 74136-5427
  CEO: Jim Flurry
  Bus: *Engaged in engineering and construction specializing in bulk liquid terminals.*

  Tel: (918) 496-7599
  Fax: (918) 496-7599

  %FO: 100

  CB&I CONSTRUCTORS, INC.
  1501 North Division St., Plainfield, Illinois 60544
  CEO: Gerald M. Glenn
  Bus: *Engaged in engineering and construction specializing in bulk liquid terminals.*

  Tel: (815) 439-6000
  Fax: (815) 439-6010

  %FO: 100

  CB&I CONSTRUCTORS, INC.
  9550 Hickman Rd., Clive, Iowa 50325
  CEO: Paul Brown
  Bus: *Engaged in engineering and construction specializing in bulk liquid terminals.*

  Tel: (515) 254-9228
  Fax: (515) 254-9228

  %FO: 100

  CB&I CONSTRUCTORS, INC.
  1603 Carmody Ct., Sewickley, Pennsylvania 15143
  CEO: Mike Braden
  Bus: *Engaged in engineering and construction specializing in bulk liquid terminals.*

  Tel: (724) 933-4450
  Fax: (724) 933-4486

  %FO: 100

  CB&I CONSTRUCTORS, INC.
  700 South 550 East, Provo, Utah 84606-6100
  CEO: Tom Langston, Pres.
  Bus: *Engaged in engineering and construction specializing in bulk liquid terminals.*

  Tel: (801) 373-8150
  Fax: (801) 373-8150

  %FO: 100

CB&I CONSTRUCTORS, INC.
250 West 1st St., Suite 210, Claremont, California 91711
CEO: William Jordan
Bus: *Engaged in engineering and construction specializing in bulk liquid terminals.*

Tel: (909) 624-4000
Fax: (909) 624-4000

%FO: 100

CHICAGO BRIDGE AND IRON COMPANY
2103 Research Forest Dr., The Woodlands, Texas 77380
CEO: Gerald M. Glenn, CEO
Bus: *Engaged in engineering and construction specializing in bulk liquid terminals.*

Tel: (832) 513-1400
Fax: (832) 513-1400

%FO: 100

MORSE CONSTRUCTION GROUP, INC.
5500 South First Ave., Everett, Washington 98203
CEO: Karen Glenn
Bus: *Engaged in engineering and construction specializing in bulk liquid terminals.*

Tel: (425) 258-2731
Fax: (425) 259-6355

%FO: 100

● **CHN GLOBAL NV**
Schiphol Blvd. 217, Tower B, 10th Fl., NL-118 BH Schiphol Airport, Netherlands
CEO: Harold D. Boyanovsky, Pres. & CEO
Bus: *Mfr. agricultural and construction equipment.*

Tel: 31-20-446-0429
Fax: 31-20-446-0436
www.newholland.com

Rev: $11,545
Emp: 25,700

NAICS: 333111, 333120

CNH GLOBAL
100 S. Saunders Rd., Ste. 200, Lake Forest, Illinois 60045-2502
CEO: Paolo Monferino, Pres.
Bus: *Mfr./sales agricultural and construction equipment.*

Tel: (847) 735-9200
Fax: (847) 735-9200

%FO: 100

● **CORE LABORATORIES**
Herenracht 424, NL-1017 BZ Amsterdam, Netherlands
CEO: David M. Demshur, Pres. & CEO
Bus: *Provides reservoir management services and geological and petroleum engineering services.*

Tel: 31-20-420-3191
Fax: 31-20-627-9886
www.corelab.com

Rev: $427
Emp: 4,500

NAICS: 211111, 221310, 541330

CORE LABORATORIES, INC.
6316 Windfern, Houston, Texas 77040
CEO: David M. Demshur, COO
Bus: *Provides reservoir management services and geological and petroleum engineering services.*

Tel: (713) 328-2673
Fax: (713) 328-2150

%FO: 100

CORE LABORATORIES, INC.
3430 Unicorn Rd., Bakersfield, California 93308-682
CEO: Bryon Bell
Bus: *Provides reservoir management services and geological and petroleum engineering services.*

Tel: (661) 392-8600
Fax: (661) 392-0824

%FO: 100

PROTECNICS
131 Credit Dr., Scott, Louisiana 70583
CEO: Brent Bolin   Tel: (337) 264-1958   %FO: 100
Bus: *Provides reservoir management services*   Fax: (337) 264-1958
        and geological and petroleum engineering
        services.

● **CSM N.V.**
Nienoord 13, NL-1112 XE Diemen, Netherlands
CEO: Gerard J. Hoetmer, CEO   Tel: 31-20-590-6911   Rev: $4,740
Bus: *Development, production, sale and distribution of* Fax: 31-20-695-1942   Emp: 13,614
        bakery supplies and food ingredients.   www.csmnv.com
NAICS: 311942

BAKEMARK EAST
217 Edee Rd., Saratoga Springs, New York 12866
CEO: Bert Grant   Tel: (518) 584-4282   %FO: 100
Bus: *Mfr. ingredients for bakery products.*   Fax: (518) 584-4816

BAKEMARK EAST
1400 William St., Buffalo, New York 14206
CEO: Micheal Pinkowski   Tel: (716) 842-1200   %FO: 100
Bus: *Mfr. ingredients for bakery products.*   Fax: (716) 856-0986

BAKEMARK EAST
120 Victoria Rd., Youngstown, Ohio 44515
CEO: Timothy Dove   Tel: (330) 793-3925   %FO: 100
Bus: *Mfr. icing products, toppings and fruit*   Fax: (330) 793-1643
        fillings for the bakery and ice cream
        industries.

BAKEMARK INGREDIENTS INC.
1933 North Meacham Rd., Schaumburg, Illinois 60173
CEO: Brad H. Weaver   Tel: (847) 925-2100   %FO: 100
Bus: *Mfr. icing products, toppings and fruit*   Fax: (847) 925-2100
        fillings for the bakery and ice cream
        industries.

BAKEMARK INGREDIENTS INC.
7351 Crider Ave., Pico Rivera, California 90660
CEO: Rik Bennett, Mgr.   Tel: (562) 949-1054   %FO: 100
Bus: *Mfr. ingredients for bakery products.*   Fax: (562) 949-1257

BAKER & BAKER
1301 Estes Ave., Elk Grove Village, Illinois 60007
CEO: Paul V. Barron   Tel: (847) 593-5700   %FO: 100
Bus: *Mfr. ingredients for bakery products.*   Fax: (847) 593-0749

H. C. BRILL
3301 Montreal Industrial Way, Tucker, Georgia 30084
CEO: Eric Conley   Tel: (770) 938-3823   %FO: 100
Bus: *Mfr. icing products, toppings and fruit*   Fax: (770) 939-2934
        fillings for the bakery and ice cream
        industries.

HENRY & HENRY INC.
3765 Walden Ave., Lancaster, New York 14086
CEO: Laura McKenrick, Mgr.   Tel: (716) 685-4000   %FO: 100
Bus: *Mfr. icing products, toppings and fruit*   Fax: (716) 685-0160
fillings for the bakery and ice cream
industries.

● **DAMCO INTERNATIONAL B.V.**
Albert Plesmanweg 161, NL3088 GC Rotterdam, Netherlands
CEO: W. R. Oord, Mng. Dir.   Tel: 31-10-428-8801
Bus: *Air and sea freight forwarders.*   Fax: 31-10-428-8882   Emp: 500
                                                www.damcomar.com
    NAICS: 488510

    C.H.POWELL COMPANY/ DAMCO
    47 Harvard St., Westwood, Massachusetts 02090
    CEO: Peter H. Powell, CEO   Tel: (781) 410-3200   %FO: 100
    Bus: *Air and sea freight forwarders.*   Fax: (781) 410-3223   Emp: 200

    DAMCO SEA & AIR
    20013 Rancho Way, Rancho Dominquez, California 90220
    CEO: G. E. Villate, NVOCC Mgr.   Tel: (310) 900-0300   %FO: 100
    Bus: *Air and sea freight forwarders.*   Fax: (310) 900-0307

    DAMCO SEA & AIR
    24 Drayton St., Savannah, Georgia 31401
    CEO: Debbie Barbee, Rep.   Tel: (912) 233-8402   %FO: 100
    Bus: *Air and sea freight forwarders.*   Fax: (912) 233-9440

    DAMCO SEA & AIR
    c/o C.H. Powell Company, 5356 GA Hwy. 85, Ste. 500, Forest Park, Georgia 30297
    CEO: D.J. Garren, Mgr.   Tel: (404) 767-3373   %FO: 100
    Bus: *Air and sea freight forwarders.*   Fax: (404) 669-0413

    DAMCO SEA & AIR
    10 North Calvert St., Ste. 530, Baltimore, Maryland 21202
    CEO: J.I. Balcerowicz, Mgr.   Tel: (410) 752-5136   %FO: 100
    Bus: *Air and sea freight forwarders.*   Fax: (410) 752-6106

    DAMCO SEA & AIR
    478 Wando Park Blvd., Mount Pleasant, South Carolina 29464
    CEO: A.H. Powell, NVOCC Mgr.   Tel: (843) 856-2460   %FO: 100
    Bus: *Air and sea freight forwarders.*   Fax: (843) 856-2485

    DAMCO SEA & AIR
    1395 E. Irving Park Rd., Itasca, Illinois 60143
    CEO: Charles Powell, Pres.   Tel: (630) 773-9398   %FO: 100
    Bus: *Air and sea freight forwarders.*   Fax: (630) 773-9357   Emp: 20

    DAMCO SEA & AIR
    c/o C.H. Powell Company, 6 Northway Ct., Greer, South Carolina 29651
    CEO: J.R. Godfrey, Sales Dir.   Tel: (864) 879-7163   %FO: 100
    Bus: *Air and sea freight forwarders.*   Fax: (864) 879-2124

DAMCO SEA & AIR
3340-D Greens Rd., Ste. 710, Houston, Texas 77032
CEO: C. S. Johnson, Mgr.   Tel: (281) 442-5363   %FO: 100
Bus: *Air and sea freight forwarders.*   Fax: (281) 442-5365

DAMCO SEA & AIR
8268-70 NW 14th St., Miami, Florida 33126
CEO: Ana Maria Chavez, NVOCC Mgr.   Tel: (305) 599-8199   %FO: 100
Bus: *Air and sea freight forwarders.*   Fax: (305) 599-1066

DAMCO SEA & AIR
Executive Tower Bldg., 3500 N. Causeway Blvd., Ste. 410, Metairie, Louisiana 70002
CEO: Nancy Bertucci, Mgr.   Tel: (504) 834-1440   %FO: 100
Bus: *Air and sea freight forwarders.*   Fax: (504) 834-1504

DAMCO SEA & AIR
208 East Plume St., Monticello Arcade, Ste. 310, Norfolk, Virginia 23510
CEO: Richard Powell, Mgr.   Tel: (757) 626-1346   %FO: 100
Bus: *Air and sea freight forwarders.*   Fax: (757) 626-1644

DAMCO SEA & AIR
19231 36th Ave. West, Ste. J, Lynnwood, Washington 98036
CEO: Chiharu Brown, Mgr.   Tel: (425) 774-3363   %FO: 100
Bus: *Air and sea freight forwarders.*   Fax: (425) 774-8316

DAMCO SEA & AIR
c/o C.H. Powell Company, 4477 Woodson Rd., Ste. 123, St. Louis, Missouri 63134
CEO: J. O. Boedicker, Mgr.   Tel: (314) 427-5055   %FO: 100
Bus: *Air and sea freight forwarders.*   Fax: (314) 427-1005

DAMCO SEA & AIR
158-12 Rockaway Blvd., Jamaica, New York 11434
CEO: P.A. Bernacki, Dir.   Tel: (718) 276-4948   %FO: 100
Bus: *Air and sea freight forwarders.*   Fax: (718) 276-0563

DAMCO SEA & AIR
2 Hudson Place, 3/F, Hoboken, New Jersey 07030
CEO: Mary Theodorou, Mgr.   Tel: (207) 876-9860   %FO: 100
Bus: *Air and sea freight forwarders.*   Fax: (201) 876-9845

INTERCONTINENTAL TRANSPORT SERVICES
440 McClellan Hwy., East Boston, Massachusetts 02128
CEO: J.V. Costello, Mgr.   Tel: (617) 569-4400
Bus: *Air & sea freight forwarders.*   Fax: (617) 523-6813

● **DE BRAUW BLACKSTONE WESTBROEK NV**
Tripolis 300, Burgerweeshuispad 301, NL-1076 HR Amsterdam, Netherlands
CEO: Paul Klemann, Prtn.   Tel: 31-20-577-1771
Bus: *International law firm.*   Fax: 31-20-577-1775   Emp: 2,200
                                           www.dbbw.nl
NAICS: 541110

DE BRAUW BLACKSTONE WESTBROEK PC
650 Fifth Ave., 4/F., New York, New York 10019-6108
CEO: Bernard Spoor, CEO   Tel: (212) 259-4100   %FO: 100
Bus: *International law firm.*   Fax: (212) 259-4111   Emp: 120

● **DELFT INSTRUMENTS N.V.**
Delftechpark 39, PO Box 103, NL-2628 XJ Delft, Netherlands
CEO: Markus J. Dekker, Pres.   Tel: 31-15-2601-200   Rev: $203
Bus: *Mfr. instruments for the medical, space, industrial*   Fax: 31-15-2601-222   Emp: 1,194
     and scientific industries.   www.delftinstruments.com
NAICS: 334516, 339112

     ENRAF INC.
     4333 West Sam Houston Pkwy. North, Ste. 190, Houston, Texas 77043-1219
     CEO: Mark Tippie, Pres.   Tel: (832) 467-3422   %FO: 100
     Bus: *Sales/service of tank gauge systems.*   Fax: (832) 467-3441

     MTS-DELFT
     206 East Garfield Rd., Aurora, Ohio 44202
     CEO: Gary Kaufman   Tel: (330) 995-9712   %FO: 100
     Bus: *Medical technology services*   Fax: (330) 562-2988

     NUCLETRON CORPORATION
     8671 Robert Fulton Dr., Columbia, Maryland 21046
     CEO: Paula Waddell   Tel: (410) 312-4100   %FO: 100
     Bus: *Radiation oncology.*   Fax: (410) 312-4199

● **DELI UNIVERSAL, INC.**
Wijnhaven 65, NL-3011 WJ Rotterdam, Netherlands
CEO: Jan Willem van Gelder, CEO   Tel: 31-10-402-1700
Bus: *Import, sales/distribution of coffee, dried nuts*   Fax: 31-10-411-7694
     and fruits, sunflower/birdseed, and agricultural   www.deli-universal.nl
     commodities.
NAICS: 311423, 311911, 311920

     GLOBAL LABORATORY SERVICES INC.
     2107 Black Creek Rd., Wilson, North Carolina 27893
     CEO: Amy Walker, Pres.   Tel: (252) 234-4950   %FO: 100
     Bus: *Laboratory services.*   Fax: (252) 234-4959

     HARKEMA INC.
     PO Box 382, Canton, Connecticut 06107
     CEO: Joep Van Huystee   Tel: (860) 693-8378   %FO: 100
     Bus: *Agriculture.*   Fax: (860) 693-0882

     IMPERIAL COMMODITIES CORPORATION
     17 Battery Place, Ste. 636, 6/F, New York, New York 10004-1101
     CEO: John M. Morley, Pres.   Tel: (212) 837-9400   %FO: 100
     Bus: *Mfr. polymers.*   Fax: (212) 269-9878

     MOMENTUM TECHNOLOGIES INC.
     1507 Boettler Rd., Uniontown, Ohio 44685
     CEO: Jeremy Elliot, Mgr.   Tel: (330) 896-5900   %FO: 100
     Bus: *Laboratory and polymer distribution services.* Fax: (330) 896-9943

RED RIVER COMMODITIES INC.
PO Box 3022, Fargo, North Dakota 58102
CEO: Robert A. Majkrzak, Pres.   Tel: (701) 282-2600   %FO: 100
Bus: *Mfr./sales/distribution/warehousing of*   Fax: (701) 282-5325
      processors of sunflower and bird seed

TOBACCO RAG PROCESSORS
4744 Potato House Ct., Wilson, North Carolina 27893
CEO: Bob Johnson   Tel: (252) 265-0081   %FO: 100
Bus: *Tobacco processors.*   Fax: (252) 265-0081

UNIVERSAL CORP.
1501 North Hamilton St., Richmond, Virginia 23230-3925
CEO: Jack Mm Van De Winkel, Pres.   Tel: (804) 359-9311   %FO: 100
Bus: *Import/export, sales/distribution of dried*   Fax: (804) 320-1896
      nuts and fruits

UNIVERSAL LEAF NORTH AMERICA
800 Tiffany Blvd., Rocky Mount, North Carolina 27804
CEO: Brenda Brewer, HR   Tel: (252) 212-3700   %FO: 100
Bus: *Tobacco processors.*   Fax: (252) 212-3700

● **DRAKA HOLDING NV**
Rhijnspoorplein 22, NL-1018 TX Amsterdam, Netherlands
CEO: Garo Artinian, Chmn. & CEO   Tel: 31-20-568-9898   Rev: $1,783
Bus: *Mfr. of wire and cables.*   Fax: 31-20-624-5633   Emp: 7,862
                                                www.drakaholding.com
NAICS: 331222, 331422, 333922, 334210, 334290, 335921

BIW CABLE SYSTEMS INC.
22 Joseph E. Warner Blvd., North Dighton, Massachusetts 02764
CEO: Tom Zambarono   Tel: (508) 822-5444
Bus: *Manufacturer of wire and cables.*   Fax: (508) 822-1944

DRAKA CABLES
One Tamaqua Blvd., Schuylkill Haven, Pennsylvania 17972
CEO: Michael J. Homa Jr.   Tel: (570) 385-4381   %FO: 100
Bus: *Mfr. instrumentation cables.*   Fax: (570) 385-1092

DRAKA COMTEQ AMERICAS INC.
2512 Penny Rd., Claremont, North Carolina 28610
CEO: Romano Valussi   Tel: (828) 459-9821   %FO: 50
Bus: *Manufacturer of wire and cables.*   Fax: (828) 459-9312

DRAKA ELEVATOR PRODUCTS INC.
2151 N. Church St., Rocky Mountain, North Carolina 27802-1237
CEO: John S. Moore, Pres.   Tel: (252) 984-5100   %FO: 100
Bus: *Mfr. elevator cables and wire rope.*   Fax: (252) 972-6001   Emp: 200

DRAKA USA CORPORATION
9 Forge Park, Franklin, Massachusetts 02038
CEO: Joseph S. Dixon, Pres. & CEO   Tel: (508) 520-1200   %FO: 100
Bus: *Mfr. industrial cables.*   Fax: (508) 541-6862

DRAKA USA INC.
1610 Greens Rd., Ste. 200, Houston, Texas 77032
CEO: Bill Foe, Gen. Mgr.
Bus: *Distribution center.*
Tel: (281) 209-1070
Fax: (281) 209-3857
%FO: 100

TAMAQUA CABLE PRODUCTS CORP.
1 Tamaqua Blvd., Schuylkill Haven, Pennsylvania 17972
CEO: Andrew Hemingway
Bus: *Manufacturer of wire and cables.*
Tel: (570) 385-4381
Fax: (570) 385-1092
%FO: 100

● **DUTCH SPACE INDUSTRY DSI (FORMERLY FOKKER SPACE BV)**
PO Box 3, NL-4630AA Hoogerheide, Netherlands
CEO: Pieter G. Winters, Pres. & CEO
Bus: *Specialist in advanced robotics technology
supplying solar arrays. (65% JV of Saab
Ericsson Space, Sweden and 35% JV of Stock,*
NAICS: 237130
Tel: 31-164-618207
Fax: 31-164-618666
www.fokkerservices.com
Rev: $100
Emp: 400

FOKKER SPACE, INC.
5169 Southridge Pkwy., Ste. 100, Atlanta, Georgia 30349
CEO: Jan Narlinge, Office Services Mgr.
Bus: *Mfr./sales/distribution and service of
aircraft parts.*
Tel: (770) 991-4373
Fax: (770) 991-4360
%FO: 100
Emp: 22

● **ENV INTERNATIONAL, SUB. FRANCE TELECOM**
Heathrowstraat 10, NL-1043 GL Amsterdam, Netherlands
CEO: Charles Dehelly, CEO
Bus: *Operates telecommunications data networks.*
NAICS: 517910, 518210, 561499
Tel: 31-20-581-8283
Fax: 31-20-688-0388
www.equant.com
Rev: $2,914
Emp: 9,313

EQUANT INC.
Jamboree Center, 1 Park Plaza, Ste. 560, Irvine, California 92614
CEO: John Powell, Mgr.
Bus: *Provider of managed data network services.*
Tel: (949) 660-4160
Fax: (949) 660-4160
%FO: 100

EQUANT INC.
5741 Rio Vista Dr., Clearwater, Florida 33760
CEO: John Yves Charlier, Pres.
Bus: *Provider of managed data network services.*
Tel: (727) 533-3600
Fax: (727) 533-3600
%FO: 100
Emp: 350

EQUANT INC.
400 Galleria Pkwy., Atlanta, Georgia 30339
CEO: Charles Dehelly, Pres.
Bus: *Provider of managed data network services.*
Tel: (678) 346-3000
Fax: (678) 346-3636
%FO: 100
Emp: 400

EQUANT INC.
1 Park Plaza, Ste. 560, Ste. 720, Irvine, California 92614
CEO: John Powell
Bus: *Provider of managed data network services.*
Tel: (949) 660-4160
Fax: (949) 660-4160
%FO: 100

EQUANT INC.
455 Market St., Ste. 910, San Francisco, California 94105
CEO: Bruce Smith, Pres.　　　　　　　　　Tel: (415) 357-6000　　　　%FO: 100
Bus: *Provider of managed data network services.*　Fax: (415) 357-6000

EQUANT INC.
2355 Dulles Corner Blvd., Bldg. 3, Herndon, Virginia 20171
CEO: Mack Treece, Pres.　　　　　　　　Tel: (866) 849-4185
Bus: *Telephone communications*　　　　Fax: (866) 849-4185　　　Emp: 2,000

EQUANT INC.
3 Park Ave., 25/F, New York, New York 10016
CEO: Shawn Connely　　　　　　　　　Tel: (212) 251-2000　　　　%FO: 100
Bus: *Provider of managed data network services.*　Fax: (212) 251-2000

EQUANT INC.
8 New England Executive Park, 3/F West, Burlington, Massachusetts 01803
CEO: Gene Duran　　　　　　　　　　Tel: (866) 849-4185　　　　%FO: 100
Bus: *Provider of managed data network services.*　Fax: (866) 849-4185

- **ERIKS GROUP N.V.**
PO Box 280, NL-1810 BK Alkmaar, Netherlands
CEO: Hans Kreuger, Pres.　　　　　　　　Tel: 31-72-5475-888　　　Rev: $282
Bus: *Distribution and selling of mechanical engineering*　Fax: 31-72-5475-889　　Emp: 1,574
components.　　　　　　　　　　　　www.eriks.com
NAICS: 334519, 336350, 551112

  ERIKS MIDWEST INC.
  5330 South Emmer Dr., New Berlin, Wisconsin 53151
  CEO: Mark Yerrick, Pres.　　　　　　Tel: (262) 785-1333　　　%FO: 100
  Bus: *Sealing elements.*　　　　　　Fax: (262) 785-1756

  ERIKS SOUTHWEST, INC.
  14837 Trinity Boulevard, Ft. Worth, Texas 76155
  CEO: Shawn Courtney, Pres.　　　　　Tel: (817) 267-8837　　　%FO: 100
  Bus: *Airline industry materials*　　　Fax: (817) 571-4700

  ERIKS WEST, INC.
  14600 Interuban Ave., South, Seattle, Washington 98168
  CEO: Cindy Scheelsmith, Pres.　　　　Tel: (206) 243-9660　　　%FO: 100
  Bus: *Sealing elements.*　　　　　　Fax: (206) 243-4718

- **EUROPEAN AERONAUTIC DEFENCE AND SPACE COMPANY EADS NV**
Le Carre, Beechavenue 130-132, NL-1119 PR Schiphol-Rijk, Netherlands
CEO: Noel Forgeard, CEO　　　　　　　Tel: 31-20-655-4800　　　Rev: $43,322
Bus: *Aerospace.*　　　　　　　　　　Fax:　　　　　　　　　　Emp: 110,662
　　　　　　　　　　　　　　　　　www.eads-nv.com
NAICS: 332995, 334511, 336411, 336412, 336413, 336414, 336415, 336419, 811219, 927110

  AIRBUS NORTH AMERICA HOLDINGS, INC.
  198 Van Buren St., Ste. 300, Herndon, Virginia 20170
  CEO: Henri Courpron, Pres. & CEO　　　Tel: (703) 834-3400　　　%FO: 100
  Bus: *Aircraft manufacture.*　　　　　Fax: (703) 834-3340

AMERICAN EUROCOPTER CORPORATION
2701 Forum Dr., Grand Prairie, Texas 75052-7099
CEO: Marc Paganini, Pres. & CEO
Bus: *Designs helicopters and provides instruction facilities.*

Tel: (972) 641-0000
Fax: (972) 641-3550

%FO: 100

EADS NORTH AMERICA
1616 N. Ft. Myers Dr., Ste. 1600, Arlington, Virginia 22209
CEO: Ralph D. Crosby Jr., Chmn. & CEO
Bus: *Aerospace & defense.*

Tel: (703) 236-3300
Fax: (703) 236-3301

EADS TELECOM
2811 Internet Blvd., Frisco, Texas 75034
CEO: Philippe Lecat, Pres.
Bus: *Telephone & telegraph apparatus*

Tel: (469) 365-3000
Fax:

Emp: 400

MBDA
5701 Lindero Canyon Rd., Ste. 4-100, Westlake Village, California 91362
CEO: John Smith, Pres.
Bus: *Search & navigation equipment*

Tel: (818) 991-0300
Fax: (818) 991-4669

Emp: 90

RACAL INSTRUMENTS
4 Goodyear St., Irvine, California 92618
CEO: Gordon Taylor, Pres.
Bus: *Aerospace & defense.*

Tel: (949) 859-8999
Fax: (949) 859-7139

● **EXACT HOLDING N.V.**
Poortweg 6, NL-2612 PA Delft, Netherlands
CEO: Rajesh Patel, CEO
Bus: *Developer of software for CRM, ERP, and HR management applications.*
NAICS: 511210

Tel: 31-15-261-3714
Fax: 31-15-262-5461
www.exactsoftware.com

Rev: $290
Emp: 2,153

ALLIANCE / MFG US
281 South Magnolia Ave., Ste. 201, Goleta, California 93117
CEO: James Kent, VP North America
Bus: *Developer of software for CRM, ERP and HR resource management applications.*

Tel: (805) 683-6363
Fax: (805) 696-6718

%FO: 100

EXACT JOBBOSS
7701 York Ave. South, Ste. 350, Minneapolis, Minnesota 55435
CEO: James Kent, VP North America
Bus: *Developer of software for CRM, ERP and HR resource management applications.*

Tel: (800) 777-4334
Fax: (866) 451-0363

%FO: 100

EXACT SOFTWARE BOSTON
300 Brickstone Sq., Andover, Massachusetts 01810
CEO: James P. Kent, Jr., VP North America
Bus: *Developer of software for CRM, ERP and HR resource management applications.*

Tel: (978) 474-4900
Fax: (978) 474-4944

%FO: 100

EXACT SOFTWARE LATIN AMERICA INC.
PO Box 451363, Sunrise, Florida 33345-1363
CEO: Sergio Castro
Bus: *Developer of software for CRM, ERP and HR resource management applications.*

Tel: (954) 385-1450
Fax:

%FO: 100

EXACT SOFTWARE NA INC.
8800 Lyra Dr., Ste. 350, Columbus, Ohio 43240
CEO: James Kent, VP North America   Tel: (614) 410-2600   %FO: 100
Bus: *Developer of software for CRM, ERP and*   Fax: (866) 544-5456
    HR resource management applications.

EXACT SOFTWARE NJ
31-00 Broadway, Fair Lawn, New Jersey 07410
CEO: James Kent, VP North America   Tel: (201) 703-9100   %FO: 100
Bus: *Developer of software for CRM, ERP and*   Fax: (201) 703-0330
    HR resource management applications.

EXACT SOFTWARE SAN FRANCISCO
7020 Koll Center Pkwy, Ste. 118, Pleasanton, California 94566
CEO: James Kent, VP North America   Tel: (925) 846-9714   %FO: 100
Bus: *Developer of software for CRM, ERP and*   Fax: (925) 846-3018
    HR resource management applications.

MAX ERP
1065 East Hillsdale Rd., Ste. 301, Foster City, California 94404
CEO: James Kent, VP North America   Tel: (650) 345-6000   %FO: 100
Bus: *Developer of software for CRM, ERP and*   Fax: (650) 345-3079
    HR resource management applications.

● **FEADSHIP HOLLAND**
PO Box 5238, NL-2000 GE Haarlem, Netherlands
CEO: Hein Velema, Pres.   Tel: 31-23-524-7000
Bus: *Design, engineering and construction of world*   Fax: 31-23-524-8639   Emp: 300
    class yachts.   www.feadship.nl
NAICS: 336611

    FEADSHIP AMERICA INC.
    801 Seabreeze Blvd., Bahia Mar, Ft. Lauderdale, Florida 33316
    CEO: Don Kenniston, Pres.   Tel: (954) 761-1830   %FO: 100
    Bus: *Sales, distribution and service of yachts.*   Fax: (954) 761-3412

● **FENESTRAE BV**
Loire 128-130, PO Box 24016, NL-2491 The Hague, Netherlands
CEO: Wim G. de Koning, CEO   Tel: 31-70-301-5100
Bus: *Fax server software manufacture.*   Fax: 31-70-301-5151
    www.fenestrae.com
NAICS: 511210

    FENESTRAE INC.
    420 Technology Pkwy., Ste. 200, Norcross, Georgia 30092
    CEO: Dominic Telaro   Tel: (770) 622-5445   %FO: 100
    Bus: *Fax server software manufacture and sales.*   Fax: (770) 622-5465

● **FORTIS N.V.**
Archimedslaan 6, NL-3584 BA Utrecht, Netherlands
CEO: Jean-Paul Votron, CEO   Tel: 31-30-257-6576
Bus: *Provides specialty insurance and investment*   Fax: 31-30-257-7838
    products to businesses, associations, financial   www.fortis.com
    service organizations and individuals.
NAICS: 522110, 522120, 522130, 522291, 522292, 523110, 523910, 523999, 524113, 524126, 525110, 525190, 525910, 525920, 525990

FORTIS CAPITAL CORPORATION
3 Stamford Plaza, 301 Tresser Blvd., Stamford, Connecticut 06901
CEO: Jackues Thys, Chmn.
Bus: *Security broker & dealer*
Tel: (203) 705-5700
Fax: (203) 705-5900
Emp: 97

FORTIS INVESTMENTS
75 State St., Ste. 27, Boston, Massachusetts 02109
CEO: Richard Wohanka, Pres.
Bus: *Investment management services.*
Tel: (617) 478-7200
Fax: (617) 439-4174
Emp: 65

FORTIS INVESTMENTS
150 East 52nd St., 20/F, New York, New York 10022
CEO: Chris McCall
Bus: *Investment management services.*
Tel: (212) 521-9920
Fax: (212) 521-9921

INFORMATION BANKING
141 West Jackson Blvd., Ste. 1800, Chicago, Illinois 60604
CEO: Russell Levens, Pres.
Bus: *Security & commodity services*
Tel: (312) 612-1600
Fax: (312) 612-1601
Emp: 49

INFORMATION BANKING
520 Madison Ave., 3/F, New York, New York 10022
CEO: Lisa Welden
Bus: *Security & commodity services*
Tel: (212) 418-6816
Fax: (212) 759-8609

MEES PIERSON
520 Madison Ave., 3/F, New York, New York 10022
CEO: Marije van der Lint
Bus: *Offers private banking in investment, trust, finance and insurance services.*
Tel: (212) 891-2680
Fax: (212) 891-2681

● **FUGRO N.V.**
Veurse Achterweg 10, NL-2264 SG Leidschendam, Netherlands
CEO: Gert-Jan Kramer, Pres. & CEO
Bus: *Oil and gas exploration and production services.*
Tel: 31-70-311-1422
Fax: 31-70-320-2703
www.fugro.com

NAICS: 211111, 213112, 541360

FUGRO AIRBORNE SURVEYS INC.
6100 Hillcroft, Houston, Texas 77081
CEO: Mike Carson, Mgr.
Bus: *Airborne survey.*
Tel: (713) 369-6121
Fax: (713) 369-6110
%FO: 100

FUGRO CHANCE INC.
200 Dulles Dr., Lafayette, Louisiana 70506
CEO: P. J. Stutes, Mgr.
Bus: *Marine survey.*
Tel: (337) 237-1300
Fax: (337) 268-3272
%FO: 100

FUGRO CHANCE INC.
6100 Hillcroft, Houston, Texas 77081
CEO: R. J. Williams, Mgr.
Bus: *Marine survey.*
Tel: (713) 346-3700
Fax: (713) 346-3671
%FO: 100

FUGRO CONSULTANTS BRE
8613 Cross Park Dr., Austin, Texas 78754
CEO: John A. Wooley, Mgr.   Tel: (512) 977-1800   %FO: 100
Bus: *Onshore geotechnical services.*   Fax: (512) 973-9966

FUGRO CONSULTANTS LP
11009 Osgood, San Antonio, Texas 78233
CEO: P. G. King, Mgr.   Tel: (210) 655-9516   %FO: 100
Bus: *Onshore geotechnical services.*   Fax: (210) 655-9519

FUGRO CONSULTANTS LP
4252 Rhoda Dr., Baton Rouge, Louisiana 70816
CEO: B. Cotton, Mgr.   Tel: (225) 292-5082   %FO: 100
Bus: *Onshore geotechnical services.*   Fax: (225) 292-8084

FUGRO CONSULTANTS LP
115 Topeka, Waco, Texas 76712
CEO: R. E. Weathers, Mgr.   Tel: (254) 399-9299   %FO: 100
Bus: *Onshore geotechnical services.*   Fax: (254) 399-9993

FUGRO CONSULTANTS LP
7031 West Oakland St., Chandler, Arizona 85226
CEO: T. C. Wesling, Mgr.   Tel: (480) 961-1169   %FO: 100
Bus: *Onshore geotechnical services.*   Fax: (480) 940-0952

FUGRO CONSULTANTS LP
2410 East Pasadena Freeway, Pasadena, Texas 77506
CEO: M. Jafari, Mgr.   Tel: (713) 475-0100   %FO: 100
Bus: *Onshore geotechnical services.*   Fax: (713) 475-0107

FUGRO CONSULTANTS LP
6100 Hillcroft, Houston, Texas 77081
CEO: J. M. Cibor, Mgr.   Tel: (713) 369-5400   %FO: 100
Bus: *Onshore geotechnical services.*   Fax: (713) 369-5518

FUGRO CONSULTANTS LP
2517 East Loop 820 North, Fort Worth, Texas 76118
CEO: F. K. Cook, Mgr.   Tel: (817) 284-9595   %FO: 100
Bus: *Onshore geotechnical services.*   Fax: (817) 284-4480

FUGRO CONSULTANTS LP
1205 North Tancahua St., Corpus Christi, Texas 78401
CEO: W. C. Rushing   Tel: (361) 882-5411   %FO: 100
Bus: *Onshore geotechnical services.*   Fax: (361) 882-4028

FUGRO CONSULTANTS LP
4252 Rhoda Dr., Baton Rouge, Louisiana 70816
CEO: B. E. Cotton, Mgr.   Tel: (225) 292-5084   %FO: 100
Bus: *Onshore geotechnical services.*   Fax: (225) 292-8084

FUGRO CONSULTANTS LP
1850 IH-10 South, Beaumont, Texas 77707
CEO: U. K. Backu, Mgr.   Tel: (409) 840-5551   %FO: 100
Bus: *Onshore geotechnical services.*   Fax: (409) 840-5553

FUGRO CONSULTANTS LP
916 Sampson St., Ste. E Lake Charles, Westlake, Louisiana 70669
CEO: D. W. Duhon, Mgr.
Bus: *Onshore geotechnical services.*
Tel: (337) 439-1731
Fax: (337) 433-3313
%FO: 100

FUGRO GEOSCIENCES INC.
6105 Rookin, Houston, Texas 77074
CEO: R. Yilmaz, Mgr.
Bus: *Onshore geotechnical and environmental services.*
Tel: (713) 346-4000
Fax: (713) 346-4002
%FO: 100

FUGRO GEOSERVICES INC.
200 Dulles Dr., Lafayette, Louisiana 70506
CEO: T. D. Hampton, Mgr.
Bus: *Marine survey services.*
Tel: (337) 237-2636
Fax: (337) 268-3221
%FO: 100

FUGRO GEOSERVICES INC.
404 East Main St., Patterson, Louisiana 70392
CEO: P. Fontaine, Mgr.
Bus: *Marine survey services.*
Tel: (985) 395-6737
Fax: (985) 395-2833
%FO: 100

FUGRO GEOSERVICES INC.
6100 Hillcroft, Houston, Texas 77081
CEO: T. K. Hamilton, Mgr.
Bus: *Marine survey services.*
Tel: (713) 369-5800
Fax: (713) 369-5811
%FO: 100

FUGRO GLOBAL ENVIRONMENTAL & OCEAN SCIENCES INC.
6100 Hillcroft, Houston, Texas 77081
CEO: J. R. van Smirren, Mgr.
Bus: *Marine survey services.*
Tel: (713) 346-3600
Fax: (713) 346-3605
%FO: 100

FUGRO INC.
6100 Hillcroft, Houston, Texas 77081
CEO: J. E. Kasparek, Mgr.
Bus: *Geological engineering services.*
Tel: (713) 346-4050
Fax: (713) 346-4054
%FO: 100

FUGRO MULTI CLIENT SERVICES
6100 Hillcroft, Houston, Texas 77081
CEO: K. Mohn, Mgr.
Bus: *Development and production services.*
Tel: (713) 369-5859
Fax: (713) 369-5860
%FO: 100

FUGRO PELAGOS INC.
615 E. 82nd Ave., Ste. 304, Anchorage, Alaska 99518
CEO: E. J. Saade, Mgr.
Bus: *Marine survey services.*
Tel: (907) 258-1799
Fax: (907) 258-3422
%FO: 100

FUGRO PELAGOS INC.
7225 Stennis Airport Dr., Ste. 100, Kiln, Mississippi 39556
CEO: E. Saade, Mgr.
Bus: *Marine survey services.*
Tel: (228) 252-1111
Fax: (228) 252-1133
%FO: 100

FUGRO PELAGOS INC.
3738 Ruffin Rd., San Diego, California 92123
CEO: E. Saade, Mgr.
Bus: *Marine survey services.*
Tel: (858) 292-8922
Fax: (858) 292-5308
%FO: 100

FUGRO ROBERTSON INC.
6100 Hillcroft, 5/F, Houston, Texas 77081
CEO: M. E. Weber, Mgr. Tel: (713) 369-6199 %FO: 100
Bus: *Development and production services.* Fax: (713) 369-6110

FUGRO SEAFLOOR SERVICES
2727 Alaskan Way, Pier 69, Seattle, Washington 98121-1107
CEO: D. M. Hussong, Mgr. Tel: (206) 441-9305 %FO: 100
Bus: *Marine survey services.* Fax: (206) 441-9308

FUGRO SEISMIC IMAGING INC.
6100 Hillcroft, Houston, Texas 77081
CEO: A. Conway, Mgr. Tel: (713) 369-5808 %FO: 100
Bus: *Seismic and gravity surveys.* Fax: (713) 369-5811

FUGRO SOUTH INC.
2880 Virgo Lane, Dallas, Texas 75229
CEO: Hugh T. Kelly, Mgr. Tel: (972) 484-8301 %FO: 100
Bus: *Onshore geotechnical services.* Fax: (972) 620-7328

FUGRO WEST INC.
1000 Broadway, Ste. 200, Oakland, California 94607
CEO: J. Grant, Mgr. Tel: (510) 268-0461 %FO: 100
Bus: *Onshore geotechnical services.* Fax: (510) 268-0137

FUGRO WEST INC.
3738 Ruffin Rd., San Diego, California 92123
CEO: T. Dunne, Mgr. Tel: (805) 650-7000 %FO: 100
Bus: *Onshore geotechnical services.* Fax: (805) 650-7010

FUGRO WEST INC.
4820 McGrath St., Ste. 100, Ventura, California 93003
CEO: T. Dunne, Mgr. Tel: (805) 650-7000 %FO: 100
Bus: *Onshore geotechnical services.* Fax: (805) 650-7010

FUGRO WEST INC.
211 East Victoria St., Ste. D, Santa Barbara, California 93101
CEO: K. M. Clements, Mgr. Tel: (805) 963-4450 %FO: 100
Bus: *Onshore geotechnical services.* Fax: (805) 564-1327

FUGRO WEST INC.
4820 McGrath St., Ste. 100, Ventura, California 93003
CEO: R. Villa, Mgr. Tel: (805) 650-7000 %FO: 100
Bus: *Marine survey services.* Fax: (805) 658-6679

FUGRO WEST INC.
660 Clarion Ct., Ste. A, San Luis Obispo, California 93401
CEO: J. D. Blanchard, Mgr. Tel: (805) 542-0797 %FO: 100
Bus: *Onshore geotechnical services.* Fax: (805) 542-9311

FUGRO-GEOTEAM AS
6100 Hillcroft (77081), Houston, Texas 77274
CEO: B. Hottman, Mgr. Tel: (713) 369-5863 %FO: 100
Bus: *Geological engineering services.* Fax: (713) 369-5860

FUGRO-JASON INC.
6100 Hillcroft, Ste. 200, Houston, Texas 77081
CEO: D. E. Adams, Mgr.   Tel: (713) 369-6900   %FO: 100
Bus: *Development and production services.*   Fax: (713) 369-6936

FUGRO-LCT INC.
Box 740010, Houston, Texas 77274
CEO: Brian Anderson, Mgr.   Tel: (713) 369-6100   %FO: 100
Bus: *Development and production services.*   Fax: (713) 369-6110

FUGRO-MCCLELLAND MARINE GEOSCIENCES INC.
6100 Hillcroft, Houston, Texas 77081
CEO: W. S. Rainey, Mgr.   Tel: (713) 369-5600   %FO: 100
Bus: *Marine geotechnical services.*   Fax: (713) 369-5570

JOHN CHANCE LAND SURVEYS INC.
200 Dulles Dr., Lafayette, Louisiana 70506
CEO: C. G. Rhinehart, Mgr.   Tel: (337) 237-1300   %FO: 100
Bus: *Onshore survey services.*   Fax: (337) 268-3281

OMNISTAR INC.
8200 Westglen Dr., Houston, Texas 77063
CEO: S. J. Waits, Mgr.   Tel: (713) 785-5850   %FO: 100
Bus: *Positioning services.*   Fax: (713) 785-5164

PETCOM INC.
1600 North Collins, Ste. 1700, Richardson, Texas 75080
CEO: Mike Barnett, Mgr.   Tel: (214) 368-2191   %FO: 100
Bus: *Development and production services.*   Fax: (214) 368-5281

● **GAMMA HOLDING NV**
Panovenweg 12, NL-5708 HR Helmond, Netherlands
CEO: Meint Veninga, CEO   Tel: 31-492-56-6600   Rev: $1,174
Bus: *Mfr. textiles for car seats, mattress ticking,*   Fax: 31-492-56-6700   Emp: 9,072
  automobile upholstery.   www.gammaholding.com
NAICS: 313111, 313311, 313320, 314999

    DIMENSION POLYANT SAILCLOTH
    78 Highland Dr., Putnam, Connecticut 06260
    CEO: Rich McGhee, VP   Tel: (860) 963-7413   %FO: 100
    Bus: *Mfr. sailcloth.*   Fax: (860) 928-0161

    VERSEIDAG USA INC.
    4 Aspen Dr., Randolph, New Jersey 07869
    CEO: Garland Drew, Pres.   Tel: (973) 252-1189   %FO: 100
    Bus: *Mfr. textile products.*   Fax: (973) 252-1109

● **GETRONICS NV**
Rembrandttoren, Amstelphlein 1, NL-1096 HA Amsterdam, Netherlands
CEO: Klaas Wagenaar, Chmn. & CEO   Tel: 31-20-586-1412   Rev: $3,353
Bus: *Information technology service provider including*   Fax: 31-20-586-1568   Emp: 22,079
  systems integration, networking, consulting and   www.getronics.com
  human resources services.
NAICS: 541511, 541512, 541519

GETRONICS INC.
22425 East Appleway Ave., Liberty Lake, Washington 99019
CEO: Ray Cazier, Mgr.   Tel: (509) 927-5600   %FO: 100
Bus: *Information technology services.*   Fax: (509) 927-5754

GETRONICS INC.
836 North St., Tewksbury, Massachusetts 01876
CEO: Kevin Roche, Mgr.   Tel: (978) 625-5000   %FO: 100
Bus: *Information technology services.*   Fax: (978) 625-5000

GETRONICS INC.
9009 West Loop South 500, Houston, Texas 77096
CEO: Ray Chattery, VP   Tel: (713) 852-5600
Bus: *Computer system design*   Fax:

GETRONICS INC.
290 Concord Rd., Billerica, Massachusetts 01821
CEO: Kevin Roche   Tel: (978) 625-5000   %FO: 100
Bus: *Computer maintenance & repair.*   Fax: (978) 858-6090   Emp: 3,800

GETRONICS INC.
8110 Anderson Rd., Ste. 100, Tampa, Florida 33634
CEO: Andy Horvath   Tel: (813) 884-2500
Bus: *Information technology services.*   Fax:

● **GRANARIA HOLDINGS B.V**
PO Box 233, NL-2501 CE The Hague, Netherlands
CEO: Joel P. Wyler, Chmn.   Tel: 31-70-312-1100   Rev: $3,400
Bus: *Industry operations include food processing, real* Fax: 31-70-312-1150   Emp: 7,000
estate investment & manufacturing.   www.granaria.nl.
NAICS: 311615, 311712, 531210

   EAGLE-PICHER INDUSTRIES, INC.
   3402 E. University Dr., Phoenix, Arizona 85034
   CEO: Bert Iedema, Pres. & CEO   Tel: (602) 794-9600   %FO: 100
   Bus: *Mfr. industrial products for automotive,* Fax: (602) 794-9601   Emp: 3,900
   defense, aerospace & construction

● **GRASSO PRODUCTS N.V.**
Parallelweg 27, NL-5223 Hertogenbosch, Netherlands
CEO: Frans-Joseph van Laarhoven, Gen. Mgr.   Tel: 31-73-6203-911
Bus: *Compressors and components for industrial* Fax: 31-73-6214-320   Emp: 1,400
refrigeration installations manufacture and sales. www.grasso-global.com.
NAICS: 423830

   FES SYSTEMS INC.
   3475 Board Rd., York, Pennsylvania 17405
   CEO: Ronald Eberhard, CEO   Tel: (717) 767-6411   %FO: 100
   Bus: *Sales of compressors and components for* Fax: (717) 764-3627   Emp: 250
   industrial refrigeration installations.

FES SYSTEMS INC.
1101 N. Governor St., PO Box 4799, Evansville, Indiana 47724
CEO: Roland Doggen, CEO
Bus: *Sales of compressors and components for industrial refrigeration installations.*
Tel: (812) 465-6600
Fax: (812) 465-6610
%FO: 100
Emp: 10

● **GUCCI GROUP N.V.**
Rembrandt Tower, 1 Amstelplein, NL-1096 HA Amsterdam, Netherlands
CEO: Robert Polet, Chmn. & Pres. & CEO
Bus: *Design/mfr. clothing and leather goods. (JV of Pinault-Printemps-Redoute, France and)*
Tel: 31-20-462-1700
Fax: 31-20-465-3569
www.guccigroup.com
Rev: $3,227
Emp: 11,254
NAICS: 315211, 315212, 315222, 315223, 315224, 315993, 315999, 316991, 316992, 325620, 334518, 446120, 448150

GUCCI AMERICA, INC.
50 Hartz Way, Secaucus, New Jersey 07094
CEO: William Franz, Pres.
Bus: *Sales/distribution of designer clothing and leather goods.*
Tel: (201) 867-8800
Fax: (201) 392-2679
%FO: 100
Emp: 800

GUCCI AMERICA, INC.
347 North Rodeo Dr., Beverly Hills, California 90210
CEO: Nora Bedrossian, Mgr.
Bus: *Sales/distribution of designer clothing and leather goods.*
Tel: (310) 278-3451
Fax:
%FO: 100
Emp: 30

GUCCI AMERICA, INC.
685 Fifth Ave., 10/F, New York, New York 10022
CEO: Kamal Abbasi, Mgr.
Bus: *Sales/distribution of designer clothing and leather goods.*
Tel: (212) 826-2600
Fax: (212) 230-0894
%FO: 100
Emp: 60

● **HAGEMEYER N.V.**
Rijksweg 69, NL-1411GE Naarden, Netherlands
CEO: Rudi W.A. da Becker, CEO
Bus: *Gourmet and specialty foods, indoor plants, ceramics and decorative articles.*
Tel: 31-35-695-7611
Fax: 31-35-694-4396
www.hagemeyer.com
Rev: $7,402
Emp: 17,680
NAICS: 333293, 334111, 334112, 334113, 334119, 444190

HAGEMEYER NORTH AMERICA, INC.
330 W. Montague Ave., Ste. 400 B, Charleston, South Carolina 29418
CEO: David G. Gabriel, Pres. & CEO
Bus: *Industrial machinery & equipment distribution*
Tel: (843) 745-2400
Fax: (843) 745-6942

● **JAMES HARDIE INDUSTRIES LTD.**
4th Level, Atrium Unit 04-07, Strawinskylaan 3077, NL-1077 Amsterdam, Netherlands
CEO: Meredith Hellicar, Chmn.
Bus: *Mfr. fiber cement siding, backer board and pipe.*
Tel: 31-20-301-2984
Fax: 31-20-301-2984
www.jameshardie.com
Rev: $1,210
Emp: 3,073
NAICS: 327390

JAMES HARDIE INDUSTRIES USA
26300 LaAlameda, Ste. 250, Mission Viejo, California 92691
CEO: Louis Gries, VP
Bus: *Mfr./sales building products, including fiber cement and gypsum.*
Tel: (949) 348-1800
Fax: (949) 367-1294
%FO: 100

● **HEAD NV**
Rokin 55, NL-1012 KK Amsterdam, Netherlands
CEO: Johan Eiasch, Chmn. & CEO
Bus: *Branded sports equipment manufacture.*
Tel: 31-20-625-1291
Fax: 31-20-625-0956
www.head.com
Rev: $467
Emp: 2,472

NAICS: 339920

HEAD USA INC./ HTM USA HOLDINGS, INC.
Shore Pointe, 1 Selleck St., Norwalk, Connecticut 06855
CEO: David Haggerty, Pres.
Bus: *Branded sports equipment manufacture and sales.*
Tel: (203) 855-8666
Fax: (230) 855-8660
%FO: 100
Emp: 133

HEAD/PENN RACQUET SPORTS
306 South 45th Ave., Phoenix, Arizona 85043
CEO: David Haggerty, Pres.
Bus: *Racquet equipment sales.*
Tel: (602) 269-1492
Fax: (602) 269-1492
%FO: 100
Emp: 302

● **HEINEKEN N.V.**
Tweede Weteringsplantsoen 21, NL-1017 ZD Amsterdam, Netherlands
CEO: Jean Francois van Boxmeer, Chmn. & CEO
Bus: *Mfr. Heineken, Buckler and Amstel light beers.*
Tel: 31-20-523-9239
Fax: 31-20-626-3503
www.heinekeninternational.com
Rev: $13,647
Emp: 61,271

NAICS: 312111, 312120, 312130, 424810

HEINEKEN U.S.A., INC.
360 Hamilton Ave., Ste. 1103, Ste. 1103, White Plains, New York 10601
CEO: Frans van der Minne, Pres. & CEO
Bus: *Import/sales/distribution of Heineken, Buckler, and Amstel light beers.*
Tel: (914) 681-4100
Fax: (914) 681-1900
%FO: 100

● **HOLMATRO INDUSTRIAL EQUIPMENT BV**
PO Box 33, NL-4940AA Raamsdonksveer, Netherlands
CEO: William Swain, Pres.
Bus: *High-pressure hydraulic equipment manufacture.*
Tel: 31-16-258-9200
Fax: 31-16-252-2482
www.holmatro.com

NAICS: 333996

HOLMATRO INC.
505 McCormick Dr., Glen Burnie, Maryland 21061
CEO: William Swayne, Pres.
Bus: *Mfr./sale/distribution/service and warehousing of industrial and rescue equipment.*
Tel: (410) 768-9662
Fax: (410) 768-4878
%FO: 100
Emp: 30

- **HUNTER DOUGLAS N.V.**
Piekstraat 2, NL-3071 EL Rotterdam, Netherlands
CEO: Ralph Sonnenberg, Pres. & CEO
Bus: *Mfr./sale/distribute window covering,*
architectural products, metals trading, precision
NAICS: 314121, 337920, 339999, 444190

Tel: 31-10-486-9911
Fax: 31-10-485-0621
www.hunterdouglasgroup.com

Rev: $2,077
Emp: 15,913

BYTHEWAYS
2750 Redding Ave., Sacramento, California 95830
CEO: Mervin Bytheways Jr., Pres.
Bus: *Sale of home furnishings.*

Tel: (916) 453-1212
Fax: (916) 453-0920

Emp: 300

HUNTER DOUGLAS ARCHITECTURAL PRODUCTS
5015 Oakbrook Pkwy., Ste. 100, Norcross, Georgia 30093
CEO: David Hagan, Operations Mgr.
Bus: *Mfr./sales/distribution & warehousing of*
architectural products.

Tel: (770) 806-9557
Fax: (770) 806-0214

%FO: 100
Emp: 28

HUNTER DOUGLAS INC.
2 Park Way& Rte. 17 South, Upper Saddle River, New Jersey 07458
CEO: Marvin Hopkins, Pres. & CEO
Bus: *Mfr./sale/distribute window covering,*
architectural products.

Tel: (201) 327-8200
Fax: (201) 327-7938

%FO: 100
Emp: 7,501

HUNTER DOUGLAS WINDOW FASHIONS
1 Duette Way, Broomfield, Colorado 80020
CEO: Marv Hopkins, Pres.
Bus: *Mfr. of window treatments.*

Tel: (303) 466-1848
Fax: (303) 876-3387

Emp: 950

RICHMOND TEXTILES
900 N. Franklin, Ste. 200, Chicago, Illinois 60610
CEO: Paul Richmond, CEO
Bus: *Textile converter.*

Tel: (312) 944-8787
Fax: (312) 944-8910

Emp: 12

TIMBER BLINDS
800 East Elm St., McKinney, Texas 75063
CEO: Mike Hayes, Partner
Bus: *Mfr. of blinds.*

Tel: (877) 846-2378
Fax: (877) 846-2378

Emp: 280

TURNILS
Peachtree North, 1327 Northbrook Pkwy., Ste. 410, Suwannee, Georgia 30024
CEO: Debbie Holmberg, Mgr.
Bus: *Sale of home furnishing.*

Tel: (770) 995-2222
Fax: (770) 995-2210

- **IFCO SYSTEMS NV**
Rivierstaete, Amsteldijk 166, NL-1079 LH Amsterdam, Netherlands
CEO: Karl Pohler, CEO & Mng. Dir.
Bus: *Holding company engaged in supply chain*
solutions: round-trip container management (RTC), www.ifcosystems.de
pallet management & commercial container
services.
NAICS: 321920, 322211, 322214, 532411

Tel: 31-20-504-1772
Fax: 31-20-646-0793

Rev: $417
Emp: 3,312

IFCO SYSTEMS NORTH AMERICA, INC.
6829 Flintlock Rd., Houston, Texas 77040
CEO: David S. Russell, Pres.   Tel: (713) 332-6145   %FO: 100
Bus: *Engaged in supply chain solutions,*   Fax: (713) 332-6146   Emp: 3,000
including round-trip container management
(RTC), pallet management services &
industrial container services.

IFCO SYSTEMS NORTH AMERICA, INC.(RPC DIV)
5401 W. Kennedy Blvd., Tampa, Florida 33609
CEO: Tel: (813) 287-8940   %FO: 100
Bus: *Engaged in supply chain solutions,*   Fax: (813) 286-2070
including round-trip container management
(RTC), pallet management services &
industrial container services.

IFCO SYSTEMS WOOD CRATING & PACKAGING DIV.
2312 D. St., Pine Mountain Valley, Georgia 31823
CEO: David Russell   Tel: (706) 628-5032
Bus: *Engaged in supply chain solutions,*   Fax: (706) 628-5157
including round-trip container management
(RTC), pallet management services &
industrial container services.

● **INALFA ROOF SYSTEMS BV**
Smakterweg 70, NL-5804 AH Venray, Netherlands
CEO: Frank Boekholtz, Dir.   Tel: 31-478-555-100   Rev: $544
Bus: *Design and manufacture of automobile roof* Fax: 31-478-555-101   Emp: 1,800
                                            www.inalfa-roofsystems.nl
NAICS: 336399

INALFA ROOF SYSTEMS INC.
10350 N. Holly Rd., Holly, Michigan 48442
CEO: Ron Rouse, Plant Mgr.   Tel: (810) 953-4166   %FO: 100
Bus: *Automobile sunroofs manufacture.*   Fax: (810) 953-4166

INALFA ROOF SYSTEMS INC.
12500 East Nine Mile Rd., Warren, Michigan 48089
CEO: Will Jacobs   Tel: (586) 758-6620   %FO: 100
Bus: *Automobile parts manufacture.*   Fax: (586) 758-6043

INALFA ROOF SYSTEMS INC.
1370 Pacific Dr., Auburn Hills, Michigan 48326
CEO: Michael S. Smith, Mgr.   Tel: (248) 371-3060   %FO: 100
Bus: *Automobile sunroofs manufacture.*   Fax: (248) 371-3019

● **ING GROEP N.V.**
ING House, Amstelveenseweg 500, NL-1081 KL Amsterdam, Netherlands
CEO: Michel Tilmant, CEO   Tel: 31-20-54-15-411   Rev: $115,324
Bus: *Commercial and investment banking and* Fax: 31-20-54-15-412   Emp: 113,039
insurance services.   www.ing.com
NAICS: 522110, 522120, 522130, 522190, 522291, 522292, 522310, 523110, 523130, 523140, 523910, 523920,
523930, 523991, 523999, 524113, 524114,
        524126, 524130, 524210, 524292, 524298, 525110, 525120, 525190, 525910, 525920, 525990, 531390

FINANCIAL NETWORK INVESTMENT CORP.
200 N. Sepulvida, Ste. 1300, Torrance, California 90245
CEO: Stephen B. Benton
Bus: *Insurance, financial markets, Investing*
Tel: (310) 326-3100
Fax: (310) 784-1121
%FO: 100

ING ADVISORS
5780 Powers Ferry Rd. NW, Atlanta, Georgia 30327
CEO: Tom Balachowski, Pres.
Bus: *Financial advisors.*
Tel: (770) 690-4600
Fax: (770) 690-4899
Emp: 800

ING BANK
1 South Orange St., Wilmington, Delaware 19801
CEO: Arkadi Kuhlmann, Pres. & CEO
Bus: *Insurance services.*
Tel: (302) 658-2200
Fax:
Emp: 996

ING CAPITAL ADVISORS, LLC
333 South Grand Ave., Ste. 4120, Los Angeles, California 90071
CEO: Michael Hatley, Pres.
Bus: *Financial & investment banking services*
Tel: (213) 621-3700
Fax: (213) 621-3795
%FO: 100
Emp: 35

ING CLARION PARTNERS
601 13th St. NW, Washington, District of Columbia 20005
CEO: Robert D. Greer, Jr., Mgr.
Bus: *Investment advisory services.*
Tel: (202) 393-1957
Fax: (202) 393-2025

ING CLARION PARTNERS
230 Park Ave., 12/F, New York, New York 10169
CEO: Stephen J. Furnary, Chmn.
Bus: *Securities broker/dealer & investment management services.*
Tel: (212) 883-2500
Fax: (212) 883-2700
%FO: 100
Emp: 175

ING CLARION PARTNERS
1001 Fourth Ave., Seattle, Washington 98154
CEO: Stephen P. Latimer, mgr
Bus: *Investment advisory services.*
Tel: (206) 622-9200
Fax: (206) 622-5950

ING CLARION PARTNERS ATLANTA
2410 Paces Ferry Road, Suite 200, Atlanta, Georgia 30339
CEO: Thomas Flanigan, CEO
Bus: *Investment advisory services.*
Tel: (404) 691-4007
Fax: (404) 691-4779
%FO: 100

ING CLARION PARTNERS BOSTON
One Federal Street, 18th Floor, Boston, Massachusetts 02110
CEO: Mark C. Weld, mgr
Bus: *Investment advisory services.*
Tel: (617) 482-6700
Fax: (617) 482-6555

ING CLARION PARTNERS CHICAGO
209 S. LaSalle Street, Suite 405, Chicago, Illinois 60604
CEO: Denise Stewart
Bus: *Investment advisory services.*
Tel: (312) 553-6150
Fax: (312) 553-6151
%FO: 100

ING CLARION PARTNERS DALLAS
3141 Hood Street, Suite 700, Dallas, Texas 75219
CEO: James C. Hendricks
Bus: *Investment advisory services.*
Tel: (214) 647-4940
Fax: (214) 647-4941
%FO: 100

ING CLARION REAL ESTATE SECURITIES
259 North Rednor-Chester Rd., Ste. 205, Radnor, Pennsylvania 19087
CEO: T. Ritson Ferguson
Bus: *Real estate services.*
Tel: (610) 995-2500
Fax: (610) 964-0410

ING EMPLOYEE BENEFITS
100 Washington Ave. S, Minneapolis, Minnesota 55401
CEO: Curt Olson
Bus: *Insurance services.*
Tel: (612) 372-5322
Fax: (612) 372-1015

ING FINANCIAL HOLDINGS CORP.
1325 Ave. of the Americas, New York, New York 10019
CEO: Thomas J. McInerney, CEO
Bus: *Life insurance services.*
Tel: (646) 424-6000
Fax: (646) 424-6018

ING FINANCIAL PARTNERS
909 Locust St., Des Moines, Iowa 50306-1635
CEO: Bill Lowe, Pres.
Bus: *Proprietary insurance and investment products.*
Tel: (515) 698-7000
Fax: (515) 698-7886

ING FUNDS
7337 East Doubletree Ranch Rd., Scottsdale, Arizona 85258
CEO: Jim Henessey, Pres.
Bus: *Security broker & dealer.*
Tel: (480) 477-3000
Fax:
Emp: 250

ING INVESTMENT
100 Washington Ave. South, Ste. 1635, Minneapolis, Minnesota 55401
CEO: Tedd Elsen, mgr
Bus: *Investment services.*
Tel: (612) 342-3736
Fax:

ING INVESTMENT MANAGEMENT AMERICAS
10 State House Sq., Hartford, Connecticut 06103
CEO: Robert W. Crispin, Chmn. & CEO
Bus: *Investment services.*
Tel: (860) 275-2705
Fax: (860) 275-3822
%FO: 100

ING INVESTMENT MANAGEMENT AMERICAS
10 State House Sq., Hartford, Connecticut 06103
CEO: Robert W. Crispin
Bus: *Life insurance services.*
Tel: (860) 275-3720
Fax: (860) 275-3720
%FO: 100

ING LIFE INSURANCE
151 Farmington Ave., Hartford, Connecticut 06156
CEO: Thomas J. McInerney, Prtn.
Bus: *Investment advisory services.*
Tel: (860) 723-4646
Fax:
Emp: 2,000

ING REAL ESTATE CLARION
335 Madison Ave., New York, New York 10017
CEO: C. Stephen Cordes, member
Bus: *Real estate services.*
Tel: (212) 883-2500
Fax: (212) 883-2700
Emp: 173

MULTI-FINANCIAL SECURITIES CORP.
PO Box 5120, Denver, Colorado 80217
CEO: Jack Conley, Chmn.
Bus: *Securities broker.*
Tel: (303) 446-8400
Fax: (303) 571-4400
Emp: 60

POMONA CAPITAL
780 Third Ave, New York, New York 10017
CEO: Michael D. Granoff, Pres.   Tel: (212) 593-3639
Bus: *Investment advisory services*   Fax: (212) 593-3987   Emp: 14\

PRIMEVEST FINANCIAL SERVICES, INC.
400 First St. South, Ste. 300, St. Cloud, Minnesota 56301
CEO: Randall Ciccati, Pres. & CEO   Tel: (320) 656-4300   %FO: 100
Bus: *Corporate banking.*   Fax: (320) 656-4002   Emp: 267

● **KAAK GROUP**
Varsseveldsewg 20 A, NL-7061 GA Terborg, Netherlands
CEO: Johan H. B. Kaak, Dir.   Tel: 31-315-33-9111   Rev: $83
Bus: *Mfr. of dough processing equipment for baking*   Fax: 31-315-33-9355   Emp: 600
    industries.   www.benier.com
NAICS: 332212, 333294, 337127, 523991

    KAAK GROUP NORTH AMERICA
    351 Thornton Rd., Ste. 123, Lithia Springs, Georgia 30122
    CEO: Peter C. F. Oud, CEO   Tel: (770) 745-2200   %FO: 100
    Bus: *Sales, distribution and service of machinery* Fax: (770) 745-0050   Emp: 15
        for the baking business.

● **KIPP & ZONEN INC.**
Rontgenweg 1, NL-2624 BD Delft, Netherlands
CEO: James Yuel, Pres.   Tel: 31-15-269-8000
Bus: *Mfr. instruments for scientific research.* Fax: 31-15-262-0351
                                                 www.kippzonen.com
NAICS: 334516, 339999

    KIPP & ZONEN INC.
    125 Wilbur Place, Bohemia, New York 11716
    CEO: Jim Yuel, Pres.   Tel: (516) 589-2065   %FO: 100
    Bus: *Mfr. instruments for scientific research.* Fax: (516) 589-2068

● **KLM ROYAL DUTCH AIRLINES**
Amsterdamseweg 55, NL-1182GP Amsterdam, Netherlands
CEO: Leo M. van Wijk, Pres. & CEO   Tel: 31-20-649-9123   Rev: $7,154
Bus: *International commercial air transport services.* Fax: 31-20-649-2324   Emp: 31,182
                                                 www.klm.nl
NAICS: 481111, 481112, 481212

    KLM-ROYAL DUTCH AIRLINES
    2491 Winchester Rd., Memphis, Tennessee 38116
    CEO: Todd Smoyer, Mgr.   Tel: (901) 922-2235   %FO: 100
    Bus: *International commercial air transport* Fax: Emp: 13
        services.

    KLM-ROYAL DUTCH AIRLINES
    11001 AVI Blvd., Ste. 216, Los Angeles, California 90045
    CEO: Dave Janzow, Mgr.   Tel: (323) 646-4010   %FO: 100
    Bus: *Air transport services.*   Fax: Emp: 15

KLM-ROYAL DUTCH AIRLINES
500 W. Cypress Creek Rd., Ft. Lauderdale, Florida 33309
CEO: Annette Tardelo, Mgr.   Tel: (954) 771-6344   %FO: 100
Bus: *International commercial air transport*   Fax: Emp: 3
services.

KLM-ROYAL DUTCH AIRLINES CARGO
8 East Greenway Plaza, Ste. 940, Houston, Texas 77046
CEO: Joe Painter, Pres.   Tel: (713) 572-3377   %FO: 100
Bus: *International commercial air transport cargo* Fax: Emp: 4
services.

● **KONINKLIJKE BAM GROEP NV**
Runnenburg 9, NL-3981 AZ Bunnik, Netherlands
CEO: Wim van Vonno, Chmn.   Tel: 31-30-659-89-88   Rev: $10,187
Bus: *Construction, dredging, civil engineering and* Fax: 31-30-659-89-43 Emp: 22,986
mechanical and electrical services.   www.bam.nl
NAICS: 236210, 236220, 237130, 237310, 237990

   FCI CONSTRUCTORS INC.
   2385 Business Park Dr., Vista, California 92081
   CEO: Garry K. Crabtree, Pres. & CEO   Tel: (760) 727-9767   %FO: 100
   Bus: *Provider of design/build and construction* Fax: (760) 727-9892   Emp: 300
   services for transportation and heavy civil
   projects.

   FLATIRON CONSTRUCTION CORPORATION
   10090 I-25 Frontage Rd., Longmont, Colorado 80504
   CEO: Garry K. Crabtree, Pres. & CEO   Tel: (303) 485-4050   %FO: 100
   Bus: *Provider of design/build and construction* Fax: (303) 485-3922
   services for transportation and heavy civil
   projects.

● **KONINKLIJKE KPN NV**
Maanplein 5, NL-2515 CK The Hague, Netherlands
CEO: A. U. Scheepbouwer, CEO   Tel: 31-70-343-4343   Rev: $16,393
Bus: *Fixed line and mobile telephone services.* Fax: 31-70-332-4485   Emp: 31,116
                                              www.kpn.com
NAICS: 517910

   KPN INC.
   494 8th Ave., 23/F, New York, New York 10001
   CEO: Feddo Hazewindus   Tel: (212) 560-9898   %FO: 100
   Bus: *Telecommunications.*   Fax: (212) 560-0770

● **KPMG INTERNATIONAL**
Burgemeester Rijnderslaan 10, NL-1185 MC Amsterdam, Netherlands
CEO: Robert W. Alspaugh, CEO   Tel: 31-20-656-7890   Rev: $13,440
Bus: *Accounting and financial services.*   Fax: 31-20-656-7700   Emp: 93,983
                                              www.kpmg.com
NAICS: 523930, 524210, 541110, 541199, 541211, 541213, 541219, 541611, 541618

KPMG LLP
345 Park Ave., New York, New York 10154-0102
CEO: Timothy P. Flynn, Chmn. & CEO
Bus: *Accounting and financial services.*

Tel: (212) 758-9700
Fax: (212) 758-9819

%FO: 100
Emp: 18,200

● **LEASEPLAN CORPORATION N.V.**
P.J. Oudweg 41, P.O. Box 3001, NL-1300 EB Almere, Netherlands
CEO: Hugo M. Levecke, Chmn.
Bus: *Corporate fleet leasing and management.*

Tel: 31-365-272700
Fax: 31-365-2710
www.leaseplan.com

Rev: $613
Emp: 7,378

NAICS: 523991, 532112, 551112

LEASE PLAN USA
1165 Sanctuary Pkwy., Alpharetta, Georgia 30004
CEO: Robert E. Harper, VP
Bus: *Engaged in vehicle leasing and fleet
    management solutions.*

Tel: (770) 933-9090
Fax: (678) 202-8700

%FO: 100
Emp: 14

● **MARTINAIR HOLLAND N.V.**
Martinair Bldg., Schipol Airport, PO Box 7507, NL-1118 ZG Amsterdam, Netherlands
CEO: Arie Verberk, CEO
Bus: *Passenger and cargo airline.*

Tel: 31-20-60-11-222
Fax: 31-20-60-1160
www.martinair.nl

Rev: $811
Emp: 2,300

NAICS: 481112

MARTINAIR OF THE AMERICAS
5550 Glades Rd., Ste. 500, Boca Raton, Florida 33431
CEO: Gerrit Draai, VP
Bus: *Airline sales/marketing and service.*

Tel: (561) 391-6165
Fax: (561) 391-2188

%FO: 100
Emp: 150

● **MITTAL STEEL COMPANY N.V.**
Hofplein 20, 15/F, NL-3032 Rotterdam, Netherlands
CEO: Lakshmi N. Mittal, Chmn. & CEO
Bus: *Mfr. steel and iron.*

Tel: 31-10-217-8800
Fax: 31-10-217-8850
www.mittalsteel.com

Rev: $22,197
Emp: 164,393

NAICS: 331111, 331210, 331221

MITTAL STEEL GEORGETOWN USA
420 Hazard St., Georgetown, South Carolina 29440
CEO: Brian Kurtz
Bus: *Mfr. high-carbon steel wire rod products.*

Tel: (843) 546-2525
Fax: (843) 527-3134

%FO: 100

MITTAL STEEL SPARROWS POINT USA
5111 N. Point Blvd., Baltimore, Maryland 21219
CEO: Steve Painter
Bus: *Mfr. cold-rolled steel shapes.*

Tel: (410) 388-3000
Fax: (410) 388-5288

%FO: 100

MITTAL STEEL USA BAR PRODUCTS
3300 Dickey Rd., East Chicago, Indiana 46312
CEO: Louis Schorsch, Pres.
Bus: *Sales and marketing of special quality
    carbon, alloy and free machining bar
    products.*

Tel: (219) 399-1200
Fax: (219) 399-5544

%FO: 100

MITTAL STEEL USA INC.
4020 Kinross Lakes Pkwy., Richfield, Ohio 44286
CEO: Rodney B. Mott
Bus: *Mfr. hot- and cold-rolled steel and hot-
dipped and electrolytic galvanized steel.*

Tel: (330) 659-9100
Fax: (330) 659-9135

%FO: 100

MITTAL STEEL USA INC.
30 West Monroe St., Chicago, Illinois 60603
CEO: Stephen Rogers
Bus: *Marketing/sales of flat-rolled steel
products.*

Tel: (312) 346-0300
Fax: (312) 899-3562

%FO: 100

MITTAL STEEL USA INC.
3210 Watling St., East Chicago, Indiana 46312
CEO: Michael G. Rippey, Pres. & CEO
Bus: *Mfr. flat-rolled steels and alloy bar products
for industrial industries.*

Tel: (219) 399-1200
Fax: (219) 399-5544

%FO: 100

MITTAL STEEL WEIRTON USA
400 Three Springs Dr., Weirton, West Virginia 26062
CEO: Brian James
Bus: *Mfr. hot- and cold-rolled steel and hot-
dipped and electrolytic galvanized steel.*

Tel: (304) 797-2000
Fax: (304) 797-2792

%FO: 100

● **NAUTA DUTILH**
Strawinskylaan 1999, NL-1077 XV Amsterdam, Netherlands
CEO: Marc Blom, Mng. Prtn.
Bus: *International law firm.*

Tel: 31-20-717-1000
Fax: 31-20-717-1111
www.nautadutilh.com

Emp: 400

NAICS: 541110

NAUTA DUTILH
One Rockefeller Plaza, Ste. 1528, New York, New York 10020
CEO: E. Van Schifgarde, Mng. Prtn.
Bus: *International law firm.*

Tel: (212) 218-2990
Fax: (212) 218-2999

%FO: 100

● **NEW SKIES SATELLITES NV**
Rooseveltplantsoen 4, NL-2517 KR The Hague, Netherlands
CEO: Daniel S. Goldberg, Pres. & CEO
Bus: *Engaged in satellite communications.*

Tel: 31-70-306-4100
Fax: 31-70-306-4101
www.newskies.com

Rev: $35
Emp: 262

NAICS: 517410, 517910, 518210, 519190, 561499

NEW SKIES SATELLITES, INC.
2001 L St. NW, Ste. 800, Washington, District of Columbia 20036
CEO: Robert W. Ross, CEO
Bus: *Engaged in satellite communications.*

Tel: (202) 478-7100
Fax: (202) 478-7101

%FO: 100
Emp: 30

● **NUCLETRON B.V.**
Waardgelder 1, NL-3905 TH Veenendaal, Netherlands
CEO: Egbert H. de Groot, CEO
Bus: *Mfr. medical, industrial and defense imaging and
optical instruments.*

Tel: 31-318-557-133
Fax: 31-318-550-485
www.nucletron.com

NAICS: 333314, 339111, 339112, 339113, 339114, 339115

NUCLETRON INC.
8671 Robert Fullerton Dr., Columbia, Maryland 21046
CEO: Jack Coats, Pres.
Bus: *Mfr./distributor medical, industrial and
    defense imaging and optical instruments.*

Tel: (410) 312-4100
Fax: (410) 312-4199

%FO: 100
Emp: 110

● **NUTRECO HOLDING NV**
Prins Frederiklann 4, NL-3818 KC Amersfoort, Netherlands
CEO: Wout Dekker, CEO
Bus: *Animal feed and fish feed production.*

Tel: 31-33-422-6100
Fax: 31-33-422-6101
www.nutreco.com

Rev: $5,262
Emp: 12,400

NAICS: 115210

BG MARINE HARVEST AMERICAS
1600 S. Federal Hwy., Pompano Beach, Florida 33062
CEO: Patty Mann
Bus: *Animal feed and fish feed production.*

Tel: (954) 782-4015
Fax: (954) 782-5897

%FO: 100

BG MARINE HARVEST AMERICAS
14220 Interurban Ave. S, Ste. 150, Seattle, Washington 98168
CEO: Fernando Nuez
Bus: *Animal feed and fish feed production.*

Tel: (206) 762-0676
Fax: (206) 762-7491

%FO: 100

BG MARINE HARVEST AMERICAS
350 Long Beach Blvd., Stratford, Connecticut 06615
CEO: John Tuttle
Bus: *Animal feed and fish feed production.*

Tel: (203) 345-0201
Fax: (203) 345-0210

%FO: 100

BG MARINE HARVEST AMERICAS
2730 E. 37th St., Vernon, California 90058
CEO: Elizabeth Hernandez
Bus: *Animal feed and fish feed production.*

Tel: (323) 277-4600
Fax: (323) 277-4610

%FO: 100

TROUW NUTRITION USA INC.
PO Box 219, Highland, Illinois 62249
CEO: Bruce Crutcher
Bus: *Animal feed and fish feed production.*

Tel: (618) 654-2070
Fax: (618) 654-6700

%FO: 100

● **OCE NEDERLAND N.V.**
St. Urbanusweg 43, NL-5900 MA Venlo, Netherlands
CEO: R. L. van Iperen, Chmn. & CEO
Bus: *Reprographics, copiers, printers, office*

Tel: 31-77-359-2222
Fax: 31-77-354-4700
www.oce.com

Rev: $3,522
Emp: 21,315

NAICS: 333293, 333315, 334119

ARKWRIGHT INC.
538 Main St., PO Box 139, Fiskeville, Rhode Island 02823
CEO: John R. Health, Pres.
Bus: *Sales/service office automation equipment.*

Tel: (401) 821-1000
Fax: (401) 826-3926

%FO: 100
Emp: 400

OCE BUSINESS SERVICES, INC.
855 Ave. of the Americas, New York, New York 10001
CEO: Joseph R. Marciano, Pres. & CEO
Bus: *Sales/service of copier systems.*

Tel: (212) 502-2100
Fax: (212) 502-2113

%FO: 100
Emp: 5,500

OCE DIGITAL DOCUMENT SYSTEMS
Oce North America Inc., 5600 Broken Sound Blvd., Boca Raton, Florida 33487
CEO: Nel Baboyian, Pres. Tel: (800) 877-6232 %FO: 100
Bus: *Mfr. printing systems.* Fax:

OCE DISPLAY GRAPHICS SYSTEMS
2811 Orchard Pkwy., San Jose, California 95134
CEO: Wilbert Verheyen, CEO Tel: (408) 232-4000 %FO: 100
Bus: *Mfr. of computer peripheral equipment &* Fax: Emp: 100
 printing trades machinery.

OCE DOCUMENT TECHNOLOGIES
4330 East-West Hwy., Ste. 304, Bethesda, Maryland 20814
CEO: Michael Breithaupt, Webmaster Tel: (301) 652-9732 %FO: 100
Bus: *Document interpretation, character* Fax: (301) 652-7088
 recognition, & document management.

OCE FINANCIAL SERVICES, INC.
5600 Broken Sound Blvd., Boca Raton, Florida 33487
CEO: H. Werner Krause, Pres. Tel: (561) 997-3100 %FO: 100
Bus: *Sale of computers/peripherals.* Fax: Emp: 700

OCE GROUPWARE TECHNOLOGY, INC.
812 Huron Rd., Ste. 790, Cleveland, Ohio 44115
CEO: Eric Wagoner, Pres. Tel: (216) 687-9970 %FO: 100
Bus: *Computer software development.* Fax: (216) 687-0170 Emp: 60

OCE IMAGING SUPPLIES
1800 Bruning Dr. West, Itasca, Illinois 60143
CEO: S. J. Lee, Mgr. Tel: (800) 323-4827 %FO: 100
Bus: *Mfr. imaging supplies.* Fax:

OCE NORTH AMERICA, INC.
5450 North Cumberland Ave., Chicago, Illinois 60656
CEO: Givanni Pelizzari, CEO Tel: (773) 714-8500 %FO: 100
Bus: *Sales/service of reprographic equipment.* Fax: (773) 714-4056 Emp: 2,400

OCE REPROGRAPHIC TECHNOLOGIES, INC.
1850 N. Central Ave., Ste. 1500, Phoenix, Arizona 85004
CEO: Eric Wagner, Mgr. Tel: (602) 744-1300 %FO: 100
Bus: *Prepackaged software services.* Fax: Emp: 35

OCE WIDE FORMAT PRINTING SYSTEMS
5450 North Cumberland Ave., Chicago, Illinois 60656
CEO: Ran Delli, CEO Tel: (800) 714-4427 %FO: 100
Bus: *Mfr. mid/high volume copiers.* Fax:

ONYX GRAPHICS CORPORATION
6915 South High Tech Dr., Midvale, Utah 84084
CEO: Rakech Kumar, Mgr. Tel: (801) 568-9900 %FO: 100
Bus: *Sales software RIPS for large format inkjet* Fax: Emp: 60
 and electrostatic printers.

- **PANALYTICAL BV**
  Lelyweg 1, NL-7602 EA Almelo, Netherlands
  CEO: Peter N. T. van Velzen, CEO
  Bus: *X-ray instrumentation systems manufacture.*

  Tel: 31-546-534-444
  Fax: 31-546-534-598
  www.panalytical.com

  NAICS: 333295, 334413, 334516, 423450

  PANALYTICAL INC.
  12 Michigan Ave., Natick, Massachusetts 01760
  CEO: Stephen Piela, Pres.
  Bus: *X-ray instrumentation systems manufacture.*

  Tel: (508) 647-1100
  Fax: (508) 647-1115

  %FO: 100

- **PHARMING GROUP NV**
  Archimedesweg 4, NL-2333 CN Leiden, Netherlands
  CEO: Francis J. Pinto, CEO
  Bus: *Pharmaceutical manufacture.*

  Tel: 31-71-5247-400
  Fax: 31-71-5216-507
  www.pharming.com

  Rev: $1
  Emp: 40

  NAICS: 325412

  PHARMING HEALTHCARE, INC.
  6938 Hickory Lane, DeForest, Wisconsin 53532
  CEO: Samir Singh
  Bus: *Pharmaceutical manufacture.*

  Tel: (908) 720-6224
  Fax: (201) 437-6574

- **PHILIPS LIGHTING BV**
  Bldg. EDW-113, NL-5600 JM Eindhoven, Netherlands
  CEO: Theo van Deursen, CEO
  Bus: *Mfr. automotive lighting and lamps*

  Tel: 31-40-27-56476
  Fax: 3-140-27-57052
  www.lighting-philips.com

  Rev: $6,173
  Emp: 44,000

  NAICS: 335110, 335121, 335122, 335129, 335931

  PHILIPS LIGHTING COMPANY
  200 Franklin Sq. Dr., Somerset, New Jersey 08875
  CEO: Steve Goldmacher
  Bus: *Mfr. lighting products.*

  Tel: (732) 563-3000
  Fax: (732) 563-3523

  %FO: 100

- **PHILIPS SEMICONDUCTORS**
  Hurksestraat 19, PB 218, NL-5600 MD Eindhoven, Netherlands
  CEO: Frans A. van Houten, CEO
  Bus: *Mfr. semiconductors and logic devices.*

  Tel: 31-31-4027-82537
  Fax: 31-40-2788-399
  www.semiconductors.philips.com

  Rev: $7,453
  Emp: 35,116

  NAICS: 334413, 334414, 334415

  PHILIPS SEMICONDUCTORS
  730 Boston Post Rd., Ste. 251, Sudbury, Massachusetts 01776
  CEO: David Longden
  Bus: *Semiconductor manufacture.*

  Tel: (978) 579-7932
  Fax: (978) 579-9457

  %FO: 100

  PHILIPS SEMICONDUCTORS
  345 Scarborough Rd., Briarcliff Manor, New York 10510
  CEO: Diego Olego
  Bus: *Semiconductor manufacture.*

  Tel: (914) 945-6000
  Fax: (914) 945-6375

  %FO: 100

Netherlands

PHILIPS SEMICONDUCTORS
3595 Kenton Rd., Marietta, Georgia 30066
CEO: Phil Anzalone   Tel: (770) 904-6611   %FO: 100
Bus: *Semiconductor manufacture.*   Fax: (770) 919-7403

PHILIPS SEMICONDUCTORS
25 Forbes Blvd.., Unit 4, Foxboro, Massachusetts 02035
CEO: Larry Covington   Tel: (508) 337-7900   %FO: 100
Bus: *Semiconductor manufacture.*   Fax: (508) 337-7900

PHILIPS SEMICONDUCTORS
1109 McKay Dr., San Jose, California 95131
CEO: Scott McGregor   Tel: (408) 434-3000   %FO: 100
Bus: *Semiconductor manufacture.*   Fax: (408) 922-5252

● **PIE MEDICAL EQUIPMENT BV**
PO Box 1132, NL-6201 BC Maastricht, Netherlands
CEO: Claudio Bertolini, Pres.   Tel: 31-43-382-4600
Bus: *Mfr. diagnostic ultrasound systems.* Fax: 31-43-382-4601   Emp: 200
                                            www.piemedical.com
NAICS: 334510

BIOSOUND ESAOTE INC.
8000 Castleway Dr., Indianapolis, Indiana 46250
CEO: Claudio Bertolini, Pres.   Tel: (317) 849-1793   %FO: 100
Bus: *Mfr. diagnostic ultrasound systems.* Fax: (317) 841-8616

PHARVISION, DIV. CLASSIC MEDICAL SUPPLY
19900 Mona Rd., Ste. 105, Tequesta, Florida 33469
CEO: Steve DuMond   Tel: (561) 746-9527   %FO: 100
Bus: *Mfr. diagnostic ultrasound systems.* Fax: (561) 746-4212

● **PON HOLDINGS BV**
Putterstraatweg 5, NL-3862 Nijkerk, Netherlands
CEO: K. Borsje, CEO   Tel: 31-247-5211
Bus: *Sale, lease and distribution of automobiles, tires,* Fax: 31-245-8613
  building materials, and construction equipment. www.pon.nl
NAICS: 326211

LEVEELIFT INC.
6320 Kentucky Dam Rd., Paducah, Kentucky 42003
CEO: M. Miles, Reg. Mgr.   Tel: (270) 898-2255   %FO: 100
Bus: *Sales and service of material handling*   Fax: (270) 898-8667
  equipment.

LEVEELIFT INC.
922 Division St., Evansville, Indiana 47711
CEO: M. Miles, Reg. Mgr.   Tel: (812) 425-8164   %FO: 100
Bus: *Sales and service of material handling*   Fax: (812) 436-4792
  equipment.

Netherlands

LEVEELIFT INC.
6198 Nashville Rd., Bowling Green, Kentucky 42101
CEO: M. Miles, Reg. Mgr.　　　　　　Tel: (270) 782-9990　　%FO: 100
Bus: *Sales and service of material handling*　Fax: (270) 270-4210
　　equipment.

LEVEELIFT INC.
2921 South Floyd St., Louisville, Kentucky 40209
CEO: M. Miles, Reg. Mgr.　　　　　　Tel: (502) 636-2000　　%FO: 100
Bus: *Sales and service of material handling*　Fax: (502) 636-1871
　　equipment.

MATERIAL HANDLING SERVICES
315 E. Fullerton Ave., Carol Stream, Illinois 60188
CEO: Jean Gardecki　　　　　　　　Tel: (630) 665-7200　　%FO: 100
Bus: *Material handling equipment sales and lease.* Fax: (630) 665-4669

MATERIAL HANDLING SERVICES
4414 11th St., Rockford, Illinois 61109
CEO: Burt Anderson　　　　　　　　Tel: (815) 397-4450　　%FO: 100
Bus: *Material handling equipment sales and lease.* Fax: (815) 397-4456

MATERIAL HANDLING SERVICES
1800 W. Hawthorne Ln., Suite M, Chicago, Illinois 60185
CEO: Jasper van den Driest　　　　　Tel: (630) 562-4900　　%FO: 100
Bus: *Material handling equipment sales and lease.* Fax: (630) 665-4780

PON NORTH AMERICA, INC.
230 Park Ave., Ste. 1000, New York, New York 10169
CEO: D. Atkinson　　　　　　　　　Tel: (212) 808-6560　　%FO: 100
Bus: *Bicycle, auto and tire equipment*　Fax: (212) 808-3020
　　manufacture.

PON SERVICES COMPANY
10600 Corporate Dr., Stafford, Texas 77477
CEO: D. Atkinson　　　　　　　　　Tel: (281) 275-4329　　%FO: 100
Bus: *Bicycle, auto and tire equipment*　Fax: (281) 565-8499
　　manufacture.

PORTMAN EQUIPMENT COMPANY
1342 Jamike Dr., Erlanger, Kentucky 41018
CEO: Wym C. Portman　　　　　　　Tel: (859) 371-2200　　%FO: 100
Bus: *Material handling equipment sales and lease.* Fax: (859) 371-2248

W&O SUPPLY
3333 SW 2nd Ave., Ft. Lauderdale, Florida 33315
CEO: K. D. Huff, Reg. Mgr.　　　　　Tel: (954) 462-8008　　%FO: 100
Bus: *Provider of total piping solutions to the*　Fax: (954) 467-3236
　　marine industry.

W&O SUPPLY
2390 Boswell Rd., Ste. 400, Chula Vista, California 91914
CEO: K. D. Huff, Reg. Mgr.　　　　　Tel: (619) 656-7420　　%FO: 100
Bus: *Provider of total piping solutions to the*　Fax: (619) 421-7518
　　marine industry.

W&O SUPPLY
3485 Evergreen Ave., Jacksonville, Florida 32206
CEO: K. D. Huff, Reg. Mgr.   Tel: (904) 354-3800   %FO: 100
Bus: *Provider of total piping solutions to the*   Fax: (904) 354-5321
marine industry.

W&O SUPPLY
2220 Michigan Ave., Mobile, Alabama 36615
CEO: K. D. Huff, Reg. Mgr.   Tel: (251) 433-2816   %FO: 100
Bus: *Provider of total piping solutions to the*   Fax: (251) 438-1210
marine industry.

W&O SUPPLY
800 W. 14th St., Long Beach, California 90813
CEO: K. D. Huff, Reg. Mgr.   Tel: (562) 435-6359   %FO: 100
Bus: *Provider of total piping solutions to the*   Fax: (562) 436-5679
marine industry.

W&O SUPPLY
1902 "B" 43rd St. North, Tampa, Florida 33605
CEO: K. D. Huff, Reg. Mgr.   Tel: (813) 248-3267   %FO: 100
Bus: *Provider of total piping solutions to the*   Fax: (813) 248-3267
marine industry.

ZY-TECH GLOBAL INDUSTRIES
600 SE Maritime Ave., Ste. 210, Vancouver, Washington 98661
CEO: Ray Baker, Pres.   Tel: (360) 696-5838   %FO: 100
Bus: *Mfr. material handling equipment.*   Fax: (360) 696-5833

● **Provimi Pet Food PL**
Veerlaan 17-23, NL-3072 AN Rotterdam, Netherlands
CEO: Wim Troost, Chmn. & CEO   Tel: 31-10-423-9500   Rev: $2,155
Bus: *Animal feed and nutrition.*   Fax: 31-10-423-9624   Emp: 8,170
                                                www.provimi.com
NAICS: 311119

AKEY INC.
PO Box 5002, Lewisburg, Ohio 45338
CEO: Dwight Armstrong, Mgr.   Tel: (937) 962-7038   %FO: 100
Bus: *Animal feed and nutrition.*   Fax: (937) 962-4031

PROGRESSIVE NUTRITION INC.
5264 Council Street NE, Cedar Rapids, Iowa 52406
CEO: Dwight Armstrong   Tel: (319) 393-3310   %FO: 100
Bus: *Animal feed and nutrition.*   Fax: (319) 393-6388

SUNGLO FEEDS INC.
300 North Main St., Hesston, Kansas 67062
CEO: Jon Previant, Gen. Mgr.   Tel: (800) 366-1354   %FO: 100
Bus: *Animal feed and nutrition.*   Fax:

VIGORTONE AG PRODUCTS INC.
775 N .Hwy., Lamar, Missouri 64759
CEO: Rebecca Haskins   Tel: (417) 398-0012   %FO: 100
Bus: *Animal feed and nutrition.*   Fax: (417) 398-0012

- **PURAC BIOCHEM, DIV. CSM NV**
  PO Box 21, Arkelsedijk 46, NL-4200 AA Gorinchem, Netherlands
  CEO: R. R. Hendriks, Chmn.   Tel: 31-18-369-5695   Rev: $43
  Bus: *Produces natural lactic acid, lactates, lactitol,*   Fax: 31-18-369-5600   Emp: 450
  lactides and polylactides.   www.purac.com
  NAICS: 325199
  > **PURAC AMERICA INC.**
  > 111 Barclay Boulevard, Lincolnshire, Illinois 60069
  > CEO: Claudia Bratrude, Mktg.   Tel: (847) 634-6330   %FO: 100
  > Bus: *Bakery supplies and food ingredients.*   Fax: (847) 634-1992

- **QIAGEN N.V.**
  Spoorstraat 50, NL-5911 KJ Venlo, Netherlands
  CEO: Peer M. Schatz, CEO & Mng. Dir.   Tel: 31-77-320-8400   Rev: $381
  Bus: *Mfr. products for drug screening, diagnostics and*   Fax: 31-77-320-8409   Emp: 1,322
  development of genetic vaccinations. (JV of   www.qiagen.com
  Quiagen Germany)
  NAICS: 334516
  > **QIAGEN INC.**
  > 27220 Turnberry Lane, Valencia, California 91355
  > CEO: Metin Colpan, Pres.   Tel: (800) 426-8157
  > Bus: *Biotechnological research*   Fax: (800) 718-2056
  >
  > **QIAGEN SCIENCES**
  > 19300 Germantown Rd., Germantown, Maryland 20874
  > CEO: Peer Schatz, CEO   Tel: (240) 686-7700   %FO: 100
  > Bus: *Chemical preparations*   Fax: (240) 686-1618   Emp: 170

- **RABOBANK NEDERLAND**
  Croeselaan 18, NL-3521 CB Utrecht, Netherlands
  CEO: Hubertus Heemskerk, Chmn. & CEO   Tel: 31-30-216-0000   Rev: $31,270
  Bus: *Banking and financial services.*   Fax: 31-30-216-1916   Emp: 56,690
                                                     www.rabobank.com
  NAICS: 522110, 522220, 522298, 523110, 523920, 523991, 524210, 525110, 525920
  > **RABO AG SERVICES, INC.**
  > 1309 Technology Pkwy., Cedar Falls, Iowa 50613
  > CEO: Kevin D. Schipper, CEO   Tel: (319) 277-0261
  > Bus: *Agricultural lending.*   Fax: (319) 277-0144
  >
  > **RABOBANK INTERNATIONAL**
  > 13355 Noel Rd., One Galleria Tower, Ste. 1000, Lock Box 69, Dallas, Texas 75240
  > CEO: Bruce Baccus, Mgr.   Tel: (972) 419-6300
  > Bus: *Financial services.*   Fax: (972) 419-6315
  >
  > **RABOBANK INTERNATIONAL**
  > 4 Embarcadero, Ste. 3200, San Francisco, California 94111
  > CEO: Robert W. Mitchell, Mgr.   Tel: (415) 782-9800
  > Bus: *Financial services.*   Fax: (415) 986-8349

RABOBANK INTERNATIONAL
One Atlantic Centre, 1201 West Peachtree St. N.W., Ste. 3450, Atlanta, Georgia 30309
CEO: Adrianne Weststrate, Mgr.   Tel: (404) 872-9005   %FO: 100
Bus: *Banking and financial services.*   Fax: (404) 877-9150

RABOBANK INTERNATIONAL
245 Park Ave., New York, New York 10167
CEO: Cor Broekhuyse, Chmn.   Tel: (212) 916-7800   %FO: 100
Bus: *Engaged in investment banking.*   Fax: (212) 818-0233   Emp: 843

RABOBANK INTERNATIONAL
123 North Wacker Dr., Ste. 2100, Chicago, Illinois 60606
CEO: Bruce Baccas, Mgr.   Tel: (312) 408-8200   %FO: 100
Bus: *Banking and financial services.*   Fax: (312) 408-8240

RABOBANK INTERNATIONAL
1825 I St., NW, Ste. 400, Washington, District of Columbia 20006
CEO: Inge Skjelford, Mng. Dir.   Tel: (202) 429-2053
Bus: *Financial services.*   Fax: (202) 822-4999

VIB CORP.
1448 Main St., El Centro, California 92243
CEO: Dennis L. Kern, Pres. & CEO   Tel: (760) 337-3200
Bus: *Regional banks & thrifts*   Fax: (760) 337-3229   Emp: 490

● **RANDSTAD HOLDING NV**
Diemermere 25, NL-1112 TC Diemen, Netherlands
CEO: Ben Noteboom, Chmn. & CEO   Tel: 31-20-569-5911   Rev: $6,599
Bus: *Engaged in office staffing, temporary staffing,*   Fax: 31-20-569-5520   Emp: 218,280
   cleaning staffing and security personnel staffing.   www.randstad.com
   NAICS: 561310, 561320

   RANDSTAD NORTH AMERICA
   2015 South Park Place, SE, Atlanta, Georgia 30339
   CEO: James H. Reese, CEO   Tel: (770) 937-7000   %FO: 100
   Bus: *Engaged in temporary office, cleaning and*   Fax: (770) 937-7100   Emp: 2,362
      security personnel staffing.

● **ROYAL AHOLD N.V.**
Albert Heijnweg 1, NL-1507 EH Zaandam, Netherlands
CEO: Anders C. Moberg, Pres. & CEO   Tel: 31-75-659-9111   Rev: $70,439
Bus: *Engaged in international food and beverage*   Fax: 31-75-659-8350   Emp: 206,441
   retailing,ifor food chains Stop & Shop, Tops,   www.ahold.com
   Giant Food and Peapod stores.
   NAICS: 445110, 722310

   AHOLD USA INC.
   1385 Hancock St., Quincy Center Plaza, Quincy, Massachusetts 02169
   CEO: Don Gabrys, EVP   Tel: (781) 380-8000   %FO: 100
   Bus: *Retail food chain*   Fax: (781) 770-8190   Emp: 170,000

ALLEN FOODS
8543 Page Ave., St. Louis, Missouri 63114
CEO: Ken Craft, Pres.   Tel: (314) 426-4100
Bus: *Wholesale food distributors.*   Fax: (314) 426-0391

GIANT FOOD LLC
1385 Hancock St., Quincy Center Plaza, Quincy, Massachusetts 02169
CEO: Marc E. Smith, Pres. & CEO   Tel: (780) 380-8000
Bus: *Grocery Retail*   Fax: (617) 770-8190   Emp: 18,270

GIANT FOOD STORES LLC
1149 Harrisburg Pike, Carlisle, Pennsylvania 17013
CEO: Anthony Schiano, Pres. & CEO   Tel: (717) 249-4000
Bus: *Grocery retail*   Fax: (717) 960-1327

PEAPOD
9933 Woods Dr., Ste. 375, Skokie, Illinois 60077
CEO: Andrew B. Parkinson, Pres.   Tel: (847) 583-9400   %FO: 100
Bus: *Online grocery shopping service.*   Fax: (847) 583-9494   Emp: 158

THE STOP & SHOP SUPERMARKET COMPANY
1385 Hancock St., Quincy Center Plaza, Quincy, Massachusetts 02169
CEO: Marc E. Smith, Pres. & CEO   Tel: (781) 380-8000
Bus: *Grocery retail*   Fax: (617) 770-8190   Emp: 40,877

TOPS MARKETS LLC
6363 Main St., Williamsville, New York 14221
CEO: Anthony Schiano, Pres. & CEO   Tel: (716) 635-5000   %FO: 100
Bus: *Retail food chain.*   Fax:

U.S. FOODSERVICE
9755 Patuxent Woods Dr., Columbia, Maryland 21046
CEO: Lawrence S. Benjamin, Pres. & CEO   Tel: (410) 312-7100   %FO: 100
Bus: *Engaged in restaurant, hotel and school*   Fax: (410) 312-7591   Emp: 23,282
food distribution.

● **ROYAL DSM NV**
Het Overloon 1, NL-6411 TE Heerlen, Netherlands
CEO: Peter A. Elverding, Chmn.   Tel: 31-45-578-8111   Rev: $10,574
Bus: *Mfr. of life sciences and performance materials.*   Fax: 31-45-571-9753   Emp: 24,180
                                            www.dsm.nl
NAICS: 311942, 325192, 325211, 325221, 325311, 325312, 325411, 325412, 325414

DSM DESOTECH INC.
1122 St. Charles St., Elgin, Illinois 60120
CEO: Steve Hartig   Tel: (847) 697-0400   %FO: 100
Bus: *High-quality ultraviolet light and electron*   Fax: (847) 695-1748
beam (UV/EB) curable materials

DSM ELASTOMERS AMERICA
31 Fuller St., Leominster, Massachusetts 01453
CEO: Tony De Vrught, Dir.   Tel: (978) 534-1010   %FO: 100
Bus: *Mfr. laminated plastic sheets.*   Fax: (978) 534-1010

DSM ENGINEERING PLASTICS, INC.
2215 Hillsboro Lane, Naperville, Illinois 60564
CEO: John McMullan   Tel: (630) 904-5234   %FO: 100
Bus: *Compounder of reinforced thermoplastics*   Fax: (630) 904-5234
and additives.

DSM ENGINEERING PLASTICS, INC.
PO Box 3333, Evansville, Indiana 47732
CEO: Auke Rottier   Tel: (812) 424-3831   %FO: 100
Bus: *Compounder of reinforced thermoplastics*   Fax: (812) 435-7709
and additives.

DSM PHARMACEUTICALS, INC.
5900 NW Greenville Boulevard, Greenville, North Carolina 27835
CEO: Leendert H. Staal, Pres. & CEO   Tel: (252) 707-2307   %FO: 100
Bus: *Contract manufacturing and development.*   Fax: (252) 707-2046

DSM SOMOS
2 Penn's Way, Ste. 401, New Castle, Delaware 19720
CEO: Steve Hartig   Tel: (302) 326-8100   %FO: 100
Bus: *Ultraviolet light manufacture.*   Fax: (302) 326-8121

• **ROYAL DUTCH/SHELL GROUP OF COMPANIES**
Carel van Bylandtlaan 30, NL-2596 HR The Hague, Netherlands
CEO: Jeroen van der Veer, Chmn.   Tel: 31-70-377-9111   Rev: $201,728
Bus: *Oil and natural gas exploration and production.*   Fax: 31-70-377-3115   Emp: 119,000
                                            www.shell.com
NAICS: 211111, 211112, 213111, 221210, 324110, 324191, 324199, 333132, 424710, 424720, 445120, 447110,
447190, 454311, 454312, 454319, 486110,
        486210, 486910, 541360

AERA ENERGY
10000 Ming Ave., Bakersfield, California 93311
CEO: Eugene J. Voiland, Pres. & CEO   Tel: (661) 665-5000
Bus: *Oil & gas exploration & production*   Fax: (661) 665-5042   Emp: 1,100

BASELL NORTH AMERICA
912 Appleton Rd., Elkton, Maryland 21921
CEO: Randy Woelfel, Pres.   Tel: (410) 996-1600
Bus: *Plastic & fiber manufacturing*   Fax: (410) 996-2121   Emp: 1,500

INFINEUM INTERNATIONAL LTD.
1900 E. Linden Ave., Linden, New Jersey 07036
CEO: Mark Struglinski, Pres.   Tel: (908) 474-0100
Bus: *Commercial physical research*   Fax: (908) 474-6117   Emp: 700

INTERGEN
15 Wayside Rd., Burlington, Massachusetts 01803
CEO: Marvin Odum, CEO   Tel: (781) 993-3000
Bus: *Power production*   Fax: (781) 993-3005   Emp: 210

JIFFY LUBE INTERNATIONAL
700 Milam St., Houston, Texas 77002
CEO: Larry Burch, Pres.   Tel: (713) 546-4100   %FO: 100
Bus: *Automotive service & collision repair*   Fax: Emp: 26,000

MOTIVA ENTERPRISES LLC
700 Milam St., Houston, Texas 77002
CEO: William B. Welte, Pres. & CEO
Bus: *Gasoline retail marketer.*
Tel: (713) 277-8000
Fax: (713) 277-7600
%FO: 50
Emp: 3,600

SHELL CHEMICALS
910 Louisiana St., Houston, Texas 77002
CEO: Stacy Methvin, VP
Bus: *Mfr. chemicals.*
Tel: (713) 241-6161
Fax: (713) 241-2909
%FO: 100

SHELL EXPLORATION AND PRODUCTION COMPANY
200 N. Dairy Ashford St., Houston, Texas 77079
CEO: Raoul Restucci, CEO
Bus: *Produces oil and natural gas.*
Tel: (713) 241-6161
Fax: (713) 241-6946
%FO: 100
Emp: 25

SHELL GLOBAL SOLUTIONS INTERNATIONAL
Westhollow Technology Center, 3333 Hwy. 6 South, Houston, Texas 77082
CEO: Graeme Sweeney, Pres.
Bus: *Crude petroleum & natural gas*
Tel: (281) 544-8844
Fax: (281) 544-8930
Emp: 15

SHELL HYDROGEN
700 Milam St., Houston, Texas 77002
CEO: Graeme Sweeney
Bus: *Energy exploration and production.*
Tel: (713) 277-3155
Fax:

SHELL MARTINEZ REFINERY
3485 Pacheco Blvd., Martinez, California 94553
CEO: Aamir Farid, Mgr.
Bus: *Petroleum refining*
Tel: (925) 313-3000
Fax: (925) 313-5613
Emp: 900

SHELL OIL COMPANY
One Shell Plaza, 910 Louisana St., Houston, Texas 77002
CEO: John D. Hofmeister, Pres.
Bus: *Global oil/gas company; JV with UK.*
Tel: (713) 241-6161
Fax: (713) 241-4044
%FO: 100
Emp: 20,474

SHELL OIL PRODUCTS
1100 Louisiana St., Houston, Texas 77210
CEO: Lynn Laverty Elsenhans, Pres. & CEO
Bus: *Petroleum products marketing.*
Tel: (713) 277-7000
Fax: (713) 277-7856
%FO: 100

SHELL PIPELINE CO.
2 Shell Plaza, Houston, Texas 77002
CEO: John Hollowell, Pres.
Bus: *Petroleum exploration, refining and sales.*
Tel: (713) 277-7600
Fax: (713) 241-6988
Emp: 540

SHELL SOLAR
4650 Adohr Ln., Camarillo, California 93011
CEO: Karen de Segundo, CEO
Bus: *Power generation & storage*
Tel: (805) 482-6800
Fax: (805) 388-6395
Emp: 496

WOODSIDE PETROLEUM LTD.
Sage Plaza, 5151 San Felipe, 12/F, Houston, Texas 77056
CEO: Don Voelte, CEO & Mng. Dir.
Bus: *Oil & gas exploration & production*
Tel: (713) 963-8490
Fax: (713) 969-8868
Emp: 2,219

- **ROYAL NUMICO N.V.**
WTC Schiphol Airport Tower E, Schiphol Blvd. 105, NL-1118 BG Schiphol Airport, Netherlands
CEO: Jan Bennink, Pres. & CEO   Tel: 31-20-456-9000   Rev: $3,955
Bus: *Baby food products, dietary and clinical*   Fax: 31-20-456-8000   Emp: 10,889
  nutritional products and supplements   www.numico.com
NAICS: 311422, 311423, 311999

  SHS NORTH AMERICA
  Human Genome Sciences Campus, 9900 Belward Campus Dr., Ste. 100, Rockville, Maryland 20850
  CEO: Jennifer Devaney   Tel: (301) 795-2300
  Bus: *specialized clinical nutrition*   Fax: (301) 795-2301

- **ROYAL P&O NEDLLOYD NV**
Boompjes 40, NL-3011XB Rotterdam, Netherlands
CEO: Philip N. Green, CEO   Tel: 31-10-400-6111   Rev: $1,906
Bus: *International shipping and transport services.*   Fax: 31-10-400-6075   Emp: 13,500
    www.ponl.com
NAICS: 483111

  NEDLLOYD LINES
  3875 Faber Place Dr.., Ste. 200, Charleston, South Carolina 29405
  CEO: Chuck Csernic, Gen. Mgr.   Tel: (843) 566-7400   %FO: 100
  Bus: *Marine cargo handling*   Fax: (843) 566-7411

  P&O NEDLLOYD
  1 Meadowlands Plaza, 14/F, East Rutherford, New Jersey 07073
  CEO: Michael White   Tel: (201) 896-6200
  Bus: *Freight transport services.*   Fax: (201) 896-6342   Emp: 800

  P&O NEDLLOYD LINES
  2500 Cumberland Pkwy., Ste. 400, Atlanta, Georgia 30339
  CEO: Less Cutrona, VP   Tel: (678) 309-7100   %FO: 100
  Bus: *Freight transportation arrangements.*   Fax: (678) 309-7113

  P&O NEDLLOYD LINES
  6 Hutton Centre Dr., Ste. 520, Santa Ana, California 92707
  CEO: Tel: (714) 754-6000   %FO: 100
  Bus: *International shipping and transport*   Fax: (714) 754-6001
    services.

  P&O NEDLLOYD LTD.
  Port Centre 1, 415 Portcentre Pkwy., 2/F, Portsmouth, Virginia 23704
  CEO: Tom Dushatinski, Sales   Tel: (757) 398-5400
  Bus: *Water transportation*   Fax: (757) 398-5410

  P&O NEDLLOYD LTD.
  4700 West Sam Houston Pkwy. N, Houston, Texas 77041
  CEO: Bob Porche, Mgr.   Tel: (832) 467-7000   %FO: 100
  Bus: *Freight transportation arrangements.*   Fax: (832) 467-7010

  P&O NEDLLOYD LTD.
  2001 York Rd., Ste. 500, Oak Brook, Illinois 60523
  CEO: Mike Maselli, Mgr.   Tel: (630) 891-7700
  Bus: *Deep sea foreign trans. of freight*   Fax: (630) 891-7710

- **ROYAL PHILIPS ELECTRONICS N.V.**
Breitner Center, Amstelplein 2, NL-1096 BC Amsterdam, Netherlands
CEO: Gerard Kleisterlee, CEO
Bus: *Mfr. consumer electronics, lighting components, appliances, professional system, communications and information system, medical imaging equipment.*
Tel: 31-20-59-77-777
Fax: 31-20-59-77-070
www.philips.com
Rev: $41,070
Emp: 161,586
NAICS: 333314, 334310, 334413, 335110, 335121, 335122, 335129, 339113

  PHILIPS CONSUMER ELECTRONICS NORTH AMERICA
  64 Perimeter Center East, Atlanta, Georgia 30346
  CEO: Lou Ann Thomas, Pres.
  Bus: *Mfr. digital convergence products for Televisions, audio equipment, PC monitors and peripherals.*
  Tel: (770) 821-2400
  Fax: (770) 821-2250
  %FO: 100

  PHILIPS ELECTRONICS NORTH AMERICA CORPORATION
  1251 Ave. of the Americas, New York, New York 10020
  CEO: Paul Zeven, CEO
  Bus: *Holding company.*
  Tel: (212) 536-0500
  Fax: (212) 536-0559
  %FO: 100
  Emp: 27,144

  PHILIPS GLOBAL PACS
  5000 Marina Blvd., Ste. 1000, Brisbane, California 94005
  CEO: Mark Reis
  Bus: *Distribution and management of diagnostic-quality digital medical images.*
  Tel: (650) 228-5555
  Fax: (650) 228-5580
  %FO: 100

  PHILIPS MEDICAL SYSTEMS
  710 Bridgeport Ave., Shelton, Connecticut 06484
  CEO: Brent Shafer
  Bus: *Mfr. medical imaging equipment.*
  Tel: (203) 926-7674
  Fax: (203) 929-6099
  %FO: 100

  PHILIPS MEDICAL SYSTEMS
  3000 Minuteman Rd., Andover, Massachusetts 01810
  CEO: Heidi Wilson
  Bus: *Mfr. medical imaging equipment.*
  Tel: (978) 687-1501
  Fax: (978) 687-1501
  %FO: 100
  Emp: 10,000

- **ROYAL TEN CATE NV**
Egbert Gorterstraat 3, NL-7607 GB Almelo, Netherlands
CEO: Louis De Vries, Chmn.
Bus: *Mfr. of industrial, agricultural and erosion control fabrics, fire hoses and geotextiles.*
Tel: 31-54-654-4911
Fax: 31-546-514145
www.tencate.com
Rev: $874
Emp: 3,270
NAICS: 313210, 313221, 313230, 313312, 314912, 325211

  MIRATECH INC.
  10822 NE 148th Ln., #J-201, Bothell, Washington 98011
  CEO: Stephen Martin
  Bus: *Sale of Mirafi construction products.*
  Tel: (425) 488-4178
  Fax: (425) 488-5948
  %FO: 100

  MIRATECH INC.
  435 Country Club Rd., Phoenixville, Pennsylvania 19460
  CEO: Peter Kaye
  Bus: *Mining and mineral processing.*
  Tel: (610) 935-5863
  Fax: (610) 917-0742
  %FO: 100

MIRATECH INC.
3680 Mount Olive Rd., Commerce, Georgia 30529
CEO: Tom Stephens   Tel: (706) 693-1897   %FO: 100
Bus: *marketing and support of the*   Fax: (706) 693-1896
      geocontainment technology.

MIRATECH INC.
3971 Iroquois Ct., Rhinelander, Wisconsin 54501
CEO: Glenn Lundin   Tel: (715) 369-2598   %FO: 100
Bus: *Sale of Mirafi construction products.*   Fax: (715) 369-5263

ROYAL TEN CATE (USA) INC.
26071 Merit Cir., Ste. 109, Laguna Hills, California 92653
CEO: Chip McCallum   Tel: (949) 716-3950   %FO: 100
Bus: *Mfr. construction products.*   Fax: (949) 716-3951

ROYAL TEN CATE (USA) INC.
365 South Holland Dr., Pendergrass, Georgia 30567-4625
CEO: David C. Clarke, Pres.   Tel: (706) 693-2226   %FO: 100
Bus: *U.S. holding company.*   Fax: (706) 693-2226

TEN CATE NICOLON INC.
258 Spielman Hwy., Burlington, Connecticut 06013
CEO: Jeff Harris   Tel: (860) 675-9200   %FO: 100
Bus: *Sale of Mirafi construction products.*   Fax: (860) 675-9201

● **ROYAL VOLKER WESSELS STEVIN NV**
Oostmaasiaan 71, NL-3063 AN Rotterdam, Netherlands
CEO: Herman J. Hazewinkel, CEO   Tel: 31-10-4244-244   Rev: $5,271
Bus: *Construction services, property development,*   Fax: 31-10-4244-233   Emp: 16,600
      building materials, mechanical and electrical   www.volkerwessels.com
      installation and traffic engineering.
NAICS: 236220

     VOLKERWESSELS NORTH AMERICA (VWS US CORP.)
     825 Fifth Ave., Ste. 201, Kirkland, Washington 98083-2909
     CEO: J. P. Leenhouts   Tel: (425) 202-3600   %FO: 100
     Bus: *Construction services.*   Fax: (425) 202-3600

● **ROYAL VOPAK NV**
Westerlaan 10, NL-3016 CK Rotterdam, Netherlands
CEO: Charles van den Driest, Chmn.   Tel: 31-10-400-2911   Rev: $945
Bus: *Transportation services and tank storage for oil,*   Fax: 31-10-413-9829   Emp: 4,004
      gases, and chemicals.   www.vopak.com
NAICS: 221210, 424710, 484230, 486110, 486210, 486910

     VOPAK DEER PARK
     2759 Battleground Rd., Deer Park, Texas 77536
     CEO: Jimmy Brasher, Mgr.   Tel: (281) 604-6000
     Bus: *Marine cargo handling*   Fax: (281) 604-6100

VOPAK TERMINAL GALENA PARK
1500 Clinton Dr., Galena Park, Texas 77547
CEO: Jimmy Ritter, Mgr.
Bus: *Special warehousing & storage*
Tel: (713) 675-9171
Fax: (713) 675-9622

VOPAK TERMINAL LONG BEACH
3601 Dock St., San Pedro, California 90731-7540
CEO: David Mahon
Bus: *Marine cargo handling.*
Tel: (310) 521-7969
Fax: (310) 831-3213

VOPAK TERMINAL LOS ANGELES
401 Canal St., Wilmington, California 90744
CEO: Mike Lacavera, Mgr.
Bus: *Oil holding company*
Tel: (310) 549-0961
Fax: (310) 549-2308

VOPAK TERMINAL SAVANNAH
Turner-Hart Sts.-GPA, Savannah, Georgia 31418-7390
CEO: Mike Mayhuegh, Mgr.
Bus: *Marine cargo handling.*
Tel: (912) 964-1811
Fax: (912) 966-2252

VOPAK TERMINAL WESTWEGO
106 Bridge City Ave., Bridge City, Louisiana 70094
CEO: Terry Hill
Bus: *Marine cargo handling.*
Tel: (504) 436-2242
Fax: (504) 436-8406

VOPAK TERMINAL WOLMINGTON
1710 Woodbine St., Wilmington, North Carolina 28401
CEO: Alfred Smeilus, Mgr.
Bus: *Special warehousing & storage*
Tel: (910) 763-0104
Fax: (910) 763-0725

VOPAK USA INC.
2000 West Loop South, Ste. 2200, Houston, Texas 77027
CEO: Eugene P.Sabatier, Pres.
Bus: *Marine cargo handling*
Tel: (713) 561-7200
Fax: (713) 561-7322
%FO: 100
Emp: 454

• SATELLITE NEWSPAPERS CORPORATION
Alexanderstraat 18, NL-2514 JM The Hague, Netherlands
CEO: Roy Piceni, Pres.
Bus: *Prints, distributes and sells newspapers through interactive vending units.*
Tel: 31-70-346-5056
Fax: 31-70-360-2376
www.pepcworldwide.com
Rev: $2,619
Emp: 1,000
NAICS: 334119, 519190

SATELLITE ENTERPRISES CORP.
980 Post Rd. East, Westport, Connecticut 06880
CEO: Philip M. Fox
Bus: *Prints, distributes and sells newspapers through interactive vending units.*
Tel: (203) 672-5912
Fax: (203) 672-1337
%FO: 100

• SEAGULL HOLDING N.V.
Korte Parallelweg 1, NL-3311 JN Dordrecht, Netherlands
CEO: Donald P. Addington, Pres. & CEO
Bus: *Software manufacture.*
Tel: 31-78-632-2800
Fax: 31-78-613-8134
www.seagullsoftware.com
Rev: $23
Emp: 185

NAICS: 511210

SEAGULL SOFTWARE INC.
3340 Peachtree Rd. NE, Ste. 900, Atlanta, Georgia 30326
CEO: Donald P. Addington, Pres. & CEO   Tel: (404) 760-1560   %FO: 100
Bus: *Mfr. of software.*   Fax: (404) 760-0061   Emp: 221

● **SHV HOLDINGS N.V.**
Rijinkade 1, P.O. Box 2065, 3500GB, NL-3511 LC Utrecht, Netherlands
CEO: P.C. Klaver, Chmn.   Tel: 31-30-233-8833   Rev: $12,893
Bus: *Energy and retail businesses.*   Fax: 31-30-233-8304   Emp: 28,200
                                                www.shv.nl
NAICS: 452910, 454312, 454319, 525990
        DAVID J. JOSEPH COMPANY
        300 Pike St., Cincinnati, Ohio 45202
        CEO: Kevin B. Grass, Pres. & CEO   Tel: (513) 419-6200   %FO: 100
        Bus: *Metal recycling and marketing of scrap iron*   Fax: (513) 419-6222
            and steel.

● **SMIT INTERNATIONALE NV**
Zalmstraat 1, NL-3016 DS Rotterdam, Netherlands
CEO: Ben Vree, Chmn.   Tel: 31-10-454-9911   Rev: $463
Bus: *Marine salvage services.*   Fax: 31-10-454-9777   Emp: 2,859
                                                www.smit.com
NAICS: 483111, 483211, 488310, 488320
        SMIT AMERICAS, INC.
        626-C Admiral Dr., PMB 309, Annapolis, Maryland 21401
        CEO: R. Fredricks, Mgr.   Tel: (410) 544-5248   %FO: 100
        Bus: *Marine salvage services.*   Fax: (410) 544-3105

        SMIT AMERICAS, INC.
        15402 Vantage Pkwy. East, Ste. 316, Houston, Texas 77032
        CEO: Roger C. Elliott, Pres.   Tel: (281) 372-3500   %FO: 100
        Bus: *Marine salvage services.*   Fax: (281) 372-3525   Emp: 18

        SMIT AMERICAS, INC.
        400 East Pratt St., Ste. 800, Baltimore, Maryland 21202
        CEO: Richard Fredricks   Tel: (410) 685-0790   %FO: 100
        Bus: *Marine salvage services.*   Fax: (410) 685-0792

● **SOBEL NV**
NCB-Weg 10, NL-5681 RH Best, Netherlands
CEO: Dirk Kloosterboer, Chmn.   Tel: 31-499-364-555   Rev: $929
Bus: *Organic products and gelatin products*   Fax: 31-499-393-084   Emp: 4,472
    manufacture.   www.sobel.nl
NAICS: 311225, 311612, 311613
        BANNER INC.
        4125 Premier Dr., PO Box 2210, High Point, North Carolina 27265
        CEO: James Warren, CEO   Tel: (336) 812-4729   %FO: 100
        Bus: *Mfr. of pharmaceutical products.* Fax: (336) 812-3718

BANNER PHARMACAPS, INC.
4100 Mendenhall Oaks Pkwy., High Point, North Carolina 27265
CEO: Roger E. Gordon, Pres. & CEO   Tel: (336) 812-3442   %FO: 100
Bus: *Healthcare products manufacture and sales.*   Fax: (336) 812-7030   Emp: 897

● **SOLVAY DRAKA B.V.**
Flevolaan 1-5, Enkhuizen, NL-1601 MA Noord-Holland, Netherlands
CEO: Marcel A. G. Lorent, Dir.   Tel: 31-22-835-5355   Rev: $93
Bus: *Mfr. of semi-finished products for medical*   Fax: 31-228-355-888   Emp: 300
     applications.   www.solvaydraka.com
NAICS: 326199, 424690

     SOLVAY DRAKA INC.
     6900 Elm St., Commerce, California 90040
     CEO: Mark Stern, VP Mktg.   Tel: (323) 725-7010
     Bus: *Industrial vinyl coated fabrics*   Fax: (323) 725-6466

     SOLVAY DRAKA, INC.
     403 Heron Dr. C, Swedesboro, New Jersey 08085
     CEO: Scott Burns, CEO   Tel: (856) 467-3800   %FO: 100
     Bus: *Industrial vinyl coated fabrics*   Fax: (856) 467-4880   Emp: 122

● **STORK N.V.**
Amersfoortsestraatweg 7, NL-1412 KA Naarden, Netherlands
CEO: Sjoerd S. Vollebregt, Chmn.   Tel: 31-35-695-7411   Rev: $2,368
Bus: *Machinery and parts textile printing, complete*   Fax: 31-35-694-1184   Emp: 20,500
     systems for poultry processing and convenience   www.stork.com
     foods.
     • *systems and services for aviation and aerospace*
NAICS: 333292, 333294, 523991, 551112

     FOKKER SERVICES INC.
     5169 Southridge Pkwy., Atlanta, Georgia 30349
     CEO: Leon Kouters, Sales   Tel: (770) 991-4600
     Bus: *Transportation equipment*   Fax: Emp: 8

     STORK CELLRAMIC, INC.
     8399 N. 87th St., Milwaukee, Wisconsin 53224
     CEO: Hhooge Venterink, Pres.   Tel: (414) 357-0260   %FO: 100
     Bus: *Thermal spray coatings and anilox rolls.*   Fax: Emp: 33

     STORK GAMCO INC.
     1024 Airport Pkwy., Gainesville, Georgia 30501
     CEO: Theo Hoen, Pres.   Tel: (770) 532-7041   %FO: 100
     Bus: *Sales/distribution/service of machinery for*   Fax: Emp: 160
     meat processing industry

     STORK MATERIALS TECHNOLOGY AND INSPECTION INC.
     15062 Bolsa Chica St., Huntington Beach, California 92649
     CEO: Jay Haber, Pres.   Tel: (714) 892-1961
     Bus: *Testing laboratories*   Fax: Emp: 141

STORK PRINTS AMERICA
3201 N. Interstate 85, Charlotte, North Carolina 28221
CEO: Copland Willis, VP   Tel: (704) 598-7171
Bus: *Process control instruments*   Fax: Emp: 14

STORK SOUTHWESTERN LABORATORIES, INC.
222 Cavalcade St., Houston, Texas 77009
CEO: Robert Jefferies, COO   Tel: (713) 692-9151
Bus: *Medical laboratories*   Fax: Emp: 112

STORK TECHNIMET INC.
2345 S. 170th St., New Berlin, Wisconsin 53151
CEO: Tijs Van Wershoven, COO   Tel: (262) 782-6344
Bus: *Testing laboratories*   Fax: Emp: 27

STORK TWIN CITY TESTING INC.
662 Cromwell Ave., St. Paul, Minnesota 55114
CEO: Matt Horton, COO   Tel: (651) 645-3601
Bus: *Business services testing laboratories.*   Fax:

STORK UNITED CORP.
1200 Westinghouse Blvd., Ste. E, Charlotte, North Carolina 28273
CEO: John Low, Mgr.   Tel: (704) 588-1131
Bus: *Testing labs.*   Fax:

● **TELE ATLAS NV**
Reitscheweg, 7F, NL-5232 BX Hertogenbosch, Netherlands
CEO: Alain A. DeTaeye, CEO   Tel: 31-73-640-2121   Rev: $174
Bus: *Develops geographic databases.*   Fax: 31-73-640-2122   Emp: 1,952
                                                 www.teleatlas.com
NAICS: 511210

    TELE ATLAS NORTH AMERICA INC.
    11 Lafayette St., Lebanon, New Hampshire 03766
    CEO: Michael J. Gerling   Tel: (603) 643-0330   %FO: 100
    Bus: *Develops geographic databases.*   Fax: (603) 653-0249

    TELE ATLAS NORTH AMERICA INC.
    100 Cambridge St., Suite 1302, Boston, Massachusetts 02114
    CEO: Michael J. Gerling   Tel: (617) 725-2809   %FO: 100
    Bus: *Develops geographic databases.*   Fax: (617) 725-2809

    TELE ATLAS NORTH AMERICA INC.
    1605 Adams Dr., Menlo Park, California 94025
    CEO: Larry Sweeney   Tel: (650) 328-3825   %FO: 100
    Bus: *Develops geographic databases.*   Fax: (650) 328-3148

    TELE ATLAS NORTH AMERICA INC.
    2000 Town Center, Suite 220, Southfield, Michigan 48075
    CEO: Larry Sweeney   Tel: (248) 213-3847   %FO: 100
    Bus: *Develops geographic databases.*   Fax: (248) 213-4815

- **TELEPLAN INTERNATIONAL NV**
  De Run 1120, NL-5503 LA Veldhoven, Netherlands
  CEO: Rolf Huber, Chmn. & CEO
  Bus: *Provides warranty services for information technology products.*
  NAICS: 423420, 423430, 423440, 518210, 532420, 532490, 541513, 541519, 811212, 811213, 811219

  Tel: 31-40-255-8670
  Fax: 31-40-255-7311
  www.teleplan-int.com

  Rev: $367
  Emp: 6,300

  TELEPLAN INTERNATIONAL
  6401 New Cut Rd., Fairdale, Kentucky 40118
  CEO: Jamie Horan
  Bus: *Provides warranty services for information technology products.*

  Tel: (502) 375-8300
  Fax: (502) 375-8510

  %FO: 100

  TELEPLAN INTERNATIONAL
  230 Weakley Rd., Calexico, California 92231
  CEO: Bill Loza
  Bus: *Provides warranty services for information technology products.*

  Tel: (760) 357-9644
  Fax: (760) 357-9647

  %FO: 100

  TELEPLAN INTERNATIONAL
  8875 Washington Blvd., Roseville, California 95678
  CEO: Jack Rockwood
  Bus: *Provides warranty services for information technology products.*

  Tel: (916) 677-4500
  Fax: (916) 677-4496

  %FO: 100

  TELEPLAN SERVICES LOGISTICS
  7000 S. 33rd St., Bldg. AA, McAllen, Texas 78503
  CEO: Larry Popkes
  Bus: *Provides warranty services for information technology products.*

  Tel: (956) 631-5554
  Fax: (956) 686-7528

  TELEPLAN SERVICES TEXAS INC.
  2800 W. Story Rd., Dallas-Irving, Texas 75038
  CEO: Ed Rogers
  Bus: *Provides warranty services for information technology products.*

  Tel: (972) 594-3400
  Fax: (972) 594-3535

  %FO: 100

  TELEPLAN VIDEOCOM SERVICES
  196 Quigley Blvd., New Castle, Delaware 19720
  CEO: Joe Neff
  Bus: *Provides warranty services for information technology products.*

  Tel: (302) 322-6088
  Fax: (302) 322-6331

  TELEPLAN WIRELESS SERVICES
  1000 Park Rd., Chanhassen, Michigan 55317
  CEO: Leo Smith
  Bus: *Provides warranty services for information technology products.*

  Tel: (952) 279-5700
  Fax: (952) 279-5727

- **TIE HOLDING NV**
  180 Beech Ave., NL-1119PS Amsterdam, Netherlands
  CEO: Dick Raman, Pres. & CEO
  Bus: *Integration software.*

  Tel: 31-20-658-9903
  Fax: 31-20-658-9902
  www.tieglobal.com

  Rev: $9
  Emp: 80

  NAICS: 511210, 541511, 541512

TIE COMMERCE INC.
24 New England Executive Park, Burlington, Massachusetts 01803
CEO: Dick Roman, Chmn.   Tel: (781) 272-4252   %FO: 100
Bus: *Integration services.*   Fax: Emp: 49

TIE COMMERCE INC.
1435 Energy Park Dr., St. Paul, Minnesota 55108
CEO: Steve Zapata, CEO   Tel: (651) 999-8600   %FO: 100
Bus: *Integration services.*   Fax: (651) 999-8845   Emp: 25

- **TNT N.V.**
Neptunusstraat 41-63, NL-2132 JA Hoofddorp, Netherlands
CEO: M. Peter Bakker, CEO   Tel: 31-20-500-6000   Rev: $17,115
Bus: *Premium mail, express and logistics services.*   Fax: 31-20-500-7000   Emp: 162,244
www.tnt.com
NAICS: 488510, 491110, 492110, 493110, 541614

    TNT LOGISTICS CORPORATION
    10751 Deerwood Park Blvd., Ste. 200, Jacksonville, Florida 32256
    CEO: Jeffery D. Hurley, Mng. Dir.   Tel: (904) 928-1400   %FO: 100
    Bus: *International transport services.*   Fax: (904) 928-1550

- **TRIPLE P N.V.**
Ir. D.S. Tuynmanweg 10, NL-4131 PN Vianen, Netherlands
CEO: Huub Crijns, CEO   Tel: 31-347-353-353   Rev: $101
Bus: *Computer software & services.*   Fax: 31-347-353-354   Emp: 346
www.triple-p.com
NAICS: 423430, 511210, 541511, 541512, 541519, 611420, 811212

    TRIPLE P USA, INC.
    11320 Random Hills Rd., Ste. 375, Fairfax, Virginia 22030
    CEO: Goly Bouroman   Tel: (703) 385-1212   %FO: 100
    Bus: *Computer software & services.*   Fax: (703) 385-2091

- **UNILEVER N.V.**
Weena 455, PO Box 760, NL-3000 DK Rotterdam, Netherlands
CEO: Antony Burgmans, Chmn.   Tel: 31-10-217-4000   Rev: $54,413
Bus: *Soaps and detergents, foods, chemicals,*   Fax: 31-10-217-4798   Emp: 223,000
personal products (J/V of UNILVER PLC, UK).   www.unilever.com
NAICS: 311411, 311520, 311920, 311999, 312111, 322291, 325199, 325611, 325612, 325613, 325620, 327910, 446120

    BEN & JERRY'S HOMEMADE INC.
    30 Community Dr., South Burlington, Vermont 05403
    CEO: Walt Freese, CEO   Tel: (802) 846-1500
    Bus: *Mfr. of ice cream.*   Fax: (802) 846-1610

    SLIM-FAST FOODS CO.
    777 S. Flagler Dr., West Tower, Ste. 1400, West Palm Beach, Florida 33401
    CEO: John Rice, Pres. & CEO   Tel: (561) 833-9920
    Bus: *Health & nutritional drinks*   Fax: (561) 822-2876

UNILEVER NORTH AMERICA
700 Sylvan Ave., Englewood Cliffs, New Jersey 07632
CEO: John W. Rice, CEO
Bus: *Mfr. beverages, food, cosmetics,*
fragrances, detergents and soaps.
Tel: (201) 894-4000
Fax: (201) 871-8079
%FO: 100

● **UNIQEMA, SUB IMPERIAL CHEMICAL**
Buurtje 1, NL-2802 BE Gouda, Netherlands
CEO: Leonard J. Berlik, CEO
Bus: *Mfr. intermediates and additives.*
Tel: 31-182-542-187
Fax: 31-182-542-286
www.uniqema.com
Rev: $1,212
Emp: 2,800

NAICS: 311942

    UNIQEMA
    1000 Uniqema Blvd., New Castle, Delaware 19720
    CEO: Amy Bollinger
    Bus: *Mfr. intermediates and additives.*
    Tel: (302) 574-5000
    Fax: (302) 574-3525
    %FO: 100

● **UNIVAR NV**
Blaak 333, 11th Fl., NL-3011 GB Rotterdam, Netherlands
CEO: Gary E. Pruitt, CEO
Bus: *Chemicals distribution.*
Tel: 31-10-275-7800
Fax: 31-10-414-6863
www.univarcorp.com
Rev: $44
Emp: 6,700

NAICS: 424690

    UNIVAR USA INC.
    27001 Trolley Industrial Dr., Taylor, Michigan 48180
    CEO: Lisa F. Fitzsimmons-Allred
    Bus: *Chemical products manufacture.*
    Tel: (313) 295-9072
    Fax: (313) 295-7078
    %FO: 100

    UNIVAR USA INC.
    1686 E. Highland Rd., Cleveland, Ohio 44087
    CEO: Mike V. Sebenoler
    Bus: *Chemical products manufacture.*
    Tel: (330) 963-2020
    Fax: (330) 425-7582
    %FO: 100

    UNIVAR USA INC.
    3950 NW Yeon Ave., Portland, Oregon 97210
    CEO: Pauline A. Benedict
    Bus: *Chemical products manufacture.*
    Tel: (503) 222-6230
    Fax: (503) 222-2714
    %FO: 100

    UNIVAR USA INC.
    2041 N. Mosley St., Wichita, Kansas 67214
    CEO: Bret D. Almire
    Bus: *Chemical products manufacture.*
    Tel: (316) 267-6292
    Fax: (316) 267-5188
    %FO: 100

    UNIVAR USA INC.
    8500 W. 68th St., Bedford Park, Illinois 60501
    CEO: George H. Coyle III
    Bus: *Chemical products manufacture.*
    Tel: (708) 728-6875
    Fax: (708) 728-6801
    %FO: 100

    UNIVAR USA INC.
    50 S. 45th Ave., Phoenix, Arizona 85043
    CEO: Debra J. Bailey
    Bus: *Chemical products manufacture.*
    Tel: (602) 484-4560
    Fax: (602) 278-9138
    %FO: 100

UNIVAR USA INC.
PO Box 25187, Albuquerque, New Mexico 87102
CEO: David Armstrong
Bus: *Chemical products manufacture.*
Tel: (505) 842-6306
Fax: (505) 243-1984
%FO: 100

UNIVAR USA INC.
One Colonial Rd., Salem, Massachusetts 01970
CEO: Michael J. Amenta
Bus: *Chemical products manufacture.*
Tel: (978) 825-2444
Fax: (978) 745-5875
%FO: 100

UNIVAR USA INC.
2145 Skyland Ct., Norcross, Georgia 30071
CEO: Chuck T. Magill
Bus: *Chemical products manufacture.*
Tel: (770) 246-7716
Fax: (770) 662-0394
%FO: 100

UNIVAR USA INC.
1925 N. Redmond Rd., Jacksonville, Arkansas 72076
CEO: Mike M. Price
Bus: *Chemical products manufacture.*
Tel: (501) 982-4402
Fax: (501) 982-0127
%FO: 100

UNIVAR USA INC.
3320 S. Council Rd., Oklahoma City, Oklahoma 73179
CEO: Mike M. Wells Jr.
Bus: *Chemical products manufacture.*
Tel: (405) 745-2376
Fax: (405) 745-4934
%FO: 100

UNIVAR USA INC.
1819 W. Burlington Ave., Burlington, Iowa 52601
CEO: Rick O. Cline
Bus: *Chemical products manufacture.*
Tel: (319) 753-2253
Fax: (319) 753-1499
%FO: 100

UNIVAR USA INC.
845 Terrace Ct., St. Paul, Minnesota 55101
CEO: Don P. Wozniak
Bus: *Chemical products manufacture.*
Tel: (651) 772-6380
Fax: (651) 774-0850
%FO: 100

UNIVAR USA INC.
PO Box 5287, Denver, Colorado 80217
CEO: Fred LeBrun
Bus: *Chemical products manufacture.*
Tel: (303) 398-7502
Fax: (303) 321-3188
%FO: 100

UNIVAR USA INC.
1707 S. 101st St., Milwaukee, Wisconsin 53214
CEO: Jeffrey A. Prier
Bus: *Chemical products manufacture.*
Tel: (414) 259-9301
Fax: (414) 259-9532
%FO: 100

UNIVAR USA INC.
9853 Highway 78, Ladson, South Carolina 29456
CEO: Joseph D. Boland
Bus: *Chemical products manufacture.*
Tel: (843) 553-5270
Fax: (843) 553-5393
%FO: 100

UNIVAR USA INC.
2100 Haffley Ave., National City, California 91950
CEO: Jeff B. Floyd
Bus: *Chemical products manufacture.*
Tel: (619) 336-6509
Fax: (619) 474-2820
%FO: 100

UNIVAR USA INC.
6800 Enterprise Dr., Louisville, Kentucky 40214
CEO: Jerry W. Whitaker
Bus: *Chemical products manufacture.*
Tel: (502) 375-9791
Fax: (502) 366-5359
%FO: 100

UNIVAR USA INC.
1176 Jordan Rd., Huntsville, Alabama 35811
CEO: Christina M. Kasprovich
Bus: *Chemical products manufacture.*
Tel: (256) 851-9170
Fax: (256) 851-9172
%FO: 100

UNIVAR USA INC.
4515 E. Wisconsin Ave., Spokane, Washington 99212
CEO: Mike A. Jilbert
Bus: *Chemical products manufacture.*
Tel: (509) 534-0405
Fax: (509) 534-2468
%FO: 100

UNIVAR USA INC.
650 W. 800 St., Salt Lake City, Utah 84104
CEO: Robin E. Cowley
Bus: *Chemical products manufacture.*
Tel: (801) 933-6115
Fax: (801) 531-1937
%FO: 100

UNIVAR USA INC.
PO Box 512062, Los Angeles, California 90051
CEO: Brian F. Rinehart
Bus: *Chemical products manufacture.*
Tel: (323) 837-7058
Fax: (323) 837-7144
%FO: 100

UNIVAR USA INC.
4650 S. Valley View, Las Vegas, Nevada 89103
CEO: Roy B. Cash
Bus: *Chemical products manufacture.*
Tel: (702) 736-7066
Fax: (702) 736-6679
%FO: 100

UNIVAR USA INC.
6100 Carillon Point, Kirkland, Washington 98033
CEO: Terry Hill, CEO
Bus: *Chemical products manufacture.*
Tel: (425) 889-3400
Fax: (425) 889-4100
%FO: 100

UNIVAR USA INC.
6049 Old 41A Hwy., Tampa, Florida 33619
CEO: Robin K. Hazel
Bus: *Chemical products manufacture.*
Tel: (813) 677-8414
Fax: (813) 671-2970
%FO: 100

UNIVAR USA INC.
150 Enterprise Rd., Johnstown, New York 12095
CEO: Steve A. Roberts
Bus: *Chemical products manufacture.*
Tel: (518) 762-3500
Fax: (518) 762-3100
%FO: 100

UNIVAR USA INC.
532 E. Emaus St., Bldg. 24, Middletown, Pennsylvania 17057
CEO: Jim Reardon
Bus: *Chemical products manufacture.*
Tel: (717) 948-5364
Fax: (717) 944-1801
%FO: 100

UNIVAR USA INC.
10889 Bekay St., Dallas, Texas 75238
CEO: Jason V. Miller
Bus: *Chemical products manufacture.*
Tel: (214) 503-5709
Fax: (214) 340-9113
%FO: 100

UNIVAR USA INC.
4351 Director Dr., San Antonio, Texas 78219
CEO: Kathy A. DeLeon   Tel: (210) 333-2310   %FO: 100
Bus: *Chemical products manufacture.*   Fax: (210) 337-1411

UNIVAR USA INC.
777 Brisbane St., Houston, Texas 77061
CEO: Michael E. Lange   Tel: (713) 641-9494   %FO: 100
Bus: *Chemical products manufacture.*   Fax: (713) 644-9565

● **VAN DER MOOLEN HOLDING NV**
Keizersgracht 307, NL-1016 ED Amsterdam, Netherlands
CEO: Friedrich M. J. Bottcher, Chmn.   Tel: 31-20-535-6789   Rev: $168
Bus: *Equities trading.*   Fax: 31-20-535-6744   Emp: 464
    www.vandermoolen.com

NAICS: 523110, 523910

    VAN DER MOOLEN SPECIALISTS USA
    45 Broadway, 32/F, New York, New York 10006
    CEO: Mark Baer, Mng. Dir.   Tel: (646) 576-3000   %FO: 100
    Bus: *Equities trades.*   Fax: (646) 576-3131

● **VAN LEEUWEN PIPE & TUBE B.V.**
Lindtsedijk 20, NL-3336 LE Zwijndrecht, Netherlands
CEO: Jacobus C. Breen, Chmn.   Tel: 31-78-625-2525   Rev: $454
Bus: *Distribution of carbon steel, weld fittings, flanges*   Fax: 31-78-625-2020   Emp: 1,000
    and pipe.   www.vanleeuwen.com
NAICS: 332919, 423510, 531210, 551112

    WILSON INDUSTRIES, INC.
    9781 Highway 124, Beaumont, Texas 77705
    CEO: Jim Rucker, Mgr.   Tel: (409) 840-5021
    Bus: *Sale of industrial supplies.*   Fax: Emp: 3

    WILSON INDUSTRIES, INC.
    15333 Hempstead Rd., 10 Nealy Blvd., Marcus Hook, Pennsylvania 19061
    CEO: Pete Colucci, Mgr.   Tel: (610) 485-5411   %FO: 100
    Bus: *Sale of industrial supplies.*   Fax: Emp: 2

● **VEDIOR NV**
Tripolis Bldg. 200, Burgerweeshuispad 201, NL-1076 GR Amsterdam, Netherlands
CEO: C.K.Z. Miles, CEO   Tel: 31-20-573-5600   Rev: $8,821
Bus: *Engaged in temporary staffing solutions.*   Fax: 31-20-573-5601   Emp: 13,043
    www.vedior.com
NAICS: 561310, 561320

    ACSYS INC.
    5 Concourse Pkwy., Ste. 2650, Atlanta, Georgia 30328
    CEO: Jack Unroe, CEO   Tel: (770) 395-0014
    Bus: *Accounting & finance staffing.*   Fax: (770) 395-6521

TRINET GROUOP
1100 San Leandro Blvd., Ste. 300, San Leandro, California 94577
CEO: Martin Babinec, Pres. & CEO   Tel: (510) 352-5000
Bus: *Outsourced human resources services.*   Fax: (510) 352-6480

VEDIOR NORTH AMERICA INC
60 Harvard Mill Square, Wakefield, Massachusetts 01880
CEO: Gregory A. Netland, Pres. & CEO   Tel: (781) 213-1500   %FO: 100
Bus: *Engaged in temporary staffing solutions.*   Fax: (781) 213-1520

● **VETUS DEN OUDEN NV**
Fokkerstr. 571, NL-3125 BD Schiedam-Holland, Netherlands
CEO: Hendrik Den Ouden, Dir.   Tel: 31-10-437-7700
Bus: *Mfr. marine equipment parts and accessories.*   Fax:
www.vetus.nl

NAICS: 334511, 336612, 339999, 423860

    VETUS DENOUDEN, INC.
    PO Box 8712, Baltimore, Maryland 21240
    CEO: Leo Van Hemert, Pres.   Tel: (410) 712-0740   %FO: 100
    Bus: *Mfr. marine equipment parts and accessories.*   Fax: (410) 712-0985

● **VITRONICS SOLTEC**
Innovatiepark, 12, NL-4906 AA Oosterhout, Netherlands
CEO: Jeroen L. Schmits, Pres.   Tel: 31-16-248-3030   Rev: $14
Bus: *Mfr. circuit board equipment.*   Fax: 31-16-248-3253   Emp: 110
www.vitronics-soltec.com

NAICS: 333992, 334413

    VITRONICS SOLTEC INC.
    2 Marin Way, Stratham, New Hampshire 03885
    CEO: Jeroen Schmits, Pres.   Tel: (603) 772-7778   %FO: 100
    Bus: *Mfr./sales/service of circuit board equipment.*   Fax: (603) 772-7776   Emp: 110

● **VNU BV**
Ceylonpoort 5-25, NL-2037 AA Haarlem, Netherlands
CEO: R.F. Van den Bergh, CEO   Tel: 31-23-546-3463   Rev: $5,157
Bus: *Publishing and business information, consumer magazines, directories, information services, and educational publishing.*   Fax: 31-23-546-3938   Emp: 39,366
www.vnu.com

NAICS: 511120, 511140, 541910, 561920

    AC NIELSEN
    150 North Martingale Rd., Schaumburg, Illinois 60173
    CEO: Tim Callahan   Tel: (847) 605-5000
    Bus: *Market research, information, analysis based on retail info.*   Fax: (847) 605-2000

    AC NIELSEN BASES
    50 West River Center Blvd., Ste. 600, Covington, Kentucky 41011
    CEO: Matt Carey   Tel: (859) 905-4000
    Bus: *Test marketing*   Fax: (859) 905-5000

AC NIELSEN HCI
50 Millstone Rd., Bldg. 100, Ste. 300, East Windsor, New Jersey 08520
CEO: Eugene M.May   Tel: (609) 630-6450
Bus: *Pharmaceutical promotion research.*   Fax: (609) 630-6456

ACNIELSEN CORPORATION
770 Broadway, New York, New York 10003
CEO: Steve M.Schmidt, Pres. & CEO   Tel: (646) 654-5000   %FO: 100
Bus: *Engaged in research and media*   Fax: (646) 654-5002
     measurement including compiling consumer
     data for businesses.

CLARITAS
5375 Mira Sorrento Place, San Diego, California 92121
CEO: Robert Nascenzi, Pres. & CEO   Tel: (858) 622-0800
Bus: *supplier of detailed consumer lifestyle*   Fax: (858) 550-5800   Emp: 470

HOLLYWOOD REPORTER INDUSTRIES
5055 Wilshire Blvd., Los Angeles, California 90036
CEO: Lynne Segall   Tel: (323) 525-2000
Bus: *Regional office for VNA*   Fax: (323) 525-2372

IMS MEDIA SOLUTIONS
770 Broadway, New York, New York 10003
CEO: Tel: (646) 654-5900   %FO: 100
Bus: *Provides information systems for the*   Fax: (646) 654-5901
     advertising industry

INTERNET MEASUREMENT DIVISION
770 Broadway, New York, New York 10003
CEO: Frank Martell   Tel: (646) 654-5000
Bus: *Publishing and business information,*   Fax:
     consumer magazines, directories,
     information services, and educational

NIELSEN / NET RATINGS
120 West 45th St., 35/F, New York, New York 10036
CEO: William R. Pulvar, Pres. & CEO   Tel: (212) 703-5900
Bus: *internet audience measurement*   Fax: (212) 703-5901   Emp: 368

NIELSEN EDI
6255 Sunset Blvd., Hollywood, California 90028
CEO: Nick King   Tel: (323) 860-4600
Bus: *Tracking box office receipts.*   Fax: (323) 860-4610

NIELSEN MEDIA RESEARCH
770 Broadway, New York, New York 10003
CEO: Susan D. Whiting, Pres. & CEO   Tel: (646) 654-8300
Bus: *Market Research Services*   Fax: (646) 654-8990

PERQ/HCI
50 Millstone Rd., Bldg. 100, Ste. 300, East Windsor, New Jersey 08520
CEO: Tel: (609) 630-6440
Bus: *measurement & analysis on promotional*   Fax: (609) 630-6456
     activities.

SCARBOROUGH RESEARCH
770 Broadway, New York, New York 10003
CEO: Robert L. Cohen, Pres. & CEO
Bus: *Market Research Services*
Tel: (646) 654-8400
Fax: (646) 654-8450

SOLUCIENT
1007 Church St., Ste. 609, Evanston, Illinois 60201
CEO: Nancy Pope Nelson
Bus: *Maintaining healthcare database*
Tel: (847) 475-7526
Fax: (847) 475-7830

SPECTRA
200 West Jackson Blvd., 28/F, Ste. 2800, Chicago, Illinois 60606
CEO: Tim Kregor, Pres.
Bus: *Provides trade consulting services.*
Tel: (312) 583-5100
Fax: (312) 583-5101
%FO: 100

SRDS
1700 Higgins Rd., Des Plaines, Illinois 60018
CEO: Tom Drouillard, Pres. & CEO
Bus: *Media Solutions*
Tel: (847) 375-5000
Fax: (847) 375-5001

TRADE DIMENSIONS USA
45 Danbury Rd., Wilton, Connecticut 06897
CEO: Scott Taylor
Bus: *Retailer information products*
Tel: (203) 563-3000
Fax: (203) 563-3006
%FO: 100

VNU INC. USA
770 Broadway, New York, New York 10003-9595
CEO: Rob V. Bergh
Bus: *Provides media and marketing consulting services.*
Tel: (646) 654-5500
Fax: (646) 654-5001
%FO: 100

● **WERELDHAVE NV**
23 Nassaulaan, PO Box 85660, NL-2514 JT The Hague, Netherlands
CEO: G.C.J. Verweij, CEO
Bus: *Real estate investments.*
Tel: 31-70-346-9325
Fax: 31-70-363-8990
www.wereldhave.nl
Rev: $120
Emp: 100

NAICS: 525930

WEST WORLD MANAGEMENT, INC.
4 Manhattanville Rd., 2/F, Purchase, New York 10577
CEO: Charles O.W. Schouten, Pres.
Bus: *Real estate investment company.*
Tel: (914) 694-5900
Fax: (914) 694-4642
%FO: 100

● **KONINKLIJKE WESSANEN NV**
Prof. E. M. Meijerslaan 2, NL-1183 AK Amsterdam, Netherlands
CEO: Ad H. A. Veenhof, CEO
Bus: *Global manufacturing and marketing of food and beverages.*
Tel: 31-20-574-9547
Fax: 31-20-547-9501
www.wessanen.com
Rev: $2,891
Emp: 8,445

NAICS: 311230, 311423, 311823, 311991, 312111, 312111, 424490

AMERICAN BEVERAGE CORPORATION
1 Daily Way, Verona, Pennsylvania 15147
CEO: Antonio Battaglia, Pres.
Bus: *Bottled cocktail mixes, fruit drinks and bottled water sales.*
Tel: (412) 828-9020
Fax: (412) 828-9195
%FO: 100

TREE OF LIFE, INC.
405 Golfway West Dr., St. Augustine, Florida 32095
CEO: Wayne Richman, Pres.
Bus: *Sales/distribution of natural and specialty foods to supermarkets and natural food*
Tel: (904) 940-2100
Fax: (604) 940-2553
%FO: 100

● **WOLTERS KLUWER N.V.**
Apollolaan 153, P.O. Box 75248, NL-1070 AE Amsterdam, Netherlands
CEO: Boudewijn Beerkens, CFO
Bus: *Legal, medical, science, educational, professional and trade publishing.*
Tel: 31-20-607-0400
Fax: 31-20-607-0490
www.wolters-kluwer.com
Rev: $4,448
Emp: 18,393
NAICS: 511120, 511130, 516110

WOLTERS KLEWER U.S. CORPORATION
111 Westport Plaza, Ste. 300, St. Louis, Missouri 63146-3014
CEO: Ken Killion
Bus: *Medical publications.*
Tel: (314) 216-2200
Fax: (314) 878-5563
%FO: 100

WOLTERS KLUWER DELAWARE CORP.
530 Walnut St., 7/F, Philadelphia, Pennsylvania 19106-3619
CEO: Peter W. Van Wel, Pres.
Bus: *Medical journals publisher.*
Tel: (215) 521-8501
Fax: (215) 521-8902
%FO: 100
Emp: 300

WOLTERS KLUWER U.S. CORPORATION
161 North Clark St., 48/F, Chicago, Illinois 60601
CEO: Peter W. Van Wel, Chmn.
Bus: *Book and journals publishing.*
Tel: (312) 425-7000
Fax: (312) 425-7023
%FO: 100
Emp: 7,020

WOLTERS KLUWERS U.S. CORP.
111 8th Ave., New York, New York 10011-5201
CEO: Noel Barrett, Mgr.
Bus: *Subscription based electronic services.*
Tel: (212) 894-8920
Fax: (212) 894-8920

● **ZUIVELCOOPERATIE CAMPINA U.A.**
Hogeweg 9, NL-5301 Zaltbommel, Netherlands
CEO: C.H. Wantenaar, Chmn.
Bus: *Develops and produces functional and nutritional ingredients for the food, nutrition and pharma industry worldwide.*
Tel: 31-418-571-300
Fax: 31-418-571-582
www.campina.com
Rev: $4,854
Emp: 7,099
NAICS: 311412, 311511, 311512, 311513, 311514, 311520

CAMPINA USA
9010 Goliad, Pharr, Texas 78577
CEO: German Perez, Pres.
Bus: *Sales/distribution of condensed powder.*
Tel: (956) 782-7660
Fax:
%FO: 100
Emp: 4

DMV INTERNATIONAL
1285 Rudy St., Onalaska, Wisconsin 54650
CEO: David Lee, Mgr.
Bus: *Mfr./sales dairy products.*

Tel: (608) 779-7676
Fax: (608) 779-7666

%FO: 100

Netherlands Antilles

- **FUEL-TECH NV**
  Castorweg 22-24, Willemstad, Curacao, Netherlands Antilles
  CEO: Ralph E. Bailey, CEO
  Bus: *Mfr. products for the reduction of nitrogen oxide in industrial power generators.*
  NAICS: 423830, 511210, 541330, 562910

  Tel: 599-9-461-3754
  Fax: 599-9-461-6501
  www.fuel-tech.com

  Rev: $30
  Emp: 92

  FUEL-TECH INC.
  695 East Main St., Stamford, Connecticut 06901
  CEO: Steven C. Argabright, CEO
  Bus: *Mfr./sales of products for the reduction of nitrogen oxide in industrial power*

  Tel: (203) 425-9830
  Fax: (203) 425-9823

  %FO: 100

- **ORTHOFIX INTERNATIONAL NV**
  7 Abraham de Veerstraat, Willemstad, Curacao, Netherlands Antilles
  CEO: Charles Federico, CEO
  Bus: *Orthopedic device manufacture.*

  NAICS: 339113

  Tel: 599-9-465-8525
  Fax: 599-9-461-6978
  www.orthofix.com

  Rev: $287
  Emp: 997

  ORTHOFIX INTERNATIONAL
  1720 Bray Central Dr., McKinney, Texas 75069
  CEO: Gary D. Henley
  Bus: *Orthopedic device manufacture and sales.*

  Tel: (469) 742-2500
  Fax: (469) 742-2500

  %FO: 100

- **SINGER NV**
  De Ruyterkade 62, Willemstad, Curacao, Netherlands Antilles
  CEO: Stephen H. Goodman, Chmn. & Pres. & CEO
  Bus: *Consumer sewing machine manufacture.*
  NAICS: 321211, 335224, 335228, 339993, 339999, 423210, 423620, 443111, 454390

  Tel: 599-9-7322-555
  Fax: 599-9-7322-500
  www.retailholdings.com

  Rev: $281
  Emp: 12,222

  SINGER SEWING MACHINE COMPANY
  1224 Heil Quaker Blvd., PO Box 7017, LaVergne, Tennessee 37086
  CEO: Don Fletcher, CEO
  Bus: *Consumer sewing machine manufacture and sales.*

  Tel: (615) 213-0880
  Fax: (615) 213-0994

  %FO: 100
  Emp: 80

- **VELCRO INDUSTRIES B.V.**
  15 Pietermaai, Willemstad, Curacao, Netherlands Antilles
  CEO: Albert John Holton, Chmn. & CEO
  Bus: *Mfr. Velcro-brand fasteners for the apparel, auto, aerospace and consumer markets.*
  NAICS: 339993

  Tel: 599-9-433-5000
  Fax: 559-800-235-6640
  www.velcro.com

  Rev: $261
  Emp: 2,900

  VELCRO USA INCORPORATED
  406 Brown Ave., Manchester, New Hampshire 03103
  CEO: A. John Holton, Pres.
  Bus: *Industrial facility.*

  Tel: (603) 669-4892
  Fax: (603) 669-9271

  %FO: 100
  Emp: 1,430

New Zealand

- **AIR NEW ZEALAND LTD.**
  29 Customs St. West, Level 19, Quay Tower, Auckland, New Zealand
  CEO: Rob Fyfe, CEO
  Bus: *Commercial air transport services.*

  Tel: 64-9-336-2400
  Fax: 64-9-336-2401
  www.airnz.co.nz

  Rev: $2,150
  Emp: 9,000

  NAICS: 481111

    AIR NEW ZEALAND
    1960 East Grand Ave., Ste. 900, El Segundo, California 90245
    CEO: Norm Thompson, VP
    Bus: *International commercial air transport services.*

    Tel: (310) 648-7000
    Fax: (310) 648-7017

    %FO: 100

- **FLETCHER BUILDING PRODUCTS INC.**
  Fletcher House, Private Bag 92-114, Auckland, New Zealand
  CEO: Ralph Waters, Pres.
  Bus: *Building materials manufacture and distribution.*

  Tel: 64-9-525-9000
  Fax: 64-9-535-9205
  www.gerardroofs.co.nz

  Rev: $2,499
  Emp: 11,000

  NAICS: 332322

    DECRA ROOFING SYSTEMS INC.
    1230 Railroad St., Corona, California 91720
    CEO: Bo Hudson, Pres.
    Bus: *Mfr. stone-coated steel roofing systems.*

    Tel: (951) 272-8180
    Fax: (951) 272-4476

    %FO: 100

    FLETCHER GRANITE COMPANY
    275 Groton Rd., Westford, Massachusetts 01886
    CEO: Delio Valadao
    Bus: *Quarrying and fabrication of fine granite products.*

    Tel: (978) 251-4031
    Fax: (978) 251-8773

    %FO: 100

- **TELECOM NEW ZEALAND LIMITED**
  Telecom House, 68 Jervois Quay, Wellington, New Zealand
  CEO: Theresa Gattung, CEO & Mng. Dir.
  Bus: *Provides telecommunications services and engaged in fiber optic cable network.*

  Tel: 64-4-801-9000
  Fax: 64-4-473-2613
  www.telecom.co.nz

  Rev: $4,004
  Emp: 6,840

  NAICS: 511140, 517110, 517212, 517910, 518111, 518210, 519190, 561499

    TELECOM NEW ZEALAND LIMITED
    251 South Lake Ave., Ste. 540, Pasadena, California 91101
    CEO: Anthony Briscoe, Chmn.
    Bus: *Engaged in telecommunications.*

    Tel: (626) 432-4300
    Fax: (626) 432-4303

    %FO: 100
    Emp: 20

- **TENON LTD.**
  Tenon House, 8 Rockridge Ave., Penrose, Auckland 1030, New Zealand
  CEO: John A. Dell, CEO
  Bus: *Processing and marketing of pine products.*

  Tel: 64-9-571-9800
  Fax: 64-9-571-9801
  www.fcf.co.nz

  Rev: $556
  Emp: 972

  NAICS: 113210, 113310, 423310

TENON USA
1352 Charwood Rd., Ste. B, Hanover, Maryland 21076
CEO: George Kelly, Sales   Tel: (410) 850-5433   %FO: 100
Bus: *Processing and marketing of pine products.*   Fax: (410) 850-5434

Nigeria

● **UNITED BANK FOR AFRICA, PLC.**
UBA House 57, Marina, PO Box 2406, Lagos, Nigeria
CEO: Kayode Sofola, Chmn.   Tel: 234-1-264-4651
Bus: *Commercial banking services.*   Fax: 234-1-264-2287
                                                             www.ubagroup.com
NAICS: 522110

    UNITED BANK FOR AFRICA, PLC
    40 East 52nd St., 20/F, New York, New York 10022
    CEO: G.H. Denniston Jr., Mgr.   Tel: (212) 308-7222   %FO: 100
    Bus: *International commercial banking services.*   Fax: (212) 688-0870   Emp: 40

Northern Ireland, U.K.

● **UPU INDUSTRIES LTD., SUB. STEVE ORR**
Quillyburn Business Park, Unit 1, Banbridge Road, Dromore, Down BT25 1BY, Northern Ireland, U.K.
CEO: Steve Orr, Mng. Dir.   Tel: 44-28-9269-9020
Bus: *Agricultural blade crop products manufacturer,*   Fax: 44-28-9269-9029
high performance round bale netting.   www.steve-orr.com
NAICS: 314991

   UPU INDUSTRIES INC.
   3000 Industrial St., Junction City, Kansas 66441
   CEO: Phillip Orr   Tel: (785) 238-6990   %FO: 100
   Bus: *Mfr. baling twine.*   Fax: (785) 238-6990

● **WARNER CHILCOTT (FORMERLY GALEN HOLDINGS)**
Old Belfast Rd., Millbrook, Larne BT40 2SH, Northern Ireland, U.K.
CEO: Roger M. Boissonneault, CEO   Tel: 44-28-3836-3620   Rev: $432
Bus: *Specialty pharmaceutical; women's healthcare*   Fax: 44-28-3835-0206   Emp: 2,000
and dermatology.   www.warnerchilcott.com
NAICS: 325411, 325412, 551112

   WARNER CHILCOTT INC.
   100 Enterprise Dr., Ste. 280, Rockaway, New Jersey 07866
   CEO: William J. Poll, SVP   Tel: (973) 442-3222   %FO: 100
   Bus: *Engaged in pharmaceuticals.*   Fax: (973) 422-3246   Emp: 5

Norway

- **AKER KVAERNER ASA**
Prof. Kohts vei 15, NO-1325 Lysaker, Norway
CEO: Inge K. Hansen, CEO
Bus: *Provider of engineering and construction
services, technology products and integrated*
NAICS: 541310, 541330, 541490

Tel: 47-67-51-3000
Fax: 47-67-51-3100
www.akerkvaerner.com

Rev: $5,873
Emp: 20,700

  AKER KVAERNER
  717 South Alvernon Way, Tucson, Arizona 85711-5351
  CEO: Les Guthrie
  Bus: *Engineering and construction services.*

  Tel: (520) 620-1530
  Fax: (520) 620-1591

  %FO: 100

  AKER KVAERNER BOWEN
  5242 College Dr., Ste. 205, Salt Lake City, Utah 84123
  CEO: Les Guthrie
  Bus: *Engineering and metal services.*

  Tel: (801) 263-8940
  Fax: (801) 268-9455

  %FO: 100

  AKER KVAERNER METALS
  12657 Alcosta Blvd., Ste. 200, San Ramon, California 94583
  CEO: Jim McGrath
  Bus: *Metal services.*

  Tel: (925) 866-1166
  Fax: (925) 866-6520

  %FO: 100

  AKER KVAERNER METALS
  1200 Penn Ave., Pittsburgh, Pennsylvania 15222-4204
  CEO: Dave Lawson
  Bus: *Engineering and metal services.*

  Tel: (412) 918-4500
  Fax: (412) 918-5000

  %FO: 100

  AKER KVAERNER OGPI
  3600 Briarpark, Houston, Texas 77042
  CEO: Les Guthrie
  Bus: *Engineering services.*

  Tel: (713) 988-2002
  Fax: (713) 772-4673

  %FO: 100

  AKER KVAERNER SONGER
  455 Racetrack Rd., Washington, Pennsylvania 15301
  CEO: Jim Miller
  Bus: *Engineering and construction services.*

  Tel: (724) 223-0800
  Fax: (724) 223-9445

  %FO: 100

  AKER KVAERNER SONGER
  1845 Willowcreek Rd., Portage, Indiana 2197637863
  CEO: Jim Miller
  Bus: *Engineering services.*

  Tel: (219) 763-7834
  Fax:

  %FO: 100

  AKER KVAERNER SUBSEA INC.
  3750 Briarpark, Houston, Texas 77042
  CEO: Lasse Torkildsen
  Bus: *Engineering services.*

  Tel: (713) 685-5700
  Fax: (713) 685-5888

  %FO: 100

AKER KVAERNER SUBSEA INC.
7611 Lake Rd. South, Bldg. 505, Middle Bay Port, Mobile, Alabama 36605
CEO: Lasse Torkildsen   Tel: (251) 443-7910   %FO: 100
Bus: *Engineering services.*   Fax: (251) 443-7918

AKER MARINE CONTRACTORS US INC.
3600 Briarpark Dr., Houston, Texas 77042
CEO: Helge Roraas   Tel: (713) 270-3045   %FO: 100
Bus: *Engineering services.*   Fax:

● **ANDERS WILHELMSEN & CO. AS**
Beddingen 8, NO-0250 Oslo, Norway
CEO: Arne Wilhelmsen, Pres.   Tel: 47-22-01-4200
Bus: *Maritime enterprise engaged in shipping and*   Fax: 47-22-01-4374
     investments.   www.norwegian-shipping.com
NAICS: 483111

    ROYAL CARIBBEAN CRUISES LTD.
    1050 Caribbean Way, Miami, Florida 33132
    CEO: Richard D. Fain, Chmn. & CEO   Tel: (305) 539-6000   %FO: 39
    Bus: *Cruise shipping line.*   Fax: (305) 374-7354   Emp: 38,870

● **BERGESEN ASA**
Drammensveien 106, NO-0204 Oslo, Norway
CEO: Helmut Sohmen, Chmn.   Tel: 47-22-1205-05   Rev: $652
Bus: *Natural liquid gas marine transportation services.*   Fax: 47-22-1205-00   Emp: 1,839
          www.bergesen.no
NAICS: 483111

    BERGESEN OFFSHORE USA INC.
    3010 Briarpark Dr., Houston, Texas 77042
    CEO: Petter Hoie   Tel: (713) 821-4224   %FO: 100
    Bus: *Natural liquid gas marine transportation*   Fax: (713) 821-3604
         services.

● **BIRDSTEP TECHNOLOGY ASA**
Bryggegate 7, NO-0250 Oslo, Norway
CEO: Jorgen Bredesen, CEO   Tel: 47-24-134700   Rev: $4
Bus: *Database software development.*   Fax: 47-24-134701   Emp: 75
          www.birdstep.com
NAICS: 541511

    BIRDSTEP TECHNOLOGY, INC.
    2101 4th Ave., Ste. 2000, Seattle, Washington 98121
    CEO: Laura Klebs, PR   Tel: (206) 748-5353   %FO: 100
    Bus: *Database software development.*   Fax: (206) 748-5200

● **CORROCEAN, INC.**
Teglgarden, NO-7485 Trondheim, Norway
CEO: Øystein I. Narvhus, CEO   Tel: 47-73-82-5000   Rev: $20
Bus: *Mfr. corrosion monitoring equipment.*   Fax: 47-73-82-5050   Emp: 175
          www.corrocean.com
NAICS: 325998

CORROCEAN, INC.
3300 Walnut Bend Lane, Houston, Texas 77042-4712
CEO: David Rees, Pres.
Bus: *Corrosion monitoring equipment.*

Tel: (713) 334-2222	%FO: 50
Fax: (713) 266-0172	Emp: 7

● **DET NORSKE VERITAS FOUNDATION**
Veritasveien 1, PO Box 300, NO-1322 Hovik, Norway
CEO: Miklos Konkoly-Thege, CEO
Bus: *Quality assurance services, ship classification and inspection.*
NAICS: 488390, 488390

Tel: 47-67-57-9900	Rev: $984
Fax: 47-67-57-9911	Emp: 6,200
www.dnv.com	

DET NORSKE PROCESS
16340 Park Ten Place, Ste. 100, Houston, Texas 77084
CEO: Ruby Frueboes
Bus: *Engaged in consulting services to the oil, gas and process industries.*

Tel: (281) 721-6600   %FO: 100
Fax: (281) 721-6906

DET NORSKE PROCESS
136 Ocean Ridge Dr., Fernandina Beach, Florida 32034
CEO: Cornelis Jan Herman
Bus: *Engaged in consulting services to the oil, gas and process industries.*

Tel: (904) 277-1606   %FO: 100
Fax: (904) 277-2883

DET NORSKE PROCESS NORTH AMERICA
30700 Telegraph Rd., Ste. 1530, Bingham Farms, Michigan 48025
CEO: Robert Djurovic
Bus: *Engaged in consulting services to the oil, gas and process industries.*

Tel: (248) 540-5591   %FO: 100
Fax: (248) 540-5597

DET NORSKE VERITAS
917 Western America Circle, Mobile, Alabama 36609-4120
CEO: Oleksandr Shulyayev
Bus: *Quality assurance services, ship classification & inspection.*

Tel: (251) 344-3384   %FO: 100
Fax: (251) 344-3384

DET NORSKE VERITAS
1600 Sawgrass Corporate Pkwy., Sunrise, Florida 33323
CEO: Bjorn Nystad, Pres.
Bus: *Ship classification.*

Tel: (954) 838-0055   %FO: 100
Fax: (954) 838-0551   Emp: 6

DET NORSKE VERITAS
1 International Blvd., Mahwah, New Jersey 07495
CEO: Abhijit Das, Mgr.
Bus: *Ship classification, certification & advisory services.*

Tel: (201) 512-8900   %FO: 100
Fax: (201) 512-8901   Emp: 500

DET NORSKE VERITAS AMERICAS
16340 Park Ten Place, Ste. 100, Houston, Texas 77084-5143
CEO: Gary Kenney, Dir.
Bus: *Quality assurance services, ship classification & inspection.*

Tel: (281) 721-6600   %FO: 100
Fax: (281) 721-6900

DET NORSKE VERITAS CERTIFICATION INC.
3805 Crestwood Pkwy., Duluth, Georgia 30096
CEO: Les Smith, Pres.   Tel: (770) 279-0001   %FO: 100
Bus: *Quality assurance services, ship*   Fax: (770) 279-0282   Emp: 13
classification & inspection.

● **DNB HOLDING (DEN NORSKE BANK) ASA**
Strandon 21, NO0021 Oslo, Norway
CEO: Svein Aaser, CEO   Tel: 47-22-48-1050   Rev: $6,402
Bus: *Financial banking services.*   Fax: 47-22-48-1870   Emp: 10,359
                                        www.dnbnor.com
NAICS: 522110, 522120, 522210, 522291, 522292, 522293, 523110, 523930, 523999, 525110, 525190, 525910, 525990, 531210

   DNB (DEN NORSKE BANK) ASA
   200 Park Ave., 31/F, New York, New York 10166
   CEO: Verit Henriksen, Mgr.   Tel: (212) 681-3800   %FO: 100
   Bus: *Commercial banking services.*   Fax: (212) 681-3900   Emp: 44

● **DYNO NOBEL**
Drammensveien 147 A, NO-0214 Oslo, Norway
CEO: Dag Mejdell, Pres. & CEO   Tel: 47-22-31-7000   Rev: $1,338
Bus: *Mfr. chemicals and military explosives.*   Fax: 47-32-31-7000   Emp: 7,200
                                        www.dynonobel.com
NAICS: 325920

   DYNO NOBEL INC.
   50 South Main, 11/F, Salt Lake City, Utah 84144-0103
   CEO: Peter I. Richards, Pres.   Tel: (801) 364-4800   %FO: 100
   Bus: *Mfr. chemicals and military explosives.*   Fax: (801) 328-6452

   ENSIGN-BICKFORD INDUSTRIES, INC.
   100 Grist Mill Rd., Simsbury, Connecticut 06070
   CEO: Robert J. Lepofsky   Tel: (860) 843-2000   %FO: 100
   Bus: *Mfr. cable filler and synthetic tapes.*   Fax: (860) 843-2600

● **EDB BUSINESS PARTNER ASA**
Nedre Skoyen Vei 26, NO-0214 Oslo, Norway
CEO: Endre Rangnes, CEO   Tel: 47-22-52-8080   Rev: $700
Bus: *Information technology (IT) consulting services.*   Fax: 47-22-77-2114   Emp: 2,480
                                        www.edbusinesspartner.com
NAICS: 541511

   TELESCIENCES INC.
   2000 Midlantic Dr., Ste. 410, Mt. Laurel, New Jersey 08054-1512
   CEO: Greg Fegley   Tel: (856) 866-1000   %FO: 100
   Bus: *Telecommunications software.*   Fax: (856) 866-0185

   TELESCIENCES INC.
   12396 World Trade Dr., Ste. 110, San Diego, California 92128
   CEO: Rich Kraus   Tel: (858) 676-1777   %FO: 100
   Bus: *Telecommunications software.*   Fax: (858) 676-1770

- **ELKEM ASA**
Hoffsveien 65 B, PO Box 5211, NO-0303 Majorstua Oslo, Norway
CEO: Ole Enger, Pres. & CEO
Bus: *Metals and materials manufactures.*

Tel: 47-22-45-0100
Fax: 47-22-45-0155
www.elkem.com

Rev: $2,770
Emp: 11,093

NAICS: 332999

ELKEM ASHTABULA
2700 Lake Rd. East, Ashtabula, Ohio 44005
CEO: Dan Korda, Mgr.
Bus: *Metals manufacture.*

Tel: (440) 993-2300
Fax: (440) 993-2302

%FO: 100

ELKEM CHARTERING INC.
2000 Old Spanish Trail, Slidell, Louisiana 70458
CEO: Kurt Jensen
Bus: *Sales, distribution steel products.*

Tel: (985) 265-0014
Fax: (985) 645-9825

%FO: 100

ELKEM METALS COMPANY
Airport Office Park, Bldg. 2, 400 Rouser Road, Moon Township, Pennsylvania 15108
CEO: Geir Kvernmo, Pres.
Bus: *Sales, distribution steel products.*

Tel: (412) 299-7200
Fax: (412) 299-7225

%FO: 100

SILCON METAL BUSINESS UNIT ELKEM ALLOY
PO Box 613, Alloy, West Virginia 25002-0613
CEO: Ed A. Mays, Mgr.
Bus: *Metals manufacture.*

Tel: (304) 779-3264
Fax: (304) 779-3368

%FO: 100

- **FAST SEARCH & TRANSFER ASA**
Oslo Atrium, Christian Frederiks Plass 6, NO-0120 Oslo, Norway
CEO: John M. Lervik, CEO
Bus: *Software development.*

Tel: 47-23-011200
Fax: 47-23-011201
www.fast.no

Rev: $64
Emp: 299

NAICS: 541511

FAST SEARCH & TRANSFER, INC.
17 Kendrick St., Needham, Massachusetts 02494
CEO: Robert Lancaster
Bus: *Software development.*

Tel: (781) 304-2400
Fax: (781) 304-2410

%FO: 100

- **HAG ASA**
Fridtjof Nansens vei 12, Majorstuen, PO Box 5055, NO-0301 Oslo, Norway
CEO: Lars I. Roiri, Pres. & CEO
Bus: *Office chairs manufacture.*

Tel: 47-22-59-5900
Fax: 47-22-59-5959
www.hag.no

Rev: $78
Emp: 377

NAICS: 337214

HAG INC.
202 Centreport Dr., Ste. 130, Greensboro, North Carolina 27409
CEO: Rune Akselberg, Pres.
Bus: *Mfr. of office furniture.*

Tel: (336) 668-9544
Fax: (336) 668-7331

%FO: 100

- **HELLY HANSEN ASA**
Solgaard Skog 139, P.O. Box 278, NO-1502 Moss, Norway
CEO: Erik Larsson, CEO
Bus: *Outdoor wear wholesale manufacturer.*
Tel: 47-69-24-9000
Fax: 47-69-24-9099
www.hellyhansen.com
Rev: $186
Emp: 680

NAICS: 315225

  HELLY HANSEN INC.
  Kenyon Center, 3326 160th Ave. SE, Ste. 200, Bellevue, Washington 98008
  CEO: Ric Long, Pres.
  Bus: *Wholesale manufacturer of outdoor wear.*
  Tel: (425) 378-8700
  Fax: (425) 649-3740
  %FO: 100
  Emp: 55

- **KONGSBERG AUTOMOTIVE HOLDING ASA**
Dyrmyrgata 45, PO Box 62, NO-3601 Kongsberg, Norway
CEO: Olav Volldal, CEO
Bus: *Mfr. seating products for the automotive and commercial vehicle industries.*
Tel: 47-32-77-0500
Fax: 47-32-77-0509
www.kongsbergautomotive.com

NAICS: 336211, 336360

  KONGSBERG AUTOMOTIVE INC.
  3000 Kefauver Dr., Milan, Tennessee 38358
  CEO: Larry Mesecher
  Bus: *Mfr. head restraints and arm rests for automobiles.*
  Tel: (731) 686-0805
  Fax: (731) 686-2340
  %FO: 100

  KONGSBERG AUTOMOTIVE INC.
  23065 Commerce Dr., Farmington Hills, Michigan 48335
  CEO: Hans Peter Havdal
  Bus: *Mfr. automobile comfort products.*
  Tel: (248) 615-3090
  Fax: (248) 615-3098
  %FO: 100

- **KONGSBERG MARITIME AS**
Strandpromenaden 50, PO Box 111, NO-3191 Horten, Norway
CEO: Torfinn Kildal, Pres. & CEO
Bus: *One-source, end-to-end supplier of integrated ship systems.*
Tel: 47-33-03-4100
Fax: 47-33-04-4424
www.km.kongsberg.com
Emp: 2,384

NAICS: 333319

  KONGSBERG MARITIME INC.
  125 James Dr. West, Ste. 110, Saint Rose, Louisiana 70087
  CEO: Pal Liset, Mgr.
  Bus: *Computer system design services, mfr. of radio & TV equipment.*
  Tel: (504) 712-2799
  Fax: (504) 712-7986
  %FO: 100
  Emp: 13

  KONGSBERG MARITIME INC.
  7225 Langtry St., Houston, Texas 77040
  CEO: Jan Roger Hellerud, Pres.
  Bus: *Provides fully integrated packages and stand-alone maritime instrumentation systems for the global maritime market.*
  Tel: (713) 934-8885
  Fax: (713) 934-8886
  %FO: 100
  Emp: 30

KONGSBERG MARITIME SIMULATION INC.
70 Essex St., PO Box 180, West Mystic, Connecticut 06388
CEO: Herbert Taylor, Pres.   Tel: (860) 536-1254   %FO: 100
Bus: *Provides fully integrated packages and* Fax: (860) 536-0923   Emp: 11
      stand-alone maritime instrumentation
      systems for the global maritime market.

KONGSBERG UNDERWATER TECHNOLOGY INC.
19210 33rd Ave. West, Ste. A, Lynnwood, Washington 98036
CEO: Tom Healy, Dir.   Tel: (425) 712-1107   %FO: 100
Bus: *Provides fully integrated packages and* Fax: (425) 712-1197   Emp: 13
      stand-alone maritime instrumentation
      systems for the global maritime market.

● **KVAERNER GROUP**
PO Box 169, Prof. Kohtsvei 15, NO-1325 Lysaker, Norway
CEO: Inge K. Hansen, Pres. & CEO   Tel: 47-67-51-3000   Rev: $4,980
Bus: *Engaged in engineering and construction and oil* Fax: 47-67-51-3410   Emp: 34,500
      and gas.   www.kvaerner.com
NAICS: 325411, 541710

  KVAERNER PHILADELPHIA SHIPYARD INC.
  2100 Kitty Hawk Ave., Philadelphia, Pennsylvania 19112
  CEO: Dave Meehan, Pres.   Tel: (215) 875-2600   %FO: 100
  Bus: *Container ships.*   Fax: (215) 875-2700

  KVAERNER USA INC.
  440 US Highway 22, Ste. 210, Bridgewater, New Jersey 08807
  CEO: George J. Pierson   Tel: (908) 429-9100   %FO: 100
  Bus: *Engineering and construction services.* Fax: (908) 429-3969

● **LAERDAL MEDICAL A/S**
PO Box 377, NO-4002 Stavanger, Norway
CEO: W. Clive Patrickson, Pres.   Tel: 47-51-51-1700
Bus: *Training and therapeutic lifesaving products* Fax: 47-51-52-3557   Emp: 700
      manufacture.   www.laerdal.com
NAICS: 339113

  LAERDAL MEDICAL CORPORATION
  PO Box 1840, Wappinger Falls, New York 12590-8840
  CEO: Terje Aasen, Pres.   Tel: (914) 297-7770   %FO: 100
  Bus: *Mfr. and sales of medical training equipment* Fax: (914) 297-1137   Emp: 200

● **MAXWARE INTERNATIONAL AS**
Haakon VII's GT 7B, NO-7041 Trondheim, Norway
CEO: Tore Wold, Pres. & CEO   Tel: 47-7320-1000
Bus: *Management software manufacture.*   Fax: 47-7321-1050
                                               www.maxware.com
NAICS: 511210, 541511, 541519, 611420

  MAXWARE INTERNATIONAL
  71 West Main St., Ste. 101, Freehold, New Jersey 07728
  CEO: Elliott Friedman, Mng. Dir.   Tel: (732) 409-5000   %FO: 100
  Bus: *Management software manufacture and*   Fax: (732) 409-0233
        sales.

- **O MUSTAD & SON A/S**
PO Box 41, NO-2801 Gjovik, Norway
CEO: Anders Haug Thomassen, VP
Bus: *Mfr. fish hooks.*
NAICS: 339920

Tel: 47-61-13-7700
Fax: 47-61-13-7951
www.mustad.no

Rev: $25
Emp: 1,121

    O MUSTAD & SON (USA) INC
    241 Grant Ave., PO Box 838, Auburn, New York 13021
    CEO: Kevin LaMontagne, Gen. Mgr.
    Bus: *Distributor fish hooks, fishing tackle.*

Tel: (315) 253-2793
Fax: (315) 253-0157

%FO: 100
Emp: 15

- **NCL CORPORATION**
Grensen 3, Vika, NO-0124 Oslo, Norway
CEO: David C. S. Veitch, Pres. & CEO
Bus: *Holding company, passenger shipping, cruise*
NAICS: 483112, 483114, 488999, 561510, 561520, 561599

Tel: 47-22-944-120
Fax: 47-22-830-014
www.ncl.com

    NORWEGIAN CRUISE LINE
    7665 Corporate Center Dr., Miami, Florida 33126
    CEO: Colin Veitch, Pres.
    Bus: *Cruise line, travel industry.*

Tel: (305) 436-4000
Fax: (305) 436-4120

%FO: 100
Emp: 12,000

- **NERA ASA**
Kokstadveien 23, P.O. Box 7090, NO-5020 Bergen, Norway
CEO: Bjorn Olafsson, CEO
Bus: *Mfr. microwave antennas, receivers and transmitters.*
NAICS: 334220

Tel: 47-55-22-5100
Fax: 47-55-22-5299
www.nera.no

Rev: $336
Emp: 1,564

    NERA AMERICA INC.
    4975 Preston Park Blvd., Ste. 600, Plano, Texas 75093
    CEO: Billy Cain, Pres.
    Bus: *Mfr. microwave antennas, receivers and transmitters.*

Tel: (972) 265-8118
Fax: (972) 265-8130

%FO: 100
Emp: 20

    NERA INC.
    200 Research Dr., Wilmington, Massachusetts 01887
    CEO: Dr. Jon Wainright
    Bus: *Mfr. microwave antennas, receivers and transmitters.*

Tel: (978) 661-8400
Fax: (978) 657-6097

%FO: 100

- **NORSK HYDRO A/S**
Bygdoy Alle 2, NO-0240 Oslo 2, Norway
CEO: Eivind Reiten, Pres. & CEO
Bus: *Mfr. aluminum products including primary metal, metal products, rolled products, extrusion.*
NAICS: 324110, 324191, 324199, 331312, 331524, 424910

Tel: 47-22-53-8100
Fax: 47-22-53-2725
www.hydro.com

Rev: $25,754
Emp: 34,600

HYDRO ALUMINIUM AS
801 International Dr., Ste. 200, Linthicum, Maryland 21090
CEO: Martin Carter, Pres.   Tel: (410) 487-4500
Bus: *metals service centers & offices.*   Fax: (410) 487-8053   Emp: 2,900

NORSK HYDRO AMERICAS, INC.
100 N. Tampa St., Ste. 3350, Tampa, Florida 33602
CEO: Odd Gullberg, Pres.   Tel: (813) 222-3880
Bus: *Mfr. fertilizers chemicals& aluminum*   Fax: Emp: 2,900
    extrusions forgings.

NORSK HYDRO AMERICAS, INC.
15995 North Barkers Landing Rd., Houston, Texas 77079
CEO: Odd S. Gullberg, Pres.   Tel: (281) 504-1100   %FO: 100
Bus: *Oil and energy.*   Fax: (281) 504-1101   Emp: 2,900

● **NORSKE SKOGINDUSTRIER ASA**
Okenoyveien 80, NO-1326 Lysaker, Norway
CEO: Jan A. Oksum, Pres. & CEO   Tel: 47-67-599-000   Rev: $4,180
Bus: *Paper and paper product manufacturer of*   Fax: 47-67-599-181   Emp: 8,181
    newsprint.   www.norske-skog.com
  NAICS: 322122, 322222, 322299, 424130

    NORSKE SKOG NORTH AMERICA
    1011 Western Ave., Ste. 700, Seattle, Washington 98104
    CEO: L. Thomas Crowley, Pres.   Tel: (206) 838-2000   %FO: 100
    Bus: *Sale of newsprint paper.*   Fax: (206) 838-2031   Emp: 11

    NORSKE SKOG USA INC.
    2507 Post Rd., Southport, Connecticut 06890
    CEO: Kaye Curran, CFO   Tel: (203) 254-5292   %FO: 100
    Bus: *Paper and paper product manufacturer of*   Fax: (203) 254-5291   Emp: 10
    newsprint.

● **ODFJELL ASA**
Conrad Mohrs veg 29, NO-5072 Bergen, Norway
CEO: Terje Storeng, Pres. & CEO   Tel: 47-55-27-0000
Bus: *Engaged in shipping.*   Fax: 47-55-28-4741
      www.odfjell.no
  NAICS: 483111, 488310, 488320, 488510, 541614

    HOYER- ODFJELL INC.
    9938 Chemical Rd., Pasadena, Texas 77507
    CEO: David Payne, Mgr.   Tel: (281) 727-3720   %FO: 100
    Bus: *Environmental Cleanup Services*   Fax:

    HOYER-ODFJELL, INC.
    16055 Apc Ctr. Blvd. 500, Houston, Texas 77062
    CEO: Cor Mol, Chmn.   Tel: (281) 853-1000
    Bus: *Freight transportation services*   Fax: Emp: 67

ODFJELL USA INC.
12211 Port Rd., Seabrook, Texas 77586
CEO: Bernt Netland, Pres.   Tel: (713) 844-2200   %FO: 100
Bus: *Freight transportation services.*   Fax: Emp: 50

• **OPERA SOFTWARE ASA**
Waldemar Thranes Gatae 98, NO-0175 Oslo, Norway
CEO: Jon S. von Tetzchner, CEO   Tel: 47-24-16-4000   Rev: $16
Bus: *Internet browser software manufacture.*   Fax: 47-24-16-4001   Emp: 195
                                                  www.opera.com
NAICS: 511210
    OPERA SOFTWARE
    2700 Pecan St. West, Ste. 400, Pflugerville, Texas 78660
    CEO: Peter Kelly   Tel: (512) 647-7145   %FO: 100
    Bus: *Internet browser software manufacture and*   Fax: (512) 647-7145
       sales.

• **ORKLA, ASA**
Karenslyst alle 6, NO-0278 Oslo, Norway
CEO: Dag J. Opedal, CEO   Tel: 47-69-2254-4000   Rev: $5,296
Bus: *Mfr. chemicals and brand-name consumer*   Fax: 47-69-2254-4490   Emp: 19,575
   products, including food/beverage,   www.orkla.com
   candy/biscuits, outerwear and footwear, and
NAICS: 311222, 311225, 311320, 311340, 311411, 311421, 311422, 311612, 311613, 311711, 311712, 311821,
311930, 311941, 311942, 312111, 316219,
        325191, 325199, 325620, 325992, 424450
    BORREGAARD LIGNOTECH USA INC.
    100 Grand Ave., Rothschild, Wisconsin 54474-1198
    CEO: Ole Kristian Lunde, Pres.   Tel: (715) 359-6544
    Bus: *Mfr. chemicals.*   Fax: (715) 355-3629

• **PETROLEUM GEO-SERVICES ASA**
Strandveien 4, NO-1326 Lysaker, Norway
CEO: Svein Rennemo, CEO   Tel: 47-6752-6400   Rev: $1,129
Bus: *Marine seismic data, onshore surveying and oil*   Fax: 47-6753-6883   Emp: 2,899
   and gas production services.   www.pgs.com
NAICS: 213112, 541330, 541360
    PETROLEUM GEO-SERVICES (PGS)
    15150 Memorial Dr., Houston, Texas 77079
    CEO: Sverre Strandenes   Tel: (281) 509-8000   %FO: 100
    Bus: *Marine seismic data, onshore surveying and*   Fax: (281) 509-8500
       oil and gas production services.

• **ROXAR ASA**
Gamle Forusvei 17 PO Box 112, NO-4065 Stavanger, Norway
CEO: Morten Brandt, CEO   Tel: 47-51-81-8800   Rev: $99
Bus: *Provides integrated field development and* Fax: 47-51-81-8801   Emp: 251
   reservoir management products and services for   www.roxar.com
   the upstream oil and gas industries.
NAICS: 334514, 511210

ROXAR, INC.
14701 St. Mary's Lane, Ste. 275, Houston, Texas 77079
CEO: Sandy Esslemont, Pres.
Bus: *Mfr. multi-phase meters for gas and oil industries.*

Tel: (713) 482-6400
Fax: (713) 482-6401

%FO: 100

● SCANDPOWER PETROLEUM TECHNOLOGY AS
PO Box 3, Gasevikvn 2-4, NO-2027 Kjeller, Norway
CEO: John Olaf Romma, CEO
Bus: *Software and consulting services to the international petroleum industry.*

Tel: 47-64-84-4400
Fax: 47-64-84-4595
www.scandpowerpt.com

NAICS: 541511, 541618

SCANDPOWER PETROLEUM TECHNOLOGY
11490 Westheimer Rd., Ste. 610, Houston, Texas 77077
CEO: Alex de Paula
Bus: *Software and consulting services to the international petroleum industry.*

Tel: (281) 496-9898
Fax: (281) 496-9950

%FO: 100
Emp: 11

● I. M. SKAUGEN ASA
Karenslyst Alle 8B, NO-0277 Oslo, Norway
CEO: Morits Skaugen Jr., CEO
Bus: *Gas and LPG marine transportation.*

Tel: 47-23-120-400
Fax: 47-23-120-401
www.skaugen.com

Rev: $110
Emp: 745

NAICS: 483111, 488390

SKAUGEN PETROTRANS, INC.
2 Houston Center, 909 Fannin, Ste. 3300, Houston, Texas 77010
CEO: Per Voie, Pres.
Bus: *Marine shipping.*

Tel: (713) 266-8000
Fax: (713) 266-0309

%FO: 10
Emp: 80

● STATOIL ASA
Forusbeen 50, NO-4035 Stavanger, Norway
CEO: Helge Lund, Pres. & CEO
Bus: *Exploration, production, refining and marketing crude oil and natural gas.*

Tel: 47-51-99-0000
Fax: 47-51-99-0050
www.statoil.com

Rev: $50,332
Emp: 23,899

NAICS: 211111, 211112, 213111, 213112, 221111, 221112, 221113, 221119, 221121, 221122, 221210, 324110, 324191, 324199, 333132, 424710, 424720, 447110, 447190, 454311, 454312, 454319, 486110, 486210, 486910, 541360

STATOIL MARKETING & TRADING INC.
225 High Ridge Rd., Ste. 16, Stamford, Connecticut 06905-3035
CEO: Luann G. Smith, Pres. & CEO
Bus: *Exploration, production, refining and marketing oil and gas, petrochemical products.*

Tel: (203) 978-6900
Fax: (203) 978-6952

%FO: 100
Emp: 41

● TANDBERG ASA
Philip Pedersens Vei 22, NO-1366 Lysaker, Norway
CEO: Andrew M. Miller, CEO
Bus: *Video conferencing systems manufacture.*

Tel: 47-67-125-125
Fax: 47-67-125-234
www.tandberg.net

Rev: $305
Emp: 589

NAICS: 334220, 334310

TANDBERG TELEVISION
4500 River Green Pkwy., Ste. 110, Duluth, Georgia 30096
CEO: Eric Cooney, Pres. & CEO Tel: (678) 812-6300 %FO: 100
Bus: *Billing & service provisioning software.* Fax: (678) 812-6400 Emp: 135

TANDBERG USA INC.
1860 Michael Faraday Dr., Ste. 250, Reston, Virginia 20190
CEO: Per Haug Kogstad, Pres. Tel: (703) 709-4281 %FO: 100
Bus: *Videoconferencing systems manufacture* Fax: (703) 709-4231 Emp: 10
and sales.

TANDBERG USA INC.
1750 Valley View Lane, Ste. 200, Dallas, Texas 75234
CEO: Naomi Armentrout, Mgr. Tel: (972) 243-7572 %FO: 100
Bus: *Motion picture & video production.* Fax: (972) 243-4026

TANDBERG USA INC.
200 Park Ave., Ste. 2005, New York, New York 10166
CEO: John Lubarsky, Dir. Tel: (212) 692-6500 %FO: 100
Bus: *Videoconferencing systems manufacture* Fax: (212) 692-6501
and sales.

● **TELENOR ASA**
Snaroyveien 30, NO-1331 Fornebu, Norway
CEO: Jon Fredrik Baksaas, Pres. & CEO Tel: 47-810-77-000 Rev: $10,067
Bus: *Telecommunications product manufacture.* Fax: 47-678-91-554 Emp: 20,900
www.telenor.com
NAICS: 511140, 515210, 517110, 517211, 517212, 517410, 517510, 517910, 518111, 518210, 519190, 541511,
561421, 561499

   TELENOR SATELLITE SERVICES
   1101 Wootton Pkwy., 10/F, Rockville, Maryland 20852
   CEO: Britt Carina Horncastle, Pres. Tel: (301) 838-7800 %FO: 100
   Bus: *Telecommunications product manufacture.* Fax: (301) 838-7701 Emp: 300

● **TFDS (TROMS FYLKES DAMPSKIBSSELSKAP AS)**
PO Box 6144, NO-9291 Tromso, Norway
CEO: Lund Ole, Chmn. Tel: 47-77-64-8100 Rev: $346
Bus: *Shipping, transportation, travel and tourism* Fax: 47-77-64-8180 Emp: 1,054
services. www.tfds.no
NAICS: 483111, 561599, 721199

   NORWEGIAN COASTAL VOYAGE INC.
   405 Park Ave., New York, New York 10022
   CEO: Rosalyn Gershell, Pres. Tel: (212) 319-1300 %FO: 100
   Bus: *Ticketing office for passenger ferries,* Fax: (212) 319-1390 Emp: 16
   cruise ships and tour packages.

● **TOMRA SYSTEMS ASA**
Drengrudshaugen 2, PO Box 278, NO-1372 Asker, Norway
CEO: Amund Skarholt, Pres. & CEO Tel: 47-66-79-9100 Rev: $380
Bus: *Reverse vending machines manufacture for* Fax: 47-66-79-9111 Emp: 2,100
plastic bottle returns. www.tomra.com
NAICS: 423930

NORTHEAST RECYCLING, INC.
234 Easthampton Rd., Northampton, Massachusetts 01060
CEO: Neil Kelley, Mgr.
Bus: *Reverse vending machines manufacture for*
aluminum recycling.
Tel: (860) 289-8301
Fax: (860) 282-7519
%FO: 100

TOMRA MAINE
897 Forest St., Portland, Maine 04103
CEO: Don Uva Jr., Mgr.
Bus: *Reverse vending machines manufacture for*
aluminum recycling.
Tel: (207) 775-7787
Fax: (207) 775-9157
%FO: 100

TOMRA MASSACHUSETTS, LLC
260 Kenneth Welch Dr., Lakeville, Massachusetts 02347
CEO: Mike DeVoe, Operations Mgr.
Bus: *Reverse vending machines manufacture for*
aluminum recycling.
Tel: (508) 946-8184
Fax: (508) 946-8154
%FO: 100
Emp: 60

TOMRA MICHIGAN
1044 Durant Dr., Howell, Michigan 48843
CEO: Debra Hall, VP
Bus: *Reverse vending machines manufacture for*
aluminum recycling.
Tel: (517) 552-9915
Fax: (517) 552-0746
%FO: 100
Emp: 72

TOMRA NORTH AMERICA, INC.
5923 Loomis Rd., Farmington, New York 14425
CEO: Peter Arquette, Mgr.
Bus: *Reverse vending machines manufacture for*
aluminum recycling.
Tel: (585) 742-3790
Fax: (585) 742-3792
%FO: 100
Emp: 16

TOMRA NORTH AMERICA, INC.
480 Lordship Blvd., Stratford, Connecticut 06615
CEO: Gregory Knoll, Pres.
Bus: *Reverse vending machines manufacture for*
aluminum recycling.
Tel: (203) 455-5000
Fax: (203) 455-5010
%FO: 100
Emp: 1,100

TOMRA NORTH AMERICA, INC.
820 First St., Ste. 200, West Des Moines, Iowa 50265
CEO: Debbie Hall, VP
Bus: *Reverse vending machines manufacture for*
aluminum recycling.
Tel: (515) 277-2100
Fax: (515) 255-2524
%FO: 100

TOMRA PACIFIC INC.
150 Klug Circle, Corona, California 92880
CEO: Scott Lamb, Pres.
Bus: *Reverse vending machines manufacture for*
aluminum recycling.
Tel: (951) 520-1700
Fax: (951) 520-1701
%FO: 100
Emp: 600

UPSTATE TOMRA, LLC
31 Opus Blvd., Rotterdam, New York 12306
CEO: Peter Arquette, Mgr.
Bus: *Reverse vending machines manufacture for*
aluminum recycling.
Tel: (518) 356-2597
Fax: (518) 357-9502
%FO: 100

WESTERN NEW YORK BICS, INC.
4284 Walden Ave., Lancaster, New York 14086
CEO: Brian Gregor, Operations Mgr.   Tel: (716) 685-7400   %FO: 100
Bus: *Reverse vending machines manufacture for* Fax: (716) 685-7409   Emp: 20
      aluminum recycling.

• **VIZRT LTD.**
Nostegaten 72, NO-5020 Bergen, Norway
CEO: Bjarne Berg, Pres. & CEO   Tel: 47-55-90-8080   Rev: $29
Bus: *3-D graphics production software.*   Fax: 47-55-90-8280   Emp: 132
      www.vizrt.com
NAICS: 511210

    CURIOUS SOFTWARE, INC.
    1118 Paseo Barranca, Santa Fe, New Mexico 87501
    CEO: Halid Hatic, Mgr.   Tel: (505) 988-7243   %FO: 100
    Bus: *Prepackaged software.*   Fax: (505) 988-1654

    VIZRT AMERICAS
    555 8th Ave., 10/F, New York, New York 10018
    CEO: Isaac Hersly, Pres.   Tel: (212) 560-0708   %FO: 100
    Bus: *3-D graphics products manufacture and* Fax: (212) 560-0709   Emp: 15
      sales.

    VIZRT USA
    5205 Trolley Square Crossing, Atlanta, Georgia 30306
    CEO: Ingrid Agasoster, Mgr.   Tel: (404) 488-6182   %FO: 100
    Bus: *Prepackaged software.*   Fax:

    VIZRT USA
    6100 Melrose Ave., Hollywood, California 90038
    CEO: Stein Gausereide, Mgr.   Tel: (323) 908-7004   %FO: 100
    Bus: *Prepackaged software.*   Fax: (601) 510-5012

• **YARA INTERNATIONAL ASA**
Bygday alle 2, NO-0202 Oslo, Norway
CEO: Thorleif Enger, CEO   Tel: 47-24-15-7000   Rev: $5,457
Bus: *Mfr. fertilizers and industrial gases.*   Fax: 47-24-15-7267   Emp: 7,067
      www.yara.com
NAICS: 325311, 325312, 325314

    YARA AMERICA INC.
    100 North America, Ste. 3200, Tampa, Florida 33602
    CEO: Terje Gronlie   Tel: (813) 222-5700   %FO: 100
    Bus: *Mfr. fertilizers and industrial gases.*   Fax: (813) 875-5735

    YARA AMERICA INC.
    6160 Stoneridge Mall Rd., Ste. 350, Pleasanton, California 94588
    CEO: Nyree Cruz   Tel: (925) 467-0100   %FO: 100
    Bus: *Mfr. fertilizers and industrial gases.*   Fax: (925) 467-0125

Pakistan

- **HABIB BANK LTD.**
  Habib Bank Plaza, 1.1. Chundrigar Rd., Karachi 75650, Pakistan
  CEO: Zakir Mahmood, Pres.   Tel: 92-21-241-8000   Rev: $25
  Bus: *General banking services.*   Fax: 92-21-241-1647   Emp: 1,462
                                            www.habibbankltd.com

  NAICS: 522110, 523110
  - **HABIB BANK LTD.**
    60 East 42nd St., Rm. 535, New York, New York 10165
    CEO: Rana A. Rashid, Mgr.   Tel: (212) 551-5000   %FO: 100
    Bus: *International banking services.*   Fax: Emp: 50

- **NATIONAL BANK OF PAKISTAN**
  NBP Bldg., I.I. Chundrigar Rd., Karachi 74200, Pakistan
  CEO: S. Ali Raza, Chmn. & Pres.   Tel: 92-921-2220
  Bus: *Commercial banking services.*   Fax: 92-921-2731
                                            www.nbp.com.pk

  NAICS: 522110
  - **NATIONAL BANK OF PAKISTAN**
    1875 Connecticut Ave. N.W., Washington, District of Columbia 20009
    CEO: Nasim Abbasi, CEO   Tel: (202) 462-7373   %FO: 100
    Bus: *International banking services.*   Fax: (202) 667-2515

  - **NATIONAL BANK OF PAKISTAN**
    100 Wall St., 21/F, PO Box 500, New York, New York 10005
    CEO: Mrafiq Bengali, CEO   Tel: (212) 344-8822   %FO: 100
    Bus: *International banking services.*   Fax: (212) 344-8826   Emp: 15

  - **NATIONAL BANK OF PAKISTAN**
    2315 West Devon Ave., Chicago, Illinois 60659
    CEO: Ali Raza   Tel: (773) 508-9728
    Bus: *International banking services.*   Fax: (773) 508-9723

- **PAKISTAN INTERNATIONAL AIRLINES CORPORATION (PIA)**
  Quaid-e-Azam International Airport, Karachi 75200, Pakistan
  CEO: Ahmad Saeed, CEO   Tel: 92-21-457-2225
  Bus: *Airline transport services.*   Fax: 92-21-457-2011
                                            www.piac.com.pk

  NAICS: 481111
  - **PAKISTAN INTERNATIONAL AIRLINES CORPORATION**
    505 Eighth Ave., 14/F., New York, New York 10018
    CEO: Salah Uddin   Tel: (212) 971-5434   %FO: 100
    Bus: *Airline services.*   Fax: (212) 760-8484

PAKISTAN INTERNATIONAL AIRLINES CORPORATION
2907 Butterfield, Ste. 110, Chicago, Illinois 60623
CEO: Shahid Jamal Naizmi   Tel: (312) 263-3082   %FO: 100
Bus: *Airline services.*   Fax: (312) 263-3082

• **UNITED BANK LIMITED**
State Life Insurance Corp. Bldg. 1, I.I. Chundrigar Rd., PO Box 4306, Karachi 74200, Pakistan
CEO: Mr. Atif R. Bokhari, Pres. & CEO   Tel: 92-21-111-825-111
Bus: *Commercial banking services.*   Fax: 92-21-241-3492
                                            www.ubl.com.pk
NAICS: 522110

UNITED BANK LIMITED
80 Broad St., 24/F, New York, New York 10004
CEO: M.A. Rauf, Gen. Mgr.   Tel: (212) 943-1275   %FO: 100
Bus: *International banking services.*   Fax: (212) 968-0557

Panama

● **BAC INTERNATIONAL BANK PANAMA**
Cl. Aquilino de la Guardia, Edificio BAC International Bank, Planta Baja, Panama
CEO: Carlos F. Pellas, Pres.
Tel: 507-213-0822
Bus: *International financial services, commercial &*
investment banking, securities and insurance
services.
Fax: 507-269-3879
www.bacbank.com
NAICS: 522110, 523110
    BAC INSURANCE GROUP
    3600 Douglas Rd., Ste. 1003, Coral Gables, Florida 33184
    CEO: Carlos Hurtado
    Bus: *Real estate loans.*
    Tel: (305) 377-1046
    Fax: (305) 375-0351
    %FO: 100

● **BANCO LATINOAMERICANO (BLADEX)**
Calle 50 y Aquillino de la Guardia, PO Box 6-1497, Panama City, Panama
CEO: Jaime Rivera, CEO
Bus: *International banking services.*
Tel: 507-210-8500
Fax: 507-269-6333
www.blx.com
Rev: $155
Emp: 129
NAICS: 522110
    BANCO LATINOAMERICANO DE EXPORTACIONES (BLADEX)
    641 Lexington Ave., 32/F, New York, New York 10022
    CEO: Jose M. Yepez, Gen. Mgr.
    Bus: *International banking services.*
    Tel: (212) 840-5400
    Fax: (212) 753-9060
    %FO: 100
    Emp: 8

● **WILLBROS GROUP, INC.**
Plaza 2000 Bldg., 50 th St., 8/F, Apartado 6307, Panama City 5, Panama
CEO: Michael F. Curran, Chmn. & Pres. & CEO
Bus: *Independent contracting serving the oil and gas*
industries.
Tel: 507-2-13-0947
Fax: 507-2-63-9294
www.willbros.com
Rev: $419
Emp: 3,300
NAICS: 213112, 237120, 237310, 237990, 541330
    WILLBROS USA, INC.
    4400 Post Oak Pkwy., Ste. 1000, Houston, Texas 77027
    CEO: Clay Etheridge, Pres.
    Bus: *Engaged in independent contracting serving*
the oil and gas industries.
    Tel: (713) 403-8000
    Fax: (713) 403-8066
    %FO: 100
    Emp: 1,200

Peru

- **BANCO DE CREDITO DEL PERU**
  Av. Centenario 156, Urb. Las Laderas Melgarejo, La Molina, Lima 27, Peru
  CEO: Javier Mayolo, Mng. Dir.   Tel: 51-1-313-2000   Rev: $1,009
  Bus: *International banking services.*   Fax: 51-1-313-2407   Emp: 7,522
                                                 www.viabcp.com

  NAICS: 522110

    BANCO DE CREDITO DEL PERU
    410 Park Ave., New York, New York 10022
    CEO: Manuel Rottero, Gen. Mgr.   Tel: (212) 644-6644   %FO: 100
    Bus: *International banking services.*   Fax: (212) 826-9852   Emp: 13

- **CREDICORP LTD.**
  Calle Centenario 156, La Molina, Lima 12, Peru
  CEO: Dionisio Romero, CEO   Tel: 51-1-349-0590   Rev: $979
  Bus: *Financial services.*   Fax: 51-1-349-0381   Emp: 9,638
                                                 www.credicorpnet.com

  NAICS: 523930

    BANCO DE CREDITO DEL PERU
    410 Park Ave., 6/F, New York, New York 10022
    CEO: Manuel Rottero   Tel: (212) 644-6644   %FO: 100
    Bus: *Financial services.*   Fax: (212) 826-9852

- **SOUTHERN PERU COPPER CORP.**
  Ave. Caminos del Inca No. 171, Chacarilla del Estanque, Santiago de Surco, Lima 33, Peru
  CEO: Oscar Gonzalez Rocha, Pres. & CEO   Tel: 51-1-372-1414   Rev: $1,716
  Bus: *Copper mining.*   Fax: 51-1-372-0262   Emp: 3,544
                                                 www.southernperu.com
  NAICS: 212222, 212234, 331411, 331423

    SOUTHERN PERU COPPER CORPORATION
    2575 East Camelback Rd., Ste. 500, Phoenix, Arizona 85016
    CEO: Oscar Gonzalez Rocha, Pres.   Tel: (602) 977-6500
    Bus: *Copper mining.*   Fax: (602) 977-6700   Emp: 3,544

Philippines

- **AMBERGRIS SOLUTIONS INC.**
  31/F, Discovery Center, 25 ADB Avenue, Ortigas Center, Pasig City 1605, Philippines
  CEO: Javier Infante, CEO
  Bus: *Operates call centers for U.S-based*

  Tel: 63-2-638-9440
  Fax: 63-2-638-9445
  www.ambergrissolutions.com

  NAICS: 517110

  > **AMBERGRIS SOLUTIONS INC.**
  > 3900 Sparks Dr.,, Grand Rapids, Michigan 49546
  > CEO: Charina Quizon
  > Bus: *Operates call centers for U.S-based
  > corporations.*
  >
  > Tel: (212) 684-5556
  > Fax: (616) 957-3635
  >
  > %FO: 100

- **BANK OF THE PHILIPPINE ISLANDS**
  BPI Bldg., Ayala Ave., Paseo de Roxas, Makati Metro Manila 1200, Philippines
  CEO: Jaime Augusto Zobel de Ayala II, Chmn.
  Bus: *Commercial banking services.*

  Tel: 63-2-818-5541
  Fax: 63-2-186-9436
  www.bpi.com.ph

  Rev: $573
  Emp: 10,425

  NAICS: 522110, 523120, 523920, 523930, 524113, 524126

  > **BANK OF THE PHILIPPINE ISLANDS**
  > 7 East 53rd St., New York, New York 10022
  > CEO: Xavier P. Loinaz, Gen. Mgr.
  > Bus: *Commercial banking services.*
  >
  > Tel: (212) 644-6700
  > Fax: (212) 752-5969
  >
  > %FO: 100

- **JOLLIBEE FOODS CORPORATION**
  5th Fl. Emerald Avenue, Ortigas Center, Pasig City 1605, Philippines
  CEO: Tony Tan Caktiong, CEO
  Bus: *Food services and restaurant chains.*

  Tel: 63-2898-8181
  Fax: 63-2634-1191
  www.jollibee.com.ph

  Emp: 6,373

  NAICS: 722211

  > **JOLLIBEE/HONEYBEE FOODS CORPORATION**
  > 4300 Sonoma Boulevard, Ste. 140, Vallejo, California 94589
  > CEO: Noli Tingzon
  > Bus: *Food services and restaurant chains.*
  >
  > Tel: (707) 557-3290
  > Fax: (707) 556-1973
  >
  > %FO: 100

- **METROPOLITAN BANK & TRUST COMPANY**
  Senator Gil Puyat Avenue, Makati, Metro Manila 1200, Philippines
  CEO: Antonio S. Abacan Jr., Pres.
  Bus: *Commercial banking services.*

  Tel: 63-2-892-3598
  Fax: 63-2-817-6248
  www.metrobank.com.ph

  Rev: $722
  Emp: 7,223

  NAICS: 522110

  > **METROPOLITAN BANK & TRUST COMPANY**
  > 2201 West Cermak Rd., Chicago, Illinois 60608-3921
  > CEO: Paul Gaughan
  > Bus: *International commercial banking services.*
  >
  > Tel: (773) 254-1000
  > Fax: (773) 254-1000
  >
  > %FO: 100

METROPOLITAN BANK & TRUST COMPANY
10 East 53rd St., New York, New York 10022
CEO: Alfred V. Madrid, VP & Gen. Mgr.   Tel: (212) 832-0855   %FO: 100
Bus: *International commercial banking services.*   Fax: (212) 832-0993

● **PHILIPPINE AIRLINES (PAL)**
Philippine Airlines Center, 1/F, Legaspi St., Legaspi Village, Makati City 0750, Philippines
CEO: Lucio C. Tan, Chmn. & CEO   Tel: 63-2-818-4914
Bus: *Commercial air transport carrier.*   Fax: 63-2-815-6481   Emp: 14,000
                                           www.philippineair.com
  NAICS: 481111

  PHILIPPINE AIRLINES
  Honolulu International Airport, 116 Mcdonnell Rd., San Francisco, California 94128
  CEO: Alfred Nethercott   Tel: (650) 877-4830   %FO: 100
  Bus: *International airline carrier.*   Fax: (650) 877-4830

  PHILIPPINE AIRLINES
  5959 W. Century Blvd., Los Angeles, California 90045
  CEO: Adrian Ingles, District Sales Mgr.   Tel: (310) 338-9000   %FO: 100
  Bus: *International airline carrier.*   Fax: (310) 338-7194   Emp: 30

  PHILIPPINE AIRLINES
  447 Sutter St., Ste. 200, San Francisco, California 94108
  CEO: Rodolfo Llora, Deputy Mgr.   Tel: (415) 217-3100   %FO: 100
  Bus: *International airline carrier.*   Fax: (415) 217-3163   Emp: 150

● **PHILIPPINE NATIONAL BANK**
PNB Financial Center, Roxas Blvd., Pasay City, Manila, Philippines
CEO: Omar Byron T. Mier, Pres.   Tel: 63-2-891-6040   Rev: $729
Bus: *Commercial banking services.*   Fax: 63-2-891-6267   Emp: 7,085
                                        www.pnb.com.ph
  NAICS: 522110

  PHILIPPINE NATIONAL BANK
  Sahara Towne Square, 2600-A S. Maryland Pkwy., Las Vegas, Nevada 89109
  CEO: Benjamin M. Sison   Tel: (702) 650-5263   %FO: 100
  Bus: *International banking services.*   Fax: (702) 650-5263

  PHILIPPINE NATIONAL BANK
  5845 N. Clark St., Chicago, Illinois 60660
  CEO: Christopher P. Ortiz   Tel: (773) 784-2953   %FO: 100
  Bus: *International banking services.*   Fax: (773) 784-2952

  PHILIPPINE NATIONAL BANK
  1145 Bishop St., Honolulu, Hawaii 96813-4296
  CEO: Luis G. David Jr.   Tel: (808) 521-1493   %FO: 100
  Bus: *International banking services.*   Fax: (808) 533-2842

  PHILIPPINE NATIONAL BANK
  3345 Wilshire Boulevard, Ste. 200, Los Angeles, California 90010
  CEO: Francisco R. Ramos   Tel: (323) 802-8050   %FO: 100
  Bus: *International banking services.*   Fax: (323) 802-8011

PHILIPPINE NATIONAL BANK
546 Fifth Ave., 8/F, New York, New York 10036
CEO: Pedro E. Reyes III, SVP & Gen. Mgr.　　　Tel:　(212) 790-9600　　　%FO: 100
Bus: *International banking services.*　　　　　Fax:　(212) 382-2238

PHILIPPINE NATIONAL BANK
11849 Bissonnet, Suite U-1, Houston, Texas 77099
CEO: Shirley Ann Camacho　　　　　　　　　Tel:　(281) 988-7575　　　%FO: 100
Bus: *International banking services.*　　　　　Fax:　(281) 988-7555

- **PSI TECHNOLOGIES HOLDINGS, INC.**
Electronics Avenue, FTI Industrial Complex, Taguig Metro, Manila 1604, Philippines
CEO: Arthur J. Young Jr., CEO　　　　　　　Tel:　63-2-838-4966　　　Rev: $79
Bus: *Mfr. semiconductors.*　　　　　　　　　Fax:　63-2-838-4648　　　Emp: 3,314
　　　　　　　　　　　　　　　　　　　　　www.psitechnologies.com
  NAICS: 334413

  PSI TECHNOLOGIES HOLDINGS, INC.
  4633 Old Ironsides Dr., Ste. 260, Santa Clara, California 95054
  CEO: B.J. Sebastian, SVP　　　　　　　　　Tel:　(408) 982-0188　　　%FO: 100
  Bus: *Semiconductor manufacture and sales.*　Fax:　(408) 982-0355

  PSI TECHNOLOGIES HOLDINGS, INC.
  721 East Citation Lane, Tempe, Arizona 85284
  CEO: Mike Gholson　　　　　　　　　　　　Tel:　(480) 838-5286　　　%FO: 100
  Bus: *Semiconductor manufacture and sales.*　Fax:　(480) 838-5292

Poland

- **MELEX VEHICLE PRODUCTION PLANT CO., LTD.**
  Wojska Polskiego 3, Podkarpackie, PL-39-300 Mielec, Poland
  CEO: Dzialowski Ryszard, Pres.   Tel: 48-17-788-0295   Rev: $38
  Bus: *Mfr. golf cars and specialty vehicles.*   Fax: 48-17-788-7945   Emp: 1,600
                                                www.melex.com
  NAICS: 336411, 336413, 336999
  - **MELEX USA**
    3208 Wellington Ct., Ste. J, Raleigh, North Carolina 27615
    CEO: Roman Gwarnicki, Pres.   Tel: (919) 872-9389   %FO: 100
    Bus: *Mfr./sale golf cars & specialty vehicles.*   Fax: Emp: 3

- **POLSKIE LINIE LOTNICZE LOT SA**
  17 Stycznia 39, 00-906 Warsaw, Poland
  CEO: Marek Grabarek, Pres. & CEO   Tel: 48-22--9572   Rev: $972
  Bus: *International commercial air transport services.*   Fax: 48-22--9573   Emp: 3,672
                                                www.lot.com
  NAICS: 481111, 481112, 481212
  - **LOT POLISH AIRLINES**
    333 North Michigan Ave., Chicago, Illinois 60601
    CEO: Marek Kawczyski, Mgr.   Tel: (312) 236-5501   %FO: 100
    Bus: *International commercial air transport*   Fax:
          services.

  - **LOT POLISH AIRLINES**
    500 5th Ave., Ste. 408, New York, New York 10110
    CEO: Krzysztos Ziebinski, Mgr.   Tel: (718) 751-4623   %FO: 100
    Bus: *International commercial air transport*   Fax: (718) 751-4625   Emp: 22
          services.

Portugal

- **BANCO COMERCIAL PORTUGUES, SA**
  Praca D. Joao I, 28, P-4000-295 Porto, Portugal
  CEO: Jorge Jardim Goncalves, Chmn.
  Bus: *General commercial banking.*

  Tel: 351-21-321-1000
  Fax: 351-21-321-1759
  www.bcp.pt

  Rev: $5,585
  Emp: 13,636

  NAICS: 522110

  - **BANCO PORTUGUES DO ATLANTICO**
    Two Wall St., New York, New York 10005
    CEO: Pedro Belo, Assoc. VP
    Bus: *International banking services.*

    Tel: (212) 306-7800
    Fax: (212) 766-8047

    %FO: 100

- **BANCO ESPIRITO SANTO, SA**
  Av. da Liberdade 195, P-1250-142 Lisbon, Portugal
  CEO: Antonio Luis Roquette Ricciardi, Chmn.
  Bus: *Investment banking and financial services.*

  Tel: 351-21-350-1713
  Fax: 351-21-359-7309
  www.bes.pt

  Rev: $5,297
  Emp: 8,241

  NAICS: 522110

  - **BANCO ESPIRITO SANTO DE LISBON**
    320 Park Ave., 29/F, New York, New York 10022
    CEO: Joaqim Garnecho, Gen. Mgr.
    Bus: *Banking services.*

    Tel: (212) 702-3400
    Fax: (212) 750-3888

    %FO: 100
    Emp: 27

- **BANCO FINANTIA**
  Rua General Firmino Miguel 5, P-1600 Lisbon, Portugal
  CEO: Antonio M. A. Guerreiro, Chmn. & CEO
  Bus: *Provides investment banking services.*

  Tel: 351-21-720-2000
  Fax: 351-21-726-9820
  www.finantia.pt

  NAICS: 523110

  - **FINANTIA USA LTD.**
    437 Madison Ave., 39/F, New York, New York 10022
    CEO: Shin Sukui, Pres.
    Bus: *Real estate agents & managers*

    Tel: (212) 891-7300
    Fax: (212) 891-7310

    %FO: 100

Qatar

● **AL JAZEERA SATELLITE CHANNEL**
PO Box 22300, Doha, Qatar
CEO: H.E. Sheikh Hamad bin Thamer Al Thani,   Tel: 974-489-2777
Bus: *Non-censored TV broadcasts.*   Fax: 974-442-6864
          www.aljazeera.net

NAICS: 515120, 515210

AL JAZEERA SATELLITE CHANNEL
529 14th St., NW, Ste. 927, Washington, District of Columbia 20045
CEO: Wadah Khanfar   Tel: (202) 393-1333   %FO: 100
Bus: *Non-censored TV broadcasts.*   Fax: (202) 293-1337

Romania

- **TAROM ROT**
Otopent Airport, Soseaua Bucuresti, Ploiesti KM 16.5, Bucharest, Romania
CEO: Rodica Miculescu, Pres.   Tel: 40-1-201-4700   Rev: $
Bus: *Commercial air transport services.*   Fax: 40-1-2014761
                                                  www.tarom.ro
NAICS: 481111
  TAROM - Romanian Air Transport
  Empire State Building, 350 Fifth Ave., Ste. 1410, New York, New York 10118
  CEO: Tel: (212) 560-0840   %FO: 100
  Bus: *Commercial air transport services.*   Fax: (212) 560-0845

Russia

● **AEROFLOT RUSSIAN AIRLINES JSC**
Leningradsky Prospectus 37, Bldg. 9, 125167 Moscow, Russia
CEO: Valery M. Okulov, CEO
Bus: *International air carrier.*

Tel: 7-095-156-8019
Fax: 7-095-155-6647
www.aeroflot.org

Rev: $1,716
Emp: 14,700

NAICS: 481111

    AEROFLOT (RUSSIAN) AIRLINES
    80 SW 8th St., Ste. 1970, Miami, Florida 33130
    CEO: Alexander Balaour, Dir.
    Bus: *International air carrier.*

Tel: (305) 577-8400
Fax: (305) 577-8400

%FO: 100

    AEROFLOT (RUSSIAN) AIRLINES
    1411 4th Ave., Ste. 420, Seattle, Washington 98101
    CEO: Gennadi Tavlinstev, Dir.
    Bus: *International air carrier.*

Tel: (206) 464-1005
Fax: (206) 464-0452

%FO: 100

    AEROFLOT (RUSSIAN) AIRLINES
    120 Montgomery St., San Francisco, California 94104
    CEO: Yuri Zakharenko, Dir.
    Bus: *International air carrier.*

Tel: (415) 403-4033
Fax: (415) 403-4033

%FO: 100

    AEROFLOT (RUSSIAN) AIRLINES
    1384 Broadway, 22/F, New York, New York 10118-0494
    CEO: Sergey Gudkov, VP
    Bus: *International air carrier.*

Tel: (212) 288-2125
Fax: (212) 288-5973

%FO: 100

    AEROFLOT (RUSSIAN) AIRLINES
    80 S.W. 8th St., Miami, Florida 33131
    CEO: Valery Okulov, Dir.
    Bus: *International air carrier.*

Tel: (305) 577-8500
Fax: (305) 579-8666

%FO: 100

● **AURIGA, INC.**
Research Computer Center, Moscow State University, Leninskie Gory, 119992 Moscow, Russia
CEO: Aleksei Sukharev, Dir.
Bus: *Provides high-quality, low cost offshore software
    development services.*

Tel: 7-095-939-1784
Fax: 7-095-939-0300
www.auriga.com

Rev: $3
Emp: 130

NAICS: 511210

    AURIGA, INC.
    1 Overlook Dr., Ste. 2, Amherst, New Hampshire 03031
    CEO: Sergei Riabov
    Bus: *Provides high-quality, low cost offshore
    software development services.*

Tel: (603) 673-2300
Fax: (603) 672-2316

%FO: 100

- **GOLDEN TELECOM, INC.**
  1 Kozhevnichesky Proezd, 2nd Fl., 115114 Moscow, Russia
  CEO: Alexander Vinogradov, CEO
  Bus: *Internet and telecom service provider.*
  Tel: 7-501-797-9300
  Fax: 7-501-797-9332
  www.goldentelecom.ru
  Rev: $584
  Emp: 3,426

  NAICS: 517212, 518111, 518210

  GOLDEN TELECOM, INC.
  2831 29th St., NW, Washington, District of Columbia 20008
  CEO: Julia Marx
  Bus: *Internet and telecom service provider.*
  Tel: (202) 332-5997
  Fax: (202) 332-4877
  %FO: 100

- **JSC SEVERSTAL**
  Mira St.30, Vologda Region, 162600 Cherepovets, Russia
  CEO: Alexey A. Mordashov, Chmn.
  Bus: *Steel production and distribution.*
  Tel: 7-8202-530-909
  Fax: 7-8202-571-276
  www.severstal.ru
  Rev: $6,648
  Emp: 54,597

  NAICS: 331111, 331210, 331221

  ROUGE INDUSTRIES INC.
  3001 Miller Rd., Dearborn, Michigan 48121-1699
  CEO: Carl L. Valdiserri, Chmn. & CEO
  Bus: *Steel production and distribution.*
  Tel: (313) 317-8900
  Fax: (313) 845-0199
  %FO: 100
  Emp: 2,705

  SEVERSTAL INC.
  51 South Grove Ave., 3/F, Elgin, Illinois 60120
  CEO: Victor Lipukhin, Pres.
  Bus: *Distributor for steel mills.*
  Tel: (847) 374-0400
  Fax:
  %FO: 100

  SEVERSTAL NORTH AMERICA, INC.
  3001 Miller Rd., Dearborn, Michigan 48121
  CEO: Vadim A. Makhov, Chmn. & CEO
  Bus: *Steel production.*
  Tel: (313) 317-8900
  Fax: (313) 337-9377
  %FO: 100
  Emp: 2,000

- **MINING METALLURGICAL COMPANY NORILSK NICKEL**
  22 Voznesensky Pereulok, 103009 Moscow, Russia
  CEO: Michael D. Prokhorov, Chmn. & Mng. Dir.
  Bus: *Mining exploration, including nickel and palladium.*
  Tel: 7-095-787-7667
  Fax: 7-095-785-5808
  www.norilsknickel.ru
  Rev: $1,832
  Emp: 100,786

  NAICS: 212234, 212299

  NORILSK NICKEL USA
  2 Penn Ctr. West, Ste. 330, Pittsburgh, Pennsylvania 15276
  CEO: Yuri Sobolev, Pres.
  Bus: *Distribution of non-ferrous metals.*
  Tel: (412) 722-1120
  Fax:
  %FO: 100
  Emp: 6

  STILLWATER MINING COMPANY
  1321 Discovery Dr., Billings, Montana 59102
  CEO: Frank McAllister, Chmn. & CEO
  Bus: *Platinum mining.*
  Tel: (406) 373-8700
  Fax: (406) 373-8701
  %FO: 100
  Emp: 1,575

- **OAO LUKOIL**
  11 Sretenski Blvd., 101 000 Moscow, Russia
  CEO: Vagit Y. Alekperov, Pres.　　　　　Tel: 7-095-927-4444　　　Rev: $22,299
  Bus: *Oil and gas exploration and production.*　　Fax: 7-095-916-0020　　　Emp: 14,000
  　　　　　　　　　　　　　　　　　　www.lukoil.com
  NAICS: 211111, 211112, 213111, 213112, 221210, 324110, 324191, 324199, 333132, 424710, 424720, 447110, 447190, 454311, 454312, 454319, 486110,
  　　　　　486210, 486910, 541360

  　　GETTY PETROLEUM MARKETING INC.
  　　1500 Hempstead Tpke., East Meadow, New York 11554
  　　CEO: Vadim Gluzman, Chmn. & CEO　　Tel: (516) 542-4900　　%FO: 100
  　　Bus: *Petroleum terminals operations.*　　Fax: (516) 832-8272

- **VAO INTOURIST**
  150 Prospect Mira, 129366 Moscow, Russia
  CEO: Aliev Abbas, Pres.　　　　　　　　Tel: 7-095-956-4207
  Bus: *Engaged in international tourism and investment*　Fax: 7-095-730-1957
  　　operations.　　　　　　　　　　www.intourist.ru
  NAICS: 523999, 561599

  　　INTOURIST USA
  　　610 5th Ave., Ste. 603, New York, New York 10020
  　　CEO: Sergey Tsapov, Mgr.　　　　Tel: (212) 757-3884　　%FO: 100
  　　Bus: *International tourism and investment*　Fax:
  　　operations.

  　　INTOURIST USA
  　　12 South Dixie Hwy., Ste. 201, Lake Worth, Florida 33460
  　　CEO: Alexey N. Mesiatsev, Pres.　　Tel: (561) 585-5305　　%FO: 100
  　　Bus: *International tourism and investment*　Fax: (561) 582-1353
  　　operations.

Saudi Arabia

- **HAJI ABDULLAH ALIREZA & CO. LTD.**
  Alirreza Centre, King Abdulaziz St., Jeddah 21411, Saudi Arabia
  CEO: Teymour A. Alireza, Pres. & CEO
  Bus: *Holding company engaged in manufacturing, energy, construction, transportation, and healthcare.*
  Tel: 966-2-647-2233
  Fax:
  www.alireza.com
  Rev: $373
  Emp: 500

  NAICS: 334518, 339911, 423940, 424720, 483111, 483212, 517110, 517310, 561510

  CORTELCO SYSTEMS CORP.
  4119 Willow Lake Blvd., Memphis, Tennessee 38118
  CEO: Stephen R. Bowling, CEO
  Bus: *Management services.*
  Tel: (901) 365-7774
  Fax:
  %FO: 100
  Emp: 260

  P-COM, INC.
  3175 S. Winchester Blvd., Campbell, California 95008
  CEO: Don Meiners, Pres.
  Bus: *Wireless broadband service equipment.*
  Tel: (408) 866-3666
  Fax: (408) 866-3655
  %FO: 100
  Emp: 125

- **THE NATIONAL SHIPPING COMPANY SAUDI ARABIA**
  Sitteen St., PO Box 8931, Riyadh 11492, Saudi Arabia
  CEO: Abdullah Abdulrahman Al-Shraim, CEO
  Bus: *International shipping and cargo services.*
  Tel: 966-1-478-5454
  Fax: 966-1-477-7478
  www.nscsa.com

  NAICS: 483111

  NSCSA (America) INC.
  399 Hoes Lane, Ste. 100, Piscataway, New Jersey 08854
  CEO: Ahmed Banaja
  Bus: *International shipping/cargo services.*
  Tel: (732) 562-8989
  Fax: (732) 562-0909
  %FO: 100

  NSCSA (America) INC.
  400 Pratt St., Ste. 400, Baltimore, Maryland 21202
  CEO: Ahmed Banaja, Pres.
  Bus: *International shipping/cargo services.*
  Tel: (410) 625-7000
  Fax: (410) 625-7050
  %FO: 100

- **RIYAD BANK**
  King Abdul Aziz Rd., PO Box 22622, Riyadh 11416, Saudi Arabia
  CEO: Talal I. Al-Qudaibi, Pres.
  Bus: *General banking services.*
  Tel: 966-1-401-3030
  Fax: 966-1-404-2707
  www.riyadbank.com
  Emp: 4,300

  NAICS: 522110, 523110

  RIYAD BANK
  700 Louisiana St., Ste. 4770, Houston, Texas 77002
  CEO: Samir Haddad, Mgr.
  Bus: *International trade & project financing services.*
  Tel: (713) 331-2001
  Fax: (713) 331-2043
  %FO: 100

● SAUDI ARABIAN AIRLINES

Saudi Arabian Bldg., Old Airport Rd., King Abul Aziz International Airport, Jeddah 21231, Saudi Arabia
CEO: Ali Ibn Abdul Rahman Ali Ibn Al Khalaf, Pres.   Tel: 966-2-686-0000   Rev: $2,500
Bus: *International commercial air transport services.*   Fax: 966-2-686-2251   Emp: 24,170
www.saudiairlines.com

NAICS: 481112, 481211, 488210

SAUDI ARABIAN AIRLINES
The Watergate, 2600 Virginia Ave. NW, Ste. 903, Washington, District of Columbia 20037
CEO: Shaima Ismati, Mgr.   Tel: (703) 661-8300   %FO: 100
Bus: *International commercial air transport
    services.*   Fax: (703) 661-8617

SAUDI ARABIAN AIRLINES
11301 West Irving Park Rd., Franklin Park, Illinois 60131
CEO: Arpine Ayvazian, Mgr.   Tel: (847) 957-0973   %FO: 100
Bus: *International commercial air transport
    services.*   Fax: (847) 957-0976

SAUDI ARABIAN AIRLINES
2029 Century Park East, Ste. 1180, Los Angeles, California 90067
CEO: Demos Sirhannas, Principal   Tel: (800) 421-3359   %FO: 100
Bus: *International commercial air transport
    services.*   Fax: (310) 556-5637

SAUDI ARABIAN AIRLINES
12555 Northborough Dr., Houston, Texas 77067
CEO: Joseph Basrari, Mgr.   Tel: (281) 873-1000   %FO: 100
Bus: *International commercial air transport
    services.*   Fax: (281) 873-1069   Emp: 65

SAUDI ARABIAN AIRLINES
8002 Kew Gardens Rd., Ste. 401, Kew Gardens, New York 11415
CEO: Nezar Sonbol, Mgr.   Tel: (212) 551-3020   %FO: 100
Bus: *International commercial air transport
    services.*   Fax: (212) 551-3021

● SAUDI ARABIAN OIL COMPANY

PO Box 5000, Dhahran 31311, Saudi Arabia
CEO: None Ali I. Al-Naimi, Chmn.   Tel: 966-3-872-0115   Rev: $116,000
Bus: *Oil exploration, transportation & refining.*   Fax: 966-3-873-8190   Emp: 54,000
www.saudiaramco.com

NAICS: 211111, 211112, 213111, 213112, 221210, 324110, 324191, 324199, 333132, 424710, 424720, 447110,
447190, 454311, 454312, 454319, 486110,
        486210, 486910, 541360

ARAMCO SERVICES CO.
9009 West Loop South, Houston, Texas 77096
CEO: Mazen Snobar, Pres.   Tel: (713) 432-4000   %FO: 100
Bus: *Management services & engineers for oil*   Fax: Emp: 450
    company.

MOTIVA ENTERPRISES LLC
700 Milam St., Houston, Texas 77002
CEO: William B. Welte, Pres. & CEO   Tel: (713) 277-8000   %FO: 50
Bus: *Oil & Gas Refining, Marketing & Distribution*   Fax: Emp: 3,600

SAUDI PETROLEUM INTERNATIONAL, INC.
527 Madison Ave., 22/F & 23/F, New York, New York 10022
CEO:
Bus: *Provides marketing and ocean transport
  support services for North and South
  America and the Caribbean*

Tel: (212) 832-4044
Fax: (212) 446-9200

%FO: 100

SAUDI REFINING, INC.
9009 West Loop South, Ste. 11081, Houston, Texas 77096-1719
CEO: S.M. Salamah, Pres.
Bus: *Oil industry service and support.*

Tel: (713) 432-4000
Fax: (713) 432-4900

%FO: 100
Emp: 8

● **SAUDI BASIC INDUSTRIES CORPORATION**
PO Box 5101, Riyadh 11422, Saudi Arabia
CEO: Mohamed H. Al-Mady, CEO
Bus: *Mfr./marketing chemicals, plastics, fertilizers &
  steels.*

Tel: 966-1-225-8000
Fax: 966-1-225-9000
www.sabic.com

Rev: $12,472
Emp: 16,000

NAICS: 325110, 325120, 325181, 325188, 325192, 325199, 325211, 325221, 325222, 325311, 325312, 325314, 326199, 331111

SABIC AMERICAS, INC.
2500 City West Blvd., Ste. 650, Destec Tower, Houston, Texas 77042
CEO: Mohammed Al-Bathi, Gen. Mgr.
Bus: *Research/development, procurement &
  recruitment petrochemical/fertilizer/steel
  industries.*

Tel: (713) 532-4999
Fax: (713) 532-4994

%FO: 100
Emp: 85

SABIC TECHNOLOGY CENTER
1600 Industrial Blvd., Sugar land, Texas 77478
CEO:
Bus: *Research/development, procurement &
  recruitment petrochemical/fertilizer/steel
  industries.*

Tel: (281) 207-5500
Fax: (281) 207-5550

Scotland, U.K.

- **ABERDEEN ASSET MANAGEMENT PLC**
  10 Queen's Terrace, Aberdeen AB10 1YG, Scotland, U.K.
  CEO: Martin J. Gilbert, Chmn. & CEO   Tel: 44-1224-631-999   Rev: $251
  Bus: *Provides financial services.*   Fax: 44-1224-647-010   Emp: 735
                                                www.aberdeen-asset.com

  NAICS: 523920

  ABERDEEN ASSET MANAGEMENT, INC.
  45 Broadway, 31/F, New York, New York 10006
  CEO: Renee Arnold, Sales   Tel: (212) 968-8800   %FO: 100
  Bus: *Financial services.*   Fax: (212) 968-8888

- **AGGREKO PLC**
  121 West Regent St., Glasgow G2 2SD, Scotland, U.K.
  CEO: Rupert Soames, CEO   Tel: 44-141-225-5900   Rev: $590
  Bus: *Temporary utility rental systems, compressors*   Fax: 44-141-225-5949   Emp: 2,127
      and accessories manufacturer.   www.aggreko.com
  NAICS: 332410, 333415, 333618

  AGGREKO INC.
  4607 W. Admiral Doyle Dr., New Iberia, Louisiana 70560
  CEO: Terry Dressel, Pres.   Tel: (337) 367-7884   %FO: 100
  Bus: *Provides temporary utility rental systems,*   Fax: (337) 367-0870
      compressors and accessories.

  AGGREKO INC.
  6747 Leopard, Corpus Christi, Texas 78409
  CEO: Mark Shedd, Sales   Tel: (361) 289-5684   %FO: 100
  Bus: *Engaged in critical air services.*   Fax: (361) 289-5687

  AGGREKO INC.
  3732 Magnolia St., Pearland, Texas 77584
  CEO: Bruce Pool, Sales   Tel: (713) 512-6700   %FO: 100
  Bus: *Engaged in event services*   Fax: (713) 512-6794

  AGGREKO INC.
  12000 Aerospace Ave., Ste. 300, Houston, Texas 77034
  CEO: George Walker   Tel: (713) 852-4500   %FO: 100
  Bus: *Generator sales.*   Fax: (713) 852-4590

- **ASCO PLC**
  Regent Centre, Regent Rd., Aberdeen AB11 5NS, Scotland, U.K.
  CEO: Claude Littner, Chmn.   Tel: 44-1224-580-396   Rev: $673
  Bus: *Provider of logistics and supply chain*   Fax: 44-1224-576-172   Emp: 1,150
      management services.   www.ascoplc.com
  NAICS: 488510, 541614

ASCO FREIGHT MANAGEMENT
13609 Industrial Rd., Ste. 107, Greensport, Houston, Texas 77105
CEO: Rick Higgens, VP   Tel: (713) 451-0008   %FO: 100
Bus: *Provider of logistics and supply chain*   Fax: (713) 451-1510
      management services.

ASCO USA LLC
3421 North Causeway Blvd., Ste. 502, Metairie, Louisiana 70009-6984
CEO: Danny M. Brown   Tel: (504) 832-8600   %FO: 100
Bus: *Provider of logistics and supply chain*   Fax: (504) 832-8620
      management services.

● **AVIAGEN LTD.**
11 Lothend Rd., Newbridge, Midlothian EH28 8SZ, Scotland, U.K.
CEO: Ian Panton, CEO   Tel: 44-131-333-1056
Bus: *Poultry-breeding.*   Fax: 44-131-333-3296
      www.aviagen.com

NAICS: 112320, 112330, 112340, 112390

   AVIAGEN INC.
   Cummings Research Park, 5015 Brandford Dr., Huntsville, Alabama 35805
   CEO: Derek Emmerson, VP North America   Tel: (256) 890-3800   %FO: 100
   Bus: *Poultry-breeding.*   Fax: (256) 890-3919

● **AXIS-SHIELD PLC**
Luna Place, Technology Park, Dundee DD2 1XA, Scotland, U.K.
CEO: Svein W. F. Lien, CEO   Tel: 44-1382-422-000   Rev: $101
Bus: *Diagnostic test mfr.*   Fax: 44-1382-561-201   Emp: 440
      www.axis-shield.com

NAICS: 325412, 325413

   AXIS-SHIELD USA
   10 Commerce Way, Norton, Massachusetts 02776
   CEO: John Sperzel   Tel: (508) 285-4870   %FO: 100
   Bus: *Supplier of point of care diagnostic*   Fax: (508) 285-4840
      products.

● **DEVRO PLC**
Gartferry Rd., Moodiesburn, Chryston, Glasgow G69 0JE, Scotland, U.K.
CEO: Graeme Y. Alexander, CEO   Tel: 44-1236-879-191   Rev: $260
Bus: *Produces collagen casings and film for sausage*   Fax: 44-1236-8111-005   Emp: 2,055
      products for the food industry.   www.devro.plc.uk
NAICS: 311612

   DEVRO-TEEPAK INC.
   915 North Michigan, Danville, Illinois 61832
   CEO: Doug Cunningham, Plant Mgr.   Tel: (217) 446-6460   %FO: 100
   Bus: *Produces collagen casings and film for*   Fax: (217) 442-2617
      sausage products.

● **FIRSTGROUP PLC**
395 King St., Aberdeen AB24 5RP, Scotland, U.K.
CEO: Moir Lockhead, CEO
Bus: *Provider of public bus services.*

Tel: 44-1224-650-100
Fax: 44-1224-650-140
www.firstgroup.com

Rev: $4,526
Emp: 61,897

NAICS: 485113, 485410, 485510

   FIRST SERVICES
   21406 Promontory Circle, San Antonio, Texas 78258
   CEO: Joy Johnson
   Bus: *Pre-owned bus sales*

Tel: (210) 481-3532
Fax: (210) 483-8940

%FO: 100

   FIRST STUDENT
   705 Central Ave., Ste. 300, Cincinnati, Ohio 45202
   CEO: Carey Paster, Pres.
   Bus: *Provider of transportation for students.*

Tel: (513) 684-8728
Fax: (513) 684-1694

%FO: 100
Emp: 13,000

   FIRSTGROUP AMERICA INC.
   705 Central Ave., Ste. 300, Cincinnati, Ohio 45202
   CEO: Bruce Ballard, Pres. & CEO
   Bus: *Provider of public transit contracting and*
      management services.

Tel: (513) 241-2200
Fax: (513) 419-3242

%FO: 100

● **HBOS PLC**
The Mound, Edinburgh EH1 1YZ, Scotland, U.K.
CEO: James R. Crosby, CEO
Bus: *General banking services.*

Tel: 44-131-470-2000
Fax: 44-131-243-5437
www.hbosplc.com

Rev: $40,111
Emp: 67,458

NAICS: 522110, 522291, 522292, 522294, 522390, 523110, 523120, 523920, 523930

   BANK OF SCOTLAND
   565 Fifth Ave., 5/F, New York, New York 10017
   CEO: Liz Wilson, Mgr.
   Bus: *International banking services.*

Tel: (212) 450-0800
Fax: (212) 557-9460

%FO: 100

   BANK OF SCOTLAND
   601 2nd Ave. S, Ste. 4380, Minneapolis, Minnesota 55402
   CEO: Katherine Oniffrey, Mgr.
   Bus: *International banking*

Tel: (612) 333-6990
Fax:

   BANK OF SCOTLAND
   660 S. Figueroa St., Los Angeles, California 90017
   CEO: Craig Wilson
   Bus: *International banking services.*

Tel: (213) 629-3057
Fax: (213) 489-3594

%FO: 100

   BANK OF SCOTLAND
   311 South Wacker Dr., Ste. 1625, Chicago, Illinois 60606
   CEO: Stephen Canpbell, Mgr.
   Bus: *International banking services.*

Tel: (312) 939-9710
Fax: (312) 939-9710

%FO: 100

   BANK OF SCOTLAND
   1420 5th Ave., Ste. 1475, Seattle, Washington 98101
   CEO: Brian Watters, Mgr.
   Bus: *International banking services.*

Tel: (206) 343-4895
Fax: (206) 343-4895

%FO: 100

BANK OF SCOTLAND
1200 Smith St., Ste. 1750, Houston, Texas 77002
CEO: Justin Alexander
Bus: *International banking services.*
Tel: (713) 651-1870
Fax: (713) 651-9714
%FO: 100

● **INDIGOVISION GORUP PLC**
Charles Darwin Bldg., The Edinburgh Tech, Bush Loan, Edinburgh EH26 0PJ, Scotland, U.K.
CEO: Oliver Vellacott, CEO
Bus: *Mfr. surveillance systems.*
Tel: 44-131-475-7200
Fax: 44-131-475-7201
www.indigovision.com
Rev: $3
Emp: 78
NAICS: 334119, 334220, 334413

INDIGOVISION USA INC.
50 Cragwood Rd., Ste. 111, South Plainfield, New Jersey 07080
CEO: Steve Wright, VP
Bus: *Mfr. surveillance systems.*
Tel: (908) 315-0288
Fax: (908) 822-0031
%FO: 100

● **J & J DENHOLM LTD.**
18 Woodside Crescent, Glasgow G3 7UL, Scotland, U.K.
CEO: John S. Denholm, Chmn.
Bus: *Management and consulting services to ship operators.*
Tel: 44-141-353-2090
Fax: 44-141-353-2190
www.denholm-group.co.uk
Rev: $178
Emp: 1,400
NAICS: 114111, 311712, 483111, 488510, 541614

ANGLO EASTERN USA INC.
10701 Corporate Dr., Ste. 138B, Stafford, Texas 77477
CEO: Captain A. Chopra
Bus: *Management and consulting services for ship operators.*
Tel: (281) 265-4814
Fax: (281) 265-7871
%FO: 100

● **JOHN WOOD GROUP PLC**
John Wood House, Greenwell Rd., Aberdeen AB12 3AX, Scotland, U.K.
CEO: Sir Ian Wood, CEO
Bus: *Oil and gas services.*
Tel: 44-1224-851-000
Fax: 44-1224-851-474
www.woodgroup.com
Rev: $2,288
Emp: 14,000
NAICS: 213112

ALLIANCE ENGINEERING
410 17th St., Ste. 1260, Denver, Colorado 80202
CEO: Bobbie Ireland
Bus: *Oil and gas services.*
Tel: (303) 350-2000
Fax: (303) 350-2000
%FO: 100

ALLIANCE WOOD GROUP ENGINEERING
16340 Park Ten Place Dr., Ste. 300, Houston, Texas 77084
CEO: Norbert Roobaert
Bus: *Engineering, design, procurement, project management and construction management of on- and offshore upstream oil and gas facilities and structures.*
Tel: (281) 828-6000
Fax: (281) 647-9701
%FO: 100

JOHN WOOD GROUP
17420 Katy Fwy., Ste. 300, Houston, Texas 77094
CEO: Bobbie Ireland
Bus: *Provider of oil and gas services.*
Tel: (281) 828-3500
Fax: (281) 828-3525
%FO: 100

JP KENNY INC.
17420 Katy Freeway, Ste. 100, Houston, Texas 77094
CEO: Alan Brackenridge   Tel: (281) 675-1000   %FO: 100
Bus: *Energy services.*   Fax: (281) 675-9827

MULTIPHASE SOLUTIONS INC.
Two Park Ten, 16300 Katy Freeway, Houston, Texas 77094
CEO: Michael Mai   Tel: (281) 646-1515   %FO: 100
Bus: *Energy services.*   Fax: (281) 646-8700

MUSTANG ENGINEERING
2830 Howe Rd., Ste. B, Martinez, California 94553
CEO: William G. Higgs   Tel: (925) 231-4151   %FO: 100
Bus: *Design and management services for oil and* Fax: (925) 231-4151
    gas markets.

MUSTANG ENGINEERING
2002 North Lois Ave., Ste. 300, Tampa, Florida 33607
CEO: Steve Beeston   Tel: (813) 876-2424   %FO: 100
Bus: *Design and management services for oil and* Fax: (813) 769-2372
    gas markets.

MUSTANG ENGINEERING
1600 Market St., Ste. 1430, Philadelphia, Pennsylvania 19103
CEO: Howard R. Otte   Tel: (267) 238-2424   %FO: 100
Bus: *Design and management services for oil and* Fax: (267) 238-2424
    gas markets.

MUSTANG ENGINEERING
1200 Highway 146 South, Ste. 200, La Porte, Texas 77571
CEO: William G. Higgs   Tel: (281) 206-6620   %FO: 100
Bus: *Design and management services for oil and* Fax: (281) 206-6621
    gas markets.

MUSTANG ENGINEERING HOLDINGS INC.
16001 Park Ten Place, Houston, Texas 77084
CEO: William G. Higgs, Co-Pres.   Tel: (713) 215-8000   %FO: 100
Bus: *Design and management services for oil and* Fax: (713) 215-8506
    gas markets.

● **MACFARLAND GROUP**
Clansman House, 21 Newton Place, Glasgow G3 7PY, Scotland, U.K.
CEO: Peter Duncan Atkinson, CEO & Mng. Dir.   Tel: 44-141-333-9666   Rev: $233
Bus: *Provides service-based packaging solutions* Fax: 44-141-333-4858   Emp: 1,349
    manufacture.   www.macfarlanegroup.net
NAICS: 322221, 322222, 322223, 322224, 326112, 326113, 326199, 561910

    MACFARLANE WESTERN FOAM, INC.
    33200 Lewis St., Union City, California 94587
    CEO: John McAuslan, Pres.   Tel: (510) 324-3626
    Bus: *Mfr. of foamed plastic products.*   Fax: (510) 324-3632   Emp: 200

● **MARTIN CURRIE LTD.**
20 Castle Terr., Saltire Court, Edinburgh EH1 2ES, Scotland, U.K.
CEO: Willie Watt, CEO   Tel: 44-131-229-5252   Rev: $84
Bus: *Engaged in investment banking services.*   Fax: 44-131-228-5959   Emp: 207
     www.martincurrie.com
NAICS: 523999

     MARTIN CURRIE INC.
     1350 Ave. of the Americas, Ste. 3010, New York, New York 10019
     CEO: Wilson Madden, VP   Tel: (212) 258-1900   %FO: 100
     Bus: *Engaged in investment banking services.*   Fax: (212) 258-1919

● **THE ROYAL BANK OF SCOTLAND GROUP PLC**
42 St. Andrew Square, Edinburgh EH2 2YE, Scotland, U.K.
CEO: Fred A. Goodwin, CEO   Tel: 44-131-556-8555   Rev: $48,729
Bus: *Financial services company; banking, insurance,*   Fax: 44-131-557-6140   Emp: 126,100
investment advisory services.   www.rbs.com
NAICS: 522110, 522210, 522291, 522310, 523110, 524210, 551111

     CITIZENS FINANCIAL GROUP, INC.
     One Citizens Plaza, Providence, Rhode Island 02903
     CEO: William J. DeBlois, Chmn. & Pres. & CEO   Tel: (401) 456-7000   %FO: 100
     Bus: *Financial services company banking,*   Fax: (401) 456-7819   Emp: 15,500
     insurance, investment advisory services.
     Holding company.

     GREENWICH CAPITAL MARKETS, INC.
     600 Steamboat Rd, Ste. 2, Greenwich, Connecticut 06830
     CEO: Benjamin Carpenter, CEO   Tel: (203) 625-2700   %FO: 100
     Bus: *Financial services company; banking,*   Fax: (203) 625-7941   Emp: 563
     insurance, investment advisory services.

     RBS LYNK INC.
     600 Morgan Falls Rd., Ste. 260, Atlanta, Georgia 30350
     CEO: Jim Jaworski, Pres. & CEO   Tel: (770) 396-1616
     Bus: *Financial services.*   Fax: (770) 399-2520

     THE ROYAL BANK OF SCOTLAND
     Travis St., Ste. 6070, Houston, Texas 77002
     CEO: Jim McBride   Tel: (713) 221-2400
     Bus: *Financial services.*   Fax: (713) 221-2400

     THE ROYAL BANK OF SCOTLAND
     110 Park Ave., 10/F, New York, New York 10178
     CEO: Garry Popofsky   Tel: (212) 401-3200
     Bus: *Financial services.*   Fax: (212) 401-3404

     THE ROYAL BANK OF SCOTLAND/ RBS LOMBARD INC.
     425 California, Ste. 2000, San Francisco, California 94104
     CEO: Marti MacInnes   Tel: (415) 249-4800
     Bus: *Financial services.*   Fax: (415) 249-4809

THE ROYAL BANK OF SCOTLAND/ RBS LOMBARD INC.
222 South Riverside Plaza, 15/F, Chicago, Illinois 60606
CEO: Laird Boulden, Pres.   Tel: (312) 589-8550
Bus: *Asset finance.*   Fax: (312) 589-8559   Emp: 19

● **SCOTTISH & NEWCASTLE, PLC.**
33 Ellersly Rd., Edinburgh EH12 6HX, Scotland, U.K.
CEO: Tony Froggatt, CEO   Tel: 44-131-528-2000   Rev: $8,537
Bus: *Mfr./owner of breweries for distribution of beers.*   Fax: 44-870-333-2121   Emp: 15,715
                                           www.scottish-newcastle.com
NAICS: 312120, 424810

    SCOTTISH & NEWCASTLE IMPORTERS
    8374 Woodlawn Ave., San Gabriel, California 91775-1734
    CEO: Paul Zappia, Mgr.   Tel: (626) 285-5391   %FO: 100
    Bus: *Importer/distributor beer*   Fax: (626) 285-5391

    SCOTTISH & NEWCASTLE IMPORTERS
    4040 Civic Center Dr., San Rafael, California 94903
    CEO: Kevin Moodie, Pres.   Tel: (415) 479-5700   %FO: 100
    Bus: *Importer/distributor beer*   Fax: Emp: 64

● **SCOTTISH POWER PLC**
One Atlantic Quay, Glasgow G2 8SP, Scotland, U.K.
CEO: Ian M. Russell, CEO   Tel: 44-141-248-8200   Rev: $12,943
Bus: *Generation, transmission and distribution of*   Fax: 44-141-248-8300   Emp: 16,142
     electricity.   www.scottishpower.plc.uk
NAICS: 221111, 221112, 221119, 221121, 221122, 424720, 486210, 523130, 523140

    PACIFICORP
    825 Northeast Multnomah St., Portland, Oregon 97232
    CEO: Judith A. Johansen, Pres. & CEO   Tel: (503) 813-5000   %FO: 100
    Bus: *Engaged in electric utility services.*   Fax: (503) 813-7247   Emp: 6,654

    PPM ATLANTIC RENEWABLE
    3311 Church St., Ste. 210, Richmond, Virginia 23233
    CEO: Theo J. de Wolff, Mng. Dir.   Tel: (804) 965-9530
    Bus: *Alternative energy sources.*   Fax: (703) 995-0770

    PPM ENERGY, INC.
    1125 NW Couch, Ste. 700, Portland, Oregon 97209
    CEO: Terry F. Hudgens, Pres. & CEO   Tel: (503) 796-7000
    Bus: *Energy & utilities.*   Fax: (503) 796-6901   Emp: 168

● **SPARROWS OFFSHORE SERVICES LIMITED**
Denmore Rd., Bridge of Don, Aberdeen AB23 8JW, Scotland, U.K.
CEO: Ken Scott, Mng. Dir.   Tel: 44-1224-704-868   Rev: $111
Bus: *Crane management and engineering services.*   Fax: 44-1224-825-191   Emp: 600
                                           www.sparrows.co.uk
NAICS: 333132

ENERGY CRANES LLC
6707 Northwinds Dr., Houston, Texas 77041
CEO: David Pearcy
Bus: *Crane management and engineering services.*
Tel: (713) 896-0002
Fax: (713) 856-5442
%FO: 100

ENERGY CRANES LLC
17621 LA Highway 82, Intracoastal City, Louisiana 70510
CEO: John Jordan
Bus: *Crane management and engineering services.*
Tel: (337) 892-0704
Fax: (337) 892-0709
%FO: 100

ENERGY CRANES LLC
5864 Kooiman Rd., Theodore, Alabama 36582
CEO: John Jordan
Bus: *Crane management and engineering services.*
Tel: (251) 654-0006
Fax: (251) 654-0273
%FO: 100

ENERGY CRANES LLC
279 Thompson Rd., Houma, Louisiana 70363
CEO: Jim Hicks
Bus: *Crane management and engineering services.*
Tel: (985) 873-7969
Fax: (985) 873-8932
%FO: 100

ENERGY CRANES LLC
29451 LA Hwy. 333, Intracoastal City, Louisiana 70510
CEO: Jim Hicks
Bus: *Crane management and engineering services.*
Tel: (337) 898-1357
Fax: (337) 898-9431
%FO: 100

● **SUBSEA 7, INC. (JV DSND AND HALLIBURTON)**
Peregrine Rd., Westhill Business Park, Westhill, Aberdeenshire AB32 6JL, Scotland, U.K.
CEO: Mel Fitzgerald, CEO
Bus: *Deep water construction ships for pipe laying and surveying.*
NAICS: 486990
Tel: 44-1224-344-300
Fax: 44-1224-344-600
www.subsea7.com
Rev: $813
Emp: 3,000

SUBSEA 7, INC.
15990 North Barkers Landing, Houston, Texas 77079
CEO: Mel Fitzgerald, member
Bus: *Subsea engineering & construction.*
Tel: (281) 966-7600
Fax: (281) 766-7623
%FO: 100
Emp: 75

● **THE WEIR GROUP PLC.**
149 Newlands Rd., Cathcart, Glasgow G44 4EX, Scotland, U.K.
CEO: Sir Robert Smith, Chmn.
Bus: *Mfr. valves, slurry pumps and process*
NAICS: 332912, 332919, 333995, 333996
Tel: 44-141-637-7111
Fax: 44-141-637-2221
www.weir.co.uk
Rev: $1,411
Emp: 7,642

WEIR FLOWAY INC.
2494 S. Railroad Ave., PO Box 164, Fresno, California 93707
CEO: Raymond Dunn, Pres.
Bus: *Mfr. slurry pumps.*
Tel: (559) 442-4000
Fax: (559) 442-3098
%FO: 100
Emp: 175

WEIR SLURRY GROUP, INC.
2701 S. Stoughton Rd., Madison, Wisconsin 53716
CEO: Chris Gilbert
Bus: *Mfr. centrifugal slurry pumps and process equipment.*
Tel: (608) 221-2261
Fax: (608) 221-5807
%FO: 100

WEIR SPECIALTY PUMPS INC.
PO Box 209, Salt Lake City, Utah 84110
CEO: Joe Roark, Prtn.   Tel: (801) 359-8731   %FO: 100
Bus: *Mfr. centrifugal slurry pumps and process* Fax: (801) 355-9303   Emp: 2,634
     equipment.

WEIR VALVES & CONTROLS USA INC.
285 Canal St., Salem, Massachusetts 01970
CEO: Chris Gilbert, Pres.   Tel: (978) 744-5690
Bus: *Industrial valves*   Fax: (978) 741-3626   Emp: 160

● **WOLFSON MICROELECTRONICS PLC**
Westfield House, 26 Westfield Rd., Edinburgh EH11 2QB, Scotland, U.K.
CEO: David Milne, CEO   Tel: 44-131-272-7000   Rev: $119
Bus: *Mfr. and sale of mixed-signal microchips.* Fax: 44-131-272-7001   Emp: 189
                               www.wolfsonmicro.com
NAICS: 334119, 334413

    WOLFSON MICROELECTRONICS INC.
    16875 W. Bernardo Dr., Ste. 280, San Diego, California 92127
    CEO: Brian McLean, CEO   Tel: (858) 676-5090   %FO: 100
    Bus: *Mfr. mixed-signal microchips.*   Fax: (858) 676-0484

● **WOOD MACKENZIE**
Kintore House, 74-77 Queen St., Edinburgh EH2 4NS, Scotland, U.K.
CEO: Paul Gregory, CEO   Tel: 44-131-243-4400   Rev: $59
Bus: *Market research and consulting services to the* Fax: 44-131-243-4495   Emp: 272
     energy, biotech, pharmaceutical and animal health www.woodmac.com
     industries.
NAICS: 541611, 621511

    WOOD MACKENZIE INC.
    30 Rowes Wharf, 2/F, Boston, Massachusetts 02110
    CEO: Matthew Calish   Tel: (617) 535-1000   %FO: 100
    Bus: *Market research and consulting services.* Fax: (617) 535-1333

    WOOD MACKENZIE INC.
    5847 San Felipe, 10/F, Houston, Texas 77057
    CEO: Bob Fleck   Tel: (713) 470-1600   %FO: 100
    Bus: *Market research and consulting services.* Fax: (713) 470-1701

Singapore

- **ASIA PULP & PAPER CO. LTD. (APP)**
  Jl. M.H. Thamrin No.51, 099253, Singapore
  CEO: Teguh Ganda Wijaya, Dir.
  Bus: *Engaged in the manufacture of paper and pulp for printing, including colored and uncoated papers.*
  NAICS: 322121, 322224

Tel: 65-6477-6118	Rev: $3,100
Fax: 65-6477-6116	Emp: 79,000
www.asiapulppaper.com	

  ASIA PULP & PAPER TRADING, INC.
  17785 Center Ct. Dr. North, Cerritos, California 90703
  CEO: Anthony Atamimi
  Bus: *Mfr. of paper and pulp for printing, including colored and uncoated papers*

Tel: (562) 916-7216	%FO: 100
Fax: (562) 916-7216	

- **BIL INTERNATIONAL LIMITED**
  16-02/03 Tung Centre, 20 Collyer Quay, 043319, Singapore
  CEO: Arun Amarsi, CEO
  Bus: *Investment management services.*
  NAICS: 523999

Tel: 65-6438-0002	Rev: $298
Fax: 65-6435-0040	Emp: 1,928
www.bilgroup.com	

  MOLOKAI PROPERTIES LTD., DIV. BIL
  745 Fort St., Mall 600, Honolulu, Hawaii 96813
  CEO: Peter Nicholas
  Bus: *Real estate property investments.*

Tel: (808) 531-0158	%FO: 30
Fax: (808) 531-0158	

- **CAPITALAND LIMITED**
  168 Robinson Rd., Capital Tower #30-01, Singapore
  CEO: Liew Mun leong, CEO
  Bus: *Resorts, hotels and real estate management.*
  NAICS: 531110, 531190, 531390

Tel: 65-6823-3200	Rev: $2,322
Fax: 65-6820-2202	Emp: 10,668
www.capitaland.com.sg	

  RAFFLES L'ERMITAGE
  9291 Burton Way, Beverly Hills, California 90210
  CEO: Jack Nader, Mgr.
  Bus: *Hotel resort.*

Tel: (310) 278-3344	%FO: 100
Fax: (310) 278-8247	

  SWISSOTEL CHICAGO
  323 East Wacker Dr., Chicago, Illinois 60601
  CEO: Matt Rose, Mgr.
  Bus: *Hotels.*

Tel: (312) 565-0565	%FO: 100
Fax: (312) 565-0540	

  SWISSOTEL DRAKE
  440 Park Ave., New York, New York 10022
  CEO: David Gibson, Mgr.
  Bus: *Hotels.*

Tel: (212) 421-0900	%FO: 100
Fax: (212) 371-4190	

- **CHARTERED SEMICONDUCTOR MANUFACTURING LTD.**
  60 Woodlands Industrial Park, Street Two, 738406, Singapore
  CEO: Song Hwee Chia, Pres. & CEO
  Bus: *Mfr. semiconductor chips.*

  Tel: 65-362-2838
  Fax: 65-362-2938
  www.csminc.com

  Rev: $932
  Emp: 3,606

  NAICS: 334413

  > **CHARTERED SEMICONDUCTOR MANUFACTURING LTD.**
  > 807 Las Cimas Pkwy., Ste. 250, Austin, Texas 78746
  > CEO: Kevin Meyer, Mng. Dir.
  > Bus: *Mfr. semiconductor chips.*
  >
  > Tel: (512) 899-4850
  > Fax: (512) 899-4850
  >
  > %FO: 100

  > **CHARTERED SEMICONDUCTOR MANUFACTURING LTD.**
  > 1450 McCandless Dr., Milpitas, California 95035
  > CEO: Pamela Rosen, Pres.
  > Bus: *Mfr. semiconductor chips.*
  >
  > Tel: (408) 941-1100
  > Fax: (408) 941-1101
  >
  > %FO: 100

- **CREATIVE TECHNOLOGY LTD.**
  31 International Business Park, 609921, Singapore
  CEO: Sim Wong Hoo, CEO
  Bus: *Mfr. digital entertainment products.*

  Tel: 65-6895-4000
  Fax: 65-6895-4999
  www.creative.com

  Rev: $815
  Emp: 4,700

  NAICS: 334112

  > **CAMBRIDGE SOUNDWORKS, INC.**
  > 100 Brickstone Sq., Andover, Massachusetts 01810
  > CEO: Michael Sullivan, PR
  > Bus: *Mfr. digital entertainment products.*
  >
  > Tel: (978) 623-4400
  > Fax: (978) 623-4400
  >
  > %FO: 100

  > **CREATIVE LABS, INC.**
  > 1901 McCarthy Boulevard, Milpitas, California 95035
  > CEO: Craig McHugh, Pres. & CEO
  > Bus: *Mfr. digital entertainment products.*
  >
  > Tel: (408) 428-6600
  > Fax: (408) 428-6611
  >
  > %FO: 100

- **DBS GROUP HOLDINGS LTD.**
  6 Shenton Way, Tower One, 068809, Singapore
  CEO: Jackson Peter Tai, Pres.
  Bus: *Commercial banking services.*

  Tel: 65-6327-2265
  Fax: 65-6221-6370
  www.dbs.com.sg

  Rev: $3,891
  Emp: 11,454

  NAICS: 522110

  > **DBS BANK LOS ANGELES AGENCY**
  > 445 South Figueroa St., Ste. 3550, Los Angeles, California 90017
  > CEO: Andrew Ko
  > Bus: *Banking services.*
  >
  > Tel: (213) 627-0222
  > Fax: (213) 627-0228

- **DENSELIGHT SEMICONDUCTORS PTE**
  6 Changi North St. 2, 498831, Singapore
  CEO: Yee-Loy Lam, CEO
  Bus: *Photonic microchips and modules manufacture.*

  Tel: 65-6415-4488
  Fax: 65-6415-4414
  www.denselight.com

  NAICS: 334413

DENSELIGHT SEMICONDUCTORS INC.
900 East Hamilton Ave., Campbell, California 95008
CEO: Sunil Phatak, VP
Bus: *Photonic microchips and modules manufacture and sales.*
Tel: (408) 879-7255
Fax: (408) 879-7256

● **FLEXTRONICS INTERNATIONAL LTD.**
2 Changi South Lane, 286123, Singapore
CEO: Michael E. Marks, CEO & Mng. Dir.
Bus: *Provides contract electronics manufacturing services.*
Tel: 65-6299-8888
Fax: 65-6543-1888
www.flextronics.com
Rev: $15,908
Emp: 82,000
NAICS: 334119, 334210, 334412, 334413, 334418

FLEXTRONICS
1 Upland Rd., Bldg. N1, Norwood, Massachusetts 02062
CEO: Juns Zhao
Bus: *Enclosure systems manufacture*
Tel: (888) 826-5121
Fax: (781) 386-6372
%FO: 100

FLEXTRONICS DESIGN
17034 Camino San Bernardo, San Diego, California 92127
CEO: Craig Wright, Mgr.
Bus: *Enclosure systems manufacture.*
Tel: (858) 674-2444
Fax: (858) 674-2445
%FO: 100

FLEXTRONICS INTERNATIONAL
2090 Fortune Dr., San Jose, California 95131
CEO: Michael McNamara, VP
Bus: *Enclosure systems manufacture.*
Tel: (408) 576-7000
Fax: (408) 576-7454
%FO: 100
Emp: 141

● **GES INTERNATIONAL LIMITED**
28 Marsiling Ln., 739152, 739152, Singapore
CEO: Daniel B. W. Yeong, Mng. Dir.
Bus: *Computer hardware design manufacture.*
Tel: 65-6732-9898
Fax: 65-6368-6225
www.ges.com.sg
Rev: $316
Emp: 1,827
NAICS: 334111, 334119, 334419

ELTECH ELECTRONICS INC.
790 Chelmsford St., Lowell, Massachusetts 01851
CEO: John Vallone, Pres.
Bus: *Computer hardware design manufacture and sales.*
Tel: (978) 459-4434
Fax: (978) 459-9925
%FO: 100

● **GLOBAL SOURCES LTD.**
1 Sims Lane #08-01, Singapore
CEO: Merle A. Hinrichs, Chmn. & CEO
Bus: *On-line import and export company providing e-commerce services.*
Tel: 65-6547-2608
Fax: 65-6547-2338
www.globalsources.com
Rev: $106
Emp: 2,017
NAICS: 511120, 516110, 519190

GLOBAL SOURCES USA, INC.
4718 E. Cactus Rd., Ste. 108, Phoenix, Arizona 85032
CEO: Merle Hinrichs, Pres.
Bus: *Engaged in on-line marketing.*
Tel: (602) 978-7501
Fax: (602) 978-7512
%FO: 100

TRADE SOURCES, INC.
Lake Amir Office Park, 1200 Bayhill Dr., Ste. 116, San Bruno, California 94066
CEO: Chuck Armitage, Gen. Mgr.   Tel: (650) 742-7900   %FO: 100
Bus: *New dealers*   Fax: (650) 742-7962

WORDRIGHT ENTERPRISES, INC.
2508 Park Place, Evanston, Illinois 60201
CEO: Judy Trusdell   Tel: (847) 869-3740   %FO: 100
Bus: *Engaged in e-commerce.*   Fax: (847) 869-3755

• **INFINITI SOLUTIONS PTE LTD.**
17 Changi Business Park Central 1, 06-09 Honeywell Bldg., 486073, Singapore
CEO: Boon Hwee Koh, Chmn.   Tel: 65-6587-7358   Rev: $55
Bus: *Pre-production microchip test services.*   Fax: 65-6784-0301   Emp: 1,669
                                         www.infinitisolutions.com
NAICS: 334413

    INFINITI SOLUTIONS PTE LTD.
    2006 Martin Ave., Santa Clara, California 95050
    CEO: George Liu, VP Operations   Tel: (408) 988-2181   %FO: 100
    Bus: *Pre-production microchip test services*   Fax: (408) 988-0885

    INFINITI SOLUTIONS PTE LTD.
    1605 Mabury Rd., San Jose, California 95133
    CEO: Ram Pratura, VP   Tel: (408) 923-7300   %FO: 100
    Bus: *Pre-production microchip test services*   Fax: (408) 251-1993

• **INNOMEDIA, INC.**
10 Science Park Rd., Ste. 03-04, Alpha Singapore Science Park II, 117684, Singapore
CEO: Kai-wa Ng, Chmn. & CEO   Tel: 65-6872-0828
Bus: *Computer telephone and videoconferencing*   Fax: 65-6872-0900
    equipment manufacture.   www.innomedia.com
NAICS: 334290, 334310

    INNOMEDIA, INC.
    186 Topaz St., Milpitas, California 95035
    CEO: Wymond Choy, VP   Tel: (408) 432-5400   %FO: 100
    Bus: *Computer telephone and videoconferencing*   Fax: (408) 432-5404
    equipment manufacture and sales.

• **INTRACO LIMITED**
348 Jalan Boon Lay, 619529, 188024, Singapore
CEO: Teng Theng Dar, CEO   Tel: 65-6586-6777   Rev: $241
Bus: *Diversified holding company; food, engineering,*   Fax: 65-6316-3128   Emp: 113
    telecommunications and automotive dealerships.   www.intraco.com.
NAICS: 112120, 334111, 334119, 334290, 334413, 423610, 423620, 423690, 424460, 424490, 517910, 523130, 523140, 541330, 561499

    INTERNATIONAL TRADE COMPANY
    6456 Hartwell St., Dearborn, Michigan 48126
    CEO: Ibrahim Mazeh, Pres.   Tel: (313) 204-6325   %FO: 100
    Bus: *Vinyls and fabrics manufacture for auto*   Fax: (313) 204-6325
    industry.

INTRACO CORPORATION
530 Stephenson Hwy., Troy, Michigan 48083
CEO: Nicola Antakli, Pres.   Tel: (248) 585-6900   %FO: 100
Bus: *Diversified holding company; food,*   Fax: (248) 585-6900   Emp: 50
engineering, telecommunications and
automotive dealerships.

INTRACO HOLDING PARTNERSHIP
2505 Second Ave., Ste. 300, Seattle, Washington 98121
CEO: Mike Miller, Pres.   Tel: (206) 625-9226   %FO: 100
Bus: *Real estate development.*   Fax: (206) 625-9226

INTRACO INC.
1014 Santee St., Los Angeles, California 90015
CEO: Sang H. Nam, Pres.   Tel: (213) 747-8809
Bus: *Costume jewelry manufacture.*   Fax: (213) 747-8809   Emp: 17

INTRACO INC.
1068 Grand Ave., St. Paul, Minnesota 55105
CEO: Sally Kahn, Mgr.   Tel: (651) 227-5819
Bus: *Women's clothing manufacture and sales.*   Fax: (651) 227-5819

INTRACO INC.
7157 Shady Oak Rd., Eden Prairie, Minnesota 55344
CEO: Danna Atherton, Pres.   Tel: (952) 253-0834   %FO: 100
Bus: *Sale of woman's clothing & accessories.*   Fax: Emp: 130

INTRACO INC.
2397 Hwy. 23, Oskaloosa, Iowa 52577
CEO: Gary Hall, CEO   Tel: (641) 673-8451   %FO: 100
Bus: *Mfr. of agricultural livestock & poultry feed*   Fax: Emp: 20
equipment.

● **KIM ENG ONG ASIA HOLDINGS LTD.**
9 Temasek Boulevard, #39-00 Suntec Tower Two, 038989, Singapore
CEO: Gloria K. Y. Lee, Chmn.   Tel: 65-6336-9090   Rev: $74
Bus: *Securities brokerage services.*   Fax: 65-6339-6003   Emp: 1,229
www.kimeng.com

NAICS: 523120, 523920, 523930

    KIM ENG SECURITIES USA INC.
    406 East 50th St., New York, New York 10022
    CEO: Khin Go   Tel: (212) 688-8886   %FO: 100
    Bus: *Securities brokerage services.*   Fax: (212) 688-3500

● **NEPTUNE ORIENT LINES LIMITED**
456 Alexandra Rd., NOL Bldg., 119962, Singapore
CEO: David Lim, Pres. & CEO   Tel: 65-6278-9000   Rev: $6,545
Bus: *Container shipping and logistics.*   Fax: 65-6278-4900   Emp: 11,304
www.nol.com.sg

NAICS: 483111, 488510, 541614

APL LIMITED
1111 Broadway, Oakland, California 94607
CEO: Ron Widdows, CEO
Bus: *Engaged in container shipping and logistics.*　Tel: (510) 272-8000　%FO: 100
Fax: (510) 272-7421

APL LOGISTICS, LTD.
1111 Broadway, Oakland, California 94607
CEO: David Lim, CEO　Tel: (510) 272-8000　%FO: 100
Bus: *Logistics services.*　Fax: (510) 272-7941　Emp: 4,000

● **OVERSEA-CHINESE BANKING CORP.**
65 Chulia St., OCBC Centre, 049513, Singapore
CEO: Cheong Choong Kong, Chmn.　Tel: 65-530-1515　Rev: $2,841
Bus: *Financial services, including consumer, corporate*　Fax: 65-533-7955
　and international banking, investment　www.ocbc.com.sg
　management, global treasury, stock broking and
　financial services.
NAICS: 522110, 523110

OVERSEA-CHINESE BANKING CORP LTD (OCBC)
1000 Wilshire Boulevard, Ste. 1940, Los Angeles, California 90017
CEO: Melvin Ang Yong Sia　Tel: (213) 624-1189　%FO: 100
Bus: *Provides loans and advances and financial*　Fax: (213) 624-1386
　services.

OVERSEA-CHINESE BANKING CORP LTD.
1700 Broadway, 18/F, New York, New York 10019
CEO: Wee Tiong Seng, Mgr.　Tel: (212) 586-6222　%FO: 100
Bus: *Provides loans and advances and financial*　Fax: (212) 586-0636　Emp: 18
　services.

● **RAFFLES HOLDINGS LTD.**
2 Stamford Rd., #06-01, Raffles City Convention Centre, 178882, Singapore
CEO: Jennie K. Y. Chua, CEO　Tel: 65-6339-8377　Rev: $322
Bus: *Worldwide hotel chain.*　Fax: 65-6339-1713　Emp: 3,283
　www.rafflesholdings.com
NAICS: 721110

RAFFLES L'ERMITAGE
9291 Burton Way, Beverly Hills, California 90210
CEO: Jack Naderkhani, Mgr.　Tel: (310) 278-3344　%FO: 100
Bus: *Luxury hotel accommodations.*　Fax: (310) 278-3344

SWISSOTEL CORPORATION
323 E. Wacker Dr., Chicago, Illinois 60601
CEO: Andreas Meinhold, VP　Tel: (312) 565-0565　%FO: 100
Bus: *Hotel chain.*　Fax: (312) 565-0540

THE DRAKE HOTEL
440 Park Ave., New York, New York 10022
CEO: Thomas Klein, Pres.　Tel: (212) 421-0900　%FO: 100
Bus: *Hotel chain.*　Fax:

● **SINGAPORE AIRLINES LTD.**
Airline House, 25 Airline Rd., 819829, Singapore
CEO: Chew Choon Seng, CEO
Bus: *International air transport services.*

Tel: 65-6541-4885
Fax: 65-6542-3002
www.singaporeair.com

Rev: $5,796
Emp: 29,734

NAICS: 481111, 481112, 481212

SINGAPORE AIRLINES LTD
100 Cummings Centre, Ste. 327G, Beverly, Massachusetts 01915
CEO: Edwin Pereira, Mgr.
Bus: *International airline.*

Tel: (800) 742-3333
Fax:

%FO: 100

SINGAPORE AIRLINES LTD
5670 Wilshire Blvd., Ste. 1800, Los Angeles, California 90036
CEO: Tee Hooi Teoh, Mgr.
Bus: *International airline.*

Tel: (323) 934-8833
Fax: (323) 934-3049

%FO: 100
Emp: 135

SINGAPORE AIRLINES LTD
122 South Michigan Ave., Ste. 1710, Chicago, Illinois 60603
CEO: Terri Steinberg, Sales
Bus: *International airline.*

Tel: (800) 742-3333
Fax: (312) 939-4079

%FO: 100

SINGAPORE AIRLINES LTD.
55 East 59th St., Ste. 20B, New York, New York 10022
CEO: Walt Meyer, Mgr.
Bus: *International air transport services.*

Tel: (212) 644-8801
Fax: (212) 888-6645

%FO: 100

SINGAPORE AIRLINES LTD.
333 Bush St., Ste. 1500, San Francisco, California 94104
CEO: Edwin Kwee, Mgr.
Bus: *International air transport services.*

Tel: (415) 781-7304
Fax: (415) 296-8080

%FO: 100

SINGAPORE AIRLINES LTD.
3400 Peachtree Rd. NE, Atlanta, Georgia 30326
CEO: Mark Hoffland, Mgr.
Bus: *International air transport services.*

Tel: (404) 233-7300
Fax: (404) 233-1707

%FO: 100

● **SINGAPORE TECHNOLOGIES ENGINEERING LTD.**
51 Cuppage Rd., #09-08 StarHub Centre, 229469, Singapore
CEO: Tan Pheng Hock, Pres. & CEO
Bus: *Holding company engaged in engineering services*
for auto, aerospace and marine.

Tel: 65-6722-1818
Fax: 65-6720-2293
www.stengg.com

Rev: $1,800
Emp: 11,619

NAICS: 333298, 336611, 541330, 811219, 811310

INTELECT TECHNOLOGIES, INC.
1225 Commerce, Richardson, Texas 75081
CEO: Kim Hock, CEO
Bus: *Mfr. & design of electronic*
telecommunication equipment.

Tel: (972) 367-2100
Fax: (972) 367-2200

%FO: 100
Emp: 15

SAN ANTONIO AEROSPACE LP (SAA)
9800 John Saunders Rd., San Antonio, Texas 78216
CEO: Tay Kok Khiang, Pres.   Tel: (210) 293-3200   %FO: 100
Bus: *Provides maintenance services for a wide*   Fax: (210) 293-2642   Emp: 543
range of narrow-body and wide-body

ST MOBILE AEROSPACE ENGINEERING INC. (MAE)
2100 9th St., Brookley Complex, Mobile, Alabama 36615
CEO: Ronnie Koh, Pres.   Tel: (251) 438-8888   %FO: 100
Bus: *Engaged in heavy maintenance and repair*   Fax: (251) 438-8892   Emp: 1,094
of narrow-body and wide-body aircraft.

VT HALTER MARINE
900 Bayou Casotte Pkwy., Pascagoula, Mississippi 39581
CEO: Boyd E. King, CEO   Tel: (228) 769-8333   %FO: 100
Bus: *Ship building & repairing.*   Fax: (228) 696-6899   Emp: 500

VT KINETICS
3800 Richardson Rd. South, Hope Hull, Alabama 36043
CEO: WU Tzu Chien, Pres.   Tel: (334) 284-8665   %FO: 100
Bus: *Design and engineering services for military* Fax: (334) 613-6302
vehicles.

VT MILTOPE
3800 Richardson Rd. South, Hope Hull, Alabama 36043
CEO: Thomas R. Dickenson, Pres. & CEO   Tel: (334) 284-8665   %FO: 100
Bus: *Industrial & military computer systems.*   Fax: (334) 613-6302

VT SYSTEMS
99 Canal Center Plaza, Ste. 210, Alexandria, Virginia 22314
CEO: John Coburn, Pres.   Tel: (703) 739-2610   %FO: 100
Bus: *Provides maintenance services for a wide*   Fax: (703) 739-2611   Emp: 665
range of narrow-body and wide-body

● SINGAPORE TELECOMMUNICATIONS LTD.
31 Exeter Rd., Comcentre, 239732, Singapore
CEO: Hsien Yang Lee, Pres. & CEO   Tel: 65-6838-3388   Rev: $7,121
Bus: *International telecommunications services &* Fax: 65-6732-8428   Emp: 19,081
equipment.   www.singtel.com
NAICS: 443112, 517110, 517211, 517212, 517410, 517510, 517910, 518111, 518210, 519190, 541519, 561421,
561499

SINGAPORE TELECOM USA
8770 West Bryn Mawr, Ste. 1302, Chicago, Illinois 60631
CEO: Lucas Chow   Tel: (773) 867-8122
Bus: *Representative office; service/sales*   Fax: (773) 867-8121
telecommunications services/equipment.

SINGAPORE TELECOM USA
363 N. Sam Houston Pkwy. East, Ste. 1100, Houston, Texas 77060
CEO: Lucas Chow   Tel: (281) 405-2626
Bus: *Representative office; service/sales*   Fax: (281) 405-2627
telecommunications services/equipment.

SINGAPORE TELECOM USA
203 Redwood Shores Pkwy., Ste. 100, Redwood City, California 94065
CEO: Lim Toon, CEO   Tel: (650) 508-6800
Bus: *Representative office; service/sales*   Fax: (650) 508-1578   Emp: 50
    telecommunications services/equipment.

SINGAPORE TELECOM USA
1 Landmark Sq., Ste. 300, Stamford, Connecticut 06901
CEO: Lisa Inoue, Mgr.   Tel: (203) 323-9690   %FO: 100
Bus: *Representative office; service/sales*   Fax: (203) 323-9948
    telecommunications services/equipment.

• **STATS CHIPPAC LTD.**
10 Ang Mo Kio St. 65, #05-17/20 Techpoint, 768442, Singapore
CEO: Tan Lay Koon, Pres. & CEO   Tel: 65-6824-7777   Rev: $769
Bus: *Mfr. lead frame and laminate packaging for*   Fax: 65-6720-7823   Emp: 11,694
    semiconductors.   www.statschippac.com
NAICS: 334413

    FASTRAMP TEST SERVICES
    1768 McCandless Dr., Milpitas, California 95035
    CEO: Mark Kelly, Pres.   Tel: (408) 586-0600   %FO: 100
    Bus: *Mfr. of semiconductors.*   Fax: (408) 586-0601   Emp: 100

    STATS CHIPPAC INC.
    1711 West Greentree, Ste. 117, Tempe, Arizona 85284
    CEO: Philip Wingate, Principal   Tel: (480) 222-1700   %FO: 100
    Bus: *Mfr. of electronic components.*   Fax: (480) 961-8181   Emp: 25

    STATS CHIPPAC LTD.
    47400 Kato Dr., Fremont, California 94538
    CEO: Jeffrey R. Osmun, Pres.   Tel: (510) 979-8000   %FO: 100
    Bus: *Mfr. integrated circuits for semiconductor*   Fax: (510) 979-8001
    manufacture.

    STATS CHIPPAC TEST SERVICES, INC.
    9868 Scranton Rd., San Diego, California 92121
    CEO: Mark Kelly, Pres.   Tel: (858) 550-8200   %FO: 100
    Bus: *Mfr. of semiconductors.*   Fax: (858) 550-8238

• **TIMES PUBLISHING LIMITED**
Times Centre, 1 New Industrial Rd., 536196, Singapore
CEO: Lai Seck Khui, Pres. & CEO   Tel: 65-6213-9288   Rev: $261
Bus: *Engaged in publishing, distribution, commercial*   Fax: 65-6284-4733
    printing, and online and retail bookstores.   www.timespublishing.sg
NAICS: 323110, 323111, 323115, 323117, 323119, 424920, 451211, 511130, 511140, 541860, 561920

    MARSHALL CAVENDISH CORPORATION
    99 White Plains Rd., Tarrytown, New York 10591
    CEO: Albert Lee, Pres.   Tel: (914) 332-8888   %FO: 100
    Bus: *Engaged in book publishing.*   Fax: (914) 332-8882   Emp: 40

- **UNITED OVERSEAS BANK LTD.**
  80 Raffles Place, UOB Plaza, 048624, Singapore
  CEO: Wee Cho Yaw, Chmn. & CEO
  Bus: *Commercial banking and financial services.*

  Tel: 65-6533-9898
  Fax: 65-6534-2334
  www.uob.com.sg

  Rev: $2,910
  Emp: 13,574

  NAICS: 522110, 523991, 525920

  UNITED OVERSEAS BANK LTD.
  777 S. Figueroa St., Ste. 518, Los Angeles, California 90017
  CEO: Chen Hoong, Gen. Mgr.
  Bus: *Commercial banking and financial services.*

  Tel: (213) 623-8042
  Fax: (213) 623-3412

  %FO: 100
  Emp: 7

  UNITED OVERSEAS BANK LTD.
  UOB Bldg., 592 Fifth Ave., 10/F, 48th St., New York, New York 10036
  CEO: Wong Kwong Yew, Gen. Mgr.
  Bus: *Commercial banking and financial services.*

  Tel: (212) 382-0088
  Fax: (212) 382-1881

  %FO: 100
  Emp: 7

- **UNITED OVERSEAS UNION BANK LTD.**
  OUB Plaza 1, 80 Raffles Place, 0104, Singapore
  CEO: Wee Cho Yaw, Chmn. & CEO
  Bus: *Commercial banking services.*

  Tel: 65-6533-9898
  Fax: 65-6534-2334
  www.oub.com.sg

  Rev: $2,910
  Emp: 13,574

  NAICS: 522110

  OVERSEAS UNION BANK, LTD.
  777 S. Figueroa St., Ste. 3988, Los Angeles, California 90017
  CEO: Hoong Chen, Mgr.
  Bus: *International banking services.*

  Tel: (213) 624-3187
  Fax: (213) 623-6407

  %FO: 100

  OVERSEAS UNION BANK, LTD.
  592 5th Ave., 10/F, New York, New York 10036
  CEO: Lyee S. Teo, VP
  Bus: *International banking services.*

  Tel: (212) 382-0088
  Fax: (212) 382-0088

  %FO: 100

- **UNITED TEST AND ASSEMBLY CENTER LTD.**
  5 Serangoon North Avenue, 554916, Singapore
  CEO: Lee Joon Chung, CEO
  Bus: *Test and assembly services for semiconductor
  devices.*

  Tel: 65-6481-0033
  Fax: 65-6551-1168
  www.utac.com.sg

  Rev: $89
  Emp: 1,026

  NAICS: 334413

  UTAC AMERICA INC.
  6601 Koll Center Pkwy., Ste. 248, Pleasanton, California 94566
  CEO: J. C. Lee
  Bus: *Test and assembly services for
  semiconductor devices.*

  Tel: (925) 461-6888
  Fax: (925) 461-6825

  %FO: 100

- **VENTURE CORPORATION LTD.**
  5006 Ang Mo Kio Avenue 5, #05-01/12 Techplace II, 569973, Singapore
  CEO: Ngit Liong Wong, Chmn. & CEO
  Bus: *Electronic services provider.*

  Tel: 65-6482-1755
  Fax: 65-6482-0122
  www.venture.com.sg

  Rev: $1,950
  Emp: 11,453

  NAICS: 333315, 333411, 334119, 334418, 334419

VM SERVICES INC.
6701 Mowry Ave., Newark, California 94560
CEO: C.T. Wong, Pres.
Bus: *Electronic services provider.*

Tel: (510) 744-3720
Fax: (510) 744-3730

%FO: 100
Emp: 170

South Africa

- **ABSA GROUP LIMITED**
  ABSA Tower East, 170 Main St., 3/F, Johannesburg 2001, South Africa
  CEO: Danie Gronje, Chmn.   Tel: 27-11-350-4000   Rev: $6,260
  Bus: *ATM operator*   Fax: 27-11-350-4928
                                    www.absa.co.za
  NAICS: 522110

  - **ABSA GROUP LIMITED**
    780 Third Ave., 42/F, New York, New York 10017
    CEO: Anne-Marie Pothas   Tel: (212) 223-4400   %FO: 100
    Bus: *ATM operations.*   Fax: (212) 223-5620

- **AECI LIMITED**
  24 The Woodlands, Woodlands Dr., Woodmead Sandton, Gauteng 2196, South Africa
  CEO: Schalk Engelbrecht   Tel: 27-11-806-8700   Rev: $1,151
  Bus: *Mfr. of explosives and decorative coatings*   Fax: 27-11-806-8701   Emp: 8,000
                                    www.aeci.co.za
  NAICS: 325211, 325221

  - **SANS FIBERS INC**
    2575 Pembroke Rd., Gastonia, North Carolina 28054
    CEO: Zach Zacharias   Tel: (704) 869-8311   %FO: 100
    Bus: *marketing and distribution of specialty nylon*   Fax: (704) 869-9697
         and polyester yarn

- **ANGLOGOLD ASHANTI LIMITED**
  11 Diagonal St., Johannesburg 2001, South Africa
  CEO: Robert M. Godsell, CEO & Exec.. Dir.   Tel: 27-11-637-6000   Rev: $2,396
  Bus: *Gold production and mining.*   Fax: 27-11-637-6399   Emp: 55,439
                                    www.anglogold.com
  NAICS: 212221

  - **ANGLOGOLD LIMITED**
    509 Madison Ave., Ste. 1914, New York, New York 10022
    CEO: Don Ewigleben, Pres. & CAO   Tel: (212) 750-7999   %FO: 100
    Bus: *Engaged in gold production and mining.*   Fax: (212) 750-5626

- **BARLOWORLD LIMITED**
  180 Katherine St., Sandton, Gauteng 2146, South Africa
  CEO: Warren A. M. Clewlow   Tel: 27-11-445-1000   Rev: $5,681
  Bus: *Global distributor of heavy equipment*   Fax: 27-11-444-3643   Emp: 25,233
                                    www.barloworld.com
  NAICS: 333120, 532412

  - **BARLOWORLD INDUSTRIAL DISTRIBUTION**
    PO Box 410050, Charlotte, North Carolina 28241-0050
    CEO: Brandon P. Diamond, CEO   Tel: (704) 587-1003   %FO: 100
    Bus: *Manufacturer of heavy equipment*   Fax: (704) 587-9269   Emp: 1,653

● **BOART LONGYEAR INC.**
204 Rivonia Rd., Morningside, Gauteng 2057, South Africa
CEO: Philip Baum, Chmn.
Bus: *Diamond drilling equipment manufacture and contract drilling services. (Sub. Anglo American plc)*
Tel: 27-11-520-9300
Fax: 27-11-783-2411
www.boartlongyear.com
NAICS: 213112, 333132

BOART LONGYEAR COMPANY
2640 West 1700 South, Salt Lake City, Utah 84104
CEO: Hans Glaessner, Gen. Mgr.
Bus: *Provides drilling products and contract services to the mining and constructions markets.*
Tel: (801) 972-6430
Fax: (801) 977-3374
%FO: 100

BOART LONGYEAR COMPANY - Core Drilling Division
300 Grayson Rd., Wytheville, Virginia 24382
CEO: Bill Dycus, Gen. Mgr.
Bus: *Core drilling contractor*
Tel: (276) 228-7811
Fax: (276) 228-6936
%FO: 100

BOART LONGYEAR COMPANY - Equipment Development Group
1155 Post Rd., Oakdale, California 95361
CEO: Reb Silay, Gen. Mgr.
Bus: *Provides drilling products and contract services to the mining and constructions markets.*
Tel: (209) 847-4238
Fax: (209) 847-6026
%FO: 100

BOART LONGYEAR COMPANY - US Products Group
2200 Centre Park Ct., Stone Mountain, Georgia 30087
CEO: Paul McCalla, Gen. Mgr.
Bus: *Provides drilling products and contract services to the mining and constructions markets.*
Tel: (770) 469-2720
Fax: (770) 498-2841
%FO: 100

BOART LONGYEAR ENVIRONMENTAL DRILLING
14950 Iris Rd., Little Falls, Minnesota 56345
CEO: Tom Oothoudt, Gen. Mgr.
Bus: *Environmental drilling services.*
Tel: (320) 632-6552
Fax: (320) 632-2915
%FO: 100

BOART LONGYEAR ENVIRONMENTAL DRILLING SERVICES
101 Alderson St., Schofield, Wisconsin 54476
CEO: Ron Thalacker, Gen. Mgr.
Bus: *Provides drilling products and contract services to the mining and constructions markets.*
Tel: (715) 359-7090
Fax: (715) 355-5715
%FO: 100

DESI
3610 E. Anne St., Phoenix, Arizona 85040
CEO: Wayne Mehlhorn, Gen. Mgr.
Bus: *Full service provider of drilling equipment and supplies.*
Tel: (800) 736-6236
Fax: (602) 437-1845
%FO: 100

GEO-TECH EXPLORATIONS INC.
19700 SW Teton Ave., Tualatin, Oregon 97062
CEO: Bill Klostermann, Gen. Mgr.
Bus: *Provides drilling services to the*
geotechnical, environmental, water and
construction industries.

Tel: (503) 692-6400
Fax: (503) 849-4759

%FO: 100

HOLT DRILLING
3820 Freeman Rd. E, Fife, Washington 98354
CEO: Randy Holt, Gen. Mgr.
Bus: *Provides drilling services to the*
geotechnical, environmental, water and
construction industries.

Tel: (253) 883-5200
Fax: (253) 883-5201

%FO: 100

LANG EXPLORATORY DRILLING, DIV. BOART LONGYEAR
2745 West California Ave., Salt Lake City, Utah 84104
CEO: Alan Lang, Pres.
Bus: *Provides drilling products and contract*
services to the mining and constructions
markets.

Tel: (801) 973-6667
Fax: (801) 973-4572

%FO: 100

SINCLAIR SERVICES
10602 Midway Ave., Cerritos, California 90703
CEO: Doug Barakat, Gen. Mgr.
Bus: *Provides drilling products and contract*
services to the mining and constructions
markets.

Tel: (800) 782-3222
Fax: (562) 403-3564

%FO: 100

● **DIMENSION DATA HOLDINGS PLC**
The Campus, 57 Sloane St., Bryanston, Sandton, Gauteng 2191, South Africa
CEO: Brett W. Dawson, CEO
Bus: *Provides design, implementation, and*
maintenance services for computer and
communications networks
NAICS: 541511, 541512, 541513, 541519, 611420

Tel: 27-11-575-0000
Fax: 27-11-576-0000
www.didata.com

Rev: $2,500
Emp: 8,563

DIMENSION DATA NORTH AMERICA, INC.
12120 Sunset Hills Rd., Ste. 550, Reston, Virginia 20190
CEO: Raul J. Fernandez
Bus: *IT services.*

Tel: (571) 203-4000
Fax: (571) 203-4001

%FO: 100

● **ELEMENT SIX**
PO Box 1770, Southdale, Gauteng 2135, South Africa
CEO: Christian Hultner
Bus: *Supplier of synthetic and industrial-grade*

NAICS: 212399, 213115

Tel: 27-11-374-6819
Fax: 27-11-374-6840
www.e6.com

DIAMOND ABRASIVES CORP
35 West 45th St., New York, New York 10036
CEO:
Bus: *Industrial abrasives.*

Tel: (212) 869-5155
Fax: (212) 764-0349

%FO: 100

● **FIRSTRAND LIMITED**
1 Merchant Place, 17/F, Rivonia Road, Gauteng, Sandton 2196, South Africa
CEO: Lauritz L. Dippenaar, CEO Tel: 27-11-282-1808 Rev: $5,002
Bus: *Banking and insurance services.* Fax: 27-11-282-8088 Emp: 35,000
  www.firstrand.co.za
NAICS: 522110, 524210

  DESTINY HEALTH, DIV. FIRSTRAND
  11785 Beltsville Dr., Ste. 220, Bethesda, Maryland 10705
  CEO: J. Scott Spiker, Pres. Tel: (301) 586-9500 %FO: JV
  Bus: *Health insurance services.* Fax: (301) 222-0330

● **FRONTRANGE LIMITED**
1 Albury Park, Albury Rd., Johannesburg 2144, South Africa
CEO: Michael J. McCloskey, CEO Tel: 27-11-325-5600 Rev: $74
Bus: *Developer of computer software* Fax: 27-11-325-5660 Emp: 403
  www.frontrange.co.za
NAICS: 511210

  FRONTRANGE SOLUTIONS INC.
  1125 Kelly Johnson Blvd., Ste.100, Colorado Springs, Colorado 80920
  CEO: David R. Smith, CEO Tel: (719) 531-5007 %FO: 100
  Bus: *Software development* Fax: (719) 536-0620

  FRONTRANGE SOLUTIONS INC.
  4120 Dublin Blvd., Ste. 200, Dublin, California 94568
  CEO: Jim O'Gara Tel: (925) 404-1800 %FO: 100
  Bus: *Computer software development* Fax:

● **GOLD FIELDS LIMITED**
24 St. Andrews Rd., Parktown, Gauteng, Johannesburg 2193, South Africa
CEO: Ian D. Cockerill, CEO Tel: 27-11-644-2400 Rev: $1,768
Bus: *Gold exploration and development.* Fax: 27-11-484-0626 Emp: 52,100
  www.goldfields.co.za
NAICS: 212221, 212299

  GOLD FIELDS LIMITED
  6400 South Fiddlers Green Circle, Ste. 1620, Englewood, Colorado 80111
  CEO: Craig J. Nelsen, Pres. Tel: (303) 796-8683 %FO: 100
  Bus: *Gold exploration and development.* Fax: (303) 796-8293 Emp: 14

● **INVESTEC LIMITED**
100 Grayston Drive, Sandown, 2/f, Sandton, Gauteng 2196, South Africa
CEO: Stephen Koseff, CEO Tel: 27-11-286-7000 Rev: $1,024
Bus: *Engaged in investment banking.* Fax: 27-11-286-7777 Emp: 4,458
  www.investec.co.za
NAICS: 523920, 523930, 523999

  INVESTEC ASSET MANAGEMENT INC.
  1055 Washington Blvd., Stamford, Connecticut 06901
  CEO: Mimi Ferrini Tel: (203) 324-0010 %FO: 100
  Bus: *Engaged in investment banking.* Fax: (203) 324-0023

INVESTEC US INCORPORATED
One Battery Park Plaza, 2/F, New York, New York 10004
CEO: Leonard E. Belvedere, Mgr.   Tel: (212) 898-6200   %FO: 100
Bus: *Trades bonds and mutual funds.*   Fax: (212) 898-6255

● **SAPPI LIMITED**
Sappi House, 48 Ameshoff St., Braamfontein, Johannesburg 2001, South Africa
CEO: Eugene van As, Chmn.   Tel: 27-11-407-8044   Rev: $4,728
Bus: *Mfr. fine paper and paper products.*   Fax: 27-11-403-8236   Emp: 16,010
                                                     www.sappi.com
    NAICS: 113110, 321113, 322110, 322222, 322299

   SAPPI FINE PAPER NORTH AMERICA
   1329 Waterville Rd., Skowhegan, Maine 04976
   CEO: John Donahue, Mng. Dir.   Tel: (207) 238-3000   %FO: 100
   Bus: *Sales of fine paper products.*   Fax: (207) 453-4532

   SAPPI FINE PAPER NORTH AMERICA
   280 Madison Ave., New York, New York 10016
   CEO: Robert R. Forsberg Jr., Reg. Sales Mgr.   Tel: (212) 683-6070   %FO: 100
   Bus: *Sales of fine paper products.*   Fax: (212) 683-8147

   SAPPI FINE PAPER NORTH AMERICA
   1340 Hickory Lane, Allentown, Pennsylvania 18106
   CEO: Ronnie Barnes, Mgr.   Tel: (610) 398-8400   %FO: 100
   Bus: *Sales of fine paper products.*   Fax: (610) 398-7895

   SAPPI FINE PAPER NORTH AMERICA
   PO Box 511, 2201 Ave. B, Cloquet, Minnesota 55720
   CEO: Tom Collins, Mng. Dir.   Tel: (218) 879-2300   %FO: 100
   Bus: *Sales of fine paper products.*   Fax: (218) 879-0648

   SAPPI FINE PAPER NORTH AMERICA
   333 South Anita Dr., Ste. 760, Orange, California 92868
   CEO: Eric Keller, Reg. Mgr.   Tel: (714) 459-0600   %FO: 100
   Bus: *Sales of fine paper products.*   Fax: (714) 456-0611

   SAPPI FINE PAPER NORTH AMERICA
   523 Leon Circle, Langhorne, Pennsylvania 19053
   CEO: Ed Hainsworth   Tel: (215) 750-0904   %FO: 100
   Bus: *Sales of fine paper products.*   Fax: (215) 750-8177

   SAPPI FINE PAPER NORTH AMERICA
   3 Long Hill Rd., Bolton, Massachusetts 01740
   CEO: Ned Schroeder, Mgr.   Tel: (978) 779-6950   %FO: 100
   Bus: *Sales of fine paper products.*   Fax: (978) 779-6367

   SAPPI FINE PAPER NORTH AMERICA
   1 Financial Way, Ste. 309, Cincinnati, Ohio 45242-5858
   CEO: Francis Hannigan, Mgr.   Tel: (513) 985-3900   %FO: 100
   Bus: *Sales of fine paper products.*   Fax: (513) 985-3910

SAPPI FINE PAPER NORTH AMERICA
280 Madison Ave., Rm. 206, New York, New York 10016-0801
CEO: Bill Fleming, Dir.   Tel: (212) 683-6070   %FO: 100
Bus: *Sales of fine paper products.*   Fax: (212) 683-8147

SAPPI FINE PAPER NORTH AMERICA
38 High St., Peterborough, New Hampshire 03458
CEO: Bernt Ruediger, Mgr.   Tel: (603) 924-4350   %FO: 100
Bus: *Sales of fine paper products.*   Fax: (603) 562-5737

SAPPI FINE PAPER NORTH AMERICA
2400 Lakeshore Dr., Muskegon, Michigan 49441
CEO: Vern Holtzlander   Tel: (231) 755-3761   %FO: 100
Bus: *Sales of fine paper products.*   Fax: (231) 759-5416

SAPPI FINE PAPER NORTH AMERICA
225 Franklin St., 28/F, Boston, Massachusetts 02110
CEO: Veronica M. Hagen, Mgr.   Tel: (617) 423-7300   %FO: 100
Bus: *Sales of fine paper products.*   Fax: (617) 423-5494   Emp: 3,268

SAPPI FINE PAPER NORTH AMERICA
89 Cumberland St., Westbrook, Maine 04092
CEO: Michael Sosnowski   Tel: (207) 856-3660   %FO: 100
Bus: *Sales of fine paper products.*   Fax: (207) 856-3770

SAPPI FINE PAPER NORTH AMERICA
3400 Peachtree Rd., NE, Atlanta, Georgia 30326
CEO: Don Titherington, Reg. Mgr.   Tel: (404) 751-2600   %FO: 100
Bus: *Sales of fine paper products.*   Fax: (404) 751-2601

SAPPI FINE PAPER NORTH AMERICA
1717 Dixie Hwy., Ste. 300, Fort Wright, Kentucky 41011
CEO: Scott D. Lich, Reg. Mgr.   Tel: (859) 426-8600   %FO: 100
Bus: *Sales of fine paper products.*   Fax: (859) 426-0700

SAPPI FINE PAPER NORTH AMERICA
199 Wells Ave., Newton, Massachusetts 02459
CEO: Eric Kibblehouse   Tel: (617) 964-0200   %FO: 100
Bus: *Sales of fine paper products.*   Fax: (617) 332-1925

SAPPI FINE PAPER NORTH AMERICA
1701 E. Woodfield Rd., Ste. 330, Schaumburg, Illinois 60173
CEO: Mike Hall, Mgr.   Tel: (847) 605-1000   %FO: 100
Bus: *Sales of fine paper products.*   Fax: (847) 605-1024

US PAPER CORPORATION
2700 Westchester Ave., Ste. 300, Purchase, New York 10577
CEO: John Swingler, Mgr.   Tel: (914) 253-8660   %FO: 100
Bus: *Sales of fine paper products.*   Fax: (914) 253-8949

● **SASOL LIMITED**
1 Sturdee Ave., Rosebank, Johannesburg 2196, South Africa

CEO: L. Patrick A. Davies, CEO	Tel: 27-11-441-3111	Rev: $9,456
Bus: *Mfr. proprietary technologies for the production*	Fax: 27-11-788-5092	Emp: 30,910
of synthetic fuels and chemical products. (JV	www.sasol.com	
with Merisol UK)		

NAICS: 211111, 211112, 212112, 213112, 324199, 325311, 325312, 325613, 325920, 447190

    MERISOL USA LLC
    11821 East Freeway, Ste. 600, Houston, Texas 77029

CEO: Colin Wright, Pres.	Tel: (713) 428-5400	%FO: JV
Bus: *Mfr. chemical products.*	Fax: (713) 455-8045	Emp: 148

    SASOL NORTH AMERICA, INC.
    900 Threadneedle, Ste. 100, Houston, Texas 77079-2990

CEO: Charles Putnik, Pres.	Tel: (281) 588-3000	%FO: JV
Bus: *Markets and distributes alpha olefins.*	Fax: (281) 588-3144	

    SASOL NORTH AMERICA, INC.
    2201 Old Spanish Trail, West Lake, Louisiana 70669

CEO: Christopher Turner, Mgr.	Tel: (337) 494-5140
Bus: *Mfr. plastic materials.*	Fax:

    SASOLCHEM, INC.
    3441 Fairfield Rd., Baltimore, Maryland 21226

CEO: Peter E. Markey, Mgr.	Tel: (410) 355-6200
Bus: *Mfr. plastic materials.*	Fax:

    SOUTHWEST ENERGY
    2040 W. Gardner Lane, Tucson, Arizona 85705

CEO: James Toole, Pres.	Tel: (520) 696-9495	
Bus: *Heavy construction mfg. explosives.*	Fax:	Emp: 100

● **SOUTH AFRICAN AIRWAYS LTD.**
Airway Park, Jones Rd., Johannesburg International Airport, Kempton Park, Johannesburg 1627, South Africa

CEO: Khaya Nggula, Pres. & CEO	Tel: 27-11-978-1111	Rev: $2,572
Bus: *Commercial air transport services.*	Fax: 27-11-978-1126	Emp: 12,556
	www.flysaa.com	

NAICS: 481111

    SOUTH AFRICAN AIRWAYS
    4531 NW 32nd Ct., Ft. Lauderdale, Florida 33319

CEO:	Tel: (954) 485-0620
Bus: *Air transport services.*	Fax:

    SOUTH AFRICAN AIRWAYS
    9841 Airport Blvd., Los Angeles, California 90045

CEO:	Tel: (310) 478-3585
Bus: *Air transport services.*	Fax:

    SOUTH AFRICAN AIRWAYS CORPORATION
    3303 Casino Rd., Everett, Washington 98203

CEO: Kathy Grundle, Mgr.	Tel: (425) 342-3765	%FO: 100
Bus: *Commercial air transport services.*	Fax: (425) 342-3765	

SOUTH AFRICAN AIRWAYS CORPORATION
901 East Ponce De Leon Blvd., Miami, Florida 33134
CEO: Vernon Nadel, Mgr.　　　　　　　Tel: (305) 461-3484　　　%FO: 100
Bus: *Commercial air transport services.*　Fax: (305) 461-3484

SOUTH AFRICAN AIRWAYS CORPORATION
200 Old Country Rd., Ste. L1, Mineola, New York 11501
CEO: Jan Vilojoen, Dir.　　　　　　　Tel: (516) 742-0311　　　%FO: 100
Bus: *Commercial air transport services.*　Fax: (516) 742-0311

SOUTH AFRICAN AIRWAYS CORPORATION
PO Box 45432, Atlanta, Georgia 30320
CEO:　　　　　　　　　　　　　　　Tel: (404) 763-8235　　　%FO: 100
Bus: *Commercial air transport services.*　Fax: (404) 763-8235

● **STANDARD BANK GROUP LIMITED**
Standard Bank Centre, 5 Simmonds Street, 9th Fl., Johannesburg 2001, South Africa
CEO: Jacko H. Maree, CEO　　　　　　Tel: 27-11-636-9111　　　Rev: $8,865
Bus: *Commercial banking services.*　　Fax: 27-11-636-5617　　　Emp: 35,820
　　　　　　　　　　　　　　　　　www.sbic.co.za
NAICS: 522110

STANDARD NEW YORK SECURITIES INC.
320 Park Ave., 19/F, New York, New York 10022
CEO: W.S. Dorson, Mng. Dir.　　　　Tel: (212) 407-5000　　　%FO: 100
Bus: *International banking services.*　Fax: (212) 407-5025　　　Emp: 45

STANDARD NEW YORK SECURITIES, INC. MAIMI
1001 Brickell Bay Dr., Ste. 3200, Miami, Florida 33131
CEO: P. Wallin, Mng. Dir.　　　　　　Tel: (305) 349-0500　　　%FO: 100
Bus: *International banking services.*　Fax: (305) 349-0559

South Korea

● **ANAM SEMICONDUCTOR INC.**
645, Songgok-dong, Ansan, Kyonggi 425110, South Korea
CEO: James J. Kim, CEO
Bus: *Assembly of semiconductor devices.*

Tel: 82-32-680-4700
Fax: 82-32-680-8105
www.aname.co.kr

Rev: $67
Emp: 4,000

NAICS: 334413

> **AMKOR TECHNOLOGY**
> 1345 Enterprise Dr., West Chester, Pennsylvania 19380
> CEO: James J. Kim, CEO
> Bus: *Sale/distribution of semiconductor devices.*
>
> Tel: (610) 431-9600
> Fax: (610) 431-5881
>
> %FO: 100
> Emp: 50

> **AMKOR TECHNOLOGY**
> 1900 South Price Rd., Chandler, Arizona 85248
> CEO: Jeff Luth, VP
> Bus: *Sale/distribution of semiconductor devices.*
>
> Tel: (480) 821-5000
> Fax: (480) 821-8276
>
> %FO: 100

● **ASIANA AIRLINES**
10-1 Hoehyun-Dong 2-Ka, Chung-Gu, Seoul, South Korea
CEO: Chan Bup Park, Pres.
Bus: *Air transport services.*

Tel: 82-2-774-4000
Fax: 82-2-758-8009
www.flyasiana.com

Emp: 49

NAICS: 481111

> **ASIANA AIRLINES**
> 2745 Armstrong Ct., Des Plaines, Illinois 60018
> CEO: D. N. Choi
> Bus: *International air transport services.*
>
> Tel: (847) 375-0200
> Fax: (847) 375-0200
>
> %FO: 100

> **ASIANA AIRLINES**
> 1420 5th Ave., Ste. 2950, Seattle, Washington 98101-4087
> CEO: Chul Sung Kang, CEO
> Bus: *International air transport services.*
>
> Tel: (206) 516-0300
> Fax: (206) 343-1939
>
> %FO: 100

> **ASIANA AIRLINES**
> 3000 Town Center, Ste. 610, Southfield, Michigan 48075-1132
> CEO: W. Huhn
> Bus: *International air transport services.*
>
> Tel: (248) 353-2621
> Fax: (248) 353-2621
>
> %FO: 100

> **ASIANA AIRLINES**
> 3530 Wilshire Blvd., Ste. 145, Los Angeles, California 90010
> CEO: S.C. Kang
> Bus: *International air transport services.*
>
> Tel: (213) 365-4500
> Fax: (213) 365-9630
>
> %FO: 100

- **CHOHUNG BANK, LTD., DIV. SHINHAN FINANCIAL**
  120, 2-Ga, Taepyung-Ro, Jung-Gu, Seoul 100-102, South Korea
  CEO: Eung Chan Ra, Chmn.   Tel: 82-2-6360-3000   Rev: $5,410
  Bus: *Commercial banking services.*   Fax: 82-2-777-1883   Emp: 17,391
  www.shinhangroup.com
  NAICS: 522110

    CHOHUNG BANK
    3000 W. Olympic Blvd., Los Angeles, California 90006
    CEO: Soo Hwan Cho, Pres.   Tel: (213) 380-8300   %FO: 100
    Bus: *International commercial banking services.*   Fax: (213) 386-2170   Emp: 20

    CHOHUNG BANK LTD
    320 Park Ave., New York, New York 10021
    CEO: Nam Soo Heo, Mgr.   Tel: (212) 935-3500   %FO: 100
    Bus: *International commercial banking services.*   Fax: (212) 355-2231   Emp: 40

- **DACOM CORPORATION, SUB LG GROUP**
  706-1 Dacom Bldg., Yeoksam 2- dong, Gangnam-gu, Seoul 125-987, South Korea
  CEO: Hong Shik Jung, CEO   Tel: 82-505-200-0220   Rev: $1,020
  Bus: *Internet services.*   Fax: 82-505-200-0221
  www.dacom.net
  NAICS: 518111

    DACOM AMERICA, INC.
    626 Wilshire Bldg., Ste. 714, Los Angeles, California 90017
    CEO: Sung Won Choi   Tel: (213) 624-5546   %FO: 100
    Bus: *Internet services.*   Fax: (213) 624-5546

- **DAELIM INDUSTRIES CO, LTD.**
  146-12 Susong-Dong, Jongno-Gu, Seoul, South Korea
  CEO: Joon Y. Lee, Chmn. & CEO   Tel: 82-2-2011-7114   Rev: $3,889
  Bus: *Construction and design services*   Fax: 82-2-2011-8000   Emp: 2,500
  www.daelim.co.kr
  NAICS: 236210, 236220, 237990, 541330, 541611

    DAELIM INDUSTRIAL CO. LTD.
    Ste. 335, 14701 St. Mary's Lane, Houston, Texas 77079
    CEO: H.D. Koon, CEO   Tel: (281) 558-4700   %FO: 100
    Bus: *Construction and design services*   Fax: (281) 558-4701

- **DAERIM CORPORATION**
  482-2 Bangbae-Dong, Seocho-Gu, Seoul, South Korea
  CEO: Jin Won Kim, Pres.   Tel: 82-2-3470-6000
  Bus: *Engaged in the processing and distribution of the*   Fax: 82-2-523-8900
  bottom fish fillet.   www.daerimi.com
  NAICS: 424460

    DAERIM AMERICA, INC.
    195-197 W. Spring Valley Ave., Maywood, New Jersey 07607
    CEO: David Lee, Pres.   Tel: (201) 587-8989   %FO: 100
    Bus: *Fresh and frozen seafood products.*   Fax: (201) 587-8959

● **DAEWOO ELECTRONICS CORP.**
686 Ahyeon-dong, Mapo-gu, Seoul, South Korea
CEO: Choong-Hoon Kim, Pres.
Bus: *Electronics manufacture, including televisions,*
  VCR's, refrigerators and washing machines.
NAICS: 334310, 335311, 423620

Tel: 82-2-360-7114
Fax: 82-2-364-5588
www.dwe.co.kr

Rev: $2,290
Emp: 5,000

  DAEWOO ELECTRONICS AMERICA INC.
  120 Chubb Ave., Lyndhurst, New Jersey 07071
  CEO: Chul Lee
  Bus: *Sales/distribution of electronics.*

  Tel: (201) 460-2000
  Fax: (201) 935-5284

  %FO: 100

● **DAEWOO HEAVY INDUSTRIES AND MACHINERY LTD.**
7-11, Hwasu-dong, Dong-gu, Inchon, South Korea
CEO: Jae-Shin Yang, Pres.
Bus: *Mfr. machinery construction equipment.*

NAICS: 333120, 333120

Tel: 82-32-760-1114
Fax: 82-32-762-1546
www.dhiltd.co.kr

Rev: $1,937
Emp: 23,300

  DAEWOO HEAVY INDUSTRIES AMERICA
  4350 Renaissance Pkwy., Cleveland, Ohio 44128
  CEO: K. H. Choi
  Bus: *Forklift, truck and compact equipment*
    manufacturer.

  Tel: (216) 595-1212
  Fax: (216) 595-1214

  %FO: 100

  DAEWOO HEAVY INDUSTRIES INC.
  2905 Shawnee Industrial Way, Ste. 100, Suwannee, Georgia 30024
  CEO: Justin Kim, Pres.
  Bus: *Construction equipment manufacturer.*

  Tel: (770) 831-2200
  Fax: (770) 831-0480

  %FO: 100

● **DAEWOO INTERNATIONAL CORPORATION**
541 5-Ga Namdaemunno, Chung-Gu, Seoul, South Korea
CEO: Lee Tae-Yong, CEO
Bus: *International trading; chemicals, textiles, metals*
  and steel.
NAICS: 424690, 484121

Tel: 82-2-759-2114
Fax: 82-2-753-9489
www.daewoo.com

Rev: $198
Emp: 890

  DAEWOO INTERNATIONAL (AMERICA) CORPORATION
  85 Challenger Rd., Ridgefield Park, New Jersey 07660
  CEO: Young Nam Ma, Pres.
  Bus: *Importing/exporting trading services; sale of*
    industrial & consumer products.

  Tel: (201) 229-4500
  Fax: (201) 440-2244

  %FO: 100
  Emp: 150

  DAEWOO INTERNATIONAL CORPORATION
  3206 North Kennicott Rd., Arlington Heights, Illinois 60004
  CEO: Y. H. Park, Pres.
  Bus: *Auto parts, electronics, textiles.*

  Tel: (847) 590-9800
  Fax: (847) 590-9814

  %FO: 100
  Emp: 5

  DAEWOO MOTOR AMERICA
  1055 West Victoria St., Compton, California 90220
  CEO: Dong Lee, Pres.
  Bus: *Mfr. auto parts, aerospace, textile.*

  Tel: (310) 884-5800
  Fax: (310) 669-2020

  %FO: 100
  Emp: 23

- **DC CHEMICAL CO. LTD**
  Oriental Chemical Bldg., 50 Sogong-dong, Jung-gu, Seoul, South Korea
  CEO: Soo Young Lee, Chmn.   Tel: 82-2-7279-500   Rev: $793
  Bus: *Mfr. chemicals and petrochemicals*   Fax: 82-2-757-4111   Emp: 1,844
                                               www.dcchem.co.kr
  NAICS: 325188, 325199

  OCI International Inc.
  910 Sylvan Ave., Englewood Cliffs, New Jersey 07632
  CEO: Mr. K.H. Kim   Tel: (201) 569-3003   %FO: 100
  Bus: *Manufacturer industrial chemicals*   Fax: (201) 569-3005

- **DONGBUANAM SEMICONDUCTOR INC.**
  Dongbu Financial Center Bldg., 32/F, 891-10 Daechi-Dong, Kangnam-Ku, Seoul, South Korea
  CEO: J.K. Kim, Chmn.   Tel: 82-2-3484-2863   Rev: $263
  Bus: *Mfr. integrated circuits*   Fax: 82-2-3484-2851   Emp: 1,800
                                               www.dsemi.com
  NAICS: 334413

  DONGBUANAM
  2953 Bunker Hill Lane, Ste. 206, Santa Clara, California 95054
  CEO: Tel: (408) 330-0330   %FO: 100
  Bus: *Manufacturer integrated circuits*   Fax: (408) 330-0340

- **DONGKUK STEEL MILL CO., LTD.**
  50 Suha-Dong, Chung-Gu, Seoul 100-210, South Korea
  CEO: Sae-joo Chang, Chmn.   Tel: 82-2-317-1114   Rev: $2,825
  Bus: *Mfr. galvanized coil and sheet, steel scrap, slab,*   Fax: 82-2-317-1391   Emp: 1,563
      plate, pipe and tubing.   www.dongkuk.co.kr
  NAICS: 331111, 331222

  DONGKUK INTERNATIONAL
  460 Bergen Boulevard, Palisades Park, New Jersey 07650
  CEO: Yung Mun, Pres.   Tel: (201) 592-8600   %FO: 100
  Bus: *Steel importing & exporting.*   Fax: (201) 592-8795   Emp: 35

  DONGKUK INT'L INC.
  19750 Magellan Dr., Torrance, California 90502
  CEO: M. H. Kim   Tel: (310) 523-9595   %FO: 100
  Bus: *Galvanized Coil and sheet/steel scrap, slab,*   Fax: (310) 523-9599
      plate, pipe, and tubing.

- **THE EXPORT-IMPORT BANK OF KOREA**
  16-1 Yoido-dong, Youngdungpo-gu, Seoul 150-010, South Korea
  CEO: Yeong Hoe Lee, Pres. & Chmn.   Tel: 82-2-784-1021
  Bus: *Government owned financial institution.*   Fax: 82-2-784-1030
                                               www.koreaexim.go.kr
  NAICS: 522293

  THE EXPORT-IMPORT BANK OF KOREA
  600 Wilshire Blvd, Los Angeles, California 90017-3212
  CEO: Jung Boo Bae, Rep.   Tel: (213) 622-4314   %FO: 100
  Bus: *Engaged in banking and finance.*   Fax: (213) 622-4314

● **HAITAI INTERNATIONAL, INC.**
321-4 Choenheung-Ri, Seongkeo-eup, Chonan, Chungchongnam-do 330830, South Korea
CEO: Young Dal Yoon, CEO
Bus: *Wholesaler/exporter of frozen concentrated orange juice (Sunkist), wheat, beans, livestock.*
NAICS: 311211, 311340, 311411, 424510, 424520

Tel: 82-2-3270-1600
Fax: 82-2-3701-7573
www.ht.co.kr

Rev: $490
Emp: 4,019

    HAITAI GLOBAL, INC.
    7227 Telegraph Rd,, Montebello, California 90640
    CEO: Taeki Min, Pres.
    Bus: *Food products, including dried laver (nori sheets).*

    Tel: (323) 724-7337
    Fax:

    %FO: 100
    Emp: 50

● **HANA BANK**
101-1 Euljiro 1-ga, Jung-gu, Seoul 100-191, South Korea
CEO: Seung Yu Kim, EVP
Bus: *Banking and financial securities services.*

NAICS: 522110

Tel: 82-2-2002-1111
Fax: 82-2-2002-1111
www.hanabank.co.kr

    HANA BANK
    650 Fifth Ave., 17/F, New York, New York 10019
    CEO: Byoung Ho Kim
    Bus: *Banking and financial securities services.*

    Tel: (212) 687-6160
    Fax: (212) 818-1721

● **HANJIN HEAVY INDUSTRIES & CONSTRUCTION CO., LTD.**
29, 5-Ga, Bongnae-dong, Youngdo-ku, Pusan 606-796, South Korea
CEO: N.H. Cho, Chmn.
Bus: *General contracting, home building and developing; in-flight catering.*
NAICS: 236210, 236220, 237110, 237310, 237990, 336611, 541310, 541330

Tel: 82-51-410-3114
Fax: 82-51-410-3337
www.hanjinsc.com

Rev: $1,865
Emp: 4,460

    HANJIN HEAVY INDUSTRIES
    8506 Osage Ave., Los Angeles, California 90045
    CEO: H.W. Kho, Mgr.
    Bus: *Producer of cargo ships, passenger ships, war ships & special-purpose ships.*

    Tel: (310) 645-9011
    Fax: (310) 645-9110

    %FO: 100

    HANJIN HEAVY INDUSTRIES
    11220 Hindry Ave., Los Angeles, California 90045
    CEO: H.W. Kho, Mgr.
    Bus: *Producer of cargo ships, passenger ships, war ships & special-purpose ships.*

    Tel: (310) 645-9011
    Fax: (310) 645-9110

    %FO: 100

● **HANJIN SHIPPING COMPANY, LTD.**
Hanjin Shipping Bldg., 25-11 Yoido-Dong, Youngdeungpo-ku, Seoul, South Korea
CEO: Won Pyo Choi, Pres. & CEO
Bus: *Containerized international shipping and cargo transport.*
NAICS: 483111, 488510, 541614

Tel: 82-2-3770-6114
Fax: 82-2-3770-6748
www.hanjin.com

Rev: $5,921
Emp: 3,600

HANJIN SHIPPING CO LTD
3010 LBJ Freeway, Ste. 726 LB44, Dallas, Texas 75234
CEO: Earl Hopper, Mgr.   Tel: (972) 247-4371   %FO: 100
Bus: *Cargo transport, containerized systems.*   Fax: (972) 247-4160

HANJIN SHIPPING COMPANY, LTD.
2128 Burnett Blvd., Wilmington, North Carolina 28401
CEO: Braxton Musseau, Mgr.   Tel: (910) 251-9377   %FO: 100
Bus: *Ocean shipping.*   Fax: (910) 251-2164

HANJIN SHIPPING COMPANY, LTD.
80 East Route 4, Ste. 490, Paramus, New Jersey 07652
CEO: Jong Sun Lee, Mng. Dir.   Tel: (201) 291-4600   %FO: 100
Bus: *Cargo transport, containerized systems.*   Fax: (201) 291-9393   Emp: 550

HANJIN SHIPPING COMPANY, LTD.
Container Port Bldg., Highway 25 N, 2/F, Ste. 201, Garden City, Georgia 31408
CEO: Jimmy Quillan, Sales   Tel: (912) 966-1220
Bus: *Freight forwarder and logistics management.* Fax: (912) 966-1217

HANJIN SHIPPING COMPANY, LTD.
PO Box 82264, Rochester, Michigan 48308
CEO: Eric Taylor, Sales   Tel: (248) 652-7932
Bus: *Freight shipping.*   Fax: (248) 652-7938

HANJIN SHIPPING COMPANY, LTD.
1030 Melrose Dr., Westlake, Ohio 44145
CEO: Jeffrey McComb, Sales   Tel: (440) 895-1504
Bus: *Freight shipping.*   Fax: (440) 895-1629

HANJIN SHIPPING COMPANY, LTD.
1415 Northloop West, Ste. 1200, Houston, Texas 77008
CEO: W K Choy, Mgr.   Tel: (832) 325-4600   %FO: 100
Bus: *Cargo transport, containerized systems.*   Fax: (713) 802-7413

HANJIN SHIPPING COMPANY, LTD.
2000 Powers Ferry Rd., Ste. 630, Marietta, Georgia 30067
CEO: Jennifer Snow, Mgr.   Tel: (678) 239-0200   %FO: 100
Bus: *Marine transportation.*   Fax: (678) 239-0229

HANJIN SHIPPING COMPANY, LTD.
950 West Elliott Rd., Ste. 201, Tempe, Arizona 85284
CEO: Shirley Harderty, Mgr.   Tel: (480) 768-3600   %FO: 100
Bus: *Ocean shipping.*   Fax: (480) 755-3311

HANJIN SHIPPING COMPANY, LTD.
401 Alaskan Way, Terminal 46, Seattle, Washington 98104
CEO: Seung K. Park, Mgr.   Tel: (206) 447-9422   %FO: 100
Bus: *Cargo transport, containerized systems.*   Fax: (206) 447-9428

HANJIN SHIPPING COMPANY, LTD.
1500 NE Irving St., Ste. 300, Portland, Oregon 97232
CEO: Jeff McEwen, Mgr.   Tel: (503) 234-4133   %FO: 100
Bus: *Cargo transport, containerized systems.*   Fax: (503) 234-4766

HANJIN SHIPPING COMPANY, LTD.
639 Granite St., Ste. 315, Braintree, Massachusetts 02184
CEO: Frank Goffredo, Mgr.   Tel: (781) 849-3130   %FO: 100
Bus: *Ocean shipping.*   Fax: (781) 849-1539

HANJIN SHIPPING COMPANY, LTD.
2200 Broening Highway, Ste. 201, Baltimore, Maryland 21224
CEO: Patrick Frank, Mgr.   Tel: (410) 633-1902   %FO: 100
Bus: *Ocean shipping.*   Fax: (410) 633-1908

HANJIN SHIPPING COMPANY, LTD.
5727 Westpark Dr., Ste. 104, Charlotte, North Carolina 28217
CEO: Reed Curtis, Mgr.   Tel: (704) 679-3850   %FO: 100
Bus: *Ocean shipping.*   Fax: (704) 679-3853

HANJIN SHIPPING COMPANY, LTD.
5050 Popular Ave., Ste. 627, Memphis, Tennessee 38157
CEO: Carolyn Williams, Customer Service Tel: (901) 259-4686   %FO: 100
Bus: *Ocean shipping.*   Fax: (901) 259-4693

HANJIN SHIPPING COMPANY, LTD.
5255 Northwest 87th Ave., Ste. 304, Miami, Florida 33178
CEO: Maria Zacarias, Mgr.   Tel: (305) 594-0220   %FO: 100
Bus: *Ocean shipping.*   Fax: (305) 594-0207   Emp: 2

HANJIN SHIPPING COMPANY, LTD.
2483 15th St. NW, Ste. B, New Brighton, Minnesota 55112
CEO: Richard Szeliga, Sales   Tel: (651) 636-7726   %FO: 100
Bus: *Ocean shipping.*   Fax: (651) 636-7692

HANJIN SHIPPING COMPANY, LTD.
Greenbrier Tower I, 860 Greenbrier Circle, Ste. 200, Chesapeake, Virginia 23320
CEO: Tim Pope, Mgr.   Tel: (757) 233-2202   %FO: 100
Bus: *Ocean shipping.*   Fax: (757) 233-2204

HANJIN SHIPPING COMPANY, LTD.
175 South West Temple, Ste. 600, Salt Lake City, Utah 84101
CEO: Brian Yi, Mgr.   Tel: (801) 258-2500   %FO: 100
Bus: *Ocean shipping.*   Fax: (801) 533-3232

HANJIN SHIPPING COMPANY, LTD.
17785 Center Ct. Dr., Ste. 750, Cerritos, California 90703
CEO: Helen Kim, Mgr.   Tel: (562) 356-6600   %FO: 100
Bus: *Ocean shipping.*   Fax: (562) 356-6807

HANJIN SHIPPING COMPANY, LTD.
270 Northland Blvd., Ste. 304, Cincinnati, Ohio 45246
CEO: Michael Murphy, Mgr.   Tel: (513) 782-3200   %FO: 100
Bus: *Ocean shipping.*   Fax: (513) 782-3003   Emp: 4

HANJIN SHIPPING COMPANY, LTD.
1211 West 22nd St., Ste. 1100, Oak Brook, Illinois 60523
CEO: Ed McQuillan, Mgr.   Tel: (630) 891-7500   %FO: 100
Bus: *Cargo transport, containerized systems.* Fax: (630) 891-7560

HANJIN SHIPPING COMPANY, LTD.
180 Montgomery St., Ste. 1938, San Francisco, California 94104
CEO: Cindy Jun, Customer Service   Tel: (415) 403-5400   %FO: 100
Bus: *Ocean shipping.*   Fax: (415) 360-4590

● **HANKOOK TIRE CO., LTD.**
#645-15 Yoksam-dong, Kangnam-gu, Seoul, South Korea
CEO: Cho Chung-Hwan, CEO   Tel: 82-2-2222-1000   Rev: $1,673
Bus: *Automotive tire, batteries, brake pads, lining and*   Fax: 82-2-2222-1100   Emp: 6,154
    wheels manufacture.   www.hanta.co.kr
NAICS: 326211, 336211

    HANKOOK TIRE AMERICA CORP.
    3867 Holcomb Bridge Rd., Ste. 7, Norcross, Georgia 30092
    CEO: James E. Blanton   Tel: (678) 291-0657   %FO: 100
    Bus: *Tire manufacture.*   Fax: (678) 291-9838

    HANKOOK TIRE AMERICA CORP.
    1450 Valley Dr., Wayne, New Jersey 07470
    CEO: J. W. Choi   Tel: (973) 633-9000   %FO: 100
    Bus: *Tire manufacture.*   Fax: (973) 633-0028

    HANKOOK TIRE TECHNICAL CENTER
    3535 Forest Lake Dr., Uniontown, Ohio 44685
    CEO: Dave Martin   Tel: (330) 896-5295   %FO: 100
    Bus: *Develops state-of-the-art tread designs and*   Fax: (330) 896-6597
    tire technologies.

● **HANWHA CORPORATION**
Hanwha Bldg., 1 Janggyo-Dong, Jung-ku, Seoul 100-797, South Korea
CEO: Seung-Youn KimWon Joon Hur, Pres. & CEO   Tel: 82-2-729-2700   Rev: $1,920
Bus: *Construction, trading of petrochemicals and*   Fax: 82-2-729-1455
    manufacture of communication equipment and   www.hanwha.co.kr
    machinery.
NAICS: 325110, 325181, 325188, 325199, 325211

    HANWHA INTERNATIONAL CORPORATION
    2559 Golden Plaza, Rt. 130, Cranbury, New Jersey 08512
    CEO: Young Tae Kim, Pres.   Tel: (609) 655-2500   %FO: 100
    Bus: *Mfr. industrial furnaces, precision*   Fax: Emp: 30
    equipment, aerospace and machine tools.

    UNIVERSAL BEARINGS, INC.
    431 North Birkey St., Bremen, Indiana 46506
    CEO: Young Tae Kim, Pres.   Tel: (574) 546-2261   %FO: 100
    Bus: *Motor vehicle parts & accessories*   Fax: Emp: 280

● **HYNIX SEMICONDUCTOR INC.**
San 136-1, Ami-Ri, Bubal-eub, Ichon, Kyounggi 467-860, South Korea
CEO: Eui-Je Woo, Chmn. & CEO   Tel: 82-31-630-4114   Rev: $3,030
Bus: *Mfr. electronic devices, including memory chips*   Fax: 82-31-630-4103   Emp: 13,000
    and semiconductors..   www.hynix.com
NAICS: 334112, 334413

HYNIX SEMICONDUCTOR AMERICA, INC.
3101 N. 1st St., San Jose, California 95134
CEO: Gary Swanson, SVP
Bus: *Mfr./sales semi-conductors.*
Tel: (408) 232-8000
Fax: (408) 232-8103
%FO: 100
Emp: 186

HYNIX SEMICONDUCTOR MANUFACTURING AMERICA, INC.
1830 Willow Creek Circle, Eugene, Oregon 97402
CEO: D. W. Baik, Pres.
Bus: *Mfr. semiconductors.*
Tel: (541) 338-5000
Fax: (541) 338-5200
%FO: 100
Emp: 933

• HYOSUNG GROUP LTD.
450 Gongdeok-dong, Mapo-gu, Seoul 121-720, South Korea
CEO: S.R. Cho, CEO
Bus: *Mfr. tires, steel products, electronics, fabrics/yarns, and musical instruments.*
NAICS: 314999
Tel: 82-2-707-7000
Fax: 82-2-707-7076
www.hyosung.co.kr

HYOSUNG AMERICA, INC.
13777 Ballantyne Corp. Plaza, Ste. 415, Charlotte, North Carolina 28277
CEO: Robert Hicks, Mgr.
Bus: *Steel products, electronics, fabrics/yarns, musical instruments.*
Tel: (704) 341-2325
Fax: (704) 341-3181
%FO: 100

HYOSUNG AMERICA, INC.
One Penn Plaza, 250 West 34th St., Ste. 2020, New York, New York 10119
CEO: Yeun Ho Suk, Pres.
Bus: *Agricultural products, chemicals, electronics, textiles and garments.*
Tel: (212) 736-7100
Fax: (212) 563-1323
%FO: 100
Emp: 60

HYOSUNG AMERICA, INC.
910 Columbia St., Brea, California 92821
CEO: Yeun Suk, Pres.
Bus: *Agricultural products, chemicals, electronics, textiles and garments.*
Tel: (714) 989-8900
Fax: (714) 989-8901
%FO: 100
Emp: 12

HYOSUNG AMERICA, INC.
1679 Over View Dr., Rock Hill, South Carolina 29780
CEO: Terry Swanner, VP
Bus: *Agricultural products, chemicals, electronics, textiles and garments.*
Tel: (803) 909-5855
Fax: (803) 909-5860
%FO: 100
Emp: 15

HYOSUNG CORP.
Pittsburgh Office Penn Center West, Bldg. Two, Ste. 406, Pittsburgh, Pennsylvania 15276
CEO: Roger Hutchins, Mgr.
Bus: *Agricultural products, chemicals, electronics, textiles and garments.*
Tel: (412) 787-1170
Fax: (412) 787-2270
%FO: 100

• HYUNDAI CORPORATION
226, 1-ga, Sinmunno, Jongno-gu, Seoul 110-786, South Korea
CEO: Juhn Myung-Hun, Pres. & CEO
Bus: *Construction, electronics, automobiles, financial services, petrochemicals and shipbuilding.*
NAICS: 237990, 325110, 333298, 334210, 334310, 336111, 336611, 423510, 541512
Tel: 82-2-390-1114
Fax: 82-2-390-2341
www.hyundaicorp.com
Rev: $1,095

HYUNDAI CORP.
879 W., 190th St., 5/F 580, Gardena, California 90248
CEO: F H Pack, Mgr.   Tel: (310) 515-1101
Bus: *New & used automobiles*   Fax: (310) 532-2017

HYUNDAI CORP.
300 Sylvan Ave., Ste. 101, Englewood Cliffs, New Jersey 07632
CEO: Yound Ook Kim, Pres.   Tel: (201) 816-4000
Bus: *New & used automobiles*   Fax: (201) 816-4036   Emp: 28

● **HYUNDAI ENGINEERING & CONSTRUCTION**
140-2 Kye-Dong, Chongro-ku, Seoul 110-793, South Korea
CEO: Lee Ji-Song, Chmn. & Pres.   Tel: 82-2-746-1114   Rev: $4,436
Bus: *General contractor involved in overseas*   Fax: 82-2-746-4846   Emp: 3,531
   construction market.   www.hdec.co.kr
NAICS: 236116, 236210, 236220, 237990

   HYUNDAI ENGINEERING & CONSTRUCTION DIV.
   300 Sylvan Ave., Englewood Cliffs, New Jersey 07632
   CEO: T.W. Kim, Gen. Mgr.   Tel: (201) 816-4063   %FO: 100
   Bus: *Management services.*   Fax: (201) 816-4070

● **HYUNDAI HEAVY INDUSTRIES CO., LTD.**
1 Jeonha-dong, Dong-gu, Ulsan, South Korea
CEO: Keh Sik Min, Chmn. & C0-CEO   Tel: 82-52-230-2361   Rev: $8,673
Bus: *Engaged in shipbuilding.*   Fax: 82-52-230-3432   Emp: 25,958
                                        www.english.hhi.co.kr
NAICS: 213112, 333992, 333999, 336611, 541330

   HYUNDAI HEAVY INDUSTRIES COMPANY
   1400 Broadfield Blvd., Ste. 330, Houston, Texas 77084
   CEO: Jang Park, Pres.   Tel: (281) 578-7097   %FO: 100
   Bus: *Production of construction equipment.*   Fax: (281) 578-8317

   HYUNDAI HEAVY INDUSTRIES COMPANY
   300 Sylvan Ave., Englewood Cliffs, New Jersey 07632
   CEO: T.W. Kim, Gen. Mgr.   Tel: (201) 816-4080   %FO: 100
   Bus: *Engaged in shipbuilding, power plant and*   Fax: (201) 816-4083
      waste treatment plant construction.

● **HYUNDAI MERCHANT MARINE CO., LTD.**
66 Chokson-dong, Chongno-gu, Seoul 110-052, South Korea
CEO: Noh Jung-ik, Pres. & CEO   Tel: 82-2-3706-5114
Bus: *Marine transportation services.* Fax: 82-2-3736-8517   Emp: 4,566
                                        www.hmm21.com
NAICS: 483111

   HYUNDAI AMERICA SHIPPING AGENCY INC.
   5050 Poplar Ave., Ste. 607, Memphis, Tennessee 38157
   CEO: Eugene Lewis, Mgr.   Tel: (901) 681-4380   %FO: 100
   Bus: *Engaged in marine transportation.*   Fax: (901) 681-4383

HYUNDAI AMERICA SHIPPING AGENCY INC.
9977 North 90th St., Ste. 270, Scottsdale, Arizona 85258
CEO: Dan Fetters, Mgr.   Tel: (480) 627-1500   %FO: 100
Bus: *Engaged in marine transportation.*   Fax: (480) 627-1580

HYUNDAI AMERICA SHIPPING AGENCY, INC.
111132 South Towne Square, Ste. 203, St. Louis, Missouri 63123
CEO: John Mack, Mgr.   Tel: (314) 416-4488   %FO: 100
Bus: *Engaged in marine transportation.*   Fax: (314) 416-4499

HYUNDAI AMERICA SHIPPING AGENCY, INC.
100 Galleria Pkwy., Ste. 1360, Atlanta, Georgia 30339
CEO: K.G. Lee, Mgr.   Tel: (770) 980-2043   %FO: 100
Bus: *Engaged in marine transportation.*   Fax: (770) 952-2083

HYUNDAI AMERICA SHIPPING AGENCY, INC.
100 Cummings Center, Ste. 427A, Beverly, Massachusetts 01915
CEO: William Cianfrocca, Mgr.   Tel: (978) 922-5050   %FO: 100
Bus: *Engaged in marine transportation.*   Fax: (978) 922-4774

HYUNDAI AMERICA SHIPPING AGENCY, INC.
24500 Center Ridge Rd., Ste. 265, Westlake, Ohio 44145
CEO: Dale Milison, Mgr.   Tel: (440) 835-0930   %FO: 100
Bus: *Engaged in marine transportation.*   Fax: (440) 835-5522

HYUNDAI AMERICA SHIPPING AGENCY, INC.
26261 Evergreen Rd., Ste. 273, Southfield, Michigan 48076
CEO: Stephen Curitore, Mgr.   Tel: (248) 799-9955   %FO: 100
Bus: *Engaged in marine transportation.*   Fax: (248) 799-9718

HYUNDAI AMERICA SHIPPING AGENCY, INC.
1235 North Loop West, Ste. 900, Houston, Texas 77008
CEO: Paul Hunter, Mgr.   Tel: (713) 861-0123   %FO: 100
Bus: *Engaged in marine transportation.*   Fax: (713) 861-3668   Emp: 6

HYUNDAI AMERICA SHIPPING AGENCY, INC.
8009 34th Ave., So. # 1460, Bloomington, Minnesota 55425
CEO: Sandy Taylor, Mgr.   Tel: (952) 893-1345   %FO: 100
Bus: *Engaged in marine transportation.*   Fax: (952) 893-1718

HYUNDAI AMERICA SHIPPING AGENCY, INC.
455 Market St., Ste. 2050, San Francisco, California 94105
CEO: Jack Goecker, Gen. Mgr.   Tel: (415) 536-2700   %FO: 100
Bus: *Engaged in marine transportation.*   Fax: (415) 536-2711   Emp: 9

HYUNDAI AMERICA SHIPPING AGENCY, INC.
121 Southwest Salmon St., Ste. 830, Portland, Oregon 97204
CEO: Tony Galati, Mgr.   Tel: (503) 224-1112   %FO: 100
Bus: *Engaged in marine transportation.*   Fax: (503) 224-3434   Emp: 15

HYUNDAI MERCHANT MARINE
7807 East Peakview Ave., Ste. 200, Englewood, Colorado 80111
CEO: Horace Harrison Jr, Pres.   Tel: (720) 488-2500   %FO: 100
Bus: *Engaged in marine transportation.*   Fax: (720) 488-2509   Emp: 520

HYUNDAI MERCHANT MARINE
333 Pierce Rd., Ste. 250, Itasca, Illinois 60143
CEO: K.S. Pahk, Pres.   Tel: (630) 274-2300   %FO: 100
Bus: *Engaged in marine transportation.*   Fax: (630) 274-2369

HYUNDAI MERCHANT MARINE
11440 Carmel Commons Blvd., Ste. 206, Charlotte, North Carolina 28226
CEO: K.S. Pahk   Tel: (704) 972-3190   %FO: 100
Bus: *Engaged in marine transportation.*   Fax: (704) 972-3191

HYUNDAI MERCHANT MARINE
6840 Fort Dent Way, Ste. 300, Seattle, Washington 98188
CEO: H. Harrison Jr., Chmn.   Tel: (206) 343-1234   %FO: 100
Bus: *Engaged in marine transportation.*   Fax: (206) 343-1212

HYUNDAI MERCHANT MARINE INC.
10 Pointe Dr., Ste. 460, Brea, California 92821
CEO: Bob Magna, Gen. Mgr.   Tel: (714) 255-2000   %FO: 100
Bus: *Engaged in marine transportation.*   Fax: (714) 255-2092   Emp: 10

HYUNDAI MERCHANT MARINE INC.
1425 Greenway Dr., Irving, Texas 75038
CEO: Bob Stevenson, Mgr.   Tel: (972) 550-2600   %FO: 100
Bus: *Engaged in marine transportation.*   Fax: (972) 550-2715   Emp: 77

HYUNDAI MERCHANT MARINE INC.
1235 North Loop W., Ste. 900, Houston, Texas 77008
CEO: Paul Hunter, Pres.   Tel: (713) 867-5801   %FO: 100
Bus: *Engaged in marine transportation.*   Fax: (713) 867-5801   Emp: 45

HYUNDAI MERCHANT MARINE INC.
300 Sylvan Ave., Englewood Cliffs, New Jersey 07632
CEO: Jim Geary, Mgr.   Tel: (201) 816-4000   %FO: 100
Bus: *Engaged in marine transportation.*   Fax: (201) 816-4061   Emp: 30

HYUNDAI MERCHANT MARINE INC.
1420 N.W. Vivion Rd., Ste. 104, Kansas City, Missouri 64118
CEO: Dennis Benson, Mgr.   Tel: (816) 746-6964   %FO: 100
Bus: *Engaged in marine transportation.*   Fax: (816) 746-8457

● **HYUNDAI MOTOR CO. LTD.**
231 Yangjae-dong, Seocho-gu, Seoul 137-938, South Korea
CEO: Mong Koo Chung, Chmn. & CEO   Tel: 82-2-3464-1114   Rev: $50,695
Bus: *Mfr./sales and service of automobiles.*   Fax: Emp: 51,471
                                    www.hyundai-motor.com
NAICS: 333298, 333923, 336111, 336112
    HYUNDAI AMERICA TECHNICAL CENTER, INC.
    5075 Venture Dr., Ann Arbor, Michigan 48108
    CEO: Won Suk Cho, Pres.   Tel: (734) 747-6600
    Bus: *Auto manufacturer*   Fax:

HYUNDAI MOTOR AMERICA
10550 Talbert Ave., Fountain Valley, California 92728
CEO: Robert Cosmai, Pres. & CEO
Bus: *U.S. headquarters. Mfr./sales automobiles and parts.*
Tel: (714) 965-3000
Fax: (714) 965-3149
%FO: 100

HYUNDAI TRANSLEAD
8880 Rio San Diego Dr., Ste. 600, San Diego, California 92108
CEO: O.S. Koh, CEO
Bus: *Rail & trucking equipment manufacturing*
Tel: (619) 574-1500
Fax: (619) 542-0301
Emp: 2,092

KIA MOTORS AMERICA
9801 Muirlands Blvd., Irvine, California 92618
CEO: Peter M. Butterfield, Pres. & CEO
Bus: *Auto manufacturing*
Tel: (949) 470-7000
Fax: (949) 470-2800
Emp: 500

● **JAMES VISION CO., LTD.**
227-5 Nowon 3 Ga, Buggu, Taegu 702-083, South Korea
CEO: Jae B. Kim, Pres.
Bus: *Mfr. optical frames and sunglasses.*
Tel: 82-53-351-9027
Fax: 82-53-351-2813
www.jamesvision.com
NAICS: 339115

JAMES EYEWEAR CORPORATION
8000 N.W. 31st St., Bay 11, Miami, Florida 33122
CEO: Jae B. Kim, Mgr.
Bus: *Optical frames & sunglasses; mobile amusement products & inflatable fun houses.*
Tel: (305) 477-6336
Fax: (305) 477-9336
%FO: 100

● **JINDO CO., LTD**
60-3 Kasan-dong, Kumchon-Gu, Seoul 153-801, South Korea
CEO: Sung-Sik Suh, CEO
Bus: *Mfr./distribution of fur, garments & containers.*
Tel: 82-2-850-8200
Fax: 82-2-838-2705
www.jindo.co.kr
Rev: $192
Emp: 312
NAICS: 332439

JINDO AMERICA, INC.
1939 Harrison St., Ste. 416, Oakland, California 94612
CEO: Sung-Sik Suh, CEO
Bus: *Shipping containers; fur and leather goods.*
Tel: (510) 834-8900
Fax: (510) 834-8950
%FO: 100

● **KIA MOTORS CORPORATION**
231,Yangjae-dong, Seocho-gu, Seoul 137-938, South Korea
CEO: Eui-Sun Chung, Pres. & CEO
Bus: *Mfr. freight cars and commercial vehicles.*
Tel: 82-2-3464-1114
Fax: 82-2-346+4-6820
www.kiamotors.com
Rev: $10,747
NAICS: 336111, 336112, 336120, 336211, 336999

KIA MOTORS AMERICA, INC.
9801 Muirlands Blvd., Irvine, California 92618
CEO: Peter M. Butterfield, Pres. & CEO
Bus: *Automotive company.*
Tel: (949) 470-7000
Fax: (949) 470-2800
%FO: 100
Emp: 500

- **KOLON INTERNATIONAL CORP.**
427-709 Kolon Tower, 1-23 Byulyang-dong, Kwachon-city, Kyunggi-Do 427040, South Korea

CEO: Lee Woong-yeul, Chmn.	Tel: 82-2-3677-3114	Rev: $1,000
Bus: *General international trading, including film, video tapes, chemical and crude fibers.*	Fax: www.kolon.co.kr	Emp: 3,117
NAICS: 325222, 423990		

  KOLON AMERICA INC
  173 Kilgore Rd., Carrollton, Georgia 30116

CEO: S. Kim	Tel: (770) 832-7700	%FO: 100
Bus: *Engaged in importing and exporting.*	Fax: (770) 832-1706	

  KOLON GLOTECH USA
  1701 Northwestern Dr., El Paso, Texas 79912

CEO: K. H. Han	Tel: (915) 877-4500
Bus: *Engaged in importing and exporting.*	Fax: (915) 877-4501

  KOLON INDUSTRIES
  3 Sperry Rd., Fairfield, New Jersey 07004

CEO: H.K. Keum, Pres.	Tel: (973) 575-2550	%FO: 100
Bus: *Video tape, polyester & nylon films.*	Fax: (973) 575-1332	Emp: 19

  KOLON INDUSTRIES
  173 Kilgore Rd., Carrollton, Georgia 30116

CEO: S. Kim	Tel: (770) 832-7700
Bus: *Engaged in importing and exporting.*	Fax: (770) 832-1706

  KOLON TTA INC
  525 7th Ave., Ste. 1409, New York, New York 10118

CEO: S. Kim	Tel: (646) 366-1430	%FO: 100
Bus: *Engaged in importing and exporting.*	Fax: (646) 366-1431	Emp: 2

- **KOOKMIN BANK**
9-1, 2-Ka, Namdaemoon-ro, Choong-ku, Seoul 100-703, South Korea

CEO: Chung-Won Kang, Pres. & CEO	Tel: 82-2-2073-7114	Rev: $11,052
Bus: *Commercial and investment banking services.*	Fax: 82-2-2073-8360 www.kookmin-bank.com	Emp: 57,724
NAICS: 522110		

  KOOKMIN BANK
  565 Fifth Ave., 24/F, New York, New York 10017

CEO: Dong-Chul Lee, Gen. Mgr.	Tel: (212) 697-6100	%FO: 100
Bus: *Wholesale & merchant banking services.*	Fax: (212) 697-1456	Emp: 9

- **KOREA DATA SYSTEMS CO., LTD.**
170 Gongdan-Dong, Kumi-Si, Kyungbuk-Do, South Korea

CEO: John Hui, Pres.	Tel: 82-546-461-3121
Bus: *Mfr. personal computer monitors.*	Fax: 82-546-461-8720 www.corneasystems.com
NAICS: 334119	

KOREA DATA SYSTEMS USA, INC.
7373 Hunt Ave., Garden Grove, California 92841-2109
CEO: Erin Rippee, VP Mktg.   Tel: (714) 379-5599 %FO: 100
Bus: *Sale PC Monitors.*   Fax: (714) 379-5595 Emp: 50

● **THE KOREA DEVELOPMENT BANK**
16-3 Youido-dong, Yongdeungpo-gu, Seoul 150-973, South Korea
CEO: Jichang Yoo, Gov.   Tel: 82-2-398-6114 Rev: $502
Bus: *Development Bank.*   Fax: 82-2-733-4768 Emp: 500
             www.kdb.co.kr
  NAICS: 522110

  THE KOREA DEVELOPMENT BANK
  320 Park Ave., 32/F, Mutual of America Life Insurance Bldg., New York, New York 10022
  CEO: Song Won Oh, Mgr.   Tel: (212) 688-7686 %FO: 100
  Bus: *International commercial banking services.* Fax: (212) 421-5028

● **KOREA EXCHANGE BANK**
181 2-Ka Ulchiro, Chung Ku, Seoul 100-793, South Korea
CEO: Richard F. Wacker, Pres. Tel: 82-2-729-8000 Rev: $5,843
Bus: *Commercial banking services.* Fax: 82-2-752-3141 Emp: 4,810
           www.keb.co.kr/english/index.htm
  NAICS: 522110, 522210, 522291, 522293, 523110, 523120, 523991, 525920

  KOREA EXCHANGE BANK
  460 Park Ave., 14/F, New York, New York 10022
  CEO: Hosung Lee, Gen. Mgr. Tel: (212) 838-4949 %FO: 100
  Bus: *Commercial banking services.* Fax: (212) 371-5290 Emp: 49

  KOREA EXCHANGE BANK
  777 S. Figueroa St., Ste. 3000, Los Angeles, California 90017
  CEO: Kim Young, Mgr.   Tel: (213) 683-0830 %FO: 100
  Bus: *Commercial banking services.* Fax: (213) 622-5378 Emp: 15

● **THE KOREA EXPRESS COMPANY LTD.**
58-12 Seosomun-Dong, Chung-ku, Seoul, South Korea
CEO: Lee kook-dong, CEO   Tel: 82-2-3782-0114
Bus: *Cargo handling, storage and transport.* Fax: 82-2-3782-0098 Emp: 10,000
           www.korex.co.kr
  NAICS: 488510

  KOREA EXPRESS USA INC.
  830 Supreme Dr., Bensenville, Illinois 60106
  CEO: Yn Joo, Mgr.   Tel: (630) 616-1630 %FO: 100
  Bus: *Engaged in cargo handling, storage and* Fax: (630) 616-1669 Emp: 5
    transport.

  KOREA EXPRESS USA INC.
  3668 Enterprise Ave., Hayward, California 94545
  CEO: Doug Jun, Mgr.   Tel: (510) 782-2424 %FO: 100
  Bus: *Engaged in cargo handling, storage and* Fax: (510) 781-1234 Emp: 10
    transport.

KOREA EXPRESS USA INC.
709 East Walnut St., Carson, California 90746
CEO: Jong S. Park, Mgr.
Bus: *Engaged in cargo handling, storage and transport.*

Tel: (310) 532-3333
Fax: (310) 532-8977

%FO: 100
Emp: 12

KOREA EXPRESS USA INC.
901 Castle Rd., Ste. 2, Secaucus, New Jersey 07094
CEO: Eock Soo Oh, Pres.
Bus: *Engaged in cargo handling, storage and transport.*

Tel: (201) 863-7505
Fax: (201) 863-5036

%FO: 100
Emp: 50

● **KOREAN AIR LINES CO., LTD.**
41-3, Seosomun, Chung-gu, Seoul 360-1, South Korea
CEO: Cho Yang Ho, Chmn. & CEO
Bus: *International passenger and cargo air transport.*

Tel: 82-2-751-7442
Fax: 82-2-751-7499
www.koreanair.com

Rev: $6,884
Emp: 14,994

NAICS: 481111, 481112, 481212

KOREAN AIR
Sea-Tac International Airport, 17801 Pacific Highway South, Room A6011M, Seattle, Washington 98158
CEO: Soon Hwa Kwon, Mgr.
Bus: *International passenger & cargo air transport.*

Tel: (206) 241-1576
Fax:

%FO: 100

KOREAN AIR
Honolulu International Airport, 300 Rodgers Blvd. #69, Honolulu, Hawaii 96819
CEO:
Bus: *International passenger & cargo air transport.*

Tel: (808) 836-1711
Fax:

%FO: 100

KOREAN AIR
1813 Wilshire Blvd., 1/F, Los Angeles, California 90057
CEO: Kyung Kim, Mgr.
Bus: *International passenger & cargo air transport.*

Tel: (310) 417-5200
Fax:

%FO: 100
Emp: 100

KOREAN AIR
2000 Powers Ferry Rd., Ste. 2-10, Marietta, Georgia 30067
CEO: H. W. Lee, Mgr.
Bus: *International passenger & cargo air transport.*

Tel: (404) 761-7691
Fax:

%FO: 100

KOREAN AIR
San Francisco International Airport, Terminal A, San Francisco, California 94128
CEO: Yangho Cho, Pres.
Bus: *International passenger & cargo air transport.*

Tel: (650) 821-0603
Fax:

%FO: 100

KOREAN AIR
4600 Postmark Dr., #NB 216, Anchorage, Alaska 99519
CEO: Jae Yol, Mgr.
Bus: *International passenger & cargo air transport.*

Tel: (907) 243-3329
Fax:

%FO: 100

KOREAN AIR LINES
O'Hare International Airport, Terminal 5, Chicago, Illinois 60666
CEO: Cho Yang-Ho   Tel: (773) 686-2730   %FO: 100
Bus: *International passenger & cargo air*   Fax:
transport.

KOREAN AIR LINES
2333 South Service Rd., Terminal D, UL17334, DFW Airport, Dallas, Texas 75261
CEO: Tim Foley, Mgr.   Tel: (972) 973-7046   %FO: 100
Bus: *International air carrier.*   Fax:

KOREAN AIR LINES
609 Fifth Ave., 12/F, New York, New York 10017
CEO: Young Ho Kim, Mgr.   Tel: (212) 326-5000   %FO: 100
Bus: *International air carrier.*   Fax: (212) 326-5090   Emp: 35

● **KUMHO TIRE CO., INC.**
57, Shinmunro 1-ga, Jongro-gu, Seoul, South Korea
CEO: Sae-Chul Oh, Pres. & CEO   Tel: 82-2-6303-8114   Rev: $1,561
Bus: *Mfr. passenger, truck and bus tires.*   Fax: 82-2-6303-8297   Emp: 5,077
                                       www.kumhotire.com
NAICS: 326211

   KUMHO AMERICA TECHNICAL CENTER
   711 South Cleveland-Massillon Rd., Akron, Ohio 44333
   CEO: Guy Edington, Mgr.   Tel: (330) 666-4030   %FO: 100
   Bus: *Sales of passenger car, truck and bus*   Fax: (330) 666-3972   Emp: 26
   tires.

   KUMHO TIRE USA, INC.
   14605 Miller Ave., Fontana, California 92336
   CEO: Jong G. Kahng, Chmn.   Tel: (909) 428-3999   %FO: 100
   Bus: *Sales of passenger car, truck and bus*   Fax: (909) 428-3989   Emp: 70
   tires.

   KUMHO TIRE USA, INC.
   10299 6th St., Rancho Cucamonga, California 91730
   CEO: Dan Davis, Mgr.   Tel: (909) 483-0284   %FO: 100
   Bus: *Sales of passenger car, truck and bus*   Fax: (909) 483-0289
   tires.

● **LG CHEM LTD.**
LG Twin Tower East, 20 Yoido-dong, Youngdungpo-gu, Seoul 150-721, South Korea
CEO: Yeo Jong-Kee, CEO   Tel: 82-2-3773-5114   Rev: $5,290
Bus: *Chemical manufacture.*   Fax: 82-2-3773-7813   Emp: 10,000
                                       www.lgchem.co.kr
NAICS: 325110, 325181, 325188, 325199

   LG CHEMICAL OF AMERICA INC.
   920 Sylvan Ave., Englewood Cliffs, New Jersey 07632
   CEO: No Ki-Ho, CEO   Tel: (201) 816-2302   %FO: 100
   Bus: *Chemical manufacture.*   Fax: (201) 816-0961

   LG SOLID SURFACE LLC
   8009 W. Olive Ave., Peoria, Arizona 85345
   CEO: Melissa Teegarden, Sales   Tel: (623) 776-7373   %FO: 100
   Bus: *Chemical manufacture.*   Fax: (623) 776-3081

- **LG ELECTRONICS**
  20 Yeouido-dong, Yeoungdeungpo-gu, Seoul 150-721, South Korea
  CEO: S.S. Kim, Chmn. & CEO
  Tel: 82-2-3777-3427
  Rev: $23,542
  Bus: *Mfr./sale home electronics, home appliances,*
  Fax: 82-2-3777-3428
  Emp: 66,614
  computer office automation and magnetics.
  www.lge.com
  NAICS: 332999, 333415, 334119, 334210, 334310, 335211, 335212, 335221, 335222, 335224

  LG ELECTRONICS, INC.
  1000 Sylvan Ave., Englewood Cliffs, New Jersey 07632
  CEO: Michael K. Ahn, Pres.
  Tel: (201) 816-2000
  %FO: 100
  Bus: *Engaged in home appliance, monitor, CD-*
  Fax: (201) 816-2188
  Emp: 75
  ROM and multi-media sales.

- **LG GROUP INTERNATIONAL, LTD.**
  LG Twin Towers, 20 Yoido-Dong, Youngdungpo-gu, Seoul 150-721, South Korea
  CEO: Koo Bon-Moo, Chmn. & CEO
  Tel: 82-2-3773-1114
  Rev: $799
  Bus: *Chemicals and energy, electronics, machinery*
  Fax: 82-2-3773-7813
  Emp: 130,000
  and metals, trade and services, finance and
  www.lg.co.kr
  public services/sports and apparel manufacturing.
  NAICS: 325110, 325120, 325188, 325199, 332999, 333319, 334119, 334290, 335999, 424320, 424710, 424720, 454319, 522210

  LG ELECTRONICS
  PO Box 24007, 201 James Record Rd., Huntsville, Alabama 35824
  CEO: Tae Seung Lee, Pres.
  Tel: (256) 772-8860
  Bus: *Household audio & video equipment.*
  Fax: (256) 772-6129
  Emp: 4,000

  LG GROUP
  1000 Sylvan Ave., Englewood Cliffs, New Jersey 07632
  CEO: Michael K. Ahn, Pres.
  Tel: (201) 816-3090
  Bus: *Consumer electronics.*
  Fax: (201) 816-3094
  Emp: 75

  LG INFOCOMM USA
  10225 Willow Creek Rd., San Diego, California 92131
  CEO: Michael K. Ahn, Pres.
  Tel: (858) 635-5300
  Bus: *Wireless telecommunications equipment.*
  Fax: (858) 635-5225

  ZENITH ELECTRONICS CORPORATION
  2000 Millbrook Dr., Lincolnshire, Illinois 60069
  CEO: Michael K. Ahn, Pres. & CEO
  Tel: (847) 941-8000
  Bus: *Consumer electronics.*
  Fax: (847) 941-8200

- **LG. PHILIPS LCD CO., LTD**
  17/F, West Tower, LG Twin Towers, 20 Yoido-dong, Youngdungpo-gu, Seoul 150-721, South Korea
  CEO: Ad Huijser, Chmn.
  Tel: 82-2-3777-0790
  Rev: $8,042
  Bus: *Produces and supplies TFT-LCDs for monitors,*
  Fax:
  Emp: 8,570
  notebook computers and various applications.
  www.lgphilips-lcd.com
  NAICS: 334411, 334413, 334419

  LG. PHILIPS LCD AMERICA INC.
  150 East Brokaw Rd., San Jose, California 95112
  CEO: C.H. Woo
  Tel: (408) 350-7723
  %FO: 100
  Bus: *Manufacturer computer display components*
  Fax: (408) 350-7724

- **MANDO CORPORATION**
  949-3, Dogok-dong, Gangnam-gu, Seoul 135-270, South Korea
  CEO: Oh Sang Soo, Pres. & CEO
  Bus: *Automobile parts manufacture.*
  Tel: 82-2-6244-2114
  Fax: 82-2-6244-2992
  www.mando.com
  Rev: $1,000
  Emp: 5,000

  NAICS: 336322, 336399

  MANDO AMERICA CORPORATION
  Northeast Opelika Industrial Park, 4201 North Park Dr., Opelika, Alabama 36801
  CEO: Gi-On Jeon, Pres.
  Bus: *Automobile parts manufacture.*
  Tel: (334) 364-3600
  Fax: (334) 364-3601
  %FO: 100

  MANDO AMERICA CORPORATION
  45901 Five Mile Rd., Plymouth, Michigan 48170
  CEO: Seok Keun Song, Mgr.
  Bus: *Automobile parts manufacture.*
  Tel: (734) 254-1030
  Fax: (734) 254-1060
  %FO: 100

- **MIRAE CORPORATION**
  9-2 Cha-Am-dong, Chonan, Chungchong-nam 330-200, South Korea
  CEO: Soon Do Kwon, Pres.
  Bus: *Semiconductor manufacturing equipment.*
  Tel: 82-41-621-5070
  Fax: 82-41-621-5090
  www.mirae.co.kr
  Rev: $80
  Emp: 294

  NAICS: 333295

  FINETRON
  30912 Catarina Dr., Westlake Village, California 91362
  CEO: J. Y. Lee
  Bus: *Semiconductor manufacturing equipment.*
  Tel: (818) 706-3543
  Fax: (818) 337-2294
  %FO: 100

  MIRAE CORPORATION
  1855 O'Toole Ave., Ste. D-101, San Jose, California 95131
  CEO: Luke Makthepharack
  Bus: *Semiconductor manufacturing equipment.*
  Tel: (408) 432-3880
  Fax: (408) 432-3883
  %FO: 100

  MIRAE CORPORATION
  103 Bay Hill Dr., Blue Bell, Pennsylvania 19422
  CEO: James D. Stevens
  Bus: *Semiconductor manufacturing equipment.*
  Tel: (610) 270-3002
  Fax: (610) 270-0588
  %FO: 100

- **POONGSAN CORPORATION**
  60-1 3-Ga Chungmooro, Chung-Gu, Seoul 100-012, South Korea
  CEO: Jin Roy Ryu, CEO
  Bus: *Supplies fabricated copper and copper alloy products.*
  Tel: 82-2-3406-5114
  Fax: 82-2-3406-5400
  www.poongsan.co.kr
  Rev: $1,200
  Emp: 4,261

  NAICS: 331421, 331422

  PMX INDUSTRIES, INC.
  5300 Willow Creek Dr., Cedar Rapids, Iowa 52404
  CEO: Jin Roy Ryu, Pres.
  Bus: *Copper and metal materials.*
  Tel: (319) 368-7700
  Fax: (319) 368-7701
  %FO: 100
  Emp: 260

- **POSCO**
  POSCO Center, 892 Daechi -4-dong, Kangnam-ku, Seoul, South Korea
  CEO: Lee Ku-Taek, Chmn. & CEO   Tel: 82-2-3457-0114   Rev: $14,925
  Bus: *Rolled steel products manufacture.*   Fax: 82-54-220-6000   Emp: 27,415
       www.posco.co.kr
  NAICS: 331221, 331222

  - **POSCO AMERICA CORPORATION**
    1800 K. St., Ste. 1110, Washington, District of Columbia 20006
    CEO: Ok Hyun Kim, Mgr.   Tel: (202) 785-5643
    Bus: *Informative retrieval service*   Fax: (202) 785-5647

  - **POSCO AMERICA CORPORATION**
    2 Executive Dr., Ste. 805, Fort Lee, New Jersey 07024
    CEO: Liza Kim   Tel: (201) 585-3060   %FO: 100
    Bus: *Rolled steel products manufacture and*   Fax: (201) 585-6001
         sales.

  - **USS-POSCO INDUSTRIES**
    900 Loveridge Rd., Pittsburg, California 94565
    CEO: Robert R. Smith, Pres.   Tel: (925) 439-6000
    Bus: *Steel service center*   Fax: (925) 439-6179   Emp: 1,000

- **PUSAN BANK**
  830-38 Bomildong Donggu, Pusan 614-829, South Korea
  CEO: Shim Hoon, Chmn. & Pres.   Tel: 82-51-642-3300   Rev: $333
  Bus: *Commercial banking services.*   Fax: 82-51-642-3151   Emp: 2,838
       www.pusanbank.co.kr
  NAICS: 522110

  - **PUSAN BANK**
    29 West 30th St., New York, New York 10001
    CEO: Yon Joo Jung, Rep.   Tel: (212) 244-2780   %FO: 100
    Bus: *International banking services.*   Fax: (212) 244-2780

- **SAMICK MUSICAL INSTRUMENTS CO., LTD.**
  424 Cheongcheon 2-dong, Bupyeong-gu, Inchon, South Korea
  CEO: Jong-Sup Kim, Chmn. & CEO   Tel: 82-32-453-3333   Rev: $108
  Bus: *Mfr. musical instruments*   Fax: 82-32-453-3376   Emp: 285
       www.samick.co.kr
  NAICS: 339992

  - **SAMICK MUSIC CORP.**
    185231 E. Railroad St., City of Industry, California 91748-1316
    CEO: Robert J. Jones, Pres. & CEO   Tel: (626) 964-4700   %FO: 100
    Bus: *Manufacturer musical instruments*   Fax: (626) 965-5224

- **SAMJIN TRADING CO., LTD.**
  1140-36 Jegidong, Dongdaimoon-ku, Seoul, South Korea
  CEO: Kang Choong-Hyuan, CEO   Tel: 82-2-968-5501
  Bus: *Oriental food, Ramen noodles, canned foods, gift*   Fax: 82-2-961-5110   Emp: 50
       and kitchenware   www.agotrade.net/samjintr/
  NAICS: 311422, 311423, 311999, 327112

SAMJIN AMERICA, INC.
3345 East Slauson Ave., Vernon, California 90058
CEO: Choong Hyun Kang, Pres.   Tel: (213) 622-5111   %FO: 100
Bus: *Oriental food, Ramen noodles, canned food,* Fax: (213) 622-5285
 gift and kitchenware.

• **SAMSUNG CORPORATION**
Samsung Plaza, 263 Seohyeon-dong, Bundang-gu,
Songnam, Kyonggi 463-721, South Korea
CEO: Pae Chong-Yeul, CEO   Tel: 82-2-2145-2114   Rev: $9,257
Bus: *Import/export, construction services, e-business* Fax: 82-2-2145-3114 Emp: 4,288
 and housing development.   www.samsungcorp.com
 NAICS: 236210, 236220, 237990, 333999, 334413, 423810, 424690, 424710, 424720, 454319, 561210

 SAMSUNG AMERICA INC
 757 North Eldridge Pkwy., Ste. 640, Houston, Texas 77079
 CEO: Andy Kim, Mgr.   Tel: (713) 953-9700   %FO: 100
 Bus: *Steel & related products*   Fax: (713) 953-9911

 SAMSUNG AMERICA INC.
 14251 East Firestone Blvd., Ste. 201, La Mirada, California 90638
 CEO: Tel: (562) 483-7244   %FO: 100
 Bus: *Import/export/mfr; textiles, sportswear* Fax: (562) 407-1864
  apparel, heavy machinery, communication
  technology and construction services.

 SAMSUNG AMERICA INC.
 3655 North First St., San Jose, California 95134
 CEO: Han Joo Kim, Pres.   Tel: (408) 544-4000
 Bus: *Electronic parts & equipment*   Fax: (408) 544-4969   Emp: 1,176

 SAMSUNG AMERICA INC.
 105 Challenger Rd., Ste. 1, Ridgefield Park, New Jersey 07660
 CEO: Jae Hyung-Lee, Pres. & CEO   Tel: (201) 229-5000   %FO: 100
 Bus: *Imp/export general merchandise.*   Fax: (201) 229-5080

 SAMSUNG AMERICA, INC.
 14251 East Firestone Blvd., Ste. 201, La Mirada, California 90638
 CEO: Jae Lee, Pres.   Tel: (562) 802-2211
 Bus: *Computers, peripherals & software*   Fax: (562) 802-3011

• **SAMSUNG ELECTRONICS CO., LTD.**
250-2-Ga, Taepyong-Ro, Jung-Gu, Seoul 100-742, South Korea
CEO: Jong-Yong Yun, Chmn. & CEO   Tel: 82-2-727-7114   Rev: $54,252
Bus: *Computer memory discs, LCD panels, micro* Fax: 82-2-727-7985 Emp: 88,447
 products.   www.samsung.com
 NAICS: 332618, 333315, 333511, 333512, 333513, 333514, 333518, 334111, 334112, 334113, 334119, 334210,
334220, 334290, 334310, 334413, 334513,
  334613, 335211, 335212, 335221, 335222, 335224, 335228, 335312, 335929, 423620, 811310
 SAMSUNG ELECTRONICS AMERICA INC.
 18600 Broadwick St., Rancho Dominguez, California 90220
 CEO: Peter Skarzynski, Pres.   Tel: (310) 537-7000   %FO: 100
 Bus: *Mfr. distributor computer monitors.*   Fax: (310) 537-1033   Emp: 9,000

SAMSUNG ELECTRONICS AMERICA INC.
105 Challenger Rd., Ridgefield Park, New Jersey 07660
CEO: Dong-Jin Oh, Pres. & CEO   Tel: (201) 229-4000   %FO: 100
Bus: *Mfr. consumer electronics, information*   Fax: (201) 229-4029
systems, storage system products and
office automation products.

SAMSUNG SEMICONDUCTOR, INC.
3655 North First St., San Jose, California 95134
CEO: Young Hwan Park, Pres. & CEO   Tel: (408) 544-4000   %FO: 100
Bus: *Semi-conducting equipment, memory, TFT*   Fax: (408) 544-4980   Emp: 1,176
LCD, ASIC and MCU.

SAMSUNG TELECOMMUNICATIONS AMERICA LLP
1130 East Arapaho Rd., Richardson, Texas 75081
CEO: Jeong Han Kim, Pres.   Tel: (972) 761-7000   %FO: 100
Bus: *Telecommunications systems, consumer*   Fax: (972) 761-7001   Emp: 600
appliances, A/V equipment, computers,
printers and semiconductors/

SYMBIAN LTD.
390 Bridge Pkwy., Ste. 201, Redwood Shores, California 94065
CEO: Jerry Panagrossi, VP   Tel: (650) 551-0240   %FO: 50
Bus: *Wireless software.*   Fax: (650) 551-0241

● **SAMSUNG FIRE & MARINE INSURANCE CO., LTD.**
Samsung Insurance Bldg. 87, Euljiro 1-ga Choong-Gu, Seoul 100-191, South Korea
CEO: Soo-Chang Lee, Pres. & CEO   Tel: 82-2-758-7037   Rev: $2,491
Bus: *Sales non-life insurance.*   Fax: 82-2-758-7831   Emp: 4,075
                                                     www.samsungfire.com.cn

NAICS: 524114, 524126

    SAMSUNG FIRE & MARINE INSURANCE CO., LTD.
    105 Challenger Rd., 5/F, Ridgefield Park, New Jersey 07660
    CEO: Soo Chang Lee, Pres. & CEO   Tel: (201) 229-6011   %FO: 100
    Bus: *Sales non-life insurance policies.*   Fax: (201) 299-6015

● **SAMSUNG LIFE INSURANCE CO., LTD.**
Samsung Life Insurance Bldg., 150 Taepyongro 2-ga Jung-gu, Seoul 100-716, South Korea
CEO: Jung-Choong Bae, Pres. & CEO   Tel: 82-2-1588-3114   Rev: $20,557
Bus: *Individual and group life insurance and real* Fax: 82-2-751-8021   Emp: 6,314
estate services.   www.samsunglife.com
NAICS: 522110, 522120, 522190, 522220, 522291, 522298, 523991, 523999, 524113, 524114, 524128, 525110,
525120, 525190, 525910, 525920, 525990,
          531110, 531120, 531190, 531311, 531312, 531390

    SAMSUNG LIFE INSURANCE CO.
    399 Park Ave., 18/F, New York, New York 10022
    CEO: Byeon-Guk Park   Tel: (212) 421-2705   %FO: 100
    Bus: *Individual and group life insurance services.* Fax: (212) 421-2665

- **SAMWHA ELECTRONICS CO., LTD.**
  587-8 Shinsa-Dong, Gangnam-Gu, 7/F, Seoul, South Korea
  CEO: Lee Keun Beom, CEO   Tel: 82-2-546-0999   Rev: $145
  Bus: *Ferrite and ceramic magnetic products*   Fax: 82-2-548-7354   Emp: 642
  manufacture.   www.samwha.co.kr
  NAICS: 331112, 334413, 334414, 334415

    SAMWHA USA
    2700 River Rd., Ste. 203, Des Plaines, Illinois 60018
    CEO: David B. Yoo   Tel: (847) 294-0081   %FO: 100
    Bus: *Ferrite and ceramic magnetic products*   Fax: (847) 294-0082
    manufacture.

    SAMWHA USA
    2555 Melksee St., San Diego, California 92154
    CEO: David B. Yoo   Tel: (619) 671-0870   %FO: 100
    Bus: *Ferrite and ceramic magnetic products*   Fax: (619) 671-0874
    manufacture.

- **SEAH STEEL CORPORATION**
  10 Bongnae-dong 1, Joong-gu, Seoul 100-161, South Korea
  CEO: Jong-Young Lee, Pres. & CEO   Tel: 82-2-3783-8114   Rev: $874
  Bus: *Iron and steel products.*   Fax: 82-2-3783-8066   Emp: 956
       www.seahsteel.co.kr
  NAICS: 331111

    SEAH STEEL CORPORATION
    9615 South Norwalk Blvd., Ste. B, Santa Fe Springs, California 90670
    CEO: Chris Sohn, Mgr.   Tel: (562) 692-0600   %FO: 100
    Bus: *Iron and steel products.*   Fax: (562) 692-9295   Emp: 141

    SEAH STEEL CORPORATION
    740 Springdale Rd., Ste. 145, Exton, Pennsylvania 19341
    CEO: Byung Joon Lee, Chmn.   Tel: (610) 280-9480   %FO: 100
    Bus: *Iron and Steel products.*   Fax: (610) 280-9484

    SEAH STEEL CORPORATION
    14550 Torrey Chase Blvd., Ste. 345, Houston, Texas 77014
    CEO: Jean Lee, Principal   Tel: (281) 873-7800   %FO: 100
    Bus: *Iron and steel products.*   Fax: (281) 873-7873   Emp: 5

- **SHINHAN FINANCIAL GROUP**
  Deakyung B/D 16/F-17/F, 120 2-Ga, Taepyung-ro, Jung-Gu, Seoul 100-102, South Korea
  CEO: In-Ho Lee, Pres. & CEO   Tel: 82-2-6360-3000   Rev: $9,472
  Bus: *Retail and international banking services.*   Fax: 82-2-777-1883   Emp: 17,391
       www.shinhangroup.com
  NAICS: 522110

    SHINHAN BANK
    800 Third Ave., 32/F, New York, New York 10022
    CEO: Suk Jin Koh, Mgr.   Tel: (212) 371-8000   %FO: 100
    Bus: *International banking services.*   Fax: (212) 371-8875   Emp: 28

● **SK GLOBAL CO., LTD.**
99 Seorin-dong, Jongro-gu, Seoul 110-110, South Korea
CEO: Shin Heon-Cheol, Pres. & CEO   Tel: 82-2-2121-5114   Rev: $16,618
Bus: *Petroleum and petrochemicals manufacture.*   Fax: 82-2-2121-7001
                                              www.sk.com
NAICS: 324110, 324191, 324199, 325110, 424710, 424720, 447190, 454311, 454312, 454319, 517212

SK CORPORATION
22-10 Route 208 South, Fair Lawn, New Jersey 07410
CEO: Keeju Choi, Mgr.   Tel: (201) 796-4288
Bus: *Mfr. petroleum & petrochemicals.*   Fax: (201) 796-2278

SK CORPORATION
1300 Post Oak Blvd., Ste. 780, Houston, Texas 77056
CEO: Heon Sub Lee   Tel: (713) 871-1184   %FO: 100
Bus: *Crude oil and petroleum products trading.*   Fax: (713) 871-8050

SK CORPORATION BIO-PHARMACEUTICAL, INC.
140 A New Dutch Lane, Fairfield, New Jersey 07006
CEO: Young Choi, Principal   Tel: (973) 227-3939   %FO: 100
Bus: *Bio-pharmaceutical research and*   Fax: (973) 227-4488   Emp: 14
    development.

SK NETWORKS
Parker Plaza, 400 Kelby St., 10/f, Fort Lee, New Jersey 07024
CEO: M. Choi, Pres. & CEO   Tel: (201) 363-8200   %FO: 100
Bus: *Petroleum & petrochemicals.*   Fax: (201) 363-8393

SK NETWORKS AMERICA
17106 South Avalon Blvd., Carson, California 90746
CEO: J. Chung   Tel: (310) 527-0400
Bus: *Petroleum & petrochemicals.*   Fax: (310) 527-0410

SK SHIPPING
920 United Airlines Bldg., 2033 6th Ave., Seattle, Washington 98121
CEO: Sang Bum Park   Tel: (206) 448-9178
Bus: *Petroleum & petrochemicals.*   Fax: (206) 448-9314

SK TELCOM
400 Kelby St., 17/F, Fort Lee, New Jersey 07024
CEO: Michael M.G. Kim   Tel: (201) 613-8000   %FO: 100
Bus: *Telecommunications.*   Fax: (201) 613-8042

SK USA
400 Kelby St., 17/F, Fort Lee, New Jersey 07024
CEO: Michael M.G. Kim   Tel: (201) 613-8000
Bus: *Petroleum & petrochemicals.*   Fax: (201) 613-8040

SKC
1 SKC Dr., Covington, Georgia 30014
CEO: Y.J. Joon, Pres.   Tel: (678) 342-1000
Bus: *Petroleum & petrochemicals.*   Fax: (678) 342-1800   Emp: 200

SKEC AMERICA
2929 Briar Park, Ste. 310, Houston, Texas 77042
CEO: Michael M.G. Kim
Bus: *Petroleum & petrochemicals.*
Tel: (713) 266-6167
Fax: (713) 266-2472

● **SKC CO., LTD.**
646-15, Yeoksam-dong, Kangnam-gu, Seoul 135-080, South Korea
CEO: Jang Suk Park, CEO
Bus: *Film and microfilm.*
Tel: 82-2-3708-5151
Fax: 82-2-752-9088
www.skc.co.kr
Rev: $713
Emp: 1,991

NAICS: 325992

SKC AMERICA INC.
1000 SKC Dr., Covington, Georgia 30014
CEO: Jeff Brown, Mgr.
Bus: *Film and microfilm.*
Tel: (678) 342-1000
Fax: (378) 342-1800
%FO: 100

SKC AMERICA INC.
850 Clark Dr., Mt. Olive, New Jersey 07828
CEO: J. K. Lee, VP
Bus: *Film and microfilm.*
Tel: (973) 347-7000
Fax: (973) 347-7522
%FO: 100

● **SKM LTD.**
Hae Sung Bldg. 1, 5/F, 942 Daechi 3-dong, Gangnam-gu, Seoul 135-283, South Korea
CEO: Mun-Seong Park, CEO
Bus: *Recording media; professional and consumer audio tapes.*
Tel: 82-2-528-3001
Fax: 82-2-528-3005
www.skm.co.kr

NAICS: 334613

SUNKYONG MAGNETIC AMERICA INC. (SKMA, INC.)
4041 Via Oro Ave., Long Beach, California 90810
CEO: Mike Ingalls, Rep.
Bus: *Professional & consumer audio tapes.*
Tel: (310) 830-6000
Fax: (310) 830-0646
%FO: 100
Emp: 20

● **SSANGYONG CORPORATION**
24-1, 2-ga, Jeo-dong, Jung-gu, Seoul 100-748, South Korea
CEO: Cho Kook-Pil, Pres. & CEO
Bus: *General trading company.*
Tel: 82-2-2270-8114
Fax: 82-2-2270-8791
www.ssytrade.co.kr
Rev: $1,005
Emp: 226

NAICS: 236210, 238130, 238140, 238210, 238220, 238220, 238310, 238320, 238340, 325211, 541330, 541519

RYRAMID STEEL & PYRAMID PROCESSING
1335 Boyles, Houston, Texas 77020
CEO: Intwook Pyo, Mgr.
Bus: *Sale of nondurable goods.*
Tel: (713) 937-9090
Fax: (713) 953-0880
%FO: 100

SSANGYONG (USA) INC.
10504 Pioneer Blvd., Santa Fe Springs, California 90670
CEO: Kevin Kim, Mgr.
Bus: *Sale of nondurable goods.*
Tel: (562) 906-0799
Fax: (562) 941-9890
%FO: 100
Emp: 50

SSANGYONG (USA) INC.
115 West Century Rd., Paramus, New Jersey 07652
CEO: Chan Woong Chung, Pres.   Tel: (201) 261-9400   %FO: 100
Bus: *import/export, general trading company.*   Fax: (201) 262-8880   Emp: 110

• **TONG YANG MAJOR CO., LTD.**
23-8 Yoido-Dong,, Youngdungpo-Ku, Seoul 150-707, South Korea
CEO: Young-in Rho, CEO   Tel: 82-2-3770-3000
Bus: *Engineering and construction services.*   Fax: 82-2-3770-3311
                                     www.tongyangmajor.com

NAICS: 236210, 236220, 541310, 541330, 541340

    TONG YANG AMERICA INC.
    590 Madison Ave., 37/F, New York, New York 10022
    CEO: Hyungro Yoon, Pres.   Tel: (212) 415-1000   %FO: 100
    Bus: *Engineering and construction services.*   Fax: (212) 821-1050

• **TRIGEM COMPUTER, INC.**
1055 Shingil-dong, Ansan, Kyonggi 425-120, South Korea
CEO: Paul Lee, Chmn. & CEO   Tel: 82-3-1489-3000   Rev: $1,863
Bus: *Manufacturing and trading of computers.*   Fax: 82-3-1489-3333   Emp: 4,000
                                     www.trigem.com

NAICS: 333313, 334111, 334113, 334119

    TG INC.
    1270 Oakmead Pkwy., Ste. 101, Sunnyvale, California 94085
    CEO: Tim Seo, Mgr.   Tel: (408) 523-1470
    Bus: *Computers, peripherals & software*   Fax: (408) 523-1474

    TRIGEM AMERICA CORPORATION
    80 Icon St., Foothill Ranch El Toro, California 92610
    CEO: Kang Burn, CEO   Tel: (949) 460-5900   %FO: 100
    Bus: *Manufacturing of computers.*   Fax: (949) 580-3677   Emp: 350

• **UNION STEEL MFG. CO., LTD.**
890 Daechi-dong, Kangnam-ku, Seoul, South Korea
CEO: Sae joo Chang, Chmn. & CEO   Tel: 82-2-3279-9114   Rev: $622
Bus: *Flat rolled galvanized steel sheets, steel pipes &*   Fax: 82-2-704-2450   Emp: 1,260
    tubes.   www.unionsteel.co.kr.
NAICS: 331111, 331221, 331222

    UNION STEEL AMERICA, INC
    19750 Magellan Dr., Torrance, California 90502
    CEO: Steven Kim, Rep.   Tel: (310) 523-9595
    Bus: *Sale of flat rolled galvanized steel sheets,*   Fax: (310) 523-9599
        steel pipes & tubes.

    UNION STEEL AMERICA, INC.
    460 Bergen Blvd., Palisades Park, New Jersey 07650
    CEO: Jin Hur, Rep.   Tel: (201) 592-8600   %FO: 100
    Bus: *Sale of flat rolled galvanized steel sheets,*   Fax: (201) 947-3999
        steel pipes & tubes.

- **WOORI FINANCE HOLDINGS**
  203 Hoehyon-dong 1-ga, Chung-gu, Seoul 100-792, South Korea
  CEO: Young-Key Hwang, Pres. & CEO   Tel: 82-2-2125-2000   Rev: $8,876
  Bus: *Commercial banking services.*   Fax: 82-2-2125-2291   Emp: 15,846
      www.woorifg.com

  NAICS: 522110

      WOORI BANK OF AMERICA
      7400 Front St., Cheltenham, Pennsylvania 19012
      CEO: Soon Deok Kim   Tel: (215) 782-2015   %FO: 100
      Bus: *Commercial banking services.*   Fax: (215) 782-8907

      WOORI BANK OF AMERICA
      225 Broad Ave., Palisades Park, New Jersey 07650
      CEO: MI Ja Dong   Tel: (201) 346-0055   %FO: 100
      Bus: *Commercial banking services.*   Fax: (201) 346-0075

      WOORI BANK OF AMERICA
      7300 Old York Rd., Elkins Park, Pennsylvania 19027
      CEO: Mee Ja Kim   Tel: (215) 782-1100   %FO: 100
      Bus: *Commercial banking services.*   Fax: (215) 782-1500

      WOORI BANK OF AMERICA
      234 Closter Dock Rd., Closter, New Jersey 07624
      CEO: Lydia Cheong   Tel: (201) 784-7012   %FO: 100
      Bus: *Commercial banking services.*   Fax: (201) 784-7013

      WOORI BANK OF AMERICA
      2053 Lemoine Ave., Fort Lee, New Jersey 07024
      CEO: Su Yeon Oh   Tel: (201) 363-9300   %FO: 100
      Bus: *Commercial banking services.*   Fax: (201) 363-0900

      WOORI BANK OF AMERICA
      2053 Lemoine Ave., Fort Lee, New Jersey 07024-5704
      CEO: Soon Hee Jeong   Tel: (201) 363-9300   %FO: 100
      Bus: *Commercial banking services.*   Fax: (201) 363-9300

      WOORI BANK OF AMERICA
      1250 Broadway, New York, New York 10001
      CEO: Jay Seung Yoo, Pres.   Tel: (212) 244-1500   %FO: 100
      Bus: *Commercial banking services.*   Fax: (212) 736-5929

- **YOUNG CHANG CO., LTD.**
  178-55 Gajwadong, Seo-ku, Inchon, South Korea
  CEO: Jae-Sup Kim, CEO   Tel: 82-32-570-1000
  Bus: *Piano manufacturing.*   Fax: 82-32-576-2340
      www.ycpiano.co.kr

  NAICS: 339992

      KURZWEIL MUSIC SYSTEMS
      10107 S. Tacoma Way, Ste. A-3, Lakewood, Washington 98499
      CEO: Jeff Dunmire   Tel: (253) 589-3580   %FO: 100
      Bus: *Piano manufacture and sales.*   Fax: (866) 589-3585

Spain

- **ABENGOA SA**
Avenida de la Buhaira 2, E-41018 Seville, Spain
CEO: Felipe Benjumea Llorente, Co-Chair
Bus: *Applied engineering and process management
services.*
NAICS: 541330, 541620, 541990

Tel: 34-954-937-111
Fax: 34-954-937-020
www.abengoa.es

Rev: $1,222
Emp: 9,550

  ABENGOA BIOENERGY CORP.
  Rural Route 2, Box 60, York, Nebraska 68467
  CEO: Brian Pasbirg, Operations Mgr.
  Bus: *Ethanol production.*

  Tel: (402) 362-2285
  Fax: (402) 362-7041

  %FO: 100

  ABENGOA BIOENERGY CORP.
  523 East Union Ave., PO Box 427, Colwich, Kansas 67030
  CEO: Asif Malik, Plant Mgr.
  Bus: *Ethanol production.*

  Tel: (316) 796-1234
  Fax: (316) 796-1523

  %FO: 100

  ABENGOA BIOENERGY CORP.
  1400 Elbridge Payne Rd., Ste. 212, Chesterfield, Missouri 63017
  CEO: Javier Salgado, CEO
  Bus: *Ethanol production.*

  Tel: (636) 728-0508
  Fax: (636) 728-1148

  %FO: 100

- **ACEITES BORGES PONT SA**
Avenida J. Trepat s/n, E-25300 Tarrega, Spain
CEO: Ramon Pont Amenos, Pres.
Bus: *Production of olive oil, seeds, oil based powders,
nuts and agricultural products.*
NAICS: 311225, 311911

Tel: 34-973-501-212
Fax: 34-973-500-060
www.aceitesborges.es

Rev: $240
Emp: 220

  BORGES OF CALIFORNIA INC.
  1424 HWY 45, Glenn, California 95943
  CEO: W. Carriere
  Bus: *Olive oil products sales and distribution.*

  Tel: (916) 934-7454
  Fax: (916) 934-7983

  STAR FINE FOODS BORGES USA
  4652 E. Date Ave., Fresno, California 93725
  CEO: Stan Lewczyk, Pres.
  Bus: *Importers, processors, packers and
distributors of specialty food products,
including olives, olive oils, walnuts and*

  Tel: (559) 498-2900
  Fax: (559) 498-2920

  %FO: 50

- **ACERINOX SA**
Santiago de Compostela, 100, E-28035 Madrid, Spain
CEO: Victoriano Munoz Cava, CEO
Bus: *Mfr. stainless steel.*

Tel: 34-91-398-5100
Fax: 34-91-398-5197
www.acerinox.es

Rev: $3,656
Emp: 6,392

NAICS: 331111

NORTH AMERICAN STAINLESS, DIV. ACERINOX
6870 Highway 42 East, Ghent, Kentucky 41045
CEO: Jose M. Cornejo, Pres.
Bus: *Distributor stainless steel.*

Tel: (502) 347-6000
Fax: (502) 347-6001

%FO: JV

● **ADEX SL**
Plaza Valle de la Jarosa, 77, E-28035 Madrid, Spain
CEO: Javier Martinez, Pres.
Bus: *Ceramic tiles manufacture and sales.*

Tel: 34-96-132-1214
Fax: 34-96-132-1214
www.adexcop.com

Emp: 40

NAICS: 327122

　ADEX USA
　2818 NW 112th Ave., Miami, Florida 33172
　CEO: Cristina Palop, Pres.
　Bus: *Ceramic tile sales and distribution.*

Tel: (305) 513-4633
Fax: (305) 513-4633

%FO: 100

● **AGE FOTOSTOCK**
Buenaventura Munoz 16, E-08018 Barcelona, Spain
CEO: Alfonso Gutierrez, Gen. Mgr.
Bus: *Photographic agency.*

Tel: 34-93-300-2552
Fax: 34-93-485-0367
www.agefotostock.com

NAICS: 541922

　AGE FOTOSTOCK AMERICA
　594 Broadway, Ste. 707, New York, New York 10012
　CEO: Susan Jones, Gen. Mgr.
　Bus: *Photographic agency.*

Tel: (212) 625-9000
Fax: (212) 965-9666

%FO: 100

● **AIR PLUS COMET**
Bahía de Pollensa, 21-23, E-28042 Madrid, Spain
CEO: Antonio Mata, Pres. & CEO
Bus: *Commercial air transport services.*

Tel: 34-91-203-6300
Fax: 34-91-329-3511
www.aircomet.com

NAICS: 481111

　AIR PLUS COMET
　420 Lexington Ave., Ste. 2631, New York, New York 10170
　CEO: Jordi Pique
　Bus: *International commercial air transport
　services.*

Tel: (212) 983-1277
Fax: (212) 983-1156

%FO: 100
Emp: 15

● **ALCALAGRÉS, DIV. GRUPO CENTUNION**
Apartado 1154, Alcala de Henares, E-28880 Madrid, Spain
CEO: Gonzalez Del Valle Chavarri, Chmn.
Bus: *Porcelain tile manufacture.*

Tel: 34-91-886-5920
Fax: 34-91-886-6248
www.centunion.com

NAICS: 327122

　ALCALAGRES USA, INC.
　8600 NW 72nd St., Miami, Florida 33166
　CEO: Guillermo Puente, Mng. Dir.
　Bus: *Porcelain tiles manufacture and sales.*

Tel: (305) 640-0555
Fax: (305) 640-0266

%FO: 100

- **ALTADIS, S.A.**
  Eloy Gonzalo 10, E-28010 Madrid, Spain
  CEO: Jean-Dominique Comolli, CEO
  Bus: *Mfr. premium cigars and cigarettes.*

  NAICS: 312221, 312229

  Tel: 34-91-360-9000
  Fax: 34-91-360-9100
  www.altadis.com

  Rev: $10,600
  Emp: 19,600

  - **ALTADIS USA, INC.**
    5900 N. Andrews Ave., Ste. 1100, Ft. Lauderdale, Florida 33309-2369
    CEO: Theo W. Folz, CEO
    Bus: *Mfr. premium cigars.*

    Tel: (954) 772-9000
    Fax: (954) 938-7811

    %FO: 100

- **AMADEUS GLOBAL TRAVEL DISTRIBUTION SA**
  Salvador de Madariaga 1, E- 28027 Madrid, Spain
  CEO: Jose Antonio Tazon, CEO
  Bus: *Engaged in travel, ticketing, e-commerce and business to business services.*

  NAICS: 454111, 541511, 561599

  Tel: 34-91-582-0100
  Fax: 34-91-582-0188
  www.amadeuslink.com

  Rev: $1,800
  Emp: 4,000

  - **AMADEUS GLOBAL TRAVEL DISTRIBUTION**
    9250 North West 36th St., Miami, Florida 33178
    CEO: Debra Iannaci, Mgr.
    Bus: *Engaged in travel, ticketing, e-commerce and business to business services.*

    Tel: (305) 499-6448
    Fax: (305) 499-6866

    %FO: 100

- **AZU-VI, SA**
  Av. Italia, 58, Villarreal, E-12540 Castellon de la Plana, Spain
  CEO: Vicente Monzonis Ortells, Mgr.
  Bus: *Ceramic tile manufacture.*

  NAICS: 327122

  Tel: 34-954-509-100
  Fax: 34-954-599-110
  www.azuvi.com.

  Rev: $450
  Emp: 59

  - **AZU-VI, INC.**
    1070 N. Kraemer Place, Anaheim, California 92806
    CEO: Ray Zuniga
    Bus: *Ceramic tile sales and distribution.*

    Tel: (714) 632-9390
    Fax: (714) 632-9315

    %FO: 100

  - **AZU-VI, INC.**
    13291 Vantage Way, Ste. 103, Jacksonville, Florida 32218
    CEO: Pasquale Parra
    Bus: *Ceramic tile sales and distribution.*

    Tel: (904) 741-0555
    Fax: (904) 741-0550

    %FO: 100

  - **AZU-VI, INC.**
    3265 South Platte River Dr., Englewood, Colorado 80110
    CEO: Kevin Genuchi
    Bus: *Ceramic tile sales and distribution.*

    Tel: (303) 783-8525
    Fax: (303) 783-8682

    %FO: 100

- **BANCO ATLANTICO, S.A.**
  Avenita Diagonal 407, E-08008 Barcelona, Spain
  CEO: Aldulmohsen Y. Al-Hunaif, Dir.
  Bus: *Commercial banking services.*

  NAICS: 522110

  Tel: 34-91-538-9084
  Fax: 34-91-538-9568
  www.batlantico.es

  Rev: $598
  Emp: 2,909

BANCO ATLANTICO, S.A.
62 William St., New York, New York 10005
CEO: Sheila M. Donovan
Bus: *International banking services.*

Tel: (212) 422-3400
Fax: (212) 422-3400

%FO: 100

BANCO ATLANTICO, S.A.
801 Brickell Ave., Ste. 801, Miami, Florida 33143
CEO: Maurice Llado
Bus: *International banking services.*

Tel: (305) 374-7515
Fax: (305) 374-4076

%FO: 100
Emp: 45

● **BANCO PASTOR S.A.**
Canton Pequeno 1, E-15003 La Coruna, Spain
CEO: Jose-Maria Arias Mosquera, Chmn. & CEO
Bus: *Banking services.*

Tel: 34-981-22-7800
Fax: 34-981-22-659
www.bancopastor.es

Rev: $903
Emp: 3,308

NAICS: 522110

BANCO PASTOR
One Biscayne Tower, 2 South Biscayne Blvd., Ste. 1620, Miami, Florida 33131
CEO: Ramon Cobian
Bus: *Banking services.*

Tel: (305) 579-5213
Fax: (305) 579-5216

%FO: 100

● **BANCO SANTANDER CENTRAL HISPANO, S.A.**
Plaza de Canalejas 1, E-28014 Madrid, Spain
CEO: Alfredo Saenz Abad, CEO
Bus: *Banking and investment products.*

Tel: 34-91-558-1111
Fax: 34-91-552-6670
www.gruposantander.com

Rev: $31,797
Emp: 103,038

NAICS: 522110, 522291, 522292, 523920

BANCO TOTTA
234 Jericho Turnpike, Mineola, New York 11501
CEO: Herculano De Sousa
Bus: *Commercial bank.*

Tel: (516) 742-2211
Fax:

BANCO TOTTA
590 5th Ave., New York, New York 10036
CEO: Herculano De Sousa
Bus: *Commercial bank.*

Tel: (212) 302-6870
Fax: (212) 302-7369

BANCO TOTTA
131 Jericho Turnpike, Mineola, New York 11501
CEO: Paulo Santos, Principal
Bus: *Commercial bank.*

Tel: (516) 294-4334
Fax:

Emp: 2

BANCO TOTTA
215 Church St., Naugatuck, Connecticut 06770
CEO: Bob Saores, Pres.
Bus: *Commercial bank.*

Tel: (203) 723-9920
Fax: (203) 729-0368

BANCO TOTTA
1351 Acushnet Ave., New Bedford, Massachusetts 02746
CEO: Valdomiro Soares, Pres.
Bus: *Commercial bank.*

Tel: (508) 993-1881
Fax: (508) 993-1891

BANCO TOTTA
71 Ferry St., Newark, New Jersey 07105
CEO: Antonio Horta Osorio
Bus: *Commercial bank.*
Tel: (973) 578-8633
Fax: (973) 578-8611

BANESPA
2 South Biscayne Blvd., 1 Biscayne Tower, Ste. 3700, Miami, Florida 33131
CEO: Antonio Horta Osorio
Bus: *Commercial bank.*
Tel: (305) 358-9167
Fax: (305) 381-6967

BANESPA
399 Park Ave., 39/F, New York, New York 10022
CEO: Antonio Horta Osorio
Bus: *Commercial bank.*
Tel: (212) 715-2800
Fax: (212) 371-1034

BANESTO
730 Fifth Ave., 7/F, New York, New York 10019
CEO: Antonio Horta Osorio
Bus: *Commercial bank.*
Tel: (212) 835-5300
Fax: (212) 262-8492

SANTANDER CENTRAL HISPANO
45 East 53rd. St., Ste. 900, New York, New York 10022
CEO: Daniel Keane, VP
Bus: *Commercial bank.*
Tel: (212) 350-3500
Fax: (212) 350-3535

SANTANDER CENTRAL HISPANO
701 Brickell Ave., Ste. 2020, Miami, Florida 33131
CEO: Carlos A. Hernandez, Pres.
Bus: *Commercial bank.*
Tel: (305) 373-2020
Fax: (305) 577-3304

SANTANDER CENTRAL HISPANO
1401 Brickell Ave., Ste. 1400, Miami, Florida 33131
CEO: Fernando Perez-Hickman, Dir.
Bus: *Commercial bank.*
Tel: (305) 530-3900
Fax: (305) 577-3304

● **BARCELO HOTELS AND RESORTS**
Josep Rover Motta 27, Palma de Mallorca, E-07006 Baleares, Spain
CEO: Simon Pedro Barcelo Vadell, Co-Pres.
Bus: *Hotels.*
Tel: 34-971-26-1700
Fax: 34-971-26-6936
www.barcelo.com
Rev: $300
Emp: 939

NAICS: 561510, 721110

BARCELO CRESTLINE CORPORATION
8405 Greensboro Dr., Ste. 500, McLean, Virginia 22102
CEO: Dave L. Durbin
Bus: *Hotels, resorts and conference centers.*
Tel: (571) 382-1800
Fax: (571) 382-1755
%FO: 100

BARCELO CRESTLINE CORPORATION
8405 Greensboro Dr., Ste. 500, McLean, Virginia 22102
CEO: Bruce D. Wardinski, Pres. & CEO
Bus: *Hotels and Motels*
Tel: (571) 382-1800
Fax: (571) 382-1755

RADISSON BARCELO HOTEL & RESORT
8444 International Dr., Orlando, Florida 32819
CEO: Andy Schiavone, Mgr.   Tel: (407) 345-0505   %FO: 100
Bus: *Hotel resort.*   Fax: (407) 352-5894

● **BBVA INTERNATIONAL**
Plaza San Nicolas 4, E-28005 Bilbao Vizcaya, Spain
CEO: Francisco Gonzalez Rodriguez, Chmn. & CEO   Tel: 34-944-875-555   Rev: $23,874
Bus: *Commercial banking services.*   Fax: 34-944-876-161   Emp: 86,197
                                                  www.bbv.es

NAICS: 522110, 523120, 523920, 523930, 524210

   BBVA
   1345 Ave. of the Americas, 45/F, New York, New York 10105
   CEO: Raymond Surguy, Mgr.   Tel: (212) 728-1500   %FO: 100
   Bus: *Commercial banking.*   Fax: (212) 333-2906

   BBVA SECURITIES INC.
   1345 Ave. of the Americas, New York, New York 10105
   CEO: Luis Ruigomez, CEO   Tel: (212) 728-2300
   Bus: *Securities broker & dealer.*   Fax:

● **CARRERA Y CARRERA, S.A.**
A.P. Correos 1 km 31.5 NI, E-28750 San Augustin de Guadalix, Spain
CEO: Sylvia Morales, CEO   Tel: 34-91-843-5193
Bus: *Mfr. of gift items.*   Fax: 34-91-843-5825
                                              www.carreraycarrera.com

NAICS: 423910, 423920, 423940, 424110, 424310

   CARRERA Y CARRERA, INC.
   45 W. 57th St., New York, New York 10019
   CEO: Eric Schwartz, Pres.   Tel: (800) 292-8229
   Bus: *Sales of jewelry.*   Fax: (212) 753-5043   Emp: 160

● **CEMENTOS PORTLAND VALDERRIVAS SA**
Calle Jose Abascal 59, E-28003 Madrid, Spain
CEO: Jaime Ferrer Garcia, Dir.   Tel: 34-91-396-01-00   Rev: $1,202
Bus: *Engaged in the production and distribution of*   Fax: 34-91-396-01-70   Emp: 2,708
     cement. (JV Fomento de Construcciones y   www.valderrivas.es
     Contratas).
NAICS: 212321, 327310, 327320, 327390, 327420

   DRAGON PRODUCTS COMPANY
   38 Preble St., PO Box 1521, Portland, Maine 04104
   CEO: Joseph M. Koch III, Pres.   Tel: (207) 774-6355   %FO: 100
   Bus: *Cement plant and sales.*   Fax: (207) 761-5694

   GIANT CEMENT HOLDING
   320-D Midland Pkwy., Summerville, South Carolina 29485
   CEO: Manuel Llop, Pres.   Tel: (843) 851-9898   %FO: 100
   Bus: *Engaged in the production and distribution*   Fax: (843) 851-9881
        of cement.

GIANT RESOURCE RECOVERY CO., INC.
Box 532, Harleyville, South Carolina 29448
CEO: Donna M. Davis
Bus: *Liquid and solid hazardous waste energy
recovery.*

Tel: (803) 773-1400
Fax: (803) 496-2228

%FO: 100

SOLITE CORP.
1504 Santa Rosa Rd., Ste. 200, Richmond, Virginia 23288
CEO: Doug Clarke
Bus: *Cement manufacture.*

Tel: (804) 673-8600
Fax:

%FO: 100

● **CEMUSA-CORPORACION EUROPEA DE MOBILIARIO URBANO**
Francisco Sancha 24, E-28034 Madrid, Spain
CEO: Agustin Usallan, CEO
Bus: *Advertising services and installation of bus*

Tel: 34-91-358-3344
Fax: 34-91-358-3344
www.cemusa.com

Rev: $58
Emp: 284

NAICS: 541810

CEMUSA INC.
645 N. Michigan Ave., Chicago, Illinois 60611
CEO: Toulla Constantinou
Bus: *Outdoor advertising services.*

Tel: (312) 867-5425
Fax: (312) 867-5956

%FO: 100

● **CHUPA CHUPS SA**
WTC Almeda Park 2, Cornellà de Llobregat, E-08940 Barcelona, Spain
CEO: Xavier Bernat Serra, Pres.
Bus: *Mfr. lollipops and confections.*

Tel: 34-93-495-2727
Fax: 34-93-495-2707
www.chupachups.com

Rev: $370
Emp: 1,950

NAICS: 311340

CHUPA CHUPS, USA
1200 Abernathy Rd. NE, Atlanta, Georgia 30328
CEO: Allan Slimming, VP
Bus: *Candy distribution and product
development.*

Tel: (770) 443-3200
Fax: (770) 481-0340

%FO: 100
Emp: 20

● **CIE AUTOMOTIVE**
Carretera de Zumarraga, s/n, E-20720 Guipuzcoa, Spain
CEO: Ignacio Martin, CEO
Bus: *Supplies automotive components and*

Tel: 34-943-025-200
Fax: 34-943-025-299
www.cieautomotive.com

Rev: $1,011
Emp: 5,800

NAICS: 336211

CIE AUTOMOTIVE USA INC.
28850 Cabot Dr., Ste. 1000, Novi, Michigan 48377
CEO: Jaime Aguirre
Bus: *Automotive components manufacture.*

Tel: (248) 848-1669
Fax: (248) 848-1639

%FO: 100

● **CODORNIU, SA**
Gran Via De Les Corts Catalanes 644, E-08010 Barcelona, Spain
CEO: Maria Del Mar Raventos Chavaud, Chmn.
Bus: *Sparkling wines manufacture.*

Tel: 34-93-505-1551
Fax: 34-93-317-9678
www.codorniu.es

Rev: $196
Emp: 515

NAICS: 111332, 312130, 424820

ARTESA WINERY
1345 Henry Rd., Napa, California 94559
CEO: Michael Kenton, Pres.   Tel: (707) 224-1668   %FO: 100
Bus: *Mfr.. sparkling wines*   Fax: (707) 224-1672   Emp: 20

● **COMEXI, SA**
Poligon Industrial de Girona, Avda. Mas Pins s/n-Riudellots de la Selva, E-17477 Girona, Spain
CEO: Manuel B. Xifra, Pres.   Tel: 34-972-47-7744
Bus: *Machinery manufacture.*   Fax: 34-972-47-7384
                                                 www.comexi.es
NAICS: 333319
    COMEXI NORTH AMERICA INC.
    360 N. Westfield St., Feeding Hills, Massachusetts 01030
    CEO: Cheryl Smith, Mgr.   Tel: (413) 789-3800
    Bus: *Public relations services*   Fax: Emp: 6

● **CONSTRUCCIONES Y AUXILIAR DE FERROCARRILES SA**
Padilla 17, E-28006 Madrid, Spain
CEO: Jose Maria Baztarrica Garijo, CEO   Tel: 34-91-435-2500   Rev: $622
Bus: *Mfr. railroad vehicles and related equipment.*   Fax: 34-91-436-0396   Emp: 3,472
                                                 www.caf.es
NAICS: 336510
    CAF INC.
    1401 K. St. NW, Ste. 803, Washington, District of Columbia 20005
    CEO: Virginia Verdeja   Tel: (202) 898-4848   %FO: 100
    Bus: *Mfr. and sales railroad vehicles and related*   Fax: (202) 216-8929
          equipment.

● **DOGI INTERNATIONAL FABRICS S.A.**
Pintor Domenech Farre 13-15, El Masnou, E-08320 Barcelona, Spain
CEO: Josep Domenech Gimenez, Chmn. & CEO   Tel: 34-93-462-80-00   Rev: $202
Bus: *Mfr. of elastic fabrics and yarns for lingerie,*   Fax: 34-93-462-80-34   Emp: 1,699
      swimwear, and sports apparel.   www.dogi.com
NAICS: 313241, 313249, 314999
    DOGI USA INC.
    1 West 34th St., Ste. 702, New York, New York 10001
    CEO: Yuri Clarry, Rep.   Tel: (212) 532-6066   %FO: 100
    Bus: *Manufacturer of elastic fabrics and yarns*   Fax: (212) 532-3035
          for lingerie, swimwear, and sports apparel.

● **ENDESA, S.A.**
Ribera de Loira, 60, E-28042 Madrid, Spain
CEO: Rafael Miranda Robredo, CEO   Tel: 34-91-213-1000   Rev: $24,471
Bus: *Mines/produces coal; generates*   Fax: 34-91-563-8181   Emp: 26,777
                                                 www.endesa.es
   NAICS: 221111, 221112, 221113, 221121, 221310, 424720, 486210, 517110, 517212, 518210, 523130, 523140,
523210

ENDESA
410 Park Ave., Ste. 410, New York, New York 10022
CEO: David Raya, Dir.
Bus: *Mines/produces coal; generates energy/electricity.*

Tel: (212) 750-7200
Fax: (212) 750-7433

%FO: 100

● **E-TRAVEL BUSINESS UNIT**
Calle Salvador de Madariaga, 1, E-28027 Madrid, Spain
CEO: Ian Wheeler, Mng. Dir.
Bus: *On-line travel arrangements.*

Tel: 34-91-582-0100
Fax: 34-91-582-0100
www.e-travel.com

Rev: $45
Emp: 130

NAICS: 561510, 561599

E-TRAVEL BUSINESS UNIT
1000 Winter St., Waltham, Massachusetts 02451
CEO: Thomas Kiessling
Bus: *On-line travel arrangements.*

Tel: (781) 622-5905
Fax: (781) 522-9900

%FO: 100

● **FAGOR ELECTRONICA**
S Coop B San Andres s/n, Apdo 33, E-20500 Mondragon, Spain
CEO: Alberto Trancho, Pres.
Bus: *Semiconductor manufacturer.*

Tel: 34-943-712526
Fax: 34-943-712893
www.fagorelectronica.es

Rev: $61
Emp: 461

NAICS: 334413

FAGOR AMERICA, INC.
2250 Estes Ave., Elk Grove Village, Illinois 60007
CEO: Ivica Simunic
Bus: *Control systems manufacture.*

Tel: (847) 981-1500
Fax: (847) 981-1500

%FO: 100

FAGOR AMERICA, INC.
1099 Wall St., Ste. 349, Lyndhurst, New Jersey 07071
CEO: Patricio Barriga, VP
Bus: *Electronic manufacture.*

Tel: (201) 804-3900
Fax: (201) 804-9898

%FO: 100

FAGOR ELECTRONIC COMPONENTS INC.
18 Railroad Ave., Andover, Massachusetts 01810
CEO: Richard Muller
Bus: *Electronic components sales.*

Tel: (978) 474-8765
Fax: (978) 475-7328

%FO: 100

● **FICOSA INTERNATIONAL**
Gran Via Carlos III, 98, E-08028 Barcelona, Spain
CEO: Jose M. Pujol Artigas, Chmn. & CEO
Bus: *Mechanical auto parts, industrial tools and equipment manufacture.*

Tel: 34-93-216-3400
Fax: 34-93-490-1063
www.ficosa.com

Rev: $5,555
Emp: 590

NAICS: 336399

FICOSA NORTH AMERICAN CORPORATION
30870 Stephenson Highway, Madison Heights, Michigan 48071
CEO: Allen Montesi, Gen. Mgr.
Bus: *Engineering and marketing services.*

Tel: (248) 307-2230
Fax: (248) 307-2244

%FO: 100
Emp: 37

- **GAMESA CORPORACION TECNOLOGICA SA**
  Parque Tecnologico de Alava, Leonardo da Vinci, 13, E-01510 Minano, Alava, Spain
  CEO: Juan I. Lopez Gandasegui, CEO   Tel: 34-945-185-772   Rev: $1,972
  Bus: *Energy services, including wind turbines;*   Fax: 34-945-185-667   Emp: 6,164
  aeronautics, including components for airplanes   www.gamesa.es
  and helicopters.
  NAICS: 335311, 336411

      NAVITAS ENERGY INC.
      3301 Broadway NE, Ste. 695, Minneapolis, Minnesota 55413
      CEO: Gregory J. Jaunich   Tel: (612) 370-1061   %FO: 100
      Bus: *Develops, owns and operates wind energy*   Fax: (612) 370-9005
      products.

- **GARRIGUES & ANDERSEN**
  José Abascal 45, E-28003 Madrid, Spain
  CEO: Jose Maria Alonso, CEO   Tel: 34-91-514-5200
  Bus: *International law firm.*   Fax: 34-91-399-2408   Emp: 1,036
  www.andersenlegal.com
  NAICS: 541110

      GARRIGUES & ANDERSEN
      410 Park Ave., Ste. 510, New York, New York 10022-9458
      CEO: Jose Ramon Villar   Tel: (212) 751-9233   %FO: 100
      Bus: *International law firm.*   Fax: (212) 355-3594

- **IBERIA AIRLINES (LINIAS AEREAS DE ESPANA)**
  Calle Velasquez 130, E-28006 Madrid, Spain
  CEO: Fernando Conte Garcia, Chmn. & CEO   Tel: 34-91-587-8787
  Bus: *International air transport.*   Fax: 34-91-587-7469
  www.iberia.com
  NAICS: 481111

      IBERIA AIRLINES OF SPAIN
      O'Hare International Airport, Terminal 3, East Lobby, Chicago, Illinois 60666
      CEO: Tel: (773) 686-0858   %FO: 100
      Bus: *International air transport.*   Fax: (773) 686-0863

      IBERIA AIRLINES OF SPAIN
      Miami International Airport, Concourse F, Miami, Florida 33159
      CEO: Cesar Alcazar, Mgr.   Tel: (305) 526-2010   %FO: 100
      Bus: *International air transport.*   Fax: (305) 871-3852   Emp: 100

      IBERIA AIRLINES OF SPAIN
      JFK International Airport Terminal 7, Jamaica, New York 11430
      CEO: Domingo Rodriguez, Mgr.   Tel: (718) 425-5474   %FO: 100
      Bus: *International air transport.*   Fax: (718) 425-5474   Emp: 25

- **INDITEX, S.A.**
  Edificio Inditex, Avenida de la Diputacion, E-15142 Arteixo, La Coruna, Spain
  CEO: Pablo Isla Alvarez de Tejera, CEO   Tel: 34-981-18-54-00   Rev: $5,708
  Bus: *Clothing (men/women/children) manufacture and*   Fax: 34-981-18-55-44   Emp: 39,760
      distribution to Inditex 600 worldwide stores.   www.inditex.com
  NAICS: 315111, 315192, 315211, 315212, 315221, 315222, 315223, 315224, 315225, 315228, 315231, 315232,
  315233, 315234, 315239, 315291, 315993,
          315999, 316992, 316993, 316999, 337121, 337124, 337125, 442110, 442299, 448110, 448120
  > **ZARA INTERNATIONAL, INC.**
  > 645 Madison Ave., 6/F, New York, New York 10022
  > CEO: Jose Castellano, Pres.   Tel: (212) 355-1415   %FO: 100
  > Bus: *Women's clothing.*   Fax: (212) 754-1128   Emp: 95

- **INDRA SISTEMAS, SA**
  Avda. Bruselas, 35, Parque, Empresarial Arroyo de la Vega, E-28108 Madrid, Spain
  CEO: Javier Monzon, Vice Chmn.   Tel: 34-91-480-5000   Rev: $933
  Bus: *Information technology services, including*   Fax: 34-91-480-5080   Emp: 6,092
      hardware, maintenance, outsourcing, and   www.indra.es
      technology development.
  NAICS: 541511, 541513, 541519
  > **INDRA SISTEMAS USA INC.**
  > 6969 University Blvd., Winter Park, Florida 32792
  > CEO: Cheryl Coiro, HR   Tel: (407) 673-1500   %FO: 100
  > Bus: *Engaged in information technology.*   Fax: (407) 673-1510

- **INSTRUMENTATION LABORATORY**
  Aragon 90, PO Box 35027, E-08015 Barcelona, Spain
  CEO: Jose M. Ruberalta, Chmn.   Tel: 34-93-401-0101   Rev: $252
  Bus: *Mfr. clinical diagnostic equipment.*   Fax: 34-93-451-3745   Emp: 1,200
                www.ilww.com
  NAICS: 334510, 423450, 424690, 621511
  > **INSTRUMENTATION LABORATORY COMPANY**
  > 101 Hartwell Ave., Lexington, Massachusetts 02421-3125
  > CEO: Jose Manent, CEO   Tel: (781) 861-0710   %FO: 100
  > Bus: *Sales/distribution of blood, urine and tissue*   Fax: (781) 861-1908   Emp: 600
  >   *diagnostic products.*

- **IVEX - INSTITUTO VALENCIANO DE LA EXPORTACION**
  Pl. America 2 7a, E-46004 Valencia, Spain
  CEO: Carmen de Miguel, Mgr.   Tel: 34-96-197-1500
  Bus: *Government owned export services provider.*   Fax: 34-96-197-1500
                www.ivex.es
  NAICS: 921190
  > **IVEX FLORIDA**
  > 1221 Brickell Ave., Ste. 1000, Miami, Florida 33131
  > CEO: Faustino Salcedo, Mgr.   Tel: (305) 358-7789   %FO: 100
  > Bus: *Government owned export services provider.* Fax: (305) 358-6844

IVEX LOS ANGELES
11300 West Olympic Blvd., Ste. 864, Los Angeles, California 90064
CEO: Jose Luis Vela, Mgr. Tel: (310) 477-3080 %FO: 100
Bus: *Government owned export services provider.* Fax: (310) 477-4959

IVEX NEW YORK
675 Third Ave., Ste. 2216, New York, New York 10017
CEO: Bisila Bokoko, Mgr. Tel: (212) 922-9000 %FO: 100
Bus: *Government owned export services provider.* Fax: (212) 922-9012

● **IZASA DISTRIBUCIONES TECNICAS, SA**
Aragon 90, E-08015 Barcelona, Spain
CEO: Alfredo Balcells Garcia, Dir. Tel: 34-93-401-0101 Rev: $614
Bus: *Instrument manufacture.* Fax: 34-93-451-3745 Emp: 192
www.ilww.com

NAICS: 423450, 424690, 621511

INSTRUMENTATION LABORATORY COMPANY
101 Hartwell Ave., Lexington, Massachusetts 02421-3125
CEO: Ramon Benet Tel: (718) 861-0710 %FO: 100
Bus: *Instrument manufacture.* Fax: (718) 861-1908

● **LLADRO COMERCIAL SA**
Crta. de Alboraya, s/n. Tavernes Blanques, E-46016 Valencia, Spain
CEO: Alain Viot, CEO Tel: 34-96-185 01 77
Bus: *Mfr. sales and marketing of high quality, hand-* Fax: 34-96-186-0420 Emp: 2,000
crafted porcelain figurines, vases, lamps and www.lladro.com
sculptures.
NAICS: 327112

LLADRÓ USA, INC.
43 West 57th St., New York, New York 10019
CEO: Jose Lladro, CEO Tel: (212) 838-9356 %FO: 100
Bus: *Sales/marketing of high quality, hand-* Fax: (212) 758-1928
crafted porcelain figurines, vases, lamps
and sculptures.

LLADRÓ USA, INC.
408 N. Rodeo Dr., Beverly Hills, California 90210
CEO: Jose Llardo Dolz, CEO Tel: (310) 385-0690 %FO: 100
Bus: *Sales/marketing of high quality, hand-* Fax: (310) 385-0682 Emp: 165
crafted porcelain figurines, vases, lamps
and sculptures.

● **ANTONIO MENGIBAR SA**
Calle Cesar Martinell i Brunet, E-08191 Barcelona, Spain
CEO: Antonio Mengibar, CEO Tel: 34-93-588-2914
Bus: *Packaging machinery manufacture.* Fax: 34-93-588-0863
www.mengibar.es
NAICS: 333298

MENGIBAR AUTOMATION, INC.
103 Steam Whistle Dr., Warminster, Pennsylvania 18974
CEO: Ger Smith, Pres.
Bus: *Sales and distribution of machinery.*
Tel: (215) 936-2200
Fax: (215) 396-6644
%FO: 100
Emp: 15

● **MERQUINSA**
Gran Vial, 17, Montmelo, E-08160 Barcelona, Spain
CEO: M. Domenech, CEO
Bus: *Polyurethane and polymers and chemicals manufacture.*
Tel: 34-93-572-1100
Fax: 34-93-572-0934
www.merquinsa.com
NAICS: 325199, 325510

  MERQUINSA NORTH AMERICA INC.
  34 Folly Mill Rd., Seabrook, New Hampshire 03874
  CEO: France Fontenot, Mgr.
  Bus: *Polyurethane and polymers and chemicals manufacture.*
  Tel: (603) 474-0971
  Fax: (603) 474-0972
  %FO: 100
  Emp: 3

● **NATRACEUTICAL SA**
Autovía A3 Salida 343, Camino de los Hornillos, E-46930 Quart de Poblet Valencia, Spain
CEO: Manuel Moreno Tarazona, Pres.
Bus: *Mfr. of cocoa, wine and cava derivatives producing vitamins and nutritionally healthy*
Tel: 34-96-159-7300
Fax: 34-96-192-0453
www.natra.es
Rev: $125
Emp: 324
NAICS: 311330, 325411

  NATRA US, INC.
  1059 Tierra del Rey, Ste. H, Chula Vista, California 91910
  CEO: Martin Brabenec
  Bus: *Mfr./distribution of cocoa derivatives.*
  Tel: (619) 397-4120
  Fax: (619) 397-4121
  %FO: 100

● **NICOLAS CORREA, SA**
Alcalde Martin Cobos, s/n, E-09007 Burgos, Spain
CEO: Jose Ignacio Nicolas-Correa, CEO
Bus: *Milling machines manufacture.*
Tel: 34-947-28-8100
Fax: 34-947-28-8117
www.correa.es
Rev: $50
Emp: 116

NAICS: 333999

  NICOLAS CORREA USA INC.
  81 East Jefryn Blvd., Deer Park, New York 11729
  CEO: Iker Goenaga
  Bus: *Milling machines manufacture and sales.*
  Tel: (631) 586-1200
  Fax: (631) 586-2180
  %FO: 100

● **PORCELANOSA, SA**
Cr. Nacional 340 Km. 56 200, Vila-Real, E-12540 Castellon, Spain
CEO: Manuel Colonques Moreno, Chmn.
Bus: *Ceramic floor and wall tiles, marble and bathroom fixtures manufacture.*
Tel: 34-96-450-7100
Fax:
www.porcelanosa.com
Rev: $970
Emp: 165
NAICS: 327122

  PORCELANOSA USA INC.
  8700 NW 13th Terr.., Miami, Florida 33172
  CEO: Jose Sorino, Pres.
  Bus: *Wholesale and retail ceramic tile*
  Tel: (305) 715-7153
  Fax:
  Emp: 21

PORCELANOSA USA INC.
1970 New Highway, Farmingdale, New York 11735
CEO: Herbert G. Lewis, Gen. Mgr.   Tel: (631) 845-7070   %FO: 100
Bus: *Ceramic tile sales and distribution.*   Fax: (631) 845-7136   Emp: 30

● **POSIMAT S.A.**
Av. Arraona 17-23, Pologono Can Salvatella, E-08210 Barcelona, Spain
CEO: Jaime Martí, Pres.   Tel: 34-93-729-7616
Bus: *Container component handling machines*   Fax: 34-93-729-1855
manufacture for bottling plants.   www.posimat.com
NAICS: 333298

   POSIMAT
   10830 NW 27th St., #1-B, Miami, Florida 33172
   CEO: James Marti   Tel: (305) 477-2029   %FO: 100
   Bus: *Container component handling machines*   Fax: (305) 477-8044   Emp: 2
   manufacture.

● **PUIG BEAUTY & FASHION GROUP SA**
Travessera de Gracia, 9, E-08021 Barcelona, Spain
CEO: Marc Puig, CEO   Tel: 34-93-400-7000   Rev: $968
Bus: *Perfumery, toiletries and cosmetic products*   Fax: 34-93-400-7010   Emp: 5,000
manufacture.   www.puig.es
NAICS: 325620

   PUIG USA INC.
   100 Almeria Ave., Ste. 320, Coral Gables, Florida 33134
   CEO: Gilles Prodhomme   Tel: (305) 774-0225   %FO: 100
   Bus: *Perfumery, toiletries and cosmetic products*   Fax: (305) 774-6859
   sales and distribution.

   PUIG USA INC.
   70 East 55th St., 17/F, New York, New York 10022
   CEO: Martha Brady, Pres.   Tel: (212) 980-9620   %FO: 100
   Bus: *Perfumery, toiletries and cosmetic products*   Fax: (212) 593-1648
   sales and distribution.

   PUIG USA INC.
   9 Skyline Dr., Hawthorne, New York 10532
   CEO: Fernando P. Aleu   Tel: (914) 347-3680   %FO: 100
   Bus: *Perfumery, toiletries and cosmetic products*   Fax: (914) 347-3680
   manufacture.

● **SERVICE POINT SOLUTIONS, SA**
Calle Solsones 2, planta 3 Esc. B,, Edificio Muntades, Parque de Negocios-Mas, Blau, El Prat de Llobregat, E-08820 Barcelona, Spain
CEO: Juan Jose Nieto, Chmn.   Tel: 34-93-508-2424
Bus: *Provides outsourcing services.*   Fax: 34-93-508-2442
   www.servicepoint.net
NAICS: 323115, 323119, 561410, 561439

SERVICE POINT USA INC.
110 Canal St., Boston, Massachusetts 02210
CEO: Terence Flynn, Mgr.　　　Tel: (617) 742-7150　　　%FO: 100
Bus: *Outsourcing services.*　　　Fax: (617) 742-7154　　　Emp: 4

SERVICE POINT USA INC.
45 Batterymarch St., Boston, Massachusetts 02110
CEO: Bill Hulme, Mgr.　　　Tel: (617) 542-1666　　　%FO: 100
Bus: *Outsourcing services.*　　　Fax: (617) 348-9216

SERVICE POINT USA INC.
601 Carlisle Dr., Herndon, Virginia 20170
CEO: Jo Lefebvre, Mgr.　　　Tel: (703) 318-6660　　　%FO: 100
Bus: *Outsourcing services.*　　　Fax: (703) 318-6662

SERVICE POINT USA INC.
285 Summer St., Boston, Massachusetts 02210
CEO: Mike McFadyen, Mgr.　　　Tel: (617) 439-9981　　　%FO: 100
Bus: *Outsourcing services.*　　　Fax: (617) 428-3795

SERVICE POINT USA INC.
150 Presidential Way, Ste. 210, Woburn, Massachusetts 01801
CEO: Steve Payne, CFO　　　Tel: (781) 935-6020　　　%FO: 100
Bus: *Outsourcing services.*　　　Fax: (781) 938-5251　　　Emp: 350

SERVICE POINT USA INC.
629 Highland Ave., Needham, Massachusetts 02494
CEO: David Gudejko, Mgr.　　　Tel: (781) 453-4013　　　%FO: 100
Bus: *Outsourcing services.*　　　Fax: (781) 536-6947　　　Emp: 10

SERVICE POINT USA INC.
303 Eddy St., Providence, Rhode Island 02903
CEO: Charlie Francis, Mgr.　　　Tel: (401) 278-4000　　　%FO: 100
Bus: *Outsourcing services.*　　　Fax: (401) 278-4045

SERVICE POINT USA INC.
8000 C Haute Ct., Springfield, Virginia 22150
CEO: Les Thomas, Mgr.　　　Tel: (703) 569-4651　　　%FO: 100
Bus: *Outsourcing services.*　　　Fax: (703) 569-7592

SERVICE POINT USA INC.
67 York Ave., Randolph, Massachusetts 02368
CEO: Rick Goldstein, Mgr.　　　Tel: (781) 963-7050　　　%FO: 100
Bus: *Outsourcing services.*　　　Fax: (781) 961-1422　　　Emp: 7

SERVICE POINT USA INC.
1000 Massachusetts Ave., Cambridge, Massachusetts 02138
CEO: Bob Curry, Mgr.　　　Tel: (617) 495-0235　　　%FO: 100
Bus: *Outsourcing services.*　　　Fax: (617) 492-7145

SERVICE POINT USA INC.
1129 20th St. NW, Washington, District of Columbia 20036
CEO: India Chisley, Mgr.　　　Tel: (202) 466-6453　　　%FO: 100
Bus: *Outsourcing services.*　　　Fax: (202) 466-6471

SERVICE POINT USA INC.
85 Willow St., Bldg. 12, New Haven, Connecticut 06511
CEO: Fred Dunn, Mgr.　　　　　　　　　　　　Tel: (203) 624-0440　　　　%FO: 100
Bus: *Outsourcing services.*　　　　　　　　Fax: (203) 624-8533

SERVICE POINT USA INC.
31A Olympia Ave., Woburn, Massachusetts 01801
CEO: Tony Fiore, Mgr.　　　　　　　　　　　　Tel: (781) 933-8700　　　　%FO: 100
Bus: *Outsourcing services.*　　　　　　　　Fax: (781) 935-3926

SERVICE POINT USA INC.
274 Summer St., Boston, Massachusetts 02210
CEO: Todd Rego, Mgr.　　　　　　　　　　　　Tel: (617) 482-9671　　　　%FO: 100
Bus: *Outsourcing services.*　　　　　　　　Fax: (617) 482-9668

SERVICE POINT USA INC.
450 South Henderson Rd., Ste. B, King of Prussia, Pennsylvania 19406
CEO: Ron Potchen, Mgr.　　　　　　　　　　　Tel: (610) 783-0990　　　　%FO: 100
Bus: *Outsourcing services.*　　　　　　　　Fax: (610) 783-1388　　　　Emp: 4

SERVICE POINT USA INC.
11 East 26th St., 10/F, New York, New York 10010
CEO: Edwina Prescott, Mgr.　　　　　　　　　Tel: (212) 213-5105　　　　%FO: 100
Bus: *Outsourcing services.*　　　　　　　　Fax: (212) 213-3847

SERVICE POINT USA INC.
1321 Arch St., Philadelphia, Pennsylvania 19107
CEO: Sam Banks, Mgr.　　　　　　　　　　　　Tel: (215) 567-0777　　　　%FO: 100
Bus: *Outsourcing services.*　　　　　　　　Fax: (215) 567-9588　　　　Emp: 25

● **SOCIEDAD GENERAL DE AGUAS DE BARCELONA, SA**
Passeig de Sant Joan, 39-43, E-08009 Barcelona, Spain
CEO: Ricardo Fornesa Ribo, Chmn.　　　　　Tel: 34-93-342-2000　　　　Rev: $3,360
Bus: *Provides water services.*　　　　　　Fax: 34-93-342-2662　　　　Emp: 37,481
　　　　　　　　　　　　　　　　　　　　　　www.agbar.es
NAICS: 221310, 221320, 236220, 237110, 237990, 524114, 541330, 562111, 562212, 621111, 621399, 622110
　　SOCIEDAD GENERAL DE AUTORES Y EDITORES
　　30 Cooper Square, 4/F, New York, New York 10003-7120
　　CEO: Emilio Garcia, Dir.　　　　　　　　　Tel: (212) 752-7230　　　　%FO: 100
　　Bus: *Provides water services.*　　　　　Fax:　　　　　　　　　　　　Emp: 7

● **SOCIEDAD GENERAL DE AUTORES Y EDITORES (SGAE)**
Fernando VI 4, E-28004 Madrid, Spain
CEO: Eduardo Bautista, Chmn.　　　　　　　Tel: 34-91-349-9550　　　　Rev: $36
Bus: *Music licensing organization.*　　　Fax: 34-91-310-2120　　　　Emp: 500
　　　　　　　　　　　　　　　　　　　　　　www.sgae.es
NAICS: 926150
　　SOCIEDAD GENERAL DE AUTORES Y EDITORES (SGAE)
　　30 Cooper Sq., 4/F, New York, New York 10003
　　CEO: Emilio Garcia, Pres.　　　　　　　　Tel: (212) 752-7230　　　　%FO: 100
　　Bus: *Music licensing organization.*　　Fax: (212) 754-4378

- **SOL MELIA SA**
Gremio Toneleros 24, Baleares, E-07009 Palma de Mallorca, Spain
CEO: Gabriel Escarrer Jaume Jr., CEO   Tel: 34-97-122-4400   Rev: $1,416
Bus: *Hotel and resorts.*   Fax: 34-97-122-4408   Emp: 36,000
   www.solmelia.com

NAICS: 721110

   SOL MELIA HOTELS & RESORTS
   6205 Brenhaven Rd., Arlington, Texas 76017
   CEO: Casimiro Ramirez   Tel: (817) 563-2522   %FO: 100
   Bus: *Hotel and resorts.*   Fax: (817) 679-5086

   SOL MELIA HOTELS & RESORTS
   1325 NE 25th Ave., Pompano Beach, Florida 33062
   CEO: Pamela Payne   Tel: (954) 943-0336   %FO: 100
   Bus: *Hotel and resorts.*   Fax: (954) 943-0416

   SOL MELIA HOTELS & RESORTS
   175 North Harbor Dr., Ste. 1414, Chicago, Illinois 60601
   CEO: Mary Paz Ramirez Grajeda   Tel: (312) 938-4460   %FO: 100
   Bus: *Hotel and resorts.*   Fax: (312) 938-4463

   SOL MELIA HOTELS & RESORTS
   1748 N. Kenmore Ave., Ste. 12, Los Angeles, California 90027
   CEO: Marc Opitz   Tel: (323) 665-8785   %FO: 100
   Bus: *Hotel and resorts.*   Fax: (323) 665-8013

   SOL MELIA HOTELS & RESORTS
   131 Corporate Place, Middletown, Rhode Island 02842
   CEO: Martin Young   Tel: (401) 849-3571   %FO: 100
   Bus: *Hotel and resorts.*   Fax: (401) 849-6281

   SOL MELIA HOTELS & RESORTS
   1016 Tailwood Rd., Ste. 1C, Annapolis, Maryland 21403
   CEO: Susan Carlson   Tel: (410) 216-9001   %FO: 100
   Bus: *Hotel and resorts.*   Fax: (410) 216-6676

- **SOS CUETARA SA**
Paseo de Castellana, 51, E-28046 Madrid, Spain
CEO: Raul Jaime Salazar Bello, CEO   Tel: 34-91-319-7900   Rev: $859
Bus: *Baked good and rice manufacture.*   Fax: 34-91-319-7071   Emp: 2,269
   www.gruposos.com

NAICS: 311211, 311212, 311223, 311225, 311330, 311340, 311821

   AMERICAN RICE, INC.
   10700 North Fwy., Houston, Texas 77037
   CEO: Lee Adams   Tel: (281) 272-8800   %FO: 100
   Bus: *Rice miller.*   Fax: (281) 272-9707

- **TELEFONICA SA**
  Gran Via 28, Planta 3, E-28013 Madrid, Spain
  CEO: Cesar Alierta Izuel, Chmn. & CEO
  Bus: *Provider of global communications services.*

  Tel: 34-91-584-0306
  Fax: 34-91-584-9347
  www.telefonica.com

  Rev: $3,898
  Emp: 173,544

  NAICS: 515210, 517212, 517510, 518111, 541513, 541519, 561421

  > **EMERGIA INC.**
  > 1221 Brickell Av., Suite 600, Miami, Florida 33121
  > CEO: Matthew Garrett
  > Bus: *Telecommunications services, data network operators, including internet, online and managed network services.*
  >
  > Tel: (305) 925-5202
  > Fax: (305) 374-8682
  >
  > %FO: 100

- **TEMOINSA SA**
  Pol. Ind. Congost-Av. Sant Julia 100, Granollers, E-08400 Barcelona, Spain
  CEO: Jose Pedret, CEO
  Bus: *Engineering and manufacture of integral railway equipment.*

  Tel: 34-93-8609-200
  Fax: 34-93-8609-213
  www.temoinsa.com

  NAICS: 237990, 482111, 482112, 485112

  > **TEMOINSA CORPORATION**
  > 1527 Military Turnpike, Plattsburg, New York 12901
  > CEO: Robert Cleary
  > Bus: *Engineering and manufacture of integral railway equipment.*
  >
  > Tel: (518) 562-0848
  > Fax: (518) 562-0910
  >
  > %FO: 100
  > Emp: 30

- **TERRA NETWORKS GROUP**
  Via Dos Castillas 33, Atica, Ed. 1, E-28224 Madrid, Spain
  CEO: Joaquin Faura Batlle, CEO
  Bus: *Telecommunications*

  Tel: 34-91-452-3000
  Fax: 34-91-452-3146
  www.terra.es

  Rev: $732
  Emp: 1,600

  NAICS: 518111, 518210, 519190

  > **TERRA NETWORKS GROUP**
  > 1201 Brickell Ave., Ste. 700, Miami, Florida 33131
  > CEO: Craig Stanford, Reg. Sales Mgr.
  > Bus: *Internet services.*
  >
  > Tel: (305) 714-8590
  > Fax: (305) 714-8590
  >
  > %FO: 100

- **TEXINTER SA**
  Angli 31(3-3), E-08017 Barcelona, Spain
  CEO: Luis Ferrer, CEO
  Bus: *Textiles manufacture.*

  Tel: 34-93-205-1055
  Fax: 34-93-280-2981
  www.texinter.com

  NAICS: 333292, 333298

  > **TEXINTER INC.**
  > 7701 SW 62 Ave., 2/F, Miami, Florida 33143
  > CEO: Peter Baugh, Pres.
  > Bus: *Plastic textile materials manufacture.*
  >
  > Tel: (305) 667-8858
  > Fax: (305) 667-7301
  >
  > %FO: 100
  > Emp: 6

- **TORRAS SA**
  Caldes de Montbui, E-08140 Barcelona, Spain
  CEO: Juan Serra Torras, Chmn.
  Bus: *Mfr. leather and knit jackets and sweaters.*

  Tel: 34-93-862-7533
  Fax: 34-93-865-4442
  www.torras.com

  Rev: $27
  Emp: 117

  NAICS: 315191

  BCN FASHIONS, INC.
  24 W. Gate Rd., PO Box 951, Suffern, New York 10901
  CEO: Juan Serra, Pres.
  Bus: *Sales/distribution leather and knit jackets/sweaters.*

  Tel: (845) 368-1775
  Fax:

  %FO: 100

- **TUBACEX, S.A.**
  Tres Cruces 8, E-01400 Llodio Alava, Spain
  CEO: Alvaro Videgain Muro, Chmn. & Pres. & CEO
  Bus: *Metals and mining, steel production.*

  Tel: 34-94-671-9300
  Fax: 34-94-672-5062
  www.tubacex.com

  Rev: $474
  Emp: 1,517

  NAICS: 331210, 332996

  SALEM TUBE INC.
  951 Fourth St., Greenville, Pennsylvania 16125
  CEO: Rufino Orce, Pres.
  Bus: *Metals & mining, steel production.*

  Tel: (724) 646-4301
  Fax: (724) 646-4311

  %FO: 100
  Emp: 110

  SCHOELLER-BLECKMANN PIPE & TUBE INC.
  5430 Brystone Dr., Houston, Texas 77041
  CEO: Matt Herbison, Pres.
  Bus: *Sale of seamless pipe & tube*

  Tel: (713) 466-9446
  Fax:

  Emp: 9

  TUBACEX INC.
  12707 North. Freeway, Ste. 100, Houston, Texas 77060
  CEO: Olga Elman, VP
  Bus: *Metals & mining, steel production.*

  Tel: (281) 875-8660
  Fax: (281) 875-8665

  %FO: 100
  Emp: 5

- **UNION FENOSA, SA**
  Ave. de San Luis, 77, E-28033 Madrid, Spain
  CEO: Honorato Lope Isla, Chmn. & CEO
  Bus: *Electricity.*

  Tel: 34-91-567-6000
  Fax: 34-91-567-6329
  www.uef.es

  Rev: $7,916
  Emp: 19,463

  NAICS: 221111, 221112, 221113, 221121, 221122, 324199, 424710, 424720, 454312, 454319, 486210, 517110, 523130, 523140, 541330, 541519, 541618, 541690, 561210

  SOLUZIONA USA
  Rose Tree Corporate Center II, 1400 North Providence Rd., St. 4005, Media, Pennsylvania 19063
  CEO: Vincent Bayarri, Pres.
  Bus: *Mfr. Customer Information System (CIS) software to utility companies.*

  Tel: (610) 892-8920
  Fax: (610) 892-8921

  %FO: 100
  Emp: 60

- **URIA & MENENDEZ**
  Jorge Juan 6, E-28001 Madrid, Spain
  CEO: Jesus Remon, Partner
  Bus: *International law firm.*

  Tel: 34-91-586-0400
  Fax: 34-91-586-0403
  www.uria.com

  NAICS: 541110
  ### URIA & MENENDEZ
  Grace Bldg., 1114 Avenue of the Americas, 26/F, New York, New York 10036
  CEO: Fernando Calbacho, Partner
  Bus: *International law firm (Spain).*

  Tel: (212) 593-1300
  Fax: (212) 593-7144

  %FO: 100
  Emp: 5

- **VISCOFAN SA**
  Iturrama, 23 Entreplanta, E-31007 Pamplona, Spain
  CEO: Juan Ignacio Villegas Diza, CEO
  Bus: *Mfr. artificial sausage casings.*

  Tel: 34-948-198-44
  Fax: 34-948-430
  www.viscofan.com

  Rev: $466
  Emp: 3,027

  NAICS: 311613
  ### VISCOFAN USA INC.
  50 County Ct., Montgomery, Alabama 36105
  CEO: Mauel Nadal Machin
  Bus: *Mfr. artificial sausage casings.*

  Tel: (334) 280-1000
  Fax: (332) 280-1900

  %FO: 100

- **ZARA INTERNATIONAL, INC.**
  Edificio Inditex, Avenida de la Diputación, E-15142 Arteixo, La Coruna, Spain
  CEO: Pablo Isla Alvarez de Tejera, CEO
  Bus: *Women's clothing chain store.*

  Tel: 34-981-18-5400
  Fax: 34-981-18-5454
  www.indetex.com

  Rev: $3,150
  Emp: 24,000

  NAICS: 448120
  ### ZARA USA INC.
  645 Madison Ave., Rm. 610, New York, New York 10022
  CEO: Carlos Mato, Mgr.
  Bus: *Retail clothing.*

  Tel: (212) 754-1120
  Fax: (212) 741-0555

  %FO: 100

Sweden

- **A&R CARTON AB**
  Adelgatan 6, SE-211 22 Malmo, Sweden
  CEO: Per Arne Lundeen, Pres. & CEO
  Bus: *Mfr. cardboard packaging and multipacks for frozen food, dry food, sweets, beverages, petfoods and non-food goods.*
  NAICS: 322130

  Tel: 46-40-661-5662
  Fax: 46-40-611-6605
  www.ar-carton.com

  Rev: $382
  Emp: 2,050

    A&R CARTON NORTH AMERICAN
    1955 Evergreen Blvd., Ste. 200, Duluth, Georgia 30096
    CEO: Brian Bailey, VP
    Bus: *Food packaging.*

    Tel: (770) 623-8235
    Fax: (770) 623-8236

    %FO: 100
    Emp: 10

- **AB SVENSK EXPORTKREDIT**
  Vastra Tradgardsgatan 11B, SE-103 27 Stockholm, Sweden
  CEO: Peter Yngwe, CEO
  Bus: *Long-term export credits and financial products.*
  NAICS: 522110, 522293

  Tel: 46-8-613-8300
  Fax: 46-20-38-94
  www.sek.se

  Rev: $777
  Emp: 147

    SWEDISH EXPORT CREDIT CORP.
    Swedish Consulate, 885 Second Ave., New York, New York 10017
    CEO: Per Akerlind
    Bus: *Long-term export credits and financial products.*

    Tel: (212) 583-2550
    Fax: (212) 583-2550

    %FO: 100

- **ABA OF SWEDEN AB**
  Wallingatan 2, Scheelegatan 28, SE-111 60 Stockholm, Sweden
  CEO: Lars Nordin, Pres.
  Bus: *Pipe and hose clamps, hose connectors and hose systems manufacture.*
  NAICS: 332722

  Tel: 46-371-58-8800
  Fax: 46-371-58-8801
  www.abagroup.com

  Rev: $675
  Emp: 830

    ABA OF AMERICA INC
    1445 Huntwood Dr., Cherry Valley, Illinois 61016
    CEO: Arne Stegvik, Pres.
    Bus: *Mfr. hose clamps.*

    Tel: (815) 332-5170
    Fax: (815) 332-9090

    %FO: 100
    Emp: 10

- **ABS GROUP, DIV. CARDO GROUP**
  Roskildevagen 1, Box 394, SE-201 23 Malmo, Sweden
  CEO: Peter Aru, CEO
  Bus: *Pumps, mixers and aerators manufacturer.*

  Tel: 46-31-706-1600
  Fax: 46-31-18-4906
  www.abspumps.com

  Rev: $320
  Emp: 2,100

  NAICS: 333911

ABS ALASKAN, INC.
2130 Van Horn Rd., Fairbanks, Alaska 99701
CEO: Jim Norman   Tel: (907) 452-2002   %FO: 100
Bus: *Renewable Energy System Design, Sales,*   Fax: (907) 451-1949
     Installation

ABS PUMPS, INC.
140 Pond View Dr., Meriden, Connecticut 06450
CEO: Gerald A. Assessor, Pres.   Tel: (203) 238-2700   %FO: 100
Bus: *Pumps and pumping equipment sales and*   Fax: (203) 238-0738
     distribution.

● **AIMPOINT AB**
Jagershillgatan 15, SE-213 75 Malmo, Sweden
CEO: Lennart Ljungfelt, Pres.   Tel: 46-40-21-0390
Bus: *Electronic gun sights and mounting systems; red*   Fax: 46-40-21-9238
     dot sights.   www.aimpoint.com
NAICS: 423990

   AIMPOINT INC.
   3989 Highway 62 West, Berryville, Arkansas 72616
   CEO: Michael Kingston, Mgr.   Tel: (870) 423-3398   %FO: 100
   Bus: *Import electronic gun sights, mounting*   Fax: (870) 423-2960   Emp: 7
        systems; red dot sights for the military

● **AKAB OF SWEDEN AB**
Bussgatan 4, Viared, SE-504 94 Boras, Sweden
CEO: Jan Karrman, Mng. Dir.   Tel: 46-33-233600
Bus: *Mfr. automatic sewing machines for home textile*   Fax: 46-33-136867   Emp: 80
     industry.   www.akab.com
NAICS: 333298, 423830

   AKAB OF AMERICA INC.
   4209 Pleasant Rd., Fort Mill, South Carolina 29715
   CEO: Ralf Stridh, Pres.   Tel: (803) 548-6815   %FO: 100
   Bus: *Mfr. automatic sewing machines for home*   Fax: (803) 548-6820   Emp: 7
        textile industry, spare parts and service.

   JENSEN USA INC.
   4211 Pleasant Rd., Fort Mill, South Carolina 29708
   CEO: Steve Carrigan   Tel: (803) 548-3653   %FO: 100
   Bus: *Automated textile systems manufacture.*   Fax: (803) 548-3653

● **AKERS AB**
PO Box 84, SE-640 60 Akers Styckebruk, Sweden
CEO: Ingvar Lundborg, Pres. & CEO   Tel: 46-159-32100   Rev: $285
Bus: *Mfr./marketing cast and forged steel rolls.*   Fax: 46-159-32101   Emp: 1,500
                                         www.akers.se
NAICS: 331221

   AKERS AMERICA INC.
   58 South Main St., Ste. 4, Poland, Ohio 44514-1978
   CEO: Robert P. DeNunzio, Pres.   Tel: (330) 757-4100   %FO: 100
   Bus: *Mfr./sale cast and forged steel rolls.*   Fax: (330) 757-4235

AKERS HYDE PARK FOUNDRY
326 First Ave., Hyde Park, Pennsylvania 15618
CEO: Lonnie Walp, Pres.
Bus: *Mfr./sale cast and forged steel rolls.*

Tel: (724) 842-1941
Fax: (724) 845-8865

%FO: 100

AKERS NATIONAL ROLL COMPANY
400 Railroad Ave., Avonmore, Pennsylvania 15641
CEO: Andrew L. Blaskovich, Pres.
Bus: *Mfr./sale cast and forged steel rolls.*

Tel: (724) 697-4533
Fax: (724) 697-4319

%FO: 100

AKERS VERTICAL SEAL COMPANY
RD 1, Box 147, Pleasantville, Pennsylvania 16341
CEO: Tom Parres, Pres.
Bus: *Mfr./sale cast and forged steel rolls and
     repair of mill components.*

Tel: (814) 589-7031
Fax: (814) 589-7628

%FO: 100

● **AKTIEBOLAGET SKF**
Hornsgatan 1, SE-415 50 Goteborg, Sweden
CEO: Tom Johnstone, Pres. & CEO
Bus: *Roller bearings, seals and special steels, and
     control measurement and testing equipment
     manufacture.*
NAICS: 332991, 334513, 339991, 423830

Tel: 46-31-337-1000
Fax: 46-31-337-2832
www.skf.com

Rev: $6,778
Emp: 39,867

CHICAGO RAWHIDE AMERICAS
900 North State St., Elgin, Illinois 60123
CEO: George Dettloff, Mgr.
Bus: *Mfr. heat testing, surface finishing and
     assembly machinery.*

Tel: (847) 742-7840
Fax: (847) 742-7845

%FO: 100

ERIN ENGINEERING & RESEARCH INC.
2175 N. California Blvd., Ste. 810, Walnut Creek, California 94596
CEO: Eugene A. Hughes, Pres.
Bus: *Consulting engineers.*

Tel: (925) 943-7077
Fax: (925) 943-7087

Emp: 105

MAGNETIC CORP.
3519 N. Union Dr., Olney, Illinois 62450
CEO: Thomas Lozser, Pres.
Bus: *Sale of electric motors.*

Tel: (618) 392-3647
Fax: (618) 392-0033

Emp: 12

MRC BEARINGS
402 Chandler St., Jamestown, New York 14701
CEO: Rolf Jacobson, Pres.
Bus: *Mfr. roller bearings.*

Tel: (716) 661-2600
Fax: (716) 661-2740

%FO: 100
Emp: 700

OVAKO STEEL, INC.
1096 Assembly Way, Ste. 312, Fort Mill, South Carolina 29708
CEO: Mikael Wiel, Pres.
Bus: *Sale of specialty steel & steel products.*

Tel: (803) 802-1500
Fax: (803) 802-1501

Emp: 9

ROLLER BEARING INDUSTRIES
125 Budco Lane, Elizabethtown, Kentucky 42701
CEO: Stephen Yonce, member
Bus: *Sale of industrial supplies*

Tel: (270) 737-5120
Fax: (270) 769-1633

Emp: 20

RUSSELL T. GILMAN INC.
1230 Cheyenne Ave., Grafton, Wisconsin 53023
CEO: Andrew Fletcher
Bus: *Mfr. heat testing, surface finishing and assembly machinery.*
Tel: (262) 377-2434
Fax: (262) 377-9438
%FO: 100

SARMA
180 West Dayton, Ste.105, Bldg. 4, Edmonds, Washington 98020
CEO: Prasar Bharati
Bus: *Roller bearings, seals and special steels, and control measurement and testing equipment manufacture.*
Tel: (425) 672-8229
Fax: (425) 672-7452

SKF AERO BEARING SERVICE CENTER
7260 Investment Dr., North Charleston, South Carolina 29418
CEO: John Bennett, Dir.
Bus: *Mfr. heat testing, surface finishing and assembly machinery.*
Tel: (843) 207-3377
Fax: (843) 207-3399
%FO: 100
Emp: 17

SKF AUTOMOTIVE DIV.
46815 Port St., Plymouth, Michigan 48185
CEO: David Rucinski, Mgr.
Bus: *Mfr. roller bearings.*
Tel: (734) 414-6800
Fax: (734) 414-6850
%FO: 100

SKF CONDITION MONITORING, INC.
5271 Viewridge Ct., San Diego, California 92123-1841
CEO: Jan Brons, Pres.
Bus: *Mfr./markets sensors, instruments, software, turn-key systems, and services for condition monitoring of plant machinery.*
Tel: (858) 496-3400
Fax: (858) 496-3531
%FO: 100
Emp: 130

SKF COUPLING SYSTEMS
1447 New Litchfield St., Torrington, Connecticut 06790
CEO: Stepan Norberg, Mgr.
Bus: *Mfr. anti-friction bearings & seals*
Tel: (860) 489-1817
Fax: (860) 489-3867

SKF LINEAR MOTION & PRECISION TECHNOLOGIES
1530 Valley Center Pkwy., Ste. 180, Bethlehem, Pennsylvania 18017
CEO: Paul Jeppeson, Mgr.
Bus: *Engaged in motion technologies.*
Tel: (800) 541-3624
Fax: (610) 861-4811
%FO: 100

SKF USA
Corporate Purchasing, 7310 Tilghman St., Ste. 650, Allentown, Pennsylvania 18106
CEO: Larry Hershman, Mgr.
Bus: *Purchasing services.*
Tel: (610) 391-8054
Fax: (610) 481-9070

SKF USA INC.
5385 McEver Rd., Flowery Branch, Georgia 30542
CEO: Ken Rasheff, Mgr.
Bus: *Mfr. heat testing, surface finishing and assembly machinery.*
Tel: (770) 967-3311
Fax: (770) 967-4258
%FO: 100

SKF USA INC.
1111 Adams Ave., Norristown, Pennsylvania 19403
CEO: Sten Malmstrom, Pres.
Bus: *Mfr./import ball and roller bearings; actuation systems. (U.S. headquarters).*
Tel: (610) 630-2800
Fax: (610) 630-2801
%FO: 100
Emp: 5,200

SKF USA INC.
1510 Gehman Rd., PO Box 332, Kulpsville, Pennsylvania 19443
CEO: Donald Poland, Mgr.   Tel: (215) 513-4400   %FO: 100
Bus: *Mfr. heat testing, surface finishing and*   Fax: (215) 513-4401
     assembly machinery.

VOGEL LUBRICATION, INC.
1008 Jefferson Ave., PO Box 3, Newport News, Virginia 23607
CEO: Nico Pohlmann, Pres.   Tel: (757) 380-8565
Bus: *Mfr. of motor vehicle parts & accessories*   Fax: (757) 380-0709   Emp: 50

• **ALFA LAVAL LTD.**
Rudeboksvagen 3, SE-226 55 Lund, Sweden
CEO: Lars Renström, CEO   Tel: 46-46-36-70-00   Rev: $1,919
Bus: *Separation (centrifuges), fluid handling (pumps*   Fax: 46-46-30-68-60   Emp: 9,358
     and valves) and heat transfer systems.   www.alfalaval.com
NAICS: 541330

    ALFA LAVAL INC.
    4405 Cox Rd., Ste. 140, Glen Allen, Virginia 23060
    CEO: Kirk E. Spitzer   Tel: (804) 545-8120   %FO: 100
    Bus: *Flow instruments and heat exchangers*   Fax:
     manufacture and sales.

    ALFA LAVAL SEPARATION INC.
    955 Mearns Rd., Warminster, Pennsylvania 18974-9998
    CEO: Alex Syed, Pres.   Tel: (215) 443-4000   %FO: 100
    Bus: *Mfr./marketing centrifuges.*   Fax: (215) 443-4205   Emp: 516

    ALFA LAVAL THERMAL INC.
    5400 International Trade Dr., Richmond, Virginia 23231
    CEO: Kirk E. Spitzer, Pres.   Tel: (804) 222-5300   %FO: 100
    Bus: *Mfr./marketing plate heat exchangers.*   Fax: (804) 236-1333

• **ALIMAK HEK GROUP AB**
Brunkebergstorg 5, SE-111 51 Stockholm, Sweden
CEO: Nils-Erik Haggstrom, Pres.   Tel: 46-8-402-1440
Bus: *Mfr. rack and pinion industrial and passenger*   Fax: 49-8-402-1459   Emp: 562
     service elevators and mast climbing work   www.alimak.com
NAICS: 333921, 333923, 336330

    ALIMAK ELEVATOR COMPANY
    3040 Amwiler Rd., Atlanta, Georgia 30360
    CEO: Hans-Olof-Lofstrand, Mgr.   Tel: (770) 441-9055   %FO: 100
    Bus: *Distribution/service industrial and*   Fax: (770) 441-9095
     passenger service elevators.

    ALIMAK ELEVATOR COMPANY
    1951-1 Johns Dr., PO Box 628, Glenview, Illinois 60025
    CEO: John E. Dreyzehner, Mgr.   Tel: (847) 998-4646   %FO: 100
    Bus: *Sales/distribution of industrial rack and*   Fax: (847) 998-4660
     pinion elevators.

ALIMAK ELEVATOR COMPANY
11912 Rivera Rd., Unit E, Santa Fe Springs, California 90670
CEO: Linda Moomau, Mgr.   Tel: (562) 698-2571   %FO: 100
Bus: *Distribution/service industrial and*   Fax: (562) 698-5513
passenger service elevators.

ALIMAK ELEVATOR COMPANY
16920 Texas Ave., Ste. C-14, Webster, Texas 77598
CEO: Franz Beichler, Mgr.   Tel: (281) 338-1114   %FO: 100
Bus: *Distribution/service industrial and*   Fax: (281) 338-0019
passenger service elevators.

INTERVEC ALIMAK ELEVATOR CO.
1100 Boston Ave., PO Box 1950, Bridgeport, Connecticut 06601
CEO: Dale Stoddard, Pres.   Tel: (203) 367-7400   %FO: 100
Bus: *Distribution/service industrial and*   Fax: (203) 367-9251   Emp: 80
passenger service elevators.

● **ASSA ABLOY AB**
Klarabergsviadukten 90, Box 70340, SE-107 23 Stockholm, Sweden
CEO: Bo Dankis, Chmn.   Tel: 46-8-698-8550   Rev: $3,313
Bus: *Door locks and hardware products sales and*   Fax: 46-8-698-8585   Emp: 28,700
manufacture.   www.assaabloy.se
NAICS: 335999

   ASSA ABLOY DOOR GROUP
   1502 12th St., Mason City, Iowa 50401
   CEO: Ben Fellows   Tel: (641) 423-1334
   Bus: *Steel door manufacture.*   Fax: (641) 423-1334

   ASSA ABLOY SECURITY INC.
   6005 Commerce Dr., Ste. 300, Irving, Texas 75063
   CEO: Jennifer Malcuit, Pres.   Tel: (972) 753-1127
   Bus: *Security lock systems manufacture.*   Fax: (972) 750-0792

   ASSA, INC.
   110 Sargent Dr., New Haven, Connecticut 06511
   CEO: Bob Cook, Gen. Mgr.   Tel: (203) 603-5959
   Bus: *Locking device assembly and manufacture.*   Fax: (203) 603-5953

● **ASSE INTERNATIONAL**
Kindstugatan 1, Box 2017, SE-103 Stockholm, Sweden
CEO: Lena Bello, Mgr.   Tel: 46-8-230300
Bus: *Educational services.*   Fax: 46-8-240543   Emp: 200
          www.asse.com
NAICS: 611410, 611630

   ASSE
   326 South Broadway, Wayzata, Minnesota 55391
   CEO: Terri Joski-Lang, Pres.   Tel: (952) 473-4373   %FO: 100
   Bus: *Worldwide educational organization*   Fax: (952) 476-7612
   providing innovative, high-quality programs.

ASSE
228 N. Coast Hwy., Laguna Beach, California 92651
CEO: Laura Hillstrom
Bus: *Worldwide educational organization
providing innovative, high-quality programs.*

Tel: (949) 494-4100
Fax: (949) 494-4100

%FO: 100

ASSE
210 North Lee St., Alexandria, Virginia 22314
CEO: Christine Riley
Bus: *Worldwide educational organization
providing innovative, high-quality programs.*

Tel: (703) 518-5022
Fax: (703) 518-5033

%FO: 100

• ATLAS COPCO AB
Sickla Industrivag 3, SE-105 23 Stockholm, Sweden
CEO: Gunner Brock, Pres. & CEO
Bus: *Mfr. power tools, mining and construction
equipment, pneumatic tools, assembly systems.*

Tel: 46-8-743-8000
Fax: 46-8-644-9045
www.atlascopco-group.com

Rev: $6,157
Emp: 25,958

NAICS: 333120, 333131, 333923, 423830

ATLAS COPCO COMPRESSORS INC
94 North Elm St., Westfield, Massachusetts 01085
CEO: Thomas J. Hinks
Bus: *Compressors manufacture.*

Tel: (413) 536-0600
Fax: (413) 536-0091

%FO: 100

ATLAS COPCO COMPTEC INC.
46 School Rd., Voorheesville, New York 12186
CEO: Bob Mann
Bus: *Compressors manufacture and sales.*

Tel: (518) 765-3344
Fax: (518) 765-3357

%FO: 100

ATLAS COPCO CONSTRUCTION TOOLS INC.
37 Capital Dr., West Springfield, Massachusetts 01089
CEO: Thomas J. Hinks
Bus: *Construction tools manufacture.*

Tel: (413) 536-0600
Fax: (413) 536-0091

ATLAS COPCO NORTH AMERICA, INC.
34 Maple Ave., Pine Brook, New Jersey 07058
CEO: Mark Cohen, Pres.
Bus: *Compressors, mining construction
equipment, pneumatic tools, assembly
systems manufacture.*

Tel: (973) 439-3400
Fax: (973) 439-9188

%FO: 100
Emp: 8,200

ATLAS COPCO TOOLS INC.
2998 Dutton Rd., Auburn Hills, Michigan 48326
CEO: Frederick Moeller
Bus: *Tools manufacture and sales.*

Tel: (248) 373-3000
Fax: (248) 373-3001

%FO: 100

• ATLET AB
Metallvagen 7, SE-435 82 Molnlycke, Sweden
CEO: Marianne Nilson, Mng. Dir.
Bus: *Lift trucks manufacture.*

Tel: 46-31-984000
Fax: 46-31-884686
www.atlet.se

Emp: 900

NAICS: 333924

ATLET INC.
1500 North Harmony Circle, Anaheim, California 92807
CEO: Mary Ann, Mgr.   Tel: (714) 701-4949
Bus: *Lift trucks and parts wholesale*   Fax: (714) 701-4950

ATLET INC.
502 Pratt Ave. North, Schaumburg, Illinois 60193
CEO: Larry Couperthwaite, Pres.   Tel: (847) 352-7373   %FO: JV
Bus: *Lift trucks sales and service.*   Fax: (847) 352-8001   Emp: 40

● **AUTOLIV INC.**
World Trade Center, Klarabergsviadukten 70, PO Box 70381, SE-107 24 Stockholm, Sweden
CEO: Lars Westerberg, Chmn.   Tel: 46-8-587-20600   Rev: $6,143
Bus: *Car safety equipment manufacture, including*   Fax: 46-8-411-7025   Emp: 39,765
      airbags and seat belts.   www.autoliv.com
NAICS: 336399

　　AUTOLIV ELECTRONICS AMERICA
　　26545 American Dr., Southfield, Michigan 48034
　　CEO: Lars Westerberg   Tel: (248) 223-0600   %FO: 100
　　Bus: *Car safety equipment manufacture, including* Fax: (248) 223-8800
　　　　　airbags and seat belts.

　　AUTOLIV INFLATORS
　　250 American Way, Brigham City, Utah 84302
　　CEO: Brian Snyder   Tel: (435) 734-6100   %FO: 100
　　Bus: *Car safety equipment manufacture, including* Fax: (435) 734-7070
　　　　　airbags and seat belts.

　　AUTOLIV INFLATORS
　　OEA Initiator Facility, 1360 North 1000 West, Tremonton, Utah 84337
　　CEO: Brian Snyder   Tel: (435) 257-1000   %FO: 100
　　Bus: *Car safety equipment manufacture, including* Fax: (435) 257-1010
　　　　　airbags and seat belts.

　　AUTOLIV INFLATORS
　　PO Box 100488, Denver, Colorado 80250
　　CEO: Tom Hartman   Tel: (303) 693-1248   %FO: 100
　　Bus: *Car safety equipment manufacture, including* Fax: (303) 699-6991
　　　　　airbags and seat belts.

　　AUTOLIV NORTH AMERICA
　　Technical Center, 1320 Pacific Drive, Auburn Hills, Michigan 48326-1569
　　CEO: Norm Markert   Tel: (248) 475-9000   %FO: 100
　　Bus: *Car safety equipment manufacture, including* Fax: (248) 475-9838
　　　　　airbags and seat belts.

　　AUTOLIV NORTH AMERICA
　　1000 West 3300 South, Ogden, Utah 84401
　　CEO: Tom Hartman   Tel: (801) 629-9800   %FO: 100
　　Bus: *Car safety equipment manufacture, including* Fax: (801) 629-9619
　　　　　airbags and seat belts.

AUTOLIV NORTH AMERICA
Pyrotechnic Processing Facility, 16700 West Hwy. 83, Promontory, Utah 84302
CEO: Lars Westerberg   Tel: (435) 471-3001   %FO: 100
Bus: *Car safety equipment manufacture, including* Fax: (435) 471-3007
       airbags and seat belts.

AUTOLIV NORTH AMERICA
Headquarters, 3350 Airport Rd., Ogden, Utah 84405
CEO: Brad Murray   Tel: (801) 625-9200   %FO: 100
Bus: *Car safety equipment manufacture, including* Fax: (801) 629-4979
       airbags and seat belts.

AUTOLIV NORTH AMERICA, SEAT BELT DIV.
410 Autoliv Belt Way, Madisonville, Kentucky 42431
CEO: Lisa Frary   Tel: (270) 326-3300   %FO: 100
Bus: *Car safety equipment manufacture, including* Fax: (270) 825-9809
       airbags and seat belts.

AUTOLIV NORTH AMERICA, STEERING WHEEL DIV.
4868 East Park 30 Dr., Columbia City, Indiana 46725
CEO: Mark Newton, Mgr.   Tel: (260) 244-4941   %FO: 100
Bus: *Car safety equipment manufacture, including* Fax: (260) 244-4951
       airbags and seat belts.

● **AVESTAPOLARIT OYJ**
Vasagatan 8-10, PO 270, SE-103 27 Stockholm, Sweden
CEO: Ossi Virolainen, CEO   Tel: 46-8-613-3600
Bus: *Mfr. stainless steel.*   Fax: 46-8-613-3669
                                          www.outokumpu.com
NAICS: 331221

AVESTA WELDING PRODUCTS INC.
3176 Abbott Rd., Orchard Park, New York 14127
CEO: Paul Carpenter   Tel: (716) 827-4400   %FO: 100
Bus: *Welding products manufacture.*   Fax: (716) 827-4404

OUTOKUMPU STAINLESS BAR INC.
425 N. Martingale Rd., Ste. 2000, Schaumburg, Illinois 60173
CEO: Michael Stateczny   Tel: (847) 517-4050   %FO: 100
Bus: *Steel manufacture and sales.*   Fax: (847) 517-2950

OUTOKUMPU STAINLESS BAR INC.
3043 Crenshaw Pkwy., Richburg, South Carolina 29729
CEO: Lou Kern, EVP   Tel: (803) 789-5383   %FO: 100
Bus: *Long products manufacture.*   Fax: (803) 789-3177

OUTOKUMPU STAINLESS PIPE INC.
1101 North Main St., Wildwood, Florida 34785
CEO: Joseph Avento, EVP   Tel: (352) 748-1313   %FO: 100
Bus: *Tubular products manufacture.*   Fax: (352) 748-6576

OUTOKUMPU STAINLESS PLATE INC.
PO Box 370, New Castle, Indiana 47362
CEO: Mike Stateczny   Tel: (765) 529-0120   %FO: 100
Bus: *Plate products manufacture.*   Fax: (765) 529-8177

- **AXEL JOHNSON AB**
  Villagatan 6, PO Box 26008, SE-100 41 Stockholm, Sweden
  CEO: Goran Ennerfelt, Pres. & CEO   Tel: 46-8-701-6100   Rev: $730
  Bus: *Food importers and retailers; supermarkets and*   Fax: 46-8-21-3026   Emp: 3,200
  department stores.   www.axel-johnson.se
       NAICS: 424410, 424480, 424490, 442110, 442299, 445110, 445120, 446120, 448110, 448120, 448130, 448140,
  448150, 452112, 452990

  ADS CORP.
  5030 Bradford Dr., Bldg. 1, Huntsville, Alabama 35805
  CEO: William Garland   Tel: (256) 430-3366
  Bus: *Mfr. of industrial machinery.*   Fax: (256) 430-6633

  AXEL JOHNSON INC
  300 Atlantic St., Stamford, Connecticut 06901
  CEO: Antonia Ax Son Johnson, Chmn.   Tel: (203) 326-5200   %FO: 100
  Bus: *Industrial machinery manufacture and sales.*   Fax: (203) 326-5280

  PARKSON CORPORATION
  2727 N.W. 62nd. St., Ft. Lauderdale, Florida 33340
  CEO: William C. Acton   Tel: (305) 974-6610   %FO: 100
  Bus: *Industrial machinery manufacture and sales.*   Fax: (305) 974-6182   Emp: 280

  SPRAGUE ENERGY CORPORATION
  Two International Dr., Ste. 200, Portsmouth, New Hampshire 03801
  CEO: John McClellan, Pres.   Tel: (603) 431-1000   %FO: 100
  Bus: *Heavy fuel oil, coal, jet fuel, gasoline*   Fax: (603) 431-5324   Emp: 450
  marketing and provides bulk material
  handling services.

- **AXIS COMMUNICATIONS AB**
  Scheelevagen 34, SE-223 69 Lund, Sweden
  CEO: Mikael Karlsson, Pres. & CEO   Tel: 46-46-2721800
  Bus: *Mfr. computer and office equipment.*   Fax: 46-46-136130   Emp: 100
       www.axis.se
       NAICS: 511210

  AXIS COMMUNICATIONS INC.
  800 El Camino Real, Ste. 180, Mountain View, California 94040
  CEO: Patrik von Bergen   Tel: (650) 903-2221   %FO: 100
  Bus: *Computer and office equipment.*   Fax: (650) 903-2224   Emp: 100

  AXIS COMMUNICATIONS INC.
  100 Apollo Dr., Chelmsford, Massachusetts 01824
  CEO: Ray Mauritsson, Pres.   Tel: (978) 614-2000   %FO: 100
  Bus: *Computer and office equipment.*   Fax: (978) 614-2100

- **BESAM AB, DIV. ASSA ABLOY**
  Box 131, SE-261 22 Landskrona, Sweden
  CEO: Juan Vargues, Pres. & CEO   Tel: 46-418-51100   Rev: $2,000
  Bus: *Mfr. automatic swing, slide, folding and revolving*   Fax: 46-418-238-00   Emp: 1,420
  doors.   www.besam.se
  NAICS: 332321

BESAM AUTOMATED ENTRANCE SYSTEMS
2140 Priest Bridge Ct., Ste. 7, Crofton, Maryland 21114
CEO: Paul Belliveau, Pres. & CEO	Tel: (443) 270-3600	%FO: 100
Bus: *Automatic doors distribution and sales.*	Fax: (443) 270-3608	Emp: 250

● **BIACORE INTERNATIONAL AB**
Rapsgatan 7, SE-75450 Uppsala, Sweden
CEO: Erik Wallden, Pres. & CEO	Tel: 46-18-675-700	Rev: $75
Bus: *Supplier of protein interaction analysis systems.*	Fax: 46-18-675-811	Emp: 342
	www.biacore.com	

NAICS: 334516, 339111

    BIACORE INC.
    200 Centennial Ave., Ste. 100, Piscataway, New Jersey 08854-3950
CEO: Jerry Williamson, Pres.	Tel: (732) 885-5618	%FO: 100
Bus: *Supplier of protein interaction analysis systems.*	Fax: (732) 885-5669	

● **BINDOMATIC AB**
Vretenborgsvägen 9, Box 42101, SE-126 12 Stockholm, Sweden
CEO: Sture Wiholm, Mng. Dir.	Tel: 46-8-709-5800	
Bus: *Mfr. binding systems.*	Fax: 46-8-188-652	
	www.bindomatic.se	

NAICS: 333313

    COVERBIND CORP
    3200 Corporate Dr., Wilmington, North Carolina 28405
CEO: Eileen Prado, Mgr.	Tel: (910) 799-4116	%FO: 100
Bus: *Mfr. binding systems.*	Fax: (910) 799-3935	

● **BIOCORE INTERNATIONAL AB**
Rapsgatan 7, SE-754 50 Uppsala, Sweden
CEO: Erik Wallden, Pres. & CEO	Tel: 46-18-675-700	Rev: $71
Bus: *Product and quality control instruments manufacture.*	Fax: 46-18-150-110	Emp: 325
	www.biacore.com	

NAICS: 334516

    BIOCORE INC.
    6125 Cornerstone CT East, San Diego, California 92121
CEO: Dr. Laure Jason-Moller	Tel: (858) 457-4151	%FO: 100
Bus: *Product and quality control instruments manufacture.*	Fax: (858) 457-4151	

    BIOCORE INC.
    200 Centennial Ave., Ste. 100, Piscataway, New Jersey 08854
CEO: Jerry Williamson, Pres.	Tel: (732) 885-5618	%FO: 100
Bus: *Product and quality control instruments manufacture.*	Fax: (732) 885-5669	

- **BIORA AB**
Medeon Science Park, SE-205 12 Malmo, Sweden
CEO: Erik WalldEn, CEO
Bus: *Mfr. products for treatment of periodontal disease and products used during oral surgery.*
NAICS: 325412
Tel: 46-40-32-1340
Fax: 46-40-32-1335
www.biora.se
Rev: $10
Emp: 75

    BIORA, INC.
    415 North LaSalle St., Ste. 615, Chicago, Illinois 60610
    CEO: Karen Williams
    Bus: *Mfr. products for use during oral surgery and for treatment of periodontal disease.*
    Tel: (312) 832-1414
    Fax: (312) 832-1429
    %FO: 100

- **BRIO AB**
Briogatan 1, SE-283 83 Osby, Sweden
CEO: Thomas Brautigam, Pres.
Bus: *Mfr./marketing specialty toys.*
NAICS: 339932
Tel: 46-479-19000
Fax: 46-479-14124
www.brio.se
Rev: $200
Emp: 1,075

    BRIO CORP
    North 120 W.18485 Freistadt Rd., Germantown, Wisconsin 53022
    CEO: Tim O'Connor, Pres.
    Bus: *Importer marketing/distribution toys.*
    Tel: (262) 250-3240
    Fax: (262) 250-3255
    %FO: 100
    Emp: 30

- **BROMMA CONQUIP AB**
Krossgatan 31-33, SE-162 50 Vallingby, Sweden
CEO: Terry E. Howell, Mng. Dir.
Bus: *Mfr. spreaders and container handling equipment.*
NAICS: 333111, 333120, 333298
Tel: 46-8-620-0900
Fax: 46-8-739-3786
www.bromma.com
Emp: 146

    BROMMA, INC.
    2285 Durham Rd., PO Box 451, Roxboro, North Carolina 27573
    CEO: Terry E. Howell, Pres.
    Bus: *Mfr. container-handling equipment & related attachments.*
    Tel: (336) 599-3141
    Fax: (336) 599-4499
    %FO: 100

- **BT INDUSTRIES AB**
Syarvargatan 8, SE-595 81 Mjolby, Sweden
CEO: Per Zaunders, CEO
Bus: *Material handling trucks manufacture.*
NAICS: 333924
Tel: 46-1-428-6000
Fax: 46-1-428-6080
www.bt-industries.com
Rev: $1,206
Emp: 7,900

    BP PRIME-MOVER INC.
    3305 North Highway 38, Muscatine, Iowa 52761
    CEO: James J. Malvaso
    Bus: *Mfr. electric lift trucks and material-handling equipment.*
    Tel: (319) 262-7700
    Fax: (319) 262-7600
    %FO: 100

BT RAYMOND INC.
South Canal St., PO Box 130, Greene, New York 12778
CEO: James J. Malvaso, Pres. & CEO
Bus: *Mfr. electric lift trucks.*

Tel: (607) 656-2311
Fax: (607) 656-9005

%FO: 100

• CARDO AB
Roskildevagen 1, Box 486, SE-201 24 Malmo, Sweden
CEO: Peter Aru, Pres. & CEO
Bus: *Mfr. centrifugal pumps, doors, brake systems and garage doors.*

Tel: 46-40-35-0400
Fax: 46-40-97-6440
www.cardo.se

Rev: $1,060
Emp: 6,200

NAICS: 238290, 335314, 336399

ABS PUMPS, INC.
140 Pond View Dr., Meriden, Connecticut 06450
CEO: Gerald Assessor, Pres.
Bus: *Mfr. centrifugal pumps.*

Tel: (203) 238-2700
Fax: (203) 238-0738

%FO: 100

MEGADOOR INC.
665 Highway 74 South, Peachtree City, Georgia 30269
CEO: Ulf Peterson
Bus: *Mfr. metal doors.*

Tel: (770) 631-2600
Fax: (770) 631-2600

%FO: 100

PUMPEX, INC.
49 Molasses Hill Rd., Lebanon, New Jersey 08833
CEO: Robert Montenegro, Pres.
Bus: *Mfr. submersible pumps.*

Tel: (908) 730-7004
Fax: (908) 730-7580

%FO: 100

• CELLMARK GROUP
O Hamngatan 17, PO Box 11927, SE-404 39 Gothenburg, Sweden
CEO: Håkan Björnhage, CEO
Bus: *Produces printing papers.*

Tel: 46-31-100300
Fax: 46-31-136421
www.cellmark.com

Rev: $1,200
Emp: 500

NAICS: 322121, 322221, 322222

AMERISOUTH HOLDINGS INC.
3799 Brownsmill Rd., Atlanta, Georgia 30354
CEO: Edward A. Collier
Bus: *Paper pulp sales and marketing.*

Tel: (404) 209-0002
Fax: (404) 209-0005

%FO: 100

CELLMARK INC.
5055 New Chapel Hill Way, Cumming, Georgia 30041
CEO: Ben C. Smith
Bus: *Recycling services.*

Tel: (770) 844-9466
Fax: (770) 844-0992

%FO: 100

CELLMARK INC.
877 B&A Blvd, Suite 307, Serverna Park, Maryland 21146
CEO: Todd Petrocelli
Bus: *Recycling services.*

Tel: (510) 544-1588
Fax: (510) 544-5002

%FO: 100

CELLMARK PACKAGING INC.
200 Tamal Plaza, Ste. 200, Corte Madera, California 94925
CEO: Paul J. Busnardo
Bus: *Paper pulp sales and marketing.*

Tel: (415) 927-1799
Fax: (415) 381-4358

%FO: 100

CELLMARK PAPER INC.
300 Atlantic St., 5/F, Stamford, Connecticut 06901
CEO: Joe P. Hoffman, Jr., Pres.   Tel: (203) 363-7800   %FO: 100
Bus: *Distributes forest products.*   Fax: (203) 363-7809

CELLMARK PULP AND PAPER INC.
2800 Ponce de Leon Blvd., Coral Gables, Florida 33134
CEO: Michel Robert   Tel: (305) 459-4100   %FO: 100
Bus: *Paper pulp sales and marketing.*   Fax: (305) 461-0221

CELLMARK PULP AND PAPER INC.
Box 641, South Norwalk, Connecticut 06856
CEO: Bengt Stenbeck   Tel: (203) 299-5050   %FO: 100
Bus: *Paper pulp sales and marketing.*   Fax: (203) 299-5055

CELLMARK PULP INC.
2112 Whalen Dr., Point Roberts, Washington 98281
CEO: Peter Fraser   Tel: (360) 945-0345   %FO: 100
Bus: *Paper pulp sales and marketing.*   Fax: (360) 945-1399

CENTRAL KENTUCKY FIBER RESOURCES, LCC
123 Buchanan St., Lexington, Kentucky 40522
CEO: David Ratliff   Tel: (859) 225-8100   %FO: 100
Bus: *Paper pulp sales and marketing.*   Fax: (859) 225-1238

PITTSBURGH RECYCLING SERVICES LLC
50 Vespucius St., Pittsburgh, Pennsylvania 15201
CEO: Vic Alfieri   Tel: (412) 420-6000   %FO: 100
Bus: *Recycling services.*   Fax: (412) 420-6009

SUNSET TRADING
16390 Pacific Coast Hwy., Huntington Beach, California 92649
CEO: Tom Curran   Tel: (562) 592-1200   %FO: 100
Bus: *Paper pulp sales and marketing.*   Fax: (562) 592-2800

TRIBORO FIBERS INC.
770 Barry St., Bronx, New York 10474
CEO: Bob Pirrello   Tel: (718) 378-4600   %FO: 100
Bus: *Paper pulp sales and marketing.*   Fax: (718) 378-2385

● **CHRIS-MARINE AB**
Stenyxegatan 3, SE-213 76 Malmo, Sweden
CEO: Leif Olsson, Mng. Dir.   Tel: 46-40-671-2600
Bus: *Mfr. of maintenance equipment for marine and*   Fax: 46-40-671-2699
      stationary diesel engines.   www.chris-marine.com
NAICS: 212319, 333618, 333991, 811310

    CHRIS-MARINE USA, INC.
    732 Parker St., Jacksonville, Florida 32202
    CEO: Kent Ekenberg, Pres.   Tel: (904) 354-8784   %FO: 100
    Bus: *Diesel engine & turbocharger repairs.*   Fax: (904) 358-7862

- **CYCORE AB**
Dragarbrunnsgatan 35, SE-753 20 Uppsala, Sweden
CEO: Jerry Pettersson, CEO
Bus: *Mfr. interactive, 3-D software.*

Tel: 46-18-656-560
Fax: 46-18-656-566
www.cycore.com

NAICS: 511210

> **CYCORE INC.**
> 3130 La Selva Dr., Ste. 100, San Mateo, California 94403
> CEO: Jim Madden, Pres. & CEO
> Bus: *Mfr. interactive, 3-D software for the internet.*
>
> Tel: (650) 627-5000
> Fax: (650) 358-8419
>
> %FO: 100

- **DELAVAL INTERNATIONAL AB**
Gustaf de Lavals vag 15, SE-147-21 Tumba, Sweden
CEO: Joakim Rosengren, Pres. & CEO
Bus: *Mfr. of dairy farm machinery.*

Tel: 46-8-530-660-00
Fax: 46-8-530-689-00
www.delaval.com

Rev: $941
Emp: 4

NAICS: 112120, 112990, 333111

> **DELAVAL INC.**
> 11100 North Congress Ave., Kansas City, Missouri 64153
> CEO: Ulf Jaern, Reg. Dir.
> Bus: *Manufacturer of farm machinery.*
>
> Tel: (816) 891-7700
> Fax: (816) 891-1606
>
> %FO: 100

- **DOMETIC AB ORIGO**
Sondrumsvagen 35, SE-302 39 Halmstad, Sweden
CEO: Anders Magnusson, CEO
Bus: *Mfr. stoves and heaters for mobile homes and*

Tel: 46-35-16-5700
Fax: 46-35-16-5710
www.origo-sweden.com

NAICS: 333414, 335221

> **ICM INTERCON MARKETING INC.**
> 1540 Northgate Blvd., Sarasota, Florida 34234
> CEO: Anders Ebbeson, Pres.
> Bus: *Mfr. of heaters.*
>
> Tel: (941) 355-4488
> Fax: (941) 355-1558
>
> %FO: 100

- **DUNI AB**
Kungsgatan 72, Box 95, SE-101 21 Stockholm, Sweden
CEO: Hans von Uthmann, CEO
Bus: *Food service and table products for airlines, trains and ferries.*

Tel: 46-8-402-1300
Fax: 46-8-206-6609
www.duni.com

Rev: $720
Emp: 4,500

NAICS: 327112

> **DUNI CORPORATION**
> 2260 Delray Rd., Thomaston, Georgia 30286
> CEO: Steve Sizemore, Pres.
> Bus: *Mfr. plastic airline food trays.*
>
> Tel: (706) 647-2205
> Fax: (706) 647-1360
>
> %FO: 100

> **DUNI CORPORATION**
> 225 Peachtree St., Ste. 400, Atlanta, Georgia 30303
> CEO: Morgan Cederblom, Pres.
> Bus: *Mfr. disposable food service and table products.*
>
> Tel: (404) 659-9100
> Fax: (404) 659-5226
>
> %FO: 100

DUNI SUPPLY CORPORATION
W 165 N5830 Ridgewood Dr., Menomonee Falls, Wisconsin 53051-5655
CEO: William Mahnke   Tel: (262) 252-7700   %FO: 100
Bus: *Mfr. disposable food service and table*   Fax: (262) 252-7710   Emp: 200
     products.

● **DUX INDUSTRIER AB**
Box 1002, SE-231 25 Trelleborg, Sweden
CEO: Anders Börgdal, Pres.   Tel: 46-410-58755
Bus: *Furniture and mattresses manufacture.*   Fax: 46-410-58755
                                               www.duxbed.com
  NAICS: 337125, 337910

  DUXIANA
  235 East 58th St., New York, New York 10022
  CEO: Bo Gustafsson, Pres.   Tel: (212) 755-2600   %FO: 100
  Bus: *Wholesale furniture and mattresses.*   Fax: (212) 755-2600

  DUXIANA
  6134 Berkshire Lane, Dallas, Texas 75225
  CEO: Serena Cole   Tel: (214) 739-8133   %FO: 100
  Bus: *Wholesale furniture and mattresses.*   Fax: (214) 739-8133

  DUXIANA LODELA
  15 West Putnam Ave., Greenwich, Connecticut 06830
  CEO: Laura Rajovic   Tel: (203) 661-7162   %FO: 100
  Bus: *Wholesale furniture and mattresses.*   Fax: (203) 661-7162

● **EKA CHEMICALS AB**
Lilla Bommen 1, SE-445 80 Goteborg, Sweden
CEO: Jan Svard, Pres.   Tel: 46-31-58-7000   Rev: $1,125
Bus: *Mfr. chemicals and allied products for the pulp*   Fax: 46-31-58-7212   Emp: 2,883
     and paper industries..   www.akzonobel.com
  NAICS: 325181, 325188

  EKA CHEMICALS, INC.
  4374 Nashville Ferry Rd. E., Columbus, Mississippi 39702
  CEO: Andy Gressett   Tel: (601) 327-0400   %FO: 100
  Bus: *Mfr. chemicals and allied products.*   Fax: (601) 329-3004

  EKA CHEMICALS, INC.
  1775 West Oak Commons Ct., Marietta, Georgia 30062
  CEO: Mario Houde, Pres.   Tel: (770) 578-0858   %FO: 100
  Bus: *Mfr. chemicals and allied products.*   Fax: (770) 578-1359   Emp: 100

  EKA CHEMICALS, INC.
  2701 Rd. N-NE, Moses Lake, Washington 98837
  CEO: Caldin Greene   Tel: (509) 765-6400   %FO: 100
  Bus: *Mfr. chemicals and allied products.*   Fax: (509) 765-5557

  EKA CHEMICALS, INC., BINDZIL/NYACOL GROUP
  1616 Marvin Griffin Rd., Augusta, Georgia 30906
  CEO: Chris Buster   Tel: (706) 790-9364   %FO: 100
  Bus: *Mfr. chemicals and allied products.*   Fax: (706) 790-0534

● **ELECTROLUX AB**
St. Goransgatan 143, SE-105 45 Stockholm, Sweden
CEO: Hans Straberg, Pres. & CEO
Bus: *Mfr. household and commercial appliances and outdoor lawn and leaf products.*
NAICS: 333112, 333991, 335212, 335221, 335222, 335224

Tel: 46-8-738-6000
Fax: 46-8-656-4478
www.electrolux.com

Rev: $18,242
Emp: 77,140

> **BEAM INDUSTRIES**
> 1700 West 2nd St., Webster City, Iowa 50595
> CEO: John Coghlan, Pres.
> Bus: *Mfr. of home appliances.*
>
> Tel: (515) 832-4620
> Fax: (515) 832-6659
>
> %FO: 100

> **ELECTROLUX HOME CARE PRODUCTS-NORTH AMERICA**
> 807 North Main St., Bloomington, Illinois 61701
> CEO: John J. Case, Pres. & CEO
> Bus: *Mfr. of home appliances.*
>
> Tel: (309) 828-2367
> Fax: (309) 823-5203
>
> %FO: 100
> Emp: 300

> **ELECTROLUX HOME PRODUCTS**
> 1219 West Glen Ave, PO Box 3900, Peoria, Illinois 61612
> CEO: Bob Barton, CEO
> Bus: *Mfr. of home products.*
>
> Tel: (309) 683-3494
> Fax: (309) 683-3494
>
> %FO: 100

> **ELECTROLUX HOME PRODUCTS**
> 20445 Emerald Pkwy., Ste. 250, Cleveland, Ohio 44135
> CEO: Johan Bygge, Pres.
> Bus: *Headquarters office for US operations.*
>
> Tel: (216) 898-1800
> Fax: (216) 898-2366
>
> %FO: 100
> Emp: 22,000

> **ELECTROLUX HOME PRODUCTS-NORTH AMERICA**
> 250 Bobby Jones Expressway, Augusta, Georgia 30907
> CEO: Keith R. McLoughlin, Pres.
> Bus: *Mfr. of home appliances.*
>
> Tel: (706) 651-1751
> Fax: (706) 651-7769
>
> %FO: 100

● **ELEKTA AB**
Birger Jarlsgatan 53, Box 7593, SE-103 93 Stockholm, Sweden
CEO: Tomas Puusepp, Pres.
Bus: *Technical instrument and supplies for medical and dental surgery manufacture and sales.*
NAICS: 334513

Tel: 46-8-587-25400
Fax: 46-8-587-25500
www.elekta.se

Rev: $200
Emp: 1,100

> **ELEKTA HOLDINGS USA**
> 4775 Peachtree Industrial Blvd., Bldg. 300, Norcross, Georgia 30092
> CEO: Hans Von Celsing, Pres.
> Bus: *Sales/distribution of surgical and medical instruments.*
>
> Tel: (770) 300-9725
> Fax: (770) 448-6338
>
> %FO: 100

> **IMPAC MEDICAL SYSTEMS INC.**
> 100 West Evelyn Ave., Mountain View, California 94041
> CEO: Joseph K. Jachinowski, Pres.
> Bus: *Provides integrated clinical and administrative management systems for cancer specialists.*
>
> Tel: (650) 286-9425
> Fax: (650) 428-0721
>
> %FO: 100
> Emp: 430

- **ELMO LEATHER AB**
  Borasvagen 13, SE-512 81 Svenljunga, Sweden
  CEO: Nalle Johansson, Chmn.
  Bus: *High quality furniture and automotive leathers
  development and manufacture.*
  NAICS: 337214

  Tel: 46-325-66-1400
  Fax: 46-325-61-1004
  www.elmoleather.com

  Emp: 369

  ELMO LEATHER OF AMERICA
  505 Thornall St., Ste. 303, Edison, New Jersey 08817
  CEO: Stefan Brunander, Pres.
  Bus: *Design/mfr./marketing high quality furniture
  and automotive leathers.*

  Tel: (732) 549-5151
  Fax: (732) 549-7990

  %FO: 100
  Emp: 50

- **ELOF HANSSON AB**
  Forsta Langgatan 17, SE-413 80 Goteborg, Sweden
  CEO: Thomas Peterson, Pres.
  Bus: *Forestry products, industrial products and
  consumer products manufacture.*
  NAICS: 322121, 322299, 333999

  Tel: 46-31-85-6000
  Fax: 46-31-12-6735
  www.elofhansson.com

  Rev: $899
  Emp: 548

  ELOF HANSSON INC
  565 Taxter Rd., Elmsford, New York 10523
  CEO: Thomas Petterson, Chmn.
  Bus: *Importer; pulp, paper products.*

  Tel: (914) 345-8380
  Fax: (914) 345-8112

  %FO: 100
  Emp: 35

- **ELTEX OF SWEDEN AB**
  Box 608, SE-343 24 Almhult, Sweden
  CEO: Staffan Ferm, Dir.
  Bus: *Mfr. stop motion equipment for textile machines.*

  Tel: 46-476-48800
  Fax: 46-476-13400
  www.eltex.se

  Emp: 180

  NAICS: 334519, 335912

  ELTEX US INC.
  1692 E. Wade Hampton Blvd., PO Box 868, Greer, South Carolina 29651
  CEO: Jonathan Bell, Pres.
  Bus: *Sales/service electronic yarn monitoring
  equipment; battery chargers; data loggers.*

  Tel: (864) 879-2131
  Fax: (864) 879-3734

  %FO: 100
  Emp: 6

- **ETON SYSTEMS AB**
  Djupdal, SE-507 71 Ganghester, Sweden
  CEO: Fredrik Satradahl, Dir.
  Bus: *Mfr. unit production systems (UPS) for the sewn-
  product industries.*
  NAICS: 333518

  Tel: 46-33-23-1200
  Fax: 46-33-24-9167
  www.eton.se

  Emp: 10

  ETON SYSTEMS, INC.
  4000 McGinnis Ferry Rd., Alpharetta, Georgia 30005
  CEO: Sven G. Bodell, Mgr.
  Bus: *Unit production systems for apparel and
  home fashion.*

  Tel: (770) 475-8022
  Fax: (770) 442-0216

  %FO: 100

● **FLEXLINK SYSTEMS AB**
Kullagergatan 50, SE-415 50 Goteborg, Sweden
CEO: Fredrik Jonsson, CEO
Bus: *Mfr. industrial machinery.*

Tel: 46-31-337-3100
Fax: 46-31-337-2233
www.flexlink.com

Rev: $84
Emp: 330

NAICS: 333298

> **FLEXLINK SYSTEMS INC.**
> 6580 Snowdrift Rd., Allentown, Pennsylvania 18106
> CEO: Paul Jarossy, Pres.
> Bus: *Mfr. plastic chain conveyors and
>   automation components.*
>
> Tel: (610) 973-8230
> Fax: (610) 973-8345
>
> %FO: 100
> Emp: 75

● **FORENINGSSPARBANKEN AB (SWEDBANK)**
Brunkebergstorg 8, SE-105 34 Stockholm, Sweden
CEO: Jan Lidén, CEO
Bus: *Commercial banking services.*

Tel: 46-8-585-90000
Fax: 46-8-796-8092
www.fsb.se

Rev: $8,320
Emp: 15,156

NAICS: 522110

> **SWEDBANK NEW YORK**
> One Penn Plaza, 15/F, New York, New York 10119
> CEO: John Matthews, Mgr.
> Bus: *Commercial banking services.*
>
> Tel: (212) 486-8400
> Fax: (212) 486-3220
>
> %FO: 100
> Emp: 30

● **FORSHEDA AB**
Lilla Bomen 1, SE-411 04 Goteborg, Sweden
CEO: G. Bark, CEO
Bus: *Automobile seat heater manufacture.*

Tel: 46-31-771-2280
Fax: 46-31-802715
www.forsheda.com

NAICS: 336391

> **FORSHEDA PALMER-CHENARD INC.**
> 366 Route 108, Somersworth, New Hampshire 03878
> CEO: Linda Currier
> Bus: *Automobile seat heater manufacture and
>   sales.*
>
> Tel: (603) 692-7400
> Fax: (603) 692-7400
>
> %FO: 100

● **GAMBRO AG**
Jakobsgatan 6, SE-103 91 Stockholm, Sweden
CEO: Soren Mellstig, Pres. & CEO
Bus: *Medical technology and healthcare; renal care
    services, blood component technology &
    cardiopulmonary care. (Gambro created by
    Incentive AB.)*

Tel: 46-8-613-6500
Fax: 46-8-611-2830
www.gambro.com

Rev: $4,024
Emp: 21,279

NAICS: 325411, 325412, 325413, 325414, 334510, 335999, 339112, 339113, 541380, 541710, 621492, 621511

> **GAMBRO BCT INC.**
> 10811 W. Collins Ave., Lakewood, Colorado 80215
> CEO: Kevin Smith, Pres.
> Bus: *Blood center operations.*
>
> Tel: (303) 232-6800
> Fax: (303) 231-4150

GAMBRO HEALTHCARE LABORATORY SERVICES
3951, SW 30th Ave., Ft. Lauderdale, Florida 33312
CEO: Mark Brown
Bus: *Laboratory services.*
Tel: (954) 585-1100
Fax: (954) 585-1181

GAMBRO HEALTHCARE PATIENT SERVICES
4510 Cox Rd., Ste. 106, Glen Allen, Virginia 23060
CEO: Lawrence J. Centella
Bus: *Dialysis providers.*
Tel: (804) 747-6188
Fax: (804) 747-0624

GAMBRO HEALTHCARE, INC.
5200 Virginia Way, Brentwood, Tennessee 37027
CEO: R. Douglas Mefford
Bus: *Engaged in medical technology and healthcare.*
Tel: (615) 341-5890
Fax: (615) 320-4260

GAMBRO USA, INC.
10810 West Collins Ave., Lakewood, Colorado 80215
CEO: Larry C. Buckelew, Pres.
Bus: *Engaged in medical technology and healthcare.*
Tel: (303) 232-6800
Fax: (303) 231-4150
%FO: 100
Emp: 10,000

● **GETINGE AB**
Ekebergsvagen 26, Halland, SE-310 44 Getinge, Sweden
CEO: Johan Malmquist, Pres. & CEO
Bus: *Sterilization, disinfection, surgical and medical products manufacture.*
NAICS: 339113, 551112
Tel: 46-35-155500
Fax: 46-35-54952
www.getinge.com
Rev: $1,174
Emp: 6,060

ARJO INC.
50 North Gary Ave., Roselle, Illinois 60172
CEO: Ross Scavuzzo, Pres.
Bus: *Sale of medical supplies & equipment.*
Tel: (800) 323-1245
Fax:
Emp: 135

GETINGE USA
1777 E. Henrietta Rd., Rochester, New York 14623
CEO: Charles Carrier, CEO
Bus: *Medical equipment & supplies.*
Tel: (585) 475-1400
Fax: (585) 272-5033
Emp: 600

LANCER SALES USA INC.
3543 State Rd. 419, Winter Springs, Florida 32708
CEO: James Fry, Pres.
Bus: *Industrial medical products and cleaning chemicals manufacture.*
Tel: (407) 327-8488
Fax: (407) 327-1229
Emp: 11

MAQUET INC.
1140 Route 22 East, Ste. 202, Bridgewater, New Jersey 08807
CEO: John Rich, Operations Mgr.
Bus: *Mfr. of medical & hospital equipment*
Tel: (908) 947-2300
Fax:
Emp: 90

PEGASUS AIRWAVE INC.
791 Park of Commerce Blvd., Ste. 500, Boca Raton, Florida 33487
CEO: R. Geoffrey D. Welch, Chmn.
Bus: *Sale & rental of hospital equipment*
Tel: (561) 989-9898
Fax:
Emp: 103

- **GRANSFORS BRUKS AB**
Gränsfors Yxsmedja, SE-820 70 Bergsjo, Sweden
CEO: Gabriel Branby, Pres.
Bus: *Axes, wrecking bars and protective material manufacture.*
NAICS: 315225, 332212

Tel: 46-652-71090
Fax: 46-652-14002
www.gransfors.com

Emp: 75

   GRANSFORS BRUKS INC.
   821 West 5th North S., PO Box 818, Summerville, South Carolina 29483
   CEO: Yvonne Caruso, Pres.
   Bus: *Mfr./marketing safety apparel for forest industry.*

   Tel: (843) 875-0240
   Fax: (843) 821-2285

   %FO: 100
   Emp: 27

- **GRINDEX AB**
Hantverkarvagen 24, Box 538, Haninge, SE-136 25 Stockholm, Sweden
CEO: Goran Holmen, Mng. Dir.
Bus: *Electronic submersible heavy duty drainage and sludge pumps manufacture.*
NAICS: 333913

Tel: 46-8-606-6600
Fax: 46-8-745-5328
www.grindex.com

Emp: 80

   GRINDEX PUMPS
   18524 South 81st Ave., Tinley Park, Illinois 60477
   CEO: Goenn Wievoruk, Gen. Mgr.
   Bus: *Sale/service drainage & sludge pumps.*

   Tel: (708) 532-9988
   Fax: (708) 532-8767

   %FO: 100

- **H&M HENNES & MAURITZ AB**
Regeringsgatan 48, SE-106 38 Stockholm, Sweden
CEO: Rolf Eriksen, CEO & Mng. Dir.
Bus: *Mfr. of reasonably priced, trendy clothing.*
NAICS: 446120, 448110, 448120, 448140

Tel: 46-8-796-5500
Fax: 46-8-24-8078
www.hm.com

Rev: $8,001
Emp: 45,000

   H&M HENNES & MAURITZ LP
   47 West 34th St., 3/F, New York, New York 10001
   CEO: Sanna Lindberg, Prtn.
   Bus: *Mfr. of reasonably priced, trendy clothing.*

   Tel: (212) 564-9922
   Fax:

   %FO: 100
   Emp: 2,500

- **HÄGGLUNDS DRIVES AB**
Bjornavagen 41, SE-890 42 Mellansel, Sweden
CEO: Per Nordgren, Pres.
Bus: *Armored and all-terrain vehicles, marine transport equipment, hydraulic drives.*
NAICS: 332995, 336111, 336399, 423120

Tel: 46-660-87-0001
Fax: 46-660-87-160
www.hagglunds.com

Rev: $319
Emp: 1,071

   HÄGGLUND DRIVES INC.
   2275 International St., Columbus, Ohio 43228
   CEO: John Duncan, Pres.
   Bus: *Mfr. hydraulic drives and motors.*

   Tel: (614) 527-7400
   Fax: (614) 527-7401

   %FO: 100
   Emp: 38

● **HALDEX AB**
Biblioteksgatan 11, SE-103 88 Stockholm, Sweden
CEO: Claes Warnander, Pres. & CEO   Tel: 46-8-545-049-50   Rev: $1,022
Bus: *Mfr. automatic brake adjusters, air dryers, drain*   Fax: 46-8-678-89-40   Emp: 4,317
  valves and air oil separators for commercial   www.haldex.com
  vehicle market.
NAICS: 336311, 336340

  HALDEX BRAKE PRODUCTS CORPORATION
  10930 N. Pomona Ave., Kansas City, Missouri 64153-4918
  CEO: Charles Kleinhagen, Pres.   Tel: (816) 891-2470   %FO: 100
  Bus: *Motor vehicle parts & accessories*   Fax: (816) 891-9447   Emp: 800

  HALDEX GARPHYTTAN CORP.
  4404 Nimtz Pkwy., South Bend, Indiana 44628
  CEO: Kirk Manning, Pres.   Tel: (574) 232-8800
  Bus: *Mfr. wire springs*   Fax: (574) 232-2565   Emp: 45

  HALDEX HYDRAULICS CORPORATION
  2222 15th St., PO Box 6166, Rockford, Illinois 61125-1166
  CEO: Jay Longbottom, Pres.   Tel: (815) 398-4400   %FO: 100
  Bus: *Motor vehicle parts & accessories*   Fax: (815) 398-5977

● **HALLDE MASKINER AB**
Box 1165, SE-164 26 Kista, Sweden
CEO: Johan Strömdahl, Pres.   Tel: 46-8-587-730-00
Bus: *Food process equipment manufacture.*   Fax: 46-8-587-730-30   Emp: 75
     www.hallde.com
NAICS: 333294

  HOBART CORP.
  701 South Ridge Ave., Troy, Ohio 45374
  CEO: John McDonough, Pres.   Tel: (937) 332-0000
  Bus: *Distribution food process equipment.*   Fax: (937) 332-3146

  PAXTON CORPORATION
  897 Bridgeport Ave., Shelton, Connecticut 06484
  CEO: Leif Jensen, Pres.   Tel: (203) 929-1800   %FO: 100
  Bus: *Distribution food process equipment.*   Fax: (203) 925-8722   Emp: 3

● **HOLMEN AB**
Strandvagen 1, P.O. Box 5407, SE-114 84 Stockholm, Sweden
CEO: Magnus Hall, Pres. & CEO   Tel: 46-8-666-2100   Rev: $2,367
Bus: *Engaged in paper business, newsprint and*   Fax: 46-8-666-2130   Emp: 4,897
  magazine paper, paperboard and packaging   www.holmen.com
NAICS: 113310, 221111, 221119, 221121, 221122, 321113, 322110, 322121, 322122, 322212, 322213

  HOLMEN PAPER, INC.
  7272 Park Circle Dr., Hanover, Maryland 21076
  CEO: Henry Olsson, Pres.   Tel: (410) 712-6900   %FO: 100
  Bus: *Pulp and paper manufacture.*   Fax: (410) 712-4846   Emp: 4

IGGESUND PAPERBOARD, INC.
1050 Wall St., Ste. 650, Lyndhurst, New Jersey 07071
CEO: Rickard Osterlindh, Pres.
Bus: *Mfr./distributor forestry products; wood, pulp, and paper.*

Tel: (201) 804-9977
Fax: (201) 804-9693

%FO: 100
Emp: 10

• ICON MEDIALAB INTERNATIONAL AB
Birger Jarlsgatan 26, SE-114 34 Stockholm, Sweden
CEO: Karin Johansson, CEO
Bus: *Media service provider including web publishing, technology and Website production.*
NAICS: 323119, 516110

Tel: 46-8-5223-9000
Fax: 46-8-5223-9097
www.iconmedialab.com

Rev: $75
Emp: 950

ICON MEDIALAB
21355 Ridgetop Cir., Ste. 155, Dulles, Virginia 20166
CEO: Patrick Cherniawski
Bus: *Media service provider of websites.*

Tel: (703) 433-0088
Fax: (703) 433-0088

%FO: 100

ICON MEDIALAB
700 Goddard Ave., Chesterfield, Missouri 63005
CEO: Louis Hawn
Bus: *Media service provider of websites.*

Tel: (636) 530-7776
Fax: (636) 530-4644

%FO: 100

ICON MEDIALAB SAN FRANCISCO
22 Fourth St., 9/F, San Francisco, California 94103
CEO: Beth Elliott
Bus: *Media service provider of websites.*

Tel: (415) 932-5500
Fax: (415) 932-5560

%FO: 100

ICON NICHOLSON
295 Lafayette St., 8/F, New York, New York 10012
CEO: Jennifer Chen
Bus: *Engaged in Internet development.*

Tel: (212) 274-0470
Fax: (212) 274-0380

%FO: 100

• IKEA INTERNATIONAL A/S
Box 640, SE-25 106 Helsingborg, Sweden
CEO: Anders Dahlvig, Pres.
Bus: *Retail and mail-order furniture and household items.*
NAICS: 442110, 442210, 442291, 442299, 454113

Tel: 46-42-267-100
Fax: 46-42-132-805
www.ikea.com

Rev: $15,425
Emp: 84,000

IKEA INTERNATIONAL
496 W. Germantown Pike, Plymouth Meeting, Pennsylvania 19462
CEO: Pernille Spiers-Lopez, Pres.
Bus: *Furniture stores*

Tel: (610) 834-0180
Fax: (610) 834-0872

Emp: 2,400

IKEA NORTH AMERICA
8352 Honeygo Blvd., Baltimore, Maryland 21236
CEO: Mike Lahey, Mgr.
Bus: *Retail and mail-order furniture & household items.*

Tel: (410) 931-4444
Fax:

%FO: 100

IKEA NORTH AMERICA
1800 E. McConnor Pkwy., Schaumburg, Illinois 60173
CEO: Kerri Molinaro, Mgr.   Tel: (847) 969-9700   %FO: 100
Bus: *Retail and mail-order furniture & household*   Fax: (847) 969-9244
     items.

IKEA NORTH AMERICA
7810 Katy Freeway, Houston, Texas 77024
CEO: Laura Coletti, Mgr.   Tel: (713) 688-7867   %FO: 100
Bus: *Retail and mail-order furniture & household*   Fax:
     items.

IKEA NORTH AMERICA
Media City Center, 600 N. San Fernando Blvd., Burbank, California 91502
CEO: Gary Ternes, Mgr.   Tel: (818) 842-4532   %FO: 100
Bus: *Retail and mail-order furniture & household*   Fax:
     items.

IKEA NORTH AMERICA
2982 El Camino Real Blvd., Tustin, California 92680
CEO: Walter Reuters, Mgr.   Tel: (714) 838-4000   %FO: 100
Bus: *Retail and mail-order furniture & household*   Fax:
     items.

IKEA NORTH AMERICA
1000 Center Dr., Elizabeth, New Jersey 07202
CEO: Robert Kay, Pres.   Tel: (908) 352-1550   %FO: 100
Bus: *Retail and mail-order furniture & household*   Fax:
     items.

IKEA NORTH AMERICA
1100 Broadway Mall, Hicksville, New York 11801
CEO: Anders Moberg, Mgr.   Tel: (516) 681-4682   %FO: 100
Bus: *Retail and mail-order furniture & household*   Fax:
     items.

IKEA NORTH AMERICA
Town Centre, 2001 Park Manor Blvd., Pittsburgh, Pennsylvania 15205
CEO: Pernille Spiers-Lopez, mgr   Tel: (412) 747-0747   %FO: 100
Bus: *Retail and mail-order furniture & household*   Fax:
     items.

IKEA NORTH AMERICA
600 SW 43rd St., Renton, Washington 98055
CEO: Bjorn Bailey, Prtn.   Tel: (425) 656-2980   %FO: 100
Bus: *Retail and mail-order furniture & household*   Fax: (425) 656-8104   Emp: 350
     items.

IKEA NORTH AMERICA
2901 Potomac Mills Cir., Woodbridge, Virginia 22192
CEO: Tel: (703) 492-1222   %FO: 100
Bus: *Retail and mail-order furniture & household*   Fax:
     items.

IKEA NORTH AMERICA
2149 Fenton Pkwy., San Diego, California 92108
CEO: Lars Ottosson, Controller
Bus: *Retail and mail-order furniture and household items.*
Tel: (619) 283-6166
Fax:
%FO: 100
Emp: 300

IKEA NORTH AMERICA HDQRTS.
400 Alan Wood Rd., Conshohocken, Pennsylvania 19428
CEO: Jan Kjellman, Pres.
Bus: *Retail and mail-order furniture & household items.*
Tel: (610) 834-1520
Fax: (610) 834-0150
%FO: 100
Emp: 200

IKEA WHOLESALE
100 Ikea Dr., Paramus, New Jersey 07652
CEO: Keith Keller, Pres.
Bus: *Home furnishings*
Tel: (201) 843-1881
Fax:
Emp: 215

● **INDUSTRIAL AND FINANCIAL SYSTEMS, IFS AB**
Teknikringen 5, SE-583 30 Linkoping, Sweden
CEO: Michael Hallen, CEO
Bus: *Engineering software applications.for enterprise, asset, financial analysis, manufacturing & supply chain management*
NAICS: 511210
Tel: 46-13-460-40-00
Fax: 46-13-460-40-01
www.ifsworld.com
Rev: $329
Emp: 2,846

IFS SOFTWARE
2801 Slater Rd., Ste. 100, Morrisville, North Carolina 27560
CEO: Cindy Jaudon, Pres.
Bus: *Mfr. Web-based software.*
Tel: (888) 437-4968
Fax: (847) 592-0201
%FO: 100

IFS SOFTWARE
501 E. Hwy. 13, Burnsville, Minnesota 55337
CEO: Cindy Jaudon, Pres.
Bus: *Mfr. Web-based software.*
Tel: (888) 437-4968
Fax: (847) 592-0201
%FO: 100

IFS SOFTWARE
100 Century Center Ct., Ste. 340, San Jose, California 95112
CEO: Cindy Jaudon, Pres.
Bus: *Mfr. Web-based software.*
Tel: (888) 437-4968
Fax: (847) 592-0201
%FO: 100

IFS SOFTWARE
10 N. Martingale Dr., Ste. 600, Schaumburg, Illinois 60173
CEO: Cindy Jaudon, Pres.
Bus: *Mfr. Web-based software.*
Tel: (847) 592-0200
Fax: (847) 592-0201
%FO: 100

IFS SOFTWARE
71 Franklin's Row, Solon, Ohio 44139
CEO: Cindy Jaudon, Pres.
Bus: *Mfr. Web-based software.*
Tel: (888) 437-4968
Fax: (847) 592-0201
%FO: 100

IFS SOFTWARE
12000 W. Park Place, Milwaukee, Wisconsin 53224
CEO: Cindy Jaudon, Pres.
Bus: *Mfr. Web-based software.*
Tel: (888) 437-4968
Fax: (847) 592-0201
%FO: 100

IFS SOFTWARE
1010 N. Finance Center Dr., Tucson, Arizona 85710
CEO: Cindy Jaudon, Pres.   Tel: (888) 437-4968   %FO: 100
Bus: *Mfr. Web-based software.*   Fax: (847) 592-0201

● **INDUSTRI-MATEMATIK INTERNATIONAL AB**
Stadsgarden 10, Box 15044, SE-104 65 Stockholm, Sweden
CEO: J. Patrick Tinley, CEO   Tel: 46-8-676-5000   Rev: $70
Bus: *High-performance supply chain and customer*   Fax: 46-8-676-5010   Emp: 530
    service software manufacture.   www.im.se
NAICS: 511210

   INDUSTRI-MATEMATIK AMERICAN OPERATIONS, INC.
   521 Fellowship Rd., Ste. 140, Mt. Laurel, New Jersey 08054
   CEO: Timothy Campbell, Pres.   Tel: (856) 793-4400   %FO: 100
   Bus: *Provides high-performance supply chain and*   Fax: (856) 793-4401   Emp: 250
       customer service software.

   INDUSTRI-MATEMATIK INTERNATIONAL CORP.
   2 Concourse Pkwy., Ste. 800, Atlanta, Georgia 30328
   CEO: Dan Bachrodt, SVP   Tel: (856) 793-4400
   Bus: *customer service software*   Fax: (856) 793-4401

● **INTENTIA INTERNATIONAL AB**
Vendevagen 89, Box 59, SE-182 15 Danderyd, Sweden
CEO: Bertrand Sciard, Pres. & CEO   Tel: 46-8-555-25-000   Rev: $451
Bus: *Mfr. software for the paper, food and beverage*   Fax: 46-8-555-25-999   Emp: 2,371
    industries.   www.intentia.com
NAICS: 511210

   INTENTIA UNITED STATES
   2 Century Plaza, Ste. 900, 1700 E. Golf Rd. 9/F, Schaumburg, Illinois 60173
   CEO: David Rode, Pres. & CEO   Tel: (847) 762-0900   %FO: 100
   Bus: *Computer software development sales &*   Fax: (847) 762-0901   Emp: 90
       consulting

● **INVESTOR AB**
Arsenalsgatan 8C, SE-103 32 Stockholm, Sweden
CEO: Marcus Wallenberg, Pres. & CEO   Tel: 46-8-614-2000   Rev: $1,562
Bus: *Industrial holding company.*   Fax: 46-8-614-2150   Emp: 720
                                                 www.investorab.com
NAICS: 523999, 551112

   INVESTOR GROWTH CAPITAL, INC.
   12 E. 49th St., 27/F, New York, New York 10017
   CEO: Henry E. Gooss, Dir.   Tel: (212) 515-9000   %FO: 100
   Bus: *Holding company.*   Fax: (212) 515-9009

   INVESTOR GROWTH CAPITAL, INC.
   258 High St., Ste. 200, Palo Alto, California 94301
   CEO: Torbjorn Wingardh   Tel: (650) 543-2100
   Bus: *Investment advice.*   Fax: (650) 543-2109

● **ITT FLYGT AB**
Gesallvagen 33, SE-174 87 Sundbyberg, Sweden
CEO: Jan Greger Andersson, Chmn.
Bus: *Mfr. pumps.*

Tel: 46-8-475-6000
Fax: 46-8-475-6900
www.flygt.com

Rev: $627
Emp: 3,041

NAICS: 333912, 423830

ITT FLYGT
2330 Yellow Springs Rd., Malvern, Pennsylvania 19355
CEO: Doug Spencer, Mgr.
Bus: *Mfr./sales electric pumps, hydro turbines, mixers.*

Tel: (610) 647-6620
Fax: (610) 647-5563

%FO: 100
Emp: 20

ITT FLYGT
N27 W23291 Roundy Dr., Pewaukee, Wisconsin 53072
CEO: James Randall, Mgr.
Bus: *Submersible pumps, mixers and accessories manufacture and sales.*

Tel: (262) 544-1922
Fax: (262) 544-1399

%FO: 100
Emp: 24

ITT FLYGT
35 Nutmeg Dr., PO Box 1004, Trumbull, Connecticut 06611
CEO: Kie Ericsson, Pres.
Bus: *Mfr./sales electric pumps, hydro turbines, mixers.*

Tel: (203) 380-4700
Fax: (203) 380-4705

%FO: 100
Emp: 215

ITT FLYGT
790-A Chadborne Rd., Fairfield, California 94534
CEO: Darrell Smith, Mgr.
Bus: *Mfr./sales electric pumps, hydro turbines, mixers.*

Tel: (707) 422-9894
Fax: (707) 422-9808

%FO: 100
Emp: 20

ITT FLYGT
90 Horizon Dr., Suwannee, Georgia 30024
CEO: J. Danny Adams, Mgr.
Bus: *Submersible pumps manufacture.*

Tel: (770) 932-4320
Fax: (770) 932-4321

%FO: 100
Emp: 19

ITT FLYGT
2400 Tarpley Rd., Carrollton, Texas 75006
CEO: Ed Bailey, Sales Mgr.
Bus: *Regional sales office.*

Tel: (972) 418-2400
Fax: (972) 416-9570

%FO: 100
Emp: 15

● **JOHNSON PUMP AB**
Nastagatan 19, PO Box 1436, SE-701 14 Orebro, Sweden
CEO: Anders Larsson, Pres.
Bus: *Mfr. pumps and pumping equipment.*

Tel: 46-19-218300
Fax: 46-19-272330
www.johnson-pump.com

Emp: 600

NAICS: 333913

JOHNSON PUMPS OF AMERICA, INC.
10509 United Pkwy., Schiller Park, Illinois 60176
CEO: Gerald A. Assessor
Bus: *Mfr./sales of pumps and pumping equipment.*

Tel: (847) 671-7867
Fax: (847) 671-7909

%FO: 100

- **KMT KAROLIN MACHINE TOOL AB**
  Box 8, Kungsgatan 66, SE-101 20 Stockholm, Sweden
  CEO: Lars Goran Bergstrom, Pres. & CEO
  Bus: *Mfr. fabrication machinery and systems, punching & beveling machinery, laser systems.*
  NAICS: 323121, 333513
  Tel: 46-8-594-21150
  Fax: 46-8-594-21159
  www.kmt.se
  Rev: $95
  Emp: 450

  CINCINNATI GRINDING TECHNOLOGIES
  155 Westheimer Dr., Middletown, Ohio 45044
  CEO: Jahon Westberg
  Bus: *Mfr. grinding machines.*
  Tel: (513) 539-8550
  Fax: (513) 539-7516
  %FO: 100

  KMT WATERJET SYSTEMS INC.
  PO Box 231, Baxter Springs, Kansas 66713
  CEO: Malcolm Macquarrie, VP Sales
  Bus: *Mfr. of ultra-high pressure (UHP) waterjet and abrasive waterjet pumps.*
  Tel: (620) 856-2151
  Fax: (620) 856-3756
  %FO: 100

  LIDKOPING MACHINE TOOLS USA
  4 Industrial Rd., Suite 3, Milford, Massachusetts 01757
  CEO: Johan Westberg
  Bus: *Mfr. grinding machines.*
  Tel: (508) 634-4301
  Fax: (508) 634-4196
  %FO: 100

  PULLMAX, INC.
  2255 Lois Dr., Unit 1, Rolling Meadows, Illinois 60008
  CEO: Tom Wessel, Pres.
  Bus: *Mfr. fabrication machinery and systems, punching and beveling machinery, laser systems.*
  Tel: (847) 952-9977
  Fax: (847) 952-9988
  %FO: 100
  Emp: 12

  UMV MACHINE TOOL INC.
  1636 Todd Farm Dr., Elgin, Illinois 60123
  CEO: Tomas Johansson
  Bus: *Mfr. machine tools.*
  Tel: (847) 214-8700
  Fax: (847) 214-8705
  %FO: 100

  UVA MACHINE COMPANY
  Box 701 520, Plymouth, Michigan 48170
  CEO: Johan Soderstrom
  Bus: *Mfr. fabrication machinery and systems.*
  Tel: (734) 454-0244
  Fax: (734) 454-0367
  %FO: 100

- **KOCKUM SONICS AB**
  Industrigatan 39, Box 1035, SE-212 10 Malmo, Sweden
  CEO: Claes Egmont Tornberg, Dir.
  Bus: *Mfr. marine signal and lighting, industrial sonic cleaning, and civil alarm equipment.*
  NAICS: 333999, 336611, 541330
  Tel: 46-40-671-8800
  Fax: 46-40-21-6513
  www.kockumsonics.com
  Rev: $192
  Emp: 1,237

  KOCKUM SONICS LLC
  1922 H Corporate Square Blvd., Slidell, Louisiana 70458
  CEO: Jeff Guillot
  Bus: *Shipbuilding*
  Tel: (985) 646-2823
  Fax: (985) 646-2883

● **LORENTZEN & WETTRE, SUB. CARDO AB**
Viderogatan 2, SE-16493 Kista, Sweden
CEO: Peter Uddfors, Pres.
Bus: *Paper industry product testing equipment quality control.*

Tel: 46-8-477-9000
Fax: 46-8-477-9199
www.lorentzen-wettre

Rev: $32
Emp: 175

NAICS: 333291, 334513, 532490

LORENTZEN & WETTRE
1055 Windward Ridge Pkwy., Ste. 160, Alpharetta, Georgia 30005
CEO: Philip Westmoreland
Bus: *Paper industry product testing equipment quality control.*

Tel: (770) 442-8015
Fax: (770) 442-6792

%FO: 100

● **MANNHEIMER SWARTLING LLP**
Norrmalmstorg 4, Box 1711, SE-111 87 Stockholm, Sweden
CEO: Peter Alhanko, Mng. Prtn.
Bus: *International law firm.*

Tel: 46-8-505-765-00
Fax: 46-8-505-765-01
www.mannheimerswartling.se

Rev: $103
Emp: 446

NAICS: 541110

MANNHEIMER SWARTLING
101 Park Ave., 25/F, New York, New York 10178
CEO: Maria Tufvessin Shuck, Partner
Bus: *International law firm.*

Tel: (212) 682-0580
Fax: (212) 682-0982

%FO: 100
Emp: 5

● **MICRONIC LASER SYSTEMS AB**
Nytorpsvagen 9, SE-183 03 Taby, Sweden
CEO: Sven Lofquist, Pres. & CEO
Bus: *Specialized laser pattern generator mfr.*

Tel: 46-8-638-5200
Fax: 46-8-638-5290
www.micronic.se

Rev: $127
Emp: 359

NAICS: 333295

MICRONIC LASER SYSTEMS INC.
1922 Zanker Rd., San Jose, California 95112-4216
CEO: Manny Ferreira, Pres.
Bus: *Specialized laser pattern generator mfr.*

Tel: (408) 392-2260
Fax: (408) 392-2261

%FO: 100

● **MORGARDSHAMMAR AB**
Smedjebacken, SE-777 82 Smedjebacken, Sweden
CEO: Franco Alzetta, Chmn.
Bus: *Mfr. equipment for steel mills & mines.*

Tel: 46-240-668500
Fax: 46-240-668501
www.morgardshammar.se

Rev: $53
Emp: 300

NAICS: 333131, 333516, 333518

MORGARDSHAMMAR INC.
9800 Southern Pines Blvd, Charlotte, North Carolina 28273-5522
CEO: Grant Philip, Pres.
Bus: *Sales/service equipment for steel mills & mines.*

Tel: (704) 522-8024
Fax: (704) 522-0264

%FO: 100
Emp: 11

- **MUNKSJO PAPER AB**
  Box 624, Barnarpsgatan, SE-551 18 Jonkoping, Sweden
  CEO: Per Rodert, CEO
  Bus: *Mfr. paper and paper products.*

  Tel: 46-36-30-33-00
  Fax: 46-36-16-26-33
  www.munksjo.com

  Rev: $605
  Emp: 1,750

  NAICS: 326112

    MUNKSJO PAPER INC.
    624 River St., Fitchburg, Massachusetts 01420
    CEO: Dennis Bunnell, Pres.
    Bus: *Mfr. paper products for interior design.*

    Tel: (978) 342-1080
    Fax: (978) 345-4268

    %FO: 100
    Emp: 154

- **THE NEDERMAN GROUP AB**
  Sydhamnsgatan 2, SE-252 28 Helsingborg, Sweden
  CEO: Sven Kristensson, Pres.
  Bus: *Environmental pollution control for dust and fume.*

  Tel: 46-42-18-8700
  Fax: 46-42-14-7971
  www.nederman.com

  Emp: 10

  NAICS: 334512

    NEDERMAN INC.
    39115 Warren Rd., Westland, Michigan 48185
    CEO: Brian Voss, Pres. & CEO
    Bus: *Environmental pollution control for dust and fume.*

    Tel: (734) 729-3344
    Fax: (734) 729-3358

    %FO: 100
    Emp: 10

- **NEFAB AB**
  Slottsgatan 14, Box 2184, SE-550 02 Jonkoping, Sweden
  CEO: Lars-Ake Rydh, Pres. & CEO
  Bus: *Mfr. of plywood and steel customized packaging solutions.*

  Tel: 46-36-34-5050
  Fax: 46-36-15-0444
  www.nefab.se

  Rev: $191
  Emp: 1,133

  NAICS: 321920, 331221

    NEFAB, INC.
    3105 North Ashland Ave., Ste. 394, Chicago, Illinois 60657
    CEO: Eric Howe, Mgr.
    Bus: *Mfr. plywood packaging systems.*

    Tel: (800) 536-7261
    Fax: (705) 748-0034

    %FO: 100

- **NOBEL BIOCARE AB**
  Bohusgatan 15, SE-402 26 Goteborg, Sweden
  CEO: Hedwig Heliane Canepa, Mgr.
  Bus: *Surgical, medical and dental supplies.*

  Tel: 46-31-81-8800
  Fax: 46-31-16-3152
  www.nobelbiocare.com

  Rev: $384
  Emp: 1,332

  NAICS: 339114

    NOBEL BIOCARE USA INC.
    22715 Savi Ranch Pkwy., Yorba Linda, California 92887
    CEO: Martin J. Dymek, Pres.
    Bus: *Distributor of surgical/medical/dental equipment.*

    Tel: (714) 282-4800
    Fax: (714) 998-9236

    %FO: 100
    Emp: 350

- **NOLATO AB**
  Box 66, SE-260 93 Torekov, Sweden
  CEO: Erik Gustav Paulsson, CEO
  Bus: *Molded rubber and plastic products manufacture.*

  Tel: 46-431-442290
  Fax: 46-431-442291
  www.nolato.se

  Rev: $208
  Emp: 1,870

  NAICS: 326199, 326299
  - **SUNNEX INC.**
    3 Huron Dr., Natick, Massachusetts 01760
    CEO: Jennifer Butler, Pres.
    Bus: *Mfr./sales machine mounts and industrial work lights.*

    Tel: (508) 651-0009
    Fax: (508) 651-0099

    %FO: 100
    Emp: 24

- **NORDEN MACHINERY AB**
  PO Box 845, SE-391 28 Kalmar, Sweden
  CEO: Bjorn Persson, CEO
  Bus: *Provides advanced packaging systems.*

  Tel: 46-480-44-7700
  Fax: 46-480-44-7764
  www.norden-pac.se

  Rev: $33
  Emp: 197

  NAICS: 423830
  - **SIRIUS MACHINERY INC.**
    230 Industrial Pkwy, Somerville, New Jersey 08876-3450
    CEO: Scott Winfield, Pres.
    Bus: *Advanced packaging systems.*

    Tel: (908) 707-8008
    Fax: (908) 707-8008

    %FO: 100

- **NOSS AB**
  Box 20, SE-601 02 Norrkoping, Sweden
  CEO: Bjorn Wikdahl, Pres.
  Bus: *Pulp and paper equipment manufacturer.*

  Tel: 46-11-231500
  Fax: 46-11-135923
  www.noss.se

  Emp: 160

  NAICS: 423830
  - **NOSS COMPANY**
    2500 Park Central Blvd., Decatur, Georgia 30035
    CEO: Michael Lostracco, Sales
    Bus: *Paper and pulp equipment.*

    Tel: (770) 981-9550
    Fax: (770) 981-3572

    %FO: 100
    Emp: 16

- **E. OHMAN J:OR FONDKOMMISSION AB**
  Berzelii Park 9, P.O. Box 7415, SE-103 91 Stockholm, Sweden
  CEO: Claes Dinkelspiel, Chmn.
  Bus: *Financial services.*

  Tel: 46-8-402-5000
  Fax: 46-8-20-0075
  www.ohman.se

  Emp: 130

  NAICS: 523110, 523120, 523910, 523920, 523930, 523991, 523999, 525110, 525910, 525920, 525990
  - **NORDIC PARTNERS, INC.**
    488 Madison Ave., Ste. 1706, New York, New York 10022
    CEO: Anders Lindquist, Pres.
    Bus: *Financial services.*

    Tel: (212) 829-4200
    Fax: (212) 829-4201

    %FO: 100
    Emp: 11

- **OMX AB**
  Tullvaktsvagen 15, SE-105 78 Stockholm, Sweden
  CEO: Magnus K. Bocker, CEO   Tel: 46-8-405-6000   Rev: $439
  Bus: *Finance and marketing, including futures and*   Fax: 46-8-405-6001   Emp: 1,355
      exchanges.   www.omgroup.com
  NAICS: 523210
    OMX US INC.
    140 Broadway, 25/F., New York, New York 10005
    CEO: Roland Tibell   Tel: (646) 428-2800   %FO: 100
    Bus: *Finance and marketing, including futures*   Fax: (646) 428-2899
        and exchanges.

- **ORREFORS KOSTA BODA AB (DIV. OF INCENTIVE AB)**
  Box 8, SE-380 40 Orrefors, Sweden
  CEO: Olle Markoo, Pres.   Tel: 46-481-34000
  Bus: *Mfr. crystal products.*   Fax: 46-481-30400   Emp: 200
                                              www.orrefors.com
  NAICS: 327211, 327212
    ORREFORS KOSTA BODA
    140 Bradford Dr. West, West Berlin, New Jersey 08091
    CEO: Oyvind Saetre   Tel: (609) 768-5400   %FO: 100
    Bus: *Sale/distribution crystal products.*   Fax: (609) 768-9726   Emp: 100

    ORREFORS KOSTA BODA
    959 N Michigan Ave., Chicago, Illinois 60611
    CEO: Amy Chuckerman   Tel: (312) 642-9160   %FO: 100
    Bus: *Sale/distribution crystal products.*   Fax: (312) 642-9160

    ORREFORS KOSTA BODA
    3333 Bristol St., Ste. 1505, Costa Mesa, California 92626
    CEO: Jim Daughtery   Tel: (714) 662-2644   %FO: 100
    Bus: *Sale/distribution crystal products.*   Fax: (714) 662-2644

- **PERBIO SCIENCE AB**
  Knutpunkten 34, SE-252 78 Helsingborg, Sweden
  CEO: Mats Fischier, CEO   Tel: 46-42-26-9090
  Bus: *Production of supplies to science researchers*   Fax: 46-42-26-9098
      and the biopharmaceutical industry.   www.perbio.com
  NAICS: 541710
    ENDOGEN INC.
    30 Commerce Way, Woburn, Massachusetts 01801-1059
    CEO: Owen A. Dempsey, CEO   Tel: (781) 937-0890   %FO: 100
    Bus: *Provides immunoassay test kits.*   Fax: (781) 937-3096

- **PERGO AB**
  Strandridaregatan 8, SE-231 25 Trelleborg, Sweden
  CEO: Anthony Sturrus, Pres. & CEO   Tel: 46-410-363100   Rev: $420
  Bus: *Mfr. laminate flooring and flooring accessories.*   Fax: 46-410-15560   Emp: 775
                                              www.pergo.com
  NAICS: 321213, 321219, 321918

PERGO INC.
3128 Highwoods Blvd., Ste. 100, Raleigh, North Carolina 27604
CEO: David Stidhem
Bus: *Mfr. laminate flooring and flooring
accessories.*

Tel: (919) 773-6000
Fax: (919) 773-6004

%FO: 100

● **PERSTORP AB**
, SE-284 80 Perstorp, Sweden
CEO: Lennart Holm, Pres. & CEO
Bus: *Mfr. specialty chemicals, analytic instruments,
decorative laminates, flooring and wood products.*
NAICS: 237990, 325188, 325199, 325998, 541330

Tel: 46-435-380-00
Fax: 46-435-381-00
www.perstorp.com

Rev: $792
Emp: 2,184

PERSTORP COMPOUNDS INC.
238 Nonotuck St., Florence, Massachusetts 01062
CEO: Per Dahlen, Pres.
Bus: *Mfr. Plastic materials & resin custom
compounding purchased resins*

Tel: (413) 584-2472
Fax: (413) 586-4089

%FO: 100
Emp: 48

PERSTORP INC.
238 Nonotuck St., Florence, Massachusetts 01062
CEO: Lennart Holm
Bus: *Holding company.*

Tel: (413) 584-2472
Fax: (413) 586-4089

%FO: 100

PERSTORP POLYOLS INC.
600 Matzinger Rd., Toledo, Ohio 43612-2695
CEO: David Wolf, Pres.
Bus: *Mfr. pentaerythritol, sodium formate,
trimethylolpropane, specialty polyols, other
chemicals.*

Tel: (419) 729-5448
Fax: (419) 729-3291

%FO: 100
Emp: 92

VYNCOLIT NORTH AMERICA, INC.
T24 Mill St., Manchester, Connecticut 06040-2316
CEO: Henny van Dijk
Bus: *Perstorp Engineering Materials*

Tel: (860) 646-5500
Fax: (860) 646-5503

%FO: 100

YLA, INC.
2970 C Bay Vista Ct., Benicia, California 94510
CEO: Brad Pletcher
Bus: *Prepreg, composite material, resins,
honeycomb, molding compounds.*

Tel: (707) 747-2750
Fax: (707) 747-2754

%FO: 61

● **PUMPEX**
PO Box 5207, Rokerigatan 20, SE-121 18 Johanneshov, Sweden
CEO: Robert Montenegro, Pres.
Bus: *Mfr. of submersible pumps.*

Tel: 46-8-725-4930
Fax: 46-8-659-3314
www.pumpex.com

NAICS: 333913

ABS GROUP
140 Pond View Dr., Meriden, Connecticut 06450
CEO: Peter Uddfors, Mgr.
Bus: *Mfr. of Wastewater pumps.*

Tel: (203) 238-2700
Fax: (203) 238-0738

● **RAPID GRANULATOR AB**
Industrivagen 4, Box 9, SE-330 10 Bredaryd, Sweden
CEO: Karl-Valter Fornell, Chmn.   Tel: 46-370-86500
Bus: *Mfr. granulators.*   Fax: 46-370-80251   Emp: 300
                                                    www.rapidgranulator.se

NAICS: 333220, 333298
   RAPID GRANULATOR, INC.
   5217 28th Ave., Rockford, Illinois 61109
   CEO: Kirk Winstead, Pres.   Tel: (815) 399-4605
   Bus: *Mfr./distribute granulators.*   Fax: Emp: 30

● **READSOFT AB**
Sodra Kyrkogatan 4, SE-252 23 Helsingborg, Sweden
CEO: Jan Andersson, Pres. & CEO   Tel: 46-42-490-2100   Rev: $54
Bus: *Mfr. document automation software.*   Fax: 46-42-490-2120   Emp: 274
                                                    www.readsoft.com

NAICS: 511210
   READSOFT USA INC.
   1414 Windsor Park Lane, Havertown, Pennsylvania 19083
   CEO: E. Stagnaro   Tel: (610) 853-0377   %FO: 100
   Bus: *Mfr. and sales document automation*   Fax: (610) 853-0378
       software.
   READSOFT USA INC.
   205 N. Michigan Ave., Ste. 3910, Chicago, Illinois 60601
   CEO: E. Stagnaro   Tel: (312) 470-9031   %FO: 100
   Bus: *Mfr. and sales document automation*   Fax: (312) 470-9075
       software.
   READSOFT USA INC.
   340 main St., Ste. 862, Worcester, Massachusetts 01608
   CEO: Robert Fresneda   Tel: (508) 754-4744   %FO: 100
   Bus: *Mfr. and sales document automation*   Fax: (508) 519-1098
       software.
   READSOFT USA INC.
   3838 N. Causeway Blvd, Ste. 2620, Metairie, Louisiana 70002
   CEO: Robert Fresneda, Pres. & CEO   Tel: (504) 841-0112   %FO: 100
   Bus: *Mfr. and sales document automation*   Fax: (504) 841-0144
       software.

● **RESULT STRATEGY AB**
Rehnsgatan 20, Plan 2, SE-113 57 Stockholm, Sweden
CEO: Ola Ahlvarsson, CEO   Tel: 46-8-458-7200
Bus: *Engaged in venture capital; develops*   Fax: 46-8-458-7229
    international business and communications   www.result.com
NAICS: 523910, 523999
   RESULT VENTURE KNOWLEDGE INTERNATIONAL
   160 Mercer St., 5/F, New York, New York 10012
   CEO: Andreas Oscarsson   Tel: (212) 979-1700   %FO: 100
   Bus: *Develops international business and*   Fax: (212) 979-1773
       communications strategies.

- **ROTTNE INDUSTRI AB**
Fabriksvagen 12, SE-360 40 Rottne, Sweden
CEO: Jarl Petersson, Mng. Dir.
Bus: *Forestry equipment manufacture.*

Tel: 46-470-75-8700
Fax: 46-470-75-8701
www.rottne.com

Rev: $33
Emp: 230

NAICS: 333319, 333999

   BLONDIN INC.
   7647 Third St. SE, Turner, Oregon 97392
   CEO: David Ehrmantrout, Pres.
   Bus: *Sales/distribution forestry equipment.*

   Tel: (503) 743-3263
   Fax: (503) 743-3763

   %FO: JV

   BLONDIN INC.
   85 Cool Spring Rd., PO Box 1287, Indiana, Pennsylvania 15701
   CEO: Rikard Olofsson, Pres.
   Bus: *Sales/distribution forestry equipment.*

   Tel: (724) 349-9240
   Fax: (724) 349-9242

   %FO: JV
   Emp: 5

- **SAAB AIRCRAFT AB**
Nobymalmsvagen 1, SE-581 88 Linkoping, Sweden
CEO: Michael Andersson, Pres.
Bus: *Design and manufacture of aircraft and parts.*

Tel: 46-13-18-2616
Fax: 46-13-18-4495
www.saabaircraft.com

Rev: $1,033
Emp: 7,890

NAICS: 336413

   SAAB AIRCRAFT LEASING INC.
   21300 Ridgetop Circle, Sterling, Virginia 20166
   CEO: Michael Magnusson, Pres.
   Bus: *Design/mfr. aircraft & parts.*

   Tel: (703) 406-7200
   Fax: (703) 406-7309

   %FO: 100

- **SAAB AUTOMOBILE AB**
, SE-461 80 Trollhattan, Sweden
CEO: Jan-Ake Jonsson, CEO
Bus: *Mfr. automobiles.*

Tel: 46-520-85000
Fax: 46-520-35016
www.saab.com

Rev: $3,500
Emp: 7,032

NAICS: 336111

   SAAB CARS USA INC.
   4405-A International Blvd., Norcross, Georgia 30093
   CEO: Jan-Willem Vester, Mgr.
   Bus: *Import/distribution/service automobiles.*

   Tel: (770) 279-0100
   Fax: (770) 279-6499

   %FO: 100
   Emp: 182

- **SAAB ERICSSON SPACE AB**
Solhusgatan, SE-405 15 Goteborg, Sweden
CEO: Bengt Mortberg, Pres. & CEO
Bus: *Design/mfr. components for satellites and launch vehicles.*

Tel: 46-31-735-0000
Fax: 46-31-735-4000
www.space.se

Rev: $65
Emp: 419

NAICS: 334111, 334220, 334413, 336411, 541990

   SAAB ERICSSON SPACE, INC.
   Pacific Corporate Towers, 222 N. Sepulveda Blvd., Ste. 2000, El Segundo, California 90245
   CEO: Michael Miller, Gen. Mgr.
   Bus: *Marketing of Saab Ericsson space products.*

   Tel: (310) 662-4760
   Fax: (310) 662-4762

   %FO: 100

- **SANDVIK AB**
Storgatan 2, SE-811 81 Sandviken, Sweden
CEO: Lars Pettersson, Pres. & CEO
Bus: *Specialty steel manufacture; drilling tools and mining and equipment tool manufacture.*
NAICS: 331111, 331210, 331221, 331222

Tel: 46-26-26-0000
Fax: 46-26-26-1022
www.sandvik.com

Rev: $5,565
Emp: 37,388

DORMER TOLS, INC.
135 Sweeten Creek Rd., Asheville, North Carolina 28803
CEO: Richard Tunstill, Dir.
Bus: *Mfr./distribution tools and tooling systems for metalworking and rock drilling.*

Tel: (828) 274-6078
Fax: (828) 274-6076

%FO: 100

KANTHAL PALM COAST
One Commerce Blvd., Palm Coast, Florida 32164
CEO: Lars Bogren, Pres.
Bus: *Wire products manufacture and sales.*

Tel: (904) 445-2000
Fax: (904) 445-2244

%FO: 100

PRECISION TWIST DRILL COMPANY
One Precision Plaza, Crystal Lake, Illinois 60039-9000
CEO: Alan Godfrey, Pres.
Bus: *Mfr./distribution tools and tooling systems for metalworking and rock drilling.*

Tel: (815) 459-2040
Fax: (815) 459-2804

%FO: 100

SANDVIK COROMANT U.S.
1702 Nevins Rd., PO Box 428, Fair Lawn, New Jersey 07410
CEO: James T. Baker, Pres.
Bus: *Mfr./distribution/service cemented carbide metalworking tools & systems.*

Tel: (201) 794-5000
Fax: (201) 794-5032

%FO: 100
Emp: 500

SANDVIK HARD MATERIALS COMPANY
510 Griffin Rd., West Branch, Michigan 48661
CEO: Tommy Erixon, Pres.
Bus: *Mfr. metal products; cemented carbide.*

Tel: (989) 345-2622
Fax: (989) 345-2622

%FO: 100
Emp: 20

SANDVIK PROCESS SYSTEMS INC
21 Campus Rd., Totowa, New Jersey 07512
CEO: Brian Spalding, Pres.
Bus: *Mfr./sale/service conveyors, handling & automatic sorting systems.*

Tel: (973) 790-1600
Fax: (973) 790-9247

%FO: 100
Emp: 100

SANDVIK SORTING SYSTEMS, INC.
500 East Burnett Ave., Louisville, Kentucky 40217
CEO: Thomas Barry, Pres.
Bus: *Design/mfr./service industrial handling systems.*

Tel: (502) 636-1414
Fax: (502) 636-1491

%FO: 100
Emp: 100

SANDVIK SPECIAL METALS CORPORATION
PO Box 6027, Kennewick, Washington 99336
CEO: Kirk P. Galbraith, Pres. & CEO
Bus: *Mfr./distribution tube products in titanium & zirconium alloys.*

Tel: (509) 586-4131
Fax: (509) 582-3552

%FO: 100
Emp: 50

UNION BUTTERFIELD CORPORATION
301 Industrial Ave., Crystal Lake, Illinois 60012
CEO: Alan Godfrey, Pres.
Bus: *Cutting tools manufacture.*

Tel: (800) 432-9482
Fax: (800) 222-8665

%FO: 100
Emp: 8

● **SAS AB**
Frosundaviks Alle 1, Solna, SE-195 87 Stockholm, Sweden
CEO: Joergen Lindegaard, Pres. & CEO
Bus: *International air transport services.*

Tel: 46-8-797-0000
Fax: 46-8-797-1603
www.scandinavian.net

Rev: $8,781
Emp: 32,481

NAICS: 481111, 481112, 481212

SCANDINAVIAN AIRLINES OF NORTH AMERICA, INC.
9 Polito Ave., 10/F, Lyndhurst, New Jersey 07071
CEO: Jorgen Lindgaard, Pres.
Bus: *Commercial air transport services.*

Tel: (201) 896-3600
Fax: (201) 896-3725

%FO: 100
Emp: 293

● **SCAN COIN AB**
Jagershillgatan 26, Skane, SE-21375 Malmo, Sweden
CEO: Nils Goran Waldenstrom, Mng. Dir.
Bus: *Mfr. coin counting sorting machinery, currency counters, coin wrappers.*

Tel: 46-40-600-0600
Fax: 46-40-600-0700
www.scancoin.com

Rev: $82
Emp: 427

NAICS: 333313, 531190

SCAN COIN INC
20145 Ashbrook Place, Ste. 110, Ashburn, Virginia 20147
CEO: Per Lundin, Pres.
Bus: *Currency handling equipment.*

Tel: (703) 729-8600
Fax: (703) 729-8606

%FO: 100
Emp: 8

● **SCANIA AB**
Jarnagatan 33-51, SE-151 87 Sodertalje, Sweden
CEO: Leif Ostling, Pres. & CEO
Bus: *Mfr. heavy-trucks, buses, industrial and marine engines.*

Tel: 46-8-55-38-1000
Fax: 46-8-55-38-1037
www.scania.com

Rev: $8,586
Emp: 29,639

NAICS: 333924, 336120, 336211, 336312

SCANIA USA INC.
121 Interpark Blvd., Ste. 601, San Antonio, Texas 78216
CEO: Claes Sundberg, Pres.
Bus: *Sales/distribution of heavy-trucks, buses and industrial and marine engines.*

Tel: (210) 403-0007
Fax: (210) 403-0211

%FO: 100

● **SEB GROUP**
Kungstradgardsgatan 8, SE-106 40 Stockholm, Sweden
CEO: Marcus Wallenberg, Chmn.
Bus: *International banking services.*

Tel: 46-8-763-8000
Fax: 46-8-763-7163
www.sebank.se

Rev: $3,504
Emp: 19,000

NAICS: 522110

SEB ASSET MANAGEMENT AMERICA INC.
263 Tresser Blvd., Stamford, Connecticut 06901
CEO: Claude Parenteau, VP Mktg.
Bus: *International banking & financial services.*

Tel: (203) 425-1431
Fax: (203) 425-1432

%FO: 100

SKANDINAVISKA ENSKILDA BANKEN - NY BRANCH
245 Park Ave., 42/F, New York, New York 10167
CEO: Elisabeth Lavers, Pres.   Tel: (212) 907-4700   %FO: 100
Bus: *International banking & financial services.*   Fax: (212) 370-1642   Emp: 50

● **SECO TOOLS AB**
Svenska Forsaijning, SE-737 82 Fagersta, Sweden
CEO: Kai Warn, CEO   Tel: 46-223-400-00   Rev: $655
Bus: *Develop and manufacture metalwork tools.*   Fax: 46-223-718-60   Emp: 3,910
                                                 www.secotools.com
NAICS: 333512, 333513

    SECO-CARBOLOY NORTH AMERICA
    3121 Cross Timbers, Ste. 111, Flower Mound, Texas 75028
    CEO: Jay Verellen, Mgr.   Tel: (972) 724-9522   %FO: 100
    Bus: *Develop and manufacture metalwork tools.*   Fax: (972) 691-5623

    SECO-CARBOLOY NORTH AMERICA
    4700 Industrial Park Dr., Lenoir City, Tennessee 37771
    CEO: Chuck Mc Keown   Tel: (865) 988-6700   %FO: 100
    Bus: *Develop and manufacture metalwork tools.*   Fax: (865) 986-4577

    SECO-CARBOLOY NORTH AMERICA
    11177 E. Eight Mile Rd., Warren, Michigan 48089
    CEO: Bruce Belden, Pres.   Tel: (586) 497-5000   %FO: 100
    Bus: *Develop and manufacture metalwork tools.*   Fax: (586) 497-5627

    SECO-CARBOLOY NORTH AMERICA
    123 NW 4th St., Ste. 220, Evansville, Indiana 47708
    CEO: Mike Parker   Tel: (812) 436-9260   %FO: 100
    Bus: *Develop and manufacture metalwork tools.*   Fax: (812) 436-9261

● **SECTRA AB**
Teknikringen 20, Mjardevi Science Park, SE-583 30 Linkoping, Sweden
CEO: Jan-Olaf Bruer, CEO   Tel: 46-1323-5200   Rev: $65
Bus: *Technologies for medical systems, secure*   Fax: 46-1321-2185   Emp: 347
    communication systems and wireless information   www.sectra.se
    systems.
NAICS: 334119, 334220, 334290, 334510, 334613, 511210

    SECTRA NORTH AMERICA INC.
    2 Enterprise Dr., Ste. 507, Shelton, Connecticut 06484
    CEO: John Goble   Tel: (203) 925-0899   %FO: 100
    Bus: *Technologies for medical systems, secure*   Fax: (203) 925-0906
    communication systems and wireless
    information systems.

● **SECURITAS AB**
Lindhagensplan 70, SE-102 28 Stockholm, Sweden
CEO: Thomas Berglund, Pres. & CEO   Tel: 46-8-657-7400   Rev: $9,025
Bus: *Provides security guards and cash transport*   Fax: 48-6-657-7072   Emp: 210,700
    services and provides and maintains alarm   www.securitasgroup.com
NAICS: 561612, 561613

LOOMIS FARGO & CO.
2500 City West Blvd., Ste. 900, Houston, Texas 77042
CEO: Clas Thelin, Pres. & CEO
Bus: *Armored vehicle services*
Tel: (713) 435-6700
Fax: (713) 435-6905
Emp: 8,000

SECURITAS SECURITY SERVICES USA, INC.
2 Campus Dr., Parsippany, New Jersey 07054
CEO: Santiago Galaz, Pres.
Bus: *Security guard services*
Tel: (973) 397-2681
Fax: (973) 397-2681
Emp: 101,000

• **SELDEN MAST AB**
Redegatan 11, SE-426 77 Vastra Frolunda, Sweden
CEO: Zeb Elliott, CEO
Bus: *Spar, masts and rigging systems for yachts manufacture.*
Tel: 46-31-69-6900
Fax: 46-31-29-7137
www.seldenmast.com
Rev: $250
Emp: 170
NAICS: 321999, 336611, 336999

SELDEN MAST INC.
4668 Franchise St., N. Charleston, South Carolina 29418
CEO: Peter Ronnback, Pres.
Bus: *Mfr. of masts and rigging systems for yachts.*
Tel: (843) 760-6278
Fax: (843) 760-1220
%FO: 100
Emp: 15

• **SKANDIA INSURANCE COMPANY LTD.**
Sveavagen 44, SE-103 50 Stockholm, Sweden
CEO: Hans-Erik Andersson, CEO
Bus: *Insurance; property and casualty.*
Tel: 46-8-788-1000
Fax: 46-8-788-3080
www.skandia.com
Rev: $15,263
Emp: 5,449
NAICS: 522110, 522120, 522130, 522291, 522292, 523991, 523999, 524113, 524114, 524126, 525110, 525120, 525190, 525910, 525920, 525990

AMERICAN SKANDIA LIFE ASSURANCE CORPORATION
One Corporate Dr., Shelton, Connecticut 06484
CEO: David R. Odenath Jr., Pres. & CEO
Bus: *Property and casualty insurance services.*
Tel: (203) 926-1888
Fax: (203) 929-8071
%FO: 100
Emp: 435

AMERICAN SKANDIA MARKETING, INC,
One Corporate Dr., Shelton, Connecticut 06484
CEO: David R. Odenath Jr., Pres.
Bus: *Investment banking services.*
Tel: (203) 926-1888
Fax: (203) 402-3240
Emp: 356

• **SKANSKA AB**
Klarabergsviadukten 90, SE-11191 Stockholm, Sweden
CEO: Stuart E. Graham, Pres. & CEO
Bus: *Engineering, construction, development and rental of real estate properties.*
Tel: 46-8-753-8800
Fax: 46-8-755-1256
www.skanska.com
Rev: $18,355
Emp: 53,803
NAICS: 236210, 236220, 237110, 237120, 237130, 237310, 237990, 561210

ATLANTIC SKANSKA
2030 Powers Ferry Rd., Ste. 444, Atlanta, Georgia 30339
CEO: Joseph LoCurto, CEO
Bus: *Commercial contractors*
Tel: (678) 460-2600
Fax: (678) 460-2638
Emp: 300

BAYSHORE CONCRETE PRODUCTS CORP.
1134 Bayshore Rd., PO Box 230, Cape Charles, Virginia 23310
CEO: John Dobbs, Pres.   Tel: (757) 331-2300
Bus: *Concrete products*   Fax: Emp: 350

FAIRFIELD SKANSKA, INC.
85 Construction Lane, Fishersville, Virginia 22939
CEO: Roger W. Farris, Pres.   Tel: (540) 337-1201
Bus: *Construction.*   Fax: (540) 337-0845   Emp: 100

GOTTLIEB SKANSKA
20 N. Central Ave., Valley Stream, New York 11580
CEO: Joseph Locurto, CEO   Tel: (516) 872-5700
Bus: *General contractors.*   Fax: (516) 872-0894   Emp: 400

KOCH SKANSKA
400 Roosevelt Ave., Carteret, New Jersey 07008
CEO: Robert W. Koch Jr., Pres.   Tel: (732) 969-1700
Bus: *Bridge & tunnel construction*   Fax: (932) 969-0197   Emp: 250

NIELSONS SKANSKA, INC.
22419 Country Rd. "G", PO Box 1660, Cortez, Colorado 81321
CEO: Charles S. Davis, Pres.   Tel: (970) 565-8000
Bus: *Heavy construction*   Fax: (970) 565-0188   Emp: 200

SKANSKA USA
16-16 Whitestone Expressway, Whitestone, New York 11357
CEO: Salvatore Mancini, Pres. & CEO   Tel: (718) 767-2600   %FO: 100
Bus: *Heavy construction, construction*   Fax: (718) 767-2663   Emp: 5,000
     management & development, rental of real
     estate.

SKANSKA USA BUILDING INC.
CONSTRUCTION COMPANY

1633 Littleton Rd., Parsippany, New Jersey 07054
CEO: Johan Karlstrom, EVP   Tel: (973) 656-6500
Bus: *Heavy construction, construction*   Fax: (973) 334-6408   Emp: 4,100
     management & development, rental of real
     estate.

SLATTERY SKANSKA INC.
16-16 Whitestone Expressway, Whitestone, New York 11357
CEO: Joseph M. LoCurto, Pres.   Tel: (718) 767-2600
Bus: *Commercial & heavy construction*   Fax: (718) 767-4030   Emp: 100

TIDEWATER SKANSKA
809 South Military Hwy., Virginia Beach, Virginia 23464
CEO: D.J. Eastwood, CEO   Tel: (757) 578-4100
Bus: *Commercial & heavy construction*   Fax: (757) 420-3551   Emp: 1,000

UNDERPINNING & FOUNDATION CONSTRUCTORS, INC.
46-36 54th Rd., Maspeth, New York 11378
CEO: Peter MacKenna, Pres.   Tel: (718) 786-6557   %FO: 100
Bus: *Provides heavy foundation construction,* Fax: (718) 786-6981   Emp: 25
     pile driving and marine construction

YEAGER SKANSKA
1995 Agua Mansa Rd., Riverside, California 92509
CEO: William V. McGuinness II, Pres. & CEO   Tel: (951) 684-5360
Bus: *Commercial & heavy construction*   Fax: (951) 684-1664   Emp: 900

● **SMEDBO AB**
Grustagsgatan 1, Box 13063, SE-250 13 Helsingborg, Sweden
CEO: Svante Andrae, Pres.   Tel: 46-42-25-1500   Rev: $150
Bus: *Mfr. brass, decorative hardware and bathroom*   Fax: 46-42-25-1515   Emp: 35
     accessories.   www.smedbo.com
NAICS: 332510

     SMEDBO INC.
     1001 Sherwood Dr., Lake Bluff, Illinois 60044
     CEO: Borje S. Jemsten, Pres.   Tel: (847) 615-0000   %FO: 100
     Bus: *Import/distribution decorative hardware,*   Fax: (847) 615-1001   Emp: 8
       bathroom accessories.

● **SMT AB (SWEDISH MACHINE TOOL TRICEPT)**
PO Box 800, Regattagatan 13, SE-72 122 Vasteras, Sweden
CEO: Per-Anders Holmström, CEO   Tel: 46-21-80-5100   Rev: $15
Bus: *Machine tool manufacture.*   Fax: 46-21-80-5111   Emp: 100
     www.smt-machine.se
NAICS: 333298, 333513

     S M T TRICEPT INC.
     2850 S. Milford Rd., Highland, Michigan 48357
     CEO: Al Bolen, Pres.   Tel: (847) 352-0013   %FO: 100
     Bus: *Sale of industrial equipment.*   Fax: (847) 352-0388   Emp: 5

     S M T TRICEPT INC.
     38236 Abruzzi Dr., Westland, Michigan 48185
     CEO: Al Bolen, Mgr.   Tel: (734) 721-7854
     Bus: *Sale of industrial supplies.*   Fax:

● **SSAB SWEDISH STEEL AB**
Birger Jarlsgatan 58, SE-11429 Stockholm, Sweden
CEO: Anders Ullberg, Pres. & CEO   Tel: 46-8-45-45-700   Rev: $2,539
Bus: *Mfr. steel.*   Fax: 46-8-45-45-725   Emp: 9,374
     www.ssab.com
NAICS: 331111, 551112

     SSAB HARDOX, INC.
     4700 Grand Ave., Pittsburgh, Pennsylvania 15225
     CEO: Louis J. Bolen, Mgr.   Tel: (412) 269-3231
     Bus: *Mfr. and sale of steel and steel products.*   Fax: (412) 269-3251   Emp: 20

● **SVENSKA CELLULOSA AKTIEBOLAGET (SCA)**
Box 7827, SE-103 97 Stockholm, Sweden
CEO: Jan Astrom, Pres. & CEO   Tel: 46-8-788-5100   Rev: $13,603
Bus: *Produces and sells absorbent hygiene products,*   Fax: 46-8-660-7430   Emp: 5,300
     packaging solutions and publication papers.   www.sca.com
NAICS: 113110, 321113, 322110, 322211, 322291

SCA NORTH AMERICA
500 Baldwin Tower Blvd., Eddystone, Pennsylvania 19022
CEO: Michael Bertrop, Pres.
Bus: *Paper product manufacturer.*

Tel: (610) 499-3700
Fax: (610) 499-3391

%FO: 100
Emp: 5,000

• SVENSKA HANDELSBANKEN
Kungstradgardsgatan 2, SE-106 70 Stockholm, Sweden
CEO: Lars O. Gronstedt, Pres. & CEO
Bus: *Commercial banking services.*

Tel: 46-8-701-1000
Fax: 46-8-701-2345
www.handelsbanken.se

Rev: $9,150
Emp: 7,836

NAICS: 522110, 522292, 524210

SVENSKA HANDELSBANKEN
875 Third Ave., 4/F, New York, New York 10022
CEO: Per Beckman, Gen. Mgr.
Bus: *Commercial banking services.*

Tel: (212) 326-5100
Fax: (212) 326-5196

%FO: 100

• SWEDISH MATCH AB
Rosenlundsgatan 36, SE-118 85 Stockholm, Sweden
CEO: Sven Hindrikes, Pres. & CEO
Bus: *Smokeless tobacco, pipe tobacco and lighters
manufacture and sales.*

Tel: 46-8-658-0200
Fax: 46-8-658-6263
www.swedishmatch.com

Rev: $1,967
Emp: 15,039

NAICS: 312229, 339999

GENERAL CIGAR HOLDINGS, INC.
387 Park Ave., South, New York, New York 10016
CEO: Edgar M. Cullman Jr., Pres. & CEO
Bus: *Sale of cigarettes, cigars & smokeless
tobacco products.*

Tel: (212) 448-3800
Fax: (212) 561-8979

SWEDISH MATCH NORTH AMERICA
7300 Beaufont Springs Dr., Ste. 400, PO Box 13297, Richmond, Virginia 23225
CEO: Lennart Freeman, Pres. & CEO
Bus: *Tobacco manufacture and sales.*

Tel: (804) 302-1700
Fax: (804) 302-1760

%FO: 100
Emp: 1,100

• SWEDTEL AB
Box 10029, SE 121 26 Stockholm-Globen, Sweden
CEO: Lennart Mikaelsson, Pres.
Bus: *Telecommunication products and services.*

Tel: 46-8-688-1100
Fax: 46-8-318-319
www.swedtel.com

NAICS: 334515, 517110

TELIA SONERA INTERNATIONAL CARRIER, INC.
2201 Cooperative Way, Ste. 302, Herndon, Virginia 20171
CEO: Tom von Weymarn, Chmn.
Bus: *Wireless network operations.*

Tel: (703) 546-4000
Fax: (703) 546-4125

%FO: 100

• TELEFONAKTIEBOLAGET LM ERICSSON
Torshamnsgatan 23, Kista, SE-164-83 Stockholm, Sweden
CEO: Carl-Henric Svanberg, Pres. & CEO
Bus: *Mfr. telecommunications systems, radio
communications and electronic defense systems.*

Tel: 46-8-719-0000
Fax: 46-8-18-4085
www.ericsson.com

Rev: $19,954
Emp: 50,534

NAICS: 334119, 334210, 334220, 334290, 336413

ERICSSON USA INC.
6300 Legacy Dr., Plano, Texas 75024
CEO: Angel Ruiz, Pres. & CEO
Bus: *Mfr./distribution/service
     telecommunications, switching & cellular*
Tel: (972) 583-0000
Fax: (972) 669-8860
%FO: 100
Emp: 8,279

SONY ERICSSON MOBILE COMMUNICATIONS
7001 Development Dr., Research Triangle Park, North Carolina 27709
CEO: San Deep, Mgr., Mgr.
Bus: *Mobile communications products.*
Tel: (919) 472-7000
Fax: (919) 472-7451
%FO: 100

SYMBIAN LTD.
390 Bridge Pkwy., Ste. 201, Redwood Shores, California 94065
CEO: Jerry Panagrossi, VP
Bus: *Mobile communications products.*
Tel: (650) 551-0240
Fax: (650) 551-0241

WIRELESS CAR, INC.
111 Pacifica, Ste. 200, Irvine, California 92618
CEO: Paul Drysch, Pres. & CEO
Bus: *Telemetry & telemetric services providers.*
Tel: (949) 930-8200
Fax: (949) 930-8299

● **TELELOGIC AB**
Kungsgatan 6, SE-203 Malmo, Sweden
CEO: Anders Lidbeck, Pres. & CEO
Bus: *Software developer for testing computer
     applications.*
NAICS: 511210
Tel: 46-40-650-0000
Fax: 46-40-650-6555
www.telelogic.com
Rev: $157
Emp: 719

TELELOGIC AMERICAS INC.
9401 Jeronimo Rd., Irivne, California 92618-1908
CEO: Scott D. Raskin, Pres.
Bus: *Software developer for testing computer
     applications.*
Tel: (919) 830-8022
Fax: (919) 830-9023
%FO: 100

● **TELIASONERA AB**
Sturegatan 1, SE-106 63 Stockholm, Sweden
CEO: Anders Igel, Pres. & CEO
Bus: *Telecommunications services.*
Tel: 46-8-504-550-00
Fax: 46-8-504-550-01
www.teliasonera.com
Rev: $12,389
Emp: 29,082

NAICS: 237130, 334290, 443112, 511140, 515210, 517110, 517211, 517212, 517410, 517910, 518111, 518210, 519190, 541219, 541512, 541519, 541690, 561421, 561499, 561621, 811213

TELIASONERA INTERNATIONAL CARRIER INC.
2201 Cooperative Way, Ste. 302, Herndon, Virginia 20171
CEO: Brian McHugh, CEO
Bus: *Telecommunications.*
Tel: (703) 546-4000
Fax: (703) 546-4125
%FO: 100
Emp: 40

● **TRELLEBORG INDUSTRI AB**
Henry Dunkers gata 2, SE-231-22 Trelleborg, Sweden
CEO: Fredrik Arp, Pres. & CEO
Bus: *Mfr. molded rubber products, wear resistant
     rubber, industrial hoses, protective clothing, v-
     belt, motor vehicle parts/equipment.*
Tel: 46-410-670-00
Fax: 46-410-427-63
www.trelleborg.com
Rev: $3,464
Emp: 21,675

NAICS: 325212, 326121, 326122, 326199, 326220, 326291, 332721, 336399, 339991

BUSAK & SHAMBAN AMERICAS
2531 Bremer Dr., Fort Wayne, Indiana 46803
CEO: Bob Dodd, Mgr.   Tel: (260) 749-9631   %FO: 100
Bus: *Mfr. of adhesives sealants, mechanical* Fax: (260) 749-4844   Emp: 350
     rubber gods & gaskets, packing & sealing
     devices.

FENTEK AMERICAS
3302 Craggy Oak Ct., Ste. 102, Williamsburg, Virginia 23188
CEO: Michael Langford, Gen. Mgr.   Tel: (757) 564-1780   %FO: 100
Bus: *Marine fendering.*   Fax: (757) 564-1781

GOODALL RUBBER COMPANY, INC.
790 Birney Hwy., Ste. 100, Aston, Pennsylvania 19014
CEO: Terry L. Taylor, Pres. & CEO   Tel: (610) 361-0800   %FO: 100
Bus: *Industrial rubber products manufacture and* Fax: (610) 361-0810 Emp: 400
     distribution.

TRELLEBORG AMERICAN VARISEAL
510 Burbank St., Broomfield, Colorado 80020
CEO: Fredrik Arp, Pres.   Tel: (303) 465-1727   %FO: 100
Bus: *Mfr. plastic products, gaskets, packing &* Fax: (303) 469-4874 Emp: 120
     sealing devices.

TRELLEBORG AUTOMOTIVE, INC.
400 Aylworth Ave., South Haven, Michigan 49090
CEO: Mark Brooks, Pres.   Tel: (269) 637-2116   %FO: 100
Bus: *Mfr. of mechanical rubber goods &*   Fax: (269) 637-8315 Emp: 1,173
     processor of urethane plastics.

TRELLEBORG FILLITE INC.
1856 Corporate Dr., Ste. 135, Norcross, Georgia 30093
CEO: Torgny U Astrom, CEO   Tel: (770) 729-8030   %FO: 100
Bus: *Mfr. of noise reduction material for*   Fax: (770) 729-1820
     automobile brake industry.

TRELLEBORG INDUSTRIAL AVS USA, INC.
200 Veterans Blvd., Ste. 3, South Haven, Michigan 49090
CEO: Mikael Bystroem   Tel: (269) 639-9891   %FO: 100
Bus: *Business services.*   Fax: (269) 639-8822

TRELLEBORG ORKOT COMPOSITES
2535 Prairie Rd., Unit D, Eugene, Oregon 97402
CEO: Joseph Abbruzzi, Pres.   Tel: (541) 688-5529   %FO: 100
Bus: *Mfr. of laminated plastic.*   Fax: (541) 688-2079   Emp: 20

TRELLEBORG RUBORE, INC.
445 Enterprise Ct., Bloomfield Hills, Michigan 48302
CEO: Ed Wojtkowicz, Mgr.   Tel: (248) 631-0197   %FO: 100
Bus: *Mfr. of mechanical rubber goods.* Fax: (248) 631-0198   Emp: 30

TRELLEBORG RUBORE, INC.
1856 Corporate Dr., Ste. 135, Norcross, Georgia 30093
CEO: Torgny U. Astrom, CEO   Tel: (770) 729-8030   %FO: 100
Bus: *Rubber hose products manufacture and* Fax: (770) 729-1820
     sales.

TRELLEBORG VIKING, INC.
170 West Rd., Ste. 1, Portsmouth, New Hampshire 03801
CEO: John Drewinka, Gen. Mgr.   Tel: (603) 436-1236   %FO: 100
Bus: *Sale of professional diving equipment &*   Fax: (603) 436-1392   Emp: 10
hazardous chemical protective suits.

TRELLEBORG WHEEL SYSTEMS AMERICAS, INC.
61 State Route 43 North, Hartville, Ohio 44632
CEO: Tim Ryan, Pres.   Tel: (330) 877-4800   %FO: 100
Bus: *Mfr. tires, inner tubes & mechanical rubber*   Fax: (330) 877-2346   Emp: 246
goods.

● **TURNILS INTERNATIONAL**
Sandbergsvagen, SE-441 39 Alingsas, Sweden
CEO: Frank Ahling, Dir.   Tel: 46-322-65-01-60
Bus: *Window coverings manufacture.*   Fax: 46-322-65-01-61
www.turnils.com

NAICS: 314121, 423220

NIBROL INC.
950 Quality Dr., Lancaster Business Park, PO Box 2649, Lancaster, South Carolina 29721-2649
CEO: Brian Porter, Mgr.   Tel: (803) 286-4500
Bus: *Mfr. drapery hardware, blinds & shades*   Fax: (803) 286-4502   Emp: 36

TURNILS NORTH AMERICA, INC.
1327 Northbrook Pkwy., Ste. 410, Suwannee, Georgia 30024
CEO: Debbie Holmberg, Mgr.   Tel: (770) 995-2222   %FO: 100
Bus: *Venetian blinds and window treatments.*   Fax: (770) 995-2210

● **VOLVO_AB**
Bergegardsvag 1, S-405 08 Gothenburg, Sweden
CEO: Leif Johansson, Pres. & CEO   Tel: 46-31-660000   Rev: $31,813
Bus: *Truck manufacture.*   Fax: 46-31-545772   Emp: 78,196
www.volvo.com

NAICS: 336120, 336211, 336412, 522291

BLUE BIRD CORPORATION
402 Blue Bird Blvd., Fort Valley, Georgia 31030
CEO: Jeffry D. Bust, Pres. & CEO   Tel: (478) 825-2021
Bus: *Mfr. of trucks, buses, & other vehicles.*   Fax: (478) 822-2457

MACK TRUCKS INC.
2100 Mack Blvd., Allentown, Pennsylvania 18105-5000
CEO: Paul L. Vikner, Pres. & CEO   Tel: (610) 709-3011   %FO: 100
Bus: *Mfr./sale Mack trucks.*   Fax: (610) 709-3308

VOLVO AERO SERVICES LP
645 Park of Commerce Way, Boca Raton, Florida 33487
CEO: Claes Malmros, Pres.   Tel: (561) 998-9330
Bus: *Aerospace & defense maintenance &*   Fax: (561) 998-9719   Emp: 275
services.

VOLVO COMMERCIAL FINANCE, LLC THE AMERICAS
7025 Albert Pick Rd., Ste. 105, Greensboro, North Carolina 27409
CEO: Jim Ryan, Pres. & CEO
Bus: *Financial services.*
Tel: (336) 931-4000
Fax: (336) 931-3773
Emp: 400

VOLVO CONSTRUCTION EQUIPMENT NORTH AMERICA, INC.
1 Volvo Dr., Asheville, North Carolina 28803
CEO: Denny Slagle, Pres.
Bus: *Industrial machinery & equipment manufacturing.*
Tel: (828) 650-2000
Fax: (828) 650-2501
Emp: 300

VOLVO GROUP NORTH AMERICA
570 Lexington Ave., 20/F, New York, New York 10022
CEO: Tomas Ericson, Pres.
Bus: *Administrative services.*
Tel: (212) 418-7400
Fax: (212) 418-7435

VOLVO TRUCKS OF NORTH AMERICA, INC.
7900 National Service Rd., Greensboro, North Carolina 27409
CEO: Peter Karlsten, Pres. & CEO
Bus: *Mfr./sale trucks.*
Tel: (336) 393-2000
Fax: (336) 393-2277
%FO: 87

WIRELESS CAR, INC.
111 Pacifica, Ste. 200, Irvine, California 92618
CEO: Gart Hallgren, COO
Bus: *Wireless communications systems.*
Tel: (949) 930-8200
Fax: (949) 930-8299
Emp: 10

• **VSM GROUP AB (FORMERLY HUSQVARNA VIKING)**
Drottninggatan 1, Jonkoping, SE-561 64 Huskvarna, Sweden
CEO: Svante Runnquist, CEO
Bus: *Develops, produces, markets and sells high quality household sewing machines and related accessories and software .*
Tel: 46-36-146000
Fax: 46-36-147444
www.husqvarnaviking.com
Rev: $131
Emp: 44
NAICS: 333292, 423830

    VSM SEWING INC.
    31000 Viking Pkwy., Westlake, Ohio 44145
    CEO: Bengt Gerborg, Pres.
    Bus: *Sales and distribution of high quality household sewing machines and related accessories and software.*
    Tel: (440) 808-6550
    Fax: (440) 808-6550
    Emp: 800

• **WALLENIUS WILHELMSEN**
P.O. Box 38193, SE-10064 Stockholm, Sweden
CEO: Ingar Skaug, Pres. & CEO
Bus: *Specialized shipping for motor vehicle and heavy cargo industries.*
Tel: 46-877-20-800
Fax: 46-864-00-594
www.2wglobal.com
NAICS: 483111, 483113, 484121, 484122, 488510, 493110, 493120, 493130, 541614

    WALLENIUS WILHELMSEN AMERICA
    PO Box 1232, 188 Broadway, Woodcliff Lake, New Jersey 07677
    CEO: Jan Eyvin Wang, Pres.
    Bus: *Transportation automobiles, trucks and rolling cargo.*
    Tel: (201) 307-1300
    Fax:
    %FO: 100
    Emp: 300

WALLENIUS WILHELMSEN LINES
PO Box 1198, Mobile, Alabama 36633
CEO: Peter Basler
Bus: *Specialized shipping for motor vehicle and heavy cargo industries.*
Tel: (251) 432-8061
Fax: (251) 432-8061
%FO: 100

WALLENIUS WILHELMSEN LINES
1311 Butterfield Rd., Downers Grove, Illinois 60515
CEO: Mark Barnwell
Bus: *Specialized shipping for motor vehicle and heavy cargo industries.*
Tel: (630) 719-1525
Fax: (630) 719-1525
%FO: 100

Switzerland

- ## THE ABB GROUP
Affolternstrasse 44, PO Box 8131, CH-8050 Zurich, Switzerland
CEO: Fred Kindle, Pres. & CEO
Bus: *Power and automation technologies.*

NAICS: 221121

Tel: 41-1-317-7111
Fax: 41-1-317-4420
www.abb.com

Rev: $23,725
Emp: 102,000

ABB AUTOMATION
29801 Euclid Ave., Wickliffe, Ohio 44092
CEO: Frank M. Smith
Bus: *Mfr. robotic cells and systems and process automation systems.*

Tel: (440) 585-8500
Fax: (440) 585-5539

%FO: 100

ABB AUTOMATION INC. / ETSI
2 Acee Dr., Natrona, Pennsylvania 15065
CEO: Andy Gavrilos
Bus: *Mfr. process automation equipment and related services.*

Tel: (724) 295-6000
Fax: (724) 295-6560

%FO: 100

ABB C-E BOILER SYSTEMS
2000 Day Hill Rd., Windsor, Connecticut 06095
CEO: John L. Marion, Pres.
Bus: *Engineers and designs utility, marine and industrial boiler systems.*

Tel: (860) 688-1911
Fax: (860) 285-5877

%FO: 100

ABB FINANCIAL SERVICES
One Stamford Plaza, 263 Tresser Blvd., Stamford, Connecticut 06901
CEO: Jeffrey A. Gilbert, Pres.
Bus: *Engaged in ABB financial services.*

Tel: (203) 961-7800
Fax: (203) 961-7943

%FO: 100

ABB FLEXIBLE AUTOMATION
1250 Brown Rd., Auburn Hills, Michigan 48326
CEO: Keith S. Hasenfratz
Bus: *Engaged in ABB financial services.*

Tel: (248) 391-8522
Fax: (248) 391-8789

%FO: 100

ABB FLEXIBLE AUTOMATION, INC.
2487 South Commerce Dr., New Berlin, Wisconsin 53151
CEO: Jeff Gelfand, Pres.
Bus: *Industrial automation systems.*

Tel: (262) 785-3400
Fax: (262) 785-3466

%FO: 100

ABB INC.
843 North Jefferson St., Lewisburg, West Virginia 24901
CEO: Gary Brewer, Pres.
Bus: *On-line process analyzers for detection, analysis and monitoring of chemical compounds.*

Tel: (304) 647-4358
Fax: (304) 645-4236

%FO: 100

ABB INSTRUMENTATION
125 East County Line Rd., Warminster, Pennsylvania 18974
CEO: Blake Doney, Pres.
Bus: *Field and control room instrumentation.*

Tel: (215) 674-6000
Fax: (215) 674-7183

%FO: 100

ABB LUMMUS GLOBAL, INC.
1515 Broad St., Bloomfield, New Jersey 07003
CEO: Gary L. Hamilton, VP
Bus: *Construction services, engineering and*
power-generation equipment.

Tel: (973) 893-1515
Fax: (973) 893-2000

%FO: 100

ABB POWER AUTOMATION
208 South Rogers Lane, Raleigh, North Carolina 27610
CEO: Randy Schrieber, Pres.
Bus: *Power engineering services.*

Tel: (919) 212-4700
Fax: (919) 212-4821

%FO: 100

ABB POWER T & D COMPANY
1021 Main Campus Dr., Raleigh, North Carolina 27606
CEO: Mary G. Flieller
Bus: *Provides electrical power transmission and*
distribution solutions.

Tel: (919) 856-3806
Fax: (919) 856-3810

%FO: 100

ABB, INC.
501 Merritt Seven, PO Box 5308, Norwalk, Connecticut 06556-5308
CEO: Dinesh C. Paliwal, Pres.
Bus: *Products/services for power, process,*
industrial automation, mass transit,
environmental control markets.

Tel: (203) 750-2200
Fax: (203) 750-2263

%FO: 100
Emp: 22,000

● **ACTELION LTD.**
Gewerbestrasse 16, CH-4123 Allschwil, Switzerland
CEO: Jean-Paul Clozel, CEO
Bus: *Drug research and manufacture.*

Tel: 41-61-565-65-65
Fax: 41-61-565-65-00
www.actelion.com

Rev: $417
Emp: 225

NAICS: 325412

ACTELION PHARMACEUTICALS INC.
601 Gateway Blvd., Ste. 100, South San Francisco, California 94080
CEO: Simon Buckingham
Bus: *Drug sales and distribution.*

Tel: (650) 624-6900
Fax: (650) 589-1501

%FO: 100

● **ACUTRONIC SCHWEIZ AG**
Techcenter Schwarz, CH-8608 Bubikon, Switzerland
CEO: Thomas W. Jung, Chmn. & CEO
Bus: *Develop motion simulation and inertial navigation*
test systems.

Tel: 41-55-253-2323
Fax: 41-55-253-2333
www.acutronic.com

NAICS: 334511

ACUTRONIC USA INC.
640 Alpha Dr., Pittsburgh, Pennsylvania 15238
CEO: Michael H. Swamp, Pres.
Bus: *Production, sales and service of motion*
simulators.

Tel: (412) 963-9400
Fax: (412) 963-0816

%FO: 100
Emp: 25

- **ADECCO SA**
Sagereistrasse 10, CH-8152 Glattbrugg, Switzerland
CEO: John Bowmer, CEO
Bus: *International recruitment, temporary employment,*
  outplacement and career and human resources
  services.
NAICS: 541612, 541990, 561320

Tel: 41-1-878-88-88
Fax: 41-1-878-87-87
www.adecco.com

Rev: $16,445
Emp: 30,000

ADECCO EMPLOYMENT SERVICES
225 Broad Hollow Rd., Melville, New York 11747-8905
CEO: Victoria Mitchell
Bus: *Staffing and career services.*

Tel: (631) 293-0009
Fax: (631) 293-3665

%FO: 100

ADECCO, INC.
100 Redwood Shores Pkwy., Redwood City, California 94065
CEO: John Bowmer, Pres.
Bus: *Recruitment, temporary employment,*
  outplacement and career and human
  resources business.

Tel: (650) 610-1000
Fax: (650) 610-1076

%FO: 100

AJILON SERVICES, INC.
210 West Pennsylvania Ave., Ste. 650, Towson, Maryland 21204-5348
CEO: Melanie Lawrence
Bus: *Recruitment, temporary employment,*
  outplacement and career and human
  resources business.

Tel: (410) 821-0435
Fax: (410) 828-0106

%FO: 100

LEE HECHT HARRISON
500 West Monroe St., Suite 3720, Chicago, Illinois 60661
CEO: Delthia Croft
Bus: *Staffing services.*

Tel: (312) 377-2300
Fax: (312) 930-9035

%FO: 100

LEE HECHT HARRISON
50 Tice Blvd., Woodcliff Lake, New Jersey 07677
CEO: Paul R. O'Donnell
Bus: *Personnel services.*

Tel: (201) 930-9333
Fax: (201) 505-1439

%FO: 100

LEE HECHT HARRISON
2777 Summer St., Ste. 4, Stamford, Connecticut 06905
CEO: Carol Amacher
Bus: *Staffing services*

Tel: (203) 975-9400
Fax: (203) 975-9400

%FO: 100

LEE HECHT HARRISON
235 Pine St., San Francisco, California 94104
CEO: Andrea Huff, Mgr.
Bus: *Recruitment, temporary employment,*
  outplacement and career and human
  resources business.

Tel: (415) 434-0125
Fax: (415) 362-3585

%FO: 100

LEE HECHT HARRISON
2200 Ross Ave., Dallas, Texas 75201
CEO: Peter O'Neill, Mgr.
Bus: *Recruitment, temporary employment,*
  outplacement and career and human
  resources business.

Tel: (972) 383-7400
Fax: (972) 383-7420

%FO: 100

LEE HECHT HARRISON
50 Tice Boulevard, Woodcliff Lake, New Jersey 07675
CEO: Stephen G. Harrison, Pres. Tel: (201) 930-9333 %FO: 100
Bus: *Recruitment, temporary employment,* Fax: (201) 307-0864
outplacement and career and human
resources business.

LEE HECHT HARRISON
100 South Wacker Dr., Ste. 1900, Chicago, Illinois 60606
CEO: Chuck Ziale, Mgr. Tel: (312) 726-1880 %FO: 100
Bus: *Recruitment, temporary employment,* Fax: (312) 726-1574
outplacement and career and human
resources business.

OLSTEN STAFFING SERVICES
111 Speen St., Framingham, Massachusetts 01701
CEO: Susan Acorn Tel: (508) 875-1970 %FO: 100
Bus: *Temporary staffing services.* Fax: (508) 875-7779

● AGIE CHARMILLES HOLDING LTD.
Bundesplatz 10, CH-6300 Zug, Switzerland
CEO: Kurt E. Stirnermann, Pres. Tel: 41-41-711-1376 Rev: $699
Bus: *Electric discharge machines (EDM) and high-* Fax: 41-41-711-1371 Emp: 13,247
speed machining (HSM) manufacturing. www.agie-charmilles.com
NAICS: 525910, 551112

AGIE LTD.
575 Bond St., Lincolnshire, Illinois 60069
CEO: Dr. Kurt E. Stirnemann, Chmn. Tel: (800) 438-5021
Bus: *Industrial machinery and equipment* Fax: (847) 478-5780 Emp: 200

CHARMILLES TECHNOLOIES CORP.
560 Bond St., Lincolnshire, Illinois 60069
CEO: Harry C. Moser, Pres. Tel: (847) 913-5300 %FO: 100
Bus: *U.S. headquarters operation for* Fax: (847) 913-5344 Emp: 125
manufacture and distribution of electric
discharge machines.

INTECH TECHNOLOGY CORPORATION
2001 West Parkes Dr., Broadview, Illinois 60155
CEO: Linda Radtke, Pres. Tel: (708) 681-6110 %FO: 100
Bus: *EDM wire, graphite, supplies and* Fax: (708) 681-0447 Emp: 53
accessories distribution.

MIKRON BOSTOMATIC CORP.
560 Bond St., Lincolnshire, Illinois 60069
CEO: Henry Moser Tel: (847) 913-5300 %FO: 100
Bus: *Precision machining systems for milling,* Fax: (847) 474-1111
profiling, contouring, and engraving
manufacture.

SYSTEM 3R USA INC.
40-D Commerce Way, Totowa, New Jersey 07512
CEO: Nick Giannotte, Pres. Tel: (973) 785-8200 %FO: 100
Bus: *Machine tools sales and service.* Fax: (973) 785-9612 Emp: 25

- **ALCON, INC., DIV. NESTLE**
  Bosch 69, Hünenberg, CH-6331 Zug, Switzerland
  CEO: Cary R. Rayment, Chmn. & Pres. & CEO
  Bus: *Eye care products manufacture and sales.*

  Tel: 41-41-785-8888
  Fax: 41-41-785-8888
  www.alconlabs.com

  Rev: $3,914
  Emp: 12,200

  NAICS: 335999, 339112
  - **ALCON, INC., DIV. NESTLE**
    6201 South Fwy., Fort Worth, Texas 76134
    CEO: Timothy R. Sear, VP
    Bus: *Eye care products manufacture and sales.*

    Tel: (817) 293-0450
    Fax: (817) 568-7201

    %FO: JV

- **ALOS AG**
  Raffelstrasse 12, CH-8045 Zurich, Switzerland
  CEO: Stephan Kopp, Chmn.
  Bus: *Mfr./sales of document management and imaging
  systems.*

  Tel: 41-1-468-7111
  Fax: 41-1-468-7100
  www.alos.ch

  Rev: $933
  Emp: 1,031

  NAICS: 334510
  - **ALOS MICROGRAPHICS CORPORATION**
    118 Bracken Rd., Montgomery, New York 12549
    CEO: Urs Kopp
    Bus: *Sales/distribution of document management
    and imaging systems*

    Tel: (845) 457-4400
    Fax: (845) 457-9083

    %FO: 100
    Emp: 40

- **ALU MENZIKEN HOLDING AG**
  Hauptstr. 35, CH-5737 Menziken, Switzerland
  CEO: Alfred M. Niederer, Pres.
  Bus: *Mfr. of aluminum products and modular assembly
  systems and components.*

  Tel: 41-62-765-2121
  Fax: 41-62-765-2145
  www.alu-menziken.com

  Rev: $160
  Emp: 850

  NAICS: 331312, 331316
  - **UNIVERSAL ALLOY CORPORATION**
    2871 La Mesa Ave., PO Box 6316, Anaheim, California 92816-6316
    CEO: Robert Lobb, Pres. & CEO
    Bus: *Mfr./sales of aluminum extrusions.*

    Tel: (714) 630-7200
    Fax: (714) 630-7207

    Emp: 600

- **ANTIQUORUM AUCTIONEERS**
  2, rue du Mont-Blanc, CH-1211 Geneva, Switzerland
  CEO: Osvaldo Patrizzi, CEO
  Bus: *Private auction house specializing in watches
  and clocks.*

  Tel: 41-22-909-2850
  Fax: 41-22-909-2860
  www.antiquorum.com

  NAICS: 561990
  - **ANTIQUORUM AUCTIONEERS**
    609 Fifth Ave., Ste. 503, New York, New York 10017
    CEO: Osvaldo Patrizzi
    Bus: *Private auction house specializing in
    watches and clocks.*

    Tel: (212) 750-1103
    Fax: (212) 750-6127

    %FO: 100

• ASCOM HOLDING AG
Belpstrasse 37, PO Box 3000, CH-3000 Bern 14, Switzerland

CEO: Juhani Anttila, CEO	Tel: 41-31-999-1111	Rev: $2,000
Bus: *Development/sales of public telephone/data switching systems, security systems, paging equipment, ticket vending machines & parking systems.*	Fax: 41-31-999-2300 www.ascom.ch	Emp: 12,000

NAICS: 334210, 334220, 561621

ASCOM TRANSPORT SYSTEMS, INC.
3100 Medlock Bridge Rd., Ste. 370, Norcross, Georgia 30071-1439

CEO: Peter Sands, Pres.	Tel: (770) 368-2003	%FO: 100
Bus: *Installs/maintains computerized parking control and toll road systems.*	Fax: (770) 368-2093	Emp: 50

ASCOM WIRELESS SOLUTIONS INC. (AWS)
598 Airport Boulevard, Ste. 300, Morrisville, North Carolina 27560

CEO: Chad West, Pres.	Tel: (919) 234-2500	%FO: 100
Bus: *Workplace wireless communication.*	Fax: (919) 234-2526	

• BACHEM AG
Haupt Str. 144, Basel Land, CH-4416 Bubendorf, Switzerland

CEO: Peter Grogg, Pres.	Tel: 41-61-935-2333	Rev: $106
Bus: *Mfr. of bulk peptide pharmaceuticals and amino acid derivatives.*	Fax: 41-61-931-2549 www.bachem.com	Emp: 520

NAICS: 551112

BACHEM BIOSCIENCE, INC.
3700 Horizon Dr., King of Prussia, Pennsylvania 19406

CEO: Peter Grogg, Chmn.	Tel: (610) 239-0300	%FO: 100
Bus: *Research, development and distribution services.*	Fax: (610) 239-0800	Emp: 26

BACHEM CALIFORNIA INC.
3132 Kashiwa St., Torrance, California 90505

CEO: Philip Ottiger, Pres.	Tel: (310) 539-4171	%FO: 100
Bus: *Synthetic peptides and peptide-related products and distribution center for catalog products.*	Fax: (310) 530-1571	Emp: 75

PENINSULA LABORATORIES INC.
305 Old Country Rd., San Carlos, California 94070

CEO: Paul Ladden, COO	Tel: (650) 592-5392	%FO: 100
Bus: *Research and polyclonal antibody and antisera production.*	Fax: (650) 595-4069	Emp: 300

• BALLY MANAGEMENT LTD.
Via Industria 1, Ticino, CH-6987 Caslano, Switzerland

CEO: Marco Franchini, Chmn. & CEO	Tel: 41-91-612-9111	Rev: $409
Bus: *Leather shoes and accessories manufacture.*	Fax: 41-91-612-9112 www.bally.ch	Emp: 3,000

NAICS: 315299, 315999, 316211, 316213, 316214, 316992, 316993, 448210

BALLY, INC.
745 Fifth Ave., New York, New York 10151
CEO: Sandie Samuells, Pres. & CEO
Bus: *Markets shoes, accessories, leather goods and apparel.*

Tel: (212) 751-3540
Fax: (212) 753-5024

%FO: 100

● **BELIMO AUTOMATION AG**
Brunnenbachstrasse 1, CH-8340 Hinwil, Switzerland
CEO: Andreas Steiner, Pres.
Bus: *Mfr./sales/marketing of air damper actuators for the HVAC industries.*
NAICS: 333995, 334512

Tel: 41-1-933-1262
Fax: 41-1-933-1241
www.belimo.com

Rev: $111
Emp: 446

BELIMO AIRCONTROLS USA INC.
43 Old Ridgebury Rd., PO Box 2928, Danbury, Connecticut 06813
CEO: Werner A. Buck, Pres.
Bus: *Mfr./sales/marketing of air damper actuators for the HVAC industries.*

Tel: (203) 791-9915
Fax: (203) 791-9919

%FO: 100
Emp: 200

● **THE BENNINGER GROUP AG**
Fabrikstrasse, Postfach 68, CH-9240 Uzwil, Switzerland
CEO: Ahmet Calik, CEO
Bus: *Mfr. textile machinery.*

Tel: 41-71-955-8585
Fax: 41-71-955-8747
www.benninger.ch.com

Emp: 830

NAICS: 333292

BENNINGER CORPORATION
885 Simuel Rd., PO Box 2627, Spartanburg, South Carolina 29304
CEO: Hans J. Balmer, Pres.
Bus: *Sales/service of textile machinery.*

Tel: (864) 578-7107
Fax: (864) 574-7033

%FO: 100
Emp: 15

● **BERNA BIOTECH LTD.**
Rehhagstrasse 79, Box 8234, CH-3018 Bern, Switzerland
CEO: Peter Giger, Chmn.
Bus: *Mfr. pharmaceuticals.*

Tel: 41-31-980-6111
Fax: 41-31-980-6775
www.bernabiotech.com

Rev: $206
Emp: 470

NAICS: 325412, 541611, 541710

BERNA PRODUCTS, INC.
4216 Ponce de Leon Boulevard, Coral Gables, Florida 33146
CEO: Andres Murai, Pres.
Bus: *Sales of pharmaceuticals.*

Tel: (305) 443-2900
Fax: (305) 567-0143

%FO: 100
Emp: 8

● **BISCHOFF TEXTIL AG**
Bogenstrasse 9, PO Box 362, CH-9000 St. Gallen, Switzerland
CEO: Karin Bischoff, CEO
Bus: *Mfr. lace, embroidery, couturier fabrics and luxury bedding.*
NAICS: 313111, 313249, 313312, 314129

Tel: 41-71-72-0111
Fax: 41-71-72-0397
www.bischoff-august.com

BISCHOFF ROYAL EMBROIDERED
1329 East Thousands Oak Boulevard, Thousand Oaks, California 91362
CEO: Maria Alejandro   Tel: (805) 379-1099   %FO: 100
Bus: *Sales/distribution of embroidered goods.*   Fax: (805) 379-3548

BISCHOFF-AUGUST INTERNATIONAL INC.
8901 J.F. Kennedy Blvd., North Bergen, New Jersey 07047
CEO: Maria Alejandro, CEO   Tel: (201) 295-3400   %FO: 100
Bus: *Sales/distribution of embroidered goods.*   Fax: (201) 861-1030   Emp: 10

● **BLASER SWISSLUBE AG**
Winterseistrasse, CH-3415 Hasle-Rüegsau, Switzerland
CEO: Peter Blaser, Pres.   Tel: 41-34-460-0101
Bus: *Mfr./distribution of metalworking fluids and*   Fax: 41-34-460-0100
    lubricants.   www.blaser-swisslube.com
NAICS: 324191

    BLASER SWISSLUBE INC.
    31 Hatfield Lane, Goshen, New York 10924
    CEO: Ulrich Krahenbuhl, Pres.   Tel: (914) 294-3200   %FO: 100
    Bus: *Sales/distribution of metalworking fluids and*   Fax: (914) 294-3102   Emp: 25
        lubricants.

● **BOBST S.A.**
Case Postale, CH-1001 Lausanne, Switzerland
CEO: Andreas Koopmann, CEO   Tel: 41-21-621-2111   Rev: $930
Bus: *Mfr. equipment and services for the folding*   Fax: 41-21-621-2070   Emp: 5,050
    carton, corrugated, and flexible packaging   www.bobstgroup.com
NAICS: 333999

    BOBST GROUP
    146 Harrison Ave., PO Box 2800, Roseland, New Jersey 07068
    CEO: Phillipe Michel, Pres.   Tel: (973) 226-8000   %FO: 100
    Bus: *Mfr./distribution, & servicing printing &*   Fax: (973) 226-8625   Emp: 350
        converting machines for paper and
        cardboard.

    BOBST GROUP USA INC.
    13325 South Point Blvd., Charlotte, North Carolina 28273
    CEO: Alain-Roger Jendly   Tel: (704) 587-2450
    Bus: *Flexible materials.*   Fax: (704) 587-2451

● **BOSCHUNG HOLDING AG**
route d'Englisberg 21, CH-1763 Granges-Paccot, Switzerland
CEO: Paul Boschung, Mng. Dir.   Tel: 41-26-460-4311
Bus: *Development, production and sales of machines*   Fax: 41-26-460-4388
    and devices for cleaning airports, highways and   www.boschung.com
    cities.
NAICS: 333319, 339999

BOSCHUNG COMPANY INC.
PO Box 8427, 930 Cass St., New Castle, Pennsylvania 16101-8427
CEO: Jay H. Bruce, member Tel: (724) 658-3300 %FO: 100
Bus: *Sales of mechanical and electronic* Fax: (724) 658-2300 Emp: 12
equipment to clean and clear airports from
ice, snow and dirt.

● **BOSSARD HOLDING AG**
Steinhauser Str. 70, CH-6301 Zug, Switzerland
CEO: Heinrich Kurt Reichlin, Pres. Tel: 41-41-749-6611 Rev: $313
Bus: *Develop and manufacture fastening technology* Fax: 41-41-749-6622 Emp: 1,277
systems, methods and elements for industry www.bossard.com
assembly.
NAICS: 525910, 551112

BOSSARD US HOLDINGS, INC.
881 Lafayette Rd., Ste. Ij, Hampton, New Hampshire 03842
CEO: Peter Vogel, Pres. Tel: (603) 926-9444 %FO: 100
Bus: *Manufacture fastening units.* Fax: (603) 926-9446

● **BOURDON-HAENNI HOLDING AG**
Bernstrasse 59, CH-3303 Jegenstorf, Switzerland
CEO: Peter Gloor, Pres. & CEO Tel: 41-31-764-9955
Bus: *Design and manufacture of scales and measuring* Fax: 41-31-764-9966
equipment. www.bourdon-haenni.ch
NAICS: 333997, 334519, 423490

BOURDON-HAENNI
3295 Cobb International Blvd., Kennesaw, Georgia 30157
CEO: Don Wise, Gen. Mgr. Tel: (770) 429-0599 %FO: 100
Bus: *Sales of pressure gauges, scales and* Fax: (770) 429-0795 Emp: 5
measuring equipment.

● **BRUDERER AG**
Stanzautomaten, CH-9320 Frasnacht, Switzerland
CEO: Markus E. Bruderer, Pres. Tel: 41-71-447-7500
Bus: *Mfr./sales high speed punching presses.* Fax: 41-71-447-7780 Emp: 750
www.bruderer-presses.com

NAICS: 333513

BRUDERER MACHINERY INC.
1200 Hendricks Causeway, Ridgefield, New Jersey 07657
CEO: Alois Rupp, Pres. Tel: (201) 941-2121 %FO: 100
Bus: *Sales high speed presses.* Fax: (201) 886-2010 Emp: 40

● **BUHLER LTD.**
Postfach, CH-9240 Uzwil, Switzerland
CEO: Calvin Grieder, Pres. & CEO Tel: 41-71-955-1111
Bus: *Mfr./sales of food processing and industrial* Fax: 41-71-955-3675 Emp: 3,000
machinery. www.buhler.ch
NAICS: 333294

BUHLER LTD.
1100 Xenium Lane North, PO Box 9497, Minneapolis, Minnesota 55441-4499
CEO: Magnus Baumann, Pres.
Bus: *Mfr./sales food processing; industrial machinery.*

Tel: (763) 847-9900
Fax: (763) 847-9911

%FO: 100
Emp: 280

SORTEX, INC.
2385 Arch- Airport Rd., Stockton, California 95206
CEO: Mike Evans, Pres.
Bus: *Color sorters and vision systems for food and agricultural products.*

Tel: (209) 983-8400
Fax: (209) 983-4800

%FO: 100

● BYSTRONIC LASER AG
Industriestrasse 21, CH-3362 Niederoenz, Switzerland
CEO: Rick Troesch, CEO
Bus: *Mfr. of machinery for cutting, breaking, grinding, drilling and handling of flat glass.*

Tel: 41-62-958-7777
Fax: 41-62-958-7676
www.bystronic.com

NAICS: 238910, 333131, 333515

BYSTRONIC INC.
185 Commerce Dr., Hauppauge, New York 11788
CEO: Marcel Bally, VP
Bus: *Sales/service of machinery for the glass industry, laser cutting machines and water jet cutting machines.*

Tel: (631) 231-1212
Fax: (631) 231-1040

%FO: 100

● BARRY CALLEBAUT AG
Westpark, Pfingstweidstrasse 60, CH-8005 Zurich, Switzerland
CEO: Patrick G. DeMaeseneire, CEO
Bus: *Chocolate confectionery manufacture.*

Tel: 41-44-801-6157
Fax: 41-44-801-6153
www.barry-callebaut.com

Rev: $3,182
Emp: 8,933

NAICS: 311320, 311330, 311340, 424450

BARRY CALLEBAUT CHADLER USA
400 Eagle Ct., Swedesboro, New Jersey 08085
CEO: Bill Mahaffy
Bus: *Manufacturing and processing Chocolate and Cocoa related products.*

Tel: (856) 467-0099
Fax: (856) 467-8024

%FO: 100

BARRY CALLEBAUT USA
1175 Commerce Blvd, Ste. D, American Canyon, California 94503
CEO: Mark Rasmussen
Bus: *Manufacturing and processing Chocolate and Cocoa related products.*

Tel: (707) 642-8200
Fax: (707) 642-8300

%FO: 100

BARRY CALLEBAUT USA
400 Industrial Park Rd., St. Albans, Vermont 05478
CEO: Lisa Matanle, HR
Bus: *Manufacturing and processing Chocolate and Cocoa related products.*

Tel: (902) 524-9711
Fax: (802) 524-1608

%FO: 100

BARRY CALLEBAUT USA
1500 Suckle Highway, Ste. A, Pennsauken, New Jersey 08110
CEO: Bruno Casabon, Dir. Sales
Bus: *Manufacturing and processing Chocolate and Cocoa related products.*

Tel: (856) 663-2260
Fax: (856) 665-0474

%FO: 100

BRACH'S CONFECTIONS INC.
19111 N. Dallas Pkwy., Dallas, Texas 75287
CEO: Charles D. Haak
Bus: *Candy manufacture, including chocolate and jelly beans.*
Tel: (972) 930-3600
Fax: (972) 930-3612
%FO: 100

BRACH'S CONFECTIONS INC.
4120 Jersey Pike, Chattanooga, Tennessee 37421
CEO: John Norton
Bus: *Manufacturing and processing Chocolate and Cocoa related products.*
Tel: (423) 899-1100
Fax: (423) 893-4484
%FO: 100

● **CARD GUARD AG**
Rheinweg 7-9, CH-8200 Schaffhausen, Switzerland
CEO: Yacov Geva, CEO
Bus: *Specializes in the design, manufacture and sale of healthcare technology monitoring systems and monitoring services.*
Tel: 41-52-632-0050
Fax: 41-52-632-0051
www.cardguard.com
NAICS: 334510, 621999

INSTROMEDIX
6779 Mesa Ridge Rd., Ste. 200, San Diego, California 92121
CEO: David Barach
Bus: *Design/mfr./sale of advanced telemedicine systems and the provision of telemedicine monitoring services.*
Tel: (858) 450-1750
Fax: (858) 450-9718
%FO: 100

LIFEWATCH INC.
1351A Abbott Ct., Buffalo Grove, Illinois 60089
CEO: Ofer Sandelson
Bus: *Ambulatory ECG monitoring.*
Tel: (877) 774-9846
Fax: (847) 720-2121
%FO: 100

● **CHOCOLADEFABRIKEN LINDT & SPRUNGLI AG**
Seestrasse 204, CH-8802 Kilchberg, Switzerland
CEO: Ernst Tanner, CEO
Bus: *Mfr./trading of chocolate products.*
Tel: 41-1-716-2233
Fax: 41-1-716-2662
www.lindt.com
Rev: $1,782
Emp: 6,293
NAICS: 311320, 445292

LINDT & SPRUENGLI INC.
68 Palmer Sq. West, Princeton, New Jersey 08542
CEO: Lindy Mayers, Pres.
Bus: *Mfr./sales of Swiss chocolates.*
Tel: (609) 279-1889
Fax: (609) 279-1889
%FO: 100

LINDT & SPRUENGLI INC.
1 Fine Chocolate Place, Stratham, New Hampshire 03885-2577
CEO: Thomas Linemayr
Bus: *Mfr./sales of Swiss chocolates.*
Tel: (603) 778-8100
Fax: (603) 778-3102
%FO: 100
Emp: 170

THE GHIRARDELLI CHOCOLATE COMPANY
1111 139th Ave., San Leandro, California 94578-2631
CEO: Ernst Tanner
Bus: *Chocolate manufacture and sales.*
Tel: (510) 483-6970
Fax: (510) 297-2649
%FO: 100

- **CIBA SPECIALTY CHEMICALS HOLDING**
  Klybeckstr. 141, CH-4002 Basel, Switzerland
  CEO: Armin Meyer, Chmn. & CEO
  Bus: *Specialty chemicals manufacture.*

  Tel: 41-61-636-1111
  Fax: 41-61-636-1212
  www.cibasc.com

  Rev: $6,158
  Emp: 19,338

  NAICS: 325131, 325132, 325211, 325510, 325998

  CIBA SPECIALITY CHEMICALS CORPORATION
  4090 Premier Dr., High Point, North Carolina 27265
  CEO: Eric Marohn, Mgr.
  Bus: *Home & fabric care, personal care.*

  Tel: (336) 801-2237
  Fax: (336) 801-2057

  CIBA SPECIALTY CHEMICALS
  250 South James St., Newport, Delaware 19804
  CEO: Colin MacKay, Mgr.
  Bus: *Coatings, electronic materials, imaging & inks, master batch, pigments for plastics.*

  Tel: (302) 992-5600
  Fax: (302) 994-3751

  CIBA SPECIALTY CHEMICALS COMPANY
  4050 Premier Dr., High Point, North Carolina 27265
  CEO: Eric Marone, Pres.
  Bus: *Colors division; pigments, textile dyes and paper chemicals manufacture.*

  Tel: (336) 801-2500
  Fax: (336) 801-2800

  %FO: 100

  CIBA SPECIALTY CHEMICALS COMPANY
  2301 Wilroy Rd., PO Box 820, Suffolk, Virginia 23439
  CEO: James J. Usilton, Pres.
  Bus: *Productions of chemicals for water treatment.*

  Tel: (757) 538-3700
  Fax: (757) 538-3989

  %FO: 100
  Emp: 450

  CIBA SPECIALTY CHEMICALS COMPANY
  540 White Plains Rd., Tarrytown, New York 10591
  CEO: Martin Riediker, Pres.
  Bus: *Mfr. specialty chemicals including water treatment products.*

  Tel: (914) 785-2000
  Fax: (914) 785-2211

  %FO: 100
  Emp: 3,000

- **CLARIANT INTERNATIONAL LTD.**
  Rothausstr. 61, Baselland, CH-4132 Muttenz, Switzerland
  CEO: Roland Losser, CEO
  Bus: *Mfr./sales of dyes and specialty chemicals*

  Tel: 41-61-469-5111
  Fax: 41-61-469-5901
  www.clariant.com

  Rev: $7,536
  Emp: 24,769

  NAICS: 325131, 325132, 325211, 325510, 325611, 325998

  CLARIANT CORPORATION
  4000 Monroe Rd., Charlotte, North Carolina 28205
  CEO: Kenneth Golder, CEO
  Bus: *Mfr./sales of dyes and specialty chemicals*

  Tel: (704) 331-7000
  Fax: (704) 331-7825

  %FO: 100
  Emp: 3,450

  CLARIANT LSM AMERICA, INC.
  2114 Larry Jeffers Rd., Elgin, South Carolina 29045
  CEO: Mark Witterholt, Mgr.
  Bus: *pharmaceutical preparations*

  Tel: (803) 438-3471
  Fax: (803) 438-4497

  %FO: 100

- **COMPAGNIE FINANCIERE RICHEMONT**
  8 Blvd. James-Fazy, CH-1201 Geneva, Switzerland
  CEO: Norbert Platt, CEO
  Bus: *Holding company for Dunhill and Winfield tobacco products, high value jewelry and watches and luxury goods subsidiary, Vendome Group.*

  Tel: 41-22-715-3500
  Fax: 41-22-715-3550
  www.richemont.com

  Rev: $4,043
  Emp: 14,871

  NAICS: 315212, 315232, 315233, 315234, 315992, 315999, 316110, 316991, 316992, 316993, 316999, 334518, 339911, 339941, 423940, 448310

  RICHEMONT NORTH AMERICA
  645 5th Ave., New York, New York 10022-5910
  CEO: Callum Barton, Pres.
  Bus: *Jewelry Manufacturing*

  Tel: (212) 593-0444
  Fax:

  %FO: 100
  Emp: 75

- **COMPAGNIE FINANCIÈRE TRADITION**
  11, rue de Langallerie, Vaud, CH-1003 Lausanne, Switzerland
  CEO: Patrick Combes, Pres.
  Bus: *International securities broker.*

  Tel: 41-21-343-5300
  Fax:
  www.traditiongroup.com

  Rev: $660
  Emp: 1,830

  NAICS: 523120

  TFS ENERGY FUTURES
  680 Washington Blvd., 5/F, Stamford, Connecticut 06901
  CEO: Emil Assentato
  Bus: *International securities broker.*

  Tel: (203) 351-9557
  Fax: (203) 351-9567

  %FO: 100

  TRADITION NORTH AMERICA
  75 Park Place, 4/F, New York, New York 10007
  CEO: Emil Assentato, Pres.
  Bus: *International securities broker.*

  Tel: (212) 797-4500
  Fax: (212) 791-3441

  %FO: 100
  Emp: 361

  TRADITION NORTH AMERICA
  865 S. Figueroa St., Ste. 1320, Los Angeles, California 90017
  CEO: Emil Assentato
  Bus: *International securities broker.*

  Tel: (213) 622-4127
  Fax: (213) 622-9561

  %FO: 100

- **CONVERIUM HOLDING AG**
  Baarerstrasse 8, CH-6300 Zug, Switzerland
  CEO: Terry G. Clarke, CEO
  Bus: *Property and casualty reinsurance services.*

  Tel: 41-41-639-9335
  Fax: 41-41-639-9334
  www.converium.com

  Rev: $3,541
  Emp: 771

  NAICS: 524130

  CONVERIUM REINSURANCE INC.
  One Canterbury Green, 11/F, PO Box 29, Stamford, Connecticut 06904
  CEO: Mary Rauscher
  Bus: *Property and casualty reinsurance services.*

  Tel: (203) 965-8800
  Fax: (203) 965-8805

  %FO: 100

  CONVERIUM REINSURANCE INC.
  One Market St., Ste. 1625, San Francisco, California 94105
  CEO: Jack Butlin
  Bus: *Property and casualty reinsurance services.*

  Tel: (415) 977-7800
  Fax: (415) 977-7838

  %FO: 100

CONVERIUM REINSURANCE INC.
311 South Wacker Dr., Ste. 4875, Chicago, Illinois 60606
CEO: Roy Scott
Bus: *Property and casualty reinsurance services.*
Tel: (312) 935-3838
Fax: (312) 935-3839
%FO: 100

CONVERIUM REINSURANCE INC.
One Chase Manhattan Plaza, New York, New York 10005
CEO: Paul E. Dassenko
Bus: *Property and casualty reinsurance services.*
Tel: (212) 898-5000
Fax: (212) 898-5052
%FO: 100

● **COTECNA INSPECTION SA**
58, rue de la Terrassiere, CH-1211 Geneva 6, Switzerland
CEO: Robert M. Massey, CEO
Bus: *Customs values inspection services for international traded goods.*
Tel: 41-22-849-6900
Fax: 41-22-849-6989
www.cotecna.com
Emp: 4,000
NAICS: 488510, 541614

COTECNA INSPECTION INC.
14505 Commerce Way, Ste. 501, Miami Lakes, Florida 33016
CEO: Manny Castillo, Mgr.
Bus: *Engaged in quality control services.*
Tel: (305) 828-8141
Fax: (305) 827-0616
%FO: 100
Emp: 40

COTECNA INSPECTION INC.
507 North Sam Houston Pkwy. East, Ste. 340, Houston, Texas 77060
CEO: Natalie Macias, Mgr.
Bus: *Engaged in quality control services.*
Tel: (281) 272-6733
Fax: (281) 272-6769
%FO: 100

COTECNA, INC.
1101 30th St., NW, Ste. 500, Washington, District of Columbia 20007
CEO: Nancy Williams, VP
Bus: *Engaged in quality control services.*
Tel: (202) 333-2540
Fax: (202) 333-2541
%FO: 100

● **CREDIT SUISSE GROUP**
Paradeplatz 8, CH-8070 Zurich, Switzerland
CEO: Ulrich Korner, CFO
Bus: *Global financial services.*
Tel: 41-44-212-1616
Fax: 41-44-333-2587
www.credit-suisse.com
Rev: $63,989
Emp: 60,532
NAICS: 522110, 522292, 522293, 523110, 523120, 523130, 523140, 524210, 525110

CREDIT SUISSE ASSET MANAGEMENT
466 Lexington Ave., New York, New York 10017
CEO: Matt Moss, CFO
Bus: *Security brokers & dealers*
Tel: (212) 875-3500
Fax: (646) 658-0728
Emp: 20

CREDIT SUISSE FIRST BOSTON
11 Madison Ave., New York, New York 10010
CEO: Brady W. Dougan, CEO
Bus: *Engaged in financial advisory services and sales/trading financial products.*
Tel: (212) 325-2000
Fax: (212) 325-6665
%FO: 100
Emp: 18,341

CSFB PRIVATE EQUITY
11 Madison Ave., New York, New York 10010
CEO: Brian D. Finn, Pres.
Bus: *Engaged in financial advisory services and*
    sales/trading financial products.

Tel: (212) 325-2000	%FO: 100
Fax: (212) 318-1188	

GENERAL CASUALTY INSURANCE COMPANIES
1 General Dr., Sun Prairie, Wisconsin 53596
CEO: Pete McPartland, Pres. & CEO
Bus: *Auto & other vehicle insurance*

Tel: (608) 837-4440
Fax: (608) 837-4418   Emp: 1,900

IMAGYN MEDICAL TECHNOLOGIES, INC.
1 Park Plaza, Ste. 1100, Irvine, California 92614
CEO: Charles A. Laverty, Chmn. & CEO
Bus: *Medical equipment & supplies*

Tel: (949) 809-0800
Fax: (949) 757-1491

METRO-GOLDWYN-MAYER INC.
10250 Constellation Blvd., Los Angeles, California 90067
CEO: Daniel J. Taylor, Pres.
Bus: *Motion picture production*

Tel: (310) 449-3000
Fax: (310) 449-8857   Emp: 1,440

MGM PICTURES
10250 Constellation Blvd., Los Angeles, California 90067
CEO: Alex Yemenidjian, Chmn. & CEO
Bus: *Motion picture production & distribution*

Tel: (310) 449-3000
Fax: (310) 449-8750

SPROUT GROUP
1 Madison Ave., 7-T/F, New York, New York 10010
CEO: Craig Slutzkin, CFO
Bus: *Venture Capital*

Tel: (212) 538-3600
Fax: (212) 538-8245   Emp: 36

UNITED ARTIST CORPORATION
10250 Constellation Blvd., Los Angeles, California 90067
CEO: Danny Rosett, Pres.
Bus: *Motion picture production & distribution*

Tel: (310) 449-3000
Fax:

WINTERTHUR SWISS INSURANCE COMPANY
2727 Turtle Creek Blvd., Dallas, Texas 75219
CEO:
Bus: *General insurance services.*

Tel: (214) 559-1222
Fax: (214) 748-9590

● **DARTFISH**
Route de la Fonderie 6 CP 53, CH-1705 Fribourg 5, Switzerland
CEO: Jean-Marie Ayer, CEO
Bus: *Develops performance enhancing sport video*
    training applications.
NAICS: 512191

Tel: 41-26-425-4850
Fax: 41-26-425-4859
www.dartfish.com

DARTFISH USA, INC.
1301 Hightower Trail, Ste. 111, Atlanta, Georgia 30350
CEO: Ron Imbriale
Bus: *Develops performance enhancing sport*
    video training applications.

Tel: (404) 685-9505   %FO: 100
Fax: (404) 685-9130

● **DAY SOFTWARE HOLDING AG**
Barfuesserplatz 6, CH-4001 Basel, Switzerland
CEO: Michael Moppert, CEO
Bus: *Management software manufacture.*

Tel: 41-61-226-9898
Fax: 41-61-226-9897
www.day.com

Rev: $12
Emp: 85

NAICS: 511210, 518210, 541511, 541512

    DAY SOFTWARE INC.
    5251 California, Ste. 110, Irvine, California 92612
    CEO: Santi Pierini
    Bus: *Management software manufacture.*

    Tel: (949) 679-2960
    Fax: (949) 679-2972

    %FO: 100

● **DKSH HOLDING LTD.**
Wiesenstrasse 8, PO Box 888, CH-8034 Zurich, Switzerland
CEO: Joerg W. Wolle, Pres. & CEO
Bus: *Logistics and supply chain management services.*

Tel: 41-1-386-7272
Fax: 41-1-386-7550
www.dksh.com

Rev: $3,372
Emp: 14,600

NAICS: 488510, 541614

    SIBER HEGNER NORTH AMERICA INC.
    300 E. Lombard St., Ste. 630, Baltimore, Maryland 21202
    CEO: Don Cox
    Bus: *Logistics and supply chain management services.*

    Tel: (410) 385-1666
    Fax: (410) 385-1266

    %FO: 100

● **DUFRY**
Hardstr. 95, CH-4020 Basel, Switzerland
CEO: Julian Diaz Gonzalez, CEO
Bus: *Watchmakers.*

Tel: 41-61-266-4215
Fax: 41-61-261-4303
www.weitnauer.ch

Rev: $568
Emp: 2,800

NAICS: 334518

    DUFRY AMERICA SERVICES, INC.
    10300 NW 19th St., Ste. 114, Miami, Florida 33172
    CEO: Manuel Sosa, VP
    Bus: *Wine & distilled beverages.*

    Tel: (305) 591-1763
    Fax: (305) 513-3964

    Emp: 32

    WEITNAUER AMERICA TRADING SERVICES INC.
    10300 NW 19th St., Ste. 214, Miami, Florida 33172
    CEO: Robert Hendry, Gen. Mgr.
    Bus: *Supplier of duty free merchandise to cruise/cargo ships, duty free retailers, airliners, military/diplomatic corps.*

    Tel: (305) 591-1763
    Fax: (305) 593-9893

    %FO: 100
    Emp: 200

● **EFTEC AG**
Hofstrasse 31, Romanshorn, CH-8590 Thurgau, Switzerland
CEO: Hans M. Feix, CEO
Bus: *Automobile sealants, adhesives and coatings manufacture. (JV of HB Fuller USA)*
NAICS: 325510, 325520

Tel: 41-71-466-4300
Fax: 44-71-466-4301
www.eftec.com

EFTEC NORTH AMERICA, INC.
31601 Research Park Dr., Madison Heights, Michigan 48071
CEO: Chet Ricker   Tel: (248) 585-2200   %FO: 100
Bus: *Automobile adhesives and sealants*   Fax: (248) 585-3699
manufacture.

● **ELMA ELECTRONICS AG**
Hofstrasse 93, Wetzikon, CH-8620 Zurich, Switzerland
CEO: Peter Neth, CEO   Tel: 41-1-933-4111
Bus: *Computer enclosures and components*   Fax: 41-1-933-4215
                                                 www.elma.ch
NAICS: 334418

    ELMA ELECTRONICS, INC.
    44350 South Grimmer Blvd., Fremont, California 94538
    CEO: Fred Ruegg, VP   Tel: (510) 656-3400   %FO: 100
    Bus: *Computer enclosures and components*   Fax: (510) 656-8008
    manufacture.

● **EMS-CHEMIE HOLDING AG**
Kugelgasse 22, CH-8708 Mannedorf, Switzerland
CEO: Magdalena Martullo-Blocher, Chmn. & CEO   Tel: 41-1-921-0000   Rev: $982
Bus: *Chemicals, including airbag igniters, coating and*   Fax: 41-1-921-0001   Emp: 2,637
sealing products and generators manufacture.   www.emschemie.com
NAICS: 325211, 325412, 541330

    EMS-CHEMIE INC.
    2060 Corporate Way, Sumter, South Carolina 29151
    CEO: Hans U. Enzinger   Tel: (803) 481-9173   %FO: 100
    Bus: *Chemicals, including airbag igniters, coating*   Fax: (803) 481-3820
    and sealing products and generators
    manufacture.

● **ENDRESS + HAUSER HOLDING AG**
Kagenstrasse 7, CH-4153 Reinach, Switzerland
CEO: Klaus Endress, CEO   Tel: 41-61-715-6111   Rev: $700
Bus: *Mfr./distribution level, pressure, flow and*   Fax: 41-61-711-0989   Emp: 2,900
moisture instrumentation and process recorders.   www.endress.com
NAICS: 334513, 551112

    A. D. INSTRUMENTS, DIV. ENDRESS + HAUSER INC.
    13900 S Lakes Dr., Ste. A, Charlotte, North Carolina 28273
    CEO: Glenn Walkop, Mgr.   Tel: (704) 522-8415   %FO: 100
    Bus: *Mfr./sales of level, pressure, flow and*   Fax: (704) 527-5005
    moisture instrumentation process recorders.

    ENDRESS + HAUSER
    11843 Bricksome Ave., Ste. B, Baton Rouge, Louisiana 70816
    CEO: Pat Fogarty   Tel: (225) 295-0100   %FO: 100
    Bus: *Mfr./sales of level, pressure, flow and*   Fax: (225) 295-0200
    moisture instrumentation process recorders.

ENDRESS + HAUSER INSTRUMENTS INC.
2350 Endress Place, PO Box 246, Greenwood, Indiana 46143
CEO: George H. Endress
Bus: *Mfr./sales of level, pressure, flow and moisture instrumentation process recorders.*
Tel: (317) 535-7138
Fax: (317) 535-8498
%FO: 100
Emp: 180

ENDRESS + HAUSER SYSTEMS & GAUGING INC.
5834 Peachtree Corners East, Norcross, Georgia 30092
CEO: Keith Coggins
Bus: *Mfr./sales of level, pressure, flow and moisture instrumentation process recorders.*
Tel: (770) 447-9202
Fax: (770) 662-8939
%FO: 100

● **ESEC HOLDING AG, SUB. UNAXIS**
Hinterbergstrasse 32, Cham, CH-6330 Zug, Switzerland
CEO: Asuri S. Raghavan, CEO
Bus: *Microchips equipment manufacture.*
Tel: 41-41-749-5111
Fax: 41-41-749-5177
www.esec.com
Rev: $107
Emp: 640

NAICS: 334413

ESEC USA, INC.
1407 W. Drivers Way, Tempe, Arizona 85284
CEO: Joe Lippincott, Mgr.
Bus: *Microchips equipment manufacture.*
Tel: (480) 893-6990
Fax: (480) 893-6793
%FO: 100

● **THE FANTASTIC CORPORATION**
PO Box 1350, CH-6301 Zug, Switzerland
CEO: Peter Ohnemus, CEO
Bus: *Produces software for rich data distribution in corporate networks.*
Tel: 41-41-728-8888
Fax: 41-41-728-8900
www.fantastic.com

NAICS: 511210

THE FANTASTIC CORPORATION, INC.
2121 South El Camino Real, 4/F, San Mateo, California 94403
CEO: Chris Wallace
Bus: *Produces software for rich data distribution in corporate networks.*
Tel: (650) 356-2100
Fax: (650) 356-2139
%FO: 100

● **FIRMENICH INTERNATIONAL SA**
Route de La Plaine 45, CH-1283 Geneva, Switzerland
CEO: Patrick Firmenich, CEO
Bus: *Flavors and fragrances manufacturer.*
Tel: 41-22-780-2211
Fax: 41-22-754-1473
www.firmenich.com
Rev: $1,282
Emp: 4,300

NAICS: 311942, 325620

FIRMENICH INTERNATIONAL
625 Madison Ave., 17/F, New York, New York 10022
CEO: Theo Spilka, VP
Bus: *Flavors and fragrances manufacturer.*
Tel: (212) 489-4800
Fax: (212) 980-4312
%FO: 100

NOVILLE FIRMENICH INC.
3 Empire Blvd., South Hackensack, New Jersey 07606
CEO: Daniel Carey, Gen. Mgr.
Bus: *Flavors and fragrances manufacturer.*
Tel: (908) 754-2222
Fax: (908) 754-0167
%FO: 100

- **GEORG FISCHER LTD.**
  Amsler-Laffon-Strasse 9, PO Box 671, CH-8201 Schaffhausen, Switzerland
  CEO: Kurt E. Stirnemann, Chmn. & CEO   Tel: 41-52-631-1111   Rev: $3,127
  Bus: *Automotive castings and products; piping* Fax: 41-52-631-2847   Emp: 12,324
       systems; machine tools manufacturing; plant www.georgfischer.com
       engineering and construction.
  NAICS: 332919, 336111, 541330

  GEORGE FISCHER SIGNET INC.
  3401 Aerojet Ave., PO Box 5770, El Monte, California 91734-1770
  CEO: Charlotte Hill, Pres.   Tel: (626) 571-2770   %FO: 100
  Bus: *Fluid sensor products manufacture.* Fax: (626) 573-2057   Emp: 110

  GEORGE FISCHER SIGNET INC.
  2882 Dow Ave., Tustin, California 92680-7285
  CEO: John Pregenzer, CEO   Tel: (714) 731-8800   %FO: 100
  Bus: *Distribution plastic piping systems, plastic* Fax: (714) 731-6201   Emp: 52
       values, fluid sensor products.

  GEORGE FISCHER SLOANE INC.
  7777 Sloane Dr., Little Rock, Arkansas 72206
  CEO: Daniel Curtis, Pres.   Tel: (501) 490-7777   %FO: 100
  Bus: *Industrial machinery manufacture and sales.* Fax: (501) 490-7100

  SENNINGER IRRIGATION INC.
  16220 East Hwy 50, Clermont, Florida 34711
  CEO: Adam Skolnik   Tel: (407) 293-5555   %FO: 100
  Bus: *Agricultural product sales.* Fax: (407) 293-5740

- **FLM HOLDING**
  Polypag AG, Tiefenackerstr. 52, CH-9450 Altstatten, Switzerland
  CEO: Stefan Miczka, Pres.   Tel: 41-71-757-6411
  Bus: *Polyurethane foam manufacture.* Fax: 41-71-757-6498   Emp: 100
                              www.polypag.ch
  NAICS: 326150

  FOMO PRODUCTS INC.
  2775 Barber Rd., Norton, Ohio 44203
  CEO: Kristin Lewis, CEO   Tel: (330) 753-4585   %FO: 100
  Bus: *Sales/distribution of polyurethane foam.* Fax: (330) 753-5199   Emp: 58

- **FORBO HOLDING AG**
  Bauelenzelgstr. 20, Egilsau, CH-8193 Zurich, Switzerland
  CEO: This E. Schneider, CEO & Mng. Dir.   Tel: 41-1-868-2525   Rev: $1,287
  Bus: *Decorative building products and construction* Fax: 41-1-868-2526   Emp: 5,585
       materials holding company. www.forbo.com
  NAICS: 325520, 326192, 327122, 333922

  FORBO ADHESIVES LLC
  4920 Gold Rd., Dallas, Texas 75237
  CEO: Charles Wieland, Gen. Mgr.   Tel: (214) 330-7295   %FO: 100
  Bus: *Adhesive products for flooring.* Fax: (214) 331-4928

FORBO ADHESIVES SYNTHETIC POLYMERS
3150 Fiberglass Rd, Kansas City, Kansas 66115
CEO: Debbie Nutter
Bus: *Mfr. adhesives & sealants.*
Tel: (913) 321-1576
Fax: (913) 321-7287
Emp: 27

FORBO ADHESIVES SYNTHETIC POLYMERS
7440 West Dupont Rd., Morris, Illinois 60450
CEO: Bob Evans, Mgr.
Bus: *Mfr. adhesives & sealants.*
Tel: (815) 357-6726
Fax: (815) 357-8320
%FO: 100

FORBO ADHESIVES, INC.
9828 J St., Omaha, Nebraska 68127
CEO: William Hatfield, Mgr.
Bus: *Mfr. adhesives & sealants.*
Tel: (402) 331-1330
Fax: (402) 331-4276

FORBO ADHESIVES, INC.
523 Davis Dr., Ste. 400, Durham, North Carolina 27713
CEO: Jack Chambers, Pres.
Bus: *Adhesives for flooring.*
Tel: (919) 433-1300
Fax: (919) 433-1301
%FO: 100
Emp: 300

FORBO LINOLEUM INC.
Humboldt Industrial Park, PO Box 667, Hazelton, Pennsylvania 18201
CEO: Dennis Darragh, Pres.
Bus: *Sale of floor covering.*
Tel: (570) 459-0771
Fax: (570) 450-0277
Emp: 94

SIEGLING AMERICA
12201 Vanstory Rd., Huntersville, North Carolina 28078
CEO: Wayne E. Hoffman, Pres.
Bus: *Mfr. of rubber & plastic hose & belting.*
Tel: (704) 948-0800
Fax: (704) 948-0995
Emp: 240

• **FRANKE HOLDING AG**
Dorfbachstr. 2, CH-4663 Aarburg, Switzerland
CEO: Michael Pieper, Pres. & CEO
Bus: *Sales/distribution of kitchen sinks and accessories, food service equipment, industrial and medical equipment.*
Tel: 41-62-787-3131
Fax: 41-62-787-3037
www.franke.com
Rev: $762
Emp: 4,042

NAICS: 332111, 332112, 332114, 332115, 332116, 332214, 332312, 332313, 332321, 332322, 332323, 332510, 332611, 332612, 332618, 332721, 332722,
332812, 332813, 332919, 332999, 333294, 333414, 333924, 334518, 336111, 336112, 336211, 336399, 337215, 339911, 339912, 339914, 423110

FRANKE COMMERICAL SYSTEMS
690 Overmyer Rd., Sparks, Nevada 89431
CEO: Jim Oliphant, Mgr.
Bus: *Mfr. food service equipment, kitchen sinks & accessories.*
Tel: (702) 359-6663
Fax: (702) 359-0407
%FO: 100

FRANKE CONSUMER PRODUCTS INC., KITCHEN DIV.
3050 Campus Dr., Ste. 500, Hatfield, Pennsylvania 19440
CEO: Tom Smith, Mgr.
Bus: *Mfr./distribution of kitchen sinks, faucets and accessories.*
Tel: (215) 822-6590
Fax: (215) 822-5873
%FO: 100

FRANKE CONTRACT GROUP
One Franke Blvd., Fayetteville, Tennessee 37334
CEO: John Smith, Mgr.
Bus: *Mfr. of food service equipment.*
Tel: (931) 433-7455
Fax: (931) 433-3309
%FO: 100

FRANKE FOODSERVICE SYSTEMS INC.
305 Tech Park Dr., LaVergne, Tennessee 37086
CEO: Bud Ward, Pres.
Bus: *Sales/distribution spare parts.*

Tel: (615) 287-8200
Fax: (615) 287-8250

%FO: 100
Emp: 334

● **CARLO GAVAZZI HOLDING AG**
Sumpfstrasse 32, CH-6312 Steinhausen, Switzerland
CEO: Werner S. Welti, Chmn.
Bus: *Automation components and electronic*

Tel: 41-41-747-4525
Fax: 41-41-740-4560
www.carlogavazzi.ch

Rev: $260
Emp: 2,240

NAICS: 335314, 551112

CARLO GAVAZZI COMPUTING SOLUTIONS
740 E. Glendale Ave., Sparks, Nevada 89431
CEO: Chris Boutilier, Pres.
Bus: *Sales of control components for the industrial automation market.*

Tel: (775) 331-8283
Fax: (775) 331-8004

%FO: 100

CARLO GAVAZZI COMPUTING SOLUTIONS
10 Mupac Dr., Brockton, Massachusetts 02301
CEO: Mads Lillelund, Mgr.
Bus: *Design/mfr./marketing of system integration products.*

Tel: (508) 588-6110
Fax: (508) 588-0498

%FO: 100

CHANNEL ACCESS LLC
170 Knowles Dr., Los Gatos, California 95032
CEO: Stephen Dow
Bus: *Design/mfr./marketing of system integration products.*

Tel: (408) 378-5500
Fax: (408) 341-0490

%FO: 100

● **GEBERIT AG**
Schachenstr. 77, St. Gallen, CH-8645 Jona, Switzerland
CEO: Albert M. Baehny, CEO
Bus: *Sanitary systems manufacture, including sinks and toilets.*
NAICS: 326191, 327111

Tel: 41-55-221-6300
Fax: 41-55-221-6747
www.geberit.com

Rev: $1,685
Emp: 5,516

DUFFIN MANUFACTURING COMPANY
PO Box 4036, 316 Warden Ave., Elyria, Ohio 44036
CEO: Mark Alan, Mng. Dir.
Bus: *Turned-part components, coatings and assemblies manufacture.*

Tel: (440) 323-4681
Fax: (440) 323-7389

%FO: 100

GEBERIT MANUFACTURING INC.
1100 Boone Dr., Michigan City, Indiana 46360
CEO: Scott Farrisee, VP & Gen. Mgr.
Bus: *Mfr. of sanitary systems.*

Tel: (219) 879-4466
Fax: (219) 872-8003

%FO: 100
Emp: 469

SYNAPSE, INC.
500 Dan Tibs Rd., Huntsville, Alabama 35806
CEO: Wade Patterson, Mng. Dir.
Bus: *Sale of electronic components.*

Tel: (256) 852-4211
Fax: (256) 852-3251

%FO: 100

THE CHICAGO FAUCET COMPANY
2100 South Clearwater Dr., Des Plaines, Illinois 60018
CEO: Keith D. Kramer, Pres. & CEO
Bus: *Mfr. & sales of handles spouts, outlets & inlets for faucets.*

Tel: (847) 803-5000
Fax: (847) 803-4499

%FO: 100

● **GIVAUDAN, S.A.**
5 Chemin de la Parfumerie, Geneve, CH-1214 Vernier, Switzerland
CEO: Gilles Andrier, CEO
Bus: *Flavors and fragrances manufacturer.*

Tel: 41-22-780-9111
Fax: 41-22-780-9150
www.givaudan.com

Rev: $2,368
Emp: 5,901

NAICS: 311942, 325620

GIVAUDAN CORP.
4705 US Hwy. 92 East, Lakeland, Florida 33801
CEO: Mike Taylor, Mgr.
Bus: *Mfr. and sales of flavors and fragrances.*

Tel: (863) 665-1040
Fax: (863) 665-2273

%FO: 100

GIVAUDAN CORPORATION
9500 Sam Neace Dr., Florence, Kentucky 41042
CEO: Mark Marasch, Mgr.
Bus: *Mfr. and sales of flavors and fragrances.*

Tel: (859) 746-5900
Fax: (859) 746-5930

%FO: 100

GIVAUDAN FLAVORS CORP.
231 Rock Industrial Dr., Bridgeton, Missouri 63044
CEO: Philip Hill, CEO
Bus: *Mfr. of food preparations.*

Tel: (314) 291-5444
Fax: (314) 291-3289

Emp: 3

GIVAUDAN FLAVORS CORP.
110 E. 69th St., Cincinnati, Ohio 45216
CEO: Tony Bowing, Mgr.
Bus: *Mfr. of flavor extracts & syrup.*

Tel: (513) 948-8000
Fax: (513) 948-5637

GIVAUDAN FLAVORS CORP.
63 Boardman Rd., New Milford, Connecticut 06776
CEO: Bruce Vibbert, Principal
Bus: *Mfr. and sales of flavors and fragrances.*

Tel: (860) 210-5300
Fax: (860) 210-5190

%FO: 100

GIVAUDAN FLAVORS CORP.
1 Merry Lane, East Hanover, New Jersey 07936
CEO: Joseph Fabbri, Mgr.
Bus: *Mfr. of industrial organic chemicals.*

Tel: (973) 386-9800
Fax: (973) 428-6312

GIVAUDAN FLAVORS CORP.
1199 Edison Dr., Cincinnati, Ohio 45216
CEO: Errol G. W. Stafford, Chmn.
Bus: *Mfr. and sales of flavors.*

Tel: (513) 948-8000
Fax: (513) 948-5637

%FO: 100
Emp: 1,350

GIVAUDAN FRAGRANCES CORP.
1775 Windsor Rd., Teaneck, New Jersey 07666
CEO: Errol Stafford, Mgr.
Bus: *Fragrances manufacture and sale.*

Tel: (201) 833-7500
Fax: (201) 833-8165

%FO: 100

GIVAUDAN FRAGRANCES CORP.
40 West 57th St., 11/F, New York, New York 10019
CEO: Art Alvarado, Mgr.   Tel: (212) 649-8800
Bus: *Mfr. of fragrances & flavors.*   Fax: (212) 649-8899

GIVAUDAN FRAGRANCES CORP.
International Trade Center, 300 Waterloo Valley Rd., Mount Olive, New Jersey 07828
CEO: John Vernieri, Mgr.   Tel: (973) 448-6500   %FO: 100
Bus: *Fragrance production.*   Fax: (973) 448-6517

NTERNATIONAL BIOFLAVORS, INC.
1730 Executive Dr., Oconomowoc, Wisconsin 53066
CEO: Jeffrey G. Farnham, Pres.   Tel: (262) 569-6200
Bus: *Mfr. of food flavorings.*   Fax: (262) 569-6202   Emp: 45

- **GLENCORE INTERNATIONAL AG**
Baarermattstr. 3, CH-6341 Zug, Switzerland
CEO: Ivan Glasenberg, CEO   Tel: 41-41-709-2000   Rev: $54,700
Bus: *Mining, smelting and refining.*   Fax: 41-41-709-3000   Emp: 3,000
                                                              www.glencore.com
  NAICS: 423510, 424720

  COLUMBIA FALLS ALUMINUM COMPANY
  2000 Aluminum Dr., Columbia Falls, Montana 59912
  CEO: Steve Knight, VP   Tel: (406) 892-8400   %FO: 100
  Bus: *Aluminum manufacture.*   Fax: (406) 892-8210

  GLENCORE COMMODITIES
  301 Tresser Blvd., 14/F, Stamford, Connecticut 06901
  CEO: Tel: (203) 328-4900
  Bus: *Commodity contracts brokers & dealers*   Fax:

  GLENCORE LTD.
  681 Anderson Dr., Pittsburgh, Pennsylvania 15220
  CEO: Bob Lincy, Mgr.   Tel: (412) 921-4800
  Bus: *Petroleum products*   Fax:

  GLENCORE LTD.
  2901 Grande Ave., Ste. E, PO Box 806, Los Olivos, California 93441
  CEO: Robert Reif, Mgr.   Tel: (805) 686-8440
  Bus: *Petroleum products*   Fax:

- **GMC SOFTWARE AG**
Postplatz 12, CH-9050 Appenell, Switzerland
CEO: Rene Mueller, CEO   Tel: 41-71-787-8530   Rev: $12
Bus: *Software manufacture and services.*   Fax: 41-71-787-8541   Emp: 120
                                                              www.gmc.net
  NAICS: 334611, 541511
  GMC SOFTWARE TECHNOLOGY, INC.
  419 Hollywood Ave., Hampton, Virginia 23661
  CEO: Adam Randolph   Tel: (800) 250-1850   %FO: 100
  Bus: *Software manufacture and services.*   Fax: (800) 250-1850

GMC SOFTWARE TECHNOLOGY, INC.
913 L St., Davis, California 95616
CEO: Brad Cecil
Bus: *Software manufacture and services.*

Tel: (530) 231-2911
Fax: (530) 231-2911

%FO: 100

GMC SOFTWARE TECHNOLOGY, INC.
294 Longview Lane, Kennett Square, Pennsylvania 19348
CEO: William McMillan
Bus: *Software manufacture and services.*

Tel: (800) 250-1850
Fax: (800) 250-1850

%FO: 100

GMC SOFTWARE TECHNOLOGY, INC.
529 Main St., Ste. 223, Charlestown, Massachusetts 02129
CEO: Hal Morrow, Pres.
Bus: *Software manufacture and services.*

Tel: (781) 356-7000
Fax: (781) 356-8585

%FO: 100

GMC SOFTWARE TECHNOLOGY, INC.
115 North 25th St., Newark, Ohio 43055
CEO: Dave Ridenbaugh, VP
Bus: *Software manufacture and services.*

Tel: (740) 344-1537
Fax: (740) 344-1537

%FO: 100

● **HABASIT AG**
Romerstrasse 1, CH-4153 Reinach-Basel, Switzerland
CEO: Giovanni Volpi, Pres.
Bus: *Mfr./distribution of power transmission and conveyor belts.*
NAICS: 326220, 332618, 335311

Tel: 41-61-715- 1515
Fax: 41-61-715-1555
www.habasit.com

Rev: $450
Emp: 2,224

HABASIT ABT INC.
150 Industrial Park Rd., Middletown, Connecticut 06457
CEO: Harry Cardillo, Pres.
Bus: *Mfr./sales of power transmission and conveyor belts.*

Tel: (860) 632-2211
Fax: (860) 632-1710

%FO: 100
Emp: 140

HABASIT BELTING INC.
1400 Clinton St., Buffalo, New York 14206
CEO: Pat Solomon, Mgr.
Bus: *Mfr./distribution of power transmission and conveyor belts.*

Tel: (716) 824-8484
Fax: (716) 827-0375

%FO: 100
Emp: 85

HABASIT BELTING INCORPORATED
305 Satellite Blvd., PO Box 80507, Suwannee, Georgia 30024
CEO: Harry Cardillo, Pres.
Bus: *Sales/distribution of power transmission and conveyor belts.*

Tel: (678) 288-3600
Fax: (678) 288-3651

%FO: 100
Emp: 270

● **HANRO LTD.**
Hauptstr. 17, CH-6840 Gotzis, Switzerland
CEO: Erhard F. Grossnigg, Gen. Mgr.
Bus: *Mfr. of sleepwear and underwear.*

NAICS: 315192

Tel: 43-5523-90-5050
Fax: 43-5523-90-5056-062
www.hanro.com

Emp: 110

HANRO USA, INC.
40 East 34th St., Ste. 207, New York, New York 10016
CEO: Cindy Kelly, Pres. & CEO   Tel: (212) 532-3320   %FO: 100
Bus: *Distributor underwear, sleepwear.*   Fax: (212) 685-4823

● **HERMANN BUHLER AG**
Spinnerei Spinning Mill, CH-8482 Sennhof Winterthur, Switzerland
CEO: Moreno Zanin, Sales Dir.   Tel: 41-52-234-0404
Bus: *Spinning mill for high quality yarns.*   Fax: 41-52-234-0494   Emp: 265
                                        www.buhleryarn.com
NAICS: 313111, 313113

    BUHLER QUALITY YARNS CORP.
    1881 Athens Hwy., PO Box 506, Jefferson, Georgia 30549
    CEO: Werner Bieri, Pres.   Tel: (706) 367-9834   %FO: 100
    Bus: *Spinning mill for high quality yarns.*   Fax: (706) 367-9837   Emp: 120

● **HOLCIM LTD.**
Zurchenstr. 156, St. Gallen, CH-8645 Jona, Switzerland
CEO: Markus Akermann, CEO & Mng. Dir.   Tel: 41-58-858-8600   Rev: $10,143
Bus: *Mfr. cement and building materials.*   Fax: 41-58-858-8609   Emp: 48,220
                                        www.holcim.com
NAICS: 212311, 212312, 212319, 212321, 327310, 327320, 327410

    AGGREGATE INDUSTRIES MANAGEMENT INC.
    13900 Piney Meetinghouse Rd., Rockville, Maryland 20850
    CEO: Peter Tom, CEO   Tel: (301) 284-3600
    Bus: *Aggregates, concrete & cement.*   Fax: (301) 284-3645

    HOLCIM GROUP SUPPORT
    6100 Blue Lagoon Dr., Ste. 250, Miami, Florida 33126
    CEO: Charles Bester, Dir.   Tel: (305) 263-7002
    Bus: *Industrial machinery & equipment.*   Fax: (305) 265-8040   Emp: 18

    HOLCIM US INC.
    6211 North Ann Arbor Rd., Dundee, Michigan 48131
    CEO: Patrick Dolberg, Pres. & CEO   Tel: (734) 529-2411   %FO: 100
    Bus: *Mfr./supplier cement, aggregates &*   Fax: (734) 529-5268   Emp: 2,389
      concrete.

    ST. LAWRENCE CEMENT COMPANY
    3 Columbia Circle, Albany, New York 12203
    CEO: Dennis Skidmore, VP   Tel: (518) 452-3563   %FO: 100
    Bus: *Mfr./supplier cement. (JV with Holderbank &*   Fax: (518) 452-3045   Emp: 2,000
      St. Lawrence Cement, Canada)

● **HUBER & SUHNER AG**
Degerscheimerstr.14, Appenzell, CH-9100 Herisau, Switzerland
CEO: Urs Kaufmann, CEO   Tel: 41-71-353-4111   Rev: $495
Bus: *Communications technology.*   Fax: 41-71-353-4444   Emp: 2,601
                                        www.hubersuhner.com
NAICS: 237130, 331222, 331422, 332618, 334515, 335921, 335931, 335999

CHAMPLAIN CABLE CORP.
175 Hercules Dr., Colchester, Vermont 05446
CEO: Richard Hall   Tel: (802) 654-4200
Bus: *Mfr. of cable & wire.*   Fax: (802) 654-4224

HUBER & SUHNER INC.
19 Thomas Dr., Essex Junction, Vermont 05452
CEO: Ian Shergold, Pres. & CEO   Tel: (802) 878-0555   %FO: 100
Bus: *Sales/distribution of microwave products* Fax: (802) 878-9880   Emp: 125
and specialty insulated cables.

HUBER & SUHNER INC.
10620 E. June St., Mesa, Arizona 85207
CEO: Aread Takacs, Mgr.   Tel: (480) 807-4353
Bus: *Mfr. Electronic parts & equipment*   Fax:

HUBER & SUHNER INC.
500 Park Blvd., Ste. 740, Itasca, Illinois 60143
CEO: Ian Shergold, Mgr.   Tel: (630) 250-0100   %FO: 100
Bus: *Sales/distribution of microwave products* Fax: (630) 250-0460
and specialty insulated cables.

● **INFICON HOLDING AG**
Hintergasse 15 B, Bad Ragaz, CH-7310 St. Gallen, Switzerland
CEO: Lukas Winkler, CEO   Tel: 41-81-300-4980   Rev: $188
Bus: *Mfr. instrumentation for semiconductor analysis,* Fax: 41-81-300-4988   Emp: 729
control, leak detection & plasma cleaning,   www.inficon.com
vacuum coatings, a/c & refrigeration & industrial
NAICS: 333295, 334513, 511210

INFICON USA INC.
Two Technology Place, East Syracuse, New York 13057
CEO: Steven Tiso, Sales Mgr.   Tel: (315) 434-1100   %FO: 100
Bus: *Mfr. instrumentation for monitoring,*   Fax: (315) 437-3803   Emp: 700
analysis, control, leak detection & plasma
cleaning in the semiconductor, vacuum
coatings, air conditioning/refrigeration &
industrial markets.

● **INFRANOR INTER AG**
Schaffhauserstr. 418, CH-8050 Zurich, Switzerland
CEO: Martin Bolsterli, CEO   Tel: 41-44-307-4500   Rev: $68
Bus: *Mfr./service systems, motors and industrial* Fax: 45-44-307-4510   Emp: 284
equipment.   www.infranor.com
NAICS: 335312

INFRANOR INC
45 Great Hill Rd., PO Box 1307, Naugatuck, Connecticut 06770
CEO: John L. Carbone, Pres.   Tel: (203) 729-8258   %FO: 100
Bus: *Mfr./service systems, motors and industrial* Fax: (203) 729-6969
equipment.

INFRANOR INC
1222 Hazlett Rd., Pittsburgh, Pennsylvania 15237
CEO: John Carbone, Mgr.
Bus: *Mfr./service systems, motors and industrial equipment.*
Tel: (412) 369-3500
Fax: (412) 369-4280
%FO: 100

● **ISOTIS SA**
Rue de Sébeillon 1, CH-1004 Lausanne, Switzerland
CEO: Pieter Wolters, CEO
Bus: *Develops and manufactures natural and synthetic bone graft materials.*
NAICS: 325411, 325414, 339112
Tel: 41-21-620-6000
Fax: 41-21-620-6060
www.isotis.com
Rev: $4
Emp: 150

ISOTIS ORTHOBIOLOGICS INC.
2 Goodyear, Irvine, California 92618
CEO: David Campagnari, VP
Bus: *Synthetic bone graft materials manufacture.*
Tel: (949) 595-8710
Fax: (949) 595-8711
%FO: 100

● **JET AVIATION MANAGEMENT AG**
Zollikerstrasse 228, PO Box 586, CH-8034 Zurich, Switzerland
CEO: Heinz Kohli, CEO
Bus: *Engaged in leasing chartered jets worldwide.*
NAICS: 481211, 481219
Tel: 41-58-158-8888
Fax: 41-58-158-8889
www.jetaviation.com
Rev: $520
Emp: 3,800

JET AVIATION INC.
7240 Hayvenhurst Ave., Ste. 248, Van Nuys, California 91406
CEO: Stergios D. Rapis, CEO
Bus: *Engaged in leasing corporate and private jets and helicopters.*
Tel: (818) 843-8400
Fax: (818) 843-6606
%FO: 100
Emp: 12

JET AVIATION INC.
1515 Perimeter Rd., West Palm Beach, Florida 33406
CEO: Thomas Hirschmann, Pres.
Bus: *Engaged in aircraft charter, management and flight support.*
Tel: (561) 233-7250
Fax: (561) 233-7279
%FO: 100
Emp: 4,000

JET AVIATION INC.
111 Charles A. Lindbergh Dr., Teterboro Airport, Teterboro, New Jersey 07608
CEO: Theo Staub, COO
Bus: *Engaged in aircraft charter, management and flight support.*
Tel: (201) 462-4026
Fax: (201) 462-4009
%FO: 100
Emp: 790

JET AVIATION INC.
116 Kestrel Dr., Spring Branch, Texas 78070
CEO: Michael Girts, Mgr.
Bus: *Engaged in leasing corporate and private jets and helicopters.*
Tel: (830) 438-7486
Fax: (830) 438-7811
%FO: 100
Emp: 20

JET AVIATION INC.
5200 West 63rd St., Bldg. A, Chicago, Illinois 60638
CEO: Jim Short, Mgr.
Bus: *Engaged in leasing corporate and private jets and helicopters.*
Tel: (773) 581-6575
Fax: (773) 581-2635
%FO: 100
Emp: 20

JET AVIATION INC.
7363 Cedar Springs, Love Field, Dallas, Texas 75235
CEO: Hames Kelly, Principal
Bus: *Engaged in leasing corporate and private jets and helicopters.*
Tel: (214) 350-8523
Fax: (214) 352-4678
%FO: 100
Emp: 70

JET AVIATION, INC.
380 Hanscom Dr., Hanscom Field, Bedford, Massachusetts 01730
CEO: Frank Giglio, Mgr.
Bus: *Engaged in leasing corporate and private jets and helicopters.*
Tel: (781) 274-0512
Fax: (781) 274-7916
%FO: 100
Emp: 60

● **JT INTERNATIONAL SA**
14 Chemin Rieu, CH-1211 Geneva 17, Switzerland
CEO: Pierre de Labouchere, CEO
Bus: *Tobacco and cigarette sales.*
Tel: 41-22-7030-111
Fax: 41-22-3472-907
www.jti.com
Rev: $3,943
Emp: 12,000

NAICS: 312229

JT INTERNATIONAL USA INC.
910 Sylvan Ave., Englewood Cliffs, New Jersey 07632
CEO: Jim Lane, Mgr.
Bus: *Tobacco and cigarette import.*
Tel: (201) 871-1210
Fax: (201) 871-1417
%FO: 100

● **JULIUS BAER HOLDING LTD.**
Bahnhofstr. 36, CH-8010 Zurich, Switzerland
CEO: Walter Knabenhans, Pres. & CEO
Bus: *Engaged in securities and investment banking.*
Tel: 41-58-888-1111
Fax: 41-58-888-5517
www.juliusbaer.com
Rev: $1,059
Emp: 1,766

NAICS: 522110, 522190, 522390, 523110, 523120, 523910, 523920, 523930, 523991, 523999, 524210, 525910, 525920, 525990

BANK JULIUS BAER
330 Madison Ave., New York, New York 10017
CEO: Bernard Silko, Mng. Dir.
Bus: *Engaged in private banking.*
Tel: (212) 297-3600
Fax: (212) 557-7839
%FO: 100
Emp: 23

JULIUS BAER INVESTMENT MANAGEMENT
1999 Ave. of the Stars, Ste. 2340, Los Angeles, California 90067
CEO: Roger Wacker, Mgr.
Bus: *Security broker*
Tel: (310) 282-0200
Fax: (310) 282-0213

JULIUS BAER INVESTMENT MANAGEMENT INC.
330 Madison Ave., New York, New York 10017
CEO: Bernard Spilko, Mng. Dir.
Bus: *Engaged in securities and investment banking.*
Tel: (212) 297-3850
Fax: (212) 557-7839
%FO: 100
Emp: 2

JULIUS BAER SECURITIES INC.
330 Madison Ave., New York, New York 10017
CEO: Bernard Spilko, Mng. Dir.
Bus: *Security broker.*
Tel: (212) 297-3800
Fax: (212) 557-7839
Emp: 43

- **KABA HOLDING AG**
Hofwisenstr. 24, CH-8153 Rumlang, Switzerland
CEO: Ulrich Graf, Chmn.
Bus: *Leading technology developers and providers in the field of access management.*
NAICS: 511210

Tel: 41-44-818-9011
Fax: 41-44-818-9018
www.kaba.com

Rev: $843
Emp: 5,900

    KABA BENZING AMERICA, INC.
    3015 North Commerce Pkwy., Miramar, Florida 33025
    CEO: John Edwards, Pres. & Gen. Mgr.
    Bus: *Time and labor management systems.*

Tel: (954) 416-1720
Fax: (954) 416-1721

%FO: 100

- **KUDELSKI SA**
Route de Geneve 22, Cheseaux-sur-Lausanne, CH-1033 Vaud, Switzerland
CEO: Andre Kudelski, Chmn. & CEO
Bus: *Mfr. digital TV access systems.*
NAICS: 334119, 334220

Tel: 41-21-732-0101
Fax: 41-21-732-0100
www.kudelski.com

Rev: $332
Emp: 1,400

    NAGRA USA INC.
    McLemore Way, Franklin, Tennessee 37064
    CEO: Virginio Trevisan, Pres.
    Bus: *Mfr./sales digital TV access systems.*

Tel: (615) 790-4165
Fax:

%FO: 100

    NAGRASTAR LLC
    90 Inverness Circle East, Englewood, Colorado 80112
    CEO: Alan Guggenheim, member
    Bus: *Mfr./sales digital TV access systems.*

Tel: (303) 706-5700
Fax: (303) 706-5719

%FO: 100
Emp: 41

    NAGRAVISION
    2041 Rosecrans Ave., El Segundo, California 90245
    CEO: Virginia Trevisan, Principal
    Bus: *Mfr./sales digital TV access systems.*

Tel: (310) 335-5225
Fax: (310) 335-5227

%FO: 100
Emp: 10

- **KUEHNE & NAGEL INTERNATIONAL AG**
Kuhne & Nagel House, Schindellegi, CH-8834 Schwyz, Switzerland
CEO: Klaus Herms, CEO
Bus: *Freight forwarding and logistics services.*
NAICS: 488510, 493110, 524210, 541614

Tel: 41-1-786-9511
Fax: 41-1-786-9595
www.kuehne-nagel.com

Rev: $8,058
Emp: 23,000

    KUEHNE & NAGEL INTERNATIONAL
    10 Exchange Place, Ste. 19, Jersey City, New Jersey 07302
    CEO: Rolf Altorfer
    Bus: *Freight forwarding and logistics services.*

Tel: (201) 413-5500
Fax: (201) 413-5777

%FO: 100

    KUEHNE & NAGEL LOGISTICS, INC.
    1 Corporate Dr., Windsor Locks, Connecticut 06096
    CEO: Marion Babich
    Bus: *Freight forwarding and logistics services.*

Tel: (860) 627-6606
Fax: (860) 627-6042

%FO: 100

KUEHNE & NAGEL LOGISTICS, INC.
1810 S. Lynhurst Dr., Ste. A, Indianapolis, Indiana 46241
CEO: Charlie Michaels
Bus: *Freight forwarding and logistics services.*
Tel: (317) 227-0100
Fax: (317) 227-0100
%FO: 100

KUEHNE & NAGEL LOGISTICS, INC.
1470 Brummel Ave., Elk Grove Village, Illinois 60007
CEO: Janet Barber
Bus: *Freight forwarding and logistics services.*
Tel: (847) 228-8500
Fax: (847) 439-7696
%FO: 100

KUEHNE & NAGEL LOGISTICS, INC.
4202 East Elwood St., Ste. 23, Phoenix, Arizona 85040
CEO: Richard Peterson
Bus: *Freight forwarding and logistics services.*
Tel: (602) 437-8108
Fax: (602) 437-4816
%FO: 100

KUEHNE & NAGEL LOGISTICS, INC.
15700 Int'l. Plaza, Ste. 100, Houston, Texas 77032
CEO: Vicky McLaughlin
Bus: *Freight forwarding and logistics services.*
Tel: (281) 449-8888
Fax: (281) 449-9630
%FO: 100

KUEHNE & NAGEL LOGISTICS, INC.
88 Black Falcon Ave., Boston, Massachusetts 02210
CEO: John Franse
Bus: *Freight forwarding and logistics services.*
Tel: (617) 261-8000
Fax: (617) 261-8000
%FO: 100

● **KUONI TRAVEL HOLDING LTD.**
Neue Hard 7, CH-8010 Zurich, Switzerland
CEO: Armin Meier, CEO
Bus: *Leisure travel firm.*
Tel: 41-44-277-4444
Fax: 41-44-271-5282
www.kuoni.com
Rev: $2,653
Emp: 7,700

NAICS: 561510, 561520, 561599

INTRAV
11969 Westline Industrial Dr., St. Louis, Missouri 63146-3220
CEO: David Dreier, CEO
Bus: *Engaged in leisure travel services.*
Tel: (314) 655-6700
Fax: (314) 655-6670
%FO: 100

● **LAMPRECHT TRANSPORT AG**
Peter-Merian Str.48, CH-4002 Basel, Switzerland
CEO: Thomas A. Lamprecht, Mng. Dir.
Bus: *Freight forwarding and logistics services.*
Tel: 41-61-284-7474
Fax: 41-61-284-7444
www.lamprecht.ch
Emp: 300

NAICS: 488510

AMERICAN LAMPRECHT TRANSPORT INC.
Ridgeview Centre Dr., Ste. 197B, Duncan, South Carolina 29334
CEO: Jean G. Dill, VP
Bus: *Air/ocean, import/export forwarding and customhouse brokers.*
Tel: (864) 433-8585
Fax: (864) 433-8555
%FO: 100

AMERICAN LAMPRECHT TRANSPORT INC.
700 Rockaway Turnpike, Lawrence, New York 11559
CEO: Thomas Lamprecht, Chmn.   Tel: (516) 239-6200   %FO: 100
Bus: *Air/ocean, import/export forwarding and*   Fax: (516) 239-0844   Emp: 25
    custom house brokerage services.

AMERICAN LAMPRECHT TRANSPORT INC.
2218 Landmeier Rd., Elk Grove Village, Chicago, Illinois 60007
CEO: Jean G. Dill   Tel: (847) 364-0555   %FO: 100
Bus: *Air/ocean, import/export forwarding and*   Fax: (847) 364-9350
    customhouse brokers.

AMERICAN LAMPRECHT TRANSPORT INC.
5757 West Century Blvd., Ste. 480, Los Angeles, California 90045
CEO: John Bruckner, Gen. Mgr.   Tel: (310) 645-4736   %FO: 100
Bus: *Air/ocean, import/export forwarding and*   Fax: (310) 645-5985
    customhouse brokers.

● **LEICA GEOSYSTEMS HOLDINGS AG**
Heinrich-Wild-Str., St. Gallen, CH-9435 Heerbrugg, Switzerland
CEO: Hans Hess, Pres. & CEO   Tel: 41-71-727-3131   Rev: $538
Bus: *Develop, manufacture and sales of microscopes*   Fax: 41-71-727-4674   Emp: 2,461
    and optoelectronic sensors, surveying instrument   www.leica-geosystems.com
    and photogrammetic equipment.
NAICS: 334519

LEICA GEOSYSTEMS HDS LLC
4550 Norris Canyon Rd., San Ramon, California 94583
CEO: Geoff Jacobs, SVP   Tel: (925) 790-2300   %FO: 100
Bus: *Mfr. of electronic test & measurement*   Fax: (925) 790-2309
    instruments.

LEICA GEOSYSTEMS INC.
8201 East 34th St., Ste. 804, Wichita, Kansas 67226
CEO: Denny Deegan, Mgr.   Tel: (316) 634-0844   %FO: 100
Bus: *Sales of microscopes and optoelectronic*   Fax:
    sensors, surveying instrument and
    photogrammetic equipment.

LEICA GEOSYSTEMS INC.
5051 Peachtree Corners Circle, Ste. 250, Norcross, Georgia 30092
CEO: Robert Williams, Pres.   Tel: (770) 326-9500   %FO: 100
Bus: *Sales of microscopes and optoelectronic*   Fax: (770) 447-0710   Emp: 142
    sensors, surveying instrument and
    photogrammetic equipment.

LEICA GEOSYSTEMS INC.
37459 Schoolcraft Rd., Livonia, Michigan 48150
CEO: Martin Nixx, Pres.   Tel: (734) 464-2221   %FO: 100
Bus: *Sales of microscopes and optoelectronic*   Fax: (734) 464-1903
    sensors, surveying instrument and
    photogrammetic equipment.

• LIEBHERR-INTERNATIONAL AG

Rue de L'industrie 45, Fribourg, CH-1630 Bulle, Switzerland

CEO: Willy Liebherr, Chmn.

Bus: *Mfr. industrial machinery, cranes, machine tools, assembly lines, automation, and aviation*

NAICS: 333120, 333131, 333513, 333611, 333923, 333999

Tel: 41-26-913-3111
Fax: 41-26-912-1240
www.liebherr.com

Rev: $123
Emp: 600

LIEBHERR AEROSPACE SALINE CO.

1465 Woodland Dr., Saline, Michigan 48176

CEO: Klaus Singler

Bus: *Mfr. aviation machinery.*

Tel: (734) 429-7225
Fax: (734) 429-2294

LIEBHERR AUTOMATION SYSTEMS CO.

1465 Woodland Dr., Saline, Michigan 48176

CEO: Klaus Singler, VP

Bus: *Mfr. industrial machinery.*

Tel: (734) 429-7225
Fax: (734) 429-2294

%FO: 100

LIEBHERR CONSTRUCTION EQUIPMENT COMPANY

4100 Chestnut Ave., Newport News, Virginia 23605

CEO: Ronald E. Jacobson, Pres.

Bus: *Mfr. construction machinery and concrete mixes.*

Tel: (757) 245-5251
Fax: (757) 928-8701

%FO: 100
Emp: 350

LIEBHERR CRANES

4100 Chestnut Ave., Newport News, Virginia 23605

CEO: Ronald Jacobson, Pres.

Bus: *Construction & mining machinery*

Tel: (757) 245-5251
Fax: (757) 928-8700

Emp: 33

LIEBHERR GEAR TECHNOLOGY CO.

1465 Woodland Dr., Saline, Michigan 48176

CEO: Peter Kozma, Pres.

Bus: *Mfr. industrial machinery.*

Tel: (734) 429-7225
Fax: (734) 429-2294

%FO: 100
Emp: 60

LIEBHERR MINING EQUIPMENT CO.

4100 Chestnut Ave., Newport News, Virginia 23605

CEO: Ronald E. Jacobson, Pres.

Bus: *Mfr. industrial machinery.*

Tel: (757) 245-5251
Fax: (757) 928-8700

%FO: 100
Emp: 350

• LOGITECH INTERNATIONAL SA

Moulin du Choc, CH-1122 Romanel-sur-Morges, Switzerland

CEO: Guerrino De Luca, Pres. & CEO

Bus: *Mfr. digital video cameras, keyboards, trackballs, 3-D game controllers and joysticks.*

NAICS: 334119

Tel: 41-21-863-5111
Fax: 41-21-863-5311
www.logitech.com

Rev: $1,483
Emp: 6,898

LOGITECH INC.

6505 Kaiser Dr., Fremont, California 94555

CEO: Guerrino De Luca, VP

Bus: *Sales/distribution of digital video cameras, keyboards, trackballs, 3-D game controllers and joysticks.*

Tel: (510) 795-8500
Fax: (510) 792-8901

%FO: 100

LOGITECH INC.
1499 SE Tech Center Dr., Ste. 350, Vancouver, Washington 98683
CEO: Mitchell Phillipi   Tel: (360) 896-2000   %FO: 100
Bus: *Sales/distribution of digital video cameras,*   Fax: (360) 896-2020
keyboards, trackballs, 3-D game controllers
and joysticks.

• **LONZA GROUP LTD.**
Muenchensteinerstr. 38, CH-4002 Basel, Switzerland
CEO: Stefan Borgas, CEO   Tel: 41-61-316-8111   Rev: $1,928
Bus: *Chemicals.*   Fax: 41-61-316-9111   Emp: 5,668
                                     www.lonza.com
NAICS: 325211, 325411, 325998, 541710

  LONZA BIOLOGICS, INC.
  101 International Dr., Portsmouth, New Hampshire 03801
  CEO: Stephan Kutzer, Pres.   Tel: (603) 334-6100   %FO: 100
  Bus: *Mfr. of bulk purified therapeutic proteins.*   Fax: (603) 610-4891   Emp: 476

  LONZA INC.
  3500 Trenton Ave., Williamsport, Pennsylvania 17701
  CEO: Howard Wilt, Pres.   Tel: (570) 321-3900   %FO: 100
  Bus: *Mfr./distribution of composite materials.*   Fax: (570) 321-3925

  LONZA INC.
  900 River Rd., Conshohocken, Pennsylvania 19428
  CEO: Charlie Nye, Mgr.   Tel: (610) 292-4300   %FO: 100
  Bus: *Mfr./distribution of composite materials.*   Fax: (610) 292-4380   Emp: 130

  LONZA INC.
  8316 West Route 24, PO Box 105, Mapleton, Illinois 61547
  CEO: Bruce Davey, Mgr.   Tel: (309) 697-7200   %FO: 100
  Bus: *Mfr./distribution of composite materials.*   Fax: (309) 697-7298   Emp: 95

  LONZA INC.
  90 Boroline Rd., Allendale, New Jersey 07401
  CEO: Stephan Kutzer, Pres. & CEO   Tel: (201) 316-9200   %FO: 100
  Bus: *Mfr. of chemicals.*   Fax: (201) 785-9989   Emp: 607

• **MEDELA HOLDING AG**
Lattichstr. 4, CH-6341 Baar, Switzerland
CEO: Carr L. Quackenbush, Pres.   Tel: 41-41-769-5151
Bus: *Breast pumps and accessories manufacture.*   Fax: 41-41-769-5100
                                     www.medela.ch
NAICS: 334510, 339111, 339112, 339113

  MEDELA, INC.
  1101 Corporate Dr., McHenry, Illinois 60050
  CEO: Carr L. Quackenbush, Pres.   Tel: (815) 363-1166   %FO: 100
  Bus: *Breast pumps and accessories manufacture*   Fax: (815) 363-1246   Emp: 300
  and sales.

- **MEDITERRANEAN SHIPPING COMPANY SA**
  40, Avenue Eugene Pittard, CH-1206 Geneva, Switzerland
  CEO: Gianluigi Aponte, Pres.   Tel: 41-22-703-8888   Rev: $1,000
  Bus: *Steamship company.*   Fax: 41-22-703-8787   Emp: 19,000
                                          www.mscgva.ch

  NAICS: 483111

  MEDITERRANEAN SHIPPING COMPANY (USA) INC.
  28045 Clemens Rd., Ste. D, Cleveland, Ohio 44145
  CEO: Thomas Sherry, Mgr.   Tel: (480) 871-6335   %FO: 100
  Bus: *Steamship agents.*   Fax: (480) 971-1155   Emp: 12

  MEDITERRANEAN SHIPPING COMPANY (USA) INC.
  100 Terminal St., 2/F, Boston, Massachusetts 02129
  CEO: Bill Eldridge, Mgr.   Tel: (617) 241-3710   %FO: 100
  Bus: *Steamship agents.*   Fax: (617) 241-3710   Emp: 18

  MEDITERRANEAN SHIPPING COMPANY (USA) INC.
  1000 North Fleet St., Elizabeth, New Jersey 07201
  CEO: Richard Rizzo, Mgr.   Tel: (908) 353-3511   %FO: 100
  Bus: *Steamship agents.*   Fax:

  MEDITERRANEAN SHIPPING COMPANY (USA) INC.
  550 Long Point Rd., Mount Pleasant, South Carolina 29464
  CEO: Jerry Baldwin, Mgr.   Tel: (843) 971-4100   %FO: 100
  Bus: *Steamship agents.*   Fax: (843) 971-4100   Emp: 200

  MEDITERRANEAN SHIPPING COMPANY (USA) INC.
  420 Fifth Ave., 8/F, New York, New York 10018
  CEO: Nicola Arena, Pres.   Tel: (212) 764-4800   %FO: 100
  Bus: *Steamship agents.*   Fax: (212) 764-8592   Emp: 700

  MEDITERRANEAN SHIPPING COMPANY (USA) INC.
  1343 Terrell Mill Rd. SE, Marietta, Georgia 30067
  CEO: Harry Hagens, Sales Mgr.   Tel: (770) 953-0037   %FO: 100
  Bus: *Steamship agents.*   Fax: (770) 953-0037

  MEDITERRANEAN SHIPPING COMPANY (USA) INC.
  10050 NW Fwy., Ste. 300, Houston, Texas 77092
  CEO: Darlene Ruiz, Dir.   Tel: (713) 681-8880   %FO: 100
  Bus: *Steamship agents.*   Fax: Emp: 90

  MEDITERRANEAN SHIPPING COMPANY (USA) INC.
  8200 NW 52nd. Terr., Ste. 301, Miami, Florida 33166
  CEO: Jose Moreno, Mgr.   Tel: (305) 477-9277   %FO: 100
  Bus: *Steamship agents.*   Fax: Emp: 15

  MEDITERRANEAN SHIPPING COMPANY (USA) INC.
  4121 Rose Lake Dr., Ste. C, Charlotte, North Carolina 28217
  CEO: Paul Hargett, Mgr.   Tel: (704) 357-8000   %FO: 100
  Bus: *Steamship agents.*   Fax: Emp: 5

MEDITERRANEAN SHIPPING COMPANY (USA) INC.
300 East Main St., Ste. 1180, Norfolk, Virginia 23510
CEO: Vito Piriano   Tel: (757) 625-0132   %FO: 100
Bus: *Steamship agents.*   Fax: Emp: 10

MEDITERRANEAN SHIPPING COMPANY (USA) INC.
10400 West Higgins Rd., Des Plaines, Illinois 60018
CEO: Patrick McKeen, Mgr.   Tel: (847) 296-5151   %FO: 100
Bus: *Steamship agents.*   Fax: (847) 296-5151   Emp: 50

● **METTLER-TOLEDO INTERNATIONAL INC.**
Im Langacher, Greifensee, CH-8606 Zurich, Switzerland
CEO: Robert F. Spoerry, Pres. & CEO   Tel: 41-1-944-2211   Rev: $1,405
Bus: *Mfr. precision weighing instruments used in* Fax: 41-1-944-3060   Emp: 8,700
    industrial, laboratory and retail food markets. www.mt.com
NAICS: 333997, 334513, 334515, 334516

    EXACT EQUIPMENT CORPORATION
    20 N. Pennsylvania Ave., Morrisville, Pennsylvania 19067
    CEO: Tom Maurer   Tel: (215) 295-2000   %FO: 100
    Bus: *Mfr. high-speed automatic wrapper*   Fax: (215) 295-2000
        machines.

    HI-SPEED CHECKWEIGHER CO. INC.
    5 Barr Rd., Ithaca, New York 14850
    CEO: Jeff Adams   Tel: (607) 257-6000   %FO: 100
    Bus: *Mfr. high-speed process weigh machines.* Fax: (607) 257-5232

    METTLER-TOLEDO AUTOCHEM INC.
    7075 Samuel Morse Dr., Columbia, Maryland 21046
    CEO: Henry Dupina   Tel: (410) 910-8100   %FO: 100
    Bus: *Mfr. automated lab reactor equipment.*   Fax: (410) 910-8100

    METTLER-TOLEDO INC.
    1900 Polaris Pkwy., Columbus, Ohio 43240
    CEO: Todd Manifold, VP   Tel: (614) 438-4511   %FO: 100
    Bus: *Sales/distribution of precision weighing* Fax: (614) 438-4900
        instruments used in industrial, laboratory
        and retail food markets.

    METTLER-TOLEDO INGOLD, INC.
    36 Middlesex Turnpike, Bedford, Massachusetts 01730
    CEO: Jeffrey Vancura   Tel: (781) 301-8800   %FO: 100
    Bus: *Liquid process analysis equipment sales.* Fax: (781) 301-8800

    SAFELINE INC.
    6005 Benjamin Rd., Tampa, Florida 33634
    CEO: Viggo Nielsen   Tel: (813) 889-9500   %FO: 100
    Bus: *Mfr. metal detection systems.*   Fax: (813) 889-9500

● **MICRONAS SEMICONDUCTOR HOLDING AG**
Technopark, Technoparkstrasse 1, CH-8005 Zurich, Switzerland
CEO: Wolfgang Kalsbach, CEO   Tel: 41-1-445-3960   Rev: $851
Bus: *Develops microchips, integrated circuits (ICs) and*   Fax: 41-1-445-3961   Emp: 1,970
     sensors.   www.micronas.com
NAICS: 334413

     MICRONAS SEMICONDUCTORS INC.
     8954 Rio San Diego Dr., Ste. 106, San Diego, California 92108-1659
     CEO: Camille Madison, Pres.   Tel: (619) 683-5500   %FO: 100
     Bus: *Mfr. semiconductors.*   Fax: (619) 683-3161

     MICRONAS SEMICONDUCTORS INC.
     26877 Northwestern Highway, Ste. 417, Southfiled, Michigan 48034
     CEO: Brian McGibbon   Tel: (248) 357-5886   %FO: 100
     Bus: *Mfr. semiconductors.*   Fax: (248) 357-5891

● **MONTRES ROLEX SA**
Rue Francois-Dussaud 3, CH-1211 Geneva 24, Switzerland
CEO: Patrick Heiniger, CEO & Mng. Dir.   Tel: 41-22-308-2200
Bus: *Mfr. of watches.*   Fax: 41-22-300-2255
     www.rolex.com

NAICS: 334518

     ROLEX WATCH, INC.
     Rolex Bldg., 665 Fifth Ave., New York, New York 10022
     CEO: Walter Fischer, Pres.   Tel: (212) 758-7700   %FO: 100
     Bus: *Import/sales/service of watches.*   Fax: (212) 371-0371   Emp: 300

● **MOTURIS LTD.**
Flughstrasse 55, CH-8152 Glattbrugg, Switzerland
CEO: Ernst Dahler, Pres.   Tel: 41-1-808-7000
Bus: *Rental of motor homes and motorcycles.*   Fax: 41-1-808-7001
     www.moturis.com

NAICS: 532120

     MOTURIS INC.
     1315 North Lake St., Aurora, Illinois 60506
     CEO: Ruedi Meier   Tel: (630) 897-7116   %FO: 100
     Bus: *Rental of motor homes and motorcycles.*   Fax: (630) 897-7129

     MOTURIS INC.
     3901 NW 16th St., Ft. Lauderdale, Florida 33311
     CEO: Neal Klass, Mgr.   Tel: (954) 587-6450   %FO: 100
     Bus: *Rental of motor homes and motorcycles.*   Fax: (954) 587-6452

     MOTURIS INC.
     274 Newburyport Turnpike, Rowley, Massachusetts 01969
     CEO: Martin Stucki, Mgr.   Tel: (978) 887-7336   %FO: 100
     Bus: *Rental of motor homes and motorcycles.*   Fax: (978) 887-7336

MOTURIS INC.
400 West Compton Blvd., Gardena, California 90248
CEO: Heinz Zberg, Mgr.   Tel: (310) 767-5988 %FO: 100
Bus: *Rental of motor homes and motorcycles.* Fax: (310) 767-5980

MOTURIS INC.
5300 Colorado Blvd., Ste. 2, Commerce City, Colorado 80022
CEO: Reto Kunz, Mgr.   Tel: (303) 295-6837 %FO: 100
Bus: *Rental of motor homes and motorcycles.* Fax: (303) 295-6849

MOTURIS INC.
11 Rockland Park Rd., Tappan, New York 10983
CEO: Martin Stucki   Tel: (845) 365-0747 %FO: 100
Bus: *Rental of motor homes and motorcycles.* Fax: (845) 365-9111

• **MOUNT10 HOLDING AG**
Grundstr. 12, Zug, CH-6343 Rotkreuz, Switzerland
CEO: Adrian Knapp, Chmn. & CEO Tel: 41-41-798-3344 Rev: $24
Bus: *Storage software manufacture.* Fax: 41-41-798-3393 Emp: 75
           www.mount10.com
NAICS: 511210

  MOUNT10 SOFTWARE, INC.
  222 North Sepulveda Blvd., Ste. 1800, El Segundo, California 90245
  CEO: Nathan Muthuswamy, Head Of Operations Tel: (800) 323-8863 %FO: 100
  Bus: *Mfr. of software.*   Fax: (323) 843-9425

• **NESTLÉ SA**
Avenue Nestle 55, CH-1800 Vevey Vaud, Switzerland
CEO: Peter Brabeck-Letmathe, Chmn. & CEO Tel: 41-21-924-2111 Rev: $76,660
Bus: *Develop/mfr. foods, beverages, pharmaceuticals* Fax: 41-21-924-4800 Emp: 253,000
  and pet foods.   www.nestle.com
NAICS: 112310, 112910, 114112, 114119, 115111, 115112, 115115, 115116, 115210, 311111, 311119, 311211,
311212, 311221, 311222, 311223, 311225,
    311230, 311311, 311312, 311313, 311320, 311330, 311340, 311411, 311412, 311421, 311422, 311423,
311511, 311512, 311513, 311514,
    311520, 311611, 311612, 311613, 311615, 311711, 311712, 311811, 311812, 311813, 311821, 311822,
311823, 311911, 311919, 311920, 311930,
    311941, 311942, 311991, 311999, 312111, 325131, 325132, 325199, 325311, 325312, 325314, 325320,
325411, 424410, 424420, 424430,
    424440, 424460, 424480, 424490, 424910, 541940, 722310, 722320, 722330, 812910

  DREYER'S GRAND ICE CREAM HOLDINGS, INC.
  5929 College Ave., Oakland, California 94618
  CEO: T. Gary Rogers, Chmn. & CEO Tel: (510) 652-8187
  Bus: *Mfr. of ice cream & frozen dessert* Fax: (510) 450-4592 Emp: 5,979

  NESTLE PURINA PETCARE COMPANY
  Checkerboard Square, St. Louis, Missouri 63164
  CEO: W. Patrick McGinnis, Pres. & CEO Tel: (314) 982-1000
  Bus: *Pet food manufacturer.* Fax: (314) 982-2134

  NESTLE USA INC.
  800 North Brand Blvd., Glendale, California 91203
  CEO: Joseph M. Weller, Chmn. & CEO Tel: (818) 549-6000 %FO: 100
  Bus: *U.S. holding company: food, beverages, pet* Fax: (818) 549-6952 Emp: 21,000
  food and pharmaceuticals.

NESTLE WATERS INC.
777 W. Putnam Ave., Greenwich, Connecticut 06830
CEO: Kim E. Jeffery, Pres. & CEO   Tel: (203) 531-4100
Bus: *Bottled water manufacture and sales.*   Fax: (230) 863-0297

POWERBAR INC.
2150 Shattuck Ave., Berkeley, California 94704
CEO: Jeff Lozito, VP Sales   Tel: (510) 843-1330
Bus: *Mfr. of healthy snack foods*   Fax: (886) 574-6420

● **NOVARTIS INTERNATIONAL AG**
Lichstr. 35, CH-4056 Basel, Switzerland
CEO: Daniel L. Vasella, Chmn. & CEO   Tel: 41-61-324-1111   Rev: $28,247
Bus: *Pharmaceutical company; research/mfr./marketing* Fax: 41-61-324-8001   Emp: 81,392
of healthcare and nutritional products.   www.novartis.com
NAICS: 325411, 325412, 339115

CIBA VISION CORP.
11460 Johns Creek Pkwy., Duluth, Georgia 30097
CEO: Joseph T. Mallof, CEO   Tel: (678) 415-3937
Bus: *Mfr. of eyewear.*   Fax: (678) 415-3001   Emp: 5,479

GERBER LIFE INSURANCE COMPANY
1311 Mamaroneck Ave., White Plains, New York 10605
CEO: Wesley David Protheroe, Pres.   Tel: (914) 272-4000   %FO: 100
Bus: *Life insurance services. Sub. of Gerber*   Fax: (914) 272-4099
products company.

GERBER PRODUCTS COMPANY
200 Kimball Dr., Parsippany, New Jersey 07054
CEO: Kurt T. Schmidt, Pres.   Tel: (973) 503-8000   %FO: 100
Bus: *Mfr./markets baby/children's nutritional*   Fax: (973) 503-8400   Emp: 6,000
products.

IDENIX PHARMACEUTICALS, INC.
60 Hampshire St., Cambridge, Massachusetts 02139
CEO: Jean-Pierre Sommadossi, Chmn. & Pres.   Tel: (617) 995-9800
Bus: *Biopharmaceuticals & biotherapeutics.*   & CEO   Fax: (617) 995-9801
Emp: 125

NOVARTIS CORPORATION
608 Fifth Ave., New York, New York 10020
CEO: Terence A. Barnett, Pres. & CEO   Tel: (212) 307-1122   %FO: 100
Bus: *Corporate administrative & financial*   Fax: (212) 246-0185
services.

NOVARTIS PHARMACEUTICALS CORPORATION
1 Health Plaza, East Hanover, New Jersey 07936
CEO: Paulo Costa, Pres.   Tel: (862) 778-8300   %FO: 100
Bus: *Develop/mfr./market pharmaceuticals.*   Fax: (973) 781-8265   Emp: 7,000

SANDOZ INC.
506 Carnegie Center, Ste. 400, Princeton, New Jersey 08540
CEO: John Sedor, Pres. & CEO   Tel: (609) 627-8500   %FO: 100
Bus: *Mfr./distribution generic pharmaceuticals.*   Fax: (609) 627-8659   Emp: 998

SYNGENTA CORPORATION
1800 Concord Pike, Wilmington, Delaware 19850
CEO: Michael Mack, Chmn. & Pres.
Bus: *Agricultural support activities & products.*
Tel: (302) 425-2000
Fax: (302) 425-2001
Emp: 5,060

SYNGENTA CROP PROTECTION, INC.
410 Swing Rd., Greensboro, North Carolina 27409
CEO: Valdemar Fischer, Pres.
Bus: *Mfr. agricultural chemicals*
Tel: (336) 632-6000
Fax: (336) 632-7353
Emp: 1,456

SYNGENTA SEEDS INC.
7500 Olson Memorial Hwy., Golden Valley, Minnesota 55427
CEO: John Sorenson, Pres. & CEO
Bus: *Agricultural support activities & products.*
Tel: (763) 593-7333
Fax: (763) 593-7218
Emp: 2,060

● **ODYSSEY ASSET MANAGEMENT SYSTEMS**
Case Postale 144, CH-1000 Lausanne 16, Switzerland
CEO: Antoine Duchateau, CEO
Bus: *Technology services to investment management firms*
NAICS: 541511, 541512, 561110, 611420
Tel: 41-21-310-00-00
Fax: 41-21-310-00-99
www.odyssey-group.com
Emp: 450

ODYSSEY ASSET MANAGEMENT SYSTEMS
245 Park Ave., 24/F, New York, New York 10167
CEO: David DeLouya, Gen. Mgr.
Bus: *Technology services to investment management firms*
Tel: (212) 672-1986
Fax: (212) 792-4001
%FO: 100
Emp: 10

● **PAISTE AG**
Kantonstr. 2, Luzern, CH-6207 Nottwil, Switzerland
CEO: Robert Paiste, Co-CEO
Bus: *Percussion accessories manufacture.*
NAICS: 339992
Tel: 41-41-939-3333
Fax: 41-41-939-3366
www.paiste.com

PAISTE AMERICA, INC.
460 Atlas St., Brea, California 92821
CEO: Erik Paiste, CEO
Bus: *Mfr./sales of percussion instruments & accessories.*
Tel: (714) 529-2222
Fax: (714) 671-5869
%FO: 100

● **PANALPINA WORLD TRANSPORT HOLDING**
Viaduktstrasse 42, CH-4002 Basel, Switzerland
CEO: Bruno Sidler, Pres.
Bus: *International forwarding agents.*
NAICS: 488510
Tel: 41-61-226-1111
Fax: 41-61-226-1101
www.panalpina.com
Rev: $5,407
Emp: 13,224

PANALPINA INC.
10 Griffin Way, Chelsea, Massachusetts 02150
CEO: Benno Forster, VP
Bus: *International freight forwarder/custom house broker.*
Tel: (617) 889-0019
Fax: (617) 889-6485
%FO: 100

PANALPINA INC.
22750 Glenn Dr., Sterling, Virginia 20164
CEO: Rainer Wildenhin   Tel: (703) 471-6480   %FO: 100
Bus: *International freight forwarder/custom house* Fax: (703) 471-6480
      broker.

PANALPINA INC.
5540 W. Century Blvd., Los Angeles, California 90045
CEO: Clive Tranter   Tel: (310) 957-4060   %FO: 100
Bus: *International freight forwarder/custom house* Fax: (310) 957-4060
      broker.

PANALPINA INC.
PO Box 45405, Atlanta, Georgia 30320
CEO: Horst R. Baumann, SVP   Tel: (770) 991-9220   %FO: 100
Bus: *International freight forwarder/custom house* Fax: (770) 991-9220   Emp: 1,000
      broker.

PANALPINA INC.
811 S. 192nd St., Seattle, Washington 98148
CEO: Erik Saathoff, VP   Tel: (208) 824-7424   %FO: 100
Bus: *International freight forwarder/custom house* Fax: (208) 824-7424
      broker.

PANALPINA INC.
950 Tower Ln., Ste. 1600, Foster City, California 94404
CEO: David Beatson   Tel: (650) 653-6600   %FO: 100
Bus: *International freight forwarder/custom house* Fax: (650) 653-6735
      broker.

● **PUBLIGROUPE LTD.**
Avenue des Toises 12, CH-1002 Lausanne, Switzerland
CEO: Hans-Peter Rohner, CEO   Tel: 41-21-317-7111   Rev: $1,560
Bus: *Advertising magazine sales.*   Fax: 41-21-317-7555   Emp: 3,675
                                                 www.publigroupe.com

NAICS: 511140, 541613, 541840, 541870, 541890

24/7 REAL MEDIA, INC.
132 W. 31 St., New York, New York 10001
CEO: David J. Moore, Chmn. & CEO   Tel: (212) 231-7100   %FO: 100
Bus: *Interactive marketing and technology.*   Fax: (212) 760-1774   Emp: 325

PUBLICITAS NORTH AMERICA INC.
261 Madison Ave., 7/F, New York, New York 10016
CEO: E. Pricco, CEO & Mng. Dir.   Tel: (212) 599-5057   %FO: 100
Bus: *Advertising magazine sales.*   Fax: (212) 599-8299

● **RESOURCE FINANCE & INVESTMENT**
World Trade Center, 10 Route de L'Aeroport, CH-1215 Geneva, Switzerland
CEO: Philip J. Garrat, CEO   Tel: 41-22-799-0800
Bus: *Mining of precious and base metals, gems, and* Fax: 41-22-799-0801
      minerals.   www.resource-finance.com
NAICS: 212231, 213115

DYNAMEX RESOURCES CORP.
PO Box 501, Portland, Oregon 97207
CEO: Cheryl Wilson, VP
Bus: *Property development for mineral deposits.*

Tel: (503) 227-5228
Fax: (503) 227-0031

%FO: 100

● **RICOLA AG**
PO Box 130, CH-4242 Laufen, Switzerland
CEO: Felix Richterich, Pres.
Bus: *Mfr. of confections.*

Tel: 41-61-765-4121
Fax: 41-61-765-4122
www.ricola.ch

NAICS: 311340

RICOLA USA, INC.
51 Gibraltar Dr., Morris Plains, New Jersey 07950
CEO: Dan Thomas, Pres.
Bus: *Distribution and marketing of Ricola
confectionery products.*

Tel: (201) 984-6811
Fax: (201) 984-6814

%FO: 100
Emp: 18

● **RIETER HOLDING LTD**
Schlosstalstr. 43, Winterthur, CH-8406 Zurich, Switzerland
CEO: Hartmut Reuter, CEO
Bus: *Supplier of systems and services to the textile,
automotive and plastics industries.*

Tel: 41-52-208-7171
Fax: 41-52-208-7060
www.rieter.com

Rev: $2,510
Emp: 13,316

NAICS: 333298, 336360, 336399

MAGEE RIETER AUTOMOTIVE
480 West Fifth St., Bloomsburg, Pennsylvania 17815
CEO: Harry M. Katerman, Pres. & CEO
Bus: *Carpets & rugs*

Tel: (570) 784-4100
Fax: (570) 784-4106

Emp: 700

RIETER AUTOMOTIVE N.A.
38555 Hills Tech Dr., Farmington Hills, Michigan 48331
CEO: David Westgate, Pres. & CEO
Bus: *Automotive parts & accessories*

Tel: (248) 848-0100
Fax: (248) 848-0130

%FO: 100

RIETER CORPORATION
PO Box 4383, Spartanburg, South Carolina 29305
CEO: Ueli Schmid, Pres.
Bus: *Industrial machinery & equipment*

Tel: (864) 582-5466
Fax: (864) 948-5284

%FO: 100
Emp: 151

RIETER GREENSBORO, INC.
PO Box 18507, Greensboro, North Carolina 27419
CEO: James Morgan, Pres.
Bus: *Industrial machinery & equipment*

Tel: (336) 668-9581
Fax:

Emp: 31

UGN INC.
2638 East 126th St., Chicago, Illinois 60633
CEO: Peterr C. Anthony, Pres.
Bus: *Motor vehicle parts & accessories*

Tel: (773) 437-2403
Fax: (773) 437-2405

Emp: 1,250

- **RIRI SA**
  Via Catenazzi 23, CH-6850 Mendrisio, Switzerland
  CEO: Livio Cossutti, Pres.
  Bus: *Mfr. zippers.*

  Tel: 41-91-640-6161
  Fax: 41-91-646-5822
  www.riri.com

  NAICS: 339993

  RIRI USA INC.
  29 West 34th St., 12/F, New York, New York 10001
  CEO: L.B. Howell, Pres.
  Bus: *Sales of zippers.*

  Tel: (212) 268-3866
  Fax: (212) 268-3868

  %FO: 100

  RIRI USA INC.
  6114 LaSalle Ave., Oakland, California 94611
  CEO: L. Howell, Pres.
  Bus: *Sales of zippers.*

  Tel: (510) 338-0059
  Fax: (510) 338-0059

  %FO: 100

- **ROCHE HOLDING AS**
  Grenzacherstr. 124, CH-4070 Basel, Switzerland
  CEO: Franz B. Humer, Chmn. & CEO
  Bus: *Research/mfr./marketing pharmaceuticals,
  medicinals, botanicals, biological products and
  drugs. (20% owned by Novartis AG)*

  Tel: 41-61-688-1111
  Fax: 41-61-691-9391
  www.roche.com

  Rev: $27,630
  Emp: 64,703

  NAICS: 325411, 325412, 325413

  GENETECH INC.
  1 DNA Way, South San Francisco, California 94080
  CEO: Arthur A. Levinson, Chmn. & Pres. & CEO
  Bus: *Biopharmaceuticals & biotherapeutics.*

  Tel: (650) 225-1000
  Fax: (650) 225-6000

  Emp: 7,646

  HOFFMANN-LA ROCHE INC.
  340 Kingsland St., Nutley, New Jersey 07110-1199
  CEO: George B. Abercrombie, Pres. & CEO
  Bus: *Mfr./distribution/research pharmaceuticals,
  chemicals, diagnostics & lab services.*

  Tel: (973) 235-5000
  Fax: (973) 235-7605

  %FO: 100

  ROCHE CAROLINA
  6173 East Old Marion Highway, Florence, South Carolina 29506
  CEO: Don Herriott, Pres.
  Bus: *Pharmaceutical preparations.*

  Tel: (843) 629-4300
  Fax: (843) 629-4353

  Emp: 280

  ROCHE COLORADO CORP.
  2075 North 55th St., Boulder, Colorado 80301
  CEO: Erik Lodewijk, Pres.
  Bus: *Medicinals & botanicals.*

  Tel: (303) 442-1926
  Fax: (303) 938-6413

  Emp: 330

  ROCHE DIAGNOSTICS CORP.
  9115 Hague Rd., Indianapolis, Indiana 46256
  CEO: Heino von Prondzynski, Pres. & CEO
  Bus: *Mfr./distribution health diagnostic
  equipment, pharmaceuticals and health
  related products.*

  Tel: (317) 521-2000
  Fax: (317) 845-2221

  %FO: 100

ROCHE MOLECULAR SYSTEMS
4300 Hacienda Dr., Pleasanton, California 94588
CEO: Heiner Dreismann, Pres. Tel: (925) 730-8200
Bus: *Commercial physical research.* Fax: (925) 225-0758 Emp: 800

ROCHE MOLECULAR SYSTEMS, INC.
1080 U.S. Highway 202, Bldg. 500, Branchburg, New Jersey 08876
CEO: Tel: (908) 253-7200
Bus: *Pharmaceutical preparations.* Fax:

ROCHE MOLECULAR SYSTEMS, INC.
1145 Atlantic Ave., Alameda, California 94501
CEO: Terrance Taford, Mgr. Tel: (510) 865-5400
Bus: *Commercial physical research.* Fax: (510) 814-2800

ROCHE PALO ALTO LLC
3431 Hillview Ave., Palo Alto, California 94304
CEO: Jim Woddy, Dir.   Tel: (650) 855-5050
Bus: *Commercial physical research.* Fax:

● **SANTEX AG**
Fliegeneggstr. 9, CH-9555 Tobel, Switzerland
CEO: Christian Strahm, Pres. Tel: 41-71-918-6666 Rev: $70
Bus: *Mfr. textile finishing machines and systems.* Fax: 41-71-918-6600 Emp: 145
           www.santex-group.com
NAICS: 333292, 333298

  AMERICAN SANTEX INC.
  Corporate Center, 100 Corporate Way, Ste. L, Spartanburg, South Carolina 29303
  CEO: Heidi Mathis, Pres. Tel: (864) 574-7222 %FO: 100
  Bus: *Textile machines manufacture, sales and* Fax: (864) 574-0804 Emp: 3
    service.

● **SANTHERA PHARMACEUTICALS AG**
Hammer Str 47, Baselland, CH-4410 Liestal, Switzerland
CEO: Klaus Schollmeier, CEO Tel: 49-61-906-8950
Bus: *Pharmaceutical development.* Fax: 49-61-906-8951
           www.santhera.com
NAICS: 325412

  SANTHERA PHARMACEUTICALS
  111 Huntington Ave., Ste. 610, Boston, Massachusetts 02199
  CEO: Mathias Woker, SVP Tel: (401) 301-1086 %FO: 100
  Bus: *Pharmaceutical development.* Fax:

● **SARNA POLYMER HOLDING INC.**
Industriestr., CH-6060 Sarnen, Switzerland
CEO: Matti Paasila, Chmn. & CEO Tel: 41-41-666-9966 Rev: $682
Bus: *Plastic components manufacture for automobile* Fax: 41-41-666-9999 Emp: 3,844
  industry.   www.sarna.com
NAICS: 326130, 326199, 339999

SARNAMOTIVE BLUE WATER, INC.
1515 Busha Hwy., Marysville, Michigan 48040
CEO: Andrew Ridgway, CEO
Bus: *Mfr. of auto parts.*

Tel: (810) 364-4550
Fax: (810) 364-4556

%FO: 100
Emp: 1,100

● **SARNAFIL AG**
Industriestr., CH-6060 Sarnen, Switzerland
CEO: Karl Brandenburg, Pres.
Bus: *Processing and application of roofing and polymeric materials.*
NAICS: 324122, 326199

Tel: 41-41-666-9966
Fax: 41-41-660-2332
www.sarnafil.com

Rev: $228
Emp: 250

    SARNAFIL INC.
    100 Dan Rd., Canton, Massachusetts 02021
    CEO: Brian Whelan, Pres.
    Bus: *Sales/distribution of roofing.*

Tel: (781) 828-5400
Fax: (781) 828-5365

%FO: 100
Emp: 200

● **SAURER LTD.**
Textilstrasse 2, Arbon, CH-9320 Thurgau, Switzerland
CEO: Heinrich Fischer, CEO
Bus: *Mfr. systems for spinning, texturizing, twisting and embroidery.*
NAICS: 333292

Tel: 41-71-447-5274
Fax: 41-71-447-5288
www.saurer.com

Rev: $1,405
Emp: 10,286

    SAURER HOLDING INC.
    1575 West 124th Ave., Denver, Colorado 80234-1707
    CEO: Heinz Backmann
    Bus: *Sale/service textile equipment, machinery and parts.*

Tel: (303) 457-1234
Fax: (303) 457-1234

%FO: 100

● **SCHINDLER HOLDING AG**
Seestr. 55, Nidwalden, CH-6052 Hergiswil, Switzerland
CEO: Alfred N. Schindler, Chmn. & CEO
Bus: *Elevators and escalators manufacture.*

Tel: 41-41-632-8550
Fax: 41-41-445-3134
www.schindler.com

Rev: $7,297
Emp: 39,443

NAICS: 333921, 423430, 541519, 811212, 811213

    SCHINDLER ELEVATOR CORP.
    20 Whippany Rd., Ste. 225, PO Box 1935, Morristown, New Jersey 07962
    CEO: Roland W. Hess, CEO
    Bus: *Designs, manufactures, installs, and services elevators, escalators, and moving*

Tel: (973) 397-3700
Fax: (973) 397-3710

%FO: 100
Emp: 6,000

● **SERONO SA**
15 bis, chemin des Mines, CP 54, CH-1211 Geneva 20, Switzerland
CEO: Ernesto Bertarelli, CEO
Bus: *Development/marketing pharmaceutical and diagnostics products.*
NAICS: 325411, 334510

Tel: 41-22-739-3000
Fax: 41-22-739-3000
www.serono.com

Rev: $2,458
Emp: 4,300

SERONO INC.
One Technology Place, Rockland, Massachusetts 02370
CEO: Stacey Minton, PR
Bus: *Mfr./research/marketing/distribution
pharmaceutical products.*

Tel: (781) 982-9000
Fax: (781) 982-9481

%FO: 100
Emp: 200

● **SEZ HOLDING LTD.**
Leutschenbachstrasse 95, CH-8050 Zurich, Switzerland
CEO: Egon Putzi, Chmn. & CEO
Bus: *Chemical spin etch systems for semiconductor
wafers.*
NAICS: 333295

Tel: 41-1-308-3948
Fax: 41-1-308-3500
www.sez.com

Rev: $269
Emp: 663

    SEZ AMERICA, INC.
    1405 Preston Ave., Austin, Texas 78703
    CEO: Adam Venn, Mgr.
    Bus: *Chemical spin etch systems for
    semiconductor wafers.*

Tel: (512) 481-0403
Fax: (512) 481-0407

%FO: 100

    SEZ AMERICA, INC.
    4829 South 40th St., Phoenix, Arizona 85040
    CEO: Egon Putzi, Pres.
    Bus: *Chemical spin etch systems for
    semiconductor wafers.*

Tel: (602) 437-5050
Fax: (602) 437-4949

%FO: 100

    SEZ AMERICA, INC.
    163 Lexington Ave., Westwood, New Jersey 07675
    CEO: Gordon Hoekstra, Mgr.
    Bus: *Chemical spin etch systems for
    semiconductor wafers.*

Tel: (201) 722-2936
Fax: (201) 263-1119

%FO: 100

● **SGS S.A.**
1 place des Alpes, PO Box 2152, CH-1211 Geneva 1, Switzerland
CEO: Daniel I. Kerpelman, CEO
Bus: *Provides inspection and monitoring services for
traded agricultural products, minerals, petroleum,
petrochemicals and consumer goods.*
NAICS: 541380, 541614, 541690, 541710

Tel: 41-22-739-9111
Fax: 41-22-739-9886
www.sgs.com

Rev: $2,549
Emp: 32,659

    SGS NORTH AMERICA INC.
    201 Rte 17 North, Rutherford, New Jersey 07070
    CEO: Christian Jilch, COO
    Bus: *Technical & scientific research services.*

Tel: (201) 508-3000
Fax: (201) 508-3193

Emp: 6,100

● **SIEGFRIED LTD.**
Untere Bruehlstr. 4, CH-4800 Zofingen, Switzerland
CEO: Douglas Guenthardt, Chmn.
Bus: *Mfr. pharmaceuticals and bulk medical chemicals.*
NAICS: 325412, 325998, 423990, 424210, 424490, 561990

Tel: 41-62-746-1111
Fax: 41-62-746-1103
www.siegfried-cms.ch

Rev: $247
Emp: 700

    SIEGFRIED ACTIVES
    4370 La Jolla Village Dr., San Diego, California 92122
    CEO: Richard Haldimann, Mgr.
    Bus: *Drug development.*

Tel: (858) 546-4343
Fax: (858) 548-4346

%FO: 100

SIEGFRIED USA INC.
33 Industrial Park Rd., Pennsville, New Jersey 08070
CEO: Donald Bell, Pres.   Tel: (877) 763-8630   %FO: 100
Bus: *Mfr. bulk medical chemicals.*   Fax: (856) 678-8201   Emp: 185

● **SIEMENS BUILDING TECHNOLOGIES**
Bellerivestr. 36, CH-8034 Zurich, Switzerland
CEO: Heinrich Hiesinger, Pres. & CEO   Tel: 41-1-385-2211   Rev: $5,785
Bus: *Building control, fire detection, engineering and*   Fax: 41-1-385-2525   Emp: 33,000
contracting.   www.sbt.siemens.com
NAICS: 334290, 334310, 334419, 334511, 334519

SIEMENS BUILDING TECHNOLGIES, INC.
1000 Deerfield Pkwy., Buffalo Grove, Illinois 60089
CEO: Daryl Dulaney, Pres. & CEO   Tel: (847) 215-1000   %FO: 100
Bus: *Provides building control solutions for*   Fax: (847) 215-1093   Emp: 8,635
commercial facilities.

● **SIG COMBIBLOC INTERNATIONAL AG**
Rolf-Dieter Rademacher Industrieplatz, CH-8212 Neuhausen Rhine Falls, Switzerland
CEO: Rademacher Rolf-Dieter, CEO   Tel: 41-52-674-7500
Bus: *Mfr. aseptic packages and filling systems.*   Fax: 41-52-674-7200   Emp: 2,250
www.sig-group.com
NAICS: 322215, 333993

SIG COMBIBLOC INC.
5327 Fisher Rd., Columbus, Ohio 43228
CEO: Ben Hamer, CEO   Tel: (614) 876-0661   %FO: 100
Bus: *Mfr./sales packaging systems for fresh and*   Fax: (614) 876-8678   Emp: 230
long-life liquid food.

● **SIG HOLDING AG**
Laufengasse 18, Neuhausen am Rheinfall, CH-8212 Schaffhausen, Switzerland
CEO: Rolf Dieter Rademacher, CEO   Tel: 41-52-674-6111   Rev: $23,780
Bus: *Mfr. packaging machines and systems.*   Fax: 41-52-674-6556   Emp: 9,014
www.sig.biz/english
NAICS: 322221, 326160, 333414

SIG BEVERAGES NORTH AMERICA
808 Stewart Ave., Ste. 200, Plano, Texas 75074
CEO: Harald Luling, Pres.   Tel: (972) 535-0535
Bus: *Mfr. of beverage equipment.*   Fax: (972) 509-8755   Emp: 75

SIG COMBIBLOC INC.
5327 Fisher Rd., Columbus, Ohio 43228
CEO: Stefan Walliser, Pres.   Tel: (614) 876-3700
Bus: *Sales/service of aseptic packaging &*   Fax: (614) 876-8678   Emp: 27
related aseptic mfr. & parts.

- **SIKA AG**
  Zugerstr. 50, Baar, CH-6341 Zug, Switzerland
  CEO: Peter Krebser, Head Of Operations
  Bus: *Specialty chemicals manufacture.*

  Tel: 41-41-768-6800
  Fax: 41-41-768-6850
  www.sika.com

  Rev: $2,262
  Emp: 9,218

  NAICS: 325211, 325510, 325520, 327390

  SIKA AUTOMOTIVE
  30800 Stephenson Hwy., Madison Heights, Michigan 48071
  CEO: William E. Loven, SVP
  Bus: *Mfr. of auto parts.*

  Tel: (248) 577-0020
  Fax: (248) 577-0980

  %FO: 100

  SIKA CORPORATION
  201 Polito Ave., Lyndhurst, New Jersey 07071
  CEO: William E. Loven, Pres. & CEO
  Bus: *Mfr. of paints & other finishing products.*

  Tel: (201) 933-8800
  Fax: (201) 804-1076

  %FO: 100
  Emp: 816

- **SOCIETE INTERNATIONALE DE TELECOMMUNICATIONS AERONAUTIQUES**
  26 Chemin de Joinville, Cointrin, CH-1216 Geneva, Switzerland
  CEO: Peter Buecking, Pres.
  Bus: *Telecommunications services cooperative.*

  Tel: 41-22-747-6111
  Fax: 41-22-747-6110
  www.sita.com

  NAICS: 517910, 518210, 561499

  SITA, INC.
  3100 Cumberland Blvd., Ste. 200, Atlanta, Georgia 30339
  CEO: Bob Thorpe, Mgr.
  Bus: *Telecommunications services cooperative.*

  Tel: (770) 850-4500
  Fax: (770) 612-2265

  %FO: 100
  Emp: 600

- **STAEUBLI AG**
  Seestrasse 238, CH-8810 Horgen, Switzerland
  CEO: Anthony Staeubli, Pres. & CEO
  Bus: *Mfr. textile machinery, robot systems, weaving
  preparation systems and quick connect*
  NAICS: 333292

  Tel: 41-43-244-2222
  Fax: 41-43-244-2245
  www.staeubli.com

  Emp: 2,000

  STAEUBLI CORPORATION
  201 Parkway West, PO Box 189, Hillside Park, Duncan, South Carolina 29334
  CEO: Joe Gemma, Pres.
  Bus: *Sales/service for textile machines, robot
  systems, weaving preparation systems and
  quick safety couplings.*

  Tel: (864) 433-1980
  Fax: (864) 433-5485

  %FO: 100
  Emp: 125

- **STMICROELECTRONICS N.V.**
  39 Chemin du Champ des Filles, Plan-Les-Ouates, CH-1228 Geneva, Switzerland
  CEO: Carlo Bozotti, Pres. & CEO
  Bus: *Semiconductor manufacture.*

  Tel: 41-22-929-29-29
  Fax: 41-22-929-29-00
  www.st.com

  Rev: $8,760
  Emp: 49,500

  NAICS: 334112, 334413, 334414, 334415

ST MICROELECTRONICS, INC.
1310 Electronics Dr., Carrollton, Texas 75006-5039
CEO: Richard J. Pieranunzi, CEO
Bus: *Mfr. semi-conductors.*
Tel: (972) 466-6000
Fax: (972) 466-8387
%FO: 100

ST MICROELECTRONICS, INC.
1000 East Bell Rd., Phoenix, Arizona 85002
CEO: John Coleman, Mgr.
Bus: *Sales/marketing of semi-conductors.*
Tel: (602) 485-6100
Fax: (602) 485-6102
%FO: 100

● STRAUMANN HOLDING AG
Peter Merian-Weg 12, CH-4052 Basel, Switzerland
CEO: Gilbert Achermann, CEO
Bus: *Manufacturer of dental implants.*
Tel: 41-61-965-1111
Fax: 41-61-965-1101
www.straumann.ch
Emp: 1,100

NAICS: 339113, 339114

STRAUMANN INC.
100 Minuteman Rd., Andover, Massachusetts 01810
CEO: Russell Olsen
Bus: *Manufacturer of dental implants.*
Tel: (781) 890-0001
Fax: (781) 890-6464
%FO: 100

● SULZER LTD.
Zurcher Str. 12, Winterthur, CH-8401 Zurich, Switzerland
CEO: Ulf Berg, CEO
Bus: *Engineering systems: textile, energy, oil, gas and chemicals, mining, water technology, wood and food products industries.*
Tel: 41-52-262-1122
Fax: 41-52-262-0101
www.sulzer.com
Rev: $1,826
Emp: 9,586

NAICS: 332919, 333911, 333996

SULZER CHEMTECH
4106 New West Dr., Pasadena, Texas 77507
CEO: Mauricio Bannwart, Pres.
Bus: *Structural metal fabrication.*
Tel: (281) 604-4100
Fax: (281) 291-0207
%FO: 100
Emp: 200

SULZER ENPRO INC.
1516 Engineers Rd., Belle Chasse, Louisiana 70037
CEO: Kristian J. Andersen, Pres.
Bus: *Oil field services.*
Tel: (504) 392-1800
Fax: (504) 392-2235
%FO: 100
Emp: 60

SULZER EUROFLAMM US INC.
240 Detrick St., 2/F, Dayton, Ohio 45404
CEO: Eric A. Schueler, Pres.
Bus: *Mfr. of automotive transmissions.*
Tel: (937) 425-7873
Fax: (937) 425-7885
%FO: 100
Emp: 36

SULZER HICKMAN
11518 Old La Porte Rd., La Porte, Texas 77571
CEO: Darayus Pardivala, Pres.
Bus: *Service of thermal turbo machinery.*
Tel: (713) 567-2700
Fax: (713) 567-2844
%FO: 100
Emp: 330

SULZER METAPLAS INC.
222 Goldstein Dr., Woonsocket, Rhode Island 02895
CEO: Jacob Evisser, Pres.
Bus: *Mfr. of thin film coating.*
Tel: (401) 766-3353
Fax: (401) 766-5646
%FO: 100
Emp: 10

SULZER METCO (US) INC.
1101 Prospect Ave., Westbury, New York 11590
CEO: Henri Steinmetz, Pres.
Bus: *Design/mfr. industrial spraying materials & systems.*

Tel: (516) 334-1300
Fax: (516) 338-2214

%FO: 100

SULZER PROCESS PUMPS INC.
155 Ahlstrom Way, Easley, South Carolina 29640
CEO: Dale Libby, Pres.
Bus: *Mfr. of pumps systems & parts.*

Tel: (864) 855-9090
Fax: (856) 855-9095

%FO: 100
Emp: 70

SULZER PUMPS HOUSTON
800 Koomey Rd, Brookshire, Texas 77423
CEO: Mauricio Gamez, Mgr.
Bus: *Mfr. pumps & pumping equipment.*

Tel: (281) 934-6014
Fax: (281) 934-6064

%FO: 100
Emp: 405

SULZER PUMPS INC.
2800 Northwest Front Ave., PO Box 10247, Portland, Oregon 97210
CEO: Cesar Montenegro, Pres.
Bus: *Design/sales/service pumps; energy industry .*

Tel: (503) 226-5200
Fax: (503) 226-5286

%FO: 100
Emp: 550

SULZER TCS INC.
One Sugar Creek Center Blvd., Ste. 380, Sugar Land, Texas 77478
CEO: Kelli Edell, Pres.
Bus: *Business consulting services.*

Tel: (281) 277-6331
Fax: (281) 277-6350

%FO: 100

SULZER US HOLDING INC.
555 Fifth Ave., New York, New York 10017
CEO: Leonardo Vannotti, Chmn.
Bus: *Import/sales/service of machinery and systems for process technology.*

Tel: (212) 949-0999
Fax: (212) 661-0533

%FO: 100

● **THE SWATCH GROUP LTD.**
Faubourg du Lac 6, CH-2501 Biel, Bern, Switzerland
CEO: G. Nicolas Hayek Jr., CEO
Bus: *Mfr./marketing of microelectronics and major brand watches including Blancpain, Omega, Longines, Hamilton, Balmain, Swatch.*

Tel: 41-32-343-6811
Fax: 41-32-343-6911
www.swatchgroup.com

Rev: $3,517
Emp: 20,949

NAICS: 333298, 333315, 333319, 334512, 334514, 334518, 334519, 335312, 339911

SWATCH GROUP
1200 Harbor Blvd., Weehawken, New Jersey 07086
CEO: Yann Gamard, CEO
Bus: *Sale/distribution and repair of watches, clocks and movements, including brands Swatch, Longines, Omega and Hamilton.*

Tel: (201) 271-1400
Fax: (201) 271-4633

%FO: 100
Emp: 700

● **SWISS REINSURANCE COMPANY**
Mythenquai 50/60, CH-8022 Zurich, Switzerland
CEO: John R. Coomber, CEO
Bus: *Insurance and reinsurance services.*

Tel: 41-43-285-2121
Fax: 41-43-285-2999
www.swissre.com

Rev: $29,326
Emp: 7,949

NAICS: 523991, 523999, 524130, 525110, 525120, 525190, 525910, 525990

SWISS RE LIFE & HEALTH AMERICA
1700 Magnavox Way, Fort Wayne, Indiana 46804
CEO: Jacques Dubois
Bus: *Insurance services.*
Tel: (260) 435-8950
Fax:

SWISS REINSURANCE
28 State St., 12/F, Boston, Massachusetts 02109
CEO: John Christopher, Mgr.
Bus: *Insurance and reinsurance services.*
Tel: (617) 367-8000
Fax: (617) 742-6569
%FO: 100

SWISS REINSURANCE AMERICA
227 West Monroe St., Ste. 3850, Chicago, Illinois 60606
CEO: William Sampson, Mgr.
Bus: *Property and casualty reinsurance*
Tel: (312) 553-4220
Fax: (312) 553-0905

SWISS REINSURANCE AMERICA
One Galleria Tower, 13355 Noel Rd., Ste. 1250, Dallas, Texas 75240
CEO: Arthur Nanney, Mgr.
Bus: *Property and casualty reinsurance*
Tel: (972) 386-7475
Fax: (972) 980-7531

SWISS REINSURANCE AMERICA
1818 Market St., Ste. 2720, Philadelphia, Pennsylvania 19103
CEO: Thomas Agnew, Mgr.
Bus: *Property and Casualty reinsurance*
Tel: (215) 567-6200
Fax: (215) 567-6581

SWISS REINSURANCE AMERICA
150 California St., 14/F, San Francisco, California 94111
CEO: Vincent Friscia, Mgr.
Bus: *Property and casualty reinsurance*
Tel: (415) 956-6900
Fax: (415) 989-2633

SWISS REINSURANCE AMERICA
The Lenox Bldg., Ste. 900, 3399 Peachtree Rd., N.E., Atlanta, Georgia 30326
CEO: Blane Dunahoo, Mgr.
Bus: *Property and casualty reinsurance*
Tel: (404) 261-6242
Fax: (404) 261-0368

SWISS REINSURANCE AMERICA COMPANY
1 Liberty Plaza, 52/F, New York, New York 10006
CEO: Joe Naggar, Mng. Prtn.
Bus: *Asset management.*
Tel: (212) 557-4000
Fax: (212) 557-4800
%FO: 100

SWISS REINSURANCE AMERICA CORPORATION
175 King St., Armonk, New York 10504
CEO: Andreas Beerli, Chmn.
Bus: *Property and casualty reinsurance*
Tel: (914) 828-8000
Fax: (914) 828-7000
%FO: 100
Emp: 428

● **SWISSCOM AG**
Alte Tiefenaustr. 6, CH-3050 Bern, Switzerland
CEO: Jens Alder, CEO
Bus: *Engaged in telecommunications; provides local, long distance and international services.*
Tel: 41-31-342-1111
Fax: 41-31-342-6411
www.swisscom.ch
Rev: $8,813
Emp: 15,952

NAICS: 517110, 517211, 517212, 517910, 518111, 518210, 519190, 524126, 524130, 541511, 541512, 541519, 561499

SWISSCOM, INC.
111 8th Ave., Ste. 307, New York, New York 10011-5204
CEO: Rajiv Sharma, Principal   Tel: (212) 633-7597   %FO: 100
Bus: *Engaged in telecommunications services.*   Fax: (212) 633-7597

SWISSCOM, INC.
2001 L St. NW, Ste. 750, Washington, District of Columbia 20036
CEO: Konnie Schaeffer   Tel: (202) 496-9101   %FO: 100
Bus: *Engaged in telecommunications services.*   Fax:

● **SWISSLOG HOLDING AG**
Webereiweg 3, CH-5033 Buchs, Switzerland
CEO: Remo Brunschwiler, CEO   Tel: 41-62-837-9537   Rev: $632
Bus: *Mfr. automated material handling systems.*   Fax: 41-62-837-9510   Emp: 2,336
    www.swisslog.com
NAICS: 541511, 541512, 541519

    SWISSLOG LOGISTICS INC.
    1401 North Batavia St., Ste. 104, Orange, California 92867
    CEO: Robert Rosales, Pres.   Tel: (714) 288-8800   %FO: 100
    Bus: *Custom computer programming.*   Fax: (714) 288-8805

    SWISSLOG LOGISTICS INC.
    101 Billerica Ave., 5 Billerica Business Center, North Billerica, Massachusetts 01862
    CEO: Steve Simmerhan, CEO   Tel: (978) 663-9840   %FO: 100
    Bus: *Computer software development.*   Fax: (978) 670-9840   Emp: 50

    SWISSLOG LOGISTICS INC.
    161 Enterprise Dr., Newport News, Virginia 23603
    CEO: Charlie Kegley, Pres.   Tel: (757) 820-3400   %FO: 100
    Bus: *Mfr. of conveyors & equipment.*   Fax: (757) 887-5588   Emp: 50

    SWISSLOG USA, INC.
    10825 East 47th Ave., Denver, Colorado 80239
    CEO: Charles Kegley, Pres.   Tel: (303) 373-7883   %FO: 100
    Bus: *Computer controlled material/ handling*   Fax: (303) 373-7932   Emp: 340
    systems & mail sorting equipment.

● **SWISSPORT INTERNATIONAL LTD.**
Flughofstr. 55, 22/F, Glattbrugg, CH-8152 Zurich, Switzerland
CEO: Joseph In Albon, Pres. & CEO   Tel: 41-43-812-2020   Rev: $1,060
Bus: *Ground handling services.*   Fax: 41-43-321-2901   Emp: 22,000
    www.swissport.com
NAICS: 488119, 488190, 488510, 541614

    SWISSPORT INTERNATIONAL LTD.
    45025 Aviation Dr., Ste. 350, Dulles, Virginia 20166
    CEO: Erich Bodenmann, CEO   Tel: (703) 742-4300   %FO: 100
    Bus: *Ground handling services.*   Fax: (703) 742-4321

    SWISSPORT INTERNATIONAL LTD.
    4305 West International Airport Rd., Anchorage, Alaska 99502
    CEO: Scott Miller, Gen. Mgr.   Tel: (907) 248-0070   %FO: 100
    Bus: *Airport services.*   Fax: Emp: 285

SWISSPORT INTERNATIONAL LTD.
1055 East Tropicana Ave, Las Vegas, Nevada 89119
CEO: Joe Hall, Mgr.   Tel: (702) 940-6340   %FO: 100
Bus: *Airport/transportation services.* Fax:

SWISSPORT INTERNATIONAL LTD.
7007 West Imperial Hwy., Los Angeles, California 90045
CEO: Armin Unternaehrer, VP   Tel: (310) 417-0258   %FO: 100
Bus: *Airport services.* Fax: Emp: 500

● **SYNGENTA AG**
Schwarzwaldalle 215, CH-4058 Basel, Switzerland
CEO: Michael P. Pragnell, CEO   Tel: 41-61-323-1111   Rev: $7,269
Bus: *Mfr. agrochemicals and seeds.* Fax: 41-61-323-1212   Emp: 19,500
    www.syngenta.com

  NAICS: 113210, 325311, 325312, 325320

SYNGENTA
7755 Office Plaza Dr. North, Ste. 105, W. Des Moines, Iowa 50266
CEO: Tel: (515) 222-1400
Bus: *Mfr. agricultural chemicals.* Fax: (515) 222-4816

SYNGENTA BIOTECHNOLOGY INC.
3054 Cornwallis Rd., Research Triangle Park, North Carolina 27709
CEO: Roger Kemble, Pres.   Tel: (919) 541-8500
Bus: *Seed research and biotechnology.* Fax: Emp: 255

SYNGENTA CORP.
2200 Concord Pike, PO Box 8353, Wilmington, Delaware 19850
CEO: Michael Mack, Chmn. & Pres.   Tel: (302) 425-2000
Bus: *Agricultural support activities & products.* Fax: (302) 425-2001   Emp: 5,060

SYNGENTA CROP PROTECTION, INC.
410 Swing Rd., PO Box 18300, Greensboro, North Carolina 27409
CEO: Valdemar Fischer, Pres.   Tel: (336) 632-6000   %FO: 100
Bus: *Mfr./sales agrochemicals.* Fax: (336) 632-7353   Emp: 1,456

SYNGENTA SEEDS INC.
11939 Sugar Mill Rd., Longmont, Colorado 80501
CEO: Keith Haagenson, Mgr.   Tel: (303) 776-1802
Bus: *Sale of farm supplies.* Fax:

SYNGENTA SEEDS INC.
PO Box 4188, Boise, Idaho 83704
CEO: Joyce Black, Mgr.   Tel: (208) 322-7272   %FO: 100
Bus: *Mfr./sales of vegetable seeds.* Fax:

SYNGENTA SEEDS INC.
5300 Katrine Ave., Downers Grove, Illinois 60515
CEO: Drew Effron   Tel: (630) 969-6300
Bus: *Sale of horticultural products.* Fax:

SYNGENTA SEEDS, INC.
7500 Olsen Memorial Hwy., Golden Valley, Minnesota 55427
CEO: John Sorenson, Pres. & CEO   Tel: (763) 593-7333
Bus: *Agricultural support activities & products.*   Fax: (763) 593-7218   Emp: 2,060

● **SYNTHES**
Glutz Biotzheim Str. 1-3, CH-4500 Solothurn, Switzerland
CEO: Hansjorg Wyss, CEO   Tel: 41-32-720-4060   Rev: $1,780
Bus: *Mfr. osteosynthesis medical devices, instruments*   Fax: 41032-720-4061   Emp: 6,711
  and implants.   www.synthes.com
NAICS: 334510, 339112, 339113

SYNTHES USA INC.
1303 Goshen Pkwy., West Chester, Pennsylvania 19380
CEO: Mike Sticklin   Tel: (610) 738-4600   %FO: 100
Bus: *Mfr. osteosynthesis medical devices,*   Fax: (610) 718-6634
  instruments and implants.

SYNTHES USA INC.
224 N. Main St., Bldg. 17-2, Horseheads, New York 14845
CEO: Ron Lerner   Tel: (607) 739-3722   %FO: 100
Bus: *Mfr. osteosynthesis medical devices,*   Fax: (607) 795-4634
  instruments and implants.

SYNTHES USA INC.
PO Box 366, 1051 Synthes Ave., Monument, Colorado 80132
CEO: Tom Freestone, Plant Mgr.   Tel: (719) 481-5300   %FO: 100
Bus: *Mfr. osteosynthesis medical devices,*   Fax: (719) 481-5300
  instruments and implants.

● **TETRA LAVAL SA**
70, ave General-Guisan, CH-1009 Pully Vaud, Switzerland
CEO: Larry G. Pillard, Chmn.   Tel: 41-21-729-2211   Rev: $12,358
Bus: *Mfr. of machines for packaging food products.*   Fax: 41-21-729-2288   Emp: 29,540
      www.tetralaval.com
NAICS: 322130, 322212, 322213, 326160, 333993

DELAVAL, INC.
11100 North Congress Ave., Kansas City, Missouri 65143
CEO: Walt Maharay, EVP   Tel: (816) 891-7700   %FO: 100
Bus: *Mfr. of farm & garden machinery.*   Fax: (816) 891-1606   Emp: 566

NOVEMBAL USA, INC.
3 Greek Lane, Edison, New Jersey 08817
CEO: John Fimelliti, Mgr.   Tel: (732) 287-4949   %FO: 100
Bus: *Mfr. of plastic products.*   Fax: (732) 287-4988   Emp: 22

SIDEL INC.
6015 31st East St., Bradenton, Florida 34203
CEO: Mary Limpert, Sales   Tel: (941) 727-1400   %FO: 100
Bus: *Sales & services of replacement parts for*   Fax: (941) 727-1200
  pet blow molding services.

SIDEL INC.
9480 Utica Ave., Ste. 605, Rancho Cucamonga, California 91730
CEO: Martin Flores, Mgr.   Tel: (909) 466-7799   %FO: 100
Bus: *Sales & services of replacement parts for*   Fax: (909) 466-8778
pet blow molding services.

SIDEL INC.
5600 Sun Ct., Norcross, Georgia 30092
CEO: Tehiery Parges, Pres.   Tel: (770) 449-8058   %FO: 100
Bus: *Sales & services of replacement parts for*   Fax: (770) 447-0084   Emp: 165
pet blow molding services.

TETRA PAK AMERICAS LTD.
1221 Brickell Ave., Ste. 1700, Miami, Florida 33131
CEO: Alan Murray   Tel: (305) 416-2460   %FO: 100
Bus: *Mfr. of sanitary food containers.*   Fax: (305) 416-2468

TETRA PAK INC.
200 South Park Blvd., Greenwood, Indiana 46143
CEO: Einar Lilleas   Tel: (317) 889-4600   %FO: 100
Bus: *Repair services.*   Fax: (317) 889-4665

TETRA PAK INC.
193 Industrial Dr., PO Box 1547, Louisa, Virginia 23093
CEO: Dan H. Scott   Tel: (540) 967-0733   %FO: 100
Bus: *Mfr. of sanitary food containers.*   Fax: (540) 967-2125

TETRA PAK CARTON CHILLED INC.
451 East Industrial Blvd., Minneapolis, Minnesota 55413
CEO: Peter Lindkvist, Mgr.   Tel: (612) 362-8500   %FO: 100
Bus: *Mfr. of food products machinery.*   Fax: (612) 623-4212   Emp: 200

TETRA PAK HOYER INC.
753 Geneva Pkwy., Lake Geneva, Wisconsin 53147
CEO: Viggo Neilsen, Pres.   Tel: (262) 249-7400   %FO: 100
Bus: *Sale of ice cream plant equipment.*   Fax: (262) 249-7500   Emp: 26

TETRA PAK INC.
101 Corporate Wood Pkwy., Vernon Hills, Illinois 60061
CEO: Brian Kennell, Pres.   Tel: (847) 955-6000   %FO: 100
Bus: *Package food product manufacture.*   Fax: (847) 955-6500   Emp: 1,001

TETRA PAK INC.
5201 Investment Dr., Fort Wayne, Indiana 46808
CEO: Frank Kopecky, Mgr.   Tel: (219) 484-7734   %FO: 100
Bus: *Mfr. of sanitary food containers.*   Fax: (219) 484-2279   Emp: 100

TETRA PAK INC.
3300 Airport Rd., Denton, Texas 76207
CEO: Charles Posey, Mgr.   Tel: (940) 565-8800   %FO: 100
Bus: *Mfr. of packaging paper/film, sanitary food* Fax: (940) 565-8420   Emp: 170
containers.

TETRA PAK INC.
1616 West 31st St., Vancouver, Washington 98660
CEO: Steve Bean, Mgr.   Tel: (360) 693-3664   %FO: 100
Bus: *Mfr. of fiber cans, drums & sanitary food* Fax: (360) 690-1207   Emp: 120
  containers.

TETRA PAK INC.
110 Erie St., Pomona, California 91768
CEO: Steve Seeley   Tel: (909) 629-5348   %FO: 100
Bus: *Mfr. of sanitary food containers.* Fax: (909) 629-4697

TETRA PAK INC.
3405 Industrial Way, PO Box 3017, Longview, Washington 98632
CEO: Steve Estes, Mgr.   Tel: (360) 636-7125   %FO: 100
Bus: *Mfr. of wood containers, paperboard mill.* Fax: (360) 636-7112   Emp: 75

TETRA PAK INC.
2200 East Malone Ave., Sikeston, Missouri 63801
CEO: Mike Tomaszewskr, Mgr.   Tel: (573) 471-1441   %FO: 100
Bus: *Mfr. of sanitary food containers.* Fax: (573) 471-9068   Emp: 136

● **TETRA PAK INTERNATIONAL SA**
70 Av. General-Guisan, CH-1009 Pully, Switzerland
CEO: Nick Shreiber, Pres. & CEO   Tel: 41-21-729-2111 Rev: $10,264
Bus: *Mfr. aseptic beverage box packaging.* Fax: 41-21-729-2244 Emp: 20,905
            www.tetrapak.com
NAICS: 322212

NOVEMBAL USA INC.
3 Greek Lane, Edison, New Jersey 08817
CEO: Alan Murray   Tel: (732) 287-4949   %FO: 100
Bus: *Mfr. aseptic beverage box packaging.* Fax: (732) 287-4988

TETRA PAK AMERICAS
1221 Brickell Ave., Ste. 1700, Miami, Florida 33131
CEO: Jacquelyn Paul   Tel: (305) 416-2460   %FO: 100
Bus: *Mfr. aseptic beverage box packaging.* Fax: (305) 416-2468

TETRA PAK CARTON CHILLED INC.
451 East Industrial Blvd., Minneapolis, Minnesota 55413
CEO: Gail Barnes   Tel: (612) 362-8500   %FO: 100
Bus: *Mfr. aseptic beverage box packaging.* Fax: (612) 623-4212

TETRA PAK DRY FOODS
451 East Industrial Blvd., Minneapolis, Minnesota 55413
CEO: Peter Lindkvist   Tel: (612) 617-3037   %FO: 100
Bus: *Mfr. aseptic beverage box packaging.* Fax: (612) 617-5739

TETRA PAK FOOD SERVICE
101 Corporate Woods Pkwy., Vernon Hills, Illinois 60061
CEO: Stephen Hellenschmidt   Tel: (847) 955-6554   %FO: 100
Bus: *Mfr. aseptic beverage box packaging.* Fax: (847) 955-3054

TETRA PAK HOYER INC.
753 Geneva Pkwy., Lake Geneva, Wisconsin 53147
CEO: Gustav Korsholm   Tel: (262) 249-7400   %FO: 100
Bus: *Mfr. aseptic beverage box packaging.*   Fax: (262) 249-7500

TETRA PAK INC.
101 Corporate Woods Pkwy., Vernon Hills, Illinois 60061
CEO: Alan Murray, Pres. & CEO   Tel: (847) 955-6000   %FO: 100
Bus: *Mfr. aseptic beverage box packaging.*   Fax: (847) 955-6500

TETRA PAK INC.
110 Erie St., Pomona, California 91768
CEO: Alan Murray   Tel: (909) 629-5348   %FO: 100
Bus: *Mfr. aseptic beverage box packaging.*   Fax: (909) 629-4697

TETRA PAK INC.
1616 W. 31st St., Vancouver, Washington 98660
CEO: Alan Murray   Tel: (360) 693-3664   %FO: 100
Bus: *Mfr. aseptic beverage box packaging.*   Fax: (360) 690-1207

TETRA PAK INC.
3300 Airport Rd., Denton, Texas 76207
CEO: Bryan Morris   Tel: (940) 565-8800   %FO: 100
Bus: *Mfr. aseptic beverage box packaging.*   Fax: (940) 565-8420

TETRA PAK INC.
2200 E. Malone Ave., Sikeston, Missouri 63801
CEO: Michelle Dorman   Tel: (573) 471-1441   %FO: 100
Bus: *Mfr. aseptic beverage box packaging.*   Fax: (573) 471-9068

TETRA PAK INC.
5201 Investment Dr., Fort Wayne, Indiana 46808
CEO: Frank Kopecky   Tel: (219) 484-7734   %FO: 100
Bus: *Mfr. aseptic beverage box packaging.*   Fax: (219) 484-2279

TETRA PAK INC. PACIFIC LAMINATION
PO Box 3017, Longview, Washington 98632
CEO: Steve Estes   Tel: (360) 636-7125   %FO: 100
Bus: *Mfr. aseptic beverage box packaging.*   Fax: (360) 636-7112

TETRA PAK PROCESSING SYSTEMS AMERICAS INC.
200 South Park Blvd., Greenwood, Indiana 46143
CEO: Einar Lilleas   Tel: (317) 885-5155   %FO: 100
Bus: *Mfr. aseptic beverage box packaging.*   Fax: (317) 889-4619

TETRA PAK TUBEX INC.
193 Industrial Dr., Box 1547, Louisa, Virginia 23093
CEO: Dan H. Scott   Tel: (540) 967-0733   %FO: 100
Bus: *Mfr. aseptic beverage box packaging.*   Fax: (540) 967-2125

● **TEUSCHER CONFISERIE**
Storchengasse 9, CH-8001 Zurich, Switzerland
CEO: Dolf Teuscher, Pres. & CEO
Bus: *Handmade Swiss chocolates.*

Tel: 41-1-211-5151
Fax: 41-1-212-2958
www.teuscher.com

NAICS: 311320, 445292

> **TEUSCHER CHOCOLATES OF SWITZERLAND**
> 307 Sutter St., San Francisco, California 94108
> CEO: Dolf Teuscher
> Bus: *Sales of handmade Swiss chocolates.*
>
> Tel: (415) 834-0850
> Fax: (415) 834-0860
> %FO: 100

> **TEUSCHER CHOCOLATES OF SWITZERLAND**
> 322 South Guadalupe St., @ Cookworks, Santa Fe, New Mexico 87501
> CEO: Dolf Teuscher
> Bus: *Sales of handmade Swiss chocolates.*
>
> Tel: (505) 988-7676
> Fax: (505) 988-1886
> %FO: 100

> **TEUSCHER CHOCOLATES OF SWITZERLAND**
> Madison Ave. @ 61st St., New York, New York 10021
> CEO: Bernard Bloom, Pres.
> Bus: *Sales of handmade Swiss chocolates.*
>
> Tel: (800) 554-0624
> Fax: (212) 751-0723
> %FO: 100

> **TEUSCHER CHOCOLATES OF SWITZERLAND**
> 5213 Alpha Rd., @ Cookworks, Dallas, Texas 75240
> CEO: Dolf Teuscher
> Bus: *Sales of handmade Swiss chocolates.*
>
> Tel: (972) 960-2665
> Fax: (972) 392-2645
> %FO: 100

> **TEUSCHER CHOCOLATES OF SWITZERLAND**
> 900 North Michigan Ave., Chicago, Illinois 60611
> CEO: Gilles Noyer, Pres.
> Bus: *Sales of handmade Swiss chocolates.*
>
> Tel: (312) 943-4400
> Fax: (312) 943-4900
> %FO: 100

> **TEUSCHER CHOCOLATES OF SWITZERLAND**
> 1089 Newport Center Dr., Newport Beach, California 92660
> CEO: Dolf Teuscher
> Bus: *Sales of handmade Swiss chocolates.*
>
> Tel: (949) 721-1801
> Fax: (949) 721-1802
> %FO: 100

> **TEUSCHER CHOCOLATES OF SWITZERLAND**
> Aladdin Hotel Desert Passage, 3663 Las Vegas Blvd. South, Las Vegas, Nevada 89109
> CEO: Hervert Pastornak, Owner
> Bus: *Sales of handmade Swiss chocolates.*
>
> Tel: (702) 866-6624
> Fax: (702) 866-6641
> %FO: 100

> **TEUSCHER CHOCOLATES OF SWITZERLAND**
> 620 Fifth Ave., Rockefeller Center, New York, New York 10020
> CEO: Dolf Teuscher, Owner
> Bus: *Sales of handmade Swiss chocolates.*
>
> Tel: (212) 246-4416
> Fax: (212) 765-8134
> %FO: 100

> **TEUSCHER CHOCOLATES OF SWITZERLAND**
> 230 Newbury St., Boston, Massachusetts 02116
> CEO: Hedy Genhart, Pres.
> Bus: *Sales of handmade Swiss chocolates.*
>
> Tel: (617) 536-1922
> Fax: (617) 536-1787
> %FO: 100

TEUSCHER CHOCOLATES OF SWITZERLAND
531 SW Broadway, Portland, Oregon 97205
CEO: Dolf Teuscher
Bus: *Sales of handmade Swiss chocolates.*

Tel: (503) 827-0587
Fax: (503) 827-0587

%FO: 100

TEUSCHER CHOCOLATES OF SWITZERLAND
Obertal Mall, Ninth St., Leavenworth, Washington 98826
CEO: Dolf Teuscher
Bus: *Sales of handmade Swiss chocolates.*

Tel: (509) 548-5144
Fax: (509) 548-5144

%FO: 100

TEUSCHER CHOCOLATES OF SWITZERLAND
9648 Brighton Way, @ Camden Dr., Beverly Hills, California 90210
CEO: Aviva Covitz, Pres.
Bus: *Sales of handmade Swiss chocolates.*

Tel: (310) 276-2776
Fax: (310) 276-5691

%FO: 100

● **THINK TOOLS AG**
Weinbergstrasse 139, CH-8006 Zurich, Switzerland
CEO: Sven Mattka, CEO
Bus: *Decision optimization software and services manufacturer.*
NAICS: 511210

Tel: 41-1-368-7888
Fax: 41-1-368-7899
www.thinktools.com

Rev: $1
Emp: 43

THINK TOOLS
300 Atlantic St., 11/F, Stamford, Connecticut 06901
CEO: Christina Mott
Bus: *Decision optimization software and services manufacturer.*

Tel: (203) 975-0351
Fax: (203) 975-0352

%FO: 100

● **UBS AG (UNION BANK OF SWITZERLAND)**
Bahnhofstr. 45, CH-8098 Zurich, Switzerland
CEO: Peter A. Wuffli, Pres. & CEO
Bus: *Banking, securities trading and underwriting, asset management and corporate finance*
NAICS: 522110, 523110, 523120, 523130, 523140, 523920, 523930, 525910

Tel: 41-44-234-4111
Fax: 41-44-234-3415
www.ubs.com

Rev: $67,424
Emp: 59,878

UBS CAPITAL MARKETS L.P.
111 Pavonia Ave. East, Jersey City, New Jersey 07310
CEO: John P. Costas, Chmn. & CEO
Bus: *Financial services*

Tel: (201) 963-9100
Fax: (201) 656-2411

UBS FINANCIAL SERVICES INC.
1251 Ave. of the Americas, New York, New York 10019
CEO: Mark B. Sutton, Chmn. & CEO
Bus: *Engaged in investment banking and asset management.*

Tel: (212) 713-2000
Fax: (212) 713-9818

%FO: 100

UBS INVESTMENT SERVICES INC.
299 Park Ave., New York, New York 10171
CEO: John P. Costas, Chmn. & CEO
Bus: *Engaged in investment banking and asset management.*

Tel: (212) 821-4000
Fax: (212) 821-3285

%FO: 100

● **UNAXIS HOLDING AG**
Churerstr. 120, Schwyz, CH-8808 Pfaffikon, Switzerland
CEO: Thomas P. Limberger, CEO   Tel: 41-58-360-9696   Rev: $1,296
Bus: *Mfr. tool & component coating equipment, vacuum*   Fax: 41-58-360-9196   Emp: 6,456
     & semiconductor equipment, coating solutions &   www.unaxis.com
     components for satellites & launch vehicles.
NAICS: 332911, 332912, 332919, 332998, 333295, 333995, 333996, 334413, 541511, 541512, 541519

    BALZERS INC.
    2511 Technology Dr., Ste. 114, Elgin, Illinois 60123
    CEO: Kent W. Connell, Pres.   Tel: (847) 844-1753
    Bus: *Mfr. of paints, coatings and other finishing*   Fax: (847) 844-3306   Emp: 283
     products.

    UNAXIS ESEC INC.
    1121 West Warner Rd., Ste. 107, Tempe, Arizona 85284
    CEO: Joe Lippincott   Tel: (480) 893-6990
    Bus: *Advanced packaging assembly.*   Fax: (480) 893-6793

    UNAXIS OPTICS USA INC.
    16080 Table Mountain Pkwy., Golden, Colorado 80403
    CEO: Joe Haggerty, Pres.   Tel: (303) 273-9700   %FO: 100
    Bus: *Optical components.*   Fax: (303) 273-2995   Emp: 98

    UNAXIS USA INC.
    10050 16th St. North, St. Petersburg, Florida 33716
    CEO: David Lishan, CEO   Tel: (727) 577-4999   %FO: 100
    Bus: *Wafer processing*   Fax: (727) 577-7035   Emp: 208

● **UNION BANCAIRE PRIVEE**
96-98, rue du Rhone, CH-1211 Geneva, Switzerland
CEO: Guy de Picciotto, CEO   Tel: 41-22-819-2111   Rev: $505
Bus: *International private investment banking services.*   Fax: 41-22-819-2432   Emp: 1,182
                                               www.ubp.ch
NAICS: 523110

    UNION BANCAIRE PRIVEE
    30 Rockefeller Center, Ste. 2800, New York, New York 10112
    CEO: Mark Kenyon, member   Tel: (212) 218-6750   %FO: 100
    Bus: *International private investment baking*   Fax: (212) 218-6755
     services.

● **VIBRO-METER SA, DIV. MEGGITT PLC**
Rte De Moncor 4, Villars-Sur Glane, CH-1752 Fribourg, Switzerland
CEO: Terence Twigger, Pres.   Tel: 41-26-407-1111   Rev: $347
Bus: *Conditioning monitoring for rotating machinery on*   Fax: 41-26-407-1731   Emp: 31,000
     land, sea and air.   www.vibro-meter.com
NAICS: 334513, 423610

    MRT-WEST
    Box 7058, Santa Rosa, California 95407
    CEO: T. Macaluso   Tel: (707) 585-6004
    Bus: *Space & Nuclear*   Fax: (707) 585-6043

VIBRO-METER CORPORATION
10 Ammon Dr., Manchester, New Hampshire 03103
CEO: Kris Kasper, VP
Bus: *Aircraft parts & equipment manufacturer*
Tel: (603) 669-0940
Fax: (603) 666-3711
%FO: 100
Emp: 200

VIBRO-METER DIVISION
1822 E. Route 66 St., PMB 209, Glendora, California 91740
CEO: Luis Reyes, Mgr.
Bus: *Aerospace.*
Tel: (626) 852-9403
Fax: (626) 852-9406
%FO: 100

VIBRO-METER INC.
2836 Woodmount Circle, Modesto, California 95355
CEO: Dave Martin
Bus: *Industrial & Marine*
Tel: (209) 595-1450
Fax: (209) 552-2236

• VITRA INTERNATIONAL AG
Klunenfeldstrasse 22, CH-4127 Birsfelden, Switzerland
CEO: Patrick Guntzburger, CEO
Bus: *Mfr. of ergonomic office chairs, sofas and desks.*
Tel: 41-61-377-0000
Fax: 41-61-377-1510
www.vitra.com

NAICS: 337121, 337211, 337214

VITRA INC.
29 Ninth Ave., New York, New York 10014
CEO: Guy Geier
Bus: *Mfr./distribution of ergonomic office chairs, sofas and desks.*
Tel: (212) 929-3626
Fax: (212) 929-6424
%FO: 100
Emp: 15

VITRA INC.
557 Pacific Ave., San Francisco, California 94133
CEO: Guy Geier, VP
Bus: *Production facility for manufacture of office furniture.*
Tel: (415) 296-0711
Fax: (415) 296-0709
%FO: 100
Emp: 30

• VOLKART BROTHERS HOLDING LTD.
PO Box 343, CH-8401 Winterthur, Switzerland
CEO: Andreas Reinhart, Pres.
Bus: *Investment and management holding company.*
Tel: 41-52-268-6868
Fax: 41-52-268-6889
www.volkart.ch

NAICS: 551112

VOLKART AMERICA, INC.,c/O GSM LLC
6840 North First Ave., Phoenix, Arizona 85013
CEO: Walter Locher
Bus: *Cotton trading.*
Tel: (602) 222-9213
Fax: (602) 222-9214
%FO: 100
Emp: 15

• VON ROLL MANAGEMENT AG
Edenstr. 20, CH-8045 Zurich, Switzerland
CEO: Alfred M. Niederer, Chmn.
Bus: *Environmental engineering and services, electrical insulation, casting, pressure pipes and*
Tel: 41-44-204-3000
Fax: 41-44-204-3012
www.vonroll.ch
NAICS: 326150, 332618

VON ROLL INC.
302 Research Dr., Ste. 130, Norcross, Georgia 30092
CEO: Mitch Gorski, VP   Tel: (770) 613-9788   %FO: 100
Bus: *Waste management, sewage treatment,*   Fax: (770) 613-9860   Emp: 10
    multiple hearth plants, recovery systems.

VON ROLL INC.
1250 St. George St., East Liverpool, Ohio 43920-5919
CEO: Fred Sigg, VP   Tel: (330) 385-7337   %FO: 100
Bus: *Waste incineration, waste management,*   Fax: (330) 385-7813   Emp: 170
    remedial consulting.

VON ROLL ISOLA INC.
1 West Campbell Rd., Schenectady, New York 12306
CEO: Jack Craig, Pres. & CEO   Tel: (518) 344-7100   %FO: 100
Bus: *Insulation materials manufacture and sales.*   Fax: (518) 344-7288   Emp: 230

- **VONTOBEL HOLDING AG**
Toedistr. 27, CH-8022 Zurich, Switzerland
CEO: Herbert J. Scheidt, CEO   Tel: 41-58-283-5900   Rev: $6,418
Bus: *Banking and financial services.*   Fax: 41-58-283-7500   Emp: 890
     www.vontobel.com
NAICS: 523110, 523120, 523920, 523930, 523991, 523999, 525110, 525120, 525190, 525910, 525920, 525990

    VONTOBEL ASSET MANAGEMENT, INC.
    450 Park Ave., 7/F, New York, New York 10022
    CEO: Heinrich Schlegal, Pres.   Tel: (212) 415-7000   %FO: 100
    Bus: *Investment advisory.*   Fax: (212) 415-7087   Emp: 26

- **WAGNER INTERNATIONAL AG**
Postfach 109, Industriestr. 22, CH-9450 Altstaetten, Switzerland
CEO: Gunter Cott, CEO   Tel: 41-71-757-2211
Bus: *Paint spray equipment manufacturer.*   Fax: 41-71-757-2222
     www.wagner-group.ch
NAICS: 325510, 423830

    WAGNER SPRAY TECH CORPORATION
    1770 Fernbrook Lane, PO Box 279, Minneapolis, Minnesota 55440
    CEO: Sean C. James, Pres.   Tel: (763) 553-7000   %FO: 100
    Bus: *Mfr. paint spray equipment.*   Fax: (763) 553-7288   Emp: 345

    WAGNER SYSTEMS
    175 Della Ct., Carol Stream, Illinois 60188
    CEO: Sean James, CEO   Tel: (630) 784-8900
    Bus: *Special industry machinery*   Fax: (630) 784-8970   Emp: 50

    WALTHER PILOT NORTH AMERICA
    46890 Continental Dr., Chesterfield, Michigan 48047
    CEO: Bill Johnesee, Owner   Tel: (877) 925-8437
    Bus: *Air & gas compressors.*   Fax: (586) 598-1457   Emp: 20

- **WINTERTHUR SWISS INSURANCE COMPANY, DIV. CREDIT SUISSE**
General Guisan-Str. 40, Winterthur, CH-8401 Zurich, Switzerland
CEO: Leonhard H. Fischer, CEO — Tel: 41-52-261-1111 — Rev: $255,263
Bus: *General insurance services.* — Fax: 41-52-261-6620 — Emp: 20,281
www.winterthur.com
NAICS: 334518, 523991, 523999, 524113, 524126, 525110, 525120, 525190, 525910, 525920, 525990

    GENERAL CASUALTY INSURANCE, DIV. WINTERTHUR
    One General Dr., Sun Prairie, Wisconsin 53596
    CEO: Pete McPartland, Pres. & CEO — Tel: (608) 837-4440 — %FO: 100
    Bus: *Insurance services.* — Fax: (608) 837-4418 — Emp: 1,900

    WINTERTHUR INSURANCE CONPANY
    2727 Turtle Creek Blvd., Dallas, Texas 75219
    CEO: John R. Pollock, Pres. — Tel: (214) 559-1222
    Bus: *Insurance services.* — Fax: (214) 748-9590

- **WRH WALTER REIST HOLDING AG**
Industriestr. 1, CH-8340 Hinwil, Switzerland
CEO: Walter Reist, Pres. — Tel: 41-1-938-7000
Bus: *Mfr. conveying and processing system for* — Fax: 41-1-938-7070 — Emp: 1,700
printing industry. — www.walter-reist-holding.ch
NAICS: 333293

    FERAG INC.
    190 Rittenhouse Circle, PO Box 137, Bristol, Pennsylvania 19007-0137
    CEO: Barry Evans — Tel: (215) 788-0892 — %FO: 100
    Bus: *Mfr. conveying and processing system for* — Fax: (215) 788-7597 — Emp: 150
    printing industry

- **DR. EGON ZEHNDER & PARTNER AG**
Toblerstr. 80, CH-8044 Zurich, Switzerland
CEO: Aage Daniel Meiland, Pres. — Tel: 41-44-267-6969 — Rev: $214
Bus: *Executive and board search; management* — Fax: 41-44-267-6967 — Emp: 1,000
consulting. — www.egonzehnder.com
NAICS: 541612, 561310

    EGON ZEHNDER INTERNATIONAL, INC.
    Courvoisier Centre 1, 501 Brickell Key Dr., Ste. 300, Miami, Florida 33131
    CEO: Gabriel Sanchez Zinny, Mgr. — Tel: (305) 329-4600
    Bus: *Executive and board research management* — Fax: (305) 358-4728
    consulting services

    EGON ZEHNDER INTERNATIONAL, INC.
    3475 Piedmont Rd., NE, Ste. 1900, Atlanta, Georgia 30305
    CEO: Jonathan Stroup, Mgr. — Tel: (404) 836-2800 — %FO: 100
    Bus: *Executive and board search, management* — Fax: (404) 876-4578
    consulting services.

    EGON ZEHNDER INTERNATIONAL, INC.
    350 Park Ave., 8/F, New York, New York 10022
    CEO: Daniel Meiland, Pres. — Tel: (212) 519-6000
    Bus: *Executive board research management* — Fax: (212) 519-6060 — Emp: 200
    consulting services

EGON ZEHNDER INTERNATIONAL, INC.
California Plaza II, 350 South Grand Ave., Ste. 3580, Los Angeles, California 90071
CEO: A. Daniel Meiland, CEO   Tel: (213) 337-1500
Bus: *Executive and board research management* Fax: (213) 621-8901
  consulting services

EGON ZEHNDER INTERNATIONAL, INC.
1400 Two Galleria Tower, 13455 Noel Rd., Dallas, Texas 75240
CEO: Brian Reinken, Mgr.   Tel: (972) 728-5910
Bus: *Executive and board research management* Fax: (972) 728-5915
  consulting services.

EGON ZEHNDER INTERNATIONAL, INC.
45 Milk St., 4/F, Boston, Massachusetts 02109
CEO: George L. Davis, Jr., Mgr.   Tel: (617) 535-3500   %FO: 100
Bus: *Executive and board search, management*   Fax: (617) 457-4949
  consulting services.

EGON ZEHNDER INTERNATIONAL, INC.
129 Page Mill Rd., Palo Alto, California 94304
CEO: Jon F. Carter   Tel: (650) 847-3000   %FO: 100
Bus: *Executive and board search, management*   Fax: (650) 847-3050
  consulting services.

EGON ZEHNDER INTERNATIONAL, INC.
1 North Wacker Dr., Ste. 2300, Chicago, Illinois 60606-2824
CEO: Jeff W. Dodson, Mgr.   Tel: (312) 260-8800   %FO: 100
Bus: *Executive and board search, management*   Fax: (312) 782-2846
  consulting services.

EGON ZEHNDER INTERNATIONAL, INC.
100 Spear St., Ste. 920, San Francisco, California 94105
CEO: Tel: (415) 228-5200   %FO: 100
Bus: *Executive and board search, management*   Fax: (415) 904-7801
  consulting services.

● **ZEHNDER HOLDING LTD.**
Moortalstr 1, Aargau, CH-5722 Granichen, Switzerland
CEO: Hans P. Zehnder, Pres.   Tel: 41-62-855-1500   Rev: $272
Bus: *Industrial group, specializing in aluminum radiators* Fax: Emp: 2,543
  and space heaters.   www.zehndergroup.com/de
NAICS: 525910, 551112

  RUNTAL NORTH AMERICA, INC.
  187 Neck Rd., Haverhill, Massachusetts 01835
  CEO: Hans Peter Zehneder, Chmn.   Tel: (973) 373-1666   %FO: 100
  Bus: *Mfr./sales of radiators and space heaters..* Fax: Emp: 45

● **ZELLWEGER LUWA AG**
Wilstrasse 11, CH-8610 Uster, Switzerland
CEO: Konrad Peter, CEO   Tel: 41-1-943-5151   Rev: $950
Bus: *Engaged in textile air engineering and*   Fax: 41-1-943-5152   Emp: 4,700
  environmental and energy engineering. www.luwa.com
NAICS: 333292, 333412

ATLAS MECHANICAL & INDUSTRIAL LLC
1380 Enterprise St., Idaho Falls, Idaho 83402
CEO: Con Mahoney
Bus: *Air conditioning products manufacture.*

Tel: (208) 523-7030
Fax: (208) 529-8743

%FO: 100

INTERMECH INC.
Box 10 458, Winston Salem, North Carolina 27108
CEO: Hugh McPherson
Bus: *Air conditioning filters manufacture.*

Tel: (336) 760-3111
Fax: (336) 760-1548

%FO: 100

LOGAN HEATING AND AIR CONDITIONING
PO Box 11064, Winston Salem, North Carolina 27116
CEO: Travis Sink
Bus: *Air conditioning products manufacture.*

Tel: (336) 785-4308
Fax: (336) 924-0278

%FO: 100

LUWA BAHNSON, INC.
1750 Stebbins Dr., Houston, Texas 77043
CEO: Raymond K. Schneider
Bus: *Engaged in textile and industrial air
engineering and building management
services.*

Tel: (713) 461-1131
Fax: (713) 461-6319

%FO: 100

LUWA ENVIRONMENTAL SPECIALITIES
4412 Tryon Rd., Ste. A, Raleigh, North Carolina 27606
CEO: Murray V. Godley, VP
Bus: *Environmental engineering services.*

Tel: (919) 829-9300
Fax: (919) 829-7357

%FO: 100

LUWA USA INC.
3901 West Point Boulevard, PO Box 10458, Winston Salem, North Carolina 27103
CEO: T. Patton, Pres.
Bus: *Engaged in textile and industrial air
engineering and building management
services.*

Tel: (336) 760-3434
Fax: (336) 760-0283

%FO: 100
Emp: 700

THOMPSON MECHANICAL CONTRACTORS INC.
Box 1370, Richland, Washington 99352
CEO: Karl Richenbach
Bus: *Mechanical contracting and piping.*

Tel: (509) 628-9141
Fax: (509) 628-9711

%FO: 100

● **ZURICH FINANCIAL SERVICES GROUP**
Mythenquai 2, CH-8022 Zurich, Switzerland
CEO: James J. Schiro, CEO
Bus: *Insurance, risk management products, investment
advisory services.*
NAICS: 524113, 524126

Tel: 41-1-625-2525
Fax: 41-1-625-2641
www.zurich.com

Rev: $59,678
Emp: 53,246

CENTRE GROUP HOLDINGS LTD.
105 East 17th St., New York, New York 10003
CEO: Richard Price, Pres.
Bus: *Insurance services.*

Tel: (917) 534-4500
Fax: (212) 898-5400

%FO: 100
Emp: 2

FARMERS GROUP, INC.
4680 Wilshire Blvd., Los Angeles, California 90010
CEO: Martin D. Feinstein, Chmn. & CEO
Bus: *Auto & vehicle insurance*

Tel: (323) 932-3200
Fax: (323) 932-3101

%FO: 100

FARMERS NEW WORLD LIFE INSURANCE COMPANY
3003 77th Ave. SE, Mercer Island, Washington 98040
CEO: C. Paul Patsis, Pres.　　　　　　　Tel:　(206) 232-8400　　　　　%FO: 100
Bus: *Financial services; property and casualty*　Fax:　(206) 236-6519　　　　　Emp: 800
　　insurance.

FOREMOST INSURANCE COMPANY
5600 Beech Tree Lane, Caledonia, Michigan 49316
CEO: F. Robert Woudstra, CFO　　　　　Tel:　(616) 942-3000
Bus: *Auto & Vehicle Insurance*　　　　　Fax:　(616) 956-3990

RISK ENTERPRISE MANAGEMENT LTD.
2540 Route 130, Ste. 109, Cranbury, New Jersey 08512
CEO: Mike Riney, Pres.　　　　　　　Tel:　(609) 495-0001
Bus: *Insurance services.*　　　　　　Fax:　(609) 495-0252　　　　　Emp: 316

UNIVERSAL UNDERWRITERS GROUP
7045 College Blvd., Overland Park, Kansas 66211
CEO: Stephen R. Smith, Pres. & CEO　　Tel:　(913) 339-1000　　　　　%FO: 100
Bus: *Financial services.*　　　　　　Fax:　(913) 391-1026　　　　　Emp: 1,321

ZC STERLING CORPORATION
210 Interstate North Pkwy., Ste. 400, Atlanta, Georgia 30339
CEO: William J. Krochalis, Pres. & CEO　Tel:　(770) 690-8400
Bus: *Insurance services.*　　　　　　Fax:　(770) 690-8240　　　　　Emp: 1,133

ZURICH
13810 FNB. Pkwy., Omaha, Nebraska 68154
CEO: Axel Lehmann, CEO　　　　　　Tel:　(402) 963-5000
Bus: *Insurance services.*　　　　　　Fax:　(402) 963-5329　　　　　Emp: 503

ZURICH CAPITAL MARKETS, INC.
105 East 17th St., New York, New York 10003
CEO: Richard Price, CEO　　　　　　Tel:　(917) 534-4900
Bus: *Management services*　　　　　　Fax:　(212) 208-3601　　　　　Emp: 20

ZURICH U.S.
North America Commercial, Zurich Towers, 1400 American Lane, Schaumburg, Illinois 60196
CEO: Axel P. Lehmann, CEO　　　　　Tel:　(847) 605-6000　　　　　%FO: 100
Bus: *Financial services.*　　　　　　Fax:　(847) 605-6011

Taiwan (ROC)

- **ACCTON TECHNOLOGY CORP.**
  1 Creation Rd. III, 3 Science Based Industrial Park, Hsinchu 300, Taiwan (ROC)
  CEO: Doo Yi-min, Chmn. & Pres.   Tel: 886-3-5770-270   Rev: $479
  Bus: *Mfr. of networking and communication equipment*   Fax: 886-3-5780-764
                                                       www.accton.com
  NAICS: 334290

  > **ACCTON TECHNOLOGY CORPORATION**
  > 2880 Lakeside Dr., Ste.200, Santa Clara, California 95054
  > CEO: Mark Graham, VP & Gen. Mgr.   Tel: (408) 330-0940   %FO: 100
  > Bus: *Manufacturer networking and*   Fax: (408) 330-0945
  >   *communication equipment*

  > **ACCTON TECHNOLOGY CORPORATION**
  > 1362 Borregas Ave., Sunnyvale, California 94089
  > CEO: Mark Graham, VP & Gen. Mgr.   Tel: (408) 747-0994   %FO: 100
  > Bus: *Manufacturer networking and*   Fax: (408) 747-0982
  >   *communication equipment*

- **ACER INC.**
  9/F, 88 Hsin Tai Wu Rd., Sec. 1, Taipei Hsien 221, Taiwan (ROC)
  CEO: J. T. Wang, Chmn.   Tel: 886-2-2696-1234   Rev: $4,622
  Bus: *Computers and peripheries manufacturer.* Fax: 886-2-8696-1777   Emp: 39,000
                                                       www.acer.com
  NAICS: 334111

  > **ACER AMERICA CORPORATION**
  > 2641 Orchard Pkwy., San Jose, California 95134
  > CEO: Rudi Schmidleithner, CEO   Tel: (408) 432-6200   %FO: 100
  > Bus: *Computers & peripherals sales.*   Fax: (408) 922-2933

- **ADI CORP.**
  14/F, No. 1, Sec. 4, Nanking East Rd., Taipei 10569, Taiwan (ROC)
  CEO: Stephen Chou,, Pres. & CEO   Tel: 886-22-2713-3337   Rev: $1,200
  Bus: *Computer peripherals and color monitors.* Fax: 886-22-2713-6555
                                                       www.adi.com.tw
  NAICS: 334111

  > **VISTAMAX, ADI SYSTEMS INC.**
  > 6723 Mowry Ave., Newark, California 94560
  > CEO: Patrick Lai, Pres.   Tel: (510) 791-1378   %FO: 100
  > Bus: *Display monitors manufacturing.*   Fax: (510) 797-5469   Emp: 60

- **ADVANCED SEMICONDUCTOR ENGINEERING, INC.**
  26 Chin 3rd Rd., Nantze Export Processing Zone, Kaohsiung, Taiwan (ROC)
  CEO: Jason C. S. Chang, CEO   Tel: 886-7-361-7131   Rev: $2,583
  Bus: *Semiconductor packaging services.*   Fax: 886-7-361-4546   Emp: 24,443
                                                       www.aseglobal.com
  NAICS: 334413

ADVANCED SEMICONDUCTOR ENGINEERING, INC.
3590 Peterson Way, Santa Clara, California 95054
CEO: Jennifer Yuen
Bus: *Semiconductor packaging services.*
Tel: (408) 986-6500
Fax: (408) 565-0289
%FO: 100

● **ASUSTEK COMPUTER, INC.**
150 Li-Teh Rd., Taipei 11248, Taiwan (ROC)
CEO: Tzu Hsien Tung, Pres.
Bus: *High quality motherboards, notebooks, VGA cards, servers, broadband modems, and optical storage devices manufacture.*
Tel: 886-2-2894-3447
Fax: 886-2-2894-3449
www.asus.com.tw
Rev: $2,000
NAICS: 541511, 541519

ASUS COMPUTER INTERNATIONAL, INC.
6737 Mowry Ave., Bldg. 2, Newark, California 94560
CEO: Margaret Chen, Pres.
Bus: *Distributes computer hardware.*
Tel: (510) 739-3777
Fax: (510) 608-4555
%FO: 100

● **AU OPTRONICS CORPORATION**
No. 1, Li-Hsin Rd. 2, Science Based Industrial Park, Hsinchu 300, Taiwan (ROC)
CEO: Hsuan Bin Chen, CEO
Bus: *Flat panel display manufacture.*
Tel: 886-3-563-2899
Fax: 886-3-563-7608
www.auo.com
Rev: $5,072
Emp: 20,000
NAICS: 334419

AU OPTRONICS CORPORATION AMERICA
1450 Birchmeadow Ln., San Jose, California 95131
CEO: Yawen Hsiao
Bus: *Flat panel display manufacture.*
Tel: (408) 433-5278
Fax: (408) 433-5278
%FO: 100

AU OPTRONICS CORPORATION AMERICA
7711 O'Connor Dr., Ste. 516, Round Rock, Texas 78681
CEO: Max Weishun Cheng
Bus: *Flat panel display manufacture.*
Tel: (512) 248-1200
Fax: (512) 248-1200
%FO: 100

● **BANK OF TAIWAN**
120 Chung Ching South Rd., Sec. 1, Taipei City, Taipei 10049, Taiwan (ROC)
CEO: Joseph Jye-Cherng Lyu, Chmn.
Bus: *Commercial banking services.*
Tel: 886-22-349-3456
Fax: 886-22-314-6699
www.bot.com.tw
Rev: $1,857
Emp: 6,762
NAICS: 522110

BANK OF TAIWAN
100 Wall St., 11/F, New York, New York 10005
CEO: Eunice Yeh, Gen. Mgr.
Bus: *International banking services.*
Tel: (212) 968-8128
Fax: (212) 968-8370
%FO: 100

BANK OF TAIWAN
601 South Figueroa St., Ste. 4525, Los Angeles, California 90017
CEO: Ivy Huang, Mgr.
Bus: *International banking services.*
Tel: (213) 629-6600
Fax: (213) 629-6610
%FO: 100

- **BENQ CORPORATION**
  157 Shan-ying Rd., Gueishan, Taoyuan 333, Taiwan (ROC)
  CEO: Kuen-Yao (K. Y.) Lee, CEO   Tel: 886-3359-5000   Rev: $3,759
  Bus: *Phone and electronics manufacture.*   Fax: 886-3359-9000   Emp: 14,772
     www.benq.com

  NAICS: 334111, 334411, 334412, 334417, 334418, 334419

  BENQ AMERICA CORPORATION
  8750 NW 36th St., Ste. 200, Miami, Florida 33178
  CEO: Stephanie Wang   Tel: (305) 421-1201   %FO: 100
  Bus: *Phone and electronics manufacture.*   Fax: (305) 421-1202

  BENQ AMERICA CORPORATION
  53 Discovery, Irvine, California 92618
  CEO: Ralph Tang   Tel: (949) 255-9500   %FO: 100
  Bus: *Phone and electronics manufacture.*   Fax: (949) 255-9600

- **CATHAY UNITED BANK**
  7 Sung Ten Rd., Taipei City, Taipei 11073, Taiwan (ROC)
  CEO: Kuo Hwa, Pres.   Tel: 886-2-8722-6666   Rev: $1,289
  Bus: *Commercial banking services.*   Fax: 886-2-8789-0349   Emp: 4,016
     www.uwccb.com.tw

  NAICS: 522110

  CATHAY UNITED BANK LTD.
  555 West Fifth St., Ste. 3850, The Gas Company Tower, Los Angeles, California 90013
  CEO: Allen Y. Peng, VP   Tel: (213) 243-1234   %FO: 100
  Bus: *International banking services.*   Fax: (213) 627-6817   Emp: 13

- **CHANG HWA COMMERCIAL BANK, LTD.**
  57 Chung Shan N. Rd., Sec. 2, Taipei City, Taiwan (ROC)
  CEO: Pao Hsin Chang, Pres.   Tel: 886-225-362-951   Rev: $1,128
  Bus: *Commercial, savings, trust & international banking*   Fax: Emp: 5,729
  services.   www.chb.com.tw
  NAICS: 522110

  CHANG HWA COMMERCIAL BANK
  333 S. Grand Ave., Ste. 600, Los Angeles, California 90071
  CEO: Chenyu Chen, Pres.   Tel: (213) 620-7200   %FO: 100
  Bus: *Bank branch operations, lending and*   Fax: (213) 620-7227   Emp: 18
  treasury services.

  CHANG HWA COMMERCIAL BANK
  685 3rd Ave., 29/F, New York, New York 10017
  CEO: Mark Lin, Gen. Mgr.   Tel: (212) 651-9770
  Bus: *Commercial bank*   Fax: (212) 651-9785

Taiwan (ROC)

● **CHI MEI OPTOELECRONICS CORPORATION**
No. 1, Chi-Yeh Rd., Tainan, Science Based Industrial Park, Tainan County 74147, Taiwan (ROC)
CEO: Jau-Yang Ho, Pres. & CEO   Tel: 886-6-505-1888   Rev: $3,206
Bus: *Mfr. research and sale of thin film transistor-liquid*   Fax: 886-6-505-1889   Emp: 13,000
crystal display panels and color filters for   www.cmo.com.tw
notebook, desktop monitor, and television
applications.
NAICS: 334411, 334413, 334419

> **INTERNATIONAL DISPLAY TECHNOLOGY USA**
> 101 Metro Dr., Ste. 510, San Jose, California 95110
> CEO: E. Raymond, Sales   Tel: (408) 573-8438   %FO: 100
> Bus: *Transistor-liquid crystal display panels*   Fax: (408) 573-9438
> *manufacture.*

● **CHINA AIRLINES**
131 Nanking Rd. East, Section 3, Taipei, Taiwan (ROC)
CEO: Wei Hsing-Hsiung, Pres.   Tel: 886-22-715-1212   Rev: $1,990
Bus: *Commercial air transport services.*   Fax: 886-22-514-6005   Emp: 9,450
www.china-airlines.com
NAICS: 481111

> **CHINA AIRLINES**
> 380 World Way, Ste. S14, Los Angeles, California 90045-5874
> CEO: Yongming Tao, CEO   Tel: (310) 215-5660   %FO: 100
> Bus: *Commercial air transport services.*   Fax: (310) 215-5660   Emp: 30

> **CHINA AIRLINES**
> 225 North Michigan Ave., Chicago, Illinois 60601-7601
> CEO: Fred Tsao, Mgr.   Tel: (312) 856-1001   %FO: 100
> Bus: *Commercial air transport services.*   Fax: (312) 856-1001   Emp: 32

● **CHINESE PETROLEUM CORPORATION**
3 Sungren Rd., Shinyi Chui, Taipei 11010, Taiwan (ROC)
CEO: Wenent P. Pan, Pres.   Tel: 886-2-8789-8989   Rev: $13,599
Bus: *Oil & gas refining, marketing, distribution,*   Fax: 886-2-8789-9000   Emp: 15,559
exploration, production, transportation & storage   www.cpc.com.tw
NAICS: 211111, 211112, 213111, 213112, 221210, 324110, 324191, 324199, 333132, 424710, 424720, 447110,
447190, 454311, 454312, 454319, 486110,
486210, 486910, 541360

> **OPICOIL AMERICA, INC.**
> 3040 Post Oak Blvd., Ste. 800, Houston, Texas 77056
> CEO: Wayne Dai, Pres.   Tel: (713) 840-7171
> Bus: *Oil & gas exploration services*   Fax: (713) 297-8108   Emp: 32

● **CHIPMOS TECHNOLOGIES LTD.**
No. 1, R & D Rd. 1, Science-Based Industrial Park, Hsinchu, Taiwan (ROC)
CEO: Shih-Jye Cheng, CEO   Tel: 886-3-577-0055   Rev: $474
Bus: *Contract testing and packaging services for chip*   Fax: 886-3-566-8989   Emp: 3,139
makers.   www.chipmos.com.tw
NAICS: 334413

CHIPMOS USA INC.
3015 Copper Rd., Santa Clara, California 95051
CEO: Hiro Yoshida
Bus: *Contract testing and packaging services for chip makers.*

Tel: (408) 481-3107
Fax: (408) 830-9405

%FO: 100

● **CMC MAGNETICS CORPORATION**
53 Ming Chuan West Rd., 15th Fl., Taipei, Taiwan (ROC)
CEO: Bob M. S. Wong, CEO
Bus: *Optical and magnetic storage media products manufacture.*
NAICS: 334112, 334613

Tel: 886-2-2598-9890
Fax: 886-2-2598-9896
www.cmcdisc.com

Rev: $555
Emp: 2,993

CMC MAGNETICS CORPORATION
4339 Clear Valley Dr., Encino, California 91436
CEO: David Karron
Bus: *Optical and magnetic storage media products manufacture.*

Tel: (818) 501-1011
Fax: (818) 501-7547

%FO: 100

● **DEE VAN ENTERPRISE CO., LTD.**
5 Pao Kao Rd., Hsin Tien, Taipei, Taiwan (ROC)
CEO: Tony S. D. Tseng, CEO
Bus: *Computer multimedia and telecommunications accessories manufacture.*
NAICS: 334111, 334416, 335311

Tel: 886-2-2917-7002
Fax: 886-2-2915-4370
www.deevan.com.tw

DEE VAN ENTERPRISE USA INC.
4020 Clipper Ct., Fremont, California 94538
CEO: Felix C. Mu-Lu
Bus: *Computer multimedia and telecommunications accessories manufacture.*

Tel: (510) 623-0628
Fax:(510) 623-0529

%FO: 100

● **D-LINK CORPORATION**
2F, No. No. 119 Pao-Chung Rd., Hsin-Tien, Taipei, Taiwan (ROC)
CEO: Ken Kao, CEO
Bus: *Mfr. data communications hardware.*

Tel: 886-22-910-2626
Fax: 886-22-910-1515
www.dlink.com.tw

Rev: $734
Emp: 3,200

NAICS: 334210

D-LINK SYSTEMS, INC.
17595 Mount Herrmann St., Fountain Valley, California 92708
CEO: Steven H. Joe
Bus: *Mfr. data communications hardware.*

Tel: (714) 885-6000
Fax: (714) 885-6000

%FO: 100

● **EVA AIRWAYS CORPORATION**
117 Chang-An Rd., 9/F, Taipei 104, Taiwan (ROC)
CEO: Steven Lin, Chmn.
Bus: *Passenger and cargo carrier.*
NAICS: 561599

Tel: 886-2-85002533
Fax: 886-3-351-0005
www.evaair.com

Rev: $2,585
Emp: 4,934

EVA AIRWAYS CORPORATION
12440 East Imperial Hwy., Ste. 250, Norwalk, California 90650
CEO: K. W. Chang   Tel: (310) 646-9818   %FO: 100
Bus: *Passenger and cargo carrier.*   Fax: (301) 646-9818

EVA AIRWAYS CORPORATION
100 Paonia Ave., Ste. 310, Jersey City, New Jersey 07310
CEO: K. W. Chang   Tel: (973) 623-3260   %FO: 100
Bus: *Passenger and cargo carrier.*   Fax: (973) 623-3260

EVA AIRWAYS CORPORATION
18000 Pacific Hwy. South, Ste. 108, Seattle, Washington 98188
CEO: K. W. Chang   Tel: (206) 242-6868   %FO: 100
Bus: *Passenger and cargo carrier.*   Fax: (206) 242-6868

EVA AIRWAYS CORPORATION
1350 Bayshore Hwy., Ste. 820, Burlingame, California 94010
CEO: K. W. Chang   Tel: (650) 360-6800   %FO: 100
Bus: *Passenger and cargo carrier.*   Fax: (850) 360-6800

● **EVERGREEN MARINE CORPORATION (TAIWAN) LTD.**
166 Minsheng East Rd., Sec 2, Taipei 10444, Taiwan (ROC)
CEO: Arnold Wang, Pres.   Tel: 886-22-505-7766   Rev: $1,550
Bus: *International container shipping and cargo*   Fax: 886-22-505-5256   Emp: 1,500
     services.   www.evergreen-marine.com
NAICS: 483111

   EVERGREEN AMERICA CORPORATION
   1 Evertrust Plaza, Jersey City, New Jersey 07302
   CEO: Thoms Chen, Pres. & CEO   Tel: (201) 761-3000   %FO: 100
   Bus: *International commercial shipping & air*   Fax: (201) 761-3010   Emp: 650
        cargo and transport - US, Canada &
        Caribbean operations.

● **FARADAY TECHNOLOGY CORPORATION**
10-2, Li-Hsin First Rd., Science-based Industrial Park, Hsinchu 200233, Taiwan (ROC)
CEO: Hsiao-Ping Lin, CEO   Tel: 886-3-578-7888   Rev: $168
Bus: *Semiconductor manufacture.*   Fax: 886-3-578-7889   Emp: 431
                                 www.faraday.com.tw
NAICS: 334413

   FARADAY TECHNOLOGY CORPORATION
   490 De Guigne Dr., Sunnyvale, California 94085-3903
   CEO: Charlie Hauck   Tel: (408) 522-8888   %FO: 100
   Bus: *Semiconductor manufacture.*   Fax: (408) 522-8889

   FARADAY TECHNOLOGY CORPORATION
   315 Huls, Clayton, Ohio 45315
   CEO: Phillip Miller   Tel: (937) 836-7749   %FO: 100
   Bus: *Semiconductor manufacture.*   Fax: (937) 836-7749

- **FIRST COMMERCIAL BANK**
  30 Chung King South Rd., Sec. 1, Taipei 100, Taiwan (ROC)
  CEO: Ann-Chi Chen, Pres.
  Bus: *General banking services.*

  Tel: 886-2-2348-1111
  Fax: 886-2-2361-0036
  www.firstbank.com.tw

  NAICS: 522110

  > **FIRST COMMERCIAL BANK**
  > 4250 Barranca Pkwy., Suite E, Irvine, California 92604
  > CEO: Daisy Hyse
  > Bus: *General banking services.*
  >
  > Tel: (949) 654-2888
  > Fax: (949) 654-2899
  >
  > %FO: 100

  > **FIRST COMMERCIAL BANK**
  > 750 Third Ave., New York, New York 10017
  > CEO: Bruce Ju
  > Bus: *General banking services.*
  >
  > Tel: (212) 599-6868
  > Fax: (212) 599-6133
  >
  > %FO: 100

  > **FIRST COMMERCIAL BANK**
  > 1309 S. Baldwin Ave., Arcadia, California 91007
  > CEO: Anne Chou
  > Bus: *General banking services.*
  >
  > Tel: (626) 254-1828
  > Fax: (662) 254-1883
  >
  > %FO: 100

- **FIRST INTERNATIONAL COMPUTER, INC.**
  No. 300, Yang Guang St., NeiHu, Taipei 114, Taiwan (ROC)
  CEO: Ming J. Chien, CEO
  Bus: *PC and servers manufacture.*

  Tel: 886-2-8571-8571
  Fax: 886-2-8571-8837
  www.fic.com.tw

  Rev: $1,900
  Emp: 4,500

  NAICS: 334111, 334119

  > **FIRST INTERNATIONAL COMPUTER OF AMERICA, INC.**
  > 5020 Brandin Ct., Fremont, California 94538-3140
  > CEO: John Villejo
  > Bus: *PC and servers manufacture.*
  >
  > Tel: (510) 252-7700
  > Fax: (510) 252-8888
  >
  > %FO: 100

- **FORMOSA PLASTICS, DIV. FORMOSAN RUBBER GROUP**
  201 TunG Hwa North Rd., Taipei, Taiwan (ROC)
  CEO: C. T. Lee, Pres.
  Bus: *Mfr. rubber, PU and PVC-coated fabrics and a wide range of logistical support equipment, plastic resins and petrochemicals.*

  Tel: 886-22-712-2211
  Fax: 886-22-712-9211
  www.fpc.com.tw

  Rev: $3,813
  Emp: 4,711

  NAICS: 325110, 325181, 325188, 325199, 325211, 325212, 325221, 325222, 334413

  > **FORMOSA PLASTICS CORPORATION**
  > 9 Peach Tree Hill Rd., Livingston, New Jersey 07039
  > CEO: Robert Chou, EVP
  > Bus: *Plastic resins and petrochemicals manufacture.*
  >
  > Tel: (973) 992-2090
  > Fax: (973) 992-9627
  >
  > %FO: 100
  > Emp: 2,700

  > **FORMOSA PLASTICS CORPORATION**
  > 201 Formosa Dr., PO Box 700, Point Comfort, Texas 77978
  > CEO: Michael W. Rivet, VP
  > Bus: *Mfr. plastic resins and petrochemicals.*
  >
  > Tel: (361) 987-7000
  > Fax: (361) 987-2721
  >
  > %FO: 100

INTEPLAST GROUP LTD.
9 Peach Tree Hill Rd., Livingston, New Jersey 07039
CEO: John D. Young
Bus: *Plastic products manufacture.*
Tel: (973) 994-8000
Fax: (973) 994-8005
%FO: 100

J-M MANUFACTURING
9 Peach Tree Hill Rd., Livingston, New Jersey 07039
CEO: Walter W. Wang
Bus: *PVC and high-density polyethylene (HDPE) pipe products manufacture.*
Tel: (973) 535-1633
Fax: (973) 535-1632
%FO: 100

● **FUBON FINANCIAL HOLDING COMPANY**
237 Chien Kuo South Rd., Section 1, Taipei, Taiwan (ROC)
CEO: Daniel Tsai, Chmn.
Bus: *Financial services.*
Tel: 886-2-6636-6636
Fax: 886-2-6636-0111
www.fubongroup.com.tw
Rev: $4,013

NAICS: 522110, 523999

TAIPEI BANK
100 Wall St., 14/F, New York, New York 10005
CEO: Sophia Jing
Bus: *Financial services.*
Tel: (212) 968-9888
Fax: (212) 968-9800
%FO: 100

TAIPEI BANK
700 South Flower St., Ste. 3300, Los Angeles, California 90017
CEO: Jason C. Chen
Bus: *Financial services.*
Tel: (213) 236-9151
Fax: (213) 236-9155
%FO: 100

● **GIANT MANUFACTURING CO., LTD.**
19 Shun-Farn Rd., Tachia, Taichung, Taiwan (ROC)
CEO: Chin-Piao Liu, Chmn. & CEO
Bus: *Bicycle manufacture.*
Tel: 886-4-2681-4771
Fax: 886-4-2681-6980
www.giant-bicycle.com
Rev: $450
Emp: 4,500

NAICS: 336991

GIANT BICYCLE USA INC.
3587 Old Conejo Rd., Newbury Park, California 91320
CEO: Skip Hess, Pres. & CEO
Bus: *Bicycle manufacture and sales.*
Tel: (805) 267-4600
Fax: (805) 376-8095
%FO: 100

● **HUA NAN BANK**
38, Sec. 1, Chung-King South Road,, Taipei, Taiwan (ROC)
CEO: Oliver Hsu Cheng-Hua, CEO
Bus: *Commercial banking services.*
Tel: 886-2-2371-3111
Fax: 886-2-2331-6741
www.hncb.com.tw

NAICS: 522110

HUA NAN COMMERCIAL BANK
330 Madison Ave., 38/F, New York, New York 10017
CEO:
Bus: *Commercial banking services.*
Tel: (212) 286-1999
Fax: (212) 286-1212

HUA NAN COMMERCIAL BANK
707 Wilshire Blvd., Ste. 3100, Los Angeles, California 90017-3501
CEO: David Chen
Bus: *Commercial banking services.*
Tel: (213) 362-6666
Fax: (213) 362-6617
%FO: 100

● **THE INTERNATIONAL COMMERCIAL BANK OF CHINA**
100 Chi Lin Rd., Taipei 104, Taiwan (ROC)
CEO: Y.T. Tsai, Pres.
Bus: *Commercial banking services.*
Tel: 886-22-563-3156
Fax: 886-22-561-1216
www.icbc.com.tw
Rev: $1,200
Emp: 3,311

NAICS: 522110

THE INTERNATIONAL COMMERCIAL BANK OF CHINA
445 S. Figueroa St., Ste. 1900, Los Angeles, California 90071
CEO: Tom Huang, Mgr.
Bus: *Commercial banking services.*
Tel: (213) 489-3000
Fax: (213) 489-1183
%FO: 100
Emp: 31

THE INTERNATIONAL COMMERCIAL BANK OF CHINA
2 North LaSalle St., Ste. 1803, Chicago, Illinois 60602
CEO: Henry Ho, Mgr.
Bus: *Commercial banking services.*
Tel: (312) 782-9900
Fax: (312) 782-2402
%FO: 100
Emp: 13

THE INTERNATIONAL COMMERCIAL BANK OF CHINA
65 Liberty St., New York, New York 10005
CEO:
Bus: *Commercial banking services.*
Tel: (212) 608-4222
Fax: (212) 608-4943
%FO: 100

● **INVENTEC CORPORATION**
66 Hou-Kang St., Taipei, Taiwan (ROC)
CEO: Kuo-yi Yeh, Chmn.
Bus: *Contract manufacturing of notebook and desktop computers.*
Tel: 886-2-2881-0721
Fax: 886-2-28837729
www.inventec.co.tw
Rev: $4,107
Emp: 2,060

NAICS: 334111, 334119, 334419

INVENTEC MANUFACTURING CORP.
6215 West by Northwest, Ste. B, Houston, Texas 77040
CEO: C. W. Lin, SVP
Bus: *Contract manufacturing and sales of notebook and desktop computers.*
Tel: (713) 996-5200
Fax: (713) 996-5314
%FO: 100

● **LITE-ON TECHNOLOGY CORPORATION**
22/F, 392 Ruey Kuang Rd., Neihu, Taipei 114, Taiwan (ROC)
CEO: Raymond Soong, Chmn.
Bus: *Consumer and computer electronic products manufacture.*
Tel: 886-02-8798-2888
Fax: 886-02-8798-2866
www.liteon.com
Rev: $2,922
Emp: 3,435

NAICS: 334210, 334411, 334413, 334417, 334419

LITE-ON TRADING USA INC.
720 South Hillview Dr., Milpitas, California 95035
CEO: K.C. Terng
Bus: *Optoelectronics.*
Tel: (408) 945-0222
Fax: (408) 945-0222
%FO: 100

LITE-ON TRADING USA INC.
17 Santa Arletta, Rancho Santa Margarita, California 92688
CEO: K.C. Terng   Tel: (949) 888-8822   %FO: 100
Bus: *Consumer and computer electronic products*   Fax: (949) 888-8466
      manufacture.

LITE-ON TRADING USA INC.
23201-117th St., Trevor, Wisconsin 53179
CEO: K.C. Terng   Tel: (262) 862-9451   %FO: 100
Bus: *Consumer and computer electronic products*   Fax: (262) 862-9460
      manufacture.

LITE-ON TRADING USA INC.
1817 W. Braker Lane, Suite 100, Austin, Texas 78758
CEO: K.C. Terng   Tel: (512) 835-6052   %FO: 100
Bus: *Consumer and computer electronic products*   Fax: (512) 835-4942
      manufacture.

● **MACRONIX INTERNATIONAL CO., LTD.**
No. 16, Li-Hsin Rd., Science-Based Industrial Park, Hsinchu, Taiwan (ROC)
CEO: Miin Wu, Chmn. & Pres.   Tel: 886-3-578-6688   Rev: $725
Bus: *Memory chips manufacture.*   Fax: 886-3-563-2888   Emp: 3,593
                                                    www.macronix.com
NAICS: 334112, 334413

   MACRONIX AMERICA, INC.
   680 N. McCarthy Blvd., Milpitas, California 95035
   CEO: Ray Mak, Chmn.   Tel: (408) 262-8887   %FO: 100
   Bus: *Memory chips manufacture.*   Fax: (408) 262-8810   Emp: 55

   MACRONIX AMERICA, INC.
   800E NW Highway, Palatine, Illinois 60067
   CEO: Alan Portnoy, Mgr.   Tel: (847) 963-1900   %FO: 100
   Bus: *Memory chips manufacture.*   Fax: (847) 963-1909

   MACRONIX COMPUTER CENTER AMERICA, INC.
   238 W. Theresia Rd., Saint Marys, Pennsylvania 15857
   CEO: Todd Anderson, Pres.   Tel: (814) 834-9117   %FO: 100
   Bus: *Retail computers & computer accessories.* Fax: Emp: 4

● **MICROTEK INTERNATIONAL INC.**
6 Industry East Rd. 3, Science-Based Industrial Park, Hsinchu, Taiwan (ROC)
CEO: Benny C. H. Hsu, Chmn. & Pres.   Tel: 886-3-577-2155   Rev: $221
Bus: *Mfr. of microcomputer simulators and desktop* Fax: 886-3-577-2598   Emp: 76
      video image processors.   www.microtek.com
NAICS: 333293, 333315, 334119

   MICROTEK
   16941 Keegan Ave., Carson, California 90746
   CEO: Benny Hsu, Chmn.   Tel: (310) 687-5800   %FO: 100
   Bus: *Sales/distribution of scanners,*   Fax: (310) 687-5984   Emp: 170
      microcomputer simulators and desktop video
      image processors.

- **MITAC INTERNATIONAL CORPORATION**
No. 200 Wen Hwa 2nd Rd., Kuei Shan Hsiang, Taoyuan, Taiwan (ROC)
CEO: Matthew F.C. Miau, Chmn.
Bus: *PC, monitor and hand-held computer manufacture.*
Tel: 886-3-328-9000
Fax: 886-3-328-9000
www.mitac.com
Rev: $4,564
Emp: 14,000

NAICS: 334111, 334119, 334417, 334419

   MITAC USA INC
   47988 Fremont Blvd., Fremont, California 94538
   CEO: Francis F. Tsai
   Bus: *PC, monitor and hand-held computer manufacture and sales.*
   Tel: (510) 252-6900
   Fax: (510) 252-6930
   %FO: 100

   MITAC USA INC
   7350 Denny Rd., Ste. 888, Houston, Texas 77040
   CEO: Miles Feuer
   Bus: *PC, monitor and hand-held computer manufacture, sales and service.*
   Tel: (713) 460-8868
   Fax: (713) 460-1103
   %FO: 100

   SYNNEX INFORMATION TECHNOLOGIES INC.
   3797 Spinnaker Ct., Fremont, California 94538
   CEO: Robert Huang
   Bus: *Provides information technology (IT) supply chain services.*
   Tel: (510) 656-3333
   Fax: (510) 440-3777
   %FO: 100

- **MOSEL VITELIC INC.**
No. 19 Li Hsin Rd., Science Based Industrial Park, Hsinchu, Taiwan (ROC)
CEO: S. J. Duan, CEO
Bus: *Mfr. memory integrated circuits.*
Tel: 886-3-579-5888
Fax: 886-3-566-5888
www.moselvitelic.com
Rev: $500
Emp: 1,075

NAICS: 334413

   MOSEL VITELIC CORPORATION
   3910 North First St., San Jose, California 95134
   CEO: John Seto, Pres.
   Bus: *Mfr. memory integrated circuits.*
   Tel: (408) 433-6000
   Fax: (408) 433-0952
   %FO: 100

- **NAN YA PLASTICS CORPORATION**
201 Tun Hwa North Rd., Taipei, Taiwan (ROC)
CEO: Yong-Ching Wang, Chmn. & CEO
Bus: *Mfr. plastics, PVC leather, sheeting, pipe; polyester fibers, laminates, plate and engineering plastics. (Sub of Formosa Plastics Corp.)*
Tel: 886-2-712-2211
Fax: 886-2-717-8533
www.npc.com.tw
Rev: $5,033
Emp: 15,998

NAICS: 325211, 325212, 325221, 325222

   NAY YA PLASTICS CORPORATION USA
   9 Peachtree Hill Rd., Livingston, New Jersey 07039
   CEO: Yong-Ching Wang, Chmn. & CEO
   Bus: *Mfr. plastics; PVC sheeting, polyester fibers.*
   Tel: (973) 992-2090
   Fax: (973) 716-7470
   %FO: 100
   Emp: 393

   NAY YA PLASTICS CORPORATION USA
   700 Hwy. 59 Loop RR, Wharton, Texas 77488
   CEO: W.T. Lin, Mgr.
   Bus: *Mfr. of rigid PVC film.*
   Tel: (979) 532-5494
   Fax: (979) 532-4836
   %FO: 100
   Emp: 350

NAY YA PLASTICS CORPORATION, AMERICA
140 East Beulah Rd., Lake City, South Carolina 29560
CEO: J.S. Tseng, Mgr.   Tel: (843) 389-7800   %FO: 100
Bus: *Mfr. plastics; PVC sheeting, polyester*   Fax: (843) 389-3559   Emp: 686
    fibers.

NAY YA PLASTICS CORPORATION, AMERICA
5561 Normandy Rd., Batchelor, Louisiana 70715
CEO: H.N. Yang, Mgr.   Tel: (225) 492-2435   %FO: 100
Bus: *Mfr. plastics; PVC sheeting, polyester*   Fax: (225) 492-2134   Emp: 259
    fibers.

● **NANYA TECHNOLOGY CORPORATION**
Hwa Ya Technology Park, 669 Fu Hsing 3rd Rd., Kueishan, Taoyuan, Taiwan (ROC)
CEO: Jih Lien, Pres.   Tel: 886-3-328-1688   Rev: $1,267
Bus: *Mfr. memory chips*   Fax: 886-3-396-0997   Emp: 3,416
                                             www.nanya.com

NAICS: 334112, 334113

    NANYA TECHNOLOGY CORPORATION
    25 Metro Dr., Ste. 230, San Jose, California 95110
    CEO: Ken Hurley, pres,   Tel: (408) 573-3888   %FO: 100
    Bus: *Manufacturer memory chips*   Fax: (408) 573-3880

● **PHIHONG ENTERPRISE COMPANY, LIMITED**
No. 568, Fu Xing San Rd., Gui Shan, Tao Yuan Hsien, Taipei, Taiwan (ROC)
CEO: Peter Lin, Chmn.   Tel: 886-3-3277288
Bus: *Power supplies, cables and voltage adapters*   Fax: 886-3-3185999
    manufacture.   www.phihong.com
NAICS: 335999

    PHIHONG USA INC.
    47800 Fremont Blvd., Fremont, California 94538
    CEO: Keith Hopwood   Tel: (510) 445-0100   %FO: 100
    Bus: *Power supplies, cables and voltage*   Fax: (510) 445-1678
    adapters manufacture and sales.

● **QUANTA COMPUTER INC.**
No. 188, Wen Hwa 2nd Rd., Kuei Shan Hsiang,, Taoyuan, Taiwan (ROC)
CEO: Barry Lam, Chmn. & CEO   Tel: 886-3-327-2345   Rev: $10,146
Bus: *Notebook computer design and manufacture.* Fax: 886-3-327-1511
                          www.quantatw.com
NAICS: 334111, 334119, 334210

    QUANTA COMPUTER USA INC.
    45630 Northport Loop East, Fremont, California 94538
    CEO: Alan Lam, Pres.   Tel: (510) 226-1001   %FO: 100
    Bus: *Notebook computer design and manufacture* Fax: (510) 226-1166   Emp: 410
    and sales.

● **RITEK CORPORATION**
No. 42, Kuan-Fu North Rd., Hsin-Chu Industrial Park, Taiwan 30316, Taiwan (ROC)
CEO: Chin Tai Yeh, Chmn.   Tel: 886-3-598-5696   Rev: $560
Bus: *Mfr. optical disc storage media devices.*   Fax: 886-3-597-9963   Emp: 3m300
                                             www.ritek.com.tw

NAICS: 334112, 334413, 334419, 334613

    ADVANCED MEDIA, INC., RITEK USA
    1440 Bridgegate Dr., Ste. 395, Diamond Bar, California 91765
    CEO: Harvey Liu   Tel: (909) 861-2269   %FO: 100
    Bus: *Optical disc storage media manufacture.*   Fax: (909) 861-2269

● **SILICON INTEGRATED SYSTEMS CORPORATION**
No. 180, Sec. 2,, Gongdaowu Rd., Hsinchu, Taiwan (ROC)
CEO: John Hsuan, Chmn.   Tel: 886-3-516-6000   Rev: $490
Bus: *Develops integrated circuits.*   Fax: 886-3-516-6668   Emp: 801
                                             www.sis.com

NAICS: 334413

    SILICON INTEGRATED SYSTEMS CORPORATION
    3303 Octavius Dr., Ste. 102, Santa Clara, California 95054
    CEO: Michele Huang, PR   Tel: (408) 987-6100   %FO: 100
    Bus: *Mfr. of semiconductors.*   Fax: (408) 987-6110

● **SILICON MOTION TECHNOLOGY CORPORATION**
No. 20-1, Taiyuan St., Jhubei City, Hsinchu 302, Taiwan (ROC)
CEO: Wallace C. Kou, Pres. & CEO   Tel: 886-3-552-6888   Rev: $69
Bus: *Developer of semiconductor products*   Fax: 886-3-552-6988   Emp: 139
                                             www.siliconmotion.com

NAICS: 334112, 334413

    SILICON MOTION TECHNOLOGY CORPORATION
    2125 Zanker Rd., San Jose, California 95131
    CEO: Julia T. Chen, Gen. Mgr.   Tel: (408) 501-5300   %FO: 100
    Bus: *Develops semiconductor products*   Fax: (408) 467-9390

● **SILICONWARE PRECISION INDUSTRIES CO., LTD.**
No. 123, Sec. 3, Da-Fong Rd., Tantzu, Taichung 427, Taiwan (ROC)
CEO: Chi Wen Tsai, Chmn. & Pres.   Tel: 886-4-2534-1525   Rev: $1,086
Bus: *Electronics manufacture.*   Fax: 886-4-2531-5575   Emp: 9,749
                                             www.spil.com.tw

NAICS: 334413

    SPIL BUSINESS DEVELOPMENT
    1735 Technology Dr., Ste. 300, San Jose, California 95110
    CEO: Bough Lin, CEO   Tel: (408) 573-5500   %FO: 100
    Bus: *Mfr. electronics.*   Fax: (408) 573-5530   Emp: 52

● **SINOPAC HOLDINGS**
No. 306, Bade Rd., Sec. 2, Taipei 104, Taiwan (ROC)
CEO: Paul C. Lo, Pres. & CEO
Bus: *Holding company for bank and securities.*

Tel: 886-2-8161-8888
Fax: 886-2-8161-8485
www.sinopac.com

Rev: $1,005
Emp: 5,820

NAICS: 522110, 523120, 551111

SINOPAC BANCORP
2 California Plaza, 350 South Grand Ave., 41/F, Los Angeles, California 90071
CEO: Paul C. Lo, Chmn.
Bus: *Banking services.*

Tel: (213) 687-1200
Fax: (213) 687-8511

%FO: 100
Emp: 372

● **TAIWAN SEMICONDUCTOR MFG. CO.**
8 Li-Hsin Rd., 6 Hsinchu Science Park, Hsinchu 300, Taiwan (ROC)
CEO: Rick Tsai, CEO
Bus: *Provides manufacturing services for advanced integrated circuits.*

Tel: 886-3-563-6688
Fax: 886-3-563-7000
www.tsmc.com.tw

Rev: $8,128
Emp: 20,167

NAICS: 334413

TSMC NORTH AMERICA
2585 Junction Ave., San Jose, California 95134
CEO: Rick Cassidy, Pres.
Bus: *Provides manufacturing services for advanced integrated circuits.*

Tel: (408) 382-8000
Fax: (408) 382-8008

%FO: 100

WAFER TECH L.L.C.
5509 N.W. Parker St., Camas, Washington 98607-9299
CEO: Steve Tso, COO
Bus: *Semiconductor and related device manufacturing*

Tel: (360) 817-3000
Fax: (360) 817-3590

Emp: 1,000

● **TATUNG CO.**
22 Chungshan North Rd., Sec. 3, Taipei, Taiwan (ROC)
CEO: Lin Weishan, Pres.
Bus: *Engaged in telecommunications.*

Tel: 886-22-592-5252
Fax: 886-22-592-1813
www.tatung.com.tw

Rev: $4,325
Emp: 35,000

NAICS: 325510, 331222, 332919, 333611, 333921, 334111, 334413, 334416, 335221, 335311, 335312, 337211, 337214

TATUNG SCIENCE & TECHNOLOGY, INC.
436 Kato Terr., Fremont, California 94539
CEO: Kam H. Chan, Pres.
Bus: *Sale of computer peripheral computer maintenance/repair mfr. Of computer terminals/electronic computers.*

Tel: (510) 687-9688
Fax: (510) 687-9588

Emp: 52

TATUNG USA CORPORATION
2850 El Presidio St., Long Beach, California 90810
CEO: Lun Kuan Lin, Chmn. & Pres. & CEO
Bus: *Engaged in telecommunications.*

Tel: (310) 637-2105
Fax: (310) 637-3588

%FO: 100
Emp: 500

- **TECO WESTINGHOUSE MOTOR COMPANY**
No. 156, 2 Sung Chiang Rd., Taipei City, Taiwan (ROC)
CEO: Mike Kuo, Chmn.
Bus: *Mfr. electric motors.*

Tel: 886-22-562-1111
Fax: 886-22-536-6862
www.tecowestinghouse.com

Rev: $634
Emp: 3,400

NAICS: 336322

> **TECO WESTINGHOUSE MOTOR COMPANY**
> 215 National Ave., Spartanburg, South Carolina 29303
> CEO: Mike Kuo
> Bus: *Mfr./supplier stock motors and motor controls.*
>
> Tel: (864) 576-0356
> Fax: (864) 574-6844
>
> %FO: 100

> **TECO WESTINGHOUSE MOTOR COMPANY**
> 5100 North IH-35, Round Rock, Texas 78681
> CEO: Mike Kuo, Pres.
> Bus: *Mfr./supplier stock motors and motor controls.*
>
> Tel: (512) 255-4141
> Fax: (512) 244-5512
>
> %FO: 100

- **ULEAD SYSTEMS, INC.**
2/F, 358 Neihu Rd., Section 1, Taipei 114, Taiwan (ROC)
CEO: Way-Zen Chen, Chmn. & Pres.
Bus: *Computer software & services.*

Tel: 886-2-2659-7588
Fax: 886-2-2659-8388
www.ulead.com

Emp: 300

NAICS: 511210, 541511, 541519

> **ULEAD SYSTEMS, INC.**
> 20000 Mariner Ave., Ste. 200, Torrance, California 90503
> CEO: Miian Fang Liaw, CEO
> Bus: *Computer software & services.*
>
> Tel: (310) 896-6388
> Fax: (310) 896-6389
>
> %FO: 100
> Emp: 35

- **UNITED MICROELECTRONICS CORPORATION**
3 Li-Hsin 2nd Rd., Science Based Industrial Park, Hsinchu 103, Taiwan (ROC)
CEO: Jackson Hu, CEO
Bus: *Mfr. of semiconductors.*

Tel: 886-3-578-2258
Fax: 886-3-577-9392
www.umc.com

Rev: $4,082
Emp: 10,642

NAICS: 334413

> **UMC USA INC.**
> 488 De Guigne Dr., Sunnyvale, California 94085
> CEO: Fu Tai Liou, Pres.
> Bus: *Sales/distribution of semiconductors.*
>
> Tel: (408) 523-7800
> Fax: (408) 733-8090
>
> %FO: 100
> Emp: 75

- **UNIVERSAL SCIENTIFIC INDUSTRIAL CO. LTD.**
351 Taiping Rd., Sec. 1, Tsao Tuen, Nan-Tou 141, Taiwan (ROC)
CEO: Harvey Wu, Pres.
Bus: *Integrated circuits and printed circuit boards design and manufacture.*

Tel: 886-49-235-0876
Fax: 886-49-232-9561
www.usi.com.tw

Rev: $1,200
Emp: 6,529

NAICS: 334111, 334119, 334413, 334418

UNIVERSAL SCIENTIFIC INDUSTRIAL CO. LTD.
3600 Peterson Way, Santa Clara, California 95054
CEO: Luke Chu, VP   Tel: (408) 235-3000   %FO: 100
Bus: *Mfr. of printed circuit boards.*   Fax: (408) 982-0126

UNIVERSAL SCIENTIFIC INDUSTRIAL CO. LTD.
2020 Garner Station Blvd., Raleigh, North Carolina 27603
CEO: Steven Su, Gen. Mgr.   Tel: (919) 771-2788   %FO: 100
Bus: *Custom computer programming.*   Fax: (919) 771-2786   Emp: 13

USI MANUFACTURING SERVICE, INC.
685-A Jarvis Dr., Morgan Hill, California 95037
CEO: Harvey Wu, CEO   Tel: (408) 776-1966   %FO: 100
Bus: *Integrated printed circuit boards design and*   Fax: (408) 778-8499   Emp: 64
      manufacture.

• **VEUTRON CORPORATION**
No. 1 - 1R&D Rd. II, Science-Based Industrial Park, Hsinchu 103, Taiwan (ROC)
CEO: Frank C. Huang, Chmn. & CEO   Tel: 886-3-577-4955   Rev: $163
Bus: *Scanners manufacture.*   Fax: 886-3-577-0140   Emp: 125
    www.veutron.com
NAICS: 333293, 333313, 333315, 334119

    UMAX TECHNOLOGIES INC.
    10460 Brockwood Rd., Dallas, Texas 75238
    CEO: Vincent Tai, Pres.   Tel: (214) 342-9799   %FO: 100
    Bus: *Scanners manufacture and sales.*   Fax: (214) 342-9046   Emp: 160

• **VIA TECHNOLOGIES, INC.**
533 Chung Cheng Rd., 8/F, Hsin-Tien, Taipei 231, Taiwan (ROC)
CEO: Wen Chi Chen, Pres. & CEO   Tel: 886-2-2218-5452   Rev: $608
Bus: *Electronics manufacture.*   Fax: 886-2-2218-5453   Emp: 1,462
    www.viatech.com
NAICS: 334119, 334413

    CENTAUR TECHNOLOGY, INC.
    9111 Jollyville Rd., Ste. 206, Austin, Texas 78759
    CEO: Glenn Henry, Pres.   Tel: (512) 418-5700
    Bus: *Microprocessors, microcontrollers & DSPs.*   Fax: (512) 794-0717   Emp: 85

    VIA TECHNOLOGIES, INC.
    940 Mission Ct., Fremont, California 94539
    CEO: Wenchi Chen, Pres.   Tel: (510) 683-3300   %FO: 100
    Bus: *PC core logic chipsets manufacture.*   Fax: (510) 687-4654   Emp: 130

• **WINBOND ELECTRONICS CORPORATION**
4, Creation Rd., 3 Science Based Industrial Park, Hsinchu 300, Taiwan (ROC)
CEO: Arthur Yu-Cheng Chiao, Chmn. & CEO   Tel: 886-3-577-0066   Rev: $1,487
Bus: *Mfr. semiconductors.*   Fax: 886-3-579-2668   Emp: 3,800
    www.winbond.com
NAICS: 334112, 334413

NEXFLASH TECHNOLOGIES, INC.
2711 N. 1st St., San Jose, California 95134
CEO: Thomas Liao, Pres. & CEO
Bus: *Mfr. memory chips & modules*
Tel: (408) 907-3600
Fax: (408) 907-3601

WINBOND AMERICA
2727 North 1st. St., San Jose, California 95134
CEO: Kuang Y. Chiu, Pres.
Bus: *Mfr. semiconductors.*
Tel: (408) 943-6666
Fax: (408) 544-1786
%FO: 100
Emp: 137

● **WISTRON CORPORATION**
88 Hsin Tai Wu Rd., Sec. 1, 21/F, Taipei 221, Taiwan (ROC)
CEO: Simon Lin, Chmn. & CEO
Bus: *Computer products contract manufacture.*
Tel: 886-2-8691-2888
Fax: 886-2-8691-2188
www.wistron.com
Rev: $2,347
Emp: 14,000

NAICS: 334111, 334119, 334412, 334418, 334419

WISTRON INFOCOMM CORP.
12 Zane Grey St., Ste. A, El Paso, Texas 79906
CEO: Joseph Hsu, Pres.
Bus: *Mfr. of personal computers.*
Tel: (915) 626-2222
Fax:
%FO: 100
Emp: 100

● **YANG MING MARINE TRANSPORT CORPORATION**
271, Ming De 1st Rd., Chidu, Keelung 206, Taiwan (ROC)
CEO: Frank F. H. Lu, Chmn.
Bus: *Cargo transportation services.*
Tel: 886-2-2455-9988
Fax: 886-2-2455-9959
www.yml.com.tw
Rev: $2,452
Emp: 1,238

NAICS: 483111, 483211, 488310, 488320

YANG MING MARINE TRANSPORT CORPORATION
Newport Office Tower, 525 Washington Blvd., 25/F, Jersey City, New Jersey 07310
CEO: Spring Wu, Pres. & CEO
Bus: *Cargo transportation services.*
Tel: (201) 222-8899
Fax: (201) 222-6699
%FO: 100
Emp: 135

● **ZYXEL COMMUNICATIONS CORPORATION**
No. 6, Innovation Rd. II Science Park, Hsinchu 300, Taiwan (ROC)
CEO: Shu-I Chu, CEO
Bus: *Computer networking equipment manufacture.*
Tel: 886-3-578-3942
Fax: 886-3-578-2439
www.zyxel.com

NAICS: 541512

ZYXEL COMMUNICATIONS CORPORATION
1130 North Miller St., Anaheim, California 92806
CEO: Howie Chu, Pres.
Bus: *Computer networking equipment manufacture and sales.*
Tel: (714) 632-0882
Fax: (714) 632-0858
%FO: 100

Thailand

- **BANGKOK BANK PUBLIC COMPANY**
  333 Silom Rd., Bangkok 10500, Thailand
  CEO: Chartsiri Sophonpanich, Chmn.
  Bus: *Banking services.*

  Tel: 66-2-231-4333
  Fax: 66-2-231-4742
  www.bbl.co.th

  Rev: $1,550
  Emp: 18,400

  NAICS: 522110

  - **BANGKOK BANK PUBLIC COMPANY LTD.**
    29 Broadway, 20/F, New York, New York 10006
    CEO: Chalit Phaphan, Mgr.
    Bus: *General banking services.*

    Tel: (212) 422-8200
    Fax: (212) 422-0728

    %FO: 100
    Emp: 40

- **BANK OF THAILAND**
  273 Samsen Rd., Bangkhunphrom, Bangkok 10200, Thailand
  CEO: Rerngchai Marakanond, Gov.
  Bus: *Government, Central Bank of Thailand.*

  Tel: 66-2-283-5353
  Fax: 66-2-280-0449
  www.bot.or.th

  NAICS: 522110

  - **BANK OF THAILAND**
    40 East 52nd St., New York, New York 10022
    CEO: Aroonsri Tiuvakul, Principal
    Bus: *Commercial banks*

    Tel: (212) 750-0310
    Fax: (212) 750-0310

    %FO: 100

  - **BANK OF THAILAND**
    1270 Ave. of the Americas, 27/F, New York, New York 10020
    CEO: Supawadee Punsri, Rep.
    Bus: *Commercial banks*

    Tel: (212) 218-7950
    Fax: (212) 218-7945

    %FO: 100

- **HANA MICROELECTRONICS CO., LTD.**
  10/4 Moo 3 Vibhadi-Ransit Rd., Kwong Talad Bangkhen, Khet Laksi, Bangkok 10210, Thailand
  CEO: Winson Moong Chu Hui, Pres. & COO
  Bus: *Electronics and semiconductors.*

  Tel: 66-2-551-1297
  Fax: 66-2-552-1299
  www.hanagroup.com

  Rev: $287
  Emp: 7,000

  NAICS: 334412, 334413, 334418, 334419

  - **HANA MICRODISPLAY TECHNOLOGIES, INC.**
    2061 Case Pkwy. South, Twinsburg, Ohio 44087
    CEO: Richard Han, CEO
    Bus: *Chip technology.*

    Tel: (330) 405-4600
    Fax: (330) 405-3448

    %FO: 100

- **KASIKORNBANK**
  1 Soi. Kasikornthai, Ratburana Rd., Bangkok 10140, Thailand
  CEO: Banthoon Lamsam, CEO
  Bus: *Commercial banking services.*

  Tel: 66-2-888-8888
  Fax: 66-2-470-11445
  www.kasikornbank.com

  Rev: $2,414

  NAICS: 522110

KASIKORNBANK USA
350 South Grand Ave., Ste. 3050, Los Angeles, California 90071
CEO: Pat Arunin, Mgr. Tel: (213) 680-9331 %FO: 100
Bus: *International banking services.* Fax: (213) 620-9362 Emp: 15

● **KRUNG THAI BANK LTD.**
35 Sukhumvit Rd., Klong Toey Nua Subdistrict, Wattana District, Bangkok 10110, Thailand
CEO: Apisak Tantivorawong, Pres. Tel: 66-2-255-2222 Rev: $2,497
Bus: *Commercial banking services.* Fax: 66-2-255-9391 Emp: 18,422
www.ktb.co.th

NAICS: 522110

  KRUNG THAI BANK
  707 Wilshire Blvd., Ste. 3150, Los Angeles, California 90017
  CEO: Somsak Nontaganak, Mgr. Tel: (213) 488-9897 %FO: 100
  Bus: *International commercial banking services.* Fax: (213) 891-0734

● **SAHA-UNION PUBLIC COMPANY LTD.**
1828 Sukhumvit Rd., Bangchak, Phrakanong Bangkok 10250, Thailand
CEO: Khun Anand Panyarachun, Chmn. Tel: 66-2-311-5111 Rev: $458
Bus: *Distributor of textile products, including garment* Fax: 66-2-332-5616 Emp: 2,100
accessories and footwear. www.sahaunion.co.th

NAICS: 313311, 313312

  SAHA-UNION INTL (USA) INC
  3530 Piedmont Rd. NE, Ste. 289, Atlanta, Georgia 30305
  CEO: Paradee Supthavichaikul Tel: (404) 365-0678 %FO: 100
  Bus: *Mfr. textiles, sewing threads.* Fax: (404) 365-0657

  SAHA-UNION INTL (USA) INC
  419 Allan St., Daly City, California 94014
  CEO: Dr. Chumpol Phornprapha, Pres. Tel: (415) 467-5330 %FO: 100
  Bus: *Mfr. textiles, sewing threads.* Fax: (415) 239-2625

● **SIAM COMMERCIAL BANK PLC**
9 Rutchadatick Rd., Latyao, Chatuchak, Bangkok 10900, Thailand
CEO: Jada Wattanasiritham, Pres. Tel: 66-2-544-5678 Rev: $981
Bus: *Commercial banking services.* Fax: 66-2-937-7763 Emp: 11,428
www.scb.co.th

NAICS: 522110

  SIAM COMMERCIAL BANK PLC - NEW YORK AGENCY
  One Exchange Pl., New York, New York 10006
  CEO: David Ramos, Mgr. Tel: (212) 344-4101 %FO: 100
  Bus: *International banking services.* Fax: (212) 747-0106 Emp: 20

● **THAI AIRWAYS INTERNATIONAL**
89 Vibhavadi-Rangsit Rd., Bangkok 10900, Thailand
CEO: Kanok Abhiradee, Pres. Tel: 66-2-545-1000 Rev: $2,936
Bus: *Commercial air transport services.* Fax: Emp: 24,222
www.thaiair.com

NAICS: 481111

Thailand

THAI AIRWAYS INTERNATIONAL
6501 W. Imperial Hwy., Los Angeles, California 90045
CEO: Geoff Gilbert, Mgr.
Bus: *International commercial air transport services.*
Tel: (310) 670-8592
Fax: (310) 670-1057

THAI AIRWAYS INTERNATIONAL
222 North Sepulveda Blvd., Ste. 100, El Segundo, California 90245
CEO: Sudhagun Divaveja, Gen. Mgr.
Bus: *International commercial air transport services.*
Tel: (800) 426-5204
Fax: (310) 322-8728
%FO: 100

THAI AIRWAYS INTERNATIONAL
Lincoln Bldg., 60 E. 42nd St., Ste. 3120, New York, New York 10165
CEO: Sudhagun Divaveja, Gen. Mgr.
Bus: *International commercial air transport services.*
Tel: (212) 949-8424
Fax: (212) 286-0082
%FO: 100

THAI AIRWAYS INTERNATIONAL
Tom Bradley International Terminal, 380 World Way, Box 32, Los Angeles, California 90045
CEO: Sudhagun Divaveja, Gen. Mgr.
Bus: *International commercial air transport services.*
Tel: (310) 646-3090
Fax: (310) 646-3094
%FO: 100

● **THAI UNION FROZEN PRODUCTS PCL**
72/1 Moo 7, Sethakit 1 Rd., Tambon Tarsrai,, Amphur Muangsamutsakorn, Samutsakorn 74000, Thailand
CEO: Kraisorn Chansiri, Chmn.
Bus: *Producer and exporter of canned tuna and pet*
Tel: 66-34-816-500
Fax: 66-34-816-886
www.thaiuniongroup.com
Rev: $1,204
Emp: 23,379
NAICS: 115210, 311111, 311312, 311421, 311711, 311712, 311919, 323117, 332431, 332439, 424460

THAI UNION INTERNATIONAL
Sorrento South Corporate Center, 9330 Scranton Rd., Ste. 500, San Diego, California 92121
CEO: Thiraphong Chansiri, Pres.
Bus: *US Holding company.*
Tel: (858) 558-9662
Fax: (858) 597-4566
%FO: 100

TRI-UNION SEAFOODS, LLC
Sorrento South Corporate Center, 9330 Scranton Blvd., Ste. 500, San Diego, California 92121
CEO: John Signorino, Pres. & CEO
Bus: *Producer and exporter of canned sea food under the "Chicken of the Sea" brand.*
Tel: (858) 558-9662
Fax: (858) 597-4282
%FO: 100
Emp: 2,200

Trinidad & Tobago

● **ANGOSTURA HOLDINGS LIMITED**
Corner, Eastern Main Rd. and Trinity Ave., Laventille, Trinidad & Tobago
CEO: Lawrence Andre Duprey, Exec. Chmn.   Tel: 868-623-1841   Rev: $167
Bus: *Beverage distiller and distributor. Producer of*   Fax: 868-623-1847   Emp: 900
sauces.   www.angostura.com
NAICS: 311941, 311942, 312140, 424820

    CRUZAN INTERNATIONAL, INC.
    222 Lakeview Ave., Ste.1500, West Palm Beach, Florida 33401
    CEO: Jay S. Maltby, Chmn. & Pres. & CEO   Tel: (561) 655-8977   %FO: 68
    Bus: *Bottles beverages; produces and imports*   Fax: (561) 655-9718   Emp: 415
    spirit, cooking wine, industrial alcohol,
    vinegar, & alcohol byproduct for animal

    WORLD HARBORS, INC.
    176 First Flight Dr., Auburn, Maine 04210
    CEO: Steven Arthurs, Pres. & CEO   Tel: (207) 786-3200   %FO: 100
    Bus: *Manufacturer of sauces and marinades*   Fax: (207) 786-3900   Emp: 20

Turkey

- **GLOBAL SECURITIES (GLMDE)**
  Rhtm Caddesi, 57 Karakoy, 34425 Istanbul, Turkey
  CEO: Mert Engindeniz, CEO   Tel: 90-212-244-5566
  Bus: *Provides investment banking and asset*   Fax: 90-212-244-5567   Emp: 300
        management services.   www.global.com.tr
  NAICS: 523110

      GLOBAL SECURITIES USA, INC.
      101 E. 52nd St., 14/F, New York, New York 10022
      CEO: Donna Pulini, Pres.   Tel: (212) 317-6800
      Bus: *Security brokers & dealers*   Fax: (212) 317-9727   Emp: 11

- **HACI OMER SABANCI HOLDING A.S.**
  Sabanci Center, 4 Levent, 34330 Istanbul, Turkey
  CEO: Celal Metin, CEO   Tel: 90-212-281-6600   Rev: $8,610
  Bus: *Financial services; banking, insurance.*   Fax: 90-212-281-0272   Emp: 30,150
        www.sabanci.com.tr
  NAICS: 311223, 311920, 312221, 322212, 325211, 326211, 333120, 452910, 518111, 522110, 523999, 524113, 524126, 551111

      EXSA AMERICAS INC.
      111 West 40th St., Ste. 300, New York, New York 10018
      CEO: Huseyin Unver, Gen. Mgr.   Tel: (212) 307-6522   %FO: 100
      Bus: *Sale of synthetic fibers, woven textiles &*   Fax: (212) 307-6710   Emp: 14
        cotton goods.

      KORDSA INTERNATIONAL LLC
      E.A. Delle Donne Corporate Center, 1013 Centre Rd., Ste. 107, Wilmington, Delaware 19805
      CEO: Peter Hemken, Gen. Mgr.   Tel: (302) 996-6810   %FO: 100
      Bus: *Mfr. of yarn & tire cord fabric.*   Fax: (302) 996-6838

- **KOÇ HOLDING A.S.**
  Nakkastepe, Azizbey Sok. No. 1, Kuzguncuk, 34674 Istanbul, Turkey
  CEO: F. Bulend Ozaydinli, CEO   Tel: 90-216-531-0000   Rev: $16,624
  Bus: *Holding company; automotive, consumer goods,*   Fax: 90-216-531-0099   Emp: 59,513
        financial, tourism and energy industry services.   www.koc.com.tr
  NAICS: 112111, 311612, 311615, 311823, 336111, 424710, 445110, 522110, 522293, 522298, 523120, 523920, 523930, 524126

      RAMERICA INTERNATIONAL, INC.
      12 E. 49th St., 17/F, New York, New York 10017
      CEO: Nur Emirgil, Mgr.   Tel: (212) 759-7216   %FO: 100
      Bus: *U.S. representative: automotive & consumer*   Fax: (212) 759-7260
        goods, financial, tourism and energy
        industry services.

● **TURKISH AIRLINES (TURK HAVA YOLLARI AO)**
Ataturk International Airport, Yesilkoy, A Block, 10/F, 34149 Istanbul, Turkey
CEO: Candan Karlitekin, Chmn.   Tel: 90-212-663-6300   Rev: $2,078
Bus: *International commercial air transport services.*   Fax: 90-212-663-4744   Emp: 10,950
                                                 www.thy.com
NAICS: 481111

TURKISH AIRLINES
6033 West Century Blvd., Los Angeles, California 90045
CEO: Turgut Atay   Tel: (310) 258-0530   %FO: 100
Bus: *International commercial air transport*   Fax: (310) 258-0530
    services.

TURKISH AIRLINES
625 North Michigan Ave., Ste. 1400, Chicago, Illinois 60611
CEO: Turgut Atay   Tel: (312) 943-7858   %FO: 100
Bus: *International commercial air transport*   Fax: (312) 943-7843
    services.

TURKISH AIRLINES
Cargo Bed 77, Jamaica, New York 11430
CEO: Fifun Onar   Tel: (718) 244-7760   %FO: 100
Bus: *International commercial air transport*   Fax: (718) 244-7760
    services.

TURKISH AIRLINES
1400 Old Country Rd., Westbury, New York 11590
CEO: Turgut Atay   Tel: (516) 247-5402   %FO: 100
Bus: *International commercial air transport*   Fax: (516) 247-5402
    services.

United Arab Emirates

● **EMIRATES AIR**
G/F., Dubai Airline Centre Bldg., Dubai, United Arab Emirates
CEO: Timothy Clark, Pres.
Bus: *Commercial air transport services.*

Tel: 971-4-295-1111
Fax: 971-4-295-2001
www.emirates.com

Rev: $600
Emp: 3,400

NAICS: 481111, 481112

> **EMIRATES AIR**
> 55 East 59th St., 5/F, New York, New York 10022
> CEO: James Baxter, VP
> Bus: *International commercial air transport services.*
>
> Tel: (212) 758-3944
> Fax: (212) 758-4434
>
> %FO: 100

> **EMIRATES AIR**
> 150 N. Martingale Rd., Ste. 840, Schaumburg, Illinois 60173
> CEO: Scott Holtz, Mgr.
> Bus: *Air transport services.*
>
> Tel: (847) 592-3470
> Fax:

● **EMIRATES SKY CARGO (DNATA)**
Airline Centre A", 3rd Fl., PO Box 686, Dubai, United Arab Emirates
CEO: Ram Menen, CEO
Bus: *Travel management services, handling agency and cargo and freight forwarding.*

Tel: 971-4-22-71-04
Fax: 971-4-28-20-49
www.sky-cargo.com

NAICS: 481111, 481112, 481212

> **SKY CARGO / EC INTERNATIONAL (GSA)**
> 147-29 182nd St., Springfield Gardens, New York 11413
> CEO: Ed Chism, Pres.
> Bus: *International freight forwarding.*
>
> Tel: (718) 340-7500
> Fax: (718) 244-6881

● **MASHREQ BANK PSC**
PO Box 1250, Omar Ibn al Khatab Rd., Dubai, United Arab Emirates
CEO: Abdul Aziz Al Ghurair, CEO
Bus: *Commercial banking services.*

Tel: 971-222-3333
Fax: 971-2226061
www.mashreqbank.com

NAICS: 522110

> **MASHREQ BANK PSC.**
> 255 Fifth Ave., 2/F, New York, New York 10016
> CEO: Shariq Azhar, Mgr.
> Bus: *Commercial banking services.*
>
> Tel: (212) 545-8200
> Fax: (212) 545-0918
>
> %FO: 100

● **NATIONAL BANK OF ABU DHABI**
One NBAD Tower, Abu Dhabi, United Arab Emirates
CEO: Michael Tomalin, CEO
Bus: *Commercial banking services.*

Tel: 971-2-666-6800
Fax: 971-2-667-2081
www.nbad.com

NAICS: 522110

ABU DHABI INTERNATIONAL BANK INC.
1020 19th St. NW, Ste. 500, Washington, District of Columbia 20036
CEO: Nagy S. Kolta, Mgr.   Tel: (202) 842-7900   %FO: 100
Bus: *International commercial banking services.*   Fax: (202) 842-7955

Venezuela

- **AEROVIAS VENEZOLANAS SA (AVENSA)**
  Torré Humbolt, Av. Rio Cavro, 25 piso, Caracas 1050, Venezuela
  CEO: I. Perez, Mgr.   Tel: 58-2-907-8000
  Bus: *Commercial air transport carrier.*   Fax: 58-2-907-8027   Emp: 2,700
                                                            www.avensa.com.ve
  NAICS: 481111

  > **AVENSA AIRLINES**
  > 4343 W. Flagler St., Miami, Florida 33134
  > CEO: Joseph Lorenzo   Tel: (305) 445-2330   %FO: 100
  > Bus: *International commercial air transport carrier.* Fax: (305) 445-2330

- **BANCO INDUSTRIAL DE VENEZUELA**
  Tercera Ave. Cruce con Francisco Solano, Torre Financiera, Caracas 1050, Venezuela
  CEO: Luis Quiaro, Pres.   Tel: 58-2-545-9222
  Bus: *Commercial banking services.*   Fax: 58-2-952-4139
                                                            www.biv.com.ve
  NAICS: 522110

  > **BANCO INDUSTRIAL DE VENEZUELA**
  > 1101 Brickell Ave., Ste. 500, Miami, Florida 33131
  > CEO: Ildelfonso Ferrer, Mgr.   Tel: (305) 374-5060   %FO: 100
  > Bus: *International banking services.*   Fax: (305) 374-5060   Emp: 14

  > **BANCO INDUSTRIAL DE VENEZUELA**
  > 900 Third Ave., 14/F, New York, New York 10022
  > CEO: Ildelfonso Ferrer   Tel: (212) 688-2299   %FO: 100
  > Bus: *International banking services.*   Fax: (212) 888-4921

- **BANCO MERCANTIL, C.A. VENEZUELA**
  Avenida Andres Bello 1, Edificio Mercantil, Caracas 1050, Venezuela
  CEO: Gustavo A. Marturet, Chmn. & CEO   Tel: 58-12-503-1111   Rev: $505
  Bus: *Commercial banking services.*   Fax: 58-12-503-1391   Emp: 7,303
                                                            www.bancomercantil.com
  NAICS: 522110

  > **COMMERCE BANK NA**
  > 220 La Hambre Circle, Coral Gables, Florida 33134
  > CEO: Guillermo Villar, Mgr.   Tel: (305) 460-4000   %FO: 100
  > Bus: *Bank agency.*   Fax: (305) 448-9027

- **THE CISNEROS GROUP OF COMPANIES**
  Edificio Venevision, Quinto Piso, Final Avenida La Salle,Colina de los Caobos, Caracas 1050, Venezuela
  CEO: Gustavo A. Cisneros, Chmn. & CEO   Tel: 58-212-781-5066   Rev: $3,500
  Bus: *Owns media conglomerates, including Spanish-*   Fax: 58-212-781-8286   Emp: 35,000
       language broadcasting and engaged in gold   www.cisneros.com
  NAICS: 312111, 312120, 334612, 445110, 446120, 451211, 451212, 451220, 511110, 512191, 515111, 515112,
       515120, 515210, 516110, 517510, 518112,
            519190, 532230

CISNEROS GROUP OF COMPANIES
36 East 61st. St., New York, New York 10021
CEO: Steven I. Bandel
Bus: *Owns media conglomerates, including Spanish-language broadcasting and engaged in gold mining.*
Tel: (305) 206-3100
Fax:
%FO: 100

● **CORP BANCA, C.A.**
Av. Principal La Castellana, Torre Corp. Banca, Caracas 1060, Venezuela
CEO: Alvaro Saieh, Pres.
Bus: *International banking services.*
Tel: 58-2-206-3299
Fax: 58-2-206-3130
www.Corpbanca.com.ve
Emp: 3,500

NAICS: 522110, 522293

CORP BANCA CA
845 Third Ave., 5/F, New York, New York 10022
CEO: Alphonse Cogollos, Dir.
Bus: *International commercial banking services.*
Tel: (212) 826-5100
Fax: (212) 644-9809
%FO: 100
Emp: 35

● **PETROLEOS DE VENEZUELA SA (PDVSA)**
Edificio Petroleos de Venezuela, Avenida Libertador , La Campina, Apartado 169, Caracas 1010-A, Venezuela
CEO: Rafael Ramirez Carreno, Pres. & CEO
Bus: *Exploration, production, distribution of petrochemicals, oil and coal.*
Tel: 58-212-708-4111
Fax: 58-212-708-4661
www.pdvsa.com.ve
Rev: $42,580
Emp: 45,683

NAICS: 211111, 211112, 213111, 221210, 324110, 324191, 324199, 333132, 424710, 424720, 445120, 447110, 447190, 454311, 454312, 454319, 486110, 486210, 486910, 541360

CITGO INVESTMENT CO.
6100 S. Yale Ave., Tulsa, Oklahoma 74136
CEO: Jerry E. Thompson, Pres.
Bus: *Financial services*
Tel: (918) 495-4000
Fax: (918) 495-4511
Emp: 1,400

CITGO PETROLEUM CORP.
1293 Eldridge Pkwy., Houston, Texas 77077
CEO: Felix Rodriguez, Pres. & CEO
Bus: *Oil & gas refining, marketing & distribution*
Tel: (832) 486-4000
Fax: (832) 486-1814
Emp: 4,000

CITGO REFINING & CHEMICALS CO., L.P.
6100 S. Yale Ave., Ste. 1200, Tulsa, Oklahoma 74136
CEO: Robert J. Kostelnik, Pres.
Bus: *Petroleum refining*
Tel: (918) 495-4000
Fax: (918) 495-4511
Emp: 503

PDV AMERICA, INC.
1 Warren Place, 6100 S. Yale Ave., Tulsa, Oklahoma 74136
CEO: Aires Barreto, CEO
Bus: *U.S. headquarters. Petroleum information systems & services.*
Tel: (918) 495-4000
Fax: (918) 495-4511
%FO: 100

Wales, U.K.

- **GYRUS GROUP PLC**
  Fortran Rd., St. Mellons, Cardiff CF3 0LT, Wales, U.K.
  CEO: Brian L. Steer, Chmn. & CEO
  Bus: *Engaged in the development, manufacturing, and marketing of bipolar electrosurgical instrumentation for the minimally invasive surgery market.*

  Tel: 44-29-2077-6300
  Fax: 44-29-2077-6301
  www.gyrusgroup.com

  Rev: $167
  Emp: 617

  NAICS: 334510, 339112, 339113

  ### GYRUS MEDICAL, INC.
  6655 Wedgwood Rd., Ste. 160, Maple Grove, Minnesota 55311
  CEO: Brian Steer, Chmn.
  Bus: *Developer/mfr./marketer of bipolar electrosurgical instrumentation for the minimally invasive surgery market.*

  Tel: (763) 416-3000
  Fax: (763) 463-1200

  %FO: 100
  Emp: 240

- **IQE (INTERNATIONAL QUANTUM EPITAXY) PLC**
  Cypress Drive, St. Mellons, Cardiff CF3 0EG, Wales, U.K.
  CEO: Andrew W. Nelson, CEO
  Bus: *Mfr. compound semiconductors.*

  Tel: 44-29-2083-9400
  Fax: 44-29-2083-9401
  www.iqeplc.com

  Rev: $30
  Emp: 247

  NAICS: 334413

  ### IQE INCORPORATED
  119 Technology Dr., Bethlehem, Pennsylvania 18015
  CEO: Debora Green, CEO
  Bus: *Mfr. compound semiconductors.*

  Tel: (610) 861-6930
  Fax: (610) 861-5273

  %FO: 100

Zimbabwe

- **AIR ZIMBABWE**
  Bulawayo Town Office, PO Box 1000, Treger House, J. Moyo Street, Bulawayo, Zimbabwe
  CEO: D. Kakono, CEO
  Bus: *Airline transport services.*

  Tel: 263-9-72051-5
  Fax: 263-9-69737
  www.airzim.co.zw

  NAICS: 481111

  AIR ZIMBABWE
  401 N. Michigan Ave., Chicago, Illinois 60611-4255
  CEO: Sam Jayaseker
  Bus: *Airlines services.*

  Tel: (312) 828-9657
  Fax: (312) 828-9657

  %FO: 100

  SITA WORLD TRAVEL INC.
  350 Fifth Ave., Ste. 1421, New York, New York 10118
  CEO: John Williams
  Bus: *Air transport and tour services.*

  Tel: (212) 279-6635
  Fax: (212) 279-6602

  %FO: 100

  SITA WORLD TRAVEL INC.
  16250 Ventura Blvd., Ste. 115, Encino, California 91436
  CEO: Sam Kordi
  Bus: *Air transport and tour services.*

  Tel: (818) 990-9215
  Fax: (818) 501-2098

  %FO: 100

ALPHABETICAL
LISTING
OF FOREIGN FIRMS

Part Two is an alphabetical listing of all the foreign firms in Part One, giving the company name, and in parentheses identifying the country, and the number of the page where the complete listing can be found in Part One.

ADECCO SA (Switzerland)	1430	AGA FOODSERVICE GROUP PLC	324
ADEPTRA, LTD. (England, U.K.)	321	(England, U.K.)	
ADEX SL (Spain)	1362	AGE FOTOSTOCK (Spain)	1362
ADF GROUP INC. (Canada)	89	AGENCE FRANCE-PRESSE (France)	580
ADI CORP. (Taiwan (ROC))	1493	AGFA-GEVAERT NV (Belgium)	39
ADIDAS-SALOMON AG (Germany)	675	AGGREGATE INDUSTRIES, PLC	324
		(England, U.K.)	
ADOLF SCHNORR GMBH & CO KG	773	AGGREKO PLC (Scotland, U.K.)	1306
(Germany)		AGGREKO PLC (Scotland, U.K.)	1306
ADVA AG OPTICAL NETWORKING	676	AGIE CHARMILLES HOLDING LTD.	1431
(Germany)		(Switzerland)	
ADVANCED COMPOSITES GROUP LTD.	322	AGNES B. (France)	580
(England, U.K.)		AGRICORE UNITED (Canada)	90
ADVANCED SEMICONDUCTOR	1493	AGRICULTURAL BANK OF CHINA (China	281
ENGINEERING, INC. (Taiwan (ROC))		PRC)	
ADVANCED SOC PLATFORM	951	AGRIUM INC. (Canada)	91
CORPORATION (Japan)		AHLI UNITED BANK B.S.C. (Bahrain)	37
ADVANTEST CORPORATION (Japan)	951	AHLSTROM CORPORATION (Finland)	563
AEA TECHNOLOGY PLC (England, U.K.)	322	AIM GROUP PLC (England, U.K.)	324
AECI LIMITED (South Africa)	1326	AIMPOINT AB (Sweden)	1382
AECON GROUP INC., JV HOCHTIEF AG	89	AIOI INSURANCE CO., INC. (Japan)	952
(Canada)		AIR CANADA (Canada) 91	
AEG ELEKTROFOTOGRAFIE GMBH	676	AIR CHINA (China PRC)	281
(Germany)		AIR FRANCE COMPAGNIE NATIONALE	580
AEGIS GROUP PLC (England, U.K.)	323	(France)	
AEGON N.V. (Netherlands)	1207	AIR INDIA LIMITED (India)	833
AEON CO., LTD. (Japan)	952	AIR JAMAICA (Jamaica)	950
AER LINGUS GROUP PLC (Ireland)	860	AIR LIQUIDE GROUP SA (France)	580
AEROFLOT RUSSIAN AIRLINES JSC	1300	AIR NAMIBIA (Namibia)	1205
(Russia)		AIR NEW ZEALAND LTD. (New Zealand)	1271
AEROLINEAS ARGENTINAS SA	3	AIR PARTNER PLC (England, U.K.)	325
(Argentina)		AIR PLUS COMET (Spain)	1362
AEROSYSTEMS INTERNATIONAL LTD.	323	AIR ZIMBABWE (Zimbabwe)	1521
(England, U.K.)		AIRBOSS OF AMERICA CORP. (Canada)	91
AEROVIAS DE MEXICO (Mexico)	1190	AIRBUS SAS (France)	581
AEROVIAS NACIONALES DE COLOMBIA	290	AIRCLAIMS LTD. (England, U.K.)	325
SA (Colombia)		AISAN INDUSTRY CO., LTD. (Japan)	952
AEROVIAS VENEZOLANAS SA	1518	AISIN SEIKI CO. LTD. (Japan)	953
(AVENSA) (Venezuela)		AIT GROUP PLC (England, U.K.)	325
AERZENER MASCHINENFABRIK GMBH	676	AIXTRON AG (Germany)	676
(Germany)		AJINOMOTO COMPANY INC. (Japan)	954
AESIGN EVERTRUST INC. (Canada)	89	AKAB OF SWEDEN AB (Sweden)	1382
AETERNA ZENTARIS INC. (Canada)	90	AKER KVAERNER ASA (Norway)	1275
AETHRA, SPA (Italy)	910	AKERS AB (Sweden)	1382
AFI INTERNATIONAL GROUP INC.	90	AKTIEBOLAGET SKF (Sweden)	1383
(Canada)			
AFM HOSPITALITY CORP. (Canada)	90		

ALLIED DOMECQ PLC., DIV PERNOD	327
AKZO NOBEL NV (Netherlands)	1208
AL JAZEERA SATELLITE CHANNEL (Qatar)	1298
ALADDIN KNOWLEDGE SYSTEMS LTD. (Israel)	875
ALAN DICK & COMPANY LTD. (England, U.K.)	326
ALBA-WALDENSIAN, INC. (Israel)	875
ALCALAGRÉS, DIV. GRUPO CENTUNION (Spain)	1362
ALCAN INC. (Canada)	92
ALCATEL SA (France)	581
ALCO HOLDINGS LIMITED (Hong Kong PRC)	808
ALCON, INC., DIV. NESTLE (Switzerland)	1432
ALDES AERAULIQUE (France)	582
ALDI GROUP (Germany)	677
ALFA LAVAL LTD. (Sweden)	1385
ALFA, S.A. de C.V. (Mexico)	1191
ALFRED DUNHILL OF LONDON (England, U.K.)	326
ALFRED KARCHER GMBH & CO. (Germany)	677
ALFRED MC ALPINE PLC (England, U.K.)	326
ALFRED TRONSER GMBH (Germany)	791
ALGOMA CENTRAL CORP. (Canada)	96
ALGORITHMICS INCORPORATED (Canada)	96
ALI GROUP (Italy)	910
ALIAS SYSTEMS INC. (Canada)	97
ALIBABA.COM CORPORATION (China PRC)	281
ALIMAK HEK GROUP AB (Sweden)	1385
ALITALIA SPA (Italy)	910
ALK-ABELLÓ LABORATORIES AS, DIV. CHR. HANSEN GROUP (Denmark)	297
ALL NIPPON AIRWAYS CO., LTD. (Japan)	954
ALLEN & OVERY (England, U.K.)	327
ALLENDE & BREA (Argentina)	3
ALLIANCE ATLANTIS COMMUNICATIONS INC. (Canada)	97
ALLIANCE PIPELINE (Canada)	98
ALLIANCE TIRE COMPANY (Israel)	876
ALLIANZ AG (Germany)	677

RICARD (England, U.K.)	
ALLIED IRISH BANKS PLC (Ireland)	860
ALLOT COMMUNICATIONS (Israel)	876
ALLSEC TECHNOLOGIES LTD. (India)	834
ALLSERVE SYSTEMS LTD. (England, U.K.)	327
ALMATIS GMBH (Germany)	678
ALOS AG (Switzerland)	1432
ALOYS F. DORNBRACHT GMBH & CO. (Germany)	706
ALPHA PRO TECH, LTD. (Canada)	98
ALPHA SPACECOM INCORPORATED (Hong Kong PRC)	808
ALPHAMERIC PLC (England, U.K.)	328
ALPINE ELECTRONICS INC. (Japan)	954
ALPS ELECTRIC CO., LTD. (Japan)	955
ALSTOM SA (France)	582
ALTADIS, S.A. (Spain)	1363
ALTANA AG (Germany)	678
ALTERIAN PLC (England, U.K.)	328
ALTIUM LIMITED (Australia)	6
ALTUS SISTEMAS DE INFORMATICA SA (Brazil)	71
ALU MENZIKEN HOLDING AG (Switzerland)	1432
ALUMA ENTERPRISES INC. (Canada)	99
ALVARION LTD. (Israel)	876
AMADA LTD. (Japan)	955
AMADEUS GLOBAL TRAVEL DISTRIBUTION SA (Spain)	1363
AMALGAMATED METAL CORPORATION PLC (England, U.K.)	328
AMANO ENZYME INC. (Japan)	955
AMARIN CORPORATION PLC (England, U.K.)	328
AMBERGRIS SOLUTIONS INC. (Philippines)	1293
AMCOR LTD. (Australia)	6
AMDOCS LIMITED (Channel Islands, U.K.)	276
AMEC, PLC (England, U.K.)	329
AMER SPORTS CORPORATION	563
AMERICA MOVIL, SA DE CV (Mexico)	1191

BANK HAPOALIM BM (Israel)	878	BCE INC. (BELL CANADA ENTERPRISES) (Canada)	108
BANK LEUMI LE ISRAEL B.M. (Israel)	878	BDO INTERNATIONAL BV (Belgium)	40
BANK MELLI IRAN (Iran)	859	BE SEMICONDUCTOR INDUSTRIES N.V. (Netherlands)	1212
BANK NEGARA MALAYSIA (Malaysia)	1186		
BANK OF BARODA (India)	834	BEATE UHSE AG (Germany)	683
BANK OF CHINA (China PRC)	282	BEAZLEY GROUP PLC (England, U.K.)	344
BANK OF INDIA (India)	834	BEGHELLI SPA (Italy)	915
BANK OF IRELAND (Ireland)	861	BEHR GROUP (Germany)	683
BANK OF MONTREAL (Canada)	106	BEIERSDORF AG (Germany)	684
BANK OF TAIWAN (Taiwan (ROC))	1494	BELIMO AUTOMATION AG (Switzerland)	1434
BANK OF THAILAND (Thailand)	1510	BELL AGUSTA AIRCRAFT (BAAC) (Italy)	915
BANK OF THE PHILIPPINE ISLANDS (Philippines)	1293	BELL GLOBEMEDIA INC. (Canada)	108
		BELL GLOBEMEDIA INC. (Canada)	108
BARALAN INTERNATIONAL SPA (Italy)	914	BELLVILLE RODAIR INTERNATIONAL (Canada)	109
BARAN GROUP (Israel)	879	BELRON (England, U.K.)	344
BARBEQUES GALORE LIMITED (Australia)	11	BELZBERG TECHNOLOGIES INC.	109
		BELZBERG TECHNOLOGIES INC. (Canada)	109
BARCELO HOTELS AND RESORTS (Spain)	1365	BENEDIKT TASCHEN (Germany)	685
BARCLAYS PLC (England, U.K.)	342	BENEDIKT TASCHEN (Germany)	685
BARCO N.V. (Belgium)	39	BÉNÉTEAU S.A. (France)	586
BARILLA HOLDING SPA (Italy)	914	BENETTON GROUP, SPA (Italy)	915
BARLOWORLD LIMITED (South Africa)	1326	BENFIELD GROUP LIMITED (England, U.K.)	345
BARRATT DEVELOPMENTS PLC (England, U.K.)	343	BENNETT ENVIRONMENTAL INC. (Canada)	110
BARRICK GOLD CORP. (Canada)	107	BENQ CORPORATION (Taiwan (ROC))	1495
BARRY CALLEBAUT AG (Switzerland)	1437	BENTELER AUTOMOTIVE GMBH & CO. (Germany)	685
BARTLE BOGLE HEGARTY LTD. (England, U.K.)	343	BERG CHILLING SYSTEMS INC. (Canada)	110
BASELL NV (Netherlands)	1212	BERGESEN ASA (Norway)	1276
BASF AKTIENGESELLSCHAFT (Germany)	681	BERMANS (England, U.K.)	345
BAT INDUSTRIES (BRITISH AMERICAN TOBACCO PLC) (England, U.K.)	355	BERMUDA DEPARTMENT OF TOURISM (Bermuda)	59
BATA SHOE ORGANIZATION (Canada)	108	BERNA BIOTECH LTD. (Switzerland)	1434
BATM ADVANCED COMMUNICATIONS LTD. (Israel)	879	BERNARD CALLEBAUT CHOCOLATERIE (Canada)	110
BAYER AG (Germany)	682	BERNDORF BAND GMBH (Austria)	29
BAYERISCHE HYPO-UND VEREINSBANK AG (HVB) (Germany)	683	BERTELSMANN AG (Germany)	686
		BERU GMBH (Germany)	688
BAYERISCHE LANDESBANK (Germany)	683	BERU GMBH (Germany)	688
BAYERISCHE MOTOREN WERKE AG (BMW AG) (Germany)	689	BESAM AB, DIV. ASSA ABLOY (Sweden)	1390
		BESPAK PLC (England, U.K.)	345
BBA GROUP, PLC. (England, U.K.)	343	BEVAN FUNNELL LIMITED (England, U.K.)	346
BBVA INTERNATIONAL (Spain)	1366	BG GROUP PLC (England, U.K.)	346
		BHARAT ELECTRONICS LTD. (India)	834

D

E

G

M

P

Q

R

S

Foreign Firms

SNIA S.P.A. (Italy)	945
SOBEL NV (Netherlands)	1256
SOBEYS CANADA INC. (Canada)	239
SOCIEDAD GENERAL DE AGUAS DE BARCELONA, SA (Spain)	1376
SOCIEDAD GENERAL DE AUTORES Y EDITORES (SGAE) (Spain)	1376
SOCIEDAD QUIMICA Y MINERA DE CHILE S.A. (Chile)	280
SOCIETE BIC (France)	587
SOCIETE DU LOUVRE (France)	653
SOCIÉTÉ GÉNÉRALE (France)	655
SOCIETE INTERNATIONALE DE TELECOMMUNICATIONS AERONAUTIQUES (Switzerland)	1474
SOCIETY FOR WORLDWIDE INTERBANK FINANCIAL TELECOMMUNICATIONS (Belgium)	49
SOCONORD GROUP (Belgium)	50
SODEXHO ALLIANCE (France)	655
SODIAAL SA (France)	656
SOFTBANK CORPORATION (Japan)	1124
SOFTCHOICE CORPORATION (Canada)	239
SOFTWARE AG (Germany)	784
SOGEFI SPA (Italy)	945
SOGETI-TRANSICIEL SA (France)	656
SOITEC SA (France)	656
SOJITZ CORPORATION (Japan)	1125
SOL MELIA SA (Spain)	1377
SOLCORP (Canada)	239
SOLO KLEINMOTOREN GMBH (Germany)	784
SOLVAY DRAKA B.V. (Netherlands)	1257
SOLVAY SA (Belgium)	50
SOMA NETWORKS, INC. (Canada)	240
SOMFY SA (France)	657
SOMPO JAPAN INSURANCE, INC.	1127
SONATA SOFTWARE LIMITED (India)	850
SONEPAR SA (France)	657
SONY CORPORATION (Japan)	1127
SONY ERICSSON MOBILE COMMUNICATIONS AB (England, U.K.)	519
SOPHEON PLC (England, U.K.)	519
SOPHOS PLC (England, U.K.)	520
SOPHUS BERENDSEN A/S (Denmark)	312
SOPRA GROUP (France)	658
SOPREMA SA (France)	658
SOS CUETARA SA (Spain)	1377
SOTHYS PARIS (France)	658
SOUTH AFRICAN AIRWAYS LTD. (South Africa)	1332
SOUTHERN PERU COPPER CORP.	1292
SPARK NETWORKS PLC (England, U.K.)	520
SPARROWS OFFSHORE SERVICES LIMITED (Scotland, U.K.)	1312
SPC ELECTRONICS CORPORATION (Japan)	1130
SPECTRAL DIAGNOSTICS INC. (Canada)	240
SPECTRIS PLC (England, U.K.)	521
SPECTRUM SIGNAL PROCESSING INC. (Canada)	240
SPEEDWARE CORPORATION INC. (Canada)	241
SPHERETEX GMBH (Germany)	784
SPIRAX SARCO ENGINEERING PLC (England, U.K.)	522
SPIRENT PLC (England, U.K.)	522
SPOT IMAGE SA (France)	658
SQUARE ENIX CO. LTD. (Japan)	1131
SR TELECOM INC. (Canada)	241
SSAB SWEDISH STEEL AB (Sweden)	1421
SSANGYONG CORPORATION (South Korea)	1358
SSL INTERNATIONAL PLC (England, U.K.)	523
ST. IVES PLC (England, U.K.)	523
ST. LAWRENCE CEMENT GROUP, INC. (Canada)	241
STADA ARZNEIMITTEL AG (Germany)	784
STAEUBLI AG (Switzerland)	1474
STAGECOACH HOLDINGS PLC (England, U.K.)	524
STANDARD BANK GROUP LIMITED (South Africa)	1333
STANDARD CHARTERED, PLC (England, U.K.)	524
STANTEC INC. (Canada)	242
STAPLA ULTRASCHALL-TECHNIK GMBH (Germany)	785

T

Firm	Page
THIES GMBH & CO. (Germany)	790
THINK TOOLS AG (Switzerland)	1485
THINKFILM COMPANY (Canada)	251
THINKPATH INC. (Canada)	251
THISTLE HOTELS LIMITED, DIV. BIL (England, U.K.)	539
THOLSTRUP CHEESE A/S (Denmark)	313
THOMSON SA (France)	662
THRILLTIME ENTERTAINMENT INTERNATIONAL, INC. (Canada)	254
THYSSEN KRUPP AG (Germany)	790
TI AUTOMOTIVE LIMITED (England, U.K.)	539
TIE HOLDING NV (Netherlands)	1259
TIGBUR LTD. (Israel)	905
TIMES PUBLISHING LIMITED	1323
TIMMINCO LIMITED (Canada)	254
TISSUE SCIENCE LABORATORIES PLC (England, U.K.)	540
TLC VISION CORPORATION (Canada)	254
TNT N.V. (Netherlands)	1260
TOA CORPORATION (Japan)	1149
TOAGOSEI CO. LTD. (Japan)	1150
TODA CORPORATION (Japan)	1150
TOHO TENAX CO., LTD. (Japan)	1150
TOHOKU ELECTRIC POWER CO., INC. (Japan)	1151
TOKAI RIKA CO., LTD. (Japan)	1151
TOKYO BROADCASTING SYSTEM, INC. (Japan)	1152
TOKYO ELECTRON LIMITED (Japan)	1152
TOKYO GAS CO., LTD. (Japan)	1153
TOKYO SEIMITSU COMPANY, LTD. (Japan)	1153
TOKYU CORPORATION (Japan)	1154
TOMEN CORPORATION (Japan)	1154
TOMKINS PLC (England, U.K.)	540
TOMMY HILFIGER CORPORATION (Hong Kong PRC)	814
TOMOEGAWA PAPER CO., LTD. (Japan)	1155
TOMRA SYSTEMS ASA (Norway)	1286
TOMY COMPANY, LTD. (Japan)	1155
TONG YANG MAJOR CO., LTD. (South Korea)	1359
TONNELLERIE DEMPTOS SA (France)	663
TOP IMAGE SYSTEMS, LTD. (Israel)	905
TOPCALL INTERNATIONAL AG (Austria)	32
TOPCON CORPORATION (Japan)	1155
TOPPAN PRINTING COMPANY, LTD. (Japan)	1156
TOPY INDUSTRIES LIMITED (Japan)	1156
TORAY INDUSTRIES INC. (Japan)	1157
TOROMONT INDUSTRIES LTD. (Canada)	254
TORRAS SA (Spain)	1379
TORSTAR CORPORATION (Canada)	255
TORYS LLP (Canada)	255
TOSHIBA CORPORATION (Japan)	1158
TOSHIBA MACHINE COMPANY, LTD. (Japan)	1159
TOSOH CORPORATION (Japan)	1160
TOTAL S.A.. (France)	663
TOTO LTD. (Japan)	1160
TOWER SEMICONDUCTOR LTD. (Israel)	906
TOYO COTTON COMPANY (Japan)	1160
TOYO SUISAN KAISHA, LTD. (Japan)	1160
TOYO TIRE & RUBBER CO., LTD.	1161
TOYOBO CO., LTD. (Japan)	1161
TOYODA GOSEI CO., LTD. (Japan)	1161
TOYODA MACHINE WORKS (Japan)	1162
TOYOSHIMA SPECIAL STEEL COMPANY, LTD. (Japan)	1162
TOYOTA INDUSTRIES CORPORATION (Japan)	1162
TOYOTA MOTOR CORPORATION	1163
TOYOTA TSUSHO CORPORATION (Japan)	1164
TQ3 TRAVEL SOLUTIONS GMBH (Germany)	791
TRACTEL SWINGSTAGE LTD. (Canada)	256
TRANSALTA CORPORATION (Canada)	256
TRANSAT A.T. INC. (Canada)	257
TRANSCANADA CORPORATION (Canada)	257
TRANSCONTINENTAL INC. (Canada)	258
TRANSGENE S.A. (France)	664
TRANSITIVE TECHNOLOGIES LTD. (England, U.K.)	541
TRANSURBAN GROUP (Australia)	25

U

W

Z

ALPHABETICAL LISTING OF AMERICAN AFFILIATES

Part Three is an alphabetical listing of all the American affiliates in Part One, giving the name, and in parentheses the country in which the foreign parent or investor is located, and the number of the page where the complete listing can be found in Part One.

American Affiliates

American Affiliates

AMERICAN SOY PRODUCTS, INC. (Japan) 1016

AMERICAN STEEL AND ALUMINUM 210
CORPORATION (Canada)
AMERICAN SUZUKI MOTOR 1139
CORPORATION (Japan)
AMERICAN TRANSPORT GROUP CSAV 278
(Chile)
American Water Heater Company (Canada) 165
AMERICAN WATER WORKS COMPANY, 504
INC. (England, U.K.)
AMERISOUTH HOLDINGS INC. (Sweden) 1393
AMERISTEEL STEEL MILL (Brazil) 75
AMERIWOOD INDUSTRIES (Canada) 141
AMIL INTERNATIONAL INSURANCE CO. 71
(Brazil)
AMKOR TECHNOLOGY (South Korea) 1334
AMMERAAL BELTECH, INC. (Netherlands) 1209
AMPLIFON USA INC. (Italy) 911
AMRI INC. (Germany) 747
AMTOTE INTERNATIONAL, INC. (Canada) 191
AMVESCAP USA INC. (England, U.K.) 330
ANACHEMIA CHEMICALS (Canada) 99
ANACHEMIA SCIENCE (Canada) 100
ANDERSON DEVELOPMENT CO. (Japan) 1055

ANDOVER CONTROLS CORP. (France) 650
ANDRITZ INC. (Austria) 28
ANGIOTECH BIOCOATINGS CORP. 100
(Canada)
ANGIOTECH PHARMACEUTICALS, INC. 100
(Canada)
ANGLE TECHNOLOGY INC. (England, 331
U.K.)
ANGLO EASTERN USA INC. (Scotland, 1309
U.K.)
ANGLO IRISH BANK CORPORATION 861
(Ireland)
ANGLOGOLD LIMITED (South Africa) 1326
ANHEUSTER-BUSCH COMPANIES, INC. 278
(Chile)
ANKER ENERGY CORPORATION, 1210
VANTRANS DIV. (Netherlands)
ANRITSU COMPANY (Japan) 956

ANSELL HEALTHCARE INC. (Australia) 9
ANSUL INCORPORATED (Bermuda) 66
ANTARCTICA SYSTEMS INC. (Canada) 100
ANTIQUORUM AUCTIONEERS 1432
(Switzerland)
ANTON/BAUER (England, U.K.) 548
AOZORA BANK (Japan) 956
APATECH INC. (England, U.K.) 331
APEM COMPONENTS INC. (France) 583
APEX SILVER MINES LIMITED (Cayman 273
Islands)
API ELECTRONICS CORP. (Canada) 101
APL LIMITED (Singapore) 1320
APL LOGISTICS, LTD. (Singapore) 1320
APM TERMINALS NORTH AMERICA 308
(Denmark)
APOLLO GOLD CORP. (Canada) 101
APPLIED DISCOVERY INC. (England, 493
U.K.)
APPLIED ENGINEERING PRODUCTS 644
(France)
APPLIED OPTICAL TECHNOLOGIES INC. 331
(England, U.K.)
APS JETCAM (Monaco) 1203
APV BAKER INC. (England, U.K.) 332
AQUADUCT (Germany) 675
AQUA-LUNG AMERICA (France) 581
AQUARION COMPANY (England, U.K.) 435
AQUIONICS INC. (England, U.K.) 412
ARAB BANKING CORPORATION 37
(Bahrain)
ARACRUZ CELULOSE USA INC. (Brazil) 71
ARAMCO SERVICES CO. (Saudi Arabia) 1304
ARAMEX INTERNATIONAL (Jordan) 1176
ARAMEX INTERNATIONAL COURIER 1176
(Jordan)
ARAUCO WOOD PRODUCTS, INC. (Chile) 277
ARBI TRANSNATIONAL, INC. (Brazil) 71
ARBORS AT NEW CASTLE (Canada) 146
ARC INTEGRATED MARKETING (France) 640
ARC INTERNATIONAL NORTH AMERICA 583
(France)
ARC WORLDWIDE (France) 640
ARCADIS G&M (Netherlands) 1210

American Affiliates

ARCELOR INTERNATIONAL AMERICA (Luxembourg) — 1183

ARCH REINSURANCE COMPANY (Bermuda) — 59

ARCHOS USA INC. (France) — 583

ARCO ALUMINUM INC. (England, U.K.) — 351

ARCOM CONTROL SYSTEMS, INC. (England, U.K.) — 521

AREL COMMUNICATIONS AND SOFTWARE INC. (Israel) — 877

AREVA ENTERPRISES INC. (France) — 584

ARGER ENTERPRISES (England, U.K.) — 451

ARIANESPACE, INC. (France) — 584

ARIANSPACE (France) — 661

ARISTOCRAT TECHNOLOGIES INC. (Australia) — 9

ARIZONA PORTLAND CEMENT (Japan) — 1140

ARJO INC. (Sweden) — 1400

ARKEMA (France) — 663

ARKOPHARMA INC. (France) — 624

ARKWRIGHT INC. (Netherlands) — 1241

ARM, INC. (England, U.K.) — 332

ARMSTRONG PUMPS INC. (Canada) — 101

ARNOLD WORLDWIDE PARTNERS (France) — 617

AROMAT CORP. (Japan) — 1041

ARQUATI USA INC. (Italy) — 911

ARROW STEEL PROCESSORS (Canada) — 230

ARROWPAK INC. (Italy) — 914

ARTESA WINERY (Spain) — 1368

ARTESIA MORTGAGE CAPITAL CORP. (Belgium) — 45

ARTESIA TECHNOLOGIES, INC. — 214

ARTHUR COX (Ireland) — 861

ARTICON-INTEGRALIS (Germany) — 679

ARTISAN COMPONENTS INC. (England, U.K.) — 332

ARUP GROUP (England, U.K.) — 333

ARVATO SYSTEMS NORTH AMERICA INC. (Germany) — 679

ARVESTA CORP. (Japan) — 1154

ASACA/SHIBA SOKU CORP. (Japan) — 957

ASACA-SHIBASOKU CORPORATION OF AMERICA (Japan) — 1118

ASAHI AMERICA (Japan) — 959

ASAHI AMERICA INC. (Japan) — 958

ASAHI BEER USA INC. (Japan) — 957

ASAHI DIAMOND AMERICA INC. (Japan) — 957

ASAHI GLASS COMPANY INC. (Japan) — 958

ASAHI GLASS FLUOROPOLYMERS USA INC. (Japan) — 958

ASAHI KASEI AMERICA, INC. (Japan) — 958

ASAP SOFTWARE (Netherlands) — 1213

ASARCO, INC. (Mexico) — 1197

ASAT INC. (Hong Kong PRC) — 808

ASC PROFILES (Mexico) — 1195

ASCENT SGI (Hong Kong PRC) — 811

ASCO FREIGHT MANAGEMENT (Scotland, U.K.) — 1307

ASCO USA LLC (Scotland, U.K.) — 1307

ASCOM TRANSPORT SYSTEMS, INC. (Switzerland) — 1433

ASCOM WIRELESS SOLUTIONS INC. (AWS) (Switzerland) — 1433

ASHTEAD TECHNOLOGY, INC. (England, U.K.) — 334

ASI ENTERTAINMENT (Australia) — 10

ASIA PULP & PAPER TRADING, INC. (Singapore) — 1315

ASIAINFO HOLDINGS, INC. (China PRC) — 282

ASIANA AIRLINES (South Korea) — 1334

ASICS AMERICA CORPORATION (Japan) — 959

ASM AMERICA INC. (Netherlands) — 1211

ASML US, INC. (Netherlands) — 1211

ASO CORPORATION (Japan) — 959

ASSA ABLOY DOOR GROUP (Sweden) — 1386

ASSA ABLOY SECURITY INC. (Sweden) — 1386

ASSA, INC. (Sweden) — 1386

ASSANTE CORPORATION (Canada) — 101

ASSE (Sweden) — 1386

ASSOCIATED HYGIENIC PRODUCTS LLC (Hong Kong PRC) — 812

ASSOCIATED NEWSPAPERS N.A., INC. (England, U.K.) — 335

ASTAR AIR CARGO, INC. (Belgium) — 45

ASTELLAS PHARMA US, INC (Japan) — 960

ASTELLAS PHARMA US, INC. (Japan) — 960

ASTELLAS VENTURE CAPITAL LLC (Japan)	960	ATTACHMENTS INTERNATIONAL INC. (Canada)	172
ASTRAZENECA PHARMACEUTICALS (England, U.K.)	335	ATTC MANUFACTURING, INC. (Japan)	953
ASTRIS FINANCE (Belgium)	45	ATTUNITY INC. (Israel)	877
ASTROCOSMOS (France)	625	AU OPTRONICS CORPORATION AMERICA (Taiwan (ROC))	1494
ASUS COMPUTER INTERNATIONAL, INC. (Taiwan (ROC))	1494	AUCHAN USA, INC. (France)	585
AT PLASTICS, FILMS (Canada)	102	AUDI OF AMERICA, INC. (Germany)	680
ATI RESEARCH, INC (Canada)	102	AUDIO SPECIALISTS GROUP (England, U.K.)	548
ATIC SERVICES (France)	584	AUDIOCODES, INC. (Israel)	877
ATKINS HANSCOMB FAITHFUL & GOULD (England, U.K.)	336	AUDIO-TECHNICA USA INC. (Japan)	960
ATLANCO (England, U.K.)	559	AUGUSTA AEROSPACE CORP. (Italy)	926
ATLANTIC BANK OF NEW YORK (Greece)	806	AURIGA, INC. (Russia)	1300
ATLANTIC PROCESS SYSTEMS (Austria)	28	AURORA HOUSE (Canada)	146
		AUSTAL USA (Australia)	10
ATLANTIC SKANSKA (Sweden)	1419	AUSTRALIA & NEW ZEALAND BANKING GROUP LTD. (Australia)	10
ATLANTIC TURBINES USA INC. (Canada)	261	AUSTRALIAN BROADCASTING CORP. (Australia)	11
ATLANTIS SUBMARINES HAWAII (Canada)	103	AUSTRIAMICROSYSTEMS USA INC. (Austria)	28
ATLANTIS SUBMARINES INC. (Canada)	103	AUSTRIAN AIRLINES GROUP (Austria)	29
ATLAS COPCO COMPRESSORS INC (Sweden)	1387	AUTHENTIC SPECIALTY FOODS INC. (Mexico)	1193
ATLAS COPCO COMPTEC INC. (Sweden)	1387	AUTO ALLIANCE INTERNATIONAL (Japan)	1041
ATLAS COPCO CONSTRUCTION TOOLS INC. (Sweden)	1387	AUTO SAFETY HOUSE (England, U.K.)	417
ATLAS COPCO NORTH AMERICA, INC. (Sweden)	1387	AUTOBACS USA (Japan)	960
ATLAS COPCO TOOLS INC. (Sweden)	1387	AUTODIE INTERNATIONAL INC. (Italy)	920
ATLAS MECHANICAL & INDUSTRIAL LLC (Switzerland)	1491	AUTOLIV ELECTRONICS AMERICA (Sweden)	1388
ATLET INC. (Sweden)	1388	AUTOLIV INFLATORS (Sweden)	1388
ATOMIC SKI USA INC. (Finland)	563	AUTOLIV NORTH AMERICA (Sweden)	1388
ATOS ORIGIN INC. (France)	584	AUTOLIV NORTH AMERICA, SEAT BELT DIV. (Sweden)	1389
ATRIUM BIOTECHNOLOGIES (Canada)	103	AUTOLIV NORTH AMERICA, STEERING WHEEL DIV. (Sweden)	1389
ATS CAROLINA (Canada)	103	
ATS MICHIGAN SALES & SERVICE INC. (Canada)	103	AUTOMODULAR ASSEMBLIES INC. (Canada)	104
ATS OHIO INC. (Canada)	104	AUTONOMY INC. (England, U.K.)	337
ATS SOUTHWEST (Canada)	104	AUTOTYPE AMERICAS INC. (England, U.K.)	337
ATS SYSTEMS CALIFORNIA, INC. (Canada)	104	
ATS SYSTEMS OREGON INC. (Canada)	104	AVALON RISK MANAGEMENT, INC. (Canada)	181

AVANADE INC. (Bermuda)	57
AVEBE AMERICA INC. (Netherlands)	1211
AVECIA BIOTECHNOLOGY INC. (England, U.K.)	337
AVECIA INC. (England, U.K.)	337
AVENSA AIRLINES (Venezuela)	1518
AVENT AMERICA INC. (England, U.K.)	337
AVENUE ENERGY INC. (Australia)	11
AVESTA WELDING PRODUCTS INC. (Sweden)	1389
AVEVA DRUG DELIVERY SYSTEMS (Japan)	1092
AVEVA INC. (England, U.K.)	338
AVIAGEN INC. (Scotland, U.K.)	1307
AVIANCA AIRLINES (Colombia)	290
AVIVA LIFE INSURANCE COMPANY (England, U.K.)	339
AVON ENGINEERED FABRICATIONS (England, U.K.)	339
AVON MILK-RITE USA (England, U.K.)	339
AVON RUBBER & PLASTICS INC. (England, U.K.)	339
AVON ZATEC (England, U.K.)	339
AVOTUS CORP. (Canada)	105
AVSEC SERVICES LLC (England, U.K.)	474
AVX CORPORATION (Japan)	1034
AW NORTH CAROLINA, INC. (Japan)	954
AXA ADVISORS (France)	585
AXA ART INSURANCE INC. (Germany)	680
AXA EQUITABLE LIFE INSURANCE CO. (France)	585
AXA FINANCIAL INC. (France)	585
AXA ROSENBERG GROUP (France)	585
AXALTO INC. (France)	586
AXCAN PHARMA INC. (Canada)	105
AXEL JOHNSON INC (Sweden)	1390
AXICAN PHARMA INC. (France)	635
AXIM (Italy)	931
AXIS COMMUNICATIONS INC. (Sweden)	1390
AXIS-SHIELD USA (Scotland, U.K.)	1307
AXL MUSICAL INSTRUMENTS CO. (China PRC)	282
AXSYS INCORPORATED (England, U.K.)	380
AXWAY, INC. (France)	658

AZCAR USA INC. (Canada)	105
AZO INC. (Germany)	681
AZTECA AMERICA (Mexico)	1202
AZU-VI, INC. (Spain)	1363

B

B&R AGENCY, DIV. ZIM (Israel)	908
B.E.A INC. (England, U.K.)	412
B+H OCEAN CARRIERS, DIV. NAVINVEST MARINE (Bermuda)	59
BAA INDIANAPOLIS INC. (England, U.K.)	340
BAA PITTSBURGH INC. (England, U.K.)	340
BAA USA (England, U.K.)	340
BABCOCK EAGLETON INC. (England, U.K.)	340
BAC INSURANCE GROUP (Panama)	1291
BACARDI MARTINI USA (Bermuda)	59
BACCARAT CRYSTAL (France)	653
BACCARAT CRYSTAL (France)	653
BACHEM BIOSCIENCE, INC. (Switzerland)	1433
BACHEM CALIFORNIA INC. (Switzerland)	1433
BACHMANN INDUSTRIES (Germany)	805
BACOU DALLOZ USA INC. (France)	586
BADGER DAYLIGHTING INC. (Canada)	106
BAE SYSTEMS ELECTRONICS & INTEGRATED SOLUTIONS (England, U.K.)	340
BAE SYSTEMS LAND & ARMAMENTS (England, U.K.)	340
BAE SYSTEMS NA (England, U.K.)	341
BAE SYSTEMS SAN DIEGO SHIP REPAIR (England, U.K.)	341
BAE SYSTEMS SHIP REPAIR (England, U.K.)	341
BAE SYSTEMS STEEL PRODUCTS DIVISION (England, U.K.)	341
BAE SYSTEMS TECHNOLOGY SOLUTIONS & SERVICES (England, U.K.)	341
BAER SUPPLY CO. (Germany)	802
BAHLSEN GMBH & CO. (Germany)	681
BAIKOWSKI MALAKOFF INC. (BMI) (France)	639
BAKEMARK EAST (Netherlands)	1216
BAKEMARK INGREDIENTS INC. (Netherlands)	1216

BAKER & BAKER (Netherlands) 1216
BAKER HUGHES INCORPORATED 551
(England, U.K.)
BAKER TILLY INTERNATIONAL LTD. 341
(England, U.K.)
BALD MOUNTAIN MINE (Canada) 218
BALDWIN INTERNATIONAL (Canada) 231
BALFOUR BEATTY CONSTRUCTION INC. 342
(England, U.K.)
BALKAN BULGARIAN AIRLINES 83
(Bulgaria)
BALLANTINE INC. (Japan) 1165
BALLARD MATERIAL PRODUCTS 106
(Canada)
BALLARD POWER SYSTEMS 106
CORPORATION (Canada)
BALLAST NEDAM CONSTRUCTION, INC. 1212
(Netherlands)
BALLI STEEL PIPE USA (England, U.K.) 342
BALLI WEBCO INTERNATIONAL 342
(England, U.K.)
BALLY, INC. (Switzerland) 1434
BALTIMORE TECHNOLOGIES INC 342
(England, U.K.)
BALZERS INC. (Switzerland) 1486
BALZERS, INC. (Liechtenstein) 1182
BANCA CARIGE USA (Italy) 913
BANCA DI ROMA (Italy) 919
BANCA MONTE DEI PASCHI DI SIENA 913
SPA. (Italy)
BANCA NAZIONALE DEL LAVORO (Italy) 913

BANCA POPOLARE DI MILANO (Italy) 914
BANCAFE INTERNATIONAL MIAMI 290
(Colombia)
BANCO ATLANTICO, S.A. (Spain) 1364
BANCO BRADESCO SA (Brazil) 72
BANCO COLPATRIA S.A. (Colombia) 291
BANCO DE CHILE (Chile) 277
BANCO DE CREDITO DEL PERU (Peru) 1292
BANCO DE GALICIA Y BUENOS AIRES 4
(Argentina)
BANCO DE LA NACION ARGENTINA 4
(Argentina)
BANCO DO BRASIL S.A. (Brazil) 72

BANCO ESPIRITO SANTO (Luxembourg) 1183
BANCO ESPIRITO SANTO DE LISBON 1297
(Portugal)
BANCO INDUSTRIAL DE VENEZUELA 1518
(Venezuela)
BANCO INTERNACIONAL DE COSTA 292
RICA, S.A. (Costa Rica)
BANCO ITAU HOLDING FINANCEIRA S.A. 73
(Brazil)
BANCO LATINOAMERICANO DE 1291
EXPORTACIONES (BLADEX) (Panama)
BANCO MERCANTIL DE SAO PAULO 73
(Brazil)
BANCO PASTOR (Spain) 1364
BANCO PORTUGUES DO ATLANTICO 1297
(Portugal)
BANCO SANTANDER (Chile) 277
BANCO TOSCANA USA (Italy) 914
BANCO TOTTA (Spain) 1364
BANCOLOMBIA S.A. (Colombia) 291
BANDAI AMERICA INC. (Japan) 1065
BANESPA (Spain) 1365
BANESTADO SA (Brazil) 72
BANESTO (Spain) 1365
BANG & OLUFSEN (Denmark) 298
BANGKOK BANK PUBLIC COMPANY 1510
LTD. (Thailand)
BANGLADESH BIMAN AIRLINES 38
CORPORATION (Bangladesh)
BANGOR HYDRO ELECTRIC COMPANY 143
(Canada)
BANJO STRATEGIC ENTERTAINMENT 196
(Canada)
BANK BNI (Indonesia) 858
BANK HAPOALIM (Israel) 878
BANK INTESA (Italy) 912
BANK JULIUS BAER (Switzerland) 1455
BANK LEUMI USA (Israel) 878
BANK MELLI IRAN (Iran) 859
BANK NEGARA MALAYSIA (Malaysia) 1186
BANK OF BARODA (India) 834
BANK OF BERMUDA (NEW YORK) LTD 59
(Bermuda)
BANK OF CHINA (China PRC) 282

American Affiliates

American Affiliates

CUNNINGHAM LINDSEY U.S., INC. (Canada) 186
CURIOUS SOFTWARE, INC. (Norway) 1288
CURTIS CIRCULATION CO. (France) 617
CURTIS CIRCULATION COMPANY (France) 624
CUSHMAN & WAKEFIELD, INC. (Japan) 1048
CUSTOM INTEGRATED TECHNOLOGY, INC. (Japan) 963
CYBERPLEX INC. (Canada) 137
CYBIO, INC. (Germany) 699
CYBOZU CORPORATION (Japan) 968
CYCORE INC. (Sweden) 1395
CYPRUS AIRWAYS LTD. (Cyprus) 294
CYRO INDUSTRIES (Germany) 709
CYRO INDUSTRIES, INC. (Germany) 768
CYTEC CARBON FIBERS LLC (Belgium) 42
CYTEC ENGINEERED MATERIALS INC. (Belgium) 42
CYTEC INDUSTRIES INC. (Belgium) 43
CZECH AIRLINES LTD. (Czech Republic) 295

D

D. F. STAUFFER BISCUIT COMPANY, INC. (Japan) 1042
DACOM AMERICA, INC. (South Korea) 1335
DAEHNFELDT INC. (Denmark) 299
DAELIM INDUSTRIAL CO. LTD. (South Korea) 1335
DAERIM AMERICA, INC. (South Korea) 1335
DAEWOO ELECTRONICS AMERICA INC. (South Korea) 1336
DAEWOO HEAVY INDUSTRIES AMERICA (South Korea) 1336
DAEWOO HEAVY INDUSTRIES INC. (South Korea) 1336
DAEWOO INTERNATIONAL (AMERICA) CORPORATION (South Korea) 1336
DAEWOO INTERNATIONAL CORPORATION (South Korea) 1336
DAEWOO MOTOR AMERICA (South Korea) 1336
DAI BAI DANG RESTAURANT (Hong Kong PRC) 810

DAI NIPPON IMS AMERICA CORP. (Japan) 968
DAICEL (USA) INC. (Japan) 969
DAICEL SAFETY SYSTEMS AMERICA, LLS (Japan) 969
DAICOLOR-USA (Japan) 972
DAIDO CORPORATION (Japan) 969
DAIDO STEEL (AMERICA) INC (Japan) 970
DAIDO STEEL (AMERICA), INC. (Japan) 970
DAIDOH INTERNATIONAL INC. (Japan) 970
DAIEI USA, INC. (Japan) 971
DAIHATSU AMERICA INC. (Japan) 971
DAIICHI CHUO SHIPPING AMERICA, INC. (Japan) 971
DAI-ICHI LIFE INSURANCE USA INC. (Japan) 971
DAIICHI PHARMACEUTICAL CORPORATION (Japan) 971
DAIKIN AMERICA INC. (Japan) 972
DAIKIN U.S. CORPORATION, INC. (Japan) 972
DAIMARU U.S.A., INC. (Japan) 972
DAIMLER-CHRYSLER NORTH AMERICA 700
DAINIPPON SCREEN ELECTRONICS INC. (Japan) 974
DAIWA CORPORATION (Japan) 975
DAIWA SB INVESTMENTS LTD. (Japan) 974
DAIWA SECURITIES AMERICA INC. (Japan) 974
DAIWA SECURITIES TRUST CO. (Japan) 974
DAK AMERICAS (Mexico) 1191
DAKOCYTOMATION INC. (Denmark) 299
DALSA CORECO (Canada) 137
DALSA CORPORATION (Canada) 137
DAMCO SEA & AIR (Netherlands) 1217
DANFOSS AUTOMATIC CONTROLS (Denmark) 300
DANFOSS BAUER (Denmark) 300
DANFOSS COMMERCIAL 300
DANFOSS COMMERCIAL COMPRESSORS LTD. (Denmark) 300
DANFOSS DRIVES (Denmark) 300
DANFOSS DRIVES (Denmark) 300
DANFOSS FLOMATIC CORPORATION (Denmark) 300
DANFOSS FLUID POWER (Denmark) 300

DANFOSS GRAHAM (Denmark)	300
DANFOSS INC. (Denmark)	300
DANFOSS TURBOCOR COMPRESSORS INC. (Canada)	138
DANFOSS WATER & WASTEWATER (Denmark)	300
DANIELI CORPORATION (Italy)	921
DANISCO (Denmark)	301
DANISCO AMERICA (Denmark)	301
DANISCO ANIMAL NUTRITION (Denmark)	301
DANISCO INGREDIENTS USA, INC. (Denmark)	301
DANISCO USA INC. (Denmark)	302
DANISCO USA, INC. (Denmark)	302
DANISH CROWN USA INC. (Denmark)	302
DANKA BUSINESS SYSTEMS (England, U.K.)	378
DANKA OFFICE IMAGING CO. (England, U.K.)	378
DANSKE BANK (Denmark)	303
DARTFISH USA, INC. (Switzerland)	1442
DASSAULT FALCON JET CORPORATION (France)	602
DASSAULT SYSTEMES OF AMERICA (France)	602
DASSAULT SYSTEMES OF AMERICA CORP. (France)	603
DATA CONNECTION CORPORATION (England, U.K.)	378
DATALEX COMMUNICATIONS USA, INC. (Ireland)	862
DATAMARK SYSTEMS GROUP INC. (Canada)	138
DATAMATICS AMERICA INC. (India)	835
DATAMIRROR CORPORATION (Canada)	138
DATAMONITOR INC. (England, U.K.)	379
DATAQUICK.COM (Canada)	190
DATAWAVE SYSTEMS, INC. (Canada)	139
DATEX-OHMEDA INC. (Finland)	569
DAVID HALSALL LTD. (England, U.K.)	379
DAVID J. JOSEPH COMPANY (Netherlands)	1256
DAVID KEIGHLEY PRODUCTIONS 70 MM INC. (Canada)	171

DAVIDE CENCI INC. (Italy)	920
DAVIDSON LADDERS INC., DIV. LOUISVILLE LADDERS (Mexico)	1196
DAVIES WARD PHILLIPS & VINEBERG LLP (Canada)	139
DAWSON-FORTE CASHMERE (England, U.K.)	379
DAY SOFTWARE INC. (Switzerland)	1443
DBA SEASIA (Japan)	1085
DBI/SALA (England, U.K.)	363
DBS BANK LOS ANGELES AGENCY (Singapore)	1316
DBT AMERICA INC. (Germany)	700
DCI MARKETING INC. (England, U.K.)	422
DDD GROUP (England, U.K.)	379
DE BRAUW BLACKSTONE WESTBROEK PC (Netherlands)	1219
DE LONGHI AMERICA, INC. (Italy)	921
DEARBORN MID-WEST CONVEYOR CO. (England, U.K.)	540
DECEUNINCK NORTH AMERICAN (Belgium)	44
DECHRA VETERINARY PRODUCTS (England, U.K.)	380
DECISION ONE MORTGAGE COMPANY, LLC (England, U.K.)	420
DECLEOR U.S.A., INC. (France)	603
DECODE GENETICS, INC. (Iceland)	830
DECRA ROOFING SYSTEMS INC. (New Zealand)	1271
DECTRON INTERNATIONALE INC. (Canada)	139
DEE VAN ENTERPRISE USA INC. (Taiwan (ROC))	1497
DEERE-HITACHI CONSTRUCTION MACHINERY CORPORATION (Japan)	995
DEGUSSA BIOACTIVES US (Germany)	701
DEGUSSA BUILDING SYSTEMS (Germany)	709
DEGUSSA CONSTRUCTION CHEMICALS AMERICAS (Germany)	701
DEGUSSA CORP. (Germany)	709
DEGUSSA CORPORATION (Germany)	701
DEGUSSA FEED ADDITIVES (Germany)	701

DPI NORTHWEST (Ireland)	869	DSM DESOTECH INC. (Netherlands)	1249
DPI ROCKY MOUNTAIN (Ireland)	869	DSM ELASTOMERS AMERICA (Netherlands)	1249
DPI SOUTHWEST (Ireland)	869	DSM ENGINEERING PLASTICS, INC. (Netherlands)	1250
DPI WEST (Ireland)	869		
DR. ALEXANDER AGHAYAN & ASSOCIATES, INC. (Iran)	859	DSM PHARMACEUTICALS, INC. (Netherlands)	1250
DR. MARTENS AIRWAIR USA (England, U.K.)	409	DSM SOMOS (Netherlands)	1250
DR. PEPPER BOTTLING COMPANY (England, U.K.)	361	DTRIC INSURANCE CO., INC. (Japan)	952
DR. REDDY'S LABORATORIES INC. (India)	848	DUCATI NORTH AMERICA INC. (Italy)	924
		DUCATI NORTH AMERICA, INC. (Italy)	924
DR. REDDY'S LABORATORIES LIMITED (India)	835	DUFFIN MANUFACTURING COMPANY (Switzerland)	1448
DRAEGER SAFETY, INC. (Germany)	707	DUFRY AMERICA SERVICES, INC. (Switzerland)	1443
DRAEGER SIEMENS MEDICAL, INC. (Germany)	707	DUNI CORPORATION (Sweden)	1395
DRAGON PRODUCTS COMPANY (Spain)	1366	DUNI SUPPLY CORPORATION (Sweden)	1396
DRAKA CABLES (Netherlands)	1220	DUNKIN' BRANDS, INC. (France)	637
DRAKA COMTEQ AMERICAS INC. (Netherlands)	1220	DUNKIN' BRANDS, INC. (England, U.K.)	327
		DUPONT (Japan)	1148
DRAKA ELEVATOR PRODUCTS INC. (Netherlands)	1220	Durango-McKinley Paper Company	1193
		DURATEX NORTH AMERICA, INC. (Brazil)	74
DRAKA USA CORPORATION (Netherlands)	1220	DUREZ CORP. (Japan)	1133
DRAKA USA INC. (Netherlands)	1221	DURKOPP ADLER AMERICA INC. (Germany)	708
DRAKE EXTRUSION (England, U.K.)	366		
DRESDNER BANK AG (Germany)	707	DURR INDUSTRIES INC. (Germany)	708
DRESDNER BANK LATIN AMERICA (Germany)	708	DUTCH FINEST FANTASIES (Germany)	683
DRESDNER KLEINWORT WASSERSTEIN (Germany)	708	DUXIANA (Sweden)	1396
		DUXIANA LODELA (Sweden)	1396
DRESDNER KLEINWORT WASSERSTEIN NA INC. (England, U.K.)	385	D-VELCO MANUFACTURING OF ARIZONA, INC. (Canada)	209
DRESHER HILL EXTENDICARE INC. (Canada)	146	DYMO CORPORATION (England, U.K.)	393
		DYNACS INC. (Canada)	190
DREYER'S GRAND ICE CREAM HOLDINGS, INC. (Switzerland)	1464	DYNAMESH, INC. (Japan)	1088
		DYNAMEX RESOURCES CORP. (Switzerland)	1468
DRYKOR, INC. (Israel)	883	DYNARIC INC. (Japan)	973
DS SMITH PLASTICS (England, U.K.)	518	DYNEA INC. (Finland)	564
DS SMITH WORLDWIDE DISPENSERS INC. (England, U.K.)	518	DYNEA OVERLAYS INC. (Finland)	565
		DYNO NOBEL INC. (Norway)	1278
DS WATER OF AMERICA (Japan)	1138	DZ BANK (Germany)	709
DS WATERS OF AMERICA (France)	602	DZ FINANCIAL MARKETS LLC (Germany)	709
DSG-CANUSA (Canada)	235		

E

E & E MAGNETIC PRODUCTS LTD. 812
(Hong Kong PRC)
E FUNDS CORPORATION (Canada) 213
E.ON NORTH AMERICA, INC. (Germany) 709
E.W. HOWELL CO., INC. (Japan) 1096

E2V TECHNOLOGIES INC. (England, U.K.) 387
EADS NORTH AMERICA (Netherlands) 1223
EADS TELECOM (Netherlands) 1223
EADS TELECOM NA (France) 606
EAGLE MANUFACTURING LLC (Canada) 186
EAGLE OPTICS, INC. (Japan) 1006
EAGLE TECHNOLOGIES SERVICES LTD. 142
(Canada)
EAGLE-PICHER INDUSTRIES, INC. 1230
(Netherlands)
EARTH SATELLITE CORP. (Canada) 190
EARTH TECH (Bermuda) 66
EARTHRISE NUTRITIONALS (Japan) 973
EAST JAPAN RAILWAY COMPANY 978
(Japan)
EASTERN BRIDGE COMPANY (France) 599
EASTERN COMPONENTS (Japan) 998
EASYSCREEN INC. (England, U.K.) 387
EBARA AMERICA CORPORATION 978
(Japan)
EBARA INTERNATIONAL (Japan) 978
EBARA TECHNOLOGIES INC. (Japan) 978
EC PIGMENTS USA (England, U.K.) 394
ECHELON BIOSCIENCES INC. (Canada) 90
ECI TELECOM, INC. (Israel) 884
ECOLAB INC. (Germany) 731
ECS, DIV. SPEEDWARE CORPORATION 241
(Canada)
ECTEL INC. (Israel) 884
ECTEL INC. USA (Israel) 884
EDAP TECHNOMED INC. (France) 606
EDDIE BAUER HOLDINGS, INC. (Germany) 760

EDGETECH CONSULTING, INC. (Canada) 142
EDGETEK MACHINE CORPORATION 496
(England, U.K.)

EDITORIAL TELEVISA CALIFORNIA (Mexico) 1193
EDITORIAL TELEVISA INTERNACIONAL 1193
(Mexico)
EDITORIAL TELEVISA NEW YORK 1193
(Mexico)
EDNA VALLEY VINEYARD (England, U.K.) 382
EDWARD LLOYD LIMITED (England, U.K.) 417

EFKA OF AMERICA INC. (Germany) 715
EFTEC NORTH AMERICA, INC. 1444
(Switzerland)
EFX COMPRESSION USA (Canada) 144
EGON ZEHNDER INTERNATIONAL, INC. 1489
(Switzerland)
EGYPTAIR (Egypt) 316
EGYPTAIR CARGO (Egypt) 316
EICON NETWORKS (Canada) 142
EIDOS INTERACTIVE USA, INC (England, 388
U.K.)
EIKI INTERNATIONAL INC. (Japan) 979
EIMCO WATER TECHNOLOGIES 164
(Canada)
EIMSKIP USA INC. (Iceland) 830
EINSON FREEMAN, INC. (England, U.K.) 556
EIRCOM USA LTD. (Ireland) 863
EISAI CORPORATION OF NORTH 979
AMERICA (Japan)
EISAI MEDICAL RESEARCH INC. (Japan) 979
EISAI RESEARCH INSTITUTE OF 979
BOSTON (Japan)
EISAI USA (Japan) 979
EISENMANN, TEMTEK-ALLIED DIV. 710
(Germany)
EKA CHEMICALS, INC. (Sweden) 1396
EKA CHEMICALS, INC., BINDZIL/NYACOL 1396
GROUP (Sweden)
EL AL ISRAEL AIRLINES (Israel) 885
ELAMEX USA INC. (Mexico) 1194
ELAN CORPORATION (Ireland) 863
ELAN HOLDINGS (Ireland) 863
ELAN PHARMA INC. (Ireland) 864
ELATERAL INC. (England, U.K.) 388
ELBIT VISION SYSTEMS (Israel) 886

FARADAY TECHNOLOGY CORPORATION (Taiwan (ROC))	1498
FARMER JACK SUPERMARKETS (Germany)	789
FARMERS GROUP, INC. (Switzerland)	1491
FARMERS NEW WORLD LIFE INSURANCE COMPANY (Switzerland)	1492
FARRAR, STRAUS & GIROUX, INC. (Germany)	721
FARRAR, STRAUS AND GIROUX (Germany)	795
FAST SEARCH & TRANSFER, INC. (Norway)	1279
FASTRAMP TEST SERVICES (Singapore)	1323
FATHAMMER USA INC. (Finland)	565
FAULTLESS CASTER (England, U.K.)	400
FAURECIA AUTOMOTIVE SEATING INC. (France)	610
FAURECIA EXHAUST SYSTEMS (France)	610
FAURECIA EXHAUST SYSTEMS, INC. (France)	639
FAURECIA INTERIOR SYSTEMS (France)	610
FAURECIA INTERIOR SYSYTEMS (France)	610
FAUSKE & ASSOCIATES (England, U.K.)	356
FCI CONSTRUCTORS INC. (Netherlands)	1238
FCX PERFORMANCE INC. (England, U.K.)	396
FCX SIMCO CONTROLS (England, U.K.)	396
FCX SIMONE ENGINEERING (England, U.K.)	396
FEADSHIP AMERICA INC. (Netherlands)	1224
FEDERAL-MOGUL PISTON RINGS (Japan)	1079
FELIX SCHOELLER TECHNICAL PAPERS INC. (Germany)	714
FENESTRAE INC. (Netherlands)	1224
FENNER DRIVES, INC. (England, U.K.)	397
FENTEK AMERICAS (Sweden)	1424
FERAG INC. (Switzerland)	1489
FERGUSON ENTERPRISES, INC. (England, U.K.)	555
FERMAG INC. (France)	626
FEROLETO STEEL COMPANY, INC. (Japan)	1164
FERRARI USA INC. (Italy)	926
FERRAZ SHAWMUT INC. (France)	626
FERRERO USA INC. (Italy)	926
FERROTEC USA CORPORATION (Japan)	981
FERRY MORSE SEED COMPANY	667
FERRY-MORSE SEED COMPANY	615
FES SYSTEMS INC. (Netherlands)	1230
FETTE AMERICA (Germany)	714
FFASTFILL INC. (England, U.K.)	397
FFE MINERALS (Denmark)	304
FHM MAGAZINE (England, U.K.)	389
FICOSA NORTH AMERICAN CORPORATION (Spain)	1369
FIDELITY AND GUARANTY LIFE INSURANCE COMPANY (England, U.K.)	475
FILA U.S.A., INC. (Italy)	926
FILTRONA EXTRUSION PHILADELPHIA INC. (England, U.K.)	398
FILTRONIC COMTEK, INC. (England, U.K.)	398
FILTRONIC SIGTEK, INC. (England, U.K.)	398
FIMAT USA INC. (France)	655
FINANCIAL MODELS COMPANY INC. (Canada)	151
FINANCIAL NETWORK INVESTMENT CORP. (Netherlands)	1235
FINANCIAL OBJECTS PLC (England,	399
FINANCIAL SECURITY ASSURANCE HOLDINGS LTD. (Belgium)	45
FINANTIA USA LTD. (Portugal)	1297
FINCENTRIC CORPORATION (Canada)	151
FINDLAW (Canada)	252
FINEOS CORPORATION (Ireland)	864
FINETEX INC. (England, U.K.)	474
FINETRON (South Korea)	1352
FINEWRAP USA, INC. (Australia)	15
FINNAIR (Finland)	566
FINNSTEEL INC. (Finland)	575
FIRCROFT ENGINEERING SERVICES INC. (England, U.K.)	399
FIREMAN'S FUND AGRIBUSINESS (Germany)	678
FIREMAN'S FUND MCGEE MARINE (Germany)	678
FIREWORKS TELEVISION, INC. (England, U.K.)	399

American Affiliates

G

GEA POWER COOLING SYSTEMS, INC. 719
(Germany)
GEA/ FES SYSTEMS INC. (Germany) 719
GEAC (Canada) 156
GEAC INTEREALTY (Canada) 157
GEAC MPC (Canada) 157
GEAC NORTH AMERICA (Canada) 157
GEAC PUBLIC SAFETY (Canada) 157
GEAC RESTAURANT SYSTEMS INC. 157
(Canada)
GEARBULK HOLDING LTD. (Japan) 1057
GEBERIT MANUFACTURING INC. 1448
(Switzerland)
GECOM CORPORATION (Japan) 1057
GEDAS USA INC. (Germany) 720
GEDEON RICHTER USA INC. (Hungary) 829

GEFRAN ISI, INC. (Italy) 927
GELITA USA INC. (Germany) 720
GEMCOM USA INC. (Canada) 157
GEMPLUS CORPORATION (Luxembourg) 1184
GEMTRON CORPORATION (Germany) 774
GENENCOR INTERNATIONAL INC. 302
(Denmark)
GENERAL CASUALTY INSURANCE 1442
COMPANIES (Switzerland)
GENERAL CASUALTY INSURANCE, DIV. 1489
WINTERTHUR (Switzerland)
GENERAL CIGAR HOLDINGS, INC. 1422
(Sweden)
GENERAL MILLS INC./ YOPLAIT (France) 656
GENERAL MINERALS CORPORATION 157
(Canada)
GENERAL MOTORS ISUZU 1009
COMMERCIAL TRUCK (Japan)
GENERAL PUMP COMPANIES INC. (Italy) 931
GENERAL SEATING OF AMERICA INC. 1069
(Japan)
GENERAL SHALE BRICK, INC. (Austria) 34
GENERALI GLOBAL (Italy) 912
GENESCAN USA, INC. (France) 609
GENESCAN, INC. (Germany) 720
GENESYS INC. (France) 613
GENETECH INC. (Switzerland) 1469
GENETIX USA INC. (England, U.K.) 405

GENPAK (Canada) 179
GENUINE PARTS COMPANY (Canada) 260
GEODIS VITESSE LOGISTICS INC. 614
(France)
GEOMETRICS, INC. (Japan) 1103
GEORGE FISCHER SIGNET INC. 1446
(Switzerland)
GEORGE FISCHER SLOANE INC. 1446
(Switzerland)
GEORGE WESTON BAKERIES (Canada) 266
GEORGIA DUCK CONVEYOR BELTING 397
(England, U.K.)
GEORGIA METAL COATINGS CO. (Japan) 1093
GEO-TECH EXPLORATIONS INC. (South 1328
Africa)
GERBER LEGENDARY BLADES (Finland) 567
GERBER LIFE INSURANCE COMPANY 1465
(Switzerland)
GERBER PRODUCTS COMPANY 1465
(Switzerland)
GERDAU (Brazil) 76
GERDAU AMERISTEEL (Brazil) 76
GERDAU AMERISTEEL CORPORATION 76
(Brazil)
GERDAU AMERISTEEL RARITAN INC. 76
(Brazil)
GERLING AMERICA INSURANCE CO. 721
(Germany)
GET ASIA LTD. (England, U.K.) 405
GETINGE USA (Sweden) 1400
GETRONICS INC. (Netherlands) 1230
GETTY PETROLEUM MARKETING INC. 1302
(Russia) 1302
GFI GROUP INC. (England, U.K.) 405
GFI SOFTWARE, INC. (Malta) 1189
GFT USA CORPORATION (Italy) 928
GIANFRANCO FERRE USA (Italy) 927
GIANT BICYCLE USA INC. (Taiwan (ROC)) 1500
GIANT CEMENT HOLDING (Spain) 1366
GIANT FOOD LLC (Netherlands) 1249
GIANT FOOD STORES LLC (Netherlands) 1249
GIANT RESOURCE RECOVERY CO., INC. 1367
(Spain)
GIBRALTAR LIFE (Japan) 989

American Affiliates

GIBRALTAR NATIONAL INSURANCE CO. INC. (Japan) — 989

GIDDINGS & LEWIS, INC. (Germany) — 790

GIESECKE & DEVRIENT AMERICA, INC. (Germany) — 722

GIESECKE & DEVRIENT CARDTECH, INC. (Germany) — 722

GIFTS & DECORATIVE ACCESSORIES MAGAZINE (England, U.K.) — 493

GIGANTE USA INC. (Mexico) — 1195

GILAT SATELLITE NETWORKING SYSTEMS (Israel) — 889

GIORGIO ARMANI CORPORATION (Italy) — 911

GIVAUDAN CORP. (Switzerland) — 1449

GIVAUDAN CORPORATION (Switzerland) — 1449

GIVAUDAN FLAVORS CORP. (Switzerland) — 1449

GIVAUDAN FRAGRANCES CORP. (Switzerland) — 1449

GIVEN IMAGING, INC. (Israel) — 889

GIW INDUSTRIES (Germany) — 747

GIW INDUSTRIES-THOMSON (Germany) — 747

GKN AEROSPACE CHEM-TRONICS, INC. (England, U.K.) — 406

GKN AEROSPACE TRANSPARENCY SYSTEMS (England, U.K.) — 406

GKN AMERICA CORP. (England, U.K.) — 406

GKN AUTOMOTIVE INC. (England, U.K.) — 406

GL CONSULTANTS INC. (France) — 614

GL&V USA (Canada) — 164

GLANBIA NUTRITIONALS, INC. (Ireland) — 865

GLASSALUM INTERNATIONAL CORP. (Italy) — 938

GLAXOSMITHKLINE (England, U.K.) — 406

GLENCOE US HOLDINGS LTD. (Bermuda) — 64

GLENCORE COMMODITIES (Switzerland) — 1450

GLENCORE LTD. (Switzerland) — 1450

GLENDINNING MANAGEMENT CONSULTANTS (England, U.K.) — 407

GLEN-GERY CORPORATION (England, U.K.) — 421

GLOBAL CROSSING INC. (Bermuda) — 60

GLOBAL INSURANCE SOLUTIONS (England, U.K.) — 407

GLOBAL LABORATORY SERVICES INC. (Netherlands) — 1219

GLOBAL NUCLEAR FUEL AMERICAS LLC (Japan) — 996

GLOBAL NUCLEAR FUEL AMERICAS, LLC (Japan) — 1158

GLOBAL SECURITIES USA, INC. (Turkey) — 1514

GLOBAL SOURCES USA, INC. (Singapore) — 1317

GLOBAL THERMOELECTRIC INC. (Canada) — 158

GLOBE & MAIL NEWS BUREAU (Canada) — 108

GLOBECAST US (France) — 612

GLOBO INTERNATIONAL (Brazil) — 77

GLOBOMAX LLC (Ireland) — 866

GLOCK INC. (Austria) — 30

GLOTEL INC. (England, U.K.) — 407

GMC SOFTWARE TECHNOLOGY, INC. (Switzerland) — 1450

GMI METAULLICS, INC. (France) — 626

GN JABRA NORTH AMERICA (Denmark) — 306

GN RESOUND CORPORATION (Denmark) — 305

GN RESOUND NORTH AMERICA (Denmark) — 305

GOLD FIELDS LIMITED (South Africa) — 1329

GOLDEN ALASKA SEAFOODS, INC. (Japan) — 1070

GOLDEN GATE FIELDS (Canada) — 191

GOLDEN SPIRIT GAMING LTD. (Canada) — 158

GOLDEN STAR RESOURCES LTD. (French Guiana) — 674

GOLDEN SUNLIGHT MINES, INC. (Canada) — 219

GOLDEN TELECOM, INC. (Russia) — 1301

GOLDER ASSOCIATES (Canada) — 158

GOLDMAN SACHS TRUST (Australia) — 16

GOLIATH THREADING TOOLS INC. (England, U.K.) — 408

GOODALL RUBBER COMPANY, INC. (Sweden) — 1424

GOODFELLOW INC. (Canada) — 162

GOODYEAR DUNLOP TIRES LTD. — 1137

GORAN CAPITAL (Canada) — 163

GORANN INC. (Ireland) — 866

GORTONS INC. (Japan) — 1082

GOTTEX INDUSTRIES, INC. (Israel) 889
GOTTLIEB SKANSKA (Sweden) 1420
GOULD ELECTRONICS INC. (Japan) 1077
GP BATTERIES INTERNATIONAL 301
LIMITED (Denmark)
GPC BIOTECH INC. (Germany) 723
GRAHAM WEBB (Germany) 800
GRANADA AMERICA (England, U.K.) 409
GRANSFORS BRUKS INC. (Sweden) 1401
GRAPHIC CONTROLS LLC (Bermuda) 66
GRAPHIC TECHNOLOGY INC. (Japan) 989
GRAPHIC TECHNOLOGY, INC. (Japan) 1092
GRAPHISOFT US INC. (Hungary) 828
GRAPHITE MATERIALS DIVISION 626
(France)
GRASS AMERICA (Germany) 803
GRASS AMERICA INC. (Austria) 30
GRAY LINE SAN FRANCISCO (England, 524
U.K.)
GREAT ATLANTIC & PACIFIC TEA 789
COMPANY INC. (A&P) (Germany)
GREAT ATLANTIC NEWS (Canada) 179
GREAT ATLANTIC NEWS LLC (Canada) 206
GREAT LAKES DOWNS (Canada) 191
GREAT MIDATLANTIC NEWS (Canada) 179
GREAT MIDWEST NEWS (Canada) 206
GREAT PACIFIC NEWS CO., INC. 206
(Canada)
GREAT PACIFIC NEWS COMPANY, INC. 179
(Canada)
GREAT-WEST LIFE & ANNUITY 163
INSURANCE COMPANY (Canada)

GREEN LIND & McNULTY, INC. (Israel) 877
GREENLIGHT MEDIA USA (Germany) 723
GREENSBORO ASSOCIATES INC. 449
(England, U.K.)
GREENWICH CAPITAL MARKETS, INC. 1311
(Scotland, U.K.)
GREY GLOBAL GROUP INC. (England, 556
U.K.)
GRIDAMERICA LLC (England, U.K.) 472
GRINDEX PUMPS (Sweden) 1401
GROB SYSTEMS,INC. (Germany) 723
GROHE AMERICA, INC. (Germany) 723

GROSFILLEX, INC. (France) 614
GROSVENOR AMERICAS INC. (England, U.K.) 409
GROSVENOR USA LIMITED (England, U.K.) 410
GROUP SERVICES INC. (France) 632
GROUP TECHNOLOGIES (Germany) 724
GROVE'S DICTIONARIES INC., DIV. 447
PALGRAVE (England, U.K.)
GROZ-BECKERT USA INC. (Germany) 724
GRUMA CORPORATION (Mexico) 1194
GRUNER+JAHR USA (Germany) 687
GRUPO TACA (El Salvador) 317
GS BATTERY (USA) INC. (Japan) 989
GS-3 (GANDEN SECURITY SERVICES 888
SOLUTIONS) (Israel)
GSSI (Japan) 1103
GST CORPORATION (Japan) 1083

GTP STEEL HEDDLE INC. (Belgium) 48
GTY TIRE COMPANY (Japan) 1161
GUARDIAN WEEKLY (England, U.K.) 411
GUCCI AMERICA, INC. (France) 637
GUERBET GROUP (France) 616
GUERLAIN, INC. (France) 616
GUITABEC USA INC. (Canada) 182
GUITAR ONE MAGAZINE (England, U.K.) 539
GULF INVESTMENT CORPORATION 37
(Bahrain)
GULFSTREAM PARK (Canada) 192
GUNOLD USA INC. (Germany) 724
GYRUS MEDICAL, INC. (Wales, U.K.) 1520

H

H&M HENNES & MAURITZ LP (Sweden) 1401
H. C. BRILL (Netherlands) 1216
H. C. BRILL (Netherlands) 1216
H. PAULIN & CO. LIMITED (Canada) 217
H. STERN JEWELERS (Brazil) 78
HAAG-STREIT USA INC. (Germany) 757
HABANERO OIL & GAS (Canada) 165
HABASIT ABT INC. (Switzerland) 1451
HABASIT BELTING INC. (Switzerland) 1451
HABASIT BELTING INCORPORATED 1451
(Switzerland)

I

ING FUNDS (Netherlands)	1236
ING INVESTMENT (Netherlands)	1236
ING INVESTMENT MANAGEMENT AMERICAS (Netherlands)	1236
ING LIFE INSURANCE (Netherlands)	1236
ING REAL ESTATE CLARION (Netherlands)	1236
INGENEO TECHNOLOGIES LTD. (Israel)	890
INGENICO CORP. (France)	621
INGENTA INC. (England, U.K.)	428
INITIAL HEALTHCARE SERVICES, INC. (England, U.K.)	496
INITIAL SECURITY SERVICES (England, U.K.)	496
INMARSAT NORTH AMERICA (England, U.K.)	428
INMETCO (Canada)	171
INNOMEDIA, INC. (Singapore)	1318
INNOVACOM US (France)	612
INNOVATIVE TECHNOLOGIES IN EDUCATION (Israel)	884
INNOVENE (England, U.K.)	352
INNOVIA FILMS INC. (England, U.K.)	429
INNOVISION GROUP INC. (England, U.K.)	429
INSIGNIA SOLUTIONS INC. (England, U.K.)	430
INSPEX INC. (Japan)	991
INSTINET CORPORATION (England,	498
INSTITUTIONAL INVESTOR INC. (England, U.K.)	393
INSTROMEDIX (Switzerland)	1438
INSTRUMARK INTERNATIONAL (Denmark)	301
INSTRUMENTARIUM IMAGING, INC. (Finland)	569
INSTRUMENTATION LABORATORY COMPANY (Spain)	1371
INSUL 8 CORPORATION (France)	604
INSURANCE CORP. OF HANNOVER (Germany)	726
INSYSTEMS CORPORATION (Canada)	172
INTAC INTERNATIONAL INC. (Hong Kong PRC)	816
INTAT PRECISION, INC. (Japan)	954
INTEC TELECOM SYSTEMS PLC (England, U.K.)	430
INTECH TECHNOLOGY CORPORATION (Switzerland)	1431
INTELECT TECHNOLOGIES, INC. (Singapore)	1321
INTELITEK INC. (Israel)	902
INTENTIA UNITED STATES (Sweden)	1406
INTEPLAST GROUP LTD. (Taiwan (ROC))	1500
INTERACTIVE DATA CORPORATION (England, U.K.)	479
INTERAUDI BANK (Lebanon)	1181
INTERBAKE FOODS INC. (Canada)	266
INTERCERAMIC USA (Mexico)	1199
INTERCONTINENTAL TRANSPORT SERVICES (Netherlands)	1218
INTERCYTEX RESEARCH (England, U.K.)	430
INTERGEN (Netherlands)	1250
INTERGRATED INFORMATION TECHNOLOGY CORP. (Canada)	208
INTERMAP TECHNOLOGIES CORPORATION (Canada)	173
INTERMECH INC. (Switzerland)	1491
INTERMEDIA FILMS EQUITIES USA, INC (Germany)	737
INTERMET CORP. (Japan)	1107
INTERNATIONAL DISPLAY TECHNOLOGY USA (Taiwan (ROC))	1496
INTERNATIONAL IMMUNOLOGY CORPORATION (Japan)	1092
INTERNATIONAL MARINE UNDERWRITERS (Bermuda)	68
INTERNATIONAL METAL SERVICE (France)	621
INTERNATIONAL MOLD STEEL (Japan)	970
INTERNATIONAL NICKEL INC. (Canada)	171
INTERNATIONAL TRADE COMPANY (Singapore)	1318
INTERNATIONAL WATER MAKERS, INC. (Canada)	139
INTERNATIONAL WINE ACCESSORIES (IWA) (Australia)	16
INTERNET INITIATIVE JAPAN INC. (Japan)	1007
	1007
INTERNET MEASUREMENT DIVISION (Netherlands)	1266

JOHN LAING INTERNATIONAL LIMITED   438
(England, U.K.)

JOHN WOOD GROUP (Scotland, U.K.)   1309
JOHNSON CONTROLS INC. (Germany)   794
JOHNSON ELECTRIC NORTH AMERICA   817
(Hong Kong PRC)
JOHNSON MATTHEY INC. (England, U.K.)   434
JOHNSON PUMPS OF AMERICA, INC.   1407
(Sweden)
JOLLIBEE/HONEYBEE FOODS   1293
CORPORATION (Philippines)
JOLLY HOTEL MADISON TOWERS (Italy)   932
JOSEF GARTNER & CO. (Italy)   938
JOSEF GARTNER USA INC. (Germany)   719
JP KENNY INC. (Scotland, U.K.)   1310
JP MANAGEMENT CONSULTING   570
(Finland)
JSP INTERNATIONAL (Japan)   1018
JSR AMERICA INC. (Japan)   1018
JSR MICRO INC. (Japan)   1018
JSW PLASTICS MACHINERY, INC. (Japan)   1014

JT INTERNATIONAL USA INC.   1455
(Switzerland)
JTB HAWAII, INC. (Japan)   1019
JTB INC. (Japan)   1019
JUDD WIRE (Japan)   1134
JUGOS DEL VALLE USA (Mexico)   1199
JULIUS BAER INVESTMENT   1455
MANAGEMENT (Switzerland)
JULIUS BAER INVESTMENT   1455
MANAGEMENT INC. (Switzerland)
JULIUS BAER SECURITIES INC.   1455
(Switzerland)
JUMO PROCESS CONTROL INC.   741
(Germany)

JUN HE LAW OFFICE (China PRC)   286
JUNGHEINRICH LIFT TRUCK CORP. USA   742
(Germany)
JUNIPER FINANCIAL CORP. (England,   343
U.K.)
JUNO LIGHTING INC. (France)   650
JURYS BOSTON HOTEL (Ireland)   870
JURYS WASHINGTON HOTEL (Ireland)   870
JVC CORPORATION (Japan)   1168

JWT (England, U.K.)   556

K

K LINE AMERICA (Japan)   1023
KAAK GROUP NORTH AMERICA   1237
(Netherlands)
KABA BENZING AMERICA, INC.   1456
(Switzerland)
KAGOME INC. (Japan)   1019
KAHALA MANDARIN ORIENTAL (Hong   818
Kong PRC)
KAI NORTH AMERICA LLC (Japan)   1010
KAJIMA U.S.A. INC. (Japan)   1019
KAMPF MACHINERY CORP. (Germany)   741
KAMPF MACHINERY CORPORATION   742
(Germany)
KANEBO, LTD. (Japan)   1020
KANEKA AMERICA CORPORATION   1020
(Japan)
KANEKA CORP. (Japan)   1020
KANEKA TEXAS HIGHTECH   1020
MATERIALS, CORPORATION (Japan)
KANEMATSU (USA) INC (Japan)   1020
KANEMATSU USA INC. (Japan)   1021
KANTHAL PALM COAST (Sweden)   1416
KAO BRANDS CO. (Japan)   1022
KAO SPECIALTIES AMERICAS (Japan)   1022
KAPLAN THALER GROUP (France)   641
KARL SCHMIDT UNISIA, INC. (Japan)   1001
KARL SCHMIDT UNISIA, ZOLLNER DIV.   743
(Germany)
KASH N' KARRY FOOD STORES, INC.   44
(Belgium)
KASIKORNBANK USA (Thailand)   1511
KAUMAGRAPH FLINT CORPORATION   486
KAUMAGRAPH FLINT CORPORATION   486
(England, U.K.)
KAUPTHING NEW YORK (Iceland)   831
KAVLICO CORP. (France)   650
KAVLICO CORP. (France)   650
KAWAI AMERICA CORPORATION (Japan)   1022
KAWASAKI HEAVY INDUSTRIES USA,   1023
INC. (Japan)
KAWASAKI HEAVY INDUSTRIES, LTD.   1023
(Japan)

KAWASAKI MICROELECTRONICS AMERICA, INC (Japan) — 1017

KAWASAKI RAIL CAR, INC. (Japan) — 1023

KAYE OF CONNECTICUT, DIV. HUB (Canada) — 148

KBA NORTH AMERICA INC. (Germany) — 745

KBC ADVANCED TECHNOLOGIES (England, U.K.) — 434

KBC ADVANCED TECHNOLOGIES INC. (England, U.K.) — 434

KBC BANK NV (Belgium) — 47

KD MANITOU INC. (France) — 631

KDDI AMERICA, INC. (Japan) — 1024

KDDI LABS USA INC. (Japan) — 1024

KEELER BRASS HARDWARE COMPANY (England, U.K.) — 401

KEELER INSTRUMENTS INC. (England, U.K.) — 413

KEIL SOFTWARE INC. (England, U.K.) — 332

KELMAN TECHNOLOGIES INC. (Canada) — 180

KEMIART USA INC. (Finland) — 572

KEMIRA CHEMICALS, INC. (Finland) — 570

KEN-MAC METALS, INC. (Germany) — 790

KENNECOTT ENERGY GROUP (Australia) — 24

KENNECOTT EXPLORATION CO. (Australia) — 24

KENNECOTT GREENS CREEK MINING CO. (Australia) — 24

KENNECOTT MINERALS CO. (Australia) — 24

KENNECOTT UTAH COPPER CORPORATION (Australia) — 24

KENTUCKY ADVANCED FORGE, LLC (Japan) — 1031

KENTUCKY UTILTIES COMPANY (Germany) — 709

KENWOOD USA CORP. (Japan) — 1024

KENYA AIRWAYS (Kenya) — 1178

KERRY BIO-SCIENCE AMERICAS (Ireland) — 870

KERRY INGREDIENTS NORTH AMERICA (Ireland) — 870

KERZNER INTERNATIONAL LIMITED (Bahamas) — 36

KESWICK HALL (Bermuda) — 62

KETTLER INTERNATIONAL INC. (Germany) — 730

KEURIG INC. (Canada) — 261

KEWILL GROUP (England, U.K.) — 437

KEYENCE CORP. OF AMERICA (Japan) — 1025

KEYSTONE BY MAAX (Canada) — 189

KEYSTONE REAL ESTATE (Canada) — 174

KHS BARTELT, INC. (Germany) — 743

KHS, INC. (Germany) — 744

KIA MOTORS AMERICA (South Korea) — 1346

KIA MOTORS AMERICA, INC. (South Korea) — 1346

KIBO GROUP INC. (Japan) — 967

KID GALAXY, INC. (Hong Kong PRC) — 818

KIEHL'S SINCE 1851 LLC (France) — 629

KIKKOMAN FOODS, INC. (Japan) — 1025

KIKKOMAN INTERNATIONAL, INC. (Japan) — 1026

KIKKOMAN MARKETING & PLANNING, INC. (Japan) — 1026

KILGORE FLARES CO., LLC (England, U.K.) — 368

KIM ENG SECURITIES USA INC. (Singapore) — 1319

KINAXIS (Canada) — 180

KINEMETRICS, INC. (Japan) — 1103

KING SUPER MARKETS, INC. (England, U.K.) — 451

KINGSPAN CORPORATION (Ireland) — 871

KINGSWAY AMERICA INC. (Canada) — 181

KINOKUNIYA BOOK STORES OF AMERICA CO., LTD (Japan) — 1026

KINROSS GOLD (Canada) — 182

KINTETSU BLUE GRASS, INC. (Japan) — 1027

KINTETSU WORLD EXPRESS, INC. (Japan) — 1027

KIPP & ZONEN INC. (Netherlands) — 1237

KIRIN BREWERY OF AMERICA (Japan) — 1028

KIRSHENBAUM BOND & PARTNERS, LLC (Canada) — 197

KITZ CORPORATION OF AMERICA (Japan) — 1028

KLEERDEX CO. (Japan) — 1116

KLINGSPOR ABRASIVES INC. (Germany) — 743

M

193

M&C SAATCHI (England, U.K.)	446
M/A-COM, INC. (Bermuda)	66
MAAX AKER (Canada)	190
MAAX PEARL (Canada)	190
MABUCHI MOTOR AMERICAN CORPORATION (Japan)	1037
MACFARLANE WESTERN FOAM, INC. (Scotland, U.K.)	1310
MACK TRUCKS INC. (Sweden)	1425
MACKENZIE MARKETING (Canada)	197
MACLAREN PERFORMANCE TECHNOLOGIES INC. (Canada)	186
MACQUARIE BANK (Australia)	18
MACQUARIE ELECTRONICS (Australia)	18
MACQUARIE INFRASTRUCTURE CO. TRUST (Australia)	18
MACRONIX AMERICA, INC. (Taiwan (ROC))	1502
MACRONIX COMPUTER CENTER AMERICA, INC. (Taiwan (ROC))	1502
MAD CATZ INTERACTIVE, INC. (Canada)	191
MADAME TUSSAUDS (England, U.K.)	544
MADGE LIMITED (England, U.K.)	448
MAERSK INC. (Denmark)	308
MAERSK SEALAND INC. (Denmark)	309
MAGAZINE SPECS (England, U.K.)	389
MAGEE RIETER AUTOMOTIVE (Switzerland)	1468
MAGELLAN AEROSPACE CORP.	191
MAGGOTTEAUX INC. (Belgium)	48
MAGIC SOFTWARE ENTERPRISES, INC. (Israel)	893
MAGNA DONNELLY (Canada)	193
MAGNA INTERNATIONAL OF AMERICA (Canada)	193
MAGNA STEYR (Canada)	193
MAGNETIC CORP. (Sweden)	1383
MAGNIFOAM TECHNOLOGY INTERNATIONAL INC. (Canada)	204
MAGOTTEAUX - PULASKI INC. (Belgium)	48
MAGSOFT CORPORATION (France)	594

MAINFRAME ENTERTAINMENT INC. (Canada)	
MAINFRAME USA (Canada)	193
MAJESCO SOFTWARE INC. (India)	844
MAKER'S MARK DISTILLERY, INC. (England, U.K.)	327
MAKHTESHIM-AGAN NORTH AMERICA (Israel)	893
MAKINO (Japan)	1037
MAKINO SEIKI (Japan)	1037
MAKITA USA INC. (Japan)	1037
MALAYAN BANKING BERHAD (MAYBANK) (Malaysia)	1186
MALAYSIA AIRLINES (Malaysia)	1187
MALEV HUNGARIAN AIRLINES (Hungary)	828
MALLINCKRODT INC. (Bermuda)	66
MALVERN INSTRUMENTS INC. (England, U.K.)	521
MAN FINANCIAL INC. (England, U.K.)	448
MAN INVESTMENTS (England, U.K.)	448
MANCHU WOK USA (Hong Kong PRC)	810
MANDARIN ORIENTAL (Hong Kong PRC)	818
MANDARIN ORIENTAL KAHALA (Hong Kong PRC)	816
MANDARIN ORIENTAL MIAMI (Hong Kong PRC)	816
MANDARIN ORIENTAL NEW YORK (Hong Kong PRC)	816
MANDARIN ORIENTAL SAN FRANCISCO	816
MANDARIN ORIENTAL SAN FRANCISCO (Hong Kong PRC)	816
MANDARIN ORIENTAL WASHINGTON DC (Hong Kong PRC)	817
MANDO AMERICA CORPORATION (South Korea)	1352
MANGELS USA INC. (Brazil)	76
MANNHEIMER SWARTLING (Sweden)	1409
MANNING, SELVAGE & LEE (France)	641
MANPOWER SOFTWARE INC. (England, U.K.)	449
MANULI HYDRAULICS INC. (Italy)	934
MANULI OIL & MARINE USA INC. (Italy)	935
MANULI RUBBER INDUSTRIES (Italy)	935
MANULI RUBBER INDUSTRIES (Italy)	935
MANULIFE FINANCIAL (Canada)	194

MANULIFE FINANCIAL CORPORATION 194
(Canada)
MANULIFE USA INC. (Canada) 194
MANULIFE WOOD LOGAN (Canada) 194
MAPEI CORP USA (Italy) 935
MAPINFO (England, U.K.) 508
MAPLE LEAF BAKERY, INC. (Canada) 195
MAPLE LEAF FOODS USA (Canada) 195
MAPLEHURST BAKERIES INC. (Canada) 267
MAQUET INC. (Sweden) 1400
MARANGONI TREAD INC. (Italy) 935
MARATHON 570
ENGINEERS/ARCHITECTS/PLANNERS
LLC (Finland)
MARATHON SENSORS INC. (England, 413
U.K.)
MARBULK SHIPPING INC. (Canada) 96
MARCOLIN USA INC. (Italy) 936
MARCONI (England, U.K.) 449
MARCONI BROADBAND ROUTING & 449
SWITCHING DIV. (England, U.K.)
MARCONI NORTH AMERICA (England, 449
U.K.)
MARCONI TEST SYSTEMS (England, 450
U.K.)
MARCUS EVANS INC. (England, U.K.) 450
MAREL USA (Iceland) 832
MARGEOTES FERTITTA POWELL LLC 197
(Canada)
MARKETFORWARD (France) 642
MARKLIN, INC. (Germany) 753
MARSHALL & SWIFT BOECKH (Canada) 190
MARSHALL CAVENDISH CORPORATION 1323
(Singapore)
MARSHALL POTTERY INC. (Italy) 922
MARSILLI NORTH AMERICA (Italy) 932
MARTEK POWER ABBOTT, INC. (France) 631
MARTEK POWER, INC. (France) 631
MARTIN CURRIE INC. (Scotland, U.K.) 1311
MARTINAIR OF THE AMERICANS 1239
(Netherlands)
MARUBENI AMERICA (Japan) 1038
MARUBENI AMERICA CORPORATION 1038
(Japan)

MARUBENI AMERICAN CORPORATION 1038
(Japan)
MARUBENI CITIZEN-CINCOM, INC. 966
(Japan)
MARUBENI-ITOCHU STEEL AMERICA 1011
INC. (Japan)
MARUHA CAPITAL INVESTMENT (Japan) 1039
MARUICHI AMERICAN CORPORATION 1039
(Japan)
MARUKAI CORPORATION (Japan) 1040
MARUZEN AMERICA INC. (Japan) 1040
MARUZEN INTERNATIONAL CO., LTD. 1041
(Japan)
MARZOLI INTERNATIONAL (Italy) 919
MASCON GLOBAL LIMITED (India) 843
MASHREQ BANK PSC. (United Arab 1516
Emirates)
MASIUS (France) 642
MASON HAYES & CURRAN (Ireland) 871
MASONITE INTERNATIONAL (Canada) 195
MASSACHUSETTS FINANCIAL 245
SERVICES COMPANY (Canada)
MASTER-HALCO INC. (Japan) 1011
MASTERTASTE (Ireland) 870
MATERIAL HANDLING SERVICES 1245
(Netherlands)
MATHESON ORMSBY PRENTICE (Ireland) 871
MATHESON TRI-GAS, INC. (Japan) 1141
MATRIKON INC. (Canada) 195
MATRIKON INTERNATIONAL, INC. 195
(Canada)
MATSUSHITA AVIONICS SYSTEMS 1041
CORPORATION (Japan)
MATSUSHITA ELECTRONIC 1041
COMPONENTS CO., LTD. (Japan)
MATSUSHITA KOTOBUKI ELECTRONICS 1041
INDUSTRIES OF AMERICA INC. (Japan)

MAUELL CORPORATION (Germany) 731
MAX ERP (Netherlands) 1224
MAXCESS TECHNOLOGIES, INC. (Japan) 1000
MAXELL CORPORATION OF AMERICA 998
(Japan)
MAXWARE INTERNATIONAL (Norway) 1281

METAL BULLETIN, INC. (England, U.K.)	454
METAL COATINGS INTERNATIONAL INC. (Japan)	1093
METAL PROCESSING SYSTEMS, INC. (Japan)	1125
METAL STORM INC. (Australia)	19
METALINK LTD. (Israel)	894
METCRAFT INC. (POWER SOAK SYSTEMS) (Canada)	143
METGLAS, INC. (Japan)	1000
METHANEX CORPORATION (Canada)	200
METL-SPAN (Mexico)	1196
METRO NEW YORK INC. (England, U.K.)	454
METRO-GOLDWYN-MAYER (Japan)	1128
METRO-GOLDWYN-MAYER INC. (Switzerland)	1442
METROPOLITAN BANK & TRUST COMPANY (Philippines)	1293
METSO AUTOMATION INC. (Finland)	571
METSO AUTOMATION MAX CONTROLS INC. (Finland)	571
METSO MINERALS (Finland)	572
METSO MINERALS INDUSTRIES INC. (Finland)	571
METSO MINERALS INDUSTRIES, INC. (Finland)	572
METSO PAPER USA, INC. (Finland)	571
METSO USA (Finland)	571
METSO USA INC. (Finland)	572
METTLER-TOLEDO AUTOCHEM INC. (Switzerland)	1462
METTLER-TOLEDO INC. (Switzerland)	1462
METTLER-TOLEDO INGOLD, INC. (Switzerland)	1462
METTON AMERICA, INC. (Japan)	1125
MEXICANA AIRLINES (Mexico)	1199
MEYER CORPORATION COMPANY (Hong Kong PRC)	819
MGE UPS SYSTEMS INC. (France)	632
MGM PICTURES (Japan)	1128
MGP LLC (Germany)	778
MIBA BEARINGS US LLC (Austria)	31
MIBA HYDRAMECHANICA CORP. (Austria)	31

MICE DALLAS (England, U.K.)	455
MICE DELTA (England, U.K.)	455
MICE DISPLAYWORKS (England, U.K.)	455
MICE ICOM (England, U.K.)	455
MICE INTERIORS (England, U.K.)	456
MICE NORTH AMERICA (England, U.K.)	456
MICE NORTHAMERICA (England, U.K.)	456
MICHAEL PAGE INTERNATIONAL INC. (England, U.K.)	457
MICHELIN NORTH AMERICA, INC. (France)	633
MICHIGAN AUTOMOTIVE COMPRESSOR, INC. (Japan)	1163
MICHIGAN METAL COATINGS CO. (Japan)	1093
MICRO FOCUS INC. (England, U.K.)	457
MICROGEN USA INC. (England, U.K.)	458
MICRONAS SEMICONDUCTORS INC. (Switzerland)	1463
MICRONIC LASER SYSTEMS INC. (Sweden)	1409
MICROSCAN SYSTEMS, INC. (England, U.K.)	521
MICROTEK (Taiwan (ROC))	1502
MIDDLE ATLANTIC WAREHOUSE DISTRIBUTOR, INC. (Canada)	261
MIDDLE EAST AIRLINES (Lebanon)	1181
MIDDLETON AEROSPACE CORPORATION (Canada)	191
MID-FLORIDA BIOLOGICALS (Canada)	121
MIDLAND MATERIALS RESEARCH (France)	626
MIELE, INC. (Germany)	756
MIKIMOTO AMERICA CO. (Japan)	1044
MIKRON BOSTOMATIC CORP. (Switzerland)	1431
MIKUNI AMERICAN CORPORATION (Japan)	1045
MILLENNIUM HOTEL (England, U.K.)	458
MILLENNIUM HOTEL PREMIER (England, U.K.)	459
MILLENNIUM RESORT MCCORMICK RANCH (England, U.K.)	459
MILLENNIUM UN PLAZA HOTEL (England, U.K.)	459

MITSUI ZINC POWDER LLC (Japan)	1057
MITSUI-SOKO CO., LTD. (Japan)	1059
MITSUKOSHI USA, INC. (Japan)	1059
MITSUMI ELECTRONICS CORP. (Japan)	1060
MITSUMI ELECTRONICS CORPORATION (Japan)	1060
MITSUMI USA, INC. (Japan)	1060
MITTAL STEEL GEORGETOWN USA (Netherlands)	1239
MITTAL STEEL SPARROWS POINT USA (Netherlands)	1239
MITTAL STEEL USA BAR PRODUCTS (Netherlands)	1239
MITTAL STEEL USA INC. (Netherlands)	1240
MITTAL STEEL WEIRTON USA (Netherlands)	1240
MIURA BOILER USA, INC. (Japan)	1061
MIZUHO CAPITAL MARKETS CORP. (Japan)	1061
MIZUHO CORPORATE BANK (Japan)	1061
MIZUHO CORPORATE BANK (USA) (Japan)	1061
MIZUHO CORPORATE BANK OF CALIFORNIA (Japan)	1061
MIZUHO SECURITIES USA, INC. (Japan)	1062
MIZUHO TRUST & BANKING CO. (USA) (Japan)	1062
MIZUNO USA INC. (Japan)	1062
MKS INTEROPERABILITY INC. (Canada)	203
MKS SOFTWARE INC. (Canada)	203
MMA/ CARAT INC. (England, U.K.)	323
MMC ELECTRONICS AMERICA INC. (Japan)	1050
MOBILE ACCESS (Israel)	894
MOBILE CLIMATE CONTROL INDUSTRIES INC. (Canada)	203
MOBIUM CREATIVE GROUP (Canada)	198
MODEC INTERNATIONAL LLC (Japan)	1056
MOLOKAI PROPERTIES LTD., DIV. BIL (Singapore)	1315
MOMENTUM TECHNOLOGIES INC. (Netherlands)	1219
MONADNOCK FOREST PRODUCTS INC. (England, U.K.)	460
MONARCH CERAMIC TILE INC., DIV. AMERICAN MARAZZI (Italy)	935
MONARCH INDUSTRIES, INC. (Canada)	204
MONEYCORP INC. (England, U.K.)	433
MONIER LIFETILE (Australia)	13
MONITOR CONTROLS INC (England, U.K.)	413
MONO (Canada)	198
MONTUPET INC. (France)	633
MOORE STEPEHENS WURTH FRAZER AND TORBET LLP (England, U.K.)	461
MOORE STEPHENS APPLE INC. (England, U.K.)	461
MOORE STEPHENS APPLE, INC. (England, U.K.)	461
MOORE STEPHENS ATKINSON, LLC (England, U.K.)	461
MOORE STEPHENS BANSLEY AND KIENER LLP (England, U.K.)	461
MOORE STEPHENS BEENE GARTER, PLC (England, U.K.)	461
MOORE STEPHENS BENSON & MCLAUGHLIN (England, U.K.)	462
MOORE STEPHENS BONADIO LLP (England, U.K.)	462
MOORE STEPHENS BROWN SMITH WALLACE LLC (England, U.K.)	462
MOORE STEPHENS DOEREN MAYHEW, PC (England, U.K.)	462
MOORE STEPHENS DUDLEY (England, U.K.)	462
MOORE STEPHENS ELLIOTT DAVIS LLC (England, U.K.)	462
MOORE STEPHENS FROST PLC (England, U.K.)	462
MOORE STEPHENS HAYS, INC. (England, U.K.)	462
MOORE STEPHENS LOVELACE, P.A. (England, U.K.)	462
MOORE STEPHENS LOVELACE, PA (England, U.K.)	462
MOORE STEPHENS MOHLER NIXON & WILLIAMS (England, U.K.)	463
MOORE STEPHENS NORTH AMERICA INC. (England, U.K.)	463
MOORE STEPHENS REILLY, PC (England, U.K.)	463

MOORE STEPHENS TILLER, LLC (England, U.K.)	463
MOORE STEPHENS TRAVIS WOLFF, LLP (England, U.K.)	463
MOORE STEPHENS WATKINS MEEGAN LLC (England, U.K.)	463
MOORE STEPHENS WATKINS MEEGAN, LLC (England, U.K.)	463
MOORE STEPHENS WURTH FRAZER & TORBET LLP (England, U.K.)	464
MORAVIA IT, INC. (Czech Republic)	295
MORGAN ADVANCED CERAMICS INC., GBC PRODUCTS (England, U.K.)	464
MORGAN ADVANCED CERAMICS INC., WESGO CERAMICS (England, U.K.)	464
MORGAN ADVANCED CERAMICS, ALBEROX PRODUCTS (England, U.K.)	464
MORGAN ADVANCED CERAMICS, CVD PRODUCTS (England, U.K.)	464
MORGAN ADVANCED CERAMICS, DIAMONEX PRODUCTS (England, U.K.)	464
MORGAN ADVANCED CERAMICS, INC., WESGO/DURAMIC PRODUCTS (England, U.K.)	464
MORGANITE CRUCIBLE INC. (England, U.K.)	465
MORGANITE, INC. (England, U.K.)	465
MORGARDSHAMMAR INC. (Sweden)	1409
MORI SEIKI USA (Japan)	1063
MORI SEIKI USA, INC. (Japan)	1063
MOROCH LEO BURNETT USA (France)	642
MORRISON HOMES, INC. (England, U.K.)	555
MORSE CONSTRUCTION GROUP, INC. (Netherlands)	1215
MORTON NIPPON COATINGS (Japan)	1078
MOSAIC SOFTWARE INC. (England, U.K.)	465
MOSAID SYSTEMS INC. (Canada)	204
MOSEBACH MANUFACTURING COMPANY (England, U.K.)	413
MOSEL VITELIC CORPORATION (Taiwan (ROC))	1503
MOSS MARITIME INC. (Italy)	943
MOTIVA ENTERPRISES LLC (Netherlands)	1251
MOTOWN RECORD COMPANY (France)	669
MOTURIS INC. (Switzerland)	1463
MOUNT10 SOFTWARE, INC. (Switzerland)	1464
MOUNTAIN CREEK (Canada)	174
MOUNTAIN PROVINCE DIAMONDS INC. (Canada)	204
MOVIE LINK (France)	669
MPHASIS (India)	844
MPHASIS CORPORATION (India)	845
MRC BEARINGS (Sweden)	1383
M-REAL USA CORPORATION (Finland)	572
MRT-WEST (Switzerland)	1486
MSI PRODUCTS INC. (England, U.K.)	398
MSM US INC. (Japan)	1052
MSNBC CABLE (France)	669
MSNBC INTERACTIVE NEWS (France)	669
M-SYSTEMS INC. (Israel)	895
M-SYSTEMS INC. (Israel)	895
MTL INC. (England, U.K.)	470
MTS INTERNATIONAL (Israel)	894
MTS-DELFT (Netherlands)	1219
MULTI-FINANCIAL SECURITIES CORP. (Netherlands)	1236
MULTIPHASE SOLUTIONS INC. (Scotland, U.K.)	1310
MUNCIE POWER PRODUCTS, INC. (Italy)	931
MUNICH AMERICAN REASSURANCE COMPANY (Germany)	758
MUNICIPAL SOLUTIONS GROUP, INC. (Canada)	204
MUNKSJO PAPER INC. (Sweden)	1410
MURATA ELECTRONICS NORTH AMERICA, INC. (Japan)	1063
MURATA MACHINERY USA, INC. (Japan)	1063
MURATEC AMERICA, INC. (Japan)	1063
MUROX, DIV. CANAM STEEL CORP. (Canada)	120
MUSIC SALES LIMITED (England, U.K.)	471
MUSTANG ENGINEERING (Scotland, U.K.)	1310
MUSTANG ENGINEERING HOLDINGS INC. (Scotland, U.K.)	1310
MWG-BIOTECH, INC. (Germany)	758
MY TRAVEL NORTH AMERICA INC. (England, U.K.)	471
MYCAL CORP. (Japan)	952

MYLLYKOSKI NORTH AMERICA INC. (Finland) — 573

MYOB US, INC. (Australia) — 19

MYRIO CORP. (Germany) — 781

MYSTICOM INC. (Israel) — 895

N

N. I. TEIJIN SHOJI USA, INC. (Japan) — 1148

N. M. ROTHSCHILD & SONS INC. (England, U.K.) — 501

NABTESCO (Japan) — 1064

NACHI AMERICA INC. (Japan) — 1064

NACHI ROBOTIC SYSTEMS INC. (Japan) — 1064

NACIONAL FINANACIERA SNC (Mexico) — 1200

NAFINSA SECURITIES, INC. (Mexico) — 1200

NAGASE AMERICA CORPORATION (Japan) — 1065

NAGASE CALIFORNIA CORPORATION (Japan) — 1065

NAGASE PLASTICS AMERICA CORP. (Japan) — 1065

NAGRA USA INC. (Switzerland) — 1456

NAGRASTAR LLC (Switzerland) — 1456

NAGRAVISION (Switzerland) — 1456

NAGY & TROCSANYI LLP (Hungary) — 829

NAMASCO CORPORATION (Germany) — 743

NAMCO AMERICA HOLDING CORP. (Japan) — 1065

NAMCO HOMETEK INC. (Japan) — 1066

NANO-OR TECHNOLOGIES LTD. (Israel) — 895

NANYA TECHNOLOGY CORPORATION (Taiwan (ROC)) — 1504

NARRAGANSETT ELECTRIC CO. (England, U.K.) — 472

NATBANK (Canada) — 205

NATIONAL AUSTRALIA BANK LTD. (Australia) — 20

NATIONAL BANK OF CANADA (Canada) — 205

NATIONAL BANK OF PAKISTAN (Pakistan) — 1289

NATIONAL CEMENT COMPANY OF ALABAMA (France) — 667

NATIONAL CEMENT COMPANY OF CALIFORNIA (France) — 667

NATIONAL EXPRESS CORP. (England, U.K.) — 471

NATIONAL GRID USA (England, U.K.) — 472

NATIONAL HEARING CENTERS (Italy) — 911

NATIONAL PROCESSING SERVICES — 215

NATIONAL STARCH & CHEMICAL COMPANY (England, U.K.) — 423

NATRA US, INC. (Spain) — 1373

NATURE AMERICA INC (England, U.K.) — 447

NATUZZI AMERICAS (Italy) — 936

NAUTA DUTILH (Netherlands) — 1240

NAVITAS ENERGY INC. (Spain) — 1370

NAY YA PLASTICS CORPORATION USA (Taiwan (ROC)) — 1503

NAY YA PLASTICS CORPORATION, AMERICA (Taiwan (ROC)) — 1504

NAZCA SAATCHI & SAATCHI (France) — 642

NBB CONTROLS, INC. (Germany) — 758

NBC TELEVISION NETWORK (France) — 670

NBC UNIVERSAL (France) — 670

NBC UNIVERSAL CABLE (France) — 670

NBC UNIVERSAL TELEVISION STUDIO (France) — 670

NBS CARD TECHNOLOGY CORPORATION (Canada) — 205

NBS TECHNOLOGIES (Canada) — 205

NCI CONSULTING (France) — 642

NCIPHER INC. (England, U.K.) — 472

NDC INFRARED ENGINEERING LTD. (England, U.K.) — 522

NDS AMERICAS INC. (England, U.K.) — 473

NEATON AUTO PRODUCTS MFG. — 1072

NEC AMERICA, INC. (Japan) — 1066

NEC DISPLAY SOLUTIONS OF AMERICA (Japan) — 1066

NEC ELECTRONICS CORP. (Japan) — 1066

NEC FIBEROPTECH (Japan) — 1066

NEC FINANCIAL SERVICES, INC. (Japan) — 1066

NEC LABORATORIES AMERICA (Japan) — 1066

NEC SOLUTIONS, INC. (Japan) — 1067

NEC SOLUTIONS, INC. (Japan) — 1067

NEC USA, INC. (Japan) — 1067

NECHO SYSTEMS CORPORATION (Canada) — 205

NEDERMAN INC. (Sweden) 1410
NEDLLOYD LINES (Netherlands) 1252
NEFAB, INC. (Sweden) 1410
NEGEVTECH INC. (Israel) 895
NELSON PROFESSIONAL SALES (France) 642
NEMETSCHEK NORTH AMERICA INC. (Germany) 758
NEOMAX AMERICA, INC. (Japan) 1000
NEOPOST INC. (France) 634
NEOPOST USA INC. (France) 634
NERA AMERICA INC. (Norway) 1282
NERA INC. (Norway) 1282
NESS GLOBAL SERVICES, INC. (Israel) 896
NESS TECHNOLOGIES INC. (Israel) 896
NESS TECHNOLOGIES, INC. (Israel) 896
NESTLE PURINA PETCARE COMPANY (Switzerland) 1464

NESTLE USA INC. (Switzerland) 1464
NESTLE WATERS INC. (Switzerland) 1465
NESTLE WATERS NORTH AMERICA (France) 634
NETAFIM IRRIGATION USA INC. (Israel) 896
NETCALL USA, INC. (England, U.K.) 473
NETG, INC. (Canada) 252
NETGALACTIC INC. (India) 845
NETVALUE USA INC. (France) 635
NETZSCH INCORPORATED (Germany) 712
NETZSCH INSTRUMENTS (Germany) 712
NEUCOLL INC. (Canada) 100
NEUMAN & ESSER USA (Germany) 759
NEW ENERGY ASSOCIATES, LLC (Germany) 781
NEW ENGLAND POWER COMPANY (England, U.K.) 472
NEW HAMPSHIRE BALL BEARINGS INC. (Japan) 1046
NEW HERBOLD INC. (Germany) 759
NEW MATHER METALS, INC. (Japan) 1069
NEW SKIES SATELLITES, INC. (Netherlands) 1240
NEW WAVE LOGISTICS (Japan) 1083
NEWARK INONE (England, U.K.) 485
NEWLONG LATIN AMERICA (Japan) 1068

NEWMARK INFRASTRUCTURE SOLUTIONS (Germany) 762
NEWMARK INTERNATIONAL INC. (Germany) 763
NEWPORT NEWS, INC. (Germany) 760
NEWPORT PRECISION, INC. (Japan) 1000
NEWTON VINEYARD LLC (France) 605
NEXANS ENERGY USA INC. (France) 635
NEXANS INC. (BERK-TEK) (France) 635
NEXANS MAGNET WIRE USA INC. (France) 635
NEXANS USA INC. (France) 635
NEXEN PETROLEUM USA INC. (Canada) 206
NEXFLASH TECHNOLOGIES, INC. (Taiwan (ROC)) 1509
NEXTEXIS BANQUES POPULAIRES (France) 633
NFJ INVESTMENT GROUP (Germany) 678
NGK INSULATORS, LTD (Japan) 1068
NGK METALS CORP. (Japan) 1068
NGK SPARK PLUGS USA, INC. (Japan) 1068
NHK INTERNATIONAL CORPORATION (Japan) 1069
NHK-ASSOCIATED SPRING SUSPENSION COMPONENTS INC. 1069
NIAGARA MOHAWK POWER CORPORATION (England, U.K.) 472
NIBROL INC. (Sweden) 1425
NICE SYSTEMS, INC. (Israel) 896
NICHIA AMERICA CORPORATION (Japan) 1069

NICHIREI USA INC. (Japan) 1070
NICOLAS CORREA USA INC. (Spain) 1373
NIDEC AMERICA CORP. (Japan) 1070
NIDEC AMERICA CORPORATION (Japan) 1071
NIEHOFF ENDEX, INC. (Germany) 753
NIELSEN / NET RATINGS (Netherlands) 1266
NIELSEN EDI (Netherlands) 1266
NIELSEN MEDIA RESEARCH (Netherlands) 1266
NIELSONS SKANSKA, INC. (Sweden) 1420
NIHILENT TECHNOLOGIES, INC. (India) 845
NIHON KEIZAI SHIMBUN AMERICA, INC. (Japan) 1072

American Affiliates

OPTIMEDIA (England, U.K.) 560

OPTIONS TAI PING CARPETS INC. (Hong 823
Kong PRC)

OPTISCAN IMAGING LTD. (Australia) 20

OPTO INTERNATIONAL INC. (England, 475
U.K.)

ORACLE CORP. (England, U.K.) 508

ORANGE US (France) 612

ORANGINA USA COMPANY INC. 361
(England, U.K.)

ORBITAL CORPORATION LTD. (Australia) 20

ORBOTECH INC. (Israel) 898

ORCKIT COMMUNICATIONS (Israel) 899

OREGON SCIENTIFIC, INC., DIV. IDT 816
(Hong Kong PRC)

OREN SEMICONDUCTOR INC. (Israel) 886

ORGANON INTERNATIONAL INC. 1209
(Netherlands)

ORICA USA INC. (Australia) 21

ORIENTAL MOTOR USA CORPORATION 1101
(Japan)

ORIENT-EXPRESS HOTELS LTD. 63
(Bermuda)

ORIX EQUIPMENT FINANCE (Japan) 1101

ORIX REAL ESTATE (Japan) 1101

ORIX USA CORP. (Japan) 1101

ORIX USA CORPORATION (Japan) 1101

ORLANDO SANFORD INTERNATIONAL, 538
INC. (England, U.K.)

ORMAT TECHNOLOGIES, INC. (Israel) 899

ORREFORS KOSTA BODA (Sweden) 1412

ORS NASCO (Ireland) 873

ORTHOFIX INTERNATIONAL (Netherlands 1270
Antilles)

ORTHOGON SYSTEMS LLC (England, 475
U.K.)

ORTOFON INC. (Denmark) 310

ORTRONICS INC. (France) 628

OSAKA GAS COMPANY, LTD. (Japan) 1102

OSLER (Canada) 216

OSMETECH (England, U.K.) 476

OSMETECH INC. (England, U.K.) 476

OSRAM SYLVANIA (Germany) 781

OSRAM SYLVANIA INC. (Germany) 759

OSSBERGER TURBINES, INC. (Germany) 759

OSSUR NORTH AMERICA (Iceland) 832

OTAY MESA METAL CORP. (Japan) 1156

OTI AMERICA, INC. (Israel) 897

OTIM USA INC. (Italy) 936

OTSUKA AMERICA, INC. (Japan) 1102

OTSUKA PHARMACEUTICAL FACTORY, 1102
INC. (Japan)

OUTBLAZE LTD. (Hong Kong PRC) 820

OUTOKUMPU ADVANCED 573
SUPERCONDUCTORS INC. (Finland)

OUTOKUMPU AMERICAN BRASS 574
(Finland)

OUTOKUMPU COPPER FRANKLIN INC. 574
(Finland)

OUTOKUMPU COPPER NIPPERT INC. 574
(Finland)

OUTOKUMPU COPPER USA, INC. 574
(Finland)

OUTOKUMPU COPPER VALLEYCAST 574
(Finland)

OUTOKUMPU HEATCRAFT USA INC. 574
(Finland)

OUTOKUMPU STAINLESS BAR INC. 1389
(Sweden)

OUTOKUMPU STAINLESS PIPE INC. 1389
(Sweden)

OUTOKUMPU STAINLESS PLATE INC. 574
(Finland)

OUTOKUMPU TECHNOLOGY INC. 574
(Finland)

OVAKO STEEL, INC. (Sweden) 1383

OVERHEAD DOOR CORPORATION 1111
(Japan)

OVERSEA-CHINESE BANKING CORP 1320
LTD (OCBC) (Singapore)

OVERSEA-CHINESE BANKING CORP 1320
LTD. (Singapore)

OVERSEAS UNION BANK, LTD. 1324
(Singapore)

OVERSEAS WIBORG CHARTERING CO. 369
(England, U.K.)

OWT INDUSTRIES, INC. (Hong Kong PRC) 824

OXFORD BIOMEDICA INC. (England, 476
U.K.)

American Affiliates

American Affiliates

RANDSTAD NORTH AMERICA (Netherlands)	1248
RAPAK INC. (England, U.K.)	518
RAPID GRANULATOR, INC. (Sweden)	1414
RATTI USA INC. (Italy)	940
RAW COMMUNICATIONS INC. (England, U.K.)	492
RAYCO-WYLIE SYSTEMS (Canada)	227
RAYMARINE USA INC. (England, U.K.)	492
RAYMOND VINEYARD AND CELLAR, INC. (Japan)	1028
RBC DAIN RAUSCHER (Canada)	230
RBC DOMINION SECURITIES, INC. (Canada)	228
RBC FINANCIAL GROUP (Canada)	230
RBC INSURANCE (Canada)	230
RBC MORTGAGE COMPANY (Canada)	230
RBS LYNK INC. (Scotland, U.K.)	1311
RCA LABEL GROUP-NASHVILLE (Germany)	687
RCA MUSIC GROUP (Germany)	687
RCS RIZZOLI CORPORATION (Italy)	941
READSOFT USA INC. (Sweden)	1414
RECKITT BENCKISER INC. (England, U.K.)	493
RECOCHEM (USA) (Canada)	228
RECORDATI CORPORATION (Italy)	941
RED BULL NORTH AMERICA, INC. (Austria)	31
RED DISTRIBUTION (Germany)	687
RED DISTRIBUTION COMPANY, DIV. EDEL MUSIC (Germany)	710
RED DOT SOLUTIONS CORP. (Canada)	169
RED LION CONTROLS INC. (England, U.K.)	522
RED MANDARIN (England, U.K.)	425
RED RIVER COMMODITIES INC. (Netherlands)	1220
RED STORM ENTERTAINMENT (France)	613
REDCATS USA (France)	637
REDDY US THERAPEUTICS INC. (India)	835
REDDY US THERAPEUTICS, INC. (India)	848
REED BUSINESS INFORMATION US (England, U.K.)	494
REED ELSEVIER GROUP (England, U.K.)	494
REED ELSEVIER INC. (England, U.K.)	494
REED ELSEVIER PUBLISHING, INC. (England, U.K.)	494
REED ELSEVIER US (England, U.K.)	494
REEVES CONSTRUCTION COMPANY (France)	590
REFLEC USA CORP. (England, U.K.)	495
REFORMED SPIRITS COMPANY (England, U.K.)	495
REGUS BUSINESS CENTERS (England, U.K.)	495
REICHHOLD, INC. (Japan)	973
REIFENHAUSER, INC. (Germany)	767
RELIANCE MEDICAL INC. (Germany)	757
REMAK OF NORTH AMERICA (Germany)	744
REMINGTON PARK (Canada)	192
REMOTE DYNAMICS INC. (England, U.K.)	460
REMY COINTREAU USA, INC. (France)	645
RENESAS TECHNOLOGY AMERICA, INC. (Japan)	1106
RENESAS TECHNOLOGY CORP. (Japan)	997
RENFERT USA INC. (Germany)	767
RENISHAW INC. (England, U.K.)	496
RENK CORPORATION (Germany)	767
RENK LABECO CORPORATION (Germany)	767
RENOLD AJAX (England, U.K.)	496
RENOLD JEFFREY (England, U.K.)	496
RENTOKIL PEST CONTROL (England, U.K.)	497
RENTOKIL, INC. (England, U.K.)	497
RESEARCH IN MOTION LIMITED (Canada)	228
RESERVE BANK OF AUSTRALIA, NY REPRESENTATIVE OFFICE (Australia)	22
RESIDENCE INN (Mexico)	1198
RESOURCE SOLUTIONS INC. (England, U.K.)	497
RESPONSE RENTALS, DIV. ASHTEAD TECHNOLOGY (England, U.K.)	334
RESTAURANT SUNTORY (Japan)	1139
RESULT VENTURE KNOWLEDGE INTERNATIONAL (Sweden)	1414

RETAIL BRAND GROUP, LLC (France) 655
RETAIL DECISIONS (England, U.K.) 497
RETALIX USA INC. (Israel) 900
REUTERS AMERICA, INC. (England, U.K.) 498
REUTERS HEALTH INFORMATION 498
(England, U.K.)
REVCAR FASTENERS INC. (Germany) 803
REXAM BEVERAGE CAN AMERICAS INC. 499
 (England, U.K.)
REXAM BEVERAGE CANS AMERICA 96
(Canada)
REXAM INC (England, U.K.) 499
REXEL INC. (France) 646
REXEL, INC. (Canada) 229
REYNOLDS AMERICAN INC. (England, 355
U.K.)
RHEEM MANUFACTURING (Japan) 1104
RHEIN CHEMIE USA INC. (Germany) 767
RHODIA INC. (France) 646
RICARDO GROUP, INC. (England, U.K.) 500
RICCHETTI CERAMIC, INC. (Italy) 927
RICHARD WOLF MEDICAL INSTRUMENT 801
CORPORATION (Germany)
RICHEMONT NORTH AMERICA 1440
(Switzerland)
RICHMOND AIRCRAFT PRODUCTS 545
(England, U.K.)
RICHMOND EVENTS INC. (England, U.K.) 500
RICHMOND TEXTILES (Netherlands) 1233
RICOH BUSINESS SYSTEMS, INC. 1107

RICOH CORPORATION (Japan) 1107
RICOLA USA, INC. (Switzerland) 1468
RIDGE VINEYARDS INC. (Japan) 1103
RIETER AUTOMOTIVE N.A. (Switzerland) 1468
RIETER CORPORATION (Switzerland) 1468
RIETER GREENSBORO, INC. (Switzerland) 1468
RIKEN OF AMERICA INC. (Japan) 1107
RINKER MATERIALS CORPORATION 15
(Australia)
RIO DOCE AMERICA INC. (Brazil) 74
RIPLEY'S ENTERTAINMENT, INC. 179
(Canada)
RIRI USA INC. (Switzerland) 1469

RISK ENTERPRISE MANAGEMENT LTD. 1492
(Switzerland)
RISK MANAGEMENT SOLUTIONS (RMSI) 377
(England, U.K.)
RIT TECHNOLOGIES, INC. (Israel) 901
RITCHIE BROS. AUCTIONEERS (Canada) 229
RITRAMA, INC. (Italy) 941
RITTAL CORPORATION (Germany) 768
RIVERDEEP INC. (Ireland) 872
RIVERSIDE MFG. CO., SUB. GFT USA 928
CORP. (Italy)
RIVERWOOD INTERNATIONAL 929
PACKAGING, INC. (Italy)
RIYAD BANK (Saudi Arabia) 1303
ROAD MACHINERY LLC (Japan) 1055
ROADRUNNER RECORDS (France) 670
ROBBINS GIOIA (England, U.K.) 536
ROBCO INC. (Japan) 1165
ROBERT BOSCH CORPORATION 691
(Germany)
ROBERT BOSCH TOOL CORPORATION 691
(Germany)
ROBERT WALTERS USA INC. (England, 550
U.K.)
ROCHE CAROLINA (Switzerland) 1469
ROCHE COLORADO CORP. (Switzerland) 1469
ROCHE DIAGNOSTICS CORP. 1469
(Switzerland)
ROCHE MOLECULAR SYSTEMS 1470
(Switzerland)
ROCHE MOLECULAR SYSTEMS, INC. 1470
(Switzerland)
ROCHE PALO ALTO LLC (Switzerland) 1470
ROCKEFELLER GROUP INC. (Japan) 1048
ROCKEY INDUSTRIAL SALES (Austria) 28
RODAIR INTERNATIONAL INC. (Canada) 109
ROEDIGER PITTSBURGH INC. (Germany) 761
ROGER CLEVELAND GOLF COMPANY, 652
INC. (France)
ROHDE & SCHWARZ (Germany) 768
ROHM AMERICA INC. (Germany) 769
ROHM ELECTRONICS USA (Japan) 1108
ROHMAX USA (Germany) 701

ROLAND BERGER STRATEGY CONSULTANTS LLC (Germany)	769	
ROLAND CORPORATION USA (Japan)	1108	
ROLEX WATCH, INC. (Switzerland)	1463	
ROLL CALL INC. (England, U.K.)	387	
ROLLER BEARING INDUSTRIES	1383	
ROLLS ROYCE COMMERCIAL MARINE INC. (England, U.K.)	500	
ROLLS ROYCE MARINE INC. (England, U.K.)	501	
ROLLS ROYCE NAVAL MARINE, INC. (England, U.K.)	501	
ROLLS-ROYCE CORP. (England, U.K.)	501	
ROLLS-ROYCE MOTOR CARS, INC. (Germany)	797	
ROLLS-ROYCE MOTOR CARS, INC. - SOUTHERN REGION (Germany)	797	
ROLLS-ROYCE NAVAL MARINE, INC. (England, U.K.)	501	
ROLLS-ROYCE, INC. (England, U.K.)	501	
ROMER CIMCORE INC. (England, U.K.)	380	
RONDELE ACQUISITION LLC (France)	614	
ROSENBAUER AMERICA (Austria)	31	
ROSENLEW INC. (Finland)	576	
ROSENTHAL USA LTD. (Germany)	769	
ROSS SYSTEMS INC. (Hong Kong PRC)	811	
ROSS SYSTEMS, INC. (Hong Kong PRC)	811	
ROSS-ELLIS U.S.A. (Canada)	258	
ROSS-ELLIS U.S.A. INC. (Canada)	258	
ROSSIGNOL (France)	652	
ROTHSCHILD NORTH AMERICA, INC. (England, U.K.)	502	
ROTORK CONTROLS INC. (England,	502	
ROUGE INDUSTRIES INC. (Russia)	1301	
ROUND MOUNTAIN GOLD (Canada)	108	
ROUTIN AMERICA, INC., c/o PRAMEX (France)	647	
ROVEMA PACKAGING MACHINES, INC. (Germany)	769	
ROWENTA / MOULINEX / KRUPS (France)	615	
ROXANE LABORATORIES, INC. (Germany)	690	
ROXAR, INC. (Norway)	1285	

ROYAL & SUN ALLIANCE USA INC. (England, U.K.)	503	
ROYAL AIR MAROC (Morocco)	1204	
ROYAL APPLIANCE MFG. (Hong Kong PRC)	824	
ROYAL CANIN USA INC. (France)	647	
ROYAL CARIBBEAN CRUISES LTD. (Norway)	1276	
ROYAL CHINA & PORCELAIN COMPANIES (England, U.K.)	503	
ROYAL CONSUMER INFORMATION PRODUCTS (Italy)	936	
ROYAL DOULTON USA INC. (England, U.K.)	503	
ROYAL JORDANIAN AIRLINES (Jordan)	1176	
ROYAL JORDANIAN AIRLINES(CARGO) (Jordan)	1176	
ROYAL JORDANIAN AIRLINES(OFFICE) (Jordan)	1177	
ROYAL JORDANIAN AIRLINES(RESERVATIONS) (Jordan)	1177	
ROYAL JORDANIAN AIRLINES(SALES) (Jordan)	1177	
ROYAL MOULDINGS INC. (Canada)	230	
ROYAL TEN CATE (USA) INC. (Netherlands)	1254	
ROYALBLUE GROUP, INC. (England, U.K.)	503	
RPC BRAMLAGE-WIKO USA, INC. (England, U.K.)	504	
RREEF FUNDS LLC (Germany)	702	
RSTAR CORPORATION (Israel)	889	
RTM PRODUCTIONS (France)	625	
RTS LIFE SCIENCE INTERNATIONAL (England, U.K.)	500	
RUETGERS ORGANICS CORPORATION (Germany)	770	
RUNTAL NORTH AMERICA, INC.	1490	
RUNTAL NORTH AMERICA, INC. (Switzerland)	1490	
RUSKIN (England, U.K.)	541	
RUSKIN (England, U.K.)	541	
RUSSEL METALS WILLIAMS BAHCALL (Canada)	231	
RUSSELL METALS INC. (Canada)	231	
RUSSELL T. GILMAN INC. (Sweden)	1384	
RUTGERS ORGANICS CORP. (Germany)	770	

SAUDI REFINING, INC. (Saudi Arabia)   1305
SAUER-DANFOSS INC. (Denmark)   301
SAURER HOLDING INC. (Switzerland)   1471
SAVIN CORPORATION (Japan)   1107
SAVINO DEL BENE USA INC. (Italy)   943
SCA NORTH AMERICA (Sweden)   1422
SCAN COIN INC (Sweden)   1417
SCAN HOUSE - SHIPCO TRANSPORT   311
(Denmark)
SCANDINAVIAN AIRLINES OF NORTH   1417
AMERICA, INC. (Sweden)
SCANDPOWER PETROLEUM   1285
TECHNOLOGY (Norway)
SCANDURA CONVEYOR BELTING USA   397
(England, U.K.)
SCANIA USA INC. (Sweden)   1417
SCAPA NORTH AMERICA (England, U.K.)   506
SCARBOROUGH RESEARCH (Netherlands)   1267
SCENE 7, INC., DIV. XCELERA INC.   275
(Cayman Islands)
SCHENCK ACCURATE (Germany)   772
SCHENCK MINING (Germany)   772
SCHENCK ROTEC CORPORATION   772
(Germany)
SCHENCK TREBEL (Germany)   772

SCHENCK WEIGHING SYSTEMS   772
(Germany)
SCHENKER INC. (Germany)   786
SCHENKER USA INC. (Germany)   772
SCHIEFFELIN & CO. (France)   605
SCHINDLER ELEVATOR CORP.   1471
(Switzerland)
SCHLEICHER & SCHUELL INC. (Germany)   773
SCHLUMBERGER (England, U.K.)   551
SCHLUMBERGER LIMITED (England,   551
U.K.)
SCHLUMBERGER-DOLL RESEARCH   551
(England, U.K.)
SCHLUMBERGERSEMA (England, U.K.)   552
SCHNEIDER NORTH AMERICA (France)   650
SCHNORR CORPORATION (Germany)   774
SCHOELLER-BLECKMANN PIPE & TUBE   1379
INC. (Spain)

SCHOKINAG CHOCOLATE NORTH   774
AMERICA, INC. (Germany)
SCHOTT GLASS TECHNOLOGIES INC.   774
(Germany)
SCHOTT LITHOTEC USA CORP.   774
(Germany)
SCHOTT NORTH AMERICA INC.   774
(Germany)
SCHRATTER FOOD (France)   588
SCHRODERS INVESTMENT   507
MANAGEMENT INC. (England, U.K.)
SCHUMAG-KIESERLING MACHINERY,   775
INC. (Germany)
SCHUNK GRAPHITE TECHNOLOGY, INC.   776
(Germany)
SCHUNK INEX CORP. (Germany)   776
SCHUNK OF NORTH AMERICA (Germany)   776
SCHUNK QUARTZ (Germany)   776
SCHWARZ PHARMA INC. (Germany)   777
SCHWARZKOPF & DEP INC. (Germany)   732
SCI FI CHANNEL (France)   670
SCIENTIFIC AMERICA (England, U.K.)   447
SCIENTIFIC AMERICAN (Germany)   721
SCIENTIFIC DESIGN COMPANY, INC.   752
(Germany)
SCIENTIFIC GENERICS INC. (England,   405
U.K.)
SCOPUS NETWORK TECHNOLOGIES   902
(Israel)
SCOR COMMERCIAL RISK RE-   651
INSURANCE (France)
SCOR LIFE RE-INSURANCE COMPANY   651
(France)
SCOR REINSURANCE (France)   651
SCOR REINSURANCE COMPANY (France)   651
SCOR U.S. CORPORATION (France)   651
SCOTIABANK (Canada)   107
SCOTSMAN GROUP, INC. (England, U.K.)   391
SCOTT WILSON (England, U.K.)   508
SCOTTISH & NEWCASTLE IMPORTERS   1312
(Scotland, U.K.)
SCREEN GEMS INC. (Japan)   1129
SDL USA INC. (England, U.K.)   508
                                                508

American Affiliates

TREE OF LIFE, INC. (Netherlands)	1268
TREEV LLC (Germany)	695
TREIBACHER SCHLEIFMITTEL INC. (Austria)	32
TRELLEBORG AMERICAN VARISEAL (Sweden)	1424
TRELLEBORG AUTOMOTIVE, INC. (Sweden)	1424
TRELLEBORG FILLITE INC. (Sweden)	1424
TRELLEBORG INDUSTRIAL AVS USA, INC. (Sweden)	1424
TRELLEBORG ORKOT COMPOSITES (Sweden)	1424
TRELLEBORG RUBORE, INC. (Sweden)	1424
TRELLEBORG VIKING, INC. (Sweden)	1425
TRELLEBORG WHEEL SYSTEMS AMERICAS, INC. (Sweden)	1425
TREND DISTRIBUTORS, INC. (Germany)	803
TREND MICRO INC. (Japan)	1164
TREVI - ICOS CORPORATION (Italy)	946
TRIBORO FIBERS INC. (Sweden)	1394
TRICO PRODUCTS (England, U.K.)	541
TRICOM USA (Dominican Republic)	315
TRIDONIC INC. (Austria)	35
TRIGEM AMERICA CORPORATION (South Korea)	1359
TRIKON TECHNOLOGIES, INC. (England, U.K.)	542
TRIM MASTERS, INC. (Japan)	1164
TRIMAC CORPORATION (Canada)	258
TRIN, INC. (Japan)	1151
TRINET GROUOP (Netherlands)	1265
TRINITY BIOTECH USA (Ireland)	872
TRINITY BIOTECH USA, INC. (Ireland)	873
TRINTECH INC. (Ireland)	873
TRIPLE P USA, INC. (Netherlands)	1260
TRIUMPH MOTORCYCLES AMERICA LTD. (England, U.K.)	543
TRI-UNION SEAFOODS, LLC (Thailand)	1512
TRIVERSITY CORPORATION (Canada)	259
TRMI, INC. (Japan)	1152
TRONSER, INC. (Germany)	791
TROUW NUTRITION USA INC. (Netherlands)	1241
TROY BUMPER (Canada)	237
TROY LAMINATING & COATING IVEX (France)	596
TRUCAST INC. (England, U.K.)	384
TRUMPF AMERICA INC. (Germany)	792
TRUSTFIN USA - UNIPLET CO. LTD. (Czech Republic)	296
TSL NORTH AMERICA (England, U.K.)	540
TSMC NORTH AMERICA (Taiwan (ROC))	1506
TSUBAKI CONVEYOR OF AMERICA INC. (Japan)	1165
T-SYSTEMS NORTH AMERICA	704
T-SYSTEMS NORTH AMERICA INC. (Germany)	792
TTI TEAM TELECOM INTERNATIONAL LTD. (Israel)	906
TTPCOM INC. (England, U.K.)	544
TTPCOM LTD. (England, U.K.)	544
TUBACEX INC. (Spain)	1379
TUCHENHAGEN (Germany)	719
TUCOWS INC. (Canada)	259
TUI AMERICA (Germany)	792
TULLETT LIBERTY INC. (England, U.K.)	373
TUNDRA SEMICONDUCTOR CORPORATION (Canada)	259
TURBOSONIC TECHNOLOGIES, INC. (Canada)	260
TURKISH AIRLINES (Turkey)	1515
TURNER CONSTRUCTION COMPANY (Germany)	734
TURNILS (Netherlands)	1233
TURNILS NORTH AMERICA, INC. (Sweden)	1425
TURQUOISE RIDGE MINE (Canada)	219
TUV RHEINLAND OF NORTH AMERICA, INC. (Germany)	792
TVB USA INC. (Hong Kong PRC)	824
TWIN MINING CORPORATION (Canada)	260
TYCO ELECTRONICS (Bermuda)	66
TYCO ENGINEERED PRODUCTS AND SERVICES, INC. (Bermuda)	66
TYCO FIRE & BUILDING PRODUCTS (Bermuda)	66
TYCO FIRE AND SECURITY SERVICES (Bermuda)	67
	67

American Affiliates

X

PART FOUR

NAICS CODES

Part Four is a numeric index of NAICS Codes with their definition. The NAICS codes for each firm are included with the Foreign Firm information.

Code	Description	Code	Description
111110	Soybean Farming	112410	Sheep Farming
111120	Oilseed (except Soybean) Farming	112420	Goat Farming
111130	Dry Pea and Bean Farming	112511	Finfish Farming and Fish Hatcheries
111140	Wheat Farming	112512	Shellfish Farming
111150	Corn Farming	112519	Other Animal Aquaculture
111160	Rice Farming	112910	Apiculture
111191	Oilseed and Grain Combination	112920	Horses and Other Equine Production
111199	All Other Grain Farming	112930	Fur-Bearing Animal and Rabbit Production
111211	Potato Farming		
111219	Other Vegetable (except Potato) and Melon Farming	112990	All Other Animal Production
		113110	Timber Tract Operations
111310	Orange Groves	113210	Forest Nurseries and Gathering of Forest Products
111320	Citrus (except Orange) Groves		
111331	Apple Orchards	113310	Logging
111332	Grape Vineyards	114111	Finfish Fishing
111333	Strawberry Farming	114112	Shellfish Fishing
111334	Berry (except Strawberry) Farming	114119	Other Marine Fishing
111335	Tree Nut Farming	114210	Hunting and Trapping
111336	Fruit and Tree Nut Combination	115111	Cotton Ginning
111339	Other Noncitrus Fruit Farming	115112	Soil Preparation, Planting, and Cultivating
111411	Mushroom Production	115113	Crop Harvesting, Primarily by Machine
111419	Other Food Crops Grown Under Cover	115114	Postharvest Crop Activities (except Cotton Ginning)
111421	Nursery and Tree Production		
111422	Floriculture Production	115115	Farm Labor Contractors and Crew Leaders
111910	Tobacco Farming		
111920	Cotton Farming	115116	Farm Management Services
111930	Sugarcane Farming	115210	Support Activities for Animal
111940	Hay Farming	115310	Support Activities for Forestry
111991	Sugar Beet Farming	211111	Crude Petroleum and Natural Gas Extraction
111992	Peanut Farming	211112	Natural Gas Liquid Extraction
111998	All Other Miscellaneous Crop Farming	212111	Bituminous Coal and Lignite Surface Mining
112111	Beef Cattle Ranching and Farming		
112112	Cattle Feedlots	212112	Bituminous Coal Underground Mining
112120	Dairy Cattle and Milk Production	212113	Anthracite Mining
112130	Dual-Purpose Cattle Ranching and Farming	212210	Iron Ore Mining
112210	Hog and Pig Farming	212221	Gold Ore Mining
112310	Chicken Egg Production	212222	Silver Ore Mining
112320	Broilers and Other Meat Type Chicken Production	212231	Lead Ore and Zinc Ore Mining
		212234	Copper Ore and Nickel Ore Mining
112330	Turkey Production	212291	Uranium-Radium-Vanadium Ore
112340	Poultry Hatcheries	212299	All Other Metal Ore Mining
112390	Other Poultry Production	212311	Dimension Stone Mining and Quarrying

212312	Crushed and Broken Limestone Mining and Quarrying	236115	New Single-Family Housing Construction (except Operative
212313	Crushed and Broken Granite Mining and Quarrying	236116	New Multifamily Housing Construction (except Operative Builders)
212319	Other Crushed and Broken Stone Mining and Quarrying	236117	New Housing Operative Builders
212321	Construction Sand and Gravel Mining	236118	Residential Remodelers
212322	Industrial Sand Mining	236210	Industrial Building Construction
212324	Kaolin and Ball Clay Mining	236220	Commercial and Institutional Building Construction
212325	Clay and Ceramic and Refractory Minerals Mining	237110	Water and Sewer Line and Related Structures Construction
212391	Potash, Soda, and Borate Mineral	237120	Oil and Gas Pipeline and Related Structures Construction
212392	Phosphate Rock Mining		
212393	Other Chemical and Fertilizer Mineral Mining	237130	Power and Communication Line and Related Structures Construction
212399	All Other Nonmetallic Mineral Mining	237210	Land Subdivision
213111	Drilling Oil and Gas Wells	237310	Highway, Street, and Bridge
213112	Support Activities for Oil and Gas Operations	237990	Other Heavy and Civil Engineering Construction
213113	Support Activities for Coal Mining	238110	Poured Concrete Foundation and Structure Contractors
213114	Support Activities for Metal Mining	238120	Structural Steel and Precast Concrete Contractors
213115	Support Activities for Nonmetallic Minerals (except Fuels)	238130	Framing Contractors
221111	Hydroelectric Power Generation	238140	Masonry Contractors
221112	Fossil Fuel Electric Power Generation	238150	Glass and Glazing Contractors
221113	Nuclear Electric Power Generation	238160	Roofing Contractors
221119	Other Electric Power Generation	238170	Siding Contractors
221121	Electric Bulk Power Transmission and Control	238190	Other Foundation, Structure, and
		238190	Other Foundation, Structure, and Building Exterior Contractors
221122	Electric Power Distribution	238210	Electrical Contractors
221210	Natural Gas Distribution	238220	Plumbing, Heating, and Air-Conditioning Contractors
221310	Water Supply and Irrigation Systems		
221320	Sewage Treatment Facilities	238290	Other Building Equipment Contractors
221330	Steam and Air-Conditioning Supply	238310	Drywall and Insulation Contractors
233320	Commercial and Institutional Building Construction	238320	Painting and Wall Covering Contractors
234910	Water, Sewer, and Pipeline	238330	Flooring Contractors
234990	All Other Heavy Construction	238340	Tile and Terrazzo Contractors
235110	Plumbing, Heating, and Air-Conditioning Contractors	238350	Finish Carpentry Contractors
		238390	Other Building Finishing Contractors
235420	Drywall, Plastering, Acoustical, and Insulation Contractors	238390	Other Building Finishing Contractors
		238910	Site Preparation Contractors
235610		238990	All Other Specialty Trade Contractors
235710	Concrete Contractors	311111	Dog and Cat Food Manufacturing
		311119	Other Animal Food Manufacturing
		311211	Flour Milling

311212	Rice Milling		311830	Tortilla Manufacturing
311213	Malt Manufacturing		311911	Roasted Nuts and Peanut Butter Manufacturing
311221	Wet Corn Milling			
311222	Soybean Processing		311919	Other Snack Food Manufacturing
311223	Other Oilseed Processing		311920	Coffee and Tea Manufacturing
311225	Fats and Oils Refining and Blending		311930	Flavoring Syrup and Concentrate Manufacturing
311230	Breakfast Cereal Manufacturing		311941	Mayonnaise, Dressing, and Other Prepared Sauce Manufacturing
311311	Sugarcane Mills			
311312	Cane Sugar Refining		311942	Spice and Extract Manufacturing
311313	Beet Sugar Manufacturing		311991	Perishable Prepared Food
311320	Chocolate and Confectionery Manufacturing from Cacao Beans		311999	All Other Miscellaneous Food Manufacturing
311330	Confectionery Manufacturing from Purchased Chocolate		312111	Soft Drink Manufacturing
			312112	Bottled Water Manufacturing
311340	Nonchocolate Confectionery Manufacturing		312113	Ice Manufacturing
			312113	Ice Manufacturing
311411	Frozen Fruit, Juice, and Vegetable Manufacturing		312120	Breweries
			312130	Wineries
311412	Frozen Specialty Food Manufacturing		312140	Distilleries
311421	Fruit and Vegetable Canning		312210	Tobacco Stemming and Redrying
311422	Specialty Canning		312221	Cigarette Manufacturing
311423	Dried and Dehydrated Food Manufacturing		312229	Other Tobacco Product Manufacturing
			313111	Yarn Spinning Mills
311511	Fluid Milk Manufacturing		313112	Yarn Texturizing, Throwing, and Twisting Mills
311512	Creamery Butter Manufacturing			
311513	Cheese Manufacturing		313113	Thread Mills
311514	Dry, Condensed, and Evaporated Dairy Product Manufacturing		313210	Broadwoven Fabric Mills
			313221	Narrow Fabric Mills
311520	Ice Cream and Frozen Dessert Manufacturing		313222	Schiffli Machine Embroidery
311611	Animal (except Poultry) Slaughtering		313230	Nonwoven Fabric Mills
311612	Meat Processed from Carcasses		313241	Weft Knit Fabric Mills
311613	Rendering and Meat Byproduct Processing		313249	Other Knit Fabric and Lace Mills
			313311	Broadwoven Fabric Finishing Mills
311615	Poultry Processing		313312	Textile and Fabric Finishing (except Broadwoven Fabric) Mills
311711	Seafood Canning			
311712	Fresh and Frozen Seafood Processing		313320	Fabric Coating Mills
311811	Retail Bakeries		314110	Carpet and Rug Mills
311812	Commercial Bakeries		314121	Curtain and Drapery Mills
311813	Frozen Cakes, Pies, and Other Pastries Manufacturing		314129	Other Household Textile Product Mills
			314911	Textile Bag Mills
311821	Cookie and Cracker Manufacturing		314912	Canvas and Related Product Mills
311822	Flour Mixes and Dough Manufacturing from Purchased Flour		314991	Rope, Cordage, and Twine Mills
			314992	Tire Cord and Tire Fabric Mills
311823	Dry Pasta Manufacturing			

314999	All Other Miscellaneous Textile Product Mills
315111	Sheer Hosiery Mills
315119	Other Hosiery and Sock Mills
315191	Outerwear Knitting Mills
315192	Underwear and Nightwear Knitting
315211	Men's and Boys' Cut and Sew Apparel Contractors
315212	Women's, Girls', and Infants' Cut and Sew Apparel Contractors
315221	Men's and Boys' Cut and Sew Underwear and Nightwear
315222	Men's and Boys' Cut and Sew Suit, Coat, and Overcoat Manufacturing
315223	Men's and Boys' Cut and Sew Shirt (except Work Shirt) Manufacturing
315224	Men's and Boys' Cut and Sew Trouser, Slack, and Jean Manufacturing
315225	Men's and Boys' Cut and Sew Work Clothing Manufacturing
315228	Men's and Boys' Cut and Sew Other Outerwear Manufacturing
315231	Women's and Girls' Cut and Sew Lingerie, Loungewear, and Nightwear Manufacturing
315232	Women's and Girls' Cut and Sew Blouse and Shirt Manufacturing
315233	Women's and Girls' Cut and Sew Dress Manufacturing
315234	Women's and Girls' Cut and Sew Suit, Coat, Tailored Jacket, and Skirt Manufacturing
315239	Women's and Girls' Cut and Sew Other Outerwear Manufacturing
315291	Infants' Cut and Sew Apparel Manufacturing
315292	Fur and Leather Apparel Manufacturing
315299	All Other Cut and Sew Apparel Manufacturing
315991	Hat, Cap, and Millinery Manufacturing
315992	Glove and Mitten Manufacturing
315993	Men's and Boys' Neckwear Manufacturing
315999	Other Apparel Accessories and Other Apparel Manufacturing
316110	Leather and Hide Tanning and
316211	Rubber and Plastics Footwear Manufacturing
316212	House Slipper Manufacturing
316213	Men's Footwear (except Athletic) Manufacturing
316214	Women's Footwear (except Athletic) Manufacturing
316219	Other Footwear Manufacturing
316991	Luggage Manufacturing
316992	Women's Handbag and Purse Manufacturing
316993	Personal Leather Good (except Women's Handbag and Purse)
316999	All Other Leather Good Manufacturing
321113	Sawmills
321114	Wood Preservation
321211	Hardwood Veneer and Plywood Manufacturing
321212	Softwood Veneer and Plywood Manufacturing
321213	Engineered Wood Member (except Truss) Manufacturing
321214	Truss Manufacturing
321219	Reconstituted Wood Product Manufacturing
321911	Wood Window and Door
321912	Cut Stock, Resawing Lumber, and Planing
321918	Other Millwork (including Flooring)
321920	Wood Container and Pallet Manufacturing
321991	Manufactured Home (Mobile Home) Manufacturing
321992	Prefabricated Wood Building Manufacturing
321999	All Other Miscellaneous Wood Product Manufacturing
322110	Pulp Mills
322121	Paper (except Newsprint) Mills
322122	Newsprint Mills
322130	Paperboard Mills
322211	Corrugated and Solid Fiber Box Manufacturing
322212	Folding Paperboard Box Manufacturing
322213	Setup Paperboard Box Manufacturing
322214	Fiber Can, Tube, Drum, and Similar Products Manufacturing

322215	Nonfolding Sanitary Food Container Manufacturing	325120	Industrial Gas Manufacturing
322221	Coated and Laminated Packaging Paper and Plastics Film	325131	Inorganic Dye and Pigment Manufacturing
322222	Coated and Laminated Paper Manufacturing	325132	Synthetic Organic Dye and Pigment Manufacturing
322223	Plastics, Foil, and Coated Paper Bag Manufacturing	325181	Alkalies and Chlorine Manufacturing
322224	Uncoated Paper and Multiwall Bag Manufacturing	325182	Carbon Black Manufacturing
		325188	All Other Basic Inorganic Chemical Manufacturing
322225	Laminated Aluminum Foil Manufacturing for Flexible Packaging Uses	325191	Gum and Wood Chemical
		325192	Cyclic Crude and Intermediate Manufacturing
322226	Surface-Coated Paperboard Manufacturing	325193	Ethyl Alcohol Manufacturing
322231	Die-Cut Paper and Paperboard Office Supplies Manufacturing	325199	All Other Basic Organic Chemical Manufacturing
322232	Envelope Manufacturing	325211	Plastics Material and Resin Manufacturing
322233	Stationery, Tablet, and Related Product Manufacturing	325212	Synthetic Rubber Manufacturing
322291	Sanitary Paper Product Manufacturing	325221	Cellulosic Organic Fiber
322299	All Other Converted Paper Product Manufacturing	325222	Noncellulosic Organic Fiber Manufacturing
323110	Commercial Lithographic Printing	325311	Nitrogenous Fertilizer Manufacturing
323111	Commercial Gravure Printing	325312	Phosphatic Fertilizer Manufacturing
323112	Commercial Flexographic Printing	325314	Fertilizer (Mixing Only) Manufacturing
323113	Commercial Screen Printing	325320	Pesticide and Other Agricultural Chemical Manufacturing
323114	Quick Printing	325411	Medicinal and Botanical Manufacturing
323115	Digital Printing	325412	Pharmaceutical Preparation Manufacturing
323116	Manifold Business Forms Printing	325413	In-Vitro Diagnostic Substance Manufacturing
323117	Books Printing		
323118	Blankbook, Looseleaf Binders, and Devices Manufacturing	325414	Biological Product (except Diagnostic) Manufacturing
323119	Other Commercial Printing	325510	Paint and Coating Manufacturing
323121	Tradebinding and Related Work	325520	Adhesive Manufacturing
323122	Prepress Services	325611	Soap and Other Detergent
324110	Petroleum Refineries	325612	Polish and Other Sanitation Good Manufacturing
324121	Asphalt Paving Mixture and Block Manufacturing	325613	Surface Active Agent Manufacturing
324122	Asphalt Shingle and Coating Materials Manufacturing	325620	Toilet Preparation Manufacturing
		325910	Printing Ink Manufacturing
324191	Petroleum Lubricating Oil and Grease Manufacturing	325920	Explosives Manufacturing
324199	All Other Petroleum and Coal Products Manufacturing	325991	Custom Compounding of Purchased Resins
325110	Petrochemical Manufacturing	325992	Photographic Film, Paper, Plate, and Chemical Manufacturing

NAICS Codes

325998	All Other Miscellaneous Chemical Product and Preparation Manufacturing
326111	Plastics Bag Manufacturing
326112	Plastics Packaging Film and Sheet (including Laminated) Manufacturing
326113	Unlaminated Plastics Film and Sheet (except Packaging) Manufacturing
326121	Unlaminated Plastics Profile Shape Manufacturing
326122	Plastics Pipe and Pipe Fitting Manufacturing
326130	Laminated Plastics Plate, Sheet (except Packaging), and Shape
326140	Polystyrene Foam Product
326150	Urethane and Other Foam Product (except Polystyrene) Manufacturing
326160	Plastics Bottle Manufacturing
326191	Plastics Plumbing Fixture
326192	Resilient Floor Covering
326199	All Other Plastics Product
326211	Tire Manufacturing (except
326212	Tire Retreading
326220	Rubber and Plastics Hoses and Belting Manufacturing
326291	Rubber Product Manufacturing for Mechanical Use
326299	All Other Rubber Product
327111	Vitreous China Plumbing Fixture and China and Earthenware Bathroom Accessories Manufacturing
327112	Vitreous China, Fine Earthenware, and Other Pottery Product
327113	Porcelain Electrical Supply Manufacturing
327121	Brick and Structural Clay Tile Manufacturing
327122	Ceramic Wall and Floor Tile Manufacturing
327123	Other Structural Clay Product Manufacturing
327124	Clay Refractory Manufacturing
327125	Nonclay Refractory Manufacturing
327211	Flat Glass Manufacturing
327212	Other Pressed and Blown Glass and Glassware Manufacturing
327213	Glass Container Manufacturing
327215	Glass Product Manufacturing Made of Purchased Glass
327310	Cement Manufacturing
327320	Ready-Mix Concrete Manufacturing
327331	Concrete Block and Brick Manufacturing
327332	Concrete Pipe Manufacturing
327390	Other Concrete Product Manufacturing
327410	Lime Manufacturing
327420	Gypsum Product Manufacturing
327910	Abrasive Product Manufacturing
327991	Cut Stone and Stone Product Manufacturing
327992	Ground or Treated Mineral and Earth Manufacturing
327993	Mineral Wool Manufacturing
327999	All Other Miscellaneous Nonmetallic Mineral Product Manufacturing
331111	Iron and Steel Mills
331112	Electrometallurgical Ferroalloy Product Manufacturing
331210	Iron and Steel Pipe and Tube Manufacturing from Purchased Steel
331221	Rolled Steel Shape Manufacturing
331222	Steel Wire Drawing
331311	Alumina Refining
331312	Primary Aluminum Production
331314	Secondary Smelting and Alloying of Aluminum
331315	Aluminum Sheet, Plate, and Foil Manufacturing
331316	Aluminum Extruded Product Manufacturing
331319	Other Aluminum Rolling and Drawing
331411	Primary Smelting and Refining of
331419	Primary Smelting and Refining of Nonferrous Metal (except Copper and Aluminum)
331421	Copper Rolling, Drawing, and Extruding
331422	Copper Wire (except Mechanical) Drawing
331423	Secondary Smelting, Refining, and Alloying of Copper
331491	Nonferrous Metal (except Copper and Aluminum) Rolling, Drawing, and Extruding

331492	Secondary Smelting, Refining, and Alloying of Nonferrous Metal (except Copper and Aluminum)	332618	Other Fabricated Wire Product Manufacturing
331511	Iron Foundries	332710	Machine Shops
331512	Steel Investment Foundries	332721	Precision Turned Product
331513	Steel Foundries (except Investment)	332722	Bolt, Nut, Screw, Rivet, and Washer Manufacturing
331521	Aluminum Die-Casting Foundries	332811	Metal Heat Treating
331522	Nonferrous (except Aluminum) Die-Casting Foundries	332812	Metal Coating, Engraving (except Jewelry and Silverware), and Allied Services to Manufacturers
331524	Aluminum Foundries (except Die-Casting)	332813	Electroplating, Plating, Polishing, Anodizing, and Coloring
331525	Copper Foundries (except Die-Casting)	332911	Industrial Valve Manufacturing
331528	Other Nonferrous Foundries (except Die-Casting)	332912	Fluid Power Valve and Hose Fitting Manufacturing
332111	Iron and Steel Forging	332913	Plumbing Fixture Fitting and Trim Manufacturing
332112	Nonferrous Forging	332919	Other Metal Valve and Pipe Fitting Manufacturing
332114	Custom Roll Forming		
332115	Crown and Closure Manufacturing	332991	Ball and Roller Bearing
332116	Metal Stamping	332992	Small Arms Ammunition Manufacturing
332117	Powder Metallurgy Part Manufacturing	332993	Ammunition (except Small Arms) Manufacturing
332211	Cutlery and Flatware (except Precious) Manufacturing	332994	Small Arms Manufacturing
332212	Hand and Edge Tool Manufacturing	332995	Other Ordnance and Accessories Manufacturing
332213	Saw Blade and Handsaw		
332214	Kitchen Utensil, Pot, and Pan Manufacturing	332996	Fabricated Pipe and Pipe Fitting Manufacturing
332311	Prefabricated Metal Building and Component Manufacturing	332997	Industrial Pattern Manufacturing
332312	Fabricated Structural Metal Manufacturing	332998	Enameled Iron and Metal Sanitary Ware Manufacturing
332313	Plate Work Manufacturing	332999	All Other Miscellaneous Fabricated Metal Product Manufacturing
332321	Metal Window and Door	333111	Farm Machinery and Equipment Manufacturing
332322	Sheet Metal Work Manufacturing		
332323	Ornamental and Architectural Metal Work Manufacturing	333112	Lawn and Garden Tractor and Home Lawn and Garden Equipment Manufacturing
332410	Power Boiler and Heat Exchanger Manufacturing		
332420	Metal Tank (Heavy Gauge) Manufacturing	333120	Construction Machinery Manufacturing
		333131	Mining Machinery and Equipment Manufacturing
332431	Metal Can Manufacturing		
332439	Other Metal Container Manufacturing	333132	Oil and Gas Field Machinery and Equipment Manufacturing
332510	Hardware Manufacturing	333210	Sawmill and Woodworking Machinery Manufacturing
332611	Spring (Heavy Gauge) Manufacturing		
332612	Spring (Light Gauge) Manufacturing	333220	Plastics and Rubber Industry Machinery Manufacturing

333291	Paper Industry Machinery	333618	Other Engine Equipment
333292	Textile Machinery Manufacturing	333911	Pump and Pumping Equipment Manufacturing
333293	Printing Machinery and Equipment Manufacturing	333912	Air and Gas Compressor
333294	Food Product Machinery Manufacturing	333913	Measuring and Dispensing Pump Manufacturing
333295	Semiconductor Machinery		
333298	All Other Industrial Machinery Manufacturing	333921	Elevator and Moving Stairway Manufacturing
333311	Automatic Vending Machine Manufacturing	333922	Conveyor and Conveying Equipment Manufacturing
333312	Commercial Laundry, Drycleaning, and Pressing Machine Manufacturing	333923	Overhead Traveling Crane, Hoist, and Monorail System Manufacturing
333313	Office Machinery Manufacturing	333924	Industrial Truck, Tractor, Trailer, and Stacker Machinery Manufacturing
333314	Optical Instrument and Lens Manufacturing	333991	Power-Driven Handtool Manufacturing
		333991	Power-Driven Handtool Manufacturing
333315	Photographic and Photocopying Equipment Manufacturing	333992	Welding and Soldering Equipment Manufacturing
333319	Other Commercial and Service Industry Machinery Manufacturing	333993	Packaging Machinery Manufacturing
		333994	Industrial Process Furnace and Oven Manufacturing
333411	Air Purification Equipment Manufacturing	333995	Fluid Power Cylinder and Actuator Manufacturing
333412	Industrial and Commercial Fan and Blower Manufacturing	333996	Fluid Power Pump and Motor Manufacturing
333414	Heating Equipment (except Warm Air Furnaces) Manufacturing	333997	Scale and Balance (except Laboratory) Manufacturing
333415	Air-Conditioning and Warm Air Heating Equipment and Commercial and Industrial Refrigeration Equipment Manufacturing	333999	All Other Miscellaneous General Purpose Machinery Manufacturing
		334111	Electronic Computer Manufacturing
333511	Industrial Mold Manufacturing	334112	Computer Storage Device
333512	Machine Tool (Metal Cutting Types) Manufacturing	334113	Computer Terminal Manufacturing
		334119	Other Computer Peripheral Equipment Manufacturing
333513	Machine Tool (Metal Forming Types) Manufacturing	334210	Telephone Apparatus Manufacturing
333514	Special Die and Tool, Die Set, Jig, and Fixture Manufacturing	334220	Radio and Television Broadcasting and Wireless Communications Equipment Manufacturing
333515	Cutting Tool and Machine Tool Accessory Manufacturing	334290	Other Communications Equipment Manufacturing
333516	Rolling Mill Machinery and Equipment Manufacturing	334310	Audio and Video Equipment Manufacturing
333518	Other Metalworking Machinery Manufacturing	334411	Electron Tube Manufacturing
333611	Turbine and Turbine Generator Set Units Manufacturing	334412	Bare Printed Circuit Board Manufacturing
333612	Speed Changer, Industrial High-Speed Drive, and Gear Manufacturing	334413	Semiconductor and Related Device Manufacturing
333613	Mechanical Power Transmission Equipment Manufacturing		

334414	Electronic Capacitor Manufacturing		335211	Electric Housewares and Household Fan Manufacturing
334415	Electronic Resistor Manufacturing			
334416	Electronic Coil, Transformer, and Other Inductor Manufacturing		335212	Household Vacuum Cleaner Manufacturing
334417	Electronic Connector Manufacturing		335221	Household Cooking Appliance Manufacturing
334418	Printed Circuit Assembly (Electronic Assembly) Manufacturing		335222	Household Refrigerator and Home
			335222	Household Refrigerator and Home Freezer Manufacturing
334419	Other Electronic Component Manufacturing		335224	Household Laundry Equipment
			335224	Household Laundry Equipment Manufacturing
334510	Electromedical and Electrotherapeutic Apparatus Manufacturing		335228	Other Major Household Appliance
			335228	Other Major Household Appliance Manufacturing
334511	Search, Detection, Navigation, Guidance, Aeronautical, and Nautical System and Instrument Manufacturing		335311	Power, Distribution, and Specialty
			335311	Power, Distribution, and Specialty Transformer Manufacturing
334512	Automatic Environmental Control Manufacturing for Residential, Commercial, and Appliance Use		335312	Motor and Generator Manufacturing
			335313	Switchgear and Switchboard Apparatus Manufacturing
334513	Instruments and Related Products Manufacturing for Measuring, Displaying, and Controlling Industrial Process Variables		335314	Relay and Industrial Control Manufacturing
			335911	Storage Battery Manufacturing
			335912	Primary Battery Manufacturing
334514	Totalizing Fluid Meter and Counting Device Manufacturing		335921	Fiber Optic Cable Manufacturing
			335929	Other Communication and Energy Wire Manufacturing
334515	Instrument Manufacturing for Measuring and Testing Electricity and Electrical Signals		335931	Current-Carrying Wiring Device Manufacturing
334516	Analytical Laboratory Instrument Manufacturing		335932	Noncurrent-Carrying Wiring Device Manufacturing
334517	Irradiation Apparatus Manufacturing		335991	Carbon and Graphite Product Manufacturing
334518	Watch, Clock, and Part Manufacturing			
334519	Other Measuring and Controlling Device Manufacturing		335999	All Other Miscellaneous Electrical Equipment and Component Manufacturing
334611	Software Reproducing			
334612	Prerecorded Compact Disc (except Software), Tape, and Record Reproducing		336111	Automobile Manufacturing
			336112	Light Truck and Utility Vehicle Manufacturing
334613	Magnetic and Optical Recording Media Manufacturing		336120	Heavy Duty Truck Manufacturing
			336211	Motor Vehicle Body Manufacturing
334920	Other Communications Equipment Manufacturing		336212	Truck Trailer Manufacturing
335110	Electric Lamp Bulb and Part Manufacturing		336213	Motor Home Manufacturing
			336214	Travel Trailer and Camper
335121	Residential Electric Lighting Fixture Manufacturing		336311	Carburetor, Piston, Piston Ring, and Valve Manufacturing
335122	Commercial, Industrial, and Institutional Electric Lighting Fixture		336312	Gasoline Engine and Engine Parts Manufacturing
335129	Other Lighting Equipment		336321	Vehicular Lighting Equipment Manufacturing

336322	Other Motor Vehicle Electrical and Electronic Equipment Manufacturing	337127	Institutional Furniture Manufacturing
336330	Motor Vehicle Steering and Suspension Components (except Spring) Manufacturing	337129	Wood Television, Radio, and Sewing Machine Cabinet Manufacturing
		337211	Wood Office Furniture Manufacturing
336340	Motor Vehicle Brake System Manufacturing	337212	Custom Architectural Woodwork and Millwork Manufacturing
336350	Motor Vehicle Transmission and Power Train Parts Manufacturing	337214	Office Furniture (except Wood) Manufacturing
336360	Motor Vehicle Seating and Interior Trim Manufacturing	337215	Showcase, Partition, Shelving, and Locker Manufacturing
336370	Motor Vehicle Metal Stamping	337910	Mattress Manufacturing
336391	Motor Vehicle Air-Conditioning Manufacturing	337920	Blind and Shade Manufacturing
		339111	Laboratory Apparatus and Furniture Manufacturing
336399	All Other Motor Vehicle Parts Manufacturing	339112	Surgical and Medical Instrument Manufacturing
336411	Aircraft Manufacturing	339113	Surgical Appliance and Supplies Manufacturing
336412	Aircraft Engine and Engine Parts Manufacturing	339114	Dental Equipment and Supplies Manufacturing
336413	Other Aircraft Parts and Auxiliary Equipment Manufacturing	339115	Ophthalmic Goods Manufacturing
336414	Guided Missile and Space Vehicle Manufacturing	339116	Dental Laboratories
336415	Guided Missile and Space Vehicle Propulsion Unit and Propulsion Unit Parts Manufacturing	339911	Jewelry (except Costume)
		339912	Silverware and Hollowware Manufacturing
336419	Other Guided Missile and Space Vehicle Parts and Auxiliary Equipment Manufacturing	339913	Jewelers' Material and Lapidary Work Manufacturing
		339914	Costume Jewelry and Novelty Manufacturing
336510	Railroad Rolling Stock Manufacturing	339920	Sporting and Athletic Goods Manufacturing
336611	Ship Building and Repairing		
336612	Boat Building	339931	Doll and Stuffed Toy Manufacturing
336991	Motorcycle, Bicycle, and Parts Manufacturing	339932	Game, Toy, and Children's Vehicle Manufacturing
336992	Military Armored Vehicle, Tank, and Tank Component Manufacturing	339941	Pen and Mechanical Pencil Manufacturing
336999	All Other Transportation Equipment Manufacturing	339942	Lead Pencil and Art Good
		339943	Marking Device Manufacturing
337110	Wood Kitchen Cabinet and Countertop Manufacturing	339944	Carbon Paper and Inked Ribbon Manufacturing
337121	Upholstered Household Furniture Manufacturing	339950	Sign Manufacturing
		339991	Gasket, Packing, and Sealing Device Manufacturing
337122	Nonupholstered Wood Household Furniture Manufacturing	339992	Musical Instrument Manufacturing
337124	Metal Household Furniture Manufacturing	339993	Fastener, Button, Needle, and Pin Manufacturing
337125	Household Furniture (except Wood and Metal) Manufacturing	339994	Broom, Brush, and Mop

339995	Burial Casket Manufacturing	422330	Women's, Children's, and Infants' Clothing and Accessories Wholesalers
339999	All Other Miscellaneous		
421120	Motor Vehicle Supplies and New Parts Wholesalers	422470	Meat and Meat Product Merchant Wholesalers
421210	Furniture Wholesalers	422490	Other Grocery and Related Products Wholesalers
421310	Lumber, Plywood, Millwork, and Wood Panel Wholesalers	422690	Other Chemical and Allied Products
		422690	Other Chemical and Allied Products Wholesalers
421320	Brick, Stone, and Related Construction Material Wholesalers	422720	Petroleum and Petroleum Products
		422720	Petroleum and Petroleum Products Wholesalers (except Bulk Stations and Terminals)
421330	Roofing, Siding, and Insulation Material Wholesalers		
		422820	Wine and Distilled Alcoholic Beverage Wholesalers
421390	Other Construction Material		
421420	Office Equipment Wholesalers	422910	Farm Supplies Wholesalers
421430	Computer and Computer Peripheral Equipment and Software Wholesalers	422990	Other Miscellaneous Nondurable Goods Wholesalers
421450	Medical, Dental, and Hospital Equipment and Supplies Wholesalers	423110	Automobile and Other Motor Vehicle Merchant Wholesalers
421510	Metal Service Centers and Offices	423120	Motor Vehicle Supplies and New Parts Merchant Wholesalers
421610	Electrical Apparatus and Equipment, Wiring Supplies, and Construction Material Wholesalers	423130	Tire and Tube Merchant Wholesalers
		423140	Motor Vehicle Parts (Used) Merchant Wholesalers
421620	Electrical Appliance, Television, and Radio Set Wholesalers	423210	Furniture Merchant Wholesalers
421690	Other Electronic Parts and Equipment Wholesalers	423220	Home Furnishing Merchant
		423220	Home Furnishing Merchant
421710	Hardware Wholesalers	423310	Lumber, Plywood, Millwork, and Wood Panel Merchant Wholesalers
421720	Plumbing and Heating Equipment and Supplies (Hydronics) Wholesalers	423320	Brick, Stone, and Related Construction
		423320	Brick, Stone, and Related Construction Material Merchant Wholesalers
421730	Warm Air Heating and Air-Conditioning Equipment and Supplies	423330	Roofing, Siding, and Insulation
		423330	Roofing, Siding, and Insulation Material Merchant Wholesalers
421810	Construction and Mining (except Oil Well) Machinery and Equipment Wholesalers	423390	Other Construction Material Merchant
		423390	Other Construction Material Merchant Wholesalers
421830	Industrial Machinery and Equipment Wholesalers	423410	Photographic Equipment and Supplies Merchant Wholesalers
421910	Sporting and Recreational Goods and Supplies Wholesalers	423420	Office Equipment Merchant
421930	Recyclable Material Wholesalers	423430	Computer and Computer Peripheral Equipment and Software Merchant Wholesalers
421990	Other Miscellaneous Durable Goods Wholesalers	423440	Other Commercial Equipment
		423440	Other Commercial Equipment Merchant Wholesalers
422110	Printing and Writing Paper Wholesalers	423450	Medical, Dental, and Hospital Equipment and Supplies Merchant Wholesalers
422120	Stationery and Office Supplies Wholesalers		
422210	Drugs & Druggists Sundries Wholesalers	423460	Ophthalmic Goods Merchant
422320	Men's and Boys' Clothing and Furnishings Wholesalers	423490	Other Professional Equipment and Supplies Merchant Wholesalers

423510	Metal Service Centers and Other Metal Merchant Wholesalers
423520	Coal and Other Mineral and Ore Merchant Wholesalers
423610	Electrical Apparatus and Equipment, Wiring Supplies, and Related Equipment Merchant Wholesalers
423620	Electrical and Electronic Appliance, Television, and Radio Set Merchant Wholesalers
423690	Other Electronic Parts and Equipment Merchant Wholesalers
423710	Hardware Merchant Wholesalers
423720	Plumbing and Heating Equipment and Supplies (Hydronics) Merchant Wholesalers
423730	Warm Air Heating and Air-Conditioning Equipment and Supplies Merchant Wholesalers
423740	Refrigeration Equipment and Supplies Merchant Wholesalers
423810	Construction and Mining (except Oil Well) Machinery and Equipment Merchant Wholesalers
423820	Farm and Garden Machinery and Equipment Merchant Wholesalers
423830	Industrial Machinery and Equipment Merchant Wholesalers
423840	Industrial Supplies Merchant
423850	Service Establishment Equipment and Supplies Merchant Wholesalers
423860	Transportation Equipment and Supplies (except Motor Vehicle) Merchant Wholesalers
423910	Sporting and Recreational Goods and Supplies Merchant Wholesalers
423920	Toy and Hobby Goods and Supplies Merchant Wholesalers
423930	Recyclable Material Merchant Wholesalers
423940	Jewelry, Watch, Precious Stone, and Precious Metal Merchant Wholesalers
423990	Other Miscellaneous Durable Goods Merchant Wholesalers
424110	Printing and Writing Paper Merchant Wholesalers
424120	Stationery and Office Supplies Merchant Wholesalers
424130	Industrial and Personal Service Paper Merchant Wholesalers
424210	Drugs and Druggists' Sundries Merchant Wholesalers
424310	Piece Goods, Notions, and Other Dry Goods Merchant Wholesalers
424320	Men's and Boys' Clothing and Furnishings Merchant Wholesalers
424330	Women's, Children's, and Infants' Clothing and Accessories Merchant Wholesalers
424340	Footwear Merchant Wholesalers
424410	General Line Grocery Merchant Wholesalers
424420	Packaged Frozen Food Merchant Wholesalers
424430	Dairy Product (except Dried or Canned) Merchant Wholesalers
424440	Poultry and Poultry Product Merchant Wholesalers
424450	Confectionery Merchant Wholesalers
424460	Fish and Seafood Merchant
424460	Fish and Seafood Merchant
424480	Fresh Fruit and Vegetable Merchant Wholesalers
424490	Other Grocery and Related Products Merchant Wholesalers
424510	Grain and Field Bean Merchant Wholesalers
424520	Livestock Merchant Wholesalers
424590	Other Farm Product Raw Material Merchant Wholesalers
424610	Plastics Materials and Basic Forms and Shapes Merchant Wholesalers
424690	Other Chemical and Allied Products Merchant Wholesalers
424710	Petroleum Bulk Stations and Terminals
424720	Petroleum and Petroleum Products Merchant Wholesalers (except Bulk Stations and Terminals)
424810	Beer and Ale Merchant Wholesalers
424820	Wine and Distilled Alcoholic Beverage Merchant Wholesalers
424910	Farm Supplies Merchant Wholesalers
424920	Book, Periodical, and Newspaper Merchant Wholesalers
424930	Flower, Nursery Stock, and Florists' Supplies Merchant Wholesalers

424940	Tobacco and Tobacco Product Merchant Wholesalers
424950	Paint, Varnish, and Supplies Merchant Wholesalers
424990	Other Miscellaneous Nondurable Goods Merchant Wholesalers
425110	Business to Business Electronic
425120	Wholesale Trade Agents and Brokers
441110	New Car Dealers
441120	Used Car Dealers
441210	Recreational Vehicle Dealers
441221	Motorcycle Dealers
441222	Boat Dealers
441229	All Other Motor Vehicle Dealers
441310	Automotive Parts and Accessories
441320	Tire Dealers
442110	Furniture Stores
442210	Floor Covering Stores
442291	Window Treatment Stores
442299	All Other Home Furnishings Stores
443111	Household Appliance Stores
443112	Radio, Television, and Other Electronics Stores
443120	Computer and Software Stores
443130	Camera and Photographic Supplies
444110	Home Centers
444120	Paint and Wallpaper Stores
444130	Hardware Stores
444190	Other Building Material Dealers
444210	Outdoor Power Equipment Stores
444220	Nursery, Garden Center, and Farm Supply Stores
445110	Supermarkets and Other Grocery (except Convenience) Stores
445120	Convenience Stores
445210	Meat Markets
445220	Fish and Seafood Markets
445230	Fruit and Vegetable Markets
445291	Baked Goods Stores
445292	Confectionery and Nut Stores
445299	All Other Specialty Food Stores
445310	Beer, Wine, and Liquor Stores
446110	Pharmacies and Drug Stores

446120	Cosmetics, Beauty Supplies, and Perfume Stores
446130	Optical Goods Stores
446191	Food (Health) Supplement Stores
446199	All Other Health and Personal Care Stores
447110	Gasoline Stations with Convenience Stores
447190	Other Gasoline Stations
448110	Men's Clothing Stores
448120	Women's Clothing Stores
448130	Children's and Infants' Clothing Stores
448140	Family Clothing Stores
448150	Clothing Accessories Stores
448190	Other Clothing Stores
448210	Shoe Stores
448310	Jewelry Stores
448320	Luggage and Leather Goods Stores
451110	Sporting Goods Stores
451120	Hobby, Toy, and Game Stores
451130	Sewing, Needlework, and Piece Goods Stores
451140	Musical Instrument and Supplies Stores
451211	Book Stores
451212	News Dealers and Newsstands
451220	Prerecorded Tape, Compact Disc, and Record Stores
452111	Department Stores (except Discount Department Stores)
452112	Discount Department Stores
452910	Warehouse Clubs and Supercenters
452990	All Other General Merchandise Stores
452990	All Other General Merchandise Stores
453110	Florists
453210	Office Supplies and Stationery Stores
453220	Gift, Novelty, and Souvenir Stores
453310	Used Merchandise Stores
453910	Pet and Pet Supplies Stores
453920	Art Dealers
453930	Manufactured (Mobile) Home Dealers
453991	Tobacco Stores
453998	All Other Miscellaneous Store Retailers (except Tobacco Stores)
454111	Electronic Shopping
454112	Electronic Auctions

454113	Mail-Order Houses		485991	Special Needs Transportation
454210	Vending Machine Operators		485999	All Other Transit and Ground
454311	Heating Oil Dealers			Passenger Transportation
454312	Liquefied Petroleum Gas (Bottled		486110	Pipeline Transportation of Crude Oil
	Gas) Dealers		486210	Pipeline Transportation of Natural Gas
454319	Other Fuel Dealers		486910	Pipeline Transportation of Refined
454390	Other Direct Selling Establishments			Petroleum Products
481111	Scheduled Passenger Air		486990	All Other Pipeline Transportation
481112	Scheduled Freight Air Transportation		487110	Scenic and Sightseeing
				Transportation, Land
481211	Nonscheduled Chartered Passenger		487210	Scenic and Sightseeing
	Air Transportation		487210	Scenic and Sightseeing
				Transportation, Water
481212	Nonscheduled Chartered Freight Air		487990	Scenic and Sightseeing
	Transportation		487990	Scenic and Sightseeing
				Transportation, Other
481219	Other Nonscheduled Air		488111	Air Traffic Control
482111	Line-Haul Railroads		488119	Other Airport Operations
482112	Short Line Railroads		488190	Other Support Activities for Air
483111	Deep Sea Freight Transportation			Transportation
483112	Deep Sea Passenger Transportation		488210	Support Activities for Rail
483113	Coastal and Great Lakes Freight		488310	Port and Harbor Operations
	Transportation		488320	Marine Cargo Handling
483114	Coastal and Great Lakes Passenger		488330	Navigational Services to Shipping
	Transportation		488330	Navigational Services to Shipping
483211	Inland Water Freight Transportation		488390	Other Support Activities for Water
483212	Inland Water Passenger			Transportation
484110	General Freight Trucking, Local		488410	Motor Vehicle Towing
484121	General Freight Trucking, Long-		488490	Other Support Activities for Road
	Distance, Truckload			Transportation
			488510	Freight Transportation Arrangement
484122	General Freight Trucking, Long-		488991	Packing and Crating
	Distance, Less Than Truckload		488991	Packing and Crating
484210	Used Household and Office Goods		488999	All Other Support Activities for
	Moving			Transportation
484220	Specialized Freight (except Used		491110	Postal Service
	Goods) Trucking, Local		492110	Couriers
484230	Specialized Freight (except Used		492210	Local Messengers and Local Delivery
	Goods) Trucking, Long-Distance		493110	General Warehousing and Storage
485111	Mixed Mode Transit Systems		493120	Refrigerated Warehousing and
485112	Commuter Rail Systems		493130	Farm Product Warehousing and
485113	Bus and Other Motor Vehicle Transit		493190	Other Warehousing and Storage
	Systems			
485119	Other Urban Transit Systems		511110	Newspaper Publishers
485210	Interurban and Rural Bus		511120	Periodical Publishers
485310	Taxi Service		511130	Book Publishers
485320	Limousine Service		511140	Directory and Mailing List Publishers
485410	School and Employee Bus		511191	Greeting Card Publishers
485510	Charter Bus Industry		511199	All Other Publishers

511210	Software Publishers		519190	All Other Information Services
512110	Motion Picture and Video Production		521110	Monetary Authorities - Central Bank
512120	Motion Picture and Video Distribution		522110	Commercial Banking
512131	Motion Picture Theaters (except Drive-Ins)		522120	Savings Institutions
			522130	Credit Unions
512132	Drive-In Motion Picture Theaters		522190	Other Depository Credit Intermediation
512191	Teleproduction and Other Postproduction Services		522210	Credit Card Issuing
512199	Other Motion Picture and Video Industries		522220	Sales Financing
			522291	Consumer Lending
512210	Record Production		522292	Real Estate Credit
512220	Integrated Record Production/Distribution		522293	International Trade Financing
			522294	Secondary Market Financing
512230	Music Publishers		522298	All Other Nondepository Credit Intermediation
512240	Sound Recording Studios			
512290	Other Sound Recording Industries		522310	Mortgage and Nonmortgage Loan Brokers
513120	Television Broadcasting			
513210	Cable Networks		522320	Financial Transactions Processing, Reserve, and Clearinghouse Activities
513220	Cable and Other Program Distribution			
513310	Wired Telecommunications Carriers		522390	Other Activities Related to Credit Intermediation
513322	Cellular and Other Wireless Telecommunications		523110	Investment Banking and Securities Dealing
514191	On-Line Information Services		523120	Securities Brokerage
514210	Data Processing Services		523130	Commodity Contracts Dealing
515111	Radio Networks		523140	Commodity Contracts Brokerage
515112	Radio Stations		523210	Securities and Commodity Exchanges
515120	Television Broadcasting		523910	Miscellaneous Intermediation
515210	Cable and Other Subscription Programming		523920	Portfolio Management
			523930	Investment Advice
516110	Internet Publishing and Broadcasting		523991	Trust, Fiduciary, and Custody Activities
517110	Wired Telecommunications Carriers		523999	Miscellaneous Financial Investment Activities
517211	Paging			
517212	Cellular and Other Wireless Telecommunications		524113	Direct Life Insurance Carriers
			524114	Direct Health and Medical Insurance Carriers
517310	Telecommunications Resellers			
517410	Satellite Telecommunications		524126	Direct Property and Casualty Insurance Carriers
517510	Cable and Other Program Distribution			
517910	Other Telecommunications		524127	Direct Title Insurance Carriers
518111	Internet Service Providers		524128	Other Direct Insurance (except Life, Health, and Medical) Carriers
518112	Web Search Portals		524130	Reinsurance Carriers
518210	Data Processing, Hosting, and Related Services		524210	Insurance Agencies and Brokerages
			524210	Insurance Agencies and Brokerages
519110	News Syndicates		524291	Claims Adjusting
519120	Libraries and Archives		524292	Third Party Administration of Insurance and Pension Funds

524298	All Other Insurance Related Activities
525110	Pension Funds
525120	Health and Welfare Funds
525190	Other Insurance Funds
525910	Open-End Investment Funds
525920	Trusts, Estates, and Agency Accounts
525930	Real Estate Investment Trusts
525990	Other Financial Vehicles
531110	Lessors of Residential Buildings and Dwellings
531120	Lessors of Nonresidential Buildings (except Miniwarehouses)
531130	Lessors of Miniwarehouses and Self-Storage Units
531190	Lessors of Other Real Estate Property
531210	Offices of Real Estate Agents and Brokers
531311	Residential Property Managers
531312	Nonresidential Property Managers
531320	Offices of Real Estate Appraisers
531390	Other Activities Related to Real Estate
532111	Passenger Car Rental
532112	Passenger Car Leasing
532120	Truck, Utility Trailer, and RV (Recreational Vehicle) Rental and Leasing
532210	Consumer Electronics and Appliances Rental
532220	Formal Wear and Costume Rental
532230	Video Tape and Disc Rental
532291	Home Health Equipment Rental
532292	Recreational Goods Rental
532299	All Other Consumer Goods Rental
532310	General Rental Centers
532411	Commercial Air, Rail, and Water Transportation Equipment Rental and Leasing
532412	Construction, Mining, and Forestry Machinery and Equipment Rental and Leasing
532420	Office Machinery and Equipment Rental and Leasing
532490	Other Commercial and Industrial Machinery and Equipment Rental and Leasing
533110	Lessors of Nonfinancial Intangible Assets (except Copyrighted Works)
541110	Offices of Lawyers
541120	Offices of Notaries
541191	Title Abstract and Settlement Offices
541199	All Other Legal Services
541211	Offices of Certified Public Accountants
541213	Tax Preparation Services
541214	Payroll Services
541219	Other Accounting Services
541310	Architectural Services
541320	Landscape Architectural Services
541330	Engineering Services
541340	Drafting Services
541350	Building Inspection Services
541360	Geophysical Surveying and Mapping Services
541370	Surveying and Mapping (except Geophysical) Services
541380	Testing Laboratories
541410	Interior Design Services
541420	Industrial Design Services
541430	Graphic Design Services
541490	Other Specialized Design Services
541511	Custom Computer Programming
541512	Computer Systems Design Services
541513	Computer Facilities Management Services
541519	Other Computer Related Services
541611	Administrative Management and General Management Consulting
541612	Human Resources and Executive Search Consulting Services
541613	Marketing Consulting Services
541614	Process, Physical Distribution, and Logistics Consulting Services
541618	Other Management Consulting
541620	Environmental Consulting Services
541690	Other Scientific and Technical Consulting Services
541710	Research and Development in the Physical, Engineering, and Life
541720	Research and Development in the Social Sciences and Humanities
541810	Advertising Agencies

541820	Public Relations Agencies
541830	Media Buying Agencies
541840	Media Representatives
541850	Display Advertising
541860	Direct Mail Advertising
541870	Advertising Material Distribution Services
541890	Other Services Related to Advertising
541910	Marketing Research and Public Opinion Polling
541921	Photography Studios, Portrait
541922	Commercial Photography
541930	Translation and Interpretation
541940	Veterinary Services
541990	All Other Professional, Scientific, and Technical Services
551111	Offices of Bank Holding Companies
551112	Offices of Other Holding Companies
551114	Corporate, Subsidiary, and Regional Managing Offices
561110	Office Administrative Services
561210	Facilities Support Services
561310	Employment Placement Agencies
561320	Temporary Help Services
561330	Professional Employer Organizations
561410	Document Preparation Services
561421	Telephone Answering Services
561422	Telemarketing Bureaus
561431	Private Mail Centers
561439	Other Business Service Centers (including Copy Shops)
561440	Collection Agencies
561450	Credit Bureaus
561491	Repossession Services
561492	Court Reporting and Stenotype
561499	All Other Business Support Services
561510	Travel Agencies
561520	Tour Operators
561591	Convention and Visitors Bureaus
561599	All Other Travel Arrangement and Reservation Services
561611	Investigation Services
561612	Security Guards and Patrol Services
561613	Armored Car Services
561621	Security Systems Services (except Locksmiths)
561622	Locksmiths
561710	Exterminating and Pest Control
561720	Janitorial Services
561730	Landscaping Services
561740	Carpet and Upholstery Cleaning
561790	Other Services to Buildings and Dwellings
561910	Packaging and Labeling Services
561920	Convention and Trade Show
561990	All Other Support Services
562111	Solid Waste Collection
562112	Hazardous Waste Collection
562119	Other Waste Collection
562211	Hazardous Waste Treatment and
562212	Solid Waste Landfill
562213	Solid Waste Combustors and
562219	Other Nonhazardous Waste Treatment and Disposal
562910	Remediation Services
562920	Materials Recovery Facilities
562991	Septic Tank and Related Services
562998	All Other Miscellaneous Waste Management Services
611110	Elementary and Secondary Schools
611210	Junior Colleges
611310	Colleges, Universities, and Professional Schools
611410	Business and Secretarial Schools
611420	Computer Training
611430	Professional and Management Development Training
611511	Cosmetology and Barber Schools
611512	Flight Training
611513	Apprenticeship Training
611519	Other Technical and Trade Schools
611610	Fine Arts Schools
611620	Sports and Recreation Instruction
611630	Language Schools
611691	Exam Preparation and Tutoring
611692	Automobile Driving Schools

611699	All Other Miscellaneous Schools and Instruction	624110	Child and Youth Services
611710	Educational Support Services	624120	Services for the Elderly and Persons with Disabilities
621111	Offices of Physicians (except Mental Health Specialists)	624190	Other Individual and Family Services
621112	Offices of Physicians, Mental Health Specialists	624210	Community Food Services
621210	Offices of Dentists	624221	Temporary Shelters
621310	Offices of Chiropractors	624229	Other Community Housing Services
621320	Offices of Optometrists	624230	Emergency and Other Relief Services
621330	Offices of Mental Health Practitioners (except Physicians)	624310	Vocational Rehabilitation Services
621340	Offices of Physical, Occupational and Speech Therapists, and Audiologists	624410	Child Day Care Services
		711110	Theater Companies and Dinner
621391	Offices of Podiatrists	711120	Dance Companies
621399	Offices of All Other Miscellaneous Health Practitioners	711130	Musical Groups and Artists
		711190	Other Performing Arts Companies
621410	Family Planning Centers	711211	Sports Teams and Clubs
621420	Outpatient Mental Health and Substance Abuse Centers	711212	Racetracks
		711219	Other Spectator Sports
621491	HMO Medical Centers	711310	Promoters of Performing Arts, Sports, and Similar Events with Facilities
621492	Kidney Dialysis Centers		
621493	Freestanding Ambulatory Surgical and Emergency Centers	711320	Promoters of Performing Arts, Sports, and Similar Events without Facilities
621498	All Other Outpatient Care Centers	711410	Agents and Managers for Artists, Athletes, Entertainers, and Other Public Figures
621511	Medical Laboratories		
621512	Diagnostic Imaging Centers	711510	Independent Artists, Writers, and Performers
621610	Home Health Care Services		
621910	Ambulance Services	712110	Museums
621991	Blood and Organ Banks	712120	Historical Sites
621999	All Other Miscellaneous Ambulatory Health Care Services	712130	Zoos and Botanical Gardens
		712190	Nature Parks and Other Similar Institutions
622110	General Medical and Surgical		
622210	Psychiatric and Substance Abuse Hospitals	713110	Amusement and Theme Parks
		713120	Amusement Arcades
622310	Specialty (except Psychiatric and Substance Abuse) Hospitals	713210	Casinos (except Casino Hotels)
		713290	Other Gambling Industries
623110	Nursing Care Facilities	713910	Golf Courses and Country Clubs
623210	Residential Mental Retardation	713920	Skiing Facilities
623220	Residential Mental Health and Substance Abuse Facilities	713930	Marinas
		713940	Fitness and Recreational Sports
623311	Continuing Care Retirement Communities	713950	Bowling Centers
		713990	All Other Amusement and Recreation Industries
623312	Homes for the Elderly		
623990	Other Residential Care Facilities	721110	Hotels (except Casino Hotels) and
		721120	Casino Hotels

721191	Bed-and-Breakfast Inns
721199	All Other Traveler Accommodation
721211	RV (Recreational Vehicle) Parks and Campgrounds
721214	Recreational and Vacation Camps (except Campgrounds)
721310	Rooming and Boarding Houses
722110	Full-Service Restaurants
722211	Limited-Service Restaurants
722212	Cafeterias
722213	Snack and Nonalcoholic Beverage Bars
722310	Food Service Contractors
722320	Caterers
722330	Mobile Food Services
722410	Drinking Places (Alcoholic Beverages)
811111	General Automotive Repair
811112	Automotive Exhaust System Repair
811113	Automotive Transmission Repair
811118	Other Automotive Mechanical and Electrical Repair and Maintenance
811121	Automotive Body, Paint, and Interior Repair and Maintenance
811122	Automotive Glass Replacement Shops
811191	Automotive Oil Change and Lubrication Shops
811192	Car Washes
811198	All Other Automotive Repair and Maintenance
811211	Consumer Electronics Repair and Maintenance
811212	Computer and Office Machine Repair and Maintenance
811213	Communication Equipment Repair and Maintenance
811219	Other Electronic and Precision Equipment Repair and Maintenance
811310	Commercial and Industrial Machinery and Equipment (except Automotive and Electronic) Repair and
811411	Home and Garden Equipment Repair and Maintenance
811412	Appliance Repair and Maintenance
811420	Reupholstery and Furniture Repair
811430	Footwear and Leather Goods Repair
811490	Other Personal and Household Goods Repair and Maintenance

812111	Barber Shops
812112	Beauty Salons
812113	Nail Salons
812191	Diet and Weight Reducing Centers
812199	Other Personal Care Services
812210	Funeral Homes and Funeral Services
812220	Cemeteries and Crematories
812310	Coin-Operated Laundries and Drycleaners
812320	Drycleaning and Laundry Services (except Coin-Operated)
812331	Linen Supply
812332	Industrial Launderers
812910	Pet Care (except Veterinary) Services
812921	Photofinishing Laboratories (except One-Hour)
812922	One-Hour Photofinishing
812930	Parking Lots and Garages
812990	All Other Personal Services
813110	Religious Organizations
813211	Grantmaking Foundations
813212	Voluntary Health Organizations
813219	Other Grantmaking and Giving
813311	Human Rights Organizations
813312	Environment, Conservation and Wildlife Organizations
813319	Other Social Advocacy Organizations
813410	Civic and Social Organizations
813910	Business Associations
813920	Professional Organizations
813930	Labor Unions and Similar Labor Organizations
813940	Political Organizations
813990	Other Similar Organizations (except Business, Professional, Labor, and Political Organizations)
814110	Private Households
921110	Executive Offices
921120	Legislative Bodies
921130	Public Finance Activities
921140	Executive and Legislative Offices, Combined
921150	American Indian and Alaska Native Tribal Governments

921190	Other General Government Support
922110	Courts
922120	Police Protection
922130	Legal Counsel and Prosecution
922140	Correctional Institutions
922150	Parole Offices and Probation Offices
922160	Fire Protection
922190	Other Justice, Public Order, and Safety Activities
923110	Administration of Education Programs
923120	Administration of Public Health Programs
923130	Administration of Human Resource Programs (except Education, Public Health, and Veterans' Affairs
923140	Administration of Veterans' Affairs
924110	Administration of Air and Water Resource and Solid Waste Management Programs
924120	Administration of Conservation
925110	Administration of Housing Programs
925120	Administration of Urban Planning and Community and Rural Development
926110	Administration of General Economic Programs
926120	Regulation and Administration of Transportation Programs
926130	Regulation and Administration of Communications, Electric, Gas, and Other Utilities
926140	Regulation of Agricultural Marketing and Commodities
926150	Regulation, Licensing, and Inspection of Miscellaneous Commercial Sectors
927110	Space Research and Technology
928110	National Security
928120	International Affairs

PART FIVE

PUBLISHER'S NOTES
RELATED PUBLICATIONS

FREQUENTLY ASKED QUESTIONS

Do you have an on-line product?

Yes. We provide our database on-line through subscription services for those who have a long term business data and contact information needs as well as one time purchases. Information may be downloaded for a single firm, a single country, the entire world, or any combination as you need it. Please visit us at: www.uniworldbp.com

How do you obtain your information?

We do proprietary research. Our primary sources of information are the parent company, annual reports, press releases and other public and private publications. Direct telephone, fax, and e-mail contact are used by our researchers for verification and clarification. Sources are monitored daily for changes in corporate governance and acquisitions.

What is your contact name editorial policy?

Company contact names change often and we monitor this on a daily basis. However, in the past few years, for reasons of security, fewer firms have willingly provided contact name information. For this reason, it is our editorial policy to publish the last known and verified contact name for a given firm.

How often is the data updated?

The World Edition hardcover reference directories are published bi-annually; however, the data is updated daily and created in custom print editions upon request from our latest data. These customer print editions are available for a fraction of the world edition hardcopy price and perfect for those interested in a single country, region, or industry.

What kind of special country/regional groups can be created?

We can create custom editions that meet your criteria with a combination of country, state, revenue range, postal code, and/or NAICS code(s). Regional or non-regional editions are possible (i.e., Asia region and Eastern Europe along with firms in Panama), as are different industries (i.e., telecommunications firms in New England along with insurance firms in the Northwest doing business in China.) As well, pre-set custom editions are also available of the more common international trade agreements (e.g., CAFTA, etc.) This information is created and printed at the time of your order, therefore, it is as up to date as possible.

A recent US customer needed to generate a pool of potential suppliers and partners in Canada, Mexico, India, and France in order to meet an RFP submitted by one of its largest manufacturing clients, likewise a California economics firm developed a strategic plan for a Japanese client based on a listing of revenues and employee size of foreign firms with offices in San Francisco. Only Uniworld offers the data in an easy to read, reference directory.

How do you decide what firms are included?

Our team of researches at the director of the Editor, monitor firms within countries with significant economic and business activities as well as firms within industries that are undergoing significant merger, acquisition, and expansion activity. These firms are given priority. Overall, firms included have revenues greater than $10 million; therefore, only larger international firms.

How long have you been publishing these books?

The Directory of American Firms Operating in Foreign Countries has been published since 1955. The Directory of Foreign Firms Operating in the United States has been published since 1969.

What is the NAICS Code?

For the first time we have included a numeric industrial classification. We have chosen the North American Industry Classification System (NAICS), which has replaced the U.S. Standard Industrial Classification (SIC). The official U.S. Census Bureau listing of all NAICS is available at the U.S. Census Bureau   http://www.census.gov/epcd/naics02/

NAICS 2002 is the same as NAICS 1997 for fourteen of the twenty sectors. Construction and wholesale trade are substantially changed, but the revisions also modify a number of retail classifications and the organization of the information sector. Very minor boundary adjustments affect administrative and support services and mining.

When will the next world edition reference book be published?

The 14th edition of the Directory of Foreign Firms Operating in the United States will be available in January, 2008. The 18th edition of the Directory of American Firms Operating in Foreign Countries was published in June 2005. These are both hardcover editions.

Do companies pay to be in the book?

No, companies cannot pay to be in the book nor do we accept any advertising.

Do you accept standing orders for yet-to-be-published directories?

Yes, many of our customers routinely place standing orders in advance of published directories.

DIRECTORY OF AMERICAN FIRMS OPERATING IN FOREIGN COUNTRIES

18th Edition
ISBN: 0-8360-0049-8

Published June 2005

First published in 1955, the Directory of American Firms Operating in Foreign Countries is the authoritative source of information on American Firms, which have branches, subsidiaries, or affiliates outside the United States. Designed to aid anyone interested in American business activities abroad, it is the only reference work of its kind.

The directory is used as a primary source of information by public, university, business, government and special libraries, banks, accounting, brokerage and investment firms, manufacturers, transportation companies, advertising and personnel agencies, researchers, embassies and many governmental agencies dealing with commerce, trade and foreign relations.

CONTENT

- >3,000 American Corporations
- >36,000 Foreign Subsidiaries, Affiliates or Branches
- 196 Countries
- Full contact information including contact names

FORMAT

- Clear and Quick Reference Format
- Volume 1/Part 1: Alphabetical listing by American Parent firm
- Volume 1/Part 2: Alphabetical listing by country
- Volume 2 and 3: continuation of alphabetical listing by country
- Available online

The overseas companies in this specialized listing are those in which American Firms have a substantial direct investment and which have been identified by the parent as a wholly or partially owned subsidiary, affiliate or branch. Franchises, representatives and non-commercial enterprises or institutions, such as hospitals, schools, etc., financed or operated by American philanthropic or religious organizations, are not included.